Anonymous

American agriculturist

Anonymous

American agriculturist

ISBN/EAN: 9783337716752

Printed in Europe, USA, Canada, Australia, Japan

Cover: Foto ©ninafisch / pixelio.de

More available books at **www.hansebooks.com**

THE

THE AMERICAN AGRICULTURIST.

FOR THE

Farm, Garden, and Household.

"Agriculture is the most Healthful, the most Useful, the most Noble Employment of Man."—WASHINGTON.

VOLUME TWENTY-SIX—FOR THE YEAR 1867

NEW-YORK:
PUBLISHED BY ORANGE JUDD & CO.,
245 BROADWAY.

CONTENTS OF VOLUME TWENTY-SIX.

☞ *The stars (*) in the following Index show where engravings occur, and the prefixed figures the number in the article. Articles referring directly or indirectly to Bees, Cattle, Insects, Manures, Trees, Weeds, etc., will be found indexed under these general heads.*

T

U

V

W

Recipes.

INDEX TO ILLUSTRATIONS IN VOLUME TWENTY-SIX.

A

B

C

D

E

F

G

H

I

J

K

L

M

O

P

R

S

T

V

W

AMERICAN AGRICULTURIST

FOR THE

Farm, Garden, and Household.

"AGRICULTURE IS THE MOST HEALTHFUL, MOST USEFUL, AND MOST NOBLE EMPLOYMENT OF MAN."—Washington.

ORANGE JUDD & CO., PUBLISHERS AND PROPRIETORS. Office, 41 Park Row, (Times Buildings.)

ESTABLISHED IN 1842. Published also in German at $1.50 a Year.

$1.50 PER ANNUM, IN ADVANCE. SINGLE NUMBER, 15 CENTS. 4 Copies for $5; 10 for $12; 20 or more, $1 each.

VOLUME XXVI—No. 1. NEW-YORK, JANUARY, 1867. NEW SERIES—No. 240.

GROUP OF KINGFISHERS—ALCYONES.—*Engraved for the American Agriculturist.*

We have had several of the most beautiful of the Kingfishers engraved for our frontispiece this month, not to remind our readers of the "halcyon days" when they went a-fishing and made the acquaintance of the brave little fellow who seemed there to be entertaining a party of [illegible], but simply to introduce this family to our readers. The Kingfishers are peculiar birds, distinguished by their short bodies, short legs, short rounded wings, large heads and bills. The central one above is our own Kingfisher, (*Alcedo alcyon*,) with its bright eye and cocked hat, and true Union-blue coat. It builds its nests in holes in banks near streams; lives upon fish which it takes from a poise in the air above the water. Its sharp, loud call, quick, arrow-like flight, brilliant manœuvres, and quick, sure plunges after its finney prey, are familiar to every country-bred American. Beneath, in the picture, flying from us, is the brilliantly colored European Kingfisher—a bird of great beauty. The upper part of the bill is black, the lower orange colored; the throat white; the crest green and blue; shoulders and wings dark green, with the edges of the feathers pale blue; the back resplendent azure; tail blue, and the whole under part bright orange; legs red, with black claws. It is much smaller than our Kingfisher; and smaller yet, but not more brilliant, is the little East Indian one, which is darting across the bottom of the picture. The spotted Kingfisher on the right is also a native of India, where it is called by the natives the "Fish Tiger." It is considerably larger than ours, and is brilliantly, but not gaily colored. The largest is the great African Kingfisher.

Contents for January, 1867.

INDEX TO "BASKET," OR SHORTER ARTICLES.

Department of Agriculture.—A bill to reorganize this, as under its present head, disgraceful concern, has been before the House of Representatives twice read and ordered printed. It provides that the President shall appoint a new commissioner within 30 days. There are many wise features in the bill, and some that are especially good to correct present abuses, but might not wear well. We are glad Congress is brought to *think* on this subject, and hope for a good result.

AMERICAN AGRICULTURIST.

NEW-YORK, JANUARY, 1867.

January seems to have been taken as a starting point for the year, because it comes in mid-winter at that time—when, for weeks before and weeks after the first of the month we have little change. The natural end of the year has been past for weeks, nature is asleep, and just now taking her soundest nap. The natural beginning of the year is weeks a-head, when the sun-shine and the mild south wind shall wake the buds and the roots, and rouse the seeds to clothe the Earth in verdure again. What better time could we have to stop and take a fresh start. Janus of the fables, after whom the month is named, is said to look forward with one face and backward with another, so we may review with profit the old year, and with diligence and fore-thought prepare for the new.

It would be unpardonable in us not to send with this first number of the New Year our cordial good wishes to all our friends.—In this we not only follow a very pleasant custom, but sincerely speak the wishes of our hearts, that the year may be a prosperous and happy one to every reader of the *Agriculturist*, to our beloved country, and to the world. We shall labor to make the *Agriculturist* more useful, more varied, more interesting, and more beautiful, to make the farmer's calling more profitable and elevating to himself and more attractive to his children, and to make our journal a welcome visitor and safe guide to all who cultivate the earth for pleasure or for profit, or rejoice in its beauties.

Hints about Farm Work.

Beginning the new year "with a conscience void of offence," and his pecuniary affairs in such condition, that he may know exactly what he owes and what is his due, and of the latter what will be paid and what may possibly be lost, the farmer is ready to take hold in earnest of his year's work. He should have, as essential to success,

Definite Plans, not only for 3 months or 6 months a-head, but for every day, and as the evening and the morning made the first and each succeeding day of the creation, so every evening properly begins the next day, as it is the best time to lay plans for work to be done. This makes the man "fore-handed." The work of every week should be planned by the Saturday night before. Winter is evening to the morning which dawns in April and culminates in July.

Buildings.—Desirable alterations and new erections may be discussed and planned, timber and stones hauled when sledding is good, and preparations completed before the frost begins to come out, immediately after which is the best time to dig cellars, etc., and do grading.

Stock of all kinds should now, in the beginning of severe weather, be well fed and groomed. It is really the most critical time, for they now feel the change of food most, and if not kept up and well cared for, will begin to run down.

Cows.—Good hay is *not* 'good enough for any body's cows,' *if* a few roots daily, and a little meal or oil-cake will make the hay go much farther, make the cattle do much better, and make their whole keeping cheaper, notwithstanding the extra work. Do not dry off cows too early, especially young cows. If possible, keep up the flow of milk by extra feeding, etc., until within 6 weeks of calving. Be careful to have no slippery places where a cow may fall on the ice; the injury may induce slinking (abortion), and this is infectious. If a cow with calf shows symptoms of sickness of any kind, remove her at once to another barn, entirely away from her companions, and keep especial watch upon cows that have slunk their calves in previous years. This is a great scourge to farmers in many sections, and every precaution should be taken to avoid it.

Oxen.—See hints in December number. Beef cattle will be greatly benefited by regular carding; they need it as much as horses, and we doubt not it would be more to the pecuniary profit of the feeder.

Young Stock.—Keep them growing, and give daily exercise and sunning in roomy yards.

Sheep.—If troubled with ticks, lice, or scab, though at this season it will not do, ordinarily, to dip them, the spots most affected may be wet with the dipping solution, (strong tobacco water, made by boiling tobacco stems, mixed with strong country soft-soap). This is best applied by a bottle having a groove cut in the side of the cork with which it is stoppered. Give sheep access to water daily. It is a great mistake to force them to eat snow or go without. Feed roots freely to all, and especially to fattening sheep. Very little grain will be a great benefit, if equally distributed. Handle your sheep and *know* their condition.

Ventilation.—Stables and cellars need good ventilation. It is better to let in the cold air in blasts than to confine the air in the stables so that the animals breath it over and over again, loaded with the exhalations of their skins and lungs, and the vapors which rise from their manure both solid and liquid. The health of the stock requires *fresh* air; economy of feeding is a secondary consideration; requiring warm stables; both may and should be had. In house cellars, especially if damp, the gases from the decay of vegetables, though slight, if not removed by frequent ventilation, may produce miasmatic diseases, typhoid fevers, etc.

Fowls usually roost as high as possible to avoid uncomfortable draughts of air. If indulged in this, they often become asphixiated and drop dead from their perches, from breathing foul air arising from the fermentation of their droppings, or being suffocated by the carbonic acid gas from the breaths of many fowls, all close to the top of the house, or from both causes. In warm quarters and well fed, they will begin to lay before the close of the month.

Ice.—See article about tools used in gathering ice on page 15. In packing, take care to have the drain clear and covered to prevent the air drawing through; and see that the floor is covered thick with straw, the ice is closely packed, and the chinks filled with snow or ice chips; also that straw or saw-dust is packed between the ice and the sides, and that, if possible, the ice is put in when very cold.

Seeds.—Keep seeds in a dry cool place away from rats, and not in tight boxes of either wood or tin. Secure all that you will need, in good time, before the stocks of seedsmen are exhausted, or they have so many orders to fill, that yours will be delayed. For the same reasons look out a-head for

Tools and Machines for spring and summer work. Send for catalogues, study what you want, correspond about strength, durability, adaptation to your particular requirements, and order in time.

Manure.—Keep it piled up compactly, so that fermentation will go on slowly in the mass. If possible, have a tank for liquid manure under the heap, and pump it up over the solid frequently. Manure sheds quickly pay for their cost in the increased value of the manure. See hints on hauling out manure in December number.

Swine confined upon manure under cover, will keep hard at work rooting it over and working it up all winter, and if it is quite strawy, they will not compact it too much, but add much to its value.

Markets.—We venture no predictions in regard to the markets, but state as facts, that our grain crop is not equal to the demand, that much corn will go South, and much to Europe; the wheat will go to Europe also—all that we can spare. Prices are now very remunerative. Hay and all fodder is high. There has been a great rush of beef, mutton and pork to market. Those who can hold on to animals intended for slaughter, will no doubt get well paid. Still, the turns of speculation and the uncertainties of winter and spring travel, involve it with risks, and lead us to hold to our oft repeated advice, sell when a *fair* price can be obtained.

Wood.—Cut fire-wood, also fencing stuff, such as needs splitting or sawing, if not cut already, as it should have been. Small stuff for fencing, posts, or poles, should be cut when the bark will peel off easily.

Work in the Horticultural Departments.

Writing up these notes for the month, has one pleasant feature, for, dry as they may seem, they allow a little play to the imagination, and we often fancy ourselves as walking in the well kept gardens and orchards of our friends, and talking with them of the things of so much interest to both of us. We do not make up these hints for the professional gardener, for he needs nothing of the kind; but to those to whom gardening is a recreation, and to those who follow it as adding much to their home comforts, we have reason to know they are useful helps. They are intended to "jog the memory" at the right time, and while they are not supposed to be full treatises upon the different branches of gardening, we are gratified to find that but few essentials are omitted. The enthusiastic cultivator, in whatever department, will avail himself of the best recorded experience, and have at least one standard work upon his favorite topic. These notes always, among other things, have the farmers' garden in view, and we aim to interest our agricultural friends in horticultural matters. If we could induce every farmer who reads the *Agriculturist* to grow one kind of fruit or vegetable more than he now has, how great the aggregate increase of comfort that would result. Why should not your home be the pleasantest in all the neighborhood—*yours*, reader, we mean—your family the most contented, your children the most intelligent and refined? Did you ever think how far a few shade trees go towards converting a house into a home? The comfort and health that grow upon currant bushes and strawberry patches, and what teachers and preachers are rose bushes and garden lilies? It is pleasing to know how welcome we are in so many thousand homes, and to be told, as we often are, that these homes are happier for our coming. The Horticultural Department, in giving its New Year's Greeting to both old and new friends, asks each one of them to acknowledge this salutation by resolving to plant either one new fruit tree or shrub, one new garden vegetable, or one new ornamental flowering plant or shrub.

Orchard and Nursery.

Did you carefully plant an orchard last autumn, and think there is nothing to do but wait for the fruit thereof? If so, in five years from now we shall have letters asking what is the matter with the orchard. The setting of a tree or plant of any kind involves a promise to take care of it. Unless these conditions are accepted, plant no more trees.

Young Trees, from the beginning, need constant supervision. Were the trees properly planted, no stakes will be needed, but if from careless planting or accident, any tree has been thrown out of the perpendicular, straighten it up and tie it to a stake.

Horses or Cattle often do much damage in young plantations, and must be kept out; indeed hogs are the only animals ever to be allowed in the orchard. There are some annoying wild animals.

Rabbits are easily kept off by anything that is distasteful to them. Blood is found to be as efficacious as anything else, and is easily obtained and applied. A small sprinkling only is necessary.

Mice will girdle small trees and shrubs. They work under cover, and all dead weeds and such rubbish must be removed from around the trees. Clasping the trees with a girdle of sheet iron or old tin, will be found to pay where mice are annoying. Tramp down loose snow.

Drains should be opened on the surface, wherever water accumulates upon the surface. In properly drained orchards this ought not to occur.

Insects can now be successfully headed off. The eggs of the Tent-caterpillar seem to be especially arranged with a view to their ready removal. If a swelling is seen near the end of a twig, it should be looked to, as it is likely that there is a deposit of eggs glued in a band around it. These clusters are readily seen while the trees are leafless, and may be removed by the aid of a step-ladder, on trees of moderate size, and on larger ones a pair of shears may be arranged at the end of a pole to work by a string. Any time and labor required to remove these eggs will be profitably expended.

Cions are to be cut at any time in winter when the trees are not frozen. Be careful to label every parcel. Saw-dust, fresh from the log, is the best possible material for preserving cions. Its amount of moisture is just that required to keep them from drying, and it is not sufficient to cause injury. It is preferable to sand, as the knife is not injured.

Root Graft at any time during winter, and set the grafted roots in boxes of sand or earth. In

Nurseries, the young stock is to be headed back and brought into shape. Never let two limbs start so near together as to form a crotch. Make every preparation for the spring trade, and have all packing material and labels ready for use.

Manure may be carted out while the ground is frozen, and be ready to spread in spring.

Labels on trees received from the nursery are, for safety, bound on tightly. In this time of leisure go over the orchard and see that no strangulation can result from tight wires.

Fruit Garden.

The general remarks about orchard trees apply to

Dwarf Trees in the garden. Some pear trees may be injured by lodging snow, which, if it remains in the tree, may do mischief. Shake it out. If any

Grape Vines were not pruned in autumn, do it now in mild spells, and do the same with

Currants and Gooseberries.—Keep the bush open and shorten in the new growth. Cuttings may be made of the prunings by dipping the lower ends in mud and setting them in a cool cellar. See that the

Winter Covering of strawberry and other plants is not blown or washed off. If leaves are used, they may require a little soil to be thrown over them.

Kitchen Garden.

The work here is that uninteresting one of preparation. There is actual work to be done, and there is thinking to be done. Are you growing the best and the earliest variety of every kind? Those who grow for market, look to earliness as the first essential, while those who provide only for home use, look for both earliness and good quality. When one tells us that this or that is the best variety, we must know what use he intends to make of it. If there is one fixed fact in gardening, it is, that the crop is in direct proportion to the amount of

Manure, which should now, while the ground is frozen, be hauled to where it is to be used. Fresh manure for hot-beds, and composted manure to apply to the ground, need different treatment. Well decomposed manure may be taken to the spot where it will be needed, and left in small heaps, while that for hot-beds should not be in so small heaps that it will be chilled through, but it should be kept in a state of fermentation. As soon as a heap shows signs of heating, it should be turned over, and each turning will much improve its quality. Plants in

Cold Frames will need attention. If the weather is very cold and the plants are frozen, it is not necessary to remove the snow from the frames, but a light fall of snow, followed by mild weather, must be immediately removed. Give air abundantly; even take off the glass entirely in mild weather, as it is the object to keep the plants as hardy as possible. If fine weather has made it safe to delay the final

Covering of celery and roots in pits, do it now. At the time we write, the middle of December, it seems as if this might be delayed for some time.

Lettuce, where there is a demand for early plants, may be forced in a hot-bed. The bed should be excavated at least 2½ feet deep, and this be filled with fermenting manure. If not already done, make

Straw Mats for covering hot-beds, these or shutters, will be needed on severe nights, later in the season.

Flower Garden and Lawn.

But little can be done here, other than the general care that every careful person will give.

Evergreens must not be allowed to suffer from an overloading of snow, and there are many close growing deciduous shrubs injured by this. Shake it out before it becomes icy, and shovel it away from the lower branches of trees and shrubs. All

Laying out of beds and walks may be planned, and in a mild season some of the work may be done. Plants that are wintered in

Pits, need air in mild weather. Water only when they seem to actually need it. Keep mice from pits.

Seedling Perennials in their first winter will do all the better for protection, no matter how hardy the old plants may be. A mulch over the bed will prevent the roots from injury. Leaves may be used, or well weathered muck.

Green and Hot-Houses.

It is not well to let any collection reach a temperature much below 40°. Plants cannot, as a general thing, be expected to flower at much below 60°. For stove plants proper, more heat is needed, according to their tropical character.

Bulbs, that were potted last autumn and kept cool, may be brought to the warmer atmosphere of the green-house or dwelling, and will soon flower. Whenever the flower has passed its prime, cut away the stalk, but allow the leaves to grow to ripen the bulb, which may be useful in out-door culture.

Camellias need an even temperature, one rather low with a moist atmosphere. If necessary, thin the buds. Keep the foliage clear by use of syringe.

Cactuses should, generally, have rest and dryness.

Manure Water, made with sheep or other droppings to the color of pale ale, or an amber color, may be used upon roses and other plants just coming into flower. Beware of over-stimulating.

Plants in cold frames, such as

Violets and other half hardy things, need plenty of air when the outside temperature will allow.

Bedding Stock of scarce kinds may be multiplied by starting the stock plants into growth and taking cuttings, which, after they are rooted, will in turn furnish cuttings for later propagation.

Apiary for January.

During winter, the colder the weather, the closer do bees crowd together in the center of the hive. If they could be observed, they would be seen filling most of the cells of the plates of comb in the middle, and forming almost a perfectly solid globe. They eat out all the honey close to them, and the outer ones of course must eat most, to keep up the vital heat, for they are most exposed to cold. Such a mass of bees throw off much moisture in their breath (so to speak), and in cold weather and in illy ventilated hives, this freezes in the top of the comb, and as it thaws and freezes often, shuts off many bees from access to their stores, unless passage ways are provided in the middle through the combs. These should have been made in the autumn. Besides, were no ice present, the bees might be fatally chilled in passing around the outside of the combs. It is therefore sometimes advisable in case of outstanding hives in long protracted severe weather, to remove the light stocks to the bee-house described last month, or to any room that can be darkened and warmed, when, after examining them to know their state, clear out dead bees, etc. If necessary, let them remain long enough to melt the ice, and allow the bees to dry themselves, and get to their stores, which requires only a few hours. Examine hives to see if they have been attacked by mice, and if so, close entrances against them with wire cloth, but not so as to prevent the egress of the bees. Watch hives that are housed against attacks of mice, but do not disturb them; look to the ventilators. If snow covers exposed hives—well; if light snows fall, sweep it away from the entrances and alighting boards, and from close around the hives. The bees fly out somewhat in mild weather, and would be chilled and die did they fall in the snow. Prepare hives, frames, honey boxes and supers for next summer's use. Painting hives should not be deferred until summer, the longer they are painted before needed, the better.

AMERICAN AGRICULTURIST.

ORANGE JUDD & Co., Publishers, 41 Park Row, N. Y. City.

ANNUAL SUBSCRIPTION TERMS (always in advance): $1.50 each for less than four copies: Four to nine copies, $1.25 each: Ten to nineteen copies, $1.20 each: Twenty copies and upwards, $1 each. Papers are addressed to each name.

Our Excellent Premiums.

EXPLANATION.

In inviting the special attention of all to the list of most valuable premiums, offered in the accompanying table, a word of explanation may be needed by the many thousands of new subscribers who now see this paper for the first time——: We employ no agents, traveling or otherwise, to attend to the collection or renewing of subscriptions, or the securing of new subscribers. As a rule, our old subscribers renew without solicitation, and they generally invite some of their neighbors and friends to join them. In this way our circulation is continually increasing. We bespeak the continuance of this good will and favor, and shall spare no effort to make the coming numbers increasingly valuable, and worthy the patronage of every man, woman and child in the entire country.

Still, it is usually convenient and desirable to have some one or more persons at every Post-Office to gather up and forward renewals, and solicit new subscribers, and to those who do this we offer a choice of good articles, of a value proportioned to their cost, and to the number of names sent in. These premium articles are a token or acknowledgment on our part of favors received, to those who act from disinterested motives—though they also afford good pay in most cases for time expended. Hundreds of persons have written us that they have, by using a few evening hours or stormy days, secured without expense just the articles desired. Frequent cases are reported to us where premium canvassers have cleared from $10 to $30 a day, by earning the premiums and selling them.

Any person so disposed can make up a premium list—the offers are open to all. It is a pleasant work. Any one who persuades a dozen, or twenty, or more of his neighbors to read about their business, does much to improve and elevate the character of the people, and to bring increased value to his own homestead, and to every other homestead around him.

Our premiums are all *really valuable articles*, such as we can cheerfully recommend to our friends. By wholesale purchases, by advertising arrangements, etc., we are able to supply them as premiums on far better terms than we could sell them, and we thus pay our canvassers much more than we could possibly do in cash. The paper is supplied to subscribers at cost, or even less. The immense circulation gives great value to our advertising columns, to which only reliable parties are admitted, and these can well afford to supply all the funds needed to pay our premiums, and also a satisfactory profit.

It will be seen then, that the premiums, by aiding to increase the circulation, thus enlarge our advertising receipts, and these, in turn, furnish not only the means of paying for further premiums, but also enable us to supply a very valuable paper *at less than its real cost*, and still receive an ample remuneration for our work.

We invite every reader who lives where no one is already actively engaged in raising a premium club, to take hold in these leisure winter days, and secure such a club. We often receive several different premium clubs from the same Post-Office.... The last column in the table shows how many subscribers are required when they are sent at the lowest club price of $1 a year for 20 or more. The next column shows the number required at the regular price of $1.50 a year. (See notes following the table.)

Men and Women of various occupations, Farmers, Gardeners, Post-masters, Merchants, Mechanics, Clergymen, Teachers, Soldiers, Boys, Girls, etc., can engage in the work of soliciting subscribers and secure good pay for it, in the excellent and desirable premium articles.

Table of Premiums and Terms, For Volume 26—(1867).

Open to all—No Competition.

No.	Names of Premium Articles.	Price of Premiums.	Number of Subscribers required at $1.50.	at $1.
1	Garden Seeds for a Family (42 kinds)	$5 00	13	37
2	Flower Seeds for a Family (100 kinds)	$5 00	13	37
3	Nursery Stock (Any kinds desired)	$20 00	30	97
4	Iona Grape Vines (12 of No. 1)	$18 00	27	90
5	Concord Grape Vines (100 of No. 1)	$12 00	19	65
6	Japan Lilies (12 Bulbs)	$6 00	15	45
7	Sewing Machine (Wheeler & Wilson)	$55 00	[illegible]	[illegible]
8	Sewing Machine (Grover & Baker)	$55 00	[illegible]	210
9	Sewing Machine (Singer's Tailoring)	$80 00	[illegible]	[illegible]
10	Sewing Machine (Florence)	$63 00	[illegible]	270
11	Sewing Machine (Willcox & Gibbs)	$55 00	[illegible]	210
12	Sewing Machine (Howe's)	$60 00	[illegible]	[illegible]
13	Washing Machine (Doty's)	$14 00	21	70
14	Clothes Wringer (Best—Universal)	$10 00	18	58
15	Tea Set (Hart's best Silver Plated)	$50 00	[illegible]	[illegible]
16	Castors and Fruit Basket (do. do.)	$30 00	44	130
17	Ice or Water Pitcher (do. do.)	$18 00	27	90
18	One Dozen Tea Spoons (do. do.)	$7 50	17	50
19	One Dozen Table Spoons (do. do.)	$15 00	[illegible]	73
20	One Dozen Dining Forks (do. do.)	$15 00	[illegible]	73
21	Piano (Best Steinway & Son's 7-octave)	$625 00	[illegible]	1550
22	Melodeon (Best 5-octave)	$112 00	[illegible]	160
23	Melodeon (Best 4-octave)	$67 00	[illegible]	[illegible]
24	Ladies' Gold Watch (Beautiful)	$100 00	138	400
25	Silver Watch (Valuable Time Keeper)	$32 50	[illegible]	[illegible]
26	Double Barrel Gun (Very good)	$30 00	[illegible]	[illegible]
27	Spencer's Breech-loading Rifle (Hunting)	$35 00	[illegible]	[illegible]
28	Tool Chest (First Quality of Tools)	$44 50	[illegible]	[illegible]
29	Case of Mathematical Instruments	$9 00	[illegible]	[illegible]
30	Case of Mathematical Instruments	$15 00	[illegible]	[illegible]
31	Morton's Best No. 6 Gold Pen (Silver Case)	$5 75	[illegible]	[illegible]
32	Morton's Best No. 5 Gold Pen, Silver Case	$4 50	[illegible]	[illegible]
33	Barometer (Woodruff's Mercurial)	$14 00	27	[illegible]
34	Barometer (Woodruff's Mercurial)	$12 00	19	65
35	Buckeye Mowing Machine, No. 2	$125 00	150	450
36	Allen's Patent Cylinder Plow, etc.	$20 50	31	100
37	The Aquarius or Water Thrower	$11 00	19	65
38	American Cyclopedia (Appleton's)	$80 00	[illegible]	[illegible]
39	Worcester's Great Illustrated Dictionary	$12 00	19	65
40	Any Back Volume Agriculturist	[illegible]	[illegible]	[illegible]
41	Any Two Back Volumes do.	[illegible]	[illegible]	[illegible]
42	Any Three do. do. do.	[illegible]	13	[illegible]
43	Any Four do. do. do.	[illegible]	15	[illegible]
44	Any Five do. do. do.	[illegible]	[illegible]	[illegible]
45	Any Six do. do. do.	[illegible]	[illegible]	[illegible]
46	Any Seven do. do. do.	[illegible]	[illegible]	[illegible]
47	Any Eight do. do. do.	[illegible]	[illegible]	[illegible]
48	Any Nine do. do. do.	[illegible]	[illegible]	[illegible]
49	Vols. XVI to XXV do.	[illegible]	27	[illegible]
50	Any Back Volume Agriculturist	[illegible]	[illegible]	[illegible]
51	Any Two Back Volumes do.	[illegible]	[illegible]	[illegible]
52	Any Three do. do. do.	[illegible]	16	[illegible]
53	Any Four do. do. do.	[illegible]	[illegible]	[illegible]
54	Any Five do. do. do.	[illegible]	[illegible]	71
55	Any Six do. do. do.	[illegible]	[illegible]	[illegible]
56	Any Seven do. do. do.	[illegible]	[illegible]	[illegible]
57	Any Eight do. do. do.	[illegible]	30	102
58	Any Nine do. do. do.	[illegible]	33	110
59	Vols. XVI to XXV do.	[illegible]	[illegible]	[illegible]
60	Genesee Farmer, 1858–1865, 8 Vols., Bound	$14 00	21	70
61	Downing's Landscape Gardening	$6 50	15	46
62	Cummings & Miller's Architect.	$10 00	18	58
63	A $10 Library (Your Choice)	$10 00	18	58
64	A $15 Library do.	$15 00	24	85
65	A $20 Library do.	$20 00	31	[illegible]
66	A $25 Library do.	$25 00	[illegible]	[illegible]
67	A $30 Library do.	$30 00	41	[illegible]
68	A $35 Library do.	$35 00	50	[illegible]
69	A $40 Library do.	$40 00	55	177
70	A $45 Library do.	$45 00	61	[illegible]
71	A $50 Library do.	$50 00	[illegible]	[illegible]
72	A $60 Library do.	$60 00	[illegible]	[illegible]
73	A $75 Library do.	$75 00	100	[illegible]
74	A $100 Library do.	$100 00	125	[illegible]
75	A Choice of Good Books (See Terms below.)			
76	Sewing Machine (Finkle & Lyon)	$60 00	80	210
77	One Dozen Pocket Lanterns	$9 00	19	48

(Nos. 40–49: In clean new Nos.—Post-paid—Unbound. Nos. 50–59: Neatly Bound, Sent Post-paid. Nos. 61–74: All sent post-paid through, by Mail or Express.)

☞ *Every article offered is new and of the very best manufacture. No charge is made for packing or boxing any of the articles in this Premium List. The forty-three Premiums,* **Nos. 1, 2, 6,** *and from* **20** *to* **32,** *and from* **40** *to* **75** *inclusive, will each be delivered* **FREE** *of all charges, by mail or express, to the Post-Office or express office nearest recipient, to any place in the United States or Territories, excepting those reached only by the Overland Mail.—The other articles cost the recipient only the freight after leaving the manufactory of each, by any conveyance that may be specified.*

☞ **We take** *so much pains to procure only good articles in all cases, that any one securing anything from our premium list, saves the risk usually run of getting poor or indifferent goods, when buying of unknown or irresponsible parties. Every thing we send out as a premium is guaranteed to be the best of its kind and price.*

Our premiums are standard articles, and enough can be obtained to supply all calls for premiums for six months. Every canvasser can take abundant time, but

As fast as subscriptions are obtained, send them along, that the subscribers may begin to receive the paper; and when all the names that can be obtained are forwarded, select the premium, and it will be promptly furnished. To save mistakes and keeping accounts, *send with each list of names, the exact subscription money* (in Post Office money orders, or drafts or checks on N. Y. City, or, if these can not be had, register money letters.)

☞ **Every name** *designed for a premium list must be so marked* WHEN *sent in.* (We can not count others.)

Old and new subscribers count in premium lists, but a part should be new names, for it is to obtain such that the premiums are in part offered. *Papers to Premium clubs need not all go to one Post Office.* Of course the extra copy, usually offered to clubs of ten or twenty, will not be furnished when a premium is called for.

Specimen Numbers of the *Agriculturist*, Cards, and Showbills, as may be needed, will be supplied to Canvassers. These should be used carefully and economically, as each extra copy of the paper, with postage (2c.) which must be prepaid, costs about 12 cents.

For Full Description of the several premiums see October *Agriculturist*, pages 349 to 352, or apply for a *Descriptive List*, which will be furnished *free* and post-paid. We have room here for only the following:

No. 63 to 74—Good Libraries.—These can be selected by the recipients, from any of the books in the list below. The books will be *delivered* free of cost, by mail or express.

No. 75—General Book Premium.—Any one not desiring the specific Book premiums, 63 to 74, on sending any number of names above 25, may select Books from the list below, to the amount of 10 cents for each subscriber sent at $1; or to the amount of 30 cents for each name sent at the (ten) club price of $1.20 each; or to the amount of 60 cents for each name at $1.50. *This offer is only for clubs of 25 or more. The books will be sent by mail or express, prepaid by us.*

No. 77 (New)—Pocket Lanterns.—This new premium is a very ingenious as well as valuable Yankee invention. It is a complete *Lantern*, large enough to afford light for walking or other purposes, and yet in less than half a minute it can be folded into a parcel 5 by 4 inches and ¾ inch in thickness, or small enough to set into the vest pocket, and yet contain 3 little sperm candles, matches, etc. We have used one for several months, carrying it in the pocket whenever going out at night, ready for use at any moment. It is manufactured by the Merriam Manufacturing Company, (Julius Ives & Co., Agents, 49 Maiden Lane, N. Y. City). The few sold thus far have been retailed at $1 each (we thought our first one purchased at that price a good investment;) but in order to introduce specimen samples generally, the manufacturers enable us to make a special offer of One Dozen of the Lanterns, for a club of 12 subscribers at $1.50 each. For larger clubs, at the same rate, or a lantern for each member. A dozen pack in a box 8¼ by 5½ by 8½ inches, and will go anywhere cheaply by express. It is described in our advertising columns.

BOOKS FOR FARMERS AND OTHERS.

[For sale at the office of the *Agriculturist*, or they will be forwarded by mail, *post-paid*, on receipt of price. ☞ *All these are included in Our Premiums, Nos. 63 to 75, above.*

Allen's (L. F.) Rural Architecture	$1 50
Allen's (R. L.) American Farm Book	1 50
Allen's Diseases of Domestic Animals	1 00
American Bird Fancier	30
American Rose Culturist	30
American Weeds and Useful Plants	1 75
Architecture, by Cummings & Miller	10 00
Barry's Fruit Garden	1 75
Bement's Poulterer's Companion	2 00
Bement's Rabbit Fancier	30
Breck's New Book of Flowers	1 75
Buist's Flower Garden Directory	1 50
Buist's Family Kitchen Gardener	1 00
Burr's Vegetables of America	5 00
Chorlton's Grape-Grower's Guide	75
Cobbett's American Gardener	75
Cole's (S. W.) American Fruit Book	75
Cole's Veterinarian	75
Dadd's Modern Horse Doctor	1 50
Dadd's (Geo. H.) American Cattle Doctor	1 50
Dana's Muck Manual	1 25
Dog and Gun (Hooper's) ....paper, 30c.. cloth..	60
Downing's Country Houses	9 00
Downing's Landscape Gardening (new Edition)	6 50
Downing's Fruits and Fruit Trees of America	3 00
Downing's Rural Essays	5 00
Eastwood on Cranberry	75
Elliott's Western Fruit Grower's Guide	1 50
Flax Culture	50
Field's (Thomas W.) Pear Culture	1 25
Flint's Milch Cows and Dairy Farming	2 50
French's Farm Drainage	1 50
Fuller's Grape Culturist	1 50
Fuller's Strawberry Culturist	20
Gray's How Plants Grow	1 25
Gray's Manual of Botany and Lessons in one Vol.	4 00
Guenon on Milch Cows	75
Harris' Insects Injurious to Vegetation, plain 4.00, col'd	5 00
Harris' Rural Annual. Bound, 8 Nos., in 2 Vols. Each	1 50
Herbert's Hints to Horsekeepers	1 75
Hop Culture	40
Husmann's Grapes and Wine	1 50
Johnston's Agricultural Chemistry	1 75
Johnston's Elements of Agricultural Chemistry	1 50
Johnson's (Prof. S. W.) Essays on Manures	1 25
Langstroth on Honey Bee	2 00
Leuchar's How to Build Hot-Houses	1 50
Mayhew's Illustrated Horse Doctor	3 50
Mayhew's Illustrated Horse Management	3 50
Mayhew's Practical Bookkeeping for Farmers	90
Blanks for do. do.	1 20
Miles on the Horse's Foot	75
My Farm of Edgewood	1 75
My Vineyard at Lakeview	1 25
Norton's Scientific Agriculture	75
Onion Culture	20
Our Farm of Four Acres (bound) 60c .... paper..	30
Pardee on Strawberry Culture	75
Peat and its Uses, by Prof. S. W. Johnson	1 25
Pedder's Land Measurer	60
Quinby's Mysteries of Bee Keeping (NEW)	1 50
Randall's Sheep Husbandry	1 50
Randall's Fine Wool Sheep Husbandry	1 00
Rivers' Miniature Fruit Garden	1 00
Richardson on the Dog, paper 30c ....cloth..	60
Rural Annual, by Joseph Harris	25
Saunders' Domestic Poultry (NEW), paper, 40c., bound	75
Schenck's Gardener's Text Book	75
Scribner's Ready Reckoner	30
Skillful Housewife	25
Stewart's (John) Stable Book	1 50
Thompson's Food of Animals	1 00
Tobacco Culture	25
Todd's (S. E.) Young Farmer's Manual	1 50
Warder's Hedges and Evergreens	1 50
Watson's American Home Garden	2 00
Woodward's Country Homes	1 50
Youatt and Spooner on the Horse	1 50
Youatt and Martin on Cattle	1 50
Youatt on the Hog	1 00
Youatt on Sheep	1 00
Youmans' Household Science	2 25

AMERICAN
AGRICULTURAL ANNUAL for 1867.

(Companion to the Am. Horticultural Annual.*)

This new Annual includes an Almanac and Calendar for each month, a review of events of agricultural interest during the past year, valuable articles from eminent agriculturists, convenient and important tables, etc. It is profusely illustrated with original engravings. Among other articles of especial value are the following:

Country Life and the Farmer's Old Age, by Rev. Wm. Clift.

Tile Draining, by Col. Geo. E. Waring, Jr., C. E., Engineer of the Drainage of the Central Park. A concise yet very explicit and detailed account of the principles of thorough land drainage and the best modes of accomplishing it. Very fully and beautifully illustrated.

The Culture of Wheat in America, by Joseph Harris, exhibiting the essence of the best practice.

The Culture of Barley, by the same writer.

Horse Training vs. "Breaking," by Samuel F. Headly. Full of valuable hints. Illustrated.

Cheap and Substantial Fences and Gates, from several writers, with numerous illustrations.

Requirements of a Good Barn, with Plans, by Dr. F. M. Hexamer, discussing the principles of economy and convenience, applicable to large or small barns.

The Profitable Culture of Potatoes, with descriptions and pictures of some of the newer and best varieties, by Wm. S. Carpenter, of Westchester Co., N. Y.

Management of Large Apiaries.—A record from the experience of Bidwell Brothers, St. Paul, Minn.

On Fattening Sheep in Winter, by John Johnston, the Veteran Farmer of Seneca Co., N. Y. Full of very valuable practical and instructive hints.

The Culture of Sorghum in the United States, by Wm. Clough, Editor of the Sorgo Journal.

Principles of Fine Wool Sheep Husbandry, by Henry Swift, Esq., of Dutchess County, N. Y.

Raising Poultry on a Large Scale, by Simeon M. Saunders, Author of Domestic Poultry.

Veterinary Medicine and Surgery, by John Busteed, M. D., President of the New York College of Veterinary Surgeons.

Recent Progress in the Science of Agriculture, by S. W. Johnson, Professor of Agricultural Chemistry at Yale College.

Agricultural Education and Agricultural Colleges in the United States.

AMERICAN
HORTICULTURAL ANNUAL for 1867.

(Companion to the Am. Agricultural Annual.*)

This important new Annual is now ready. Its plan is different from any heretofore published in this country; it aims to be a

RECORD OF HORTICULTURAL PROGRESS, for the year 1866, free from matters not legitimately Horticultural.

THE MATERIAL IS ALL NEW, and not a reproduction of old articles that have served their turn elsewhere. The volume is

LIBERALLY ILLUSTRATED, with engravings made especially for the purpose. That a Year Book of Horticulture is needed, is shown by the readiness with which

DISTINGUISHED HORTICULTURISTS have contributed to its pages. Among other contributions from experienced cultivators, there will be

THE APPLES OF 1866, by Doct. John A. Warder, (President of the Ohio State Pomological Society, Author of American Pomology, etc.) New Ohio Apples; New Indiana Varieties; Southern Varieties fruited at the North, &c. *Illustrated.*

NEW AND NOTEWORTHY PEARS, by P. Barry, author of the Fruit Garden, etc., giving descriptions of new varieties as well as of the less known ones that have been fully tested. *Illustrated.*

NEW BEDDING AND OTHER PLANTS OF 1866, by Peter Henderson, Florist, etc. An account of the newer varieties of bedding and other flowering plants, and their success and failure during the past year. *Illustrated.*

THE RARER EVERGREENS THAT HAVE PROVED VALUABLE, by Thomas Meehan, Editor of Gardener's Monthly, American Hand-book of Ornamental Trees, etc.)

NEW VEGETABLES OF 1866, by Fearing Burr, Jr., author of American Field and Garden Vegetables; and J. J. H. Gregory, Marblehead, Mass.

SMALL FRUITS IN 1866, by Andrew S. Fuller, author of the Grape Culturist, Forest Tree Culturist, etc. A valuable summary of all small fruits, excepting grapes.

HOME DECORATIONS, by A. Bridgeman. How to treat Ivy; Hanging Baskets, Rustic Stands, etc.—*Illustrated.*

NEW ROSES OF 1866, by John Saul, Florist, of Washington, D. C., and well known authority on Roses.

THE CULTIVATION OF HORSERADISH, by Peter Henderson, author of Gardening for Profit. Concise directions for growing this profitable crop.—*Illustrated.*

GRAPES IN 1866. From notes by Geo. W. Campbell, Delaware, Ohio, and other Grape Growers.

PROPAGATING GRAPES IN THE OPEN AIR, by William Patrick, Terre Haute, Ind., giving a method by which the Delaware and other difficult varieties may be grown—without artificial heat.

USEFUL SEED TABLES, by James Fleming, Seedsman, New York, giving the amount of seed to the acre, to a given length of drill, etc.

Other communications by well known authorities, besides a great amount of Editorial matter, including a Calendar for each month in the year, articles on Wine Grapes, Table Ornaments, Hedges, Farm Nurseries, Tree Labels, New Gladioluses, List of Engravings of New Fruits and Flowers published in 1866. List of Works on Horticulture for 1866. A DICTIONARY of Horticultural Terms, and a great amount of other matters of interest, both to the professional and amateur gardener.—Price 50 Cents.

* These valuable Annuals are worthy a place in every family. Price 50 cts. each. Sent post-paid for same price,

Commercial Matters—Market Prices.

Gold has again declined materially, and closes heavily, leading to great caution in business operations, especially in produce and merchandise, and most adversely influencing the market for imported articles.... Early in the month under review, breadstuffs were quite depressed in price, influenced by liberal receipts, the fall in gold, and the restricted wants of buyers, both for home use or for export. Toward the close, the receipts fell off; the home and foreign inquiry revived, accompanied by some speculative orders; and prices of the leading articles, particularly of flour, wheat and corn, close with a strong upward tendency. We enter the winter months with comparatively moderate stocks of flour and grain, on which the principal holders are not eager to realize at prevailing rates, as they confidently look for a better market later in the season. The canals of the State were to have been officially closed on the 15th inst. Since that day, the weather has been so cold as to forbid the hope of any further considerable receipts by water. Henceforward, for some months, the railroads will be the main reliance of the trade.... Provisions have been much more freely offered and purchased at materially reduced prices, especially for hog products, which have been arriving in unusually liberal quantities, but the market closes firmly on the basis of our quotations, with a fair trade demand.... Cotton has been moderately inquired for at variable prices, closing tamely and slightly in favor of buyers. Thus far, in the current cotton year, commencing with Sept. 1, the receipts at this port have been 208,000 bales, and at all the shipping ports of the country, 504,000 bales; exports from this port, 82,000 bales, and from all ports, 185,000 bales; estimated stock now here, 150,000 bales, and at all the ports, at latest mail dates, 400,000 bales.... There has been an improved inquiry for wool, chiefly within the past two weeks. Low prices were made early in the month, but the market closes with more firmness and buoyancy. Manufacturers evince more disposition to purchase. Stocks of desirable grades are moderate, and less eagerly pressed for sale.... In tobacco there has been less doing, and prices have been irregular.... In hemp and seeds, business has been light, and prices of both have been nearly nominal. ..Hay has been in better supply and less request at lower figures ...Hops have been in fair demand, and quoted a shade higher.

The following condensed, comprehensive tables, carefully prepared specially for the *American Agriculturist*, show at a glance the transactions for a month, ending Dec. 15, 1866, and the exports of Breadstuffs from this port thus far, since January 1:

1. TRANSACTIONS AT THE NEW-YORK MARKETS.

RECEIPTS.	Flour.	Wheat.	Corn.	Rye.	Barley.	Oats.
25 days *this* month	417,000	2,400,000	3,184,000	431,000	2,317,000	1,722,000
27 days *last* month	353,000	1,210,000	1,896,000	177,000	2,184,000	948,000

SALES.	Flour.	Wheat.	Corn.	Rye.	Barley.
25 days *this* month	311,000	1,012,000	2,888,000	179,000	881,000
27 days *last* month	324,000	2,015,000	3,610,000	470,000	2,135,000

2. *Comparison with same period at this time last year.*

RECEIPTS.	Flour.	Wheat.	Corn.	Rye.	Barley.	Oats.
25 days 1866...	417,000	2,400,000	3,184,000	431,000	2,317,000	1,722,000
27 days 1865...	553,000	2,916,000	1,910,000	810,000	516,000	943,000

SALES.	Flour.	Wheat.	Corn.	Rye.	Barley.
25 days 1866......	311,000	1,012,000	2,888,000	179,000	881,000
27 days 1865......	715,000	1,383,000	2,135,000	311,000	411,000

3. *Exports from New York, Jan. 1 to Dec. 15:*

	Flour.	Wheat.	Corn.	Rye.	Oats.	Barley.
1866......	987,140	440,124	10,995,640	226,000	1,156,000	1,059,371
1865......	1,181,411	2,390,000	5,017,525	170,991	11,338	—
1864......	1,983,807	12,135,944	823,398	994	41,419	—
1863......	2,454,738	14,887,816	7,308,148	436,389	195,703	—
1862......	2,889,619	24,860,341	11,331,819	1,089,856	171,262	—

4. *Stock of Breadstuffs in Store at New York, Dec. 15:*

	Flour.	Wheat.	Corn.	Rye.	Barley.	Oats.
1866...	Unknown	1,338,653	5,051,340	307,981	1,801,089	2,110,507

5. *Receipts of Breadstuffs at Albany, by the New York Canals from the opening of Navigation to Dec. 7:*

	Flour.	Wheat.	Corn.	Rye.	Barley.	Oats.
1866...	150,900	4,858,200	24,189,400	1,331,900	6,081,700	10,340,300
1865...	814,300	8,996,600	18,118,700	1,740,900	4,388,100	10,482,700
1864...	1,186,700	15,165,600	10,352,800	636,300	3,615,900	13,177,500
1863...	1,549,000	22,065,400	28,508,700	652,800	3,101,300	12,381,900

CURRENT WHOLESALE PRICES.

	Nov. 15.	Dec. 15.
PRICE OF GOLD	143¾	137⅞
FLOUR—Super to Extra State	$8 75 @ 11 40	$7 80 @ 11 30
Super to Extra Southern	12 25 @ 17 50	10 50 @ 16 85
Extra Western	9 50 @ 16 00	8 70 @ 16 50
Extra Genesee	12 50 @ 14 00	11 85 @ 15 00
Superfine Western	8 75 @ 10 50	[illegible]
RYE FLOUR	[illegible]	[illegible]
CORN MEAL	[illegible]	[illegible]
WHEAT—All kinds of White	[illegible]	[illegible]
All kinds of Red and Amber	[illegible]	[illegible]
CORN—Yellow	[illegible]	[illegible]
Mixed	[illegible]	[illegible]
OATS—Western	[illegible]	[illegible]
State	[illegible]	[illegible]
RYE	[illegible]	[illegible]
BARLEY	[illegible]	[illegible]
HAY—Bale ℔ 100 ℔	[illegible]	[illegible]
Loose	[illegible]	[illegible]
STRAW, ℔ 100 ℔	[illegible]	[illegible]
COTTON—Middlings, ℔ ℔	[illegible]	[illegible]
HOPS—Crop of 1866, ℔ ℔	[illegible]	[illegible]
FEATHERS—Live Geese, ℔ ℔	[illegible]	[illegible]
SEED—Clover, ℔ ℔	[illegible]	[illegible]
Timothy, ℔ bushel	[illegible]	[illegible]
Flax, ℔ bushel	Nominal.	[illegible]
SUGAR—Brown, ℔ ℔	[illegible]	[illegible]
MOLASSES, Cuba, ℔ gl	[illegible]	[illegible]
COFFEE—Rio (Gold price) ℔ ℔	[illegible]	[illegible]
TOBACCO, Kentucky, &c., ℔ ℔	[illegible]	[illegible]
Seed Leaf, ℔ ℔	[illegible]	[illegible]
WOOL—Domestic Fleece, ℔ ℔	[illegible]	[illegible]
Domestic, pulled, ℔ ℔	[illegible]	[illegible]
California, unwashed	[illegible]	[illegible]
TALLOW, ℔ ℔	[illegible]	[illegible]
OIL CAKE—℔ ton	[illegible]	[illegible]
PORK—Mess, ℔ barrel	[illegible]	[illegible]
Prime, ℔ barrel	[illegible]	[illegible]
BEEF—Plain mess	[illegible]	[illegible]
LARD, in barrels, ℔ ℔	[illegible]	[illegible]
BUTTER—Western, ℔ ℔	[illegible]	[illegible]
State, ℔ ℔	[illegible]	[illegible]
CHEESE	[illegible]	[illegible]
BEANS—℔ bushel	[illegible]	[illegible]
PEAS—Canada, ℔ bushel	Nominal.	[illegible]
EGGS—Fresh, ℔ dozen	[illegible]	[illegible]
POULTRY—Fowls, ℔ ℔	[illegible]	[illegible]
Turkeys, ℔ ℔	[illegible]	[illegible]
POTATOES—Mercers, ℔ bbl.	[illegible]	[illegible]
Peach Blows, ℔ barrel	[illegible]	[illegible]
POTATOES—Buckeye, ℔ bbl.	[illegible]	[illegible]
APPLES—℔ barrel	[illegible]	[illegible]
CRANBERRIES, ℔ barrel	[illegible]	[illegible]

New York Live Stock Markets.—The supply during the past five weeks has been abundant for the season, as is shown in the following table:

WEEK ENDING.	Beeves.	Cows.	Calves.	Sheep.	Swine.
Dec. 18	4,184	67	586	27,408	17,987
Dec. 11	5,567	81	959	29,911	25,118
Dec. 4	4,836	42	794	27,892	13,098
Nov. 27	4,941	57	1,328	24,169	11,189
Nov. 20	4,166	66	1,607	30,325	10,887
Total in five Weeks	23,104	311	4,674	139,681	77,080
Average per Week	3,621	62	985	27,193	17,880
do. do. last Month	6,729	188	1,729	29,408	21,008
do. do. prev's Month	6,176	162	1,511	27,814	11,899
do. do. do. 1865	5,853	118	1,370	16,091	11,023
do. do. do. 1864	5,161	145	1,511	15,315	12,676
do. do. do. 1863	5,150	129	994	9,941	21,670

Total Animals for Slaughter in past 5 Weeks.... [illegible],106

The weekly receipts of all kinds of animals, though less than the previous month, have yet been abundant for all demands.... **Beef Cattle** continued low for a time, but with diminished receipts and cold weather, have advanced a little, and just now (Dec. 22) prices range at 16c. @17c. per lb. estimated dressed weight for the first quality; good fair killing animals, 15c.@15½c.; medium 14c.@14½c.; common to poorest, 13½c.@11½c. Some "Christmas Bullocks," sold at 18c.@21c.... **Milch Cows** are in little demand at $45@$60 for poorest to common; $65 @$80 for fair to good; $90@$100 for superior or extra.... **Veal Calves** of superior quality are in demand at 13c. @14c. per lb. live weight; medium to inferior, 10c.@ 10c.... **Sheep and Lambs** have continued to arrive in large numbers (over 25,000 per week,) and prices have run very low. Present rates for sheep are, 5c.@7c. per lb. live weight for poor to very good. "Christmas Sheep" brought 8c.@10c. Lambs, ½c.@1c. above the same grades of sheep.... **Live Hogs** have come in less freely. The fall in barreled pork has kept prices very low, but they are looking up a little; latest sales, 7½c.@8¼c. per lb, live weight.

Containing a great variety of Items, including many good Hints and Suggestions which we throw into smaller type and condensed form, for want of space elsewhere.

Mark All Subscriptions sent in as *New*, or *Old*.

To Correspondents.—Just now, when everybody is sending subscription letters, we are receiving many notes of experience, hints, suggestions, inquiries, etc. This is well——nay, very desirable. Let them come without limit. But we must take time to read, digest, and use this mass of material; we only refer to the matter, to excuse any seeming, but not real, inattention.

Back Volumes Supplied.—The back volumes of the *Agriculturist* are very valuable. They contain information upon every topic connected with rural life, out-door and in-door, and the last ten volumes make up a very complete library. Each volume has a full index for ready reference to any desired topic. We have on hand, and print from stereotype plates as wanted, all the numbers and volumes for ten years past, beginning with 1857—that is, Vol. 16 to Vol. 25, inclusive. Any of these volumes sent complete (in numbers) at $1.75 each, post-paid, (or $1.50 if taken at the office). The volumes neatly bound, are supplied for $2 each, or $2.50 if to be sent by mail. Any single number of the past ten years will be supplied, post-paid, for 15 cents each.

Parsons & Co's. Sale of Grapes.—Messrs. Parson & Co., the well known nurserymen of Flushing, N. Y., have for two years held a trade sale of grape vines. They claim that the mere disposal of the vines, was not so much of an object to them, as to ascertain, by putting up a large number of vines at public sale, the state of the market and the estimation in which the different varieties are held. We attended the sale held on the 18th of Dec. last, and were surprised to find a company, not of vine buyers and planters, but one made up almost entirely of vine growers and dealers. People who should have gone to buy vines, stayed away, while those who had vines to sell and had curiosity to see how those of other people sold, attended in considerable numbers. As a consequence, but a small number of vines were sold, and those at low prices.

Of Small Consequence.—The Country Gentleman thinks that the appropriation of the literary property of another is a "*matter of small consequence.*" Is it though? Just wait awhile and see.

The American Dairymen's Association holds its Second Annual meeting at Utica, N. Y., January 9th and 10th. The meetings of the Associated Dairymen, for some years past, have been full of interest and profit to those attending. This flourishing Society was formed last year. Wm. H. Comstock is President, and Gardner B. Weeks, of Utica, Secretary.

Cornell University.—Hon. Andrew D. White, of Syracuse, has been chosen president. He is a graduate of Yale College, for some time filled a professorship in the University of Michigan, and has from its organization been a member of the Executive Committee of the University. It is an excellent appointment.

The N. Y. State Agricultural Society holds its annual meeting in Albany, February 13.

Illinois Horticultural Society.—The annual meeting was held at Champaigne, commencing Dec. 11. We were unable to be present, but have received from one of its prominent members the following summary:

On the present occasion the attendance at opening was larger than usual. The address of welcome was pleasantly offered by Mr. J. O. Cunningham, and was responded to by the President, Parker Earle, Esq., of South Pass, who gave a very agreeable address, filled with valuable suggestions for the guidance of his fellow members.

The reports of the Vice-presidents, from the various Congressional Districts, were then read. Some of these were quite encouraging as to the extent and results of horticultural operations. It was reported that at several points along the line of the Illinois Central Railroad, south of Centralia, there have been planted within a few years: 800,000 Peach Trees; 250,000 Apple Trees; 85,000 Pear Trees; 100 acres of Grape Vines; 825 acres of Strawberries; 75 acres of Raspberries, and that all of these kinds of fruits do well in that region. One gentleman stated that eighteen tons of strawberries had been shipped from a single station in one day, and it was estimated that in a few years, in a favorable season, a daily train of thirty or forty cars would be required for the transportation of the peach crop alone.

The bird question was brought up on the reading of the reports upon this subject, by committees appointed last year. This topic always excites a good deal of animated discussion. Fruit growers who suffer from the depredations of these creatures are becoming very jealous of their intrusion upon the privacy of the garden and orchard, and are hardly willing to acknowledge the services rendered by our feathered friends.

B. D. Walsh, of Rock Island, who ought to be the State Entomologist, delivered a very interesting popular lecture, illustrating the importance of a knowledge of entomology. He was listened to with marked attention.—Strong resolutions were adopted, urging the State Legislatures to act liberally in this matter, to appoint and pay State Entomologists to instruct the people by reports on injurious insects.—The members and all others were urged to sustain the *Practical Entomologist*, which is published in Philadelphia at a low price.—Much time was occupied by reports as to the *Status of Horticulture* in different sections of the State, and in revising the fruit lists.—Among the lectures read, was one by Hon. M. L. Dunlop, of Champaigne, who pointed out the great advantages which might be hoped for from the establishment of our great school, supported by the proceeds of the Congressional Land Grant.—The meeting closed with the feeling on the part of all, that the occasion had been one of profit and pleasure to those in attendance.

Mass. Agricultural College.—It is often a good thing that events happen which put a dead lock upon the proceedings of people in power, or those holding important trusts, and force them to *stop and think*. This has occurred to the Trustees of the Mass. Agricultural College, which body, unwieldy from its numbers and slow to act—its members disagreeing among themselves—has finally come to the point of stopping to think. Their president and also the president of the College, Hon. H. F. French, has resigned, Prof. Chadbourne of William's College has been appointed president; a first rate farmer, Levi Stockbridge, of Hadley, has been appointed farm-manager, and things look now as if beginning anew with more moderate ideas, the Institution might gain a healthy *growth*. A mistake too often made, is in attempting to create a great institution in a short time. Strength, vigor and sound vitality come with a gradual growth—as witness Rome and the Oak.—In the beginnings of our agricultural colleges and similar institutions, the error fallen into, has been in considering a grand building the most important thing. Set a number of earnest men, capable of teaching agriculture, down upon a good farm, with a good large house and barns upon it, and the co-operation of a good farmer; put up a few temporary buildings, if need be, for lecture rooms now, and perhaps for stables by and by; give the faculty a little money to spend upon books, apparatus and fitting up; let them know that they shall have more as fast as they can show results; let all permanent improvements be made with a view to the future; and leave the Faculty as unhampered in regard to matters of instruction and discipline as possible, and success of the most gratifying character will be almost certain in any State of the Union. The grand establishment, with all desirable surroundings, will come in good time, with that practical fitness of things to ends, which comes with gradual healthy growth.

Report of the Commissioner of Agriculture.—The opening of a new session of Congress last month was the occasion of the message from the President and reports from the Departments, and the report of "The Honorable" (what are titles worth?) Isaac Newton, Commissioner of Agriculture, comes also among them. This document has been extensively published by the daily press of the country, and we will here only call attention to the fact, that nothing of any importance has been done, with the exception of collecting and publishing statistics in regard to growing crops and the prospects, the wholesale distribution of seeds, (amounting to 992,000 packages,) and of plants (84,000,) with the reported "interesting and suggestive" operations of the experimental farm, where grains, etc., received from all over the world are tested. These, with the publication of the Annual Report, has cost $162,600.43, but how much real good is accomplished? Mr. Newton has sent away his best men. The chemist has been kept at work analysing copper, iron and silver ores, testing rhubarb wine and such things (for Mr. Newton's friends). The museum has grown, as it should, under the care of Mr. Glover; the garden improves year by year under Mr. Saunders: the farm is, we presume, in good hands, and the statistical department seems to have careful thought and labor. Mr. Newton has nothing to do with these things, except to make himself a nuisance, and interfere with their better operation, as he has with the able chemist, Dr. Erni, who, for faithfulness, has lost his position. Mr. Newton has kept his own place, though notoriously inefficient and a disgrace to the country, which has such an illiterate, thick-headed man in so responsible a place, simply by the diligent use of *means*—fruits to this Senator, flowers to the wife of another, delicacies to the White House, a sinecure clerk-ship to the lazy cousin of some one of influence, and so on.——Does agricultural education receive a thought from the Commissioner? Do the causes of the diseases which are so destructive to our animals? Hog-cholera has been among us for years, and is as yet uninvestigated; the Spanish fever threatens great damage to the cattle of our Western States; abortion in cows is on the increase at the East, and glanders and farcy are destroying thousands of horses. Why no word about these things? Does he concern himself with agricultural immigration, and the occupation of United States land under the Homestead Act? The instruction of immigrants? The projects of planting trees upon the prairies? The encouragement of emigration southward, to restock and cultivate the Southern States? and many such like things? Not he.—In his concluding sentence, Mr. Newton says, "he cannot repress the conviction that a new era is dawning upon the agriculture of our country."—May his own speedy retirement from office give force to the conviction.

Hog Cholera.—This pest grows worse and worse—its ravages have been the past year greater than ever before within our knowledge. Many a farmer's profits for the year have been swept away by the almost utter loss of his swine just maturing for the butcher. We know of no investigation of the disease by any really scientific veterinarian, and the quacks either disagree or follow the last published opinion. The anxious queries of multitudes of our correspondents, and the reports which burden the press, carry the conviction that something must be done by our General or State Governments to investigate and stay this plague if possible. The Prairie Farmer expresses the belief that the disease prevails in every county in Illinois, and over a large part of Kentucky, and our information is to the same effect.

Wire Fences.—J. Flanagin, Pawnee Co., Nebr. Wire fences answer very well after cattle are used to them, and if they are not inclined to be breachy. A fence with one rail at top and wire below is safer than all wire, although horses will get accustomed to this and jump it, as they will any wooden fence not too high. No animal likes to jump a wire fence, but they will learn to crowd it down. The use of living trees set as posts for wire fences is not new, and it works very well when plenty of ground can be given up to the rows of trees.

Don't Buy those Peach Trees.—"J. L. J.," Gallia Co., O., says, a peddler has been along with peach trees budded on a "*Persian Root*," asserting that insects will not kill the trees, they will bear fruit every year, and frost will not hurt the bloom. Now *one* of those good things would be enough for one root, but three such precious qualities is more than one root could have, and be anything less than Persian. Friend J. doubts the statement—as he evidently reads the papers—but he wishes his doubts confirmed. Suppose it were possible for a stock to confer such qualities, would you be likely to first hear of it through a peddler?—If you had such a stock, Mr. J., you could be the richest man in Ohio, and your country's benefactor at the same time. Some things are "too good to be true."

Above-ground Cellars.—"J. A. M.," Miami Co., Ind., asks for the experience of the readers of the *Agriculturist* in regard to buildings made with double walls, filled with saw-dust, and used as cellars.—We know that "bomb-proofs" made altogether above ground, by building up with logs and covering the structure with many feet of earth, make excellent cellars, and think a building walled with saw-dust, if thick enough and well roofed, would answer a good purpose. They certainly would if they contained ice houses in one end.

"Northern Coffee."—"J. R.," Southwick, Mass. This is just the old Chick Pea, *Cicer arietinum*, that in years past we have freely shown up when offered for sale as a new kind of "coffee." It is probable that it is as good as any of the substitutes. We cannot publish the offer of any one to send the seeds of anything free, unless assured that they have seeds by the ton, and a large force with nothing to do but put them up, for in our next issue we should be obliged to inform the public that the stock was long ago exhausted. Such offers are made in a liberal spirit, but it is kindness to refuse to publish them, though it may not seem so. We do not recollect a case, in which our giving such notice did not bring untold vexation to the one making the offer, and disappointment to thousands of unsupplied applicants. Every such offer through the *Agriculturist*, is seen by at least half a million people, and responded to by many thousands at least.

Doctors in Difficulties—Camellias, etc.—If one should write to a physician a hundred miles off "Doctor, I am sick, what shall I do?" he would perhaps get by return mail the advice, "get well."—Now, we get a great many letters that are no more definite than the one supposed above. As a sample: One writes that his Camellia is not doing well, is afraid he shall lose it, and asks what he shall do. How is it possible to answer? The only useful advice we can give is to send it to the nearest florist and let him take it in hand. The plant may be overwatered, may have been burned in the sun, it may want re-potting, it may have been injured, as Camellias too often are, by over-stimulating with manure; Scale may be all over it; there is no end of troubles the plant might have in the hands of one not used to plants.

Dahlias—Two Colors on One Plant.—J. Brushhurst, M. D., gives an account of a Dahlia with a light and dark flower on the same stalk, and asks if it is a common occurrence. We have had it happen a number of times with flowers that have dark petals tipped with a lighter color. Sometimes these colors split up as it were, and we had some flowers all of one, and others all of the other color. Dahlias are so constantly changing that no book, a few years old, would be of much use for varieties. The catalogues of the florists' made up every year, are the best guides as to colors, etc.

Beurré — How Pronounced.—"Querist" asks "Can the *American Agriculturist* tell us how to pronounce the word *beurre*, which forms part of the names of so many varieties of pears, as Beurré Diel, Beurre Superfin, Beurré Clairgeau, etc.? Leading fruit men differ, some calling it *bure*, others *bu-re*, others *bu-ra*, others *bu-re*, and still others *burr*. Some one proposed the question through the N. Y. Evening Post, which deals much in literary topics, but nobody has ventured an answer in that journal, and we must look to the 'authority' on all horticultural and agricultural matter, viz.: to the *Agriculturist*, to get the 'question settled.'"—Answer: The word *beurre* means butter-pear, and if one follows the French pronunciation it is *bur-ray*, as near as can be expressed in English spelling. We think, however, that most of our pomologists say *bu-ray*, which is Americanizing the word, and perhaps the next best thing to dropping it altogether. We cannot see why Clairgeau is not just as good a name to designate the pear as Beurré Clairgeau, and we hope that when our American Pomological Society convenes again this subject of names will have an overhauling. We put our own pronunciation to geographical names, and consider it affectation if one says Pah-ree for Paris—why not do the same with fruits.

Late Strawberries.—Several accounts have come to us of strawberries fruiting in autumn, and some sent us specimens. This is nothing new, nor is it at all desirable. A warm autumn will frequently start buds that should have kept quiet until spring, and the next season's crop will be so much the poorer.

Fruit in California.—At the State Fair last year, held at Sacramento, Cal., Mr. J. R. Nickerson, of Lincoln, exhibited 265 varieties of apples, 92 of pears, 30 of peaches, 12 of quinces, 240 of grapes, 5 of figs, 13 of prunes, besides blackberries and several other things. Mr. N., we make you our best pomological bow, and encourage you with the assurance that if you keep on thus, you will one day have a very choice collection of fruits.

A String of Flower Queries.—The following letter from a correspondent in Waltham, Mass., illustrates how questions pour in upon us. As this writer's queries are all in one line, the case is not so difficult, but it very often happens that we have as many in as many different departments. When the latter is the case, it rarely happens that more than one gets answered, as our editors live many miles apart: 1. Is there any hardy Evergreen climber suitable for a porch? Do any of the *Ivies* answer the demand—if so, which?—2. Why is not the common Sumach eligible as an ornamental shrub; yet no nursery has it? It is common—so is Maple—has it a further ailment?—3. Do double Portulacas seed, or must I buy more, annually?—4. Is Calystegia a desirable plant?—5. Must I say gladiolus or gladiolus?—6. Will any hardy rose flower in the garden perpetually through the summer?—7. Does any Lobelia retain the beauty of *cardinalis*?—8. And any Aquilegia the color of the *Canadensis*?—9. Why is not the Red lily, *Lilium Philadelphicum*, cultivated in gardens?—10. The seed catalogues give us the excellences, and not the faults of all the flowers.—*Answers.* (1) Only Ivy, which will not be hardy with you.—(2) It is. Nurserymen keep only those things for which there is a demand.—(3) They produce but very little seed.—(4) If you wish a task, just try to get the roots out, after it is once established. The vine and flower are pretty, and if you wish to grow it, sink a box or keg for the roots.—(5) That depends upon whether you want to use it as a botanical or common name. Gladiolus is the former, but popularly gladiolus is too well established, to hope to change it. We say Anemone and Anemone, for the Latin and English of the Wind-flower.—(6) No.—(7) Some have larger flowers, but none more brilliant.—(8) Not precisely.—(9) It is in several that we know of.—(10) Because they are catalogues, and not treatises.

Soap Inquiries.—We have a large batch of letters of inquiry about various soaps, and saponaceous preparations, advertised to "wash without rubbing," "labor-saving soaps," etc. These are nearly all answered in November, by the article on soap in general. Most of the advertised soaps do what is promised for them, but remember that anything that will dissolve out grease and filth quickly without rubbing, will also injure the fibers of the garments. The only safe soap is the common brown, or pale brown, which, on drying, does not contain any whitish or other deposit on the surface. That which shrinks greatly, contains too much water to be economical. The brown soaps, if not very dark, may be used for cotton and linen, but for woolen, use only the light colored or pale bar soap.—See November number, where the subject is fully discussed, except as to fancy soaps, and the like, which are reserved for a future chapter.

Flat or Lap Furrows.—An article in the *Agriculturist* recommending to turn furrows "flat as a floor," has provoked comment both among our subscribers and our exchanges and their correspondents. The subject is one which ought to be discussed. The writer long held to the value of lap-over flat-furrows in fall plowing, for two principal reasons, viz.: that they better drain or dry the land, and that they expose more soil to the weather during winter. In regard to these points we have changed our views, having seen it repeatedly demonstrated that the difference is not very great. Perhaps on tenacious clays on springy cold land, essential benefit might be found in lap furrows; on other land not. There are two other considerations, in fact three, which outweigh the above altogether in our mind: 1st, manure is much better covered; 2d, the land is left free from weeds, the sod is perfectly killed out of the way of the harrow, and in the best position to rot quickly and uniformly; 3d, by the action of frost alone, much fall plowed land is prepared for spring sowing of grass or grain. For grass or clover it needs no working over at all. For oats, barley or wheat, all that is necessary, is to harrow or bush in the seed, if sown broadcast, or otherwise, to go right on with the drill, and follow with the roller—this on good, common, loamy soils. We can point to a field plowed two years ago for corn, half with a lap furrow and half with a flat one, where the number of weeds and the labor of suppressing them on the lap furrowed part has been twice, if not three times, as great as on the other. And we can name farmers who once held strongly to the lap-furrows, but are now delighted with the working of their flat-furrow plows. They are not on heavy clays, but we think the principles named equally applicable to clay and sand as to loam, and especially so in spring plowing, to which the objections urged do not apply with the same force as to fall plowing.

Wash the Teeth at Night.—A few who inherit good teeth, and care nothing for "looks," neglect brushing their teeth; but none who study cleanliness and a sweet breath, or who wish to preserve their teeth, good or bad, as long as possible, should neglect to brush them well one or more times a day, with a brush so stiff as to clean them well, but not so hard as to wound and irritate the gums. They should be brushed both night and morning, but if only once, let it be done the last thing before retiring. Portions of food, sweets, etc., left on or between the teeth during the night, decay or acidify, and corrode the enamel, and thus gradually injure them. If the cavities between and in decaying teeth be thoroughly brushed out with water at night, and when rising, it will add years to their effective use and freedom from pain. Most of the tooth powders sold contain an injurious acid, which, though it gives the teeth a clean, white surface, does it at the expense of some of the natural surface. A little hard soap, pleasantly perfumed, is the best possible application. We would not recommend even the finest charcoal, or prepared chalk or clay, for though inert, they wear upon the enamel.

In Polishing or Washing Door Knobs, or other articles projecting from a painted surface, protect the paint by slipping over the articles a piece of stout pasteboard or cloth, having a hole or slit in the center large enough to slip it on.

Have you Plenty of Door Mats? Our observation is, that comparatively few housekeepers appreciate the economy of having plenty of mats at every outside door. The chief wear of carpets comes from sandy or gritty materials brought in on the boots or shoes. Uncarpeted floors are constantly soiled from the same source. Most persons keep but a single mat just inside, or outside of the door. It is far better to have two or three—one coarse, heavy one outside the door, at the bottom of the steps, another just against the door on the outside, and another finer one on the inside. Mats so placed will be a strong hint to careless, slovenly men and boys to wipe their feet clean. The cost is not much more for three mats thus used, for they will last nearly three times as long as a single one. Each fifty cents invested in mats will usually save ten times the amount in carpets, and in lessening labor and annoyance. Corn husks braided together make good home-made mats. Pieces of old carpets are far better than nothing. A good, cheap mat can be easily made by stitching two pieces of old carpet together and stuffing with a thin layer of hay or straw, knotting it through to keep the filling in place.

In Boiling Meats, never put them in cold water, but plump them into that which is boiling briskly. This will coagulate the albumen on the outside, close the pores, and prevent the water from soaking out the rich juices. If salted meats need freshening, let it be previously done with cold water, taking all needed time, with frequent changing of the water, if it is very salt.—Tough, cheap pieces of beef, can be made tender and palatable as follows: If salt, freshen as above. Put into the pot with a trifle more water than will be finally needed. Set into the top of the cooking pot a closely fitting tin pail or pan, and fill it with cold water. If this gets boiling hot, dip out some and add cold water from time to time. Boil the meat until it gets so entirely tender that the bones will drop out, even if it takes five or ten hours. The steam and aroma or flavor of the meat, will be condensed on the bottom of the covering pan or pail of water, and drop back, and thus be retained. When thoroughly done, remove the cover, and slowly simmer down thick enough to jelly when cold. Dip out the meat, remove the bones, place it in a pan, pour over it the boiled liquid, lay over it a large plate, or inverted tin platter, and put on 15 to 20 lb. weight. When cold, it will cut into nice slices, and if lean and fat or white meat be mixed, it will be beautifully marbled. The juice will jelly and compact it firmly together, and you will have nice juicy meat, good for breakfast, dinner or supper, and so tender that poor teeth can masticate it. Fresh beef, or corned beef well freshened in cold water, may be used in this way with decided economy, and it is far superior to meat boiled in an open vessel from which the flavor has constantly escaped, as you can perceive by the odor all through the house, if Bridget leaves the kitchen door open a minute or two, as she will certainly happen to do.

Cleaning Tripe.—In October, we referred to tripe as a wholesome, nutritious food, that should be more generally used, and gave some methods of preparing and cooking it. Edw. Partridge, of Waldo County, Me., sends his method of cleaning, which he thinks better than those described: "In removing the stomach, be careful to keep the outside clean. Shake the contents well out through a small hole, and put in a quantity of unslaked lime about the size of a coffee cup, with about 2 gallons of water. Place it in a tub of water and agitate 15 or 20 minutes, or until the lime is well slaked. A slight scraping will then remove the inside skin. The slaking lime takes out all odor, and makes the tripe nice and soft." After cutting up and washing well, it is ready for boiling, and may then be pickled in vinegar, or kept in salt water, to be changed daily and be cooked like souse, or broiled like steak, buttered and peppered; or be dipped in batter and fried.

Mush, or Hasty Pudding.—Salt the water sufficiently, and when boiling, stir into it sifted meal until two-thirds as thick as desired; then for the other third, use coarse wheat flour, and boil a few minutes, stirring all the time.—*Mrs. M. W., Agency City, Iowa.*—[The secret of making corn meal palatable, whether in puddings of any kind, or in cakes or corn bread, lies in cooking it thoroughly, we think. Whether pure meal, or part meal and flour, we advise to mix the hasty pudding very thin, and then cook it down by at least half an hour's boiling—an hour or more, improves it. While about it, always make a large quantity so as to be sure to have a full supply to slice up and fry for breakfast. It is economical, and is relished by almost everybody.—Ed.]

"Uncle Sam's Fried Cakes," (so-called because they were invented by our "Soldier Boy.") Take 1 quart flour, 2 tablespoonfuls shortening (butter or lard), 2 tablespoonfuls vinegar, 1 teaspoonful soda, 1 teaspoonful salt, and warm water enough to fit the dough for rolling.—*Emily C. Cook, Saratoga Co., N. Y.* [In this case the vinegar takes the usual place of cream of tartar to set the carbonic acid free from the soda. We suppose the other ingredients are first thoroughly mixed with the flour, and the vinegar afterward added with water.

Jersey Cow "Treasure."—We have received from T. A. Denison, of Hampden Co., Mass., a photograph of their family pet, a Jersey cow, of which he says: She is 5 years old, weighs 780 pounds, gives 16 quarts of milk per day at her best, and 6 quarts of milk yield 14 to 16 oz. of very hard, fine grained, high colored butter. One day's milk, 3 months before her time to calve, yielded 15 oz. of butter, when she had been giving milk more than a year. Twenty years' experience leads our correspondent to the conclusion that no breed equals the Jerseys in value as family cows.

A Great Rat Hunt.—"Rat Hunter" writes as follows: "An article in the *Agriculturist* on the subject of catching rats by ferrets, induces me to give the methods of destroying rats in Clinton Co., O. A rat hunt is decided upon—a meeting is called, and two 'captains' appointed, who choose their men alternately to any number they wish; the parties then appoint a committee of three to count the tails of the rats caught by both parties. A time is appointed for the hunt to close. Then the tails are all counted, the party having killed the least number, furnishes a free supper to both sides. A hunt of this kind was ended on the 25th Nov. at New Burlington, Ohio. Each of the sides killed over 6000 rats. A sumptuous supper was given on the evening of Nov. 29th, of which over two hundred ladies and gentlemen partook, and every thing passed off pleasantly. Let every community adopt the same plan, and there will be many rats destroyed, and few left for ferrets and patent rat traps."

Tall Buckwheat.—Wm. A. McCleary writes that he settled in the green woods, October, 1865, and after clearing a piece, raised among other crops, broom corn and buckwheat, last summer—the former grew 15 feet high, the buckwheat grew 7 feet 10 inches high, and yielded 28 bushels to the acre.

The Bee Periodicals.—Two Bee papers started in this country during the past season. One made a start *de novo*—the other revived and took a fresh start. Things did not seem to work quite rightly, or our hand and word of greeting would have been prompt and cordial. The Am. Bee Gazette, published in this city, departed this life a few weeks since; the Am. Bee Journal, of Washington, as "next of kin," inheriting its list of subscribers and worldly effects. We hope its excellent foreign department may be continued in the Journal. We have pleasure in commending the Journal to our readers, and wishing it merited success.

Beautiful Grape Leaves.—J. W. Hinks & Co., Bridgeport (Conn.) Nursery, sent us some leaves of Rogers' No. 19 grape, that were colored as beautifully as the autumn tinted leaves of the maple. They state that the foliage of several of Rogers' numbers does the same when it escapes early frosts. As far as we recollect, this peculiarity has not before been noticed.

Laurel Poisoning.—R. A. Holcomb writes, that when a lamb is poisoned by laurel, he takes a hard lump of fine salt—such as is usually to be found in a sack where the grains have caked together—as large as a walnut, puts it in the animal's mouth, and holds up the head until the salt is swallowed. For sheep and calves [illegible] more. He has tried many remedies, and considers this the simplest and most efficacious.

Heeling-in.—M. J. Skinner criticises the spelling of this word, and suggests that if it is derived from the saxon word *hele*, to cover or conceal, it should be spelt accordingly. We do not think the word has any such derivation; it is a short and convenient rendering of the old garden phrase, "laying-in-by-the-heels."

What may be Done with Small Garden Plots.—I. K. Jessup, of Staten Island, writes us, that upon an oval piece of ground, 14×177 feet, he raised 820 lbs. marrow squashes, 1 bushel tomatoes, 37 peppers, and 8 egg plants.

A Mechanical Plowman.—A few days since we were called upon to witness the operation of a contrivance, which we designate as a "mechanical plowman." The idea is not a new one. There have been other contrivances for holding and guiding the plow, and whether this one possesses merit sufficient to make it a success, the future must determine. We found a plow without handles, having a rather short beam fastened at the end into a sort of baby-carriage affair, consisting of an iron frame with adjusting screws set upon two little wheels, one of greater diameter than the other. The inventor is a German, and the plow was a common German one of modern construction, by no means superior to our good plows. Two horses were hitched close to the little carriage, and, the plow being on its side, the team was started in a patch from which Lima beans had just been removed and full of stubs of broken poles. The plow instantly righted itself, and laid a fair furrow, though the wheels had no furrow to guide them. The second time round it did perfectly good work. When it struck a stub it was partly thrown out or turned, but got at work again so quickly that one hardly noticed it. With a quick and strong jerk one might throw the plow out of the furrow, but it would get back again almost instantly. It was set to cut about 6 inches deep and 10 inches wide, and in steady going and even soil it did this, but the soil was variable, and on hard packed spots it inclined to run shallow, and where it was very mellow, it would go deeper. The depth and width of the furrows is very quickly and easily regulated by screws, and the set of the wheels is changed for different depths. The trial was made upon the farm of Mr. Breck, of New Durham, N. J., a thoroughly practical man and no way interested in the implement. He uses it in preference to good plows of his own, and, as he says, by a little practice he quickly gained facility in its management. Stones, he says, will throw it out or stop it; if thrown out, it sets itself again quicker than one held by hand, and if stopped, requires to be lifted or pulled back and eased over, as any plow would be. On the whole, the thing looks practical and handy. For a foreign-made article it is very light. Still, its strength has been well tested, and as we understand many will soon be made, we may expect to see it put to the test of hard and diverse usage. The inventor is Mr. F. Volkmann, who has U. S. Patents for the essential features. See advertisement. We can hardly over-estimate the importance of the invention, if made easily adaptable to our plows of different sizes, provided it proves practical.

Dahlia Roots.—"Subscriber"—Keep your Dahlia roots just as they come out of the ground, until spring. *Do not* pull the roots from the stem, unless you wish to destroy them. They must be kept attached until the buds are started in the spring, when they are separated in a way to give a root to each bud.

Club-Foot in Cabbage.—"Subscriber," Conn.—This is ascribed to an insect, or rather to a kind of centipede; plenty of lime in the soil is said to prevent it.

"**What can be Done** for formerly good land, now covered 3 or 4 feet deep with creek gravel?" is a question asked by an "Old Subscriber."

How to Thaw out Pumps or Water Pipes.—"The simplest way in the world."—We must repeat directions given, and repeated in years gone by. Procure a piece of india rubber pipe as long as any emergency will require. It should have a little less than a quarter of an inch bore, and walls thick enough to be quite stiff. Apply one end of this upon a common funnel, and run the other end into the water-pipe down as far as the ice. When hot water is poured in, the ice will melt before the end of the tube out of which it flows with great rapidity, and of course the tube must be pushed along down as fast as the ice melts.

Barometer in the House.—J. Mendenhall, Parke Co., Ind., asks, if the indications of the barometer are affected by the heat of the room in which it is placed. The heat expands the mercury, making it lighter, and in nice observations a correction for temperature is made. The difference is of no consequence when the barometer is observed merely as a weather indicator.

Acids and Alkalies—Poisons.—In November we gave a general article to explain to the unscientific reader the common terms "acids" and alkalies—mainly with reference to the article on "Soaps" following it. An incidental allusion was made to these substances as poisons, whereupon a hyper-critical correspondent of the Country Gentleman comes out with a column headed "dangerous advice," and garbles our remarks to sustain his anathemas. Let him go back and read, and then quote aright what we did say, viz., that if an acid is accidentally swallowed, "a strong solution of soap swallowed freely, is the best common remedy;" that is, one always at hand. That was the whole gist of our remarks, which were not intended to discuss poisons, and "Chemicus" will find it hard to create any sensation by his exclamation of "Dangerous Advice."—We may ere long give a chapter on poisons and their treatment.

Low Priced Sewing Machines.—A considerable variety of these have been offered, and the number is increasing. One sold under different names, for $5 by some, and for $10 by others, is a small affair, costing the dealers $2 to $2.50, and would be dear to any purchaser at 50 cents. We have examined most of the machines advertised, or offered by private circulars for $5 to $25, and have yet to find one that we would advise a friend to buy. A dozen or more of them have been refused admission to our columns. We saw a new one the other day which is simple, and with further improvement, it may come into practical use, but it is not yet tested enough, nor well enough manufactured, to be worth buying. One caution we advise our readers to heed, viz.: Never buy any sewing machines to be turned by hand—as most of these low-priced, but *dear*, machines are worked. We consider a table and a good pedal gearing to be worked by the foot, as *indispensable* to any useful sewing machine. Instead of purchasing any hand-worked machine, however cheap, it is better to reserve the money until it is increased by interest and otherwise to the cost of a good machine.——It would give us great pleasure to find a really practical effective machine retailed at $20 to $30; it would be a boon to multitudes of housekeepers; but we know of no such machine yet.

In Winding a Watch, always be careful to have the tube of the key thoroughly *clean*, picking out any lint gathered in from the pocket, and removing the smallest trace of dust in it. This is very important; the slightest particle of dust may fall in through the key hole and clog some of the delicate works. More watches are injured from this cause, and require frequent cleaning, than from all other reasons. A watch should never be wound or opened when dust is flying in the air, nor should it be opened with soiled fingers.——New watches, even of the best manufacture, require a year or so of wear to get all the parts smooth and in proper running order, so that a new watch can hardly be fully regulated to entirely accurate time the first year. The moving of the regulator when very near the right point, is so delicate an operation that a long time is required to adjust it exactly; one may sometimes *chance* to hit it on a first or second trial.

Hint to Watch Manufacturers.—From the great difficulty of regulating a watch exactly, referred to in the item above, we suggest to manufacturers, and inventors, the contrivance of some kind of screw, or other arrangement, by means of which a more slight change can be readily given to the length of the chain spring, than can now be made without the aid of the magnifying glass used by watch repairers. The screw on a clock pendulum is much more convenient than the index arm for regulating a watch. This hint is at the service of the American Watch Company, or of any one disposed to apply it.

Lime, Water and Fire.—S. W. Stewart, Newcastle Co., Delaware, had his barn set on fire during a heavy thunder storm. He wishes to know if the conflagration was probably due to the lightning, or to some lime that was stored there. As the barn had two good lightning rods, and as the lime was placed close to the side of the barn, where the rain could be blown through the cracks, we conclude that the lime, or rather the water, was in this case the incendiary. He thinks, that if it was due to the presence of the lime, the fact should be published for the benefit of others. We supposed it was generally known that lime, in combining with water, or in "slaking," as it is termed, evolved sufficient heat to set fire to wood and other combustibles. Only a few weeks ago, Doct. Grant, at Iona Island, had an experience of this kind. The Hudson made an unusual rise and overflowed his dock, on which was a shed having a considerable quantity of lime stored in it, and a conflagration was the result. It is not an unusual occurrence that vessels having lime as part of their cargo, are lost by fire. How small a quantity of lime will generate heat sufficient to set fire to wood, we cannot precisely state, but a few ounces will produce a glowing heat, and a pound will cook a beefsteak. It is better to lose the value of a few bushels of lime than to run any risks in storing it.

Basket Making.—W. B. Waldo suggests that some one who knows how to make willow baskets for farm use, should communicate such instructions through the *Agriculturist*, as will enable farmers who have osiers to make their own baskets. We heartily endorse this request. Who will respond?

The Indelible Pencil for marking clothing is much more convenient than ink, and equally good as to permanence—we judge after several months' trial.

Castile Soap.—"S. F. S." asks, if this could be home-made. It could be by an expert soap maker, but it would be found rather expensive. In the true article Olive oil is the only fatty material used.

Vinegar from Sorghum.—L. F. Miller, of Hardin Co., O., asks: "Will raw juice of sorghum make good vinegar?"—We have no experience, but to put the question in another form: May good vinegar be made from sorghum juice without evaporating? If so, how? The syrup is often used in making vinegar.

Large Poultry Establishment.—We are gratified to learn that a project is set on foot by honorable and responsible parties, well fitted for the undertaking, to test the question of the profit of a large poultry farm. It is proposed to lease the farm near New York, and attention will be given to raising pure breeds for sale, and also eggs and poultry for market. We think the success of this enterprise would put the trade in fancy poultry on a reliable basis.

Sliding or Balance Gates.—These gates made as described in the *Agriculturist* for June last, page 213, and in the number for November, 1864, p. 312, are so simple and excellent, that many of our readers have adopted them, and some are annoyed by persons who have patented "improvements" upon the principle which consist in swivel rollers of different patterns (we know of three.) The parties who sell these rollers, or the rights for their use, tell the public that their patent covers the use of the gate—which is not true. It only covers the rollers, which are, perhaps, an improvement for gates much used, but not for field gates opened no oftener than ordinary bars. We supposed that the principle of the gate itself was not patented until quite recently. Now it seems that it is one of those still-born patents which are given and not used—no effort being made to introduce it extensively. The Patentee is Ami C. Tell, of Galesburg, Ill., whose patent covers the principle. The fact that this principle is patent should discourage no one who wishes to use it. The roller Patentees, however, should themselves make terms for the use of the principle.

Potatoes in a Warm Cellar.—"J. W.," Rehoboth, Mass. No vegetables will keep well in a warm cellar, except sweet potatoes. The temperature should be as low as possible, and yet not freeze. A mild uniform temperature is better than a fluctuating one, averaging considerably lower. A cellar where the thermometer will stand between 40° and 40° in winter weather, will keep roots perfectly well. Keep the cellar well ventilated, the potatoes covered with straw, and watch the temperature to guard both against heat and cold.

Experience with Sorghum.—L. Grafton, of Pulaski Co., Ind., writes, giving his experience as a sorghum syrup boiler. He says that the old original black seeded sort makes the best molasses. The nicer it is stripped, the better, and green cane makes an inferior product. He appears not to hold strongly to the theory, that green cane makes sugar, while the ripe makes syrup. Cane cut when ripe, and worked up will make more syrup than if stored a while, but it improves the quality of the product to store the cane. He planted the White African cane on good black soil, and expected to make sugar. A small quantity cut early and boiled down, tasted salty. This was accounted for by its having been evaporated in a meat pot. A quantity of juice expressed with a light pressure, boiled down in an evaporating pan, had no such taste, but when a hard pressure was given, the syrup had the same "tang" again.

Arbor or Trellis.—G. T. Tanner, Bristol Co., Mass., has his vines planted, and asks if he shall put up an arbor or a trellis for them. A trellis by all means, as the vines have a much better exposure to light and air, are always accessible, and easily kept under control. If an arbor is needed for a screen, we would cover it with vines, but never build one on purpose for vines.

Do Weeds Emigrate with People? is the substance of a letter from a "Doubter." They do just as far as the people take the seeds of weeds along with them. The more civilized the people, the more agricultural and other seeds they would take from their old home, and would thus sow many weeds with their first crop. Besides, the seeds of weeds will be taken in the wool of sheep, in packing straw and other material, and in a hundred unthought of ways. Some seeds are carried by the winds, and others by streams, but the greater number are taken to a new country by human agency.

Tree Medicine.—We have in general terms expressed our opinion, that no medicine would help trees, —and have refused the advertisement of several of these tree medicines. We find the following in the Country Gentleman, of Nov. 22, in relation to one of these compounds: "J. D. Wisener, West Dresden, writes us as follows: P. S. Sheldon's patent composition for fruit trees has been tested in this vicinity, this season, on hundreds of trees. The result has been worse than failure, as it has killed quite a number of thrifty trees, and others are as good as dead. It was removed a few weeks after it was applied, or it would have been far worse for the trees. Wherever it washes down the tree, the bark dies and cracks open to the wood. There are also borers in the trees now."—The advertisement of this stuff was offered to us, and when its composition was made known, we refused to publish it, on the ground that we could not see how a well known poison could kill the borers, unless actually placed in their holes, and that injury might result from its use. The above shows that our view was correct, and all other persons having tree medicines for sale will please take notice. We have before us a circular of a "Patent Fruit Tree Invigorator," which does still more wonders, and makes "mineral gases," and "air gases" form a strong bud, besides a lot more of "gas" about keeping worms, curculios and borers from the tree.

Unnatural Grafting.—"Inquirer" takes exception to our statement, that a common chestnut will not be converted into a Spanish chestnut by grafting on the Horse-chestnut. He cites the grafting of the pear upon the Hawthorn as an instance of the union of plants as dissimilar as the Chestnut and the Horse-chestnut. The best advice we can give our friend is, to study the structure of plants a little, and he will not be so apt to be misled by similarity of names. He has seen somewhere a drawing of a Horse-chestnut stock prepared for grafting with the Chestnut. We can beat that; we have seen a drawing of a peach not only grafted on, but growing on a willow tree! The value of a drawing depends upon its source.

Death of Siebold.—Perhaps no one else has so largely contributed to our knowledge of Japan and its productions, as Philippe Francois de Siebold, who died at Munich, the 18th of Oct. last, at about the age of 70. He accompanied the expedition sent by the Dutch Government to Japan about the year 1823, and resided there for a number of years, in the enjoyment of peculiar facilities for acquiring information about the country and for procuring plants. Of late years, introductions from Japan have been numerous, but horticulturists must ever be indebted to Siebold for some of their choicest plants.

Salt as a Manure.—"The reason why salt acts as a manure," says the N. Y. Tribune, "is because it contains much of the quality of unleached ashes." Shade of Solon!—Takedst thou thy mantle with thee when thou wentest at novel writing?—In the same way a stone quarry 'contains much of the quality of' a brick meeting house. Salt contains soda; ashes contain potash. Potash and soda are about as much alike, being alkalies, as brick and stone. Ashes are alkaline, salt is not. Soluble potash (contained in ashes) is a rare, yet very desirable substance in most soils; soda (contained in salt) exists in abundance—more than the plants need. The uses of salt in agriculture are more discussed and less understood than almost every thing else. Its action may be beneficial, or the reverse, and it is often neutral.

Long Keeping Squashes.—H. L. Loomis, Westfield, Mass., writes, that a squash, a cross of the Hubbard with some other, raised in 1865, kept sound until the middle of Nov., 1866, and asks if we ever before knew a squash to keep 15 months. We have frequently known the old Winter Crookneck to keep until the same kind was ripe again, a year at least.

Coal Tar and Rats.—A. Ransom, of Ulster Co., N. Y., says that rats dislike coal tar very much, and that he is in the habit of daubing it about their holes and runs, with good results. Taking the hint from the suggestion to dip rats in red paint, he proposes to dip some in coal tar and let them go. Mr. Gilbert J. Green, says: "Coal tar, mixed with sand, to the consistency of thick mortar, is an effectual stopper to rat holes. The process is not patented, and a sure cure is warranted."

Wonderful Phenomena.—Accounts of phenomena are frequently sent to us for an explanation, which, as they are related, are inexplicable. Many persons, who would not for any consideration misrepresent a thing, are simply inaccurate observers. For instance, we have an account of a quince found two and a half feet below the surface of a gravel bed. The quince "had all the appearance of stone" when broken to get out the seeds, which were planted and grew. It is assumed that this was a petrified quince, and we are asked, "how long would a quince lie buried before it would petrify, and how long would the seeds lie in it and come out in a condition to germinate." In an ordinary gravel bed it is not probable that a quince would ever *petrify*, and no one can tell how long seeds will retain their vitality when buried below the influences that induce germination. Had this been a really *petrified* quince, containing living seeds, it would be very strange, but the probabilities are all against its being such, and the buried quince ceases to be wonderful.... Another remarkable instance is cited, of a Black Currant bush, in the crotch of a pear tree, where it grew and produced fruit for many years. To decide whether this presents anything out of the ordinary course of things, one must examine what is the real relation between the two. The crotch of the pear tree may have formed a convenient depression to retain dust, decayed leaves, etc., and thus form a soil for the bush; the case would then be no more strange than if it grew in a flower pot. We notice, almost every season, Ailanthus trees, two feet or more high, growing upon the stone window caps of buildings in New York City. Some plants, if shaded, will get along with an astonishingly small amount of soil, and the Ailanthus finds enough in the dust of the crevices of a stone or brick building to allow it to make a vigorous growth. A good observer puts objects through as searching a cross-questioning as a good lawyer does a witness. Every child should be taught some branch of natural science, if for no other purpose than to teach him how to observe accurately. The lack of this power gives rise to a large proportion of the wonderful stories that are spread abroad and handed down in print and by tradition.

Is Snow a Fertilizer?—"Farmer," of Sullivan Co., N. Y., writes: "I have frequently heard it said that snow is very beneficial to land, and hence it is sometimes called the 'poor man's manure.' Although this is a commonly received opinion, I have hitherto failed to meet with any one who could explain it upon philosophical principles, and have been led to doubt the truth of the assertion. Why is it said to be so?"—*Answer.*—Snow absorbs from the atmosphere very considerable quantities of ammonia, which is especially abundant in the air near cities, as it is set free from coal and other fuel. It is a warm covering, protecting the plants covered by it, especially such as the grasses and winter grains, from the unfavorable action of frost, for it matters little how deeply the ground is frozen, a good bed of snow lying upon it several weeks will thaw it all, and even permit a growth of grain and grass to take place under it. When it melts, the soil has the benefit of the ammonia, and any fertilizing dust that the snow may have caught, and the snow-water besides contains much oxygen—hence the effects are like those of manure, and the reason for the popular judgment, which is quite right.

F. P. Pea.—Seedsmen and all others will please take notice. In August last, we published a note from a valued correspondent, to the effect that Carter's First Crop Pea, was a late one. Our friend, by some mistake, had got the wrong sort. In September, pages 311 and 314, we gave testimony on the other side. These last articles seem to have been overlooked, as we still get many notes from Seedsmen and others, on the matter. Now, be it understood that, as far as evidence can go, Carter's First Crop Pea is a first-rate thing, and please don't write us any more about that particular pea.

Difficult to Answer.—W. L. Lent, Seneca Co., Ohio, asks: "Can grapes or Osage Orange be grown on a clay side-hill, from which the surface soil has been removed by grading?"—Generally, no; but there are some kinds of drift, often called clay, that are good grape lands. It is a local question, and difficult to answer.

Lime Water and Cream of Lime.—"L. R. V."—Lime water is a saturated solution of lime. Lime is very little soluble in water, one part requiring about 700 parts of water. A quantity of slacked lime is put into a tight vessel of water and stirred up, and after the undissolved portion has settled, the clear liquid is poured off. Cream of lime, or milk of lime, is water with enough undissolved lime in it to make a thick mixture.

Pelargonium will not Bloom.—"S. F. S.," Setauket, L. I. One of the difficult cases to answer, as you do not say whether it is in a dwelling or green-house. In either case pelargoniums need to be kept rather dry and cool until towards spring, and then be started into growth by plenty of heat, light and water.

Hubbard Squash.—"Staten Island."—This variety will sometimes come splashed with orange colored spots, and be in all other respects like the clay-colored. One of the distinctive characters of the Hubbard is its very hard shell.

Insect on Plums and Cherries.—G. Tullar, Oswego Co., N. Y. The insect that destroys your plums and cherries is the Curculio, which is able to fly as well as to climb. Any invention for preventing its ascending trees will therefore be of little use.

Snails in the Cellar.—J. W. Halloway, Macon County, Ill., finds that a toad kept in a cellar where snails are troublesome, soon disposes of them.—Another writes that he has found a land tortoise or terrapin to perform the same service.

Salt the Slugs and Snails.—J. S. Swain, of Jacksonville, Fla., says, salt sprinkled freely in the haunts of snails and slugs in the cellar, is a perfect bane to them. He has tried it with success.

Another Agriculturist Editor.—We have an announcement to make which will doubtless gratify our readers, as it does ourselves. It has been the policy of the Publishers of this journal to secure the best possible Editorial aid to be obtained, at whatever cost, and the result has justified the policy. One man, of even moderate ability and experience only, may collect enough readable matter *of some kind* to fill up a weekly sheet; but to prepare a thorough-going journal, varied in its matter, pruned of superfluous words and sentences and full of condensed thought, reliable in all its teachings, and treating on subjects so multitudinous as are embraced in the labors of the Farm, Garden, and Household, there is needed the combined thought, experience, and observation of a considerable number of first class men—the more the better. If every page or two has the entire thought and investigation of one such man, the paper must certainly be far superior to what it would be if only one man spread his thoughts and repeated himself over twenty or thirty pages each month.....While the *Agriculturist* will continue to have the editorial labors of our Associates, Messrs. THURBER, WELD, HARRIS, FITCH, and others, who have done so much to make the paper what it has been, we have at length prevailed upon Rev. Wm. CLIFT to join our Editorial Corps, and he will enter upon his duties here soon after the present number goes to press. Mr. Clift became widely and very favorably known by his "Carriage Views of Farming," and other valuble contributions to the press, some twenty years ago, and he has given us occasional editorial aid during the past fifteen years; but his practical labors as a cultivator, his pastoral and other public duties, and the care of the extensive Woodlawn Cemetery, of which he has been Comptroller or Superintendent for some time past, have left him little time to devote to his pen. In the wide and influential field upon which he now enters, he will doubtless do good service to the country.—PUBLISHERS.]

Capital, Reliable Advertisements fill all the space we can spare to that department. Many more good parties, late comers, wanted room which we could not give, and a multitude was shut out under our rules, which exclude all secret and deceptive things, and require evidence that the advertiser *has both the intention and ability to do what he promises.* It is a good time to study these business columns well, and find out what is for sale, by whom, and make arrangements for the spring stock of needed implements, etc., and the other things wanted now. It will please the advertisers, if in writing, to them for catalogues, or circulars, or sending orders, they are informed *where* their advertisements were seen. They like to know where they find the largest number of wide-awake, enterprising readers. One man tells us that last year he advertised in just 320 papers, received 2900 orders, and that he knows that over 2100 of them came from the *Agriculturist* readers.—Another says he set aside just $10,000 for advertising, and that the $600 paid the *Agriculturist* brought him more good business than the $9,400 paid elsewhere. Many others talk in the same way.

Special to Advertisers.—Our new advertising terms are announced in the proper place. A little advance is made, but not so much as the increased circulation would really warrant. Our basis for ordinary advertisements is, one cent, *or less* per line for each thousand subscribers, as we expect to print 150,000 to 200,000 or more copies the present year. The subscriptions so far are 80 per cent above the same period last year. If this ratio continues a little while longer, we shall exceed 200,000. Based on circulation alone, our terms are the cheapest in the world, to say nothing of the fact that our advertisements are select, and are trusted by the reader; that they are before the reader a month at least; and that they are beautifully printed on small pages and are thus easily seen.——To merely print 150,000 cards containing 5 square inches of reading matter, would cost at least $600. To print that card in this paper, and have a copy sent into 150,000 families, *one in a place*, costs less than $60. At our old terms the advertising would not pay much more than the expense of the paper they are printed on, as any one acquainted with the cost of such paper can readily calculate. (See note on "Capital Advertisements" above.)

"Proper Bad."—A "Rural" paper, published not a thousand miles from Rochester, annually, about the close of its subscription year, makes itself ridiculous and annoys its readers, by a billious overflow toward the *Agriculturist* and one or two other journals. This year its groans indicate almost expiring agonies. Its latest special cause of complaint arises from the fact that some extra copies of the *Agriculturist* were sent into half a dozen towns in Western New York, where the Genesee Farmer, which we purchased, formerly circulated. We guarantee that neither the Mail clerk, nor his employers, when sending those papers, had the least thought of "disturbing" or "displacing" the "Rural." They have too much compassion for their Weakly friend. They were not thinking of him at all, or they would have remembered that he had a mortgage on, owned, and possessed, all the farmers of Western New York, or claims to.——But why is he so disturbed at the apparition of an extra copy or two of our beautiful sheet in that region, where thousands of copies go regularly! Oh! we see.—One of his scattered subscribers by chance saw our paper. Is he so afraid of the *comparison?* Perhaps his conscience troubled him lest that subscriber should see how extensively the Rural has copied from our paper and books—transferring our beautiful and costly original engravings, and ideas, without a word of credit.——Pray, keep cool, friend Rural; we will sin as little as possible, though it is hard to suppress the wish to let *your* readers occasionally see a real, live, finished, *original paper*, that has had a whole month's work of preparation, and is not hastily thrown together and illustrated with borrowed or stolen engravings. If you don't stop scolding, you will get down toward a par with your competing "Rural" whose editor will fume at us until he dies, because we wont notice him, wont advertise for him, or exchange with him, and because we once showed up his sales of patent "Beehives" without any patent, and his selling the address of young ladies for sixpence each. Harris Brothers' "gift enterprise" is helping that "Rural" to subscribers. Pray don't get down to its level.

"Tim Bunker."—Old readers of the *Agriculturist* will be glad to know that a spicy letter from our old friend, of racy, practical, homely wit and wisdom—Timothy Bunker, Esq., of Hookertown, Conn.—is in type for our next number. 'Squire Bunker has been so much occupied of late, that it has interfered with the claims which readers of the *Agriculturist* seem to have upon him. We can now congratulate our readers on the promise of a letter from him every month or two.

Copeland's Country Life.—When the new and enlarged edition of this work appeared, we recommended it as a useful encyclopædia of rural affairs. A further examination of the book has resulted in our purchasing it and adding it to our list of standard publications. There is scarcely a topic relating to the management of gardens, green-houses, orchards, and all the matters pertaining to small farms and country places, that is not intelligently and pleasantly treated. It does not profess to be a work upon agriculture proper, but it is one that will meet the wants of a large class who live in the country. We do not mean to say that it would not be useful to the farmer, for it would be, in teaching him how to give his home pleasant surroundings. The work is abundantly and well illustrated. A new issue is now ready, on fine paper, in beveled boards—912 pages. Price $5.00. Sent by mail post-paid.

The American Gardener's Assistant.—By Thomas Bridgeman. New Edition, Revised, Enlarged and Illustrated, by S. Edwards Todd. New York: William Wood & Co. The work of Mr. Bridgeman first appeared many years ago, and was in its day a standard authority. The name is an honored one in American horticulture, and when a new edition of his work came to hand, we felt glad that the "Gardener's Assistant" still lived. Upon looking over the volume, we found illustrations taken boldly and bodily from the *Agriculturist*, and from books of which we hold the copyright. We were astonished to find that honorable dealers, like William Wood & Co., had thus taken the property of others. Our astonishment was at an end when we turned to the title page, and found by whom the work was revised. A committee of twelve men may decide on this matter of illustrations, and we will turn to the literary portion of the work. We doubt if so many blunders were ever before enclosed in one cover, and one hardly knows where to begin to notice a work, claiming to be "revised," in which old errors, thought to be truths in their time, are so mingled with modern blunders. As a specimen of the recklessness with which names are handled, we are told under Cabbage, p. 53, "The *Brassica rapa*, or Turnip-Cabbage, produces its bulb or protuberance," etc., and on page 186 we have *Brassica rapa*, given as the name of the Turnip.—The "reviser" is even less at home among fruits than he is among vegetables, and the article on the grape is of about as much use in the present state of grape culture, as an almanac of thirty years ago. As a matter of curiosity, we copy the names of the grapes treated of. We first have, on page 103, a "Select Descriptive List of Native Grapes," which gives notes on Alexander, Blond, Carolina Perfumed, Catawba, Cunningham, Elsinburgh, Hides Eliza, Isabella, Lufborough, Maddox, Norton's Virginia, Pond's Seedling, Scuppernong, Warren and Woodson. A "*select*" list truly! Evidently pleased with the amusement of making grape lists, the "reviser" gives us a few pages further on another (p. 111) "Select Descriptive List of Native Grapes," in which we have this time Diana, Gilbert's White Shonga, Lenoir, Missouri, Ohio, Shurtleff's Seedling, Uchee Grape, and White Scuppernong. The pears present a most melancholy array of antiquated varieties, with a number of illustrations, only one of which is referred to in the text. The list of strawberries gives some twenty-four varieties, not one-fourth of which are now extant; the Wilson, Triomphe de Gand, Scott's Seedling and Trolloppe's Victoria are represented by bad engravings, but not a word is said of them. The flowers are still worse managed, as witness the Dahlia, in which a gentleman who has been dead a number of years, is quoted as if he had given recent information. It were a waste of time and space to point out the errors of omission and commission in a work, that in competent hands, might have been made valuable. The heirs of Mr. Bridgeman must indeed feel chagrined to see their name connected with such a jumble, and certainly must feel that an alteration is not always an improvement.

The Agriculturist Book Department.—A few years ago, in response to their oft-repeated requests, the Publisher commenced supplying his subscribers with such books as they desired, sending them by mail, post-paid, without additional charge. The retiring of C. M. Saxton & Co., who were the leading agricultural Book Publishers, cut off the supply of many books, and it became necessary for Mr. Judd to issue some of these books in order to meet his engagements to furnish them. Subsequently, at the urgent request of many booksellers, and others, Mr. Judd purchased all the plates, rights to publish, etc., previously owned by Messrs. Saxton & Co., and increased the stock by other purchases, until he had control of a very large proportion of all the Agricultural and Horticultural books published in this country. A careful weeding was made, and more than half of the books were condemned, and their stereotype plates consigned to the melting pot, where it could be done without infringing upon the vested right of authors. Mr. Chase, an experienced Boston publisher, was associated in the business, so that there should be no lack of business and editorial attention to the *Agriculturist*, but *rather* greater efficiency secured.——The Firm, and all associated with them, are ambitious to have the credit of supplying *good* books. With the large editorial power employed upon the *Agriculturist*, good old books are being revised, and first rate new books, edited with the same care that is expended upon the *Agriculturist*, are being constantly prepared. The field is an extensive one. Cultivators of the soil are waking up more and more to the importance of studying their business in all its bearings, and to meet the demand for good reliable Books, Pamphlets, Annuals, etc., is an important work. The Publishers say in their circular, that "they aim to exercise so much care that their imprint upon any book shall be a guarantee of its value." The *Agriculturist* is entirely independent in its sphere, though its issue by the same publishers gives it additional resources, financial and otherwise, so that this business connection makes it possible to furnish it to subscribers at a lower rate than could be done without this aid. Those who understand the matter, will readily see that the subscription money paid cannot of itself cover the cost of supplying such a paper.

Sundry Humbugs.—Our letters, for four weeks past, describe 85 individuals, or firms, engaged in 14 different modes of swindling, or of corrupting morals. An analysis, and somewhat detailed exposure, is prepared, but we have not room for it this month. Several of these parties are consigned to the magistrates or policemen. The writers of over 200 letters, now before us, will please understand that those who have inquired about reliable parties will be answered by mail; all not thus answered may put down the parties inquired about, either as swindlers, or as being under investigation to be reported upon hereafter.——While waiting room to speak more particularly, we advise our readers to beware of all tempting offers coming by circular through the mails; of all gift enterprises, however sugar-coated by pretending to aid soldiers and their orphans, or needy artists; of all watch and jewelry tickets; of Gold and Silver Mining Companies; of recipes for washing, ink, vinegar, honey, etc.; of applications for catalogues of Female Seminaries, and lists of names of farmers and others; of low-priced sewing machines (see item elsewhere); of cheap burning fluids; of map publishers asking money for something to be issued hereafter; of wonderful new discoveries where money is to be sent; etc., etc.——Please continue to report to us all new schemes, as soon as they appear.

2,000 Good Words.—Our Assistant who receives, examines, and sorts the large number of newspapers regularly received, says that during the past year alone, more than two thousand different editorial notices have appeared in these journals, strongly commending the *Agriculturist*. Our space is too valuable to allow repeating such notices.

The Prairie Wolf.

This animal (*Canis latrans*) which is found upon the Prairies of the West, from Mexico to as far north as lat. 55°, is the type in this country of the Jackal of the Eastern world, both in appearance and habits. Although naturalists differ on the subject, it is the generally received opinion that he is the same animal as the Mexican Coyote. In size, he is a medium between the common Red Fox and the ordinary Wolf. His head is shaped more like the former animal, having its long and sharp muzzle, while the whole form of his body is more that of the Wolf, and his tail, which is bushy and tapering, and his coarse hair, are unmistakably those of the latter. He is from 36 to 40, or 42 inches in length of body, with a tail some 16 or 18 inches long. In color he is usually of a dull, yellowish gray on the back and sides, sprinkled or clouded with black, the belly and inside of the limbs being white. His ears are large and triangular, always held in an erect position, and almost entirely coated with hair. He has four toes on each foot, besides a sharp claw on the inside of the fore-foot, about two inches above the sole, and attached to the rudimentary toe, corresponding to the thumb. He has a sharp, snapping bark, which gives him the name, among the dwellers upon the prairies, of the "Barking Wolf." They live and breed in burrows, and have their young in April. They are very prolific, sometimes bringing forth 10 or more at a birth, and not often less than 8. They are very fleet of foot, more so than the ordinary Wolf, and hunt in packs, hanging on the outskirts of the herds of buffalo, on the lookout for stragglers, aged, halt, and maimed. Though small, they are a most terrible enemy when combined, and attacking in numbers. They will follow up a company of hunters for days, and loiter around their camps for the refuse of their game, of which they get quantities, as your true buffalo hunter only cares for the hump, tongue, marrow-bones, and skin. They are afraid of man, and rarely, if ever, injure the hunter or his horses, although stealing into a still camp at night, they often cause the latter to stampede. The male is an excellent watchman, for he no sooner detects their neighborhood by his keen scent, than he gives vent to his own, peculiar, musical bray, and stands like a well-bred game dog, head and tail erect, and nose pointed in the direction of his enemy. The hunter then looks out for the safety of his game or provisions, for the little thieves are as expert as the New York pickpockets, and will appropriate his most precious morsels. They are killed for their skins, which, however, are not very valuable, and are used to fill up the scanty load of some not over-successful trader.

PRAIRIE WOLF OR COYOTE.—(*Canis latrans.*)

The Red Fox.—(*Vulpes fulvus.*)

Closely allied to the wolf and the dog, is the Fox, of which there are several distinct species in this country, and among these there exists a great tendency to varieties. The skins of the common red fox show diverse shades, some being very dark, (indeed there are those called black;) others have a more or less distinctly marked cross, a stripe down the back and across the shoulders. The usual color is bright reddish brown, most intense along the saddle and shoulders. The face is nearly black, as are also the flanks; and the feet are black in front, the color extending up on the outside of the thighs. The under jaw, the edges of the upper jaw, and the throat are white, and this color extends more or less upon the belly. The brush is rendered dark by many long black hairs, occurring among the reddish ones, which are more abundant and shorter. In the darker varieties of the fox the brush is often white tipped. The head and body measure 27 to 30 inches usually, and the tail to the tips of the hairs about 15 to 17 inches. They rarely attain a weight of 15 pounds, and 8 to 10 pounds is the usual weight. The young are littered in March or April, 4 to 6 in a nest. As the old one has these to provide for just when field mice and birds are least abundant, foxes are then boldest in their attacks upon poultry, and will even attack young lambs. We think, however, that lamb is not a favorite diet by any means, and that rats, mice, and small birds and eggs are much preferred to poultry of any kind—we are willing to give the little rascals credit for all the good they do. Their habits, their great degree of sly intelligence and reasoning powers, are well known. They are active throughout the winter, and lives in burrows. In trapping the fox, to destroy the smell of iron, the trap should be smeared with fresh blood, or heated and covered with bees-wax, then set near their haunts, covered with light earth, or ashes, and fastened to a clog of 8 or 10 lbs. The surface all around should wear a natural look. Scraps of fried meat and honey may be distributed around the bed, but not on the trap, and no foot prints should be seen near. The genital organs of the female fox, or dog in heat, preserved in alcohol and smeared upon some object near the trap, will be most alluring. A fox will be very likely to follow a trail of bloody meat to the trap.

Walks and Talks on the Farm.—No. 37.

I notice from the papers that the receipts of sheep and pigs in New York are now greater than ever before, and prices have fallen a little. The best sheep only bring about 6 cts. per lb., live weight, and hundreds of poor sheep are sold as low as $3.00a$4.00 a head. It seems a pity to send such sheep to a distant market. After deducting the cost of transportation and other expenses, the prices received by the farmer must be very low. It costs no more to send a sheep to market that will bring $8.00, than one that is slow of sale at $3.00. If the expenses are a dollar a head, the farmer would get $2.00 in one case, and $7.00 in the other.

Pork will probably be lower for a few weeks. The failure of the corn crop will induce many farmers to dispose of their hogs before they are fat. The receipts will be very large, and for the time being, will depress the market. But it seems to me that after the first rush of half-fat pigs is over, it will be found that good, well-fed hogs are scarce, and the demand will be large enough to insure a fair price for the corn they have consumed. After severe cold weather sets in, however, pigs will not fat rapidly. The increase of weight alone, will hardly pay for the food. The profit of keeping them, if there is any, will be from the increase in price. With warm, comfortable pens, hogs, as a general rule, can be kept until after Christmas with advantage, on account of the advance in pork. But in a cold, dirty pen, they will eat a good deal of corn, and do little more than hold their own.

It is not half as interesting now to talk about pigs as it was last September, when our Rochester butchers were eager to buy them at 14 and 15 cents a lb. They are now a drug at 10 cents, and some have been sold as low as 8 cents. The city papers are rejoicing over the decline in prices. They *were* too high, perhaps. But to attribute high prices solely to the "speculators" is absurd. The speculators do not create the scarcity, they only avail themselves of it and buy for a rise. If it proves that there is no scarcity, they are—ruined. But if there is an actual scarcity, they are really public benefactors, as by storing away the food until it is wanted, and thus forcing up prices in the meantime, they check consumption. If prices remained low, much more would be consumed, and in the end the scarcity would be greater.

It may be that farmers, tempted by high prices, have raised too many hogs, and that they must sell them at a loss. Certain it is, that with corn worth $1.25 a bushel, there is little profit in fattening hogs at 8 cents a lb. It is a good hog that, with ordinary treatment, will give 7 lbs. of pork for a bushel of corn. Fed in a rail pen, cob and all, among the mud, it doubtless takes much more, especially in cold weather. The other day I wanted a new India rubber tube for my steamer, and a few lbs. of castings. The bill was $5.75. Now, with corn at $1.25 per bushel and pork at 8 cents a lb., how long, at the above estimate, will it take me to pay this bill out of the profits? I heard a farmer say last fall that "it took three bushels of potatoes to buy a pair of baby's shoes!"

With all the drawbacks in our business, I have no reason to complain. Farming is as pleasant and profitable as I expected—especially the former. Those who complain that the farmers charge such high prices do not understand what they are talking about. If our city friends will practice as close economy as the farmer is compelled to do, they will be able to pay him remunerative prices for his products. He asks nothing more. And when the farmer prospers, other business prospers too.

The great trouble with farmers is, that they do not cultivate their land as well as they might. One reason of this has been the low price of produce. And now that we are getting good prices, the land is in such a poor state that too many farmers have nothing to sell. I know a farmer who had six acres of Peach Blow potatoes, which yielded him 250 bushels, all told. This was not owing to the rot, or to a bad season, but solely to poor farming, past and present. The land has never been manured, and the potatoes this year were not half cultivated. He works the farm "on shares." The profits, both to the owner and farmer, will not be exorbitant even if the potatoes bring $1.00 a bushel. But if, on the other hand, the crop had been, as it might, 200 bushels per acre—say 1200 bushels, the *extra* yield at this price, would have paid for a little manure, and a good deal of cultivating. And this was all that was needed.

Working land on shares seems to be a poor business for both parties. It is to the interest of the tenant to spend as little for extra labor as possible, because the owner of the land gets half the benefit without bearing any of the cost. When the country was new and the land rich, a man could perhaps afford to give half the products, as he could get fair crops with little labor. But now that the land is more or less "run down," and it is necessary to build it up with manure and good culture, it is impossible for a man to expend the necessary labor and give half the produce for rent. It may be done for a year or two on land in high condition, but the farm must inevitably deteriorate under the system. A man might afford to rent a grass farm on shares, but not an arable farm. It is difficult to take one of our ordinary "run down" farms and raise enough from them, for a few years, to pay the cost of labor and support the teams, from the *whole* of the produce!

"What, then, is the value of a run-down farm?" Not much, these times. It would be cheaper, so far as immediate profit is concerned, to pay $100 an acre for a farm in high condition, with good buildings and fences, than to accept as a gift one of these run-down farms. It is time this matter was understood, so that those uneasy mortals who are always expecting to sell, and consequently make no efforts to keep up and improve their land, should be compelled to turn over a new leaf, or else dispose of their farms at a low figure.

The advance of farm lands has been greater in the dairy regions than in any other districts of the State—certainly far more than in the wheat growing sections of Western New York. Dairy farms in Herkimer County have changed hands at two hundred dollars an acre. And yet I have always supposed that one acre of our land was worth two of their's. Farms can be had in this section at $100 per acre—and dear enough at that! The high rates of wages and other expenses of managing an arable farm do not affect the farmers in the grass growing districts as much as they do us. We should learn from this fact, not to cultivate so much land, but to let a larger proportion lie in grass. This would reduce expenses, and yet give us heavier crops of grain. It is the one lesson which the history of agriculture clearly teaches.

We must, however, improve our grass land. Most of our pastures consist of low land, which produces little except coarse grass of very inferior quality. Nothing can be done with such land until it is drained. But if we would drain our upland, we should in many cases cut off the springs which feed the low land, and then a few surface ditches would be all that is needed to make these low pastures dry and productive.

The upland pastures must be top-dressed with manure. I am inclined to think that, for immediate effect, we can use our manure on grass land to greater advantage than in plowing it under for corn. I think I related before, that last fall I drew out some manure on an old upland timothy meadow that we intended to plow up in the spring for corn. The year before we mowed it, and the grass was hardly worth cutting. In the spring, however, I found we should hardly be able to manage so much corn ground, and abandoned the idea of breaking up this meadow. Well, we pastured the field, and you would have been astonished at the effect of the top-dressing of manure. As far as the manure went, the grass assumed a dark green hue, thickened at the bottom, and must have afforded three times as much feed as the other portion. The cows stayed pretty much all the time on the manured land, and evidently liked the grass.

The timothy on the unmanured portion was light, but what there was of it the cattle did not eat, and it went to seed, while the other portion was eaten close and gave a green succulent bite all through the season. I am fattening about 200 sheep, a dozen head or so of cattle, with ten milch cows, and some sixty head of pigs, little and big, black and white, and as Thomas says: "There will be some manure in the yard next spring, Sir, whoever lives to see it." I think of putting every bit of it on to the grass land.

When I bought this farm three years ago, I came from a temporary residence in the city, where we had a rather nice lawn and garden. And of course when we moved into the country, the first thought was to "fix up things round the home." I bought the farm the latter part of November, and the first thing I did on it was to set out a large bed of roses and one or two beds of flowering bulbs. The next, was to top-dress the "lawn." This took pretty much all the manure there was on the farm, except some loose horse litter that we used to protect the roses and other tender shrubs! All this time, the corn stalks were out in the field, and I can now very well imagine that such a mode of farming did not call forth any very flattering remarks from the passers by. One day, when I was busily engaged in attending to the roses, and a man was carting the manure and spreading it on the "lawn," a young farmer, whom I had known for some years, came along on a load of wood, and after looking on for a few minutes and ascertaining what we were driving at, remarked, "I'll tell you what I think." "Well, John, what do you think," I asked. "I think," he said, "*you've got a good many things to learn.*" I had sense enough not to press him for particulars, and he passed on. Well, I have made a great many mistakes in farming, but that was not one of them. The effect of the top-dressing on the grass was truly wonderful. We mowed it three or four times during the summer, and sowed a little guano on it in showery weather, leveled down some of the inequalities by taking the soil from under the grass without removing the sod, and batting them down with the spade, throwing the soil in the hollows and—well we have now quite a respectable "lawn" for a farm home. I advise any city man, who turns farmer, to attend to such things the first year—for if put off for more time, they will never be done at all!

I received a letter to-day from a subscriber to the *Agriculturist* in Illinois. "I would like," he says, "to get an apparatus for cooking food for a few hogs and neat cattle; and I notice that in your Walks and Talks you mention that you have one; and that D. R. Prindle, in his circular, publishes testimonials from you. Do you use his steamer, and is it a convenient apparatus, simple enough to be used without danger and without difficulty. Would his No. 3, have capacity to cook enough meal for, say 30 hogs and 10 steers? Or is there a better than his?"

I have used Prindle's steamer for two or three years. There is no difficulty or danger in using it. And it is a very simple and convenient apparatus. Still it requires some brains to manage it—and farm hands, you know, are rather deficient in that article. I have never had a man yet who did not think he could cook better and faster with an old-fashioned kettle. I have steamed a barrel of potatoes with it perfectly in ½ hour; but I have known a man to keep the steamer going all day on one barrel, and not have the potatoes cooked at night! A boy generally, after a few weeks training, manages it better than a man, because less prejudiced.

But it must be confessed the steamer has faults. You can not tell when the water is getting low; and we have several times had it get dry, with a large fire underneath; and in one case we poured water in when it had been dry for sometime, and was nearly red hot. We came near having an explosion—at least near enough to frighten the person pouring in the water, though I presume there was no real danger, as the steam was not confined. Still it blew the water all over the room, and *cracked the bottom of the steamer*, and it cost me $22 to get it repaired. The steam is conveyed from the top of the cauldron in a vulcanized rubber tube, to an iron pipe, which goes through the meal or potatoes, to the bottom of the barrel. This tube sometimes gets stopped up with the meal, partly or entirely. We obviate it by tying a piece of cloth round the pipe. You and I would have no trouble in correcting it, but those "hands!"

There would be a great saving of heat if the cauldron was set in an arch. It is now sheathed with iron, and the heat radiates from it and is lost. On the whole, I do not think it would pay to cook food for neat cattle. I have tried it for milch cows and found it too much trouble. It will pay better to cook food for hogs than for any other animal. Their stomachs are smaller, and they require more concentrated food. In steaming meal, I find that it is necessary to put in considerable water, and to be careful to have it well mixed. If any of the meal is dry, it will remain dry, no matter how long you steam it. The advantage of the steamer over a common cauldron is, that there is no danger of burning the meal. There is no absolute saving of heat; it is simply more convenient, and when the steam is up, you can cook another barrel as soon as the first is done.

Another gentleman writes me in regard to a mill for grinding grain. The one I have, on the whole, is not entirely satisfactory. It does not grind fast enough. Once, when I attended to it myself, with four horses, I ground twenty-eight bushels of peas in three hours and ten minutes. This would do very well. But it has never been done since. The men do not like it. They prefer to take the grain to the mill and wait for it to be ground. And I find that if I set two of them at grinding, one to drive, and one to attend the mill, twenty-five or thirty bushels is all that they will grind in a day! The men are not lazy either. I have as good men as can be found—married men who live in houses on the farm, and possessing more than average intelligence. It is a lack of energy and self-confidence. They think a thing "can't be done," and they are generally right, so far as they are concerned. But if you can attend to it yourself, all the time, get a good mill, and it will pay. I do not know, however, where there is a really good one. I wish the good people at the *Agriculturist* Office would look up the best one there is made, and offer it as a premium.

When I was pulling some weeds out of the potatoes last summer, the Deacon stood near and shaking his head, said: "There is too much top." But one thing struck me: Notwithstanding that it had rained almost constantly for several weeks, I found in pulling up these large weeds that *the soil was really quite dry*. The potato tops completely covered the ground, and if there was any truth in the idea that growing crops shade the ground and keep it moist, this land would have been wet; yet the soil pulled up on the roots of the weeds was dry as dust. A correspondent of the Country Gentleman mentions a fact that appears to prove that weeds which shade the ground keep it moist. He says:

"To-day I was hoeing in my garden, where the weeds were one inch high, and scarce; there the ground was *dry* half an inch. One place, not two feet distant, had many weeds about four inches high, completely shading the ground. There, not a particle of dry earth is to be found."

The fact may well be as here stated. But what does it prove? It shows, perhaps, that weeds which shade the ground, check evaporation of moisture from the *surface*, and that for half an inch deep such soil is not as dry as that which is exposed to the sun and air. But does it show that the weeds do not take up *from the soil beneath*, a large quantity of water and evaporate it through their leaves? Had the soil where the weeds grew been examined three, four, or six inches deep, it would probably have been found drier than that which was bare. One thing is certain: plants, during all their growth, take up by their roots and evaporate through their leaves an enormous quantity of water. Many experiments have been made which demonstrate this fact. Those of Lawes are the most thorough and extensive. He ascertained with the greatest accuracy, the amount of water evaporated by wheat, barley, beans, peas and clover. A Wheat plant giving in grain and straw only one pound of dry substance, evaporated during its growth, of 172 days, 247.4 lbs. of water; Barley, 257.8 lbs.; Beans, 208.8 lbs.; Peas, 250.1 lbs.; Clover (during 101 days), 209.1 lbs. In other words, an acre of wheat of 30 bushels and 1800 lbs. of straw, would evaporate during the spring and summer, 835¼ tons of water, or over *five hundred gallons a day*. A crop of clover of 2 tons per acre evaporates in 101 days, 430 tons of water, or over 1,000 gallons a day! And yet a heavy crop of clover would shade the ground completely.

This water actually passed *through* the plants. Of course the exhalation was greater as the plants increased in growth. Thus a wheat plant in March exhaled 14.1 grains of water a day; in April, 41 grains; in May 103 grains; in June 1,177 grains; in July 1,585 grains a day. After this, as the plant began to mature, the exhalation decreased.—What we want for our growing crops is not a moist surface, half an inch deep, but a warm, moist soil underneath, where the roots ramify and imbibe their food.

I wish something could be done to break up the practice of tying the lines round the back in plowing. It is very convenient, but it spoils the horses for ordinary driving. It is hard work to manage them with two hands, and no wonder. They have to pull some lazy plowman along every day by the bit, and when he wants them to back or turn round, he braces himself against the ground and pulls hard enough to spoil any decently broken horse in a week. I once saw a boy take the First Prize at one of the plowing matches of the Royal Agricultural Society, who drove his team without lines at all. Our horses are a little too lively for that, but still they might easily be trained to haw and gee, to back, to turn round, and to stop, without using the lines scarcely at all.

You "do not see how holding the lines round your back in plowing and cultivating spoils the horse for ordinary driving in a wagon and carriage." Simply because the poor horse has to pull hard on the bit all the time, and is obliged to set his neck so stiff that it soon loses all elasticity. And a stiff-necked horse is always difficult and unpleasant to drive. My men say they have to put the lines round their back to keep the horses from going so fast, and to guard against breaking the plow in case you strike a stone. In the spring I mean to get some cord lines just long enough to put on the handles of the plow, putting a short stick between the horses fastened to the inside of the bits, and then say, "If the horses go too fast at first, they will soon get tired of it, and if you strike a stone and break a plow, you can go to the barn and get another one." The light wooden stretches between the horses' heads keeps them from crowding each other, or from getting too far apart, and you can plow much straighter. And then the saving of the leather lines is quite an object these times.

Raising Clover Seed.

This is one of the most profitable crops raised by northern farmers. It is not generally large in quantity, but so far as it goes, it yields large returns for the labor and money expended on it. From three to five bushels per acre may generally be expected, and this, selling at from $8 to $12 a bushel, is a good return for the labor. The culture of clover is simple and easy. The ground should be well plowed and harrowed fine, the manuring moderate. Such lands as bring good crops of wheat, oats, and barley, will produce good crops of clover. The seed should be sown early, the earlier the better. As clover does not last usually more than one year for a full crop, it is generally best to seed down the land to timothy at the same time; the latter to form the main crop of the second year. When the clover has got well established, it is the practice of many to turn in their cattle and sheep upon it. This furnishes excellent feed, and the cropping of it does no harm to the clover, but rather helps it. The stock are kept here until the middle of June, when they are taken out, and the crop allowed to take a new start. If kept on longer, the clover would not have time to mature seed before frost. By being fed down pretty closely over the whole field, the plants now start uniformly, and all blossom and ripen their seeds nearly at once, which is a very important matter. Attention to this point can hardly be urged too much. The closer and evener the feeding off, the better and more uniform the filling and ripening of the seed. Sheep will feed closer than cattle, and they should be relied upon for finishing off. As soon as the stock are taken from the field, plaster should be applied, which will give the plants a vigorous growth. A spell of dry weather may be usually expected during the mid-summer season and then plaster will be particularly useful.

The seed will generally be ripe by the time of the first frosts, and then is the time to harvest it. It is mown, and when wilted well, raked into small cocks in which it is left to dry—the cocks being occasionally turned over by passing a rake handle under them, and with one hand on the top, inverting them. When dry enough, let it be hauled to the barn, where it may be threshed and cleaned in a mill provided for the purpose. Or after beating the seed off from the stalks it may be left in a heap with the closely adhering chaff to heat slightly, when the seed is rubbed out and separated in a common fan mill.

Fig. 1.—ELEVATION.

Houses, Cheap and Convenient.

BY NARRAGANSETT.

[We published on page 53 (Feb. '66.), the elevation and plan of a comfortable dwelling for a small family, one adapted either to the vicinity of a large city, or to the interior of a village. These designs are not intended for farm houses, although the principles of comfortable living, upon which the plans are based, are equally applicable to farm houses, cottages, or villas. Our correspondent takes the elevation of the February house, and by a re-arrangement of the inside, gives us a plan adapted to a family of a little different tastes and mode of life, and perhaps as convenient on the whole.—ED.]

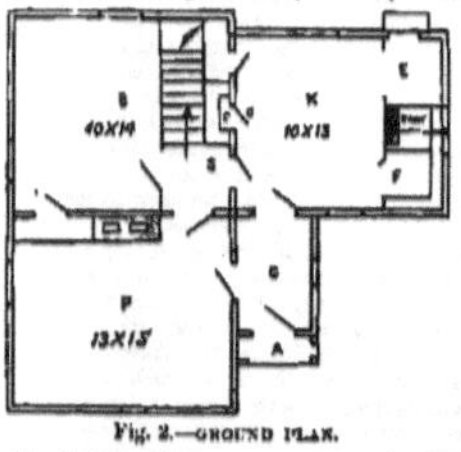

Fig. 2.—GROUND PLAN.

In this design, upon the ground floor, as seen in fig. 2, are a Parlor, Bed Room and Kitchen; *A*, Porch; *G*, Front Entry; *S*, Stairway; *F*, Pantry, connecting by slide with the sink in the Back Entry (*E*); *C, C*, marks the China Closet. Each room has independent facilities for warming; and while the rooms are in close communication with each other, they yet can be quite separate. The bed-room has a spacious closet. Upon the chamber floor (fig. 3), are three nice bed-rooms and four closets. Each room has direct access to a chimney flue. The stairway can be lighted by a glazed scuttle in the roof. This Cottage, if well built, may be made a comfortable, and as they say, a "genteel" house. It is very compact—not an inch of room is lost. If desirable, the partition between the closets over the pantry and back entry, may be moved a little to one side, making one of the closets larger; a circular window may be inserted in the gable; and to the room used for bathing, water may be carried by a force pump, and even heated by a boiler connected with the kitchen fire. Few plans of this size afford a greater amount of convenience than may be found in this simple design. True, the economy in side walls, accompanying square ground plans, is sacrificed to the greater light and airiness of the structure, but in a snug cottage like this that is a small fault.

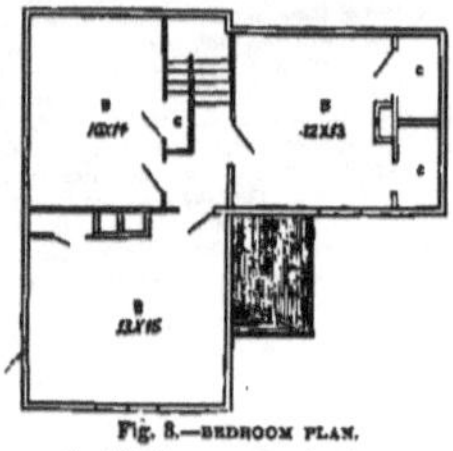

Fig. 3.—BEDROOM PLAN.

Partialities at Fairs.

One of the minor hindrances to the success of our Agricultural and Horticultural Fairs, is the real or fancied injustice done to exhibitors. When a man takes great trouble and goes to some expense in preparing to exhibit stock or grain, or fruit or flowers, and then finds his articles slighted, and the premiums given to less deserving competitors, he feels hurt, and perhaps resolves to abandon the Society and its exhibitions. Every year witnesses cases of this kind. And so it happens that good contributors fall off every year, and their places are poorly supplied by new comers, or not at all. Not only do influential supporters drop off, but with their defection the quality of the exhibitions declines, and spectators go home every year declaring the Fair a humbug, not worth attending again.

Now, to avoid such troubles, it is important, first of all, to secure good men for judges. They should be men above all mean and petty prejudices and partialities, men thoroughly competent to decide on the merits of the articles presented before them, and who will give time and thought to their examination. They should be the guests of the Society and be entertained, free of expense, during the Fair.

The time for appointing the Executive Board who will select the Judges, is at the winter meeting of the local Society. Let all the members attend this meeting, and see to it that good and true men are chosen for officers. Then, let this Board give time and careful thought to the choice of Judges. The success of the Society will depend much on this. But when the Judges have been appointed, the exhibitor should thenceforth dismiss all suspicion of partiality, and take the decision of the Judges as given in good faith. Let us ever remember that we are apt to think more highly of our own articles than we ought to think. The Judges have to look on all sides of a case in order to render due justice to all parties. Putting faith in their honor and fairness, we should bear with occasional disappointments quietly. This course is right in itself, and is the only way in which a Society and its fairs can be successfully maintained.

Nevertheless, it is important that the judges should feel their responsibilities as men, to render unbiased judgment, and we think that over every department a member of the Executive Board should preside, and while he watches narrowly the behavior of exhibitors, some of whom will leave no stone unturned to influence Judges in their favor, he should be ready to entertain objections to Judges or to their action; and in case proof is afforded of improper bias, it should be in his power to arrest proceedings and have a new committee appointed, or the unfair man removed. The position of Judge at a fair is a thankless one, and should be made as light and agreeable to honest men as possible. But the Executive Committee should avoid men who ask for appointment, or who are nominated by exhibitors in the classes they inspect.

Fig. 1.

Hitching Horses in the Stall.

There are horses that are as sober and staid while in the stall, as any one could desire, and which might be tied with a six-foot tie rope without ever getting a foot over it, and there are others which are ever restless, pawing and thrashing about, and making themselves very uneasy about something. These are frequently getting themselves and their masters into trouble in one way and another, and very frequently by getting one of their fore-legs caught over the halter strap. A correspondent, using the friendly signature of "A Quaker," sends us the following, showing forth his experience in this matter, together with illustrative drawings, which the artist and engraver have somewhat improved upon:

Fig. 2.

"Having seen and experienced much trouble

with horses getting their fore-feet over the halter strap, I employ a simple remedy. The tie-line is of rope instead of leather, with the end well wipped (wound with twine, to prevent the strands untwisting). This is passed through the hole and a figure-eight knot made a little distance from the end; the hole in the manger being made smooth, and slanting up and down; the rope runs freely in and out, just as the horse moves his head, thereby leaving no "bight" or bend to hang down. This prevents any possibility of the horses' leg being caught over it; which before was a frequent occurrence. Not only did it take time and trouble to extricate him; but there was also the liability of breaking the halter, and endangering his limbs. Aside from the above, less time is lost in tieing and untieing, and there is no danger of the horse getting loose; having tried this plan nearly two years, I am convinced of its efficacy."

Fig. 1.—ICE PLOW.

Gathering the Ice.

In gathering the ice for filling the home ice-house, all the tools that are really necessary are an ax, a shovel, one or two pike-poles, a stone-boat, ox-sled, or wagon of some kind, and a few

Fig. 2.—ICE PLANE.

boards. With the shovel, the ice is cleared of snow and broken pieces frozen on; with the edge of a board for a guide, the ice is marked off into strips of the desirable width, say 2, 2½, or 3 feet wide, using any iron point to scratch with. Then with the ax, a long narrow gutter is cut so that a start can be made, and the lines marked off are deepened so that long, narrow cakes may be detached from the main field. These are then, or previously, measured off into cakes of uniform size, and then striking blows with the ax, at first gently, to start cracks, and finally splitting blows, they are divided up into cakes of a size to be handled. It requires some judgment to get the best sized cakes, for they must be as large as can be handled easily, and yet be of a size to pack evenly in the house. Much, of course, depends upon the thickness. When the cakes are separated, the next thing is to get them out of the water. This may be done either by making "ways" or skids of boards, of about the width of the cakes. This should consist of 2 or 3 bottom boards and 2 side strips fastened together by cross-ties or cleats upon the bottom. It is shoved partly into the water, the cakes one after another floated over its sub-

Fig. 3.

merged end, and then shoved out by pike poles. The same thing is used to load with subsequently. It is best to set the ice on edge and leave it until the next morning early, when the temperature of the air is the lowest; for then ice is as dry as wood, and not only those who handle it do not get wet, but it is much better for the ice to be packed at a low temperature. If the whole of the ice could be packed at zero, the probability is that no thawing would take place for months. Hard wood wedges are sometimes useful in making the long strips of ice first cut, split off evenly. Several of these are driven into holes started by the ax on the line, and tapped smartly, one after the other. The hand ice saw, fig. 3, is very useful in gathering ice in a small way even. It is simply run through a hole in the ice, and operated by a man standing. The cakes cut with it in both directions are as true and even as possible.

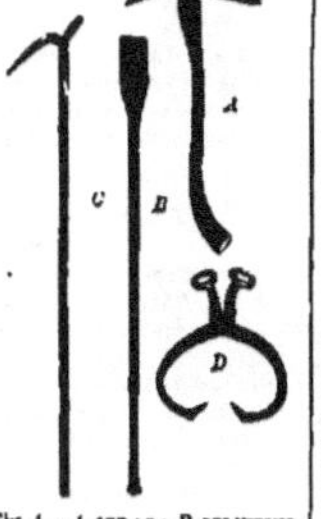

Fig. 4.—A, ICE AX; B, SPLITTING BAR; C, PIKE; D, HAND TONGS.

If much ice is to be gathered, other tools expedite matters greatly. Then, ice gatherers can not choose what time of the day to do their work, and they must handle the ice cakes when wet and dripping, as well as when cold and dry. Instead of lining off the field ice with axes, after the first scratch is made as a guide, the *ice plow* is used. This instrument works on the principle of a dozen narrow planes in a line, each cutting its way a little deeper, and so making, in once or twice passing, a groove so deep that a crack will follow it when once started. Attached to this is a guide which will run in one furrow and guide the plow in making the next. To free the ice from snow, and broken pieces, making the surface uneven, or from soft bubbly ice, an *ice plane* (fig. 2) is used. It consists of plate iron guides in a frame, and a blade which may be raised or lowered, crossing at right angles near the middle between the guides. This is little used in this country, the common road scraper being employed, before the plow is used, to throw the snow into ridges, and to scrape it off into the water, or out of the way. The strips are cut up into accurately equal-sized cakes by the *hand saw*, or better by running the plow at right angles to its former furrows. This divides the ice into perfectly square cakes. Splitting is accomplished by the broad-ended iron bar, fig. 4, called the *splitting bar*. The pike poles are much employed, and in cases where the ice-houses are close by the shore of the lake or river, canals are cut through the ice so that the cakes may be floated close to shore, and upon the long trestled ways up which the cakes are slid by horse-power, either upon cars or sliding directly upon the ways.

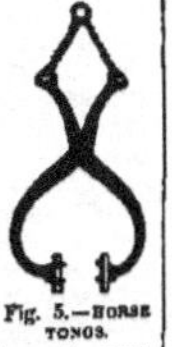

Fig. 5.—HORSE TONGS.

Tongs for lifting ice cakes are shown in *D*, fig. 4, and fig. 5, and are of different sizes, some intended simply for use in the hands, or for horse-power, where large cakes or two at a time are drawn up into the tops of the ice-houses. The approved style of ax is shown in fig. 4, *A*. *B* is a splitting bar for use on the pond or in the house, and *C* is a convenient form of pike pole. With these implements adapted especially to the purpose, the work goes on very rapidly. They may be obtained in all the cities we believe. The drawings were made from the tools of R. H. Allen & Co., 189 Water-st., New York.

Agricultural Schools.

[This subject is one attracting the serious attention of many good men in our country, and the following article is from a valued correspondent. In one particular, at least, he is surely wrong, namely, in supposing that several hours of work will interfere with the most efficient study. We will state as one incontrovertible proof, that at the Michigan Agricultural College the boys all work three hours a day, and those who are reported by the farmer as the best in the field, are uniformly the best scholars.—ED.]

It is a noteworthy fact, that agricultural colleges and schools, as thus far organized and conducted in this country, have, with a single exception perhaps, proved practical failures. Students in law schools become lawyers, medical students become physicians, and so on, but the students in our agricultural schools do not distinguish themselves as farmers, and time enough has passed for them to have done so if they would. How is this to be accounted for? We may not be able fully to explain it, but may point out some of the defects in the plans of the institutions thus far established.

It is a mistake to make an agricultural school a school also for general education. Our common schools and academies teach the rudiments of geography, grammar, arithmetic, etc.; why burden an agricultural school with these elementary and common branches? They cannot teach them any better or more economically than it is now already done elsewhere, and it only wastes time and clogs the working of the professional school to bring them into their courses of study. It not only takes up the time which should be devoted to studies strictly professional, but it lowers the standard of attainment. It tends to make a young man's education superficial, and hurries him into practical life at too early an age. The growing tendency in our country to shorten the period devoted to education, is hurtful, and should be resisted. As the country grows older, the tendency should be in the other direction.

Again, it is a mistake to connect the study of agriculture with a regular classical college, and make it a part of a course of general and classical education. This would tend to divert the mind too much from the regular studies. If a young man who intends to be a doctor, should have the science of medicine taught him in the midst of his college course, he would be very apt to neglect the other studies and give his chief thoughts to medicine. It might, in some cases, be wise to have an agricultural school in the same town with the classical college, but they should be separate institutions. In this respect, they should be organized just as our existing schools of medicine, law, theology, and practical science are—separate and independent.

It is a mistake, also, to make an agricultural school a manual labor school. The student in any and every department of knowledge should have daily exercise in the open air, for the preservation of his health. But his exercise should partake of the nature of recreation, not labor. No man can well carry on two kinds of work at once: it may be either brain-work or muscle-work, but not both in the same day. If he toils with hands the largest part of each day, his reading, during his hours of rest, should not be of the nature of study. If he toils with his head the largest part of every day, he should, for the remainder, seek some kind of diversion, amusement, not additional labor of any sort. For all kinds of labor exhaust vitality. "All work and no play makes Jack a dull boy."

An agricultural school should differ from other institutions, in that it should be established on a farm. This farm should, if practicable, present a great variety of soils, also upland, lowland, woodland. It should have all needful buildings for stock, hay and grain, a well furnished chemical laboratory, the departments of Natural Philosophy, Natural History, etc., well provided with apparatus, and collections, a well stocked library, a gymnasium, etc. The farm, and its buildings and implements, and all other needful apparatus, should not be for the student to *work* upon and with, to any great extent, but rather to afford him ample means for study. He should work enough to learn how to handle tools and implements, and to know how to perform all kinds of farm-labor.

The school should have two courses of study: the one for a year and-a-half or two years, and another for three years. The first should be designed for those who are unable or disinclined to prosecute any but the elements of agricultural science; the second for those who wish to become thoroughly educated. The conditions of membership should involve only a thorough common school education. The course of study should embrace such branches as Botany, Vegetable Chemistry, Natural Philosophy, Mechanics, Vegetable and Animal Physiology, Mineralogy and Geology, Surveying, Farriery, Principles of Stock Breeding, Culture of Fruits, Draining, Elementary Law, etc., but which should be taught in recitation, by lectures, and text-books, and illustrated by experiments in the laboratory and on the farm.

This course of study, the long or short, should be considered as only preparatory to study in the great school of experience. Actual farming on one's own land will illustrate and confirm what has been taught in an elementary way in the agricultural school.

A Word for Mules.

We are glad to see that the use of mules for all kinds of hard, rough work, is steadily gaining ground. These animals are not beautiful or musical, but they are useful and economical. They are fit for work younger than the horse, since they are put to service at three years old, though they do not reach their maturity until seven years of age. Their temper, health, and usefulness, depend very much on the manner of breaking them. The so-called stubbornness and obstinacy of this animal arises chiefly from the abuse he is wont to receive when young. He seldom if ever bites or kicks those who treat him kindly. But the fact is, that the club and whip and whip-handle and boot-toe are applied to him without mercy; and yet he is expected to be always as patient and gentle as a cow!

The mule will do more work, and require less grain than a horse; he is less liable to disease, and recovers from sickness and injury quicker than a horse. He works better when old, and holds out longer. He seldom takes fright, or runs away. He does not like overurging when drawing heavy loads, and he should never be driven very fast. In making up spans (those of 15 to 15½ hands high make most serviceable teams), those of similar dispositions should be chosen and put together, so that they will work together pleasantly and with a will. The mule seems made for work—he thrives under it, and is better in spirits and temper than when idle.

Experiments in Raising Potatoes.

"Delaware" makes the following communication. "Last spring I tried an experiment in raising potatoes from whole tubers, halves, and single eyes, planting three rows of "White Sprouts," one with each, and marked a section of thirty feet in each row, near the middle, for testing. I planted 5 lbs. of whole potatoes, 12 inches apart—yield 18 lbs. In the next row, 5 lbs. of halves, six inches apart—yielded 20 lbs., while 1 lb. 12 oz. of single eye pieces produced 10 lbs. There was no discoverable difference in the quality of the potatoes, and very little in the size. Those of the whole tubers were a shade the largest. This makes it appear that in economy of seed, the advantage is largely in favor of single eyes; for in the same proportion, the whole and half potatoes should each have yielded 28.57 lbs., instead of 18 and 20 lbs. respectively. Having reference to the ground occupied, the result is in favor of the halves first, and the whole potatoes second. The halves yielded double, and the whole ones nearly double what the single eyes yielded on the same surface of ground. Observe that, although the quantity of seed and the ground planted with whole and with half potatoes were the same, yet the distance apart was double in the first mentioned."

Milk for N. Y. City—Striking Figures.

This City is supplied with milk brought in over eight or nine railroads, and by wagons from many points in the immediate vicinity. The largest supplies come over three railroads, which during the ten months ending Nov. 1st, delivered the following supplies: Erie Railroad, 17,228,085 quarts; Harlem Railroad, 15,406,605 quarts; Hudson River Railroad, 13,007,810 quarts: Total, **45,043,400 Quarts!**—equal to 150,143 quarts per day, Sundays included. If we add as much more for milk from all other sources, condensed milk, etc., which is far too great an estimate, the supply would amount to 300,000 quarts per day. But this quantity is divided among the permanent and transient residents of New York, Brooklyn, Jersey City, Newark, and a dozen suburban cities and towns, as Hoboken, Hudson City, etc.—amounting in all to little if any short of two millions of people. The consumption therefore is *less than one third of a pint per day to each person.* It is evident therefore, that there is still opportunity to largely increase the supply of milk without overstocking the market, even if there were to be no increase in population....Taking the average retail price at 10c. per quart, the citizens paid for the milk brought on over the three principal railroads, over 4½ million dollars, of which the producers received about $2,300,000, the Railroads $800,000 for freight, and the wholesale and retail dealers $1,400,000. These are general estimates, based upon the facts as nearly as they can be ascertained....This 45,043,400 quarts of milk (brought over the three Railroads) would fill one million one hundred and twenty-five thousand ten-gallon cans!......Reckoning this milk at only wine measure, it would cover 85 acres one foot deep, or it would fill a tank covering an acre thirty-five feet deep! The reader can readily extend the figures to the number of cows, the number of milk-men or milk-maids required, the feed consumed, etc., etc.

Middle Tennessee.

A correspondent, Mr. M. F. Averselz, who refers to Dr. Hart, of Tullahoma, as willing to give particular information about this comparatively new part of the country, sends us the following letter. The land is broad, and many desirable locations are offered to enterprising settlers. Here is a plea for Tennessee:

"This beautiful country, especially the high table-lands in the Counties of Coffee, Warren, Grundy, and Marion, have many advantages, and are well worthy the attention of every one seeking a new home. The delightful climate, proverbially healthy, is very mild. The spring allows early plowing, sowing and planting. After April 1st, there is little or no danger from frost. In summer it is never too hot for out-door work, and the nights are always refreshing and cool, to such a degree that sleeping without cover is uncomfortable. The autumn is very pleasant, and the winter never severe; snow seldom lies longer than 3 or 4 days at a time, and ice rarely forms thicker than 3 or 4 inches. The land, a good deal of which, about 60 years ago, was a prairie, is now covered with White, Black, Spanish and Post Oak and Chestnuts, and near the streams Yellow Poplar, Black Walnut and Ash, having only little undergrowth, is easily cleared, and after this, on account of being level or slightly rolling, admits the use of all improved agricultural implements. The soil, although not so rich as the river bottoms, is a happy mixture of loam and sand, with a good subsoil, very easily worked, capable of holding a good deal of moisture, not liable to cake very susceptible, of lasting improvement by deep plowing, subsoiling, manuring, and a systematic natural rotation of crops. It is well adapted to the growth of all kinds of vegetables and grain. Wheat, rye, barley, oats and spring grains are sown in February. Corn, grass, clover, tobacco, flax, sorghum, yield enormously. Fruit of all kinds seldom fails; peaches grow large, and the trees last 40 years. Apples grow quite thriftily and bear well almost every year, also Cherries, Pears and Apricots. The Grape, though not yet grown extensively, is cultivated with success on the level land, and at a small cost, as thus the greatest part of deepening, loosening and cleaning the soil can be done by horse-power. Although not proper cotton land, yet this crop can be grown and pay well at present prices.

All circumstances combine to extend the farmer's work over the whole year, and as plowing can be done every month in the year, one man can put in and tend about twice as many acres of crops as at the North and West. The raising of horses, cattle, sheep, hogs and poultry, is very easy, and pays well; wild grasses abound; in the woods, a good mast of acorns falls almost every year, and only four months of winter feeding is needed—for sheep, only when snow covers the ground. Large springs of the best, purest, and healthiest water, abound in this region, and good water-power on different streams. The most remarkable of these water-powers is at Manchester, the county seat of Coffee County, a neat village before the war, beautifully situated on the McMinnville Railroad, destined by nature to become a manufacturing city of great importance. Here the Duck River, a crystal clear stream, of considerable size, falls 150 feet in one mile, creating an immense propelling power. Such valuable advantages can not fail to attract the attention of capitalists eager for a well paying investment, as with water-power, all kinds of manufactured articles may be made with less expense than were steam power employed. Before the war, a Paper-Mill, Cotton Factory, Distillery, and Saw and Grist-mill were here erected, but the most of them were badly damaged during the war, when General Bragg made here 3,000 lbs. of powder per day.

The facilities for transportation to good markets are ample; good roads intersect the country everywhere. From Tullahoma, a Depot on the Nashville and Chattanooga Railroad, a Branch Road leads to McMinnville, which will soon be in running order again, and probably extended to Cincinnati; from Decherd, another Depot on the Nashville and Chattanooga Railroad, a Railway leads to the inexhaustible Coal Mines at Tracy City, where a coal-vein of five feet is worked, and lately a bed of Iron Ore has been found, and a Foundry is to be erected. The war has devasted this country badly, and deprived the inhabitants, a very clever, polite, affable, sociable, and hospitable people, of almost every thing but their land; they are very glad that they are back again in the Union, and very desirous that Northern men of enterprise should come and help to obliterate the ravages of the war, and to develop the resources of the country. Money is very scarce here, and thus most every land owner is willing to sell a part of his generally large estates at a reasonable price under favorable conditions. Wild lands are offered at from one to six dollars per acre, and partly improved farms at five to fifteen dollars per acre. At present, labor is cheap, white men work for $1 to $1.25 per day and board themselves, or for 50 to 75 cents and board; colored men can be hired for $100 to $125 per year and board, colored women from 50 to 75 dollars.

Although agriculture is here yet in its infancy, no improved implements to be found, as much as 25 bushels wheat per acre have been raised, and Cotton brings $100 per acre. An apple orchard containing 60 acres, last year yielded 8,000 gallons of cider Brandy, and another orchard of 100 acres yielded to the owner, a year ago, $15,000."

Apple Pomace.

Hundreds of tons of what, every farmer knows, would be good food, or at least good manure, if it could be used, go annually to waste, because nobody knows what to do with it. If spread as manure, it poisons the grass or crops, and it is hard to knock it to pieces. So it lies in heaps and rots slowly, and after a while, is used as chip manure would be.

Apple pomace may be worked over again, and fair vinegar made from it, but still the pomace or spent cider-cheese is left. It is remarkable that farmers never think of adding this ingredient to the messes they cook up for their hogs. The sour juice is nearly all pressed out, there is starch, pectin, gum, sugar, and much albuminous matter, besides the seeds, left—and it will require not more than 20 minutes boiling to cook it thoroughly. It would probably be palatable simply boiled, but the addition of potatoes, or any roots, with corn meal or oil meal, would surely make it so. We regret that we are not situated so as to try the experiment carefully and report results, and hope very much that some of our readers will try it. We have no data to determine the average value of what is left of the apples, but have no doubt it is greater than that of turnips or even beets. So far as we see, it needs only to be cooked to become tender and palatable. We commend the subject to "Tuckahoe," who writes inquiring what to do with the article.

The Treatment of Tree Seeds.

Our people are at last waking up to the importance of trees, whether for fuel, timber, or shelter; indeed, so many have been the inquiries in regard to the subject, that we have offered a large premium (Oct. No.) to bring out the greatest amount of experience relating to it. The subject is already beginning to have a literature, as we last month noticed the "Forest Tree Culturist" of Mr. Fuller. Upon looking over our correspondence we find a great many queries as to the proper method of treating particular tree seeds, and we can best answer these queries in a lump. These seeds may be divided into two classes, one including those that must be sown as soon as ripe, and the other those that with proper care may be kept until the following spring. Of those that are to be sown as soon as ripe, the Elm and the Red and White (or Silver) Maples ripen their seed in the spring. As we have shown in a former number, the failure with these seeds is due to want of knowledge of the fact that they ripen in June, and that they must be sown at that time. If kept until the following spring, these seeds lose their vitality and fail, but if sown as soon as mature, they make strong young plants the first year. Other seeds needing immediate sowing ripen in autumn, and these are to be treated as nearly as posible as nature treats them. If, late in autumn, we look beneath the fallen leaves of an oak tree, a plenty of acorns will be found from which the radicle has protruded, showing that germination has already commenced. This will give the hint as to the proper treatment of acorns, which are to be planted shallow and the bed protected with a good covering of leaves, or other mulch. Chestnuts, Horse Chestnuts and Buckeyes, Tulip Tree, Hickories and Walnuts are treated in the same way. Hickories and Walnuts are said to do well if kept mixed with earth in a cool cellar during winter, and we have succeeded perfectly well with Horse Chestnuts put in a box of earth and exposed to the weather all winter.

Seeds that are kept over winter should be preserved at a low and even temperature, and of course be quite dry before they are put away, to prevent mould. The following are among the commonly planted seeds that are usually to be had of seed dealers: Honey Locust, Osage Orange, the Ashes, Larch, Deciduous Cypress, Maples (except Red and White), Spruces, Pines and other evergreens. Honey Locust, if fresh, will grow without preparation, but if old, it should be scalded. Osage Orange must be sprouted; the others merely need to be sown in a light rich soil. Evergreens are very tender when young, and are apt to be sun-scorched. These are best sown in beds where they can be shaded by a lattice work screen made of laths.

Young trees, like other young plants, require care, and no one need sow the seeds with the expectation that they will take care of themselves. Weeding, cultivation, and thinning must be duly attended to, and if the little trees are likely to suffer from drouth, the ground should be covered with a good mulch of saw-dust. If they are left in the seed-bed over the first winter, they will need to be covered with leaves.

American Wines.

Those who have only seen the sugared liquids often presented as wines, can have no idea of the wine producing capabilities of our native grapes; and very few are aware of the large amount of capital already invested in wine making, or of the excellent quality of the wines produced at first class establishments. At Hammondsport, N. Y., the Pleasant Valley Wine Company, the oldest in that vicinity, has already established a reputation for its Still and Sparkling Catawba, and other wines, and it proposes to compete, in the way of sparkling wines, with the products of the French vineyards, at the Paris Exposition. The Urbana Wine Co., at the same place, though not yet fully in operation, has the capital and means to carry on the business on an extensive scale. At the exhibition of the Lake Shore Grape Grower's Association, we saw about a hundred samples wine, some of them from well known makers, and others from those of less reputation. The character of these wines was of a high average, and some samples remarkably fine. Aside from the well-known Catawba and Delaware, the first prizes for which were taken by W. P. Anderson & Co., Cincinnati, there were some kinds not often seen. A specimen of Clinton showed that the wine making capabilities of this grape have been overlooked. This, and a creditable sample of Concord, were shown by the Lake Shore Wine Co., Brocton, N. Y., and took a well deserved premium. Norton's Virginia, of which but little is known at the East, gives a dark red wine, of a peculiar flavor that is usually unpleasant to those who are unaccustomed to it, but it is highly esteemed by many. W. P. Anderson & Co. took the premium in this class. The wine which deservedly attracted the most attention, both on account of its rarity and fine quality, was that from Ives' Seedling, exhibited by J. M. M'Cullough, Cincinnati. It is a red wine, somewhat like Burgundy, and gives promise that we shall not long depend on foreign countries for a supply of wines of this character. Many other noteworthy samples were exhibited which we should be glad to speak of, if we had space. In the discussions of the convention, very strong grounds were taken against the addition of anything—even grape sugar—to grape juice in order to *make* wine. It is probable that the many plantations of Iona will in the coming season be in bearing, and this variety be sufficiently abundant to allow it to be made into wine in a quantity large enough to give it a fair trial. From a sample made in a small way, as well as tests, we have seen of the must, something remarkable may be looked for.

VARIEGATED EVERGREENS are becoming quite numerous; among the recent ones are a silver leaved variety of *Cupressus Lawsoniana*; said to be very fine, and a variety of *Sequoia gigantea* (Wellingtonia of the English), with yellow markings upon the leaves. The Golden Yew, a marked variety of the European Yew, is represented in this country by some fine specimens. In the spring nothing is more beautiful in the way of "foliage plants," than this shrub.

[COPYRIGHT SECURED.]

THE BULL STABLE.—FROM A PAINTING BY BRASCASSAT.—*Engraved for the American Agriculturist.*

Who has not stood at the door of a bull stable and looked in upon his Lordship, lazy and warm in his bed of straw, as we are supposed to see Monsieur Taureau here? The soft flank, the gnarly massive neck, the wrinkled, curly, hair-padded forehead, the stout, short horns, are all so natural and familiar that one almost expects him to sway himself up, and then hollow his back, and stretch, and snuff. In standing near or handling a bull we have always the same feeling we have in standing near a locomotive engine, or a steam boiler—that it is safe now, but a little indiscretion on our part might produce an explosion at any moment. There is a wonderful amount of power slumbering in both. The bull may be never so sleepy and quiet, it is not safe to give him a chance to show himself wide-awake and able to use his power. To this end, while still a calf, or just growing out of calf-ship, the bull should have a ring put in his nose, and be always led by it with a leading pole.

Notwithstanding the familiar look of the bull here pictured, it is not rash to say that his like was never seen in America. He is obviously of none of the British breeds: every point is continental. Of the Continental breeds we have in this country, those which came from the north of France left their descendants chiefly in Canada. These somewhat resemble the cattle of the Channel Islands, (Alderneys, etc.,) and are usually marked by the mealy muzzle, which this one has not. We have also the Dutch cattle, those of modern importation, having much better beef points than are here shown, and the descendants of the cows brought over by the early Dutch settlers, in which the black and white spots are sharply defined, and which, indeed, have something of this look, but are not so coarse as this fellow, handsome and picturesque though he is. With the Spanish cattle of the South, he bears no affiliation. We must look rather to the common stock of the Swiss border for the model which the artist had in mind, or before his eye, rather, for this is no fancy piece. We remember well to have seen animals very like him at the cattle shows, and in the farm-yards, and pastures of that French-German-Swiss region of the upper Rhine. The monstrous coarseness of the root of the tail, accompanying rather large head and great flabby dewlaps, is a marked feature of some of the large Swiss breeds. Their tails often stand up several inches above the line of their backs. They are round buttocked too, and narrow above the hock. We present the picture, however, primarily as a beautiful and interesting work of art, and not as a model for the breeder.

The Imperial Dahlia.—(*Dahlia imperialis.*)

All the double Dahlias of our gardens, whether of the tall growing or dwarf sorts, though they number their varieties by hundreds, all belong to one species, *Dahlia variabilis*. This species is rightly called *variable*, as it has run into all the sports of color that we can conceive any one plant capable of. Besides this, there are some half-dozen other species cultivated in European collections, but as none of these seem disposed to make double flowers, they have not obtained popularity. We have been much interested in one of these rare species, cultivated this year by Mr. Henderson, the *Dahlia imperialis*. This, like the common one, is a native of Mexico, but has quite a different aspect from that. It is a very stately looking plant, with palish leaves that are more divided than those of the ordinary plant. It produces an abundance of flowers, which, though single, are very beautiful. A small yellow disk is surrounded by a single row of rays, four inches long, which together form a sort of bell, and look much more like a lily than they do like a head of composite flowers. This lily-like appearance is heightened by these rays being pure white, except just at the base, where they are touched with a rich crimson. The engraving is about half size, and though it gives the general form of leaf and flower, it fails to convey the color, upon which the effect so much depends. In France, this is valued to plant out in the open ground of their winter gardens, where it attains an enormous size. As it requires a long season, it will be necessary to start it early and get a good growth before putting in the open ground.

IMPERIAL DAHLIA.—(*Dahlia imperialis.*)

The Cabbage in its Varieties.

In preparing the engravings for the work upon gardening, noticed in another article, we were particularly struck with the wonderful variety presented by the cabbage plant, *Brassica oleracea*. Perhaps no cultivated plant presents us with such a wide range of varieties, and certainly no one of our garden vegetables affords so many useful forms. In one or another shape it, as Beecher says of the apple, "belts the year," for with a properly managed garden a family need be no time in the year without fresh vegetable food from some form of this useful plant.

The original, or wild plant of the cabbage, is found on the coast of England, France, etc., and would hardly be recognized by those who have only known the garden forms. Its great tendency to change is shown in the first generation, as seeds of the wild plant will, if sown in rich soil, give plants varying much in their foliage and other peculiarities.

Fig. 1.—BORECOLE OR KALE.

The nearest to the wild state of the plant is the Borecole, or Kale, (fig. 1,) which never makes a head, but only a cluster of loose leaves, in different sorts beautifully cut and curled, and often presenting fine colors. This is a very useful, but much neglected variety. It is quite hardy, and where the thermometer does not go much below zero, it will stand out without any protection. After a freezing it is very tender and well flavored. In the Savoy Cabbages (fig. 2) we have the leaves broader, still much curled and wrinkled, but formed into a more or less compact head. These are the richest of all cabbages, and so distinct in appearance and flavor from the smoother and harder forms, that in the English gardens they are not called cabbages, but Savoys. For family use, though they do not grow so large as other cabbages, they are late and stand severe frosts. We then come to the cabbage proper, including early and late sorts, which present us with a great variety, from the loose Early York, to the enormous and compactly folded Drumheads (fig. 3). In the Cauliflower and Broccoli, which are very much alike, the leaves do not fold, but surround a center, which is a mass of fleshy flower stems and undeveloped flower buds, all so closely crowded together that their parts are not distinguishable (fig. 4). This when cooked is of almost melting tenderness, and may be considered thus far the crowning achievement of the remarkable *Brassica*, in the way of varieties. A curious variety is presented in the Brussels Sprouts, (fig. 5,) a vegetable not so much grown as it would be, were it known that it is easily raised in any garden soil, and that it is a most excellent vegetable. In this the stem grows tall, and instead of producing a head at the top, it forms a great number of small heads, about the size of walnuts, along the stem. Still another variation is presented by the Kohlrabi, (fig. 6,) in which the leaf is rejected, but the

Fig. 2.—SAVOY CABBAGE.

stem, which swells out like a turnip, is the eatable portion. This, if taken early and before it becomes stringy, is esteemed by many. Then again we have an always acceptable vegetable

Fig. 3.—DRUMHEAD CABBAGE.

in the form of "cabbage sprouts" or greens, obtained by setting out cabbage stumps in spring.

These are all the forms of the plant grown with us, but there are others more or less known. As illustrations of the manner in which a single plant may vary in cultivation, and be thus adapted to different seasons and uses, they are interesting and curious, but we had another object in view in presenting them; they include plants little known beyond a certain few, that *should* be known and grown by all. In the majority of farmers' gardens, the late cabbage is the only one that finds a place. Here are six distinct sorts, each differing in flavor, and in season, all of which might, with no more care than is required for the common cabbage, be grown and thus add largely to the variety upon the table. Our city markets are supplied with cabbages in June, from plants that have been wintered over. The seed is sown in September, and the young plants are set in cold frames where they pass the winter, and are transferred to the open ground in early spring. The cabbage is quite hardy, and more plants are lost by keeping the frames too closely covered, and thus weakening them, than there are by actual freezing. Any one with a few sashes at command, can put together a rough frame of boards of the proper size for the sashes; he should set the young plants rather closely, down to their leaves, and have them well established before cold weather comes on. He can afterwards, by a little attention to airing, carry plants through the winter without any difficulty. Kohl-rabi does not transplant as readily as do the other varieties, and the safest way with this is, to sow it in drills where it is to stand, and afterwards thin to the required distance. We have not room to treat at length of their cultivation now, but in our notes for the month these things are always noticed.

Fig. 4.—CAULIFLOWER.

Fig. 5.—BRUSSELS SPROUTS.

Fig. 6.—KOHL-RABI.

Sports, as Affecting Fruits.

That plants will sport—that is, deviate from their ordinary ways, and produce leaves and flowers different in form and color from the ordinary—is a well known horticultural fact. It is also well known, that many of our varieties have been obtained by perpetuating these sports by cuttings, grafts, etc. Some of our variegated leaved Geraniums or Pelargoniums, and other plants with marked foliage, have been obtained in this way, and some of our fine Roses are sports from other varieties. That the quality of fruit may be affected by sporting is not so well established; yet some cases have come to our notice that look as if this were the case, and which we wish to put on record, with a view of calling out other and similar facts. At our grape exhibition, in 1863, a dish of Isabellas was presented, the berries in which were of a size so great that the judges decided that such fruit could only be produced by ringing the vines, and excluded the dish from competition. Since then the exhibitor has assured us that no ringing was practised, but that one part of the vine always bore just such fruit, while the other portion produced that of only ordinary size. Recently, Mr. Albert Granger, of Washington Heights, N. Y., brought us some bunches of grapes, for an opinion, which we gave to the effect that the fruit was an indifferent Isabella. The account that he gave of the fruit was so remarkable, that we requested him to make his statement in writing, which is as follows:

"In the spring of 1860, I procured 9 Catawba vines from Dr. Underhill, Croton Point. I set them all, they lived and thrived, and, in 1862–63, fruited, bearing Catawba grapes. In Nov., 1863, the trellis on which they grew was partially destroyed by fire (catching from a burning barn,) and one of the vines was burnt down to within one foot of the ground. I left the stump standing. In the spring of 1864 several buds appeared just above the ground; I let them all grow, and in the summer broke off all but two thrifty canes that sprung from opposite sides of the stump. These two canes grew well that year, and in 1865 the vine again bore Catawba grapes. This year it has borne very prolifically, and, as it had the best exposure of any of my vines, the fruit commenced changing two weeks earlier than on any other vine on the same trellis. The beautiful tints of the berries—the semi-transparency so to speak—was matter of remark; but to my surprise the fruit soon lost that character of color, and changed to the color of an Isabella. When ripe, they were found not to possess a single characteristic of a Catawba, but are pronounced by all persons who have partaken of the fruit to be Isabella grapes, and so they appear and taste to me. There can be no question about the history of the vine, and the fact that it bore, in 1862–3–5 Catawba grapes; to this I would affirm."

From a long conversation with the writer of the above, we cannot see where he could have made any error in his observations, and that, as far as evidence can be relied on to establish an occurrence, the above must be accepted. Before this article was in type, we found in a foreign journal an observation bearing on this point by M. Carriere, the well-known horticulturist, of the *Jardin des Plantes*, Paris. "A Black Hamburgh was cut down, when it produced three suckers, one of which was layered, and after a time produced much smaller berries, ripening at least a fortnight sooner than the others. This phenomenon occurs every year. Of the remaining two suckers from the same stock, one gives every year fine grapes, while the other, although it sets abundance of fruit, only ripens a few, and those of inferior quality."

These facts appear to us to show that in some cases, vines at least do sport to an extent that essentially modifies the quality of the fruit, and that this helps us to understand how there may be so many vines with fruit, differing much in quality, all called Isabella. The subject is an interesting one, and one that has a practical bearing. It should induce propagators, at least those who grow vines, to be careful as to the sources whence they obtain the wood, from which they propagate stock for sale.

Western Apples—Grimes' Golden Pippin.

The number of new, or rather unpublished apples that turn up every year, is something alarming to one who tries to keep the run of such matters. The Western States give us annually a batch of new sorts, that are slow in making their way eastward; indeed, there are so many peculiarly western varieties, that a large orchard might be stocked with a good assortment of choice kinds, not one of which a New England orchardist ever saw, if he ever heard of them. Of good apples, we have a sufficient number of varieties, and probably some of these

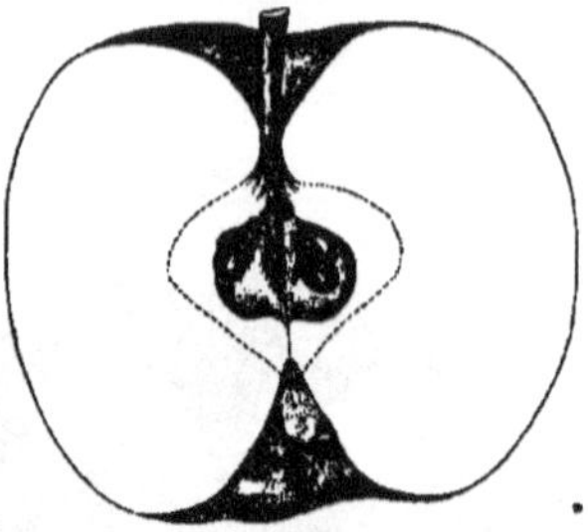

GRIMES' GOLDEN PIPPIN.

will never be excelled as far as quality is concerned, and could we only get the fruit of those, there would be but little temptation to look after others. However this accumulation of varieties may bother the pomologist, one good results from it; it allows more attention to be paid to the character of the tree, than if the lists were limited. A new variety, the tree of which is hardy when young, comes into bearing early, and bears regularly, must supplant an old sort, no matter if the fruit is a little better, provided the tree lacks these desirable qualities. This is just what our Western friends are doing, with their abundance of material—studying the qualities of the trees as to hardiness and healthfulness, as well as those of their fruit.

Doct. J. A. Warder, of Ohio, in making up some notes on new apples for the *Horticultural Annual for* 1867, refers to the Grimes' Golden Pippin as one of the varieties that are remarkable for the characters of the tree as well as those of the fruit. Specimens did not reach us in time to illustrate this, with the others, for the *Annual*, but we have since received specimens from S. B. Marshall, Massillon, O., which enable us to give an outline of the fruit, to which we append an account abridged from the more extended one furnished by Doct. Warder.

The original tree stands in Brooks Co., West Virginia, not far from the Ohio River; it was known to the boatmen in 1804, and is still in vigorous fruiting, having borne about twelve barrels the past season, all perfect and smooth. Orchard trees of this variety in Smithfield Co., O., have not failed to produce a crop for the past eighteen years. Mr. Marshall, who sent us the specimens, writes that it the hardiest tree in his nursery; that the branches neither split nor break, and that it is a regular and uniform bearer, being never affected by the severest winters. We append a description and note by Doct. Warder, with the remark that, while our Western friends are responsible for the statements about the tree, we are able to corroborate all they have said about the superior quality and richness of the fruit:

"Tree, hardy, vigorous, healthy, productive; branches, strong, spreading, shoots stout, dark; foliage, healthy, dark green, fruit, medium, globular, cylindrical, regularly or slightly angular; surface, smooth, yellow, bronzy or slighted russeted; dots, numerous, minute, yellow; basin, abrupt, deep, folded; eye, large, generally open; cavity, wide, regular, green; stem, long, slender, curved; core, small, closed, meeting the eye; seeds, numerous, angular, brown; flesh, yellow, breaking, very fine-grained, quite juicy; flavor, sub-acid, aromatic, rich. Use, table, its size being very convenient, and kitchen. Season, December or March. Quality, best.

"This delicious winter keeping apple should be extensively disseminated by nurserymen, who will find nothing to complain of in its habit in the nursery, while the planter will be gratified by a noble and productive tree, that comes early into bearing, and annually furnishes him choice fruit that rivals the Newtown Pippin in its good qualities. Indeed this variety may well be recommended as a substitute for that old favorite in regions where that does not succeed. In its peculiarities of richness and flavor, however, it more nearly resembles that charming amateur fruit, the Newark Pippin, which is unfortunately little known in the markets, though it is quite an old variety."

Fig. 1.—BEURRE GRIS D'HIVER.

A Couple of Old, but Little Known, Pears.

A good pear is a good thing; but what is a good pear? The select lists of the amateur pomologist are not the lists of the fruit dealer, and nurseryman. We have a democratic way in our pomology as well as in our politics, and vote for or against things without regard to presidents or precedents. Pomologists say that

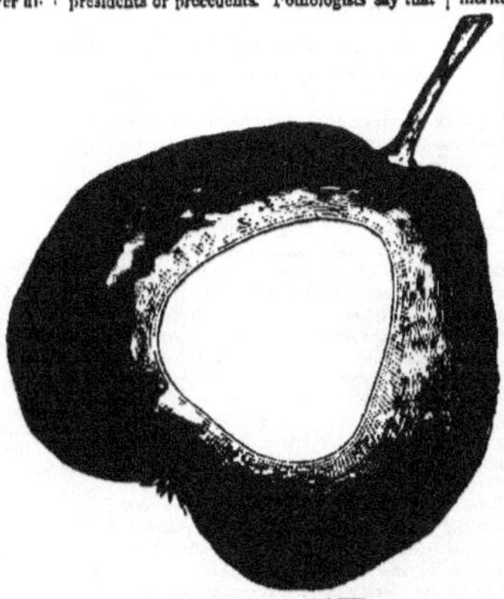

Fig. 2.—JOSEPHINE DE MALINES.

the Bartlett is a third rate, or, at best, a second rate pear; the people say that the Bartlett is the pear for their money, and the nurseryman is obliged to grow the trees, and the orchadist produce the fruit. We were led to the above remarks upon thinking how many really good pears there were, in comparison with those that found their way to the markets. One reason perhaps is, that we have been too hasty in our judgments, and have condemned many worthy varieties before they had time to show what they could do. At all events there are many old sorts that have been overshadowed by newer comers, which have been quietly gaining strength year by year, and though they do not find a place in the "select lists" of fruits, are well known, to those who have been patient with them, to be of the greatest excellence. Among the late varieties that are likely to be held higher in popular favor than they have yet been, are the two of which we present figures.

BEURRE GRIS D'HIVER.—This is a French pear, and is given in some of their works as Beurré de Luçon; first known in 1839. The tree is a very vigorous grower and does much better on pear than it does upon quince roots. The size and shape are sufficiently well given in the engraving. The skin russet, with sometimes a ruddy cheek in the sun. The flesh is melting, juicy and vinous. Quality, best. An early winter pear that keeps through December. Mr. Barry informs us that it brings the highest price.

JOSEPHINE DE MALINES.—A Belgian variety made known about 1830. The tree is hardy, but only a moderate grower, and does not give its best fruit until it has acquired age, but when sufficiently old, is very productive. The fruit is yellowish green, sprinkled with russet. Flesh slightly rose tinted, melting, sweet, vinous, and agreeably perfumed. Keeps until January, and with care will last even into March. It is justly regarded as one of the best winter varieties.

There are several other varieties now in unmerited neglect, that we hope to bring to the notice of our readers. More attention should be given to late varieties, both for market and home consumption. Well kept late varieties bring astonishing prices; while at home, nothing can be more refreshing as a dessert fruit, than a properly ripened, melting winter pear.

"Gardening for Profit" * — Small Places near Towns and Villages.

The regular "salt" used only to ocean sailing, looks with great contempt upon the short waves of our inland lakes; yet we always attained the result, if not the real object, of sailing—sickness—sooner on the fresh wave than on the briny one. So farmers of five hundred or a thousand acres would see ruin before them were they told they could have only ten. Yet many do get comparatively rich off of ten acres, and some who have only five, pocket more money in a year than those who have five hundred. But there is this to be borne in mind, that these small places must be near a market, the land must be good, and kept up to the very top of fertility, its occupant must work hard, and he must *know how*. This knowing how is perhaps the hardest of the conditions, but we have cornered one of our most successful market gardeners until he has recorded his eighteen years' expe-

* Gardening for Profit, by Peter Henderson, South Bergen, N. J. New York: Orange Judd & Co.

rience in a book, the title of which is given above.—Mr. H. writes pointedly, gives the "tricks of the trade," so to speak, without any reservation, tells his failures as well as his successes, makes a book that is the best guide, short of actual experience, and has the rare merit of stopping when he has nothing more to say. To be successful in market gardening, besides the requisites above mentioned, there must be a sufficient capital to employ all the necessary working force, and procure the required amount of manure and other appliances. Every mile from market lessens the profits, and every mile nearer the market increases the value of the land. Every foot is made to pay, and two and often three crops are taken from the same ground each year. Thus: In spring the land is planted to early cabbages, with lettuce between the cabbages; the lettuce comes off before it is in the way of the cabbages, which, after they have matured, are followed by celery or other late crops. In this way, by various combinations and rotations, the land is kept always at work. Though the leading object of this work is to furnish a hand-book on market garden, yet the private garden is not overlooked, and the cultivator "for profit," whether he gets it in consuming or marketing his produce, will find it of great value. One commendable feature in the work is, that the author confines the lists of varieties to the few that he considers best; suitable illustrations are given where needed, and the chapters upon frames and houses for forcing vegetables will meet a long felt want.

Those who have places near towns and villages will generally find it profitable to raise garden crops. Even if there is no regular market, we know from experience that a demand is easily made, and we have no doubt that in all large villages and towns, vegetables a little earlier or better than usual, will meet with a ready and remunerative sale. The raising of plants under glass can be made to pay in almost every thickly populated community, as people are willing to pay a good price for tomato, cabbage, pepper and other plants. Mr. Henderson's work gives ample directions for raising these, as well as for wintering cabbage and other plants for sale, or for setting in the spring.

A NEW VARIETY OF THE PAMPAS GRASS (*Gynerium*) has been raised in the Paris Garden. Instead of the silvery white panicles of the ordinary form, it has its flower clusters of a rich purple color. It will probably be a long time before this becomes generally distributed, but it will form a marked contrast with the original plant. A striped leaved variety is also among the newer plants. This, by the way, is a most stately ornamental plant, and should be more common than it is. It may be kept by placing the roots in a cellar for the winter. Around New York it passes the winter safely if covered with a box or cask, then filled in with leaves.

ASTILBE JAPONICA.

A Valuable Herbaceous Plant.

(*Astilbe Japonica—not Spiræa Japonica.*)

Under the incorrect name of *Spiræa Japonica* we have for years grown a plant that we knew could not be a *Spiræa*, but neglected until last summer to look up its true name. It is curious, as well as provoking, to see how an incorrect name will stick, after it once gets into the catalogues. A remarkable instance of this is *Dicentra*, which the best of florists will call *Dielytra*, a name that first came into use through a misprint, and the above plant is an illustration of how the botanists sometimes keep a name unsettled. As many who are not botanists are puzzled at the way in which names are confused and changed, we will briefly state what happened to this. As the plant is in general appearance like some Spiræas, it was without sufficient care, called *Spiræa Japonica*. After the French botanists found out it was not a *Spiræa*, they called it *Hoteia*, making a new genus in 1836, and naming it after a Japanese botanist—for they have botanists, after their way, in Japan—named Ho-Tei. When Hooker and Bentham came to overhaul genera for their great work, they found our plant did not need a new genus at all, but would fit very well in the old genus *Astilbe*, published some thirty years before, and here it will doubtless rest.

But to get back to our plant, of which our engraving shows some flowering stems, with their leaves, of the natural size. The radical leaves are like those which are represented, but much larger, and as they form a dense tuft of dark green, shining, and handsomely cut foliage, the plant itself would be worth growing, even if it did not bloom. In June it throws up stems about 18 inches in hight, which bear spikes of very small flowers of the purest white, and when these are set off by the unusually dark and somewhat fern-like foliage, the plant has an aspect of delicacy and neatness that is most pleasing. The flowers of the *Astilbe* are among the few of those of our herbaceous perennials that are sufficiently refined in their character to use in a bouquet, and for this purpose they are always in demand among florists. The leaves are also a serviceable green in large bouquets. *Astilbe* is perfectly hardy, grows rapidly, and multiplies readily by division of the clumps after flowering is over; it likes a good soil, and does rather better if in a partially shaded place. This is an excellent plant to force for green-house decoration in winter, and it is one of the many forced perennial herbaceous plants sold in our flower markets in spring. Though in the nurseries and in works on floriculture the plant is classed under the herbaceous Spiræas, under its old name of *Spiræa Japonica*, it does not belong in the same family, but to the Saxifrage Family. It is catalogued by the principal nurserymen at 25 cts. a plant. A beautiful variety, with the leaves elegantly veined with golden yellow, was sent from Japan by Mr. Hogg; it is yet quite scarce.

MARKET GARDENING IN PARIS.—At the "Great Exposition" to be held in Paris the present year, market gardening will be a prominent horticultural feature. A portion of the grounds is appropriated to the use, under the direction of a committee of the most celebrated market gardeners near Paris. It is proposed to have a model garden to illustrate all the processes of cultivation employed in supplying Paris with its *legumes*, or, as a Jersey-man would say, "garden truck." Extensive programmes are put forth for displays in other departments of horticulture, but we see nothing at once so novel and so useful as this.

VIOLETS IN ENGLAND.—Violets are attracting much attention in England just now; several new varieties are offered, and some old and lately neglected ones have suddenly become popular. We hope our florists will have a Violet fever.

THE HOUSEHOLD.

(☞ For other Household Items, see "Basket" pages.)

The Housekeeping "Prize Articles."

We are in trouble about these, as the reader will see.—Every other department of human labor has been freely written about, in books and periodicals; a few receipt-book books, and occasional newspaper items, embrace most that has been printed about Household *work* and *cares*. After a dozen years of oft repeated invitations, we began to fear our good Marthas either could not do it, or that they *would* not be induced to pen down their own experiences for the benefit of others. So, in November, we threw out a positive challenge in the form of a $100 Greenback, hoping somebody would accept the banter. Well, it has been done, and by nearly four-score of our fair readers—and to our utter overwhelment! *Seventy-six* fair competitors! and from almost every State in the Union, we are told, though we are in utter ignorance of the name or residence of any one of the writers, and have our curiosity tantalized to the highest pitch, for one of the Publishers took the Essays in charge as they came in, numbered them in the order of reception, privately recorded the address of the writers, and only handed the Essays themselves to us Editors ("the Bachelor" included). We look over the beautifully written manuscripts, one after another, and wonder *who* wrote this one and that one, but the only response is "No. 1," "No. 5," "No. 14," "No. 26," "No. 34," "No. 43," "No. 56," "No. 74," as the case may be. We beg Mr. Chase to just tell us who wrote *this* very beautiful one. But he answers "No; decide upon the *merits* of the Essays themselves, and not of the writer. They are all supposed to be written by married housekeepers"—which of course we (especially "the Bachelor,") don't like to believe. As we look on this vast collection of more than two thousand pages of manuscript, and think of the labor and toil and time and thought, they have cost, we would regret having thrown out the challenge, were we not sure that great general good will come of it. Our own appreciation of the amount of thought, skill, and patience, and the degree of domestic talent to be found among Housekeepers, is greatly heightened, and we shall strive anew to secure a higher appreciation on the part of others. We are carefully considering how this mass of information can be turned to good account for others, and in some degree to the benefit of, at least, a part of the writers.

But what about the selection of the Prize Essay? Of course, we men-folks can not do that. Well, Dec. 1st these numbered Essays were handed over to a Committee of Intelligent Housekeepers, in good repute for their practical acquaintance with every day work. They have been busy reading for nearly two weeks! and have only got to No. 65. They read each Essay carefully through, make notes upon it, and mark it "A," "B" or "C." They report that nearly one third are marked "A," and that to go over and over these, and reduce the choice to *one*, will require the work and consideration of many days, if not weeks, yet. It is therefore impossible to announce the award, this month, or begin the publication of the Prize Article, or articles if more than one is selected.—While waiting, we will give a few extracts, taken at random, from some of the Essays. As so small a portion of each is taken, these extracts will not at all affect the value of any one for future use in this paper, or elsewhere. The numbers merely indicate the order in which the Essays came in. We have not the slightest idea of the name of any writer.—Eds.]

Extracts from Prize Essays.

[From No. 44.]—"....We had always two wells, one in the yard, the other in the cellar, and used either at pleasure. It was long after the house was rebuilt, that a pleasant innovation came in the shape of a pump. The relief from carrying water up stairs is very great. We are not a demonstrative family, but we felt that our water-pail had fallen in more pleasant places, if we did not tell of it. From an oversight at the first, in the location of our kitchen, we had compelled upon ourselves 731 *miles travel* in the fifteen years, for the one item of water. Without a cent more expense at first, we might have so arranged that we could have pumped water and poured it into the kettle on the stove, the dish-pan in the sink beneath, or the hand-basin in an adjoining sink, *without taking a single step*.......Our table arrangements are equally incomplete. A dish-closet adjoining the dish-sink, and in convenient proximity to the table, would leave the circuit from closet to table, from table to sink, and from sink to closet again, a matter of less steps in a week than we now find necessary for one meal. As it is, we traverse an average of 180 feet in simply *bringing* the dishes for each meal. Returning them to their places involves a distance of 240 more. This foots up in the little annual journey to our commissary, 103 miles! Counting our fifteen years' blunder, it amounts to 1,558 miles! and this not for the meals only—the 731 miles for water, and 1,558 for dishes, giving a total of **2,278** miles! and the *time* absorbed in this long pedestrian journey might have been *absolute leisure*, and the work have been as well performed. A review of all our mistakes might not prove interesting. We made a dozen or so, each having an unfortunate effect on our domestic enjoyment...." (How many thousands of families are doing the same to-day?—Ed.)

[From No. 3.]—"....It is the little things of this life that annoy a body; my annoyance is (I'm ashamed to confess,) no larger than the 'swill pail.' It is a 'necessary nuisance,' always needed, yet always in the way—an unsightly object to man or woman-kind. John acted in this, as in every thing else, very clever with me. He built a box, just large enough for the pail to set in, and covered it with a lid on leather hinges, and set this box in one corner of the wood-house, just by the kitchen door ...John brought home fifty pounds of beef last week, and I concluded to '*corn*' it. My way is this: I have it cut into pieces of five or six pounds, and rub each piece with sugar, two pounds will do for 100 lbs. of meat; then pack tightly in the barrel; take sufficient rain water to corn well. To every 100 lbs. of meat, take 10 pounds salt, 4 ounces saltpetre, and 2 gallons molasses; put these in about half the water, and heat until the scum rises, skim, stirring meanwhile to dissolve the ingredients, then mix with the rest of the water, and when cold, pour over the beef. This is the base of an Eastern 'Boiled Dinner.'...."

[From No. 15.]—"....A house in the country is not a *house* merely, 'to keep and to dress.' It is a garden, a farm—a little realm complete in itself—and a woman's presence should be felt throughout—especially in the arranging and ornamenting the grounds adjoining the house, should her taste be apparent. And first of all, it is desirable to produce a *harmonious* effect, so that regarding the home from without or from within, each object shall appear to be a part of a beautiful whole. Then, be the design simple or elaborate, it matters not, provided the home be an exponent of the owner's tastes and means....We chose *our* home because of its proximity to institutions we love, and not, as may fairly be presumed, for the beauty of its location.—We built our house in an open field, on a rise of ground *made by grading*, but which now often elicits the remark, 'How fortunate you were in finding such a pretty building spot,'—the observer little dreaming that our cellar bottom is a part of the original surface. There being no previous improvements to modify our plans, we gave the public road a wide berth, and immediately set about shutting it from view, by setting forest trees along our whole front, and on either side of the carriage way. An amusing conversation occurred between the original owner of our fields, and my husband, Mr. Max, while thus engaged. To give the story point, it must be premised that this stickler for 'fruit,' had scarcely managed in the course of twenty years to cover his house lot with enough trees to supply his family with apples. ——'See here, neighbor,' said he, 'What kind o' fruit do you expect them are trees to bear.'——'They would have borne *dollars* for you, had you set them here twenty years since,' was the rather tart reply, for the bare and desolate appearance of our fields was a serious drawback to our happiness that first year. Well! the trees have already borne—not dollars nor apples—but the pleasant assurance to us, that our home is growing in beauty every year. Next, grass was desirable, thick, soft and velvety. Thanks to our peculiar soil, we soon had this to our liking; and it is not woody and rough, if it is sometimes high enough for meadow. A few evergreens scattered here and there was all we attempted further, that spring, for showy parterres and graveled walks were not to be thought of. Trees will grow while we are at work or asleep, or enjoying our noonday rest. Many hardy climbers, roses, and ornamental shrubs, will do the same, and thank us for the privilege. We will put out a few of these each spring and autumn—no more than we can take good care of—and in time we shall be satisfied....Such was our conclusion, and steadily we have worked upon it. The care of the grounds has been our recreation....Our winter sitting-room opens to the south; the smoothly shorn lawn, and a variety of shapeful evergreens are in view from here, so that no sense of desolation mars the prospect. The rooms that open to the north and east, are our principal summer resort. Opposite these I grow my showy annuals and bed my petted exotics. The breath of the Sweet Briar, Lilac, Missouri Currant, and innumerable roses in their season, floats in at our open window. There are always flowers for as many bouquets as I like, from early spring until the Chrysanthemums are frozen, and yet we spend but very little time among them! How can we when we do not have it to spend?...."

[From No. 49.]—"....I am fully convinced that there are not only many *men* of many minds, but many women

[Copyright Secured.]

A STUDY IN PHYSIOGNOMY.

Our Artist has been amusing himself, as children sometimes do, by "making up faces," and has succeeded so well, we think our readers will be pleased to examine his production. An interesting part of the performance is, that one feature is in many instances, made to do double duty, presenting the singular fact of several persons having but one nose, one pair of eyes, etc., among them. The picture was intended for the Boys and Girls' Department, but other matters fully occupied that space, and probably their mothers will not object to a little "spice" in their own part of the paper.

also. In talking of renewing fine shirts, quite an item in these days, Mrs. Thorn says when the edge of a bosom begins to wear, she makes a delicate button-hole stitch the length of the bosom, works over the button-holes carefully as soon as they give way, patches the cuffs which never show it, and in this way she makes a shirt last one-third longer than she once did. Mrs. May, who owns a sewing-machine, and seems to think there is sport in making button-holes, stitches a strip of linen to match the middle fold, cuts out the old one with its worn button-holes and (having allowed for it in cutting) sets the new one in under the first plait. Mrs. Jones says that just as soon as this is all done, the bosom will give way in other places. She long ago discarded her practice of lining the bosoms throughout. Now she makes but one fine shirt at a time—so that she never has new ones altogether—allows an extra bosom and pair of wristbands to every two shirts, sets them into shirt No. 1, as that needs it, and then into shirt No. 2. Now hear old Mrs. Simpkins: "What's the use of a farmer's having fine shirts, anyhow? The land! what is the world coming to? *My* husband never had a fine shirt in all his life. He puts on his standing collar and stock, and one of those false bosoms ('*hypocrites*,' some call them), over his every-day shirt, when he goes to meeting, or takes a load to town, and then he is dressed fit for a king. At any rate, that old Alfred the Great, my Josms used to read about, would have thought it fit for *him*. I suppose Kings now-a-days would not think so, they've all got so grand—kings, parsons and their wives, farmer folks, and all.'.... !"

[FROM No. 20.]—"....A good housekeeper makes a good servant—a good *housekeeper*, you understand, not a good woman. Look at Aunt Debby, one of the best women in the world, and was there ever such an abominable muddle as her *housekeeping*! Sometimes Aunt Debby does a certain piece of work, sometimes it is left for Sarah Jane—trimming the lamps for instance. Sarah Jane leaves them for Aunt Debby, and Aunt Debby leaves them for Sarah Jane; if Aunt Debby sets out to do them, she must, in the first place, find her scissors. Accordingly, she runs up stairs and down to rummage the pockets of her dresses, then she pokes over the little heaps of strings and dried orange peel lying promiscuous in the cupboard; possibly her search is uninterrupted, but generally the butcher comes, or a neighbor drops in; the scissors are discovered after a time, but then the lamps are forgotten......"

[FROM No. 17.]—"....I will give my rule for bread-making—a certain one for me. Of course, the flour must be good; it should always be sifted just before using. We use baker's yeast, and get it fresh every week, as it is more convenient. For three loaves of bread, take 3 pints of milk or luke warm water (according to taste). Boil and mash 5 good sized potatoes, add 1 cup of yeast and a little salt. Stir all together at night with as much flour as you can stir in with a spoon. Leave it in a warm place to rise, and in the morning, when light, *knead it well*, adding sufficient flour. Let it rise until light and full of air-holes, and mould it out into loaves; then let it rise again to the point from which it was last worked down, and bake.——If I can not, through the medium of this Essay, teach a novice to make bread, I wish I could impress it upon those who *do* know how, to give more attention to it. If you know when bread is light, attend to it immediately, and not put it off, because you are doing something else, as the fermentation passes so rapidly into the acetous stage, from which no saleratus or legerdemain of that kind, can redeem it into good bread. Bread should be baked about an hour, and as cook stoves are so very different, every one should know best how to temper her own oven. The heat should be directed to the bottom as much as possible, for if the top crust forms too rapidly, it will press down the bread and prevent the expansion of the loaf, and so make a heavy streak. Or if not so bad as that, there will be great ugly cracks in the crust. When it is cut, if there are large air-holes in it, you may conclude it was not kneaded enough, and try to have it better next time........A tin of raised biscuit may be easily made by taking enough of the bread dough when ready for moulding into loaves, and working in nearly a cup of butter. But to make capital raised biscuits, try the following rule, for it is certain: Six cups of milk, 1 of yeast, and a little flour stirred in at night. In the morning add 1 cup of butter, and let it rise the same as bread. For rusks, add 1 cup of sugar and 2 eggs, and varnish the tops, when done, with the white of an egg.......With regard to pie-making, probably it would have been much better for us, if no pies had ever come into existence; but since they have, and since people will eat them, we had better make them as nicely as possible. Every body knows that it takes equal parts of lard and water mixed in flour, to make crust, but every body does not know *how* to mix it. It requires a deftness that can be gained only by practice. Put the lard into the flour cold, and rub it in smoothly, adding the water by degrees and roll out neatly and quickly as possible. If you want the upper crust particularly flaky, roll it out partially and dot here and there with lard. Then make it in a lump and roll out again for the pie. All pies are better baked in earthen dishes. There must always be an opening in the upper crust. Apple pies are especially nice, when made in these dishes, the apples sliced in without a bottom crust, sweetened, and a nice top crust, but you may sigh in vain at hotels, and at the many private tables, for any thing so simple and so delicious....What we call 'Tued Pie,' (though I'm sure I don't know why) is delicious. The apples are stewed and then placed in a crust and baked. The top crust and some of the apple is then taken off. Sweeten and put on sweet cream or butter. Replace the top crust and put the apple over it, and season the same as the lower part; to be eaten warm...."

[FROM No. 11.]—(*Extracts from Vine Leroy's Experience.*)

"....'Come to supper, Mother, Aunt Peggy, Eva, and all.'—'In a minute, dear.'—'Five o'clock precisely.' Josey is always very punctual, I can trust her to get meals for us, with no fear of her not having them ready in season. Shall I take your work Peggy? Come Eva, we will go and see what Josey has got good for supper.——'Has *she* been getting supper all alone, Aunt Vine?'——Yes, dear; she does it often.——I had become so interested in the story of 'A Summer,' in Leslie Goldthwaite's Life, I had not missed her. 'I wish you would take a magazine for me,' said Eva to her mother, Aunt Peggy. 'Do you know that that magazine costs two dollars a year? I will tell you sometime how the children pay for their magazines.' 'You have got a very nice supper, daughter, and have set the table very nicely.'——'You don't mean to say Vine, that Josey has made *them* short-cakes,' said Aunt Peggy.——'Oh, yes, she has made a good many.'—'Why don't you never let me help you so, Ma,' said Eva.—'You will never let me bake any, and I am as old as Josey.'——'Well, I never could bear to see girls of your age mussing in dough,' said Aunt Peggy.——'My! how short and good these biscuits are.'——'Yes, I often tell Vine, that Josey can beat her making short-cakes.'——'Now, Papa, I don't like you to praise my cooking so in company.'——'But it must be you don't have such good one's as these very often, or you could *not* make so much butter,' said Aunt Peggy.——'We only have them about twice a week.'——'Twice a week, and short as this! You must milk all cream from your cows.'——'Let me tell her, Ma, how I made them,' said Josey. 'In the first place, mother always strains her buttermilk; and I take a bowlful of the dried cream we get from it, and a quart of buttermilk, in which I put two teaspoonfuls of soda, and a little salt. And here is a berry short-cake I have made; father likes them so well.'——'A berry short-cake in January! I never heard of such a thing,' said Aunt Peggy.——'Yes, when rolling my biscuit I roll a strip about two inches thick, and put it in a long tin and bake it with them. When it is done, I take it out on a platter, split it open and butter it, then put my stewed berries in it while hot. I had the berries hot, too, and sweetened well, with a good deal of juice. I think strawberries are better, but they were not plentiful last season, and red raspberries were, so we use them. Black raspberries are excellent to make them of, too, and any of them are better still, if kept by canning.'——'I wish Eva could cook like this,' said Aunt Peggy.——'And *I* wish my Ma would sometimes make such a short-cake as this, or let *me* learn how,' responded Eva. * * * 'Heigho! there goes seven o'clock, and I must be off, it is the evening for the 'Farmer's Club,' so you must excuse me. There's a kiss for you Vine, now let me kiss you Peggy,' said Mr. Leroy, in a playful manner.——'Well! I declare! I don't believe you ever will leave off your boyish capers. Now you have been married fifteen years, and you kiss your wife like a boy, just because you are to leave her for a couple of hours. My husband hasn't kissed me since I married him.'——'I hope my husband will never be too dignified to kiss me.'——'And I guess I never will. Even the name of Joshua has never made a prophet of me. Good evening to you.'...."

Good Bread.—Mrs. M. W., writes, that after keeping house 12 years, and trying all sorts of bread recipes, and finding them all to fail some times, she adopted the directions published in the *Agriculturist* two years ago, (Feb. 1865), and she has never since failed to have good bread. Several others have written similarly, and we repeat the substance of the directions for the benefit of at least a hundred thousand present readers who did not have that number of the paper; Requisites, good flour, good potatoes, and good hops.—For stock yeast, good for 4 to 6 weeks, boil 2 or 3 handfuls of hops, 1½ hours, in 2 quarts water; strain the liquor on to 2 tablespoonfuls of flour, previously wet with cold water; stir well and leave until lukewarm; add ½ cup yeast, let it stand 15 to 20 hours, then bottle for use—to be shaken every time any is to be taken out.——Make a ferment thus: Wash clean and boil soft 2 quarts of potatoes, and mash fine while hot, with 1 quart of flour; reduce with cold water, and add half a cup of the stock yeast from the bottle; let it ferment 8 or 10 hours, or until it begins to fall at the top, then strain. This will keep two weeks in cold weather, but must not freeze or heat.——For baking, in the evening lay the sponge with ½ ferment, ½ water, and ½ milk if you have it, otherwise use ⅔ds water; add a little salt; cover with a cloth in a warm place until morning, then knead in flour until it works free from the hands and board. Let it rise again in pans, then bake.—The sponge should be a little too soft to knead, but the more flour you add in kneading, the longer will it be in rising; in summer it should be quite stiff. It should always rise until it has a delicate, silky touch to the hand, or until it begins to fall at the top, which is a sure test. If worked too soon, it will be tough and dark colored; if not kneaded enough, it will be coarse-grained, while that properly kneaded will be fine-grained, light, and showy. When cold keep bread in a stone jar; it will thus remain moist much longer.

About the Winter Fashions.

BY MADAME DEMOREST.

If women are not healthy, and do not dress sensibly, it certainly is not the fault of fashion. This much abused goddess is, at least just now, doing every thing possible to render the clothing of both women and children healthy, convenient, and economical.—The trailed dresses which are so generally worn in the drawing-room, are hereafter to be confined to such privileged localities, and dresses looped up or shortened, so as to form a mere upper skirt to the petticoat, worn in the street.

These short dresses are the novelty of the season; they are always cut gored, and are vandyked out, or shaped in battlements, or square teeth, over a petticoat, ornamented with a plaiting: a flat, single plaiting, called "*Marie Antoinette*," is the most in vogue. A striped Balmoral petticoat is very good wear, the plaiting edged with a contrasting color, and put on with a narrow braid also of the contrasting color. This may be worn with all kinds of dresses, long or short, and with all dark or neutral colors. With a short dress cut out square, and bound, or edged with a flat silk, or jet braid, a short *sac*, or loose paletot is worn, also cut out square, and edged to match. If the dress is vandyked, a peplum basquine, or "Ristori" paletot is worn, both describing points to match with dress.

Ladies should be careful in changing the style of a walking dress, to change also the size and shape of their hooped skirts to agree with it. A short dress is of course narrow, and requires a very narrow hoop, of the proper gored shape. If one can not be purchased, it is better to cut a short gored skirt (six gores) in cotton cloth, and insert in casings, five or six springs. A flounce made to button on and take off, will transform this into a handsome "dress" hooped skirt, the whole at a less cost than a good skeleton hoop, besides which, the indelicacy of skeleton hoops is avoided.

Ladies who do not like the short dresses, or who consider them unsuited to their age, will find the "Boscobel" Dress Looper, a very graceful, convenient, and ornamental adjunct, extremely simple, and efficient in raising dresses without injury out of contact with the dirt of the streets. This useful novelty is made in all styles, and contributes a sufficient trimming to any dress.

An inexpensive, and very lady-like accessory to a handsome gored dress, consists of a dress peplum, which is attached to a waist-band, and forms a sort of pointed basque to the skirt, relieving it entirely of the look of plainness, which is to many so objectionable. The dress peplum opens on the sides, in front, and at the back, and may be trimmed with fringe, with braid, with gimp, with Cluny lace, or with anything adapted to the material, and in harmony with the other parts of the dress.

There is a simple and excellent Shoulder Brace, and skirt supporter, which ladies should always wear, in conjunction with a heavy hoop, or Balmoral skirt. It is composed only of bands of elastic, arranged so as to support the back and relieve the hips of the weight upon them, and this it does effectually, at the same time greatly promoting a fine walking *pose*, and symmetry of form.

Bonnets are still worn very small, [ridiculously so—ED.] although the last Parisian advices indicate a considerable enlargement. A decided change, however, will not take place until spring. In the meantime, ladies may be thankful, that with little skill, trouble or expense, they can make their own bonnets.

A novel little invention has been introduced recently, which has such direct bearing upon the health of women, and children, that I can not forbear an allusion to it. This is a new Stocking Suspender, superseding the old elastics, which form a tight ligature around the limbs, causing congestion, rush of blood to the head, cold feet, and various evils. The new Suspender has no "machinery," requires no sewing on of buttons, is cheap, and keeps the stocking neat, and accurately in place.

BOYS & GIRLS' COLUMNS.

A Happy New Year!!!

To all the girls and boys of the *Agriculturist* family. A few years ago it took some 25,000 greetings to go all round, and give each family a share of our good wishes—now, 150,000 congratulations are not enough to distribute to the throng, in return for the welcomes they send us from all over the land. Kind feeling and the words of cheer which it prompts, come from a spring which can not be exhausted; they increase in the giving. But words are cheap—one little boy of our acquaintance, in reply to the salutation, "I wish you a happy New Year," was accustomed to ask, "What are you going to give me to make me happy?" This, of course, was not a very polite question, but it was very "common-sense-ical." A true friend will find many ways to bestow benefits upon those he loves, besides kind words, although these alone, are of great value. Well, 1866 has, we trust, proved that little folks are high in our regard. The pictures, puzzles, stories, and other good things which the *Agriculturist* has given them, need no further acknowledgment than we have received already in many thousands of pleasant letters, telling us how much enjoyment our monthly visits give.

THE BEAUTIFUL HOLIDAY PICTURE (*next page*) is an earnest of what may be expected in 1867. There the old year is represented going out sorrowfully, as if regretting that more good has not been done, while the New Year, 1867, coming from the Horn of Plenty, indicates that we may look for abundant good things to follow; and we shall certainly try to do our part in keeping the horn well supplied.

All will feel like joining the joyous group who are so gleefully welcoming Santa Claus, and not a few will rejoice with those in the corners who are examining their holiday gifts, or joining in the sports of the season. Do not neglect to study the scene in the upper right hand corner of the sketch. It represents two little street sweepers, such as swarm in large cities, enjoying the Christmas pie which some kind hearted friend has given them. The stable where they find shelter, and the manger, will bring to mind the story and the example of Him, "who though he was rich, for our sakes became poor," and will, we trust, lead many to bestow some good upon the poor of their own neighborhoods. To begin the year with good-will shown to the needy, will be a most worthy way of exhibiting our gratitude for good received, and our own worthiness of expected blessings. God loves those who remember his poor. No surer way of making this a happy year can be found than keeping the resolution, to

DO GOOD TO SOME ONE EVERY DAY THIS YEAR.

Street Beggars.

In most large cities, street begging is a regular profession, having its own peculiar arts and mysteries, and requiring a special training to make it successful. A professional beggar studies appropriate dress, gesture, and manner of speech, as certainly, if not as thoroughly as the actors in a theatre, and many of them attain a degree of perfection in this part of their art, that might make their fortunes if practiced on the stage. For example, notice that poor, tottering, white-haired old man, that has just entered our office; he has frequently called before. He is the very picture of a recent emigrant. His dress is scanty, but neat; apparently a great effort is being made to be decent, though poor. He wears wooden clogs, which give notice of his approach, as he hobbles toward you, and stretches out his long thin hand, that in itself has a most appealing look. In reply to a question, he mumbles over some strange jargon, that no one present can understand. Most persons at once think, "here is a case of real misfortune, an aged stranger in a foreign land, who has no doubt lost the little all he depended on to make him comfortable in old age." The whole appearance of the man is carefully studied and arranged to produce just this effect, and until known as a professional beggar, few can turn him away, without at least a trifle. Yet on some fine afternoon, in walking up Broadway, you may meet a well dressed, respectable looking old gentleman, walking erect, carrying a nice cane, rather for ornament than support, the picture of one who has laid by enough to make him easy for the rest of his earthly journey, and if you are sharp at scrutinizing countenances, you may recognize our poor pauper, for it is the same. He is said to be already wealthy from begging, but he keeps at his trade, part of the time, perhaps from mere habit.

Thousands of our readers have seen a one-legged man clad in an old military dress, stumping painfully along Park Row, not on crutches, but seated on the pavement, and moving himself by means of his hands, which are protected by thick leather mittens. He never asked for even a penny—that is in words—but his appealing look to the passers by, said more plainly than words could speak, "For the love of humanity, and in gratitude to your country's defenders, please aid a poor maimed soldier," and hundreds daily answered the appeal. A few weeks ago this man was arrested by the police, as a vagrant, having no visible means of support, and consigned to the place on Blackwell's Island, provided for such cases. Just as he was about being sent up, his lawyer brought into court, deeds, mortgages, etc., proving him to be worth over twenty thousand dollars! This disclosure will probably put an end to his further begging operations.

These are but two examples out of hundreds here that could be described—some of them we may yet notice. The large majority of street beggars are impostors, and though it seems harsh, we believe it to be a safe rule to give to none of them, unless their cases have been first investigated and found worthy of help. If one desires to help the poor, as all should do, a little inquiry in almost any neighborhood will bring out deserving cases enough to employ all the resources of charity.

A Game!—"Boys," said a facetious farmer to his sons, "we had a pretty hard day's work yesterday, now let's have a game of chopping wood."

Singular Cure for Laziness.

A friend, whose name we are not at liberty to give, but who is well and widely known as a business man of sterling worth, was last year erecting a large building. One of his excellent peculiarities is, to allow no intemperance or profanity among his men, and to insist that every man shall work for the liberal pay he is willing to give. One day, this gentleman noticed that one of the builders was continually shirking, seeming to care only to pass away the time and draw his pay. Calling his foreman, who had the hiring as well as the overseeing of the men, our friend asked whether the lazy hand had been engaged for the season, or only for a short time. "For the season," was the reply, "but I can discharge him, I suppose."—"Oh! no," said Mr. ——, "but I want you to go down to the village hotel and engage the best room you can find; let this man go there and occupy it; every month send his bill to me, and I will pay it."—The foreman informed the hired man of the instructions given, and he at once went to the owner. "I understand you are not satisfied with my work," said he.—"I find no fault with your work," was the reply, "but because you *don't work*." "I will leave, if you insist on it," said the man.—"Not at all—I don't turn you away, but I have given orders to have the best room at the hotel put at your service, since you want to play the gentleman at my expense, and I promise you I will pay the bill promptly every month, but I will not have your *bad example* among my men." The poor fellow, utterly dumb-founded at such novel treatment, scarcely knew how to reply, but looked as though he would like to sink into the ground. Finally, he asked, "Are you willing to try me for a week."——"Certainly," said Mr. ——, "I am always willing to help a man who wants to reform." The man returned to his work, cured of his laziness, and from that day forth, no more industrious hand was to be found on the place.

Stories About Parrots.

As our young readers well know, the parrot may be taught to repeat many words. It is generally supposed that they attach no meaning to what they say, but simply utter the sounds, as they would any other notes. This may be so, but some incidents seem to show that they may sometimes know the use of language. A lady friend of the writer occupied part of a house where was kept a very talkative parrot. One day the lady came down stairs dressed in a short-gown and petticoat, the weather being intensely warm, when the parrot immediately cried out, "What frock you got on?".... Another friend relates that a parrot belonging to his landlady one day annoyed her very much by its continued talking and screeching. At last she seized the stick with which she had been stirring the clothes, and raised it threateningly, when the bird immediately cried out, "You saucy thing, poll won't speak another word," and remained silent almost the whole day.——A bird show was held at the Museum in New-York several years since, to which a parrot was sent that had been taught to repeat the Lord's Prayer. This was advertised extensively, and hundreds of persons went to hear the wonder, but to their disappointment, and the vexation of the owner, Poll would not utter a word during the exhibition, although fully able to do what had been expected. After the show, the parrot was taken home, and upon reaching its place, it exclaimed, "I suppose I can talk now," and became as voluble as ever. The bird's silence was not remarkable, as song birds will seldom sing freely, for some time after being taken to a new place; the speech on going home certainly seemed to indicate intelligence. A gentleman had taught his parrot to say, "Get your gun, John," which was well remembered one night by the bird, for burglars entered the house, and Poll, hearing a noise, screamed out at the top of her voice, "Get your gun, John," awakening her owner, and at the same time putting the robbers to flight.

Answers to Problems and Puzzles.

The following are answers to the puzzles, etc., in the December number, page 441. No. 239 and 240. Mathematical Problems.—These were incorrectly stated last month, and are given properly below under the numbers 246, 247. No. 242. Geographical Problem.—We shall discuss this next month.——No. 240. Illustrated Rebus.—Iona Grape Vine (eye on a grape-vine).——No. 243. Conundrum.—It is papa-veraceous.——No. 244. Illustrated Rebus.—From infancy to adolescence a man's future position and stand in life are usually taken.

The following have sent in correct answers up to Dec. 1st.: George and William Fenik, John Norway, Joseph S. Bonaparte, Christian Wine, J. Celiff, Clara Greiner, Julia Greiner, Avery L. Rand, James P. Veatch, A. Jackson, Andrew Jackson, Delmer D. Bryant, Jennie Cooper, J. B. Conant, Nellie J. Cox, Alfred Hawksworth, John E. Wittmor, B. J. Hammer, Sarah Purdy, Fred. Stanley, R. L. Selden, Frank B. Bourne, H. Mattie Comiler, John H. Lehman, Samuel M. Edwards, Peter Smith, Nettie Waldron, H. S. Loper, D. Luther Roth, Mrs. Wm. Baum, "H. D. S.," Sarah F. Winser, Martin Keeney, James Ratleff.

New Puzzles to be Answered.

No. 245. *Mathematical Problem*, to be solved arithmetically. The crew of a ship consisted of Sailors and Soldiers. There were 22 sailors to every 3 guns and 10 over. The whole number of men was 5 times the number of soldiers and guns together. After an engagement in which one-fifth were slain, there lacked 5 to be 13 men to every 2 guns. How many guns, sailors and soldiers at first?

No. 246. *Illustrated Proverb.*—Usually found to be true.

No. 247. *Mathematical Problem.*—A man has a triangular piece of ground whose sides measure respectively, 500, 400 and 300 feet each. How can he divide it equally among his four sons, giving each a plot of the same form?

No. 248. *Mathematical Problem*, to be solved arithmetically. John and Charles, set out from C, and D, at the same time, to travel to E, the road from C to E, passing through D. John travels 7 miles an hour, and at that rate he would overtake Charles 3 miles before he arrives at E. But, after arriving at D, John travels 6½ miles an hour in consequence of which, he overtakes Charles just as he enters E. Supposing Charles, to travel 5 miles an hour, what are the distances between C, D, and E?

No. 249. *Illustrated Rebus.*—Well worth remembering.

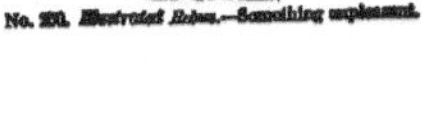

No. 250. *Illustrated Rebus.*—Something unpleasant.

[COPYRIGHT SECURED.]

HERE WE COME WITH A MERRY CHRISTMAS AND A HAPPY NEW YEAR!!!—*Designed and Engraved for the American Agriculturist.* (*See Page* 25.)

(Business Notices $2.50 per Agate Line of Space.)

FLORENCE

LOCK-STITCH SEWING MACHINES.

Highest Premium, Fair of American Institute, 1865.
CELEBRATED REVERSIBLE FEED MOVEMENT.
UNIFORM SELF-ADJUSTING TENSION,
FOUR SEPARATE DISTINCT STITCHES,
WILL GATHER AND SEW A RUFFLE AT ONCE.
OFFICES OF THE COMPANY.
505 Broadway, N. Y., and [illegible], England.

PRINCIPAL AGENCIES.

141 Washington-st., Boston. [illegible], N. Y.
630 Chestnut-st., Phila. [illegible], Havana,
100 [illegible] Cuba,
26 West Fourth-st., Cin. [illegible] Binghamton, N. Y.
43 Public Square, [illegible], N. Y.
[illegible], Newark, N. J.
7 North Pennsylvania-st., [illegible], Nashville, Tenn.
Indianapolis, 2 Yates Block, E. Genesee-st.,
Cor. Jeff. and Woodward Av., Syracuse, N. Y.
Detroit, [illegible] Rochester, N. Y.
[illegible] Montgomery-st., San Fran. 51 North Fifth-st., St. Louis, Mo.
[illegible], Troy, N. Y.
372 to 376 Main-st., Hartford, Cor. Genesee, Columbia, and
Conn. Seneca-sts., Utica, N. Y.
529 Broadway, Albany, N. Y.

WHEELER & WILSON ROTARY HOOK LOCK STITCH SEWING MACHINES.

625 BROADWAY.

"WOMAN'S GREATEST BOON. We would advise a man to forego a [illegible] with a flail, rather than to [illegible] the wife wear her health [illegible] away in the everlasting 'stitch, stitch, stitch,' when a Sewing Machine [illegible]. The WHEELER & WILSON is an invaluable [illegible] every household. We have had several [illegible], and after a six years' service, the WHEELER & WILSON has taken the [illegible] the best, where all kinds of sewing are to be done in a family."
[illegible] Jan. 1865.

THE GREAT FAMILY SEWING MACHINE.

GROVER & BAKER'S

HIGHEST PREMIUM
Elastic Stitch
SEWING MACHINE.
495 Broadway, New York.

TAKE YOUR CHOICE!

We have already given away more than

FOUR HUNDRED SEWING MACHINES!

as premiums for new subscribers to the NEW YORK OBSERVER. [illegible] for one year, $[illegible], we [illegible] a $55 MACHINE, Wheeler & Wilson, or Grover & Baker. [illegible] circulars and [illegible]; they will be sent FREE.—Terms, $3.50 a year, in advance.

SIDNEY E. MORSE, JR. & CO.,
[illegible] Park Row, New York.

SOMETHING NEW.—An ingenious little article, just patented, needed in every household. AGENTS WANTED. Sample [illegible] Address W. A. BOARDMAN, [illegible] avenue, New Haven, Conn.

A MODEL PAPER. The *Watchman & Reflector*, of Boston, has an extensive reputation for ability and enterprise. It has not been surpassed in merit by any religious journal in the country. But it aspires to higher excellence, and proposes to [illegible], with the opening of the New Year, one of the most comprehensive family papers in the world. It will be greatly enlarged, and published on a double sheet: one sheet devoted [illegible] to religious matter; the other to literary, [illegible], monetary and agricultural articles. This latter department will be new and peculiar, with a rich variety of [illegible] articles on current, moral, social and [illegible] questions; [illegible] the leading men of the age in thought [illegible] reviews of important books; tales for the family [illegible] horticultural and gardening matter for farmers; [illegible] and reports of the markets for business [illegible].

[illegible] has a more comprehensive [illegible] to meet the wants of all families and of all the [illegible] a family; and as the editorial staff will consist of [illegible] and experts used to the several departments, [illegible] will be assisted by [illegible] contributors, many of them [illegible] Watchman & Reflector [illegible] family paper, unequalled in merit and in [illegible] enterprising conductors deserve the largest success.

For Specimen [illegible]

FORD, OLMSTEAD & CO.,
Publishers, Boston, Mass.

Our Young Folks

Is very highly praised by numerous State Superintendents of Schools and other distinguished Educators, for "the freshness, vigor, and variety of its pages," "its simplicity and purity of style," "its high moral tone," "pure and ennobling sentiment," "elevating and refining influences," "life-like and attractive illustrations," as "unquestionably the best juvenile magazine published in this country."

TERMS: $2.00 a year; large discount to Clubs. Specimen number, 20 cents.

Every Saturday

Has the best and freshest selections from the most popular Foreign Periodicals, including frequently articles by HENRY KINGSLEY, EDMUND YATES, ALEXANDER SMITH, Miss ROSSETTI, MATTHEW ARNOLD, ROBERT BUCHANAN, FRANCES POWER COBBE, EDMOND ABOUT, ALEXANDER DUMAS, ANTHONY TROLLOPE, JEAN INGELOW, and other eminent writers. TERMS: Single Number, 10 cents. Yearly subscription, $5.00.

TICKNOR & FIELDS, Publishers, Boston.

HEADQUARTERS

FOR

U. S. MAPS

IS AT

H. H. LLOYD & CO.'S,

21 John-St., New York.

P. S.—We have 5 sizes of U. S. Maps, the largest, a Copper plate, 6x6 ft., made in 12 styles, and a vast variety of other Maps, Charts, Prints, Photographs, Engravings, &c., &c.

"Fighting against WRONG and for the GOOD, the TRUE and the BEAUTIFUL."

FOR BOYS AND GIRLS.

THE LITTLE CORPORAL

Is acknowledged by the leading papers to be the

Best Juvenile Paper in America.

The New York *Tribune* says: The only literary periodical which has ever succeeded in our Western States, is THE LITTLE CORPORAL. Its subscription list at the end of the first year numbered 35,000, and if it continues to be conducted with the same ability and enterprise which are now devoted to it, there is no reason why the second year should not close with a roll of 70,000 subscribers. It is an admirable periodical, lively, entertaining, instructive, unexceptionable in tone, and charmingly printed. It is published at the low price of $1.00 a year.

We offer a

Magnificent List of Premiums!

The price of the Corporal is one dollar a year, in advance; sample copy, telling all about the premiums, ten cents. Address ALFRED L. SEWELL, Publisher, Chicago, Ill.

For Marking Linen.

CLARK'S PATENT INDELIBLE PENCIL.

1866. Greatly Improved. 1866.

Warranted superior to all Indelible Inks. Agents wanted. Circulars and sample Pencil sent post-paid, on receipt of Fifty Cents.

For sale by Stationers, Booksellers, and Druggists.

Address

The Indelible Pencil Co.,
Northampton, Mass.

THE AUTOMATIC ORGAN. This is the name which has been given by Messrs. Prince & Co., of Buffalo, N. Y., to one of the varieties of the popular instruments manufactured by them. The Automatic Organ is designed for a parlor instrument, and is preferred by many over the Piano cased Melodeon. It is certainly a superb instrument, combining great power and sweetness, and finished in that exquisite style for which the Organs and Melodeons of Prince & Co. are so justly celebrated. The Automatic Organ is made with from two to eight stops, and from two to six or more sets of reeds. The large Organ with eight stops, though not equal to the Organ Melodeon with pedal bass, has the volume, power, and sweetness sufficient for any ordinary sized Church. Send for full descriptive Catalogue, which will be forwarded free of postage. Address Prince & Co., Buffalo, N. Y.

HERALD OF HEALTH, November and December numbers free to new subscribers for 1867.
Dio Lewis says, "It cannot fail to succeed."
The New York Tribune says, "It deserves a [illegible] welcome, as an efficient aid to the progress of popular education."
Demorest's Monthly says, "It has greatly improved under its new management."
[illegible] a number. A Wheeler & Wilson's Sewing Machine, worth $55, for [illegible] subscribers.
MILLER, WOOD & CO.,
No. 15 Laight-st., New York.

THE CHILDREN'S HOUR.—A new illustrated magazine for the [illegible]. Edited by T. S. ARTHUR, 323 Walnut-street, Philadelphia, Pa. $1.25 a year; 6 copies, $[illegible]. Specimen numbers, 10 cents.

THE HORTICULTURIST.

TWENTY-SECOND ANNUAL VOLUME—1867.

A Monthly Magazine, devoted to the ORCHARD, VINEYARD, GARDEN, and NURSERY; to *Culture under Glass, Landscape Gardening, Rural Architecture, and the Embellishment and Improvement of Country, Suburban and City Homes. Handsomely Illustrated.*

1867—Two Dollars and Fifty Cents; 1866 bound and post-paid, and 1867—$4.50; 1865 and 1866 bound and post-paid, and 1867—$6.

The three volumes contain 1,200 royal octavo pages.

GEO. E. & F. W. WOODWARD,
Publishers, 37 Park Row, New York.

Now Ready.

The Illustrated
HORTICULTURIST ALMANAC for 1867.

Containing a Calendar of Operations in the ORCHARD, VINEYARD, FARM, GARDEN and GREEN-HOUSE, for every month in the year.—Price, TEN CENTS, post paid.
60 cents per doz.; $5 per 100; $40 per 1,000.
GEO. E. & F. W. WOODWARD, 37 Park Row, N. Y.

New Books, Fine Paper, Extra Bindings.

WOODWARD'S ARCHITECTURE AND RURAL ART.

170 Original and Practical Designs and Plans for Low-priced COTTAGES, FARM HOUSES, BARNS, &c., with numerous plans for laying out small plots of ground. 12mo. 120 pages.

Paper covers, 75 cents; cloth, $1.00. Post-paid.

WOODWARD'S COUNTRY HOMES.

Eighth Edition, revised and enlarged. A new and original work with 150 designs and plans for Country Houses of moderate cost, with a full illustrated description of the manner of constructing "Balloon Frames." 12mo. 192 pages. Cloth, extra.—Post-paid, $1.50.

MANUAL OF THE HOUSE:

OR, HOW TO BUILD COUNTRY HOUSES AND OUTBUILDINGS;
With 126 Designs and Plans,
By D. H. Jacques.
12mo. 176 pages.
Cloth, extra—post-paid, $1.50.

FULLER'S FOREST TREE CULTURIST.

A new Work on the PROPAGATION, CULTIVATION, AND MANAGEMENT OF FOREST TREES.
By Andrew S. Fuller,
Author of the Grape Culturist.
Fully Illustrated.
Post-paid, $1.50.

GRAPES AND WINE.

A New and Practical Work on the CULTIVATION of NATIVE GRAPES AND MANUFACTURE OF AMERICAN WINE;
By GEORGE HUSMANN,
of Missouri.
Fully Illustrated.
Cloth, extra—post-paid, $1.50.

Woodward's Graperies, &c., 60 designs, post-paid,		$1.50
Manual of the Farm, Agriculture, Illustrated, post-paid,		$1.00
Manual of the Garden, Horticulture, do.	do.	$1.00
Manual of the Barn Yard, Domestic Animals,	do.	$1.00

GEO. E. & F. W. WOODWARD, Publishers,
And Dealers in all works on Architecture & Agriculture,
37 PARK ROW, New York.

Illustrated Priced Catalogue sent Free.

GARDENING FOR PROFIT.

A Work, instructive alike to the Amateur or Market Gardener, detailing the practical experience of nearly 20 years' Gardening for the New York Market.

By PETER HENDERSON,
(of HENDERSON & FLEMING.)
Price, $1.50, by mail pre-paid.

Seed and Plant Catalogues for 1867, will be mailed to our customers as usual, to others on receipt of 10 cents.

HENDERSON & FLEMING,
Seedsmen and Market Gardeners,
67 Nassau-st., New York.

FIRST MORTGAGE BONDS

OF THE

SOUTH WEST PACIFIC R. R. CO.

Principal and Interest guaranteed by the Atlantic and Pacific Railroad Company, in Coupon Bonds of

$1,000 EACH,

TWENTY YEARS TO RUN.

Due September 15, 1886.

INTEREST AT THE RATE OF 7 PER CENT. PER ANNUM, PAYABLE IN THE CITY OF NEW YORK, ON THE FIRST DAYS OF JANUARY AND JULY.

These Bonds are issued on 77 miles of completed road, now in operation to Rolla, in the State of Missouri, which cost to construct	$4,500,000
And 23 miles of road graded, with material on hand, to be completed by January 1, 1867, at a cost of	500,000
Together with 200,000 acres of land, now being disposed of at a minimum of $5 per acre, (maximum $15.)	1,200,000
Say present total value of	$6,200,000

The amount of Bonds issued is $2,000,000, secured by mortgage to John P. Yelverton and Chas. H. Ward, of New York, as Trustees of the above-named property.

By a provision of this Mortgage, when Lands are sold to the amount of $40,000, it is to constitute a Special Fund for the redemption of a like amount of these Bonds, at a rate not exceeding 105 per cent. They are also receivable at PAR by the Company in payment of its sales of Lands.

At St. Louis this road connects with all the Eastern Railways, and runs west through the most attractive parts of the State of Missouri via Franklin, St. James, Rolla, Lebanon, Marshfield, Granby (Lead Mines), and Neosho, to the west line of the State. At Springfield it will connect with the great ATLANTIC AND PACIFIC RAILROAD (its eastern terminus), to the Pacific.

When completed, it will present a road of 310 miles in length, costing about	$12,000,000
With 1,030,000 acres of Land valued at	10,000,000
Showing a total value of	$22,000,000

With a total amount of Bonds authorized, with the guarantee as above, of $7,250,000, which may be issued at a rate not exceeding $25,000 per mile of completed work as it progresses.

Of the present issue of $2,000,000 of Bonds, the sum of $500,000 is now offered for sale at the low rate of 80 per cent., after 1st January, the rate will be 85 per cent.

For further particulars apply to

WARD & CO. BANKERS,
No. 54 Wall Street, New York.

Highly Important to Manufacturers and Capitalists.—*The New Self-Holding Volkmann Plow.*—The most competent judges who have examined the new Patented Self-Holding Volkmann Plow, are of opinion that it is superior to any plow now in use, and that it must therefore, soon supersede every other plow. For a description of its peculiar features we refer to the N. Y. Semi-Weekly Tribune of Nov. 13, the Semi-Weekly Times, Nov. 9, the N. Y. Independent, Nov. 15, the Artisan, Dec. 5, and other leading papers. Mr. Volkmann, the inventor, is ready to entertain offers for the sale of State rights, or for the formation of a partnership. Address J. VOLKMANN, No. 111 West Thirty-eighth Street, New York City.

KNOX FRUIT FARM & NURSERIES.

One Hundred and Fifty Acres in Grapes, Strawberries, Blackberries, Raspberries, Currants, Gooseberries, &c., &c.

Send for our Catalogue, which is a valuable Treatise on their Cultivation.

We were among the very first to engage in growing **SMALL FRUITS**, on a large scale, and for many years have been making a collection, which is unsurpassed if equaled anywhere.

GRAPES.

The Concord is decidedly the most popular grape in the country. It is now generally planted, and gives greater satisfaction than any other. The

GREELEY PRIZE

has just been awarded it as the grape of the greatest value. For full description SEE CATALOGUE.

Hartford Prolific and Creveling, are the best *very* early grapes yet thoroughly tested, and are very profitable.

Ives is destined to be, if it is not now, the leading wine grape of the country. For full description of this invaluable grape, SEE CATALOGUE.

Rentz is nearly of the same value, and is a most vigorous grower.

Martha is a **White Concord**, and is destined to be among White grapes, what its parent, the Concord is among the colored varieties.

Black Hawk promises to be a grape of very great merit—perhaps the earliest of all.

For description of above, and **Iona, Israella, Adirondac**, and all other desirable kinds, as well as much valuable information on Grape Culture, send **10 Cents for Catalogue.**

Our vines are grown in the open air, *from* bearing wood taken from our extensive Vineyards.

STRAWBERRIES.

For many years we have given earnest attention to the cultivation of Strawberries. Our long and varied experience gives us great advantages, in the selection of such varieties as will give the best satisfaction to the grower, whether for home or market purposes; our collection, in variety, quality, and quantity, is unsurpassed, if equaled anywhere. We call special attention to the

JUCUNDA—OUR NO. 700.

After thoroughly testing this variety for seven years, we unhesitatingly say, that for UNIFORM AND LARGE SIZE, BEAUTY OF FORM AND COLOR, ENORMOUS YIELD, LONG CONTINUANCE IN BEARING, GREAT PROFIT, HEALTH AND VIGOR OF PLANT, and other desirable qualities, it is the most valuable Strawberry of which we have any knowledge. All who have seen it on our grounds, prize it alike highly.

Our present stock of plants of **Jucunda**, and all other valuable varieties is the largest and best we have ever offered.

Send 10 Cents for Catalogue, which is a complete Manual on the Strawberry.

CURRANTS.

The demand for this valuable *fruit* is greatly increasing every year. We have taken special pains to make the best possible collection, and our stock is, perhaps, much the largest in the country.

We offer very superior plants of
Versaillaise.—The best of all.
Fertile de Angers.—Very similar to the above.
Cherry.—Excellent *for* jelly.
Victoria.—Very late and good.
White Grape.—Superior for Wine.
La Hative.—Vigorous grower and very good.
Black Naples.—Good for Jams and Jellies.

We can furnish any other desirable kinds.

Also,

Raspberries, Blackberries, Gooseberries, &c., &c.

Send 10 cents for our **Descriptive and Illustrated Catalogue with Supplement.**

It contains **Descriptions and Illustrations** of the leading varieties of

Grapes, Strawberries, Raspberries, Blackberries, Gooseberries, Currants, &c.—Select Lists of Fruits, made up with great care.

Letters from Eminent Fruit Growers, and **Reports of various Committees**, who have visited our grounds, including the **Report of the Ad Interim Committee** of the **Ohio Pomological Society, 1865**, written by the President, DR. JNO. A. WARDER, from which we extract:

"Four things struck all the visitors as especially worthy of note: The modes of propagation and culture of the soil, the varieties under culture and trial, the wonderfully abundant product of magnificent berries, and the excellent and successful mode of harvesting and marketing the fruit, all of which may properly be introduced into this Report for the benefit of our fellow members."

Much valuable information, in each of these points, is contained in this Report, and other parts of the Catalogue.

J. KNOX,
Box 155, Pittsburgh, Pa.

L. L. WHITLOCK,

Room 6, { 115 Nassau-street, 37 Park Row, } New-York.

All kinds of Trees, Shrubs, &c., bought and sold on Commission. Producers are requested to send a list of Stock they have for sale.

Advantages in Buying of L. L. Whitlock.
1.—He keeps a list of the cheapest Stock in the Market.
2.—He buys Stock for you at Wholesale price.
3.—His twelve years' experience enables him to know how to select good Stock.

FOR TERMS, PRICE-LIST, &C., SEND A STAMP.
Office Hours, from 11 A. M., to 1 P. M.

HUTCHINSON'S PATENT UNIVERSAL EAGLE PLOW.—Makes three furrows any size or depth, while the driver rides, and without leaving his seat, has full command of the Plow. STATE or COUNTY RIGHTS for sale on reasonable terms. For descriptive Circular, apply to

HUTCHINSON & CO.,
Care A. WINCHESTER, 700 Chestnut street,
Philadelphia, Pa.

THE "THREE WARRANTS."—Please read my advertisement headed "Farmers and Gardeners."
JAMES J. H. GREGORY, Marblehead, Mass.

WE WANT AN AGENT IN EVERY COUNTY
TO SELL OUR
POPULAR SUBSCRIPTION BOOKS

They are the most popular books now published, and many Agents are making $10 to $20 a day. Send for Circulars giving full particulars to RICHARDSON & CO., Publishers, 540 Broadway, New York.

VICK'S ILLUSTRATED CATALOGUE of Seeds and FLORAL GUIDE FOR 1867,

Is now published. It contains nearly 100 pages, 100 fine Illustrations on Wood, of choice Flowers and Vegetables, and a beautiful Colored Flower Plate for Frontispiece. Also, descriptions of the finest flowers grown, with full and plain directions for culture.

Sent to all who desire, postage paid, for 15 cents—not half the cost. Sent free to all my customers of 1866, without being ordered. Address

JAMES VICK,
Rochester, N. Y.

☞ As will be seen by an advertisement in another column, HENRY WARD BEECHER is engaged in writing a story for the *New York Ledger*. The circulation of the *Ledger* is larger by one hundred thousand copies than that of any weekly or daily paper in the country.

B. T. BABBITT,

Manufacturer of and Dealer in

YEAST POWDER, SOAP POWDER, CONCENTRATED POTASH, ARROW ROOT, WASHING BLUE, SODA-ASH, etc.

SOAPS, SALERATUS, STARCH, SUPER-CARBONATE OF SODA, SAL-SODA, CREAM TARTER,

Nos. 64, 65, 66, 67, 68, 69, 70, 72 and 74 Washington Street, NEW YORK.

SUPERIOR GARDEN AND FLOWER SEEDS.

B. K. BLISS'

CELEBRATED SEED CATALOGUE,

and Guide to the Flower and Kitchen Garden.

Beautifully Illustrated with upwards of One Hundred Engravings.

The **Thirteenth Edition with Supplement for 1867**, is now in press, and will be ready for distribution early in January. It will contain 1[illegible] pages of closely printed matter, and upward of *One Hundred finely executed engravings of Flowers and Vegetables*, and a descriptive list of *Two Thousand varieties of Garden and Flower Seeds*, embracing all the **NEW VARIETIES** worthy of cultivation, introduced the past season—both of European and Home production, with explicit directions for their culture, also a list of **One Hundred and twenty-five varieties of French Hybrid Gladiolus**, including the leading novelties of the past season, with many other **Summer Flowering Bulbs**, consisting of **Amaryllis, Tuberoses, Tigridias—Lilies** in great variety, etc. To which is added a list of a few of the choicest varieties of **Grapes, Strawberries, Raspberries** and other **Small Fruits, Bedding Plants, etc., etc.**, cultivated at his gardens, with much other useful information upon the subject of gardening generally, which will be found useful to all engaged in the delightful occupation of gardening. A copy of the Catalogue will be mailed to all applicants enclosing **Twenty-five Cents**. Our regular customers supplied without charge. Address

B. K. BLISS,
Lock Box No. 11,
P. O. Springfield, Mass.

STRIPED LEAVED JAPANESE MAIZE.

The experience of the past season fully confirms all that we stated in reference to this beautiful plant, when introducing it to the public last spring; and we are in receipt of many flattering letters from the leading Florists in Europe, all of whom agree that it is the finest plant for decorative purposes that has been introduced for many years. Certificates of Merit and numerous Prizes have been awarded to Exhibitors at the various English and Continental exhibitions, not the least of which was that of the "Royal Horticultural Society's International Show," all grown from seed furnished by us last spring to our European correspondents.

"Cosmos," Agricultural Editor of the Saturday Evening Post, writes us that it is superior to any other for table use, as green corn.

Packets containing about 40 seeds, 25 cents.

Prices to the Trade, in bulk or in packets, will be given upon application.

B. K. BLISS,
Springfield, Mass.

A Cough, A Cold, or A Sore Throat,

REQUIRES IMMEDIATE ATTENTION AND SHOULD BE CHECKED.

IF ALLOWED TO CONTINUE,

Irritation of the Lungs, a Permanent Throat Disease, or Consumption,

IS OFTEN THE RESULT.

BROWN'S BRONCHIAL TROCHES

HAVING A DIRECT INFLUENCE TO THE PARTS, GIVE IMMEDIATE RELIEF.

For Bronchitis, Asthma, Catarrh, Consumptive and Throat Diseases,

TROCHES ARE USED WITH ALWAYS GOOD SUCCESS.

SINGERS AND PUBLIC SPEAKERS

will find *Troches* useful in clearing the voice when taken before Singing or Speaking, and relieving the throat after an unusual exertion of the vocal organs. The *Troches* are recommended and prescribed by Physicians, and have had testimonials from eminent men throughout the country. Being an article of true merit, and having *proved* their efficacy by a test of many years, each year finds them in new localities in various parts of the world, and the *Troches* are universally pronounced better than other articles.

OBTAIN only "BROWN'S BRONCHIAL TROCHES," and do not take any of the *Worthless Imitations* that may be offered.

SOLD EVERYWHERE.

DEMOREST'S BED-CLOTHES CLASPS are real Guardian Angels, at 25 cents each. Every parent should secure these invaluable protectors. No. 473 Broadway. Mailed post free.

Thorough-bred Poultry.

FOWLS, of all the valuable choice breeds, furnished at reasonable prices. They are carefully selected from the progeny of the most recent importations, and their purity is guaranteed. Orders sent by mail promptly filled.

Circulars, with full descriptive list, will be forwarded to any address on receipt of stamp. American Live Stock Co., No. 190 Water-st., New York City.

A. T. SCHAUFFLER, Superintendent.

New and Rare Vegetables.

I present to the Public my Annual List of New and Rare Seed for 1867, many of which I send out the first time this season.

MARBLEHEAD MAMMOTH DRUMHEAD CABBAGE.—(*The largest Cabbage in the world. Weighs from thirty to sixty pounds to the head, and is tender and sweet. No cabbage does so well in the South as this.*) CANNON BALL CABBAGE.—(*About as round and hard as a cannon ball. An early sort, and the hardest heading of all Cabbage.*) STONE MASON CABBAGE.—(*Standard variety of Winter Drumhead Cabbage in Boston market. Under good cultivation every plant on an acre will make a large and hard head. It is remarkably tender and sweet. In half ounce packages.*) LENORMAND'S MAMMOTH CAULIFLOWER.—(*A new variety, the largest of all the Cauliflower family. Very reliable for heading.*) VERY EARLY ERFURT CAULIFLOWER.—(*New, remarkably early, and fine for hot-beds.*) NEW YORK IMPROVED EXTRA LARGE PURPLE EGG PLANT.—(*This grows to a larger size, and is of a richer color, than the Common Large Purple Egg Plant.*) STRIPED GAUDELOUPE EGG PLANT.—(*An elegant variety for the table. The stripings of white, purple and yellow give it a magnificent appearance.*) ORNAMENTAL KALE.—(*The great variety in color, and structure of the leaves, make them elegant ornaments for the flower garden and among shrubbery.*) MAMMOTH SWEET CORN.—(*The largest of all Sweet Corn. Sweet, and excellent for the table. The ears weigh, as gathered, from two to three pounds each.*) MAMMOTH FRENCH SQUASH.—(*Sometimes grown to weigh over two hundred pounds. They grow well proportioned, and are finely colored.*) VEGETABLE CATERPILLARS.—(*Vegetable curiosities, the seed-vessels resembling caterpillars.*) VEGETABLE SNAILS.—(*A French Oddity, the seed vessels of which resemble snails.*) VEGETABLE WORMS.—(*Another curious vegetable product.*) SNAKE CUCUMBER.—(*A very long variety which grows coiled up, having the appearance of a large snake.*) COMMODORE NUTT PEA.—(*A new dwarf Sugar Pea, grows about one foot high, with pods eatable.*) LAXTON'S PROLIFIC EARLY LONG POD PEA.—(*A new and quite distinct variety. Many of the pods contain from ten to twelve Peas each.*) DWARF INDIAN CHIEF BEAN.—(*Those who have grown the Pole Indian Chief will be pleased to find a bush variety of this fine String Bean.*) GIANT WAX BEAN.—(*A new Pole Bean, being an improvement on the Indian Chief, it bring a larger and longer Podded Bean than that choice variety. The Wax Beans (so called because the pods are of a wax color,) are the best of all String Beans.*) NORBITON'S GIANT CUCUMBER.—(*A new English variety, the finest, longest, and most prolific Cucumber in cultivation.*) WARD'S NECTAR MELON.—(*When compared with all other sorts, this has been awarded the palm as the best of all green-fleshed Melons.*)

Each of the above sent to any part of the United States, and warranted to reach the purchaser, at twenty-five cents per package.

AMERICAN TURBAN SQUASH.—(*The dryest, finest grained, and best flavored of all Fall Squashes. The packages contain about fifty seed.*) HUBBARD SQUASH.—(*I was the original introducer of this, and the seed is* TRUE.) YOKOHAMA SQUASH.—(*A new variety from Japan; very prolific. The quality resembles a fine Crookneck, but is much superior.*) BOSTON MARROW SQUASH.—(*My variety took the premium for purity at the Annual Fair of the Massachusetts Horticultural Society in 1865.*) PARA SQUASH.—(*A bush Squash from South America, which can be kept into winter. Oblong in shape, of good size, fine-grained, and excellent quality, far superior to any standard variety of bush Squash.*) IMPROVED GREEN GLOBE SAVOY CABBAGE.—(*For family use, the Savoys are the richest of all Cabbages. The heads of this variety are large, hard, and of most excellent quality, the stumps short. Remarkably reliable for heading.*) PANCALIER SAVOY.—(*The French consider this the earliest Cabbage grown.*) SMALL EARLY ULM SAVOY.—(*Very early and reliable.*) BURNELL'S KING OF THE DWARFS.—(*In England this is considered the earliest of Cabbages. Very dwarf, fine quality, and sweet.*) LARGE BRUNSWICK SHORT STEM.—(*A very large and very early Drumhead, much sought for by market gardeners.*) LITTLE PIXIE CABBAGE.—(*An early dwarf; stump, short; heads, pointed, and very hard, fine quality, and very sweet.*) TILDEN'S NEW TOMATO.—(*Large, round or oblong; color, rich scarlet; vines, dwarf, and very productive.*) EARLY YORK TOMATO.—(*Very early, and remarkably prolific, has yielded at the rate of over one thousand bushels per acre. Fruit of good market size; flat, round shape; quality, excellent.*) COOK'S FAVORITE TOMATO.—(*A large, apple-shaped variety; very prolific; quality, superior; decidedly the best of the apple-shaped Tomatoes.*) MAMMOTH CHIHUAHUA TOMATO.—(*Enormously large, weighing from two to three pounds. Some single specimens will heap a quart measure.*) NEW MEXICAN TOMATO.—(*Very large, round Tomato; a great bearer; resembles, in color, Lester's Perfected, but an improvement on it, in always being round.*) TREE TOMATO.—(*A French variety; grows erect in the form of a bush.*) MCLEAN'S ADVANCER PEA.—(*A new English wrinkled Pea. A decided improvement on the Champion of England; bears well, with Peas equally sweet, is much larger, and does not run nearly as high.*) MCLEAN'S LITTLE GEM.—(*A new dwarf wrinkled Pea; grows about one foot high, very early, only a few days later than the Dan O'Rourke; a decided acquisition.*) VILMORIN'S NEW, WRINKLED, EDIBLE, PODDED PEA.—(*The first wrinkled sort yet found, the pods of which can be eaten.*) CARTER'S FIRST CROP.—(*A new English Pea, sent out as the earliest of all varieties.*) HAIR'S DWARF MAMMOTH.—(*A wrinkled Pea, larger than Champion of England, growing only half its hight; quality, fully equal to the Champion.*) TOM THUMB PEA.—(*As early as Dan O'Rourke, grows ten inches high, and is remarkably prolific.*) DREW'S NEW DWARF PEA.—(*Peas, very large, egg-shaped; each plant forms quite a bush. Peas should be planted about a foot apart. Early, dwarf, and very prolific.*) BROWN'S NEW DWARF MARROWFAT.—(*Warranted to be the earliest and most dwarf Marrowfat Pea grown. A capital Pea for market gardeners.*) FORTY DAYS' CORN.—(*Earlier than any Sweet Corn. Desirable as an early sort.*) BATES' EXTRA EARLY SWEET CORN.—(*A variety of wrinkled kerneled Sugar Corn; earlier than Darling's Early, and excellent for table use.*) MAMMOTH FLINT CORN.—(*Ears grow sixteen inches long; stalks very tall and stout, and matures as far North as Central New England.*) CROSBY'S EARLY.—(*The earliest of all twelve rowed Sweet Corn. The Massachusetts Horticultural Society offered special premiums for this new Corn at their last Annual Fair. It is of good size for market, and a decided acquisition.*) MEXICAN SWEET CORN.—(*I still find this to be the sweetest and most tender of all varieties of Sweet Corn. Nothing can equal it for the table.*) GOLDEN SWEET CORN.—(*A Sweet Corn of golden color; early, of good size, and excellent quality for the table; flavor, fine, and distinct from any other variety.*) YARD LONG BEAN.—(*A curious Bean; pods growing over two feet long; foliage, a rich, dark, glossy green.*) CONCORD BEAN.—(*This new Bean is probably the earliest Pole Bean grown; very prolific, and of excellent quality, either as a string or shell Bean.*) FEJEE BEAN.—(*A new bush Bean; the earliest and hardiest of all beans; very prolific, and worthy of general cultivation.*) INTERMEDIATE HORTICULTURAL BEAN.—(*An excellent bush Bean for marketmen. Pods of the same rich color as the Pole Horticultural.*) CALIFORNIA BEAN.—(*A very early, large, flat Pole Bean; excellent, either green or baked.*) MOTTLED CRANBERRY.—(*An improvement in health, vigor, and productiveness on the old fashioned Cranberry. Few Pole Beans will yield equal to this. Pods, long, large, and well filled.*) SIMM'S EARLY BEET.—(*A new, early sort, well shaped; as early as Bassano, and darker.*) NEW TURNIP BEET.—(*Round, flat-shaped, very early, and very nice.*) CASTLENANDARY BEET.—(*A famous French variety; flesh, a deep purple color, very tender and sweet.*) CRAPAUDINE BEET.—(*Rough skinned; color, very dark purple. Esteemed by the French as the best of all Beets for table use.*) WHYTE'S VERY DEEP RED BEET.—(*Medium size, dark color, very sweet, and excellent for table use.*) YELLOW OVOID MANGEL WURTZEL.—(*For cattle. Of seventeen varieties tested, the crop of this exceeded all.*) EARLY CRACKER ONION.—(*Earliest of all the yellow sort; quality, very delicate and sweet.*) HOOD'S NEW DWARF IMPERIAL PURPLE CELERY.—(*A choice new English variety.*) TURNER'S INCOMPARABLE DWARF WHITE CELERY.—(*A first class English variety.*) READ'S MATCHLESS CELERY.—(*A premium English variety, fine, solid and red.*) BOSTON MARKET CELERY.—(*True. This is the short, compact, solid variety, so often admired by strangers in the markets of Boston.*) TRUE BOSTON CURLED LETTUCE.—(*The most elegant of all the Lettuce family, grows in the form of a Rosette.*) WHEELER'S TOM THUMB LETTUCE.—(*A choice new variety, in high favor with those who have grown it.*) PERPIGNAN LETTUCE.—(*This is an excellent Lettuce for standing the summer heat. Heads, compact, attaining to seven inches in diameter.*) NEAPOLITAN CABBAGE LETTUCE.—(*One of the finest Cabbage Lettuces yet introduced.*) SIX VARIETIES OF CABBAGE LETTUCE.—(*Six of the choicest varieties in one package.*) ORANGE WATERMELON.—(*When fully ripe the skin will peel off like an Orange.*) ALLEN'S SUPERB MUSK MELON.—(*Quality, superior; by some called the "Queen of Melons."*) LARGE PERSIAN MUSK MELON.—(*A fine, large variety.*) WHITE JAPANESE MELON.—(*Flesh, greenish white, very thick meated; one of the earliest and sweetest of all melons.*) DWARF BROOM CORN.—(*This is thought to make a better brush than the common tall sorts.*) CHUFAS, OR GROUND ALMONDS.—(*These taste very much like a Cocoanut; are very prolific, yielding 100 to 1.*) ORNAMENTAL GOURDS.—(*Many varieties in one package.*) NEW JERSEY HYBRID CUCUMBER.—(*A remarkably long variety; an improvement on the White Spined.*) IMPROVED LONG GREEN CUCUMBER.—(*This is the longest of all the Long Greens.*) CHINESE SCARLET EGG PLANT.—(*Of magnificent scarlet color, and highly ornamental.*) MAMMOTH MILLET.—(*Extra tall; seed heads much larger than any other variety.*) SURRY WHITE WHEAT.—(*A new English Winter Wheat, highly recommended for poor soils, remarkably free from blight and rust.*) OTAHEITIAN SUGAR CANE.—(*This yields more Sugar than any other variety of Sugar Cane grown in the North.*)

Any of the above varieties will be forwarded, post-paid, and warranted to reach the purchaser at fifteen cents each.

EARLY SEBEC POTATOES.—(*Coming rapidly into favor in Boston and vicinity as a first class, early market Potato. Large size, excellent quality, and remarkably productive.*) EARLY GOODRICH.—(*True.*) SHAKER'S FANCY.—(*A new variety of white-fleshed Potatoes, considered as early as Early Goodrich, yielding equally well, and rapidly gaining favor in Pennsylvania. This and the Early Sebec are of better shape for market purposes than the Early Goodrich.*)

Four pound packages of either of these varieties sent to any address, warranted to reach the purchaser, on receipt of one dollar. All orders for Potatoes will be put on file, and be filled as soon as danger from freezing is past.

Catalogues containing over two hundred varieties of warranted Garden Seeds, one hundred and twenty-five of which are of my own growing, sent gratis to all applicants.

I warrant three things; 1st. That my seed is genuine. 2d. That your money shall reach me. 3d. That my seed shall reach you. Can the Public ask for anything fairer than this?

JAMES J. H. GREGORY,
Marblehead, Mass.

New Seed Catalogue!!

J. M. THORBURN & CO.'S

ANNUAL DESCRIPTIVE PRICED CATALOGUE OF

Kitchen, Garden and Agricultural Seeds

For 1867,

Is Now Ready for Mailing.

J. M. THORBURN & CO.,
15 John-st., New York.

PREMIUM CHESTER WHITE PIGS.

Progeny of Hogs that have taken State and United States Premiums, sent in pairs (not akin) by Express, to all parts of the United States, Canada, Cuba, South America. For Circulars and prices, Address N. P. BOYER & CO., Gum Tree, Chester Co., Pa.

To The Seed Trade!

Our WHOLESALE CATALOGUE OF Garden, Agricultural and Flower Seeds, &c.,

For Large Dealers Only,

Is Now Ready for Mailing.

J. M. THORBURN & CO.,
15 John-st., New York.

MY WHOLESALE and RETAIL CATALOGUE OF SEEDS and Fruit and Ornamental Trees, Shrubs, Evergreens, Grapes, Strawberries, &c., will be sent gratis to any address. Agents Wanted. Seeds and Plants carefully sent by mail, pre-paid, to any part of the United States and Canadas. B. M. WATSON, Old Colony Nurseries and Seed Establishment, Plymouth, Mass.

Shaker Fancy Potatoes.

The earliest and best Potato now under cultivation, being a No. 1 Potato, early or late. Orders now received to be delivered as soon as the weather in the spring will admit. Price, $10.00 per Barrel; or $3.00 per Bushel. Circular sent on receipt of stamp.

JOHN BORLAND & CO.,
Morrisville, Bucks Co., Pa.

YELLOW NANSEMOND SWEET POTATOES for sale, or to sprout on shares. A premium offered. For directions, particulars, &c., address, with stamp,
ALFRED LEE, Kokomo, Ind.

WHITE CALIFORNIA SPRING SEED Wheat which yields from 50 to 80 bushels to the Acre, for sale by
C. B. ROGERS,
No. 133 Market-st., Philadelphia, Pa.

BLOOMINGTON NURSERY,

Osage Orange Hedge Plants.—Strong, selected, one year, packed in good order, 1,000, $3; 5,000, $13; 10,000, $25. **Apple and Pear Trees**, all sizes. **Early Richmond Cherry. Apple Root Grafts**, best quality. **Kittatinny and Wilson's Early Blackberry.**

Grapes.—Iona, Ives, Israella, Norton's, Concord, Hartford, Rogers' Hybrids, &c., &c.

Nursery Stocks, general assortment.

Evergreens, immense stock, mostly medium and small, just right for shipping.

Shrubs, Roses, Green-house, Bedding and Garden Plants. Send red stamp each for 3 Catalogues, Wholesale, Retail and Bedding Plants.

F. K. PHOENIX, Bloomington, Ill.

Sing Sing Grape Vines.

I have a few thousand Grape Vines yet unsold. Good single eyes, one year old, grown under glass and out-door, at the following prices, if the cash come with the order:

Iona No. 1, per 100, $85, per 1,000, $800.
Iona No. 2, per 100, $65, per 1,000, $600.
Iona No. 3, per 100, $45, per 1,000, $400.
Israella No. 1, per 100, $85.
Israella No. 2, per 100, $70.
Israella No. 3, per 100, $50.
Adirondac No. 1, per 100, $70.
Adirondac No. 2, per 100, $50.
Adirondac No. 3, per 100, $40.
Allen's Hybrid, No. 1, per 100, $40.
Allen's Hybrid, No. 2, per 100, $30.
Allen's Hybrid, No. 3, per 100, $20.
My Vines are as good, if not better, than any others offered.
First class, wood grown under glass, of Iona and Israella:
Iona, per 1,000 buds, $30.
Israella, per 1,000 buds, $25.

J. F. DELIOT, Vine Grower,
Sing Sing, New York.

GRAPE VINES.

Iona, Israella, Adirondac, Concord, Diana, Hartford, Rogers', &c., &c. *Prices too low to Advertise in this Paper without injury to the Trade.* By the use of my patent process, I am enabled to produce the largest and best vines for future growth and productiveness, grown on the American Continent. See cut in Sept. No., page 334. Send for Terms to those forming Clubs, which is worthy of *particular attention.*

If Illustrated and Descriptive Catalogue is wished, send two red stamps. Address
F. L. PERRY, Canandaigua, N. Y.

GRAPES! GRAPE WOOD!

Catawba and Isabella cuttings, roots and layers, Concords and Hartford Prolifics, Ives Seedling, Rentz, Delaware, Iona, Rogers' and other varieties. Wood—all cut before the frost and stored in cellars, Delaware at $3.75 per 1,000 buds, and Catawba and Isabella cuttings, three buds, at $2 per 1,000. Price list for spring of '67 and account of the Ives Seedling sent to any address. M. H. LEWIS & CO., Sandusky, Ohio.

GRAPE WOOD OF IONA, ISRAELLA, and other popular varieties, at current rates. Also, a few hundred very choice Iona layers. Address,
A. BUSHNELL,
Peekskill, Westchester County, N. Y.

15,000 HALE'S Early Peach Trees; 300,000 Agriculturist Strawberry Plants; 15,000 Osage Orange, one year old; 150 bushels Peach Pits. Send for Circular. For sale by ISAAC PULLEN, Hightstown, N. J.

THE MOST SPARKLING AND BRILLIANT MAGAZINE ever issued, will be found in the January number of DEMOREST'S MONTHLY, now ready.

PHILADELPHIA.
The *Largest, Best, and most Productive, Hardy* Raspberry. Stood unprotected, 16 degrees below, and 106 degrees above zero, and averaged over $12 per bushel the past summer.

Metcalf's Early and Agriculturist Strawberries.
Wilson's Early and Kittatinny Blackberries.
Other Vines, Plants and Trees for Sale.
Send for Catalogues GRATIS.
WILLIAM PARRY, Cinnaminson, N. J.

Silver Leaved Maple Trees Given Away.

To any person sending me nine Subscriptions to the American Agriculturist at $1.50 each, for 1867, I will send them 500 trees as above; for 15 names, at $1.50 each, 1,000 trees; 40 names, $1.50 each, 3,000 trees. The trees are all first-class, one year, 1 to 1½ feet, are worth the sum required, should the paper not be wanted, (which of course will be). Trees shipped early in spring, well packed. Send along Greenbacks or P. O. Orders, to
J. H. GRAVES, Dement, Ogle Co., Illinois.

Valuable and Important Catalogue
For the Spring of 1867.

Containing instructions from fifteen years of practical experience in the cultivation of Small Fruits. Tells how to plant, grow and market. How to make the cheapest and best shipping boxes and stands, and baskets to gather the fruit. How to gather, and many other important and valuable hints, which will prove invaluable to the market grower, as well as the amateur and those growing but a small bed for family use. Sent to all applicants as soon as issued in Dec., on receipt of 10cts. Address A. M. PURDY South Bend, Ind.

CRANBERRY PLANTS, bearing vines in parcels of 100 cuts, for price and culture, send for Circular. Trowbridge's Grafting Wax. Nurserymen and Grafters [illegible] of best quality, and cheaper to purchase than to make [illegible] for Nurserymen, and in one, one-half and one-quarter pound rolls for retailing, with directions for use. Liberal discount to Nurserymen and Dealers. Tree Varnish, an indispensable article in trimming trees, causing the wound to heal sound. $3 per dozen; 30 cents single bottle.
F. TROWBRIDGE, Milford or New Haven, Conn.

Burroughs' Nurseries.
WALTHAM, VT.
SOLON BURROUGHS, Proprietor.

Post Office Address, Vergennes, Vt.—Fruit and Ornamental Trees, Grape Vines, Evergreens, Roses, &c., &c. Send 1 stamp for Grape Catalogue, or 2 stamps for General Catalogue.

STRAWBERRY, RASPBERRY, AND BLACKBERRY Plants, Good Roots, Best Varieties. Inducements offered to those wishing a few of each variety. Catalogue gratis; send for one. JOHN S. COLLINS, Moorestown, N. J.

TO FARMERS AND PLANTERS.

The LODI MANUFACTURING CO., having the exclusive control of the night soil of New York City, have received therefrom the past season, some [illegible] tons of night soil, which they have manufactured into an *extra fine article of Poudrette of superior quality, (put up in bright new packages,)* (which they offer for sale at the usual price.) For

CORN, TOBACCO AND COTTON

This article has no superior, taking into consideration its price, and the effects derived therefrom. It is equal, pound for pound, to the best brands of Super-phosphates in market sold at $60 per ton, while the Poudrette costs only $20. It matures the crop two to three weeks earlier, does not injure the seed when brought into contact with it, and is cheaper by 50 per cent. than any other fertilizer offered for sale. Send for a Pamphlet. Address
THE LODI MANUFACTURING CO.,
66 Cortlandt-st., New York.

ROCKY MOUNT, Edgecombe Co., N. C., Nov. 13, 1866.
JAMES R. DEY, Pres't.—Sir: In regard to the results of our experience in the use of your improved Poudrette on this year's cotton crop, we beg leave to say that the season has been unfavorable to the action of all Fertilizers. Several kinds were used by us, and with the *exception* of your [illegible], with little or no effect to the crop. Where the Poudrette was applied it gave us near a *half Bale* more [illegible] much earlier. We would recommend it not only as a manure suitable for the growth of cotton, but for the improvement of the soil.
Yours, very respectfully,
HENRY P. STULTS & BRO.

AMMONIATED PACIFIC GUANO.

The attention of Farmers and Agriculturalists is called to this article, as superior to anything else offered in the market, equal to Peruvian Guano, and costing much less.

We offer this fertilizer in lots to suit all purchasers. A liberal discount made to the Trade.

Pamphlets with copies of Analysis by Dr. Liebig, of Baltimore, and Dr. Jackson, Massachusetts State Assayer, and [illegible] from Agricultural dealers, showing its value, and directions for use, can be obtained from
J. O. BAKER & CO., SELLING AGENTS,
131 Pearl-st., New-York.

Thorough-bred Chester White Pigs

For Sale: from 10 weeks to 1 year old. For growth and [illegible], can not be excelled in the *United States*. For description and Prices, send for Circular. Address
JAMES YOUNG, Jr. & CO.,
Marshallton, Chester Co., Pa.

WANTED.—A good thorough-bred Durham Bull, from a [illegible] milk strain. Address T. C., Box 317, Warsaw, Ind.

DEMOREST'S MONTHLY MAGAZINE is unquestionably the most useful, sparkling, and popular Magazine, and offers the most liberal terms and premiums for clubs. Send for circular. Back numbers, 10c., post free. No. 473 Broadway. The January number, with extraordinary Holiday attractions, now ready. Sold everywhere.

Lane's Purchasing Agency,
FOR PURCHASING

at the lowest regular price, any thing to be procured in New York City, and at other accessible points.

Orders for Books for private and public Libraries carefully attended to. Special attention given to the selection of Circulating Libraries, and Libraries for Farmers' Clubs. Valuable Books can be purchased by me at the frequent Auction Sales, much below the regular prices.
HARVEY B. LANE, 151 Nassau-street, New York.

HALSTED & PUTNAM
68
Pearl-Street,
NEW-YORK.

Produce Commission Merchants,

For the sale of Country produce of all kinds.
Send for WEEKLY PRICE CURRENT, Marking Plate and Circular with Packing and Shipping directions.

NURSERY FOR SALE.

We offer for sale a Nursery containing 120 Acres of land selected for its favorable location and soil, well improved, underdrained, &c. Situated a short distance from Toledo, Ohio, in a pleasant neighborhood. All its surroundings making it a desirable place for the business and a residence.

There is on the premises an ELEGANT RESIDENCE, surrounded by a fine PARK, laid out and ornamented with Walks, Shrubbery, &c.—Also, THREE TENEMENT HOUSES, an Office, Packing House, Corn Crib, Root Cellar, Barn, Stabling room for ten horses, large Cistern, Propagating House heated by Hitchings Boiler No. 5, Green-Houses, Growing Houses, Forcing Pits, Sash for Hot Beds, &c.—Also, an ORCHARD, containing 2500 Fruit Trees of the best and finest varieties, most of which are in bearing.—Also, a VINEYARD of one acre of vines in bearing—and two acres of vines, two and three years old, all of the best and most suitable varieties for this climate.—The STOCK EMBRACES the BEST COLLECTION of Green and Hot House Plants in the West, over 50,000 Grape Vines, 1 and 2 years old,—A large and fine stock of ORNAMENTAL TREES, SHRUBS, &c.—A large stock of FRUIT TREES of vigorous growth, and embracing all kinds and varieties grown and sold in this Market.—The location of this Nursery is in every way desirable, being near the flourishing City of TOLEDO, Ohio, in the midst of a fast improving country—with means of transportation almost unequaled; in fact, possessing advantages in every particular not excelled in the West.

Address, or inquire of
VON BLESSINGH & BAY,
Real Estate Agents, No. 7 Lenks Block,
Toledo, Ohio.

SUPERIOR FARM LAND.—20,000 Acres, Franklin Tract, at Newfield, Gloucester County, New Jersey, on the Railroad running from Philadelphia to Cape May, 30 miles South of Philadelphia—adjoining the Vineland Tract, and 2 miles North of the Vineland Station—for sale at low prices and on easy terms in lots to suit purchasers. Circulars, with reports of Solon Robinson, Hon. William Parry, and others, with full information and map, sent to applicants, free. Address MORRIS & CO., Newfield, Gloucester Co., N. J. Improved Farms also for Sale.

Farms in South Jersey,

Of all sizes and excellent quality, well improved, good buildings, fruit, etc., for SALE at $25 to $10 per acre. Also, excellent Timber Land at $15 to $30 per acre, near churches, schools, mills, also, railroad and navigation leading to Philadelphia and New York. Descriptive Catalogues sent free. Apply to T. HOYT, Manumuskin, Cumberland Co., N. J.

FARM AND COAL LANDS.—160 Acres, 3½ and 4 miles from La Salle and Peru, Illinois, ½ mile from Illinois Central Railroad, underlaid by three veins of coal. Farm well improved, good house, orchard of 130 choice bearing trees; good out-buildings. Soil, rich and deep. Price, $100 per acre; one-fourth cash.
THOS. W. HENNESSEY,
La Salle, Illinois.

187 ACRES, 6 miles of Richmond, Va. The Wood and Timber on it will pay first cost. Sandy loam, every acre good for Garden or meadow. 1½ miles of York River R. R. 100 acres cleared; no buildings. $15 per acre, or will be divided.
A. VAN DOREN,
Manchester, Chesterfield County, Virginia.

FOR SALE LOW, Fruit and Garden Farm, ¾ hour's drive from Washington, D. C., on Potomac, 131 acres, 50 cleared, 30 of second growth, balance heavy timber. Good buildings, etc.; 1,000 peach and pear trees. J. DEVLIN, 1,190 Broadway, N. Y.

WANTED—10,000 FARMERS TO ACT AS Agents for the great AMERICAN STOCK JOURNAL. THE FARMERS' AND STOCK BREEDERS' ADVERTISER. Splendid Inducements. Copies free. Address
N. P. BOYER & CO., Gum Tree, Chester Co., Pa.

WANTED.—A situation by a practical Nurseryman and Fruit Grower, to take charge of a Fruit Farm or Garden, and manage the culture and marketing of the same. Reference Unexceptionable. Address, Box 91, Strasburg, Lancaster County, Penn.

WANTED!

Good Agents in every Town and County to sell "HOME," a Religious Book for every family, by Rev. W. K. Tweedie, D. D., Author of "Seed-time and Harvest; or, Sow Well and Reap Well." "Lamp to the Path," "Meditations, etc., etc." This Book will undoubtedly have a large sale, and Agents, both *Male and Female*, will find it a book particularly adapted to their sales. Address
H. FENTON & CO.,
Springfield, Mass.

K Prizes Give N 4 ans. 2 the Prize Pus.
MERRY L. MAY'S Monthly.

Greenback or other valuable prizes distributed every month. A chance is afforded Base Ball Players to get a magnificent solid silver-mounted rosewood Bat free, by a little exertion. Sold by all dealers, 15 cents. None free. 3 months for 25 cents, or $1.25 a year. Try it. HANEY & CO, 109 Nassau-st., N. Y. Also, any of the following cheap, good and popular books, sent, post paid, on receipt of price: ROGUES AND ROGUERIES, exposing all tricks and traps of great cities, and all swindles and humbugs, 25 cents.—SECRETS WORTH KNOWING, tells how to make hundreds of articles in universal use, made at trifling cost, and sold at immense profits, 25c.—HANDBOOK OF VENTRILOQUISM, plain and simple, and how to make the Magic Whistle, to imitate birds, animals, insects, &c., 15c.—HOW TO MAKE A BAD MEMORY GOOD and a Good One Better, 15c.—TOM TRUMP, WIFE AND BABY, comic, illustrated, 15c.—JEFF DAVIS, comic, illustrated, 10c.—LETTER WRITING SIMPLIFIED, 15c.

DEMOREST'S "YOUNG AMERICA," THE most sparkling Juvenile Magazine ever issued. The Jan. No. has an extraordinary display of Novelties, Toys, Engravings, &c. *Harper's Weekly*, 15 cents; mailed from No. 473 Broadway. Yearly, $1.50, with a beautiful premium.

THE VANISHING PICTURE TRICK, 25 cents. —How to Write Letters Correctly, 15 cts.—Guide to Etiquette, 15 cts.—Bridal Etiquette, 15 cts.—Courtship Made Easy, 15 cts. Housekeepers' Own Book, 15 cts.—Rarey's How to Buy, Tame and Keep Horses, 15 cts.—Knowlson's Farrier, 15 cts.—Home Cook Book, 30 cts.—Parlor Magician, 30 cts.—Parlor Theatricals, 30 cts.—Parlor Pantomimes, 25 cts.—500 Puzzles, 30 cts.—Fireside Games, 30 cts.—Laws of Love, 30 cts.—Love Oracle, 30 cts.—Comic Courtship, 30 cts.—Great Fortune Teller, 60 cts. Thousands of other Books, Pictures, Albums, Games, Yankee Notions. Send stamp for Mammoth Catalogue. W. C. WEMYSS, 575 Broadway, N. Y. City.

New Agricultural Paper.

MORRIS' RURAL ADVERTISER, which has just completed its third volume, will be issued on the first day of year 1867, merged in a large Quarto of sixteen pages each, under the title of the

Practical Farmer & Rural Advertiser,

issued monthly, at $1.00 per annum payable in advance. Devoted to Agriculture, Horticulture, and every branch of Rural Economy.
PASCHALL MORRIS,
Editor and Publisher, 1120 Market st.,
Philadelphia.

AGENTS WANTED FOR WEDGWOOD'S GOVERNMENT & LAWS of U. S.

A Comprehensive View of the Rise, Progress and Present Organization of the State and National Governments.

It contains the law which every citizen should possess to discharge, with intelligence and fidelity, his duties to the State and to the Nation, and to conduct his private affairs with safety to himself and justice to others.

STRICTLY A SUBSCRIPTION BOOK.—Reliable, active men and women, who wish to do good and make money, can do both by canvassing for this book. Some Agents make over $100 per week. A circular, giving Title-page, Table of Contents, Testimonials and Specimen pages, with Agency documents, sent on application. Territory assigned, and liberal inducements offered. J. W. SCHERMERHORN & CO., Publishers, 430 Broome-street, New York.

FOREST TREES.

A new and much improved edition of Michaux & Nuttall's "North American Sylva," complete in 5 Imperial Octavo volumes, with 277 beautifully Colored plates, true to nature, accompanied with letter-press descriptions of all our "North American Forest Trees." The most elegant and scientific work ever published on this subject. Experienced Agents wanted to sell valuable illustrated works in all parts of the United States.
Address
RICE, RUTTER & CO.,
525 Minor-st., Philadelphia.

1000 Agents and Canvassers Wanted.

MACKENZIE'S 10,000 RECEIPTS, or UNIVERSAL ENCYCLOPÆDIA, containing Receipts in Agriculture, Brewing, Cooking, Carving, Cements, Cosmetics, Dyeing, Distillation, Farriery, Fire-Works, Inks, Medicine, Metallurgy, Perfumery, Poisons and Antidotes, Preserving, Photography, Tanning, Varnishes, Wines, &c., &c., &c., &c.
☞ Liberal terms and exclusive territory given.
Apply to T. ELLWOOD ZELL & CO., Publishers,
Philadelphia.

AGENTS WANTED!—In all parts of the United States to sell "THE LIVES OF THE PRESIDENTS," a new work, by John S. C. Abbott, the great historian. The work is finely illustrated, complete in one volume, and ready for subscribers. The author, the theme, and the elegant style in which it is issued, combine to render it one of the best books for Agents ever published in this country. Exclusive territory may be secured by addressing
B. B. RUSSELL & CO., Publishers,
Boston, Mass.

Books for the Million.

Send stamp for Catalogue to CARTER, COLLINS & RICHARDSON, 41 John st., N. Y.

SCHOOL TEACHERS WANTED.—The subscriber wishes to employ for each town in the United States, male teachers who have formerly been engaged either in Day Schools, or Sunday Schools, who can devote their exclusive time to the business, to canvass for the "Illustrated History of the Bible," by John Kitto, D. D., F. S. A., edited by Alvan Bond, D. D., of Norwich, Conn.

This is the best selling book I have ever published. Agents make from $100 to $200 per month, and say "*they never have a book to sell so well.*" Apply immediately in person or by letter to the publisher.
HENRY BILL, Norwich, Conn.

CORN.—HOW TO RAISE 100 BUSHELS PER ACRE.—Useful and practical hints for every farmer, by M. P. Parsons. Sent, post-paid, for 25 cents, by H. WATKIN, box 2718, Cincinnati, O.

No one Need be in the Dark!

Canvassers Wanted to Sell

OPEN—FOR USE. CLOSED—FOR THE POCKET.

The Folding Pocket Lanterns.

ARE MOST APPRECIATED IN THE GREATEST EMERGENCIES.

LIBERAL TERMS TO DEALERS AND CANVASSERS.

JULIUS IVES & CO., 49 Maiden Lane, N. Y.

Manufacturers and Dealers in Kerosene Goods generally.

IVES' PATENT LAMPS,

THE SAFEST, MOST CONVENIENT, AND IN EVERY WAY

THE BEST LAMP EVER USED.

CHANDELIERS, BRACKETS, HANGING AND TABLE LAMPS OF ALL KINDS, CAN BE LIGHTED AS QUICKLY AS GAS, FILLED AND TRIMMED SAFELY AND NEATLY, ALL WITHOUT REMOVING THE SHADE, GLOBE OR CHIMNEY OR UNSCREWING THE BURNER.

The Substantial Value of the Improvements

EFFECTED BY

MASON & HAMLIN,

In instruments of this Class, and the superiority of their CABINET ORGANS, have been acknowledged by the award ... within a few years, of

Fifty-six Gold and Silver Medals,

... at the principal Industrial ... the sharpest competition.

THEIR INSTRUMENTS HAVE THUS BEEN

Repeatedly Declared the Best

At the following, among other Fairs:

MASSACHUSETTS CHARITABLE MECHANIC ASSOCIATION, BOSTON.
FRANKLIN INSTITUTE, PHILADELPHIA.
AMERICAN INSTITUTE, NEW YORK.
MARYLAND INSTITUTE, BALTIMORE.
MECHANICS' INSTITUTE, CINCINNATI.
UNITED STATES FAIR, CHICAGO.
MECHANICS' FAIR, SAN FRANCISCO.

AND AT THE STATE FAIRS OF

NEW YORK	IOWA
PENNSYLVANIA	VERMONT.
OHIO	KANSAS.
INDIANA.	RHODE ISLAND.
ILLINOIS	

At ... other State where Fairs are held.

M. & H. ... been allowed to publish in their Circulars ... of

More than Two Hundred and Fifty of the Most Eminent Musicians in the Country.

... the M. & H. Cabinet Organs to all ...

... with full particulars as to styles ... sent free to any address.

Warerooms, 596 Broadway, New York.
154 Tremont Street, Boston.

GEO. A. PRINCE & CO.'S MELODEONS,

GEO. A. PRINCE & CO.'S AUTOMATIC ORGANS

GEO. A. PRINCE & CO.'S SCHOOL ORGANS,

... the principal trade stores throughout ... Canada, and the British Provinces. No ... instruments ever obtained the same popularity.

... Send to the manufacturers at Buffalo, N. Y., for an ILLUSTRATED CATALOGUE and Price List, which will be mailed to any address, free of charge.

PRINCE & CO.'S

PATENT

MELODEONS,
AUTOMATIC ORGANS,
SCHOOL ORGANS.

Catalogues and Price List sent on application. All orders and communications should be addressed to

F. P. WHITING,
2 Fulton Street, New York.

PIANOS AND ORGANS.—HIGHLY important to those intending to purchase unparalleled inducements. Money Saved. Send for Circulars.
SIGERJA OIT, 281 Broadway, New York.

IS WATER POISONED!!! BY LEAD PIPE.

The Manchester (N. H.) Mirror and Farmer, of recent date, notices the death of two citizens of that place by lead poison, from water drawn through lead pipe. They say: "The disease manifests itself in different ways: lead colic, a painful affection of the joints, disease of the brain, as in the case of Mr. Sargent; partial or general paralysis, as in the case of Dr. Tibbetts."

The mortuary statistics of this city indicate a larger increase of *deaths* by paralysis, since the introduction of the Croton Water, *in proportion to the population*, than any other disease of this class. The statistics show THE DEATHS, in 1838, to be 92, population about 375,000, in 1865, 291, population about 1,000,000. The same is true as regards consumption of the bowels, want of action of the kidneys, disease of the heart, etc., etc.

Dr. Hayes, of Boston, says: "Lead, as a material for pipes, cannot safely be used *for* conducting water which is to be used for domestic purposes;" and all the leading Chemists and Physicians of the country assert the same thing.

LEAD ENCASED BLOCK TIN PIPES,

Entirely prevent water, and other liquids that flow through them, from becoming impregnated with poisonous solutions of lead.

It is the only safe and durable pipe made for domestic use.

It costs but little more than lead pipe, and possesses all the mechanical qualities required by Plumbers.

The following distinguished Chemists and Physicians have unqualifiedly endorsed and recommended this pipe for general use:

Prof. Torrey, U. S. Assay Office, N. Y.
Prof. Doremus, College of the City of New York.
Prof. Chandler, School of Mines, Columbia College.
Prof. Draper, University Medical College.
Prof. Horsford, late of Harvard College.
Prof. Silliman, Yale College.
Dr. Hayes, State Assayer, Mass.
Prof. Booth, U. S. Mint, Philadelphia.
Dr. Poley, successor to J. R. Chilton & Co.

Willard Parker, M. D.,	Dr. Percy, N. Y. Med. College,
James Anderson, M. D.,	James R. Wood, M. D.,
Jared Linsly, M. D.,	Alfred C. Post, M. D.,
Lewis A. Sayre, M. D.,	F. G. Thomas, M. D.,
James Crane, M. D.	M. G. Echeverria, M. D.,

And many others.

We also manufacture

TIN PLATED SHEET LEAD,

For Lining Water Tanks, &c., &c.

For Pamphlets, and further information, address,

The Colwells, Shaw & Willard Mfg. Co.,
(Sole Manufacturers.)
Foot of West Twenty-seventh-st., New York.

GREAT SALE OF CLOTHING AT RAYMOND'S,

Nos. 121, 123 & 125 Fulton-st.

The days of high prices having passed, to meet the demand of the times RAYMOND is selling off his immense stock of Clothing for Men and Boys

AT

GREATLY REDUCED PRICES.

Persons desiring fine Clothing, at a reasonable figure, will find it greatly to their interest to call and examine the superb stock of

Overcoats, Business and Dress Suits,

now offered, before purchasing elsewhere.

DEGRAAF & TAYLOR,

87 & 89 Bowery, and 65 Christie-street, New York, still continue to be the largest dealers in

Parlor, Dining and Bed-room Furniture,

of any house in the City.

Prices reduced 20 per cent.

Colgate's Aromatic Vegetable Soap.

A superior Toilet Soap, prepared from refined Vegetable Oils in combination with Glycerine, and especially designed for the use of Ladies and for the Nursery. Its perfume is exquisite, and its washing properties unrivalled. For sale by all Druggists.

THE UNIVERSAL CLOTHES WRINGER

AND

DOTY'S CLOTHES WASHER.

THE UNIVERSAL WRINGER *was awarded the First Premium by the unanimous vote of the Committee of the GREAT NEW ENGLAND FAIR of 1866, after the most scrutinizing trial of the various machines of numerous competitors.*

It was pronounced superior to all others at the WORLD'S FAIR IN LONDON, 1862.

Took the First Premium at the last two Great Fairs of the AMERICAN INSTITUTE in New York City, 1863 and 1865. At each of the following State Fairs it also received the

FIRST PREMIUM;

NEW YORK	[illegible]		[illegible]
VERMONT	[illegible]		[illegible]
NEW HAMPSHIRE			[illegible]
PENNSYLVANIA	[illegible]		[illegible]
OHIO			[illegible]
MICHIGAN	[illegible]		[illegible]
INDIANA	[illegible]	[illegible]	[illegible]
ILLINOIS	[illegible]	[illegible]	[illegible]
IOWA	[illegible]	[illegible]	[illegible]
WISCONSIN	[illegible]	[illegible]	[illegible]
MINNESOTA			[illegible]
MISSOURI			[illegible]
KENTUCKY		[illegible]	[illegible]
CONN. RIVER VALLEY FAIR			[illegible]
CHAMPLAIN VALLEY FAIR			[illegible]
MECHANICS' INSTITUTE, Boston			[illegible]

And at most of the County and Institute Fairs throughout the country where it was exhibited.

The manufacturers WARRANT it FAR superior to all others.

There have been more than half a million UNIVERSAL CLOTHES WRINGERS sold, which amounts to more than those sold by *all other makers*. We warrant them to be all they are represented to be. They are so well made and durable as to seldom need repairing, and with ordinary care will last many years. Those received for repairs will not average more than one in every two hundred sold. The UNIVERSAL CLOTHES WRINGER has given really *universal* satisfaction. It wrings clothes almost dry without injury to the most delicate garments.

In selling the UNIVERSAL WRINGER, we find a large demand for a good Washing Machine, and knowing

DOTY'S WASHING MACHINE

to be the best, we bought the patent, and now offer it to the public, *knowing* that it will *give satisfaction* wherever used.

DOTY'S CLOTHES WASHER was awarded the FIRST PREMIUM at the GREAT NEW ENGLAND FAIR of 1866, after the most thorough trial with numerous competitors.

It has taken the

FIRST PREMIUMS

At the State Fairs of

NEW YORK, PENNSYLVANIA, VERMONT, MICHIGAN, WISCONSIN, and IOWA.

Also, at the last GREAT FAIR OF THE AMERICAN INSTITUTE.

A supply of the Wringers and Washers are always kept on hand in Chicago, Cincinnati, Cleveland, Louisville and St. Louis, boxed ready for shipment, at about New York prices.

Circulars, giving wholesale and retail prices, sent free.

Large profits are made selling these Machines. Exclusive right of sale given, with no charge for the patent right.

On receipt of the price from places where no one is selling, we will send one Washer and one Wringer, either or both, free of freight charges. Family Size Washer, $14; No. 1½ Wringer, $10; No. 2 Wringer, $8.50.

R. C. BROWNING, General Agent,
No. 32 Cortlandt St., New York,
(Opposite Merchants' Hotel).

SAVONINE.

NOTICE.—whenever an article of actual value, and acknowledged as such by the Public, becomes "*a Household Necessity*," it is a notorious fact numberless counterfeits immediately appear, and claims are made of "*priority of invention*." An action on this head has already commenced in the Supreme Court of New York. Now, therefore, TAKE NOTICE that any one counterfeiting, or, in any manner, making use of the Trade Mark hereunder, and, duly registered, will be prosecuted, and, without further notice, by the

GLAMORGAN SOAP CO.,
45 Broadway, N. Y.

SAVONINE

MME. DEMOREST'S BENOITON DRESS LOOPERS—Convenient, efficient and durable, requiring no sewing, and very ornamental. $1 per set; sold everywhere, or mailed, post free, on receipt of price. No. 473 Broadway, N. Y.

EXTREMES

MEET.

VERMONT & LOUISIANA.

Gothic Furnace vs. Zero Refrigerator.

"Your Furnace gives perfect satisfaction. We warm our Store, 100×25 ft., Carpet rooms in 2d story, and Public Hall in 3d story, 75×50 ft.—none but a powerful Furnace would do this." J. JAY JOSLIN, Poultney, Vermont.
Dec. 12th, 1866.

"LESLEY'S ZERO-Refrigerator has just received the first Premium at the Louisiana State Fair, over all others."
Nov., 1866. J. D. STRONG, New Orleans, La.

The above for sale by ALEX. M. LESLEY, 605 Sixth-Avenue, New York.

PYLE'S SALERATUS AND CREAM TARTAR,

Are the best in market. All first-class Grocers keep them.

FARMERS ATTENTION.

Hogs Bristles Wanted, by DAVID McMURRAY, Jr., Manufacturer of Brushes, Troy, N. Y.
Established 1825.

THE LODI MANUFACTURING COMPANY, 66 Cortlandt street, New York, wish to engage some smart young men as county Canvassers, to distribute advertisements and to procure orders for their celebrated Poudrette. A liberal commission allowed.

Gregory's Seed Catalogue,

Containing One Hundred and twenty-five varieties that I grow myself, besides many kinds imported from France and England, and grown by the best Seed growers in the United States. Farmers and Gardeners will find in my Catalogue many new and rare vegetables, some of which are not to be found in any other Seed Catalogue. As the original introducer of the Hubbard Squash, Marblehead Mammoth Cabbage, Boston Curled Lettuce, and many other new vegetables, I invite the patronage of the public. Catalogues sent *gratis* to all. Those who purchased seed last season will receive it without writing for it.
JAMES J. H. GREGORY, Marblehead, Mass.

WALTON'S SERIES OF ARITHMETICS

CONSISTS OF

I. Walton's Pictorial Primary Arithmetic.
II. Walton's Intellectual Arithmetic.
III. Walton's Written Arithmetic.

The Pictorial Primary Arithmetic,

On the plan of Object-Lessons, is appropriately illustrated, and presents the elementary combinations of numbers in a series of simple and progressive lessons, calculated to interest and develop the mind of the young learner.

The Intellectual Arithmetic

Forms a connecting link between the Primary and Written Arithmetics, reviewing the former, and illustrating with small numbers nearly all the principles applied in the latter. This book contains also *An Introduction to* WRITTEN ARITHMETIC, and is well adapted to meet the wants of the large class of students who can devote but little time to the study of arithmetic.

The Written Arithmetic,

For Common and Higher Schools, is a thoroughly analytical and progressive work; it presents the science of numbers in a philosophical manner, and affords a more full and varied practice than any other book of its class. Its original and thorough system of reviews commends it to every practical teacher. A distinguishing feature of this Arithmetic is its adaptation to the present wants of business life.
BREWER & TILESTON, Publishers, 131 Washington-street, Boston.

THE MOTHERS' JOURNAL, And FAMILY VISITANT.

A Monthly Magazine, for Mothers and the Household. With nothing light or trashy, it is practical in purpose, substantial in matter, attractive in style. To aid Mothers in their noble, but difficult work, and to make the family healthy, happy, useful, and good, is the object of the JOURNAL. Price $1.50 per year. Five copies, $7. Single Numbers, *Fifteen cents.* Send by mail, directed to "MOTHERS' JOURNAL, 503 Broadway, New York."

Merry's Museum.

The Children's Old Favorite.

THE JANUARY NUMBER, 1867, commences the Twenty-seventh Year of this popular favorite of the young folks everywhere, and is filled with the choicest Stories, Pictures, and Puzzles. In addition to its present unequaled list of writers for that class in America, a number of others have been secured, and no pains will be spared to make it worthy of its reputation of being the first magazine for Young People in the land. Its moral tone will be unexceptionable, and the literary matter interesting and instructive. Valuable Premiums given for obtaining new subscribers. Terms, $1.50 a year in advance. Single copies, 15 cents. Send for it. Address
H. B. FULLER, Publisher, 177 William Street, New York.

1867.

10 Copies for $15.

A NEWSPAPER

Now, as always, pledged to the advocacy of the Great Principles of

Free Soil, Free Speech, Free Labor, Free Men and Free Trade!

THE "EVENING POST,"

NEW-YORK,

Combines all the essential elements of a

First-Class Metropolitan Newspaper.

ITS LITERARY and MISCELLANEOUS SELECTIONS are prepared with great care, and constitute its chief attractions to the

FAMILY CIRCLE.

ITS SOUND POLITICAL VIEWS on all the great questions of the day recommend it to all who prize

TRUTH ABOVE PARTY.

ITS AGRICULTURAL AND HORTICULTURAL articles are full and interesting.

ITS MONEY AND MARKET REPORTS are invaluable to *Farmers or Country Merchants.*

It is printed on entirely new type, and good white paper.

PLEASANT WORDS.

The following complimentary expressions are selected from numerous notices of the recent improvements in the EVENING POST:

Though in its sixty-sixth year, the EVENING POST has all the freshness and vigor of its more youthful competitors. Mr. Bryant's writings have always been its principal charm, and it is gratifying to know that his pen is still as active as ever.—*American Agriculturist.*

The New York EVENING POST is one of the most dignified and able newspapers in the country—a creditable exponent of American thought.—*Albany Evening Journal.*

The New York EVENING POST is one of the soundest, as it has always been one of the ablest and most dignified of American newspapers.—*Rochester Democrat.*

THE EVENING POST is an honor to American journalism. Having definite convictions, and a broad comprehensive political creed, it is not so much the organ of any party as it is the educator of statesmen. Dignified, direct, and forcible in style, its editorials are frequently models of linguistic purity and elegance. With its political philosophy is allied a practical comprehension, which has secured for the POST a confidence sparingly reposed in journals of a more impetuous or more servile temper. We are glad that a paper so deserving of appreciation as the POST, receives it with ever augmenting measures.—*Christian Intelligencer.*

TERMS TO MAIL SUBSCRIBERS.

Evening Post—Semi-Weekly.

One copy, 1 year	$4.00
Two copies, 1 year	7.00
Five copies or over, for each copy	3.00

Evening Post—Weekly.

Single copy, 1 year	$2.00
Five copies	9.00
Ten copies addressed to names of subscribers	17.50
Twenty copies, addressed to names of subscribers	34.00
Ten copies to one person's address	**$15.00**

☞ Additions may be made to a club, at any time, at club rates.

POSTMASTERS or others acting as Club Agents can learn further particulars on application.

CLERGYMEN are supplied by Mail with the Daily at $10; Semi-Weekly at $3; or Weekly at $1.50 per annum.

REMITTANCES should be made, if possible, by Draft or Post-Office order, payable in New York.

☞ Specimen copies sent free.

WILLIAM C. BRYANT & CO.,
PUBLISHERS,
41 Nassau Street, New York.

REV. HENRY WARD BEECHER,

will furnish REGULAR CONTRIBUTIONS to the columns of

THE METHODIST.

Consisting of Fortnightly SERMONS, and "Lecture-Room Talks," reported expressly for "THE METHODIST," revised by Mr. Beecher, and protected by Copy-right. [These Sermons are now published in THE METHODIST instead of in the *Independent*, as formerly.]

Also a series of valuable and instructive Sermons, by the most eminent Pulpit Orators of the Methodist and other Churches.

THE METHODIST is an eight-page Weekly Newspaper, now in its seventh year of highly successful publication. It is Religious and Literary; Independent, Fraternal, Loyal and Progressive.

It is Edited, as heretofore, by

REV. GEORGE R. CROOKS, D.D.

Assisted by able Editorial Contributors:

TERMS: $2.50 per year, payable in advance.

Twenty cents must be added by Subscribers in the British Provinces, to pre-pay postage.

Liberal Premiums are allowed to those forming Clubs of subscribers.

Specimen Numbers sent free, on application.—Address

THE METHODIST,
114 Nassau-street, New York.

THE AMERICAN

JOURNAL OF HORTICULTURE,

AND FLORIST'S COMPANION,

ILLUSTRATED.

We shall commence with the coming year the publication of an Illustrated Monthly Magazine devoted to Horticulture. For a long time the demand has been felt for a Journal in this department, of high tone and liberal ideas, employing not only the best talent in America, but the selection of all that is good from the English, French, German and other foreign works. This demand we design to supply.

An important and novel feature of the Magazine will be the department of FLORICULTURE. Receiving contributions from all of the known talent in America, with copious extracts from the best foreign works, it will be an Encyclopedia of Floriculture. To the lady who has only a window for her garden, or the front of a city residence, as well as to the proprietor of the largest garden and green-house, it will be a necessary companion and guide. Every novelty introduced will receive proper attention in our columns.

The subscription price will be $3.00 per annum, so that it may be within the reach of all who desire such a work.

Each number of the magazine will contain 64 pages of reading matter, including illustrations.

THUS IT WILL BE SEEN THAT FOR THREE DOLLARS WE GIVE NEARLY EIGHT HUNDRED OCTAVO PAGES OF ILLUSTRATED HORTICULTURAL MATTER, SELECTED FROM THE BEST THE COUNTRY CAN PRODUCE.

The January number will be ready about December 1st.

TERMS: Three dollars per annum, strictly in advance. Liberal terms will be made with those desiring to form clubs, or to act as agents in enlisting subscribers.

Sample numbers sent by mail on receipt of 30 cents.

Agents wanted in every city and town in the country.

J. E. TILTON & CO.,
PUBLISHERS, BOSTON.

Prospectus with list of contributors, sent on application.

TAXIDERMISTS' MANUAL,

GIVING full instruction in Skinning, Mounting and Preserving Birds, Animals, Reptiles, Fishes, Insects, Eggs, Skeletons, &c. Sent by mail, postpaid, on receipt of $1.00.

ADDRESS S. H. SYLVESTER, TAXIDERMIST, **Middleboro', Mass.**

BOOK AGENTS WANTED.—Agents are now wanted to solicit orders in each town in the United States, for **The Illustrated History of the Bible,** by John Kitto, D. D., F. S. A., Edited by Alvan Bond, D. D., of Norwich, Conn.

This is the best selling book now published. Agents make from $100 to $300 per month, and say "*they never knew a book to sell so well.*"

For further information apply immediately to the publisher. HENRY BILL, Norwich, Conn.

THE HOG BREEDERS' MANUAL, tells you how to cure Hog Cholera, and all diseases of Hogs, only 25 cents. Address N. P. BOYER & CO., Gum Tree, Chester Co., Pa.

AGENTS WANTED everywhere for "Phillips' Excelsior Sticking Paper." Send 2 red stamps and get sample and terms. L. W. PHILLIPS, E. Bridgewater, Mass.

IONA AND ISRAELLA

[*Continued from next page* (36), *which see.*]

And the wine from the Delaware, although most excellent of its class (resembling the alcoholic Sherry), was too rich and "heady," or intoxicating for general use. It could not supply the want that is *felt* for the finest German Wines, which are more healthful and restorative, but less stimulating, and though greatly coveted, are but rarely obtained in this country. Their use is greatly restricted by their exceeding costliness.

The following from Mr. Mottier, will be conclusive for wine making to those who know his cautious manner of forming and expressing opinions, and his ability to judge.

DR. C. W. GRANT,—

Dear Sir: I have to express to you my very great satisfaction at the trial of the Iona Wine, and also of the juice. The Wine of 1864 was far better than any American production that I ever tasted, of that age, and I think equals the very finest Hocks of Germany. That of this fall that has just finished its fermentation, I think, promises at least equally well. I never doubted the great excellence of the Iona for Wine—its fruit plainly indicates that; as it appears to me now, it is of the very highest promise, and I shall plant very largely of it.

Signed, (Yours, respectfully,
JOHN E. MOTTIER.)*

The must (juice) of the IONA has registered by the scale from 88 to 120 degrees, where that of Catawba could scarcely rise above 70, and the wine at two years old, is able to bare comparison in pure refinement and all good qualities, with the most excellent of Europe, at that age. While this can be said of no other American Wine, except that of the Delaware, there is a general concurrence among good judges in awarding great superiority to the IONA over that. In purity and richness, it equals the Delaware, and greatly excels it in sustaining and restorative power, without the strong disposition to intoxication, from which the Delaware is not exempt. It has been well characterized as "generous and animating, smooth, rich, refined and pure, leaving the mouth cool and the head clear, in no degree heavy or oppressive, with delightful bouquet, and not a trace of native foxiness."

Its juice never requires sugar or any admixture to prevent acidification, and the wine is most simply made, requiring only that its juice should be pressed and set to ferment in an open vessel, either in a warm upper room or cellar. It is so fixed and enduring in its character that it does not require a cellar to keep it from acetous fermentation, and a little of its rich juice added to that of Catawba, prevents the disposition of that to form vinegar, and adds greatly to its refinement and richness.

An all important characteristic that belongs to the IONA, it may be said alone, of all our native kinds, is its habit of ripening *thoroughly* and *uniformly*, quite to the center, and *as soon* at the center as at any other portion. To say that this characteristic added to the Catawba, would tenfold its value for wine, and change its character entirely for the table, is saying less than the fair plain truth. The Catawba, merely for the want of this one of the peculiar characteristics of the IONA, must become of little value as soon as enough vines of the IONA can be planted to supply its place.

But the IONA has other exclusive characteristics of exceeding importance. Its skin is pleasantly spicy and good to eat, in place of the acrid foxiness of the Catawba. Its juice is perfectly pure, smooth to the tongue, in place of the harsh impurity of the Catawba, (our other natives being greatly more harsh and impure,) at the same time greatly exceeding it in richness. It ripens three weeks earlier, and is exempt from rot, where the Catawba is rendered worthless by it. I leave all that are inferior to the Catawba out of the comparison.

The planting of vines in vineyards as well as in gardens, is now being so extensively done, that we are called upon to look attentively and intelligently at the conditions of profit and success in the undertaking.

It is only in the production of *good* articles of any kind that it is safe to put trust for permanent profit, and especially if the good are *greatly better* than the inferior, and cost no more.

The best varieties of grapes which we designate as European (but originated in Asia), differ greatly from our ordinary American kinds in their quality, and in the construction or physical character of the fruit. In order to get a true notion of the Grape as the best of fruits, which it truly is in its best kinds, in perfect condition, it will be necessary to note the prominent points of these somewhat critically that we may bring them in our minds into just comparison with our own kinds. This will enable us rightly to estimate the value and importance of some of our new varieties (when we know also the habit and character of the vines), both for fruit and for wine.

The skins of the foreign kinds generally grow inseparably fast to the flesh, but are good to eat, and the *flesh* or substance of the berries ripens uniformly from the circumference to the center, and the entire substance is equally rich and good. This fruit is *eaten*, and all the substance deliberately enjoyed in the mouth, instead of *being* swallowed chiefly whole, and in the rich spirited kinds, it is literally *eating* wine. All persons who have had knowledge of these, have most earnestly desired their cultivation in this country, for their pure, rich, animating spirit, and for their exquisite refinement of flavor.

But these can be grown only in expensive glass houses in this country.

In contrast to these, the skins of American grapes let the fruit slip out from them when burst by pressure, like a bullet from a gun. The skins are too unpleasant for eating, being sharp and acrid to the lips, with the offensive odor of the excreta of the Fox. There is always a tough, unripe acid portion in which the seeds are imbedded, that must be swallowed whole like coated pills. The only portion which ripens is that between the skin and bullet center, and even this portion, as in the Catawba and Isabella, is neither refined or rich in flavor, when compared with Frontignan or Muscat of Alexandria, which are equally good from circumference to the center.

To say that a grape is as good as Muscat of Alexandria, is to give it the highest possible commendation, and this is certified of the IONA. Both are raisin grapes.

It is equally important that grapes for making good wine should be pure and refined in flavor, without any foxiness or unripeness at the center, and *indispensable* that they should be high flavored and spirited.

The stories of high prices for wine from Concord and kindred kinds, are doubtless true to the letter, but tend to propagate notions of great and disastrous untruth.

(*These may seem to be minute details, but they show the only foundation upon which Grape Culture can permanently stand. Continued next month. For Pamphlet in which the subject is treated at length, send stamp.*)

*(*Mr. Mottier has already taken Six Thousand vines of IONA this Fall, and expects to take more in the Spring.*)

The Present State of Grape Culture.

The past has been acknowledged, by general consent, to have been the most unfavorable season for Grape Culture, (both for the propagation of plants and production of fruit,) that has occurred since these became an important branch of cultivation, and more interest from those that are alive to the importance of the subject, has centered in the IONA, than in all of the other kinds, for that is the only one before the public that has promised, by its assemblage of excellences, to make our country eminent in grape producing for all purposes.

If this were to come short in any important point of the high expectations raised by its past history, it would be an astounding disappointment. From a very extended survey, we shall see that it has fully **sustained its high promises in every particular**, although vines have failed in some instances from improper treatment.

It is true, there have been instances of failure of the vines from being frozen out, as of all other kinds, from a vicious plan of planting, but in no instance within my knowledge, where the simple directions of the Manual have been followed. Of that I shall treat farther soon.

Three years ago it had begun to be clearly apparent to those who were most intimately acquainted with grapes, and who were also most thoroughly conversant with vine culture throughout this country and in Europe, that the IONA was the grape to complete the revolution both for Fruit and for Wine, that had been already well undertaken by the *Delaware*.

The richness, purity, and refinement of flavor of the Delaware, apparently left little to be hoped for, better in these respects. As a fruit, it was exquisite, and its wine was of a rich, refined character, heretofore unapproached by the productions of this country. The Catawba, before the introduction of the Delaware, had justly stood high above all other Native kinds, both for Fruit and for Wine, but with strong points of excellence, it had very great and radical defects for both purposes, in the quality of its fruit as well as in the habit and character of the vine.

Its Southern origin, and consequent lateness in ripening and sensitiveness to atmospheric changes, inducing mildew and rot, restricted its cultivation to a very narrow limit, and then in only a few favored localities could its fruit be hoped for with any degree of constancy that rendered its cultivation valuable commercially, or worthy of much attention in the *Fruit-garden*.

In addition to these discouragements, were the serious defects in the fruit itself, when in best condition—it always having a large, tough, unripe acid portion, that must be swallowed together with the seeds—and quickly to avoid its unpleasantness.

The better portion, too, had always some astringency from excess of Tannic-acid, and the skin was somewhat acrid with a considerable degree of disagreeable and unwholesome foxy odor, even under the most favorable influences of season and climate. As a fruit, it could measurably satisfy the cravings of persons who had known nothing better, but was not good enough to afford much, if any, enjoyment to those who had known the real excellence of Grapes, as existing in the best foreign kinds.

As a Table-grape, the Isabella was always associated with the Catawba, but by its earlier ripening, it was adapted to a much more extended region.

The native defects in this were the same as those in the Catawba, but with much less of excellence, the Isabella being comparatively feeble-flavored—that is, having in a given quantity of juice, less sugar, and what is more important, less of the acids that are indispensable constituents of *good* grapes. The acids of unripeness in the tough, unripe center, are not here intended, for these are the bane of our ordinary natives, and especially for wine-making.

The Isabella has thus too little richness for making *real* wine—while the Catawba in its best condition, as cultivated in some favored localities, produces wine of good quality, that has, like the grape, strong points of excellence, with its very positive native defects—in unpleasant aroma, and want of refinement. Mr. John E. Mottier, has exhibited the best Catawba wine probably that the grape is capable of producing, in the vintages of '59 and '63, and our comparisons are made with that.

These two kinds had led a large portion of our people to a knowledge of much better grapes than the wild ones of the woods, and Catawba wine, had given a good idea of an exhilarating and refreshing beverage, with little tendency to intoxicate. But the adulterated imitations (falsely represented as pure Catawba, because of the alcoholic strength being added in the form of sugar,) had been manifold more in quantity than the pure wine.

The strong desire to have grapes and wine acting constantly had induced some progress; yet, the advance had been slow, because no grape had appeared of the requisite quality and character to bear comparison with the best of vine-growing countries.

But after the propagation of the Delaware had been undertaken in earnest, as rapidly as plants for the purpose could be supplied, the knowledge of good grapes was spread abroad over the country. At the time we have named (three years ago), the Delaware, which had been extensively disseminated, had borne much of its fine fruit, and made great progress in "educating the American taste," and those who had been foremost in learning from the Delaware how *good* grapes can be, were ready to take the IONA from the same recommendation, although the originator hesitated then to represent it as surpassing the Delaware in excellence of quality. The claim for it was, that it "deserved to *stand by the side* of the Delaware for quality, while in size of bunch and berry, it greatly exceeded it." Without detracting at all from the merits of the Delaware (it has not been over-praised), it is now by extensive trial, clearly established by the most abundant proof, that the IONA surpasses the Delaware in quality, for Wine and Fruit, as well as in its bright transparent beauty, and in the large size of its bunches and berries, and in addition that it is an excellent raisin grape, and *our only one that has sufficient richness of substance for that purpose*.

The Delaware was one of the greatest accessions to our enjoyment in fruits, and must ever maintain a very high position.

But a table grape as pure and refined as that, and more "spirited and exhilarating," and much larger in size for full free use, was yet wanted, that would ripen *thoroughly to the center*, which was not the case with the Delaware. [*Continued on preceding page (35) which see.*]

AMERICAN AGRICULTURIST

FOR THE

Farm, Garden, and Household.

"AGRICULTURE IS THE MOST HEALTHFUL, MOST USEFUL, AND MOST NOBLE EMPLOYMENT OF MAN."—WASHINGTON.

ORANGE JUDD & CO., PUBLISHERS AND PROPRIETORS. Office, 41 Park Row, (Times Buildings.)

ESTABLISHED IN 1842.

Published also in German at $1.50 a Year.

$1.50 PER ANNUM, IN ADVANCE. SINGLE NUMBER, 15 CENTS. 4 Copies for $5; 10 for $12; 20 or more, $1 each.

VOLUME XXVI—No. 2. NEW-YORK, FEBRUARY, 1867. NEW SERIES—No. 241.

[COPYRIGHT SECURED.]

HEAD OF "BARON," INFANTADO MERINO RAM.—BRED AND OWNED BY WM. CHAMBERLAIN.—*Drawn from Life for the American Agriculturist.*

The fine Ram, whose head is portrayed above, is of the breed known in this country as Silesian *Merino*. He was bred by his owner, Mr. Wm. Chamberlain, of Red Hook, N. Y., from pure Infantado stock, and has a documentary pedigree running back to 1811, when his ancestors were imported from Spain into Silesia. The wool is fine and very dense, with comparatively little grease or yolk, and the fleece, which usually weighs about 16½ pounds, covers the carcass remarkably, and grows well down to the hoofs. We regret not to be able to state the weight of cleansed wool, for we are confident it would compare most favorably with that of fleeces which, in the grease, would weigh a great deal more. He took the first prize in his class at the last show of the New York State Agricultural Society, where the artist secured the sketch for the above engraving. It was very gratifying to us to witness the satisfaction of several wool manufacturers (some of whom we asked concerning their opinion of Mr. Chamberlain's Silesians,) when they examined the fleece of this ram and other sheep of the same stock. It confirmed us in a long held opinion that it will pay for farmers to produce such wool as manufacturers want to buy. The wool of these sheep is of great uniformity and excellent quality, opening brilliantly, but the yolk gives it a dark crust at the surface. This kind of Merinos have compact, well-formed carcasses, and are not given to wrinkles nor grease in the excessive fashion of those popularly known as the Vermont or American Merinos. The Infantado's were imported also into this country about the same time that "Baron's" ancestors were taken to Silesia, and from 1813 to about 1845 were bred pure by Stephen Atwood of Connecticut. As now known, the two families both claiming much the same parentage, present notable differences, though many similarities, and breeders of good judgement are divided in their preferences.

Contents for February, 1867.

Back Volumes Supplied.—The back volumes of the *Agriculturist* are very valuable. They contain information upon every topic connected with rural life, out-door and in-door, and the last ten volumes make up a very complete library. Each volume has a full index for ready reference to any desired topic. We have on hand, and print from stereotype plates as wanted, all the numbers and volumes for ten years past, beginning with 1857—that is, Vol. 16 to Vol. 25, inclusive. Any of these volumes sent complete (in numbers) at $1.75 each, post-paid, (or $1.50 if taken at the office). The volumes neatly bound, are supplied for $2 each, or $2.50 if to be sent by mail. Any single numbers of the past ten years will be supplied, post-paid, for 15 cents each.

AMERICAN AGRICULTURIST.

NEW-YORK, FEBRUARY, 1867.

We hope our readers will not think that we are unseasonably "harping upon one string," when we again insist upon the necessity of laying definite plans for work to be done. This makes the difference between success and failure—between thrift and unthrift, provided of course, that such plans are made, as may be, and are, carried out. An old farmer knows by experience what may be done, by what has been, and it is well for the young farmer not to undertake too much. Depend upon it, time will not hang heavy on your hands. Do what you undertake, thoroughly well, but do not "putter" and fuss to no account. Especially regard four things: *First*: "Your own *health* and that of the family, especially that of the good wife—relieving her in every possible way, by servants, by washing machine and wringer, by sewing machine, by your own helpful care, solicitude, and interest in her work and cares. *Second—System*: Having every thing go according to a preconcerted plan. *Third—Time*: Being prompt, up early, having chores done, breakfast ready at the moment, and the work of the day begun as nearly as possible at the same hour daily—and so through the day. Besides, allowing full resting spells, permit no loitering of men or teams. *Fourth*: If you employ one or more hands, impose a strict *responsibility* in regard to certain work, and enforce the same. Thus things will go smoothly.

There is one thing farmers are very apt to neglect, and that is, the Kitchen Garden—many of them hardly glance at the *hints* in another column. A good vegetable garden is the most profitable part of any farm. Manure will pay best applied there, and labor will produce more comfort, food and gratification if expended in the garden than elsewhere. And in the neighborhood of villages there are always quick sales for fresh vegetables, and by the preparation of a little more ground and a small additional cost for seed and tillage, no inconsiderable income may be derived. Think of this while making plans for March and April work.

Hints About Work.

At the North we are pretty much cut off from proper field work, yet, as the *Agriculturist* goes Southward, it soon comes upon bare fields and soil in which no frost remains long. There spring begins in good earnest a month or six weeks earlier than in our latitude (41°), and "spring plowing," etc., is there winter work. We adapt these hints to our own latitude, but are apt to anticipate a little, chiefly in order to have plenty of leeway in case the season is especially early.

Field Work.—Dead furrows in *grain fields* and furrows plowed for surface draining should be clear, so that the ground will not wash much in thaws. If grain is badly harmed by frost put on an even light dressing of muck or soil or simply roll.

Grass and Clover Seed may be sown if the ground is bare and the frost is out. It is best to be done on a very light snow in case the surface is not frozen. Any kind of grass or clover seed may be sown.

Manure may be hauled out to the distant fields when there is good sledding, but it should only be such as is well composed and which will neither wash nor deteriorate essentially by exposure. It may easily be put in this condition by the use of [illegible], but very little that is hauled to the field in the winter time is so protected from the action of the weather, and half to two-thirds is wasted.

Buildings.—Timber may be prepared for any repairs, or for new buildings which may be desired. (Pine, Spruce, and Hemlock, may be cut at this season.) Stables and cellars should be opened and aired on warm dry days. A little salt sprinkled around posts, which form the foundations of corn cribs and similar structures will prevent their being harmed by the frost. This is true of gate posts.

The Wood Lot affords plenty of work in cutting fire wood, getting out framing stuff, cedar bean poles, stakes, and such things. Avoid cutting trees that are full of sap at this season, or as soon as the weather is warmer—as the maple, beach, etc.

Ice.—Review what has previously been said about storing ice, it is not too late so long as good ice can be procured. Pack only solid ice, removing all the soft snow ice that may be attached to the cakes.

Secure Seed of each kind of grain it is proposed to sow this spring. If you can do so, select seed grain from a large quantity by repeated winnowings. Send for catalogues of seedmen, study them, and order early. At the same time also

Secure Good Farm Hands.—February is usually the time to make the best engagements.

Working Stock, if not employed, should not be fed too much grain, but roots should be in a measure substituted, and if hard worked, feed accordingly.

Horses ought to be kept sharp-caulked, as ice is more dangerous if it exists only in spots than when it covers the ground. Feed four quarts of carrots with a handful of ashes and half as much ginger daily if they get "off their feed" for lack of exercise. They are approaching the time when they shed their coats, and as they are then liable to take colds, they should be well fed and in good condition. The tax upon the system in renewing the coat is considerable. Brood mares, with foal, need especial care, lest they slip and fall, or in playing strain themselves, or get kicked.

Colts.—When there is a foot of snow on the ground the time is particularly favorable to training and breaking colts to saddle and harness. Gentleness, firmness and sugar are the specifics, with the common sense use of which, we warrant it easy to break any colt not made vicious by bad boys or men.

Oxen should come out in fine condition for spring work on little besides corn stalks if these are properly prepared, namely: cut up, soaked and salted with a very little meal upon them.

Beef Stock may have a little increase of meal or oil cake when they begin to shed their coats.

Cows that are giving milk may well have wheat bran and oil-cake meal on their cut and soaked stalks. The earlier they are dried off, the better will the calf be, in all likelihood, but if milked until nearly time for the new milk to "spring" a tendency to give much milk is increased.

Calves intended for veal may very early be taught to nibble hay, and finally to eat a good deal, and with what skimmed milk they can get in their boiled gruel, they will make rapid progress.

The Currycomb should not be neglected, its exercise on all kinds neat stock and horses is a great prevention of disease and vermin, and is productive of thrift.

Sheep should be kept so assorted in flocks that all can get the proper allowance of feed. Provide a warm shed, feed straw and hay in racks, and grain in troughs; of course, feed some roots, or hemlock boughs, or both. House ewes near yeaning time, where they will have room, warmth, and comfort. Visit all the stock personally the last thing at night and first thing in the morning. See that they have water enough, at least twice a day, better three times. Give salt frequently, and let them stand several hours in the yards every day if fair.

Poultry.—Set one or two clutches of the earliest eggs, mating the finest pullets with the best old cock, as early in the month as possible, provided you can furnish the chicks warm, dry, light quarters. Kept clean, and attended with care, they will make fine birds, either to improve your own flock, or for the fall shows.

Swine.—Keep the shoats at work at the manure. We often think of the saying of a Massachusetts farmer, that for corn, a cob that a hog had breathed on is worth a bushel of yard manure. Breeding sows near farrowing, should be well sheltered, and have warm nests away from other swine and be fed well, but not with heating food; a few raw potatoes or other roots are promotive of milk, and make an excellent addition to their diet.

Work in the Horticultural Departments.

The "note of preparation" should be sounding in every department. Occasional mild days will allow of some out of door work, and the tool-house and repairs in the work shop will give abundant indoor employment. Have everything ready, not only the tools and appliances, but have all *plans* made for the opening season. This month, catalogues of the dealers are ready, and if trees or other nursery stuff or seeds, etc., are to be purchased, our advertising columns will show where the articles are to be had. Order early, as the stock of some things is often exhausted later in the season. In sending an order to nurserymen or seedsmen write plainly, and put only one article upon a line. Mistakes are usually as much the fault of the purchaser as of the seller, who is often puzzled to find out what is wanted. If any correspondence is necessary, have it separate from the order. Give clear directions how the articles are to be sent, and do not omit to given the address in full. A dealer of our acquaintance recently received an order inclosing money, but no name was signed; a few days after he received a letter from the same writer, which informed him that an order had been sent a few days before, but that the name had been forgotten, and *this* letter of explanation also had no name to it.

Orchard and Nursery.

The principal items of out door work were indicated last month. As the severity of the weather moderates, the knife may be used in shaping

Young Trees.—Cut them back to secure a stocky growth, and a well balanced form. Do not cut so close to a bud as to endanger it, nor so far above as to leave a stub. The treatment of young trees that have been badly formed is noticed on page 62. Though February is not the best possible month for

Pruning, there are many who are obliged to do it now; select a time when the wood is not frozen, and observe the precautions mentioned on page 62.

Old trees and neglected young ones may have a a wash of soft soap, mixed with water enough to apply with a brush. If there is much loose bark, or a great accumulation of moss, a blunt scraper may be used. Some are made for this use. Every cluster of

Caterpillar's Eggs removed now is clear gain; the Tent-caterpillar's were described in January.

Cions are to be cut on mild days, and kept in saw-dust or moss until wanted. Earth or sand will keep them as well, but they are less pleasant to use than when preserved in moss or saw-dust. Cions are readily sent by mail; tie them in a bundle, wrap in oiled silk, and over all put a stout brown paper, and tie securely. Mark "cuttings only," and put no writing in the package. Postage is 2 cents for 4 oz.

Grafting should be deferred until the buds of the stock begin to swell—which they will do this month in some parts of the South. Root grafting ought to be finished up, and the grafted roots ready to set out.

Nursery trees will be received by some of our southern readers, and if long on the way may have suffered from drying, or they may be frozen. Completely bury all dried or shrivelled trees, and if not too far gone they will become plump in a few days. Any packages, the contents of which are likely to be frozen when they are received, should be allowed to thaw gradually in a cool place before opening.

Manure may be spread in the orchard wherever the ground is not frozen.

Fruit Garden.

Continue to exercise oversight, and see that no injury comes to trees and plants by animals. If

Grape Vines were not pruned in autumn, take advantage of the first thaw, and do it this month. The wood from winter pruning is not so good for cuttings as that removed in fall, and if used for this purpose must be carefully selected.

Currants may also be pruned, and the cuttings buried until the weather allows of their being set.

Dwarf trees treat as noticed above, under Orchard.

Kitchen Garden.

As there is but little to be done here, in northern localities, our notes for January are equally good now. Make every preparation for spring work.

Manure, whether for garden use or for hot-beds, should be accumulated. When the heap becomes hot it should be turned to avoid injury.

Hot-beds are to be made at the South, and at the North, if very early plants are wanted. For the simplest form of hot-bed see page 63. Prepare

Straw-covers, as described on page 63, or straw mats; the last are made by stretching a warp of five tarred strings, the width of the sash and a foot longer, then laying on handfuls of straw, each of which is to be bound to the warp by a small string.

Cold Frames need more close attention as the weather gets milder. Open them whenever the weather is not severe, and harden off the cabbage and other plants to fit them for early transplanting.

Root crops still in the ground, such as horse-radish, parsnips and salsify are to be dug and marketed whenever the ground is sufficiently thawed.

Onions, if frozen, should be kept so by a covering of hay to prevent alternate freezing and thawing.

Poles and brush that may be needed for beans, peas and other climbers, are best cut before vegetation starts, and while the swamps are frozen.

Rhubarb is easily forced where there is plenty of manure. Cover the roots with boxes or barrels, and surround them well with heating material. The leaves soon start, and when grown in the dark in this way are exceedingly tender. Do not forget that all labor is lost unless you have good

Seeds.—If there is any doubt about the quality of seeds, be at any trouble or expense to procure those of a reliable character. Buy of responsible parties only. The postal arrangements, for all except points reached by the over-land mail, are such that it makes but little difference where one lives, as the mail puts him in reach of all the seed stores in the country. See "Basket" item on page 50.

Flower Garden and Lawn.

The mild days will allow pruning to be done.

Ornamental trees, as a general thing, should be left to assume their natural form, but it sometimes becomes necessary to remove branches that are in the way, and others that have become injured by winds or snow. All pruning of them should be done with as much care as with fruit trees—for which see article on page 62.

Shrubs, too, will need the knife and the shears. They ought not to be cut into formal shapes, but left still in their natural form. Those that bloom upon the new growth may be shortened at pleasure, while those that have their flower buds ready formed only need to have crowded branches thinned out.

Repairs of fences and of trellises, arbors, and all garden fixtures may be made and painting done.

Pits and cellars where plants are stored will need looking to. Give air on mild days; if the plants become very dry and likely to suffer, water moderately.

Dahlias, Cannas, and other roots, stored in the cellar for winter must not be allowed to be damp enough to mould or rot. If this occurs, separate the affected ones and remove to a dryer place.

Green and Hot-Houses.

The variable weather this month will demand care with the fires to secure that uniformity of temperature so necessary to success.

Insects are easily kept in check if taken in time. Burn tobacco occasionally at night at closing the house to keep the green fly in check.

Camellias and other shrubs that have done flowering may be trimmed into shape. The camellia, especially, is often neglected in this respect.

Bulbs are to be brought into the green house to supply the place of those that have gone out of flower.

Propagation of all kinds of bedding stuff may be commenced, and seeds of annuals may be sown.

Roses coming into flower may have very weak liquid manure, not more highly colored than tea.

The Apiary for February.

Bee culture requires, in its most successful management, the right thing to be done promptly at the right time, hence, all necessary appliances should be in readiness before wanted. Bees do not wait our convenience, and so we must closely observe their habits and accommodate ourselves to them. A knowledge of them can be gained from the standard works on Bee Culture, but practice, in connection with the theoretical knowledge, is essential to success. It is easily gained, and so, young bee keepers need not be discouraged by a lack of success for a year or two. Bee keepers in most of the United States and Canada encounter two draw backs—namely, cold winters, and an interrupted and irregular succession of flowers. These may be obviated, to a considerable extent, by protection in winter, and by cultivating honey producing flowers, adapted to bee pasturage. Success depends to a great degree in being able to know what is going on within the hive—for this moveable frame hives are necessary. Then it is proved that Italian Bees are superior to the common or black ones, not only because they are more industrious, better workers and breeders, but especially because more easily handled (if pure), hence, it is best to have them if they can be obtained.

MEMORANDA, FURNISHED BY M. QUINBY.

Only the light newly fallen snow is dangerous to bees; if a warm, bright day should come the day after snow has fallen, shade the hive to discourage the bees leaving. Should bees that are housed become uneasy, and some of them, leaving the hive, discharge filth on its sides, it is well to put them out some good warm day, and return at night. If bees are to be changed to any new stand or bee-house, let it be done this month, or next, at least, before they fly out to mark the locality. It is worse to move a short distance than a great one. Separate stands and roofs are approved by many, and if adopted, should be crowded with hives, to secure all possible advantages. This involves the necessity of making artificial swarms, and rearing and introducing laying queens to all the hives as they need them; this is not a difficult operation. See that no full colony is without one longer than two to seven days. Those intending to do this, should prepare now a few miniature moveable comb hives, with a few of the combs filled with dry combs. Directions for raising and introducing queens will be given at the proper season. This month is a good time for purchasing more stocks, if wanted, as they may be moved safely by sleigh.

When purchased stocks have been housed during the winter, they should have at least one fair day on which to fly, before starting on a journey.

The Indiana Horticultural Society.—The annual meeting of this Society was held at Indianapolis on January 8th. We extract the following from the letter of a correspondent who was present: The veteran President, J. D. G. Nelson, of Fort Wayne, opened the meeting with some interesting and encouraging statements as to the status of Horticulture in the State. Sundry papers and reports were presented by the officers of the society and from county societies. The following members were elected to office: *President*, J. D. G. Nelson, Fort Wayne. *Vice-Presidents*, A. Furnas, Danville; Calvin Fletcher, Indianapolis; J. C. Shoemaker, Rome; E. C. Siler, Parke County. *Secretary*, S. W. Pearson, Plainfield. *Corresponding Secretary*, Jos. Gilbert, Terre Haute. *Treasurer*, J. S. Dunlop, Indianapolis.—Committees were appointed to examine and award premiums upon the specimens on the table. The show of fruits was very extensive and fine. Quite an array of native wines was also on exhibition. Several papers of interest were read during the course of the sessions—but the great work of the meeting has been the revision of the Fruit Catalogues, the result of which can only be seen in the official report, soon to be printed. In the course of the discussions, insects came in for a share of consideration, and many testified to the advantage they had gained from reading the *Practical Entomologist*. One evening was devoted to the memory of the late Secretary, Geo. M. Beeler, and to the presenting an eulogy of him to a large and attentive audience of his fellow-citizens and admirers.

AMERICAN AGRICULTURIST.
ORANGE JUDD & Co., Publishers, 41 Park Row, N. Y. City.
ANNUAL SUBSCRIPTION TERMS (always in advance): $1.50 each for less than four copies: Four to nine copies, $1.25 each: Ten to nineteen copies, $1.20 each: Twenty copies and upwards, $1 each. Papers are addressed to each name.

DO YOU WANT,

Without Expense:

Do YOU WANT a fine assortment of 40 kinds of first-rate Garden Seeds for spring use—enough for any family?

Do YOU WANT 100 papers of Flower Seeds, of choice kinds—just such as will beautifully adorn your homestead?

Do YOU WANT a good lot of Nursery Stock, your own selection from the best nurseries in the country, such as Fruit Trees, Ornamental Trees, Shrubs, Plants, etc.?

Do YOU WANT a dozen No. 1 Iona Grape Vines; or 100 No. 1 Concord Vines which are good everywhere?

Do YOU WANT a dozen bulbs of the beautiful Japan Lilies, which you can plant for bloom next spring?

Do YOU WANT for your wife, or a friend, a first-rate Sewing Machine, your choice from the *seven* best kinds?

Do YOU WANT one of the Best Washing Machines?

Do YOU WANT one of the Best Clothes-Wringers?

Do YOU WANT a splendid, Silver-plated Tea-Set, of beautiful form—heavily plated on the best white metal?

Do YOU WANT a *best* Silver-plated Castor and Fruit Basket combined, one of the most beautiful ever made?

Do YOU WANT a dozen of the *best* Silver-plated Teaspoons, or a dozen Tablespoons, or Dining Forks?

Do YOU WANT one of Steinway & Sons most excellent $625 Pianos, an instrument—commended by everybody?

Do YOU WANT one of Geo. A. Prince & Co.'s first-rate Portable Melodeons, 4 or 5 octave, sold at $67 and $112?

Do YOU WANT a most beautiful and valuable Lady's Gold Watch—one warranted by Benedict Brothers?

Do YOU WANT a really good Silver Watch, Hunting case, of excellent make, and a correct Time-keeper?

Do YOU WANT a really first-rate Double Barrel Gun?

Do YOU WANT one of Spencer's Breech-loading, Hunting Rifles, that shoots seven times with once loading?

Do YOU WANT a chest of the very best Tools made?

Do YOU WANT a very excellent set of Mathematical Instruments for drawing plans, sketches, etc.?

Do YOU WANT one of Morton's Gold Pens, the best made?

Do YOU WANT one of Woodruff's Improved Barometers—the best weather prophet, or guide, we know of?

Do YOU WANT a first-rate Premium Buckeye Mower?

Do YOU WANT one of Allen's excellent Cylinder Plows?

Do YOU WANT an Aquarius or Water Thrower?

Do YOU WANT a set of 16 great Volumes of Appleton's New Cyclopedia, which is a whole library in itself?

Do YOU WANT one of Worcester's Great Dictionaries?

Do YOU WANT from one to ten of the past valuable Volumes of the *American Agriculturist*, bound or unbound?

Do YOU WANT from one to eight of the Volumes of the valuable old Genesee Farmer, neatly bound?

Do YOU WANT Downing's Splendid Work on Landscape Gardening and Rural Architecture—a beautiful volume?

Do YOU WANT from $10 to $100 worth of Good Books?

Do YOU WANT, for yourself and friends, a dozen of the most ingenious portable Pocket Lanterns ever made?

Well, all these good articles are offered in our Premium List to any and all persons who make up clubs of subscribers to the *Agriculturist*, according to the table in the next column. Thousands of persons have already received from one to half a dozen of these premiums, and in most cases by only a few evenings in canvassing. Frequent cases are reported to us where premium canvassers have cleared from $10 to $30 a day, by earning the premiums and selling them.—There are in our country more than five million families, and single persons, who ought to have the *Agriculturist*, and who would be greatly benefited by reading it. A good many such persons live in *your* neighborhood. It only needs you or some other enterprising person to call upon them, show a copy of the paper and ask them to join a club. There is plenty of time to do this—five months if you desire. In more than two thousand places such clubs have already been made up, but there are more than **20,000** other Post-offices in the United States and British America, where clubs can just as easily be raised, and the premiums secured without expense. Human nature, and the people are about the same everywhere; it only needs the same enterprising person in each town to get up the desired club. Who will do it in *your* town. Can not *you* do it? *Try it.* If you chance to fail in getting a large club this year, even a few subscribers will open the way for many more next year, and every subscriber you get will help develop taste, good culture, and increased comfort and interest in the Household. *Try it this month.*

Men and Women of various occupations, Farmers, Gardeners, Post-masters, Merchants, Mechanics, Clergymen, Teachers, Soldiers, Boys, Girls, etc., can engage in the work of soliciting subscribers and secure good pay for it, in the excellent and desirable premium articles.

Any person so disposed can make up a premium list—the offers are open to all. It is a pleasant work. Any one who persuades a dozen, or twenty, or more of his neighbors to read about their business, does much to improve and elevate the character of the people, and to bring increased value to his own homestead, and to every other homestead around him.

Our premiums are all *really valuable articles*, such as we can cheerfully recommend to our friends. By wholesale purchases, by advertising arrangements, etc., we are able to supply them as premiums on far better terms than we could sell them, and we thus pay our canvassers much more than we could possibly do in cash.

We invite every reader who lives where no one is already actively engaged in raising a premium club, to take hold in these leisure winter days, and secure such a club. We often receive several different premium clubs from the same Post-Office.....The last column in the table shows how many subscribers are required when they are sent at the lowest club price of $1 a year for 20 or more. The next column shows the number required at the regular price of $1.50 a year. (See notes following the table.)

Our premiums are standard articles, and enough can be obtained to supply all calls for premiums for six months. Every canvasser can take abundant time, but

As fast as subscriptions are obtained, send them along, that the subscribers may begin to receive the paper; and when all the names that can be obtained are forwarded, select the premium, and it will be promptly furnished. To save mistakes and keeping accounts, *send with each list of names, the exact subscription money.*

Remit in Post Office money orders, drafts or checks on N. Y. City. If these can not be had, register money letters.

☞ **Every name** *designed for a premium list must be so marked* WHEN *sent in.* (We can not count others.)

Old and new subscribers count in premium lists, but a part should be new names, for it is to obtain such that the premiums are in part offered. *Papers to Premium clubs need not all go to one Post Office.*

Table of Premiums and Terms, For Volume 26—(1867).

Open to all—No Competition.

No.	Names of Premium Articles.	Price of Premiums.	Number of Subscribers required at $1.50	at $1.
1	Garden Seeds for a Family (40 kinds)	$5 00	13	37
2	Flower Seeds for a Family (100 kinds)	$5 00	13	37
3	Nursery Stock (Any kinds desired)	$20 00	30	[illegible]
4	Iona Grape Vines (12 of No. 1)	$18 00	27	90
5	Concord Grape Vines (100 of No. 1)	$12 00	19	65
6	Japan Lilies (12 Bulbs)	$6 00	15	45
7	Sewing Machine (Wheeler & Wilson)	$55 00	60	[illegible]
8	Sewing Machine (Grover & Baker)	$55 00	60	[illegible]
9	Sewing Machine (Singer's Tailoring)	[illegible]	[illegible]	[illegible]
10	Sewing Machine (Florence)	[illegible]	[illegible]	[illegible]
11	Sewing Machine (Willcox & Gibbs)	$55 00	60	[illegible]
12	Sewing Machine (Howe's)	$60 00	[illegible]	[illegible]
13	Washing Machine (Doty's)	$14 00	21	70
14	Clothes Wringer (Best—Universal)	$10 00	18	[illegible]
15	Tea Set (Hart's best Silver Plated)	$50 00	[illegible]	[illegible]
16	Castors and Fruit Basket (do. do.)	$30 00	44	140
17	Ice or Water Pitcher (do. do.)	$18 00	27	90
18	One Dozen Tea Spoons (do. do.)	$7 50	17	[illegible]
19	One Dozen Table Spoons (do. do.)	$15 00	[illegible]	[illegible]
20	One Dozen Dining Forks (do. do.)	$15 00	[illegible]	[illegible]
21	Piano (Best Steinway & Son's 7-octave)	$625 00	320	[illegible]
22	Melodeon, 5-octave (G. A. Prince & Co.'s)	$112 00	[illegible]	[illegible]
23	Melodeon, 4-octave (do. do.)	$67 00	[illegible]	[illegible]
24	Ladies' Gold Watch (Beautiful)	$100 00	130	[illegible]
25	Silver Watch (Valuable Time Keeper)	[illegible]	[illegible]	[illegible]
26	Double Barrel Gun (Very good)	$30 00	46	150
27	Spencer's Breech-loading Rifle (Hunting)	$55 00	70	[illegible]
28	Tool Chest (First Quality of Tools)	[illegible]	[illegible]	[illegible]
29	Case of Mathematical Instruments	$9 00	18	55
30	Case of Mathematical Instruments	$15 00	[illegible]	[illegible]
31	Morton's Best No. 6 Gold Pen (Silver Case)	$5 75	14	[illegible]
32	Morton's Best No. 5 Gold Pen (Silver Case)	$4 50	[illegible]	[illegible]
33	Barometer (Woodruff's Mercurial)	$18 00	27	[illegible]
34	Barometer (Woodruff's Mercurial)	$12 00	19	[illegible]
35	Buckeye Mowing Machine, No. 2	$125 00	150	[illegible]
36	Allen's Patent Cylinder Plow, &c.	$20 50	31	[illegible]
37	The Aquarius or Water Thrower	$11 00	19	[illegible]
38	American Cyclopedia (Appleton's)	$80 00	[illegible]	[illegible]
39	Worcester's Great Illustrated Dictionary	$12 00	19	[illegible]
40	Any Back Volume Agriculturist (In clean new Nos. Post-paid.—Unbound.)	[illegible]	[illegible]	[illegible]
41	Any Two Back Volumes do.	[illegible]	[illegible]	[illegible]
42	Any Three do. do. do.	[illegible]	[illegible]	[illegible]
43	Any Four do. do. do.	[illegible]	[illegible]	[illegible]
44	Any Five do. do. do.	[illegible]	[illegible]	[illegible]
45	Any Six do. do. do.	[illegible]	[illegible]	[illegible]
46	Any Seven do. do. do.	[illegible]	[illegible]	[illegible]
47	Any Eight do. do. do.	[illegible]	[illegible]	[illegible]
48	Any Nine do. do. do.	[illegible]	[illegible]	[illegible]
49	Vols. XVI to XXV do.	[illegible]	[illegible]	[illegible]
50	Any Back Volume Agriculturist (Neatly Bound, Sent Post-paid.)	[illegible]	[illegible]	[illegible]
51	Any Two Back Volumes do.	[illegible]	[illegible]	[illegible]
52	Any Three do. do. do.	[illegible]	[illegible]	[illegible]
53	Any Four do. do. do.	[illegible]	[illegible]	[illegible]
54	Any Five do. do. do.	[illegible]	[illegible]	[illegible]
55	Any Six do. do. do.	[illegible]	[illegible]	[illegible]
56	Any Seven do. do. do.	[illegible]	[illegible]	[illegible]
57	Any Eight do. do. do.	[illegible]	[illegible]	[illegible]
58	Any Nine do. do. do.	[illegible]	[illegible]	[illegible]
59	Vols. XVI to XXV do.	[illegible]	[illegible]	[illegible]
60	Genesee Farmer, 1858-1865, 8 Vols., Bound	[illegible]	[illegible]	[illegible]
61	Downing's Landscape Gardening (All post-paid through, by Mail or Express.)	[illegible]	[illegible]	[illegible]
62	Cummings & Miller's Architect.	[illegible]	[illegible]	[illegible]
63	A $10 Library (Your Choice)	$10 00	[illegible]	[illegible]
64	A $15 Library do.	$15 00	[illegible]	[illegible]
65	A $20 Library do.	$20 00	[illegible]	[illegible]
66	A $25 Library do.	$25 00	[illegible]	[illegible]
67	A $30 Library do.	$30 00	[illegible]	[illegible]
68	A $35 Library do.	$35 00	[illegible]	[illegible]
69	A $40 Library do.	$40 00	[illegible]	[illegible]
70	A $45 Library do.	$45 00	[illegible]	[illegible]
71	A $50 Library do.	$50 00	[illegible]	[illegible]
72	A $60 Library do.	$60 00	[illegible]	[illegible]
73	A $75 Library do.	$75 00	100	[illegible]
74	A $100 Library do.	$100 00	125	[illegible]
75	A Choice of Good Books (See Terms below.)			
76	Sewing Machine (Finkle & Lyon)	$60 00	[illegible]	[illegible]
77	One Dozen Pocket Lanterns	$9 00	12	[illegible]

☞ *Every article offered is new and of the very best manufacture. No charge is made for packing or boxing any of the articles in this Premium List. The forty-three Premiums,* **Nos. 1, 2, 6,** *and from* **29** *to* **32,** *and from* **40** *to* **75** *inclusive, will each be delivered* **FREE** *of all charges, by mail or express, (at the Post-Office or express office nearest recipient), to any place in the United States or Territories, excepting those reached only by the Overland Mail.—The other articles cost the recipient only the freight after leaving the manufactory of each, by any conveyance that may be specified.*

☞ **We take** *so much pains to procure only good articles in all cases, that any one securing anything from our premium list, saves the risk usually run of getting poor or indifferent goods, when buying of unknown or irresponsible parties. Every thing we send out as a premium is guaranteed to be the best of its kind and price.*

Specimen Numbers of the *Agriculturist*, Cards, and Showbills, as may be needed, will be supplied to Canvassers. These should be used carefully and economically, as each extra copy of the paper, with postage (2c.) which must be prepaid, costs about 12 cents.

For Full Description of the several premiums see October *Agriculturist*, pages 349 to 352, or apply for a *Descriptive List*, which will be furnished *free* and post-paid. We have room here for only the following:

No. 63 to 74—Good Libraries.—These can be selected by the *recipients*, from any of the books in the list in the next column. The books will be *delivered* free of cost, by mail or express.

No. 75—General Book Premium.—Any one not desiring the specific Book premiums, 63 to 74, on sending any number of names above 25, may select Books from the list (next page), to the amount of 10 cents for each subscriber sent at $1: or to the amount of 30 cents for each name sent at the (ten) club price of $1.20 each: or to the amount of 60 cents for each name at

$1.50. *This offer is only for clubs of 25 or more. The books will be sent by mail or express, prepaid by us.*

BOOKS FOR FARMERS AND OTHERS.

[For sale at the office of the *Agriculturist*, or they will be forwarded by mail, post-paid, on receipt of price. ☞ *All these are included in Our Premiums, Nos. 60 to 73, above.*

Title	Price
Allen's (L. F.) Rural Architecture	$1 50
Allen's (R. L.) American Farm Book	1 50
American Agricultural Annual, 1867, paper, 50c.; cloth	75
Allen's Diseases of Domestic Animals	1 00
American Horticultural Annual, 1867, paper, 50c.; cloth	75
American Bird Fancier	30
American Rose Culturist	30
American Weeds and Useful Plants	1 75
Architecture, by Cummings & Miller	10 00
Barry's Fruit Garden	1 75
Bement's Poulterer's Companion	2 00
Bement's Rabbit Fancier	30
Breck's New Book of Flowers	1 75
Buist's Flower Garden Directory	1 50
Buist's Family Kitchen Gardener	1 00
Burr's Vegetables of America	5 00
Chorlton's Grape-Grower's Guide	75
Cobbett's American Gardener	75
Cole's (S. W.) American Fruit Book	75
Cole's Veterinarian	75
Dadd's Modern Horse Doctor	1 50
Dadd's (Geo. H.) American Cattle Doctor	1 50
Dana's Muck Manual	1 25
Dog and Gun (Hooper's) paper, 30c. cloth	60
Downing's Country Houses	8 00
Downing's Landscape Gardening (new Edition)	6 50
Downing's Fruits and Fruit Trees of America	3 00
Downing's Rural Essays	5 00
Eastwood on Cranberry	75
Elliott's Western Fruit Grower's Guide	1 50
Flax Culture	50
Field's (Thomas W.) Pear Culture	1 25
Flint's Milch Cows and Dairy Farming	2 50
French's Farm Drainage	1 50
Fuller's Grape Culturist	1 50
Fuller's Strawberry Culturist	20
Gardening for Profit, by Peter Henderson	1 50
Gray's How Plants Grow	1 25
Gray's Manual of Botany and Lessons in one Vol.	4 00
Guenon on Milch Cows	75
Harris' Insects Injurious to Vegetation, plain $4 00, col'd	5 00
Harris' Rural Annual. Bound, 8 Nos., in 2 Vols. Each	1 50
Herbert's Hints to Horsekeepers	1 75
Hop Culture	40
Husmann's Grapes and Wine	1 50
Johnson's Agricultural Chemistry	1 75
Johnston's Elements of Agricultural Chemistry	1 50
Johnson's (Prof. S. W.) Essays on Manures	1 25
Langstroth on Honey Bee	2 00
Leuchar's How to Build Hot-Houses	1 50
Mayhew's Illustrated Horse Doctor	3 50
Mayhew's Illustrated Horse Management	3 50
Mayhew's Practical Bookkeeping for Farmers	90
Blanks for do. do.	1 20
Miles on the Horse's Foot	75
My Farm of Edgewood	1 75
My Vineyard at Lakeview	1 25
Norton's Scientific Agriculture	75
Onion Culture	20
Our Farm of Four Acres (bound) 60c paper	30
Pardee on Strawberry Culture	75
Peat and its Uses, by Prof. S. W. Johnson	1 25
Pedder's Land Measurer	60
Quinby's Mysteries of Bee Keeping (new)	1 50
Randall's Sheep Husbandry	1 50
Randall's Fine Wool Sheep Husbandry	1 00
Rivers' Miniature Fruit Garden	1 00
Richardson on the Dog, paper 30c. cloth	60
Rural Annual, by Joseph Harris	25
Saunders' Domestic Poultry (new), paper, 40c., bound	75
Schenck's Gardener's Text Book	75
Scribner's Ready Reckoner	30
Skillful Housewife	75
Stewart's John] Stable Book	1 50
Thompson's Food of Animals	1 00
Tobacco Culture	25
Todd's (S. E.) Young Farmer's Manual	1 50
Warder's Hedges and Evergreens	1 50
Watson's American Home Garden	2 00
Woodward's Country Homes	1 50
Youatt and Spooner on the Horse	1 50
Youatt and Martin on Cattle	1 50
Youatt on the Hog	1 00
Youatt on Sheep	1 00
Youmans' Household Science	2 00

Commercial Matters—Market Prices.

The following condensed, comprehensive tables, carefully prepared specially for the *American Agriculturist*, show at a glance the transactions for a month, ending Jan. 22, 1867, and also for the year ending Dec. 31:

1. TRANSACTIONS AT THE NEW-YORK MARKETS.

RECEIPTS.	Flour.	Wheat.	Corn.	Rye.	Barley.	Oats.
20 days this m'th	299,000	1,475,000	2,078,000	814,000	1,890,000	1,327,000
25 days last m'th	317,000	2,100,000	2,714,000	681,000	2,211,000	1,752,000

SALES.	Flour.	Wheat.	Corn.	Rye.	Barley.
20 days this month	248,500	681,000	1,782,000	219,000	546,000
25 days last month	211,000	1,012,000	2,581,000	178,000	801,000

2. *Comparison with same period at this time last year.*

RECEIPTS.	Flour.	Wheat.	Corn.	Rye.	Barley.	Oats.
20 days 1867	299,000	1,475,000	2,074,000	314,000	1,898,000	1,327,000
25 days 1866	125,000	81,500	139,000	11,300	10,500	81,000

SALES.	Flour.	Wheat.	Corn.	Rye.	Barley.
20 days 1867	248,500	681,000	1,782,000	219,000	546,000
25 days 1866	216,000	4,3,000	982,000	85,000	46,000

3. *Exports from New York, Jan. 1, to Jan. 19:*

	Flour.	Wheat.	Corn.	Rye.	Oats.
1867	17,898	12,939	194,821	15,912	14,398
1866	35,971	50,344	83,700	15,419	2,911
1865	47,744	48,864	74,300	1,885	161

4. *Receipts of Breadstuffs in New York in each of the last four years:*

	Flour.	Wheat.	Corn.	Rye.	Barley.	Oats.
1866	3,730,000	5,790,912	22,140,380	1,811,988	3,680,485	9,811,064
1865	[illegible]	8,189,950	13,565,257	569,672	3,199,054	9,631,855
1864	[illegible]	15,854,159	7,164,965	491,865	3,541,401	12,953,388
1863	4,574,008	19,997,856	14,234,588	449,587	2,153,865	11,076,085

5. *Exports from New-York during each of 8 years past:*

	Flour, bus.	Wheat, bus.	Corn, bus.	Rye, bus.	Barley, bus.	Oats, bus.
1866	900,834	873,869	11,079,864	288,648	1,329,942	1,160,993
1865	1,402,144	2,527,978	4,596,410	190,314	—	84,867
1864	1,914,562	12,195,428	946,831	598	150	47,135
1863	2,857,398	15,171,609	7,339,431	416,388	80,439	136,556
1862	2,911,316	25,544,736	12,079,848	1,041,548	47,061	210,688
1861	3,110,341	24,699,814	12,960,860	1,030,465	3,377	160,875
1860	1,836,309	13,529,089	4,085,092	435	8,140	165,076
1859	1,468,516	291,567	491,808	—	6,550	3,565

6. *Comparative Stock of Flour in New-York, Jan. 1:*

	1865.	1866.	1867.
Western and State Flour, bbls.	485,935	708,279	630,367
Canadian Flour, bbls.	4,950	22,810	2,700
Southern Flour, bbls.	87,463	99,256	17,359
Grand total, bbls.	568,348	731,505	650,929

7. *Comparative Stock of Grain in New-York, Jan. 1:*

	1864.	1865.	1866.	1867.
Wheat, bush.	3,830,141	1,807,356	3,946,109	2,678,811
Corn, bush.	1,751,630	461,414	4,501,784	4,713,908
Rye, bush.	87,460	312,896	518,486	777,408
Barley, bush.	881,700	308,184	1,089,937	2,340,286
Oats, bush.	3,411,636	3,016,301	2,346,024	8,470,244

8. *Receipts of Breadstuffs at Albany, by the New York Canals in each of the last seven years:*

	Flour, bus.	Wheat, bus.	Corn, bus.	Rye, bus.	Barley, bus.	Oats, bus.
1860	1,189,100	11,178,000	14,158,300	373,100	2,687,800	6,180,000
1861	1,193,238	28,946,087	23,328,784	872,791	3,233,856	3,976,808
1862	1,524,800	32,687,969	23,978,844	719,897	2,563,688	3,940,028
1863	1,340,900	22,200,900	20,683,600	470,500	3,100,400	12,138,500
1864	1,185,200	15,465,600	10,892,400	830,300	2,425,900	12,177,500
1865	1,011,000	10,579,930	18,690,900	1,251,906	4,551,678	10,417,300
1866	450,000	6,824,700	34,165,000	1,531,200	6,801,800	10,740,300

9. *Receipts at Chicago for three years:*

	Flour.	Wheat.	Corn.	Rye.	Barley.	Oats.
1866	1,931,200	11,560,501	35,033,781	1,175,616	1,500,300	10,848,730
1865	1,146,541	9,465,618	25,175,690	1,168,109	1,305,714	10,317,960
1864	1,161,764	11,257,190	18,833,917	900,116	740,446	18,653,911

10. *Shipments from Chicago for three years:*

	Flour.	Wheat.	Corn.	Rye.	Barley.	Oats.
1866	1,797,100	8,4[illegible]	33,390,351	1,580,131	1,015,371	9,035,695
1865	1,033,327	8,8[illegible]	24,615,159	838,221	44,913	9,542,645
1864	1,153,668	10,515,389	12,551,965	794,765	261,145	14,504,637

CURRENT WHOLESALE PRICES.

	Dec. 15.		Jan. 22.	
PRICE OF GOLD	137¼		135¼	
FLOUR—Super to Extra State	$7 80	@11 50	$9 40	@12 40
Super to Extra Southern	10 50	@18 25	11 75	@17 00
Extra Western	8 75	@16 50	10 15	@17 00
Extra Genesee	11 80	@15 00	12 45	@15 00
Superfine Western	7 35	@ 9 70	9 40	@10 50
RYE FLOUR	5 75	@ 7 15	6 65	@ 8 00
CORN MEAL	5 25	@ 5 80	5 00	@ 5 85
WHEAT—All kinds of White	2 70	@ 3 30	3 00	@ 3 35
All kinds of Red and Amber	1 85	@ 3 00	2 00	@ 3 25
CORN—Yellow	1 04	@ 1 12	1 12	@ 1 15
Mixed	1 00	@ 1 12	1 14	@ 1 15
OATS—Western	64	@ 66	62	@ 65
State	70	@ —	62	@ 65
RYE	1 15	@ 1 30	1 15	@ 1 30
BARLEY	85	@ 1 30	95	@ 1 25
HAY—Bale ℔ 100 ℔	95	@ 1 55	1 15	@ 1 55
Loose	1 00	@ 1 60	1 40	@ 1 70
STRAW, ℔ 100 ℔	85	@ 1 00	85	@ 1 25
COTTON—Middlings, ℔ ℔	31	@ 35	31½	@ 33½
HOPS—Crop of 1866, ℔ ℔	35	@ 65	35	@ 70
FEATHERS—Live Geese, ℔ ℔	50	@ 1 00	55	@ 85
SEED—Clover, ℔ ℔	13½	@ 15½	13½	@ 15
Timothy, ℔ bushel	3 25	@ 3 62½	3 00	@ 3 75
Flax, ℔ bushel	2 75	@ 3 10	2 60	@ 2 85
SUGAR—Brown, ℔ ℔	8	@ 12½	9	@ 13½
MOLASSES, Cuba, ℔ gal	42	@ 55	37	@ 55
COFFEE—Rio, (Gold price) ℔ ℔	16	@ 18½	15	@ 19
TOBACCO, Kentucky, &c. ℔ ℔	4	@ 27	4	@ 25
Seed Leaf, ℔ ℔	5	@ 60	5	@ 60
WOOL—Domestic Fleece, ℔ ℔	37½	@ 65	35	@ 65
Domestic, pulled, ℔ ℔	35	@ 55	35	@ 50
California, unwashed	20	@ 40	22	@ 40
TALLOW, ℔ ℔	11½	@ 11½	11½	@ 11½
OIL CAKE—℔ ton	55 00	@ 58	55 00	@57 00
PORK—Mess, ℔ barrel	21 50	@ 22 25	19 75	@ 21 00
Prime, ℔ barrel	16 50	@ —	16 75	@ 17 00
BEEF—Plain mess	18 00	@ 17 50	12 00	@ 18 00
LARD, in barrels, ℔ ℔	12½	@ 13½	11½	@ 12½
BUTTER—Western, ℔ ℔	15	@ 35	15	@ 32
State, ℔ ℔	20	@ 50	25	@ 48
CHEESE	11	@ 17	16	@ 18
BEANS—℔ bushel	1 75	@ 3 35	1 75	@ 3 25
PEAS—Canada, ℔ bushel	1 15	@ 1 35	1 25	@ 1 40
EGGS—Fresh, ℔ dozen	35	@ 40	30	@ 35
POULTRY—Fowls, ℔ ℔	14	@ 18	12	@ 13
Turkeys, ℔ ℔	15	@ 20	15	@ 18
POTATOES—Mercers, ℔ bbl.	3 25	@ 3 50	2 75	@ 3 00
Peach Blows, ℔ barrel	2 75	@ 3 00	2 25	@ 3 00
POTATOES—Buckeye, ℔ bbl.	1 25	@ 1 75	1 50	@ 2 00
APPLES—℔ barrel	2 00	@ 5 00	3 00	@ 5 00
CRANBERRIES, ℔ barrel	10 00	@14 00	13 00	@15 00

Gold has been down to 131¼, up to 137½, and closes at 135¼.... Breadstuffs have been less freely offered, and also in less active request. Prices improved early in the month, but have been variable and rather depressed for two weeks past. There is now more firmness apparent, and holders evince more confidence in the immediate future, though the demand is not very brisk. The export business has been checked by the scarcity of desirable freight room. Receipts from the interior have recently been very light, and the available supplies have been diminishing since the opening of the new year. We give, in the accompanying tabular statements, a comparative exhibit of the stocks of flour and grain on hand at this port, Jan. 1, in each of the last three years. This, with the comparisons of the receipts at, and exports from the port, for three years, constitutes an interesting feature.... Provisions have been in better request, but at irregular prices, the market closing slightly in favor of sellers.... Cotton has been in fair demand, opening buoyantly, but closing heavily. Thus far, in the current cotton year, commencing with Sept. 1, the receipts at this port have been 191,000 bales, and at all the shipping ports of the country, 880,000 bales; exports from this port, 138,300 bales, and from all ports, 375,000 bales; estimated stock now here, 185,000 bales, and at all the ports, at latest mail dates, 516,000 bales.... Wool has been in moderate request for manufacturing purposes, and there has been more firmness, without any remarkable buoyancy in prices. The stock of domestic fleece in this market on January 1st, was 4,450,000 lbs.; of domestic pulled, 600,000 lbs.; of Texas, California and Oregon, 2,080,000 lbs., making the total stock of domestic wool here at the opening of the new year 7,830,000 lbs., against 4,500,000 lbs. Jan. 1, 1866, and 4,700,000 lbs. Jan. 1, 1865. The total stock of foreign here on the 1st of Jan., 1867, was 25,480 bales, or equal to 14,802,500 lbs. The imports of foreign wool at this port, in 1866, reached 58,794 bales, against 58,420 bales in 1865, and 113,068 bales in 1864. The total arrivals of foreign and domestic wools at this port in 1866 were 150,705 bales, equal to 59,088,818 lbs, against 50,409,305 lbs. in 1865, and 77,889,442 lbs. in 1864. The clip of wool in the United States, in 1866, has been estimated at 137,000,000 lbs., yielding about fifty per cent. of clean, pure wool.... Tobacco has been in more demand at steady rates. Hay and Hops have been in better request and firmer.... Seeds, Rice and Hemp have been quiet and rather heavy in price.

New York Live Stock Markets.—The supply during the past five weeks has continued fair for the season, as is shown in the following table:

WEEK ENDING.	*Beeves.*	*Cows.*	*Calves.*	*Sheep.*	*Swine.*
Dec. 25	6,369	54	580	24,050	15,650
Jan. 1	4,000	66	800	11,870	23,350
Jan. 8	3,821	60	455	16,856	19,000
Jan. 15	4,600	60	380	19,500	20,598
Jan. 22	5,628	50	505	14,581	16,258
Total in five Weeks	24,300	300	2,190	86,350	96,736
Average per Week	4,848	60	438	17,270	19,330
do. do. *last Month*	5,021	63	823	21,133	17,390
do. do. *prev's Month*	6,770	103	1,320	29,495	20,580
Average per Week, 1866	5,748	94	1,300	30,000	18,000
do. do. do. 1865	5,255	118	1,500	16,091	11,023
do. do. do. 1864	5,161	115	1,511	15,315	12,676
do. do. do. 1863	5,150	129	694	9,941	21,670
Total in 1866	298,880	4,885	67,422	1,040,000	672,000
Total in 1865	270,274	6,161	77,391	836,733	573,197
Total in 1864	267,609	7,603	75,621	782,462	660,270
Total in 1863	264,091	6,470	35,709	519,316	1,101,617

The supply has been fully up to the requirements, at least until just now, when the severe storms are interfering with transportation.... **Beef Cattle** have not varied greatly in value during a month. A few extra animals command 17c.@18c. ℔ ℔, estimated dressed weight; good or first quality, 15½c.@16½c.; medium, 14½c.@15½c.; common to poorest, 11c.@12c.... **Milch Cows.**—The receipts have been light, but the demand is small. Extras, when sold, bring $90@$110; good, $80@$85; common, $60@$75; poor, $50@$45.... **Veal Calves.**—Receipts light. Really good animals sell readily at 13c.@14c. ℔ ℔, live weight; other grades, 13½c.@10c., according to quality; some of the poorest 9c.... **Sheep and Lambs.**—The supply has been very large for the season, and prices have continued very low until within a few days. The present rates are 7c.@7½c. ℔ ℔, for superior lots, some extras, 8c.; good, fair sheep, 6c.@7c., and poor, 5½c.@6c.... **Live Hogs.**—The supply has been ample, and with large receipts of dressed hogs, and the heavy decline in barrelled pork, prices have ruled very low, sometimes as low as 6½c. ℔ ℔, live weight. The latest sales were at 7c.@7½c.

the members of an intelligent farmer's family can be filled, at a very reasonable price.

We have frequently commended the *American Agriculturist* to our readers as the best paper of its class in the country, and we are glad to know that its value in the future will be greatly enhanced by a liberal expenditure on the part of the publishers in several departments that will add greatly to its interest in the family circle.

The two journals, one monthly, the other *weekly* or *semi-weekly*, as the subscriber prefers, furnish a full supply of interesting reading matter, relative to all that occurs in the world of literature, art, science, politics, and what is spoken of and discussed in the great centres of civilization. Address WM. C. BRYANT & CO., PUBLISHERS OF THE EVENING POST, 41 Nassau Str., Cor. Liberty, New York, or: ORANGE JUDD & CO., PUBLISHERS AMER. AGRICULTURIST, 41 Park Row, N.Y.

The "Evening Post," New-York, A Newspaper.

Now, as always, pledged to the advocacy of the Great Principles of FREE SOIL, FREE SPEECH, FREE LABOR, FREE MEN and FREE TRADE!

PLEASANT WORDS. The following complimentary expressions are selected from numerous notices of this Journal:

"The" EVENING POST of New York city—where else? for this paper has the proud cognomen of "The" EVENING POST—is one of the most ably edited, racy and high toned papers in the country. We heartily bear witness to the ability, character and culture displayed in its management, and wish it even more prosperity in the next than it has experienced in the last half century.—*Chicago Post.*

The EVENING POST is a pattern of typographical style and neatness, and the favorite of the *literati* of Gotham. Its editorials, able and high-toned, are written in the interest of no party, are always up to the times, and often a little ahead. It is an acknowledged leader, and wields a powerful influence upon the mind of the nation.—*Boston Voice.*

The New York EVENING POST is one of the largest newspapers of the United States, and always one of the best and most entertaining; its friends and readers are of the most substantial class in the country.—*Taunton (Mass.) Gazette.*

The EVENING POST is edited with as much ability as any paper in the country, and its instincts and principles are all in favor of freedom and the progressive party of the day.—*Hallowell Gazette.*

The EVENING POST is one of the very best papers we receive; its editorials are thoughtful and dignified, its news judiciously and carefully selected, and a general culture and literary taste characterize its contents. As a good family and *newspaper*, it has no superior.—*Ashtabula Sentinel.*

The EVENING POST is an honor to American journalism. Dignified, direct, and forcible in style, its editorials are frequently models of linguistic purity and elegance.—*Christian Intelligencer.*

REMITTANCES should be made, if possible, by draft or Post-office order, payable in N. Y. Specimen copies free.

WILLIAM C. BRYANT & CO., PUBLISHERS, 41 Nassau Street, New-York.

Containing a great variety of Items, including many good Hints and Suggestions which we throw into smaller type and condensed form, for want of space elsewhere.

"& CO."—Another Agriculturist Publisher.—Last month, page 10, an addition to our editorial corps was noted, and we now have another pleasant announcement. In October, 1863, it was stated that the previous Publisher had associated with himself MR. LUCIUS A. CHASE, of Boston. The copartnership thus formed, has gone on pleasantly and very prosperously for nearly a year and a half. But the business and editorial cares have *increased* so rapidly, that, with the experienced and very effective aid of his partner, Mr. JUDD has not found even the partial relief from severe labor that he has for years needed. The copartnership has therefore been still further enlarged by the addition of MR. SAMUEL BURNHAM, JR., who has for a number of years past superintended the issuing of the extensive book and periodical publications of the American Tract Society, at Boston, Mass. (Our readers who also read the "Child at Home," will be glad to recognize Mr. B. as the "Uncle Paul" and "Victor" of that paper.) That Mr. Burnham's labors have been appreciated there, is pleasantly attested by the great *surprise* boxes, containing silver plate and other valuables, which have just followed him here, sent as tokens of regard and esteem by his late associates in the Tract House, and among business men of Boston, and by the teachers and scholars of the Sabbath School of Dr. Kirk's church, of which he has been the superintendent for several years past. The present firm of ORANGE JUDD & Co., will thus consist hereafter of Messrs. Orange Judd, Lucius A. Chase and Samuel Burnham, Jr. With this new aid, therefore, unless our friends insist upon increasing the business of this office far beyond the present bounds, which indeed they seem inclined to do, Mr. Judd may secure that relief from unremitting and severe application, which he has so long needed, though he will, as the senior and largest proprietor, continue to superintend and advise in both editorial and business matters. We fear it will be difficult for him not to still endeavor to "*hold the plow and drive*;" but the associate editors and publishers intend to enforce upon him less labor and more leisure; for, in common with our readers, we desire that his period of public usefulness may be long extended. ....We give a hearty welcome to the incoming partner, and trust he may find his new field of labor as pleasant and useful as his former one. Thus reinforced in both the business and editorial departments, with all the previous working force continued, we expect the *Agriculturist*, in its new Quarter Century, will exhibit the results of increased energy and efficiency, and, with its adjunct book department, will accomplish much towards the diffusion of sound information, and the development and improvement of the important interests of the Farm, Garden, and Household.—ASSOCIATE EDITORS.

A Literary Newspaper.—The New York Evening Post—edited almost as long as we can remember by our favorite American Poet, WM. CULLEN BRYANT, whose "Thanatopsis" we learned "to speak in public on the stage" when a youth—is one of the best family, literary and general Newspapers in our country. We do not endorse or agree with all its political and financial views by any means; but aside from these peculiarities, we prefer it to almost any other journal in the country, as a literary and family newspaper, always safe from any thing that could possibly injure the morals of even the youngest member of a household. It is full of intelligence from all parts of the world. The Post, together with the *Agriculturist*, will supply most that is needed in a family, aside from the Religious Journals. The Evening Post is published Daily, Semi-Weekly, and Weekly. The subscription price of the Weekly, (which, like the other editions, is a very large sheet), is $2 a year; and of the Semi-Weekly, $4.—In accordance with a proposition from the publishers, we will be happy to receive any subscriptions for that paper, in combination with the *Agriculturist*, as follows:—One copy of the *Agriculturist* and one copy of the Weekly Evening Post, one year for $2.50. One copy of the *Agriculturist* and one copy of the Semi-Weekly Post, one year for $4. By this arrangement, a saving will be made to the subscribers.

This Number Late.—The immense press of business at the opening of the year—far greater this year than ever before—the necessity of re-making up the paper to increase its size beyond what was at first designed, some temporary ill health among our editorial corps, etc., have all combined to keep back the present number behind the usual time of going to press; and though we make duplicate Electrotype plates of the pages, and shall use double presses on the forms, it will take some time into February, to get the last numbers into the mail bags. The March number is in active preparation, and we expect to get it off in time to reach most of our readers by the first day of the month. The process of printing Engravings in the beautiful style of this journal, is necessarily slow. The utmost capacity of any presses yet made, which can print in our style, does not exceed 10,000 to 12,000 copies per day, and this requires five presses for the five forms—one on each side of each sheet, the extra sheet being turned and cut.

Phrenology, etc.—A Subscriber objects to our advertising the Phrenological Journal, Journal of Health, and some other like things, and thus endorsing them. We do not *endorse* any of these things. Our rules require that Advertisers must be men who have both the *ability* and *intention* to do what they promise to do; that everything must be above board, that the readers may be able to know just what is offered. Any thing of a secret or deceptive character, or of an immoral tendency, is excluded. On matters of opinion, respecting politics, health theories, and the like, we suppose our readers intelligent enough to judge as to what they want. To meet everybody's views and wishes, we should need to leave everything out. We have heard from the man who objects to planting apple trees even, on temperance principles, but we must advertise trees, nevertheless.

Our Horticultural Annual, *both in Beauty and Intrinsic Value*, excels even the expectations of the Publishers, and it will give great pleasure to every reader. Its contents have been pretty fully referred to already. The first 24 pages gives on each left hand page a complete almanac adapted to the four leading sections of the country, and on the corresponding right hand page a calendar of operations for the month, which is valuable as a guide to the work to be done. The following 122 pages are filled with original and useful information, and many superb engravings on a great variety of topics. The work is in very neat style, and is ornamental as well as useful. This, with the Agricultural Annual, noticed elsewhere, may well find a place in every family. Taking into account their intrinsic value and size, these are among the cheapest volumes ever issued. Price, in illustrated paper covers, 50 cents; neatly bound in cloth, 75 cents. Sent post-paid at the same prices.

American Agricultural Annual Now Ready.—After some delays from unforeseen causes, we are now happy to lay this New Annual before the public. It contains a number of exceedingly valuable essays on subjects which are of universal interest to agriculturists. Prof. Johnson's article upon Recent Progress in Agricultural Science, is exceedingly valuable. Dr. Dusteed's notes upon the results arrived at by the Congress of Veterinarians, present facts which should have an important influence upon our Legislators, and have not been made public in this country in any other form. Col. Waring presents the most recent and soundest views of the very important subject of Drainage; and the same may be said of Mr. Clough's article on Sorghum. The practical views of Mr. John Johnston on Sheep-feeding; Mr. Carpenter on Potatoes; Dr. Hexamer on Barns; Mr. Headley on Horse-Training, etc., will commend themselves to every discriminating man. There are, besides, numerous other articles, practical, explicit, and thorough, on Wheat, Barley, Agricultural Education, Poultry, etc. The subjects are very fully illustrated with engravings, of a high order of excellence. A Calendar of Operations, and numerous useful tables, rules for measurements of capacity, etc., are prefixed. This new Annual is certainly of great value, and every cultivator of the largest or smallest portion of land, would do well to secure a copy of this first of the Annual series. Price, in paper covers, 50 cents; neatly bound in cloth, 75 cents. Sent post-paid, by mail, at the same price.

Sundry Humbugs.—The past month has brought in the usual supply of letters reporting attempts to defraud the people. Our Assistant who takes charge of and classifies the letters in this department, sums up the reports for the first half of January, thus: 5 different Medical Swindlers; 11 Sellers of vile Medical publications and instruments; 6 humbug sellers of Ink and Washing Mixture Recipes; 28 operators in Lottery, Gift Enterprise, Watch, and Jewelry Tickets, (reported in 192 letters); sundry *prospective* publications and periodicals, *promised* in return for lists of names of persons; cheap, good-for-nothing Sewing Machines; some complaints of a Map Publisher, who keeps the money sent him and don't send the maps; ditto, a Corn Husking Machine maker, etc., etc., in all 66 operators, though many of the concerns are run by the same individuals under different names....The result of the Crosby House Lottery will make a multitude sick of such schemes, but there are thirty or more similar enterprises in the country, including several that "come the benevolent dodge" by attaching to their schemes some pretended benefit for soldiers, orphans, widows, etc., etc. We unhesitatingly pronounce each and all of these affairs detestable and unworthy of the slightest countenance or favor. For every dollar that goes to a good object, several other dollars find their way into the pockets of the operators—no matter how specious their statements and pretenses. It is high time that both the law and the good sense of the country should put a stop to this new form of the old lotteries, *alias* "Gift Enterprises," "Artists' Unions," "Benevolent Enterprises," "Prize Concerts," etc. Chicago is a present "head centre" in this line....The Jewelry, Watch, and Dry Goods Ticket men still continue their operations. They send out circulars with tickets pretending to give the recipient a claim to some valuable article, or prize, for a small sum. Nine out of ten of these pocket the money sent them, and make no response to the letters of their victims, or when hard pressed, pretend the money has been lost by mail or otherwise. A few send out galvanized, showy articles "marked" at a high figure, but almost or quite worthless for use. Some do send out cheap but very taking articles, costing *almost* as much as they receive at first, so as to *bait* customers, and then they do the swindling afterwards. We warn the readers that every man who sends a circular and tickets, is a swindler, and every pretense of making you his special helper, is a fraud. Every other person in your own neighborhood whose address can be got, receives the same "private and confidential" offer as yourself. ....Carey, Vandegrift & Co., of Sidney, Ohio, complain of the classification we gave their "Soldiers' Monument Association," in October, and claim that "its object is legitimate, and benevolent, its purposes honorable, and that all its pledges or promises will be carried out in good faith." We have no information to the contrary, and give them the benefit of their statement. *But* their *modus operandi* is in the highest degree objectional, certainly, and "the end does not sanctify the means." They have a scheme that is neither more nor less than a lottery. They try to dazzle the minds of people with the hope of getting for $1, a $15,000 prize, also fine houses, a farm, carriages, pianos, etc., and on their lottery circulars, they print an article from the August *Agriculturist*, in a way to make *us* appear to endorse enterprises like theirs. ... To show the extent to which people are pestered by the humbug operators, a subscriber sends us *twenty-one* circulars, *from* as many different parties, most of which have recently been sent to him by mail. There must be many victims to these swindling schemes, or the operators could not pay the enormous expense they incur for printing, and the postage on the millions of circulars they have sent out. ...A circular about "Jackson's Universal Washing Compound," quotes a tremendous puff from the "Agriculturist." *Some* paper bearing this name may have said what is quoted—but not the *American* "Agriculturist." We never heard of this compound before, but we condemn all the recipes for washing compounds, that are sold around the country. Let Mr. Johnson tell *what* "Agriculturist" he quotes. ...Several subscribers inquire about sundry "Mutual Coal Companies." There may be one or more good ones: after repeated solicitations, we have not gained confidence enough in any one to invest, though we have to use a good deal of coal. ... John L. Andrews, of Marion Co., O., like a good many other unhung villains, offers for $50 to *lie* a $500 ticket through a bogus "Benefit Association." Anybody that will trust to a confessed liar, *ought* to be cheated.—Richard Adams, Buffalo, N. Y., is another like Andrews; so is ... F. Sherwood, Providence, N. Y., *alias* Batavia, N. Y., *alias* Huron, N. Y. ...Dr. Thos. Andrews, *alias* E. Andrews, of Albany, is scattering poison among the people, in the form of Pamphlets and Circulars, called "Good Samaritans," in which he offers murderous medicines, etc. Let every body, married or unmarried, beware of trusting a word to his statements, as they value their health, their lives, and their souls. There are many others of this class.—In the same catalogue is a monster who assumes the name of a pretended firm of French ladies, and dates from a room in the "Bible House," N. Y. City. He sends a pamphlet about "Married Life," said to be "by a Married Woman." After a great deal of palaver, he comes to the gist of the matter, which is to advertise sundry villainous articles of "French" origin. None but very foolish, and insane people will risk their lives, health and money, by giving the slightest heed to this specious pretender. We are sad to know that thousands of women, and men too, are enduring terrible anguish of body and mind, and dragging out a miserable existence, while many other thousands have gone down to early graves, because they have been lured by the false statements of these very demons on earth, who, to put money in their own pockets, would sell sugar-coated arsenic to infants and idiots. We have little, if any more charity for the Heralds, the Timeses, and other journals, which publish the advertisements of these Madame Restelles, and the like, who make a business of murdering the unborn innocents in hecatombs, and the fair daughters of our land almost by the million. ...We have hundreds of circulars pretending to be sent out from Nassau-street, Cedar-street, Third-Avenue, Sixth-Avenue, etc., offering vile publications, obscene pictures, etc. None of these parties are ever to be found at the places they hail from, or if found, they have nothing for sale or to show to *callers*—they must be addressed by mail—and they never make any return for money sent them, unless it is when they hope to make a larger sum out of their victims.

The American Pomological Society.—Col. Marshall P. Wilder, President of the American Pomological Society, informs us that, after corresponding with the Western associates, he has fixed upon September 11th, as the day for the next meeting. It is found that this date will conflict as little as any with other pomological meetings.

American Pomology.—Doct. Warder's work has been delayed, by the great number of illustrations and the inconvenience that attends the wide distance between publisher and printer. The book is now approaching completion, and will be one that will be welcomed by every fruit-grower. Its introductory chapters upon propagation, the nursery, planting, pruning, etc., are so full that they might well have formed a work of themselves. The descriptive list of apples contains all the new introductions and peculiarly western varieties. The illustrations, all made expressly for the work, are from original drawings, and are in a style superior to that of any pomological work heretofore published. Over 250 varieties of apples will be figured, the majority of which were never before illustrated. In this work Doct. Warder presents his classification of apples, in which he attempts to bring the great mass of material into something like system. How far this will prove useful to the pomologist will be proven by experience, and we have no doubt that the author will welcome any suggestions that will facilitate his object:—to aid in the determination of an unknown variety of fruit. We hope to have the work ready during the present month.

Fuller's Small Fruit Culturist.—Growers of small fruits will be glad to know that Mr. A. S. Fuller's work is in hand, as all who are familiar with his works upon the grape and strawberry, will anticipate a valuable and practical treatise upon a subject that has of late years assumed great importance. There is a directness and independence about Mr. Fuller's writings that give them a deserved popularity, and his forthcoming work will, no doubt, meet with the same favor that has attended his other productions. We have no work exclusively devoted to small fruits, and the one under notice will be very full in all particulars, from propagating the plants to marketing the fruit. The illustrations are all ready, and will be numerous and fine.

To "Authors."—Letters, concerning the publication of books, have been of late quite numerous, and perhaps a general statement of our position may save many the trouble of writing and us that of answering. No one need make a book unless he has something new to say, or can present old facts better than they have been given before. There are books enough; we wish better ones than any now extant. We cannot decide upon the publication of any work without first seeing the manuscript. In each case the manuscript will be submitted to competent judges, whose decision will be final, and no certificates or commendations from other parties can be of any use. Mere compilations of any kind are not wanted at any rate—we are not in the paste and scissors line.

My Vineyard at Lakeview.—We have just one request to make of the author of this book—viz., that he will allow us to give his name and thus put many inquisitive people out of misery. Writers upon grape culture suspect this or that person of the authorship, and we get numerous letters asking as a special favor the name of the author. We are under a pledge of secrecy which we shall keep until the author relieves us from it, and when he does, many will be amused at the wildness of their guesses. We can relieve the anxious ones to this extent. The author *does* live on the shores of Lake Erie, and more than one of those who have been so desirous to know who he is, have met him and talked grapes with him the present winter. His book is none the less valuable because it has not his name, and is growing in favor because it relates experience in grape culture, and rests its popularity upon its own merits. Price, by mail, $1.25.

N. Y. Live Stock Markets in 1866.—The following interesting statistics, prepared from the records kept at the Office of the *American Agriculturist*, will give the reader some idea of the magnitude of the dealings in neat Cattle, Sheep and Swine, destined for slaughter, at the Metropolitan markets. To assist the memory, we give the nearest round numbers, which differ but slightly from the actual figures: **Beef Cattle.**—Receipts **300,000** head; value, about **$32,000,000.** We estimate the cattle—good, bad and indifferent—to average 700 lbs. dressed weight each, and the average of all sales at a trifle over 15 cents per lb. The weight of dressed beef amounted in round numbers to 210,000,000 lbs. This equals 140 lbs. to each of one and a half million of people, adults and children included, which is about the population supplied regularly by the New York city markets, including Brooklyn, Jersey City, and a score of smaller suburban cities and villages.... Over half of these cattle are credited to the single State of Illinois, one sixth to Ohio, one-eighth to New York, one-ninth to Kentucky, and one-thirtieth to Indiana, or about nine-tenths to these five States.... To bring them all by railway, 15 to the car, would require 20,000 cars. Allowing 60 feet to a car, the cattle trains would stretch away nearly 200 miles.... The price of extra cattle declined about 4 cents per lb. net from January to December, medium grades about 2 cents.... The actual weekly average receipts were 5,758, against 5,255 in 1865, an increase of about 500 head per week, which has been our estimate all along through the year of the probable increase, as our readers will remember.... **Veal Calves.**—Receipts **62,000,** or an average per week of about 1,200 head. This is 15,000, or 300 per week, less than in 1865, the decrease being doubtless due to the stringent measures adopted by the Board of Health to shut out young calves, or "bobs," that were so largely sold in previous years.... **Sheep and Lambs.**—Receipts **1,000,000,** (or more nearly 1,030,000,) averaging very nearly 20,000 per week. This is about 200,000, or 4,000 per week in excess of any former year.... The price of the various grades ran down from 8@10 cents per lb., live weight, in January, to 4½@7c. in December.... **Live Hogs.**—Receipts, **666,000,** which is 90,000 above 1865, about the same as in 1864, and nearly half a million less than in 1862 and 1863. The prices ranged between 10c. and 12c. per lb., live weight, for the first ten months, but declined from 9¼c@10½c. in October, to 6@7c. at the close of the year.... **Milch Cows.**—Receipts, scant **5,000,** the lowest number in any other one of a dozen years past.... The total receipts in 1866 of Cattle, Sheep, and Swine destined for slaughter were, according to our statistics, fully **2,000,000** head.

Look Over the Table of Contents.—Our readers who do not read the Table of Contents in each number of the *Agriculturist*, are apt to overlook valuable articles. For instance, many did not see the Market Reports in the December number, because they were not in the part of the paper where usually found.

Gardening for Profit.—The rapid sale of this work shows that a treatise of this kind was needed, and that Mr. Henderson's recorded experience is eagerly sought after. As this is the only work in which the practice of commercial gardening is given, it has a value above that of any other on vegetable gardening, while for the private garden it is as useful a guide as any other. The value of the book is increased by a full chapter on the construction of the best form of houses for forcing or forwarding vegetables. As the same style of house is used by Mr. H. in his extensive propagation of plants, he has added an appendix on the "Propagation of Plants by Cuttings."—A neat volume of about 250 pages, on excellent paper, and well illustrated. Sent by mail for $1.50.

New Work on Draining in Press.—Orange Judd & Co. have now in press and will publish early in the spring, a work entitled "DRAINING FOR PROFIT AND DRAINAGE FOR HEALTH," by Geo. E. Waring, Jr., of New York, Engineer of the Drainage of the Central Park. This is a very thorough, complete, and practical treatise, simply and easily followed. The subject of thorough farm drainage is discussed in all its bearings, and also that more extensive land drainage by which the sanitary condition of any district may be greatly improved—even to the banishment of fever and ague, typhoid and malarious fevers, as shown by New York experience.

Breck's New Book of Flowers.—There are plenty of works in the style of a dictionary which tell something about flowering plants, what family they belong to, and give some points of their history. Whoever really loves flowers, and is not satisfied with these unsympathetic works, will turn with pleasure to Breck's New Book of Flowers, where he speaks of them in a familiar, talky way, and as if he loved them. This is not a book made up by re-arranging antiquated English works on gardening, but one which was *written*, and written too because the author had something to say. It is the only flower-book that *records personal* experience, and when that experience is that of a veteran cultivator like Mr. Breck, we care not how personal it is, for the more it tells just what he has done, the more the novice feels that he can do the same. In this work all the genera and the leading species are noticed, and their proper treatment given. *Varieties* come upon us in numbers every year, and for these the cultivator must consult the frequent issues of the florist and seedsmen. Besides the annuals and herbaceous perennials, this work contains a descriptive list of the choicest flowering shrubs. A handsome volume of 480 pages, finely bound, well printed and illustrated. Sent by mail, post-paid, for $1.75.

40 PAGES!—Our old advertising patrons who have for years past done business with our readers, and learned by experience the value of the *Agriculturist* as a medium of communication with their customers, seem more anxious than ever to secure space in our columns. They will doubtless find many other agreeable business acquaintances among tens of thousands of new subscribers this year.——These, with some new advertisers, have crowded in upon us so much that to make room for a part of them only, we have added more space, and issue 40 pages—the limit of single postage rates. This is a double advantage to the readers, as they get an extra page of reading matter for every added page of advertisements, and as our advertisers are all believed to be responsible, reliable men, the advertisements are themselves of great value to the readers—showing, as they do, what is for sale, where, and by whom. We advise a careful reading of all the advertisements, (there are no stale, long-standing ones among them).—Advertisers express so much pleasure at learning where they find so large a class of wide-awake enterprising readers as they meet through this journal, that we are induced to repeat the request that every one writing for circulars, or otherwise, or sending orders to our advertisers, will inform them in what Journal their advertisements were seen.

Advertisers, who Want Space, must send their orders in early. Those coming after the 5th of the preceding month, have no certainty, and in future will have but little likelihood of finding admission on any terms. It takes almost a month to work off our immense edition, and print the Engravings well.

Hops in California.—Daniel Flint, of Sacramento Co., Cal., writes: "Last year I grew on five acres of ground 12,000 lbs. of No. 1 hops. The largest yield was on one and one-half acres, which produced 4600 lbs., or a little over 3000 lbs. to the acre. My hills are planted seven feet each way, 888 to the acre, or 1332 on the one and one-half acres, nearly 3½ lbs. to the hill."

A Good Crop of Clover Seed.—A correspondent in York Co., Pa., in reference to an article in the *Agriculturist* for January, states, that one of his neighbors, Mr. Joseph Irwin, raised 36 bushels of clover seed from 9 acres, and sold it for $9.15 per bushel. The first crop of hay yielded 20 tons, which he estimates at $10 per ton, or $200. The seed brought $329.40, making $529.40 as the produce of the nine acres in one season.

Comfort for Cows in "Stanchions."—Our readers know that we have always objected to the use of Stanchions for fastening cows in stables on the ground of inhumanity, and because the cows' discomfort detracts from their value to their owners. Mr. L. Safford, Newtonville, Massachusetts, has invented and patented a style of Stanchion which, to a considerable extent, obviates this objection, and, giving the cows comfort, adds to the profit of keeping them, while all of the conveniences of stanchions are retained. It is simply a contrivance by which each set of Stanchions is hung like a door, so that the cow can swing it half around and lie at ease when she likes. We heartily advise those using, or wishing to use stanchions, to address the inventor.—See advertisement.

Meat for Fowls to make them Lay.—One subscriber asks, what food will induce fowls to lay? another asks about scrap cake; another about hogs' lights and similar offal. To those we would say: It is the nature of fowls in good health to lay, and they cannot help it—the eggs will come. Scanty fare will reduce their laying propensity, and on very short commons, eggs cease altogether. Rich food promotes the tendency; certain seeds, like buckwheat, sunflower and hemp seeds increase it, and meat of any kind does the same. All this, however, forces the fowl into an unnatural state, and ordinarily shortens her life. The eggs, besides, have often a poor flavor. Occasional feedings of fresh meat, like the lights of hogs chopped fine, are very good in winter when the fowls find no insect food. They need, besides, hearty food in cold weather, especially if they are not kept in warm houses. In very cold weather, hens running about and roosting in exposed places, will not lay, though richly fed; their food goes to keeping them warm.

Chicken Ailments — Gapes.—"Hoosier" writes as follows: I notice a great many articles on chicken ailments, especially gapes, but do not remember seeing lime recommended as a cure. In the summer my chickens, a fine brood of eighty or more, took to gaping, and every chick, least unto the greatest, went around squeaking as though they wished to discharge their "windpipes." I "tried the horse hair, feather, and turpentine," and almost everything I heard tell of, but nothing availed to stop the dire disease. Next I turned my attention toward the diet and drink. First, I removed the entire village to a clean grassy spot; each time I fed them, I put a good quantity of lime in the feed, which was a mixture of cornmeal and wheat bran. The drinking vessels were cleaned thoroughly each morning, and filled with clear, fresh water, pretty well whitened with lime. In less than a week the chickens quit dying, and began to improve amazingly. Not another chick died after the first week of this new course of treatment. The tonic and anti-acid properties of the lime imparted an invigorating influence upon the systems of the chicks. Give fowls plenty of lime to eat, lime and ashes to wallow in, and they will never be lousy, nor lay soft-shelled eggs.

Sorghum Vinegar.—"J. S. C.," writes: We have never succeeded in making vinegar from Sorghum juice without boiling; but if it be boiled away one-third or one-half, 't will make good vinegar. We have made Sorghum vinegar for a number of years, and we made the *best* from the white skimmings and washings of the finishing pan. As soon as the juice begins to thicken up in boiling, or when it gets to be very thin syrup, a whitish scum rises, which, if saved and diluted with rain water, will make a *number one* vinegar. Vinegar can be made from *good* Sorghum syrup, (one gallon of syrup to two of rain water), but it will not work as quick and is no better than that made from the skimmings. The reason of this I suppose is, that the skimmings contain something that acts as a ferment. Keep the skimmings until the following spring, add about as much water as you have skimmings; be sure and leave it sweet enough, for the sweeter it is the better the vinegar will be; then, if it is too sweet to work well, add more water; put it in vinegar or whiskey casks, and set in a sunny place to work.

Prize Essays on Housekeeping.—By reference to the Household department it will be seen that instead of a single first prize of $100, we have awarded three such prizes. The names of two of the successful ones are given with the instalments of their essays; the other is Miss Eva M. Collins, of Rochester, N. Y.

Molasses Cake.—By Mrs. Nellie Foster.—Take of Sorghum molasses 2 cupsfuls; 1 cup of butter, melted; yolks of 4 eggs, half cup of milk, 3 cups of flour, half teaspoonful of soda dissolved in a small quantity of the milk. Thoroughly stir as each article is added; whites of 4 eggs beaten. A very fine light molasses cake.

Cooking Tripe.—Letty Ermine says: Dip the salted pieces of tripe in corn meal, and fry in butter. Let the butter (a small portion) be quite hot before putting in the tripe, and then it will become a handsome brown color. Another way is, to cut the tripe in very small squares or strips, and stew it in milk, at last adding a little butter, pepper and salt.

Rice Pudding.—L. Stanley, of Maine, gives the following recipe: Take one cupful of rice, boil it in a small quantity of water until tender; when done, it should be almost dry. Then add one cup of sugar, one cup of raisins, previously boiled 15 minutes, two eggs and three pints of milk; salt and spice to taste.

Door Mats.—Letty Ermine writes: "In a recent item upon 'door mats' you do not mention one variety. Take any such pieces as might be used for rag-carpet—pantaloons, sacks, old flannels, pieces of baize, etc., cut into strips, and braid the easy three-strand braid. Sew this braid with carpet thread, in circular or oval shapes, to lay by the doors in the dining room, at the foot of the back stairs, etc. They are so firm, that they are not easily *kicked up*. A large oval is very agreeable laid by the dining room stove. By a trifling effort, the red flannel, and the brown and black clothes and green baize can be made into a very tasteful little matter."

Warts on Hands.—"Moorestown," N. J. These excrescences are sometimes very obstinate, and again disappear so readily that a number of absurd remedies have acquired a popular reputation. The surgeon disposes of them by means of various caustics, but these are not recommended for domestic use, unless one understands the nature of the articles and exercises proper care. Perhaps the safest general remedy is strong acetic acid, applied to the warts every few days.

To Color Brown.—By L. Stanley, of Maine.—Make a dye of common alder bark. First dip the articles in this, then wring them out and dip them into weak lye. This will make the color light or dark, according to the strength of the alder dye. It is a fast color.

A Good Paper Cutter.—Grandmother's Knitting-needle, if it is stiff enough. Try it on the *Agriculturist*. It will not do so well on the last novel.

Painting Floors.—This is sometimes done in alternate squares or diamonds of different colors to imitate variegated marbles. But if the floors are much used, the paint soon wears off in patches and looks badly. One color we think in better taste, and the natural color of the wood, kept perfectly clean, the best taste of all

Manufactured Manures—Information Wanted from Farmers.—That there are some good "artificial fertilizers" made, we have no doubt; but we are quite sure that there is a very large amount of cheating in this line, besides a great deal of really worthless stuff sold by innocent dealers who are working under false theories. One of the common frauds is the manufacture of a good article until a reputation is established and "certificates" obtained, and then often adulterate or depreciate the fertilizer. In order to collect some information on the subject, we solicit from *each* of our readers who have used any kind of special or manufactured fertilizer, a report on the results. Let us know briefly: 1st, about the date of first using; 2d, the name of the fertilizer; 3d the manufacturer's name; 4th, the seller's name; 5th, did it appear to pay; 6th, did it pay so well that its use was continued more than one year, and if so, how many years; 7th, if still in use, is it as good as when first sold. We want the failures all reported as well as the successes; the manufacturers take good care to learn of, and give us the latter. The plainest farmer can write out brief answers to the above simple questions. We do not want these reports for publication in detail, but to gather some general results that will be given, if we can have full reports from all our readers.

Brazilian Sugar Cane.—Mr. Charles J. Smith, U. S. Consul at Para, Brazil, has left at the *Agriculturist* office a few specimens of Sugar Cane, 15½ feet high, and carrying a diameter of 2 inches to a hight of nearly 10 feet from the ground. We never saw finer cane.

Pears in California.—Daniel Flint, Sacramento, asks if any one can beat him in raising pears. In February he set a cion of the Bartlett, and in September following he cut off the limb and exhibited it at the State Fair. It contained 12 pears and weighed 12 pounds. This will do, even for California, a State from which we look for great things in horticulture.

Trouble with Strawberry Plants.—J. Arnold, Paris, C. W. We do not recognize the worm that killed your strawberry plants, from the description. Next year send specimens to B. D. Walsh, Editor Practical Entomologist, Rock Island, Ill. He or some of his associates will be glad to study them up for you.

Bait for Slugs.—L. Langwor, Rutland Co., Vt., says, that a spoonful of malt placed here and there, and covered by a flower pot or other dish to prevent their access to it, will prove very attractive to slugs, which will assemble around the bait during the night and may be killed in the morning. Next to malt, he has found grated carrots used in the same way to be the most attractive bait.

New Hand-weeder.—Mr Geo. P. Allen, of Woodbury, Conn., is the inventor and patentee of the little implement which we represent in the accompanying engraving. It is a scuffle-hoe, consisting of a thin steel blade, with two cutting edges. These edges consist of a series of acute teeth sharpened from the under side. Held naturally, by a man standing erect, the blade lies perfectly flat upon the ground, and raising or lowering the handle gives it a tendency to enter, if shoved or drawn. The common straight-bladed scuffle-hoe, though sharp, often meets with considerable resistance from roots of grass and weeds, and frequently slips over them; even hard lumps of soil obstruct its movement. This one readily passes through the clods, and cuts any kind of roots with ease. It is especially adapted to hoeing among garden vegetables, carrots, onions, and other root crops in the field. We ourselves used one of these weeders last year with entire satisfaction.

The Apple as a Pear Stock.—"T. J. P." proposes to set out apple trees the coming spring, and the following spring to graft them with pears. The apple is not a good pear stock—the trees are generally short lived. We cannot advise our friend to proceed in this way, and we do not see any reason why he should not set out pear trees at once. The answer to the question "will pears pay?" will depend very much upon the locality, and no clue to the place is given to this in the letter.

Shrub for a Grave.—J. B. Bowman, Blair Co., Penn. Plants with white flowers are generally preferred for cemetery decorations. Among the best of these are St. Peter's Wreath, *Spiræa hypericifolia*, the Mock Orange *Philadelphus*, and *Deutzia gracilis*. These are all readily obtained from the nurseries and are hardy.

How Far Apart?—"J. W. B.," Iowa, wishes to set an orchard, and is told by some to set his trees 18 feet apart, and by others to put them at the distance of two rods. Both may be right, as there is a great difference in the habit of trees. Two rods is the old rule, and is applicable to all large-growing varieties, such as the Fall Pippin, Tallman's Sweet, etc., while the Red Astrachan and others may be set at half that distance. Those who advocate close planting claim that the trees protect one another. We cannot tell what your troublesome vine is, from the description; send specimens

Muck Composts.—"M. M. S.," Nashua, N. H., uses this: "To each cord of dry muck add 1 bushel of live ashes, and 1 quart of salt, and mix well, and pile in shed. [illegible]" "W. T. S.," Westchester Co., N. Y., proceeds as follows: "Slake lime with as much strong brine (an old meat or fish brine preferred, or brine made from the refuse salt of a packing house), as it will take up and not become wet. This is scattered over layers of muck dried by a few weeks exposure to the air, using about ½ bushel to the cubic yard."—This is a large proportion. It is usual to recommend the lime and salt mixture at the rate of 1 or 2 bushels to the cord (128 cubic feet).

Supply of Guano.—A correspondent of the N. Y. Times says: During the month of November, 1866, 38 vessels of [illegible] tons loaded guano at the Chinchas, principally [illegible] Europe. It is estimated that there are about 800,000 tons [illegible] guano on the Guanape Islands, which the Peruvians have commenced to work. The Islands are within seven miles of the main land. The guano at the Chinchas will be exhausted in about two years.

Hen Manure.—"W. H. S., of Buffalo," W. Va., inquires about the use of this article. It is one of the best kinds of manure, better than much that is sold under the name of guano. It is good spread and plowed-in in field or garden. It is more commonly used as a fertilizer in the hill for all kinds of farm and garden crops. It is quite too strong to [illegible] itself, and should either be [illegible] with four or five times its bulk of muck or loam, or [illegible] mixed with earth in the hill at the time of planting. Undiluted it will destroy most seeds that it comes in contact with.

Spring Wheat on New Land.—A. A. C[illegible], of West Virginia, has some land grubbed and cleared this winter, and asks what is the best variety of spring wheat to sow, time of sowing, quantity per acre, etc. Sow the best kind that can be obtained in the neighborhood, and as early as the land is in fit condition to work—a bushel and a half to two bushels per acre.

Spring Wheat in Wisconsin.—A Farmer's Club in Fond du Lac Co., Wisconsin, passed an unanimous vote that the *Fife* was the best and most profitable variety of spring wheat to sow in that County. We mention the fact, not for the purpose of creating a demand for seed of this well known and excellent variety, but rather to commend the action of the club. If farmers in different parts of the country, when they meet together, would take a lesson from our horticultural friends, and take a vote as to what are the best varieties of seeds, etc., they would soon be in possession of much useful information. Let the vote be intelligently and honestly taken.

Sowing Winter Wheat in Spring.—John G[illegible], of Minnesota, writes us, that the crop of spring wheat in 1865 was very heavy and badly lodged, and in harvesting, several bushels per acre were shelled out and sprouted, and grew on the ground. There was a heavy fall of snow which remained all winter and until the first of April. The spring wheat which came up the fall previous, did not winter-kill, and many farmers left a few acres to see what it would come to. Mr. G. says, his wheat was cut with a "header," leaving a very high stubble, which he burnt, then harrowed the ground once and left ten acres to grow to wheat. He had 124 bushels of uncommonly fine wheat. He asks the opinion of the *American Agriculturist*, whether it will be safe to use this wheat for seed the coming spring? We should be afraid to risk too much of it. Spring wheat can be obtained by sowing winter wheat in the spring, and continuing to do so until the desired habit is established. But until this habit be formed, there is danger that a good portion of the wheat would not mature. How far this spring variety has been changed into a winter wheat, by once sowing in the fall, is uncertain, and we would not like to risk sowing a large area. Sow a few acres, *as early as possible*, and if the season is favorable, the probabilities are, that you will get wheat of better quality than the proper spring varieties will yield.

Corn Planter and Manure Sower.—Mr. J. B. Grinnell, York Co., Pa., wants to know where he can get a good corn planter that drops two rows at a time and sows guano, plaster, etc., at the same time. We do not know of one that we can recommend. There may be one; certainly such a planter is much needed. On many soils it is very beneficial to drop a little plaster or superphosphate with the seed, to give the plants an early start. This is important on all crops, but especially so with corn. A strong, vigorous growing young plant is almost invariably followed, on good land, by a large yield. Peruvian guano, however, should not be dropped with the seed, as a good article will certainly injure it. Ordinary superphosphate will not hurt any seeds, but there are some superphosphates, which are impregnated with the liquid from gas-works to furnish ammonia, which will destroy seed, and should be used with great care.

Wheat in Maine.—M. R. Allen, of York Co., Me., wishes "to raise wheat enough the coming season for home consumption," but says, he "is ignorant of the right way to proceed." Soil, a sandy loam. Proposes to use bone-dust or superphosphate. A mixture of superphosphate and Peruvian guano, half and half, would be better—say 100 lbs. of each per acre. If fine bone-dust, 200 lbs. per acre. Sow these manures broadcast and harrow them in before putting in the wheat. Break up the manures fine, and run them through a sieve to take out all the lumps. If mixed with equal parts of sifted coal ashes (*not* wood ashes), or with fine sand, it will enable you to distribute the manures more evenly. Make the ground as mellow as possible. Spring wheat differs from winter wheat, we think, in requiring a looser and mellower soil. Sow as soon as the snow goes off and the land can be got ready, or else do not sow until rather late. Where the midge is troublesome, late sown wheat sometimes escapes, while that which is sown moderately early, is destroyed. We should prefer, however, to sow early, as late sown frequently gives only a light yield. Make the land rich, mellow and dry; sow early and rather thick—say 2½ to 3 bushels per acre. Thick seeding, we think, favors early ripening.

Good for Egypt!—"Zero," writing from South Pass, in Southern Illinois, says, that seeing a notice a year or two since in the old Genesee Farmer of a turnip measuring about 8 or 9 inches across, he measured some of his that beat "Father Harris" by 1 inch; but he "thought it would be too bad to brag over the old gentleman about *one* inch," so he let it go. "But," he adds, "the story I have now I can't hold. Ezra Pierce raised a crop of Strapleaf turnips, a great many among which weighed 10 to 11 lbs. each, and one, 13 lbs. cleansed weight, 'no grease nor dust.' This one measured 34 inches around. Will not 'Egypt' beat the world for large turnips? We have a kind of sweet potatoes, called 'Bermudas,' which weigh 8 to 12 lbs. If you have statements of any big things, please publish them, so as to give us a chance to get ahead another year."

Warts on Cows' Teats.—J. E. Blake, wants to know how these may be removed. If the warts are drawn out, and a waxed linen or silk thread is tied close down to the roots, they dry up and drop off after a while—generally without making a sore. If suppuration takes place, it may be treated like any cut or wound.

Application for Chapped Hands and Calf-bitten Teats.—Dr. "Hoosier," of Rush Co., Ind., sends us the following sensible note: "It is about this time of the year that the young folks, and often old ones, are complaining of chapped-hands and lips. Now, this state of the human economy is quite annoying, especially to the ladies; consequently, almost everybody is hunting after heal-all ointments, and soothing lotions. I have used a simple mixture for many years, with great success. It is made as follows: Take 1 oz. Glycerine, add 15 grains of Tannin, shake thoroughly, and it will soon dissolve. Apply this preparation to the chapped surface, once or twice a day. A few applications will suffice to cure. This mixture is valuable, also, for the chapped and calf-bitten teats of cows. Rub the teats just before milking. It is readily washed off."

Driving Horses to Plow.—W. F. Brown says: "At the West, we always use the single line on the *near* or left-hand horse, and couple the other by a jockey stick, about four feet long, fastened to the hames' ring of the line horse, and to the bit of the off horse. The jockey stick has a chain about six inches long, at each end, with a T or cross piece attached to slip through the rings. Any patient man can teach a horse in one or two days to go better than with double lines. A pull on the line means *haw*, and a jerk, *gee*. The horse soon catches your idea by these signals, and obeys as readily as by the bit, in the ordinary way. The line is buckled into a ring on a rein buckled to the bit, and passes between the hames, and is kept to its place by the rein that you check the horse's head up with, that being put over it. The rein is held by a loop over the left hand." This method of driving remedies the difficulty complained of by our friend who "walks and talks" on the farm. [Will he please take notice, and will Mr. Brown please try again.—Eds.]

Cooking Food for Stock.—W. F. Brown, of Ohio, recommends the Sorghum pan as the best vessel out for this purpose. He says: "My pan is 11 feet long and about 3 wide at the bottom. The sides, (made of 2-inch stuff) are sloped at an angle of 45 degrees. The sheet iron bottom (No. 18 iron, I believe,) is heavy, and is riveted together, and then nailed on to the wood with common shingle nails. The pan holds about 250 gallons. The furnace is built of brick, and made wide enough so that the wooden sides of the pan will come just outside of the wall. The flue is made 2 bricks by 3, that is 2 feet by 18 inches, and about 10 feet high, with furnace door and grate. That part of the flue or chimney which is exposed to the weather, should be built with lime mortar, but the furnace will last twice as long if laid up with common clay. The door and space under the pan should be made large so as to take in brush, corn stalks, or any light material for fuel. A quick, blazing fire is better for boiling than one made of solid wood. A large scoop holding about 2 gallons, is very convenient for emptying the pan.——In making mush, have an old broom cut off to within six inches of the handle, and stir briskly with this to keep the material from burning. Put out the fire as soon as the mush is cooked. It will take but little wood, and not over 45 minutes to cook six barrels of mush.——In boiling potatoes, it would pay to have a cover to the pan."

Carrots for Spring Feed.—"M. H. S.," says: Four quarts of oats, with 6 or 8 good-sized Carrots, will go farther in feeding a horse than eight quarts of oats without the Carrots. Alone, the roots are excellent feed for cows in the spring before grass comes. Also chopped fine, and mixed with ground oats, they make the best of food for sheep having early lambs.

Working Cows in the Yoke.—Chas. W. Treadwell, of Rockingham County, N. H., has sent us a beautiful card photograph of a floral car drawn by a pair of cows, which figured at the late County Fair. He says they use the cows for all kinds of light work, plowing old land, harrowing, hauling wood, etc., and find them serviceable and uninjured in their milk. They are 5 years old, well broken, give 14 quarts of milk each a day. Moderate labor will cause a cow to eat more, digest it better, and probably improve her health were she to be kept in a stable. In the pasture she gets an equivalent amount of exercise, and with it the better health and appetite. Much labor immediately reduces the yield of milk, and impairs the quality of that which is obtained.

Fat Pigs—How to Make Them.—Mr. Allen, of Missouri, wants to know how it is possible to make pigs weigh from 250 to 300 lbs. dressed, in nine months from birth. This is rather more than the average performance of Yankee pigs, but it is by no means unusual, even with the mongrel stock found in their yards. The pigs are dropped about the first of March from a large thrifty sow. The mother has a plenty of straw for her bed, and a nice warm sty, with a small yard attached. After she is nicely over the birth of her litter, she is well fed with skim milk, boiled potatoes, and a provender made of Indian corn and oats ground together. This is cooked and is fed warm three times a day, and with great punctuality and as much as she will eat up clean. She never has a chance to waste an ounce of flesh in squealing for her meals. This is a matter of great importance. The pigs fed on such a mother should not be more than six, if to get the best results. The pigs have all the milk the mother affords, and as soon as they begin to feed from the trough, they share her messes, which are increased in quantity as the pigs grow. The rule is to give just as much of the swill as they will eat up clean. On dairy farms they have all the skim milk, and whey they can drink in addition to the provender. The pigs are kept growing every hour from birth until they are slaughtered. They sometimes have clover, grass, weeds, or green corn stalks thrown into the pen for a little change of diet, but the staple is the provender and plenty of it. The last few weeks the potatoes are dropped, and they are fed almost wholly on corn meal or raw corn. Pork, thus made, is of splendid quality, and it is by no means uncommon to have pigs so treated weigh from 200 to 300 lbs. dressed, at nine months old.

Raising Calves by Hand.—A California correspondent says: "I have taken calves from one to two days old to as many weeks, and taught them first to drink milk warm from the cow. When they are used to this, add a handful of corn meal, (or better still oil meal), and stir well while they are drinking. All milk may be withheld at perhaps three weeks old, by giving more tea and meal; barley or wheat meal will do perhaps better than corn. Tea is the best substitute for milk, and should be made from good sweet hay, and not steeped too long. If the calves are troubled with scours, stop the meal a day or two, and give a little new milk. If they are constipated, give a little more oil meal or rye meal."

Fine Devon Steers.—A correspondent at Port Byron has a pair that weighed 1540 lbs. at one year old, and 2534 at twenty-one months old. This speaks well for the stock, and for the care taken of them.

Plants by Mail.—It is a great convenience to those who live at a distance from seedsmen and nurseries to be able to obtain plants and seeds through the mail. The ordering of seeds to be received in this way is very common, and, some seedsmen do an almost exclusively mail business. Parcels of plants of moderate size are also easily transmitted by post, and though there have been some loss of plants by this mode of conveyance, it has generally been due either to improper packing or to sending them in too warm a season. But few nurserymen, doing a large business, care to be troubled with small orders by mail at the season when they are crowded with large orders, and we find that it is mainly the dealers in small fruits who offer to transmit plants by post. One of the first to go into the business of mailing plants was Mr. Knox, of Pittsburg, Pa., and, as will be seen by his advertisement, he is so well pleased with his experience in this matter that he not only offers to mail plants, but to guarantee their safe arrival. His offers of collections of vines, etc., by mail, are worthy the attention of those intending to plant. We received plants from Mr. K. by mail long before we ever knew him, and had reason to be satisfied with the condition in which they reached us. We have before spoken of the extent of Mr. Knox's small fruit establishment, at which there are abundant facilities for producing and packing plants, and his reputation is a sufficient guarantee that he will do what he promises.

Bad for Tree-Peddlers.—At the Annual Meeting of the Illinois Horticultural Society, the following resolutions were passed:

WHEREAS, The progress of horticulture has been very much impeded by tree-peddlers, through their ignorance and dishonesty in selling trees untrue to name, at enormous and unusual prices, sometimes delivered in cold and freezing weather, by which farmers and amateur fruit-growers have been discouraged and disgusted; therefore,

Resolved, That this Society as a body of fruit-growers, farmers, legitimate nurserymen and others, do emphatically denounce the business as empirical and injurious to the best interests of horticulture and the prosperity of the State.

Resolved, That there is no good reason why the authorized traveling agents of reliable nurserymen should not be treated with the same respect as the traveling agents of any other useful business, and that these agents be not confounded with the tree-peddlers.

Standard Dwarfs.—I. H. Ellis, Butler Co., Iowa, says that there are agents selling "standard dwarf" fruit trees, and asks if there is any such thing. A dwarf tree is generally considered to mean one grafted upon a dwarfing stock. Thus, the pear is dwarfed by working on the quince, the apple on the *Paradise* apple, etc. Trees on free stocks may be made dwarfs by properly pruning branches and roots. It is a matter as much of training as of stock, and we know of "dwarf" trees—i. e., originally on quince roots—that have become standards. The agent who pretends to have a new sort of trees called "standard dwarfs" is not to be believed.

Report of the Department of Agriculture for 1865.—This document is received. It is a volume of 608 pages, in the usual style, full of pictures, with much valuable information and many blunders. We shall, perhaps, take space to review it at another time.

American Seeds.—An importer of English seeds said to us a few days ago that "All American seed raising is a myth." Now we would like to have some statistics about American seeds. We believe that the amount of garden seeds raised in this country is far from being "mythical," and we know that for many things our gardeners will pay any price for American seeds, when they know who raised them, rather than take imported ones. Do Brill, of Newark, N. J.; Gregory, of Marblehead, Mass.; Macomber, of Rhode Island, the various onion seed-growers of Connecticut, the different Shaker communities and others think that seed growing is a myth? As soon as American grown seeds can be had, of reliable growers, the importations will decrease; and here is a profitable kind of culture that our wide awake small farmers will do well to look into. We do not advise ignorant people, who would grow cabbage seed from "stumps," to go into seed-growing, but those who know the conditions necessary to success and who have a reputation for truthfulness, may well give this attention. We know people at the West who will not plant a carrot or a beet seed, unless they know that it has been raised by a "Shaker," so thoroughly has the name of these people become identified with reliability. Flower seed-raising is certainly not a "myth," for we saw last autumn a delivery of 75 pounds of one kind—Phlox Drummondii—at Thorburn's, in John St., from a grower in New Jersey, and this was not all of this one kind of seed that he expected to deliver. Does James Vick, with his 25 acres at Rochester, devoted to flower seed raising, consider that American grown seeds are all a "myth?" There are a few, and but a few, varieties of seeds that can be better raised in other climates than ours; but we believe that the majority of all garden and flower seeds can be raised better here than abroad.

Where Can I Get It?—A letter from Dayton, O., asks: "Where can good seed of all kinds be procured." This is a sample of many letters that are passed by unnoticed, as our advertising columns give all needed information. We do not allow any one to advertise whom we know to be unreliable, or against whom there are strong suspicions. We believe that *all* advertisers, whose notices are admitted into our columns, will deal fairly, and we cannot recommend one nurseryman or seedsman in preference to another. Buy of the nearest nurseryman or seedsman, if he have the required articles.

Come West is the advice of the St. Louis Democrat to the thousands of unemployed workmen in our Atlantic cities. It says: "A few dollars would place them in Missouri where all kinds of labor are in demand and are paid high wages, where the climate and the soil combine with inexhaustible mineral wealth to offer sure employment and prosperity to a million of industrious workers, and where rich land sells for five dollars an acre. If he does not fancy the cultivation of the soil, pushing railroads are waiting for workmen of every kind. Buildings, going up in every part of the State, are hindered by lack of workmen; mines are lying idle with inexhaustible wealth, scarcely hidden by earth's russet carpet, for want of laborers." This is wholesome advice to the class indicated. New York could with great benefit to itself and to the country spare fifty thousand, who are barely living; here they are consumers and add nothing to the wealth of the country. Their room is better than their company. There the fertile earth pines for their company and would hail their coming with joy. But let the tillers of the soil in the East stay at home, and help us supply the greedy home market.

Whole or Half Sheets.—"O. A. J." asks if it is necessary to write letters on a whole sheet, when a half sheet will answer as well. In all business letters it is customary to use only a half sheet. In other letters, as in matters of etiquette generally, it is difficult to lay down a rule. Those who wish to follow the usages of good society, will write all letters of ceremony, notes of invitation, etc., and will address all officials and dignitaries on a whole sheet, be it large or small. We do not say that this is absolutely necessary, but it is an established custom, as is taking off one's hat in entering a house—and it is better to fall in with it than to appear odd. In some countries the amount of respect of the writer for the recipient of the letter is indicated by the width of the blank margin at the left hand side of the sheet, and we have seen this carried to the extent of leaving a margin half the width of the page.

Unwarranted.—John Vanderbilt & Bros. have sent us a circular of "Hunt's Hoosier Fodder Cutter," in which the *Agriculturist* is made to figure in an unwarranted manner. Hunt's Cutter may be, for all we know, the best in existence, but we have nothing just now to do with that. It publishes, among others, a certificate dated at the Office of the American Agriculturalist, and signed by "S. Edwards Todd, Ag. Editor of Am. Agriculturalist," etc. S. Edwards Todd is not and never was the "Agricultural Editor" of the *Agriculturist*, (without the *al*), and this use of the name of the paper to give apparent value to any certificate whatever, is unwarranted by us.

Fruit Preserving Houses.—Houses built on Nyce's plan appear to be quite successful. Mr. W. S. Carpenter brought us, about Jan. 20, specimens of pears taken from a house of this kind. Duchesse d'Angouleme and other autumn varieties were as fresh and green as if first taken from the tree.

Noteworthy Catalogues.—A dealer's catalogue may be a mere list of the stock on hand, or it may be a pamphlet of real value and one worthy of preservation for future reference. We have before referred to the efforts on the part of our dealers, in the way of catalogues, and some of them give very useful directions for culture, but are generally inexcusably loose in respect to names. As an illustration of a nearly perfect catalogue, we cite that of Andre Leroy, of Angers, France, to whose Agents, Messrs. Bruguiere & Thebaud, 51 Cedar St., N. Y., we are indebted for a copy. Though this catalogue is badly translated, we advise our nurserymen to consult it as a model. The fruits, etc., have their names correctly given, the authority for the name usually appended, synonyms, if any, follow, and then, there are columns giving a clue to the quality, size, texture, fertility, time of maturity and form, with a column for "remarks" where these are necessary. All through the catalogue we find the names in accordance with the best botanical authorities, and all correctly spelled, points in which it affords a marked contrast with any American catalogue we have yet seen. Another pleasing catalogue is that of William Thompson, Ipswich, Eng., in which flower seeds are presented in their botanical families and under their correct names.

Several of our dealers have put out catalogues this year that are more noteworthy for the attempt to render them useful as hand-books, or for the pains taken to illustrate them than for any great attempt at accuracy. Among those useful as giving directions for cultivation, we mention those of A. M. Purdy, South Bend, Ind., and J. Knox, Pittsburg, Pa., for small fruits, and James Vick, Rochester, for flowers. Mr. V. has given a great number of illustrations in his catalogue, and has a noticeably well done frontispiece printed in colors; this catalogue is nearer correct in its names than any that have come to us this year. Peter Henderson's Catalogue of New Plants is also well illustrated, and, as usual, contains all the domestic and foreign novelties. We are always interested in catalogues, as they serve to mark our horticultural progress, and we preserve a file of them with great care.

Documents, etc., Received.—Report of the Committee on Roads, Dedham, Mass ... The Income Taxpayers' Guide and Pocket Register, F. H. Stauffer, Asst. Assessor, Mt. Joy, Pa ... Message, etc., of Gov. of Vermont, from H. Clark, Sec'y .... Index, Charter, and Regulations of St. Louis Public School Library ... Texas Geological Survey—Preliminary Report—by S. B. Buckley .... Address by Hon. Anson S. Miller, of Ill., at Saratoga, before N. Y. State Agl. Soc., from Col. B. P. Johnson .... Report of Sec'y of Iowa State Ag'l Society for 1865, from J. M. Shaffer, Sec'y ... Census Returns of the different Counties of the State of Iowa, for 1865 ... Revelations of the Paraguayan War and the Alliances of the Atlantic and Pacific .... Message of the Gov. of Michigan, Catalogue of Michigan State Agl. College, etc., from Prof. M. Miles Lansing .... Report of the State Agl. College, Mich., by the Pres't, Prof. T. C. Abbot .... A Few Things to be thought of before proceeding to Plan Buildings for the National Agricultural Colleges, from the author, F. Law Olmstead.

Catalogues Acknowledged. — All dealers will find it to their advantage to send us catalogues of their stock, as in preparing the list of nurserymen and others for our Annuals, we only include those who take pains to make themselves known. Some of the catalogues issued this year are very creditably illustrated, and many of them are valuable as hand-books upon the management of fruit, vegetable and flower gardens.

AGRICULTURAL IMPLEMENTS. — John Vanderbilt & Brothers, 23 Fulton St., New York .... Griffing & Company Agricultural and Horticultural Implements, 58 and 60 Cortland St. N. Y.

GENERAL NURSERY STOCK.—Walnut Hills Nurseries, J. S. Cook, Cincinnati, O .... "The Evergreens," Saml. Edwards, La Moille, Ill .... J. C. Plumb, Madison, Wis .... Walworth (Wayne Co., N. Y.) Nurseries, T. G. Yeomans.

GRAPES AND OTHER SMALL FRUITS. — South Bend (Ind.) Nursery, A. M. Purdy .... "The Best Three Market Berries," (*Ill.*) William Parry, Cinnaminson, Burlington Co., N. J .... A. M. Burns, Manhattan, Kansas .... A. J. Hatfield, Niles, Berrien Co., Mich .... Alfred Wells, Ithica, Tompkins Co., N. Y .... Holton & Zundell, Haverstraw, N. Y .... J. Knox, Pittsburg, Pa.

FLORISTS PLANTS, ROOTS, BULBS, ETC.—Peter Henderson (*Ill.*), South Bergen, N. J., and 67 Nassau St., N. Y. .... Wm. F. Basset, Hammonton, N. J.

SEEDS.—John Vanderbilt & Brothers, 23 Fulton St., N. Y .... Saml. T. Thorburn, Albany, N. Y .... Henderson & Fleming, 67 Nassau St., N. Y .... William Thompson, Ipswich, Engl .... Frederick William Wendel, Erfurt, Prussia. J. C. Wendel, Ag't, Boston .... Waite, Burnel & Co., London, Eng .... Illustrated Catalogue and Floral Guide, Jas. Vick, Rochester, N. Y .... Henry A. Dreer, Phila., Pa .... J. M. Thorburn & Co., 15 John St., N. Y .... E. Newbury (*Ill.*), Brooklyn, Conn .... Beisig & Hexamer, Newcastle, Westchester Co., N. Y., Seed Potatoes.

The American Naturalist.—This is the title of a new popular illustrated magazine of Natural History, to be published by the Essex Institute, Salem, Mass. It will be issued monthly at $3 per year. The list of persons who have promised to contribute to its pages comprises the names of those who stand at the head of their different departments of science. Some half dozen periodicals, devoted to popular science, are published in England, but, with the exception of the Practical Entomologist, we have not one in this country. The American Journal of Science serves as a medium for scientific men, but one which should aim to popularize science is greatly needed, and if the one now proposed is well managed, it will meet a long felt want. We wish this enterprise much success, and advise such of our readers as desire to know more about it to send to the Editors of the American Naturalist, Salem, Mass., for a circular.

Walks and Talks on the Farm—No. 38.

My best paying crop on the farm last year was Beans. They cost but little labor and bring a good price. I have just sold them to the seed store for $3 25 per bushel. The early kind turned out better than last year, but the late sort was nipped by the frost, and is not so good. I had to have them picked over by hand at a cost of 15 cents per bushel.

Beans have always been, theoretically, a favorite crop with me. And I am now more than ever convinced that, on wheat farms at least, they should always form a part of the rotation. True, we cannot always hope to get such a high price for them as they have brought this year. But I think they will pay to grow even for feeding out on the farm to sheep. They are very nutritious, and nothing except oil cake makes such rich manure. The vines are excellent fodder. I was fortunate in getting the crop well cured. The growth of vines was unusually large—completely covering the ground, and though the frost struck them before they were pulled, I find that the sheep ate them with avidity. In fact, they seem to like them fully as well as clover hay.

John Johnson writes me that he is fattening over three hundred sheep. Like nearly all of us, he paid more for them than they could have been bought for later in the season. But he thinks that there is not *one eighth* as many sheep being fattened this winter as last, and consequently they are likely yet to bring a fair price. He urges me to feed a little oil cake, and I am doing so. I bought a few tons of it at $50 per ton. It is a high price, but less than it has been for several years. If it were not for the manure I question if it would pay. But if, as Mr. Lawes estimates, the manure from a ton of oil cake is worth $28, and you can buy cattle or sheep ill-fed for two or three cents less per lb. than you can get for them when fat in the spring, we may be sure that we can afford to buy oil cake enough at least to use up all our fodder.

Feeding straw and stalks alone to any kind of stock is of rather doubtful economy. We must feed a little grain or cake with it to get out its full value. With hay, the case is somewhat different, as it contains both grain and straw—or rather, it is cut while all the juices which would go to form grain are still in the stems and leaves. But for fattening animals, it is still desirable to feed out a little grain or roots in addition.

Farmers feel the high taxes this winter more than ever before. They are higher in this town than at any time during the war. The effect, as a general rule, is to check improvements. There is less work being done than for some time past, and wages will come down. But it is no use holding back. The taxes must be paid, and we shall have to get the money out of the land. If we stop work we shall be worse off instead of better. After all, the money paid for State and county taxes does not leave the country. It soon finds its way back again into circulation. If farmers only had to pay high taxes, or if they were merely local, it would be all loss and no gain, but as they are general, all over the country, we will not complain. Let us lend all our energies to make the land as productive as possible, and we shall find it less difficult to pay the high taxes than we anticipated. Our County, State and National debt is really a mortgage on our farms, but as everybody's farm is thus mortgaged it does not affect any one farmer as an ordinary mortgage would. Let us be cheerful then, and keep on working. The prospects of farmers are as good now, compared with other occupations (except office holders), as ever.

How much do you suppose I paid the Doctor for that cow? One hundred and ten dollars! I am a little ashamed of it, but try to persuade myself that I should not have given so much to any one else. She comes in very early, is a well built cow, with a trace of Shorthorn blood in her, and is in high condition. The latter point I think more of than the generality of farmers. I like to see a milch cow pretty fleshy in the spring, for if she is a good milker you will get all the fat she has stored up during the winter back again in the form of butter before the season is over. This cow gave, last summer, two lbs. of butter a day. And if she will do this for me, I would rather give $130 for her than $60 for one that will give only one pound of butter a day. For of course she will not eat *as much again* food.

The high price of cows will prove a boon to farmers if it teaches us to *feed* our milch cows better. In the dairy districts I presume they have paid more attention to this point, but there are not a few farmers that have treated their milch cows and young stock during the winter months as though they did not care whether they lived or died. And even now, while cows are so scarce and high, I can take you to several farmers in this "highly enlightened community," in this "centre of the garden of the Empire State," where cows, colts and young cattle are wintered in the field with no other shelter than a rail fence!

Neighbor Sloe has sold all his straw to the paper makers, and now lets his cattle run in the fields to pick up what grass they can find under the snow. It's a *fact*.

I was glad to see the *Agriculturist*, last month, recommending currying cows and fattening cattle. Animals that are stabled need it more than those in the yards, but it is beneficial to both. When I want a little recreation I take a currycomb and card the cows. They like it beyond anything. I have seen them stop eating their corn meal as soon as I commenced. I wish the practice was general. A man that curries his cows will not be apt to starve them.

There is another thing in the *Agriculturist* this month (January), that I like—the allusion in "Hints about Work," to future prices of farm products. We are all interested in this matter, and there is no way in which the *Agriculturist* could benefit its readers more than by giving all the facts which have any bearing on the subject. Of course, no one can predict with any degree of certainty what prices will be a year or a month from this time, but still some idea can be formed by a careful consideration of the facts. But the difficulty is to *get the facts*. These the *Agriculturist* could give us even more fully than it now does. The advice it gives to "sell when you can get a fair price" is certainly correct; and, on the other hand, hold on to any article that is below the cost of production, if there is a chance for a rise.

"What do you find to do on the farm in winter?" asked a city friend. "What do you people in the city *ever* find to do?" I replied. Whatever sources of discontent there may be in farm life, want of occupation is not one of them. I do not pretend to do much work myself. I would like to do more than I do, but cannot afford it. There are but few men who can work both with their hands and their brains. But there is no lack of work for man and horse, provided it is properly laid out. In stormy weather you can grind grain, chaff fodder, thresh beans, and if you have a tool-house, with a stove in it, you can repair tools and implements, paint wagon wheels, cultivators, harrows, plows, &c., and get everything ready for spring.

We have been latterly busy drawing stones to build fences. There are hundreds of tons of stones on my farm that have been taken out of the land and drawn into large heaps. It is no little labor to draw these stones on a wagon or a stone-boat in the summer, even if we had time; but with sleds it is less work to load, not having to lift them so high, and you can draw a much heavier load. In the summer time it would cost me nearly as much to draw the stones as to build the fence; and when the ground is wet in the spring and fall it is still more expensive, and, besides, injures the land. It is rather cold work handling stones, but the winter is *the* time for moving such heavy materials.

Did I tell you of a discovery the Deacon made last summer? He has a small ditch running through one of his fields which carries off the water from ten or fifteen acres of my farm. Last summer he observed that there was a hole in this ditch into which the water soaked away. He took a crow-bar and enlarged the hole. I have two long underdrains discharging into the ditch, and during the heavy rains of last fall there was a great quantity of water discharged, but this hole *took every drop* of it. I presume the hole goes down to a fissure in the rock. If it was opened out and then stoned up so as to prevent choking, I see no reason why it should not prove a permanent outlet for all the water. There is on my farm a low spot from which there is no outlet, into which flows a considerable quantity of water, which all disappears.

The great difficulty in draining is to get a good outlet. There is scarcely any land that cannot be readily drained if the natural water courses were kept free from obstructions, and the ditches which run into them were deepened and widened and kept clean. But as this must be done by the several farmers through whose land the water courses run, any one of them can seriously damage all the rest by his negligence or obstinacy. This matter demands the immediate attention of our legislators. A well considered law, compelling farmers to clean out water courses, &c., or in case of refusal authorizing the proper authorities to do the work and assess the expense on the property benefited, would do much for agricultural improvement.

The Deacon last night was telling me of an interesting fact in regard to wheat, which he observed on his farm some years ago. He and another farmer had bought some wood which lay back of my present farm. By going across my farm they could save a mile or so of travel. They obtained permission from the owner to draw their wood during the winter, on condition that they should pay for any damage done to a piece of wheat they had to go over. Before spring the snow broke through occasionally, and they expected to have to pay considerable damage. But during the summer the wheat on the track was far superior to the rest of the field. The snow being pressed hard, did not melt in the spring for a long time after it had all disappeared from the rest of the field. There may have been some droppings from the horses, which could have done no harm, but still I have no doubt it was the late coming of snow and ice in the spring that was of so much benefit to the wheat. "At harvest," said the Deacon, "the wheat was so good that the men told me they got all their bands from this track to tie up the bundles from the rest of the field."

But what a wretched picture of farming is this—the straw not long enough to tie up the wheat! This, mark you, was on the farm I now own, and if I ever have a crop of wheat that I cannot bind, it must not be ascribed to "book farming." For my predictions certainly are not open to such an accusation. If not strictly "practical" farmers, they did not ruin themselves by taking agricultural papers or farming according to the books. Some of them spend more time at the card table and the grog shop than I do in my library. Those of my good friends who shake their heads at some of my performances will agree with me in one thing: It is better to buy bone dust than whisky; better to spend your evenings at home, reading the experience of the best farmers of the past and the present than to be expending the hours in smoking in a grocery at the "corners."

I do not know a more striking instance of the benefits of drainage on a small scale than one not half a mile from me. A city man, three or four years ago, bought a farm of some seventy-five acres. The house was situated on the top of an easterly slope, some forty or fifty rods from the road. He moved out to the farm the 1st of May. The young ladies, who had had no experience of farm life, came out in a carriage, and when they came to turn up the private road that led to the house the horses mired, and the driver had to get out, and lay down rails for the ladies to walk on across this mud hole. Their feelings can be imagined. A quite respectable family had lived on the farm since the county was first settled—lived, thrived and died. They had pulled through that mud hole for thirty or forty years, without any attempt to drain it. Our city friend immediately cut a ditch along the side of the road a distance perhaps of fifty rods, down to a natural water-course. He then put in some three or four underdrains, running up and down the slope in front of the house, and which discharge into the new ditch. The affect was magical. These underdrains run winter and summer, day and night, and carry off all the water. The meadow is one of the handsomest and most productive in the neighborhood. The young ladies have surrounded the house with evergreens and ornamental trees and shrubs. The mud hole has disappeared, and in its place is a nice gravel road, firm and dry at the wettest seasons of the year, and I question if the whole expense of the improvement amounted to two hundred dollars.

"But did your city friend make farming pay?" Yes, Sir. He has received more money from his apple orchard alone than he paid for the farm! He has everything very comfortable around him, is an active, energetic man, cultivates his land thoroughly, raises large crops and enjoys farm life——well, about as much as I do.

I am glad so many city people are turning their attention to farming. The country needs new blood. But there can be little doubt that many of these new comers will soon leave us. I have a neighbor who came from the city last spring. He bought a farm that would be productive if thoroughly underdrained, but without, it is not worth cultivating. He has worked hard all summer, managed the land as well as any one could, but his corn was not worth husking, and the whole farm receipts were so small, he is about to return to the city in disgust.

Our agriculture has much to hope from young men who, having a love for farming, the necessary capital, a good education, and abundant energy, make up their minds to study farming at some Agricultural College, or with some good practical farmer, and then settle down in the country for life, determined to "make farming pay." It will not be many years before our Agricultural Colleges turn out hundreds of such men. And the more of them the better.

Milking Stools—A Hint.

We published some time since an article about milking stools, which brought several communications in regard to them, among others, some advocating the use of one-legged stools. These are very common articles of cow-yard furniture in some places, but probably unused in others, they have their advantage, however, upon side hills or uneven ground.

There are multitudes of people who use 3-legged stools while milking, for the very good reason that they will stand firmly wherever they are set down. And if the idea of a one-legged stool were suggested to them, it might not be entertained for the reason that such a stool will not stand alone. The quality of firmness is good, but that of being *level* is better. A one-legged stool will be level, or as nearly level as the milker wishes, at all times, and to enforce this fact we have had this illustration made. The artist has probably never milked a dozen cows morning and night, winter and summer, during some of the best years of his life, or he would have given his milkman a better position, and provided a bigger pail for the *show* of milk.

Convenient Tools in the Garden.

There are some implements very convenient and even necessary to have in the garden that are not usually kept by the dealers in garden tools, and they must be home made, if had at all. At this time of comparative leisure it is well to have all the tools repaired and to purchase or make such as are likely to be wanted.

Fig. 1.—ROLLER.

A ROLLER of some kind is an implement so useful that no large garden should be without it. Those of iron, for rolling gravel, are too heavy for the main purpose for which a roller is required, that of rolling the soil after sowing seed. Figure 1, shows the form of roller used in market gardens in the vicinity of New York.

It is a cylinder of hard wood about 5 feet long and 9 inches in diameter. It is bored through its whole length to receive a rod of 2-inch round iron; this rod makes the roller sufficiently heavy, and being a few inches longer than the roller, its projecting ends furnish arms to which to attach the handle. It is of great importance, after sowing seeds, to pack the soil closely in contact with them, or to "firm" it, as the gardeners say. In a small way this can be done by means of a strip of board, but when a large sowing is made, the roller is necessary. Moreover, the smooth surface left by the roller allows the first hoeing to be done with greater facility, than when it is left lumpy and uneven.

THE MARKER is another very convenient implement, used for tracing lines upon the surface of the ground, as a guide in setting plants or for making drills in which to sow seeds. The double marker shown in figure 2, has one set of teeth at 9 inches apart, and another at 12 inches distant. A marker of this kind will lay out lines at the distances ordinarily required, as by using every mark, or every alternate one, we can have rows at nine, twelve, eighteen, and twenty-four inches distant as may be needed.

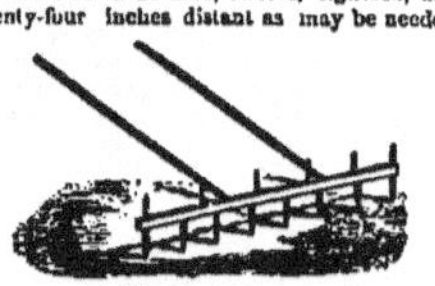

Fig. 2.—MARKER.

THE CULTIVATOR most in use in our market gardens is simply a harrow, made in the form of a cultivator, and adjustable to different widths.

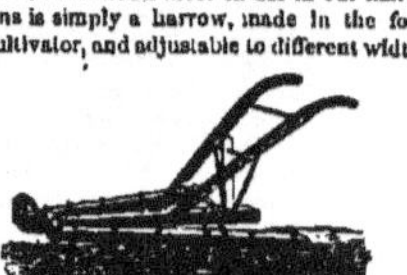

Fig. 3.—CULTIVATOR.

The teeth are like ordinary harrow teeth; and when unusually deep culture is required, a weight is put upon the implement to make it enter the soil to a considerably greater depth.

THE DIBBLER, or Dibble, fig. 4, is of great use in transplanting. It is made from a bit of hard wood that has a convenient curve to fit the hand, and will be all the more durable if the point is shod with iron. The foregoing engravings are from Mr. Peter Henderson's new work "Gardening for Profit."

Fig. 4.

A GARDEN LINE is necessary where one would lay out his work with accuracy, and a wooden reel may be made to wind it upon. The iron reels, as generally sold, soon get out of order and become useless. We have found two stakes of hard wood, properly pointed, to be more satisfactory than any kind of reel. One of these stakes is made fast to each end of the line; when not in use the line is wound upon one of the stakes in the manner that a boy winds up a kite string.

The Beaver.—(*Castor Canadensis.*)

The beaver is another of those interesting quadrupeds which the march of civilization exterminates. We are reminded constantly of the fact that they were once abundant throughout the Northern States, by the creeks, ponds and meadows which bear the marks of their wonderful engineering. It is a pleasant fancy that all the trades have their representatives among the brute creation; the Beaver is the civil engineer. Old beaver dams still stand, and, in not a few locations, are now busy mill-sites. The accumulated deposits of silt and rubbish carried down by the dammed-up streams, and deposited in the slack water above the dams, form more permanent monuments to the beaver's industry, than the dams, which have, in the most cases, rotted and been washed away, while the deposits above them have become covered by swamp vegetation, and, as "beaver meadows," perpetuate the memory of the industrious colonies once established upon them. The Beaver belongs to the family of the *rodents*—gnawers—distinguished by two pairs of very strong, sharp, cutting, front teeth. They are found in both hemispheres, but most abundantly in North America, and are hunted and trapped for their fur, which is very valuable if taken in the winter season. They are from 2 to 3 feet in length, exclusive of the tail, which measures about a foot, is of oval form, flattened laterally, and covered with semi-horny scales instead of fur. The hind feet are webbed; but the fore-feet are not. The body is low, squat on the hind feet, the ears small and rounded, and the fur is exceedingly fine, soft and close, thickly interspersed with coarse hairs. These hairs are removed by the process of "plucking," when the fur is prepared for use.

THE BEAVER.—(*Castor Canadensis.*)

It is absurd to exaggerate psychological qualities in animals, especially if so remarkable as those possessed by the beaver. Nevertheless this has been done by most of the old writers who have listened to the trappers' marvelous tales. Beavers act in concert in felling small trees and floating them, and logs cut from them, down stream to form their dams. The trees are anchored by stones and gravel piled upon those parts of their tops which rest upon the bottom; and the dams are finished by building-in logs, stones and boughs, the interstices being filled with gravel and mud. The dams are built or repaired in the summer when the water is low, and in the autumn the beavers, in families of 4 old, and 6 or 8 young ones, construct their lodges, which are made of sticks, stones and mud, piled in a broad circle, a chamber about 7 feet wide being left in the center, the floor of which is above usual high water. As the structure rises, it is contracted into a dome, the cavity being about 3 feet high, and the thickness of the walls above and around being often from five to seven feet.

The entrances to these lodges are all below the water level when the dam is full, and near and about them canals and channels are formed which communicate with their stores of food, which consists of the bark stripped from the logs used for their dams, and that of logs and boughs of the willow, aspen, poplar, and other soft wooded non-resinous trees.

Beavers are not only valuable for their fur, but for the drug *Castor*, or *Castoreum*, which is found in sacks near the root of the tail, and is used in medicine. It is used also by the hunters as a means of attracting beavers to the trap.

Beavers are easily domesticated, and as their food is willow bark, they might perhaps be economically bred and fed on the bark stripped from willows used for basket making. If not domesticated, this interesting animal will soon be extinct in the United States.

Shrew Mole and Star-nosed Mole.

The common American Mole is the Shrew Mole (*Scalops aquaticus*), though the Star-nosed Mole (*Condylura cristata*) is not rare. The former is found in many gardens and fields where it does much benefit by destroying grubs and worms in the soil, and some harm also in disturbing the roots of plants by its subterranean galleries. The question whether moles are, on the whole, friends or enemies, is worthy of discussion. For our own part, considering their most ravenous appetites and the great amount of food they require to sustain life, which may easily be seen when one is caught alive and fed, we are inclined to regard them as friends. The family name, *Talpidæ*, covers a number of similar genera in different parts of the world. They agree in living a short distance below the surface of the ground, having stout, clumsy bodies, without apparent neck or external ears, exceedingly small eyes and short legs, the fore-feet being generally very broad and armed with strong claws. In all, the senses of smell, hearing, and feeling, are very acute. They are able to move swiftly about in their galleries, and to extend them with great ease and rapidity. The fur of the Shrew Mole, and of moles in general, is of exquisite fineness, and lies in no particular direction. The Star-nosed Mole has coarser fur, and the termination of its snout is a very remarkable fringe of fleshy points. We have besides, three other moles in the United States, the *Silver Mole* of the Prairies; the *Hairy-tailed Mole* of the New England and Middle States, and the *Oregon Mole* found all along the Pacific coast.

SHREW MOLE, (*Scalops aquaticus*), AND STAR-NOSED MOLE, (*Condylura cristata.*)

Dealing in Fancy Poultry—Poultry Clubs.

In common business transactions, the buyer is generally expected to decide for himself whether quality and price in the thing he buys are such as to make the purchase desirable—and the practice of "beating down," is as old as the time of Solomon, who wrote, "'It is naught; it is naught,' saith the buyer—and when he is gone then he boasteth." But when a man orders by mail, and sends the money in advance for a good article which he expects to receive by express, he throws himself entirely on the honor of the seller. This is the usual way of buying the different kinds of fancy poultry of professional breeders. No one would think of buying a horse in this way, except of a tried friend, or of a dealer of proved honor, or of such a reputation that his interest would tally with his integrity, and we are sorry to be obliged to rank poultry dealers and horse dealers in the same class, with a few honorable exceptions.

Many people buy fancy poultry, who do so for the sake of gaining by experience a knowledge of the breeds and their qualities. In their orders they exhibit their ignorance, and the dealers take advantage of this, demand pay in advance, and send fowls utterly worthless as breeders. Some of these breeders of fancy poultry are so ignorant as actually not to know how to select the best birds of their own flocks, and will actually breed from accidental crosses to keep up their breeding stock. This is true of a Jersey breeder who sells many fowls in N. Y. City by auction, and otherwise advertises extensively. Birds bought of such an one will only by accident give satisfaction. We saw at the N. Y. State Fair some fine Black Spanish fowls, and a friend ordered some on the strength of our statement of the excellence of the parent stock. They came and were worthless for breeding purposes, fit only for the pot or for layers. There are several places in New York City, where fancy poultry are kept caged for days and weeks. People who buy fowls or turkeys from these pens, or dens, will be almost sure to carry vermin and disease (roup) to their yards.

In a dealer in fancy poultry, ignorance of what constitutes a pure-bred fowl, or a healthy fowl, or a well shaped fowl, is a crime. It causes fraudulent dealing. He knows that he inevitably, in his ordinary course of dealing, must cheat his customers, and besides send disease and death among their fowls at home.

Fowls bred from the best stock will not always be equal to their parents, and in many cases those a little inferior may not communicate their bad points to their offspring; these therefore, have a value above common "dunghills." The nearer birds approach the ideal of perfection, the higher should the price rise. The breeder who would set any price for the very best, and selling, continue to breed from his own inferior stock, should be tabooed.

Know what you want, and see before you buy, or before you pay for what you order; if you order by mail and receive by express, is the best advice we can give. Breeders who know they send a good article will not object to this practice. They sometimes suggest it. We have known of some who requested purchasers, if not pleased, to replenish the food and water stores, clean out the coop, and return the birds.

The remedy for much of this cheating is the association of poultry fanciers, in correspondence, and in visiting each other's yards, in poultry clubs, and in other ways. We are now too much every man for himself. The Grey Dorkings have often proved failures in this country for want of the ability of breeders, by exchange or otherwise, to get fresh blood. They do not bear in-and-in breeding, and the same is true of much other poultry. We recommend, therefore, the formation of Poultry Clubs, or other associations of amateur poultry breeders.

Impurities of Cross-bred Drones.

BY BIDWELL BROS., ST. PAUL, MINN.

The best Apiarians, both in this country and Europe, consider that a pure Italian queen, in mating with a less pure or black drone, though producing cross-bred queens and workers, will nevertheless produce pure Italian drones. In our experience we have not found it so.

The great multiplication of Italian bees in Europe as well as America, is by what is termed Italianizing, that is, removing a black queen and substituting an Italian in her place. Her progeny in time replace the black bees. Queens for the remaining hives of the apiary are reared by removing the Italian queen and compelling the queenless bees to rear one or more "forced queens" from her worker eggs or larvæ. After hatching, these fly out to meet the drones, which at that time are for the greater part black drones, the progeny of the previous black queens, or belonging to neighboring hives. The drones of these "hybrid queens," so-called—(Italian queens which mate black drones), are claimed to be pure Italians, and are allowed the second season to mate with queens subsequently reared from eggs of the original pure queen, thereby affecting, we claim, in a degree, the greater part of the apiary.

In bee-breeding these facts are established, viz.: Queens that have never met the drones will lay fertile eggs which will all hatch into drones. Queens never meet the male but once, and after this they are called "fecundated queens." Their eggs are directly influenced by the fecundative principle, or not, at volition. Those eggs which are thus fecundated produce workers or queens; those which are not fecundated, as is the case with the eggs of the non-fecundated queens, produce drones. From these premises, and from the fact that an Italian queen crossed with a black drone produces drones more or less closely resembling pure Italians, apiarians argue that the drone progeny must be of the original purity of the virgin queen, and advise the use of such drones in apiaries.

Now, we claim that *a pure Italian queen, in mating with a less pure drone, or with a black drone, is tainted*, and remains a cross-bred ever after. Certain it is that the seed of the drone forms a part of her system, requiring the blood or fluids of her body to circulate into it and back into her for its nutrition and development.

An Italian queen having mated an Italian drone, produces handsomer, and hence purer drones than similar and sister queens having mated black drones; this we have observed in many different apiaries. Our experience on this point is as follows: In raising Italian queens in the summer of '65, the first queen that mated with a black drone produced drones of an inferior color, and apparently less pure than those of sister queens mating with Italian drones. We were compelled to remove her from our apiary. We repeated the experiment afterwards with similar results. To prove that this queen must have mated with a black drone, we offer, that, 1st, its mother was the only Italian queen within 20 miles, and the nearest cross-bred queens were 18 miles; 2d, black drones were in an adjoining apiary; 3d, the queen was one of 5 sisters reared from the aforesaid queen, all hatching on the same day, and reared from eggs laid on the same day, and their brothers (the drones) were hatched 6 days before them; 4th, 4 of the sisters, after impregnation, all produced progeny similar to their mother, and this one different. Fertile Italian workers, and unfecundated queens, have better drones than queens, reared from similar eggs, and mated with a black drone. Another marked characteristic of such cross-breeding is, that the bees are more irritable and unmanagable. Continued cross-breeding with only occasional additions of strains of black blood, together with the imperfections of forced queens and drones, will rapidly reduce the standard of purity of Italians. The evidences of this degeneration are unfortunately too apparent in very many apiaries.

Bringing up Worn-out Land.

It is ever and anon asserted that the only systematic and intelligent way to bring up land that has been run down, is to have the soil carefully analysed by a professional agricultural chemist, to ascertain the lacking mineral ingredients, and then to purchase and apply the same.

Theoretically, this is all very well. But let us remember two or three things. It will be necessary to analyse nearly every field of a farm, if not different portions of the same field, because the soils will be more or less unlike. Then, too, these analyses are expensive. And lastly, they are very liable to fatal errors.—Prof. S. W. Johnson writes: "I do not doubt that in many cases a careful *investigation* of a soil—chemical, physical, and historical—by a genuine *scientific farmer*, one familiar with science and practice, would afford safe and nearly accurate data for its proper treatment. But this would be always expensive, and in nine cases out of ten, would not *pay*. Soil analysis, at the best, is a chance game; and where one wins, a hundred may lose."

Instead, then, of looking abroad for some special process of reconstruction, let the farmer turn to the farm itself and his own brains, and see what they can do. If our farm is exhausted, it is because it has been abused, and to restore it, it must receive kind treatment. Let us see. Some parts of it may need draining. Other parts will need deeper plowing, and all will doubtless need more manure and cleaner tillage.

The owners of such farms generally complain that they have not manure enough on their premises, and can not afford to buy more. Then let them try plowing under green manure, such as peas, buckwheat, and, best of all, clover. Marvelous results have been achieved in this way. And muck has done and will yet do as great wonders. Many a farm has a bed of this, and whoever has it, has a mine of wealth. Get it out every leisure day, and after it has drained, stack it up with alternate layers of lime or ashes. In a few months, it will be nearly as efficacious as so much barn-yard dung. Dr. Dana classes it with cow-manure in value. Now, these two sources of fertility are enough, with deeper plowing and cleaner culture, to set any "worn-out" farm on a career of improvement. But, as "every little helps," the farmer should save the droppings of his poultry-house, the slops and waste from kitchen and chamber, the contents of the privy, all bones and chips and sods and leaves:—In short, whatsoever will decay, and so become a fertilizer. These several items amount in the aggregate to a good deal in a year's time. And the farmer who neglects to save them should be ashamed to complain of his worn-out land. It is by economy of this sort that some of the poorest farms of the country have been reclaimed and made profitable. And there are many more waiting to be reclaimed by just such simple means. There are farms, however, which this will not regenerate, and these in 99 cases in 100, need bone-dust. Green manure and bone-dust will cure 9-10ths of the ills that well drained and plowed land is heir to. Lime is often a great help, and ashes still better. These facts are easier learned by experiment than by chemical analysis. •

Manures—How and When Applied?

A long established custom—a "rut" that the wheels of every-day practice have run in for years, has something which entitles it to respect. We should not switch off upon a side track, or no track at all, just because we find ourselves running our practice in the old ruts. These were formed probably for some good reason, and should be departed from only for a good reason. The interest in the subject of manuring land is increasing over the whole country, even on the rich prairies, where the ideas advanced from time to time by the *Agriculturist*, have so often provoked derision, manure is getting to have a recognized value; everywhere else it is the very life of farming. It is gratifying to hear a farmer say, "Five years ago, do the best I could, I could not make over 70 loads of good manure, but now I keep double the stock I did then, and make 300 loads of better quality." Such a man can not leave the accumulations of the whole year until April and May before he gets it out, but there must be a system of almost constantly getting it to the field, and getting it under ground. The farmer whose remarks we quote, has, on an average, 25 ox-cart loads of manure per month to dispose of.

For some crops, corn for instance, manure may be applied fresh and plowed in. For others, as flax or wheat, such rank manure would be fatal to a good crop. Applied in the autumn, manure will generally become so incorporated with the soil before spring, that its rank character will be entirely lost, and if examined it will be found much of the consistency of manure that has lain 6 months or more in the yard.

For corn and root crops, it is best to have the manure diffused through the soil. For wheat and the other cereals, the upper layer of the soil to the depth of say 4 inches, should contain the manure applied, especially for that crop. There are two ways of securing this surface enrichment, which, in the case of the small grains, should never consist of rank unfermented manure. One way is to make a compost, work it over, and when of a uniform consistency, apply it on the plowed surface and harrow it in, or work it in with a cultivator. The other is to plow in a good dressing of manure spread evenly over the surface, turning it well under. If this be done in autumn, the spring plowing and harrowing, if done aright, will bring it again to the surface, well incorporated with the soil, and making usually a nice seed bed. If it be done in the spring, a crop of corn or early potatoes may be raised, or on some soils a summer small grain crop, and the manure be brought to the surface for the especial benefit of a wheat crop in August or September.——There are such great differences in soils, exposures, and the general adaptation of districts to certain crops, that only general rules will apply universally.

"Inquirer," who omits the State from his address, says it is customary with farmers in his neighborhood to manure in spring, on corn stubble for oats, and follow with wheat, seeding to clover and timothy. This to be followed by corn. Sometimes, it seems, the oats grow rank and lodge, but usually the crop is good. The reason evidently is that sometimes they plow the manure in so deep, the oats get but little, and if the plowing is too shallow, they fall badly. When they manure before plowing for wheat, the clover and timothy do better than when the manuring is before plowing for oats, but the wheat is not materially affected. Instead of this, try coarse manure and plenty of it for the corn—none for the oats, a fine compost for the wheat kept near the surface. The rotation is not a good one, but we are not on that subject now.

Dead Animals—What Becomes of Them?

We do not eat horses and mules, and we eat only a portion of cattle, sheep, and swine. Without considering the immense waste of offal which take place in the slaughter houses all over the country, from the little "one-horse" affairs of the villages, to the monster abattoirs of the cities, where good sized brooks of blood flow out to be lost, think of what becomes of the horses, etc., the whole number of which in the United States may be estimated at 10,000,000.

Their average age is, say 12 years, and the weight of those that die, about three to the ton. We have then annually the immense amount of 280,000 tons of dead horse-flesh, nine-tenths of which is worse than wasted, being left on the surface, or so slightly buried that it is dug up by dogs, and pollutes the air for miles around. Its value, where barn-yard manure is worth $1 a load, is not less than $10 per ton, for if properly managed, it will make not less than 15 loads of good manure, and where manure is worth more, the value is of course proportionally increased. The way to save this waste and economize it as manure, is as follows:

Take 3 loads of dry, weathered swamp muck mixed with lime, in proportion of 1 bushel of slaked lime to the load, as a bed—on this, kill the old horse, or drag the dead one. Then skin him; remove hoofs and shin bones, if you have a market for them, and cut him up with axes and knives into pieces weighing 6 to 18 pounds, leaving the big bones uncut, but dividing the principal joints. Spread the pieces evenly, sprinkle well with lime, cover 6 inches deep with muck and add more lime. Then cover with a foot or 18 inches of muck, and leave it. Look out for dogs; they will frequently dig out the bones, and see how many you can add to the heap. After about 3 months of warm weather, or 6 months or more of cold weather, examine the heap to see if it is well decomposed, and as soon as it is in such a condition as not to be particularly offensive, work it over, adding more muck, without lime. A new fermentation will commence, and when this is over, the manure will be fit for use. In shoveling it out, the big bones should be thrown to one side, to be put into another compost heap, or into the horse-manure heap, where they will gradually decay, so as to be easily broken up with a sledge hammer, or even mashed with a shovel; this takes some time, however. The labor is not great to pitch them out and work them over again, and finally the land gets their full value. If at any time the odor of ammonia is perceived, gypsum should be sprinkled freely over the heap, and more muck thrown on. If muck is not to be obtained easily, use sods or bogs which have been laid up with a little ashes or lime until they crumble, or even good soil may be used with almost equally good results. The manure resulting is excellent for corn, potatoes, or grass, and if not too strong, and if it has lain long enough, is good for wheat or any purpose.

Like Produces Like—Old Mares as Mule Breeders.

This law prevails in the vegetable and animal economy. Would that farmers always bore this in mind, and practised accordingly. It seems to be well understood that if we would maintain and improve the quality of our corn and wheat, and other grains, we must save our best each year for seed. But in raising stock, in numerous districts in our country, less care is taken. Every year we see calves raised from the meanest scrub and grade bulls, and cows of no especially valuable qualities either for flesh or milk. Every year we see poor old broken down mares used to raise horses from. We do not suppose that *all* diseases and infirmities are propagated from one generation to another, but many are; and where no specific disease is entailed, general inferiority certainly descends, which sooner or later will breed many evils. It is no doubt true that bad management and harsh usage will spoil the best descended colt; but a colt propagated from a diseased dam will break down under work and exposure much quicker than one of sound and vigorous parentage. It is abundantly proven that the various diseases of the wind passages are quite likely to be propagated. Readers of the *Agriculturist* will make note of facts like these, and practice accordingly in raising stock; but there are thousands who do not read, and who live and work on in needless ignorance of their own interests. Quietly argue with such people, and prove by your own experience that it pays over and over again to use thorough-bred bulls and rams, and the best stallions and mares for stock, and show the man that says, "the old mare is pretty well broken down, I know, but I can get two or three colts and some work out of her yet," that the colts which cost him $100 to $150 each to raise, if from a sound and fine dam, and by a superior sire, might sell for $300 to $700 a piece, instead of barely bringing their cost, if even that—the difference being two or three times what the old mare is worth. There is one use for which we commend old mares that cannot work, and can breed, and that is for raising mules. These will indeed, to a certain extent, inherit the impaired constitutions of their dams, but being prevailingly used for so much slower work, they will be much less injuriously affected than horses, while their evil stops with them. We might profitably make a much more extensive use of mules than we do at the North, and there is a steady demand for young mules for shipment. While we object to prostituting our best mares to this purpose, as they used to do in Kentucky with their fine thorough-breds, yet we believe there are thousands of mares that would raise good mules, that it would never pay to raise colts from; and that the mules would bring a much higher price than horses raised from the same mares. Certainly they would, if we regard the fact that they may be marketed 2 to 3 years old.

How to Bring Swamp Meadows into Tame Grasses, etc.

First, shut off the water. This we discussed with considerable detail in our last-year's volume. A wall of puddled clay, not less than 14 inches wide, should extend from the hard pan of the meadows to the height desired, protected by an embankment wide and solid enough to resist the action of both frost and water.—This embankment, with its impervious clay wall within it, must be provided with tide-gates to let water out, but not in, and these must be muskrat proof. Ditches within the embankment convey the surface and spring water to the main drains and the outlets. These may be open or covered, according to the depth to which the water can be drawn down below the surface. If possible, they should be tile drains, laid at least below the action of frost and the reach of the plow. If the soil is of a black mucky character, containing little inorganic matter, a liberal dressing, say 30 to 50 loads to the acre, of the surface soil of the neighboring upland is all that is required to prepare it for timothy and clover. Thirty to fifty bushels of dry slacked lime, harrowed in after plowing, will fit it for potatoes or cabbages, and 20 bushels of lime, and an equal quantity of leached ashes, will be an excellent preparation of most land of this sort for a good corn crop, which, however, may well be quickened by dropping a handful of some good fertilizer in the hill.

This is a tolerably fair showing for profit, for the crops from such land are very good, and the culture is quite easy for several years; the limings, moreover, will last for several years, and little manure will be required. But, but—there is always a *but*, and well it is if you find it out in time—there are places where the muskrats will undermine the dykes and let in the water.

"A Young Jersey Farmer" writes us in distress, endorsing our views about dykes and salt meadows, but is in despair on account of the muskrats. He suggests the availability of a thin concrete wall in the middle of the dyke. This, he says, he knows will stop them. But the question still is how deep it must needs be to prove effective, for they will burrow. He proposes that the wall should be constructed simply by filling a narrow ditch with cement concrete, and allowing it to remain where it is formed; or making long thin concrete slabs, cast in moulds and fitted close together in the trench. The suggestions strike us as eminently practical and sensible. There has been a plan proposed for dyking the extensive Newark meadows which consists in driving prepared iron plates into the swamp to the required depth, which is supposed to be economical because no digging will be necessary, nor will any moving of earth be needed, except to raise an embankment high enough to shut out the tides. This is not so thorough to appearance as the concrete wall plan; and neither plan so surely water tight as the clay wall. In these works there is nothing like thoroughness—getting well down to the hard pan, or to an impervious stratum for one thing, and using a rat proof wall for another. The value of these lands is so great, that projects of reclaiming them should readily command not only the co-operation of owners, but capital enough to secure the best skill and most thorough work. If our readers meet with decided success, or have important facts to communicate, we hope they will tell them to one another through the *American Agriculturist*, for it is a subject which interests many thousands of its readers.

Fig. 1.—WOODEN WHEELBARROW.

About Wheelbarrows.

Our correspondent, Gilbert J. Greene, Hudson, N. Y., sends us some practical notions about wheelbarrows which, however, need a word of preface in favor of one-wheeled barrows, for which he has nothing to say. The fact is they are just as useful in their place as two wheeled ones. In "navvy" work for instance, such as grading roads, parks, etc., digging cellars, making railroads and canals, where gangs of a number of men each go back and forth on the same track, which can ordinarily be only of the width of a single board, and where of necessity they must dump at the side, the navvy-barrow is by far the most convenient form. The fact that it will only carry a small load is counter-balanced by the fact that such a load is all that can be easily moved up and down the inclines which ordinarily exist where such work is done; besides, the barrows may be filled without the laborers being obliged to shift the position of the barrow, and this expedites the work materially.

Fig. 2.—IRON WHEELBARROW.

Fig. 3.—TWO-WHEELED BARROW.

The common wheelbarrow with side boards, for ordinary use about the barn and garden, has not so specific an adaptation to its uses; nevertheless, this has a great advantage over the two wheeled one in going through narrow garden walks, and in the convenience with which rails, stakes, bean-poles, and such things may be loaded upon it. Two-wheeled barrows find in Mr. Greene an able champion. He writes:

"I would contribute a small sum to erect a monument to the memory of the man who invented the wheelbarrows, but it would be on the condition that no more should be built with a single wheel; how he came to adopt the single wheel is past my comprehension, unless it be that he had but one wheel and could not get another. A two-wheeled barrow possesses so many advantages over a single wheeled one that to me it is surprising that it has not long since been adopted. 500 pounds can be carried upon a two wheeled barrow as easily as 150 can be on a single wheeled one. It is more reliable, as it is not easily upset while being loaded or in wheeling it. It is very much more easily turned round, and more easily unloaded. The wheels being on the sides, the load is balanced upon the axle, and there need be little or no weight upon the hands. There are no sideboards to take out or put on each time you unload it. The two wheels do not cut in the ground so much as one does. The body and frame being solid, and resting upon an axle, it is stronger than the other. Fig. 1 represents a wooden two-wheeled barrow of the form I prefer for ordinary use. The wheels are twenty-six inches high, with iron axle. The body is similar in shape to that of the single wheeled barrows. When constructed of iron (fig. 2) they are made of an oval or dishing form. Fig. 3 represents a two wheeled barrow in the position of being unloaded; the load being nearly balanced upon the axle, the handles are easily raised and the load dumped over the front. Such a barrow can be made so as to sell for $12 to $16, but would cost a man, tolerably handy with tools, a good deal less if he made it himself."

[Pretty broad wheels are advisable if heavy loads are to be wheeled over soft ground, or if neat garden walks are to be travelled over.—ED.]

Feeding at the Stack in Winter.

We still see examples of this barbarous and unthrifty custom in our journeyings. Truth compels us to say that some of our neighbors practice it. If the country only had a society for the suppression of cruelty to brutes, as your city has, somebody would get into trouble.—What is laying a turtle on his back, or boring a hole through one of his flippers, in comparison with keeping one of the mammalia, with a nervous organization like that of man, under slow torture during the whole winter? With the best of food at the stack, the shelterless beast shivers and pines. With corn stalks and bog hay, it loses much of the flesh laid on in summer. It takes a good part of the spring and summer, in flush feed, to make up for the loss, and the profit of the animal to the farmer is nowhere.

The animal system is only a living stove, to be kept in heat by food. The lower the temperature the more wood it takes to keep up the heat of the stove. The colder the weather the more hay and provender it takes to keep up animal heat. At least a third of the fodder consumed at the stack is required to keep up animal heat, and so is wasted. Boards in the shape of good tight stables are much cheaper than hay. Do not keep any more stock than you can stable. Slow torture at the stack ought to be abolished by statute. The man who practices it needs an overseer to keep him out of the poor house. CONNECTICUT.

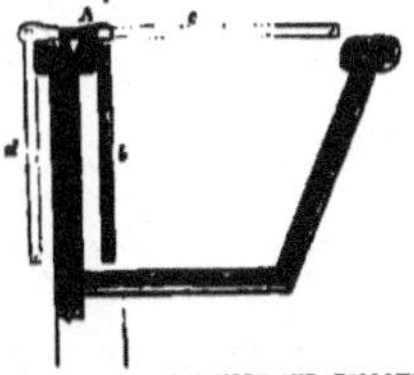

Fig. 1.—SECTION OF MANGER AND FOLLOWER.

How to Hang "Followers" in Horse Mangers.

Where there is a feeding alley, "followers," as they are usually hung, are a nuisance, in fact cannot be used. The Follower, as it is called, is a rack laid in the manger, which rests upon the fodder and prevents the horse throwing it out. Fig. 1 exhibits a section of a manger with a follower adapted to use in connection with a feeding alley. It is hung on double-jointed hinges, made of pieces of heavy plate iron, with holes punched in each end, measuring, from the edge of one hole to the center of the other, half the width of the manger-front.

Fig. 2 represents the follower hanging over the front of the manger into the alley. The engraver has represented an extra bar across the top, which is unnecessary.

Fig. 2.—FOLLOWER TURNED BACK.

The follower is made of 7/8-inch round iron, of a rectangular shape, to fit the manger, not reaching quite to the bottom as it hangs when the manger is empty, and having a free space of some 3 or 4 inches between the follower and the edge, and an equal space on the sides. Rather an elaborate hinge to be screwed on the front rail, is shown in fig. 2; but this is not necessary, as a much simpler contrivance, which any blacksmith will make, will answer equally well. With a follower of this kind, the hay, cut feed, or anything of that kind, may be thrown in from the feeding alley, the follower being turned over outside the manger and hanging in the alley, entirely out of the way. The use of a follower may not be apparent to farmers who have a great abundance of hay and no market for it; but in districts where hay is worth from 1 to 1½ cents per pound, even small daily wastes will be seriously felt at the end of the season.

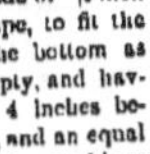

Fig. 3.

COMPOSTING MANURE.—Much can be done at this season to prepare manures for the field, or for spreading wherever they are wanted. With all that has been written and said upon the compost heap, few are aware of the importance of absolute fineness in fertilizing matter.

One element in the immediate effects of guano is the extreme fineness to which the particles are reduced. The success of liquid manures is owing, in part, to the same cause. The finer we can make our fertilizers the better for immediate results. In the compost heap at this season, there are three agencies at work to reduce the coarser particles of the manure, viz.: manipulation, fermentation, and frost. After the heap is formed in the usual manner with alternate layers of fresh manure and other material, and gone through with the first fermentation, it should be carefully forked or shoveled over, changing the whole mass, from top to bottom, and breaking all the lumps. The more thoroughly this is done the better. A new fermentation takes place inside, while the surface freezes and thaws with the changes of the weather. Labor upon the compost heap now will tell upon the growing crops next summer.

Barn Doors, Fastenings, Etc.

The discussion of any subject in the columns of the *Agriculturist* has the effect to set people thinking, and as a result we gather a crop of suggestions and new ideas which are often very valuable. We discussed barn-door fastenings not long since, and after the first publication had numerous suggestions, of which our readers had the benefit. Next to loose floors and springy cellars—swinging great doors are the greatest nuisance that a man can encumber his barn with. They are not only unwieldy, ever slamming and getting out of order, hard to fasten open, or shut, but really dangerous to life and limb to both men and animals. Sliding doors are the only suitable ones for outside barn-doors, large or small, and they are so easily hung and kept in repair, if well made, that, in point of economy simply, they are superior. Besides, they may be opened wide enough for a cat to enter, or to give a little change of air, or as easily, opened wide enough for a horse or for a load of hay. No wind moves them; there is no sagging, and no trouble from snow-drifts outside, or from snow and rain blowing in over the top. These doors are hung by cast iron "hangers,"—groved wheels bolted fast to the top of the door. These run upon an iron rod, well supported upon a bar or rail, crossing over the doorway, and extending to a distance beyond equal to the width of the door. This is protected by a little roof-like door-cap which, however, need not extend much beyond the width of the door. These doors may indeed be constructed and braced in the usual way, but are best made of two thicknesses of well-seasoned 5/8-in., clear, matched stuff. On the inside, boards of any convenient width may be used, and should be horizontal. The outside should be of boards only 4 or 5 inches wide, and put on at an angle of 45°. To give additional strength, a board 10 or 12 inches wide may be put across the top, outside, and 8-inch battens across the bottom and sides.

Fig. 1.—LATCH.

Fig. 2.—LATCH.

It is a matter of considerable interest to know how to fasten these doors securely and easily. They are usually fastened on the inside with a hasp and pin, or with a hook; if these are not securely pinned they can be opened with a knife from the outside, and simple inspection does not tell whether they are secure or not. Dr. Hexamer, of Westchester Co., many of whose contrivances for saving steps and labor about the barn are very good, uses latches on the following plan. Figure 1 shows the latch of a double barn-door, which is simply a flat hook and staple with a pendant piece of iron, of the shape shown, above the staple, and so hung that when the hook is in it must be fastened. It is easily seen from the inside whether it is so or not, and an attempt to open the door from the outside will also reveal the fact.

Figure 2 is a self-fastening latch for a single sliding door. The catch is in a gain in the inside of the post against which the door shuts, and the latch may be in a similar gain, or in a mortice in the door. This arrangement may sometimes be conveniently reversed by putting the latch in a mortice in the door post, in which case there should be a strong outside batten projecting as far as the latch does, to guard animals and men from harm from it, as well as to protect it from injury.

One door of every barn should lock from the outside. This will seem folly to many people, but we know that many barns are burnt by the pipe-fire of wandering "tramps," who always sleep in unlocked barns if they can, and that harness and other things are stolen in all parts of the country, more or less. It is usually best to lock one of the small doors, which should be hung on the inside, and locked with a strong hasp and good padlock, chained to the door.

Tim. Bunker on the Food Question.

"I knew we should catch it to-day," said Seth Twiggs, as he came into our house on the evening of Thanksgiving day, and seating himself comfortably upon the settle, blew a ring of smoke out of his mouth, as if it had been shot out of a rifle: "The Parson ginerally hits the nail on the head, and hit it square to-day, no mistake. We have sent off too many of our boys to the city. There isn't so much breadstuff raised in Hookertown as there was fifty years ago, and if it keeps on at this rate, somebody has got to starve bye and bye."

"That is to say, if every place is just like Hookertown," I responded.

Neighbor Twiggs' remark had reference to Mr. Spooner's Thanksgiving sermon, which was pretty much like all his sermons, whether on Sundays or not, "a word in season." You see, Mr. Spooner, like myself, belongs to the old school of folks, who have got so accustomed to making up our own minds on public questions, that we can't afford to take our opinions second hand. You see, most people around here in Connecticut have got a dreadful hankering after city life and fashions. They want something better than farming for their sons and daughters, though, according to my notion, farming, taking the long run, pays better than any other calling upon the face of the earth. The boys that grow up around here are smart, and would probably do well at almost any thing, if they had a fair chance. But Hookertown can't hold 'em any more than a pot can hold boiling water. Some of them have gone down South to try their fortunes, some to the West, but more to the City, which threatens to swallow up the country, which is a good deal like a man swallowing his own stomach. You see this state of things makes rather a dull look for the old parish, and worries the minister, and it works out in his sermons on Thanksgivings, and Fasts, and sometimes on Sundays. Some grumble about political preaching, and secular preaching, etc., but for my part, if a man has got any thing to say to make folks better, I never could see why it wan't jest as well to say it on Sunday as any other time. But the grumbling don't trouble Mr. Spooner much. He is independent as a wood-chopper, and knows he can get his bread and take care of himself, if the Hookertown people turn him out of the pulpit to-morrow, which they have no notion of doing. He speaks right square out, and nobody has any more doubt as to which side of a question he is on, than they have about sunrise.

Well, you see this food question is what the philosophers call a poser. If bread and meat are all the while getting dearer, and labor is growing cheaper, and that is the settled tendency of society, you see the time is coming when labor won't buy bread, and somebody must perish. That is the way things are working now, and wise men should be looking for a remedy.

Mr. Spooner showed this very clearly. It has been the tendency in Europe for a great many years—England hasn't raised her own breadstuffs for more than 30 years. The great mass of her people are gathered in cities, and large manufacturing towns, and there is not land enough left to raise a full supply of food for her population, even with their improved husbandry. She has to bring large quantities of wheat and other grains from the ports of the Mediterranean, and from across the Atlantic, to make up the deficiency. Now, if there should be short crops in these countries and in America, or if she should be at war with enemies strong enough to blockade her ports, nothing could prevent great distress and starvation.

The same social disease is beginning to work in this country. The price of food has more than doubled within a very few years, not only in cities but in the farming districts. Flour in Hookertown has been selling this fall at $15 a barrel; butter at 45 cents, and beefsteak at 30 cents per lb., and these things are just about a fair sample of everything else. Eight years ago these things could have been bought for less than half the money. This shows that mouths have multiplied faster than food. There are more consumers than producers. Farm labor in the same time has increased in value, but it has not kept pace with the increased price of food. Wheat has gone up from $1 to $2.50 a bushel—labor from five Yankee shillings to nine, which is an increase of more than one-half, and the labor is not near so good. The native born hired man of a generation ago, who worked for $12 a month and board, the year round, has pretty much disappeared, and we have in his stead the unskilled immigrant. This shows that labor is not comparatively as well rewarded. His day's work will not buy him as many comforts as it did 20 years ago. This shows that something is "rotten in Denmark," for the condition of the laboring class, and not that of the rich, is the measure of the prosperity of a country. It is a bad state of society where only a few are growing rich, and the many are just getting a living or suffering for the comforts of life.

Then, Mr. Spooner said, the Societies in the cities for the aid of children, were another indication of the same evil. Thousands are left every year in circumstances of extreme want, and there is no efficient remedy for their case but to find homes for them in the country, where they can help themselves. Thousands are sent off every year through these Societies, and a little is thus done to restore the disturbed balance of society.

The pith of the discourse was, that Hookertown was the center of the Universe, that farming was the best business, that those who were engaged in it should be content with such things as they had, and be thankful for them. He had some sly thrusts at clam-shell bonnets, silks, satins, and ribbons, fast men, and fast women, and the general extravagance of the times. These I suppose, were meant as sauce for the Thanksgiving turkey, and to help digestion.

"Well, Squire, what are you gwine to do about it. Food is getting higher every year, and labor don't keep up with it. The rich are growing richer, and the poor poorer. What are you gwine to do about it?" asked Seth Twiggs, as he knocked out the ashes of his third pipe and loaded again.

"Well," said I, "I am not going to whine about it. Of all remedies for a great public evil that of whining is the poorest. I have faith to believe that there is some way of deliverance from this and all other social evils. The high price of food is not going to last forever among this great people, with territory enough to raise breadstuffs for the world, were it only half tilled.

"All that Mr. Spooner says is as true as preaching. Things are a little unsettled just now, but they will come right after awhile. I have noticed that there is a tendency in Christian society to correct its own evils. Sometimes we have an outbreak of burglaries, bank robberies, and shop-lifting, and it seems as if society was going to ruin. But when the people get waked up, and a few of the thieves are convicted and sent to State's Prison, the times improve wonderfully. People are not going to live in miserable tenement houses, and suffer all the miseries of city poverty without learning something. Native born Americans certainly are not. I have noticed that many go to the city, do not succeed there, and come back agin wiser, if not better men. They find that their genius does not lie in the direction of trade, but they have a decided tact for making corn and potatoes grow. They support their families comfortably, and on the whole, are no worse for their city experience. Then I have noticed again, that a good many who succeed in the city, acquire a competence, and before they are spoiled, retire to the country to lead an industrious rural life. They become large producers of breadstuffs, and supply the city markets with fat cattle, sheep and swine. They rejoice in their well tilled farms, and in their flocks and herds. Then again, I have noticed that some of our very best small farmers and gardeners are city bred people, tradesmen, or mechanics, who from failure of health or disgust with the city, come into the country, near good markets, to support their families from the soil. They have thrifty habits, some capital, and succeed admirably by making the most of a little land. Thousands in these ways are changed from consumers into producers, every year. If multitudes flock to the city, multitudes come back to the country.

"And then there is a growing tendency among our city people to scatter themselves in the neighboring towns. A large part of the men who do business in New York, live out from five to fifty miles in the country. Some have small homesteads, but they are all to some extent cultivators, and draw a part of their support from the soil. And this tendency is on the increase, and will grow with the increased facilities for travel that every large city is making for itself. This will not only help to unburden the city, but will add to the production of the country, and help to make food cheaper."

"I shouldn't wonder if we had New Yorkers living in Hookertown, yet," said Seth.

"Stranger things have happened," said I.

"I shall beat'em on cabbage tho', if the smartest of 'em come," said Seth, with an extra puff.

"It takes Dutchmen for cabbage. You should not brag!" I continued.

"Then there is another thing in connection with this food question, which I have thought of a good deal. No man has begun to conceive of the great change which our improved farming tools are destined to make in the productiveness of human labor. A man is multiplied ten fold. We should have had a famine during the war, if it had not been for them, and food would have been a great deal dearer than it now is. The horse reaper and mower mean cheaper grain, and cheaper meats of every kind, that consume hay and grain. Every year is adding to these improved tools, and extending the fields of their usefulness. They come very slowly into use, but they are certainly coming; and they can not fail to do two things; to make farming pay better, and to cheapen the price of food. A vast deal of brain power is lavished upon these inventions, and it will have its reward in relieving the sweat of the brow.

"And then when steam gets into the field, as it must, upon the prairies at least, what may we not expect in the way of cheap Johnnycakes and bacon?"

"May I be there to see," exclaimed Seth, rising to go. "That is what other folks will do about it;—but what do you mean to do about it, Squire Bunker?"

"Do?" said I. "Why, I'll stick to the old farm, set my neighbors a good example, and die in the furrow. And if that ain't enough, I'll blow my trumpet in the *Agriculturist*, and set all the people from Maine to Texas, thinking on the food question."

"Good!" said Seth, as he went out. "That paper is the best tool yet out, to make bread cheap. It believes in brain manure."

Hookertown, Conn., Dec. 5th. } Yours to command,
TIMOTHY BUNKER, Esq.

The Best Style of Family or Dairy Cows, and How Obtained.

We have before us an article from a gentleman who has a rather large herd of milch cows, the surplus of which he advertises and puts upon the market and finds ready sale for at remunerative prices. It is natural that he should advocate such cows as he breeds, or at least breed such as he advocates, if he is a fair-minded man, and such we know him to be. The subject he proposes cannot but be discussed with profit, and we hope those who may disagree with him will respond. He writes:

"The subject that probably interests more of the readers of the *Agriculturist* than almost any other is, 'What is the most desirable kind of cows for family use or dairy purposes? In other words, what breed will produce the most value in milk, butter, and cheese, on a given amount of feed?' I will give you my experience for what it is worth. I have tried nearly all the various breeds, Alderneys, Ayrshires, Short Horns, Madagascars and natives, and I became satisfied, some six years ago, that 'Alderneys' gave the *richest milk* and produced the *best butter*, but thought 'thorough breds' too delicate in constitution for the general use of farmers. I then commenced crossing the "Alderneys" with all these breeds, and after careful observation I am convinced that Alderneys crossed with Ayrshires produce the best and most desirable cow to be had for all purposes. The Ayrshires are of good size, extremely hardy, and good milkers, but the quality of milk is no better than the Devons, natives, etc.; but cross the Alderneys with them and you get a hardy animal, with the rich milking quality of the Alderney. You increase the size over the thorough-bred Alderney. Half Alderney and half Ayrshire is, I think, the very best cow extant. I have now in my herd several heifers of this cross, three years old last spring, that the past season gave 12 to 14 quarts milk per day each, and made 12 pounds of splendid butter per week on good pasture. If the farmers in the dairy sections of our country would try the crossing of their present breeds of cows with thorough-bred Alderney bulls, they would greatly improve their stock, increase both the quantity and quality of their butter, and benefit the *millions* of *consumers* of these articles of necessity and luxury in every family. T. F.

Night Soil as a Manure.

The use of night soil as a fertilizer has frequently been advocated in these columns, and we have endeavored to show how a generally wasted article might be turned to account. Recently we have had sent to us, by several correspondents, an article that originally appeared in the *Springfield Republican*, which we quote:

"Very severe prohibitions have been issued in France, England and Germany, against the use of poudrette, imperfectly prepared, it having been proven by careful experiments that the fœcal matter of sinks cannot be converted with safety into garden manure under five years' careful preparation. Pestilential and other diseases are propagated by vegetables grown in soil thus manured. Yet, it is stated that these death-dispensing deposits are absolutely used in the market gardens around our large American cities in their natural state, and many of the fruits and vegetables so grown can be told by the nostrils or the taste before they are cooked, and in the process of cooking. It is the opinion of skillful medical observers, that nearly all the novel diseases which now afflict many American cities, owe their origin to the organic diseased matter taken up by vegetables and fruits grown in soil dressed by the fœcal matter of the sinks, and transferred to the stomach. Galloping consumption in persons whose families have never been subject to this terrible disease have been traced to the use of vegetables grown by poudrette."

These are serious charges, which if true would warrant the denunciation contained in the article, and our readers need not be told that if there were the least foundation for such an alarming report we should not only not advocate the use of night soil, but be among the first to condemn it. Let us look a little at the alleged facts in the above statement. Are there any "prohibitions" in France, England and Germany? As to the last named country, we cannot speak so positively, but in England, the use of city sewage has been attended with such profitable results, that one of the important problems of the day is, to increase its employment, and prevent a fearful waste. In olden times, 1789, there was a prohibition in France, but the restriction was long ago removed, and we are quite certain that it has not been renewed, as the most recent French work on gardening, only a few weeks old, speaks of the use of night soil. The work of M. Gressent, 1865, gives plans of some of the celebrated market gardens, in which are tanks for holding liquid manure, made from this "death dispensing deposit." Joigneaux, in the most recent and most elaborate work on gardening yet published in France, says that the exclusive use of fæcal matters may give a bad flavor to vegetables, but advises their use when composted with other matters. It is very probable that a plant, especially an edible root, if grown in ground containing a large quantity of recent night soil, would have an unpleasant flavor. Yet we have eaten vegetables from a garden where this manure was used exclusively for a series of years, and though our prejudices kept us on the lookout for something unpleasant in their flavor, we failed to detect it.

In China and Japan their success in gardening—for their agriculture is almost all gardening—has for centuries depended upon the use of this manure, as they have scarcely any other.

As to the medical view of the case, no names being given to the "medical observers" we attach no weight to their "opinion." As far as negative testimony to this point goes, we have consulted with two of the most eminent physicians—men who are known everywhere as among the first in their profession—and they have never heard of, or read of, any disease being attributed to the use of vegetables treated with this manure.

In all cases we have advised the composting and deordorizing of the night soil, and we believe that when prepared thus, it may be used with as much safety as any other fertilizer. We regret that a paper so generally correct as the *Springfield Republican* should have given what seems to us an unfounded and needless alarm.

Sense at the "Farmers' Club."—Doubtless many who read the reports of the so-called Farmers' Club, really believe that a meeting of farmers assembles in New York to discuss farming matters. It is simply a miscellaneous gathering, including persons, who, by carrying on business in the city, are enabled to keep up a farm in the suburbs; doctors whose practice does not seem to occupy all their time; men who have given up farming to earn a living by their wits, and everlasting talkers, who are always delighted with the sound of their own voices. These people get together and discuss, with equal gravity, the influence of the moon, or the last invention in the way of bitters. The reports of what they do are about the funniest reading extant, and were it not for their comical character, it would be a great waste of paper on the part of the *Tribune* to publish them. These reports, however, have some good things put in by the reporter, or from his correspondence; these save the whole thing from being utterly ridiculous. Of late, the Club, having exhausted agriculture, have turned their attention to medicine—and as the talkers there seem to know as much about one subject as they do about another, they discoursed about curing fever and ague as glibly as they would the sticking of pigs. There is no knowing but the Club would have exhausted medicine and tried its facile hand at theology, had not a live farmer happened in, who entertained the singular notion that a Farmers' Club was for the purpose of discussing farming. We read in the report: "Dr. Hexamer inveighed at some length against the discussion of medical questions by a Farmers' Club." Keep on, Doctor, with your "inveighing;" you used to be a good practitioner before you turned farmer, and if you will only cure the Farmers' Club of *cacoethes loquendi*, we shall believe that your skill is equal to the most desperate cases.

How New York is Supplied with Flowers.

In a large city the sale of cut flowers, in the form of bouquets, baskets, table decorations, and the like, in the aggregate amounts to a very large sum. Every wedding, party, or similar occasion makes a great demand for flowers, and during the holidays all the sources of supply are taxed to their utmost. It would not be extravagant to estimate the expenditure for flowers in New York City on New Years day at from thirty thousand to forty thousand Dollars. The little bunch of violets offered on the streets, by the flower girls, for a dime, as well as the choice bouquet furnished at the florists' stores for $20 and upwards, all require flowers, and for a good part of the year flowers that are grown under glass. In all sorts of odd and out of the way places we find small greenhouses, in which these are produced. The neighborhood of Hoboken, N. J., is especially noted for the quantity of flowers produced by the German growers. These are frequently mechanics, shoemakers, tailors, etc., who have small glass structures, and generally grow but one or a few kinds of flowers. One will grow violets, another carnations, another heliotropes, and so on. By giving attention to only one or two varieties, these humble cultivators often attain greater perfection in their products than do larger establishments where there are many varieties. The flowers are gathered from these places by middlemen, who bring them to New York for sale to the bouquet makers. These flowers are cut with great care, and the buyer gets flowers only, without any extra buds, and seldom any stem. Indeed, the bouquet maker can furnish a better stem, for his purposes, from a bit of broom corn or a sliver of wood, than the one naturally belonging to the flower. The green-houses referred to are, however, small affairs when compared with the large establishments, in which sufficient capital allows the erection of the best houses and the use of all the modern appliances.

One of the most extensive florists' establishments in the vicinity of New York, is that of John Henderson & Co., Flushing, L. I., where the production of cut flowers is made the leading business. The range of glass is extensive, there being twelve houses, each 100 feet long, built on the low roofed plan, described in Oct., 1865; these houses are all side by side, on what is called the ridge and furrow system. Besides houses there is about as much area occupied by buildings of other styles. The camellia house is very spacious, and the camellias are planted out in the open ground of the house. Each of the twelve buildings above referred to is generally occupied by one kind of plant. To look through a house a hundred feet long, entirely filled with Carnations, Bouvardias, or other plants, has a singular effect. Those who pet a single plant with great care will experience no great amount of pleasure at seeing things they have learned to regard as individuals, massed into such crowds, and with no more personal identity than a soldier in an army. In looking through such an establishment, one almost gets tired of flowers. A sheet of scarlet is seen in one house, a broad bed of white in another, lavender color in another, and one goes away with his senses of sight and smell so overwhelmed by quantity that he has lost all idea of quality. It is only when the individual flowers get out of the crowded green-houses, and passing through the hands of the expert bouquet-maker are worked up into beautiful combinations, that they again seem to us objects of beauty, and not stock in trade.

[COPYRIGHT SECURED.]

HEAD OF A CALF.—PAINTED BY ROSA BONHEUR.—*Engraved for the American Agriculturist.*

We have had the pleasure repeatedly of presenting our readers with engravings of animals from the chaste pencil of that really wonderful woman, Rosa Bonheur, whose success as an animal painter is so remarkable. This is due altogether to her faithful study of nature, and great familiarity with the animals which she paints. Her studio is said to be located almost in the very midst of her animals, a number of which she maintains in luxurious idleness for the purpose of getting "studies" of them in all their different attitudes and positions. There is something so young and green, and playful and "butty" in that calf's head, that we enjoy looking at it, now, as much as we did when we first saw the picture, although there is something painful to be obliged to repress the desire to rub the fellow behind the horns and scratch its soft ears. Mademoiselle Rosa's history is somewhat remarkable, showing that distinction comes almost surely from faithfully following out natural inclinations. Her father was a painter. Rosa was a poor scholar and very sensitive, and so was taken from school and allowed to draw and paint. She was so fond of animals that she could not be prevented attending markets and fairs, and making her studies at butchers' stalls, and most likely at the abbatoirs, too. So soon she became distinguished for her freedom from conventionality—or imitation of other artists—and for her bold, life-like delineations of animals.

We need in this country artists of high character and integrity, who shall give to the study of our domestic animals the same careful labor. Several who might distinguish themselves with comparatively little trouble, are so taken up with painting scenes from the war, or with other subjects for which there is great demand, that cattle and sheep are neglected; or if studied, the lean kine and the dung-smeared, the scabby, tag-rag sheep at the end of a hard winter, and starey, half starved calves are taken as fit models. Pictures of such will sell to city gentlemen of fortune, who hardly know how an animal should look, or who remember the cattle on the run-down farm of their boyhood, which they left in disgust at 16; but they will not be bought by anybody in whose breast emotions of pity and indignation are excited at the sight, and they will spoil the sale, to such people, of the fine pictures in which they are introduced. We need true artists who will study well the points of fine animals, and portray them. The great beauty of well bred stock with requisite skill can be placed upon the canvas and upon the engraver's block.

Violets New and Old.

A bunch of Violets on Christmas day! how beautiful they are, and then, how they fill the room with an odor, more grateful than any incense that will be burned in celebrating the holiday. What a pity it seems, that our native violets—or at least the showy ones—have no odor. For the violet of poetry we have to go across the water, and right beautiful things do we receive. The name given to the European species, *Viola odorata*, is strikingly appropriate, for no flower excels it in the abundance, and at the same time the delicacy, of its perfume. A single little flower will manifest its presence to the senses, while a handful of them do not give of a fragrance strong enough to be oppressive. The original single species has been greatly improved upon, and we have now plants that bloom more abundantly, and that give flowers of different shades, down to white, and even double ones, some of which are very large. One of the best of the older varieties is the Neapolitan, double, of a pure violet color, a free bloomer and very fragrant. A quite recent variety is *La Reine des Violettes*—or Queen of Violets—a very large flower, as double as a rose, and looking as unlike a violet as need be. As we have seen it, it does not appear to be a very free bloomer. The English florists announce three or four other new varieties not yet tested in this country.

The Russian Violet belongs to another species, and has already given some well marked varieties, one of the latest of which is called the Czar. Mr George Such, of South Amboy, N. J., sent us materials for the accompanying illustration, and the following notes upon the variety

"This fine flower was obtained from seed by Mr. Graham, of Crawford, in England. It is an improvement on the old Russian Violet, the flowers being very large and sweet, of a fine deep blue. The plant is remarkable for extreme luxuriance of growth; some plants in pots having produced more than one hundred and thirty flowers to a root, many of the blooms measuring an inch and a quarter in depth.

"A writer in the *London Cottage Gardener*, says: 'I have now (Nov. 3d), some splendid plants with full-blown flowers, which from their wonderful size and sweetness, cannot be surpassed; nor, indeed, can any violet come near the Czar.' Another, under the heading of 'New things I have tried,' says, 'the Czar Violet has proved not only hardy, but very prolific. Its flowers are not only larger than the older kinds, but are decidedly superior in fragance.' Mr. Graham, the raiser, says, 'the Czar Violet is now in bloom (October 1st), and will continue so through the winter, even during frost and under snow, until May.'

"*Viola cornuta*, which is now much used in England as a bedding plant, is not a novelty, having been introduced from Spain in 1776. It was figured in the *Botanical Magazine*; but with this exception, has remained for ninety years almost unnoticed. The flowers are slightly fragrant, of a delicate slate-blue, a color very useful for toning down, and rendering more effective the brilliant and glowing colors.

"In England, *Viola cornuta* is 'extremely hardy,' thriving without care in any common garden soil, and flowering abundantly throughout the summer. On light and dry soils, however, the flowers are not so large as those from plants on heavier and moister ground. There are three or four varieties of this violet, the true one being of better habit of growth and more free flowering than the others."

Violets when grown in the garden do much better in a partially shaded place. They may be had almost any time in the winter if one has a frame and a few sashes, as it takes only a slight heat, that of the sun, to start them into flower. The plants are set in the frame in good soil, in August or September, and when cool weather comes on they are covered at night. By a proper management of the sashes, flowers

NEW RUSSIAN VIOLET—THE CZAR.

may be had until early winter. For later flowers, the plants are covered with leaves, which, by excluding the light keep them dormant. When wanted to bloom, the leaves are removed and a few days of sun will bring them out.

Propagating the Blackberry.

BY A. S. FULLER.

The most common method of propagating the blackberry is by cuttings of the roots, which may be made in the fall or early in spring—the former being preferable.

Take up the roots when the plants have ceased growing, and cut them into pieces of from one to three inches in length. Then prepare some boxes, by boring holes in the bottom to

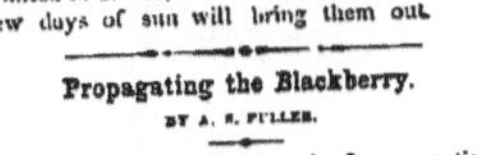

Fig. 1.—BURYING CUTTINGS.

insure a good drainage, and place a layer of straw over the holes to prevent the soil from falling through; over this put a layer of roots, then another layer of soil, and so on alternately until the box is full.

Bury the boxes containing the roots, on a dry knoll or slight elevation in the garden, bank them up with soil, and cover so deeply that the roots will not be frozen. In addition to this, it is well to cover the whole with boards to carry off the water, and if the soil is naturally tenacious and wet, a small excavation should be made at a point that will be under the center of the box when put in place, as shown in figure 1.

This arrangement will allow any surplus moisture which may accumulate in the boxes to drain off. Early in spring, so soon as the weather and soil will permit, take out the roots and plant them in good rich soil, placing the pieces about three or four inches apart, in drills, and covering them two to four inches deep, according to the nature of the soil. If it is a heavy one, two inches will be sufficient. When the plants are to be cultivated with the plow or cultivator, the drills should be three feet apart; but the best method is to place them not more than eighteen inches or two feet apart, and cultivate entirely with the hoe or fork. In a naturally dry and porous soil, it is a good plan to cover the entire surface, at the time of planting, with a liberal dressing of some coarse material as a mulch. This will ensure a supply of moisture, and often save a large portion of the cuttings, if not the entire stock. Cuttings made in the fall and placed where they will not freeze during winter, have an advantage over those made in the spring, from the fact that the peculiar process which always precedes the formation of roots, called the *callus*, has sufficient time for full development before actual root growth commences. The new roots are usually emitted from the ends of the cuttings where the callus appears. The callus is always produced first, roots succeed it, but what relation the callus bears to the root is not fully known; it appears to hold the same relation to it that the cotyledons of some seeds do to the germ, *i. e.* it supplies the roots with necessary food until they are sufficiently advanced and able to extract it from the soil themselves.

The buds from which the stems are produced are distinctly adventitious, that is they do not arise from any previously formed or latent bud, but are developed from the matter between the bark and wood. From this point the bud originates; first, by a very minute aggregation of cells, which assumes a conical shape, pressing outward through the bark and up to the surface, where the leaves are spread out to the light and air. Sometimes several buds will be produced on a very small piece of root; but when this occurs all will be comparatively feeble if they continue to grow. In a majority of such cases the strongest of them will take the lead and the others fail.

Figure 2 shows a piece of root with two shoots, one of which has reached the surface, and the leaves expanding. Plants grown in this manner are much better than those produced in the natural manner from suckers, because they are more abundantly supplied with fibrous roots. Root cuttings of from one to three inches in length, planted in good soil, will make plants one to three feet high the first season. Plants may also be taken up, and the roots made into cuttings, in the spring, and planted in the same manner as described for those made in the fall.

When the variety is very scarce, then any small roots may be used for propagating, but in such cases it is best not to attempt it in the open ground, but place them in a propagating house. Cut the roots into pieces of from one-half to one inch long, mix with sand, and place in a warm situation, but not in so high a temperature as to force the formation of buds. When the callus is formed, and buds begin to show themselves upon the surface, which they should do in four to six weeks, place them in soil composed of equal parts of leaf mold and sand, and in a position where they will receive a heat of seventy-five to ninety degrees.

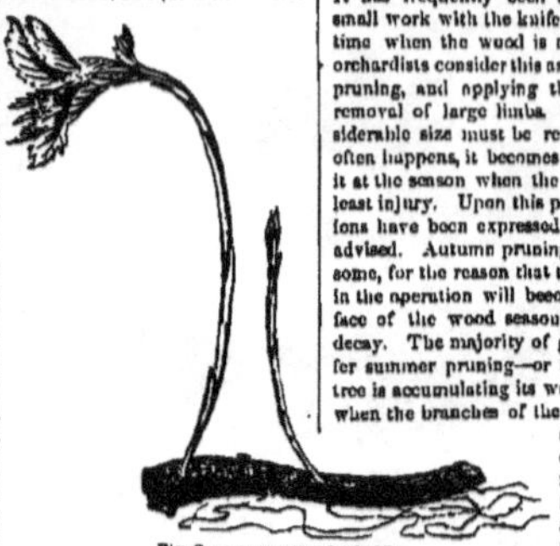

Fig. 2.—BLACKBERRY SHOOT.

When the plants have made a growth of four to six inches, they may be potted singly, or planted out into the open ground, provided the weather is warm and there is no danger of their becoming checked by cold. The blackberry may also be propagated from green wood in summer, in the propagating-house, or early in Spring by cuttings from plants forced for the purpose.

The same process used by propagators in multiplying grapes and other plants from green wood is equally applicable to the blackberry.

Single bud cuttings may be made of the mature wood in the fall, always choosing the medium sized branches, and those that have not become very hard; or in other words, not fully ripe. Plant in boxes or pots, and place in a temperature of from 80 to 100 degrees. This is not quite so certain a method as the others, still, with some varieties, very good plants can be produced by an experienced propagator.

Layering the branches in summer is often practiced with success, especially with some varieties. In making layers, that portion to be covered should be stripped of its leaves, and then a small incision made on the branch, and on the under side, as is usually done when layering woody plants. Root cuttings, however, produce the very best plants, and the number that can be made from the roots of one large stool, if given proper care, is much greater than one would suppose who has never tried it.

DANA'S HOVEY PEAR.—The London Gardener's Chronicle gives a description and (very poor) figure of this American variety, and says: "Its flesh is melting and juicy, its flavor more delicious than that of any pear known, being that of the Winter Nelis, with a slight smack of the Seckel; its season is December until January. When this pretty and delicious pear becomes known, a dish of them at dessert will be as much sought after as a dish of old Golden Pippins in the last Century."

Ways and Means in Pruning.

Notwithstanding the fact that in our notes for the month there is always a timely word upon all the important operations in the orchard, we have many letters asking about pruning, especially as to the time at which it is to be done. It has frequently been stated here that the small work with the knife may be done at any time when the wood is not frozen; but most orchardists consider this as trimming rather than pruning, and applying the latter term to the removal of large limbs. When limbs of considerable size must be removed, and this too often happens, it becomes of importance to do it at the season when the tree will sustain the least injury. Upon this point a variety of opinions have been expressed and different seasons advised. Autumn pruning is recommended by some, for the reason that the wounds thus made in the operation will become dry and the surface of the wood seasoned and secured from decay. The majority of good orchardists prefer summer pruning—or that done when the tree is accumulating its woody deposit. This is when the branches of the year have ceased to elongate, and the forces of growth are directed to preparing for the vegetation of another year. At this time the process of healing goes on more rapidly than at any other, but it has the disadvantage of being a season when there is so much other work to be done that the labor cannot be given to the orchard. Another, but a minor disadvantage is, that the trees being covered with foliage the effect of the removal is not so readily observed. The season in which there is most leisure, and perhaps the next best to the one last mentioned, is after the severity of winter is over, but before the swelling of the buds indicates the awakening of vegetation. Though late winter is not the best season, it is preferable to do the work then than to neglect it altogether. As soon as the tree starts into growth no wound should be made, as there will be a disagreeable and injurious out-pouring of sap.

As to the operation itself, it should be done with judgment and care. Cutting away a limb without a clear idea of the object to be gained—going into a tree with an axe and chopping here and there, is not pruning, but butchery. Having determined upon the removal of a limb, it should be sawed off neatly, close to the main branch. It is not rare to see a butt of a foot or more in length left by the pruner; this is a most mischievous practice, as a crowd of small branches will usually spring from the base of this stump, as shown in the engraving, while the upper end, having no supply of sap, will decay. Works upon orchard culture generally recommend that the wound be made no larger than the base of the limb removed. In France, where tree culture is made a profession, the most recent writers advocate pruning close to the trunk, and covering the wound with some preparation.

BAD PRUNING.

In France coal-tar is used on all trees except stone-fruits—but while we mention this as a matter of interest, we do not advise its use. It may be that our coal-tar is different from theirs—at all events so much injury has been done to plants in this country by the various products of coal and petroleum that we advise great caution in their use. Grafting wax, made warm enough to apply with a brush is cheap, safe, and efficacious, as is the shellac and alcohol paint, but the materials for this are now very expensive.

The rough surface left by the saw should be smoothed with a knife or drawing knife before using the wax. Limbs of considerable size may be neatly removed by means of a large, stout, and sharp chisel, driven from below by a wooden mallet.

The Care of Young Trees.

There would be much less said about pruning and much less pruning to be done, were it generally known—and the knowledge acted upon—that we have it in our power to form the tree while young, and so regulate the young growth that the removal of large limbs would be a rare necessity. The too common method is, to trim the trees up, to a small head, at planting, and then let them grow until they come into fruit, when it is discovered that pruning is needed, and there is a great lopping off of useless limbs, that with proper treatment would never have grown. Those who will have their trees trimmed high, doubtless have good reasons for the practice, but the best experience teaches that low headed trees are, other things being equal, more exempt from those troubles dependent upon climatic influences, than those trained to a tall naked trunk. Our present object is not to discuss the general subject of pruning young trees, but to point out a trouble that often arises from allowing them to have their own way. We refer to the formation of crotches, or a division of the trunk into two nearly equal branches, which may again subdivide in a similar manner, and thus render the tree liable to split. In forming the young tree in the nursery this is avoided by all intelligent growers; but all trees are not treated as they should be, even in the nursery, and we often see young orchards containing examples of very bad management. When a crotched tree of this kind is discovered, it is best to remedy the defect even at the considerable sacrifice of one-half of the present growth. The manner of treatment is to cut away one of the branches that form the fork, retaining the one that can be most readily brought to the upright position; in removing the limb, enough of its base is left to afford a support to which the remaining one may be secured, and this is then brought as nearly erect as possible and tied to the butt, as in the engraving. When the erect position has become established, the supporting portion is cut away even with the trunk; if this be done at the usual season of pruning, the wound will soon heal over.

EARLY MAY AND EARLY RICHMOND CHERRY.—This popular and early market cherry has also been called Kentish. It seems to be established that it is a Virginia seedling, long known in the State where it originated, as the Early May. The elder Prince procured the variety from Richmond, Va., and called it the "Richmond." The Illinois State Hort'l Society, at its recent meeting, voted to adopt the name Early May.

Profits from Small Places.

In January, we alluded to some of the methods by which, in thickly peopled districts, and in towns and villages, small tracts of land might be rendered profitable. The raising for sale of such plants as are usually transplanted, was hinted at as a considerable source of profit. Tomatoes, egg plants, peppers, early cabbages, cauliflowers, cucumbers and melons, will usually meet with a ready sale, if produced under glass a little earlier than they can be raised in the open ground; while late cabbages, celery, asparagus roots, etc., may be raised without the use of glass. Let one make a business of supplying good plants and he will soon find that the majority of his neighbors will prefer to buy plants to raising them. Then, there are always a certain number of people who forgot to sow at the proper time, or who had "bad luck" with their seeds, who would be glad to make up for their neglect by purchase. The earliest plants are raised in hot-beds, but these are not absolutely necessary, as cold frames are more easily managed, and will bring forward many things sufficiently early. For hot-beds or cold frames, sashes will be required in number according to the extent of the operations. The usual size is 3 × 6 feet, but any other size may be made to answer. Beginners had better try a *mild* hot-bed, with a gentle heat to start the seeds. Choose a sheltered place, facing the south, fix on the size of the bed for the number of sashes to be used, and make an excavation about two feet deep. Then drive down stakes and board up the sides of the pit, allowing the boards at the front to come 12 inches above the surface, while those at the rear are 18 inches above. Put cross-pieces 3 inches wide from front to rear, as far apart as the sashes require; in the center of each cross-piece, nail a strip an inch square, running the whole length; this will serve as a guide for the sash to run against. Fill the trench with fermenting manure that has previously been turned over several times, throwing it in gradually and beating it down firmly with the fork; cover it with 6 inches of good light soil, and put on the sashes. The bed will soon become very hot, and when the thermometer shows that the heat is declining below 100°, the seeds may be sown. Plants from warm countries, such as tomatoes, egg plants and peppers, need the hot-bed more than do cabbages, etc. The plants, as soon as up, require air during the middle of the day, and to be covered at night. Cold frames are far preferable for those who have had no experience with plants under glass. A frame like the above is used, but no excavation is needed. It is put over well prepared, light, rich soil, and the sashes kept on during the day; shutters or mats are put over them at night, and when the soil, from receiving heat by day and being prevented from giving it off at night, has become well warmed, the seeds may be sown. After the plants are up, the beds will need daily care. Give air, by tilting the sash, or removing it altogether, according to the weather. Close the sash early in the afternoon, before the soil begins to cool, and cover the glass at night to retain the heat. Plants in frames will need thinning, weeding and watering. Watering should not be done with cold water, but it should always be brought to the temperature of the earth in the frames. Where means will allow, it is better to have extra frames into which the plants may be transplanted when large enough, in order to give them room. Tomatoes in particular, are benefited by this treatment. Whenever the weather will allow, keep the glass off altogether, except at night. Cucumbers and melons may be planted on inverted sods cut into pieces 3 inches square, and the plants be raised to a size that will render them safe from the attacks of insects when they are put out. By the use of cold frames, plants may be had ready for sale two or three weeks earlier than if the seeds were sown in the open ground. The chief precautions are, to avoid burning the plants by keeping the sashes closed during the day, and to avoid chilling them by delaying the covering too late at night. The end of February is quite early enough to make hot-beds in the latitude of New York, and cold frames may be started in March. There are other things that may be profitably raised by the occupants of village and town lots that will be noticed another month.

BEURRE CLAIRGEAU.

A Noble Pear—The Beurre Clairgeau.

In a note on pears in January, it was remarked that the most popular fruits were not those that had the highest rank with the pomologist. The Beurré Clairgeau is one of those pears that, without ranking as "*best*," has so many good qualities that when it becomes better known, it will doubtless hold a high place in popular estimation. Like many other valuable fruits, this was a chance seedling, found at Nantes, France, about 1839, by Pierre Clairgeau, a gardener, by whose name the fruit is now known.

The tree is a handsome one, a good grower, and a remarkably abundant bearer. It does not grow well upon Quince Stock, though there are reports of its success when double worked. The fruit is of large size, and what is an important quality, hangs well upon the tree. The form of the fruit is shown in the engraving, from which will be seen the peculiar insertion of the stem, which is very short in proportion to the size of the fruit, and the somewhat curved form of the pear. The skin is yellow, with green and brown dots, and upon the sunny side it is washed with vermillion; some specimens are more or less russeted. When well ripened and colored, no pear can make a finer show. The flesh is very white, fine, juicy, and melting, vinous, and with a delicate perfume. Pomologists differ in their views as to quality; while those of France consider it of first quality, it does not rank with us as more than second rate. The fruit is generally above the medium size, and some very large specimens have been grown. One received a prize at the Horticultural Society of Paris, that weighed one kilogramme—or about two and a quarter pounds. The fruit ripens in October, and will, with care, keep into December.

The size and great beauty of this variety make it a valuable market fruit, while the excellent qualities of the tree commend it to the planter.

Straw Covers for Hot-Beds and Cold Frames.

Some covering for the sashes of a hot-bed or cold frame is absolutely necessary to prevent the loss of heat by radiation at night. Shutters, made of light boards, and straw mats are most generally used. We have before described the manner of making straw mats, which are on many accounts the most convenient covering. We have used straw covers, or frames filled with straw, with much satisfaction, and though they are less conveniently stored away than are the mats, they are made with greater rapidity. For the frames, take three pieces of inch-board 3 inches wide, and as long as the sash; lay down two of these as far apart as the width of the sash, and the other one midway between the two; cross pieces, of half-inch stuff, 3 inches wide, are nailed on at each end, and similar pieces are nailed on between the end pieces at distances of a foot. Now turn the frame over and fill it with straight straw regularly laid in, and nail a cross piece over the straw at each end. The straw is to be further secured by a tarred string over it, opposite the cross pieces, on the other side, fastening each piece of string securely by tacks or small nails. Sometimes the frames are made with wooden cross pieces above, instead of the strings, but this renders the frame heavier, and does not allow the water to run off so readily.

Frames of this kind, when not in use, should be put under cover—taking care that they be thoroughly dried before they are put away. The covering and uncovering the beds is best done by two persons, as then the straw frames may be lifted; shoving them wears the paint off the sashes; this may be avoided by nailing strips upon the sashes to slide upon.

Hollies—American and European.

There is, perhaps, no indigenous evergreen tree less generally known than our native Holly, *Ilex opaca.* The reasons for this probably are, that it is found, in its wild state, chiefly near the coast, and its growth is so slow that nurserymen find but little inducement to raise it for sale. Indeed it grows so slowly, that we seldom see it in cultivation, other than as a shrub, while under favorable circumstances it forms a tree 30 to 40 feet high. Eastern Massachusetts is its northern limit, as a native tree, and it is found all along the coast as far as Florida. There are, or were a few years ago, at the Highlands of Neversink, the well-known landmark at the entrance of the harbor of New York, some remarkable specimens of this tree, the trunks of which were as large as a man's body. The tree, when developed under favorable circumstances, is a very symmetrical one, with an erect trunk, of a light ash-gray color, and nearly horizontal branches. The leaves are of the size and shape of those shown in the engraving, of a very thick leathery texture; they are sharp-pointed and their wavy margins bear sharp spines; their green color is not so dark as that of the European Holly, and their surface is less shining. The flowers are not showy, being of a greenish white. These are succeeded by bright scarlet berries, which remain on all winter, and give the tree a brilliant appearance. From its intrinsic beauty, as well as from the traditional association of Holly with Christmas, this is one of the evergreens most sought after for holiday decorations. The wood of the tree is very hard, and is used for making small articles in which this quality is required, such as screws, whip-handles, etc. It is considered to take color better than any other wood, and is used for fancy cabinet work. The Holly may be raised from seeds, but they require to lie in the rot-heap a year before planting them. Where it is found growing wild, there are usually plenty of young seedlings that may be removed in early spring. Naturally, our Holly grows in a great variety of situations, and seems to flourish in both dry and rocky soils, and in low lands. In cultivation it does best in a partial shade. Were it not for its very slow growth, this Holly would be an admirable hedge-plant, but we do not find it used for that purpose, and when met with in cultivation, which is rarely, it is found chiefly as an ornamental shrub, or at most, as a small tree.

The European Holly, *Ilex aquifolium*, has the same general character as our own, but its foliage, as shown in figure 2, is of a different shape, and of a shining green that makes it a much handsomer plant. It is largely employed in Europe as a hedge-plant, as well as an ornamental tree or shrub. There are many varieties, having leaves in shape and size different from the ordinary, as well as several with the leaves blotched and margined with white and yellow.

Fig. 1.—AMERICAN HOLLY.

Some of these striking varieties are among the most highly prized shrubs for the lawn. The European Holly is not hardy enough with us, to be recommended for general cultivation, though in some sheltered localities it succeeds tolerably well. We have four other evergreen species of *Ilex*, all shrubs; these, except the Ink-berry, are mostly southern. The Black Alder, so conspicuous in autumn for its numerous scarlet berries, was formerly called *Prinos*, but is now put in the same genus as the Holly, and called *Ilex verticillata.*

Fig. 2.—EUROPEAN HOLLY.

The Use of a Straw Bed.

Last year we gave an account of growing potatoes under straw in the larger way, we now present the garden experience of "Hoosier," Rush County, Ind.: "Last summer I planted my potatoes under straw, just as an experiment. I planted the 'Peach Blows,' and, by the way, there no better potatoes. The potatoes were planted in drills, two feet apart, the distance between the potatoes being about six inches; covered them with a light coat of soil, then about six inches of old straw. They came up finely and grew well. The bugs made an assault on the vines, but I opened my light artillery—a little coal oil and a brushy switch —upon the greedy host, and shortly not a 'blistering imp' could be found. This fall, when potato digging time came round, I had an easy job of it. With a fork I turned over the straw, and there clear and bright lay the crimson crew. Picking them up was an easy matter, and soon they were beyond the chilly winds and withering frosts. They turned out exceedingly well, but the ground mice, moles, and rats, left many proofs of their festivals.

"I did not find a single decayed potato among the lot, a rare thing for this year, for 'King Rot' has swept, scourge like, over the land. Next year all the potatoes I plant, early and late, shall have a straw bed over them. The straw enriches the soil, keeps it mellow, and makes an excellent garden plat, free from weeds and grass.

THE "BIG TREE" OF CALIFORNIA.—It is a singular fact that some trees make a more rapid growth, and flourish better in every way, in a country quite different from their own. Our most rapid growing deciduous and evergreen trees are foreigners, and in California, that land of remarkable trees, an *Eucalyptus* from Australia is found to excel in vigor any of the native trees, and will probably become the leading tree of the country. In Great Britain, the *Sequoia gigantea*, the California "Big Tree," which with us is at best uncertain, flourishes remarkably. Some statistics have been published by the Scottish Arboricultural Society, giving the hight and age of trees of this species, in different parts of the kingdom. Several at the age of five years are twelve feet high, others at seven years are eighteen feet, and trees ten years old are about twenty-one feet in hight.

THE HOUSEHOLD.

(☞ For other Household Items, see "Basket" pages.)

Household Ornaments.

Household ornaments are not perhaps so essential in the country as in the city, where people are necessarily cut off from the fields and woods with their thousand beautiful things. But every where pretty articles of furniture are prized, and perform an important office in the education of children. The only objection to them in many houses is their cost. We frequently give illustrations of such ornaments, and show how they may be constructed. Any one ingenious with the knife or handy with the needle can learn to make them, and thus add to their own usefulness, while they adorn their houses.

Fig. 1, shows a match safe, made from a common cigar box, or any other thin bit of board. It is easy to have black walnut, butternut, oak, or other ornamental wood sawed thin for this purpose. The shield should first be marked out with a pencil according to the design. The cutting can all be done with a sharp penknife, and will afford very good amusement for a winter evening. The large star in the centre forms the hole to hang up the box when finished. The box, made as shown in fig. 1, can be put together, and fastened to the shield with a little glue. Such a match safe, hung up over the mantle piece or near the stove where the fire is to be kindled or lamps lighted, will help essentially in the formation of orderly habits. There will always be a place for the matches, and the matches can be kept in their place. By enlarging the pattern, boxes can be made that will answer other purposes.

Fig. 1.—MATCH SAFE.

Fig. 2, shows a bracket shelf, consisting of three parts, and made like No. 1. The article may be suspended upon the wall in any convenient place by small brass rings near each end of the shelf, or upon brass headed pins or common nails fitted for the tops of the groves under the shelf. The pins give the firmest support. *B*, in fig. 3, gives a side view of the bracket, which goes under the middle of the shelf to support *A*. This may be fastened to the back and to the shelf with small wooden pins and glue, or with the glue alone. The pins make the best job. After the work with the knife is done, fine sand paper may be applied to give it a finish. It may also be varnished, or rubbed over with linseed oil.

Fig. 2.—BRACKET.

Fig. 4, shows a pattern of a pen wiper, and calls for the needle and scissors. It may be made of any convenient size or material. The foundation piece may be of broadcloth, the top of silk, and the intermediate pieces, for the process of wiping, of less valuable cloth. The mice are the nicest part of the work, and require mouse colored velvet, and some beads for the eyes. The bag of malt may be filled with any substance that will present a smooth surface. If shot or sand are put in it, the article will serve the double purpose of pen wiper and paper holder, quite as good if not as pretty as the manufactured glass ones that cost a dollar or more.

Fig. 3.

Fig. 5, shows another pattern of the same article, with a little different material to imitate the poodle dog's hair. The idea shown in these illustrations

Fig. 4.—PEN-WIPER.

will suggest many other patterns for the use of our readers. Such articles are a great convenience upon the writing desk and table, and look much better than a white rag or old piece of newspaper bedaubed with writing ink. They help to cultivate

Fig. 5.—PIN CUSHION.

habits of order and neatness, and indirectly adorn the persons making them as much as the room.

Leaves from the Diary of a Young Housekeeper.

PRIZE ESSAY BY MRS. LAURA E. LYMAN, STAMFORD, CT.*

Dec. 26, 18—.—It is now a month since I became a happy bride. We have been visiting our relatives, my sister Emeline and Edward's married brother, where I have been taking notes as to their modes of housekeeping, hoping to become better prepared for the responsibilities I have assumed. A few days ago we came here to our new home, and, while Edward has driven over to the village with a load of wheat, I have been folding and stitching together some sheets of paper, on which I design to keep a record of my success, perplexities and observations as a housekeeper. This idea was suggested by looking over Edward's farm books with him last night, in which he has an admirably-kept journal of everything he has done, and everything he has learned since he purchased the farm three years ago. Another motive that stimulates me in this enterprise is the perfect manner in which he keeps up everything on the place, and I am sure I can do nothing that will more directly conduce to his happiness than to show him, within doors, the same evidences of care, system, and order, which he has stamped upon every part of the premises.

Day before yesterday we walked all over the farm, and through the outbuildings. I noticed that the fences are all in good order, the gates on their hinges, and the bar posts upright, which, I have heard my father say, are invariable signs of good farming. His implements are all in order; the dirt scraped off the ploughshares, the harrows well stowed away, the cellars thoroughly protected from frost, and the axes ground sharp for a winter's foray among the timber. Now, I am determined to equal him in my department if I can; especially as I find that, in the plan of the addition which he has made to the old farm-house he found here, he has made for me the best arrangements for doing my work easily and rapidly, that I ever saw. He has a map of his farm and buildings, which he spreads out before him when he plans the next year's crops and improvements on the place. Why should not I map out my domain, especially as it is a realm that I love to call my own? The old part of the house is very much in the usual style—two large rooms below, and two above, with halls between, and bed rooms adjoining; but this *L*, which Edward planned, and much of which he built with his own hands, is a gem of a place for a diligent housekeeper, who knows what she wants. Here is the plan:

A is the principal door opening on the north side, *B* another door leading into the old house; *C* the bed-room door, and *D* leads into the wood-house. There are two windows on the south side, between which stands my work table, and one on the north, throwing light on Edward's business desk, which occupies the corner between the doors *A* and *B*. At the right of *B* is my dining table, over which hangs a fruit picture, which I painted when I was a school girl. At the window on the left of my work table Edward has fastened a couple of shelves, where I can have my geraniums, and they are blooming now in that sunny exposure. *S* is my stove, standing just midway between the sink and the pantry.

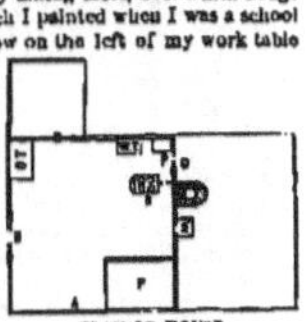

PLAN OF HOUSE.

There is a pump in the sink, as well as a waste water pipe. At the right of and just behind the stove is a small sliding door, marked *w*, which opens into a box in the wood-house, containing split wood and kindling. Edward fills it when he does his morning chores. I never saw such an arrangement anywhere else, and I find it in the highest degree convenient. There is no running out into the wood-house after an armful of wood, and there is no litter of chips or dirt about my stove. The pantry has a north window in it, and a wide shelf running all along just below the window seat. This serves as a cover to my barrels, which will just slip under it; and here, without moving more than a step, I can lay my hand upon everything necessary to do all my cooking. By opening the door the heat from the stove makes it comfortable to work in, and at night prevents my milk and provisions from freezing. In the summer, by keeping the door shut and the window open, I shall find it a cool place for my milk. This arrangement of sink, stove, pantry and working table enables me to keep all my work in one end of the kitchen. My wood, water, provisions and stove are so near each other that a step or two will bring me within reach of everything that I need. I can accomplish twice as much in an hour here as I could in mother's kitchen,

* The Committee of Judges, on the Prize Essays, as noted last month, gave long and patient attention to the seventy-nine essays sent in. The numbers refer to the marks upon the manuscript to distinguish them, the Committee being entirely ignorant of the names of the writers. The publishers very cheerfully acceded to the recommendation of the Committee, and will give three prizes of $100 each, instead of the one offered. We print the opening chapters of two of the Essays. The third one is very fully and prettily illustrated, and it will be reserved for use hereafter, as the engravings will need time for preparation. Our thanks are due to the great number of intelligent and enterprising housekeepers who have contributed their efforts. We are only sorry they could not each receive a first prize.—EDS.]

REPORT OF THE COMMITTEE.

To Messrs. O. Judd & Co.—The ladies assigned the task of examining the articles offered for your prize, have felt very much embarrassed by the richness and variety of the materials presented. There were seventy-nine of the competitors, representing almost every section of the country, and every variety of country housekeeping. These communications have all been read, and the merits of the few that came near to the required standard of excellence, have been thoroughly discussed. After mature deliberation, we have come to the unanimous conclusion that the communications marked No. 43, No. 26, and No. 1, are of equal merit, and, availing ourselves of your permission, we assign a premium of one hundred dollars to each of these three, instead of to only a single one, as at first offered.

Several others show very marked excellencies, and contain many valuable hints, that we should like to see embodied in a volume on household economy. We have no doubt that from the material here presented a more complete work on housekeeping can be compiled, than has yet been given to the public. Yours, Respectfully, THE COMMITTEE.

which was built in the old style, and without any reference to economy of labor, or value of time.

In that, the pantry was in one corner of the room and the sink and pump in the opposite corner, with the stove half-way between; every stick of wood had to be brought up half a dozen stairs, and when the table was set there was no part of the room where one who was sewing or reading could be out of the way. I like the finish of the wood work, too; it is chestnut cut on the place, rubbed with oil and varnished. The grain is handsome, does not show dirt, and can be easily cleaned. The hard-finished walls are painted of a light chestnut color and varnished, so that I shall never need to whitewash them, but only to wipe them down in spring and fall with a wet cloth.

Just outside of the kitchen, in the wood-house, is a large cauldron set in masonry, where I can have my washing done, and where a large quantity of water can be heated for butchering, and other farm purposes. Only last night Edward was talking with me about a girl, and said I should have one if I wanted. I told him he had prevented the necessity of any such help by his plan for the kitchen. What do I want of a Biddy, when, in an hour after each meal, my work is all done up, and the kitchen is as quiet and neat as a parlor?

Dec. 28.—I picked up a volume of *Hall's Journal of Health* last evening, and was so deeply impressed by a well-written article which it contains on the subject of ventilation that I have determined to make a change in one feature of my household economy. Mother used to have us make up our beds the first thing in the morning, but I am satisfied that if I want to keep my bedding, which is now very nice and new, perfectly sweet and wholesome, I must air it every day. So this morning, notwithstanding the cold, while Edward was lighting the fire, I opened the window, which, fortunately, has a southern exposure, laid the blankets and pillows where the air and the sun will fall upon them, and there I mean to let them stay until I have done all my other work.

Dec. 30.—My washerwoman has just gone. This is Monday, and I always did like the plan of having the washing and ironing done up in the early part of the week. She has been at work all day, consumed a good deal of wood, and now her last clothes are frozen on the line, where they must stay all night. If she had had two hours of midday sun upon them, they would have been dry. There must be some improvement on this. I will talk to Edward about it, whether it is not best to buy a wringer, and perhaps a Doty washer, so she can do the washing in the forenoon, and part of the ironing at least in the afternoon. I have heard that washerwomen don't generally like these inventions. Very well; I'll learn to use them and do the washing myself; or, what may be better still, I will pay her a whole day's wages for half a day's work. I am sure that poor women ought not to be made to suffer for want of employment by the multiplication of labor-saving machines.

Mem.—Find out about the different kinds of soap; which is the best, and what soaps are injurious to fabrics. I presume I can learn something on the subject by looking over Edward's *Agriculturists.*

Jan. 28.—The weather has moderated very much, and I asked Edward if the hams did not require attention. He thought they did, and I went to my cook-book for instructions. This is the first time I ever had anything to do with the curing of hams. Following a suggestion I found in Mrs. Child's "Frugal Housewife," I rubbed over them a mixture of saltpetre and molasses, using an ounce of saltpetre and a quart of molasses to eight hams.

Jan. 30.—I have just been looking over Edward's wardrobe to see if I cannot fix him up a suit of plain but warm clothing that he can wear in the woods, so as to save the business suit he bought last fall. I find I can get him out a good substantial vest, buttoning up to the chin, from the skirts of an old pilot-cloth coat that he has worn threadbare and thrown aside. He was talking yesterday about a new every-day vest, and this will surprise him. I can get a pattern by ripping up an old vest, and the coat linings will do for the back of the vest; and as to how to make it, Mrs. Wilson will tell me, and I will go over and see her about it as soon as Edward goes away after dinner.

Leaves from My Journal.

PRIZE ESSAY BY MRS. MCLELLAN, OF OHIO.

January, 1867.—A shade of sadness steals over me, as for the first time I write the new year. How many memories gather around the past, tender and sad as well as joyous. How many questionings and anxieties about the future. But when shall I learn that truest happiness is found in the right improvement of the present. "In the morning sow thy seed, and in the evening withhold not thy hand."

Hannah has gone home for a few weeks. She needs some time for fitting up her wardrobe, as well as a change from the unceasing treadmill of housework. I can spare her better now than at any other time, but must be busy to accomplish all I have in hand.

I have become so interested in making little frames for pictures. I make them of pasteboard, of any shape I fancy, and cover them with cones, acorns, seeds and shells, putting them on with glue, and finishing with a coat of varnish. Some choice engraving or photograph can in this way be provided with a pretty frame at trifling expense. My husband said to a young friend to-day, that I had got so taken up with *fancy work*, he supposed I should want to do nothing else now! I knew he didn't mean it, by the roguish twinkle of his eye. Besides he is just as much interested as I, giving me a hint here and there about the frames, and insisting upon varnishing them, though I really wanted to do it myself. I intend next to make some lamp brackets, like one described so pleasantly in the August *Agriculturist* last year.—I know I should like them, for hav'nt I so often had to run up-stairs and hold the lamp for Nellie, while she dressed her hair?

I had poor bread to-day. I have no patience with myself when that happens. The provoking part of it is, that I can always tell *exactly* what was the trouble, when too late to remedy it. To-day I let it rise too long. A neighbor came in for a little while. Being without help, I should have asked her to sit a few minutes in the kitchen, while I molded it; but I foolishly waited until she went away. If bread rises until it passes from the saccharine to the vinous fermentation, it is past help. It has lost its wholesome and nutritious quality. No art can restore it. Bread must not be neglected or forgotten. It must have a chief place in the mind until safely out of the oven. Two things are absolutely essential to good bread—flour No. 1 and light sweet yeast. With these no housekeeper should be satisfied with bread of only medium quality. It is far better, after testing a rule and finding it good, to abide by it than to experiment with new recipes. Here, literally, "practice makes perfect." This is my recipe: Boil twelve peeled potatoes, and mash them well. Add a quart of the water they were boiled in, while hot, and a cup of sugar. When cool, add a quart of cold water, and a half pint of fresh yeast. Let it stand in a warm place twelve hours, after that shut it up tightly, and keep it in a cool place. It will rise quickly and make delightful bread.

I called round upon my young friend Lizzie Mason to-day. Her mother was a dear mate of mine in our girlhood days. I should love Lizzie for her mother's sake, but I love her for her own as well. It more than repays me for any little advice or encouragement I may give her, to enjoy the freshness and heartiness of her first year at housekeeping, and to have a good laugh over some of her failures and mishaps. They carry me back to days of "auld lang syne." No medicine is so good for a care worn housekeeper as a merry laugh. But to-day Lizzie wore a troubled brow. Baby was fretful, and such *piles* of work stared her in the face, while really she could do none of it. Mr. Mason and baby both needed warmer clothing at once, and the housework was getting sadly behind. "Why, Lizzie," I said, "what a heavy burden you are carrying about. Do throw it off at once. The wrinkles are on your face already!" "That is just what Henry told me at dinner," she replied. "He said he would rather hire all the sewing done than have me so troubled about it. But you know he is just beginning for himself, and I want to help him all I can. It seems shiftless for me to hire sewing with only my little family to care for." Well, Lizzie, I used to say just the same, but I look at it differently now. Young wives and mothers are too proud, and too ambitious. They want to do every thing themselves, and be esteemed model housekeepers, when in fact they are not yet through with the alphabet. You are not strong. Your little one is worrisome. The care of that as well as of your house is new care. You make *hard work* of it. By degrees you will get along easier. You will learn where to take the advantage of your work, and how to favor yourself some, while at the same time you will accomplish more. It is a new thing for you to have the long night of refreshing sleep, parcelled up into naps so broken and unquiet, that the morning finds you even more weary than bed-time. It is just here that so many young wives break down; and becoming discouraged at the prospect before them, indulge in a complaining spirit, and an inefficiency, fatal alike to their own happiness, and to all with whom they are associated. Settle some points in your mind, the sooner the better. First, take proper care of your own health. This is the greatest kindness to your husband in a pecuniary as well as domestic sense. You cannot violate nature's laws with impunity. Exercise in the fresh air every day; if nothing more than a brisk walk on your piazza, throwing your arms backward and forward, receiving into the lungs that which shall change the torpid and impure blood to a life giving current, imparting energy and strength to the system. Take good care of your child. Make it comfortable and happy as far as in your power. Prepare wholesome and nutritious food for your table. If Mr. Mason provides abundant material, he has a right to expect that on your part it shall be turned to good account. Next in order is sewing. Have one or two garments ready, and sew when you can. *Don't think* of others, until these are done. Select that which is most difficult and irksome, and hire some one to do it *for you*. You will not, by and by, with half a dozen little ones around you, carry such a load as you are sinking under to-day. I think my long lecture did her good, for she told me in parting that she should not forget it, though the "half dozen little ones" she should banish from her memory, with the piles of sewing I had said must have such a fate. From the brow of the hill, as I looked back, I saw her on the porch, going through with such evolutions and attitudes, that a stranger would at once have pronounced her crazy!

February.—"A place for every thing, and every thing in its place." How invaluable this rule to the housekeeper. For every article in common use about a house, a place should be assigned, and each member of the family distinctly understand it must be found there. Any one in the dark should be able to put hands upon it. How much time and patience is thus saved. Hannah, though a good girl in many respects, cannot have the bump of order well developed, at least, if there is any truth in phrenology. How annoying to be questioned as to the whereabouts of missing articles, and then find them in some out of the way place, where she has carelessly left them. To-day, after she had commenced washing, the floor was covered with water. I found she had left the tubs in the wood-shed all the week, instead of taking them to their true place in the cellar. Then she had a long hunt for the indigo bag. Had I not taken it from the pantry? She was so sure she put it there last Monday. She would have been just as sure the tubs were in the cellar before commencing washing.

Finality on Rats.—The only effectual remedy is cement on the bottom and sides of the cellar. They cannot get through this, and so cannot find entrance to the house. Now is a good time to invest in sand, water and lime.

BOYS & GIRLS' COLUMNS.

The Eyes may Deceive.

Most persons readily believe what they "see with their own eyes," but even these reliable witnesses may give a wrong impression. This is often the case when a person is much influenced by fear, hope, anger, or any passion or strong excitement. Great love makes a mother think her children are handsome, although they may be homely in the eyes of others. Hatred makes even beautiful objects appear ugly. The snake is really a beautiful and singularly graceful creature; yet it looks hideous to most persons, because of their fear or their superstition. A recent incident shows how fear may deceive the eyes. A woman who had great dread of robbers, always looked carefully under her bed before retiring. One night she came running down stairs and alarmed the family by wildly declaring that somebody was under her bed, as she plainly saw his face. Some of her friends immediately made examination, and found she had indeed seen a face, but it was only her own reflected from a looking glass which had been stowed away there during the day! Had not the matter been investigated, she would always have been persuaded that a stranger had hid himself in her room. Hundreds of persons have been deceived by their eyes, while under the influence of fear, into seeing ghosts, as they supposed. When very improbable stories are related by persons who claim to have been eye-witnesses, it will be well to remember that the eyes can not always be trusted.

A Curious Bouquet.

Our artist having succeeded in *making up faces* in a rather curious manner last month, (see Jan. No., page 27) has tried his hand again, and sends in this sketch of a bouquet, where he says, girls and boys with sharp eyes will find many curious features, which do not appear at first sight. Study every flower and leaf carefully, see how

many portraits you can find and point them out to your friends. There are said to be a good many of them.

A New Plaything.

Our young friends who are afraid of harmless snakes, may, perhaps, overcome their dislike by making such a one as we recently saw; it is shown in the engraving. Take a straight piece of soft pine wood two feet long. Whittle it into the form of a snake, supposing him to be stretched out, and frozen stiff. Next cut out a little groove along the top of the back, and another exactly under it along the belly, just wide and deep enough to allow a piece of fine strong cord, like a small fishing line, to lie in below the surface, as shown at *C*, fig. 2. Also, bore a hole to pass the line through the head from the top to the under groove. With a fine saw cut down through on each

Fig. 1.—THE SNAKE COMPLETE.

side of the snake, nearly to the middle, making the cuts exactly opposite, and an inch apart, except at the head and

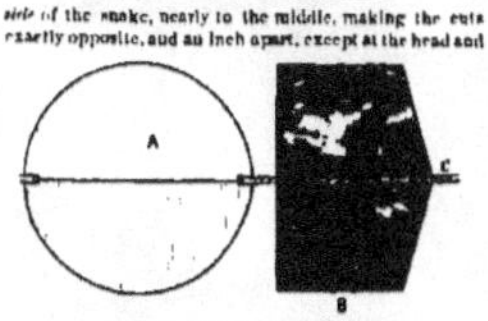

Fig. 2.—SECTION OF BLOCKS.

tail, each of which may be left about two inches long. Fig. 1 shows nearly how these cuts should be made. Then cut the *front* edge of each division beveling about one-quarter of an inch down to the centre. This will separate the snake into inch pieces. (*B*), fig. 2, gives the shape of each piece, looking from the top. (*A*), fig. 2, represents the *back* end of each piece. Arrange the pieces in proper order, in a straight line, from head to tail, and, with a fine brush partially fill the top groove with glue. Then pass the cord through the hole in the head piece, crowd it down snugly into the glue, bringing each piece close up to the one before it. Turn the snake over, glue the under groove, and fasten the other part of the string down into the groove of the belly part, throughout the whole length, the same as on the top part. Leave it until perfectly dry, and you will have a wooden snake that will squirm alarmingly. Two pin heads for eyes, and a little paint skillfully applied will complete the resemblance to nature, and make an amusing plaything. Do not selfishly use it to frighten the timid.

Ants—Strong Little People.

The patient industry of the ants is an old lesson with us, and in some lands their power for good or evil rivals that of the fairies, especially if we include the African "termites" which generally go by the name of white ants. All at once a swarm of small, winged creatures, not unlike a cloud of snow flakes, fill the air. They are eagerly snapped up by dogs and other animals; and, moreover, great numbers are caught by the native negroes who eat them as a great delicacy. The bodies of the insects are about half an inch long, and of a whitish color, so that when boiled or roasted they resemble grains of rice. Those which escape this use, waste no time fluttering around, like idling butterflies, but making a first and last flight, alight by instinct upon a spot suitable for their future labors. Dropping the now useless wings, the industrious ants set about their work with a good will, and grain by grain the soil is bored and lifted and placed. Chamber after chamber is built, each connected with others by covered galleries or bridges, until a hill arises thirty or forty feet high, with a base in proportion, every particle of which has been carried by the tiny workers. While building their houses the ants do great good by removing old logs and other decaying matter, which they dispose of with wonderful rapidity. The hills thus formed become, in the way of soil, almost as good as hot beds, and the natives make gardens upon their sides. Some parts of the country are overflowed a large portion of the year, and only the ant hills, covered with trees, rise above the reedy surface of the marsh.

There is also another family of ants, which do as much in their way as the termites. These black ants, or soldiers, as they are called, build no hills, but dig out their homes under ground. They prey upon all kinds of small creatures, and will, in a short time, make way with the carcass of a large animal. Not unfrequently they go on a raid into a village, and overrun the huts in their paths, so that the natives are obliged to retire until the little invaders have cleared the huts of every species of vermin which infest their not over neat dwellings.

The black ants constantly make war upon the termites, and it has been thought that they carried off the white ants to work for them. But as the little hard legs of the termites are often seen near the holes of the soldier ants, these small cannibals probably eat their captives.

These black ants store away such quantities of the small kinds of grain used there, that the natives often dig for it in times of drouth and scarcity.

Nothing can stop an army of ants when once started, and it is very interesting to watch their wonderful ingenuity in getting over obstacles. For instance, if a stream of water is in the way, one ant clings to another until a chain is formed, firm at one end, and floating in the air, long enough for the free end to reach the opposite side of the stream. Then the whole army passes over on this living suspension bridge.

Besides the soldiers and termites, there is a small red ant much dreaded by those who have felt their bite. Not content with their burning sting, they twist the little crooked claw about in the wound, and such is the fierceness of their attack, that an ant can rarely be pulled away from the flesh without being torn apart.

Very little people, if they did all they could as faithfully as the very little insects, might be surprised to find how much they are worth in the household. And like the ants, if they don't do good they do harm. Old folks at least know how much discomfort and mischief may be accomplished in a home by a five year old child.

Answers to Problems and Puzzles.

The following are answers to the puzzles, etc., in the January number, page 25: No. 245, *Mathematical Problem.*—90 guns, 670 sailors, 55 soldiers.... No. 246. *Illustrated Rebus.*—Ill news flies fast (*fly's fast.*) .... No. 247. *Mathematical Problem.*—Draw a triangle with the apex of its angles bisecting the sides of the given triangle, and the four required parts will be found.... No. 248. *Mathematical Problem.*—Distance from *C* to *D*, 14 miles; from *D* to *E*, 40 miles; from *C* to *E*, 54 miles.... No. 249. *Illustrated Rebus.*—Effeminacy and cowardice go hand in hand with indolence and luxury.... No. 250. *Illustrated Rebus.*—To be elbowed.

No. 251—*Illustrated Rebus.*

The following have sent correct answers up to January 12th: "J. T. N. W.," Robert Robertson, M. Olden, J. E. Bonsall, "R. D. W.," Henry Colgate, J. Morris Leeds, Edmund J. Young, Alice Sull, "E. M.," James M. Evans, J. W. Diddle, Emma Findley, M. D. Wires, W. James Haskell, Mollie E. Jacoby, J. C. Norton, E. Leonard, Clarence C. Howard, H. P. Guirrant, Eli Mendenhale, J. T. Norton, Samuel Yeakle, Jr., "Old Rusty," Jennie Cook, Eugene Lane, Almeron, O. Meade, "A. H. S.," Willie and Bertie, W. S. Carver, Irwin Chase, Ella Staples, Emma Sturmwald, John Andes, J. K. Hallock, A. H. Mahaffey, Frank A. Lawrence, William Worden Marryatt, Franklin Belford, James and Edward Jones.

No. 252. *Illustrated Rebus.*—For Farmers' boys to study.

[COPYRIGHT SECURED.]

A HARE-BRAINED TEAM.—FROM AN ORIGINAL PAINTING BY OTTO EBERLEIN.—*Drawn and engraved for the American Agriculturist.*

A fine ride this little fellow was taking across the fields, with his strong and well trained team of dogs. They had often carried him safely before, and he could not have expected such a ludicrous and somewhat dangerous experience as he is now having. The dogs did very well until strong temptation came before them; then they could see nothing but the hare, and forgetful of the voice and the lines of the driver, away they rushed, leaving their unlucky young master to look out for the consequences. Probably after this he will be careful how he takes them over that road again. We have seen many a lad thus run away with, not by dogs, but by his own thoughts, when he had left the places and companions which his parents judged safe for him to have, and got into the way of temptations among bad company. One poor young man we know, was lately thrown down from a fine position in a bank, being run away with by his passion for gambling—his character ruined for life; another is losing his good name in the bar-rooms, where his appetites have drawn him; and many more are in danger of having their honesty shaken out of them by taking short cuts "across lots" in their haste to get rich. The "old ways" are safest, in driving a team, or in making the journey of life.

A Master Workman's Tools.

The great natural philosopher, Dr. Wollaston, was once called on by a scientific foreigner who desired to see his laboratory, and inspect the apparatus with which he had made his splendid discoveries. "Certainly," was the reply, and he immediately brought out a small tray containing some glass tubes, a simple blow-pipe, or bent metal tube worth a few pence, three common watch glasses, a slip of platinum, and a few other similar things. On another occasion, shortly after Wollaston had inspected a grand galvanic battery, he met a friend in the street, and seizing him by the button he led him into a quiet corner, when, after looking carefully about him as if engaged in some strange mystery, he took from his pocket a tailor's thimble, in which he had constructed a galvanic arrangement, and pouring into it the contents of a small vial, he instantly caused a bit of platinum wire to become quite hot.—Our young readers are familiar with the experiment of Dr. Franklin, who, with only a common kite, proved that the lightning in the clouds was of the same nature as the electric spark which had been produced by various contrivances. These and many similar incidents show the value of "brains," that with an educated power of thinking, the highest results can be gained with the simplest materials.

Cotton on the Gallows.

Less than one hundred and fifty years ago, the masses of the people of Great Britain believed that the introduction of cotton clothing and its manufacture would ruin the kingdom. Woolen and linen garments were then almost universally worn, and large manufacturers, employing many thousand workmen, were engaged in supplying the demand for them. It was thought that the woolen and flax machinery would be useless and a total loss, and the workmen thrown out of employment, if cotton should take the place of the fabrics then worn. Even Parliament shared this belief, and in 1721, passed an Act imposing a penalty of five pounds upon the seller of a piece of calico. The common people on one occasion, took a singular way to show their prejudice against the new fiber, and to bring it into disrepute. One Michael Carmody was executed at Cork, in Ireland, for felony; upon which the journeymen weavers (who were short of work, and who attributed the "hard times" to the introduction of cotton manufacture,) assembled in a body and dressed the criminal, the hangman, and the gallows, in cotton, in order to bring the wearing of it into disgrace; and at the place of execution the criminal made the following remarkable speech:—"Give ear, O good people, to the words of a dying sinner. I confess I have been guilty of what necessity compelled me to commit, which starving condition I was in, I am well assured, was occasioned by the scarcity of money, that has proceeded from the great discouragement of our woolen manufactures. Therefore, good Christians, consider that if you go on to suppress your own goods by wearing such cottons as I am now clothed in, you will bring your country into misery, which will consequently swarm with such unhappy malefactors as your present object is, and the blood of every miserable felon that will hang, after this warning, will lay at your doors."—Nevertheless, happily for Great Britain, the wearing of cottons continued to be extended, so that in thirty years afterward, their yearly manufacture was estimated at $1,000,000, and at the present day nearly 400,000 steam looms are at work there upon cottons, directly employing at least 500,000 work people, besides the millions engaged elsewhere in producing the staple.

A Curious Book-Worm.—A friend recently at a book sale in New York, describes a book that he saw containing a singular mark made by a small worm. The insect had first bored through the outside cover, near the bottom, then worked his way through the pages on the margin below the print, until it came to the last page, where it had excavated a snug burrow for raising a family; then it, or one of its progeny, continued on and made its way out through the back cover, leaving through all its course a small hole as if made with a large pin.

(Business Notices [illegible] per Agate Line of Space.)

Advertisements, to be sure of insertion, must be received **BEFORE** the 5th of the preceding month.

TERMS— (cash before insertion):
Ordinary Pages, $1.50 *per line*. *Open Pages*—$2 *per line*.
Business Notices—$2.50 per line of space, each insertion.

Henderson & Fleming's
SELECTED SEEDS & PLANTS
FOR
MARKET GARDENERS AND OTHERS.

	Quart.	*Bush.*
Beans (Bush), Valentine, Refugee	40c.	$10.00
Beans (Pole), Lima, Sera	75c.	14.00
	Ounce.	*lb.*
Beets, Short Top Round, Long Blood	15c.	$1.00
Cabbage (Early), *true Jersey* Wakefield	$1.00	12.00
" (Late), Flat Dutch, Drumhead	50c.	$3.00
Carrot, Early Horn, Long Orange	15c.	$1.50
Cauliflower, Early Paris and Half-Early	$1.50	16.00
Celery, New Dwarf White	$1.00	$12.00
" White Solid	30c.	$3.00
	Quart.	*Bush.*
Corn, Dwarf Prolific, Asylum	30c.	$6.00
	Ounce.	*lb.*
Cucumber, White Spine, Long Green	15c.	$1.50
" Forcing varieties	25c. per packet.	
	Ounce.	*lb.*
Egg Plant, New York Improved Purple	75c.	$7.50
Lettuce, Simpson, Butter	40c.	$1.00
Melon, Citron, Nutmeg and Skillman	20c.	$1.20
" (Water), Ice Cream & Mountain Sprout	15c.	$1.50
Okra, Tall and Dwarf	15c.	$1.50
Onions, White, Weggets Red	30c.	$3.00
" Large Red, Yellow Dutch	20c.	$1.50
Parsley, Extra Dwarf Curled	15c.	$1.50
	Quart.	*Bush.*
Peas (Early), Dan. O'Rourke, "Extra Early."	30c.	$7.00
" (Late) Champion, British Queen	50c.	$8.00
	Ounce.	*lb.*
Pumpkin, Cheese	10c.	75
Radish, Scarlet Turnip, Long Scarlet	15c.	$1.50
Salsify (or Oyster Plant)	20c.	$2.00
Spinach, Round and Prickly	10c.	75
Squash (Bush), Summer Crookneck	10c.	75
" (Late), Boston Marrow, Hubbard	20c.	$2.50
Tomato, Early Smooth Red, Fejee	30c.	$4.00
Turnip, Red Top, Yellow Aberdeen	10c.	$1.00
Herbs, Thyme and Sweet Marjoram	50c.	$6.00
" Sage and Summer Savory	30c.	$4.00

The above sent by mail to any address on receipt of the prices annexed, with the addition of 8c. per lb. for postage. In packets at 5c. each, or 75c. per dozen, free by mail.

Plants and Roots for Market Gardeners and Others.

Onion Sets, Yellow, 40c. per quart, $2.00 per peck, $8.00 per Bushel.
Onion Sets, White, 60c. per quart, $3.00 per peck, $9.00 per Bushel.

		Per Bush.	*Per Bbl.*
Potatoes—	Early Goodrich (true)	$3.00	$8.00
"	Early Cottage	3.00	7.50
"	Gleason	3.00	7.50
"	Sebec	3.00	7.50
"	Harrison	7.50	15.00
"	Cusco	2.00	5.00

Asparagus, (2 years old,) $1.50 per 100; $10.00 per 1,000
" (1 year old,) $1.00 " $7.50 "
Rhubarb, Victoria and Linnæus, $3 per doz.; $15 per 100
Cabbage Plants (Cold Frame), Wakefield, $1.50 per 100; $10.00 per 1,000
" " (Hot-bed), Wakefield, 75 cents per 100; $4.00 per 1,000
Cauliflower, (Cold Frame), $3 per 100; $20.00 per 1,000
" (Hot-bed), $1 " $15.00 per 1,000
Horseradish Sets, $1.00 per 100; $7.50 per 1,000.

HENDERSON & FLEMING,
Seedsmen and Market Gardeners,
67 Nassau-st., New York.

Our General Catalogue of Flower and Vegetable Seeds

is now ready, containing descriptions and plain directions for cultivation. Mailed on receipt of 10 cents.

New Vegetable Seeds, &c.!

BRIDGEMAN'S
ANNUAL DESCRIPTIVE
PRICED CATALOGUE
of
KITCHEN GARDEN
and
AGRICULTURAL SEEDS,
for 1867, is Now Ready,
and mailed free to all applicants.

ALFRED BRIDGEMAN,
No. 876 Broadway, New York.

New and Rare Vegetables.

I present to the Public my Annual List of New and Rare Seed for 1867, many of which I send out the first time this season.

MARBLEHEAD MAMMOTH DRUMHEAD CABBAGE.—(*The largest Cabbage in the world. Weighs from thirty to sixty pounds to the head, and is tender and sweet. No cabbage does so well in the South as this.*) CANNON BALL CABBAGE.—(*About as round and hard as a cannon ball. An early sort, and the hardest heading of all Cabbage.*) STONE MASON CABBAGE.—(*Standard variety of Winter Drumhead Cabbage in Boston market. Under good cultivation every plant on an acre will make a large and hard head. It is remarkably tender and sweet. In half-ounce packages.*) LENORMAND'S MAMMOTH CAULIFLOWER.—(*A new variety, the largest of all the Cauliflower family. Very reliable for heading.*) VERY EARLY ERFURT CAULIFLOWER.—(*New, remarkably early, and fine for hot-beds.*) NEW YORK IMPROVED EXTRA LARGE PURPLE EGG PLANT.—(*This grows to a larger size, and is of a richer color than the Common Large Purple Egg Plant.*) STRIPED GAUDELOUPE EGG PLANT.—(*An elegant variety for the table. The stripings of white, purple and yellow give it a magnificent appearance.*) ORNAMENTAL KALE.—(*The great variety in color, and structure of the leaves, make them elegant ornaments for the flower garden and among shrubbery.*) MAMMOTH SWEET CORN.—(*The largest of all Sweet Corn. Sweet, and excellent for the table. The ears weigh, as gathered, from two to three pounds each.*) MAMMOTH FRENCH SQUASH.—(*Sometimes grown to weigh over two hundred pounds. They grow well-proportioned, and are finely colored.*) VEGETABLE CATERPILLARS.—(*Vegetable curiosities, the seed-vessels resembling caterpillars.*) VEGETABLE SNAILS.—(*A French Oddity, the seed vessels of which resemble snails.*) VEGETABLE WORMS.—(*Another curious vegetable product.*) SNAKE CUCUMBER.—(*A very long variety which grows coiled up, having the appearance of a large snake.*)

LAXTON'S PROLIFIC EARLY LONG POD PEA.—(*A new and quite distinct variety. Many of the pods contain from ten to twelve Peas each.*) DWARF INDIAN CHIEF BEAN.—(*Those who have grown the Pole Indian Chief will be pleased to find a bush variety of this fine String Bean.*) GIANT WAX BEAN.—(*A new Pole Bean, being an improvement on the Indian Chief, it being a larger and longer Podded Bean than that choice variety. The Wax Beans (so called because the pods are of a wax color,) are the best of all String Beans.*) NORBITON'S GIANT CUCUMBER.—(*A new English variety, the finest, longest, and most prolific Cucumber in cultivation.*) WARD'S NECTAR MELON.—(*When compared with all other sorts, this has been awarded the palm as the best of all green-fleshed Melons.*)

Each of the above sent to any part of the United States, and warranted to reach the purchaser, at twenty-five cents per package.

AMERICAN TURBAN SQUASH.—(*The dryest, finest grained, and best flavored of all Fall Squashes. The packages contain about fifty seed.*) HUBBARD SQUASH.—(*I was the original introducer of this, and the seed is* TRUE.) YOKOHAMA SQUASH.—(*A new variety from Japan; very prolific. The quality resembles a fine Crookneck, but is much superior.*) BOSTON MARROW SQUASH.—(*My variety took the premium for purity at the Annual Fair of the Massachusetts Horticultural Society in 1865.*) PARA SQUASH.—(*A bush Squash from South America, which can be kept into winter. Oblong in shape, of good size, fine-grained, and excellent quality; far superior to any standard variety of bush Squash.*) IMPROVED GREEN GLOBE SAVOY CABBAGE.—(*For family use, the Savoys are the richest of all Cabbages. The heads of this variety are large, hard, and of most excellent quality, the stumps short. Remarkably reliable for heading.*) PANCALIER SAVOY.—(*The French consider this the earliest Cabbage grown.*) SMALL EARLY ULM SAVOY.—(*Very early and reliable.*) BUNNELL'S KING OF THE DWARFS.—(*In England this is considered the earliest of Cabbages. Very dwarf, fine quality, and sweet.*) LARGE BRUNSWICK SHORT STEM.—(*A very large and very early Drumhead, much sought for by market gardeners.*) LITTLE PIXIE CABBAGE.—(*An early dwarf; stump, short; heads, pointed, and very hard, fine quality, and very sweet.*) TILDEN'S NEW TOMATO.—(*Large, round or oblong; color, rich scarlet; vines, dwarf, and very productive.*) EARLY YORK TOMATO.—(*Very early, and remarkably prolific; has yielded at the rate of over one thousand bushels per acre. Fruit of good market size; flat, round shape; quality, excellent.*) COOK'S FAVORITE TOMATO.—(*A large, apple-shaped variety; very prolific; quality, superior; decidedly the best of the apple-shaped Tomatoes.*) MAMMOTH CHIHUAHUA TOMATO.—(*Enormously large, weighing from two to three pounds. Some single specimens will heap a quart measure.*) NEW MEXICAN TOMATO.—(*Very large, round Tomato; a great bearer; resembles, in color, Lester's Perfected, but an improvement on it, in always being round.*) TREE TOMATO.—(*A French variety; grows erect in the form of a bush.*) MCLEAN'S ADVANCER PEA.—(*A new English wrinkled Pea. A decided improvement on the Champion of England; bears well, with Peas equally sweet; is much larger, and does not run nearly as high.*) MCLEAN'S LITTLE GEM.—(*A new dwarf wrinkled Pea; grows about one foot high, very early, only a few days later than the Dan O'Rourke; a decided acquisition.*) VILMORIN'S NEW, WRINKLED, EDIBLE, PODDED PEA.—(*The first wrinkled sort yet found, the pods of which can be eaten.*) CARTER'S FIRST CROP.—(*A new English Pea, sent out as the earliest of all varieties.*) HAIR'S DWARF MAMMOTH.—(*A wrinkled Pea, larger than Champion of England, growing only half its hight; quality, fully equal to the Champion.*) TOM THUMB PEA.—(*As early as Dan O'Rourke, grows ten inches high, and is remarkably prolific.*) DREW'S NEW DWARF PEA.—(*Peas, very large, egg-shaped; each plant forms quite a bush. Peas should be planted about a foot apart. Early, dwarf, and very prolific.*) BROWN'S NEW DWARF MARROWFAT.—(*Warranted to be the earliest and most dwarf Marrowfat Pea grown. A capital Pea for market gardeners.*) FORTY DAYS' CORN.—(*Earlier than any Sweet Corn. Desirable as an early sort.*) BATES' EXTRA EARLY SWEET CORN.—(*A variety of wrinkled bronzed Sugar Corn; earlier than Darling's Early, and excellent for table use.*) MAMMOTH FLINT CORN.—(*Ears grow sixteen inches long; stalks very tall and stout, and matures as far North as Central New England.*) CROSBY'S EARLY.—(*The earliest of all twelve rowed Sweet Corn. The Massachusetts Horticultural Society offered special premiums for this new Corn at their last Annual Fair. It is of good size for market, and a decided acquisition.*) MEXICAN SWEET CORN.—(*I still find this to be the sweetest and most tender of all varieties of Sweet Corn. Nothing can equal it for the table.*) GOLDEN SWEET CORN.—(*A Sweet Corn of golden color; early, of good size, and excellent quality for the table; flavor, fine, and distinct from any other variety.*) YARD LONG BEAN.—(*A curious Bean; pods growing over two feet long; foliage, a rich, dark, glossy green.*) CONCORD BEAN.—(*This new Bean is probably the earliest Pole Bean grown; very prolific, and of excellent quality, either as a string or shell Bean.*) FEJEE BEAN.—(*A new bush Bean; the earliest and hardiest of all beans; very prolific and worthy of general cultivation.*) INTERMEDIATE HORTICULTURAL BEAN.—(*An excellent bush Bean for marketmen. Pods of the same rich color as the Pole Horticultural.*) CALIFORNIA BEAN.—(*A very early, large, flat Pole Bean; excellent, either green or baked.*) MOTTLED CRANBERRY.—(*An improvement in health, vigor, and productiveness on the old-fashioned Cranberry. Few Pole Beans will yield equal to this. Pods, long, large, and well filled.*) SIMON'S EARLY BEET.—(*A new, early sort, well shaped; as early as Bassano, and darker.*) NEW TURNIP BEET.—(*Round, flat-shaped, very early, and very nice.*) CASTLENANDARY BEET.—(*A famous French variety; flesh, a deep purple color, very tender and sweet.*) CHAPAUDINE BEET.—(*Rough skinned; color, very dark purple; Esteemed by the French as the best of all Beets for table use.*) WHYTE'S VERY DEEP RED BEET.—(*Medium size, dark color, very sweet, and excellent for table use.*) YELLOW OVOID MANGEL WURTZEL.—(*For cattle. Of seventeen varieties tested, the crop of this exceeded all.*) EARLY CRACKER ONION.—(*Earliest of all the yellow sort; quality, very delicate and sweet.*) HOOD'S NEW DWARF IMPERIAL PURPLE CELERY.—(*A choice new English variety.*) TURNER'S INCOMPARABLE DWARF WHITE CELERY.—(*A first class English variety.*) READ'S MATCHLESS CELERY.—(*A premium English variety, fine, solid and red.*) BOSTON MARKET CELERY.—(*True. This is the short, compact, solid variety, so often admired by strangers in the markets of Boston.*) TRUE BOSTON CURLED LETTUCE.—(*The most elegant of all the Lettuce family, grows in the form of a Rosette.*) WHEELER'S TOM THUMB LETTUCE.—(*A choice new variety, in high favor with those who have grown it.*) PERPIGNAN LETTUCE.—(*This is an excellent lettuce for standing the summer heat. Heads, compact, attaining to seven inches in diameter.*) NEAPOLITAN CABBAGE LETTUCE.—(*One of the finest Cabbage Lettuces yet introduced.*) SIX VARIETIES OF CABBAGE LETTUCE.—(*Six of the choicest varieties in one package.*) ORANGE WATERMELON.—(*When fully ripe the skin will peel off like an Orange.*) ALLEN'S SUPERB MUSK MELON.—(*Quality, superior; by some called the "Queen of Melons."*) LARGE PERSIAN MUSK MELON.—(*A fine, large variety.*) WHITE JAPANESE MELON.—(*Flesh, greenish white, very thick-meated; one of the earliest and sweetest of all melons.*) DWARF BROOM CORN.—(*This is thought to make a better brush than the common tall sorts.*) CHUFAS, OR GROUND ALMONDS.—(*These taste very much like a Cocoanut; are very prolific, yielding 100 to 1.*) ORNAMENTAL GOURDS.—(*Many varieties in one package.*) NEW JERSEY HYBRID CUCUMBER.—(*A remarkably long variety; an improvement on the White Spined.*) IMPROVED LONG GREEN CUCUMBER.—(*This is the longest of all the Long Greens.*) CHINESE SCARLET EGG PLANT.—(*Of magnificent scarlet color, and highly ornamental.*) MAMMOTH MILLET.—(*Extra tall; seed heads much larger than any other variety.*) SCRBY WHITE WHEAT.—(*A new English Winter Wheat, highly recommended for poor soils, remarkably free from blight and rust.*) OTAHEITIAN SUGAR CANE.—(*This yields more Sugar than any other variety of Sugar Cane grown in the North.*)

Any of the above varieties will be forwarded, post-paid, and warranted to reach the purchaser at fifteen cents each.

EARLY SEBEC POTATOES.—(*Coming rapidly into favor in Boston and vicinity as a first class early market Potato. Large size, excellent quality, and remarkably productive.*) EARLY GOODRICH.—(*True.*) SHAKER'S FANCY.—(*A new variety of white-fleshed Potatoes, considered as early as Early Goodrich, yielding equally well, and rapidly gaining favor in Pennsylvania. This and the Early Sebec are of better shape for market purposes than the Early Goodrich.*

Four pound packages of either of these varieties sent to any address, warranted to reach the purchaser, on receipt of one dollar. All orders for Potatoes will be put on file, and be filled as soon as danger from freezing is past.

Catalogues containing over two hundred varieties of warranted Garden Seeds, one hundred and twenty-five of which are of my own growing, sent, gratis, to all applicants.

I warrant three things: 1st. That my seed shall be genuine. 2d. That your money shall reach me. 3d. That my seed shall reach you. Can the Public ask for anything fairer than this?

JAMES J. H. GREGORY,
Marblehead, Mass.

PARSONS & CO.,

offer a large assortment of the best

TREES AND SHRUBS,

both for Streets and Lawns.

PEAR TREES of large size.

PEACH TREES, very fine, at $120 per 1,000.

APPLE, PLUM and other Fruit Trees.

STRAWBERRIES of the different sorts.

ROSES on their own roots, not budded or grafted, and as strong, healthy and vigorous as need be desired. The finest Hybrid Perpetuals and Mosses at $30 per 100; $150 per 1,000.

TRITOMA UVARIA, $25 per 100.
(See *American Agriculturist*, October No., 1866, page 368.)

LINNÆUS RHUBARB, $5 per 100.

EVERGREENS

In very large variety, including hardy Rhododendrons of all the best kinds, from white to purple.

For Catalogues, &c., apply to

PARSONS & CO., Flushing, N. Y.

JUCUNDA, OR 700.---GROWN BY J. KNOX, PITTSBURGH, PA.

"The [illegible] we give (as above), are drawn from Nature; and we can say, are not exaggerations of the specimens which were selected at Pittsburgh, when we were there in June, [illegible] Philadelphia the next day." THOMAS MEEHAN, Editor *Gardeners' Monthly.*

"The above Engraving is a faithful representation, drawn from actual specimens of fine fruit grown on the Knox Fruit Farm, at Pittsburgh." A. W. HARRISON.

"Its flowers are perfect, and fruitful to an enormous extent. Last year counted trusses that had ninety per cent. of perfect fruit upon them, as compared with the number of flowers. [illegible] of value in this variety is the great number of extra large berries. I saw great quantities, ten to twelve berries of which filled a pint. These, you must remem[illegible] [illegible] for the exhibition tables, but there were bushels of them sold every day in market, which brought one dollar per quart. This is equal to four or [illegible] cents each, and may be considered rather profitable." GEORGE M. BEELER, *late Secretary Indiana Hort. Society.*

"I entirely [illegible] to the statement there made (at the meeting of the Ohio Pomological Society, held in Cincinnati, December, 1865) as to its great productiveness, its large and uniform [illegible] [illegible] but, more especially, as to its *brilliant color, perfect form,* and *extreme beauty,* and consider it the most remarkable fruit of its class that has ever [illegible]." DR. JOHN A. WARDER.

For further [illegible] in reference to this the most valuable of all our Strawberries, send 10 Cents for our Catalogue.

Our stock of [illegible] and vigorous plants is very large this season, which we offer at the following greatly reduced prices:

12 Plants	$1.00.	1000 Plants	$40.00.
100 "	$5.00.	3000 "	$100.00.

For Vines and Plants BY MAIL, see extraordinary inducements on page 77.——ORDER EARLY.

GRAPE VINES.

CONCORD.

The most valuable grape in the country. More popular [illegible], and is being more generally planted than all [illegible]. Very valuable for the table and for market purposes. [illegible] palates, and sells very readily at [illegible] [illegible] Average yield about 1[illegible]0 gallons per [illegible] GEORGE HUSMANN.

[illegible] present [illegible] supplies

200,000	[illegible], 1 year old Vines.	
25,000	" 2 " " "	
3,000	" 3 " " "	

[illegible] are grown in the best possible manner, from [illegible] bearing vineyards. For prices [illegible] information, send 10 Cts. for Catalogue.

IVES.

[illegible] great American wine grape. Average annual yield [illegible] 600 gallons per acre, which sells at from $1.50 [illegible] per gallon.

60,000

[illegible] Vines for sale.

SEVEN

[illegible] *healthy, hardy, vig*[illegible] *productive, of good quality, and very profitable*

HARTFORD and CREVELING. } Best *very early*, yet thoroughly tested.

MARTHA—WHITE CONCORD.—Best White.

BLACK HAWK.—Perhaps the earliest of all grapes of any merit.

IVES and RENTZ. } Best American wine grapes.

Samples of each sent by mail, post paid, on receipt of retail price. For full description, prices and much other valuable information on Grape Culture, send 10 Cents for Catalogues.

STRAWBERRIES.

SEVEN

varieties of largest size—best quality, and greatest yield.

JUCUNDA—OUR NO. 700. Largest and most valuable of all.

FILLMORE.—Next in value.

GOLDEN SEEDED. BURR'S NEW PINE. } Best very early.

WILSON.—Best for canning.

TRIOMPHE DE GAND.

AGRICULTURIST.

☞ Two dozen of JUCUNDA—Our No. 700, and one dozen each of the other varieties, sent by mail, post paid and their safe carriage guaranteed for five dollars.

For special terms of Plants and Vines

"BY MAIL,"

See page 77 of this Number of *Agriculturist.*

CURRANTS.

If proper attention were given the Currant—in the selection of varieties, and its culture, it would undoubtedly prove to be not only one of our greatest Home comforts, but also a most profitable market fruit.

SEVEN

Best Varieties by Mail.

For $3, we will send by mail, post-paid, and guarantee their safe carriage, 6 each Versaillaise and Fertile de Angers; 4 each of Cherry, White Grape, Victoria, Short Bunch Red and La Hative.

Full descriptions of these, and other desirable varieties, may be found in our Catalogue, which will be sent to all applicants enclosing Ten Cents.

☞ EARLY ORDERS ARE SOLICITED.

J. KNOX,

Box 155, Pittsburgh, Pa.

RARE and BEAUTIFUL FLOWERS,
Select Vegetables.
B. K. BLISS,
Importer and Dealer in Garden, Field and Flower Seeds,

Would invite attention to his large and well selected assortment of the above, comprising the newest and most approved varieties, both of European and Home Productions, the quality of which cannot be surpassed. For a list of which, see his

Illustrated Seed Catalogue and Guide to the Flower and Kitchen Garden.

THE THIRTEENTH ANNUAL EDITION, enlarged and improved, contains 124 pages of closely printed matter, *Beautifully Illustrated* with 100 engravings, also a splendid frontispiece of a group of recent novelties—and a descriptive list of TWO THOUSAND VARIETIES OF GARDEN AND FLOWER SEEDS, embracing all the *new varieties* worthy of cultivation introduced the past season—with explicit directions for their culture—also a list of ONE HUNDRED AND TWENTY-FIVE VARIETIES OF FRENCH HYBRID GLADIOLUS, including the leading novelties of the past season, with many other SUMMER FLOWERING BULBS—consisting of AMARYLLIS, TUBEROSES, TIGRIDIAS—LILIES in great variety, etc. To which is added a list of the choicest varieties of GRAPES, STRAWBERRIES, RASPBERRIES, and other SMALL FRUITS, BEDDING PLANTS, etc., etc., cultivated at his gardens, with much other useful information upon the subject of gardening generally, which will be found useful to all engaged in the delightful occupation of gardening. A copy of the Catalogue will be mailed to all applicants enclosing TWENTY-FIVE CENTS. Our regular customers supplied without charge. Address

B. K. BLISS,
Drawer No. 11, P. O. Springfield, Mass.

Seeds for the Farm & Garden.

The following seeds, the purity and vitality of which cannot be excelled, will be mailed post-paid, to any address, upon receipt of price affixed:

	pr oz.	pr lb.
BEETS—Early Bassano, New Rough Skinned.	$0 15	$1.00
Early Blood Turnip, Orange, Long Blood.	15	1.00
Long Red, Yellow Globe Mangel, White Sugar	10	75
CABBAGE—Early York, Large York, Battersea	25	2.00
French Sugar Loaf, Red Dutch, Wakefield	35	4.00
Premium Flat Dutch, Fr. Ox Heart Drumhead, Stone Mason, Drumhead Savoy, Winningstadt.	40	5.00
True Jersey Wakefield, Imp'd American Savoy, Little Pixie, New Dw'f Ulm, Large Brunswick.	50	6.00
Marblehead Mammoth, enormous heads, pkt.	25	
CAULIFLOWER—Half Early Paris, sure to head.	1.25	15.00
Early Dutch, London, Asiatic, Walcheren	75	8.00
Carter's Mammoth, Lenormands, Early Erfurt, pkt	25	
CELERY—White Solid, Crystal White, Red Solid	35	3.00
New Dw'f White, Mammoth Red, Nonsuch	40	4.00
Hood's Dw'f Purple, Incomparable Crimson, pkt.	25	
CARROT—Bliss' Imp'd Long Orange, ex. deep col.	20	1.50
Fr. Long Orange, White Belgian, Altringham	15	1.25
Early Horn, Extra Early Short	20	1.50
CUCUMBER—Gen'l Grant, 20 to 30 inches long, pkt.	25	
Extra Early Russian, Long Green Prickly	25	2.00
Early Frame, White Spine, Short Green	15	1.25
CORN—Crosby's Ex. Early Sugar or Boston Market, pkt.		25
Darling's, Red Cob, Evergreen, Mammoth, qt.	50	
Tuscarora, Early Burlington, Smith's White, qt.	50	
EGG PLANT—Improved N. Y. Purple, very large	75	
White, Striped Guadaloupe, Scarlet Fruited, pkt	10	
KOHL RABI—Early White and Purple Vienna	40	4.50
LETTUCE—Curled Silesia, Butter, Cabbage	25	3.00
Large India (extra fine), White and Green Cos.	45	4.00
Perpignan, a new German sort, stands a long time without running to seed, fine solid head, pkt.	15	
MUSKMELON—Green Citron, Nutmeg, Large Yellow,	15	1.25
Early White Japan, delicious flavor	50	4.00
WATERMELON—Mountain Sweet, Black Spanish	15	1.50
Orange, Goodwin Imperial	40	4.00
PARSNIP—Long Smooth White, Hollow Crown	15	80
Student, improved from the wild variety	20	1.50
PEAS—Carter's First Crop, Little Gem, pkt	15	qt. 1.00
Dan'l O'Rourke, ex. early, Champion of England,		qt. 50
Tom Thumb, grows 8 inches high, very early		qt. 75
Vilmorin's New Edible Podded, Drew's New Dw'f, Brown's Dw'f Marrow, Laxton's Prolific		pkt. 15
PEPPERS—Large Sweet Mountain, Sweet Spanish.	50	5.00
RADISH—New French Breakfast, fine and crisp	25	2.50
Fr. Olive Shaped, Scarlet Turnip, Long Scarlet.	15	1.25
Raphanus caudatus, a great novelty, per seed	50	
Madras Edible Pod, fine for pickles, pkt	15	
SALSIFY, or Vegetable Oysters, very fine	20	1.75
SPINACH—Round, Prickly, Flanders, Lettuce	15	75
SQUASH—Early Summer Crookneck, Scallop	10	1.00
Boston Marrow (true), Yokohama, Turban, pkt.	15	
Hubbard (true), Canada Crookneck (true)	25	2.00
TURNIP—Early Flat Dutch, Red Top, Yellow Globe, Cow Horn, Sweet German, Long White French	10	1.00
RUTA BAGA—Purple Top, Laing's, Dale's Hybrid.	10	75
Sutton's Champion, a superb variety, pkt	25	
White's Ex. fine Purple Top Yellow Hybrid	10	75
SWEET AND POT HERBS—Sage, Summer Savory, Thyme, Lavender, Rosemary, Sweet Marjoram, etc., pkt. 10		

For a more full and complete list of Seeds, with directions for culture, see our Catalogue and "Guide to the Flower and Kitchen Garden," which will be mailed to all applicants on receipt of Twenty-five Cents. Address

B. K. BLISS, Springfield, Mass.

PRIZE CUCUMBERS FOR FORCING.

General Grant.—A new and superb variety either for exhibition or the table, perfect in form, solid and crisp, and of a most agreeable flavor. Many specimens were grown the past summer averaging 24 to 30 inches in length. It succeeds well also in the open ground. Packets containing 10 seeds, 25 cents. Also the following English and German varieties, at 25 cents per packet: Ayre's Perpetual Black Spine; Cuthill's Black Spine; Ipswich Standard; Weeden's Symmetry; Victory of Bath; Giant of Arnstadt; Roman Emperor; Minster Abbey; Lord Kenyon's Favorite; Ne Plus Ultra; Carter's Champion; Colney Hatch. Either of the above varieties will be mailed to applicants upon receipt of price affixed. Address B. K. BLISS, Springfield, Mass.

CHOICE VARIETIES of the TOMATO.

The following varieties of this valuable esculent will be mailed to applicants upon receipt of the price affixed:

Mappay's Superior.—Fruit of a beautiful deep red color, round, slightly flattened, without crease or wrinkle; flesh almost as solid as beef steak, delicious flavor, average weight, 9 to 12 ounces each, packet, 25 cents.

Tilden's New Seedling.—A new and truly valuable variety, oval shaped, the color a brilliant scarlet, skin smooth, glossy, and rarely wrinkled, very productive, an excellent market variety, packet, 15 cents.

Tilden's Harrison's Improved, packet, 25 cents.

Extra Early York, the earliest variety, very prolific, of good size, and fine quality, packet, 15 cents.

The Cook's Favorite.—Fruit of medium size, roundish or oval, smooth, of a rich deep color, fine flavor, very solid and prolific, an excellent market variety, pkt. 15c.

Lester's Perfected, fruit of large size, pinkish red, remarkably solid and of fine flavor, packet, 10 cents.

Mammoth Chihuahua, often weighs 2 and 3 lbs. 25c.

New Erect French, or Tree Tomato, grows upright like a bush, fruit solid and of fine quality, very ornamental, fine for pot culture, packet, 10 cents.

Also, the following varieties at 10 cents per packet:

Early Apple; Pear Shaped; Yellow Plum; Red and Yellow Cherry; Fejee Island; New White; Large Yellow; Strawberry. One packet each of the 18 varieties, $1.00.

Address B. K. BLISS, Springfield, Mass.

SEED POTATOES.

New English varieties not before offered in this Country.

Patterson's Celebrated Seedlings.

These have acquired a notoriety in England, not surpassed by Goodrich Seedlings of this country. We have selected the following from many varieties received, and tested the past year, and can confidently recommend them:

PATTERSON'S REGENT; SEEDLING ROCK; FORFARSHIRE RED; IRISH BLUE; SCOTCH BLUE; KING OF THE POTATOES; PRINCE OF WALES; SEEDLING BLUE, PAT'NS BLUE.

A writer in the "London Gardener's Chronicle," after describing his success with the above varieties, closes with the following remarks: "As to the quality of the above varieties, we are in a position to speak from experience, and we can only say that we have never tasted any potatoes equal to them. They contain an extraordinary amount of farinaceous matter, are pure white inside, and almost as solid as bread."

As our stock of the above is very small, we can only offer them in sample packages of One Pound Each, which will be sent by Mail upon receipt of One Dollar.

One package each of the nine new varieties will be mailed post-paid upon receipt of *Seven Dollars.*

	Peck.	Bush.	Bbl.
EARLY SEBEC, or Boston Market	$1.25	$2.00	$5.00
EARLY GOODRICH	1.00	3.00	7.00
EARLY STEVENS	75	2.00	5.00
EARLY SOVEREIGN	1.00	3.50	6.00
HARRISON	1.50	5.00	12.50
CALICO	1.00	2.50	5.00
GLEASON	1.00	2.50	5.00
CUZCO	75	2.00	5.00
NEW WHITE PEACH BLOW	75	2.00	5.00
DELMAHOY	75	2.50	6.00
GARNET CHILI	75	2.00	5.00
SUTTON'S EARLY RACE HORSE. } earliest	1.00	4.00	
EARLY HANDSWORTH. } known.	1.25	5.00	

Upon receipt of $1.00, we will mail post-paid, a four pound package of either of the above 13 varieties, to any address in the Union—6 packages for $5.00.—*No less than $1 worth, nor more than one variety in a package, will be sent by mail.* Our descriptive cultural Catalogue of Potatoes mailed to all applicants. Address

B. K. BLISS, Springfield, Mass.

Collections of Kitchen Garden Seeds.

A COMPLETE ASSORTMENT OF VEGETABLE SEEDS FOR ONE YEAR'S SUPPLY, FOR A LARGE OR SMALL GARDEN.

The following Collections are made up in the most liberal manner, care being taken to give a sufficient quantity of all the finest varieties and most useful sorts of Vegetables required in the Kitchen Garden.

Assortment No. 5, contains 55 varieties.........$3.00
No. 6, " 32 " 2.00
No. 7, " 15 " 1.00

The above are prepared expressly for sending by mail, and will be sent post-paid, upon receipt of prices annexed:

Larger Collections which can be safely sent by express to any part of the country, as follows:

No. 1, $20.00; No. 2, $15.00, No. 3, $10.00; No. 4, $5.00.

For a List of the contents of each Collection, see Catalogue pages 89 and 90. Address B. K. BLISS, Springfield, Mass.

Connecticut Seed Leaf Tobacco Seed.

Be Sure and Get the Best.

A superior lot raised expressly for the subscriber by one of the most successful cultivators in the Valley of the Connecticut.—Packets with *full directions for culture, curing, packing, &c.*, will be mailed, post-paid, to all applicants at the following rates: 1 ounce, 25 cents; 4 ounces, $1; 1 lb., $3.50. Address B. K. BLISS, Springfield, Mass.

New Crop Onion Seed.

Mailed post-paid, upon receipt of price affixed. Prices for larger quantities upon application.

	per oz.	¼ lb.	per lb.
Large Red Wethersfield	15c.	45c.	$1.25
Early Red "	15c.	45c.	1.50
Yellow Danvers	15c.	50c.	1.50
Large Yellow Dutch	15c.	50c.	1.25
White Portugal	25c.	80c.	3.00
Potato Onion Sets, per quart			50

Address B. K. BLISS, Springfield, Mass.

CHICORY SEED.—The great substitute for Coffee. Packets containing 1 ounce, 15 cents; 4 ounces, 40 cents; 1 pound, $1, by mail post-paid, with directions for culture. Address B. K. BLISS, Springfield, Mass.

KNOX'S NURSERY AT YOUR DOOR.—See Advertisement "By Mail," page 77.

ALL THE NURSERIES IN ONE!!!

The cheapest Trees, Plants, Vines, &c., are for sale by

L. L. WHITLOCK, 37 Park Row, New York.

1. It is being proved every day that in all kinds of business, the producer and the salesman are in all respects, distinct in their business, and that the purchaser must sooner or later, pay not only the first cost of the article, but also the cost of selling that article, whether sold direct or by Agent, or on Commission.

2. In my business, the purchaser pays the Commission direct to me, instead of the producer.

3. The producer being at no expense, will, in most cases, send a list of all the stock he has for sale, in this way, it will come into direct competition with all others, of the same kind and quality.

4. Purchasers will find the cheapest trees and greatest variety on my books.

5. Nurserymen will, in this way, be able to sell surplus stock at very low prices, without injuring their own business in the future, or the trade, by advertising in their Catalogues at low rates.

6. Producers' names are not seen on my books, every thing being known by numbers, as a matter of self interest, and a benefit to persons selling stock low.

7. No charge made for advertising in my Catalogues, &c.

8. Persons wishing anything under One Hundred Dollars worth, will be charged the usual retail prices of our best Nurserymen, delivered in this city free of expense.

One Hundred Dollars or over, will be considered a wholesale order, and purchasers given every advantage of buying their trees at the lowest wholesale price, whether they want one or one hundred of a kind.

9. I have been engaged in the Horticultural trade for the past twelve years, and consider my services in selecting trees worth more than I ask, but in addition to this I pay my own expenses, and give the advantage of my complete lists of stock for sale, at less money than one could send a man to select them for him, even if he knew where they could be bought, and then he would be obliged to pay retail price for each article.

Send a stamp for a new Price List out February 15th.

Orders, to secure the best selection, should be received by the 1st of March.

All Nurserymen or producers of Horticultural stock of any kind, are invited to send a full statement of what they want to sell, and cheapest wholesale price.

Best reference given on application. Address

L. L. WHITLOCK, 37 Park Row, New York.

American Gate Company,

Manufacturers of

Self-Acting Hand and Carriage Gates. The best ever invented. Also the best **Gate Latch** and **Gate Hangings.**

For Circulars send to

AMERICAN GATE COMPANY,
25 Bank Street,
Cleveland, Ohio.

PLANT-LICE,

Their friends and their enemies. Illustrated. Also BIRDS versus INSECTS. See **Practical Entomologist** for January, 1867. Send a TWO CENT stamp for a copy.

Address PRACTICAL ENTOMOLOGIST,
Philadelphia, Pa.

Eagle Seed Sower.

Farmers and Dealers, your attention is invited to the *Best Hand Seed Sower* in use; it drops the Seed by a Reciprocating Seed Box, which keeps the Seed in constant agitation, and insures an even dropping of the Seed.

Send for Illustrated Circular. Address

E. D. & O. B. REYNOLDS,
North Bridgewater, Mass.

My Illustrated Catalogue of New and Rare Plants for 1867,

is now ready, and sent to my customers of past years, gratis—to all others, on receipt of 10 cents.

PETER HENDERSON,
67 Nassau-st., New York

1867.

THORBURN'S ANNUAL DESCRIPTIVE CATALOGUE OF GARDEN, FIELD, FRUIT, &c., SEEDS, NOW READY. Will be distributed or sent by mail (FREE) to applicants.

SAMUEL T. THORBURN, Seedsman,
46 Hudson-st., Albany, N. Y.

WE WANT AN AGENT IN EVERY COUNTY TO SELL OUR POPULAR SUBSCRIPTION BOOKS

They are the most popular books now published, and many Agents are making $10 to $20 a day. Send for Circulars giving full particulars to RICHARDSON & CO., Publishers, 540 Broadway, New York.

Fort Edward Institute, N. Y.

Sixty dollars for thirteen weeks. Best sustained Boarding Seminary in the State. A few vacancies. Spring term, March 21. Address REV. J. E. KING, D. D.

PARTNER WANTED in the Nursery Business, near New York. The *right man* with $5,000 to $10,000 capital, will find an excellent opening. Address "NURSERY," *Agriculturist Office,* 41 Park Row, New York.

THE "THREE WARRANTS."—Please read my advertisement headed "Farmers and Gardeners."

JAMES J. H. GREGORY, Marblehead, Mass.

Marblehead Mammoth Cabbages!

As some cultivators have an impression that these cabbages cannot be fully matured outside of Marblehead, I invite their attention to the following list of weights to which they have been grown by some of my customers.

H. A. Terry, Crescent City, Iowa, has grown them weighing 40 lbs., measuring 56 inches around the solid head. Thos. A. Lambert, Oceanside, C. W., exhibited three cabbages weighing respectively, 40, 42½, and 41 lbs. John W. Dean, St. Michaels, Md., has grown them weighing 31 lbs. R. M. Shurk, Preston, Minn., has raised them weighing 30 lbs. when trimmed. E. H. E..., Ross Green, Ind., has grown them weighing over 30 lbs. A. L. Garrison, Des Moines, Iowa, has raised them weighing 30 lbs. James B. Allen, Union Bridge, N. Y., has grown them weighing 30 lbs., when stripped of loose leaves. Wm. Lee, Jr., Denver City, Colorado, has grown them weighing 45 and 50 lbs., as a penalty for which the miners of the Mountains call him the "Big Cabbage Man." Col. De Lacon, Ogdensburgh, N. Y., has raised them weighing 50 lbs. Leonard Cheat, Denver City, Col., raised one, which when trimmed of waste leaves, weighed 48 lbs. P. Sweeney, Loretto, Penn., has grown them weighing 43 lbs. Sam'l H. Grasser, Blooming Prairie, Wis., has raised them weighing 43 lbs. M. D. Clark, Elyria, Ohio, has grown them weighing 33 lbs. Chas. W. Olsen, Little Sioux, Iowa, produced quite a lot which weighed from 30 to 40 lbs. Hundreds of others have written me that they have "taken all the prizes at the County Fair," "Raised the largest Cabbage ever seen in the country," "Had astonished all their neighbors," "That in sweetness, crispness, and tenderness, they were unequaled." As the original Introducer of the Mammoth Cabbage, I am prepared to supply pure seed in packages containing about 800 seeds, at 25 cents per package, 5 packages for $1, and large quantities at a proportionate discount. Catalogue of over 200 varieties containing many new and rare vegetables, sent gratis to any address.

JAMES J. H. GREGORY, Marblehead, Mass.

PURE CANE SEED.

Regular Sorgo—By Mail, 40 cts. per lb.; by Express, 25 lbs. or less, 25 cts. per lb.; over 25 lbs., 15 cts. per lb.

Liberian, Oomseeana and Neeazana. By Mail, 50 cts. per lb.; by Express, 25 lbs. or less, 35 cts. per lb.; over 25 lbs. 25 cts. per lb. Package included.

Address BLYMYER, NORTON & CO., Successors to CLARK SORGO MACHINE CO., CINCINNATI, OHIO.

THE TILDEN TOMATO.

TRUE. TRUE.

GET THE GENUINE.

Seed will Give Satisfaction.

The undersigned, originator of this truly valuable addition to the Vegetable Garden, has grown it seven years as a field crop, i. e., by the Acre. It shows no tendency whatever to deteriorate, as no other varieties are grown within one mile of his place, and the utmost care is exercised in saving seed, using none but the best specimens. Single packets containing seed enough for 300 plants, postage paid, 25 cents.

5 packets, 50 cts.; 12 packets, $1.00; 100 packets, $12.50.

Address HENRY TILDEN, Davenport, Iowa.

1867. THORBURN'S ANNUAL 1867.

Descriptive Catalogue

of Flower Seeds, now ready. Will be mailed Free to all applicants. SAMUEL T. THORBURN, Seedsman, No. 48 Hudson-st., Albany, N. Y.

EUROPEAN SEEDS—GROWTH 1866.

My Catalogue for the Trade only, is Now Ready. Sent free on application. THOMAS McELROY, 71 Pine st., New York European Seed Grower and Importer.

Farmers and Gardeners!

Many of you have thus far found the purchase of Garden Seed the most unsatisfactory and most vexing of all your investments. Now, *if you will stand by me*, I propose to change all this, and make a revolution in the seed business by my three warrants:—1st, I will warrant my seed to be what it purports to be in kind and quality: 2d, I will warrant that the money you send for seed shall reach me; and 3d, I will warrant that the seed you order shall reach you.

Thus, you see, I take all the risks on myself. I know that in doing this I shall make some losses, but I have confidence that the good sense of the farmers and gardeners of the United States will stand by me in this new movement, and so far increase my business as to enable me to bear all such losses and continue the business on the "three warrants" basis. Stand by me and I will stand by you! Catalogues sent gratis to all. See the advertisement headed "Gregory's Seed Catalogue."

JAMES J. H. GREGORY, Marblehead, Mass.

FLOWER SEEDS BY MAIL.—The Subscriber raises about one hundred kinds of Flower seeds, selected from over one thousand varieties, of the most showy and attractive. He will furnish, neatly put up, any 35 kinds on the list for $1, and send by mail, with postage pre-paid.

C. R. GARRETSON, Flushing, N. Y.

Extra Early York Tomato.

After testing fifteen varieties I have found none that will come are favorably with this for family and market purposes. It is very early—grows to a good market size, lays its fruit in large clusters, well open to the sun, makes but little vine, and is most remarkably prolific, having yielded the past season at the rate of 1000 bushels per acre. Packages containing over 300 seeds, 15 cents each, or 8 for $1. Packages of Tilden's New Seedling Tomato (500 seeds), 15 cents; 8 packets for $1. Catalogue gratis to all.

JAMES J. H. GREGORY, Marblehead, Mass.

SUGAR TROUGH GOURD SEED.

Having the past season raised a very fine lot of these valuable gourds, I offer fresh pure seed for the spring planting. They averaged this year about 8 gallons each, and I have just measured one holding 8 gallons. They have a very hard shell, and will last for years, and for keeping lard are superior to any thing I have ever tried, and are good for many household purposes. Send your orders early. Directions will accompany each package. Price 25 cts. per package of 25 seeds. Address WALDO F. BROWN, Oxford, Butler Co., Ohio.

SEED POTATOES.

Early Goodrich, Harison, Cuzco, Gleason, Coppermine, Calico, Monitor, Pinkeye Rustycoat, White Peach Blow, Flake, Climax, Holbrook, Early Cottage, Sebec, and other varieties will be mailed, in packages containing 4 pounds of either variety, post-paid to any address, upon receipt of One Dollar. For larger quantities and Circular, Address

REISIG & HEXAMER, New Castle, Westchester Co., N. Y.

Potatoes, Choice New Varieties, Early and Late.

E. C. ALLEN, West Meriden, Conn., having raised especially for seed, offers for sale by the bbl. four desirable, productive sorts of the NEW GOODRICH SEEDLINGS, first obtained direct from Mr. Goodrich and his successor—viz. CALLAO, EARLY GOODRICH, GLEASON and CALICO. The CALLAO is very fine quality, early, white flesh, beautiful and productive. Prices for either sort given on application, stating number of bbls. wanted. Orders promptly filled, avoiding shipments in freezing weather. Potatoes can reach New York in less than one day.

Seed Potatoes by Mail as Heretofore.

Early Goodrich,	Jackson White,	Monitor,	Rusty Coat,
Coppermine,	W. Peach Blow,	Gleason,	Cusco,
White Sprout,	Harison,	Chili,	Calico, &c.

4 lb. packages of any kind, $1. Address

See next No. E. WILLIAMS, Montclair, N. J.

SEED POTATOES.

	Per Peck.	Per Bush.	Per bbl.
Early Goodrich and Gleason....	85 cts.	$2.25	$6.00
Calico....................	75 cts.	$2.00	$5.00

Any two or the three kinds sent in a barrel if desired. Orders filled in the order received, and the tubers forwarded by Rail or Express, as directed, as soon as all danger of freezing is past in the spring. Address

G. D. TALCOTT, Owego, Tioga Co., N. Y.

5000 BUSHELS NANSEMOND AND BERMUDA SEED SWEET POTATOES for sale at $13.00 per bbl. of 3 bush. each. (A reasonable discount on large orders and to seed dealers.) Responsible Agents wanted to sprout our Potatoes on Shares. Address

TEN BROOK PIERCE & CO., Rockville, Ind., or South Pass, Union Co., Ill.

YELLOW NANSEMOND SWEET POTATOES for sale, or to sprout on shares. A premium offered. For directions, particulars, &c., address, with stamp,

ALFRED LEE, Kokomo, Ind.

Early Goodrich and Gleason Potatoes, $2 per bush. $5 per bbl., $45 ten bbls. L. R. WELLS, New Britain, Ct.

WHITE ONION SETS!—500 Bushels in fine shipping order, for sale by ROBERT BUIST, Jr., PHILADELPHIA, PA.

Striped Leaved Japanese Maize.

Package containing about 40 seeds of this new ornamental plant sent to any address, for 25 cents. Dealers supplied with packages of seed in bulk at a liberal discount.

JAMES J. H. GREGORY, Marblehead, Mass.

PRIME NEW RED CLOVER SEED, at 18 cents per pound, for sale by GEO. A. DEITZ, Grower and Importer of Seed Wheat and Grass Seeds, Chambersburg, Pa. No extra charge for bags or package.

BLOOMINGTON NURSERY.

Osage Orange Hedge Plants.—Strong, selected, one year, packed in good order, 1,000, $3; 5,000, $13; 10,000, $25. **Apple and Pear Trees**, all sizes. **Early Richmond Cherry. Apple Root Grafts**, best quality. **Kittatinny and Wilson's Early Blackberry.**

Grapes.—Iona, Ives, Israella, Norton's, Concord, Hartford, Rogers' Hybrids, &c., &c.

Nursery Stocks, general assortment. **Sweet Brier Seedlings**, $7.50 per 100. **Peach Seeds**, fresh, frozen, packed, $3 per bush. **Osage Orange and Pear Seeds.**

Evergreens, Shade Trees, immense stock, all sizes.

Althea, Dbl. Named, fine collection, 2 ft., 100, $12.

Roses and Dahlias, extra large, fine collection. **Green-house, Bedding and Garden Plants.** Send red stamp each for 3 Catalogues, Wholesale, Retail and Bedding Plants.

F. K. PHŒNIX, Bloomington, Ill.

PLANTS FOR SALE.

20,000 Jucunda or "Knox's 700" Strawberry, grown from Knox's Stock. Price $4 per 100, or $30 per 1000.

20,000 Wilson's Albany Seedling, $8 per 1000.

5000 Wilson's Early Blackberry, grown from the original stock. This berry is very desirable both for its earliness and great productiveness. 1 plant $1.50, 1 dozen plants $15, 50 plants $50, 100 plants $85, 1000 plants $800.

10,000 Concord Grapes, 25 cts. per vine; $150 per 1000.

5,000 Philadelphia Raspberry, $25 per 100; $200 per 1000.

Plants delivered in Philadelphia free of charge.

Cash orders filed and filled in the order they are received.

Address EDWARD REEVE, Medford, Burlington County, N. J.

12th mo., 31st, 1866.

25,000 APPLE, 3 to 5 yrs., 15,000 Cherry, 1 and 2 yrs., $25 to $40 per 100; 5000 Stand. Pear, 4 to 10 ft.; 2000 Dw'f Pear, bearing; 1000 Apricot, $20 to $30 per 100; Calycanthus, $3 per doz., $20 to $30 per 100; 200,000 Wilson Strawberry, very low. Houghton Seedling Gooseberry, Osage Orange, Linnæus Rhubarb, in large quantities at low rates. Large lot Bartlett and other Pear cions. 125,000 root grafted Apples, and a general stock of Trees and Plants. Address WAMPLER & TILLOTSON, Trotwood, near Dayton, Ohio.

NATIVE EVERGREENS OF THE FOLLOWING varieties, 5 to 12 inches high, at $7 per 1000: Balsam Fir, Arbor Vitæ, White Pine, Spruce and Hemlock. Packing free. JAMES A. ROOT, Skaneateles, N. Y.

Strong, Well Rooted Plants, Warranted Genuine.

The Wilson Early Blackberry.

AVERAGE SIZE.

Most profitable variety yet introduced. Why? Because as large and productive as any other, sweet, firm, and yields its whole crop when most needed between Raspberries and the later Blackberries, Peaches, &c. Price, 1 plant $1.50; 12, $15; 100, $100; 1000, $800.

Kittatinny Blackberry, 1 plant $1; 12, $10; 50, $35; 100, $60. Raspberries, Phil. Rasp. needs only to be tried to be liked. 3 plants $1; 12, $3; 100, $20; 1000, $100; 2000, $150. Clark & Doolittle, 1 plant $1; 12, $10. Any of the above sent free by mail upon receipt of price. Strawberries.—Metcalf's Early, said to be 8 days earlier than Albany. 12 plants $1; 100, $6; 1000, $50. Ida, 12, 50c.; 100, $2; 1000, $15; 5000, $60. Rippawam, 12, $1.25; 50, $4; 100, $7; $1000, $60. Jucunda, or No. 700, 12, 50c.; 100, $2.50; 1000, $20; 5000, $100. Agriculturist, 12, 40c.; 100, $1.50; 1000, $10. Phila. Strawberry, 12, $2; 50, $7; 100, $12; 1000, $100. New Jersey Scarlet, 12, 30c.; 100, $1.50; 1000, $10; 5000, $40. Durand Seedling, 12, $1, 100, $25. Stinger, Starr's, and Mead's Seedlings, 12, $2; 100, $10. Lady Finger, and Triomphe de Gand, 12, 30c.; 100, $1; 1000, $6. Russell, Buffalo, Green Prolific, Byberry Seedling, and Lennig's White, 12, 30c.; 100, $1.50; 1000, $10. Downer, French, Cutter, and Albany Seedlings, 12, 20c.; 100, 80c.; 1000, $5; 5000, $20; 10,000, $35. Brooklyn Scarlet, and Monitor, 12, 30c.; 100, $2. The 31 varieties, 3 plants each, $5; 12, $15. Every family should have a variety.

$2.00 List, Post-paid.

No. 1.—12 Metcalf, 12 French, 12 Agriculturist, 12 Russell, 12 Cutter.

$5.00 List, Post-paid.

No. 1.—12 Metcalf, 12 Rippawam, 12 Ida, 12 Philadelphia, 1 Wilson Early Blackberry, 1 Kittatinny Blackberry.

$10.00 List, Post-paid.

No. 1.—12 Metcalf, 12 French, 12 Agriculturist, 12 Jucunda, 12 Russell, 12 Ida, 12 Philadelphia Raspberry, 4 Wilson Early Blackberry, 4 Kittatinny Blackberry.

$15.00 List.

No. 1.—12 Metcalf, 12 Rippawam, 12 Agriculturist, 12 Ida, 12 Philadelphia, 12 French, 6 Doolittle Raspberry, 6 Philadelphia Raspberry, 6 Wilson Early Blackberry, 6 Kittatinny Blackberry, and 100 Asparagus Roots.

$30.00 List.

No. 1.—12 Metcalf, 12 French, 12 Starr, 12 Philadelphia, 12 Agriculturist, 12 Rippawam Strawberry, 12 Doolittle, 12 Philadelphia Raspberry, 8 Wilson Early, 8 Kittatinny Blackberry, and 100 Asparagus Roots.

For further particulars, Testimonials, &c., send for Catalogue. JOHN S. COLLINS, Moorestown, N. J.

Imported NURSERY STOCKS for sale by G. RAOUX, 42 Cedar-st., New York City.

APPLES, Common, Doucin and Paradise.
CHERRY, Mahaleb and Mazzard.
PEARS, 1 and 2 years.
QUINCE, Angers and Fontenay.
NORWAY SPRUCE, 2 and 3 yrs., transp'd, 1 foot high.
AUSTRIAN AND SCOTCH PINES.
ROSES, Dwarf and Standard, grafted, new and old sorts.
GLADIOLUS, Mixed.
HERBACEOUS PÆONIES, Named sorts.
NEW STRAWBERRY, Gloede's Perpetual, fine.

STRAWBERRIES.

Agriculturist.—I have a large stock of very fine plants of this magnificent variety, at 30c. per doz., $1.00 per 100, or $12.00 per 1000.

Great Ripawam.—This variety took the first prize over all other varieties for the largest berry at the great show of the American Institute. It is wonderfully productive, very large, scarlet, fine flavored, and promises to be one of the best market berries known. Plants, $2.00 per doz., $10.00 per 100, or $90.00 per 1000.

Golden Queen.—A monstrous berry, very handsome, productive and good. (Said by some to be Trollop's Victoria.) With me it is much more productive than that variety. Plants, $1.00 per doz., $5.00 per 100, or $40.00 per 1000.

Ida.—The most productive strawberry known, literally covering the ground with its fruit. Berry, scarlet, medium size, one of the most profitable for market. Plants, $1.00 per doz., $3.00 per 100, or $20.00 per 1000.

New Jersey Scarlet.—One of the earliest to ripen. Fruit large, scarlet, fine, and very productive, valuable. Plants, 50 cts. per doz., $1.00 per 100.

Lenning's White.—The best white berry known. Fruit very large, finest flavor, and very productive. Should be in every collection. Plants, $1.00 per doz., $3.00 per 100, $25.00 per 1000.

Mead's Seedling.—This is put down as one of the finest berries in cultivation. Fruit very large and productive. Plants, $1.00 per doz., $6.00 per 100.

Jucunda, or Knox's 700.—A very large and beautiful berry. Should be in every collection. Plants, $1.00 per doz., $3.00 per 100, $40.00 per 1000.

White Alpine.—A valuable, very productive white berry, so sweet that it requires no sugar for the table. Plants, $1.00 per doz., $3.00 per 100.

Also Wilson, Russell, Buffalo, Austin, Downer's Prolific, French Seedling, Green Prolific, and many others, at low prices. All plants will be delivered in rotation as ordered. Address WM. S. CARPENTER, 156 Reade-st., New York.

500,000 Red Cedar Seedlings.

Would you have a wall of LIVING GREEN to shelter your homes from the STORMS OF WINTER, then PLANT the Red Cedar. EARLY orders filled at following low prices. Send stamp for Circular. Correspondence solicited. 4 to 8 inches high, per 1000, $5.50; 4 to 8 inches, per 10,000, $40. 8 to 12 " per 1000, $10; 20 to 30 inches high, per 100, $15. Address JNO. M. HUNTER & CO., Ashley, Washington Co., Ill.

BY MAIL.

A COMPLETE ASSORTMENT OF GRAPES, STRAWBERRIES, RASPBERRIES, BLACKBERRIES, GOOSEBERRIES, AND CURRANTS.

FOR $10.00,

We will send to any Post-Office address in the United States, the whole of the following list.

GRAPE VINES.

6 **CONCORD.** The most valuable Grape in America.
2 **IVES.** The best American wine grape.
1 **HARTFORD.** } The best very early grapes yet
1 **CREVELING.** } thoroughly tested.
1 **IONA.**

STRAWBERRY PLANTS.

12 **JUCUNDA—our No. 700.** Greatly the most valuable of all our strawberries. See Cut on page 71.
12 **FILLMORE.** Second only to Jucunda.
12 **BURR'S NEW PINE, or** } The best very
12 **GOLDEN SEEDED.** } early varieties
12 **WILSON.** The best for canning.
12 **AGRICULTURIST.**

RASPBERRIES.

3 **BRINCKLE'S ORANGE.** The finest flavored.
3 **IMPROVED BLACK CAP.** Very good and an enormous bearer.

BLACKBERRIES.

2 **ROCHELLE.** Very good and productive.

GOOSEBERRIES.

2 **AMERICAN SEEDLING.** Very good and a great bearer.

CURRANTS.

3 **VERSAILLAISE.** The most valuable.
3 **WHITE GRAPE.** The best for wine.

FOR $20.00,

We will send to any Post-Office address in the United States, the whole of the following list.

GRAPE VINES.

12 **CONCORD.**
6 **IVES.**
6 **CREVELING.**
1 **HARTFORD.**
1 **IONA.**

STRAWBERRY PLANTS.

25 **JUCUNDA—our No. 700.**
25 **FILLMORE.**
25 **BURR'S NEW PINE, or**
25 **GOLDEN SEEDED.**
25 **WILSON.**
25 **AGRICULTURIST.**

RASPBERRIES.

6 **BRINCKLE'S ORANGE.**
6 **IMPROVED BLACK CAP.**

BLACKBERRIES.

6 **ROCHELLE.**

GOOSEBERRIES.

6 **AMERICAN SEEDLING.**

CURRANTS.

6 **VERSAILLAISE.**
6 **WHITE GRAPE.**

THE ABOVE VINES AND PLANTS WILL BE:

1. **All No. 1.**
2. **Carefully Marked.**
3. **Safely Packed.**
4. **Post Paid.**
5. **Their Safe Carriage Guaranteed.**
6. **Accompanying each package there will be Printed Instructions for their management and cultivation.**

The purchaser is at liberty to omit any of the varieties named in these lists, and increase others to the same amount.

We are induced to make the above offers,

1. Because there are many points throughout the country which cannot be easily reached except by mail.

2. Where there are express facilities the charges are often unreasonable.

By the above arrangement wherever there is a Post-Office, parties ordering may be sure of getting a first-class article delivered to them as safely as their letters, and **free of charge.**

Our present stock of vines and plants is much the largest and best we have ever offered. It is important to know as soon as possible, what portion of it to reserve for mail orders. We therefore solicit early orders, and make the following additional **most liberal proposals:**

For every $10 order as above, accompanied by the cash, received previous to March 1st, we will add vines and plants to the amount of $1.

And for every $20 order, as above, accompanied by the cash, received previous to March 1st, we will add vines and plants to the amount of $2.50.

Thus, every family throughout the length and breadth of the country, has the opportunity of securing, by a small outlay, a complete and valuable selection of **Small Fruits.**

All orders will be filled in rotation as received, or at times designated, as far as practicable.

Our Descriptive and Illustrated Catalogue is a valuable treatise on small **Fruit Culture,** and will be sent to all applicants enclosing 10 Cents.

J. KNOX,
Box 155, Pittsburgh, Pa.

VEGETABLES AND FLOWER SEEDS.

J. KNOX, HORTICULTURIST AND SEEDSMAN,

WAREHOUSE, No. 137 Liberty Street, Pittsburgh, Pa.

150 Acres Appropriated to the Culture of Grapes, Strawberries, Currants, Raspberries, &c.

This Season's supply of Seeds has been chosen with more than usual care, and grown by experienced Seedsmen in Europe and the United States. I am enabled through early contracts to offer Seeds of first quality, at reasonable rates.

Descriptive Catalogues mailed upon receipt of postage. They contain much valuable Horticultural information.

For convenience and economy, I will send by mail, **post-paid, upon receipt of the annexed prices—Reliable Collections** for **Small** or **Large Gardens.**

FLOWER SEEDS.

ASSORTMENT NO. 1.—20 Select kinds	....	$1.00
" " 2.—30 " "	....	2.00
" " 3.—100 " "	....	4.00
" " 4.—6 " "	....	1.00

The last Collection embraces the new and charming Prussian varieties of **Pansies, Zinnias, Balsams, Ten Week Stocks, Hunt's Sweet William, General Negley's Amateur Collection of Phlox Drummondii, and Japan Pinks.** These present the gems of all the sub-varieties, and have gained first **Prizes** at our Exhibitions.

VEGETABLE SEEDS.

ASSORTMENT NO. 1.—Intended for a small garden, a quarter of an acre	....	$5.00
" " 2.—For half an acre	....	10.00
" " 3.—For one acre	....	20.00

SPECIAL COLLECTION,

Including the following new and highly approved varieties:
Mappay's Tomato.
Le Normand Cauliflower.
Covent Garden Radish. Tennis Ball Lettuce.
Improved White Spine Cucumber.
New Dwarf Sugar Corn.
Winningstadt Cabbage.
Newington Wonder (Dwarf) Beans.
Early Red Onion, Extra.
Students Parsnip.
Citron Melon, Negley's Hybrids, *fine.*
Early Scarlet Short Horn Carrot.
Sweet Potato Squash.
Cole's Crystal White Celery.
Peas, Daniel O'Rourke, and Hairs.
Dwarf Mammoth. $2.00.

☞ Insure promptness and certainty by early orders.

SILVERS'

PATENT EXCELSIOR BROOM.

5000 Agents Wanted.

We Charge Nothing for the Right to Sell it.

DESCRIPTION.

A single brush or stalk is represented by A; B represents two brushes with their stems bent and passed through the malleable iron loop C; these brushes are arranged alternately until the loop is filled, as represented by D; the seamless metallic band F, made of polished sheet brass or German silver, is then passed over the filled loop, after which it is firmly screwed into the ferruled handle, and thus held in a compact form as represented by the cut.

This celebrated broom has now been before the public for one year, and has proved itself to be as represented—the cheapest, simplest, most beautiful, durable and ELASTIC in the United States. It has been awarded the first premium wherever exhibited, including the New York, Ohio, and Kentucky State Fairs of 1866, and is highly recommended by the leading Journals, and scientific men of the country, as the following unsolicited notices of the press and testimonials will show.

[From the Scientific American.]

SILVERS' METHOD OF CONSTRUCTING A BROOM MAKES A MUCH BETTER ARTICLE THAN THE OLD-FASHIONED ONE, FOR THE SHANK IS STIFF AND HELD FAST, THUS OBTAINING A SPRING OR ELASTICITY WHICH IS VALUED BY HOUSEKEEPERS.

[From the American Agriculturist, after 3 Month's Test.]

SILVERS' PATENT BROOM.—This is a novelty, certainly. By means of a cap and screw, the brush can be removed at any time. We have no broom corn at hand to test the removal of the old brush and the putting in of new, but we do not see why it can not be readily done by any one, and farmers thus raise a little plot of broom corn and make their own brooms, after buying a patent handle. The one we are using has a superior elasticity.

[From the Boston Cultivator.]

Everybody who sees it says it is *perfection*, and that it will soon supersede all others. Let every farmer plant a small piece of broom corn, grow the brush and make his own brooms hereafter, as all can do.

[From a Report of the American Institute "Farmers' Club," in the New York Weekly Tribune.]

Silvers' Patent Broom was exhibited. An iron screw-bolt, some six inches long, has an open head. The stalks of the brush are scarfed off and put in this loop, alternately from each side, until there is enough for a broom. Then a metallic cap is slipped down over the brush, to hold it in proper shape and keep it firm in the loop. The handle is then screwed on, and the broom is finished. When the broom is worn out, unscrew, shake out the old brush and insert new. *A child ten years old can make a new broom in ten minutes.* These new contrivances will tempt farmers to grow their own broom corn.

EMPORIUM OF FASHION, 473 Broadway,
New York, June, 1866.

MR. SILVERS: The beauty and practical utility of your "Excelsior Broom Head" are too SELF-EVIDENT to require commendation. I cordially indorse all you claim for it.

MME. DEMOREST.

[From Prof. O. S. Fowler, the Celebrated Phrenologist.]

DEAR SIRS: In my judgment your broom embodies the very best sweeping instrument extant. You will save dollars to every cleanly family, and thousands per annum to our country by its introduction—in doing which you are public benefactors.

[From E. P. Cooley, the Noted Corn Broom and Brush Manufacturer, 294 Pearl Street, New York.]

Silvers' is the only Patent Broom I have ever seen that is of any account. This patent, for simplicity, durability, beauty, elasticity and cheapness, seems perfection itself.

[From Miles Greenwood & Co., Cincinnati.]

Having examined Silvers' Patent Excelsior Broom Head, we have no hesitation in recommending it as being one of the most perfect we have seen.

THE ELASTICITY of this Broom is so great that it will wear twice as long, sweep with half the effort, AND DOES NOT WEAR OUT THE CARPET one fourth as fast as the ordinary broom. It is fast becoming a universal favorite, AND IS THE ONLY PATENT BROOM EQUALLY ADAPTED TO CITY AND COUNTRY, as the filled loops D will soon be supplied by all dealers at two-thirds the cost of the common broom.

TO AGENTS.—We want an Agent in every County in the United States. We charge nothing for the right to sell, but let it stand on its own merits. All of our Agents are doing well. Mr. Geo. A. Wetherell sold 1100 in Athens Co., Ohio, and expects to sell as many more in Morgan Co. William Marvin made $31 in the first day's canvass in Ulster Co., N. Y. A. Goodale, Agent for Orange Co., N. Y., writes that he expects it will supersede all others in his County, as the ladies say they will use no other when the "SILVERS" is to be procured.

For Illustrated Circular, Terms, &c., Address

C. A. CLEGG & CO.,
200 Broadway, New York,
Proprietors and Manufacturers.

See Advertisement "ALL NURSERIES IN ONE," on page 73.

GET WELL AND KEEP WELL.—Read the Advertisement of Herald of Health, page 72.

KNOX'S NURSERY AT YOUR DOOR.—See Advertisement "By Mail," page 77.

PORTABLE AND STATIONARY ENGINES,

CIRCULAR SAW AND GRIST MILLS.

The Old and Extensive Establishment, the Mount Vernon Iron Works, has for sale:

20	*Portable* Engines Mounted on Wheels	of	8	Horse	Power.
25	do. do. do. do.		10	do.	do.
17	do. do.		15	do.	do.
40	*Portable* and 10 *Stationary* Engines	of	20	Horse	Power.
10	do. and 22 do. do.	of	25	do.	do.
15	do. and 11 do. do.	of	30	do.	do.
11	*Stationary* Engines	of	35	do.	do.
9	do. do.	of	40	do.	do.
7	do. do.	of	50	do.	do.
5	do. do.	of	65	do.	do.
3	do. do.	of	80	do.	do.
2	do. do.	of	100	do.	do.

Also, 250 CIRCULAR SAW MILLS of all sizes, and 150 HERD & DUCKWORTH'S SUPERIOR PATENT FLOURING AND FEED MILLS, with BOLTS and other fixtures.

All are being erected with modern improvements, AND THE GREATEST STRENGTH AND DURABILITY IS GUARANTEED.

THIS FIRM WAS THE FIRST TO COMMENCE THE PRACTICE OF FURNISHING THE ENTIRE MACHINERY AND COMPLETE FIXTURES FOR GRIST AND SAW MILLS, AND MILL WRIGHTS, TO ERECT AND PUT THEM IN RUNNING ORDER; hence, their great success and reputation for getting up the BEST MILLS IN THE WORLD.

Deliveries made in any of the principal cities of the United States.

For Information or Circulars Address

C. & J. COOPER,
Mount Vernon, Ohio.

The Great National Field Trial of Mowers & Reapers.

THE PREMIUM MACHINE.

In the important features of lightness of draft, and freedom from side draft, the "BUCKEYE MOWER," (built by ADRIANCE, PLATT & CO., 165 Greenwich St., New York,) surpassed all competitors, and was declared by the Judges, to be superior in mechanical construction, facility of management, portability, strength, and durability. The "BUCKEYE MOWER" was the only machine which received the highest mark (10) for perfect work in every kind of grass, and on all varieties of surface.

MAPLE SUGAR.

To make the **Best Quality** with the greatest

Saving of Labor and Fuel,

Use the Celebrated

COOK'S EVAPORATOR.

Maple Circular and Descriptive Pamphlet sent free of charge, on application.

PURE SORGO AND IMPHEE SEED of the best varieties. Send for Circular. BLYMYER, BATES & DAY, Mansfield, Ohio.

Important to Farmers.

Will be sent anywhere free of express charges for $3, one of McConaughey's Patent Corn Droppers, one of the most complete machines ever invented for dropping corn, sorgo, and other seeds. Agents wanted to introduce it.
Patented March 27, 1860, and Dec. 4, 1866.
THOS. B. McCONAUGHEY, Newark, Delaware.

THE HOG BREEDERS' MANUAL.

A Treatise on Breeding, Feeding, and General Management of Hogs. Particulars of all Diseases, Remedies, &c. Sent free of postage for 25 cents. Every farmer should have a copy. Address N. P. BOYER & CO., Gum Tree, Chester Co., Pa.

THE VANISHING PICTURE TRICK, 25 cents.—How to Write Letters Correctly, 15 cts.—Guide to Etiquette, 15 cts.—Bridal Etiquette, 15 cts.—Courtship Made Easy, 15 cts.—Housekeepers' Own Book, 15 cts.—Barry's How to Buy, Tame and Keep Horses, 15 cts.—Knowlson's Farrier, 15 cts.—Home Cook Book, 30 cts.—Parlor Magician, 30 cts.—Parlor Theatricals, 30 cts.—Parlor Pantomimes, 25 cts.—Puzzles, 30 cts.—Fireside Games, 30 cts.—Laws of Love, 30 cts.—Love Oracle, 30 cts.—Comic Courtship, 30 cts.—Great Fortune-Teller, 50 cts. Thousands of other Books, Pictures, Albums, Games, Yankee Notions. Send stamp for Mammoth Catalogue. W. C. WEMYSS, 575 Broadway, N. Y. City.

DEMOREST'S MONTHLY MAGAZINE.—Splendid attractions in the February Number. Now Ready. The February number contains a beautiful Engraving of the Ascent of the Matterhorn, in Oil Colors, worth many times the cost of the Magazine. Also, New Music, Entertaining Stories, and other novelties. Single copies 30 cents, *mailed free*; Yearly, $3, with a valuable premium. No. 473 Broadway, New York. Splendid Premiums and for Terms Clubs. Now is the time to subscribe.

YOUR SON WOULD BE GREATLY benefited by reading the PHRENOLOGICAL JOURNAL.

THE NEW MAGAZINE FOR 1867.

THE RIVERSIDE MAGAZINE

FOR YOUNG PEOPLE,
BRILLIANTLY ILLUSTRATED BY THE BEST AMERICAN ARTISTS.
FEBRUARY NUMBER NOW READY.
TWO FULL-PAGE ILLUSTRATIONS
AND NUMEROUS ENGRAVINGS.
A SUPERIOR NUMBER.

Subscription, $2 50 per annum, in advance.
A liberal discount to Clubs.
Sample numbers, one by mail, prepaid, for 20 cents.
Clergymen and Teachers furnished one year for $2 00.
Send your subscriptions direct to

HURD & HOUGHTON, Publishers,
459 Broome st., New York.

*** Agents and Canvassers wanted in all parts of the country. Apply as above.

THE GAME OF LOTO

Given Away with No. 10 of

Send 5 Cents and you will receive in return No. 10, post-paid, with the GAME OF LOTO on a separate sheet.
FRANK LESLIE, 537 Pearl-st., New York.

AMERICAN RE-PRINT OF LONDON SOCIETY;

A Popular Magazine.
BRILLIANTLY ILLUSTRATED.
Messrs. HURD & HOUGHTON

Have now ready the January number of this deservedly popular magazine—reprinted in this country by special arrangement with the London publishers.

The Programme for 1867 will contain many readable and entertaining topics, amply illustrated by eminent artists.

TERMS OF SUBSCRIPTION.

Single numbers	$0 40
One copy, one year	4 50
Two copies, one year	8 50
Five copies, one year	20 00
Ten copies, one year	40 00

And an extra copy gratis.

CLUBBING WITH THE RIVERSIDE MAGAZINE FOR YOUNG PEOPLE:

The *Riverside Magazine* ($2 50 per annum) and *London Society* ($4 50 per annum) sent to one address for six dollars.
☞ All subscriptions are payable in advance.
HURD & HOUGHTON, Publishers,
459 Broome-st., New York.

Sample copies of the January number, sent by mail prepaid, on receipt of 30 cents.

Agents Wanted for Headley's Great Work.

The only book issued on our Navy during the Rebellion. Agents find no competition.

Comprising popular Biographies of our Naval Heroes, by Hon. J. T. HEADLEY, the distinguished Author and Historian—complete in one large volume—handsomely illustrated on steel. The best paying agency of the day. In connection with this work our Agents can take orders for five of Headley's Standard Works of our own publication. Call or send at once for circulars and terms. Address E. B. TREAT & CO., Publishers, 654 Broadway, New York.

THE MOTHERS' JOURNAL, And FAMILY VISITANT.

A Monthly Magazine, for Mothers and the Household. With nothing light or trashy, it is practical in purpose, substantial in matter, attractive in style. To aid Mothers in their noble, but difficult work, and to make the family healthy, happy, useful, and good, is the object of the JOURNAL. Price $1.50 per year. Five copies, $7. Single Numbers, *fifteen cents*. Send by mail, directed to "MOTHERS' JOURNAL, 500 Broadway, New York."

(CONTINUED FROM PAGE 66, WHICH SEE.)

wine. * * * No! the Concord won't make wine, even in the West. You may set that down as a sure thing."

EXTRACT FROM WILLIAM GRIFFITH, LATE PRESIDENT OF LAKE-SHORE WINE CO.

Northeast, Jan. 10, 1867.

"DR. C. GRANT.—While sending my order for another ten thousand No. 1 Iona vines, I cannot forbear offering a few remarks. Last year, after (as I thought) becoming thoroughly acquainted with the Iona both for fruit and for wine, I felt constrained to say: "If C. W. Grant had gotten it up to order, I know not in what respect he could have improved it." But we lost a thousand fine vines by the freezing and thawing of our open rainy winter. Did that change my opinion of the Iona? Not at all! Why should it? All other kinds that received the same treatment in planting, Concord included, shared the same fate, while the Iona under the treatment that you recommend, passed unscathed. Between bad treatment and multitudes of poor plants, and *other difficulties* that should not attach to it, the Iona has a heavy weight not its own to carry. An extended tour of observation has added great weight of confirmation to my own experience. * * * * I shall take much pleasure in disseminating knowledge of it. It needs but to be thoroughly known to take precedence of all other kinds *for all purposes*. In the amount of enjoyment it can yield for fruit or wine, there is none to compete with it.

In the next number I shall give some interesting facts concerning the Greeley prizes, showing that no "*Greeley prize*" has ever been awarded to any except the Iona Grape, or could be. See Downing & Mead's report, also pamphlet, for which send stamp.

IONA, Jan. 10, 1867.

C. W. GRANT.

N. B.—For Advertisement of Iona and Israella, see January number, page 33.

INCOME TAX PAYER'S GUIDE. Sent by mail on receipt of 25 cts. Incomes must soon be returned—be as well posted as the assessor—SAVE MONEY.
F. H. STAUFFER, Publisher, Mount Joy, Pa.

ALMANACS FOR 1867.

Frank Leslie's

ILLUSTRATED ALMANAC,

With Over Sixty Illustrations.
And full of useful information.
Sixty-Four Pages, Large Octavo. Price 50 Cents.

FRANK LESLIE'S
ILLUSTRATED LADY'S ALMANAC,

With over Seventy Illustrations. Full of useful information and pleasant reading for the ladies. Sixty-Four pages, Large Octavo. Price, 50 Cents.

On receipt of 50 Cents, either of these beautiful Almanacs will be sent post-paid, to any part of the United States or Canada. Address

FRANK LESLIE, 537 Pearl-st., New York.

LIFE OF ANDY JOHNSON,

By PETROLEUM V. NASBY, including Andy's trip to the West and his "orations." With 33 comic illustrations. This book is very funny and has made a big hit. Sent free for 30 cts. Also, Secrets Worth Knowing, tells how to make medicines, perfumery, toilet articles, soaps, dyes, candies, wines, delicious beverages, manufacturers' secrets and hundreds of articles in universal use, made at trifling cost and sold at immense profits, including most of the good advertised money making secrets, 25 cts.—How to Make Bad Memory Good and Good Better, valuable to professional men, teachers and students, especially when preparing for examination, 15.—Handbook of Phonography, a new practical work for self instruction, 25.—Handbook of Ventriloquism, plain and simple, and really teaching the art, also how to make the Magic Whistle, 15.—Rogues and Rogueries, exposing all tricks and traps of great cities and all swindles and humbugs, 25.—Also send Ten cents for samples of our Hundred Dollar Prize Puzzles, Magic Wells, Puzzle Pictures, &c. HANEY & CO., office MERRYMAN'S MONTHLY, (15 cents, 8 for $1, post-paid,) 100 Nassau-st., New York.

Photographs—1000 Subjects.

Price 15 cents each. Agents wanted. Send stamp for Catalogue to CARTER, COLLINS & RICHARDSON, 42 John-st., New York.

To Small Fruit Growers.

Send for Specimen Copy of the Hammonton Culturist, A Monthly Journal, devoted to the Interest of Fruit Culture. Terms, 25 cents per Annum. 16 pp. Address E. MALTACE, Publisher, No. 904 Market-st., Philadelphia. (Box 1888.)

SCHOOL TEACHERS SHOULD read the PHRENOLOGICAL JOURNAL, and learn to classify and teach their students according to temperaments and capacity. Also to govern them wisely. Only $2 a year. FOWLER & WELLS, New York.

IF YOU are not well supplied with berries, see J. S. COLLINS' Advertisement, page 76, this No., to be supplied by mail.

To Advertisers.

Agricultural and Religious Papers
The Best Advertising Mediums.

We have COMPLETE LISTS of both classes, and can insert advertisements in any of them at PUBLISHERS' LOWEST CASH RATES.
CARLTON & SMITH, 171 Broadway, New York.

GET WELL AND KEEP WELL.—Read the Advertisement of Herald of Health, page 72.

IONA AND ISRAELLA.

CONTINUED FROM JANUARY NO., PAGE 33.

If it is true that persons who have eaten no better grapes than Concord, can have no idea of *good grapes*, still further are those from any just idea of the goodness of real wine, or of what are the principal constituents of its excellence who have only drank the syrups made from the juice of that or any of its class. Several years since I felt called upon to make the declaration that Concord *had not* made wine, and could not make wine. This stands unshaken at the present moment by anything that the Concord has produced in *any quarter*. Poor vinegar and various syrups and confections have been made from Concord grapes, but no *wine*.

The excellence of wine *must* exist in the grape, and only those kinds which possess the requisite characteristic qualities can make *wine*. Those qualities, and in proper proportion, have never been found to exist in the Concord. It is unnecessary to note here its nauseating odor which is even more prominent and offensive in the wine than in the grapes.

I have not space allowed me here at present to complete this Essay, but quite enough to write a *full* history of the Concord grape to be read two years hence. "The more it was known, the less it was esteemed. Numerous fortunes were made by the propagators of it, and more pecuniary interest centered in it in this respect, than in all other kinds combined," which "The most *capable* and *impartial* Committee that ever sat in judgment upon grapes, made their best effort to conserve." The Committee was made thus *impartial* and *capable* by weeding out of it Charles Downing and Peter B. Mead, who were manifestly unsuited to the emergency.

A few Objections against the IONA briefly noted:

"It was destroyed last winter in large numbers, by being thrown out and frozen." This is sadly true; and all other kinds, Concord and Delaware included, by their side, suffered just the same, that were subjected to the same treatment, while all, treated according to the directions of my Manual, withstood without injury. Mr. Wm. Griffith, (late President of the Lake Shore Wine Co.) who was the largest sufferer by the unprecedented winter, writes: "The loss was not from want of hardiness in the kinds, and I have lost no jot of faith in the Iona. The ten thousand I had *from you* last season made a very handsome, even growth, and are now having a healthful sleep preparatory to a vigorous start next spring. I hereby send an order for another ten thousand vines, to be sent in early spring."

Mr. Mottier was also a large loser, but he has given a public statement, that *any* kind, under like circumstances, must have failed equally. (For full account, see Pamphlet.) His recent order, greatly enlarged over former years, shows, in connection with his notes, the present state of his mind on the subject.

It has been alledged, as a *great fault*, that it did not receive the award of the Greeley prize; but I think that has been clearly shown to be a grievous *misfortune* rather, not *chiefly* to the grape—*far* otherwise.

It is charged that although unqualifiedly best for the table, it may not be equally excellent for wine. I offer the following from the Secretary and Manager of the Pleasant Valley Wine Co., who is *capable* certainly, but perhaps neither "impartial nor disinterested":

PLEASANT VALLEY, Jan., 1867.

DR. C. W. GRANT.

I have tried the Iona wine by the severest tests that could be furnished, and all of the trials have been very satisfactory.

Taking the best Catawba wine that has been made as "*very good*," I should place Delaware next above it in rank; Diana, for some qualities, next above that, and Iona above all.

Placing Iona by the side of the finest wines of Germany, that are not excelled in the world, it does not suffer in comparison in any respect, while it has some important characteristics entirely its own that, in my estimation, place it above that of all other grapes with which I am acquainted. I intend to plant largely of it, and of that only, and from my own experience and extended observation, confidently recommend the same to my friends.

Enclosed find order for 10,000 Iona vines No. 1, Vineyard Class.

C. D. CHAMPLIN, Secretary,
Pleasant Valley Wine Co.

An extract from Dr. Charles J. May, Hancock Co., Ill.: "I propose to plant Iona, and only that hereafter, although Delaware does admirably here, and makes excellent wine—*real* wine, which the Concord never has done. It is true, immense yields of the Concord are recorded, both in this vicinity and in Missouri. But did you ever believe that here in the West, the Concord does make a good wine? Did you *for one* moment believe that our soil and climate had so changed its nature? I ask you this, because for a time I thought it might be *possible*. I could not bring myself to *believe* it, but thought it possible. Well, we have grown Concord grapes in their highest perfection; we have made wine from selected berries, using only the ripest and most perfect; we have made the wine in our best arched cellars, and have used everything known to the present age of wine-making, to make it perfect, except sugar, and the result is, wine that will make a pig squeal. I speak now of pure

(*CONTINUED ON PAGE 79, WHICH SEE.*)

AMERICAN AGRICULTURIST

FOR THE

Farm, Garden, and Household.

"AGRICULTURE IS THE MOST HEALTHFUL, MOST USEFUL, AND MOST NOBLE EMPLOYMENT OF MAN."—Washington.

ORANGE JUDD & CO., PUBLISHERS AND PROPRIETORS. Office, 41 Park Row, (Times Buildings.)

ESTABLISHED IN 1842. Published also in German at $1.50 a Year.

$1.50 PER ANNUM, IN ADVANCE. SINGLE NUMBER, 15 CENTS. 4 Copies for $5; 10 for $12; 20 or more, $1 each.

VOLUME XXVI—No. 3. NEW-YORK, MARCH, 1867. NEW SERIES—No. 242.

THE BALD EAGLE.—(*Haliætus leucocephalus.*)—*Drawn and Engraved for the American Agriculturist.*

The Bald or White Headed Eagle, is, without dispute, one of the most striking and beautiful of the eagles, from his dark heavy plumage, white head and tail. There is nothing particularly noble about the bird, and many have considered it unfortunate that he was made the national emblem. Bald Eagles are occasionally seen in all the States of the Union. In winter they are frequently quite common along the coast. We have seen them in groups along the Sound coast of Connecticut, so tired as to be easily approached, probably having been blown by some storm far out to sea, and having made the coast at that point. This eagle lives upon fish, birds, and such animals as it can catch and overpower. Often it lets the Fish Hawk catch the fish, and then pursues the hawk, thus impeded in its flight, forces it to let its prey fall, when, adroitly turning, the eagle robber catches it in the air. In certain feats of flight, it surpasses all other birds—soaring in circles out of sight, without perceptibly moving its wings; closing its wings and dropping perpendicularly from immense heights, and with the sound of a rushing wind.

The length of these birds is about 35 to 40 inches, and the spread of the wings about seven feet. The plumage of the body and wings is brownish black, that of the thickly feathered head and the tail being white, in adult birds only; the feet are yellow, and the beak a paler yellow

Contents for March, 1867.

INDEX TO "BASKET," OR SHORTER ARTICLES.

Back Volumes Supplied.—The back volumes of the *Agriculturist* are very valuable. They contain information upon every topic connected with rural life, out-door and in-door, and the last ten volumes make up a very complete library. Each volume has a full index for ready reference to any desired topic. We have on hand, and print from stereotype plates as wanted, all the numbers and volumes for ten years past, beginning with 1857—that is, Vol. 16 to Vol. 25, inclusive. Any of these volumes sent complete (in numbers) at $1.75 each, post-paid, (or $1.50 if taken at the office). The volumes neatly bound, are supplied for $2 each, or $2.50 if to be sent by mail. Any single numbers of the past ten years will be supplied, post-paid, for 15 cents each.

AMERICAN AGRICULTURIST.

NEW-YORK, MARCH, 1867.

Good or ill success in the farming operations of the season depend very much upon this month—much upon the weather of this most variable and uncertain of all changeable periods, and more upon the farmer's own ability, promptness and diligence to take advantage of events. There are many things in the future that we may calculate upon with great certainty, and, planning to take advantage of *them*, be able to turn the uncertainties to our good also. We shall have in March 31 days and nights—many frosty nights and cold days; some storms and rainy days, cold, clear, drying northwest winds lapping up the water over the fields and drying the fall-plowed furrows. We shall have sunshine too, warming the ground and breaking the frost fetters. The snow on the hills will melt and the streams will swell, sweeping off fences and bridges, perhaps. The roads will be broken up, traveling hindered, and mails detained, going to mill with grain and to town for needed articles, will be a labor to be undertaken only by the pressure of necessity. Poultry will be laying, and clucking or setting. Foxes, minks and other vermin will be prowling about. Calves, lambs and pigs will be coming into the world; stock will be hungry, and we hope, satisfied also. There is work to be done and time to do it in.

Hints About Work.

Plans for the Month.—We shall all accomplish double the work, if it be well laid out, and it will be better done.—"What do we want done?"—"How and when shall we do it?"—Let us make a list of the things we want to do most, and then see how fast we can cancel them off as *done*.

Hired Labor.—If a farmer does not hire any labor now, let it be his aim to employ as many men as he profitably can, and make arrangements to do so as soon as he can. Hired men are often very disagreeable associates, and the worst companions for one's children, but this need not be; lookout at once for good, steady, moral men, and sacrifice the profits of the farm rather than have a vicious, bad fellow about, though his work be never so needed. If we do our part to make the men comfortable and do them good, few will ill reward it.

Buildings.—The winds will find out any insecure weather boards and shingles, and play mischief with the exposed hay stacks and with thatched roofs. Have nails and hammer at hand; stop leaks; see that door and shutter fastenings are secure, and that board fences, posts of which are loosened by the frost, are not prostrated by the wind.

Cellars.—Over-haul the roots, put them in bins or boxes, or make fresh heaps of sound ones only; clean out cellars, air and white wash; stop rat-holes with coal tar and mortar, said to be rat-proof.

Draining.—While the frost is coming out of the ground, and the soil of plowed side-hills is liable to slide, look to it that no water finds its way upon such spots, or great damage may ensue. Open surface drains with the hoe, pick, or mattock, so that surface water may flow off upon sward ground or where it will not wash off the soil. Such water from cart paths, roads, or plowed fields brings with it, upon the meadows and pastures, a wealth of enrichment, not to be lost. The advantage of

Irrigation can hardly be over-estimated. If a brook can be turned to flow at will (your will) over a piece of meadow, even in the crudest and simplest way, by all means try it, and then profit by experience to extend the system, or rather, profit by the experience of others and use the best system.

Grain Fields are especially liable to injury from washing, and surface drains on them should be kept free. Top-dressings of plaster, bonedust, superphosphate, guano, fine fowl-house compost, home-made poudrette and such things are applied with great advantage at this season.

Clover and Grass Seed may be sown on winter grain; best on a still day, after a light snow, which may have fallen on frost-cracked and thawing ground.

Plowing should be done as soon as the ground is dry enough, but not one hour before; better wait a week or two than compact the soil, so that it will dry into hard clods, which will last for months.

Peas may be sown as soon as the ground is dry enough to plow well, often in March, in this latitude; they may be sown broad cast, alone or mixed with oats, or in drills. On warm, early spots the drill culture may be recommended. The soil should be in good order for a heavy crop of oats, and deeply plowed, then plow shallow (4-inch) furrows, and in every third furrow scatter the peas, throwing in twelve to fifteen to the running foot. If you have time these may be picked for marketing green, and if not, the crop will be ripe enough to cut and cure, and leave the ground for summer plowing, and wheat, cabbages or turnips may follow.

Seeds.—Procure, and test the vitality of all seeds.

Horses need very thorough grooming, and the feet and legs should be washed and kept clean, long fetlocks trimmed off, and any redness or cracking of the skin or heels treated with pine tar and grease, or an ointment of lard and turpentine. These applications are either of them very good for chafed shoulders, sprains, or harness galls. Blanket carefully if exposed to the wind or cold when warm.

Working Oxen.—Protect from storms; feed well; use the card freely; impose hard labor gradually; have well fitting yokes, and if their necks become tender, give a day or two of rest, and grease the spot, rubbing the grease well in. A wet towel on the neck, with a piece of blanket bound over it, kept on one night, and the neck greased well the next day, will, it is said, cure a very tender neck between Saturday night and Monday morning.

Cows.—Give good care, personal attention, and roomy box stalls to cows about to calve. They may need assistance, and suffer much or even die for lack of it. If milk is worth much the

Calves should be removed from their dams at once, and brought up on skimmed milk gruel. The cow misses the calf least if she never even licks it; but we would rather she should worry more, when she loses her calf after a day or two, than deprive her of the satisfaction of loving and licking it awhile.

Lice, from many causes, show themselves, especially among ill-kept stock, more in spring than at any other season. They cannot stand regular carding and brushing, but if very bad, should be treated to an application of alum water, with a good rubbing, and subsequent carding and greasing, on the same day of two or three weeks in succession. Mercurial ointment (unguentum), is sure death to the lice, and to the ox too, if too much be used. A lump as big as a hazelnut, rubbed up with a table-spoonful or more of lard is enough for an ox. Rub it in behind the horns and along the spine, then spread it by thoroughly rubbing with straw. Keep the animal from exposure to wet or storms.

Sheep.—Mutton sheep may be yeaning this month. Separate ewes and give them warm quarters, with a few extra roots or other feed.

Hogs.—Isolate breeding sows, give warm pens and treatment as before directed. Keep others at work in the manure, giving sods, etc., to be worked over.

Poultry.—Give chance to run and scratch and dust themselves. Save eggs for setting, and make sure of a few clutches of early chickens for winter layers.

Field work of a miscellaneous kind there will be no lack of. Get out and cart off stones loosened by the frost. Reset fence posts, or walls, where needed, with spuds, spades, and hoes; clear out the bull-thistles, docks, and all biennial weeds that show themselves. Remove also any rubbish from fields and fence rows. Open ditches and mend roads.

Manure.—Haul out while the ground is frozen or after it is settled. Spread at once, whether for plowing under or for top dressing, but put it on no spots where flowing surface water will wash it away. It is best to plow it under at once, unless it be well made compost, which will bear weathering.

Work in the Horticultural Departments.

The next worst thing to being too late, is being too early. As soon as the snows disappear, the enthusiastic cultivator is desirous of beginning out of door operations. He has read and planned all winter, and now wishes to execute. How tedious it is to wait until the ground is in "working order," and ready to receive trees, vines, or seeds. Yet we must wait, and the time required for soil to be fit to work will depend upon its natural or artificial drainage. Let this springs' experience of those who have to wait for the waters to subside, emphasize our often repeated injunction, to drain the orchard, vineyard, or kitchen garden, if the soil be at all retentive. Look over the notes of the two preceeding months and see if some preparatory work is not there suggested which is still undone, and do not delay sending orders to nurserymen and seedmen.

Orchard and Nursery.

Many trees will be purchased this month, and we would give a word of caution against the common practice of ordering large trees. A small, well grown tree with an abundance of small roots, is greatly to be preferred to a tall, much branched one, with its large roots chopped off in the digging. Some of the best western orchardists prefer trees one year from the bud or graft, to any other.

Heel-in at once trees that arrive before you are ready to plant; bury their roots well in a sandy place, and they may remain for weeks without injury.

Plant whenever the soil is ready, taking care to first trim mutilated roots, and shorten back the top; planting will generally be left until next month.

Insects are always to be looked after. See notes for January and the article on the canker-worm, on page 102. If small cottony spots, looking like mould, are seen, they are the far too common Woolly-Aphis, and for this the best remedy is the

Soft Soap Wash, which may be applied with advantage, even if no insects are visible. Make as strong as it will work; it removes not only insects and their eggs, but parasitic plants and loose bark as well.

Girdled trees must be attended to as soon as the injury is discovered. Where the girdling is complete, the tree may often be saved by connecting the bark above and below the wound, by means of cions whittled to a thin chamfer at each end, and inserted beneath the bark. Cover with wax or grafting clay, or simply bandage securely, and put a mound of earth around the tree large enough to cover the wounded portion.

Grafting should not be done too soon. It is time enough when the swelling of the buds shows that vegetation is active. Continue to secure cions, and preserve as heretofore directed. Cut back

Stocks budded last year, if the bud is sound.

Fruit Garden.

Trees in this department will need the care indicated under Orchard.

Grape vines that were laid down may be uncovered as soon as severe weather is over. In planting new vines, cut them back to two or three buds, provided the nurseryman has not done it before sending them. In any system of training, a single cane is all that should be grown the first year.

Cuttings of currant, grape, etc., are to be set out as soon as the soil is ready. It cannot be too often repeated, that much of the success of this kind of propagation, depends upon pressing the soil firmly around the lower end of the cuttings.

Currants.—Set out plants early. The Versailles is the best red, and the White Grape the best white. There are many varieties, only such in name. Plant

Gooseberries—only the American sorts are to be commended for general cultivation, and among these the Houghton is one of the most reliable. Some of the English sorts will do for amateurs to pet.

Strawberries should have the beds all ready for them, and the plants be set as early as they can be had. The Wilson is the variety still the most generally reliable, though there are many better sorts that succeed in favorable situations.

Blackberries.—The sooner they are planted the better. Kittatinny and Wilson's Early are among the newer kinds, and the New Rochelle is now so well known as to need no description.

Raspberries, also need early planting, as, like blackberries, the shoots push early, and are liable to be broken if they have made much growth. The Philadelphia and the Clark are two of the most promising new sorts. For the many older varieties, of these and other plants, consult the catalogues.

Kitchen Garden.

Except where glass, as hot-beds or cold-frames, is in use, the work in this latitude is still mainly preparatory, and but little is gained, as a general thing, by commencing gardening operations before next month. In dry or well drained soils,

Plowing may be done, but only when their condition will admit of thorough pulverization. Recollect that ground for a garden can hardly be too thoroughly worked or too highly enriched.

Manure, especially if well rotted, should be applied with a liberal hand; on stiff soils, coarser manure may be used, and on sandy ones, apply peat with ashes, or peat with lime, if at command. One of the best gardens we ever worked, was so sandy that it would blow when dry, but by the aid of muck and ashes we gained astonishing crops. As to

Hot-beds, we have already said sufficient in the article, Profits from Small Places, p. 63, where some hints on cold-frames, and a substitute, will be found. The novice, in the use of glass, especially if over a hot-bed, needs to be told of the importance of

Airing.—He will learn it after having a crop or two scorched by the sun, but that is rather expensive knowledge. Not only seedlings, but plants that have been wintered and escaped damage from cold, are now liable to be burned; hence,

Cold-frames will need frequent attention, and in the case of lettuce and cabbage wintered over, if the plants are properly hardened, the glass may be removed altogether, and used over other frames.

Seeds.—By all means order at once, and if roots of any kind, or cabbage or other plants, have been wintered over for seed-raising, put them out, the last of the month, in a dry rich spot, and do not plant allied varieties near each other. More attention to seed-raising would lessen the complaints of bad seed. It would be a good thing if the members of local clubs would each agree to raise one or two sorts of seeds. By doing thus, greater purity and perfection could be attained, and each community could raise nearly all its own seed.

Old seeds should be tried, if any doubt exists as to their reliability. Count out a dozen or twenty, put them in a box or pot of earth in a warm place, keep moist, but not too wet, and see the proportion that starts. If half the number grow, it will be safe to plant them. Look over the article on page 53, (last month,) and see if you have all the needed

Conveniences in the Garden.—Those mentioned and figured there are great helps to save labor.

Asparagus.—Remove the litter from old beds as soon as severe weather is over, and if there is not a good dressing of short manure left on the bed, put on some good manure and fork it in. Apply a dressing of 2 to 3 pounds of salt to the square yard. Sow seed for new plants as early as the soil is ready, in a rich bed, in rows a foot apart. Where new plantations are to be made, have the ground highly manured and deeply worked. Set good one or two year old plants, and cover the crowns 2 or 3 inches. The best way for family gardens is to have beds five feet wide, one row in the center, and one a foot from each edge, the plants nine inches in the row.

Rhubarb should have the bed manured the same as for asparagus; plants may be forced as directed last month. Make new beds before the plants start. Divide old roots, as soon as the frost is out, with a sharp spade, to have a piece of root with each eye.

Onions.—Of the Potato variety, Top onions and sets may be got in early. Put the Potato and Top sorts, 4 or 5 inches apart, in one foot rows. Sets may be put in 9 inch rows, and 3 inches apart. All these bulbs need to be covered, and all the better if the ground is rolled to pack it closely around them.

Peas should be sown early. We hear good accounts of Carter's First Crop, and there are several other early ones offered. Daniel O'Rourke, where it can be had good, is the best known early sort.

Roots, such as Parsnip and Salsify, should be taken out of the ground before they begin to grow, and all plants protected during the winter, such as

Spinach, uncovered and thinned for use as soon as it starts to grow. Sow in a warm corner seeds of early varieties of

Carrot, radish, cress, lettuce, and other things, according to locality and season.

Chives come very early in spring, and are in such demand that, near large cities, they are forwarded in frames. Cut the leaves as soon as large enough.

Flower Garden and Lawn.

Considerable preparatory work can be done here, and if any new improvements are to be made, have them well under way.

Roads should receive more attention than they generally do; in this we include drives and paths of all kinds. A good, dry road or walk is a great comfort, and the reverse is a nuisance. The best part of a road is out of sight. Those who are troubled to get rid of their stone, need have no anxiety as long as there is a bad road on the place. Excavate 2 or 3 feet, fill in with large stones, upon these put smaller ones, diminishing the size as the surface is reached, and finish off with coarse gravel, and then a coat of finer; roll well, and there will be a road that will need little mending, and fit to travel in all weathers; besides, such a road does much towards draining the ground through which it passes, and may be built with a view to drainage.

Lawns are seldom seen in a satisfactory state of perfection. Here the work must begin low down, and drains be put in where they would be required for a garden crop. Manure, plow, subsoil, grade and level with great care, sow and roll. Do the work as soon as the season will admit of it. Blue Grass or June Grass we have found to be satisfactory. In using the mixed seeds, sold under the name of Lawn Grass, we have not been successful. The White Clover, generally, killed out everything else, but this was on the light and poor soil.

Roots, of herbaceous perennials, of all kinds that have been in place two or three years, will do all the better if divided and reset. Do this early, and be liberal with the surplus. Do all necessary

Transplanting of shrubs and hardy herbaceous plants before vegetation starts, and finish up the

Pruning of shrubs, if not done. Do not hurry to

Uncover tender plants, that have been protected by straw or other shelter. There will still be a succession of warm days and cold nights that will be more injurious to them than steady severe cold.

Plant hedges, edging, shrubs and trees on the lawn as soon as the ground can be worked, and the plants be procured. Set out the various

Climbers wherever they are appropriate, and if means are lacking to buy, go to the woods and fence rows and get Virginia Creeper and Waxwork, that are everywhere common. Every country home should have a veranda, with several climbers upon it.

Hardy Annuals.—All those that come from self-sown seeds, such as Larkspur, Whitlavia, Candytuft, and most of the California things, do best when warm, as soon as frost leaves, but the

Tender Annuals must be kept back until the ground is well warmed, unless sown under glass.

Green and Hot-Houses.

The heat of the sun will render less fuel necessary. Give air freely on mild days, but close up early, before the air gets chilly.

Propagation will demand the chief attention, as a large stock of bedding plants is needed in most gardens where there is a green-house. Verbenas, Bouvardias, Pelargoniums, Fuchsias, Ageratums, and all such things may be multiplied in any quantity. The chief point in propagating from cuttings is to keep the temperature of the house 10° to 15° lower than that of the cutting bench, which should be from 65° to 75°. Put in a good stock of *Chrysanthemums*, for they are generally forgotten, as they do not bloom until quite late. The best plants are raised from cuttings. Sow seeds of *Tender Annuals*, and when large enough, pot them off and set strong plants for use out of doors.

Camellias, and other hard-wooded shrubs, will now be making a new growth, and will need more care in watering, and may be put in a warmer place. Prune, if not already done. The Camellia "breaks" very readily, and may be cut at will, with the probability that branches will start in abundance.

Azaleas will now be in bloom, and those that are in demand may be brought in a warmer place. Give sufficient water when in flower. Keep the better of the green fly and of other insects by *Fumigation* with tobacco, and whenever an insect of any kind appears on a plant, do not rest until that plant has been attended to; *principiis obsta*, or in plain English, "nip in the bud," should be the motto of the gardener in treating insects.

Forcing Plants, that have been kept in cold frames, may be brought forward, if not already done.

Bulbs, such as Tuberoses and Lilies, may be had in flower earlier, if they are started in pots ready to turn out into the ground in warm weather.

Cold Grapery.

Avoid starting the vines before their growth can be pushed rapidly, and to this end the house must be kept cool by opening the doors and ventilators. While preserving a low temperature, avoid sudden changes. In northern localities, it is not safe to start the vines before next month generally.

Apiary in March.—*Prepared by M. Quinby.*—In consequence of the scanty stores provided in most places, the last season, bees may yet be in danger of starving. If your hives have moveable combs lift them out, and if there is no sealed honey, the bees should be fed. To examine box hives, invert them, if possible, in the sun. Sealed honey will be near the top, and may be seen by clear sunlight. This should be done in the cool morning. Should the bees be disturbed, use smoke to quiet them, and drive them from places you want to inspect. Sealed honey is best to feed bees; strained honey will do, but it is scented farther. If none of any kind is to be had, sugar may be used. Add hot water and make a syrup about the consistence of honey. Feeding is done best at the top of the hive at this season. The feed may be put in a shallow dish, sprinkling cut straw upon it, to prevent the bees from drowning. Or a piece of old honey comb may be laid on the top, and a few spoonfuls poured into the cells every day or two. Trail a little down into the hive, till the bees learn the way to the feed dish; feed at night. Cover all with a tight, close-fitting box. This is the season when bees are disposed to pillage. Feeding is apt to induce it. A queenless hive is in danger of robbery; so is a colony very much weakened. The true condition of every stock should be ascertained now. Change bottom boards. Have one clean and dry on which set the hive. Examine among the chips, dead bees and filth, for young immature bees or eggs; any seen indicate the presence of a queen. Clean this bottom board and use it for the next hive. A queenless colony should be united with a weak one containing a queen. All weak colonies should have their entrances contracted, to allow room for only one bee to pass. Dead bees in masses between the combs should be removed before becoming moldy, or, if already so, cut out the combs as far as the mold extends. Feeding flour as food for young bees takes attention from robbing. Rye, ground fine and unbolted, seems to be the best; mix with bran or cut hay. An average of three or four pounds to the hive is sufficient. Place it in the sun, but out of the wind.

In setting out bees from the cellar, endeavor to have each occupy the stand of the last year. Choose a warm day, but not too warm. It sometimes happens in large apiaries, where a few are set out at a time, that the first ones, having been out a day or two and everything in order, commence robbing.

AMERICAN AGRICULTURIST.

ORANGE JUDD & CO., Publishers, 41 Park Row, N. Y. City.

ANNUAL SUBSCRIPTION TERMS (always in advance): $1.50 each for less than four copies: Four to nine copies, $1.25 each: Ten to nineteen copies, $1.20 each: Twenty copies and upwards, $1 each. Papers are addressed to each name.

FORWARD: MARCH!!!!

LAST (1866) MARCH,

A Great Many Persons filled up their Premium Clubs, which had been previously begun, and received the valuable articles they desired from our list.

A Great Many Others started *new* Club lists *after* the first of March, and filled them up in a brief time, and these also received very valuable articles.

THIS (1867) MARCH,

Three Thousand Persons, at least, may fill up the Premium Clubs for which they have already sent some names, and receive the desired premiums.

Seventeen Thousand Others, (one at each P. O.) may start now and make up a *new* Premium Club, and secure the excellent premiums.... This is

A GOOD MONTH

To Secure Subscribers. People are beginning in earnest to plan out the SPRING WORK, in the FIELD, in the ORCHARD, in the GARDEN, around the HOUSE, and in the HOUSE. They feel, or ought to feel, the necessity of gathering every hint and suggestion they can obtain from others. They will get a great many *valuable and profitable* hints from the *Agriculturist*, if some one will show them the paper, explain what it is, and ask them to subscribe for a year ...More than

70,000 Premium Names

have been sent in already this year, besides the regular subscribers; and we have had the pleasure of sending out a very large number of the excellent articles named in the table (next column.) *But the supply of premiums is unlimited, and all who want them may get them* ...At nearly

EVERY POST OFFICE

in the United States and British Provinces, there are persons enough who would be benefited by the *Agriculturist*, to make up one or more *large premium clubs*. From some single post-offices, even in small country towns, we have received premium lists of one, two, and three hundred subscribers, gathered by enterprising persons. It only needs some one to show the paper, explain its advantages, and tell how cheap it is, to secure a subscription in every family. Why! for less than 3 cents a week (or less than the cost of a cigar), *each* subscriber gets a paper containing, during the year, over *Ten Thousand Dollars worth of original Engravings*, besides reading matter that costs nearly or quite *Fifteen Thousand Dollars*. In a multitude of cases reported to us, single hints in this paper have been worth scores of dollars, and often hundreds.

We have abundant evidence that during 1866 this paper saved to the people of the country *millions of dollars*, by its exposures of Humbugs alone. The New York swindlers have confessed that their business has nearly ceased to pay in the Northern and Middle States "on account of the muss raised by that Judd's paper," and now they have gone to work vigorously down South, where its circulation was disturbed by the war, and is not yet fully restored, though it is rapidly finding its way everywhere there. Let us have a good premium club at every post-office in all the land, and the humbug business will die of starvation.

Well, look over our premium list, choose the premium you would like, take a copy of the paper, sally out among neighbors and friends, in your own neighborhood and elsewhere (*for premium clubs need not be all at one post-office*), and in a brief time the desired number of subscribers can be gathered, and the premium secured. A full description of the premiums will be sent free to any one desiring it. Any Specimen numbers, cards and show bills needed, will be supplied free.

Our premiums are all *really valuable articles*, such as we can cheerfully recommend to our friends. By wholesale purchases, by advertising arrangements, etc., we are able to supply them as premiums on far better terms than we could buy and sell them, and we thus pay our canvassers much more than we could possibly do in cash.

☞ **We take** *so much pains to procure only good articles in all cases, that any one securing anything from our premium list, saves the risk usually run of getting poor or indifferent goods, when buying of unknown or irresponsible parties. Every thing we send out as a premium is guaranteed to be the best of its kind and price.*

☞ *Every article offered is new and of the very best manufacture. No charge is made for packing or boxing any of the articles in this Premium List. The forty-three Premiums,* **Nos. 1, 2, 6,** *and from* **29** *to* **32,** *and from* **40** *to* **75** *inclusive, will each be delivered* **FREE** *of all charges, by mail or express, (at the Post-Office or express office nearest recipient), to any place in the United States or Territories, excepting those reached only by the Overland Mail.—The other articles cost the recipient only the freight after leaving the manufactory of each, by any conveyance that may be specified.*

Table of Premiums and Terms, For Volume 26—(1867).

Open to all—No Competition.

No.	Names of Premium Articles.	Price of Premiums.	Number of Subscribers required at $1.50	at $1.
1	Garden Seeds for a Family (40 kinds)	$5 00	13	37
2	Flower Seeds for a Family (100 kinds)	$5 00	13	37
3	Nursery Stock (Any kinds desired)	$20 00	30	[illegible]
4	Iona Grape Vines (12 of No. 1)	$18 00	27	[illegible]
5	Concord Grape Vines (100 of No. 1)	$12 00	19	[illegible]
6	Japan Lilies (12 Bulbs)	$8 00	15	45
7	Sewing Machine (Wheeler & Wilson)	$55 00	60	240
8	Sewing Machine (Grover & Baker)	$55 00	60	[illegible]
9	Sewing Machine (Singer's Tailoring)	$80 00	95	[illegible]
10	Sewing Machine (Florence)	$63 00	70	[illegible]
11	Sewing Machine (Willcox & Gibbs)	$55 00	60	[illegible]
12	Sewing Machine (Howe's)	$60 00	67	[illegible]
13	Washing Machine (Doty's)	$14 00	21	[illegible]
14	Clothes Wringer (Best—Universal)	$10 00	18	[illegible]
15	Tea Set (Hart's best Silver Plated)	$50 00	60	[illegible]
16	Castors and Fruit Basket (do. do.)	$30 00	44	[illegible]
17	Ice or Water Pitcher (do. do.)	$18 00	27	[illegible]
18	One Dozen Tea Spoons (do. do.)	$7 50	17	[illegible]
19	One Dozen Table Spoons (do. do.)	$15 00	22	[illegible]
20	One Dozen Dining Forks (do. do.)	$15 00	[illegible]	[illegible]
21	Piano (Best Steinway & Son's 7-octave)	$625 00	520	1500
22	Melodeon, 5-octave (G. A. Prince & Co.'s)	$112 00	138	400
23	Melodeon, 4-octave (do. do.)	$67 00	[illegible]	[illegible]
24	Ladies' Gold Watch (Beautiful)	$100 00	130	400
25	Silver Watch (Valuable Time Keeper)	$32 50	46	[illegible]
26	Double Barrel Gun (Very good)	$30 00	46	[illegible]
27	Spencer's Breech-loading Rifle (Hunting)	$55 00	70	[illegible]
28	Tool Chest (First Quality of Tools)	$44 50	60	[illegible]
29	Case of Mathematical Instruments	$9 00	14	[illegible]
30	Case of Mathematical Instruments	$16 00	[illegible]	[illegible]
31	Morton's Best No. 6 Gold Pen (Silver Case)	$5 75	14	[illegible]
32	Morton's Best No. 5 Gold Pen (Silver Case)	$4 50	11	[illegible]
33	Barometer (Woodruff's Mercurial)	$18 00	27	[illegible]
34	Barometer (Woodruff's Mercurial)	$12 00	19	[illegible]
35	Buckeye Mowing Machine, No. 2	$125 00	150	[illegible]
36	Allen's Patent Cylinder Plow, etc	$20 50	31	[illegible]
37	The Aquarius or Water Thrower	$11 00	19	[illegible]
38	American Cyclopedia (Appleton's)	$80 00	96	[illegible]
39	Worcester's Great Illustrated Dictionary	$12 00	19	[illegible]
40	Any Back Volume Agriculturist	$1 75		[illegible]
41	Any Two Back Volumes do.	$3 50		[illegible]
42	Any Three do. do. do.	$5 25	13	[illegible]
43	Any Four do. do. do.	$7 00	15	[illegible]
44	Any Five do. do. do.	$8 75	17	[illegible]
45	Any Six do. do. do.	$10 50	19	[illegible]
46	Any Seven do. do. do.	$12 25	21	[illegible]
47	Any Eight do. do. do.	$14 00	23	[illegible]
48	Any Nine do. do. do.	$15 75	25	[illegible]
49	Vols. XVI to XXV do.	$17 50	27	[illegible]
50	Any Back Volume Agriculturist	$2 50		[illegible]
51	Any Two Back Volumes do.	$5 00		[illegible]
52	Any Three do. do. do.	$7 50	16	[illegible]
53	Any Four do. do. do.	$10 00	18	[illegible]
54	Any Five do. do. do.	$12 50	21	[illegible]
55	Any Six do. do. do.	$15 00	24	[illegible]
56	Any Seven do. do. do.	$17 50	27	[illegible]
57	Any Eight do. do. do.	$20 00	30	[illegible]
58	Any Nine do. do. do.	$22 50	33	[illegible]
59	Vols. XVI to XXV do.	$25 00	36	[illegible]
60	Genesee Farmer, 1858–1865, 8 Vols., Bound	$14 00	21	[illegible]
61	Downing's Landscape Gardening	$6 50	15	[illegible]
62	Cummings & Miller's Architect.	$10 00	18	[illegible]
63	A $10 Library (Your Choice)	$10 00	18	[illegible]
64	A $15 Library do.	$15 00	24	[illegible]
65	A $20 Library do.	$20 00	31	[illegible]
66	A $25 Library do.	$25 00	38	[illegible]
67	A $30 Library do.	$30 00	44	[illegible]
68	A $35 Library do.	$35 00	50	[illegible]
69	A $40 Library do.	$40 00	56	[illegible]
70	A $45 Library do.	$45 00	62	[illegible]
71	A $50 Library do.	$50 00	68	[illegible]
72	A $60 Library do.	$60 00	80	[illegible]
73	A $75 Library do.	$75 00	100	[illegible]
74	A $100 Library do.	$100 00	125	[illegible]
75	A Choice of Good Books (See Terms below.)			
76	Sewing Machine (Finkle & Lyon)	$60 00	70	240
77	One Dozen Pocket Lanterns	$9 00	13	[illegible]

(Nos. 40–49: In cloth cases, Post-paid—Unbound. Nos. 50–59: Neatly Bound, Sent Post-paid. Nos. 60–74: All sent paid through, by Mail or Express.)

Old and new subscribers count in premium lists.

Our premiums are standard articles, and enough can be obtained to supply all calls for premiums for six months. Every canvasser can take abundant time, but

As fast as subscriptions are obtained, send them along, that the subscribers may begin to receive the paper, and when all the names that can be obtained are forwarded, select the premium, and it will be promptly furnished. To save mistakes and keeping accounts, *send with each list of names, the exact subscription money.*

Remit in Post Office money orders, drafts or checks on N. Y. City. If these can not be had, register money letters.

☞ **Every name** *designed for a premium list must be so marked* WHEN *sent in.* (We can not count others.)

For Full Description of the several premiums see October *Agriculturist*, pages 319 to 332, or apply for a *Descriptive List*, which will be furnished *free* and post-paid. We have room here for only the following:

No. 63 to 74 Good Libraries.—These can be selected by the recipients, from any of the books named in the list in this column. The books will be *delivered free of cost*, by mail or express.

No. 75—General Book Premium.—Any one not desiring the specific Book premiums, 63 to 74, on sending any number of names above 25, may select Books from the list (below), to the amount of 10 cents for each subscriber sent at $1: or to the amount of 30 cents for each name sent at the (ten) club price of $1.20 each: or to the amount of 60 cents for each name at $1.50. *This offer is only for clubs of 25 or more. The books will be sent by mail or express, prepaid by us.*

BOOKS FOR FARMERS AND OTHERS.

[For sale at the office of the *Agriculturist*, or they will be forwarded by mail, *post-paid*, on receipt of price. ☞ *All these are included in Our Premiums, Nos. 63 to 73, above.*

Allen's (L. F.) Rural Architecture	$1 50
Allen's (R. L.) American Farm Book	1 50
American Agricultural Annual, 1867, paper, 50c.; cloth	75
Allen's Diseases of Domestic Animals	1 00
American Horticultural Annual, 1867, paper, 50c.; cloth	75
American Bird Fancier	30
American Rose Culturist	30
American Weeds and Useful Plants	1 75
Architecture, by Cummings & Miller	10 00
Barry's Fruit Garden	1 75
Bement's Poulterer's Companion	2 00
Bement's Rabbit Fancier	30
Breck's New Book of Flowers	1 75
Buist's Flower Garden Directory	1 50
Buist's Family Kitchen Gardener	1 00
Burr's Vegetables of America	5 00
Chorlton's Grape-Grower's Guide	75
Cobbett's American Gardener	75
Cole's (S. W.) American Fruit Book	75
Cole's Veterinarian	75
Dadd's Modern Horse Doctor	1 50
Dadd's (Geo. H.) American Cattle Doctor	1 50
Dana's Muck Manual	1 25
Dog and Gun (Hooper's) ....paper, 30c.. cloth	60
Downing's Country Houses	8 00
Downing's Landscape Gardening (new Edition)	6 50
Downing's Fruits and Fruit Trees of America	3 00
Downing's Rural Essays	5 00
Eastwood on Cranberry	75
Elliott's Western Fruit Grower's Guide	1 50
Flax Culture	50
Field's (Thomas W.) Pear Culture	1 25
Flint's Milch Cows and Dairy Farming	2 50
French's Farm Drainage	1 50
Fuller's Grape Culturist	1 50
Fuller's Strawberry Culturist	20
Gardening for Profit, by Peter Henderson	1 50
Gray's How Plants Grow	1 25
Gray's Manual of Botany and Lessons in one Vol.	4 00
Guenon on Milch Cows	75
Harris' Insects Injurious to Vegetation, plain 4.00, col'd	6 00
Harris' Rural Annual. Bound, 8 Nos., in 2 Vols. Each	1 50
Herbert's Hints to Housekeepers	1 75
Hop Culture	40
Husmann's Grapes and Wine	1 50
Johnston's Agricultural Chemistry	1 75
Johnston's Elements of Agricultural Chemistry	1 50
Johnson's (Prof. S. W.) Essays on Manures	1 25
Langstroth on Honey Bee	2 00
Leuchar's How to Build Hot-Houses	1 50
Mayhew's Illustrated Horse Doctor	3 50
Mayhew's Illustrated Horse Management	3 50
Mayhew's Practical Bookkeeping for Farmers	[illegible]
Blanks for do. do.	1 [illegible]
Miles on the Horse's Foot	75
My Farm of Edgewood	1 75
My Vineyard at Lakeview	1 25
Norton's Scientific Agriculture	75
Onion Culture	20
Our Farm of Four Acres (bound) 60c ....paper..	30
Pardee on Strawberry Culture	75
Peat and its Uses, by Prof. S. W. Johnson	1 25
Pedder's Land Measurer	60
Quinby's Mysteries of Bee Keeping (NEW)	1 50
Randall's Sheep Husbandry	1 50
Randall's Fine Wool Sheep Husbandry	1 00
Rivers' Miniature Fruit Garden	1 00
Richardson on the Dog, paper 30c..........cloth..	60
Rural Annual, by Joseph Harris	25
Saunders' Domestic Poultry (NEW), paper, 40c., bound	75
Schenck's Gardener's Text Book	75
Scribner's Ready Reckoner	30
Skillful Housewife	75
Stewart's (John) Stable Book	1 50
Thompson's Food of Animals	1 00
Tobacco Culture	25
Todd's (S. E.) Young Farmer's Manual	1 50
Warder's Hedges and Evergreens	1 50
Watson's American Home Garden	2 00
Woodward's Country Homes	1 50
Youatt and Spooner on the Horse	1 50
Youatt and Martin on Cattle	1 50
Youatt on the Hog	1 00
Youatt on Sheep	1 00
Youmans' Household Science	2 25

Commercial Matters—Market Prices.

The following condensed, comprehensive tables, carefully prepared specially for the *American Agriculturist*, show at a glance the transactions for a month, ending Feb. 16, 1867, and also for the same month last year:

1. TRANSACTIONS AT THE NEW-YORK MARKETS.

RECEIPTS.	*Flour.*	*Wheat.*	*Corn.*	*Rye.*	*Barley.*	*Oats.*
24 days *this* m'th	101,000	85,000	14,000	3,600	57,000	124,000
30 days *last* m'th	290,000	1,473,000	2,078,000	514,000	1,050,000	1,227,000

SALES.	*Flour.*	*Wheat.*	*Corn.*	*Rye.*	*Barley.*
24 days *this* month,	192,000	515,000	993,000	317,000	405,000
30 days *last* month,	248,300	681,000	1,722,000	298,000	546,000

2. *Comparison with same period at this time last year.*

RECEIPTS.	*Flour.*	*Wheat.*	*Corn.*	*Rye.*	*Barley.*	*Oats.*
24 days 1867....	101,000	85,000	142,000	3,600	57,000	124,000
25 days 1866....	104,300	31,500	311,000	6,500	60,500	204,000

SALES.	*Flour.*	*Wheat.*	*Corn.*	*Rye.*	*Barley.*
24 days 1867....	192,000	515,000	993,000	317,000	406,000
25 days 1866..	251,000	312,548	836,000	69,000	101,000

3. *Exports from New York, Jan. 1, to Feb. 14:*

	Flour.	*Wheat.*	*Corn.*	*Rye.*	*Oats.*
1867........	32,920	16,798	778,286	73,731	25,442
1866........	121,251	61,028	816,574	25,127	19,025
1865........	194,225	68,644	53,404	141	9,298

Gold has fluctuated frequently during the month, but only to the extent of 4@5 per cent., closing very little higher than one month ago.... The produce and merchandise markets have been quiet. The demand for breadstuffs, whether for home use or for export, has been restricted to the supplying of the pressing wants of buyers. The receipts have been light, yet receivers have been very eager to sell, and there have been few realizations on the part of speculative holders. Prices have accordingly declined, closing very decidedly in favor of purchasers. There have been considerable arrivals of flour and wheat from California, which have added to the depression of the market. Stocks have been reduced, but this has not been sufficient to strengthen, or sustain the confidence of holders..... The business in Provisions has been more active, but, in the instance of hog products, at a reduced range of prices. Beef has been quite firm. Butter heavy. Cheese rather buoyant..... Cotton has been in moderate request and has been easier in price, on more liberal receipts. The receipts at all the shipping ports of the country, thus far, this season, have been 1,131,000 bales; exports from the ports, 530,000 bales; estimated stock at latest mail dates, 665,000 bales..... Wool has been more sought after, and prices of desirable lots have been well supported, on a rather moderately supplied market.... Hay, Hops, Seeds and Tobacco, have been comparatively quiet.

New York Live Stock Markets.—The supply during the past four weeks has been small, especially of beef cattle, as shown in the following table:

WEEK ENDING.	*Beeves.*	*Cows.*	*Calves.*	*Sheep.*	*Swine.*
Jan. 22	3,990	50	308	18,303	18,250
Jan. 29	4,184	46	690	20,071	7,947
Feb. 5	1,740	82	425	19,032	4,732
Feb. 12	8,075	59	656	23,109	11,450
Total in four Weeks....	18,950	247	2,039	79,012	43,379
Average per Week......	4,737	62	510	19,753	11,845
do. do. *last Month*..	4,910	69	438	17,770	19,250
do. do. *prev's Month*.	5,311	63	833	21,105	11,500
Average per Week, 1866.	5,718	94	1,200	20,000	15,000
do. do. do. 1865	5,255	118	1,500	16,091	11,023
do. do. do. 1864.....	5,161	145	1,511	15,315	12,676
do. do. do. 1863	5,150	129	694	9,941	21,670
Total in 1866	298,880	4,885	61,150	1,040,000	672,000
Total in 1865	270,274	6,161	77,991	836,733	573,197
Total in 1864	267,919	7,603	75,621	782,462	660,270
Total in 1863	264,091	6,170	35,700	519,316	1,101,617

The transportation of animals to market has been greatly impeded by snow on the railroads, and the supply has been moderate.... **Beef Cattle** have fluctuated in price somewhat, though not much advance has occurred until this week, when a light supply, with little surplus to fall back upon, enabled sellers to put up prices. Two or three bullocks of very extra quality sold at full 18c. ℔ ℔, net weight, estimating dressed weight 63 to 64 ℔s to the 100 ℔s live weight; good or first quality, 16½c.@17½c.; medium, 15c.@16c.; inferior to worst, 11c.@12c. These prices are not expected to continue, as the railroads again carry cattle through regularly..... **Milch Cows,** though at present in limited numbers, are quite abundant for the very light demand. Really good cows sell at $80@$90; a few extras at fancy prices, or $100@$125; common, $60@$70; poor, $50@$60. These prices include each cow's own young calf, as no cow will be purchased without this guarantee of fresh milk.... **Veal Calves** are beginning to come in more freely. An occasional extra brings 13½c.@14c. ℔ ℔, live weight; the range of good calves average about 12½c., while common to poor sell at 10c.@8½c. ....**Sheep** continue in very abundant supply, averaging about 20,000 per week, despite snow blockades. Prices temporarily went up to 7½c.@8½c. ℔ ℔, live weight, for first class to extras, last week; but the present rates are 6½c.@7c. for good medium wool, 85 to 90 ℔ sheep; some extras bring 7¾c.@7¾c.; while common and poor lots sell at 6¼c.@5¾c..... **Live Hogs** have come in very unevenly, varying from 18,250 to 4,732 per week, and prices have fluctuated considerably. Present rates ℔ ℔, live weight, are 7¾c.@8½c. for the different grades; dressed hogs 9c.@9½c.

CURRENT WHOLESALE PRICES.

	Jan. 22.	Feb. 14.
PRICE OF GOLD	133¾	136¾
FLOUR—Super to Extra State	$9 40 @12 40	$8 80 @11 25
Super to Extra Southern	11 75 @17 00	10 67 @16 50
Extra Western	10 15 @17 00	9 90 @16 25
Extra Genesee	12 65 @15 00	11 75 @15 25
Superfine Western	9 40 @10 50	8 80 @10 [illegible]
RYE FLOUR	6 40 @ 8 00	7 00 @ [illegible]
CORN MEAL	5 00 @ 5 50	4 90 @ [illegible]
WHEAT—All kinds of White	[illegible]	[illegible]
All kinds of Red and Amber	[illegible]	[illegible]
CORN—Yellow	1 12 @ 1 20	1 10 @ 1 12
Mixed	1 08 @ 1 20	1 10 @ 1 13
OATS—Western	[illegible] @ 61	[illegible]
State	[illegible] @ 70	67 @ [illegible]
RYE	1 15 @ 1 30	1 15 @ 1 [illegible]
BARLEY	[illegible]	[illegible]
HAY—Bale ℔ 100 ℔	1 [illegible] @ 1 65	1 [illegible] @ 1 [illegible]
Loose	1 50 @ 1 70	1 55 @ 1 [illegible]
STRAW, ℔ 100 ℔	75 @ 1 25	[illegible]
COTTON—Middlings, ℔ ℔	31½ @ 33½	[illegible] @ 31½
HOPS—Crop of 1866, ℔ ℔	35 @ 70	[illegible]
FEATHERS—Live Geese, ℔ ℔	85 @ 85	[illegible]
SEED—Clover, ℔ ℔	13½ @ 15	13 @ 15
Timothy, ℔ bushel	3 30 @ 3 75	3 [illegible] @ 3 [illegible]
Flax, ℔ bushel	3 00 @ 3 25	3 [illegible] @ 3 [illegible]
SUGAR—Brown, ℔ ℔	9 @ 12¾	9 @ 12¾
MOLASSES, Cuba, ℔ gl	37 @ 50	40 @ [illegible]
COFFEE—Rio, (Gold price) ℔ ℔	15 @ 18	15½ @ 19
TOBACCO, Kentucky, &c., ℔ ℔	4 @ [illegible]	4 @ [illegible]
Seed Leaf, ℔ ℔	5 @ [illegible]	5 @ [illegible]
WOOL—Domestic Fleece, ℔ ℔	45 @ [illegible]	40 @ [illegible]
Domestic, pulled, ℔ ℔	30 @ 55	30 @ [illegible]
California, unwashed	27 @ 40	27 @ 40
TALLOW, ℔ ℔	11½ @ 11¾	11 @ 11½
OIL CAKE—℔ ton	52 50 @57 00	51 00 @56 00
PORK—Mess, ℔ barrel	19 00 @21 50	19 61 @19 75
Prime, ℔ barrel	16 75 @17 00	16 03 @17 00
BEEF—Plain mess	12 00 @18 00	12 00 @18 00
LARD, in barrels, ℔ ℔	12½ @ 13¾	11 @ 13
BUTTER—Western, ℔ ℔	15 @ 35	15 @ 35
State, ℔ ℔	30 @ 48	[illegible] @ 45
CHEESE	9 @ [illegible]	[illegible] @ 21
BEANS—℔ bushel	2 75 @ 3 50	[illegible]
PEAS—Canada, ℔ bushel	1 [illegible] @ 1 [illegible]	1 [illegible] @ 1 [illegible]
EGGS—Fresh, ℔ dozen	35 @ 42	[illegible]
POULTRY—Fowls, ℔ ℔	13 @ 15	17 @ 18
Turkeys, ℔ ℔	12 @ [illegible]	[illegible]
POTATOES—Mercers, ℔ bbl.	2 50 @ [illegible]	2 50 @ [illegible]
Peach Blows, ℔ barrel	3 00 @ [illegible]	3 00 @ [illegible]
POTATOES—Buckeye, ℔ bbl.	2 25 @ 2 50	2 00 @ [illegible]
APPLES—℔ barrel	3 50 @ 7 50	3 50 @ 9 10
CRANBERRIES, ℔ barrel	15 00 @20 00	23 00 @28 00

OUR BASKET

Containing a great variety of Items, including many good Hints and Suggestions which we throw into smaller type and condensed form, for want of space elsewhere.

Forty Pages Again.—To accomodate advertisers, we, for the first two months of the year, gave four extra pages of advertising, and had to leave out many advertisements. This month we give them four more. This is a gain to the readers, as for each page added to the business part of the paper, we give an extra one of reading matter. Thirty-two pages is all we promise.

Read the Advertisements.—They contain a large amount of really useful information, and one going through these business pages very often gets new ideas that prove profitable. A gentleman informed us recently that an advertisement in this paper, some years ago, set him to thinking about a new enterprise from which he has derived more than $30,000 profit. The present mail and express facilities render it quite easy to procure seeds, plants, etc., from any part of the country; and to go through our advertising pages is almost equivalent to a visit to an immense "variety store." We have rejected far more advertisements than we have inserted, our aim being to admit none but parties whom we have reason to believe will honestly do what they promise in their advertisements. Please gratify the advertisers, by always stating *where* their advertisements were seen, when ordering, or sending for catalogues, etc.

Supplying the Evening Post.—As announced last month, we send the *American Agriculturist* with the Weekly Evening Post for $2.50, and with the Semi-weekly Post at $4.00 a year. It is essential to this arrangement that the subscriptions to both papers *come at the same time.* We cannot receive additions of $1 each to former subscriptions, and send the Post. If any present subscriber to the *Agriculturist* wishes to get the Post at the reduced rate, he can send $2.50 with a new name for the *Agriculturist*, or we will extend his own subscription a year beyond the time to which it is already paid.

The Agricultural Annual, though rather late in making its appearance, has been very well received. It is a very neat volume, in both cloth and paper covers, printed on excellent paper, the illustrations being well engraved and well printed. The Annual is valuable as an almanac and calendar of operations. Some of the tables are not to be found elsewhere, and are well worth the price of the book. For instance, one table shows concisely the action that has been taken in all the States and British Provinces on the weight of the bushel. There are simple rules for finding the cubical contents of round, square, hopper-shaped, and firkin-shaped vessels. The articles upon draining, horse-training, poultry, potatoes, scientific progress, veterinary subjects, agricultural education, etc., etc., have been before alluded to. There is altogether a great deal of information for fifty cents, and such as every farmer wants.

Fuller's Grape Culturist—New and Enlarged Edition.—Mr. Fuller's work met the general want of a plain and practical treatise on grape culture. As it was based upon established principles, it at once took rank as a standard work. Most of the treatises that have appeared since are nothing more than Fuller modified and diluted. When the structure and mode of growth of the vine is once understood, all systems of training become plain, and one may be followed as readily as another. Mr. Fuller gives this knowledge of the vine most clearly, and illustrates it so plainly that no one can fail to understand it, and for this reason his book has become remarkably popular, and has not been, nor is it likely to be superseded by any other work on the same subject. The teachings of the work are all from actual practice, and the illustrations are mainly from growing vines. As some of the illustrations of unusual methods of training have been said to be fancy sketches, we will state that we know them to be genuine, as we have seen the vines, from which they were taken, growing in Mr. Fuller's grounds. To bring this work up to the times in respect to varieties, a considerable portion of the matter has been re-written. An additional list of varieties, including synonyms, has been given, and important additions have been made all through the volume. Garden culture is treated as well as that of the vineyard, and the book is equally adapted to the owner of a single vine, or the one who has thousands of vines. Ready March 1st. Well illustrated. Price, by mail, $1.50.

S. S. Lessons for Every Sunday in the Year, consist of four volumes, containing 52 lessons each. No. 1 embraces the period from the Birth of Christ to the end of Acts; No. 2, the rest of the New Testament. No. 3, From Adam to Elijah; No. 4, From Elijah to Christ. The lessons are connected by a running history. The value of these books is attested by the demand for above half a million copies already. They are non-sectarian, and are used by all denominations of Christians. They are designed to secure the learning of portions of the Scriptures, to give a connected view of Sacred History, and especially to aid S. S. teachers and scholars who have not the aid of commentaries and reference books. The full scope of the books is stated in the preface to No. 1. They are sold at a remarkably low price, viz., 15 cents each. We send full sample copies, (Nos. 1, 2, 3, and 4,) post paid, for 75 cents.

A "Staple" Article.—While looking around among the iron workers for other articles, we came across one that we have often felt the want of, and had we known that it was made for sale it would have saved much trouble. It is simply a small staple to be used for fastening wire to posts for trellises and fences. The engraving shows the size and form; the two ends are chamfered in opposite directions, so that, when driven, the points tend to spread, and hold with great firmness. These staples, which will be welcomed by all who use horizontal trellises, are made by machinery by H. C. Richardson, Williamsburg, N. Y., and are sold at wholesale at only fifteen cents per pound, about one hundred making a pound.

The Grandest Excursion of this or any other age, is projected for the present year. About one hundred persons will go on board a large Steamship June 1st, and visit the Azore Islands and Gibraltar; stop eighteen days at Marseilles and Genoa, to allow all desiring it to go up by railway to Paris and visit the Exhibition, and thence eastward to the Rhine, and down through Switzerland to the ship again. Several days will be allowed at Genoa, Leghorn, Naples, etc., to visit the Quadrilateral fortifications, Venice, Florence, Rome, and other Italian cities. The company will visit Caprera, the home of Garibaldi, Palermo in Sicily, Athens, Corinth, Constantinople, the Crimea, see Vesuvius and other volcanoes, sail over St. Paul's Route in the Mediterranean, visit Beirout and Joppa, giving time to go down through Palestine from Beirout to Jerusalem, and also from Joppa over, and spend some time around Jerusalem; next to Alexandria, the Pyramids, etc., in Egypt; thence westward through the Mediterranean, stopping at various points of interest; from Gibraltar southward to the Madeira Islands; across to the Bermudas, and thence home, after an absence of 4½ to 5 months. The excursionists will have their home constantly aboard the ship, where physicians, books, music, etc., are to be provided free. The expedition is to be under the charge of Capt. Duncan—the Captain who has been eighteen years at sea, about half the time as master of large ships—who never swore an oath—never drank a glass of liquor, and though he has crossed the Atlantic *fifty-eight* times, never suffered a shipwreck, nor lost a man by accident. The company is to be select—every applicant's name is submitted to a committee. If any wish to join the grand excursion, let them send their credentials to Capt. C. C. Duncan, 117 Wall street, New York, who will send all particulars, and inform them if there are any vacancies. The expense will be about $1,250 for adults, for all expenses on the water, and as much, or a little more, as they choose to spend in land excursions.

Sundry Humbugs.—We have a large box full of letters recently received, describing various swindles. In two other paragraphs we describe the "ticket operators, and Southern swindlers, and have room for but few words here." Some of the operators have stolen our cards, or got *fac similes* of them printed, and enclose them in their circulars in a way to make us seem to indorse *their* operations. Others pretend to have obtained the addresses of individuals from us. Once for all we say: *No names of our subscribers have ever been furnished to any person for any purpose whatever, good or bad. No person except those employed to post books and write wrappers, are ever permitted even to look into our books.* Some postmasters, we suspect, have furnished to applicants the names of subscribers to this and other journals at their offices....We again caution our readers against the pretended cheap sewing machine operators.....Harris & Brothers, of Boston, whom we exposed in October, have been "put under bonds."....The "Howard Association," of Philadelphia, is to be avoided always....The "American Artists' Association," Pine st., New York, has been often hunted after, but never found "at home."——Ditto, Hodge of 107 Broadway—no such man there——ditto, the Tea Company at 109 Water street——ditto, somebody at 512 Broadway....Milnor & Co. 206, alias 210 Bowery, appear to be the same as Parkinson & Co. 206 Broadway, whom we showed up some time since. There is quite an assortment of swindlers in several upper rooms of 201, 206 and 208 Broadway, all entered by one flight of stairs....(Rev.) Edward Wilson, of Williamsburg, and J.T. Inman, Station D, Bible House, continue to come the "pious dodge." Our letters contain circulars of about 50 gift and other swindles, of a character similar to those already described in this and previous numbers....We may stop here, by repeating, that all the gift enterprises, for benevolent or other purposes, the Art Union Associations, etc., are downright swindles.....W. Purdy, a base wretch, of P——, N. J., offers vile pictures, books, instruments, etc. Any of his class who thus offer to steal the morals of the ignorant, will not hesitate to steal any money sent them. Among such fellows rank "Reeves & Co.," of Nassau street; Beach, Putney & Co.; Somers & Co., Dr. Andrews, Birch & Co., White & Co., and many others. ....Gilbert & Co. offer stationery parcels, with watch premiums, jewelry, etc., and refer to Cutter, Tower & Co., and Saml. Raynor & Co., both of which firms "don't know anything of this Gilbert," or have given no permission to refer to them.....Beware of "Manufacturers' Associations" who sell by tickets.....See our previous notes on Humbugs for answers to many letters recently sent to us.

Ticket Swindlers—How They Operate.—Among the numerous methods of cheating people, the following is one of the most common: The operator hires a small upper room so as to have a place to receive letters. He buys from some other operator the names and P. O. address of a great many thousands of people, which have been obtained from postmasters and others under honest pretences. He then gets out a very plausible circular, or advertisement, pretending to have on hand a great many thousands of dollars worth of watches, jewelry, dry goods, etc., a bankrupt stock, or the consignment of some failing foreign house, which he claims must be sold, or will be sold at wonderfully low rates. He pretends to put them all together, to be sold by lot, at a uniform price of $1, $2, or $3, or $5, or $10 each. He sends out sealed tickets for these things, pretending that they have been drawn by lot, and that he does not know what any sealed envelope contains. Sometimes pay for the tickets is first asked; sometimes they are sent, pretending that somebody has ordered and paid for them. Sometimes he pretends to desire the recipient to act as agent, and promises special facilities. *Every* person opening these tickets is sure to find among them at least one calling for a watch or other valuable article, "marked at" $20, $30, $40, $50 or $75, or more, to be obtained by remitting a tenth of its "marked" value. The recipient thinks he has drawn a valuable prize, and so sends on the money. This is usually the last he hears of it. No answer is returned to the letters of inquiry he may write; or if hard pressed, the operator pretends the money has been lost by mail, or that he has sent the articles, and that they have been lost. He operates at a distance, so that few people can call in person to trouble him. If one calls, the operator pretends that "the boss is out." If cornered, he hands over the watch, which is usually a showy, but nearly or quite valueless affair. Sometimes one of these taking-looking prizes is sent out as a bait, but in 99 cases in 100 nothing is returned for money sent them. This is an outline of one mode of operating. The same rascal operates in half a dozen or more places, under as many different names; and, with few exceptions, the name is changed every month or two. We have tickets and circulars, ostensibly from over 200 different operators, though not over half a dozen men are at the bottom of the whole of them. A man by the name of Todd has operated under 40 or 50 names probably, but never in his own real name. We say, positively, if you give heed to a single one of these circulars or ticket enterprises, you will lose all the money you invest.

Look Out for Humbugs at the South.—We learn from sundry sources, that a score or more of the most expert swindlers of this city—the gift enterprise men, the watch and jewelry ticket men, etc.—having become discouraged by meeting the *Agriculturist's* exposures at every turn throughout the North, are now directing their efforts especially to the Southern States. (The *Agriculturist*, shut out from those States by the war, and by the prejudice of many of the people, does not circulate so largely in those States as at the North, where it goes to nearly every post office. It is, however, now making rapid headway all through the South.) These Humbug operators, through the aid of postmasters and others, unwittingly given, have gathered up the names and address of more than a hundred thousand Southern people, and they are plying them with their circulars, and plausibly told, but nefarious schemes. See descriptions elsewhere. Southern Newspapers should sound the alarm at once. We are sorry to see that quite a number of them are, unsuspectingly we trust, aiding the swindlers, by publishing their advertisements. Let every one of our readers who has friends or acquaintances at the South, send them a copy or two of this journal, or better send them the paper for a year. A few numbers at any post office would soon head off the swindlers.

Sample Heads of Grain from Germany.—We are indebted to Mr. Ferdinand Hunderpfund, florist, of 197 Broadway, New York, for samples of the mature heads of nearly or quite 100 kinds of Grain—Oats, Millet, Wheat, Rye and Barley. Both summer and winter varieties. Many of them possess extraordinary beauty. They were raised at the Agricultural and Garden School at Karlsruhe, in Baden, and were accompanied by samples of seed which we shall try, and hope to report upon in due time, if any appear to be especially valuable.

190 Different Kinds of Beans.—The same gentleman has left at our office a collection of 190 samples of Beans. Most of them are true beans, though some are of a different but allied species. These also are from the gardens of the Karlsruhe School, of which institution Mr. Hunderpfund was a pupil.

The Officers of the N. Y. State Agricultural Society for 1867, elected at the annual meeting February 15th are as follows: *President*, Gen. Marsena R. Patrick. *Vice-Presidents*, 1st District, Thomas H. Faile, Jr., New York; 2d District, Samuel Thorn, Dutchess; 3d District, Adam Thayer, Rensselaer; 4th District, Milo Ingoldsby, Washington; 5th District, Samuel Campbell, Oneida; 6th District, Joseph McGraw, Jr., Tompkins; 7th District, H. T. E. Foster, Seneca; 8th District, J. H. Plumb, Erie. *Corresponding Secretary*, B. P. Johnson, Albany. *Recording Secretary*, Erastus Corning, Jr., Albany. *Treasurer*, Luther H. Tucker, Jr., Albany. *Executive Committee*, George H. Brown, Dutchess; John Havens, N. Y.; S. T. Taber, Queens; T. L. Harrison, St. Lawrence; W. M. Ely, Broome; James Geddes, Onondaga; W. Chamberlain, Dutchess; J. G. Masters, Erie.

How Often May a Mare Have Colts?—"J. B. S. H.," Hartford County, Conn. It is as natural for a mare to have foals as it is to live, and if she is kept well, as you say you keep yours, she may have a foal every year, as regularly as a cow has calves. Only do not overwork her when she is heavy with foal.

Map of Maryland.—Mr. S. J. Martenet, Baltimore, has published a large map of Maryland and an Atlas of County maps, each County being accompanied by a concise account of its peculiarities, with statistics of population, productions, etc. Such a map will be of great use to those who contemplate a removal to the State.

Bommer's Manure Method.—Yes, we did get hold of some old pamphlets which were formerly sold, with the patent, for $10, and offer them for 25 cents, without any patent. We told our readers that the patent was so old that it had become public property. Is it not, then, absurd to claim that we put it out as something new, or intimate that we tried to deceive about it. Our readers know that the method is old. They may well wonder, as we do, that a patent was ever granted, and that it was pronounced valid. That does not alter the case, nor make the method of less value, to whoever does not know it. We remember well to have seen what, we presume, was the very same method, in use in Switzerland, 12 years ago, and saw it also described, substantially, by an enthusiastic Swiss agriculturist, who termed Switzerland "the native country of the proud dung heap;" and we have often described, and urged upon our readers, practice very similar to Bommer's. Nevertheless, we think the book is worth much more than its price (25c) to every farmer in the country. We would be happy to sell to the *Country Gentleman* as many copies as he wants for his readers, at the usual discount, one-third off, for cash.

Hope for the Farmers' Club.—The people who assemble under the name of the "Farmers' Club" did not like the article, last month, headed "Sense at the Farmers' Club." Of course they didn't. It was intended as medicine, and they were expected to squirm under its operation, but it did them much good. In the report of the meeting of January 22d, there were only six "medical" articles, and in that of January 29th, only two!—a recovery more rapid than that of any patient who will follow their published prescriptions. Here is a specimen of the effects produced by our strictures, from the report of the meeting of January 29th:

"*Management of the Club.*—An agricultural paper in this city speaks of our club as being more comic than wise, and as having better talkers than farmers. Now and then, there is an Ishmaelite boy skulking through the lots. When he sees other boys enjoying themselves together, nothing pleases him more than to throw a stone. What can he expect?"

"Boys enjoying themselves together" is a capital figure, and shows that the club posses the rare ability "to see ourselves as others see us." "Ishmaelite" is also good, and hints at a commendable kind of reading.

Sweet Potatoes.—Several, who have made inquiries about Sweet Potato culture, will be glad to know that we have an article in type from an experienced cultivator which will appear in season.

Catalogues Acknowledged.—Seeds.—A. Bridgeman, 878 Broadway, N. Y., Vegetable Seeds.... J. M. Thorburn & Co., Flower Seeds and Spring Bulbs.... James J. H. Gregory, Marblehead, Mass., including many novelties.... Collins, Anderson & Co., Vegetables and Flowers, with very full descriptions.

General Nursery Stock.—J. W. Dodge & Son, Pomona Nursery, Cumberland County, Tenn.... Husmann & Manwaring, Hermann, Mo.... Calvin S. Goddard, Evergreens and Fruit Trees, Portland, Me.... John Saul, Washington, D. C.; Roses a specialty.

Small Fruits.—William Hacker, Philadelphia, Pa.... Thomas C. Andrews, Moorestown, Burlington County, N. J.... Johnston's Nursery, South Bend, Ind.... Geo. W. Campbell, Delaware, O., full description of grapes.

Florists' Plants.—Ellwanger & Barry, Rochester, N. Y.... Joseph W. Vestal, Cambridge City, Wayne Co., Ind.

Wines.—F. C. Brehm, Waterloo, New York.

The Western New York Fruit Growers' Society.—The interruption of travel by the great snow storm, prevented our attending the meeting in January, as we had intended. We observe by the report in the *Country Gentleman*, that the time was chiefly occupied in discussing the grape question. A great deal was said about different varieties, but we do not find that anything new was elicited. A vote was taken on the question "What one variety of grapes is best for garden culture in Western New York?" The Delaware was the choice of the majority. We do not see any report of the vote on the next best. It would be well if it were stated what are the limits of "Western New York," for which the Delaware is considered the best.

Large Barley—Selecting Seed.—C. A. Brown, Stockbridge, Vermont, sowed the product of an accidental head of barley found in a field of wheat; the product of four grains was 1,411 grains; one stool had twenty three large, fine, full heads. Any grain growing by itself in good soil, will develope wonderfully. Selection of heavy seed will do much. Culling the large, full, ripe heads, and saving for sowing only the heaviest grains from them, will greatly improve the result, but the climax is reached by very thin sowing in drills, giving hand culture, weeding and hoeing, and continuing this with the most careful culling of heads and selection of seed by weight year after year. The improvement is rapid.

The Surprise Oats.—This, which claims to be a new variety of oat, is put before the public with apparent good faith on the part of the proprietors. The claim is that one Van Olinda, near Sandwich, DeKalb County, Ill., found some strangely bearded oats growing among some other grain (Patent-Office wheat if we mistake not.) We have seen what purports to be some of this original seed, and it looks almost exactly like the wild oat, from which it is known that our cultivated varieties sprung, and to which it is supposed that, under some circumstances, they revert. After several years of care and culture the result is claimed to be that a very plump, heavy, prolific, early variety is established free from the bristly beards, and every way a first-rate oat. We have no means of knowing whether the surveyor, who claims to have measured the 125 square rods of ground on which 375 bushels of oats grew, knew anything about his business or not, or whether he is an honest man. We don't know whether the weight of the oats was taken properly or not. They may have been weighed in bags, no deductions made, and the total weight simply divided by thirty-two, the weight of the legal bushel of oats. The statements in the circular are unsatisfactory and meager, and there is a concealment of the fact that the 133 bushels per acre, means bushels of 32 pounds each, weighed as soon as thrashed. If the weighing had been done in December the results would have required a different statement, and we presume also that the 45 pounds which the measured bushel is said to weigh may be subject to the same drawback. We have admitted the advertisement because the proprietors appeared to be fair, honest men, and certainly showed us a very excellent sample of oats.

Selecting Grain Seed for Sowing.—Take out the screens, except perhaps the top one, and arrange the fan-mill for giving the strongest and evenest blast. Then run the grain through, saving the heaviest half, and repeating the operation upon this several times.

Good Seeds.—"Where can I get good seeds?" is the purport of a dozen letters now on file. One says that he is poorer by a thousand dollars than he would have been if he had had good seeds last year. We believe that all the seedmen who advertise with us intend to send good seeds. Much of their stock, imported and otherwise, is bought upon good faith in others, and they may sometimes be deceived. One writes us that Tom Thumb Peas grew from eight inches to five feet, and were growing yet. We do not know a seedman who would intentionally mix seeds. Much of the failure is attributable to the sower, who sows too early, or too deeply. There is not a seedman of our acquaintance who has not been denounced to us as a swindler, and not one who has not been praised to us as the best of all his craft. There is no business in which a reputation is more essential, simply as a business investment, than that of the seedman, and no one who expected to continue long in the business would, simply as a matter of policy, sell a thing if known to be untrue. Seedmen are human and may err, and be deceived, and so with the purchasers. Let us encourage home grown seeds, and then we can be able to trace everything to its source.

A Span-roof Cold Grapery.—"Constant Reader." Much will depend upon your notions as to style. Make out a plain statement of just what you want, and send to John Ellis, White Plains, N. Y., or Messrs. Woodward, No. 37 Park Row, N. Y., and they will give you estimates, and, of course, will expect to be paid for their trouble.

Red Legged Locust.—What shall they do in Kansas? L. A. Alderson, of Atchison, thus states the case: "Last September we were visited by the Red Legged Locust (*Acrydium femur-rubrum*), the same insect that committed such depredation in Utah, Colorado and Montana. They spread over our entire State, and before cold weather they advanced about fifty miles into Missouri. They devoured all our buckwheat, turnips, tobacco, and most of the green fodder, and all the young wheat that had been sown. (Several farmers have sown since their disappearance.) The surface of the earth is filled with their *larva*, and as further West, they will doubtless appear in force in the spring. The *Agriculturist* is extensively read in Kansas, and you would do us a great favor by informing us through its columns what crops, if any, we may be able to raise next summer. It is said they will not destroy sorghum. I have noticed the Castor Oil Bean untouched by them; but I have seen them feasting upon a pod of red pepper and a quid of tobacco. As a general rule the young hatched from the *larva* of the preceeding fall, leave about the first of July; but this is too late for most of our crops."

Beans, Peas, Millet, Oats, to cut for fodder, Corn for fodder, Buckwheat, Turnips, Rutabagas and Tobacco if the seed beds can be protected, are what we think of as most likely to produce a crop after July 1st; but their success depends on your having no second crop of locusts, and these are usually most abundant in August and later.

Use for Hickory Withe.—W. G. Waring, of Tyrone, Pa., says, that when plowing he broke a clevis, and adapting a strong withe, cut from a neighboring hickory, to the situation, it held well, endured the draft all day, and saved an hour's time of man and team.

Sensible.—At a meeting of delegates from seventy-five of the Ohio County Agricultural Societies recently held at Columbus, Ohio, the following resolution was adopted. We hope that the agriculturists of other States will do likewise. "That the Convention adhere to the resolutions adopted at the session of 1865, and again indorsed in 1866, in favor of one College under the Congressional grant, and opposed to the division of the fund.

The American Journal of Horticulture and Florists Companion.—Boston, J. E. Tilton & Co. Monthly, 64 pages, at $3 per year. The January and February numbers of this journal have been received. We did not notice the first number, as the publishers apologized for its want of variety and stated that it had been "issued under many disadvantages." The second number contains no such apology, and we suppose it is intended as a specimen of what we may expect, and as several have asked our opinion upon it, we will say that it is a very handsome magazine, on excellent paper and in beautiful type, and is wonderfully cheap. The publishers deserve much credit for giving so many pages for so little money. Why it is called an "*American* Journal of Horticulture," we are at loss to understand, as it is most intensely *Bostonese*. The February issue has the bad taste to give the biography of our revered friend Col. Wilder. We hope that the day is far distant when any one shall have the right to make up his record, and we cannot conceive why he should be thus afflicted. The issue is all about Boston and its suburbs, and though Boston is our pet city, and its people are good to know, we can't see why they call it an "American" journal. The articles on Garden Architecture will attract attention for the reason that the illustrations are *nearly as good* as those in *Hughes' Garden Architecture*, recently published in London. We supposed that Boston was the headquarters for pears, and they figure such novelties as the Bartlett, Seckel and Urbaniste! But we cannot give the space to an extended criticism. It is pleasant reading about horticulture, and will no doubt be acceptable to the large class who like to have the "road to learning" graded and rolled. Its wordiness is its most objectionable feature, and its diffused light, as compared with the other Horticultural monthlies, is as that of moonlight to sunlight.

Queries.—"Young Farmer" asks the following questions:

Is Johnston's Agricultural Chemistry a distinct work from his Elements of Agricultural Chemistry, or an enlargement of the same. *Answer.*—A distinct work, the former much the fuller and larger. The full title is "Lectures on Agricultural Chemistry and Geology."

Cabbages.—I have seven acres for cabbage in 1867. This land without manure, with a year or two rest, I deem unsurpassed for cabbage, but having been cultivated without rest in corn, I think manure is needed. What kind shall I use? *Answer.*—Lime, or a muck and lime compost, with super-phosphate, bone dust and ashes.

Stable Manure and Lime.—I have about twenty loads stable manure (not compost), and an indefinite quantity of air-slacked lime; in composting, shall I put in lime, and what proportion? *Answer.*—Use no lime with stable manure; the lime will prove a damage.

Lime.—How shall I apply my lime broadcast. What amount per acre, and what machine, if any, shall I use?—*Answer.*—Spread from small heaps with a shovel, or from the tail of a cart. The amount applied may vary from the least quantity you can spread evenly to 300 to 500 bushels. Heavy lands and those of a moist and mucky character, or dark from vegetable mold, will bear much more than light soils; 50 to 100 bushels is a common dose. Small quantities are best applied mixed with muck or soil, and in garden culture this is almost always best. The effects of the lime on the soil in the compost are similar to those which it produces on the soil in the field.

Gas Tar for Posts in Stables.—This is one of the best safe guards against decay, and for a time at least would resist the action of liquid manure.

Miles on the Horse's Foot.—Good shoeing must be systematic. The Miles system has stood the test of thousands of miles under the horse's foot, and that after all is the best test. It has the approval of the best Veterinarians, and many a man who has given the book to his blacksmith, and insisted on the horse-shoeing being done just right, has been rewarded in his own case, and thanked by his neighbors, and by the smith, again and again. See book list. Price, 75 cents.

Single Lines and Left-Hand Plows.—P. P. Wisler, Bucks Co., says: It would be a rare sight to see double lines to drive a plow team in Lancaster County, Pa. More than three-fourths of a century ago, the left hand plow was introduced into that County, and at the present time there are scarcely any right hand plows and double lines seen in that region. The farmers use the left hand plow and single line altogether: drive the leader, or near horse, in the *furrow*, and tie a jockey stick to the inside ring of his harness, and the other end of the stick tied to the outside ring in the blind halter of the off horse, and a tying strap to the inside ring of the same, fastened to the furrow horse, to keep the off horse from going too fast, and make him walk true to his work. This is the modern style of plowing, and quite an improvement on the old plan of using a right hand plow, and double lines cast over the neck or "*round the back of the plowman*," with the horses' heads tied together, to harass and baffle them in fly time. With a good leader in a left hand plow, I have set boys, twelve years old, in the middle of a square field to plow what is called 'haw round,' after giving them a start. They would plow the whole field without using any lines. The horses turning at the corners like a perfect machine, and the horse on the land side, pressing against the jockey stick, would walk so true, that, in stiff sod without stones, the plow boy could leave the plow to run alone for several feet on a stretch, which makes it a light task, compared to the old plan.

Farm Proverbs.—"D. E." writes: 1. Use diligence, industry, integrity, and proper improvement of time, to make farming pay. 2. Choose a farm with a soil either naturally dry or drained, not too level nor yet too steep, well fenced in proper sized fields, not too large. 3. Good, snug buildings, with dry, if not clean, yards and cellars, especially barn and stabling. 4. Economy in accumulating, saving, and properly using all manures and fertilizers possible, no matter how rich your land may be naturally. 5. A good and tolerably fast team, better smart than large. 6. Your farming implements well made, of good material, not too heavy. 7. Have work done in season. 8. Always sow good clean seeds. 9. Do not harvest before your crop is fit to harvest. 10. Don't keep more live stock on your farm than you can keep well. 11. House all things as much as possible—animals, utensils, and crops. 12. Sell when you can get a fair price, and do not store for rats and speculators.

Hints to Horsekeepers.—There are few books which all who own or use the horse, peruse with greater satisfaction than this. We may truly say that we know of no book better worth its price. It is full, yet very much condensed; pleasant reading, yet exceedingly pithy and terse. Price, $1.75. See Book List.

Cotton Planters' Manual.—This little volume contains much that is valuable, especially to the novice in cotton culture. It is the collated experience of veteran planters. A single good hint from an experienced cultivator might enable a farmer to make a crop by avoiding erroneous practice, or providing beforehand against difficulties or damages which might otherwise be unthought of until too late. See our Book List.

Poultry Book.—The little work on Domestic Poultry, by Mr. Saunders, which we published more than a year ago, and which was subsequently thoroughly revised, receiving important additions, has reached its seventh thousand. In the appendix is an account of Mr. Geyelin's visit to the poultry yards of France, which, in connection with the great interest now-a-days being taken in French fowls, has a peculiar importance.

Home-Made Binding.—"W. H. W." I have stitched three volumes; taking an awl and pricking the holes, sewing with strong thread. Pasting a piece of strong cotton cloth over the back with a strong paste, made by scalding a thin batter of flour, wet up cold, and adding a piece of glue about two inches square, dissolved in hot water, to a half pint of paste. Take pasteboard, such as is used by book-binders, of a suitable size, sew to the papers already stitched, including fly leaves. On the back, with your paste, put a strip of enamelled cloth, cut to the proper length and width. Now cover the whole sides, turning over the edges, with marbled paper; finish by pasting the fly-leaf to inside of cover, and, if neatly done, you have a book handsome enough for any farmer's library, at a cost of only a few cents.

Always Too Late.—Notices of the winter meetings of several of the Western Horticultural Societies, to be held in January, were received after our paper was printed and being mailed. Nothing of this kind is sure to be noticed that reaches us later than the 10th of the preceding month. Will Secretaries of Horticultural Societies please send notices in season?

"Cornea Restorers" and "Eye Sharpeners."—Several have lately asked our opinion of these things, probably new subscribers, as we had an item upon the matter last year. An application was made to us to advertise a thing of this kind, and while our impressions were all adverse to it, we took the trouble, in justice to the advertisers as well as to our readers, to consult one of our most eminent oculists, who confirmed our impressions by his opinion that it "would do more harm than good." If one wishes a watch repaired or a piano tuned, he goes to some one who understands their mechanism and does not tinker them himself. An eye is more valuable than all the watches and pianos that were ever made. Do not trifle with it.

Cheated by the "Doctors."—J. W. Way, sends the names of two quacks, who warranted to cure him for certain sums, and who got his money but left him no better. He wishes us to publish the names of these as a warning to other sufferers. If we were to publish the names of all the quack doctors, of whom we have complaints, it would not do a particle of good, as these chaps don't remain long under one name. If any one who has read the *Agriculturist* for a year, will employ a "Doctor," who advertises that he can do this or that, or who will warrant a cure for a given sum, we cannot pity him very much, as he has already had abundant warning. Nor can we, as J. W. W. requests, publish the names of reliable Doctors. We have no doubt that there are several in his own town who could give him good advice, and in his case he needs that rather than medicine.

Bluffton Wine Company.—A Company for carrying on the culture of the grape and wine making on the large scale has been organized in Missouri. George Husmann is President, and Dr. L. D. Morse, Secretary. The lands of the Company are chiefly in Montgomery County, and have a front of about three miles on the Missouri River. Mr. Samuel Miller, of Avon, Pa., the originator of the Martha, Black Hawk, and other seedlings, is Superintendent of out-door propagation and cultivation.

Teeth and Hair.—"A. A." asks if Zozodont is good for the teeth, and what kind of a hair restorative we would recommend. As we do not know the composition of Zozodont, we can't say, and do not recommend any "hair restorative," believing them to be of no other use than to put money in the venders pockets. If there is any disease of the scalp, go to a physician, if not, keep it clean and healthy by washing and friction, and if the hair don't grow no fertilizer will make it grow.

Lathing Upon Adobe Walls.—"West" writes "please tell us if an adobe wall, without studding, may be furred for lathing by nailing strips directly on the sun-dried brick. Will not the bricks be cracked inevitably in the process? To avoid the cost of timber, such as studding, would be a great reason for adopting the adobe." It would be easy in laying up the Adobe to put into the wall strips of board; say, a foot or 18 inches apart, for the purpose of holding the nails. This would be the safer course and less expensive than furring in the regular way.—Ed.

Raising Calves Without Milk.—"C. V. B.," of Beaver Dam, Wisconsin, Nov. 5, writes: In regard to bringing up calves without milk the plan I have always found to work well is to feed on "Bean Soup," prepared as for family use, and with the same quantity of salt—say, two tablespoonfuls in each mess (of two quarts.) I have always found the calves to thrive upon this as well as upon milk. I take them from the cow at one week old, and they are never troubled with scours, nor with the opposite tendency.

Dry Earth.—Fine dry soil may be obtained by raking over a loamy spot, taking the stones off, and letting it dry in the sun until it may be dashed through a screen with eight holes to the inch; then covering it at night, and exposing it another day to the sun. Thus dried it may be barreled, and is as powerful a deodorizer as gypsum or plaster, an excellent disinfectant and drier for use in privies, hen-houses, or any foul places. The best we ever used was road dust swept up and barreled on hot days. It was employed in the hen-house. There are laws against taking dirt from the roads, but if the dust were to be replaced by gravel, no objection could be urged.

Agriculture in Hamilton College.—A correspondent informs us that the trustees of Hamilton College, Clinton, N. Y., have received a bequest of $30,000 from the late Silas D. Childs, of Utica, N. Y., for a Department of Agricultural Chemistry. A well-timed generosity. The immutable laws of Vegetation, Animal Physiology, and Agricultural Chemistry are better worth the study of young men than the shifting statutes that are made and unmade by human legislators.

Peat and Muck.—"L. F. H.," Ohio. The sample sent is apparently a very fair article of peat. You can test its value as fuel thus: Cut out 100 cakes, (like bricks, 2+4+8); dry them thoroughly; weigh a bushel; make a fire in a clean stove, or on a hearth, save and weigh the ashes. If the ashes are more than 10 per cent. of the peat, it will not be very good fuel. Composted with lime or ashes, or manure, after being exposed one winter, or after being treated with lime or ashes, it will make good manure. Three loads of fine muck, with one load of good dung and litter, with a barrel or two of yard liquor pumped over the heap twice or thrice in four weeks, will be better than four loads of barn-yard manure.

Temperature of Cream for Churning.—John B. Larover, Union County, Ill. The temperature is very important in churning, for it is hard work to bring butter if the cream is above 70 degrees, or below 58 degrees F. The best temperature to begin churning is at about 62 degrees, for the friction of the agitation will raise it a little, and 65 is as high as it should ever be at the close. The richness of the milk and cream depends upon the feed and upon the cow; salting the cows regularly, or having it always before them, makes the butter come well, other things being equal. Butter comes easiest when the cream is slightly sour. Then look to the temperature, and make it right by setting the vessel holding cream in an outer vessel of hot or cold water, or lower a tin pail of water into the cream, stirring the cream until it is of a uniform and right temperature from top to bottom. Then, not filling the churn too full, churn steadily, giving thorough agitation until the butter comes.

"Can the Ethiopian Change His Skin?"—"A. T.," of New York City (farm in New Jersey) asks: "Did you ever know of a Spanish cock changing his color? I have one, a splendid fellow, which came into the world raven black, and so remained for nearly a year, when he dropped that garb, and took on another, and is now as white as snow. It occurred about the time Mr. Lincoln issued his Emancipation Proclamation." This change is not a very rare occurrence with Black Spanish fowls, and has given rise to the so-called "White Spanish" breed, in which the white color is fixed. We have heard of none changing back again.

Experience With Ferrets.—Mr. Jacob Flanagan, after an experience of some years with these animals, falls back upon the cat as the best rat catcher. He says: "A ferret can seldom climb to a hay mow, they are so clumsy. I do not think they can smell a rat, and are nearly blind. I have seen them within one foot of a rat and not touch it; but if the rat squeals, they will attack immediately. I thought it might be better if they were trained, and engaged a professional rat catcher to come with his ferrets and dogs; but he did no permanent good. I kept ferrets for three or four years, but to no profit. They would dig out occasionally, and get over the fence around their pen, and kill a good lot of chickens. So I killed the ferrets and bought a young *black* cat, and always feed her in the barn twice a day, and in no other place. Since the cat came I have hardly seen a rat or mouse about the barn, except in the cat's mouth." [We attach more importance to the confinement to the barn than to the color, though dark colors are best.—Ed.]

Chicory.—L. B. Tifft, Connecticut. Chicory is cured by cutting up into pieces an inch or two in length, and drying thoroughly in a kiln at a temperature below that of boiling water. After it is dry it may be marketed. For use it is roasted like coffee, care being taken not to char it, and ground to a coarse meal.

Osage Orange on Timothy Sod.—"J. B. R.," Gentry County, Mo. A good Timothy sod, plowed in the fall, the soil being naturally rich, would, we should think, make a very good seed bed for an Osage Orange nursery, if dry, worked deep, and kept clean

Turning in Green Crops.—B. M. French asks: "Why will not Ragweed plowed in, be as beneficial to the soil as any cultivated crop?" Because they do not furnish as much vegetable matter. The great advantage of clover as a green crop, is the large mass of roots and leaves it furnishes. So of buckwheat, peas, and other crops used for this purpose. Weeds are better turned under than left to go to seed, but hoed crops should be kept upon the ground until the weeds are subdued. Clean cultivation and high manuring will soon finish them. If Mr. F. can not use clover on account of its winter killing, try buckwheat, or what is better, drain his land. The cereals do not exhaust land, when they are turned under, but when they are suffered to go to seed, and both stalk and kernel are removed from the soil. Under draining is a remedy for winter killing.

Cockle Instead of Wheat.—A Subscriber asks: "What are the merits and demerits of cockle as an article of food for cattle?"—We have been shy of the article since Job and his friends held their discussion. "Let cockles grow instead of barley," was about as bitter a curse as those old time farmers could invoke on their neighbors' fields, and their cockle and ours, if not the same plant, we guess are of about equal value for fodder. We most decidedly prefer the cereals.

Draining to Dry up Springs.—"B. M. F." asks: "Where springs come out near the base of a hill, will a drain above, five or six feet deep, cut off the water and dry up the spring?" Certainly, if you tap the feeder of the spring, and provide an outlet for your drain. The spring is a natural outlet for an underground drain.

Pumpkins instead of Roots.—"B. M. F." We have never made accurate experiments of the comparative value of these for feeding purposes. Both are very good. Large quantities of pumpkins and squashes are raised in the Eastern States, and fed to milch cows, and fattening cattle, and hogs, both cooked and raw. They pay well. They are not as easily kept as roots, but are raised with less trouble, as they are generally a stolen crop with corn and potatoes, which is very doubtful economy.

Pipe for Liquid Manure.—"B. M. F." This should be protected with a strainer at the upper end. Its liability to obstructions will depend very much upon the fall. The more rapid the descent, the less trouble you will have with sediments. Two inch glazed tile would probably be much cheaper than lead or iron, and would be less likely to be obstructed by sediment.

Plowing Pasture and Meadow.—All land, that is not already too wet, is benefitted by irrigation. Land plowed in winter produces much more grass. It may stand on all winter without injuring the grass. In the summer the water should be carried over the ground in small ditches, and let on at intervals. Draining and irrigation should go together to secure the best results.

Premium Washer and Wringer.—Next to the sewing-machine, the Washer and Wringer have always been favorite premiums with those obtaining clubs of subscribers for the *American Agriculturist*, and hundreds of them have been sent out in this way. The following testimonial to their excellence from so competent a source, is worthy of note. Mrs. Laura E. Lyman, authoress of one of our prize Housekeeping Essays, writes, "I have for some time been using the Doty Washer. It is in the highest degree a labor-saving machine, and also a great saver of clothes, as it dispenses almost entirely with the old mode of rubbing them on the wash-board. With two children, a girl of twelve and a boy of seven, the washing can be done with no fatigue on my part and little on theirs. With the Washer and Wringer there is avoided the inconvenience and danger to health of having the hands immersed, now in hot, and then in cold water. Doty, for his invention, deserves the gratitude of every housekeeper."

Vermont Agricultural Society—Significant Wool Resolutions.—The State Agricultural Society, of Vermont, held its annual meeting on the 9d of January, and in the resolutions passed respecting the tariff bill, now before Congress, praying its passage, a remarkable admission was made, namely: "Our own wools are lying on our hands uncalled for at any prices that would pay over half the cost of production." We would ask Vermont farmers if they think this fact an especial recommendation for the greasy Merinos they are so proud of? Other people can sell their wool. But we hear that the clips of two or perhaps three years are chiefly still in first hands in Vermont. Why? Not because of low tariffs, but because, if manufacturers can buy wool they will let grease alone. When it is bought and sent to the New York market, it is avoided by all manufacturers, and the purchase of these greasy fleeces, cleansing them thoroughly, and returning them to the market, constitutes a lucrative business. If Vermont wool growers, will but tub-wash these fleeces, they will save a large amount of excellent manure for use upon their farms, and find a ready sale, at a fair price, for the stock now on hand. We do not argue against the tariff, but only against grease.

Experience with Sorghum.—H. K. Smith, of Putnam Co., Ill., writes: "L. Grafton's experience in the January 'Basket' is in some ways very different from my own. I have worked at it on 'Cook's' Evap. for 7 years, and prefer the original black-seeded Sorghum. *Green cane is not fit to work.* It will *not make sugar* for me, and *but little* syrup. What syrup I make when the seed is *entirely ripe* makes a great deal of sugar, often ½ to ⅔ of the barrel will be *grained*, but *never a grain* when the cane is at all green. My molasses (not syrup) will not keep over summer if the cane is not ripe, but works, sours, and forms more or less *jelly*. I can tell 'Grafton' just what makes the 'salty taste' in the molasses. I have had half a dozen lots that were grown on a *pig pen site*, where *rich manure* had been hauled out, or an old straw pile, and they universally tasted *salty*; one so much so that we could scarcely taste it. We never manure in Illinois for cane. It grows a *good crop* upon land that has been farmed steadily, and without manure, for 25 or 30 years, and which will not raise good corn or wheat. Three years ago I cut the seed of some Sorghum when it *was in bloom*, let it stand three weeks, worked up two-thirds of the lower end of stalks, it made a beautiful molasses; 6 gallons to a barrel of 30 gallons, which nearly all grained, forming *very fine* crystals. We think it improves the quality of the cane to store it *in cool weather*. We make a great deal of molasses here in Illinois. To show you that I have had experience in evaporating, I will state that my molasses always commands the highest price in market. I can always get all that I wish to work, and more, at *one-half* the equivalent price."

Am. Dairymens' Association.—The second meeting of this association under its present organization was held at Utica, N.Y., on the 9th of January. The attendance of dairymen was large, and included many from Canada and from the Western States. The feature of the meeting was Mr. X. A. Willard's report of his observations abroad, in regard to cheese-making there. Mr. Willard is a thoroughly practical man of culture, and probably better informed in regard to cheese-making than any other man in America. His address was very interesting, and his observations and conclusions, when given to the public, as it doubtless will be, will be productive of great good. Officers for the current year were elected. The President is George Williams, of Oneida, N. Y., and the Secretary Geo. B. Weeks, of Verona, N. Y.

The American Cow Milker.—"J. J.," of Spring Valley, Colorado, and others, ask if we have yet found out whether or not the cow milker is a success. We have visited the office once and again, in order to find out when we could go to see the milker in use. We were told that none were in use hereabouts, that the employes at the great milk stables would mob any one attempting to introduce them, and that they had been out only a few months, and had not been tried very long any where, etc. Each time they told about the same story. The same machine, to all appearance, was exhibited at the World's Fair in London, in 1862, and we have tried in vain ever since to know of a fair trial being made. We have written to their agents at a distance and got no reply, and on the whole, have not as much faith in it as in the more tedious hand process.

The Horticultural Laws of Illinois.—Every one with much experience in fruit growing knows that certain marauders consider all kinds of fruit as "free plunder," that these thieves have a way of taking one's choicest specimens, and that it is very difficult to meet such fellows with the "common law." To remedy the difficulty of convicting fruit thieves, the State of Illinois has passed some very stringent laws, which we copy, in the hope that these, or similar laws, may be enacted in States in which the Legislature is now in session:

AN ACT TO PUNISH FRUIT THIEVES.—*Be it enacted by the People of the State of Illinois, represented in the General Assembly*, That if any person or persons shall hereafter enter the inclosure of any person, without the leave or license of such owner, and pick, destroy, or carry away the fruit of any apple, plum, peach, pear, or other fruit tree or bush, such person or persons shall be guilty of a misdemeanor, and upon conviction thereof, may be fined any sum not less than ten dollars, nor more than fifty dollars, and may be imprisoned in the county jail for any period not exceeding twenty days. The penalties incurred by a violation of this act may be enforced by indictment in any court having jurisdiction of misdemeanors in the county where the offense is committed, or the fine may be recovered in action for debt before any justice of the peace of such county.

AN ACT FOR THE PROTECTION OF FRUIT, AND ORNAMENTAL TREES, SHRUBBERY AND VEGETABLE PRODUCTS. SECTION 1. *Be it enacted by the People of the State of Illinois, represented in the General Assembly*, That if any person or persons, in this State, shall willfully, maliciously and without lawful authority, cut down, root up, sever, injure, peel or destroy any fruit or ornamental tree, cultivated root or plant, fruit or other vegetable production, grape, strawberry or cranberry vines, currant, gooseberry, raspberry, or cultivated blackberry bushes, standing or growing on or being attached to the land of another, or shall, willfully and without lawful authority, cut down, root up, destroy or injure any fruit or ornamental tree or shrubbery, planted or growing on any street, lane, or alley, or public grounds, in any city, borough or incorporated town in said State, every such person so offending, shall be deemed guilty of a misdemeanor, and, on conviction thereof, shall be punished by a fine of not more than five hundred dollars, or by imprisonment in the jail of the county not exceeding three months, or both, at the discretion of the court, and shall, moreover, be liable in double the amount of damages to the party injured. This law to take effect from and after its passage.

Annual Meeting of the Connecticut State Board of Agriculture.—This body was authorized by the last Legislature of the State, and was duly organized at its first session in New Haven, on the 8th of January, his Excellency Governor Hawley in the chair. It is composed of certain *ex officio* members, besides the Governor, and two representatives from each of the eight County Agricultural Societies, making about twenty members. By special invitation, the *American Agriculturist* was also represented at the meetings, which were continued with unabated interest for three days. A circular, issued by T. S. Gold, Secretary of the Board, proposing certain questions upon drainage, irrigation, and fruit culture, called forth a good many replies, and led to the attendance of some of the most distinguished farmers and fruit growers in the State. The Board had also made provision for lectures by Professors Johnson and Brewer, of the Yale Scientific School, which added much to the interest of the occasion. These were interspersed by discussions upon the topics indicated, and by reports from the various Agricultural Fairs held in the several Counties of the State. The County Societies are all kept up, and fairs are usually held, but not with uniform success. The following resolutions, looking to the improvement of these Societies, were introduced, and much the liveliest session was spent in their discussion. As they are of general interest and very suggestive of the wants of similar Societies in all parts of the country, we give them in full:—

Resolved, That we regard permanent buildings, as well for live stock as for manufactural goods, essential to the permanent success of our Agricultural Societies, thereby enabling them to continue their Fairs for a longer period in each year.

Resolved, That the location of these buildings in regard to facility of access by rail or steamer, is of the first importance.

Resolved, That we recommend to the Agricultural Societies the practice of securing contributions of stock and manufactures by personal solicitations of breeders and manufacturers, and devoting some time previous to the days of the Fair to this object.

Resolved, That we recommend the publication of the proceedings of Societies, and their distribution through the country.

Resolved, That we recommend to breeders the importance of explaining at the Fairs the qualities in the stock that they consider of chief value, with statements of their practice and success.

The County fairs are doing a good work, and they ought to be kept up in all the States where they are in existence, and to be organized where they are not. A County embraces usually just about territory enough to bring together a good representation of the several branches of agriculture, horticulture, and manufactures, and to make an interesting exhibition. A single town does not give variety enough, and the expense is a very serious objection. The impression left upon our mind by the meetings is, that the agricultural and horticultural interests of the State are in a thriving condition. The organization of this Board by the Legislature, after the example of Massachusetts, as one of the permanent institutions of the State, with its Secretary and Annual Volume of Transactions, is a cheering indication. The facilities afforded for the meetings at the Hall of the Sheffield Scientific School, the gratuitous lectures given by Professors Johnson and Brewer, and the cordial welcome of all the Professors to the Board, and their guests, show that science is ready to extend its aid to these interests. Our thanks are due to the Board for their generous hospitality, and to the Yale Professors for numerous favors.

Valuable Experiments with Potatoes.

Dr. Hexamer, of New Castle, N. Y., furnishes us again (see last vol., p. 98) with an account of some very important experiments of his with potatoes, and also with the tally of his crops reduced to bushels per acre for each sort. We should preface the specifications of these results by stating that Dr. H. is an accurate and scientific experimenter and observer, and a good farmer. His results have a scientific value.

RESULTS OF EXPERIMENTS.

1. Out of 70 hills of potatoes, peeled so that no eyes were visible, 35 grew. Some produced very large potatoes. The planted potatoes remained, mostly, hard and firm till digging time.

2. Out of 80 hills, pieces cut without eyes, 13 hills grew. All of these sprouted on the cut surfaces, none through skin. (One large potato, cut in two lengthwise, sprouted on the cut side near, but below the skin, and there was no sprout proceeding from a visible eye.)

3. Out of 100 whole potatoes, 98 grew from the small end, and 2 at the side. With more than half the number of potatoes planted whole, only one eye grew, the rest remaining dormant.

4. A potato does not always expend *all* germinating power in one year.

5. Wet rot and dry rot are one and the same disease. Potatoes affected with the rot, will rot dry when they are kept dry, and the same will rot wet when they are kept in a moist place.

YIELD OF POTATOES IN 1866.

The following list is arranged in order of productiveness, and gives the number of years the seed has been planted on the farm, and the amount of assorted, marketable potatoes:

Variety.	Years planted	Bu. per acre.	Remarks.
Cusco	3d year	[illegible]	No rot.
Monitor	1st year	253	Rotted badly.
Pinkeye Rustycoat	3d year	240	No rot.
White Peach Blow	3d year	225	Rot.
Fluke	3d year	215	No rot.
Peach Blow	3d year	200	Much rot.
Mercer	3d year	180	Much rot.
Bulkley's Seedling	3d year	168	Much rot.
Garnet Chili	3d year	166	Rot.
Buckeye	3d year	150	Eaten by grubs.
Early Goodrich	2d year	145	No rot.
Prairie Seedling	3d year	125	Rotted badly.
Early Cottage	3d year	118	No rot.
Colebrook	1st year	109	Rot.
Blue Mercer	3d year	105	Rotted.
Gleason	1st year	95	No rot, poor location.
Jackson White	1st year	90	Rot.
Dykeman	3d year	85	Little rot.
Prince Albert	3d year	80	Rotted badly.
White Rock	3d year	75	No rot.
Rough and Ready	3d year	62	Rotted.
Early Sovereign	2d year	57	No rot.
Early June	3d year	53	Poor location, no rot.

Cow Stables—Not New but Good.

By Gilbert J. Green.

Enclosed I send you a rough sketch of my idea of a cow stable. I would always *tie* cows, believing it to be the easiest and best plan. This is best done by having a strap buckled around the horns, and always left there; upon this strap in front, is a ring two inches in diameter. In the stable is a rope or chain two feet long, or less, with a ring sliding upon an upright pole beside the manger, on the other end a snap hook. When the cow enters the stable, this hook is snapped into the ring upon the strap, and the cow is securely, as well as comfortably, fastened.

I would arrange the front of the manger, (see figure.) with two diverging boards, having them to touch at the bottom, and widen to the full width of the stall above. These prevent the cow from throwing the hay out of her manger with her head, and getting it under her feet. The stall should be 40 inches wide between the partitions, and 50 inches long between the manger and the gutter, which should be 7 inches deep and two feet wide. The manger should be two feet in width and 17 inches high, in front of the cow. The partition should extend across the manger, and be five feet in length and four or more in height. The floor (as well as the bottom of the gutter), should be made of asphaltum or coal tar, two inches higher in front than it is behind. Such a stable is clean, durable and convenient, the cows have plenty of room, their heads are not closely confined, you scrape over no broken planks or rough stones in cleaning out the stalls, but a smooth, even floor, that absorbs no moisture, generates no foul odors, and is easy for the cow to stand or lie upon, even without litter.

MANGER FOR COWS.

Walks and Talks on the Farm—No. 39.

The winter so far has not been favorable for wheat. Severe winds and little snow, with sudden freezing and snowing. One morning the thermometer on my stoop marked 8° below zero, and the next day we had a thaw, followed by high winds, and then a hard frost. This, with bare ground, will severely try our winter wheat, especially where the land is not drained.

The Doctor has bought a stack of nice clover hay at $9 a ton, delivered. He is not feeding his cows so much corn-pudding this winter. It costs too much, and clover hay and carrots are much cheaper. A little grain in addition, however, is a great improvement. The Doctor raised a splendid crop of carrots, and lectures me for not growing more on my farm. I tell him that as soon as I get my land clean and rich I propose to beat him in raising root crops. All my efforts at present are directed to this one object—to get my land clean and rich. There is no profit in farming until this is accomplished. Fortunately in making land clean you do a good deal towards making it rich. And when it is once rich, this very process of keeping it rich will do a good deal towards keeping it clean.

I told the Doctor that the manure from the clover would be worth as much as he paid for the hay. A practical farmer who heard the remark thought this an extravagant estimate. He draws a good deal of manure from the city, and says he has made up his mind to sell everything from the farm that brings a good price—straw, hay, grain, roots, and anything that can be turned into money. He thinks a farmer cannot afford to make manure by feeding stock. That the only way land can be profitably manured, from the farm itself, is by turning under green clover.

Situated as he is, near the city, it may be cheaper to buy manure than to make it by feeding stock. But he cannot afford to sell clover hay for nine dollars a ton. The cutting, curing and stacking cost, say two dollars a ton, and weighing and delivering it to the purchaser at least a dollar more, so that he does not net over six dollars per ton. A farmer who wants manure had certainly better plow in the clover than sell it at such a price. But I do not think he need do either. Hay is always worth something to feed out to cows and sheep. Some years it is worth more, some less, but, taking one year with another, it is worth at least the expense of cutting and curing, and drawing back the manure. The real question to be considered in determining whether it is better to plow in the clover, or to make it into hay and feed it out is: can you harvest the clover and draw back the manure for what the hay is worth to feed out?

"I would really like to know how you make it out that the manure from a ton of clover is worth $9.00?"

"We know how much nitrogen, phosphoric acid, potash, etc., the clover contains, and we know about how much is retained in the increase of the animal eating the clover, and consequently we know how much would be left in the manure. We know, furthermore, how much these ingredients cost when purchased in the form of Peruvian guano, or other artificial manures; and from these and other data, it is easy to determine the value of the manure made from any article used as food."

"That may be all very well, but still I do not believe the manure from a ton of clover hay is worth $9.00. It cannot be. *There is not bulk enough.* I do not believe you would get, after it was fed out, over half a load of manure, and I can buy good stable manure for a dollar a load."

"Well, suppose you can, and that it costs you another dollar to draw it; I question if you get manure cheaper than you would from clover hay at nine dollars a ton. You do not draw much more than a ton of this fresh horse litter to a load."

"Probably not, taking one load with another."

"Very well. A ton of this fresh manure, then, costs you two dollars by the time it is deposited in your barn yard, or in the field."

"This is rather too high an estimate. I have not much for my man and team to do in winter, except to draw manure. But let that pass."

"The question then is, what is the real value of this ton of fresh manure, calculated on the same estimate that we apply to the manure made from clover hay. Nitrogen, phosphoric acid and potash are, confessedly the most valuable ingredients in any manure. A ton of ordinary barnyard manure contains: Nitrogen, 6 lbs.; Phosphoric acid, 4 lbs.; Potash and Soda, 11 lbs."

Fresh, solid horse droppings, without any admixture of straw, would contain a little more nitrogen than the above estimate—say 10⅓ lbs.—and would be proportionally more valuable. On the other hand, solid cow dung, unmixed with straw, contains, according to the best analyses, less than 4½ lbs. of nitrogen to the ton.

Now a ton of good clover hay contains about 50 lbs. of nitrogen. And if we assume that 3 lbs. of this nitrogen is retained in the animal, or otherwise disposed of by the vital functions, we shall have 47 lbs. of nitrogen in the manure made from a ton of clover hay. The clover, too, is exceedingly rich in potash.

To sum up the matter, that it may be understood at a glance, we put the figures side by side:

	A ton of ordinary manure contains	Manure from a ton of clover hay contains
Nitrogen	6 lbs.	47 lbs.
Phosphoric acid	4 lbs.	12 lbs.
Potash and soda	11 lbs.	40 lbs.

In the manure made from a ton of clover hay we got nearly four times as much potash and soda, three times as much phosphoric acid, and nearly six times as much nitrogen. The latter is the ingredient of most value, and we shall not be far wrong in concluding that the manure from a ton of clover hay is worth five times as much as a ton of common manure.

"This mode of reckoning is not satisfactory,

I would like some practical proof. Manure from clover is not a new thing, and I have never noticed that it was so much more valuable than stable manure, as these figures indicate. In fact, I don't believe it. There is not bulk enough."

"You think highly of green clover plowed under for manure. Now, how many tons of green clover does it take to make a ton of clover hay?"

"Probably five or six."

"Very well. Now, how much manure do you suppose that five or six tons of green clover would make, if thrown into a heap in the barn yard and allowed to rot, with water enough to keep it moist? *Would it not make more than half a load?*"

I did not press the question. It seemed to throw new light on the subject. Of course, a ton of hay made from five tons of green clover is worth just as much for manure as if the five tons had been fed out in the green state. The four tons of water dispelled from the grass in curing has no value as a manure.

The farmer who sells clover hay will soon impoverish his land. He cannot grow too much of it, but every pound should be plowed under or fed out on the farm, and the manure carefully preserved. The former practice was all very well when the country was new, and butter, beef and mutton sold for almost nothing; but now that there is an increasing demand for these articles, the practice of plowing under so much valuable food is a loss to the farmer and to the consumers of meat. When fed to animals, we get back in the manure nearly or quite 95 per cent. of all the elements of plant-food (except carbonaceous matter) that the food contains. And this carbonaceous matter has no manurial value. We can spare all that the animal can digest from the food without the slightest injury to the manure. If anything, it is improved by the processes of mastication and digestion. The only ingredients of any value that we lose are the nitrogen, phosphoric acid, potash, &c., and this loss is not over 5 per cent. The food of horses, cattle and sheep contains so much indigestible woody-fibre (carbonaceous matter) that, even after the animals have taken out all they can digest, there is still left in the manure more than enough to meet the demand from the crops to which the manure is applied. A ton of *dry* horse dung contains 1,622 lbs. of this carbonaceous matter; dry sheep dung, 1,608 lbs., and dry cow dung, 1,714 lbs. On the other hand, a ton of dry, solid excrement of the pig contains only 1,108 lbs. of carbonaceous matter. This is owing to the fact that pigs are supplied with food containing less woody fibre. But even in the case of pigs it will be seen that more than half the dung consists of carbonaceous matter. In ordinary barn-yard manure, where straw is used freely, the proportion is even still greater. We need not plow in clover, therefore, for the sake of getting carbonaceous matter. And this is practically about all that we lose when it is fed to animals.

Manure made solely from straw and cornstalks is hardly worth the labor of drawing it out to the field and spreading it. The manure from a ton of wheat straw is worth $2.68, while that from a ton of clover is worth $9.64. This is Mr. Lawes' estimate, and it is undoubtedly a close approximation to the truth. The price will fluctuate according to circumstances, but if the manure from a ton of straw is worth $2.08, that from a ton of clover is worth $9.61.

Now, then, ten tons of straw, half of it fed to cows or sheep, and the other half used as litter, would give us about 28 tons of manure. Assuming that there was no loss from leaching, &c., this 28 tons would be worth, say $27.

On the other hand, 5 tons of clover hay, and 5 tons of straw for litter, would give 28 tons of manure, worth $61.60. Add a couple of tons of oil-cake to the hay and straw, and you would then get 29 or 30 tons of manure, worth $101.08.

When it costs so much to draw out and spread manure, it should be our aim to make it as rich as possible. The addition of oil-cake to the ordinary food does not, according to Mr. Lawes, add more than 11 lbs. additional weight to each ton of the manure, "a quantity which," he truly says, "is so small that neither the man that loaded the cart, nor the horse that drew the dung to the field, would detect it." And yet, as before stated, the substitution of clover hay for straw, and the addition of the oil-cake, would make one load more than three times as valuable as that made from straw alone. Ordinary barn-yard manure contains 70 per cent. of water; and in the spring it doubtless contains a good deal more; and it will readily be seen that the addition of a few tons of oil-cake to the feed adds very little to the weight of the manure. If it costs half a dollar a ton to draw the manure to the field and spread it, the net value of the straw made manure would be less than 47 cents, while that from the half hay and half straw manure would be $1.77, and that from the manure, with oil-cake added to the feed, would be $3.11. In other words, after deducting the expense of handling the manure, the net value of the oil-cake dung is nearly *seven times* as great as that of the straw made dung.

I believe there is no error in these figures, and they show the importance of paying more attention to the subject of high feeding, viewed merely from the effect of the food on the value of the manure.

A Canadian farmer writes me that he thinks I "unduly magnify the trouble of storing roots for winter use." "Any one," he says, "who has a dry side-hill near the barn, can make a cellar, with 350 feet of rough 2 inch plank, capable of holding seven or eight hundred bushels of roots." I do not think that this proves anything. Seven or eight hundred bushels of roots are better than nothing, but, after all, what do they amount to? They are equal, perhaps, to 4 tons of clover hay. If, on a farm of 200 acres, we could raise, and readily store away, *twenty thousand* bushels of roots, they would amount to something. In England, double this amount is not uncommon. I have seen a hundred thousand bushels of Swedes grown in one field! At least, there was a splendid crop, and there were 120 acres in the field, and there were on the same farm several other fields of turnips 80 to 100 acres each! Now, when I "magnify the trouble of keeping roots" in this climate, I had reference to growing them as a general crop, on the same scale as we grow clover or corn. It is not easy to see how this can be done without a great change in our system of winter feeding. But I do not despair of seeing the change effected. There is no difficulty in raising the roots. The trouble is in storing them and feeding them out. A few hundred bushels, to be used occasionally, as a kind of tonic, are useful; but so far as the mere supply of nutriment is concerned, they are now, as most farm buildings are arranged, more plague than profit. We must have system and regularity in feeding, and we must either have a large supply of roots, or feed them out in such small quantities that they can go but a short way towards supplying the necessary food. I have 20 head of cattle and 200 sheep. If they were allowed all the roots they would eat, which is the English rule, "seven or eight hundred bushels" would not last them two weeks. Raising a few roots for a condiment is all very well, and need involve little trouble in preserving them. But this was not what I had reference to. I want to see a dozen acres of roots to the hundred acres. To store and feed out such a quantity will tax our ingenuity. But it will yet be done.

For the American Agriculturist.

Shall We Have An Efficient Dog Law?

Many of our State Legislatures are now in session, and others will be soon, and we wish to call their attention to one of the most important interests of their constituents—sheep raising. It is hardly possible to exaggerate the importance of this subject. It concerns the people of the city and country alike. For the only wholesome meat that is within the means of all in the city is the flesh of sheep, and the price of this must depend upon the supply of the flocks afforded by our farms. With mutton at present prices, we believe that sheep are one of the best crops of the farmer. We can afford to raise them without counting the wool and pelts. As a means of renovating old pastures, and keeping the soil in good heart, the sheep surpasses all other animals. No meat is more wholesome than mutton, and, but for dogs, it could be upon every man's table in town and country, at much less cost than we now have it.

The dog is the natural enemy of the sheep, and needs to be kept under by efficient legislation in all the States. The whole dog tribe, Tray, Blanche and Sweetheart, hound, cur and spaniel, should be made expensive luxuries, to be kept in kennels and leading strings, or exterminated. We never go down to the dog pound in your city, on a July morning, where they drown them by the hundred, without a feeling of grim satisfaction, "served 'em right." These animals destroy sheep by the thousand, and in districts where their growth is unchecked, they make sheep raising almost an impossibility. The business is so precarious that no man wants to embark his capital in it. He must either keep a man to watch his flock all the time, and yard them at night within a dog-proof fence, or give up the business. The dogs destroy vast multitudes, but the chief evil that they do is that of inspiring apprehension, and making flocks insecure. They operate as a constant check upon production.

Now, we want a State law, in every sheep growing State, that shall do for country dogs, what the city ordinance does for its canine population, in summer. The statute should outlaw the whole tribe. It should brand the dog as an enemy to the commonwealth. It should say to his owner, "Take care of that animal or we will do it for you." It should make the dog contraband. His owner should pay a heavy tax on him; should keep him muzzled; and a large bounty should be offered on all dogs running at large. The taxes should go to a fund to pay for the damages done to the farmers' flocks by dogs.

They have a curious dog law in Connecticut, leaving it optional with the towns to enforce the provisions of the statute. One town may make clean work with the dogs, and the next may offer a premium on puppies, and look to its neighbors' sheep pastures for dog feed. This makes a farce of legislation against these animals. We want one law, for a whole State, that will make a sheep as secure as a cow in the remotest pasture upon the farm. Then we can have cheap mutton whether wool is protected or not. We earnestly hope that this matter may

SIC SEMPER CANIBUS.

be taken up for discussion in our farmers' clubs, and agricultural societies, and that measures may be taken to secure efficient legislation, and mete out exact justice to our dog population. Failing in this, we suggest a resort to cold lead, hemp, strychnine, anything that will abate the crying nuisance. CONNECTICUT.

[Our artist has caught our correspondent's idea, and illustrated the "hemp."—EDS.]

Willows and Withes.

Mr. W. G. Waring, of Tyrone, Pa., writes: "Having had occasion lately to use a great many long, strong withes, and becoming fatigued with the necessary twisting, we contrived a little machine for doing it, which works with such ease and completeness that we think a description of it will be welcome to very many. In an evening hour, by the warm fireside, we can comfortably prepare enough to use the next day, and in superior condition for quick, secure work. We use them for binding fodder, straw, bags, bundles of trees, roots, brush or poles, and for connecting portable fence panels and gates, etc. The machine is very simple. In fig. 1, *a* is a piece of hard seasoned wood, as thick as a broom handle, and four or five inches long. It is fitted into a carpenter's brace as a bit. A hole is bored into the end two or three inches deep, and then burned into a triangular form with an old saw file. The brace and bit are then fitted across the top of the V of one end of a saw-horse, using two staples of wire or hickory to keep it in place, and the butt of a willow rod is dressed with three cuts of a knife, so as to nearly fit the triangular hole in the wooden bit, into which it is then inserted. A strip of board as long as the withes is laid with one end resting on the tie-piece (*b*) of the saw-horse, and the other end resting upon a stool. While a boy sits on the horse end, you sit on the stool; this steadies all. You take the small end of the withe in your hands, as in fig. 2; the boy turns, and that end will immediately be twisted. The hand *a* advances as the twisting progresses, and the bend which it gives to the rod aids the twist to splinter, and makes the rod easy to hold. The boy now places *his* hand at *a*, and continues to twist, while *you* use your right hand to knot the small end *b* into a loop, as in fig. 3, securing it by passing the point through the loop, as seen under the thumb. The withe is now completed, and much sooner than described. You may pull it out of the bit, and then lay it aside to untwist; or, if you wish to preserve the open form of the loop, convenient for inserting the butt end when tying, and also to keep the cord-like form of the withe, you must have at one side a piece of plank nearly as long as the withes—at one end a little upright pin on which you string the loops successively, while the boy sticks the butt into a hole in the other end of the plank to prevent untwisting. If you have warmed the rods before twisting, either over the stove, or more equally, and without danger of scorching, by standing them, excepting two or three inches of the butt, in a vessel (like a piece of tin spout-tube), filled with hot water or steam, then they will retain their twist perfectly when taken off the plank in the morning, and they may be carried on the pin to the field like a string of fish. They will be found exceedingly handy and pleasant to use. The loop form is most useful for drawing loose bundles into compact bales, and the tying is done by simply grasping the butt end, which has been passed through the loop and drawn tight, giving it three or four twists, sweeping round so as to produce a kink just at the loop. That ties the knot, and it is secured from opening by merely slipping the butt into the bale as at *d*, fig. 4. If it is to be opened soon, a large loop (*c*) affords means of doing it quickly and conveniently. To connect gates, fences, etc., or for rings around calves' necks to hold them by, the withe is woven into a ring like

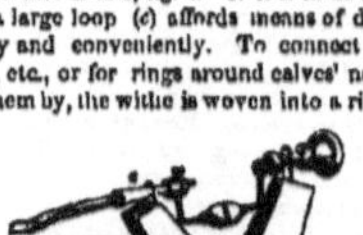

Fig. 1.—WITHE-TWISTER.

a basket handle without forming a loop. To tie large shocks of corn fodder, two withes can be spliced in a second by passing the point of each through the loop of the other. A dried withe can be used again if soaked awhile.

"No ties equal these for security and quickness of application, and a rod or two of ground—good, deep, moist soil—should be planted with the sorts of willow that yield the cleanest, longest, toughest rods, and these should be cut down every fall, to secure a growth of strong annual sprouts.

"The pleasantest willow to use, on account of its leathery softness and smoothness, clean shoots, and bright varnished bark, is the Varnished Willow (*Salix decipiens*). The foliage is handsome, and the growth erect; shoots clean and long. The Goat Willow (*S. caprea*) yields

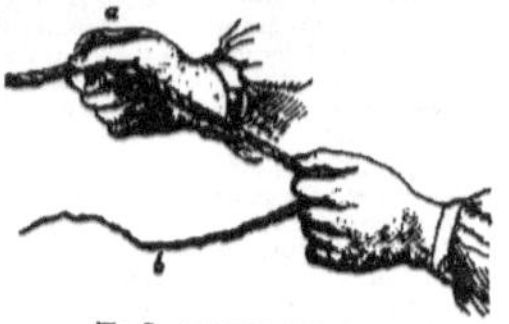

Fig. 2.—TWISTING THE WITHE.

very strong withes, of moderate length. The leaves are large, broad and dark, sometimes almost round. The Beveridge, Comewell, and the strikingly beautiful variety called Kilmarnock, (a drooping variety), are Goat Willows.

"The Russell Willow, and the tall White or Gray and Yellow Willows are of strong growth, and are used for a great variety of purposes, as charcoal, from which crayons and gunpowder are made, tan, boards for barrows and carts, turners' and coopers' work, handles for hoes and

Fig. 3.—LOOPING.

rakes, hedge stakes and hoops, as well as withes, and they grow on any soil; whereas some willows do not thrive on dry soil. For tying young shoots of vines, or espalier trees, the little twigs of the Yellow Willow or *S. vitellina* are superior and very neat. They can be tied like a shoestring, and are fit to use as early as August. These willows branch much, and having the curious quality of snapping or breaking off at the base, they do not yield very long rods.

Cuttings of all the willows grow freely in deep mellow soil, kept clean and moist by a liberal mulch of old leaves, tan, or chaff. They should be set early in April, five inches deep to secure constant moisture without being watered, the base pressed firmly down into the sand or mellow mould, and only one or two buds exposed above ground. The cuttings are easily kept in damp sand in a cellar, or out of doors."

Fig. 4.—BUNDLE.

[Our correspondent adds that, in his own experience he has found it tantalizing to learn about things, and have no hint how to procure them. In this case, though some of these varieties are common in swamps and moist grounds, yet if any one wants such as he describes, the lad whose hands are figured will procure them for a small fee.—ED.]

The Canada Lynx.—(*Lynx Canadensis.*)

This peculiar cat-like animal was once common during severe winters in all the Northern States. And, probably on account of the scarcity of prey in the forests of Canada, which are its congenial haunts, single individuals are now occasionally shot; but it is very timid, avoiding men and preying only upon birds and small, or defenceless animals. The resemblance between it and the Wild-cat or Bay Lynx, (*Lynx rufus*), is quite striking, but it is much larger and of different habits. The Canada Lynx is about 3 feet long to the tail, which is scarcely 6 inches long and much concealed in fur. The head is cat-like, and the ears are large, triangular and tipped with a tuft of coarse black hairs. The general color is clouded gray, somewhat reddish and wavy on the back and sides, and of a lighter gray on the belly. The legs are robust, and the feet immensely large, appearing especially so in winter when covered with long fur. The track in the snow being about 9 inches long—almost like that of a bear. The long, dense, fine fur is much prized, and for this the Lynx is hunted, being trapped with ease in the almost inaccessible solitudes in which it abounds. The creature is a great coward, never attacks men, and when cornered does not make a hard fight, if any, and is easily killed. Its large and softly padded feet present so much surface that even a very slight crust upon the snow supports it, and it is thus enabled to follow successfully those animals whose progress is impeded by snow. When small game becomes scarce, it occasionally attacks deer, and, owing to the same cause, sometimes it is driven by hunger to the vicinity of human habitations, and the sheep, pigs, and calves fall victims to its rapacity. There is no reason to suppose that lynxes have acuter vision than many other animals of the feline family. They have large eyes, capable, like those of the common cat, of great contraction and expansion of the pupils, so that they can use them well in the full glare of the sun upon the snow, and in dark nights also. The animal swims and climbs well, exhibits some strategy in catching its prey, but, on the whole, has little cunning or sagacity. This is especially evinced by the blundering way in which it falls into traps, or is caught under "dead falls," which are logs, or blocks of stone or ice, supported by a "figure 4," or other trip, and which fall, when the trip or trigger is touched, killing by their weight any animal caught beneath them.

CANADA LYNX (*Lynx Canadensis.*)

Our artist has presented us also the picture of the European Lynx, (the *Felis Lynx* of Linnæus). It is an animal of the same genus, and so closely resembles our Lynx that Linnæus regarded both as of the same species. It ranges over the cold parts of Europe and Asia, and we know no reason why it should not also extend across Behrings Straits into North America. Its habits are much like the Canada Lynx, and its color similar, but perhaps a little more inclined to reddish-brown, and more brightly marked. Both have a peculiar galloping run when in open ground, shown in the engraving of the Canada Lynx, and when confined exhibit a surly, snarly and utterly unfriendly disposition. It has few enemies, (besides man), and multiplies fast, though the females have but 2 young a year.

EUROPEAN LYNX.

Tim Bunker on Horse-Racing at Fairs.

MR. EDITOR—You will recollect that I had my say on this subject some years ago, when the thing was first started. I worked about as hard as any body to get our County Agricultural Society agoing. It cost me a year's labor riding, walking, writing, and elbowing folks around before I could get 'em waked up to it. Some folks are made all breechin, and it takes a locomotive to get 'em started. And when I got the thing on its legs, I hated to see it start off in the wrong direction. We had grand fairs for a few years, before the horse fever struck on. Every kind of stock was brought out, and there was no end to the show of vegetables, fruits, farm products, and home manufactures. We had sometimes ten thousand people out to see the show, and we made money enough to get up buildings, and have first-rate accommodations upon the grounds for exhibitors. Then the young folks thought they knew everything, and nothing would satisfy 'em but fancy horses and racing. I opposed it then, and have been dead set agin it ever since.

I shouldn't have said anything more about it now, if the thing hadn't a come up at the last meeting of our County Society, when we was arranging for the fair next fall. You see the horse has been gaining all the while since he got on the track, until more premiums were offered for fast horses than for everything else. Of course folks who had nothing but fine cattle, fruits, or vegetables to show, did not care to come to a fair where everybody was horse crazy, and would'nt see anything else, if it was as bright as the sun in the heavens. You see a good many of 'em had got disgusted with racing, when they saw it was ruining everything else, and spoiling our fairs. The last two or three years they have been pretty slim, and might as well have been called horse races. Jockeys and gamblers took possession of the track, and had everything their own way.

As soon as we got together, I see we were going to have a pretty fight on the horse question. All the horse men were there, with Cicero Smith at their head, and the old fogies were around pretty thick also. Cicero Smith is the son of

Deacon Smith in our town, who don't walk exactly in the footsteps of his father. The deacon sent him to college some years ago, and thought he was going to make a lawyer or doctor of him. But he fell into a very common error of furnishing him with all the money he wanted, and gratified all his boyish whims and fancies. In college, he wanted a fast horse, and had him. The result was that he spent more time with his horse than with his tutors. He cultivated the acquaintance of jockeys, and betting men, more than men of letters, became dissipated, got into all manner of college scrapes, and was expelled. He has been loafing about Hookertown ever since, fond of a dog and gun, of a horse and buggy—but mighty shy of a hoe and shovel, a yoke of cattle and a dung cart. He was just the fellow to head the jockeys in this struggle to get possession of the fair next fall.

Cicero moved to offer a thousand dollars premium for the fastest horse in the race, best two in three, open to all comers. He supported his motion in a telling speech, and waxed eloquent. He wanted to know who did not admire a fast horse. He thought the horse the most graceful and noble of all animals. He never saw a blood horse in motion but he thought of Job's magnificent description: "the glory of his nostrils is terrible. He paweth in the valley, and rejoiceth in his strength: he goeth on to meet the armed men. He swalloweth the ground with fierceness and rage; neither believeth he that it is the sound of the trumpet." He thought the moral influence of fast horses was very good in the community. Everybody had a passion for a fine horse, and it was the legitimate business of Agricultural Societies to meet the popular taste. Nothing would draw a crowd, or fill up the treasury, like the sports of the turf. He thought the prejudice against racing a foolish superstition that was fast dying out. He thought the morals of the community would be greatly aided by cultivating fast horses. He had himself been saved from destruction by owning a fast horse. This provided a wholesome outlet for boyish spirits, and prevented the young from illegitimate pleasures."

Seth Twiggs jumped up as soon as Cicero got through, and said: "He couldn't see things exactly in that light. Perhaps it was because he hadn't been to college. He was glad if there was anything that made Cicero think of any part of the Bible, for he tho't he needed it. He hoped he would read a little further, and learn that the "horse was a vain thing for safety." We had been trying to save ourselves by horseflesh, as a society, for some years, and could'nt come it. The fairs grew worse and worse every year. Multitudes were disgusted and wouldn't go nigh 'em. There wasn't one man in ten in Hookertown that took anything to the fair, because it was managed by jockeys, and fast men, who offered all the premiums to fast horses. For his part, he wanted to carry up his carrots, and pumpkins; but all the pumpkins that stood any chance now was horses. He didn't think horse flesh was jest the kind of medicine for saving fast young men, if Cicero was a fair sample of the cure. In his opinion, there was considerable room for improvement."

Jake Frink said: "I bet on the wrong hoss at the last fair, and I'm agin havin any more racin unless they'll tell who is gwine to win. The scound'rels know all aboout it aforehand, and it is a blam'd contrivance to cheat a feller eout of his money. It *is* neow, and no mistake."

Jotham Sparrowgrass said: "That was a fact," bringing his cane down with great emphasis, which brought down the house. Cicero began to look more like a sheep than a horse.

Then Mr. Spooner, our minister, got up and said: "He deplored the evils of horse racing, whether at the fairs or elsewhere. It was quite manifest that that evil existed in the Society, and had turned a great many against it. The managers of the Society were responsible for this. They ought to arrange the premiums so as to call out all the products of the soil, and encourage every branch of industry. The annual fair ought to be a school where the people go to learn something about their business, and have a good talk with their neighbors. He did not want to see it turned into a scene of excitement and betting, where black-legs were thicker than blackberries, and well-meaning men were fleeced of their money."

Judge Jones said: "That is my view of the case precisely. The main thing is not to draw a crowd. We want to make the fair help the cause of agriculture. If the crowd come to see the race, and bet, you gain nothing, but lose much. A gambling spirit is fostered, which is exceedingly unfriendly to industry. The man who makes ten dollars on a bet, in six minutes, don't like to work six days to make the same money at the plow-tail. It seems a one-horse way of making money. He wants to try his luck again, and he keeps trying until he is ruined. We used to have full fairs, and money enough, before horse racing was tried. We had, perhaps, as many people now, but they were a very different sort of folks. He wanted to see the solid, substantial men and women of the county—a fair representation of its wealth, and moral worth—at the exhibition. For my part, I have been ashamed to be in the company I found there for the last three years, and I sha'nt go again till we have a change in the management."

Cicero saw the tide was against him and didn't rally. He was voted down by a large majority. New managers were put in, and next fall, Mr. Editor, if you will come up to Hookertown, we'll show you a fair that "aint all hoss."

The way I look at the horse question is jest this: Speed in a horse is only one of his good qualities. The jockeys make it everything, because that gives the animal his whole value for their purposes. He is just as much an implement of gambling as a pack of cards. I want to see speed encouraged, but strength, beauty, docility and bottom, quite as much. And other domestic animals are quite as important to the farmer as the horse. We want to arrange the premiums so as to call out every form of industry, and make every man feel that he has had fair play. We want premiums, but we want fair play more. Give the horse a fair chance, but don't forget Seth Twiggs' pumpkins.

Hookertown, Conn., February 1st. } Yours to command,
TIMOTHY BUNKER, Esq.

Vinegar from Apple Pomace.

An Illinois subscriber in commenting upon an article in the January issue on Apple Pomace, says the best thing that can be done with it is to make it into vinegar. It is the practice in his section to make a leach, as for ashes, only on a much larger scale. This may be made in the shape of an inverted pyramid, placed upon a stone or plank platform, and furnished with a trough, or spout at the bottom, to carry off the liquid. Any stout boards an inch or more thick will answer for this purpose. It is a good plan to have this large leach stand near the cider press, and throw the apple pomace into it, as fast as it accumulates. It need not stand under cover. In a large leach all the rain that falls will be needed to carry off the valuable properties of the pomace. So much of the liquid is exposed to the atmosphere, in the leaching, that it very soon turns to vinegar, and it may be kept running as long as good vinegar is made. This pays much better than feeding, and has given good satisfaction in the region where it has been tried. It economizes an article that is generally treated as a nuisance where much cider is made.

Take Care of the Tools.

Father! where is the auger?" cries out John Smith, Jr. "Don't 'zactly know, son: let me see, where did I use it last? Either in the barn, or wood-shed, or down cellar, and there I left it; look till you find it?" And so the boy runs till he is out of breath and patience, meanwhile thinking, if not speaking hard thoughts about his slack father. A half dozen places have to be searched before the tool is found, and if haply it is found, it is quite likely to be broken, or rusted, or much out of order.

"Father! where is the hand saw?" inquires James Brown. "Why do you ask, James? it is where it always is, when not in use, hanging on the hook near the window, in the tool-room." James goes, where he should have gone at first, and he finds it in perfect trim; and he puts it back again in its place, when he is done with it, knowing that he will get a sound reprimand if he does not return it to its place.

Now, we do but repeat what we have often said, that on the farm there should be a place for everything, and everything in its place. There is no use in trying to carry on a farm or to do anything else well, without system and order. And the care of tools is an important part of that system. One cannot accomplish much without a set of tools, larger or smaller—as for *borrowing* them unnecessarily, that should be regarded as next to stealing them. And the purchase of tools should be followed up by scrupulous care of them. A tool-room is a great convenience. It may be an apartment by itself in the carriage-house or wood-house. Here let there be a row of pegs for saws; there is the bench for planes; yonder is a drawer with separate compartments for screws, washers, nuts, rivets, &c. Here is a place for bolts, there for chains. The hammers, chisels, screw-driver, auger, broad axe, adz, files—all have their appointed locality, and are kept there and no where else. The law should be laid down and enforced, that whoever uses a tool must put it back, so that it can always be found at a moment's notice; nay, even if it be in the dark.

And this care of tools should lead and will lead on to system with regard to other things about the premises. Here is a corner for extra plow handles, and there a box for plow points; there are bolts of all sizes, ready in case of a break down; yonder are hooks with extra pieces of harness. Notice, too, the crow-bar, beetle and wedges, and log chains, the grindstone always in its place, and always in order; the scythes, hoes, spades, shovels, forks, rakes, and what-not have so long been kept in their respective places that they would almost cry out if carelessly left in an unaccustomed spot.

The time spent in keeping such a room in order is not lost. The time spent in carrying back tools after using them is not lost. If tools are not carried back, they would many of them be lost. And then the moral influence of system and order is almost beyond computation.

For the American Agriculturist.

How to Start a County Agricultural Society.

We have hundreds of these societies in all the older States, working efficiently for the promotion of the farmer's interests. Little need be said in their favor where they are known. But there are many counties, especially in the newer States, where a society has not yet been organized, though there are wealth and population enough to sustain one. The want of it is seen and felt, and multitudes are ready to coöperate as soon as the leaders appear. The first thing to be done then, is for a few energetic men, a half dozen is enough, to resolve that a County Society shall be formed, issue a call for a meeting at some central point, a village or city with railroad communication if possible, and invite a delegation from every town in the county. At the meeting adopt a constitution, with the usual provisions, and determine to have a fair the next fall, at the most convenient point.

To call out a good representation of the industry of the county, a large premium list must be made out for all classes of stock, farm products and manufactured articles, amounting to at least fifteen hundred or two thousand dollars; the more the better. The raising of this sum of money is generally the point of embarrassment. The money is not in hand, and the fair, which is to raise it by the sale of admission tickets, is an untried experiment. It may be a failure from lack of interest, from rain, or other causes, and leave the managers in debt. To divide up the responsibility equally, let a delegate be appointed from each town, to canvass his own district for members. These should be of two kinds, annual and for life. The annual memberships should be not less than a dollar each, carrying with them four admission tickets for the fair, at twenty-five cents each. The life memberships should not be less than five dollars, carrying with them one ticket of admission every year, or some other equivalent privilege. A spirited canvasser would be able to secure at least a hundred dollars, or more, for these memberships in each town, and if there were twenty towns in the county, enough would be raised to cover the premium list before the fair came off. You might safely calculate on an advance of fifty per cent. for the attendance of those who were not members.

Then a show bill should be issued on a large sheet, announcing the fair and list of premiums, and be posted at all places of public resort in the county; railroad depots, postoffices, hotels, blacksmith shops, etc. A few weeks before the time of the fair, the managers should see that the county is canvassed for exhibitors. If a man has a fine herd of blood stock, visit him, and make him promise to come out. Secure the attendance of every man that has anything to show. If there are manufacturers of any kind, get them out with their goods. People like to be noticed, and many a men will bring out their best, if asked, who would otherwise stay at home.

Then, at the holding of the fair, let all the arrangements be as complete as possible; so that stock and goods exhibited may not be injured, and may be seen to good advantage. It is essential to the success of the fair that it should be held in some large enclosure, and if this is not at hand it must be extemporized with a high board fence. This, the lumber merchant or builder will attend to on contract. It is desirable that shelter should be provided for stock. Owners will not exhibit freely, and for successive days, unless their cattle can be made comfortable, and be well supplied with water, hay, and provender. A large tent will answer for the exhibition of fruits, vegetables, butter and cheese, but a building is better. The society should look forward to permanent grounds and buildings, and realize them as soon as possible. The starting of a County Agricultural Society involves a good deal of labor and expense, but it will pay a hundred fold. A few energetic men, in any county with ten thousand people, can accomplish it. It will aid their enterprise, if they sprinkle liberally among their premiums some good paper devoted to their art, like the *American Agriculturist*. CONNECTICUT.

Buildings for Agricultural Fairs.

At a recent meeting of the Connecticut State Board of Agriculture, the fact dropped out that there was but one County Agricultural Society in the State, that had permanent grounds and buildings to accommodate stock, and all classes of goods offered for exhibition; and that was the most flourishing of all. Is there not a logical connexion between the buildings and this success. We think the importance of permanent buildings is greatly overlooked. We regard the housing of an Agricultural Society as essential to its success as the building of a church edifice is to the prosperity of a church. It may dwell in tents for a time as a matter of necessity, but it is never assured of a permanent existence until it has a home. Permanent buildings are an expression of the faith of its founders in its vitality, and impart confidence of its success to the community in which they are placed. It is a living power among them, and invites their co-operation.

These buildings should be located at some central point in the county, or near some city or village easily accessible by rail or steamer. This, with a good exhibition and good weather, will secure a large attendance. The people will come if the place is easily accessible. Such a location also materially affects the character of the exhibition. Most railroads will, on application, carry stock, farm products, and goods for the fair, at reduced price, or free of charge; relying upon passenger tickets for their profits. This, of course, is an inducement for people to bring out their products.

The buildings need not be of an expensive character, but substantial and neat; affording perfect protection to all goods and stock entrusted to the care of the Society. When there are nothing but tents or temporary buildings, goods are frequently damaged, and though the owners be remunerated, it always operates disastrously to the Society. The community want entire confidence in the managers of the Society, and the assurance that everything will be properly cared for. Articles like paintings, and heir looms of various kinds are frequently exhibited, and they have a value to their owners much beyond what they would bring in money. People who have the best articles to exhibit, will not forward them, unless they have security for their protection against damage from the elements.

Stock of all kinds want protection in permanent sheds or stalls. It is found to be desirable at most country fairs to have the exhibition continued through two or more days. This arrangement gives not only a better opportunity to examine the animals, and to see the various products of the farm, but affords a very important safeguard against failure from bad weather. If one day should prove stormy, and forbid attendance, the next may be fair, and draw the crowd. With good accommodations for stock, the owners of fine animals, who are raising principally to sell, will have no objection to exhibit a second or-third day. They can be made as comfortable at the fair as at home; and the more they are known the better for the owners' interests. If there is no shelter, and provisions for feeding and watering are bad, it will be difficult to get them out.

Permanent buildings are the capital that an Agricultural Society needs to do business with; and immediate measures should be taken in every county where there is a Society to secure them. Wisely managed, they would pay for themselves in a very few years, and make the prosperity of the Institution permanent. We will thank any of our friends for drawings and descriptions of suitable inclosures and buildings for the use of county or other agricultural fairs, with estimates of their cost.

Shall we have the Address at Fairs,

That depends entirely upon the character of the address. If the speaker is a distinguished politician, who will improve the occasion to air his views of the political situation, and talk buncombe, it wont pay. If he is a reformer, or monomaniac, who will trot out his favorite hobby, and show off his antics, his services may be dispensed with. Farmers and their wives come together on such occasions to learn something about their business, and unless the speaker has some experience in their calling, he should take other occasions to dispense his wisdom. There are men in almost every county who have studied the principles of husbandry, and practiced them so far as to make them intelligent critics of the practice of others. Sometimes the members of the learned professions have given special attention to the farm and garden, and can give a good address. Whoever is invited should have something pertinent to say, and be invited for that reason. If the address is not at hand, an "experience meeting" of farmers and fruit growers should be provided for. A few practical questions offered for discussion will draw out the views of farmers from all parts of the State or county, and make the meeting one of great interest. Every one who comes to the fair should have the memory of things heard, as well as things seen, to carry home with him.

BREEDING YOUNG MARES.—"W. M. B.," of Nelson County, Virginia, asks: "Does breeding stop the growth of a young mare, that has not attained her full size, or does is it materially injure her in any respect?"

The best horse breeders hold, we believe, with few, if any, exceptions, that having a colt not only does not hurt a young mare, but, on the contrary does her good, gives her constitution, bottom, and a vigor of digestive organs, and firmness of muscle, which last her through life with good treatment. Thoroughbred or warm blooded mares that have proper care, gain sufficient maturity at 2 to 2½ years, and cold blooded mares 3 to 3½, to take the horse. Of course, the fillies diet should be liberal, and regular, and her grooming thorough. For two growing horses stand at her rack. Thoroughbred horses arrive at maturity fully a year earlier than others. They grow faster, are fit for work quicker, and, as stated, are not injured by breeding considerably earlier, than it would be safe to breed a common mare.

Country Houses with City Conveniences.

It is generally supposed that city houses are far more convenient than country dwellings. Servant girls lay special stress upon this, when asked to go to the country. But, with the single exception of gas-light, every city convenience may be equally well secured in any country place. To illustrate this, and also to furnish good house-plans, we present engravings and descriptions of some houses now being completed in Flushing, eight miles distant by Railroad from the Hunter's Point Ferry, opposite 34th-street New-York. These houses, by the way, are almost as quickly reached, and with far more comfort, than any city residence above 40th-street, while they are in a healthful location, and have the benefit of country air, the pleasure of a garden, etc., and, being supplied with gas from the village, they have *all* the conveniences of city houses. The proprietor, in their erection, has attempted to introduce every improvement, and to construct every part as if to be occupied by his own family. (The general superintendence and carpenter work, is done by John Donald; the mason work by James & Patrick Carroll; the painting by P. Thornton; the tin-work by Benj. Field; and the slating and roofing by J. S. Moseley, of the Union Roofing Co., of New York.)

Fig. 6.

ELEVATION.—Fig. 1 shows the general appearance from a front corner view. The basement walls are 3½ feet stone-wall below the surface, and 4 feet brick-wall above, cemented and laid off into stone blocks. The siding is of 10-inch boards, half-tongue and lap, with a v groove at the lap, and another v groove cut along the center of each board, giving it the appearance of 4½-inch siding, an end section of which is seen in fig. 6. This new style of siding is the finest and best we have seen. The roofing is French, or half French style, the fronting all round covered with slate, black (*B*), green (*G*), and red (*R*)—as shown by these letters in fig. 7. The top part on one house is tin, and on the others, H. W. Johns' Patent Roofing. The window caps and cornices are alike on all sides, which gives almost a front view, when seen from any direction. The walls are filled in with brick, from cellar to roof.

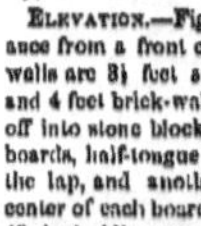

Fig. 7.—SLATE.

FIRST FLOOR (Fig. 2).—The Parlor *A*, *B*, with Bay Window at *O*, is divided by sliding doors, so that *A*, 14×20 feet, can be used for the parlor, and *B*, 14×10 as a Library or Sitting-room; or the whole be thrown into one large parlor when desired. *A*, is spacious enough except for large gatherings. The Main Hall, *E*, is six feet wide. Many err in making this too narrow; it is the first room entered, and its capacity gives the first impression in regard to the whole house. At the front is a small closet (*c*, *c*, *c*,) for cloaks, umbrellas, etc., leaving plenty of room for a hat-stand between that and the parlor door. *N*, is a covered piazza. *C*, is the general family room, or sitting-room, or may be used as a Dining Room, when *D*, is used as a Kitchen. *D*, is the Dining-Room, but is provided with a medium size cooking-range at *J*, so that for a small family, or with a scarcity of help, or at special seasons of the year, *D* may be used as a Kitchen. *I*, is a common Dish closet, and *K*, a China closet, with doors opening into both *D*, and *C*. By the side of this is *D*, *W*, a dumb-waiter from the room below, which, when not in use, shuts down even with the floor, and occupies no room. The Sink in the corner is neatly enclosed, with a door to open to its front. G, is a rear hall extending out to a small piazza and steps. Under this at the left, is seen the outside entrance to the Basement. A closet from G, furnishes a place for hats, garments, umbrellas, etc. *F*, is a general pantry and flour room for *D*. Ventilators, throughout the house, are placed in the base-boards of the rooms, in accordance with the principles explained in September *Agriculturist*, 1864. The suggestions

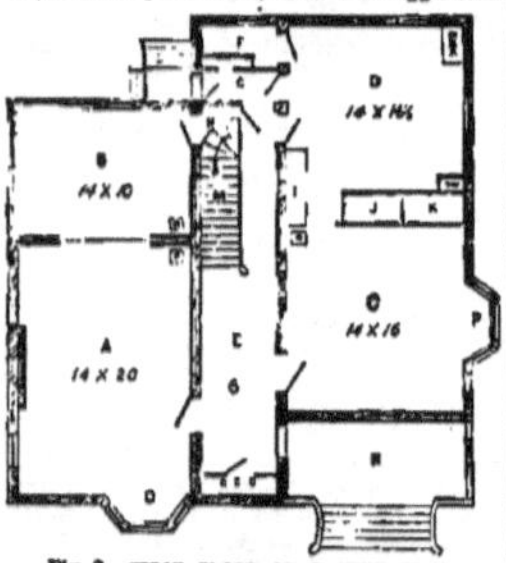

Fig. 2.—FIRST FLOOR OR GROUND PLAN.

published in this journal for several years past, have been consulted in constructing these houses.

SECOND STORY (Fig. 3).—*Q*, *R*, are front and rear chambers, with connecting closets, s, s, and a double door passage containing drawers and shelves. *U*, is the family chamber or bed-room, connected with *W*, and with the hall bed-room, *T*, so that a child, sick or well, occupying either *W* or *T*, will be in hearing and easy reach of *U*. This room, *U*, is specially fitted for the convenience of the lady of the house, even if she be an invalid. The wash-stand and basin, E, E, has cold and hot water brought to it by pipes from the Attic reservoir, and the basement-boiler (*I*, fig. 4). A bell wire extends to the servants' room on the third-floor. One speaking-tube extends to the basement Kitchen, and another to the Dining-Room (*D*, fig. 2), so that the lady can give directions to those rooms without calling through the halls. We commend this arrangement to every housekeeper. A small sum will connect two distant rooms with tubings so that free conversation can be held, and thus *save a great number of steps.* The lady, while dressing herself or children, can give full directions to the kitchen or dining-room, and make inquiries. From this room, *U*, another speaking tube extends to and opens over the outside front door bell-knob, so that in case the bell is rung at night, instant inquiry can be made of the caller as to "what's the matter," without a long journey through the halls. Such a tube should at least extend from every Physician's sleeping-room to

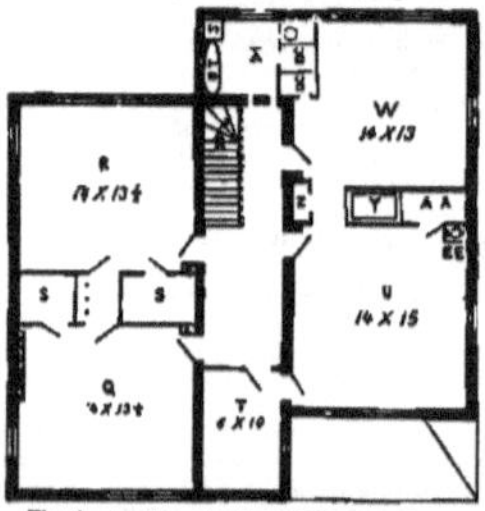

Fig. 3.—SECOND FLOOR OR CHAMBER PLAN.

his door-bell. The tubing costs but 5 or 6 cents a foot, and is easily put in, along the corners of rooms, or, as in these houses, behind the lathing, when done at the time of building.... *W*, is another bed-room, large enough for two beds if desired.—*X*, is a bath-room, with wash basin, *S*, and bath-tub, *B*, *T*, both of which are supplied with cold water pipes from the Attic reservoir, and hot water from the boiler tank in the basement.—A water closet here is supplied with water from the Attic, and with a large waste pipe runing underground to the privy vault, at the end of the grape arbor which extends back from the rear door. The closets *A*, *A*, *Z*, D C, D C, are shown in the plan: there can hardly be too many of these, as every housekeeper knows.

BASEMENT (Fig. 4).—*K*, is the Kitchen, supplied with stationary wash-tubs, *w*, *w*; sink, *w*; force-pump which draws water for the Kitchen from a large cistern outside, which is filled from a filtering cistern. This pump is connected by a pipe with the Attic reservoir, so that if in a long drouth that should fail, it can be refilled from below, and thus a supply of water and pressure always be secured to the hot water tank. *K*, is supplied with a large "Challenge" cooking-range, *J*, having a water back and a large tight thirty-five gallon boiler, *I*, seen at the left, which is kept filled and under pressure from the Attic reservoir.——*H*,

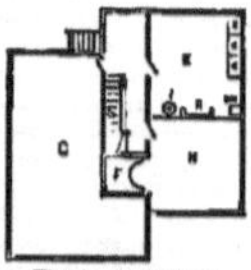

Fig. 4.—BASEMENT.

is the coal cellar, receiving coal directly from the cart. *F*, is a large Sanford & Truslow's Heater or furnace (with extra evaporating pans), which sends warm air to nearly every room in the house, including two Attic rooms and the bath-room. (An opening over the bath-room admits warm air enough to the Attic reservoir to prevent its freezing in very cold weather.) *R, R, R*, indicate the warm air registers from the furnace, shown in several of the rooms.

ATTIC OR THIRD STORY (Fig. 5).—This is 8 feet high, the full size of the house for 4 feet high, then inclined inward at the sides, under the slating. Two Rooms, *R, R*, are finished off; the large room *D*, is also lathed and plastered, and furnishes a convenient place for drying clothes, storage, and other purposes; or if needed, it can easily be divided into several rooms. The 8 dormer windows furnish abundant light and air. The Reservoir, *T*, is of plank, lined with tinned lead, 8 × 8 × 4 feet. All the water from the upper roof runs into this reservoir, and when full, it overflows through a pipe down to the filtering cistern.

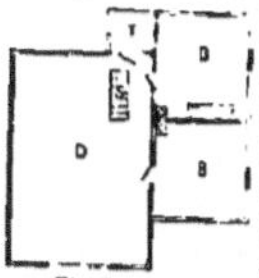

Fig. 5.—ATTIC.

PAINTING, COST, ETC.—The outside color is light drab, with dark trimmings; the doors throughout the house, inside and out, grained Walnut; the parlor and chamber above white; the halls, sitting, and dining-room, etc., grained in oak; outside of all sashes, dark green; inside grained to match the rooms. Every room from cellar to attic is supplied with gas pipes, built in the walls.—Without the land, the cost of such a house at *this* time, all complete as here described, is from $5,000 to $7,000, according to the locality, expense of lumber, bricks, etc. This includes all the fixtures named—the furnaces, double cooking-ranges, extra style painting, plumbing, fancy slate roofing, drainage, waste pipes, double filtering cisterns, grape arbor, front fence, etc.

Coal Tar and Asphaltum for Floors.

BY GILBERT J. GREEN, HUDSON, N. Y.

A floor properly made of Asphaltum or coal tar, or both combined, so far surpasses all other floors for stables, that it has but to be seen to be generally adopted. The cheapness of these floors, their ease of construction, durability, freedom from moisture, and their cleanliness, recommend their adoption by all good farmers. The way in which I have constructed floors for cow or horse stable, as well as floors for barns, carriage house, poultry houses, pig pens, or other out-buildings and barn-yards, is about as follows, varied somewhat to circumstances.

I first prepare the floor by removing sufficient earth to allow coarse sand or gravel to be laid upon it to the depth of about two inches, this gravel or sand should be free from clay or other earthy matter, and be perfectly dry, by being exposed to the sun, or dried over a fire. If it is summer time, and the floor or stable will not be needed for immediate use, I would use nothing but coal tar, boiled in a kettle from fifteen minutes to half an hour, this I pour upon the gravel hot, and leave until it is cold, I then mix fine dry sand with hot coal tar, to the consistency of thin mortar, and spread it over the floor to the depth of half an inch, I then take a hot smoothing iron, holding it with a pair of blacksmith's, tongs, and iron it down smooth. If it can remain twenty days without being used, in warm weather; it will make a hard solid floor, that may always be kept clean and dry.

If it is desirable to use the floor at once, I would use one-half or two-thirds of Asphaltum and the remainder coal tar, this can be used the moment it is cold, but it lacks the strength and elasticity of a floor made wholly of coal tar, still I have known pavements made wholly of Asphaltum and gravel that have endured many years of severe use, and are still good.

The cost of such a floor with Asphaltum or coal tar at eight cents per gallon, (the usual price), will be about three cents per foot, about half the cost of plank, with the floor timber included. It will last longer than any hemlock floor will in a stable, and can be much more easily repaired.

A floor of Asphaltum or coal tar, like a piece of India rubber, neither attracts or absorbs moisture, and is therefore easily cleaned and always dry. The edge of such floors should be protected by a joist or piece of timber, so that it will not be broken off by cattle's feet nor wheels of wagons. It is equally useful as a floor for pig pens, or any out-buildings, and I believe it superior to stone or brick for sidewalks. It is smooth but not slippery! Hard, but still sufficiently elastic; the sun does not injuriously soften it, and frost will not injure it. For pavements or floors where heavy loads will pass over it, it should be thicker than above recommended, or else the earth beneath it should be very solid.

Fig. 1.—SECTION OF HEN HOUSE.

A Good and Cheap Hen-House.

We have an urgent appeal to publish a plan for a cheap Fowl-house, "with all the modern improvements." Modern improvements are *costly* as a rule—but nevertheless we may have a warm, snug hen-house, which should be neat and convenient, and yet not be very costly. The accompanying plan is used with entire satisfaction by an acquaintance, who is so particular in his views, that we may safely commend it to our readers:

The house is 10 feet wide and 12 feet long; a passage-way 4 feet wide passes along the south side, in which are windows; this is formed by a partition 3 feet high, (see fig. 1), which extend from near the door to the rear, and supports the lower side of a sloping floor, which rises to the eaves on the north side. Above this sloping floor the roosts are fixed and the droppings of the birds fall upon the floor, which being sprinkled with plaster, they roll down, or are easily scraped off. There is a ledge at the front edge which prevents their going to the floor. Under this sloping floor the space is divided by a partition, making a nest room about 6 feet square and a setting room 6 × 5 feet, which is also used for a store room for grain, eggs, etc. This setting room is entered by another door, and lighted by a pane in the gable end. The nest boxes above through the partition into the setting room, but there is no access for the fowls, except when setting. At these times hens are moved, if

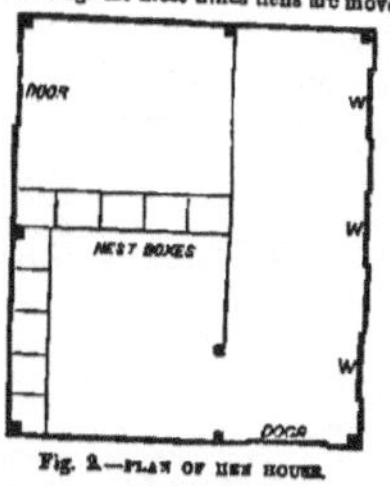

Fig. 2.—PLAN OF HEN HOUSE.

they happen to be in boxes against the side building, and made to occupy those in the partition. The back end of the 4-foot passage-way, (see plan, Fig. 2), is used as a feeding floor, and here stands the water fountain.

We made once a small hen-house, and lighted it by placing some of the roof boards, which went up and down, ten inches apart, and fastening 8 × 10 glass between them, slipping the glass into the groves in the boards, which were common flooring. The panes lapped about half an inch, were fastened by tacks, and little water came through. Windows in a fowl-house must be protected by slats or by wire. The use of plaster on the sloping floor under the roosts is very well—nothing can be better; but fine, dry road dust, swept up on a hot day, is as good.

Simple Farm Gates.

There is almost no end to the devices for farm gates, but after all the simplest, strongest and lightest, of the old better patterns, are the most reliable, and, on the whole, the best. The posts should be of locust, or cedar timber, if possible, and set very firmly, being securely braced either above or under the ground, and protected by coal tar beneath the surface, and by paint above, from the action of the elements. The long, hard-wood latch, in common use, is probably the best for all kinds of farm gates.

A LIGHT FARM GATE is described by W. S. Gilchrist, Warren County, N. Y.—"I send you the plan of gates which we have had in use for the past ten years, and for that time have never, *with the aid of paint*, required any repairs. My experience proves that the lighter a gate can be made, the longer it will last, besides being much more convenient in use. I, therefore, use well seasoned pine lumber (cedar if to be had); the hinge-piece (*a*) and latch-piece (*b*) of 3 × 3 scantling; the rail (*c*) 3 × 3 also, tapered to 2 inches; the slats of $^3/_4$-inch seasoned pine or, if to be had, cedar, by all means avoiding the use of green or heavy lumber; the braces of good clear

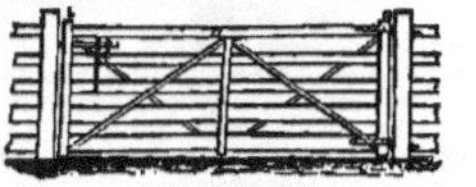

LIGHT FARM GATE.

stuff, and straight grained lumber, $1 \times 1^1/_2$ inches, of any description; the whole securely nailed or pinned. Any one of ordinary mechanical skill in the use of tools, should be able to build a gate after the accompanying sketch."

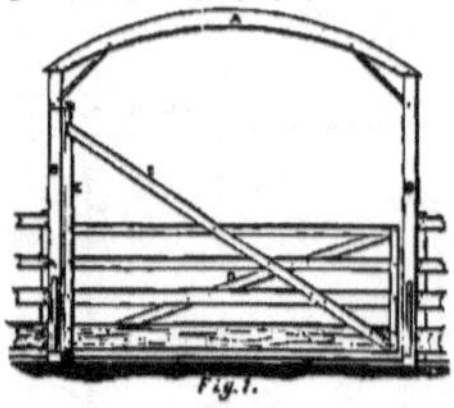

FRAME GATE.

Frame Gate.—Seth Clark, of Wellsboro', Pa., writes, "I have made several gates of this kind for myself and my neighbors, and they give general satisfaction. Figure 1 represents the gate and the frame in which it hangs (which should be a little wider and higher than the barn doors). The cross piece (*A*) may be made either straight or slightly arching, and in either case is mortised upon, and braced, as shown, into the posts. The posts (*B*) (5×5 studs) are framed into sills, as seen in Figures 2 and 3,

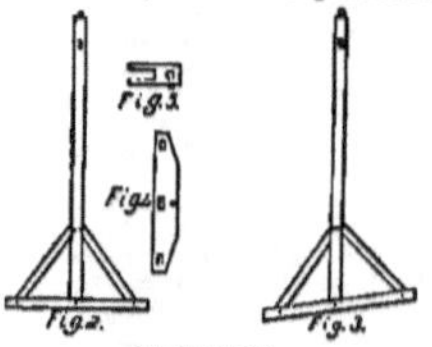

BRACED POSTS.

which effectually prevents a tendency to lean to either side. The hinge-piece (*E*) of the gate rests on a pivot inserted in the sill (Fig. 4), which should be wide enough to receive the post and hinge-piece without crowding. The upper hinge is of wood, and is shown in Figure 5. Figure 3 shows how the posts are framed and braced on sloping ground, which does not interfere with the gate if it swings open down the slope. The long braces of the gate (*C* and *D*, Fig. 1,) are placed on opposite sides, and the gate is made very light. The gate may be hung upon iron hinges if preferred. Such a frame will last as long as the best posts set in the ground, and has the advantage of being always erect."

An excellent gate is one framed much like this, except that the cross-piece (*A*) is straight, and instead of being at the top, is three feet from the bottom of the posts, and well beneath the surface of the road, being strongly braced into the posts below, they being set a little more than three feet in the ground. The posts extend five feet above the ground, and the gate is hung to them in any desirable way. The hinge-piece of the gate, if hung as above described, should rest on a block, pinned to the post and resting upon the cross-piece. A gate made after this plan is very convenient and firm.

Fall Plowing to Kill Grubs.—"H. E. H." writes, "I am turning over a heavy sod (in December), to kill grub-worms, so that they will not destroy my corn, next June. Will I accomplished the object? Is fall plowing ever an injury to the soil?" You will probably disturb and kill a good many grub-worms. Your corn will not be so weedy as if plowed in the spring. And the fall plowing will have done nothing but good. A very light sandy soil naturally dry and warm is not benefitted by fall plowing—for the frosts and weathering cause the organic matters in it to decompose rapidly, and these are essential to its integrity, but all loamy and clayey soils, or those rich in organic matter, and most gravelly soils are decidedly benefitted by fall plowing, if it be not done when the ground is wet, and even this is much less injurious than plowing wet soil in spring.

Building in Cold Climates.

The house room of all sorts should be contained within four walls for this (unless it be an octagon or some other *gon*), gives the most room per foot of wall, admits of the most thorough warming, and the least radiation of heat into "universal space," there being the least outside surface for radiation; and the advantage is as decided in summer, for then there is the least surface for absorption of solar heat. There should be as few windows and doors as possible on the north side, and few on the west side; and on those sides should be the halls, pantries, and other small rooms, and the wood-house apartments, to serve as air-chamber bulwarks between the north-western winds and the living rooms on the south side, where the sun brings light, heat and health. Cistern, cistern-pump and drain should never be on the north side. Outside walls should be lathed and plastered between studding, as well as on the face of it; the economy of double walls is great, in the course of time. The cellar wall should be lathed and plastered from sill to a lower level than outside surface of the ground. Keep a sharp eye on carpenters, lest they fur out the outside base or drip-board, in a way to let the wind blow up behind the siding. Finally, front the house east, so that the front verandah may be shady in the afternoon for out-door sitting in summer, and so that the sitting-room, back of the parlor, may have a sunny outlook in winter. H. W. P.

Cranberry Culture.

Mr. Gilbert Conant, of Ipswich, Mass., received a premium from the Essex Agricultural Society for his success with cranberries. We give the essential portions of his report, which is somewhat peculiar, as it describes a method of growing cranberries without setting the plants. This can, of course, be useful only in localities where cranberries grow spontaneously, but it shows how a natural and unproductive patch may be converted into a cultivated cranberry meadow.

"In the summer of 1861 I prepared about an acre of meadow, by cutting a ditch to drain it, and in the fall I plowed it from four to six inches deep, according to the hight of different parts of the meadow. Since then I have flowed it annually about the first of November, and let the water off about the first of May.

"The first summer after preparing the meadow as stated, vines sprang up and grew considerably on the lowest parts of it. The second summer the vines increased and grew rapidly. In the fall of that year I gathered about a half bushel of cranberries. In 1864 the vines blossomed full, and after the berries were set, gave promise of a fine crop; but an early frost, while they were quite green, injured them so that I gathered but about a bushel. In 1865 the vines had increased in some spots on the meadow, so that they had almost killed out the grass, and in the fall, when the berries were ripe, they lay so thick that the vines were scarcely visible. I gathered twenty bushels of cranberries, worth three and a half dollars per bushel. The expense of gathering and marketing these berries was less than ten dollars. This year there are but very few cranberries in this section of country, though my vines are bearing better than I have seen any others on fresh meadow.

"The expense of draining this meadow was nothing. The peat taken from the ditch paid the expense. It cost me but $5 to flow it. This was done by a small flood-gate at the bridge. I spread upon the ice in the winter of 1863 two loads of yellow sand, which cost but $2.50, making the whole amount that it has cost me to prepare the meadow, but $7.50. I would here state that the vines on the spot upon which the sand was spread were far more prolific last year than any other vines upon the meadow.

"I have had experience in preparing several other pieces of meadow in the same manner, for the cultivation of the cranberry, and in every case have been successful. I neither plant vines nor sow the seed. Whenever any meadow adapted to the cultivation of the cranberry is prepared in the manner that I have prepared mine, vines will spring up and bear spontaneously."

John Johnston on Drainage.

In a recent letter this pioneer of drainage says: "I commenced in 1838, and have drained 280 acres, laid over 200,000 tile. Drains should run directly down the slopes. You never can make thorough work by running them across the slopes. My drains are from twenty-five to perhaps forty feet apart—very few of the latter, generally about thirty-three feet. In soft soils, and where you have to go four feet deep and lower, before getting on hard bottom, drains might be fifty or sixty feet apart, and dry the land perfectly; while in stiff clays, eighteen or twenty feet may be rather too wide. I estimate that the excess of two wheat crops on drained land will pay the whole cost of the improvement. I took up the first drain after twenty years, and found the tile as good as ever. Although I paid twenty-five cents a rod, and board, for digging some of the drains, two and a half feet deep, I got the great majority dug at twelve to fifteen cents per rod, without board. The internal drains need not be over thirteen inches wide at the surface, and wide enough at the bottom to take in a two or three inch tile. Main drains cost much more." We must add that, however much we value John Johnston's experience, 2½ foot draining is considered too superficial to be ever recommended if one can go lower.

Garden Irrigation, How Practised.

BY "TESUQUE," NEW MEXICO.

The subject of irrigation has of late attracted considerable attention in parts of the country where it is not, as it is in New Mexico, absolutely essential. The following article, prepared at our request by a gentleman living near Santa Fe, gives very clearly the plan of irrigating a garden as practised in that country. The writer promises to resume the subject, and we hope to be able to present the details of operations upon a larger scale.—[Eds.]

I submit a few general principles, as practised here, in the hope of seeing in your paper some hints by which we can improve upon our present system. But, before I venture farther, I would advise those who make a practice of keeping their land clean *only* where it is planted, and of allowing fence corners, etc., to raise their own crops of weeds, not to irrigate, because, if they do not keep their ditches and all water avenues clean and free from weeds, they will assuredly bring such crops upon their land every time they water it, as will soon disgust them with the whole system.

The first thing to be done is to get the water to the highest part of the land to be cultivated. Here this is done by communities; each community having its own peculiar by-laws as regards compensation of the Major domo, division of the water, etc., all being governed by the general laws of the Territory as regards the election of the Major domo, and the fines for delinquency in working the "Ascequias," as the canals are called, or for stealing water, &c.

The advantages of irrigating by open ditches are many; principally, that you get your water on the land at a much higher temperature than from a well. I have seen persons here, when short of water, use their wells, and give their crops of cucumbers, peppers, tomatoes, &c., such a "back-set" as often to lose the whole crop. We are here 8,000 feet or more above the sea level, and have to take the greatest care as regards the temperature of the water and the time for irrigating, or it would be impossible to raise any of the more delicate vegetables. Again, by ditches, if well made at the outset, the advantage is that they are *always there*, whereas if one has complicated machinery it is liable to be out of order when needed, and before the repairs can be made the good time has gone by.

In preparing for irrigating a garden, which can be laid under water from one line, as in figure 1, run the main ditch as near level as possible, because, as the water has to run in this ditch to feed all the smaller ones, it will cut away, if sloping, much more than the smaller ditches. Those ditches which slope much should be well paved or lined with plank. In figure 1, *A*, *B*, *C*, *D* is a plot of ground having a slight fall from *B* to *A*, and a greater fall from *B* to *D*, the lowest point being at *C*; *m*, the main ditch, entering the plot at *B* and leaving at *A*; *c*, *c* and *c* are the cross ditches, numbered in the order in which they would be used when irrigating the whole plot; *n* is a ditch of the same size as the main ditch, and is used for running off that part of the stream which is surplus when irrigating; it is also used as a channel for the whole stream when breakage occurs, and the gardener has fear that the water may

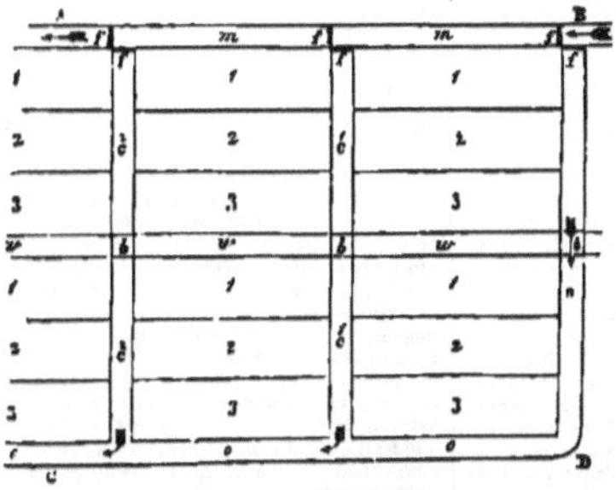

Fig. 1.—PLAN OF IRRIGATION.

get the upperhand while he is repairing borders. This ditch, to a practiced irrigator, is almost unnecessary, except in cases where neighbors above him, using from the same stream, may let all the water upon him without warning; but, in any case, it is better to have it, as it can

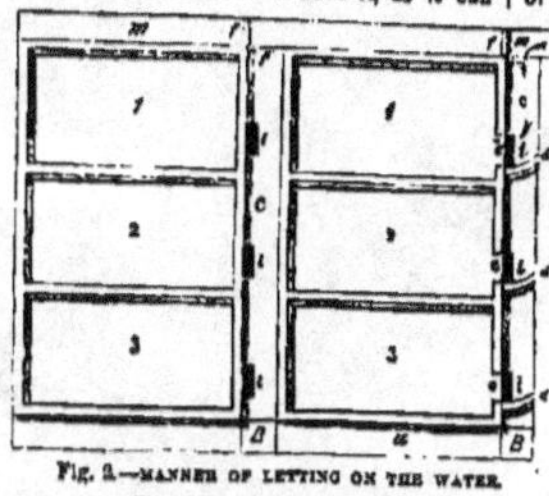

Fig. 2.—MANNER OF LETTING ON THE WATER.

be used also to irrigate the right hand row of beds. The points where flood-gates are necessary to regulate the amount of water are marked *f*; *w* is a walk, bridging the cross ditches at the points *b*, which must be enlarged or added to according to taste or convenience; but all walks or roads should be made on a level with the border above them, and in fact serve to form the border, as they give strength to the beds. *o* is a continuation of the ditch; *n* serves also as an outlet for the water when one tier of beds has been watered, until the next tier has been started. The same principle marked in this plot will apply equally to a garden of fifty acres or more, and the larger the garden the more will the labor be lessened by following some such system.

Now, let us suppose the main ditch dug, and water running through it: the first thing will be to make the upper row of beds (marked 1); commencing on the right hand, make the first bed; of course the land has been ploughed well long ago. For vegetables of most kinds, no bed should exceed ten feet by twenty, and before the first season is over the gardener will find that, by making small beds, he has saved much labor. The first line of beds is made with borders, or raised margins, from six to nine inches above the level and at least six inches across the top, and the cross ditches finished down to the lower edge of the completed beds. The next thing is to ascertain that they are perfectly level, and this is best done by opening them, as in figure 2, and letting in the water *slowly*, and if there is a corner higher or lower than the rest of the bed the water will surely find it for you. Leveling the beds well previous to planting is absolutely necessary, for if you have to irrigate very young plants, (which, in many cases, will give them a two weeks' start over those left later,) and the beds have not been exactly levelled, some of the plants will be drenched or covered with sediment, while others will get no water.

While beds No. 1 are filling you can be making the next row, and so on, until your plot is all terraced; and if, wherever the fall increases, the beds be made narrower, much labor will thereby be saved. Next put in the flood-gates, (see figure 3,) and sink boxes in the cross ditches, at the points where you open the beds, or make holes and line them with brick; these boxes, or holes, are so placed that when the border of a bed is opened for irrigation, the water has to run over the hole to get into the bed, so that all sand which would otherwise go into the bed is caught; and whenever these holes fill with sand before you have water enough in the bed, clean it promptly. It is better, where the lay of the land will admit of it, to water the beds from the lower corners. But always commence to water those beds which are the highest, so that if a border breaks the water will run into a dry bed; whereas, on the other hand, if you commence at the lower beds, and the same accident should occur, the water runs into beds already full, and may burst a dozen borders before you can stop it. Another reason for irrigating from the top beds is, that while one bed is filling you can open as many below as you choose, and in this way you are ahead of your work, always ready to spare a few minutes to remedy any accident, and also have perfect command of the water.—When the plants are strong enough to allow of a good stream being used, one man can, in this way, easily water from 150 to 200 beds in a day.

In figure 2, is shown the method of letting on the water. First, break the border of bed 1

Fig. 3.—FLOOD GATE.

at the point *e*, throwing the soil across the cross ditch *c*, so as to form the dam *d*, then open the floodgate marked by the dotted line *f*, until the amount of water needed passes; and if the whole of the water running in the main ditch, is used, shut the flood-gate in *m*; but if not, open all the flood-gates on the main ditch enough to allow the surplus water to pass on. Now, while the first bed is receiving the water, open other beds in succession, as indicated by 2, 3, and when the first bed has received sufficient, draw the first dam over again to its place in the border, and allow the water to flow into the next bed, and so on to the end of the work; always taking care to keep your boxes (*b*) clean, and never leave any of the beds open to the ditches when not irrigating. This is a slovenly fashion, and often from a heavy rain, or by the leaking of a flood-gate, is the means of ruining the beds so left, and of course the plants they contain.

Figure 3 shows the flood-gate in general use here; it is a square box, open at the top, except the braces for strengthening it, with a door sliding between cleats nailed on the inside and bottom, and having a frame (*f*) through which the handle slides, and which is bored so as to be fastened at any height by a peg or nail. It is set in its place so that the end (*a*) at which the water enters shall be a little below the level of the ditch, marked by the dotted line *l*, *l*. By this means the water is not so apt to lift the gate out of place, and it also catches much sand, and so helps the boxes in the cross ditches.

[COPYRIGHT SECURED.]

SQUIRRELS OF THE NORTHERN AND EASTERN STATES.—*Drawn and engraved for the American Agriculturist*

A Squirrel Congress was probably never convened, and so, in all likelihood, no such committee-meeting was held as our artist has represented. Of all hard things to draw and engrave, one of the most so is a squirrel's tail,—so light and airy, and graceful and thin, and delicate,—each hair distinctly banded, of two or three colors, and all, one moment in elegant confusion, and the next, jerked into the most precise order. Our artist, we have no doubt, agrees with us. This beautiful group represents the common American species of this family.

The squirrels of our northern woods are the following: The Great Gray Squirrel, called also Cat or Fox Squirrel (*Sciurus cinereus*); the Common or Little Gray Squirrel (*Sciurus Carolinensis*); the Black Squirrel, a variety of the same species; the Red Squirrel (*Sciurus Hudsonicus*); the Flying Squirrel (*Pteromys volucella*), and the Striped Squirrel or Chipmunk (*Tamias Striatus*). The two species of Gray Squirrels are much alike, except in size, the Great Gray being much heavier, more robust, having a broader head. The color of the Little Gray Squirrel varies greatly, it being sometimes red, and again becoming quite black, so that the variety was long regarded as a distinct species.

The squirrels are so familiar to our readers that a particular description of them would be unnecessary, even had we space, and we might easily fill this number of the *Agriculturist* with the accounts of different kinds; for, besides those we have named, there are several other distinct species inhabiting the United States.

These lively, agile, and beautiful denizens of our forests, retreat reluctantly before the approach of civilization, and most of them need only a little encouragement to become familiar as door-yard pets. They are all easily domesticated, and are playful and mischievous. The Gray and Black Squirrels retreat together to the mountains and thick woods from near settlements; but the Red and Striped ones remain in the stone-walls and open woods, and even in our barns and granaries, when not driven off.

The introduction of squirrels into city parks and pleasure-grounds of late years has been productive of much gratification; but these pets are destructive to the birds, whose eggs and young they devour; they eat also the buds of trees. They are on the whole undesirable, and cannot be recommended as useful tenants of such places, except in the midst of large cities, where birds are at best only occasional residents.

The Flying Squirrel is one of the most interesting of our quadrupeds. Possessed of all the other powers of its family: climbing, running, jumping from limb to limb and from tree to tree, as freely as any of them—it has another distinguishing peculiarity—namely, that of flying, or, more properly, sliding on the air from one elevation to a lesser one. In these flights it is supported by the thin double skin, which is stretched between its fore and hind legs, and no doubt also by the broad tail. This species is perhaps more easily domesticated, and more gentle, docile and affectionate than any of the others. The extreme length of the different species of squirrels is as follows: Large Gray, 24 to 20 in.; Little Gray and Black, 20 to 23 inches; Red, 13 to 15 inches; Chipmunk, 9 to 10 inches; Flying Squirrel the same size or a little less.

Oranges North and South.

The climate of the Gulf States is so well adapted to the culture of the Orange and its relatives, that it is probable this will become, before long, an important branch of horticulture in that portion of the country. In some parts of Florida the bitter Orange has become so thoroughly established that it forms natural groves, and is there known as the "Wild Orange," producing a yield of a bitter and sour fruit, and affording an abundance of stocks upon which to graft the finer kinds. Sometime ago, Doctor C. J. Kenworthy, an enthusiastic traveler and horticulturist, brought us a collection of the various oranges and lemons from the St. John's River, Florida. The Sweet and Mandarin oranges were of excellent quality, and the specimens of the wild variety were so remarkably fruitful—as many being placed upon the stems as they would hold—that we had an engraving made of one of the branches, somewhat reduced in size. — Doctor K. has furnished the following notes upon their cultivation: "I have tasted fruit from almost every orange producing country of the world, and for size, thinness of skin, amount of juice, and richness of flavor, I have never met with any to equal some I gathered during a visit to the banks of the St. John's River, Florida. I arrived at the conclusion that (independent of climatic influences), soil and manure had much to do with the superiority of the fruit. The soil where they attain the greatest perfection is light and sandy, closely resembling that found in many of the poorer portions of New Jersey. The only manure used, is a remarkable deposit found along the banks of the St. John's River, and known as 'shell bank.' These deposits vary from a few inches to several feet in thickness, and consist almost entirely of the remains of snail shells. This deposit contains a large amount of calcareous and animal matter in a decomposed state, furnishing an ample supply of food for the nourishment of the tree. About once in four years, a bushel of 'shell bank' is forked in around each tree, and I was surprised at the deep green of the leaves, the luxuriance of growth, and the size of the fruit. I neglected to measure the oranges, but one of the lemons from the same locality, left at your office, measured five and one half inches in length, and eleven inches in circumference.

"The soil generally used as compost for the orange tribe, when grown in pots, is composed of loam and rotten dung, and it is but seldom that we see a healthy plant under green-house culture. I am of the opinion that the orange tribe in pots should test light silicious soils, and use a manure containing an excess of calcareous and animal matter. In Florida, where the wild orange attains its greatest perfection, the soil is always light, and the trees are usually shaded by the evergreen oaks."

CLUSTER OF WILD ORANGES.

The orange affords a remarkable instance of the production of several different odors, or flavors by the same plant. The leaves are aromatic; the young fruit, when of the size of a large pea, furnish a very strong and different flavor from that of the leaves; the character of the oil contained in the rind of the ripe fruit is well known, and the odor of the flowers, still different from either, is among the most highly prized perfumes. So beautiful and fragrant are orange blossoms, that we often find the tree in cultivation at the North for these alone. In a cool green-house, suited to camellias, there is little difficulty with the orange; but in the dwelling house, where its cultivation is often attempted, it seldom succeeds. Since the introduction of the modern methods of heating and lighting our houses, we now seldom see, as we formerly did, fine home-grown specimens of orange and lemon trees. They cannot endure a hot and dry atmosphere during the winter. They should be kept where they will not freeze, have very little water, and be kept clear of insects until spring. As soon as the weather is mild enough they may be set out of doors, and sheltered from the wind.

Concord and Discord Among Grapes.

When the "Greeley Prize" for the best grape for general cultivation was awarded to the "Concord," we supposed that the business was ended, and that the folly of a few men, some of them not particularly interested in grape culture, attempting to decide upon one grape for a wide extent of country, embracing almost every diversity of soil and climate, would soon be forgotten. Had we been on the committee, with the imperative necessity of finding a verdict, we should, perhaps, have done as they did; but we hope never to be placed in so useless a predicament. To see the folly of any such decision upon any one fruit, one has only to compare, one year with another, the proceedings at the annual meetings of the Ohio, Indiana, Illinois, or any other live State Pomological Societies. At these meetings a large share of the time is occupied in the revision of the fruit lists for one State only, and we find that the status of such generally cultivated fruits as apples and pears is very difficult to fix. A large State like that of Illinois is divided into three fruit regions, as those varieties suited to one extreme fail in the opposite end of the State. In some grape regions, the distance of a mile or less will make a difference of one or two hundred dollars an acre in the price of land, because some is favorably situated for grape culture and other is not. Now, can it be possible to fix upon one grape, one apple, or one pear, that will do everywhere? And can there be a more unfortunate position in which to place pomologists who have a reputation at stake? When we announced the award of this prize, it was stated that it would cause much dissatisfaction, and the same would have been the result, no matter what grape had received it. Already we find discussions in the various journals, and conflict of opinion as to the justice of the award and the merits of the Concord. A marked illustration of the different views taken by people living not only in the same State, but in the same County, has just come to hand. At the meeting of the Warsaw (Hancock Co., Illinois) Horticultural

Society, the Standing Committee on Grapes made a report, in which they say:

"The Concord not only keeps its place in public favor, but is gaining ground every year. The Committee congratulate Dr. Warder and other members of the Committee, on their moral courage in awarding to the Concord the Greeley prize of one hundred dollars, as the best grape for general cultivation. It makes a good wine, and as a tablegrape is generally preferred to the Catawba, and sells for more money, all the time. It is easily propagated, not subject to disease, and will endure a greater degree of cold and neglect, and bear more fruit than any other grape known to this Committee.

"We would say to persons wishing to plant a few vines to raise grapes for family use—plant mostly of the Concord." Again: "At Dr. Warner's vineyard, Sept. 20th, the Concord, gathered from the lower wire, six inches to one foot from the ground, weighed 66 degrees. From the second wire, three to four feet from the ground, weighed 76 degrees. From the top wire, five to six feet from the ground, weighed 78 degrees. This result is an instance to the contrary of the old theory that 'the nearer the ground the heavier the must.' On Oct. 15th, the grapes off the same vines, all pressed together, yielded a must averaging 83 degrees. * * * In conclusion, we would advise every one that has a home to plant grapevines. If they have not room for vines, plant a vine, and let that be a Concord. Give it plenty of room and sunshine, and it will bear grapes every year. —GEO. D. WORTHEN, CHRISTIAN LAISLER, WILLIAM BANDER."

Within a day or two after the receipt of this report, there came a communication from Mr. C. J. May, of Warsaw, Hancock Co., Ill., the same place in which the above meeting was held, who speaks of the Concord as follows:

"The Concord has been quite extensively planted. Many persons have planted largely of it, because men in whom they *have* had confidence recommended it through our agricultural papers, as being a first-class grape for the table, and that in the West it so changed its natural qualities as to make a wine better than Catawba, and that there was a greater demand for it at better prices. Those who have fruited it for the past two years know that it will not make a wine equal to the Catawba; in fact, that it will not make wine at all—that is, wine that will keep even through the first summer, unless extraordinary means are used to prevent its acetous fermentation. Sugar is generally used to bring the must up to 75 or 80, it weighing in its natural state about 60. The Catawba often weighs 85. It is well known that a must weighing only 60 will not make even a passable wine. Had the Concord all the sugar necessary to make a good wine, it would still be worthless because of its intense foxy flavor, which would alone destroy its value for wine. Concord will not make wine. It is an impossibility. As a market grape it has some value—now selling at a fair price in all our city markets, but selling for a comparatively larger price in our Western cities, where such grapes as the Delaware are as yet little known. As soon as the taste of the people has been educated by the use of good grapes, the Concord will find its level, and sell for its true value only. I have planted the Concord quite largely, and have many vines in full bearing. I believed, as others have done, that the Concord would make a passable wine, and planted it for that purpose. I believed it, because men in whom I had confidence—men who were said to have grown it for some years, positively stated that it would make a wine of good quality. But finding that it will not do what has been claimed for it, I think it full time that the truth should be known. It has been put before the people as our best native grape—as a grape possessing qualities that it never had a shadow of claim too. Many will plant it because those qualities have been claimed for it by men who should know its true value, and the result will be that every man who plants Concord vines will, within four years, find he has made a mistake, and will be badly disappointed. Is it not necessary to real success in any and every calling that our aim should be high? If success in the cultivation of the Concord is our highest aim, shall we reach a shining mark though we are successful?——"It has indeed been a 'noble' grape—royal even to those engaged in the propagation of it, and with every facility for reaping a grand harvest in this way, ought not I also to thrust in my sickle? leaving the truth to come out afterwards."

Such contradictory testimony as this, coming from one and the same locality, is certainly puzzling to one who knows nothing about fruit, and yet wishes to plant vines. The great trouble in the whole matter is, that grape culture is in that tentative state that it requires considerable more knowledge than individuals or even committees are supposed to possess, to say with confidence that any one of our grapes is the best for any State or county. That we have yet the universal grape, no one believes; indeed one of the very committee who decided the Greeley Prize said to us, a few days ago, that he knew of a grape that in five years would quite supersede the Concord; and we know of several grapes that are accumulating strength to enter the contest for eminence. Our opinion with regard to the many varieties now offered is already recorded. We doubt not that the Hartford and Concord *will more generally succeed than any others;* but they are inferior in quality to Catawba, Iona, and a dozen others we could name.

Remedy for the Canker Worm

The *Phalæna vernata* of the naturalists, or Canker Worm of New England, belongs to the order of *Lepidoptera*, and the class of *Geometers*, or earth measurers, so named from their habit of walking by successive spans. The male moth of the canker worm, as described by Harris, (Fig. 1), has very narrow antennæ, and almost downy edging on each side, hardly to be seen with the naked eye. The minute feelers do not extend beyond the mouth. The wings are large, very thin and silky; and when the insect is at rest, the fore wings are turned back, entirely cover the hind wings, and overlap on their inner edges. The fore wings are ash colored, with a distinct whitish spot on the front edge near the tip; they are crossed by two jagged whitish bands, along the sides of which there are several blackish dots. The wings expand about one inch and a quarter.

Fig. 1.

The female moth is wingless, (Fig. 2), and its antennæ are short, slender and naked. Its body approaches to an oval form, but tapers, and is turned up behind. It is dark ash colored above, and gray beneath. It is now known, contrary to the former opinion, that these moths come out of the ground in the autumn and during the winter, under favorable circumstances; but the general time is about the middle of March. If the weather continues very soft and mild they may all be expected to come out of the ground in about a week. If there are cold snaps, and long intervals of frozen weather, their rising will be delayed until better weather. A little observation will teach the fruit grower when to expect them, and when to apply his remedies. The sluggish females instinctively seek the nearest tree, and crawl up the trunk to deposite their eggs. They are followed a few days after by the males for the purpose of pairing. Soon after this the females lay their eggs, which are shown in Fig. 3, of the natural size and magnified. These are laid upon the ends of the branches, close by the buds, for the convenience of feeding the broods when they hatch out. The eggs are set on end, in rows, and form clusters of from sixty to a hundred or more. They are glued to each other, and to the bark, by a grayish varnish, which is water-proof. This being done, the moths soon die.

Fig. 2.

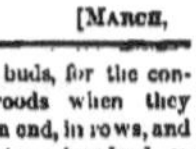

Fig. 3.

The eggs hatch from the first to the middle of May, or about the time the currant blooms and the apple shows its first leaves. When in sufficient numbers they devour the young leaves as fast as they grow, and by June the whole orchard presents a russet, burnt appearance, as if scorched by fire. They are terribly destructive. The seem to like the apple and elm trees best, but are found upon the cherry, plum, and lindens, and other cultivated trees and shrubs, when their favorite food is wanting. The worms feed for about four weeks, and when full grown measure about one inch in length. (Fig. 4.) They are ash colored on the back, and black on the sides, with a yellowish line on the belly, but vary somewhat in shades of coloring, depending perhaps upon the quality of their food. When full grown, they either crawl down the trunk, or descend by a web, and immediately burrow in the soil if they find it soft enough, and turn to chrysalids in their cells. The chrysalis (fig. 5) is of a light brown color, and varies somewhat in size according to the sex, the female being the larger.

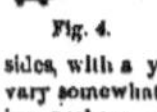

Fig. 4.

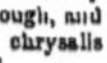

Fig. 5.

It will be seen from the character of the insect here described, that the most available method of destroying it must be by attacks upon the wingless mother, as she ascends the trees in spring. Various methods are given to accomplish this, but we like best that presented by Ralph W. Robinson, of Hampton, member of the Connecticut State Board of Agriculture. It involves a good deal of labor, but that is the price of good apples by any or all methods. He who will not take the trouble must go without apples—and ought to. Mr. Robinson says:

"I take a sufficient quantity of common tar, and an equal quantity of urine, (the latter to be increased or diminished, according to circumstances, or the judgment of him who applies it.) Heat it in an iron kettle, and stir it until well mixed. I then, with a brush, or swab, made of old rags for the purpose, apply it around the trunk of the tree, on a space about three inches wide, in the best place I can find between the ground and the limbs. The females stick fast in this tar, and the millers coming to pair with them, stick fast also, where their destruction is sure. The application should be repeated every evening (unless the ground be frozen), until they have done running, which is usually in from one to four weeks.

"Last year the ground did not thaw out until late in March, and kept so until they finished their running, which was five days. The reason of mixing urine with the tar is this: If tar is put on clear, it hardens so rapidly that the grubs crawl over it; whereas if softened with urine, it remains soft for a longer time, and completes the work of destruction more effectually.

"I think also that clear tar is more liable to injure the trees. It is recommended by some to put a strip of cloth about three inches wide around the tree, and put the tar upon that, but mixing it as I do, and then scraping it all *clear* from the tree as soon as they have done running (which may be done advantageously on a warm day), I consider there is no danger of injury. I cannot see that *my* trees have been injured, and I have practised it for five years, at the same time keeping the better of the enemy."

A Committee of the Essex (Massachusetts) Agricultural Society recommend printer's ink as a substitute for tar, it being quite as effectual and less expensive. They advise to first surround the tree with tarred paper and smear this with the ink, diluted with oil, thin enough to apply with a brush. They say that it needs renewing less oftener than tar—only once every two or three weeks. The same Committee also give the sensible advice to cut down all the old and unfruitful apple trees, of which hundreds are found in every community, cumbering the ground, and only serving as nurseries of worms.

All the Year Round.

The statement that a day laborer, in a large city like New York, has a greater variety upon his table, the year round, than many wealthy farmers, may seem strange, but it is nevertheless true. This variety does not consist so much in the meats as in the vegetables. Indeed the one thing that the city dweller misses, when he makes a visit to his country friends, is a variety of vegetables. The city markets and green groceries present a great assortment, and the tables of even those in moderate circumstances generally have some one or more of the products of the market gardens upon them. There is no reason why every one who has sufficient land should not have fresh vegetables all the year round. Aside from the roots that are in the cellar, or left in the ground, there is the cabbage, raw or cooked, as the main reliance for winter. In using the cabbages, save the stumps, to set out as soon as the ground is open, for most excellent greens. This month the Kale or Borecole that has been wintered out, will be an agreeable change from the cabbage. In April, winter spinach will be ready to cut, and the tender shoots of asparagus will give the first real fore-taste of the host of good things that follow soon after. Besides, lettuce, cresses and other salad plants, should grace the breakfast table, for their refreshing look if nothing more. There is "no end" of excellent vegetables to go with the dinner, and where there are plenty it makes little difference whether the meat is fresh or salt. It has been a custom with us to publish, each year, a list of the most desirable vegetables, as well as to make a note of the new ones offered for sale. We find that our different advertisers have given a very full account of the novelties, at least, and in the "Notes for the Month," we indicate reliable and readily obtainable sorts. If the farmer passes by the notes on the "Kitchen Garden," as something beneath his notice, she who provides for the table, and wishes her family to have a variety of healthful food, will read them—and have the vegetables too, or she is not the woman we take her to be. If a hot-bed or cold frame can be managed, all the better; but without these helps to greater earliness, a little forethought and painstaking will give every farmer fresh vegetables "all the year round."

Profits from Small Places.

The raising of early seedlings of culinary plants was referred to last month. Another way in which a small tract of land may be turned to profitable account, is the propagation of small fruits. We may safely say that, in a small way, more profit is to be derived from the growing of plants than of fruit. Within our knowledge there are several instances of eminent success with these small fruit nurseries of moderate extent. To be successful requires a knowledge of varieties, and the methods of propagation required for each. There is nothing about these that an intelligent man cannot learn; and scarcely one that has not been sufficiently treated of in our own pages. One must not only raise the plants, but let it be known that he has them. Strawberry, blackberry, raspberry, currant and other plants are in demand, are easily raised in a small way, and are profitable. Take the strawberry, for instance; we have not known a season for several years in which there was not a scarcity among the leading varieties. If strawberry plants are grown, we would advise the main planting to be of a few of the leading varieties, and enough of the novelties to get a start and be ready to take advantage of a demand for any of them; yet we would not invest enough in any one of the newer sorts to feel disappointed if the latest novelty proved a failure—as in the majority of instances it will.

There is always a scarcity of currants, of the finer kinds; these are raised readily from cuttings, and grow to good plants in a year. Whatever kind of propagation one engages in, strict integrity is essential to success—the most scrupulous care in procuring genuine stock, with which to make a beginning, and the greatest pains to keep each sort distinct and true to its name. Attention to these things will soon establish a reputation for accuracy, without which no propagator can hope to retain his customers.

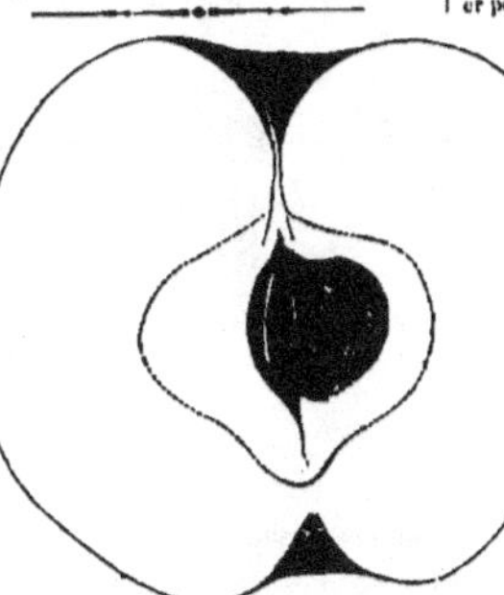

A New Apple—Dodge's Crimson.

Pomologists in Ohio, Illinois, and other Western States, find their best apples, or rather their best keepers to be of southern origin, while those known as long keepers at the East, are only autumn sorts with them; hence a great interest attaches to all southern varieties. Mr. J. W. Dodge, well known as an artist before he became a fruit grower, has brought us a collection of fine apples from his fruit farm and nursery at Pomona, Cumberland County, Tennessee, which comprises fine specimens of well known varieties, and others not familiar to eastern fruit growers. In the collection is a seedling raised by Mr. D., which he calls Dodge's Crimson, and as it has not before been published, we give a description and figure of it. Mr. D.'s place is on the table of the Cumberland mountain, and 2,000 feet above the sea level.

The tree is a good grower, with a round or spreading head and slender and tapering limbs which droop, but never break, with the weight of the fruit; bark very dark; it is an annual bearer.

Fruit medium to large, roundish oblong, tapering slightly towards the eye; smooth and even in form; color very dark crimson, sometimes nearly black, and on the tree covered by an abundant bloom; dots minute, few and inconspicuous; basin rather deep, a little irregular; eye very small, closed, segments of calix with tips reflexed; cavity deep, acute, somewhat irregular; stem very stout; core open, not meeting the eye; seeds roundish, light colored; flesh white, juicy, tender, at first a brisk acid; use—cooking, or table, very fine for jelly; season, November to March; a good keeper.

Cedar and Thorn Seeds—Stratification.

There are on file, some dozen or more complaints of want of success with the seeds of Red Cedar, Thorns, Dogwoods, etc., from persons who have sown the seeds and failed to get any plants. The trouble is, that these seeds do not come up until the second year after they are put in the ground, and if they are sown in a bed and left for a year, the weeds take such complete possession that the young trees, if they do start, have but little chance. To avoid this difficulty, the English propagator puts his seeds in "a rot heap" for a year, and the French "stratify" them, both names meaning the same thing. The manner of proceeding depends upon the quantity of seed; if small, a common flower pot, box, or keg is employed, and the seeds are placed in the receptacle with sand, or sandy earth, in alternate layers. The vessel containing the seeds is buried in a well drained place where the seeds will not be enveloped by standing water, nor dry out during summer. If a large quantity of seeds are to be operated upon, a heap is built up, putting alternate layers of seeds and earth, and making a mound with sloping sides to carry off the water. The seeds are usually ready the second spring after burying, and should be sown as soon as they show signs of germinating. Seeds of trees which form a strong tap-root, even if they are not long in germinating, are best treated by stratifying; such as Walnuts, Chestnuts, Horsechestnuts, and even Peaches. They are kept in this situation until the radicle pushes, when they are carefully planted, previously pinching off the lower extremity of the young root. This promotes the branching of lateral roots, and avoids the formation of a long tap-root. Trees from seeds treated thus, are much more readily and safely transplanted than those that have not received this early root pruning. Those who buried peach pits last autumn will do well to observe this precaution, when they plant this spring, as they will obtain much better trees.

NEW TREES.—A golden leaved variety of the common European Alder is advertised by the French nurserymen under the name of *Alnus aurea*, as being a permanent variety and very showy shrub.—Also a remarkable Walnut, from the North of China, *Juglans macrophylla*, the leaves of which are said to be three feet long.

Hobbies in Horticulture.

An old friend of ours, whom it is a delight to visit, always has some hobby, which, for the time, he rides bravely. The last time we were at his place, he was riding Chinese Primroses; his new seedlings were just coming into flower, and the pleasure he took in observing the difference in the shades of color, or the promise that some plants gave of being a little more double, or otherwise different from others, was something pleasant to see. In this country we have but little of this devotion to one particular genus or family of plants. Abroad, they have their chrysanthemum, auricula, gooseberry and other shows, and even societies devoted to some special culture. In our desire to do a little of everything, we do but little well, and are disposed to sneer at people who estimate gooseberries by grain weights and count the pips of a flower truss. Yet great perfection comes out of this devotion to a single thing. Years ago, we knew a journeyman shoemaker who carried all the prizes for asters away from under the noses of "gentlemen's gardeners," and, in his own humble way, did as much for the improvement of this flower as Truffaut, or any of the foreign florists. What can be pleasanter, for those who have leisure and taste, to take a plant, or several plants, and see what they are capable of, and by selections and crossings make them do their utmost. We suggest this not only for flowers, but for fruits, as there are many fruits that have not yet been half developed.—Who has crossed a peach? and yet what a chance the Golden Dwarf presents for experiments. Who will give us a raspberry as hardy and prolific as the Philadelphia, and as fine flavored as Brinckle's Orange? Where is the sweet and high flavored strawberry as surely productive as the Wilson? Then, in flowers too, are we to stop with what the Japanese have done with the lilies? Will not some one put odor into our native violets by a lucky hybridizing? There is a whole host of hobbies waiting for some one to mount them. We ask those who are on the look out for every "new importation," and spend their money freely for the results of foreign skill and patience, to try their hand at the home production of "novelties" in fruits and flowers. Let what Snow has done with the Verbena, and other of our florists with the Carnation, encourage the belief that success is not confined to any country.

The Sweet-Scented Shrub, or Carolina Allspice.—(*Calycanthus floridus.*)

For those who prefer fragrance to beauty of flowers there is no common shrub from which more enjoyment may be derived than from the *Calycanthus*. It is not particular as to soil or treatment, remains in flower for several months, and diffuses a strong fruit-like odor that is to most persons very agreeable. It is a shrub that has already become popular, and we notice it now as one of those good old things that every lover of shrubbery should have. It grows from six to nine feet high, and naturally forms a roundish clump. The character of the leaves and flowers are given in the engraving. The flowers are of a brownish purple color, with but little difference in appearance between the calyx and corolla. The parts of the calyx are united below, and form a kind of cup which encloses the pistils, a fact that gives origin to the botanical name. The bark and leaves have an aromatic odor, which doubtless suggested the name of Carolina Allspice, while the fragrance of the flowers, compared by some to that of strawberries, and by others to that of apples, has given it the name of Sweet-Scented Shrub. The flowers give off their odor more powerfully when crushed or slightly wilted. There are several varieties which are ranked by some botanists as species. *Calycanthus glaucus, laevigatus, inodorus*, etc., are put down by

THE SWEET-SCENTED SHRUB (*Calycanthus floridus.*)

some as distinct species, and by others as only varieties of *C. floridus*. It is found in most of the Southern States, one variety extending as far north as the mountains of Pennsylvania. *C. occidentalis*, of California, is much larger in all its parts than our Eastern plant, and has brighter colored flowers. This is prized in Europe as an ornamental shrub, but we have not noticed it in cultivation with us. The Calycanthus readily multiplies itself by an abundance of suckers, or it may be propagated by layering.

"Getting a Few Turns Ahead."

A man employed in a ship-yard to turn a grindstone was found by the men, when they came to their work, busily engaged in turning the stone. When asked why he was turning when no one was holding, he replied, "I am getting a few turns ahead." The idea was a good one, but not well carried out. Getting "a few turns ahead" can be done in many operations, and in none more satisfactorily than in the garden. Whoever cleaned up and burned all rubbish last autumn, got "a few turns ahead" of him who has to do it this spring, when all is so soaked that it won't burn. Now, before garden operations, in most places, fairly begin, something can be done to forward plants, and have them ready earlier than they would be in the natural course of things. Those who have hot-beds or cold-frames have already read what we have said last month on page 68. If there is no disposition to try glass, or not the ability to command it, there are the kitchen windows. We last year advised the use of boxes, and can only briefly say now, that they are much better than pots. Get a long box six inches deep; filled with light soil, sow the seeds of early cabbage, tomatoes, etc. Keep it moist and exposed to full light in the kitchen window, where cooking and washing are going on, and the air is always moist, and the young plants will soon be up and need thinning. Thin, and transplant the thinnings to another box like the first. Open the window on mild days, or set the boxes out of doors during the middle of the day, and there will be a lot of hardy plants ready to put out by the time a less wide-awake neighbor is just sowing his seed. On a larger scale, make a bed as soon as the ground thaws, put a frame around it of nine inch boards, and have some shutters made, of boards battened together, to cover it. Open the frame, when the sun is warm, in the morning, and cover it as soon as the heat declines in the afternoon. In a short time the soil will get well warmed, and lettuce, radishes, cabbage, and other things, may be forwarded considerably without glass. Get ahead of your work in every possible way; having tools ready, manure in sufficiency, seeds procured, and wherever forethought will do it, be a "few turns ahead" in the garden.

Earliness in Vegetables.

If we can get a variety of any vegetable a few days or a week earlier than any before known, it is a great gain, especially with the cultivator for market. Much that is said by venders of seeds, about extreme earliness, that experience fails to sustain. One, this year, advertises a tomato thirty days earlier than any other sort. Now, a tomato a whole month in advance of any we now have, would be, near New York, worth a small fortune, and we doubt not it would be proportionately valuable elsewhere, and few would be willing to part with the seeds of so precious a variety. While we hope that all that is said of this tomato may be true, we would not have any one deterred, by our doubts in this case, from striving for great earliness, or testing this, and all other things claiming to be in advance of ordinary varieties.

Much can be done in most vegetables by selecting, year after year, the earliest for seed. We know of an instance in which this plan of selecting the earliest Sweet Corn for seed, for several years in succession, resulted in establishing a variety of great earliness. If in saving peas for seed we took the very first pods for next year's crop, instead of using them upon the table, we should not be running after "First Crops," "Expresses," and other new sorts of peas—and the same with other vegetables.

THE HOUSEHOLD.

(☞ For other Household Items, see "Basket" pages.)

Home-Made Household Ornaments.

We present this month some ornaments a little more elaborate than those given in the last number: Fig. 1, is a rustic flower stand, made to hold two eight-inch pots, with Geraniums, Fuchias, or any other flowers suitable for the living-room or parlor. The foundation of the stand is a piece of board about 20 inches long, and ½ inch thick. Pine or some soft wood is the best. This is cut out on the front in the shape of a capital B, only the indenture is not quite so deep, and the edge upon which the slats are to be nailed, are left a little flaring, so as to give the required shape to the stand, the top of which should incline outward, about an inch from a perpendicular line. A strip of rattan or willow, three-eighths of an inch diameter, is first nailed with small brads upon the lower edge of the board, against which the slats are to fit. The slats are made of light and dark colored wood, with the bark on, split from sticks 1 to 1½ inches in diameter, and whittled down to a ¼ inch in thickness. They are

Fig. 1.—RUSTIC FLOWER STAND.

made a little narrower at the bottom than at the top, to provide for the flare of the stand, and are picketed at the top as shown in the sketch. These slats are fastened to the board at the bottom, with small brads about ¾ inch long, and at the top, to a strip of rattan, willow, or any other lithe wood, about half an inch in diameter, whittled flat upon one side, to fit neatly to the slats. The nails or brads at the top should be much smaller than those at the bottom. The bottom of the stand is finished by nailing strips upon it in the same style as those at the side, fitting them neatly to the rattan or willow on the edge. If the slats have not been previously finished, rub slightly with fine sand paper to remove any roughness, but not to disturb the original bark color.

You now want a pot of warm glue, and a good selection of acorns, in the cups and out of them. A row of these should be fastened around the bottom, next to the willow band, taking care to put them so that they will not hit the floor or window ledge, when the stand is in its place. The rosettes at the sides are made of acorns, and the cones of the Black Spruce, and those in front of single acorns, with the scales of the Norway Spruce cone placed around them. The ornaments seen between the rosettes are made of sprigs of the oak, with acorns having cups on them, and small spruce cones at the bottom. In the arrangement of these there is room for the home artist to display his taste. These are fastened on with glue, and after they have dried a few days, the whole should receive a coat of varnish. The inside bottom of the board should have paper pasted upon it, when it is ready for use. This flower stand is open upon one side as shown, and may stand in the window, or upon the mantle piece.

Fig. 2.—RUSTIC BASKET.

Fig. 2, represents a rustic basket in the same general style of work, varied by handles and legs. It is about eight inches across the top, and the same in height. The handles, the edging at the bottom, and the band upon the inside, to which the slats are fastened, are made of rattan, but willow will answer. The slats are made of dogwood and hazlenut, about a ½-inch through, and are fastened with brads or tacks. The legs are about ¾ inch in diameter, and raise the basket about an inch from the stand or shelf. It may be appropriately used to hold a flower pot, a vase with a bouquet, or for the work-table to hold knitting or sewing when laid aside. All wood that is used for this kind of work should be first thoroughly seasoned. We have several varieties well adapted to this work. The main thing in the selection is to have uniformity of size and a pretty contrast in the color.

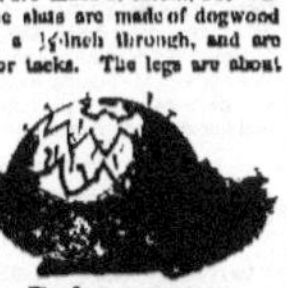

Fig. 3.—PIN CUSHION.

Fig. 3 represents a pin-cushion. The foundation is a bit of pine board, cut or turned in a lathe, round, about seven inches in diameter. It is furnished with legs ½ or ⅝ inch long, and the underside is covered with morocco paper. The pin-cushion on top is any pretty pattern of worsted work, stuffed with wool. The border of rustic work, about 1½ inches wide, is quite elaborate, presenting a dozen varieties or more of acorns, cones, seeds, and berries gathered from the woods. The top and bottom courses are made of the scales of the cone of the Norway Spruce, turned inside out, and fastened to the paste board with thread and needle. There are three courses at the bottom, and two at the top. The space between is filled in with acorns of several varieties of oak, beech nuts, hard hack seeds, black spruce cones, dried berries, seeds of weeds, and buds of evergreen trees stripped of their foliage. Almost any small shrub or weed, whose seeds hold on in the winter, will furnish appropriate material for this kind of work. They may be fastened on with needle or glue, as can be done to best advantage. When tastefully wrought up, they make beautiful pin-cushions. They not only ornament the toilet table at home, but command a ready sale at fairs, and are a source of profit to the maker.

Leaves from the Diary of a Young Housekeeper.—No. II.

PRIZE ESSAY BY MRS LAURA E. LYMAN, STAMFORD, CT.

Jan. 31.—For a few days past I have been sending broth and other delicacies to a poor family about half a mile down the road; two of whom are sick, a little girl and the father. He was a Union prisoner at Salisbury, N. C., and was released at the close of the war with a shattered constitution and a gloomy future.

There are three or four girls in the family, one about twelve years of age, and Edward has been talking about the propriety of our taking her when the father dies, as, poor man, he must before many days. Edward says that next summer, when he has a number of farm laborers, I shall need some help, and it will be a great advantage to the girl if she can be taken into a good family, where she can learn the best ways of doing work, and so become useful to me as long as she stays, and able to command good wages in service.

I should prefer to take a girl who has a more thrifty and energetic mother than she seems to have; for the family belongs in that great class of the shiftless and the improvident, who always were poor and always will be. But I really feel, that all who can give such children a lift ought to do so, and perhaps I may put this girl in the way of becoming an excellent housekeeper, and eventually the mistress of a home of her own.

Feb. 25.—The poor soldier died. Edward and I went to the funeral, and it made my heart ache to see those five little ill-clad orphans shivering on the heap of frozen dirt at their father's grave, their feet only half protected from the snows of mid-winter, and their future apparently as dark as the lowering skies above them.

The next day we went down in a sleigh, and got Sue with her little bundle of clothes, tied up in an old handkerchief. She has been here ten days, and I've been thinking a good deal as to how, both for her own sake as well as for mine, I can make the most of her. She is cheerful and always willing, but has no ideas of thrift, economy, or neatness. To teach her these, and, at the same time, divert her mind from her grief and loneliness, I have devoted a good deal of time to her. I find I must not expect very much, and must have great patience with her dull perception, and her weak memory.

On one point I have been very successful, and this gives me encouragement that the same system in other departments will be equally effective.

She seemed to have no idea as to how a table should be set. So, to assist her conception, I wrote out in a very clear hand the following list, and pasted it on the inside of the closet door: "Table-cloth, napkins, mats, plates, knives, forks, spoons, glasses, cups, saucers, sugar and milk, butter, salt, the castor, bread, water, the dishes from the stove, chairs." Just under this paper I drew a little outline picture of the table, with all the dishes on it in their proper places. The effect was magical. She now looks upon table setting as pastime, and does it as well as I could if I were expecting Miss Leslie herself to dine with us.

Raised as she has been, in an atmosphere of improvidence, it is not strange that I could not get her to remember to put on her dishwater at the right time. But she looked so mortified at being constantly reminded of it, that I changed my tactics, and told her she should have a penny every time she remembered it, and forfeit one every time she forgot. For two days now there has been plenty of hot dishwater at the right time, at an expense of three cents a day, but the value of that habit alone, when once fixed, cannot be estimated. It has always been a topic of conversation, and a ground of complaint with my housekeeping acquaintances who employ help, that they have to work almost as hard to get the servant to do the work well, as if they did it all themselves, besides the greater waste and trial of patience. But I think if servants were kindly and fully instructed in what is expected of them, they would certainly try to please. My success with Sue about the table makes me believe that similar painstaking will make her equally reliable and thorough in all kinds of work. So I am writing out a catechism in questions and answers, explaining exactly how and when everything she has to do must be done; how, for instance, she can wash her dishes in the quickest and best way; what she must do first, and what next when she gets up in the morning. This catechism she recites to me every night after tea, and I have promised her that as she learns what I have written, and carries it out, I will instruct her as thoroughly in washing, ironing, and bread-making.

March 3rd.—Yesterday we returned from a visit to our relatives, which was very pleasant. We went to Edward's home first, where we stayed a week, and then to mine, where we spent another week.

Edward had prepared me somewhat to find things a little different from what they are in my home, but the contrast was far greater than I imagined. There never was a more amiable woman than his mother, and few men are so thoroughly sensible as his father. But how such an order-loving, systematic man as my husband, ever grow up in such a family, is past my power of conjecture. While he was talking, one of the girls came up to tell us breakfast was just ready, and we went down. A savory meal was smoking on the table, and the fragrant coffee most gratefully greeted our olfactories, as we entered the dining room. Whatever defects my new mother possesses, she is an excellent cook, perfectly at home in the culinary department. There is no lack in the store-room, for Edward's father is well off, and provides his family with all they need. We sat down, and one after another the family gathered round the table. Jane was still in bed, and Julia was not quite ready. The boys were busy about something, and we were nearly half done eating before the entire family assembled at the table. It seemed so strange to me, for my father would never ask the blessing until every child was in his place, and we were as obedient to the ring of the breakfast bell as it was possible to be. But here, every one came when ready, and all left when they had finished, as though they were at a hotel. Jane made her appearance after we were quite through, her hair in curl papers, and with a soiled morning dress carelessly wrapped around her. She said she had laid awake reading Victor Hugo's "Toilers of the Sea," until a late hour, and didn't feel like getting up early. At last everybody was done eating, and I helped clear away, expecting that the table would at once be put in its place, and the dishes washed up and put away. Edward went out with his father to look about the place, and the boys were busy with their sleds and skates. Edward's mother was taking care of the milk, which had set through breakfast unstrained, while Julia devoted herself to her canary bird, and Jane dreamily addressed herself to the task of washing the dishes, talking all the time about the novel she had read the night before. It was ten o'clock before every thing was put away, and then it was most time to begin to get dinner.

It was very different at my home; we were all made to get up early, and while mother moved about the house, putting everything in order, and superintending the several domestic departments, one of us girls got the breakfast, another took care of the milk, and the other trimmed the lamps and helped generally. The boys brought in wood and did the various chores that boys usually do. We all sat down to table together, and after breakfast and prayers were over, one of us girls cleared away the breakfast dishes, another swept the floor, or made the necessary preparations for dinner, and thus by a division of labor, our work was all done up by nine o'clock, floors swept, beds made, and everything in order. Mother had us take turns in the different departments. I had entire charge of the table one week, while Emeline attended to the chamber-work and sweeping, and Jennette was responsible for the work not included in these divisions. Thus, by a system of rotation in office, we all became familiar with the entire household routine, while Mother directed and supervised all.

March 10th.—I was not half done writing in my Diary, when Edward came in with bad news, and a funny time we have had! The old mother pig suddenly died, leaving ten poor little orphan babies only three days old. "What shall be done with them?" we both exclaimed. My sister Jennette, who came home with me to stay a month or two, and who is extremely fond of animals, suggested that we bring them into the house and raise them by hand. So we took the two bushel basket, filled it half full of soft oat straw, and the bereaved family was established in a warm corner back of the kitchen stove. I scalded a quart of new milk, added a little water, as I had seen mother do for human babies, and Jennette and I spread large aprons in our laps, and began to feed them. We had to open their little mouths with our fingers and pour the milk down their musical throats. Such a squealing as they made! but they relished the sweetened lacteal very much. In two hours, we repeated the operation, passing them all back into basket No. 1. At night we took turns in feeding them every two hours. They soon learned to squeal the moment they heard the rattling of the spoon, but by feeding them the last thing at night, and the first thing in the morning, we secured good rest last night, and they are growing so fast!

I meant to have written more about my visit, but the advent of the ten baby pigs so unexpectedly into my kitchen, quite banished all thoughts of writing from my head. And I have been occupied with Jennette, and in teaching Sue, and in making and receiving visits.—Who should come to see me the other day, but Bettie Hannum! She was married the week after I was, and went right to housekeeping. Such doleful accounts as she gave of her experience in cooking! She used to say, she thought my mother was very hard on her girls to make them do so much housework, that it would be time enough to learn how when she had a house to keep, and her mother wanted her to enjoy herself while she was free from domestic care. She sees her mother's mistake now.

Leaves from My Journal.

PRIZE ESSAY BY MRS. B. McCLELLAN, OF OHIO.

I have been making a "shoe bag" for Lizzie to-day. I made a small one, too, for Hannah's room, though I don't know as she will take the trouble to use it. As it is quite fanciful, she will like it for an ornament at any rate. Lizzie's is of green delaine, bound with crimson braid, and lined with cambric of the same color. It is really pretty. A good size is three quarters of a yard in length, and half a yard in width. This gives room for three tiers of bags, with three in a row. The lower ones are the deepest; and the upper, being the smallest, furnish a nice place for the shoes of the little ones, or for stockings as well. One of the lower corner bags is just the place for "father's" slippers. The bag should be tacked upon the inside of the closet door of the bed-room.—A "string bag" is most convenient in the pantry; made of calico, a quarter of a yard square, and hung by a stout cord to its own nail. Let every string around store bundles and every thing else find place in it. Though within reach of "Charlie," who has such unheard of uses for strings, it will always be running overfull. Another useful bag about house, is one for patches and pieces of all sorts. This should be large and square, so that, upon drawing it wide open, the whole contents can be seen, without being at the trouble to empty it. The old-fashioned "rag bag," though not ornamental, must have some good corner for safe keeping. Not a shred should be carelessly thrown away. Its contents will keep the tin mended, and now and then furnish a bright addition in that line, which the careful housekeeper, with a self-satisfied shrug, will pronounce "clear gain."

I called to-day upon two of my friends, and have been thinking so much about them, I must tell my Journal some of my thoughts to night. They are both considered very superior housekeepers, but view life and its duties from quite opposite standpoints. Mrs. W. is an inveterate scrubber. Her house, from attic to cellar, and everything in it, is just as clean as soap and sand, and hard rubbing can make it. She has a large family, and usually does the work herself, for she can not find help neat enough to suit her. Of course she has no time for any thing else. She is jaded and worn, and so annoyed by dirt, that I fear her children do not find home either bright or happy. She seldom goes out, but she mourns that her *cares* allow her no time for enjoyment.

The home of Mrs. Y. is equally neat, but much more inviting. She is often called overnice. Perhaps she is. But she says she has found that keeping every thing in order, and doing every thing at the right time, *saves* work and time too, and she does it for that. At any rate, she *has* time for many a work of love. She visits the poor and the sick, with hands and heart full, for their relief and comfort. She is kind and polite to all, intelligent and beloved. If a choice bouquet is wanted, or a delicate cake, a garden herb, or the very best recipe for any thing in the housekeeping line, it is well understood that Mrs. Y. is the one to supply it. "Her children rise up and call her blessed, her husband also, and he praiseth her." Her home is relieved from the stiffness and exactness of too scrupulous order, by the atmosphere of love, with which it seems ever surrounded.

March.—One of my neighbors told me to-day, that her Pickled Peppers were covered with a white scum. She had scalded the vinegar, and then put on new, but all to no purpose. She had come to the conclusion that the vinegar was poor. That may be the trouble, as Peppers keep better than other pickles. But for the past two years I have put horseradish root among mine for this very purpose, and it has been "just the thing." It adds a fine element to their flavor, and has wholly prevented the white scum. Tomatoes are favorite pickles with us. I choose those of small size, slice them and scald a few minutes in strong salt water. After draining, I pack them in a jar, sprinkling among them cloves, cinnamon, peppers, and horseradish. The vinegar should be scalded, and poured over them hot. They keep well until they are eaten up! When blustering March comes round, pickles find a good market. I don't know why it is, but the appetite becomes dainty, and craves something sour and stimulating. Now is the time for the housekeeper to bring out from her hoarded treasures the *canned red cherries.* How splendid their color! How delicious and acceptable their flavor! Mr. Frisby declares, again and again, that they "go to the very spot." However, they must not be dealt out too generously. Currants, blackberries, and jellies, give a good variety. Apples, too, must be freely used, for they will soon become insipid, and there is scarcely an end to the different modes in which they may be prepared for the table. Cut into halves, removing the cores and skins, and filling the space with a little butter and sugar, and baking in a pan, in which has been poured a little water, they make an excellent dessert to be eaten with cream and sugar, or served as sauce for the tea-table. "Yankee Pie" is another favorite dish. Slice apples into a quart basin, or pudding dish, which has been well buttered. Add a little water, and cover with crust about half an inch thick, made up as for soda-biscuit. It requires about three-quarters of an hour to bake. Place the plate to receive it upside down upon its top, and reverse the whole. The apples, white and soft, will thus be upon the crust, and may have a dressing of butter, sugar, and nutmeg. But the crowning dish of all is fresh apple-pie. (That is, provided I make it myself!) *Too much* apple is usually put in a pie. Let the plate be only even full, but of a quality that is tender, tart, and juicy. Add sugar, butter, salt and a *little* nutmeg. This last gives a lemon flavor if used in small quantity.

Mr. G. took dinner with us to-day. He came round to his favorite topic—comparing the women of the present generation with our wonderful grandmothers and great-grandmothers of the olden time. He enjoys it so well, and is so perfectly *set* in his opinion, that I don't take the trouble to have any argument with him. One fact, however, is noticeable. He never alludes to the sturdy old *grandfathers*, who were a match for their wives any time. Who ever heard of them with false shirt bosoms and wristbands, with paper collars, and all manner of fancy neckties, with kid gloves, or stove-pipe hats, or cloth boots, or bosom pins, even if they wore miniature *links*, or *rule* and *compass* set in gold! Were they found at the Theatre, or Opera, or even at the counting-room, until the small hours of the night! By nine o'clock they and their families were in bed, and long before the morning light crimsoned the east, they were up and at work, milking the cows, and feeding the cattle. How, in the dead of winter, with good homespun suit, and cowhide boots, and mittens that "mother" had knit, they were off with an ox-team to the woods, cutting and drawing, with never flinching patience, the year's supply of firewood. How heartily they breakfasted, and dined, and supped upon "*potluck,*" with a good mug of cider for a condiment. Who ever heard then of bronchitis, or dyspepsia, or a voyage to Europe, or dumb-bells, or fishing-smacks, for health? I do hope Mrs. G. doesn't try very hard to be like our grandmothers, for I am sure her husband don't remind me *in the least* of the grandfather's of yore.

A blessed old man of eighty-three was mine, when he went to rest. A fresh, rosy face, and a heart full of love, had he. His teeth were as sound as a nut, but his head was bald. He wore a wig of young brown hair. Ah, me! human nature was the same then as now, after all!

BOYS & GIRLS' COLUMNS.

Learn to Use What You Know.

George Barnard's father brought home from the war an empty bomb-shell as a relic from the battle-field. George was a bright boy, though a small one, and was much interested in his father's story about the shell; but he wanted to make the relic useful. He therefore filled it with various seeds, pouring them in carefully through the fuse-hole, and buried it in his garden, with the top out of ground. One morning his father discovered the buried shell. "Why, George, what's this? Are you expecting a crop of bomb-shells by and by?" he asked. "Oh, no, father, its full of seeds. I thought they would do well in such a nice, warm place, but they don't start yet." "Nor will they, my boy, if you live to be a hundred years old. The seeds need to be dropped in the ground, Georgie, where they can have room and nourishment, and a chance to put out roots below and sprouts above." George took up the shell and "unloaded" it. That evening Mr. Barnard told his older children of George's operations. "It makes me think," said he, "of a learned man who can't use his learning for himself, nor give any body else the benefit of it,—one whose head is stuffed as full of book-knowledge, or ideas, as that shell was of seeds—good enough in themselves, but not one of which can get fairly out. Now, I want you all to be intelligent boys and girls; but I want you, when you learn a good thing, to think *how to use it*, so as to make it of service to yourselves and others. You have, perhaps, learned some things to-day, which may be made valuable if you try to think *how* they may be made so. I have heard wise men say that they had known persons, with comparatively little knowledge, to make themselves of far more value to the community, from understanding how to use what they had learned, than others whose heads were full. The knowledge of these last was like gold in a mountain—precious if it could be got out, but useless while it lay buried."

UNCLE PAUL.

Curious Geographical Problem.

In the December *Agriculturist* (page 411), the following problem appeared: "Suppose a person to start from New York on Monday noon, and travel westward at the same rate the earth revolves eastward, thus passing around the globe in 24 hours. It would, of course, be noon the whole length of his journey. At what point in his journey would he find the inhabitants calling it *Tuesday* noon, supposing the whole of his route to be inhabited!" A discussion of this problem was intended for the Feb. number, but was crowded out by other matter. The following communication from Mr. J. D. Pulsifer, Auburn, Me., treats the matter so clearly that it is presented, instead of the comments of the editor:

"Your problem (No. 242) is a very interesting one, but does not admit of a *certain* solution. The traveler will pass over two Continents and two oceans. On the Western Continent it will be Monday noon; on the Eastern Continent it will be Tuesday noon; on the Atlantic Ocean, it will be Tuesday noon. On the Pacific Ocean, at a point somewhere, the change is instantaneous from Monday to Tuesday. Where that point is, has not, to my knowledge, ever been settled.

The reason why the change does not occur on the Atlantic Ocean is owing to the fact that America was discovered by crossing that ocean. If the discovery had been made by sailing from Asia eastward to California, custom would have thrown the change of day on to the Atlantic Ocean. In making a complete circle the day must be changed. *Where* it is changed is immaterial and conventional. We may, if we please, fix upon the central line of the Mississippi River; all east of that line in the problem supposed, shall be Monday, all west Tuesday; but that is not the line fixed upon. The Pacific Ocean—a very wide line—is the one fixed upon. This is, however, contrary to the definition of a line, length without breadth. When sufficient authority shall have fixed upon some line of longitude in the Pacific where the change occurs, your problem will admit of a more exact solution." Several others have written upon the subject, some of them quite understandingly, especially one who signs himself "Rusticus;" his views are substantially the same as those given above. A large number laughed (on paper) at the problem, and answered "way at New York of course"! If that were true, then it would be Tuesday noon at New York, and Monday noon at Boston, and all places east of this city.

A Borer Under Water.

Many of our young readers may have seen the work of the *borer*, or worm which bites its way into trees, a nibble at a time, leaving sawdust behind it. These insects are very destructive to apple and peach orchards; pine and other trees also suffer from their attacks. With sharp eyes you may find them, perhaps, at work in your neighborhood. A similar class of creatures live in the waters of the ocean. The *teredo* or ship borer, is a small shell-fish, that has the best kind of an apparatus for boring wood, which it uses very effectually. A ship's bottom, unprotected by metal, would soon be pierced by millions of holes made by these minute workers. They attack piles driven to form wharves, etc., and in a few weeks a stout stick of timber may be dangerously weakened. In February, 1861, a great inundation occurred in Holland, caused by the breaking of the embankments which prevented the overflow of the sea; villages were destroyed, many lives were lost, and nearly 40,000 acres of land were flooded. It is believed by good authorities that the piles which gave strength to the embankment had been so weakened by the *teredo* as to give way under the great pressure of a high tide. Where it is needed, protection is given against these borers by sheathing the wood with metal, or *kyanizing* it—that is, filling the pores of the wood with some substance poisonous to the *teredo*.——It is stated by a gentleman, in the "Adelphi Academy Record," that "previous to some thirty years since, the augers in general use for boring the holes to receive the fastenings of vessels were so made that, in using, it was necessary to frequently draw them out to remove the borings, and this made nearly one-third of the work. About that time a distinguished Naval Officer invented the auger now in general use, which continuously delivers the borings from the orifice. Upon examination of the boring apparatus of the *teredo*, this gentleman was surprised to find it similarly constructed! One more interesting fact concerning the *teredo*, and we leave it. The creature not only works through the hardest wood, but lines the little tube it leaves with a beautiful casing of fretted shell work, extending to the length of one to two feet.

Don't be a Coward.

This picture history of Timid Timothy, is for the amusement of those boys and girls who are afraid "something will catch them" in the dark, or when left alone. You can see how he was frightened at a mouse, his shadow, etc. The story says he grew more and more like a hare, a most timid creature, until, finally, no one could see any difference between him and that animal, and away he ran into the woods. We don't say the story is true, but if you will carefully observe men, you will be surprised to see how much they grow to look like the animals which they resemble in habits and character.

New Puzzles to be Answered.

No. 253. *Illustrated Rebus.*—A beautiful song.

No. 251. *Illustrated Rebus.*—For the young to remember.

No. 255. *Word Square.*—The proper definitions of the following words, viz.: *Apology, Jump, Rest, Monkeys*, written one under the other will form a *word square*—that is, the words will be the same whether read across or downward. Find these definitions and form the square.

No. 256. *Illustrated Rebus.*—A true proposition.

No. 257. *Anagrams.*—Make single words from each of the following: 1, Fat reward; 2, One drum; 3, Red paper; 4, Sophy, I cry; 5, Set on a dish.

Answers to Problems and Puzzles.

The following are answers to the puzzles, etc., in the February number, page 67; No. 251. *Illustrated Rebus.*—A little darkey (*dark e*) in bed, with nothing over it ......No. 252. *Illustrated Rebus.*—*A* straight furrow, and a well made fence are sure (*rr's ever*) signs of an excellent farmer. The following have sent in correct answers to puzzles, etc., in previous numbers, up to Feb. 1st, at which time this part of the paper is finished: L. W. Gates, Ada Stanton, Mary A. Rhodes, Alfred Hawkesworth, Mary and Lizzie Brumbaugh, Thos. R. Gurnee, Jos. Ball, W. S. Flinn, Isaac A. Chapman, Sarah D. Veatch, W. B. Drew, James Hoffman, J. B. Daniels, C. D. Bishop, F. Schnebley, T. S. Cadwallader, E. G. S., John Wertz, Frank Painter, Theodore W. Bellis, Leonora Barrus, Reuben Pickett, Mrs. H. A. Rhodehamel, Sylvania Sherman, Isaac T. McLain, Mrs. Ruth A. Clute, John B. Demster, Abraham J. Greiner, D. F. Albaugh, Hannah Fawcett, Annie McGrew, William Foulk, Charles W. Stewart, Ella C. McWilliams, Jonathan Smith, Wilson Everly, Thomas Bellsmith, George D. Watson, F. Brush.

[COPYRIGHT SECURED.]

S U S P E N S E.—FROM A PAINTING BY SIR EDWIN LANDSEER.—*Engraved for the American Agriculturist.*

Perhaps the artist, in painting this picture, had in mind the story of the dog that was his master's constant companion, until the death of the latter. Then it was found impossible to console the poor brute. When driven from the room where the body lay, the dog took refuge outside, under the window, and remained there night and day, until the funeral; and when the grave received his master, he refused to leave the spot, and actually died there of grief and starvation. Such cases are no doubt very rare, but one would expect it from a dog like this, if from any. The character of an animal, like that of a child, will depend much upon training. By kind treatment you may make your pets confiding, faithful, and almost every way agreeable; by abuse, they will become cowardly, sneaking, cross, and it may be dangerous. The picture will bear studying a long time, so well has the artist filled it with expression, and we are happy to be able to aid in improving the taste of our young friends, by presenting to them so fine a work of art. Every boy and girl can see what the dog in the picture is thinking of—"Do dogs think?" Yes, in their own way. How plainly this one says by his look, "I wish master would come." A human face could not express feelings more plainly. He is a faithful creature; no sneaking, sheep-killing, cur ever gave such a look as that.

A Hit at the Editors.

"Sheridan" pleasantly writes to the Editors: "In your Jan. number, under your 'Study of Physiognomy,' you charge your artist with childishly amusing himself by 'making faces.' My man 'Dan' questions your ingenuousness, and gives it as his 'notion' that you all '*put your heads together*' to produce that picture." Some of the Editors feel flattered by the above. One of them suggests that "Dan" probably got his idea from the fact that the faces were certainly members of a *press*.

How Large is the Earth?

"Twenty-five thousand miles in circumference," promptly answer thousands of our young readers. How do you know? "The geography says so." "How did the geographers find it out?" "Perhaps they measured it," suggests some thoughtful little girl. Yes, that is true; but perhaps in a different way from what you may suppose. Let us see if we can make it plain. Here is a

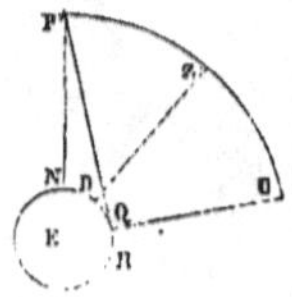

round ball, E, representing the earth. P, is a point, at a distance above it. Now, suppose a fly to be at R. He could not see the point P, because it would be hidden from him by the circumference of the body E. If he crawls up over the surface, when he arrives at Q, the point P, will be just in sight above the horizon. The point O, will be over his head. When he arrives at D, Z, will be exactly overhead, and P, will appear to be half way up to over his head. When he arrives at N, the point P will be directly above him. Now, suppose the circumference of the body E, to be divided into 360 parts, or degrees, and suppose another circle to be drawn around E, passing through the point P, and this also to be divided into 360 parts, or degrees. Then as the fly crawls from Q, towards N, the point P will appear one degree nearer over his head, every time he passes over a degree of the circumference of E. Now, suppose E to be the earth, N, the North Pole, P, the North Star (which is directly over the North Pole), and Q, a point near the Equator. Let a man start from Q, where he could see the North Star just above the horizon, and travel toward the North Pole, then each degree north he traveled, the star would seem to rise one degree above the horizon, until he came to the North Pole, when the star would be directly above his head. If, when he has traveled one degree, he measures the space he has passed over, and multiplies the distance by 360, it will give the entire distance around the globe; and this is just the way it has been ascertained, except that it was not necessary to start from the equator—any point will answer equally well, as by traveling north until the North Star appears to have risen one degree higher, a degree on the earth's surface can be ascertained.

"Uncle Paul," whose first sketch appears in another column, will be readily recognized by thousands of girls and boys, who have often enjoyed his writings in the "Child at Home." He is "our" Uncle Paul now, and appears very happy to find himself with so numerous and so bright a company of children as belong to the *Agriculturist* family. Give him a hearty welcome.

(Business Notices ... per Agate Line of Space.)

FLORENCE

LOCK-STITCH SEWING MACHINES.

Highest Premium, Fair of American Institute, 1865.
CELEBRATED REVERSIBLE FEED MOVEMENT,
UNIFORM SELF ADJUSTING TENSION,
FOUR SEPARATE DISTINCT STITCHES,
WILL GATHER AND SEW A RUFFLE AT ONCE.
OFFICES OF THE COMPANY.
505 Broadway, N. Y., ... Boston, England.

PRINCIPAL AGENCIES.

141 Washington-st., Boston. ... Buffalo, N. Y.
... Utica,
26 West ... Binghamton, N. Y.
45 Public Square, Cleveland. ... N. Y.
1... ... Newark, N. J.
... North Pennsylvania ... Troy, N. Y.
... 2 Yates Block, ...
Cor. J st. and ... N. Y.
... Rochester, N. Y.
... North Fifth-st., St. Louis, Mo.
... River-st., Troy, N. Y.
... to 5... Main-st., Hartford, Cor. Genesee, Columbia, and Seneca-sts., Utica, N. Y.
629 Broadway, Albany, N. Y.

WHEELER & WILSON ROTARY HOOK

LOCK STITCH

SEWING MACHINES.

625 BROADWAY.

"Woman's Greatest Boon. We would advise a man to forego a ... and thresh wheat with a flail, rather than to see the wife wear her health, vigor and life away in the everlasting ... stitch, stitch, when a Sewing Machine ... The WHEELER & WILSON is an ... We have had several ... and after ... six year's service, the WHEELER & WILSON has taken the precedence as the best, where all kinds of sewing are ... in a family."

Rural ... Agriculturist, Jan 1866.

THE GREAT FAMILY SEWING MACHINE.

GROVER & BAKER'S

HIGHEST PREMIUM
Elastic Stitch
SEWING MACHINE.
495 Broadway, New York.

THIS MEDALLION IS EMBEDDED IN EVERY GENUINE HOWE SEWING MACHINE.

The Howe Machine Co.'s Sewing Machines,

699 Broadway, Cor. Fourth-st., N. Y.

For Families and Manufacturers.

These World-Renowned Sewing Machines.

Were awarded the highest premium at the World's Fair in London, and six first premiums at the N. Y. State Fair of 1866.

These machines are made under the immediate supervision of the President of the Company, ELIAS HOWE, Jr., the original inventor of the Sewing Machine.

The Stitch invented by MR. HOWE, *and made on this Machine, is the most popular and durable, and all Sewing Machines ... the principle invented by him.*

SEND FOR CIRCULAR.

A CHECKER BOARD GIVEN AWAY.

FRANK LESLIE'S BOYS' AND GIRLS' WEEKLY

With No. ... will be given gratis,

A Beautifully Illustrated Comic Checker Board.

Send Five Cents, and you will receive in return No. 15, with the Checker Board, post-paid.

FRANK LESLIE, 537 Pearl-st., New York.

My Catalogue of New and Fine Plants,

is now ready, containing new Double Geraniums, Beaton's Geraniums, new Dahlias, new Fuchsias, new Heliotropes, new Verbenas, new Chrysanthemums, superb new Gladiolus, the Czar Violet, and many other novelties.

Address GEORGE SUCH, South Amboy, New Jersey.

THE LITTLE CORPORAL

Is acknowledged by the leading papers to be the

Best Juvenile Paper in America.

The American Phrenological Journal, of New York, says: "*The Little Corporal.*"—Mr. Sewell's Western Juvenile surpasses, both in real merit and in circulation, any similar attempt, East or West. Its success excites the cupidity of others, and we now have a swarm of juvenile journals launched on the uncertain sea of experiment. While we wish well to all good endeavors, we must award the credit to *The Little Corporal* of leading the van."

We offer a MAGNIFICENT LIST of PREMIUMS!

The price of the Corporal is one dollar a year, in advance; sample copy, telling all about the premiums, ten cents.

Address ALFRED L. SEWELL, Publisher, Chicago, Ill.

HEADQUARTERS FOR MAPS

IS AT

H. H. LLOYD & CO.'S,

21 John-St., New York.

P. S.—We have 5 sizes of U. S. Maps, (the largest, a Copper plate, 6x6 ft.,) made in 12 styles, and a vast variety of other Maps, Charts, Prints, Photographs, Engravings, &c., &c.

Harper & Brothers ... say: "We have already spoken of the reliable character of the house of H. H. Lloyd & Co. *This is not J. T. Lloyd.*"

BUCKEYE MOWER & REAPER

AWARDED FIRST PRIZE

GRAND GOLD MEDAL

at Great National Field Trial,

Held at Auburn, July, 1866,

for perfect work, lightness of draft, freedom from side draft, superiority in mechanical construction, FACILITY OF MANAGEMENT, portability, strength and durability.

Manufactured by ADRIANCE, PLATT & CO.,
165 Greenwich-st., New York.
(Manufactory, Po'keepsie.)

BRICK and Shingle MACHINES.

We have the simplest, and we believe the most powerful Brick Machine in America, works *every kind of clay*, and with only one pair of Mules makes 2,000 good brick per hour, or 1,500 by Steam Power.—Satisfaction guaranteed.—Our Re-pressing Machine, with *One Man and a Boy*, will re-press 4,000 per day. The Empire Shingle Machine pleases every one that uses it. ABRAM REQUA, General Agent, 141 Broadway, New York.

KNOX'S NURSERY AT YOUR DOOR.—A Liberal Offer. See Advertisement on page 117.

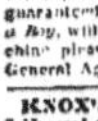

AGENTS wanted for Hue's patent scissors-sharpener, and Hue's patent knife-sharpener—articles wanted in every family. Samples sent by mail for 50 cents each. Address PECK & SEYMOUR, 13 ...-st., New York.

GET WELL AND KEEP WELL.—Read the Advertisement of Herald of Health, page 114.

The "Franklin" Brick Machine,

Justly celebrated for perfect simplicity, great strength, and immense compressing power, is GUARANTEED, with eight men and two horses, to self temper the clay and make 3,000 to 3,500 elegant bricks per hour. J. H. RENICK, Proprietor, No. 71 Broadway, New York, Room 39.

CONVENIENCE FOR ALL.—Hall's Patent Burner. Light and trim without removing or tipping chimney.—Usual size, burning ⅝ inch wick, sent by mail for 35 cents. Agents Wanted, both Gentlemen and Ladies, in every town. Address N. H. LOOMIS, Agent, Room 22, No. ... Park Row, New York.

PEACH TREES of fine quality, at $120 per 1000.
PARSONS & CO., Flushing, N. Y.

NOW READY:

Woodward's Record of Horticulture For 1866,

EDITED BY ANDREW S. FULLER,

Author of the

FOREST TREE AND GRAPE CULTURIST,

Fully Illustrated, Extra Morocco Cloth, Bevelled *edges*, post-paid, one dollar.

WOODWARD'S COUNTRY HOMES.

150 designs and plans for Country Houses of moderate cost, with a full Illustrated description of the manner of constructing "Balloon Frames."

12mo. 192 pages. Cloth, extra.—Post-paid, $1.50.

WOODWARD'S ARCHITECTURE AND RURAL ART.

178 Designs and Plans for Country Houses, Cottages, Farm Houses, Barns, Out-Buildings, Grounds, &c. Paper, 75 cents; Cloth, $1.00, post-paid.

JACQUES'S MANUAL OF THE HOUSE.

How to Build Dwellings, Barns, and Out-Buildings of all kinds. 126 Designs and Plans, $1.50, post-paid.

Fuller's Forest Tree Culturist.—A new work on the cultivation and management of Forest Trees, by the author of the Grape Culturist; fully illustrated, post-paid, $1.50

Husmann's Grapes and Wine.—A new and practical work on the Cultivation of the Native Grape and Manufacture of American Wine, fully illustrated, post-paid, $1.50.

The Illustrated

HORTICULTURIST ALMANAC

for 1867. Price, TEN CENTS, post-paid.

GEO. E. & F. W. WOODWARD, Publishers,

And Dealers in all works on Architecture & Agriculture,

37 PARK ROW, New York.

Illustrated Priced Catalogue sent Free.

B. T. BABBITT'S SOAP AND SALERATUS FACTORY.

We had an opportunity lately of passing through this great establishment, which is one of the largest in the country, embracing Nos. 64, 65, 66, 67, 68, 69, 70, 72 and 74 Washington-st. The space occupied by it seems incredible. Nine buildings of four or five stories, with a depth of from 90 to 100 feet each, and most extensive steam power are embraced. Mr. Babbitt laid the ground work of this immense business some twenty years ago, making a very humble start in a single store. With untiring effort, enterprise, and personal supervision, in twenty-three years he has become one of the millionaires of New York. He is still an active and *hard working* man. The manufacture of soap—an article so necessary—is always profitable. Soaps of all kinds find a ready market everywhere, and though millions of pounds are poured out of the immense boilers daily, it is soon consumed. This mammoth house gives constant employment to over 200 persons, and huge engines with thousands of pounds of steam keep its machinery in motion. Steam is conducted through the entire block by pipes, some of which cross the street and supply power to two buildings on the opposite side. A boiler which is said to be the largest in the world, and which rises from the ground floor to the fifth story of one of the buildings, it is said will make at one time nearly 200 tons of the best soap, which at the present prices would bring $32,000. Here is soap for the million in one turn of this monster pot. The grease, etc., is melted by the agency of pipes filled with steam, which run throughout the base and sides of the boiler.

Mr. Babbitt is an extensive manufacturer of saleratus, of which from fifteen to eighteen tons are turned out daily. In addition to this, another article universally used—the STAR YEAST POWDER—is said to possess superior qualities, adding twenty pounds and more to a barrel of flour when made into bread. Mr. Babbitt believes that bread made with this Yeast Powder will prevent indigestion and dyspepsia.

We are pleased to see that his custom is wide-spread in all parts of this country, and we are informed that he has upward of 10,000 regular customers in the United States and foreign countries, which we do not doubt, seeing the number of wagons, drays and carts continually loading and unloading, and the immense piles of boxes, both inside and outside of the buildings, labeled Soap, Saleratus, Yeast Powder, Sal Soda, Soap Powder, Super Carbonate of Soda, and Concentrated Potash, all of which articles are manufactured by him. With a man of his energy and enterprising spirit, there is no such word as "fail."—*De Bow's Review.*

MARK YOUR CLOTHING!

Clark's Patent Indelible Pencil.

"The Indelible Pencil for marking clothing is much more convenient than ink, and equally good as to permanence—we judge after several month's trial."—*Am. Agriculturist.*

"The Indelible Pencil is invaluable for marking linen."—*Chicago Tribune.*

"Remarkable for the ease and neatness with which it can be used."—*Detroit Tribune.*

Manufactured and Sold at Wholesale by THE INDELIBLE PENCIL CO., Northampton, Mass. Sold post-paid on receipt of price. Pairs—50 cents single, $4 per dozen. A liberal discount made to dealers. AGENTS WANTED. EVERY PENCIL WARRANTED.

See Advertisement "ALL NURSERIES IN ONE," on page 112. Observe the low Prices.

THE GREAT COMMERCIAL ENTERPRISES OF NEW YORK.

During the past ten years the moneyed men of this metropolis have projected many gigantic enterprises, designed to keep pace with the growing wants and tastes of the rapidly advancing civilization of this city and country. Many of these enterprises have rewarded the projectors with liberal returns for their investments—others have been but partially completed—while others, from lack of skill and judgment, were necessarily abandoned either before or after completion. Among all these enterprises there is none more worthy of notice and commendation, and none that has met with better success than that of THE GREAT AMERICAN TEA COMPANY. The founders of the Company believed that the consumers of tea and coffee were paying too many and too large profits on these articles. They projected the enterprise for the purpose of affording the consumers an opportunity of obtaining these *necessaries* at the very lowest prices. They believed that an immense trade could be built up by the ONE PRICE system, and SMALL PROFITS. They based their rate of profit upon a sale of at least *one thousand chests per week*. The sales at the present time are about double that amount, and increasing daily, which proves unmistakably that the public approve their efforts. This Company do not rest content with their success, but continually strive to improve their facilities for supplying their trade.

This Company have now the most complete, best arranged, and most attractive warehouses in this city or in the world. They are located with especial reference to convening the inhabitants of the metropolis and neighboring cities. Their stores have been fitted up with the latest improvements, and with original designs of prismatic and crystal lights and reflectors, which display with grand effect the superb original oil paintings of Chinese notables, &c., and give brilliancy to the elaborate and unique scenery that decorates the walls.

Among other improvements, we have added to our establishments steam and caloric engines, cylinders, &c., for roasting and grinding our coffee; four printing presses for the purpose of printing our tea and coffee bags, circulars, &c.

Persons have traveled hundreds of miles, in some instances, to examine the establishments of this Company, and have expressed themselves not only highly pleased and delighted, but considered that they were amply repaid for their time and expense, by what they saw and learned, by a visit to the store at Nos. 31 and 33 Vesey Street alone, without even visiting any of the other splendid establishments of the Company.

Whenever heads or members of clubs come to the city, we shall be happy to have them call upon us and make themselves known.

NOTICES OF THE PRESS.

From the New York Tribune.

A SUCCESSFUL ENTERPRISE.—THE GREAT AMERICAN TEA COMPANY commenced business in 1860 in this city. They now occupy six large stores and employ about 200 persons, their sales of Tea and Coffee amounting to $90,000 per week. Their success shows what ability and enterprise will accomplish. It is simple enough. Their sales being large, they are of course in a position to sell their goods for a smaller profit on each pound. In their advertisements in the *Tribune*, from time to time, they fully explain their system of doing business, and from the many letters received from all parts of the country, we judge that their customers are well satisfied.

From the Christian Advocate and Journal, N. Y.

* * * * Last of all, be sure not to go home from your holiday foragings without calling at the store of The Great American Tea Company, 31 and 33 Vesey Street, corner of Church, and lay in a supply of their choice goods, paying for them not the most extravagant prices.

From the Christian Intelligencer, N. Y.

THE GREAT AMERICAN TEA COMPANY.—Patrons of this company express much satisfaction with the qualities of the teas which they obtain and with the prices at which they are enabled to effect their purchases. The business of the company is conducted on a plan so accurate and comprehensive, that people living at remote distances from this city can give their orders, and have them filled according to advertised terms.

From the N. Y. Day Book.

THE GREAT AMERICAN TEA COMPANY.—Our readers will see in our advertising columns a novel suggestion in relation to getting Tea at cheap rates. The Great American Tea Company offers great inducements to purchasers, and we know the articles it sells are of superior quality.

From the Evangelist, N. Y. City.

TEAS.—The attention of persons who purpose attending the May Anniversaries is directed to the advertisement of THE GREAT AMERICAN TEA CO., Nos. 31 and 33 Vesey Street. It will be seen that this Company have made arrangements to supply families with the choicest new crop of Black, Green and Japan Teas at the wholesale prices. The Company guarantee all the goods they sell to give entire satisfaction. Those who wish to economize are requested to read the advertisement of the Company in another column of this paper.

From the American Agriculturist.

THE GREAT AMERICAN TEA CO.—*To Queries.*—Before admitting the advertisement, we learned that a large number of our clerks and others had for several months been buying their tea and coffee from this company, without its being known who they were, and that they had been highly pleased with their purchases, both as to quality and price, and were all recommending their *friends* to the same course. As we have published the advertisements for many months, and received no complaints, we conclude "there is no humbug about the establishment."

From the Brooklyn (E. D.) Daily Times.

THE GREAT AMERICAN TEA CO.'S STORE.—The Great American Tea Company opened their new and magnificent store on Saturday night, at 133 Grand street. The store was literally run down with customers and thronged until the hour of closing. We regard the opening of this new establishment in our midst as a public benefit. The company has such a thorough organization, possesses such unrivalled facilities for purchasing cheaply, and deals in such enormous quantities of tea and coffee, that they can well afford to undersell any other dealers in the country, and yet make a good profit. Precisely the same tea that is sold elsewhere for $1.50 can be had of them for $1.00, and good judges pronounce it even superior. We suppose that hereafter the "Great American Tea Company" will monopolize the business in this place, as the other dealers appear to be too antiquated and old-fogyish even to make their places of business known to the public. The company, on the other hand, knowing that they can sell a better article a third or a half cheaper than anybody else, are bound to spread the information abroad, and the tremendous business which is done at their New York warehouses, at their Western District branch, and now at their Eastern District establishment, shows what enterprise will effect.

COMPLIMENTARY LETTERS FROM CLUBS.

Xenia, Dallas Co., Iowa, Nov. 8, 1866.

Great American Tea Company:

Sirs: The order that I sent to your house the fore part of the summer gave universal satisfaction, and all of the Club have been trying for some time to get me to make up another. The complimentary package which I received was the best tea I have drank in Iowa. Please fill the following order, and express to me at Boonsborough, Iowa.

ZERAH K. COTTRELL.

Franconia, N. H., Nov. 10, 1866.

The Great America Tea Company:

Gentlemen: My last order for tea of 59 pounds came to hand in due time all right, and has given entire satisfaction, and, if you continue to send us as good tea as you have sent, you are sure of a permanent trade in this place. The Imperial was the best of anything we have had in this place. Several of the club have told me it was better than the tea they had paid $2 a pound for. I send you another order for $68.63. Please forward as before by express to Franconia, N. H., Grafton County. I thank you for the complimentary package. Address

PRIEST YOUNG, Franconia, N. H.

Elk Horn, Wis., Nov. 10, 1866.

Great American Tea Company:

My order for tea was filled and the tea arrived safely, *promptly*—good *weight* and good *quality*. We are all well satisfied, and others wish they had joined us. I shall doubtless send another order before long, for we have paid *large* profits to *small* traders about long enough.

Respectfully yours, &c., O. HAND.

Fairmount, Illinois, Nov. 12, 1866.

Great American Tea Company:

Gentlemen: Your Advocate fell into my hands yesterday morning, and I at once opened a club in my shop, and hasten to send it now, as it has reached the required size ($30), and it will take faster and easier after we receive the first bill. I have cut out and posted up in my shop the price list, and some other items, and shall keep a club open perpetually. My shop is in a public place and adjacent to the depot, and I can, ere long, buy of you about all the tea that is used in this town and vicinity. I shall aim to keep some tea on hand to supply such persons as cannot wait for return bill, and also that I may keep the club open longer and thereby increase the size of the bill. I would say that we are all heartily glad that your enterprise is an actual success.

Yours truly, H. M. ROBINSON.

Waterbury, Nov. 13, 1866.

The Great American Tea Company:

Gentlemen: My order of last month of $149.99 came in good order, and, as usual, gave satisfaction. Inclosed I send you an order not quite as large, but pretty good for one shop. *The Merchants growl a good deal*, but as long as we can get such tea of you as we have had you will get our money. Accept my thanks for the complimentary package. Please send as before by express, C. O. D., and oblige

Yours, THEODORE COLLINS.

New London, Nov. 15, 1866.

Great American Tea Company:

Sirs: I herewith send you another club. We are well satisfied with that which we received before, and much obliged for the complimentary package. We find that it is 50 per cent. cheaper than we can get it here, and at least 50 per cent. better. Please send me two or three blanks for clubs and circulars to go with them, as I know of some in adjoining towns who would like to get up clubs.

Yours truly, L. M. DAY.

Ohio and Mississippi Railroad Line,
Aurora Station, Nov. 10, 1866.

Great American Tea Company:

Gents: Here is your sixth club from these "diggins," making an aggregate amount of nearly $700. Some of the country storekeepers here say that your tea is of no account, but the *people* who use it think otherwise, as is demonstrated by the increasing demand for it. We send inclosed an order for $191.63, and next month we expect to beat that.

Yours, &c., E. H. LONG.

Lowell, Nov. 20, 1866.

Great American Tea Company:

Gents: I herewith send second order of Merrimac Club for tea and coffee. In regard to first order, would say your promptness in answering it and quality of goods sent gave entire satisfaction, as you will see by an increase of $24 in this order, C. O. D.

Respectfully yours, — D. GORDON,
159 Colburn Street, Lowell, Mass.

Great American Tea Company,
31 and 33 Vesey Street, New York.

November 23, 1866.

To The Great American Tea Co.:

The tea I received gives good satisfaction. My thanks to you for the complimentary package sent me.

Yours respectfully, EDMOND ESTEY.

St. Peter, Minn., Nov. 26, 1866.

Great American Tea Company:

It has been one month since I commenced getting up a club for tea, and this is my third order, and amounts to nearly $200. All are well satisfied, and say that the tea is as good as we get here at $2.50. I will send your circulars to all the different towns in my reach, and try and get the whole trade turned in the tea line so that the consumers can save these great profits. Yours truly,

W. O. POWELL.

Fountain Green, Ill., Nov. 29, 1866.

Great American Tea Company,
31 and 33 Vesey Street, New York:

Gentlemen: The tea you sent me the middle of this month was received in good order and gave general satisfaction. The present order is mostly for other parties who are not yet satisfied that it is possible for tea of a good quality to be furnished at your figures after paying former prices. I am sure, however, that a few experiments, resulting as favorably as my first, will give people confidence and insure you a liberal patronage from this locality. Wishing you success, I am, gentlemen

Your most ob't servant, J. M. FOY.

EVIDENCE AFTER A YEAR'S TRIAL.

Treasury Department,
Fourth Auditor's Office, Dec. 1, 1865.

Great America Tea Co., Nos. 31 & 33 Vesey st., N. Y.

Inclosed herewith I send you our regular list for December. It is now twelve months since we began the use of your Teas and Coffees, and I am pleased in being able to say that the satisfaction derived from the use of said articles by the members of this Club, instead of being confined to individual instances, is universal, and I think I may safely say without exception. Thanking you for the many favors received at your hands, I am, sirs, very respectfully, your obedient servant, L. CASS CARPENTER.

Bernardstown, Franklin Co., Mass., Dec. 3, 1866.

To the Great American Tea Company,
31 and 33 Vesey Street, New York:

Gentlemen, The tea that I ordered from you gives general satisfaction, and I this day mail you another club order, No. 3, for tea and coffee, amounting to $39.10, which you will please fill and send to my address, by express. Please accept my thanks for the complimentary package.

Respectfully yours, E. D. RICHARDSON.

William Penn Works, near Shenandoah City,
Schuylkill Co., Pa., Dec. 6, 1866.

Gents: We received our orders of Tea and Coffee all right, and each package put up so nice as to give us but little trouble. They have given great satisfaction both as regards weight and quality; and so cheap that we have saved fifty cents per lb., beside getting a better quality; and we are all satisfied that they are as good—both Tea and Coffee—as your advertisement represented them to be.

I remain, yours, THOMAS ROGERS.

Indianapolis, Ind., Dec. 7, 1866.

Great American Tea Company, 31 and 33 Vesey st., New York:

Gents: Yours of the 1st inst. is before me, and I would state that the tea has been received, and gave entire satisfaction. The money has been forwarded per Adams' Express. You may expect another order.

Respectfully, &c., WILLIS G. OVERSTREET.

Lake Forest, Dec. 12, 1866.

Proprietors Great American Tea Co., 31 and 33 Vesey st., N. Y.

Sirs: The box of tea I ordered of you two weeks ago came safely to hand. All are well pleased with their goods, and their reputation have spread from house to house. Every one here now proposes to save nearly $1.00 per pound on his teas. The Gunpowder I got I have given samples of, and all those who have tried pronounce it superior to any they have had for years. Retailing tea here now is far below par; every one says "send to New York, and save money by it." The express charges were 3½ cents per pound, so we can safely say we save 70 cents per pound at $1.25 per pound.

I send you, by this mail, another order, twice as large as the first; it is filled out in one of your blank sheets; should it not reach you, let me know immediately. Please fill order as soon as possible, for we want it before Christmas, and oblige, J. M. SIMPSON, Lake Forest, Lake Co., Ill.

Joliet, Ill., Dec. 13, 1866.

Great American Tea Company,
31 and 33 Vesey Street, New York:

Gents: The invoice of teas you sent to me came duly to hand, and I have this day paid the amount to the express agent. So far as I have heard, all in the club are well satisfied. Already I have found others desirous of sending, and ere long I think I shall give you another order. Thanking you for the complimentary package, I am

Yours truly, F. K. BAILEY.

New Haven, Dec. 14, 1866.

To The Great American Tea Co.:

Sirs: This will convince you that your goods have given perfect satisfaction, as I have added somewhat to the club. Please accept our especial thanks for the complimentary package, also for the nice manner in which the whole was put up. Yours truly, Mrs. L. BLOSS.

Please return as soon as convenient. Direct as before to Justin Bloss, New Haven, Vermont.

N. B.—For Price List of Teas, how to get up Clubs, &c., see the last page of this paper.

Rare and Beautiful Flowers----Select Garden Vegetables.

B. K. BLISS,

Seed and Agricultural Warehouse, Springfield, Mass.,

Importer and Dealer in Garden, Field and Flower Seeds, Agricultural Implements, Fertilizers, &c., &c.

The attention of all who are interested in the culture of FLOWERS or VEGETABLES is invited to our large and well selected assortment of the above—comprising the newest and most approved varieties, both of European and Home production, the quality of which cannot be surpassed.—For a list of which, see our

New Illustrated Seed Catalogue and Guide to the Flower and Kitchen Garden.

The Thirteenth Annual Edition, enlarged and improved, contains 124 pages of closely printed matter—BEAUTIFULLY ILLUSTRATED WITH 100 ENGRAVINGS, and a descriptive list of TWENTY-FIVE HUNDRED VARIETIES OF FLOWER, VEGETABLE AND AGRICULTURAL SEEDS, including all the leading novelties of the past season, with explicit directions for their culture; also a list of

ONE HUNDRED AND TWENTY-FIVE VARIETIES OF FRENCH HYBRID GLADIOLUS,

Embracing many new sorts now offered for the first time in this country—with many other SUMMER FLOWERING BULBS, consisting of AMARYLLIS, TUBEROSES, TIGRIDIAS, LILIES, etc. To which is added a list of the choicest varieties of GRAPES, STRAWBERRIES, RASPBERRIES, CURRANTS and other SMALL FRUITS, BEDDING PLANTS, etc., cultivated at his gardens, with much other useful information upon the subject of gardening generally. A copy will be mailed to all applicants upon receipt of 25 Cents.

Our New Illustrated Plant Catalogue, just published, contains a list of many new and rare plants, not before offered in this country—also a Descriptive list of all the leading varieties of DAHLIAS, HOLLYHOCKS, ROSES, CANNAS, CARNATIONS, PICOTEES, VERBENAS, HELIOTROPES, PETUNIAS, GERANIUMS and other BEDDING PLANTS. **Price, 10 Cents.**

Our Regular Customers supplied with both Seed and Plant Catalogues without charge.

N. B.—We would invite particular attention to the following COLLECTIONS OF SEEDS—also to the SPECIAL VARIETIES enumerated—the purity and vitality of which cannot be excelled—all of which (with the exception of those noted) will be mailed, post-paid, to any address in the Union upon receipt of price affixed.

Collections of Flower Seeds by Mail.

The following collections have been sent out from our establishment for the past 13 years, and are now favorably known in every section of the country. They contain the most showy varieties in our large assortment, with full directions for culture. Each packet contains a mixture of the different colors and varieties of its species, so that a greater display can be made at a much less price than when ordered in separate packets. Those unacquainted with Flowers as well as the experienced cultivator may order without fear of disappointment.

No. 1—	Contains twenty choice varieties of Annuals	$1 00
No. 2—	" " " of Biennials and Perennials	1 00
No. 3—	Contains ten extra fine varieties of Annuals and Perennials, embracing many of the new and choicest in cultivation	1 00
No. 4—	Contains five very choice varieties selected from Prize Flowers of English Pansies, German Carnation and Picotee Pinks, Verbenas, Truffaut's French Asters, Double Hollyhocks	1 00
	Any one remitting $3 00 will receive the four assortments.	
No. 5—	Contains fifteen very select varieties of Greenhouse seeds	$3 00
No. 6—	Contains one hundred varieties of Annuals, Biennials, and Perennials, including many new and choice varieties	5 00
No. 7—	Contains fifty varieties of Annuals, Biennials, and Perennials	2 50
No. 8—	Contains twenty varieties of hardy Annuals, Biennials, and Perennials, for sowing in the autumn	1 00

The seeds contained in the above assortments are of our own selection. Purchasers who prefer to make their selection from the Catalogue, will be entitled to a discount proportionate to the quantity ordered.

SEEDS of FLORISTS' FLOWERS.

QUALITY UNSURPASSED.

	p'kt.
ANTIRRHINUM (Snapdragon), finest hybridized	[illegible]
ASTERS, Truffaut's Peony flowered, the finest grown	[illegible]
AURICULA, from the finest prize varieties	[illegible]
BALSAMS, [illegible] and Smith's prize, unequaled, each	[illegible]
BELLIS PERENNIS, Double Daisy, a general favorite	[illegible]
CALCEOLARIA, Herbaceous and Shrubby varieties saved from [illegible] spotted and mottled flowers, each	[illegible]
CARNATIONS, from the newest and best named sorts	[illegible]
CARNATION, [illegible]	[illegible]
CARNATION & PICOTEE PINKS, from named varieties, each	[illegible]
do. [illegible] flowering for pot culture	[illegible]
GERANIUMS, scarlet, from finest variegated foliaged vars.	[illegible]
do. [illegible] all the newest varieties	[illegible]
PELARGONIUMS, [illegible] Eng. and French prize flowers	[illegible]
GLADIOLUS, [illegible] collection of 125 varieties	[illegible]
GLOXINIAS, from the finest erect and drooping varieties	[illegible]
HOLLYHOCKS, from our own collection of 75 varieties, producing flowers fully double, of every shade of color	[illegible]
LANTANA, from named flowers	[illegible]
MIMULUS, from the finest new hybridized varieties	[illegible]
do. New Double flowering "Bull's"	[illegible]
PANSIES, from the finest English show flowers	[illegible]
do. New Fancy, beautifully edged, marbled & varieg'd.	[illegible]
do. Blue, Yellow, White, Black, Bronze, Striped, Yellow margined; Violet bordered with white; Marbled purple, in separate packets, each	25
(The collection of eleven varieties of Pansies ..$1 50)	
PETUNIAS, Double, carefully hybridized by a noted German Florist	25
PETUNIAS, BUCHANAN'S Hybrids, from the finest mottled and variegated varieties	25
PORTULACAS, New Double, in many colors, producing flowers as double as Roses, a most desirable acquisition	50
PRIMULA SINENSIS, (Chinese Primrose), saved from the finest fringed varieties, Rose and White, each	25
STOCKS, New German, large flowering, finest mixed	25
do. Scarlet and White Intermediate, (Covent Garden varieties), each	25
do. New White Wall flower leaved, fine for pots	[illegible]
SWEET WILLIAMS, HUNT'S PERFECTION and AURICULA FLOWERED, beautifully margined, laced and mottled, most [illegible] for beauty, each	25
THUNBERGIA, fine [illegible] hybridized bedding varieties	[illegible]
do. [illegible] and its hybrids for green-house	[illegible]
WALLFLOWERS, finest double, much improved	[illegible]
The foregoing collection of 40 varieties for	$1[illegible].00

Splendid Novelty from Japan.

JAPANESE STRIPED LEAVED MAIZE.

The experience of the past season fully confirms all that has been said of this beautiful plant, and it is now acknowledged by all the leading Florists both in our own country and Europe as the most valuable plant for decorative purposes introduced for many years. The variegation appears [illegible] the plant is about four inches in height, and in a short time it is beautifully striped or ribboned with alternate stripes of green and white, and in its earlier stages of growth [illegible] with rose colors. Nothing in the way of a [illegible] plant can exceed in gracefulness and beauty a group of three to five plants of this variety of the Zea. Price, 25 cts. per packet; 5 packets for $1. The trade supplied upon liberal terms. B. K. BLISS, Springfield, Mass.

CHOICE VARIETIES of the TOMATO.

Keyes' Early Prolific.—Said to be 20 days earlier than any other Tomato. Plant, dwarf, compact, vigorous, enormously productive. Fruit very solid, and of superior flavor. Packet, 25 cents.

Mappay's Superior.—Fruit of a beautiful deep red color, round, slightly flattened, without crease or wrinkle; flesh almost as solid as beef steak, delicious flavor, average weight, 8 to 12 ounces each, packet, 25 cents.

Tilden's (Harrison's Improved).—A new and truly valuable variety, oval shaped, the color a brilliant scarlet, skin smooth, glossy, and rarely wrinkled, very productive, an excellent market variety, packet, 25 cents.

Extra Early York, the earliest variety, very prolific, of good size, and fine quality, packet, 15 cents.

The Cook's Favorite.—Fruit of medium size, roundish or oval, smooth, of a rich deep color, fine flavor, very solid and prolific, an excellent market variety, pkt, 15c.

Mammoth Chihuahua, often weighs 2 and 3 lbs. 25c.

Also, the following varieties at 10 cents per packet:

Early Apple; Pear Shaped; Yellow Plum; Red and Yellow Cherry; Fejee Island; New White; Large Yellow; Strawberry; New Erect French; Lester's Perfected.

SEED POTATOES.

New English varieties not before offered in this Country.

Patterson's Celebrated Seedlings.

These have acquired a notoriety in England, not surpassed by Goodrich Seedlings of this country. We have selected the following from many varieties received, and tested the past year, and can confidently recommend them:

PATTERSON'S REGENT; SEEDLING ROCK; FORFARSHIRE RED; IRISH BLUE; SCOTCH BLUE; KING OF THE POTATOES; PRINCE OF WALES; BERRY BLUE, PAT'NS BLUE.

A writer in the "London Gardener's Chronicle," after describing his success with the above varieties, closes with the following remarks: "As to the quality of the above varieties, we are in a position to speak from experience, and we can only say that we have never tasted any potatoes equal to them. They contain an extraordinary amount of farinaceous matter, are pure white inside, and almost as solid as bread."

As our stock of the above is very small, we can only offer them in sample packages of **One Pound Each, which will be sent by Mail upon receipt of One Dollar.**

One package each of the nine new varieties will be mailed post-paid upon receipt of *Seven Dollars.*

	Peck.	Bush.	Bbl.
EARLY RESEC, or Boston Market	$2.75	$4.00	$5.00
EARLY GOODRICH	1.00	3.00	7.00
EARLY STEVENS	[illegible]	2.00	5.00
EARLY SOVEREIGN	1.00	2.50	6.00
HARISON	1.50	5.00	12.50
CALICO	1.00	2.50	5.00
GLEASON	1.00	2.50	5.50
CUZCO	.75	2.00	5.00
NEW WHITE PEACH BLOW	.75	2.00	6.00
DELMAHOY	.75	2.50	8.00
GARNET CHILI	.75	2.00	5.00

Upon receipt of $1.00, we will mail post-paid, a four pound package of either of the above 11 varieties, to any address in the Union—4 packages for $3.00.—*No less than $1 worth, nor more than one variety in a package, will be sent by mail.* Our descriptive cultural Catalogue of Potatoes mailed to all applicants.

Collections of Kitchen Garden Seeds.

A COMPLETE ASSORTMENT OF VEGETABLE SEEDS FOR ONE YEAR'S SUPPLY, FOR A LARGE OR SMALL GARDEN.

The following Collections are made up in the most liberal manner, care being taken to give a sufficient quantity of all the finest varieties and most useful sorts of Vegetables required in the Kitchen Garden.

Assortment No. 5,	contains 55	varieties	$3.00
" No. 6,	" 33	"	2.00
" No. 7,	" 15	"	1.00

The above are prepared expressly for sending by mail, and will be sent post-paid, upon receipt of prices annexed.

Larger Collections which can be safely sent by express to any part of the country, as follows:

No. 1, $20.00; No. 2, $15.00; No. 3, $10.00; No. 4, $5.00.

For a List of the contents of each Collection, see Catalogue pages 85 and 86.

Connecticut Seed Leaf Tobacco Seed.

Be Sure and Get the Best.

A superior lot raised expressly for the subscriber by one of the most successful cultivators in the Valley of the Connecticut.—Packets with *full directions for culture, curing, packing, etc.,* will be mailed, post-paid, to all applicants at the following rates: 1 ounce, 25 cents; 4 ounces, $1; 1 lb., $1.50.

Seeds for the Farm & Garden.

	per oz.	per lb.
BEETS—Early Bassano, New Rough Skinned	$0.15	$1.00
Early Blood Turnip, Orange, Long Blood	15	80
Long Red, Yellow Globe Mangel, White Sugar	10	75
CABBAGE—Early York, Large York, Battersea	25	2.50
French Sugar Loaf, Red Dutch, Wakefield	35	4.00
Premium Flat Dutch, Fr. Ox Heart, Drumhead, Stone Mason, Drumhead Savoy, Winningstadt	40	5.00
True Jersey Wakefield, Imp'd American Savoy, Little Pixie, New Dw'f Ulm, Large Brunswick	50	6.00
Marblehead Mammoth, enormous heads, pkt.	25	
CAULIFLOWER—Half Early Paris, sure to head	1.25	15.00
Early Dutch, London, Asiatic, Walcheren	75	8.00
Carter's Mammoth, Lenormands, Early Erfurt, pkt	25	
CELERY—White Solid, Crystal White, Red Solid	35	3.00
New Dw'f White, Mammoth Red, Nonsuch	40	4.00
Hood's Dw'f Purple, Incomparable Crimson, pkt.	25	
CARROT—Bliss' Imp'd Long Orange, ex. deep col.	20	1.50
Fr. Long Orange, White Belgian, Altringham	15	1.25
Early Horn, Extra Early Short	20	1.50
CUCUMBER—Gen. Grant, 24 to 30 inches in length,	pkt.	25
Extra Early Russian, Long Green Prickly	25	2.00
Early Frame, White Spine, Short Green	15	1.25
CORN—Crosby's Ex. Early Sugar or Boston Market,	pkt.	25
Darling's, Red Cob, Evergreen, Mammoth, qt.	50	
Tuscarora, Early Burlington, Smith's White, qt.	30	
EGG PLANT—Improved N. Y. Purple, very large	75	
White, Striped Guadeloupe, Scarlet Fruited, pkt	10	
KOHL RABI—Early White and Purple Vienna	40	4.00
LETTUCE—Curled Silesia, Butter, Cabbage	25	3.00
Large India (extra fine), White and Green Cos	40	4.00
Perpignan, a new German sort, stands a long time without running to seed, fine solid head, pkt.	15	
MUSKMELON—Green Citron, Nutmeg, Large Yellow,	15	1.25
Early White Japan, delicious flavor	50	
WATERMELON—Mountain Sweet, Black Spanish	15	1.50
PARSNIP—Long Smooth White, Hollow Crown	15	80
Student, improved from the wild variety	20	1.50
PEAS—Carter's First Crop, Little Gem, pkt	15	qt. 1.00
Dan'l O'Rourke, ex. early, Champion of England,	qt.	50
Tom Thumb, grows 8 inches high, very early	qt.	75
Vilmorin's New Edible Podded, Drew's New Dw'f, Brown's Dw'f Marrow, Laxton's Prolific	pkt.	15
PEPPERS—Large Sweet Mountain, Sweet Spanish	50	5.00
RADISH—New French Breakfast, fine and crisp	25	2.50
Fr. Olive Shaped, Scarlet Turnip, Long Scarlet	15	1.25
Raphanus caudatus, a great novelty, per seed	50	
Madras Edible Pod, fine for pickles, pkt	15	
SALSIFY, or Vegetable Oysters, very fine	20	1.75
SPINACH—Round, Prickly, Flanders, Lettuce	10	75
SQUASH—Early Summer Crookneck, Scallop,	10	1.00
Boston Marrow (true), Yokohama, Turban, pkt.	15	
Hubbard (true), Canada Crookneck (true)	20	2.00
TURNIP—Early Flat Dutch, Red Top, Yellow Globe, Cow Horn, Sweet German, Long White French	10	1.00
RUTA BAGA—Purple Top, Laing's, Dale's Hybrid,	10	75
Sutton's Champion, a superb variety, pkt.	25	
Waite's Eclipse Purple Top Yellow Hybrid	15	75

For a more full and complete list of Seeds, with directions for culture, see our Catalogue and "Guide to the Flower and Kitchen Garden."

New Crop Onion Seed.

Prices for larger quantities upon application.

	per oz.	¼ lb.	per lb.
Large Red Wethersfield	15c.	45c.	$1.50
Early Red "	15c.	45c.	1.50
Yellow Danvers	15c.	50c.	1.50
Large Yellow Dutch	15c.	50c.	1.50
White Portugal	25c.	65c.	2.00
Potato Onion Sets, per quart			60

CHICORY SEED.—The great substitute for Coffee. Packets containing 1 ounce, 15 cents; 4 ounces, 40 cents; 1 pound, $1, by mail post-paid, with directions for culture.

A NEW FORAGE PLANT.

Bromus Schraderi.—A new forage plant from Australia, particularly recommended for resisting the drouth better than any other variety, and will thrive on any soil except where there is superabundance of moisture, yields two good crops in a season, and is much liked by cattle, who will walk over everything else to reach it, and will eat it down as close as they can bite. Trial packets, 25 cts. Per pound, $1.25.

GIANT ASPARAGUS ROOTS BY MAIL.

Extra, strong, one year old Roots, carefully packed, and mailed, post-paid, at $1.25 per 100; $5.00 for 500; $10.50 per 1,000.

We earnestly request our correspondents to give their *Name, Post-office Address, County* and *State* distinctly written in full. All orders should be addressed as follows:

B. K. BLISS, Springfield, Massachusetts.

Be particular and name the *State in full,* as there is a Springfield in almost every State in the Union.

Advertisements, to be sure of insertion, must be received BEFORE the 5th of the preceding month.

TERMS—(cash before insertion):
Ordinary Pages, $1.50 *per line. Open Pages*—$2 *per line. Business Notices*—$2.50 per line of space, each insertion.

THE PATENT YANKEE BLADE.

STATE and COUNTY RIGHTS for Sale.

It is the best **Seam Ripper** ever invented.
Also, a complete **Eraser**, for the Desk.
Also, a neat **Paper Cutter.**
Also, a first-rate **Letter Opener.**
Also, a capital **Nail Cleaner and Trimmer.**
Also, useful for many other purposes.

It is well recommended by American Agriculturist, N. Y. Tribune, Independent, Moore's Demorest, and hundreds more.

Thousands are in use all over the country, giving general satisfaction, and one is wanted in every family. Price, $1 for 3, sent by mail, post-paid. Liberal discount by the quantity.

In response to many applications I now offer State and County Rights for sale on very reasonable terms. Address W. A. FITCH, 151 Nassau-street, New York.

SOUTHWEST PACIFIC RAILROAD CO.

Seven Per Cent. FIRST MORTGAGE BONDS.

$2,000,000 IN COUPON BONDS OF $1,000 EACH.

TWENTY YEARS TO RUN.

Principal and Interest Guaranteed by the Atlantic and Pacific Railroad Co.,

And secured by property valued at $7,500,000, consisting of 90 miles of completed road and 250,000 acres of rich agricultural and mineral lands on the line of the road. (By a provision of the mortgage, when lands are sold to the amount of $10,000, it is to constitute a fund for the redemption of a like amount of bonds, which are also received by the Company at PAR in payment for land.) This land is now being disposed of at rates of from $3 to $10 per acre.

The climate is remarkably salubrious, and the mean temperature the same as in Virginia. The winters last about six weeks, and stock can be kept on the range the year through. For particulars respecting lands address Colonel A. ALBERT, Land Agent at St. Louis, Mo.

This Company has recently been merged with the Atlantic and Pacific Railroad Co., having a land grant of 53 millions of acres, thereby adding to the fullest to the security of these Bonds.

The road of the latter Company, when completed, will form a direct and continuous railway from St. Louis to San Francisco, shorter by 500 miles from New York to the Pacific than by any other route.

Of the present issue of Bonds, a limited amount is now offered for sale at the low rate of 80 per cent., subject to advance at the option of the Company.

For further particulars apply to

WARD & CO., 54 Wall Street, *NEW YORK.*

No One Need Fear Pickpockets.

Hickman's Safety Pocket is a sure preventive against their depredations. $1,000 will be given to any one who will successfully cut, pick or in any way purloin the contents of one. Can be attached to any garment in two minutes, are *neatly made, very light, and no inconvenience whatever.* Money, watches and other valuables can be secured in them, while you can go in to any crowd with entire safety. *Remember, they can no more rob you than they can take the coat off your back.*

PRICES: Sent by mail, post-paid, Large Size, $2.50; Small Size, $2.00. When sent by express, and receiver paying charges, 50 cents will be deducted from each size.

LIBERAL TERMS TO DEALERS AND CANVASSERS. This Pocket is a NECESSITY, No HUMBUG and MUST TAKE.

T. S. LAMBORN, Marshalton, Chester Co., Pa.

Patent Self-Closing Pocket Books, Pocket Memorandums and Diaries; in which a Steel Spring supersedes Elastic Bands, Tucks or Straps. A great improvement. For sale everywhere.

LAWYERS SHOULD READ THE PHRENOLOGICAL JOURNAL, that they may read the character of clients and culprits. $2 a year.

KNOX'S NURSERY AT YOUR DOOR.—A Liberal Offer. See Advertisement on page 117.

GARDENING FOR PROFIT.

A Work, instructive alike to the Amateur or Market Gardener, detailing the practical experience of nearly 20 years' Gardening for the New York Market,

By PETER HENDERSON,
(of HENDERSON & FLEMING.)

Price, $1.50, by mail pre-paid.

Or with our New Illustrated Seed and Plant Catalogues for 1867, $1.75.

HENDERSON & FLEMING,
Seedsmen and Market Gardeners,
67 Nassau-st., New York.

All the Nurseries in One.

37 Park Row, N. Y. City.

The Cheapest in the Market. Among which is the following first class stock:

STANDARD APPLE .... each..	5 to 8	cents.
DWARF and STANDARD PEARS..	25	"
do. do. CHERRIES..	25 to 30	"
STANDARD PLUMS	19	"
do. PEACHES........	9 to 11	"
CLINTON GRAPE........	4	"
CATAWBA........	5	"
CONCORD........	8	"
DELAWARE........	15	"
IONA........	35	"
ISRAELLA........	50	"
ADIRONDAC........	80	"
DOOLITTLE RASPBERRY........	1½	"
EARLY WILSON BLACKBERRY..	70	"
WILSON'S ALBANY STRAWBERRY..	$3 p.	1000
AGRICULTURIST........	$5 p.	1000
SHADE TREES, 6 to 12 feet........	15 to 25	cents.
ARBOR VITÆ, 5 to 6 feet........	20	"
NORWAY SPRUCE, 1 to 2 feet........	8	"
DECIDUOUS SHRUBS........	5 to 10	"
ROSES........	5 to 30	"
BEDDING PLANTS........	4	"

The above prices are for orders of one hundred dollars and over, to which my commission of ten per cent. is added.

Orders under $100 at the regular prices

For particulars send stamp for price list.

L. L. WHITLOCK,
37 Park Row, N. Y.

THE HERALD OF HEALTH JOURNAL OF PHYSICAL CULTURE.

(FOR A FULL PROSPECTUS AND PREMIUMS OF THIS MAGAZINE, SEE AGRICULTURIST FOR FEB., p. 74.)

The March Number contains:

Length of Days,
BY REV. H. W. BELLOWS.
Permanent Results in Life,
BY HENRY WARD BEECHER.
The Value of Fruit as Food,
BY F. R. ELLIOT.
Letters to Ladies,
BY MRS. R. B. GLEASON, M. D.
Vitality, its Phenomena,
BY GEO. F. TAYLOR, M. D.
Weak Lungs and How to Make them Strong.

Alcoholic Medication, How to Bathe, Home Treatment, Liver Complaint, Longevity, Healthy Cookery, and 50 other articles.

No other Magazine attempts to popularize the Science of Physiology and make it Applicable to PHYSICAL and MENTAL IMPROVEMENT. If it is important to understand politics, agriculture, science, how much more to know ourselves.

$2.00 a Year. One Number, 20 Cents.

MILLER, WOOD & CO.,
15 Laight-street, New York.

WE WANT AN AGENT IN EVERY COUNTY TO SELL OUR POPULAR SUBSCRIPTION BOOKS

They are the most popular books now published, and many Agents are making $10 to $20 a day. Send for Circulars, giving full particulars, to RICHARDSON & CO., Publishers, 540 Broadway, New York.

AMERICAN REIN HOLDER.

Last and Greatest Novelty.

SAVES LIVES, LIMBS AND ACCIDENTS.
SIMPLE, CHEAP, DURABLE AND ORNAMENTAL.
Great Inducement to Agents.
They are making from $100 to $200 per month.
Write for Descriptive Circular and Terms to
AMERICAN REIN HOLDER CO., Binghamton, N. Y.

no **O** garden **K**omplete **B** without **B**it.

DOTY'S Clothes Washer,

using boiling-hot suds, saves three-fourths the labor and time—takes out all the dirt—no sore hands—no fœtid air—no injury to the clothes.

"It really merits all the good that can be said of it."—*Rural New Yorker.*

"Doty's Washer, *the best.*"—*Orange Judd.* (See Premium List.)

"Would not be parted with under any consideration."—*Solon Robinson.*

"Could not be persuaded to do without it."—*Rev. Bishop Scott.*

The Universal Clothes Wringer, WITH COG-WHEELS,

wrings clothes almost dry, without injury to the most delicate garments, and never gets tired or out of order.

This wringer is so well known, and so unanimously acknowledged to be *the best*, that recommendations are not quoted.

On receipt of the price from places where no one is selling, we will send one Washer and one Wringer, either or both, free of freight charges. Family Size Washer, $14; No. 1½ Wringer, $10; No. 2 Wringer, $8.50.

☞ Exclusive right of sale given to the first responsible applicant from each town.

Send for illustrated circulars, giving wholesale and retail terms.

R. C. BROWNING, General Agent,
No. 32 Cortlandt-st., New York,
(Opposite Merchants' Hotel.)

SOMETHING NEW.

Apple Catsup! Apple Catsup!

This new condiment is prepared from the pulp of the Apple, together with Spices and Vinegar. All of the materials are of the best quality, and manipulated with the greatest care in its production, combining in its manifold uses, rendering it *par excellence* in value to every housekeeper. In point of piquancy and flavor for giving zest and relish to food, and for healthfulness and aperitive value it is not excelled by anything of the kind made, adding another economic value to that king of all fruit, the Apple. This Catsup is made heavy and rich, and can be reduced, by adding vinegar or wine, to any quality desired. It can be used for flavoring Soups and Gravies, Oysters, Clams, Fish, Meat, &c. PRICE FIFTY CENTS PER BOTTLE. For sale by SAMUEL T. THORBURN, 46 Hudson-st., Albany, N. Y.

LASH'S WASHER AND WRINGER.

Best and Cheapest.

See page 73 of Feb. No. of *Agriculturist.*

J. S. LASH & CO.,
727 Market-st., Philadelphia.

CANE SEED.

Regular Sorgo, or the original Chinese Cane.

Liberian, a new and a very popular variety. Does not blow down.

Oomseeana—Sometimes called the *Otaheitan*. Best for Sugar.

Neeazana, or White Imphee, a short stout cane, stands up well and is generally liked.

The Cane from which the above Seed was produced, was grown and the Seed harvested and cured under our immediate observation. The Seed is all true to the varieties designated, and absolutely free from admixture with base and worthless Canes.

The Cane from which the seed was produced yielded from two to three hundred gallons of Syrup per acre.

Send for Circular.

BLYMYER, DAY & CO., Mansfield, O.

THE AMERICAN NATURALIST; A Popular, Illustrated, Monthly Magazine of Natural History.—Published by the Essex Institute.

Contents of the first number (March, 1867):—Introductory; The Land Snails of New England, (with a plate); The Volcano of Kilauea, Hawaiian Islands, in 1864-5, (with a plate); The Fossil Reptiles of New Jersey; The American Silk Worm, (with Illustrations); Winter Notes of an Ornithologist; Reports of the Meetings of Scientific Societies; Natural History Miscellany; Reviews; Natural History Calendar, Answers to Correspondents; Glossary for the Number.

TERMS: $3 per year. Clubs supplied at liberal rates. Single copies, 35 cents.

EDITORS: ALPHEUS S. PACKARD, Jr., in connection with EDWARD S. MORSE, ALPHEUS HYATT, and FREDERIC W. PUTNAM. ☞ For Prospectus, etc., address

A. S. PACKARD, Jr., Salem, Mass.

The list of contributors embraces the best scientific talent in the country.

EDITORS SHOULD READ THE PHRENOLOGICAL JOURNAL and learn how to make more perfect newspapers. Only $2 a year.

BEDDING PLANTS, &C., BY MAIL.

Strong and healthy Plants of the following varieties will be securely packed and mailed, post-paid, to any address in the United States, upon receipt of the price affixed.—*Selection of varieties to be left with us.* When a less number than the set unit specified is ordered, an additional charge will be made at the rate of 50 cents per dozen.

12 Hardy Carnations and Picotees, assorted	$2.75		
12 Monthly " " "	3.00		
12 Florists' Pinks...ass'd.	$2.50	12 Fuchsias, assorted	2.00
12 Scarlet Geraniums, "	2.25	12 Heliotropes, "	2.00
12 Lantanas, "	2.00	12 Petunias, "	2.00
12 Phloxes, "	2.00	12 Pansies, "	2.00
6 Salvias, "	1.25	12 Verbenas, "	1.50
12 Dahlias (pot roots), "	2.50	6 Pot Roses, "	2.00
6 H. P. Roses, "	2.50	6 Feverfews	1.25
3 Tritomas, "	1.50	1 Daphne Cneorum	50
1 Lilium Auratum	5.00	3 Japan Lilies (3 var.)	1.50
12 Gladiolus, assorted	2.00	12 Italian Tuberoses	2.00
4 Ornamental Foliage Plants, distinct	1.25		
12 Chrysanthemums, large Flowering	2.50		
12 " Pomponed	2.50		

D. K. BLISS, Springfield, Mass.

CHINESE SUGAR CANE.

Imported Seed.

In consequence of so much of the seed of this valuable plant that is raised in this country being deteriorated by hybridization with other varieties, we have just imported a supply from Messrs. Vilmorin & Co., of Paris, grown from the *original stock*, which may be relied upon as *perfectly pure.* 4 ounces, 25 cents; 8 ounces, 40 cents; one lb., 75 cents.

D. K. BLISS, Springfield, Mass.

The Best and most Hardy Hedge Plant.

HONEY LOCUST, OR THREE THORNED ACACIA.

Fresh Seed with directions for culture, will be mailed to any address, at the following prices: 1 oz., 15 cents; 4 ozs., 50 cents; 1 pound, $1.50. Prices in larger quantities will be given upon application. B. K. BLISS, Springfield, Mass.

Grape Vines at Reduced Prices.

Strong one year old plants.

	Each.	Doz.	Hundred.
Iona	75	$7.50	$50.00
Delaware	40	4.00	25.00
Diana	40	4.00	25.00
Concord	25	2.50	15.00

One each of the following varieties post-paid, per mail, upon receipt of $1.00.

Iona, Israella, Delaware, Diana, Concord, Creveling, Union Village. D. K. BLISS, Springfield, Mass.

THE IONA AND ISRAELLA GRAPES.

Surpass all others in excellence and value for every purpose.

The ISRAELLA, although BEST and EARLIEST of all BLACK GRAPES of good size, is also one of the very best for late keeping. The berries do not fall from the bunch when ripe—do not crack, and bear carriage very long distances without injury.

The IONA, also VERY EARLY, has all of the delicacy, purity and refinement in flavor, uniform tenderness of flesh and transparent beauty, that characterize the best European varieties, and surpasses them in RICH VINOUS SPIRIT, while in HARDINESS and CONSTANCY of PRODUCTION and PERFECTION of RIPENING, it is unequalled among our most enduring natives.

For a full account of the characteristics of these seedlings, with their origin and history, see Pamphlet with engravings, representing the vines in bearing, which contains other important matter concerning grapes. It is sent with Price List and Club propositions for a two-cent stamp.

A beautiful colored representation of a bunch of the Iona, with branch and leaf, will be sent for $1.50.

The same will be sent to agents of clubs for $1.00. Plain Lithographs of the same twenty cents. Club propositions and price lists sent with Pamphlet, when requested, without charge.

The "Manual of the Vine" is sent for 50 cents. It contains about 150 engravings, and is intended to be the most practical, thorough and comprehensive treatise on the vine in the language. It contains an important chapter on "Ripening, Taste, and Propagation," with many engravings. "I tell every one it is the only book to be safely trusted in all matters belonging to grapes."—JOHN E. MOTTIER.

"I have made failures in following the directions of others, but never in following the directions of the 'Manual.'"

C. I. MAY.

All interested in grapes are invited to visit Iona, with assurance that endeavors will be made to render the visit pleasant and profitable. Inspection of the plants convinces every one not only of their surpassing quality, but of their unequaled cheapness, also six sample vines sent free by mail to any applicant at dozen prices. See advertisement on page 30, January No.

C. W. GRANT, Iona,
(near Peekskill,) Westchester Co., N. Y.

THE "THREE WARRANTS."—Please read my advertisement headed "Farmers and Gardeners."
JAMES J. H. GREGORY, Marblehead, Mass.

CONTINUAL LEVER and Screw Press, with Grinder attached, for Pressing Cheese, Wine, Cider and Lard, &c. ..d ires WILLIAM C. REA. Pleasant Run, New Jersey.

New and Rare Vegetables.

I present to the Public my Annual List of New and Rare Seed for 1867, many of which I send out the first time this season.

MARBLEHEAD MAMMOTH DRUMHEAD CABBAGE.—(*The largest Cabbage in the world. Weighs from thirty to sixty pounds to the head, and is tender and sweet. No cabbage does so well in the South as this.*) CANNON BALL CABBAGE.—(*About as round and hard as a cannon ball. An early sort, and the hardest heading of all Cabbage.*) STONE MASON CABBAGE.—(*Standard variety of Winter Drumhead Cabbage in Boston market. Under good cultivation every plant on an acre will make a large and hard head. It is remarkably tender and sweet. In half-ounce packages.*) LENORMAND'S MAMMOTH CAULIFLOWER.—(*A new variety, the largest of all the Cauliflower family. Very reliable for heading.*) VERY EARLY ERFURT CAULIFLOWER.—(*New, remarkably early, and fine for hot-beds.*) NEW YORK IMPROVED EXTRA LARGE PURPLE EGG PLANT.—(*This grows to a larger size, and is of a richer color than the Common Large Purple Egg Plant.*) STRIPED GAUDELOUPE EGG PLANT.—(*An elegant variety for the table. The stripings of white, purple and yellow give it a magnificent appearance.*) ORNAMENTAL KALE.—(*The great variety in color, and structure of the leaves, make them elegant ornaments for the flower garden and among shrubbery.*) MAMMOTH SWEET CORN.—(*The largest of all Sweet Corn. Sweet, and excellent for the table. The ears weigh, as gathered, from two to three pounds each.*) MAMMOTH FRENCH SQUASH.—(*Sometimes grown to weigh over two hundred pounds. They grow well-proportioned, and are finely colored.*) VEGETABLE CATERPILLARS.—(*Vegetable curiosities, the seed-vessels resembling caterpillars.*) VEGETABLE SNAILS.—(*A French Oddity, the seed vessels of which resemble snails.*) VEGETABLE WORMS.—(*Another curious vegetable product.*) SNAKE CUCUMBER.—(*A very long variety which grows coiled up, having the appearance of a large snake.*)

LAXTON'S PROLIFIC EARLY LONG POD PEA.—(*A new and quite distinct variety. Many of the pods contain from ten to twelve Peas each.*) DWARF INDIAN CHIEF BEAN.—(*Those who have grown the Pole Indian Chief will be pleased to find a bush variety of this fine String Bean.*) GIANT WAX BEAN.—(*A new Pole Bean, being an improvement on the Indian Chief, it being a larger and longer Podded Bean than that choice variety. The Wax Beans (so called because the pods are of a wax color,) are the best of all String Beans.*) NORBITON'S GIANT CUCUMBER.—(*A new English variety, the finest, longest, and most prolific Cucumber in cultivation.*) WARD'S NECTAR MELON.—(*When compared with all other sorts, this has been awarded the palm as the best of all green-fleshed Melons.*)

Each of the above sent to any part of the United States, and warranted to reach the purchaser, at twenty-five cents per package.

AMERICAN TURBAN SQUASH.—(*The dryest, finest grained, and best flavored of all Fall Squashes. The packages contain about fifty seed.*) HUBBARD SQUASH.—(*I was the original introducer of this, and the seed is TRUE.*) YOKOHAMA SQUASH.—(*A new variety from Japan; very prolific. The quality resembles a fine Crookneck, but is much superior.*) BOSTON MARROW SQUASH.—(*My variety took the premium for purity at the Annual Fair of the Massachusetts Horticultural Society in 1866.*) PARA SQUASH.—(*A bush Squash from South America, which can be kept into winter. Oblong in shape, of good size, fine-grained, and excellent quality; far superior to any standard variety of bush Squash.*) IMPROVED GREEN GLOBE SAVOY CABBAGE.—(*For family use, the Savoys are the richest of all Cabbages. The heads of this variety are large, hard, and of most excellent quality, the stumps short. Remarkably reliable for heading.*) PANCALIER SAVOY.—(*The French consider this the earliest Cabbage grown.*) SMALL EARLY ULM SAVOY.—(*Very early and reliable.*) BURNELL'S KING OF THE DWARFS.—(*In England this is considered the earliest of Cabbages. Very dwarf, fine quality, and sweet.*) LARGE BRUNSWICK SHORT STEM.—(*A very large and very early Drumhead, much sought for by market gardeners.*) LITTLE PIXIE CABBAGE.—(*An early dwarf; stump, short; heads, pointed, and very hard, fine quality, and very sweet.*) TILDEN'S NEW TOMATO.—(*Large, round or oblong; color, rich scarlet; vines, dwarf, and very productive.*) EARLY YORK TOMATO.—(*Very early, and remarkably prolific; has yielded at the rate of over one thousand bushels per acre. Fruit of good market size; flat, round shape; quality, excellent.*) COOK'S FAVORITE TOMATO.—(*A large, apple-shaped variety; very prolific; quality, superior; decidedly the best of the apple-shaped Tomatoes.*) MAMMOTH CHIHUAHUA TOMATO.—(*Enormously large, weighing from two to three pounds. Some single specimens will heap a quart measure.*) NEW MEXICAN TOMATO.—(*Very large, round Tomato; a great bearer; resembles, in color, Lester's Perfected, but an improvement on it, in always being round.*) TREE TOMATO.—(*A French variety; grows erect in the form of a bush.*) MCLEAN'S ADVANCER PEA.—(*A new English wrinkled Pea. A decided improvement on the Champion of England; bears well, with Peas equally sweet; is much larger, and does not run nearly as high.*) MCLEAN'S LITTLE GEM.—(*A new dwarf wrinkled Pea; grows about one foot high, very early, only a few days later than the Dan O'Rourke; a decided acquisition.*) VILMORIN'S NEW, WRINKLED, EDIBLE PODDED PEA.—(*The first wrinkled sort yet found, the pods of which can be eaten.*) CARTER'S FIRST CROP.—(*A new English Pea, sent out as the earliest of all varieties.*) HAIR'S DWARF MAMMOTH.—(*A wrinkled Pea, larger than Champion of England, growing only half its hight; quality, fully equal to the Champion.*) TOM THUMB PEA.—(*As early as Dan O'Rourke, grows ten inches high, and is remarkably prolific.*) DREW'S NEW DWARF PEA.—(*Peas, very large, egg-shaped; each plant forms quite a bush. Peas should be planted about a foot apart. Early, dwarf, and very prolific.*) BROWN'S NEW DWARF MARROWFAT.—(*Warranted to be the earliest and most dwarf Marrowfat Pea grown. A capital Pea for market gardeners.*) FORTY DAYS' CORN.—(*Earlier than any Sweet Corn. Desirable as an early sort.*) BATES' EXTRA EARLY SWEET CORN.—(*A variety of wrinkled kernaled Sugar Corn; earlier than Darling's Early, and excellent for table use.*) MAMMOTH FLINT CORN.—(*Ears grow sixteen inches long; stalks very tall and stout, and matures as far North as Central New England.*) CROSBY'S EARLY.—(*The earliest of all twelve rowed Sweet Corn. The Massachusetts Horticultural Society offered special premiums for this new Corn at their last Annual Fair. It is of good size for market, and a decided acquisition.*) MEXICAN SWEET CORN.—(*I still find this to be the sweetest and most tender of all varieties of Sweet Corn. Nothing can equal it for the table.*) GOLDEN SWEET CORN.—(*A Sweet Corn of golden color; early, of good size, and excellent quality for the table; flavor, fine, and distinct from any other variety.*) YARD LONG BEAN.—(*A curious Bean; pods growing over two feet long; foliage, a rich, dark, glossy green.*) CONCORD BEAN.—(*This new Bean is probably the earliest Pole Bean grown; very prolific, and of excellent quality, either as a string or shell Bean.*) FEJEE BEAN.—(*A new bush Bean; the earliest and hardiest of all beans; very prolific and worthy of general cultivation.*) INTERMEDIATE HORTICULTURAL BEAN.—(*An excellent bush Bean for marketmen. Pods of the same rich color as the Pole Horticultural.*) CALIFORNIA BEAN.—(*A very early, large, flat Pole Bean; excellent, either green or baked.*) MOTTLED CRANBERRY.—(*An improvement in health, vigor, and productiveness on the old-fashioned Cranberry. Few Pole Beans will yield equal to this. Pods, long, large, and well filled.*) SIMON'S EARLY BEET.—(*A new, early sort, well shaped; as early as Bassano, and darker.*) NEW TURNIP BEET.—(*Round, flat-shaped, very early, and very nice.*) CASTLENANDARY BEET.—(*A famous French variety; flesh, a deep purple color, very tender and sweet.*) CRAPAUDINE BEET.—(*Rough skinned; color, very dark purple. Esteemed by the French as the best of all Beets for table use.*) WHYTE'S VERY D... RED BEET.—(*Medium size, dark color, very sweet, and excellent for table use.*) YELLOW OVOID MANGEL WURTZEL.—(*For cattle. Of seventeen varieties tested, the crop of this exceeded all.*) EARLY CRACKER ONION.—(*Earliest of all the yellow sort; quality, very delicate and sweet.*) HOOD'S NEW DWARF IMPERIAL PURPLE CELERY.—(*A choice new English variety.*) TURNER'S INCOMPARABLE DWARF WHITE CELERY.—(*A first class English variety.*) READ'S MATCHLESS CELERY.—(*A premium English variety, fine, solid and red.*) BOSTON MARKET CELERY.—(*True. This is the short, compact, solid variety, so often admired by strangers in the markets of Boston.*) TRUE BOSTON CURLED LETTUCE.—(*The most elegant of all the Lettuce family, grows in the form of a Rosette.*) WHEELER'S TOM THUMB LETTUCE.—(*A choice new variety, in high favor with those who have grown it.*) PERPIGNAN LETTUCE.—(*This is an excellent Lettuce for standing the summer heat. Heads, compact, attaining to seven inches in diameter.*) NEAPOLITAN CABBAGE LETTUCE.—(*One of the finest Cabbage Lettuces yet introduced.*) SIX VARIETIES OF CABBAGE LETTUCE.—(*Six of the choicest varieties in one package.*) ORANGE WATERMELON.—(*When fully ripe the skin will peel off like an Orange.*) ALLEN'S SUPERB MUSK MELON.—(*Quality, superior; by some called the "Queen of Melons."*) LARGE PERSIAN MUSK MELON.—(*A fine, large variety.*) DWARF BROOM CORN.—(*This is thought to make a better brush than the common tall sorts.*) CHUFAS, OR GROUND ALMONDS.—(*These taste very much like a Cocoanut; are very prolific, yielding 100 to 1.*) ORNAMENTAL GOURDS.—(*Many varieties in one package.*) NEW JERSEY HYBRID CUCUMBER.—(*A remarkably long variety; an improvement on the White Spined.*) IMPROVED LONG GREEN CUCUMBER.—(*This is the longest of all the Long Greens.*) CHINESE SCARLET EGG PLANT.—(*Of magnificent scarlet color, and highly ornamental.*) MAMMOTH MILLET.—(*Extra tall; seed heads much larger than any other variety.*) SURRY WHITE WHEAT.—(*A new English Winter Wheat, highly recommended for poor soils, remarkably free from blight and rust.*) OTAHEITIAN SUGAR CANE.—(*This yields more Sugar than any other variety of Sugar Cane grown in the North.*)

Any of the above varieties will be forwarded, post-paid, and warranted to reach the purchaser at fifteen cents each.

EARLY SEBEC POTATOES.—(*Coming rapidly into favor in Boston and vicinity as a first class early market Potato. Large size, excellent quality, and remarkably productive.*) EARLY GOODRICH.—(*True.*) SHAKER'S FANCY.—(*A new variety of white-fleshed Potatoes, considered as early as Early Goodrich, yielding equally well, and rapidly gaining favor in Pennsylvania. This and the Early Sebec are of better shape for market purposes than the Early Goodrich.*

Four pound packages of either of these varieties sent to any address, warranted to reach the purchaser, on receipt of one dollar. All orders for Potatoes will be put on file, and be filled as soon as danger from freezing is past.

Catalogues containing over two hundred varieties of warranted Garden Seeds, one hundred and twenty-five of which are of my own growing, sent, gratis, to all applicants.

I warrant three things: 1st. That my seed is genuine. 2d. That your money shall reach me. 3d. That my seed shall reach you. Can the Public ask for anything fairer than this?

JAMES J. H. GREGORY,
Marblehead, Mass.

Flower Seeds in Collections.

The 5 collections that should be sown in every Garden in the country are:

12 Varieties of Finest German Asters for	$1.00
12 " " " Stocks "	1.25
8 " " French Camellia Balsams for	1.25
10 " " Beautiful Phlox Drummondii for	75
6 " " " Portulaca for	40

ALSO COLLECTIONS OF

100 " " Annuals, Biennials and Perennials, for	5.00
50 " " " " "	2.50
20 " " "	1.00
10 " " "	50
20 " " More Rare Annuals,	2.00
10 " " "	1.00
25 " " Choice Green-House Seeds,	4.00
10 " " " " "	2.00
40 " " Hardy Biennials and Perennials,	1.00

ALL STRICTLY OUR OWN SELECTION.

☞ Send for our Flower Seed Catalogue.

J. M. THORBURN & CO.,
15 John-st., New York.

Fort Edward Institute, N. Y.

Sixty dollars for thirteen weeks. Best sustained Boarding Seminary in the State. A few vacancies. Spring term, March 21. Address REV. J. E. KING, D. D.

KNOX'S NURSERY AT YOUR DOOR.—A Liberal Offer. See Advertisement on page 117.

GRAPE VINES AT REDUCED RATES.
PARSONS & CO.

Offer their vines for the Spring at the following very low rates:

DELAWARE	1 year,	No. 1, $20 per 100;	$150 per 1000.
"	"	No. 2, $15 "	$100 " "
"	"	No. 3, $10 "	$70 " "
"	2 years,	No. 1, $25 "	$180 " "
"	"	No. 2, $15 "	$120 " "
IONA	1 year,	No. 1, $35 "	$300 " "
"	"	No. 2, $25 "	$200 " "
"	"	No. 3, $20 "	$130 " "
"	2 years,	No. 1, $100 "	$750 " "
IVES' SEEDLING	1 year,	No. 1, $25 "	$200 " "
NORTON'S VIRGINIA	"	No. 1, $25 "	$150 " "
CONCORD	"	No. 3, $8 "	$60 " "
ISRAELLA	"	No. 1, $40 "	No. 2, $60 per 100.
CREVELING	"	No. 1, $20 "	
DIANA	"	No. 1, $15 "	
ROGERS' 4, 15, 19	"	No. 1, $40 "	

ADIRONDAC, ALLEN'S HYBRID and REBECCA, $30 per 100.

For other Vines, see Retail Catalogue.

Address PARSONS & CO., Flushing, N. Y.

All the vines we offer are grown without bottom heat, from well ripened wood, and in good, deep soil, not injured by extra manuring.

In classifying we make no *extras*. Our No. 1 plants are the largest and best of our stock, and their average quality is not allowed to be diminished by selecting the largest for retailing as *extras*.

It accords neither with our taste nor our principles to assert that our vines have never been approached in quality by those of any other propagators. The vines must speak for themselves, and those who wish to purchase largely are sufficiently wise to accept the evidence of the vines rather than the assertion of the grower. To account for the abundant roots of our plants it is only necessary to say that ours is the *open border culture.*

We have discarded the pot-culture because the roots are thereby inevitably cramped, and in value as far as possible from the model roots of our figure, while the costs of pots and the labor necessary to insure this forced cramping compels the grower to sell at prices so high as to forbid purchase for extensive planting.

We have reduced our prices *very low*, because we deem it more profitable to sell a thousand DELAWARES at 10 cents each, or a thousand IONAS at 20 cents each, than one-third of that quantity at double those rates.

Those who wish to plant many acres cannot afford to buy at the high rates at which some valuable varieties have been hitherto sold, and our large culture demands for its outlet extensive planting. Our plan is thus by low prices to insure large sales.

Our present stock of DELAWARE and IONA remaining from the culture of last year, is about 100,000 plants.

For the excellence of those varieties it is not necessary for us to vouch.

Their surpassing qualities are known to all, and the general opinion of the DELAWARE was well expressed at the late Convention of Fruit Growers, at Rochester, where the Delaware ranked first and the Iona next by large majorities.

Of IVES' SEEDLING, we have remaining only 20,000. The freedom of this variety from rot or mildew, and its very rapid, hardy growth, make it one of the most reliable varieties—one of the few which are absolutely safe.

PARSONS & CO.

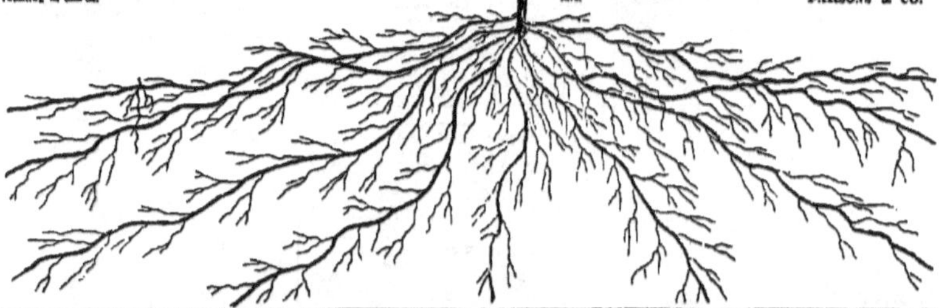

SWEET CORN FOR SEED.

Russell's Improved Sweet Corn is now for Sale

At the Wooden Willow Ware and House Furnishing Store,

NO. 243 STATE-ST., NEW HAVEN, CONN.

This Corn has large ears, fine and delicious flavor, and is three weeks earlier than any other Sweet Corn in the State, of equal size and quality. It needs no recommendation to those who have eaten it. Those who have not, are referred to Hon. James E. English and Hon. John Woodruff of this State. It has brought fifty cents per dozen ears in New Haven the last three years. The greatest trouble has been, I could not raise enough to supply the demand. This year I have thought it best to let the public have the seed, and all those that want can have it, by ordering or calling soon. It will require about forty ears to plant one acre. Those that raise early corn for New York and other cities, will get more than double for their crop, if they plant this corn, as all the markets cannot be supplied this year. I sold in eighteen hundred and sixty-four, two hundred and thirteen dollars worth raised on three quarters of an acre of ground, besides what we ate and gave away. I will send it to any place in the United States for three dollars per dozen, or at the same rate for any number of ears, any way I may be directed, or will send a package or any number of packages, each containing enough to plant about sixty hills, for twenty-five cents per package, by mail postage paid.

All orders addressed to CALVIN RUSSELL, New Haven, Conn., with money enclosed, will be attended to promptly.

CALVIN RUSSELL.

The undersigned, having used in our families the above described corn, do most cheerfully concur in all that is stated as to its good qualities.

JAMES E. ENGLISH.
JOHN WOODRUFF.

New Haven, Feb. 4, 1866.

The undersigned certify that we sold for Calvin Russell what early sweet corn he brought to market in 1866, for fifty cents per dozen, which did'nt half supply the demand, while any other corn in market was selling for less than one half the above price.

SHEFFELE & DASSEHMAN.

BRIDGEMAN'S

ANNUAL DESCRIPTIVE
PRICED CATALOGUE
of
KITCHEN GARDEN
and
AGRICULTURAL SEEDS.
Also his
NEW DESCRIPTIVE CATALOGUE OF
FLOWER SEEDS,

including novelties for 1867, are now ready; and mailed free to all applicants.

ALFRED BRIDGEMAN,
No. 876 Broadway, New York.

Dwarf Pear Trees.

3,000 *Bartletts, Duchesse d' Angoulemes and Louise Bonne de Jerseys*, 3 to 7 *years old*, 4 to 10 *feet high, in bearing condition* at ½ price, to thin out orchards.

WILLIAM Y. BEACH, Wallingford, Conn.

Novelties in Vegetable Seeds.

	⅌ PACKET.
BLACK WAX BEAN BEANS. *Same style of pods as the German Wax Pole, and equal to it in quality, very desirable*	25 cts.
GIANT WAX POLE BEANS. *Pods from 6 to 9 inches long, fine for succotash*	25 cts.
TRIMBLE'S CELEBRATED SUGAR CORN. *The sweetest variety in cultivation*	25 cts.
BLACK PEKIN EGG PLANT. *A great acquisition, fruit round, black and most delicious flavor; the foliage is bronze and very ornamental*	25 cts.
GIANT CASTLE LEEK. *Extra large and solid*	25 cts.
	⅌ QUART.
NEW DWARF WATERLOO PEAS, *growing but 1½ feet high, a very great cropper*	2.00
MCLEAN'S WONDERFUL PEAS. *New wrinkled variety growing 2 feet high*	1.00
MCLEAN'S EPICUREAN PEAS. *Another new wrinkled variety, growing 2 feet high*	1.00
	⅌ PACKET.
NEW WHORTLEBERRY TOMATO. *A new and entirely distinct variety, from California, producing edible fruit of the size, color and general appearance of the Whortleberry, very desirable for pickling and preserving*	25 cts.
ALSO	
	⅌ QUART.
THE CELEBRATED NAPOLEAN PEAS. *The finest dwarf wrinkled marrow variety in cultivation, growing 3 feet high*	75 cts.

All of the above by mail on receipt of the amount annexed.

☞ Send for our Vegetable Seed Catalogue.

J. M. THORBURN & CO.,
15 John Street, New York.

O. K. B. B.

The quality of the KITTATINNY is thus expressed by the Editor of the N. Y. World on receipt of some fruit. "We confess to being skeptical when told a better blackberry than the Lawton had been found. * * But justice compels us to acknowledge that never before have we tasted such Blackberries as those sent us by Mr. Williams. In the first place, the berries are large, deep colored, and firm in flesh, even when fully ripe—good marketing qualities. Second, they are sweet, juicy, melting in the mouth, more like a new Pine Strawberry than like a Blackberry, and are of excellent flavor." The quality of my plants is so much superior to those usually sent out, even at higher prices, as to elicit universal commendation. For the above article in full and other testimonials see my New Catalogue, now ready, for 2 stamps. Order early as the stock is very limited.

Address E. WILLIAMS, Montclair, N. J.

SING SING GRAPE VINES.
The Best in the Market.

All my large stock of No. 1 and No. 2, Iona and Israella Vines is sold, except a small quantity I have reserved to use in filling retail orders.

As has been the case every season, the demand *for really good vines*, has been beyond my ability to supply. That my vines sell so readily at *full rates*, argues well that the *quality* of vines offered will hereafter have much to do with their sale. Buy good vines at a good price, rather than vines advertised at reduced rates. You may be sure that with the present great demand for vines, all of good quality will be sought after at good prices.—Send for Price List.

J. F. DELIOT, Vine Grower, Sing Sing, N. Y.

GRAPE VINES.

Good Plants! Low Prices!! Delaware, Iona, Israella, Adirondac, Concord, Hartford, Creveling, Allen's White Hybrid, Rebecca, Maxatawney, Union Village, Ives' Seedling, and many others. Kirtland Raspberry, the best, hardy, early, red kind; Agriculturist and Jucunda Strawberries; Houghton Gooseberry, Currants, &c. Send stamp for full Catalogue, to

GEO. W. CAMPBELL,
Delaware, Ohio.

4,000 Acres in Grapes!

At Sandusky, Kelly's Island and vicinity. Midst which are

The Sandusky Grape Nurseries,

M. H. LEWIS & CO., Proprietors.

Plants sent by mail, by Express or by freight at *low rates*. All our roots lifted before severe frost, and kept in perfect condition over winter in frost-proof cellars in sand.

Grape Wood cut in the fall and stored in cellar in moss and sand.—IVES SEEDLING, a few 1000 eyes from Col. Waring's Vineyard; Delaware, Iona, Rogers' No. 15, Catawba and Israella.—Our Circular and Price List sent to all applicants GRATIS.—It contains an illustration, natural size, of the Ives Seedling, its history and what the most disinterested authorities say of it. Address, *at once*,

M. H. LEWIS & CO., Sandusky, Ohio.

WESTCHESTER COUNTY NURSERIES,
Pleasantville, N. Y.

(On Harlem Railroad.)

EDWARD J. CARPENTER, Prop'r.

The Subscriber begs to inform his friends and the public that he has established a NEW NURSERY near Pleasantville, and has a finely grown stock of TREES, PLANTS, &c., and respectfully solicits EASTERN BUYERS before giving their orders to WESTERN AGENTS to call and examine this stock of Trees. Our planting now covers over twenty acres of ground, well stocked with the choicest varieties.

NORTON'S VIRGINIA SEEDLING LAYERS For Sale. No. 1 at $200, No. 2, $100 per 1000. Concord at $100 per 1000. Clinton at $75 per 1000. Terms cash on delivery, or collected by express. The plants may also be ordered from Mr. John Trumpy, Brooklyn, Cuyahoga Co., O., or Messrs. Schwill & Bros., Seed Merchants, No. 69 and 71 Maine-st., Cincinnati, O.

GEORGE NESTEL,
Mascoutah, St. Clair Co., Ill.

PEACH TREES.—A few thousand very fine trees, 1 year from bud. Address G. H. DANTA, Tappantown, N. Y.

JUCUNDA, OUR 700.—GROWN BY J. KNOX, PITTSBURGH, PA.

"The illustrations we give (as above), are drawn from Nature; and we can say, are not exaggerations of the specimens which were selected at Pittsburgh, when we were there in June, and sent to Philadelphia the next day." THOMAS MEEHAN, Editor *Gardeners' Monthly*.

"The above Engraving is a faithful representation, drawn from actual specimens of fine fruit grown on the KNOX FRUIT FARM, at Pittsburgh." A. W. HARRISON.

"Its flowers are perfect, and fruitful to an enormous extent. I last year counted trusses that had ninety per cent. of perfect fruit upon them, as compared with the number of flowers. A most remarkable point of value in this variety is the great number of extra large berries. I saw great quantities, ten to twelve berries of which filled a pint. These, you must remember, were not merely a few selected ones for the exhibition tables, but there were bushels of them sold every day in market, which brought one dollar per quart. This is equal to four or five cents each, and may be considered rather profitable." GEORGE M. BEELER, *late Secretary Indiana Hort. Society*.

"I entirely concur in the statement there made (at the meeting of the Ohio Pomological Society, held in Cincinnati, December, 1865,) as to its great productiveness, its large and uniform size, and its protracted fruitage, but, more especially, as to its *brilliant color, perfect form,* and *extreme beauty*, and consider it the most remarkable fruit of its class that has ever come under my observation." DR. JOHN A. WARDER.

For further information, in reference to this, the most valuable of all our Strawberries, send **10 Cents for our Catalogue.**

Our stock of well-rooted and vigorous plants is very large this season, which we offer at the following greatly reduced prices:

12 Plants	$1.00.	1000 Plants	$40.00.
100 "	$5.00.	3000 "	$100.00.

For Vines and Plants **BY MAIL**, see extraordinary inducements on page 77, February No. of *Agriculturist*.——**ORDER EARLY.**

SEVEN VARIETIES OF GRAPES,

which are reliable, healthy, hardy, vigorous, productive, of good quality, and very valuable.

CONCORD.—Best known and most popular.

HARTFORD. / **CREVELING.** } Best *very early*, yet thoroughly tested.

MARTHA—WHITE CONCORD.—Best White.

BLACK HAWK.—Perhaps the earliest of all grapes of any merit.

IVES. / **RENTZ.** } Best American wine grapes.

For $12 we will send to any Post-Office address in the United States, post-paid, and guarantee their safe carriage, one each of the above seven valuable kinds.

For full description and much valuable information on Grape Culture, send **10 Cents for Catalogue.**

SEVEN VARIETIES OF STRAWBERRIES

Of largest size, best quality and greatest yield.

JUCUNDA—OUR NO. 700.—Largest and most valuable of all.

FILLMORE.—Next in value.

GOLDEN SEEDED. / **BURR'S NEW PINE.** } Best very early.

WILSON.—Best for canning.

TRIOMPHE DE GAND.

AGRICULTURIST.

The above list comprises the best *early, medium and late* maturing varieties, and makes a very complete collection.

For $5 we will send to any Post-Office address in the United States, post-paid, and guarantee their safe carriage, 2 dozen of Jucunda—our No. 700, and 1 dozen each of the other varieties.

For full description of the above and all other desirable kinds, also minute instructions for strawberry culture, send **10 cents for our Catalogue.**

SEVEN BEST VARIETIES OF CURRANTS.

For $5 we will send by mail to any Post-Office address in the United States, post-paid, and guarantee their safe carriage

6 **VERSAILLAISE.**—The best of all.

6 **FERTILE DE ANGERS.**—Very similar to above.

4 **CHERRY.**—Best for jams and jellies.

4 **WHITE GRAPE.**—Best for wine.

4 **VICTORIA.**—Good and very late.

4 **SHORT BUNCH RED.**—Very productive and good.

4 **LA HATIVE.**—Vigorous grower, and very good.

Full descriptions of these, and other desirable varieties, may be found in our Catalogue, which will be sent to all applicants enclosing 10 cents.

☞ **EARLY ORDERS ARE SOLICITED.**

J. KNOX,

Box 155, Pittsburgh, Pa.

(*Continued from page 109, which see.*)

(Business Notices $2.50 per Agate Line of Space.)

The Immense Profits

OF THE

TEA TRADE.

The Proprietors of "THE GREAT AMERICAN TEA COMPANY," became fully convinced, several years ago, that the consumers of Tea and Coffee were paying too many and too large profits, on these articles of every day consumption, and therefore organized THE GREAT AMERICAN TEA COMPANY, to do away, as far as possible, with these enormous drains upon the Consumers, and to supply them with these necessaries at the smallest possible price.

To give our readers an idea of the profits which have been made in the Tea trade, we will start with the American houses, leaving out of the account entirely the profits of the Chinese factors.

1st.—The American House in China or Japan makes large profits on their sales or shipments—and some of the richest retired merchants in this country have made their immense fortunes through their houses in China.

2d.—The Banker makes large profits upon the foreign exchange used in the purchase of Teas.

3d.—The Importer makes a profit of 30 to 50 per cent. in many cases.

4th.—On its arrival here it is sold by the cargo, and the Purchaser sells it to the Speculator in invoices of 1,000 to 2,000 packages, at an average profit of about 10 per cent.

5th.—The Speculator sells it to the Wholesale Tea Dealer in lines at a profit of 10 to 15 per cent.

6th.—The Wholesale Tea Dealer sells it to the Wholesale Grocer in lots to suit his trade, at a profit of about 10 per cent.

7th.—The Wholesale Grocer sells it to the Retail Dealer at a profit of 15 to 25 per cent.

8th.—The Retailer sells it to the consumer for *all the profit he can get.*

When you have added to these *eight* profits as many brokerages, cartages, storages, cooperages, and waste, and add the original cost of the tea, it will be perceived what the consumer has to pay. And now we propose to show why we can sell so very much lower than small dealers.

We propose to do away with all these various profits and brokerages, cartages, storages, cooperages, and waste, with the exception of a small commission paid for purchasing to our correspondents in China and Japan, one cartage, and a small profit to ourselves—which, on our large sales, will amply pay us.

Some parties inquire of us how they shall proceed to get up a club. The answer is simply this: Let each person wishing to join in a club, say how much tea or coffee he wants, and select the kind and price from our Price List, as published in the paper or in our circulars. Write the names, kinds, and amounts plainly on a list, and when the club is complete send it to us by mail, and we will put each party's goods in separate packages, and mark the name upon them, with the cost, so there need be no confusion in their distribution—each party getting exactly what he orders, and no more. The cost of transportation the members of the club can divide equitably among themselves.

The funds to pay for the goods ordered can be sent by drafts on New York, by Post-Office money orders, or by Express, as may suit the convenience of the club. Or, if the amount ordered exceeds thirty dollars, we will, if desired, send the goods by Express, to "*collect on delivery.*"

Parties getting their Teas from us may confidently rely upon getting them pure and fresh, as they come direct from the Custom House Stores to our warehouses.

The Company have selected the following kinds from their Stock, which they recommend to meet the wants of clubs. They are sold at Cargo Prices, the same as the Company sell them in New York, as the List of prices will show.

Hereafter we will send a complimentary package to the party getting up the club. Our profits are small, but we will be as liberal as we can afford. We send no complimentary package for clubs of less than $30.

All goods sold are warranted to give satisfaction.

PRICE LIST:

YOUNG HYSON (Green), 80c., 90c., $1, $1.10, best $1.25 per pound.

GREEN TEAS, 80c., 90c., $1, $1.10, best $1.25 per pound.

MIXED, 70c., 80c., 90c., best $1 per pound.

JAPAN, $1, $1.10, best $1.25 per pound.

OOLONG (Black), 70c., 80c., 90c., best $1 per pound.

IMPERIAL (Green), best $1.25 per pound.

ENGLISH BREAKFAST (Black), 80c., 90c., $1, $1.10, best $1.20 per pound.

GUNPOWDER (Gunpowder), $1.25, best $1.50 per lb.

P. S.—All towns, villages, or manufactories, where a large number of men are engaged, by CLUBBING together, can reduce the cost of their Teas and Coffees about one-third by sending directly to the

GREAT AMERICAN TEA COMPANY,
31 and 33 VESEY-STREET, corner of Church.
Post Office Box, 5,643 New-York City.

☞ We call special notice to the fact that our Vesey Street Store is at Nos. 31 and 33 Vesey Street, corner of Church Street—*large double store.*

From the Methodist, N. Y. City.

THE GREAT AMERICAN TEA COMPANY.—In noticing the operations of this large and enterprising establishment, it may be proper for us to offer a remark in explanation of the reasons which induce us to call the attention of the community to a concern which has reached its eminence in public favor. It is our undeviating rule to exercise a scrupulous judgment in relation to business enterprises—never recommending any except such as we believe have been proved worthy and reliable, and whose system of business, uprightness of dealing with their customers, and ample capital to fulfill their engagements are fully established. Upon these principles we call attention to the advertisement of the GREAT AMERICAN TEA COMPANY, published in our advertising columns. The Company have several very large stores, located in different parts of the city, stocked with the best and most serviceable goods, which they are content to sell at merely living profits, as they have proved by their prices for the past five or six years. They have but *one price*, which is no small consideration to those who are dependent to any considerable degree upon servants or children to make purchases, or to those who wish to order from the country. By these rules alone the company propose in the future to conduct their vast and rapidly augmenting trade. Believing that the ability and disposition of the Company are ample to perform all they promise, warrants us in calling special attention to them in our columns. It is a trite saying "that the honest strivings of honest men are sure to be commended, their business efforts encouraged, and ultimately adequately compensated."

Clergymen and Gentlemen of the religious and secular press of very careful speech, have emphatically indorsed and recommended the GREAT AMERICAN TEA COMPANY, as also commendatory letters of our customers.

On page 110 of this paper, we give their own words, so that consumers of Tea may rely upon our statements and manner of doing business.

VALUABLE PUBLICATIONS BY LUTHER TUCKER & SON, ALBANY, N. Y.

"**The Cultivator and Country Gentleman**"—a LARGE WEEKLY JOURNAL, 16 pages, quarto, devoted to the Practice and Science of Agriculture and Horticulture at large, and to all the various Departments of Rural and Domestic Economy. Only **$2.50** per year, with favorable Terms to Clubs.

*** SPECIMEN COPIES sent free, or on receipt of 50 cents, we will forward the Five Numbers for January, stitched and trimmed in paper cover, post-paid—80 pages, and very cheap at the price.

"**Rural Affairs**," in FOUR HANDSOME VOLUMES, muslin, containing about **1300** pages of Reading Matter, and over **1700 Engravings**, including all Agricultural and Horticultural Subjects, and very valuable PLANS OF FARM AND COUNTRY HOUSES, and Outbuildings.

*** Sent postage paid for $6, or either Volume alone for $1.50.—Send for one and you will want all.

Address, with remittances, or for further information, LUTHER TUCKER & SON, ALBANY, N. Y.

Imported Crevecœur Fowls,

Direct from the Jardin d'Acclimatation, Paris, selected with great care; the finest in the country. Orders received for fowls only, progeny of above, to be delivered after Sept. 1st. Send for Circular. Also, limited number of

HOUDANS,
of same importation.

DUCKS.

Pieta and Aylesbury Ducks and Eggs from the best imported Stock. Send for Circular.

A. M. HALSTED & CO., 68 Pearl St., New York.

To Farmers and Agents.

On receipt of $1.50 we will send by mail or express, prepaid, the Brass Metallic parts, or for $2.00 one of the Celebrated Silvers' Patent Excelsior Brooms complete—with full instructions how to fill it.—Universally acknowledged to be the cheapest, best and most beautiful Broom in the world, and the only one accepted for the "Paris Exposition" of 1867.

An Agent wanted in every county. For full particulars, see February Agriculturist, page 77, or send for Illustrated Circular to G. A. CLEGG & CO.,
205 Broadway, N. Y.

KNOX'S NURSERY AT YOUR DOOR.—A Liberal Offer. See Advertisement on page 117.

SOUTHERN LANDS.

Great Bargains in Maryland, Virginia and Cotton growing States. Farms of all sizes and at all prices, from $3 to $100 per acre. Large Tracts of Timber on Railroad and Water. *Never failing Water Powers.* Mill Sites, etc., etc.

For sale by WM. H. NEWTON, Att'y and Broker.
23 Lexington-st., Baltimore, Maryland.

☞ *Send 25 Cents for Catalogue.*

GET WELL AND KEEP WELL.—Read the Advertisement of Herald of Health, page 112.

See Advertisement "ALL NURSERIES IN ONE," on page 112. Observe the low Prices.

MR. GREELEY'S PROPOSITION FOR GRAPE-PRIZE.

So much has been well done within the last few years in American Fruit growing that it seems feasible, to do still more or at least to realize more extensively and rapidly the benefit of past improvements. Perhaps the most signal improvement has been made in the production of Grapes * * * Still, we are growing far too many inferior grapes, while our established favorites are too generally deficient in one or more respects. * * * *They have some notable defect as a table fruit.* * * * But it is plausibly claimed that several substantially new or little known varieties of domestic origin of high quality, fulfill all the requisites of *a choice table fruit.* It is time these claims were tested and passed upon by disinterested and capable judges. As a humble contribution to this end, I hereby offer a premium of One hundred dollars for the best plate of native grapes, weighing not less than six pounds of any variety known to the growers or propagators of the country. I require as follows of the grapes competing for the premium: The berries must be at least of good medium size, and not liable to fall from the stem when ripe: The flesh must be melting and tender quite to the center; The flavor must be pure, vinous, and exhilarating: The vine must be healthy, productive, of good *habit of growth for training in gardens and yards*, as well as in vineyards, with leaves as hardy and well adapted to our climate as those of the Delaware. *In short, what is sought is a vine embodying all of the best qualities of the most approved American and foreign varieties so far as possible.*

I propose to pay this premium on the Award of the Fruit Department of the American Institute, and invite competition for it at the annual fair of the Institute soon to open; but if a *thoroughly satisfactory Grape* should not now be presented, the Institute will of course postpone the award till the proper claimant shall have appeared.

Signed, HORACE GREELEY.

The Committee, consisting of Peter B. Mead, Chairman, R. G. Pardee and Francis Brill, reported (see report in pamphlet) that "the Iona fully met Mr. Greeley's requirements, and that no other grape in cultivation could."

[This the committee knew to be true in Sept., 1864, and thousands of others in all parts of the country now affirm the same *from their own experience.*]

This appears to be the only committee that ever adjudicated the Greeley prize, although another committee—or rather a portion of it—(*apparently after enjoying a party and forgetting their errand*) made another report, which embodies an apology for giving it to so poor a grape as the Concord. See what one of them at the late meeting "of Fruit-growers Society of Western N. Y." says about it when asked to explain.

Extract from letter giving report: "The Concord ripened well, but the berries fell from the bunch some, and I don't think so much of it on that account. There are several grapes that I always eat in preference to the Concord—in fact, I seldom eat that—but the public—the great masses—are not so well educated in their taste, and are ready to gulp down any black grape of good size, regardless of quality. For that reason I recommended the Concord for the Million." Mr. William Griffith, of North East, Pa., who believed the Iona best of all grapes for table and for wine, denounced the doctrine of Mr. Committee-man, saying "he (committee-man) little knew the American people," and closed by saying "that 999,000 out of every million and part of the other thousand were already dissatisfied with that award, and that 'the million' in all coming years would rebuke the finding of that Greeley Committee." (*It is also stated that only three of the Committee ever saw the grapes last fall, on exhibition for the premium.*) The Convention, on voting for "best variety," gave one vote for Concord—the man explained "*that it was because the birds would'nt touch that.*"

Mr. F. R. Elliot (Author of Fruit Growers' Guide) said, "of all the grapes that *had* had any reputation at the West, Concord was the poorest in quality."

It will be seen that Mr. Greeley's requirements specify very judiciously and accurately the distinctive qualities of a good grape, without which his offer of a munificent premium would have been entirely wanting in that clear significance and practical good sense, for which he is so eminently distinguished. It was not to have been expected that any one of Concord's "hundred head of friends" should have placed before the public an analysis of the qualities of a good grape so directly in contrast to that from which they were reaping such golden harvests, which could last only while the "ignorance of the million" should continue, but when we consider how utterly wanting in all of these essential qualities the Concord is, and in fitness for "Market" also, we cannot fail to wonder that the portion of the committee reporting should omit to state such important facts, to avoid the appearance of collusion with what will be regarded as the most enormous swindle that has been perpetrated in fruit-culture, when the history of the dissemination of the Concord shall be known. The latter is in very unenviable contrast with the former committee.

Now, Mr. Public, we have finished our little essay, and at an expenditure of some thousands of dollars have spread it before you. Please let some one of your philosophers weigh it in his scales, using for weights all that has appeared on the subject of grapes in all of the magazines and papers during the past three years.—Note the result and make your calculations accordingly.

C. W. GRANT.

MEAD ON GRAPE CULTURE AND WINE MAKING.

Harper and Brother will publish, on or before the first of March, "American Grape Culture," an elementary work, by Peter B. Mead, intended specially to meet the wants of the present time.

It is the work of a thorough practitioner of the most extended knowledge of the subject, and who, at the same time, is able to express his ideas in a clear, intelligent, and scholarly manner.

The work is most profusely illustrated with the best engravings ever produced for the purpose, and we are happy to be able to offer it so opportunely to the American public.

HARPER & BROTHER,
Franklin Square, N. Y.

Sent by mail on receipt of price.

PREFACE.

The present volume has been prepared in compliance with the urgent request of friends in various parts of the country.

(*Continued on page 119, which see.*)

AMERICAN AGRICULTURIST

FOR THE

Farm, Garden, and Household.

"AGRICULTURE IS THE MOST HEALTHFUL, MOST USEFUL, AND MOST NOBLE EMPLOYMENT OF MAN."—WASHINGTON.

ORANGE JUDD & CO., PUBLISHERS AND PROPRIETORS. Office, 41 Park Row, (Times Buildings.)

ESTABLISHED IN 1842.

Published also in German at $1.50 a Year.

$1.50 PER ANNUM, IN ADVANCE. SINGLE NUMBER, 15 CENTS. 4 Copies for $5; 10 for $12; 20 or more, $1 each.

VOLUME XXVI.—No. 4. NEW-YORK, APRIL, 1867. NEW SERIES—No. 243.

SOUTHDOWN RAM.—PROPERTY OF AMASA BEMIS & SON, SOUTH BURKE, VT.—*Drawn from Life and Engraved for the American Agriculturist.*

Every lover of good mutton has an affection for anything that looks like a Southdown Sheep. Among the Southdowns there is an aristocracy of pedigree, form and excellence, and so we honor the name of Jonas Webb, of Babraham, England, as a benefactor of the race, on account of the degree of excellence to which his careful breeding brought this favorite mutton breed.

The Ram above portrayed was sketched by our artist at the New England and Vermont Fair last fall, as the winner of the first prize in his class. He is known as "No. 19" of Bemis & Son's flock; is three years old; was bred by J. C. Taylor of some of his best stock, imported in 1860. Mr. T. having secured at Mr. Webb's sale the very choice ones of the flock. This blood tells wherever it has been scattered,—even where it is used upon common flocks, and the grades show little of the Southdown look. The butcher's knife develops the beautifully marbled chops and thick loins which characterize the breed. Southdown mutton, or that of grade Southdowns, always commands the very highest market price in all our large cities. In fact, it is rarely found in the common markets—the sheep being sold to butchers having private stalls. In New York good Southdown mutton brings a price at retail equal to good beef. Early lambs, half Southdown, meet a quick market from green-pea time until late in the season.

Contents for April, 1867.

INDEX TO "BASKET," OR SHORTER ARTICLES.

Back Volumes Supplied.—The back volumes of the *Agriculturist* are very valuable. They contain information upon every topic connected with rural life, out-door and in-door, and the last ten volumes make up a very complete library. Each volume has a full Index for ready reference to any desired topic. We have on hand, and print from stereotype plates as wanted, all the numbers and volumes for ten years past, beginning with 1857—that is, Vol. 16 to Vol. 25, inclusive. Any of these volumes sent complete (in numbers) at $1.75 each, post-paid, (or $1.50 if taken at the office). The volumes neatly bound, are supplied for $2 each, or $2.50 if to be sent by mail. Any single numbers of the past ten years will be supplied, post-paid, for 15 cents each.

AMERICAN AGRICULTURIST.

NEW-YORK, APRIL, 1867.

Extreme views and practices are held and followed, with small profit to any one, and least of all to him who suddenly adopts them. However at variance any man's system of farming is with sound philosophy, if he has hitherto met with any sort of success, and is not absolutely running backward, we would surely *not* advise him to cast loose from his moorings and adopt all new practices, to accord with the views of a sounder agricultural faith, to which he may have become a convert. Rashness is the usual precursor of failure, but progressive conservatism uniformly leads to success. Deep plowing is an excellent practice, but only when there is a soil to plow. He who lifts several inches of untempered subsoil and mingles it with a shallow surface soil, will repent his deed when the sickly, yellow grain testifies to the poison presented to the plants with their food, or to the difficulty they have in picking up a living among the mass of rubbish. In the spring, especially, the soil should not be plowed much deeper than heretofore. In the autumn the plow may very well be put down quite deeply, provided there is enough plant food in the soil, or added to it, to warrant it; for the freezing and thawing of winter, and the action of the atmosphere will essentially modify its character. These influences are wanting at this season, and deeper plowing than usual must either be accompanied with thorough liming or the use of unleached ashes, or very heavy manuring; and even then it is not to be recommended for small grains. It is well, however, at every plowing to run the plow a little deeper than before; and if the soil is neither water soaked nor leachy, even quite shallow subsoiling will prove of great benefit. We advocate most earnestly deepening of the soil, but not rashly, nor too much in spring plowing.

The failures of certain crops year after year admonish us not to put our trust too much in any single staple. Influences, which are injurious to one class of crops, benefit others, and so, judiciously dividing our interests, we are surer of success.

Double cropping of the land is one of the essential features of "high" or "intensive" farming. It is equivalent to getting double interest for the money invested in the land, and in the labor of weeding and clearing the same, and for the buildings, fences, roads and superintendence of the farm, it gives quicker returns for the investment in manure, and in all points is a great gain. It requires that the land should be rich and in good tilth, reasonably free from weeds, and that there should be a proper rotation of crops followed, and labor enough at command. It affords also a means of profitably employing many hands the season through, for whom there would otherwise be little to do most of the time. The practice should be commenced in the garden and extended to the field, when familiarity has given confidence in it.

We entreat farmers not to neglect their gardens. Many are too apt to read the hints about farm work and slight the other columns. The kitchen garden, if well cultivated, better rewards labor than any portion of the farm of five times its extent.

Hints About Work.

Review the hints for last month; many of them will be found equally applicable to this, especially if the season be backward. Besides, the weather of March, in the latitude of Philadelphia and St. Louis, is that of April near Boston or St. Paul.

Tillage.—The preparation of the soil for the seed is the important work of this month. Manure is to be hauled and spread, and the ground is to be plowed. The waste of manure which occurs after it is spread is very little in weather which will not allow plowing, and not very great in full, hot sunshine, if it does not lie long. It is much worse to dump the manure in small heaps and leave it for some time exposed to the action of rains, for the goodness washes out into the soil and enriches it in spots, to the serious damage of the crop.

Plowing and any other working of the soil should never be done when the clods will not crumble. Dryness is essential to useful tillage. It is much better to delay work than to leave the land lumpy and hard. There are many spots on which

Draining may be done in the spring—especially where there is a good fall, and work may progress from the outlet. The necessity for drainage is now obvious, and though partial drainage is never to be recommended where thorough work will be undertaken, yet as a demonstration of the fact that "burying crockery" will pay, it is worth while often to try the experiment "just to see." Remember that the full effects of draining are often not witnessed until the third or fourth season.

Spring Grains.—Prepare seed by selecting with the fan-mill the heaviest grain—the more times it is fanned, the better will be the seed; then, when the soil is nearly or quite ready, prepare the seed by pickling to destroy the seed of smut, which may be attached to it. This is useful for barley, and imperatively necessary for wheat. Add to a strong brine pulverized "blue stone," (sulphate of copper,) until no more is dissolved; into this throw the grain, stir thoroughly, and after five minutes scoop it out, throw into a basket, let it drip back into the tub of pickle, then put in a heap upon a floor; after 24 hours shovel it over, sprinkling on dry slaked lime, thus drying it. Sow 5 to 7 pecks of wheat, 2 bushels to 2½ of barley, 2½ of oats. The ground should have been plowed in the fall for wheat and barley. Oats do tolerably well on a sward plowed in spring. For all either very fine compost or some concentrated fertilizer, such as a mixture of superphosphate of lime and Peruvian guano—say 100 lbs. of each—should be used. Sow, as a rule, those kinds of grain which are in highest repute in your own neighborhoods.

Root Crops.—Prepare the soil for sowing carrots, beets and mangels, and onions, the earlier the better. It should be deep and rich, plowed in the fall and as free from weeds as possible, especially for onions, which require the finest and mellowest soil, enriched with good, fine compost. The other root crops need also rich soil, deeper than onion soil, but not less rich, though the enrichment need not be of so fine a quality. These crops can not be sown too early, after danger for hard freezing is passed and the soil is warm and dry enough. Beet seed ought to be soaked 24 hours.

Potatoes.—At least a portion of the crop should be planted very early for security against the rot. The Early Cottage, White Peachblow, Cuzco and Fluke are commendable kinds. Plant deep, in drills 2½ to 3 feet apart, cover with the plow. Harrow as often as weeds appear, until the tops show very plainly, and once after that, driving with the rows. It is sometimes well to turn furrows upon the rows to cover them a few days after this, and when a new crop of weeds appears to harrow again. Superphosphate, castor pomace, leached or unleached ashes are good used in the drill. It is usually poor practice to plant in hills.

Peas.—See notes for last month.

Pea Nuts or Ground Nuts, for profitable culture, require a rather long season. Sow in rows three to four feet apart in deep, mellow, rather sandy soil, in a good condition; drop two shelled kernels in a hill, and put the hills one foot apart. Plant as early as there is a chance for the young plants to escape frosts, to which they are as sensitive as beans—cover two inches deep. Use horse hoes at first, and hand hoes after they begin to run. At all events keep the weeds down. After first hoeing, thin to one plant in each hill. Crop, in the warmer States, 50 to 150 bushels per acre.

Flax.—See pamphlet "Flax Culture." Sow on very mellow soil, free from weeds, one and a half bushels per acre, (for seed and lint both,) as evenly as possible. Selecting the heaviest seed, soak in warm water two or three hours, roll in gypsum and sow two ways. Cover with a brush or light harrow.

Manure makes fast in compost heaps, if occasionally worked over with the addition of muck or any vegetable mold, and thus the quantity available for corn may be greatly increased.

Liquid Manure has great effect upon grass, and no better application can be made upon winter grain, though the labor attending its application is considerable. A liquid manure distributor is a rare, but needed, article on American farms. In buying

Concentrated Manures do not purchase any because they are cheap. The adulteration of guano is notorious. The farmer can much better afford to mix in the sand on his own farm than to pay $65 in gold a ton for sand, and cart it a dozen miles besides. The other popular manures, superphosphate, etc., are quite as liable to adulteration, or even more so. After all, it is best to make one's own fertilizers, or buy only of reliable parties.

Home-made Fertilizers.—1st, Poudrette. Mix dry soil, muck or peat with the contents of the privy every three days, remove and work over the contents, once a fortnight adding more. 2d, Guano. Sprinkle plaster under the hen-roosts, and also earth or muck, cleaning all out once a week. Mix in a dry place, moistening with chamber ley, barnyard leachings, or simply water, and cover the heap with soil pressed down. Work over, adding more soil, or muck and plaster, as often as it heats well.

Horses.—Feed according to the amount of labor required of them. Groom daily and thoroughly. Give air and sunlight in the stables, feed and water regularly, blanket only when exposed after labor.

Oxen.—See hints for March. Warbles, or grubs in the back, often become very obvious at this season and later; destroy such as show their heads. We have never known of harm to result from killing the grubs by pressure or by puncturing the skin before their heads protrude. Feed grain if hard worked, and do not neglect carding regularly.

Cows and Calves.—If allowed to run together, it is best to put two calves upon one cow, as a rule, and to have these of different ages, so that both shall not be removed at once when fit for veal. The calves should be fed gruel besides, and some veal raisers allow them free access to dry corn meal, or better, linseed-cake meal, and corn meal mixed.

Sheep.—Give ewes and lambs the attention they require at lambing time. The flock should have the personal supervision of the owner. Give, if possible, shelter of some sort, and at least keep the flock of ewes as near as possible to the house and closely watched. Distribute the lambs among the ewes having most milk, not necessarily leaving twins with their own dams.

Swine.—See hints in former numbers for treatment of breeding sows. Employ all hogs in making manure, supplying sods and all vegetable refuse.

Work in the Horticultural Departments.

Frequent showers and the increasing warmth of the sun remove the last vestiges of snow and ice, and this is emphatically a working month. As so many things have to be hinted at this month, we shall assume that preparatory work is generally done or in progress, and refer the reader to preceding months for whatever relates to that.

Orchard and Nursery.

Assuming that the land for the new orchard has been plowed and subsoiled, and if need be, drained, and that the needed trees have been ordered.

Planting may be done as soon as the trees come to hand. Do not leave the roots exposed any longer than necessary, and if planting can not be done at once, cover the roots with earth. Trim mutilated roots, shorten the tops and, at the same time, remove useless branches. Do not plant too deeply; make a broad opening for the roots, spread them in a natural position, cover with fine soil, press it down firmly with the foot, and the tree will not need to be staked to keep it in position.

Shrivelled Trees are to be buried, root and branch, until the bark becomes plump, and those that have started in the package, must be cut back severely.

Old Orchards are often brought in a state of fruitfulness by generous manuring and cultivation.

Grafting may be carried on as soon as the buds begin to swell. It is better to wait for the first indications of life in the tree than to do it earlier. Cions may be cut if the buds have not started.

Root Grafts should be planted in nursery rows as soon as the soil is in proper condition.

Seeds and Pits, for raising young nursery stock, are to be sown as early as possible. Peaches that have been buried in heaps, should be looked to. If they were dried too long before they were put with earth, they will need to be carefully cracked.

Insects.—Continue to destroy eggs, and use the soap wash heretofore recommended. When protectors are used to stop the ascent of the Canker-worm, see that the tar, oil, or other adhesive material is properly renewed. See p. 102, last month.

Fruit Garden.

Planting, grafting and general care of trees in the fruit garden is the same as for those in the orchard. Only dwarf trees are in place here, and they should be models of health and fruitfulness. Those who wish to try at the different methods of training, should consult Rivers' Miniature Fruit Garden.

Figs may be ripened in well sheltered gardens, but they must be taken up and wintered in the cellar, or be laid down and well protected with earth.

Quinces, so beautiful whether in flower or in fruit, may be trained to form handsome pyramids, if the leading branch be kept tied up to a stake.

Currants should be in abundance in every family garden. They will bear under neglect, but will amply repay manuring and care. The Cherry and White Grape are the best; there is a great confusion in names, and any of the large fruited sorts are good.

Gooseberries.—Houghton and the American Seedling are the common sorts free from mildew, and are more valuable green than when ripe.

Blackberries are now considered necessary in the garden. The Kittatinny and Wilson's Early are the newest sorts, and both good. Dorchester and New Rochelle are older sorts.

Raspberries.—New varieties are so numerous that it is difficult to say which is best for general cultivation. The finest sorts all need covering in winter. The Black-caps are hardy and popular.

Grapes.—Plant strong one or two year old vines on well drained soil, and allow only a single cane to grow the first year. We have given considerable space of late to the discussion of the leading varieties. A garden of considerable extent should contain several of the standard sorts.

Strawberries.—Remove the mulch from over the crowns, but leave the ground covered. Set new beds as soon as the soil can be worked. For garden culture, beds 4 feet wide are the best; one row of plants in the center and a row 18 inches from it on each side. The plants may be from a foot to 18 inches in the row, according to their habit of growth; the latter distance is none too much for the strong growing kinds that make large stools.

Kitchen Garden.

Many of the hints of last month will be timely now. The care there suggested in the management of glass is more necessary now, as the plants are more liable to suffer from extremes of heat and cold.

Asparagus.—Fork over the beds if not already done, and if new plantations are needed, make early, as directed last month. Treat beds of

Rhubarb in a similar manner; both do much better when planted early before the growth starts.

Beans may be planted where there is no longer danger of frost, but it is generally too early at the North. The Early Valentine is a favorite garden sort.

Beets.—Sow in rows a foot or 13 inches apart, or, if preferred, two feet apart, with radishes between. Several early kinds are better than the old Bassano.

Cabbages.—Set out the plants from cold frames. Our market gardeners put the rows 24 to 28 inches apart, with the plants sixteen inches in the rows, and then set lettuce in rows equi-distant between the cabbages, but this economy of land is not usually necessary in private gardens. Harden off the plants in hot-beds by exposure. Sow seeds in open ground in drills 4 inches apart, and sprinkle with flour of bone or air slacked lime as soon as up. The Wakefield and Early York are the most common early sorts, and there are several other and newer kinds described in the catalogues.

Cauliflower is planted and treated same as cabbage.

Carrots.—Sow Early Horn in 15-inch drills, using plenty of seed to ensure a good start.

Celery.—Sow seed in a rich, mellow soil, in drills 8 inches apart—cover lightly with soil.

Chives.—Propagate by breaking up the old clumps and setting the bulbs 6 inches apart.

Cress.—Whoever would keep up a supply of this pungent salad—well called pepper grass—should make a sowing every eight or ten days.

Cucumbers may be sown in cold frames from which other plants have been removed. Next month will be early enough to start on sods under glass those to be planted in the open ground.

Egg Plant.—Sow in hot-bed and keep warm. They are slow to recover if they once get chilled.

Garlic.—Break up the bulbs into sets and plant 6 inches apart in rows a foot apart.

Horseradish.—See very full article on page 141.

Herbs.—Have a plenty of these for home use or for market. Thyme, Sage, Sweet Marjoram, and Summer Savory are the most used. Prepare a bed of rich and finely worked soil, and sow seeds in rows 4 inches apart, and keep free of weeds.

Leeks.—Sow in rows a foot apart, in fine rich soil, and keep clear of weeds from the start.

Lettuce.—Set out plants from cold frames one foot apart each way, or the same distance between rows of early cabbages. Sow in the open ground in drills 8 inches apart. The Curled Silesia is most commonly used, but many prefer a variety of it, the Curled Simpson, as it is rather earlier.

Mustard.—For salads sow thickly in foot rows.

Onions.—Sets are put out as early as the ground can be worked. If the onions are to be pulled green, the rows may be 9 inches apart, but if they are to be left to ripen, make them 15 inches. Potato and Top Onions are also to be put at this distance. Put the sets 3 or 4 inches apart in the rows, cover, and roll. Seeds, or "black seed" as it is often called, is sown in 15-inch drills in highly manured soil. Onion sets are raised by planting the seed very thickly in rather wide 9-inch rows in poor soil.

Parsley.—For early, sow in cold frames between the rows of lettuce; for later, sow in the open ground in rows a foot apart. It germinates slowly.

Parsnips.—Sow in deep soil in rows 15 inches apart. Be sure that the seed is of last year's growth.

Peas.—The early and "extra early" kinds are so numerous that one is at loss to choose between them. Dan. O'Rourke is the old standard sort. Some of the dwarfs are very convenient for garden culture, but the taller kinds are more prolific. Tom Thumb and other dwarfs may be sown in rows a foot apart. The taller growing kinds are usually put 3 or 4 feet apart, and supplied with brush before they are tall enough to fall over.

Peppers.—Sow Squash and Mountain Sweet varieties in hot-bed, and treat the same as egg plants.

Potatoes.—The Early Goodrich is perhaps the best for garden culture. Plant this, or other early sort, in well manured soil in drills 6 inches deep and 2 feet apart; drop seed—cut or not, as may be preferred—a foot apart in the drills.

Radishes.—Sow in any spare spaces in the frames, or in light soil in the open ground. Market growers, after sowing their beets, sow the ground broadcast with radish seed. The radishes come off by the time the beets are large enough to thin. The Scarlet Turnip and the Scarlet Short Top are among the best. The French Breakfast is a new sort.

Salsify.—Sow and treat the same as carrots. The same culture for Scorzonera, or Black Salsify.

Sea Kale.—A plant, the young shoots of which are eaten. A perennial, and grown in beds much in the way of asparagus. The plants are started from seed sown this month; keep well weeded.

Spinach.—The plants wintered over may be thinned for use. Sow seed in 15-inch drills.

Seeds.—Whatever roots, bulbs, etc., are to produce seed should be looked over, the best specimens selected and set in a rich soil. Keep related varieties at a good distance from one another.

Swiss Chard.—Excellent for greens, and is grown the same as the beet, of which it is a variety, with large and eatable leaves which are cooked as spinach.

Sweet Potatoes.—The manner of starting these without a regular hot-bed is given on page 143. Those who have a hot-bed have only to lay the potatoes on the rich mould of the bed and cover them with 2 inches of rich compost. Those who wish only a few plants had better buy of those who advertise them for sale. They go well by express.

Tomatoes.—Those well up in the hot-beds should be transplanted to another hot-bed or potted, and kept under glass. Seeds may be sown under glass.

Turnips.—Sow early varieties as directed for beets, on light, well enriched soil.

Window Boxes, as we have often mentioned, are very useful in getting a few early plants. A box 5 or 6 inches deep, filled with good soil, and set in the kitchen window, will give quite a stock of young plants. The box may be set out in the sun for a few hours during the warm portion of the day.

Flower Garden and Lawn.

The preparatory work of road and path making, and repairing old walks, should be out of the way, as the ground will be in good condition to be forked over for planting. In old beds it is well to take out a portion of the earth and replace it with some fresh soil from a pasture. In all planting of

Ornamental Trees, take as much pains in the preparation of the soil and the tree as if it were a choice fruit tree. A single specimen is in small places often better than several. The Weeping and Copper Beech, the Cut-leaved Birch, and a score of others among deciduous trees, make glorious specimens. Don't plant exactly such varieties as your neighbor has. In many of our villages one person sets the fashion and all others copy it. The custom of staking the trees is a bad one, but if they need to be anchored put some large stones over the roots. Then have plenty of

Shrubs.—There are so many beautiful ones that we are at a loss to designate them. Everyone wants Lilacs and Snowballs, just for the old associations, and does not wish to be without Weigelas, Japan Quince, Spiræas, and a host of others, native and exotic. Where, to make a division,

Hedges are desirable, it is for the most part best to use evergreens, as they are pleasing all the year round, but if deciduous ones are preferred, set them early. If properly attended to, any woody thing, from a beech tree to a barberry bush, will make a garden hedge, and if neglected, nothing will make a hedge of its own accord. The Japan Quince is very ornamental as a hedge, and when in flower, is in a blaze of glory. Most of the line

Edgings, as a general thing, are an abomination. Nothing is neater when well kept, but they are so seldom seen thus. Reset box, digging a trench with one perpendicular side, and split up the old plants, preserving as much root as possible to the divisions. Set them regularly, crowd the earth against them firmly, and clip the tops evenly to about two inches. Why don't some one make a cheap and neat edging tile and advertise it?

Roses, for general culture, should always be on their own roots. The catalogues give the varieties. The "perpetuals" are not perpetual at all, but the China sorts bloom all summer, though they are not hardy in winter. Don't forget the various

Climbing Roses and Wistarias, Honeysuckles, Clematises and other vines. The old clumps of

Herbaceous Plants, such as Phloxes, Dicentras, and others, if they have become large, should be divided and reset. Those from seed last year, as well as

Biennials, such as Sweet Williams, Hollyhocks, etc., must be transplanted to the borders.

Hardy Annuals are to be sown early. By a ridiculous misprint we were made, last month, to say that they "do best when *warm* as soon as the frost leaves," when we wrote it **sown**, and very plainly. By hardy annuals, we mean Larkspurs, Gilias, Whitlavias, Candytufts, Sweet Alyssums, and all things that come readily from seeds that were self-sown last season. Sow seeds of

Tender Annuals, such as Asters, Balsams, Everlasting flowers, etc., under glass, or in window boxes. The coverings should be gradually removed, as the weather gets warmer, from the beds of

Bulbs, to give Hyacinths, Crown Imperials, and the rest of them, a chance to show themselves. Do not be too anxious to get out

Bedding Plants that have been raised in the atmosphere of a green-house; they are generally warm weather plants, and stand still in cool weather.

Buying Plants.—Those who live near towns and cities will often be tempted to buy plants that have been forced. Many of our common herbaceous plants are potted and forced. These plants are at their best when you buy them, and you will get no more satisfaction from them this year.

Green and Hot-Houses.

As the plants will all go out of the green-house as soon as the weather suits, they should be gradually hardened off by abundant ventilation at all seasonable times, at the same time avoiding the ill effects of the sudden changes of temperature.

Camellias, making their new growth, need more warmth. Keep them free of insects.

Pelargoniums now coming into flower, should have all possible light, and a plenty of water, as should other plants now blooming.

Propagating of bedding stuff for out of door planting, should be pushed rapidly. The great element of "luck" is to keep the air of the house 10° to 15° cooler than the sand on the bench. If potted cuttings have filled the pots with roots, shake out the earth and repot in the same pots. Sow

Seeds of those annuals that have very fine seeds, such as Lobelias, in pots or pans with scarcely any covering of earth. Put the roots of

Dahlias in a warm place where they will sprout.

Cannas and *Colocasia*, or Caladium esculentum, so valuable as foliage plants, may be forwarded.

Tuberoses.—Usually very unsatisfactory if put out as dry bulbs, if started with a little heat, and then planted out in warm weather, will flower finely.

Plants in Pits and Frames must not be allowed to suffer by being kept too close, nor for want of water.

Cold Grapery.

April is usually the month for uncovering and putting up the vines. In order to insure an even breaking of the buds along the whole length of the vine, it is not put up in place at once, but is suspended so that the upper end shall bend downward, and the whole vine hang in the form of a bow. This counteracts the tendency of the upper buds to get the advantage of the lower ones. When all have taken an equal start, which can be secured by altering the curvature of the vine, and the shoots have grown 2 or 3 inches long, the vine may be put in place. Fork over the inside borders and syringe the house thoroughly. If any injury has happened to the vines in winter, which will be indicated by cracking and bleeding, and a failure of the upper buds to start, the vine must be cut back, and a strong lower shoot selected to be trained in place of the vine cut away. Keep the temperature of the house at about 65° until near the end of the month, when it may increase to 70° or 80°, and the syringe be used to wet all parts of the house and vines, morning and evening. Avoid sudden changes of temperature within the house.

Apiary in April.

The full notes by Mr. Quinby, given last month, are in good measure applicable to this, especially, if on account of the weather, or for other reason, or no reason, the suggestions were neglected. Mr. Q.'s memoranda for April have not come to hand. ——Be sure that each hive contains a laying queen, and food (honey) enough to last them until flowers are abundant. If all the stocks are strong and well provided, there will be little danger of robbing. The bees will be busy gathering pollen and nursing the young brood. But if severe frosts and rains cut off the supply of pollen, they will very likely begin to rob. At such times watch the hives and contract the entrances. Robber bees may be detected by their greasy look, and by the ferment of excitement the robber-colony is in. In the robbed colony there is great excitement also: bees leave with full honey sacks, and if flour be dusted upon them as they leave, they may be tracked to the hive in which they belong. It is sometimes advised to change two such hives, placing each on the other's stand. April is a favorable time to transfer bees to movable comb-hives. This is best done by driving the bees from their hive, inverted, into a box of about the same size placed above it, and when nearly all have gone up, set the bees at one side and open the old box hive by prying off one side, so as to expose the flat sides of the combs. Then cut the combs out one after another, and laying them upon a soft cushion of some kind; cut them to fit snugly, and tie them into several of the frames of a movable comb-hive. The combs may be tied into the frames by fastening splints on each side, or by winding strings or wire round and round, which are removed after the bees fasten the combs to the frames. Arrange the combs as nearly in the same relative position that they had originally as possible. Finally, shake the bees upon the top frame and put down the cover. Injury may happen to the brood if this be done in the open air; hence the hive should be removed to the workshop. Put new hives and old ones in order for use. All filth and refuse, dead bees, etc., must be carefully cleaned out, and the bottom boards kept clean. Salt sprinkled under the hives will keep away the ants, and the moth worms must be sought out and killed. Wrens, if their boxes are set near, or among the hives, will help keep moths in check. Study carefully the progeny of Italian queens; see which have the brightest colors, and which queen is best to select as the mother of new queens for "Italianizing" your stock, or for improving the breed, if it is already Italianized. There is a great difference in queens, and the stock which contains the best one should lack nothing—neither bees nor honey, nor empty brood cells for her to lay in; and according to the needs of your apiary, she should be furnished with worker or with drone comb in which to lay. With proper care, the Italianizing of an apiary may proceed very rapidly.

Interesting Emigration Statistics for 1866.—During 10 months, from Jan. 1st to Oct. 31st, 1866, there arrived at the port of New York alone **200,723** Emigrants or New Settlers from different parts of the Old World—much the largest proportion of them from Germany, Ireland and England—as follows:

Jan. 10,861	Mar. 14,204	May 41,530	July 29,772	Sep. 18,483
Feb. 6,108	Apr. 26,418	June 34,183	Aug. 17,438	Oct. 19,397

The destination of these new comers is also interesting. Large numbers stop in New York City, and are set down to this State, though many of them afterwards move on westward and to New England. Why Indiana received a greater number than any other State is not clear to us. So far as ascertained, their destination was as follows:

New York	68,563	California	1,467	Mississippi	54
Indiana	72,801	Kentucky	1,430	New Brunswick	50
Pennsylvania	21,818	Virginia	897	Oregon	37
Illinois	19,925	Dist. Columbia	790	Nova Scotia	33
Ohio	11,147	Tennessee	490	Colorado	30
Massachusetts	10,719	Kansas	418	Arkansas	25
Wisconsin	7,063	Louisiana	304	South America	20
New Jersey	6,998	Maine	311	West Indies	15
Missouri	4,360	Vermont	270	Mexico	11
Iowa	4,078	Delaware	209	British Columbia	10
Michigan	3,415	Georgia	183	Florida	8
Connecticut	3,361	New Hampshire	169	Pr. Edward's Isl.	8
Minnesota	3,247	South Carolina	148	Central America	8
Utah	3,083	North Carolina	135	Cuba	5
Rhode Island	2,171	Nebraska	97	Nevada	4
Maryland	1,628	Texas	86	Australia	3
Canada	1,361	Alabama	58	Idaho	1

AMERICAN AGRICULTURIST.

ORANGE JUDD & Co., Publishers, 41 Park Row, N. Y. City.

ANNUAL SUBSCRIPTION TERMS (always in advance): $1.50 each for less than four copies: Four to nine copies, $1.25 each: Ten to nineteen copies, $1.20 each: Twenty copies and upwards, $1 each. Papers are addressed to each name.

They are Coming.

Yes, 500–600–700 a day! We refer to the subscription names for premium lists. During March our premium canvassers have been very active and *very successful*, and we have been sending out at a rapid rate the good premiums offered in the table (next column.)

Many lists of names partly filled during December, January and February, have been completed, and many *new* premium clubs have been started and part of them already filled. The work can go on just as well **all through April.** The supply of premiums is unlimited, and almost everybody desiring it, can get one or more valuable articles. All that is needed to get a subscriber in every family, is, to show the paper, explain that it is the most beautifully Illustrated Paper in the country, and yet published at less than half the cost of other Periodicals and Illustrated Journals, while its reading matter is all carefully prepared and very *instructive* and *useful*. It costs less than half a cent a day! In most places the eggs from a single hen would pay the subscription. Each subscriber gets during the year, for only $1.50, a great *volume* of about **430** large pages, containing over *Ten Thousand Dollars worth of original Engravings*, besides reading matter that costs nearly or quite *Fifteen Thousand Dollars!* In a multitude of cases reported to us, single hints in this paper have been worth scores of dollars, and often hundreds.

Now, look over our premium list, choose the premium you would like, take a copy of the paper, sally out among neighbors and friends, in your own neighborhood and elsewhere (*for premium clubs need not be all at one post-office*), and in a brief time the desired number of subscribers can be gathered, and the premium secured. A full description of the premiums will be sent free to any one desiring it. Any Specimen numbers, cards and show bills needed, will be supplied free.

☞ **We take** *so much pains to procure only good articles in all cases, that any one securing anything from our premium list, saves the risk usually run of getting poor or indifferent goods, when buying of unknown or irresponsible parties. Every thing we send out as a premium is guaranteed to be the best of its kind and price.*

Old and new subscribers count in premium lists. *Our premiums* are standard articles, and enough can be obtained to supply all calls for premiums for six months. Every canvasser can take abundant time, but

As fast as subscriptions are obtained, send them along, that the subscribers may begin to receive the paper; and when all the names that can be obtained are forwarded, select the premium, and it will be promptly furnished. To save mistakes and keeping accounts, *send with each list of names, the exact subscription money.*

Remit in Post-Office money orders, drafts or checks on N. Y. City, if these can not be had, register money letters.

☞ *Every name designed for a premium list must be so marked when sent in.* (We can not count others.)

☞ *Every article offered is new and of the very best manufacture. No charge is made for packing or boxing any of the articles in this Premium List. The forty-three Premiums,* **Nos. 1, 2, 6,** *and from* **29** *to* **32,** *and from* **40** *to* **75** *inclusive, will each be delivered* **FREE** *of all charges, by mail or express, (at the Post-Office or express office nearest recipient), to any place in the United States or Territories, excepting those reached only by the Overland Mail.—The other articles cost the recipient only the freight after leaving the manufactory of each, by any conveyance that may be specified.*

Table of Premiums and Terms, For Volume 26—(1867).

Open to all—No Competition.

No.	*Names of Premium Articles.*	*Price of Premiums.*	*Number of Subscribers required* at $1.50	at $1.
1	*Garden Seeds for a Family* (40 kinds)	$5 00	13	37
2	*Flower Seeds for a Family* (100 kinds)	$5 00	13	37
3	*Nursery Stock* (Any kinds desired)	$20 00	30	[illegible]
4	*Iona Grape Vines* (12 of No. 1)	$18 00	27	[illegible]
5	*Concord Grape Vines* (100 of No. 1)	$12 00	19	65
6	*Japan Lilies* (12 Bulbs)	$8 00	15	45
7	*Sewing Machine* (Wheeler & Wilson)	$55 00	60	210
8	*Sewing Machine* (Grover & Baker)	$55 00	60	210
9	*Sewing Machine* (Singer's Tailoring)	[illegible]	[illegible]	[illegible]
10	*Sewing Machine* (Florence)	[illegible]	[illegible]	270
11	*Sewing Machine* (Willcox & Gibbs)	[illegible]	60	210
12	*Sewing Machine* (Howe's)	[illegible]	[illegible]	210
13	*Washing Machine* (Doty's)	$14 00	21	70
14	*Clothes Wringer* (Best—Universal)	$10 00	18	58
15	*Tea Set* (Hart's best Silver Plated)	[illegible]	[illegible]	[illegible]
16	*Castor and Fruit Basket* (do. do.)	$30 00	45	145
17	*Ice or Water Pitcher* (do. do.)	[illegible]	[illegible]	[illegible]
18	*One Dozen Tea Spoons* (do. do.)	[illegible]	17	[illegible]
19	*One Dozen Table Spoons* (do. do.)	$15 00	22	[illegible]
20	*One Dozen Dining Forks* (do. do.)	$15 00	22	[illegible]
21	*Piano* (Best Steinway & Son's 7-octave)	$625 00	[illegible]	1550
22	*Melodeon, 5-octave* (G. A. Prince & Co.'s)	$112 00	138	400
23	*Melodeon, 4-octave* (do. do.)	$67 00	78	[illegible]
24	*Ladies' Gold Watch* (Beautiful)	$110 00	130	400
25	*Silver Watch* (Valuable Time Keeper)	[illegible]	48	[illegible]
26	*Double Barrel Gun* (Very good)	$30 00	46	150
27	*Spencer's Breech-loading Rifle* (Hunting)	[illegible]	[illegible]	[illegible]
28	*Tool Chest* (First Quality of Tools)	[illegible]	[illegible]	[illegible]
29	*Case of Mathematical Instruments*	$9 00	19	[illegible]
30	*Case of Mathematical Instruments*	$15 00	22	[illegible]
31	*Morton's Best No. 6 Gold Pen* (Silver Case)	[illegible]	14	[illegible]
32	*Morton's Best No. 5 Gold Pen* (Silver Case)	[illegible]	11	[illegible]
33	*Barometer* (Woodruff's Mercurial)	$18 00	27	[illegible]
34	*Barometer* (Woodruff's Mercurial)	[illegible]	19	[illegible]
35	*Buckeye Mowing Machine, No. 2.*	$125 00	150	[illegible]
36	*Allen's Patent Cylinder Plow, etc.*	[illegible]	31	100
37	*The Aquarius or Water Thrower*	$11 00	19	65
38	*American Cyclopedia* (Appleton's)	[illegible]	[illegible]	[illegible]
39	*Worcester's Great Illustrated Dictionary*	$12 00	19	[illegible]
40	*Any Back Volume Agriculturist* (In clean new Nos. Post-paid—Un-bound.)	[illegible]	[illegible]	[illegible]
41	*Any Two Back Volumes* do.	[illegible]	[illegible]	[illegible]
42	*Any Three* do. do. do.	[illegible]	13	[illegible]
43	*Any Four* do. do. do.	[illegible]	15	[illegible]
44	*Any Five* do. do. do.	[illegible]	17	[illegible]
45	*Any Six* do. do. do.	$10 [illegible]	19	[illegible]
46	*Any Seven* do. do. do.	[illegible]	[illegible]	[illegible]
47	*Any Eight* do. do. do.	[illegible]	[illegible]	[illegible]
48	*Any Nine* do. do. do.	[illegible]	[illegible]	[illegible]
49	*Vols. XVI to XXV* do.	[illegible]	[illegible]	[illegible]
50	*Any Back Volume Agriculturist* (Neatly Bound, Not Post-paid.)	[illegible]	[illegible]	[illegible]
51	*Any Two Back Volumes* do.	[illegible]	[illegible]	[illegible]
52	*Any Three* do. do. do.	[illegible]	18	[illegible]
53	*Any Four* do. do. do.	$10 [illegible]	[illegible]	[illegible]
54	*Any Five* do. do. do.	[illegible]	21	[illegible]
55	*Any Six* do. do. do.	[illegible]	[illegible]	[illegible]
56	*Any Seven* do. do. do.	[illegible]	[illegible]	[illegible]
57	*Any Eight* do. do. do.	[illegible]	[illegible]	[illegible]
58	*Any Nine* do. do. do.	[illegible]	[illegible]	[illegible]
59	*Vols. XVI to XXV* do.	[illegible]	[illegible]	[illegible]
60	*Genesee Farmer, 1838-1865, 8 Vols.* Bound	[illegible]	21	[illegible]
61	*Downing's Landscape Gardening* (All sent post-paid through, by Mail or Express.)	[illegible]	15	[illegible]
62	*Cummings & Miller's Architect.*	$10 00	18	[illegible]
63	*A $10 Library* (Your Choice)	$10 00	18	[illegible]
64	*A $15 Library* do.	$15 00	[illegible]	[illegible]
65	*A $20 Library* do.	[illegible]	[illegible]	[illegible]
66	*A $25 Library* do.	[illegible]	[illegible]	[illegible]
67	*A $30 Library* do.	$30 00	[illegible]	[illegible]
68	*A $35 Library* do.	[illegible]	[illegible]	[illegible]
69	*A $40 Library* do.	[illegible]	[illegible]	[illegible]
70	*A $45 Library* do.	[illegible]	[illegible]	[illegible]
71	*A $50 Library* do.	[illegible]	[illegible]	[illegible]
72	*A $60 Library* do.	[illegible]	[illegible]	[illegible]
73	*A $75 Library* do.	[illegible]	110	[illegible]
74	*A $100 Library* do.	$100 00	150	[illegible]
75	*A Choice of Good Books* (See Terms below.)			
76	*Sewing Machine* (Finkle & Lyon)	[illegible]	60	210
77	*One Dozen Pocket Lanterns*	[illegible]	13	[illegible]

For Full Description of the several premiums see October *Agriculturist*, pages 319 to 35[illegible], or apply for a *Descriptive List*, which will be furnished *free* and post-paid. We have room here for only the following:

No. 63 to 74—Good Libraries.—These can be selected by the recipients, from any of the books named in the list in this column. The books will be *delivered* free of cost, by mail or express.

No. 75—General Book Premium.—Any one not desiring the specific Book premiums, 63 to 74, on sending any number of names above 25, may select Books from the list (below), to the amount of 10 cents for each subscriber sent at $1: or to the amount of 30 cents for each name sent at the (ten) club price of $1.20 each: or to the amount of 60 cents for each name at $1.50. *This offer is only for clubs of 25 or more. The books will be sent by mail or express, prepaid by us.*

BOOKS FOR FARMERS AND OTHERS.

(For sale at the office of the *Agriculturist*, or they will be forwarded by mail, *post-paid*, on receipt of price. ☞ *All these are included in Our Premiums, Nos. 63 to 75, above.*

- Allen's (L. F.) Rural Architecture ... $1 50
- Allen's (R. L.) American Farm Book ... 1 50
- American Agricultural Annual, 1867, paper, 50c.; cloth ... 75
- Allen's Diseases of Domestic Animals ... 1 00
- American Horticultural Annual, 1867, paper, 50c.; cloth ... 75
- American Bird Fancier ... [illegible]
- American Rose Culturist ... [illegible]
- American Weeds and Useful Plants ... 1 [illegible]
- Architecture, by Cummings & Miller ... 10 00
- Barry's Fruit Garden ... 1 75
- Bement's Poulterer's Companion ... 2 00
- Bement's Rabbit Fancier ... 30
- Breck's New Book of Flowers ... 1 75
- Buist's Flower Garden Directory ... 1 50
- Buist's Family Kitchen Gardener ... 1 00
- Burr's Vegetables of America ... 5 00
- Chorlton's Grape-Grower's Guide ... [illegible]
- Cobbett's American Gardener ... [illegible]
- Cole's (S. W.) American Fruit Book ... [illegible]
- Cole's Veterinarian ... [illegible]
- Dadd's Modern Horse Doctor ... 1 50
- Dadd's (Geo. H.) American Cattle Doctor ... 1 50
- Dana's Muck Manual ... 1 25
- Dog and Gun (Hooper's) ... paper, 30c. ... cloth ... [illegible]
- Downing's Country Houses ... [illegible]
- Downing's Landscape Gardening (new Edition) ... [illegible]
- Downing's Fruits and Fruit Trees of America ... [illegible]
- Downing's Rural Essays ... [illegible]
- Eastwood on Cranberry ... [illegible]
- Elliott's Western Fruit Grower's Guide ... 1 [illegible]
- Flax Culture ... [illegible]
- Field's (Thomas W.) Pear Culture ... [illegible]
- Flint's Milch Cows and Dairy Farming ... [illegible]
- French's Farm Drainage ... [illegible]
- Fuller's Grape Culturist, (Revised Edition) ... [illegible]
- Fuller's Strawberry Culturist ... [illegible]
- Gardening for Profit, by Peter Henderson ... [illegible]
- Gray's How Plants Grow ... [illegible]
- Gray's Manual of Botany and Lessons in one Vol. ... 4 [illegible]
- Guenon on Milch Cows ... [illegible]
- Harris' Insects Injurious to Vegetation, plain $4.00, col'd ... [illegible]
- Harris' Rural Annual. Bound, 8 Nos., in 2 Vols. Each ... [illegible]
- Herbert's Hints to Horsekeepers ... [illegible]
- Hop Culture ... [illegible]
- Husmann's Grapes and Wine ... [illegible]
- Johnston's Agricultural Chemistry ... [illegible]
- Johnston's Elements of Agricultural Chemistry ... [illegible]
- Johnson's (Prof. S. W.) Essays on Manures ... [illegible]
- Langstroth on Honey Bee ... [illegible]
- Leuchar's How to Build Hot-Houses ... [illegible]
- Mayhew's Illustrated Horse Doctor ... [illegible]
- Mayhew's Illustrated Horse Management ... [illegible]
- Mayhew's Practical Bookkeeping for Farmers ... [illegible]
- Blanks for do. do. ... [illegible]
- Miles on the Horse's Foot ... [illegible]
- My Farm of Edgewood ... [illegible]
- My Vineyard at Lakeview ... [illegible]
- Norton's Scientific Agriculture ... [illegible]
- Onion Culture ... [illegible]
- Our Farm of Four Acres (bound) 60c ... paper ... [illegible]
- Pardee on Strawberry Culture ... [illegible]
- Peat and Its Uses, by Prof. S. W. Johnson ... [illegible]
- Pedder's Land Measurer ... [illegible]
- Quinby's Mysteries of Bee Keeping (NEW) ... [illegible]
- Randall's Sheep Husbandry ... [illegible]
- Randall's Fine Wool Sheep Husbandry ... [illegible]
- Rivers' Miniature Fruit Garden ... [illegible]
- Richardson on the Dog, paper 30c ... cloth ... [illegible]
- Rural Annual, by Joseph Harris ... [illegible]
- Saunders' Domestic Poultry (NEW), paper, 40c., bound ... [illegible]
- Schenck's Gardener's Text Book ... [illegible]
- Scribner's Ready Reckoner ... [illegible]
- Skillful Housewife ... [illegible]
- Stewart's (John) Stable Book ... [illegible]
- Thompson's Food of Animals ... [illegible]
- Tobacco Culture ... [illegible]
- Todd's (S. E.) Young Farmer's Manual ... [illegible]
- Warder's Hedges and Evergreens ... [illegible]
- Watson's American Home Garden ... [illegible]
- Woodward's Country Homes ... [illegible]
- Youatt and Spooner on the Horse ... 1 50
- Youatt and Martin on Cattle ... [illegible]
- Youatt on the Hog ... [illegible]
- Youatt on Sheep ... [illegible]
- Youmans' Household Science ... [illegible]

Commercial Matters—Market Prices.

The following condensed, comprehensive tables, carefully prepared specially for the *American Agriculturist*, show at a glance the transactions for the month, ending March 15, 1867, and also for the same month last year:

1. TRANSACTIONS AT THE NEW-YORK MARKETS.

RECEIPTS.	*Flour.*	*Wheat.*	*Corn.*	*Rye.*	*Barley.*	*Oats.*
27 days *this* m'th	111,000	94,000	138,000	15,000	47,500	78,000
24 days *last* m'th	101,000	85,000	14,000	8,600	51,000	134,000

SALES.	*Flour.*	*Wheat.*	*Corn.*	*Rye.*	*Barley.*
27 days *this* month,	161,500	1,565,000	238,000	316,000	885,000
24 days *last* month,	182,000	815,000	985,000	317,000	650,000

2. *Comparison with same period at this time last year.*

RECEIPTS.	*Flour.*	*Wheat.*	*Corn.*	*Rye.*	*Barley.*	*Oats.*
27 days 1867	111,000	94,000	138,000	15,000	47,500	78,000
24 days 1866	177,000	13,700	161,000	8,400	88,000	181,000

SALES.	*Flour.*	*Wheat.*	*Corn.*	*Rye.*	*Barley.*
27 days 1867	161,000	1,565,000	238,000	316,000	885,000
24 days 1866	201,000	617,000	844,000	189,500	101,000

3. *Exports from New York, Jan. 1 to March 15:*

	Flour.	*Wheat.*	*Corn.*	*Rye.*	*Oats.*	*Barley.*
1867	71,793	18,396	1,842,249	114,858	45,981	325,877
1866	210,283	67,710	1,765,987	78,173	192,271	......
1865	374,130	123,980	191,046	161	16,643	......

Gold has declined since our last from 140⅝ to 133, leading to corresponding depression in most financial and commercial values. Within the past few days it has been more freely dealt in by speculative buyers at rising prices, thus stimulating business in other departments.... The month under review, (February 18 to March 15,) opened with a dull and heavy market for nearly all kinds of Breadstuffs. Liberal receipts of Flour and Wheat from California influenced prices unfavorably, making holders eager to sell and buyers reluctant to purchase more than was necessary to supply pressing wants. Subsequently the demand improved, fostered, in part, by more encouraging foreign news, which led to rather extensive export operations, especially in Corn. Prices rallied pretty sharply, and toward the close the tendency was upward. The principal receivers evince less disposition to press supplies on the market, and less anxiety to realize at the ruling figures, as they generally look for the establishment of even better rates, in view of the current light arrivals and the gradual absorption of the stocks available at this center.... Provisions have been much brisker, and hog products firmer in price. Beef has been steady. Butter, Cheese and Eggs have favored buyers decidedly. ....Cotton has been more freely offered and more sought after at reduced quotations, closing with partially renewed firmness.... Wool has advanced 3c.@5c. ℔ since the passage of the Wool Tariff, so-called, but at the improved prices trade has been very moderate.... Hay has been scarce and stiffly held, with a fair inquiry, partly for export ...Hops, Seeds and Tobacco have been comparatively quiet at about previous figures.

CURRENT WHOLESALE PRICES.

	Feb. 15.	March 15.
PRICE OF GOLD	136¾	134¾
FLOUR—Super to Extra State	$9 80 @ 11 25	$9 80 @ 12 40
Super to Extra Southern	10 [illegible] @ 16 [illegible]	10 [illegible] @ 16 [illegible]
Extra Western	[illegible]	[illegible]
Extra Genesee	[illegible]	[illegible]
Superfine Western	[illegible]	[illegible]
RYE FLOUR	[illegible]	[illegible]
CORN MEAL	[illegible]	[illegible]
WHEAT—All kinds of White	[illegible]	[illegible]
All kinds of Red and Amber	[illegible]	[illegible]
CORN—Yellow	[illegible]	[illegible]
Mixed	[illegible]	[illegible]
OATS—Western	[illegible]	[illegible]
State	[illegible]	[illegible]
RYE	[illegible]	[illegible]
BARLEY	[illegible]	[illegible]
HAY—Bale ℔ 100 lb.	[illegible]	[illegible]
Loose	[illegible]	[illegible]
STRAW, ℔ 100 lb.	[illegible]	[illegible]
COTTON—Middlings, ℔ lb.	[illegible] @ 31½	[illegible] @ 31½
HOPS—Crop of 1866, ℔ lb.	[illegible]	[illegible] @ 70
FEATHERS—Live Geese, ℔ lb.	[illegible]	[illegible]
SEED—Clover, ℔ lb.	15 @ [illegible]	14½ @ 15½
Timothy, ℔ bushel	[illegible]	[illegible]
Flax, ℔ bushel	[illegible]	[illegible]
SUGAR—Brown, ℔ lb.	9 @ 12½	9½ @ 12½
MOLASSES, Cuba, ℔ gl.	[illegible]	[illegible]
COFFEE—Rio, (Gold price) ℔ lb.	15½ @ 19	15½ @ 19
TOBACCO, Kentucky, &c., ℔ lb.	[illegible]	[illegible]
Seed Leaf, ℔ lb.	[illegible]	[illegible]
WOOL—Domestic Fleece, ℔ lb.	[illegible]	[illegible]
Domestic, pulled, ℔ lb.	[illegible]	[illegible]
California, unwashed	[illegible]	[illegible]
TALLOW, ℔ lb.	11 @ 11½	10¾ @ 11½
OIL CAKE—℔ ton	[illegible]	[illegible]
PORK—Mess, ℔ barrel	[illegible]	[illegible]
Prime, ℔ barrel	[illegible]	[illegible]
BEEF—Plain mess	[illegible]	[illegible]
LARD, in barrels, ℔ lb.	[illegible]	[illegible] @ 13½
BUTTER—Western, ℔ lb.	[illegible]	[illegible]
State, ℔ lb.	[illegible]	[illegible]
CHEESE	[illegible]	[illegible]
BEANS—℔ bushel	[illegible]	[illegible]
PEAS—Canada, ℔ bushel	[illegible]	[illegible]
EGGS—Fresh, ℔ dozen	[illegible]	[illegible]
POULTRY—Fowls, ℔ lb.	17 @ 19	17 @ [illegible]
Turkeys, ℔ lb.	18 @ 20	[illegible]
POTATOES—Mercers, ℔ bbl.	[illegible]	[illegible]
Peach Blows, ℔ barrel	[illegible]	[illegible]
POTATOES—Buckeye, ℔ bbl.	[illegible]	[illegible]
APPLES—℔ barrel	[illegible]	[illegible]
CRANBERRIES, ℔ barrel	25 00 @ 29 00	17 00 @ 21 00

New York Live Stock Markets.—The supply during the past four weeks has been only moderate as is shown in the following table of receipts:

WEEK ENDING.	*Beeves.*	*Cows.*	*Calves.*	*Sheep.*	*Swine.*
Feb'y. 19	4,714	66	637	13,936	15,250
Feb'y. 26	5,165	91	609	9,967	13,770
March 5	6,190	63	646	13,871	13,870
March 12	5,903	78	789	13,038	16,960
Total in four Weeks	20,364	299	2,481	56,815	59,850
Average per Week	5,090	75	625	11,211	14,959
do. do. *last Month*	4,767	67	510	19,739	11,343
do. do. *prev's Month*	4,346	69	436	17,770	19,250
Average per Week, 1866	5,748	94	1,200	20,000	13,000
do. do. do. 1865	5,255	118	1,500	16,091	11,023
do. do. do. 1864	5,161	145	1,511	15,315	12,676
do. do. do. 1863	5,150	129	694	9,941	21,670
Total in 1866	298,880	4,885	62,420	1,040,000	672,000
Total in 1865	270,274	6,161	77,991	836,733	573,197
Total in 1864	267,609	7,603	75,621	782,462	660,270
Total in 1863	264,091	6,470	35,705	519,316	1,101,617

The heavy snow storms reduced the supply of animals materially, the last half of February....**Beef Cattle** run more than a thousand head below last year's weekly average. Prices went up correspondingly, the best reaching fully 18c. ℔ lb, estimated dressed weight, the last week in February, but fell back 1c.@1¼c. ℔ lb, (March 5th,) and continue about the same this week—viz: 16¼c.@17c. for first quality cattle, and 17½c. for a few extras; medium good qualities 16c., fair to inferior 15¼c.@14¼c.; low grades, 12c.@14c....**Milch Cows** are in very little demand here. A really good milker with her young calf by her side, and sure of being sold for no defect, will bring $80@$90, calf included, where a purchaser happens to come along, and an occasional fancy animal goes at $100 and upwards; but the most of the sales are at $75@$70 for fair animals, and $65@$30 for inferior to lowest grade....**Veal Calves** have been selling well, 13c.@14c. ℔ lb live weight for the best grades, but the seizure by the Sanitary Police of some 500 carcasses of dressed young calves has turned the appetites of most persons against veal, and 12c.@13c. are the highest present rates, with plenty of sales at 10c.@11c. for common, and 9c. and below for poor. It will be useless hereafter to send a calf here under four or five weeks old at least....**Sheep.**—The new tariff on wool is leading farmers to keep their sheep, to get the spring clip of wool, and our markets are scantily supplied. Prices have rapidly advanced to 9¼c.@10c. ℔ lb live weight for good sheep; 10¼c.@10½c. for extras, and 9c.@7½c. for inferior to poorest....**Live Hogs** advanced materially two or three weeks ago, but with warmer weather approaching, with the Lent season present, and with fair supplies, the market is declining. The latest sales stand at 7¾c.@8¼c. ℔ lb live weight, for the different grades.

Hop Culture.—There is increasing interest taken in this crop, which is frequently so profitable. We cannot better satisfy our readers than by referring them to our little manual of hop culture, for which see book list. The authors of the prize essays will be able to give information as to how and where sets may be obtained.

Containing a great variety of Items, including many good Hints and Suggestions which we throw into smaller type and condensed form, for want of space elsewhere.

SPECIAL TO ADVERTISERS.—Owing to the greatly increased circulation of the *American Agriculturist*, it is necessary to send the paper to press much earlier than formerly, in order to have the numbers reach all subscribers by the first of the month. For this reason, to insure the insertion of an advertisement, *send it in by the* **first** of the month preceding publication, and never later than the 10th. Advertisers will please make a note of this, to prevent future disappointment.

No Plants for Sale. No Seeds for Sale. No Cuttings for Sale.—We wish we had a thousand acres with hundreds of people with nothing to do but make cuttings, save seeds, and do all sorts of kind things. But the trouble is we havn't, and if we were to supply all the grafts of the Beurré Clairgeau pear that have been asked for, our one tree would only serve as a bean-pole. So with seeds; we notice a plant, and hundreds of people think we have seeds to sell or give away. We are not in the nursery or seed business, but have only private grounds for our own amusement and instruction. The dealers advertise, and each nurseryman or seedsman is supposed to have a general assortment. Will our friends just see how impossible it is to answer their many requests for plants, cuttings, seeds, and the like?

American Pomology.—Part I. Apples, by Dr. J. A. Warder.—To pomologists a work by Dr. Warder will need no commendation. Though a citizen of Ohio, he is so sure to be at any pomological gathering, be it East or West, that the whole country claims him, and if any one has a right to entitle his work *American* Pomology it is certainly Dr. Warder. The present is the first instalment of a work that will cover the whole ground. The author has taken the "bull by the horns," and attempted to bring apples into something like order. We leave criticism of the work to other hands, and content ourselves with giving an idea of its contents. This volume has over 750 pages, the first 375 of which are devoted to the discussion of the general subjects of propagation, nursery culture, selection and planting, cultivation of orchards, care of fruit, insects, and the like. The remainder is occupied with descriptions of apples. With the richness of material at hand, the trouble was to decide what to leave out. It will be found that while the old and standard varieties are not neglected, the new and promising sorts have prominence. A list of selections for different localities by eminent orchardists is a valuable portion of the volume, while the Analytical Index or *Catalogue Raisonné*, as the French would say, gives evidence of a fearful amount of labor. This differs from any fruit book heretofore published in this country, in presenting a classification of apples. The author gives principal European systems and modestly puts forth his own to be tested by practice. He divides apples into four classes, according to their forms. Each of these classes is sub-divided by other obvious characters, and it would seem that any apple described in the book might be easily identified. Should this stand the test of experience it will prove a great advance in pomology, and we trust it will be given a trial. Fruit-growers will welcome this book as a valuable and long-wished for addition to pomological literature, and it will prove equally useful to the novice and the experienced orchardist. The work has 293 illustrations, and is printed on good paper, well bound, and sent by mail at $3. Ready on April 1st, or shortly after.

S. S. Question-Books—Advance in Price.—The manufacturers find it necessary, in order to cover cost, to increase the price of "*Lessons for Every Sunday in the Year*" to 15 cents per copy. They are still the cheapest books in the market, however. The postage is 4 cents per copy, or 3 cents each in parcels of ten or more. We send full sample copies, (Nos. 1, 2, 3, and 4,) post-paid, for 75 cents.

A Horticultural "Gift Enterprise."—Several have sent us circulars of the "New England Vine Growers' Association," at South Norwalk, Conn., asking our opinion thereof. This circular, in brief, starts with the announcement that the object of the Association is—we can't use all their adjectives—the promotion of Grape Culture. It will receive "subscriptions" from everybody at $3 each. (It would'nt look well to say sell tickets.) For this $3, one gets 1 Iona, 1 Delaware, and 1 Concord grape vine. The circular says: "This being a discount from "Nursery prices," which simply is not true. Besides these vines, a "subscriber" has a chance in the "award of premiums"—why not say lottery and be done with it? These are: First, "A farm of 40 acres, title perfect; second, 15 acres of land near a thriving New England village." We will not discuss the vagueness of these premiums as it is self evident. We have a letter from the secretary of this "Association" referring to very respectable people. We advise him to get out of a disreputable scheme, or he will not be able to refer to some of these again. That precious humbug, the "Orphans' Home Lottery," leaves its slimy train behind it, and though it was countenanced by wives of officers whose patriotism outweighed their discretion, it is now a common by-word of reproach. In behalf of horticulture we denounce this project, and beg every right-thinking man to withdraw his name from it. New England enterprise needs no such "stimulating" for any "lucrative branch of husbandry." (See catalogues.) Better that Connecticut should never bear grapes, other than on her State shield, than that their culture should be forced by a *lottery*, and it is "only this and nothing more."

The Grape Culturist, by A. S. Fuller, New and Revised Edition, N. Y., Orange Judd & Co., 1867.—When this work first appeared in 1864, and before the publishers of the *Agriculturist* had any interest in it, the following appeared in a notice on page 101, vol. XXIII: "This treatise covers the whole ground of garden and vineyard culture, from starting the plants from eyes or cuttings, to the established fruiting vine. The whole is told in a plain style from the author's own experience; his system of pruning is very simple and easily understood, and the reasons are given for preferring it to others; he, however, gives the other modes in practice and illustrates the whole in a most liberal manner. * * * This most useful manual will be equally valuable to one who cultivates a single vine and to the vinyardist." After three years, and having in the interval read all its successors, we cannot express its character better than to repeat and emphasize this commendation. Mr. Fuller, in his writings, as well as in his nursery, tells the "secrets," as some consider them, of horticulture so freely that some grape-growers blame him. This, however, only gives him the stronger hold on "the people," for whom he writes, as is seen by the large sale that attends every book that bears his name. The new edition is brought up to the present time by additions. Some parts have been entirely re-written and new illustrations added. It still continues to be *the* Grape Book. Price, $1.50 by mail.

Humbug Plants, Seeds, Etc.—At this season it is well to avoid all circulars and advertisements of wonderful corn, and other seeds and plants, brought before the public just at the planting season, too late to admit of an inquiry into their real merits. We see several such things advertised with got up "certificates," and have rejected sundry such advertisements offered at prodigious pay. Don't waste money, time, soil, and labor on any of these before unheard of things.

SUNDRY HUMBUGS.—Hundreds of letters this month show great activity among the "Ticket" and Circular operators. Many ask an immediate answer by letter, but we cannot respond individually to half of them. Many swindlers, previously shown up by us are still inquired about. We cannot repeat all we have written; those interested should look over our back numbers; several hundred operators have been described within a year. We give below the present names of several operators, but most of these names will soon be changed to others, if not already done. Three or four men, like Tuttle and Todd, have used quite a number of different names within two years past....A huge swindle, with large plans and employing a great many clerks, was recently started at 69 Broadway, under the name of the "*Bankers' and Merchants' Grand Presentation Entertainment*," ostensibly by "Clark, Webster & Co.," but probably by a large Chicago operator, with J. D. Miller, the "Sand River Petroleum Prize Co." man. The police stepped in and seized an immense mass of circulars, etc., and nipped the swindling scheme, though about 20,000 circulars had already gone out. All of these Gift Enterprises, etc., are to be carefully avoided, no matter how pretentious or plausible, or how good an object they may *profess* to be aiming at....We continue to receive circulars issued by "Harris Brothers," of Boston, offering a copy of the *American Agriculturist* to subscribers to the so-called "National Distribution," *alias* lottery, for a home for disabled soldiers. In October last we exposed this swindling concern. The managers have been put under "bonds" in the Boston Courts. As before stated, we recognize no certificate issued by them....A vile villain, calling himself "A. B. Channing, M. D.," sends circulars to young men, and even to lads as young as 13 years, offering disgusting books, instruments, etc. He refuses to deliver those things in person, and can only be reached by mail. Of course any such man would pocket any money sent him. If to be found, he should be summarily locked up. It is now positively unsafe for parents or guardians to allow any mail matter to go into the hands of young people without being previously examined. . A letter from South Carolina says the writer sent $10 to Whitman & Co., N. Y., for a lottery ticket, but can get no response—says further he has not the means to take the *Agriculturist*. If he had invested $1.50 of the $10, in this journal, its warnings would have saved him $8.50 sent to the bogus lottery man . *Hazard & Moore*, 120 Broadway, are grand fellows to furnish watches; they offer 431 watches valued at $100 to $450 each, and a lot more at *from* $40 to $275 each, all for $12 each, to persons green enough to bite at their bait. We pity those who are foolish enough to believe that these fellows will, for $12, furnish watches worth any such money as they would make people believe. A hatfull of their tickets have been sent to us by subscribers—all calling for $45 to $17 watches on paying only $12. Could they not let us have one of those $300, or $325, or $450 tickets offered at the same price? We hope our readers are too well informed to *hazard* any *more* money with that properly named concern ... *Garland & Co.*, (Todd,) 119 Broadway, right opposite the above, appropriate, *on paper*, the whole *outside* of a splendid building. They have, inside, one room better fitted up than the rickety attics usually occupied by the "grand establishments" of the gift men. Moreover, "Garland & Co." strike for smaller fish than Hazard & Moore, and ask only $5 each for their $35, $45, $50 and $55 watches, their $30 to $65 pistols, music boxes, vest chains, etc. We have tickets of their's enough to get rich in an hour ("over the left"). Why, right here is one lot as a sample: 16 tickets calling for $538 valuation in watches, etc., all new articles, to be given us on paying $5 each, and $1 more for each ticket—only $96 in all, or nearly *six dollars* for one!!! Good place this New York is: benevolent fellows just do a large *losing* business to make other people happy—$538 "valuation" all for $96!! We must call at 119 and 120 Broadway and get rich; $5 for $1 will pay vastly better than publishing the *Agriculturist*. (When it *does*, we'll surely let our readers know, for these fellows have an unlimited supply, and we want *our* readers to have *all* the good chances.).... *Marcus Grandin* (grand humbug) locates his P. O. at Danville, N. J., and tries to imitate city swindlers. Having less rent to pay than on Broadway, he offers $110 watches for $5, and asks only 25 cents for tickets. We have lots of the fellow's tickets: 100 of these promise us $11,000 worth of gold watches for only $25!! Our head is turned with the *prospective* wealth! *When* we get any of it we will tell our readers; when they get anything but loss from Marcus Tullus, Cicero, Grandin, or any others of these ticket chaps, will they please tell us? ...*Similar to the above* are the following: Mackay, Puff & Co., 81 Nassau street, N. Y., *alias* 838 Walnut street, Philadelphia.—Carey, Bonner & Co., 619 Chestnut street, Philadelphia, *alias* 333 Broadway, N. Y., *alias* 48 Exchange Building, Boston.—Vincent, Willis & Co., and J. Birch & Co., Williamsburg, N. Y.—Richard Ayres & Co., 81 Nassau street, N. Y.—J. Hickling & Co, 163 Broadway, N. Y.—Jas. Prendegast & Co., 38 John street, N. Y.—Jason H. Tuttle, Bevans, N. J., *alias* Flatbrookville, N. J., *alias* New York City, *alias* a good many other places, *alias* the express parcel swindler, *alias* Reeves & Co., *alias* other names, *alias* the man who put "U. S. Sanitary Commission" on his different named envelopes, and was stopped by the agent of the U. S. Sanitary Commission, (see N. Y. City Police Reports,) *alias* one of the most extensive, various, and barefaced villians out of jail, unless we except L. Todd . The half dozen "*Doctors*" inquired about in many letters before us, are, every one of them, either quacks or impostors, and by no means to be trusted with your money or health ...The so-called "*Howard Association*," of Philadelphia, is a myth, we repeat again, as persons keep asking about it.... Don't trust your precious *eyes* to one of these advertising men who offer to cure by prescription or by instruments. If you must *give* them your money, don't use their apparatus or medicine ... Beware of the *Ink* and *Washing Compounds* offered to "agents" and others.... The low-priced sewing-machines, of half a dozen kinds, offered with great display of claims and recommendations, are not worth buying. A pretended "Company" in this city sends out worthless machines at $15 each. We hear of cases where poor soldiers' widows have been thus swindled out of money borrowed to help them to a machine to earn their living. The "Medallion and Franklin" machine, of Boston, we know nothing about. A Pennsylvania subscriber complains that in order to get their improvements, he is required to buy a *new* machine—says the old one drops a stitch so often that it is worthless... Hundreds of *Recipes* for effective, but dangerous to clothes, washing compounds, for coffee extracts, for making honey, etc., etc. We would on no account invest a dime in any one of those sent to us. The same of recipes for making cheap oils, etc... The "Royal Havana Lottery" was fully exposed last May, page 172. . Cosmopolitan Art Association, for relief of soldiers, etc., is a humbug.... "Manufacturers' Association," 197 Broadway, N. Y., offering $80,000 prizes for $5, is a humbug. . But space fails us to go through the long catalogue of humbugs, vile publications, medicines, and instruments, etc., etc., etc., now before us. No response given here, or by letter, in reference to any particular scheme, sent to us, implies that it is also a humbug.

Personal.—An Indiana correspondent asks: "What has become of A. S. Fuller, has he quit the nursery business? I have not seen his card in the *Agriculturist* for some months."——When we last saw Mr. Fuller he went out of the door of 41 Park Row, with a basket on his arm, contents unknown. We presume he went directly to his present residence in Ridgewood, N. J. He says he does not dare to advertise in the *Agriculturist*, as a single advertisement made a demand for all the stock he could raise last year. The same correspondent asks "Who is Timothy Bunker?" We thought every one knew he was Justice of the Peace at Hookertown, Conn. He is one of our valued contributors, and for all further particulars we must refer to Mrs. Sally Bunker, of Hookertown, who has enjoyed his acquaintance much longer than we have.

Horse Hay-Fork Trial.—A trial of horse-hay forks was held under the auspices of the Farmers' Club of the American Institute, on the farm of Josiah Macy, in the town of Rye. The trial continued two days. Sixteen forks were tested, each one having a weighed load of good hay to unload over the beam. Many did the work very handsomely, while some failed, but in our opinion more from bad management than from any inherent difficulty. Still there was a great difference in the forks. Of the "forks" presented there were but two real forks; five were Grappling Claws, and nine were harpoons, or of similar construction. There was far too great a difference in the weight of the loads and in the manner in which they were loaded; and it was currently reported and believed that while some of the exhibitors took the loads furnished them without a question, others had been sharp enough to be present early and load their own hay. The bare fact that the loads varied in weight from 544 lbs. to 2,150 lbs., as reported, shows that there was no accuracy attempted. Blodgett's Cat's-Claw Harpoon was first tried, and did very good work, impressing us as favorably as any harpoon fork. Sprouts' Harpoon and Hay Knife was better manipulated, and showed off better than any of its class. Davidson's Harpoon and Knife was not worked so well, but is a good implement. The Ames Plow Co.'s Harpoon is of exceedingly simple construction, appeared very well, but was not well worked. That harpoons are better adapted to good long upland hay, timothy or orchard grass predominating, is evident; the grappling forks or claws are adapted, (if they have fingers enough,) to hay, straw, fine hay and even manure. They are heavier than the harpoons, not nearly so easily managed, and make cleaner work. We are satisfied that any effort to make them lighter by a reduction of the number of fingers below two on each side, and perhaps we should say three, is a damage to their efficiency. Raymond's Grappling Fork was attached to a "traveller," called the "Hick's Car," and did excellently well. There were other grapples which appeared well, but which, for some cause did not work very well. Plumb's "Railway Hay Elevator and Carrier" is a simple traveller furnished with an immense wooden headed fork, with the handle set at right angles to the tines. It was a fixture of the barn, and though clumsy did good work. The old Palmer (revolving head) Fork, a true fork also, did its work very well. Before purchasing, a man must decide between the harpoons, taking big "grips" and the true forks, with their smaller gripe. The Farmers' Club deserves the thanks of the public for affording this opportunity of seeing the hay pitchers all together, and manufacturers will be not the least benefited.

The following is the report of awards: "First award in Class No. 1 was given to "Palmer's Excelsior Sickle-tined Fork," entered by Palmer & Wackenhagen, Hudson, New York: second prize, Class No. 1, to John H. Champman, Utica, New York; Second Class, first prize, Harpoon Forks, to C. C. Blodgett, Watertown, Jefferson County, New York; second prize to S. C. & L. B. Sprout, Muncy, Pennsylvania."

Catalogues, Etc.—We have been furnished with a large number, but our list of acknowledgments has been crowded out by the press of matter.

Why It Pays?—Many have asked how can men afford to pay the rates charged for advertising in the *American Agriculturist*. First, we may answer, that this is the cheapest way to reach so many people. To merely print 100,000 large cards would cost at least $5 per thousand, or $500; to have the same card electrotyped, fastened into the page as an advertisement, neatly printed and distributed into 100,000 families, one in a place, costs one-fifth to one-tenth less than the bare printing of the cards. The paper is seen by many others than the subscribers. Probably seldom less than 250,000 different families read the *Agriculturist* regularly. It would seem to be impossible that any man engaged in respectable business should not find among all these readers enough patrons who also desire to find him, to make his business well pay the cost of an advertisement and a fair profit. Again: aside from the immense circulation of itself, making this the cheapest medium in the country, people have confidence in the parties whose cards are admitted into these columns and patronize them. Our rule is to admit none who are not believed to be entirely reliable, so that our readers may safely send their orders, if wanting the goods offered, and at the prices asked. There is also a great advantage in having the matter clearly printed, and *permanently* placed in the hands of subscribers, as most of them preserve the numbers to bind up, and the advertisements are printed in every edition issued. These considerations are fully appreciated by advertisers, as our crowded columns bear witness (while several pages have been left out for want of room,) and we are happy to know that "I saw your advertisement in the *American Agriculturist*," is becoming a stereotyped phrase in many business establishments, from its frequent occurrence in letters received from all over the country.

Prize Essays on Housekeeping.—Several competitors for the $100 prize have desired the return of their manuscripts, upon the supposition that we had no further use for them. It is proposed to issue a volume on housekeeping, made up in part of selections from these essays. As soon as the editor, who has this matter in charge, finds time to make the selection, the remaining manuscript will be returned to their authors, in all cases where they are desired. If any object to this use of their essays, we shall return them immediately.

Scalding Peas to Kill the Bug.—This practice is good, but caution is advisable. Peas will stand boiling hot water, provided not more than a few quarts are scalded at a time and the amount of water is just about sufficient to cover them. A subscriber reports pouring boiling water over about *two bushels* of peas, and attributes the partial failure of the crop to this.—He is no doubt right. So much hot water retained heat enough to both kill the bugs, and *cook* the peas.

Works in Preparation.—We shall shortly publish a translation of Dr. Friederich Mohr's Work on the Grape, the German title of which is "*Der Weinstock und der Wein.*" That portion treating of the vine will only be issued at present. "Horticola," in a notice of the original, in the *Gardeners' Monthly* says: "His work does not interfere with any extant." It is a setting forth of general principles upon the understanding or neglect of which the success or failure of all culture and training depend. We shall also shortly publish a manual of Squash Culture, by the authority in such matters—James J. H. Gregory, of Marblehead, Mass.

How it Sells!—Gardening for Profit has had a remarkable run. Every land owner, whether of one lot or a farm, should have it. $1.50 by mail.

The American Naturalist.—The first number is out. We welcome it as a long needed helper.

Wet Cellars.—Harrison County, Ind. We have several appeals from the West—among others three from the above-named county, for information in regard to water-tight cellars. The land, we presume, is flat and heavy, or holds water like a sponge, so wherever there is a hole it is of course filled. Well, the cure is very simply stated. No one has any trouble in firm soil to make a tight cistern. All our friends have to do is to make big square cisterns and put their houses over them. Round cisterns will bear great pressure from the outside: large square ones will not, unless securely walled. Besides, if the floors are very large, and water has access under them, the pressure might lift the floors of the cellars in spots. This is obviated by flagging with flat stones or laying a course of bricks or of planks upon the front layer of cement. Partition walls of stone or brick will not only secure both the outer or foundation walls and the floor, but add greatly to the coolness of the cellar. These walls should be carried up at the same time that the foundation walls are laid and bedded, but carried up in cement. One-third good hydraulic lime (or cement) and two-thirds sharp, clean sand, make a good cement mortar.

Horse Racing at Fairs.—Last autumn, great exertions were made to give a good start to an Agricultural Society in Minnesota. Nothing but want of space prevented our responding to the request to lend it our strong aid. Of the Fair held, a lady friend writes incidently :...."I was sorry you could not visit us last fall, though I suspect you would not have been pleased with the fair. The display was said to be very creditable to our young State, but like Tim Bunker's State Fair, the *prize money* was mostly paid to horse racers; and the housewives, to whose handiwork premiums were awarded, are obliged to content themselves with *paper diplomas* instead of the promised premiums. I think the effect will not be favorable to future fairs. Many say; 'the horse jockeys take all the prizes; I will not try again.'—Last year I made 300 lbs. of premium butter from one cow, and husband proposed taking 'Cherry,' her calf, and a crock of the butter over to the fair. He was too busy, however, and would have lost his labor." The people were too much occupied with the fast horses to pay any attention to such trivial matters as 300 lbs. of good butter from one cow, besides the family supply of milk.'

The Monthly Report of the Agricultural Department for January contains several interesting and valuable articles. One on the "Rate of Wages of Farm Laborers in the United States" has been prepared with great labor and pains. There is also an important article on wool consumption, and one on the Red Bug or Cotton Stainer, besides minor items, tables, etc. Now, why should not the people who are taxed for this publication, and are sufficiently desirous to get it, write for it and be supplied?—They will be informed that the supply is exhausted. We claim that subscriptions should be taken at cost for this and similar publications, and so all who wished could be supplied, provided they applied in advance; 5 cents a number or 50 cents a year would more than cover the cost of printing, etc.

Prescribing at a Distance.—The London *Lancet* records a case of an Englishman, in this country, who, being seized with a renewed attack of an illness from which he had suffered at home, consulted his physician in London, by means of the Atlantic cable, a prescription was returned by the same channel. This is as in the olden times, when physicians wrote in *cabalistics*.

Peat as Fuel.—A word of caution is necessary to the enthusiastic people who are rushing into peat enterprises, buying peat machines and peat bogs at fabulous prices. Remember Multicaulis and Petroleum. There is undoubtedly great wealth in our peat swamps. It is a question to be solved, whether they are worth more for manure, or for fuel. In estimating the value for fuel, it will not do to put a cord of uncondensed peat higher in value than a cord of wood. Then it is to be remembered that peat in drying shrinks into from ½ to ⅙ of its original bulk, and the better the article the more shrinkage. If it costs three dollars a cord to manufacture peat and two dollars to get it to market, and wood is worth only four dollars a cord, you do not gain much by buying peat, or putting it into the market. This whole business is too much a matter of experiment for farmers to venture upon largely. It will be safer for capitalists to make the experiments. While the article is so valuable for manure, we should not advise haste in selling peat bogs, even at the high figures sometimes reported.

Grapes—A Correction.—In our catalogue of Grapes, in the Horticultural Annual, Roger's Hybrids were omitted by the loss of a slip containing the notes. This omission occurs only in the first two thousand, and is remedied in those printed since. That which Doct. Grant proposed to call "Washington," and is so recorded in the Annual, is to be known as *Eumelan*.

The Miner Plum.—This variety is advertised as of "excellent flavor," and "never injured by the curculio." Can some one—not interested in its sale—give us an account of this plum, and its real value?

Keeping Pickles in Salt.—M. Roberts. A quart of salt to a gallon of water will make a brine strong enough. There is no danger of getting them too salt, as they will only absorb about so much, and the soaking before putting into vinegar will take it all out. The greening of pickles by putting them in a brass kettle is a custom much more honored in the breach than in the observance. Pickles are made for the stomach rather than the eye, and should not be poisonous, that they may be green.

Salt in Whitewash.—Salt is a good addition to whitewash, but if put into that used upon fences or buildings which cattle can get at they will be likely to lick it off. Wash made of water lime is less glaring.

Sorghum Vinegar.—"J. W. Y.," says a good vinegar can be made from sorghum juice without evaporating, by letting it stand in the sun a few days, exposed as much as possible to the air. With the syrup at a dollar a gallon it is not a very cheap source of vinegar. The skimmings are much cheaper as recommended in Feb. number, page 48. Why would not the bagasse, or pressed cane, treated in a leach like the apple pomace, make a good vinegar? Has this ever been tried?

Hoe Cake.—Hawkey gives the following: Mix a little salt with sifted meal, and pour boiling water upon it, sufficient to dip the batter out on a common cooking stove griddle. This should be tested by throwing a pinch of meal on it, and it is hot enough when the meal begins to turn brown. As soon as this is the case, dip the batter or mush out of the pan upon the griddle until it is covered all over exactly half an inch thick. Cook it with a lively fire, and when baked enough to turn without sticking, turn the cake over and bake it on the other side.

Mice—How to get rid of them.—"C. T. P." Keep a good cat. Color not important. Set the common wire spring traps. Use any of the rat poisons made of phosphoric paste. Use arsenic spread on a paper, and mixed with meal—where nothing else can get it.

Ventilation in Houses.—Mrs. C. C. Allen. See March No. *Agriculturist*, 1867, and Sept No., 1864.

Maryland Recipe for Hams.—For one hundred pounds of hams, eight pounds of fine salt, two pounds of brown sugar, two ounces of saltpetre, 1½ ounces of potash, four gallons of soft water. The brine must be boiled and cooled. The meat must be well washed before being cut up, then lie in a cool place for some days. Rub each piece with fine salt, and pack the whole down. Let it remain two or three days, according to the weather. The brine should then be poured into the cask at the sides. Leave the hams six weeks in the brine. Take out and rinse in cold water. Hang up to dry four or five days, then smoke with hickory wood.

Cornmeal Pudding—Mrs. L. A. Muller.—Two cups of cornmeal, one cup of grated bread, one cup of molasses, and one of sour milk, two tablespoonfuls of butter, a half a teaspoonful of ginger, do. of cinnamon, one teaspoonful of baking soda, or a half a teaspoonful of saleratus, three eggs; after the batter is made, one cup of sliced apple—the apple must be of a kind that will cook quickly—and can be added or left out as preferred. Bake half an hour in a moderately hot oven. Cream and sugar for sauce, as any other is apt to alter the flavor.

Corn Muffins.—One and a half pint of cornmeal, a half pint of wheat flour, one pint of sour or thick milk, two pints of sweet milk, two eggs, a small teaspoonful of salt, do. of baking soda. Bake twenty minutes in a tolerably hot oven. To be made up just before baking, and must be well beaten. If preferred, use *all* sweet milk, and *raise* with a tablespoonful of yeast.

Newport Cake.—Three eggs, 1 quart of flour, 2 teaspoonfuls of cream tartar, 1 of soda, 2 tablespoonfuls melted butter, 3 of sugar, 1 cup of milk. Bake in a long tin pan and cut in slices; eaten hot with butter.

Corn Biscuit.—One and a half pint of cold mush, one and a half pint of wheat flour, one cup of butter, nearly a pint of sour cream, a small teaspoonful of baking soda, do. of salt. First rub flour and butter together, then add mush, then the other ingredients.

Rye Bread.—"C. H." wants a recipe. "A quart of water and as much milk. Two teaspoonfuls of salt and a teacup of Indian meal. A teacupful of home brewed yeast, or half as much distillery yeast. Make it as stiff as wheat bread with rye flour.—*Miss Beecher*.

To Keep Smoked Meat—By J. C. E.—Make a dark, tight closet in the north end of the garret, or in any out-building. If there is any appearance of fly or worm, during the summer, dust the hams with air slacked lime. Some allow their hams to hang in the smoke-house during the summer, starting a smoke occasionally to keep off insects. The house should be tight.

Cooking Cabbage—H. B. Stanley.—Cut it fine, but not cross cut it. Put it in the frying pan, add a little salt and pepper, with some cream and a large piece of butter. Cook it slowly for ten minutes. Then add a half teacupful of vinegar, and turn it over immediately into the dish from which it is to be served.

Influence of the Moon on Meat.—"I. P. C. S." It is one of the many foolish superstitions that the world has not yet outgrown. "Kill your pork when the moon is increasing and it will swell in the pot." Stuff your pigs with good sound corn, or corn meal, for two months before slaughter, and the moon can't help its swelling in the pot. The meat of lean, half fed animals always shrinks in cooking.

Poor Man's Pudding.—Set 2 quart skim milk over a kettle of hot water, until it is scalding hot, then stir into it a pint of corn meal, and immediately after set the pan off; add a teacup of syrup or molasses, a teaspoonful of salt, and one of allspice; put in a buttered pan; bake slow one hour. Good, warm or cold, with cold cream or without.—*M. W. C.*

Pumpkin Johnny Cake.—Take 1 bowl of corn meal, 1½ teacups of stewed pumpkin; add 3 tablespoonfuls of sugar, 1 teaspoonful of soda, and 2 eggs. Mix well and bake in a moderate oven.—*Mrs. M. E. R.*—[We have pleasant memories of this. Hubbard or Boston Marrow Squash is an improvement on the pumpkin.—Ed.]

Frothy Cream and no Butter.—"J. E.," of East Fairfield, Ohio, says: "Our cow calved about the middle of Fourth month last; will calve again 27th of Fifth month; gave in the summer forty pounds of milk per day. We have failed to get butter for the past two months; nice thick cream, slightly sour and *sufficiently warm*, gets thin and froths in a few minutes and bids defiance to "patience and perseverance." We have tried all the remedies we have heard of, both for cow and cream. Salted the cow, etc., all to no purpose. We understand that it has been a failing with the cow heretofore. We could get good butter in 15 to 30 or 45 minutes during the summer and fall and early winter." Has not your cream frozen occasionally? Buy a thermometer and begin churning when the temperature of the cream is 60°, having scalded out the churn so that it will not cool the cream. Feed the cow a little linseed or cotton seed cake meal and some roots if you can. It will not do to warm cream by pouring much hot water into it.

Eggs for Setting.—"C. E. G.," Buffalo, N. Y. Eggs will often hatch after being transported hundreds of miles by rail, at other times a few miles of waggon or railroad travel will ruin them. No reliance can be placed on eggs transported far, unless they be carried in the hands, and packed with great care at that.

What are Corn Cobs Good For?—"L. F. L.," of Torrington, Conn., asks: "Are corn cobs of any use as nourishment for animals, or as a manure for vegetables? I shell a large amount of corn and have tried cobs as manure in various ways, have put them in my pig-pen for a season, and from there to my garden, have put them in a heap to heat and rot, and then to the garden, and have applied them in a natural state with bad rather than good results. I have used them as fuel, they make very strong ashes and will form a hard crust over the ashes in the stove, some of it is white, some green, etc., of which I send you a sample for your opinion; if it is fit for feed for stock of any kind, then our farmers should grind their cobs with their corn."—*Ans.* We suppose they have a little value as manure but are slow to decompose, and believe it to be much better to burn them and apply the ashes which are very valuable. It is worse than useless to grind cobs with the corn unless the corn is very soft and immature. After the corn ripens well the cobs contain a very small proportion of nutriment—not so much as straw.

The N. Y. State Agr'l Society held its Annual Meeting at Albany, on the 13th and 14th of February, for the election of officers, as announced in our last issue. The report of the Treasurer, Luther H. Tucker, Esq., showed the finances of the Society in a healthy condition. There was an interesting and instructive Address by X. A. Willard, on the Agriculture of Great Britain, and another by Dr. Fitch, on the recent discoveries in Entomology, dwelling particularly upon the canker worm, the joint worm, and the grape-beetle. The address of the retiring President, J. Stanton Gould, was a scholarly performance, full of practical wisdom which we hope to see carried out in the future operations of the Society. We exceedingly regretted that there were not better arrangements made for discussion of topics of practical interest to farmers and horticulturists. There were present at the meeting a hundred or more gentlemen from various parts of the State, and some from abroad, distinguished farmers, nurserymen, and horticulturists, whose last year's experience we very much wanted to obtain. Yet there were no arrangements made for discussions and experience meetings. We had but three sessions in the two days, when we could easily have had twice as many of two hours each, and have got much useful information and spread it before our readers. We beg leave to suggest a change in this respect at the next Annual Meeting. We know the Committees are necessarily busy, but the rest of the members should have work laid out for them in meetings for discussion.

Patent Office Reports.—"W." asks where he can obtain them. If "W." lives in a large city he can probably find them at any dealers in waste paper.

Slow Torture at the Stock.—An intelligent "Iowa Farmer" takes "Connecticut" to task for his plea for shelter for cattle. We agree with Connecticut in regard to the desirableness of shelter, yet believe with Iowa that such stock as we get from Iowa and Illinois do not appear to have led lives of extreme suffering. He writes: "Now I do not uphold slow torture or any kind of torture for the dumb brutes, but it does not follow because they are not in warm stables that they are uncomfortable. That depends very much upon climate, natural shelter and food. In the report of the live stock market of New York for the week ending Feb. 2—and I believe it is so during the year—nearly one half of the cattle were from Illinois, numbering 2,062, while only 97 were from Connecticut. I do not suppose one half of these Illinois steers were ever inside a stable, and yet when they left the Sucker State they were fine, fat, sleek fellows, and did not look as though they were suffering slow torture, but enjoying themselves about as well as bovines usually do. A fat animal rarely suffers from cold. But few of the men that have fed these steers are at present in much danger of going to the poor house."

Draining Marshes into Wells.—"M. M." This is sometimes done with success. If the swamp lies upon a clay hard pan, impervious to water, and there is a stratum of dry gravel beneath, it would be best to dig through the hard pan and watch the results. If the water disappears in the immediate vicinity of the well, it will pay to dig others. We should not rely upon one well to drain several acres. You want to empty your basin rapidly after showers, especially in summer. Wells at frequent intervals would also help to improve the character of the subsoil more rapidly. But if the wells fail, break through the hills and put down a covered drain deep enough to take off all the water. Marsh land is, as a general thing, poor property:—knock the bottom out of it, and it makes the best grass land in the world.

Selling Land for Quarries.—Mrs. N. E. B. An undeveloped quarry cannot be worth very much more than the value of the land for other purposes. It costs large sums of money to test the value of the slate, granite or marble, as the case may be; and all this investment is a dead loss if the stone prove worthless. Even when the value is proved, nearly the whole cost of a stone is for the labor expended in dressing it, and in getting it to market. And yet a stone quarry may be worth more to a community than a gold mine. It may make a steady market for labor and foster industrious habits.

Flat or Lap Furrows—Double Plows.—In our discussion of Flat and Lap Furrows we have had no reference to the furrows turned by double plows—that is, large plows, with a "skimmer" plow or "jointer" on the beam. "Rastus," of Westport, N. Y., writes thus: "In the number for January I see an article in which the writer gives the flat furrow the preference. Such is not the theory or practice of our first-class farmers in this section; the lap furrow better drains the land and gives us a warmer, livelier and quicker seed bed. That the grass and weeds are more troublesome with lap than with flat furrows may be true if sod-land be plowed with the common plow. But we obviate that difficulty in this manner: we attach to the beam of the plow, in the same manner as a coulter, what is termed a 'jointer,' which cuts two or three inches deep: as the plow moves on, the jointer deposits in the bottom of the furrow all the grass, which otherwise would form the joint or lap of the furrow and thus it is buried out of the way of the harrow, and where it will rot quickly. Corn land prepared in this manner will require but little hand labor. Instead of a sod in the lap of the furrow, we have a ridge of mellow soil, and the cultivator or horse-hoe, in the hands of a careful laborer, will destroy all the weeds that make their appearance between the rows. In preparing stubble land for wheat the same plow is used; the jointer turns down the stubble, the plow covers it up, and the field has the appearance of a summer fallow. The jointer may be attached to any plow with a proper length of beam."—We hope this will beguile no one into employing lap furrows (in the common sense) in spring plowing, unless he can not make flat ones.

The Wheat Failure.—"J. B.," Richmond, Ind., writes: "The partial failure of the wheat crop during the past few years in some sections, suggests the question if with a soil of unimpaired fertility, all the modern appliances of machinery, and various periodicals and books that treat of systematic and scientific agriculture, are we falling far behind our less favored neighbors of the extreme North and Northwest in the production and quality not only of wheat, but of other cereals? We admit the seasons have been of late unfavorable, but is this the only cause of failure? Have not other causes over which we had control had more to do with it? Have we not been too careless about the improvement and selection of seed, the choice and preparation of soil? Has not successive and exhaustive cropping of the land, with a want of intelligent and searching investigation into this soil deterioration and diminution of one of our great staple crops, contributed to the result?—While some of our farmers have been allured by the specious representations and promises of adventurers and irresponsible dealers in "wine plants," tobacco, etc., they have neglected the culture of those more substantial and permanent sources of wealth upon which rest the real happiness and prosperity of the country. During a recent visit to Canada I was informed that the farmers meet at stated periods in their several districts for the buying, selling and exchange of choice grain, etc. Could not such a wise system be instituted here? Cannot something be done before we risk another failure?"—[It would be hard to set a limit to what a good, active township or county farmers' club might accomplish in this way.—Ed.]

Pump for Well.—"E. A. P." The distance of the well from the house is not a matter of so much importance as the *depth* of the well. The suction pump will only raise water twenty-nine feet in a perpendicular hight, and the pump must be very perfect to draw this whole distance. The deeper the well, the more force it will require at the pump handle. The lead encased block tin pipe is a good article. The nearest village plumber will tell you the cost of the article and of suitable pumps.

What to Do With Slaughter-House Bones.—It is a difficult thing to say what a farmer should do with bones and offal that he can collect at a slaughter-house. They may all be thrown into a heap with stable manure, to fill all the interstices and give compactness to the heaps. This, if watered a little to start fermentation, and covered with earth or muck, will heat, and many soft bones and all the gristle and flesh will become free from the hard bones, which may be thrown out when the heap is forked over. The softened bones should be thrown to one side and mashed with a sledge. Those that remain hard, though they would yield to repeated operations, may better be left to dry and then sent to a bone mill, if one can be easily reached. There should be one in every neighborhood. If this can not be done, which is usually the case, the bones may be broken up somewhat with a sledge, and either rotted again, or treated at once with sulphuric acid and water. First wet the bones, which should be on a hard clay floor, somewhat dishing, or in a half-hogshead tub, then pour upon and over the heaps gradually oil of vitriol, to the amount of half the weight of the bones, adding more water occasionally. There will be intense heat generated, and the mass should be shoveled over or stirred well frequently, more water added if it dries at all; and so, after a while, the hard bones will yield. It may be necessary to add more acid, and finally the mass may be dried off by mixing the mashed bones, or adding muck or dry soil.

Corn Blight.—"Will corn blight if planted three years in succession upon the same piece of ground?" Not if you put on plenty of manure. Corn is said to have been planted on some of the bottom lands of the Scioto Valley for 40 years in succession, without any evidence of blight. But rotation of crops is ordinarily the true policy.

The skimmings of Sorghum Juice are said to be good food for milch cows, and it will pay better to use it in this manner than for vinegar.

Coal Ashes.—"H. S. F.," Bellows Fall, Ct., asks, "whether coal ashes can be used in any way." The best use to be made of them is on roads and walks, either by themselves or with gravel. They soon pack very firm. They contain a slight amount of fertilizing material and may be used on stiff soils where sand would be beneficial.

Farming by Professional Men.—We have received a letter from a city lawyer asking information upon this topic, which will soon be answered by a gentleman of experience. It is entirely practicable for a business man in the city to live in the country, and derive a large part of the support of his family from the cultivation of the soil, or to quit the city altogether upon a very moderate income. Just how this can be done can not be told in a basket article.

Louisiana State Fair in May.—An Association proposes holding a State Agricultural Fair in Baton Rouge, La., during the week beginning Monday, May 6th. Mr. Clayton Evarts, of Baton Rouge, is Corresponding Secretary and will give further information.

Apples for Wisconsin.—At the annual meeting of the Wisconsin Horticultural Society the following list of five varieties was adopted: Red Astrachan, Duchess of Oldenburgh, Fameuse, Tallman Sweeting, Golden Russet. For a second five: Fall Stripe, St. Lawrence, Perry Russet, Red Romanite, and Willow-twig.

How to Make Hens Lay.—It is well enough to start hens in laying by giving them stimulating food, but we do not believe in keeping it up after they begin to lay generally. Much meat fat will induce disease sooner or later. M. J. Skinner, of Northampton Co., Pa., says he takes a common milkpot full of thickened milk, adds a tablespoonful of Cayenne pepper, and a handful of wheat bran, stirs it up and feeds it to the chickens every morning, and since he has done so has greatly increased his supply of eggs. It is a good practice, and not so injurious as feeding much meat.

Stale Fish for Manure.—Mackerel and other kinds of salt fish, which are spoiled for food, may often be bought very cheap for manure. They are best mashed up with soil or muck, and used after laying a few weeks and being worked over once or twice. Use at least three parts muck to one of fish.

Cure for Cribbing Horses.—We published in the December number a suggestion from a Volunteer Officer in regard to a cure for cribbing being effected by separating the crowding front teeth. He attributed the habit or disease of cribbing or wind-sucking to the painful crowding of the teeth. Since making that statement we have received several letters confirming the view. One correspondent says: "I am satisfied from experience the view is correct." Our friends of the N. Y. College of Veterinary Surgeons, however, say it is entirely incorrect, and that they have seen horses' teeth filed out—that is, a thin file run up between all the front teeth on the upper jaw without producing the least effect.

Improved King Philip Corn, "Holdon" Dutton Corn and other standard eastern varieties, may be obtained of all dealers in agricultural seeds.

Breaking Horses to Single Line.—"J. L.," Chester Co., Pa., says the best way to break a horse to the single line that he has found is, to put him before a hoe-harrow in working corn, and attach *single* and *double lines*. When the single line will not answer, use the others. Have the single line loose from the harrow and folded around the hand. You can make a good leader of almost any horse in this way in a short time.

Two Eggs a Day from One Hen.—"J. G. S.," Philadelphia. It may be that your observation is correct. There is nothing in the nature of things to render it impossible for a hen to lay two eggs in one day. Two yolks in one shell are common. The occurrence of one perfect egg inclosed in another, (there being room in the outer shell for the first egg, and for a yolk and white of ordinary size), is not very rare. Hens will sometimes lay a sound egg and a soft shelled one the same day; but whether or not there is any absolute proof that a hen has laid two good eggs in one day we do not know.

Black Spanish.—"*Can the Ethiopian Change his Skin?*"—J. H. Mabbett, of South Bergen, N. J., states that he has a Black Spanish hen, about one half of whose feathers came white at the second moulting; at the third she was *entirely white*; at the fourth she still remained *white*; at the fifth, which was last fall, about one half of her plumage came *black*. The hen now looks as she did at the second moulting. He says: "I have taken no little interest in watching the changes in her plumage, and intend to keep her as a curiosity until she dies. I presume she will be black again this fall. It is a freak of nature, and one I think of rather rare occurrence. Having made Black Spanish a specialty for the past six years, I have only heard of a very few from true stock that have made this change in plumage, and think, unless they come in contact with some white fowls, they will not become more abundant than 'white crows.'"

Threshing Conveniently in Single Floored Barns.—John Larkin, of East Brandywine, Chester Co., Pa., furnishes us with the following plan he adopted to do his threshing last fall, by which he says he was enabled to perform the same in about half the time formerly required. He has an endless chain one-horse power and thresher, and instead of having them both on one floor, as is the custom with most farmers in that section, he put the thresher up on poles, or square pieces of timber that had been put across the front part of the barn, about eight feet above the floor for mowing wheat on. He placed a couple of planks cross-ways of these, and screw-bolted them down. The thresher was then placed on these, and after adjusting the strap, was fastened down the same as on the floor. Two or three temporary posts were put up from the floor beneath and nailed fast to the cross-pieces, a few loose boards laid down for a floor, etc.

The strap from the horse power was passed up between the cross-pieces, and one of them was left in front of the thresher to support a platform for the person tending the machine to stand on, and a light strip was attached to the brake and extended up to the platform, to start and stop the machine without going down. The space under the shaker was left open for the grain to fall through to the floor beneath. The great benefit of this arrangement is that you have no caving-up to do while threshing, and the straw is easily thrown off into the bays on each side and avoids throwing the unthreshed grain so far *down*, and then having to *pitch the straw up*.——This plan certainly has great advantages in a single floored barn, but if the horse power can be placed on the floor below, the merits of this arrangement will not be so striking.

Suggestions about Threshing Machines.—J. F. Dilworth, of Port Penn, Del., offers some suggestions to makers of threshing machines, which are worth their attention, for many large grain raisers doubtless find similar difficulty. He writes: "Since steam has been brought into use for threshing grain, we have power sufficient to do a great deal more work if we had the threshers. We have been using the Pitts, Geiger, and Westenhouse machines; two of them are made in New York, and one in Virginia. They are all deficient in ability to separate and clean. We are now using the Westenhouse machine, which is a very good one, with an eight-horse engine; but when we feed the cylinder (36 inches, and large enough,) to its full capacity, it wastes a great deal of grain, by carrying it over with the straw—more with oats than wheat. The fan also is defective, not being near large enough; we want a fan capable of threshing and cleaning from the chaff sixty or seventy bushels of wheat, and one hundred to one hundred and twenty of oats per hour. The cylinder of the Westenhouse machine is able to do that amount of threshing with the power we use, and the consequence is the separating and cleaning capacity of the machine is overtaxed, and grain is wasted. Now, the separating might be done either by lengthening the straw carrier, (making two might be preferable, as it would give more strength,) or putting revolving prongs between the elevator and straw carrier, so arranged that they would not catch the straw, yet shake all the grain out. The fan would have to be made larger; in other words, we want a more elaborate machine; a little additional weight would be no objection; it would be on trucks, and there would be no trouble in moving it about. Last summer I had to carry my grain fan to the yard, and take the grain from the thresher, and put it through it before sending to market; this trouble might all be avoided by having an additional fan attached; it need not be large, and could be arranged on top of the machine, with elevators to carry the grain from where it is deposited by the first cleaning to the fan above, the tailings from that conducted to the cylinder, and the grain run into bags ready for market."

Economy of Feeding Turnips.—"C. E. T.," of Topsfield, Mass., writes as follows:—"Owing to the scarcity and high price of English hay, I have kept my few sheep this winter on low meadow hay, mostly 'buckhorn,' with about one quart of sliced turnips to each per day. They like this fare extremely well, are in good order, and the lambs so far (Feb. 18) are strong and active. I also give to my oxen, and other stock, which consume coarse hay, and to cows not in milk, a few turnips daily, much to their gratification and apparent benefit. By so doing I have been enabled to use up most of my coarse hay, and with a little English I estimate one ton of coarse hay and one ton of turnips fully equivalent to one ton best English hay for sustenance of cattle."

The Pine Barrens of the South.

"X. Y." writes as follows: Along the whole extent of the Atlantic coast, from New Jersey to Georgia, and thence along the Gulf to the Mississippi River, stretches a strip of sandy land, varying from fifty to one hundred miles in width, and known as the "Pine Barrens." On this land, the cultivation of the common agricultural staples is not remunerative; hence the land, while not suited to the production of wheat and corn, may produce other plants of value, and it would be much better to search out such plants as are suited to the soil, than to condemn the land as utterly worthless. By cultivating only, or at least chiefly, such plants as prosper in a sandy soil, we believe the cultivation of the Pine lands can be made remunerative. The watermelon, muskmelon, squash, sweet potato, &c., are known to thrive better and produce more abundantly in sandy soil than in clayey or even loamy upland, but others have not had so extensive a trial. The groundnut or peanut delights in a warm, sandy soil. It yields abundantly, and the demand for it, for making oil, is unlimited. It is equal to corn for fattening pork. The Scuppernong grape is said to thrive luxuriantly on the dryest sands, sending down its long roots to the marl beds, and bearing heavy crops. If this grape thrives, may not some kinds of the improved grapes be equally suited to such soil? Field beans will often pay where scarcely any other crop will, and some of the pole beans, if not even the Lima bean, may be cultivated, and should be tried on a moderate scale by way of experiment. There need be no fear of over stocking the market with this delicious vegetable. The castor oil bean will pay well on moist bottom lands. We import annually several millions of dollars worth of liquorice. This plant luxuriates in a sandy soil, and, once planted, requires scarcely any cultivation. Instead of importing, we ought to export it largely. The peach, apricot and nectarine are known to succeed well. South of Norfolk the fig stands the winter in the open air, and ought to be cultivated largely. Some years since a planter near Mobile planted a large field with figs, for the purpose of feeding pigs, saying the yield per acre was greater than that of corn, and the pork was sweeter, while the trees required no attention or labor. The arrow-root of Bermuda, and the tapioca or Manihot of Brazil, are also worthy of trial, and will richly reward the labor bestowed upon them if found to succeed. Madder will pay when labor and capital are more abundant. For forage, different kinds of millet and sorghum promise well.

Walks and Talks on the Farm—No. 40.

I have just lost the best cow I had. It was the one I paid the Doctor one hundred and ten dollars for last fall. She died of puerperal or milk fever. It is seldom that this disease occurs later than four days after calving. But this cow was not attacked till the eighth day. She had a hard time calving, and did not cleanse for three days, and then not till we had given her a dose of ergot. After that she appeared perfectly well, and I thought all danger was past. She ate heartily, and gave her usual quantity of milk the morning before she was taken sick. But the next morning she refused her food, and gave only about two quarts of milk, and in half an hour afterwards was trembling all over, and so weak that she could hardly stand. She seemed to be paralyzed across the loins. We put her into a warm basement cellar, where she could not be disturbed. She had barely strength enough to walk in, and had an inclination to stick her head in the ground, which is said to be one of the symptoms of the disease. She soon fell down, perfectly prostrated; our efforts to restore her proved of no avail, and she died in two days and a half from the time of the attack.

In England this disease is called "the Drop," and is most troublesome in dairies where the cows are kept in high condition. Mr. Spooner, an eminent veterinary surgeon, states that, so far as his experience goes, common cows, when highly fed, are more liable to the disease than Shorthorns or Herefords. He says: "In a rather large suckling dairy of Shorthorns, in the vicinity of the writer, the disease is scarcely known but by name; whilst in another, consisting for the most part of Norman and cross-bred animals, the loss has been most disheartening to the owners. One thing, however, is clear: that the mortality is greater among cows that are highly kept." The Shorthorns, however, that escaped were fed just as high as the common cows, and were quite as fat. The reason why highly fed Shorthorns escape, while highly fed common cows are attacked, is due probably to the fact that the Shorthorns are more accustomed to high feeding. They have been bred for the purpose of converting a large amount of food into beef and butter. What would be an unnatural state of fatness in a common cow would be no more than the ordinary condition of a good Shorthorn. I have a thoroughbred Essex sow that, compared with ordinary sows, was excessively fat, and the Deacon and some of my other neighbors said it was impossible for such a sow to breed. But at ten months old she had a fine litter of six pigs. I have no doubt that a common sow as fat as she was would not have bred. As long as an animal is growing rapidly it should be allowed liberal feed. And in the case of animals that have been bred for generations for the sole purpose of producing a large amount of flesh and fat in a short time, a fleshy condition is perfectly natural and will not prove injurious, unless carried to excess.

A common cow cannot be stimulated to take on fat or give milk with as much safety as a Shorthorn, Hereford or Devon. It is perfectly true, as is sometimes said in opposition to improved breeds, that "they will not stand starvation as well as the natives." And, on the other hand, the so-called "natives" will not stand high feeding as well as the improved breeds. And this is probably the true explanation of the fact mentioned by Mr. Spooner. Those of us, who, like the Doctor, wish to feed high for the purpose of getting a large quantity of rich milk, must get cows that have considerable Shorthorn, Ayrshire or Devon blood in them.

Stephens, in his Book of the Farm, recommends giving cows four pounds of oil-cake a day for a month before and a month after calving, for the purpose of preventing costiveness. Before he adopted this practice he lost two or three cows, but none afterwards. I gave my cow a little after she calved, made into a mash with warm water, but none before; and there I think was the mistake. She was a great milker and had been used to high feeding, and probably needed richer food than we gave her. But she was rather fleshy and I was afraid to give her grain. I am satisfied now that it would have been better to have given her a little corn meal or oil-cake for a month or two before calving.

Misfortunes rarely come singly. I had a number of nice early lambs that we kept in the basement cellar, and when the cow was taken sick we turned them out to make room for the cow. There were two sows in the yard and they got into the pen and ate up five of the lambs.

Have just been reading the Agricultural Annual for 1867. It is quite a book, and I am glad that it is bound in cloth as well as paper. Works of this kind, which are designed for reference, are well worth an extra quarter when bound in cloth. Paper covered books are a nuisance. They are always lying round loose, and are never to be found when wanted.

The editor writes me that he intends to make the next volume much better than this. I suspect he is "fishing for a compliment," or else he is a more modest man than New Yorkers are supposed to be! Certainly this Annual is a most valuable work, though I presume, with more time for its preparation, the next volume will be better. The "Calendar of Operations" contains many excellent hints, and will be very valuable to young farmers, and those of more experience read them with advantage.

The article on "Tile Draining," by George E. Waring, Jr., Engineer of the Draining of the Central Park, has given me several new ideas which I hope to profit by. I had not thought of putting in "silt basins" in those parts of the drain where there is less fall, and where there is, consequently, more likelihood of the drain choking up from the deposit of fine sand. Of course, in ordinary draining, we need not make such expensive affairs as those used in the Central Park. A hole, dug two or three feet below the drain, and stoned up to keep the soil from falling in, is all that we can afford. But after drains are covered up and are fairly working there is not much danger of their filling up with sediment. The water filters through the soil and is as clear as the purest spring water. The chief danger is from the surface water washing away the soil, more or less, and running in large quantities into the drains. I have several places on my farm where this occurs. Of course this water is not clear and may choke up the drains.

Another important point which Mr. Waring calls particular attention to is "securing the outlet." Of course it is not necessary to have such finished work as that represented in fig. 2, page 53. But I have had one or two drains which discharge large quantities of water into a deep open ditch, which, from neglecting to secure the outlet with stones, &c., have given me more trouble than a little. The soil is continually falling in, and the tiles are carried by the force of the water into the ditch. I have now built them up, rudely, with stones, but the work would have been better done at the first.

The only objection to Mr. Waring's article is that it represents underdraining as a work requiring such accuracy that few farmers would be able to carry it out alone. I have used a surveyor's level more or less in laying out drains, but where a man is acquainted with the land it is not indispensable. Water is a good level, and in two or three cases has shown me outlets, during the wet weather in the spring, that I was unable to discover with the level.

When drains are cut during dry weather, a level, measuring staff, boring rod, &c., are necessary; but in ordinary farm practice draining is seldom done at such seasons. The work can be done much more easily in the spring, when the ground is wet and soft, than in the summer, when it is dry and hard. And in digging a drain where there is water, there is no necessity for a level to determine the grade. Cut the drain so that the water will run away from you, and a little experience will enable any man to clean out the bottom of the drain *better* than it can be done with a level in a dry season. Where the water runs fast, deepen the drain a little, and you will soon get a sufficiently accurate grade.

The "Finishing Scoop" is an important tool, but there is not one man in ten that knows how to use it. The artist, in fig. 9, has not given the exact shape. The blade, or scoop, should be the same width its whole length, and it should be *perfectly straight at the bottom*. It should be bright and sharp, with a wrought iron shank that can be bent to the desired angle, and if long enough and perfectly straight a skillful man can make the bottom of the drain as level as a carpenter can a piece of board with a planer. Many farmers take an old scoop shovel, bend up the sides and uses this to clean out the ditches. But it is too short to make good work. Good "finishing scoops" are not easily to be found. There is not one to be had in Rochester.

Prof. Johnson's account of the experiments made in Saxony on the ripening of rye and spring wheat should attract attention. The results differ entirely from those obtained by Mr. Hannam in England. Mr. H. found that wheat cut two weeks before it was fully ripe gave a better sample, worth 6 cents a bushel more in market, and yielded 4 per cent. more than the same wheat allowed to get fully ripe. Nearly all our agricultural writers have accepted these experiments as decisive on the point, and the majority of farmers cut their wheat at an earlier period than was the case twenty years ago.

The experiments quoted by Prof. Johnson seem to prove that there is a decided gain in allowing grain to get fully ripe before cutting. One hundred grains of rye cut July 16th, when the "kernels were firm, past the milk, straw, yellow and pretty dry," weighed 203 grains; while a hundred grains, cut July 30th, when the crop was "dead ripe," weighed 223 grains. In other words, a crop of rye that would yield 30 bushels per acre, cut at the ordinary time, would yield 33 bushels if allowed to get dead ripe.

The experiments on spring wheat do not show so great a gain, but "the advantage of allowing the grain to become dead ripe, instead of cutting just as it passes out of the milk, is about 5 per cent." On a crop of 30 bushels we gain a bushel and a half by allowing it to get fully ripe.

Of course it is very easy to lose this amount by shelling. But now that we have reaping machines which give us complete control of the crop, we need not be in such a hurry to cut our grain. We need not wait till it is dead ripe, but should let it get as near ripe as we can without running any risk of shelling. This conclusion carries us back again to the opinions of practical farmers when I was a boy. I can well recollect how my father opposed the new doctrine at first, but gradually relaxed a little and cut earlier, to avoid the risk of shelling. As usual, the truth probably lies between the two extremes.

It has been supposed that by allowing grain to get dead ripe there was a loss of starch—that it was changed into woody fibre or bran. But it seems that the rye cut July 18th, when out of the milk, contained 72.2 per cent. of starch, while that cut July 20th, when dead ripe, contained 73.7 per cent—a notable increase.

Prof. Johnson says, in ripening, "the grain becomes slightly, the straw and chaff considerably, *poorer in gluten* or nitrogenous matters." We suppose he does not mean that the grain contains any less gluten, but rather that it contains more starch; and this would give a less *percentage* of gluten. Just as in a fat ox there is no less meat (nitrogen) than in the same ox when thin, although the *percentage* would be less. And so in a fat kernel of wheat, there is no less gluten, but proportionally more starch.

The most interesting part of Mr. Carpenter's article on potatoes is the statement in regard to three neighboring farmers, who planted the same variety of potato (the Pinkeye Rusty Coat).

No. 1—Planted whole potatoes in hills 3 feet apart. Yield 80 bushels per acre.

No. 2—Planted whole potatoes in rows 3 feet apart and 15 inches apart in the rows. Yield 100 bushels per acre.

No. 3—Planted the same distance apart as No. 2, but with sets cut to only two eyes. Yield two hundred and sixty (260) bushels per acre.

The explanation of this astonishing difference is not so much (probably) to planting sets with only two eyes, as to the fact that No. 1 and No. 2, although they cultivated the land thoroughly up to July 1st, let the weeds grow up and choke the crop afterwards, while No. 3 kept his land free from weeds. All through the season No. 1 and No. 2 had to "mow the weeds at digging time," while in No. 3 "no weeds were to be seen." This is the great lesson that we must all learn—that the land must be clean to produce maximum crops. If you take the weeds into partnership you cannot have the whole profits. They are the worst of partners. They do no work, put in no capital, bear none of the expenses, pay no taxes and have very extravagant habits.

It seems that Mr. Carpenter has been eminently successful as a potato grower. His success seems to be due to three things: 1st. Change of seed; 2nd. Close planting, and 3rd, to thorough cultivation. He plants in narrow rows, only from two feet to two feet nine inches apart, cuts to two eyes and drops the sets from twelve to sixteen inches apart in the rows. He covers the seed with a plow from four to six inches deep. I do the same thing, and some of my neighbors told me I would smother them, or that, at all events, they would be a week or ten days later in getting through the soil than if covered lightly with a hoe. They may be a little longer in coming up, but you can plant that much earlier, and then harrow the ground to kill the weeds just as the potatoes are breaking the ground. If planted deep there is no danger of pulling up the sets or of doing any serious damage to the shoots. With Peachblows and other rampant growers three feet between the rows is near enough. If the land is in good order the tops will completely cover the ground. Flukes could be planted as close together as Mr. Carpenter recommends with decided advantage.

Mr. C. puts ashes and plaster on the rows after the potatoes are up., I have known plaster produce a good effect; but on my soil ashes have never been of much benefit to the potatoes. I should have more faith in 250 pounds of good Peruvian guano, sown broadcast and harrowed in before planting. The ashes and plaster might then be applied afterwards on top with more probability of proving beneficial. I have known 300 pounds of Peruvian guano give an *increase* of nearly one hundred bushels per acre. This, however, was on land which, without guano, produced only 98 bushels per acre. On rich land the effect might not be so marked; I do not see why we cannot raise 300 bushels per acre.

MEASUREMENT OF UNHUSKED CORN IN THE CRIB.—A Missouri correspondent propounds a question, which we must say, in our belief, defies mathematics or ordinary guessing. He asks for a rule for the measurement of unhusked corn in the crib. Were the cribs equally well packed down, the corn ears year after year, in any district, very uniform in size and well filled, (for nubbins and half-filled ears have nearly as much husk as good ones), there might, perhaps, be a rule given. But the fact is, no two kinds of corn can be relied upon to have the same amount of husk; on different land the same kind of corn will not have the same quantity of husk and cob in proportion to the grain; even on the same field, in different years, the production will vary greatly. After all, the variation will not be so much in the number of ears produced, as in the amount of shelled corn they will yield; while the unhusked ears will have much the same apparent size and amount of husks.

Fig. 1.—EXTERIOR OF CHEESE ROOM.

How Cheddar Cheese is Made.

BY EVA M. COLLINS.

Mr. Editor: You expressed a desire to go through our cheese-rooms again, and to see how the Cheddar Cheese was made. If you can spare a few moments this morning, and will imagine yourself at my elbow, I will take you around with pleasure. We have a dairy of 40 cows. You remember they used to be milked in a yard.

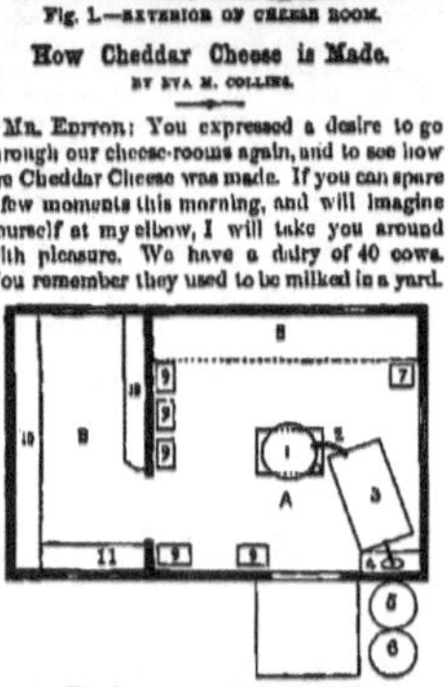

Fig. 2.—PLAN OF CHEESE ROOM.

A, Cheese Room; B, Curing Room; 1, Furnace with large kettle and closely fitting cover; 2, Steam pipe from furnace to steam chamber under vat; 3, Vat for milk; 4, Sink with strainer; 5, Tank for sweet whey; 6, Tank for sour whey; 7, Curd mill; 8, large table, formerly work bench; 9, Cheese presses; 10, Shelves; 11, Shelf under window.

Now father has milking stables. These are a decided improvement. Most of the cows have learned to drink whey, so we at present do not keep so many pigs as we formerly did.

Do you recognize, in fig. 1, the old door-way to the cheese-room? Do you remember washing your hands in the tank of sour whey in front, after your blackberrying excursion with Willie

Fig. 3.—INSIDE OF CHEESE ROOM.

and I? That stands there still—one of the fixtures. They cannot feed out whey sweet, as it would kill cows or pigs. Father talked about having it carried in pipes, but it would require so much grading that it was not finally done.

Figure 2 is a plan of the cheese-rooms; fig. 3 shows the inside and a view of the vat, and method of heating the milk by steam. The evening's milk is strained into the vat, and kept cool with covered pails of ice water till morning, when the cream is removed, heated to 80°, and returned to the milk. Frequently both butter and cheese are made from the same milk, but the practice is unknown in our dairy. A ball of annotto, an inch in diameter, is rubbed up in a bowl with a little warm water, in which has been dissolved a half teaspoonful of soda to brighten the annotto, as a high color is desirable in Cheddar Cheese, and the whole is thoroughly mixed with the milk. The morning's milk has been strained into the vat, the whole heated to 90°, the rennet added, the curd has come, and there Mary stands cutting it up with a wooden knife, fig. 4, into parallelopipedons (isn't that learned!) an inch square at the top. Mary cuts up an entire rennet, puts it into a pitcher with a quart of water and a half pint of salt, and uses about a gill to bring the curd, adding a little water occasionally as that in the pitcher gets low. A good strong rennet will last a week. Calves' rennets differ so much in strength that the only rule possible is to use as little as will do. Mary keeps two pitchers for rennet, and prepares the second one a day or two before she begins to use from it, when, if there is still any liquid remaining in the first, it is carefully strained into the second.

Fig. 4.—WOODEN KNIFE.

In about half an hour Mary will begin to break up the curd with her hand; moving it gently for twenty minutes, meanwhile increasing the heat to 96°, when one end of the vat is raised by means of the screw, and the process of drawing off the whey commences, and is continued for an hour or two. When it is sufficiently dry, it is weighed, salted in the proportion of 1 oz. dry salt to 5 lbs. curd, cooled off, and pressed in large hoops for half an hour, when it is removed and ground into lumps, the size of a pea, in the curd mill, fig. 5, of which fig. 6 is the cylinder. This turns against a curved surface with similar teeth. By this mill the curd is not really ground, but picked fine. Cotton bags, fig. 7, are then filled with the curd and pressed in seven inch tin hoops, fig. 8, strongly banded with iron, under 1,000 lbs. weight to 20 lbs. curd, for two days. Once during this time the cheeses are taken out, turned, and the bags replaced by bandages. We have one press which holds eight hoops, fig. 9; the others only four. They are then bandaged anew, immersed in a kettle of scalding brine to make a rind impervious to the flies, and stored away in the curing-room, where they are daily turned, and, after the first morning, dressed down with whey, butter and annotto for a month or six weeks. This is the room which you used to say reminded you of pine apples, strawberries and roses. They are taken from this room to the stone cheese-house, where the process of curing still goes on. By and by the shelves, from the floor to the ceiling, will be filled with beautiful little Cheddar Cheeses, fig. 10, just alike, each weighing from 10 to 12 lbs., and about the color of a horse chestnut. The Cheddar Cheeses are made extensively in England, and are imported for this market. The name is taken from the town of Cheddar, in the northern part of England, where they are manufactured on a large scale. Mr. F. W. Collins introduced the idea of making them in this country, in his dairy in Morris, Otsego County, N. Y., in 1862, since which time he has confined his dairy to the production of foreign cheese, mostly of that stamp. The wholesale price has been regulated by the exchange on gold, and consequently has vacillated widely. In 1862 it was 16 cents per lb.; in 1863, 25; in 1864, 40; in 1865, 30; in 1866, it has ranged from 33 to 35 cents per pound.

Fig. 5.—CURD MILL.

Fig. 6.—CYLINDER.

Fig. 7.

Fig. 8.

[The manufacture of the finer varieties of cheese is receiving great attention in the dairy districts. The introduction of the factory system by Jesse Williams, of Rome, a few years since, has had the happiest influence in the improvement of the quality of American cheese, and in the demand for it in other countries, especially England. In 1857 the total export of American cheese amounted to but 6½ millions of pounds. In 1864 the exports from this port alone were estimated at fifty millions of pounds. It only needs suitable care in the management of the dairy to give us the command of the cheese markets of the world. The Cheddar is the highest style of English cheese. It will be seen from the prices named by our correspondent that they are nearly a third higher than the average price of ordinary qualities of cheese in those years. This is a pretty strong argument for absolute cleanliness in the milking stables, and the greatest nicety in the dairy-room.—Eds.]

Fig. 9.

Fig. 10.

Thill and Pole Harrows.—It is very desirable to give corn, sorghum, potatoes, and all root crops very early culture. This cannot be well done with implements having teeth which shovel, scrape, slice, or otherwise move much the soil. The best hoe for many purposes is the potato hook, and harrows of various sizes are the best implements for the tillage of such crops. Potatoes require little care, and if planted deep may be harrowed without reference to the rows, but for other crops the teeth must be guided to stir the soil and not touch the plants. Why not bolt a pair of thills and a handle or pair of plow handles to a light (A) harrow? Clods and stones will have much less influence upon it than if drawn simply by the clevis. The thills may be very narrow. With a pole, using two horses, and taking out the middle teeth, the harrow being run astride the rows, the work of corn hoeing might be greatly facilitated. The full efficacy of a harrow is secured only when every tooth does its work and no one follows in the track of another. This may be better secured by using thills and poles than by any other way.

The Opossum.—(*Didelphis Virginiana.*)

This is one of those peculiarly American "institutions," which, after the discovery of the Western World, added much to the interest with which naturalists regarded America. New flowers and shrubs, new trees and animals were expected, but as a general thing these followed in some measure the old familiar forms of Europe. But this wonderful genus (*Didelphis*) in many important respects was an entire anomaly. In the first place, the teeth are more numerous than those of any other then known animal; the hind feet are hand-like, being furnished with a sort of nailless thumb, so that the animal can grasp a branch; the naked tail is prehensile, enabling the animal to use it in climbing or to suspend itself by it, as in the picture, and, more astonishing than all, the females have a belly pouch in which the young are reared. This pouch is common to the order of marsupial animals, which is the prevailing type of the mammalia of Australia—the kangaroo, for example. The Opossum Family includes ten or twelve genera and perhaps fifty species, some of which are not much larger than a common mouse; but the Opossum is the only one found in the United States, and from its size is one of the most important and interesting. Its head is long, the nose straight and pointed, teeth numerous and sharp, ears thin, dark at base and bordered with white; fur gray, composed of fine soft wool, with many long white hairs; color on the back and legs darker. The Opossum weighs 10 to 14 pounds, is quick and active among the branches of trees, but clumsy on the ground. When pressed to close quarters it feigns death, and shows no fight, but watches an opportunity to escape. From this well known habit comes the expression "playing 'possum." A nocturnal animal, crafty and stealthy in its motions, feeding upon fruits and vegetables to some extent, but particularly fond of eggs and young birds, the nest of many a poor bird is robbed. Young mice are greedily devoured, and many reptiles also. In fact there is little animal food not acceptable, provided the Opossum does not have to fight for it. The birth of the young seems to be a matter of mystery. When first discovered they are minute, blind, naked, shapeless things, weighing only a single grain each, and each attached to a teat, of course within the protecting marsupial pouch. After some fifty days, having gained sight and fur, and being about as large as little mice, they begin to run in and out, though remaining most of the time attached to the teats; when their size is so great that the pouch will not hold them, they are said to cling to the mother's back, coiling their tails around hers for additional security. The Opossum is found in all the Atlantic States south of New-York, occasionally in this State, but not east of the Hudson River; and southward and westward. Its flesh is excellent, usually very fat, and resembling that of a sucking pig.

OPOSSUM.—(*Didelphis Virginiana.*)

The Green Turtle (*Chelonia Midas.*)

This animal belongs to the family of Loggerhead Turtles. It is common in our markets, but rarely appears upon the coasts of the Atlantic States, except Florida, though occasional specimens have been found as far north as Long Island. It is an inhabitant of the deep sea in the neighborhood of the West India Islands. It is well represented in our engraving, and has little the look of our land or fresh water tortoises. The feet are really fins, and are exclusively used for swimming, except when they come upon the shore to lay their eggs. These they lay in hollows dug in the dry sand, high on the beach. One hundred and fifty to two hundred eggs are laid in a place, they are covered with sand and left to be hatched by the sun. At these times the turtles are taken, and shipped in great numbers to the markets of the United States and Europe. They weigh from two hundred to four hundred pounds. Considerable pains is now taken on many of the West India Islands to prevent the destruction of the eggs and of the turtles before the eggs are laid. When the young hatch they shuffle away down to the water and are seen no more until they appear of full size, living apparently continually under water. They feed upon a kind of sea weed called turtle grass. The general color of this turtle is olive green, and the fat has a greenish hue. They never bite, we believe, but sometimes strike with their "flippers." In market the fore and hind fins on the same side are usually tied together by a cord passed through the leathery web. The flesh of these animals is savory and tender, being cut into steaks for broiling or frying, and those parts unfit for steaks are used for the popular "green turtle soup."

GREEN TURTLE AND SALT WATER TERRAPIN.

THE SALT WATER TERRAPIN (*Malacoclemmys palustris.*)—The little fellow at the left of the picture is another favorite of the epicure. The Salt Water Terrapin inhabits the salt water marshes from Rhode Island to South America, during our Northern winters burying itself in the mud. Taken at this time it is fat and delicious, and greedily sought for in our City markets. Each plate of the upper shell is marked with deep striæ parallel with the sides. These are deepest in the males, and the males are considerably less in size than their companions. These Terrapins are very active on shore, and expert swimmers—on the alert and ever suspicious of danger, except when hybernating. They are about 7½ inches long, the shell being of an olive green color, with darker concentric markings on the scales. The under shell or *sternum* is yellowish green, with dusky markings, and the legs and neck of a light brown, inclining to white, with innumerable black dots.

Carrot Culture.

BY M. H. SILVERTHORN.

Select a good rich piece of clover sod, with deep loam or gravel soil; put on twenty loads of good manure to the acre and spread evenly over the ground. Then plow the ground about six inches deep. I once failed entirely to raise a crop because I plowed my ground too deep; the seed would not germinate in the soil turned up. I do not think it advisable to undertake the culture of carrots on clay soil with a stiff subsoil, as the cost of them will exceed the profit.

After plowing, harrow fine; harrow the last time the short way of the piece; then drill in the seed the long way, in rows, two feet apart.

I prefer to raise my own seed, as it grows much more sure than seed purchased at the stores—use fresh seed. I usually raise the White Belgian, as I can grow more to the acre than of any other kind. Still I consider there is more nutriment in the same amount of the Orange carrot. The best tool that I have yet used is of my own invention.

The frame is similar to that of a common cultivator, and about the same length, but only about two-thirds as heavy—in this I have eight teeth. The teeth are about ten inches long from the shoulder to the point. The blade is similar to the coulter on a plow, except it is only about 1¼ inches wide and brought to an edge. These, with a good cultivator shovel for the front tooth, complete the implement.

With this cultivator and a horse, you can commence to work your carrots as soon as they are up, cutting up the ground deep and very close to the carrots without covering them up, thus saving five-sixths of the labor usually spent with the hoe, and leaving the ground in much better condition than it otherwise could be. After the carrots are about as big as a pipe stem, I take my hoe the narrow way, and cut the rows into hills, leaving them, when thinned out, about six inches apart. After this you have no more to do with the hoe, but use the cultivator occasionally. To harvest, plow around the patch, just as close to the row as you can without cutting the roots. Now let your team stand, take a good butcher knife, catch the top of the carrot in the right hand, pulling it out of the ground, after which take the root in the left, and turn the top down—now, with one clip, cut off the top and throw the carrots in piles on the plowed ground, and tramp the tops in the furrows—now, plow about twice around, and you are ready to pull and cut as before. In this way myself and one other hand have harvested and buried one hundred bushels in half a day.

Carrots should remain in the ground as long as they can be left, and be got out while the ground is dry, as they generally improve till freezing weather, and they keep much more fresh than when harvested before they are fully matured. Still they should be dug when the ground is dry, for the carrots come out clean, and need no washing before feeding. Dirty carrots never should be fed to any kind of stock.

Every person should have a good root cellar attached to the barn. After your carrots are harvested, put in the cellar about what will last till midwinter, and bury the balance, as they keep much fresher when buried than in a cellar.

Carrots have no great fattening properties, but when fed with grain they are much better than *either* fed separately. I have always found it more advantageous to feed, say to a horse, four quarts of oats and six to eight good sized carrots than eight quarts of oats with no carrots, or than double the amount of carrots with no oats. Carrots alone, are most excellent feed for cows in the spring, before grass comes; chopped fine and mixed with ground oats, they make the best of feed for sheep having early lambs.

[Deeper plowing than six inches is advisable in rich sandy loams, and in all heavy loams sub-soiling will pay. The tops of carrots make excellent feed, and we think it pays better to feed them than to turn them under. In some districts they are sold to dyers, at a good price.]

Driving Horses at Plowing.

[The following sensible notions about plowing are from "T. C.," of Paulding County, Ohio. The docility of the horse, under proper training, is such that lines need only be used at plowing, in an emergency; but horses can seldom be trusted without some control upon their heads.—Eds.]

"The subject of driving horses before the plow is an important one to every farmer, for good driving and good plowing go together, and good, easy plowing is no small item in farming. I have seen one man take a team to plow, and permit them to walk so fast that they had to stop every few rods to breathe, and thereby lose more time and injure the team more, and not make as good work by far as if they had been driven more slowly; and I fear this is the practice of thousands of the readers of the *American Agriculturist.* I have seen another man take two old horses that had been used singly in a buggy, one much lighter and much faster than the other, and (neither of which had been used to plowing), hitch them to the plow, and in a short time have them go step by step with each other, what pace he wished, and so straight as to surprise his employer. While the former plowman made bad work by letting some slices fall back, setting some on edge, and leaving dead furrows from two to three feet wide, the latter would turn all well over, and in finishing up would leave a dead furrow only the breadth of the plow, and as straight as need be, without making any 'turns' or short furrows. The good plowman did his work much easier to himself and team than the other. Both pieces were in corn, and that best plowed was easiest tended.

"The best way that I know of to tie horses that are in the habit of going too fast is the following: Use the cord lines, (those thick at the hind ends are best for lazy horses), instead of the short stick between their heads. I prefer a coupling strap, with a spring hook at each end, and buckle in the middle, or a cord line will do. We do not want horses always the same distance apart, especially in finishing up, and besides the stick is not pleasant to a tender-mouthed horse when turning round, especially if the driver does not believe in it, or if he is not kind to his team. If one horse is faster than the other, instead of hanging the check rein on the harness as usual, put it back between the hames, tie a short line to the middle of it, and tie the other end of the short line to the other horse's wiffletree, or to his trace forward of it. When the fast horse steps forward he steps into his 'bit'; if he has a tender mouth he may 'rear,' but by the time his feet are off the ground the other horse makes a step, and his rein is slack, and he will learn to go slow before he gets tired. If both horses are too fast, tie them both in the same way. As to driving, every good plowman establishes a communication between himself and his team peculiar to himself—not, however, by putting the lines round the back, nor by hanging them on the 'handles,' unless they have more practice than is usual on small farms. The boy that took the prize without lines had practice. The place for the lines is in the plowman's hands, where he can let one slip through his fingers, or gather it in, as needed. With lines, properly used, words are seldom needed; and with sufficient practice words properly spoken do away to a great extent with the use of lines. 'Come' and 'gee' are all the words necessary, besides speaking to each horse by name; they should be spoken to kindly. If a horse is lazy, a stroke with a cord line shows him his pace much quicker than unkind words. I know of no surer way to break up a bad practice than that which induced the boy to drive his team without lines—namely, the offer of a prize."

Screens for Shelter.

Screens are planted for two purposes: the concealment of objects offensive to the taste, and the shelter of buildings, gardens and orchards from the winds. It is of screens as a shelter that we purpose to say a few words here. The importance of shelter in our northern climate is but little understood. It answers several economic as well as esthetic purposes. No country home has its appropriate surroundings until evergreens are planted. It is cheerless and desolate in winter—it lacks the highest charm in summer. By the shelter of evergreens, we may change the temperature of the seasons, and give gardens and orchards the climate of regions four or five degrees further south. The violence of the prevailing winds may be completely broken, so that the thermometer will not sink so low in winter, and the snow, instead of drifting in heaps and leaving many places bare, will spread its soft covering evenly over all delicate plants and preserve them. Many of the difficulties with which the gardener and orchardist have to contend, may be obviated by the shelter of trees. One reason why grapes and other small fruits do better in cities and villages than in the country, is the fact that they have the shelter of yards and buildings. Train an Isabella upon a trellis in an open field, and you may not get a crop once in five years. Put it upon the south or east side of a building, and, with suitable feeding and pruning, the crop is generally as sure as that of Indian corn.

One of the best examples of the ameliorating influences of shelter upon climate that has ever fallen under our observation, was upon the farm of the late Judge Meech, of Shelburne, Vt. His homestead was near the shores of Champlain, and swept by the severe lake winds in the winter and spring. He inclosed about two acres with a screen of American Arbor

Vitæ, that being the most common evergreen of the region. Within this inclosure he could raise the grape, the peach, and other fruits that would not mature outside. The effect of the screen was to give his garden the climate of New York.

There can be no doubt of the economy of planting screens in cold climates around gardens and orchards, wherever there is sufficient room for them. A screen, unlike a hedge, does not require close planting, and not much shearing or attention of any kind, after it is once established. As to the plants that will serve this purpose, deciduous trees are better than nothing, but they are not nearly so effective as evergreens; and if one is to be at the expense of planting it is better economy to plant the best.

There are several varieties of evergreens that make perfect shelter, and we should be governed in their selection mainly by the cost of the plants and the facility of transplanting. We put at the head of the list the Norway Spruce, and this conifer has been so extensively imported for

SCREEN OF NORWAY SPRUCE.

the last dozen years or more, that almost every well established nursery has a large stock, and they are as cheap as any other tree. Many nurseries have evergreen trees fit for no other purpose than screens, or to be cut up for stakes and poles. The Hemlock is another admirable tree for this purpose, and if we could find plants that had been properly grown, we should prefer them to the Norway Spruce. The foliage is more beautiful, they are a perpetual feast to the eye, but unfortunately they are exceedingly impatient of removal. It is rare to find a nurseryman that knows how to grow a Hemlock, and hardly ten per cent. of plants taken from the woods, with ordinary treatment, will live. Next to this we place the American Arbor Vitæ, which is abundant and easily transplanted. The White and Black Spruce, and the Red Cedar, also, make good screens. So much depends upon keeping the roots of evergreens moist during transportation that we should be governed mainly by location and price in selecting any one of the varieties here mentioned.

If the soil is rich enough to bear sixty bushels of corn to the acre, it will require nothing but mechanical preparation—plowing with the surface and subsoil plow. It will pay to loosen the soil to the depth of eighteen inches. If enriching is called for, use no fresh manures, but a compost made of peat and ashes, or muck and lime. Ashes are always a good dressing for evergreens. The distance of planting will be determined somewhat by the size of the trees, and the immediate objects aimed at. With Norway Spruces ten or twelve feet high, an effective shelter may be made at once. We have succeeded admirably with trees of this size, losing less than five per cent.—planting them so that the limbs just touched. They were put out, with good balls of earth, the same day they were taken up. It is safer, however, to plant smaller trees, and closer together, even if you have to take out the alternate trees two or three years later. A screen for an apple orchard may be left to grow twenty-five or thirty feet high, and in this case the trees should be at least ten feet apart to give the requisite strength at the base. The screen will require much less attention than the hedge, but it is good policy to keep the ground cultivated for a few years after the planting, and to bring out the bottom limbs well by shearing those above. All the different kinds of evergreens we have named bear the shears well, and can be readily trained in the way they should go, with a little timely attention.

Smallness of Cob Very Desirable in Seed Corn.

The selection of seed corn is one of the most important things which a farmer does at this season. Coarse cobs accompany late maturity, as a rule; fine cobs, well tipped out, indicate perfect maturity, adaptation to the season and soil, and a fixedness of character which it is important to maintain. The curing of corn takes place to a great extent after husking, and the presence of a great, soft, moist cob in each ear gives a tendency to mold, which should be sedulously avoided. The old experiment of fitting a paper cone to an ear of corn, then withdrawing the ear, shelling it and returning the kernels to the cone, is interesting and instructive. If the kernels will all go easily into the cone, the cob is too large, and we should say, the corn unfit for seed. The cone should be made of brown paper, dampened, bound tightly around the ear, coming no higher than the kernels, but covering all; the ends are trimmed off, and it is allowed to dry before the ear is drawn out. One may easily judge by the eye which ears have the smallest cobs—those which are best tipped out, which have the kernels in the closest rows, and all the rows running unbroken from end to end. These ears will not be found among the biggest round, nor among the longest, usually, but among those of medium size. A friend used to say, as he showed off his seed corn, "every ear as regular and solid as a white-oak pin." And so they were, as nearly as corn ears could be, firm, close, hard and solid.

Cotton Culture.

BY F. G. DWIGHT.

[Our offer of two premiums for prize essays upon this subject has been responded to, and the first premium has been awarded to Joseph B. Lyman, a recent cotton planter in Louisiana, and the second to F. G. Dwight, whose experience has been in the Atlantic Seaboard Cotton States. Both essays will be probably published in one volume, in season for the next year's operations. For the immediate benefit of our readers in the cotton growing districts, and of the large class who are contemplating a removal thither, we give in this issue the first of a series of articles culled from these essays.—Eds.]

Bedding Up.—After the fields have all been plowed the work of bedding commences. One hand leads off with a scooter plow, and marks rows, running through the whole length or width of the field; others follow with turn plows, and throw two or more furrows on each side of the marks, making a slightly elevated bed, the number of furrows to be turned depending on the width of the spaces between the rows. A small water furrow is left between the beds to serve as a drain after heavy rains. Where the land is not likely to wash, and there is a good deep subsoil to readily absorb rains, *flat culture* is often practiced. In this case the land is thoroughly plowed as before, and if possible cross plowed, bedding up being dispensed with until seeding time, when slight beds are thrown up in the process of planting.

Cotton Rows.—In marking out rows, it is recommended that they should be laid out east and west, in order to be as much as possible exposed to the sun at all hours of the day—cotton being of all others a hot weather plant. This distinction can be observed on level ground, or such as is slightly rolling, but where there is much fall, attention must be paid to safeguards against the land washing. On hilly lands, curves should be followed around the sides on a level.

The probable productiveness of the soil must determine the distance between the rows; the poorer the soil the nearer should they be. On land that is not well known to be *very* good, it is safest to let the distance be about 20 inches or two feet, so that in getting twice as many rows on poor soil as would be put on land admitting of four-foot distance, the difference in the yield of a crop grown on good and only tolerably good land would not be very great.

Planting.—The cotton plant in its early growth is very tender, particularly when in a crowded state, it cannot withstand frost and is even very sensitive to cool weather. As early planting is generally recommended and will be found to be the most successful, caution must be exercised not to plant *too* early. To replant is discouraging work, involving much loss of time. In the Gulf States from the 25th March to the 10th April is the usual planting season.

Details.—The hands that are selected to drop the seed must be furnished with bags or "wallets" large enough to hold about half a bushel of seed. These are suspended at the right or left side by a rope or strap over the shoulder. With the scuter plow, a seed furrow is opened to the depth of three or four inches in the middle of the bed, the hands following the plow and dropping the seed as even as possible.

Careful supervision is needed. The best of the freedmen are not easily impressed with the importance of dropping the seed regularly. They soon get careless, and if you are not on the alert, the young plants will come up in patches. Light furrows are thrown towards the opened row to cover the seed, one on each side. If left in this condition the seed would be covered too deeply; and after one field is planted, the wooden scraper, fastened to a plow stock, is drawn over the seed row, taking off all unevenness of surface, removing the excess of covering, and leaving the bed in a neat condition, somewhat elevated above the water furrow.

In Flat Culture, where there has been no previous "bedding up," the seed furrows are opened at proper distances. Seed dropped and covered as before; then successive furrows are thrown towards the seed row until the space between the rows is plowed up, leaving a shallow water furrow midway between the beds.

Again, on very good land, and where the soil is in fine working order, the labor of plowing previous to planting is sometimes dispensed with. This "short cut" way, however, is not to be recommended. Whenever this *must* be done, the process is simply to open furrows at the proper distance apart, drop the seed and cover as before. One or two furrows are then thrown up with the turn plow to complete a bed, and the middle broken out with the sweeps; the wooden scraper being used to level off the beds.

Your Personal Supervision.—Every day during "planting season" is necessary to look after the furrow opening, planting, covering, plowing and scraping off. Permit no carelessness or slighting on the part of any one engaged in the work; it must all be done well and promptly. See that the seed furrows are opened in a straight line, to facilitate the after culture.

The seed dropper should walk with a regular gait along the side of the furrow, letting the seed fall from his hand *evenly*, and as much as possible *right in the middle*. Let him stop when empty, and as soon as he has another handful, step on. In covering the seed row, the plow hand must be "wide awake," keep his plow under control, and see that the soil is sufficiently thrown over to cover *all* the seed. The most experienced hand should hold the scraper, otherwise too much soil will be "knocked off" here or not enough there, leaving the seed exposed in one place, and in another covered with earth so deeply as to endanger its never coming up.

DEPTH TO COVER SEED.—It need be but *thinly* covered. In light, dry soil an inch to two inches will be enough; in heavier soil less.

Fig. 1.—HAY BARRACK AND COW STABLE.

Jersey Hay Barracks—Roofed Stacks—The Poor Man's Barn.

Last year we presented our readers some rather elaborate barn plans, and many complained that they were extensive and expensive, and had little interest for them. They were wrong in this, for the plans were full of good hints for all. It occurred to us the other day that the structures, of which we give some engravings, were really very philosophically devised, and that many whose means do not permit them to build such barns as they would like to, might be profited by a lesson from the "Jersey Dutch." The affair called in New Jersey a "Hay Barrack" is really a stack cover—a light square roof, made to be raised and lowered, and set at any desired height between four corner posts. These posts are about eight inches in diameter, and twenty-three to twenty-four feet long, and are set 3 to 3½ feet in the ground. The roof is made upon the ground and then raised to its place, where it is held by pins. Thatched roofs are made by fastening four substantial rails (square or round) together by gains and pins near the ends; to these rails light poles, many of which reach the peak of the roof, are fastened, and upon them thatch is laid, usually in a coarse manner. It is important that the roof should be very light. Hence thatched roofs are preferred, and barracks 12+12 are better than those of larger size.

Another kind of roof is that seen in fig. 2, where boards, the upper ends of which are not only sawed to fit, but chamfered off to match, are simply nailed together upon the ridges, and to the plates forming a "hip-roof." Sometimes

Fig. 2.—BOARD ROOF TO BARRACK.

they are battened on the ridges, and over the cracks between the boards, and sometimes not. Either of these roofs will last many years, and, as stack covers, save many times their cost. The lower part of the hay or straw stack is often protected from the cattle by perpendicular boarding, nailed to rails or studs set between the posts. This siding extends six to eight feet from the ground, as seen on the sides of fig. 1, and the transition is easy from this to the cow stable, which is there represented. In this case there are four strong rails or joists spiked to the posts at the desired height (say seven feet), and a flooring of boards or rails—the tighter the better—is laid upon them, and the hay, straw or grain is put above. Thus a 12+12 feet stable is made, and a door is swung as shown. There is room for three cows and a horse to stand comfortably. Holes may be cut or bored for ventilation if needed. If the side boarding is double, and leaves or straw are stuffed into the space between the sides, the stable will be a very warm one. If two or three barracks are placed close together, forming an angle or three sides of a hollow square, cows or horses may be very well protected in our severest winters.

Another plan for a shed under the stack is seen in fig. 3. Common fence rails are set up against the rails which support the hay, and a few slabs driven into the ground on each side and nailed together to contract the entrance. The sloping sides may be thatched with spruce or hemlock boughs and sods, and thus made very warm and comfortable. This makes an excellent fowl-house also; and if the south side

Fig. 3.—BARRACK WITH SHED BENEATH.

were to be glazed, two or three sashes being inserted, and the whole made tight, it would be as good a winter laying house as could be desired.

We remarked that the affair is philosophically devised. Well made stacks keep hay as well as it can be kept in a barn. The difficulty is that it is expensive to thatch and rope a stack so as to make it shed water perfectly, besides vermin have a little freer swing at the grain and grass seed; and when a stack is cut into or partly taken down, it is at once more or less seriously exposed to detriment by the weather. All trouble about covering and protecting against rain after the stack is used from is removed by this contrivance, and the warm, snug little stable beneath, for a poor man, or for any one as a temporary expedient, may often be very convenient.

Design in Feeding Stock.

Some farmers fail to adapt their food to the particular wants of their stock, as if all that was needed was to give them enough to eat. But different kinds of food produce different results.

For example: if I have a steer, which is already well developed in bone and muscle, but which I wish to fatten for market, I should give him linseed or cotton-seed oil-cake, or Indian meal, or shorts. If I wish to encourage the growth of colts or calves, or other young animals, I should give them a variety of feed, but especially good hay, ground oats, or oats in the sheaf, cut tolerably fine. Corn meal, barley, and buckwheat are also useful for this purpose. A working team, whether horses or oxen, demand food which will supply the waste of muscle and a fair amount of fat. When spring work is about to commence, after seeing that my teams are reasonably fat, I should give them oil-cake, oats, and good, bright hay, or cut straw. Oats (ground) will supply muscle, and give greater power of endurance, in hard work or fast driving, than will corn meal. Then, to make the bill of fare complete, I should give an occasional meal of carrots, or potatoes, or turnips. These will aid the digestion, sharpen the appetite and promote the general health. If feeding for milk, I would continue this bill of fare in a measure, and give oil-cake, corn meal, shorts, or bran, with good hay or stalks cut fine, and roots, such as beets or carrots. G.

The Sheep's Foot—Biflex Canal—Fouls.

If we examine a sheep's foot externally we find the hoof or horny portion presenting three distinct forms. First, the outer walls, hard, horny, sometimes smooth, as is usually the case with the mutton breeds, as the Southdowns and Cottswolds—in others, much corrugated and rough, as with the Merinos. Second, the inner walls, or walls of the cleft, less firm, somewhat scaly and fissured on the surface. Third, the sole, of much the consistence of the walls of the cleft, but thicker, and elastic from resting upon a soft, spongy cushion, which covers the bone, and forms in a measure the base of the heel. If we spread open the cleft between the toes, and examine it closely, we find a small hole, apparently in the skin, shown in fig. 1, into which the head of a pin may be easily passed. It is the mouth of what is called the "Biflex Canal," and is a peculiarity of the foot of the sheep, other cloven footed animals not having it. The canal, as shown in section in fig. 2, is about an inch and a half in length, curved like a horseshoe, and has but one opening. The sheep books are particularly vague in their allusions to the Biflex or Interdigital Canal, and it will, we doubt not, surprise many of our sheep raisers to know that this canal exists, and others that it is not an "issue" or mouth of some tube connected with a secretory gland, but an inflection of the skin, the canal walls being like the adjacent skin, and really forming a curious little sack, lined with hairs, and secreting a sort of yolky, gummy substance. Its use seems to be to provide an elastic cushion to spread the toes apart, and perhaps also a viscid secretion to protect the tender skin between the toes, where it is so easily

Fig. 1.—MOUTH OF BIFLEX CANAL.

washed away, and where abrasions and slight injuries are liable to occur. Were the skin between the toes formed to exude enough of this secretion, it would, of necessity, be more tender and liable to injury and disease than it now is.

We know of no disease of the Biflex Canal, except stoppage at its mouth, which causes inflammation and swelling, and similar inflammation caused by some foreign substance being introduced. Instead of lancing and trying to cut out the "worm," as some people think it is, the sensible treatment is to procure a fine pointed ear syringe, and, after opening the mouth, wash it out with castile soap and warm water, and grease the parts with tar mixed with lard. This Biflex Canal has been charged with being the cause of the rot, and though this view is generally scouted at now-a-days, we are by no means sure that it may not be guilty sometimes, to a certain degree; for certainly any cause which will render the skin harsh and inflamed, or subject to injury

Fig. 2.—BIFLEX CANAL.

Fig. 3.—STRUCTURE OF FOOT.

from long grass or vines of any kind caught between the toes, puts the foot in the best condition to be poisoned by the virus of the hoof-rot coming in contact with the inflamed part.

FOULS.—When this condition of inflammation of the skin in the cleft of the foot, from any cause, becomes established, and a wet soil keeps the hoofs moist, and greasy or yolky matter from the Biflex Canal is constantly washed out, the then disease known as "the Fouls" occurs. It is easily cured by cleaning and greasing the parts, and putting the sheep on dry pastures. If, however, it is neglected, it is liable to introduce hoof-rot—the subject of another article.

If we examine the internal structure of the foot we find that the horn is attached to the sensitive portion above, at the crown of the hoof and at the sole, by what is called a papillated surface. Lower down we find that the horn on its inner surface is split into an almost infinite number of delicate leaves or *lamellæ*. Between these leaves of hoof are sensitive leaves of the vascular membrane which covers the whole surface of the horn. These two sets of lamellæ, or leaves, are as if we were to take two books and lay the leaves of each, leaf for leaf, between those of the other. The structure is very beautiful and easily seen in the hoof of a horse, which, after the flesh has decayed, may be washed out and will show the horny lamellæ very clearly. The sensitive lamellæ are seen in figure 3, as also the papillated structure at the crown and sole. From this papillated surface the hoof grows, and it is an inflammation of this which constitutes the hoof-rot. The same membrane—full of the papillæ by which horn is formed—covers the whole foot and secretes horn at all points; where it is the thickest and most vascular, as at the crown and sole, there most horn is formed, but on the lamellæ, little.

Adobe and Concrete Buildings.

The name *adobe* is applied to building material in the form of bricks, but unburned. It is not necessarily clay, but it must be of a clayey or loamy nature, and so firm when dried in the sun as to be easily handled, and to sustain considerable weight without crushing. This is distinguished from concrete by its containing no lime or cement, and being always used in the form of bricks. The concrete is a mortar of sand and lime, usually hydraulic lime or cement, in part at least, especially such as is used for foundations, in which the proportion of cement preponderates. This is laid up in the walls as it is to remain, and the largest possible quantity of gravel and larger stones is worked in. The present high price of building materials leads farmers to look anxiously for some good substitute for stone, brick and wood. The need for the dissemination of knowledge on this subject is great, especially throughout the Prairie States. A correspondent in Iowa pleads for information, definite and full, about adobe building, which we shall try to give, and would be glad to give also particulars of the experience of any of our readers who have tried, and either approve or condemn this material. Our correspondent writes as follows:—

"The high price of the material would be but a small evil, provided we could obtain it. The fact is that now throughout the Northwest we go without farm buildings nearly altogether. Tumble-down stables, made of poles and straw, ornament at least one-half of the farms. The sides, which are of straw, slip down and are not repaired, letting the cold wind in without hindrance, and the water drips through the covering for days after every rain. Even of those well-to-do farmers who have barns not one in ten has shelter sufficient to protect *all* of his domestic animals. I sometimes dream of warm stables, filled with rows of contented cattle, nice and cosy, with the straw up to their knees, but alas! save only the 'straw up to their knees,' I fear it must ever be only a dream throughout all Prairiedom. If you would take hold of the matter and show us what to do, and how to do it, you would in that particular alone confer an immense blessing upon the country."

A Simple Ventilator.

"H. W. P." sends us a drawing of a simple apparatus, devised by the writer (and by others, very possibly), to be fastened with small screw-bolts to the back of a stove—in this case a sheet-iron air-tight—for the purpose of introducing to the room a constant supply of fresh warmed air in winter. It works admirably. The box is 9 x 10 x 2½ inches, made of sheet-iron. The pipe of zinc, 4 inches diameter, with a damper, descends beneath the floor, and thence runs under the floor and through the north wall of the building, to secure the force of the prevailing north-westerly winds. A west wall would, no doubt, be equally well. A strong current of air rushes in, is thrown against the back of the stove and the underside of the stove pipe, whence, perfectly warmed, it diffuses itself through the room, is cooled by contact with walls and windows, descends to the floor, and is drawn off by the draft of the stove, or through an opening in the chimney near the floor, thus giving place to a new supply. Tight double windows render the system more complete and add vastly to economy and comfort.

SIMPLE VENTILATOR.

Home-made Baskets.

BY SALIX.

I observe your call for information as to how willow baskets are made. Having often, when a boy, seen my father's plowmen make baskets for farm purposes during the long winter evenings, I will endeavor to tell you how it was done.

The willows were never peeled, but were soaked in water in a long pig trough. The

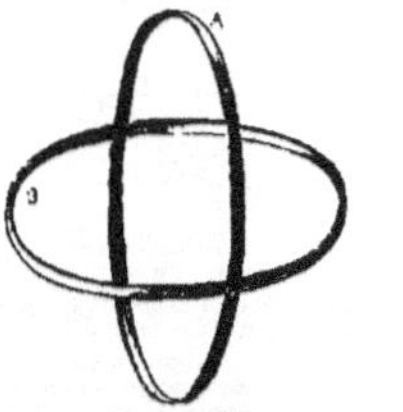

Fig. 1.—HOOPS.

hoops, ribs and handles were generally made of split ash. Two ash splints were bent into hoops and placed one within the other, but at right angles, as shown in figure 1, *a* and *b*. If the two hoops are round, of the same size and cross in the middle, the basket will be round—that is hemispherical. If the inner hoop, which forms the top of the basket, be the larger, the basket will be more or less oval. Having arranged the hoops, take the willow rods and weave them, as in figure 2. As the semi-circle enlarges, insert the ribs, bent as shown in figure 3, and of such size and form as to regulate the shape or contour of the basket, as shown at *d*, *d*, figure 4. The splints, if well soaked, can be easily bent into any shape. Weave willows

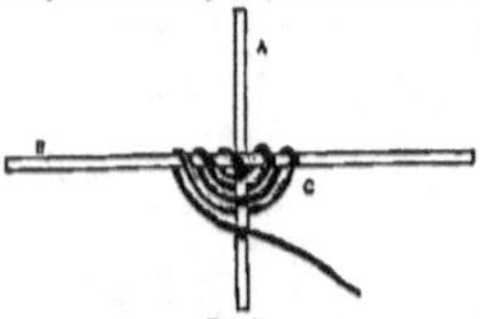

Fig. 2.

among these ribs or hoops—it being simply done—out and in, out and in, until the semi-circle reaches down the side of the basket to about the dotted line (fig. 4). Then commence on the ends of the basket and weave willows down the ends and along the bottom, as seen on the right hand end at *e*, (fig. 4,) putting in more of the ribs (fig. 3), if the work is large and consequently open. When you have the ends and sides well woven, the basket is finished, so far as strength is concerned. You can not pull it apart. But there will be gores or vacant spots left. Fill these up with weaving, and your basket is done.—It matters little where a willow ends, provided it does not end at the top without going round the upper hoop. The wet willow twigs will bend easily and take any form, and yet when dry they will be hard and stiff, and can not be unwoven. Push the several layers of willow close together and pull them tight, and they will hold very firmly.

Fig. 3.

After the basket is dry, trim off all straggling ends with a sharp knife. A little practice, and perhaps the spoiling of a few baskets made with materials that are quite cheap, will enable you to make an article worth a dozen of what you

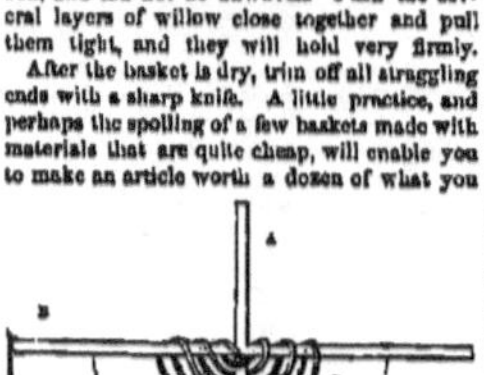

Fig. 4.

can buy. Do not give it up if you cannot make a neat job at first. A little care and patience, with a modium of practice, will set you all right.

[Several kinds of willow may be employed. The common white and yellow willows answer very well, but the basket osiers are superior on account of the slenderness of the rods. The white willow rods are strong and pliable, but not so delicate and long. When peeled and bleached with the fumes of burning sulphur, very beautiful work may be produced. Rods for basket making are best cut in the autumn, for the good of the stock, but may be cut for use at any time after they are sufficiently grown, and before they branch in the spring.—Ed.]

Investing in the Farm.

Leonard D. Clift, of Carmel, Putnam Co., one of the best farmers New York has ever produced, was wont to say of his own course in life: "I have pursued a different policy from farmers generally. Some of them have skinned their farms, brought up their children in ignorance, given little or nothing in charity, and have reached old age with barren farms, uncultured children, and narrow views of life, but they have *cash in bank!* On the contrary, my surplus earnings have gone to enrich my farm, until it is capable of yielding an abundant support; my children have been educated, and now occupy respectable positions in society. I have felt it a privilege to give in charity; my table has been bountifully supplied, and my house open to the stranger. All this I have, but not money in bank; and I am satisfied with my choice."

He went to his rest on the 9th of September last, at the age of 73—patriot, sage, counsellor and friend, leaving his beautiful homestead and his good works as his fitting monument. This farm was the work of his lifetime, and we wish to commend to our readers that sound policy which made his one of the model farms of the Empire State. It took the premium in 1855 as one of the best grazing farms, and the report of the Visiting Committee may be found in the Transactions of the State Ag. Soc. for that year.

He reprobated that policy of skinning the soil which, we are sorry to say, has been the prevailing style of husbandry even in the North and East, and which is still the worst feature of farming all over the country. Men have no faith in the capacity of the soil to reward them for the labor and money they expend upon it. They get a good crop of grain or roots from the land, and instead of investing the proceeds in more manure, more improvements or more stock, they invest in more land or more bank stock. Many a man has pursued this course with his farm until its fertility has been almost exhausted. He has transferred all its fatness to the bank, and it will not now sustain ten animals so well as it would fifty, fifty years ago. He may have grown rich in money by the process, but his farm is ruined. Go through the older farming districts of any of our seaboard States, and we doubt if the majority of the farms will carry the stock they grazed and fattened two generations back. They have lost so much in fertility that not even the improved tools and husbandry of the present day can make them pay so well as they did then.

The Carmel farmer had faith in his business, and felt that his surplus earnings were safer and better invested in the soil, under his own management, than in the bank, under the management of others. He literally cast his bread not only upon the land, but upon the waters of his farm, not doubting that it would return again.

He put money into dams and sluice ways; and the brook that had run to waste for ages was turned over his meadows, and set every blade of grass it fertilized to coining money for him. He demonstrated that irrigation alone would keep up the fertility of meadows, improving the quality and increasing the quantity of the grass. He gave us one of the best conducted experiments in irrigation—worth millions to the State, if his example were only faithfully followed. The stream that was barren to others became a Pactolus for him, flowing over sands of gold. He had faith in drains, and the rough land was cleared of its stones, and sluice ways for the passage of water were formed beneath the surface, making the drained field of fourfold value for all its future history. He believed in improved stock and invested largely in it both for milk and beef. He expected to get more milk and more beef from a given number of cattle, from the fact that they had been bred respectively for those qualities; and he succeeded in his object. He had faith in homemade manures, and worked his muck mines, and turned the stable, stye and barn-yard to good account. He brought up a rough farm, worth less than five thousand dollars, to a valuation of fifty thousand. He claimed that it would pay the interest on that, well managed; and that perhaps is the best test of value.

We believe this course—investing in the farm rather than in the bank—is better both for the farmer and for society. It is certainly much safer; for banks fail much more frequently than well managed farms. The dividends of the latter never fail entirely. The good, substantial living, and the comfortable home are always secure. It makes better society, farming becomes an improving and improvable art, and intelligence is as much a growth of the pursuit as farm products are of the soil. It puts the farmer's capital into his business, where he needs it, and where he can manage it himself. He ventures everything upon his business, lives wholly by it while he lives, and at death hands over a cultivated homestead and a living business to his heirs. This policy glorifies husbandry and hastens the Agricultural Millennium. We look with longing for the dawn of that day.

Stone Fences.

In some regions a stone wall is the cheapest fence that can be made. In many respects, too, it is the best for farm purposes. It has a look of honest stability that is truly pleasing, but is rarely advisable, except where adjoining fields will furnish stones enough to inclose them, and the fields will be greatly improved by their removal. Every wall will tumble down some time or other. On springy soils, draining is indispensable. A trench should be dug a foot or more deep with plow and scraper. Then draw the larger stones for the foundation, and dump them in the trench, which will save much hand-lifting. Afterwards draw the smaller, scattering them along the entire line. Of course, the stones should be laid so as to bind as much as possible, and inclining inwards somewhat. If practicable, find enough flat stones to cover the top of the fence, and help to throw off the rain, and to prevent Jack Frost from tearing it into pieces.

Mangel-Wurtzels for Sheep.—"Will it pay in Missouri to raise mangels to feed sheep when good hay may be put up for $3.00 per ton and corn is worth 40 cents per bushel?" No—unless you can feed them off on the ground. If so, yes; for then you will manure your land at the same time for a good crop of corn to follow, or for some other crop perhaps, and so doubly save and doubly gain. You will save the labor of harvesting the crop and of making and hauling out manure; you will gain the clearing of the land of weeds, if the crop is well attended to, and the value of the roots as feed, besides the security of not placing all your dependence for winter fodder on hay and corn, and the introduction of something like a sensible system of rotation, which is a gain all round.

Sweet Potato Culture.

BY W. W. RATHBONE, MARIETTA, OHIO.

The following article gives the method of preparing the land for sweet potatoes; that portion relating to setting the plants and cultivation will be given another month.

The Yellow Nansemond is the only variety worthy of general culture in the Northern and Middle States. Of robust habit, it matures early, and is fit for the table as soon as of sufficient size. Soil is poor that will not produce remunerative crops of corn and Irish potatoes. Yet I have grown 102½ bushels of Nansemonds per acre, without manure, on a side hill, the same land having failed in corn and Irish potatoes.

SOIL AND PREPARATION.—Sandy and gravelly soils are generally selected, and many think other soils will not answer. I have not a rod of sandy soil, and grow fifteen acres per annum. My soil is mellow, if properly treated—very cloddy, if mismanaged by plowing when wet.

I have produced good crops on red clay land, and raise annually several acres on a yellow loam. Where the soil is poorest, with very hard sub-soil, the Nansemonds grow of a rounded form, while in the richer, deeper and mellower soil they are more elongated. There is many a field laid by as too poor for corn or wheat, or, as many would say, good only for beans, that would produce excellent sweet potatoes, with but a slight dressing of well rotted manure, and leached or unleached ashes. On no other crop does manure tell so plainly. The sweet potato is well adapted to thin soils, especially as it is not an exhaustive crop. I have known it to be raised fifteen years on the same plot of land, showing no diminution of yield. The coating of vines seems to add more to the soil than is extracted by the potatoes. On rich soils too much vine is produced at the expense of the roots.

By saving none but the largest potatoes for planting, I notice a constant increase in the yield per acre. As for fifty years the small and refuse potatoes have been saved for seed, the wonder is that a crop can be raised at all.

A southern aspect is best, yet any other will answer. I always prefer rolling land, and in many years' experience in cultivating side hills, I entirely dissent from the practice almost universally recommended by writers, viz: "Make the ridges run parallel to the hill to avoid washing." It is nonsense to try to dam up the quantity of water that falls in our summer showers. My experience with the sweet potato proves it best to *get rid of all surface water as soon as possible.* Therefore, run the ridges from top to bottom of all inclinations, in order that each ditch may carry its own water, and the quantity will never be sufficient to do much damage.

In very light soils, especially if sandy, ridges are by many preferred to hills, but on loamy and clayey soils make hills by all means. I prefer them in all cases, because you are more certain of a good crop; the sun, reaching all sides of the hill, ripens the potatoes sooner; more bushels of *large* potatoes can be had; and early in the season the large tubers can easily be found, by the bursting of the hills, and grabbled; which, if the operation be done by first cutting the potato loose before pulling, is a positive benefit to those remaining. I have thus passed over a crop three times before digging, and finally taken out large potatoes on the 10th of October that were very small on the 20th of September.

Many who attempt sweet potato growing make *great ridges*, 2½, or 3 feet broad at the base; and some flatten them on the top, fearing drought. Better throw away the plants at once than place them in or on such a mass of earth.

NEW MODE OF MAKING RIDGES.—For twelve years I followed the stereotyped plan of throwing two heavy furrows together with a two horse team; it was killing work, and made crooked rows. Eight years ago I invented an easy method, by which ridges can be made as straight as the furrow by a marking out plow. This has been worth much to me, as by it many more hills can be planted per acre, and experienced growers know that the narrow ridges give the greatest product.

From the 1st to the 15th of May, when danger of hard frosts is over, the land, having been plowed, harrowed and rolled, should be ridged.

With two horses and a plow, turning a furrow slice to the right hand, begin on the left hand side of the field, throwing a furrow as the team passes down the hill. Drive back to place of beginning without plowing. Set the clevis over to the extreme left of the beam. The near horse is now to walk in the furrow first made, while the off horse walks on the land to be ridged, and the plow is held off to follow, cutting along and taking off part of the first furrow slice, leaving a ridge as you go, never to be over eighteen inches in diameter at the base. When at the foot of the hill, come back, dressing up lightly in the same furrow—*i. e.*, the one last passed down in, letting the near horse walk in the last furrow, and the off horse in the next one to the right. When passing up hill crooked places can be straightened. In the figure 1 and 2 show finished ridges. The nigh horse walks at *B*, and the off one at *A*, the perpendicular line shows where the plow is to be set to turn the next ridge.

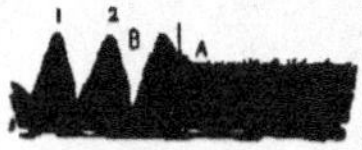

MANNER OF MAKING RIDGES.

This mode of making ridges will be valuable to all persons who wish to ridge land in autumn, to expose it to the action of frost or for aeration. I can expose four acres *per diem*, by going entirely round the field—the return furrow would be useless. And more; I can make the ridges sharp, two feet from tip to tip, and therefore more readily permeated by frost and air.

For and Against Dogs.

The affection with which man regards the animals which are dependent upon or attached to him varies greatly, and is nearly in proportion to the affection they show in return. The sheep is more valuable to man than the dog, but the dog returns with the strongest manifestations of affection man's kindness to him, while the sheep barely recognises its owner, and even pet lambs, however fondled, show no love in return, except a love for the food they get. It is not then to be wondered at that man should love the dog, which, of all other animals, exhibits qualities the most loveable. His affection for his master is often such as few friends or even brethren show for each other; his intelligence and docility place him in these respects foremost among brutes; his faithfulness, the offspring of his intelligence and affection, renders him a worthy type of this almost divine virtue. David could use no stronger words than "If He slay me yet will I trust in him," and this is the constant attitude of the meanest cur towards the master to whom he has attached himself. No cruelty will drive him away, no abuse will weaken his love, nor will severity, and all harsh treatment combined, prevent the exercise of his faithfulness. Taking this view of the relations of the dog to his master, well may he be to man an amplification of the traits, love, joy, long suffering, gentleness, faith, meekness. "*Against such*," says the Apostle Paul, "*there is no law*." All dogs do not exhibit those qualities equally, yet all in a considerable degree, and like men, their good behavior and intelligence depend much upon their bringing up. But dogs are enemies to all the world except their masters, their families and friends, so while we all that have opportunity love a dog, we, as a rule, dislike dogs in general. They are dangerous, ugly brutes, cross, apt to bite severely and subject to a distressing malady, which prompts the most peaceable to bite, and which, by their bite, is communicated with fearful certainty to man and other animals, causing inexpressible distress, and, almost certainly, the most terrible of deaths. Dogs are naturally beasts of prey, and no civilization or association with man will destroy their natural instincts to pursue the weaker animals. So they are the natural enemies of sheep, and the statistics of the immense destruction they cause are sufficient to condemn the entire race in an economical point of view, notwithstanding, that when trained from birth, they become such docile and faithful guardians of the flock, defending their charge, even against their own kind, and with their own lives.

Our laws may be too severe to be rigidly enforced, for the people will not sustain them if they aim at the absolute extinction of dogs. While, therefore, we agree very well with "Connecticut," and the hang-dog picture in our last number, we sympathize very fully with him who loves a dog; in fact, there is one animated little piece of dog flesh which would weigh heavily against a great many pounds of mutton in the estimation of the writer. Well has he earned the affection with which he is regarded.

No law could be executed which is too severe, yet the people demand the greatest possible security for their flocks, and against the undue multiplication of dogs, which so greatly enhances the danger from madness—hydrophobia.

The picture on the next page, needs barely a word of comment. Our artist has grouped a number of beautiful designs—chiefly from Sir Edwin Landseer's paintings, with some of his own. They exhibit different traits and phases of canine character and expression, and show the dog in his various relations to man—of servant, guard, play fellow, companion and friend. We are proud to call attention to this picture as a successful effort of both artist and engravers. The central figure is that of the Skye Terrier. The beggar's dog, though a mongrel, is in good part of Scotch Terrier blood; the next, to the right, is the Mastiff—then comes a pair of Smooth Rat-terriers, in a very spirited attitude; next we have one of a group by Jardin, which represents a rough-haired Pointer, common in Europe. The rag and bone pickers' drudge is a common cur, and the scene—dogs working hard at drawing a hand-cart—is common in our cities. Next is a fancy group of a Newfoundland's and two Hound's heads. The two lower corners show a contrast between the life of dogs in humble circles, and in those of wealth and luxury. The one a common cur of bull-dogish aspect; the other the Scotch Greyhound. The dog with a hare we are at a loss to name, it probably represents a cross between the Shepherd and Terrier—said to be a very good cross for hunting singly, if trained. The dog with doves is a portrait; and the group on the right shows a Retriever (with the duck), and a Cocker Spaniel.

Window Gardening.

There is a love of plants so interwoven in the make up of many people, that it will gratify itself under the most adverse surroundings. To those who are blessed with this love—for it is a blessing—no brick and mortar of the city, nor newness of a backwoods dwelling prove any obstacle. As we go about the streets of our large towns, we admire the well kept places, but not the less do we stop to note the humble efforts at horticulture that are made upon window-sills, or upon some favoring roof. What pleasure often grows in a discarded sauce-pan or other domestic utensil, which, having served well in its proper sphere, is glorified by being the home of a fuchsia or an aster! In making up the Horticultural Annual, we were obliged to omit an article on window gardening, prepared for it by Mr. John Henderson, the well known florist of Flushing, L. I. The article was upon inside and outside window gardens, and we now present his drawing of an outside garden, and make use of some of his material:

"Another mode of having plants and flowers, and for spring and summer the best of all, is to have boxes neatly made of wood to fit on the outside of the window, and then filled with flowering plants, thus making a kind of miniature garden, and at the same time forming an excellent screen. Shades may be dispensed with, as the plants are sufficiently close to prevent persons seeing into

WINDOW GARDEN.

the room, but, at the same time, not preventing those inside from observing through the foliage and flowers everything taking place outside. These boxes can be made quite plain or ornamented, and afterwards painted a light green. Stocks, scarlet geraniums, and mignonette succeed well, grown in boxes of this description. The outer edges, next the street, should be planted with the pretty blue lobelia, verbenas, and other trailing plants, which, falling over the sides of the boxes, add much to their effect. The ends of the boxes may be planted with morning glories (*Convolvulus major*), and Canary bird flower (*Tropæolum peregrinum*), to be trained on wires up and around the windows."

Boxes of this kind are sold by the London dealers ready stocked with plants. They have a great advantage over pots, as they do not dry out so readily, and they can be made much more secure. The edging of the box, shown in the engraving, can be readily made of willow or rattan. Besides the plants mentioned above, almost any of our annual and bedding plants may be grown; water them as often as may be needed, taking care to avoid over watering.

AMERICAN ATRAGENE—(*Atragene Americana.*)

A Native Climber.—(*Atragene Americana.*)

The pleasure we take in illustrating and describing native plants, is somewhat detracted from, by the knowledge that they are, as a general thing, quite difficult to procure. Very few of them are kept in our nurseries, and unless one happens to know their native localities, he has but little chance of obtaining them. The very beautiful native climber that we now notice, is not, as far as we are aware, in the catalogues of any of our nurserymen, though we find it in those of Leroy, and other large European growers. The Atragene, though a native plant, seems to be so little known, that it has received no popular name; but its botanical name is a rather pretty one, and there is no reason why it, as in numerous other instances, should not become the common name. As will be seen from the engraving, the plant is in the general appearance of its leaves and flowers, much like a *Clematis*; indeed it is by some botanists put in that genus, the chief difference being that this has small petals inside the showy calyx, while Clematis has none. It is a half woody vine, growing in good soil, to the hight of eight or nine feet. It climbs by the twining of the stalks of its opposite leaves. The flowers are solitary, two to three inches across, and of a purplish color. It is found in shady, rocky places, from Canada to Virginia, and though not particularly common, does not rank as a rare plant. We have seen it growing near New Haven, Conn., and have received fine specimens from a correspondent in Canada, whose address has been mislaid, or we would acknowledge it.—If any of our nurserymen would make a specialty of supplying such of our native plants as are desirable for cultivation, he would find his account in it. Who will take the hint and act upon it?

How the Horseradish is Grown for Marketing.

The method of growing Horseradish as advised by the older works on gardening is quite different from that practiced in the vicinity of New York. Even the recent French and English works advise the old plan of allowing the roots to remain two and three years before digging them. We have a faster and better way of managing this plant, as will be seen in the following article, prepared for our Horticultural Annual, by Peter Henderson, author of Gardening for Profit.

Perhaps there is no vegetable, the cultivation of which is so generally neglected, as that of Horseradish. From the fact that it will grow in almost any soil, and under almost any circumstances, it is for that reason very generally neg-

Fig. 3.—HORSERADISH MILL.

lected when grown for private use. For the past twenty years it has been quite extensively grown for market purposes in the vicinity of New-York, and there are probably to-day not less than two hundred acres occupied in its cultivation. One grower, alone, on Long Island, grew last season forty acres of this root.

Although, as we have said, it may be grown on any soil, or in any situation, yet, when grown for sale, the best soils are chosen, and the highest degree of cultivation is given it. It is almost always grown as a second crop; that is, it is planted between the spring crop of early beets and cabbages, after they have been sown or planted, in the following manner. The sets, or small roots, are taken from the main root, at the time of digging the crop, and prepared in lengths of from five to seven inches; they are cut as in figure 1, the lower end with a slope, so that it can readily be distinguished at planting. These sets are tied in convenient bundles and kept in boxes of sand, in a cool cellar, or in a

Fig. 1.—HORSERADISH SET.

pit. These are planted between the rows of beets or cabbages, (which are set two feet apart,) at a distance of 15 inches between each plant.

In planting, a hole is made with a light crowbar, and the set of Horseradish dropped in deep enough for its top to be two inches *under* the surface; planted thus deeply, it does not usually grow much, until the crops of beets or cabbages have been marketed; but should the tops grow, so as to interfere with the summer crop, they are hoed off; we have often done this twice in a season, without any injury to the Horseradish crop. The main growth and development of the root being made during the late summer and fall months, the cutting off of the leaves that first start, in a plant of this vigorous nature, is of no injury. There is but little further labor required with it. After cabbages are off, the stumps are dug up, and the plow is run through between the rows of the Horseradish, which soon grows luxuriantly enough to crowd down weeds of any kind. The crop is dug up during the late fall or winter months, and meets a ready sale to those who manufacture it. It is prepared for market by removing the green tops and the small roots, which last are preserved, for next season's planting. The roots are preserved in pits, and when wanted for market are washed and sold by weight. Fig. 2 shows a root as ready for market, much reduced in size. It has thus far been a most profitable crop, and always a safe one, for its hardy nature renders it free from the risk of injury from frost, which attends many other vegetables we cultivate. On the highly cultivated grounds on which it is grown, it yields a large profit —from 12,000 to 15,000 roots are grown on an acre, which average ½ of a pound each. Prices have ranged, during the past twenty years, from $100 to $200 per ton. Even at the minimum rate, it will be seen that it averages from $500 to $600 per acre. Those who retail it in our markets, usually supply it in the ground or grated state. They have a mill, or rather a revolving grater, against which the washed and scraped roots are pressed, and rapidly reduced to a condition fit for the table. Figure 3, on preceeding page, shows a common form of the grater, which works by a treadle, and is boxed in. The grater consists of a sheet of tin in which rough holes are punched. A similar machine is used by those who put Horseradish up in bottles with vinegar. We do not know where these mills are sold, but any ingenious mechanic can make a revolving grater, which is all that is required.

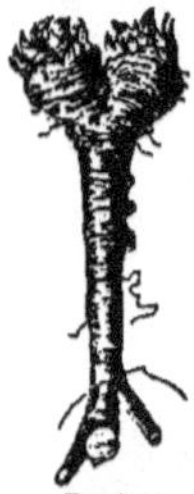

Fig. 2.

Preparing Trees for Removal.

Messrs. Bidwell Brothers, St. Paul, Minn., from whom our readers have had valuable suggestions on other rural subjects, give their method of treating trees that are to be removed from their native localities. While the plan is not altogether new, it is none the less worthy of being followed:

"So common has become the practice of setting out trees resembling bean poles, that the more valuable kinds are in a great measure neglected, and of these few kinds set out as shade trees, nearly half are lost for want of skill in transplanting. By the plan we recommend, the longer lived and slower growing kinds are as readily transplanted as the others, and if followed will result in our having a greater variety of shade and ornamental trees.

"As soon as the frost is out of the ground in the spring, select the trees to be removed, and, if necessary, clear away around them to give them the full benefit of sun and air. In selecting, avoid crotched trees, and all deformed ones. With a fine saw and sharp knife, trim the tree into shape, removing all superfluous or dead limbs, then with a sharp spade dig a circular trench around the tree, of such diameter as to cut off all the leading roots. After the roots have been cut by the spade, smooth the ends with the knife, after which fill up the trench. The tree is to be allowed to remain where it stands until the following fall or spring, when it may be removed. The tree will be found to have made a fine growth of limbs and a mass of fibrous roots, and if transplanted with care to injure neither top nor roots, and mulched after removal, it will well repay the extra trouble."

Notes on Grapes and Grape Culture.

Our estimate of the importance of grape culture may be inferred from the space we give to it. We endeavor to keep the readers of the *Agriculturist* advised as to progress in this branch, and to give them the status of varieties in different parts of the country. To do this involves a great deal of travel, and a careful reading of the reports of the horticultural gatherings that we are unable to attend, besides any amount of "grape talk" with those who visit us. All this is pleasant, but there is another side. There are those, who, if we express a favorable opinion of a variety, seem to think we are unduly favoring the grower or growers thereof, as if we did not know a man from a grape vine. These notes, as well as all other articles, are written solely for the benefit of the readers of the paper, and if any grower of vines or other plants, breeder of animals, or inventor of machines derives any benefit because we think well of an article he has on sale, so much the better for him. We try to make these grape notes without prejudice and without any reference to anything but grapes. We sometimes have made a judgment on specimens from young vines, that we have had cause to modify. In this way we have spoken disparagingly of Roger's Hybrids as a class, but with last year's experience we gladly admit that several of the numbers of which we had fruit, from old vines, give promise of value, and we shall watch them the present year with a great deal of interest. In an article last month we showed the different estimation in which the Concord was held by people residing in the same town, and in almost every meeting of fruit-growers we find a similar conflict of opinion; and not only are certain varieties denounced, but the persons who introduced them, or advocated them, come in for a share of condemnation. The following notes are from Dr. C. J. May, Hancock County, Ill., whose article is too long to allow us to produce it entire. His views of the Concord were given last month:

"The vineyards are mostly on the bluffs, which rise from three to four hundred feet above the river, and extend about four miles back to the prairie. The vineyard region is about thirty miles in length. The exposure most generally chosen is the south, southeast and east, though some are in ground inclining towards the north. There seems to be very little difference in the success, except that those vineyards facing south and east ripen their fruit a few days earlier than those that have a northern exposure.

The Catawba was first planted, and probably nine-tenths of all vines to-day are of that variety. Here the Catawba seems to find all that is necessary for it to produce its best results, the vines constantly bearing crops of fruit and ripening so thoroughly that we are usually able to let the fruit intended for wine remain on the vine six weeks after it is in good condition for market. It is then, of course, so well ripened that its hard acid center nearly disappears, and is in condition to make as good a wine as the Catawba is capable of making under the most favorable conditions. No where in our country does the Catawba reach a higher perfection than here, in no place is it more free from disease, and of course other varieties do equally well.

I have one hundred Delaware vines that bore their second crop the past season, averaging twelve pounds to the vine. They all ripened their wood and fruit perfectly, and there is a prospect of their bearing even a larger crop next season. This is no more than others have done in all parts of our county, wherever good vines have been planted and well cared for. But this is undoubtedly too large a crop per vine for so many vines to the acre as I have planted, though they seem now well able to carry it. Eight pounds per vine will afford enough profit to satisfy the largest desires.

The Delaware is with us a very rapid growing vine, provided good plants are used; comes into bearing early, and sets more fruit than it should be permitted to carry; especially while the vines are young each cane will generally have four bunches, but not more than three should be suffered to remain. Planted four feet apart in rows, and the rows six feet apart, the trellis may be all covered and the vines in full bearing the third season with us, without apparent injury to the vines from haste. If planted at greater distances in the rows, longer time for covering the trellises will be required and more thinning.

The Iona is another variety of which too much cannot be said in its favor. I procured vines of Dr. Grant in the spring of 1864. These vines made a large growth the season of planting, showing no sign of disease—there was not a spot of mildew on any of them. The canes in the fall were cut back to eighteen inches, and the next season (that of '65) all the vines set fruit, and were permitted to carry from four to six clusters each, though I knew so much fruit would impair any variety of grape on vines so young, yet I could not wait. Though this was the season which damaged the Catawba so badly, yet the fruit on these young vines showed not a sign of rot, neither did the foliage mildew; and here I may say neither did the Delaware. The fruit ripened about the first of September, and was of superior quality—the clusters were large and perfect. I this year grew two canes from as near the ground as possible, and in the fall these canes were cut back to four feet each, the vines were not in the least injured by the following winter, and in the spring of 1866 set a very large number of bunches, many of which I removed. They ripened their fruit August 24th, though they were eatable ten days earlier. There was no disease of any kind about them. And this season there was none on any variety except the Rebecca, which has never failed to mildew badly. The quantity of fruit produced by the Iona was about ten pounds per vine; the quality was superior to all other varieties. A small quantity of expressed juice or must from fruit fairly ripe, and no more, weighed 120°. I know that others have found it to weigh 130° from fruit not more thoroughly ripened than our Catawba grapes usually are when intended for wine. The very best Catawba must I have ever seen weighed 87°. I am satisfied from my own experience that there is no grape now before the people possessing so many good qualities and so few, if any, bad ones as the Iona.

I have fruited the Israella two years, and find it all that has been claimed for it. It is our best early grape, bearing large crops of excellent fruit. It will be the very best early market grape we have. Its beauty, size and goodness will commend it to buyers, while the compact bunch, the berries of which never drop, even when more than ripe, will cause it to become a favorite with those who grow grapes for market. It is in all respects as healthy, hardy and as large a grower and bearer as the Concord.

Starting Sweet Potato Plants.

J. W. C., Lower Pennsneck, Salem County, N. J., who last year grew 170,000 hills of sweet potatoes, gives the readers of the *Agriculturist* his method of raising the plants for setting:

Select a high piece of ground, sheltered from cold winds by a fence or bushes, and dig a pit fifteen inches deep, five feet wide, and two feet in length for each bushel of tubers—ten bushels requiring a trench five feet wide and twenty feet long. Upon the margins of the pit, set on edge boards, six inches wide, and hold them in place by driving stakes inside of the pit, and banking earth against them on the outside. Fill the pit twelve inches deep with coarse hay or cornstalks, or other litter, and dampen it by the use of one pail of water to every three feet in length of the bed. Upon the litter place four inches of good horse manure, level off well and then put on four inches of light sandy soil, and it is ready to receive the seed potatoes.

We differ here in one practice. As to time of planting, some plant immediately, and others wait for the heat to rise in the bed. I prefer to plant the day the bed is made, as there is no delay nor loss of heat in case a cold storm should come. Lay in the whole potatoes as close as may be, without their touching one another, and cover them with light soil about two inches deep. When this is done, the bed will be filled to within two inches of the top of the slats on the edges; now cover the whole with hay, allowing it to be one foot high on the edges, and four feet high in the center. After the bed has been prepared thus it may be left to itself for a few days, but in three to five days it must be examined; make a hole in the hay and thrust in your arm; if the temperature is more than blood heat, leave holes open here and there in the hay. If the heat increases, turn the hay over and air it; and if this does not moderate the heat sufficiently, remove the hay altogether. If the sun shines hot after the hay has been removed, we put rails across the bed and throw on a little hay, to prevent damage from too great an increase of heat. In eight or ten days after the heat starts, the hay may be left off entirely in the middle of the day, as the plants will need airing, and to be covered up at night. When the nights become warm, the covering is left off entirely. In this neighborhood we make the beds from the first to the middle of April.

Grape Culture and Vine Training.

BY DR. C. J. MAY, WARSAW, ILL.

The following synopsis of vine culture is well put and seasonable, and the method of training is worthy the attention of those who find it necessary to protect their vines during the winter. The caution not to allow the vines to bear too large a crop cannot be too often repeated, as much of the failure of certain varieties is due to over cropping. We know of several large vineyards on their road to ruin from overbearing:

The conditions of success in vine growing are few and simple. First, a situation should be chosen that either needs no artificial draining, or that can be thoroughly drained; the ground for the vineyards should incline enough to run off all surface water, or wet ground will cause the fruit to rot, and the vines to kill in winter. The ground should be prepared to the depth of at least twenty inches; two feet will be found better yet. Good strong healthy vines must be procured for planting. The vines should be staked and tied up, and the laterals pinched out even the first season. The vine should be trained so as to bring the fruit as near the ground as possible, and keep clear of it, the earth reflecting back the heat absorbed during the day, and thus keeping the surrounding air at a more even temperature. The vine grower should be as careful not to let his vines bear *too large a crop* as to get a good crop from them; and to secure this I know of no better method of training than the double or single arms. No one who has once thoroughly tried these will train his vines in any other way. These are the most simple and the most easily understood, and less troublesome than any other methods. Any one who will choose a reasonably favorable location, *and take interest enough in his vines to try and see how much he can do for them, and yet do all things understandingly, can be successful in grape culture*, and can grow such varieties as Delaware and Iona, and also Catawba, where the season is long enough to ripen it, as well as he can grow the Concord. In all cases the vines should be laid down and covered with earth in winter to insure the best results.

The experience of the last fifteen years has at last convinced our vine growers that, by covering their vines in the fall, they are as certain of a large crop of grapes every year as of a crop of corn; for, with the exception of an occasional winter so cold as to injure, and sometimes entirely destroy the fruit buds of the vine, there is, nineteen years out of twenty, no danger to be feared. By covering the vines, even this uncertainty is removed, and it has been found that, even in years when we have no severe cold weather, covering the vines causes them to produce better fruit and more of it, thus paying for the expense of covering, though the winter may have been in all respects most favorable.

That the vines may be covered easily, they should be trained with that purpose in view, although almost any vine may be covered without injury if care is used in bending down the canes. My method of training is the arm and spur system, the only difference being that in place of growing up a single cane, and taking the two arms from it at one foot from the ground, I grow each arm from as near the ground as possible, and train them at an angle up to the first wire, which is one foot from the ground; then along the wire. These arms, when untied from the trellis, readily go to the ground their whole length, and, of course, are easily covered. This is done by one man bending down the arms, while another, with a spade, throws on enough earth to hold the arm in its place; then, with a plow, throw a furrow on it from each side, continuing the plowing until all the ground is turned, leaving a dead furrow in the middle between the rows. This is all done very rapidly, two men covering one thousand vines per day ready for the plow, so that covering is, after all, but a small matter, compared with the value of the crop, which is ren-

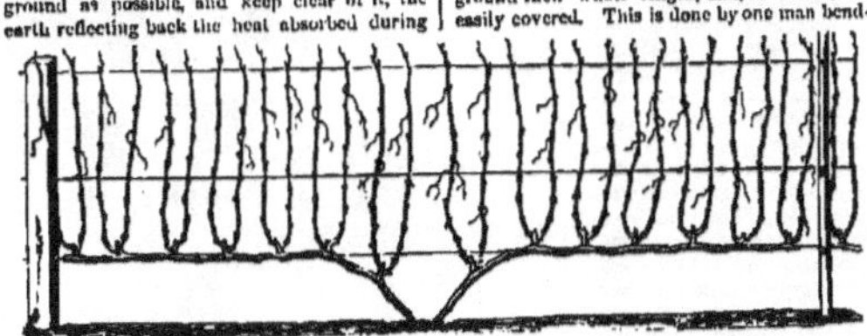

Fig. 1.—VINE TRAINED WITH TWO ARMS.

Fig. 2.—VINES TRAINED WITH ONE ARM.

dered as certain as man can be of anything. There are not probably one thousand bearing vines in our county not covered this winter. I have never seen my method of taking the arms from the ground at an angle up to the first wire, and then along it, recommended in any books on grape culture, or in any of the Agricultural or Horticultural papers; but I have trained over three thousand vines in this way for three years. The accompanying drawings on the preceding page will show it much better than I can in words. Figure 1 represents a vine with two arms, as I would train all vines planted at a greater distance in the row than four feet. Figure 2 shows vines with a single arm, trained as I do my Delawares last planted, four feet apart in the row. To those who think that vines can not be successfully trained by the arm and spur system, I would say, that I can show them a vineyard of about six thousand vines, all trained in this way. Some of them have been in bearing three years, and none have failed to produce good crops each year. I tried upright wires, but have discarded them, and now use three No. 12 wires—the first one foot from the ground, the second fifteen inches above that; to this the shoots are tied as soon as possible; they will then readily go to the upper wire, which is within one or two inches of the top of the posts. My posts are five and a half feet in length, and are set in the ground eighteen inches, so that my trellis is just four feet high. In making my trellis now, I set a post, four inches square, once in every one hundred feet, and two inch white oak stakes, of the same length as the posts, once in twelve feet. These have about twenty inches of their lower ends coated with coal tar; they are driven into the ground eighteen inches, and the wire fastened to them by staples, as to the posts. The first and last posts of a row need to be longer, to be set deeper for bracing when no lath is used at the bottom. The stakes of this size will last as long as the posts, and make equally as good a trellis. As one post will make four of these stakes, it is quite a saving with us, where white oak timber is very costly.

The Judas-tree.—(*Cercis Canadensis.*)

The Judas-tree or Red-bud, as it is sometimes called, is a native tree that should not be overlooked. Its very oddity should commend it, for in early spring, before it unfolds its leaves, it robes itself, trunk and limbs, in a sheet of pink. The small pea-shaped flowers appear in the greatest profusion, in small clusters upon the trunk and limbs, and give the tree a most striking appearance. The rounded leaves come a little later, and the flowers are succeeded by flat, many-seeded pods. The tree is found wild from New York, South and West. The largest specimen we have seen was on the ground now occupied by Central Park. It was as large and much the shape of a good sized apple tree. The engraving will give a good idea of the size and shape of the flowers and leaves. The European species, *Cercis Siliquastrum*, is sometimes seen in cultivation. It has larger flowers than our own, and according to tradition, is the tree upon which Judas hanged himself—whence

JUDAS-TREE.—(*Cercis Canadensis.*)

the common name. The flowers of this have an agreeable acid taste, and in some parts of Europe they are used in salads or made into fritters. The flowers of our own species are also sour, and might be similarly employed. The wood of both species is hard, variegated in color and takes a high polish. The trees are not only ornamental in flower, but their foliage is of a pleasing shade of green. The Japan species, *Cercis Japonica*, is a valuable introduction. It blooms when but a mere shrub, and is completely covered with bright, rose-colored flowers, and is one of our most ornamental early flowering shrubs. It is perfectly hardy in the vicinity New York. All three of the species may be had at any of our larger nurseries, and they are readily propagated by sowing the seeds.

Nut Bearing Trees—Grafting, Etc.

A request for the experience of those who have attempted to graft nut-bearing trees has brought out several letters—some to the effect that all their attempts have failed, while others state that they may be grafted as easily as other trees. Mr. E. L. Allyn, New London County, Conn., having some Pig-nut seedlings, says:

"I let them grow four or five years, and kept them trimmed as I would apple trees. They were from an inch to an inch and a half in diameter. About the 20th of April I cut the trees close to the ground, except one, which was left about four feet high, and grafted them from the "Shagbark." The wood was of the previous year's growth, set in the same manner, and at the same time that I graft my apple trees. My Walnut cions nearly all grew, and most of them very thriftily. The larger trees bore at four or five years from the graft, the fruit being equal, if not superior, to that of the old tree. These trees are now from 25 to 30 feet high, some 7 or 8 inches in diameter, and have borne nearly half a bushel of fine nuts apiece in a season. *The cions were cut at the time they were inserted.*"

"G. M. C.," Bucks County, Penn., writes us: "There is no more difficulty in grafting chestnuts than cherries; indeed, of the two, I think I have been the most successful with the chestnut. I have trees which I think have not been grafted more than five years, and which have now borne two years. A neighbor has one which bore the second year; these, of course, are very thrifty. Much depends on getting grafts from early bearing trees; but because the trees grow wild in our forests it will not do to set them out and expect them to do well without any further care; they will appreciate a good soil, and good mulching; in many situations, the latter seems indispensable while the trees are small."—"A subscriber," Havre de Grace, Maryland, and W. Marble, Middlesburg, Mass., give similar accounts of their success with the chestnut. Judging from all these reports, the conditions of success seem to be the use of young stock, and recently cut cions.

How to Help the Growth of Evergreens.—We frequently see Evergreens in a languishing condition. If alive, they make no wood, and the bottom limbs show signs of decay. The trouble is frequently in the character of the soil, which is too dry and gravelly. Almost all the evergreens prefer a moist, loamy soil, or even a muck or peat, like that upon the mountains where they grow. The dryness of soil may be entirely relieved by trenching and working in peat or muck. We have seen evergreens making a luxuriant growth upon a pure gravel bed treated in this way. Peat that had been exposed to the atmosphere for one season was thoroughly incorporated with the soil, the ground being covered to the depth of six inches before the trenching began. This is somewhat expensive, but much cheaper than unthrifty trees about the dwelling. The soil should be kept cultivated around all hedges and evergreens several years after planting, and when well established, enrich with old manure.

THE HOUSEHOLD.

(☞ For other Household Items, see "Basket" pages.)

Home-Made Household Ornaments.

The Cone Bracket, fig. 1, may be made at a trifling expense, by any one of moderate skill and taste. Cut the bracket of any desired shape from pine, or if it can be procured walnut is better, as it needs no staining, and the glue adheres more firmly. If

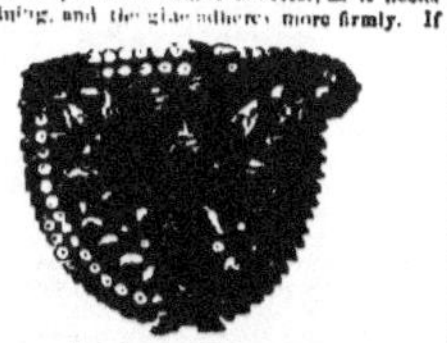

Fig. 1.—CONE BRACKET.

of pine, stain with powdered umber mixed with a little water. After the two pieces of the bracket are nailed together, a piece of wood two inches square and one inch thick, glued to the center of the lower piece close to the top, gives strength to the bracket, and raises the work in the center. Have a good assortment of cones, acorns, etc., at hand, and dispose them on the frame to suit the fancy; this may be done in a great variety of ways. The engraving shows one, the central figure of

Fig. 2. BRACKET.

which is a large open pine-cone; at the top and bottom, smaller cones not open; at the sides, butternuts, spruce and hemlock cones, with large and small acorns. The border is made of inverted acorn-cups—a row on the edge of the frame and one on the surface: these must be of uniform size and shape. Now have good hot glue and fasten each piece, beginning at the center. When this is done, let the work dry thoroughly, after which varnish with thin furniture varnish, and it is complete. Fig. 2 shows a bracket to be cut with a narrow saw and penknife. It can all be done with the knife, but the saw makes much more rapid work. It is finer work than that shown in former illustrations, but it requires little skill after the pattern is marked upon the board. This should be of thin stuff, about three-eighths of an inch in thickness, after it is planed down. The shelf is fastened by glue, and by small brads or screws driven in at the back. The support underneath may be put on with glue or with a small brass hinge. A board seven or eight inches wide is sufficiently large for work of this pattern. Pine, white wood, black walnut and butternut are suitable woods for this kind of work. The latter, we think, is quite overlooked as an ornamental wood. It is nearly as dark and handsome in the grain as black walnut, and in many parts of the country much more accessible.

Fig. 3.

Fig. 3 is a "cornucopia" made of perforated card board. The board is cut square, of any desirable size; six or eight inches will do for lamp lighters or papers. It is worked with bright scarlet worsted, single thread, six holes square, in alternate squares, as shown in figure 3. Beads of suitable size to match are then sewed upon the vacant squares. The inside is lined with tissue paper and the edges bound with ribbon. It is then drawn together in cornucopia shape, sewed up at the edges, and furnished with three bows. It will save labor to slip in an extra lining of tissue paper, which can be removed as often as soiled, and replaced. This is a convenient article for shaving paper, to have near the glass where "my lord" attends his morning toilet. There is nothing like having these little conveniences handy to keep him good natured.

Leaves from the Diary of a Young Housekeeper.—No. III.

PRIZE ESSAY BY MRS. LAURA E. LYMAN, STAMFORD, CT.

April 3.—When I was looking over Edward's wardrobe I found a great deal of old flannel—some red, some blue, some gray—and a variety of worn out clothing. It will make me just such a rug to lay before my kitchen stove as I have been wishing for all winter. I talked with Jennette about it, and we determined to devote these rainy days, when we can not visit and are not likely to have company, to making the rug. I explained what I wanted to Edward, and he made me some frames, and a hook to work it with out of an old fork. Our grocer gave us a coffee bag, saying that he never sold trifles like that to a regular customer. I ripped it open, hemmed around with strong linen thread and sewed it into the frame. It is about two yards long and one wide. Then Jennie and I displayed our taste in drawing a pattern. As our variety of colors was limited, black predominating, and I intended it only for the kitchen, I could not expatiate in a brilliant cornucopia, such as I made for a parlor rug before I was married. So we decided to make a wide, variegated border into which everything would work, and have the centre-piece three diamonds, filled around with black, (fig. 1.)

We worked the diamonds first, using our most brilliant colors. The rags we cut into strips from a quarter to half an inch wide and pulled from the underside through the foundation, holding the strip in the left hand and the hook in our right. Edward made us some hooks out of two old-fashioned forks, by breaking off the tines and filing down the shank into the shape of an enormous crochet needle. Mrs. Wilson came in while we were at work and was so delighted with the idea of a rug in this style, which she had never seen before, that she is going to have one. She has so many bright colors from the little girls' woolen dresses they have worn and laid aside, that she can make a splendid thing of hers. I told her when she was ready I would bring over my worsted patterns and help her draw the design for the centre.

The hook is of this shape, fig. 2, with the handle on the upper end, of course. When the points of the hook got dull we sharpened them with the file. Jennie and I worked pretty steadily, and in less than a week our rug was done, the surface trimmed off evenly, and laid before the stove. Mother has rugs of this sort that have been in use for ten years, and are still serviceable. It is an excellent plan to make rag carpets out of worn clothing, but I need rugs also to save my carpets.

April 10.—I find I must have another bed for the summer, and have been casting about in my mind to get one up. I know Edward wants to buy ten acres more of land, and so I am unwilling to suggest any unavoidable outlay for family expenses. I asked him if he had any special use for that pile of husks in the corn house. "No," he said, "only to throw into the barn-yard for manure." I told him I thought there were enough to make an excellent mattress, and at an expense of ten yards of ticking we could manufacture an article that would be as good as one costing eight dollars. He assented, and the next rainy day, when he can not plow, we will all go out and make a frolic of picking over and splitting up the husks. Edward says he can make a mattress needle out of an old umbrella brace, and so our new bed will cost us a trifle over three dollars.

April 15.—Jennette said she would stay a few days longer if I would undertake my house-cleaning. Edward didn't have much done to the old part of the house before we were married, and I have been thinking all winter what a good cleaning that dingy paint and brown ceiling would get as soon as the weather became warm enough. So the other day we began, taking one room at a time, so as not to have any more disorder than we could possibly help. I could leave the dinner getting entirely to Sue, with some instruction, and she was very proud of the trust. Instead of using strong soap suds for cleaning paint, I tried a recipe that I found in an old number of the Genesee Farmer, I believe. Sue went down to the paint shop and got five pounds of Spanish whiting; I had a bucket of warm water, and, squeezing my flannel wash cloth nearly dry, pressed it on to some whiting I had put on an old plate, and rubbed the paint with it; then washed my cloth out and wiped it dry. Jennette followed me with a dry flannel cloth, rubbing the clean paint, which by this process was very easily cleaned, and looked better than any old paint I ever saw cleaned by the common method of soap suds.

April 17.—Edward has been at work around the door all day, and the yard is so much improved!

Fig. 1.—RUG PATTERN.

The wood is all cut and piled in the woodhouse, for he says that, when seasoned under cover, it gives out more heat in burning than when used green, and does not consume so fast. The chips are raked into a large pile, the sleigh and sled stored away for the season, the sap buckets piled away in the woodhouse loft, some of the gate posts that were heaved by the frost have been set upright, and three or four pickets that were off nailed on the front fence. In the garden a place has been spaded for early peas and for onions. On the south shelf of our kitchen window some of my flowers have given way temporarily to boxes of rich dirt, in which we have cabbages just peeping out, and tomatoes an inch high. I mean to have at least fifty plants of grape tomatoes. Mother sent me the seed, and she has preserves made of them which are delicious. They are very prolific, and when ripe have a delicate flavor not found in the other varieties. I brought with me from home some flower seeds, and a few choice cuttings of tea and bouquet roses. They are growing well in pots, but the ground on the north and west sides of the house, where I intend to plant them, is not quite warm enough yet.

Fig. 2.

April 25.—House cleaning and white-washing all done! And my walls and ceilings look so well! I had a few pounds of Spanish whiting left, which I added to my slaked lime, and put in also a few handfuls of salt and a little dissolved white glue. Edward helped us by doing some of the whitewashing one rainy forenoon, and Jennie and I did the rest inside. I had considerable left, to which I added two handfuls of brown sugar, some more salt, and ochre enough to make a pale straw color, with which Sue has covered the masonry around the caldron in the woodhouse, the back fences and outhouses. She looks upon it as fun, and, after a little instruction in dipping and rapping out her brush, succeeded in doing very good work. The first of May will find the premises inside and out in as perfect condition as to cleanliness as a sanitary inspector could wish.

I must not forget to ask Edward when he goes to Syracuse to get a little sulphuric acid, or some chloride of lime for disinfecting purposes. I asked Mr. Reynolds for some, and he said there was no demand for such strange chemicals in this plain farming community. Then, said I, with a laugh, if you neglect preventives, you will be safe in getting a gross or two of cholera remedies.

April 30.—Jennette was so anxious I should go part way home with her, and visit a friend of ours who lives near the railroad, that Edward consented to spare me two days, and I got back home last night. I never thought Sue White would make such an admirable housekeeper and mother as I found her to be. At school she was one of the most learned and intellectual students in the whole Academy, and quite a literary character. I expected to find her house rather neglected, and her two boys resembling the children of literary people generally. But Sue has consummate sense as well as ability, and she has applied it to the regulation of her household and to the training of her boys, while she still reads a good deal, and frequently contributes to the Monthlies.

I never saw more intelligent children. The oldest is not quite seven and the youngest just five. At morning prayers their father opened to the lesson for the day, in Chronicles I believe, and asked the boys "what the chapter was about yesterday morning." The youngest boy happened to remember first what it was, and gave a very graphic account of the destruction of the host of Sennacherib. Then the elder added something more about Hezekiah, showing the utmost interest in the Scriptural narrative. I was very much pleased with Mr. White's mode of conducting family devotions. As he read, he put every thing into language the children could understand, and they listened as to an Arabian Nights' tale. Then they all sung a few verses of the boys' selection, and at the conclusion of the devotions all joined in repeating the Lord's prayer. Then the little boys went to their mother for a kiss, the customary reward for good behavior in prayer time. She told me afterward, in speaking of their family training, that they had commenced at Genesis, and had read to that morning's lesson in the same way, explaining everything a child could be made to understand, and requiring from the children an account each morning of the lesson which had been read the previous day.

When Mr. White came in to dinner, the boys gathered round him and said: "Papa, won't you please tell us a story while dinner is getting ready?" "What kind of a story—a bear story?" "No, Papa, a historical story." So he told them in a most graceful and simple style the story of John Smith and Pocahontas. They ran to get the little magnetic globe their mother had earned by a contribution to one of the magazines, to find Virginia, and then the Atlas, as the divisions into States were not marked on the globe. I was equally surprised and delighted to find how much they knew of geography, all taught them from the globe by their mother principally, as Mr. White is away much of the time. Sue said they never told their boys fairy tales or taught them Mother Goose's melodies, but translated into child language the innumerable stories scattered through all the books, Homer stories, Milton stories, geographical stories, Shakspeare stories, historical stories.

My visit was only too short. I found that Sue had carried into housekeeping the same mental activity which characterized her at school—that she was constantly applying the principles of chemistry and physiology which she had learned at the Academy, to every-day life in the kitchen and nursery.

I intend to imitate her example, and, instead of regretting that I can not carry my scientific and literary studies further, endeavor to apply all the knowledge I possess to the duties of daily life.

Leaves from my Journal.—No. III.

PRIZE ESSAY BY MRS. B. McLELLAN, OF OHIO.

April.—I partly uncovered some of my bulbs to-day. They are crowding their heads out into the world again, but looked so delicate that I hid them away as soon as possible. The air is too chilly; we shall have frost yet. My house-plants have afforded us much pleasure through the long, cold winter; I have no good place for them. At the south window of the sitting-room I make room for a few, but it is too warm. Roses, geraniums, and some running plants, have grown well. They make the winter sitting-room fragrant and cheery, and are a pleasant reminder of the beauty of summer. By April, one tires of the confinement of house. Somehow, things look faded, and not overnice.

The fresh springing grass, the young willows by the brook, the trailing arbutus with its pink fragrant blossoms looking out from some lingering snowdrift in the woods, seem more beautiful than ever before. But winter clothing must not be recklessly cast off. The ground is damp and cold. Warm weather is not yet here, and nothing is gained by trying to forestall its coming.

While making sponge cake to-day, I thought of the time, now long ago, when I said to a lady friend in my family that I quite despaired of ever being able to make sponge cake. She at once volunteered to teach me I gladly engaged in the process, though with rather a tedious time in prospect. According to her direction it must be stirred "*two hours by the clock.*" The cake would by no means compare favorably with that made and baked to-day in just forty minutes. The rule is so simple, I wish every housekeeper had it. It has been in the *Agriculturist*, but will bear to be published a second time. Six eggs, well beaten together, two cups of sugar, two of flour, two teaspoonfuls cream of tartar, and one of soda, with a little salt. It should bake quickly as possible without burning, being careful to have the oven right when it *goes in*, instead of making the fire afterwards. It is much nicer to be kept a few days before eating, in the cellar in a stone jar. A "Farmer's Fruit Cake" was noticed in the *Agriculturist* for January, 1865, which I had the curiosity to try. I was surprised, as well as all others who have tasted it, at its excellence. The apple prepared as directed has much the taste of citron, and the whole would pass for rich fruit cake, while it can be eaten without injury. Tarts are very easily made, and filled with nice jelly, are a great ornament to the table, as well as highly relished. A small piece of pie-crust left from pie-making, with which the young housekeeper don't know what in the world to do, will make a plate full. The crust is to be rolled very thin, and baked quickly in patty pans.

I have been ironing shirts and collars. Hannah can't make them look nicely. I rather think she don't care to learn, for I have given her faithful lessons. The gloss and smoothness must be put on *while* drying, just as in polishing a stove or boot, and the harder the pressure the better. Muslins, laces and embroideries need working and clapping in the hands until they are very clear from starch, and if ironed when quite damp will look nearly as well as new. It is a good rule to have ironing finished by Wednesday night, as Thursday must be partly occupied with baking.

I was at Lizzie's just after dinner. I found her *cleaning the gridiron.* It had got sadly burned while she cooked a small piece of steak, and she was scraping it with a knife, while Georgey, in high glee, evidently thought she was at work for his benefit. Is there no way, she inquired, that I can cook a piece of meat, no bigger than the palm of my hand, without such a bother as this? Yes, indeed, I replied. Take that little stew pan, with a long handle, and, putting it over a good fire until it is hot, place the steak in it, covering tightly. Of course it will adhere to it at first, but in a moment or two becomes juicy, when it must be turned, keeping it covered as far as possible. Turn it every half minute, and in three it will be done. Upon putting it into a dish, add butter, pepper and salt, cover still, and by the time you have placed your other dishes upon the table, there will be a sufficiency of gravy; and I question whether Henry could tell that it was not broiled on the gridiron after the former fashion.

I was a long time learning how to roast meat. But once when employing a washerwoman who had formerly been cook in a large boarding establishment, she said to me bluntly: "Why, Mrs. Frisby, you roast your meat to death. It is as tough as leather, and I reckon has not much better taste!" After this, according to her direction, I put the meat into a *hot* oven at eleven, and it was in readiness for dinner at twelve. The roast is thus quickly browned over and its juices retained. Before, I had cooked it two hours in an oven of only moderate heat. Many and many a time have I thus obtained most useful information from persons whose experience had taught them more than can be learned from books. When first married, I studied my cook-book so constantly that my husband called it my "Library." Though valuable, of course, it often failed to inform me about some little point most essential to success. Salt or fresh meat when *boiled* is seldom cooked long enough. It should be just ready to drop from the bone when taken up. As it becomes cold, it hardens somewhat. A beef bone, with a little lean meat upon it, will make an excellent soup. Boil very thoroughly, and, removing the bone, add such vegetables as you fancy, chopped finely together. A little rice thrown in, is an improvement. This is a convenient dinner for ironing day. But, Lizzie, I came to take you away from gridirons and dishwater a few days. We have decided upon a few improvements at home, and shall be "topsy turvy" a while. I want a little visit from you first—I shall take Georgy in his wagon with me, and you may follow at your leisure. Go round by the store and tell Henry as much.

How Women Can Help Us,

And at the same time help themselves. There are multitudes of ladies among our readers who are longing for "something to do," and are willing to do it. They have heard of woman's rights possibly, and of the enlargement of her sphere of usefulness. We should like to accomplish this latter, and our own, at the same time. We are aiming at a reformatory work, on the farm and in the household. We seek to lighten woman's burdens in every home we enter, and to cheer her in every department of her toils. And we have abundant evidence, in the kindly appreciation of the *Agriculturist* in the families where it is read, that we are successful in this work. Every such family can pursue its labors more intelligently and profitably. There is an atmosphere of cheerfulness and thrift in these homes, that we do not find where no paper is taken. Now we want to enter the millions of homes of cultivators where no agricultural paper is read, and introduce this new atmosphere. We want to teach better methods of husbandry and housekeeping, and to make the whole family, men, women, and children, better and happier in their home duties and toils.

In this matter the ladies can help us as others can not. Many of them have the leisure and special adaptation to the work, and we offer large premiums in useful articles as a reward. If they would take a subscription paper and go around among their friends and acquaintances and ask them to subscribe, they would get well paid for their trouble, and enlarge our field of usefulness. We greatly desire to have a hearing in every one of the five millions of homes that are sustained by the products of the farm and garden. We have a good deal to say that will aid production, and digestion. Will the ladies help us?

Lime Soap.—The substance that forms in flocculent masses in hard water when soap is used in it, is lime soap, which is insoluble in water. An acquaintance tried to remove some mortar spots from his clothes by rubbing soap upon them; the result was the gumming up of his clothes with lime soap, which no washing would remove, and no fluid that he could apply would dissolve. We recommend him to soak the spots in vinegar, or some other dilute acid. This will decompose the soap, leaving a lime salt, to be washed out, and the grease remaining in the cloth. Then he can remove the grease with benzine, or in any other way. The acid may discharge the color of the garment, for some delicate colors are affected at once by acid, but many colors will not be changed. Where hard water is continuously used for washing, the fabrics become harsh and disagreeable from this lime-soap. The use of soda will in a good measure prevent its formation.

BOYS & GIRLS' COLUMNS.

The Doctor Talks to the Boys and Girls.

When you read about the tricks of magicians, who show a human head floating in the air, and who take out of a man's hat articles enough to fill a hand-cart, your young eyes open wide with astonishment. These things are indeed wonderful as showing what ingenuity can do, but they are only tricks, and a person as ingenious as the one who invented them can easily find out how they are done. Right around you are things more wonderful than any thing the conjuror can show, and if you will only open your eyes at *this*, and learn how to use them, you will not regret that you can not see the magician display his skill. Some of the things that I shall talk to you about have been carefully watched by the most learned men, who have told us very plainly what they have seen in egg and seed, in bud and flower; but *how* the seed becomes a plant or the egg brings forth a living animal—these have never been found out. Wise heads—philosophers as they are often called—are not, as many suppose, always engaged in looking at the stars, and measuring mountains; many of the most learned poke around mud holes and ponds and find animals and other objects for their study; many think that curious things

Fig. 1.

are only to be found by travelers in distant countries—but you need not go out of your own neighborhood nor off of your own farm to search for curious objects, or to see more wonders than all the showmen can display.

Every boy and girl in the country knows frog-spawn. It is a mass of clear jelly, to be found in early spring in almost every pool of water. If you can find some of this frog-spawn—and you can readily do so by a little search—take home a little of it and place it in a saucer or bowl of rain water, and look carefully at it. It is a mass of clear jelly, with some dark spots distributed

Fig. 2.

Fig. 3.

through it. It is really a collection of transparent eggs surrounded and held together by a jelly-like substance, and the spots are the yolks of the eggs (fig. 1). Keep the vessel containing the spawn and water in a warm window, and look at it carefully every day and change the water every day or two. The round spots, or yolk, soon cease to be round, and will have this outline, fig. 2, and later like this, fig. 3; but unless one has a microscope and knows how to use it, all the minute changes that take place can not be followed. Still a great change may be seen without any help but your own eyes. The spots will rapidly increase in size, and you will soon see them of the shape of fig. 4, and you will be able to make out that the little animal has a head and a

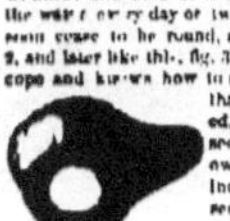

Fig. 4.

tail. Which is the head, is made more certain by the appearance of eyes, and the tail shows its character by having a tendency to wiggle, and growing longer. Fig. 5 shows an older and larger animal than fig. 4, and as the little fellow has been growing all the while, you will wonder what he has fed on. The transparent jelly of the egg has thus far contributed to his growth, but he has done no feeding proper, as he has no mouth. As a mouth is the next thing needed, a little opening appears in the head, and the internal arrangements of the animal having been completed, he jerks himself out of the cavity of the egg that has heretofore been his prison, and when strong enough goes forth to see the little world you have made for him in a bowl. The figures given here-

Fig. 5.

with are all more or less larger than the natural size.

But, you will say, this is not a frog. It is only a tadpole or pollywog. True, but is it not a wonderful change. A mass of jelly into living animals; and is it not also curious that the frog is not born a frog, but that he is at first an animal quite unlike a frog. It is equally interesting to watch the changes of the tadpole on his way to frog-hood, but we can not do so now. Put some of the tadpoles where they can take care of themselves, and keep a few to study. They will do best in a glass jar, in which you must change the water every day or two. Any fruit can will do, and you can avoid the trouble of changing the water by putting in some plants. Place an inch or so of gravel in the bottom of the jar, and then place in it any of the plants that are found growing entirely under water. Every deep brook or pond will furnish a number of these, and it does not make much difference which is taken, only those with the finest leaves are the best. Tie the plants to a bit of stone to hold them down, fill the jar

Fig. 6.

with rain or river water, and put in the tadpoles. If this is kept in full light, the water will not need changing.

A New and Useful Toy.

One of the best toys for children we have ever seen is a set of improved builders' blocks, invented and patented by a subscriber to the *Agriculturist*, Mr. Charles M. Crandall, Montrose, Pa. They are so really pleasing and useful, that we publish an engraving, showing how they work. They are plain bass-wood pieces, most of them of the shape shown in the figure, notched to fit each other firmly, so that when a building is put together it can be taken up whole and moved about without falling to pieces. They can be joined in almost endless combinations. We have seen churches, factories, windmills, fences, cradles, and other furniture made with them. The little house shown in the picture was put up by a boy in a few minutes. Besides the many hours'

amusement they will afford, playing with these blocks will develop skill and taste in planning and executing, and we think Mr. Crandall has done the children a real service in bringing out so capital a plaything. The blocks are very durable, but if any split, they are still serviceable in making new designs. All information about prices, etc., can be had by addressing the inventor.

Plant Something, a grape-vine, strawberry plant, a rose-bush, or even a beet or a carrot—something to care for and watch and study day by day. It will give more pleasure than any toy, besides adding something to your knowledge. It may perhaps be the beginning of a successful career as a fruit grower, a gardener, or a botanist.

The Boy who kept "Blowing."

Those who read the story of Timid Timothy in the March *Agriculturist*, page 107, will readily see the meaning of the similar picture given here. Boys who brag or

"blow" a great deal may here see themselves as others see them, on the way to become mere porpoises in society, amusing perhaps to those about them, but not counted as valuable fish. "Let another praise thee and not thyself."

New Puzzles to be Answered.

No. 258. *A Clock Problem*, suggested by David Rue, Jr.—Suppose the striking part of a clock to be out of order so that at one o'clock it strikes three, at the next hour it strikes five, thus gaining two strokes each hour, in how many hours from one o'clock will it strike the time correctly, and how many strokes will it have given in all, counting the three made at the beginning? Of course it never strikes more strokes than twelve at one time.

No. 259. *Illustrated Rebus.*—A very obvious truth.

No. 260. *Mathematical Problem*, by J. S. Chandler.—Two wheels, one four (4) feet and the other four feet and one inch (4 feet 1 inch) in diameter, were put on an axle-tree, which brought them just four (4) feet apart; both were then started at the same rate of speed, but as one wheel was larger than the other, they soon came back to the point from which they started, describing a perfect circle in their course. What was the diameter of the smaller and what the diameter of the larger circle?

Answers to Problems and Puzzles.

The following are answers to the puzzles, etc., in the March number, page 107. No. 253. *Illustrated Rebus.*—The last rose of summer....No. 254. *Illustrated Rebus.*—The proper study of mankind is man....No. 255. *Word Square.* The proper definitions are: Plea, leap, ease, apes....No. 256. *Illustrated Rebus.*—To the wise, nothing is accidental....No. 257. *Anagrams.*—1, Afterward; 2, Mourned; 3, Prepared; 4, Hypocrisy; 5, Astonished.

The following have sent in correct answers, up to March 1st. R. L. Wells, C. H. Cannon, Oliver Coombs, Willie Lesher, George Kemper, "J. G. S.," Chs. E. McLenegan, E. Van Syckel, Jr., A. A. Boyden, Charles A. Farmer, "H," Wm. A. Fulton, A. J. Walling, James and Libbie Bartlett, Owen E. Brumbaugh, Irvin Clark.

[COPYRIGHT SECURED.]

GREAT EXCITEMENT IN THE MONKEY FAMILY.—*Drawn and Engraved for the American Agriculturist.*

In the *Agriculturist* for May, 1868 (page 193), we gave an amusing picture representing an honest dog and a thievish monkey left near the dinner table after the family had finished their meal. It gave the monkey a bad reputation, and, according to our artist's account, several members of the monkey family have had a serious talk about it. You may see in the picture that the dog-nosed ape is examining the *Agriculturist* and studying the picture with much interest. He thinks there may be some truth in it, but is sure it does not mean *him*, for he gives a sidewise look at his neighbor, who is chattering away very angrily, having discovered his own portrait. If he could speak, he would no doubt give us as harsh a scolding as many a man has done when his character has been shown up among the humbugs. But we will not be too severe upon the poor monkey, by comparing him with some of the knavish swindlers who have been exposed.

"I Wasn't Watching."

A little girl went with a friend into a book-bindery. She was much pleased to see how the titles and pictures in gilt were put upon the backs and sides of the covers; and for some time she watched the man who was doing this work, thrusting the covers one by one under the press, with the gold leaf upon them. But at length she noticed that a part of three of this man's fingers was gone. Her sympathy was excited and she whispered a request that her friend would ask how the accident happened. "I was at work here at the press," was the reply, "and not attending to what I was about I got my fingers under the press and it crushed them. *I wasn't watching*, and I shall have to carry this mark to remember it as long as I live."

I'll tell you what I thought when the little girl told me the story: There are many things that boys and girls are tempted to say and do, and that they will say and do if they are not on the watch. They are things that always make a wound that leaves a scar,—not on the outside; not where you can see it,—but *on the heart*. When a boy uses a profane or obscene word; when he does an act that he would blush to have known at home; when a girl says or does any of those things which none of you need be told are only *bad*, then scars upon the heart are being made that will sooner or later cause bitter sorrow. "I wasn't watching" will have to be said about them. Try not to get these scars upon your hearts. There is one strong and willing Friend, you know, who is always ready to help you.

UNCLE PAUL.

A Home-loving Cat.

A lady correspondent sends to the *Agriculturist* the following, which she says is true: "Father H. had a favorite cat which he took with him when he removed from the house which he had long occupied to another, half a mile away, across a river. A few days after the river became greatly swollen by the spring freshets, and the bridge was swept away. Kitty evidently did not like the change. All the coaxing and petting she received failed to reconcile her to the new home. She disappeared, and what was her master's surprise, on crossing the swollen stream in a boat, to find kitty at the old house. He carried her back with him, and the second time she was gone and re-appeared at the deserted home. There she remained for a year alone, greeting members of the family on their occasional visits with great affection. At the end of the year the family returned there to live, to the great apparent satisfaction of the faithful old sentinel."

A Novel Bird Catcher.

Effie Johnson contributes the following to the *Agriculturist*: "One of our friends, a neighbor living a short distance from us, had a beautiful bird—a pet canary. One of the seed cups of its cage accidentally getting turned one day, the bird escaped to the woods, only a few yards from the house. Toward evening Mrs. W. and her husband walked out toward the woods, talking of the lost bird, and wishing it would come home again. The house dog, a large, noble looking animal, walked by their side, looking up into their faces as if he understood all they were saying, then suddenly started off, and in a few moments returned and laid the bird at their *feet*. Mrs. W. screamed out thinking her pet was dead, and the frightened bird flew away again. The dog started after it, and the *second* time caught it and brought it to his mistress. He held it carefully inside his lower jaw, and did not injure it at all; but when Mrs. W. took it in her hand it lay motionless from fright for a moment. She placed it in its cage, and soon it was hopping about, with ruffled feathers it is true, but as well and sprightly as ever. Whenever Mr. or Mrs. W. told the story the dog would look up, wagging his tail with an extremely satisfied air, as much as to say 'Wasn't that pretty well done for a dog?'"

How to "Finish" a Boy.—Give him plenty of money, nothing to do, let him choose his own playmates, spend his evenings where he pleases, come home when he gets ready, and he will very soon finish himself.

(Business Notices $2.50 per Agate Line of Space.)

FLORENCE

LOCK-STITCH SEWING MACHINES.

Highest Premium, Fair of American Institute, 1865
CELEBRATED REVERSIBLE FEED MOVEMENT.
UNIFORM SELF ADJUSTING TENSION.
FOUR SEPARATE DISTINCT STITCHES.
WILL GATHER AND SEW A RUFFLE AT ONCE.
OFFICES OF THE COMPANY
505 Broadway, N. Y., and 73 Cheapside, London, England.

PRINCIPAL AGENCIES.

[illegible]

WHEELER & WILSON
ROTARY HOOK

LOCK STITCH

SEWING MACHINES.
625 BROADWAY.

"Woman's Greatest Boon. We would advise a man to [illegible] wheat with a flail, rather [illegible] WHEELER & WILSON [illegible] We have had several [illegible] six year's service, the WHEELER & WILSON has taken the preference [illegible] the best [illegible] a family."
[illegible]

THE GREAT FAMILY SEWING MACHINE.

GROVER & BAKER'S

HIGHEST PREMIUM
Elastic Stitch
SEWING MACHINE.
195 Broadway, New York.

THIS MEDALLION IS EMBEDDED IN EVERY GENUINE HOWE SEWING MACHINE.

The Howe Machine Co.'s Sewing Machines,

699 Broadway, Cor. Fourth-st., N. Y.

For Families and Manufacturers.

These World-Renowned Sewing Machines

Were awarded the highest premium at the World's Fair in London, and six first premiums at the N. Y. State Fair of 1866.

These machines are made under the immediate supervision of the President of the Company, ELIAS HOWE, Jr., the original Inventor of the Sewing Machine.

The Stitch invented by **MR. HOWE,** *and made on this Machine, is the most popular and durable, and all Sewing Machines are subject to the principle invented by him.*

SEND FOR CIRCULAR.

FRANKLIN BRICK MACHINE.

Justly celebrated for perfect simplicity, great strength, and [illegible] J. H. RENICK, Proprietor, [illegible]

HUDSON RIVER INSTITUTE, at Claverack, [illegible] *Every facility for the very best Christian Education.*
REV. ALONZO FLACK, A. M., Principal.

The Herald of Health.

The March Number contains:

Length of Days,
(By Rev. H. W. Bellows.)

The Value of Fruit as Food,
(By F. R. Elliott.)

Letters to Ladies,
(By Mrs. R. B. Gleason, M. D.)

Vitality, Its Phenomena,
(By Geo. F. Taylor, M. D.)

Weak Lungs and How to Make Them Strong.

No other Magazine attempts to popularize the Science of Physiology and make it Applicable to PHYSICAL AND MENTAL IMPROVEMENT. If it is important to understand Politics, Agriculture, Science, how much more to know ourselves.

Articles in the January No. on

"Human Development."
(By Henry Ward Beecher.)

"The Sacredness of the Body."
(By Rev. O. B. Frothingham.)

"How to Train up a Child."

The February No. contains:

Sources of Muscular Power,
(By Prof. R. King Browne.)

Buildings for the Poor,
(By Horace Greeley.)

Body and Brain.

How to Bathe.

Memory, and How to Improve It.

The April Number is larger, richer and better than any preceding one. Prof. Rufus King Browne commences in it an illustrated Series of Papers on the **Physiological Anatomy and Physiology of Man,** derived from his extensive Microscopic investigations.

Henry Ward Beecher furnishes a discourse, preached by request, to **Medical Students.** It is one of great power, and should be read by every man and woman.

Moses Coit Tyler commences a Series of Papers called

The Brawnville Athletic Club.

Nothing before published on Health Topics is so fascinating. Besides these, the April Number contains a **long list** of articles on Health, and all subjects relating to Human Welfare. See February *Agriculturist*, page 72, for Prospectus, etc.

(From the Country Gentleman.)

"The Herald of Health" is a Monthly, very carefully edited, and with a very able corps of contributors. We call attention to it, with the conviction that its *extended circulation would be a source of great benefit to the country at large, as well as to individuals.*

2.00 a Year. 20 Cents a Number.

For 30 subscribers and $60.00 we give for a premium **Wheeler & Wilson's Sewing Machine,** worth $55.

For Ten Subscribers and $20, each Subscriber shall receive, post-paid, a handsome Steel Engraving of **"LINCOLN AT HOME,"** 19x24 inches, and worth One Dollar.

Address **MILLER, WOOD & CO.,**
15 Laight-street, New York City.

THE LITTLE CORPORAL

Is acknowledged by the leading papers to be the

Best Juvenile Paper in America.

The American Phrenological Journal, of New York, says: "*The Little Corporal.*"—Mr. Sewell's Western juvenile surpasses, both in real merit and in circulation, any similar attempt, East or West. His success excites the cupidity of others, and we now have a swarm of juvenile journals launched on the uncertain sea of experiment. While we wish well to all good endeavors, we must award the credit to *The Little Corporal* of leading the van."

We offer a **MAGNIFICENT LIST of PREMIUMS!**

The price of the Corporal is one dollar a year, in advance; sample copy, telling all about the premiums, ten cents.
Address ALFRED L. SEWELL, Publisher, Chicago, Ill.

Book Agents Wanted.

To solicit orders, in each town in the United States and Canada, [illegible] subscription book ever published, being THE ILLUSTRATED HISTORY OF THE BIBLE, by *John Kitto, D. D., F. S. A. Edited by Rev. Alvan Bond, D. D., of Norwich, Conn.* Over 700 closely printed Royal Octavo pages—more than 100 full page engravings. Recommended by the leading Clergy of all denominations of Christians. 50,000 Copies already printed. Six large power presses running on the work. Everybody wants it. Experienced Agents say they never knew a book sell so well. No competition. Experienced Agents, School Teachers, Sabbath School Teachers, retired Clergymen, and others are wanted to introduce this great work into every household in the land. For Circulars, etc., apply immediately to the Publisher, HENRY BILL, Norwich, Conn.

RURAL IMPROVEMENTS.

ROBERT MORRIS COPELAND, Author of Country Life, furnishes plans, &c., for all kinds of Rural Improvements. Refers to John M. Fisher, Nathaniel Thayer, Boston; Francis G. Shaw, New York; Rufus Waterman, Providence, R. I.
Office, 41 Barrister's Hall, Boston.

BUCKEYE MOWER & REAPER

Pronounced by the Judges at the

GREAT NATIONAL FIELD TRIAL

at Auburn, in July last, to be superior to all others in

Every Desirable Point.

Order early to secure Machines.
Manufactured by
ADRIANCE, PLATT & CO.,
165 Greenwich-st., New York.
(Manufactory, Poughkeepsie.)

To My Patrons:

It is due to myself that I should explain the reasons for non-appearance of my spring advertisements. My supply of plants, extensive as it was, was almost exhausted by fall sales. I expect to offer a *very* large and superior lot of plants to the public next fall. Shall issue 10,000 of a new edition of my *Manual* next summer. Also expect to be able to offer a fine stock of a new Grape *of large size, fine flavor,* and perfectly *hardy vine.*

J. H. FOSTER, Jr.

The Eureka Brick Machine

makes 3,000 *splendid Brick per hour, with only nine men and one pair horses, or 4,000 per hour by steam power. Has no complex machinery to be getting out of order or breaking down.* Its great simplicity and marvelous power command the approval of every expert, *at sight.*
We challenge the world to produce its equal.
Also, The Empire Shingle Machine, the best in the world.
Satisfaction guaranteed to all purchasers.
ABRAM REQUA, General Agent,
No. 141 Broadway, New York.

MARK YOUR CLOTHING!

Clark's Patent Indelible Pencil.

"The Indelible Pencil for marking clothing is much more convenient than ink, and equally good as to permanence—we judge after several month's trial."—*Am. Agriculturist.*

"The Indelible Pencil is invaluable for marking linen."—*Chicago Tribune.*

"Remarkable for the ease and neatness with which it can be used."—*Detroit Tribune.*

Manufactured and Sold at Wholesale by
THE INDELIBLE PENCIL CO., Northampton, Mass.
Price—50 cents single, $3 per dozen. Sent post-paid on receipt of price.
A liberal discount made to dealers.
EVERY PENCIL WARRANTED. AGENTS WANTED.

EMPIRE SPRING BED CO.,
63 Liberty-st.,
NEW YORK.

MANUAL'S PATENT ADJUSTABLE

Spring Bed Bottom.

One Mattress—No Bugs—No Noise—Perfect Rest—Cheap.
$5.00 to $7.00 at retail—Durable—Fit any bedstead. Anybody can do it.
"I DO NOT WANT A BETTER BED."—N. C. Meeker, Agricultural Editor Tribune.
Address as above. Agents wanted.

50 PER-CENT SAVED BY USING

D. T. BABBITT'S STAR YEAST POWDER. Light Biscuit or any kind of Cake may be made with this Yeast Powder in fifteen minutes. No shortening required when sweet milk is used.
I will send a sample package free by mail on receipt of fifteen cents to pay postage.
Nos. 64, 65, 66, 67, 68, 69, 70, 72, and 74 Washington Street, New York.

SQUIRE'S PATENT FRUIT JAR.

Fruits Preserved Without Sugar.
The Only Jar for Preserving Vegetables.
The Newest, Most Convenient and Economical Jar extant.

This Jar is constructed so that the contents can be cooked in it, and all handling of Hot Fruit or Hot Jars or Tempering of Jars avoided; the contents retain all their natural flavor, and the labor of preserving is lessened more than one-half. Pamphlets sent on application.
J. B. BARTLETT, Wholesale Manufacturer,
69 Murray-street, New York.

ROSES.

We offer very fine plants of the best sorts, such as have been found to succeed in our climate, at

$40 per 100; $350 per 1000.

They are on their own roots, and embrace the different classes, but are largely composed of Hybrid Perpetuals.
For Catalogues, address
PARSONS & CO., Flushing, N. Y.

THE GREAT AMERICAN TEA COMPANY,

Since their organization, have created a new era in the Tea Trade. They have introduced their selection of Teas and Coffees, and have sold them at the smallest profits possible. They warrant all the goods they sell to be perfectly satisfactory. If they do not prove so, the purchaser has the privilege of returning them within 30 days at the expense of the Company, and have the money refunded.

The Company have selected the following kinds from their stock, which they recommend to meet the wants of Clubs. They are sold at Cargo Prices, the same as the Company sell them in New-York, as the list of prices will show.

PRICE LIST:

YOUNG HYSON (Green), 80c., 90c., $1, $1.10, best $1.25 ℔ lb.
GREEN TEAS, 80c., 90c., $1, $1.10, best $1.25 ℔ lb.
MIXED, 70c., 80c., 90c., best $1 ℔ lb.
JAPAN, $1, $1.10, best $1.25 ℔ lb.
OOLONG (Black), 70c., 80c., 90c., best $1 ℔ lb.
IMPERIAL (Green), best $1.25 ℔ lb.
ENGLISH BREAKFAST (Black), 80c., 90c., $1, $1.10, best $1.20 ℔ lb.
GUNPOWDER (Green), $1.25, best $1.50.

COFFEE DEPARTMENT.

Our Coffee Department is very extensive—the largest, perhaps, in the country. We run three engines constantly, and sometimes four or five in roasting and grinding our Coffee. Our Coffee buyers are experts, who examine most of the Coffees imported, and select the best and finest flavors for our trade. We employ the most experienced and skillful roasters, who exercise the greatest care that it shall be cooked in a perfect manner. It is always fresh, for our orders crowd our facilities to their utmost capacity. A considerable portion of the Coffee put upon the market of late years is picked while the pods are green, and subjected to artificial heat to open the pods. This is not so good as that which ripens in the natural way upon the plant. Our Coffee buyer thoroughly understands this business, and can readily distinguish the naturally ripened from the artificially cured; and he only buys the Coffee which is naturally ripened. We examine the cargoes as soon as they arrive, and our trade is so large that it requires all the finest lots. This is what gives our Coffee a superior flavor to many others, and the same flavor it used to have in days long gone by. It is a common saying that most Coffee does not taste as well as it formerly did. The reason for it is that a considerable portion of it is picked before it is fully ripe. We sell none but the fully ripe, rich flavored Coffee.

COFFEES ROASTED AND GROUND DAILY.

GROUND COFFEE, 20c., 25c., 30c., 35c., best 40c. per pound. Hotels, Saloons, Boarding-house Keepers, and Families who use large quantities of Coffee can economize in that article by using our FRENCH BREAKFAST AND DINNER COFFEE, which we sell at the low price of 30c. per pound, and warrant to give perfect satisfaction.

Consumers can save from 50c. to $1 per pound by purchasing their Teas of

THE GREAT AMERICAN TEA COMPANY.
Nos. 31 and 33 VESEY-ST.,
No. 640 BROADWAY, corner of Bleecker-st.
No. 461 EIGHTH-AVE., north corner of Thirty-fourth-st.
No. 299 SPRING-St.
No. 205 FULTON-ST., BROOKLYN, corner of Concord-st.
No. 135 GRAND-ST., WILLIAMSBURGH.

COUNTRY CLUBS, Hand and Wagon Pedlers, and small stores (of which class we are supplying many thousands, all of which are doing well), can have their orders promptly and faithfully filled, and in case of Clubs can have each party's name marked on their package and directed by sending their orders to Nos. 31 and 33 Vesey-st.

Our friends are getting up Clubs in most towns throughout the country, and for which we feel very grateful. Some of our Clubs send orders weekly, and some not so often; while others keep a standing order to be supplied with a given quantity each week, or stated periods. And in all cases (where sufficient time has elapsed) Clubs have repeated their orders.

Parties sending Club or other orders for less than $30 had better send Post-Office drafts, or money with their orders, to save the expense of collecting by express; but larger orders we will forward by express, to collect on delivery.

We return thanks to parties who have taken an interest in getting up Clubs; and when any of them come to New-York we shall be happy to have them call upon us and make themselves known.

Hereafter we will send a complimentary package to the party getting up the Club. Our profits are small, but we will be as liberal as we can afford. We send no complimentary package for Clubs of less than $30.

N.B.—All villages and towns where a large number reside by *clubbing* together can reduce the cost of their Teas and Coffees about one-third by sending directly to the

GREAT AMERICAN TEA COMPANY,
Nos. 31 and 33 VESEY-ST
Post-Office Box, No. 5,643, New-York City.

GETTING UP CLUBS.

Some parties inquire of us how they shall proceed to get up a club. The answer is simply this: Let each person wishing to join in a club, say how much tea or coffee he wants, and select the kind and price from our Price List, as published in the paper or in our circulars. Write the names, kinds, and amounts plainly on a list, and when the club is complete send it to us by mail, and we will put each party's goods in separate packages, and mark the name upon them, with the cost, so there need be no confusion in their distribution—each party getting exactly what he orders, and no more. The cost of transportation the members of the club can divide equitably among themselves.

The funds to pay for the goods ordered can be sent by drafts on New York, by Post-Office money orders, or by Express, as may suit the convenience of the club. Or, if the amount ordered exceeds thirty dollars, we will, if desired, send the goods by Express, to "*collect on delivery.*"

We publish some of our Club Lists to show how it is done and as matter of reference.

After the first Club we send blanks.

Direct your orders plainly, THE GREAT AMERICAN TEA COMPANY, Nos. 31 and 33 Vesey st., Post Office Box, 5,643—as some parties imitate our name as near as they dare do.

From The Great American Tea Company's Advocate.

A Word with Our Customers.

We have no doubt that our customers, scattered throughout the length and breadth of the land, as they are, embracing every State in the Union, except those on the Pacific shores, will be interested to learn how we have succeeded in our great enterprise of furnishing Teas and Coffees, to all, at the smallest possible profits. To afford them this information we propose to give a *few facts* connected with our business.

Years ago, in the early stage of our enterprise, we based our calculations and graded our rates of profit upon the basis of a trade of $100,000 per week. This amount we expected to reach by enterprise and fair dealing. We well knew that it could be accomplished only by filling every order promptly, and to the letter; and at uniform prices. These principles we have adhered to strictly, and have carried out the ONE PRICE SYSTEM in all our transactions.

After years of anxiety and incessant toil, we are enabled to say, without boasting, that our standard of sales, which we erected years ago, has been reached. The *New York Tribune*, in an editorial published in their paper several months ago, placed the amount of our sales at that time at $90,000 per week. Our business increases regularly and constantly, and never faster than at the present time. We therefore look confidently forward to a large increase during the present year, over and above the average of $100,000 per week. At the present time our sales are fully equal to 2,000 chests per week, which is equal to about one-fifth of all the Teas imported into this country. This we consider a great success for a *speciality*—probably the greatest ever achieved in this country, in any similar mercantile enterprise.

With our increased trade we increase our facilities, so that all our orders will be filled as promptly and correctly as heretofore, and perhaps more so, because our system becomes more and more perfect with time and practice.

We employ at least two hundred persons constantly, and by our perfect system of division of labor into departments, we make a great saving of expense, of which we give consumers the benefit, by furnishing them with the great necessaries of life—TEAS AND COFFEES—at the unprecedented low figures which we publish in our Price List in another column.

While we feel sure that we have given, and as we shall continue to give, our customers the fullest and amplest return for their money, we thank them, one and all, for their patronage.

COMPLIMENTARY LETTERS.

In order to give our friends in the country an idea of the magnitude of our business, we publish the following letters which we have received from two of the principal Express Companies of this country, and from other sources. The facts which they state show conclusively that no other Tea House in this city or country can compare with us in magnitude of business.

UNITED STATES EXPRESS OFFICE, No. 82 BROADWAY, NEW-YORK, Jan. 1, 1867.

To the Great American Tea Company:

GENTLEMEN: Accept the compliments of the season.

We thank you for the patronage we have received from your house.

Perhaps you would be gratified to learn that we have expressed more goods from your Company during the past year than from any other Tea or Grocery House in this city during the same time.

We solicit a continuance of your patronage, and pledge ourselves to give your goods dispatch, careful attention, and we will do so at the very lowest rates. Yours, &c.,

C. P. THAYER, General Agent.

OFFICE OF THE AMERICAN EXPRESS COMPANY, Nos. 122 and 124 Broadway, cor. Cedar-st., NEW-YORK, January 10, 1867.

To the Great American Tea Company, Nos. 31 & 33 Vesey-st.:

GENTLEMEN: We are pleased to acknowledge our indebtedness to you for the liberal patronage we have received at your hands during the last year.

We consider your business of as much importance to us as that of any other house in the city, and shall be happy in the future, as we have been in the past, to receive your consignments, hoping that by dealing out "safety and dispatch" we will merit them.

With many thanks for past favors, we wish you, gentlemen, "A Happy New-Year."

Yours respectfully,
JAS. C. FARGO, Manager.

NEW-YORK, Jan. 5, 1867.

To the Great American Tea Co.:

GENTS: I am happy to say that your orders for packing boxes have increased more than two-hundred per cent. within the past year. I am now manufacturing more boxes for you than for any other concern, although I am supplying the largest manufacturing establishments in this city.

Hoping to receive a continuance of your patronage, I am,
Respectfully yours,
J. H. SWIFT,
Packing Box Manufacturer,
Nos. 92, 94, 96, 98, and 100 Norfolk-st., New-York City.

PAPER WAREHOUSE, No. 29 BEEKMAN-ST., NEW-YORK, Dec. 24, 1866.

The Great American Tea Co.:

GENTLEMEN: We can send you but four hundred thousand paper bags to-day, and will endeavor to give you seven hundred thousand more before the 31st. After the 1st of January we shall increase our production so as to meet your large orders more promptly.

Respectfully yours,
WILLIAM H. AMES & CO.

Complimentary Letters from Clubs.

TOLEDO, Ohio, Jan. 12, 1867.

Great American Tea Company, Nos. 31 and 33 Vesey-st., N. Y.

GENTLEMEN: The two boxes of Tea I ordered from you were received yesterday by M. U. Express Co., and have been delivered to the subscribers. I was much pleased with the manner in which you put up the packages with the subscriber's name on each. I would say that the quality of your Tea is superior, giving entire satisfaction. "Some of the club" say that it is the finest flavored Tea they have ever tasted. Your Company deserve credit for their perseverance in overcoming the difficulties incurred in establishing such a trade, and in breaking down the monopolies that have so long kept the consumer paying such high prices. With thanks for the complimentary package, I am most truly yours,

DAVID CARRUTHERS.

NEW-HAVEN, Dec. 14, 1866.

To the Great American Tea Company:

SIRS: This will convince you that your goods have given perfect satisfaction, as I have added somewhat to the Club. Please accept our especial thanks for the complimentary package, also for the nice manner in which the whole was put up.

Yours truly,
Mrs. L. BLOSS.

Please return as soon as convenient. Direct as before to Justin Bloss, New-Haven, Vermont.

CLUB ORDERS.

LAKE PLEASANT, Erie Co., Pa., Jan. 12, 1867.

Great American Tea Company, Nos. 31 & 33 Vesey-st., N. Y.

GENTLEMEN: The Tea you sent me last month arrived safely and in good order, and gives good satisfaction. Please send the within order, the sixth I have sent within less than a year. The first order I sent last Spring was an experiment, to see if good tea could be sold at retail in New-York for the low price of $1.25 per pound. We found the Tea to be of good quality, and since then we have continued to send to you for our Tea, and shall do so as long as you do as well by us as you have in the past.

Yours truly,
W. F. WILLIAMS.

12 lbs.	Japan	at	$1.25	$15.00
2	Gunpowder	at	1.50	3.00
5	Gunpowder	at	1.25	6.25
7	Imperial	at	1.25	8.75
				$33.00

LAKEVILLE, N. Y., Jan. 3, 1867.

The Great American Tea Co., Nos. 31 and 33 Vesey-st.:

This is the third Club that has been sent from this place since about the 12th of December, 1866. Your Teas have given universal satisfaction. I shall do my best to keep the ball rolling. Yours respectfully, WILLIAM KIMBARK.

1 lb	Young Hyson	C. R. Ames	at	$1.10	$1.10
1	Young Hyson	J. N. Hillman	at	1.00	1.00
1	Gunpowder	J. N. Hillman	at	1.25	1.25
4	Young Hyson	James Clark	at	1.10	4.40
1	Young Hyson	James Clark	at	1.25	1.25
1	Young Hyson	James H. Clark	at	1.00	1.00
1	Young Hyson	James H. Clark	at	1.10	1.10
1	Imperial	Wm. P. Wattle	at	1.25	1.25
1	G. and B. mixed	Wm. P. Wattle	at	1.00	1.00
1	Young Hyson	Edward Butler	at	1.25	1.25
1	Young Hyson	John Gardner	at	1.10	1.10
1	Gunpowder	John Gardner	at	1.50	1.50
1	G. and B. mixed	W. H. Kimbark	at	1.00	1.00
1	G. and B. mixed	Geo. Hillman	at	1.00	1.00
1	Young Hyson	Geo. Hillman	at	1.25	1.25
1	Young Hyson	Geo. Hillman	at	1.10	1.10
1	Young Hyson	N. W. Bearsley	at	1.10	1.10
1	Young Hyson	N. W. Bearsley	at	1.25	1.25
1	Uncolored Japan	N. W. Bearsley	at	1.25	1.25
1	Young Hyson	Wm. Taylor	at	1.00	1.00
1	Young Hyson	Wm. Taylor	at	1.10	1.10
1	Young Hyson	Revillo Bigelow	at	1.25	1.25
1	G. & B. Mix	Revillo Bigelow	at	1.00	1.00
1	Young Hyson	B. V. Valkenburg	at	1.10	1.10
1	Gunpowder	W. Eddy	at	1.50	1.50
6	Young Hyson	Emerson Pease	at	80	4.80
1	Gunpowder	David Alvord	at	1.25	1.25
1	Gunpowder	David Alvord	at	1.50	1.50
2	Uncolored Japan	David Alvord	at	1.25	2.50
1	Uncolored Japan	Nelson Griswold	at	1.25	1.25
1	Uncolored Japan	James Hill	at	1.25	1.25
1	Young Hyson	James Hill	at	1.10	1.10
1	Young Hyson	Edward Savery	at	1.10	1.10
1	Green and Black	Edward Savery	at	1.00	1.00
1	Uncolored Japan	C. Crossett	at	1.10	1.10
1	Young Hyson	Wm. Radford	at	1.10	1.10
1	Young Hyson	Wm. Radford	at	1.25	1.25
2	Young Hyson	Wm. Drake	at	1.10	2.20
1	G. & B. Mix	Wm. Drake	at	1.00	1.00
1	Uncolored Japan	Wm. Drake	at	1.25	1.25
1	Uncolored Japan	James Hanna	at	1.25	1.25
1	Young Hyson	B. Gilbert	at	1.00	1.00
					$58.00

WILLIAMSTOWN, Orange Co., Vt., Jan., 1867.

To the Great American Tea Co., Nos. 31 & 33 Vesey-st., N. Y.

GENTLEMEN: The Tea I ordered before gives good satisfaction, and I send you another order amounting to $41.00, which you will please fill and send to my address by express. Many thanks for the complimentary package.

Respectfully yours,
ALEXANDER SMITH.

4 lb.	Young Hyson	C. A. Earl	at	$1.25	$5.00
1	Black, best E. B.	C. A. Earl	at	1.20	1.20
4	Young Hyson	John Clarke	at	1.25	5.00
3	Young Hyson	H. B. Harrington	at	1.25	3.75
2	Young Hyson	D. D. Martin	at	1.25	2.50
2	Young Hyson	A. B. Martin	at	1.25	2.50
2	Young Hyson	Mrs. Wakefield	at	1.25	2.50
2	Young Hyson	Wallace Martin	at	1.25	2.50
1	Young Hyson	L. H. Merrill	at	1.25	1.25
1	Best Japan	L. H. Merrill	at	1.25	1.25
2	Young Hyson	D. M. Harrington	at	1.25	2.50
1	Young Hyson	F. Goodrich	at	1.25	1.25
2	Japan	F. Harrington	at	1.25	2.50
2	Young Hyson	S. H. Bohonon	at	1.25	2.50
2	Young Hyson	Enos Town	at	1.25	2.50
2	Young Hyson	Alex. Smith	at	1.25	2.50
1	Japan	Alex. Smith	at	1.25	1.25
1	Coffee, best	A. C. Boswell	at	40	40
					$41.00

Rare and Beautiful Flowers----Select Garden Vegetables.

B. K. BLISS,

Seed and Agricultural Warehouse, Springfield, Mass.,

Importer and Dealer in Garden, Field and Flower Seeds, Agricultural Implements, Fertilizers, &c., &c.

The attention of all who are interested in the culture of FLOWERS or VEGETABLES is invited to our large and well selected assortment of the above—comprising the newest and most approved varieties, both of European and Home production, the quality of which cannot be surpassed.—For a list of which, see our

New Illustrated Seed Catalogue and Guide to the Flower and Kitchen Garden,

The Thirteenth Annual Edition, enlarged and improved, contains 121 pages of closely printed matter—BEAUTIFULLY ILLUSTRATED WITH 100 ENGRAVINGS, and a descriptive list of TWENTY-FIVE HUNDRED VARIETIES OF FLOWER, VEGETABLE AND AGRICULTURAL SEEDS, including all the leading novelties of the past season, with explicit directions for their culture; also a list of

ONE HUNDRED AND TWENTY-FIVE VARIETIES OF FRENCH HYBRID GLADIOLUS,

Embracing many new sorts now offered for the first time in this country—with many other SUMMER FLOWERING BULBS, consisting of AMARYLLIS, TUBEROSES, TIGRIDIAS, LILIES, etc. To which is added a list of the choicest varieties of GRAPES, STRAWBERRIES, RASPBERRIES, CURRANTS and other SMALL FRUITS, BEDDING PLANTS, etc., cultivated at his gardens, with much other useful information upon the subject of gardening generally.—A copy will be mailed to all applicants upon receipt of 25 Cents.

Our New Illustrated Plant Catalogue, just published, contains a list of many new and rare plants, not before offered in this country—also a Descriptive list of all the leading varieties of DAHLIAS, HOLLYHOCKS, ROSES, CANNAS, CARNATIONS, PICOTEES, VERBENAS, HELIOTROPES, PETUNIAS, GERANIUMS and other BEDDING PLANTS. **Price, 10 Cents.**

Our Regular Customers supplied with both Seed and Plant Catalogues without charge.

N. B.—We would invite particular attention to the following COLLECTIONS OF SEEDS—also to the SPECIAL VARIETIES enumerated—the purity and vitality of which cannot be excelled—all of which (with the exception of those noted) will be mailed, post-paid, to any address in the Union upon receipt of price affixed.

Splendid Novelty from Japan.

JAPANESE STRIPED LEAVED MAIZE.

The experience of the past season fully confirms all that has been said of this beautiful plant, and it is now acknowledged by all the leading Florists both in our own country and Europe as the most valuable plant for decorative purposes introduced for many years. The variegation appears when the plant is about four inches in height, and in a short time it is beautifully striped or ribboned with alternate stripes of green and white, and in its earlier stages of growth is also striped with rose color. Nothing in the way of a *foliage plant* can exceed in gracefulness and beauty a group of three to five plants of this variety of the Zea. Price 25 cts. per packet; 5 packets for $1. The trade supplied upon liberal terms. B. K. BLISS, Springfield, Mass.

Collections of Kitchen Garden Seeds.

A COMPLETE ASSORTMENT OF VEGETABLE SEEDS FOR ONE YEAR'S SUPPLY, FOR A LARGE OR SMALL GARDEN.

The following Collections are made up in the most liberal manner, care being taken to give a sufficient quantity of all the finest varieties and most useful sorts of Vegetables required in the Kitchen Garden.

Assortment	No. 5, contains 55 varieties	....	$3.00
"	No. 6, "	35 "	2.00
"	No. 7, "	15 "	1.00

The above are prepared expressly for sending by mail, and will be sent post-paid, upon receipt of prices annexed.

Larger Collections which can be safely sent by express to any part of the country, as follows:

No. 1, $20.00; No. 2, $15.00; No. 3, $10.00; No. 4, $5.00.

For a list of the contents of each Collection, see Catalogue pages 96 and 97.

HOVEY & CO.'s ILLUSTRATED GUIDE

TO THE

FLOWER AND VEGETABLE GARDEN FOR 1867,

is now ready, containing more than 130 pages, and 80 elegant engravings, with

A SPLENDID COLORED PLATE,

and detailed descriptions of more than

2500 Varieties of Flower and Vegetable Seeds,

with full and complete directions for their cultivation. Sent free to all applicants on the receipt of 25 cts. Address HOVEY & CO., 53 North Market-st., Boston.

New Russian Mammoth Sunflower.

The largest variety yet introduced, well adapted for planting in shrubberies.

For Poultry Feeders it is invaluable.

25 cts. per packet. Prices per oz. on application.

WASHBURN & CO., Seed Merchants, Horticultural Hall, Boston, Mass.

Striped Leaved Japanese Maize.

Package containing about 40 seeds of this new ornamental plant sent to any address, for 25 cents. Dealers supplied with packages or seed in bulk at a liberal discount.

JAMES J. H. GREGORY, Marblehead, Mass.

SUPERIOR LONG BRUSH BROOM CORN SEED—(New)—For sale by SAML. T. THORBURN, Seedsman, 8 Hudson-street, Albany, N. Y. $10 per bushel; 40 cents per quart. The seed grows well.

BEDDING PLANTS, &C., BY MAIL.

Strong and healthy Plants of the following varieties will be securely packed and mailed, post-paid, to any address in the United States, upon receipt of the price affixed. *Selection of varieties to be left with us.*—When a less number than the amount specified is ordered, an additional charge will be made at the rate of 50 cents per dozen.

12 Hardy Carnations and Picotees, assorted	$2.50		
12 Monthly " " "	3.00		
12 Florists' Pinks ... ass'd.	$2.50	12 Fuchsias, assorted	2.00
12 Scarlet Geraniums "	2.50	12 Heliotropes, "	2.00
12 Lantanas, "	2.00	12 Petunias, "	2.00
12 Phloxes, "	2.0	12 Pansies, "	2.00
8 Salvias, "	1.50	12 Verbenas, "	1.50
12 Dahlias (pot roots), "	2.50	6 Pot Roses, "	2.00
6 H. P. Roses, "	2.50	6 Feverfews	1.25
3 Tritomas, "	1.25	1 Daphne Cneorum	75
1 Lilium Auratum	5.0	3 Japan Lilies (3 var.)	1.50
12 Gladiolus, assorted	2.0	12 Italian Tuberoses	2.00
4 Ornamental Foliage Plants, distinct	1.25		
12 Chrysanthemums, large Flowering	2.50		
12 " Pomponed	2.50		

Imported Chinese Sugar Cane Seed.

In consequence of so much of the seed of this valuable plant that is raised in this country being deteriorated by hybridization with other varieties, we have just imported a supply from Messrs. Vilmorin & Co., of Paris, grown from the *original stock*, which may be relied upon as *perfectly pure.* 4 ounces, 25 cents; 8 ounces, 40 cents; one lb. 75 cents.

The Best and most Hardy Hedge Plant.

HONEY LOCUST, OR THREE THORNED ACACIA.

Fresh Seed with directions for culture, will be mailed to any address, at the following prices: 1 oz., 15 cents; 4 ozs., 35 cents; 1 pound, $1.00. Prices in larger quantities will be given upon application.

Connecticut Seed Leaf Tobacco Seed.

Be Sure and Get the Best.

A superior lot raised expressly for the subscriber by one of the most successful cultivators in the Valley of the Connecticut. Packets with *full directions for culture, curing, packing, &c.*, will be mailed, post-paid, to all applicants at the following rates: 1 ounce, 35 cents; 4 ounces, $1; 1 lb., $3.50.

Improved Long Orange Carrot.

This variety originated in this vicinity several years since, and is rapidly superseding all others wherever it has been tested. It resembles the Long Orange in shape—but is superior in every respect, being *larger, better flavored, of a deeper orange color*, and more sure to produce a crop. Mailed, post-paid, upon receipt of price.

4 ounces, 50 cents; 8 ounces, 80 cents; one pound, $1.50.

Dreer's Garden Calendar for 1867,

with select lists of Seeds and Plants, and directions for their cultivation, mailed upon the receipt of a stamp.

Address H. A. DREER, 714 Chestnut-st., Philadelphia, Pa.

Assortment of Imported Choicest Flower and Garden Seeds,

from Frederic William Wendel, Nursery and Seed Establishment, Erfurt, Prussia, for sale by his Sole Agent for the United States, Theodore Ch. Wendel, 518 Washington-st., Boston, Mass. Correspondence in English and German.

For catalogues in English and German, as required, please address THEODORE CH. WENDEL, 518 Washington-st., Boston, Mass.

OSAGE ORANGE SEED,

Just received on Consignment from Texas, and guaranteed fresh and new, for sale in quantities to suit, by pound or bushel. PLANT & BRO., St. Louis, Mo.

Collections of Flower Seeds by Mail.

The following collections have been sent out from our establishment for the past 15 years, and are now favorably known in every section of the country. They contain the most showy varieties in our large assortment, with full directions for culture. Each packet contains a mixture of the different colors and varieties of its species, so that a greater display can be made at a much less price than when ordered in separate packets. Those unacquainted with Flowers as well as the experienced cultivator may order without fear of disappointment.

No. 1—Contains twenty choice varieties of Annuals.....$1 00

No. 2— " " " of Biennials and Perennials.. 1 00

No. 3—Contains ten extra fine varieties of Annuals and Perennials, embracing many of the new and choicest in cultivation.......... 1 00

No. 4—Contains five very choice varieties selected from PRIZE FLOWERS of English Pansies, German Carnation and Picotee Pinks, Verbenas, Truffaut's French Asters, Double Hollyhocks 1 00

Any one remitting $3.50 will receive the four assortments.

No. 5—Contains fifteen very select varieties of Greenhouse Seeds.......... $3 00

No. 6—Contains one hundred varieties of Annuals, Biennials, and Perennials, including many new and choice varieties.......... 5 00

No. 7—Contains fifty varieties of Annuals, Biennials, and Perennials.......... 2 50

No. 8—Contains twenty varieties of hardy Annuals, Biennials, and Perennials, for sowing in the autumn.. 1 00

The seeds contained in the above assortments are of our own selection. Purchasers who prefer to make their selection from the Catalogue, will be entitled to a discount proportionate to the quantity ordered.

A New Early Cabbage.

Large Early Schweinfurt.

A New German variety—very early, of large size, the heads are large—firm and close, very tender and most excellent flavor—try it—per packet, 25 cents.

GIANT ASPARAGUS ROOTS BY MAIL.

Extra, *strong*, one year old Roots, carefully packed, and mailed, post-paid, at $1.25 per 100; $4.00 for 500; $10.50 per 1,000.

We earnestly request our correspondents to give their *Name, Post-office Address, County* and *State* distinctly written in full. All orders should be addressed as follows:

B. K. BLISS, Springfield, Massachusetts.

Be particular and name the *State in full*, as there is a Springfield in almost every State in the Union.

The New Vegetable, "Raphanus Caudatus."

I have received from Mr. Bull, of Chelsea, a few thousand seeds of this new vegetable.

The price in England is *one shilling* sterling, or twenty-five cents each. I will furnish those who desire to give it a trial with seeds in small quantities at 25 cents a seed.

Address JAMES VICK, Rochester, N. Y.

Farmers and Gardeners!

Many of you have thus far found the purchase of Garden Seed the most unsatisfactory and most vexing of all your investments. Now, *if you will stand by me*, I propose to change all this, and make a revolution in the seed business by my three warrants.—1st. I will warrant my seed to be what it purports to be in kind and quality: 2d. I will warrant that the money you send for seed shall reach me; and 3d. I will warrant that the seed you order shall reach you.

Thus you see, I take all the risks on myself. I know that in doing this I shall make some losses, but I have confidence that the good sense of the farmers and gardeners of the United States will stand by me in this new movement, and so far increase my business as to enable me to bear all such losses and continue the business on the "three warrants" basis. Stand by me and I will stand by you! Catalogues sent gratis to all. See the advertisement headed "Gregory's Seed Catalogue."

JAMES J. H. GREGORY, Marblehead, Mass.

CRANBERRY TRACT, (part in bearing,) near N. Y., for sale cheap. Address M. D. Beach, Toms River, N. J.

Just Published.

New Edition Revised and Enlarged.

WELLS'

EVERY MAN HIS OWN LAWYER

and Business Form Book.

A complete Guide in all matters of Law, and Business Negotiations for every State in the Union.

With Legal Forms, and Full Instructions for Proceeding, without legal assistance, in Suits and Business transactions of every description.

Together with the different State Laws, concerning the Collection of Debts, Property exempt from Execution, Lien Laws, Usury, License to Sell Goods, Qualification of Voters, Limitation of Actions, &c.

Also, *the General Bankrupt Law, with Forms and full instructions* to enable the insolvent debtor to take full benefit of the Act without legal assistance.

Also, *Pension Laws*, with full instructions and forms to enable every Discharged Soldier and Sailor to procure Back Pay, Pensions, Bounties and all war claims.

Also, *Patent Laws*, with full instructions to inventors.

Also, *Excise Laws, Stamp Duties, Post-office and Custom House Regulations, the whole action of the Government in relation to Reconstruction, and the Freedmen, Constitution of the United States, with Amendments, State Seals, with descriptions, &c.*

This work, prepared some years ago, was received with great favor by the public, attaining a larger sale, it is believed, than any work of the kind ever published. Lapse of time has brought material changes in the statutes of many of the States; the War has not only altered the legal condition of some of them, but has introduced the Internal Revenue System, National Banks, new Post-Office and Custom-House Regulations, Amendments to the Constitution of the United States, Emancipation of Slaves, General Bankrupt Law, &c.

The subject of Pensions, Bounties and War Claims, has assumed a new and greatly increased importance.

These various changes have led the publisher to make a new and thoroughly revised edition, reproducing the whole work, with special reference to making the work complete and reliable, without regard to expense. So critical and thorough has been the revision, that the most implicit reliance can be placed upon the work, as authority on all the subjects of which it treats.

Over two hundred and fifty pages new matter have been added to meet the requirements of the times.

The utility of such a work, none will now question. The sale of hundreds of thousands of copies of the former edition, and the constant demand for it have settled that point. The professional man, the farmer, the mechanic, the manufacturer, the merchant, the sailor, each requires a convenient, comprehensive and reliable work which will enable him to draw up any instrument in writing that may be required, in a legal form, which will furnish such local information as is needed for the various avocations of life, a book that everybody can understand, and that will enable every man or woman to be his or her own lawyer.

There is no class of the community, male or female, who have, or expect to have, any property, or who have any rights or privileges which require protection, who will not be greatly benefited and advantaged by the possession of this book. It will save them money, save them trouble, save them time, save them litigation and lawyers' fees, and give them information that nobody can afford to be without.

12mo., 650 pages. PRICE, HANDSOMELY BOUND, $2.00.

Sent post paid, on receipt of price.

A good, reliable agent wanted in every town in the United States. Also a responsible man at all prominent points, as General Agent. Also, a few wide awake men to travel in establishing agencies. Address,

BENJ. W. HITCHCOCK, Publisher,
14 Chambers-st., New York.

Papers giving this advertisement a conspicuous insertion, will receive a copy of the work.

SCHOOL TEACHERS WANTED.—The Subscriber wishes to employ for each town in the United States, one or two teachers who have formerly been engaged, either in Day Schools or Sunday Schools, who can devote their exclusive time to the business, to canvass for the "*Illustrated History of the Bible*," by John Kitto, D. D., F. S. A., revised by Alvan Bond, D. D., of Norwich, Conn.

This is the best selling book I have ever published. Agents make from $100 to $200 per month, and say "they never knew a book to sell so well." Apply immediately in person or by letter to the publisher.

HENRY BILL, Norwich, Conn.

EMPLOYMENT.

THE AUBURN PUBLISHING Co. offer THE BEST HISTORY OF THE REBELLION. *Latest, Cheapest, most Complete.*

THE BEST ILLUSTRATED NATURAL HISTORY.
THE BEST WORK ON THE DOMESTIC ANIMALS.
THE BEST WORK ON THE FARM AND GARDENS.
THE BEST FAMILY RECEIPT BOOK, &c., &c.

The best *Terms*, and the *most reliable Instructions* to Agents. Address E. G. STORKE, Publishing Agent,
Auburn, N. Y.

---

500 Large Double Column Pages in THE AMERICAN STOCK JOURNAL.

TO BOOK AGENTS.—We are now ready to employ additional Canvassers for GREELEY'S HISTORY complete. The popularity of this work is unprecedented. For more than four months past the demand has far exceeded our utmost ability to supply, although we have printed and bound a much greater number of volumes than were ever before issued of any single work in so short a time and of equal size in the whole history of book-making. The great superiority of GREELEY'S HISTORY is everywhere admitted, even by the author's political opponents. Experienced Canvassers can secure good territory on favorable terms. Address O. D. CASE & Co., Hartford, Conn., Cleveland, O., or Detroit, Mich.

Thoroughbred Chester White Pigs

For Sale; from 10 weeks to 1 year old. For growth and quality cannot be excelled in the *United States*. For Description and Prices, send for Circular. Address

JAMES YOUNG, Jr., & CO.,
Marshallton, Chester Co., Pa.

SEND FOR DESCRIPTION of the finest *Thoroughbred Spanish Merino Sheep, Chester White Pigs, and Imported Fowls* in America. L. B. SILVER, SALEM, Ohio.

15 Months for $1.00—THE AMERICAN STOCK JOURNAL.

Important to Owners of Horses.

Advice and Prescriptions for Sick and Injured Horses given Free.

The Editor of WILKES' SPIRIT OF THE TIMES desires to inform the owners of horses throughout the United States, that he has regularly engaged upon his paper, one of the ablest and most experienced professional veterinarians in the United States, whose special duty it shall be to answer, gratis, all questions relative to sick or injured horses which may be addressed to the SPIRIT, *whether by subscribers or not*. These answers will in all cases contain a prescription for the injury described, and will be printed, in connection with the question asked, in the following number of the SPIRIT. No answers, however, will be given by mail, it being a part of the object of the editor, to submit the ability of the professor, who has assumed this department of the SPIRIT, to the keenest criticism of the general public. By adding this useful department to the SPIRIT, the editor contributes to those of his readers and subscribers, who own horses, a horse-doctor free, and not only to his subscribers, *but to every horse-owner in the United States who may choose to direct an inquiry to the SPIRIT by mail*. The subscription price of the SPIRIT is $5 a year; but single copies may be bought *from* news agents from week to week by those who desire to use it temporarily only, for veterinarian questions, at fifteen cents per copy. The SPIRIT OF THE TIMES is a high-toned gentleman's paper, which (with the old SPIRIT, whose business and title it inherits) is of forty years' standing, and is devoted to Hunting, Fishing, Racing, Field Sports, Literature, and the Stage.

GEORGE WILKES, Editor and Proprietor,
201 William-st., New York.

☞ Dealers will continue to procure their supplies as heretofore.

Everybody Should Send for THE AMERICAN STOCK JOURNAL.

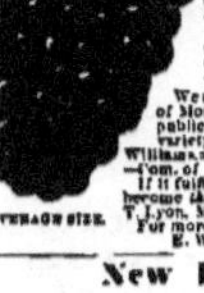

AVERAGE SIZE.

See O, March, K, page B, 116 B.

By mail, $4 ⅌ ½ doz., $10 ⅌ doz.

The *best* Blackberry I have yet seen.—C. Downing, N. Y.

A large, handsome, high flavored, delicious fruit.—P. J. Mead, N. Y.

Its great *hardiness* and *superior* quality make it the *most* desirable variety yet introduced.—W. S. Carpenter, N. Y.

We deem it due both to E. Williams, of Mont Clair, and the Horticultural public to state that we regard this variety, recently introduced by Mr. Williams, as worthy *of unqualified praise*.—Com. of Investigation.

If it fulfills its present promise it must become *the* "Berry for the Million."—T. T. Lyon, Mich.

For more of the same send address to
E. WILLIAMS, Mont Clair, N. J.

New Patent.

PROTECTOR FRUIT JARS.

They are made air tight with certainty and ease.

Readily opened, without injury to the covers.

Each Cover will fit all the Jars.

Handsome in Style—Low in Price; they are all that are needed for use by Families or Fruit Preservers.

Send for Circular and Price List.

F. J. BODINE, Philadelphia, Pa.

Crystal White Blackberry.

Originated in Kentucky. **Very Delicious, Large Size, Productive**, and on account of its beautiful, glossy white and attractive appearance, very desirable indeed. $2 per doz.; $8 per 100. Also, a very **large** stock of **all** the **newer** and **old** sorts of **Small Fruits** at the **lowest advertised rates, and Express charges pre-paid.** ☞ Instructive Catalogues, (notice of which see Feb. No. of *Agriculturist*, under heading of *Noteworthy Catalogues*,) sent on receipt of 10 cents, also, *Wholesale List*. Address A. M. PURDY, South Bend, Ind.

GARDEN SEEDS.

OUR DESCRIPTIVE CATALOGUE

of every Standard and Improved variety of

Vegetable and Agricultural Seeds for 1867, with directions *for their Cultivation*, has just been published, and will be mailed *free* on application to

C. G. CRANE & CO., 30 Broad-st., Newark, N. J.
J. C. KUMERLE, Seedsman,
(formerly Brill & Kumerle.)

Every Stock Breeder Should Send for THE AMERICAN STOCK JOURNAL.

THE FARMERS' REGISTER AND JOURNAL OF FRUIT CULTURE, a reliable and practical monthly publication of 16 pages. Only 50 cents a year. Don't fail to send stamp for sample, and —— *Then subscribe.*

D. HESTON, Publisher,
511 Market-st., Philadelphia, Pa.

MAKE YOUR GRAPE VINES PAY.

FULLER'S

GRAPE CULTURIST.

New Edition, Revised and Enlarged.

BY ANDREW S. FULLER.

Mr. Fuller's work met the general want of a plain and practical treatise on grape culture. As it was based upon established principles, it at once took rank as a standard work. Most of the treatises that have appeared since are nothing more than Fuller modified and diluted. When the structure and mode of growth of the vine is once understood, all systems of training become plain, and one may be followed as readily as another. Mr. Fuller gives this knowledge of the vine most clearly, and illustrates it so plainly that no one can fail to understand it, *and for this reason his book has become remarkably popular, and has not been, nor is it likely to be superseded by any other work on the same subject.* The teachings of the work are all from actual practice, and the illustrations are mainly from growing vines. To bring this work up to the times in respect to varieties, a considerable portion of the matter has been re-written. An additional list of varieties, including synonyms, has been given, and important additions have been made all through the volume. Garden culture is treated as well as that of the vineyard, and the book is equally adapted *to the owner of a single vine or the one who has thousands of vines.* Well illustrated.

SENT POST-PAID. PRICE, $1.50.

ORANGE JUDD & CO.,
41 Park Row, New-York.

NEW GRAPES,

Of Iona, Israella, Adirondac, Strong Rooted Plants grown in borders at reduced prices.

Also, Concord, Delaware, Hartford, Prolific, Diana, Isabella, Catawba, and a general assortment of Fruit and Ornamental Trees. Send red stamp for price list. W. T. SMITH, Geneva Nursery, Geneva, N. Y.

Lilium Lancifolium.

Japan Lilies, all the varieties, strong bulbs, very cheap to the trade; also, other varieties of Lilies, &c. Prices on application.

FRANCIS BRILL,
590 Ferry Street, Newark, N. J.

VIOLA ODORATA.

I have several thousand of the double English sweet violets, which I will send, "post-paid," at the following rates:

Single Roots .... 50 cents.
Dozen " .... $1.25.

Money and plants at my risk.
Address S. P. WAKELEE, Rochester, N. Y.
Care JAMES VICK.

MY WHOLESALE and RETAIL CATALOGUE of Seeds and Fruit and Ornamental Trees, Shrubs, Evergreens, Grapes, Strawberries, &c., will be sent gratis to any address. Agents Wanted. Seeds and Plants carefully sent by mail, pre-paid, to any part of the United States and Canadas. B. M. WATSON, Old Colony Nurseries and Seed Establishment, Plymouth, Mass.

HARRISON, E. GOODRICH, GLEASON AND MONITOR Potatoes by mail, post-paid, 1 lb. of each, $1.50, or 4 lbs. of either for $1.

F. SUTTON, Beverly, Burlington Co., N. J.

GET WELL AND KEEP WELL.—Read the Advertisement of Herald of Health, page 149.

AMMONIATED PACIFIC GUANO.

The attention of Farmers and Agriculturalists is called to this article, as superior to anything else offered in the market. Equal to Peruvian Guano, and costing much less.

We offer this *fertilizer* in lots to suit all purchasers. A liberal discount made to the Trade.

Pamphlets with copies of Analysis by Dr. Liebig, of Baltimore, and Dr. Jackson, Massachusetts State Assayer, and testimonials from Agriculturalists, showing its value, and directions for use, can be obtained from

J. O. BAKER & CO., Selling Agents,
131 Pearl-st., New York.

Every Farmer Should Send for THE AMERICAN STOCK JOURNAL.

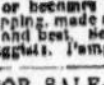

A Comfort, Blessing and Relief at SEELEY'S "Hard Rubber Truss" Establishment, 1347 Chestnut street, Philadelphia. This Truss cures the most difficult Ruptures, frees the cord from all pressure, never rusts, (the fine steel spring being coated with hard rubber,) breaks, limbers or becomes filthy, used in bathing, fitted to form, no strapping, made any power required, cleanest, lightest, easiest and best. Sent by mail or express, and for sale by all Druggists. Pamphlets free.

FOR SALE—Short Horn Heifer, 2 years old, calves in June—4 South Down Ewes, all in lamb, Brahma Fowls, $4.50 a pair; do. Eggs, $1 a dozen. L. N. I., Box 19, Claremont, N. H.

FOR SALE—A Fine Thorough-Bred AYRSHIRE Bull. ALFRED M. TREDWELL, Madison, Morris Co., New Jersey.

See Advertisement "ALL NURSERIES IN ONE," on page 152. Observe the low Prices.

1 8 6 7.

Rochester Commercial Nurseries,

ESTABLISHED, 1830.

W. S. LITTLE,

(FORMERLY H. E. HOOKER & CO.)

PROPRIETOR.

The New Circular of Prices *(by the dozen, 100 and 1000,)* **for the Spring of 1867—Just Published.**

I offer our usual large and fine assortment of every description of

HARDY TREES AND PLANTS,

including

Standard and Dwarf Fruit Trees, Vines, etc.,

and

Hardy Ornamental Trees and Shrubs, and Roses.

I mention the following

(Extract.)

SPECIALTIES & NOVELTIES.

☞ The following articles are particularly noted, because my stock of them is uncommonly good, on account of which, I believe, I can offer special inducements to purchasers:

Arbor Vitæ, Siberian and Hovell—A fine lot, one and two years old. See page 3.

Beech & Elm—PURPLE-LEAVED—Good Plants, of different sizes. See page 4.

Berberry—PURPLE-LEAVED—For hedges—a handsome stock. See page 5.

Deutzia, Crenata—FLORE PLENA—A new double-flowering Deutzia, perfectly hardy, and a decided acquisition. See page 5. Small 1 year old plants, for Nurserymen.

Grape Vines—DELAWARE LAYERS OF BEARING WOOD—A very large lot of *fine well rooted vines.*

CATAWBA—Strong Vines, 2 and 3 years old, in large quantity.

IONA, ADIRONDAC, and all the newer sorts—excellent vines, in large quantity.

Japan Quince—A very extensive stock of this fine flowering shrub, especially adapted for making beautiful hedges. See page 5.

Juniper, Irish—A great quantity of fine young Plants of this popular Evergreen. See page 5.

Pansy—A NEW DOUBLE-FLOWERING pansy; quite unique. Price, $3.00 per doz.

Peach—*Van Buren's Golden Dwarf—a real dwarf,* very hardy, and a decided acquisition. See page 8.

Pine, Dwarf—PINUS MONTANA—Good, stocky young Plants of this handsome Evergreen, now rapidly coming into favor. See page 5.

Smaller Plants, same age as the others noted, $15 per 100.

Roses—*Strong Plants, on their own roots, grown from cuttings,* (not root grafted.) One of the finest assortments of *Hybrid Perpetuals* that can be found. See above.

Address **WM. S. LITTLE,**
Commercial Nurseries,
Rochester, N. Y.

IMPORTED NURSERY STOCK

for sale by **C. RAOUX,** 42 Cedar-st., New York City.

APPLES, Common, Doucin and Paradise.
CHERRY, Mahaleb and Mazzard.
PEARS, 1 and 2 years.
QUINCE, Angers and Fontenay.
NORWAY SPRUCE, 2 and 3 yrs., transp'd, 1 foot high.
AUSTRIAN AND SCOTCH PINES.
ROSES, Dwarf and Standard, grafted, new and old sorts.
GLADIOLUS, Mixed.
HERBACEOUS PÆONIES, Named sorts.
NEW STRAWBERRY, Gloede's Perpetual Pine.

Keyes' Early Prolific Tomato.

This is the most distinct and valuable variety yet produced. 25 cents per packet.

MAUPAY'S SUPERIOR TOMATO.

Is of medium size, perfectly solid, average weight 9 to 12 oz. each. This variety does not sport, and for delicate flavor it is unapproachable. 25 cts. per packet.

WASHBURN & CO., Seed Merchants,
Horticultural Hall, Boston, Mass.

Goodrich Seedling Potatoes.

Early Goodrich, Harison, Gleason, Calico,—Four of the best varieties, 2 lbs. (or 32 eyes) of each, or *four lbs.* of either (including box), by mail, post-paid, *One Dollar.*—As we use

Wardwell's Patent Wooden Boxes

for sending plants, &c., by mail, we can easily send different varieties without danger of their being mixed together, or destroyed by the roughest usage, or longest detention of the mails. And for $1 you can get *four* varieties, and seed enough for from 5 to 9 bushels next fall—an opportunity seldom offered. Also, Grape Vines, Strawberries, Roses, Dahlias, and other plants, all warranted to go safely in Wardwell's Patent Wooden Boxes.

Potatoes by Express.—One peck of each of the best 4 varieties, $4; ½ peck of do, $2.50, in one box, carefully separated, also by the bushel. Other varieties at cheaper rates. Warranted true to name. Send for Plant and Potato Catalogue. Directions given for raising a large quantity (potatoes) from a little seed. Address

WARDWELL & CO., West Dresden, Yates Co., N. Y.

Early Goodrich Potatoes.

Gleason, Calico, Monitor, Harison, &c., &c., for sale by

R. H. ALLEN & CO.,
189 & 191 Water-st., New York.

Our Annual Catalogue of Field and Garden Seeds can be had on application.

See the Advertisement of AMERICAN STOCK JOURNAL, F. & S. B. A.

FRUIT AND ORNAMENTAL TREES

for the Spring of 1867.

ELLWANGER & BARRY have the pleasure of offering for Spring planting, their usual large and well grown stock of

Standard and Dwarf Fruit Trees.
Ornamental Trees, Shrubs and Plants.
Green-house and Hot-house Plants.
Bedding Plants, including the splendid large leaved Cannas, Colocasia, &c.
Pear, Quince, and Cherry Trees.

Each of these departments contains all of real value, old and new.

The following Catalogues, which give full particulars, will be sent pre-paid upon the receipt of postage stamps, as follows:

No. 1.—A Descriptive and Illustrated Catalogue of Fruits. 10 Cents.

No. 2.—A Descriptive and Illustrated Catalogue of Ornamental Trees, Shrubs, Roses, &c., &c. 10 Cents.

No. 3.—A Catalogue of Dahlias, Verbenas, Petunias, and select new Green house and Bedding Plants, published every Spring. 5 Cents.

No. 4.—A Wholesale Catalogue or Trade List. 3 Cents.

ELLWANGER & BARRY,
Mount Hope Nurseries,
Rochester, N. Y.

ORNAMENTAL TREES AND SHRUBS,

Evergreen Trees, Rhododendrons, &c.

Fruit Trees and Plants.

A large assortment of these at low prices, of fine form and well rooted, will be found priced in Catalogue of

PARSONS & CO., Flushing, N. Y.

---

100 VARIETIES OF BEAUTIFUL FRENCH HYBRID GLADIOLUS.

No description can give an idea of the brilliancy of color of the hybrid productions of the Gladiolus: and from their free flowering habit, and strong trusses of bloom, form the most desirable hardy flowering Bulbs of the garden. The proper season for planting in this latitude is May, June and July. They thrive well in any good garden soil, and are admirably adapted for clumping and bedding.

MY OWN SELECTION.

12 Named Varieties	$2.00
12 Fine Named Varieties	3.00
12 Extra Fine do.	5.00
12 Very Best do.	10.00
12 Mixtures	1.50
100 Mixtures	9.00

For sale by SAMUEL T. THORBURN, Seedsman,
46 Hudson-street, Albany, N. Y.

HUBBARD AND TURBAN.

My specimens of these two squashes received the two prizes offered for the best squash for family use, at the last exhibition at the rooms of the American Agriculturist. As this was open to competitors in all parts of the United States, the Hubbard and Turban can fairly be ranked as the two best varieties for table use, and hundreds of letters received this season speak of them as "the sweetest, dryest and best flavored squashes known." Both kinds can be kept through the winter. As the original introducer of these two squashes, I send packages of the purest seed in the market to any address, at 15 cents each.—Ounce packages, Hubbard, 30; Turban, 25.—Pound packets, Hubbard, $4.00; Turban, $2.50.—All warranted to reach the purchaser. *If any person, after trying these, does not find them to be what I represent, I will refund his money.*

JAMES J. H. GREGORY,
Marblehead, Mass.

SEED POTATOES.

Early Goodrich, Harison, Cuzco, Gleason, Coppermine, Calico, Monitor, Pinkeye-Rustycoat, White Peach Blow, Fluke, Union, Holbrook, Early Cottage, Sebec, and other varieties will be mailed, in packages containing 4 pounds of either variety, post-paid to any address, upon receipt of One Dollar. For larger quantities and Circular, Address

REISIG & HEXAMER, New Castle,
Westchester Co., N. Y.

GOODRICH POTATOES FOR ALL.

By using Wardwell's Patent Wooden Boxes, we can place these valuable Potatoes within the reach of all. We offer EARLY GOODRICH, HARISON, GLEASON and CALICO, FOUR of the very best varieties, warranted genuine, and each variety by itself—30 eyes of each for $1; 15 eyes of each for 75 cts.; 10 eyes of each for 50 cts., by mail, post-paid.—An outlay in cash of 10 or 15 cts. per bushel for Potatoes next fall.—Our Circular will also be sent free, with directions, &c. Address

WARDWELL & CO.,
West Dresden, Yates Co., N. Y.

Seed Sweet Potatoes,

$3.50 per bushel; $10 per barrel of 3 bushels. Plants in May and June $4 per thousand.

Strawberry Plants.

Wilson's Albany and Triomphe de Gand, $4; Russell's Prolific, $5 per thousand; Metcalf's Early, $1 per dozen, $6 per hundred—by mail, pre-paid. ☞ The potatoes or plants will be safely packed and delivered where ordered in New York city free of expense. Address

P. PHILLIPS, Matawan, Monmouth Co., N. J.

Keyes' Early Prolific Tomato.

The Earliest Variety yet Produced.

See advertisement in the Agriculturist for January. The greatest acquisition to our varieties of Tomatoes. Seeds, 25 cts. per packet. Address

HOVEY & CO., 53 North Market-st., Boston.

BLOOMINGTON NURSERY.

Osage Orange Hedge Plants.—Strong, selected, one year, packed in good order, 1,000, $3; 5,000, $13; 10,000, $25. **Apple and Pear Trees,** all sizes. **Early Richmond Cherry. Apple Root Grafts,** best quality. **Kittatinny and Wilson's Early Blackberry.**

Grapes.—Iona, Ives, Israella, Norton's, Concord, Hartford, Rogers' Hybrids, &c., &c.

Nursery Stocks, general assortment. **Sweet Brier Seedlings,** $1.50 per 100. **Peach Seeds,** fresh, frozen packed, $3 per bush. **Osage Orange and Pear Seeds.**

Evergreens, Shade Trees, immense stock, all sizes.

Althea, Dbl. Named, fine collection, 2 ft., 100, $12.

Roses and Dahlias, extra large, fine collection, **Green-house, Bedding and Garden Plants.** Send red stamp each for 3 Catalogues, Wholesale, Retail and Bedding Plants.

F. K. PHŒNIX, Bloomington, Ill.

JOHN SAUL'S

Catalogue of

BEAUTIFUL NEW AND RARE PLANTS,

For 1867, is Now Ready.

Many new and valuable Plants are offered this season for the first time.

Catalogues mailed on application.

JOHN SAUL, Washington City, D. C.

CHOICE SEED BY MAIL, PRE-PAID,

All in Papers, at 5 Cents Each.

BEETS—Extra Early Turnip, Bassano, and Long Blood, 80 cts. per lb., 10 cts. per oz. CABBAGE—True Early Wakefield and Red Dutch, $4.00 per lb., 37 cts. per oz.; Large Earliest York, Extra Large Drumhead, Premium Flat Dutch, Large Drumhead Savoy, $2.50 per lb., 25 cts. per oz. CARROTS—Long Orange, $1.10 per lb., 10 cts. per oz.; Early Horn, $1.50 per lb., 15 cts. per oz. CELERY—Red and White Solid, $2.50 per lb., 25 cts. per oz. CHICORY, $2.00 per lb., 25 cts. per oz. CUCUMBER, fine sorts, $1.25 per lb., 15 cts. per oz. LETTUCE, fine sorts, $2.50 per lb., 25 cts. per oz. MELONS, fine sorts, $1.50 per lb., 25 cts. per oz. ONIONS, fine sorts, $1.25 per lb., 20 cts. per oz. PARSNIP, best, long, smooth, white, 80 cts. per lb., 10 cts. per oz. RADISH, fine sorts, $1.00 per lb., 10 cts. per oz. SQUASH, $2.00 per lb., 25 cts. per oz. TURNIPS, best sorts, 75 cts. per lb., 10 cts. per oz. TOMATOES, fine sorts, $2.50 per lb., 25 cts. per oz., and all other seeds.

Also, Beans, Peas, Corn, Tree Seed and Flower Seeds of the choicest kinds. Priced descriptive catalogues of all useful Trees, Plants, Shrubs, Hedge Plants, Flower and Garden Seeds, will be sent to any address. Also, Wholesale Trade List. Agents Wanted. B. M. WATSON,

Old Colony Nurseries and Seed Establishment,
Plymouth, Mass.

THE NEW EARLY TOMATOES.

Including the new Californian Whortleberry fruited Tomato (now first offered), Keyes' New Early Prolific Tomato (Hovey), Tilden's Early Tomato, the New Extra Early Red Solid Tomato (fine), and the Early York Tomato, will be sent to any address, prepaid, for $1.00, or single for 25 cts. each. My new catalogue of new and choice Garden Seeds, including the true Mongri Radish from Japan (now first offered), with edible pods, three feet in length. Several new and very desirable sorts of Cauliflowers, Cabbage, Celery, Cucumbers, Egg Plants, Early Peas, Melons, Sweet Corn, and Turnips, will be sent to any address, prepaid.

The true Early Sebec, the Early White Forcing, and the Harison Potatoes, will be sent by mail, prepaid, in four pound packages only, for $1 each.

Wholesale List to the trade. Agents wanted.

B. M. WATSON, Old Colony Nurseries and
Seed Establishment, Plymouth, Mass.

The New Double White Clarkia,

with very large beautifully imbricated flowers (petals entire);—the new Solferino Balsam;—the new *Desmodium gyrans,* a remarkable whirling plant, with perpetually moving leaflets;—the new golden and silver margined Pansies;—the new Nemophila, with flowers two inches across;—a new hardy Salvia (chionantha), with large white flowers;—Wigandia Vigieri (finer than W. caracasana);—the new and charming Whitlavia gloxinioides;—the new Portulaca in all colors, as double as roses;—the new Gigantic Sunflower;—several new rapid growing annual climbers, with showy fruits and foliage, for the piazza, etc., and many other new Flower and Garden Seeds now first offered, with all the finest old and really useful sorts, will be sent prepaid by mail to any part of the U. S. or Canada. Priced descriptive catalogue of the above, containing the most select and practically useful Trees, Plants, Shrubs, Fruits, Evergreens, Hedge Plants, Bulbs, Roses, Climbers, and Seeds, will be sent to any plain address.

Wholesale List to the trade. Agents wanted.

B. M. WATSON, Old Colony Nursery and
Seed Establishment, Plymouth, Mass.

Gregory's Seed Catalogue,

Containing One Hundred and twenty-five varieties that I grew myself, besides many kinds imported from France and England, and grown by the best seed growers in the United States. Farmers and Gardeners will find in my Catalogue many new and rare vegetables, some of which are not to be found in any other Seed Catalogue. As the original introducer of the Hubbard Squash, Marblehead Mammoth Cabbage, Boston Curled Lettuce, and many other new vegetables, I invite the patronage of the public. Catalogues sent *gratis* to all. Those who purchased seed last season will receive it without writing for it.

JAMES J. H. GREGORY,
Marblehead, Mass.

NEW MAMMOTH PRIZE SQUASH.

Awarded the Silver Medal at the Mass. Horticultural Society. Weight, 145 lbs. Described by Mr. Meehan in Gardeners' Monthly, page 373, as perfect monsters in size. Per packet 25 cts.

WASHBURN & CO.,
Seed Merchants, Horticultural Hall,
Boston, Mass.

LATAKIA TOBACCO.

The Finest Smoking Tobacco Known.

Introduced by Bayard Taylor, and superior to the Cuba. Has the rich and aromatic flavor of dried Rose Leaves. Packets of Seeds, warranted true, sent free for 25 cents. Address

HOVEY & CO., 53 North Market-st., Boston.

GRAPE VINES FROM THE KNOX VINEYARDS.

The largest and best Stock we have ever offered, including all the Old and New Varieties of any merit.

What we do not, and what we do claim for our Vines:

We do not claim that they are superior to all other Vines in the market. Other propagators, with similar advantages, may produce equally as good.

We do claim that the quality of our Vines is unsurpassed by any in the Country, and that they will give entire satisfaction to the purchaser in their **growth and yield of fruit.** We found this claim on the following facts:

First.—Our Vines are grown from Mature Wood, taken from our bearing Vineyards, thus securing health and correctness. We use no green wood in propagating, and grow **Grapes as well as Vines.**

Second.—We start our Vines in propagating houses, and as early as the weather will admit turn them out into the open ground, where they are carefully cultivated during the entire growing season.

We regard this system of producing Vines as the very best, and much preferable to that of growing them under glass, with their roots cramped in pots.

We secure by our mode, healthy, stocky and well rooted Vines.

Third.—Our soil is peculiarly well adapted to the production of Vines of the best quality, and we use no stimulants to excite an unnatural growth.

THE CONCORD

did not need the strong endorsement it has received the past year, as the PEOPLE had already decided that it is THE Grape of America. But it is worthy of note that in addition to its continuance in well-doing, it has been awarded, without any effort or management on the part of its friends, the

GREELEY PRIZE

as the Grape of the greatest value. The eminent Pomologists who made the award took ample time and unusual pains to arrive at a correct conclusion, and however *interested parties* may demur, the PEOPLE are well satisfied with the decision. As evidence of this, at a late trade sale of vines—largely advertised all over the country—while other leading varieties would not sell, in quantity, at *one-third* the Catalogue prices, all the Concords offered were sold at twenty-three per cent. above Catalogue prices.

Our opinion of the Concord is well known, and we unhesitatingly re-affirm all we have said in its favor, and pronounce it the most valuable Grape in America yet tested. It is to be hoped that seedlings from it will take the highest rank among the Grapes of the country.

The proper place to determine the merits of a Grape is in the Vineyard, when in fruit.

For a number of years we have held on our grounds, during the fruiting season, Grape Exhibitions, which have been largely attended by the most prominent fruit growers of the country, all of whom, in their examination of our Vineyards, have been enthusiastic in their praise of the Concord. We refer to such men as Dr. Jno. A. Warder, Author of "*American Pomology;*" Geo. Husmann, Author of "*Grapes and Wine;*" Wm. Saunders, *Supt. of Gov't Gardens, Washington City;* Prof. G. Thurber, *Editor of American Agriculturist;* A. Thomson, of *Delaware;* R. E. Mason, of *St. Louis*, and many others.

Our **Grape Show** this Year will be on the 16th and 17th of October. **Strawberry Show**, 12th and 13th of June. Both promise to be of unusual interest.

The Concord is no longer on trial. If it were, overwhelming evidence could be produced in its favor from all parts of the country.

Propagators aware of its great popularity, and the immense demand there will be for Vines, are making every effort to increase their Stock.

Notwithstanding we publish that we will not part with any Cuttings—needing all for our own use—we have the most urgent orders for Wood.

William Griffith, of *North East, Pa.*, writes under date of Jan. 18th, 1867: "I want a portion of your immense Stock of Concord Wood, say 200,000 Cuttings."

As we sell no Wood, and have greatly increased our facilities for growing Vines, our customers may reasonably expect to be supplied.

Our Stock of Concords this season is very large and superior, which we offer on most favorable terms.

For further information send 10 cents for Catalogue.

We have also a large supply of

HARTFORD, CREVELING, IVES, RENTZ, ELSINGBURG, MAXATAWNY, DELAWARE, DIANA, ROGERS' HYBRIDS, IONA, ISRAELLA and ADIRONDACK.

Also a limited quantity of

MARTHA and BLACK HAWK,

(Seedlings of the Concord,) which we think will prove the **two most valuable new Grapes now before the public.**

For description of above, and much other valuable information on Grape Culture, send 10 cts. for Catalogue.

STRAWBERRIES.

Wishing to have the

JUCUNDA—OUR NO. 700,

The most valuable of all our Strawberries, tested as soon as possible very generally throughout the country, we will send Plants at the following Prices:

BY MAIL—$1 per dozen; $5 per 100.

BY EXPRESS—$40 per 1000; $100 per 3000.

All other desirable varieties for sale. Also

Raspberries, Blackberries, Gooseberries, Currants, &c.

All orders shall receive prompt and careful attention.

J. KNOX,

Box 155, Pittsburgh, Pa.

Marblehead Mammoth Cabbages!

As some cultivators have an impression that these cabbages cannot be fully matured outside of Marblehead, I invite their attention to the following list of weights to which they have been grown by some of my customers:

H. S. Terry, Crescent City, Iowa, has grown them weighing 40 lbs., measuring 56 inches around the solid head. Thos. A. Lambert, Beauharnois, C. W., exhibited three cabbages weighing respectively, 40, 42½ and 41 lbs. John W. Dean, St. Michaels, Md., has grown them weighing 37 lbs. S. M. Shuck, Preston, Minn., has raised them weighing 33 lbs. when trimmed. E. H. Kess, Eliza Green, Ind., has grown them weighing over 30 lbs. A. E. Garrison, Des Moines, Iowa, has raised them weighing 33 lbs. James E. Allen, Union Springs, N. Y., has grown them weighing 30 lbs., when stripped of loose leaves. Wm. Lee, Jr., Denver City, Colorado, has grown them weighing 45 and 50 lbs., as a penalty for which the miners of the Mountains call him the "Big Cabbage Man." Collins Eaton, Ogdensburgh, N. Y., has raised them weighing 50 lbs. Leonard Choat, Denver City, Col., raised one, which when trimmed of waste leaves, weighed 46 lbs. P. Sweeney, Loretto, Penn., has grown them weighing 4- lbs. Sam'l D. Ormsbee, Rolling Prairie, Wis., has raised them weighing 31 lbs. M. D. Clark, Elyria, Ohio, has grown them weighing 35 lbs. Chas. W. Oden, Little Sioux, Iowa, produced quite a lot which weighed from 30 to 60 lbs. Hundreds of others have written me that they have "taken all the prizes at the County Fairs." "Raised the largest Cabbage ever seen in the country." "Had astonished all their neighbors." "That in sweetness, crispness, and tenderness, they were unequaled." As the original introducer of the Mammoth Cabbage, I am prepared to supply pure seed in packages containing about 200 seeds, at 25 cents per package, 5 packages for $1, and larger quantities at a proportionate discount. Catalogue of over 200 varieties containing many new and rare vegetables, sent gratis to any address.

JAMES J. H. GREGORY, Marblehead, Mass.

COLLECTIONS OF FLOWER SEEDS.

100 Varieties of Annuals, Biennials and Perennials, for	$5.00
50 Varieties of Annuals, Biennials and Perennials, for	2.50
20 Varieties of Annuals, for	1.00
10 Varieties of Annuals, for	.50
20 Varieties of More Rare Annuals, for	2.00
10 Varieties of More Rare Annuals, for	1.00
20 Varieties of Choice Green-House Seeds, for	4.00
40 Varieties of Choice Green-House Seeds, for	7.00
20 Varieties of Hardy Biennials and Perennials	1.00
20 Varieties of American Seeds, for European Culture	2.00

ALL STRICTLY MY OWN SELECTIONS.

Fresh and true to name. Sent by mail for price named. For sale by SAMUEL T. THORBURN, Seedsman, 48 Hudson street, Albany, N. Y.

UNRIVALLED GARDEN SEEDS, of my own growing, and warranted A No. 1, for sale by FRANCIS BRILL. Catalogues gratis. 600 Ferry St., Newark, N. J.

SEND FOR CATALOGUE of STRAWBERRIES, RASPBERRIES AND BLACKBERRIES, which contains prices to suit the wholesale, prices to suit the retail, and $10 worth sent for $10 to those who wish a variety list. Also, leading varieties of Potatoes. Address THOS. C. ANDREWS, Moorestown, N. J.

Tomatoes and Potatoes.

MAUPAY'S SUPERIOR and TILDEN, the two best market varieties. Sent by mail in 25 cent packages. GOODRICH and other seedling Potatoes. A full assortment of Garden and Field Seeds of choicest quality. Apply for Circulars.

WILLIAM HACKER, Seed Grower and Importer, 460 Market Street, Philadelphia, Pa.

MARBLEHEAD MAMMOTH AND STONE MASON CABBAGE, (Gregory Seed,) for sale by SAMUEL T. THORBURN, Seedsman, 48 Hudson-st., Albany, N. Y. Price 25 cents per packet.

Potato Onion Sets!

Eleven Dollars a Barrel; Five Dollars a Bushel. JAMES J. H. GREGORY, Marblehead, Mass.

SUGAR CANE SEED.—Regular Sorgo, Liberian Oomseeana and Neenzana, best varieties. D. S. MESSLER & CO., 183 Market-st., Philadelphia, Pa. General Agents for Cook's Evaporators and Cane Mills. SEND FOR CIRCULAR.

$1 PER lb., SENT FREE BY MAIL.—Danvers Globe Onion Seed, Red or Yellow, of my own raising, warranted. Address J. HODGES, Barrington Centre, R. I.

Carrot and Mangold Wurtzel.

I have Long Red Mangold Wurtzel, Yellow Globe Mangold Wurtzel, and White Sugar Beet; also Long Orange and Improved Short Horn Carrot Seed—every seed warranted to be grown last season. *I grew them myself and know all about them.* The Carrot seed is extra clean, free from stick and the beard all off. Either of the varieties of Mangold Seed sent pre-paid to any address for $1.00 a pound. Long Orange Carrot, $1.25. Improved Short Horn, $1.37. Get *good seed, farmers!*—Catalogues, containing over 100 varieties of seed of my own growing, sent gratis to all.

JAMES J. H. GREGORY, Marblehead, Mass.

C. B. ROGERS,

Wholesale Dealer in Field and Garden Seeds, No. 133 Market-st., Philadelphia, Pa.

THE "THREE WARRANTS."—Please read my advertisement headed "Farmers and Gardeners."

JAMES J. H. GREGORY, Marblehead, Mass.

Vegetable and Flower Seeds.

Novelties and Specialties.

The largest collection ever offered in America. See Our New Amateur Guide, now ready, mailed free for 25 cts.

WASHBURN & CO., Seed Merchants, Horticultural Hall, Boston, Mass.

Strawberries and Small Fruits.

Stinger's Seedling Strawberry, a new variety of great excellence; Philadelphia Raspberry, and other Small Fruits. Circulars on application.

WILLIAM HACKER, Seed Grower and Importer, 460 Market Street, Philadelphia, Pa.

GRAPE VINES.

DELAWARES, 2 years old at special rates, very low—and all the other leading varieties.

J. W. HELMER, Lockport, N. Y.

Grape Vines by Mail,

AT THE FOLLOWING RATES:

IONA, three years old, $2.50 each.
" two years old, $2.00 each; $18 per dozen.
" one year old, $1.00 each; $10 per dozen.
" " " " No. 2, 75 cents each; $6 per dozen.

ISRAELLA, three years old, $2.50 each.
" one year old, $1.00 each; $10 per dozen.

ALLEN'S HYBRID, three years old, $2.50 each.
" " one year old, 75 cts. each; $7 per doz.

DELAWARE, three years old, $1.50 each.
" two years old, $1.00 each; $10 per dozen.
" one year old, 50 cents each; 4 per dozen.

DIANA, two years old, 50 cents each; $4 per dozen.

All raised from strong wood of bearing vines.

CHARLES S. MASON, West Hartford, Conn.

GRAPE VINES.—Strawberries, Raspberries and Blackberries, old and new varieties, in large or small quantities and at reduced prices. *No charge for packing and charges pre-paid*, all stock sent out warranted true to name. Send for spring Catalogue. HATFIELD'S FRUIT FARM AND NURSERIES, Box 210, Niles, Michigan.

Iona Vines for Early Fruiting.

EXTRA LAYERS OF IONA *for early bearing*, at $3 each, or $24 per doz. Also Iona and Israella, grown from single eye, and wood of both these varieties for propagation. Address A. BURNELL, Peekskill, Westchester Co., N. Y.

SING SING GRAPE VINES.

The Best in the Market.

All my large stock of No. 1 and No. 2, Iona and Israella Vines is sold, except a small quantity I have reserved to use in filling retail orders.

As has been the case every season, the demand *for really good vines*, has been beyond my ability to supply. That my vines sell so readily at *full rates*, argues well that the *quality* of vines offered will hereafter have much to do with their sale. Buy good vines at a good price, rather than vines advertised at reduced rates. You may be sure that with the present great demand for vines, all of good quality will be sought after at good prices.—Send for Price List.

J. F. DELIOT, Vine Grower, Sing Sing, N. Y.

Iona and Israella Grape Vines,

By the single vine or 10,000. In point of quality we challenge the country.

Mr. Charles Downing says of this stock: "The vines are certainly as fine, if not the finest one year old plants I ever saw."—Send for Price List, which will be found *satisfactory*.

Good wood for propagating.

BOLTON & ZUNDELL, Haverstraw, Rockland Co., N. Y.

GRAPE VINES
AT
REDUCED PRICES.

Iona No. 1, $35 per 100; $300 per 1000.
Delaware No. 1, $20 per 100; $150 per 1000.
Ives' Seedling, $15 per 100; $200 per 1000.
Norton's Virginia, $25 per 100; $150 per 1000.

These are really No. 1 plants, none having been selected from them to sell as extras.

We offer also a good stock of the smaller sizes of these sorts, as well as fine plants of almost all the other varieties of vines, and for prices refer to our Descriptive Catalogue of Grape Vines.

PARSONS & CO., Flushing, N. Y.

Adirondac Grape Nursery and Vineyard.

Superior Vines of one, two, and three years at reduced prices.

Adirondac, Iona, Israella, Allen's Hybrid, Concord, Creveling, Cuyahoga, Delaware, Diana, Hartford Prolific, Isabella, Loome's Honey, N. Muscadine, Rebecca, Rogers' Hybrid, Sherman, To Kalon, Maxatawny, and Union Village.

Vines securely packed (and if not too bulky) will be sent by mail, *prepaid, and at our risk*. Larger packages by Express, with additional vines to the probable amount of Express charges. Our New Spring Catalogue sent to all applicants.

JOHN W. BAILEY & CO.,
Plattsburgh, Clinton Co., N. Y.

GRAPE VINES.

	Hundred.	*Thousand.*
Ionas, Extra large	$100	$900
" No. 1, Extra fine	80	600
" No. 2, "	60	500
Israellas, Extra large	100	800
" No. 1, Extra fine	80	700
" No. 2, "	60	500
Adirondacs, No. 1	60	
" No. 2	45	
Delaware Layers for immediate bearing	60	

HUSTED & HAZELTON,
Delaware, O.

IONA GRAPE VINES.

RYDER & CO. (successors to J. F. Deliot & Ryder) now offer their remnant stock of Vines at such prices that those wanting good Vines cannot object. Vines from three to six feet before cut back. Price, $40 to $50 per 100. Also extra under glass wood, $30 per 1000 eyes; from vineyard, $20. Samples sent free on receipt of price. Sing Sing, N. Y.

GRAPES! GRAPES! GRAPES!

300,000 Concord, **100,000** Catawba from Vines never mildewed or rotted, 20,000 Hartford, 10,000 Delaware; Norton's Virginia, Diana, Clinton, and all other good sorts of Grape Vines, Currants, Raspberry, Strawberry, and other Plants, cheaper than anywhere else, for sale.

DR. H. SCHRODER, Bloomington, Illinois.

IONA GRAPE VINES, 2 years old, transplanted and grown in open air, of EXTRA size and quality. Samples at WHOLESALE rates, (SINGLE vines by MAIL,) $1.10 each.

A. HAMMOND, Nurseryman,
Geneva, N. Y.

1,000,000 Grape Vine Cuttings for Sale.

Norton's Virginia, 12 Dollars per 1000 Cuttings, by 10,000 or more, only 10 Dollars. Concord and other sorts cheaper. Send stamp for Catalogue and Essay on Grape Culture, to

DR. H. SCHRODER, Bloomington, Illinois.

The Clarke Raspberry.—The most valuable variety of the Antwerp class yet originated. Perfectly hardy—the greatest bearer—the best flavor and quality—large as the largest—bright crimson color—and will be the leading market variety. Send for Circulars giving full particulars and origin. Prices, $1 each by the 100 or more, by express; $15 per dozen; $1.50 each for less number, sent free by mail; cash with the orders. Address

ELIZUR E. CLARKE, New Haven, Conn.

Strawberry Plants.

Agriculturist, 12 plants, 50 cts.; 100, $3; 1000, $10; 10,000, $80.
Golden Queen, very large and fine, extra, $1 doz.; $5 100.
Hippawain, a monstrous berry, $1 doz.; $5 100.
Knox 700, true fruit very large, $1 doz.; $5 100.
Bond's Seedling, 6 inches in circumference, $1 doz.; $6 100.
Leaning's White, a splendid, white berry, $1 doz.; $5 100.
White Alpine, sweet enough without sugar, $1 doz.; $5 100.

The above 7 varieties have been selected from over 100 kinds, nearly all of them will weigh one ounce each. This is a splendid collection for family or market purposes. I will send the above 7 varieties, 1 doz. each, for $5, free by mail. All other desirable kinds can be furnished by the 100 or 1000 at low rates.

A NEW RASPBERRY.

Scarlet Seedling, perfectly hardy as far north as Canada. Fruit large, first quality, very firm, fine for market. Much better than the Philadelphia. 12 plants, $1; 100, $15.

Address WM. S. CARPENTER, 156 Reade-st., N. Y.

The Best Three Market Berries.

Plants by Mail Post-paid.

For $10 we will send to any Post-office in the United States:
12 Plants Philadelphia Raspberry.
8 " Wilson's Early Blackberry.
8 " Kittatinny "

Send P. O. Stamp for Catalogues.

WILLIAM PARRY,
Cinnaminson, N. J.

KITTATINNY BLACKBERRIES.

Now ready, young plants, warranted fresh and sure to grow with *fair treatment*—$2.50 per dozen, $15 per hundred, $120 per thousand.

Wilson's Early Blackberry,

Young plants, $1.50 per dozen, ready April 15th.
Send red stamp for Catalogue.

F. K. PHŒNIX, Bloomington, Ill.

STRAWBERRY PLANTS.

Strong, healthy plants, well rooted, carefully packed to carry safely.
Wilson's Albany, $5 per 1000. Send for Price List.

O. J. TILLSON, Highland, N. Y.

DURAND'S SEEDLING STRAWBERRY,

Will undoubtedly prove to be the best and most profitable variety yet known. Plants strong; blossoms, perfect; fruit, large, bright scarlet; flesh, very firm; flavor, excellent, very prolific; early, and continues long in bearing; will carry better than any other variety. Circulars with prices, &c., free.

FRANCIS BRILL,
500 Ferry St., Newark, N. J.

STRAWBERRY PLANTS.

Agriculturist, Jucunda, Lennig's White, New Jersey Scarlet, $1 per doz., $2 per fifty, $3 per hundred. Sent by mail post-paid. For other varieties and circular address

REISIG & HEXAMER, Newcastle, Westchester Co., N. Y.

9,999 SUBSCRIBERS WANTED TO SEND for $10 post-paid List of Berry Plants, offered in Feb. No., page 73, by JOHN S. COLLINS, Moorestown, N. J., or send for a 12 paged Descriptive Catalogue gratis.

THE PHILADELPHIA STRAWBERRY, $10 per 100; Jucunda, $20 per 1000; Agriculturist, $10 per 1000; French, Downer and Cutter, $30 for 10,000, and others at low rates. Send for Catalogue.

THOS. C. ANDREWS, Moorestown, N. J.

SEND ME **$10** BY MAIL, and I will guarantee to reach you by mail, 1 dozen each Metcalf, French, Agriculturist, Jucunda or 700, Russell and Iris Strawberries, 12 Philadelphia Raspberries, 4 Wilson Early and 4 Kittatinny Blackberries. Catalogue contains 11 other variety Lists, Wholesale Prices, Testimonials, &c., 12 pages, sent gratis.

JOHN S. COLLINS, Moorestown, N. J.

---

500 Plants by Mail for $5.

100 each of Agriculturist, New Jersey Scarlet, Byberry, Wilson's Albany and French's Seedling. 100 plants (*your own selection*) for $2. Warranted genuine and postage prepaid. P. SUTTON, Beverly, Burlington Co., N. J.

NATIVE EVERGREENS—Balsam Fir, Arbor Vitæ, Hemlock, White and Norway Pine, 5 to 12 inches high. $6 per 1000; $25 per 5000; $40 per 10,000. Packing free. For price of larger sizes, apply to

JOHN UECKE, Green Bay, Wisconsin.

NATIVE EVERGREEN PLANTS.
The following varieties, 5 to 12 inches high at $7 per 1000: Balsam Fir, White Spruce, Arbor Vitæ, White Pine, and Hemlock. Packing free.

JAMES A. ROOT, Skaneateles, N. Y.

SMALL NATIVE EVERGREENS at Wholesale. Address, from March 1st to June 1st, A. F. CHAPMAN, Tree Dealer, 144 Fulton-st., New York. Any other time Portland, Me. 100,000 Arbor Vitæ, 6 to 12 inches, at $3 per 1000.

100,000 ARBOR VITÆ, and other Hedge Plants; Apple, Pear, Quince, Cherry, Mahaleb, Paradise stocks. Price Catalogue now ready.

B. M. WATSON, Plymouth, Mass.

25,000 Osage Hedge Plants for Sale.

Strong, one year old. Address

H. M. ENGLE, Marietta, Pa.

ARBOR VITÆ PLANTS, 6 to 12 inches high, for sale at $5 per 1000, by

L. B. CHAPMAN, 51 Cortlandt-st., N. Y.

SOUTH DOWN CO.'S PATENT

SheepWashTobacco

THE BEST KNOWN REMEDY FOR

TICKS, SCAB, VERMIN & FOOT ROT,

should be used by all Farmers on

SHEEP, ANIMALS & PLANTS.

☞ This pure preparation has been successfully used for years, and never fails to produce the desired effect when used according to directions.

It will not injure the most delicate Animal.
It will improve the Quality and Quantity of Wool.
It kills TICKS on Sheep.
It cures SCAB on Sheep.
It cures all SKIN DISEASES on Animals.
It kills all VERMIN that infest Animals, Trees, Plants and Vines.

☞ For FOOT-ROT it is a sure cure, used as a poultice.

☞ ONE POUND of this Extract will make TWELVE GALLONS of Wash, and contains the strength of EIGHT POUNDS of TOBACCO, as prepared by farmers.

Sold by all Druggists and Country and Agricultural Stores.

JAMES F. LEVIN,
23 Central Wharf, Boston, Mass.

For sale by DUDLEY & STAFFORD, New York; BLISS & SHARP, Chicago; E. M. LIVERMORE, Cleveland, Ohio.

PURE CHESTER WHITE HOGS.
Send for Circular.

W. H. FURMAN, Cedar Rapids, Iowa.

THE AMERICAN STOCK JOURNAL.

Farmers' and Stock Breeders' Advertiser.

$50,000 worth of Premiums offered to Subscribers for 1867.
Only $1.00 a year.
Address N. P. BOYER & CO., Gum Tree, Chester Co., Pa.

Full Blood and Grade Alderney and Ayrshire Stock for Sale.

Persons wishing to purchase the very best Family Cows, or to improve the Stock on their Farms, are invited to examine my Herd, which now numbers One Hundred and Eighteen head of all descriptions, Cows, Heifers and Bulls.

THOMAS FITCH, Breeder, New London, Conn.

ITALIAN QUEEN BEES for Sale throughout the summer. Send for Circular to

M. QUINBY, St. Johnsville, N. Y.

FANCY FOWLS' EGGS OF MOST VARIETIES, PLATA DUCKS, birds and eggs, Aylesbury Ducks, eggs only. Send for Circular. A. M. HALSTED,

Agent, 68 Pearl-st., New York.

FANCY FOWLS.

Eggs from Brahmas, the second step from Imported Stock—live weight from 18 to 25 lbs. per pair, when mature; also Pure White Faced Black Spanish, Yellow Legged Leghorn, White Crested Black Poland, and White Call Duck at $1.50 per dozen. Golden Spangled Hamburg, $2.00 per dozen, boxed and delivered at express on receipt of price.

ALEX. RANKIN, Rochester, Mass.

BRAHMA POOTRAS, bred from stock weighing 24 lbs. per pair at maturity. Warranted pure. Can be seen on owner's premises. Price, $8 per pair; $12 per trio. Eggs, $2 per dozen.

J. M. HALSTED, 68 Pearl-st., New York.

EGGS FOR SETTING, from White-faced Black Spanish, Brahma, White Leghorn, Bolton Gray and Dominique Fowls, bred with care and warranted pure, at $1 per dozen. Address

N. A. SHUTE, Exeter, N. H.

EGGS from Brahma Fowls, weighing 26 lbs. a pair, live weight. Also, Eggs from White Leghorn Fowls, with yellow legs, pure bred. For sale by

HENRY VINE, Schenectady, N. Y.

BUFF COCHINS.

Pure Blooded Buff Cochins' Eggs for sale, $2.50 per dozen. Address CHAS. F. NETTLETON, Birmingham, Conn.

A FEW PAIRS choice Black Spanish, White Leghorn and Brahma Fowls, also trio imported Polands for sale, by G. W. FARLEE, Cresskill, Bergen Co., N. J.

PURE BLOOD WHITE CANTON and BRAHMA POOTRA EGGS for Sale, at $2.00 per doz., by

L. B. SPENCER, Claremont, N. H.

BRAHMA EGGS for Setting at $1.50 per doz.

B. F. HOLBROOK, Natick, Mass.

THE HOG BREEDERS' MANUAL.

A Treatise on Breeding, Feeding, and General Management of Hogs. Particulars of all Diseases, Remedies, &c. Sent free of postage for 25 cents. Every farmer should have a copy. Address N. P. BOYER & CO.,

Gum Tree, Chester Co., Pa.

ITALIAN BEES.

Extra Queens. The golden Italian Bees.

"KELLEY'S ISLAND APIARY."

Our Circular and Price List sent to all applicants GRATIS.

W. A. FLANDERS & Co., Shelby, Ohio.

Combing Wool Sheep and Berkshire Pigs for Sale. Send for Circular, L. CONVERSE, Bucyrus, O.

CHESTER WHITE PIGS FOR SALE.—Sent by Express to all parts of the U. S. For Circulars address H. TEMPLE & CO., Marshallton, Chester Co., Pa.

GOODYEAR'S INDIA RUBBER

GLOVE MANUFACTURING CO.,

WAREHOUSE, 205 BROADWAY, NEW YORK.
One door below Fulton street.
Western Warehouse, 417 North Fourth-st., St. Louis, Mo.
Factories, Naugatuck, Conn.

Manufacturers of and dealers in
INDIA RUBBER GOODS
of every description, including
RUBBER CLOTHING,
HOSE, BELTING AND PACKING,
BOOTS AND SHOES,
FINE VULCANITE ARTICLES,
COMBS AND FANCY ARTICLES,
DRUGGISTS' ARTICLES, etc., etc.,
And a full variety of everything
of RUBBER MANUFACTURE.

GEO. M. ALLERTON, Vice-President.
H. G. ALLERTON, Treasurer.
ROB'T S. WALKER, Secretary.

South Jersey Farms For Sale,

Atco, Camden Co., N. J., in a fertile, healthful and highly improving location, being located at the Junction of the Raritan and Camden and Atlantic Railroads, accessible by several daily trains to both New York and Philadelphia.

Apply to GEO. W. HANCOCK, Atco, Camden Co., N. J.
N. B.—First class Hotel accommodations.

A GOOD REFRIGERATOR.—Judge Storer, of Cincinnati, O., says: "The Zero Refrigerator gives perfect satisfaction. It has preserved meats, vegetables, milk and butter during the hottest months of our variable climate."

ALEX. M. LESLEY, Manufacturer,
No. 605 Sixth Avenue, New York.

SENT 3 MONTHS FREE.—THE AMERICAN STOCK JOURNAL. The Oct., Nov., and Dec. Numbers of 1866 sent free to all subscribers for 1867. Only $1.00 a year. Send stamp for a specimen copy and circular, with list of splendid premiums to Agents. Address

N. P. BOYER & CO., Gum Tree, Chester Co., Pa.

PERUVIAN GUANO SUBSTITUTE!

BAUGH'S RAW BONE Super-Phosphate of Lime.

BAUGH & SONS,
Sole Proprietors & Manufacturers,
Delaware River Chemical Works,
PHILADELPHIA, U. S. A.

For Corn, Oats, Potatoes, Garden Vegetables, and every Crop and Plant.

Especially recommended to the growers of **Strawberries, Raspberries, Blackberries, And All Small Fruits.**

BAUGH'S RAW BONE SUPER-PHOSPHATE OF LIME,

is very prompt in its action - is lasting in effect to a degree unattained by any [illegible] manure in the market. As a Substitute for Peruvian Guano and Stable Manure it is eminently a success, and is offered to the Agriculturists of the Northern and Eastern States as a fertilizer that will cheaply restore to the soil those essentials which have been drained from it by constant cropping and light manuring.

☞ Our NEW PAMPHLET "*How to Maintain the Fertility of American Farms*,"—[illegible] pages, giving full information in regard to the use of manure, &c., will be furnished gratis on application.

BAUGH BROTHERS & CO.,
GENERAL WHOLESALE AGENTS,
No. 181 Pearl-st. and No. 4 Cedar-st.,
NEW YORK.

TO FARMERS AND PLANTERS.

The Lodi Manufacturing Company, (Established since 1840,) having the exclusive control of all the night-soil of New York City, offer for sale their Celebrated Poudrette, warranted the best fertilizer for the price in this country. Experience has shown that it has no equal for Corn, Cotton, Tobacco and Vegetables. It prevents worms from destroying the seeds. It ripens the crop from two to three weeks earlier, and adds from ⅓ to ½ to the yield.

☞ It is of better quality and much finer than ever made heretofore.

Price, $2.00 per Barrel—Cash.

The Company are also manufacturing *Double Refined Poudrette*, as fine as flour, concentrated and free from nearly all extraneous matter—samples of which will be sent by mail on receipt of 3-cent stamp.

It is packed in new barrels and shipped without extra charge for package or cartage in New York City.

Price for the *double refined Poudrette*, $25 per Ton.

The Company's Farmers' Almanac, giving further particulars, will be sent *free* by addressing
THE LODI MANUFACTURING COMPANY,
66 Cortlandt-st., N. Y.

MILLER & SMITH'S STANDARD Super-Phosphate of Lime

is offered in the assurance that it is the best, and most economical *Fertilizer* in the market.

The *Manufacturers* introduce their **Super-Phosphate**, with the **guarantee** that it is *perfectly free* **from adulteration.**

The great superiority claimed over other Fertilizers in the market is:

FIRST, That it is manufactured chiefly from **Pure Bone.**

SECOND, That a sufficient quantity of acid has been used to convert the *insoluble* Bone into **Super-Phosphate of Lime.**

THIRD, That the Bone being **unburned** retains the **Ammonia**, and is a **true Raw Bone Super-Phosphate.**

For Sale by
WILLIAMS & TYLER,
SOLE AGENTS FOR THE MANUFACTURERS,
No. 129 Broad-st., NEW YORK.
No. 6 Commercial-st., BOSTON, Mass.

The American Stock Journal.

Farmers' and Stock Breeders' Advertiser.

A first class Monthly Journal, devoted to Farming and Stock Breeding. Each number contains 24 large double column pages, illustrated with numerous engravings.

Only $1.00 a year. Specimen copies free.

Address N. P. BOYER & CO., Gum Tree, Chester Co., Pa.

MIRTH FOR THE MELANCHOLY! Gravities for the Gay! Fun, Fact and Fancy six months for 25 cts. Address Humanism Magazine, Loudon Ridge, N. H.

GET WELL, AND KEEP WELL.—Read the Advertisement of Herald of Health, page 149.

WOODWARD'S ARCHITECTURE AND RURAL ART.

178 Designs. $1, post-paid.
Woodward's COUNTRY HOMES.
150 Designs. $1 50, post-paid.
Manual of the House.'
126 Designs. $1 50, post-paid.

Woodward's Record of Horticulture for 1866. Edited by A. S. Fuller, fully illustrated....$1.00, post-paid.

Fuller's Forest Tree Culturist. A new work on the cultivation and management of Forest Trees. Fully illustrated ....$1.50, post-paid.

Husmann's Grapes and Wine. A practical work on the Cultivation of the Native Grape and Manufacture of Wine, illustrated....$1.50, post-paid.

Horticulturist Almanac, 1867...10 cents, post-paid.

GEO. E. & F. W. WOODWARD, No. 37 Park-row, N. Y.

$2 50.

AGRICULTURE, NEWS AND LITERATURE.

FOR THE FARM AND FIRESIDE.

FOR **$2 50 A YEAR,**	YOU CAN GET BOTH THE **AMERICAN AGRICULTURIST** AND THE **WEEKLY EVENING POST.**
FOR **$4 00 A YEAR,**	YOU CAN GET BOTH THE **AMERICAN AGRICULTURIST** AND THE **SEMI-WEEKLY EVENING POST.**

The two journals, one monthly, the other *semi-weekly* or *weekly*, as the subscriber prefers, will furnish the different members of an intelligent family in the country with a full supply of interesting reading matter on agricultural and horticultural subjects, and keep them fully informed of all that occurs in the world of literature, art, science, politics, and what is spoken of and discussed in the great centres of civilization.

☞ Remit by Draft or Post-office Order to
WM. C. BRYANT & CO.,
PUBLISHERS OF THE EVENING POST,
41 Nassau Street, New York,
or, **ORANGE JUDD & CO.,**
PUBLISHERS OF THE AMERICAN AGRICULTURIST,
41 Park Row, New York.

GET THE BEST WEBSTER'S DICTIONARY UNABRIDGED NEW ILLUSTRATED

OVER 3000 FINE ENGRAVINGS.

10,000 *Words and Meanings not in other Dictionaries.*

A necessity to every intelligent family, student, teacher and professional man. What Library is complete without the best English Dictionary?

"Superior, in most respects, to any other English Dictionary known to me."—*Hon. George P. Marsh.*

"All young persons should have a standard Dictionary at their elbows. And while you are about it, GET THE BEST; that Dictionary is NOAH WEBSTER'S—*the great work, unabridged.* If you are too poor, save the amount from off your back to put it into your head."—*Phrenolog. Jour.*

"*Every farmer* should give his sons two or three square rods of ground, well prepared, with the avails of which they may buy it. Every *mechanic* should put a receiving box in some conspicuous place in the house to catch the stray pennies for the like purpose. Lay it upon your table by the side of the Bible; it is a better expounder than many which claim to be expounders. It is a great labor saver; it has saved us time enough in one year's use to pay for itself; and that must be deemed good property which will clear itself once a year. If you have any doubt about the precise meaning of the word *clear*, in the last sentence, look at Webster's nine definitions of the v. t."—*Massachusetts Life Boat.*

In one vol. of 1,840 Royal Quarto Pages.
Published by G. & C. MERRIAM, Springfield, Mass.
SOLD BY ALL BOOKSELLERS.

MR. TOODLE'S ELEPHANT HUNT. Price 5 cents.
DAY'S AMERICAN READY RECKONER. Price 50 cents.
AMERICAN HOME COOK BOOK. Price 30 cents.
MARTINE'S HAND BOOK OF ETIQUETTE. Price 50 cts.
MARTINE'S SENSIBLE LETTER WRITER. Price 50 cts.
All sent free of Postage by DICK & FITZGERALD, 18 Ann-st., New York.

TO ADVERTISERS.

Our readers will find the advertising columns of THE WEEKLY TRIBUNE exceedingly interesting, representing as they do nearly all the branches of business.

THE WEEKLY TRIBUNE'S circulation is steadily increasing and is greater than that of any other newspaper.

Notwithstanding its large size, the pressure of news is so great that we are compelled to allow but a small space for Advertisements. This is a manifest advantage to all whose notices appear in THE WEEKLY TRIBUNE, as they are conspicuous and mostly read with as much interest as the news.

That it is the most economical medium for advertising is well known, and conclusively proved by those whose advertisements frequently or continuously appear in its columns.

Circulating as it does among the thrifty, industrious body of the people, the Farmers, the Mechanics, the Merchants, the Manufacturers throughout the country, it is eagerly read by their wives, sons and daughters, so that it is reasonable to suppose each advertisement in it is read every week by at least half a million of the most intelligent portion of the community.

The great advantage that must accrue to any one who takes this method of making known his wants, his merchandise or manufactures, it is very easy to understand but can hardly be overestimated.

Every person having a farm for sale should advertise in THE TRIBUNE. Make the advertisement as short as possible, stating the advantages offered. Farmers wishing to purchase farms can always find chances by inserting a short advertisement in THE WEEKLY TRIBUNE.

Implement Manufacturers and Seedsmen find THE WEEKLY TRIBUNE especially valuable as an advertising medium, circulating, as it does, mainly among the better farmers in all parts of the country, in every State and Territory.

Terms for advertising in THE WEEKLY TRIBUNE are $1.20 per line for ordinary advertisements, and $2.00 per line for items in the news columns, prefixed by the word "Announcement." Nothing is inserted for less than $5.00. Cuts and Large Type charged double rates for space occupied.

SEND FOR A SPECIMEN COPY.

Address THE TRIBUNE, New York.

OUR SCHOOLDAY VISITOR.

A FIRST-CLASS ILLUSTRATED MAGAZINE.

32 large double column pages every month. Some of the ABLEST AMERICAN WRITERS contribute regularly. "A most valuable aid in the cause of Juvenile education."—*New York Tribune.* "We take pleasure in commending it."—*N. Y. Independent.* "One of the most attractive and cheapest periodicals published."—*Phrenological Journal.* "Variety enough to suit every shade of juvenile taste."—*Pittsburgh Commercial.* "The most sprightly and interesting magazine for the young."—*Christian Standard*, Cleveland, O. "It has no equal in our knowledge."—*Rural New-Yorker.* "The music is worth the subscription price."—*Canada Christian Advocate.*

☞ Terms $1.25 a year. To clubs $1.00. Valuable premiums for clubs. Specimen numbers ten cents. Agents wanted in every school, and at every post-office in the United States. The attention of Teachers is particularly invited. Address J. W. DAUGHADAY & CO., Publishers, 424 Walnut Street, Philadelphia, Pa.

JUST PUBLISHED.

SCHOOLDAY DIALOGUES.

A Book for the School, the Family, and the Literary Circle.

Compiled by ALEXANDER CLARK, A. M.,
Editor of OUR SCHOOLDAY VISITOR.

New Original Dialogues, Tableaux, &c.

The most entertaining and instructive book of Dialogues yet issued. 12mo. 252 pages. Price, post-paid, $1.50. A liberal discount to Agents.

J. W. DAUGHADAY & CO., Publishers,
424 WALNUT ST., Philadelphia, Pa.

THE AMERICAN NATURALIST;

A Popular, Illustrated, Monthly Magazine of Natural History.—Published by the Essex Institute.

Contents of Vol. 1, No. 2.—April, 1867.—THE MOSS-ANIMALS, OR FRESH WATER POLYZOA, *with a plate.* By Alpheus Hyatt.—THE FERTILIZATION OF FLOWERING PLANTS. By J. T. Rothrock.—INSECTS AND THEIR ALLIES, *with illustrations.* By A. S. Packard, M. D.—THE AMERICAN SILK WORM, *with illustrations.* By L. Trouvelot. Continued.—THE LAND SNAILS OF NEW ENGLAND, *with illustrations.* By E. S. Morse. Continued.—THE TARANTULA KILLERS OF TEXAS, *with a cut.* By G. Lincecum, M. D.—REVIEWS.—NATURAL HISTORY MISCELLANY.—CORRESPONDENCE.—NATURAL HISTORY CALENDAR. Birds, Reptiles and Insects.—REPORTS OF THE MEETINGS OF SCIENTIFIC SOCIETIES.—BOOKS RECEIVED AND GLOSSARY FOR THE NUMBER.

TERMS: $3 per year. Clubs supplied at liberal rates. Single copies, 35 cents.

EDITORS: ALPHEUS S. PACKARD, Jr., in connection with EDWARD S. MORSE, ALPHEUS HYATT, and FREDERIC W. PUTNAM. ☞ For Prospectus, etc., address
A. S. PACKARD, Jr., Salem, Mass.

The list of contributors embraces the best scientific talent in the country.

200 Farms in Virginia For Sale.

Settlement of Exclusively Northern Farmers.

Valley land, heavily timbered, well watered. Soil and climate unsurpassed for Grains and Fruits. Title perfect. Price only $5.00 per acre.
Send for Descriptive Circulars. Address
T. B. WIGFALL, Hillsville P. O.,
Carroll Co., Virginia.

See Advertisement, "ALL NURSERIES IN ONE," on page 152. Observe the low Prices.

(Business Notices $2.50 per Agate Line of Space.)

The Immense Profits

OF THE

TEA TRADE.

The Proprietors of "THE GREAT AMERICAN TEA COMPANY," became fully convinced, several years ago, that the consumers of Tea and Coffee were paying too many and too large profits, on these articles of every day consumption, and therefore organized THE GREAT AMERICAN TEA COMPANY, to do away, as far as possible, with those enormous drains upon the Consumers, and to supply them with these necessaries at the smallest possible price.

To give our readers an idea of the profits which have been made in the Tea trade, we will start with the American houses, leaving out of the account entirely the profits of the Chinese factors.

1st.—The American House in China or Japan makes large profits on their sales or shipments—and some of the richest retired merchants in this country have made their immense fortunes through their houses in China.

2d.—The Banker makes large profits upon the foreign exchange used in the purchase of Teas.

3d.—The Importer makes a profit of 30 to 50 per cent. in many cases.

4th.—On its arrival here it is sold by the cargo, and the Purchaser sells it to the Speculator in invoices of 1,000 to 2,000 packages, at an average profit of about 10 per cent.

5th.—The Speculator sells it to the Wholesale Tea Dealer in lines at a profit of 10 to 15 per cent.

6th.—The Wholesale Tea Dealer sells it to the Wholesale Grocer in lots to suit his trade, at a profit of about 10 per cent.

7th.—The Wholesale Grocer sells it to the Retail Dealer at a profit of 15 to 25 per cent.

8th.—The Retailer sells it to the consumer for *all the profit he can get.*

When you have added to these *eight* profits as many brokerages, cartages, storages, cooperages, and waste, and add the original cost of the tea, it will be perceived what the consumer has to pay. And now we propose to show why we can sell so very much lower than small dealers.

We propose to do away with all these various profits and brokerages, cartages, storages, cooperages, and waste, with the exception of a small commission paid for purchasing to our correspondents in China and Japan, one cartage, and a small profit to ourselves—which, on our large sales, will amply pay us.

Some parties inquire of us how they shall proceed to get up a club. The answer is simply this: Let each person wishing to join in a club, say how much tea or coffee he wants, and select the kind and price from our Price List, as published in the paper or in our circulars. Write the names, kinds, and amounts plainly on a list, and when the club is complete send it to us by mail, and we will put each party's goods in separate packages, and mark the name upon them, with the cost, so there need be no confusion in their distribution—each party getting exactly what he orders, and no more. The cost of transportation the members of the club can divide equitably among themselves.

The funds to pay for the goods ordered can be sent by drafts on New York, by Post-Office money orders, or by Express, as may suit the convenience of the club. Or, if the amount ordered exceeds thirty dollars, we will, if desired, send the goods by Express, to *"collect on delivery."*

Parties getting their Teas from us may confidently rely upon getting them pure and fresh, as they come direct from the Custom House Stores to our warehouses.

The Company have selected the following kinds from their stock, which they recommend to meet the wants of clubs. They are sold at Cargo Prices, the same as the Company sell them in New York, as the List of prices will show.

Hereafter we will send a complimentary package to the party getting up the club. Our profits are small, but we will be as liberal as we can afford. We send no complimentary package for clubs of less than $30.

All goods sold are warranted to give satisfaction.

PRICE LIST:

YOUNG HYSON (Green), 80c., 90c., $1, $1.10, best $1.25 per pound.

GREEN TEAS, 80c., 90c., $1, $1.10, best $1.25 per pound.

MIXED, 70c., 80c., 90c., best $1 per pound.

JAPAN, $1, $1.10, best $1.25 per pound.

OOLONG (Black), 70c., 80c., 90c., best $1 per pound

IMPERIAL (Green), best $1.25 per pound.

ENGLISH BREAKFAST (Black), 80c., 90c., $1, $1.10, best $1.20 per pound.

GUNPOWDER (Green) $1.25, best $1.50 per lb.

P. S.—All towns, villages, or manufactories, where a large number of men are engaged, by CLUBBING together, can reduce the cost of their Teas and Coffees about one-third by sending directly to the

GREAT AMERICAN TEA COMPANY,
31 and 33 Vesey-Street.,
Post Office Box, 5,643 New-York City.

☞ We call special notice to the fact that *our Vesey Street Store* is at Nos. 31 and 33 Vesey Street, a *large double store.*

From Moore's Rural New Yorker.

THE GREAT AMERICAN TEA COMPANY.

EDS. RURAL NEW-YORKER:—Seeing that the Great American Tea Company advertise extensively in your columns, I thought it would not be improper to inquire of you concerning them,—whether they are sufficiently reliable for farmers to depend on them for their teas,—whether they have a large amount of capital in it, or not, &c. Or, is it one of the many humbugs with which our country is infested now-a-days? Please answer through the RURAL, and you will greatly oblige many of its constant readers.—M. W., West Liberty, Iowa, Dec., 1866.

REMARKS.—The above inquiry was received some weeks ago, and although we were confident the Company alluded to was reliable, we wished to "make assurance doubly sure," and therefore wrote to an intelligent friend in New York city for information on the subject, inclosing the note of M. W. To our letter of inquiry we have received substantially this reply:—"I am confident the Great American Tea Company is '*reliable*' in *every sense* of the word. The Company has, I believe, *eight* large stores in this city and Brooklyn. It sells, probably, one third of all the tea imported in New York. In furnishing farmers by the club system, every pound of tea is warranted to give satisfaction, or money returned. Satisfaction is always given, so far as it would appear from the testimony of the subscribers to the religious papers of this and other cities, and the Company is indorsed and recommended by the editors of the same papers, and other influential journals. I learn that nearly fifty persons, from the offices of these papers, are buying constantly of the Company, and you know printers and editors are not likely to patronise humbugs. If any person is fearful that he will not be treated fairly by the Company, let him write to any one of the thousands of persons whose names have been published as its customers. I have taken time to find out that the statements here made are correct."

In confirmation of the statement of our correspondent, we will only add that several prominent religious and other journals of New York strongly indorse and commend the Great American Tea Company, and that, though we have advertised it for months, we have never received a complaint from any of the large number of RURAL readers who must be its customers. We therefore feel like commending the Company as eminently reliable and worthy of confidence.

On page 153 of the *Agriculturist*, the Company publish their mode of doing business, and other matters interesting to consumers of Teas and Coffees. It is worthy of perusal.

COAL.

The subscriber respectfully informs parties wanting Coal the ensuing season, that he personally attends to filling orders, *free of charge*, for all the best kinds of

AMERICAN OR FOREIGN COAL,

on the market, to suit the various purposes they are designed for, at the lowest wholesale prices.

Purchases made at the PUBLIC AUCTION SALES on a small commission.

GEO. W. PECK, Broker,
110 Wall-street, New York.

A NEW GRAPE.

SALEM.

The subscriber now offers for sale for the first time the above grape, named SALEM from the place of its origin. It is a variety considered not only superior to any of the former well-known numbers, but also to any hardy grape at present before the public, combining, as nearly as possible, every quality desired in an out-door grape; being one of the hardiest, healthiest and most vigorous of vines, and producing enormous crops of beautiful and high-flavored fruit.

Like the other well-known kinds, Nos. 4 and 15, this is a hybrid between the native and Black Hamburg; bunch large and compact; berry large as Hamburg, of a light chestnut or Catawba color, thin-skinned, perfectly free from hard pulp, very sweet and sprightly, with a most exquisite aromatic flavor, not equalled by any other out-door grape for wine or table; as early as Delaware or Hartford, having never failed to ripen in the most unfavorable season for the past six years.

Taking all its qualities into consideration, earliness, hardiness, and great vigor of vine, size and quality of fruit, it is pronounced by a few of the best judges who have tried it to have no equal among all the numerous varieties now before the public; and I can, with confidence, recommend it as the best of all my collection, and now offer it for the first time.

E. S. ROGERS,
Salem, Mass.

NOTICE.

The subscriber would here state that he has disposed of his entire Stock of Vines and Wood of the Salem Grape to J. L. Waring, of "Amenia Vineyard," Amenia, Dutchess County, N. Y., to whom all orders for the same must hereafter be addressed.

E. S. ROGERS.

Salem, Mass., March 2, 1867.

The undersigned will dispose of a few layers of the Salem, with two eyes, at $5 each, and next autumn be prepared to supply One Year Old Vines in quantity.

The demand for this valuable Grape will be large, it is therefore advisable for those who wish to secure them to apply early.

J. L. WARING,
Amenia Vineyard,
Amenia, Dutchess County, N. Y.

MISSOURI REAL ESTATE for sale or Exchange for property in or near New York city. Address J. M. COVINGTON, Office of the Scientific American, 37 Park Row, New York.

SPRING VETCHES—For sale by
SAMUEL T. THORBURN, Seedsman,
40 Hudson-street, Albany, N. Y.
Price $5.00 per bushel; 20 cents per quart.

PEACH TREES.—Fine Trees of the best sorts, $100 per 1000. PARSONS & CO., Flushing, N. Y.

IONA VINES.

All who have read our article, published as advertisement in the three last numbers of the *Agriculturist*, have had reason to see that the Iona Grape must soon supersede all others for all purposes. Like the famous Pinot of France and Germany, it gives good results wherever any good grape will thrive, and, like that, it combines all of the excellent qualities to be found in the best grapes of any country. In size and productiveness it is entirely unlike the Pinot. That is small and unproductive, and does not permit of that generous treatment generally designated as "high culture," by which its productiveness might be increased.

The Iona is large and extremely productive; and although thriving under the most moderate culture, is as well able to bear generous treatment, with the best results, as the Delaware. This has been fully shown by extensive trial in all parts of the country. A full statement of its unequaled wine-producing qualities would require an extended essay. No grape but the Delaware can stand one moment in comparison with it, and that falls far below it. This is fully admitted by every wine-maker who has taken pains to become informed on the subject. Excellent wine, like that which brings seventy-five dollars per dozen at wholesale, can be made from it in every *family* that will provide the grapes.

Under the prescribed conditions of treatment, which are plain and simple, and just those that all grapes require, it is the most constant in the production of thoroughly ripened crops of any grape in cultivation, and has often attained full success by the side of Concords that have failed. It ripens as early as Delaware, and earlier than Concord.

The plants that I offer for gardens are better and cheaper, probably, than will again be offered. Their quality is unapproachable by any in market, and the quality of my vineyard vines, and their prices, are such that few who see them fail to purchase.

There can not be a more opportune time than the present for the purchase of vines, and the vine to plant is the Iona. If those offered at trebly reduced prices are good vines, buy them at once; the country has need immediately of one hundred times as many as are now for sale, to banish false wines, and introduce true wines in their place.

But to learn whether mine are not the cheapest in the market, send for samples, or call and examine my stock. I promise to make very advantageous trades; and nearly all who have called, after thorough examination elsewhere, have practically admitted it by making large purchases. *My largest sales have been to persons who have looked in vain for vines of satisfactory quality at "reduced rates."*

Send two cents for pamphlet and price list, with inducements to clubs, and engravings of Iona and Israella. Manual of the Vine sent for 50 cents.

C. W. GRANT,
Iona, near Peekskill, N. Y.

FROM HENRY WARD BEECHER.

BROOKLYN, Feb. 7, 1867.

W. L. BRADLEY, BOSTON:

DEAR SIR: I tried several barrels of your XL Superphosphate of Lime during the season of 1866, on my farm at Peekskill. The soil is a sandy loam, on a clay and gravel subsoil. I found it to be excellent upon all garden vegetables, peas, beets, lettuce, cabbages, &c.

The onions, of which I raised several acres, were so much influenced by it, that the difference between those which had received your Phosphate and those on which I had used another favorite brand was distinguishable at a long distance off. I used it upon grass with very satisfactory results.

My foreman, T. J. Turner, who more particularly noticed the detailed effects, speaks very highly of it.

If its quality is faithfully kept up to the standard, it can not but satisfy every reasonable expectation.

HENRY WARD BEECHER.

Manufactured by W. L. BRADLEY, Boston, and sold by all Dealers.

McCLEES, LEFFERTS & Co.,

100 Beekman Street, N. Y.,

Manufacturers of Galvanized, Best Charcoal, Best Refined and Common Sheet Iron.

Iron Wire of all descriptions, made of the Best Refined Charcoal Iron.

GALVANIZED WIRE

For Fences, Grape Trellis, Clothes Line, and Garden purposes.

GALVANIZED STAPLES.

THE CHRISTIAN.

This is a large, live, eight-page MONTHLY religious and family PAPER, containing sermons, tracts, tales, sketches, poetry, MUSIC, pictures, etc., suited to OLD and YOUNG. LARGE PRINT, good paper, no controversy, sectarianism, politics, puffing, pills, or patent medicines. A healthy family sheet. ONLY 60 CTS. A YEAR. TEN COPIES FOR $5. THREE SPECIMENS sent for 10 CTS. Also, 100 new, stirring, practical tracts for $1, post-paid. Address all orders to H. L. HASTINGS, SCRIPTURAL TRACT REPOSITORY, No. 19 Lindall st., Boston, Mass.

AGENTS wanted for Hum' patent scissors sharpener, and Hum' patent knife sharpener—articles wanted in every family. Samples sent by mail for 50 cents each. Address

PECK & SEYMOUR,
13 Gold-st., New York.

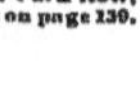

G. E. & F. W. WOODWARD, No. 37 Park Row, N. Y. See advertisement of Books on page 139.

AMERICAN AGRICULTURIST

FOR THE

Farm, Garden, and Household.

"AGRICULTURE IS THE MOST HEALTHFUL, MOST USEFUL, AND MOST NOBLE EMPLOYMENT OF MAN."—WASHINGTON.

ORANGE JUDD & CO., PUBLISHERS AND PROPRIETORS. Office, 41 Park Row, (Times Buildings.)

ESTABLISHED IN 1842. Published also in German at $1.50 a Year.

$1.50 PER ANNUM, IN ADVANCE. SINGLE NUMBER, 15 CENTS. 4 Copies for $5; 10 for $12; 20 or more, $1 each.

VOLUME XXVI—No. 5. NEW-YORK, MAY, 1867. NEW SERIES—No. 244.

THE MOOSE—MALE AND FEMALE.—(*Alce Americanus.*)—*Drawn and Engraved for the American Agriculturist.*

This is the largest of the deer family, as well as the most ungainly and awkward. It has none of the grace of other deer, but moves its ponderous body (weighing often ten or twelve hundred weight) with a plunging, reckless gait, often, it is said, meeting with mishaps, and falling from treading on its own feet. The forests of Maine, Northern New York, and Michigan, are its southern limits. The Elk of Europe and Asia (*Alce malchis*) is closely allied to the Moose, but a distinct species. The animal we call Elk should be called the American Stag, and the Moose is really the American Elk. The form is well shown in the engraving. Very high at the withers, and sloping to the tail, the fore legs long and stiff, the head enormous, ears large, the nose and upper lip pendulous, the horns flat, palmated, ending in numerous tips, and very large. The Moose is a semi-arctic and semi-aquatic animal, feeds upon water plants, moss, and twigs, and remains in winter in what are called "yards," where the snow is kept trodden down. The males are called bulls, and the females cows; they are hunted in canoes upon the lakes, or on snow shoes, when deep snows impede the going of the animal. The flesh and hide are both of value, but as a general thing the animal is more hunted for sport than for profit. They are taken in pit-falls also and by nooses. The strength of the animal is in proportion to its size, and its speed is very considerable. The Moose, as well as its European congener, has been repeatedly tamed, and, like the rein-deer, made to draw wagons and sledges. During the breeding season, however, the males become utterly unmanageable and so dangerous that their use has to be dispensed with. We find no record of the use of emasculated animals, but see no reason why they might not be made as docile as oxen, while at the same time they would be profitable for their meat, as they feed on a great variety of coarse herbage, green and dry. Domestication would doubtless also change their fierce nature. It seems a pity that so valuable an animal should become extinct.

Contents for May, 1867.

INDEX TO "BASKET," OR SHORTER ARTICLES.

Peruvian Maize.—We learn from Mr. E. G. Squier, that he ordered a supply of the Peruvian Maize, (see p. 219, 1866,) as he supposed in abundant time for it to arrive early this spring. Up to this time we have heard nothing further of it. If it does not come by or before the first of May, it will be too late to give it a fair trial this year, which we shall very much regret.

Back Volumes Supplied.—The back volumes of the *Agriculturist* are very valuable. They contain information upon every topic connected with rural life, out-door and in-door, and the last ten volumes make up a very complete library. Each volume has a full index for ready reference to any desired topic. We have on hand, and print from stereotype plates as wanted, all the numbers and volumes for ten years past, beginning with 1857—that is, Vol. 16 to Vol. 25, inclusive. Any of these volumes sent complete (in numbers) at $1.75 each, post-paid, (or $1.50 if taken at the office). The volumes neatly bound, are supplied for $2 each, or $2.50 if to be sent by mail. Any single numbers of the past ten years will be supplied, post-paid, for 15 cents each.

AMERICAN AGRICULTURIST.

NEW-YORK, MAY, 1867.

April is called "fickle, frail and fair,"—"tearful" and "sighing."—We talk about April showers and May flowers, and about smiling and blushing May, as if April were the cold and rainy month in which sunshine was the exception and drizzly spring rains the rule—and even that rule not to be depended upon. Not so. May is the fickle sister, whose smiles are capricious, whose promises are frail. We usually have fine dry weather in April, which enables us to finish up a great deal of work and get ready for May planting. So it has been this year. The spring was very late in March, but the warm weather early in April dried the ground, enabled farmers to plow, haul manure, and get their spring grain in very well. We fear in consequence of so fine an April, a cold May, but the long lingering of winter gives hope against this. Nevertheless we must repeat our caution against too early planting the main crops of Indian corn, beans and roots, except potatoes, for you will lose seed, by its rotting in the ground; or the weeds will get such a start that carrots, parsnips, mangel wurtzels or beets will be choked, if they come up, before they can be hoed. Sow all such seeds when the ground is dry and warm, and not before.

Take care to cultivate no more land than you can do well by, without working yourself to death, or overworking either teams or men. This will secure thoroughness, and larger profits if not larger crops. Make provision for work to fill up all the "spare time," so that you will not have any. That is—for rainy days, and days when the ground is wet and can not be worked. A few roods of carrots or beets, for stock, are excellent for this, because they *must* be hand-weeded and thinned out on damp and rainy days. Give men and teams always good long "noon spells," but exact promptness to begin work, and willingness to stick to it and do it well.

To "Gentlemen Farmers" let us say—know how to handle every tool, and if you do not now, practice "on the sly" until you can show any awkward man how he should do his work. You gain much by beating a workman at his own trade, and it is very easy to do it, if you have a modicum of knack and common sense. You may almost always calculate with certainty, on mind against muscle, with a quill or a crowbar. Learn to judge accurately and justly of a good day's or hour's work, not by what you can do yourself, but by what an active, thorough man can do, when you are with him. Bear down as hard as you please on the shirks; they will wince, but stand it, and perhaps do better. If you are unjust to a faithful man, he will be very apt to "flare up" and quit, as he should, if he can not serve you without lowering his own self-respect. Elevate your men, by your just dealings with them, interest in them, and care for their improvement. Furnish them reading for Sundays and evenings. Give them such papers as this, and such books as the Agricultural and Horticultural Annuals, Herbert's Hints to Horse-keepers, Johnson on Peat, the Hop, Flax, Onion or Tobacco culture handbooks, etc., etc. point out particular views as expressed in other books, which you use as guides to practice.—The practice will surely pay.

Hints About Work.

What would you give if your land—all of it—were now dry enough to plow? Would it not be worth $5 an acre to you more this very year and every year? Five dollars is ten per cent. interest on $50, which it would cost to drain it, grade it, and put it in excellent shape—and after all in nine cases in ten, $5 would not represent half the profit. The article on draining in the Agricultural Annual is full of good ideas and suggestions to any one who wishes to be thorough in his farming, and this is the season when a man's needs press upon him the consideration of this very important subject.

Spring Grains.—It is seldom worth while to sow oats, barley or spring wheat, unless it can be done during the dry warm spells which we always get, some time in March or April. This weather sometimes lingers into May, being broken up more or less, and sometimes comes all together, four or five weeks of it. If you are caught by cold rains, coming the last of April or early in May, let the spring grains go, and put something else in the land. Corn manured in the hill, or, if the soil is fit, roots of some kind. This is a general rule, but when the rains are early and apparently over before the middle of the month, good crops of wheat are occasionally obtained, and oats may be profitably sown when straw for fodder is the principal desideratum, but the early sown always yield the best grain.

Root Crops.—See hints given last month in regard to roots that will bear early sowing. In field culture do not put the drills too close, 20 inches is near enough for carrots, and 2 feet for mangels and beets. The soil for *Parsnips* must be deep and well enriched throughout—no shallow culture will do at all. They do well in heavy, clayey loam. Sow when the ground is warm, in drills, 20 inches to 2 feet apart, according to the depth and richness of the soil, and the size to which the roots will grow. The tops will in a measure correspond, and should have space to expand. Delay sowing *Rutabagas* (Swedish turnips) until June. All these crops should be hoed by horse power; and there are several horse hoes, well adapted to the purpose. Weeding in the drills, and thinning the very young plants, must be done by hand, and on rainy days, or towards night. On fair days, only when the ground is moist. Should the hot sun strike the young plants within 12 to 15 hours after the soil about them has been disturbed, a great many might disappear at once. Never let the weeds get a start, if you do, a dry hot spell in June would almost entirely prevent proper weeding, and the crop would be lost. Soak beet seed in hot water, keeping it blood warm 24 hours.

Corn.—Be in no hurry about planting. There is a tendency to err in planting too large varieties, and those that need a long season. This leads to planting too far apart. On soils properly manured 3½ × 3½ feet is far apart enough for the hills of our largest flint corn, and 4 feet each way, right for dent corn. The little northern varieties should be much closer; sown in drills, 3 feet apart, and stalks left 8 inches apart in the drills, very heavy crops are often obtained. The roots of corn wander a good way, hence on only moderately enriched land the plants must stand further apart. Corn rarely begins to grow before the middle of June, and if well up by the last of this month or the first of next, it is well enough.

Broom Corn.—Use a little manure in the hill, planting on a good sward. Lime slaked with brine is advisable, harrowed in at the rate of about 20 to 50 bushels to the acre, if the sod is infested with wire or cut worms. Ashes and plaster mixed, in the hill, or dropped upon it, is a good application. The culture is, in short, much like corn, except more seed is sown. The plant does not do so well on stiff soils, and should not be exposed to early frosts. The hills should stand 2½ feet apart, in rows 3 feet apart. Plant before the main crop of corn (1st to 15th of this month).

Flax.—Go through and weed carefully by hand, when the plants are 2 to 4 inches high, let the weeders be bare-foot; children are best employed.

Hemp may be sown any time this month. Use 4 to 6 pecks of heavy, bright seed, for broad-cast sowing. Be thorough in keeping the grass down.

Cotton.—See articles on culture in this and previous numbers.

Castor Bean.—An article on the cultivation of this plant on page 171 will repay perusal.

Tobacco.—The seed-bed, which, having been well prepared in a warm place and rich soil, will be just now showing its covering of minute round leaves, close to the surface, should be watered with dilute liquid manure, from the barn yard, or with guano water, very dilute, and any weeds, showing themselves, should be pulled out. Tobacco sowed May 1st will be a little late, but will do very well to fill out after the first planting—as is usually needed.

Potatoes.—See hints given last month. Late planted potatoes often escape rot, but are sometimes the worst victims. The newer kinds, as a rule, are least affected, but they succumb after a few years.

Cows.—Consider the advantages of having beets or parsnips to feed the cows before the pastures are ready for grazing, and make sure of some for next year. New milch-cows need succulent food before grass comes, but do not hurt the pastures for all summer by feeding them off too early in the season.

Calves may be let run as soon as they can get a "bite" of grass, and being fed regularly besides, they will pick up a good part of their living and improve fast on skim-milk and a little meal.

Brood must not be allowed to fall away in the least, but their meal, if anything, be increased. At first, let them have but an hour or two a day at grass, making no difference in their feed. Gradually increase the grass and decrease the meal.

Horses and Working Oxen, should have well fitting harness and yokes, long noons to feed, and hard work every day. Plan to keep them employed or they grow soft, and you lose the cost of their keep.

Sheep.—Shear, without washing, in May, the earlier the better, if you can give the naked animals protection against storms. There is much less risk of hurting the sheep, than is incurred by washing them. The flock should be thoroughly and carefully "tagged," and the clip may be tub-washed in a Doty washing machine, to advantage. Thus a large quantity of excellent manurial liquid is saved for the garden, and with merinos, this is quite an object, on account of the great amount of yolk, rich in potash. Do not change suddenly from hay to grass.

Soiling.—Sow corn in drills 3 feet to 3½ feet apart, dropping about 12 kernels to the running foot, on well manured sod land, laid *flat*. This will furnish either green fodder for cows in dry weather, or it may be cut and cured for winter feed, for either of which it will pay better than almost any fodder crop. Sow as early as the 15th, and keep the ground stirred until the crop shades the ground.

Birds.—Protect them on every part of the farm.

Implements.—Be in time about ordering those you need, secure strength when that is needed, but lightness and durability combined for all hand tools. Every farmer needs a good horse rake, of which there are several, a good horse hay-fork, (see page 176), and it will pay most farmers to have a mowing machine, and a combined mower and reaper, such as the "Buckeye" or Allen's "Clipper." The neighbors will be glad to hire it. Don't lend such a tool, nor let it without your own man to go with it, even if *you* are "your own man."

Work in the Horticultural Departments.

The willows and poplars have hung out their tassels—like banners of the advancing host, and admonish us, that these "notes" will reach the reader when he is surrounded by early flowers, and buds full of promise—hence they must be many, and each one brief, for in this working month one has little time to read long stories.

Orchard and Nursery.

The utility of heeling-in trees in a cool and shady place, will now be appreciated, as planting can be continued long after trees in the nursery have started to grow. In many cases

Trees from the nursery will arrive now, after a long detention on the way. When opened they may be shriveled and apparently worthless; if packed close and damp, their buds may have pushed out long white shoots. If shriveled, bury for a week, root and branch. If growth has taken place, cut back to a dormant bud; don't be afraid to use the knife freely—you will be glad next autumn.

Grafting can still be done, except with stone fruits, but when vegetation is active, use care.

Root-grafts.—If not yet set out, should not be delayed. Put in rows, 4 feet apart, and 12 inches in the row, pressing the soil firmly about them.

Planting in Orchard.—Many ask about this. Cultivate *for the orchard*. If any crop will leave the land cleaner and *richer* than before, grow it. Root-crops are best. Never grow grain, and of all things, don't try so greedy a weed as tobacco. The same remark holds as to setting strawberries, and other small fruits, between the rows of young trees. It may be profitably done, if the trees are not robbed.

Nursery Trees must be looked to. If suckers or useless shoots are rubbed off, as soon as they push, much future cutting will be avoided.

Mulching of young trees is to be done before dry weather comes on, straw, bog, hay salt, hay, etc., may be used. If no mulch is applied, keep the ground mellow by frequent stirring.

Insects.—"I shall move upon your works at once," should indicate the character of the warfare. When a "tent" is visible, however small the nest, be sure that caterpillars are there. Pull it down with the fingers, rub it off with a brush, swab it out with soft soap,—anything, but let it get large enough to do as a correspondent suggests—fire blank cartridges at it. The curculio begins its work as soon as plums and cherries are large enough to sting. Jar the trees, catch the insect on a sheet, and burn or scald.

Seedlings of all kinds of trees are to be kept weeded and thinned, whenever too crowded. Some of the hardiest forest trees, as oaks, need shading in their youth. This is especially true of young evergreens. A lattice of lath is best.

Fruit Garden.

Planting of all kinds may continue, provided the stock can be had in a sufficiently dormant condition, with the precautions noticed under orchard.

Grape Vines are frequently left down until danger of frost is over, and put up after the shoots have pushed. Great care in handling will be required. Vines trained on the arm system should have the arm bent in a curve to insure an equal starting of the buds. With newly planted vines let only one cane grow the first year; select the strongest that start, and cut off the rest. Put down

Layers of last year's wood. Leave the cane uncovered in the trench until the buds are well advanced, and cover with soil as the growth proceeds.

Cuttings of the grape, currant, and any others not yet planted, should be put in at once, and mulched with tan-bark or leaves.

Currants.—If the sickly appearance of the plants shows that the borer has entered them, cut away the affected part, if it takes the whole bush, and burn. Look out for the worm on the leaves; if it appears, dust with the powder of white hellebore at once. Mulching is of great benefit to this crop.

Insects.—Besides those mentioned under orchard, the annoying Rose-bug will often prove very destructive to the blossoms of the grape. This fellow seems to defy every application, and the only way is to shake him off early in the morning, and catch on a cloth or in a pan of water. Burn or scald.

Strawberries.—Plant, if not already done, even if it be late. Keep the beds clean. If they are mulched, pull up the weeds that force their way through. Put on a mulch before the fruit ripens, if not already done. Should there be a dry time, water, if practicable. Those who have facilities for irrigation should provide for this.

Packages.—If fruit is to be marketed, have baskets and crates ready and distinctly marked. There are so many kinds of baskets now in the market that one has a wide range in selection. If in doubt which to buy, take the advice of your commission merchant, as local prejudice has much to do with the matter; a style of basket that is approved in one market may not take in another.

Kitchen Garden.

The first radishes, cress, or lettuce of one's own garden! No after crop ever seems so welcome as these first fruits of our spring sowing. Those who live in mild climates, or who use glass, may now enjoy these. The rest have to wait a little longer.

Asparagus.—Cut from established beds, taking care not to injure the root, nor trample the beds. When marketed it is bunched in bundles 6 to 8 inches in diameter, according to the season; have the tops even; cut the butts even; tie closely with two bass strings, and keep moist to prevent wilting. If the beetle appears, or its blackish caterpillar, each less than one-half an inch long, cut or burn every shoot on which it is found, if it takes the whole. It is a serious trouble, and demands severe treatment, or the plantation is done for.

Beans.—Plant when all danger of frost is over, in rows 2 feet apart. Early Valentine is the most popular early. Mohawk, China and others are good. Of pole beans the Lima is most esteemed, and needs a warm soil. Plant 5 or 6 around the poles, which should be 4 feet apart, and 6 or 8 feet high. Press the beans into the soil with the eye down. The Cranberry, London Horticultural and White Runner are good sorts for snaps or to shell. The New Giant Wax Podded, for snaps only, is as near perfection as we expect to see in a bean.

Beets.—The early sowings should be thinned to from 4 to 6 inches, according to the distance between rows. Sow early sorts, if not already done.

Cabbage and its varieties, Broccoli, Brussels Sprouts, Cauliflower and Kohlrabi, all need nearly the same treatment when young. Sow in a well prepared seed-bed in rows 6 inches apart. As soon as up, dust with air-slacked lime, to keep off the fly; thin if the plants become too much crowded. Keep those from cold-frames well hoed. The hoe-fork is excellent for this work. Kohlrabi is not so readily transplanted as the others, and it is better to sow the seed, when the crop is to stand, in rows 18 inches apart, and then thin to 8 or 10 inches. For early cabbages, Wakefield and Early York; medium, the Winningstadt, especially for poor soils; later, any of the Drumheads, and for family use the Savoys, though small, the best of all cabbages.

Carrots.—Treat the same as beets, but they need closer attention as to weeding, which should be done very early. Early Horn and Long Orange.

Celery.—Sow as directed last month; loosen the soil between the rows as soon as up, and pull weeds as soon as they appear. The same treatment is followed with Celeriac, or Turnip-rooted Celery.

Cress or *Peppergrass.*—Sow every 8 or 10 days.

Corn.—The time to plant is governed by locality. Darling's Early is one of the earliest, but not so good as many others, of which each locality has its favorite sort. In gardens, rows 4 feet apart, or more, for the tall sorts, are better than hills.

Cucumbers.—Plants started under glass may be put out as soon as the weather is warm. In most localities, it is soon enough to start seeds on sods. Plant in manured hills when the soil is warm, and use plenty of seed. Leave the main crop for pickles until next month. Early Russian and Cluster, earliest. White Spine the best for family or market.

Egg Plants.—Transplant when large enough to another hot-bed, or pot and keep under glass. Do not put out of doors until settled warm weather.

Herbs, sow. See article on page 183.

Leeks.—Sow, if not done. Weed as soon as up.

Lettuce.—The crop from wintered plants will now be ready for use or sale. Sow seeds for succession. Transplant when large enough 1 foot apart each way.

Martynia.—Sow when the soil gets well warmed.

Melons.—Treat in all respects like cucumbers.

Mustard.—Sow for salad or greens every 10 days.

Nasturtium.—When the soil is warm sow, and provide brush or other support for them to climb upon.

Okra.—Sow where it is to grow. Very tender, and is best left until June. Dwarf is best.

Onions.—See last month. Loosen the soil between the rows; keep clear of weeds from the start.

Parsley.—Sow in open ground. See last month.

Peas.—Put brush to the tall sorts, before they fall over. Earth up in hoeing. Sow late sorts.

Peppers or *Capsicums* in all respects like egg plants.

Potatoes.—Hoe as soon as up. Finish planting.

Radishes.—A constant supply will require sowings at intervals of 10 days or 2 weeks. If insects trouble, sift on air slaked lime as soon as up.

Rhubarb.—Do not remove the leaves from plants set last fall or this spring. Older plants will now give a crop. Remove the leaves with a slight side-wise pull—never cut. Remove flower stalks.

Salsify or *Oyster Plant* is grown the same as carrots.

Spinach.—Sow as directed last month. Hoe and thin. New Zealand Spinach, valuable during the hot months, is a branching plant, and quite different from true spinach. Sow, and when large enough transplant to 3 feet each way in rich soil.

Sweet Potatoes.—See articles in this and April Nos.

Squashes.—The early sorts are managed the same as cucumbers. Out of door planting of late sorts must not be done too soon. Have the soil thoroughly enriched. Summer Crook-neck is best early.—Boston Marrow, Turban, Yokohama and Hubbard are all fine late. See Basket, page 109.

Tomatoes.—Transplant when danger of frost is over, 3 to 4 feet apart, according to richness of soil. In small gardens it conduces to neatness, and perhaps productiveness, to train the plants to some kind of trellis; on the large scale it will not pay.

Turnips.—Sow, and sift lime over young plants.

Winter Cherry.—This is called Strawberry Tomato. Excellent for preserves. Grown same as tomatoes.

General Management.—As soon as seeds germinate and the rows are visible, break the surface of the soil with a light scuffle hoe. Use the rake among recently set plants in preference to the hoe. A frequent raking, to destroy weeds as soon as they start from the seed, will save much hard work. Never let a weed go to seed. Have a handy, but out of sight, place to deposit rubbish—or rather two places: A pit for decomposable matter, weeds, without seeds, and all green stuff, and a heap for brush sticks, and old weeds—everything that can be converted into ashes. A deal of fertilizing matter will be ready next spring if everything is carefully saved.

Flower Garden and Lawn.

Greater success usually attend the planting of *Evergreens* this month than in any other, and and screens, hedges and single trees will be largely planted. It seems trite to repeat so often, that success depends upon not allowing the roots to dry—yet we do it with emphasis. Get trees from the nearest available nursery; if near enough, go for them, get them dug, bring them home and plant them out on the same day—all the better if it is a damp one. If packed, great care must be taken of the roots. Plenty of damp moss must be used; some nurserymen claim that a ball of clay is best to preserve the roots. For the success of the rarer kinds, see our Horticultural Annual. Those useful, cheap, and to be had everywhere, the trees "for the million," as the cant term is—are Norway Spruce, Arbor Vitæ, Hemlock, Red Cedar, White Pine, Austrian Pine, and Scotch Pine. The first four are useful for hedges and screens, as well as to plant singly. The Norway, is the one tree for all purposes, whether for beauty, hardiness, ease of removal, or rapidity of growth. Hemlock, more graceful, but rather less easy to manage. Red Cedar, a rather slow grower, but fine for screens. See article in April, page 134. For low hedges, 2 to 3 feet apart is the proper distance for either. Never trim off the lower branches of an evergreen, they may be cut back at the sides or top, like any other trees. The pines are esteemed in the order in which we have named them. Price varies with the size. 50 cents each for trees for planting singly, down to 10 and 5 cents each, for small hedge plants. As these trees retain their leaves during winter, they convey an impression of hardiness that leads to their neglect. Cultivate near a hedge, or screen, as carefully as if it were a row of cabbages, and they will be much less slow, than they have the credit of being. When plants are well established, give an annual dressing of good compost, with a plenty of vegetable matter in it.

Deciduous Trees.—In cooler localities most ornamental, may still be set, as may

Flowering Shrubs.—We are sometimes asked to make selections of them, but when we do so, the list is so long, that we are afraid to publish it. Any thing that bears flowers, is better than no shrub. See page 181 for several white flowering ones.

Edgings.—Box should have been set last month. Thrift, Ivy, Stone-crop, and various others are used.

Annuals.—Sow hardy sorts at once, and tender ones near the end of the month. Set out those started under glass as soon as the weather is settled. Have a plenty of Asters and standard things, and don't rely upon novelties, but just try a few.

Perennials.—Have a seed bed for these, and weed and thin carefully. Sow seeds of those coming in bloom as soon as ripe. Transplant seedlings.

Bulbs.—Gladioluses, Japan Lilies, Tigridias, and others may be planted in warm rich soil.

Tuberoses.—Better buy bulbs that have been started in the green-house, as they flower before frost. Give a rich, warm place to secure early flowers.

Climbers.—Plant seeds of Sweet Pea, Cypress Vine, (first scalding,) Canary-bird flower, etc., and get Cobæa, Maurandia, Lophosperum, and "German Ivy," (Senecio,) from the florists. Use these to hide unsightly fences and other objects.

Dahlias.—Set the roots in a spent hot bed and cover with soil, and when the buds have started divide so as to have a piece of root to each bud. Those who have no glass can set the roots in a warm exposure, and cover with a mat at night.

Lawns.—Mow as soon as the grass is long enough. Root up any coarse weeds. Roll frequently.

Roses will soon be attacked by their enemies. Hand picking will do a good deal, and whale-oil soap for the slugs. No help for the rose bug but to shake him off, catch or kill. Turn potted roses into the border.

Bedding Plants are generally put out too soon. They are mostly tender, and should not be exposed to cold nights. Verbenas, Lantanas, Salvias, Geraniums, Gazanias, etc., may be used in abundance.

Green and Hot-Houses.

Judgment must be exercised in bringing out plants, and sudden changes avoided. Those pots that are not plunged should be sheltered from strong winds, and Camellias and the like shaded in part. A layer of coal ashes, upon which to place the pots, will prevent worms from getting in. Let the plants remaining in the house be shaded as needed. Bring out those things that have been wintered in the cellar and place in the borders.

Cactuses are splendid for verandahs, and for turning into the border, where they make a grand show.

Fuchsias, when planted out, need partial shade and to be well staked. A few specimens should be grown tall for out of door flowering.

Lantanas do not show half their beauty when grown as bedding plants. When trained as small trees nothing can be finer in the garden.

Cuttings of shrubs grown from green wood are to be made, as soon as the growth gets a little firm, to replace those overgrown from being put out.

Cold Grapery.

The vines, if not already started, should be put up as noticed last month. Warmth and moisture being under the control of the cultivator, the starting may be hastened or retarded. When growth has commenced, the temperature of the house may reach 85° at mid-day. Use the syringe to preserve a proper moisture in the air. Select the strongest shoots for fruiting, and rub out the rest.

Apiary in May.—*Prepared by M. Quinby.*

The readers of the *American Agriculturist* are scattered over so wide a range of country, that it will not be expected, that remarks applying to any one section, will serve for all. Bee keepers report the average quantity of honey on hand this year, compared with last, is not more than one pound in ten or twenty. Last year, all throughout the period of fruit blossoms, the weather was cold and windy, and very unfavorable for the production of honey. Very many of the best stocks starved outright, from the 1st to the middle of June. Should the weather prove similar this year, ten times the number will starve, or need feeding. But the chances are that this year will be much better. A close watch must be kept continually of weather, bees, and honey. See directions in "Apiary" heretofore in regard to feeding. Feeding bees moderately at this season, just before, and immediately after fruit blossoms, is a good investment, although it may not be needed to prevent starving. The best brown sugar made into a syrup is probably the best and cheapest material for the present time. It will not be scented by robbers as readily as honey. Swarms, in some places, very much favored, may issue the last of this month. Italians are quite apt to swarm before they are expected to. Hives should be in order to receive them. As not over three or four swarms in a thousand will leave for the woods, without first clustering, it is not strange that many persons think they have compelled them to do, with tin kettle music, just what they would have instinctively done, without interference. Make no noise to quiet the swarms. When they leave, after clustering, it is often owing to bad management,—as allowing them to hang clustered too long, not getting *all the bees to enter the hive*, raising the hive too high from the bottom, leaving it in the hot sun, smell of new paint, etc.

Bees that swarm out naturally are quite as apt to divide nearly right as when artificial swarms are made. Yet, with the movable comb-frames, the divided colonies are so readily made equal, that I recommend artificial swarms whenever the master has the requisite skill to provide queens properly. A weak colony can be strengthened by giving it a comb or two well filled with sealed brood. After they have hatched, if not strong enough, give another. Strong stocks only pay. Artificial swarms are readily made as follows: First, have a queen ready; then be sure that your stock can spare a good swarm, and that the bees are getting honey. Operate in the middle of the day. Lift out combs till you find the one with the queen upon it, and put that, with the bees that adhere to it, into the new hive. Set it on the old stand, and the old hive on a new stand, at least 20 feet distant. All the old bees will adhere to the old place. The old hive will be nearly destitute of honey gatherers for a few days, but nurses enough will be left to mature the brood, and they will accept a mature queen two days after the removal, and in three or four weeks will be strong enough to divide again, having gained a good swarm by having a laying queen so soon after the old one was gone. If surplus honey is an object, instead of an increase of stocks, both old and young are in the best condition to produce it. Strong colonies are not destroyed by worms.

Carrying or Sending Money Abroad.—Nearly all of the payments of money between distant points in our own country and between this and foreign countries, are made by a system of exchanges. One western man sends wheat, pork, etc., to New York, and makes a draft upon it. Another buys goods in New York, and sends a draft for the pay. These drafts are exchanged or balanced by banks and bankers at the two points, and only money enough is sent either way to pay, from time to time, the difference between the aggregate amounts of the drafts or indebtedness. So with our foreign trade; we send abroad cotton, grain, etc., and buy manufactured articles and other things, and only gold enough goes across the ocean to balance accounts.—A person going abroad does not want to carry all the money he may need there. He therefore buys a "Draft" on London or Paris, which is cashed on presentation and identification; or he deposits the money here, and takes a "Letter of Credit" for $250 in gold or any higher sum, and then draws the money as he needs it; or he buys "Circular Notes," of $25 to $100 each, which are good at almost any point. Messrs. Duncan, Sherman & Co. have "correspondents" or agencies in more than 300 different cities or towns in Europe and elsewhere in foreign countries, any one of whom will cash their Circular Notes or Letters of Credit. We found these very convenient when abroad, as we obtained any sum at any point by calling at their agency, and received it in the currency of the country we happened to be in. Their business card will be found in our advertising columns.

AMERICAN AGRICULTURIST.

ORANGE JUDD & Co., Publishers, 41 Park Row, N. Y. City.

ANNUAL SUBSCRIPTION TERMS (always in advance): $1.50 each for less than four copies: Four to nine copies, $1.25 each: Ten to nineteen copies, $1.20 each: Twenty copies and upwards, $1 each. Papers are addressed to each name.

See Here—Extra

PREMIUMS!

Accessible To

EVERYBODY!!!

We have prepared TWO most excellent and valuable Annuals, viz. the **Agricultural Annual No. 1,** and the **Horticultural Annual No. 1.** Though of large size, and costly, they are sold at only **50 Cents each,** and many thousands have been disposed of already. They are designed for *general* use, and one or both of them should be found in every Family in America. But they were originated and executed too late to be ready at the beginning of the year, and so they did not get so large a general distribution as they really merit. We design to make these Annuals a "permanent institution," that is, to issue both of them at the beginning of every year, and we have begun the preparation of material that will make the next numbers (for 1868), much superior even to the valuable volumes of this year.

Now we want everybody to get the FIRST number, so as to have the series complete from the beginning, for we know everybody will want the future numbers. THEREFORE, we make the following offer: To every person who shall, *after May 1st*, send us a subscriber to the *Agriculturist* for this year, at the regular rate ($1.50), we will present and send post-paid, either a copy of the *No. 1 Agricultural Annual* or of *No. 1 Horticultural Annual*, whichever is desired, (if applied for at the time of subscribing.) They are each in neat ornamental covers, beautiful inside and outside, and full of valuable information, including a full almanac, calendar of operations for each month, all finely illustrated, and contain many useful articles and suggestions.

Each present subscriber, not already supplied, can thus get one or both of these annuals *free* of expense, simply by procuring and forwarding one or two subscribers—(If the new subscriber thus obtained wants one of the annuals, he can get it for himself by furnishing another subscriber, and so on.) We shall keep the Annuals on the press until June 30, and print all that may be called for under this offer. This extra premium is entirely distinct from our regular premiums offered on this page.

2 2 2 2 2 2 2 2 2 2 2 2

2 TWO MONTHS 2

2 2 2 2 2 2 2 2 2 2 2 2

yet remain for all to secure the *general* premiums offered in the table in another column. There are many good things, and thousands can still get them. "Where there is a will, there is a way."....A subscriber writes: "I sort o' half tried to get up a premium club in January, but not succeeding so well at first as I thought I ought to, I gave it up, and only sent a few names obtained. But April 1st, on seeing that many others were successful, I started out again, *determined* to succeed any way, and get either a Sewing Machine, or a Gold Pen at least. The first man I asked said 'No!' but I opened the four numbers, and showed him the 140 engravings, pointed out the many articles on farming and gardening, the prize articles in the household, the talks with the children, the hundreds of condensed 'meaty' Basket items, the Calendar of Work to be done, given in each number, and then dwelt on the humbug exposures, reading him a few extracts. I then told him, there would be three times as much during the year, and I did not know how much more, as the Editors were constantly bringing out something new. I argued the advantages of keeping up with the times, the improved taste, which the beautiful engravings would give to himself and family—told him how many hundreds of dollars I had got from a single hint the *Agriculturist* gave me four years ago, etc., etc. He seemed interested, but answered that 'he could not afford it.' I told him I was sure he would be richer a year hence, though *he* might not see it now. I explained that though it was $1.50 a year, this was less than *half a cent* for each working day, and his working hours would be so much happier with more to think about. He finally came down, and subscribed, partly to get rid of me or to oblige me. Thus successful, I kept on every evening, and on two rainy days. I gained confidence and experience, and where you had only five subscribers, and where everybody said 'no' last January, I have now got more than subscribers enough for both Sewing Machine and Gold Pen! The time taken from my work has been slight, and I have learned not a little of business tact. Indeed I have been thus paid for my time and effort, aside from the premiums. Just tell my experience to others, (omitting my name), and encourage them to go and do likewise. They will like it; it will pay them in a double way; it will benefit the people they persuade to read, and it will help extend the benign influence that the good old *Agriculturist* is exerting in the country....Keep up your war upon the humbugs; our Postmaster says, you have saved the people of this place many hundreds of dollars...."

We commend the above example to others. The experience of our friend is that of very many. There is not one of the twenty thousand towns in our country, where a like determined effort would not be similarly successful. Human nature is the same everywhere. **May** is as favorable a month as any other in the year for securing subscribers. The work of scattering the paper among those who do not now read, is a good one, aside from the premiums, and we could appeal to the reader to work "for the good of the cause;" but we gladly pay for the work. The premiums offered are good and desirable, and we like to send them. Let us have the pleasure of sending hundreds or thousands of them this month. Will you have one of them?

If so, look over our premium list, choose the premium you would like, take a copy of the paper, sally out among neighbors and friends, in your own neighborhood and elsewhere (*for premium clubs need not be all at one post-office*), and in a brief time the desired number of subscribers can be gathered, and the premium secured. A full description of the premiums will be sent free to any one desiring it. Any Specimen numbers, cards and show bills needed, will be supplied free.

☞ **We take** *so much pains to procure only good articles in all cases, that any one securing anything from our premium list, saves the risk usually run of getting poor or indifferent goods, when buying of unknown or irresponsible parties. Every thing we send out as a premium is guaranteed to be the best of its kind and price.*

Old and new subscribers count in premium lists.

Our premiums are standard articles, and enough can be obtained to supply all calls for premiums for six months. Every canvasser can take abundant time, but

As fast as subscriptions are obtained, send them along, that the subscribers may begin to receive the paper; and when all the names that can be obtained are forwarded, select the premium, and it will be promptly furnished. To save mistakes and keeping accounts, *send with each list of names, the exact subscription money.*

Remit in Post-Office money orders, drafts or checks on N. Y. City; if these can not be had, register money letters.

☞ *Every name designed for a premium list must be so marked* WHEN *sent in.* (We can not count others.)

☞ *Every article offered is new and of the very best manufacture. No charge is made for packing or boxing any of the articles in this Premium List. The forty-three Premiums, Nos.* **1, 2, 6,** *and from* **29** *to* **32,** *and from* **40** *to* **75** *inclusive, will each be delivered* **FREE** *of all charges, by mail or express, (at the Post-Office or express office nearest recipient), to any place in the United States or Territories, excepting those reached only by the Overland Mail.—The other articles cost the recipient only the freight after leaving the manufactory of each, by any conveyance that may be specified.*

Table of Premiums and Terms, For Volume 26—(1867).

Open to all—No Competition.

No.	Names of Premium Articles.	Price of Premiums.	Number of Subscribers required at $1.50	at $1.
1	Garden Seeds for a Family (40 kinds)	$5 00	13	37
2	Flower Seeds for a Family (100 kinds)	$5 00	13	37
3	Nursery Stock (Any kinds desired)	$20 00	30	97
4	Iona Grape Vines (12 of No. 1)	$18 00	27	90
5	Concord Grape Vines (100 of No. 1)	$12 00	19	65
6	Japan Lilies (12 Bulbs)	[illegible]	15	45
7	Sewing Machine (Wheeler & Wilson)	$55 00	60	240
8	Sewing Machine (Grover & Baker)	$55 00	60	[illegible]
9	Sewing Machine (Singer's Tailoring)	$80 00	[illegible]	[illegible]
10	Sewing Machine (Florence)	$73 00	70	[illegible]
11	Sewing Machine (Willcox & Gibbs)	$55 00	60	[illegible]
12	Sewing Machine (Howe's)	$60 00	67	270
13	Washing Machine (Doty's)	$14 00	21	70
14	Clothes Wringer (Best—Universal)	$10 00	18	58
15	Tea Set (Hart's best Silver Plated)	$50 00	66	[illegible]
16	Castors and Fruit Basket (do. do.)	$30 00	41	140
17	Ice or Water Pitcher (do. do.)	$18 00	27	90
18	One Dozen Tea Spoons (do. do.)	$7 50	17	[illegible]
19	One Dozen Table Spoons (do. do.)	$15 00	[illegible]	[illegible]
20	One Dozen Dining Forks (do. do.)	$15 00	[illegible]	[illegible]
21	Piano (Best Steinway & Son's 7-octave)	$625 00	[illegible]	1550
22	Melodeon, 5-octave (G. A. Prince & Co.'s)	$112 00	138	400
23	Melodeon, 4-octave (do. do.)	[illegible]	[illegible]	[illegible]
24	Ladies' Gold Watch (Beautiful)	$100 00	[illegible]	400
25	Silver Watch (Valuable Time Keeper)	[illegible]	48	[illegible]
26	Double Barrel Gun (Very good)	$30 00	46	150
27	Spencer's Breech-loading Rifle (Hunting)	[illegible]	[illegible]	[illegible]
28	Tool Chest (First Quality of Tools)	[illegible]	60	[illegible]
29	Case of Mathematical Instruments	$9 00	[illegible]	[illegible]
30	Case of Mathematical Instruments	$15 00	[illegible]	[illegible]
31	Morton's Best No. 6 Gold Pen (Silver Case)	[illegible]	14	42
32	Morton's Best No. 5 Gold Pen (Silver Case)	[illegible]	11	[illegible]
33	Barometer (Woodruff's Mercurial)	$18 00	[illegible]	[illegible]
34	Barometer (Woodruff's Mercurial)	$12 00	19	[illegible]
35	Buckeye Mowing Machine, No. 2	$125 00	150	450
36	Allen's Patent Cylinder Plow, etc.	[illegible]	31	100
37	The Aquarius or Water Thrower	$11 00	19	[illegible]
38	American Cyclopedia (Appleton's)	$80 00	[illegible]	[illegible]
39	Worcester's Great Illustrated Dictionary	$12 00	19	[illegible]
40	Any Back Volume Agriculturist (In clean new Nos. Post-paid—Unbound.)	[illegible]	[illegible]	[illegible]
41	Any Two Back Volumes do.	[illegible]	[illegible]	[illegible]
42	Any Three do. do. do.	[illegible]	13	[illegible]
43	Any Four do. do. do.	[illegible]	15	47
44	Any Five do. do. do.	[illegible]	17	[illegible]
45	Any Six do. do. do.	[illegible]	19	[illegible]
46	Any Seven do. do. do.	[illegible]	[illegible]	[illegible]
47	Any Eight do. do. do.	[illegible]	[illegible]	71
48	Any Nine do. do. do.	[illegible]	[illegible]	[illegible]
49	Vols. XVI to XXV do.	[illegible]	27	[illegible]
50	Any Back Volume Agriculturist (Neatly Bound. Sent Post-paid.)	[illegible]	[illegible]	[illegible]
51	Any Two Back Volumes do.	[illegible]	[illegible]	[illegible]
52	Any Three do. do. do.	[illegible]	16	[illegible]
53	Any Four do. do. do.	$10 00	[illegible]	[illegible]
54	Any Five do. do. do.	[illegible]	[illegible]	[illegible]
55	Any Six do. do. do.	[illegible]	[illegible]	[illegible]
56	Any Seven do. do. do.	[illegible]	[illegible]	[illegible]
57	Any Eight do. do. do.	[illegible]	[illegible]	[illegible]
58	Any Nine do. do. do.	[illegible]	[illegible]	116
59	Vols. XVI to XXV do.	[illegible]	[illegible]	[illegible]
60	Genesee Farmer, 1858-1865, 8 Vols., Bound	[illegible]	[illegible]	[illegible]
61	Downing's Landscape Gardening (All sent paid through, by Mail or Express.)	[illegible]	[illegible]	[illegible]
62	Cummings & Miller's Architect.	[illegible]	[illegible]	[illegible]
63	A $10 Library (Your Choice)	[illegible]	[illegible]	[illegible]
64	A $15 Library do.	[illegible]	[illegible]	[illegible]
65	A $20 Library do.	[illegible]	[illegible]	[illegible]
66	A $25 Library do.	[illegible]	[illegible]	[illegible]
67	A $30 Library do.	[illegible]	41	[illegible]
68	A $35 Library do.	[illegible]	[illegible]	[illegible]
69	A $40 Library do.	[illegible]	[illegible]	[illegible]
70	A $45 Library do.	[illegible]	[illegible]	[illegible]
71	A $50 Library do.	[illegible]	[illegible]	[illegible]
72	A $60 Library do.	[illegible]	[illegible]	[illegible]
73	A $75 Library do.	[illegible]	[illegible]	[illegible]
74	A $100 Library do.	$100 00	[illegible]	[illegible]
75	A Choice of Good Books (See Terms below.)			
76	Sewing Machine (Finkle & Lyon)	$60 00	60	[illegible]
77	One Dozen Pocket Lanterns	[illegible]	18	[illegible]

For Full Description of the several premiums see October *Agriculturist*, pages 349 to 352, or apply for a *Descriptive List*, which will be furnished *free* and post-paid. We have room here for only the following:

No. 63 to 74—Good Libraries.—These can be selected by the recipients, from any of the books named in the list in this column. The books will be *delivered* free of cost, by mail or express.

No. 75—General Book Premium.—Any one not desiring the specific Book premiums, 63 to 74, on sending any number of names above 25, may select Books from the list (below), to the amount of 10 cents for each subscriber sent at $1: or to the amount of 30 cents for each name sent at the (ten) club price of $1.20 each: or to the amount of 60 cents for each name at $1.50. *This offer is only for clubs of 25 or more. The books will be sent by mail or express, prepaid by us.*

BOOKS FOR FARMERS AND OTHERS.

[For sale at the office of the *Agriculturist*, or they will be forwarded by mail, *post-paid*, on receipt of price. ☞ *All these are included in Our Premiums, Nos. 63 to 75, above.*

Allen's (L. F.) Rural Architecture	$1 50
Allen's (R. L.) American Farm Book	1 50
American Agricultural Annual, 1867, paper, 50c.; cloth	75
Allen's Diseases of Domestic Animals	1 00
American Horticultural Annual, 1867, paper, 50c.; cloth	75
American Bird Fancier	30
American Rose Culturist	30
American Weeds and Useful Plants	1 75
Architecture, by Cummings & Miller	10 00
Barry's Fruit Garden	1 75
Bement's Poulterer's Companion	2 00
Bement's Rabbit Fancier	30

Breck's New Book of Flowers	1 75
Buist's Flower Garden Directory	1 50
Buist's Family Kitchen Gardener	1 00
Burr's Vegetables of America	5 00
Chorlton's Grape-Grower's Guide	75
Cobbett's American Gardener	75
Cole's (S. W.) American Fruit Book	75
Cole's Veterinarian	75
Dadd's Modern Horse Doctor	1 50
Dadd's (Geo. H.) American Cattle Doctor	1 50
Dana's Muck Manual	1 25
Dog and Gun (Hooper's)..........paper, 30c....cloth	60
Downing's Country Houses	6 00
Downing's Landscape Gardening (new Edition)	6 50
Downing's Fruits and Fruit Trees of America	5 00
Downing's Rural Essays	5 00
Eastwood on Cranberry	75
Elliott's Western Fruit Grower's Guide	1 50
Flax Culture	50
Field's (Thomas W.) Pear Culture	1 25
Flint's Milch Cows and Dairy Farming	2 50
French's Farm Drainage	1 50
Fuller's Grape Culturist, (Revised Edition)	1 50
Fuller's Strawberry Culturist	20
Gardening for Profit, by Peter Henderson	1 50
Gray's How Plants Grow	1 25
Gray's Manual of Botany and Lessons in one Vol.	4 00
Guenon on Milch Cows	75
Harris' Insects Injurious to Vegetation, plain 4.00, col'd	5 00
Harris' Rural Annual. Bound, 8 Nos., in 2 Vols. Each	1 50
Herbert's Hints to Horsekeepers	1 75
Hop Culture	40
Husmann's Grapes and Wine	1 50
Johnston's Agricultural Chemistry	1 75
Johnston's Elements of Agricultural Chemistry	1 50
Johnson's (Prof. S. W.) Essays on Manures	1 25
Langstroth on Honey Bee	2 00
Leuchar's How to Build Hot-Houses	1 50
Mayhew's Illustrated Horse Doctor	3 50
Mayhew's Illustrated Horse Management	3 50
Mayhew's Practical Bookkeeping for Farmers	90
Blanks for do. do.	1 20
Miles on the Horse's Foot	75
My Farm of Edgewood	1 75
My Vineyard at Lakeview	1 25
Norton's Scientific Agriculture	75
Onion Culture	20
Our Farm of Four Acres (bound) 60c.........paper	30
Pardee on Strawberry Culture	75
Peat and its Uses, by Prof. S. W. Johnson	1 25
Pedder's Land Measurer	60
Quinby's Mysteries of Bee Keeping (new)	1 50
Randall's Sheep Husbandry	1 50
Randall's Fine Wool Sheep Husbandry	1 00
Rivers' Miniature Fruit Garden	1 00
Richardson on the Dog, paper 30c.........cloth	60
Rural Annual, by Joseph Harris	25
Saunders' Domestic Poultry (new), paper, 40c., bound	75
Schenck's Gardener's Text Book	75
Scribner's Ready Reckoner	30
Skillful Housewife	75
Stewart's (John) Stable Book	1 50
Thompson's Food of Animals	1 00
Tobacco Culture	25
Todd's (S. E.) Young Farmer's Manual	1 50
Warder's Hedges and Evergreens	1 50
Watson's American Home Garden	2 00
Woodward's Country Homes	1 50
Youatt and Spooner on the Horse	1 50
Youatt and Martin on Cattle	1 50
Youatt on the Hog	1 00
Youatt on Sheep	1 00
Youmans' Household Science	2 25

Commercial Matters—Market Prices.

The *following* condensed, comprehensive tables, carefully prepared specially for the *American Agriculturist*, show at a glance the transactions for the month, ending April 15, 1867, and also for the same month last year:

1. TRANSACTIONS AT THE NEW-YORK MARKETS.

RECEIPTS.	*Flour.*	*Wheat.*	*Corn.*	*Rye.*	*Barley.*	*Oats.*
26 days *this* m'th	151,000	150,000	141,000	8,970	54,000	51,000
27 days *last* m'th	111,000	94,000	150,000	15,000	47,200	78,000

SALES.	*Flour.*	*Wheat.*	*Corn.*	*Rye.*	*Barley.*
26 days *this* month,	273,000	1,040,000	2,911,000	500,000	700,000
27 days *last* month,	304,500	1,563,000	230,000	516,000	925,000

2. *Comparison with same period at this time last year.*

RECEIPTS.	*Flour.*	*Wheat.*	*Corn.*	*Rye.*	*Barley.*	*Oats.*
26 days 1867...	151,000	150,000	141,000	8,970	54,000	51,000
24 days 1866...	167,500	9,300	54,000	4,100	131,000	117,000

SALES.	*Flour.*	*Wheat.*	*Corn.*	*Rye.*	*Barley.*
26 days 1867......	273,000	1,040,000	2,911,000	500,000	700,000
24 days 1866......	238,500	809,000	1,418,000	337,000	874,000

3. *Exports from New York, Jan. 1 to April 15:*

	Flour.	*Wheat.*	*Corn.*	*Rye.*	*Oats.*	*Barley.*
1867.....	114,838	82,712	1,091,820	127,370	28,735	753,520
1866.....	283,125	108,457	1,421,248	125,920	891,400	......
1865.....	850,250	155,704	120,749	111	24,303	......

Gold has fluctuated considerably during the month. The extremes have been 132⅞ and 138¼. The warlike news from Europe has been the main cause of the rise. The latest advices thence have been of a more pacific tenor, and the drift of gold has been downward. The price on Monday, the 15th of April, was 135....Breadstuffs have been in much more demand, for home use, shipment, and on speculative account, and, with light receipts, prices have favored sellers decidedly. The most active foreign call has been for corn, which has been quite excited and variable through the month. The milling demand has been good at buoyant rates. Rye has advanced materially. Barley has been almost out of season. There have been considerable arrivals of flour and wheat from California during the month, which have met with a more ready market at more remunerative prices. Our millers have about overcome their prejudices against California wheat, and are buying quite freely at the highest ruling prices.....There has been a fair degree of activity in provisions, at, however, irregular prices, most articles in the line closing heavily....Cotton has been decidedly depressed, by liberal receipts, and adverse foreign news. The demand for it has been quite moderate....Wool has been rather lightly dealt in at the improved prices noticed in our last....In other agricultural products business has been restricted, and prices have been unsettled.

CURRENT WHOLESALE PRICES.

	March 15.	April 15.
PRICE OF GOLD	134¾	135
FLOUR—Super to Extra State	$8 60 @11 40	$10 25 @13 60
Super to Extra Southern	10 30 @16 50	12 00 @17 75
Extra Western	10 00 @16 50	11 60 @18 75
Extra Genesee	12 00 @14 50	13 65 @15 75
Superfine Western	8 65 @10 15	10 25 @11 45
RYE FLOUR	6 50 @ 8 00	7 00 @ 8 75
CORN MEAL	4 90 @ 5 50	5 25 @ 6 25
WHEAT—All kinds of White	2 90 @ 3 25	3 10 @ 3 45
All kinds of Red and Amber	2 40 @ 3 10	2 30 @ 3 35
CORN—Yellow	1 11 @ 1 11	1 28 @ 1 31
Mixed	1 13 @ 1 15	1 29 @ 1 31
OATS—Western	62 @ 69	73 @ 75
State	72 @ 72	74 @ 79
RYE	1 30 @ 1 35	1 50 @ 1 62
BARLEY	85 @ 1 25	80 @ 1 22
HAY—Bale ₱ 100 lb	1 45 @ 1 85	1 30 @ 1 90
Loose	1 50 @ 1 93	1 35 @ 1 85
STRAW, ₱ 100 lb	1 30 @ 1 60	1 15 @ 1 35
COTTON—Middlings, ₱ lb	30 @ 31½	27 @ 28½
HOPS—Crop of 1866, ₱ lb	25 @ 70	30 @ 63
FEATHERS—Live Geese, ₱ lb	78 @ 85	75 @ 85
SEED—Clover, ₱ lb	12½ @ 14½	17 @ 18
Timothy, ₱ bushel	3 65 @ 4 00	3 70 @ 4 00
Flax, ₱ bushel	2 80 @ 3 00	2 65 @ 3 00
SUGAR—Brown, ₱ lb	9½ @ 13½	9¾ @ 12¾
MOLASSES, Cuba, ₱ gl	43 @ 65	49 @ 57½
COFFEE—Rio, (Gold price) ₱ lb	15½ @ 18	16 @ 19½
TOBACCO, Kentucky, &c., ₱ lb	4½ @ 23	4½ @ 21
Seed Leaf, ₱ lb	8 @ 65	8 @ 65
WOOL—Domestic Fleece, ₱ lb	40 @ 70	40 @ 70
Domestic, pulled, ₱ lb	30 @ 58	30 @ 58
California, unwashed	22 @ 42	25 @ 42
TALLOW, ₱ lb	10¾ @ 11½	11½ @ 11¾
OIL CAKE—₱ ton	38 50 @56 00	48 00 @57 00
PORK—Mess, ₱ barrel	24 00 @23 50	21 00 @23 25
Prime, ₱ barrel	17 00 @18 00	19 00 @19 25
BEEF—Plain mess	12 00 @18 00	13 00 @18 00
LARD, in barrels, ₱ lb	12 @ 13½	12¼ @ 13¼
BUTTER—Western, ₱ lb	12 @ 32	11 @ 28
State, ₱ lb	25 @ 45	20 @ 40
CHEESE	10 @ 20	10 @ 18
BEANS—₱ bushel	2 75 @ 3 50	2 25 @ 3 70
PEAS—Canada, ₱ bushel	1 40 @ 1 60	1 35 @ 1 40
EGGS—Fresh, ₱ dozen	25 @ 29	23 @ 26
POULTRY—Fowls, ₱ lb	17 @ 22	18 @ 22
Turkeys, ₱ lb	20 @ 24	24 @ 25
POTATOES—Mercers, ₱ bbl	3 00 @ 3 25	3 50 @ 3 75
Peach Blows, ₱ barrel	2 25 @ 2 75	2 75 @ 3 00
POTATOES—Buckeye, ₱ bbl	2 00 @ 2 25	2 00 @ 2 60
APPLES—₱ barrel	3 50 @ 7 50	3 50 @ 7 50
CRANBERRIES, ₱ barrel	17 00 @21 00	12 00 @20 00

New York Live Stock Markets.—The supply during the past four weeks has been fair for the season, as is shown in the following table:

WEEK ENDING.	*Beeves.*	*Cows.*	*Calves.*	*Sheep.*	*Swine.*
March 19	5,393	73	1,005	11,569	14,238
March 26	5,010	89	906	13,810	14,330
April 2	3,921	98	1,216	17,025	11,699
April 9	4,704	79	1,604	10,937	16,138
Total in four Weeks	19,035	336	4,731	53,820	56,410
Average per Week	4,759	84	1,183	13,235	11,853
do. do. *last Month*	5,096	78	625	14,811	14,360
do. do. *prev's Month*	4,737	62	510	19,738	11,343
Average per Week, 1866	5,718	94	1,200	20,000	13,000
do. do. do. 1865	5,255	118	1,500	16,091	11,023
do. do. do. 1864	5,161	145	1,511	15,315	12,676
do. do. do. 1863	5,150	129	694	9,941	21,670
Total in 1866	298,880	4,885	62,420	1,040,000	672,000
Total in 1865	270,274	6,161	77,991	836,733	573,197
Total in 1864	267,609	7,603	75,621	782,462	660,270
Total in 1863	264,091	6,470	35,709	519,316	1,101,617

The Lenten season extending over the past four weeks has diminished the consumption of beef, so that the supply, though moderate, has generally been equal to the demand....**Beef Cattle** were a little higher the first of April, and remain a trifle above our previous quotations, the present rates being equivalent to 17½c.@18c. ₱ lb., dressed weight, for the few of the best or extra cattle; 16½c.@17½c. for first quality; 16c.@15c. for medium grades, and 14c.@13½c. for inferior to very poor...**Milch Cows** are very slow of sale now, and it does not pay to send them here. Very good cows seldom bring over $75@$80, calf included, though occasional extra or fancy cows sell at $90@$100 and upward; common to poor range from $70 to $30, according to quality. ....**Veal Calves** are coming in freely, live, and "hog-dressed," that is, with head, feet, and entrails removed, but the skin left on most of the carcass. Live range from 12c. ₱ lb. live weight, for the best or extras, down to 7c. for the worst....**Sheep and Lambs** have not been very plentiful, but prices are a little lower than one month ago, the latest sales being at 9½c.@10c. ₱ lb. live weight for extras, 9c.@9½c. for first quality, and from that down to 7c.@7½c. for poor. Some sheared sheep, and a few lambs have appeared, but not in quantity enough to establish a price....**Live Hogs** have been abundant for the demand, most of the time, and prices have not varied much during a month; the latest sales range between 7½c.@8c. ₱ lb. live weight, for good, and 7c.@8½c. for poor, rough lots.

Take Notice!—All Subscriptions begin with the Volume, unless otherwise desired and specified when subscribing. All subscriptions received up to June 15th are entered down for the entire volume, and the numbers from January 1st are forwarded. We keep on hand, or print from our electrotype plates, as needed, the entire numbers of the volume, to supply to new subscribers, and to others desiring them. Subscriptions received *after* June 15th, begin at the middle of the volume, unless otherwise desired or specified.

Containing a great variety of Items, including many good Hints and Suggestions which we throw into smaller type and condensed form, for want of space elsewhere.

Good Half Dollar Easily Earned.—The special premiums offered by the Publishers on page 165, are worthy of attention. The *Annuals* are richly worth their price, (50 cents), and almost everybody can each find at least one more who may, with a little explanation, be convinced that it will be for his or her interest and profit to take the *Agriculturist* for the present year.—The Annuals are not only useful now, but they will grow increasingly so from year to year as the series goes on. It is designed to make these works so beautiful and valuable that they will be indispensible to every family.

We Commend the Experience of a Subscriber, as detailed under the head "Two Months" on page 165, to the attention of others. What one man has done, many others can do.

Answers to Correspondents.—We are not under *obligations* to answer any questions, but being rather good-natured, we prefer to do it, and do it when we can, and it is a pleasure to assist our friends when it is possible to do so. Many letters go unanswered for various reasons, and the great numbers to which we do reply are written by the editors, away from the office in time that properly belongs to them for other uses. When one writes us a letter upon a matter that is solely for his own benefit, and in a few days after demands "an explanation" why his first is unanswered, we submit that it is pushing good nature. Will our friends understand that we answer all that we can as fast as we can, and that no one is willingly neglected. We show some preferences though: a letter with prepaid postage is likely to be taken up before an unpaid one. Inquiries, where to buy seeds, plants, or any other thing already advertised in our columns, are not answered. Inquiries, about "doctors," are not answered. Those who ask us questions involving the writing of a full volume in reply—like a Brooklyn correspondent who asks us to write to him directions to propagate and cultivate small fruits—we must pass by. Those who ask advice in matters totally unconnected with the objects of our paper—such as desiring us to advocate the construction of a certain railroad, etc., must go unanswered, as must requests for seeds, grafts, and the like. With a hundred letters before him, all reasonable persons will see that one must make some discrimination. Do not send more than money or stamps enough to cover the return postage—it only makes us trouble; and we can't be hired for 25 cents to write a letter. So much for replies by mail.

As to replies in the paper: the first choice is for those of *general* interest. Next, those that have but one subject. Don't mix Agriculture, Horticulture, Household, etc., all on one page—at least separate them by a space so that they can be cut apart and distributed to the editors.

Again, please always put the name on the letter, which will not be used if some other signature or initials are given. It often happens, that inquiries are made which are of interest to the writer and to no one else—such as those in a Taunton, Mass., letter, inquiring about distinguished botanists and others. We have not space for such matters in the paper, but would gladly reply by letter did we know the writer's address, which is not given.

N. B.—A great many letters are answered in the "Notes about Work." All the necessary points in about fifty letters are covered in this way in the present issue. We try to have those in mind in making up this portion of the paper, which is always newly written. Continue to ask us questions, then, and believe that no sensible one is unconsidered or neglected because there is no personal answer by "return mail," or in "next month's Basket." We cannot write on *every* subject in *every* paper.

Great Sale of Duchess and Oxford Shorthorns.—Mr. Samuel Thorn, of Thorndale, Duchess Co., N. Y., has recently sold to Mr. James O. Sheldon, of Geneva, N. Y., his entire herd of Shorthorns, with the exception of two bulls, the 6th and 12th Dukes of Thorndale. This sale is the largest ever made of animals of the Oxford-Duchess tribe, the number sold, old and young, being 40, and the average price paid $1,000 a head. Mr. Thorne's reputation as a careful, discreet, and successful breeder, is known wherever this most favorite family of Shorthorns, (the Duchesses,) is admired, and in the regard of both American and English breeders, this breed has long stood foremost among those of American Shorthorns. Mr. Sheldon has been for some years forming a herd of Duchess of Oxfords, which bears a most excellent reputation, and with this addition to it, becomes the owner of more fine animals of these families than any other breeder in the world.

Osage Orange.—An article on this was crowded out. In brief we can answer many questions about starting the plants.—Soak the seeds 5 or 6 days in blood-warm water, changing each day. Don't cook the seeds, as our Delaware friend did. Then keep the seeds damp, and in a warm place, until they sprout, stirring now and then to prevent heating. Sow in well prepared soil; rows, a foot apart; cover an inch deep and roll; keep well weeded, and thin where too crowded.

A Good Repeating Shot-gun.—This, long a desideratum, seems now to have been accomplished, and the favorite double-barreled fowling piece seems to be doomed. This engraving represents *Roper's Repeating Shot-gun*, manufactured at Amherst, Mass., under the supervision of Mr. C. M. Spencer, whose name is world-famous as the inventor of the repeating rifle, the terrible seven-shooter of our mounted riflemen. This gun is light and handy, very neatly made, strong and accurate, as we judge from careful inspection, and from examination of several sheets of paper, shot at, at different distances. Metallic cartridges, using the common cap, are loaded before hand and inserted, four at a time in the magazine. The cartridge cases are light, of steel, and may be used many times without perceptible wear, and a large number, ready charged, be conveniently carried.

American Pomology — Apples.—Doctor Warder's book is now before the public, and will receive the attention it deserves. It is in fact the only work where the newer fruits can be found, and will mark an era in pomological literature, in importance second only to the appearance of Downing's work, over 20 years ago. The catalogue of all the recorded varieties occupies 25 pages, and condenses a wonderful amount of information in a very small space. One can see at a glance the origin, shape, color, quality, season, etc., of any of the many hundreds of apples there enumerated. We trust that the work will meet with a welcome that will encourage its author to bring out his vast accumulation of materials upon other fruits at once. A handsome volume of 744 pages. By mail $3.

Sundry Humbugs.—Since our last we have received about **200** letters from different parts of the country with swindling schemes and circulars, and accounts of impositions and cheating by the humbug operators. Many of these refer to parties described in this journal last month and previously. Others are concerning parties who have merely changed their places and names. Very many of those letters ask responses by mail, but the number is so large that it is out of the question to write to the half of them. Some ask the return of tickets, &c., that they have previously forwarded; but this is not practicable. We have thousands of such tickets, and cannot afford time to hunt up any particular man's document, unless it be of special importance. Look for our exposures in past numbers before writing. Remember that if we do not reply to any inquiry, either by letter or in a following number, it is an indication that the parties inquired about are either swindlers, or at best of doubtful character. This response must answer for many letters asking replies, but which we cannot take time to respond to by letter... We mention a few new names, reserving others for more time and room than we now have, and others for further investigation.... We say, unhesitatingly, that, without exception, every "gift enterprise" now before the country is a fraud, and that the investors in them will find it so in 9,999 cases out of every 10,000. We have accounts of more than fifty such gift enterprises now under way in various places. The soldiers', widows' and orphans' "sympathy schemes" are by far the most numerous. They literally "steal the livery of heaven to serve the devil"—that is their own pockets. ...*I. D. Bowman & Co.*, (Van Allen,) we refer to here, not to pronounce them humbugs, but to say the use of Mr. Judd's name on their circulars as reference was wholly unauthorized, and would have been refused if asked for. Mr. J. does not indorse anything which he has not examined with the greatest care, and even then he aims to avoid being annoyed with a multitude of letters of inquiry as to the genuineness of any and every claimed indorsement, by refusing his signature.——The "ink powder" was submitted by us to a good chemist, and reported "to answer for common writing purposes, but not permanent in its character," and his advertisement was therefore declined....."*Aliases*." — We publish a multiplicity of names of swindlers, but the operators are comparatively few in number, and they change their "business" firms and names at convenience, and often run several names and places at the same time. In our calls upon the swindling gentry in various disguises, personally and by proxy, the same individual will on successive days turn up in several localities. For illustration, an old post-office clerk, whose real name is, or was, Thomas Fletcher, afterwards was employed in a provost marshal's office; again he appeared as "Whitman & Co."; anon as D. H. Kellum & Co., etc., etc. After having tried various other names until they became too well known, he lately took up his own again.... *A Masonic Gift Scheme*.—Geo. W. Holmes & Co., are trying to persuade all good Masons to send them $300,000 for as many tickets, promising chances at $10 silk hats, $75 plated tea sets, $1,500 pianos, $25,000 house, etc., etc., *reckoned* at $300,000 in all, and costing perhaps half as much. They don't tell how much is to go to a "Hall and Asylum fund," and leave the "time and place of distribution to be hereafter named." No intelligent Mason will bite at this bait.... *Nursery Gift*.—Smith Whittier, dating at Chicago, says he has "lost the head of his family," (he ought to lose his own head,) and wants 50,000 farmers and others to console him by sending in $100,000 at $2 each, and promises to give them a chance—a fifty-thousandth chance—to draw his wonderful *fruit farm* of 34 acres, somewhere in St. Joseph, Mich.—he don't tell exactly where. Plenty of other widowers would like a similar *consolation*. Go to digging, Smith Whittier, and not try to humbug honest people out of their hard earned dollars by your big picture and great promises. *Sam'l Birchfield & Co.*, of Philadelphia, ask people to send them $4 each for a soldiers' orphans' home, offering in return $9 pictures, and a bonus of about half a million dollars worth of gifts. That may do to catch very "green-horns," but not anybody else. Before investing for charity's sake, better write to Jay Cooke & Co., and ask them if the reference to Geo. A. Cooke is allowed, or worth anything *if* allowed.... *Of Gift Enterprises*, the meanest are those that solicit patronage ostensibly to aid soldiers, or their widows, and orphans. A score or more of them are now operating. Among others, Tudor, Gates & Co., of Mulberry, O., *alias* Cincinnati, give the pretended full indorsement of Governors, members of Congress, etc. None but very foolish people will pay $1 for one chance in 300,000 of drawing a valuable prize, even if sure that $250,000 worth is to be drawn for. When one wishes to aid soldiers and their families, better send the *whole* money to responsible parties, and not let the ticket operators pocket three-fourths or nine-tenths of the money paid in to them.... The "*Nassau Association*" offer 12 *silver* spoons for $3 in currency, and to throw in gift tickets for watches and other articles, "marked" from $250.00 to $4.00 each. Very tiny *silver* spoons they would be at $3 for 12, to say nothing of the "gifts." Lead spoons, very thinly plated with silver, can be bought for a trifle, and are worth no more. Where do the green-horns live who keep such enterprises agoing?... *Lotteries*.—T. J. Furniss, of Cedar street, New York, like many others, pretends to assure a great many people of his ability to send them valuable prizes. Let everybody having an itching to try these fellows, remember, 1st, that *if* they can pick out lucky numbers, then the whole lottery is in every way a swindle, and you will be surely swindled; 2d, that if conducted fairly the pretended agent is a liar, and will cheat you; 3d, that if he had the ability to select lucky numbers, he would surely keep them himself, for he would make far more thus than by the commissions he could hope for from any customers you could possibly send; 4th, that at least nine in every ten of these lottery "agents" keep every dime sent them, and you can never find them or get a word from them; and, finally, that all lotteries are unfair swindles, however regularly conducted, because of every $5 paid in, the managers and agents pocket from $3 to $4, and leave only $1 to $2 to be drawn for by the tickets... Frank, Mars & Co., William-st., and J. E. Brennan & Co., Nassau-st., are match swindlers with T. J. Furniss. ....Beware of *New Tea Companies*. The so-called "Great American Tea Company," 31 & 33 Vesey st., advertised in our columns, though doing an immense business all over the country, has not even been complained of to us more than two or three times in as many years. On this account, as well as for other reasons we have previously stated, we believe general satisfaction is given to their customers. But stimulated by their success, several of the swindling fraternity have started or pretend to have started other "Tea Companies,"—some copying very nearly the advertisements, etc., of the old company. Some of these we know to be humbugs, (one was noted last month,) and as to others we have not evidence sufficient to warrant us in admitting their advertisements... *Every man* offering watches, jewelry, etc., by *ticket* is to be carefully avoided. Nine out of ten of the most plausible of these fellows will send nothing for your money, and not one in a hundred will give you your money's worth.... *Every stealer of morals, modesty, and virtue*, will be quite likely to steal your money if sent to him. These fellows know you will not make a fuss about money sent for immodest or immoral books and instruments, and they will keep it and send nothing, unless pretty sure of making a bigger haul afterwards.... *Plants, etc.*—Don't spend your money, time, and soil, on any of the wonderful foreign corns, seeds, plants, etc., that just now turns up exclusively in the hands of some one individual. Egyptian corn, Dourah corn, etc., which were tried and condemned years ago, are "up" for speculation again.... Want of space compels us to stop here, leaving about 50 letters unanswered—but they are all humbugs, so don't be troubled about losing some great money making chance.... See last month's exposures for sundry names in these letters. ....P. S.—*Harris Brothers*, of Boston, received something towards their just deserts in the Superior Court on April 15th, viz.: a fine of **$14,000** ($7000 each).—Good for Boston: Now let N. Y. City take hold of her lottery and "gift enterprise" swindlers.

Mr. Judd not an Office-Seeker.—The following appeared in a New York daily morning paper on April 4th: "OFFICE SEEKERS.—The halls and ante-rooms of the Executive Mansion were literally blocked to-day by the crowds of office-seekers. The crowd exceeded anything of the kind for months past. The President was almost exhausted by 3 P. M., and not one-third had obtained interviews. Orange Judd, the publisher of the *Agriculturist*, and Horace Capron, of Illinois, are prominent candidates for the position of Commissioner of Agriculture. The President is determined to remove Newton."——Similar telegrams have appeared in many other journals. From the above, it would appear that Mr. Judd was one of the "crowd" of candidates knocking at the Presidential door for office. We take the liberty to say that so far from this being the case, he was quietly at home looking after his gardeners and builders, and entirely ignorant of any efforts making, or to be made by anybody, to get him into office, *nolens volens*. The *Agriculturist* "Office," with its half million of patrons and friends, is abundantly satisfactory so far as position, usefulness, and pay are concerned. In short, he is not an aspirant to any Government office.

Worse than Humbug.—The *Murder* of the unborn, is beginning to attract, in some degree, the attention which its great importance imperatively demands. The prevalence and recent great increase of this crime, the general ignorance as to its criminality, and of its terrible consequences upon the guilty actors themselves, forbid longer silence on the part of medical men, ministers and editors, who have until now feared lest public effort should make known and increase an evil which it aimed to diminish. Dr. Storer's Essay, "Why Not," published by Messrs. Lee & Shepard, of Boston, should be in the hands of every Physician, Clergyman, Editor, and of all other intelligent persons of either sex, in the country. (Price 50 cts.) Dr. Todd recently furnished an article on the subject to the *Congregationalist*, at Boston, and we hear he is preparing a longer essay for publication. The *Christian Advocate*, of New York, also published an article from an intelligent lady, entitled: "Fashionable Murder." The *Northwestern Christian Advocate*, of Chicago, Ill., of March 13, devoted 7¼ editorial columns to a bold and outspoken discussion of the subject, which is being copied at the West, and is worthily awakening much attention. We learn that one of the editors, Rev. Arthur Edwards, Chicago, is preparing a cheap Pamphlet or Tract designed for extensive circulation. We wrote somewhat sharply on one phase of the subject—the medical advertisements—in May, last year, and we are very glad to see these further efforts to check a wide spread, growing, and terrible evil—crime! It behooves every woman—every man indeed—to become enlightened upon this subject.—— What shall we say of those journals, even such papers as claim and find admission into the best families, that yet, for the sake of the money consideration, daily spread before their readers the advertisements of such monsters—such murderers—as Restell, Mauriceau, and many others, who offer their services and medicines to all, married and unmarried, and promise for a small consideration to assist them not only to the most criminal deeds, but to the almost certain destruction of their own future health and happiness—very often of their lives. If the publishers of such journals lack the conscience or the intelligence required to reject these advertisements, their sheets should be banished from the household by every one who would not nurse a viper in his domestic circle.—An editor, with whom we recently remonstrated, excused himself by pleading ignorance of the character of an advertisement. Any editor, so simple or ignorant as not to know the intent of advertisements "to remove irregularities from whatever cause," "monthly pills," etc., and the like, has woefully mistaken his calling as an enlightener of the public.

Small Wooden Boxes for Butter.—W. B. Guernsey, of Norwich, N. Y., has brought to our notice an apparently excellent device for marketing butter in small packages. Two round boxes of equal hight, made of maple veneer with maple bands, very light and strong, fit together almost air-tight, one forming the box, the other the cover. They are protected by a tasteless inodorous varnish, and butter, being packed in them when made, and filling them completely, is said to keep as well or better than in firkins; and the cost is about the same, pound for pound. These, if they will work, will afford a most profitable means for marketing butter, both for the producer and consumer. We shall test and report.

A Winter of Snows.—Wishing to preserve some record of the remarkable winter just past, we requested Prof. O. W. Morris, of the Deaf and Dumb Asylum, N. Y., to give us the data. Prof. M. is an accurate meteorological observer, and has charge of one of the stations of the Smithsonian Institute: — "Farmers generally predict good crops when the snow falls early, and the ground is covered by it during the winter, whether the same snow continues or melts, and is followed by other falls. The ground has been covered nearly all the time since the first of any depth came, and it had suffered but little from freezing and thawing. The popular saying, 'That there will be as many snow storms as the date indicated in the month when the first falls,' is not borne out in this winter, for it first fell on the 22d November, and there have been 26 distinct times when snow has fallen. The quantity is very much more than common, as the aggregate is 6 feet and 10 inches. The weather for this latitude has also been unusually cold, the thermometer on one morning fall to 13 degrees below zero, and a longer continuance of cold weather also; for, in Jan., there were 17 mornings that the thermometer was below freezing point. We have also had very high winds, doing much damage on the sea, and also on the land. Last year, our first thunder storm occurred on the 21st April; but this year, we had very heavy thunder and vivid lightning on the 2d of February, and again on the 9th."

Hydraulic Rams deliver at usual hights about one-seventh to one-eighth the amount of water required to run them. They cost from $8 (for a ram adapted to a brook furnishing 3 quarts to 2 gallons of water per minute—having a ½-inch drive-pipe, and ⅜-inch discharge), to $150, (for one adapted to a flow of 25 to 75 gallons per minute, having a 4-inch drive-pipe and 2-inch discharge). Water rams are applied to raising water for the purposes of supplying dwellings and stock-yards, gardens, etc.; for irrigation, ornamental fountains, etc., etc., and when well set, require little care. They may be supplied by plumbers generally; Douglas' is esteemed.

The American Pomological Society.—We have space for only the following portions of the circular:—The undersigned give notice that its Eleventh Session will commence in the City of St. Louis, Mo., on Wednesday, Sept. 11th, at 11 o'clock, A. M., at Mercantile Library Hall, and will continue several days. All Horticultural, Pomological, Agricultural, and other kindred institutions in the United States and British Provinces, are invited to send delegations as large as they may deem expedient; and all other persons interested in the cultivation of fruits are invited to be present and take seats in the Convention.

Among the prominent subjects which will come before the Society at this session, will be that of the revision of the Society's Catalogue of Fruits. The several State Pomological and Horticultural Associations are requested to compile lists for their own States or Districts, and forward them, at as early a day as possible, to P. Barry, of Rochester, N. Y., Chairman of the Committee on the Revision of the Catalogue.

Members and delegates are requested to contribute specimens of the fruits of their respective districts, and to communicate in regard to them whatever may aid in promoting the objects of the Society and the science of American Pomology; and as the fruits of the South and Southwest will then have attained their size, it is desirable that a grand display from these sections be made.

Each contributor is requested to come prepared with a complete list of his collection, and to present the same with his fruits, that a report of all the varieties entered may be submitted to the meeting as soon as practicable.

Packages of fruits, with the name of the contributor, may be addressed as follows: "American Pomological Society," care of C. M. Saxton, corner Fifth and Walnut Streets, St. Louis, Mo. MARSHALL P. WILDER, Pres't.
JAMES VICK, Sec'y.

Still Another.—New Agricultural papers multiply so rapidly of late that we can hardly keep the run of them. The latest accession to the ranks is the New England Homestead, a 16 page monthly, published by Henry M. Burt & Co., at Northampton, Mass. A taking title, and a good looking and cleverly edited sheet. The editors in their first issue show a virtue that we commend to others much longer in the harness—when they quote, they give full credit for articles taken from other journals. It starts with our good wishes.

Showers of Brimstone.—C. Wade, of Todd County, Kentucky, sends a sample of a yellow substance that fell with a rain on the 11th of March. It is a pale, sulphur colored powder, and its appearance somewhat alarmed some persons, though Mr. W. rightly conjectures that it is the pollen of some kind of a flower. A glance at a portion under the microscope at once showed it to be the pollen of some pine. As this pollen is of a very peculiar shape, we give an illustration of its appearance under the microscope.

It must be very early for the pines to be in blossom in Kentucky, and it would be interesting to know how far the winds had carried it. This phenomenon has been noticed many times before. Many years ago a copious shower of it fell in Troy, N. Y., and caused great alarm among a certain class. Showers of brimstone, blood, and the like, soon lose their mystery under the microscope.

The American Fruit Culturist, by John J. Thomas; New York: William Wood & Co.—There are a few people—just a few—whose writings we feel safe in recommending, without even seeing them, and John J. Thomas is one of these. But we think too highly of the author to pass his book by without an examination, and after a perusal we are able to commend it as one of the most useful of the recent additions to horticultural literature. Many horticultural books are ground out by the job, but this is not of that kind; the author knows just what he is writing about, and puts that knowledge in so plain and pleasant a way that others can benefit by it. As the scope of the book includes all kinds of fruit, the author does not attempt too much with any, but gives the leading varieties of each, and directions for their propagation and culture. The book contains 511 pages, produced in handsome style, and liberally illustrated. We can send it by mail, at publishers' price—$3.

Gravel-wall (Concrete) Houses—Gables.—Aliquis will find no difficulty in putting up gables of concrete, if he will make large bricks, the width of the wall and twice as long, of the concrete, and lay them up like a flight of steps on each side. They may be made rectangular or with one end beveled at the desired angle for the roof. The wall between them may be laid up in concrete the same as the walls of the building.

The Roller Whiffletree — illustrated herewith, is a simple and effective device for preventing injury to trees, when plowing among them. Its working can be readily seen by the figure. It is patented by a subscriber to the *American Agriculturist.*

Dog Law in Connecticut.—A correspondent informs us, that the dog law in the above state has been perfected so as to apply to the whole state without reference to town action. Dogs are registered, taxed, collared, and watched by select men. Outlawed dogs given over to death. Good, we are glad to hear it. Three cheers for the Nutmeg State, if she will only live up to the law.

Plastering vs. Weather-boarding.—J. R. Chambers. If the plaster be made of cement, and good, clean, sharp sand, it will last for ages. Brick and stone buildings are finished in this way, and stand the weather. The American Building Block Company put up the walls of large buildings with an artificial stone, made of cement, sand and lime. Consult a builder.

A Strawberry Exhibition will be held by the American Institute in New York in June—time not yet fixed. Liberal premiums are offered and a large show expected. Another will be held in Pittsburgh, Pa., by Mr. Knox on June 12th and 13th, on which occasion we are sure that at least "700 Strawberries" can be seen.

Poultry Matters.—We have certainly been growing careless in neglecting poultry in this country. The prizes of our Agricultural Societies are given freely to unworthy subjects, and ignorance of their business is the rule and not the exception among poultry breeders; real "fanciers" are rare, while those who take a fancy to keep a certain kind or kinds of poultry, do so for a year or two and then neglect them. Worcester, Mass., sustains the only Poultry Club in the country; there may be others, but they are very quiet. Poultry fanciers are those who breed, not for the sake of multiplying poultry, but for securing perfection in points of purity and excellence, and for improving upon the various breeds now known, and who are on the alert to introduce new and improved breeds. Such persons gain much by being associated, and we would be very glad to chronicle the formation of a

New York Poultry Club, which the following letter from an enthusiastic poultry breeder suggests:

MESSRS. EDITORS:—Noticing an editorial suggestion in the *American Agriculturist*, in reference to a poultry club, I wish you would again call attention to the matter. It seems hardly creditable to our great metropolis and neighboring cities that there is no association of the kind. Thousands of persons residing within fifty miles of the city are interested in poultry, and if these will only take an active interest in forming a club, it may be made not only a *pleasure* but a *benefit* to every one connected with it. We certainly need such a club here, and I, for one, will do all I can to further the object. Will any of your readers assist? If so, I hope to hear from them.
Yours, A. M. HALSTED, 69 Pearl street.

Importations.—A number of our prominent poultry fanciers have been importing from England, France and Belgium quite extensively of late. Since the list published in the American Agricultural Annual was prepared, we hear of importations by Mr. Halsted, above named, of Crevecœur, Houdan and La Fleche fowls; by Mr. Benj. Haines, Jr., of Elizabeth, N. J., of Crevecœur, Golden-Pencilled and Silver-Spangled Hamburg, Gray and White Dorking, Silver-Pencilled and Black Poland, Golden and Silver Seabright, Game and Black African Bantam, and Black Spanish fowls, besides Rouen and Aylesbury Ducks; by Mrs. Saunders, Brahma, Cochin, Gray Dorking, Houdan and Crevecœur fowls, Toulouse Geese and Aylesbury Ducks; by Capt. Singleton, Dark Brahma and Cochin China fowls.

A New Corn Dropper.—A subscriber sends the following: Boys and men in dropping corn often drop 20 or more grains where 5 only are needed. I propose to obviate this by fastening a small cup, holding 5 or 6 grains, on the

thumb, and a flat piece on the fingers of a glove or mitten, as shown in the illustration. This is, of course, for planting on the small scale only. Unpatented.

Angora or Cashmere Goats, Fleeces, etc.—We have many inquiries in regard to these interesting animals and their beautiful, silky fleeces, and shall endeavor to satisfy our readers as soon as we can satisfy ourselves. The animals are the subject of wild speculation at present, and what their economical value will be, when people sober down, it is hard to say. This much is certain: They are as hardy and easy to keep, probably as mischievous also, and may be made to yield as good milk, with proper selection and breeding, as the common milking goat. They have not, it is said, so strong an odor, and their flesh is claimed to be superior,—these two propositions we will not vouch for. Their fleeces vary greatly in length and fineness. They are wonderfully silky and beautiful,—and just now fringes and tassels made from them are very fashionable. The hair, or wool, takes color easily, and may be woven into beautiful and durable fabrics. The demand now is chiefly for fancy-work, fringes, tassels, etc., and for the skins for muffs, tippets, and capes for ladies. The fleece is said to sell, in New York, Lowell, and wherever there is a demand, for $1 to $4 per pound, according to quality, but so far as we can learn, the demand is uncertain. We are glad to know that efforts are being made to introduce a stock of the very best animals that can be purchased in Asia, and also to introduce looms and foreign weavers.

To Bring up Sandy Land.—"J. C. M." You have no clay, can get muck, and any "hand manures" which can be bought in New York market. Your best plan would probably be to cart muck as soon as the roads are settled; use this to increase your manure heaps, compost it with shell lime, 10 bushels to the cord, plant corn with the manure compost, potatoes with the lime compost, with plaster and ashes when they first come up. Plow other land and sow 100 to 150 weight of Peruvian guano, to the acre; sow buckwheat and plow it in when in full blossom with a flat furrow; then put on 50 bushels of lime to the acre, harrow, and sow buckwheat again, (if before the first of August, sow corn or sorghum,) and plow under as soon as growth is checked by the frost. Clover will probably not take well on the soil now, but may be used as a green manure crop after this treatment, or on land after manuring and taking off a corn or other crop.

Going to Paris, London, etc.—Several subscribers in different parts of the country have from time to time asked about the methods and expenses of getting to the Exhibition at Paris this summer. There are many steamers advertised, but it is hardly in our line to go into particulars. In remembrance, however, of a most delightful voyage in the world-renowned "Great Eastern," in 1862, without the least sea-sickness or other discomfort, we can commend a voyage in her as a most desirable thing. This Leviathan of the deep has even been greatly improved (not "*enlarged*," as editors say), and will leave New York for Brest May 28 and July 9. (For circulars, etc., address Wells & Fargo's Express Company, New York City.) A railway extends through a beautiful part of France from Brest to Paris. First class fares to Brest are $100, $125 and $140 each in gold—the different rates depending upon the size and location of state rooms. This fare includes all necessary expense on ship-board. Railroad fare from Brest to Paris $7.50. This makes the trip to Paris, at present prices of gold, about $144, or $178, or $200 in our currency. One may allow about $5 a day in Paris for expenses, sight seeing, riding, etc., or $100 for twenty days. The round trip will therefore cost from $400 to $500 currency, according to style of going, extras, etc. A $100 or more, taken along to use in purchases, etc., if desired, will not come amiss. —When in Paris, one will want to run over to London, which can be done by several routes, in 14 to 16 hours, and for $6 to $8 in gold, according to the route and accommodations chosen. As much more will take one up through the heart of England to Liverpool.—Another very pleasant, short trip, for one pressed for time, is to go from Paris to Lyons; thence to Geneva, Switzerland—a romantic ride up into or among the Alps—; thence to Frankfort, Germany, diverging to Strasburg if time serves, thence to Mayence; thence down the most interesting portion of the Rhine by steamer to Cologne; thence to Brussels, thence to Paris, or to London *via* Ostend. We give partly from memory, and partly from our notes made in passing over portions of the route in 1862, an approximate table of the distances, first and second class fares (the latter about equal to our first class cars), in gold, and the through time by express trains, not allowing for stopping to rest or for sight seeing. Starting from Paris:

Paris	*Miles.*	*Hours.*	*1st Class.*	*2d Class.*
To Lyons	316	11	$11.00	$8.00
To Geneva	197	8	3.50	2.50
To Frankfort....	323	16	9.00	6.50
To Mayence....	21	1	80	50
To Cologne....	187	10	2.00	1.50
To Brussels	150	8	5.00	4.00
To Paris	215	10	7.00	5.50
Or to London ...	240	11	10.00	7.50

Slow Torture at the Stack.—An "Iowa Farmer" should cypher on the problem of the cost of fattening steers in the field rather than in the barn in the winter. One third of the food at least goes to keep up animal heat, and is wasted. Corn is cheap in Iowa, but is it cheaper than boards? In the East, store cattle and cows have little to eat except corn stalks, straw and hay, and this often of poor quality. If kept at the stack through the winter, they grow poor and suffer.

Fence Posts.—H. T. Lake, Portage Co., O. We know nothing better to preserve posts than to dip the butts in hot coal tar, let them drip, and then roll in sand.

What Manures shall We Buy?—"J. M." Peruvian guano, at present prices, is out of the reach of most cultivators, and yet it is so reliable, and so certain to produce immediate results, that some will buy it at any price. Superphosphate of lime is always good for certain crops, if you get a genuine article, and for this you have to rely upon the integrity of the manufacturer. Bone dust is in the same category. The cheapest manures in the market, this spring, we think, are the fish guanos, or the dried pomace from the fish-oil factories. These are of two kinds, the refuse as it comes from the press, deprived of all the oil, and the refuse still further dried and ground to a coarse powder, so that it can be sown in drills or broadcast. The latter involves considerable more labor in its preparation, and stands higher in the market. It has about 9 per cent. of ammonia. It is better for certain purposes; is more conveniently applied either in the hill or to growing crops, and can be more evenly distributed upon the surface for harrowing or plowing in. The unground refuse is lumpy, and needs to be mixed with large quantities of turf, loam, peat, or muck in compost, and to be thoroughly worked over, in order to use it economically. We have used both varieties with excellent results, and at present prices, we think we get more fertilizing material, for the money, in fish guano than in any other article in the market. The market is generally at the factories, and, for the most part, the article is kept in first hands for sale; so that there is not much chance for adulteration without detection. Until quite recently the local demand has taken it up about as fast as made. The fish-oil factories are increasing, and as the refuse multiplies, it has to go farther from home for a market. It is coming into use on the cotton plantations, and wherever it is fairly tried the demand for the article increases.

The Price of Farm Labor—as given in the Monthly Report of the Agricultural Department is: In the Eastern States $31.30 per month; in the Middle States, $30.07 per month; in the Western States, $28.91; in the Southern States, $16.00; in Oregon, $35.75; in California, $45.71. In Massachusetts the price is $39.94 per month, which is higher than in any other State except California. This is attributed to the great variety of industry in the State, only about one-fourth of the people being employed in agriculture. This makes a very lively demand for all farm products. The greater variety of occupations in a State the better for laborers. There has been an advance in the price of labor of about seventy per cent. in the last forty years, notwithstanding an immigration of 5,000,000 of people. The greatest want of the country is labor to develope our resources.

Where Farms are Advertised.—G. Ober. Farms for sale are frequently put into the hands of real estate agents in the neighboring cities, who advertise in the daily or weekly papers. A visit to a reading room in the city, where all the papers are kept, would give you the desired information. The cheapest farms will generally be advertised in the local papers in regions where there is the least enterprise.

Boston Marrow Squash for Milch Cows in Winter.—At the annual meeting of the N. Y. State Agricultural Society, Judge Osborn, of Albany, made interesting statements in regard to his mode of cultivating, preserving, and feeding this important crop. He thought it very valuable as a part of the winter feed of milch cows. After the fall feed was over, he fed with cabbage until about the 1st of January, and then with squashes for two months, and followed with mangels and then with carrots. He thought one pound of the squash equal in nutriment value to five pounds of pumpkin. The cows were very fond of them, and they imparted no disagreeable flavor to the butter. He sometimes fed fifty pounds of squash to a cow in a day.

He cultivated the Marrow among his corn, reserving every fourth row for this purpose, running clear across the field. The rows were four feet apart. The squashes thus had a fourth part of the land, and as much sunshine and manure as the corn had. He did not approve of the too common method of stealing a crop by planting pumpkins in the same hill with the corn or potatoes. He had two methods of guarding the vines against destruction by bugs. As soon as the vines began to run vigorously, he covered all about the roots with fine manure to induce the formation of new rootlets near the surface. This hastened the growth, disturbed the bugs, and helped the starting of new roots. A little later in the season he covered the vines at the joints, so as to make them strike roots there. If they lost their first roots by the bugs, as they sometimes did, they would be nourished by the joint roots and perfect their fruit. Plaster was used to prevent injury by the striped bugs in the early stages of the growth of the vines. It required considerable labor to guard the squashes against freezing after they were gathered in the fall. His rule was to keep just ahead of the frost in protecting them. They were gathered into heaps in the field and covered when frost threatened. As the cold increased, they were carried to the cellar and laid upon shelves where they could be easily examined. The defective ones were removed as fast as decay made its appearance. He thought this squash was not in perfect condition for eating until the 1st of January.

National Trial of Plows, Harrows and Cultivators.—There will be a great trial of these implements held under the auspices of the New York State Agricultural Society near Utica, N. Y., on the 7th of May and days following, by a committee consisting of nearly the same gentlemen who officiated as Judges at the trial of Mowers, Reapers and other hay and grain harvesting implements, at Auburn last year. The programme was not received until after the April number of the *Agriculturist* was in the hands of our subscribers. According to the terms it announces, entries must be made two weeks before the trial, and $20 entrance fee paid for plows, ($5 if for exhibition only). The plows must be exactly as they are sold to farmers, and they are arranged under ten gold medal classes, as follows: I. Stiff-soil sod-plow; II. Stiff-soil stubble-plow; III. Light-soil sod-plows; IV. A plow which will plow 12 inches deep in stubble land, inverting the soil—("raise the *lowest* soil to *surface* of the *furrow*"—*Programme*); that is, probably, 'raise the lowest soil to the surface of the furrow slice.' For a plow which will turn a furrow of this kind, not less than five inches wide—the *large* gold medal. V. Michigan (sod and trench) plow; VI. Sub-soil plow in connection with an ordinary (?) plow; VII. Ditching plow for opening drains; VIII. Machine for excavating ditches; IX. Steel plow for soils that will not scour; X. Swing or side-hill plow. A medal is offered for the best Harrow, and "Cultivators" are divided into two classes in each of which two gold medals are offered. The New York State Society by this action will place the public under renewed obligations to it and its public spirited officers. The trial will, we doubt not, result in great good.

The New Registered Letter System, which is to be a very great improvement in the matter of security, goes into operation June 1st, as we learn from official sources. We state by request, that some Post-masters are erroneously attempting to carry it out now; they should wait for the new "Register Package Envelopes," the chief feature of the new system.

Unanswered Letters, Special Note. In addition to the usual business and editorial letters, referred to Mr. Judd for advice and direction, he is in the constant receipt of many letters marked "Personal," on various topics, including friendly epistles he would like to answer, personal inquiries, offers of implements, etc. He has kept these along, responding as fast as possible—to the most important first—but they have accumulated beyond his hope of getting to the bottom of the drawer. He *must* soon have more time for rest, or cease to write at all. Will his correspondents please kindly excuse this seeming, but by no means designed or desired, lack of courtesy or attention to their favors and requests.

The Small Fruit Culturist.—By A. S. Fuller. The only work devoted to small fruits. Special treatises of this kind have the advantage that the author can more thoroughly discuss his subject, and go into greater detail than in a work embracing both large and small fruits. Mr. F. has been so long identified with the culture of small fruits, that it is unnecessary to speak of his qualifications as a teacher. The work covers the whole ground of propagation, culture, varieties, packing for market, etc. While many will differ with the author in his estimation of the value of some varieties, all will agree as to the thoroughness, and clearness, of the practical part of the work—except perhaps those few growers, who wish to keep the secrets of the trade to themselves, these should recollect that the work was written for the people. The work is most abundantly illustrated. About 300 pages, $1.50 by mail.

Medicines to Try.—We ask those who send us specimens of this kind to excuse us. We have no desire to compete with the Farmers' Club.

A Card.

BAROMETER CHALLENGE TO SOLON ROBINSON OF THE TRIBUNE.

Sir:—In your "reports" of the New York Farmers' Club you have more than once spoken of the Barometer in a manner to convey the impression that it is worthless to farmers, and its sale to them a humbug and swindle. You have said that "in your opinion it is utterly worthless to farmers; that it does not predict rain at all; that the rules laid down in scientific works for the observation of the Barometer are utterly fallacious, and that persons who depend upon the Barometer will fail fifty-nine times out of sixty in their weather predictions!" Now, you have told me, in presence of witnesses, in effect, that "you knew *nothing at all* about mercurial Barometers, or their operation, that all the chance you ever had to observe the movements of a Barometer, was from a few weeks' use of an imperfect Aneroid, and that you did not feel competent to decide upon their merits." Knowing your reputation as a writer of *fiction*, (Me-won-i-toc, &c.) I, of course, know how to appreciate the first of the above statements, but appearing, as it did, in a widely circulated journal, the public is liable to be led into hurtful error, from the great difficulty in discriminating facts from fiction in your "reports." To get at the truth of the matter, I make you these propositions:

1st. There are many thousands of Woodruff's Barometers in the hands of practical farmers in this country. You may procure as many certificates as you can from persons using *my Barometers* to prove your point, and if I do not show *forty* certificates from farmers of its value and practical utility for every *one* you can produce to the contrary, then I will yield the point.

2d. I will place one of my Barometers in the hands of a practical, disinterested man, who shall keep a record of its movements three times a day for three months, and from its movements alone, daily predict the coming weather, in strict accordance with a printed "card of directions," which I will furnish, and for every time he fails to predict correctly the coming weather, I will furfeit the sum of *five dollars*, while for every time he predicts correctly, you shall forfeit the sum of *one dollar*. If at the end of three months the balance of forfeitures is against me, you shall pocket it. If the balance of forfeits is in my favor, it shall be used to advertise the result in the *American Agriculturist*. In both cases, and whatever the result, you are to publish this challenge, and the results arrived at, in the *Tribune*. You cannot object to the fairness of this proposition, for, as you publicly state that the Barometer fails fifty-nine times out of sixty, and you gain five dollars for each failure, and I but one dollar for each success, if your statement is true, you will get $295 for every time I get $1. I make this offer in good faith, and will act up to it, and, if you require it, will deposit $300 in advance as security. I do not make the proposition as a betting or gambling scheme at all, but to call out evidence and thorough investigation, that we may have more tangible and certain proof than random individual statements, if the facts are as you have stated. Your connection with the *Tribune* gives wide circulation to your statements, and it is important to the public that they do not lead to error. Yours, very truly,

CHARLES WILDER.

Peterboro', N. H., April 2d, 1867.

Walks and Talks on the Farm—No. 41.

A few days ago I got a letter from John Johnston. After he had sealed the envelope, he wrote on the outside: "Write the name of your farm plain; I cannot make it out."

I call it "Moreton Farm." One has to have a name of some kind, you know. Rose Hill, Sunnyside, and similar names would be too sentimental. "Edgewood" I like, but Ike Marvel has appropriated that. Henry Ward Beecher's Farm in Lennox, before he bought it, was called "Mount Desolation." But when I saw it, a dozen years ago, it was a lovely spot. If I could have got those glorious old elms by adopting the name, I would have done so. But there was no hope of that, and so I finally adopted a name which has no meaning in itself, but which, to me, revives the pleasantest recollections of my early days. Moreton was the place were my forefathers lived and died. The old thatched home is still there, but the family is gone. Not one remains, and the farm is in other hands. My uncle John, the last occupier, was a good specimen of an English farmer. His father died when he was sixteen years old, and he and my father carried on the farm jointly for a dozen years or so. The farm contained 260 acres, half of it high rolling land, and the other half low and wet. The latter produced little but rushes and coarse grass. My uncle cut a deep ditch through this land, and underdrained into it. The effect was magical. It produced enormous crops, and for eight or ten years previous to the close of the war in 1815, the price of farm produce ruled fearfully high. He has sold wheat at $5 a bushel. Of course he made money. But I have heard him say that he did even better later in life, although prices were much lower. This was because his land became richer and richer, and he grew heavier crops. I hope such will be the case in this country.

On this two hundred and sixty-eight-acre farm he raised 40 acres of wheat, 40 acres of barley, 40 acres of turnips, 5 acres of vetches, and sometimes more, cut green for the horses in summer, and six or eight acres of potatoes for fattening pigs. I think his wheat in later years would average, one year with another, 30 bushels per acre, and the barley 40 bushels. In addition to this he kept, on an average, 44 milch cows. He raised a dozen of his best calves every year; had a dozen two year olds, and fatted for the butcher every winter a dozen cows;—their place in the dairy being supplied by the dozen three year old heifers he had raised. He made cheese, and it was of excellent quality, although the night's milk was skimmed in the morning before it was put into the vat with the new morning's milk. And in this way he got about 100 lbs. of butter a week, in addition to the cheese. He kept nine horses, 150 large Southdown and Leicester sheep, and many pigs.

My land is naturally richer than the old Farm. Why cannot I make it equally productive?

In the dairy districts of this State, the farms are kept too exclusively to grass; and in the wheat region, too exclusively to grain. If we could combine the two should we not obtain better results? My uncle was a wheat grower, and his wife a Cheshire dairyman's daughter. In Cheshire the land is devoted pretty exclusively to the dairy. But at Moreton they combined the two systems, and I believe they made nearly as much cheese, butter, mutton, wool, and pork, as if the whole farm had been devoted solely to these; and on the other hand they obtained as much wheat and barley as if the farm had been devoted exclusively to grain.

Now I do not see why my farm, and much of the land in Western New York, will not produce as good cheese as the land at Moreton, and certainly as good meat. I asked Mr. Willard to visit Moreton and examine the matter. I do not know whether he did so or not. Sanford Howard did so, and I wish he would give his views on this subject. At Ingersoll, C. W., there is a large and flourishing cheese factory, and if I mistake not, it is as much a wheat growing section as Western New York. We want manure on our wheat farms, and wool growing is not very profitable, and cattle can be fatted cheaper at the west than here, and so with pork. But if we could make cheese, the problem would be solved. We could feed high, make rich manure, and raise good wheat.

Donald G. Mitchel, in his *Wet Days at Edgewood*, a book I am never weary of reading, quotes a maxim from Columella, which he says is broad enough to cover all possible conditions: "Whoever would devote himself to the pursuit of agriculture, should understand that he must summon to his aid—prudence in business, a faculty of spending, and a determination to work."

My uncle had all these. He had prudence, but it did not degenerate into parsimony. He fed his land and his stock with a liberal hand. He was not afraid to lay out money in improvements. He could look ahead and was willing to wait. He had confidence in good farming.

As an instance of his "faculty of spending." When guano was first introduced, he heard on good authority of its astonishing effect, and ordered five tons to give it a trial. It proved to be all that could be desired and the next year he ordered ten tons.

I once tried to persuade one of our Monroe County potato growers to use guano, and finally succeeded. "When you send for yours, you may order *fifty pounds* for me. I have not as much faith in these things as you have, but am willing to try it."

I want to raise a good crop of corn this year. The field has been in grass for some years. I am plowing under some 25 loads of manure per acre, and have a heap of last year's manure in the field, thoroughly rotted, that I intended to spread on the surface after plowing and harrow it in thoroughly before planting. "Would it not be better to put it in the hill?" Possibly it might, but the roots extend farther than we imagine, and will find it. Besides, I do not plant in hills. I shall drill in the corn. The Deacon does not believe in drilling. He thinks corn does far better in hills. But John Johnston writes me that he has drilled in all his corn since 1846, and few men have better crops.

I wrote Mr. Johnston that my underdrains were running freely, while the surface was frozen as solid as a rock, and asked him how the water got into the drains. He replies: "Don't you know that when we have much snow it draws the frost out of the ground, and the tile drains discharge all the water there is in the land? Some of mine have discharged water all winter. Where the snow blows off, they don't. You will learn much if you keep farming and draining! Some of my wheat made a good growth under the snow this winter. I suppose thousands of farmers never notice this fact." The above appears to be a partial explanation, but does not, it seems to me, cover all the facts.

I have just received the April *Agriculturist*. As Mr. Johnston says, I do not write very "plain" and the printers doubtless are often troubled to make out my meaning. They sometimes guess at it, and do not always hit it. Speaking of underdrains filling up with sediment, they make me say: "The chief danger is from the surface water washing away the soil, more or less, and running in large quantities into the drain." What I intended to say was, that where the drains run through the valleys of rolling land, the water in the spring runs along the surface of the frozen land and accumulates in the valleys over the drains. The soil over the drain is not frozen as hard as the rest of the land, and in several instances on my farm, the water soaks through this soft soil and makes a hole down to the drain, small, probably, at first, but soon wearing larger. These holes are usually about the size of a rat-hole, running perpendicularly down to the tiles. But where there are larger tiles the holes are sometimes larger. What I was afraid of was that this water, being more or less muddy, might, in a drain that has little fall, deposit silt, and choke it up. But I have recently been examining the matter, and find there is less danger from this source than I expected. The water being two or three feet above the drain, must be forced through the tiles with considerable rapidity, and carry the sediment with it.

While my hand is in, I may say that the argument in favor of feeding clover hay and oilcake in the March No. is rendered obscure by the omission of a line. It should have been stated that "the manure from a ton of oilcake is worth $19.72." Several gentlemen have written me about my remarks on this subject. If they will supply this line, and take a pencil and go over the calculation, they will come to the same conclusion that I did—namely, that, after deducting the expense of carting and spreading the manure, the net value of a load of clover hay and oilcake dung, with part straw for litter, is *seven times* as great as the manure obtained from feeding straw alone. And if this is true, are we not making a mistake in allowing American oilcake to be shipped to England?

Cotton-seed cake, which I understand is being made extensively, is more valuable for manure even than Linseed oilcake. It contains 6½ per cent. of nitrogen, 7 per cent. of phosphate of lime, and over 3 per cent. of potash, and these figures show that the manure obtained for a ton of it is worth $27.86. This is on the supposition that the husks are removed from the cotton before the oil is expressed. If this is not the case, the cake will be of far less value for manure, and of no value at all for feed. It is the "*decorticated* cotton-seed cake" that we need. It is valuable feed, and affords the richest manure, of any known vegetable food that has been investigated.

A correspondent asks me how I plant and cultivate beans. Last year I turned over an old sod, harrowed it thoroughly, marked it out in rows 2 feet 5 inches apart, with a common wooden marker, then drilled in the beans with the "Corn and Bean Planter." We finished the whole field of twelve acres in a day and a half. Of course it is not necessary to mark out the land before planting. The drill will do its own marking, but I find it better to mark the land first, as the drill can be guided so much straighter. The drill sows two rows at a time, and when the land is marked in advance, the tubes, or "hoes," run in the marks, and you can see the least deviation. I set two men at it, one to drive the horse and the other to guide the drill. Too much pains cannot be taken to plant straight. A little extra labor in doing this will be saved five times over in the after culture. Of course this is equally true of corn, potatoes, and all other hoed crops. The drill drops five or six beans in a hill, about 14 inches apart. I have no doubt the beans would do just as well, and perhaps better, if dropped a single bean at a time, two inches or so apart. They do very well planted so in the garden, but having them in hills is more convenient in hoeing. I hoed mine only once last year, but kept the cultivator running frequently between the rows. This is the great point, and it is here where so many fail. It is said to rust the leaves if cultivated when the dew is on. This may or may not be so. I do not know. But I do know that frequent cultivation will make all the difference between a good crop and a poor one. One of my neighbors told a friend that "there was the grandest field of beans he ever saw in his life on the north road." "They are Mr. Harris'." "Not they, he hasn't got a field on his farm that will produce such a crop as that." But they *were* my beans, and what is more, they were planted on the roughest and most neglected field on the farm—a field that had not been plowed for fifteen years, and produced little else than thistles and teasels. There was a great growth of beans, and it was caused by nothing but *frequent cultivation*. I do not know how often they were cultivated, but I think eight or nine times. At all events, not a weed was suffered to show its head between the rows.

"What is the best variety?" I have not had experience enough to tell. Hayward thinks the Marrow is the most profitable. It yields nearly or quite as well as the medium, and brings a higher price. The only objection to it is that the beans are apt to split open.

I question whether there is anything gained by scalding seed-peas to kill the pea-bug. Of course it will kill the bugs, but whether the next crop will be any more likely to escape, is somewhat doubtful. Two years ago I got my seed-peas from Canada. A finer sample could not be desired, and there was not, apparently, a bug in the whole fifty bushels. I sowed them on twelve acres and had a splendid crop. But a more buggy lot of peas I never saw. We thrashed them rather late in the fall, but on a warm, sunny day, and the bugs, or more correctly weevils, flew above the stock and round the heads of the men by thousands. The partly dormant bugs might have been gathered from under the fanning mill by the bushel.

This crop, as I have said, was grown from seed free from bugs. And it seems to me clear that simply destroying all the bugs there may be in the seed, will not insure a crop from their depredations as a consequence.

I may mention that the next year I sowed these buggy peas, and they grew apparently as well as sound ones. I presume they were as buggy as the previous crop, but I fed the peas to the pigs early in the fall, before the bugs were fully developed. This is really the only plan we can adopt, with safety, in this section. It is no use trying to raise peas for market, although I did sell a load or two to the *coffee* manufacturers in the city. They prefer, however, to get sound peas from Canada, though for my own part, I think a certain proportion of bugs in the peas, after they were roasted and ground, would make about as good coffee as the sound peas. But then, you know, people have their prejudices, and it is well to humor them.

One of my neighbors last year sowed his peas in June. They escaped the bug. But the crop was hardly worth harvesting. Better sow early, on rich land, raise a heavy crop, and feed them out very, early in the fall, to the pigs. The crop will pay very well for this purpose, and a good smothering crop of peas leaves the land in good condition for wheat. And no crop that we raise makes richer manure than peas.

Origin of Forced Drones.

BY BIDWELL BROS., ST. PAUL, MINN.

[By Forced Drones, those are meant, which, being reared in worker cells, are of small size and lower vitality than those raised in drone cells. Worker bees are imperfectly developed females, and Fertile Workers are those which are sometimes found laying eggs. These eggs not having any impregnation, if they hatch, all produce drones. Forced queens are those reared in case of the loss of a queen from eggs or larvæ which would have become worker bees, if hatched and fed in the usual way.—Ed.]

We found the origin of, and gained ability to recognize fertile workers, in trying to answer a question often put to us, much in this way: "Why do my bees, having reared forced queens, which were all removed before they commenced to lay, or lost in their flight to meet the drones, refuse again to rear queens, though worker eggs and larvæ be repeatedly given them, and destroy queen cells or kill queens, but persist in rearing drones in worker and drone cells?"

On removing a queen from a hive to induce the bees to replace the queen by rearing others from worker eggs or larvæ—as they will, several,—sometimes many common worker bees commence to consume large quantities of honey and pollen for the purpose of secreting jelly, to feed the selected worker larvæ to convert them into queens. This food, we suppose, developes their dormant ovaries, so that they may thereafter lay eggs. At first they are noticeable from their singular and uneasy motions, and are continually eating. We have often, in cool weather, separated the honey and pollen from these bees, by intervening empty combs, and always found these particular bees first at the stores. After several days, they have the appearance of robber bees—a black color, which in time has an oily look. We once tried to see if a high temperature gave robber bees their dark, greasy appearance, and allowed a stock of bees to steal or rob a pail of honey, first placing a thermometer in their hive; in 20 minutes the temperature arose from 64° to 108°. We had often observed the bees to take on that color, in hot, close weather, and confined a swarm on a hot noon-day, and the temperature arose to 131°, melting the combs with the great heat, the bees all becoming of this dark color and greasy lustre. One of our hottest days last summer indicated a temperature of 128° in the sun, and the brown of nearly all bees in close locations turned black.

When bees lose their young queens, they feed and caress the bees above described, and they, after some days, commence to lay eggs in worker, drone, and queen cells, often 10 to 15 eggs in a cell, laying more when the weather is cool than when it is hot. When one egg in a cell hatches, the remainder are consumed by the nursing bees. As drone larvæ are fed similar food to that fed to workers, drones mature in worker cells; yet these do not attain more than two-thirds the size of natural drones; while the larvæ from eggs laid in queen cells, doubtless from a difference in food, die before maturity. Unfecundated queens—those forced queens reared early or late in the season, and not meeting the drones or having met this kind of small drones, and the seed becoming exhausted, are worse than fertile workers, as they are more prolific, and more frequently lay in worker cells.

Although forced drones are apparently able to fulfill the office of male bees as well as forced queens that of a queen, they ought equally to be avoided as causing the degeneration of the stock.

[The Messrs. Bidwell answer the question proposed in their first paragraph, but do not tell what to do in such a case. We suppose the cure is simply to introduce an impregnated queen, kill the fertile workers, or break up the colony.]

Culture of the Castor Oil Bean.

BY S. B. STEWART, CLEAR CREEK LANDING, ILL.

[Although we are not familiar with the culture of the castor oil bean, except as an ornamental plant, we have no doubt it might be profitably cultivated in parts of the Union where now it is unknown. The geographical limits of its profitable employment as a farm crop, are, we should judge, nearly coincident with those of the Sweet potato, or the larger varieties of Dent corn. The following communication to the *Agriculturist* will be read with interest, and, though so late in the season, may form the basis of experiments, with a view to planting more largely another year.—Ed.]

"I plant what we call the Florida Beans; they are smaller than the Spanish Beans, and do better in this latitude; then, there is more oil to the bushel, (so say the oil factory men). They can be raised about 100 miles north of us, with success. A fair crop here is from 16 to 20 bushels per acre; 100 miles north, 10 to 12 bushels per acre. The soil is prepared first, the same as for corn, then lay your ground off both ways, seven feet apart each way, plant as soon as the frost is out of the ground and it will do to plow. Before planting, soak the beans say from 12 to 20 hours in warm water—about as warm as the hand will bear when beans are first put in—plant and cover same as corn, dropping two beans in each hill. They require about a week longer to come up than corn, and when the plants first come out of the ground, they are red. Castor beans are usually planted here on our poorest soil; still, a much better yield can be had from rich land. Our object in planting on poor soil is, that a crop raised on a piece of land one year, is equal in its effects to a crop of clover plowed in towards enriching, or "bringing land to," as it is often termed. Plow or use a cultivator (*the latter is the best*,) when the plants stand about 3 or 4 inches high, going close to the plant, leaving the middle of the row until you have gone both ways of the rows, and the beans have fresh loose dirt about the hills; then go through and clean the middle with a cultivator or plow. When the stalk is 7 to 10 inches high, go through and thin out, leaving one stalk in a hill; then plow or cultivate as corn, only be careful not to plow after the stalk is so high that the whiffletrees will break the branches and thus injure the plant. In fact, when the plants average 12 to 18 inches high, they can take care of themselves if the weeds are kept from the middle, between the rows. No stock will eat them excepting young colts, and if the land is grassy it is often well to turn in sheep or hogs.

I planted last year on the 9th of May (rather late); and began to gather the 14th of August. One can easily tell by watching, when the spikes are ripe enough to cut, viz.: when the bottom pods begin to crack; then cut the spikes and draw to a dry house—drying yards are nuisances. St. Louis, New Orleans, or New York are good markets—either of the latter preferable.

[This plant is a native of tropical countries, and where no frost stops its growth, attains the size of a small tree. The leaves are very large, and the contrasts of color in the leaves, stems and leafstalks, make it quite ornamental. The fruit is borne on spikes growing in the axils of the leaves and branches, and the seeds are inclosed in burs somewhat like miniature horse-chestnut burs. These, when ripe and dry, explode or "pop," throwing the seeds to a distance

CASTOR BEAN DRYING HOUSE.

of 12 or 15 feet, sometimes. When the gathering takes place, the spikes are cut when brown, and the bottom pod begins to crack open, and are spread in the sun, when no kiln or drying house is at hand. The ground where they are dried is called a "yard," and is prepared by leveling and rolling hard a piece with a good southern exposure. The ground so prepared is fenced with boards, to prevent the loss of seeds, or it is made to extend 12 to 15 feet on every side wider than the space covered by the spikes when spread out to dry. They are spread thin, and turned occasionally. In case of rain, the spikes are raked up and covered, and the beans are swept up. When all the pods have dried and shed their seeds, they are raked off, the beans winnowed, put in sacks and kept in a dry place. Ten acres of castor beans will justify the building of a drying house of 12×20 feet.—ED.]

DRYING HOUSE OR KILN.—The kiln or drying house is usually a frame or log building, but the material is unimportant. The one figured is about 20 feet long by 12 wide. The drying floor is 6 feet in the clear above the ground floor, and is made of slats a quarter of an inch apart. The floor above the stove is tight. The stove is set near the door and a 6×6 foot space is left around it. A pipe passes under the floor to the rear, where it passes through the floor, and returns above the spikes, and both the space around the stove and that through which the pipe passes, are surrounded by a boxing. The spikes being frequently stirred, the beans drop through the floor and accumulate below. There is a window above the drying floor for taking in the green spikes and removing the dry ones, which are used as fuel; and there is for convenience a window also, below the floor.

The Crevecœur Fowl.

This breed derives its name from Crevecœur, a town of Normandy, France, where for several years past, they have been extensively raised for the Paris markets, being highly valued both for weight and delicacy of flesh. The hens are low on the legs, with large fleshy thighs, the wings large, and the body square; the abdomen is voluminous and pendant, especially in those which are more than a year old; they walk slowly, scratch but little, and rarely fly. Their plumage is black, except white feathers may appear in the tuft on the head; the tuft is large, and the comb small, upright, two-horned; while a large cravat of feathers under the neck gives to them a matronly air, the tuft and singularly shaped comb present a grotesque but not unpleasing appearance. They are very tame, mumble little; in this resembling the Brahmas.

The cocks, which are similar in form to the hens, have a brilliant black plumage; their heads are handsomely surmounted with beautiful tufts, and large toothed, two-horned combs, which together form a kind of crown; they have also dense cravats of feathers, and are adorned with pendant wattles of large size.

The chickens are of great precocity, being frequently put up to fatten at the early age of three months. The hen produces large eggs, and is an excellent layer, but scarcely ever sits. Such is the description given in French works on fowls. So far as the appearance is concerned it is correct, as seen in recent importations. The accompanying illustration was made from pure bred birds, imported from the Jardin d'Acclimatation, Paris, and owned by A. M. Halsted. Mr. Jas. E. Mallory of Tarrytown, N. Y., who has some of the same stock, regards the likeness as quite faithful. If the breed proves to be as hardy and valuable here as it has in France, it will be an excellent addition to our present stock.

GROUP OF IMPORTED CREVECŒUR FOWLS.—*Drawn from Life for the American Agriculturist.*

Baskets for Sitting Hens' Nests.

The use of baskets for hens' nests is mentioned by some of the very earliest writers upon agriculture in our language, and in some respects they are peculiarly advantageous. Boxes are very apt to get musty and damp; baskets on the contrary, give free ventilation to the nest and its contents. They afford no safer lodging places for vermin than boxes, and may very easily be

moved, cleaned and washed. The one which we figure is in the style of those in common use in France, where poultry are reared so much more systematically than in this country. It represents a home-made willow or wicker affair with a cover to shut the hen in, she being taken off or allowed to go off once a day to feed, and a label is attached for any memoranda which may be desirable—at least, for a record of the kind of eggs and the date of setting the hen

The American Black Bear.

(*Ursus Americanus.*)

Bears are not very uncommon over a considerable portion of the Northern United States, and the one we represent is the only species ever seen wild in America south of the Arctic regions, and east of the Great Plains. The Yellow bear and the Cinnamon bear being regarded as varieties of this species. The American Black Bear is seldom more than 6 feet in length, and 3 feet in hight at the shoulders, and is characterized by its long, straight, shining black coat, high, oval, rounded ears, short tail, short feet, and short blunt claws, covered by the hair. Its color is dark brown to nearly or quite black, with a yellowish, dusky brown patch on each side of the muzzle. The food of this bear is almost exclusively of a vegetable nature, namely: wild cherries, berries, grapes, nuts, acorns, honey, sundry roots, and such things. It eats eggs also, and some insects, and when very hungry, small quadrupeds and birds—though it seldom takes animal food from choice. When sore pressed, bears sometimes enter farm-yards and do considerable damage, being partial to pigs and poultry—taking also it is said, sometimes a sheep or a calf. The chief damage they do to the farmer is, however, in his potato fields, corn fields, and orchards—preferring the corn in its green state, when fit for boiling, and eating large quantities of sweet apples, peaches or other fruit. The bear is timid and will seldom attack a man, never, unless provoked or in defence of its young. The female has two young at a time, bringing them forth very early in the spring. Continued severe weather not unfrequently forces them out from their retirement soon after this, in search of food, and at such times they are often captured, the old one submitting, at least at first, with a poor grace to restraint or confinement, but the young ones becoming and remaining as tame as puppies. Bears are naturally docile and imitative; they climb trees with ease, are very quick in many of their motions. They are protected by a thick hide, a very thick coat of furry hair, and almost as thick a coating of fat as a well fed porker, and thus possess a triple defence against blows and against cold, as well as against the attacks of dogs or other animals. The flesh is delicate and savory, the steaks having much the flavor of pork. During the winter the meat is still common in the markets, even of our eastern cities; the grease is in considerable request for hair oil, and brings a good price, and the skins are valuable and salable according to size and the quality of the fur.

THE AMERICAN BLACK BEAR.—(*Ursus Americanus.*)

The Polar Bear (*Ursus maritimus.*)

The White or Polar Bear is regarded as the largest, most powerful, and, with the exception of the Grizzly Bear of the Rocky Mountains, as the fiercest of the bears. They are courageous in defence of their mates, and of their young, for which they manifest the most touching affection; savage when attacked, and very tenacious of life. The food of Polar Bears is wholly animal, they live chiefly upon fish, and are altogether maritime in their habits. The prominent characteristics of this bear are large size, and great length of body, (which varies considerably, occasionally reaching a length of nine feet with a hight of four feet, and weight of 1,500 pounds), the neck is also proportionally long; a small head; very small ears; soles of the feet very large; the line of the forehead and nose remarkably straight, and the coat of fine long fur of a nearly white color. These bears range and rule within the North Polar Circle, upon the ice-bound coasts and floating ice. They do not live long in menageries or zoological collections on account of their suffering from the heat, but they always form a very attractive feature in these exhibitions. The flesh is not savory. The habits of the Polar Bear are little understood. Whether they hibernate, or not, is not settled. It would seem probable that when the long arctic winter night shuts down, the well fed and fat ones retire into winter quarters, but those not in so good condition, wander as prompted by hunger in search of food. It is an interesting fact that the shape and character of the teeth of this purely carnivorous bear vary scarcely at all from those of the almost purely vegetable eaters of the same genus. These animals are hunted by the inhabitants of those regions where they abound, for the flesh which doubtless compares favorably with that of the seals, walrusses and oily fish, and for the skins which form an article of commerce, making very fine sleigh robes, etc.

THE POLAR BEAR.—(*Ursus maritimus.*)

THE "TEXAS MURRAIN." — This disease, also called "Spanish Fever," which had entirely disappeared during the war, has, this year, done in some sections terrible injury. It is known only in the track of Texas cattle, or those with which they have come in contact, its period of incubation is very short usually, but with the Texas stock very long, so that apparently healthy cattle communicate the disease, and cattle die after taking it, while the original animals are still well, to all appearance. The fatal symptom is extreme thirst; death follows soon after drinking. A severe frost is said to put an end to the disease.

Large Root Crops.

We notice in the Report of the Massachusetts Horticultural Society, that the farm connected with the Deer Island House of Industry raised extraordinary root crops. An acre in mangolds produced 73 *tons of roots*, carefully weighed, and 5 tons in *tops*, by estimate. This acre was planted with potatoes in 1863, carrots in 1864, onions in 1865, and with mangolds in 1866. The manure, each previous year, had been 20 cords of compost of sea kelp and stable manure. In the fall of 1865 it was heavily coated with sea-weed (*Laminaria*), and the weed plowed in and re-plowed in the spring of 1866. The seed was sown in drills 30 inches apart. Mr. Payson, the manager of the farm, estimates the value of mangolds as equal to sugar beets, and the yield as one-third greater. The rotation and the adaptation of marine manures to mangolds, are noticeable points in this statement. On the same farm and with similar treatment, 29 tons of carrots were grown to the acre. Our shore farmers who neglect sea-weed and root crops are not living up to their privileges.

Tim Bunker on Jim Crow.

MR. EDITOR:—It may seem an ungracious task to say a word agin this gentleman, when everybody is writing up people of color in gineral. Folks who, a year ago, could not express their disgust of the negro, in language strong enough, are now bawling for universal suffrage. Such sudden conversions I never saw in camp meeting. But I have been in favor of their voting this twenty years; so I've no prejudice agin color to influence my opinion on the crow question. You said you wanted all the Hookertown news, especially if it had any bearing on farming. Now you see, we have had a big ferment in the Farmer's Club up here on this question, which is certainly as old as I am, and I guess as old as the country. I thought it had been settled several times, but it is one of them questions that don't stay settled. I expect it is because we haven't got upon the right foundation yet. I have always noticed that any unsound opinion kept working in the public mind like bad food in the stomach. It won't stay down. Hookertown has spoke and I rather think Jim Crow is settled forever.

You see, these creatures had been uncommon plenty last season, and we had all suffered more or less from their depredations in planting time, and this had been put down as one of the things that was to be discussed and settled in the Club this winter. "Jim Crow, shall he jump or no?" In old times in Connecticut they said no, and offered a premium on crows, and the boys used to hunt them, and bring the young ones by the basketfull to get their pocket money. Then the men, who were science on birds, thought the crows killed a good many grubs, and paid their way and said we must not kill them.

Deacon Smith was chairman for the evening and stated the question. He said "it was admitted that the crow did some good and a great deal of mischief. The point was to find out whether he did more good or hurt."

Jotham Sparrowgrass said "he did not think there was any question at all about it. He knew what he was about when he went to the Legislature in Hartford, well nigh fifty years ago, and got the law passed to give a bounty on foxes and crows. He said both of 'em were the farmer's enemies, and he didn't know which was the worst. He said our fathers understood their cases, and killed them off as fast as they could lay hands on them. Talk about crows destroying bugs! He has shot 'em many a time, and he always found more corn and carrion in their crops than anything else."

Cicero Smith said "he was astonished to hear such sentiments from his venerable friend. He thought the crow had not been made in vain. If it had not been for some good end he would never have been brought into existence, and been made so hardy and so prolific. He was a very long-lived and very shy bird, so that with all the warfare which men had made upon them they were as numerous as ever. They were the farmers' friends, picking up a multitude of grubs and worms that preyed upon his crops, and acting the part of a scavenger in removing dead animals, that would otherwise pollute the atmosphere; they pulled up some corn, to be sure, but every laborer was worthy of his hire."

Mr. Spooner, our minister, said "he found some difficulty with Mr. Smith's argument. A good many creatures had been made for a different state of the world than existed at present, and if we admitted that they were originally useful, it would not follow that they could not very well be spared now. He said they had found over in Shadtown, and in many other places, the remains of extinct birds, beasts and fishes. These fossils had had their day, and died out, or been killed off, because they had become nuisances. He was inclined to think that it was about time for man, who was lord of nature, to dispense with the services of the crow; he could join the great company of fossils without disturbing the balance of nature. He admitted he had been useful in the earlier ages, when animal life was more abundant, and the air was likely to be tainted with the effluvia of dead animals. But the farmer did not need such a scavenger now. Dead animals were exceedingly valuable for the compost heap, and he must be a very foolish cultivator who would allow them to waste unburied. Wolves and bears, and other wild animals had disappeared from the State, without any suspicion that the Almighty had made a mistake in their creation. He thought that the crows could all be killed off without interfering with the divine purposes, according to which man has the responsibility of subduing nature, and ruling over it."

Jake Frink said "he was agin crows, and had been from the start. He never had been on more than one side of this question. They pulled up his corn whether it was tar'd or not, and strings and scare crows had n't any more influence on 'em than on the wind. He had seen 'em light right on a stuffed man. He never'd found but one thing to fix 'em, and that was corn soaked in New England rum. That made the critters so drunk you could knock 'em over as easy as lame geese."

Seth Twiggs thought "that was the best use neighbor Frink could put his rum to. If he kept it, he was mighty afraid that somebody besides the crows would become extinct. His opinion was that 'carrion crow' expressed the character of the bird as well as his habits. He not only pulled up his corn, and bothered him to death with planting over, but he destroyed the eggs and young birds in his orchard. He was a thievish, blood thirsty fellow, ready to kill any thing, that has not strength enough to defend itself against his attacks. He knew a good many of the small birds lived mostly on insects, for he had watched them when feeding their young. He thought the crow destroyed the grub killers, instead of the grubs, and he was glad to see folks getting waked up to his true character. He should go strong for smoking him out."

You see which way the current is setting up here. Every crow thinks his own young the whitest, they say; and I am perhaps a little prejudiced in favor of Hookertown, but it strikes me that there is about as much good common sense in our Club as there is in any scientific society. I have to admit that I have been on both sides of this question, but have found hard bottom at last. Our fathers were right in killing crows. The birds belong to the fossil age. There is no music in his caw. He prefers a dead carcass to a living one, and will devour a half pound of putrid flesh a day. We can make a better use of the flesh than to bestow it on this sneaking thief. He destroys our song birds and worm eaters in the nest. He is the pest of our corn fields and the scourge of our orchards, where the farmer's true friends build their nests. A strong petition is going up to the Legislature from Hookertown this spring for a big bounty on crows.

Hookertown, Conn.,
March 1st.
Yours to command,
TIMOTHY BUNKER, Esq.

The Pennsylvania Agricultural College.

[We have of late refrained from any allusion to the Agricultural College of Pennsylvania, for the reason that reports came to us, from various sources, of its utter inefficiency and demoralization. The trustees have made a new start, and their appointments, as far as we are informed, are highly commendable. The following account of its condition and prospects is by a scientific friend, who is in no way connected with the College, and we give it without adopting his views in some particulars.—EDS.]

Some time since accident led us into the neighborhood of the Agricultural College, and we availed ourselves of an opportunity offered for going through the building, and being made familiar with its workings.

We start out with the statement that it this session begins its course under new and more promising auspices. First in the list of reforms, we find the abolition of compulsory labor. In theory, I am aware, wiseacres will tell us the move was a bad one, and likely to frustrate entirely the original design. But we do not so see it. Boys are boys, (no doubt all will admit,) whether found in the streets of their native towns, or under the protecting ægis of a literary institution, and to convince a hundred or more of them that there existed a necessity of doing well the work assigned them, would, we imagine, be a task likely to baffle the most practical men. We contend that loose habits of working will be more likely engendered than correct ones. The best evidence of the truthfulness of this statement may be taken from the opinions of those in the vicinity of such institutions. While labor is no longer compulsory, the students may, on demand, have portions of ground assigned them, and, in the care of such, their agricultural propensities may be thoroughly ventilated. As a ready and accomplished guide over these operations, the Professor of Agriculture may exercise his authority. Here at once is instituted a generous rivalry, instead of the slip-shod habits induced by making all men, men of all work, and then lumping the result. The time allotted for completing the course of study is too short to allow of from three to four hours outside labor per day.

A glance at the curriculum shows a new feature. While the literary course is quite equal to that of our best colleges, and may be adopted by all so inclined, there exists also a course of study more polytechnic in its nature, and which is more advanced in its requirements than that of some older and more pretentious institutions I could name. Let us glance *en passant* at the course of study insisted on as the requisite for obtaining the scientific diploma of the College: Anatomy, Physiology, Botany, Entomology, Zoology, Shades and Shadows, and Perspective Drawing, Physics, Principles and Practice of Road Making, Chemistry (laboratory practice two years), Meteorology, Practical Astronomy, Physical Geography, *Geology, Hygiene (lectures), Mineralogy. We have here selected from the list of studies *only such as are entirely omitted or passed over with the merest smattering in most colleges.* They are here *brought out practically* into a desired prominence. Correlated with these we find an item (not always noticed in college graduates), a decent acquaintance with our mother tongue imperatively demanded. Mathematics, Logic, Rhetoric, and the Constitution of the United States, come in to supply the polish. Ere long a competent Professor of Modern Language will take a place in the institution. A course of Agriculture adds to most of the above Horticultural and Agricultural practice, Lectures on Domestic Animals, their diseases and cures; Soils, Manures, Rotation of Crops, Drainage and Tillage, Grain, Grass, Root and other Crops, Agricultural Implements and Farm Buildings. Connected with the institute exercises proper, we have military exercises from the *School of the Soldier*, up to lectures on *Higher Tactics*, under supervision of acknowledged competency. These military exercises are obligatory. Cases of conscience alone are excepted.

One fact more is worthy of note—chairs are not filled by superannuated "good fellows," who have no other visible means of support. The fitness of things seems to have been considered in making the recent appointments.

The State appropriation of the land scrip being now made to this College, it is placed on a secure footing, and may be expected to run an extensive career of public usefulness.

Such an institution has long been wanted to meet an existing necessity. Dead languages are placed in their proper position, and studies which really confer mental power in *a measure substituted.* For those who wish to take up Latin and Greek every facility is provided, but diplomas may now be merited without giving to them the major part of a four years' course.

Let us hope that ere long we may not the less "gaze at the stars," but that we may fall less frequently into the mudholes of our own ignorance; that we shall have more men whose minds are rounded by proper educational courses, and fewer men made angular by contractions derived from some of the liberal studies.

Dog Statistics.

We have received several communications in reply to our correspondent's article on a dog law, signed "Connecticut," in our March issue, some wise and some otherwise. It seems to us, that "I. H. P." in his "word for dogs" admits all that "Connecticut" claims, and that they are substantially agreed. "It is really discreditable," he says, "that almost the only dogs in the country which are treated with any care, are lap dogs, the most useless, and bull dogs, the least sagacious. The natural fruit of such neglect is a race of nondescripts of all kinds, deteriorated in body and brain." It is because of this nondescript character of our dog population that "Connecticut" and all friends of sheep want efficient dog laws in all our States. Ninety-nine out of every hundred of our dogs are worthless curs which need clearing out as much as the old Canaanites did to make way for something civilized, that can keep company with our domestic animals. The destruction occasioned among sheep by these animals is appalling, and only needs to be better known to secure the requisite legislation. The Department of Agriculture has made a beginning of gathering statistics upon this subject. In 373 counties reported, there was an estimated loss of 77,834 sheep killed, besides many others injured. Some counties suffered to the extent of 2000 or 3000, and the average number per county was 208.

From this, the number killed in the whole country is estimated at **500,000**, worth at least **$2,000,000**, while the injury to those not killed is another million, making a loss to the country of *three millions of dollars*, as the direct result of dogs killing sheep. But this is only a small part of the pecuniary damage inflicted upon us by these wretched curs. In many districts admirably adapted to sheep, farmers dare not embark in the business from fear of the dogs. In the counties where 8000 sheep are annually slain by the dogs, we think this kind of husbandry can not pay very well. The counties where few are slain, we apprehend, are the ones where the dogs have made sheep husbandry unprofitable. The pastures are desolate and growing up to brush for want of cropping. Millions of dollars are lost to the country every year from this cause, and we have, as a consequence, to pay dear for wool and mutton.

Then we have to add to this the enormous tax of supporting our dog population. We have no reliable statistics on this subject, but estimate one dog to a family, say seven millions in the whole country. Some families have none, but others have six, a dog to each child, and glory in them! The food that an average cur will devour would keep a pig, and is worth at least ten dollars a year. People who are paying 70 *millions of dollars a year* for the support of curs, to say nothing of damages, ought to make inquiries about dog laws.

Pleuro-Pneumonia or Lung Murrain.

The pleuro-pneumonia is one of the most fatal and distressing maladies which ever attack cattle. At all times liable to spread rapidly among animals coming near or in contact with those diseased, it frequently assumes the form of a contagious epidemic, being taken by almost every animal coming within striking distance. This was remarkably the case in Massachusetts a few years since, and the disease every now and then breaks out somewhere with alarming violence, but happily it appears to be more easily controlled here than in Europe, where the pole ax, or absolute isolation are the only approved ways of checking its ravages. This disease has been confounded with the Rinderpest or Steppe Murrain, which has lately wrought such distress in England, and has not yet stayed its march of destruction, but it has few or no symptoms in common with that, except contagiousness and fatality. The disease exists almost constantly among the swill-milk stables of New York and Brooklyn, and probably other cities, and certainly should come under the careful investigation of the Board of Health. The following description is furnished by Dr. Busteed, of the N. Y. College of Veterinary Surgeons:

Pleuro-Pneumonia of Cattle.—A malignant form of inflammation of the lungs, of an eminently contagious character, peculiar to the ox-tribe, has existed within the memory of man in the mountain regions of Central Europe.

Symptoms.—From the time that an animal is exposed to the contagion to the first manifestation of symptoms, a certain period elapses; this is the period of incubation. It varies from a fortnight to forty days, or even two months. Some credit may be given to reports of even longer periods. During this period cows are found to thrive fast, and often to yield much milk. The first signs, proving that the animal has been seized, can scarcely be detected by any but a professional man; though, if a proprietor of cattle were extremely careful, and had painstaking individuals about his stock, he would invariably notice a slight shiver usher in the disorder, which for several days, even after the shivering fit, would limit itself to slight interference with breathing, detected readily on auscultation. Perhaps a cough might be noticed, and a diminution of the appetite and milk secretion. Though the amount of milk may not be much diminished at first, milk-maids sometimes say that a clever milker can tell when the cow is taken ill. The animal becomes costive, and the shivering fits recur. The cough becomes more constant and oppressive, the pulse full and frequent, usually numbering about 80 per minute at first, and rising to upwards of 100. The temperature of the body rises, and all the symptoms of acute fever set in. A moan or grunt, in the early part of the disease, indicates a dangerous attack, and the nostrils rise spasmodically at each inspiration; the air rushes through the inflamed windpipe and bronchial tubes, so as to produce a loud, coarse, respiratory murmur; and the spasmodic action of the abdominal muscles indicates the difficulty the animal experiences also in the act of expiration. Pressure over the spaces between the ribs and on the spine, induce the pain and shrinking characteristic of pleurisy, and a deep moan not unfrequently follows such an experiment. The eyes are bloodshot, mouth clammy, skin dry and tightly bound to the subcutaneous tissues, and the urine is scanty and high-colored.

On auscultation, the characteristic, dry, sonorous râle of ordinary bronchitis may be detected along the windpipe and in the bronchial tubes. A loud sound of this description is not unfrequently detected at the interior part of either side of the chest, while the respiratory murmur is entirely lost posteriorly, from consolidation of the lung. A decided leathery friction sound is detected over a considerable portion of the thoracic surface. As the disease advances, and gangrene, with the production of cavities in the lungs, ensues, loud, cavernous râles are heard, more or less circumscribed, occasionally attended by a decided metallic noise. When one lung alone is affected, the morbid sounds are confined to one side, and on the healthy side the respiratory murmur is uniformly louder than is natural all over. By carefully auscultating diseased cows from day to day, interesting changes can be discovered during the animal's lifetime. Frequently the abnormal sounds indicate progressive destruction; but at other times portions of lung that have been totally impervious to air, become the seat of sibilant râles, and gradually a healthy respiratory murmur proves that, by absorption of the materials that have been plugging the lung-tissue, resolution is fast advancing. I have seen some very remarkable cases of this description.

Unfortunately, we often find a rapid destruction of lung-tissue, and speedy dissolution. In other cases, the general symptoms of hectic or consumption attend lingering cases, in which the temperature of the body becomes low; the animal has a dainty appetite, or refuses all nourishment. It has a discharge from the eyes, and a fœtid, sanious discharge from the nose. Not unfrequently it coughs up disorganized lung-tissue and putrid pus. Great prostration, and indeed typhous symptoms set in. There is a fœtid diarrhœa, and the animal sinks in the most emaciated state, often dying from suffocation, in consequence of the complete destruction of the structures concerned in respiration.

Treatment.—Stop all communication with the ascertained source of the disease. Do not disturb the cows from their byres, or the oxen from their stalls, as removing animals from their old quarters tends to spread disease, and does no good to the cattle. Allow water, feed judiciously, and give carbonate of ammonia, preparations of iron, gentian, or other tonics, sparingly.

Horse Hay-Forks, Grapples and Harpoons.

The subject of Horse Hay-Forks has been brought prominently before the public in the great "Auburn Trial" of mowers and reapers, and hay and grain harvesting implements, held in July, by the N. Y. State Ag'l Society, the report of which is just published, and recently by a trial of some 16 Forks at Rye, under the auspices of the American Institute Farmers' Club, the report of which appeared in the *American Agriculturist* for April, page 127.

In common parlance, every thing used to pitch hay off a load is called a fork, though

Fig. 1.—GLADDING HORSE HAY FORK. Fig. 2.

some have not the remotest resemblance to that implement in its normal form. They all, that will work at all, present to the farmer the great advantage of being able to do this fatiguing and lung-trying work by horse-power, and very quickly, all, with proper appliances, carrying the hay up into the ridge of the roof and along to where it may be wanted. Some are arranged expressly for, and sold with these "travelers," others with or without the ropes and blocks (pulleys) needed in the simplest operations.

We observe three very distinct varieties of hay pitchers, namely: *First*, the forks proper, illustrated by figures 1 and 3, having long or short straight handles, or short handles at right angles to the direction of the tines; *Second*, the "grappling forks," or grapples, which are like two forks working together, and grasping their load between them, one of these is shown in figure 5, but they vary exceedingly, having 4 and 4 fingers, or tines, opposed to each other, 3 and 3, 2 and 2, 1 and 1, 1 and 3, 1 and 2, respectively. *Third*, Harpoons, shown in figures 7 to 14. These are a comparatively new invention, and their introduction struck dismay into

Fig. 3.—THE PALMER FORK.

the hearts of patentees of some of the good old horse-forks, but they are more limited in their application than was supposed. The principle on which they work is obvious. They are thrust perpendicularly into the hay, then opened, exposing the barbs or shoulders of the head or spurs, as a spear or harpoon, which lay hold upon the hay when the upward draft comes.

When one buys such a tool, he should study beforehand what uses he wishes to put it to. If he pitches chiefly timothy and clover hay, or any long, coarse hay, of which he can, without difficulty, take up heavy forkfuls with the common pitch fork, then let him think where he wishes to pitch it, if over the great beam, or into windows from the outside, or from the barn floor a long way back. If he has much short, fine hay to pitch, he should be aware that the harpoons and grapples with few fingers are less adapted to do this work than other kinds of forks. If he wishes to use his hay fork for loading coarse manure, certain kinds are very well adapted to this work—and these in turn are usually not so rapid at unloading coarse hay as others. Loose straw and grain, as oats and barley, are best handled by grapples, though the true *forks* manage them very well, and on the whole, we think that for definite ends, each kind

Fig. 4.

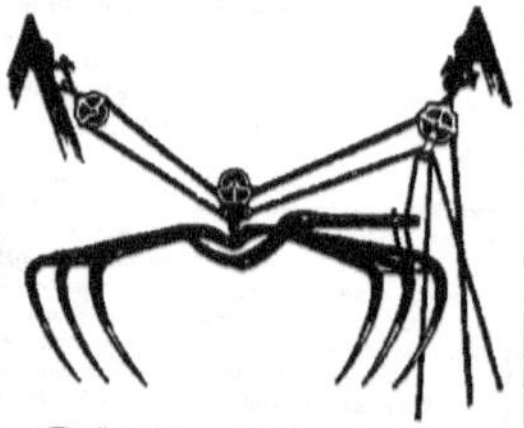

Fig. 5.—THE RAYMOND GRAPPLING FORK.

of fork has its especial claims upon the farmer.

Fig. 1 represents the Gladding Fork, as made by J. L. Mansfield & Co., Clockville, N. Y., price $11. This fork took the first premium at the Auburn trial, and is well adapted to all common purposes, will take its load over high beams into windows, and other narrow places, takes up a good load, though not very large, and is easily tripped. The rope whereby it is tripped passes through the handle, and is attached to the catch which holds the head in position. The handle being hinged upon the cross head, when tripped, the head drops, depositing its load as shown in fig. 2. An iron brace may be and is attached, which supports the long handle in a nearly horizontal position when not loaded. This is a slight modification of one of the original styles of horse fork, which was simply a large fork, such as this would be with a fixed handle. It was loaded as this is, the man on the load holding the handle down by means of a cord attached to the end, thus balancing the load, and when he wished, he dropped the hay by letting go the cord, when the handle would fly up. There were many objections to this form, chiefly obviated by the Gladding fork.

Fig. 6.

Fig. 7. Fig. 8.

Figures 3 and 4 represent the Palmer Fork (price $12, with pulleys). This took the first prize at the recent Farmers' Club trial. The tines are sickle shaped, and the short handle fixed in the head piece. When the fork enters the hay, it is in the position shown in figure 4; it is loaded by pressing the bail forward or the handle backward, so that the hinged-brace becomes straight and rigid, and holds the fork in the position shown in figure 3. Thus it is lifted, and the load is dropped by drawing upon the trip cord, which causes the brace to double up, and lets the handle up and the tines down, dropping their load. This is an excellent and useful implement, adapted to all varieties of work, well made and easily operated, and is found in most well furnished agricultural implement stores.

Fig. 5 shows Raymond's Grappling Fork, made by Chapman, Hawley & Co., Utica, N. Y. (price $20). This implement took the second premium at the Auburn trial, and also at the Farmers' Club trial. It is loaded by being lowered down upon the hay, and will take up a pretty good load if simply lifted, each head should, however, be shoved down into the hay, which they enter easily. The heads draw together when they rise, and the load is dropped by drawing the heads apart, by means of the cord and lever seen upon one side. The arrangement of the three pulleys, etc., looks a little complicated, but it is easily managed. The pulleys may be set at any distance apart, and the hay conveyed to the extreme end of the barn before it is dumped. This attachment, indispensable to this one, is applicable to any fork, and enables a single horse to move forkfuls which he otherwise could not lift. This fork is said to be especially good for loading manure, and it works well in oats, barley and rowen hay. Fig. 6 is a clamp or grapple for attaching the pulleys to the rafters, an exceedingly simple and efficient little affair. It is lifted to its place, and detached, by means of a pole with an iron

Fig. 9.— SPROUT'S FORK. —Fig. 10.

head adapted to the purpose, and might be useful for many other things about the farm.

Figs. 7 and 8 represent Blodgett's Harpoon Fork, (made by C. C. Blodgett, Watertown, N. Y.,) which received the first prize in the class of Harpoons at the Farmers' Club trial. It consists of a smooth shaft like a gun barrel with a pointed end, out of which, by a simple mechanism, two prongs or "cat's claws" are thrown, when the implement has been thrust down into the hay. Our figures were made from very poor engravings, but illustrate the principle. An improvement has been made which does away with the lever and pulley outside the shaft, and brings the machinery necessary to throw out and draw in the "cat's claws" all within the ring-handle to which the lifting rope is attached. This is apparently simple and strong, not so long as many of the harpoons, but is capable of lifting very heavy forkfuls.

Figs. 9 and 10 exhibit Sprout's Harpoon Fork and Hay-knife, made by A. B. Sprout, Muncy, Pa., (price $9 for fork alone, $11 for fork and 3 pulleys). This is a remarkable implement. It consists of two flat pieces of steel working together, being riveted like a pair of shears, (in fact Mr. Sprout claimed at Rye that they were

Fig. 11.— WALKER FORK. —Fig. 12

good to trim trees and hedges). The rounded points of these are ground sharp, and are notched an inch or inch and a half above the ends as shown in the cuts. When the blades are closed together, the implement enters the hay with great ease, it is then opened, as shown, and will lift very heavy loads, carrying them securely. The report of the Committee at Auburn commends this fork highly, making an award to it, equal in amount to a second premium, and states that it picks up scattering hay upon the floor, "better than either of the other forms." It received the second prize in its class at the trial at Rye. This "Fork," (more knife, or pair of shears,) is an excellent hay knife, and might be no bad investment if bought for this purpose alone.

Figs. 11 and 12 represent the Walker Harpoon Fork, made by Wheeler, Mellick & Co., Albany. (price $10 and $1 each for pulleys). This is also a harpoon, entering the hay like a spear as in fig. 11. The head is turned to one side by means of a lever, as shown in fig. 12, and when the load is lifted and brought over the right place, a jerk on the trip-cord, causes the head to resume its former position and the load falls. On the whole a very neat and efficient tool, lifting immense forkfuls, and easily worked.

Figs. 13 and 14.

Figs. 13 and 14 show another very simple harpoon, made by the Ames Plow Company of Boston, and of 53 Beekman St., New York (price $5). It was not well operated at Rye, but lifted good loads, and was apparently not hard to work. Its construction is exceedingly simple, being a straight harpoon with a movable shield, covering the barbs, which is shoved down when the fork is loaded, after it has entered the hay, and drawn up, crowding the hay off from the barbs when it is unloaded. The workmanship is excellent, and, with one or two slight modifications, we think bids fair to become a favorite.

Any of these forks would be, at least, awkward things to have fall from the top of the barn upon the mow where men where mowing away hay, or upon the cart, and there is not the least danger of such a catastrophy if they are well secured to the lifting rope. Careless hands frequently endanger their own lives and those of others by either not knowing how or not half doing a job. It is best always to tie a regular bowline knot (figured on page 305, October, 1855) this is perfectly secure. In dragging down over the beams most of these forks present themselves very awkwardly to the man on the load. In fact it almost makes one shudder to see such a sharp edged affair as Sprout's come swaying down, performing girations about a man's head. The simply sharp pointed ones are bad enough, but when it comes to two-edged swords we can but utter a word of warning.

Two—or ten Per Cent on Investments? —It is estimated that the property invested in agriculture does not pay over two per cent. interest annually. This may be near the truth for the whole country. The property embraces vast tracts of wild land that pay nothing, and in the southern parts of the country large districts that are barely scratched by the plow, paying much less than two per cent. For the northern States the estimate is much below the truth. There are, possibly, farmers here who do not get two per cent. a year on the cash value of their farms, yet we think them rare. There are others who make their farms pay seven per cent. and more, but these are also exceptions. The farms of the northern States probably do not pay much over four per cent., but this is owing more to the way their capital is invested than to any defect in the business. Full one-half of this capital is invested in land that is not used, and so does not pay any interest. If one-half of a man's farm is in woodland that he does not need for timber or fuel, in swamps, in pastures that are not grazed, so far as immediate returns are concerned, he might as well be without it. Land pays no interest that has not capital and labor expended upon it. If this change were made, and the dead capital were made active, the farm would pay better than bank stock. The smallest, best worked farms pay best. Good gardens pay twenty per cent.

A Poultry Fancier's View.

BY A. M. DECKER, GLENS FALLS, N. Y.

My belief is, that with judicious management, there can be made a clear profit of from two to five dollars on each hen. The first question which arises is, "What breed is the best?" As for me, I put the Brahma Pootra, with its large size, rich feather, and quietness, ahead. If I could keep but one kind it should be the pure Brahma. They will not get over a common fence, are always at home, and together. The chicks are very hardy and sure to live, which can not be said of most other pure breeds. Brahmas will keep a family in eggs the year round better than any other fowl, if provided with good quarters.

Next to the Brahmas, I put the White Leghorns, then come the White-faced Black Spanish, Sicilians, Golden Penciled Hamburghs, and Silver Penciled Hamburghs. These six varieties constitute my choice. There are other breeds, perhaps, equally as good, but none better.

I can not put the Spanish ahead, unless it might be for a warm climate. I am a fancier of the pure White-faced Black Spanish, but more for fancy than profit. They lay the nicest eggs of any fowl and a great many of them, but

Fig. 1.—PERSPECTIVE ELEVATION OF FOWL HOUSE.

their long and continued spell of moulting in the fall takes off a great deal from their good qualities, besides they are too tender for a cold climate, unless one has pride enough in them to keep them in a warm place, which is very essential in making fowls of any kind lay in winter.

I have a plan for building a very cheap poultry house, which I submit to your readers.

It is 60 feet long and 12 feet wide, divided into six different apartments to keep the different kinds separate. *A* is the laying room, *B*, roosts, *C*, scratching room, etc., *E*, door. The partitions should be of lattice work, the building filled in at least six inches with saw-dust or tan-bark (roof and all). Yards to be made in front in proportion, double windows. These rooms are suitable for from six to twelve fowls, which is as many as should ever go together, they will be found more profitable than a large flock. Fowls kept in such a house and provided with a variety of food—grains of different kinds,

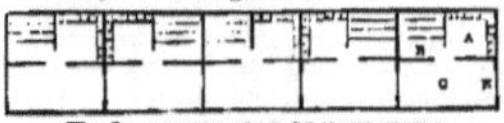

Fig. 2.—GROUND PLAN OF FOWL HOUSE.

boiled potatoes, meat, gravel, lime and ashes, they will do about as well as if running at large, destroying your garden, and doing more damage to yourself and your neighbors than they are all worth. I would also paint the roosts, etc., occasionally with gas tar, which is a sure cure for vermin. If not put on too thick it will dry in a short time. It also keeps the fowls healthy.

The manure will (if taken care of) nearly pay the care taken in their keeping. It should not be allowed to remain a great while in the house.

The Culture of Indian Corn.

The culture of Indian corn is to be undertaken not alone because it is profitable to raise the grain for sale, or for feeding, but because it is one of the best crops we have to subdue weeds, and to amend the soil by the thorough tillage which it requires, and which it enables us to apply with profit. In fact, for many eastern farmers, it is this consideration alone which gives a margin for profit in connection with the corn crop. How mistaken then is the practice which half does this work. In the vicinity of railroads, by which we can obtain western corn, where land is worth 100 to 150 dollars an acre, and where manure is worth $2 an ox-cart load, no man can afford to raise corn, except as a cleaning and tillage crop as part pay for labor.

The accompanying engraving is made from a drawing sent us by a subscriber who has used the implement it represents with satisfaction. It is a harrow for going astride the rows of corn and destroying the weeds while yet the corn is very small and liable to be covered up if the cultivator teeth were used. The teeth are of square iron, the beams of 4 x 4 stuff, 4 feet long,

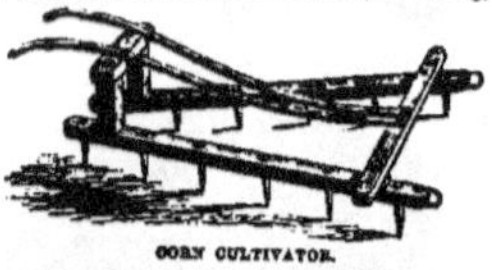

CORN CULTIVATOR.

connected at both ends as shown; at the rear, the teeth are brought within one foot; at the front they are spread 3 to 4½ feet apart. There are several holes in the front cross-piece which allow of adjustment to sweep different breadths. The two cross-pieces connecting the beams are elevated respectively 4 and 8 inches above them, and raised high enough to clear the corn. They are banded at their ends and bolted through the beams with bolts strong enough to stand any ordinary strains. The implement strikes us as an efficient one, but requires two horses, and these should draw upon a pole. It is especially useful when the corn is very small and most in danger from weeds and grass.

A New Way of Trapping Rats.

BY L. L. LANGSTROTH, OXFORD, OHIO.

Get a common round wire-trap. Bait it with the most inviting food, and wait patiently until a rat is caught. Instead of killing this rat, and waiting perhaps for weeks before you are fortunate enough to trap another, keep him alive and feed him much as you would a pet squirrel. In a few days he will become quite reconciled to his cage, and you are now ready for business. At night, bait the trap well and set it where the rats resort most. Some one or more of them, seeing a rat quite at home in the midst of plenty, will enter the trap without any suspicion of harm. Next morning, pump or pour water thoroughly over the trap to clean it, and to make the killing of your prey more easy. Have an empty barrel into which drop the contents of your cage; the prisoners being well soaked, will be so heavy and slow that you can easily knock them on the head. Treat your partially tamed rat, however, "as if you loved him," and return him to his cage; this is easily done by lowering the cage into the barrel. Repeat the operation from night to night, and you will be surprised to see how easy a matter it is to outwit so cunning an animal as an "old rat."

Be careful not to keep a large one for your tame rat. He will frighten off all the younger fry, as none of them will dare to enter. The only difficult thing in the matter is to get your first rat. I have had a wire trap well baited for weeks before I could entice one to enter it. To get the first, is something like Astor's recipe for getting rich: "Get a thousand dollars clear of the world, and it is all very easy." Since I caught my first rat, I have failed but once for many nights in getting from one to four to keep him company. If your readers will try my plan, I think that something may be done to abate one of the most intolerable nuisances of this country. To say that millions of dollars worth of our property are annually destroyed by rats, would not be an extravagant assertion.

Foot Rot in Sheep.

This distressing and destructive malady is seldom properly understood or treated, and the result is that, though checked, it breaks out again and again. This is because so few farmers read and inform themselves thoroughly about their business, and because even those well informed perform surgical operations in so careless a manner. In the April number of the *American Agriculturist*, we explained the structure of the sheep's foot and the origin of the disease known as *the fouls*. This never need be confounded with foot rot, though we doubt not it is often the precursor of it, for it puts the foot in excellent preparation to take it easily.

Contagiousness of Hoof Rot.—There are some medical men, we believe, who deny that any disease is contagious, and they deny the contagiousness of hoof-rot. They are, we presume, right just so far:—were a perfectly healthy foot, sound and clean, to be exposed to the contagious virus, it would probably escape; if, however, it were anywise sore, inflamed or wounded, it would probably take it at once. The disease is often long in reaching that point which causes the sheep to go lame, and it progresses gradually, first causing limping; then the lifting of one foot; then severe lameness of both forefeet; then going upon the knees, which brings the feet in contact with the breast. It does not involve other parts of the system until far advanced. Then the feet become masses of rottenness; maggots breed in them and work into the flesh, and this corruption is communicated to the breast. During the whole course of the disease, until near the last, the sheep has good appetite and digestion, and is in no other way affected.

On this account the cure is, theoretically, very simple and sure. In practice, it is just as simple, if thoroughly done. The well cleaned hoofs, softened by soaking in dewy grass or on a rainy day, or otherwise, are pared with cutting pliers and very sharp knives until *every particle* of diseased matter is taken away, even if it involves the removal of *all* the hoof; they are then washed with warm water and soap, and smeared with some caustic paste, or fluid, or the sheep forced to stand in a hot, saturated solution of blue vitriol for ten minutes.

In discussing the origin of hoof-rot, most writers take sides, either denying its contagiousness, or asserting it most vehemently. For ourselves, we can see no other sensible belief than that it may be originated whenever the hoofs, being softened by moisture, are penetrated by foreign substances like gritty soil or sand, and especially when such things, finding their way through cracks in the hoof, thus come in contact with the sensitive lamellæ, or the papillary tissues, where they induce acute inflammation. The natural growth of the hoof adapts it to the wear and tear of gravelly and rocky hill sides, and on such localities the outer walls wear off fast, so that they are nearly even with the sole, and the foot is neat and trim; but on soft ground, in stables or in yards, the growth of the outer walls is so much more rapid than the wear, that they grow long, curl under the sole, and turn up in front, throw the wear back upon the heels, and keep them more or less inflamed, and are themselves liable to cracks and splits, which, if foreign substances work in, readily involve the sensitive portion of the hoof in inflammation. Where the horn-forming tissue becomes inflamed, the character of the horn formed is changed; its quantity is greatly increased, but it is softer, owing to the mixture of pus and foreign matter, and in portions has a fungoid appearance. The walls of the hoof become detached from the foot in spots of larger or smaller extent, owing to the fact that as soon as the lamellæ become diseased the horn they secrete has no consistence, and hence the walls have no hold upon the foot. The pus which constantly exudes from the sores has the quality of inducing the same disease, if it comes in contact with inflamed or wounded surfaces of the feet of other sheep. We see, then, good reasons for the views that the hoof-rot originates only in wet locations, or on ground which is not dry, and where sheep's hoofs are liable to crack from over-growth and softening by water, and exposed to grit, and that where the malady is otherwise unknown, it may be communicated to a sound flock by the introduction of one sheep having the disease.

Cotton Culture.—(*Continued from page 136.*)

BY F. G. DWIGHT.

COTTON COMING.—If a warm rain sets in immediately after planting, your cotton rows will, in about a week or ten days, be well marked; and the chances of a "good stand" will be discussed; then, too, the tell-tale plants will betray where there has been careless dropping.

By having the plants in a straight line, instead of scattering from three to six inches in width, *all* the after work would be easier. Siding and plowing could be more effectually done, and the whole field have a neater appearance.

When there are heavy rains, followed by much wind and a bright sun, directly after planting, and any part of your land is of such a nature as to form a crust on the surface, it is sometimes necessary to go over it with the scraper, to break up and "knock off" the thin crust formed on the surface, so that the young plants can push their way through.

This practice, however, cannot be recommended; cotton is not or should not be covered so deeply as to admit of much scraping off after the beds are leveled in the first place at planting. In any event, judgment must be exercised to know when such a scraping might be injurious to the seed row, by cutting off the tops of the young plants, should the seed have been in the ground long enough to be sending up young shoots, and any meddling with the surface does more harm than good. When any danger is feared from such a crust, an adjustable horse hoe run between the rows will be found sufficient to break up or crack the surface, and permit the plants to force their way through.

FIGHT GRASS.—Should, however, the young grass and weeds come up so thickly, four or five days after planting, as to threaten to overrun the beds and choke off the young plants as soon as they appear, it is best not to delay one hour in commencing to "fight grass," but to run the wooden scraper, in the hands of a careful man, over the beds, and "knock off" ***very lightly*** this first coat of weeds, etc., even at the risk of breaking off some of the forward plants near the surface. The hoes, plows, sweeps, and horse plows must be kept moving—judiciously—over the fields, early and late, as long as and wherever there is any grass to kill.

CLEAN CULTURE.—Upon the clean cultivation of your cotton land depends, in a great measure, the success of the crop. Let none of your hands forget that the ground must be kept stirred, and that every single weed and blade of grass must be cut up, and demolished.

A COTTON PLANTER NEEDED.—Perhaps no other improved implement in the cultivation of cotton is so much needed as a good one-horse planter, of simple and durable construction. Much labor, not only in planting and covering, but in all the after cultivation—"chopping out," "siding," etc.—would be saved by such an implement. If the seed could be sown ***straight*** in one continuous row, the seed not more than two or three inches apart in the row—so as to be sure of a "stand," the process of "chopping out" would be simpler and require less care.

The difficulties that might be experienced in dropping cotton seed through a planter, would be owing to the lint that covers them, causing the seed to hang together in bunches. But by rolling in ashes, as recommended, this difficulty may be somewhat overcome, and enable the seed to be dropped through a small opening or tube, with more certainty. The sales for such a planter would be immense, and make the inventor rich. May we soon see it in the field.

CAUTION.—Never work cotton during a spell of rainy weather, unless you are behind-hand with the work, and must take advantage of every moment in fair or foul weather to "catch up." You can not effectively kill grass in wet weather; you may plow it around, push it about and turn it upside down—but your plants are only partially relieved; the moist soil and warm rains enable it to take a fresh hold the instant almost that it is uprooted.—Hot, sunny weather, is the best time to work among cotton—no matter how hot,—then all grass turned up or displaced only partially, and buried under the burning sand, will be effectually disposed of.

CHOPPING OUT.—It is a common rule, not to begin working cotton until the greater part of the young plants can show *two pairs of leaves*, mostly when they are four or five inches in hight. But if the grass is very rank and threatens to outgrow the cotton, it will be prudent *not to wait for four leaves*, but to open the fight at once; even though the plants are but two or three inches in hight and have but two leaves.

The first work then in order will be "chopping out," or scraping out of the rows some of the over-abundant plants that have come up too crowded, giving them a careful thinning wherever they stand in bunches, to prevent a spindling, and consequently delicate growth.

At the same time scrape off and pull up all the grass around and among the plants; and let the sweep follow the hoes, running through the middles to destroy the grass not reached by the hoes, and to throw a little loose soil toward the plants, using care not to cover them.—For this a horse-hoe or cultivator is well adapted; it should be used by a careful man and run along lightly.

The hoe hands confine their labors only to the grass in the immediate vicinity of the rows, about and among the plants, leaving the middles for the sweep or hoe-harrow.

It is not advisable to remove many plants at this first working, except where they are much crowded; a late frost may nip many of them, or early grasshoppers may thin them out, so that if the hoe hands remove too many, the chances of a "stand" may be endangered.

SIDING.—After all the fields have been gone over with this first operation, it will be found necessary, in consequence of the rapid growth of weeds and grass, and to keep the soil well stirred, to at once proceed with the next work.

The small turn plows are now run along *close* to the young plants, up one side of the row and down the other, as near as an average of three inches, throwing a light furrow away *from* the plants towards the middle of the space between the rows, covering the grass, and leaving the plants on a slight elevation or ridge. Be careful not to run the plows too deep, as there is danger of hurting the roots; besides it is an injury to the young plants to set them up too high and dry on a sandy ridge,—the hoe hands may not come along for a day or two, and the hot withering sun may dry out the tender roots.

Do not let the ridge—made by the plows (run up one side of the row and down the other)—be cut *too narrow*. The plant has not only a tap root, but numerous fine and delicate side roots, that in young plants are hardly noticed. These tender feeders are of vital importance to the growth of the stalk, and none of them can be rudely cut or broken without proportionately injuring the plant itself.

After the plows have sided the rows and left the plants on a ridge, the hoe hands come along as soon as the work on hand permits,—the sooner the better,—and scrape off the grass remaining on this plant ridge; at the same time chopping out and again reducing the over-abundant plants, where they stand too crowded, and endeavoring as much as possible to have the plants standing in the rows at intervals of six or eight inches, in pairs, or three or four near together, always cutting out the weaker and letting the strongest plants stand, at the same time leveling the ground about the rows and drawing up soil to the stems, where the plows in "siding" have run too close to the plants or too deep.

A Look into the Sea.

Those who live at the sea side have an opportunity to observe forms of animal and vegetable life which, to those residing far inland, must seem very strange. Indeed those who live upon the very beach overlook many of the curious forms that grow near them. These animals and plants are best observed when grown in a glass tank or aquarium, and we have in our seaboard towns many who devote much time to marine aquaria. Our Superintendent of Engraving is well known as an enthusiast in this way, and he is so much pleased with an aquarium of one of his friends that he has produced a beautiful picture of it, presented on the succeeding page, and has furnished us with the following note of its contents: "The engraving represents the interior of an aquarium in the possession of Mr. W. E. Damon, and gives at one view a number of remarkable forms of animal life that are but little known. The two prominent figures in the center of the aquarium are Sea Anemones. These belong to the class of Polyps, and are two of the finest species found on our coast. It is almost impossible to describe the beauties of these flower-like gems of the ocean, nor is it strange that they were considered for so long a time as marine plants. Their tentacles expand like the petals of a flower, and at other times they remain closed for hours, only to seem more beautiful when again opened. On account of their bodies being coated with slime, and being of a soft pulpy nature to the touch, they are named by our fishermen "Halibut slime," and are brought up on the trawls in large numbers, they are attracted by the bait, and the fishermen imagine that they are the slime from the bodies of the Halibut. It is only in still water and in perfect security that they unfold their thousand tentacles, and display their beautifully organized disk. Each tentacle is a hand, by which it can seize any small fish, and convey it to its mouth; if the fish is strong and hard to hold, the Anemone will bring every hand to bear, so that the fish is entirely surrounded and held fast till dead, when it will slowly disappear into the mouth and down one of the many stomachs of the Anemone. Their manner of reproduction is very curious—they throw off a piece from the base. I have often cut pieces off with a penknife, which in about two weeks became perfect Anemones, but always having only six tentacles, which, in the course of time, increased to the proper number. Another way of multiplying is by budding off from the sides of the stalk (as shown in engraving.) These buds fall off from the parent, make an attachment on some stone or shell, and in course of time become perfectly organized Anemones. They also reproduce by ejecting young from the mouth or orifice at the disk. Two smaller varieties are also figured, of great delicacy and beauty.

The fish shown in the engraving is the Stickleback (*Gasterosteus*,) and one of the most lively and interesting fish known for the aquarium.

The male fish, about the month of March, begins to take on the most brilliant hues, of blue, orange and green; it then commences to build its nest for the reception of the spawn. As soon as the female has spawned, she is driven away by the male fish, who carefully guards the nest, and ventilates the spawn by ejecting water from his mouth into one of the orifices of the nest. I had one Stickleback that every day, as the sun reached a certain spot in the tank, would take the spawn out of the nest and give it a half hour's sunning, then take it back and deposit it in the nest, and when the young were

INTERIOR OF A SALT WATER AQUARIUM.—*(See preceding page.)* —*Drawn and Engraved for the American Agriculturist.*

hatched out and wandered too far from the nest, would take them in his mouth and bring them back. I have often amused myself by placing small sticks in the nest, and watching the male fish tug at them until they were loosened, and then carry them off in his mouth to the farthest extremity of the tank. There is no fish so easily domesticated, and that will bring forth young so readily in either fresh or salt water aquarium.

At the left of the picture is a most curious animal, the Sea-horse, (*Hippocampus Hudsonius*).—The male fish is furnished with a pouch for the reception of the spawn, in which it is hatched. The young sea-horses cling together in a mass, by means of their prehensile tails. The natural food of the Sea-horse, is the Serpula, noticed below. Mr. Damon had for a year three Sea-horses which were so tame, that they would follow his hand around the tank to be fed; he at first fed them on the hinder parts of shrimp, afterwards on Serpula, which they eat greedily.

Serpula contortuplicata, shown near the Sea-horse, consists of a mass of twisted tubes formed of hard shell, each of which contains an animal. When these are out feeding and fully expanded with their "stoppers" of white and orange, in connection with their feather like branchiæ of rich brown and crimson, they present a body of rich color. On the slightest disturbance, the entire mass of serpula disappears, and the color of the whole instantaneously changes from a brilliant orange or crimson to the dull grey of their cells. They venture out one by one and the mass of shell becomes brilliant again. When any of the cells become broken, the serpula in a few days build them up. If one is cut in half, each half becomes a perfect animal. They live entirely at the bottom, and do not thrive well in a strong light.

Star-fish, one of which is shown at the left hand, (*Asteracanthion*,) are very common, and the great enemy of the oyster and clam. Every fisherman considers it his duty to destroy them.

The small Hermit Crab (*Pagurus longicarpus*) is found in great numbers on our coast. The hinder part of the body is soft and unprotected, so that it becomes necessary for them to inhabit some empty shell, generally that of the Buccinum, when they grow too large for the shell, they take possession of a new one that fits them better; when they are about making this change, they first carefully examine the interior and exterior of the shell with their claws, and finding it all right they jerk themselves out of the old shell and into the new so quickly, that the change is hard to detect. Should a Hermit Crab have one of his claws crushed or broken, it will amputate it down to the next perfect joint, eating all the flesh that is torn off through amputating. In about three days, a small, soft fleshy point makes its appearance, which is the new claw; this increases in size until it has attained nearly its natural proportions, but is soft and without shell, until the next moulting or shedding season, when it becomes a perfect claw, shell and all. One of these Crabs, inhabiting a small shell, is shown in the center foreground of the picture.

The Spider Crab, or Sea Spider, (*Labinica canaliculata*) is interesting, in spite of its homely look, of which it seems to be conscious, from the fact of its dressing itself up with sea-weed or algæ, of the most brilliant colors. This it only does at the fall of the year, as the bedding time approaches, so that it may be more securely hid from the numerous bottom fish who prey upon the smaller crustaceans. One is seen at the extreme right of the picture. There are several equally curious objects shown, that can only be named: The Shrimp, which the Stickleback seems to be after; Tubularias, long horn-like tubes, seen just under the Shrimp; Barnacles, between the two Crabs, etc. Of course, there must be some vegetation to keep up the balance between animal and vegetable life, and for this nothing is so useful as the *Ulva*, or Sea-lettuce, some broad fronds of which are seen floating behind the Sea-horse and Serpula.

The Silver-Striped Bamboo.

The name Bamboo is associated with the gigantic tropical and subtropical grasses, the stems of which grow 50 feet or more high, and are celebrated for their general use by the Orientals, to whom they serve for everything from a penholder to a mast. There are, however, some very humble bamboos, and at least one hardy one. *Bambusa Metake.* This is a Japanese species, two or three feet high, and endured the winter with us several degrees north of New York City. Recently Mr. E. Bauman, Florist and Landscape Gardener at Rahway, N. J., has brought to our notice a still more dwarf species, which has been introduced by the European florists under the name of *Bambusa Fortunii alba vittata.* The engraving is made from a pot plant, of the natural size. From the abundance of buds at the base it is no doubt a vigorous grower, and is said to continue dwarf and stocky and not exceed about a foot in hight. Should this prove hardy, as Mr. Bauman thinks it will, it will be a valuable addition to our "foliage plants" of which we now have a great number, with but few hardy ones. The leaves are very distinctly marked, both the green and the white stripes being clear. The plant is apparently well adapted to form edgings in decorative planting, and a single plant would prove very ornamental in the border. A variety with green and yellow stripes is noticed in Europe, and either this, or the one under notice, is advertised as *Bambusa Japonica variegata.* There is much confusion in florists' names, both in this country and Europe.

SILVER-STRIPED BAMBOO.

The Sex of the Strawberry.

From the fact that there are some varieties of strawberry, which, being pistillate, require the presence of some other sort to make them fruitful, many suppose that it is necessary in all cases to plant two kinds in order to bear fruit. We have several letters asking what variety should be planted with the Triomphe de Gand and other sorts that will fruit without aid. As this matter of the sex of strawberries has been muddled so much, we will try to make it plain. The great majority of flowers with which we are familiar, are perfect, i. e., have both pistils,

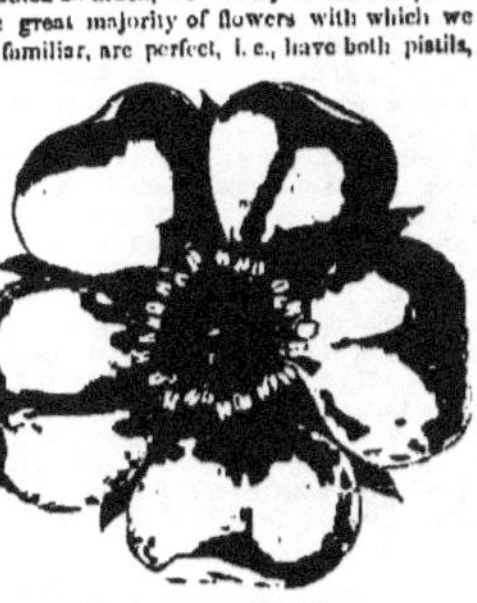

Fig. 1.—PERFECT FLOWERS.

the organs that are to become the fruit, and stamens, the fertilizing organs, in the same flower. Other plants constantly have their stamens and pistils in separate flowers of the same plant, as the cucumber, squash, and all of that family—and the Indian corn, in which the tassel contains the stamens, and the ear the pistils, the elongated portion of which is the silk. In still another set of plants the flowers of one will bear pistils only, and the flowers of another will produce nothing but stamens. The hemp, hop, and willows are common instances of plants of this kind. The pistils, in each one of these classes are the portions that become fruit,

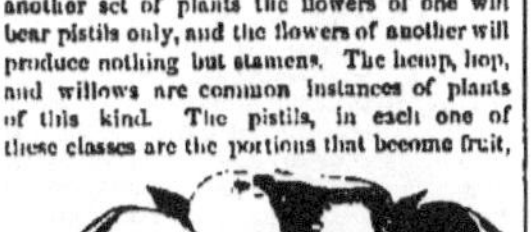

Fig. 2.—SECTION OF FLOWER.

but they only do this after they have received the influence of the pollen, a fine dust produced by the stamens. The pistils of perfect flowers, that have both stamens and pistils, may readily become fertilized by the pollen of the same flower, while in separated flowers, those in which the stamens are in one and the pistils are in another, no fruit will be produced unless pollen is brought to the pistils by some agency, such as insects or winds, from a staminate one. Some plants that ordinarily produce perfect flowers do sometimes have separated ones, the stamens and sometimes the pistils being suppressed or abortive, when the flower becomes pistillate or staminate as the case may be. This happens in both the wild and the cultivated state with the strawberry and with the grape. In the strawberry it is usually the stamens that are wanting, and in the grape it is more common to have the pistils absent, if either one. The engravings (figs. 1, 2, 3), of strawberry flowers, very much enlarged, prepared for Fuller's Small Fruit Culturist, show the different parts quite distinctly, and a careful inspection of them will enable any one to tell a perfect—or hermaphrodite, as it is often called—from a pistillate flower. In fig. 1, the small knob in the center is the pistils, which are surrounded by numerous stamens. The same flower is shown in figure 2, as cut down through the center. The conical elevation in the center of this cut flower is the enlarged end of the stem of the flower, on which the pistils are placed, this is called the *receptacle.* The stamens are arranged around this, and outside of these the showy parts of the flower, the petals and calyx. As the pistils ripen, to produce the fruit proper—seeds we usually call them—the receptacle enlarges, becoming often of enormous size compared to what it was in the flower, and very often inclosing the seed-like fruits in deep pits or cavities, while in other cases these remain upon the surface. In several cultivated varieties of the strawberry, the stamens are altogether wanting, as in fig. 3, and then the plant is said to be pistillate. It is evident that plants of this character need the help of those that produce stamens. The general tendency of strawberry cultivators is to discard pistillate sorts altogether, though there are a very few, like Hovey's Seedling, that in some localities are so excellent and productive, that it is desirable to grow them. Where this is the case, it is only necessary to plant adjacent beds of some perfect variety that blossoms at the same time, and the insects and winds will look after the fertilization. When a perfect variety is planted to fertilize a pistillate or imperfect one, great care should be taken to prevent the runners of one bed reaching across into the other bed. It is from carelessness in this respect, that there is so much confusion in regard to varieties, and this has also given rise to the common belief that pistillate plants become changed when fertilized by another sort. While we are not prepared to assert that the flavor of a pistillate sort may not be modified somewhat, according to the variety by which it was fertilized, yet we have no proof that the plant itself undergoes any change. To answer many inquiries, we may say that, practically, as far as the value of the fruit is concerned, strawberries in proximity do not mix. As regards the seeds, the case is different; here the crossing is the rule rather than the exception. And this is apt to take place even with perfect flowers, as insects

Fig. 3.—PISTILLATE FLOWER.

will often bring pollen and fertilize the pistils of a flower, before its own pollen is ready.

When the pistils are absent, making a truly staminate flower, of course no fruit is borne, and the plants are perfectly useless. They have been recommended for fertilizing the pistillate ones, but as this office can be as well performed by the perfect flowers—which produce enough pollen for their own pistils and to spare, it is a mere waste of ground to employ them. The term "staminate" is often applied to perfect flowers; it belongs to those only bearing stamens.

The Spring Adonis.—(*Adonis vernalis.*)

The names of many of our cultivated plants—if we trace them to their origin—take us back to the days of mythological fables, when gods and goddesses had the uncomfortable power of transforming mortals into beasts and flowers. The Adonis is said to be so called in memory of the young man beloved of Venus, and to have sprung either from his blood, or from the

SPRING ADONIS—(*Adonis vernalis.*)

tears shed by the goddess at his death. Which is the true story of its origin, it is too late at this day to settle, but whether it was blood or salt water, we would like to see the plant itself oftener than we do. We only meet it in those gardens where good old things, that have been grown by lovers of flowers for centuries—and ought to be prized on that very account—have not been thrown aside for modern introductions. We like the new things too, but don't believe in discarding old friends to make place for them.

This Adonis is a hardy perennial, and comes in bloom with the flowers of May. Its stems are about a foot in hight, and clothed with delicate and finely cut foliage. Each branch is terminated by a large yellow flower, the petals of which are marked with greenish lines. The plant belongs to the same family with the Buttercups, Pæony, etc.—the Ranunculus or Crowfoot Family. In looking over the catalogues to see if the seeds were generally kept by seedsmen, we were surprised to find it only in that of Jas. Vick of Rochester. Being a perennial, it will not flower the first year from seed, but after that it is easily managed, it being only necessary to divide the clumps when they get too large. There are some annual species that are worth cultivating. One of them, *Adonis autumnalis*, blooms in autumn, with a small dark red and purple flower and fine foliage. It has the popular name of Pheasant's-eye.

Tree Doctoring and our "Doctrine."

Just now we have "no end" of circulars of "Patent Tree Invigorators," "Apple worm Annihilators" and the like, with many letters of inquiry. These tree medicines divide themselves into two classes, those that are put *into* the tree and those that are put *on* the ditto. The internal remedies proposed to drive away worms are sulphur and calomel. A hole is to be bored into the tree, the stuff introduced and the hole plugged up. Some ask us if the use of these materials will hurt the tree. Probably no more than if the hole had been entirely filled by a nicely fitting plug—as both are very insoluble—and the amount of benefit would in either case probably be about the same.

The external remedies are more numerous, and are generally "patent" preparations. If there is anything too stupid to get a patent we should like to see it. What principle governs the issuing of patents we are at loss to discover—except it be a general desire to get the fees, and be rid of bores. In the circulars before us, one proposes to "treat" the trees to rid them of worms, and will send the article for a consideration. Another not only kills the borer, but his medicine contributes to the growth of the tree, and so on. Now on general principles we don't believe that there is any *specific* virtue in them. The whole secret of their success lies in the fact that one who has invested money in them *will look after his trees*—while if we tell him month after month to use soft soap wash and other simple remedies, he will not think it worth while. There is nothing like a few dollars, to wake up some people. We copied last January a communication from the Country Gentleman, of Mr. Wisner, who had used Mr. Sheldon's composition to the injury of his trees. Mr. Sheldon writes that Mr. Wisner admits to have made the composition with the wrong ingredients, and we give him the benefit of this statement. With our present information, "certificates of well known persons" included, we can see nothing to induce us to recommend any of these patented or secret things whatever. Our doctrine is constant attention. If one loves his trees and looks after them, he will not need any "annihilator," or "invigorator." Give a soft soap wash in the spring, probe and kill all the borers that are in the tree, and keep others from entering by placing some mechanical obstruction around the trunk in July, either stiff paper, a mound of earth, or whatever will keep the insects away. If canker worms are in the vicinity, then something must be used to prevent their ascent,—see March *Agriculturist*. Tent caterpillars are easily kept down by destruction of eggs and nests—it is only lazy people who suffer. If a tree "invigorator" be needed, just try what virtue there is in manure.

Cultivating Orchards.

Apple orchards left to themselves bear only on alternate years, with such uniformity, that "bearing years" have come to be regarded as the order of nature, rather than a human device. The trees, in average soil, do not have aliment enough to give full crops every year. Cultivation and manuring will change all this, and give us remunerative crops every season. Possibly manuring might do this even if the orchard were left in grass. But the danger is, if the orchard is left unplowed, it will not get the manure.

The common objection offered to plowing is the damage done to the roots of the trees. We have no doubt that an orchard might be plowed so deep and so near the trunk of the trees as to damage it past hope of recovery. But discretion is to be used, and the plow is to be kept so near the surface under the trees, as not to break off the large roots. It has also been ascertained that grain crops are not good for orchards. We have known orchards to be made barren for several years in consequence of a crop of rye. Grain crops, unless buckwheat be an exception, take from the soil what the tree needs, and shade the land too much. Root crops are the most desirable, because they require a good deal of manure and thorough tillage to make them profitable. The frequent stirring of the soil, and the fertilizers, are the wants of the apple tree, and the root crop enables the farmer to give these to his orchard, and at the same time he is remunerated for his labor.

Potatoes, carrots, beets, turnips, are all good crops for the orchard, if you put on manure enough to make them pay. A surplus must be left in the soil to make the apple crop. But will an orchard thus fed bear every year? We have no doubt of it. The apple crop may be made as sure as the root crops. We once plowed up beneath an old apple tree that had an inveterate habit of bearing only every other year, and planted with potatoes, manuring liberally. We had a full crop of apples the second year, and shall always think the manure and the cultivation made the change. Horticulturists who make a specialty of apples, and manure every year, succeed in getting crops every season, with very rare exceptions. David Lyman, Esq., of Middlefield, Conn., stated, at a recent meeting of the State Board of Agriculture, that he cultivated his orchards, and got crops every year. They were not always full crops, but were enough to pay for the trouble. Judging from the appearance of his orchards, which we visited a few years since in the apple season, we think *that* a very modest statement. We have rarely seen so fine a show of apples, even at the county fairs, as could have been gathered from his trees. The secret of his success is cultivation and manure, and a reasonable watch against the encroachments of insects. The plowing late in the fall as well as in the spring, he thinks a great safeguard against their depredations. Multitudes of the chrysalides are unearthed and destroyed. If this was attended to, and the windfalls picked up and fed to the pigs, we think there would be little damage from the attacks of insects. The apple is so fine a fruit, and so easily kept, it is so much both food and luxury, that no pains should be spared to keep our orchards in the best condition. We are tired of seeing apples quoted at $7 a barrel, but even at that price they are much cheaper than pills.

SWEET HERBS.—Those who like seasoning should not forget these little matters in "making the garden." Sage is the staple article, and is so readily grown from seed that it is not worth while to make divisions or cuttings of the old plants, and the same may be said of Thyme. Make a seed bed of good light soil and sow Sage, Thyme, Sweet Marjoram, and Summer Savory, when the ground gets warm. Keep the plants well weeded, and thin if crowded. By the time that early crops of peas, cabbages, etc., come off, there will be a plenty of good plants to set out and occupy the ground, and give an abundant supply for home use and for sale.

Raspberries and Black Caps.

The great trouble with the cultivation of the common raspberries, even when they pass the winter safely by being protected or otherwise, is that the manner of growth is not understood. In private gardens we frequently see the raspberry bed a dense thicket, with new canes struggling with the old ones, and all in an uninviting and unfruitful condition. The majority of private growers do not seem to be aware that the stems of the raspberry are biennial, i. e., they grow one year and bear fruit the next, and then die. With some of the varieties called ever-bearing, the young growth flowers and fruits in the autumn of the same year. When a raspberry cane of the ordinary kind has fruited, it is no longer of any use, and should be cut out. The large cultivators usually leave the pruning out of the old canes until the time to cover them, but it is much better to remove them as soon as fruiting is over, to allow the new growth a plenty of room. Those who plant raspberries this spring, and wish the best results, should cut the old canes back to a few inches, leaving just enough to serve as a convenient handle in planting, and look to the new growth of this year to produce fruit the next. If the canes be left their full length at transplanting, a poor crop of fruit may be had the first season, at the risk of the future good of the plants. The plants are set four feet apart each way for the more moderate growers, and the taller kinds five or six feet apart. The varieties are numerous, and every year brings additions to the list. Along the Hudson River the Hudson River Antwerp is the great market berry. In Southern New Jersey, the Philadelphia is the profitable market fruit, and at the West, the Purple Cane enjoys great popularity. Choice sorts for garden culture are: Brinckle's Orange, Franconia, Clark, (said to be hardy,) Fastolf, and French.

The Black Caps, of which there are now many named varieties, are becoming very popular. Though not to be compared in flavor of fruit with the others, they have many good qualities. They are hardy, very productive, and throw up no suckers. They are propagated by rooting from the tops of the pendent branches. Of this class the Doolittle's Improved, is, perhaps, the best known, and doubtless many others, including native seedlings, are just as good.

Sweet Potato Culture.

BY W. W. RATHBONE, MARIETTA, OHIO.

In April, page 189, we gave Mr. Rathbone's manner of preparing the land for Sweet Potatoes, and now add the remainder of his article, upon setting the plants. The plants should always be set down to the first leaf, and if the upper portion is destroyed by a late frost, they will start from below and make a good growth. The ridges being made, they will stand 30 to 36 inches from top to top; let them be sharp pointed. To mark the distances for plants, I use a revolving wheel, with fans every three feet, resembling a reaping machine fan, marking two rows at once. I keep the plants well set up on the ridge, and cut between them at the second and third hoeing to *make the hills.* Make the hills pointed and high. Do not be afraid of dry weather. We always get the best crops when "everything is burnt up."

MODE OF SETTING PLANTS.—One plant per hill is plenty. Put fifteen inches apart if to be kept in the ridge. I have two modes of setting. First, if the weather be dry, don't wait for rain, nor the "dark of the moon." Let one boy drop the plants, another pour from a water-pot, with the rose off, sufficient water to float the rootlets, and immediately fill up with mellow earth. One can water for three to set. Never set plants after heavy rains. A second method of planting, which I prefer when the earth is sufficiently moist, is to dip the roots in a puddle of clay of the consistence of thick cream. The plants thus treated generally live well, and the objectionable hard lump formed about the plants in many soils when watered in the hill is obviated.

AFTER CULTIVATION.—After every rain break up the crust of soil in contact with the plants. I do this rapidly with both hands—clasping, raising and pressing the earth on the tips of the hills. It answers all the purposes of a regular hoeing, breaking up the ant holes and giving health to the young plant. Keep the surface clear of weeds. Be careful in working among the plants, not to hoe too deeply. The earliest potatoes lie immediately beneath the surface.

After heavy rains the vines root at the joints. On sunny days they may be upturned on the hill or ridge. But in no case cut off the vines. I have cut every alternate row in a large patch to fully test this point, and on harvesting found fully 100 per cent. in favor of the uncut hills. A frost that merely blackens the *leaves* does not hurt sweet potatoes, but if the *vines* are frozen it does. Upon digging, the potatoes should be carefully handled and put away in boxes or barrels, with alternate layers of leaves, (some prefer cut straw,) in a warm, dry place to keep.

In conclusion, I repeat, if good plants are set as indicated, on moderately fertile land, with good surface drainage on small high hills, the surface kept well cleaned, any reader of the *Agriculturist* south of 43° north latitude can raise good Nansemond sweet potatoes.

THE AILANTHUS.—We hear so much against the Ailanthus, that we are quite disposed to take its part. It will grow every where, is a rapid grower, and is very seldom troubled by insects. We know that it makes good fuel, and we cannot see why its timber should not be useful for a great many purposes. We have had a couple of blocks upon our desk for some time, the one varnished and the other plain, and of the great many who have examined them, not one has guessed the kind of wood. Its disagreeable quality is an unpleasant odor when in flower, and its great nakedness in winter renders it less suitable as a wind-break than many others. Despite all the abuse it has had, were we upon a tree-less prairie, we should plant the Ailanthus, notwithstanding it has been condemned by several pomological societies. It is the tree that converts the brick and brown-stone streets of New York into beautiful avenues of tropical foliage, it grows among the pavements as if it rather enjoyed a hard life, and it is especially adapted to rocky and sterile soil.

Cranberry Culture.

To answer numerous letters we condense recent articles upon this subject, some of which came to us, and others appeared in papers, published in New Jersey, a State some portions of which present remarkable facilities for cranberry culture. The essentials seem to be, 1st, a sandy peat soil; where the deposit of peat or muck is shallow, with sand beneath, then a proper soil may be made by plowing. If the peat is very deep, then sand must be put on to the depth of four to eight inches. 2nd.—The bog must be so situated that it can be drained, ditching is the common method. 3d.—The land must be capable of being flowed at will. This is not considered so essential in New-Jersey, as the other two conditions, but is considered desirable as a means of protecting the vines from frost and insects. 4th.—The land must be cleaned of all stumps as well as tussocks of sedge and other vegetation, and the surface made as level as possible. The sanding is of course the last thing to be done before planting. These are in brief the New Jersey essentials. Mr. Orrin C. Cook, of South Milford, Mass., who last year sent us the largest and finest berries we ever saw, has quite different notions. He says: "In selecting land for the cranberry, wet swamp land is the best, as it requires more moisture than is found on high lands, but any land that will grow potatoes will raise good cranberries. I raise my best berries on a hard clay soil. To prepare the ground for the plants, take out all the roots, brush, and tufts of coarse grass, plow deep, and, if not too wet, harrow. Having made the land as level as possible, set the plants one foot apart each way. We set the plants in the fall, from the middle of September until the ground freezes, and in the Spring until the 25th of May. We neither plow nor hoe among the plants, but in the fall go through and pull all the brush and grass that may have started. In three years the vines will cover the ground, at which time a full crop may be expected. There is no crop that we can raise here with so little trouble as the cranberry; after they get to bearing there is no trouble beyond picking the crop and marketing it. One acre will yield from fifty to one hundred bushels, and these sell from $7 to $10 per barrel of three bushels each."

We have heretofore expressed our disbelief in the success of the upland culture of the cranberry, but last autumn a gentleman from Long Island, whose address we have mislaid, brought us very fine specimens of berries, raised on upland. We should be glad if Mr. Cook's statement that "any land that will grow potatoes will raise good cranberries" were generally applicable. Some unfortunate attempts of this kind that we have seen, have made us cautious in advising any one to invest in cranberries on high ground, and we should be glad of more reports, whether of success or failure.

Mr. Gilbert Conant, whose report was quoted in the March *Agriculturist*, says, that in the article we copied, the word "plowed" in the third line of the quotation should be *flowed.*

The question is often asked, will it do to set wild plants, or must the cultivated ones be purchased. The cranberry, like all other fruits, varies from the seed, and seedlings will differ in the size and shape of the fruit, and in the productiveness of the vines. Wild plants may give good results and may not. The advantage of cultivated vines is that they are produced from runners of a sort known to be fruitful. Several different kinds are sold by dealers.

THE ROUGH DEUTZIA.—(*Deutzia scabra.*)

Some Beautiful White-Flowering Shrubs.

While shrubs with gaily colored flowers excite our admiration, we believe that we derive more satisfaction from those the flowers of which are white. A Japan Quince, in a blaze of scarlet, or a Forsythia hung with its golden bells, is pleasant to look upon, but there is a tenderness and purity about a Deutzia or Silver-bell that call forth another sentiment than admiration. Pure white and green form a combination, whether in plant or bouquet, that is always pleasing. Among the white-flowering shrubs, are the old Snow-ball, now but little grown, and its more dwarf, but more beautiful Japanese brother, *Viburnum plicatum*. Then we have the Fringe-tree, the two Silver-bells, any number of varieties of Spiræa, and Philadelphus, or Syringa as it is often called. Besides these are the Double-flowering Plum and Cherry, that come early, and our native and beautiful Clethra that flowers late, and if it were not in every swamp, would be in every garden; our fragrant White Azalea, and a host of others that we cannot now enumerate. Among the white flowering shrubs, well enough known to be in all good collections, but yet not sufficiently popularized to be grown every where, as are Lilacs and Snowballs, are the *Deutzias*. These shrubs have no common name, aside from their botanical one, which is fortunately one readily popularized. The species most common in cultivation are *Deutzia scabra*, *D. crenata* and *D. gracilis*, all natives of Japan. The first two grow six or eight feet high, and differ only in the shape of the leaves and some minute characters of the flowers. They are so much alike that one is frequently sold for the other. The leaves are rough, and when examined by a strong magnifier, this roughness is found to be due to transparent star-shaped hairs, which are very pretty microscopic objects. *Deutzia gracilis*, grows about two feet high and forms a large tuft of slender arching branches, and when these are loaded with pure white flowers, nothing can be more graceful. This is a most valuable shrub, for cemetery decoration, and is valuable for forcing. The florists around New-York force it in large quantities, and at this time (March) we find it freely used in bouquets and flower baskets. All these species are hardy as far north as Boston. The Deutzias are nearly related to the Syringas, (*Philadelphus*), but have smaller flowers, of a more delicate texture, and the plants are more graceful in habit. We give an engraving of a flowering branch of *D. scabra*, much reduced in size. The swamps of Virginia and southward furnish another white-flowered shrub that should be better known, the American Storax, *Styrax Americana*. It belongs to the same family with the popular Silver-bell (*Halesia*), has good foliage, and is in May covered with neat flowers that look much like small orange blossoms. The specimen from which our engraving is taken was from a large shrub in the grounds of that pioneer in horticulture, the late Thomas Hogg. The advancing tide of "improvement" has gradually encroached upon these grounds, and this season will probably obliterate a spot dear to all horticulturists. We shall hereafter, when this collection is scattered, hardly know where to find many old favorites.

AMERICAN STORAX.—(*Styrax Americana.*)

Thinning Out Ornamental Trees.

This is one of the matters most likely to be overlooked, and yet most necessary to be done this spring. It has already been neglected several years, on account of the reluctance very naturally felt to destroy a work that nature has been twenty years in building up. As a rule, the shade trees on our streets and avenues are planted too near each other. The tree that wants fifty feet of space for its full development is scarcely allowed twenty. This would be of little consequence, if the planter only had the nerve to remove them when they began to worry and devour each other. But he prizes his own handiwork; he is a tender hearted man, and perhaps lacking in taste. How can he be expected to destroy in a day what he has been so many years nursing and watching with pride. He can cut out dead limbs, and occasionally a live one if a straggler. But to put the grub ax to the root is more than he can bear.

Yet this is just the severe remedy that is needed among the beautiful plantations of shade trees in our suburban towns and villages. The trees stand too thick, and are destroying one another. The fight is as real as that of the Kilkenny cats, though less noisy. The top branches already interlock, and begin to die for want of light and air. The roots are meeting beneath the surface, and struggling for aliment. Neither of the adjacent trees has aliment enough nor room enough to develop after its own law of growth. It can not do justice to itself, nor show forth the beauty and glory of its kind. Every dead branch and distorted limb cries out "make room," and room can only be had by the destruction of its neighbor. This must be had or the tree is spoiled of its beauty. Make this, and the gaps will soon be filled with more comely and healthful trees. One handsome, well developed elm or maple is worth a whole row of decaying, distorted trees, struggling for the mastery. This is not the less important with evergreens than with deciduous trees. The perfection of an evergreen consists in its being a perfect pyramid, with its base resting on the ground, and care should be taken that they are never so crowded by close planting that they lose their lower branches.

Trouble with Seed.

We expect to have every seedman of our acquaintance denounced as an imposter—that has been the way heretofore, and will probably be the case this year. Disappointment and vexation may be avoided by a little thought. Those who have had no experience in gardening, whether with flowers or vegetables, are generally in too much of a hurry. They sow their seeds—of all kinds, the first fine day, a cold rain comes and soaks the ground for several days, the seeds decay, and the seedsman is blamed. This is one way in which seeds fail. Another is, the directions to sow shallow are followed, the seeds start and a dry time comes on, and the germinating plants perish for want of sufficient moisture, when a watering at the proper time would have saved them. The smaller the seeds the more care they require, and it is much better to sow very small ones, such as Lobelia, in boxes with a pane of glass over them to prevent evaporation, than to risk them in the open border. It is well also to sow only a portion at one time; if the first sown escapes accidents, the other portion may be sown to give a supply of plants for a later bloom.

THE HOUSEHOLD.

(For other Household items, see "Basket" pages.)

Work-Baskets and Bags.

PRIZE ESSAY BY MISS EVA E. COLLINS, ROCHESTER, N. Y.

Every lady, whether a woman or little girl, should have a convenient receptacle for the implements which are necessary for her use in sewing. A household work-box, basket, or bag, is a household nuisance. Each person should have her own thimble, wax, thread, needles scissors, etc., and a place to keep them; and the manner in which she keeps the latter is a pretty sure index to her habits of neatness and order in other respects. So great a variety in the style of these articles lies within reach of each of us, that our individuality can in no way be better discerned than in the choice we make. Our minister tells us that copying is a suicidal act, and that the spirit of the aphorism is applicable to the commonest incidents of daily life. Why not, then, to our selection of an article which presents so great a variety of forms?—not that he can mean, in this case, that we should each have a work-box unlike those we see about us, in order to express our individuality, for it would be but another form of the same act, and equally suicidal in its nature; rather that each should sufficiently understand her own needs and preferences, as to have a choice even in so small an item as this. Grandmother thinks there is nothing quite so convenient as her work-bag, fig. 1, the magical properties of which are universally acknowledged; though none of us would think of constructing such another with a hope of its wonderful properties being inherent in bags of that description, as everything that belongs to Grandmother partakes of the same nature. It consists of a round piece of box-board, covered, and surrounded with pockets. Turned wrong side out, (fig. 2.) and emptied of its contents, it is easy to see how it is made. The pockets, fig. 3, are eight in number. These, and the inside of the bottom board are of gray merino. The upper edge of the pocket is scalloped with dark blue saddler's silk, which is the outside color. A rubber cord holds the gray pockets so tightly drawn up that the bag stands of its own accord, when the strings, figure 4, which are run in the outside from opposite directions, are loosened.

Fig. 1.—GRANDMOTHER'S BAG.

Fig. 2.—BAG REVERSED.

Fig. 3.—BAG OPEN.

Fig. 4.—BAG STRINGS.

Fig. 5.—WORK BASKET.

Fig. 6.—POCKETS.

Mother's work-basket is made on the same principle. It is a basket lined with pockets, fig. 5, instead of a bag. The inside is made separately, and afterwards fastened firmly to the basket at the bottom of the pockets. The top could be simply made fast with coarse thread to the basket, though that would not look so neatly finished as it would wound with ribbon over the top of the basket, and through the material of the lining, with bows tied over between the pockets, where the strain upon the lining is greatest, in the way mother's basket is finished off. The pockets, fig. 6, are made in a straight piece, just long enough to fit the top of the basket. The bottom of the row of pockets, fig. 7, is slightly gathered to fit a circle of the same material which fits the bottom of the basket.

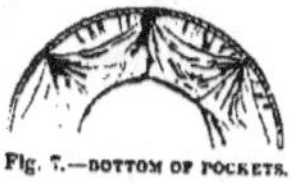

Fig. 7.—BOTTOM OF POCKETS.

Fig. 8.

Fig. 9.

Katie has a standing work-basket of willow, with three compartments. She has various nice little contrivances to hold her work, among which are "crabs." A crab like this is composed of three pieces of stiff pasteboard of an oval shape, two inches in width by three in length, neatly covered with silk, and sewed together at two of the edges. By a slight pressure at the ends it opens, and reveals a cozy little room large enough for small work, and convenient to carry in a dress pocket. In this crab, which is brown on the outside and blue within, I see Katie has a bunch of tape trimming, and a spool of thread, No. 50. In another gray and pink one there is some ruffling, narrow lace, and 100 thread; while stowed away in the drab crab I discover her tatting shuttle, fig. 8. It is one Grandfather made from the centers of two old fine-tooth combs, placing a couple of strips of ivory between the outside pieces, and riveting the whole firmly together. Katie says it is entirely owing to her supply of crabs that she always has a variety of light work ready for any emergency. Her needle-book, figure 9, although large, is appropriate to her basket, which is large and roomy. It is of bronze morocco, bound and lined with blue, with leaves for needles at one end, and a place for the thimble in the side of the broad flat cushion at the other end of the case, fig. 10. There is a morocco pocket between the silk pocket and cushion. My needle-case, fig. 11, is smaller, and is therefore better suited to my work-box, fig. 12, where every inch of space is precious, and accordingly economized. It rolls up into quite a small compass, and lies under the tray, or sometimes in the tray, beside my button-box. Between these and the cushion, is a narrow depressed division for knife, pencil, stiletto, buttons, tape, needle-book, etc. The scissors, tape-measure, emery, thimble, shuttle and pin-case belong in the division opposite the thread; while under the tray is a ball of welting cord, box of hooks and eyes, case of skeins of silk, fig. 13, scissors' sharpener, sticks and roll of tape, papers of floss and French cotton, Afghan needles, a crab or two, and a dozen little bundles of work in various stages of development, besides a thousand and one other articles, which do not legitimately belong to the box, yet are most conveniently kept here.

Fig. 10.—NEEDLE-BOOK, OPEN.

Fig. 11.—NEEDLE-CASE.

Fig. 12.—WORK BOX.

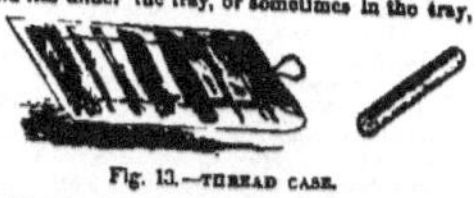

Fig. 13.—THREAD CASE.

Fig. 14.—WORK BOX.

Jennie's work-box, fig. 14, which is a tidy little affair, is a hexagon of stiff pasteboard covered with silk—gray on the outside, and scarlet within. On three of the side pieces are fastened pockets of the same material with which the basket is lined. On one side a covered strip of thin pasteboard, fig. 15, is fastened for a thimble case, over which hangs an emery, fig. 16, made from two round pieces of strong linen, stuffed with emery and wool, and covered with scarlet silk. The tomato shape is produced by drawing a double thread of green silk six times through the center of the emery—each time passing over the surface at an angle of sixty degrees from the last thread. A tuft of green is fastened with the string to the center of one side of the emery to increase its resemblance to a tomato. Jennie made several such boxes for her little friends a few months ago, some of which were very delicate in color—light blue and salmon—sea green and gray—and were prettier than her's, though scarcely as well adapted as her's for daily use.

Fig. 15.

Fig. 16.

Leaves from My Journal.—No. IV.

PRIZE ESSAY BY MRS. D. M'CLELLAN, OF OHIO.

May.—Lizzie and I have some pleasant chats together. I made her laugh to-day while telling her about putting up and taking down stoves in these premises. That is a job I absolutely dread. I believe I am very apt to lose my temper. Such fitting of pipes, lugging up stairs and down, into bedroom and parlor, scattering the grimy contents, and bedaubing every door and passage-way, one calling here and another in exactly the opposite direction, all doors open and all faces awry, to say nothing of seeing every one lift enough to break his back in two, I long ago placed it in my calendar as a day of all the year the worst. "Well, well, Mrs. Frisby," said a poor woman who was helping me at such a time, and to whom I was expressing my mind pretty freely, "I tell you it is harder where there are no stoves, and nothing to put in them either!" Was not this a reproof for my impatient spirit! Formerly the pipes of both sitting-room and parlor stoves were carried to the chambers above, and after making sundry circumlocutions, and turning various sharp corners, found their way into the roaring chimney. What times we had then! I made such a "fuss" that a mason appeared, who, by making a jog in the parlor, built up a little chimney to receive at once the abbreviated pipes. I imagine that *some one else* was quite as disgusted as I with the former process. That might have helped to make my stirring words more weighty, and to bring about so happy a result. Now and then when, on a freezing day, I go up to the chambers and see the cold black stoves standing like grim sentinels to keep all comfort at bay, I almost think the softened air of the twisting pipes would be a luxury, but I am not the one to say so. No, no; not I! by no manner of means.

When through with stoves, we had a talk about house cleaning. Lizzie appealed to my experience here. Docile and diligent pupil as she is, I am proud in any respect to be her teacher. She little knows in how many sweet and gentle ways she is mine. But I discoursed something in this wise. Some of my neighbors are through with house cleaning. But health is too precious to be risked in empty rooms, with open windows, until the weather is mild enough to do so without chill. It is not a pleasant "job," but with a little pains-taking, and a hearty effort to keep good natured, it need only produce a healthful breeze in the atmosphere at home. I think we housekeepers are too apt to assume that the male portion of the household are now only incumbrances, to be treated with cold dinners and got out of the way with all possible dispatch. By far the easier way to accomplish house cleaning is to take one or two rooms at a time, and "get them to rights" before disturbing others. But if, perchance, the good man of the house, truly reading the signs of the times, in the kindness of his heart should bring to the rescue a couple of stout Irishmen, to take down stoves, and shake carpets, then all hands to the work, in double quick time. He must be allowed to fret a little at the general discomfort, and the impossibility of finding any thing he wants. But use some "*policy*" here. Show him the heap of dust taken from under the sitting-room carpet, and the moths that have made their nest under another in a dark corner of the bedroom, and ask him if it will not be healthier and better for the children to have this all removed before the warm days of summer are here. To your great delight he will very likely propose a fresh coat of paint for a room looking rather the worse for wear, or bring home a wall paper embellished with a dainty vine of violets and rosebuds, while just in his rear you will catch the glimpse of a man armed with brushes and pails, who receives some very decided orders to give the whole house a thorough going over, with some white preparation in the aforesaid pails. Don't forget just here to thank him for his thoughtfulness, while you say it is exactly what you wanted to have done, and take some pains to have a warm dinner ready, which, though spread in the kitchen, shall be eaten with good relish, and enlivened with cheerful conversation, into which the subject of the work on hand had better not be introduced. It would not be strange if, just "to be even" with you, he should then suggest, (as this is by no means the labor of a day,) that to-morrow you give him a cold lunch for dinner, and never mind about him, if you only won't get sick, before this hubbub is over.

We spent part of to-day in the woods, and came home with Georgy's hat wreathed with flowers, though his chubby hands made some displacement of their artistic arrangement. Lizzie is so busy preparing for a visit to her old home she hardly allows herself time for recreation. It may be well to tell her that sad story of my past history.

A Coffee Roaster.

A, in Fig. 1, is a cylinder of sheet iron, (Russia is the best) 8 or 9 inches in diameter, and 6 inches deep, wired at each end. About an inch from the lower end there is securely fastened a bottom of wire-cloth, about 7×7 mesh, or such as is used for market wheat screens in fan-mills. The wire bottom is represented by the dotted line *B*. Just beneath the wire bottom there is a cross piece *C*, rivetted to support the wire and make a bearing for the end of the rod *F*, to which is attached the stirrer *J*. The upper end of the rod *F*, is supported by a cross piece similar to *C*, but which is fastened by lugs rivetted to the sides, that it may be removable.

Fig. 1.—COFFEE ROASTER.

The cover *D*, is of tin, to reflect the heat, and is divided in the center, one part overlapping the other, in order that one part of the cover may be lifted off easily to observe the process of roasting.

Figure 2 shows the under side of the apparatus. In roasting, the apparatus is placed on top the stove, over a pretty hot fire, leaving half the cover off at first that the moisture may escape, then close tightly, and continue stirring until done, which will usually be found to be the case when the coffee begins to pop, sometimes sooner. It will be found to be of great advantage to add a small bit of butter, say as large as a filbert, about the time the coffee begins to change color. Coffee can be browned in this way in from ten to twelve minutes and as evenly done as in the best of roasters. Since we used it we have not had burnt coffee in the house.

Fig. 2.—BOTTOM OF ROASTER.

Independence of Servants.

We have received an essay of thirteen pages in a beautiful hand writing, and happily expressed, containing the fair writer's experience with servants. Her afflictions and inflictions from this source are so much matters of course in housekeeping that we should not add much to the knowledge of our readers by publishing them. Paul's description of his perils by sea and land is not more graphic than the experience of many of our housekeepers in this line. They are not limited to "three shipwrecks" or to "a night and a day in the deep." Wrecks of stoves, chairs, tables, crockery, and hardware lie all along their household voyaging, thicker than stranded ships on Hatteras or Absecom, and the better part of their time they are not only in the deep, but in "hot water." There are good servants no doubt, models of neatness, faithfulness, patience, skill and industry, but they are about as scarce as Solomon's virtuous woman. Who can find them? They are advertised, we know, of every nationality, and every variety of capacity, but housekeepers suspect, after a few trials, that the keepers of Intelligence offices use a more than poetic license. A normal school for the training of servants is one of the great wants of the age. We shall get along to that some time in the millennium probably, but in the meantime what are we to do? Some are ready to declare their independence, and where that is feasible we like the plan.

A Southern lady of true grit writes us: "I am so much interested in the Essays on Housekeeping that I almost envy Mrs. Lyman her conveniences. We Southern ladies know nothing of such things, and if we buy any of the labor-saving machines they are almost useless to us. I bought a stove and paid $35 for it, and in three years it was burned up, and since then I have gone back to the fireplace. Our servants never take care of any thing, and it is fret and worry all the time with them. I have resolved to learn all I can from the *Agriculturist* about the labor-saving machines, and I think a few more of those admirable essays will put me on the right track, and you will have occasion to hear of my experience, for I am resolved to do my work myself, rather than wear out my patience and temper with servants, who neglect and waste every thing committed to their care." This lady's experience is probably confined to servants, trained under the old *regime*. The training of free labor is a long step upward, and that stove would have lasted in any northern home at least a dozen years, and by that time there would have been a new pattern of stove, so much improved that we could afford to sell the old one for old iron. But with the average grade of service that we get under free labor, there are a multitude of families where the housekeeper would do quite as well without servants as with them, if she could have suitable conveniences like our prize essay kitchen and its appurtenances. It is far within bounds to say that a kitchen may be so arranged as to save one half the necessary work of cooking and washing. It is much cheaper in the end, to bring water into the house by pipes where you want to use it, and to carry it off in the same way, than to furnish muscle to bring and empty every pailfull as it is needed. Pumps, lead pipe, tanks and reservoirs are much cheaper than labor. Then there is a great saving in a cook stove or range with its assortment of cooking utensils. Another saving is in a good washing machine and wringer, and another still in the new patent dish washer. Fitted out with these appliances, a woman in good health and without small children, can often do her own work with less worry without a servant than with one.

But, then, she must not have too high a standard of housekeeping, or too many claims of society upon her. The meals must necessarily be served in the kitchen, and she must spend the most of her time there. There can not be much time left for company, or for reading, or for the accomplishments of life. It can not be denied that servants are a necessary accompaniment of the most desirable style of living. A woman of cultivation and refinement can not do justice to her children, to her social position, and to her own self-culture and at the same time drudge in the kitchen. Servants are a necessity, if one has the means of supporting them. Our essayists offer many valuable hints upon their training and treatment.

Graham Pudding.—Mrs. "N. E. B."—Stir Graham flour gradually into boiling water with a little salt, and make about as thick as hasty pudding, or mush, and free from lumps. Eat with tolerably rich milk and sugar, and with the addition of canned peaches or other preserved fruits. If there be any of the pudding left over it may be cut in slices and fried in lard or dripping, and is very good. We have been having the above pudding for breakfast daily for years, and our "boys" are not willing to do without it. It is good for the teeth.

Rhubarb Pudding.—One cup sour milk, one teaspoonful soda, make a stiff batter with flour, and add some cropped stalks of pie plant. Boil in cloths and serve with cream and sugar for dinner.

Corn Starch Pudding.—One quart boiling milk, three spoonfuls corn starch, mixed with a little cold milk, sweeten and flavor with lemon if liked. Pour it into the boiling milk, stir well for two or three minutes. Pour into moulds. When cool, turn out and surround with large ripe strawberries to be eaten with cream and sugar. The above always presents a beautiful appearance

Potato Yeast.—Boil one pint of hops in two quarts of water, strain the water from the hops, grate five good sized potatoes, put in a kettle, add one cup of sugar, one tablespoonfull of salt, one of ginger, boil ten minutes, add more water if too thick. Strain through a colander, cool, add yeast to rise, bottle. It will keep a number of weeks.

BOYS & GIRLS' COLUMNS.

Boy Training.

"There! it may lay there, for what I care, and a plague on all grammars, I say!"

These words burst out with something of the same force which dashed a well-thumbed book across the room. Hal believed that his uncomfortable feelings were owing entirely to a "plaguey hard lesson" for to-morrow, but it is possible that circumstances may have aggravated the hardship; as for instance, a bright sun, smooth, hard snow, and other signs of a first-rate skating time. After looking out of the window a moment, Hal again broke forth with all the indignation of twelve years: "It's a real dog's life to be a boy! school, school, work, work, from one day's end to another. Stupid books! and what's the good of it all, I'd like to know!" — "What is the good, sure enough?" said a voice behind him. Hal had forgotten the quiet reader by the fire. He colored a little, but answered: "I'm sure I can't see, Cousin Ralph. Reading and writing are well enough, or learning a trade, and all that; but to be studying so much stuff, and shut up all the pleasantest days of one's life - I tell you what, I'd rather be a savage at once. What a jolly time! Free all day, in the real wild woods, hunting and fishing—why, what is their work, we call play."

"Stop a moment, Hal. We are speaking of boys—do you think savage boys have nothing to learn?" —

"Nothing like Latin grammar, I'll bet my head! It is only fun to learn to make arrows, to hunt and to fight—I would change work with them, any day."

"Be not so sure of that. Hear a specimen of boy training I have just been reading. 'All the boys over ten years are chosen to be companions of the son of the chief. They are taken to some lonely spot in the forest where huts are built for them. The old men go out daily to teach them their war dances and their notions of law and government. Much beating is necessary to bring them up to the required perfection, so that when they return from the forest their backs have many scars. When the boys have reached the age of fourteen, the great ceremony of their lives takes place. They all stand naked, in an open space, each with a pair of sandals as a shield on his hands. Facing the boys stand the men of the tribe armed with long wands of tough wood. They put such questions to the boys as "Will you guard the chief well? Will you guard the cattle well?" and while the boys answer "Yes," rush at them, each aiming a blow at the back of a boy, causing the blood to squirt out of a wound often eighteen inches long. Thus the boys' backs are seamed with wounds, the scars of which remain through life. This is their initiation into manhood.'"

"Horrible!" said Hal, with a sigh, "why that is suffering for worse than nothing."

"Yes, and you may be sure that the demands of ignorance and superstition are harder than any which civilization imposes upon us."

Hal thought a moment, still unwilling to admit the expediency of school education, and then he said, "But any way, I wish I had lived in old times—the real, grand old times, you know, when there were knights and tournaments, and men did such brave deeds. There were no school books then, and a man might be brave and true and make a great name for himself without even learning how to read. Riding, and fighting and punishing all bad people. Oh! I could be happy while I was a boy with only thinking of such a life. And those men were not savages—they lived in castles, and were Christians—they had to say ever so many prayers, and do each man his best for God and his lady—Oh, Ralph! was it not easier and pleasanter to become a great man then, than to study up to it as we have to do now!"——"As to the desirableness of that life, Hal, we will not argue just now, we will keep to the boys and see what their work was." And Cousin Ralph, taking a book from the shelf, read as follows: "Young Roland passed his earliest years with his mother and her attendants, who taught him the pater nosters, and Ave Marias, besides the first ideas of that devotion to women which belonged to the age of chivalry. But at the age of seven years his education began in earnest, as was usual then. Though the father might be capable of conducting the education of his son, it was always intrusted to some other knight, lest the tenderness of the parents should spare any of the trials and hardships necessary to the after career. So the little Roland, at that early age, left the indulgences of his own home to shift for himself in a strange household. The first place he was to fill was that of page to his new lord, his duty being to accompany the knight on excursions, do his errands, serve him at the table and pour out his drink, though the boy was of as noble blood as the man he served. At the same time great care was taken in the training of the boy. Every moment not devoted to the service of his lord was given to the practice of severe gymnastics or horsemanship; while the custom of waiting upon visitors, and listening to their conversation helped to give the grace of manner so necessary to a knight of renown. Meanwhile the young page had to encounter the jeers of his companions at his awkwardness, and bear with sore and aching limbs from his violent exercise, besides the carefully concealed pain of home sickness. Seven years of this hard service brought Roland to his fourteenth year, the eagerly expected time when he was to exchange the short dagger of the page for the sword of the 'squire.' This was a religious ceremony and conducted with due solemnity. His exercises now became more severe still, such as springing upon horseback armed, turning somersets in heavy armor, besides careful instruction in managing his horse and arms. As squire he continued to follow his lord to battle; held his stirrup, lance, shield, or gauntlets; cleaned his armor, and took care of his horse. In battle the squire waited at a distance ready to furnish a fresh horse or to draw his master from the field if wounded. If a noble squire had done well during his service, the honor of knight-hood was conferred at the age of twenty-one. Roland prepared for this great occasion by long fasts with numerous prayers and masses."

Hal had flinched at the idea of giving up the indulgences of home almost before the end of baby-hood, fidgeted at services altogether menial in his eyes, and finally wound up with a prolonged "whe——e——w!"——There, Hal, I think you will never have to bear harder training than that, and, whatever of good or of romantic interest, it is well to keep from the "old times," you may be sure that true faith, in an "excelsior" ever before us, is the best aid to insure a manhood worth having.

"**Baby Ned**" one day saw his father punish his older brother; his tender little heart was much grieved. His mother explained to him that Wally was naughty, and Papa "slapped" him to make him good. The next day he came into the dairy as she was "patting butter" with the ladle. "Lap but, (slap butter) mama?" asked Ned. "Yes," said his mother. "Is *not but f*" (naughty butter,) asked the little fellow earnestly. H.

The Fate of "Greedy Dick."

All the boys and girls who are careful to keep clean hands and faces, hair combed, clothes brushed, and all things about them as neat as their work will allow, and who love to share their *good* things with their companions, can afford to laugh at the unhappy fate of poor Greedy Dick. He didn't do any of these things, and our artist traces him at last to a barrel of lard. There we leave him, a warning to those who chance to need it!

New Puzzles to be Answered.

No. 261. *Arithmetical Problem.*—Five hundred dollars at interest at ten per cent. per annum, is to be paid up in five equal, annual payments. Required the amount of each payment.

No. 262. *Word Square.*—With the following letters, *R, R, S, S, P, L, A, A, A, A, E, E, E, E, I, I,* form a word square, that is, a square arranged so that the words will be the same, whether read across or downward.

No. 263. *Illustrated Rebus.*—Very good advice.

No. 264—*Geographical Enigma.*—By Myron A. Eddy.

I am composed of 28 letters. My 1, 7, 13, 23, 15, 19, 22, 27, is a lake in Nevada. My 3, 10, 21, 12, 25, is a lake in Russia. My 4, 16, 24, 17, 2, 21, is a lake in Canada. My 6, 11, 11, 15, 26, 27, 12, is a lake in China. My 7, 15, 4, 28, 12, 11, is a lake in New York. My 8, 11, 24, 3, is a lake in Lombardy and Venice. My 9, 24, 4, 4, 26, 1, 5, 21, is a lake in Florida. My 14, 12, 25, 24, 16, is a lake in Ethiopia. My 15, 13, 18, 28, is a lake in California. My 18, 21, 11, 11, is a lake in Nicaragua. My 20, 25, 12, 16, 11, 2, is a lake in Wisconsin. My 24, 19, 4, 9, is a lake in Ireland. My whole is the name and location of a lake in the U. S.

No. 265. *Arithmetical Problem*, to be solved mentally. If 0 cats catch 0 rats in 0 minutes, how long will it take 50 cats to catch 100 rats?

Answers to Problems and Puzzles.

The following are answers to the puzzles, etc., in the April number, page 117. No. 258. *Clock Problem.*—It will strike correctly at 11 o'clock; the number of strokes will be 71....No. 259. *Illustrated Rebus.*—Foul weather stops plain sailing ...No. 260. *Mathematical Problem.*—Diameter of smaller circle, 381 feet; of larger circle, 382 feet.

The Doctor's Talks.

How do the young frogs, or rather tadpoles get on? They probably swim about lively enough by means of their long tails and act much more like little fish than they do like frogs. It is quite curious that frogs, which live partly on land and partly in the water, and toads which live upon land altogether, should be, in the early part of their lives, so much like fishes. They are like fishes not only because they live in the water, but in the manner of their breathing. Every boy and girl knows that land animals breathe with lungs, and that fishes do the same with their gills. Fishes do not need so much air as land animals do; they get all that they need from the water which is constantly passing over their gills. The tadpole is a long while in getting ready to breathe air. A great many curious changes go on in the arrangement of its heart and lungs and all that, which we will not undertake to explain just now. Being fish-like in its

Fig. 1.

manner of living, the tadpole breathes by an arrangement like gills. When examined quite young, the gills are seen on the outside of the head; curiously fringed attachments floating in the water, but they do not last a great while in this condition, as arrangements are soon made to inclose the gills and have them do their work out of sight. The small spot on the head of figure 1 shows where the gills are placed. The tadpole swims around by means of its tail, its mouth improving as it grows, and getting into a condition to allow the animal to feed on the vegetable matter that it finds in the water. After a while, a most curious change takes place, two hinder legs appear, (fig. 2,) showing that the animal, though it has its birth in the water, is destined to live upon land. Later still, the fore-legs may be seen under the skin, and they finally break through. When the tadpole is ready to leave the water it has no further need of a tail; this is not jerked off as is generally supposed, but gradually disappears, its substance being taken up—absorbed as we

Fig. 2.

say—by the other parts of the body. All this while that the animal has been providing itself with legs, to enable it to live on land, its interior arrangements have undergone a change no less wonderful, lungs have grown to take the place of gills, and its very simple spiral intestine has become a stomach, etc. The time required for the tadpole to complete all these changes varies in the different kinds, and it is governed also by the amount of light and heat the young animals enjoy. Sooner or later the young frog or toad, as the case may be, gives up his fish-like ways and takes to the land, where he breathes air and no longer lives on plants, but takes to animal food in the form of insects, etc. The toad never returns to the water, but the frog does not abandon his youthful ways so readily, but is in water or on land as best pleases him.

To See Three Thumbs.—Look steadily, for a short time at a white wall, and then place the tips of the thumbs together and closing the fingers over the palms, raise the hands up in front of the face and about a foot from it. If you look steadily at the wall, and not at the hands, a small thumb will be seen between the other two. The engraving shows the appearance as well as the position of the hands.

A Childish Conceit.—One night in a thunder shower we thought the little ones were all asleep, when a little voice from the "trundle-bed" called out, "Oh, mother, the dark is winking! first it shuts up, and then it shuts down." H.

Please Don't waste time, paper, and postage stamps, by writing out and sending to the *Agriculturist* old puzzles, such as "I understand, you undertake, to overthrow my undertaking." That rebus amused us thirty years ago, and has been a household favorite throughout the country ever since. It has been sent here for publication from one place or another about twice a week, for several years! Many other equally ancient friends pay us similar visits, and are politely received in our (waste) basket. Good, new problems are always acceptable, though not always published at once.

COPYRIGHT SECURED.

A LIFE-LIKE PORTRAIT. — *Engraved for the American Agriculturist.*

This little fellow in the picture, no doubt, finds it much easier to play off a joke upon his grandmother than to be an artist in colors. He has stationed his sister behind a picture frame, and called the old lady to admire the fine portrait. It is a harmless, funny deception, for grandmother's spectacles will soon enable her to see through the frame and the joke at the same time, and she will join the hearty laugh the children are ready to give when the right time comes. As long as love of fun does not lead to making others feel unpleasant, for the sake of sport, it is not blame-worthy, if indulged in at proper times. If carried beyond that point, it may become a serious wrong. By such means friends have become enemies for life. Especially should care be taken not to wound the feelings of the aged. A child who makes sport of the infirmities of old people, should remember that he may one day be in the same condition, and also that the burdens of age are hard enough to bear, without the addition of unkindness from those who should show respect. To needlessly add sorrow to grey hairs has always been counted one of the most inexcusable crimes.

"Handsome Is that Handsome Does."

A short time ago I was visiting at the house of a friend; the oldest son, who has given an arm to his country, was looking over a box of old letters, etc., when his little sister, who was standing by him, took up a photograph with the exclamation, "Oh, what a homely woman!" "That!" said Edward, with a look of hurt surprise, "that is the *handsomest woman I ever saw!* You will not think her homely Mrs. S.," he said as he passed the picture to me. It was the face of a woman apparently about forty-five or fifty years old, a thin and slightly wrinkled face, with a good deal of kindness, but no beauty in it. I told him what I thought of it, but I was sorry for my frankness, when I saw that there were tears in his eyes, as he laid the picture carefully away, saying: "She took care of me when I was in the Hospital, at the time that I lost my arm, and she looked *beautiful* to me I can tell you." "Yes," he added earnestly, "I would give more to see her now than I would to see any other woman I ever saw, young or old." Our ideas of beauty are greatly influenced by the knowledge of the persons character. H.

More About the Geographical Problem.—(*See March No., page* 107.)—A correspondent at Easton, Md., writes: "Your Geographical Problem is a simple question in navigation, and I will answer it in as few words as possible. The point at which the day of the week changes is the anti-meridian of Greenwich. Ships' chronometers are set to Greenwich time, the navigator sailing, say to the westward, finds his time as shown by the sun, becoming daily slower than the chronometer until when he reaches 180° west longitude, there is just 12 hours' difference. By jumping a day at this point, he makes his time 12 hours *fast*, but the difference *lessens* as he sails westward. All circumnavigators make it a practice thus to change the day at this line."

(Business Notices $2.50 per Agate Line of Space.)

FLORENCE

LOCK-STITCH SEWING MACHINES.

[illegible] of American Institute, [illegible]
CELEBRATED REVERSIBLE FEED MOVEMENT.
UNIFORM SELF-ADJUSTING TENSION.
FOUR SEPARATE [illegible] STITCHES.
WILL GATHER AND SEW A RUFFLE AT ONCE.
OFFICES OF THE COMPANY.
505 Broadway, N. Y., [illegible], London, England.

PRINCIPAL AGENCIES.

141 Washington-st., Boston. [illegible] Main-st., Buffalo, N. Y.
[illegible] Chestnut-st., Philadelphia. [illegible], Havana,
100 Washington-st., Chicago. Cuba.
[illegible] West Fourth-st., Cincinnati. [illegible] Court-st., Binghamton, N.Y.
[illegible] Public Square, Cleveland. [illegible], N. Y.
[illegible], Baltimore. [illegible], Newark, N. J.
[illegible] North Pennsylvania-st., [illegible], Nashville, Tenn.
[illegible], [illegible].
Cor. Jeff. and Woodward Av., [illegible]. Syracuse, N. Y.
[illegible] Rochester, N. Y.
[illegible], San Francisco. [illegible] North Fifth-st., St. Louis, Mo.
[illegible], Troy, N. Y.
[illegible] to [illegible] Main-st., Hartford. Cor. [illegible], and [illegible], Utica, N. Y.
529 Broadway, Albany, N. Y.

The Howe Machine Co.'s Sewing Machines,

699 Broadway, Cor. Fourth-st., New York.

For Families and Manufacturers.

These World-Renowned Sewing Machines

Were awarded the highest premium at the World's Fair in London, and six first premiums at the N. Y. State Fair of 1866.

These machines are made under the immediate supervision of the President of the Company, ELIAS HOWE, Jr., the original inventor of the Sewing Machine.

The Stitch invented by **MR. HOWE**, *and made on this Machine, is the most popular and durable, and all Sewing Machines are subject to the principle invented by him.*

SEND FOR CIRCULAR.

WHEELER & WILSON ROTARY HOOK LOCK STITCH SEWING MACHINES.

625 BROADWAY.

"WOMAN'S GREATEST BOON.—We would advise a man to forego a Thresher, and thresh wheat with a flail, rather than to [illegible] away in the [illegible] Sewing Machine [illegible] WHEELER & WILSON is an invaluable [illegible]. We have had several [illegible] years' service, the WHEELER & WILSON [illegible] the best, [illegible] family." [illegible], 1865.

THE GREAT FAMILY SEWING MACHINE.

GROVER & BAKER'S

HIGHEST PREMIUM Elastic Stitch SEWING MACHINE.

195 Broadway, New York.

FRANKLIN BRICK MACHINE.

[illegible] celebrated for perfect simplicity, great strength, and [illegible] power; [illegible], with [illegible] [illegible] NICK, Proprietor, [illegible].

POMONA'S HOME NURSERY

AND SMALL FRUIT FARM, [illegible] to Glendale P. O., [illegible] [illegible] very large [illegible] extra good [illegible] will [illegible] [illegible] four "Manual of Grape [illegible]," *for free distribution.* J. H. FOSTER, Jr. [illegible], Canton and Atlantic Railroad, [illegible].

THE FIRST MORTGAGE BONDS

OF THE CENTRAL PACIFIC RAILROAD COMPANY present unusual inducements to investors, among which are the following:

First—The rate of interest is six per cent. IN GOLD.
Second—The principal is payable IN GOLD at maturity.
Third—The cost, NINETY-FIVE PER CENT. and accrued interest, is TEN PER CENT. less than that of the cheapest six per cent. Gold-bearing Bonds of the Government.
Fourth—Owing to the liberal grants and loans by which the Government fosters this great national enterprise, its success is certain, and its financial stability is altogether independent of the contingencies which attend ordinary railroad enterprises. The SECURITY of its FIRST MORTGAGE BONDS is therefore AMPLE, and gives them a character for safety and reliability equaled only by that of the obligations of the Government itself. **Fifth**—The earnings of the completed portion of the road are already largely in excess of the interest obligations which the Company will incur on twice the distance, rendering the uninterrupted payment of the interest ABSOLUTELY CERTAIN. **Sixth**—At the present rate of gold they pay nearly 8½ per cent. on the amount invested.

For further particulars apply to

FISK & HATCH, Bankers,
No. 5 Nassau-st., New York.

AMERICAN WALTHAM WATCHES.

We claim and are prepared to prove that the American Watches manufactured at Waltham, Massachusetts, are not only equal, but far superior, to the watches of England, Switzerland and France. We also claim that they are CHEAPER, MORE ACCURATE, MORE DURABLE, and more easily kept in order and repaired than any other watches in the market.

Because in each one of the very numerous parts of which a watch is made up, we attain, by mechanical power, nearly *absolute* mathematical precision and uniformity, making every watch of any one style a true copy of its model.

This similarity in structure reduces the cost of production; it secures uniformity in results; it *infallibly* perpetuates any excellence that may be once achieved, and makes it easy to repair any injury sustained, or replace any part that may be lost or destroyed.

In addition to these mechanical advantages, our Watches are simpler in structure, and therefore stronger, and less likely to be injured than foreign watches.

How they run under the hardest trial watches can have, is shown by the following letter.

PENN. RAILROAD COMPANY,
OFFICE OF THE GENERAL SUPERINTENDENT,
ALTOONA, PA., 15th Dec., 1866.

Gentlemen: The watches manufactured by you have been in use on this railroad for several years by our enginemen, to whom we furnish watches as part of our equipment. There are now some three hundred of them carried on our line, and we consider them good and reliable time keepers. Indeed, I have great satisfaction in saying your watches give us less trouble, and have worn and do wear much longer without repairs than any watches we have ever had in use on this road. As you are aware, we formerly trusted to those of English manufacture, of acknowledged good reputation, but as a class they never kept time as correctly, nor have they done as good service, as yours.

In these statements I am sustained by my predecessor, Mr. Lewis, whose experience extended over a series of years.

Respectfully,
EDWARD H. WILLIAMS,
General Superintendent.

American Watch Co., Waltham.

Any of the grades of Waltham Watches may be purchased of Watch Dealers generally throughout the country.

ROBBINS & APPLETON,
Agents for the American Watch Company,
No. 182 Broadway, New York; or,
ROBBINS, APPLETON & CO.,
No. 158 Washington-st., Boston.

Book Agents Wanted,

To solicit orders in each town in the United States and Canada, for the most popular subscription book ever published, being THE ILLUSTRATED HISTORY OF THE BIBLE, by *John Kitto, D. D., F. S. A.*, *Edited by Rev. Alvan Bond, D. D., of Norwich, Conn.*—Over 700 closely printed Royal Octavo pages, more than [illegible] full page engravings. Recommended by the leading clergy of all denominations of Christians. [illegible] already printed. Six large power presses running on the work. Everybody wants it. Experienced Agents say they never knew a book sell so well. No competition. Experienced Agents, School Teachers, Sabbath School Teachers, retired Clergymen, and others, are wanted to introduce this great work into every household in the land. For circulars, etc., apply immediately to the Publisher. HENRY BILL, Norwich, Conn.

BUY THE BEST!

J. W. BRADLEY'S
CELEBRATED

DUPLEX ELLIPTIC

(OR DOUBLE SPRING)

SKIRTS.

THEY will not BEND or BREAK like the Single Springs, but WILL PRESERVE their PERFECT and GRACEFUL SHAPE in all CROWDED ASSEMBLAGES, CHURCHES, THEATRES, RAILROAD CARS, and for PROMENADE or HOUSE DRESS, where three or four ordinary skirts are THROWN ASIDE as USELESS.

EACH HOOP is composed of TWO FINELY-TEMPERED Steel Springs, BRAIDED TIGHTLY and FIRMLY together, EDGE to EDGE, forming one hoop, thus making the STRONGEST and MOST FLEXIBLE, as well as the MOST DURABLE and STYLISH SKIRT EVER MADE. In fact, they are superior to all others, COMBINING COMFORT, ECONOMY, LIGHTNESS, ELEGANCE, and DURABILITY.

This POPULAR SKIRT is UNIVERSALLY RECOMMENDED by the FASHION MAGAZINES and OPINIONS of the PRESS GENERALLY.

At WHOLESALE, by the Exclusive Manufacturers and SOLE OWNERS of PATENT,

WESTS, BRADLEY & CARY,
WAREROOMS AND OFFICE,
Nos. 97 Chambers, and 79 and 81 Reade sts., N. Y.
ALSO, at WHOLESALE by the LEADING JOBBERS.

New Patent.

PROTECTOR FRUIT JARS.

They are made air tight with certainty and ease.
Readily opened, without injury to the covers.
Each Cover will fit all the Jars.
Handsome in Style—Low in Price; they are all that are needed for use by Families or Fruit Preservers.
Send for Circular and Price List.
F. & J. BODINE, Philadelphia, Pa.

The Premium Machine!

BUCKEYE MOWER & REAPER

See extract from Official Report of Great Auburn Field Trial, on page 197.

WOODWARD'S

RECORD OF HORTICULTURE for 1866.

Edited by ANDREW S. FULLER.

This work will be issued annually, and record all that is new and valuable in Horticulture.—Morocco cloth, beveled edges, post-paid, $1.00. GEO. E. & F. W. WOODWARD, Publishers, 37 Park Row, N. Y.

THE LITTLE CORPORAL

Is acknowledged by the leading papers to be the

Best Juvenile Paper in America.

We offer a **MAGNIFICENT LIST of PREMIUMS!**
Subscribe at any time during the year.

The price of the Corporal is one dollar a year, in advance; sample copy, telling all about the premiums, ten cents.
Address ALFRED L. SEWELL, Publisher, Chicago, Ill.

EMPLOYMENT! YOUNG MEN may better their condition by taking an Agency for our Pictorial Books. Send stamp for particulars to S. R. WELLS, 389 Broadway, New York.

MARK YOUR CLOTHING!

Clark's Patent Indelible Pencil.

"The Indelible Pencil for marking clothing is much more convenient than ink, and equally good as to permanence—we judge after several month's trial."—*Am. Agriculturist.*

"The Indelible Pencil is invaluable for marking linen."—*Chicago Tribune.*

"Remarkable for the ease and neatness with which it can be used."—*Detroit Tribune.*

Manufactured and Sold at Wholesale by
THE INDELIBLE PENCIL CO., Northampton, Mass.
PRICES—40 cents single, $4 per dozen. Sent post-paid on receipt of price.
A liberal discount made to dealers.
EVERY PENCIL WARRANTED. AGENTS WANTED.

THE TRADE AND AGENTS Supplied with Chromos, Photographs, Albums, Colored Prints, etc.
Send for Catalogue.
WHITING BROTHERS, Publishers,
811 Broadway, New York.

THE GREAT AMERICAN TEA COMPANY,

Since their organization, have created a new era in the Tea Trade. They have introduced their selection of Teas and Coffees, and have sold them at the smallest profits possible. They warrant all the goods they sell to be perfectly satisfactory. If they do not prove so, the purchaser has the privilege of returning them within 30 days at the expense of the Company, and have the money refunded.

The Company have selected the following kinds from their stock, which they recommend, to meet the wants of Clubs. They are sold at Cargo Prices, the same as the Company sell them in New York, as the list of prices will show.

PRICE LIST:

YOUNG HYSON (Green), 80c., 90c., $1, $1.10, best $1.25 ℔ lb.
GREEN TEAS, 80c., 90c., $1, $1.10, best $1.25 ℔ lb.
MIXED, 70c., 80c., 90c., best $1 ℔ lb.
JAPAN, $1, $1.10, best $1.25 ℔ lb.
OOLONG (Black), 70c., 80c., 90c., best $1 ℔ lb.
IMPERIAL (Green), best $1.25 ℔ lb.
ENGLISH BREAKFAST (Black), 80c., 90c., $1, $1.10, best $1.20 ℔ lb.
GUNPOWDER (Green), $1.25, best $1.50.

COFFEE DEPARTMENT.

Our Coffee Department is very extensive—the largest, perhaps, in the country. We run three engines constantly, and sometimes four or five in roasting and grinding our Coffee. Our Coffee buyers are experts, who examine most of the Coffees imported, and select the best and finest flavors for our trade. We employ the most experienced and skillful roasters, who exercise the greatest care that it shall be cooked in a perfect manner. It is always fresh, for our orders crowd our facilities to their utmost capacity. A considerable portion of the Coffee put upon the market of late years is picked while the pods are green, and subjected to artificial heat to open the pods. This is not so good as that which ripens in the natural way upon the plant. Our Coffee buyer thoroughly understands this business, and can readily distinguish the naturally ripened from the artificially cured; and he only buys the Coffee which is naturally ripened. We examine the cargoes as soon as they arrive, and our trade is so large that it requires all the finest lots. This is what gives our Coffee a superior flavor to many others, and the same flavor it used to have in days long gone by. It is a common saying that most Coffee does not taste as well as it formerly did. The reason for it is, that a considerable portion of it is picked before it is fully ripe. We sell none but the fully ripe, rich flavored Coffee.

COFFEES ROASTED AND GROUND DAILY.

GROUND COFFEE, 20c., 25c., 30c., 35c., best 40c. per pound. Hotels, Saloons, Boarding-house keepers, and Families who use large quantities of Coffee can economize in that article by using our FRENCH BREAKFAST AND DINNER COFFEE, which we sell at the low price of 30c. per pound, and warrant to give perfect satisfaction.

Consumers can save from 50c. to $1 per pound by purchasing their Teas of

THE GREAT AMERICAN TEA COMPANY,
Nos. 31 and 33 VESEY-ST.
No. 640 BROADWAY, corner of Bleecker-st.
No. 461 EIGHTH-AVE. north corner of Thirty-fourth-st.
No. 250 SPRING-ST.
No. 205 FULTON ST., BROOKLYN, corner of Concord-st.
No. 133 GRAND-ST., WILLIAMSBURGH.

COUNTRY CLUBS, Hand and Wagon Pedlers, and small stores (of which class we are supplying many thousands, all of which are doing well), can have their orders promptly and faithfully filled, and in case of Clubs can have each party's name marked on their package and directed by sending their orders to Nos. 31 and 33 Vesey-st.

Our friends are getting up Clubs in most towns throughout the country, and for which we feel very grateful. Some of our Clubs send orders weekly, and some not so often; while others keep a standing order to be supplied with a given quantity each week, or stated periods. And in all cases (where sufficient time has elapsed) Clubs have repeated their orders.

Parties sending Clubs or other orders for less than $30 had better send Post-Office drafts, or money with their orders, to save the expense of collecting by express; but larger orders we will forward by express, to collect on delivery.

We return thanks to parties who have taken an interest in getting up Clubs; and when any of them come to New York we shall be happy to have them call upon us and make themselves known.

Hereafter we will send a complimentary package to the party getting up the Club. Our profits are small, but we will be as liberal as we can afford. We send no complimentary package for Clubs of less than $30.

N. B.—All villages and towns where a large number reside, by *clubbing* together, can reduce the cost of their Teas and Coffees about one third by sending directly to the

GREAT AMERICAN TEA COMPANY,
Nos. 31 and 33 VESEY-ST.
Post-Office Box, No. 5,643, New York City.

GETTING UP CLUBS.

Some parties inquire of us how they shall proceed to get up a club. The answer is simply this: Let each person wishing to join in a club, say how much tea or coffee he wants, and select the kind and price from our Price List, as published in the paper or in our circulars. Write the names, kinds, and amounts plainly on a list, and when the club is complete send it to us by mail, and we will put each party's goods in separate packages, and mark the name upon them, with the cost, so there need be no confusion in their distribution—each party getting exactly what he orders, and no more. The cost of transportation the members of the club can divide equitably among themselves.

The funds to pay for the goods ordered can be sent by drafts on New York, by Post-Office money orders, or by Express, as may suit the convenience of the club. Or, if the amount ordered exceeds thirty dollars, we will, if desired, send the goods by Express, to "*collect on delivery.*"

We publish some of our Club Lists to show how it is done and as a matter of reference.

After the first Club we send blanks.

Direct your orders plainly, THE GREAT AMERICAN TEA COMPANY, Nos. 31 and 33 Vesey-st., Post-Office Box, 5,643—as some parties imitate our name as near as they dare do.

From The Great American Tea Company's Advocate.

A Word with Our Customers.

We have no doubt that our customers, scattered throughout the length and breadth of the land, as they are, embracing every State in the Union, except those on the Pacific shores, will be interested to learn how we have succeeded in our great enterprise of furnishing Teas and Coffees, to all, at the smallest possible profits. To afford them this information we propose to give a few facts connected with our business.

Years ago, in the early stage of our enterprise, we based our calculations and graded our rates of profit upon the basis of a trade of $100,000 per week. This amount we expected to reach by enterprise and fair dealing. We well knew that it could be accomplished only by filling every order promptly, and to the letter; and at uniform prices. These principles we have adhered to strictly, and have carried out the ONE PRICE SYSTEM in all our transactions.

After years of anxiety and incessant toil, we are enabled to say, without boasting, that our standard of sales, which we erected years ago, has been reached. The *New York Tribune*, in an editorial published in their paper several months ago, placed the amount of our sales at that time at $90,000 per week. Our business increases regularly and constantly, and never faster than at the present time. We therefore look confidently forward to a large increase during the present year, over and above the average of $100,000 per week. At the present time our sales are fully equal to 2,000 chests per week, which is equal to about one-fifth of all the Teas imported into this country. This we consider a great success for a *specialty*—probably the greatest ever achieved in this country, in any similar mercantile enterprise.

With our increased trade we increase our facilities, so that all our orders will be filled as promptly and correctly as heretofore, and perhaps more so, because our system becomes more and more perfect with time and practice.

We employ at least two hundred persons constantly, and by our perfect system of division of labor into departments, we make a great saving of expense, of which we give consumers the benefit, by furnishing them with the great necessaries of life—TEAS AND COFFEES—at the unprecedented low figures which we publish in our Price List in another column.

While we feel sure that we have given, and as we shall continue to give, our customers the fullest and amplest return for their money, we thank them, one and all, for their patronage.

Complimentary Letters from Clubs.

Cedar Rapids, Iowa, March 12, 1867.
Great American Tea Co., 31 and 33 Vesey-st., N. Y.

Gentlemen: I have received my first box of Tea, $11.25, and with pleasure inform you that it has given the purchasers a feeling of old times, as they have experienced in drinking Tea before the war, satisfying them the Company is not a "Humbug." I send to-day my second order, $12.40. Please forward to me with bill for collection.

A. C. MESSENGER.

Woonsocket, R. I., Feb. 4, 1867.
To the Great American Tea Co., Nos. 31 and 33 Vesey-st., N. Y.

Gentlemen: I now send you my 5th order for Teas, which I hope will be as good as heretofore; it is just one year since I sent my first order of $20, which I think was the first order you got from here as a club. During the year I have sent you upwards of $100, and I have not heard a complaint yet from any one, but all speaking well of your Teas, and are well satisfied. Accept my thanks for the complimentary package. Inclosed you will find $124.35 for this order. Hoping you will forward as soon as possible, I remain,

Yours respectfully, JAMES WOODHOUSE.

Direct the Teas for me, Woonsocket, R. I., by Earl's Express.

Geneva, N. Y., Feb. 22, 1867.
The Great American Tea Co., Nos. 31 and 33 Vesey-st., N. Y.

Gents: We have now been receiving Tea from you about one year, and find, in footing up our books, we have received of you Tea and Coffee, to the amount of $7,211.25 for this small village and vicinity. The public have perfect confidence in your Tea and Coffee, and the misrepresentations against you which we had to contend with at first, are now harmless. We congratulate you on the general success of your enterprise, hoping the hitherto pleasant relations which have existed, may continue between yourselves and

Yours respectfully, LUM & SON.

Angola, N. Y., Feb. 16, 1866.
The Great American Tea Company.

Gents: Your Box sent me by Express has been received. Your bill was paid on delivery. I found no mistakes, and I am glad to inform you that the Tea is giving good satisfaction. I had to make some effort to raise the club I sent you, but as the ice is broken, and nobody drowned, you may expect soon to receive a much larger club order from this place.

Yours truly, JOHN M. SLATER.

Stoughton, Dane Co., Wis., Feb. 25th, 1867.
To the Great American Tea Co., Nos. 31 and 33 Vesey-st., N. Y.

Gentlemen: The Tea I ordered came to hand all right, and gives general satisfaction. Please accept my thanks for the complimentary package.

Some of my neighbors that appeared to be afraid of being humbugged when I got up the club, are now forming a club, and you will probably hear from them soon. The ball is now started in this vicinity, and will probably turn the Tea trade in a new channel. I expect to send another club order before the Tea that we now have is all consumed.

Yours truly, E. E. ROBERTS.

Second National Bank of Detroit.
Detroit, Feb. 24th, 1867.
To the Great American Tea Co., Nos. 31 and 33 Vesey-st., N. Y.

Gentlemen: I received in good order Box of Teas and Coffees from your House yesterday. They are quite satisfactory to all parties. For the complimentary package of Tea please accept my thanks. I shall send you in future with all future orders, a draft on the Mercantile National Bank, N. Y., and thus save for myself 75 cents for return of money. I hope to send you another order in ten days.

Yours truly, R. WATSON LEAGE.

Office of the Northwestern Record,
Sheboygan Falls, Wis., Feb. 28th, 1867.
Great American Tea Co., Nos. 31 and 33 Vesey-st., N. Y.

Gents: The last order I sent you for Teas was on my own responsibility, but I incurred no risk, as it all went off in a very short time to members of former clubs. There are three clubs now forming in this county. All who purchase once are sure to keep doing so, and the trade is increasing here. Another order from this place soon.

Yours truly, S. D. LITTLEFIELD,
Editor *Record*.

Treasury Department, Third Auditor's Office,
March 2, 1867.
Great American Tea Co., Nos. 31 and 33 Vesey-st., N. Y.

Gentlemen: I have the pleasure of enclosing you our second order, $130.18, which is more than double the first one, and the next one may increase proportionately if these give as much satisfaction as the first.

You will please forward as before, by The Adams Express Company, C. O. D. Very respectfully,
Your obedient servant,
H. C. HILL.

CLUB ORDERS.

Homer, Winona Co., Minn., Feb., 1867.
To the Great American Tea Co., Nos. 31 and 33 Vesey-st., N. Y.

Gentlemen: The Box of Tea came to hand all right, and has given general satisfaction as the accompanying order will show. I hope the next time to increase the list still more.

Very respectfully, C. W. MERRITT.

2 lbs.	Best Green	E. B. Hoffman	at	$1.25	$2.50
2	Best Young Hyson	Patrick May	at	1.25	2.50
3	" "	S. Eldridge	at	1.25	3.75
1	Best Japan	C. E. Richardson	at	1.25	1.25
1	" "		at	1.00	1.00
1	Best Oolong	Jacob Beech	at	1.00	1.00
2	Best Japan	Wm. Chalmers	at	1.25	2.50
2	Best Young Hyson	S. M. Fall	at	1.25	2.50
2	Best Green	Tom Gallien	at	1.25	2.50
1	" "	N. B. Sandford	at	1.25	1.25
1	Best Young Hyson	W. Harrison	at	1.25	1.25
2	Best Imperial	S. A. Alling	at	1.25	2.50
3	Best Japan	"	at	1.25	3.75
5	" "	S. H. Branch	at	1.25	6.25
5	Best Young Hyson	"	at	1.25	6.25
8	" "	Mrs. Grant	at	1.25	10.00
1	Best Oolong	Mr. Gates	at	1.00	1.00
					$51.35

Oxford, Chenango Co., N. Y., Feb. 21, 1867.
To the Great American Tea Co., 31 & 33 Vesey-st., N. Y.

Gents: The Teas which you sent me proved perfectly satisfactory to all concerned, please accept my thanks for the complimentary package.

Yours truly, DAVY D. McGEORGE.

1 lb.	Young Hyson	M. C. Ward	at	$1.00	$1.00
1½	Imperial	John Lord	at	1.25	1.50
2	French Breakfast Coffee	"	at	30	60
3	Oolong	C. M. Haine	at	1.00	
3	Mixed	"	at	1.00	6.00
1	Oolong	Solomon Morry	at	1.00	1.00
1	Gunpowder	John Gordon	at	1.50	
2	Imperial	"	at	1.25	4.00
5	Imperial	William Doty	at	1.25	6.25
1	Uncolored Japan	Lewis Ketchum	at	1.00	
1	Young Hyson	"	at	1.25	2.25
2	Young Hyson	F. T. Seely	at	1.25	2.50
3	Oolong	Samuel Kinney	at	1.00	3.00
1	Green	Daniel Jacobs	at	1.00	1.00
2	Oolong	Chauncy Haine	at	1.00	
2	Young Hyson	"	at	1.00	4.00
2	Young Hyson	F. W. Comstock	at	1.25	2.50
2	Imperial	Martin Beadle	at	1.25	2.50
2	Oolong	D. D. McGeorge	at	1.00	2.00
					$40.18

The Best are the Cheapest.

The MASON & HAMLIN CABINET ORGANS are acknowledged to be the best instruments of this class in the world. It is the policy of these makers to produce none but *the very best work*. They aim at success, not by using poor material and economizing in workmanship, so that their instruments can be sold at a little less price; but by producing the most durable, reliable, and in all respects the best work possible, and selling it at the very lowest rates at which such work can possibly be afforded, and at the same prices to all.

They now manufacture more than sixty different styles of Organs, varying in price from $55 to $1,000 each. These instruments contain all the latest improvements, some of which are not to be found in other instruments, the right to their exclusive use having been purchased by M. & H., in some cases at very large expense.

MASON & HAMLIN have been awarded several times as many highest premiums, at Industrial Fairs, as any other maker, having received fifty-six within a few years.

They present in their circulars the printed testimony of a large majority of the most eminent Organists, Pianists, Singers and Composers in the country to the superiority of the instruments of their make.

It is certainly economy in purchasing an instrument of this class to *get the best*, although the first cost may be a little more, as a poor instrument will soon get out of order and become comparatively worthless.

☞ It should be remembered that the recommendations of dealers are not always reliable, as there is great temptation for them to recommend those instruments on which they can make the largest profit; and makers of inferior work can afford the largest discounts. Mason & Hamlin have fixed their retail prices so low that they can afford only very small discounts at wholesale, and hence the temptation to dealers to recommend and sell other instruments is great.

Circulars with full descriptions, illustrations, and prices of the different styles, with hints on what constitutes, and how to select a good instrument, sent free to any one desiring them. Address MASON & HAMLIN,
596 Broadway, New York,
Or, 154 Tremont-st., Boston.

ESTABLISHED, 1845
PRINCE & CO'S MELODEONS AND AUTOMATIC ORGANS

The Standard Instrument.
OVER 40,000 IN USE!!
Illustrated Catalogues sent free on application.
☞ Address all orders and communications to
WHITING BROTHERS,
811 BROADWAY, NEW YORK.

PETER COOPER'S
GELATINE
WILL MAKE
DELICIOUS JELLIES
WITH GREAT EASE.
ALSO,
BLANC MANCE,
CHARLOTTE RUSSE, Etc.
DIRECTIONS FOR USE WITH THE PACKAGES.
For sale by Grocers and Druggists. Depot, No. 17 Burling-Slip, New York.

AGENTS WANTED EVERYWHERE. For the Sale of "Jackson's Universal Washing Compound," which is unequalled by anything of the kind in use. Intelligent energetic agents, Ladies and Gentlemen, are wanted to represent us in every City and County, a *rare opportunity to make money*, and *permanent employment* the year round is offered to every person having a *few hours daily to spare*. For further particulars please call on, or address G. W. JACKSON & CO., [illegible] South-st., Baltimore, Md.

South Jersey Farms For Sale,

Atco, Camden Co., N. J., in a fertile healthful and highly improving [illegible], being located at the Junction of the Raritan and [illegible] and Atlantic Railroads, accessible by several daily trains to both New York and Philadelphia.
Apply to [illegible] W. HANCOCK, Atco, Camden Co., N. J.
N. B.—[illegible]

Stereopticons and Magic Lanterns,

With the Improved Lime Light, illuminating brilliantly two hundred square feet of canvas, and magnifying the views to that size, at an expense of less than one dollar for a whole evening's exhibition. Easily managed and [illegible] well.

Illustrated priced catalogue of the apparatus, with list of over two thousand artistically colored photographic views on glass, of the War, Scripture History, Choice Statuary, etc., etc., forwarded on application. T. H. McALLISTER, Optician, (of late firm of McAllister & Bro., Phila.,) 49 Nassau-street, New York.

ROPER'S NEW AMERICAN BREECH LOADING REPEATING SHOT GUN, firing four shots in two seconds, using ordinary ammunition. Manufactured by ROPER REPEATING RIFLE CO., Amherst, Mass. Under personal supervision of C. M. SPENCER, Inventor of the famous SPENCER RIFLE. ☞ Send for Circular.

IMPORTANT TO SHOEMAKERS.—SANDERS' improvement on Pegging Awl Handles, Pat. April, 1864. This improvement springs the awl out of the hardest leather. The Commissioner of Patents remarked that he would not be surprised if it would equal the Telegraph in its benefits. Samples sent by mail for $1, and to Clubs for $1.50 per dozen. Address F. A. SANDERS, Panhandle, Brooke Co., West Va.

Patent Excelsior Neck-tie Holder,

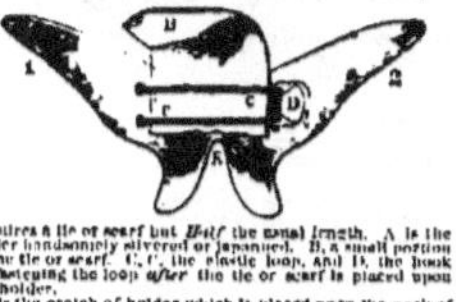

Requires a tie or scarf but *Half* the usual length. A is the holder handsomely silvered or japanned. B, a small portion of the tie or scarf. C, C, the elastic loop, and D, the hook for fastening the loop *after* the tie or scarf is placed upon the holder.

E is the crotch of holder which is placed upon the neck of the collar button, when the wings of the holder, 1 and 2, are *afterwards* slipped under the collar. The knot or bow is tied *after* the holder is upon the neck. If not to be had at your furnishing store, samples will be sent, post-paid, to any address upon receipt of 25 cts. These Holders are handsomely finished in the most workmanlike manner, and are neat and durable.

State whether to send large or small size, black or white Holder. Address WM. H. HART, Jr., Patentee,
No. 32 North Fifth-st., Philadelphia, Pa.

P. T. BARNUM'S
PATENT

Elastic Strap and Buckles
for Pants, Vest and Drawers.

Just out, and what every man needs. No Pants, Vest, or Drawers perfect without this attachment. Applied in a moment by any one. For sale by Tailors and Notion Dealers. Liberal discount to the trade. Samples sent by mail on receipt of 25 cents. Agents wanted everywhere.
Office of the Company 650 Broadway. Address
THE BARNUM ELASTIC STRAP AND BUCKLE CO.
650 BROADWAY, N. Y.

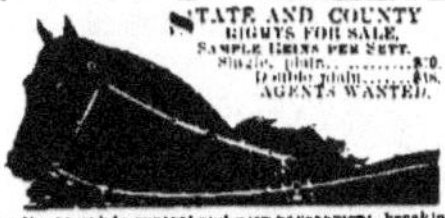

STATE AND COUNTY RIGHTS FOR SALE.
SAMPLE REINS PER SETT.
Single, plain..........$10.
Double plain.........$18.
AGENTS WANTED.

For the complete control and easy government, breaking, training and imparting the very best possible style to old, young, spirited, unruly, hard or tender mouthed Horses.
CLARK CHECK AND REIN CO.,
No. 113 BROADWAY, NEW YORK.

LADIES' and GENTLEMEN'S PEARL CUFF Buttons, $1; Red Ivory, $1; Pearl Studs, $1; a set Ladies' Breast Pins, $1. Say what letters you want on them. Emblematic Masonic sets, Buttons and Studs, $3, full set. W. C. WEMYSS, 575 Broadway, N. Y.

STARTLING AND IMPORTANT DISCOVERY. Oil burns *from* a [illegible], without light, smoke or bad odor, in MORRILL'S NEW OIL STOVE. The best and cheapest Stove for all kinds of cooking, heating and mechanical purposes. Price from $5 to $20. Will sell everywhere. Agents wanted. Dealers supplied. Send for Illustrated catalogue, "Come and see."
MORRILL PETROLEUM STOVE CO.,
16 Congress-street, Boston.

Marbleized Slate Mantels,

Superior in appearance, more durable, half the price of marble. T. B. Stewart, 603 4th av., bet. 34th & 36th sts., N. Y.

687 ACRES, 6 miles of Richmond, Va. The Wood and Timber on it will pay first cost. Sandy loam, every acre good for Garden or meadow. 1½ miles of York River R. R. 100 acres cleared; no buildings. $15 per acre, or will be divided. Address A. VAN DOREN,
Falmouth, Stafford County, Virginia.

Spear's Preserving Solution

Will effectually prevent fermentation or decay, and preserve all kinds of Fruits, Vegetables, Jellies, Tomatoes, Cider, Milk, Syrups, &c., &c., in a perfectly fresh and wholesome condition, without sugar, and without hermetically sealing or air tighting; hence a saving of sugar—and from 50 to 75 per cent. in the cost of jars. The solution is warranted to contain nothing injurious to health. Fruits, preserved by this solution, are equal to any "canned" fruits, while the use of the solution admits of keeping the fruits, &c., in vessels of any size, and of using them at long intervals when opened. It saves sugar. It will preserve milk sweet from 12 to 36 hours longer than it will naturally keep—causing it to furnish more and better cream, and make more butter in warm weather. One bottle will preserve 128 pounds of fruits, or 48 gallons of cider, or 128 gallons of milk. Price, $1. Full directions for using with each bottle. Sold by all merchants; ask for a circular with full particulars.
L. P. WORRAL, Gen. Agt., No. 91 Hudson-st., N. Y.

H. W. JOHNS'
IMPROVED ROOFING

Has been in use nearly ten years, and forms a handsome and reliable roof. Can be applied by any one. **Elastic Mineral Cement,** for Repairing Leaky Shingle and other Roofs. **Preservative Paints, Roofing, Cement, &c.** Exclusive right to sell and apply will be given. Send for descriptive circular, prices, &c., to
H. W. JOHNS, 78 William St., N. Y.

PAINTS for FARMERS and others.—The Grafton Mineral Paint Co. are now manufacturing the Best, Cheapest and most Durable Paint in use; two coats well put on, mixed with pure Linseed Oil, will last 10 or 15 years; it is of a light brown or beautiful chocolate color, and can be changed to green, lead, stone, drab, olive or cream, to suit the taste of the consumer. It is valuable for Houses, Barns, Fences, Carriage and Car-makers, Pails and Wooden-ware, Agricultural Implements, Canal Boats, Vessels and Ships' Bottoms, Canvas, Metal and Shingle Roofs, (it being Fire and Water proof), Floor Oil Cloth Manuf. (one Manuf. having used in the past year 500 bbls.,) and as a paint is unsurpassed for body, durability, elasticity, and adhesiveness. Send for a circular, which gives particulars. Price 2 cts. per lb., or $4 per bbl., of 300 lbs., which will supply a farmer for years to come. None genuine unless branded in a trade mark Grafton Mineral Paint Work. Address
DANIEL BIDWELL, 254 Pearl-st., New York.

THE NEW BREAD MIXER.—Approved by the Tribune. Send stamp for Circular.
J. M. STANYAN, Milford, N. H.

THE NEW EDITION REVISED AND ENLARGED of WELLS'S EVERY MAN HIS OWN LAWYER and BUSINESS FORM BOOK, embraces 650 12mo. pages of important information indispensable to every man and business woman, and sold at the low price of $2; and sent post paid on receipt of price. Agents wanted everywhere. Address
BENJ. W. HITCHCOCK, Publisher,
No. 14 Chambers street, New York.

AGENTS wanted to engage in a good paying business! Now ready: THE LOST CAUSE, a complete Southern History of the War; patronized by tens of thousands eager to hear the other side. One agent sold 220 in one week. Address E. B. TREAT & CO., Publishers, No. 654 Broadway, New York.

AGENTS WANTED TO SELL THE "COTTAGE Bible and Family Expositor."—1,500 pages, 800 *pages comments*,—21 steel engravings and maps. Send for Circulars and see the *Great Advantages* offered.
Address BRAINARD & SAMPSON, Hartford, Conn.

SAYS L. F. WHEELER, of New York, in reference to the ZERO Refrigerator, "All that is necessary to make it very salable, is a knowledge of its merits."
ALEX. M. LESLEY, 605 Sixth Avenue, New York.

IOWA.—ALL THE INFORMATION WANTED, by every one who thinks of seeking a home in the West, is given in a little book of 157 pages. Price $1.00.
Address B. M. OLWIG, Des Moines, Iowa.

GOLD PENS, 50 cents to $4; Pens in Silver cases, $1 to $4; Pens repaired for 50 cents; also, Fountain Pen sent by mail. Send stamp for Circular. GEORGE F. HAWKES, Manufacturer, 64 Nassau-st., New York.

AMMONIATED PACIFIC GUANO.

The attention of Farmers and Agriculturists is called to this article, as superior to anything else offered in the market. Equal to Peruvian Guano, and costing much less.

We offer this fertilizer in lots to suit all purchasers. A liberal discount made to the Trade.

Pamphlets with copies of Analysis by Dr. Liebig, of Baltimore, and Dr. Jackson, Massachusetts State Assayer, and testimonials from Agriculturists, showing its value, and directions for use, can be obtained from
J. O. BAKER & CO., Selling Agents,
131 Pearl-st., New York.

FISH GUANO.

The cheapest and best fertilizer in use, manufactured and sold by the "Mystic Oil Company," Mystic Bridge, Conn. It is pressed very dry, put up in barrels, and sent to any part of the United States for thirty dollars per ton, in quantities less than 25 tons. For 25 tons and upwards, $25 per ton. Orders may be addressed to WM. CLIFT, Jr., 57 E. 34th st., N. Y., or D. S. MILLS, Pres't, Mystic Bridge, Conn.

SCHOOL TEACHERS WANTED.—The Subscriber wishes to employ for each town in the United States, male teachers who have formerly been engaged, either in Day Schools or Sunday Schools, who can devote their exclusive time to the business, to canvass for the "*Illustrated History of the Bible*," by John Kitto, D. D., F. S. A., edited by Alvan Bond, D. D., of Norwich, Conn.

This is the best selling book I have ever published. Agents make from $100 to $200 per month, and say "they never knew a book to sell so well." Apply immediately in person or by letter to the publisher
HENRY BILL, Norwich, Conn.

NEW BOOKS.

Saunders' Domestic Poultry.

By S. M. Saunders,

New Edition Revised and Enlarged.

This Book contains Articles on the Preferable Breeds of Farm-Yard Poultry, Their History and Leading Characteristics, with Complete Instructions for Breeding and Fattening, and Preparing for Exhibition at Poultry Shows, etc., etc., derived from the Author's Experience and Observation.

The work is compact, full of valuable hints and information, and beautifully illustrated.

An appendix contains an account of *Poultry breeding on a large scale*, as practiced in the neighborhood of Paris, and is a very important addition to the work.

Price, paper 40 cts., cloth 75 cts.

ORANGE JUDD & CO., 41 Park Row.

Money in the Swamps.

PEAT! PEAT! PEAT!

FUEL—MANURE.

WHERE TO FIND IT.

HOW TO MAKE AND USE IT.

ITS VALUE.

A NEW WORK ON PEAT,

THOROUGH AND PRACTICAL;

By Prof. Samuel W. Johnson, of Yale College.

It gives a full history of **PEAT, MUCK,** etc., telling what they are, where found, and how to estimate their value.

It describes the various methods of using Peat for manure, as an absorbent, as an ameliorator of the soil, etc. and it is especially explicit in regard to the

USE OF PEAT AS FUEL,

describing minutely the various processes employed in preparing it to burn, from the simplest to the most complicated; such as are in use in this country, and Europe. It is illustrated with many Engravings of machines, etc.

The work is invaluable to those having Peat or Muck swamps, or wishing to invest in Peat Companies.

SENT POST-PAID, - - PRICE $1.25

ORANGE JUDD & CO., 41 Park Row.

HINTS TO HORSE-KEEPERS,

A COMPLETE

MANUAL FOR HORSEMEN.

BY THE LATE HENRY WILLIAM HERBERT.

(FRANK FORESTER.)

Beautifully Illustrated.

HOW TO BREED A HORSE.—

CHOICE OF STALLION.—National Value of the Horse—The best class of Horses the cheapest for all purposes—What constitutes excellence—Blood; what it gives, should be on the side of the Sire—Breed up, not down—Diseases and Defects Hereditary—General Rules.

CHOICE OF THE MARE.—Size, Symmetry and Soundness more important than Blood—Points of the Brood Mare—Diseases Hereditary—Condition of the Mare—Should have moderate work when with Foal—Food and care during gestation—Health and temper.

MUTUAL ADAPTATION OF SIRE AND DAM.—First consideration in Improvement of "cold" Blood—Relative size of Sire and Dam—Defects in either Parent—How Remedied in Progeny—Bloods which "hit."

CANADIAN BLOOD.—The Canadian originally the French Norman—Characteristics—Hardihood—Speed—Mode of Improvement—Crossing with Thorough-breds.

NORMAN BLOOD.—Origin and History of the Percheron Norman—A pure race—Characteristics and Points.

MODERN ARAB BLOOD.—English and American Thorough-breds derived from Oriental Blood—are now superior to the Modern Arabs—Nolan Arab.

PONIES — DIFFERENT BREEDS,

CHARACTERISTICS AND UTILITY.—Origin—Different Breeds, Shetlands and Scots—Galloways and Narragansetts—Mustangs and Indians—Profit of raising Ponies.

HOW TO BREED MULES.

Value of Mules—Their History and Natural History—The Mule and Hinny—Thorough-blood wasted in the Dam for Mules—The Mule in the United States—Large size not Desirable—Varieties of the Ass—The kind of Mares to be selected.

HOW TO BUY A HORSE.

Of whom to Buy it—Extraordinary Cheapness and Extraordinary Excellence not consistent with each other—Points to be regarded—How to Examine the Eye—Broken Wind—Roaring—Whistling—Broken Knees—To examine the Legs—Splents—Damaged Back Sinews—Spavins—Ringbones—Curbs—How to tell the Age of a Horse.

HOW TO FEED A HORSE.

Consequences of Improper Feeding—Different Food for different conditions—Food for the Brood Mare—for the Foal—For Working Horses—Green Food—Carrots—Corn—Feeding Horses in Training—While Travelling—Summering Horses—The Best Method—Management of Omnibus Horses in New York.

HOW TO STABLE AND GROOM A HORSE.—Requisites for a good Stable—The economy of Proper Arrangements—Ventilation—Grooming; its necessity for all descriptions of Horses—How Performed—Clothing—Treatment when brought in from Work.

HOW TO BREAK, AND USE A HORSE.—What is required in a well-broken Horse—His education should commence when a Colt—Bitting—Putting in Harness—How to Use a Horse—Travelling—Working—Pleasure Horses—Punishment.

HOW TO PHYSIC A HORSE—

SIMPLE REMEDIES FOR SIMPLE AILMENTS.—Causes of Ailments—Medicines to be given only by the order of the Master—Depletion and Purging—Spasmodic Colic—Inflammation of the Bowels—Inflammation of the Lungs—How to Bleed—Balls and Purgatives—Costiveness—Cough—Bronchitis—Distemper—Worms—Diseases of the Feet—Scratches—Thrush—Broken Knees.

FARRIERY, ETC.

Castration—Docking and Nicking—Blood-letting—Treatment of Sprains and Wounds—Galls of the Skin—Cracked Heels—Clipping and Singeing—Administering Medicines—Diseases of the Foot.

HOW TO SHOE A HORSE.

Unskillful Shoers—Anatomy of the Foot Illustrated—The Foot of a Colt—Preparation of the Foot—Removing the Old Shoe—Paring the Foot—The Shoe—Fitting the Shoe—Nailing—Number of Nails—Diseases of the Foot.

BAUCHER'S METHOD OF TRAINING HORSES.—What Constitutes a Well-trained Horse—To make him come at your call—The Philosophy of Training—Flexions of the Jaw—Flexions of the Neck—Flexions of the Croup—Backing—The Paces—Leaping.

HOW TO RIDE A HORSE.

The Saddle—The Girths—The Stirrups—Saddle-Cloths—The Crupper—The Martingale—The Bridle—Spurs—Mounting and Dismounting—The Seat—The Hands—The Legs—The Paces—Hints for Special Cases—The Art of Falling—Riding with Ladies.

LADIES' RIDING—WRITTEN BY A LADY.—Learning to Ride—The Side-saddle—The Girths—The Stirrup—The Bridle—The Martingale—The Bit—The Dress—Mounting and Dismounting—The Position—The Hands—The Leg and Whip—Accidents.

HOW TO DRIVE A HORSE.

The Art of Driving—Pleasure Driving—How to Hold the Reins—Driving a Pair—Four-in-hand Driving—Driving Working Horses—Plowing—Three-a-breast.

RAREY'S SYSTEM OF HORSE-TAMING.—Rarey's System a New Discovery—Previous System—Principles of this System—Instructions for practicing Rarey's Method—To Stable the Horse—To Approach the Horse—Tying up the Leg—Laying the Horse Down—Finale—Vices and Bad Habits—Rearing—Kicking—Baulking—Pulling on the Halter—Shying.

VETERINARY HOMŒOPATHY.

Principles of the System—Table of Remedies—General Directions—Treatment of a Sick Animal—Diet—Remedies for Specific Cases—Glossary of Diseases.

12mo. 425 p.—Sent by mail post-paid. $1.75.

ORANGE JUDD & CO.,
41 PARK ROW, NEW-YORK.

New Book of Flowers.

By Joseph Breck, Practical Horticulturist.

Beautifully Illustrated.

This work, while preserving scientific accuracy, is written in a familiar style, and with the enthusiasm of a life-long lover of flowers. Its teachings are eminently practical, and cover all branches of out of door gardening.

Bulbs.

The cultivation of bulbs, whether in-doors or in the open ground, is clearly described, and such instructions are given as will insure success with these favorite plants.

Annuals.

All the finer Annuals are described, and the peculiar treatment necessary for each given in full.

Herbaceous Perennials.

This justly favorite class of plants is given here more at length than in any work with which we are acquainted.

Bedding Plants.

The treatment of the popular kinds of bedding plants is given, together with that of Dahlias, Chrysanthemums and such as usually fall under the head of florist's flowers.

Flowering Shrubs.

A separate section is devoted to the hardy flowering shrubs, including a very full chapter upon the

Rose.

We have no work which is so safe a guide to the novice in gardening, or that imparts the necessary information in a style so free from technicalities. Not the least interesting part of the work is the author's personal experience, as he tells not only how he succeeded, but the mistakes he committed. Thus far it is

"The Book of Flowers."

SENT POST-PAID. PRICE, $1.75.

ORANGE JUDD & CO., 41 Park Row.

WARDER'S

Hedges and Evergreens.

This is the only book wholly devoted to the cultivation, pruning, and management of plants suitable for American hedging, especially the Maclura, or OSAGE ORANGE; illustrated with engravings of plants, implements, and processes; to which is added a *Treatise on Evergreens*, their varieties, propagation, culture, etc. By J. A. Warder. 12mo, 291 pp. SENT POST-PAID. PRICE $1.50

ORANGE JUDD & CO., 41 Park Row.

BUIST'S

American Flower-Garden Directory.

Containing Practical Directions for the Culture of Plants in the Flower-Garden, Hot-House, Green-House, Rooms or Parlor Windows, FOR EVERY MONTH IN THE YEAR, with descriptions of most desirable plants, soils, transplanting, erecting a Hot-House, a Green-House, laying out a Flower-Garden, etc., etc. By Robert Buist, a practical Nurseryman and Seed-Grower of Philadelphia. Cloth, 12mo. SENT POST-PAID. PRICE $1.50

ORANGE JUDD & CO., 41 Park Row.

BOMMER'S

Method of Manure Making.

COMPLETE AND CLEAR IN ITS DIRECTIONS.

Carries Conviction of its usefulness, and the correctness of its principles.

GIVES GREAT SATISFACTION.

Abundance of Good Manure depends simply upon systematic and well applied labor.

ENGLISH AND GERMAN. PRICE, 25 cts.

ORANGE JUDD & CO., 41 Park Row.

Quinby's Bee Keeping.

By M. QUINBY, Practical Bee-keeper. Fully Illustrated. Entirely new. The result of 35 years' of successful experience—with directions for all contingencies that can ordinarily occur; treating of Breeding, Movable-Comb and other Hives, Pasturage, Robbing, Feeding, Swarming, Queens, Diseases, Anger, Enemies, Wax, Transferring, Sagacity, Wintering, Care of Honey, Italian Bees, Purchasing, etc. Bee-keepers will find this new work of Mr. Quinby's fully up to the times in all practical matter.

Sent Post-paid. Price $1.50.

Gratifying Opinions of the Press.

From the Christian Intelligencer.

"Quinby's Work is the very best. It has long been regarded as of the highest authority in the matters concerning which it treats."

From Moore's Rural New Yorker.

"This is a newly written and illustrated edition of Mr. Q.'s former work. *That* has proved of value to thousands of Bee-keepers, and *this*, with its riper experience and added knowledge, can not fail of giving better satisfaction. Thirty-five years experience!——What beginner in bee-keeping will not bring this to his aid? We notice the author has no Patent Hive to introduce, and expresses his opinions freely on the merits and demerits of the various hives seeking popular favor."

From the Vermont Farmer.

"The book is written in familiar style, with the endeavor to be practical rather than scientific, thereby making it a guide to the tyro in Apiarian knowledge, as well as a standard work of reference for the more experienced bee-keepers."

From the N. Y. Christian Advocate.

"All bee-keepers should have this manual, and others may read it as a book of wonders."

SENT POST-PAID. PRICE $1.50.

ORANGE JUDD & CO., 41 Park Row.

FLAX CULTURE.

A NEW AND VERY VALUABLE WORK, consisting of *full* directions, from selection of ground and seed to preparation and marketing of crop, as given by a number of experienced growers. 8vo, paper. PRICE 50 Cents.

HOP CULTURE.

PRACTICAL DETAILS *fully* given, from the Selection and Preparation of the SOIL, SETTING and CULTIVATION of the Plants, to PICKING, DRYING, PRESSING, and MARKETING the Crop. By Ten Experienced Cultivators. Illustrated with over forty engravings. Edited by PROF. GEORGE THURBER. 8vo, paper. PRICE 40 Cents.

TOBACCO CULTURE.

This is by far the most useful and valuable work ever issued on this subject. It contains full details for the Selecting and Preparing of the Seed and Soil, Harvesting, Curing, and Marketing the Crop, with Illustrative Engravings of the operations. The work was prepared by FOURTEEN EXPERIENCED TOBACCO GROWERS, residing in different parts of the country. It also contains Notes on the Tobacco Worm, with Illustrations. Octavo, 48 pp., in neat paper covers. PRICE 25 Cents.

ONIONS.

How to Raise them Profitably.

Practical Details, given very plainly by *Seventeen Onion Growers* of long experience, residing in different parts of the country. No more valuable work of its size was ever issued. Octavo, 32 pp. Neat paper covers. Price 20 *cents*.

NEW-YORK:

ORANGE JUDD & CO., 41 Park Row.

BOOKS FOR FARMERS and OTHERS.

(For sale at the Office of the *Agriculturist*, or they will be forwarded by mail, *post-paid*, on receipt of price.

Allen's (L. F.) Rural Architecture	$1 50
Allen's (R. L.) American Farm Book	1 50
Allen's Diseases of Domestic Animals	1 00
American Agricultural Annual, 1867..pa., 50 cts..cloth	75
American Horticultural Annual, 1867..pa., 50 cts..cloth	75
American Bird Fancier	30
American Rose Culturist	30
American Weeds and Useful Plants	1 75
Architecture, by Cummings & Miller	10 00
Art of Saw Filing....(Holly)	75
Barry's Fruit Garden	1 75
Bement's Poulterer's Companion	2 00
Bement's Rabbit Fancier	30
Bommer's Method for Making Manures	25
Boussingault's Rural Economy	1 60
Breck's New Book of Flowers	1 75
Bridgeman's Fruit Cultivator's Manual	75
Bridgeman's Florist's Guide	75
Buist's Flower Garden Directory	1 50
Buist's Family Kitchen Gardener	1 00
Burr's Garden Vegetables	2 50
Burr's Vegetables of America	5 00
Canary Birds ....cloth	75
Carpenters and Joiners' Hand Book..(Holly)	75
Chorlton's Grape-Grower's Guide	75
Cobbett's American Gardener	75
Cole's (S. W.) American Fruit Book	75
Cole's Veterinarian	75
Cotton Planters' Manual (Turner)	1 50
Country Life, by R. M. Copeland	5 00
Dadd's Modern Horse Doctor	1 50
Dadd's (Geo. H.) American Cattle Doctor	1 50
Dana's Muck Manual	1 25
Dog and Gun (Hooper's)....paper, 30c....cloth	60
Downing's Cottage Residences	8 00
Downing's Country Houses	8 00
Downing's Landscape Gardening	6 50
Downing's Fruits and Fruit Trees of America	3 00
Downing's Rural Essays	5 00
Eastwood on Cranberry	75
Elliott's Western Fruit Grower's Guide	1 50
Flax Culture	50
Field's (Thomas W.) Pear Culture	1 25
Fish Culture	1 25
Flint (Charles L.) on Grasses	2 50
Flint's Milch Cows and Dairy Farming	2 50
French's Farm Drainage	1 50
Fuller's Forest Tree Culturist	1 50
Fuller's Grape Culturist	1 50
Fuller's Strawberry Culturist	20
Gardening for Profit, by Peter Henderson	1 50
Gray's How Plants Grow	1 25
Gray's Manual of Botany and Lessons in one Vol.	4 00
Guenon on Milch Cows	75
Haraszthy's Grape Culture, &c.	5 00
Harris' Insects Injurious to Vegetation, plain 4.00, col'd	6 00
Harris' Rural Annual. Bound, 8 Nos., in 2 Vols. Each	1 50
Hatfield's American House Carpenter	3 50
Herbert's Hints to Horsekeepers	1 75
High Farming Without Manure	35
Hop Culture	40
How to Buy a Farm and Where to Find One	1 75
Husmann's Grapes & Wine	1 50
Jennings' Horse Training Made Easy	1 25
Jennings on Cattle	1 75
Jennings on Swine and Poultry	1 75
Jennings on the Horse and his Diseases	1 75
Johnston's Agricultural Chemistry	1 75
Johnston's Elements of Agricultural Chemistry	1 50
Johnson's (Prof. S. W.) Essays on Manures	1 25
Kemp's Landscape Gardening	2 00
Klippart's Land Drainage	1 50
Langstroth on the Honey Bee	2 00
Leuchar's How to Build Hot-houses	1 50
Liebig's Familiar Letters on Chemistry	50
Liebig's Natural Laws of Husbandry	1 75
Loudon's (Downing's) Ladies' Flower Garden	2 00
Manual of Agriculture by G. Emerson and C. L. Flint	1 50
Mayhew's Illustrated Horse Doctor	3 00
Mayhew's Illustrated Horse Management	3 50
Mayhew's Practical Book-Keeping for Farmers	90
Blanks for do. do.	1 20
McMahon's American Gardener	2 50
Miles on the Horse's Foot	75
Morrell's American Shepherd	1 75
My Farm of Edgewood	1 75
My Vineyard at Lakeview	1 25
New Clock and Watch Maker's Manual	2 00
Norton's Scientific Agriculture	75
Onion Culture	20
Our Farm of Four Acres (bound) 60c....(paper)	30
Pardee on Strawberry Culture	75
Parlor Gardener, by C. J. Randolph	1 00
Parsons on the Rose	1 50
Parkman's Book of Roses	3 00
Peat and its Uses, by Prof. S. W. Johnson	1 25
Pedder's Land Measurer	60
Quinby's Mysteries of Bee-keeping (NEW.)	1 50
Quincy, (Hon. Josiah) on Soiling Cattle	1 25
Rabbit Fancier	30
Rand's Bulbs	3 00
Rand's Flowers for Parlor and Garden	3 00
Rand's Garden Flowers	3 00
Randall's Sheep Husbandry	1 50
Randall's Fine Wool Sheep Husbandry	1 00
Rivers' Miniature Fruit Garden	1 00
Richardson on the Dog....paper 30 cents.....cloth	60
Rural Affairs....(bound)....4 Vols....each	1 50
Rural Annual (by Joseph Harris)	25
Rural Register (by J. J. Thomas)	30
Rust, Smut, Mildew and Mould	1 00
Saunder's Domestic Poultry (NEW)..paper, 40 c...bound	75
Saxton's Farmers' Library. 3 Vols. cloth 8 50...morocco	9 50
Schenck's Gardener's Text Book	75
Scribner's Ready Reckoner	30
Silloway's Modern Carpentry	2 00
Skillful Housewife	75
Stewart's (John) Stable Book	1 50
Strong's Grape Culture	3 00
Ten Acres Enough	1 50
Tenny's Natural History, Zoology	3 00
Thompson's Food of Animals	1 00
Tobacco Culture	25
Todd's (S. E.) Young Farmer's Manual	1 50
Vaux's Villas and Cottages	3 00
Villas and Farm Cottages, (Cleaveland and Backus)	4 00
Warder's Hedges and Evergreens	1 50
Watson's American Home Garden	2 00
Wax Flowers (Art of Making)	2 00
Wet Days at Edgewood	1 75
Wetherell on the Manufacture of Vinegar	1 50
Wheat Plant (John Klippart's)	1 50
Woodward's Country Homes	1 50
Woodward's Graperies	1 50
Woodward's Homes for the Million, paper, 75c., cloth	1 00
Youatt and Spooner on the Horse	1 50
Youatt and Martin on Cattle	1 50
Youatt on the Hog	1 00
Youatt on Sheep	1 00
Youmans' Household Science	2 25

GRAPE CULTURIST.

By ANDREW S. FULLER.

New Edition, Revised and Enlarged.

This is the best Book published on Hardy Grape Culture.

CONTENTS.

INTRODUCTORY.—BOTANICAL CHARACTER OF THE Vine, Propagation by Seed.—4 *Illustrations.*

GROWING FROM SEED—GATHER WHEN FULLY RIPE.

PROPAGATION BY SINGLE BUDS.—MODE OF OPERATION, Planting in Beds, Single Buds in Open Air, Starting in Hot-Beds, Form of Single Bud Cutting—3 *Illustrations.*

CUTTINGS OF UNRIPE WOOD.—THOUSANDS OF VINES are Annually Produced from Green Cuttings.—4 *Illust.*

PROPAGATING HOUSE.—PERFECTION SHOULD BE our Aim, Span Roofed Propagating House, Lean-to Propagating House, Single Roofed House, Flues.—2 *Ill.*

CUTTINGS IN OPEN AIR.—TIME TO MAKE CUTTINGS, Selection of Cuttings, Form of Cuttings, Mallet Cuttings.

LAYERING THE VINE.—THIS IS ONE OF THE MOST Certain and Convenient Methods in Use.—1 *Illustration.*

GRAFTING THE GRAPE.—THIS IS AN OLD BUT VERY Uncertain Mode of Propagating the Grape, but Can be Used Successfully.—4 *Illustrations.*

HYBRIDIZING AND CROSSING.—THESE ARE OPERATIONS that Should Demand the Attention of Every One Who Undertakes to Produce New Varieties, Mode of Operation.—3 *Illustrations.*

TRANSPLANTING—VINES WILL OFTEN REQUIRE ONE Season of Nursery Culture before being Planted in the Vineyard, Heeling-in.—3 *Illustrations.*

SOIL AND SITUATION.—MUCH DEPENDS UPON THEM. Preparing the Soil, Manures and their Operations.

STEM APPENDAGES.—SPINES, HAIRS, LATERALS, Forms of Leaves, Tendrils, Buds.—7 *Illustrations.*

PLANTING THE VINE.—A GREAT DIVERSITY OF Opinion, My Own Rule, Root Pruning, How to Plant.

GRAPE TRELLISES.—2 *Illustrations.*

TIME TO PRUNE VINES.—PRUNING AND TRAINING, Opposite Arms, Oblique Arms, A Plan for Poor Soils.

GARDEN CULTURE.—POSITION OF BORDER, TRAINing the Vines, Four Tiers of Arms, Double Stem, Trellises in Gardens, Training to Stakes, Girdling the Vine, Removing the Leaves.—5 *Illustrations.*

GATHERING THE FRUIT.—PRESERVING THE FRUIT, Wine Making, Pruning Shears.—1 *Illustration.*

INSECTS.—ROSE CHAFER, GRAPE VINE FLEA BEETle, Spotted Pelidnota, Tree Beetle, Caterpillars, Yellow Bear, Hog Caterpillar, Grape Vine Sphinx, Blue Caterpillar, Procris Americana, Leaf Rollers, Thrips, Aphis, Red Spider, Vine Scale, Diseases, Mildew, Sun Scald.—18 *Illus.*

DESCRIPTION OF (*nearly Seventy*) VARIETIES.

REVIEW OF VARIOUS SYSTEMS OF PRUNING AND Training, Reversing the Arms, Single Arm System, Bow System, Long Rod Spur System, Upright Canes, Thomery System.—Index.

SENT POST-PAID. - - - PRICE $1.50

ORANGE JUDD & CO., 41 Park Row.

A GREAT SUCCESS.

The Gothic Free Fruit Box,

For marketing Strawberries, Raspberries, Blackberries, Grapes, and all small fruits.

Price, $15 per 1000, for either size, quarts or pints. Sample Boxes of 100 sent upon receipt of $2.50.

This Box was unanimously commended at the meeting of the "Farmers' Club" of the American Institute, held at their Rooms, April 2d, 1867, and is thus recommended by all the prominent Hotel keepers of New York, Philadelphia, Baltimore, and Washington.

This is to certify, That we consider the GOTHIC FRUIT-BOX the best fruit package yet offered to the public; combining, as it does, in a greater degree than any other that we have examined, perfect ventilation, convenience, as well as compactness and beauty of form, and cheapness.

We would, therefore, recommend its use to all fruit growers and dealers, as a matter of economy and self-interest.

Influenced ourselves by such motives, we propose to give the preference hereafter, in our purchases of fruits, to those dealers who pack them in the GOTHIC FRUIT-BOX.

Signed: Hitchcock, Darling & Co., Fifth Avenue Hotel; S. Leland & Co., Metropolitan; Pierson & Co., Astor House; Spotts & Hawks, St. Nicholas Hotel, and 23 others.——PHILADELPHIA.—J. E. Kingsley & Co., Continental Hotel; R. Washington, St. Lawrence Hotel; H. A. Hoeckley, Markoe House; Wm. H. Baker, Ashland House, and 17 others.——BALTIMORE.—Dennis Barnum per Joseph Dorsey, Barnum's Hotel; R. B. Coleman, Eutaw House; Wm. C. Bonner, Howard House, and 5 others.——WASHINGTON.—Sykes, Chadwick & Co., Willard's Hotel; Sprague & Co., Kirkwood House; A. R. Potts, Metropolitan Hotel; H. S. Benson, National Hotel.

J. O. MEEKER, Agent,
82 John Street,
New York.

INGERSOLL'S IMPROVED
HORSE AND HAND POWER
HAY AND COTTON PRESSES.

These machines have been tested in the most thorough manner throughout this and foreign countries to the number of over 800.

THE HORSE POWER is worked by either wheel or capstan, and in many respects possesses unequalled advantages. We invite those wanting such machines to write for a catalogue containing full information with cuts, prices, &c., or call and examine personally.

Orders promptly attended to, by addressing

INGERSOLL & DOUGHERTY, Greenpoint, Kings Co., L. I.

Nansemond Sweet Potato Plants.

Of best quality, during May and June. Put up to carry safely long distances. Price, 500, $2.25;—1000, $3.50;—5000, $15.00;—10,000, $25.00. This variety is successfully grown at the North. Send for our Circular of directions, etc. Address

Murray & Co.,
Foster's Crossings,
Warren Co., Ohio.

SWEET POTATO PLANTS FOR SALE.—Well hardened and ready for shipment. Send your orders early if you wish to make sure of plants. Price per 100, 75 cents; 500, $3; 1000, $5. Catalogue of Flowers, Plants and Vines sent on application.

Address I. J. SIMONSON & BRO.,
64 Cortlandt-st., New York.

SWEET POTATO PLANTS,

Safely packed and delivered where ordered, in New York City at $4 per thousand. Address P. PHILLIPS,
Matawan, Monmouth Co., N. J.

NANSEMOND SWEET POTATO PLANTS.—Ready in season, May and June. Send stamp for Circular with directions for cultivation and prices.
D. CUMMINS, Conneaut, Ohio.

NANSEMOND SWEET POTATO PLANTS, 50 cents per 100; $4 per 1000, for sale by
A. M. HALSTED, Rye, N. Y.

Carrot and Mangold Wurtzel.

I have Long Red Mangold Wurtzel, Yellow Globe Mangold Wurtzel, and White Sugar Beet; also Long Orange and Improved Short Horn Carrot Seed—every seed warranted to be grown last season. *I grew them myself and know all about them.* The Carrot seed is extra clean—free from stick and the beard all off. Either of the varieties of Mangold Seed sent pre-paid to any address for $1.00 a pound, Long Orange Carrot, $1.25. Improved Short Horn, $1.25. Get *good seed*, farmers!—Catalogues, containing over 100 varieties of seed of my own growing, sent gratis to all.

JAMES J. H. GREGORY, Marblehead, Mass.

BEDDING PLANTS.

Our Catalogue of Bedding Plants, comprising the largest stock in the country, is now ready and mailed free on the receipt of 5 cents. HOVEY & Co.,
53 North Market-st., Boston.

Striped Leaved Japanese Maize.

Package containing about 40 seeds of this new ornamental plant sent to any address, for 25 cents. Dealers supplied with packages or seed in bulk at a liberal discount.

JAMES J. H. GREGORY, Marblehead, Mass.

ROSES, Carnations, Verbenas, and all varieties of Bedding Plants in large quantities to the trade. Also Grape Vines, Pear Trees. GEO. W. WILSON, Malden, Mass.

By mail, post-paid, at 25 cts. per lb., genuine Bunch Field Bean (white). Address J. BENNETT, Bunnian, Indiana.

SOUTH DOWN CO.'S PATENT

SheepWashTobacco

THE BEST KNOWN REMEDY FOR

TICKS, SCAB, VERMIN & FOOT ROT,

should be used by all Farmers on

SHEEP, ANIMALS & PLANTS.

☞ This pure preparation has been successfully used for years, and never fails to produce the desired effect when used according to directions.

It will not injure the most delicate Animal.
It will improve the Quality and Quantity of Wool.
It kills TICKS on Sheep.
It cures SCAB on Sheep.
It cures all SKIN DISEASES on Animals.
It kills all VERMIN that infest Animals, Trees, Plants and Vines.

☞ *For* FOOT-ROT it is a sure cure, used as a poultice.

☞ **ONE POUND of this Extract will make TWELVE GALLONS of Wash, and contains the strength of EIGHT POUNDS of TOBACCO, as prepared by farmers.**

Sold by all Druggists and Country and Agricultural Stores.

JAMES F. LEVIN,
23 Central Wharf, Boston, Mass.

For sale by DUDLEY & STAFFORD, New York; BLISS & SHARP, Chicago; E. M. LIVERMORE, Cleveland, Ohio.

Have You any Children?

SUBSCRIBE AT ONCE FOR THE

RIVERSIDE MAGAZINE
FOR YOUNG PEOPLE,

AN ENTERTAINING AND INSTRUCTIVE MONTHLY, ELEGANTLY ILLUSTRATED.

YOU WILL GET YOUR

MONEY'S WORTH!

Enclose $2.50 by Mail to

HURD & HOUGHTON,
PUBLISHERS,
459 Broome-street, New York.

Send for a Sample Copy which will be sent pre-paid on receipt of 20 cents.

CLUB RATES.

Three copies, $6.50; Five copies, $10; Ten copies, $20, and an Extra copy gratis; Single copies, 25 cents.

AGENTS and CANVASSERS wanted in every part of the Country. *Clergymen and Teachers supplied with the Magazine one year for $2.*

THE AMERICAN REPRINT OF

LONDON SOCIETY.

RICHLY ILLUSTRATED.

PROGRAMME FOR 1867.

PLAYING FOR HIGH STAKES. By MISS THOMAS. With Illustrations.

SKETCHES FROM THE BENCH AND THE BAR. BIOGRAPHICAL AND ANECDOTAL. Accompanied by Portraits.

ENGLISH CARICATURE. NOTES ON THE MASTERS OF HUMORISTIC ART IN ENGLAND. With Illustrations drawn from the Salient Points of Famous Caricatures. (*Several Papers and Numerous Illustrations.*)

THE OLD LONDON HOSTELRIES, AND THE MEN WHO FREQUENTED THEM. LA BELLE SAUVAGE AND THE PRETTY WIDOW. THE SARACEN'S HEAD. JACK STRAW'S CASTLE, etc., etc.

LONDON MEN: A SERIES OF CHARACTER PORTRAITS. 1. MR. PEPYS. 2. CHARLES LAMB. 3. DOUGLAS JERROLD.

ARTISTS' NOTES FROM CHOICE PICTURES. The Paintings rendered on wood by W. LUSON THOMAS. No. 1. HONEYWOOD AND THE BAILIFFS.

&c. &c. &c. &c. &c.

TERMS OF SUBSCRIPTION:

Single numbers, 40 cents. One copy one year, $4.50; Two copies, $8.50; Five copies, $20.00; Ten copies, $40.00, and an extra copy gratis.

THE RIVERSIDE MAGAZINE ($2.50 per annum) and LONDON SOCIETY ($4.50 per annum) sent to one address for $6.00.

☞ *All Subscriptions are payable in advance.*

The January number of LONDON SOCIETY will be sent to any address on receipt of 30 cents.

HURD & HOUGHTON, Publishers,
459 BROOME STREET, NEW YORK.

$100 FOR A BRICK MACHINE SIMple; $160 with Tempering Box and Moulds, warranted to make 13,000 brick per day, of a superior quality. Address FREY & SHECKLER,
Bucyrus, O.

WANTED: AGENTS

For a New Work of surpassing interest and value to every one interested in the Horse or Mule.

THE RESULT OF TWENTY YEARS' ORIGINAL INVESTIGATIONS AND HIGHLY SUCCESSFUL PRACTICE.

Over Ten Thousand (10,000) Copies Sold in Two Months!

THE AMERICAN FARMER'S HORSE BOOK.

BY

ROBERT STEWART, M. D., V. S.

One Agent; a Veterinary Surgeon, writes: "I have examined the book carefully, and it is everything I could wish. Send me on more books immediately, for I can hardly keep the sample I have got." *Another says:* "One gentleman, on my delivering his book, after examining it, handed me $5.00 and said I need not give him back any change, as he considered it worth more than $5.00." *Another writes:* "I think it the best book published on the Horse in this country. I have been doctoring horses for my neighbors off and on for the last five years, and have read Youatt, Dadd, and others, on the Horse, but I like Dr. Stewart's book the best, on account of its *plain, simple language*, and its *sound sense* on all subjects pertaining to the Horse." *Another writes, March 4th:* "Prospects good. Those that have received the work are highly pleased with it. The beauty of the work, they say, is, they *can understand* it, it *being so very plain*. I was called some few days ago to our County Infirmary, to see one of their valuable horses, and found the animal dangerously ill with lung fever. I thought it a good chance to try Dr. Stewart's remedy, and I must say that I never had an animal recover so quickly under any other treatment." *Another report reads:* "The work takes well. Every one admires it. If there is not a large number sold, I think the fault will be with the Agents." *Another Agent; a Veterinarian of long practice, writes, after having read the book:* "I am fully convinced of its excellency. Having all my life been familiar with the horse and nearly all his diseases, I feel free to recommend the work to the public." *The same person writes in a subsequent letter:* "My mare has had a violent attack of Distemper, but thanks to the Horse Book, I treated her according to Dr. Stewart's directions, and she will soon be ready for the road." *Another says:* "It is a most gratifying success. All who have received or seen it, are highly pleased with it."

The work is written from a standpoint DISTINCTIVELY AMERICAN, and covers the WHOLE GROUND of

Stock Raising and Stock Management,

including the treatment of the Diseases of the Horse, (especially the AMERICAN Horse,) more satisfactorily than any other book extant.

☞ **Sold only by Subscription.**

☞ *Send for Circulars, giving full particulars, terms, &c.*

For Territory in the Western or South Western States, address either

C. F. VENT & CO., CINCINNATI, OHIO.
J. S. GOODMAN & CO., CHICAGO, ILLS.
ZEIGLER, McCURDY & CO., ST. LOUIS, MO.

Applications from the *New England States, Eastern New York, Northern N. J., the Southern Sea Board* and *Gulf States*, should be addressed to the

NATIONAL PUBLISHING COMPANY,

at either PHILADELPHIA, RICHMOND, ATLANTA or NEW ORLEANS.

Those from *Pa., Md., Del., and Southern N. J.* to
ZEIGLER, McCURDY & CO., PHILADELPHIA.

Those from *Western N. Y.* to
E. H. CUSHMAN, ROCHESTER, N. Y.

Those from *Canada* to
R. CARSWELL, TORONTO.

IMPORTANT TO OWNERS OF STOCK.

THE AMERICAN STOCK JOURNAL & FARMERS' AND STOCK BREEDERS' ADVERTISER.

A first class Monthly Journal devoted to Farming and Stock Breeding. Each number contains 36 large double column pages, illustrated with numerous engravings.

Only $1.00 a year. Specimen copies free.

HORSE AND CATTLE DOCTOR FREE.

The publishers of THE AMERICAN STOCK JOURNAL have established a Veterinary Department in the columns of the Journal, which is placed under the charge of a distinguished Veterinary Professor, whose duty it is to receive questions as to the *ailments* or *injuries* of all kinds of stock, and to answer in *print* in connection with the question, how they should be treated *for a cure*. These prescriptions are given *gratis*, and thus every subscriber to the Journal has always at his command a Veterinary Surgeon *free of charge*. Every Farmer and Stock Breeder should subscribe for it. We will send until the 1st of January for 50 cents. Address

N. P. BOYER & CO., Gum Tree, Chester Co., Pa.

AGENTS WANTED

For the Best Selling and Most Useful Book of the Day.

Our Agents are making from $100 to $300 PER MONTH, in selling

Dr. MACKENZIE'S
Universal Encyclopædia,

or **10,000 RECIPES** in all the USEFUL ARTS, such as AGRICULTURE, BREWING, WINE MAKING, COOKING, CEMENTS, FARRIERY, MEDICINE, DOMESTIC ECONOMY, FARMING IMPLEMENTS, &c., &c., &c.

New, reliable, and useful discoveries added in each edition, making it the MOST COMPLETE book of the kind EVER ISSUED. No similar work has been published, equaling this in completeness, variety of matter, and reliability.

Extracts from the Press.

"One of the most important family works ever published."—*Rural American*, N. Y., Sept. 1, 1866.

"Contains immense number of practical receipts and other information."—*N. Y. Tribune*, May, 1866.

Circulars giving full description and terms to Agents, copies of letters from our Canvassers, showing what they are doing; recommendations and opinions of the press, *sent free* by the publishers.

T. ELLWOOD ZELL & COMPANY,
(Established in 1819.)
Nos. 17 and 19 South Sixth St., Philadelphia.

CORRECT LETTER WRITING, CONVERSAtion, Courtship, Marriage and Bridal Etiquette. 5 books, sent, postage paid for 75 cts. W. C. WEMYSS, 575 B'dway, N. Y.

Two Gold Medals
AWARDED ONE MACHINE.

Harder's Premium Railway Horse Power and Combined Thresher and Cleaner, at the Great National Trial, Auburn, July, 1866, for *"Slow and easy movement of horses, mechanical construction of the very best kind, thorough and conscientious workmanship, and material in every place, nothing slighted, excellent work, &c.,"* as shown by Official Report of Judges. Threshers, Separators, Feeding Mills, Wood Saws, Seed Sowers and Planters, &c., all of the best in market. Circulars with prices, full information, and Judges' Report of Auburn Trial, sent free. Send in orders early, as our rule is "first come, first served." Address

R. & M. HARDER,
Cobleskill, Schoharie Co., N. Y.

NEW PATENT SOLID
CAST STEEL PLOWS.

MADE ONLY BY
COLLINS & Co.,
Hartford, Conn.

These Plows are made of a superior quality of Cast Steel, recast in moulds into the exact shape required for the Mouldboards, Landsides and Shares. These are then highly tempered, ground and polished.

Every Plow is warranted to *scour* in any soil. Any section can at any time be replaced by a duplicate, or if the Share is worn, Steel can readily be welded on to the point.

(Send for a Circular.)

FOR SALE BY
COLLINS & CO., 212 Water-st., New-York.

The American Naturalist.

A POPULAR ILLUSTRATED MONTHLY MAGAZINE OF NATURAL HISTORY.

Published by the Essex Institute.

Contents of Vol. 1, No. 2, April, 1867.

THE MOSS-ANIMALS, OR FRESH WATER POLYZOA. By Alpheus Hyatt. *With a plate.* p. 57.—THE FERTILIZATION OF FLOWERING PLANTS. By J. T. Rothrock. p. 64.—INSECTS AND THEIR ALLIES. By A. S. Packard, Jr., M. D. *Illustrated.* p. 7[illegible]—THE AMERICAN SILK WORM. By L. Trouvelot. Continued. *Illustrated.* p. 8[illegible]—THE LAND SNAILS OF NEW ENGLAND. By E. S. Morse. Continued. *Illustrated.* p. 9[illegible].—REVIEWS: *Preliminary Report of the Geological Survey of Kansas.* [illegible] *Annual Report of the Smithsonian Institution for 18[illegible]; The American Journal of Conchology,* p. [illegible] The Tertiary Flora of [illegible] Plants by [illegible] [illegible] of Butterflies. p. [illegible]—GEOLOGY: The First Appearance of Man on our Planet; The Forest in [illegible] p. [illegible] CORRESPONDENTS. Wasps as "Marriage [illegible]" to [illegible]. *Illustrated.* p. 10[illegible]—NATURAL HISTORY CALENDAR. New England Reptiles in April; the [illegible] Calendar for April; The Insects of Early Spring. p. [illegible]—PROCEEDINGS OF SCIENTIFIC SOCIETIES. p. [illegible]—GLOSSARY FOR THE NUMBER.

Address the Editors of *The American Naturalist,* ESSEX INSTITUTE, SALEM, Mass.

TERMS:

$3 per year. Clubs supplied at liberal rates. Single numbers 35 cents.

The "Louisiana Baptist"

Is one of the best advertising mediums in the South or West. It is published weekly, and being a RELIGIOUS and LITERARY Journal, it circulates extensively in Louisiana, Mississippi, Missouri, Arkansas and Texas; also, to a considerable extent in all the Southern States east of the Mississippi River. Address WELLS & McKINLY, Mt. Lebanon, La.

AGENTS and all seeking profitable employment should secure at once the agency for J. T. Headley's latest and best work, FARRAGUT AND OUR NAVAL COMMANDERS. Just out; very popular; selling rapidly; no competition. Address E. B. TREAT & Co., Publishers, No. 654 Broadway, New York.

THE MAY No. of DEMOREST'S MONTHLY MAGAZINE, with Elegant Designs for the Spring and Summer Fashions, Music, Poetry, Entertaining Stories, Engravings, Household Matters, Full Size Patterns, and other useful and entertaining Novelties. Single copies, 30 cents; yearly, $3, with a valuable Premium. Address W. JENNINGS DEMOREST, No. 473 Broadway, New York. Ready 15th inst.

IF YOU
WISH to KNOW ALL ABOUT

WESTERN FARMING,
WESTERN ORCHARDING,
WESTERN TREE PLANTING,
WESTERN HEDGING,
WESTERN STOCK RAISING,
WESTERN FARMS, SOIL,
CLIMATE and PEOPLE, MARKETS, &c.

SUBSCRIBE FOR
"THE PRAIRIE FARMER."

IT COSTS BUT
Two Dollars per Year.

PUBLISHED WEEKLY
IN A NEAT OCTAVO FORM OF 16 PAGES.

Address EMERY & CO.,
192 Lake street, Chicago, Ills.

CARPENTERS & BUILDERS.

CARPENTERS AND BUILDERS send for Catalogue of new Architectural works, inclosing stamp.
A. J. BICKNELL, Publisher, Troy, N. Y.

UNQUALIFIED PRAISE
IS BESTOWED UPON
THE AMERICAN
JOURNAL OF HORTICULTURE
—AND—
FLORISTS' COMPANION.

PUBLISHED THE FIRST OF EACH MONTH, AND CONTAINING
Articles on the Horticultural Interests of All Sections of the Union,
BY THE ABLEST WRITERS OF THE DAY.

☞ **Price Three Dollars per Annum.** ☜
SAMPLE COPIES 30 CENTS.

J. E. TILTON & CO., Publishers,
BOSTON.

NASBY'S LIFE of ANDY JOHNSON, including his wonderful rise from alderman to president, with his western trip and orations. The greatest hit of the season. Only 15 cents.—**Comic Jeff. Davis,** by Mr Arrow, 10 cts.—**RECONSTRUCTION,** by Orpheus C. Kerr, 15 cts. All these illustrated by numerous very funny pictures. They sell very rapidly, and are pronounced "tip-top." Sent free on receipt of price, or all for 35 cts. We will supply dealers and those wishing to sell, at following prices, and send *goods free by mail:* Andy, $1 per doz. Jeff., 60 cts. Reconstruction, $1. HANEY & CO., 119 (removed from 109) Nassau-st., New York.

AGENTS, and all who want a good paying business should secure at once the agency for the People's Edition of Irving's great work, THE LIFE OF WASHINGTON; five volumes complete in one, at less than half the former price. Address E. B. TREAT & CO., Publishers, No. 654 Broadway, New York.

MME. DEMOREST'S MAMMOTH BULLETIN OF LADIES' FASHIONS for the Spring and Summer of 1867; over 40 Figures, price, plain, $1.50; Elegantly colored, $3; either accompanied with full descriptions, or with 10 to large patterns of the principal figures, 50 cents extra. Mailed free. No. 473 Broadway, New York.

NEW PHYSIOGNOMY; or, "Signs of Character," 1,000 illustrations; entertaining, instructive, and amusing. Ladies enjoy it. All should read it. Newsmen and Booksellers have it, or will get it. $5. S. R. WELLS, No. 389 Broadway, N. Y. AGENTS WANTED.

MUNSON'S COMPLETE PHONOGRAPHER, the latest and best work on Phonography, teaches the whole Art as recently simplified and otherwise improved, and also Reporting. No teacher is required. Price, post-paid, $4.25. Address H. H. JOHNSTON & CO., No. 64 Nassau-st., New York.

DUNCAN'S Masonic Monitor.—Complete Guide from Entered Apprentice to Royal Arch. Illustrated with Grips, Signs, Pass-words, Lectures, "Working," &c. All masons, and those about becoming such, should have this work. Bound cloth and gold, $2.50. W. C. WEMYSS, 575 B'dway, N.Y.

"THE CHILDREN'S HOUR." Edited by T. S. Arthur, Philadelphia, Pa., $1.25 a year. Sample Copies, 10 cents. *"Its exquisite beauty surpasses our anticipations."* —LADY'S BOOK.

TRUSSES, &c.—MARSH & CO.'S Radical Cure Truss Office, only at No. 2 Vesey st. Also supporters, bandages, silks, elastic stockings, &c.

A LADY ATTENDANT.

100,000 ARBOR VITÆ, HEDGE SIZE, AT Wholesale and Retail. Small Evergreens at Wholesale. A. P. CHAPMAN, 134 Fulton-st., New York.

A WHOLE YEAR.

YOU CAN'T DO BETTER.
YOU CAN'T DO BETTER.
YOU CAN'T DO BETTER.

FOR $2.50 A YEAR
FOR $2.50 A YEAR
FOR $2.50 A YEAR

YOU CAN GET BOTH
YOU CAN GET BOTH
YOU CAN GET BOTH

THE WEEKLY EVENING POST
THE WEEKLY EVENING POST
THE WEEKLY EVENING POST

and the

AMERICAN AGRICULTURIST.
AMERICAN AGRICULTURIST.
AMERICAN AGRICULTURIST.

THEY ARE THE BEST PAPERS.
THEY ARE THE BEST PAPERS.
THEY ARE THE BEST PAPERS.

THE EVENING POST contains:

I. THE NEWS OF THE DAY.
II. FULL MARKET REPORTS.
III. A GOOD STORY.
IV. EDITORIALS ON CURRENT TOPICS.
V. LITERARY AND ART GOSSIP.
VI. INTERESTING MISCELLANY.

REMITTANCES should be made, if possible, by draft or Post-Office order, payable in New York.

☞ Specimen copies sent free.

Address WM. C. BRYANT & CO., Publishers of *The Evening Post,* 41 Nassau-st., New-York.

Or,

ORANGE JUDD & CO., *American Agriculturist,* 41 Park Row, New York.

SOMETHING NEW.

THREE IN ONE.

English's Patent Combined Knife, Tweezer and Ear Spoon.

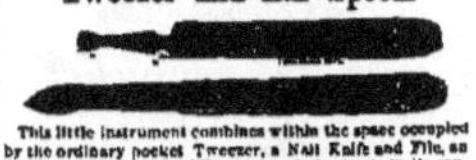

This little instrument combines within the space occupied by the ordinary pocket Tweezer, a Nail Knife and File, an Ear Spoon, and a pair of Tweezers. It is simple in its construction, being made of three simple pieces of steel, and in the most durable and workman-like manner: making one of the most useful and convenient articles for the pocket ever presented to the public.

Ladies will find this article to be a very useful and convenient adjunct to the Sewing Machine.

RETAIL PRICE, 50 CTS. EACH.

For sale by Dealers in Hardware, Notions, and Fancy Articles Generally.

Samples sent by mail to any address on receipt of 50 cents.

Address B. C. ENGLISH, Springfield, Mass.

A SERIES OF ARTICLES written by Hiram Woodruff, on the Trotting Horse of America, are now being published weekly in Wilkes' Spirit of the Times.

MONITOR MOWER,

With **"Independent Self-Rake Reaper Attachment."** The most Simple, Practical, Lightest Draft, and easiest managed machine in the World. See Report of FARMERS' CLUB OF AMERICAN INSTITUTE, in N. Y. Weekly Tribune, Dec. 12, 1866. For Descriptive Circulars, &c. Address F. NISHWITZ, Williamsburgh, L. I.

500,000 ARBOR VITÆ, 6 to 12 inches high, for sale at $5.00 per 1,000. A. P. CHAPMAN, 134 Fulton-st., New York.

BRAHMA POOTRAS, bred from stock weighing 21 lbs. per pair at maturity. Warranted pure. Can be seen on owner's premises. Price, $8 per pair; $12 per trio. Eggs, $2 per dozen.
J. M. HALSTED, 68 Pearl-st., New York.

AMERICAN AGRICULTURIST

FOR THE

Farm, Garden, and Household.

"AGRICULTURE IS THE MOST HEALTHFUL, MOST USEFUL, AND MOST NOBLE EMPLOYMENT OF MAN."—Washington

ORANGE JUDD & CO., PUBLISHERS AND PROPRIETORS. Office, 41 Park Row, (Times Buildings.)

ESTABLISHED IN 1842. Published also in German at $1.50 a Year.

$1.50 PER ANNUM, IN ADVANCE. SINGLE NUMBER, 15 CENTS. 4 Copies for $5; 10 for $12; 20 or more, $1 each

VOLUME XXVI—No. 6. NEW-YORK, JUNE, 1867. NEW SERIES—No. 245.

[COPYRIGHT SECURED.]

OUR FEATHERED FRIENDS.—*Drawn and Engraved for the American Agriculturist.*

The usefulness of birds, and the damage which some kinds do, are, and will continue to be, subjects of discussion. That they fall legitimately under the dominion of man, and may be encouraged by him if they aid him, and suppressed if they injure him, can hardly be questioned. Regarded among the most beautiful and interesting objects of creation, every one is drawn toward birds, though there are a few we can not but regard with dislike. In the group in the above engraving will be recognized some of the most beautiful and most common of the small birds, native to the larger part of the Union, and could we show colors in our printing the collection would be brilliant indeed.

The center of the group is the Blue Jay, (*Cyanura cristata*), closely related to the Crow, easily tamed, and having many of the characteristics of its relatives, ravens and magpies. Above, on the right, is the Baltimore Oriole, or Fire Hang-nest, (*Icterus Baltimore*), in color, gold and black, weaving a pendant pocket for a nest; on the right, the Red-winged Blackbird, (*Agelaius phoeniceus*), and Red-headed Woodpecker, (*Melanerpes erythrocephalus.*) Below, from right to left, the common Yellowbird, (*Chrysomitris tristis*), so pretty and so readily domesticated; the chatty and very useful House Wren, (*Troglodytes aedon*); and the beautiful Cedar Bird, or Wax-wing, (*Ampelis cedrorum*).

Contents for June, 1867.

INDEX TO "BASKET," OR SHORTER ARTICLES.

Back Volumes Supplied.—The back volumes of the *Agriculturist* are very valuable. They contain information upon every topic connected with rural life, out-door and in-door, and the last ten volumes make up a very complete library. Each volume has a full index for ready reference to any desired topic. We have on hand, and print from stereotype plates as wanted, all the numbers and volumes for ten years past, beginning with 1857—that is, Vol. 16 to Vol. 25, inclusive. Any of these volumes sent complete (in numbers) at $1.75 each, post-paid, (or $1.50 if taken at the office). The volumes neatly bound, are supplied for $2 each, or $2.50 if to be sent by mail. Any single numbers of the past ten years will be supplied, post-paid, for 15 cents each.

AMERICAN AGRICULTURIST.

NEW-YORK, JUNE, 1867.

June is a month of severe labor, constant care, and unremitting diligence. Throughout the Northern and Middle States the advance of the season is astonishing. It bursts upon us every year with as surprising a fervor as if we had not experienced the same thing ever since we can recollect. The last of May finds the Corn, and similar crops, Sorghum and Broom corn, puny and shivering in their narrow blades, pale, and living apparently on the hope of sunshine coming by and by. June comes, solsticial warmth infuses new life into the plants, they unfurl their broad green banners to the warm, moist airs, and atmosphere, and soil and sunshine favor their making amends for the delays of May. Over a considerable portion of the Northern States, in fact, so far as our exchanges and correspondents inform us, the season has been over the whole country, as with us, unusually backward. A less breadth of Spring grains, especially of oats, has been sown, but on the whole the grain crops promise remarkably well. The planting of potatoes and sowing of roots have been also much delayed. April work was crowded into May, and it is no more than to be expected that May work will hinder and complicate the proper labors for this month. If we remember distinctly, we have before alluded to the great necessity, in successful farming, of working with *a definite plan* for each month and each day, but we venture to throw out the hint again. A plan makes all the difference between success and failure—between a thrifty, fore-handed well-to-do man, and the shiftless, thriftless, worked-to-death plodder, who toils on his weary days and years, almost literally "taking no thought for the morrow."

Do not over work yourselves, your wives, your sons, or your cattle. Many a farmer has spurred up his growing son to do man's work at 15, and seen the boy broken down at 20, an old man at 30, and very likely, having learned no wisdom by experience, at 40 putting his own boys through the same *time-honored* course. Feed work-cattle of all sorts in a good degree in proportion to the amount of work required of them, and they will seldom be ailing if there is steady, hard work to do, and they are not strained by extra loads or overwork.

Hints About Work.

Clearing up.—It is to be taken for granted that however late the season, the manure has been hauled out and, except small quantities of rich compost for especial purposes, or the recent accumulations of fertilizing materials, the barn yards and manure sheds are quite cleaned out. Barns at the East at least have been woefully empty for two or three months, and ought long ago to have been swept and cleaned of hay-seed and litter of all kinds; Old hay and straw compactly packed at one side, yet conveniently come-at-able, and the whole establishment put in order for the coming crops. If this has not been done, do it the first rainy day.

Cattle stalls, cow byres and calf pens are empty now, for the most part, and it is a good time, and good wet weather work, to lift the floors, renewing them, cleaning and drying the beams and sills, painting those parts where wood becomes moistened by manure, when quite dry, with hot coal tar, sanding thoroughly before relaying the floors. Make gutters at the same time to carry off the liquids. These should be one part cement and three of good sharp, clean sand. The more time cement gutters, floors or walls have to harden before frost, the better.

Pastures.—Look to the water supply in pastures. Nothing dries up the fountains of milk like a lack of water. See also that the grass is not fed off too close, for any rain may be the last for some weeks, and then permanent damage would be sustained by over-stocked land.

Mowing land.—Early in the month it is usually well to go through the meadows and pastures, and pull or cut up with a spud the rankest of the weeds, or those most damaging to the grass and hay.

Clover, if cut early when just coming into blossom, and given a light dressing of plaster or of any fine compost, will, if the stools are strong, make a vigorous second growth, and ripen a paying crop of seed. Every farmer might raise his own clover seed in most parts of the country.

Haying will begin in favored spots—warm, moist, sunny meadows—and there are many meadows which it is worth while to cut early, in order to get this much out of the way before the main crop of grass is suffering for cutting. Such are especially those meadows which you can rely upon for a good after-math. Cut close on thick sods, but not on thin or open ones. Cut with the machine when the dew is all off the grass, and if a tedder is used, keep it in motion through the grass all the time, after it has lain about an hour; the more the grass is tossed and aired the quicker it will dry. Rake it up while the sun is still very hot, having all in winrows before four o'clock, and leaving it in cocks big enough to retain the heat well into the night. A good part will need but very little sunning the next day, and ought usually to be simply opened and shaken up after the dew is off and the ground hot. Where mowing machines and hay tedders can not be used, cut while the dew is on, turn once, rake up while warm, give the cocks a daily airing and sunning, but do the curing of the hay in the cocks, leaving them well made to shed rain and to hold the heat of the hay. Never let any dew fall on the loose hay.

Corn.—Early maturing kinds will do very well planted the first week in June; soak in warm water until it nearly sprouts, then stir it about with a little previously warmed *pine* tar until every kernal is coated, then sprinkle with plaster or lime.

Hoeing.—The use of hoeing is not only to kill the weeds, and a clean field is often an unproductive one, but the thorough working and stirring of the soil is equal to a dressing of manure on land in poor heart. The use of mere weeders and surface workers effects but little except the destruction of the weeds. It is most useful to cultivate deeply, and the one horse plow discreetly used between the rows, not to hill up too much, but to mellow and work the soil before the roots get into it, is preferable to any of the cultivators. These implements are most useful after the roots begin to fill the soil more. First the harrow, then the plow, last the cultivator. This doctrine applies equally to corn and potatoes. Frequent and thorough stirring by horse power so as not to hurt the roots, will insure good crops on any good soil.

Root Crops.—Carrots, and parsnips, and beets, may be sowed as late as early in June with fair success. Rutabagas are preferably sown about the 20th in good deep soil, well manured and dressed with bone dust or superphosphate of lime.

White Field Beans may be planted any time during the month. It is best to put them in drills. Blue-pod or White Marrowfat are good varieties, the latter much the largest, the former yielding the surest.

Green Forage Crops.—Indian corn, sown in drills about two feet apart, is probably the most reliable crop for furnishing green fodder during the summer. The cost of the seed is an item which, of itself, may deter farmers from using it extensively, especially when Sorghum will do nearly as well both for green and dry use. Millet and Hungarian grass if cut before the seed ripens, afford good fodder also, and will do well on soil somewhat exposed to drought. Peas and oats together may be sowed even in June for cutting and curing as hay or feeding green. This crop requires a good well mellowed soil, but is not especially exhausting. The seed required is about two bushels of each kind to the acre.

Cabbages.—Sow for late crop in seed beds, near the land on which they are to be grown, such varieties as Flat Dutch, Drumhead, Late Bergen, etc. There is ordinarily a good market for cabbages in all our larger cities, and they are fully equal to maugels for cattle, and as sure a crop. A crop of cabbages is one of the best for killing weeds. New land, with a plenty of good manure, is to be preferred. Mr. Henderson says that lime in any form, (bones or otherwise), will prevent club-foot.

Tobacco.—Select the largest plants from the seed beds, and, on a rainy day, transplant them to the field, so as to make the general planting about the 20th. The land should be very rich and mellow, warm, and well tilled. The plants may suffer from attacks of cut worms and grubs, and all missing ones must be reset, as fast as vacancies occur.

Animals of all kinds must have clean airy quarters, or in hot weather they will be exposed to lung diseases from exhalations of fermenting manure, etc. Use plaster freely in stables and fowl houses to arrest ammonia; dry soil is almost equally as good.

Fowls, if confined, should have fresh water and fresh sods daily, and every few days their scratching ground should be forked up and freshened. Especially provide good dusting boxes, and fresh water.

Cattle.—In providing for an increase of stock in the natural way, let no penny-wise policy interfere with the employment of the very best male animals. Use only well-bred bulls of one of the approved breeds, Shorthorn, Devon, Ayrshire, Alderney, etc., if they can be found within a reasonable distance.

Sheep.—We approve of early shearing, without washing, as explained last month. Tub washing has fewer objections than stream washing, and one important recommendation of it, to us, is, that the greater part of the yolk, or grease, may be saved for manurial purposes. This advantage is, however, we believe, generally overlooked. "Beware of dogs." Secure through legislation on the subject, if possible, and the carrying out of good laws. Dip the entire flock in some approved dip, as soon as the sores caused by shearing are *entirely* well, and there are no sun scalds or other open or tender spots on the sheep. The dips all have some very active poison, arsenic, tobacco, etc., as their bases, and must be used with great care.

Orchard and Nursery.

If the often repeated injunctions to make war on *Insects* have been followed, the orchard will be nearly free from these pests. If a nest or cluster of eggs has escaped, the insects will be the more readily seen on account of their rarity.

Moths may be killed in great numbers by keeping fires or putting lanterns in the orchard at night.

The Black-knot, which superficial observers ascribe to Curculio, but which might as well be charged to lobsters, will appear on cherries and plums, bursting up through the bark. Cut and burn at its first appearance, and don't wait until it gets old and black.

Pruning is best done this month, if trees have been so neglected as to need it. Make an open and well balanced head, and remove all limbs that crowd and chafe others. If melted grafting wax be brushed over the wounds, it will facilitate their healing. The rubbing off of superfluous shoots, as they start on young trees, will save much cutting next year. Remove suckers.

Grafts will need looking to, and will be making a vigorous growth. If some of the shoots get the lead of others, pinch their growing points. A graft should be treated just as if it were a young tree — indeed it is a young tree planted in another instead of being planted in the soil. Where two grafts have been set, and only one is needed, cut out the weaker one of the two.

Shoots from buds or stock grafts will often be so vigorous and succulent as to be easily broken by the wind, all such should be properly staked until the stem becomes strong and woody.

Borers.—June is the time when most of the eggs are laid, especially of the peach-tree borer. If it were generally understood that the egg of the borer was laid on the outside of the trunk, there hatched, and that the maggot worked its way into the tree, the remedies would be more intelligently applied. Any impediment will prevent the insect from depositing its eggs, and the various remedies of growing tansy close to the tree, piling stones around it, heaping tobacco stems, earth, or ashes, around it, all act upon the same principle—that of imposing an obstacle to the parent insect. The simplest way is wrap the base of the tree with brown paper for a foot or so above the ground, letting the lower edge of the paper go below the surface of the soil. Of course all borers already in the tree must be probed out. A wound or depression in the bark will show where they have entered; one who has a proper regard for his trees will examine them frequently, and if there are any signs of the borer, not rest content until it has been killed. The point of a knife will frequently do the work, but if the grub has penetrated deeply, cut a hole with a gouge and follow him up with a wire or flexible strip of whalebone. Don't leave the tree until you are sure that every grub in it is dead.

The Curculio will now need attention if one would have plums or cherries. All "applications" have so far been found useless. Nothing serves save jarring the trees and catching and killing the insect. This should be done every morning, early. Various contrivances for catching the insect have been proposed, but any one with a little ingenuity can arrange a convenient cloth for the purpose. A sudden jar is needed to throw the insect down, and it is a good plan to saw off a useless limb and leave a butt against which to strike with a wooden mallet.

The Slug, a green slimy and disgusting thing, now appears on the leaves of cherry and pear trees. It is soft, and seems to be easily killed by any dry powder. Dusting lime over the trees is the old and effectual remedy, and Thomas, who is good authority, says that dry road dust will answer as well. We sometime ago suggested the use of white hellebore, but have not heard of its trial.

Aphides, or plant lice, often gather in such quantities on the young growth of fruit trees as to blacken them. They of course do much injury, and should be treated to an infusion of tobacco mixed with soft soap, which is readily applied by means of a syringe or garden engine.

Mulch newly transplanted trees before the drouth comes on, it will often save those that would otherwise perish, especially stone fruits.

Layers should be made as noted on page 222.

Seed beds of fruit and ornamental trees will need special care this month. Thin where the plants are too much crowded, and shade by means of a lattice of lath. If evergreen seedlings show signs of "damping off," as the gardeners call it, or rotting, sprinkle an inch or so of fine dry sand over the bed.

Evergreens may be removed this month if sufficient care be taken to keep the roots from drying. Single trees, hedges, or screens may be trimmed, always keeping the upper branches shorter than the lower ones. Have the tree "furnished" to the ground.

Thinning of fruit may be commenced as soon as it is seen what the "set" is. There is but little danger of removing too much. Most of our careful cultivators find it necessary to thin two or three times. There is no danger of taking off too much.

Cultivation.—That is a frequent stirring of the soil, around newly planted trees, is of the greatest importance. It is now conceded that *mellow* earth is one of the most valuable kinds of mulch. Besides, it is of importance to keep down

Weeds, which should never be seen in a well-kept Nursery or Orchard. As to whether he should grow

Crops in the Orchard, see our notes last month.

Fruit Garden.

The notes in regard to pruning, insects, thinning fruit, and cultivation, given under Orchard, apply with even more force to the Fruit garden, where we suppose the highest culture is practised.

Dwarf trees will need to be formed by pinching, and whatever system is followed should be faithfully carried out. Every grower of dwarf trees, which he means to keep as dwarfs, should read Rivers' Miniature Fruit Garden. If one wishes to

Exhibit fruit at any of the coming fairs, he should begin to prepare his specimens. The fine shows made of large fruit are produced by severe thinning and high feeding and mulching. We have not much sympathy with this culture, but if one is to practise it, it is well to begin in season.

Currants will now be making many useless shoots, which should be rubbed out as they start. Mulching the soil will increase the size of the fruit. On the first appearance of the currant worm, dust the bushes with white hellebore. The same remarks as to general treatment, apply to

Gooseberries, which, if marketed, as well as currants, bring better prices when green than when ripe. If mildew appears on the bushes, use sulphur freely.

Raspberries and Blackberries of those varieties disposed to make suckers, should have all removed that are not needed for new plants. Tie up the new growth to stakes or trellises, or in field culture stop the canes at the hight of four or five feet, and make them self-supporting.

Grapes should have all superfluous shoots rubbed off. Do not let young vines overbear. One bunch to the shoot is enough for the first year. More failure of varieties is due to over fruiting, when the vine is young, than to any real fault of the variety. On old vines pinch off the fruiting shoot at three leaves beyond the last cluster. Never remove leaves to expose the fruit to the sun. The leaves do the work, and the berries develop best when shaded. Keep young vines to a single cane. Use sulphur freely on the first appearance of mildew. For the larger insect pests, such as beetles and caterpillars, hand picking is the only remedy.

Strawberries must be mulched before the fruit gets large. Use straw, dry hay, corn stalks, or similar material. Saw-dust is bad, as it soils the fruit almost as much as earth. In hill or row culture, keep the runners off and keep all plantations free of weeds. See article on picking on page 230.

Kitchen Garden.

The most important crop to be looked after this month is weeds. A sharp steel rake or a hoe-rake should be kept in constant use, and in a properly managed garden no weed will get so large that it cannot be demolished by the use of one of these. It takes but little time to go over the garden with a rake, and if it be frequently done, it will save much subsequent digging with the hoe. Very few people have an idea of how a garden should be kept, and they would get a good lesson if they could but see some of the market gardens around New York City, where gardening is not pursued for pleasure, but on high priced lands and for the money that is to be made out of it.

Replanting will be necessary when late cold rains have caused the early sowing to rot, or where late frosts have destroyed the crop. Most things, in northern climates, sown the first of June, will in the end do as well as if put in earlier.

Asparagus should not be cut too late. When peas are ready, stop cutting, hoe over the bed, and if there is any good compost at hand, give it a top dressing, and then let the tops have their own way, and grow to give strength to the roots.

Beans may still be planted for snaps or dried beans. Limas in cold localities may still be planted. The best for late plantings is the small lima. See notes under this head last month.

Cabbages, Cauliflowers, Broccoli, and Brussels Sprouts.—The early cabbages and cauliflowers from cold frames will be ready for use or market, and the ground may be cleared for other crops. In whatever condition the crops may be, they should be kept well hoed until they get too large to work among. Set out plants for late crops, and look out for the cut worm. Its holes are easily found, and when its retreat is discovered, dig out and destroy. In small plantings it may be well to wrap the stem of the plant with a leaf or bit of paper as a prevention, but on a large scale this is not practicable. See article on transplanting on page 221.

Beets.—Keep down the weeds and thin freely. Four to six inches is the proper distance. The early sorts will now be ready for use. The thinnings of the beet crop make excellent greens. Sow seeds of the Long Blood for a late crop.

Carrots may still be sown. The early ones must be thinned and weeded. Early carrots, even if not larger than a finger, bring a good price in the market.

Celery.—Keep the seed beds well weeded and cut back the plants to make them grow stocky. For early celery, some plants may be set in well manured trenches, but n our warm climate there is but little satisfaction in raising early celery.

Corn should be planted at intervals of about two weeks, and a succession of good sweet corn may be had until frost stops its growth. The variety called Stowell's Evergreen is the best for late.

Capsicums.—This month is early enough to put out this tropical plant. Give it a warm exposure and rich food, and it will reward you for the care in time with its pungent fruit.

Cucumbers.—Set out plants started under glass. Sow for pickles in well prepared land about 4 feet apart, giving a shovelful of good manure to each hill. Put in plenty of seed to give the bugs a fair chance to leave some plants to grow.

Egg Plants are dainty and uncertain. Sometimes a plant will give 6 or 8 fine fruit, and again it will be satisfied with yielding only one. Give them all the hoeing you can, all the liquid or other manure you can spare, let them have the warmest exposure, and then if they will, they will, and if they wont, they wont. We know of no more freaky plant.

Endive may be sown for a late salad. When the plants are large enough to handle, put them out a foot apart each way.

Lettuce in the warm months is apt to run to seed. The India is the best for summer sowing.

Melons.—The directions as to cucumbers apply to them. Earlier fruit may be had by thinning as soon as the crop has set. More fruit is usually set upon a vine than will ripen.

Onions.—No crop needs more care in weeding and thinning than this. In marketing, it will pay to send very young onions for sale. For ripe bulbs, thin to 3 or 4 inches. Potato onions are ripe when the tops fall over. Several remedies have been suggested for the maggot. Hot water seems to be the most generally successful application.

Parsnips should be thinned and hoed as soon as they are large enough to handle.

Peas.—Plant for late crops. Stick brush to those that need it. In field culture hoe earth up to the stems and let them run.

Radishes may be sowed for succession wherever there is a vacant spot in light soil.

Rhubarb.—Keep the flower stalks down and remove all weeds from the beds. Now that fruit is in season, the plants may have a rest, and all the better if they have a good dressing of manure. If it is desirable to dry or bottle a supply for winter, now is the time to do it.

Ruta Bagas.—Sow the latter part of the month, and as soon as the plants show themselves, give them a dusting of lime or ashes, to keep off the fly.

Salsify.—This is a most neglected vegetable, of culture as easy as that of carrots. It is capable of being cooked in several ways, and is liked by most people, and will afford an acceptable variety at the farmer's table. It may be sown now and treated like parsnips, and, as it is perfectly hardy, like that, may be left in the ground all winter.

Spinach.—Sow for succession. See last month.

Squashes.—Sow the running kinds, Marrow, Yokohoma, Turban, Hubbard, and others, in well manured soil. Let the runners take root. If a vine appears to wilt, look near the root for a borer, cut him out and cover the wounded part with soil.

Sweet Potatoes.—Plant, if not already done, according to directions in April and May numbers, where the best methods of cultivation are given.

Tomatoes.—It is not too late in most places at the North to put these out with expectations of a crop. A light warm soil is best. We have published most of the proposed methods of training, but our own experience, and that of others, has shown us that any elaborate system of training is only of use in gardens where space is valuable. For general crops, any arrangement of brush or rails, that will keep the fruit from the ground, is all the training that will pay. Those who wish to have the plants look neatly, will use some kind of a trellis.

Liquid manure is a grand thing judiciously applied. An infusion of sheep or barn-yard manure, of the color of "boarding-house tea," which means nothing too strong, may be used with great advantage. In European gardens they have a systematic use of liquid manure, and there as well as in Japan—a country from which we have yet much to learn—much of their horticultural success depends upon the use of human fæces in a liquid form. Stimulants of this kind should not be applied in a dry time, unless a proportionate amount of watering, by irrigation or otherwise, be done. The plant cannot grow in a time of drouth, and manure at this time is only an injury.

Last month's notes should be looked over. Several things mentioned there, and now seasonable, have been omitted here for want of room.

Weeds.—We end these notes as we began, with the injunction to never let a weed get too large to be *raked* out. Don't raise any weed seed.

Flower Garden and Lawn.

Impatience is the great fault of all lovers of flowers; from the boy or girl who plants seeds one day and digs them up the next, to the older one who has read all about gardening and has invested untold sums in plants, all are impatient. Those who have, despite our frequent caution not to be in a hurry, put out their verbenas, heliotropes and the like, and have seen what work these cold May storms have made with them, will probably recollect that these plants are raised in a warm propagating house, and that the change is a little too severe. We do not advise, in the climate of New York, the putting out of any of these things before the 20th of May, and the first of June is full soon enough, as that time the soil gets warm, the cold nights are over, and the plants have only to go on and grow. If put out too early they get a chill, from which they are a long while in recovering. So

Bedding Plants may still be satisfactorily put out. Those of a low growing habit should be pegged down by some of the modes given on page 219.

Green-house Plants that have grown too large are often turned into the borders with advantage, and cuttings taken for a new stock for the green-house. Among the most desirable these are the

Abutilons, which make admirable plants out of doors as well as in the house, and make good house plants in one year from cuttings.

Fuchsias should also be more freely used in places where they will not be hurt by the sun.

Oleanders, *Oranges*, and the like, do well when turned out into the borders, and the next winter seem to grow all the better for the root pruning they get when taken up in fall. We have not tried yet the hardiness of many of our green-house plants. There are, doubtless, many now considered tender that will prove hardy when put out.

Bulbs should have all the time they require for leaf-growth, and not be lifted until the leaves show signs of decay. When taken up, let the bulbs dry off and the leaves thoroughly wither before they are removed. Wrap the bulbs in paper, label, and store in a cool place, free from vermin.

Annuals.—Those already up will need transplanting. It is not too late now to sow most kinds with the prospect of satisfactory flowers, though the plants may not perfect seed. Asters are now so numerous in varieties, and all so fine, that one can hardly go amiss, and nothing gives a finer show.

Tagetes signata pumila.—Though as a general thing, we prefer a flower of some other color than yellow, is one of the finest of the later annuals. Its foliage is so delicately cut, and its habit is so compact, that we do not notice the very strongly marked "yaller" of the numerous blossoms. Of course every one will have Candytuft, Mignonette, double Zinnia, and the whole class of

Everlasting Flowers, which not only give pleasure while they are growing, but are pleasing after they are plucked. Helichrysums, Acrocliniums, Rhodanthes, and all the rest, are fine in the garden and the dried flowers are pleasing in the parlor in winter.

Herbaceous Perennials are generally multiplied by division of the roots, but when one has command of a propagating house, he can multiply them by divisions of the stems before they flower.

Tie up all plants that need support. Much of the neatness of a garden depends upon sticks and strings, and these should be used in a manner that will be effective and not obtrusive.

Green and Hot-Houses.

The plants will, of course, be taken out according to their hardiness. The old custom of clearing the houses is now giving way to proper shading and ventilating, and keeping many of the plants inside, where they do better than if exposed to burning suns, drenching rains and cold winds out of doors. It is of benefit to many of the

Green-house Shrubs to turn them out altogether, as it gives them a new root growth, and they are finer plants when potted for the next winter.

Plants in Pots should be placed on planks or a layer of coal ashes, so that worms may not enter the pots, and if the pots are plunged, some ashes should be placed at the bottom of the hole for the same purpose. Camellias and other plants, with evergreen leaves, should have the shade of an evergreen screen or be placed under a lattice. Do not neglect to give potted plants the necessary water.

Houses may now be repaired, and the plants left in them made to make the best possible display. Do not neglect to provide means for

Shading, which is necessary for even tropical plants. Whitewash upon the outside will usually last long enough, or muslin screens may be put on the inside.

Potting Soil of the best kind is made by stacking up sods from a pasture and allowing them to rot. It is well to turn the heap over occasionally and pick out the worms and grubs.

Cold Grapery.

When the vines are in flower, watering must be discontinued, and sudden changes of temperature avoided. The temperature should be from 85 to 90 at mid-day, and allowed to sink very gradually at night. Perfect fertilization is secured by giving the bunches a gentle flirt with the finger when they are in full flower. Leave only one bunch to a shoot, and stop the shoot at the third leaf beyond the bunch. Avoid over-cropping, especially on young vines. Thin the berries when they are as large as peas, removing one-half or more. As the bunches increase in weight, they will need to be supported by tying up to the vines.

Apiary in June.—*Prepared by M. Quinby.*

Swarms may be expected throughout this month. Any colony that was good early in the season, and has not increased enough to swarm by July, should be examined for the cause. If diseased, and bees enough are left, drive out into a clean hive, to begin anew. If queenless, or if the queen be barren, or a drone layer, give the stock a new queen, first removing the old one. In a good season the apiarian, if he understands his business, can control his bees, according as he wants surplus honey, or increase of stocks. He should not expect an excess of both. When swarms are wanted, make them as directed last month. Any hive, containing clean combs, where bees have died last winter, may be used again for new swarms. Be careful to remove all clusters of dead bees, moldy or soiled combs, before the bees are introduced. If kept long in warm weather, worms will appear; use a little smoke of brimstone to destroy them, even if very small. Sulphured hives may be used the next day, if needed, without harm to the bees. Light hives, set away partly full last fall, where they have frozen, will not need smoking—no worms hatch. If colonies are multiplied, and no box honey is made, it should not be carried too far. With the movable combs very much can be done toward equalizing and strengthening the weak stocks, yet, *if all are weak*, it is very difficult. A hive that does not swarm, can be made to assist others, by frequently giving them a comb or two filled with sealed brood. A hive, kept especially for this purpose, pays well. You will get *more bees* and *surplus honey* from one strong hive, than from a half dozen weak ones. When the increase of colonies is limited to one from each stock, it will, as a rule, give the best satisfaction. There will be enough bees to keep all strong, at all times, and chances for surplus honey are very good. To do this, (arrest swarming,) where they are allowed to swarm naturally, examine all the combs a week after the swarm issues, and remove all the queen cells but one, leaving this to hatch—or, if you have a laying queen, introduce her, which is much better. Where stocks are plenty, and box honey is the object, swarms should be prevented. This can usually be done by removing the old queen, and in due time destroying all royal cells but one, or introducing a young queen, reared in some other way. As soon as the hive is full of bees, plenty of boxes, with clean, white comb in them—the more, the better—as heretofore directed, should be immediately put on, and as fast as filled, removed, and replaced by others—without waiting for every cell to be sealed.

Those Two Extra

PREMIUMS!

FOR YOU!

We have prepared two most excellent and valuable Annuals, viz. the **Agricultural Annual No. 1**, and the **Horticultural Annual No. 1**. Though of large size, and costly, they are sold at only **50 Cents each**, and many thousands have been disposed of already. They are designed for *general* use, and one or both of them should be found in every Family in America. But they were originated and executed too late to be ready at the beginning of the year, and so they did not get so large a general distribution as they really merit. We design to make these Annuals a "permanent institution," that is, to issue both of them at the beginning of every year, and we have begun the preparation of material that will make the next numbers (for 1868), much superior even to the valuable volumes of this year.

Now we want everybody to get the FIRST number, so as to have the series complete from the beginning, for we know everybody will want the future numbers. THEREFORE, we make the following offer: To every person who shall, *after May 1st*, send us a subscriber to the *Agriculturist* for this year, at the regular rate ($1.50), we will present and send post-paid, either a copy of the *No. 1 Agricultural Annual* or of *No. 1 Horticultural Annual*, whichever is desired, (*if applied for at the time of subscribing.*) They are each in neat ornamental covers, beautiful inside and outside, and full of valuable information, including a full almanac, calendar of operations for each month, all finely illustrated, and contain many useful articles and suggestions.

Each present subscriber, not already supplied, can thus get one or both of these annuals *free* of expense, simply by procuring and forwarding one or two subscribers—(If the new subscriber thus obtained wants one of the annuals, he can get it for himself by furnishing another subscriber, and so on.) We shall keep the Annuals on the press until June 30, and print all that may be called for under this offer. This extra premium is entirely distinct from our regular premiums offered on this page.

AMERICAN AGRICULTURIST.

ORANGE JUDD & Co., Publishers, 41 Park Row, N. Y. City.

ANNUAL SUBSCRIPTION TERMS (always in advance): $1.50 each for less than four copies: Four to nine copies, $1.25 each: Ten to nineteen copies, $1.20 each: Twenty copies and upwards, $1 each. Papers are addressed to each

ALL THIS MONTH

Can be used in filling up premium lists begun, and in making *new* lists of subscribers, to secure the valuable articles in the table below. **Take Notice,** that two subscribers sent in for the *rest of this year*, (the second half of the present volume,) may count as one full subscriber towards a premium. Large numbers of premium names were sent in last year during **June**, and the same may be done this month.

Look over our premium list, choose the premium you would like, take a copy of the paper, sally out among neighbors and friends, in your own neighborhood and elsewhere (*for premium clubs need not be all at one post-office*), and in a brief time the desired number of subscribers can be gathered, and the premium secured.

Table of Premiums and Terms, For Volume 26—(1867).

Open to all—No Competition.

No. Names of Premium Articles.		Price of Premium.	Number of Subscribers required at $1.50	at $1.
1—*Garden Seeds for a Family (40 kinds)*		$5 00	13	37
2—*Flower Seeds for a Family (100 kinds)*		$5 00	13	37
3—*Nursery Stock (Any kinds desired)*		$20 00	30	97
4—*Iona Grape Vines (12 of No. 1)*		$18 00	27	90
5—*Concord Grape Vines (100 of No. 1)*		$12 00	19	65
6—*Japan Lilies (12 Bulbs)*		$8 00	13	45
7—*Sewing Machine (Wheeler & Wilson)*		$55 00	60	210
8—*Sewing Machine (Grover & Baker)*		$55 00	60	240
9—*Sewing Machine (Singer's Tailoring)*		$80 00	98	320
10—*Sewing Machine (Florence)*		$63 00	70	270
11—*Sewing Machine (Willcox & Gibbs)*		$55 00	60	240
12—*Sewing Machine (Howe's)*		$60 00	67	270
13—*Washing Machine (Doty's)*		$14 00	21	70
14—*Clothes Wringer (Best—Universal)*		$10 00	18	58
15—*Tea Set (Hart's best Silver Plated)*		$50 00	65	225
16—*Casters and Fruit Basket (do. do.)*		$30 00	44	140
17—*Ice or Water Pitcher (do. do.)*		$18 00	27	90
18—*One Dozen Tea Spoons (do. do.)*		$7 50	17	50
19—*One Dozen Table Spoons (do. do.)*		$15 00	22	73
20—*One Dozen Dining Forks (do. do.)*		$15 00	22	73
21—*Piano (Best Steinway & Son's 7-octave)*		$625 00	520	1550
22—*Melodeon, 5-octave (G. A. Prince & Co.'s)*		$112 00	138	400
23—*Melodeon, 4-octave (do. do.)*		$67 00	78	295
24—*Ladies' Gold Watch (Beautiful)*		$100 00	130	400
25—*Silver Watch (Valuable Time Keeper)*		$32 50	48	158
26—*Double Barrel Gun (Very good)*		$30 00	46	150
27—*Spencer's Breech-loading Rifle (Hunting)*		$46 00	70	235
28—*Tool Chest (First Quality of Tools)*		$44 50	60	190
29—*Case of Mathematical Instruments*		$9 00	18	55
30—*Case of Mathematical Instruments*		$15 00	22	75
31—*Morton's Best No. 6 Gold Pen (Silver Case)*		$3 75	14	42
32—*Morton's Best No. 5 Gold Pen (Silver Case)*		$1 50	11	35
33—*Barometer (Woodruff's Mercurial)*		$18 00	27	90
34—*Barometer (Woodruff's Mercurial)*		$12 00	19	65
35—*Buckeye Mowing Machine, No. 2.*		$125 00	150	450
36—*Allen's Patent Cylinder Plow, etc.*		$20 50	31	100
37—*The Aquarius or Water Thrower*		$11 00	19	53
38—*American Cyclopedia (Appleton's)*		$80 00	96	325
39—*Worcester's Great Illustrated Dictionary*		$12 00	19	65
40—*Any Back Volume Agriculturist*	*In clean new Nos. Post-paid—Unbound.*	$1 75	[illegible]	20
41—*Any Two Back Volumes do.*		$3 50	[illegible]	29
42—*Any Three do. do. do.*		$5 25	13	38
43—*Any Four do. do. do.*		$7 00	15	47
44—*Any Five do. do. do.*		$8 75	17	54
45—*Any Six do. do. do.*		$10 50	19	61
46—*Any Seven do. do. do.*		$12 25	21	68
47—*Any Eight do. do. do.*		$14 00	23	74
48—*Any Nine do. do. do.*		$15 75	25	82
49—*Vols. XVI to XXV do.*		$17 50	27	88
50—*Any Back Volume Agriculturist*	*Neatly Bound. Sent Post-paid.*	$2 50	[illegible]	24
51—*Any Two Back Volumes do.*		$5 00	[illegible]	38
52—*Any Three do. do. do.*		$7 50	16	49
53—*Any Four do. do. do.*		$10 00	18	60
54—*Any Five do. do. do.*		$12 50	21	71
55—*Any Six do. do. do.*		$15 00	24	82
56—*Any Seven do. do. do.*		$17 50	27	92
57—*Any Eight do. do. do.*		$20 00	30	102
58—*Any Nine do. do. do.*		$22 50	33	110
59—*Vols. XVI to XXV do.*		$25 00	36	118
60—*Genesee Farmer, 1858–1865, 8 Vols., Bound*		$14 00	21	70
61—*Downing's Landscape Gardening*	*All sent paid through, by Mail or Express.*	$6 50	13	45
62—*Cummings & Miller's Architect.*		$10 00	18	58
63—*A $10 Library (Your Choice)*		$10 00	18	58
64—*A $15 Library do.*		$15 00	24	85
65—*A $20 Library do.*		$20 00	31	106
66—*A $25 Library do.*		$25 00	38	125
67—*A $30 Library do.*		$30 00	44	144
68—*A $35 Library do.*		$35 00	50	162
69—*A $40 Library do.*		$40 00	56	177
70—*A $45 Library do.*		$45 00	62	192
71—*A $50 Library do.*		$50 00	68	207
72—*A $60 Library do.*		$60 00	80	237
73—*A $75 Library do.*		$75 00	100	282
74—*A $100 Library do.*		$100 00	125	360
75—*A Choice of Good Books (See Terms below.)*		..	..	..
76—*Sewing Machine (Finkle & Lyon)*		$60 00	60	210
77—*One Dozen Pocket Lanterns*		$9 00	13	45

☞ *Every article offered is new and of the very best manufacture. No charge is made for packing or boxing any of the articles in this Premium List. The forty-three Premiums,* **Nos. 1, 2, 6,** *and from* **20** *to* **32,** *and from* **40** *to* **75** *inclusive, will each be delivered* **FREE** *of all charges, by mail or express, (at the Post-Office or express office nearest recipient), to any place in the United States or Territories, excepting those reached only by the Overland Mail.—The other articles cost the recipient only the freight after leaving the manufactory of each, by any conveyance that may be specified.*

☞ **We take** *so much pains to procure only good articles in all cases, that any one securing anything from our premium list, saves the risk usually run of getting poor or indifferent goods, when buying of unknown or irresponsible parties. Every thing we send out as a premium is guaranteed to be the best of its kind and price.*

Old and *new* subscribers count in premium lists.

Our premiums are standard articles, and enough can be obtained to supply all calls for premiums for six months. Every canvasser can take abundant time, but

As fast as subscriptions are obtained, send them along, that the subscribers may begin to receive the paper; and when all the names that can be obtained are forwarded, select the premium, and it will be promptly furnished. To save mistakes and keeping accounts, *send with each list of names, the exact subscription money.*

Remit in Post-Office money orders, drafts or checks on N. Y. City; if these can not be had, register money letters.

☞ *Every name designed for a premium list must be so marked* WHEN *sent in.* (We can not count others.)

For Full Description of the several premiums see October *Agriculturist*, pages 340 to 352, or apply for a *Descriptive List*, which will be furnished *free* and post-paid. We have room here for only the following:

No. 63 to 74—Good Libraries.—These can be selected by the recipients, from any of the books named in the list in this column. The books will be *delivered* free of cost, by mail or express.

No. 75—General Book Premium.—Any one not desiring the specific Book premiums, 63 to 74, on sending any number of names above 25, may select Books from the list (below), to the amount of 10 cents for each subscriber sent at $1: or to the amount of 30 cents for each name sent at the (ten) club price of $1.20 each: or to the amount of 60 cents for each name at $1.50. *This offer is only for clubs of 25 or more. The books will be sent by mail or express, prepaid by us.*

BOOKS FOR FARMERS AND OTHERS.

(For sale at the office of the *Agriculturist*, or they will be forwarded by mail, *post-paid*, on receipt of price. ☞ *All these are included in our Premiums, Nos. 63 to 73, above.*)

Allen's (L. F.) Rural Architecture	$1 50
Allen's (R. L.) American Farm Book	1 50
American Agricultural Annual, 1867, paper, 50c.; cloth	75
Allen's Diseases of Domestic Animals	1 00
American Horticultural Annual, 1867, paper, 50c.; cloth	75
American Bird Fancier	30
American Pomology—Apples	3 00
American Rose Culturist	30
American Weeds and Useful Plants	1 75
Architecture, by Cummings & Miller	10 00
Barry's Fruit Garden	1 75
Bement's Poulterer's Companion	2 00
Bement's Rabbit Fancier	30
Breck's New Book of Flowers	1 75
Buist's Flower Garden Directory	1 50
Buist's Family Kitchen Gardener	1 00
Burr's Vegetables of America	5 00
Chorlton's Grape-Grower's Guide	75
Cobbett's American Gardener	75
Cole's (S. W.) American Fruit Book	75
Cole's Veterinarian	75
Dadd's Modern Horse Doctor	1 50
Dadd's (Geo. H.) American Cattle Doctor	1 50
Dana's Muck Manual	1 25
Dog and Gun (Hooper's) ....paper, 30c....cloth	60
Downing's Country Houses	8 00
Downing's Landscape Gardening (new Edition)	6 50
Downing's Fruits and Fruit Trees of America	3 00
Downing's Rural Essays	5 00
Draining for Profit and Draining for Health	1 50
Eastwood on Cranberry	75
Elliott's Western Fruit Grower's Guide	1 50
Flax Culture	50
Field's (Thomas W.) Pear Culture	1 25
Flint's Milch Cows and Dairy Farming	2 50
French's Farm Drainage	1 50
Fuller's Grape Culturist, (Revised Edition)	1 50
Fuller's Strawberry Culturist	20
Gardening for Profit, by Peter Henderson	1 50
Gray's How Plants Grow	1 25
Gray's Manual of Botany and Lessons in one Vol.	4 00
Guenon on Milch Cows	75
Harris' Insects Injurious to Vegetation, plain $4.00, col'd	5 00
Harris' Rural Annual. Bound, 8 Nos., in 2 Vols. Each	1 50
Herbert's Hints to Horsekeepers	1 75
Hop Culture	40
Husmann's Grapes and Wine	1 50
Johnston's Agricultural Chemistry	1 75
Johnston's Elements of Agricultural Chemistry	1 25
Johnson's (Prof. S. W.) Essays on Manures	1 25
Langstroth on Honey Bee	2 00
Leuchar's How to Build Hot-Houses	1 50
Mayhew's Illustrated Horse Doctor	3 50
Mayhew's Illustrated Horse Management	3 50
Mayhew's Practical Bookkeeping for Farmers	90
Blanks for do. do.	1 20
Miles on the Horse's Foot	75
My Farm of Edgewood	1 75
My Vineyard at Lakeview	1 25
Norton's Scientific Agriculture	75
Onion Culture	20
Our Farm of Four Acres (bound) 60c. ....paper	30
Pardee on Strawberry Culture	75
Peat and its Uses, by Prof. S. W. Johnson	1 25
Pedder's Land Measurer	60
Quinby's Mysteries of Bee Keeping (NEW)	1 50
Randall's Sheep Husbandry	1 50
Randall's Fine Wool Sheep Husbandry	1 00
Rivers' Miniature Fruit Garden	1 00
Richardson on the Dog, paper 30c. ....cloth	60
Rural Annual, by Joseph Harris	25
Saunders' Domestic Poultry (NEW), paper, 40c., bound	75
Schenck's Gardener's Text Book	75
Scribner's Ready Reckoner	30
Skillful Housewife	75
Small Fruit Culturist	1 00
Stewart's (John) Stable Book	1 50

Thompson's Food of Animals	[illegible]
Tobacco Culture	[illegible]
Todd's (S. E.) Young Farmer's Manual	[illegible]
Warder's Hedges and Evergreens	[illegible]
Watson's American Home Garden	[illegible]
Woodward's Country Homes	[illegible]
Youatt and Spooner on the Horse	[illegible]
Youatt and Martin on Cattle	[illegible]
Youatt on the Hog	[illegible]
Youatt on Sheep	[illegible]
Youmans' Household Science	[illegible]

Commercial Matters—Market Prices.

The following condensed, comprehensive tables, carefully prepared specially for the *American Agriculturist*, show at a glance the transactions for the month, ending May 13, 1867, and also for the same month last year:

1. TRANSACTIONS AT THE NEW-YORK MARKETS.

RECEIPTS.	Flour.	Wheat.	Corn.	Rye.	Barley.	Oats.
26 days this m'th	131,700	224,000	196,000	4,700	98,000	81,000
26 days last m'th	154,000	123,000	141,000	3,800	54,000	61,000

SALES.	Flour.	Wheat.	Corn.	Rye.	Barley.
26 days this month,	281,000	1,087,000	6,298,000	825,000	41,000
26 days last month,	324,000	1,040,000	3,914,000	846,000	709,000

2. *Comparison with same period at this time last year.*

RECEIPTS.	Flour.	Wheat.	Corn.	Rye.	Barley.	Oats.
21 days 1867...	131,700	224,000	196,000	4,700	98,000	81,000
25 days 1866...	153,000	5,300	88,000	1,100	107,000	31,000

SALES.	Flour.	Wheat.	Corn.	Rye.	Barley.
26 days 1867.....	281,000	1,087,000	6,298,000	725,000	411,000
25 days 1866.....	438,000	1,761,000	7,345,000	363,000	95,000

3. *Exports from New York, Jan. 1 to May 13:*

	Flour.	Wheat.	Corn.	Rye.	Oats.	Barley.
1867.....	180,471	89,439	2,012,114	197,284	96,790	794,790
1866.....	831,650	109,967	2,168,516	171,976	616,830	......
1865.....	682,033	219,940	140,767	111	24,913	......

CURRENT WHOLESALE PRICES.

	April 13.	May 13.
PRICE OF GOLD	133	136⅜
FLOUR—Super to Extra State	$10 25 @ 16 50	$11 50 @ 15 00
Super to Extra Southern	12 00 @ 17 75	12 75 @ 19 00
Extra Western	11 50 @ 18 75	12 00 @ 18 75
Extra Genesee	13 50 @ 15 75	15 00 @ 17 00
Superfine Western	10 25 @ 11 45	11 50 @ 12 75
RYE FLOUR	[illegible]	[illegible]
CORN MEAL	[illegible]	[illegible]
WHEAT—All kinds of White	[illegible]	[illegible]
All kinds of Red and Amber	[illegible]	[illegible]
CORN—Yellow	[illegible]	[illegible]
Mixed	[illegible]	[illegible]
OATS—Western	[illegible]	[illegible]
State	[illegible]	[illegible]
RYE	[illegible]	[illegible]
BARLEY	[illegible]	[illegible]
HAY—Bale ℔ 100 ℔	[illegible]	[illegible]
Loose	[illegible]	[illegible]
STRAW, ℔ 100 ℔	[illegible]	[illegible]
COTTON—Middlings, ℔ ℔	[illegible]	[illegible]
HOPS—Crop of 1866, ℔ ℔	[illegible]	[illegible]
FEATHERS—Live Geese, ℔ ℔	[illegible]	[illegible]
SEED—Clover, ℔ ℔	[illegible]	[illegible]
Timothy, ℔ bushel	[illegible]	[illegible]
Flax, ℔ bushel	[illegible]	[illegible]
SUGAR—Brown, ℔ ℔	[illegible]	[illegible]
MOLASSES, Cuba, ℔ gal	[illegible]	[illegible]
COFFEE—Rio (Gold price) ℔ ℔	[illegible]	[illegible]
TOBACCO, Kentucky, &c. ℔ ℔	[illegible]	[illegible]
Seed Leaf, ℔ ℔	[illegible]	[illegible]
WOOL—Domestic Fleece, ℔ ℔	[illegible]	[illegible]
Domestic, pulled, ℔ ℔	[illegible]	[illegible]
California, unwashed	[illegible]	[illegible]
TALLOW, ℔ ℔	[illegible]	[illegible]
OIL CAKE—℔ ton	[illegible]	[illegible]
PORK—Mess, ℔ barrel	[illegible]	[illegible]
Prime, ℔ barrel	[illegible]	[illegible]
BEEF—Plain mess	[illegible]	[illegible]
LARD, in barrels, ℔ ℔	[illegible]	[illegible]
BUTTER—Western, ℔ ℔	[illegible]	[illegible]
State, ℔ ℔	[illegible]	[illegible]
CHEESE	[illegible]	[illegible]
BEANS—℔ bushel	[illegible]	[illegible]
PEAS—Canada, ℔ bushel	[illegible]	[illegible]
EGGS—Fresh, ℔ dozen	[illegible]	[illegible]
POULTRY—Fowls, ℔ ℔	[illegible]	[illegible]
Turkeys, ℔ ℔	[illegible]	[illegible]
POTATOES—Mercers, ℔ bbl.	[illegible]	[illegible]
Peach Blows, ℔ barrel	[illegible]	[illegible]
POTATOES—Buckeye, ℔ bbl.	[illegible]	[illegible]
APPLES—℔ barrel	[illegible]	[illegible]
CRANBERRIES, ℔ barrel	12 00 @ 20 00	10 00 @ 18 00

Since our last, there have been frequent fluctuations in gold,—the market closing buoyantly at 136⅜....Breadstuffs have been in quite brisk demand, most of the month, at advancing prices. Much of the business has been on speculative account. Toward the close, the inquiry began to diminish, and prices to recede, especially for Corn, which, from the high prices reached through speculative management, has suddenly declined 20c@25c. per bushel, closing decidedly in favor of purchasers. California has sent hither further liberal supplies of Flour and Wheat, which are in high favor with buyers. Mixed Corn of last year's crop has been coming forward quite freely, adding to the depression in the market at the close....Provisions have been in fair demand at generally well maintained figures... Cotton has been in less demand at variable prices, closing pretty firmly, on more favorable reports from Liverpool....A very light business has been transacted in Wool, which has been tending downward. Holders have evinced more disposition to realize...Hay has been in better supply, and has receded 15c.@20c. per 100 ℔s, within a few weeks. At the reduced rates, the demand has been fair....Tobacco has been moderately dealt in at steady quotations.... Seeds have been dull and lower....Other agricultural products have been quiet.

New York Live Stock Markets.—

WEEK ENDING.	*Beeves.*	*Cows.*	*Calves.*	*Sheep.*	*Swine.*
April 16	4,978	20	1,443	9,391	16,979
April 23	5,183	70	2,007	10,181	17,171
April 30	5,163	62	2,880	9,976	14,387
May 7	5,637	25	2,759	12,878	23,091
May 14	6,043	67	1,874	13,171	17,719
Total in five Weeks....	27,224	307	10,287	55,081	73,012
Average per Week.....	5,445	61	2,117	11,019	11,879
do. do. *last Month*...	4,750	84	1,183	13,381	11,852
do. do. *prev's Month*.	5,086	76	823	11,211	14,258
Average per Week, 1866	5,748	91	1,200	20,000	13,000
do. do. do. 1865	5,255	118	1,500	16,091	11,023
do. do. do. 1864	5,161	115	1,511	15,315	12,676
do. do. do. 1863	5,150	129	694	9,941	21,670
Total in 1866	298,880	4,885	62,420	1,040,000	672,000
Total in 1865	270,271	6,161	77,991	836,733	573,197
Total in 1864	267,609	7,880	75,621	782,461	660,270
Total in 1863	264,091	6,470	35,705	519,316	1,101,617

As with wheat, so with live stock, prices have been, and still are, higher than any one could have calculated upon. The comparatively light run of shad this year has helped out the meat markets; a heavy run would have made a very material difference in the value of cattle.... **Beef Cattle** have continued to increase in supply from 4,800, April 16, to 6,000 this week, yet prices have gone up, so that the sales this week are higher than for a year past. Plenty of first quality bullocks sold yesterday at rates equivalent to 18c@18¼c. ℔ ℔. for the dressed weight; good, fair lots, 16½c@17½c., and the poor at 13½c@16c....**Milch Cows** have been little called for, until within a few days, but beef is so high that milkmen are selling off their poorer milkers, when in anything like selling order, and buying fresh ones. Some families going to the country for the summer, are also taking good cows. Present rates are $60@$75 for poorer cows, $80@$90 for good; and $95 to $125 for extra, or fancy animals—calves always included....**Veal Calves** have been plentiful, but the supply is less this week, and, influenced by the high price of beef, the best calves sell at 10½c@11½c. or 12c. ℔ ℔ live weight; common to poor, 10c@8....**Sheep and Lambs.**—Sheep are in good supply, and prices declining from the rates two weeks ago. Sheared sell at 7c@9c. ℔ ℔., live weight, according to quality. Spring lambs are scarcer than usual at this season, and bring 15c. to 18c. ℔ ℔, live weight....**Live Hogs** have been abundant and lower, but these are also now influenced by the beef market, and prices rather better, the latest sales being at 7½c@8c. ℔ ℔, live weight. The supply during the past five weeks has been quite fair for the season, as is shown in the following table:

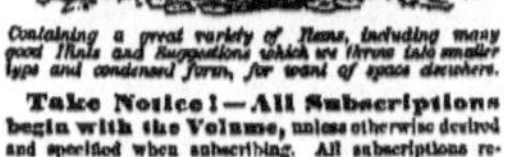

Containing a great variety of Items, including many good Hints and Suggestions which we throw into smaller type and condensed form, for want of space elsewhere.

Take Notice!—All Subscriptions begin with the Volume, unless otherwise desired and specified when subscribing. All subscriptions received up to June 15th are entered down for the entire volume, and the numbers from January 1st are forwarded. We keep on hand, or print from our electrotype plates, as needed, the entire numbers of the volume, to supply to new subscribers, and to others desiring them. Subscriptions received *after* June 15th, begin at the middle of the volume, unless otherwise desired or specified.

"41 Park Row To Let."—A subscriber writes, anxiously, that he sees our present office is "To Let," and asks if we are going to "suspend," or "contract."—*Far from it*; on the contrary, we are *expanding*. Our present quarters—though occupying the whole of the first floor through from Park Row to Nassau Street, and the large basement under our own floor, and part of that under the Times Office—are becoming too limited. Besides, our lease extends only 3 years longer, and we do not care to erect costly machinery with no certainty of having it remain. To remedy these difficulties and secure a *permanent* home for the *Agriculturist*, the Publishers have *purchased* the large buildings right across the Park from the Old Office, viz.: 245 *Broadway*, with an L opening upon Murray Street. This gives us 5 large floors, 25 feet on Broadway, 114½ feet deep, with the extension to Murray Street, 12½ feet wide, giving an ample rear entrance, hatchways, etc. There are 5 stories, (to which we shall probably add a sixth Mansard story for printing rooms,) and ample basements under the whole for steam-engines, presses, etc. The new building is most admirably located, facing the open Park between the grand New Post Office to be built, and the old City Hall and new County Court House.—As we have control of the old office for three years, and the lease is very valuable, we may remain here sometime yet, and move across the Park when the right kind of a customer comes along to take our present lease; or we may let the new office, until we need it for immediate occupancy. So, until further notice, our readers may expect to find us in the accustomed place. In the mean time, 41 Park Row, or 245 Broadway, in whole or in part, will be for lease for a time—only one of them, whichever is first called for.

Agricultural and Farmers' Columns.—It has of late became quite the fashion for the secular as well as the religious press to employ some penny-a-liner, with a smattering of agricultural and horticultural affairs, to furnish matter to fill a column or two with talk on these subjects, which is generally "talk" of the concentrated essence of ignorance. These writers are employed at so much a week and the perquisites; as they are generally "on the make," it is not to be supposed that their notices of this machine or that fruit, are given without a consideration. A publisher recently told us that he gave one of these chaps five copies of a work, as he wrote for five different papers. As this "writer" is a "purchasing agent," we suppose that the copies will be turned into cash when his purchasing agency gets an order for the work. It is interesting to see how these fellows get on committees for award of premiums for agricultural implements, and then to see how the owners of these implements hold protracted interviews with them. Of course committee men only seek for the best implements, and makers of implements only seek for the best committee men, and so it is all right. These "column" writers are highly amusing and we would not have them stop on any account, as they would deprive us of a laugh at least once a week.

Fine Engravings.—We take much pleasure in referring to the beautiful engraving on page 220. As a specimen of the art, it has not been excelled, if it has been equalled, by any engraving published in any journal of the country. Where the sheet is printed on both sides, much of the beauty of an engraving is injured, and, as we are often written to for nice impressions of our illustrations, we have had a limited number of copies of this carefully printed on fine, heavy paper, fit for framing. These will be sent post-paid for 50 cts. each. Copies of "Suspense," the much admired dog picture, that appeared in March last, may be had on the same terms.

Gift Enterprises, or Lotteries—"Harris Brothers."—Of the "*Ohio Benevolent Gift Enterprise*," by Tudor, Gates & Co., referred to last month, Mr. Gates writes, "we have in our possession the originals from which our Indorsements are printed." This being the case, the word "pretended" should be stricken out of our remarks, but this makes it so much the worse for the "Governors, Members of Congress, etc."; for we believe they misuse their official position and reputation by giving their names to indorse any Gift Enterprise, however plausible it may seem, or however good its real objects. If Mr. Gates, or Gov. Cox, or Treasurer Warner, or Senator Sherman, etc., can tell us wherein the Ohio Benevolent Gift Enterprise differs in principle or operation, from the Havana or Covington Lotteries, they will perhaps lessen the force of our objections. The best that can be said is, that the profits go to a good object instead of to private pockets. But this makes the matter worse, for the people are led into lottery operations and practices, partly by their sympathies, and partly by the sugar coating of quasi-respectability given to the scheme. The end does not sanctify the means. If Lotteries (*alias* "*Gift Enterprises*",) are proper to aid soldiers, then they are also proper for building up schools and churches, paying government debts, etc., and we may at once go back to the custom of the last century. Lotteries offer mainly money prizes to be distributed by lot (the kind of lot is not essential); the gift enterprises offer money, and country seats, farms, houses and other "gifts" in addition. They stimulate people to false hopes of acquiring riches. The judgment of enlightened people has banished lotteries and lottery dealers from most of our States; the benevolent and other gift enterprises are merely bringing back old customs under new names. We commend to Messrs. Tudor, Gates & Co. the recent decision of the Massachusetts Courts in the case of Harris Brothers, whose scheme was ostensibly every way like that of the "Ohio Benevolent Gift Enterprise," in form, means, and proposed objects, except that the Boston operators attempted to make this journal appear to indorse their scheme. The result was they were fined $14,000, and subjected themselves to a further forfeiture of, in all, about $30,000.

[*From The Boston Daily Herald, April 16, 1867.*]

In the Superior Criminal Court, this morning, before Judge Morton, Luther M. Harris and James W. Harris appeared for sentence on an indictment charging them with promoting a lottery, (found at the June term, 1865,) and on which they were found guilty, and the exceptions taken, overruled; also on an indictment, found the present year, for having in their possession for sale, and offering to sell, certain lottery tickets; and on a third indictment charging them with promoting a lottery known as the "Rural Home" swindle. On the last indictment a verdict of guilty was taken and exceptions filed and allowed, but which the Harris Brothers waived to-day. District Attorney Sanger stated to the Court that at the time of the search about $24,000 of U. S. securities were found in the defendants' trunk; also that a large number of letters were found at the Post Office freighted to these brothers, respecting the lottery business, and that the clerk at the Dead Letter Office testified to receiving on an average of five letters a day respecting Harris Brothers' schemes, and that Harnden's Express Company also testified to money packages coming very frequently for the defendants. He also showed a number of letters which had been received by the Chief of Police, the Mayor of this city and the Governor of this State, from parties who had received them from Harris Brothers, and requesting that prosecutions might be made. The District Attorney claimed that this money had been illegally gotten, and that the maximum fine should be imposed.

Chas. H. Hudson, Esq., who appeared in connection with Geo. Starkweather, Esq., as defendants' counsel, stated to the Court that he had but recently been brought into the case, and, as far as he was able to ascertain, he felt sure that the defendants believed that they were doing a legitimate business within the law, and very likely they have been reputed to be doing more than they really were. Mr. Hudson did not deem the business done by the defendants any more of a lottery than Fire Insurance companies, of one of which the District Attorney is President. Inasmuch as the indictments under which the defendants might be sent to the State Prison had been laid on file on account of doubtful questions of law, Mr. H. did not feel like urging the matter of clemency with too much persistency.

Judge Morton said he could not but characterize the business carried on by the defendants,—to call it by its right name,—as an extensive swindle, and he was unable to see how he could do otherwise than impose the maximum fine, as, in his opinion, to do less would be offering a premium to swindlers.

The prisoners (for their bail had been surrendered) were then fined, each, on the first indictment, $2,000; on the second, $2,000 on two counts; and on the "Rural Home" indictment $2,000, making a total of $14,000, with costs, which will amount to about two hundred dollars.—Under the 8th section of chapter 162 of the General Statutes, of Mass.,] the defendants forfeit to the Commonwealth—about $50,000 worth of property, which includes the $23,000 in U. S. securities, the "Rural Home" at Woburn, valued at $13,000, and the fine of $14,000 and costs.

Washing Compounds of any kind we cannot commend. We do not say there cannot be a good one, but we do not know any one which we are willing to recommend. We regret that the admission by oversight or mistake of an advertisement of such compounds should make us appear to recommend them. It will not be likely to occur again, at least until we find one we can positively indorse from a knowledge of its composition and use. Our advice is, buy none of these things, patented or unpatented, but use good soap, made at home, or by some well known or well recommended manufacturer. See our last volume, page 403, (November Number).

Weighing on the Farm.—Too much "guessing" is practised in disposing of bulky farm products, whereby the buyer, but more frequently the seller, is the loser. Dealers are usually expert from long practice and have the farmer at a disadvantage. A drover soon learns to weigh a bullock with his eye, so as to come *within* fifty lbs. of his weight every time. A Fairbanks or other good scale on the farm will change this, and put both parties on the same footing. (We name the Fairbanks as of well-known reliability.) In addition to insuring fair dealing, such an apparatus will enable one to conduct many interesting and profitable experiments in feeding stock, etc., and to ascertain their comparative thrift at any time.

Sundry Humbugs.—We have no "truce" to offer to the swindling fraternity, but it would seem that after the many exposures given in these columns, little more need be said, just now, to guard *our* readers against the multitudinous schemes constantly resorted to to filch money from the unwary. No regular reader of the *Agriculturist* can be pitied, if, after what has been said, he throws his money away upon any one of these "confidence men" who pretend to solicit his services as an agent for any ticket or lottery scheme. We earnestly caution the reader against *every one* of these gift enterprises, ticket schemes, prize concerts, secret medicines, Union Associations, artists' unions, jewelry associations, five dollar sewing machines, express parcel men, soldiers' orphans and widows' "distributions" of various kinds, cheap oil manufacturers, ink and washing compounds, honey recipes, wonderful corn and other seeds before unheard of, *every* advertising doctor, Howard Association, advice to the married, ditto to the unmarried; eye cures, vile instruments, Union book companies, silent friends, cheap money, $100 to $300 a month salary or wages, "greenbax," magic wands, hunter's secret, cider recipes, vinegar recipes, complexion beautifiers, love powders, price and prize associations and parcels, farms sold by lot or tickets, Elixirs, etc., etc., etc. We have before us hundreds of these letters, circulars, and advertisements, all of them humbugs. Scarcely one in a hundred of the operators will ever send any return for money forwarded them by mail, or even acknowledge its receipt. Perhaps in one case in ten thousand, a showy article is sent as a blind to draw the foolish recipient into a larger investment, to his loss.

The Fair of the N. E. Agricultural Society, is to be held this year, at Providence, R. I., beginning September 3d. It is to be upon the new Sprague Park, and, by the reports, the buildings and accommodations promise to be of unusual elegance and convenience. We hope for a large attendance.

The Paris Exposition.—We hear from the daily papers, that this exhibition is rich in this and that, but we learn very little about American agricultural implements. In the first World's Fair in London, 1851, we astonished the world with our implements. We do not know what has been sent to the present Paris Show. There was an American Commission to select articles to send over; this Commission was composed of a great many nobodies, with just a few somebodies to give it respectability. We do not know who made up this "Commission"—but their fitness for the work is shown by the fact that Mr. Greeley, a life-long advocate of total abstinence, was put on the sub-committee on fermented drinks, or liquors, we have forgotten which. If all the other sub-committees were made up with equal fitness, there will be a show well worth going to Paris to see. Of course, there must have been a choice in the agricultural implements, and the man who was most *convincing* probably had the preference. Now that the Show is fairly open, we look with interest for the results. We are glad to learn that Mr. Ruggles and Prof. Joy, are going over, as they will save the American Department from utter contempt. These gentlemen will worthily represent the scientific interests of our community. Who shall represent our agricultural interests? We learn that the Department of Agriculture has appointed some one to represent its insignificance, but who shall represent our noble body of farmers? Can not some State Society send out a proper person? At all events, we would say to European farmers, that the Department of Agriculture of this country, is in the charge of a man who is kept there in spite of the recorded protest of every or nearly every Agricultural Society in the country. It is our National disgrace, our repulsive sore. Whoever may be sent to represent this miserable concern, no more represents American Agriculture than a lump of clay represents a Sevres Vase.

American Pomology.—The reception given to this work everywhere must be very gratifying to its distinguished author, as it certainly is to his publishers. Very few, who have not tried to classify any thing, can have any idea of the difficulties of the task, and when it comes to putting in order things that are so nearly alike, as are the different varieties of apples, the difficulty is greatly increased. We look upon Dr. Warder's Catalogue of Apples as a remarkable result of patient labor in classifying life-long observations, and this, which is in size a very small portion of his book, should entitle him to the gratitude of every true pomologist.

Manure Making—Bommer's Method.—There is so much good sense, albeit mingled with comparatively harmless error, in the old patent method of Bommer for making (or rather increasing the value and quantity of) manure, that we are not surprised that a considerable edition of the old pamphlets should have been sold, at the low price we offered them at. The old patented process is fully described, and all that used to be sold for $10, may now be had for 25 cents, for to accommodate those who constantly order it, we bought the old plates and had a new edition printed. The aim of the author is to explain the best method of preparing vegetable and mineral composts; to augment and improve the manure of the farm; to prepare fertilizing liquid for irrigation; to convert into manure the refuse of manufactories, distilleries and kitchens; to revive hot beds without changing the litter.

At the Paris Exhibition. — The *American Agriculturist* will be represented by Mr. Judd in person—wind and tide favoring. He will probably also extend his trip to St. Petersburg, perhaps to have a little chat about our new Northwestern Farm.—The *Agriculturist* is abundantly provided for editorially and otherwise, and matters will go on as usual during his absence.

The Department of Agriculture.—We have, at last, seen one journal that praises the present management of the Department of Agriculture. It is the "Watchman and Reflector," of Boston, and we are sorry to see it "*reflecting*" the stupidity of the National Seed Shop. The article says: "Mr. Newton has been denounced by several agricultural societies by votes, asking his removal. These votes were procured, undoubtedly, in most cases, by the management of aspirants for Mr Newton's place, and it is time somebody asked for him at least, fair play." Some Boston Societies are involved in this matter, and probably the "Watchman and Reflector" knows what means were used to influence their votes—but we do not believe that any influence was needed to procure from any respectable association an endorsement of the present official's stupidity. Now, editorially, we wish to answer a number of printed slurs and private inquiries. As Mr. Judd is away, we speak for him, and say we are sure he has never desired, or sought for the office of Commissioner, and we believe he would refuse it if forced upon him. He has too long been at the head of a far more powerful and vastly more useful "Department" than that at Washington, to take an inferior position. Besides this, he could not afford to hold any office in Washington, from that of President, *down* to that of the head of the Department of Agriculture.—Snarlers will please be quiet on this subject.

Blackberries.—For those wishing that really charming new blackberry, the Kittatinny, there is yet ample time and opportunity, as may be seen by noticing Mr. Phoenix's advertisement in this number. From samples shown at this office, as well as the very liberal price and offer Mr. P. makes, we can heartily recommend them to the notice of amateurs and planters, who would keep up with the times and enjoy the fruit next year.

Abortion in Cows.—The N. Y. Legislature, at its last Session, made provision for a commission to investigate the subject of abortion in cows. They made an appropriation so disproportioned to the talent to be engaged in the work, that we are ashamed to say how much—or rather how little—they did appropriate. Prof. John C. Dalton, M. D., has been appointed commissioner, than which no better appointment could be made, and the whole subject is sure of a thorough search. Doct. Dalton has secured the services of Docts. Carmalt, Haigh, and others, known for their devotion to animal physiology, and we await their report with much interest.

Tight Boxes, Barrels, Pails, etc.—Macferran & Co., 721 Chestnut-st., Philadelphia, manufacture a style of hooped ware with an arrangement whereby the upper hoop may be instantly and powerfully tightened by means of a lever, thus fastening the head in, air-tight. These vessels are of various sizes, and useful as fur cases, sugar boxes, slop barrels, milk and butter pails, meat barrels, etc. For these purposes, they are obviously most excellent. In regard to the churns with heads on this principle, we can, at present, only say they are exceedingly convenient.

Benedict's Time Tables, issued monthly by Benedict Bros., 171 Broadway, at 25 cents per copy, contains a Map of the City, and gives in convenient form the time tables on all the Railroads and Steamboats leaving New York for American Ports.

Fuller's Small Fruit Culturist.—Though too late for those who wish to plant this Spring, this work, which is a "Culturist," will be useful to all who grow fruits. We have heretofore had no work especially devoted to small fruits, and certainly no treatises anywhere that give the information contained in this. It is to the advantage of special works that the author can say all that he has to say on any subject, and not be restricted as to space, as he must be in those works that cover the culture of all fruits—great and small. It is not possible for Mr. Fuller to follow in the track of another, and in the present work he gives his own experience and his own views with the freedom that characterizes all his other writings. He will win the esteem of all true lovers of horticulture by the searching criticism he has given to varieties, while those who believe in names rather than things, will of course be offended. The work is especially valuable for the sifting it has given the varieties of Currants and Raspberries, and if it were for this alone, it would be a valuable addition to our horticultural literature. But besides these, it treats of all the small fruits, including several kinds generally slighted or passed over by other authors, and describes the propagation and culture of all in his usual clear and vigorous manner. The chapter on gathering and packing fruit is a valuable one, and in it are figured all the baskets and boxes now in common use. The book is very finely and thoroughly illustrated, and makes an admirable companion to his Grape Culturist; about 275 pages, sent by mail for $1.50.

Fruit Preserving Solution.—This compound, advertised in another column, was tried last year by one of the editors, and was much liked. Fruit put up with it kept well, had no unpleasant taste, and, being cooked less than is usual in other methods, retained much of its flavor.

Electricity — Lightning. — Electrical phenomena are so strange, and so little understood by the general public, that they stand ready to accept electrical action as the cause of any obscure occurrence. Electricity is the great refuge of the would-be scientific, who say that this and that is due to electricity, and that ends all further questioning. A western writer on pruning, in the Gardener's Monthly, will not have the terminal buds cut from the trees in pruning, because they act as "prime conductors" of electricity, which is a very "scientific" way of talking profound nonsense. We have before us two curious illustrations of the way in which electricity is treated. One upon the pear blight, in which the writer refers this malady to the effect of lightning upon the leaves, and another, by a lady, who considers the potato-rot due to the absence of sufficient lightning in certain years. The last named writer accompanies her article by observations, which show that, in her section of country, the years with the most lightning were the freest from the rot. Now, as the rot is a well known parasitic fungus, brought, comparatively recently, from abroad, and, as in this country, before this unwelcome guest was introduced here, we probably had years quite as deficient in lightning, as we have since had, we cannot regard this view as at all satisfactory. If those who are so ready to ascribe this and that to electricity, would just take the trouble to first study some of the elementary laws of this branch of physics, they would be less apt to run into speculations respecting the influence of electricity.

Storm Signals during Harvest.—The following plan to aid in preventing injury to grain and hay crops from storms during harvest, is presented to the readers of the *Agriculturist* by A. Watson, Esq., of Washington, who has placed himself, extensively in communication with reading farmers through the newspapers. The subject is one of importance, and needs the practical thoughts of the agriculturists of the country. He estimates the extent of the damage as one-third the value of the crops, and proposes that all the County Seats throughout the land should be connected by telegraph lines, (which would require the construction of but few new ones,) and that cannons should be fired at the county town, in a way to make known, accurately, the distance of every telegraphed storm, and the rapidity of its approach. Our cotemporaries, whose comments upon this plan we have seen, seem to overlook the fact that thunder showers and storms, which do a great part of the damage, are exceedingly local phenomena, extending, often, over but a few miles in width, and soon exhausting their force. The regular "North-easters" might very well be telegraphed, for they pursue a somewhat regular and known course, from south-west to north-east, along the coast, and directions somewhat varying from this at different parts of the country, inland, we believe.

There may, also, be other well defined classes of storms, whose approach might be announced, and which might be avoided by the use of the telegraph. The firing of cannon at the county court-houses, by county officials, is entirely impracticable, at present, but as there is a telegraph office at almost every railroad station, there might, and should, be a Storm Bulletin at every station, and every person going to and fro should carry the news of approaching storms to his neighbors.

At the Smithsonian Institution in Washington, the meteorologists, aided by able observers in all parts of the country, and by the officers of the telegraph companies, keep a very close watch of the storms, at the time they are in progress. The real problem to be solved, then, is—how to convey the information thus gathered to the farmers. We think it may be easily and simply done, and would earnestly recommend the officers of our railroads to move in this matter, and, as soon as possible, co-operating with the Smithsonian, to have a thorough meteorologist appointed, whose duty it should be to learn the movements and character of storms throughout the country, and communicate definite information along all the lines of railroad telegraphs in the country, which information should be immediately and clearly bulletined at the various stations, by the railroad or telegraph employees. This may be done at once, and the result would doubtless pay the railroad companies thirty-fold for their small expenditure in the increase of agricultural wealth.

Draining for Profit, and Draining for Health, is the title of a new work on this most important subject, by Col. Geo. E. Waring, Jr., published by Orange Judd & Co., which will be issued *early in the present month.* The theory and practice of thorough draining has, within a few years, made great progress, both on the small scale involving the freeing of a few acres only from superfluous water, and opening the sub-soil to the benign influences of air and moisture, and warmth together, and also in enterprises of great magnitude, affecting the sanitary condition of whole districts of country. The progress made has been chiefly in Great Britain, and on the Continent. Col. Waring's work is compact, fully illustrated, very clear, both in its arguments and in its directions for practice, and, throughout, readable. We are confident that it will be at once recognized as the standard American authority on this subject. It is thoroughly American, and tells what everybody wants to know, (omitting those things which people generally know, or which are of little service,) in regard to thoroughly draining the land. It is needless for us to allude to the extraordinary qualifications of Col. Waring for writing such a work. He has been, practically, very successful as a draining engineer, and few, either in this country, or abroad, have such monuments of their skill to point to as has he, the most important of which is the New York Central Park. In this book he embodies and condenses the studies and results of many years. Our book-list, page 205, gives the price at $1.50.

The Poultry Book, by W. B. Tegetmeier, F. Z. S., with pictures by Harrison Wier, printed in colors by Leighton Bros., 350 pages, Royal Octavo. Cloth, gilt edged. Geo. Routledge & Sons, London, 1867. ——This work which we have been receiving and admiring in numbers for a year is now complete, and issued in very attractive style. Instruction by the eye, through accurate and beautiful engravings, is vastly more impressive and better retained in the mind of the learner or reader, if the subject be adapted to pictorial illustration, than if language be used alone. In this work not only are all the more valuable breeds of useful and ornamental poultry most beautifully represented by large colored lithographs, having the effect and richness of oil paintings, but the letter-press gives very full accounts of each breed, together with excellent instruction in regard to the rearing and care of poultry, their breeding, use, diseases, etc. The engravings are chiefly from the very accurate pencil of Mr. Harrison Wier, whose drawings every poultry fancier is more or less familiar with, from the very free manner in which they have been copied by almost every writer on this subject. One of the most valuable parts of the book is the Appendix, which contains the "Standard of excellence in exhibition birds," which is received, very generally, as the guide of judges at Poultry Shows in Great Britain. We have this elegant work on our table for sale at the moderate price of $9.

Cider Vinegar.—"H. F." The quickest way of making it, is the process by which the cider may be most exposed to the atmosphere. The cider should have passed though the alcoholic fermentation. The harder it is the better. Manufacturers on a large scale have a platform covered with oak-shavings over which the cider runs slowly from one vessel into another. Do not attempt to make cider vinegar out of anything else but *apple juice.* "First catch your hare." The tongue is a good enough test of the strength of cider vinegar for domestic uses.

Plant Lice. — "Charlie," Medina, Mich., writes: "Mother has a rose-bush, which is being devoured by thousands of lice. What shall she do?"—The answer to this will be a reply to many similar letters. Kill the lice. But how?—We have told how ever so many times, but we will repeat it.—Use tobacco smoke. As Charlie is probably a good little boy, and does not use either pipe or cigars, we must teach him the horticultural use of tobacco, and advise him, at the same time, not to learn any other use of it. Put the plant under a barrel or box, and then take a few live coals in a convenient dish, put some tobacco-stems, or other tobacco on them, and place it under the barrel or box, so as to fill it with smoke. Take care that there is not enough fire to set the tobacco in a blaze, or you will kill the plant. Our way with house plants is simply to make a cone or tent with a newspaper, and put it over the plant, light a little tobacco in the bottom of a pipe, and then fill up the pipe with tobacco. Introduce the bowl under the paper covering, and blow through the pipe-stem. Most copious clouds of smoke will fill the paper cover, and in a few minutes every *aphis* can be shaken off. Give the plant a good showering, and it will not mind the treatment.

Hair for Manure.—L. A. Wickey, York County, Pa. Hair may be used in composts which undergo fermentation. It is a very powerful manure, nearly as much so as Peruvian guano, more lasting in its effects if applied in its raw state, but if composted first with anything that will cause its decay—as horse manure, or a muck and lime compost—it will quicken the action of the manure almost as much as an equal quantity of guano. It is valuable for its nitrogen (ammonia), but does not supply phosphoric acid. Two cts. per pound is not dear for it.

Black Birds vs. Robins.—"E. W. T.," Canandaigua, N. Y., writes: "I have watched the progress of public sentiment relating to birds with some interest. While the law punishes the killing of a robin, it gives no protection to the blackbird,—and for years no epithet has seemed sufficiently severe to apply to the brute who would injure the favorite. The blackbird is constantly destroying the enemies of the fruit, and is therefore a valuable friend. I have watched the robin carefully for twenty years, and have never perceived, in a single instance, a worthy act of his in this direction. He will destroy the harmless angle-worm in countless numbers; but if any other worm or insect, I have not been able to detect it. On the other hand, there is not so pestiferous an enemy to the fruit grower, even the curculio, as the robin. First—He takes the strawberries—every one his keen optics can espy. Next he gormandises upon the raspberries, as long as they last. Then the cherries fall a prey. Then the grapes vanish through his insatiable maw; and a large portion of the delicious Bartlett pear falls picked and ruined by this omnivorous pest. A glimmering of better times is seen in the changed tone of our fruit growers' societies."——[This indictment of cock-robin must stand upon its own merits. There is a great difference of opinion about the habits of this bird. There is no doubt about the damage he does among the fruit. It is a question if he does not destroy insects enough to pay for this damage. We want more facts to determine this point, and shall be glad to hear from any of our correspondents who have carefully studied his habits to ascertain his food.—EDS.]

Keeping Eggs.—"Down East" and others. There is always some risk in keeping eggs a long time, and those not absolutely fresh will never sell well. When eggs stand long in one position the yolk gets down against the shell, and if there is any evaporation it soon either adheres to the shell or the air gets to it, and it decays, or becomes tainted a little. Eggs may be greased, and packed in oats in barrels headed up tight, kept cool and dry, and rolled or inverted or both every few days; thus they will keep, and when wanted for market must be rolled in bran or meal to get the grease off, and perhaps dipped in lime water to give them a fresh look. How long they may be kept thus we do not know, but several months at least. Eggs will keep in lime water, but it is difficult to turn or roll the barrels, and so the yolks get against the shell, and besides the shells look very chalky, and their sale is hurt. The best way is probably to pack the fresh eggs in barrels with meal or bran, setting them on end, using no grease, for the meal absorbs it and it turns rancid. Head up the barrels and invert once a week, and keep in a cool dry place.

How to Use Fish Guano.—This article is reckoned among the concentrated fertilizers, and is very rich in ammonia. It is to be used with the same precautions as Peruvian guano. It will destroy seeds, if brought in immediate contact with them. If applied in the hill, it should be mixed with the soil. It may be sown broadcast, and plowed or harrowed in, with safety. If applied as a top-dressing, it should be intimately mixed with ten times its bulk of loam, peat, or muck, and be allowed to remain in bulk ten days or more.

Oil Cake.—"Kentucky." This is the residue left after expressing the oil from Linseed, (Flax seed), and is in the form given it by the cylinder of the press—much like a thin cheese and very hard. When ground, it is called oil meal. It is simply Flax seed less the greater part of the oil.

Record of Horticulture and "Independent" Criticism.—Messrs. Woodward, of the Horticulturist, have put out a neat volume of 125 pages, (price $1.00,) called the Record of Horticulture. The editor is Mr. A. S. Fuller, who gives his notes on horticultural progress, reviews books, and contributes several valuable articles. The book is strongly individual, and, as Mr. Fuller is a known enemy to all shams, many authors and pretenders of various kinds will feel that their toes are trodden upon. Mr. Fuller is a genuine horticultural iconoclast, and we are glad that we have at least one horticulturist, who has the courage to strip off the borrowed plumes from over-rated writers, and overpraised fruits. He may not always be right, but he evidently means to be, and for that we honor him, and always welcome any contribution from his pen, as we are sure that it will be practical and vigorous. One of the most useful portions of this Record is the chapter on the propagation of Bulbs. Mr. Rand's work on Bulbs is singularly deficient in directions to the novice on the subject of propagation, and this Record is an almost indispensable supplement to that work.... The "Independent" of May 2d contains a most remarkable article on this "Record."—We do not call it criticism, out of respect to critics. The Independent has the reputation of being a religious paper. We occasionally read its Farmer's Column—upon the principle that the deacon always read the theater bills, that he might keep posted as to what the devil was doing. After we have read the "Farmer's Column," we are satisfied—just as Mrs. Squeer's boys didn't want any breakfast after their brimstone and molasses—and have no desire to see what the rest of the paper may contain. The Independent's notice of the Record of Horticulture is too long, or we would reproduce it, in order that our readers might see what stuff a "religious" paper can publish, and the number of direct and inferential—what-you-may-call-'ems, that can be put into a column. Half of the article is devoted to showing that this is not a fit book for a farmer, and gives the Independent's views on farmers' books in general. Now, Mr. Fuller did not write this book for farmers, but for horticulturists. If he did write a book for farmers, it would not be of that character that would have to lie over a year, before he could find a publisher so regardless of the good of the community, as to publish it. The Independent says: "Well, what do we find within these pretty covers, costing $1.50 of the farmer's hard earned money?" The price "$1.50" is within one-third of the truth, which is pretty good for the Independent. Farther along in the article we get a clue to "what's the matter." Mr. Fuller, in his Record, gives a justly severe castigation to the "Reviser" of Bridgeman's Gardener's Assistant. The Independent says: "As he has made some false statements in which our integrity is assailed, it is proper to explain the matter in this place." We, for the first time, learn, that that book was revised by the Independent. We supposed it was done by a chap, who took it as a job. Was it done by Mr. Henry C. Bowen, the "responsible man," by Theodore Tilton, or some subordinate? No clue is given in the article—the editorial "our" leaving us quite in the dark. We read: "The publisher of Bridgeman's Gardener brought the wood cuts, ready made, to the reviser, before he commenced his task; a portion of the illustrations were purchased by the publisher of other publishers. The reviser had nothing to do with the illustrations, only to insert them in their proper places." Now, here is a direct statement, which must be either true or false. The publishers, Messrs. William Wood & Co., say, that they know nothing of the source of at least 20 of the illustrations of Bridgeman's Gardener. We believe Messrs. Wood tell the truth, but then the Independent is a "religious" newspaper, and what does it tell? Certain cuts which appear in Bridgeman's book, were originally drawn and engraved for the *Agriculturist*. We never sold, gave away, or loaned them to Messrs. Wood, who knew nothing of them, until they saw them in the book, and these, certainly, were not the illustrations "purchased by the publisher of other publishers." We do not *know* how these cuts transferred themselves from the engraving room of the *Agriculturist* to the pages of Bridgeman's book. The Independent calls it "purchasing;" other people have a different name for it. Mr. Fuller's statements in regard to this book are none too severe, except in the fact that they are true, but this case would show that the way to get abuse from the Independent is to tell the truth. The Independent may be gratified to learn, that the publishers of Bridgeman's Gardener's Assistant, finding that its revision of that originally excellent and useful work has been quite as severely criticised by the horticultural and agricultural press, as it has been by Mr. Fuller, in his Record of Horticulture, have concluded to have the work done over again. The Independent calls Mr. Fuller's book a book of "slanders." We have no name to apply to the paper that can so unfairly treat a valuable contribution to our horticultural literature.—But then what does the Independent know about horticulture.

The State Sheep Fair. — The Third Annual Fair of the State Sheep Breeders' and Wool Growers' Association opened at Auburn, Wednesday, May 8th, but, owing to a fierce north-east storm, little was done until Thursday P. M. There were numerous entries of fine wooled sheep of middle wools, and a few of fine wools. The storm was a severe trial to the faith and patience of the exhibitors, and of the multitudes who were waiting for better weather, to see the flocks. Among the noticeable sheep at the show, were "Kilpatrick," and "Blucher," fine wools, owned by W. R. Sanford, of Vermont, the *former* valued at twelve thousand dollars in gold, and the latter at ten thousand in currency. Mr. Freeman, of Bemis Heights, had a "Dew Drop" glistening in one of the pens. Mr. Lynch, of Monroe County, had a ram of "Frank" manners, with five other South Downs and lambs, very good animals. The ram was two years old, and weighed 200 lbs. J. Bowers, of the same county, showed good, fine wooled sheep. J. D. Wing, of Washington, Dutchess County, showed the best lot of Cotswolds we have ever seen, three yearling rams, and three two year olds, "Ottawa" and "Golden Fleece." These very fine animals were recently imported from England, having been selected by Mr. Wing from the best flocks in the Cotswold district, without regard to cost, with a view to establish a purely bred flock. This breed is said to make grade wethers, that will weigh two hundred lbs., dressed. On Friday, there was a comparatively large attendance of spectators, and many of the finest sheep were sheared, and, on the whole, this fair, though the weather was of the ugliest type, brought together many of the best breeders of the State, and will give a new impulse to this very important branch of industry. We are indebted to Hon. H. S. Randall, the President of the Association, for numerous courtesies, which we are happy to acknowledge here.

National Trial of Plows, Harrows, and Cultivators.—This trial, announced in our last issue, to come off at Utica, May 7th, under the auspices of the New York State Agricultural Society, was necessarily postponed for a few days, on account of the weather. Three days of incessant rain made plowing hopeless. We found the most of the judges present, and a large number of competitors for the prizes, possessing their souls with exemplary patience. There had been thirty entries on the first day of the show, and ample arrangements had been made by the Society to have the implements subjected to the most thorough tests. In the character of the gentlemen, who have consented to act as judges in this important trial, the public have the assurance, that, when a decision is reached, it will be impartial and worthy of confidence. Eleven points are submitted as the tests of a good plow. 1. Pulverizing power. 2. Non-liability to choke in stubble. 3. Lightness of draft, considered in connection with pulverizing power. 4. Ease of holding. 5. Durability. 6. Cheapness. 7. Excellence of mechanical work. 8. Excellence of material. 9. Thorough inversion and burial of weeds. 10. Even distribution of wear. 11. Regularity or trueness of turning and carrying the furrow slice on sod.—To procure all the data, and accurately determine these points, will, necessarily, involve a good deal of time and labor. We look forward to the decision as an important event in the history of agricultural improvement.

Address of J. Stanton Gould on retiring from the Presidency of the New-York State Agricultural Society.—We had the pleasure of listening to the address of the retiring President of the N. Y. State Agricultural Society, and have since read it with renewed satisfaction. It abounds in good common sense and valuable suggestions. The State would be richer by millions, if these hints could be heeded by our farmers.

The Rhode Island Horticultural Society.—This Society will hold its 23d Summer Exhibition at Providence, on June 26th and 27th. The list of premiums is evidently prepared with great care, and the amounts are liberal. The President, Hon. Jas. Y. Smith, offers several liberal premiums, among which are two for children. But few persons outside of Rhode Island know how wide-awake its people are in horticultural matters, and while we remind all Rhode Island readers, and those in the adjacent "suburbs" of Massachusetts and Connecticut, of this exhibition, we take the privilege of one of the "fathers" of the society, to invite horticulturists from elsewhere to visit the exhibition, and be astonished at what little Rhody can do in the way of fruits, etc.

Horticultural Show in Queens Co.—For once, the Queens Co., N. Y., people have allowed us to know that they intend to hold a show, and we take pleasure in making the announcement, as we should have done many times before, had they given us the data. The Agricultural Society will hold a Horticultural show on June 21st, at Mineola, on the L. I. R. R. The Society has remarkably fine grounds, offers a large list of premiums, and several special premiums, by gentlemen interested in horticultural matters, are announced.

Catalogues. — Our acknowledgments of these have been crowded out from month to month, until the list is too long for us to give it room. We could not publish some, and leave out others. We thank those who have sent us these documents, and shall accredit them all in the next year of our Annuals. We may as well say here, that we wish to give in our Annuals the name of every dealer in implements, plants, seeds, and the like. Those who send catalogues or cards will be recorded. Those who do not take pains to make themselves known, must not complain.

American Short-horn Herd-Book.—Hon. Lewis F. Allen, of Black Rock, Erie Co., N. Y., informs us that he is now at work upon the 8th Volume of this publication. He expects to put it to press soon, and will receive pedigrees for insertion during the present month. Every breeder of pure Short-horns should see to it at once, that all his stock worthy of use as breeding animals, have their pedigrees recorded. It adds essentially to their value and to that of their progeny. The seventh volume contained upwards of 3,500 approved pedigrees, and the present volume is likely to exceed its predecessor. Breeders of Short-horns in the United States and British possessions should send to Mr. Allen, for Circular, with terms, etc.

Household Recipes.

Of late we have not given our usual number of recipes, though we have many in type. We present here an instalment of these, to let those who are so kind as to send them know, that their favors are not unappreciated.

Webster Cake.—Take 1 cup butter, ¾ cup molasses, ¾ cup sugar, 3 cups flour, 1 gill sweet milk, 1 teaspoon saleratus, 2 eggs, add currants and citron, and spice, cloves and nutmeg.—*Mrs. L. P. C., New Haven, Mo.*

Silver Cake.—Take the whites of six eggs, two and one-half cups of flour, one and one-half cups of sugar, half cup of butter, two-thirds of a cup of cream or sweet milk, half teaspoonful of cream of tartar, and a little soda.

Corn Cake.—Three cups of corn meal, one cup of wheat, two tablespoonfuls of sugar, two teaspoonfuls of cream of tartar, one teaspoonful of salt. Mix well together; while dry, add one teaspoonful of soda, dissolved in warm water. Mix the whole to a thin batter with milk or water, and bake in a quick oven.

Tapioca Pudding.—Four tablespoonfuls of tapioca, 1 quart milk, 4 eggs (leaving out the whites of two for icing); sweeten to taste and flavor with vanilla. Soak the tapioca over night in a *little* water, boil the milk and pour over the tapioca; when it is lukewarm, add the sugar and eggs, well beaten. Bake about one hour; ice it when cool.—*Mrs. H. H. McL.*

Brown Bread—By Mrs. Evans.—3 small pints of cornmeal, 3 small pints of bran flour, 1 pint of molasses, 1 tea spoonful of salt, 1 tea spoonful of saleratus, 1 quart of milk, pour into a three quart bucket with tight fitting lid, which has been well greased, and set it into a pot of boiling water, and boil four hours.

Ginger Snaps.—One cup of molasses, one of sugar, one of shortening, one egg, one tablespoonful of ginger, one of vinegar, one teaspoonful of saleratus.

Molasses Cookies.—One cup of molasses, half cup of butter, half cup of water, four eggs, one teaspoonful of soda, one of ginger.

Lemon Butter for Tarts.—"A M. R." One pound pulverized white sugar, whites of six eggs and yolks of two, three lemons, including grated rind and juice. Cook twenty minutes over a slow fire, stirring all the while.

Cooking Cauliflower.—"D. W." This is very much improved by being boiled in a large quantity of water. Some add a little grated nutmeg to the drawn butter, and use only cider vinegar.

Pickling Beef and Tongues.—Carolus. Rub the beef hams slightly with fine salt, and let them lay 24 hours then cover with the following cold pickle: For hundred pounds of meat, 6 gallons of soft water, 6 lbs. fine salt, 1½ ounces of saleratus, 3 ounces saltpetre, and 1½ lbs. of sugar. Beef for drying to be left in this brine for 9 days, tongues 5 weeks. This is the Darlington recipe.

Tomato Vinegar.—"C. H. P." No great skill is required to make the article. Express the juice, and put in any clean vessel exposed to the air in a warm place and it will soon become vinegar. It will make a stronger vinegar if molasses is added to the juice

To Preserve Furs.—Wrap them in paper of several thicknesses or in cotton cloth, *early in the spring*, before the moth miller begins to fly. It is only necessary so to secure them that no moth can get access to them. A *tight* box, with paper pasted on where the lid covers it, is equally effective.

To Remove Tea Stains from Table Cloth.—"Nannie." Lay the cloth in an earthen crock, or porcelain kettle, and cover with clean, cold, soft water. Put the kettle on the back of the stove, where it will heat slowly to a scald. After an hour or more lift out your cloth and wash with soap in the usual manner.

Carrot Juice in Butter.—M. Alden. This is sometimes added to butter to give it color, but cows fed on oats and clover hay ought to make butter of good color without it. The juice will not improve the keeping qualities of the butter, unless *fed* to the cows.

Best Kind of Cucumbers for Pickling.—"R. F. O." We have never been able to detect any difference in the favor of cucumbers after they were pickled. They are mainly a sponge to hold vinegar, and the best kind is the most fruitful. The White Spine is good enough, but in the pickle districts they raise their own seed, and improve them by selecting the fruit of the third or fourth blossom from the root. This whole subject was thoroughly discussed by Timothy Bunker, Esq., in vols. for 1865 and 1866, which see.

Farm Fences.

Every man needs some fences upon his farm; a permanent one surrounding his garden, at least, and movable ones, or hurdles, for confining stock, or for forming lanes where animals are to be driven near to tempting crops.

The preservation of the timber in fence making is a great desideratum to all who build fences. We believe no cheaper, or more effectual, way can be pursued than the plan recommended after numerous, carefully conducted experiments by different persons, of painting the slats, and soaking the posts in hot coal tar, and, after allowing all to drip off that will do so in a few minutes, to thoroughly sand the timber, and let

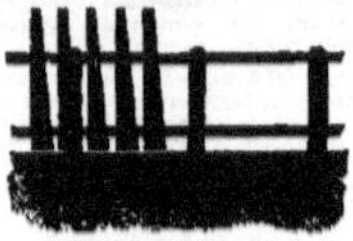

Fig. 1.—PICKET FENCE.

Fig. 2.

it get so dry, before using, that hammering will not jar it off. It is best to have a few slats unpainted, to be used if necessary to saw any, and these might be painted subsequently. The labor of protecting thus both the above-ground and the underground parts of the fence, is so considerable, that only the bottoms of the posts and underground sills of gates are usually thus protected. It is, however, very important that those parts of the posts, slats and pickets, which come in contact, should be coated with coal tar, so that water shall not find in these spots an opportunity to soak and rot the wood.

PICKET FENCE.—G. J. Greene, of Hudson, N. Y., writes: "I like picket fences for these reasons; they do not take much lumber; they make a closer fence, especially at the bottom; they are easier kept in repair; and cattle will not so readily interfere with, or break them down, as other kinds of fence; a steer that thinks nothing of jumping over a rail fence five feet high, can scarcely be driven over a picket fence four feet high. Fig. 1 represents a section of picket fence. I herewith send you a rough sketch of a fence, which, I think, has some good points. As the posts are the foundation of the fence, I have given them more attention than the rest. No good posts should be split; if the timber is large, it should be

Fig. 3.

sawed, 4×5 inches square at the bottom, and 2×4 inches at the top. They are neater, more readily used, and make a better fence. If the timber is six or seven inches in diameter, I would saw them through, as represented in fig. 2, making two good posts, each with a straight side, out of timber which would otherwise have made but one.

Fig. 4.

I set posts thirty-two inches deep; three feet would be better. Half the ills that a fence is heir to, arise from the posts not being set deep enough. Figure 3 represents a post as I would like to set it. Near the bottom, two notches are cut in the opposite sides; after the post is placed in the hole, and the dirt filled in to the notches, two short pieces of board, or stones, are placed in the notches against the posts, and the tops of them are crowded or pounded into the solid earth with a rammer, as shown; the hole is then filled up. The post will not be thrown up by frost, will not readily sag over, and if the part which enters the ground be thoroughly coated with coal tar and sand, as described on page

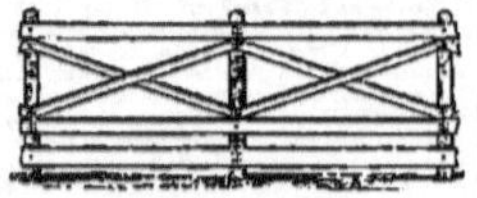

Fig. 5.—BOARD FENCE.

94 of the *American Agriculturist* for 1866, I believe there will be no occasion to replace it during the present century.

Fig. 4 represents a board sawed into pickets. Boards ten inches in width, and twelve feet long will make twelve pickets, three inches wide at the bottom and two inches at the top. The bottom bars may be let into the posts or nailed upon them, and the top bars either nailed upon the tops of the posts, which should be sawed off even, or they may be nailed upon the sides of the posts. A strip half an inch thick, and two inches wide, nailed, as a batten, over the pickets at the top and bottom bars, will prevent their being knocked off, and will add much to the appearance, and but little to the cost."

BOARD FENCE.—A. A. Gauer, Albion, Iowa, sends the description of a fence common there,

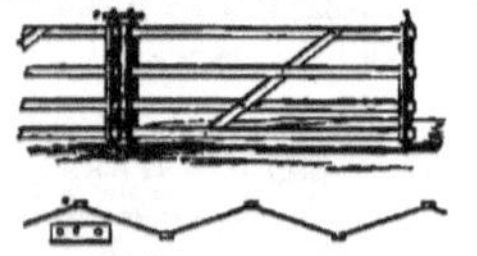

Fig. 6.—PORTABLE FENCE.

and a neat looking one for a fence of such simple construction, (Fig. 5). It is made of boards. The lower rail is six inches wide, the other two horizontal rails, five inches, and the two that cross, three or four inches wide. This is a simple and attractive variation of a plain board fence, and requires but little lumber. Posts 2×4 at the top, and 4×4 at the butts, would be abundantly strong if well set, and protected from rotting by paint or coal tar. Battens over the strips at the posts would add both to the looks and durability.

PORTABLE FENCE OR HURDLE.—Contributed by H. A. Hawkins, Vinden, Ill.—I inclose a sketch of a portable fence, which is a favorite hereabouts. There are two uprights of hard wood to each length, and upon them the horizontal strips, of any light, durable lumber, are nailed, and braced by a diagonal brace strip. The ends of the uprights are rounded so as to enter two-inch, round holes in a cap or yoke. By these caps the lengths are united, and the fence is kept upright and firm by being placed zigzag or worm-fence fashion. [Figure 6 represents what might be a modification of this fence, one and a quarter, or one and a half, inch soft wood boards being used as posts, and the rails morticed and pinned into them. It was made to illustrate the fence described, and the discrepancy was unnoticed at first. However, this idea may be of account to some one.]

FLOUR AT TWENTY DOLLARS A BARREL.—Flour at twenty dollars a barrel argues the need of more wheat growers. Probably no man anticipated, twenty years ago, that California would be shipping wheat to New York, and that grain would form part of the Western freight of boats on the Erie Canal. Yet such are the facts. The land that received so largely of our products during the early days of the gold fever is now returning them in kind, and the good people of interior New York are eating bread made of California flour! All bread stuffs are unusually high, and yet we have untold millions of acres in the sea-board States, that are lying idle, or, at least, producing a scanty crop of grass, for want of willing hands to till them. And if we look at the West, whole townships and counties are waiting for the coming settlers, to turn up the virgin soil, and put in the seed. Why should not the multitudes at the East, struggling for a bare living, take possession of these acres, erect their cottages, and live independently upon the prairies? They would soon support their families in comfort, and keep wheat, henceforth, at living prices.

A Remedy for Strikes.

These endeavors of mechanics to force capitalists to pay them higher wages are becoming very common in our cities and villages. These efforts are about as rational as to force the sun to give more heat,—the clouds to give more rain. The rain generally falls because it cannot help it, and wages come down for the same reason. If there is great competition in the manufacturer's business, he is forced to sell his products at a less price, he makes less profits and must reduce the price of labor or stop his business. As a rule, capital gives what it can afford for labor. If there is great demand for woolen goods, there is great demand for hands to make them, and the manufacturer will give wages enough to induce hands to work. Multitudes rush into the business and it is soon overdone. Wages are reduced by manufacturers, and the operatives strike to resist the fall, or to secure higher wages. This is the cause generally of strikes in all the trades. They are greatly over-done. Too many people are crowding into them for a livelihood, under the mistaken idea that it is easier and more respectable to live in a city or village, than to live in the country and till the soil. Almost all business pursuits in the city suffer from this cause.

Political economists will differ somewhat about the remedy for these strikes. Near all agree that their tendency is evil, inflicting upon the mechanic great loss of time, and prejudicing the employer against his hands, by attempting to force him to give wages that his business will not justify. Some advise mechanics to associated effort, and thus become their own employers. But this is no remedy in a business that is already overdone. In some kinds of business it may be a help. But the real difficulty that underlies these strikes is the over-stocking of all mechanical pursuits. The farm is deserted for the work-shop, and the artisan suffers. Rents are made high by the multitudes that crowd into the city to compete for dwellings, and food is made dear by the desertion of the farm. The remedy is found in a return to the tilling of the soil, where rents and food are cheap, and labor is well rewarded. There is no danger that this business will ever be over-crowded. We could spare thousands of our working population with mutual advantage to the city and the country. There are some who will always cling to cities, no matter in what poverty they may live, but many others would be glad of a rural life, could they only find means of transportation.

The Black Snake.—(*Bascanion constrictor.*)

The Black Snake is the largest of our common snakes, though there are stories of other species occasionally equalling its largest size, and from its active habits and fondness for cultivated land, it is well known to farmers and farmers' boys. It is perfectly harmless, yet has such a threatening way of resenting an attack, and so often turns and gives chase to a fleeing enemy, that it is regarded not only as an enemy, but often with a sort of terror. It will never stand to fight, but gets away marvelously quick after the first blow is dealt, unless it be effectually detained. This snake is 4 to 6 feet long, the tail being about one-fifth. The head is small, the teeth numerous, and all about of a size. It has no fangs and no venom. The scales of the back are diamond shaped. Its color is bluish black above, light slate color beneath; chin and throat white. The young are speckled, black and white above. The snake lives upon toads, frogs, lizards, small birds, and eggs of birds,—for which it climbs trees of considerable hight,—mice and their young, as also the young of larger quadrupeds when it can get them. It does little harm in the hay and grain fields, for if cut open, its belly will be often found to contain several mice. Still it probably does not discriminate well between shrews and mice, and the former are voracious insect eaters. It destroys also many toads which are among our best friends, and it would be hard to tell how many birds, including young and eggs, a single black snake annually destroys. On the whole, then, it is an enemy, and though innocent of ability to harm man, it is hardly worth while to attempt to conquer our repugnance to "the form of the serpent," and save the lives of these animals when we can, on account of any good they may do us.

BLACK SNAKE.—(*Bascanion constrictor.*) MILK OR CHICKEN SNAKE.—(*Ophibolus eximius.*)

The Milk Snake or Chicken Snake.—This beautiful serpent (*Ophibolus eximius*) is the familiar representative of its genus throughout the northern and middle States, extending into Ohio and probably further westward. The back is thick; head and tail short, and eyes small. It is of a greyish ash color, "with a dorsal series of upwards of fifty transverse, elliptical, chocolate blotches, and with two other alternating series on each side." The length is from two feet to three and a half. It is very familiar in its habits, being frequently found about the foundations of barns and cow stables, spring houses, etc. Its food is such small birds and animals as it can overpower, and it is said to be very fond of milk. The idea that it will milk a cow is as absurd as the one, so universal in Europe, that a bird much resembling our Whip-poor-will sucks goats. The Milk-Snake is entirely harmless, but shares with its kindred the aversion with which these graceful and beautiful creatures are almost universally regarded.

The Garden Toad—and Tree Frogs.

The Batrachians are cold-blooded reptiles, destitute of scales; their young are usually hatched in an immature condition from eggs laid in the water, and undergo several changes before becoming perfected animals. To this class belong Toads, Frogs, Tree-toads, etc., which fall under the subdivision of tailless batrachians. We present a representation of the common Garden Toad, (*Bufo Americanus*), of the Green Tree-frog of the South, (*Hyla viridis*,) and of the Squirrel Tree-toad, (*Hyla squirrella*,) also of the South, but found occasionally in the Middle States. There is something about toads, even tree-toads, which excites disgust, and they have been almost universally despised and persecuted. The fact is, they are among the most faithful friends of the gardener and orchardist. Living upon insects, they do much towards reducing the number of those that attack cultivated plants, and should be carefully preserved in gardens, and shielded from harm. The common toad is covered with warts from which, and especially from two large glands behind the head on each side, an acrid fluid exudes, which, while it causes smarting to tender skin, and makes a dog drop the toad and often froth at the mouth, and appear in great distress, is really harmless, neither producing warts nor other evil. If the toad has a jewel in its head, as it was once believed to have, that jewel is its tongue, for by it, darting it out to a considerable distance, it draws the unsuspecting flies and beetles into its mouth. This motion of the tongue is so rapid that it can scarcely be followed by the eye. Toads lay their eggs in the spring, in shallow pools, and while thus engaged, their note—a prolonged trill—may be heard both day and night. The eggs are enclosed in jelly, which holds them in clusters, and protects them from fish, and the young, when hatched, are the little dark-colored tadpoles or polli-

GREEN TREE FROG. SQUIRREL TREE-TOAD. GARDEN TOAD.

wogs with which we are all so familiar. These, as we all know, have, at first, tails, but no legs, then hind-legs, then fore-legs, then the tail is absorbed, and the little toads come up from the water, often in great numbers. Tree-toads and frogs undergo the same transformations. The common northern tree-toad, (*Hyla versicolor*,) lives chiefly in open woods upon decayed mossy trees, the color of which it closely resembles. The ends of its toes are flattened into roundish disks, with which, partly by means of the pressure of the air, but chiefly by a sticky secretion, it is able to walk upon the under sides of smooth substances. All these animals are not properly amphibious, but live in comfort only in a moist atmosphere, resorting to the water only at breeding time. On moist days and evenings they are most active, and the tree-toads are especially noisy when a rain storm is approaching.

Walks and Talks on the Farm.—No. 42.

In making out my income tax, the Assessor demurred to the large sum I had expended for labor. He is himself a farmer and "could not understand," he said, "how so much money could be spent."

"I have not spent quite $8 an acre, and if I could have afforded it, and could have got the right kind of men, and could have bestowed the necessary supervision, I would have spent double the amount."

"Well," he replied, "I can't allow it. I never heard of such a case. Mr. Black sold $3,000 from his farm last year, and only deducts $300 for hired help."

"How large a farm has he?"

"One hundred acres."

"His own labor and that of his children would be worth at least $500 in addition to the $300; and this brings it up to my figures, or $8 an acre. This farm is probably the most favorable one for your purpose that you can select. The small farmers, taking their own time into account, really employ more labor than the large farmers—and this is one reason why their farms are more productive. I confess, however, that I am unable to see how a man can, on a farm of 100 acres, get such large returns, and expend only $300 for hired help."

"He has a splendid wheat farm. Not an acre of it that is not naturally underdrained. He grows large crops of clover and plows them in for wheat, and this is better than guano or phosphates. You can spend all the money you like on your farm, and never make it as good as his."

"That may be, but I think I have a legal right to spend it, and if I *do* spend it, I do not see why you should not allow it. Everybody can not have the best farms. Some of us must take the poor ones, or let them remain untilled and unproductive. And the man who takes a run down farm, and endeavors to bring it up, injures no one but himself; and it is hardly fair to tax him for every little improvement that he makes, or subject him to ridicule and abuse."

In my case they do both. If I set out a few evergreens and ornamental shrubs around the house, and raise grass and a few flowers under the dining-room window, instead of potatoes and cabbage, they call it fancy farming and a great waste of land, and yet at the same time put an additional thousand dollars tax on the farm.

It would seem as though the farmers themselves, the local Assessors, Railroad Companies, and the Government itself, were all opposed to improved agriculture. Last year I ordered a ton of raw-bone phosphate from Philadelphia, and the Erie Railroad Company charged me $22 for freight! I do not know, but I presume they would have carried a ton of whiskey or tobacco for half the money. Of all improvements most needed in American agriculture, underdraining confessedly stands at the head, and yet it is this very improvement that the Government specially singles out as one which cannot be deducted from the Income tax. According to John Johnston's experience, he sometimes got the whole of his money back in one year, and always in two, and it would certainly be wise in the Government to encourage the practice of underdraining, by allowing money so expended to be deducted in making the returns of income. If a farmer spends $1000 in underdraining, and the *profits*, as Mr. Johnston states, are $500 a year, the Government in ten years would get $250 in additional tax. If put into Five-Twenties, the Government would get $50 the first year and *that would be all*.

One would think that when wheat brings $3.25 a bushel, people would begin to realize the importance of fostering agricultural improvement, and stimulating production. In England, manures are allowed to be transported free of toll, and many of the landlords pay for all the tiles that their tenants will lay in underdrains. And even in Canada, agricultural papers are allowed to go through the mails free of postage.

But a truce to fault-finding. The man who has once commenced to underdrain, will stick to it, tax or no tax. I have been laying some *brush drains* this spring, in low, mucky land, where I thought tiles would fill up. Mr. Messenger, of Long Island, who drained a twenty-acre swamp ten years ago with brush drains, informs me that the drains still work to perfection; and a correspondent of the Irish Farmers' Gazette says he has some brush drains still effective on his farm that were laid forty three years ago. The way to lay them is to secure the outlet with stones, or in other words, to lay a foot or two of the drain with stones, where it discharges into the main ditch. Lay the brush on the stones with the but ends extended up the drain. Keep on in this way, extending the brush two or three inches each time, so that the thick stems will be on the bottom of the drain, and the bushy branches will rest on the top of the others. Trample them in firm until they are lower than the plow reaches, and then cover them with soil.

Ditching on low, mucky land, is very pleasant work. There are, as the men expressed it, "not stones enough to clean the spades," and it is easy work to dig a rod in an hour, 2½ feet deep. One man dug seven rods in an afternoon, and finished it all ready for the brush. In my case, I am troubled to get a good fall, and I make it a rule to have the drains cut so that the water will follow the ditches up into the land to be drained. Where brush is used, there may be two or three inches of water in the bottom of the drains, without damage. Being cut deeper than is necessary, any loose soil that may work through the brush can settle on the bottom, and still leave fall for the water. In the spring and fall I expect the water will set back occasionally in the open ditches higher than the drains are laid, but as it passes off, I think the drains will work again. In fact, there are cases where underdrains laid three feet deep discharge into a water course dammed up, so that the water is two feet above the tiles, and yet the land is effectively drained. Of course, in this case the "water-line" would be only a foot below the surface, but the water for two feet below that, until it reached the tiles, would be constantly changing, and this is said to be just as good as if all the water was removed. It is *stagnant* water that is injurious. In a dry season, when the surface soil absorbed the water from below, the water from the main ditch would flow up the tiles into the land, and in rainy weather, when the "water-line" in the land became higher than the water in the ditch, the tiles would discharge. In either case, stagnation would be avoided. Of course, it is absolutely necessary that the main ditch should be kept clean, down to the tiles. If stopped up with dirt, they will be useless. There are thousands of acres of such land, now producing nothing but rushes and coarse grass, which, if they could be drained in this way, would make the most productive meadows. And it will pay. Take my own case. There is a stream running through the south part of the farm, which, at high water, is fifteen or twenty feet wide, and four or five feet deep. In the summer season it is not over a foot deep. Now, even supposing the land to be not over a foot higher than the surface of the brook at high water, there is still a chance for drainage. Mark out the ditches in the spring or fall during high water, when you can see the lowest land, and the next summer cut a main ditch through the land, nearly or quite as deep as the natural stream. Cut it, in fact, so that the water will follow you, unless you find, as you probably will, that you have more fall than is needed. Let this ditch be six feet wide at the top, and two feet or so at the bottom. Sow grass seed at once, on the sides, to prevent the soil from washing in. Then cut your brush drains at right angles to this main ditch, 2½ feet to 3 feet deep, through the lowest parts of the land, and I feel confident that the water will find its way into the brook, and the land, from being little else than a swamp, will become the most productive meadow on the farm. It may be necessary, and probably will be, to scour out the main ditch every summer, so as to keep it free down to the drains, but the expense will be little compared to the advantages. The water will set back when we have a flood, as it does now, but instead of remaining on the land until the middle of summer, it will pass off rapidly, as the water in the brook declines, and even in the meantime there will be a constant change of water in the soil, and thus we shall get rid of the injurious effects of stagnation, and the exclusion of atmospheric air.

The expense of draining forty or fifty acres of such land is little, as compared with the expense of draining the like extent of rolling upland, the knolls of which, in this section, are usually full of large stones. And then, what a grand chance there is to irrigate! Much of this low land can be irrigated at a very trifling cost. And those who have never witnessed its effects, will be astonished at the immense crops of grass that can be produced by irrigation. But of course, you must drain before you can irrigate. In other words, you must get rid of stagnant water. You can not well have too much water early in the spring, provided it is constantly moving over the land. Irrigating may be done in a very simple manner. Dam up the water in the brook until it will overflow the banks. This will show you the level. Then cut a shallow ditch into the land, as high up as the water will follow you and overflow, if dammed up. It should, however, be deep enough to convey the water to a more distant part of the land, and sub-conduits should be cut to distribute the water on all parts of the field that are low enough. A little experience will soon enable any one to do this in a simple manner. The water itself is the best teacher. *Only commence*, and you will soon have a system of ditches that will distribute the water all over the land.

"Floating up," as it is called, was practiced in England many years ago with considerable advantage, but it was found that irrigation produced much better results, and the former practice has been pretty much abandoned. "Floating up" is simply damming up a stream till the water overflows on the land. The water is allowed to remain on the field only four or five days, as a longer period makes the grass coarse. The weir is then raised, and the water allowed to flow off. There are places where this practice can be adopted with advantage, but irrigation is much better. What is meant by irrigation is conveying the water in a main ditch along the highest portion of the meadow, and then distributing it in small gutters on the land below, in such a way that the water will run all over the grass, half an inch or so deep, being careful that it never settles in pools or becomes stagnant. The more rapidly the water passes off, provided it does not wash away the soil, the better. Of course there are a great many little details to be attended to, but when the general principles are understood, the details of the system will easily be carried out by any intelligent farmer.

Mr. Howard, in his lecture on Things in America, says: "The grass of America has nowhere the splendid, rich green of our English pastures. Whether this arises wholly from the climate, I have some doubt. I think want of care in preparing the land, selection of seed and subsequent stocking have something to do with the miserable condition and appearance of American pastures." I think he is right. If we took as much pains with our meadows, as they do in England, we should raise as large crops. I am astonished at the effect a little top-dressing has on meadows. Even a little soil alone, spread on the grass, will impart a rich, green color. I suppose it acts as a mulch. Our clover is frequently *better* than it is in England, and our permanent meadows are brown because they are permanently neglected.

The main difficulty in all our agricultural improvements is the high price of labor. And yet, compared with the cost of living, the men do not get exorbitant wages. The trouble is, that we do not provide steady employment. We hire extra help by the day, and pay high wages. But the men are out of employ one third of the time, and it consequently follows, that a man who gets $1.50 a day and loses one third of his time, receives no more in a week than the man who has steady employment at $1.00 a day. One works four days at $1.50 for each day, and the other six days at $1.00 per day.

This spring, work was rather slack, and I employed several men at $1.00 a day. As they board themselves, I thought this cheap, and made a point to furnish them steady work. Last Saturday night they told me that they could work no longer at this price, that every one else was paying $1.25. I agreed to pay it. On Monday it commenced to rain, and at noon they asked me what they should do. I told them they could keep on spreading manure. "But it rains too hard." "I am sorry for it," I replied, "but I cannot help it; I have no in-door work I can afford to do at $1.25 a day." The consequence was, they had to go home. They lost another day during the week. And the result is that to-night, (Saturday, April 27.), instead of paying them $6.00, I only paid them $5.31. They got less money, and I lose a day and three quarters work. I had plenty to do, and this loss of time is an injury to me, and no advantage to them. There is so much work to be done in this country, and so few, comparatively, to do it, that we can, as a community, ill afford to waste time. But as long as farmers continue to pay such high rates for occasional day-work, the men dislike to engage by the month at fair wages. I am satisfied that this is one of the greatest evils of our present American system of farming.

I have lost another horse. He was old and not very valuable, and had he seen fit to have departed last fall, I should not have regretted it so very much. But having given him plenty of hay and grain all winter, and not demanded much labor in return, it is very unkind in him to give me the slip just as the busy season is coming on. Yesterday he was plowing in a three horse team, and was apparently well when he came home. The man watered him before putting him in the stall, (a bad practice), and in half an hour he was taken with violent pains, and only lived till 3 o'clock in the morning. I am having him skinned and opened, to see if we can ascertain what was the trouble. I acted on the supposition that it was a severe attack of spasmodic colic, and gave him injections of warm water and soap, with a dose of laudanum and ether, two table-spoonfuls each, in a pint of water. I repeated every two hours, with an ounce of ether in the interim. I find this almost invariably a cure for colic. It seemed to relieve "Old Dick," but did not cure him.

Abortion in Cows.

In inquiring into the causes of this scourge, for such it really is, in some sections of the country, it is very important to take note of such considerations as are presented herewith by our correspondent, as well as to consider that there is such strong nervous sympathy among cows, (though, perhaps, it is a peculiar influence, due to odor or something of that kind), that when one cow in a herd "slinks" her calf, one or two others are very apt to do the same. This subject is attracting the attention of distinguished physiologists, and of our State Agricultural Societies and Boards of Agriculture, so that we hope some light may be thrown upon the hidden cause, or causes, of so much trouble. We would be very glad of facts which will help to a better knowledge. "M. A. C.," in the article which follows, though "only a woman," as she says, writes forcible common sense in a way to surprise those, if any there be, who hold woman in as light esteem as some of them seem to hold themselves.

"I see you say that Abortion in cows, and Hog-cholera are on the increase. I am 'only a *woman*,' and as a matter of course, women are not entitled to much consideration, but I have been living on a farm from childhood, and have seen more or less of the diseases common to the cow family. My father farmed for thirty years, and kept from eight to twenty cows. All that time, he superintended his affairs himself, and but two cows and one steer died in all those years. One cow and a steer died from the effects of eating too much clover. In the last twenty years, since I have been large enough to know anything about a cow, we have had but two cows slink their calves, and these catastrophes were both caused by the unruly horn of a malicious cow belonging to the herd; they were both young cows, and neither of them were ever unfortunate again, although retained until they were old cows, and I think if those gentlemen who have so much trouble with their cows, will keep a sharp look out, they will find, as I have, that a heavy boot or brogan on the foot of some ill-tempered hireling, or the horn of some unruly member of the herd 'planted' in the *side* of their cows, is the cause of a great amount of the disappointments and trouble they experience. Of course I would not say that such is the cause in all cases, but it is in a great many. One of my neighbors was all the time complaining of his cows in the same way, and could not imagine what was the matter. I happened to pass his stable one day, and saw a German he had hired, kick a cow unmercifully, for no reason but that she was afraid him, and when he came into the stable she jumped around and set her foot on his toes. As a matter of course that was not the first kicking she had received. All the cows in the stable were in a continuous uproar, when this man was about. I thought I had found the secret of at least one stable besides my own."

New Manner of Dissolving Bones for Farming Purposes.

We have received the following translation of an article by Prof. Ilienkoff, Moscow, Russia, from a friend in Washington. The process is not altogether new, but as the success of such operations depends often upon minute details, we are glad to publish it. Prof. I. says: "It was a matter of importance with me to discover a method by means of which every farmer might be enabled to prepare bones for his meadows and fields. As great masses of salts are accumulating in the ashes of every household, and most of them with those burning wood, I used alkalies in connection with unslaked lime, which soon dissolved the bones. To my friend and pupil, Mr. Alex. Engelhart, to whom I communicated my discovery, belongs the honor of having introduced a new and convenient process for gaining manure for agricultural use. I give it in an extract:

'Suppose you have 4,000 pounds of bones, you need 4,000 *pounds of ashes*, (averaging 10 per cent. of carbonate of potash), 600 pounds of unslaked lime, and some 4,500 lbs. (55½ gallons) of water. Dig a hole some two feet deep, large enough to receive the bones and one half their volume besides; parallel to this, you dig another one, 25 per cent. larger, both being filled with bones. First, slake the lime and mix with your ashes, covering 2,000 pounds of the bones in the smaller one. Then it is filled with water, and left. When it gets dry, add, continually, water enough to keep it wet. When the bones crumble in your fingers, then take the whole mass out, and spread it over those bones in the second hole, leaving the decomposition to go on. When this is done, let the mass dry; and to make it fit for use, add *peat powder or mellow garden soil* until it is well dried and powdery. Let it be shoveled over several times, and then apply to your fields.

'Thus you get a fertilizer averaging 13 per cent. of phosphate of lime; 2 per cent. of alkalies, and 6 per cent. of nitrogen.'"

[The pits used in this process must of course be dug in soil, to a great degree impervious to water. Clayey soil will answer, if first sprinkled and then pounded, or clay may be "puddled" in a basin in any soil, and a water-tight pit be made. If the bones are tolerably fresh, there will be very little loss of ammonia. We have known the softening of the bones to be complete on a small scale.—Ed.]

Fig. 1. ELEVATION OF BARN.

Good Farm Barn.

The accompanying plan of a barn is presented in compliance with the often expressed wishes of readers of the *Agriculturist*, that we would give less elaborate and expensive plans than some which have been presented heretofore. Here is one for a barn 40 × 55 feet, with a large shed for cattle attached. It is, on the whole, a good plan, but not nearly so philosophical and labor-saving as the one in the Agricultural Annual, neither is it so expensive. This plan, like that, is susceptible of modification to accommodate a smaller farm, or a smaller number of animals, as we will explain. First is the 13-foot barn floor—of good medium width—if wider, the room would not be wasted. On the left are the horse stalls, 3 feet wide. There might be five stalls 4 feet wide, but for a large horse, the width ought to be about 5 feet. The whole space given to horses is 15 × 20 feet. Then the floor widens 7 feet, and the rest of the left side is devoted to cattle stalls—25 feet, giving room for six cow and ox stalls, and two passage ways, one of which may be closed and made a stall for a cow. The 7-foot space affords abundant room for hay-cutter, feed-box and accompaniments, located close to both cattle and horses, and if cattle are fed in the shed on feed prepared in the feed box, a passage at the rear conducts conveniently to their mangers. A three-foot square trunk extends from over the 7 × 25-foot space in front of the cow stalls to the roof, securing abundant ventilation, and affording a shute, through which hay, or straw, may be readily dropped from the mow, or corn cobs, and other matters, from the granary.

The right side of the barn floor is occupied by a hay bay. There is a tight ceiling of matched boards over the stables, at a hight of 8 feet. The posts are 16 feet to the eaves. The roof is what is usually called half-pitch, more lasting than if flatter. A substantial, tight floor is laid upon the straining beams of the roof. This may be extended, if desired, through the entire length of the barn, or only from one end to over the barn floor. In it is a large trap door directly over the threshing floor; and a small gable with a door in it, over the great doors, affords communication with the front of the barn, so that grain in bags or barrels may be raised or lowered as well here as through the trap door. This floor is the granary or corn loft—easily made rat-proof, close under the roof, and consequently very hot in sunshiny, autumn weather. Corn in the ear is easily hoisted by horse-power from the wagons; and, if spread on the floor not more than a foot thick, will cure much sooner and more perfectly than if in cribs. This grain floor is reached by a stairway from the floor over the stables; under the stairs is a shute or shutes for conducting the shelled corn, etc., to the feeding floor. This arrangement requires strong posts and roof-framing, but not stronger than for a slate roof of a less pitch—and such a roof will support double the weight likely to be placed on such a floor—for not only is it constructed to bear the weight of the slates, but of 2 feet of snow, and the force of high winds in addition. The weight of grain will only give increased steadiness, a large part being borne by the posts — the floor preventing all racking. The shed is 30 × 40 feet, with 12-foot front, and 8-foot rear posts; open in front, and having windows in the back. At the rear, a passage way 4 feet wide communicates with the cow stable in the barn, and forms the feeding alley to the loose boxes and stalls in the shed. Cattle will not suffer in such a shed, left entirely open, in the severest winter weather, but it is best to close the front by boarding, and doors, having large windows for light and air. The hog pens are placed contiguous to the barn-yard, so that the swine may be allowed the free range of the compost heaps, at least in their own corner. In the hog house is a steam boiler, and a pipe, boxed and packed in sawdust, and laid underground, crosses the yard to the feeding floor, for steaming and cooking the fodder for the cattle. By this arrangement the hogs are located at a considerable distance from the granary and root cellar, but this is not a serious inconvenience, and it is best to remove any source of danger from fire as far away as possible.

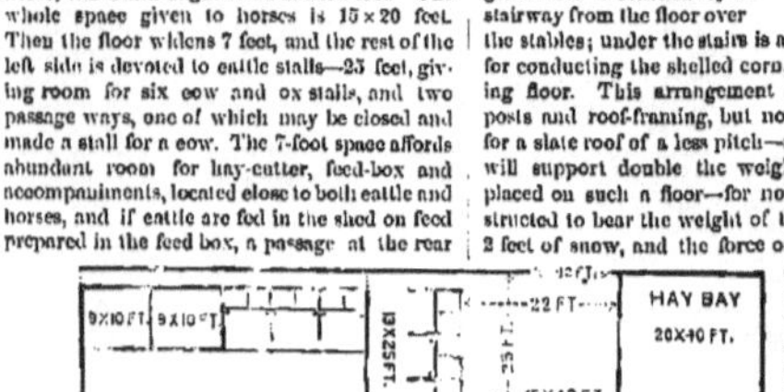

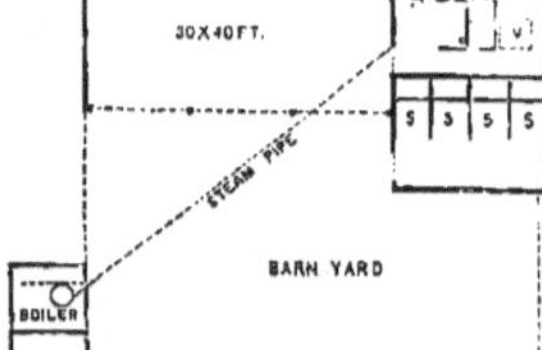

Fig. 2.—PLAN OF BARN.

The root cellar is 7 feet deep under the hay bay, on the right side of the barn. There are two shutes from the floor to the cellar, and there is a stairway as indicated. Besides, access is had by a cellar-way on the eastern side.

We think this plan will please many of our readers. It may be easily reduced, making it, say 30 × 42 feet. The floor, 13 feet; bay, 15 feet; 4 horse stalls, 18 feet, and 4 cow stalls, 12 feet, in a line across the left side; the floor being 15 feet wide in front of the cow stable, and other contractions made on the same principle.

The manure will be, of necessity, only in part under cover. The sheep barn and yard will be on the east side, accessible to the root cellar. It is not represented in the plan given.

Decker's Plow Clevis.

Mr. J. W. Decker, of Orange Co., N. Y., invented, sometime since, the simple contrivance which we figure, for the purpose of regulating at will, and without stopping, the depth of the furrow in plowing. His success, as he reports to us, was complete, so much so that the clevis was soon adopted by his neighbors. A plow with this attachment was exhibited a few years since at the Orange County Fair, where it attracted considerable attention, and elicited general commendation. Mr. Decker thinks, though he does not wish to take out a patent for his invention, that it is worthy of being more widely known and generally used. He allows us, therefore, to illustrate it, and present it to the readers of the *American Agriculturist*. See figure 1.

Fig. 1.—PLOW WITH CLEVIS ATTACHED.

The construction of the Clevis may be seen from fig. 2. The draft-rod is a piece of wrought

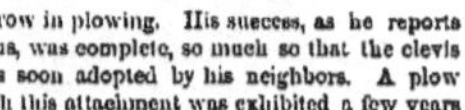

Fig. 2.—CLEVIS.

iron, similar to a common clevis, but much longer, with three notches for the ring, and fastened well back on the beam, by a bolt passing horizontally through it. This is set for the deepest plowing when against the bottom of the beam, and it is depressed for lighter work by drawing upon a light chain attached to a lever which moves two cast iron cams. There are thin plates of iron of a form indicated by drawing a circle touching the sides of a square, and cutting off three corners of the square to the line of the circle. These plates have square holes near the angle, and fit upon a bolt having a cylindrical body with square ends, to which they, together with the forked lever, are fastened tightly by means of a nut.

INDIAN CORN IN DRILLS.—Is the practice of growing this crop in hills sustained by good reason? Flat culture is much the best practice, even when rows both ways are retained. The advantage of cultivating in two directions no longer remains, when the plow is exchanged for a cultivator that will run astride the row, and disturb the soil so near to the corn, that there is no use for the hoe after the first weeding. On the contrary, it is a waste of labor. Planting in drills, secures a more even distribution of the crop upon the ground, so that each plant has its fair share of the soil and sunlight. The growth is more symmetrical, more ears set, and they are more perfectly filled. Carefully conducted experiments claim a difference of more than twenty-five per cent. in favor of drill planting. If there is this difference, we can hardly afford to continue the usual practice.

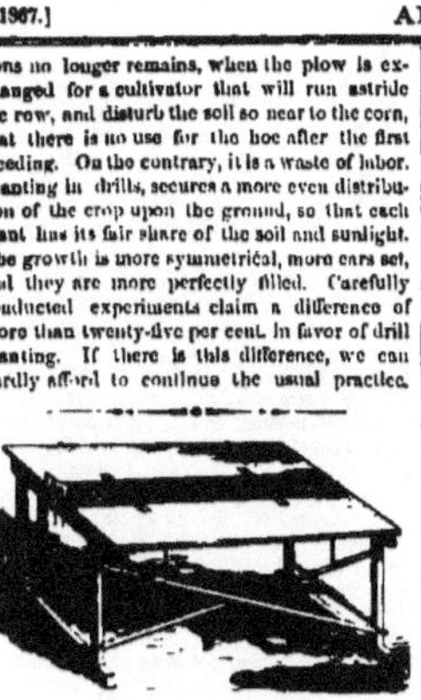

FLEECE FOLDING TABLE.

Folding Fleeces.

Wool is a bulky article, and it is essential to fold and compress it into small compass to get it to market. The usual practice of rolling and tying is strongly objected to by the manufacturer, but it is difficult to find another convenient way. Fleeces may be rolled, and not tied, and thus packed in bags, but this method interferes with inspection by buyers and their agents. Farmers are now hardly prepared to follow the advice of one of our largest wool buyers—though we doubt not it is sound—viz.: to remove the flank wool and all the coarser parts, and then, to roll carefully the fleeces and pack in bags, placing all the tags and flanks in the mouths, to mark the bags with their own names, and sell either to traveling buyers, or, as many do now, put the wool in the hands of good commission houses. In this way, the annoyance of strings would be avoided, and the name and reputation of the flock would go with the wool to the manufacturer, who would be very likely to order the clips of such-and-such farmers, year after year.

An Ohio subscriber sends us a plan of a neat folding table used in Erie Co., which we publish with his drawing, which makes it clear.

FLEECE-FOLDING TABLE, by "*Western Reserve.*"—A good machine for folding and tying up fleeces of wool is a capital thing; it saves much time, and the work is done so much easier and better than it can be without one, that it will pay for itself in a very short time.

The Table I describe is much used in this vicinity, and is considered the *very best* of all like contrivances. Any person, handy with tools, can make one in a short time. Take three boards, plump one inch thick, and four feet long, one eight, the other two fourteen inches wide; fasten them together with table-butts, put on the same as on a common table—the 8-inch one being in the middle, as seen in the drawing. Then take a block eight inches long, six wide, and five thick, bevel off one edge until two sides are nearly obliterated, and hollow this bevel so that the block will be of the form shown, one and one-quarter inches at one edge, but somewhat triangular. Then cut three small notches in one edge, two inches apart, and half an inch deep. Fasten this block on one end of the eight-inch board, the hollow side in, with heavy screws. Now, get a heavy piece of harness leather eight inches wide, and three feet long. Sew, in one end, with a waxed-end, a half-inch iron rod, with an eye bent in the middle and three links attached; cut three long slits in the leather, corresponding to the notches in the block, two inches apart, to within six inches of each end; and now fasten the other end to the 8-inch board, close up to the block, and bore three holes through the board one foot from the block, and directly under the slits in the leather. Fasten the table to a frame made of 3×3 scantling, just high enough so that one can stand up to it and work conveniently and comfortably.

To use it, draw the ends of the twine up through the holes in the bed piece, through the slits in the strap, and up over the block, letting the ends hang down about six inches; lay the fleece inside down, shoulders towards the block; crowd the wool close together; fold in the sides until it is about the width of the strap. Then raise the leaves, hook them together, and taking hold of the end of the strap, bring it over the wool to the front end. Fasten the chain to the hook on the lever, and with your foot upon it, fetch it down snug, and fasten it. Tie the twine over the fleece; unhook the leaves and let them down; then loosen the lever, unhook the strap, and throw it back on the table, take hold of the fleece, draw it over to the front, so that the twine will lie in the notches of the block, cut loose, and you are ready to fold another fleece in one half of the time it takes to tell how. If pains is taken to roll in the ends and sides well, the fleece, after it is tied, will be as round and white as a snowball.

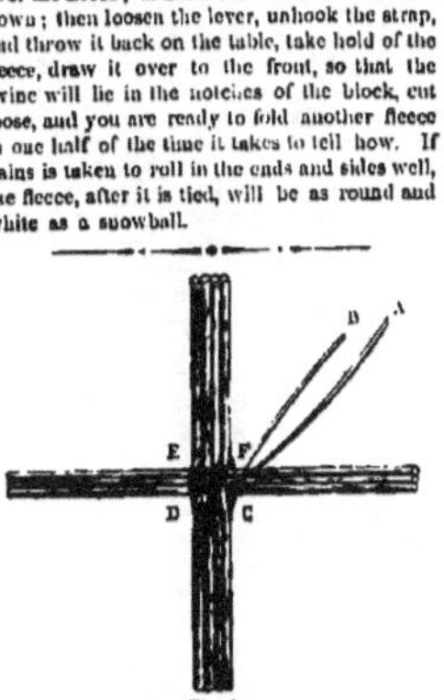

Fig. 1.

Basket Making.

"A Subscriber," of Peoria Co., Ill., writes us a letter in German, describing his method of making a *Half-Bushel Basket*. It is, in most points, clear, and as our former article on basket making set so many people thinking, and weaving willows, we publish this to give them some new ideas on the same subject. The willow rods are worked either peeled, or with the bark on, and soaked so as to be thoroughly flexible. Our correspondent writes:

"We begin by taking seven pieces of willow, $^3/_8$ to $^1/_2$ inch thick, and 14 inches long. Four of these are split in the center, and the three are passed through the middle, as shown in figure 1. Then we put in by their tips, two willows (*A* above, and *B* below,) as shown. *A* is drawn down at the angle *F*, turned under *E*, brought up at *C*. *B* is bent up at *F*; down at *C*; passed under the four rods; bent up at *D*, and so carried around twice. Then we spread the seven rods apart, as in fig. 2, and weave the willows between them. When *B*, in fig. 1, becomes too short to weave further, we bend the but down and put in another willow beside it, and continue with this until *A* becomes too short, then supply it by another in the same way, and continue. The willows are held by the left hand, while the right does the weaving. The willows used for the center of the bottom need not be so thick as those towards the outside, and in weaving, all are laid in by the tips, and the buts

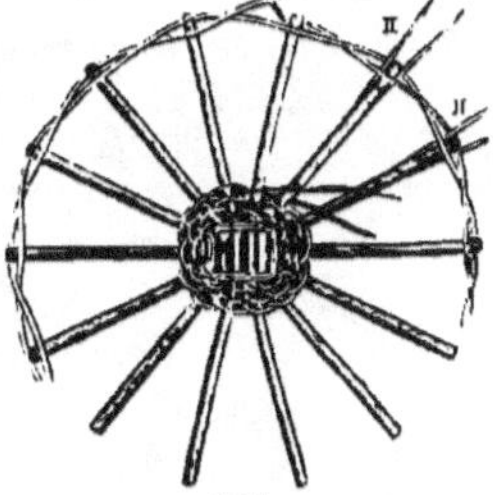

Fig. 2.

are left sticking down (outside). When we have woven a few inches, we place the bottom on the knee and press the center upward, to take the form shown in fig. 3. We then weave on, using four willows instead of two. At the last round on the bottom, the willow is cut off, bent, and stuck in horizontally, as shown at *G*, fig. 2, and all the ends cut off. This finishes the bottom of the basket.

We now take 28 willows, (*H*, fig. 2), sharpen the buts, and stick them in, one on each side of the frame rods of the bottom, as shown. They are bent up and tied together at the tops. We now take 28 weaving willows, (*I*, fig. 3), not so stout as the upright ones, (*H*), and insert them in the bottom, in the same manner, (see fig. 3); with these we weave around the basket, with each one passing two uprights, both in weaving out, and in, until all the 28 are inserted; then we weave, passing on the outside two, and inside one upright, twice around. When this is done, it is best to take a piece of wood, and, holding it upon the weaving, strike it with a hammer, to settle all firmly together. After this, we weave on until the willows *I* are exhausted, but out and in over one upright. Then we take off the strings, and 28 willows are again taken. They are laid so that the buts will stand out 3 or 4 inches from the inside, which enables one to cut them off easily. We weave these simply

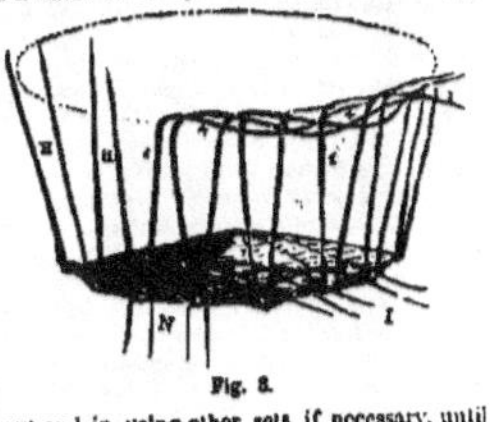

Fig. 3.

out and in, using other sets, if necessary, until the basket reaches the hight of 8 inches. (Three sets will probably reach.) Before proceeding further, four willows, (*M*, figure 4), are woven around once, and beaten together. Figure 4 shows how this set is woven in.

In topping off, one upright (*H*) is bent inside to the right, around two others. It is bent down hard upon the weaving. The second, third, fourth, and fifth, are thus bent. Before bending down the sixth, the end

Fig. 4.

of the willow first bent down is drawn within the basket, having passed inside around two and outside around three. (The course of the willows is shown in fig. 3, 4 being the first bent down, and 2 the sixth.) Then the sixth is bent down; the second is woven in, and the seventh is bent down, and so on, until the top is finished, when the ends are cut off, outside and in.

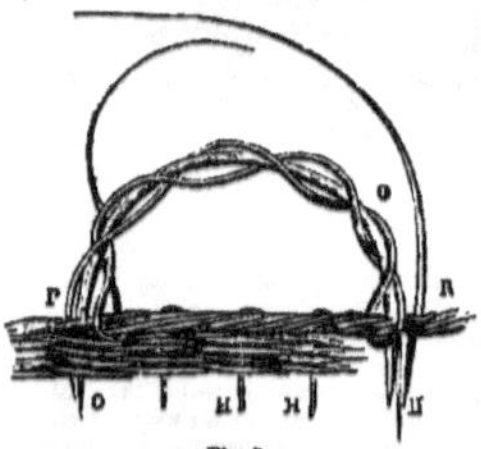

Fig. 5.

To finish off the bottom, we again take 28 willows, (*N*, fig. 3), and insert them in the bottom (as before, with the *H* and *I* willows). Then these willows are laid down and woven in precisely as the top was finished off.

To make the handles, we take for each a stout, willow stick, (*O*), bend it, sharpen it at both ends, and insert it, as shown in fig. 5. Then take two long willows, (*P* and *R*), and twist them. *P* is inserted on one side, wound around *O* three times, stuck through the rim, and drawn tight; it is then wound back around *O*, again drawn through the rim and the end secured. *R* is proceeded with in the same way, until the handle is finished. Beginners should have a good basket before their eyes to guide them."

When to Sell Hay.

The high price of this article, $30 a ton, and upward in the markets of the sea-board States, makes many farmers anxious to sell, and suspicious of the wisdom of the old maxim, "Never sell hay, but feed it all out on the farm." This is the true policy for farmers who depend upon the resources of their own farms for manure. But for those who are located near cities and villages, or near the sea, hay may be sold with advantage to the farm. The economy of selling depends mainly upon the facility of procuring good manure. After the land is in good heart, the making of this crop costs much less than most other farm crops. With improved tools, the mowing machine, the horse-rake, loader, and pitch-fork, it will not cost over $3 a ton to cut, make, and store. It costs still less if the hay is sold to be delivered directly from the field, as the labor of one handling is saved. Hay shrinks about one-third in weight between harvest and the following spring, and the price may be regulated accordingly. The quantity of hay that may be produced upon an acre depends chiefly upon the application of manure. With no very large outlay, the farmers indicated may bring up their fields from an average product of one ton to the acre, to two. The shore farmer has an inexhaustible source of fertility in the sea, and has no excuse for a small hay crop. Fish are a very cheap manure, whether applied fresh or after the oil is extracted. Rock weed, kelp, eel-grass, and mud from the creeks, will pay for carting a long distance. We have taken mud from salt water ditches and spread it, after a few weeks' exposure upon the bank of the ditch, directly upon mowing land, and seen nearly as good results from it as from a similar quantity of stable manure.

The price of stable manure in cities and villages varies from nothing to $12 a cord, according to location. It is highest, generally, where there is the most demand for it by gardeners and truck farmers. It will not pay for the hay crop at the highest price, perhaps not at $6 a cord, unless the price of hay remains very high. But in most places it can be had for less than that. Night soil can often be had for the carting, and in manufacturing villages there are factory wastes that make excellent fertilizers. The farmer's market wagon or cart should never come home empty. Hay may be sold freely where manures obtained away from the farm are applied still more freely. One advantage of this crop is, that on most soils the land need not be plowed to keep up its fertility. By top dressing alone the grass may be maintained for years in the greatest luxuriance. Some farms are favorably situated for irrigation, and by this means alone produce satisfactory grass crops. As a rule, *sell hay only when all the money you get for it may be immediately re-invested in good manures.*

Breeding Pure, Grade, and Cross-bred Stock.

"Is a pure-bred female injured for the future bearing of pure stock by having half-blood young?" It is certainly very undesirable, as a general thing, to lose the service of a valuable cow or other animal for one year—for by breeding a pure-bred cow to a scrub or grade bull, she is made for one year no better than any other cow. Her value above common cows is, in that she may bear full blooded calves, and as she can not ordinarily be expected to bear more than eight or ten in her life, the loss is considerable. Aside from this, there is a wide-spread opinion prevailing, strengthened by much that has been written on this subject, that if a heifer be covered by a bull of a different breed or by a scrub (or "native") bull, not only will her calf be an inferior "grade," but she, liable to take an *impression*, which will never leave her, or which will last for many years, and will cause her subsequent calves to bear some resemblance to the first one, or to its sire. This is accepted by many people as true, and though it is very hard to prove a negative, we must say we have *no* evidence to convince us of its truth. We can, moreover, cite numerous instances, one of which occurred in one of the best Short-horn herds in the country, in which no such effect was observable, though a well-bred Short-horn heifer had a calf by a little, dark, scrub bull, and her subsequent calves by superior sires were most closely scrutinized; and another, in one of the best flocks of Merino sheep,—many pure ewes, young and old, being accidentally crossed with a South-down buck—equally without effect. If a single case can be named, which will bear investigation, in which it is shown that such an impression has probably been made on any cow or ewe, we would be glad to know it.

There is another influence, which in the opinion of many breeders, effects the young—though very seldom operating disadvantageously—or observably in any way. We refer to the effects of association, or those circumstances which act upon the mind of the dam, during pregnancy. Careful breeders are so suspicious of these effects that they advise keeping female animals of different breeds separate, allowing choice animals to associate only with fine specimens of their own kind, and especially advising to keep breeding females from associating with deformed or crippled beasts of any kind.

When a "grade" animal is spoken of, it is always inferred that pure males have been used upon females of mixed or uncertain or grade blood. Thus, the first progeny of such breeding is a half-blood; the progeny of this half-blood with a male of the same breed as its sire, is a quarter-blood; and so we may go on in a *gradation*, always approaching the pure-blooded, so that we often speak of grade animals of seven eighths, or fifteen sixteenths pure blood. By "crosses" or "cross-bred" stock, is meant such as result from breeding one full-blood upon another—thus inferior cows of one breed are frequently bred to bulls of another breed in the hope of uniting the good qualities of the two breeds. Thus, among the Short-horns, are often found deep milkers, and the Jerseys almost uniformly give very rich milk, thus crossing the two breeds either by using the little Jersey bull with the big Short-horn cow (which would be most sensible, usually,) or the reverse, we might expect to raise a deep milker, giving rich milk. Such cross-bred animals, if males, are worthless for breeding purposes; if females, should be bred to one or the other of the original breeds. There are many cows of pure blood and unexceptionable pedigree among even the best herds, which are not up to the standard of excellence which every good breeder adopts. Such are low in value, and very properly subjects for experiments in cross-breeding. This explanation will satisfy those inquiries prompted in a recent article on crossing Jerseys and Ayrshires for milch cows. The breeder who experimented thus probably had cows of imperfect record or of inferior points which he chose to use in this way.

The Influence of Tobacco Upon Other Farm Crops.

Many a farmer's golden visions from the tobacco crop are growing dim. The crops of 1865 and 1866, in the Connecticut River Valley and, to a large extent, elsewhere, are mainly now on hand, and a proposition is made to the cultivators to grow no tobacco this year, in order to sell the old crop at high figures. There has manifestly been an overproduction, induced by the high prices during the war. It is a good time for the growers to pause and consider both the moral bearings of the crop, and its influence upon other products of the farm. The current of opinion as elicited at the last meeting of the Connecticut State Board of Agriculture, at New Haven, was decidedly against the crop, on economical grounds. It is not denied that a large sum of money may be realized by it, from a small plot of ground. But the general confession is that it ruins all the rest of the farm, by leading the cultivator to neglect it. It demands large quantities of manure, and all he can make goes to the tobacco patch, and he buys a good deal besides. The meadows run out, the pastures become barren, the orchard fruitless, and if the cultivator accumulates funds in the bank, as he may, it is by the ruin of his farm. Ten acres may be splendid, but the other hundred have gone to mulleins and hardhack. The influence of this crop upon the community is quite as disastrous as it is upon the farm. The tobacco growing district grows poorer. Other farm crops decrease in quality and quantity. Less stock is raised, less beef, pork, butter and other necessaries of life. The lands are all the while decreasing in agricultural value, and less capable of sustaining a thrifty population. If a man makes money by the crop, sells out, and goes to the city, the community loses by the depreciation the farm has undergone. The value of its taxable property is all the while diminishing, we apprehend, under the influence of this crop. Other crops, as a rule, bless the farm, and tend to make it more productive. They help to sustain animal life, and if consumed upon the soil, return more to it than was taken from it. But tobacco is a blight upon the land that raises it.

Comparative Production in Good and Bad Farming.

J. Stanton Gould, in his address before the N. Y. State Agricultural Society, stated that the average production of winter wheat in this State in 1865 was 12.30 bushels to the acre; oats, 17.16 bushels; barley, 16.27. corn, 28.44; potatoes, 94.80; hay, 0.91 tons. The production upon the farm of James Geddes, and six of his nearest neighbors, was: of winter wheat, 26 bushels to the acre; oats, 50 bushels; barley, 39.13; corn, 45; hay, 2 tons to the acre.

This shows a difference of nearly one half in favor of good farming, which consists mainly in drainage, deeper plowing, more manure, and more thorough cultivation. The largest item is manure, and this pays the farmer better for his labor, and increases the value of his farm. Statistics show, that the average production of farm crops decreased from 1855 to 1865, with the exception of wheat, corn, and potatoes. The crops on the farms of Mr. Geddes and his neighbors, show an increasing average. If the farm crops of the State should be brought up to Mr. Geddes' standard, the yearly increased product would be worth 75 millions of dollars. Good farming would soon pay our national debt.

Firewood on the Prairies.—The impression, once entertained, that trees would not flourish on the prairies, is found to be erroneous. Wherever young trees have been planted and cultivated, and protected from the ravages of vermin and cattle, they grow with astonishing rapidity. It is now calculated that a prairie farmer need wait only five years to grow wood enough from the seed and from transplanted seedlings to supply his own fire perpetually, and to keep up his fences. In a few years longer, the trees will give him abundance of timber for his own use, and to sell. A few trees recently measured in Iowa gave the following results: No. 1, planted 20 years, measured 10 inches above the ground, 91 inches in circumference, and is estimated to contain 1½ cords of wood. No. 2, planted 16 years, measured 70 inches, and will make a cord of wood. No. 3 measured 4 inches at 21 years of age. No. 4, 75 inches, and No. 5, 80 inches. It is estimated that some single acres of prairie-planted forest, 20 years out, will now cut 300 cords of wood to the acre. Facts like these account for the change that is taking place in public opinion in regard to the value of these lands. It is found in practice to be much easier to get wood upon the prairies than to get cleared fields in the timbered districts. The labor of clearing a farm upon heavy timbered land is immense, and many of the stumps linger through the first generation.

Labor Essential in Agricultural Colleges.

Messrs. Editors:—In the article on Agricultural Schools in your January number, objection is made to making such institutions "manual labor schools," and to requiring of the students more labor than "enough to *learn how* to perform all kinds of farm labor." The *italics* are mine. If the writer means that the work on the farm should be for the student's instruction and not for his own profit (money) or the school's, I agree with him; I only urge that *for this purpose, much labor is essential.* I remember when a boy, to have seen a shoemaker bristle a thread hundreds of times, and I thought I *knew how* to do it, but *when I tried, I couldn't.* Are there not enough schools now that send out young men and women who *know how* to do almost everything, but who, when put to the test, *can do nothing?* The commercial colleges advertise their actual business departments as their chief attraction, medical student's dissect, law students plead, midshipmen do the work of sailors as well as officers, young chemists work many hours in the laboratory for practice, and with all these the longer and harder the drill, the better. 'Tis a pretty race of farmers we educate(?), who walk out with kid gloves, cane, and sun umbrella, to witness the operations of farming, and *learn how.* In sober earnest, is it safe to let our young farmers taste the sweets of idleness, to let their muscles grow soft and their bones weak through inaction? Farmers must work with their own hands. Where is the college graduate who has any pursuit requiring manual labor? In their long course of study they have lost both taste for it, and strength. Is it worth nothing to retain habits of industry and strength? Is three hours too much time for healthy exercise, too much for learning how to do all the operations of the farm, and practising upon them until all be *both well understood and easily done* in the best manner? I have it from the best authority that many of the graduates of the Michigan Agricultural College are proving themselves to be good practical farmers. They labor there three hours per day. C. W. J.

Encourage the Boys.

A lad from Iowa writes us, that he thinks farmers' sons ought to have a chance to earn something for themselves, to be allowed to make little ventures in stock-raising for pocket money, and to keep them contented at home. We think so too. We suppose a great many farmers do this, certainly the great majority of our readers do. But many work their boys with as little consideration as they work hired men. They take no pains to make farm life attractive, and the boys are off at the earliest opportunity. They have no joyous memories to bind them to the spot that ought to be the dearest on earth. To learn the worth of money they must have money as the result of their labors. To form habits of faithfulness, carefulness and economy, these and other virtues must be rewarded. They should have responsibilities put upon them while they are very young, and be encouraged to make money and to save it. Give them a hen, a goose, or turkey, a lamb, or pig, and let them have all they can make by good care and feeding. A boy of ten or twelve years of age, with a little instruction, can manage the poultry. Let him take it on shares and see what he can make out of it. Give him a patch for a garden, and, if near a market, let him sell what he can raise. Give him a half dozen apple trees or pear trees, teach him to graft them, if they need it, and let the fruit be his. Give the boys an interest in your business, and make them intelligent in it, and they will not be in haste to leave the homestead. Encourage them to read agricultural papers and books, and the appetite will grow by what it feeds upon. The farm will be the scene of cheerful, well rewarded labor, and will always be loved.

To Prevent Ruts in Roads.

The art of road-making is yet in its infancy in this country. The roads are not laid out, made, or repaired with reference to economy of draft in using them. Deep ruts are soon worn in them by the common vehicles that pass over them; and these grow worse and worse, until they are almost impassable in spring. Broad cart tires are a partial remedy for these. Longer yokes, both for oxen, and for double horse wagons and carts, compelling the teams to walk in the same line with the wheels that come after them, would be a still better remedy. On most country roads there are two toe-paths and two ruts, and it is noticeable that the toe-paths are always in much the better order. Longer yokes would bring the paths and ruts together. The feet of the teams would break down the sides of the ruts, and fill them as fast as they were formed. This would improve the road bed, and make the draft of loads easier. We cannot shorten the axle trees without increasing the danger of upsetting, but we can lengthen the yokes with safety. Legislation is needed.

Decrease of Population in Agricultural Districts.—The census of 1865, in Rhode Island, shows a decrease of population in five years, in the four farming counties, of 3,878, and an increase in Providence co., made up of the city of Providence and suburbs, of 14,223. To be sure, these were years of war, but the draft upon the country for soldiers was no greater than upon the city, and the decrease can not be fairly attributed to this cause. It is another indication of that unhealthy public sentiment, which prompts men to abandon the slow gains and the substantial comforts of rural life for the rash speculations and unwholesome excitements of the city. The same process is going on in all the older States. The only increase of population is in the cities and villages. If people could better their condition by the change, nothing could be said against it, but this is rarely the case. Ninety-five in a hundred who undertake business in the city fail. On the farm, comparatively few fail, and the failures are usually traceable to moral, rather than commercial or natural causes. Society must be in an unhealthy condition where production does not exceed consumption. Rhode Island, with its unrivaled facilities for sea manures, aside from the stable, the best and cheapest in the world, ought to feed its own population and show a substantial increase in the farming districts for generations.

[COPYRIGHT SECURED.]

MOUNTAIN SHEEP. (*Ovis montana.*)—FROM STUDIES BY WM. H. BEARD.—*Drawn and Engraved for the American Agriculturist.*

The Rocky Mountain Sheep or Big Horn.

(*Ovis montana.*)

This is a giant sheep, one of the Mouflons, and closely allied to the Argali of Siberia, (*Caprovis Argali*), but not so large, and to the Aoudad or Bearded Argali of Northern Africa. It is found in the Rocky Mountains, and is of a solitary disposition, being not often found in larger flocks than 12 or 15, although sometimes perhaps as many as thirty may be found together. The male is remarkable for its immense horns. The writer of this has seen a pair measuring 3 feet 4 inches in length, and used as rockers for a chair. They are of great strength, presenting an appearance as if they were transversely grooved. These animals jump from great hights, and are said to land on their horns. Old hunters affirm this to be true, and are ready to swear that they have seen them do so. The writer has seen them jump, and thinks it may be so. At all events, the horns always present a decidedly battered appearance, which, however, may come from their conflicts with one another. They are very difficult to approach, and upon the first appearance of danger, the one first perceiving it utters a peculiar cry, sounding like a whistle, when they all scamper off to their hiding places in the rocks, from which they can not be hunted out. They frequent the most inaccessible places, and never come into the valleys to feed, preferring to crop the small tufts of grass and herbage to be found upon the crags. Their wool or hair is short and thick, and would hardly be profitable for any manufacturing purpose, even if it could be obtained in large quantity. The flesh is excellent, being considered far superior in flavor to the finest mountain venison. Their color is variable, changing with the season, from nearly white to a yellowish brown. The largest one ever seen by the writer, was nearly 3 feet 6 inches in hight at the shoulders, but this is an unusual size. They have been known to weigh as much as 350 pounds, but one of 225 to 250 pounds is about the average. The female differs from the male in size, and in the shape of the horns, which are small, and resemble a goat's horns going straight back instead of curling, like those of the male. Our engraving is composed, by permission, from sketches recently made by one of our first artists.

Fremontia Californica.

The English and other European horticulturists were last year much pleased with the flowering of one of our California shrubs, the Fremontia, and—as we wish to keep our readers advised of whatever is receiving attention at home or abroad—we arranged to have it engraved. A Boston Horticultural Journal has recently brought out a figure, purporting to be the Fremontia, accompanied by an article "adapted" from a French periodical, which gives so incorrect a representation of the flower that we are induced to publish our engraving, which we intended to reserve until some of our nurserymen should announce that plants could be had. Why a journal styling itself "American," should go abroad for an account of an American plant, discovered by an American explorer, first described by one of our own botanists, in one of

FREMONTIA CALIFORNICA.

VARIEGATED ASTILBE.

our own publications, we are at a loss to understand. Boston people stand preeminent in horticulture, but they have hard work with their botany. Hovey's Magazine will persist in calling things by wrong names, and gets properly called to account by the Gardener's Monthly, and now this "American" Journal gives us an engraving which must be a puzzler to any one who wished to make out the structure of the flowers. We will not assert that nature *could* not produce such a flower as they figure, but we can safely say that she never did. The engraving we present is from the original specimen, brought home by Gen. (then Col.) Fremont, and was not discovered in his expedition to the "Rocky Mountains," but in that made some years later to California. It grows along the sides of the Sierra Nevada, and upon the Coast Range, being rather unequally distributed. It may be properly claimed as a shrub, but it sometimes forms a small tree from 20 to 30 feet high. We have a section of a trunk of Fremontia, 5½ inches in diameter, with very hard and close grained wood. The form of the leaves is shown in the engraving; the older ones are often 3 inches in diameter, green above, and of a rusty color on the under side. The flowers, which are of a bright golden yellow, are succeeded by a downy capsule, that much resembles that borne by the common Rose of Sharon (*Hibiscus Syriacus*). The shrub was first described by Doct. Torrey, in the Smithsonian Contributions in 1850—and properly bears the name of one to whom we are so much indebted for a knowledge of the vegetation of the far West. Although this shrub has been so long known to botanists, as is usually the case with American plants, it first appears in cultivation in the gardens of Europe. We hope it may soon be found in those of this country, and prove hardy.

A Variegated Astilbe.

In a notice of *Astilbe Japonica*, (*Spiræa Japonica* of some catalogues,) given in January last, (page 22,) allusion was made to a variegated leaved form. Mr. Peter Henderson has recently afforded us an opportunity to see this variety in great perfection. We were so pleased with the plant that, notwithstanding the difficulty of adequately representing its beauty in black and white, we give an engraving of a single leaf. Imagine golden lines in place of the white, and a dark green instead of the black, and a tuft of such leaves a foot across, and some idea may be had of this most beautiful production. The plant will doubtless be hardy, and we hope that it will soon be abundant enough to become accessible to all, as it is one of the most beautiful of what the gardeners will persist in calling by the absurd name of "foliaged plants."

The Horticultural Value of Cats.

Puss has a bad name among our fruit-growing friends, and a still worse name among the little birds that seek shelter in our gardens and orchards, if they had a chance to speak their sentiments. If they could hold a convention and assert "bird's rights," puss would either be banished, kept in close quarters, or furnished with a bell necklace to warn all useful birds of her stealthy approach. The ostensible use of cats is to keep rats and mice in check. When well trained, they do this. But a great many cats of low breeding, or spoiled in education, fail in this essential point. They will not attack even when the rat squeals, as Mr. Deanagou would say. They are dainty, aristocratic animals, that have forgotten what they were made for, like certain bipeds of a higher order. They eschew rat sirloin and affect chicken, and feathered game in general. The sparrows, thrushes, wrens and martins that make constant warfare upon insects, are kept in mortal fear by puss. She runs her long claws into the boxes where they build their nests, climbs into the trees and gobbles whole broods of young robins. Cats with kittens are especially ravenous and destructive among the birds. They depopulate the garden, and wander off to distant meadows and woods after the tender, half grown game. One cat will readily destroy two hundred birds in a single season. It is easy to see how much cats may do to destroy the balance of nature, and leave insects to multiply without let or hindrance from our useful feathered friends.

We cannot in all cases get along without cats, but we may do much to keep their increase within proper limits, and much to protect the birds against their attacks. The birds that breed in boxes, like the martins, wrens, English sparrows and blue-birds, may have their homes isolated on poles, or in other ways, so that cats can not get at them. A piece of sheet iron or old tin, a foot wide or more, around the body of a tree a few feet from the ground, will be proof against pussy's claws, and make the birdlings in the branches above secure. The robins sometimes build in the wall, or on fences very near the ground, but will build in trees if they have them. Evergreen trees are favorite breeding places for several kinds of birds. If the old tin is not convenient, pare pussy's nails occasionally. The tin is the least trouble, and if you put it up to shield the nests, you will have your reward in abundant bird songs all through the summer, in fewer insects, and more fruit.

CONNECTICUT.

Grape Trellises.

Many persons who have planted vines, will this season, for the first time, put up trellises, and we have many letters asking what kind shall be made. We have published so much upon this subject that it seems like repetition to introduce it again. Mr. Knox's trellis, of wooden slats, was figured in April, 1863, p. 116. Mr. Fuller's trellis, of horizontal wooden strips at top and bottom, and vertical wires, was figured and described in August, 1863, page 244. In April last, we gave Dr. May's illustrations of the trellis of horizontal wires, most in use in the West. Of course the form of trellis will depend much upon the system of training. Where the double arm and spur system is followed, Mr. Fuller thinks that he demonstrates the superiority and cheapness of vertical wires. But this is not the system adopted in the large vineyards of the West, and there they use horizontal wires, and the hints of Doct. May will be found useful. In small vineyards, where horizontal wires are used, it will be found convenient to have a contrivance for tightening them. A screw swivel, such as is often used for tightening the frames of wood saws, can be easily adapted to this purpose, and a person, with a little ingenuity, can be relieved from all trouble from the sagging of the wires. There is one advantage in the vertical supports of Messrs. Knox and Fuller,—the one using wooden slats, and the other upright wires. There is not that constant strain upon the posts at the ends of the rows that there is when horizontal wires are employed. They also admit of a saving of timber, as short locust posts can be put in the ground, to which uprights of less durable wood can be spiked. An inspection of the trellises of both these vine-growers, shows that the plan of either is perfectly practical, according to their modes of training, though in the method of training followed at Hammondsport, and other large grape-growing regions, where the long-arm system is not followed, they consider it better and cheaper to use horizontal wires.

Wanted—A Horticultural Society.

For once, we write a local article. We need a Horticultural Society, just here in New York, the commercial emporium, the center to which everything that is transportable and worth selling, tends. We would not ignore the valuable services of horticultural associations elsewhere, but one is needed here. We have only that anomalous association, the Farmers' Club, which will give a remedy for itch, with the same facility that it discusses the latest pear. It will have a Strawberry Show this month, to which we hope all our readers within reach will contribute and make a visit. All these things are well, and it is well to offer liberal premiums for the best quart of this and that variety of fruit.

The prizes will be very welcome to those who get them, and the public will be gratified by the sight of a fine display. We ask for more than this—a society whose mature judgment on a new fruit or flower, shall outweigh all dollars—whose simple certificate shall be more valuable than green-backs. Who cares to know who can raise the largest quart of Triomphe de Gand?—any one can do great things if he coaxes properly. What we do want to know is this; is this new fruit or flower, so praised, worth buying; is this a new thing or some old one with a new name. Then again, as many meritorious things have died for want of proper notice as there have been miserable ones puffed into undue notoriety. Let us have a society to settle things. It needs some money, but more brains. It needs a class of men with knowledge, and without any interest in the mercantile aspects of the matter.

Have we these?—New York can not be so badly off as to say no! Good Mr. Greeley tried to do something when he offered premiums that must have dissatisfied as many as they pleased, no matter how they were decided. Under proper advice, such liberality might have produced some good result. Now, it is interminable bickering. Are there not enough pomologists and florists in and around New York to give us such a society? We don't mean those who always want to say "I," and make their own little patch the criterion for the rest of the world, and talk the thing to death, as other societies have been killed—but good, zealous horticulturists, who believe that horticulture is something beyond dollars—that it is an important element in our National prosperity, that it is a great humanizing influence, now often perverted, and that it belongs to the great city of the Union, which has liberally provided for other elevating arts, to do something for horticulture.

This is a subject that we have long had under consideration, and are induced to speak now by looking over Fuller's Small Fruit Culturist, and seeing—to use a vulgarism—the "perfect slathering" the author, with the aid of Mr. Downing, gives the nursery names of currants. We can not expect that such work will be done by private individuals at their own expense, nor that the decision of individuals, however eminent they may be, will carry the weight of the dictum of a society—such a society as we hope to see sooner or later established.

Picking Berries for Market.

The success of small fruit culture depends upon several other things than the choice of suitable soil and productive varieties. There must be ready access to market, and abundant labor to gather the crops, just at the right time. So perishable are most of the small fruits, that a day's delay in either picking, or in transportation, may seriously reduce the returns. Both forethought and capital must have been employed in providing an abundant stock of baskets, crates and other packages—enough to allow the grower to go on with gathering in spite of any delay in returning packages. As many hands are needed to gather the berries, the cultivation of small fruits must of necessity be carried on in thickly settled communities. In the great berry regions, picking time levels social distinctions, and the poor and well to do, young and old, black and white, find plenty of work, at paying prices. The season begins with strawberries, then come raspberries, which, followed by blackberries, prolong the season through several weeks. A shed or shanty is erected in the field for "headquarters," where empty baskets are to be had, and to which the fruit is brought. Each picker has a basket stand or tray, which is a shallow box with a handle, and large enough to hold from 6 to 12 baskets, according to the size. A row or bed is assigned to each picker, who is expected to gather all the fruit, good or bad, that is ripe at the time. Assorting is done by the picker, who reserves one or two baskets for the inferior berries, and puts only good ones in the others. This is found to be much better than assorting the berries after they are brought in, as it saves one handling. The baskets are rounded up, in order that they may be at least level full when they reach the consumer. When a picker has filled all the baskets, she (or he) brings them to headquarters and receives as many tickets as there are full baskets, fills up the stand with empty baskets, and starts anew. The basket are put at once into the crates, (the inferior berries being kept separate,) which, as soon as full, are fastened up, and are ready to go off. When the picker accumulates tickets, (representing each a basket,) enough to amount to a half dollar or a dollar, they are exchanged for one of these denominations. These larger tickets are redeemed by the proprietor. In some places they pass as currency at the stores. The price paid varies from two to five cents a quart, and the pickers earn from $1.50 to $3 a day. Those who live within an easy distance of market, find it much better to send fruit by their own conveyances than to forward it by rail.

Picking commences as soon as the dew is off, and the fruit is started for market in time to reach its destination early the following morning.

Garden Irrigation.—2d Article.

BY "TESUQUE," NEW MEXICO.

Those who have their gardens laid out for irrigation, as described in the March number, will soon begin to use the water; and in the month of May, in climates such as New Mexico, will use it pretty freely.

Parsnips, carrots, beets, radishes, and all root crops should have water, and have the beds well filled with it, at most, five or six days after being sown. By watering them at this time, the ground is well soaked, and, besides giving the seed an early start, it obviates the necessity of watering the plants when just appearing, and when, very likely, there are frosty nights; and at such times very young plants are more or less injured, or at least put back.

Early peas *should get water often*, and always be watered two or three days before picking for market, if you wish them to fill well.

Turnips will speak as plainly as any vegetable need, when they require water, and in dry climates do not leave them any longer without it, after the leaves begin to call for it, than you would your best cow; don't put it off for a day or two, or you may insure a crop of pithy, strong flavored roots, entirely unfit for the table.

Cabbages, cauliflowers, broccoli, and the rest of the cabbage tribe, should be transplanted into beds well watered overnight; and the day after transplanting, another slight watering is necessary; after the plants are well established they are not apt, in an ordinary season, to need irrigating oftener than every two weeks, until they commence heading, and then, every ten days. If lice are found on any of the plants in a bed, pull the plants up previous to irrigating, as the lice are liable to wash from one to the other.

When the lice have commenced on plants that are not higher than the borders, by filling the bed so that the plants are immersed for a few minutes, and then letting the water off rapidly at the opposite side, into the ditch that is not being used, one can often thoroughly cleanse the bed of these pests. Onions need water about as often as cabbage, but not so much at once. Spinach should be watered over night, when picking for market, and immediately after, in hot weather. Lettuce, we transplant in wet beds, and irrigate in all respects as directed for cabbage. Cucumbers need water in this climate, at least once a week, but not heavy waterings.

Celery, in trenches, must have a sink at the end of each trench to serve as explained in the March number, and when hilling up the plants, leave each side of the trench lower than the center, until you are on a level with the surface; by this means you can run the water on without covering the hills, for if you allow water to go down into the heart of the plant, for a few times, it will cause your celery to rot; throughout the growing season celery will require water nearly as often as cabbage.

Pepper: water often until it has attained the growth at which you expect it to mature, then give it but very little, as it retards the ripening.

Tomatoes need more care in the watering than any other vegetable; when the plants are first put out, they should be transplanted into wet beds, as for cabbage; then see that they are erect before irrigating, and let on the water *slowly*, taking care *not to cover the crowns of the plants;* and at no time let over two inches of water on your plants, or they will either wither, or stop growing entirely; tomatoes need water often to get an early crop, but in very limited quantities.

And now, supposing that your garden is able to wait a day or so, and that there is nothing that can be hurt by so waiting, then, the best times for irrigating are: cloudy days, and moonlight nights; but if the plants really need water, irrigate them at any time.

It is well, with your crops that have to be thinned, to take them in rotation; and the beds of carrots, beets, etc., which you intend to thin next day should be watered the night before; or even better, early the same morning; by this method you can work among them much easier, as you can pull out those which need removing without injuring the rest.

Hot-beds can be irrigated as soon as the plants are up, by cutting a hole in the back board of the frame, the bottom of which should be on a level with the soil; by spouts from the asecquia you can water many hot-beds while you would be sprinkling one. The above remarks as regards time between waterings, etc., must not, in all cases, be closely followed, as difference in climate, soil, situation, etc., will cause a difference in the need of water; I have shown here as nearly as possible what is required in this section of country, but it is a thing in which every man must rely on his own judgment, taking care, in a dry climate, never to miss seeing his whole crop, at least every two days, as plants that to-day look fresh and appear to be doing well, may to-morrow show signs of distress. It is well for beginners to rather overdo their irrigating than to err on the other side, and to bear in mind that the great cause of cabbage lice, and many other troubles to the gardener in all climates, is—drouth.

BEDDING PLANTS, such as Verbenas, Lantanas, Gazanias, etc., make a much better show if pegged down. Hair-pins, hooked sticks, etc., are used, as well as a strip of lawn matting put over them, with both ends thrust into the ground.

Flower Garden Experience.

If persons, instead of writing us essays on the beauty of flowers and the pleasures of gardening, would tell us their experience and the circumstances that led to their success or failure, we should print more of their letters than we do. Miss O. M. Luke, Trumbull Co., Ohio, gives us a clever bit of flower garden experience, from which we extract the following, with the remark that her plan of protecting seedlings with leaf mold is an excellent one, and followed by some of our best growers.

"I have always been a great lover of flowers, and have tried various experiments on some of them, marking, with the greatest pleasure, each new feature, which my experiments produce.

"Sweet Williams and Pinks are my hobbies now. Some seeds of these were sent to me by a friend, two years ago last August. Two weeks after I received them, I had a bed made about 8 feet long, and 1 foot wide, upon which I spread one peck of leached ashes, one of stone-coal cinders, and about the same of well rotted chip manure, being careful to have them all raked through the soil. Then, after sowing my seeds, I covered them very slightly by raking the compost over them. The plants came up very thick, and grew about two inches before winter. I thought best to protect them during the winter by a covering of leaf muck from the woods. In the spring, after removing the muck from their tops, they looked very green. I watered them during the summer season about once a week with soapsuds.

"They grew thriftily and needed very little weeding. The second winter, I protected them by a covering of brush and straw, removing it in the spring, and last June they blossomed. I wish every reader of the *American Agriculturist* could have seen them. The Sweet William stalks were all about two-and-a-half feet high, and measured about two-and-a-half inches around. Such a variety of colors I had never before seen. They were ringed, streaked, speckled and plain, of almost every shade; some were double, others measured an inch-and-a-half across each flower, with a fine deep fringe around their edges. There was one stalk with three different varieties of colors growing on the same stem; but on different little branches. Every one who saw them said they never had seen any thing like them before."

Transplanting Seedlings.

There will be much transplanting done this month, in both the kitchen and flower garden, and with varying success. There are some who seem to do the work very roughly and always succeed, while others appear to be very painstaking and have bad luck. A plant, in its removal from the seed-bed, will lose more or less of its root fibres, and as all the leaves usually remain, the present surface of the leaves is all out of proportion to that of the roots, and unless in a very damp time, the plant will wilt from the loss of moisture by evaporation. It is always preferable to do the work on a damp day, not so much on account of the moisture in the ground as of that in the air. The few last hours of day-light are to be preferred, as plants set at that time have a chance to recover, in a measure, during the cool night. The soil in which the plants are to be placed should have been recently worked, so that only fresh and mellow earth can come in contact with the roots. Water the seed-bed thoroughly, and take up the plants with care, and set them out as soon as possible. Much of the success depends on bringing the soil in close contact with the roots. Where a dibber is used for making the holes, an unskillful workman is very apt not to properly fill the hole made by the dibber, and as a consequence, a portion of the roots are surrounded by air instead of earth. For this reason, those who have but little transplanting to do, and are not practised in the use of the dibber, had better make broader holes with the point of a garden trowel, and when the plant is set, fill the earth in carefully, and crowd it down firmly. Always have the ground marked off beforehand, so that no time need be lost in looking out for the proper distances; besides the work will be more regular.

In larger operations, there is a division of labor; one carries a basket containing the plants, which are kept thoroughly wetted, and drops them at the proper places, and another sets them.

When plants are brought from a distance, and must be put out without waiting for favorable weather, it is best to make rather large holes with a trowel, fill each with water, and set the plants. By a division of labor it may be done much more rapidly than one would suppose. In a very light soil, in a hot, dry time, we have practised this without the loss of a plant.

Seedlings that are to be kept out of the ground for any great length of time should have their roots puddled, by mixing up a thin mud of loam, and enveloping the roots in it.

A Fruit Critic Criticised.

The farmer of Edgewood, in a recent number of the American Journal of Horticulture, advances some very sceptical and heterodox notions in pomology, calculated to discourage improvement in this fine art. He says: "I doubt very much if the finest flavored fruits can be grown as easily as the grosser tasting ones." And again, "in the pear line, it is quite possible that, with great nicety of treatment, both in garden culture and in the ripening process, (which last counts for a great deal,) a higher and finer flavor may be given to the Beurré Diel, or the Flemish Beauty, or the Beurré d'Anjou, or even the Duchess, than belongs ordinarily to the Bartlett. But put the Bartlett in comparison with either, under fair average treatment, and upon ordinary garden lands, and I think two luscious Bartletts will present themselves, to one of either the other names." The idea here advanced, that the finer kinds of pears require specially nice treatment in order to succeed, is mischievous, and is certainly not sustained by facts. The Seckel, the highest flavored of all pears, is even more hardy than the Bartlett, and will bear good fruit in almost any soil that is adapted to the pear. It is improved in size by high cultivation, but that is true of all pears—and of the Bartlett as well. We do not think the flavor of the Seckel is improved by its size. The Flemish Beauty and the Beurré Diel, upon ordinary garden lands, and with the fair average treatment, have always borne as well as the Bartlett, in our experience. The Beurré d'Anjou is a newer pear, but it is notoriously a good grower and bearer, and may prove itself adapted to as wide a range of soil and climate as the Bartlett. The Duchess is more fastidious about its soil, but where it finds congenial aliment, it is as easily raised, ripens as well, and keeps better than the Bartlett. We found four large, well grown trees, upon pear stock standing in a common meadow, three years ago, in Westchester County. They have never had any special care, apparently; they stand in sward land, and yet for three years in succession, they have borne abundant crops. A cow-pasture seedling could not be more hardy, or bear with more uniformity. This variety, we are told, does very well at New Haven, and is comparatively worthless at Hartford. This depends, we suppose, not at all upon treatment or culture, but upon the original character of the soil. The Paradise d'Automne, the Muskingum, the St. Ghislain, pears of exquisite flavor, are quite as successful with us as the Bartlett. In soil that suits them, without any special manipulation or culture, we think they can be grown with as much uniformity and in as large quantity. This, we think, is true of many other pears of the first quality. Farmers, and beginners in fruit culture, should not be discouraged from trying to grow the best varieties, by the idea that they require specially nice treatment. They will do better with this than without it, as the Bartlett will, but they are quite as likely to succeed with ordinary care. The best are quite as likely to succeed in your soil and climate as inferior varieties. Therefore, plant them. A great deal of horticultural writing is an account of local experience, valuable as far as it goes, but it should be distinctly stated that they are only individual opinions. No one man is able to lay down rules for the whole extent of this vast country.

Propagation by Layers.

Many plants are multiplied in this way more readily than in any other. Indeed, there are some plants that will make natural layers without any help, as they put out roots whenever the joints of the prostrate branches come in contact with the soil. Among our herbaceous plants, the Verbena and squash are familiar illustrations. Most of our climbing plants are readily multiplied in this way, and one can increase his stock of Wistarias, Honeysuckles, etc., very rapidly, to say nothing of the Grape, a plant notoriously of easy propagation by layers. With many of our shrubs, such as the Wiegela, the present season's growth may be layered as soon as it gets firm, as may that of roses and many others. Give well prepared soil, and if there is likely to be suffering from drouth, put over a mulch. Moss is excellent for this purpose, and a large flat stone is not bad.

The necessity for making a cut in the part layered, will depend upon the facility with which the plant forms roots. If a cut is to be made, let it be on the upper side of the branch, and not on the under side, as is recommended in the older works. The hint we got, long ago, from our contemporary of the Gardeners' Monthly, and have practiced it so successfully, that we wonder we did not think of it ourselves.

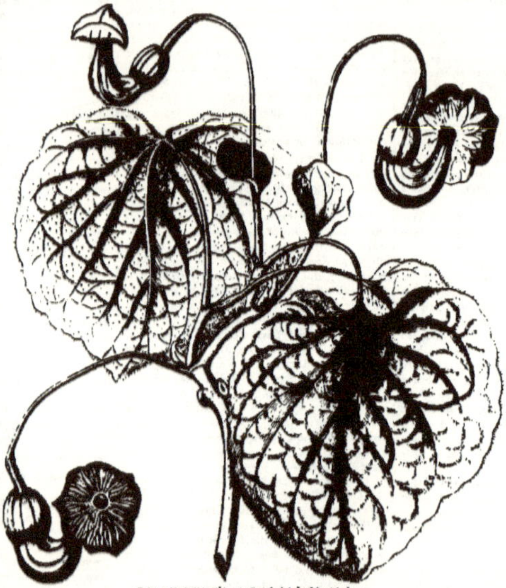

THE DUTCHMAN'S PIPE (*Aristolochia Sipho.*)

The Dutchman's Pipe.—(*Aristolochia Sipho.*)

This is a climber that we very much admire, for a fine specimen of it is among the earliest plants we remember. Though a native of our Northern States, and one that is very valuable for covering a moderate space with copious foliage, it is very little in use in this country. The vigorous growth of its twining branches, and the luxuriance of its foliage—the heart-shaped leaves being often a foot across—make it a valuable plant. Its remarkable flowers, though not showy, will attract the attention of the curious. They have a brownish-purple color, and a shape so singularly like that of a pipe, as to suggest its common name. The readers of last year's *Agriculturist* will recollect that the flower of this plant was cited by Professor Gray among those in which the fertilization must, of necessity, be effected by the agency of insects.

The engraving gives a very good representation of the flower of the natural size, and of the young leaves. This species is found from Pennsylvania, southward and westward, but is hardy in most parts of New England and Northern New York. Though it is readily multiplied from cuttings of the partly ripened wood, our nurserymen charge 75 cents a plant, which is more than they do for many exotic things. A low species, about a foot high, is *Aristolochia Serpentaria*, the Virginia Snakeroot, which formerly had a reputation as a remedy for the bite of poisonous snakes, and it is a little remarkable that species of *Aristolochia* growing in widely separated countries, have a reputation as "Snakeroots." Some tropical species, with very large flowers, are grown as curious ornaments of the Green-house. The writer discovered in Napa Valley, California, a new species, which is called *Aristolochia tomentosa*, in the report of the Mexican Boundary Survey. It is a very vigorous climber, with downy leaves, and very large flowers. We hope some of our many subscribers in that beautiful Valley, will be so kind as to send us some roots or seeds of this species.

Zinc Labels and the Ink.

Zinc labels, marked with an ink containing a salt of copper, have long been in use, and have great durability. The old ink consisted of sulphate of copper, salammoniac and lampblack, mixed with water. The only use of the lampblack is to make the ink visible at the instant of writing. Our friend, Horticola, whose hints we have before presented, sends us a specimen of a zinc label written with his ink, which seems to be as legible and as indelible a label, as one could wish. He is very curious in the way of inks, and has tried all that have been proposed. He has finally settled down upon a formula, which, reduced to convenient quantities to order from an apothecary, is: Sulphate of copper, 6 grains; water, 1 ounce; dissolve, and add sal-ammoniac, 3 grains, and sulphuric acid, 20 drops. This may be used with a quill or gold pen, or even with those steel pens that have a coating of copper or similar metal on them. Zinc, and all other labels, should be tied in a manner that will not constrict the growing limb. Lead wire answers very well. Horticola is very much pleased with his experience with a peculiarly dressed leather for tying, known among dealers as lace-leather.

Red Paint in the Garden.—In looking over the proofs of Mohr's work on the grape, we notice many little practical hints. Among others, he recommends that the handles of pruning knives and all other implements liable to be lost, be painted of a bright red. The handles of knives and other small tools are usually of a color so near that of the soil, or that of the branches of trees and vines, that it is not easy to find them, if carelessly misplaced. He also recommends the same color for wires used for low trellises for vines, etc., as wires of the ordinary color are not readily seen by strangers.

Seeds of Wild Plants.—Those who wish to introduce the early flowering wild plants into their grounds, should look out for seeds as soon as they ripen, and if it is desirable to remove the roots, put a mark of some kind near the plant, so that it will be seen when the foliage is dead.

THE HOUSEHOLD.

[illegible]

Fig. 1.—OUR RUSTIC SEATS.

Stumps, Quilts, and Counterpanes.

PRIZE ESSAY BY MISS EVA M. COLLINS.

Jennie and I have spent the morning among the hemlocks. We started out after breakfast with knives and baskets, for moss, with which to decorate our stump. An old sugar maple, standing by the south sitting-room door, had been dying by inches for years; with the exception of the year it was struck by lightning, when it took a long stride in its process of decay. Its size sensibly diminished as its dead branches were one after another cut away, while the size of the hollow in its trunk was as visibly augmented, (Fig. 2,) until it would admit almost any of us but father. Last fall we discovered a number of new fissures through to the outside, and that it had become so open that Jennie could no longer hide there; it was but a shell, and the first frost proved a feather too much in its cap, and one morning we found it scattered about on the ground in particles, somewhat larger than those of the "One-hoss shay," of poetic fame. Father spoke once of having the roots dug out, but the majority exclaimed against the measure, and triumphed as usual. It was such a beautiful stump, of historic fame! All that was left of the very tree into which our great, great grandmother climbed, when she was a little girl at home alone, to hide away from the unfriendly Indians, whom she heard coming, and who killed her dog, that now lies buried under the tree, and stole all the bread; and no one knows what might have become of her had she made a lisp of a sound. It reminds us too of the wolves she was so courageously driving away with fire-brands, when she was boiling sugar, in the night, but which turned out to be our great, great grandfather, from over the creek, who was merely testing the bravery of the pretty maiden, and had come through the wood—a meadow now—to sit up and watch the syrup with her. Oh! the stump tells us many a tale of the past, and it seems almost like sacrilege not to cherish it still. Soon after the tree fell Ralph filled the bottom of the stump with earth and muck, and carefully transplanted a wild honeysuckle there. The flowers are now filling the air with the sweetest fragrance. This spring, he drove in a strong, branching stick for a support for the Ivy, which used to run wild over the tree, and fastened rude seats among the roots. Katie has planted a rose tree on the other side, and Jennie and I have added our gift of moss. The stump is already a pleasing rustic ornament, and has the present appearance of Fig. 1, and promises to be a favorite family retreat in the warm summer days to come, and an eloquent stump speaker of the past.

Fig. 2.—[illegible]

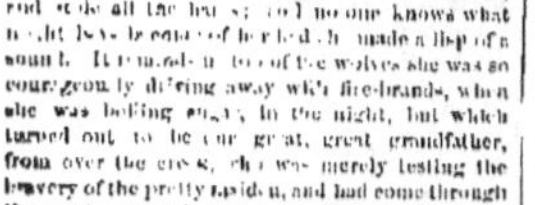

Fig. 3.—PATTERN FOR QUILT.

I had been saving paper rags all winter, having in view a white spread for my bed. The idea has prevailed with us that patchwork quilts alone were suitable in rooms that were commonly used. A patchwork quilt is a perpetual annoyance to me. The three that I pieced myself before I was five years old, my only ones indeed, were stored away on a shelf in the upper hall closet—carefully folded wrong side out, because I could never bear to see a feature of one of them—until the Sanitary Commission absorbed them. I only hope their presence afforded as signal relief to some poor soldiers, as their absence to "a friend." However, I totally relinquished my purpose of buying a spread, the first time I had an opportunity to price them, and let the rags go for tin as usual, but did not renounce my intention of having one nevertheless. We have some coarse, heavy, double-width sheets, which Charlie had at College, but which have been used

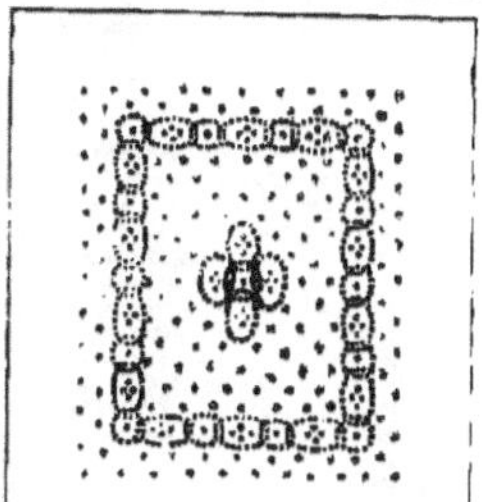

Fig. 4.—THE QUILT COMPLETED.

very little since, on account of being so heavy. I thought the groundwork of the counterpane I was examining, was not very unlike Charlie's sheets, barring the price; so I told our storekeeper "I would not take any to-day," and hastened home to see what could be done with one of them. After

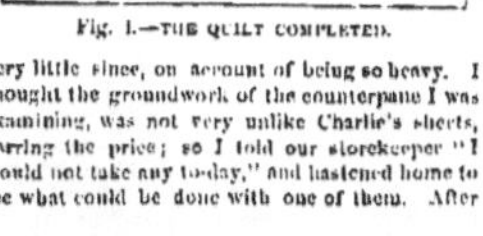

Fig. 5.—HOW IT LOOKS.

spreading it over the bed, and looking at it from all sides, I removed it to my large work table—the floor—and, bearing in mind the dimensions of the bed, with a large bowl and small meat-platter, drew a design in dots, and worked in double candle wicking with a darning needle over a smaller table, like that shown in Fig. 3. The wicking is merely drawn once through the cloth at each dot *, and the ends are trimmed off about a third of an inch in length. It was some trouble to make it, and when finished it looked as in Fig. 4. It took all my leisure time for three or four days; but it pays capitally, because I am so well satisfied with it, and it looks so nicely on my bed, (Fig 5). Mary says she has

Fig. 6.—WHIPPING IT OUT.

seen wick spreads before, and that they will wash. It is only necessary to fasten them strongly with clothes' pins to a high line, Fig. 6, and frequently whip them out while drying. Katie and Jennie are thinking of making one for their room, but say they shall improvise a prettier pattern than mine.

Leaves from the Diary of a Young Housekeeper.—No. IV.

PRIZE ESSAY BY MRS. LAURA E. LYMAN, STAMFORD, CT.

June 10th.—Mother has been passing a week with me. She seemed very much pleased with all my household arrangements. I took a deal of pride in showing her that the efforts she had made to teach me the art of housekeeping, had not been fruitless, and that the maxims she used to inculcate were not forgotten in my economy. How many thousand times I have heard her repeat: "A place for everything, and everything in its place;" "A time for everything, and everything in its time;" "Once well done is twice done." I took her into my linen closet and showed her my sheets, snowy white and folded nicely, with sprigs of lavender between. I gave her a peep into my cedar chest, where my woolens, furs, and winter clothing were stowed away, secure from the moths; and showed her my bags, hanging each upon its own proper nail, with a label stitched upon it; one with all my paper patterns in it; another filled with pieces of silk; another with new calico pieces, and another with old; my two rag-bags, one for white and the other for colored; my barrel, in which all woolens destined for rugs and carpets are kept; my button bags, and all the series so arranged, that in the darkest night I can lay my hands on everything in the house which can possibly be called for; my old linen pieces clean and tied up in a roll ready for bandages or sore fingers; my woolen pieces for patches and my worn domestic for linings. All these little evidences that I remembered the lessons of thrift, order, and economy she had taught me, were exceedingly gratifying to her.

In exploring the attic, she discovered two or three old-fashioned, rush-bottomed chairs, the frames of which were still sound as ever, though the rushes had long since disappeared. These, she said, could, with a little ingenuity, be covered, and with a coat of varnish, do service for another generation. So we carried these specimens of a past age down into the kitchen, and stitched over the seat a piece of strong canvas which we covered with some furniture calico, and I have three new chairs in my kitchen which afford decidedly the most comfortable seats in it, except my sewing chair. The coat of varnish which I put on them makes them look like new.

Mother was very much pleased with my milk room, and said it would answer admirably for all the months, except the hottest. Her father was an old-fashioned New Hampshire farmer, and she was brought up to wash and pick wool, card, spin and weave, and go through all the routine of household industry on a farm. She could bake and brew, scour and dye, and she is very proud of repeating almost the only compliment that my Puritan grandfather ever paid her. She had been away three or four months teaching a district school, at nine shillings a week, and upon her return the old gentleman quietly remarked: "Now, Hannah's got back, and all the dye pots will be going." Father was a merchant who kept a cow and a horse, and lived in a snug way, so we children knew little of mother's farming accomplishments.

I am sure we modern housekeepers cannot be too grateful to the inventors of the Cotton Gin, the Spinning Jennies, and Power Looms, for relieving us from the endless task of manufacturing all the domestic fabrics, and giving us so much more time for the improvement of our minds and the elegant accomplishments of modern society.

We have quite a flock of sheep that were clipped a short time since, and mother suggests that before the wool is taken to market, I look it over and select a few of the coarsest fleeces and all the ragged and unsightly ends, to make me a wool mattress for next winter. This laid upon the shuck mattress, which Jeanette and I manufactured last spring, will give me another excellent bed, almost as luxurious as a feather bed, equally warm, and more wholesome. By winter, my six geese will have yielded feathers enough for a bolster and pillows.

June 12th.—My poultry has been interesting me a good deal of late. I have three broods of chickens now, one, three, and five weeks old, and another hen will be off in a few days. Sue finds her pastime in egg-hunting, and her sagacity amuses me. I believe she knows the cackle of every individual biddy on the place, and from which one every egg comes. My oldest chickens, two or three of them, began to have the gapes, and farmer Jones' wife, who has a genius for raising chickens, told me to give them black pepper, and the worst cases to treat with a pretty strong dose of black pepper and sweet oil. She always mixes pepper with their meal, and never loses any, she says, from gapes. I tried her remedy and have lost no chickens yet, except one, that a weasel caught.

June 20th.—Such a lively time as we have had. A day or two after mother went home, cousin Eliza and her husband paid me a visit. They live in New York, and while John was off fishing, an amusement which he pursued with wonderful zest, Eliza and I were comparing city with rural housekeeping. She was very much, and very favorably, impressed with the abundance of eggs, butter and milk, which, in the city, are so expensive, but with us are matters of course; and she was constantly remarking the immense advantage I enjoyed in confining all, or nearly all, my work to one floor. Whether one has servants, or does the work herself, this is a grand desideratum. In the former case she can look after them so much better, and know how everything is going on; and in the latter case, she is saved so many trips up and down stairs.

While Eliza enjoyed the abundance of eggs, cream and butter, and their compounds, John was particularly delighted with my brown bread. He says he can't get used to baker's bread, or learn to like it, or even consider it wholesome; but none of their city domestics know how to make good bread, and he has been enjoining upon Eliza to take lessons of me in the sacred art. I have taught her especially how to make Boston brown bread and Graham, and no doubt, the use of these plain, but palatable and nutritious compounds will add years to John's life, as well as money to his Bank account.

He kept the table supplied with trout and perch while he was here, and Edward killed a fat wether. I never liked mutton till now, and I think Edward's way of butchering accounts for the difference in flavor between this and all I have ever eaten. As soon as the animal is dead, he makes all haste to cut him open and remove the entrails, and then to take off the skin as quickly as possible. The sheep have been ranging in a wild and rocky pasture on the back part of the farm, which probably accounts for the very fine flavor of the mutton. John said it tasted almost as good as venison. I find the best way to cook mutton is to bake it. I generally cut little gashes in it, and fill them with bread crumbs, moistened with milk and spiced with garden thyme.

After reading a good deal on the subject in the books Sue White lent me, we have decided never to butcher a calf or a lamb for our table. Veal is said to be the most indigestible and least nutritious of all the meats, and my author says, the young of any animal is less wholesome and far less nutritive, than when it has attained its growth.

My investigations in this department of knowledge have led me to these conclusions: That venison is the most perfect of all meats, being the easiest of digestion, and at the same time the most delicious and the most nourishing. Next to this ranks good mutton, and for mutton, wethers are the best. Third in value for the table is beef; tender roasting pieces and broiled sirloin steaks being the choice parts. Turkey and chicken are very highly esteemed and their flavor is delicious, as is especially that of partridge and quail; but they are not so readily digested as the first three.

June 27th.—The memorable litter of pigs that Jenny and I took so much pains with last spring, has suffered a divison. Edward had promised five of them to one of our neighbors, and he came today for them. They have been running wild for two months in the pasture, and it was no easy task to catch them. Edward has some pleasant surprise in store for me I know, by the way he speaks of those pigs. He is duly alive to the fact, that Jenny and I saved him at least fifty dollars by our assiduous care and devotion to that interesting family.

I have learned something new about butter lately, from an old farmer's wife. Now I weigh my butter before salting, and allow an ounce of salt to a pound of butter; I roll my salt, and dry it thoroughly in the oven before putting it into the butter. I find, too, that a little crushed sugar and saltpetre, worked in with the salt, improve the flavor and preserve the butter. I have a fifty pound firkin nearly full, and I am very ambitious that in market it shall rank as "prime." The firkin is of hemlock, a wood that imparts no taste, and it was perfectly new. I rinsed it with scalding hot water, and placed it in the sun until it was entirely dry. Next October, I mean to try for the prize in butter at our County Fair. Edward thinks he'll take one on those Chester White Pigs.

June 30th.—To-day I have been busy all day in putting up strawberries. Sue picked several quarts, having a fine flavor, though they were not large, in a pasture which has recently been cleared. These I preserved, allowing pound for pound. Those which I gathered from our strawberry bed, being large and very fine looking as well as delicious, I put up "in their own juice." I allowed three-quarters of a pound of sugar to a pint of water, and when it was boiling, put in my strawberries and let them scald through; then skimmed them out and put them into glass jars, placed in my tin boiler with water in it, which I raised gradually to the boiling point to prevent the jars from breaking. When I had filled each jar, I poured juice enough in it to cover the berries, and then put on the rubber cover which had a screw in it, which I turned until the mouth was perfectly sealed. Mother has kept strawberries in this way for two years.

Fashion Gossip.

BY AN EXPERT.

The authority that prophesied walking-dresses were to be a short lived caprice of Gothamite fashionables, has proved at fault. "Cleanliness is next to godliness," sayeth wisdom, and this virtue of the new mode must compensate for its want of grace and style. Gray, Bismarck, and green poplins or Alpacas, are pretty for this month, and serviceable for travelling suits. We advise short dresses for country wear. Muslins, with sacques or peplums to match, will look simple, neat and rustic. Suits have been adapted for carriage costume. They should be enriched with effective trimmings. The most casual observer must have remarked that for elegance, evening dresses, and a toilet for any ceremonial occasion, require trains and the peculiar flow of drapery produced by the fashionable gored skirts.

Gored robes are destined for such a lengthened existence, that one need not hesitate about cutting up even the richest materials in this style. The idea is certainly more economical than a preponderance of folds about the hips, which in no wise added to the symmetry of the figure. Much less material is required, and a plain surface will outwear one that has innumerable creases. A walking-dress is not complete without its accompanying peplum, but a well provided wardrobe should have a cloak of black silk for extra times. Make fine qualities into loose sacques, deeply dented, or otherwise cut around the bottom, and trim profusely with jet galloons and lace. Jet embroideries are more *distingué* than *passementerie*. Amber is not sufficiently chaste and elegant for mantles. Satin folds and piping form a new and beautiful ornamentation. Superb shawls, for Park riding, are made of black Cashmere or Almaro cloth, trimmed with jet and Cluny. Amber *bijouterie* can be worn by brunettes, but never by blondes. Mention has been made of the re-introduction of cameos. Stone cameos are always valuable, and having nearly as much prestige as pearls and diamonds, descend as heirlooms through families of note. Each successive era of popularity, however, adds its variation of appearance. To-day we have engravings fine and transparent as mists, and shapes all stars, angles and parallelograms, with a pearl or diamond glittering upon every point. Mosaics of a very beautiful order are also set in this way. Jasper silks are new, and adapted for suits or *demi-toilette*. The foundation color is dark, and overshot with scintillations of purple. Black and white striped silks are festooned with jet ornaments over gray silk petticoats. Later, *piqués* and muslins will be used as substitutes. Organdies are fresh, fair, and lovely to look upon. A most effective design simulates a tunic caught up at intervals with vines of roses trailing from the belt. Knots of blue flowers and grasses form a border upon the lower part of the skirt. The waist is all white or sprinkled with tiny bouquets. White organdies for dinner toilet are made with *bouillons* divided by narrow straw braids. The under slip should be of *taffetas*. Lace peplums are pretty over low corsages. Very wide sleeves are not so well for thin materials as half close shapes, because with a little wear, the stiffening is lost, and they are apt to look "stringy." Tulle sleeves with wide silk ones should be puffed lengthwise or crosswise as the fancy may dictate. Maltese lace is more worn than Cluny. It makes beautiful ruffs for the throat and wrists. We saw the following new spring patterns at Mme. Demorest's: The "Nicole Dress," to be made of French poplin in two choice shades of green. The under skirt should be the lighter, and trimmed around the bottom a finger deep, with black braid set on obliquely. The upper skirt is dented, and finished with black cable cord, which is formed in the same shape up a seam on each side. These side dents are connected across the back breadths by chains of cord, fastened with loops and tassels. The waist is plain, of the color of the upper skirt, and tastefully decorated with cord. The "Vicky dress" is of orange chambery. The skirt is divided into shallow scollops by two narrow rows of black braid. Below, it is closely barred with horizontal stripes of the same. The waist is trimmed to simulate a bodice. The sleeves are half close. This dress is accompanied with a graceful sacque, scolloped around the bottom and the edge of the flowing sleeves, and ornamented with black braid. The "Cluny dress" is made of blue *taffetas*, with oblique bands of black forming a border. A Gabrielle finished with narrow ruffles of Cluny is worn with this. One of the prettiest of wide sleeves is named the "Juvia." It is opened in three diamond shapes upon the outside, each being separated by a full rosette. A design full of grace and character is called the "Rosa." The bottom is intersected by deep notches, which are filled with rich loops of ribbon, attached by jet or silver buckles, or, if preferred, rosettes of straw. If the latter is used, straw gimps must be employed as waist and skirt trimmings.

For young ladies especially, rosettes are more dressy for high bodies and belt fastenings than buttons or clasps.

Many coat sleeves, variously distinguished with bows, plaitings, or rows of braid fancifully arranged, are retained in vogue. The "Fadette" is most popular. Four rows of braid or velvet form a cap at the top and a cuff. Two similar sections extend half way across at the elbow. Jet buttons separate each band.

Gold and silver embroideries appear upon parasols. Flower patterns are pretty, also Grecian borders. Crimped fringe and lace serve as a finish. It is noticeable that often in a single toilet, fringe, lace and satin pipings are used as trimmings.

This is not good taste, strictly speaking, and it is very bad, when one mantle is thus martyred. French taste has disfigured in this manner some of the costliest importations. Short circles have been adopted by very young ladies, instead of sacques or basquines. The last named should be half fitting, with flowing sleeves. It is a matter of individual caprice whether the side pieces shall be as long as the front and back, or finished out with flounces of lace.—Long sash fronts are exceedingly modish.

BOYS & GIRLS' COLUMNS.

The Doctor's Talks.

Perhaps you think I am to talk again about pollywogs. That is quite a mistake; I don't intend to confine myself to any particular subject, but say, now and then, a word

Fig. 1.

Fig. 2.

about animals, plants, stones, or any common thing that will teach you to use your eyes, and see that there are plenty of things worth the trouble of looking at closely.

Have you watched the trees this spring, and seen how the naked branches soon became clothed with leaves that now, in this warm June, cast a pleasant shade? You hardly noticed the trees when they were bare, but you admire them now that they are in full leaf. Did you ever think how all this came about, and how much work the trees did, beforehand, to prepare for this spread of foliage you now enjoy so much? Next winter, if you look at the trees, you will think of this, and notice the plump buds on the ends of the stems, and the smaller ones along their sides. Buds do not look very interesting, but those of most of our forest trees in winter already have, within them, the leaves that will so delight you in summer. I have had drawn, figure 2, a bud of a Horsechestnut tree, or Buckeye, because that is a large bud, and was handy. In winter, it looks as in the engraving, a scaly knob, all covered with a water-proof varnish. If you pick it open, you will find within it the very delicate young leaves, and these are very curiously packed away in a mass of cotton-like hairs, so as to perfectly protect them from the cold. As soon as the weather is warm enough, the scales fall open and the stem upon which the little leaves are placed pushes out; the leaves themselves rapidly enlarge, and soon the tree has its naked limbs hidden by the green covering. Figure 1 shows the shoot just pushing. Most of our forest trees make their growth in a very short time; the new shoots push rapidly in spring and unfold their leaves, and then remain quiet. But what is the tree doing all the summer? It is doing several things, and among the most important of these, it is preparing a very great number of buds for the growth of another year. At the ends of the branches and at the points where the leaves join the stem, there are quietly and slowly forming these curious buds. The buds are within and without composed of leaves, and the scales which look so dark and unlike leaves, are only leaves formed in a particular way to serve a particular purpose. In the Buckeye, in figure 1, we can see, in early spring, that, while the outer scales are very unlike leaves, the inner ones have a slight leaf-like look, and so along up to perfect leaves. Is not it strange that the tree should seem to know that something would be needed of it next spring and work away during summer to pack up carefully the young leaves, so that they will be protected from the rains and frosts of winter?

Do Cats Love Music.

Several incidents which have been communicated to the *Agriculturist*, seem to prove that cats enjoy sweet sounds, although they make horrid work when they try their own voices. One writes, that when the ladies of the family sing, the household cat will at once jump into the lap of one of the party and remain there until the music ceases. Three persons in different parts of the country have written that their cats have been detected running over the keys of the piano, apparently enjoying the sound. It would be a rare performance for one to be taught to play a tune, but we think that can hardly be expected.

Respect the Aged.

"Take my place, sir, if you please," said a boy, rising from the seat he had occupied in a crowded street car, and addressing an old gentleman who had just entered.— "Thank you, my boy, but I'm sorry you should have to stand," was the reply.—"I shall not mind it, sir; and I'm sure you need the seat more than I," returned the youth; and the old man took his place, a look of weariness, that had been noticed in his face when he came in, leaving it as he did so. It was a little thing for the boy to do, but it was a kind, respectful act, and some of those who saw it felt that it promised well for the boy's future.

Another old man was walking down the street some days later, when another boy came by, apparently in great haste. "Come, hurry up, old '76, or you'll never get where you're going;" were the rude words he spoke, as he rushed by. The old man made no reply, but looked sadly after the boy, and moved slowly on. "*I* should never speak like that," my young reader will say, and perhaps with a feeling of indignation against this boy. Well, I trust you would not. There are very many ways in which the young may show respect for the old, or rudeness to them. When you see an aged man or woman, never forget what kind of treatment they may rightly expect from you. Remember that they were young and strong and merry once like you. But that was long ago. For them the busy day of life is nearly past, and night is near. Try to make them happier. You will be glad some day to remember that you did so. UNCLE PAUL.

"Baby Ned," though not two years old, eats his dinner at the table with the family; and his mother finds it very difficult to keep him still long enough for "the blessing." One day, after much training, he folded his little hands and sat very quietly until just at the close of the service, as his mother was beginning inwardly to congratulate herself that for once, he had kept still, he suddenly called out "'at 'ill do (that will do) papa, pass plates now." Of course there was a smile.—H.

A Pattern Building.

The accompanying figure shows one of the hundreds of buildings, which may be made with Crandall's improved building blocks, noticed in a previous number of the

Agriculturist. It is here given as a pattern for some of our young friends, who have procured a set of the blocks to work by. No doubt, some of you could build a more tasteful structure, and if you succeed in making one that looks better, and will send a drawing or photograph of it, we may have it engraved, and call it the model building, until some one else succeeds in showing something more elegant. This will exercise the ingenuity and taste of all who may make the trial, whether successfully or not.

New Puzzles to be Answered.

No. 267. *Word Puzzle.*—Mace, Nutmegs, Raisins, Rice, Sugar, Tea, Salt, Lettuce—half the letters in these words, with half a letter added, will name a well-known newspaper. What is it?

No. 268. *Bible Question.*—What family of eight persons lived on a mountain, and all believed in the Word of God?

Answers to Problems and Puzzles.

The following are answers to the puzzles, etc., in the May number, page 187. No. 262. *Word Square.*—PEAR, EASE, ASIA, REAL.... No. 263. *Illustrated Rebus.*—Bear and forbear; with long-suffering overcome your foes.... No. 264.—*Geographical Enigma.*—No correct answers received.... No. 265. *Arithmetical Problem.* Twelve minutes.—The following have sent in correct answers. "S. G.," Jane, Robert and S. H. McNeel, George and Mary Carver, H. T. McCrea, Maggie Underwood, Henrietta Clayton, F. W. Livingston, McIntosh Robertson, Nannie J. Winn, Kate Fuller, Mary V. Caper, Augustus C. Busby, N. T. Wikoff, L. M. Wright, Jas. M. Danser, I. R. Webber, R. W. Fair, Wm. H. Elliott, Mrs. C. Eddy, Mary E. Reigart, F. C. Haines, Ephraim A. Chapman, "W. H. H.," H. C. Twilley, "T. D. S.," Wm. A. Fulton, Mrs. O. Mefford, Charles E. Hawkins, Matthias Barricklow, Samuel F. Seib, Isaac T. McLain, E. P. Brown, Belcher and Samuel, T. E. Lockwood, Andrew Jackson, Algernon R. McChesney, W. S. Nogus, S. Gussie Kilgore, Alice Suit, Laura Dickson, Hugh W. Kay, M. Mullaney, Bessie, Clara H. Schirenck, Harry S. Watkins, E. Lane.

No. 266. *Illustrated Rebus.*—This is ingeniously made so as to read in three ways.

THE FIRST LESSON.—From the Original Painting by Merle.—*Engraved for the American Agriculturist by J. L. [illegible]*

Knowledge gives pleasure, but the way to get it is not always easy. The child in the picture "don't want to learn its letters;" boys and girls usually like *to know*, but they do not often like to study. How many wish that learning could be done like breathing, without work, and because one could not help it. But that would not be the best way. *Study makes the mind strong*, just as work with the hands gives a stouter grip. It is not an easy thing for a little beginner to learn the alphabet; his mind has not been trained to attend, to observe, and to remember; but in a few years, by having duly fixed his thoughts upon some task, he will readily see through problems he can not now understand. Let those who can not learn quickly, and who find school duties hard, take courage by remembering that every resolute mastery of a lesson adds vigor to the brain-power, and helps make a mind that no difficulty can withstand. Those who learn easily, and carry away all the honor and prizes at school, are by no means always the most successful in life; but the boy who schools himself to conquer laziness, and trains his mind to severe application, whether he stands at the head or the foot of his class now, will by and by gain *power* to be prepared to take the front rank in any calling.

Spanish Puzzle.

Take six checker-men, three of each color, (pennies or buttons will do), and place them thus: The space left between the two colors should equal the diameter of a checker. The puzzle is, by moving and jumping, to put the whites in where the blacks [illegible] now are. Commence by moving one of the men that are next the middle, towards the opposite color. Suppose you begin by moving *Black* towards *White*. Then jump White over Black, and so on. There will never be but *one* open space, across which to move, or into which to jump. It is not allowed to jump or move a man backward—that is, each color must always advance towards the opposite side. The men must be kept in line, and a mark made at the ends, to show the limit beyond which the men must not go. The men of the same color, that is, all the whites, or blacks, are placed touching each other, although the engraving represents them as separated by a short space. To explain the puzzle, in giving an answer, the men may be numbered 1, 2, 3, etc.

(Business Notices $1.50 per Agate Line [illegible] Space.)

The Howe Machine Co.'s Sewing Machines,

699 Broadway, Cor. Fourth-st., New York.

For Families and Manufacturers.

These World-Renowned Sewing Machines

Were awarded the highest premium at the World's Fair in London, and six first premiums at the N. Y. State Fair of 1866.

These machines are made under the immediate supervision of the President of the Company, ELIAS HOWE, Jr., the original inventor of the Sewing Machine.

The Stitch invented by MR. HOWE, *and made on this Machine, is the most popular and durable, and all Sewing Machines are subject to the principle invented by him.*

SEND FOR CIRCULAR.

WHEELER & WILSON ROTARY HOOK

LOCK STITCH

SEWING MACHINES.

625 BROADWAY.

"WOMAN'S GREATEST BOON.—We would advise a man to forego a [illegible] and [illegible] wheat with a flail, rather than to see the wife wear her health, vigor and life away in the everlasting 'stitch, stitch, stitch,' when a Sewing Machine can be obtained. The WHEELER & WILSON is an [illegible] every household. We have had several different kinds [illegible], and after a six years' service, the WHEELER & WILSON has taken the precedence as the best, where all kinds of sewing are to be done in a family."

[American Agriculturist, Jan. 1865.

THE GREAT FAMILY SEWING MACHINE.

GROVER & BAKER'S

HIGHEST PREMIUM

Elastic Stitch

SEWING MACHINE.

495 Broadway, New York.

FLORENCE

LOCK-STITCH SEWING MACHINES.

Highest Premium, Fair of American Institute, 1865.
CELEBRATED REVERSIBLE FEED MOVEMENT.
UNIFORM SELF-ADJUSTING TENSION,
FOUR SEPARATE DISTINCT STITCHES.
WILL GATHER AND SEW A RUFFLE AT ONCE.
OFFICES OF THE COMPANY.
505 Broadway, N. Y., and 97 Cheapside, London, England.

THE EUREKA

BRICK MACHINE

makes 2,000 splendid Brick per hour, with only nine men and one pair horses, or 3,500 per hour by steam power. Has no complex machinery to be getting out of order or breaking down. Its great simplicity and marvelous power command the approval of every expert, at sight.

We challenge the world to produce its equal.

Satisfaction guaranteed to all purchasers.

ABRAM REQUA, General Agent,
No. 141 Broadway, New York.

FRANKLIN BRICK MACHINE.

Justly celebrated for perfect simplicity, great strength, and immense compressing power, [illegible] with eight men and two horses, [illegible]. J. H. RENICK, Proprietor, No. [illegible] Broadway, New York. [illegible]

PURE ITALIAN

Queens for sale. [illegible] Queens shipped. Send for Circular to A. FAIRFIELD [illegible], Maquoketa, Iowa.

FERD. F. MAYER, Chemist,

Has removed his Office to [illegible] Cedar-st., New York.

SILVERS' CELEBRATED

PATENT EXCELSIOR BROOM,

WHICH HAS TAKEN THE FIRST PREMIUMS AT THE NEW YORK, OHIO AND KENTUCKY STATE FAIRS, is unequaled for durability, lightness, elegance, and elasticity, and is generally acknowledged the most beautiful Broom in the world. It is the only one accepted for

THE PARIS EXPOSITION.

The ladies pronounce it THE MOST VALUABLE IN USE, when applied to Tapestry, Wilton, Brussels or Ingrain Carpets. It [illegible] to [illegible] that it sweeps with half the effort, and does not wear out the carpet one-fourth as fast as the old fashioned broom, therefore, MONEY and TIME are saved by its USE.

In the short period this broom has been before the public, it has received the highest commendations from people of all classes, and there is now no reason to doubt that in a short time it will entirely supersede the old-fashioned tied-broom as a household implement.

We present the following testimonials as evidence of the value of this invention:

[From the Hon. Horace Greeley.]

OFFICE OF THE TRIBUNE, NEW YORK, May 3, 1867.

Messrs. C. A. Clegg & Co.: Your broom is a good implement, and will, I [illegible] very large class, be acceptable and useful. To be able to renew a broom in ten minutes and at a few cents cost, will be [illegible] at once convenient and economical. I WISH IT ENTIRE SUCCESS. Yours,

HORACE GREELEY.

[From the American Agriculturist, after 3 Months' Test.]

SILVERS' PATENT BROOM.—This is a novelty, certainly. By means of a cap and screw, the brush can be removed at any time. We have no broom corn at hand to test the removal of the old brush and the putting in of new, but we do not see why it can not be readily done by any one, and farmers that raise a little plot of broom corn and make their own brooms, after buying a patent handle. **The one we are using has a superior elasticity.**

[From the New York Weekly Tribune, of May 8th, 1867.]

PATENT BROOMS.—Within a few years several patents have been issued for improved brooms. The end aimed at by all has been to make a broom which could be renewed at small cost by inserting a new brush. To combine this quality with elasticity, lightness, durability, and beauty, was difficult and seemingly impossible. An Ohio inventor conceived a plan which, it was thought, would answer, but a brass cap such as his broom required was declared impossible to make. One thought differently. A skillful worker in brass was employed, who after eight months' study and labor produced the cap now used on Silvers' Patent Broom. With the improved cap we shall not be surprised if this broom becomes popular among housekeepers in city and country.

For cut of Broom and valuable testimonials, see full column on page [illegible] of February No. *Agriculturist.*

TO FARMERS—AGENTS WANTED.

The Brass Metallic parts will be sent to Farmers (where we have no Agents) with full instructions for making their own Brooms, by mail or express prepaid, for $1.50.

Agents wanted in every city and county in the United States, to whom exclusive right of sale will be given, without any charge for Patent. Send for Illustrated Circular.

Over 200 Agents are already engaged in selling this Broom exclusively, and are making from $5 to $20 per day.

Address, stating first, second, and third choice of Counties,
C. A. CLEGG & CO., No. 206 Broadway, New York.

HERALD OF HEALTH.

The HERALD OF HEALTH is one of the grandest monthlies now before the public. It teaches the very things every family should know in order to make life complete, or how to live healthfully, beautifully, and how to secure for children complete symmetrical and beautiful bodies in which to set the immortal soul. Our list of contributors enrolls many of the leading men of the age. Turn to the February and April *Agriculturist* and see full prospectus, contributors, subjects, etc. By all means get this monthly. $2.00 a year; 20 cents a number. We will send AS SAMPLES 4 numbers for 50 cents. Address MILLER, WOOD & CO.,
15 Laight-st., New York.

THE LITTLE CORPORAL

Is acknowledged by the leading papers to be the

Best Juvenile Paper in America.

We offer a MAGNIFICENT LIST of PREMIUMS!

Subscribe at any time during the year.

The price of [illegible] one dollar a year, in advance; sample copy, with [illegible], [illegible] cents.
Address ALFRED L. SEWELL, Publisher, Chicago, Ill.

THE CHURCH UNION.

A NEW RELIGIOUS WEEKLY.

Devoted to the Unity of the Church. Advocates open communion and free Pulpit. Opposes Ritualism in every form. Publishes Sermons from every branch of the Church, including the sermons of

REV. HENRY WARD BEECHER.

Offers $1.00 per Subscriber to Agents, and will send to Clergymen who act as Agents free.

TERMS $2.50.

Address

PUBLISHER CHURCH UNION,
103 Fulton-st., New York.

Book Agents Wanted.

To solicit orders in each town in the United States and Canada, for the most popular subscription book ever published, being THE ILLUSTRATED HISTORY OF THE BIBLE, by *John Kitto, D. D., F. S. A., Edited by Rev. Alvan Bond, D. D., of Norwich, Conn.* Over 700 closely printed Royal Octavo pages, more than 100 full page engravings. Recommended by the leading clergy of all denominations of Christians. No other work [illegible]. Six large power presses running on the work. Everybody wants it. Experienced Agents say they never knew a book sell so well. No competition. Experienced Agents, School Teachers, Sabbath School Teachers, retired Clergymen, and others, are wanted to introduce this great work into every household in the land. For Circulars, etc., apply immediately to the Publisher, HENRY BILL, Norwich, Conn.

BUY THE BEST!

J. W. BRADLEY'S

CELEBRATED

DUPLEX ELLIPTIC

(OR DOUBLE SPRING)

SKIRTS.

THEY will not BEND or BREAK like the Single Springs, but WILL PRESERVE their PERFECT and GRACEFUL SHAPE in all CROWDED ASSEMBLAGES, CHURCHES, THEATRES, RAILROAD CARS, and for PROMENADE or HOUSE DRESS, where three or four ordinary skirts are THROWN ASIDE as USELESS.

EACH HOOP is composed of TWO FINELY-TEMPERED Steel Springs, BRAIDED TIGHTLY and FIRMLY together, EDGE to EDGE, forming one hoop, thus making the STRONGEST and MOST FLEXIBLE, as well as the MOST DURABLE and STYLISH SKIRT EVER MADE. In fact, they are superior to all others, COMBINING COMFORT, ECONOMY, LIGHTNESS, ELEGANCE, and DURABILITY.

This POPULAR SKIRT is UNIVERSALLY RECOMMENDED by the FASHION MAGAZINES and OPINIONS of the PRESS GENERALLY.

At WHOLESALE, by the Exclusive Manufacturers and SOLE OWNERS of PATENT,

WESTS, BRADLEY & CARY,

WAREROOMS AND OFFICE,
Nos. 97 Chambers, and 79 and 81 Reade sts., N. Y.

ALSO, at WHOLESALE by the LEADING JOBBERS.

Indelible.

Important to Gardeners, Nurserymen, Farmers, &c.

THE INDELIBLE PENCIL CO. (NORTHAMPTON, MASS.), have now ready for sale their new

HORTICULTURAL PENCIL,

for INDELIBLE writing on wood. Invaluable for making

DURABLE LABELS,

or for marking Tools, &c., &c.

PRICES:—75 cents single; $6 per dozen. Sent post-paid by mail or express on receipt of price.

ALSO FOR SALE,

THE INDELIBLE PENCIL for marking Linen, &c. PRICES:—50 cents single; $3 per dozen. Sent pre-paid as above.

A Liberal Discount made to Dealers.

EVERY PENCIL WARRANTED. AGENTS WANTED.

---

50 PERCENT.

Saved by Using B. T. Babbitt's Labor-saving Soap.

The SOAP is made from clean and pure materials, contains no adulteration of any kind, will not injure the most delicate fabric, and is especially adapted for woolens, which will not shrink after being washed with this SOAP. It may be used in hard or soft waters. It will remove paint, grease, tar, and stains of all kinds. One pound warranted equal to two pounds of ordinary family Soap. Directions sent with each bar for making three gallons of handsome Soft Soap from one pound of this Soap. Each bar is wrapped in a circular containing full directions for use, printed in English and German. Ask your grocer for "B. T. BABBITT'S SOAP," and take no other. B. T. BABBITT.

Nos. 64, 65, 66, 67, 68, 69, 70, 72 and 74 Washington-St., New York.

SQUIRE'S PATENT FRUIT JAR.

Fruits Preserved Without Sugar.

The Only Jar for Preserving Vegetables.

The Neatest, Most Convenient and Economical Jar extant.

This Jar is constructed so that the contents can be cooked in it, and all handling of Hot Fruit or Hot Jars or Tempering of Jars avoided; the contents retain all their natural flavor, and the labor of preserving is lessened more than one-half. Pamphlets sent on application.

J. B. BARTLETT, Wholesale Manufacturer,
69 Murray street, New York.

POMONA'S HOME NURSERIES,

Removed to Glendale P. O., Camden Co., N. J. We beg the indulgence of a few customers, who will receive their plants late. If the plants do not live, they will be more than duplicated in fall. The delay was unavoidable, and the first that has occurred in our very happy business relations with our customers. We shall offer, at prices to defy competition, next fall, *One Million Strawberry Plants*, 75,000 *Wilson Early Blackberry*, 20,000 *Philadelphia and other Raspberries*, 25,000 *Rochelle and other Blackberries*, with a general assortment of Nursery Stock. J. H. FOSTER, JR.

$600.—$600.—$600.

I have Agents making *Six Hundred Dollars* each month, selling and putting up my "Patent Door Bells." I want five more *good Agents.*

A. F. TAYLOR, New Britain, Conn.

Silver Tips for Children's Shoes.

They protect the toe from wear, and are highly ornamental. Applied to the most genteel shoes made. Buy no others.

SCALES.

THE ACKNOWLEDGED STANDARD.

FAIRBANKS & CO.

No. 252 BROADWAY, NEW YORK.

Turnip Seed by Mail.

The following varieties, the quality of which can not be excelled, will be mailed *post-paid*, to any address in the Union upon receipt of price affixed:

	per oz.	4 ozs.	8 ozs.	pound
Early White Dutch	10 cts.	20 cts.	30 cts.	$1.00
White Strap Leaf	10 "	25 "	30 "	1.00
Red Top Strap Leaf	10 "	25 "	30 "	1.00
Large White Globe	10 "	20 "	35 "	75
Large White Norfolk	10 "	20 "	35 "	75
Yellow Aberdeen	10 "	25 "	50 "	1.00
Golden Ball (Robertson's)	10 "	25 "	50 "	1.00
Large Yellow Globe, extra	10 "	25 "	45 "	1.00
Long White French	10 "	25 "	50 "	1.00
Long White or Cow Horn	10 "	25 "	50 "	1.00
Yellow Finland	15 "	30 "	50 "	75
Waite's Eclipse, fine	10 "	25 "	50 "	1.00
German Yellow	15 "	30 "	50 "	1.00
Sweet German	10 "	25 "	50 "	1.00
Improved Ruta Baga	10 "	25 "	50 "	1.00
Skirving's do.	10 "	20 "	45 "	75
Laing's do.	10 "	20 "	45 "	75
Dale's Hybrid	10 "	20 "	45 "	75

Packets for retailing, full size, per dozen..............50 cts.
do do. half size, do ....25 cts.

Prices to dealers by the quantity given upon application.

Our celebrated Seed Catalogue and *Guide to the Vegetable and Flower Garden*, containing 130 *pages, beautifully illustrated*, will be mailed to all applicants enclosing 25 cents.

Address B. K. BLISS, Springfield, Mass.

REMINGTON'S FOOT-ROT REMEDY.

1000 TESTS—NOT ONE FAILURE.—Two months ago I applied Remington's Foot-Rot medicine to a flock of sheep, and they have kept perfectly sound since, and I have no doubt that if properly applied that it will make a sure cure. JOHN JOHNSTON.

Geneva, N. Y., Feb. 16, 1867.

One thorough application is generally sufficient; rarely the second may be needed. The best remedy we have ever used. T. C. MAXWELL & BROS.,

Nurseries, Geneva, N. Y., April 10, 1867.

The best cure I have ever used.—

Geneva, April 16, 1867. ROB'T J. SWAN.

I cured 50 sheep for 50 cents. If taken in time one application is sufficient. In the worst cases two applications are sufficient. H. D. BENNETT.

Geneva, April 6, 1867.

I took 100 maggots from one foot and cured with one application. JOHN E. BOOTHE.

Canandaigua, April 1, 1867.

Warranted if used according to directions. For sale by Druggists. Price, $1.00. C. REMINGTON, Ag't,
Manufacturer, GENEVA, N. Y.

CHEAPEST POWER

Known to the World.

One Hundred per cent. gained by grinding and cooking food for stock. The entire corn crop of the country can be ground right on every man's farm at an expense to the farmer of less than one cent per bushel. A large, dry prairie farm can be made equal to those having natural water privileges and thus increased in value $1000. Halliday's Self-Regulating Wind Machine guaranteed to do this, and furnished on trial, on the "no-cure, no-pay," principle. 200,000 dollars' worth now in successful operation from a small size for pumping water on ordinary farms, up to 40-horse power grain-grinding mill. Engraving and price list sent by addressing EDWARD BURNHAM, 151 East 23d-st., New York, or JOHN BURNHAM, Gen'l Ag't., Batavia, Illinois.

Normal Academy of Music,

At Meadville, Pa.

The 8th Term of 6 weeks will commence July 2d. For Circulars giving Terms, &c., and particulars as to the donations of Free Scholarships, address THEODORE E. PERKINS, care of Brown & Perkins, 420 Broome-st., New York.

CARPENTER'S PORTRAIT OF LINCOLN.
HOURS AT HOME.

To get this standard Steel Engraving, and the only authentic likeness of President Lincoln, send the name of one new subscriber for two years, or those of two new subscribers for one year ($6), to our popular monthly, Hours at Home.
C. SCRIBNER & CO., New York.

5 MORE GOOD AGENTS WANTED TO SELL "*Taylor's Patent Door Bell.*" *See page 237.*

Not too Late to Plant

The Kittatinny Blackberry.

A YEAR SAVED BY PLANTING NOW.

The plants of our growth may be safely put out until July 1st.

They are YOUNG, STRONG, WELL-ROOTED, and WARRANTED TO GROW, with fair treatment.

They will make strong-bearing plants for next year.

The price is WITHIN THE REACH OF ALL.

They are sent by mail, and safe arrival guaranteed, at $7.50 per dozen; $13.00 per hundred; $120 per thousand.

CASH ORDERS WILL RECEIVE PROMPT ATTENTION.

F. K. PHOENIX, Bloomington, Ill.

U. S. MAIL

AND POST OFFICE ASSISTANT,

Contains all new Postal Laws and Regulations, Table of Foreign Postages, Answers to Correspondents on Doubtful Postal Questions, Miscellaneous Postal Information, &c., &c. Indispensable to Post-masters, especially at Small Offices. Edited by J. GAYLER, Special Agent of the Post Office Department. Published monthly in New York, at $1 per year. Address "PUBLISHER U. S. MAIL," New York.

The Premium Machine.

BUCKEYE
MOWER & REAPER

Declared by the Judges at

THE GREAT NATIONAL FIELD TRIAL,

held at Auburn, in July last, to be superior to all competitors in lightness of draft, freedom from side draft, perfection of mechanical construction, portability, facility of management, strength and durability.

Descriptive Circulars, and synopsis of Official Report of Auburn Trial, forwarded by mail.

Manufactured by ADRIANCE, PLATT & CO.,
(Manufactory, Po'keepsie.) 165 Greenwich-st., N. Y.

HURD'S PATENT

AMERICAN HOG TAMER,

TO PREVENT

HOGS FROM ROOTING,

Every Farmer Should Have it.

IT SAVES MANY TIMES ITS COST.

Price, with 3 Knives, delivered free at nearest Express Office, $1.00. Address
THE PRAIRIE FARMER CO.,
197 Lake-st., Chicago.

FOREIGN RELISHES, SAUCES, ETC.—English Pickles, Sauces and Condiments. Foreign preserved and dried Fruits, Alimentary Conserves, French Peas, Truffles, Mushrooms, Asparagus, Mustard, Vinegar, Olives, Holland Herrings, Canton Ginger, English, French and Swiss Cheese;—sold retail at wholesale prices, by the Importer, EDWARD B. J. SINGLETON, 185 Pearl-st., cor. of Cedar, New York. Orders executed for any part of the U. S. strictly for Cash, at lowest prices.

BRETT'S PATENT GAUGE or REST, for grinding MOWING MACHINE KNIVES, saves time and muscle, and preserves a true bevel. A mowing machine cannot be kept in first-rate order without it. Agents wanted in every County. Address
BRETT, SEXTON & ALLEN,
Geneva, Ohio.

Partner Wanted with a capital of $1000 to take an active part in Grape Nursery and importing, now established. For particulars address RYDER & CO., Sing Sing, N. Y.

To Merchants and Peddlers Everywhere!

A New and Good Thing for Every Family.
DOTY'S EVERLASTING CLOTHES-PIN!

(Patented March 26, 1867.)

Ingeniously constructed of a single piece of non-rusting, elastic wire, so shaped that it

ADJUSTS ITSELF TO ANY SIZE LINE.

ADVANTAGES OVER OTHER CLOTHES-PINS:

I.—CANNOT BE SHAKEN OFF THE LINE.
II.—WILL NOT FREEZE CLOTHES TO THE LINE.
III.—WILL NOT MARK THE WHITEST FABRIC.
IV.—WILL NOT SPLIT, ROT, RUST, OR WEAR OUT IN A LIFE TIME.

Although their first cost is greater than the common wooden pins, their purchase is TRUE ECONOMY, being serviceable *far longer*, and *more convenient.*

Housekeepers, who have had fine garments lost in snow, or draggled in mud by the wooden pin working loose and shaking off, or who have, on bitter cold days, had to thaw or wrench from the line, clothes frozen fast by the dampness held by wooden pins, will appreciate the merits of "DOTY'S EVERLASTING" pins.

Retail Price, 30 cents per dozen. Three dozen, boxed and mailed, POST PAID, for $1.20. Send two red stamps for sample pin and wholesale terms and circulars.
DOTY'S CLOTHES-PIN CO.,
32 Courtlandt-st., New York.

THE
UNIVERSAL

CLOTHES WRINGER,

Cannot be surpassed or equaled by any other Wringer for durability, till the expiration of the patent for the "COG-WHEEL REGULATOR" or "STOP-GEAR." *No other Wringer is licensed under this Patent.* It being now universally conceded that Cogs are necessary to prevent the Rolls from being broken or torn loose, many attempts have been made to get a Cog-Wheel arrangement which shall equal the UNIVERSAL, and yet avoid the "Stop-Gear" patent, but *without success.*

Any Cog-Wheel Wringer having Cogs, whether at one or both ends of the roll, which can play apart and fly out of gear when a large article is passing through, is COMPARATIVELY WORTHLESS, as the Cogs are then of no aid *when most needed*, and an arrangement of Cog-Wheels in *fixed* bearings, the upper one acting on a roll in *movable* bearings, must prove a *mechanical failure* in use, and we warn all persons not to purchase such Wringers as an "improvement on the Universal," which they are sometimes represented to be by the salesmen.

Many who sell the UNIVERSAL WRINGER, keep also the

DOTY

WASHING MACHINE,

which, though but recently introduced, is really as great a LABOR and CLOTHES SAVER as the Wringer, and is destined to win public favor and patronage everywhere.

It washes *perfectly*, without *wearing* or *rubbing* the clothes at all.

Those keeping the Wringer for sale, will order the Washer for customers, if they have not got a supply on hand. On receipt of the Retail price, *from places where no one is selling*, we will send either or both machines from New York.

Prices—Family Washer, $14. No. 1½ Wringer, $10. No. 2 Wringer, $8.50.

A supply of the Wringers and Washers are always kept on hand in Chicago, Cincinnati, Cleveland, Janesville and St. Louis, boxed ready for shipment, at about New York prices.

Circulars, giving wholesale and retail prices, sent free.

Large profits are made selling these machines. Exclusive right of sale given, with no charge for the patent right.

R. C. BROWNING, General Agent,
No. 32 Courtlandt-st.,
(Opposite Merchants' Hotel,) New York.

ORANGE ORCHARDS.—For Sale a magnificent Tract on the St. Johns' River, East Florida. Healthy, beautiful, and accessible. Containing hundreds of natural Orange Trees, and with every thing else in climate, soil, and position required for the highest success in that culture. The most safe, easy, agreeable, and profitable crop in the world. Address
H. R. DAVIS, "AGRICULTURIST" Office, New York.

BLUNT & NICHOLS,
LATE
E. & G. W. BLUNT,
179 Water-street, New York,
IMPORTERS AND MANUFACTURERS OF
Mathematical, Surveying and Nautical Instruments,
Fine Watches, Marine and Pocket Chronometers, Charts and Nautical Books, Telescopes, Marine Glasses, Opera Glasses. Catalogues sent free.

THE NEW YORK MIRROR.—Just *the* paper for the Farmer, Business man and Family. Contains full MARKET REPORTS, PRICES CURRENT of all Merchantable articles, besides Agricultural and Domestic Items, Stories, Poems, Miscellaneous reading, sketches of old N. Y. Houses, etc. $1 per Annum. To Clubs of ten, only $10. Send for specimen. Address N. Y. MIRROR, 21 Ann-st., New York.

EVERY MAN HIS OWN HOUSE PAINTER and Paper Hanger.—All Housekeepers, Farmers and Painters must have the Book. Send 25 cents by mail to THOS. SMITH, Baldwin City, Kansas, and it will be sent free of postage to any address.

THE JUNE No. of DEMOREST'S MONTHLY MAGAZINE, with Elegant Fashions; Music, Poems, Entertaining Stories, Engravings, Household Matters, Full Size Patterns, and other useful and entertaining Novelties. Single copies, 30 cents; yearly, $3, with a valuable Premium. Address W. JENNINGS DEMOREST, No. 473 Broadway, New York.

Hot-House, Cold Grapery, etc.; with Plans for the Construction and Heating. By WM. CHORLTON. Cloth, 12mo, 204 pp.

Cobbett's American Gardener............75

A Treatise on the Laying Out and Management of Gardens. Though an old work, it is one which will find a place in every considerable library, as the production of a remarkable man. While it is marked by the author's peculiarities, it is so full of plain common-sense, that it is worthy of being kept in print. By WILLIAM COBBETT. Cloth, 12mo., 230 pp.

Cole's American Fruit Book.......... 75

Containing Directions for Raising, Propagating, and Managing Fruit-Trees, Shrubs, and Plants, with descriptions of the best varieties of fruit, etc. 18mo, 283 pp.

Cole's American Veterinarian..........75

Diseases of *Domestic Animals*, showing the *Causes*, *Symptoms*, and *Remedies*, and rules for *Restoring* and *Preserving Health* by good management, with directions for *Training* and *Breeding*. By S. W. COLE. Cloth, 18mo., 288 pp.

Copeland's Country Life..........$5.00.

An elegant Octavo Volume, containing 926 pages, and 250 Engravings. It is a Compendium of Agricultural and Horticultural Practical Knowledge; embracing Descriptions, Hints, Suggestions and Details of great value to every one interested in Fruit. Flowers, Vegetables, or Farm Crops. It describes and illustrates nearly the whole range of topics of interest to the Farmer, the Gardener, the Fruit Culturist, and the Amateur. By ROBERT MORRIS COPELAND. Cloth, beveled boards, 8vo., 926 pp.

Cotton-Planter's Manual.. ....$1.50.

This is the only popular work published on the subject. It is a compilation of facts from the best authorities on the CULTURE OF COTTON, its Natural History, Chemical Analysis, Trade, and Consumption, with a history of Cotton and the Cotton-Gin. Cloth, 12mo, 320 pp.

Dadd's American Cattle-Doctor....$1.50.

To Help Every Man to be his own Cattle-Doctor. A work by GEO. H. DADD, M. D., Veterinary Practitioner; giving the necessary information for preserving the Health and Curing the Diseases of OXEN, COWS, SHEEP, and SWINE, with a great variety of original Recipes, and valuable information on Farm and Dairy Management. 12mo, 359 pp.

Dadd's Modern Horse Doctor......$1.50

CONTAINING PRACTICAL OBSERVATIONS ON THE CAUSES, NATURE, AND TREATMENT of Diseases and Lameness of HORSES; embracing the most recent and improved Methods, according to an enlightened system of Veterinary Practice, for Preservation and Restoration of Health. Illustrated. By GEO. H. DADD, M.D., Veterinary Surgeon. Cloth, 12mo., 432 pp.

Dana's Muck Manual.....,.........$1.25

A Manual for Farmers; treating of Soils, Manures, Composts, etc., and especially of the important subject of using MUCK, the great natural fertilizer of the country. By SAMUEL L. DANA. Cloth, 12mo., 312 pp.

Downing's Landscape Gardening and Rural Architecture $6.50

The most complete and valuable work ever issued on Landscape Gardening in North-America, for the Improvement of Country Residences; containing full Directions for everything connected with the Laying out and adorning the Rural Home, the Grounds, the Gardens, the Buildings, the Trees and Plants, etc., with principles of taste so stated as to adapt the work to all classes. Splendidly Illustrated with many Steel and fine Wood Engravings. By the late A. J. DOWNING. New Edition, Enlarged, Newly Illustrated and Revised, with Supplement, by HENRY WINTHROP SARGENT. Octavo, 531 pp. Extra cloth, gilt, beveled bds.

Eastwood's Complete Cranberry Manual 75

Giving directions for the cultivation in different localities, with illustrations and descriptions of varieties. By BENJ. EASTWOOD, Cloth, 12mo, 120 pp.

Elliott's Western Fruit Grower's Guide 1.50

The previous Edition of this work was Thoroughly Revised; embracing all the new and valuable Fruits, with the latest improvements in their Cultivation; especially adapted to the wants of Western Fruit-Growers; full Illustrations. By F. R. ELLIOTT, of Ohio. Cloth, 12mo, 503 pp.

Field's Pear Culture................$1.25

THE PEAR GARDEN; a Treatise on the Propagation and Cultivation of the Pear Tree, with Instructions for Management from the Seedling to the Bearing Tree. By THOMAS W. FIELD. Illustrations. Cloth, 12mo, 286 pp.

Flax Culture........................ 50

A new and very valuable work, consisting of full directions, from selection of ground and seed to preparation and marketing of crop, as given by a number of experienced growers. 8vo, paper.

French's Farm Drainage............... 1.50

The Principles, Process, and Effects of Draining Land with Stones, Wood, Drain-Plows, Open Ditches, and especially with Tiles; including Tables of Rainfall, Evaporation, Filtration, Excavation, Capacity of Pipes, cost and number to the acre. With over 100 Illustrations. The best work on Draining published. By Judge FRENCH, of New Hampshire, President of Mass. Agricultural College. Cloth, 12mo, 384 pp.

Fuller's Grape Culturist.............$1.50

This is the latest and most practical work issued on the Culture of the Hardy Grapes, with full directions for all departments of Propagation, culture, etc., with one hundred and five excellent engravings, illustrating the various operations of Planting, Training, Grafting, etc. New edition, revised and enlarged. By ANDREW S. FULLER, Practical Horticulturist. Cloth, 12mo, 262 pp.

Fuller's Illustrated Strawberry Culturist.......................*Paper*,.. 20

A new, practical little work, meeting with universal favor. It gives a full list of varieties, down to the latest valuable seedlings. Paper, 12mo, 48 pp.

Guenon's Treatise on Milch Cows.... 75.

An interesting work, giving new and peculiar directions, and many illustrative engravings, for determining by natural marks or external signs, the quality and quantity of milk a cow will give, length of time she will continue in milk, etc., with introductory remarks of forty pages on the Cow and Dairy. Sixty-third thousand. 8vo, 88 pp.

Herbert's Hints to Horse-Keepers.. $1.75

This is the best practical work on the Horse, prepared in this country. A COMPLETE MANUAL for HORSEMEN, embracing: How to Breed a Horse; How to Buy a Horse; How to Break a Horse; How to Use a Horse; How to Feed a Horse; How to Physic a Horse (Allopathy or Homœopathy); How to Groom a Horse; How to Drive a Horse; How to Ride a Horse, etc., and Chapters on MULES and PONIES, etc. By the late HENRY WILLIAM HERBERT, (Frank Forester.) Beautifully illustrated throughout. Cloth, 12mo., 425 pp.

Hooper's Dog and Gun...... ....30.

"A Few Loose Chapters on Shooting," with some Anecdotes and Incidents, Notes on Guns, Choosing and Training Dogs; about Game, etc. By J. J. HOOPER, Montgomery, Ala. Neat paper covers; 12mo, 105 pp.

Hop Culture..................................40

PRACTICAL DETAILS fully given, from the Selection and Preparation of the SOIL, SETTING and CULTIVATION of the Plants, to PICKING, DRYING, PRESSING and MARKETING the Crop. Plain Directions by Ten Experienced Cultivators. Illustrated with over forty engravings. Edited by PROF. GEORGE THURBER, Editor of the *American Agriculturist*. 8vo., paper.

Johnston's Agricultural Chemistry.. 1.75

LECTURES ON THE APPLICATION OF CHEMISTRY AND GEOLOGY TO AGRICULTURE. New edition, with an Appendix, containing the Author's Experiments in Practical Agriculture. By the late JAS. F. W. JOHNSTON, M.A., F.R.SS. L. and E., etc., etc. This is an American edition of the large and extensive English work. Cloth, large 12mo, 709 pp.

Leuchars' How to Build Hot-Houses..$1.50

GREEN-HOUSES, GRAPERIES, etc. etc., and how to Ventilate them. Illustrated with numerous Engravings. This is the only work published in this country, specially devoted to this subject. By ROBERT B. LEUCHARS, Garden Architect. Cloth, 12mo., 366 pp.

My Vineyard at Lakeview........$1.25.

This book is especially valuable as giving an account of the processes actually followed in celebrated Grape Regions in Western New York, and on the shores and islands of Lake Erie. To any one who wishes to grow grapes, whether a single vine or a vineyard, it is full of valuable teachings. It tells just what the beginner in grape culture wishes to know, with the charm that always attends the relation of personal experience. Cloth, 12mo., 143 pp.

Norton's Elements of Scientific Agriculture............ 75

A valuable and popular treatise on the Connection between Science and the art of Practical Farming. By the late JOHN P. NORTON, M.A., Professor of Scientific Agriculture in Yale College. Cloth, 12mo, 218 pp.

Onions: How to Raise them Profitably, *Paper*........,......,...,.........20

Being the Practical Details, from Selection of Seed and Preparation of Ground to Harvesting and Marketing the Crop, given very plainly by *Seventeen Practical Onion Growers* of long experience, residing in different parts of the country. No more valuable work of its size was ever issued. Octavo, 32 pp. Neat paper covers.

Our Farm of Four Acres, and the Money we Made by it.................30

From the Twelfth London Edition, with an introduction for the American Edition. This work has already had an immense sale, both in England and in this country. It is written by a lady, and while conveying many useful suggestions, it has almost the interest of a romance. 12mo, 126 pp. New Edition. Price in neat paper covers, 30c.; bound, 60 cents.

Pardee on Strawberry Culture........ 75

A Manual for the Cultivation of the Strawberry; with a Description of the Best Varieties. Also, Notes on the Raspberry, Blackberry, Currant, Gooseberry, and Grape. By R. G. PARDEE. Cloth, 12mo, 157 pp.

Peat and its Uses ....$1.25.

A New Work on Peat, thorough and Practical; it gives a full history of Peat, Muck, etc., telling what they are, where found, and how to estimate their value. It describes the various methods of using Peat for manure, as an absorbent, as an ameliorator of the soil, etc.; and it is especially explicit in regard to the use of Peat as Fuel, describing minutely the various processes employed in preparing it to burn, from the simplest to the most complicated; such as are in use in this country, and Europe. It is illustrated with many Engravings of machines, etc. The work is invaluable to those having Peat or Muck swamps, or wishing to invest in Peat Companies. By PROF. SAMUEL W. JOHNSON, of Yale College. Cloth, 12mo., 168 pp.

Pedder's Land-Measurer for Farmers..60

A convenient Pocket Companion, showing at once the contents of any piece of land, when its length and width are known, up to 1,500 feet either way, with various other useful farm tables. Cloth, 18mo, 144 pp.

Quinby's Mysteries of Bee-Keeping Explained..............................$1.50

Newly written throughout, containing the results of thirty-five years of successful experience, with *full, plain*, and *practical Directions for all details of Bee Culture*; including also a Description and Manner of Using the Movable Comb and Box Hives, with the most approved modes of Propagating and Treating the Italian Bee, etc., etc., with numerous illustrations. By M. QUINBY, Practical Bee-keeper.

Randall's Fine-Wool Sheep Husbandry $1.

Giving Prominent Characteristics of Different Breeds; Principles of breeding correctly; practical and concise rules for Selecting the Best, and making the best Crosses for Wool and Mutton. By HON. HENRY S. RANDALL, LL.D. 12mo, 160 pp.

Randall's Sheep Husbandry........$1.50

With an account of the different Breeds of Sheep; Selecting the Best for Wool and for Mutton; Rules for Crossing; Practical Details for Rearing; Summer and Winter Management, Treating Diseases; with New Chapters by Henry S. Randall and G. W. Kendall on Sheep Husbandry in Texas, with Portraits of different Breeds, Illustrations of Sheep Folds, and other Articles in Sheep Husband. Octavo, 338 pp.

Richardson on Dogs..*Paper*, 30, *Cloth*,..60.

Or, Dogs; Their Origin and Varieties. Directions as to their Management. Simple Instructions for Treatment under Disease, etc., etc., with numerous engravings. By H. D. Richardson, author of sundry works on animals. 18mo, 127 pp. Neat paper covers, 30c.; bound, 60c.

Saunders's Domestic Poultry........ 75.

A New Practical Treatise on the *Preferable Breeds of Farm-Yard Poultry*, their History and Leading Characteristics; with *Complete Instructions for Breeding* and *Fattening*, including Preparing for Exhibition at Poultry Shows, etc. Very fully Illustrated. By Simon M. Saunders. 12mo, 104 pp. Paper, 40c.; cloth, 75c.

Schenck's Gardener's Text Book 75

Directions for the Forming and Management of the Kitchen Garden, the Culture and Use of Vegetables, Fruits, and Medicinal Herbs. Cloth, 18mo., 306 pp.

Skillful Housewife,.... 75

Or, Complete Guide to Domestic Cookery, Taste, Comfort, and Economy, embracing 659 Recipes, with many valuable hints pertaining to household duties, the care of health, *Education of Children*, Gardening, Birds. By Mrs. L. G. Abell. Cloth, 18mo., 216 pp.

Stewart's Stable Book..............$1.50

A treatise on the Management of Horses, in relation to Stabling, Grooming, Feeding, Watering, and Working, Construction of Stables, Ventilation, Appendages of of Stables, Management of the Feet and of Diseased and Defective Horses. By John Stewart, Veterinary Surgeon. With Notes and Additions, adapting it to American food and climate. By A. B. Allen, former Editor of *American Agriculturist*. Cloth, 12mo., 378 pp.

The Miniature Fruit Garden..... $1.00.

On the Culture of Pyramidal and Bush Fruit Trees, Dwarf Apples and Pears are beautiful ornaments, besides being useful in giving abundant crops of fruit; they can be grown in Small Gardens and City Yards, and be readily removed. Root Pruning is fully explained. There are directions also, concerning Dwarf Cherries and Plums, Figs and Filberts. It is a valuable work for the cultivator. By Thomas Rivers. Cloth, 18mo., 143 pp.

Thompson's Food of Animals......$1.00.

Experimental Researches on the Food of Animals, the value of different kinds for feeding and fattening purposes, with remarks upon the food of Man; being details of important experiments made by the British Government. By Robert Dundas Thompson, M. D. Cloth, 12mo, 172 pp.

Tobacco Culture; Full Practical Details.25

This is by far the most useful and valuable work ever issued on this subject. It contains full details of every process from the Selection and Preparation of the Seed and Soil, to the Harvesting, Curing, and Marketing the Crop, with Illustrative Engravings of the operations. The work was prepared by *Fourteen Experienced Tobacco Growers*, residing in different parts of the country. It also contains Notes on the Tobacco Worm, with Illustrations. Octavo, 48 pp., in neat paper covers.

Youatt and Martin on Cattle .....$1.50.

Being a treatise on their Breeds, Management, Diseases; a full history of the various races; their origin, breeding, and merits, their capacity for Beef and Milk. By W. Youatt and W. C. L. Martin. A complete guide for the Farmer, the Amateur, and Veterinary Surgeon, with many illustrations. Edited by Ambrose Stevens. Cloth, 12mo., 469 pp.

Youatt and Martin on the Hog.....$1.00

A treatise on the Breeds, Management, and Medical Treatment of Swine, with directions for salting pork, and curing bacon and hams. By Wm. Youatt, V.S., and W. C. L. Martin. American edition, edited by Ambrose Stevens. Illustrated with engravings. Cloth, 12 mo., 221 pp.

Youatt and Spooner on the Horse..$1.50

The Structure and Diseases of the Horse, Remedies, Rules to Buyers, Breakers, Shoers, etc. Youatt's work somewhat simplified and brought down by W. C. Spooner, M.R.C.V.S.; to which is prefixed an account of the Breeds in the United States and Canadas, by Hon. Henry S. Randall. Illustrated with numerous engravings. Cloth, 12mo., 483 pp.

Youatt on Sheep.............. ...$1.00.

With details for Breeding and Rearing; Notes on Different Breeds; Summer and Winter Management; Characteristics of different Kinds of Wool, with Portraits of different Breeds of Sheep. Octavo, 160 pp.

Warder's Hedges and Evergreens...$1.50

This is the only book wholly devoted to the Cultivation, Pruning and Management of Plants suitable for American hedging, especially the Maclura, or OSAGE ORANGE; illustrated with engravings of plants, implements, and processes; to which is added a *Treatise on Evergreens*, their varieties, propagation, culture, etc. By J. A. Warder. 12mo., 291 pp.

HAVE YOU A GARDEN?

MAKE YOUR GARDEN PAY.

MAKE IT PAY.
MAKE IT PAY.
MAKE IT PAY.
MAKE IT PAY.

MAKE YOUR GARDEN PAY

By Reading the New Book,

GARDENING FOR PROFIT.

FIND OUT who are the men that are fitted for the Busi-
FIND OUT ness of Gardening.
FIND OUT
FIND OUT the amount of Capital required and the Work-
FIND OUT ing Force per acre.
FIND OUT
FIND OUT what are the Profits of Market Gardening.
FIND OUT
FIND OUT the best Location, Situation and Manner of
FIND OUT Laying Out a Garden.
FIND OUT
FIND OUT all about Soils, Drainage and Preparation; and
FIND OUT about Manures and Implements.
FIND OUT
FIND OUT the uses and management of Cold Frames.
FIND OUT
FIND OUT the formation and management of Hot Beds.
FIND OUT
FIND OUT about Forcing Pits, or Green-houses; Seeds and
FIND OUT Seed raising.
FIND OUT
FIND OUT How, When and Where to sow seeds.
FIND OUT
FIND OUT about Transplanting; about Insects; about the
FIND OUT Packing of Vegetables for Shipping, and the
FIND OUT Preservation of Vegetables in Winter.
FIND OUT
FIND OUT the most valuable kinds of Vegetables and the
FIND OUT Culture proper for each, with very many other
FIND OUT things that the owner of a Garden, *large or*
FIND OUT *small*, will be glad to know.
FIND OUT
FIND OUT how to make from $300 to $1000 per acre on
FIND OUT your land. It has been done, and you can
FIND OUT learn **How to Do It.**

FIND OUT ALL THIS BY READING

GARDENING FOR PROFIT

IN THE MARKET AND FAMILY GARDEN.

BY PETER HENDERSON.

Published by ORANGE JUDD & CO., No. 41 Park Row, New York.

Sent post-paid, on receipt of price. PRICE $1.50.

NEW BOOKS.

Saunders' Domestic Poultry.

By S. M. Saunders.

New Edition Revised and Enlarged.

This Book contains Articles on the Preferable Breeds of Farm-Yard Poultry, Their History and Leading Characteristics, with Complete Instructions for Breeding and Fattening, and Preparing for Exhibition at Poultry Shows, etc., etc., derived from the Author's Experience and Observation.

The work is compact, full of valuable hints and information, and beautifully illustrated.

An appendix contains an account of *Poultry breeding on a large scale*, as practiced in the neighborhood of Paris, and is a very important addition to the work.

Price, paper 40 cts., cloth 75 cts.

ORANGE JUDD & CO., Publishers.

Money in the Swamps.

PEAT! PEAT! PEAT!

FUEL—MANURE.

WHERE TO FIND IT.

HOW TO MAKE AND USE IT.

ITS VALUE.

A NEW WORK ON PEAT,

THOROUGH AND PRACTICAL;

By PROF. SAMUEL W. JOHNSON, of Yale College.

It gives a full history of PEAT, MUCK, etc., telling what they are, where found, and how to estimate their value.

It describes the various methods of using Peat for manure, as an absorbent, as an ameliorator of the soil, etc., and it is especially explicit in regard to the

USE OF PEAT AS FUEL,

describing minutely the various processes employed in preparing it to burn, from the simplest to the most complicated; such as are in use in this country, and Europe. It is illustrated with many Engravings of machines, etc.

The work is invaluable to those having Peat or Muck swamps, or wishing to invest in Peat Companies.

SENT POST-PAID. PRICE $1.25

ORANGE JUDD & CO., No. 41 Park Row New York.

THE

RARITAN BAY

Mining and Manufacturing Company.

CAPITAL, 150,000 Shares of $10 Each.

WORKING-CAPITAL RESERVED,

60,000 Shares.

TRUSTEES.

SAM'L BONNELL, Jr., ANDW. G. BININGER,
WM. H. TALMAGE, FREDERIC A. POTTS,
CHARLES C. ALGER, H. H. HOUSTON,
HENRY H. KEELER.

S. BONNELL, Jr., President, 111 BROADWAY.
A. G. BININGER, Treasurer, 81 LIBERTY-ST.

A LIMITED NUMBER OF SHARES
OF THE
CAPITAL STOCK
For Sale at the Office of

BELL, FARIS & CO.,

BANKERS, 14 NEW-ST., NEW YORK.

1,000 Agents Wanted

TO SELL

THREE POPULAR BOOKS.

1.

THE SOLDIER'S STORY

Of his captivity at Andersonville, Belle Isle, and other Rebel Prisons.
By W. L. GOSS.
Illustrated by Thomas Nast. 12mo, Cloth. Price $2.00.

2.

THE NEGRO

IN THE AMERICAN REBELLION.
His Heroism and his Loyalty.
By WM. WELLS BROWN,
Author of "The Black Man."
12mo. Cloth. Price, $2.00.

3.

Complete Practical Fruit Books.

Practical and Scientific Fruit Culture.
By CHAS. R. BAKER,
Of the Dorchester Nurseries.
Crown, 8vo., Cloth. $1.00.
Terms most liberal. Address
LEE & SHEPARD, Publishers, Boston.

The Murder of The Unborn!

READ
WHY NOT?
A Book for Every Woman.
By Prof. H. R. STORER, M. D.
A Prize Essay—A New Edition,
Revised and Enlarged.
16mo, Paper, 50 cents. Cloth, $1.00.
Sold by all Booksellers, and sent by mail, post-paid, on receipt of price.
LEE & SHEPARD, Publishers, Boston.

The Pulpit Against Abortion.

Serpents in the Dove's Nest.

By the Rev. JOHN TODD, D. D.
Containing
1. Fashionable Murder.
2. The Cloud with a Dark Lining.
16mo, Paper, 30 cents. Cloth, 50 cents.
Sent by mail, post paid, on receipt of price, and for sale by all Booksellers.
LEE & SHEPARD, Publishers, Boston.

How to Make Sugar Cheaper.

Beet Root Sugar,

and Cultivation of the Beet.
By E. B. GRANT.
16mo, Cloth. Price, $1.25.

How to Make Fuel Cheaper.

Peat as an Article of Fuel.

By T. H. LEAVITT.
12mo, Cloth. $1.75.
Sold by all Booksellers and Newsdealers.
LEE & SHEPARD, Publishers, Boston.

Ho for the West!

SECOND EDITION.

Mr. ALBERT D. RICHARDSON'S

Work,

Our New States and Territories.

It is one of the most interesting books of Travel, and useful compendium of information regarding the new domain beyond the plains, that has yet been given to the public.

It is beautifully illustrated from sketches and photographs of scenery, towns, mining operations, persons, &c., and altogether forms a book of great interest and value.

All who look westward with longing eyes should read it. One volume, Octavo, paper covers, price FIFTY CENTS. Sold by all Newsdealers; or, sent *post paid* to any address on receipt of price.

BEADLE AND COMPANY, Publishers,
118 William-st., New York.

NORTH RIVER AGRICULTURAL "WORKS"
GRIFFING & CO. PROPRIETORS
58 & 60
CORTLANDT ST. NEW-YORK

A Farm at Public Sale.

I will offer at Public Sale, on Saturday, June 15th, a desirable and well improved farm, located near Chambersburg, Franklin Co., Pa., adjoining lands of Hon. Thaddeus Stevens, and others, containing 149 acres, more or less, about 100 or 110 acres are in a high state of cultivation, balance splendid Pine Timber. Soil superior for all crops, consisting of tumbling sandstone, except a few acres on which are excellent Limestone Quarries. Good 2 story Brick House, Frame Bank Barn, with other necessary Out-Buildings (new), 2 choice Apple Orchards, soft and pure water in abundance. There is also Iron on the Farm.

For further particulars, address undersigned.

JAMES M. RENFREW,
Chambersburg, Pa.

FOR SALE.—THE CELEBRATED "POMONA" FRUIT-FARM and NURSERY of J. W. DODGE, on the Cumberland Table lands of East Tennessee. Unequaled as a Fruit Growing region. SEVEN FIRST PREMIUMS awarded by the State and Division Fairs to Fruit from the POMONA ORCHARDS. Fine opportunity for Nursery business. Can be made a superior Stock or Dairy Farm. For full particulars, description, terms and price—which will be low—address J. W. DODGE & SON,
Pomona, Cumberland Co., Tennessee.

THE MASSENA SPRING, ST. LAWRENCE CO., N. Y. The United States Hotel at this favorite watering place, is now open. Terms very reasonable.
CROCKER & CO.

BEWARE of IMITATIONS.
Ask for Baisley's
PAT. STEP LADDER
With Double Sides, and secured by Screws, Manufactured only by
W. T. & J. MERSEREAU,
62 Duane St.
Sold by all House Furnishing Dealers

Not too Late to Plant

The Kittatinny Blackberry.

See Advertisement on page 229.

MUNN & CO., NO. 37 PARK ROW, NEW YORK, Publishers of the SCIENTIFIC AMERICAN, Solicitors of American and Foreign Patents.
TWENTY-TWO years' experience in obtaining Patents.
THIRTY THOUSAND Applications for Patents made at their agency.
CONSULTATIONS AND ADVICE to Inventors free.
PAMPHLETS Containing Laws of all Countries free.
A HANDSOME BOUND VOLUME, Containing 150 Mechanical Engravings, and the U. S. Census by Counties, with Hints and Receipts for Mechanics, mailed on receipt of 25 cents.

MME. DEMOREST'S MAMMOTH BULLETIN of LADIES' FASHIONS for the Spring and Summer of 1867, over 70 Figures, price, plain, $1.50; Elegantly colored, $4; either accompanied with full descriptions, or with 10 full-size patterns of the principal figures, 50 cents extra. Mailed free. No. 473 Broadway, New York.

AGENTS wanted to engage in a good paying business! Now ready; THE LOST CAUSE, a complete Southern History of the War; patronized by tens of thousands eager to hear the other side. One agent sold 210 in one week. Address E. B. TREAT & CO., Publishers, No. 654 Broadway, New York.

DEMOREST'S "YOUNG AMERICA," the most sparkling Juvenile Magazine ever issued. The June No. has an extraordinary display of Novelties, Toys, Engravings, &c.

Duncan's Illustrated Masonic Monitor.—Teachings, "Workings," &c. $2.50. W. C. WEMYSS, 575 Broadway, N. Y.

IMPERIAL ORGANS AND MELODEONS sent by express to any part of the country. Send for Catalogue. SMITH, COLE & CO., 181 Broadway, New York.

GRANVILLE (Ohio) FEMALE COLLEGE.—33d year begins Sept. 10th. Advantages unsurpassed, terms low. Send for Catalogue. W. P. KERR, Granville, Ohio.

FOR SALE CHEAP.—A young Alderney Bull, 1 year old, out of imported stock. 1 Prince Albert Boar, same age; from recent importation, by
J. M. HALSTED, 68 Pearl-st., New York.

Sweet Potato Plants

Safely packed and delivered where ordered in New York City, at $3.50 per thousand.—500, $2. Address
P. PHILLIPS, Matawan, Monmouth Co., N. J.

IMPORTANT TO BREEDERS OF FINE STOCK.—For want of sufficient accommodations, and to make room for my brood Mares and their progeny, I have determined to offer for sale the whole of my recent importation of Short Horns and Devons:—I have also six very handsome Young Jersey, or Alderney Bulls, out of my imported cows, and sired by my imported Bulls:—Also, of different ages, about thirty pure bred Berkshire and Windsor (Suffolk) Pigs. For further particulars, Address
R. W. CAMERON, 41 South William Street, New York.

Great Economy in Painting.

DOTY'S PATENT

COMPOUND PAINT OIL,

Four years tested. Fully as durable, covers as well, easier to spread, quicker to dry, and in no respect inferior to pure Linseed Oil, yet is much cheaper! This compound is warranted to render White Lead WHITER, on either inside or outside work, and is FULLY AS DURABLE as Linseed Oil, and as good for all colored paints ground in oil. Four years' use has fully established this.

32 Cortlandt st., New York, May 9th, 1867.

This Certifies that I have recently had one of my brick dwellings, No. 106 Washington-st., Brooklyn, painted with "DOTY'S COMPOUND PAINT OIL," and it is the emphatic decision of both the painter and myself, that it covered full as well, spread easier, and dried much quicker than Linseed Oil Paint. I should use it again, in preference to Linseed Oil, if both were the same price. H. C. BROWNING.

Price, by the Barrel (40 gallons)..............$24 00
5 Gallons for trial, put up in good tin can....... 6 00
10 " " " " " 11 00

These cans may be shipped as common Railroad Freight, or by Express. Plenty of Testimonials as to Durability, in Circulars.

DOTY'S PAINT OIL CO.,
32 Cortlandt st., New York.

WANTED; ONE THOUSAND TONS of OKRA STALKS.—The stalks to be as clean and dry as good hay, to be baled in the same manner, and to be delivered in New York by 1st Sept. next, or as soon afterwards as possible. Persons wishing to contract for any part of the above, will please address, stating price, without delay, Box 4,011, New York P. O., for further particulars.

GRINDING MILLS.—Cheapest and best in the world. Burr Stones from 8 inches to 4 feet.
EDWARD HARRISON, New Haven, Conn.

Not too Late to Plant

The Kittatinny Blackberry.

See Advertisement on page 229.

DAVIS, COLLAMORE & CO.,

479 Broadway, below Broome-st.

White China well selected seconds. Dining Set with cups and saucers, Fruit Basket, &c., 113 pieces.	$33.
Tea Sets, 44 of same..........	6.50
Fine Stone China Chamber Sets, 11 pieces..........	$4.
Parisian Stone China, Dining Set. Nearly as fine as China—105 pieces..........	$22.

Plated Ware, Cutlery, Tea Trays, &c.

CRESYLIC SOAP.

A PERFECT DISINFECTANT
(Patented).

For Disinfecting, Deodorizing, and Purifying Cellars, Hospitals, Tenement Houses, &c. Also, for Exterminating Roaches, Bugs, and Insects of all kinds.

Manufactured solely by
JAMES BUCHAN & CO.,
190 Elizabeth-st., New York.

A RARE CHANCE!

GENESEE FARMER.

BACK VOLUMES COMPLETE,

from 1858 to 1865 inclusive.

A RARE CHANCE!

There are among the readers of the *American Agriculturist*:

1st.—Many old readers of the Genesee Farmer whose sets of back volumes and numbers are incomplete.—

WE CAN FILL THEM.

A RARE CHANCE!

2d.—Many who did not keep their numbers.—

WE CAN SUPPLY FULL SETS from 1858 to 1865.

A RARE CHANCE!

3d.—Thousands of reading Farmers who know the value of such sets as reference works. They may have the *Agriculturist* from first to last, and if so, they will be the more likely to want the Genesee Farmer.—

WE CAN SUPPLY IT.

A RARE CHANCE!

4th.—Others who do not know the great value of old volumes of an agricultural journal of such sterling merit as the Genesee Farmer, which stood second to none in America, for soundness of doctrine and practical sense.

We Would be Glad to Supply it to Them.

A RARE CHANCE!

The opportunity of obtaining so valuable a set of Back Volumes, well bound, at so low a price, ought not to be neglected.

Single Numbers, Post-Paid.......... 10
Unbound, Single Vols., Post-Paid.......... $1.00
" Sets, Eight Vols., Post-Paid.......... 5.00
Bound, Single Vols., " 1.40
" Sets, Eight Vols., " 9.00

ALSO,—ALSO,—

THE RURAL ANNUAL,

from 1856 to 1866.

A RARE CHANCE!

These Annuals are volumes of 120 pages, 12mo., full of admirable short articles on Horticultural and Agricultural topics. Tables, facts, etc., fully illustrated. They may be had either bound or in paper.

Single Numbers, Post-Paid.......... 15
Sets, Eleven Numbers, Post-Paid.......... $1.50

ALSO.

Tucker's Register of Rural Affairs for 1866.

POST-PAID, 15 CENTS.

THE GREAT AMERICAN TEA COMPANY

(Established, 1861).

Is commended by the leading newspapers, religious and secular, in this and other cities, viz.:

AMERICAN AGRICULTURIST, Orange Judd, Editor.
CHRISTIAN ADVOCATE, New York City, Daniel Curry, D. D., Editor.
CHRISTIAN ADVOCATE, Cincinnati, Ohio, J. M. Reid, D. D., Editor.
CHRISTIAN ADVOCATE, Chicago, Ill. Thomas M. Eddy, D. D., Editor.
CHRISTIAN INTELLIGENCER, E. S. Porter, D. D., Editor.
EVANGELIST, New York City, Dr. H. M. Field & J. G. Craighead, Editors.
EXAMINER and CHRONICLE, New York City, Edward Bright, Editor.
INDEPENDENT, New York City, Wm. C. Bowen, Publisher.
MOORE'S RURAL NEW-YORKER, D. D. T. Moore, Editor and Proprietor.
THE METHODIST,—Geo. R. Crooks, Editor.
TRIBUNE, New York City, Horace Greeley, Editor.

We call attention to the above list as a positive guaranty of our manner of doing business; as well as to the hundreds of thousands of persons in our published Club Lists in former editions of the leading papers of the country.

THE IMMENSE PROFITS OF THE TEA TRADE GREATLY REDUCED.

The Proprietors of "THE GREAT AMERICAN TEA COMPANY," became fully convinced, several years ago, that the consumers of Tea and Coffee were paying too many, and too large profits on these articles of every day consumption, and therefore organized THE GREAT AMERICAN TEA COMPANY, to do away, as far as possible, with these enormous drains upon the Consumers, and to supply them with these necessaries at the smallest possible price.

To give our readers an idea of the profits which have been made in the Tea trade, we will start with the American houses, leaving out of the account entirely the profits of the Chinese factors.

1st.—The American House in China or Japan makes large profits on their sales or shipments—and some of the richest retired merchants in this country have made their immense fortunes through their houses in China.

2d.—The Banker makes large profits upon the foreign exchange used in the purchase of Teas.

3d.—The Importer makes a profit of 30 to 50 per cent. in many cases.

4th.—On its arrival here it is sold by the cargo, and the Purchaser sells it to the Speculator in invoices of 1,000 to 2,000 packages, at an average profit of about 10 per cent.

5th.—The Speculator sells it to the Wholesale Tea Dealer in lines, at a profit of 10 to 15 per cent.

6th.—The Wholesale Tea Dealer sells it to the Wholesale Grocer in lots to suit his trade, at a profit of about 10 per cent.

7th.—The Wholesale Grocer sells it to the Retail Dealer at a profit of 15 to 25 per cent.

8th.—The Retailer sells it to the consumer for *all the profit he can get.*

When you have added to these *eight* profits as many brokerages, cartages, storages, cooperages, and waste, and add the original cost of the tea, it will be perceived what the consumer has to pay. And now we propose to show why we can sell so very much lower than small dealers.

We propose to do away with all these various profits and brokerages, cartages, storages, cooperages, and waste, with the exception of a small commission paid for purchasing to our correspondents in China and Japan, one cartage, and a small profit to ourselves—which, on our large sales, will amply pay us.

COUNTRY CLUBS, Hand and Wagon Pedlers, and small stores (of which class we are supplying many thousands, all of which are doing well), can have their orders promptly and faithfully filled, and in case of Clubs can have each party's name marked on their package and directed, by sending their orders to Nos. 31 and 33 Vesey-st.

Our friends are getting up Clubs in most towns throughout the country, and for this we feel very grateful. Some of our Clubs send orders weekly, and some not so often; while others keep a standing order to be supplied with a given quantity each week, or stated periods. And in all cases (where sufficient time has elapsed) Clubs have repeated their orders.

Parties sending Clubs or other orders for less than $30 had better send Post-Office drafts, or money with their orders, to save the expense of collecting by express; but larger orders we will forward by express, to collect on delivery.

We return thanks to parties who have taken an interest in getting up Clubs; and when any of them come to New York we shall be happy to have them call upon us and make themselves known.

Hereafter we will send a complimentary package to the party getting up the Club. Our profits are small, but we will be as liberal as we can afford. We send no complimentary package for a Club less than $30.

Complimentary Letters from Clubs.

Pittsfield, Ill., March 26, 1867.
Great American Tea Co., 31 and 33 Vesey-st., N. Y.

Gents: The package of Tea came safe to hand in good order, has been delivered, and gives general satisfaction. Many thanks for complimentary package. I expect to order a large club in a few days, and if it gives as general satisfaction as the one just received, you will have the entire custom of the Tea consumers in this neighborhood.

Yours with respect,
W. C. HEMPHILL, Pittsfield, Ill.

Putnam Junction, March 7, 1867.
To the Great American Tea Co., Nos. 31 and 33 Vesey-st., N. Y.

Gents: The package of Tea and Coffee (35¾ lbs.) ordered by me from your House one week ago to-day, by M. U. Express, came to hand yesterday in best of order, and proves very satisfactory. Also receipt for $64.38, in payment for above, came by mail to-day. Please accept thanks for complimentary package. You may expect another order before many days. Yours truly,
JAMES L. MONTAGUE.

White Haven, Pa., March 26th, 1867.
To the Great American Tea Co., Nos. 31 and 33 Vesey-st., N. Y.

Sirs: The Tea I sent for has arrived in good condition. We are well satisfied with it, and do not hesitate to say that it is, at least, as good a quality of Tea as we ever tasted. We could have done no better for ourselves, had we been at your Store and made the selection, than you have done for us. When this supply is exhausted, we shall, no doubt, send for some more.

Yours most respectfully,
JAMES M. SALMON

Cedar Rapids, Iowa, March 12, 1867.
Great American Tea Co., 31 and 33 Vesey-st., N. Y.

Gentlemen: I have received my first box of Tea, $44.25, and with pleasure inform you that it has given the purchasers a feeling of old times, as they have experienced in drinking Tea before the war; satisfying them the Company is not a "Humbug." I send to-day my second order, $121.40. Please forward to me with bill for collection.

A. C. MESSENGER.

Woonsocket, R. I., Feb. 4, 1867.
To the Great American Tea Co., Nos. 31 and 33 Vesey-st., N. Y.

Gentleman: I now send you my 5th order for Teas, which I hope will be as good as heretofore; it is just one year since I sent my first order of $30, which I think was the first order you got from here as a club. During the year, I have sent you upwards of $400, and I have not heard a complaint yet from any one, but all speaking well of your Teas, and are well satisfied. Accept my thanks for the complimentary package. Inclosed you will find $134.35 for this order. Hoping you will forward as soon as possible, I remain,

Yours respectfully, JAMES WOODHOUSE.
Direct the Teas for me, Woonsocket, R. I., by Earl's Express.

Geneva, N. Y., Feb. 14, 1867.
The Great American Tea Co., Nos. 31 and 33 Vesey-st., N. Y.

Gents: We have now been receiving Tea from you about one year, and find, in footing up our books, we have received of you Tea and Coffee, to the amount of $7,841.35 for this small village and vicinity. The public have perfect confidence in your Tea and Coffee, and the misrepresentations against you which we had to contend with at first, are now harmless. We congratulate you on the general success of your enterprise, hoping the hitherto pleasant relations which have existed, may continue between yourselves and

Yours respectfully, LUM & SON.

Treasury Department, Third Auditor's Office,
March 2, 1867.
Great American Tea Co., Nos. 31 and 33 Vesey-st., N. Y.

Gentlemen: I have the pleasure of enclosing you our second order, $130.15, which is more than double the first one, and the next one may increase proportionately, if these give as much satisfaction as the first.

You will please forward as before, by the Adams' Express Company, C. O. D. Very respectfully,
Your obedient servant,
H. C. HILL.

Angola, N. Y., Feb. 16, 1867.
The Great American Tea Company.

Gents: Your Box sent me by Express has been received. Your bill was paid on delivery. I found no mistakes, and I am glad to inform you that the Tea is giving good satisfaction. I had to make some effort to raise the club I sent you, but as the ice is broken, and nobody drowned, you may expect soon to receive a much larger club order from this place.

Yours truly, JOHN M. SLATER.

Olivet, Mich., Jan. 28, 1867.
To the Great American Tea Co., Nos. 31 and 33 Vesey-st., N. Y.

Sirs: The goods which I ordered for Olivet Tea Club, No. 1, were received in due time, and have given good satisfaction. Really the exhilarating power seems to be contagious, for most of the fair matrons in our neighborhood are inquiring when I send again. Enclosed I send O. T. C. No. 2. I shall probably send again in a few days. Mrs. Ingersoll, who was principal mover in Club No. 1, sends her respects for the complimentary package, and says she drinks her tea with more relish than she has for many years before.

Very truly yours, E. I. INGERSOLL.

6 lbs. Japan	H. Shallier	at $1.00	$6.00
5 do. Japan	L. Andrews	at 1.25	6.25
2 do. 1 Japan & 1 Imperial	Mrs. Keys	at [illegible]	[illegible]
[illegible] do. Imperial	L. D. Butler	at [illegible]	[illegible]
[illegible] do. Imperial	Simon Cole	at [illegible]	[illegible]
2 do. 1 Imperial & 1 Japan	N. Brooks	at [illegible]	[illegible]
[illegible] do. Imperial	J. M. Bradnor	at [illegible]	[illegible]
[illegible] do. Japan	E. Bordwell	at [illegible]	[illegible]
[illegible] do. Imperial	J. Barns	at [illegible]	[illegible]
and 18 others.			
Total			$87.00

COFFEE DEPARTMENT.

Our Coffee Department is very extensive—the largest, perhaps, in the country. We run three engines constantly, and sometimes four or five, in roasting and grinding our Coffee. Our Coffee buyers are experts, who examine most of the Coffees imported, and select the best and finest flavors for our trade. We employ the most experienced and skillful roasters, who exercise the greatest care that it shall be cooked in a perfect manner. It is always fresh, for our orders crowd our facilities to their utmost capacity. A considerable portion of the Coffee put upon the market of late years is picked while the pods are green, and subjected to artificial heat, to open the pods. This is not so good as that which ripens in the natural way upon the plant. Our Coffee buyer thoroughly understands this business, and can readily distinguish the naturally ripened from the artificially cured; and he only buys the Coffee which is naturally ripened. We examine the cargoes as soon as they arrive, and our trade is so large that it requires all the finest lots. This is what gives our Coffee a superior flavor to many others, and the same flavor it used to have in days long gone by. It is a common saying that most Coffee does not taste as well as it formerly did. The reason for it is, that a considerable portion of it is picked before it is fully ripe. We sell none but the fully ripe, rich flavored Coffee.

GETTING UP CLUBS.

Some parties inquire of us how they shall proceed to get up a club. The answer is simply this: Let each person wishing to join in a club, say how much tea or coffee he wants, and select the kind and price from our Price List, as published in the paper or in our circulars. Write the names, kinds, and amounts plainly on a list, and when the club is complete, send it to us by mail, and we will put each party's goods in separate packages, and mark the name upon them, with the cost, so there need be no confusion in their distribution—each party getting exactly what he orders, and no more. The cost of transportation, the members of the club can divide equitably among themselves.

The funds to pay for the goods ordered can be sent by drafts on New York, by Post-Office money orders, or by Express, as may suit the convenience of the club. Or, if the amount ordered exceeds thirty dollars, we will, if desired, send the goods by Express, to *"collect on delivery."*

We publish a small Club to show how it is done and as a matter of reference.

After the first Club we send blanks.

Direct your orders plainly, THE GREAT AMERICAN TEA COMPANY, Nos. 31 and 33 Vesey-st., Post-Office Box, 5,643—as some parties imitate our name as nearly as they dare do.

The Company have selected the following kinds from their stock, which they recommend, to meet the wants of Clubs. They are sold at Cargo Prices, the same as the Company sell them in New York, as the list of prices will show.

PRICE LIST:

YOUNG HYSON (Green), 80c., 90c., $1, $1.10, best $1.25 ℔ lb.
GREEN TEAS, 80c., 90c., $1, $1.10, best $1.25 ℔ lb.
MIXED, 70c., 80c., 90c., best $1 ℔ lb.
JAPAN, 90c., $1, $1.10, best $1.25 ℔ lb.
OOLONG (Black), 70c., 80c., 90c., best $1 ℔ lb.
IMPERIAL (Green), best $1.25 ℔ lb.
ENGLISH BREAKFAST (Black), 80c., 90c., $1, $1.10, best $1.20 ℔ lb.
GUNPOWDER (Green), $1.25, best $1.50.

COFFEES ROASTED AND GROUND DAILY.

GROUND COFFEE, 20c., 25c., 30c., 35c., best 40c. per pound. Hotels, Saloons, Boarding-house keepers, and Families who use large quantities of Coffee can economize in that article by using our FRENCH BREAKFAST AND DINNER COFFEE, which we sell at the low price of 30c. per pound, and warrant to give perfect satisfaction.

Parties getting their Teas from us may confidently rely upon getting them pure and fresh, as they come direct from the Custom House Stores to our warehouses.

We warrant all the goods we sell to give entire satisfaction. If they are not satisfactory, they can be returned at our expense within 30 days, and have the money refunded.

N. B.—All villages and towns where a large number reside, by *clubbing* together, can reduce the cost of their Teas and Coffees about one-third by sending directly to us.

BEWARE of all concerns that advertise themselves as branches of our Establishment, or copy our name either wholly or in part, as they are *bogus* or *imitations*. We have no branches, and do not, in any case, authorize the use of our name. The numbers of our House are advertised above.

TAKE NOTICE.—Clubs and quantity buyers only are furnished from our Wholesale and Club Department.

Post-Office orders and Drafts, make payable to the order of Great American Tea Company. Direct letters and orders to

GREAT AMERICAN TEA COMP'Y,
Nos. 31 and 33 VESEY-ST.,
NEW YORK.
Post-Office Box, 5,643, New York City.

AMERICAN AGRICULTURIST

FOR THE

Farm, Garden, and Household.

"AGRICULTURE IS THE MOST HEALTHFUL, MOST USEFUL, AND MOST NOBLE EMPLOYMENT OF MAN."—Washington.

ORANGE JUDD & CO., PUBLISHERS AND PROPRIETORS. Office, 41 Park Row, (Times Buildings.)

ESTABLISHED IN 1842. Published also in German at $1.50 a Year.

$1.50 PER ANNUM, IN ADVANCE. SINGLE NUMBER, 15 CENTS. 4 Copies for $5; 10 for $12; 20 or more, $1 each.

VOLUME XXVI—No. 7. NEW-YORK, JULY, 1867. NEW SERIES—No. 246.

[COPYRIGHT SECURED.]

THE PRONG-HORN ANTELOPE OF THE GREAT PLAINS.—*From studies, by J. E. Hayes.*

This beautiful and spirited animal is found in immense herds along the base of the Rocky Mountains, from Mexico to the River Saskatchawan, and eastward to the Missouri River. They are larger than a common sheep, exceedingly agile, fleet, and of a graceful carriage. Their flesh is valued, as a change from buffalo beef and salt pork, by the traveler and hunter, but it is not very good. The hair is coarse and brittle, and the pelt valueless. The horns are black, firm, and might be useful if obtained in sufficient numbers. The color above is yellowish brown; the belly white, as is also a square patch on the rump; other markings are somewhat irregular, but prevailingly, as shown in the engraving. The herds of these animals are often many miles in extent, and, from an elevation, appear like the shadow of a moving cloud, as they pass over the prairie. They live and thrive upon the dry prairie grasses, and, like the buffalo, are more or less migratory—moving with the supply of pasturage. The variety of horn "patterns," so to speak, among the antelopes, is very great. That no two should be alike would be expected, but the cause for such great dissimilarity in the horns of animals, so much alike in nature and habits, it is impossible to know. Some are very straight, some curve outward, some backward, some inward, some are twisted, others spiral, like a corkscrew; some have prongs, and others curious crooks and bends. There is but one other American antelope, and that is known as the Rocky Mountain Goat.

Contents for July, 1867.

INDEX TO "BASKET," OR SHORTER ARTICLES.

AMERICAN AGRICULTURIST.

NEW-YORK, JULY, 1867.

The weather—how much depends upon the weather! Millions of dollars' worth of hay will be exposed to damage from rain; millions of bushels of grain will be in condition to suffer likewise. The lack of rain may bring a blight, if not a failure, to other crops. By the blessing of Heaven we are in little danger from a general famine in this broad land, with its diverse soils and different climates, bound together, not alone by a Constitution, but by potent and ever strengthening net-works of rail-ways and of commercial interests. The plenty of one section quickly supplies the want of another. How to judge beforehand of weather probabilities, and how to shape his plans so that protracted storms, or even hard showers, shall do little damage to crops, and cause little loss of time to himself and his hands, is a study to which the farmer may well give considerable thought. One thing we may certainly do, namely: always have work for our regular hands on rainy days. It is more difficult to find work for teams. We have no doubt that the time is not distant when the coming of all great storms will be told by telegraph, so much in advance, that wide-awake *farmers*, in neighborhoods receiving a daily mail, may easily prepare for their approach. The habit of closely watching the clouds and changes of the wind, and the indicated currents of the air, high above the earth, is a valuable one. The barometer, taken in connection with other indications, is a very important premonitor of approaching storms. So also are thermometers and hygrometers, the one indicating the temperature, and the other the amount of moisture in the air. No one of these is of reliability alone, and all indications must be weighed with the judgment which experience gives. It is great folly for a farmer to buy a barometer, and think he can tell when a storm is coming, by its ups and downs. As well might he go by the wind alone, much better might he be guided by the clouds. All the signs should be taken together, the energy of the indications considered, and past experience, after all, taken as the surest guide. To gain experience, no way can compare with that of keeping a record of observations. See basket note on weather. The labors of this month are at all times severe. The facilities for using horse-power, in securing the bulky summer crops, are every year greater, yet human muscle is not dispensed with, but only made more efficient. Nevertheless, every year the farmer's success depends less on *brawn*, and more on *brain*.

Hints About Work.

Animals.—Cows at pasture must not lack pure and fresh water—stagnant pools are a poor source of supply. No stock ought to be forced to drink from them, and, least of all, milch cows. Calves are better pastured by themselves than with other stock. Young horses often get the bad habit of running after, and striking them, if they feed together. An old horse will take care of himself among cows, but colts, of one or two years old, are heedless, and, if pastured with cattle, may be hurt by their horns, without any real malice on the part of cows. Working stock should not lie over night in the pasture. It is very well for them to have a few hours, in which to graze, during some part of the day, but both cattle and horses work better on good hay, and some provender, corn and oats, rye-shorts, and the like. The amount of feed may be graduated in accordance with the average amount of work required, but it should be uniform. All animals, not at pasture, should have some green feed—perhaps one-third of all they eat. This should be cut, wilted, and brought to the yard or stables for them, and be ready when the day's work is done.

Harness and Yoke Galls.—Wash with castile soap and cold water, and, if possible, bind on a piece of sacking, wet with water, to remain over night. Relieve pressure upon the sore spots by shifting the harness, or by padding, and protect from flies with grease and pine tar mixed, during the day.

Sheep are distressed by the gad-fly this month and next, and should be protected by tarring their noses. Daub the tar on their noses, extending up, where they will not rub it off in feeding. The fly lays eggs in the nostrils, which hatch, and, the worms ascending, cause the "grub in the head."

Hogs.—Provide swine with roomy pens, to work over all the litter and weeds that can be gathered, besides sods, muck, etc. The amount of excellent manure made, as noted on another page, is enormous.

Weeds.—Suffer none to go to seed, is easily written, but very hard to carry out. Still, the nearer we can live up to this injunction, the easier will it be to carry it out, year after year. Many weeds, pulled or cut up in blossom, will ripen seed while dying, but few, the seeds of which are not fully mature, will survive the hog pen, in root or seed. It is never too late to pull docks in the mowing. Canada thistles, cut a few times below the surface, will disappear. Carrots are biennial, and, perhaps, in a few cases, will live a third year, if they cannot blossom the second; and we have strong faith, though not positive assurance, that the seeds will not germinate after the third year. So, two years' cultivation will almost always clean them out.

Mowings.—If grass lodges badly, cut it without reference to fitness. Timothy is fittest when it is just out of bloom; orchard grass and clover bloom at the same time, and should be cut when the latter is in fullest flower. Cut all grasses before the seed will shell after curing. The best time to manure grass is just after mowing; the best manure fine muck compost, with a modicum of ashes, bone dust and plaster. Spread with a shovel from the cart, and go over the land with an iron toothed horse-rake, to spread and knock the lumps to pieces, and work them into the sward. See hints of last month.

Grain Harvesting.—Barley should become nearly ripe before it is cut, and it ought to be bound and shocked the same day, and protected from dews and rains as much as possible. Thus the brightest and most marketable grain is obtained. Oats ripen so unevenly that it is often best to cut them while many are hardly out of the milk, to save those that are getting too ripe. The best time is when the kernel is in the dough state. What is lost by early cutting, in the grain, is gained in the straw. Wheat ought to get nearly ripe, according to the latest doctrine, to give the greatest weight of grain and the best quality. The happy medium between sufficient ripeness and liability to shell out is the point to be sought in determining when to cut. The older and perhaps safer theory, favored cutting while the grain was in the dough. Make all preparations early, engage extra hands to be ready to cut, and harvest at the right time; have sharp and good tools.

Hay and Grain Caps.—The cheapness of fabrics will now permit the economical use of caps for hay cocks and shocks of grain. Four feet square is a good size, and loops for pins at the corners are the best fastening. Once using sometimes pays the cost.

Hoeing.—Hoe to kill weeds, to stir the soil, to replace earth washed off by rains. The stirring of the soil is a great security against the effects of drought. It enables the plants to get the full advantage of showers and dews. It enables the air to circulate freely through the upper stratum of earth, and to penetrate lower, taking moisture with it, and depositing it in the cool soil below the surface. Work the soil as deeply as convenient, and not disturb the roots of crops. As a rule, avoid raising hills, either about corn or potatoes. Perfectly flat culture requires, however, deeper soil than we ordinarily have on all fields.

Turnips after Corn.—With the last hoeing of corn, if the soil be tolerably deep, and the culture flat, turnip seed may be sown and hoed in lightly. (A potato hook, or "claw hoe," is the best thing to hoe corn with, especially the last time, if there are not many weeds to *cut* up. It leaves the surface in excellent shape.) The corn is cut up and removed when the kernels are glazed, and the turnips often make a good crop, having 6 weeks to grow.

Turnips Alone.—Turnips may be sown any time this month. On tolerably mellow soil, it is best to sow in drills, and give as much cultivation as other cares admit of. Rutabagas will make a good crop sowed before the 15th or 20th—better for the table than if sowed earlier. They do best in drills, too, thinned to 6 or 8 inches apart. In sowing turnips broadcast, use as little seed as possible. One pound to the acre, if it can be evenly distributed, is better than more, though two pounds is the usual quantity. Sod land, or newly broken up land, should be plowed repeatedly and harrowed, to rot and kill sods and weeds, then freshly harrowed before the seed is sown.

Buckwheat is a valuable crop, especially as a weed killer. Three pecks of seed is enough for good land; more is required on poor. Sow about the middle of the month, and see article on page 253.

Tobacco.—The cultivation of this crop adds greatly to the cares and labors of July. Not a weed must be allowed to grow. Missing plants, and those destroyed by the cut worm, may be reset during the first part of this month to advantage. Every plant and leaf even must be examined for leaf worms, and topping should commence as soon as plants begin to run up. Break the tops off or pinch out the "button" just above the broad leaves. It may be done as soon as the flower stem can be taken hold of without injury to the upper leaves. The "suckers," or axillary branches, will start, after this, at once, and must be kept pinched off.

Cabbages.—Set out cabbages on land left vacant by early potatoes and peas, or on fallow ground well worked, limed and dunged. Keep well hoed.

Soiling Crops—Corn, sorghum, peas and oats, etc., may be sowed, for soiling, any time this month.

Butter.—If the feed is good, the butter may be equal to that made last month, provided the dairy is cool, or, rather, of the right temperature, which is about 58° to 60° Fahrenheit. If the pastures are short and dry, feed green fodder freely—corn, sorghum, etc. It may be necessary to increase the salt in the butter a little in the hottest weather.

Ditching.—Times of unusual, or even of usual, summer dryness, may often be most profitably employed in ditching and draining swamps, cutting the bogs, and drying and burning the same.

Orchard and Nursery.

The promise for fruit is everywhere good; even

Peaches, so often a failure, bid fair to be abundant. Old trees, that have not borne in years, are now well set with young fruit.

Thinning is now of the greatest importance. A well grown peach or pear is better, and will bring more in the market, than three half developed ones. It is often advisable to take off from one-half to three-fourths of the young fruit. Not only is the present season's crop all the better in quality, but that of the next year is more sure.

Insects.—The whole army of tent-caterpillars, borers, currant worms, pear slugs, and the like, is to be fought perseveringly. It is unnecessary to repeat the remedies given in the preceding months.

Pruning may still be done, according to the hints given last month, and on young trees future pruning avoided by rubbing off superfluous shoots.

Budding will commence with the cherry and plum. The time varies with the season and locality. When well formed buds can be obtained, and the bark of the stock parts readily from the wood, the operation may be performed.

Layers may be put down as soon as the present season's growth gets firm. Very good grape vines may be made by carefully laying the shoots of the present summer. Do not do it to excess.

Young Orchards, when root crops are not grown between the rows, should be thoroughly cultivated, unless the ground is regularly mulched.

Grafts should be looked after, all robber shoots be rubbed off, and if any of the shoots on the graft are too rampant, they should be stopped by pinching.

Seed-beds will need the shading and care suggested last month, and

Seeds collected as they ripen. Cherry pits are to be washed clean and preserved in sand.

Fruit Garden.

Picking of the small fruits will now occupy much of the grower's attention. That which is to be marketed must be picked before it is "dead ripe," while that for home use may be allowed to reach full maturity before it is gathered.

Blackberries are generally allowed to have their own way too much, and they become very difficult to work amongst. The new canes should be stopped by pinching or cutting, when they get 3½ or 4 feet high, and when the side branches are 18 inches long, these should be pinched in the same way.

Raspberries.—As soon as the crop is off, cut away the old canes, and keep down all suckers not needed to furnish a stock of new plants.

Currants are to be watched, and the bushes dusted with white hellebore, if a late brood of worms appears. See that the branches of those in the tree form do not break down from the weight of fruit.

Dwarf Trees will need to have the fruit thinned, especially varieties producing that of a large size. Treat insects as heretofore directed. The red spider is often injurious to pear trees, and they should be drenched with strong soap suds on its first appearance. Control the form of the tree by rubbing out shoots not needed to form branches, and by shortening the growth of others.

Grape Vines.—Do not allow young vines to overbear. A desire to taste the fruit of one's own vine is usually too strong to allow one to remove the first clusters. As a general thing, a vine should never be allowed to bear the first year. Upon the first appearance of mildew—whitish spots upon the leaves—use sulphur freely. Pinch off bearing shoots at the third leaf from the last cluster, and pinch laterals to one leaf. By all means, have one of the many excellent works on grape culture as a hand book for frequent consultation.

Kitchen Garden.

These notes are written during the usual cold and wet spell early in June, when the ground is soaked by cold rains, and within doors a fire is not uncomfortable. Early sowings, if the plants were up, have escaped, but seeds that were already in the ground, if at all delicate, will come slowly, and, in some cases, may rot altogether. It is not too late to replant many things, with a fair prospect of a crop, and to those who for any cause have been deprived of early vegetables, the late ones will be welcome.

Transplanting of the late crops of cabbage, cauliflower, celery, etc., will be done this month. See hints given last month on page 231. Occupy the

Vacant places with quick growing or late maturing crops, as recommended on page 256.

Asparagus.—The cutting has greatly exhausted the roots, and the aim should now be to promote a growth of tops, to give them strength for another season's effort. Manuring will pay now as well as at any other time. If the beetle appears, a small black beetle and black grub—there will be no difficulty in recognizing them—cut and burn, if it takes the whole crop of tops. You will lose your own crop at any rate, and it will be a satisfaction to know that you have done your part in preventing the pest from spreading to the gardens of your neighbors.

Beans.—Plant string varieties for succession and pickles. Keep the running sorts, such as Limas and other pole varieties, at a moderate height. Six or seven feet is high enough.

Beets will make a crop if sown now, unless an unusually dry spell should occur. The thinnings of beets, at any season, make capital greens, and are by many preferred to any others. Collect and wash, and they will keep good for several days.

Cabbage, Cauliflower, and all their relatives, that have been sown in open ground for a late crop, may now be transplanted. It is said that a plenty of lime on the land will prevent club-foot. In transplanting, put out only perfect plants. It often happens that plants from the seed-bed have diseased roots or malformed tops. All such should be rejected. If slugs are troublesome, as they often are in wet seasons, use lime, or turn the ducks in among them.

Celery.—There are many who prefer to grow in trenches. Such should gradually earth up the plants. The crop for winter is best set this month. In the flat culture, practiced by our market gardeners, they put out the plants by the middle of this month, in rows three feet apart, and the plants six inches distant. The earthing up of these plants is done later in the season.

Carrots need only to be kept clear of weeds until the tops become too large to work amongst.

Corn.—Every one who loves sweet corn should provide for a late supply. Seed sown even now will give ears for late use, and to dry for winter.

Cucumbers.—Select good specimens of the early sorts for seed, and if seed be sown now in well manured soil, there will be a good supply of pickles.

Egg Plants.—These warm-blooded fellows need all the coaxing that can be given to them. Sometimes a plant will content itself with producing one fruit, and its next neighbor will bear a half dozen. Hoe as often as may be, and give liquid manure when the weather is not very dry. Keep the fruit from contact with the ground by a handful of mulch of some kind. Near the coast we use salt hay for this purpose, but any other material, even a shingle or tile, will answer as well.

Endive.—The main crop of this desirable late salad may be sown. It is treated, as far as sowing and planting are concerned, just like lettuce, but before it is used it must be blanched, by exclusion of light. This is done by tying the leaves together, by covering the separate plants with a flower pot, or by putting a board over a whole row.

Herbs.—The time to cut these is just as they come into flower, as at that period of their growth they are in full perfection. Our market gardeners, however, pay no regard to the flowering period; they have seed beds of Thyme, Sweet Marjoram, Summer Savory, and Sage, from which they take plants during the present month, and set them in rows a foot apart each way. Keep well cultivated.

Lettuce.—The Silesian will give a fair crop, if sown in a partially shaded place.

Melons.—Cultivate the soil as long as the vines will allow of its being done. More fruit is usually set than will ripen. Take off the late fruit and thus improve the quality of the rest.

Onions.—Thin if crowded, and keep thoroughly weeded. If one has not the force to properly attend to the crop, he should not attempt to raise onions from seed on the large scale.

Peas.—Sow seed from the very best. A late sowing may be made for a venture, but we have never been very successful with late plantings of peas.

Potatoes.—Dig the early sorts. Their tops make capital manure for late turnips, if buried in the rows as they are dug. Cabbages, turnips, late peas and beans, or spinach, may follow the early crop.

Rhubarb.—Cut off every flower stock as soon as it shows itself. Now that fruit is plenty, the bed should have a rest.

Seeds.—Gather as soon as they ripen. Cabbage, cucumbers, peas, and others, should have been harvested by this time. Save the best of everything for seed, if you raise your own seed. If you can not do this, buy seed for sowing every year.

Sweet Potatoes.—At the North it is not advisable to let the vines root; at the South these roots from the stems form potatoes. We have to get our potatoes from the main plant. Our climate does not allow us to make layers. Hence our advice to move the tops while the plants are growing. Keep the ground well worked, and free from weeds.

Squashes.—Every one who grows squashes, to any extent, will have Mr. Gregory's work on his favorite subject. They will find there set forth the necessity of high manuring the whole ground for the running varieties, keeping this clean as long as possible, and then allowing the vines to root at the joints. Insects, of course, must be killed as they appear. The more bugs the fewer squashes.

Tomatoes.—Except in nice garden culture, we cannot look for any systems of training. Something to keep the fruit from the ground, be it brush or rails, is all that the farmer will attempt. Those who are able to give much time to the matter, can get a great deal of amusement out of the tomato, as it bears cutting to any extent, and may be trained in whatever manner that suits any one's fancy.

Weeds.—There is no specific for destroying weeds, and the only remedy is frequent working of the soil. Use the rake among recently set plants, the scuffle hoe among seedlings, and, later in the season, the hoe fork is an admirable implement. All of these are better than the common hoe, yet that is so much better than nothing, our advice is to scratch the soil frequently with whatever implement is at hand.

Flower Garden and Lawn.

There is much to do, yet it can all be summed up in the injunction to keep everything about the garden neat and orderly. The beauty of the

Lawn will depend upon frequent mowing and rolling. If the work is done often enough, the cut grass need not be raked off. With newly seeded grass, it should always be left to serve as a mulch. Wherever grass borders a road or bed, keep the

Verges or Margins neatly trimmed. This may be done tolerably well with a sharp spade, but it is better to have a regular cutter, like a chopping-knife on a hoe handle, and cut to a line.

Bulbs—the spring flowering ones, such as Hyacinths, Tulips, etc., will now need attention. As soon as the foliage begins to fall down and turn yellow, take up the bulbs and stack them until the leaves are quite withered; then pull the leaves off, and put the bulbs in paper bags, and store in a dry and cool place, away from rats and mice.

Neatness is, in a great measure, secured by the use of sticks and strings. Plants that are sprawling, and of unpleasant aspect, may be converted into objects of beauty by proper staking. Use as inconspicuous sticks as possible, and tie with bast, bark, or other soft material.

Dahlias will especially need care in tying, and, if large side branches are allowed to grow, they must also be supported by stakes.

Shrubs, of most kinds, may be propagated by making layers of this year's wood. Some can only be propagated from cuttings of young wood, with the aid of bottom heat, in a hot-bed, or otherwise.

Annuals must be transplanted from the seed bed, and make late sowings of the quick growing kinds.

Roses will need especial care. The rose bug must be shaken off. Pick off the leaf roller, and drench the slug with solution of whale oil soap. Keep the climbers and pillar roses well tied up.

Bedding plants, at least those of low growth, like Verbenas, make a better effect when pegged down; and even those of a naturally upright habit, like Ageratum, may be treated in this way.

Seeds should be saved as fast as they ripen, and of most herbaceous perennials it is best to sow them at once, as they are more sure to germinate, and a stock can be raised for flowering next year.

Green and Hot-Houses.

All plants left in the house should be properly cared for, as to watering and shading. The latter is necessary with even tropical plants. An inside screen of muslin may be used, or the glass may be coated on the outside with ordinary whitewash, or a mixture of whiting with glue water. Either of these will usually last the season, and be washed off by autumnal rains, when they are no longer needed. With proper attention to watering, shading and ventilation, many things do better in doors than if put out.

Insects must, of course, be looked out for, whether the plants are in doors or out. Plants set out of doors should be put on a foundation impermeable to worms. A layer of coal ashes is excellent for this.

Potted plants, set out, must not be allowed to be whipped about by the wind, burned up by the sun, nor suffer for want of water.

Alterations and Repairs may now be made, as well as at any other time, and new buildings be erected.

Cold Grapery.

The things to be attended to are roots and shoots. As to the former, sufficient moisture should be provided; mulch the outside borders, and, if this does not avail, give very weak liquid manure. The shoots should have already been shortened to the third leaf from the last bunch. Their welfare as to temperature must be regarded, and the house not allowed to get hotter than 90° to 95° at midday, and this should decrease to 85° during the night. Pinching the laterals and thinning the berries will afford the grower an abundance of pleasant work. Thinning of the berries on the bunch should be done with slender scissors, made for the purpose. One-half of the berries set, or even more, according to the variety, should be removed, to allow those that remain to attain their proper development. Mildew will often appear upon the leaves. At the first manifestation of mildew, stop sprinkling the vines and keep the house as dry as possible, and scatter sulphur abundantly over the floor of the house.

Apiary in July.—*Prepared by M. Quinby.*

The season through the spring months has been so backward, that it is doubtful if bees will have done swarming, in many places, by July 1st. This alone should be no cause of discouragement. Their prosperity should be measured by the advance of the season, not by the day of the month. Bees collect honey as they have opportunity during the blooming of any set of flowers. The first harvest of much account, in spring, is from fruit blossoms, dandelions, etc. If the weather be unfavorable, they pass out of bloom, and the bees gain nothing. Thus, if there be good weather, it makes but little difference whether apples blossom the 10th of May or 1st of June. So of clover and basswood. It is late only when the flowers are gone, and the bees have, for any reason, failed to keep pace. Swarms may be considered early two weeks after apple blossoms are gone, and late when issuing after basswood blossoms disappear. At any time, except late in the season, one good, first swarm contains all the bees necessary for profit. If two unite, and are hived together, put on surplus boxes at once, or (if in the movable-comb hive), divide as soon as combs are made. It has been recommended to give a comb containing brood, to prevent absconding, but this must not be relied upon. As soon as the hives are full, divide or put on surplus boxes. A hot day may force a few outside, when not very much crowded. This point can be determined early in the morning. The best surplus honey of the season is generally obtained this month.

Take off boxes as soon as full. If honey is being obtained plentifully, the boxes may be set down by the hive, for the bees to creep out; if it is scarce, the bees will rob them of the honey, to prevent which, put the boxes in a barrel or box, and cover with a thin cloth. The bees will collect on the under side, and, by turning it over a few times, they will fly off, and cannot return to carry away the honey. Always keep the combs vertical, and out of the sun, and avoid sudden jars.

Loss of queens will be frequent this month. Swarming hives of black bees will often indicate such loss by their troubled actions, running about morning and evening for two or three days. The Italians seldom manifest these signs. When a loss of queen occurs, and they have the means, they rear twice the number of queens that others do. When a queen has been lost, first endeavor to supply a fertile one, next, a queen cell ready to hatch; lastly, give brood. If a stock is reduced, give combs taken from strong stocks filled with sealed brood.

More moth worms appear this month and next than at all other times. Small young stocks and weak old ones suffer most. The Italians are seldom disturbed. Catch moths in shallow dishes of sweetened water, set among the hives at night. Pick out and feed to the chickens. Split elder stems, scrape out the pith, lay pieces under and around the hives, and twice a week kill the worms in them. Any very weak stock that *cannot* be strengthened, should be broken up, and the combs saved from the moths. A hive that does not breed bees, must not be allowed to breed moths.

Commercial Matters—Market Prices.

The following condensed, comprehensive tables, carefully prepared specially for the *American Agriculturist*, show at a glance the transactions for the month, ending June 14, 1867, and also for the same month last year:

1. TRANSACTIONS AT THE NEW-YORK MARKETS.

RECEIPTS.	*Flour.*	*Wheat.*	*Corn.*	*Rye.*	*Barley.*	*Oats.*
25 days *this* m'th	142,000	215,000	1,541,000	24,000	83,000	457,000
26 days *last* m'th	131,700	224,000	195,000	4,700	89,000	34,000

SALES.	*Flour.*	*Wheat.*	*Corn.*	*Rye.*	*Barley.*
26 days *this* month,	173,000	870,000	1,765,000	246,000	168,000
26 days *last* month,	281,000	1,087,000	5,280,000	525,000	41,000

2. *Comparison with same period at this time last year.*

RECEIPTS.	*Flour.*	*Wheat.*	*Corn.*	*Rye.*	*Barley.*	*Oats.*
25 days 1867....	112,000	215,000	1,511,000	21,000	83,000	457,000
24 days 1866....	202,000	285,000	1,091,000	47,000	81,000	518,000

SALES.	*Flour.*	*Wheat.*	*Corn.*	*Rye.*	*Barley.*
25 days 1867......	173,000	828,000	1,765,000	216,000	169,000
22 days 1866......	271,000	607,000	2,138,000	174,000	48,000

3. *Exports from New York, Jan. 1 to June 14:*

	Flour.	*Wheat.*	*Corn.*	*Rye.*	*Oats.*	*Barley.*
1867.....	189,707	34,000	3,078,186	138,564	94,120	608,220
1866.....	627,917	129,892	5,119,851	111,936	747,358	....
1865.....	567,611	336,001	288,163	111	41,142	....

4. *Receipts at head of tide water at Albany, each season to June 8th:*

	Flour, bbls.	*Wheat, bush.*	*Corn, bush.*	*Rye, bush.*	*Barley, bush.*	*Oats, bush.*
1867....	17,100	21,700	592,100	28,000	98,200	278,000
1866....	31,200	317,200	2,080,700	64,300	41,700	884,700
1865....	94,100	847,900	733,800	51,000	111,300	1,344,300

5. *Stock of grain in store at New York:*

1867.	Wheat, bush.	Corn, bush.	Rye, bush.	Barley, bush.	Oats, bush.	Malt, bush.
June 14..	578,970	217,796	117,287	68,601	979,965	17,871
May 15...	731,890	261,094	199,804	145,706	895,434	16,161

CURRENT WHOLESALE PRICES.

	May 15.	June 14.
PRICE OF GOLD	136¾	137
FLOUR—Super to Extra State	$11 00 @ 15 00	$ 8 80 @ 12 00
Super to Extra Southern	13 70 @ 19 00	10 80 @ 15 50
Extra Western	12 70 @ 19 75	10 40 @ 16 50
Extra Genesee	15 00 @ 17 00	12 00 @ [illegible]
Superfine Western	11 00 @ 12 70	8 00 @ 9 40
RYE FLOUR	8 60 @ 9 65	6 25 @ 9 15
CORN MEAL	6 15 @ 6 75	5 50 @ 6 20
WHEAT—All kinds of White	3 25 @ 3 65	2 25 @ 2 70
All kinds of Red and Amber	2 50 @ 3 45	1 72 @ 2 43
CORN—Yellow	[illegible] @ 1 25	[illegible] @ 1 10
Mixed	[illegible] @ 1 21	[illegible] @ 1 10
OATS—Western	85 @ 88	70 @ 90
State	88 @ [illegible]	72 @ [illegible]
RYE	1 60 @ 1 75	1 35 @ 1 50
BARLEY	90 @ 1 80	1 00 @ 1 25
HAY—Bale ₱ 100 lb	1 75 @ 2 10	1 20 @ 1 60
Loose	1 40 @ 2 10	45 @ 1 80
STRAW, ₱ 100 lb	75 @ 1 15	90 @ 1 00
COTTON—Middlings, ₱ lb	28 @ 29½	25 @ 26½
HOPS—Crop of 1866, ₱ lb	30 @ 65	30 @ 55
FEATHERS—Live Geese, ₱ lb	75 @ 85	75 @ 90
SEED—Clover, ₱ lb	13½ @ 13	11 @ 13
Timothy, ₱ bushel	3 00 @ 3 40	2 75 @ 3 00
Flax, ₱ bushel	2 75 @ 3 00	3 10 @ 3 25
SUGAR—Brown, ₱ lb	9½ @ 12¾	9½ @ 12½
MOLASSES, Cuba, ₱ gal	45 @ 60	41 @ 60
COFFEE—Rio, (Gold price) ₱ lb	15½ @ 19	13½ @ 19
TOBACCO, Kentucky, &c., ₱ lb	4½ @ 22	4 @ 20
Seed Leaf, ₱ lb	5 @ 65	5 @ 53
WOOL—Domestic Fleece, ₱ lb	35 @ 70	40 @ 75
Domestic, pulled, ₱ lb	29 @ 57	30 @ 52½
California, unwashed	20 @ 48	22 @ 35
TALLOW, ₱ lb	11 @ 11¼	11 @ 11¼
OIL CAKE—₱ ton	50 00 @ 52 00	50 00 @ 55 00
PORK—Mess, ₱ barrel	22 00 @ 23 23	21 50 @ 21 75
Prime, ₱ barrel	19 00 @ 19 25	18 50 @ 18 75
BEEF—Plain mess	14 00 @ 23 00	14 50 @ 21 00
LARD, in barrels, ₱ lb	13¼ @ 13½	12 @ 13
BUTTER—Western, ₱ lb	10 @ 22	10 @ 21
State, ₱ lb	15 @ 35	15 @ 28
CHEESE	10 @ 19	7 @ 16
BEANS—₱ bushel	1 50 @ 3 60	2 00 @ 4 00
PEAS—Canada, ₱ bushel	1 35 @ 1 60	1 35 @ 1 40
EGGS—Fresh, ₱ dozen	18 @ 21	20½ @ 23½
POULTRY—Fowls, ₱ lb	21 @ 23	15 @ 18
Turkeys, ₱ lb	24 @ 25	19 @ 26
POTATOES—Mercers, ₱ bbl	8 00 @ 8 50	8 00 @ 3 25
Peach Blows, ₱ barrel	2 50 @ 3 00	2 50 @ 2 75
POTATOES—Buckeyes, ₱ bbl	2 00 @ 2 50	1 87 @ 2 00
APPLES—₱ barrel	5 00 @ 7 00	3 50 @ [illegible]
CRANBERRIES, ₱ barrel	10 00 @ 16 00	12 00 @ 20 00

Gold has been unusually steady in price, since our last, having been in full supply and moderate demand, closing tamely at 137....Much more liberal receipts of Breadstuffs have been reported, during the month, making holders, especially on speculative account, quite eager to realize, and thus depressing prices very seriously. The demand has not been anything like active, and has been wholly insufficient to absorb the available offerings. The reduced foreign quotations, and the highly encouraging crop news, have tended to influence the market, most adversely, for the interests of sellers. Toward the close, there was a partial rally in corn, in consequence of the slightly improved figures reported from Liverpool, but in other kinds of bread-stuffs, trade was dull, at drooping rates. Provisions have been in better supply, and lower in price on a restricted inquiry. Cotton has been heavy and lower, but closes with more firmness, on a livelier demand. Hay has been in better supply, and quoted down, decidedly. The inquiry for it has been moderate. Hops have been quiet, but steady. Seeds have been very dull, and quoted lower. Tobacco has been in active demand, closing steady at our revised rates.... Wool has been quiet. Fine grades, having been scarce and in some request, have been held with more firmness. Low and medium grades have been offered freely, at easier and irregular prices, but have been very quiet.

New York Live Stock Markets.—

WEEK ENDING.	Beeves.	Cows.	Calves.	Sheep.	Swine.
May 21	5,977	74	2,424	12,415	21,482
May 28	4,218	92	2,171	16,9[illegible]	18,197
June 4	5,098	91	1,7[illegible]	15,151	[illegible]
June 11	5,788	71	1,9[illegible]	13,[illegible]	16,[illegible]
Total in four Weeks	20,[illegible]	331	8,073	[illegible]	[illegible]
Average per Week	5,179	86	2,0[illegible]	14,[illegible]	19,[illegible]
do. *do. last Month*	5,113	61	2,117	11,[illegible]	11,[illegible]
do. *do. prev's Month*	4,[illegible]	81	1,158	13,[illegible]	14,[illegible]
Average per Week, 1866	5,718	91	1,300	20,000	13,000
do. do. do. 1865	5,255	118	1,500	16,[illegible]	11,0[illegible]
do. do. do. 1864	5,161	115	1,511	15,[illegible]	12,[illegible]
do. do. do. 1863	5,150	129	691	9,911	21,[illegible]
Total in 1866	298,[illegible]	4,885	62,[illegible]	1,0[illegible]	6[illegible]
Total in 1865	[illegible]	6,1[illegible]	7[illegible]	[illegible]	5[illegible]
Total in 1864	[illegible]	7,6[illegible]	7[illegible]	[illegible]	[illegible]
Total in 1863	264,091	6,470	35,705	519,316	1,101,617

Beef Cattle.—By reference to the above figures, it will be noticed that the supply of beef fluctuated from 5,977 to 4,218, the extremes being on the two consecutive weeks ending May 21 and 28. The small supply on the latter week brought prices up, increased the number of beeves a little, and the first week in June a few very choice beeves sold in market at 20c., estimated dressed weight, while 17½c. represents about the average that week, poorest stock bringing 15c.@16c. A marked increase in the supply the next week, (the last we report), and the feeling that settled warm weather was upon us, brought prices down, and now we quote extras, 19c., average, about 17c., poorest, 15c. ...**Milch Cows** have been in little demand, and unless exceedingly good or fair beef, sell low. **Calves.**—The supply has been about equal to the demand, and prices have changed but little for those of good quality, while, as the weather grows warmer, thin calves sell very slowly. 14½c. ℔ live weight, is the usual price. **Sheep and Lambs.**—The supply of really good mutton is very light, but the number of poor, thin, worthless sheep, very large. The former sell quickly at 8c. or more, per pound, live weight, while there are grades quoted between 5c. and 6c. ℔; below this, sheep sell by the head, often at barely enough to pay transportation from Ohio. Why will not farmers hold on to such stock, and give them three or four months good pasturing, when they would be fair mutton? Now, butchers are afraid to buy, or do it on the sly, because the mutton is liable to be seized by the health police, as diseased or unhealthy meat. **Swine.**—The supply has fluctuated considerably, and prices have had their ups and downs. As we go to press, the market is rather short, 1,500 less than last week, and prices have advanced fully ½c., and are at present, 7c.@7¼c. ℔, live weight, for the general run, 7½ cents for choice.

Weather Observations.—It is interesting to watch the weather, and this interest is increased and made useful by keeping a record of Appearances, of Temperature, of the Barometer, and of the Hygrometer, for one's own reference. Though it is rather humiliating practice for any one to write down his translation of daily weather indications, and then see how his prophecies turn out, it is nevertheless useful; and in this way, almost any one will become a very accurate judge of the prospect of fair or foul weather. In keeping a record of the Barometer or Thermometer, rule off a sheet in quarter or half-inch squares. Write the days of the month at the top of the sheet, above each column of squares, and let each row of squares, or each line rather, down the sheet, stand for tenths of an inch of the Barometer, or degrees of the Thermometer. The record is kept by simply making dots in the squares, to indicate the day and about the time of the day when the observation is made, and the hight at which the mercury stood. It is enough to examine the Thermometer at 7 o'clock A. M., and 9 o'clock P. M. The Barometer's record being made at the same time, and at 12 o'clock noon, also. An idea of how to keep such a record may be gained more fully by reference to each number of the *American Agriculturist*, for the first half of the year 1864. If the dots, as they are made daily, be finally connected by a line, the fluctuations will be seen at a glance. This is precisely on the plan of the tables showing the fluctuations in gold, or any particular kind of stock or merchandise. Similar records may be kept of the amount of moisture in the air, and of the relative amount of cloud in the sky. In the latter case the most convenient way is to establish the numbers 0 to 10, to indicate relative degrees of fairness and cloudyness 0 being used to indicate a *perfectly* clear sky, and 10, one as black and stormy as *possible*.

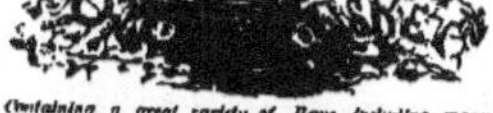

Containing a great variety of Items, including many good Hints and Suggestions which we throw into smaller type and condensed form, for want of space elsewhere.

Chances Yet for the Premiums.—The present number begins the last half of Vol. 26. Any of the premiums may yet be obtained. One lady took a second *Gold Watch* last week, which is the fifth premium she has received, and for which she commenced canvassing the last of April. Quite a number of subscriptions ran out with the last month. If they subscribe again, remember, their names will count on another premium list, the same as new subscribers. Please continue your efforts, and send in more subscribers as fast as obtained, stating whether or not the back numbers are wanted. All subscriptions received after this date, will commence with the July number, unless otherwise ordered. Back numbers will be furnished, if desired.

Registered Letters.—We would remind our subscribers that by the new registration system, which went into operation June 1st, *prepayment of the registry fee of 20 cents*, **in stamps**, *is required*, in addition to the regular postage. Post office orders, drafts, checks, and inclosures in registered letters, may be sent us at our risk. We thus answer repeated inquiries.

Deceptive Circular.—A "Washing Compound" manufacturer, sends out a circular containing, among other "puffs," an extract from "The Agriculturist." No such an article as this "puff" has ever been published in *this* journal, wherever else it may have appeared. Nor do we know of any paper of the above title. The extract is well calculated to deceive, especially as we understand that in answering letters of inquiry, the proprietor refers to a number of this paper.

The Crops.—The promise of June is rarely to be relied upon, yet it is a great satisfaction to begin the season with pleasant anticipations. From our correspondence and other sources of information throughout the country, we have very favorable reports of both grain and fruit crops, on the whole. Wheat and all the small grains are looking very well, corn is backward for the season, and a large part was not even planted by the first of June, yet this indicates no failure, and but little danger to the crop. Potatoes rarely looked better, though they lay long in the ground. Fruit prospects are generally flattering, also, and, as we write, the market is fairly flooded with strawberries, which are decidedly above the average in quality. It is hardly time to speak with confidence of the apple crop, and pears, though generally promising well, are a partial failure in some localities, where a severe cold North-easter blasted the bloom before the fruit was fairly out. There are a few localities, an extensive one in Missouri, where hail-stones have done serious damage, but the coldness of the season, it would appear, has not been favorable to hail, which usually occurs, we believe, in times of great heat. The reports of the grass crop, which is, indeed, the most important crop of the country, show more variation than those of any other. At the East, the crop is excellent. At the West, the promise of hay and present condition of the pastures appears to be not quite so good.

A New York Poultry Club.—A call has been issued by several amateur poultry breeders, of New York and vicinity, for a meeting of amateur and professional poultry breeders, to which all interested are invited, to organize a Poultry Club. The meeting is to be held July 10th, at Room No. 24, Cooper Union Building, Eighth-street and Fourth-avenue. We cordially wish the movement distinguished success.

Birds and Eggs—Ornithology and Oology.—Nichols & Noyes, of Boston, have just published a work on the Birds of New England, by Edward A. Samuels. The title page states that it comprises "a complete history of their habits, times of arrival and departure, their distribution, food, songs, times of breeding, and a careful and accurate description of their nests and eggs." To a very satisfactory extent the book (which is an 8vo. of 583 pages,) fulfils the promise of its title page. Mr. Samuels shows that he has been a close observer, his style is familiar and easy, and he quotes freely from standard authors. The observations indicating the value of birds to man are the most satisfactory we ever met with. The good and the evil done, directly or indirectly, by all our common birds, are carefully compared in a very unprejudiced way. The engravings of the eggs are remarkably fine—they are wood cuts, but the effects produced seem to us superior to anything that could have been done on steel or stone. Some of the small engravings of birds are fair, but many of the full page cuts are execrable in execution, yet doubtless accurate as regards markings of plumage, and other characteristics. There is a plain edition, one with the eggs colored, and one with all the plates colored. It is a useful and needed book.

Do You Want a "Time-keeper" for $3?—J. Birch & Co., Williamsburgh, N. Y., are benevolent people, they send out "time-keepers," "gentlemen's breast-pins," etc., for the very moderate sum of $3.30. As such liberality as this should be known, we give them the benefit of an advertisement. A friend of ours received the following:

PRIZE CERTIFICATE.

On receipt of this certificate with $3.30 to pay for postage and package, we will send to your address, by return mail, one

MAGNIFICENT GOLD CASED TIMEPIECE,

MARKED $50.

Elegant Engraved Patent Gold Cases, regular action, bridge balance, and warranted a good timer.

If this article does not suit, you can change it for any other article of the same marked value on the list.

Address J. BIRCH & CO.,
Williamsburgh, New York.

He sent the money, $3.30, and received his "time-keeper." That others may see what a valuable article it is,

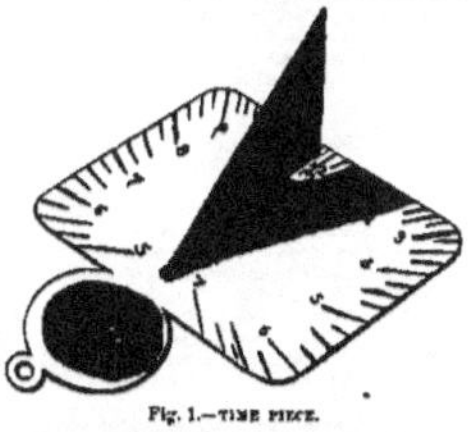

Fig. 1.—TIME PIECE.

we give an engraving of it of the natural size. A toy sun-dial, with a compass that points nowhere. Then, the "engraved patent gold case" is worthy of an illustration, which we give, in figure 2. A pasteboard box, covered with the cheapest kind of gilt paper. This is

Fig. 2.—GOLD CASE.

about a fair specimen of the articles sent out by these gift enterprises, if they send anything at all. Messrs. J. Birch & Co. finding that they were dealing with one who would expose them, returned Mr. C. the money he sent them, supposing he would keep quiet. The whole sell is a very neat one. The "time-keeper" with its gold case must have cost, altogether, at least 30 cents.

Sundry Humbugs.—The number of letters in reference to these has been, of late, very large, and much time has been consumed in investigating them. A. A. Kelley's First Grand N. Am. Gift Concert, which was advertised to take place at the Wabash Avenue Rink, Chicago, Ill., *but was postponed*, as Mr. Kelley says, because he was *not allowed* to go on, is now advertised to take place in New York," and is really the greatest enterprise ever inaugurated in the world," so says the circular. The Pacific Rail Road enterprise dwindles into insignificance beside this wonderful Gift Concert. Kelley was arrested on June 12th, and taken before the Police Court on a charge of selling lottery tickets, and admitted to bail. "He is said to have cleared a fortune by his dazzling scheme," and says himself that he has plenty of money. The ministers usually say, in making their appointments, "Providence permitting," but Kelley says, "Under any circumstances the Concert will now be given, as above stated, in good faith." We have examined the circulars, tickets, etc., of this concern, and do not see that it essentially differs from the hundreds of others which have, from time to time, been shown up in the *American Agriculturist*. We have never found a single person so stupid as to imagine that the public was ever benefited by such enterprises, and very rarely an individual, while we have thousands of complaints from people who have squandered their money, and seek advice when it is too late. We invite all parties to inform us of the *results* of their investments in this and other lotteries, if they *will* try them in spite of all our previous warnings. A. A. Kelley & Co. have another enterprise, Kelley's Weekly, and on the circular we find: "On Saturday, August 10, 1867, we will distribute half a million dollars of the *profits* in shares, including $100,000 in greenbacks, to our patrons, from a subscription amounting to $1,500,000." Please notice, they will distribute $500,000 of the profits from a subscription list amounting to **$1,500,000**. We think this would exceed in immensity "the greatest enterprise ever inaugurated in the world." A million and a half for subscriptions to a weekly paper before August 10, 1867, would be one of the wonders of the world, too wonderful to be comprehended by common mortals..... Clark, Webster & Co., Bankers. "The Bankers and Merchants Grand Presentation Entertainment. Capital, $1,987,148." They don't deal in *round* sums like most large companies. We have visited this banking establishment. The usual appurtenances of such institutions are not to be seen there. No Gold, no Greenbacks, no Government Stocks, or even stamps in sight. No big books, no paying or receiving tellers' signs. They told us they would sell 100 tickets at 40 per cent. discount, and when we inquired who some of the "New York bankers and merchants" were, who had formed this immense company, the man who understood that part of the business was out. We asked *for references*, and three were given, neither of whom knew Clark, or Webster, or Co. We inquired of ten of the prominent bankers in Wall street and vicinity, and none of them knew Clark, Webster & Co., bankers, not even the runner boys. Is it possible that people send their money to these *bankers?*....Wright, Bro. & Co. send out tickets, and offer watches at $30 to $100, either for $10. We have seen the watches, and don't want them at half the money. Buy watches and all other things of regular, established dealers, and pay a fair price, for if you send money to buy articles represented to be worth four or five times the price asked, you will surely be cheated.....T. R. Dawley & Co. propose to sell 5,000,000 newspapers, @ 10 cents each, make $50,000, and distribute it among their patrons, all in greenbacks, in sums of $1 to $10,000. This will do for the Japs or Celestials. We have this month letters from more than a score of different parties, all of whom desire to sell tickets for distribution—lotteries—of various articles, valued at prices from $1 to $75,000. Tickets are sent, in many cases, with the circulars, and all you have to do is to send $2, $3, or $10, and get articles of five or ten times the value of the little currency forwarded. Now all the probabilities are, that one will get nothing at all, but in some cases things are sent. We have just visited C. H. Garland & Co.'s (Todd) place, and presented a package of tickets, paid our $3 on one which assured us of a "Fine Silver Hunting Case American Watch," and we got it. We wish all our readers could see this chronometer. It looks very like our grandfather's old iron tobacco box, opens and shuts with the same kind of grating sound that makes one involuntarily grate his teeth. It will not keep half as good time. This watch is like Paddy's, which took "a dale of a while to knock off an hour's time," and as for silver, a distinguished dealer tells us there is not a particle in it. The only indication of where and by whom it was made on case, face, or movement, is London, Cooper. We shall hang it up for a show, and callers can see $15 worth of Gift-Enterprise-Concert-Distribution-Lottery property, and we consider it a fair representation of all *schemes* for raising money, from Soldiers' Homes up to professional gambling, which is what it pretends to be. Beware of all sellers of rights of any kind; see that they are authorized by well known business houses before making purchases. A fellow in Ohio takes *old* feathers, and proposes to bring back new ones, but don't. People careless enough to trust such a person deserve to be swindled, and it may do them good. Look out for sellers of hay-lifters, reapers, and horse powers—a large number of honest farmers have been *sold* by them....A. D. Bowman & Co., C. L. Van Allen. A friend from Massachusetts writes: "I have seen a circular from A. D. Bowman & Co., in which they refer to Mr. Judd as one that knows them." We do, and have seen—*him;* that is, we have seen a man who told us in presence of witnesses that he was A. D. Bowman. We have seen the *same man* again, under similar circumstances, and he told us that he was C. L. Van Allen. Perhaps his *old*, at 43 New street, and his *last*, at 48 Broad street, are the same—who knows? or who cares to? Knowing him, we don't *very* strongly recommend him.

Bowen's Single Lens Microscopes.—These have been extensively advertised at 50 cents each, and, as the circular and advertisement give people to expect a useful instrument, we think it only fair to show—as Mr. Bowen has failed to do it—just what may be expected for the money, even though we do give Mr. Bowen the benefit of an illustration and an advertisement. The "powerful lens" consists of a globular glass bead, and

the "neat and simple setting" is a bit of the size and shape of the engraving, rather roughly cut out of a piece of a cigar box, or similar wood. We can not see what possible use such an implement can be to any one. If our readers think differently, they can get one of them for 50 cents. They probably do not cost 3 cents.

The Grape Vine Flea-beetle.—At the time of our writing, the season is very backward, and it is not possible to give any estimate of the "set" of the grape crop. This year there is less complaint of the

insect that attacks the buds than there was last year. This insect is the Grape Vine Flea-beetle, (*Haltica chalybea*,) which has the unpleasant habit of perforating the buds of the vine, and thus impairing their vitality, if not destroying them altogether. The engraving shows the shape of the little beetle, but it is enlarged about four times beyond the natural size. The color is variable, it being steel blue, deep green, or even violet. They begin their depredations in April, and continue them through the month of May. Shaking them *from* the vines, and crushing them, is the best way of disposing of them.

Metcalf's Early Strawberry.—People who originate new things are often very slow in making them known. This strawberry is an instance. It originated in Michigan. A concern in that State has the control of the stock, and yet they have never sent us a description or a berry. Yet, in spite of their neglect, we have tried to keep the run of it, and—no thanks to them—we are glad to say that it is a really early berry. It ripened with Mr. Dory 10 days before the Agriculturist, and Mr. E. Williams, of Mont Clair, N. J., sent us a box of ripe berries on June 12th. We have had one of these berries engraved, which we shall present, with other new strawberries, at the proper time. It is a berry of fair size, rather sour, but of good flavor. It will be valuable, if it proves to be only 5 days earlier than any variety we now have. As we write *for* the people only, we don't care whether the Michigan *folks* like this notice or not. If they have a good and early berry we want it.

A Use for Sumach Berries.—Everybody knows the "Shoemaker's bob"—a cluster of small dark red berries, that grows upon the common Smooth Sumach. These contain a great amount of malic acid, and have often been used for an acid drink in *fevers*. The Rev. R. G. Hofland, has discovered that an infusion of these, with a proper amount of sugar, when fermented, makes a "wine," and "Rhus wine" has become an article in trade, and has the countenance of physicians, who ought to know better than to lend their names to *anything*. The process of making this wine has not been communicated to us. The article is about like that from rhubarb, or "wine plant." What we consider of more importance is the vinegar made from the same source. Should the Sumach prove to be a valuable vinegar producing plant, it would be less of a nuisance than it now is.

Horse Radish.—The article in our Horticultural Annual, on the cultivation of horse radish, by Mr. Henderson, has brought out many letters of inquiry, which we must answer in a lump. Mr. Henderson's estimates pre-suppose ground, in the highest possible condition, as to manure and deep tillage, and his prices are those of the New York market for the last few years. We do not know who has any sets for sale—those who have will probably advertise them in season. It is not practicable to raise the plants from seed. Although it flowers freely, we never knew it to produce seed in this country, and it very seldom does so in England.

Commercial Enterprise.—Among the many things for which New-York merchants are famous, is the magnitude of their enterprises, and the far-reaching character of their ventures. The operations of the present day throw those of a few years past quite into the shade, and often equal those of a similar kind in the commercial marts of the Old World. The recent large operations by the Great American Tea Company have taken the trade by surprise, and are rather a novelty in this market. The taking up of two cargoes within a week, comprising 12,881 packages Black, and 22,810 packages of Japan, for immediate consumption, at a cost of about a million and a half of dollars, indicates the extensive nature of the Company's business, and deserves a passing notice at our hands. The consumption of tea in this country is largely on the increase.—*Shipping and Commercial List, N. Y., May 15th*, 1867.

Bees—Queens from Italy.—It is some time since we have heard of an importation of Italian bees, but recently had the pleasure of seeing three little colonies, each with its queen-mother, in fine condition, just received by Rev. E. Van Slyke, through Rev. G. Kleine, of Hanover, Germany, from the shores of Lago Maggiore, in Northern Italy. They came from the famed establishment of Dr. Blumhoff, and are now at the apiary of Mr. Quinby, whose property they are. Their progeny will help decide the question of the deterioration of Americo-Italians. We do not believe that Italian bees deteriorate, if bred pure. If Italian queens breed with black drones, we are inclined to think in opposition to the opinions of most bee-keepers and writers, that their drone progeny will be more or less tainted. There is, however, another question for bee-keepers to study upon. May not bees be improved by breeding, as sheep or swine or cattle are, by careful selection, and so by sufficient care may we not beat the Italians themselves by and by?

Diseased Peach Leaves.—F. T. Foster, Preble Co., O. The leaves sent are affected with "curl." It is a general impression that this is produced by a plant louse or aphis, but there is room for doubt on this subject.

Soap on Oil Stones.—F. S. P. writes that an oil stone, on which the oil has become so hardened as to render the stone useless with oil, may be made all right by the use of soft soap. This reminds us that we have long used soap, instead of oil, upon a fine "oil stone," with great satisfaction. The soap may dry upon the stone, and when wanted for use it needs wetting only.

Special Advertising Agency.—As most of our advertisers are aware, matters relating to that department have for several years been under the immediate superintendence of Mr. W. A. Fitch, one of the Associate Editors. As a matter of convenience, to those desiring to extend their advertising beyond the columns of the *Agriculturist*, he has arranged to receive advertisements for other journals at their regular rates. His experience in this line, and knowledge of the best mediums, give him excellent facilities for conducting such business satisfactorily, and thus to save much time and correspondence required in arranging with different parties.

A Good Piano.—In company with musical experts of high authority, we have examined the Mathushek Piano, advertised on another page, and believe it to be well worthy the attention of those desiring to secure a good instrument. One of the party present, the musical editor of the Weekly Review, a leading authority in such matters, speaking of the smaller-sized piano, said, "It can speak with such power and sonority that we must look at the thing, in order to believe it possible. Throughout the whole scale the tone is even, very full, sonorous, brilliant, and melodious." All were greatly pleased with its performance, and gave high testimonials.

The Flowering Almond as a Wall Plant.—Miss O. M. Luke, Trumbull Co., Ohio, writes an account of her training of a Flowering Almond: "Five years ago last spring it was a little slip, one foot high. I set it close to the east side of the house, having the soil previously enriched with leached ashes, leaf muck, etc. Father said I was not giving my shrub any room to branch. That was just what I intended not to do. I pinched off all side shoots at their first appearance, and kept it trained to the house, in the same manner as a grape vine. The third year, I let two branches grow each way. I have continued training my Flowering Almond each year, and now I have a beautiful climber, a little over twelve feet high, and three inches around. The three branches on each side are two and a half feet long, and a little over one inch around. It blossoms about the 10th of May, long before other plants bud."

Sailed for Europe.—On Wednesday, May 8th, on the Steamer Tripoli, Orange Judd, Esq., wife, and three children. We have since heard of the safe arrival of the steamer.

Married.—At Munson, Mass., on June 15th, Mr. A. W. Roberts, Superintendent of the Engraving Department of the *American Agriculturist*, to Miss Ida Beattie.

Perseverance and Pianos.—We have had the pleasure of presenting a magnificent Steinway Piano to Mrs. Annie Flagg, of Bloomington, Ill. This lady commenced canvassing about the 1st of October, 1866, and allowed nothing to discourage her in her attempts to earn the prize. On May 4th she was here, selected a piano, and expressed her entire satisfaction. A beautiful little two-year old, who accompanied the mother all the way from Illinois, showed that it was not a trip to while away time, but a real business transaction, with a view to adding new attractions to a pleasant home, that stimulated this successful operation. $650, earned in seven months, besides attending to the cares of a family, are indications of the kind of stuff we should be pleased to see more of in the world. Mrs. Flagg's judgment in working for the **Steinway Piano** we can approve most heartily, as each of our partners has one of them in his own house, and desires no better instrument.

Still More Grape Literature.—"Mead's American Grape Culture and Wine Making." By Peter B. Mead. New York: Harper & Brothers. It is a very handsome volume of some 480 pages, and very liberally illustrated. When we have perused it, we shall be able to say something of its contents. Vineyard Culture, by Du Breuil, with notes by J. A. Warder, is another work soon to be issued by Robert Clark & Co., Cincinnati. Du Breuil is high authority, and the value of the work to Americans will be greatly enhanced by the copious notes of Dr. Warder. We have the specimen sheets only, and must defer a more extended notice until the work is out. It is beautifully printed.

Mohr on the Grape Vine.—The translation of Mohr's work, by "Horticola," is now ready, and forms a neat little work of 129 pages. It is a very plain discussion of the structure of the vine, and the principles involved in its pruning, training and cultivation generally. As the propagation of American varieties is different from that pursued in Europe, the translator has given an account of our methods, and added some brief notes on the leading American varieties.

Tennessee Lands.—The advertisement of Mr. Dodge will be an answer to many letters asking where southern lands can be bought. Mr. D., well known as an artist before he became a fruit grower, is, on account of the ill health of a member of his family, prevented from returning to his estate, from which he was driven by the fortunes of war. We have no personal knowledge of the property, but from the references he gives to those who have seen it, and the fruit we have seen from it, we think it worthy of the attention of those who are seeking a location in the Southern States.

Notes of Travel—Crops, Use of Lime, etc.—One of the Editors, traveling in Pennsylvania, writes us, from the Valley of the Lehigh, as we go to press, "that the crops are everywhere looking very finely, and it is admitted, on all hands, that the grain harvests were never more promising. The country, all along the line of the railroad, from Easton to far above Catasauqua, is a succession of wheat and rye fields, and blooming meadows—very encouraging to people who have been paying $35 dollars a ton for hay. Wheat is quite as generally grown in this section as rye, and many of the fields are so rank in growth that the straw is lodged in spots. The prevailing rock is limestone, and the practice of liming the land, once in four or five years, is almost universal. This, and the turning in of green crops, is the main reliance for keeping the ground in good heart. All the manure that is made is applied to the land, but a much greater breadth is cultivated than can be fertilized by this method. Indian corn is much more largely cultivated than on the sea-board. It is not uncommon to find 30 and 40 acres raised on a two hundred acre farm, with about as much in wheat or rye. It is much more a grain than a grass region. As the lime is generally quarried, and burnt, upon the farm, and always in the immediate vicinity, it makes a very cheap dressing for the land. It is rarely more than ten cents a bushel at the kiln, and the quantity, when slaked upon the field where it is used, is about double. Thirty bushels to the acre is considered a fair dressing, though much more than this is often used. Whatever the philosophy of its action upon the soil, its beneficial effects are everywhere apparent, and its influence, upon fields underlaid with lime rock, is quite as apparent as upon the adjacent districts, where another rock prevails. Liming the land is a cardinal doctrine with every farmer in this region."

To Officers and Members of Horticultural Societies.—We are desirous of being able to furnish *early* as complete and accurate a list as possible of the Autumn Fairs, and, besides, wish for our Annuals a list of the officers of all the principal agricultural, and kindred societies, in North America. We take the liberty, then, of asking to have the *circulars, posters, reports*, or marked newspapers, containing information about such societies, which will be of value to us, sent to the address of the *American Agriculturist*. In case such printed information can not be obtained, please drop us a line. Advertisements and notices in county papers, etc., are likely to be overlooked unless distinctly marked. As this item may not meet the eye of officers, a private member, or any one interested, in any particular society, will do us a great favor by giving the information at as early a day as possible.

Gregory on Squashes.—We have just published a treatise by Mr. Jas. J. H. Gregory, of Marblehead, Mass., on the Culture of Squashes. We have a liking for these books on special culture, as the author has a chance to say all he has to say on the subject. We can not see how Mr. Gregory could have treated the matter more in detail. The title of his work is "Squashes and How to Grow Them," and he not only tells how to grow them, but gives all the details of harvesting, storing and keeping, marketing, saving seed—in fact, all that a practical man who wields a vigorous pen can tell on the subject. We announced this work some time ago, but the illness of Mr. Gregory, prevented its earlier publication. We would inform certain parties (see page 254,) that this work was written by Mr. Gregory, and not by one of our Editors, and shall keep the manuscript for some time, to satisfy any stupids who may attribute this work to other than the author. Until we read this work we had no idea of the importance of the squash crop, but it would seem that it ranks next to the potato, and that it will pay every farmer to cultivate squashes, rather than the comparatively valueless pumpkin. About 70 pp., paper covers, 30c.

Silver-leaved Maple.—J. W. B., Bonaparte, Iowa., asks if "what the nurserymen sell as soft, or white maple, are one and the same." The silver-leaved maple is *Acer dasycarpum*, and is often called white maple. The name soft maple is at the East usually applied to *Acer rubrum*, the red or swamp maple. The silver-leaved maple, a common tree at the West, is one of the most valuable for planting in belts, and it is of rapid growth, does not throw up suckers, and is useful as fuel.

Where can I get it?—A large number of our letters may be condensed into "Where can I get this, that, or the other thing?" If the thing inquired about is out of the usual way, we take a little pains to find out, and write the party thus inquiring, but when it is for common nursery or seed stock, we cannot notice their letters. Every nurseryman or seedsman has or can get from his neighbors all the usual articles of trade, and it is useless for us to say that common articles may be had at any particular place. If one has a good thing to sell, he knows enough to advertise it, and there is little danger of any dealer keeping long in obscurity. The demand for new breeds of animals of all kinds, including fowls, is something wonderful, and it is the same with plants. We do our best to answer these queries, but we cannot satisfy those who ask us where many common things can be had. We suppose that we have had fifty inquiries this season for tree seed. The best that we can do, is to send the letter to a reliable dealer, with the request that he will forward his catalogue to the writer.

More Grape Vines.—Some parties, we notice, have already begun to advertise their stock of vines for the fall trade, and others are preparing to do so. Judging from the indications, the number propagated this year will be large, though not, we think, in excess of the demand. Every spring thus far has shown a scarcity of the leading kinds, and grape growing in this country has only fairly commenced. There is an advantage in securing vines for planting early; the first comers can select from better stock, and, as a rule, prices have also been higher in spring than in the fall.

Grape Queries.—G. F. C., Atchison, Kansas, writes: "I have a small, prosperous vineyard, of 200 vines, (Concord and Hartford Prolific,) now one year old, and would like to know (1.) whether it is best to give them an annual coating of manure, and cultivate them during the season, or (2.) whether it is best to give them a permanent mulch of saw dust. In cultivating them, the spade or plow will cut off some of the surplus roots. Does this (3.) injure the vine? They made a vigorous growth of from 10 to 14 feet last season, (1 cane.) I cut them back to about three feet, and will grow two arms this season, for training to trellis. Is it best (4.) to let them bear fruit this season? If so, how much, without injury to the vine?" *Answer.*—1. In proper grape soils but little manure is needed, and, as the vines were manured at planting, we should say no to the manure, and yes to the cultivation. 2. Saw dust is not advisable as a "permanent mulch," as it soon begins to decay, and be infested by troublesome fungi. 3. Use a hoe-fork, and keep the surface loose. 4. That depends upon the strength of the vine. In the long run, it is best for the vineyard not to bear until it is three years old.

Hungarian Grass.—If a farmer is likely to have less hay than his necessities require, we recommended Indian corn, sown in drills, cut, and well cured, before the kernels fills out the ears, as the best substitute; yet, as this requires a good deal of manure, or land in good tilth and heart, Hungarian grass may be used with great satisfaction and on poorer soil. It needs thoroughly drained land, and if the soil be mellow, and in fair heart, even though corn or potatoes would suffer from drought upon it, this crop will probably do well. It is best to sow between the 15th of June and the 15th of July. Half a bushel per acre is enough. Cut when just out of blossom. The hard shell of the seed, and the bristly husk of the ripened grain, are said to injure horses; hence cut early. It is cured and stored like hay.

What France Sends to England.—France exported to England from January, 1866, to October, 1866, eggs to the value of $7,100,000; butter and cheese, $18,800,000; poultry, $800,000; feathers, $2,400,000. Why cannot the United States help to supply poor John?

Mixing Manure with "Live" Ashes.—"M. A." This is never advisable, and can only be done with safety where there is a large quantity of muck, charcoal or loam present to absorb the ammonia that is released by the mixing of the manure and ashes.

Quinces.—P. H. Perrin. Angers is best for pear stocks; it is distinct from the Orange or Apple Quince, and we cannot find, that Thomas, in either his old or new work, says, that they are the same.

Aeration in Churning—A new Churn.—New churns are too common. Good ones are rare. The *quick* churns usually make poor butter—pale, soft, and lardy. The article advertised as "The Dasher Churn," has been put through its paces, and for the last six weeks has reigned supreme in our small dairy. The butter comes, almost every time, before the churner knows it, say in five minutes, or less, waxy—firm, sweet, odorous. The milk and cream are well taken care of, the cow's food is good, and the mistress of the dairy understands her business. Therefore the reason that we have so good butter is not *all* in the churn. The distinguishing feature of this churn is the admission of a constant current of air at the axle, which is dashed through the cream, and passes out of pipes in the cover. It is as simple and easily managed as any churn we ever used, and is well and durably made.

The Hoove is the distension of the rumen of cattle by the gases, produced by the fermentation of food. The effects eating too freely of red clover are often of the most serious character. The production of great quantities of gas in the paunch inflates it and the animal, like a bladder, and all efforts to reduce it sometimes fail. Great care should, therefore, be exercised that fences are strong, and that cows, or other cattle, or sheep at pasture, can not break into a clover field. When clover is to be fed off, the usual way is to accustom animals to it, gradually turning them in an hour or two daily for a few days, then leaving them in altogether. This is right, but it is not absolute security. Experienced farmers believe that there is little danger after a few days, provided the cattle are well salted, or have, constantly, access to salt. "An ounce of prevention is worth a pound of cure." Relief is often quickly afforded by tying a small, firm hay rope, rather tightly, through the mouth, and over behind the horns, or over one horn and behind the other. The animal's effort to shake off the rope, permits an escape of the gas, which will, ordinarily, not form again if a dose of soda or hartshorn be administered. One to one and one-half ounces of either may be given, in a pint of water.

The Miner Plum.—A call for information on this variety has brought out a number of replies—all too long to publish. We have three histories of its origin, all different, but all agree in their testimony as to its health and hardiness. Mr. N. C. Goldsmith, Middletown, N. Y., sums it up as follows: "The fruit is not of exquisite flavor, and the skin is a little tough. The tree is hardy, healthy, thrifty, long lived, ornamental, regularly productive, and begins to bear two or three years after transplanting; the fruit almost uniformly fair, good size, good flavor, retaining its firmness and flavor, and never injured by the curculio." It is but right to say that, while we have a number of letters in favor of this plum, we have two letters by those who say that it is only the common Wild Plum. We hope those who offer to send us specimens of the fruit will remember it next autumn.

Wasted Thunder.—The London Gardener's Chronicle criticises the taste of a catalogue of one of our seed venders, and says: "We question whether any respectable English firm would have the bad taste to issue such an advertisement as that we subjoin, and which is taken from a trans-Atlantic seed catalogue." Now, it happens that the catalogue in question is published by one who was born and brought up in England. He showed his good taste by coming to this country, and perhaps after a while he will forget the things brought up to, and not again offend his former brothers.

Pears in Maine.—The Maine Farmer advises farmers, and fruit growers in general, to abandon pears and plant apples instead. It says: "You can buy, in a few years, from the product of the apple trees, more pears than you can possibly raise by setting out pear trees, and do it, too, at a much less expense." But if fruit growers, in general, do not raise pears, in what market shall the Maine Farmer buy or exchange? Is the case really so discouraging?

Orchards on Gravel.—J. C., Sacramento Co., Cal., writes: "In the January number an 'Old Subscriber' asks, 'What can be done with a piece of land, formerly good, but now covered 4 feet with creek gravel?' If the gravel is not too coarse, why not set fruit trees on it? Most of the best orchards about Placerville, Eldorado Co., are set out on ground formed by laying in a brush dam and stopping the tailings that run from the miners' sluice boxes, which is nothing but slum, or sediment and gravel. It invariably makes fine trees."

Asparagus.—"Subscriber," Woodbury, N. J., asks: "Why will Long Island and Pennsylvania asparagus bring more in market than that from New Jersey? In Philadelphia, last week, the one was selling at 25 and 30 cents per bunch, (retail,) and the other at 06 cents. I am aware that in Pennsylvania it is cut near the surface of the ground, and Jersey asparagus is cut as far below as possible, the first looking green, the latter of course mostly white." Our correspondent is one of those rare queriets who answers his own questions. Every one who knows anything about asparagus, will pay twice as much for the green as he will for the white. Blanching is a very good thing for celery, but a very poor one for asparagus.

Soap and Candles.—A useful book of 108 pages, 12mo., on the Art of Manufacturing Soaps and Candles of all sorts, by Dr. Ott, has just been published by Lindsay & Blakiston, of Philadelphia. Though it contains many valuable and interesting facts, and would give a novice a pleasant insight into those arts, yet it strikes us as being adapted to be most useful to practical soap and candle men than to others. In the minor matter of language, there occur several rather funny blunders. The reader will be surprised to see, for instance, that "Potasse" (potash) "is called in commerce," among other names, "hydrated protoxide of potassium," and the soap boiler, in his apron and paper cap, will hardly recognise himself under the title of "Savonnier." However, we must say the book gives evidence that the author has pretty thoroughly "read up" on the subject, and condensed many valuable facts in a neatly printed and well illustrated volume.

Patent Brooms.—Broom corn brush furnishes an admirable material for house brooms. The hair brooms of Europe disappear before them, or are retained only for special uses. The desirableness of some contrivance which shall do away with the necessity of transporting and marketing the long handle is obvious, as also of one which shall enable any person, who can raise or obtain the brush, to fill his own brooms as they wear out, with fresh brushes. That gross impositions have been practised in vending patent brooms and "rights," we doubt not, and have been the more cautious and thorough in investigating the merits of a new one. Silver's Patent Broom, so far, is the best brought to our notice. It consists of a "loop" of maleable iron, terminating in a shank with a screw thread cut upon it, a brass cap, and broom stick, or handle, with a ferruled end. Into the loop the thin shaved stems of the brush are thrust from one side and the other, until it is full; over this the cap is drawn, the screw shank protruding; this is screwed into the handle, and holds all fast. The brooms have been tested by several months' use in our families, and the writer has, without instruction, and with entire ease, prepared the brush and filled the brooms to his perfect satisfaction. The ladies pronounce the brooms much superior in elasticity and durability to the old ones, and they are adopted as a family institution. For other information, see advertisement.

Temperature for Churning.—J. L. Philips. In cold weather the cream should be about 65°, not higher, when you begin churning. In warm weather 63° is about right, for in the course of the operation the temperature will rise, but should not get above 67°. Avoid adding much of either hot or cold water to secure the proper degree of warmth.

Patent Broom and Dust Pan.—Mr. J. S. Clough has done a good job for housekeepers, and they will all rise up and call him blessed as soon as they add these to their household furniture. These two articles, so wont to pull apart, are happily wedded, and hang by one ring upon the nail. The handle of the brush is a little longer than the handle of the tin pan, through which it passes, and the twain are one, for hanging up. The pan is improved by a lip, bent down a little, making it easier to gather up the dust.

The Patent Blacking Brush Holder is another bright idea by the same inventive genius. It is a tin cylinder box, about three inches in diameter, and seven or eight inches long, fitted to hold boot brush and blacking. This is a nice travelling companion, and also very "handy to have in the house."

Mutual Exchange.—C. R. Do farmers ever think of the vast amount they might gain annually, by a system of general exchange of fruits and flowers with their near neighbors, (and distant ones by mail?) I speak more particularly of small fruits. Suppose one farmer had an abundance of one kind of fruit only, (say Lawton blackberry). By exchanging it with a half dozen others, who possessed some of his "heart's desire," he would find himself far better off, and no money spent either, but a trifling amount in postage, at the rate of eight cents per pound. I think farmers should make known their wants through the press, stating, at the same time, what they could exchange for the same.

Milch Cows and Dairy Farming.—The receipt of a copy of this excellent work from the publishers, indicates that their presses are running again, to supply the demand. The binding is modern and neat. We have it as a standard work on our list.

To Separate Honey from Wax.—Mrs. L. A. Muller. Put the honey, comb and all, in a tin pan, on, or in, a moderately warm stove, adding to each pound of honey a tablespoonful of water. Stir it occasionally with a piece of wire; if anything large is used there will be an accumulation of dirty, cold wax continually added to the hot mass. When the contents of the pan are perfectly liquid—it must not boil—set it where it can cool undisturbed. Then take a knife, and pass it carefully around the pan, to detach the cake of wax, etc., on the top, and rapidly, with *great* care, lift off the cake. Don't let it drain into the pan an instant, but place in another utensil. Any one thus clarifying honey will find, on putting aside the cake of wax, that every particle of impurity, that would have to be strained from the honey, will have adhered to the cake of wax, and nothing remains beneath but the golden-colored honey, clear as water. If the honey should, in time, candy, heat it again with a very little water and white sugar. Keep in jars, tied up, in a cool place. Break up the wax cake and wash in cold water till cleansed from the honey. Then melt and strain it. To bleach the wax, boil it, after straining, for an hour, in plenty of water, in which use a few drops of chloride of soda. When quite cold, lift off the wax and leave it to dry and whiten in the open air.

Appleton's American Annual Encyclopedia.—The new American Encyclopedia is well known. From the time of its completion, about 1860, its publishers have issued an annual volume in similar style—large double columned octavo pages, in fair type, containing 800 pages, more or less, in each volume. These are a general history of the most notable things which come to pass in the world for the year, and from an American and popular stand point. The range of subjects is limitless, but such are chosen as are of most general interest and importance: wars and political changes, education, philanthropy, religion, science, art, manufactures, mines, obituaries, literature, law, medicine and philosophy, in short anything that affects the history of the day. Many of the most important United States public documents are given in full, and, as a contemporaneous history of our own country, the Annual Encyclopedia has, and will have, great value. The volume for 1866 is just out.

Tightening the Screws on Dogs.—Massachusetts has amended her dog law, making it $15 fine to keep an unlicensed dog; $5 to go to the informer, and making it incumbent on police officers to kill all such dogs. Sheep will stand some chance in the old Bay State.

Rat Premiums.—An Ohio County Agricultural Society offers a premium of $10 for the greatest number of rat tails, not less than one thousand strong, on a string. The rats to be caught by one family between March 15, 1867, and the time of the fair. We like this idea, and commend it to the attention of our agricultural societies. The depredations of these animals are a heavy tax upon our farmers, amounting to millions every year. The premiums would stimulate the boys to great activity in destroying them. The Norway rat was a terrible present to this country.

Sheep as Lawn Mowers.—In a recent ride through the Central Park, we were struck with the exceeding beauty and freshness of the large lawn near the Mall, where scores of South Downs were quietly feeding, adding picturesqueness to the scene, while they pursued their utilitarian labors. Downing quite early called the attention of rural improvers to this use of sheep. They would not, perhaps, in any case, entirely save the use of the mower, but after two or three cuttings in the early summer, they would keep the lawn in passable condition for the rest of the season. But this is only one item in their use. They return to the soil what grows upon it, with important additions, and would save the expense of all other top dressing. Sheep will keep good land constantly improving. They also form an element of beauty in any landscape, and when they have done serving the eye, they go to serve the table.

To Keep Meat Almost as Good as Fresh for a Long Time.—Mrs. L. A. Muller. Take enough water to cover the meat, make it moderately salt, and to each bucketful of water—the common wooden bucket—take one large tablespoonful of sulphite of lime, and one teaspoonful of saltpetre. It is all-important to keep every particle of meat *under* water by a press. Soak the meat in *fresh* water over night, before using it, and it will be almost as good as fresh. I found veal kept in this way, at the end of six weeks, as good as when first butchered, and beef, at the end of ten weeks, fresh enough to make excellent soup and roasts. As the season advances, and the heat increases, use more of the sulphite.

Re-packing Salt Pork.—W. Williams. Exposure to the air was undoubtedly the cause of the spoiling of the meat in removal. We would not have pork five minutes out of the brine, if we could help it, before it is cooked. In changing from one vessel to another there is a good deal of exposure. The only safety for pork is in packing it in good, clean barrels, with plenty of salt, as close as possible, and in keeping it covered with brine till used. Pork is often spoiled through the carelessness of servants. Keep a board and weight upon it constantly, and do not fail to look at the barrel every time you visit the cellar, if you want sweet pork. If the brine is not strong enough, add more salt on top. We always keep two or three inches of coarse salt on top. The bottom will always take care of itself.

Sowing Barley Early.—J. S. C., of Vt., objects to this practice, and says that he sowed May 1st, and got 1¼ bushels to the acre, while that sowed June 10th yielded 25 bushels. One swallow does not make a summer, and Vermont, though a great State, is a little too far north to be a rule for the whole country. It is quite possible that late sowing may be advisable in colder climates. We shall be glad to have any facts which our correspondents may have, bearing upon this point.

Chess Again.—"M. N.," Annapolis, Ill., wishes us to say something about the conversion of wheat into chess, or cheat. We have only space to briefly sum up the subject: While chess often appears in places where wheat was expected to grow, there is not the slightest proof that the one changes into the other, and, as far as negative evidence can go, all the authentic experiments to convert wheat into chess have proved failures. When we can be shown anything like a transition, a plant that is part wheat and part chess, we shall be willing to discuss the subject, but, until then, we can use our space better.

Comparative Nutritive Value of Different Kinds of Corn.—In response to several inquiries, we answer: That the nutritive value may probably be come at with considerable accuracy, by weighing a carefully *measured*, well shaken down bushel. This will not give accurately the fattening value, which depends in a good degree upon the amount of oil contained in the corn, but by no means wholly up in this. Different varieties vary greatly in the oil which they contain. The Dent corn contains generally less oil than the Flint, the Flint less than the little Pop corn.

Cost of Getting Crops to Market.—It is estimated by an intelligent Iowa farmer, that it costs fully eighty per cent. of the value of the wheat crop to get it to an Eastern market, which always determines the producer's price; pork, 25 per cent.; beef, 15 per cent.; and wool, 4 per cent. This is a pretty strong argument for raising sheep, and killing dogs on the prairies.

Shall we Milk Before Calving?—"G." writes: "I have a fine heifer which has just dropped her first calf. Her bag got very large and felt hard some days beforehand, and I am still afraid that I am going to have trouble with it. A man who keeps many cows told me I ought to have milked her when it first filled with milk. My uncle, last year, milked a cow a fortnight before calving, taking as much as a pailful a day. Is it the best way? Is there danger if it is neglected?"——It is not to be recommended as a general practice, if it can be avoided, but if the bag swells and feels hot, by all means draw the milk, and knead the bag when empty, washing it with warm soap and water, and perhaps greasing it to prevent inflammation or garget.

Duty on Imported Breeding Animals.—The wise provision in our Revenue laws, admitting breeding animals duty *free*, is frustrated in a measure, by the very absurd, illiterate, and unjust decision which decides that *birds* are not animals, and hence that fowls and poultry of all kinds imported for breeding purposes, are subject to pay duty. If birds are not animals, what are they? and what are animals? Webster defines animal as "an organized body, endowed with life, sensation, and power of voluntary motion," and that is the common acceptation. The humblest forms of animals are distinguished from vegetables, by having distinct mouths and stomachs. An oyster is an animal as truly as a man, and a bird as truly as an ox. This matter ought at once to be tested in the Courts, if the Treasury Department continues to beg the question, and allow its employees in the Custom Houses to interpret plain English to suit themselves. It is fair to suppose that Congress meant animals when it used the word in an important law—and that if our law-makers had intended to admit *free quadrupeds* only, they would have said so.

"Big Things"—Monster Hogs.—Ivory Lord, of Saco, Me., writes: "Zero of Egypt desires to see the 'big things' reported, so as to know how to proceed this year in order to beat them. Well, try this, O: March 7th, 1861, Richard S. Rogers, of South Danvers, Mass., killed a hog 34 months old, the live weight of which was 1,108 lbs., and dead weight 944 lbs. The last 18 months he was fed all the Indian meal and milk he could eat. He could stand and walk to his last day, and of his own accord walked up an inclined plane into a cart to be hauled to the butcher. Mr. Rogers estimated the cost of this huge grunter at 25 cents per lb.; he received 8 cents per lb. for him. This is the greatest weight of a porker that has ever come to my knowledge." [In 1842, December 21st, Benj. Rogers, Mansfield, Burlington County, N. J., killed a hog which weighed 1,611 lbs. In 1863, A. H. Benham, McLean, Tompkins County, N. Y., had a hog which weighed 1,335 lbs., which was exhibited in our office, and killed in New York, December 19th, weighing, alive, 1,278 lbs., dressed, 1,174 lbs.—Ed.]

Horse-Racing at Fairs may far better be Broken up than Permitted.—F. K. Phœnix, of Bloomington, Ill., writes: "Last year our County Fair managers determined to do without horse-racing. The sporting people prophesied and threatened, but the result was very much *the best Fair, and the best receipts* ever known in the Society's history—and that too, in despite of some very unfavorable weather. I think we shall hear no more in favor of connecting the two in our Society—the issue has been made and victory won."

Cure for the "Gapes in Chickens."—J. H. Mabbett writes: "Take a four or eight ounce vial and fill it with *large grains of wheat;* then fill the vial with turpentine and let it stand, corked tightly. When you see any of your chicks begin to droop and gasp, catch them and give each one grain of the wheat. If in the morning, give another at night. If in the afternoon, give one the next morning. I have never found this to fail in my 'family.' Handle them gently, and don't, for mercy's sake, put a feather down their windpipes."—[The turpentine kills or paralyzes the worms, which are the cause of gapes, and they are coughed up.—Ed.]

Potatoes Under Straw.—This method of growing potatoes seems to answer well in some places and not in others. We have given the experience of those who have failed and those who have succeeded. The following from J. Cass, Sacramento County, California, will interest those who live in a similar climate:

"For the last three years my potatoes have invariably run to vines and set no potatoes. Last year I tried the covering with straw and I had splendid potatoes; the ground kept moist all Summer, and we could get a mess any time by rooting in the straw with our hands. I planted as follows: Old ground that was in assorted vegetables the year previous, was ploughed in, and half potatoes, cut lengthwise, dropped 15 inches apart, in every third furrow, and put about 8 inches of old wheat straw on them; it seemed to check the growth of vines and made the potatoes set."

Suffolk Pigs.—We have frequent inquiries for this excellent breed, many of them from the West. Berkshires, Yorkshires or Seftons, and other pure breeds, are also in more or less request. Breeders of valuable kinds of stock would do well to advertise.

Cure for Lice on Cattle.—Isaac Schauber, Saratoga County, N. Y., says: "A *few* applications of good cider vinegar along the back bone, on the head, and other places where the lice gather, will soon finish them."——It will give them a check, which cleanliness and good keeping will make more or less permanent. It is, however, a safe and convenient application.

Plastic Slate Roofing.—We are constantly receiving inquiries in regard to this material. The fact is, we know very little about it. What we do know, is favorable. The claim of the venders, that it re-forms stone, is absurd; but the slate flour mingled with the gas tar remains suspended in it, and the tar is said not to separate and run, as do most tar roofs, when they are exposed to great heat of the sun in summer.

Over-Cropped Land.—What is the best plan to recuperate land that is still rich, but from frequent cropping with wheat fails to bring remunerative crops? O. P. S.——The land wants a rotation of crops, and clover turned in the summer before wheat is sown. If the clover does not grow stout enough, sow a little plaster early in the spring. The clover is a good manure for wheat.

Comparative Value of Hay and other Food.—According to experiments conducted in France and Germany, 100 lbs. of good hay is equal in alimentary value to

400 lbs.	of green clover.	45 lbs.	of wheat.
275 "	green Indian corn.	51 "	barley.
374 "	wheat straw.	56 "	oats.
419 "	rye straw.	57 "	Indian corn.
195 "	oat straw.	62 "	sunflower seed.
400 "	dried corn stalks.	69 "	linseed cake.
275 "	carrots.	105 "	wheat bran.
54 "	rye.	65 "	dried oak leaves.

Farmer's Fruit Cake.—Contributed by Mrs. E. Smith, Plymouth Co., Mass. Soak 3 cups of dried apples over night in warm water; chop (slightly) in the morning, and then simmer 2 hours in 2 cups of molasses. Add 2 eggs, 1 cup of sugar, 1 cup of sweet milk, ¾ cup of butter, 1¼ teaspoonfuls of soda, flour to make a rather thick batter; spice to suit the taste. Bake in a quick oven. Republished by request of a subscriber.

Fire and Water-proof Wash.—"A. S. K.," of Fitchburg, Mass., sends us the following recipe, of which he says: "For roofs of houses, barns and other buildings, or for brick-work, this preparation is unequaled." Dry-slake common stone lime in a close vessel, and when cool, pass eight quarts through a fine sieve; add to it one quart of fine salt, and two gallons *pure water*. Boil and skim. Then, to every four gallons of this mixture, add one and a quarter pounds of alum, three-fourths of a pound copperas, half a pound potash, and five quarts fine beach sand. The wash will now admit any coloring matter that may be desired, and may be applied with a paint or whitewash brush in the same manner as oil paints. He adds: "It looks better than any other kind of paint, will stop leaks in roofs, prevent moss from growing, and, when laid upon brick-work, will render it impenetrable to rain or moisture." [The "Chemistry" of this wash is not quite obvious, but as really good washes for out-door work are rare, we give it publicity on our correspondent's authority.]

Housekeepers with Small Children and Smaller Help.

A lady correspondent at the West, puts the following question:

"In your reply to the Southern lady who had determined to do her own work—after speaking of the arranged kitchen—you add: 'Fitted out with these appliances, a woman in good health and without small children, can often do her own work with less worry without a servant than with one.' Now, here let me ask: What would a woman do with very few of these appliances, and six or eight small children—say under ten years old?

In those essays I have met with a good many things that coincide with my experience, my thinkings, plannings, and doings—and yet when I have read them through, I have felt as though there was something wanting. A wish came up that some one who had six or eight small children to *care for* and *do for*, in addition to her other duties, would write on the subject.

It seemed to me I might learn many a lesson. I wish to make my system of housekeeping as good as I can under my present circumstances.

But for want of such a paper, I intend to make the most of those published."

As the women with eight small children is likely to be busy for some time, we will answer for her, for this case demands immediate consideration. Eight small children and no help! It is a hard case, and requires considerable philosophy, and some piety, to get along with it smoothly. *Do not despair.* Your case might be worse in two particulars; you might have no children at all, and you might have more. We know of a women who has twenty-five, all comely and doing well. The saddest people we know of are childless husbands and wives, and the most cheerless homes are those where there is no cradle to rock, and no playthings to put up when evening comes. Better a dozen than none. You need the education which will come of training them to thrifty and virtuous habits. Do not doubt for a moment that they will live, grow up, and be useful and happy, and that they will all rise up and call you blessed. The kind Providence that has given them being, has a work for them to do, and will in some way provide for their training. *Do not worry.* Worry kills a great many more people than work. There must necessarily be a different standard of attainment in such a home, from that which prevails where money and servants are plenty. There can not be so many or so fine dresses, playthings, books and amusements. They can not be kept in such absolute cleanliness and order, as if each child had a nurse, and a governess devoted her whole time to their education. If you do the best you can under the circumstances, duty is discharged—a matter of thanksgiving.

Look at the Sunny Side.—There is such a side in every lot in life. Most children grow up in homes where there are no servants, and turn out passably well. Men and women of the highest culture and social position, more often than otherwise, began life in this condition, and the early habits of self help and industry there formed, determined their characters and success. To be born in affluence is generally a calamity. The children of the rich are most appropriately objects of compassion. What shall be done for such, to make them useful and happy, is a much more difficult problem to solve than the proper training of the children of the poor. The men who make our laws and mould public opinion, as a rule, grow up under the necessity of labor. Their mothers filled the offices of nurse, cook, and laundress in their homes, and to this day it is the honest conviction of these distinguished men, that their mothers were the best women and the most savory cooks in the world.

Cultivate Self-Help in your Children.—Mothers sometimes err in excessive tenderness and devotion. Children love occupation and will have it. The passion for dressing dolls may as well be turned to dressing something more substantial. A little girl can soon learn to dress and wash herself, and then to perform these offices for her younger brothers and sisters. Play should never be forestalled, but it may be so judiciously mixed up with healthful labors that the toil will not be irksome. The boy may as well pull on his first boots, as have another do it for him. If he is taught that it is manly to help himself and to keep his clothes and person clean, he will glory in the use of brushes for the hair, the teeth, the clothes, and boots. He will soon learn to measure manhood by usefulness, and not by the amount of dirty work other people do for him. Some people indeed, get too much out of their children, but that is not the tendency or peril of American Society. They can be made much more helpful with pleasure and profit to themselves, and to the world.

Buy Labor-Saving Machines.—A large part of the labor in the family can be saved by them, and they pay for themselves many times over every year. It is difficult to see how a housekeeper can get along without them. Most people are too poor to do without them. They save what is more precious than money—health and life. We forbear to say more, lest there should be nothing left for the woman with the eight small children to say. We yield the floor until she speaks.

Experience with French Fowls.

We have published several articles concerning the important additions made to our poultry yards, in the introduction of French breeds, more particularly referring to the Crevecœurs and Houdans. This has produced testimony for and against these breeds, from those that have them. That they are non-sitters can hardly be held as a disadvantage. Moreover, it is said that the Crevecœur is not as hardy as the Houdan. This appears from the following extract from a letter of Mr. J. L. S., of Cincinnati, one of our most successful amateur poultry raisers: "My yard is in a thriving condition, excepting the Crevecœurs, and they, wretched chickens, are trying to see how fast they can die. No disease comes amiss to them, be it old and common, or new, and, what renders this more strange to me, is, that my young ones are large, better feathered, and, up to a certain age, easier to raise than any chickens I have. I began the season with fourteen 'Crevé.' hens. I now have five left. They average about an egg and a half a day. They do not bear confinement well." Our impression is that Crevecœurs suffer from dampness, and this is strengthened by the fact that in Holland, a damp country, the breed does not thrive. A dry bank, fully exposed to the south, would suit them best.

Another party gives his experience as follows: "I am greatly pleased with my Crevecœurs, having made two importations, and have not as yet lost a bird. When the first lot arrived, 3 of them were sick with roup; one hen seemed a hopeless case, but by good care she recovered, and is now presenting her egg per day with great regularity, and all are thriving. With decent care, I see no reason why they should not prove entirely satisfactory as to hardiness. Fifty-five of the young chickens are coming on finely; have lost none by disease. My second importation of hens laid all the way, and are at it yet."

A third party, having both the Crevecœur and Houdan, is of opinion that both will succeed well, judging from his own trial thus far. It is, however, too early to form any decided opinion. Several seasons must elapse before the point of hardiness can be determined satisfactorily. The reputation for early maturity, large size, excellence of flavor, and fecundity, gained by these breeds, in France and England, seems to be sustained here thus far.

The Houdans are preferred to the Crevecœurs by Mr. Turhorst, one of the oldest and most experienced of poultry breeders in Great Britain, who declares them a most valuable addition to the poultry yard. Mr. John Baily, one of the contributors to the poultry columns of the Journal of Horticulture and Cottage Gardener, says, Aug. 17, 1866: "I have never had a case of illness with a Houdan, and believe them to be hardiest of fowl." And again, April 25th, 1867, "We have kept them for many years; they are very hardy, more so than the La Fleche and Crevecœurs. They bear close confinement.

A National Tax on Dogs.

Among the 16,000 articles taxed by our Solons at Washington, it seems strange that so large and important an interest as dogs should have escaped notice. A more legitimate object to raise revenue from can not be found in the whole list. Our Government very properly taxes luxuries, with a view to bring the burdens of taxation upon those who are best able to bear them. Among these luxuries are brandies, wines, silks, gold watches, gold and silver ware, carriages, pianos, etc. Dogs are a luxury, as we see in the white-haired poodle, that rides out with his mistress and sleeps in her boudoir upon the softest of cushions, and has his hair daily perfumed with the choicest extracts of Lubin. They are considered the appropriate appendage of every genteel establishment; setters and pointers for sporting gentlemen, whether they fancy hunting or not; and the big speckled dog under the carriage, the admiration of small boys, and a terror to all evil doers among smaller dogs. The Government also taxes nuisances with a view to abate them. Dogs are a nuisance of the most troublesome and expensive kind. We have in the nation, according to the best statisticians, one to a family, or about 7,000,000. We think a hundred thousand of these may be occasionally useful and ornamental—well bred dogs—that pay their way. The rest are pests and abominations. They run mad and bite multitudes of men, and every season we have deaths from that dreadful disease, the hydrophobia. The public health suffers every season in all our large cities from apprehensions of mad dogs, and the city authorities have to make open warfare upon the race. They are a burdensome pest, costing the nation at least seventy millions of dollars to support them, a very large tax upon an over-taxed people. They are a very destructive pest—killing at least a half million of sheep every year, worth at present prices at least two millions of dollars, and ruining others to the value of a million dollars more. They make sheep raising so insecure, that large tracts of land lie waste for want of this stock to crop them, and every man has to pay a heavy tax in the shape of dear wool and mutton on account of dogs. But for these wretched curs, our forty million of sheep could be doubled in a short time, and cheap wool and mutton be made the heritage of every American citizen forever. If our legislators want to tax luxuries and abate nuisances, they will accomplish both objects in taxing dogs.

Another object of the Government should be to afford incidental protection to home interests. A heavy tax on dogs will help several important interests. It will give us a better race of dogs. Of course, only the best breeds will be spared, and the best specimens of their kind, and the canine race will be perpetuated in these lines—purely bred—well trained—well cared for—used legitimately, and a nuisance to nobody. It will also give us cheap wool and mutton, two very great blessings for any nation. Whatever the tariff may be on foreign wools, we can compete with the world on any kind of wool, if the Government will only clean out the race of curs. We have untold acres that are lying waste for want of sheep, and men dare not invest in them, for fear of the dogs.

Other Governments very wisely legislate against dogs, both to abate a nuisance and to protect the wool grower. Great Britain lays a tax of twelve shillings (three dollars) on dogs, and derives a handsome revenue from this source. In Bavaria, the canine population has been very much reduced by taxation. In Baden, the dog-revenue amounts to a hundred thousand thalers. France has a dog tax, and on this point Bismark agrees with Napoleon. At the International Congress of Veterinary Surgeons, in Vienna, in 1865, the subject was discussed, interesting statistics of hydrophobia were presented, and a resolution was adopted favoring taxation, and recommending that the tax be as high as possible. The foremost States of Europe appreciate the relation of dogs to wool and mutton. In most of our Northern States, laws upon this subject have been passed, and in Massachusetts and Connecticut, which have the best laws, the number of dogs has been greatly reduced, and a corresponding security given to sheep. It is demonstrated not only that dog laws are needed, but that wise legislation will be sustained by public opinion, and accomplish its object. National laws need not interfere with State laws, or supersede them. Properly drawn, they would work harmoniously with them, and by making curs expensive luxuries, help to exterminate them. Perhaps the only thing needed is a tax of three dollars.

This course would infringe upon no man's rights. We concede to the American citizen the largest liberty consistent with the public good. It is the undoubted privilege of the citizen to keep panthers if he fancies them, but he should keep them in a cage, and not in his neighbor's barn-yard. We have as good a right to raise calves as he has panthers, and he must take care of his wild beasts, or we can not get along peaceably together. He may keep rattlesnakes, if he pleases, but he should keep them where he can have the exclusive enjoyment of their musical rattle. We do not like the music too near—sudden death by poison is not pleasant. He may have dogs if he likes. We concede that it is none of our business whether he has a legitimate use for them or not, whether he can afford them or not. But he must not compel us to board them on sheep that cost a thousand dollars a carcass, and that are more valuable to us living than dead. If dogs are worth having, pay for them and take care of them like a man. Sheep raisers have rights as well as dog owners. Let us have fair play in this matter, and a national dog law that will give us both cheap wool and cheap mutton.

Wool Grower's Associations, State and County Agricultural Societies, and Farmer's Clubs should move early in this matter, and demand suitable legislation at the next session of Congress. Whatever reluctance there may be among Congressmen to offend dog owners who have votes, they can not withstand an enlightened public sentiment. The friends of cheap wool and mutton are in the vast majority in this country, and they have only to make their wishes known by united action to secure the needed legislation. Whatever measure ought to be carried, can be, by the activity of its friends.

The Puma.—(*Felis Concolor.*)

The Jaguar of South America is the largest of the Leopard family of cats, being also the most beautiful in its marking. The Puma approaches it in size, and is also closely affiliated to it. The geographical range of this animal is very great, probably greater than that of any other cat in a wild state, being from Canada to Patagonia. It rejoices in more titles than is quite fair in this hemisphere of republican ideas, and it is hard to say which is the most correct common name. No less than three Latin generic names have been given to it, *Felis, Leopardus* and *Puma*, but Linnaeus' name, *F. concolor*, is now accepted by the best authorities. We know the animal in books and newspapers as Puma, Cougar and American Lion; in common conversation as Catamount, Panther and Painter. It is not very uncommon throughout the still wild parts of the United States, and is a destructive pest to the flocks and herds of the South American plains. The creature has a lion-like face, but the head is small, and it is totally lacking in courage. In craft, however, it is great; and there are repeated records of men and boys having fallen victims to its covert attacks. Its usual mode of taking its prey, in wooded districts, is, to conceal itself among the branches of a tree overhanging deer paths and springs, and drop or jump upon its victims. The form of the panther is admirably shown in the above spirited engraving from one of Wier's drawings. Its color is tawny or brownish-yellow on the back, and ashy-white beneath. Its weight sometimes reaches 150 pounds; it is 4 to 4½ feet in length, exclusive of the tail, which is over 2 feet, and tipped with black, but not tufted. A subscriber in Claremont, N. H., sent us recently a photograph of a large Cougar taken near there last winter. A Cougar is not long in making its presence known in any district. Calves and young cattle in woody pastures are usually its first victims, but its depredations are extended to farm yards, where it slaughters many more than its needs require. The men of any region thus visited promptly turn out for a "Painter hunt." The hunters should go in couples, for, though easily killed if noticed, unseen a panther is dangerous.

PUMA.—(*Felis Concolor.*)

Lizards and Tritons.

People generally make no very accurate distinction between the Newts, Salamanders, and Tritons, and those animals of a finer organization properly called Lizards or Saurians. In the accompanying engraving are represented three quite similarly formed, yet very different animals. The upper one is the PINE LIZARD or BROWN SWIFT, (*Tropidolepsis undulatus*), a lizard of the Iguana family. It resides in pine woods, dwelling chiefly in the trees, yet frequently found upon the ground. It is about 7 or 8 inches long, covered with pointed scales, gray upon the back and sides, marked above with undulating dark bands; below on each side is a band of green, surrounded with black. This little animal lives altogether upon insects, and in order to take them, has to be exceedingly agile in its motions, not being provided with a long glutinous tongue. It is not uncommon throughout the greater part of the United States. The middle figure is of the BLUE-TAILED SKINK, (*Scincus fasciatus*), the common representative in the Northern States of the Skink family, which may be regarded as one of the connecting links between the Lizards and Snakes, for the closely allied family of the Glass Snakes have still more snake-like bodies, and either no external legs and feet, or very small and almost useless ones. The Skinks have cylindrical bodies, with smooth scales. They have snaky heads, covered with thin angular plates, and flat, notched tongues, and there is little difference in size between the neck and the body, at the abdomen. From this point there is a gradual taper to the tip of the tail. They are well toothed, but not venomous, though they bite severely. The Red-headed Skink of the Southern States passes popularly under the name of Scorpion. It closely resembles this one, but is considerably larger. The length of the Blue-tailed Skink is about 8 inches; its head is bluish-black, its body striped with six straw-colored lines, and the tail is of a beautiful ultramarine blue. The throat and belly are white. These are also insect eaters, hence, our friends. The spotted creature in the foreground of this group is the TIGER TRITON, (*Triton tigrinus*), and may represent the numerous class of tailed batrachians. It is not properly a lizard at all, but much more nearly related to the frogs and toads. Its eggs are laid in the water, and the young pass through a state of existence similar to the tadpole condition. It is about 6½ inches long, bluish-black above, marked with brilliant lemon-colored blotches of irregular outlines; below it is ashy with paler blotches. It is found in New England and the

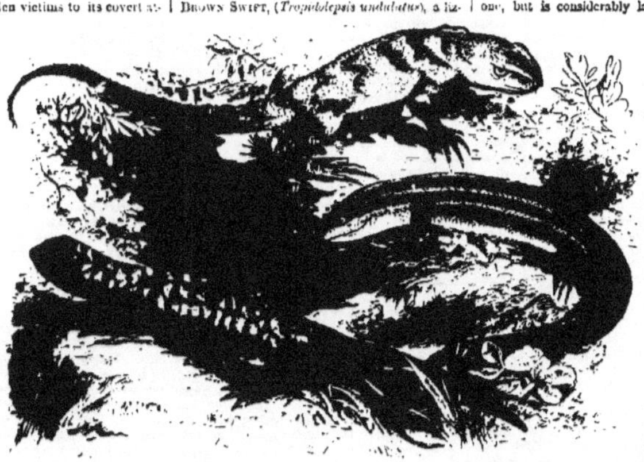

TIGER TRITON. PINE LIZARD. BLUE-TAILED SKINK.

Middle States, and is amphibious. This, also, is entirely innocent. A peculiarly interesting characteristic of the Tritons is the ease with which they *break*, and the facility with which the wounded part heals, or is *replaced*. Amputated tails or limbs will grow again, and if these are cut off they will be soon replaced by others.

Tim Bunker on the Eight Hour Law.

BIG FERMENT IN HOOKERTOWN.

MR. EDITOR.—We have been having considerable doings up here lately, and as you wanted me to keep you posted on Connecticut news in general, and Hookertown in particular, I send you some notes I took on the Eight Hour Convention. It was got up by Cicero Smith, and a few of the fellows that work with him, when they do anything, which is not often.

Big posters were stuck up on all the sign posts in town, calling upon mechanics and working people in general, to meet in the town hall, and assert their rights, just as if somebody had been trying to take away their rights. There was a full house. Shadtown was well represented by the fishermen, and the White Oakes turned out strong. Kier Frink and the coal men came down in their carts, and Hookertown-street has not seen such a collection of broken down wagons, and gaunt, raw-boned horses, in many a day. It reminded one of the early days of the war, when they were holding big meetings to drum up recruits.

Judge Loring was appointed chairman, and Cicero Smith introduced a long string of resolutions, recommending eight hours as a legal day's work, and pledging the meeting to vote for no man that was not in favor of an eight hour law. He said the time had come for the heavy burdens of labor to be lifted from the working classes; that they now did all the work, got poor pay, and had to live in humble abodes, on scant fare, and endure all the ills of poverty. They were ground down by capital to the lowest depths, and had no time for the cultivation of their minds, and for social enjoyments. He hoped to see the day when the men who did the work should have the money, and the fine houses, and the fast horses, and enjoy life like human beings. He was in favor of paying the laborer as much for his eight hours as he now received for ten, and if that was not enough, he would go as far as the farthcrest in relieving his wants, and meeting his wishes. The only true foundation for a State was to glorify labor.

Seth Twiggs said he should like the latter part of the gentleman's speech better, if he would illustrate it in his life. If any body got one hour's work out of Smith, it would be so much clear gain. "There is as many as two ways of glorifying labor. One is to make stump speeches to working people, and the other is to pitch in and work yourself." He thought a man who held a plow, or chopped wood all day, honored labor enough sight better than a man who was everlastingly talking about work and doing nothing. He didn't value the working of the jaws near so much as some other parts of the body.

Uncle Jotham Sparrowgrass said he didn't know as he understood this eight hour movement, but as far as he did, he didn't think much of it. "It ain't any thing new. It was tried over on the Island more than forty years ago. There was a set of fellows then trying to get rid of work, and they come nearer to saying what they meant than folks did now. They wanted to divide up property equally all round, and said nothing about working for it. When I was a boy, folks who got ahead any, used to get up early in the morning and work as long as they could see, and milk the cows in the dark. If they got the chores done by nine o'clock and got ready for bed, they did pretty well. They hadn't much time to feel abused and talk about their rights. The main pint was to get a living and get ahead in the world. They may have carried work a leetle too far, but arter all, they were firts-rate people, and better neighbors I never expect to find in this world." It seemed to him that the question was whether folks should work and thrive, or try to get a living without work. For one, he was in favor of work, and if he could find any thing to do that paid, he shouldn't be particular about the hours.

George Washington Tucker said he was glad there was somebody to consider poor folks. He had always worked hard and had nothing to show for it. He never owned a foot of land, and couldn't expect to without some change of times. He wanted more pay and less work, and he thought the eight hour plan was the best one that had ever been tried to relieve poor folks.

Jake Frink said he was a good deal bothered about the question. "Heaven knows I've hard work enough to git along. I've been trying to pay for my farm this thirty years, and hain't made it eout yit. And I've worked like a dog a good part of the time. But how working eight hours instead of twelve is gwine to help me, I can't exactly see. I rather guess there would be less corn in my bin, and pork in my cellar in the fall, than there is now. I have to hire some help in summer, and if a man quits in the middle of the arternoon, and leaves me to git up the hay and grain, I don't see how I'm gwine to be benefited. It looks considerable like a humbug. I bo't some patent manure onc't."

Dea. Little said he didn't like the looks of this question. "They tried the same thing in Sodom, and it didn't work well. The land was rich and produced big crops, and they had nothing to do but look on and see 'em grow. They come very near getting rid o' work, and took to serving the devil so that no decent man could live among them." Work was a good thing for sinners, and he never expected to live without it. He thought if his friend Tucker would pull harder at the hoe handle, and not so much at the bottle, he would be able to own land and a house, and to be quite comfortable. Idleness clothed a man in rags in Solomon's time, and he didn't expect to see a lazy man's wardrobe improve any in our day. "If you want any thing, work for it, and if you work long and hard enough, you are pretty sure to get it."

Rev. Mr. Spooner said he was troubled about the moral aspects of this movement. It was nothing new that men tried to escape the curse of toil. Nothing has called forth more ingenuity, but the curse still remains, and he doubted if man would ever be able to repeal the law, 'Six days shalt thou labor.' Eight hours was not a day's work under this law, whatever the civil statute might make it. The average length of the day was about twelve hours. Men were able to work more than eight hours, and did generally, without injury to health, and with much advantage to their fortunes. That was pretty good evidence that they ought to work more. Some people, he supposed, worked too long and too hard, but there was a far larger number who were ruined by idleness, and the vices that grew out of it. He thought the great want of the country now was more labor. If this measure was made a practical thing, it would take one-fifth from all the labor in the country, and that meant, when we come to sift it down, a deduction of one-fifth from every man's income. It was labor that gave value to capital. Men who had money could not loan it unless its use could be made productive by labor. The country was not ready for any such reduction of production and of income. The agitation of the question he thought was mischievous, and would only tend to embarrass the relations of capital and labor.

Last Sunday, Mr. Spooner preached a Sermon from St. Paul: "Neither did we eat any man's bread for nought, but wrought with labor and travail, night and day, that we might not be chargeable to any of you," in which he laid out the eight hour law in its grave clothes. Paul was a gentleman and believed in paying his way, which the eight hour folks don't. If we are going to have any thing besides victuals and clothes, we've got to work more than eight hours for it. Quitting work the middle of the arternoon in haying time won't go down. Even Jake Frink can see the bearing of that nonsense.

Hookertown, Conn., June 15, 1867. } Yours to command,
TIMOTHY BUNKER, Esq.

Raise Your Own Wheat.

With the best brands of family flour at $20, and a large importation of wheat from California, it becomes the farmers of the sea-board States to inquire if they cannot get their flour cheaper at home. We know some farmers can do better than to raise their own flour, even at the present high prices, but the great majority cannot. Wheat, at $2 a bushel even, would pay as well as anything else they raise, if they would only prepare the soil properly. On many of these farms wheat has not been raised for the last 30 or 40 years, and the present owners have come to regard it as an unprofitable crop. Yet these same farms formerly produced fine crops of wheat, and this grain was a prime article for export in all the sea-board States. The soil and climate have not changed, and the winters, as meteorological records clearly show, furnish about the same amount of cold and snow as they did a hundred years ago. With a suitable preparation of the soil, these old fields and meadows will produce this grain as well as they ever did. It is not true, as is too often supposed, that we must have a new soil to produce this crop to advantage. In England, there are farms that have grown wheat for a thousand years, and the yield is as bountiful as ever. There they have a regular rotation, and bountiful manuring, and get 40 bushels to the acre. There are some farmers at the East that keep up the good old custom of making their own breadstuffs, and thrive by it. We visited such a district at the east end of Long Island, where, as a rule, the farmers grow wheat enough for the supply of their own families, and the crop is found to be about as sure as anything they can raise. Their soil is not particularly rich, or better adapted to wheat than other sections. Their only advantage is ready access to sea manures, especially fish guano and the refuse of the oil factories. But with any other good manure, wheat may be raised to advantage. Try a simple acre, and make yourself independent of the West for your flour. Do not sow upon poor exhausted meadow, and fail, and say it is impossible to grow wheat. If your soil is not already rich enough to produce 50 bushels of corn to the acre, manure with fine compost. Get the best seed and prepare it with brine and lime, and sow early, and put it in with a cultivator two or three inches deep. Upon soil, naturally or artificially, well drained, it will stand the winter and give you a good crop. There is great satisfaction in growing your own wheat. You get it in the best condition; you can have it fresh ground, and not be troubled with sour, musty flour, and poor bread. You can have it unbolted for Graham bread and biscuit, and furnish the raw material for the enamel of your children's teeth. The dentists may suffer for lack of custom, but you "will put money in your purse" and health in your bones.

Fatal Accidents from Mowing Machines.

The great number of serious and fatal accidents which are reported every year as arising from carelessness in handling mowing machines, or from drivers being thrown off from their seats in front of them, has led to much thought, both on the part of conscientious manufacturers and others, to prevent such occurrences. Some mowing machines are peculiarly liable to throw the driver off on going over rough ground, or when the cutter bar strikes a fixed obstacle. They should be avoided by purchasers, as one would any treacherous dangerous thing. When accidents occur and are reported in the papers, the name of the machine should always be given. We should like to publish a list showing the number of each machine in use, and number of accidents to those using them, could a fair one be made out.

Some years ago a lady of Burlington, N. J., invented an arrangement for throwing the knives out of gear the instant the driver's weight was taken from the seat. We never knew of its being put to use. There have been several other guards contrived, generally, however, not applicable to all machines.

We have received a suggestion in a letter from Mr. J. S. Hammond, of Scarsdale, which we regard as eminently practical and sensible, and believe it will be the means of saving many lives and limbs. He writes:

"As the mowing season is rapidly approaching, I desire to make known a simple device, which I have employed during two seasons, to prevent being thrown from my mowing machine. It is well known that serious accidents have been thus produced. It is this: I take a strong leather strap, about 30 inches long, and, passing one end between the bars on the *left* side of the seat, (generally of open iron work,) buckle, so as to make a loop. Put the left arm through this loop. Let the loop be long enough to allow free use of the arm in driving, and at the same time to steady the body. The *right* arm must be free to work the machine. Should the machine strike any hidden obstacle, the strap will prevent the rider from being thrown to the right side, or forward, upon the knives, and will in most cases enable him to keep his seat. Properly adjusted it will not interfere with the management of the team or the machine.

Animals as Weather Guages.

"A. S. B.," writes: "I have observed this spring that the robins and some one or two other birds, (but especially the robins), seem to be building their nests higher than usual, and more on the outside of the trees, or further out on the limbs. The robin, as a general thing, builds its nest close to the trunk or main body of the tree, and I have known them not to build more than 8 to 10 feet from the ground, and I may say generally they are not inclined to build much above the center of the tree, but this year the contrary seems to be their habit. I have noticed this fact to one or two others, and to a Doctor to whom I have noticed it, told me he had observed some two or three robins building higher and nearer the tops of the trees than he had ever noticed their doing before. I would ask, does it indicate a warm or cold summer, a wet or dry one, heavy or light winds? I had thought, perhaps, it indicated a cloudy, cold, wet, summer. I would like others to make some observation of this in their part of the country, and see if it is so with them."

It is quite common to forecast the season from certain indications among animals, and many people, intelligent in other respects, have abiding faith in these signs. Thus, when partridges and quails have their feathers very low down on their legs, it is said to indicate a severe winter, and when muskrats build their nests very high, it will be a wet winter. These signs are very numerous, but being of a skeptical turn, we do not believe them. If our correspondent's observation is correct, it might indicate that the cats in his neighborhood had been more active than usual, and the birds were anxious to get out of the way. It has always seemed to us that the robin was very loose in its notions of locating its nest, and studied small fruits rather than the weather. If a strawberry bed were near, we have noticed that cock-robin and his bride pitched into the first red cedar, apple tree, or fence corner, at hand, where there was a little screen from observation. If the cherry trees were tall, they would not object to a tall berth in the neighboring spruce or maple. Men know very little about the coming seasons, and birds and beasts still less. We shall be glad to receive any facts in regard to the location of birds' nests this season—whether they sustain our theory or magnify bird forecast.

Large vs. Small Cotton Plantations.

We have received from a gentleman in Georgia, a communication to prove that cotton cannot be grown profitably henceforth upon large plantations. The argument, condensed, is this: It cannot be done, first, because under the slave system, the planter's chief profit was the increase of his slaves. This being gone, no money can be made with free labor. Second, compulsory labor was more reliable than that of freedmen. Third, cotton was grown at a loss last year. Fourth, capital invested in tools, stock and machinery is too insecure to tempt large capitalists. Fifth, the freedmen will be a tax upon the production of cotton. They will be henceforth full consumers and only partial producers, instead of full producers and partial consumers. Sixth, the small farmer will have an advantage in laboring with his own hands, and in the more intelligent direction of the few hands under him. He corroborates his own argument by the detailed cost and profit of working two cotton plantations in his vicinity, which we give in full:

PLANTATION NO. 1, BARNWELL DISTRICT, S. C.

Employing 18 laborers, cultivating 320 acres, viz.: 180 in corn, 140 in cotton, the planter furnishing land, stock, implements, etc., etc., and furnishing each laborer with shelter, 150 pounds of bacon and 12 bushels of corn, and allowing the laborers one-third of the produce raised. This plantation overlooked by the proprietor.

140 acres may yield 35 bales cotton, weighing [illegible] each, and may yield the planter 20 cents per lb. in net charges, making		$[illegible] 00
180 acres in corn may yield 10 bushels per acre, worth $1 per bushel		1,800 00
[illegible] blades, worth $1 per 100lbs		720 00
1,500 bushels cotton seed, worth 20 cents per bushel		300 00
Gross yield		$[illegible] 00
Deduct one-third, being laborers' share		2,[illegible] 00
		$[illegible]
Deduct 2,700lbs. bacon at 17 cents	$459 00	
Deduct 216 bushels corn at $1 [illegible]	$[illegible] 00	
Provisions furnished laborers		[illegible] 00
		$4,[illegible] 00
Deduct for interest and insurance of 9 mules, costing $150 each, equal to $1,350 at 20 per cent. per annum	$270	
Deduct for wear of gin, gin house and gear, screw, implements, wagon, cart, etc., at 20 per cent. on $200	40—	310 00
		$3,[illegible] 00
Deduct planter's share of corn, blades and cotton seed, which must be reserved as outfit for next year		1,541 00
		$2,118 00
Deduct rent of land, or interest on its cost, estimated as equal to one-sixth of what it will produce		1,2[illegible] 00
Planter's profits		$[illegible] 00

Being his return for his individual services, and with this sum he must pay State and local taxes, purchase flour, coffee, sugar, clothing, etc., and pay the doctor's charges.

PLANTATION NO. 2, BURKE COUNTY, GEORGIA.

Employing 15 laborers in number, regarded by proprietor as equalling 10 good operatives; cultivating 225 acres, viz.: 100 in corn, 125 in cotton, and overlooked by an agent.

Cotton		$[illegible] 00
Corn		1,250 00
Blades		750 00
Cotton seed		[illegible]
Gross yield		$[illegible] 00
Deduct wages paid in money	$[illegible] 00	
Do. provisions furnished laborers	667 00	
Do. interest on stock and implements	431 00	
Do salary and rations of agent	[illegible] 00	
Do. outfit of corn, blades and cotton seed for next year	1,900 00	
Deduct rent of plantation, estimated at one-fifth of its production	1,350 00—	5,[illegible] 00
Proprietor's net profit		$[illegible]

1. As to the first argument, it is what the logicians called a non sequitur. There is so much difference between slave and free labor that it is quite difficult to reason from one to the other, especially in a community where free labor has not yet had a fair trial. 2. When this trial has fairly been made, we have no doubt that planters generally will concede that free labor is both more reliable and more economical. At present the freedmen labor under two very great disadvantages. The carelessness and idleness resulting from their former slavery, and insecurity of payment. When the dollar is made certain, the work will be. The stimulus of the dollar is much more effective than that of the lash. Labor in the free States is much more secure, and more profitable, than it ever was in the South, and it is owing to this fact, mainly, that land is worth so much more in the North. Under the working of freedom a reliable class of laborers will be trained in the South. If the planter has the capital to pay his hands every week, there will be little trouble about the work. 3. Last year was exceptional, as all admit, yet, with all its disadvantages, nearly two millions of bales of cotton were raised. Had the season been favorable, the product would have been double, or fully up to the average of cotton production before the war. This is quite as much as could have been expected. We think the results of last year, under the circumstances, are encouraging, both to the large and the small planter. We may fairly prophesy from it five millions of bales, as the annual crop within three years. 4. The insecurity of capital invested does not arise from the use of free labor. On the contrary, it is made more secure by it, as the history of all free labor communities proves. The only hesitation that capitalists now have in investing in cotton plantations, arises from the unsettled state of the country. There is a fear of mobs, of regulators, of social

ostracism, but none of free labor. These apprehensions, we think, will soon be removed. 5. No doubt the freedmen will be much better consumers than they have been. As fast as they earn the means they will want land and cottages of their own, better furniture, clothing, and food, books and papers. This will be no tax on cotton growing, but by these they will be made more industrious and skillful laborers, and so will produce cotton at less cost per pound. Nothing pays so well as skilled labor. This kind of labor will manage the new tools that are soon to come into the cotton field, and diminish the cost of production at least one half. The freedmen will be better consumers, and for that reason better producers. 6. Small planters will, no doubt, greatly multiply in the South, but it will be for the want of capital rather than because large capital can not be made to pay. With capital enough one could get a better interest from fifty hands than from five. The production would be quite as large per hand, and the cost of overseeing much less.

The tables of expense and profit, we think, are fairly open to criticism. When cotton is 30 cents a pound the planter will receive more than 20 cents a pound nett. In these estimates no manure is included. This should be used, so that the product will be at least one bale of cotton to the acre, and 30 bushels of corn. If he should apply, say, one ton of fish guano to the acre, costing $85 delivered, and should get thereby one bale, instead of one-third of a bale, it would make a great difference in the look of the balance sheet. The cost of cultivation would not be increased. A little extra would have to be allowed for picking, baling and transportation. Our premium essays on cotton will show this fully.

Fig. 1.—FISH-STAIRS AT LOWELL, MASS.

Re-stocking our Fresh Waters with Fish.

We are glad to learn that this good cause is making progress. There are not nearly as many fish in our rivers as formerly, and from many of them the salmon has entirely disappeared, and shad are not caught in sufficient numbers to pay for setting nets and se.. :s. Commissioners have been appointed in five of the New England States, two from each State, to act jointly in this matter, to arrest destruction by improvident methods, and to provide for the re-stocking of the rivers. H. A. Bellows, of New Hampshire, is Chairman, and Theodore Lyman, of Massachusetts, the Secretary of this Commission. The causes of the destruction of fish, as set forth by these gentlemen, are as follows, namely:

1. Impassable dams. Over these, fish-ways may be built with little waste of water.

2. Pollution of water by lime, dyes, soap, sawdust, and other mill refuse. Much of all these should not be thrown at all into the water.

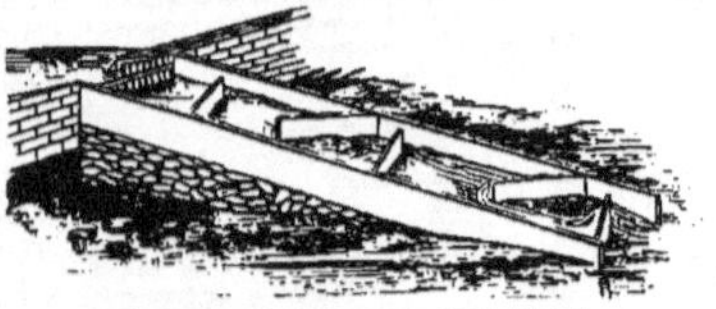

Fig. 2.—FOSTER'S FISH-WAY FOR SMALL STREAMS.

As to the dirty water from wool or cloth washing, it may be confined to one side of the river by a plank screen placed opposite the race-way.

3. Destruction of young fish by mill-wheels, which may be avoided by a lattice placed across the mouth of the canal, or flume above the mill.

4. Destructive modes of fishing, among which we may include gill-nets, weirs, very long seines, pots, set-hooks, fire-fishing, and fishing through the ice; all of which should be forbidden by law.

5. Fishing too much, and at wrong seasons. For migratory fish, certain days in each week should be "closed,"—that is to say, no fishing should then be allowed; and the taking of trout on their spawning beds should be rigorously interdicted.

Massachusetts and New Hampshire have already passed laws for the opening of the Merrimack and the Connecticut to sea fish, and for the encouragement of the breeding of valuable fresh water fish. Fish-ways have been erected upon the Merrimack, and many thousand salmon eggs have been planted in its upper waters. We regard the impassable dams as the greatest hinderance to the multiplication of the migratory fish. The rich manufacturing companies that profit by these dams should be compelled by law to provide fish-ways over them. The times when the fish wish to use them are generally times of abundant water, so that the interests of manufacturers would suffer little from loss of power. As to the second cause, much of the mill refuse is valuable as a fertilizer, and should not be run into the river, but into the compost heap. We earnestly commend this object to the favor of our readers. In many ways the people may aid it, especially by demanding suitable legislation to help it. We should like to, and now even hope, that we may see the day when fresh salmon will be the poor man's dish again, instead of a luxury hard to get at a dollar a pound.

Fish-ways, fish-stairs, Salmon-steps, etc., are names which convey distinctly the object of the various structures, which are erected for the purpose of allowing fish to pass over dams to spawn. Figure 1 represents the fish-stairs at Lowell, on the Merrimack, in Massachusetts. They consist of nine tanks, in which the water stands one foot deep, and through which it flows, falling from each, one foot into the one below. The tanks are of heavy plank, bolted together, and placed upon substantial masonry. An opening in the flush-boards of the dam permits a suitable stream of water to pass down the stairs, to afford the fish an easy passage to their breeding grounds. Figure 2 shows "Foster's" fish-way, which is better adapted (so say the Commissioners), to small streams, as it uses little water. On a basis of masonry, a straight, sloping flume conducts the water, from the flood-gate on the dam, to the still water below. The water, in its course through this flume, or trough, is interrupted by a series of "cross bulk-heads," extending alternately from one side and the other, nearly across. They have an upward slant, and thus, repeatedly, check the flow of the water, dam it back, and make a series of still pools, with a constant flow of deep water between them. Both these stairs are known to be sufficient for the passage of Salmon and Ale-wives, but Foster's, it appears, have not been thoroughly tested for shad, which are the most fastidious.

Using Three Horses Abreast.

People, who have tested it, agree very well that it is a fact, that three horses working abreast, will pull, if well harnessed or "yoked," much more than if drawing in any other way. The usual method of arranging the whiffle-trees and "eveners," is that shown in fig. 1, and when the team is used for hauling logs, or any similar work, it is very well. When used to draw a cart, the center horse works in shafts, while the horse on each side is attached to an independent whiffle-tree, hooked upon an outrigger, with a chain running back to the end of the axle outside the wheel. In backing or turning, there is a great advantage in this arrangement, for one or both of the side horses may be taken around and made to pull back, thus turning or backing easily, except in very cramped places. The side horses are guided by a short rein, fastened to the hames-ring of the horse in the shafts. See figure 2.

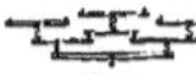

Fig. 1.

In plowing, the advantage of three horses is, perhaps, more apparent than at any other work. Experienced plowmen are strenuous advocates of this practice, but agree that much depends upon the correct proportions of the whiffle-trees and eveners, and upon the length of the traces.

This system of whiffle-trees is shown in fig. 3. If the three horses are of about similar weight, and of medium size, the whiffle-trees may be 24

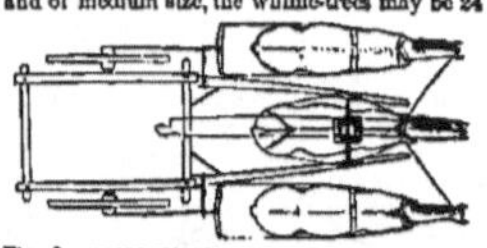

Fig. 2.—THREE HORSES ABREAST BEFORE A CART.

inches long, the simple evener 30 inches, and the irregular one 45 inches—that is, measuring between the draft-points. This will bring the horses very close, too close, if they are not driven with long traces; but it will allow them to draw very directly, and it is the only way, we know, in which the off horse can be made to walk in the furrow. If the nigh horse is a strong one, and may be made to do a little more than his fair share of the work, this will make it bette. all around, for the pair can be worked on a longer evener, and the irregular evener may be hitched to the plow, so as to favor the pair, and bring the off horse into the furrow. (A, is the furrow; B, the land; C, the furrow-slice.)

In arranging eveners for a horse at one side to pull against two, evenly, as in fig. 3, the draft-band, or clevis, should be placed exactly one-third the distance between the draft-point, at which the two horses draw, and that at

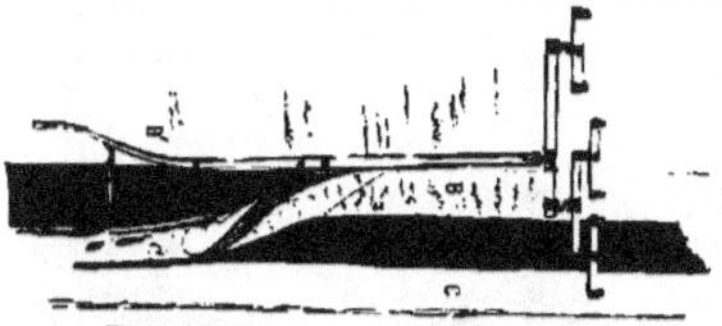

Fig. 3.—PLOW DRAWN BY THREE HORSES ABREAST.

which the single horse is attached; and when, as in fig. 1, the middle horse pulls against two, the same arrangement should be observed with reference to the two unequal eveners.

Left-hand Plows.

How true it is, that the mingling of men of different habits and different notions is productive of good to all concerned, provided always we choose the good and eschew the evil. This is one great value of such a journal as ours. It touches many people, and stirs them up to cast in their ideas into the common stock. It is a sort of mill, where ideas are taken in, winnowed, screened, ground, bolted, and thrown out upon the market in the best shape the millers can put them.

We confess, we never have been able to see any real advantage in left-hand plows, and regarded their use as simply a habit, until a recent letter from an Indiana subscriber, Mr. Delos Wood, throws light on the subject. In New England and the Middle States, so far as we know, the term "leader" is applied to the front horse, in what we have heard called a "three-cattle team," that is, either a pair of oxen or horses, with one horse before them. So, sometimes since, when a western correspondent advocated left-hand plows, because the leader could go in the furrow, we dissented, saying, that in no case should the leader walk in the

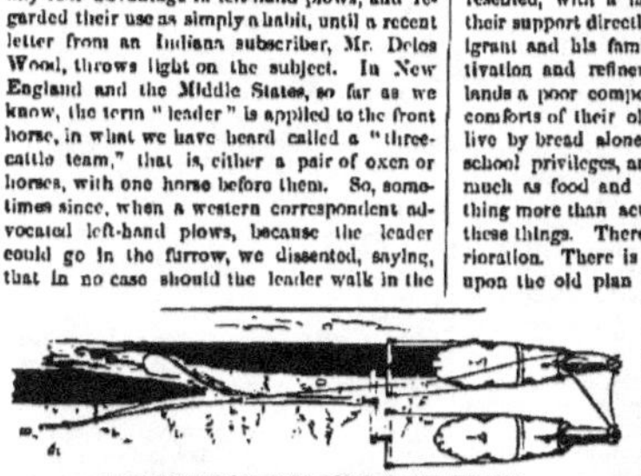

LEFT-HAND PLOW—NIGH HORSE IN THE FURROW.

furrow. Mr. Wood shows us that the western plowman, who drives with one line, calls the nigh horse, (to which the rein is of course attached,) the "leader." The advantage of driving with one line is great. We think this is demonstrated by the discussions on driving horses to plow, which lately appeared in our columns. If then the nigh horse can be driven in the furrow, great additional accuracy is secured.

To illustrate this, we figure a bird's-eye view of a pair of horses plowing with a left-hand plow, driven by one line attached to the nigh horse; he, walking in the furrow, and the off horse being guided by a "jocky stick" from the hames-ring of the other, and by a short rein between the heads.

Whither and How to Emigrate.

We have frequent inquiries as to the location of cheap lands, and the best place for an emigrant to go to. This depends so much upon the character of the man and his circumstances, that no one rule can be given that will meet the wants of all. The old style of emigration was for every man to look out for himself. He thought everything depended upon cheap land, and he pitched his tent or log cabin in the wilderness, without much reference to neighbors or surroundings. He left behind him the comforts of civilized life, church, school, mills, roads, bridges, laws, and with his wife and children, lived alone in the clearings for years. This led of necessity to much hardship, and often to prolonged suffering and death.

In modern times, we emigrate into new regions in large companies, and if a man is under the necessity of going alone, he goes into a place where much of the pioneer work has already been done, and he will find some of the comforts of civilized life. As a rule, it is much better for one who wants to emigrate to join some good company, and cast in his lot with them. This gives, at once, the very great advantage of cheap lands without the loss of the privileges of civilized life. It provides at once for the division of labor, and necessitates no violent change of business or of habits. A company should always be organized with reference to the wants of their future location. The trades and the professions should be represented, with a large proportion who draw their support directly from the soil. If the emigrant and his family are people of social cultivation and refinement, they will find cheap lands a poor compensation for the loss of the comforts of their old homes. "Man shall not live by bread alone." We want church and school privileges, and good neighbors, quite as much as food and clothing. There is something more than acute suffering in the loss of these things. There is mental and moral deterioration. There is no doubt that emigration upon the old plan tends to barbarism. Children grow up healthy and vigorous it may be, but with uncultivated minds and hearts, ignorant, boorish, and often vicious. The single emigrant, or a few families going together, we think, will do better in the older and more densely settled States, than to push out into the wilderness.

There are still wild lands in many of these States, and cheap lands in them all, waiting for willing hands to till them. They have been cleared and have some improvements upon them, cheap houses and barns, that will answer until better can be built. These improvements can generally be purchased for much less than they have cost, because the owners, for various reasons, want to sell and go further. It is an expensive process to clear heavily timbered land, and still more expensive to settle upon the prairie and buy all your fuel and building material. In the Northern States, church and school privileges will be found within reach of cheap lands, by which we mean those that sell for twenty dollars and less. At Columbus, Ohio, they have a fashion of reporting the destination of emigrants who are going west. Of a recent company of 610, 163 were for Ohio, 160 for Ind., 131 for Mo., 87 for Ill., 89 for Ky., 21 for Wis., and 0 for Iowa. In all these States there are good openings for emigration.

The prospects for Emigration to the Southern States are rapidly improving. The indications now are that civil government will soon be in a settled condition, and the people there will give a cordial welcome to immigrants from all lands. For men accustomed to the varied husbandry of the Northern States, we think the prospects in Virginia are exceedingly inviting. For those who are accustomed to market gardening, the region around Norfolk, and the mouths of the James and York Rivers, presents strong attractions. It is within twenty four hours of New York, and "garden truck" and fruits can be put into Washington Market, in about as good condition as if raised in Jersey, or on Long Island; the season is two or three weeks earlier, and the prices more than double.

New Mole, Rat, or Gopher Trap.

A subscriber sends us by mail, an ingenious contrivance, which we figure, not so much as a sure mole trap, for we have some doubts of its efficacy, yet, on general principles, as a good trap. Moles are much more suspicious than other quadrupedal vermin, and would be quite likely to turn their galleries around such an object. We have no doubt rats, gophers, squirrels, and other small animals would enter it readily. The construction is evident from the cut. A stick is formed or made hollow, having a uniform bore, of a size to accommodate the animal. (Half a 2-inch drain pipe would do well.) The ends are squared, and a groove is cut close to each end. On the side which is to be uppermost, three small holes are bored, one at each end, entering the grooves, and one in the middle. Beneath the middle one a piece is cut out of the tube as shown in fig. 1. The trap is set by placing in each groove a noose of cord or wire, passing through the holes in the top, and connected by a cord in which a fast loop, (a common bowline,) is tied. To this loop a spring pole is attached by a cord, which, being continued down, enters the hole in the middle of the trap, and is there secured by a tapering plug set in from below. This arrangement is clearly seen in section in fig. 2. The plug must be of such size and so inserted that while it will considerably obstruct the bore, and will hold the cord firmly, it will be loosened with the least touch. The size of the trap must be calculated, so that an animal touching the plug will stand with its hinder parts beyond the noose, at one end or the other. The loosening of the plug will spring the pole and draw the nooses—while the trap may be jerked out of or off the ground, provided it is not fastened down.

Fig. 1.—TRAP.

Fig. 2.

Turnips—Their Place on the Farm.

The amount of turnips which may be raised upon an acre of good land is very great, yet other crops may produce more nutriment, for a very large proportion of the root is water. Nevertheless, were the question to be, How may the greatest quantity of food be produced upon an acre *after the first of July?* we should hardly hesitate in saying, by sowing common turnips in drills, 14 to 20 inches apart, according to the soil. Turnips are always good to have, but their quick growth and our ability to sow them as a second crop—after taking off potatoes, grain, onions, or corn, (being sowed at the last hoeing,) etc.,—make them an invaluable aid to the farmer in supplying deficiencies in either grain, hay, roots, or any kind of forage. Superphosphate of lime is required as a specific for turnips, and on any tolerably good soil, 500 pounds will almost insure a fine crop. Lime, ashes, plaster, guano, bone dust, are each excellent in moderate quantities, harrowed in before sowing, or scattered broadcast, when the crop is hoed. On sward land it is best to turn under some fresh manure to insure fermentation and quicker rotting of the sod. Turnips may be sown at any time in July, and should be thinned to, at least, 6 inches apart. There are no better varieties than the Cow-horn, and Purple-top Strap-Leaf—the former long, the latter flat. Broadcast sowing gives poor results compared with drilling in the seed with a machine.

Walks and Talks on the Farm.—No. 43.

Farmers in this section are waking up on the subject of underdraining. The Rochester Brick and Tile Co. have sold every tile they had—culls and all. I wanted a load the other day, but not a tile was to be had. The fact is an encouraging one. Underdraining is the first step in improved farming, and the farmer who makes one drain is pretty sure to keep on till the whole farm is drained. And this is not all. Other improvements are sure to follow. He can, and will, plow earlier. The crops will be sown in good season. He will feel encouraged, and this in itself is a great point gained. The prospect of a good crop leads to renewed efforts. Weeds will be killed before they obtain full possession of the ground. The cultivator will be kept moving. The effect is soon seen on the crops, and their luxuriant growth cheers the farmer, and he will put forth an energy that will surprise none more than himself.

Some years ago we used to have what was then called "a lightning express" train from Albany to Buffalo. It made few stops and ran at great speed. Everything gave way to it. The engineer and conductor had a pride in making good time, and generally succeeded. But one day, when Henry Ward Beecher happened to be on board, something gave way about the engine, which delayed them half an hour. They lost the right of way, and he describes the changed aspect of passengers and officials in his own inimitable style: The engine was the same embodiment of energy and power. But instead of the proud and noble steed that commanded the admiration of all its fellows, whose coming was looked for with interest, and to whom all other trains respectfully stood aside, it moved on in an uncertain, sneaking sort of way, waiting at this station for a dirty cattle train, and at the next for a slow string of dingy coal cars. It was capable of great things, but had lost the right of way, and fell behind later and later. The few minutes lost became hours. It was no use grumbling. The other trains were not to blame; they were on time. The trouble arose from the lost half hour. No effort could make up for this. It is just so in farming.

This spring I proposed sowing forty acres of barley and oats. The first half of April was delightful weather, and we got about a dozen acres of land in good order, and drilled in the barley on the 18th of April. I had eight acres more that were plowed last fall, that I thought of getting in without again plowing. But there were some potato heaps on the land which had been covered with manure. This we spread on the land, and we found that neither the gang-plow nor the cultivator would make a good job of it, and we were obliged to plow. This was on the 20th of April. But for this, we could have got in the barley, as the weather was splendid. On the 22d of April it *snowed*. The next day it rained, and the next. We managed to plow on sod for potatoes, but could not work the barley land. On the 28th of April we had ice half an inch thick. May came in with a severe rain storm, and it was only by watching our opportunities that we were able to get in the barley this week. After that it was rain, rain, rain! We were off the track. Had the land been all drained, and had we plowed more last fall, the barley and oats could have been put in during the fine weather in April. But we missed the opportunity, and no after efforts were of any avail. We had lost the right of way. The rains were not so bad. Had the barley been in, and the land drained, they would have done more good than harm. As it was, we had to give up all idea of sowing barley and finally of sowing oats. There was nothing for it but to plant the land with corn. Part of the field was sown and seeded down, and it is a serious inconvenience to plant corn on the other part, and not to be able to seed it down. It gives me more work than I had calculated for this year, and next year part of the land will be in grass and the other part in crops. And all this for want of a little underdraining. It is no use to complain about the weather. Better anticipate such seasons and be prepared for them.

But farmers *are* improving. There can be no doubt about it. They are underdraining more, and working their land better. At present prices, farm products will pay for good culture, and the prospects are favorable. I feel quite encouraged, and expect to see agriculture command the intelligence and capital which its importance demands.

The Doctor says he was talking, the other day, with one of the oldest and most experienced millers in Western New York, and he remarked that it was "surprising how the quality of our wheat was affected for the worse by the practice of manuring the land instead of plowing in clover." There may be some truth in this observation, simply from the fact that the manure we use is not worthy of the name. It is composed principally of straw and corn stalks, and what little plant food it originally contained is half washed away before it gets back to the land. But the idea that rich, carefully preserved manure will not produce wheat of as good quality as green clover plowed under, is contrary to sound theory and practical experience. The truth is, that too many farmers neither manure their land nor plow in clover, and of course there is a great falling off in the quantity and quality of the wheat. To make clover into hay and sell it, is one of the surest methods of impoverishing the farm. It is a good deal worse even than selling timothy hay or straw. It is almost as bad as raising turnips and selling them. Whether it is better to plow under clover or to make it into hay and return the manure, depends on circumstances. Plowing it under is the quickest method of enriching the land. But consuming it on the land by sheep, or making it into hay and returning the manure, accomplishes the same object in the end, and you get the value of the food in addition. There is a little loss, but not enough to affect the question.

I got a letter to-day from a subscriber of the *Agriculturist*, asking whether I still used True's Potato Planter, and whether I would advise him to get one to plant three acres. The Planter does the work as well as can reasonably be expected. Last year I planted three acres with it, and the remainder of the field by hand, and, if anything, that planted by the machine was the better crop, owing to the sets being larger. The machine cuts the potatoes, drops them and covers them, all at one operation, and it will plant five or six acres in a day. The objection to it is that you require round potatoes, and they should be all of the same size. When you have a good many potatoes to plant, and it is difficult to get extra hands, the Planter will prove very useful. I have just finished planting twenty acres of potatoes, but did not use the machine, not because it does not work well, but because I wanted to use smaller potatoes than it is safe to cut with the machine. Larger sized potatoes are doubtless better for seed, but I had a quantity of potatoes that were rather too small to sell well, and concluded to plant them. I think it better to plant good sized potatoes, but I was offered a dollar a bushel for all the marketable potatoes, and concluded to risk small seed. For a year or two at least, the yield of potatoes depends a good deal more on the richness of the soil, and on good culture, than on the size of the seed. Another reason why I did not use the Planter, was that it drops the seed in drills, and you can only cultivate one way. I think this not a serious objection, but it is easier to dig the potatoes when in hills than when in drills. And the great labor of the potato crop is in digging. A really good potato digger is much needed. I dug several acres with one last fall, but it did not work at all satisfactorily, and I have seen none that do. As a general rule, where you have only a few acres to plant, either of corn or potatoes, it is hardly worth while attempting to do it by machinery.

The best thing I have tried for sore shoulders in horses is crude petroleum. It seems to have great healing properties. I had been using it for paint, merely rubbing it on the wood with a rag, and was astonished how soon a sore, that happened to be on my hand, got well. Since then I have used it for sores of all kinds on animals, and am satisfied that it is excellent. I rub it, not merely on the sore itself, but for some distance round it. It has a slight exciting action on the skin for a few minutes, and, when rubbed on the parts near the sore, probably has a tendency to scatter the inflammation.

Petroleum, just now, is one of my hobbies. Dr. Eddy took out a patent for its use as a paint for preserving wood, and gave me a "farm right." If he would be equally generous with other farmers, I would advise every one of them to buy a barrel of petroleum at once, and use it freely. That it will preserve wood I have no doubt, although, of course, I have not used it long enough to ascertain the fact. It is just the thing for painting wagons, and all kinds of farm implements and tools. On my farm it is particularly needed, for I find it next to impossible to get things put under cover, and the exposure to rain and wind, and sun, cracks the wood and opens the pores. Petroleum is better than ordinary paint, because it will penetrate deeper into these pores, and it seems to close them up, and makes the wood look firmer.

We are digging a ditch through the swamp. I thought it would be a slow, tedious job, and dreaded to commence, but it is not half the work I expected. This loose, mucky soil can be thrown out with little labor. I do not propose to finish the ditch at once. We cut down the brush and clear away the old logs, roots, &c., for a space of eight or ten feet, where the ditch is to be, and with potato hooks and spades make a course for the water, and then in dry weather we can make the ditch deeper. There are thousands of acres of such land, that could be easily drained, if the work was once commenced.

If I had any inventive talent, I would try and get up an implement for preparing heavy land for corn. It is now a difficult matter to get the "clay spots" sufficiently mellow for planting. Had we an implement something like Crosskill's Clod Crusher, that would take two rows at a time, and crush the clods to powder for a space of eight or nine inches, where the corn was to be planted, it would be just the thing. It would consist of two narrow rollers, with iron teeth, three or four inches long, like sheep's claws. Being so narrow, and sufficiently heavy, it would cut into the hardest ground, and crush the clods. The rollers, of course, should be set the same distance apart, as the corn is to be planted; and in order to keep the rows straight, I would go twice in a row, as it would then do its own marking, and could be guided so as to crush a space of sixteen or eighteen inches. It would give a mellow soil to plant in, and the first, and perhaps the second, cultivating should be done with side blades, or shares, set so as to draw away the soil from the plants, so that there would be no danger of smothering them with the clods. After two or three cultivatings, the tramping of the horse, and the action of the center teeth, would break the clods between the rows. I feel confident that the thing could be done. Of course, if we had plenty of time, and the right kind of weather, it would be better to work over the whole land, and make it mellow, before planting. But as this is not often the case on such soils, an implement of this kind would be useful. It would get over six or eight acres in a day, and leave a foot or more of fine soil, in which we could plant at once. With our present implements it takes nearly as long to harrow, and roll, and prepare such land for corn, as it does to plow it. And then, by the time you have it all harrowed and marked both ways, we not unfrequently have a heavy rain, and the land has to be gone over again! Anything that will enable us to get the crops in rapidly, is an especial advantage in our short seasons. Once get the corn planted in a nice hill of mellow soil, and there is no difficulty in afterwards making the intervening space loose and fine, by the use of the cultivator. I was going to say that one cultivating in hot weather, is worth a dozen harrowings when the ground is cold and wet in the spring. But this is hardly true. One cultivating does comparatively little good; we need half a dozen. If you were making superphosphate from bones, and should smash up the bones with a hammer into pieces an inch or so in diameter, you would do comparatively little good; because the acid could not "dissolve" them. But repeat the process long enough to make the bones into a fine powder, and you could then readily convert them into a good superphosphate. It is so with cultivating once or twice. It is better than nothing, but as the object of cultivating is to make the soil fine and mellow, anything which stops short of this is as unwise as it is to give a fatting pig only food enough to keep him alive. In tightening a bolt, the last turn of the nut is far more effectual than the first, and it is precisely the same in killing weeds and cultivating land. Unless you accomplish the object, you lose nearly all the benefit of your labor.

The Value of the Corn Husk.

A NEW INDUSTRY.

Everybody is familiar with husk mats, and it is well known that excellent mattrasses can be made from this article, but a very small proportion of the crop is saved for these purposes. It is not generally known that the husk is applied in foreign countries to many other important uses. Some writers even assert that the value of the husk crop, if utilized, would be nearly equal that of the oat and barley crops of the country combined. We have seen most excellent husk letter paper, and it is said better paper can be made from it than from either linen or cotton rags; and, because it has great hardness and firmness, exceeding that of the best hand made English drawing papers, that it is especially adapted for pencil-drawing, water-colors, and short-hand writing, for which latter purpose it is extensively used. Its durability, it is claimed, renders it peculiarly valuable for documents, records, bank notes, bonds, etc.

Corn husks contain a long, straight, strong, flax-like fabric, which can be spun, like flax, into a thread, and the thread, like linen thread, woven into cloth of great tenacity and strength, which excels all the coarse materials in common use, in resisting decomposition. This will furnish an excellent substitute for coarse flax and hemp cloths, jute and gunny cloths, and bagging.

Again, in the course of extracting the corn fibre, long fibres are found at the bottom of the boiler in a spongy condition, filled with a glutinous substance, which, on closer examination, proves to be a nutritious dough. This may be dried and baked, and furnishes a good, wholesome, sweet bread, especially when mixed with wheat flour. It possesses the peculiarity, that it keeps perfectly sweet for months, although exposed to the air. It will not mould, and excels almost all known vegetable substances in its resistance to decomposition. Mixed with wheat flour, it would probably make a very good material for ship bread and crackers. Cattle eat it voraciously. Of this farinaceous substance there are 15 pounds in a hundred pounds of husks; of the long fibre, suitable for spinning, a hundred pounds of husks furnishes 25 pounds, while, at the same time, 20 pounds of paper is afforded from the 100 pounds of raw material—the entire valuable products being 60 per cent. of the weight of husks.

These interesting manufactures are chiefly conducted under the patronage of the Austrian government, and it is stated that the knapsacks for the Imperial army, wagon tops, floor cloths, fire buckets, and paper of all varieties, from the coarsest wrapping to the finest bank note paper used by the government, are manufactured at the Imperial mills. Beside these, there are two private mills in operation near Vienna, conducted on an extensive scale, the owners of which, it is said, became independently rich in the two first years of their workings, their mills being several times extended and kept running night and day to fill all their different orders.

The importance of saving the husks will be fully appreciated, when it is remembered that they are simply incidental to the production of a most important cereal, everywhere cultivated, and that they cost nothing beyond the care attending their collection and preservation.

The chief reason of the inattention hitherto bestowed by capitalists on this article is traceable mainly to the difficulty of procuring a sufficient supply of husks. We are satisfied that the demand will abundantly warrant farmers in saving and storing all the husks they can. They are easily baled and marketed, like baled hay, and will bring a good price for mattrasses alone.

Our friends, who contemplate starting the husk manufacture in this country, must not, however, wait for the farmers to accumulate husks, but appoint responsible agents who will contract for the material at the farms. Farmers are beginning to appreciate their value as fodder, and probably will not be disposed to sell them for less than the price of hay.

BUCKWHEAT.—This crop occupies a position in our farming which it would be very difficult to supply. Common millet is in some respects very much like it, especially as it may be sown in July, and a crop of hay or grain harvested, and as it also does well upon sandy soils. Buckwheat is a plant which makes the most of *few* privileges—a sort of self-made crop. If it has to struggle moderately, it does well. But if it has all its needs supplied, and especially if on freshly manured land, it is very likely to fail. It does not bear fermenting manure well at all, as it runs to tops and the seed blasts. It affords one of the most valuable green manure crops to be used on light leachy lands, for with 100 to 150 pounds of good guano, or 3 to 5 cwt. of bonedust, a heavy crop of manure may be produced on almost any soil. When sowed for the grain, it is not advisable to sow too early, as the first flowers are apt to blight in hot, dry weather. In cool weather, reasonably moist, the grain fills best, but frost is fatal. It is usual, in order to avoid extremes, to sow from the 5th to the 25th of July, according to latitude. The last of the month being preferred, where frosts hold off well. It is sown on sod without manure, at the rate of a bushel to a bushel and-a-half to the acre. It is best to prepare the land well by plowing some weeks beforehand, and harrowing to get a uniform surface. We have no idea how long the plant will continue to grow and blossom, if frosts hold off. It is customary to cut, and cure in small isolated gavels, as soon as the first seeds are ripe, before they will shell out in handling. The straw is as good sheep fodder as need be, and the grain nutritious and fattening.

THE JEWEL IN TOADS.—Shakespeare and other poets locate this "precious jewel in his head," but they cultivated the flowers of poesy, and were poor observers in the garden. Watching these ugly animals among the squash and cucumber vines, we shall discover the jewel in the stomach, in the shape of a healthy appetite for bugs and worms. The quantity they will devour is enormous. "Their big bellies with fat black bug lined," proclaim their virtues. Toads are among our best friends, and they should have the full freedom of the garden.

Fig. 1.—ADULT SHAD—¼ NATURAL SIZE.—DRAWN FROM LIFE

Shad and Ale-wives.

These fish appear simultaneously in spring and early summer along our coast, and are the object of very extensive fisheries. The capital employed in the Delaware River and Bay, New York Bay and the adjoining Newark and Raritan Bays, in the Hudson and Connecticut Rivers, aside from that invested in Rhode Island, Massachusetts and New Hampshire, is estimated to amount to not less than $5,000,000.

Fig. 2.—YOUNG SHAD IN AUGUST.

THE SHAD (*Alausa prastabilis*) is at present our most important river fish, for, though great numbers are taken in salt water, they are seeking the mouths of the rivers, which they enter and ascend as far as they can, or until they find, far above tide-water, in the smaller streams, suitable breeding places. When they enter the rivers they are very fat, and the females full of spawn. After laying their eggs, which is chiefly accomplished during the month of June, they return towards the coast, emaciated and weak, falling an easy prey to carniverous fish, and being entirely unfit for the table. "Thin as a June shad" has passed into a proverb, although the shad that are late in ascending, (and many enter the rivers as late as July,) are among the fattest and best of the season.

The fine engraving at the head of this article was drawn from a large female shad taken in New York Bay, and is a very accurate representation of the fish. The color is dark-bluish or brownish-black on the head and neck, the sides lighter and growing silvery along the belly. The irregular row of spots along the side, back of the large dusky spot behind the opercule, are very indistinct when the fish is just taken, but plainly visible when the scales are removed, and show through the scales more and more distinctly for several hours. In stale fish a striped appearance is noted. The size of the shad renders it unlikely for any one at all familiar with it to mistake an adult one, its congeners being all smaller. Shad vary considerably in size, weight, and appearance, so that those of different rivers are easily recognized by the fishermen and market men. The common size is 20 to 22 inches in length, and about 6 inches in depth. The weight varies from 3 to 7 pounds. Those of the Connecticut are broader backed than others, somewhat slimy, and, being heavier also, are regarded as superior to any others seeking the New York market.

The two smaller cuts represent the young shad; fig. 2, the fry during the month of August; fig. 3, one ready to seek the sea. Our knowledge of this interesting fish, after it leaves our rivers, and before it returns, heavy with roe, is very limited. It is even uncertain how long a time is required for it to attain maturity, and it is believed by some that the shad spawns but once, rarely, if ever, returning a second time to our rivers. It is doubtful also whether these fish eat anything after leaving salt water, as the stomachs are found empty, or containing only food which they obtained in salt water—though said to rise for gay flies in fresh. The rapid decrease of shad within the past few years has finally aroused the attention of the legislators of New England, and though repeated previous enactments have been made to foster and regulate the Shad and Ale-wife fishery, it would seem that they have been to a considerable extent inoperative, and it is to be hoped that more stringent laws, well carried out, will make these fish as abundant as formerly. The great necessity seems to be proper fish-stairs over dams, and we present in this number an article on them. The subject is quite as important to farmers as to any other class of our people, (except, perhaps, fishermen,) and should be pressed upon the consideration of their representatives.

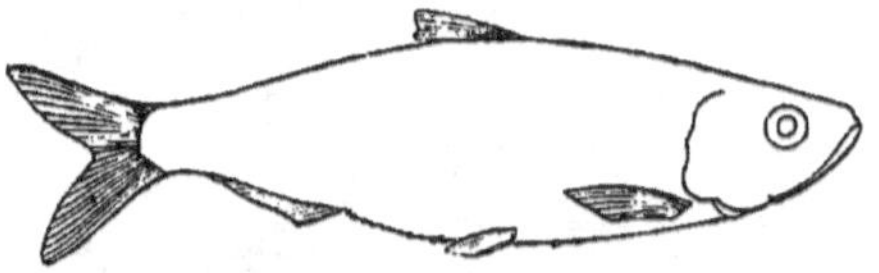

Fig. 3.—SHAD SEEKING THE SEA, IN SEPTEMBER.

THE ALE-WIFE (*Alausa tyranus*) receives its curious name from the custom, prevalent in Europe, of old women peddling smoked herring from ale house to ale house, the herring taking the name, and the customers taking "ale wives" with their mugs of beer or ale. They are caught with the shad, resemble them considerably, but are smaller, being only about 8 or 10 inches long, and more brilliant and silvery.

Raising Seedling Strawberries.

BY SETH BOYDEN, NEWARK, N. J.

[The writer of the following is a well known raiser of seedling strawberries; the Agriculturist, Boyden's Mammoth, and others, are the results. He says that he is about "retiring from the field," and gives the manner in which he produced such remarkable seedlings. — EDS.]

The strawberry plant is progressive, and with care and perseverance, will become a variety of fruit of much greater value than at present. The strawberry plant grows in almost every soil, but best in a moist, compact one. Much light stable or other manures put into the soil is an injury; plants set in such soil will make but few roots, and those that come in contact with the manure will soon turn black, while a plant set in compact soil will be vigorous, and have ten times the amount of roots. If the soil is in a low state of cultivation, it may be brought up by bone dust, liquid manure from the barn yard, poudrette, or well rotted manure, free from straw, well mixed in, and the soil finely pulverized and again pressed with a light roller.

The young plants should be set as soon as they have roots enough to sustain them. After the ground has become firm, they may be heavily top-dressed with coarse manure (though some varieties will not bear as much as others,) lightly applied near the plant, and profusely watered, (do not put the water on the plant, but on the manure a foot from it.)

There are two classes of strawberry plants, the perfect and imperfect flowered. The imperfect flower has no stamens, and requires the presence of a staminate blossom to complete its operations. The perfect flower has all the parts necessary for perfecting seed.

In selecting plants for producing improved varieties, take one or two varieties of the perfect flowered class, and also two or three of the imperfect flowered ones; these are to produce the seeds by crossing with the perfect flowers. Set them fifteen inches apart, top-dress and water freely. At the commencement of freezing weather, protect them with straw, leaves or tan.

It is desirable to gain a week or two in ripening the berries by putting a cold bed frame and sash over the plants in March. When the berries are ripe, select the best from the imperfect flowered plants. These are more eccentric and more liable to produce extra varieties.

VIRGINIAN LUNGWORT.

SHOWY LADY'S SLIPPER.

The seed from the perfect flowered plant produces progeny of nearly the same variety as the parent, but generally inferior in quality.

The strawberry seed, like many other seeds, remains until the following spring before they germinate; but, if artificial aid is applied, the strawberry seed may be brought forward and produce bearing plants for the next season. This of course saves a year in arriving at results.

Put the berries in a cloth and rub them until they are disengaged from the fruit, then wash them out and put them in ten times the quantity of fine dry washed sand, set them in a dry place a week, and stir them up a few times; now tie up the parcel in a cloth, and put it between two pieces of ice, change their position so they may freeze and thaw every day during a week or ten days. This has the effect of winter upon the seeds, and they are ready to germinate when brought into a genial temperature. Now keep them warm and wet for a week, and the seeds will be ready to plant. The bed must be prepared level, with a raised border, so that it can be flooded with water half an inch deep every day until the young plants begin to appear. Make the bed smooth, with a slight degree of firmness; distribute the seed and sand evenly over the bed, then sift light sandy loam on it to the depth of one-fourth of an inch, and commence the watering. Shade the bed from the midday sun, as the strawberry plant is a cool weather plant, making most of its growth in spring and fall. The surface of the bed should never approach dryness. If everything has been carefully performed, the young plants will begin to appear in eight or ten days. The watering may then be changed to sprinkling, like rain. When the plants are two or three inches high, and of sufficient size to determine which are the most thriving, they may be removed with a ball of earth to the prepared rows, top-dressed and watered. Allow each plant to make one or two runner plants. This will exhibit the character of the plant more accurately. Probably not one-third of the young plants will be worth moving to the rows. No inferior variety or sterile beds of the same variety should be near. They can not be too far off. The best variety, set with inferior varieties and neglected, will return to its primitive condition. Some specimens of good strawberry cultivation may be seen near Irvington, N. Y. The experiment of growing new varieties of strawberries is interesting amusement for those that have a little leisure time to fill up, and their cultivation produces an enjoyment rarely found in any other horticultural pursuit.

Our Native Lady's Slippers.

It is only those who ramble in the woods that know the beautiful things that their recesses contain. We never showed any of our native Lady's Slippers to a town dweller, that he did not express surprise that so curious a plant should grow wild. These plants belong to the genus *Cypripedium*, and are members of the Orchis family, remarkable alike for the beauty and singular structure of its flowers. In the Northern States we have in all six species of *Cypripedium*, some rarer than others, but all beautiful. Indeed, these natives of our woods are in Europe prized as rarities, and while they are almost entirely neglected here, they are there cultivated with the greatest care. Without going into the intimate structure of these plants, we may say that one of their striking characters is to have one of the petals very much enlarged, and formed into a curiously inflated bag or sac, much like the body of some huge spider. Perhaps the commonest species is the Stemless Lady's Slipper, *Cypripedium acaule*, found in evergreen woods in most of the Northern States. It has two broad leaves close to the ground, and from between them arises a naked stem about a foot high, bearing a flower nearly two inches long, of a pale purplish color and beautifully veined. Then we have two yellow species, *C. pubescens* and *C. parviflorum*, the latter fragrant and smaller than the former, which is without odor. Unlike the first mentioned species, these have leafy stems, and are found in damp woods, especially in the Northern States. The most beautiful of all the genus is the Showy Lady's Slipper, *Cypripedium spectabile*, one of the most beautiful of our native flowers, and one that need not be ashamed to show itself by the side of those of any country. Our engraving shows the general aspect of the plant. The stem often grows to the hight of two feet, and frequently bears three flowers. The sepals and petals are white, and the large lip is of the purest white, more or less shaded with a beautiful purple. These plants are well worth transferring from their native localities to the garden, and will grow well if given a peaty soil in a partially shaded place. The roots are generally very much matted, and may be taken up in a mass at almost any season, even when they are in flower.

Virginian Lungwort.—(*Mertensia Virginica.*)

As spring flowers are coming on, we have rather more than the usual number sent for names. One of the most frequently sent, in former years as well as in the present one, is the Virginian Lungwort, or Virginian Cowslip, as it is sometimes called. We present a figure of it, which is from an English work published early in the present century. It is much prized in the European gardens, but like many others of our native plants, is only rarely seen in cultivation in our gardens. We have endeavored to cultivate a taste for our native shrubs and herbaceous plants, and have to a certain extent been successful, at least if we may judge from the inquiries as to where the things we bring to notice may be had. Some nurseryman or florist will yet find it to his interest to propagate our native plants and offer them for sale. It is only because people do not know where to find them that they are so seldom cultivated. The Lungwort was formerly called *Pulmonaria Virginica*, and is found in the Western part of New York and in most of the Western States. The root-leaves, not shown in the engraving, are from four to six inches long; the stem is from one to two feet high, and terminates by a cluster of trumpet shaped flowers of a very rich purplish blue color. It belongs to the Borage family, which includes the beautiful Forget-me-not, Heliotrope and several other choice garden plants.

Spare Corners in the garden can be filled with something more profitable than the burdock, plantain, and grass, which are so frequently left to occupy them. A few radishes, half a dozen heads of lettuce, a cabbage, or a cauliflower can be put almost anywhere, and their being planted will give sufficient motive to keep the ground around them clean, which would otherwise be left as a nursery for growing weeds.

Some of the Less Known Pears.

As a people, we are as much in a hurry about fruits as we are with other matters, and many varieties have been condemned without a fair hearing. This is especially the case with pears, many of which, though condemned at first, have, by the good qualities they presented after the trees became old, commanded recognition. Mr. P. Barry prepared for our Horticultural Annual a long list of these reclaimed varieties, with illustrations. In the abundance of material at hand for that work, we were obliged to omit a number of these pears, and we give the en-

Fig. 1.—Beurre Berckmans.

gravings of some of them now, with Mr. Barry's notes upon their productiveness and quality:

Beurre Berckmans.—One of Bivort's new varieties; medium size, pale yellow, melting, juicy, sweet, excellent. Ripe in October and November. Keeps well. Tree very productive.

Fig. 2.—Bonne Sophie.

Bonne Sophie.—A new variety of much promise; medium size, melting, delicious. September and October. Tree an abundant bearer.

Souvenir D'Esperen.—An excellent late autumn or early winter pear, from Belgium, resembling the Winter Nelis, but the tree is a vigorous erect grower. Fruit large pyriform, obovate, tapering to the crown; color dull yellow, with a mottled red cheek. Flesh melting and vinous.

Making Manure in Summer.

With manure enough and labor enough, no man knows what may be the limits to the products and profits of the cultivation of the earth, in the garden or the field. We make most manure in winter, because then our stock is confined, and all the droppings, with the litter and waste of fodder, are readily accumulated. Cows yarded every night, leave their droppings and urine where they may be used, to compost with muck, litter, etc., to greater advantage, in summer than in winter, because the temperature of the season keeps the compost heaps in a more active fermentation. Thus, the value of the manure made in summer from a given number of cows, or other animals, may be nearly as great as in winter, though, if they are pastured, they may be in the yard less than half the time.

Swine used simply as pork producers or breeders, are oftentimes of profit, but on three-quarters of the farms west of the Alleghanies, if the value of the manure made by pigs were left out of the calculation, they would show a loss on the balance sheet of the farm. To employ them as manure makers to the best advantage, in connection with either private or market gardens, give them a covered yard, having a tight bottom, and open on the south for the sun to come in; give them also the free use of their rooting powers, until they are taken up to fatten; feed them well, and supply them daily with sods, weeds, peat, bog parings, etc., and it matters little how much you give them, they will work up an incredible amount and make better manure of it than the best exposed barn-yard manure you can make or buy. Every gardener, and not less every farmer, ought to begin the growing season with half grown hogs, not with a lot of little pigs. They should receive as regular attention as the rows of vegetables or plants, for they are preparing the raw material with which to produce next year's crop.

The accumulations in the hog-pen should be leveled off, and mixed somewhat by hand, but the hogs ordinarily do this themselves tolerably well. If left thus water-soaked, and trodden hard, the manure will be of the rankest, strongest character imaginable, and besides so tough and stringy that it can only be gotten out with great labor. It is best, therefore, to take time, some rainy day, about once a month, to clear the pen out, and lay the materials up in a compact compost heap, well trodden, and if possible, under cover. The action of the air will cause rapid and usually complete fermentation, and once or twice working over of the heap at times, to check excessive heating, will insure an abundance of fine and excellent compost.

About Horticultural and other Patents.

The greatest embodying of stupidity, (the Agricultural Department always excepted), is the U. S. Patent Office. In "Walks and Talks," Mr. Harris speaks of having the "right" to use petroleum as a vehicle for paint, given him. If we had a barrel of petroleum, we should use it as we pleased, and should like to see any jury of twelve honest men who would say that we had not a perfect right to mix it with any known substance. So with a patent for saving paint, that has been sent us with permission to use it. It is merely to fill the pores of the wood with some powder that will prevent it from absorbing the paint. We have known this to be done

Fig. 3.—Souvenir D'Esperen.

since we were a boy, to prevent wood from absorbing varnish. Can one make us pay for the right to use a similar process with paint? How would you, reader, if you were on a jury give a verdict in such a case? The fact is, our patent laws are brought into contempt by allowing patents for the most trivial and frequently absurd things. Now, most of the patents issued, as far as concerns horticulture at least, though not so much in agriculture, are for the way of doing things. Any one who patents a *process*—after he has accepted the accumulated experience of years, and is unwilling to contribute his small mite to the general stock of knowledge, should be shut out of the community of true horticulturists.

Crops for the Orchard.

If a man would sit down to really *think* about his orchard, and study its needs and prospects, its expense to him and the returns he may reasonably expect, he would not be likely to blunder much in its management. The first thought might be, do I want fruit, or do I want grass, grain, potatoes, etc., the most? We suppose he wants *fruit* in his orchard; if so, he may reasonably ask if he can afford to expend the amount of labor necessary to maintain his fruit trees, and nothing else upon the land, from the time they are first set out. If one does this, plants trees only, and keeps the ground plowed and *clean*, for surely weeds are worse than even a corn crop—he will, if the land is in proper condition, have good trees, but at a heavy expense for several years. He may rather revolve the question, What may I cultivate with least injury to the trees, and at most profit to myself, and thus make use of the otherwise wasted energies of the soil, manure and sunshine? This question cannot be answered off-hand, for there are many things to be considered. When we manure the soil of an orchard, we must apply more manure than the trees need, because they should find it wherever their roots wander, and these do not fill the whole soil. Trees probably draw most upon the fertility of the soil at the period of their most rapid growth. Hence, if we put a crop upon the land to use up the excess of manure, it is a poor plan to employ one, the roots of which will voraciously wrangle with those of the fruit trees for food and moisture, during this period. This will lead to the interdiction of corn and all grains, and seed producing plants, except buckwheat, for those all make their growth when the trees have a prior right to the soil. The same principle will allow the use of all root crops which gain considerable size only after midsummer, and mature later, even after the trees have ripened their fruit. Cabbages, etc., are in the same category with vegetables. Onions would seem to be an exception, but, though they require a good soil, they are not an exhausting crop, and may be used in young orchards, before much shade is cast.

As to grass—permanent grass—while the trees are growing, it is doubly injurious, first, in covering the ground so as to prevent its being worked, and preventing also the action of the sun upon it—a very important thing; second, in taking plant food from the soil at all times, but most just when the trees are growing fastest. After the trees have attained their growth, if the space for several feet around them be kept clear, grass does little or no harm if well and frequently manured. The moderate check it exercises upon the trees making wood may promote a tendency to fruit. Even in old apple orchards, sward should not be suffered to lie many years without breaking up; at which time, lime or ashes should be liberally applied, with other manure, a crop of potatoes raised, and the land seeded down again without the use of any grain crop. The idea that grass seeding will not do well, unless it be made with some small grain crop, is absurd. Grain, of whatever kind, is usually an injury to the grass.

Drying Fruit, Hops, etc.

The prospect of an abundant supply of fruit in most sections of the country, has led many fruit growers to look about for means to preserve their surplus fruit by drying. Several have sent requests for plans for drying kilns or houses. In June, 1866, we gave plans for a small house, of a style much in use at the West.

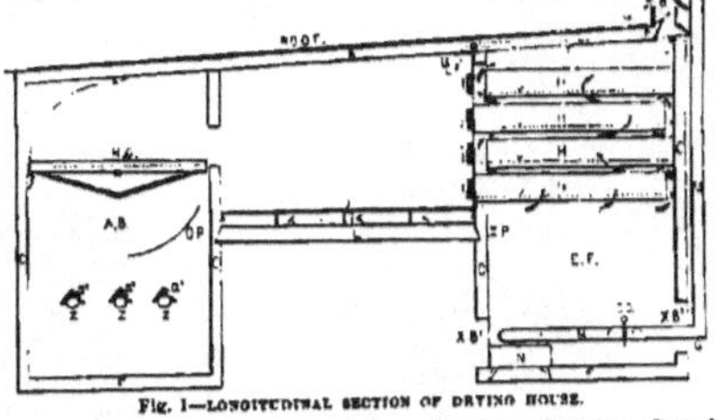

Fig. 1—LONGITUDINAL SECTION OF DRYING HOUSE.

Mr. W. H. Wilmot, of Lawn Ridge, Ill., finds the frame and sash of a common hot bed to answer excellently. The suggestion is not a recent one, but it may be new to many. He says: "Take the frames and glass used for hot beds, or 'cold frames,' and place them over a clean gravel bed; inside arrange shelves on which to place the fruit. After this you need not give the fruit a thought, except to take it out when dried. It is secure from flies and other insects, rains or dew, chickens and *small children*, nor can it be burned up. After once trying it I think no one would dispense with it." Of course, this would answer for a small quantity only.

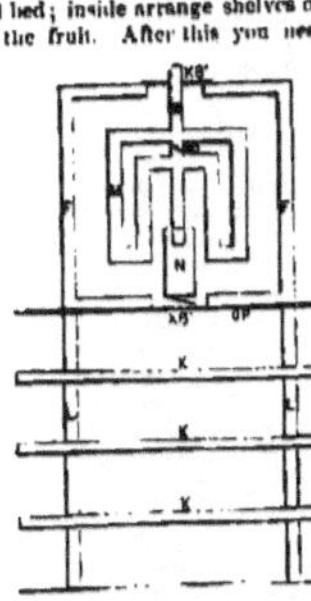

Fig. 2.—GROUND PLAN.

Mr. A. W. Decrow, of Bangor, Me., sends us an account of a drying kiln which he built for drying hops, but which, he says, answers equally well for fruit or other articles that require to be dried by artificial heat. His kiln is not patented, and as he has taken some pains to give detailed plans, we are sure that our readers will be glad to see them. Fig. 1, gives a longitudinal section of the house; *E F* is the kiln, heated by the stove, *N*. The drawers, *H H*, hold the material to be dried by the hot air, which circulates as shown by the arrows, and finally passes off by ventilator, *B*. The platform, *J*, extends between the kiln and the store-room, *A B*, which, in the drawing, is arranged especially for hops, and has a movable platform, *H G*, upon which the hops are emptied from the drawers, and passed to the room below by tilting.

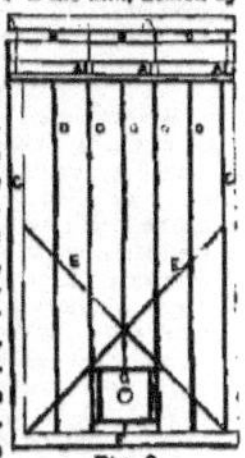
Fig. 3.

In drying hops, ventilators, shown at *Z*, are provided. In figure 2 is shown a ground plan of the houses, the store room, *A*, *B*, in fig. 1, being left out. The stove is shown at *N*, with the manner of arranging the pipe, to save all the heat possible.

Figure 3 gives the framing of the rear end, or end of the kiln room, and a similar construction is followed on the sides of the building. *A*, rafters; the outside ones being 4 × 6, and the others, 3 × 6. *B*, ventilator. *C*, posts, 4 × 4. *D*, studs, 2 × 4. *E*, braces, 2 × 4. *F*, sills, 6 × 9. *G*, place for exit of pipe, made of bricks or sheet iron. The drawers, *H*, in fig. 1, are 8 feet square and 13 inches deep. The bottoms of the drawers are of slat work, arranged as shown in fig. 4. The slats are 1 inch wide, ½ inch thick, and are placed 8 inches apart. Over the slats is placed a cloth of very open texture. The drawers, when in place, rest upon cleats, sufficiently far apart to allow of a free circulation of air.

Fig. 4.

The success of all those houses in which hot air is used for drying, depends upon keeping up a constant current of air, heated considerably above the ordinary temperature—hence there should be free opening for the air to pass out, and, what is too often neglected, an abundant supply of fresh air from without to the stove room.

WHITEWASHED OR WHITE PAINTED GARDEN fences may be neat and attractive in themselves but for that reason they are unsuitable. Any surrounding of this kind, that draws attention from the living plants, is as impertinent as a gaudy bonnet over a pretty face. Carpentry and horticulture should not painfully strive for mastery. Green, drab, or other unattractive color, is suitable, and not abominable; white not to be mentioned. The same idea applies to poles, trellises, etc., used for supports, and to the still greater absurdity of whitewashing the trunks of trees. A tallow candle is a poor model to follow in trying to improve the looks of one of the most harmoniously beautiful of nature's productions. Use colored washes.

A Hopeful Sign.

The census shows that N. Y. city made but little increase of population for the last five years. With all due allowance for the influence of the war and for the rapacity of landlords, we can but think that the attractions of country life are better appreciated. Rents for dwellings are unparalleled, and this cause has driven multitudes from the island. Once in the country, in the enjoyment of its independence and healthful breezes, they have learned to like it, and, as they say, would not go back to the city again for anything. To people who have always lived in the city, the hardening process is a little uncomfortable, but is soon over. It involves more labor to keep house in the country, but this does not necessarily come upon the housekeeper. Country life has its compensations, and we think the balance is decidedly in its favor. We do not have the Croton coming into every room in the house in the country, but then we do not have the water bills to pay for, and the plumber's bills, and the annoyance of bursting pipes, and flooded carpets and spoiled papering and plastering, and the endless list of bills to get things set right again. We do not have gas, but then we have the bliss of paying for just what light we get, and *no more*. We occasionally miss a good lecture in the country, but we have more than we can hear. In social advantages, in religious privileges, in schools, in all the means of rational enjoyment we are on a par with the resident of Fifth Avenue. We can beat him on eggs and vegetables, for we know the hens and the soil that make them, and have no occasion to take the word of the green grocer for their quality. We can beat him on dawns and sunsets, clouds and breezes, easy, and as to high art, he is just nowhere. We have the originals of the sublime mountains, the fine landscapes, the cattle and fruit pictures they make such a fuss about at the Academy exhibitions; and it costs us nothing to frame, hang and take care of them. We can but think these things are better understood than they used to be, and that the seed we have been sowing in the *Agriculturist* for the last dozen years or more is springing up. There is a good time coming.

VIOLA CORNUTA.—This old violet is attracting a great deal of attention abroad, and some of our own florists have made a trial of it. In planting an ornamental bed, we made use of this as an edging, and though not in full flower, it promises so well, that we are much pleased with it. If half what is said of it abroad should prove true with us, it will be a valuable addition to our gardens. We shall watch the behavior of our plants during the summer with interest, and probably our readers will hear more about it.

THE BLOOD-RED AMARANTH.—Under the name of *Amarantus sanguineus*, Mr. Peter Henderson grows a variety of *A. paniculatus*, which, as a "foliage plant," is not excelled in brilliancy by any of the plants with colored leaves that we have yet seen. It grows 3 or 4 feet high, and has large leaves, is an annual, and has a pleasing habit. There is not a particle of green about the plant, and in a good light, it is a "foliage plant" of great brilliancy.

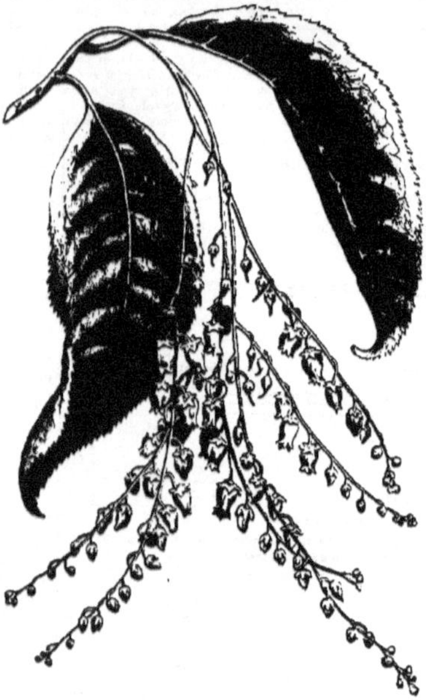

THE SORREL-TREE.—(*Oxydendrum arboreum.*)

The Sorrel-tree.—(*Oxydendrum arboreum.*)

When we state that this is a most beautiful native small tree, it is equivalent to saying that it is not commonly found in cultivation. Were it from abroad, and only to be had at five dollars the plant, it would be found almost everywhere. We shall keep "pitching into" you, Messrs. Nurserymen, until you take a little interest in our native plants—not that by any means we would have you neglect the foreign ones, only give our home-made things a chance to be known. This tree was formerly called *Andromeda arborea*, but when that large genus was divided up, this received the name of *Oxydendrum*, which means "Sour-tree"—and indeed it bears the name of Sour-wood in some parts of the country. The leaves of the tree have a remarkably sour taste; they are deciduous, have a bright shiny green color, and in shape, bear much resemblance to those of the peach. The engraving gives a representation of a twig at flowering time, and shows the form of the leaves as well as the loose panicle of small white flowers. It is found growing wild in most of the Southern and Middle States, Pennsylvania and Ohio being its northern limits. It grows wild in rich woods, and in cultivation should have a soil with a good deal of vegetable mould to correspond to its natural localities. The tree flowers when quite small, but it attains when old the hight of 40 to 60 feet. It seems to be quite hardy, as we have seen it endure the very cold winters near Boston and in Michigan.

Books, and How They Are Made.

We have heard several times of late that Mr. Fuller's Grape Book, and Mr. Henderson's Garden Book, were written by one of the editors of the *Agriculturist*. These allegations come so direct from people who ought to know better, that we feel bound to notice them, and if, after this disclaimer, we hear anything more on the subject, we shall mention the names of those who circulate these reports. In the first place, it is a miserable imputation upon both the authors and the editors. It implies that the authors cannot write, as well as that the editors are willing to allow what they write to be issued over another name. Now we distinctly repudiate both these charges. We have never published a work of which the author did not furnish the full manuscript. We exercise a critical supervision over all the works we publish, (would that others did the same,) but it is only to make the author say what he means, and in the best possible manner, that any corrections or changes have been made at all in not only these works, but any works that we publish. We would have certain persons understand that we publish only reliable works from competent authors, and that our books are not made against time and by the job, to fit certain furnished illustrations; that we are not in the "book making" business. We have, in our safe, the manuscript of more books than we can get out in many months, and some of them of great value, but we must submit them all to editorial supervision. One rule is, to never accept a manuscript until we have read it. We have had some experience in the matter, and we never yet saw the manuscript that some one other than the author could not improve. So correct an author as Bancroft has his History put in type, and, before he prints it, he subjects the proofs to judicious friends. He means to be correct, and if some publishers of horticultural books, we know of, would take the pains to have their works properly edited, both the authors and publishers would fare better, and the public would be saved much nonsense.

YOUNG GRAPE VINES.—The great trouble with inexperienced cultivators is, that they will allow a young vine to have its own way. It is the inexorable law, that a vine cannot yield both fruit and wood. If the vine is grown for present satisfaction only, then let it fruit if it will, but if future crops are regarded, then remove all the fruit that sets the first year after planting, and pinch the laterals to get a good wood growth.

THE HOUSEHOLD.

(☞ For other Household Items, see "Basket" pages.)

Dashes at House-Keeping with a Free Pencil.

PRIZE ESSAY BY MISS EVA M. COLLINS, ROCHESTER.

TIDIES.

Untidy tidies are the occasion of all the animadversions heaped upon these articles in general, by the generality of gentlemen. Tidies half fastened in their places with pins, or tidies not fastened at all, hanging by the eyelids, ready to fall upon our

Fig. 1.—DIAMOND-PATTERN TIDY.

shoulders, or walk away upon our back, deserve everything that may be said of this failing in their mistress; but, at the same time, a fresh, pretty tidy, either white or in colors, agreeing with or harmonizing the prevailing colors of the room, adorns both the room, and also, as was remarked of a different ornament, not long ago in the *Agriculturist*, the mistress of the apartment herself. The first requisite is that the tidy should be appropriate to its place. A plain, substantial, white tidy, that evidently not only may be, but is, frequently changed and washed, is far prettier in a common sitting room than the most elaborate article in colors which can not be subjected to the same renovating process. I would that all the rooms in a farmer's house were common sitting rooms; at least, that there were fewer best rooms which scarcely ever see the beautiful sunlight—fewer parlors wrapped in covers, because too nice for use, and stowed away in the darkness and gloom of perpetual night. But this useless appendage, the dark parlor, is fast becoming obsolete. Cheerful, open, light parlors, are superseding it, and soon, even [illegible] the most conservative regions, this prison room, in which every comfort of the house is confined; where the sofas and easy chairs are too nice for the tired father to rest upon at noon; where the senseless birds and flowers upon the carpets are too exquisite for little boots to crush; where the elegant bindings of the books are their only merit, will be the exception, and not the rule. There is a great variety of patterns for tidies, so simple that any child can make them, and still pretty and serviceable. Any little girl who can knit a garter can make, with a very little assistance from mamma, or sister, a charming little tidy of this description, fig. 1. All that is required is a skein of red woolen yarn, one of white cotton yarn, and two knitting needles. The red yarn should be of a bright scarlet color, and the white should be of the same size as the red. Set up the number of stitches desired in the width of the strip—eighteen stitches is a very good width—and knit until the square is perfect, which will be about twenty-nine times across the needle; then exchange the red for the white ball, twist the threads together for a few stitches, and knit twenty-nine times across with the white. Knit the red and white blocks alternately until the strip will extend from corner to corner of the tidy in view, beginning and ending with the red. The strips upon each side of the central strip will contain two blocks less than that, and the next ones two less than those. If the little child does not knit very evenly, it is better to let the strips run directly across the tidy, fig. 3. A crocheted shell edge of either the white or red yarn, or both, forms a pretty finish, and will serve to give employment to many a dull afternoon. The strips should be neatly sewed together over and over, and pressed under a damp cloth.

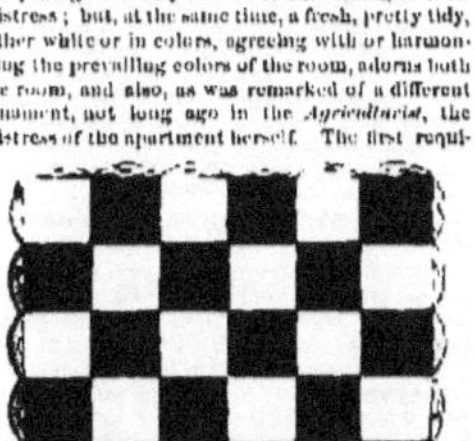

Fig. 2.—BLOCK PATTERN TIDY.

Fig. 3.

Fig. 4.

A more showy tidy is made by knitting thirteen red and six white blocks of the shape shown in fig. 3. In knitting the first point, set up one stitch and widen the second stitch in each row; make the last point by narrowing the same. The blocks are sewed together in the form of a honey-comb, fig. 4. A white initial letter embroidered in the central block produces a happy effect, and a white crocheted plain border makes a nice finish, provided all the angles are accurately preserved; if the border can not be neatly crocheted, the tidy looks better without it. These tidies, figs. 4 and 5, may be made in triangular blocks, or diamonds, to accommodate different tastes, or different chairs. The beauty or merit of these tidies consists in their being bright and cheerful in effect, where bright colors are appropriate, and yet, unlike the usual worsted Afghan tidies, they will wash and look as well as new ones, when soiled.

Fig. 5.

Sometimes a heavy tidy looks out of place. A very pretty and delicate one is made on a square frame, as in fig. 6, made of pine sticks nailed together at the corners, with large-headed pins, or even common tacks driven in almost to their heads at intervals of half an inch, all around. Fasten one end of a spool of white cotton thread, number eight, to a corner tack, and wind the thread upon the tacks, three times in a place, both diagonally and horizontally over the frame, each way, which will make such a net-work as this, fig. 7, held in its place by the tacks or pins. Then, begin again with a corner tack, fasten the thread to it, and with a needle weave the thread three or four times at the first intersection, fasten the thread in the center, and slip the needle through to the next crossing of the threads. When every crossing has been fastened in this manner, cut the tidy from the tacks, leaving the ends of the thread to form a fringed edge. When this tidy becomes soiled, it should be basted between two pieces of old and thin cloth, and, protected in this way, it can be washed, boiled, and starched, as easily as a more substantial one.

Fig. 6.

Fig. 7.

Any pattern may be formed in crochet, by drawing the designs upon paper, and copying them as nearly as possible upon checkered paper, fig. 8. Paper properly ruled is sold for this purpose, but this is probably only to be had in large cities, and we country people must rule it ourselves, which is not a very difficult job. A little practice will render one expert in making designs for working.

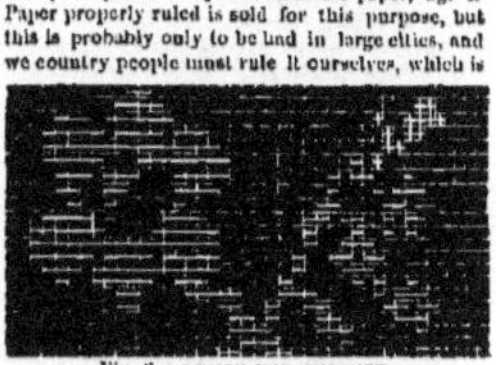

Fig. 8.—DESIGN FOR CROCHET.

Leaves from the Diary of a Young House-keeper.—No. VII.

PRIZE ESSAY BY MRS. LAURA E. LYMAN, STAMFORD, CT.

July 2d.—I have been occupied for several days in protecting my house from flies. There came a rainy day when Edward could not work out doors, and he and the hired men fitted some light pine frames for my windows, and two or three of the doors, which I have covered with fly netting, and now I can have all the ventilation I wish, without the annoyance and discomfort of these household pests. A finer netting will keep out mosquitos as well. The door frames are on hinges, so we can go in and out with ease. This is so much better than fly traps and fly poisons, and now that they are made, they will, with care, last several seasons. In some houses that I have visited, I have noticed that the parlors are kept darkened all the time—but for my part, I believe in sunlight and free ventilation, both for health and enjoyment.

What was my annoyance in going to my closet yesterday, where I keep my preserves and cake, to find it infested with great black ants. I employed the speediest and most certain way of killing them that I could think of. Taking a large sponge, I saturated it with molasses mixed with a little water, and laid it on a plate in the closet, after removing every other sweet thing. They took the bait greedily, and when there were about a thousand of them reveling upon the sweets, and penetrating every pore of the sponge, I plunged it into a bucket of hot water. Their scalded carcasses floated on the surface, reminding one of the destruction of Pharaoh's host in the Red Sea. A few successive massacres of that kind have, I believe, nearly exterminated the tribe. This mode of destroying them is certainly harmless to every body but the ants themselves, and I prefer it to using red precipitate.

July 7th.—Living on an old place has a good many advantages as well as some disadvantages. Our predecessors were certainly fond of fruit, for we have cherries, currants, apples, pears, and plums, in abundance, a few quince bushes, and two or three grape vines that promise very well. So we shall, in all probability, have plenty of fruit.

The currants have occupied me lately. As soon

as they began to turn red we used them freely on the table, and yet there are a great many on the bushes that are growing dead ripe. Yesterday I picked several quarts of them, and made my currant jelly. I intend to dry some of the nicest and largest of them for cake, and the rest will make me five or six gallons of wine. I shall be certain, in offering wine of my own manufacture to my guests, that it contains neither logwood nor Elderberry, or any other dirty drug, and it will be perfectly harmless, as well as in the last degree palatable, if I succeed well. I have put up fifteen pounds of cherries. I prepared them in the Shaker style, taking out all the stones and boiling my syrup down until it was quite thick.

July 11th.—Yesterday afternoon I had my house full of company, and of course, took a great deal of pride in my tea-table. I have had so much plain cooking to do for the workmen, that it was a real pleasure to try my skill in cakes and custards. I find that good cake depends, first, upon the quality of the materials, then upon the order in which the ingredients are mixed, and then upon thorough combination. When Eliza was here she told me of a contrivance for sale in New York, for stirring cake and bread. If Edward goes down to the metropolis next winter, I guess he will buy one for me. It consists of a funnel-shaped, tin vessel, large enough to hold two or three gallons, and fastened securely in a hole in the shelf, or set in a block which is screwed to the shelf. In the middle, and fastened to the bottom, is a round piece of wood about the size of a broomstick, terminating in a handle at the top. A small as well as a large quantity can be stirred in this, and with vastly more ease, Eliza says, than can be done in the ordinary way.

I think that this, and all other labor-saving inventions in woman's department, should be patronised. The time and strength I could save by having such a bread and cake stirrer, I could invest in enterprises in and around the house that would repay the outlay. It is only within a few years that wringers, washers, sewing and knitting machines have been invented, but what a vast amount of toil they have already saved, and the movement of invention in this direction is still onward. When I get this bread-stirrer, we shall observe the difference in the quality of the bread, for kneading a long time is essential to good bread.

July 15th.—The weather is very sultry and oppressive, and I have had a great deal of trouble with my butter and cream. I find that when the thermometer is above 90°, it is very difficult to make a superior quality of butter without the best arrangements. So Edward suggests that during the remainder of this month, and the next, I make only enough butter for family use, and make the rest of the milk into cheese. I have no practical experience in this line, but fortunately our Irish dairyman has been familiar from boyhood with the process, as conducted in the old country. Edward has bought me a neat little press, and Farmer Jones' wife will let me have a rennet. It will impose some additional labor upon me, but Sue is doing a great deal of my housework, and I have an ambition to master every department of domestic industry.

July 17th.—Amid all my other engagements I have not been obliged entirely to neglect my flowers, and I am surprised to see how much can be accomplished in keeping a flower garden in fine condition, by a little labor every day. My mornings have been so occupied that I have devoted a few moments every evening after tea, to my roses and verbenas. I make it a rule never to pass a weed without pulling it up, and I have placed it as a reward for rapid kitchen-work, that Sue shall have a half hour in the garden if she will make time for it. With such girls as Sue, whose intentions are always good, is it not best to stimulate by rewards of this sort, as much as possible, and not discourage and dishearten them by constant faultfinding? I make it a rule to praise her whenever she does a piece of work rapidly and well, and be as sparing of censure as I may.

July 20th.—Sue reports that the cucumbers are big enough to pickle. I tell her that she may go out early every other morning and pick all that are of the length of her forefinger; in that way I will prevent any from getting too large, and have my pickles of uniform size, which improves their appearance and their value in market. Those that accidentally escape her notice and reach a large size, we can use on the table, or let them ripen and make them into sweet pickle, for which my sister Emeline gave me an excellent receipt.

A few of them I shall pickle at once, but most of them will be put down in rock salt until spring, when we shall have abundance of vinegar, and time to prepare them for market.

July 22d.—I've been having some experience in sickness within a day or two. One of our workmen came in at noon, with a terrible headache from the heat of the sun, amounting almost to sunstroke. I made a pallet on the floor for him, in a cool, dark room, upstairs, put a cloth wrung from cold water, over his forehead and eyes, and left a basin of cold water beside him, to be used in keeping the cloth cool and moist. Perfect quiet and rest will restore him sooner than anything else. He was not very well in the morning, and ate a light breakfast, then, just before noon, he pitched on a big load of hay, with the thermometer at 95°. Poor fellow! I feel so sorry for him, and my sympathy seems to be as grateful to him as the cold water to his forehead. I have just carried him a glass of iced lemonade, which he received very thankfully. He says he has never been the same man since that summer at Vicksburg. Edward has told him not to worry about his loss of time, that a few days illness shall make no difference with his wages.

July 27th.—My patient is recovering. His headache and giddiness lasted two or three days, during which time I gave him gruel, toasted bread, soft boiled eggs, and lemonade. Now that the headache is gone, I have put him on a rich diet, for that is what he wants to build up his strength. We got three or four pounds of sirloin steak, which I keep hung in the well, giving him a nice cut of it, broiled, twice a day, with just as much Graham bread and as many boiled eggs as he will eat, and all the buttermilk he wants to drink.

Leaves from My Journal.—No. V.

PRIZE ESSAY BY MRS. B. M'CLELLAN, OF OHIO.

While seated at our sewing this morning, I said to Lizzie: "I never told you of a visit we made to our friends many years ago. I don't often speak of it now, though in all its details it is as fresh in my mind as the events of yesterday. Mr. Frisby was worn with incessant business, and Alice, the pet lamb of our flock, was teething and delicate. We proposed to take our own conveyance, and thus at our leisure, visit friends scattered here and there in the beautiful Valley of the Connecticut. Carrie was now five, and for these two little ones, I had all a fond mother's pride and ambition. How unweariedly I labored by day and night, to have all in readiness for our outfit! I remember especially one afternoon, feeling really impatient, while hurrying to finish some garments, assisted by a sewing girl, when my husband came in and proposed that we should lay by our work and attend a church lecture. —Ah, how did the cares of this world choke the Word, till it became unfruitful! But everything being in readiness, and quite to my liking, we commenced the journey. It was in June. Golden days, transparent in brightness and beauty. The first drive brought us to a friend's where we purposed to stop a while. That night Mr. Frisby was taken sick, and for two weeks lay prostrate with disease. Alice, the while, needed tender care and nursing, so unlike her former playful self. When Mr. Frisby was able to ride, we started for my former mountain home. Its clear bracing air would cure both the sick ones, I said. But Alice still drooped, and after three weeks lingering, painful sickness, 'slept that sleep that knows no waking.' We robed her in the white muslin I had so carefully wrought, and which she had never worn till now, and laid her to rest by 'the graves of our fathers.' With sorrowing hearts we retraced our way. As we drew near home, the words of Naomi came to my mind: 'I went out full, and the Lord hath brought me home again empty.' Then looking at the dear ones still spared, I exclaimed: Oh no, *not empty, not empty!* The Lord hath dealt very mercifully with me. Blessed be His name.

Thus without long and weary pilgrimage,
Through devious paths of pain, and tears and sin,
Her little feet have reached the Home of Rest
And stand forever safe on Zion's hill."

Sabbath.—"Our Father" know what these restless, grovelling, grasping natures needed, and gave us this sweet day, forever pointing from the dust and din of earth to heavenly mansions and immortal life. The sermon this morning was from those words of Jesus: "She hath done what she could." Precious testimony, to that grateful penitent, whose costly offering was esteemed a sacrifice of love. I saw the tears gather in Lizzie's eyes, and believe I read her thoughts. To the young housekeeper whose time and strength are taxed to the utmost in her own little circle, those ever recurring questions, "What shall we eat, what shall we drink, and wherewithal shall we be clothed," seem to be absorbing every other. Her life appears so barren of fruit to the Saviour's praise, that despondency may wrap its dark folds about her heart and shut out the bright light and hope of heaven. How little does she estimate at its real value the simple routine of her daily life! To make one more happy home in the land, one more center of healthful saving influence, from which may go forth "streams to make glad the city of our God"—are not angels even "ministering spirits" in such a work as this?

I passed a humble home to-day, and though entirely a stranger to its occupants, decided in my own mind that it was bright and happy within. That fine running rose, "The Queen of the Prairie," had been trained over one side of the house, till it had surrounded the chamber windows. It was loaded with roses. Every spot of ground was turned to the best account. Vegetables were more forward than I had seen before, with flowers here and there interspersed. Under an elm tree was a rude swing for the children; a martin box surmounted the wood-shed, while about the whole place was that indescribable air of order and thrift, which we so surely connect with true enjoyment.

We are having a heavy rain. I have had a feather bed and pillows put out on the grass. The feathers are getting heavy, the pillows somewhat yellow. If the rain is long enough, it will do them as much good as the corn in the meadow. They will need turning over two or three times, and take some days to dry, but will then be about as nice as now. Feather beds are out of date now, but for old people, in cold weather, they are a comfort, and, renewed in this way, and properly aired, need not be unhealthy.

Sour milk is an excellent bleacher. Place the garment in an earthen bowl or wooden pail, and cover entirely with the milk. Let it remain two or three days, taking pains now and then to shake it thoroughly. Then after washing and boiling, it will be found of the purest white. For table-cloths and napkins, that have become stained and yellow, this is a good cure. Iron rust needs more severe treatment, and can be removed with oxalic acid dissolved in water, and applied to the spot in the strong sunlight. It is a powerful poison, and will take the color out of anything on which it is carelessly dropped. Mildew I had supposed past remedy, but have tried the cure found in the *Agriculturist* for September, 1866. Stir ½ lb. of chloride of lime in a gallon of cold water. After settling an hour, pour off the clear liquid, and soak the mildewed cotton or linen in it two hours; wash well and expose to the sun—and it works like a charm. I only fear that leaving a garment of delicate material so long in the solution of lime, may rot it; but of this I cannot yet judge. The same fear has been expressed in regard to the oxalic acid, but I have often used it without the least injury to the linen.

Green Corn Pudding.—Grate the corn off from 6 ears, and mix with ½ pint sweet milk, ½ cup sugar, 1 tablespoonful flour, 2 eggs beaten, 1 tablespoonful butter, and add a little salt.

BOYS & GIRLS' COLUMNS.

Instructive Experiments.

Take a wide-mouthed bottle—a fruit preserving jar will answer the purpose well—put it in a pail of water, allow it to fill, turn it upside down, and lift it partly from the water, but keep its mouth under the surface, so that the water will not run out from it. Have a tube, (a clean tobacco pipe will do), place the lower end under the surface of the water, and under the mouth of the jar, so that when you blow through it, the bubbles will rise up into the jar, and drive the water down and out. Take a long full breath, and hold it in the lungs as long as can be

done with out inconvenience, and then blow through the pipe into the jar. Repeat this until the breath has filled the jar and expelled all the water from it. Be careful to keep the jar upright, with its mouth under water, so as to retain what was sent there from the lungs. Next, cover the mouth of the jar with a piece of thick, wet paper, such as a bit of an old book cover, and then carefully turn the jar right side up, when you can set it on the table or other convenient place. The wet paper, if it rests snugly on the mouth of the jar, will keep the contents from being mixed with the air for a little while. Have a short piece of candle attached to a bit of wire so that it can be lowered to the bottom of the jar. Light the candle, let it down, and the flame will go out as suddenly as though it had been dipped under water. The experiment may be repeated several times without refilling the jar with breath. If the candle be placed in such a jar containing only common air, it will continue to burn. The experiment then proves that what comes from the lungs is different from air, as it will not support a flame.

2d Experiment. Fill the jar with breath as before, and set it on the table. Light a short piece of candle and set it in the bottom of a glass tumbler. Pour the breath out of the jar into the tumbler, exactly as though you were filling the latter with water, and if the experiment is properly managed, the flame will be extinguished, though nothing can be seen to pass from the jar into the tumbler. This proves that breath from the lungs is heavier than air, otherwise it would not run out from the jar and into the tumbler like water.

Having performed these experiments satisfactorily try and find out the reason for the flame being extinguished, and what breath is; at another time we may have more to say on the subject.

The Kind-Hearted Tanner.

William Savery, an eminent minister among the Quakers, was a tanner by trade. One night a quantity of hides were stolen from his tannery, and he had reason to believe that the thief was a quarrelsome, drunken neighbor, called John Smith. Next week the following advertisement appeared in the country newspaper:

"Whoever stole a quantity of hides on the fifth of this month, is hereby informed that the owner has a sincere desire to be his friend. If poverty tempted him to this false step, the owner will keep the whole transaction secret, and will gladly put him in the way of obtaining money by means more likely to bring him peace of mind!"

This singular advertisement attracted considerable attention, but the culprit alone knew who had made the kind offer. When he read it his heart melted within him, and he was filled with sorrow for what he had done. A few nights afterwards, as the tanner's family were about retiring to rest, they heard a timid knock, and when the door was opened there stood John Smith, with a load of hides on his shoulders. Without looking up he said: "I have brought these back, Mr. Savery; where shall I put them?"—"Wait till I can get a lantern, and I will go to the barn with thee," he replied, "then perhaps thou wilt come in, and tell me how this happened. We will see what can be done for thee."—As soon as they were gone out, his wife prepared some hot coffee, and placed pies and meat on the table. When they returned from the barn, she said: "Neighbor Smith, I thought some hot supper would be good for thee."—He turned his back towards her, and did not speak. After leaning against the fire-place in silence a few moments, he said in a choked voice: "It is the first time I ever stole anything, and I have felt very bad about it. I am sure I didn't once think I should ever come to what I am. But I took to drinking and then to quarreling. Since I began to go down hill everybody gives me a kick. You are the first man that has ever offered me a helping hand. My wife is sickly, and my children starving. You have sent them many a meal. God bless you! but yet I stole the hides. But I tell you the truth when I say it is the first time I was ever a thief."—"Let it be the last, my friend," replied William Savery. "The secret lies between ourselves. Thou art still young, and it is in thy power to make up for lost time. Promise me that thou wilt not drink any intoxicating liquor for a year, and I will employ thee to-morrow on good wages. Thy little boy can pick up stones. But eat a bit now, and drink some hot coffee; perhaps it will keep thee from craving anything stronger to-night. Doubtless thou wilt find it hard at first, but keep up a brave heart for the sake of thy wife and children, and it will become easy. When thou hast need of coffee, tell Mary, and she will give it thee."

The poor fellow tried to eat and drink, but the food seemed to choke him. After vainly trying to compose his feelings, he bowed his head on the table, and wept like a child. After awhile he ate and drank, and his host parted with him for the night, with the friendly words, "try to do well, John, and thou wilt always find a friend in me." John entered into his employ the next day, and remained with him many years a sober, honest, and steady man. The secret of the theft was kept between them; but after John's death, William Savery told the story, to prove that evil might be overcome with good.

No. 269. *Puzzle Picture.*—An old-time proverb; we do not endorse it as being altogether true now-a-days.

Iron at $20,000 per Pound.

A gentleman visiting the American Watch Company's factory at Waltham, Mass., relates that a small vial, such as homœopathic pills are kept in, was handed to him, which was filled with what seemed to be grains of coarse sand, of the color of blue tempered steel. On examination under a microscope they proved to be perfect screws, of which it required 30,000 to make a pound. Microscopic bits of steel, with the points exquisitely polished were also shown, so small that fifty weighed only a single grain. These were said to be worth $20,000 per pound. These, as well as every other of the running parts of the watch, are made entirely by machinery, which turns out each different piece exactly like its fellow.

The following is his description of the method of making the fine screws: What you do see at a first glance is a thin thread of steel, finer than the most delicate of pins, slowly pushing its way through a little hole in a machine, and being grasped by a tiny tool which runs round it, as if embracing it; and then, presto! change! out comes a knife and cuts off its head. All this is done so quickly that you have to wait and watch the operation, *after* you know what it is all about, before you can see the process I have described. The bits thus beheaded with a hug, look exactly like little grains of powder. But they are screws. You notice that when you take a microscope and examine them. They are complete—*almost*. Not quite yet. A girl picks them up, one by one, with a dainty tool, and places them in rows, one in every hole in a flat piece of steel. This little plate, as soon as it is filled, is placed under another machine, and it would do any Irishman's soul good to see *it* work. It beats Donnybrook Fair "all hollow." I never had a more convincing proof of the superiority of mechanical over manual labor. For while a good hearty man with a stout bit of shillelah may break half a dozen heads of a day—with *fair luck*—this machine, without so much as saying "By yer lave," comes out of its hole, and runs along each row, quietly splitting the head of each one of them exactly in the center. And now the screw is made.

New Puzzles to be Answered.

No. 270.—*Illustrated Rebus.*—Realized this year.

No. 271. *Arithmetical Problem.*—*A* and *B* each sold a hog to one dealer, for which he paid them $35, remarking that *A*'s hog was worth ½ per cent. per lb. more than *B*'s, but that they might settle that between themselves. *A*'s hog weighed 400 lbs., *B*'s, 300 lbs.; how much money should each receive?

Answers to Problems and Puzzles.

The following are answers to the puzzles, etc., in the June number, page 223. No. 263. *Illustrated Rebus.*—1st Reading, (across the whole of each line). Keep pushing, 'tis wiser to struggle and climb; to keep your eyes open; to conquer all fear; than be watching the seasons of tide and of time; of aid and of fortune; be steadfast to this; in life's earnest battle they only prevail, marching right onward, who will not say fail.—2d Reading, (half way across each line). Keep pushing: 'tis wiser to keep your eyes open, than be watching the seasons of aid and of fortune. In life's earnest battle, marching right onward.—3d Reading, (commencing at the middle of each line and reading to the end). To struggle and climb, to conquer all fear of tide and of time, be steadfast to this, they only prevail, who will not say fail.... No. 267. *Word Puzzle.*—*American Agriculturist.* No. 268. *Bible Question.*—Noah and his family.. No. 264. *Geographical Enigma*, in May number, page 187.—Mooselocknoguntic Lake, in Maine.... *The Spanish Puzzle.*—Place the men as directed on page 226; we will call them *A, B, C,—D, E, F*, the first three representing the black men. Move *C* towards *D*, jump *D* over *C*; move *E* towards *C*, and jump *C* over *E*; then jump *B* over *D*; move *A* towards *D*, and jump *D* over *A*; jump *E* over *B*, and *F* over *C*; move *C* to the end place; jump *B* over *F*, and *A* over *E*; move *E* towards *D*, and jump *F* over *A*; finish by moving *A* towards *B*.—The following have sent in correct answers: H. J. Meixel, John Meyers, Jr., Sam'l L. Moore, W. E. Uplegrove, Orlando D. Outhout, "S.," M. E. Grigsby, William D. Reese, Mamie and Lenie Close, Thos. D. Smedley, John D. Haviland, Emma Randall and P. E. Randall, Alice McMichael, "Stupid," J. Fred. Scott, J. M. Whitman, Mary Keller, Sam'l Wolf, Jr., J. F. Day, J. Milton Snyder, Wm. Anderson, "Jeames," "S. L. C.," Mickey and Bird, "J. T. H.," Ida and Bertha Challis, Frank H. Marston, "G. H. C." (Thanks for friendly criticism.)

[COPYRIGHT SECURED.]

"MANY A SLIP BETWEEN CUP AND LIP."—*Drawn and Engraved for the American Agriculturist.*

Not quite, Mr. Reynard! You have only a few feathers for dinner, instead of the fine fat duck you were counting on, and now the bird has the use of his wings, he's out of danger from your sharp teeth. The old story of counting chickens before they are hatched is here repeated, with the addition that it's not always safe to count upon them even after they are full feathered. "Many a slip between cup and lip," should also be remembered. We know many men who were as rich over their oil-wells as this fox over his duck—until their visions suddenly flew away, because the oil wouldn't flow, and they have now only a few scraps of paper called "Certificates of Stock," worth about as much as so many ducks' feathers. Not a few of our young, inexperienced friends have other equally valuable documents,—"tickets" for some "Grand Presentation" or "Distribution," which flew away, or rather the managers did, just *before* the "prizes" were distributed. Perhaps a better way to state it would be, the foxy managers pounced upon these silly ducks, tore out a few greenbacks from their pockets, and then let them go. If they will imitate the duck, and keep out of the cunning sharpers' way hereafter it will be well.

Independence Day.

Pop! fizz! snap! bang! hurrah! Hail Columbia!!! That's about the way the boys' thoughts run now, and in a few days they will let them out from fire-crackers, pistols, cannon, and every thing that can make a noise, including their own throats for the shouting chorus. It is well to celebrate the Nation's birthday. People differ as to the best way of doing it. Young folks who don't know what weak nerves are, believe in loud noises; perhaps it is well that they do. Men and women are so full of thoughts about work and business, they talk [illegible] to observe our Great Anniversary, if the children did not disturb their quiet. We believe this Jubilee had great effect in keeping patriotism alive during the eighty years of prevailing peace following the Revolution. The Fourth of July orations, the display of the Stars and Stripes, and the general waking up of recollections of the past, and prophecies of the future, aroused the whole people once a year at least. Some day, perhaps five hundred years or more hence, when people have forgotten all about war, there will be less powder burning in celebrating such occasions. That will be when everybody knows how to keep up his own independent right of self-government. The wrongs which nations commit, and which cause wars, are only the great sum of the evil doings of the men and women who make up the nation. One great national sin of the United States is now done away with, and can not again bring on war. Other evils remain, ignorance, too great desire for wealth, love of pleasure, impatience of any restraint—these are dangers that are now to be averted. Laws alone will not prevent their growth and the ruin they may bring. It is necessary for men and women, boys and girls, each to declare their Independence and maintain their Freedom from wrong doing. This will keep the national life pure, and make the country strong enough to stand like the pyramids, or like the living Banyan tree, which no storm can uproot, but whose growth increases century by century.

Educated Senses.

The eye, the ear, the fingers, all the servants of the soul, work more skillfully when properly trained. Perhaps the Indian has the keenest senses, made so by long practice. He must be on the alert, for his life depends on being able to outwit the animals that furnish his table and his clothing, and also to elude his wary enemies. From infancy his eyes are taught to "look sharp," and his ears to "keep open," until not a bent twig or a pressed bunch of moss, or the rustle of a leaf, escapes his notice. But the most wonderful acuteness of the senses, produced by education, is seen where some of them have double duty to perform, as in the case of the blind. Hearing and touch divide between them the work usually done by the eye. A writer says: "To the seeing, touch is an auxiliary; but to the blind boy, it is the primary sense of all. By it he knows his own clothes, and almost all the property that he possesses—his tools, box, bed, hat, fiddle, cupboard, seat in chapel, schoolroom and workshop; by it he reads his chapter in St. John or in Robinson Crusoe; he plays chess or dominoes; works a sum in long division, or writes a letter [illegible] to his mother which she can read with her eyes, and he with his fingers. By the help of touch he weaves a rug of colored wools; or fringes with delicate green and red, a door mat for a lady's boudoir; by touch he sees any curiosity, which you describe to him, and which having once handled, he always speaks of as having seen. He thinks he can read a good deal of your character by touch when you shake hands with him; and when he has heard you talk for a few minutes he will make a good guess as to your age, temper, ability and stature. One blind man at times guessed even more than this. He had been sitting one day and pleasantly chatting with some visitors for an hour, when one of them wished the company good morning, and left the room. 'What white teeth that lady has!' said the sarcastic professor. 'How can you possibly tell that?' said a friend. 'Because,' was the ready answer, 'for the last half-hour she has done nothing but laugh.' This was shrewd enough; but specially characteristic of him as a blind man."

(Business Notices [illegible] Line [illegible] Space.)

Piano for a Life Time.

Those wanting [illegible] Piano [illegible] instruments [illegible] and which WILL REMAIN [illegible] LIFE TIME, will please call and examine, or send for a [illegible] newly invented

MATHUSHEK PIANOS,

constructed on an entirely new plan, the invention of Mr. Frederick Mathushek, who is well known among manufacturers as the "Father" of improvements in Pianos. By [illegible], the power and tone of the instrument are wonderfully increased, so much so, that the smallest [illegible] "square" form, only *four feet nine inches long and two feet eight inches wide*, equals the full sized piano as [illegible] made. The peculiar construction [illegible] DURABILITY. Address BARLOW, DOEHLER & CO., 694 Broadway, New York.

The Howe Machine Co.'s Sewing Machines, 699 Broadway, Cor. Fourth-st., New York.

For Families and Manufacturers.

These World-Renowned Sewing Machines

Were awarded the highest premium at the World's Fair in London, and [illegible] first premiums at the N. Y. State Fair of [illegible].

These machines are made under the immediate supervision of the President of the Company, ELIAS HOWE, Jr., the original inventor of the Sewing Machine.

The Stitch invented by MR. HOWE, *and made on this Machine, is the most popular and durable, and all Sewing Machines are [illegible] the principle invented by him.*

SEND FOR CIRCULAR.

WHEELER & WILSON ROTARY HOOK LOCK STITCH SEWING MACHINES.

625 BROADWAY.

"WOMAN'S GREATEST BOON.—We would advise a man to forego a "Thresher" and thresh wheat with a flail, rather than to see [illegible] vigor and life away in the everlasting "stitch, stitch, stitch," when a Sewing Machine can be obtained. The WHEELER & WILSON is an [illegible]. We have had several [illegible] years' service, the [illegible] WHEELER & WILSON has [illegible] the preference as the best, where all kinds [illegible] done in a family."—*American Agriculturist, Jan. 1865.*

THE GREAT FAMILY SEWING MACHINE.

GROVER & BAKER'S

HIGHEST PREMIUM Elastic Stitch SEWING MACHINE. 495 Broadway, New York.

FRANKLIN BRICK MACHINE.

Justly celebrated for perfect simplicity, great strength, and [illegible] with eight [illegible] clay and make 1000 [illegible] J. H. RENICK, Proprietor, No. [illegible] Broadway, New York, Room 24.

JOHN W. DOUGLASS,

(Late of R. H. ALLEN & CO.)

Dealer in Agricultural Implements, Machinery, Seeds, Fertilizers, &c., No. [illegible] Water-st., New York. Send for Circular.

$600.—$600.—$600.

I have Agents making *Six Hundred Dollars* each month, selling and putting on my "Patent Door Bells." I want five more *good Agents.*

A. E. TAYLOR, New Britain, Conn.

HERALD OF HEALTH.—In order to let those who have [illegible] this [illegible] judge of its merits, we will send [illegible] for [illegible] cents. [illegible] cents a number. MILLER, WOOD & CO., [illegible] Laight-st., New York.

AMERICAN WATCHES.

The true value of Machinery applied to Watch making is not that by its use Watches are made rapidly, but that they are made perfectly. Very few people know why a Waltham Watch should be superior to any other. In the first place, the Watch is regarded at Waltham as only a machine to be constructed like any other machine on mechanical principles. The Factory is indeed little else but a vast machine shop, the principle work in which is not upon watches, but upon machinery to make them with. If the watches are good, it is because the machinery is good. Of course there must be no fault in the principle or plan of the movement, none in the sizes or shapes of the pieces of which it is composed, nothing wanting in their properties, and no error in their positions. These points once thoroughly settled and fixed in the case of every part of each variety of watch, it rests wholly with the machinery constructed with infinite variety of form and function expressly for the purpose to produce the finished pieces. The method established in every department is in short that of the reduplication of parts by mechanical means, and carried out on the system of the finest sub-division of labor. By means of multiplying gauges and microscopes, tests and inspection for the detection of wear in cutting tools and for faults and flaws in steel or stone, are made to accompany the work in every stage from beginning to end. It follows that the Watch goes together a perfect machine itself. Every part is found to fit properly in its place. Every pin may be pushed till it pinches, and every screw turned home. Instead of a sluggish and feeble action, the balance, even under the pressure of the lightest mainspring, vibrates with a wide and free motion, and the beat has the clear and ringing sound always characteristic of the Waltham Watch. The machine is a timekeeper from the start.

This system is unknown in foreign countries and is entirely original with the Waltham Company. The Company claim that under it they produce watches which cannot be equaled for every quality which makes a watch valuable. Simple in plan and correct in principle, the movement is not only beautifully finished, substantial, accurate and cheap, but is uniform to the smallest details, not easily damaged, easily repaired and always as good as new. There are different grades of finish on the different kinds, as there are different sizes and shapes to suit all tastes and wants, but every Watch that bears the genuine trade mark of "WALTHAM," is guaranteed to be a good one, and nobody need be afraid to buy it.

From The N. Y. Tribune.

"The American Watch Company, of Waltham, Mass., established in 1850, has grown into proportions which entitle it to a rank among the manufacturing enterprises of America. The quality of these instruments has been thoroughly tested by minute comparisons, and the result is decidedly in favor of the home-made over the imported.

"The first duty of a watch is to keep good time. Its other uses are decorative and subsidiary. The simpler its mechanism the more trustworthy its action, and the system upon which watches are constructed by the American Company is the very perfection of simplicity.

"An important question is that of the relative costliness of European and American Watches. It appears that the advantage of cheapness is also with us. The difference in price is not excessive, but is sufficient to be an object to any purchaser. The virtue of superior durability, however, is one which ought to be well considered in this regard. American instruments will outlast all others. It has been estimated that we pay Europe [illegible] a year for watches, and a like sum for keeping them in order. At our own doors watches are manufactured at a less price, of better quality, less likely to become disordered, and so arranged that in case of injury by violence, the injury may cheaply and expeditiously be repaired."

From The N. Y. Times.

"AMERICAN WALTHAM WATCHES.—This country has reason to be proud of this splendid specimen of American operative genius and enterprise. That it will work a revolution in the watch manufacturing of the world no one can doubt who examines the operations of the Waltham Establishment, for it turns out watch movements at just about one half the cost of imported movements. Besides the uniform reliability of the machine made watches must give them a great advantage over all others wherever known. A poor time-piece of the machine make will be as rare in the future as a good one of hand-make has been heretofore, for machinery is arbitrary in its performance, and can make a perfect article just as easy as one that is worthless. It will be a cause of congratulation if this highly useful American enterprise shall have the effect of driving out of market the thousands of trashy foreign articles, miscalled time-keepers, by furnishing so excellent and economical a substitute."

From The N. Y. Herald.

"We notice with regret, (writing of the Paris Exposition), the absence of specimens of American manufacture, which, although only comparatively of recent birth among us, is already producing results of the most satisfactory character. The Watches manufactured by the Waltham Company are certainly, so far as strength, durability, and excellence as time-keepers are concerned, as good as anything produced by the French or Swiss manufacturers."

From The N. Y. World.

"We have had one of the works of this Company in a case for some considerable time, and, comparing them with former first class works of different manufacture possessed by us, they have established, in our opinion, their superiority over any ever introduced for correctness as time-pieces."

From The Scientific American.

"It is believed that a Waltham Watch is worth double the price of many of the imported watches made by hand."

From Harper's Weekly.

"The beauty, the precision, the greater cheapness, the uniform excellence of a watch constructed by machinery so exquisite that the mere spectacle of its operation is poetic, gradually give the American Watches a public preference which will not be deceived."

EVERY WATCH FULLY WARRANTED.

FOR SALE BY ALL FIRST-CLASS DEALERS IN THE UNITED STATES AND BRITISH PROVINCES.

For further information address the Agents,

ROBBINS & APPLETON, No. 182 Broadway, New York.

AMERICAN WATCHES in every variety at Manufacturers' prices a specialty with us since their introduction.

T. B. BYNNER & CO., 189 Broadway, and 155 and 157 Fulton-st., New York.

BUY THE BEST!

J. W. BRADLEY'S CELEBRATED

DUPLEX ELLIPTIC

(Or DOUBLE SPRING)

SKIRTS.

THEY will not BEND or BREAK like the Single Springs, but WILL PRESERVE their PERFECT and GRACEFUL SHAPE in all CROWDED ASSEMBLAGES, CHURCHES, THEATRES, RAILROAD CARS, and for PROMENADE or HOUSE DRESS, where three or four ordinary skirts are THROWN ASIDE as USELESS.

EACH HOOP is composed of TWO FINELY-TEMPERED Steel Springs, BRAIDED TIGHTLY and FIRMLY together, EDGE to EDGE, forming one hoop, thus making the STRONGEST and MOST FLEXIBLE, as well as the MOST DURABLE and STYLISH SKIRT EVER MADE. In fact, they are superior to all others, COMBINING COMFORT, ECONOMY, LIGHTNESS, ELEGANCE, and DURABILITY.

This POPULAR SKIRT is UNIVERSALLY RECOMMENDED by the FASHION MAGAZINES and OPINIONS of the PRESS GENERALLY.

At WHOLESALE, by the Exclusive Manufacturers and SOLE OWNERS of PATENT,

WESTS, BRADLEY & CARY,

WAREROOMS AND OFFICE,

Nos. 97 Chambers, and 79 and 81 Reade-sts., N. Y.

ALSO, at WHOLESALE by the LEADING JOBBERS.

THE INDELIBLE PENCIL CO.

(NORTHAMPTON, MASS.)

Manufacturers of the Improved Patent

Indelible,

PENCIL, for MARKING CLOTHING, &c., have now ready for sale their new

HORTICULTURAL PENCIL,

For writing on wood. Invaluable for making durable TREE and GARDEN TAGS or LABELS, or marking TOOLS, &c.

PRICES: *Horticultural*, single, 75 cents; two for $1.00; per doz., $5.00. *Clothing Pencil*, single, 50 cents; three for $1.00, per doz., $3.00. Sent pre-paid by mail or express on receipt of price.

A Liberal Discount made to Dealers.

Every Pencil Warranted.

THE LITTLE CORPORAL

is acknowledged by the leading papers to be the

Best Juvenile Paper in America.

We offer a MAGNIFICENT LIST of PREMIUMS! Subscribe at any time during the year.

The price of the Corporal is one dollar a year, in advance; sample copy, telling all about the premiums, ten cents. Address ALFRED L. SEWELL, Publisher, Chicago, Ill.

Book Agents Wanted.

To solicit orders, in each town in the United States and Canada, for the most popular subscription book ever published, being THE ILLUSTRATED HISTORY OF THE BIBLE, by *John Kitto, D. D., F. S. A., Edited by Rev. Alvan Bond, D. D., of Norwich, Conn.*—over 700 closely printed Royal Octavo pages—more than 250 full page engravings. Recommended by the leading Clergy of all denominations of Christians. 30,000 Copies already printed. Six large power presses running on the work. Everybody wants it. Experienced Agents say they never knew a book sell so well. No competition. Experienced Agents, School Teachers, Sabbath School Teachers, retired Clergymen, and others, are wanted to introduce this great work into every household in the land. *For Circulars, etc.,* apply immediately to the Publisher, HENRY BILL, Norwich, Conn.

---

50 PER CENT

Saved by Using B. T. Babbitt's Laborsaving Soap.

The SOAP is made from clean and pure materials, contains no adulteration of any kind, will not injure the most delicate fabric, and is especially adapted for woolens, which will not shrink after being washed with this SOAP. It may be used in hard or soft waters. It will remove paint, grease, tar, and stains of all kinds. One pound warranted equal to two pounds of ordinary family Soap. Directions sent with each bar for making three gallons of handsome Soft Soap from one pound of this Soap. Each bar is wrapped in a circular containing full directions for use, printed in English and German. Ask your grocer for "B. T. BABBITT'S SOAP," and take no other. B. T. BABBITT.

Nos. 64, 65, 66, 67, 68, 69, 70, 72 and 74 Washington-St., New York.

Silver Tips for Children's Shoes.

They protect the toe from wear, and are highly ornamental. Applied to the most genteel shoes made. Buy no others.

Advertisements, to be sure of insertion, must be received BEFORE the 5th of the preceding month.

TERMS—(cash before insertion):

Ordinary Pages, $1.50 *per line. Open Pages*—$2 *per line.*
Business Notices—$2.50 per line of space, each insertion.

FERD. F. MAYER, Chemist,

Has removed his Office to 52 Cedar-st., New York.

GRAPE VINES.

The Subscriber would call the attention of Dealers and Planters to his extensive stock of Grape vines, and especially to the Concord and Iona varieties.

Our vines have always been unsurpassed by any in market and our aim is not only to keep up their well known standard of excellence, but to produce, if possible, still better plants than we have had heretofore.

Having a very large number in course of propagation, we are enabled to sell at very low prices where quantities are taken, and all parties intending to purchase will find it greatly to their interest to examine our stock and prices before purchasing elsewhere. Last year the demand for our plants was so large that we were not able to fill one half of our orders. Therefore, send your orders in early to secure the best plants. Address G. E. MEISSNER,
Richmond P. O., Staten Island, N. Y.

SQUIRE'S PATENT FRUIT JAR.

Fruits Preserved Without Sugar.
The Only Jar for Preserving Vegetables.
The Newest, Most Convenient and Economical Jar extant.

This Jar is constructed so that the contents can be cooked in it, and all handling of Hot Fruit or Hot Jars or Tempering of Jars avoided; the contents retain all their natural flavor, and the labor of preserving is lessened more than one-half. Pamphlets sent on application.

J. H. BARTLETT, Wholesale Manufacturer,
[illegible] Murray-street, New York.

NEW BOOK BY THE AUTHOR OF "MY FARM OF EDGEWOOD."
Just Published by C. SCRIBNER & CO.,
654 Broadway, New York.

RURAL STUDIES—WITH PRACTICAL *Hints for Country Places*, by D. G. MITCHELL, (Ik Marvel)—with many Illustrations. One Vol.
(*Copies sent by mail post-paid, on receipt of price,* $1.75.)

The author has sought to demonstrate:

1st. *Why a man should go, if at all, into the country.*
2d. *What sort of a homestead he should seek there.*
3d. *What he should do when in possession of it.*

"I have especially sought to excite the ambition of those holders of humble estates who believe that nothing can be done in the way of adornment of country property except under the eye of accomplished gardeners, and to show that the proper appliance of small means will produce effects whose charms must in their way stand unrivaled."

THE GREAT PICTORIAL DOUBLE NUMBER of the PHRENOLOGICAL JOURNAL AND LIFE ILLUSTRATED for July, contains portraits with Biographical sketches of CHIEF JUSTICE CHASE, MRS. HARRIET BEECHER STOWE, MRS. LA VERT, EDWARD CARSWELL, and others; articles on Eloquence, QUEEN ELIZABETH, Studies in Physiognomy, MAN-MONKEYS AND GORILLAS, profusely illustrated; and a great variety of matter, agreeable and instructive. A NEW VOLUME—the 44th—ENLARGED, $3 a year, 30 cts. a number. Address
S. R. WELLS, 389 Broadway, New York.

THE EUREKA BRICK MACHINE

makes 3,000 *splendid Brick per hour, with only nine men and one pair horses, or* 4,500 *per hour by steam power. Has no complex machinery to be getting out of order or breaking down.* Its great simplicity and marvelous power command the approval of every expert, *at sight.*
We challenge the world to produce its equal.
Satisfaction guaranteed to all purchasers.
ABRAM REQUA, General Agent,
No. 141 Broadway, New York.

CELERY PLANTS.

"Incomparable Dwarf."

This variety is so much superior in flavor, ease of culture, and hardiness, that for the past six years we have grown it to the exclusion of all other varieties, for the New York market. It is planted one third closer than the tall growing sorts—from 30,000 to 40,000 being grown on an acre.

Dwarf variety, strong plants now ready, price; $1 per 100; $4 per 500; $[illegible] per 1,000; $[illegible] per 10,000; $[illegible] per 50,000.
Large Solid, suitable for light soils, price; 75c. per 100; $3 per 500; $5 per 1,000; $45 per 10,000; $150 per 50,000.

Safely packed (without extra charge,) to any distance not exceeding three days in the transit. Plain printed directions for culture and winter preservation, accompanying each package.
HENDERSON & FLEMING,
SEEDSMEN AND MARKET GARDENERS,
67 Nassau-st., New York.

Seasonable Implements, etc.

Hutchinson's Patent Wine and Cider Mill, $24; Wine Press No. 1, $[illegible], No. 2, $10; Wethersfield Seed Sowers, $8; Harrington's Patent Combined Seed Sower and Cultivator, $15; Nonpareil Washing Machines, No. 2, with Wringer, $[illegible]; and all other Agricultural Implements, etc., for sale by JOHN W. DOUGLASS, (late of R. H. Allen & Co.), 181 Water-st., N. Y.

5 MORE GOOD AGENTS WANTED TO SELL "*Taylor's Patent Door Bells.*" *See page 263.*

SPEAR'S PRESERVING SOLUTION

Will effectually prevent fermentation or decay, and preserve all kinds of fruits, vegetables, cider, milk, &c., &c., in a perfectly fresh and wholesome condition, without sugar—and without air-tighting—hence a saving of sugar, and from 50 to 75 per cent. in the cost of jars.

The solution is warranted to contain nothing injurious to health.

Fruits preserved by it are equal to the best "canned" fruits, while its use admits of keeping the fruit, &c., in large vessels, and using them at long intervals when opened.

It will preserve milk sweet from 12 to 36 hours longer than it will naturally keep, causing it to furnish more cream in hot weather.

Give it a trial and be convinced of its merits and great advantages over all other methods.

One bottle will preserve 128 lbs. of fruit, or 48 gallons of cider, or 128 gallons of milk. Full directions for using with each bottle. Price, $1 per bottle; 6 bottles for $5; or 12 bottles for $9. Good discount to dealers, ask your Merchant for it, or form club and send price for 6 or 12 bottles, and receive it by express from the nearest one of the following Wholesale Agents: John M. Maris & Co., and Johnson, Holloway & Cowden, Philadelphia; C. W. Burgess & Son, Baltimore, Md.; Charles H. Atwood, Boston, Mass.; Burnhams & Van Schaack, Chicago; A. B. Eaton & Son, Cincinnati; Valentine Gerber, St. Louis, Mo.; Elliott & Co., Berrien Springs, Mich.; Roe, Whitman & Co., South Bend, Ind.; Johnson & Bro., New Haven, Conn.; Young & Lyons, Providence, R. I.; or to
L. P. WORRALL, General Agent,
No. 91 Hudson-st., New York.

DOTY'S WASHING MACHINE and the UNIVERSAL CLOTHES WRINGER

are so well known as **the best**, that recommendations are not deemed necessary.
(See back numbers of *Agriculturist.*)
R. C. BROWNING, General Agent,
32 Cortlandt-st., N. Y. (opposite Merchants' Hotel).

HOW TO MAKE MONEY.—Buy a State right for BAKER'S COMBINATION KITCHEN TABLE. One of the most taking Patents out. Send for a Circular.
W. M. BAKER, Fortville, Ind.

COOK'S EVAPORATOR.

Patented June 22, 1858. Re-issued December 24, 1859.
Manufactured by BLYMYER, DAY & CO.,
MANSFIELD, OHIO.

OVER SIXTEEN THOUSAND IN USE.

For Sorghum and Maple.

It is the most rapid boiler known; the most thorough defecator, and the greatest economizer of fuel, in proportion to the work accomplished. It has taken 53 *State Fair First Premiums, and survived one hundred and fifty competitors.*

VICTOR CANE MILL.

Manufactured by BLYMYER, NORTON & CO.,
CINCINNATI, OHIO.

The oldest Cane Mill makers in the United States.

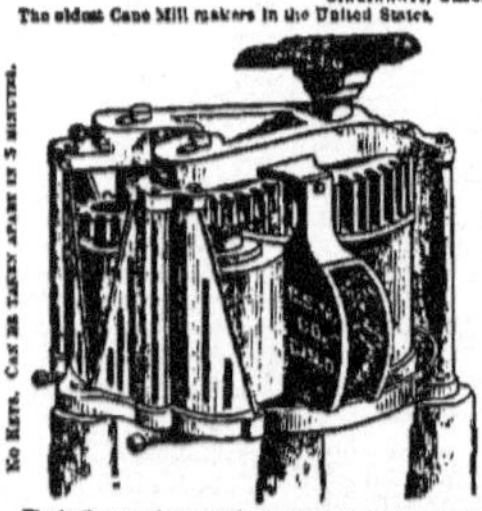

The testimony of thousands of operators, from every State in the Union, West and South of Vermont and New Hampshire, and the award of FIRST PREMIUMS over all the leading Mills in the country, at FIFTEEN State Fairs, prove it to be all we have claimed for it—*The Victor Mill.*

SORGO HAND BOOK
and Descriptive Catalogue sent free.
BLYMYER, DAY & CO., MANSFIELD, O.
BLYMYER, NORTON & CO., CINCINNATI, O.

Manufacturers of Sorgo Machinery, Drag Saws, Church and Plantation Bells, Corn Shellers, Cutting Boxes, Horse Hay Forks, Hand Corn Planters, Garden Cultivators, Cider Mills, &c.

CONTINENTAL LIFE INSURANCE CO. OF NEW YORK.

OFFICE: 26 NASSAU STREET.

OFFICERS:

President: JUSTUS LAWRENCE.
Vice-President: G. HILTON SCRIBNER.
Secretary: J. P. ROGERS.
Actuary: R. C. FROST.
Medical Examiner: E. D. WHEELER, M.D.

DIRECTORS:

JAMES B. COLGATE, of Trevor & Colgate, Bankers.
CHAUNCEY M. DEPEW, (late Secretary of State).
JUSTUS LAWRENCE, President.
G. HILTON SCRIBNER, Vice-President.
JOSEPH T. SANGER, Merchant, No. 25 Liberty Street.
M. B. WYNKOOP, of Wynkoop & Hallenbeck, 113 Fulton st.
Rev. HENRY C. FISH, D. D., Newark, N. J.
RICHARD W. BOGART, of O. M. Bogart & Co., Bankers.
LUTHER W. FROST, New York.

Policies issued during first year,	[illegible]
Amount Insured,	$7,404,600
Annual Premium,	430,310.20

Present Assets nearly **Half a Million Dollars.**

Organized on the Mutual Plan. PROFITS of the COMPANY Annually Divided. One-third of the Premium may remain unpaid as a LOAN. No notes required. Policies non-forfeitable. Thirty days grace allowed in payment of Premiums. Insured have the widest liberty to travel without extra charge.

Great Economy in Painting.

DOTY'S PATENT COMPOUND PAINT OIL, four years tested. Fully as durable, covers as well, easier to spread, quicker to dry, and in no respect inferior to pure Linseed Oil, yet much cheaper! Warranted to render White Lead WHITER, either inside or outside, and FULLY AS DURABLE as Linseed Oil, and as good for all colored paints. Four years' use has fully established this.

PRICE, by the Barrel (40 gallons)	$38 00
5 Gallons for trial, put up in good oak keg	6 00
10 " " " " "	11 00

Shipped as common Railroad Freight, or by Express. Testimonials as to Durability, in Circulars. Agents wanted everywhere. Exclusive sale given.
DOTY'S PAINT OIL CO., 32 Cortlandt-st., New York.

CRESYLIC SOAP.

A PERFECT DISINFECTANT
(Patented).

For Disinfecting, Deodorizing, and Purifying Cellars, Hospitals, Tenement Houses, &c. Also, for Exterminating Roaches, Bugs, and Insects of all kinds.
Manufactured solely by
JAMES BUCHAN & CO.,
190 Elizabeth-st., New York.

To Merchants & Peddlers Everywhere!

A New and Good Thing for Every Family.
DOTY'S EVERLASTING CLOTHES-PIN!

Retail Price, 30 cents per dozen. Send two red stamps for sample Pin and wholesale terms and circulars.
DOTY'S CLOTHES PIN CO., 32 Cortlandt-st., New York.

Normal Academy of Music,

At Meadville, Pa.

The 8th Term of 8 weeks will commence July 2d. For Circulars giving Terms, &c., and particulars as to the donations of Free Scholarships, address THEODORE E. PERKINS, care of Brown & Perkins, 420 Broome-st., New York.

GOLD MEDAL THRESHING MACHINE.—Persons intending to purchase a Threshing Machine, will do well to send for Circulars and Judges' Report of the Machine, awarded Two GOLD MEDALS at the Great National Trial, Auburn, N. Y., July, 1866. Manufactured by R. & M. HARDER, Cobleskill, N. Y. See their advertisement in June number of the Agriculturist.

THE ORIGINAL STOCK of Wilson Early Blackberry, including the *Mother Plant*, may again be seen in fruit at JOHN S. COLLINS'S Small Fruit Nursery, one mile South-West of Moorestown, New Jersey.

Approved Fertilizers.

Peruvian Guano; Ground Bone (*Best*); Coe's Superphosphate of Lime, Plaster, etc., etc., in any quantity.

FARM AND GARDEN IMPLEMENTS.

Swift's Improved Lawn Mower, Plows, Harrows, Threshing Machines, Fan Mills, and all other Agricultural Implements, for sale by JOHN W. DOUGLASS, (late of R. H. Allen & Co.), 181 Water-st., New York. Send for Circular.

EVERYBODY should send for THE AMERICAN STOCK JOURNAL.—Only 50 cents for 6 months. Address
N. P. BOYER & CO., Gum Tree, Chester Co., Pa.

DRAINING FOR PROFIT

AND

DRAINING FOR HEALTH.

By GEO. E. WARING, Jr.,

ENGINEER OF THE DRAINAGE OF CENTRAL PARK, NEW YORK.

Illustrated.

TABLE OF CONTENTS:

LAND TO BE DRAINED AND THE REASONS WHY.—Indications of the need of draining.—Sources of water.—Objections to too much water.—Wet sub-soil.

HOW DRAINS ACT AND HOW THEY AFFECT THE SOIL.—Characteristics of well laid tile drain.—Surface-water and rain water beneficial, springs and soakage water injurious.—Cracking of stiff clays. Evaporation and filtration.—Rain fall.—Evaporation.—Temperature.—Drought.—Porosity or mellowness.—Chemical action in the soil.

HOW TO GO TO WORK TO LAY OUT A SYSTEM OF DRAINS.—Amateur draining.—Maps.—Leveling instruments.—Outlets and location of drains. Main drains.—Spring water.—Fall.—Tiles.—Depth and distance apart.—Direction of laterals.—Collars.—Discharge of water from drains.

HOW TO MAKE THE DRAINS.—Tools.—Marking the lines.—Water courses.—Outlet.—Silt Basins.—Opening the ditches.—Grading. Tile laying.—Connections.—Covering the tile and filling in.—Collecting the water of springs.—Amending the map.

HOW TO TAKE CARE OF DRAINS AND DRAINED LAND.—Removing obstructions.—Mistake of substituting large tiles for small ones which have become obstructed.—Heavy lands should not be trampled while wet.

WHAT DRAINING COSTS.

Draining, expensive work.—Their permanence and lasting effects.—Cheapness versus economy.—Details of cost. (1. Engineering and Superintendence.—2. Digging the ditches.—3. Grading the bottoms.—4. Tile and tile laying.—5. Covering and filling.—6. Outlets and Silt Basins.)

WILL IT PAY?

Increased crops required to pay cost of draining.—(Corn, Wheat, Rye, Oats, Potatoes, Barley, Hay, Cotton, Tobacco.)—Instances of profit.—Benefit of draining in facilitating farm work.

HOW TO MAKE DRAINING TILES.

Materials.—Preparation of earths.—Moulding tile machines.—Drying and rolling.—Burning.—Kilns.—General arrangement of a Tile y.

THE RECLAIMING OF SALT MARSHES.—Extent of marshes on the Atlantic Coast.—The English Fens. Harlaem Lake.—The exclusion of sea water. Removal of the causes of inundation from the upland. Removal of rain fall and water of filtration.—Embankments.—Muskrats.—Rivers and Creeks.—Outlet of drainage.

MALARIAL DISEASES.

Fever and Ague.—Neuralgia. Vicinity of New York. Dr. Bartlett on Periodical Fever. Dr. Metcalf's Report to U. S. Sanitary Commission.—La Roche on the effects of Malarial Fever. Dr. Salisbury on the "Cause of Malarial Fevers." English experience. Reports to the British Parliament.—Cause of Malaria removed by draining.

HOUSE AND TOWN DRAINAGE.

Sewerage.—The use of pipes.—The new outfall sewers in London. The use of steam pumps to secure outlets. Utilization of sewage matters in agriculture.—Effects of imperfect house drainage on health.—Typhoid fever.—The Westminster fever in London. Epidemic at the Maplewood Young Ladies Institute in Pittsfield, Mass. Lambeth Square, London. Back drainage.—Water supply.—General Board of Health, England.

SENT POST-PAID. PRICE, $1.50.

ORANGE JUDD & CO.,
41 Park Row New-York.

A NEW WORK.

SMALL FRUIT CULTURIST.

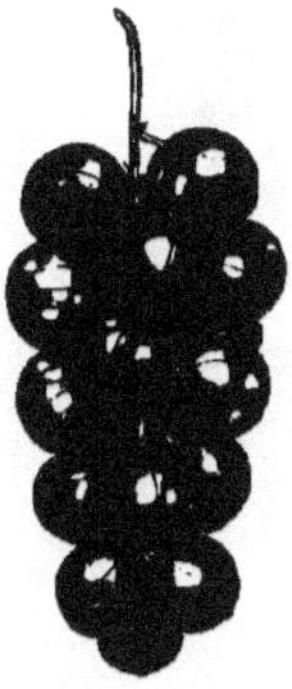

By ANDREW S. FULLER,

PRACTICAL HORTICULTURIST, RIDGEWOOD, BERGEN CO., N. J.

A new work, and the only one devoted to Small Fruits. Special treatises of this kind have the advantage that the author can more thoroughly discuss his subject, and go into greater detail, than in a work embracing both large and small fruits. The work covers the whole ground of Propagation, Culture, Varieties, Packing for Market, etc.

CONTENTS: INTRODUCTION—I. BARBERRY—II. STRAWBERRY—III. RASPBERRY—IV. BLACKBERRY—V. DWARF CHERRY—VI. CURRANT—VII. GOOSEBERRY—VIII. CORNELIAN CHERRY—IX. CRANBERRY—X. HUCKLEBERRY—XI. SHEPERDIA—XII. PREPARATION FOR GATHERING FRUIT.

We predict that this work will bring Mr. Fuller many enemies, as he has given his opinion about varieties without reserve. On the other hand it will the more strongly endear him to all true lovers of horticulture, as these wish to have the merits of fruit given without reference to the persons who introduce them.

While very full on all the small fruits, the Currants and Raspberries have been more carefully elaborated than ever before, and in this important part of his book, the author has had the invaluable counsel of Charles Downing. The chapter on gathering and packing fruit is a valuable one, and in it are figured all the baskets and boxes now in common use. The book is very finely and thoroughly illustrated, and makes an admirable companion to his Grape Culturist.

SENT POST-PAID. PRICE, $1.50

NEW YORK:

ORANGE JUDD & CO.,
41 PARK ROW.

HINTS TO HORSE-KEEPERS,

A COMPLETE

MANUAL FOR HORSEMEN.

BY THE LATE HENRY WILLIAM HERBERT.
(FRANK FORESTER.)

Beautifully Illustrated.

HOW TO BREED A HORSE.—

CHOICE OF STALLION.—National Value of the Horse—The best class of Horses the cheapest for all purposes—What constitutes excellence—Blood; what it gives, should be on the side of the Sire—Breed up, not down—Diseases and Defects Hereditary—General Rules.

CHOICE OF THE MARE.—Size, Symmetry and Soundness more important than Blood—Points of the Brood Mare—Diseases Hereditary—Condition of the Mare—Should have moderate work when with Foal—Food and care during gestation—Health and temper.

MUTUAL ADAPTATION OF SIRE AND DAM.—First consideration in Improvement of "cold" Blood—Relative size of Sire and Dam—Defects in either Parent—How Remedied in Progeny—Bloods which "hit."

CANADIAN BLOOD.—The Canadian originally the French Norman—Characteristics—Hardihood—Speed—Mode of Improvement—Crossing with Thorough-breds.

NORMAN BLOOD.—Origin and History of the Percheron Norman—A pure race—Characteristics and Points.

MODERN ARAB BLOOD.—English and American Thorough-breds derived from Oriental Blood—are now superior to the Modern Arabs—Nolan Arab.

PONIES — DIFFERENT BREEDS, CHARACTERISTICS AND UTILITY.—Origin—Different Breeds—Shetlands and Scots—Galloways and Narragansetts—Mustangs and Indians—Profit of raising Ponies.

HOW TO BREED MULES.

Value of Mules—Their History and Natural History—The Mule and Hinney—Thorough-blood wasted in the Dam for Mules—The Mule in the United States—Large size not Desirable—Varieties of the Ass—The kind of Mares to be selected.

HOW TO BUY A HORSE.

Of whom to Buy it—Extraordinary Cheapness and Extraordinary Excellence not consistent with each other—Points to be regarded—How to Examine the Eye—Broken Wind—Roaring—Whistling—Broken Knees—To examine the Legs—Splents—Damaged Back Sinews—Spavins—Ringbones—Curbs—How to tell the Age of a Horse.

HOW TO FEED A HORSE.

Consequences of Improper Feeding—Different Food for different conditions—Food for the Brood Mare—for the Foal—For Working Horses—Green Food—Carrots—Corn—Feeding Horses in Training—While Travelling—Summering Horses—The Best Method—Management of Omnibus Horses in New York.

HOW TO STABLE AND GROOM A HORSE.—Requisites for a good Stable—The economy of Proper Arrangements—Ventilation—Grooming; its necessity for all descriptions of Horses—How Performed—Clothing—Treatment when brought in from Work.

HOW TO BREAK, AND USE A HORSE.—What is required in a well-broken Horse—His education should commence when a Colt—Bitting—Putting in Harness—How to Use a Horse—Travelling—Working—Pleasure Horses—Punishment.

HOW TO PHYSIC A HORSE—SIMPLE REMEDIES FOR SIMPLE AILMENTS.—Causes of Ailments—Medicines to be given only by the order of the Master—Depletion and Purging—Spasmodic Colic—Inflammation of the Bowels—Inflammation of the Lungs—How to Bleed—Balls and Purgatives—Costiveness—Cough—Bronchitis—Distemper—Worms—Diseases of the Feet—Scratches—Thrush—Broken Knees.

FARRIERY, ETC.

Castration—Docking and Nicking—Blood-letting—Treatment of Strains and Wounds—Galls of the Skin—Cracked Heels—Clipping and Singeing—Administering Medicines—Diseases of the Feet.

HOW TO SHOE A HORSE.

Unskillful Shoers—Anatomy of the Foot Illustrated—The Foot of a Colt—Preparation of the Foot—Removing the Old Shoe—Paring the Foot—The Shoe—Fitting the Shoe—Nailing—Number of Nails—Diseases of the Foot.

BAUCHER'S METHOD OF TRAINING HORSES.—What Constitutes a Well-trained Horse—To make him come at your call—The Philosophy of Training—Flexions of the Jaw—Flexions of the Neck—Flexions of the Croup—Backing—The Paces—Leaping.

HOW TO RIDE A HORSE.

The Saddle—The Girths—The Stirrups—Saddle-Cloths—The Crupper—The Martingale—The Bridle—Spurs—Mounting and Dismounting—The Seat—The Hands—The Legs—The Paces—Hints for Special Cases—The Art of Falling—Riding with Ladies.

LADIES' RIDING—WRITTEN BY A LADY.—Learning to Ride—The Side-saddle—The Girths—The Stirrup—The Bridle—The Martingale—The Bit—The Dress—Mounting and Dismounting—The Position—The Hands—The Leg and Whip—Accidents.

HOW TO DRIVE A HORSE.

The Art of Driving—Pleasure Driving—How to Hold the Reins—Driving a Pair—Four-in-hand Driving—Driving Working Horses—Plowing—Three-a-breast.

RAREY'S SYSTEM OF HORSE-TAMING.—Rarey's System a New Discovery—Previous System—Principles of this System—Instructions for practicing Rarey's Method—To Stable the Horse—To Approach the Horse—Tying up the Leg—Laying the Horse Down—Finale—Vices and Bad Habits—Rearing—Kicking—Baulking—Pulling on the Halter—Shying.

VETERINARY HOMŒOPATHY.

Principles of the System—Table of Remedies—General Directions—Treatment of a Sick Animal—Diet—Remedies for Specific Cases—Glossary of Diseases.

12mo. 425 p.—Sent by mail post-paid. $1.75.

ORANGE JUDD & CO.,
41 Park Row, New York.

American Bird-Fancier ....*Paper*,.. 30.

Field, Cage, and House-Birds, breeding, rearing, etc. Paper, 12mo, 107 pp.

American Farm-Book.(R. L. ALLEN).$1.50

OR A COMPEND OF AMERICAN AGRICULTURE; Being a Practical Treatise on Soils, Manures, Draining, Irrigation, Grasses, Grain, Roots, Fruits, Cotton, Tobacco, Sugar-Cane, Rice, and every Staple Product of the United States, with the best methods of Planting, Cultivating, and Preparation for Market. Over one hundred engravings. By R. L. ALLEN. Cloth, 12mo, 325 pp.

American Rose Culturist 30

(Including the Dahlia.) Being a Practical Treatise on the Propagation, Cultivation, and Management of THE ROSE, to which are added full directions for the treatment of the Dahlia. In neat paper covers. 12mo, 96 pp.

American Weeds, and Useful Plants.$1.75

An Important Work for every Cultivator—Farmer, Gardener, etc.; being an Enumeration and Description, (with accurate illustrations), of the WEEDS and PLANTS found in American Fields and Gardens, which meet the observation, or require the attention of Cultivators; with practical suggestions for their Eradication when needed. While *practical* in its character, it includes both the common and botanical names and characters of the Weeds and Plants, with a Popular Account of the Structure of Plants. By WM. DARLINGTON, M.D., and Prof. GEO. THURBER. Thoroughly Illustrated with 277 Engravings. 12mo., 460 pp.

Annuals.............*Paper*, 50, *Cloth*, 75

THE AMERICAN HORTICULTURAL ANNUAL FOR 1867. A YEAR BOOK FOR THE GARDENER, THE FRUIT GROWER, AND THE AMATEUR. It is a beautifully illustrated volume of 168 pages. It contains an Almanac and Calendar for each month, giving hints for work in the various departments, with useful tables, and an article on Growing Grape Vines from cuttings, by William Patrick; How Horseradish is Grown for Market, by P. Henderson; Home Decorations, by A. Bridgeman; The New Apples of 1866, by Dr. J. A. Warder; New or Noteworthy Pears, by P. Barry; Small Fruits in 1866, by A. S. Fuller; Rare Valuable Evergreens, by T. Meehan, with valuable contributions by other writers.

THE AMERICAN AGRICULTURAL ANNUAL FOR 1867. A companion volume to the Horticultural Annual, and containing besides an Almanac with hints about work for each month, an Essay on Draining, by Col. Geo. E. Waring, jr.; articles on the Culture of Sorghum, by Wm. Clough; Some of the Newest and Best Potatoes, by Wm. S. Carpenter; How to Train a Horse, by S. F. Headley; Essential Features of a Good Barn, with Plan, by Dr. F. M. Hexamer; Recent Scientific Progress in Agriculture, by Prof. S. W. Johnson, of Yale College; The Culture of Wheat, by Joseph Harris, and other valuable essays upon subjects of interest to agriculturists. Finely Illustrated.

Bement's Rabbit Fancier 30

BREEDING, REARING, FEEDING, AND GENERAL MANAGEMENT of Rabbits; their Diseases and Remedies; Full Directions for the Construction of Hutches, Rabbitries, etc.; Recipes for Cooking and Dressing for the Table. Numerous Illustrations. By C. N. BEMENT, author of *Poulterer's Companion*, etc. 12mo, 101 pp., in neat illustrated paper covers.

Boussingault's Rural Economy.... .$1.60

Rural Economy in its relations with Chemistry, Physics, and Meteorology; or CHEMISTRY APPLIED TO AGRICULTURE in the Principles of Farm Management, the Preservation and Use of Manures, the Nutrition and Food of Animals, and the General Economy of Agriculture. By J. B. BOUSSINGAULT, Member of Institute of France, etc. Translated, with Introduction and Notes, by GEORGE LAW, Agriculturist. Cloth, 12mo, 507 pp.

Buist's American Flower Garden Directory..............................$1.50

Containing Practical Directions for the Culture of Plants in the Flower-Garden, Hot-House, Green-House, Rooms for Parlor-Windows, FOR EVERY MONTH IN THE YEAR with descriptions of most desirable plants, soils, transplanting, erecting a Hot-House, a Green-House, laying out a Flower-Garden, etc., etc. By ROBERT BUIST, a practical Nurseryman and Seed-Grower of Philadelphia. Cloth, 12mo, 342 pp.

Buist's Family Kitchen-Gardener....$1.00

An excellent Practical work, containing Plain and Accurate Descriptions of all the Different Species and Varieties of Culinary Vegetables, with their Botanical English, French, and German Names, alphabetically arranged; with full Directions for the Best Mode of Cultivating them in the Garden or under Glass. By ROBERT BUIST. Cloth, 12mo., 216 pp.

Chorlton's Grape-Grower's Guide 75

INTENDED ESPECIALLY FOR THE AMERICAN CLIMATE; being a practical Treatise, with Engravings, on the Cultivation of the Grape-Vine in each Department of Hot-House, Cold Grapery, etc.; with Plans for the Construction and Heating. By WM. CHORLTON. Cloth, 12mo, 204 pp.

Cobbett's American Gardener 75

A Treatise on the Laying Out and Management of Gardens. Though an old work, it is one which will find a place in every considerable library, as the production of a remarkable man. While it is marked by the author's peculiarities, it is so full of plain common-sense, that it is worthy of being kept in print. By WILLIAM COBBETT. Cloth, 12mo., 230 pp.

Cole's American Fruit Book 75

Containing Directions for Raising, Propagating, and Managing Fruit-Trees, Shrubs, and Plants, with descriptions of the best varieties of fruit, etc. 18mo, 288 pp.

Cole's American Veterinarian..........75

Diseases of *Domestic Animals*, showing the *Causes*, *Symptoms*, and *Remedies*, and rules for *Restoring* and *Preserving Health* by good management, with directions for *Training* and *Breeding*. By S. W. COLE. Cloth, 18mo., 288 pp.

Copeland's Country Life..........$5.00

An elegant Octavo Volume, containing 926 pages, and 250 Engravings. It is a Compendium of Agricultural and Horticultural Practical Knowledge; embracing Descriptions, Hints, Suggestions and Details of great value to every one interested in Fruit, Flowers, Vegetables, or Farm Crops. It describes and illustrates nearly the whole range of topics of interest to the Farmer, the Gardener, the Fruit Culturist, and the Amateur. By ROBERT MORRIS COPELAND. Cloth, beveled boards, 8vo., 926 pp.

Cotton-Planter's Manual.. ....$1.50

This is the only popular work published on the subject. It is a compilation of facts from the best authorities on the CULTURE OF COTTON, its Natural History, Chemical Analysis, Trade, and Consumption, with a history of Cotton and the Cotton-Gin. Cloth, 12mo, 341 pp.

Dadd's American Cattle-Doctor.. .$1.50.

To Help Every Man to be his own Cattle-Doctor. A work by GEO. H. DADD, M. D., Veterinary Practitioner; giving the necessary information for preserving the Health and Curing the Diseases of OXEN, COWS, SHEEP, and SWINE, with a great variety of original Recipes, and valuable information on Farm and Dairy Management. 12mo, 359 pp.

Dana's Muck Manual......, ...$1.25

A Manual for Farmers; treating of Soils, Manures, Composts, etc., and especially of the important subject of using MUCK, the great natural fertilizer of the country. By SAMUEL L. DANA. Cloth, 12mo., 312 pp.

Downing's Landscape Gardening and Rural Architecture.........$6.50

The most complete and valuable work ever issued on Landscape Gardening in North-America, for the Improvement of Country Residences; containing full Directions for everything connected with the Laying out and adorning the Rural Home, the Grounds, the Gardens, the Buildings, the Trees and Plants, etc., with principles of taste so stated as to adapt the work to all classes. Splendidly Illustrated with many Steel and fine Wood Engravings. By the late A. J. DOWNING. New Edition, Enlarged, Newly Illustrated and Revised, with Supplement, by HENRY WINTHROP SARGENT. Octavo. 534 pp. Extra cloth, gilt, beveled bds.

Dadd's Modern Horse Doctor......$1.50

CONTAINING PRACTICAL OBSERVATIONS ON THE CAUSES, NATURE, AND TREATMENT of Diseases and Lameness of HORSES; embracing the most recent and improved Methods, according to an enlightened system of Veterinary Practice, for Preservation and Restoration of Health. Illustrated. By GEO. H. DADD, M.D., Veterinary Surgeon. Cloth, 12mo., 432 pp.

Eastwood's Complete Cranberry Manual 75

Giving directions for the cultivation in different localities, with illustrations and descriptions of varieties. By BENJ. EASTWOOD. Cloth, 12mo, 120 pp.

Elliott's Western Fruit Grower's Guide 1.50

The previous Edition of this work was Thoroughly Revised; embracing all the new and valuable Fruits, with the latest improvements in their Cultivation; especially adapted to the wants of Western Fruit-Growers; full Illustrations. By F. R. ELLIOTT, of Ohio. Cloth, 12mo, 503 pp.

Field's Pear Culture.............. $1.25

THE PEAR GARDEN; a Treatise on the Propagation and Cultivation of the Pear Tree, with instructions for Management from the Seedling to the Bearing Tree. By THOMAS W. FIELD. Illustrations. Cloth, 12mo, 286 pp.

Flax Culture........................ 50

A new and very valuable work, consisting of full directions, from selection of ground and seed to preparation and marketing of crop, as given by a number of experienced growers. 8vo, paper.

French's Farm Drainage............ 1.50

The Principles, Process, and Effects of Draining Land with Stones, Wood, Drain-Plows, Open Ditches, and especially with Tiles; including Tables of Rainfall, Evaporation, Filtration, Excavation, Capacity of Pipes, cost and number to the acre. With over 100 illustrations. The best work on Draining published. By Judge FRENCH, of New Hampshire, President of Mass. Agricultural College. Cloth, 12mo, 384 pp.

Fuller's Illustrated Strawberry Culturist...................*Paper*,.. 20

A new, practical little work, meeting with universal favor. It gives a full list of varieties, down to the latest valuable seedlings. Paper, 12mo, 48 pp.

GARDENING FOR PROFIT;

In the Market and Family Garden.

BY PETER HENDERSON.

A new, finely illustrated work on Market and Family Gardening, and the first ever prepared by a Market Gardener in this country. The author is well known, and he here records his *successful experience* of eighteen years.

The Louisville (Ky.) *Journal* says of this work:

"We know of no manual on any subject that surpasses this. Every part of it displays the hand of a man thoroughly at home with his subject; it is full of sound, excellent sense, expressed in clear and concise language. We say a great deal when we say that Mr. Henderson is as complete as a writer on gardening as he is a practitioner in his gentle but laborious art."

William Saunders, Esq., of the Department of Agriculture, Washington, writes:

"It is the most practically useful work of any on the same subject. In these days of book-writing, it is refreshing to meet a work that has common sense and practical experience for its basis."

Hon. Horace Greeley thus speaks of this book in the *New York Tribune*:

"READING FOR BOYS.—This work would probably not be selected by most boys as the book for their money, wherein they would evince their usual greenness. There are marvels of transformation and rapid production recorded therein, which might well shame the dull fancy of the author of **Aladdin** or of **Kalouiala**. To know that a few rods of good land may well employ and will surely reward the constant labor of a stout man—that there are choice gold-fields all around us for those that *know how to dig*—that $1,000 may be wisely and profitably expended in draining, subsoiling, fertilizing, and deeply pulverizing a single acre—that he who would get rich by gardening must pile on manures by the hundreds of tons—that great crops always pay; half crops never—such are a few of the important truths succinctly set forth and tersely enforced in Mr. Henderson's little volume. There is no theory about it—one who has made himself rich by market-gardening, plainly tells our young men how *they* can get rich as easily as he did, and without wandering to California or Montana for it either."

SENT POST-PAID. PRICE, $1.50.

ORANGE JUDD & CO.,
41 Park Row, New-York.

Just Published.

A NEW WORK ON APPLES.

AMERICAN POMOLOGY.

APPLES.

BY DOCT. JOHN A. WARDER,

PRESIDENT OHIO POMOLOGICAL SOCIETY; VICE-PRESIDENT AMERICAN POMOLOGICAL SOCIETY, ETC.

293 Illustrations.

To pomologists a work by Dr. Warder will need no commendation. Though a citizen of Ohio, he is so sure to be at any pomological gathering, be it East or West, that the whole country claims him, and if any one has a right to entitle his work *American* Pomology it is certainly Dr. Warder. The present is the first instalment of a work intended to cover the whole ground. In it the author has attempted the difficult task of bringing apples into something like order.

This volume has about 750 pages, the first 375 of which are devoted to the discussion of the general subjects of propagation, nursery culture, selection and planting, cultivation of orchards, care of fruit, insects, and the like; the remainder is occupied with descriptions of apples. With the richness of material at hand, the trouble was to decide what to leave out. It will be found that while the old and standard varieties are not neglected, the new and promising sorts, especially those of the South and West, have prominence. A list of selections for different localities by eminent orchardists is a valuable portion of the volume, while the Analytical Index or *Catalogue Raisonné*, as the French would say, is the most extended American fruit list ever published, and gives evidence of a fearful amount of labor.

This differs from any fruit book heretofore published in this country, in its complete classification of apples. The author gives the principal European systems and modestly puts forth his own to be tested by practice. He divides apples into four classes, according to their forms. Each of these classes is sub-divided by other obvious characters, and it would seem that any apple described in the book might be easily identified. We trust that this will prove a great help to the pomologist.

Fruit-growers will welcome this book as a valuable and long-wished for addition to pomological literature, and it will be found equally useful to the novice and the experienced orchardist. The work has 293 Illustrations, is printed on good paper and well bound.

SENT POST-PAID, PRICE $3.00.

NEW YORK:

ORANGE JUDD & CO., 41 Park Row.

The Miniature Fruit Garden,

OR THE CULTURE OF

Pyramidal and Bush Fruit Trees.

BY THOMAS RIVERS.

Nothing is more gratifying than the cultivation of dwarf fruit trees, and this work tells how to do it successfully.

Dwarf Apples and Pears

are beautiful ornaments, besides being useful in giving abundant crops of fruit; they can be grown in

Small Gardens and City Yards,

and be readily removed. The work also gives the manner of training upon walls and trellises.

Root Pruning

is fully explained, and methods of protection from frosts are given.

Dwarf Cherries and Plums

are treated of as are other dwarf trees. Directions are also given for growing

Figs and Filberts.

This little work is full of suggestions to the cultivator, and like all the writings of its venerable author, bears the marks of long experience in the practice of fruit growing.

SENT POST-PAID. - - - PRICE, $1.00

ORANGE JUDD & CO., 41 Park Row.

My Vineyard at Lakeview;

Or, Successful Grape Culture.

To any one who wishes to grow grapes, whether a single vine or a vineyard, this book is full of valuable teachings. The author gives not only his success, but what is of quite as much importance, his failure. It tells just what the beginner in grape culture wishes to know, with the charm that always attends the relation of personal experience.

It is especially valuable as giving an account of the processes actually followed in

Celebrated Grape Regions

in Western New York and on the shores and islands of Lake Erie.

This book is noticed by a writer in the Horticulturist for August last as follows: "Two works very different in character and value have just been published and seem to demand a passing notice. The better and less pretentious of the two is 'My Vineyard at Lakeview,' a charming little book that professes to give the actual experience of a western grape grower, detailing not only his successes, but his blunders and failures. It is written in a pleasant style, without any attempt at display, and contains much advice that will prove useful to a beginner--the more useful, because derived from the experience of a man who had no leisure for fanciful experiments, but has been obliged to make his vineyard support himself and his family."

SENT POST-PAID. - - - PRICE $1.50.

ORANGE JUDD & CO., 41 Park Row.

BY

Cummings & Miller.

Carpenters, Builders, and Stone Cutters;

Your attention is invited to a NEW and PRACTICAL WORK ON ARCHITECTURE, giving in detail on a working drawing scale, the exterior and interior of various classes of buildings—with 382 designs and 714 illustrations, containing street fronts, suburban houses, cottages, cut stone work, &c., &c. It is 11 by 14 inches in size, containing only practical work, designs and illustrations that separately would cost hundreds of dollars.

SENT POST-PAID. Price $10.00.

ORANGE JUDD & CO., 41 Park Row.

DOWNING'S

Landscape Gardening and Rural Architecture.

The most complete and valuable work ever issued on Landscape Gardening in North America, for the Improvement of Country Residences; containing full Directions for every thing connected with Laying out and adorning the Rural Home, the Grounds, the Gardens, the Buildings, the Trees and Plants, etc., with principles of taste so stated as to adapt the work to all classes. Splendidly Illustrated with many Steel and fine Wood Engravings. By the late A. J. DOWNING. Enlarged, Newly Illustrated and Revised, with Supplement, by HENRY WINTHROP SARGENT. Octavo. 534 pp. Extra cloth, gilt, beveled bds.

SENT POST-PAID. PRICE $6.50.

ORANGE JUDD & CO., 41 Park Row.

ENDLESS AMUSEMENT

FOR

BOYS AND GIRLS.

Crandall's Improved Building Blocks, described in April number of the *American Agriculturist*, page 147, furnish a most attractive amusement for children. They are very simple in construction, will stand years of childrens' handling without breaking, and give renewed pleasure daily

CHURCHES,
DWELLINGS,
BARNS,
MILLS,
FENCES,
FURNITURE, etc.,

in almost endless variety, can be built with them, and when finished, the structure remains firm so that it can be carried about without falling to pieces.

For developing the ingenuity and taste of children they are unequaled. Having given these blocks a practical trial in their own families, the publishers of the *Agriculturist* were so well pleased with them, that they consented to take the general agency for their sale.

They are retailed at *Two Dollars* per set, of one hundred and thirty pieces, put up in a neat box, and accompanied with a card giving various designs of buildings. A liberal discount will be made to dealers. Address

ORANGE JUDD & CO.,
41 Park Row, New York.

Clipper Mower and Reaper.

This *Celebrated* and *unequaled* machine, heretofore made by H. L. Allen, of N. Y. City, is now manufactured by **The Clipper Mower and Reaper Company**, at their Works at Yonkers, N. Y., where they have unsurpassed facilities for the business. The Machine needs no encomium. Farmers throughout all sections of the country who have used it, are ready and willing to testify to its greatly superior qualities for all work, combining, as it does, more points of excellence than any machine yet made.

Its principal characteristics are: *Simplicity of construction, Durability, Ease of Draft, Portability and Completeness of Finish in all its parts.*

These Machines are made of Four Sizes, to meet the wants of any farmer, as follows:

No. 1, One-Horse machine (30 in. wheel), 3½ ft. Swath.
(The only practical One-horse machine in market.)
No. 2, Two-Horse (light) 30 in. wheel, 4 ft. Swath.
No. 3, " " (medium) 32 in. wheel, 4½ feet Swath.
No. 4, " " (large) 36 in. wheel, 4½ and 5 ft. Swath.
Made also as a Combined Mower and Reaper.

Address THE CLIPPER MOWER & REAPER CO.,
Nos. 12 & 14 Cliff-st., New York City

Sulky Revolving Hay Rake.

Send for description of this great improvement before buying any, to BLYMYER, DAY & CO., Mansfield, Ohio, or, BLYMYER, NORTON & CO., Cincinnati, Ohio.

IMPROVED FOOT LATHES.—Elegant, durable, cheap and portable. Just the thing for the Artisan or Amateur. Send for descriptive circular.
S. K. BALDWIN, Laconia, N. H.

GRINDING MILLS.—Cheapest and best in the world. Burr Stones from 8 inches to 4 feet.
EDWARD HARRISON, New Haven, Conn.

CONTINUAL LEVER and Screw Press, with Grinder attached, for Pressing Cheese, Wines, Cider, and Lard, &c. Address WILLIAM C. REA.
Pleasant Run, New Jersey.

Seymour's Grain Drill,

With Fertilizer Attachment and Grass Seeder. Warranted to Sow or Drill all Grains, Seeds, and Fertilizers, in the most perfect manner. Is light of draft, easy to operate, and is very simple and durable. Send for Circular.
Address P. & C. H. SEYMOUR,
East Bloomfield, N. Y.

PAINTS for FARMERS and others.—The Grafton Mineral Paint Co. are now manufacturing the Best, Cheapest and most Durable Paint in use; two coats well put on, mixed with pure Linseed Oil, will last 10 or 15 years; it is of a light brown or beautiful chocolate color, and can be changed to green, lead, stone, olive, drab or cream, to suit the taste of the consumer. It is valuable for Houses, Barns, Fences, Agricultural Implements, Carriage and Car-makers, Pails and Wooden-ware, Canvas, Metal and Shingle Roofs, (it being Fire and Water proof), Bridges, Burial Cases, Canal Boats, Ships and Ships' Bottoms, Floor Oil Cloths, (one Manuf. having used 5000 bbls., the past year), and as a paint for any purpose, is unsurpassed for body, durability, elasticity, and adhesiveness. Price $4 per bbl., of 300 lbs., which will supply a farmer for years to come. Warranted in all cases as above. Send for a circular, which gives full particulars. None genuine unless branded in a trade mark, Grafton Mineral Paint. Address DANIEL BIDWELL,
Proprietor, 251 Pearl-st., New York.

WHEELER'S PATENT CHAMPION ROOFING.—The best, cheapest and most durable; it can be manufactured and applied by any one. State, County and Town Rights for sale at reasonable rates.
Farm Rights, $1.50. Address W. W. GRIFFES,
Schenectady, N. Y. P. O. Box 711.

Elegance, Durability and Cheapness.

LARMORE'S WIRE FENCE WITH CAST IRON POSTS.

Also, Larmore's Wrought Iron Single and Double Trees. Can be made by any Blacksmith. Is lighter than wood and cannot be broken. State, County and Township Rights for sale. T. H. HUNT, Genl. Agt.,
Harrison Junction, Hamilton Co., Ohio

STENCIL TOOLS AND STOCK, cheapest and best. M. J. METCALF & SON, 101 Union-st., Boston, Mass.

H. W. JOHNS'

IMPROVED ROOFING

Has been in use nearly ten years, and forms a handsome and reliable roof. Can be applied by any one. **Elastic Mineral Cement**, for Repairing Leaky Shingle and other Roofs. **Preservative Paints, Roofing, Cement,** &c. Exclusive right to sell and apply will be given. Send for descriptive circular, prices, &c., to
H. W. JOHNS, 78 William St., N. Y.

THE HOG BREEDERS' MANUAL.

A Treatise on Breeding, Feeding, and General Management of Hogs. Particulars of all Diseases, Remedies, &c. Sent free of postage for 25 cents. Every farmer should have a copy. Address N. P. BOYER & CO.,
Gum Tree, Chester Co., Pa.

"$100 FOR A BRICK MACHINE SIMple; $160 with Tempering Box and Moulds, warranted to make 15,000 brick per day, of a superior quality. Address FREY & SHECKLER,
Bucyrus, O.

Chase's Patent Skiving Machine,

an indispensable article for Shoemakers, Harness and Belt makers, &c. Manufactured by JOHN W. CHASE, North Weare, N. H. Send for list of prices.

Poudrette on Buckwheat.

Double Refined Poudrette is the best Fertilizer in the world for Buckwheat—sown at the rate of 400 pounds to the acre it will double the crop—Price $25.00 per ton.
Apply to
THE LODI MANUF'G CO.,
66 Cortlandt-st., New York.

OFFICE OF "Passaic Carbon Works,"
129 FRONT STREET, (CORNER MAIDEN LANE).

LISTER BROTHERS,

MANUFACTURERS OF

PURE BONE DUST,

Fresh Bone Superphosphate of Lime,

Animal Charcoal, Ivory Black, &c.

Orders for the above articles manufactured at our Works on the *Passaic River, N. J.*, should be addressed to
LISTER BROTHERS, 129 Front-st., New York.

GREEN-HOUSE AND HOT-BED SASH.—The undersigned would respectively call your attention to their extensive facilities for manufacturing Sashes for Florists and Gardeners, by which means we are enabled to furnish our patrons at a much lower rate of prices than any other establishment in the city. Particular attention paid to all orders, and furnished at the shortest notice. N. B.—Hot-bed Sashes constantly on hand. WM. H. COLES & CO., Office: 79 Nassau-st., New York.

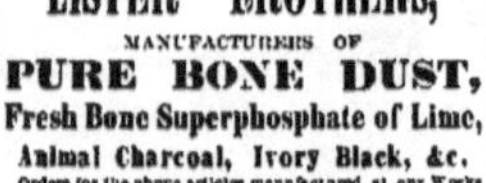

PERRY'S GRAPE VINES

Are rapidly attaining the merit they justly deserve. Planters and Dealers, and those wishing to form clubs for the sale of the only vines in the country grown by my improvement, and to which none others can compare in health and vigor, either for Garden or Vineyard planting, should send immediately for my Price List or my liberal terms to Clubs. Planters will please state about the number of each variety they wish, and whether for spring or fall planting. My Illustrated and Descriptive Catalogue contains as correct a description of the different varieties of grapes I grow, as ten years' experience in propagating and fruiting vines will admit. Price 10 cents, less than cost. Address
F. L. PERRY, Canandaigua, N. Y.

Bell's Berry Presses.

We would call the attention of Farmers and Housekeepers to these presses—they are capable of expressing the juice from all kinds of berries, are cheap and durable, and of sizes to suit, and should be in possession of every housekeeper and farmer. Call and see them.
PETER C. DENSEL, Agent,
at Lorton's Clock Store, No. 1 Cortlandt-st., New York.

10,000 lbs. of Imported Swede and Ruta-baga Turnip Seed. 10,000 American Purple Top and White Flat Turnip Seed for sale low to the Trade. To Farmers—One pound or more sent by mail on receipt of 75 cents. For sale by C. B. ROGERS,
No. 133 Market-st., Philadelphia, Pa.

The Best are the Cheapest.

The MASON & HAMLIN CABINET ORGANS are acknowledged to be the best instruments of this class in the world. It is the policy of these makers to produce *none but the very best work*. They aim at success, not by using poor material and economizing in workmanship, so that their instruments can be sold at a little less price; but by producing the most durable, reliable, and in all respects the best work possible, and selling it at the very lowest rates at which such work can possibly be afforded, and at the same prices to all.

They now manufacture more than sixty different styles of Organs, varying in price from $75 to $1,000 each. These instruments contain all the latest improvements, some of which are not to be found in other instruments, the right to their exclusive use having been purchased by M. & H., in some cases at very large expense.

MASON & HAMLIN have been awarded several times as many highest premiums, at Industrial Fairs, as any other maker, having received fifty-six within a few years.

They present in their Circulars the printed testimony of a large majority of the most eminent Organists, Pianists, Singers and Composers in the country to the superiority of the instruments of their make.

It is certainly economy in purchasing an instrument of this class to *get the best*, although the first cost may be a little more, as a poor instrument will soon get out of order and become comparatively worthless.

☞ It should be remembered that the recommendations of dealers are not always reliable, as there is great temptation for them to recommend those instruments on which they can make the largest profit; and makers of inferior work can afford the largest discounts. Mason & Hamlin have fixed their retail prices so low that they can afford only very small discounts at wholesale, and hence the temptation to dealers to recommend and sell other instruments is great.

Circulars with full descriptions, illustrations, and prices of the different styles, with hints on what constitutes, and how to select a good instrument, sent free to any one desiring them. Address MASON & HAMLIN,
596 Broadway, New York,
Or, 154 Tremont-st., Boston.

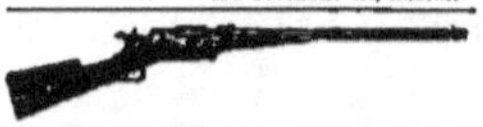

ROPER'S NEW AMERICAN BREECH LOADING REPEATING SHOT GUN, firing four shots in two seconds, using ordinary ammunition. Manufactured by ROPER REPEATING RIFLE CO., Amherst, Mass. Under personal supervision of C. M. SPENCER, Inventor of the famous SPENCER RIFLE. ☞ Send for Circular. ☜

LAMB KNITTING MACHINE

The only *Family Machine* that sets up its own work, knits all sizes, widens and narrows, knits the heel into the stocking, and narrows off the toe complete—producing all varieties of knit goods, from an infant's stocking, mitten or glove, to a lady's shawl or hood.

It is *simple, durable* and *easily operated*. Agents wanted. Send for a Circular and Sample of Work.

Address (inclosing stamp)
LAMB KNITTING MACHINE CO.,
Rochester, N. Y., or Springfield, Mass.

INVALIDS' WHEEL CHAIRS,

for in or out-door use, $20 to $40. INVALIDS' CARRIAGES to order. PATENT CANTERING HORSES, $12 to $25. CHILD'S CARRIAGES, Swings, etc. Send for Circulars.
S. W. SMITH,
90 William-st.,
NEW YORK.

Stereopticons and Magic Lanterns,

With the Improved Lime Light, illuminating brilliantly two hundred square feet of canvas, and magnifying the views to that size, at an expense of less than one dollar for a whole evening's exhibition. Easily managed and pays well.

Illustrated priced catalogue of the apparatus, with list of over two thousand artistically colored photographic views on glass, of the War, Scripture History, Choice Statuary, etc., etc., forwarded on application. T. H. McALLISTER, Optician, (of late firm of McAllister & Bro., Phila.,) 49 Nassau street, New York.

HOMES FOR THOUSANDS.—Enclose two 3-cent stamps and address ITH. S. BEALL,
Real Estate Agent, Mt. Ayr, Iowa.

TURNIP SEED! TURNIP SEED!

By Mail.

	℔ lb.	℔ oz.
Early Dutch	$1.50	10
German Teltow [illegible]	2.00	20
Red Top Strap Leaf	1.00	10
White Strap Leaf Flat	1.00	10
White Flat, Globe	.75	10
White Norfolk	.75	10
Cow Horn	1.00	10
Long White French	1.00	10
Long White Tankard	1.00	10
Veitch's New Long White	1.50	10
Long Yellow French	1.50	10
Yellow Malta	1.50	10
Yellow Stone	1.00	10
Yellow Aberdeen	1.00	10
Robertson's Golden Ball	1.50	10
New Yellow Finland	2.50	20
Dale's Hybrid	.75	10
Improved Yellow Swedish, or Ruta Baga	1.00	10
White Ruta Baga	1.00	10
Laing's Ruta Baga	1.00	10

ALSO

SEEDS OF

	℔ lb.	℔ oz.
Corn Salad	$1.00	15
Green Curled Endive	2.50	30
Brown Dutch Lettuce	4.00	40
Chinese Winter Radish	4.00	30
Black Spanish "	1.50	15
Round Spinach	.75	10
Prickly "	.75	10

All the above mailed free of postage, on receipt of the amount annexed.

J. M. THORBURN & CO.,
15 John-st., New York.

TO FARMERS AND STOCK RAISERS.

I HAVE FOUND the most practical results from giving one to two feeds a day of Root Crops; Turnips, Sugar Beets and Mangel Wurzel. They render the corn less heating. A bushel of Roots is equal to a bushel of Corn fed alone. N. C. N. American Stock Journal.

Large Orange Carrot	per lb.,	$1.00
Large White Field Carrots	"	1.00
Large Yellow Altringham Carrots	"	1.00
White Sugar Beets	"	[illegible]
Long Red Mangel Wurzel	"	[illegible]
Yellow Globe "	"	[illegible]
Red Top Strap Leaved Turnip	"	[illegible]
White "	"	[illegible]
Long White French "	"	1.00
Yellow Aberdeen "	"	[illegible]
Yellow Martha "	"	1.00
Robertson's Golden Ball "	"	1.00
Red Tankard "	"	[illegible]
White Tankard "	"	[illegible]
Orange Jelly "	"	1.00
Waite's Hybrid Eclipse "	"	1.00
Skirving's Improved Ruta Baga	"	.75
Purple top " "	"	.75

Forwarded per mail, 8 cents per lb. additional.

WASHBURN & CO.,
Seed Merchants,
Horticultural Hall, Boston, Mass.

PURE NEW CROP TURNIP SEED of my own raising, sent by mail. Purple-top Flat, 1 lb., 60 cents; 4 lbs., $2.00. Yellow or Swedish, 1 lb., 75 cts; 4 lbs., $2.00.
JOHN S. COLLINS, Moorestown, New Jersey.

PETER COOPER'S
GELATINE
WILL MAKE
DELICIOUS JELLIES
WITH GREAT EASE.
ALSO,
BLANC MANGE, CHARLOTTE RUSSE, Etc.

DIRECTIONS FOR USE WITH THE PACKAGES.

For sale by Grocers and Druggists. Depot, No. 17 Burling-Slip, New York.

THE PERPETUAL (WATCH CHARM) CALENDER—size of a two cent piece—with plain, masonic and temperance emblems, needed by every body every where. Price by mail, electroplate, with enameled figures and letters, 50 cents, gold, ditto., $1.50.

Address
E. MADEN, 161 Broadway,
Room 3, New York, P. O. Box, 5578.
Active Agents wanted every where.

PATENT BOOKHOLDER, Writing-Desk and Ladies Work-Table Combined. Convenient, portable, and easily adjusted. Sent anywhere, paid, on receipt of $5. Also several valuable Patents for sale.
JOHN CONNACHER & CO., 9th Broadway, New York.

FOR SALE.—A splendid Estate of 1,000 acres prime land, on the Potomac River, 13 miles from its mouth, 120 miles from Washington and Baltimore. 500 acres open, under good Chestnut fence. Land very productive. Fine for stock raising, Grasses, Corn, Wheat, &c. Finest body of land in Eastern Virginia. Apply to W. H. HARDING, Real Estate Agent, No. 4 N. Green-st., Baltimore, Md.

Turnip Seed by Mail.

The following varieties, the quality of which can not be excelled, will be mailed *post-paid*, to any address in the Union upon receipt of price affixed:

	per oz.	¼ lb.	8 oz.	pound
Early White Dutch	10 cts.	25 cts.	60 cts.	$1.00
White Strap Leaf	10 "	25 "	60 "	1.00
Red Top Strap Leaf	10 "	35 "	60 "	1.00
Large White Globe	10 "	30 "	45 "	75
Large White Norfolk	10 "	30 "	45 "	75
Yellow Aberdeen	10 "	25 "	60 "	1.00
Golden Ball (Robertson's)	10 "	25 "	55 "	1.00
Large Yellow Globe, extra	10 "	35 "	60 "	1.00
Long White French	10 "	35 "	65 "	1.10
Long White or Cow Horn	10 "	35 "	65 "	1.10
Yellow Finland	15 "	50 "	90 "	1.75
Waite's Eclipse, fine	10 "	35 "	60 "	1.00
German Teltow	15 "	50 "	90 "	1.75
Improved Ruta Baga	10 "	35 "	60 "	1.00
Skirving's do.	10 "	30 "	45 "	75
Laing's do.	10 "	30 "	45 "	75
Dale's Hybrid	10 "	30 "	45 "	75

Packets for retailing, full size, per dozen.............60 cts.
do do. half size, do ....35 cts.

Prices to dealers by the quantity given upon application. Our celebrated Seed Catalogue and *Guide to the Vegetable and Flower Garden*, containing 130 pages, *beautifully illustrated*, will be mailed to all applicants enclosing 25 cents.
Address B. K. BLISS, Springfield, Mass.

Winter Seed Wheat for 1867,

FOR SALE BY

GEORGE A. DEITZ,

IMPORTER AND GROWER OF

SEED WHEAT & GRASS SEEDS.
CHAMBERSBURGH, PA.

Italian Red Mediterranean,	$2.25	℔ peck.	$8.00	℔ bush.
Italian White "	2.25	"	8.00	"
Hungarian Red "	2.00	"	8.00	"
French Red "	2.00	"	8.00	"
Hallet's Eng'h Red "	2.25	"	8.00	"
German Red "	2.25	"	8.00	"
Hallet's Eng. White, "	2.25	"	8.50	"
Diehl's White,	1.50	"	6.00	"
Canada White,	1.50	"	5.00	"
Boughton White,	1.50	"	5.00	"
California White,	1.50	"	5.00	"
Blue Stem White,	2.00	"	7.00	"
Egyptian Red Mediterranean,	1.50	"	5.00	"
Red Chaff "	1.50	"	5.00	"
White Chaff "	1.50	"	5.00	"
Lancaster Red Chaff "	1.50	"	5.00	"

☞ Four pounds of either of the above varieties will be sent by mail (free of Postage) for one dollar. G. A. D.

The Land of Low Taxes!

REAL ESTATE AGENCY,

SIMON J. MARTENET, No. 6 South-st., Baltimore. *Author and Publisher of the large new MAP and ATLAS of MARYLAND.*

Persons desiring to locate, or purchase property in Baltimore, or the State of Maryland, by consulting this Agency, will have the benefit of the advertisers thorough knowledge of the City and State, acquired in eighteen years experience at Surveying in Baltimore, and ten years spent in getting up his State Map and Atlas. MARYLAND TAXES about one-third that of Northern States.

Fruit-Farm and Nursery for Sale.

The CELEBRATED POMONA FRUIT-FARM AND NURSERY of J. W. Dodge, on the Cumberland Table Lands of East Tennessee. Unequaled as a fruit growing region. Beautiful Tract of 400 acres, with rich Prairie. Good improvements, large Orchards of finest Fruits. SEVEN FIRST PREMIUMS awarded by the State and Division Fairs, to fruit from the POMONA ORCHARDS. Fine opportunity for Nursery business. Can be made a superior stock or Dairy Farm. Must be sold immediately. Price moderate. For particular description, terms, &c., address J. W. DODGE & SON,
Pomona, Cumberland County, Tennessee.

CHEAP FARMS.

Enterprising men do well in moving to the Eastern Shore of Maryland. Land sells at great bargains; the climate is mild; growing seasons long; soil good; close to Balt. & Phila. markets. Send for free price and descriptive list of farms.
MANCHA & ZOOK, Greensboro, Md.

FRANKLIN TRACT.—20,000 ACRES on Railroad, Gloucester Co., New Jersey, 25 miles south of Philadelphia, good soil, mild, healthful climate. Low prices, in lots to suit purchasers. Pamphlets with map and full information sent free. Address MORRIS & CO., Newfield, Gloucester Co., N.J. Improved Farms for sale.

MEAD'S GRAPE CULTURE.

American Grape Culture and Wine-Making.

By PETER B. MEAD.

Profusely Illustrated. 8vo, Cloth, $3 00.

It is the best book on the subject that we have seen.—*Evening Post.*

There is no cultivator so advanced that he will not find his own ideas quickened into greater clearness and accuracy by reading it, and beginners will find it a thorough and safe guide in all that relates to the vine.—*From Letter of* Dr. C. W. GRANT.

HARPER & BROTHERS *will send the above work by mail, postage prepaid, to any part of the United States, on receipt of $3 00.*

SCHOOL TEACHERS WANTED.—The Subscriber wishes to employ for each town in the United States, male teachers who have formerly been engaged, either in Day schools or Sunday Schools, who can devote their exclusive time to the business, to canvass for the "*Illustrated History of the Bible*," by John Kitto, D. D., F. S. A., edited by Alvan Bond, D. D., of Norwich, Conn.

This is the best selling book I have ever published. Agents make from $100 to $200 per month, and say "they never knew a book to sell so well." Apply immediately in person or by letter to the publisher.
HENRY BILL, Norwich, Conn.

Chester White Pigs.

$12 to $15 each; $20 to $25 per pair, 8 to 12 weeks old. CASHMERE ANGORA GOATS!—Arrive this fall from Asia! *Engage now.* Send for terms.

EGGS: for 6 weeks to come of over 100 varieties of fowls! This year's fowls can be engaged now, at *low rates*. *Breeders and Fanciers* come and visit us and our stock, and see if we have not *extra superior specimens*. Send for Catalogue, Terms, &c., with 2 stamps (6 cents). Address
"THE COX FARMS," care J. C. COX & CO.,
Osborn, Greene Co., Ohio.

N. B.—Best of *References given*, if necessary, but our stock shows for itself, when people come to see it.

THOMAS FITCH,
of New London, Conn.,

Breeder of *Alderney* and *Ayrshire* Stock of all descriptions, has constantly on hand and for sale the best Animals of each of the above breeds, at reasonable prices. Warranted as represented.

PREMIUM CHESTER WHITE PIGS for Sale.—Sent by Express to all parts of the United States. For Circulars and Prices, Address N. P. BOYER & CO.,
Gum Tree, Chester Co., Pa.

PREMIUM CHESTER WHITE PIGS for SALE by the Original Shipper. Send for a Circular on their Breeding and management. Address
THOS. WOOD, Doe Run, Chester Co., Pa.

PURE BRED BERKSHIRE PIGS boxed and shipped to any part of the United States, from Tivoli, Peoria Co., Illinois, by S. B. EMERY.

FANCY FOWLS' EGGS OF MOST VARIETIES, PLATA DUCKS, birds and eggs, Aylesbury Ducks, eggs only. Send for Circular. A. M. HALSTED,
Agent, 68 Pearl st., New York.

BRAHMA POOTRAS, bred from stock weighing 21 lbs. to 28 lbs. per pair, at maturity. Warranted pure. Price $8 per pair; $12 per trio. Eggs, $1 per dozen. Address N. P. BOYER & CO., Gum Tree, Chester Co., Pa.

AMERICAN STOCK JOURNAL, a first class monthly, containing 36 large double column pages, only 50 cents for 6 months. Try it! Will save every farmer many dollars, as we offer a Horse and Cattle Doctor free. Address N. P. BOYER & CO., Gum Tree, Chester Co., Pa.

ITALIAN BEES—New Importation just received. Queens, progeny of above, ready for delivery after July 20, 1867. Send for Circular. M. QUINBY, St. Johnsville, N. Y.

$1. $1. $1. $1. $1.

You have a Wheeler & Wilson Sewing Machine? Send for a pair of **Patent Sewing Machine Castors.** Ladies can, themselves, immediately attach them to the legs of either end of the machine, and will not then need to call upon husband, father or brother to do the lifting.

The machine stands firmly on the floor, but by slightly tipping it, it will rest upon the castors and move easily about the room. It being desirable to move it every day for the purpose of sweeping where it stands, or for a more convenient position for working than the one it usually occupies, you will find it just the thing wanted. We send them by mail, postage paid, to any part of the U. S. on receipt of $1. Agents wanted in every Town or County in the U. S.
Most excellent inducements offered.

Address H. B. FANTON, 491 Broadway, New York.

INGERSOLL'S IMPROVED
HORSE AND HAND POWER
HAY AND COTTON PRESSES,

These machines have been tested in the most thorough manner throughout this and foreign countries to the number of over 800.

THE HORSE POWER is worked by either wheel or capstan, and in many respects possesses unequalled advantages. We invite those wanting such machines to write for a catalogue containing full information with cuts, prices, &c., or call and examine personally.

Orders promptly attended to, by addressing
INGERSOLL & DOUGHERTY, Greenpoint, Kings Co., L. I.

A Clean Sweep Every Day
FOR ALL TIME.
The Silver's Patent Broom

Enables every farmer to use brush of his own raising, and have a better broom in every respect than can be bought at the store. *It is so simple that a child can put it together.* The parts (except the brush,) will *last a life time*, and the brush can be renewed in a *few* minutes.—See editorial description in this number of the *Agriculturist*, also cut of Broom on page 57, February number, and recommendations, etc., on page 217, June number.

Those who do not raise their own brush, will also find it the cheapest as well as the best article in the market, it being adapted to city and country.

AGENTS WANTED throughout the country; exclusive territory given. Sample, and full instructions for putting together, sent prepaid, on receipt of $1.50.

Address C. A. CLEGG & CO.,
506 Broadway, New York.

SPECIAL
ADVERTISING AGENCY.

Advertisements from reliable parties only, inserted in the Agricultural, Religious, and other first-class mediums throughout the country, by the undersigned.

An experience of several years in conducting the advertising department of the American Agriculturist, gives superior facilities for satisfactory transaction of such business.

W. A. FITCH, 151 Nassau-st., New York.

AMERICAN AGRICULTURIST

FOR THE

Farm, Garden, and Household.

"AGRICULTURE IS THE MOST HEALTHFUL, MOST USEFUL, AND MOST NOBLE EMPLOYMENT OF MAN."—WASHINGTON.

ORANGE JUDD & CO., PUBLISHERS AND PROPRIETORS. Office, 41 Park Row, (Times Buildings.)

ESTABLISHED IN 1842. Published also in German at $1.50 a Year.

$1.50 PER ANNUM, IN ADVANCE. SINGLE NUMBER, 15 CENTS. 4 Copies for $5; 10 for $12; 20 or more, $1 each.

Entered according to Act of Congress in July, 1867, by ORANGE JUDD & CO., in the Clerk's Office of the District Court of the United States for the Southern District of New-York.

VOLUME XXVI—No. 8. NEW-YORK, AUGUST, 1867. NEW SERIES—No. 247.

[COPYRIGHT SECURED.]

BELGIAN BULLS.—FROM A PAINTING BY DE HAAS.—*Copied for the American Agriculturist.*

Flemish, Belgian, and Dutch painters are perhaps tempted to devote themselves to animal painting, more than the artists who live among more diversified natural scenery. De Haas is a much [illegible] favorite, and his pictures have great power of showing [illegible], and a [illegible], which is [illegible] is a genuine experience, or real scene. In the rugged outlines of these bulls there is no taming down of bad [illegible] points to suit a "thorough-bred" [illegible] effort to make an ugly beast [illegible]. There is an awkward [illegible] in the swaying round of the great carcass of the [illegible] is very natural, and a soft[illegible] of the [illegible] one, which does not [illegible] at all [illegible] of the swelling muscles beneath, as the bulls arrange the preliminaries, and take positions for a grand tussle. We [illegible] tirely the effect [illegible] best [illegible] through a roll of paper, these fine effects will come out much plainer than otherwise. The original is owned by Mr. George Jones, one of the proprietors of the *N. Y. Times*, and is valued at $2,000. Its size is only 20 by 30 inches.

We never witness two steers, or cows even, with locked horns, trying one another's pluck, but we think of the poor adaptation of our best yokes, to secure for us the full power of the willing ox. There is a concentration of force in the forehead of the bull, or of any animal of the ox kind, which we hardly find in any other creature, except, perhaps, the elephant. The horse draws properly by his shoulders, but the ox's shoulders are not [illegible]. We make him draw by the top of his neck, where the projecting spines of his backbone are somewhat protected by a [illegible] band, and by [illegible] part of his hide [illegible] no circumstance can he exert his full strength upon the yoke. If yoked by the head, a practice prevalent over most of Europe, and among Spanish Americans, the forehead, pressing against a padded yoke, becomes the point of power. The concentrated energies of every muscle and sinew of the body operate through the forehead upon the load, just as in a fight between bulls, they each concentrate, with the greatest ease, their whole muscular strength in their heads. It is safe to say that in this country we *never* make use of the whole strength of our oxen. This subject has been repeatedly alluded to in the *American Agriculturist*, in the hope that some one, who uses oxen in farm work, would so break his steers, and report the results. The experiment needs to be made with care, and the animals well broken, before being tried with heavy loads. No one who has watched a fight can doubt the correctness of this principle of yoking.

Contents for August, 1867.

INDEX TO "BASKET," OR SHORTER ARTICLES.

Back Volumes Supplied.—The back volumes of the *Agriculturist* are very valuable. They contain information upon every topic connected with rural life, out-door and in-door, and the last ten volumes make up a very complete library. Each volume has a full index for ready reference to any desired topic. We have on hand, and print from stereotype plates as wanted, all the numbers and volumes for ten years past, beginning with 1857—that is, Vol. 16 to Vol. 25, inclusive. Any of these volumes sent complete (in numbers) at $1.75 each, post-paid, (or $1.50 if taken at the office). The volumes, neatly bound, are supplied for $2 each, or $2.50 if to be sent by mail. Any single numbers of the past ten years will be supplied, post-paid, for 15 cents each.

AMERICAN AGRICULTURIST.

NEW-YORK, AUGUST, 1867.

After the rush and weariness of harvest is over, together with the anxieties attendant on the press of summer work, when the crops are growing well, when corn is beyond hoeing, and buckwheat and turnips all sowed, farmers and their families ought to enjoy a few holidays. The Fourth of July finds us in the midst of hoeing, and haying, and cutting grain. We need an August festival, and as there is none in our national or popular calendar, we ought to take each his independent little play spell for a visit to a friend; or in neighborhood parties, to go into the mountains, or to the sea-side, and bake clams, catch fish, and make chowder.

Farmers ought to visit one another, and the agricultural clubs and societies of adjoining towns or counties can do few wiser things than appoint committees to visit and report upon the farming practices of their neighbors in the districts which lie just beyond the circuit of ordinary communication. The relaxation will be conducive to happiness and health, and to the enlargement of ideas. The crop of new thoughts which will be sown or garnered in new fields, will be worth more to any wide awake man, or women, than months of plodding at home.

The long continuance of rains and prevailingly wet weather has in some measure disturbed the regularity of the harvest. Grain, as usual, has been deemed of more importance than grass, and so the latter has suffered, if either. In many cases, both have been caught; cutting at the proper time has been delayed, and injury has occurred to crops that grew and matured finely. Too ripe grass makes poor hay. The remedy is one which very few farmers will apply. It is to cook or steam the hay. If this is done, the hardest and ripest hay becomes digestible and is readily eaten, and seeds of sorrel, dock, and daisies are killed. Those who steam their fodder express the view that even very poor food is thus made equal to the best uncooked. Certain it is, that with a slight flavoring of oil-cake or corn meal, all is eaten up, and the stock thrive.

If we have any dry weather this summer, it will probably come in August, and afford opportunity to do the usual drought work. The muck swamps will call for a good deal of labor from all who value swamp muck as they should, in their barn-yards and compost heaps. In draining swamps, the outlet is first determined upon and, if the ditch is to be an open one, as is usually the case, the trench is begun at that place. This is different from the way of laying tile-drains, because, if the tiles were laid first at the outlet, they would be filled up with silt from the muddy water which would flow through them as long as any work was done at the drains above, and longer too. Swamps covered with alders and other shrubs and small trees, are best cut over in winter, and then the next summer, when dry, they may be drained, the stumps and roots pulled out by oxen, and laid in heaps to dry, while the rest of the land is grubbed over or plowed, if dry enough. A man of a little contrivance will devise several ways of using the power of oxen or horses to great advantage in this work. Chains and strong levers, and perhaps a pair of blocks and tackle, singly or in combination, will tear out any of the stumps and roots of common peaty swamps. The peat or muck should be thrown out in heaps to dry, and it is best to top the heaps with that which is most earthy and crumbly, as this prevents the more dense or "fat" portions from baking into hard lumps. Thus treated, after a few weeks it may become dry enough to compost with lime, and be made fit to use in the stables as an absorbent of liquid manure. If, however, it bakes very hard and lumpy, though composted, it will hardly be made fine and dry enough, but will have to be exposed to freezing through the cold season. After that, it will probably need no other treatment to be made fit for use.

In regard to the draining of lands in general, the American farmer can have no safer or better guide than the work of Col. Waring just published, which is especially full in regard to the preliminary examination and surveys needed. Much land besides the swamps proper, is best drained in August.

The hospitalities of the country are extended to the city in the heat of summer. If bestowed and accepted with that consideration which husbands should exercise for their wives, and friends for friends, these visits of city cousins, of sons with their families, and of old friends with wives and babies, will bring great enjoyment and good to all.

The man or woman who overworks and breaks down in the hot weather, has much less chance to build up again, and become strong and well, than if the prostration occurred in the more bracing weather of other seasons. Farmers, beware of overworking your sons, allow no excuse for laziness, but impose only light work, not straining to back or muscles. The small stature and crooked forms of many once promising and handsome boys tell too plainly against their fathers, who willingly accepted all the hard farm work which the energy and pride of their sons prompted them to perform.

Hints About Work.

Animals at Pasture.—Look to the water supply, and see that no animals suffer for it. Nothing but absolute starvation pulls them down in condition faster than thirst. In the very hottest and dryest weather, horses get little good in the field, unless they have thickets and woods to stand in, and get away from flies. It is best to stable horses during the heat of the day, if one has no use for them, and turn them out towards night. Flies are exceedingly annoying on damp days, when storms are approaching, and at such times horses should be taken in. Give salt regularly, or keep it in sheltered troughs, always accessible to cattle and sheep at pasture, away from the sea shore, where, from 10 to 20 miles inland, it is regarded as unnecessary.

Sheep should have their noses tarred; rams should be separated from the ewes, and lambs of suitable age and vigor, weaned. In weaning lambs, put the ewes on the dryest pastures, but leave the lambs where they are accustomed to be, with a few large wethers for flock-leaders. They should be out of hearing of one another's calls. The ewes should be driven several evenings into pens and examined, and if their bags are tender, caking, or hot, they should be milked.

Milch Cows need regular feeding with some green fodder as the pastures get dry; yarded, and thus fed in the evening, the gain in manure, to say nothing of the milk, pays well for the trouble.

Swine.—Give plenty of green food. If there are no weeds to pull or mow for them, then cut clover or grass. The trimmings along fences, and sods cut wherever the ordinary field culture cannot extend, are excellent. Some fresh earth, either upon the roots of weeds or in sods is essential to health. Charcoal is very beneficial, and plenty of fresh water desirable. At all events, the hogs should have daily a good drink of pure water, no matter how liquid their usual food, and last, not least, they should have a dry, clean, bed at all seasons.

Wounds upon animals, at this season of flies and quick putrefaction, need the most prompt attention. We know of no better application than hot pine tar, (not hot enough to burn.) It may be put on alone, or as a plaster upon a piece of cotton cloth. Look especially to the heads of rams.

Poultry.—It is desirable to shorten the moulting season as much as possible. To this end feed well and give range, or green food, daily. Make the most liberal provision for their dust-baths; a box with mixture of coal and wood ashes, sifted, and kept where it will never get wet is best. Give them the range of stubble fields, if possible.

Corn.—Little good will be done by plowing or hoeing after the first of August. Weeds should be pulled by hand if they grow large. Let the suckers alone; they are often needed for fertilizing the tips of the ears. If corn is blown down, it is usually best to let it get up as it best can, yet if the field be entered at once, certainly within 12 hours, it may be helped a good deal. Take care not to crack the stalk, bend it, or injure the roots as is often done.

Tobacco needs constant attention, worming, and suckering, to throw the whole growth into the leaves until they are ripe. This may be known by a certain turgid and swollen look which the surface assumes, quite distinct from that of the growing leaf. The plants must then be cut at the ground, in the heat of the forenoon, turned repeatedly and with great care not to break the leaves, and, when wilted enough to handle easily without breaking, hung in airy sheds, or buildings made for the purpose. We believe the best mode of hanging to be that described in the *Agriculturist* for March, 1864, (p. 76,) as practiced by Mr. Joseph Reader, of Bordentown, N. J. The plants are hung upon long cords by taking half hitches about the butts. The cords are drawn up as fast as the plants are put on, and fastened at the top of the building, as close as they can hang, and a moderate circulation of air, above, below, and through the plants, given.

Turnips.—Sow early in the month, and up to the 10th or 15th below latitude 40°, putting them in wherever there is ground not otherwise occupied. A sprinkling of bone-dust or superphosphate of lime, with wood-ashes, will tell finely upon the crop.

Buckwheat may be sowed on ground not liable to early frost, as late as the first of the month, perhaps, and make a crop—but sowed any time before the 20th, it will make a fine mass of green manure to be plowed in as soon as it is touched by frosts, or when blossoming freely, if frosts hold off.

Wheat.—Land intended for winter wheat will probably need once or twice plowing and harrowing, and if a good dressing of fine compost can be applied, all the better. Sow at the end of this month or first of next. Use the drill. Put wheat on well drained or naturally dry land. If it does not winter-kill, water in the soil will prevent the crop being profitable. Wheat needs thorough tillage.

Oats.—Harvest before fully ripe, and thus secure better straw for feeding, and equally good grain.

Seed Grain.—The selection should be made at harvest time, when the best grain is allowed to get fully ripe before cutting. If this is not done, select at once the best sheaves, have them threshed, and cull out the best kernels by repeated winnowings.

Stacks.—Examine as soon as they have time to settle, and re-top, thatch or straighten them up, if necessary, using braces set against upright planks.

Grass and Clover.—If the object in bringing any field under the plow is to get it in good grass again, it is often best to sow the seed by itself as soon as the land is in proper condition. Grain detracts from the subsequent grass crops. Timothy, orchard grass, and blue grass may be sown by themselves in August or September. Use an abundance of seed, bush it, and roll it in, with a light dressing of ashes, guano, or fine compost. Clover may also be sown now, but spring sowing is usually preferred. Roll clover seed in gypsum, and sow both together or separately; one ton to ten acres is the common rule.

Water.—Look out for a water supply when springs are low, and tile-drains are generally dry or discharging very little water. Take levels, and see if you may not bring water in pipes to the house or stock-yard, and dig basins in the pastures. If wells are to be dug, or if digging them has been suspended on account of much water, a time of drought is favorable for this work. No farmer should be satisfied until he has good wells or running water close to, or in, his barn or stock-yards.

Implements for which there is no more use this season, should be cleaned, painted, the steel parts covered with linseed oil, and put away.

Brush in Pastures and Fence Rows.—Cut close to the ground, and lay the tops off to give the sun a fair chance at the roots. It will pay to lift a fence after cutting off the brush, and tear up the ground with a heavy plow, and then re-set the fence. Should rains occur, or if the ground be moist, and the brush start again freely, enclose sheep upon the land, stocking so heavily that they eat everything off close, and give the roots no chance to breathe.

Weeds.—Go over grass land, cutting docks, dandelions, burdocks, thistles, nettles, wild teazles, mulleins, with a "spud." Wild carrots and asters must be mowed off as soon as they throw up their seed stalks, and long before the first blossom.

Bogs.—Cut the heads or tussocks at the surface level, splitting the big ones, and lay them up to dry for burning. Much good bedding stuff may be cut from bog land this month; it should all be secured.

Orchard and Nursery.

The attention of the fruit grower will now be demanded by the early ripening products of his orchard. In the southern fruit regions, the harvest has already begun, and supplies are rapidly coming forward by rail. Peaches, this year, are more abundant than they have been in years past, and only the best prices will be brought by selected fruit. In gathering the larger fruits for marketing, a knowledge of the manner of ripening of the different varieties is important. As a general rule, the fruit should remain upon the tree until it is well formed, but not until it softens or mellows. It should reach the retailer in sound condition.

Assorting.—This is a more profitable operation than is generally supposed, and the larger the fruit, the better does it pay to make at least two qualities by selection. Where careful thinning has been done, there will be less to go with the second quality.

Careful handling, at every step, from gathering the fruit from the branch, to the final delivery of the packages, is essential to its reaching the distant market and the customer in good order.

Pears are, almost without exception, improved by early picking and ripening in-doors.

Ladders of various kinds should be in readiness, and should be self-supporting. We have, during the past year, figured several ladders of this kind.

Insects, especially the moths, may be sensibly diminished if the fallen fruit be gathered up, and fed to the swine. Plant lice are easily killed by strong soap, or tobacco water, and some prefer a mixture of the two. The great trouble is, that these pests come in such numbers, and are usually on the very ends of the twigs, where they seem so inaccessible, that they are generally allowed to have their own way. There are now many efficient and cheap engines for throwing washes into trees.

Budding will continue, and may be done wherever the bark of the stock runs freely, and good buds can be obtained. The maturity of buds may be hastened by pinching off the ends of those shoots from which they are to be taken. The usual order is cherry, plum, pear, apple, cherry on dwarf (Mahaleb) stock, peach, and quince. The stocks budded earlier should be looked to, and the tying not allowed to become too tight.

Layer Shrubs, protect seed beds from scorching, and *gather tree seeds* as directed last month.

Fruit Garden.

As the fruits ripen in succession, the surplus will need to be preserved in some form. Bottling or canning is of course the best plan, but drying is better than no method of preserving. Some hints on this matter are given in our household pages.

Blackberries are to be kept low and in a compact form, as recommended on page 294.

Dwarf Trees.—Pinch in rampant shoots, especially on young fruit trees, and continue to rub out those that push where they are not wanted. Fruit may still be thinned, especially of those kinds that grow in clusters, and are apt to harbor insects. Pick early varieties of pears for house ripening.

Grapes.—Mildew should not be allowed to get the upper hand. The timely dusting of sulphur will usually arrest it. We last year figured the bellows used for the purpose. Keep growing shoots tied up to stakes and trellises. We know of no better way to deal with caterpillars than hand picking. Where the number of vines is not large, frequent and persistent search will soon free them of these destructive agents.

Raspberries.—The general way is to remove the old canes in spring, but in garden culture it is but little trouble to cut them away as soon as the fruit is off, and give the new canes full scope.

Strawberries.—In a large way spring planting is preferable, but small beds may with proper care be advantageously made in autumn. Indeed, where the precaution has been taken to start the runners in small pots, they may be set at any time. Where plants are grown in row or hill culture, the runners are to be kept off, and weeds pulled from the rows.

Weeds.—Clean culture is as necessary in the fruit garden, as elsewhere. A mellow soil is secured by frequent working, and there will be much less suffering from drouth if the soil is stirred or mulched.

Water only when absolutely necessary, as it sometimes will be with trees set last spring; remove the surface soil from over the roots, water abundantly; when it has soaked away, replace the earth.

Kitchen Garden.

If weeds have been industriously kept down, this month will be one of comparative leisure to the gardener. Still he must look out for his future interests in the careful saving of seeds, and occupy ground cleared of early crops with such late ones as may be desirable and which have time to grow.

Asparagus.—Old beds will only need to have the coarse weeds pulled out. Seed beds, properly hoed and thinned, will give better plants at a year old than those neglected and over-crowded will furnish at the end of two years.

Beans.—The bush varieties may be planted for late crops, and to give a supply for salting.

Beets.—Give plenty of room in the rows, and thin.

Cabbages and Cauliflowers.—Plants, especially in the warmer States, may be set for a late crop. Lime will destroy slugs, and also prevent club-foot.

Carrots.—Hoe, thin, and weed, and if young roots are desired, seed of the early sorts may be sown.

Celery.—Plants may still be set with the prospect of fair-sized roots by frost. Keep the earlier planted free of weeds, and the soil mellow by frequent use of the cultivator or hoe. At the end of the month commence to earth up the more advanced plantings.

Corn.—Save seed from the finest and earliest ears.

Cucumbers will need picking over every day, or every two days at least, if small pickles are wanted.

Egg Plants.—Caterpillars will often make great havoc with the leaves, and must be picked off. Give liquid manure, and keep the heavy fruits from contact with the ground by the use of mulch.

Endive.—Transplant a foot apart each way, and sow seeds for the latest crops and for winter use.

Herbs.—Cut and dry as they begin to flower.

Lettuce.—Sow small quantities for succession.

Melons.—Increase the size and quality of the fruit by preventing the vines from overbearing. Save seed only from those varieties that have grown at a distance from other plants of the same nature.

Onions.—Harvest as soon as the tops fall over. Those that are to be stored for winter should be thoroughly dried. Take up onion sets, dry them, and spread with their tops on in an airy loft, putting them not over four inches deep.

Radishes.—Sow early sorts, if wanted so late in the season. The best winter radish is the Chinese Rose-colored Winter, which may be sown now or later, and treated in all respects like turnips. If sown too early, it will get overgrown.

Spinach.—Some may be sown for fall cutting, but the crop for next spring's use should not be put in until next month.

Squashes.—Seed of the early kinds should be secured. Let the vines of the running sorts take root at the joints. Crush all the eggs found on the underside of the leaves. Examine often.

Sweet Potatoes.—If the soil be kept mellow and free from weeds, there is no difficulty in getting a satisfactory crop. At the North, it is not advisable to allow the vines to root at the joints, nor is it well to clip them, as it diminishes the crop.

Tomatoes.—The great enemy to the tomato is the

one that causes such annoyance to the tobacco grower. A large and most voracious green "worm," the larva of one of the Sphinges. It spares neither leaves nor green fruit, but eats its way in the most unrelenting manner, until nothing but the firmer stems are left. Fortunately, its copious droppings give unmistakable evidence of its presence, and he must be a careless cultivator who allows the "worm" to get much the better of him. Pick off the fellow and crush him, using gloves if you are squeamish; though repulsive, it is harmless.

Turnips.—Ruta-bagas may be sown early in the month, and the early sorts at the end. As soon as up, dust with lime, or a mixture of equal parts of plaster and ashes, to keep away the "flea," or fly.

Weeds.—We only repeat our frequent caution to always keep a little ahead of these.

Flower Garden and Lawn.

This is the month in which the lover of flowers perhaps gets less return for his labor than in any other. All the early flowering things are gone, and there are not enough of the later ones in bloom to give the garden a very attractive appearance.

Lawns are to be mowed, and if the clip is light, leave it, especially on new lawns, to serve as a mulch to the roots. See that the roots of the grass do not run into beds cut in the lawn, and give

Grass Edgings the same care. Coarse weeds, like plantains, thistles and dandelions in lawns and edgings, must be pulled up by hand.

Chrysanthemums.—These, so appreciated in autumn, their season of bloom, are too often neglected in their early growth. Thin out useless branches, and leave only a few strong ones. We prefer to grow them with three good stems, and then pinch these to make them throw out laterals. The hairy caterpillars seem to be very partial to these plants, and they should not be allowed to suffer from their depredations.

Roses.—The free use of the knife on the constant bloomers will keep up a new growth and a succession of flowers. Of course, the slug and all other enemies, must be kept in check by whale oil soap or tobacco water. Tobacco smoke is the best thing for Aphis. We use a "crinoline," made of stiff paper, which is simply to confine the smoke for a few minutes; as soon as the lice are stupefied, a smart showering will finish them.

Fuchsias, as bedders, are a mere provocation; they do well until hot weather, and then shed leaves and buds, and go into a state of rest. There are a few varieties that will not do this, but of these we unfortunately have lost the names. With those that thus unpleasantly strip themselves, the best way is to prune them rather severely, and when the heat moderates, they will push anew and give late flowers. Start new stock from cuttings.

Dahlias.—These are grand for a few weeks before frost, but, except the dwarfs, or "Bouquet Dahlias," we think that in small grounds they are more trouble than they are satisfaction. It is all sticks and strings, and picking off grasshoppers, and looking after borers. It is best not to allow the tall-growing sorts to bloom in this hot weather.

Gladiolus is a great boon to the gardener, as it is good single, in groups, or in beds. Keep the stems erect by neat stakes, and as fast as the lower flowers are past their prime, pull them off.

"*Foliage Plants,*" a name that we despise, but which we use for want of a better, may be made much more effective by judicious cutting. Coleus—the best of them—is much better when cut back and kept bushy. This remark does not apply to Cannas and things that do not branch freely.

Propagation of bedding stuff for another year should now go on. There are but few things of which the old plants are of much value, and it is much better to lay in a stock of new plants to winter over in the green-house. Those who have no green-house had better buy each year. Those who have, should start a stock of plants.

Seeds.—As a general rule, sow seeds of perennials as soon as ripe. Some of the hardy annuals, such as Pansies, Larkspurs, etc., are best when fall sown. It is by taking advantage of every accidental perfection that improvement is made. Like does not always produce like, but the seeds of the best flowers are most likely to give good results.

Green and Hot-Houses.

Now that the most of the plants are out, all repairs may be made. Have the heating apparatus in order long before there is any need of it. See that the plants that are left in the house do not get sun-burned, overrun by insects, or suffer for proper watering. Lay in supplies of all needed articles, such as loam, sand, moss, and pots. The plants out-of-doors must not be neglected. Insects will make havoc, sun will scorch the evergreen things, worms will get into the pots, heavy winds will break down tender things, and dogs and cats, and other domestic animals, will do mischief if they have access to the plants. Many good florists are coming to the belief that, take it altogether, the majority of hot-house plants are safer in doors than out, if properly shaded and well ventilated.

Cold Grapery.

As the fruit is ripening, sudden changes of temperature will be injurious and must be avoided, though free ventilation is to be practised. Stop watering when the fruit begins to ripen, and when it is ripe, keep the upper ventilators open at night. If mildew appears, use sulphur freely, upon the floors, and keep the air of the house very dry.

Apiary in August.—*Prepared by M. Quinby.*

Look well to the weak colonies now, whether old or new, as all such are liable to injury from the moth worm. Ascertain the cause of weakness; if it is an old stock, and has over-swarmed, or is queenless, or if the queen is barren, supply the deficiency. If it lack bees, give a comb or two, filled with sealed brood; this will hatch without any further attention from the bees. If the stock be a new one which never was strong, it is easily helped in this way. Any colony intended for winter should be made strong this month. If without movable combs to operate with, it is generally best to break up the hive, and secure the contents. This also is the best thing to do with a badly diseased hive. Where there is much buckwheat, it would sometimes pay to drive out the bees to begin again in an empty hive. If they made only a few combs, this would be more valuable for another year than many think. In sections where there is no buckwheat, and the honey sources are clover and basswood, more honey will be obtained by taking up all condemned colonies early in the month. Since the commencement of fruit blossoms, the season here has been propitious. June was a swarming month. Very many stocks will store entirely too much honey in the hive to make it safe for winter. The remedy for those in the old box hive is only partial. Boxes for surplus should at once be added, and room to work inside given to all. The boxes should be furnished with all the clean, nice, white comb you can supply, that they may be tempted to fill them. With movable comb hives, the matter is easily controlled by removing full combs, and replacing them with empty frames or empty combs. Put the empty ones near the centre, alternating with full ones, moving full ones outward. The full combs can be set away, and given to any late swarms that do not obtain sufficient winter stores. When not wanted thus, they may be saved for the table. This honey may not be of the purest quality, yet the quantity obtained in this way, over any method of boxing, ought to compensate considerably. Set shallow dishes with sweetened water among the hives at night to take moths.

Cider.—What is the best steam or horse-power cider-press? Those who have good ones would do well to advertise. We have inquiries for them every year, and would be glad to learn, from those who have good ones in use, how they work, and which is best.

Commercial Matters—Market Prices

The following condensed, comprehensive tables, carefully prepared specially for the *American Agriculturist*, show at a glance the transactions for the month, ending July 15, 1867, and also for the same month last year:

1. TRANSACTIONS AT THE NEW-YORK MARKETS.

RECEIPTS.	*Flour.*	*Wheat.*	*Corn.*	*Rye.*	*Barley.*	*Oats.*
26 days *this* m'th	134,000	121,000	983,000	67,000	29,000	381,000
25 days *last* m'th	142,000	213,000	1,341,000	24,000	63,000	437,000

SALES.	*Flour.*	*Wheat.*	*Corn.*	*Rye.*	*Barley.*
26 days *this* month,	271,000	576,000	1,880,000	167,000	74,000
25 days *last* month,	113,000	829,000	1,764,000	246,000	160,000

2. *Comparison with same period at this time last year.*

RECEIPTS.	*Flour.*	*Wheat.*	*Corn.*	*Rye.*	*Barley.*	*Oats.*
21 days 1867....	134,000	121,000	983,000	67,000	29,000	381,000
21 days 1866....	291,000	538,000	4,050,000	109,000	67,000	1,311,000

SALES.	*Flour.*	*Wheat.*	*Corn.*	*Rye.*	*Barley.*
26 days 1867.....	271,000	576,000	1,880,000	167,000	74,000
21 days 1866....	283,000	430,000	3,612,800	199,000	—

3. *Exports from New York, Jan. 1 to July 15:*

	Flour.	*Wheat.*	*Corn.*	*Rye.*	*Oats.*	*Barley.*
1867.....	270,011	60,989	4,423,462	135,561	101,250	960,726
1866.....	491,437	111,551	4,780,118	187,190	[illegible]	......
1865.....	781,000	819,429	[illegible]	111	43,247	......

4. *Stock of grain in store at New York:*

1867.	Wheat, bush.	Corn, bush.	Rye, bush.	Barley, bush.	Oats, bush.	Malt, bush.
July 15...	113,500	180,790	54,946	21,330	206,773	31,700
June 14...	374,279	217,704	117,257	60,643	[illegible]	14,711
May 15...	131,330	203,004	190,804	113,706	608,191	16,101

Business has been influenced very slightly by the rise in gold during the past month.... An active demand prevailed for the leading kinds of produce. Breadstuffs have have been quite freely purchased for home use, shipment, and on speculation; but prices have been unusually variable. Toward the close, the demand has been good for desirable lots of flour, wheat, and oats, at steady rates. Corn has been in better supply and heavy. A considerable amount of new wheat has been received from the South, chiefly in small quantities. Most of it has been in fine order, and quick of sale, to the local millers. The receipts of California wheat have been less extensive.... Provisions have been in fair request. Pork and lard closed in favor of sellers, under a partial revival of the speculative demand. Beef has been very scarce, and wanted. Butter and cheese have been quiet and heavy in price, under liberal offerings.... Hay, hops, and cotton have been less active, and are depressed in price.... Wool has been unusually dull. Manufacturers have been reluctant to purchase freely, in view of the extreme depression in the market for goods. Holders have been rather eager to realize, and prices have declined, closing irregularly. Stocks are moderate for the season, but are largely in excess of the current wants of the trade.... Tobacco has been in active demand, chiefly for export, at former range.

CURRENT WHOLESALE PRICES.

	June 11.	July 12.
PRICE OF GOLD	137	139[illegible]
FLOUR—Super to Extra State	$ 10 [illegible] @ 17 00	$ 7 00 @ [illegible]
Super to Extra Southern	10 30 @ 15 50	9 [illegible] @ [illegible]
Extra Western	[illegible] @ 16 50	[illegible]
Extra Genesee	[illegible]	[illegible]
Superfine Western	[illegible]	[illegible]
RYE FLOUR	[illegible]	[illegible]
CORN MEAL	[illegible]	[illegible]
WHEAT—All kinds of White	[illegible]	[illegible]
All kinds of Red and Amber	[illegible]	[illegible]
CORN—Yellow	[illegible]	[illegible]
Mixed	[illegible]	[illegible]
OATS—Western	[illegible]	[illegible]
State	[illegible]	[illegible]
RYE	[illegible]	[illegible]
BARLEY	[illegible] @ 1 25	Nominal.
HAY—Bale, ⅌ 100 lb	[illegible]	[illegible] @ 1 40
Loose	[illegible]	[illegible]
STRAW, ⅌ 100 lb	[illegible]	[illegible]
COTTON—Middlings, ⅌ lb	[illegible]	[illegible]
HOPS—Crop of 1866, ⅌ lb	[illegible] @ 65	[illegible] @ 65
FEATHERS—Live Geese, ⅌ lb	[illegible] @ 80	[illegible] @ 80
SEED—Clover, ⅌ lb	11 @ 13	11 @ 12½
Timothy, ⅌ bushel	3 [illegible] @ 3 [illegible]	3 [illegible] @ 3 25
Flax, ⅌ bushel	3 10 @ 3 25	3 10 @ 3 [illegible]
SUGAR—Brown, ⅌ lb	9¾ @ 12½	10½ @ 13
MOLASSES, Cuba, ⅌ gal	47 @ 80	[illegible] @ 55
COFFEE—Rio, (Gold price) ⅌ lb	13½ @ 19	14 @ 18½
TOBACCO, Kentucky, &c., ⅌ lb	4 @ [illegible]	4 @ 30
Seed Leaf, ⅌ lb	3 @ [illegible]	4 @ [illegible]
WOOL—Domestic Fleece, ⅌ lb	[illegible]	40 @ [illegible]
Domestic, pulled, ⅌ lb	30 @ 52½	30 @ 55
California, unwashed,	22 @ 38	17 @ 30
TALLOW, ⅌ lb	11 @ 11½	11½ @ 11½
OIL CAKE—⅌ ton	50 00 @ 55 00	50 00 @ 54 00
PORK—Mess, ⅌ barrel	21 50 @ 21 75	23 00 @ 23 12
Prime, ⅌ barrel	18 70 @ 18 75	19 50 @ 19 75
BEEF—Plain mess	11 50 @ 21 00	18 00 @ 24 00
LARD, in barrels, ⅌ lb	12 @ 13	12 @ 13½
BUTTER—Western, ⅌ lb	10 @ 21	13 @ 21
State, ⅌ lb	15 @ 28	14 @ 30
CHEESE	7 @ 16	7 @ 13½
BEANS—⅌ bushel	3 00 @ 4 00	3 00 @ 4 0[illegible]
PEAS—Canada, ⅌ bushel	1 [illegible] @ 1 40	1 20 @ 1 25
EGGS—Fresh, ⅌ dozen	20½ @ 23½	17 @ 21
POULTRY—Fowls, ⅌ lb	15 @ 15	16 @ 18
Turkeys, ⅌ lb	15 @ 25	15 @ 20
POTATOES—Mercers, ⅌ bbl	3 00 @ 3 25	
Peach Blows, ⅌ barrel	3 50 @ 3 75	2 25 @ 2 50
POTATOES—Buckeye, ⅌ bbl	3 [illegible] @ 4 00	
New Southern, ⅌ barrel		3 00 @ 6 50
APPLES—⅌ barrel	5 50 @ 7 70	4 00 @ 5 00
CRANBERRIES, ⅌ barrel	12 00 @ 20 00	

New York Live Stock Markets.—

WEEK ENDING.	Beeves.	Cows.	Calves.	Sheep.	Swine.
June 18	[illegible]	77	[illegible]	21,909	17,835
June 25	[illegible]	14	[illegible]	[illegible]	15,917
July 2	6,911	53	2,845	19,149	[illegible]
July 9	[illegible]	21	1,647	[illegible]	[illegible]
July 16	[illegible]	53	[illegible]	[illegible]	[illegible]
Total in five Weeks	[illegible]	[illegible]	10,841	[illegible]	[illegible]
Average per Week	[illegible]	41	2,411	[illegible]	[illegible]
do. do. last Month	5,179	[illegible]	[illegible]	14,461	[illegible]
do. do. prev's Month	5,415	[illegible]	2,117	11,012	[illegible]
Average per Week, 1866	5,749	94	1,270	20,000	[illegible]
do. do. do. 1865	5,255	119	1,500	[illegible]	11,023
do. do. do. 1864	5,161	115	[illegible]	15,315	[illegible]
do. do. do. 1863	5,150	129	694	9,941	21,670
Total in 1866	[illegible]	[illegible]	[illegible]	1,040,000	672,000
Total in 1865	[illegible]	6,161	[illegible]	[illegible]	[illegible]
Total in 1864	[illegible]	[illegible]	[illegible]	[illegible]	[illegible]
Total in 1863	264,091	6,470	35,705	519,316	1,101,617

Beef Cattle.—The five weeks which our report covers are remarkable for the fluctuations in prices of beef animals. The decline in prices commenced at the close of our last report. They continued easily dropping a little, until a rush of stock, coming unexpectedly and undesired on a holiday week, caused a collapse in the market, such as has very rarely been observed. This will be fairly shown by the estimated average of prices for each week. June 18th, 17c., June 25th, 16@16¼c., July 2d, 13@13½c. July 9th, 15¾c., July 16th, 16@16¼c. This is accounted for by a reduction of railroad tolls, the hot weather, together with the abundance and excellence of lamb, salmon, and small fruits in market, which lessened the demand for beef for the city trade. We quote at present, extra beef, 17½@17¾c. per lb., estimated dressed weight; good average bullocks, 13½@16¼c., and poor, 11½@15½c. **Milch Cows.**—The supply and demand are both so small that it seems almost a farce to continue the enumeration and estimate of prices. A really good cow will bring—say $80 to $120, and this variation depends both on the quality of the cow and the chances of a purchaser, poor cows selling at a little less than they are worth for beef, generally. **Calves.**—The price of veal has been influenced in a measure by that of beef, the closing quotations being the result of a continual though gradual decline. We may state the general range of prices as about 8 to 12 cents per pound, live weight; 11c. being about the average, and very choice calves bringing a little more than 12c., and grass calves, 4 to 7c. **Sheep and Lambs.**—There has been an improvement in the quality of both sheep and lambs since last month, but we are getting too many poor, thin lots of sheep now. Prices about 6½@7¾c. for good mutton sheep, live weight, the poorer grades selling at 4@5c. Lambs bring 8@12c., according to size and fatness. The stock of the week was large, but as those figures have been approached gradually, only a very short supply of sheep or falling off in some other department would cause a marked improvement at once.... **Swine.**—The market has been subject to a fluctuating supply, and prices have varied accordingly. They now stand at 7¼@7¾c. for good, fair hogs.

The Fairs for 1867.

State Agricultural Fairs.

New England	Providence, R. I.	Sept. 3- 7
California		Sept. 9-13
New Hampshire	Nashua	Sept. 10-12
Michigan	Detroit	Sept. 10-13
Vermont	Brattleboro	Sept. 10-13
Kentucky	Louisville	Sept. 17-20
Ohio	Dayton	Sept. 23-27
Wisconsin	Madison	Sept. 23-27
Canada West	Kingston	Sept. 23-27
Kansas	Lawrence	Sept. 24-27
Pennsylvania	Pittsburgh	Sept. 24-27
Indiana	Terre Haute	Sept. 30-Oct. 4
Illinois	Quincy	Sept. 30-Oct. 5
New York	Buffalo	Oct. 1- 4
Minnesota	Rochester	Oct. 1- 4
Iowa	Clinton	Oct. 1- 4
Missouri	St. Louis	Oct. 7-12
Tenn. Ag'l & Mech. Ass.	Clarksville	Oct. 15-19
Maryland	Baltimore	Oct. 29-31

Horticultural Meetings and Fairs.

American Pomological	St. Louis	Sept. 11-14
Queens Co., N. Y.	Mineola, L. I.	Sept. 25-27

Horse Fairs.

N. Y. Horse Fair	Buffalo, N. Y.	Aug. 13-16
U. S. Horse Exhibition	Springfield, Mass.	Aug. 27-30
Orange Co. Horse Fair	Goshen, N. Y.	Sept. 11-12

County and Local Fairs.

NEW YORK.

Cayuga Co.		Sept. 17-19
Duchess Co.	Washington Hollow	Sept. 17-20
Putnam Co.	Carmel	Sept. 18-20
Ulster Co.	(Fair Grounds)	Sept. 24-26

PENNSYLVANIA.

Bucks Co.		Sept. 24-26
Cumberland Co.		Oct. 1- 4
Chester Co.	Westchester	Sept. 26-28
Susquehanna Co., Pa.	Montrose	Sept. 11-12
Union Co.		Oct. 2- 4
Warren Co.	Youngsville	Sept. 18-20

OHIO.

Ashtabula Co.	Jefferson	Oct. 9-11
Athens Co.	Athens	Oct. 2- 4
Belmont Co.	St. Clairsville	Sept. 25-27
Champaign Co.	Urbana	Oct. 1- 4
Clarke Co.	Springfield	Sept. 10-13
Clermont Co.	Boston	Sept. 17-20
Clinton Co.	Wilmington	Sept. 18-20
Cuyahoga Co.	Newburgh	Oct. 8-11
Defiance Co.	Defiance	Oct. 15-17
Delaware Co.	(Fair Grounds)	Sept. 24-26
Erie Co.	Sandusky	Oct. 1- 4
Franklin Co.	Columbus	Sept. 10-13
Fulton Co.	Ottokee	Sept. 25-27
Geauga Co.	Burton	Sept. 18-20
Geauga, (Free)	Claridon	Sept. 23-25
Greene Co.	Xenia	Sept. 4- 6
Guernsey Co.	Cambridge	Oct. 1- 3
Hamilton Co.	Carthage	Sept. 3- 6
Hancock Co.	Findlay	Oct. 3- 5
Harrison Co.	Cadiz	Oct. 2- 4
Huron Co.	Norwalk	Oct. 2- 4
Jackson Co.	Jackson	Oct. 2- 4
Lake Co.	Painesville	Oct. 2- 4
Lawrence Co.	Ironton	Sept. 25-27
Lorain Co.	Elyria	Oct. 1- 4
Lucas Co.	Toledo	Oct. 2- 4
Madison Co.	London	Sept. 18-20
Marion Co.	Marion	Oct. 1- 4
Medina Co.	Medina	Oct. 2- 4
Miami Co.	Troy	Oct. 2- 5
Morgan Co.	McConnellsville	Oct. 1- 3
Morrow Co.	Mt. Gilead	Oct. 2- 4
Portage Co.	Ravenna	Oct. 18-20
Preble Co.	Eaton	Sept. 17-20
Putnam Co.	Ottawa	Oct. 2- 4
Richland Co.	Mansfield	Oct. 2- 4
Sandusky Co.	Fremont	Oct. 2- 4
Seneca Co.	Tiffin	Oct. 9-12
Stark Co.	Canton	Oct. 1- 4
Trumbull Co.	Warren	Sept. 17-19
Tuscarawas Co.	Canal Dover	Sept. 25-27
Union Co.	Marysville	Oct. 9-11
Van Wert Co.	Van Wert	Oct. 3- 5
Warren Co.	Lebanon	Sept. 11-13
Wayne Co.	Wooster	Oct. 9-11
Wyandotte Co.	Upper Sandusky	Oct. 1- 3

TOWN, OR INDEPENDENT FAIRS.

Jamestown "Union,"	Greene Co.	Aug. 28-30
Uhricksville	Tuscarawas Co.	Sept. 10-12
Richfield	Summit Co.	Sept. 18-20
Blanchester	Clinton Co.	Sept. 21-27
Orwell	Ashtabula Co.	Sept. 24-26
Conneaut	Ashtabula Co.	Sept. 25-27
Garrettsville	Portage Co.	Oct. 1- 3

ILLINOIS.

De Kalb Co.	De Kalb	Sept. 25-28
Greene Co.	Carrollton	Oct. 15-18
Henderson Co.	Biggsville	Oct. 9-11
Jo Daviess Co.	Galena	Sept. 24-27
Mercer Co.	Millersburgh	Sept. 24-26
Montgomery Co.	Hillsboro	Oct. 1- 4
Pike Co.	Pittsfield	Sept. 24-27
Stark Co.	Toulon	Sept. 24-26

INDIANA.

Morgan Co.	Martinsville	Sept. 3- 7
Spencer Co.	Rockport	Oct. 2- 5

IOWA.

Kossuth Co.	Algona	Sept. 27
Mahaska Co.	Oskaloosa	Sept. 11-13

MAINE.

Franklin Co.	Farmington	Oct. 1- 3
York Co.	Saco and Biddeford	Oct. 8-10

MISSOURI.

Jefferson Co.	De Soto	Sept. 25-27
Pike Co.	Ashley	Sept. 17-20
St. Louis Ag'l & Mech.	St. Louis	Oct. 7-12

MASS.—Franklin Co., Greenfield	Sept. 27-28
N. J.—Hunterdon Co., (Flemington?)	Sept. 24-26
KY.—Washington Co.	Oct. 18-21
Mason & Bracken Co., Germantown	Sept. 10-14
TENN.—Maury Co., (At old grounds)	Oct. 8-12
WIS.—Outagamie Co., Grand Chute	Sept. 17-19
NEB.—Douglass Co., Omaha	Sept. 24-26

Crop Reports and Prospects.

The high prices which have prevailed thus far during the year for all kinds of provisions, make the crop prospects a theme of unusual interest. Everybody watches the weather, and consults the papers, and dreams at night of the crops. In the main the reports from all parts of the country are favorable, and there is every indication of a bountiful harvest. As we go to press, we are in the midst of the summer fruits, of which there has been an abundance, with the exception of cherries, which have been a failure in the east. Forty cents a pound in the retail market would indicate a general dearth of this fruit throughout the land. Strawberries were never better. They have been so abundant, and the prices ruled so low in the glut of the market, that in some places we have heard of, they were left to rot upon the vines. But these were not the largest and best kinds. Fine berries always sell well in the New York market. Raspberries have been abundant, and sold at good prices. We have never known a glut of this fruit. Currants have been plenty and cheap. The market is improving for this fruit, and we have seen large quantities of the Cherry and other large varieties at 10 to 20 cents per pound at wholesale.

The wheat harvest of the South is gathered, and has been a great relief to the necessities of the famishing districts. The reports made to the Agricultural Department at Washington show an increased acreage of twenty per cent. devoted to this grain, and the yield has been among the best upon record. In the large wheat growing districts of Pennsylvania, and the States lying west, they are gathering the wheat crop, under the most favorable auspices, as we go to press. It is admitted on all hands that the wheat never looked better, and, in recent years, has not been less troubled with insects, rust, or falling down. Reports from the newspapers in Missouri are highly favorable. The weather is fine, and the yield of wheat bountiful. In Central and Southern Illinois the harvest is glorious, and the earth burdened with countless stacks of the golden sheaves. All through Southern Kansas there is an unusually large crop. In Western New York, the appearance of the crop is said to be encouraging. The wheat crop is heavier than it has been for years, and the area of ground sown having been enlarged, there will be a handsome yield. From these and many other reports, we think the yield of this grain cannot be less than two hundred millions of bushels, and from present appearances, it will be gathered in good condition.

Rye is much less cultivated, but has a good report from all quarters. Oats and barley are doing well in the sections where they are raised.

It is too early to prophesy concerning Indian corn, which is the king cereal of our country. Its prospects have been somewhat damaged by the cold and rain of May and June, but it is now looking of good color. Reports generally are favorable. July and August make the corn crop.

The season has been very favorable for grass and hay. Butter and cheese have been plenty, and of good quality. The hay crop will be abundant wherever the soil is in good condition. We are now in the midst of the hay harvest, and it is generally admitted to be abundant.

The large promise of apples and pears will not be realized in the East, probably not more than an average crop, which indicates a good market in New York for all the fruit the West can send us. Of grapes it is too early to speak, though the vines are said to be looking well. Peaches in Jersey and Delaware will be plenty.

The great crops of the South, corn, cotton, and tobacco, are doing quite as well as could be expected under the circumstances. In the Mississippi Valley there were extensive breaks in the levees, and wide spread destruction therefrom. In other parts on the sea-board there have been excessive rains and overflows, but the damage is confined to the low lands in the river valleys. In some parts there are complaints from the freedmen, that they are diverted from their labor by political speakers, who are anxious to indoctrinate them in their duties as citizens. But notwithstanding these drawbacks, the reports from the South are in the main of a cheerful character. The freedmen are better paid, and work better than last year. The feeling for the future, growing out of the prospects of the crops, is very hopeful and jubilant. In North Mississippi they have devoted three-fourths of their land to breadstuffs; the cotton looks healthy, but suffers for lack of the boc. About Jackson, they are trying German laborers, and are pleased with the change. In Western Tennessee, two-thirds of the land is said to be in corn and the small grains, which last have been gathered with a fair yield. We have recently conversed with a large planter, from Southwestern Georgia, who reports the negroes as working well generally; oats a good crop, and, being fed unthreshed, a great relief to working animals; wheat very good, corn looking well, and fruits abundant. The cotton crop is promising, and planters in his section estimate it at not less than three millions of bales. We have seen this estimate made in other responsible quarters. The apprehension is felt that the crop may be so large as to carry prices down below a remunerative point. In spite of the tax, which we think a great blunder on the part of the Government, cotton is likely to be the main crop in the Gulf States for generations to come. On the whole, the crop prospects are eminently satisfactory, and indicate a profitable trade for the coming fall and winter.

THE CROPS OF EUROPE.—The prices of grain in this country depend very much upon those of Europe. Almost all our surplus crosses the Atlantic, and a heavy European demand, or the prospect of wars, which will interrupt the regular supplies, at once puts our prices up. It is still too early to be able to judge of the wheat crop of Europe. By the last advices the weather was so good, that, though the stock of wheat in first hands was reduced so low that its amount could hardly be estimated, yet markets were dull, and the general expectation of a full harvest caused an unsettled state of prices, which will no doubt continue until the question is settled, and the harvest in good part over. In Great Britain, a large part of the hay had been secured in unusually good order, and though the weather was cold and unfavorable for grains, yet, with an abundance of hay, farmers were feeling very well satisfied.

A New Era in Poultry Breeding in America.

We have expressed ourselves plainly in regard to the sad demoralization of most poultry breeders who raise birds for sale. That the grossest frauds are intentionally and unintentionally practiced, will not be denied. One reason is that poultry fanciers in this country have no sure standard of excellence to guide them. Judges at fairs decide awards upon the same principles that they would judge of hogs or sheep, without knowing the very accurate and uniform points of color, of form and feather, by which the various breeds of poultry are raised and judged of in Europe, and among poultry fanciers of intelligence in this country. Now a society of energetic men has been formed to disseminate knowledge, to correct faulty standards, and establish good ones. We know many of the gentlemen who formed the society, and believe that it was done from the real love of beautiful domestic poultry and their breeding. Some have, and will have, birds for sale, others have not, and never will have, but in the society they meet as lovers of poultry, and breeders, and not as merchants. We hope much from their exhibitions and from their annual reports, but more from the spirit of honorable rivalry, of thoroughly honest dealing, and of fair investigation, which seems to animate all. The members of the society are now located at the North, East, and West, others will join from the South, and by interchange of birds, and opinions, and free discussions at the gatherings of the society, it is not too much to expect a new era in poultry breeding in America. We append a brief report of the meeting for organization.

THE AMERICAN POULTRY SOCIETY.—Pursuant to the call noticed in the July number of the *American Agriculturist*, a meeting was held at the Cooper Institute, in this city, July 10th. Those present represented several States of the Union, and much enthusiasm prevailed, all agreeing in the desirability of establishing a Poultry Society, national in character. A committee, consisting of Messrs. A. M. Halsted, S. M. Saunders, and J. C. Thompson, submitted a draft of a constitution, which, after thorough discussion, was unanimously adopted. The first article indicates the purpose of the society. It is as follows: "This association shall be called 'The American Poultry Society.' Its object shall be to increase interest in, and promote the improvement of poultry breeding and management in this country, by adopting standards of excellence, by public discussions and exhibitions, by collecting and disseminating intelligence, and by such other reasons as may be deemed advisable." The terms of membership fixed upon, are the the payment of $5 a year. The names of thirty-eight gentlemen were enrolled as members, and the following officers were chosen to hold their places until the annual election, to be held the second Wednesday in October. *President*, J. G. Finnie, Esq., 11 Wall-st., New York; *Vice President*, James E. Mallory, Tarrytown, N. Y.; *Recording Secretary*, W. A. Fitch, *American Agriculturist* Office, New York; *Corresponding Secretary*, C. M. Saunders, corner Cedar and Pearl-streets, New York; *Treasurer*, J. C. Thompson, Tompkinsville, Staten Island, N. Y.; *Auditor*, A. M. Halsted, 68 Pearl-st., New York. These form the Executive Committee.

Editorial Jottings in Europe.

[MR. JUDD, in making a summer's tour on the other side of the Atlantic, went for the express purpose of securing *rest*, though expecting to glean much information which will be indirectly useful to our readers hereafter. He expressed the determination to abandon his pen and everything that has the slightest connection with work for the mind. Still, he sends home occasional social letters, and we shall take the liberty to give some brief extracts that will interest others, perhaps, as well as ourselves.—ASSOCIATE EDITORS.]

.... *Mid-Atlantic, June 3d*, 1867.—For five days we have been driven eastward by both steam and wind power, about 300 miles every 24 hours. Our good ship, the "Tripoli," tossed and rolled by the waves, like a floating cork, though built wholly of iron, keeps her straight onward course, regardless of wind or tide. As usual, I refuse any tribute to Old Neptune. Most of our company make at least an hourly contribution. I already begin to feel the exhilaration of absolute freedom from business cares, and every day's journey is adding to the broad sea wall that separates me from routine work. I really *feel* free for once—the first time in a dozen years, or more. Five years ago to-day I was in precisely the same latitude and longitude, and for the same object, but the depressing anxiety for the fate of the armies and of our country, gave little reason for calm quietude, and the disasters to our soldiers on the Peninsula, magnified by the interested London editors who were holders of Confederate Bonds, so distressed me that I hastened home, worse jaded than when I set out. God grant that no troubles, political or financial, may this year interfere with the quietude and rest I seek.

.... *Cork, Ireland, June 10th*.—All well. Yesterday afternoon we were landed at Queenstown, in less than 11 days' running time from New York, despite several days of severe storm. I could wish every friend crossing the ocean might have as good a ship as the Tripoli, and as good officers as Capt. Martyn and his associates.... Not a single profane word has been heard from officer, crew, or passengers, and not even a discourteous look. Everything possible to be done, has been done to make every one comfortable, and at a meeting of the passengers on Saturday, a unanimous and hearty vote of thanks was given to Captain and men ...To-day we rode out 15 miles through the country, visiting "Blarney Castle," and kissing the "Blarney stone" *of course*. This *is* a beautiful region. I am sure that without something wrong in the political, social, and religious condition of the country, no Irishman would ever leave such a fertile and lovely land as this.

.... *Londonderry, Ireland, June 14th*.—During the last four days I have passed through the entire length of the "Emerald Isle"—a distance of full 300 miles as we traveled—and stopped nearly a day each at Dublin and Belfast. I confess, I have fallen in love with the country. You need never think of Ireland as a poor barren country. Nowhere in America can you travel 300 miles and see so beautiful, so fertile, and so well cultivated a region as that I have just traversed. With few exceptions there is a succession of thoroughly tilled fields, clothed with luxuriant crops. I suppose there are barren sections on the island, but I have not seen them. The farther we came north, the more beautiful has the country appeared, and right here, away up to the very shores of the Northern Ocean, and as far north as Hudson Bay in America, the farms fairly rival in beauty and luxuriance, and good culture, the finest regions of South-eastern Pennsylvania, or the Genesee Valley in Western New York. The living hedges, instead of *fences*, of course increase the attractiveness of the rural scenery....Had I not seen scores, if not hundreds, of beggars, everywhere in the streets of the *towns* I have passed through, I should wonder greatly whence come the millions of poor that have flocked from these shores to our own land. There is another explanation. Every now and then the attentive and polite railway officials have pointed out to me a village and its surrounding country, remarking that "they *belonged* to such and such" a "lord," or "baron," or "earl," etc. Divide the soil among the *people*, as in America, and there will be a different state of things.

... *The "Giant's Causeway*."—The sun rises here now a little after 3 o'clock, A. M., and sets about 9 P. M., and the twilight continues nearly all night. I am writing this by *daylight*, at 9¼ P. M.! Last night I stopped at Portrush, some 40 miles northeast of Londonderry, and taking advantage of the early sunrise, rode 7 miles east to the noted "Giant's Causeway," a mass of regular columns *four or five thousand* in number, just out from the sea, presenting a most wonderful exhibition. Let no one fail to see this natural phenomenon. It far exceeds my previous conceptions. I will not attempt a description, when so many abler pens have failed....

Containing a great variety of Items, including many good Hints and Suggestions which we throw into smaller type and condensed form, for want of space elsewhere.

How to Remit without danger of loss.—**Checks on New-York Banks or Bankers** are best for large sums; make them payable in all cases to the order of Orange Judd & Co.

Post Office Money Orders may now be obtained at nearly every county seat, in all the cities, and in many of the large towns. We consider them perfectly safe, and the best means of remitting fifty dollars or less, as many hundreds have been sent to us without any loss.

Registered Letters, under the new system, which went into effect June 1st, are a very safe means of sending small sums of money where P. O. Money Orders cannot be easily obtained. *Observe*, the Registry fee, as well as postage, must be paid in stamps at the office where the letter is mailed, or it will be liable to be sent to the Dead Letter Office. *Buy and affix the stamps both for postage and registry, put in the money and seal the letter in the presence of the postmaster, and take his receipt for it.* Letters sent in this way to us are at our risk.

Fairs.—Who are the Officers?—We desire to have, and to keep regularly, the names of the officers of *all* the Agricultural Societies in the United States. Will those interested in such institutions, please forward them, and also notify us when changes are made? Also please state time and place for holding next exhibition; we shall publish as complete a list as can be made. Be particular to give in each instance not only the name of *town*, but that of COUNTY, and STATE.

The Death of the Commissioner of Agriculture.—The Hon. Isaac Newton died at Washington, in June last. Though we have at times felt it our duty to be rather severe on his official acts, we believe that he did as well as he knew how, and that he was socially a kind man, but placed in a position for which he was naturally unfitted. Rumor has mentioned the names of some dozen or more, as likely to be nominated as his successor, but at the time of our writing, no nomination for the position has yet been sent to the Senate.

Chemistry of the Farm and the Sea.—This title covers a series of familiar, short, and interesting essays by Dr. Jos. R. Nichols, of Boston, editor of the Boston Journal of Chemistry. The subjects treated, besides those named in the title, are the chemistry of a bowl of milk, of the dwelling, of a kernel of corn, and of the sun, obscure sources of disease, the action of water on lead pipes, and bread and bread-making. Published by A. Williams & Co., Boston, of 123 pages, 8vo.

Sundry Humbugs.—The number of letters received during the last month from parties who have been inundated with piles of circulars from the various swindling shops, is not as large as in some previous months, and they come from fewer sources than is usual; but several of the old offenders are still operating, notwithstanding they have been arrested, and held for trial under bonds, and their places cleared of the thousands of circulars, envelopes, etc., which was the bulk and substance of all they contained. The wonder is that people can be so easily taken in and swindled; in fact, it appears as if they were not only willing but desirous of being humbugged, and of paying for the operation. One of our correspondents writes that he sent forty-five dollars to Stoddard, Maguire & Co., Baltimore, whose circular is word for word like C. H. Garland & Co.'s, and received goods which he invoices thus:

2 Brass Watches, worth		$0.00
1 White Watch	"	0.05
1 Pistol	"	0.25
12 White Spoons	"	0.10
1 Brass Chain	"	0.00
1 Plated Pin	"	0.10
Grand total		$0.50

Such trades are of daily occurrence, and yet the people are infatuated with the idea that somebody is going to give *them*, as a particular favor, five, ten, or a hundred times the value of *their* money, for the sake of inducing others to try the same operation, and get gulled.... *J. E. Brennan & Co.* send out their circulars, representing that they are determined to send a good prize to your neighborhood, and have accidentally met with your name, etc., etc., and if you will send them twenty dollars in gold, they will send a package of tickets, and if these don't draw eleven hundred dollars in gold, clear of all expenses, they will send another certificate in their Brilliant Extra Lottery Scheme.... *Frank Hess & Co.* send a circular precisely similar, only for *two dollars* they want you to draw *twelve* hundred in gold. Of course, whoever "goes in" loses his coin.... A. A. Kelley, who was shown up in the July number, is still selling his lottery tickets, and swindling all those who are foolish enough to buy. May 22d, 1867, Kelley issued a flaming circular, headed "Important Announcement! To the patrons and agents of Kelley's First Grand North American Gift Concert. Of 500,000 tickets issued, only a few remain unsold. The delay in its completion has been unavoidable, and we have been compelled to extend the time of the first concert to Saturday, July 13, 1867, *when it will positively take place at any cost, without further postponement, at Cooper Institute, New York City.*" Now, TAKE NOTICE. Saturday, July 13th, an advertisement appeared in the New York Herald, headed "Kelley's Grand North American Gift Concert. A card. To TICKET HOLDERS, ETC. We have found it absolutely necessary, in justice to our patrons, to extend the time of the first concert for a *few days*, owing to the detention of our mail, containing thousands of letters, by the postmaster of Chicago, etc., etc." Peter Cooper, Esq., informs us that Kelley has never even engaged the hall for his grand enterprise, and furthermore that he cannot have it for any such purpose. Kelley in his last advertisement says, "Our sales have been immense, our success complete." Of course it has; success to him is to fill his pocket with other people's money, but this promise that his "Grand Gift Concert *will positively take place without further postponement, July 13, at Cooper Institute,*" while the hall was not secured, and the concert did *not* take place, we hold up as a mirror in which our readers may see the man.... Matthew Westbrook sends a great variety of circulars, offering fortunes for very little money. Among the lot thus advertised are the "Continental Tea Company," "The Metropolitan Jewelers' Association," "American Album Watch," "Sporting Greenbacks"—and vile things, too vile for decent people to read. On one of his circulars we find: "Our stock consists in part of 1100 pianos, 600 melodeons, 700 cabinet organs," etc., etc., etc. Matthew was arrested July 3d, in the afternoon, for selling lottery tickets, etc., had an examination, was held for trial, and, for want of ready bail, was sent to the lock-up, protesting most earnestly against this method of celebrating *Independence*. In clearing out his place, the officers failed to find any of that big stock of musical instruments, etc., the particulars with regard to which are seen in the *small bills*. The stock consisted of a pile of circulars, as usual, worth three cents per pound, electrotype plates of the Sporting Greenbacks, a few pounds of tea, etc. ...Many other smaller concerns of similar character are still sending out their circulars, and gulling the people. Most of them have been already shown up in our columns, but are still out of the penitentiary, though they ought to be in it, because, as Mr. Beecher said in his sermon, of July 14: "If a man wants to have justice in the courts of New York, it would seem as if he should go there with his purse in his hand. We have heard of corrupt judges. We have heard men speaking of the judiciary of the city of New York, which stinks like Sodom and Gomorrah. They buy and sell justice, they are seeking for pelf, they sell the sanctity of their ermine." We warn all our readers against lotteries of every kind. Anything and everything that has *prizes* to be drawn for is a violation of the civil and moral law, and here we mean to include all such drawings at church and charitable festivals, fairs, etc. Those who sell a hundred tickets, more or less, at $1 each, for a share in a twenty dollar Bible to be drawn or raffled for, are violators of the State laws, and such practices should be discountenanced by all good people. A cause that cannot be sustained by honest and honorable means is not worth sustaining at all. We caution our readers again against quack doctors, (don't write to us about them, we don't know them, and don't want to,) quack medicines, quack traders, and quackery of every kind. Millions of dollars would be saved annually to honest people by heeding this warning.

Manure Frauds—The South Chiefly Victimized.—Our attention is seldom called to fraudulent dealing in pretended fertilizers, when we do not find that the planters and farmers of the Southern States are the great sufferers. A case of most glaring fraud has lately come to our notice in this way. A gentleman having a deposit of excellent shell-marl in Virginia, where it is easy to load vessels with it, was brought in contact with a Baltimore chemist, who proposed to him to manufacture it into a fertilizer fully equal to Peruvian guano, at a very low rate. A sample was furnished of a "manipulated" fertilizer he was then making, and selling for $40 or $30 per ton retail, and the manipulator agreed to make an article equally valuable, using the marl as a basis. He took also some of the marl and prepared a sample of what he would furnish. This was sent by us to Prof. Johnson, of the Sheffield Scientific School, New Haven, for analysis, and we soon learned that it was, as we presumed it would prove, *of no value* as a high-priced fertilizer. It is probable that the rascally "chemist" had added nothing whatever of manurial value to the marl. The marl itself has value where it can be liberally applied, and the cost of transportation is not much. Our friend was thus saved the loss and shame of being involved, with his friends, in so disgraceful an enterprise, but the fact remains that the chemist continues to make and supply to the southern trade, the worthless article of his own, at a high price. The man actually pretended to court investigation, and to be perfectly willing to have the stuff analyzed, thinking in this way to bluff off investigation, by a show of honesty and conscious rectitude. His name is Carey, as we understand, and the "fertilizer" is called "French Manipulated Guano," or some similar name. There are more birds of the same feather.

Draining—Agricultural and Sanitary.—Among the Book Advertisements of this number will be found a notice of "*Draining for Profit and Draining for Health*," by Col. Geo. E. Waring, Jr., whose Essay on Tile Draining in our Agricultural Annual for 1867, has attracted such favorable attention. After a careful reading of this work, we are impelled to speak more strongly concerning it than is our custom with regard to the publishing firm with which we are associated, for we think that both the importance of the subject and the merits of the work demand that it be commended to the notice of all our readers. The *New York Tribune* says of this volume:—"Every page is lucid and practical; and he who works with this essay in hand can hardly fail to drain thoroughly and permanently. We exhort every one who meditates draining even one acre to obtain Col. Waring's treatise, for it will save him many times the cost." It might have gone still further, and added that every one who *owns* an acre of land that, at any time during the growing season is too wet for the best cultivation, will find therein arguments to convince him that he cannot afford to have it undrained. The questions of cost and profit are discussed with great fairness, and in a manner to induce even the most "practical" farmer to drain his wet lands. In fact, of all the books and essays on draining that have been published in this country or in England, none is so readable, clear in its directions for practical work, and convincing in its arguments for the necessity and *profit* of tile drainage and improved sewerage as this. Col. Waring's experience during the four years that he held the position of Agricultural Engineer in the Central Park in New York, and in an extensive private practice, has fitted him particularly well for the preparation of a manual of the art of draining, and he has performed the task with entire fidelity.

Massachusetts Agricultural College.—The Old Bay State, after some preliminary difficulties, is soon to have a college for farmers' boys in complete running order. It is not surprising that there should be differences of opinion among highly intelligent men as to the organization of an Agricultural College. In this country it is an untried experiment mainly, and the few agricultural schools that have been started have not done much to dispel the popular prejudice against agricultural education. The abiding conviction of farmers is, that education, beyond the rudiments, is a dangerous thing for a farmer's son, and if he attempts to master the science of his calling, he is pretty sure to have a call to some other business soon after he opens his books. The great majority do not believe that a young farmer can have any education, to fit him for his business, half so good as that which he can get upon the farm; and if that be the case, agricultural schools and colleges are humbugs. They may make scholars, but they fail to make farmers. The Trustees of the Massachusetts Agricultural College have another idea, and are going to give it a fair trial. It will succeed in Massachusetts if anywhere. Through the efforts of Prof. Clark, of Amherst, they have secured 400 acres of land, admirably adapted to their purposes, about a mile north of the literary institution, and just a convenient distance from the village. Any one who has ever had occasion to buy five contiguous *farms* for any public enterprise will know how to appreciate the professor's labors in this behalf. The site for the principal buildings has been selected, and a dormitory, built to accommodate 48 students, a dining hall and a laboratory, are now in a state of forwardness, and will be ready for use before the beginning of the college year, which is October 1st. It is expected that a corps of instructors will then be on hand, and, what is rarer in these enterprises, a body of students to meet them. There is to be a *regular* and a *special* course of instruction, the first to embrace four years, and to ground the student thoroughly in the science and practice of agriculture. This proposes to take boys of 14 years of age and upward, and to give them a good education cheaper than they can get it elsewhere, and in one of the most healthful and beautiful regions in the country, distinguished for the high moral and social cultivation of its people. The special course will be arranged for the fall and winter, for the benefit of those who can devote but a few weeks or months to agricultural studies. A spot has been selected for propagating houses and a botanic garden, in which it is designed to have specimens of all the trees, shrubs, and flowers that will flourish in that soil and climate. The Pinetum is to be upon the north and east side of a hill, that overlooks the whole farm—a natural locality for pines and hemlocks. It is proposed to have here all the new varieties of evergreens that promise to be hardy, and to serve for ornamental planting. About twenty thousand dollars have been given for this Botanic garden, but this is not half enough. We hope some gentleman of liberal ideas, who has a spare fifty thousand dollars, will endow this garden, and enable the trustees to give us a good arboretum, and thus do well what has never been done at all in this country. This school of agriculture has no connexion with the literary institution in the same place, known as Amherst College, except the privilege of access to its cabinets and libraries, which are among the best in New England. We are happy to commend this new institution to our readers, and shall be greatly disappointed if it does not meet a want that has long been felt for the sons of farmers, and of men in other pursuits.

Barley—Early Sowed.—"L.," of Middlefield, Mass., gives his experience in answer to the objections of J. S. C. to sowing barley early, (p. 244, July No.,) as follows: "Seeing a suggestion a few years since about sowing carrots early, to have them get a start of the weeds, I sowed about 90 square rods of very weedy ground with 2½ bushels of barley that had foul seed in it, as early as I could work the ground, and harvested 20 bushels of extra clean barley. I don't think there was half a pint of foul seed in the whole lot. Whether it was the result of sowing early or not, I can't tell, but think it was that and the heavy seeding together, for, after raking off the barley, the stubble was pretty full of weeds."

Should Animals be Shown in their Natural Condition?—Mr. A. C. Clarke, of Henderson, Jefferson Co., N. Y., writes: "I find the following useful and truthful statement in 'Walks and Talks,' of the April No. of the *Agriculturist*, p. 130, 'In the case of animals that have been bred for generations for the sole purpose of producing a large amount of flesh and fat in a short time, *a fleshy condition is perfectly natural and will not prove injurious*, unless carried to excess.' To what animal can this truth apply so well as to the hog? The same author says, 'I have a thorough-bred Essex sow, that, compared with ordinary sows, was excessively fat, and at ten months old had a fine litter of six pigs.' I ask, is it not better, then, to breed hogs whose natural condition is *fat* rather than *lean*? The Agricultural Society of the State of New York offers a premium for hogs 'not too fat to breed.' I have been denied a premium on an 'improved Cheshire sow,' because she was 'too fat to breed,' and yet within two weeks after she had a litter of ten *fat* pigs that sold, at six weeks of age, at $20 a piece, and the pigs of the lean sow, that took the premium, were not worth, and would not sell for, more than $2.50 a piece. Now, the *natural* condition of the improved Cheshire hog is fat. Though a large breed, I have bred a great many of them that, at one year of age, on coarse food and no extra care, would weigh from 500 to 700 pounds. The pigs are fat, many exceeding 350 pounds, and some 400 pounds, at nine months old. A neighbor fattened one last fall that weighed at nine months and six days 429 pounds. Would not the judges who inspect hogs for a premium at our State Fairs do well to take into consideration *the natural condition of the animal?*" Certainly, but Mr. C. will admit that an improved Cheshire sow may be too fat to breed, and, if so, ought not to show as a breeding sow.

Pork Raising.—Bidwell Bro's, of Minnesota, suggest that great good might result by calling attention to the unprofitable course pursued by many in pork raising. They say: "In the fall all the largest pigs are fatted and killed, while the smaller ones are left to winter over. These have pigs the next season, and so the evil is continued. From severe cold or want of proper food in winter, or both, they become stunted, and make no heavier pork than spring pigs. The same cause reduces the number of pigs in their farrows. We ought to select the largest and best sows for breeding, and keep them year after year. They should come in early in spring, and be well fed, and the size and number of their progeny will be increased, and early maturity secured."

The Fairs.—The managers of Agricultural Fairs make a great mistake in not putting forth their announcements in time for exhibitors to be able to study their rules over months beforehand. We would gladly publish in August a full list of fairs, with the names of secretaries, so that the thousands of owners of valuable patented articles, who look to our journal for information, may be able to get it, and form their plans to go, or send their agents, to as many fairs as possible. This is just as important with reference to the county as to State fairs, for the time must all be filled up. The secretary of the State Board of Ohio, has set others an example by publishing early a full list of county and town fairs of his State. If the secretaries of other State Agricultural Societies and Boards of Agriculture would do the same, the cause of agricultural progress would be promoted.

Special to Agricultural Societies.—Mr. W. A. Fitch, who has charge of the Advertising Department of the *American Agriculturist*, desires to receive proposals from the Executive Committees of Agricultural Societies for the insertion of one or more pages of suitable advertisements in their Annual Circular and Premium Lists. His address is 131 Nassau-st., New York.

Death of Thomas Brown.—An open-handed, free-hearted, big-souled man, fair-minded, just and honorable, a warm, true friend, and genial companion, was Thomas Brown. He was a lawyer of Cleveland, Ohio, established the Ohio Farmer, which is now in its 16th volume, a protectionist and liberal politician, a warm personal friend of Chief Justice Chase, by whom, while Secretary of the Treasury, he was made one of the special agents of the Treasury Department, which office he held at the time of his death, having exercised its functions with great success and credit to himself, both at San Francisco and in New York. His interest in agricultural subjects never abated. All who knew him will mourn his death, which took place in Brooklyn, N. Y., June 13th, cutting short a vigorous manhood in its very prime.

Death of John A. King.—This distinguished citizen, ex-Governor of the State of New York, ex-President of the State Agricultural Society, the recipient from the people of many offices of trust and honor, died on the 8th of July, at his home in Jamaica, L. I. He was born in 1788, has long been prominent as a friend of improved agriculture, and was an active member of the Queens Co. Society, and of the State Agricultural Society, while his health permitted. He was a good farmer and neighbor, a liberal, polished Christian gentleman, bringing down to our, perhaps, too democratic times, the dignity of bearing and grace of manner which characterized the "old regime." Mr. King united with his friends and neighbors in celebrating our National Anniversary just passed, and made a short address, alluding to himself as passing away, and his work as done. A day or two only elapsed before he encountered a paralytic stroke, to which his life soon yielded.

A Portable Pump invented by Mr. N. Page, Jr., was exhibited at this office a few days since. The instrument is very simple, of little weight, requires very little exertion to operate it, and is susceptible of many uses, not only as a convenient pump of small capacity, but also for syringing in Green-houses, watering plants, washing wagons, windows, etc. It is so constructed as to throw a single stream thirty to forty feet, which, without change of nozzle, may be instantly changed to a coarse spray or fine mist, at the will of the operator. An advertisement of it appears on page 307.

Leached and Unleached Ashes.—E. C. Long, Erie Co., N. Y. At the prices you name (three and twelve cents per bushel,) it will probably pay to buy both leached and unleached ashes for manure. Leached ashes usually contain but very little potash, but they are valuable for other ingredients, and on much farm land where the mechanical as well as the chemical effects of ashes are desirable, produce marked good effects.

Subjects on which Subscribers need Information.—"Rheumatism" affecting turkeys, curling up their feet. Their health otherwise being good. Cause and cure wanted.

Cause of the sudden death of calves, taken, some sucking, and others after having been weaned. Symptoms;—They refuse to eat or suck, fall, go into spasms, and soon die, frothing at the mouth.

Reason of ewes eating their lambs, and the cure. In regard to this, C. F. H., of Nebraska, writes:—"I have been troubled for three seasons by ewes eating their lambs. Last year, I found out the guilty one, and knocked her in the head; she was eating the lambs of other ewes. I thought I was rid of the trouble, but this season it appeared to be as bad as ever. I killed the one I caught at it, but that does not seem to prevent the difficulty. They eat off their feet as soon as they are born.

The Double Deutzia.—Two years ago this month, we figured the Double Deutzia, then a recent introduction from Japan. Our figure, which was taken from a green-house specimen, scarcely did justice to the shrub. Now that it is becoming more common, fine specimens may be seen, and certainly nothing can be more beautiful; the flowers are very double, and the outer petals have just a tinge of pink. It is perfectly hardy, a free bloomer, and the flowers are admirable for bouquets.

Fill up the Clubs, and select the premiums. All subscriptions sent in this month, whether commencing with January or July, will count on the premium lists. A few thousand more names may yet be added to this year's list by a little vigorous effort. *Will you have a premium?* See also Special Premiums, p. 270.

Geyelin's Poultry Breeding.—An English book of G. K. Geyelin, C.E., entitled "Poultry Breeding in a Commercial Point of View," etc., has been republished by A. Williams & Co., Boston, Mass., with an introductory preface, by Chas. L. Flint, Secretary of the Massachusetts Board of Agriculture. All contributions of new ideas on the subject of poultry raising, from persons who have given real *thought* to the subject, are of value, and for this reason we place a high estimate upon all that Mr. Geyelin writes. It is not usual for practical men, or those who have put their theories and plans to the test of real use, "in a commercial point of view," to write out their *views*, and say not a single word about their results. There is a real practical and excellent chapter in this book on poultry breeding in France—the report of a visit of Mr. G. K. G., in search of the fabled monster poultry establishments of that country. This chapter was given to the American public, more than a year ago, in an appendix to Saunders' Domestic Poultry. Mr. Geyelin's connection with the establishment of the National Poultry Co., at Bromley, Kent, was not of long continuance, and so, we suppose, his ideas were never thoroughly carried out, still, in many respects, they seem feasible. If any egg-hatching machine will work well, we think the one he describes will be likely to. It displays great ingenuity, as does also his Artificial Hen, and his plan for a large establishment, made up of small independent sections. The book is a neat 12mo. of 127 pages, for sale at our counter, or sent by mail, for $1.25.

Things by Mail.—Many persons seem to think that they have only to do up a fruit, flower, or insect, in some kind of package, put on the requisite stamps, and place it in the mail to insure its safe delivery. It is the exception that these things reach us in any tolerable condition, and many well-meaning people doubtless wonder why we do not notice their fruit, flowers, etc., while the fact is, their fruit has been converted into "jam" in the mail bags, and their flowers reduced to an unrecognizable pulp. It is quite useless to send fruit, fresh flowers, or insects, by mail, unless they are put in a tin, or other, box so strong that all the pounding the mail bags get, will not crush it. No strawberry has been received this year by mail in good condition. With dried plants we have less trouble, though these are often crushed when put in common envelopes. They should be placed between stiff papers or pasteboards.

The American Naturalist. — We made a brief announcement of the appearance of this journal, and intended before this to call more particular attention to it. The editors have gained by their experience, and each number is better than the preceding one. We have, in the July number now before us, articles on the Sea-Horse and its Young, Recent Bird Tracks, Jelly Fishes, Agency of Insects in Fertilizing Plants, Ice Marks and Ancient Glaciers in the White Mountains, besides a host of smaller items. The whole story is pleasantly told, and those of our readers who have a taste for natural history, cannot do better than send $3 to the editors of the American Naturalist, Salem, Mass., as a year's subscription to this, our best popular scientific journal.

Prong-horn — A Correction. — The spirited drawing of the Prong-horn Antelope, on the first page of the July *Agriculturist*, was erroneously credited. The artist who made the drawing is William J. Hays.

Schrœder's Bromus. — In July, 1866, we gave a figure of this grass, and showed what the thing put out under the name of *Bromus Schraderi* really was. We also, upon general principles, expressed our doubts as to its value. In the Agricultural Gazette, (English), for June 20, we find an article upon those plants that have been forced upon the community by means of "testimonials," which says: "Schrœder's Bromus, then, is another example of a plant unduly urged upon the attention of cultivators—another example of the way in which advertising seedsmen injure themselves, one another, and those with whom they deal, by those extravagant announcements to which we thus call their attention, as damaging the agency by which alone satisfactory business relations can be established between them."

Additional Strawberry Notes. — We have figured on page 291 most of the novelties of the present season. We intended in those notes to say a word about the unfavorable circumstances under which many of the sorts were exhibited at the American Institute. In many instances the rains had prevented the fruit from ripening properly. This was particularly noticeable with *Durand's Seedling*, a variety of which we gave a figure last year, and expressed a favorable opinion. Though good-sized berries were shown, they were flavorless, the flavor having been washed out.

Abraham Lincoln.—There is some trick about this berry somewhere. If there is a distinct sort with this name, we do not know it. We hear that the Agriculturist has been sold under this name, and we know that, at the show of the American Institute, the berry shown, under that name, was not different from the Jucunda. There is some trickery in this. If any one has a true and distinct seedling that he has called Abraham Lincoln, we shall be glad to get it, and if it is distinct, to make it known.

Doctor Nicaise.—We have known of this variety through the French Horticultural Journals, but never had the pleasure of seeing the fruit until Messrs. Frost & Co., the well-known nurserymen of Rochester, sent us specimens. To insure their delivery, Messrs. F. & Co. wrapped each berry in cotton batting. This quite dried out the specimens and took away their flavor.—We can only say that the fruit is very large, has a good flesh, but under the circumstances cannot give an opinion as to its quality.

New Music Store.—We have received a package of music published by C. H. Ditson & Co., 711 Broadway, New York, and O. Ditson & Co., Boston. It gives us pleasure to notice the establishment in this city of a branch of that old and justly distinguished music publishing house, Oliver Ditson & Co., and we heartily wish to the new firm a like honorable and successful career. Purchasers of music, musical instruments, etc., will find these firms worthy of their patronage.

The Results of the Harvest.—In the cities business is very dull, and were it not that men have been cautious in their dealings, and have long looked for a time of financial trouble, there would before this have been serious embarrassment. One hears on every corner reference to the crops; every traveler is inquired of; the newspapers stretch out long columns of dry facts, and estimates of probabilities, and the weather and its influence is discussed on all sides. The farmer has the responsibility of *gathering well* the good crops vouchsafed by a bountiful Providence. With plenty here of all the ordinary crops, prices will range low enough to enable us to ship wheat and flour and corn to Europe, no matter how good the crops are there. With the wheat and corn, our debts to Europe will be paid, gold will even begin to flow this way, perhaps, and business of all kinds will revive. The farmers who can demand and get the money, cash down, for their grain, if they sell at fair prices, will be the first benefited, for they will be able to take advantage of the prevailing low prices of articles of clothing, etc. Very soon, with a buoyant money market, goods now held very low, will be "marked up." The results of the harvest of spring grains, and the prospects of the corn crop, will attract public attention after this, as of great importance. We hope our readers will favor us with brief statements of the weather as affecting these crops, and the results as soon as known.

A Lady's Invention.—The Garment Conformator, advertised in another column, is an ingenious arrangement for fitting dresses, etc. Ladies of our acquaintance who have tried it, say it works admirably, and especially in fitting forms of irregular shape.

Plea and Testimony for the Robins.—"B. Bros.," St. Paul, Minn., writes: "We observe your correspondent's indictment against the robin, and would ourselves feel guilty to have sentence passed upon him without giving our testimony in his favor. They reached here about the middle of April, and busied themselves eating sumach berries until it became warm enough for the appearance of insects. We had two or three acres of borage plowed late in the fall, which, on the first days of warm weather in May, was almost alive with squash bugs. The robins left the sumach, and for several days remained the greater part of the time on the plowed ground, eating millions of the bugs as they appeared on the surface. So well satisfied were we with the destruction of the bugs that we planted an acre of squashes, which are growing finely, unmolested."

Strawberry Show of the American Institute.—The American Institute arranged for an exhibition of Strawberries on June 18th, but the unfavorable weather induced a postponement until the 20th. In consequence of this change, the show was not so large as the very liberal premiums should have brought out. The quality of the fruit more than compensated for the lack in quantity. Several new berries were shown, most of which are noticed on page 291. Though some of the principal prizes were, for reasons satisfactory to the judges, not awarded, we must commend the liberality that proposed them, and we hope that such generous efforts in behalf of horticulture may in the future lead to satisfactory results.

The following are the premiums awarded:

Premium Offered by Dudley S. Gregory, $50. For the best collection (not less than 25) of named varieties in bearing, to be exhibited in pots not more than 10 inches in diameter—Reisig & Hexamer, New Castle, N. Y.

Premium Offered by Salem H. Wales, Esq., $25. For the best collection (not less than 20) of named varieties, one plant each—Reisig & Hexamer, New Castle, N. Y.

Premium Offered by Wm. H. Butler, Esq., $12. For the best collection (not less than 12) of named varieties, one plant each—Frank Brill, Newark, N. J.

Premium Offered by Nathan C. Ely, Esq., $6. For the best collection (not less than 6) of named varieties, one plant each—E. Williams, Montclair, N. J.

For the best plant (in fruit) of any kind, to be exhibited in a pot not more than 10 inches in diameter, $5—S. Spingstead, Unionport, N. Y.

For the 3 heaviest berries—S. Spingstead, Unionport, N. Y.

For the best quart of Agriculturist, $3, James M. Betts, Stamford, Conn.; for the best quart of Austin, $3, Frank Brill, Newark, N. J.; for the best quart of Durand's Seedlings, $3, Frank Brill, Newark, N. J.; for the best quart of Green Prolific, $3, Frank Brill, Newark, N. J.; for the best quart of Ida, $3, E. Williams, Montclair, N. J.; for the best quart of Jucunda, $3, Frank Brill, Newark, N. J.; for the best quart of Lennig's White, $3, Frank Brill, Newark, N. J.; for the best quart of Rippowam, $3, J. W. Faulkner, Stamford, Conn.; for the best quart of Russell's Prolific, $3, E. Marshall, Poughkeepsie, N. Y.; for the best quart of Triomphe de Gand, $3, Mrs. R. A. Kerr, Marlborough, N. Y.; for the best quart of Wilson's Albany, $3, E. Marshall, Poughkeepsie, N. Y.; La Constante was exhibited by O. Cleveland, Jersey City, but he being a manager, was debarred from receiving a premium.

H. Beecher & Sons, Westville, Conn., for the best fruit basket, $3.

Twenty-eight varieties of seedlings were exhibited in small quantities; all were presented by T. R. Peck of Waterloo, N. Y., and some of them show good qualities.

THE GREELEY PRIZE.—Regarding the prize of $50 offered by Mr. Greeley, the Judges, John Ellis, Thomas Meehan, Geo. Thurber, and J. J. Thomas, say that several fruits of great promise were offered for this prize, among which were No. 14, Chas. Downing; a seedling of remarkable size and beauty, No. 30 of Seth Boyden's Seedling, Romeyn's Seedling, a very prolific variety, and Durand's Seedling; but before this premium can be awarded, according to the terms specified, the plants should be examined on the ground to ascertain how they have wintered, and again in fruiting time, by a committee appointed for this purpose.

Notes on Farming in the Grain Districts of Pennsylvania and New Jersey.—Almost every State has its distinct phases of agriculture, occasioned by its soil and climate, or by its first settlers. Grain growing, which is the leading business in the husbandry of the best portions of these States, is secured by the peculiarities of the soil mainly. The soil which is under the plow is easily tilled, and comparatively free from boulders or large stones. There is nothing to interfere with the plow, the harrow, or the cultivator. For the most part, corn is not touched with the hand-hoe after planting, and even the planting is often done by the drill. Lime is almost everywhere cheap, and with the small quantities of manure made, serves to keep up the fertility of the land with very moderate applications. The farms underlaid with limestone are said to be subject to drought in summer, making them unreliable for pasture. Rye or wheat, oats and corn, are easily raised, and probably pay better than dairy farming. They take less capital, involve less labor, and require less skill. The rotation, corn on a limed sod, oats or a summer fallow, manure and winter grain, either rye or wheat, clover, and timothy are common, making a five or six years' course. There is a uniformity in following this course, without much regard to the nationality of the original settlers.

We come upon the characteristic PENNSYLVANIA BARN, long before we enter the State at Easton, travelling by the Morris and Essex railroad. It is planted, if possible, upon a side hill, and has one or two stories below the barn floor, where the hay and grain are delivered. The best model has stone gables, and the walls of the lower stories are of stone or brick, laid in mortar, and made rat proof. The entrance to the main floor is directly from the ground on the upper side, or by a broad drive-way of gentle ascent where this is necessary. It is of large capacity, frequently 50 by 100 feet, and will hold several hundred tons of hay and grain. There are deep bays on either side of the floor for hay, and immediately beneath the floor is the granary into which the wheat, oats, and rye are received, when they are threshed. The threshing and cutting of straw, corn fodder, and hay, is all done by horse power. The cut feed is conveyed by a shoot to the stables in the basement, where it is mixed with meal, and fed to the animals. The whole basement is occupied with stalls for cattle and horses. There is a large cistern in the side hill, catching all the water from the barn, and furnishing an abundant supply for the stock. A pipe brings the water from the cistern, immediately in front of the feeding stalls, so that little time is lost in watering. Sometimes a neighboring spring, instead of a cistern, furnishes the water. There is one grand defect in this style of barn—the want of some means near the stalls for the preservation and composting of manures, and with this supplied, we do not know that it could be changed for the better. Manures are not prized so highly as they are further east, and for this perhaps the lime is at fault. It is a great labor to clean out the stables in this kind of barn. The manure is carried out by wheel-barrow or other contrivance, and deposited in the open yard, where, mixed with straw, it lies exposed till the annual clearing out comes in August or September, for the oat stubble or summer fallow. A barn cellar underneath the stables would save largely in labor, and in the value of manure. We think, on many of these farms, from two to five hundred dollars are lost every year for want of a cellar.

PORK RAISING is quite an important item in the business of the grain farm. The pigs are sometimes fed in clover through the summer, but quite as frequently run at large, and the manure is wasted. They are generally fed upon raw corn, and in large inclosures when shut up for fattening. We did not find the small pen well filled with muck or loam, upon which the eastern farmer relies for several cords of his best manure. We believe it pays to have swine sheltered, and to feed with ground and cooked food.

RAISING ROOTS receives very little attention in the grain growing districts. Potatoes are raised for the table, and the yield is quite as generous as in the Eastern States, but we did not see any large fields of carrots, parsnips, beets, mangels, or turnips. Perhaps the climate is not so favorable, but we could not learn that experiments had been tried to test the matter. We think some of the roots would be found to succeed very well, and that they would be found to be a very profitable addition to the stores for the winter feeding of cattle. We suspect room will yet be found in the model barn of this region for a root cellar, and that carrots will become a part of the daily rations of the horse.

THE BREEDING OF HORSES is a common branch of business upon the grain farm, and generally pays well. They are not of any distinct breed, but are larger than those raised at the east. There is a great demand in the seaboard cities for a large horse, weighing from twelve to fifteen hundred pounds, for trucks and heavy wagons, which Pennsylvania, more than any other State, supplies. Almost all the work upon the farm is done by horse-power, and this requires a large force, which, on the eastern farm, is supplied by oxen. The young horses are kept until of suitable age for service, and then sold for from two to five hundred dollars each. Strength and size are qualities sought more than beauty and speed. The horses for exportation are a large item in the wealth of the State.

FARMING BY PROXY is much more common than at the East. The land owner, instead of renting his farm for a stipulated price, or upon shares, hires a foreman or farmer to oversee and board the laborers. He is not a resident upon the farm, but visits it as often as suits his convenience, and gives such directions as he chooses to the foreman. The compensation of the foreman varies according to circumstances. We found one who received 300 dollars a year, house rent, fuel, and the use of two cows. He agreed to board laborers at three dollars a week, and the laborers worked for 16 dollars a month (wet and dry) and board. Another on a somewhat larger farm received 700 dollars a year with house rent, fuel, and other privileges. He boarded the laborers at a stipulated price, made all the purchases, and sold all the products of the farm, and kept the accounts. Land owners who pursue this course, are generally men of business in the neighboring villages or cities, who see the farm frequently, and keep close watch of the management. They have a farm account, and know the profit or loss of the business. We found one gentleman who farmed in this way, making from 7 to 8 per cent. on his capital, and he could show the figures. He spent money freely, and got it back again.

The Picnic, and How to Go to it.

The picnic is an institution in our cities and villages, and nothing is more common than a general turn out of friends and neighbors for some rural retreat in the dog-days. It is quite as much needed upon the farm, and now that the hay and grain harvests are mainly over, a good time generally should be inaugurated by the young men and maidens of the farm. "All work makes Jack a dull boy." Who should go? Everybody that has done good solid work through the hay harvest and behaved himself; the commodore, who has bossed the work, and done the thinking, and had the tools all ready in season; his wife, who has spread a bountiful table and sent savory luncheon to the field; little Bess, who has mixed the sweetened water, tempered with lemons or with vinegar, and brought it to the field; little Bob, who has rode horse to plow, and raked after the cart all summer; the old folks who have happy memories of harvest days; the good dominie, who has sweat in his pulpit to make your Sabbaths profitable, and you better every day in the week; the doctor, who has taught you to observe the laws of health, and prescribed apples and pears instead of pills—every honest worker, old and young, ought to have a day's release from toil. Where should they go? To any pleasant spot, not too far off to make it a weariness—some river bank, some island, some sea-side resort, some hill or mountain, where there is grateful shade and fine scenery. How should they go? With their own teams, if possible. The railway and steamer will do for poor people who cannot support an establishment of their own. We like independence and a home made picnic. What shall they do? Enjoy nature and society. Do not impose upon anybody the necessity of a lecture, or a speech, or be tied up to any programme. Singing is in order, so is swinging, and silence and quiet, if people like them better. Only get the people together, and let your committee see that each family brings its offering to the festival, and it will take care of itself.

Top Dressing Grass Lands.

A very interesting experiment has been made with various kinds of manures applied to grass, at the State Agricultural College of Michigan. The manures were applied to the plots, from May 5th to 10th, 1864, and the products were carefully cut, dried, and weighed, in July and October of the year 1864 and 1865. The soil was a light sandy loam.

2 bush. of plaster per acre	gave	an	increase	of 4,158 lb	of hay
5 " " wood ashes	"	"	"	" 3,942 lb	"
20 loads of muck	"	"	"	" 4,683 lb	"
20 " and 3 bushels of salt				" 3,318 lb	"
5 bushels of salt	"	"	"	" 4,184 lb	"
20 loads of horse manure	"	"	"	" 5,023 lb	"
20 " " cow	"	"	"	" 4,874 lb	"

This experiment covers two years, and seems to have been carefully made. It gives, without much doubt, the approximate value of these manures as top dressings for light sandy loams. It shows that two bushels of plaster are worth a little more than two tons of hay, and five bushels of ashes produce nearly the same quantity. Estimating hay at 15 dollars a ton, this is a very good price for plaster and ashes. Farmers who want to get ahead should certainly invest.

The experiment also shows the great value of muck in comparison with stable manure, and it is for the sake of the muck argument that we give place to this experiment this month. The muck is shown to be nearly as valuable as the cow and horse manure, and when composted with salt, is even more so. We wish a compost made of one-third fresh horse dung, and two-thirds muck, had been introduced in the experiment. Something of the value of the horse and cow dung was probably lost by evaporation, which the composting would have saved. We think such a compost would have shown better results than either of the manures specified. Muck must be worth about a dollar and a half a load, delivered upon the field, for top dressing, and if the farmer can furnish it for fifty cents, as many can, he has a strong inducement to enter the muck swamps, which are usually accessible this month and the next. How can farmers be content to do without manure when there is so much profit in applying it with a liberal hand? Muck and its composts can be spread upon grass land with safety at any time after mowing.

Cutting and Curing Grain.

The high price and scarcity of wheat flour of the best qualities, in comparison with the abundance and low price of poor flour, indicate more strongly than any statement we can make, the immense losses our farmers have sustained on account of bad management and unfavorable weather in harvest time. In our opinion, a very serious loss accrues, annually, from the notion, which teachers of agriculture have believed and promulgated for years, that grain ought to be cut before it is ripe, in order to get the most fine flour. The latest thorough experiments seem to disprove this, and so we presume the advocacy of not cutting wheat before it is ripe will be general, and farmers may swing over into the other extreme, and meet with loss from shelling. This is not, however, the great fault of our grain harvesting, especially at the West. Labor is scarce and high; as much as possible is done by horse-power, but the work of binding and shocking is not yet done by machinery, and this is what is slighted. The bundles are poorly made, and they are poorly shocked. The shocks are wet through and through by heavy rains, and more or less by every passing shower. The grain grows, and the shocks mould or become "musty," of course. The market is spoiled, the merchant embarrassed, and the farmer gets poor pay and goes behindhand year after year. Meanwhile he buys a barometer, studies the weather, grumbles, and, perhaps, honestly thinks he does his best, and that the weather must take all the blame. The prosperity, thrift, happiness of any particular agricultural region depends directly upon the good farming, measured by the profits, of its individual farmers. It is therefore for every man's interest to improve his own practice and that of his neighbors as much as possible.

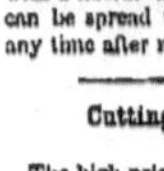

Fig. 1.

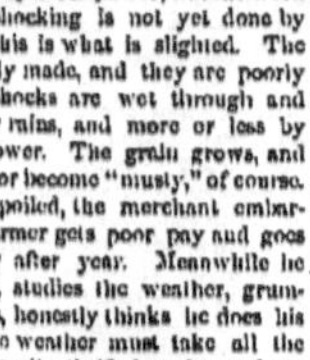

Fig. 2.

In the matter of shocking grain, great improvements are to be made before the country can feel that an abundant crop on the field can be reckoned upon as sure to add materially to the wealth of the nation. We received a communication from John Molony, Jr., of Dubuque Co., Iowa, a few weeks since, on shocking grain, and since then have taken pains to assure ourselves of the fact, that the common practice in shocking grain over large sections of the Western States is shockingly careless. Mr. Molony writes: "I think there is more grain lost by bad shocking and wet weather following, than in any other way. I generally have a hand to gather the sheaves in piles, twelve in a place, six on the right and six on the left, with a place in the middle for the shock—buts all turned in, and the rows straight through the field. I then commence by taking one sheaf in each hand, by the heads, and set them down firmly on the ground, closing the heads together; then setting two more pairs in the same way, I have six in a double row; I then put two up on each side, making ten in all in the shock, and two left for caps. This makes a round shock, (see fig. 1). I put my arms around the top of the shock and squeeze the heads together—kicking in the buts if they are slanting too much. I then take one of the remaining sheaves, and pull the band back within a few inches of the but; then put the but against my chest, the left hand holding up the sheaf, and with the right hand divide the sheaf into three parts, bending the straw first to the right, then to the left, then bend the middle straight down. I put it on the shock and prepare the other cap in the same manner, and place it across the first, and press down firmly, pushing in any heads that may protrude from under the caps, (see fig. 2). We had a fair chance to test my plan last harvest, it being very wet here. The shocks that I put up were perfectly safe, while those that my help put up were nearly all spoiled. The men could not be induced to put the shocks up as I did, but threw from 20 to 25 in a shock—dung pile would be the right name—setting the sheaves down so lightly as hardly to break the stubble, and resting very easily and insecurely against each other. They would break no caps, but only throw five or six on top. With the first wind, down came the shocks; or the weight of so many wet bundles on top spread them and caused them to fall. It is a poor policy to make a shock so large that the cap will not cover it well, and it looks like go-ahead farming to see the shocks of uniform size and in straight rows. My help and others laugh at me, and say that I am too particular, but I find advantage in it, and don't care."

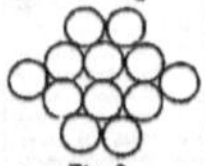

Fig. 3.

Fig. 4.

The method differs little from the common Eastern practice, in which the number of bundles varies from 10 to 14 in a shock, 12 being usual. When 14 are used, 12 are set as in figure 3. The cap sheaf is made by taking two, having the longest straw, slipping the bands towards the buts a little, then binding them together. It is opened, set over the top of the shock, and well packed down, as shown in fig. 4. This makes, if well done, a very secure thatching, as well as very substantial shock. The use of cotton cloth hay-caps offers an advantage in making shocks stand firmer, but little, if any, better security against rain. These caps which will add to the firmness of the shocks, should be at least 4 feet square, with loops in the corners, and wooden pins passing through these loops should enter the sheaves near the bands. The time required to put the caps on and off, and to take care of them, is fully equal to that necessarily spent in making good shocks. A good set of caps will often pay for themselves in a single season.

MONEY IN OYSTER SHELLS.—Large quantities of these shells are thrown into the streets in the country villages and market towns. They make a good road bed, but can be more usefully employed in improving the soil. They are easily decomposed by fire and water. Pile any combustible material in a row, about ten feet across and three feet high, as compactly as possible. Brush, turf, peat, or old roots will answer the purpose. Upon these pile your oyster shells, a foot thick or more; then pile on more brush and another layer of the shells. Bank the sides with old turf or sods, and put sods on the top. Fire the heap on the windward side, and with a little attention the whole mass will burn down and make a splendid ruin for the farmer's purposes. Clay burned by the same rude process makes an admirable dressing for the soil.

Southwestern Georgia for Fruit.

We have seen very fine specimens of fall pears from Albany, Georgia, brought north by a resident of that place, in good eating condition July 1st. The early varieties of pears and apples ripen there about the 1st of June, and peaches from the 1st to the 20th of that month. The Catawba grape grows in the greatest perfection, and is ready for market about the 20th of July. This gentleman says there is a large district, embracing several counties, between Albany and Savannah, where these and other northern fruits grow in the greatest perfection. These lands can now be bought from 1 to 10 dollars per acre, without improvements, and from five to thirty with improvements. The wild lands are mainly covered with a heavy growth of yellow pine. The diseases and insects which so greatly annoy the fruit grower at the North, are hardly known in this region. Would not this be a good opening for northern emigration in large colonies? A projected railroad will bring this fine fruit region within 10 hours of Savannah, and 3½ days of New York, and make it another feeder of our city markets. Our fall fruits in midsummer will be worth looking at.

INSECT ENEMIES.—The appearance and disappearance of insects, which destroy our crops, are governed by laws which we understand very imperfectly. Last year over large portions of New England the fruit trees and elms were deprived of their leaves by the Canker-worm, where this year scarcely one is to be found. The good people of the States west of the Missouri were making the plans to do battle with the locusts where they were so abundant last year; yet they have been very generally disappointed. Still, in other localities the locusts (grass-hoppers) have appeared, and eaten almost every green thing. The ten-lined spearman, or striped potato-beetle, is, in spite of every effort to stay its progress, moving steadily eastward—now crossing Northern and Middle Illinois. Each year its ravages become more extensive. The only hope of checking them, seems to be in attacking them in their winter quarters. How little do we know about what so nearly concerns us;

Shrews or Shrew Mice.

Among the shrews we find the most minute of our native quadrupeds. Some, like one shown in the engraving, are not very small. They are remarkable for their great shyness and activity, and, when seen, are usually mistaken for mice, which they somewhat resemble in size and form. They are all insect eaters, hence should never be killed when recognized. Several of the species burrow, forming extensive galleries under ground like the mole. They are found usually in fence rows and old stumps, and about moist, boggy meadows, wherever their food abounds. When wounded, they emit a strong musky odor, which, however, does not deter hawks and owls from swallowing them, and it is from the crops of these birds that naturalists obtain some of their rarest specimens, as we are informed by Mr. John W. Bell, the well known N. Y. taxidermist. The largest of the group in the engraving is the "mole shrew," (*Blarina talpoides*.) which is 5 or 6 inches long, including the tail, which is about one inch long. It is found from Nova Scotia to Georgia, and westward, probably, to the Mississippi River. It is shaped a good deal like a mole, having no visible ears, small bright eyes, pointed muzzle, 30 teeth, and large fore-paws. The fur is of a uniform glossy slate color, a little darker above than below. It makes burrows, and in its habits is like the mole. The little one above on the right is the "Broad-Nosed" or "Long-Eared Shrew," (*Sorex platyrhinus*,) which often is found in the Eastern States. It is only two inches long to the tail, which is about 1¼ inch long; it weighs about 50 grains. The ears are large, the nose flat, but pointed, the body chestnut-gray above, and ashy beneath. The one opposite is "Forster's Shrew," (*Sorex Forsteri*) a species found along the Atlantic coast, and more or less inland. Its tracks are often very noticeable in the winter upon the snow, and these little creatures have been seen as far north as the 67th degree of latitude, very actively running about when the thermometer indicated 40° to 50° below zero. Full grown individuals are 1¼ inches long to the tail, which measures about an inch and one-third. The color is smoky brown, with a pale ash-colored belly. These animals are now classified in three genera, and although not less than 20 species exist in the United States, yet they are strangers to most people. Most of them belong to the Pacific coast and north-western Territories. They are readily distinguished from mice by the number and closeness of the teeth, and their very sharp pointed noses. We do not know that they do any damage, except by burrowing.

GROUP OF SHREW MICE.

COPPERHEAD. RATTLESNAKE.

Rattlesnake and Copperhead.

The common rattlesnake is a sluggish, heavily moving, and, except for its rattle and bite, an uninteresting serpent of 3 to 4 feet long. It is brown above, light colored beneath, and marked with two rows of confluent brown spots from its head to near the tail, where the color becomes nearly black. The scientific name is *Crotalus durissus*. This one is common to a large part of the United States, and there are other species in the Southern States, on the prairies, and on the great plains. The reputed charming power of this snake, and probably of any snake, is a pure fiction. It takes its food by lying in wait for its victims, and killing them by its bite. It eats squirrels, birds, and such small animals. When alarmed, it at once coils itself up, vibrates the rattle on its tail, and, if menaced, strikes. The mouth is furnished with sharp teeth, and the upper jaw carries two long, curved, grooved fangs, above which are little glands, secreting the poison that is ejected simultaneously with the bite. The bite so speedily fatal to small animals, is not so dangerous to human life as is generally believed, for comparatively few cases of death to adults or active boys occur, though it is not very uncommon to hear of persons being bitten; still the bite is accompanied by much suffering. When a person is bitten, his own mouth or that of a companion should be at once applied, and the venom sucked out if possible, (when swallowed, it is harmless). A poultice of wet tobacco should be applied if nothing better is at hand, and the patient kept thoroughly under the influence of alcoholic stimulants, (even drunk). The rattles are formed by a succession of loose, horny shells, of such a shape that, though each is entirely loose from the others, it cannot become detached, unless broken. The number of rattles does not indicate the age, for one to four are added in a year, and often some are lost. The rattlesnake never pursues, and it is very seldom that men not fool-hardy or utterly careless are bitten by them.

"The Copperhead," (*Ancistrodon contortrix*,) is, next to the rattlesnake, the most venomous of our serpents, but more dangerous, as it gives no warning of its presence or alarm, as the other does. It has a thick, triangular head, and a body continuing quite thick to near the tail. The general color is light brown with transverse bars forked on the sides, which gives an appearance as of crossing diagonal lines; beneath it is flesh-colored, spotted and blotched more or less. The fangs and poison are similar to those of the rattlesnake, and like it also, if a fang is broken off, another will grow to supply its place. "Chunkhead" and "Deaf Adder" are common names. It frequents low and moist places more than the rattlesnake.

The Use of Machinery Upon the Farm.

One of the most cheering indications of the times is the rapid introduction of improved implements in husbandry, especially of those thus are moved by horse-power. In this matter the West is far ahead of the East, and the grain growing districts greatly excel the dairy regions. Corn, where it is grown upon a large scale, is now very generally cultivated by horse-power, without the use of the hand hoe. Five times cultivating is much better than three times hoeing, and much cheaper. Some drill in their corn, one kernel in a place and one foot apart, by a horse drill, and claim that they not only do the work at much less expense, but get a much larger crop. There is no hand labor about it until you come to the harvesting, and even this, we anticipate, will soon be done by machinery. Potatoes are cut, dropped, and covered, cultivated and dug by horse-power, and, we think, will soon be bagged and binned in the same way. Wheat is put in by the horse drill, and cut by the horse reaper. The hay harvest is now all secured by horse power. These machines are not indeed universally introduced, but their economy is so apparent, and they put the hay and grain harvests so completely into the power of the farmer, that no man can long afford to do without them. The manufacture of these machines has become a vast business, giving employment to tens of thousands of men, and the demand for them is constantly increasing. They are a powerful argument for the clearing out of stumps and boulders, and for making the rough ways smooth. The man who clings to the time-honored tools, and the good old ways, will be badly beaten in the market.

Ox-Yokes—How to Make Them.

Mr. E. O. Shultz, of Oconto Co., Wis., furnishes some directions about yoke-making, accompanied with a model, which we picture in fig. 1. He writes: "There is no need of having an ox's neck so sore as to require treatment, or to stop his work, if we have a yoke that is fit for a team to work in. There is not one man in ten that can make a yoke. Any one can make a stick with holes bored in it, no matter how, so that a pair of bows can be put in.

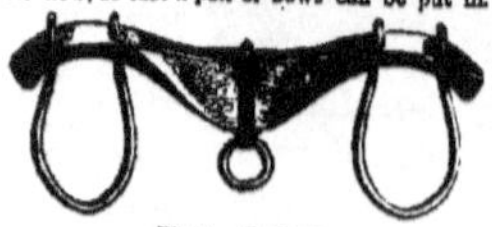

Fig. 1.—OX YOKE.

The oxen can suffer the consequences. If there is a law against cruelty to animals, this is one case which should be investigated. I have made a great many yokes, and any one who has used one of them, comes to me if he wants another. There is no place where oxen are made to draw so hard as they are in the lumber woods, and I

Fig. 2.—YOKE MARKED OUT.

have not seen a single ox laid up, and have heard of but very few that were sore enough to require treatment, where my yoke was used.

Not being able to make a sketch of anything so that it can be understood, I have resorted to cutting a small model which corresponds with a finished ox-yoke, and will show you the principle, the main thing being the shape of the neck. I make them all of the same size and shape, (with the slight variation in breadth and depth noted below), and I have yet to see the pair of oxen that one will not fit. I will give you my plan and I think it will benefit some, at least, of your subscribers to follow it.

Yellow birch is about the best timber you can use. Find a log large enough to split, in order

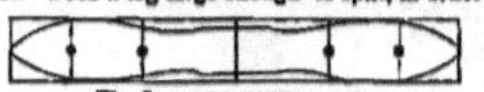

Fig. 3.—YOKE MARKED OUT.

to work the heart out, as such an one will not be so liable to check in seasoning; square it 8 × 10, then lay your yoke out, (as in figs. 2 and 3). Beginning where the staple is to come, measure 11 inches each way, then 9 inches, and then 8 inches, on each side, making in all 56 inches. Be sure and bore your holes with three-quarters of an inch slant to the foot, to each hole, and you will have no bother in getting a well shouldered bow in. Work the neck out so that the holes will come even on the under side, say like this, (fig. 4), not

Fig. 4.

Fig. 5.

thus, (fig. 5), then shape it both ways alike, so that whichever way the yoke lies on the neck there shall be no lump or ridge. The model will show you how it should be; make yokes just like it, and I warrant there will be no sore necks. For a yoke to draw on a chain, the stick should be 8½ × 11 inches, and the yoke will not roll up on their necks; to use on a tongue, 8 × 10 is the right size; if oxen draw very high, make them 8½ × 12 to draw on a chain, and 8 × 11 on the tongue. The holes should always be made as I have stated above."

Large Fields Wanted.

One of the great nuisances in the New England States and in the dairy regions generally, is the small size of the cultivated fields. One, two, and three acre lots are common, and ten acre lots and upward, are rare. In many cases the cost of fencing has been much greater than the cost of the land, and the keeping up of these fences is a large tax upon the farmer, and the principal labor of repairs comes in the spring, when he is most busy. The fences are always in the way of plowing and cultivation, and of no particular advantage in pasturage, the chief argument for them. We see no reason for any more divisions in the arable part of the farm than there are crops in the rotation. The permanent pasture ,and woodlands might come under a different rule. In the grain districts recently visited, we were struck with the large size of the fields, even on two and three hundred acre farms. Fields of twenty, thirty, and even fifty acres, are not uncommon. This feature adds beauty to the landscape, as well as facilitates the cultivation. We are coming more and more into the use of machines and horse-power in the cultivation and harvesting of our crops, and this only makes the fences a more intolerable nuisance. We want a clean sweep for the grain drills, the cultivators, the mowers and reapers, the tedders and rakes that are ready to relieve aching human muscles. The kindest thing that could happen to the average dairy farm would be to have three-fourths of its fences quietly sink out of sight. Fortunately, most of these farms need draining, and the stones are needed to help carry off the superfluous water.

Future Prospects of Cotton in the South.

Those who have held that "Cotton is King," now that the king is dethroned, seem determined that he shall not be even a citizen among us. They prophesy evil of the plant, and advocate the growing of other crops in the Cotton States. "Let us raise the cereals and the meats that we consume at home, and let the world take care of itself. If we grow cotton, let it be only in such quantity as we can manufacture at home." This outcry of disappointed ambition is very natural and very foolish. The vindictive feelings of a people will have very little to do with the crops they raise. These will be governed mainly by commercial considerations Men will raise that by which they think they can make the most money, whether it accords with their political views or not. We cultivate land to get ahead in the world, and to sustain our families, and not to build up or demolish political theories. It is the best economy for the commonwealth and for the individual that every locality should raise the crops for which it has the best natural or acquired facilities. The new lands in the north-west will grow wheat very largely, because it pays better than any thing else. In the valleys of the Susquehanna and its tributaries, they will follow the rotation, corn, oats, wheat, clover, and timothy, because these crops suit the soil and climate, and pay better than dairy farming. In New York they will raise butter and cheese. About our large cities, they will follow truck farming. In the cotton belt, they will continue to grow cotton for the same reason. The plant flourishes there better than in any other region where it has been tried, and can be raised most economically. When men can make from fifty to a hundred dollars per acre by putting in this crop, they will not plant corn and oats to get half as much. Men will follow dollars rather than dogmas in their industries. We expect to see cotton flourish in the South more extensively than ever. With all the destruction of the war, a very large capital is still invested in lands, gins, gin-houses, presses, and sheds, and the people have the requisite skill to raise and send it to market. The plantations may gradually grow smaller under the new order of things, but the old crops, with some slight variations, will be continued. Last year, with an almost unparalleled drouth and other hindrances in the matter of deficient capital and disorganized labor, nearly two millions of bales were raised. With favorable weather, at least three millions of bales would have been sent to market last year. Within a very short period, we expect to see the old time cotton crops greatly exceeded. Violent partisans may wail because thereof, but they cannot help it.

Liming Land.

This practice, which is so common in British agriculture, is but little known in our country outside of New Jersey and Pennsylvania. In a recent visit to the grain growing districts of these States, we found lime as highly esteemed as manure, and a regular part of their rotation, as we have noticed elsewhere. Where lime can be had at ten cents a bushel and under, as it can in all the limestone regions of Pennsylvania, the practice is almost universal. It is used a good deal on farms, far distant from the lime-kilns, where it costs at the depot or canal twenty cents a bushel and upwards. The conviction of its utility in these States may be said to be universal, and if it is not used, it is either owing to the high price of the article, or to the fact that agriculture receives little attention.

It is applied by some to the sod immediately after mowing, and this sod is turned under either in the fall or in the spring for corn. It is claimed that the lime stimulates the growth of grass, and affects favorably every crop in the rotation. It would be impossible, without liming, to keep up the grain farms to their present degree of productiveness. It is also claimed for the summer application and the spring plowing, that it distributes the lime more equally, and keeps it near the surface. The lime which has been carried down by the fall and winter rains, is brought to the surface again when the sod is inverted. By this method also, the lime has more time to act upon the inert material in the soil, and to prepare plant food for the subsequent crop. Other farmers are quite as certain that the best time to apply lime is upon the inverted sod in the spring, while the ground is preparing for corn. They want to keep the lime as near the surface as possible, and have no fears of its late action upon the crop. The quantity applied to the acre is from thirty to a hundred bushels, depending somewhat upon the character of the soil, the price of the lime, and the theoretical views of the planter. The better the soil, that is, the more clay and vegetable matter it contains, the more lime it will bear. Some think a hundred bushels quite too much, and that so much has a tendency to turn the stalks yellow, and to diminish the yield. Smaller quantities, say from 30 to 50 bushels, are more commonly applied. The lime is usually brought from the lime-kiln or depot in its caustic state, and is dropped upon the land in heaps where it is to be used. It is there slaked by the application of water, and is about doubled in quantity by this process. It is then spread as evenly as possible over the land. This makes a cheap dressing for the land even at twenty cents a bushel. The effect is very clearly marked wherever it is used. It keeps up the fertility of the soil, and makes remunerative crops even without manure. Of course, with manure the crops are larger and pay better. The question very naturally arises, if liming land will pay in other districts where it is not now used? Without answering this question at once in the affirmative, we think the results in these States are such as to encourage every farmer who can get lime at a reasonable price to make the experiment. We have abundance of lime rock in regions where it is not burned at all. The conviction is quite common that it will not pay to use lime upon limestone soils, but in Pennsylvania the effects of the application are quite as marked upon these soils as upon any other. Then it is supposed that it is a difficult and expensive process to burn lime. Very much of this article is made upon the farms where it is used without even a kiln for burning, as we shall show in an illustrated article next month. The lime can be made by the most unskilled labor, and with the roughest and cheapest kinds of fuel. Wherever there is lime rock and cheap fuel, we have no doubt the lime can be furnished at less than twenty cents a bushel. In the vicinity of cities and large towns, oyster shells accumulate in quantities, and can be put to better use than road making and grading. They are easily reduced with brush or peat, and afford cheap lime and generally of better quality than the rock yields. We desire to have the experiment made in other States on a scale large enough to settle the question. We believe many of our farmers will doubtless find it to their interest to use lime.

When to Turn in Clover.

In the regions where green crops are turned under for manure, there is a diversity of practice. Some plow when the crop is in its most succulent state. The rule for clover is when the heads are about half turned brown. The reason offered for this practice is, that the bulk of the crop is then the greatest, and it undergoes most rapid decomposition in the soil. Others do not plow in clover until late in fall, and after it has been well pastured. The reasons they give for this practice are: 1st, that turning in the clover green, makes the soil sour, and has a tendency to bring in sorrel. 2. It has a bad influence upon subsequent crops. 3. In waiting until fall, you have the advantage of pasturing, and if the cattle are kept upon the pasture, as they should be, everything the field produces is returned to it. 4. More carbonaceous matter is returned to the soil. What you lose in tops, you gain in the roots of the clover, which have four or five months longer to grow. 5. Better crops follow. Some of the best farmers in Pennsylvania follow this method altogether. Others still wait until the following spring, and turn in the clover just as it begins to grow.

Buckwheat as a Green Crop.

Where this grain is sowed the 1st of August, it will be in condition to plow in for a rye crop the last of September. We have seen rye taken from a field four years in succession, with no other manure than buckwheat turned in at the time of sowing the rye. There was a constant increase in the yield of the grain, showing the benefit of the green crop. If the land is not strong enough to give a good growth of buckwheat, some manure will be necessary. A continued succession of grain crops does not show good husbandry, but it may answer for remote fields, where stable manure can not be applied economically. The green crops and the grain should come in a regular rotation, and if the soil is thin, several green crops may be turned in, in succession, with profit.

Plan for a Fixed or Movable Fence.

We need not apologize for again introducing the subject of fences, for it is one which concerns every farmer, and the cost of keeping up good fences is (or would be) a drain upon many farms, which cancels nearly all the profits. Mr. W. T. Millar, of Jefferson Co., Wis., advocates the use of iron posts 2½ feet long, made of inch rod, inserted in large stones. (Fig. 1.) A hole 3 inches deep is drilled in the stone, the bar inserted, and the remaining space filled up with melted sulphur or lead.

Fig. 1.

The stones used are of such a size that by the aid of the posts, which would afford a powerful leverage, several might be easily loaded upon a stone-boat, and distributed along the line of the fence. Mr. Millar attaches the panels to the posts by putting one on each side, and bolting or pinning them together. (Fig. 2.) The panels of a movable fence might be securely hooked together by a common iron hook and staple, and those of a permanent fence might be fastened best by withes of galvanized iron wire. The posts need not be more than 2½ to 3 feet long to support the panels of a 4 or 4½-foot fence. The advantages claimed are that the posts will last long, that they will stand on the top of the ground, that they may be easily moved and reset, or straightened up, and that they may be made in winter. Two furrows or more,

Fig. 2.—IRON POST FENCE.

turned together along the line, would be a good substitute for the bottom rail. The strips of which the fence is made should be narrow, to present little surface to the wind.

The plan of using iron posts is not novel, for posts of several forms have long been used, driven into the ground and braced. The ends in the ground rust rapidly; the part above also rusts, unless painted with coal tar. When stones can not be obtained, it is very easy to improvise them with gravel and hydraulic cement. Simply dig a pit, say two feet long, a foot deep, and a foot wide. Fill this with the concrete, and insert the post in the middle, as in fig. 3. This would, we think, be cheaper and better than drilling holes in very hard stones. Wooden posts may be set in the same way—that is, by digging holes, setting in the posts, and filling up with concrete. Use a peck of lime and a quart of cement to 2½ to 3 bushels of gravel, mixed coarse and fine, some of the stones being as large as one's fist. Thus set, gate or fence posts will last a life time.

Fig. 3.

WORK THE MUCK MINES.—The spring has been so wet that it would not be strange if we had a dry summer or autumn, making ponds and swamps accessible. Drawing out muck to some spot easily reached, always pays the farmer well. He should keep on hand a large bank of muck, and the larger and older the better. The sunshine, rains, and frosts, are always improving it, as the rank growth of weeds on such heaps abundantly proves. It is always available then for the yards, stables, or privies, or wherever deodorizers are wanted. Composts can be made on short notice, and top-dressings administered just at the right time for grass field or garden.

Fig. 1.—PERSPECTIVE ELEVATION OF BARN—FROM THE NORTH-WEST.

The Barn of Mr. David Lyman.

With the increase of wealth, and we must add of good sense and enlarged ideas, among the farmers of the country, there is a gradual but very decided improvement in farm architecture. The old system was to build small barns and add others on three sides of a yard, and perhaps of several yards, and to add sheds and pig-pens, and corn-houses, and such minor structures as might seem desirable. Thus, in the course of a few years the group of roofs, big and little, span and lean-to, in the rear of a large farmer's dwelling, would present the appearance of a small crowded village. One of our neighbors has some 25 or 30 roofs pertaining to his barns. Many a farmer is shocked at the idea of investing $12,000 to $15,000 in a barn, and to spend $20,000 to $25,000 would seem utterly unwarrantable extravagance anywhere. Yet we doubt if the group of buildings referred to could be put up for an average of $1,000 apiece, while, compared with a well arranged barn, they are inconvenient and extremely expensive to keep in good repair.

Among the many large and expensive barns recently erected, we have seen none which is more thoroughly satisfactory to old school farmers with broad ideas, than one built by Mr. David Lyman, of Middlefield, Connecticut. Mr. Lyman is an active farmer and manufacturer, employing the water power adjacent to the old homestead of his fathers, and tilling the broad acres of the farm on which he was born, a family possession for four generations. He needs a very large barn for his farm purposes simply, and has built one, of which we give a view, and plans. The elevation of the building, (figure 1), shows entrances to its two main stories; there is an other story below.

THE UPPER, OR HAY FLOOR.—This floor is shown in fig. 2; all the hay, grain, and straw is stored upon it, and it maintains the same level throughout. Two threshing floors cross the building, and are entered from the high ground on the west by a very easy ascent. The main entrance crosses over an engine-room, (seen in figs. 1 and 3,) which is of stone, arched above, and roomy as well as secure.

By means of Plumb's Hay-Fork and Traveler, of which no less than six railways and travelers are fixtures over the bays, the hay is taken from the loads and dropped in any part of the immense bays. The forks are worked by one horse, attached to Dedrick's hoisting machine, of which Mr. Lyman has two, placed near the great doors during the haying season, as indicated by the figures marked *H, P*, in the plan, fig. 2. A peculiarity of the Plumb-Fork and attachments is, that the traveler on which the fork moves, is brought back over the load, by means of a heavy weight hung, and rising up and down, on the outside of the barn. The timbers containing pulleys over which the ropes pass which suspend these weights, are shown in

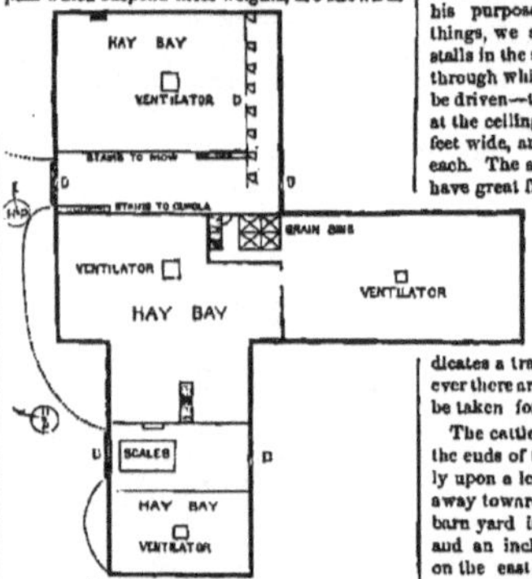

Fig. 2.—PLAN OF HAY FLOOR.

the view, fig. 1, near the high windows in the gable. The hoisting machine consists of a drum, which is turned by a horse driven in a circle; on this the rope is wound. By the movement of a lever, the drum is set loose, and the rope unwinds, thus lowering the fork to the load without backing the horse.

On this floor are the bins for grain and ground feed, provided with shutes connecting them with the feeding floor. There are hay scales, also, a fixture in one of the floors, which afford the means of being very accurate in many things, in regard to which guess work is ordinarily the rule. Not only are hay, grain, and all products sold by weight, weighed here, but beeves bought to fatten are weighed when brought in, and when turned off fat, and the gain accurately known. The great ventilators, so conspicuous in the view, (fig. 1), pass from the feeding floor through this one to the roof, and being furnished with doors at different elevations, quite to the top of the mow, thus form convenient shutes to throw down hay or straw. A long flight of stairs passes from the principal barn floor to the cupola, from which a magnificent view is had of the whole farm and surrounding country, not the least impressive feature in which is a permanent mowing lot of 100 acres, without a fence, all under-drained, which lies contiguous to the barn, and will do its share towards filling its capacious bays and mows.

THE FEEDING FLOOR is entered by several doors. Those in the main building are seen in the view, and the plan, fig. 3. Two double doors open upon a spacious floor in the rear of the horse stalls and extending through the middle of the main barn. The northwest corner is occupied by a large harness and tool room, in which is a chimney for a stove. On the right of the front entrance is the wagon and carriage room, closed by a sliding door, or partition. There is room on the open part of this floor, (behind the horse stalls, and adjacent), to drive in three wagons at a time, and let the horses stand hitched; and while the stables are being cleaned out, several of the horses may be hitched to pendant chains in different parts of the floor, and so be out of the way, and not interfere with one another. There seems to be a good deal of waste room here. Mr. Lyman assures us that he would not have less on any account; and for his purposes, considering his way of doing things, we agree with him. Between the ox-stalls in the south wing, is a 10-foot passage way through which carts with roots or green feed may be driven—the stairs in the middle, being hinged at the ceiling and fastened up. The stalls are 7 feet wide, and arranged to tie up two cattle in each. The animals are fastened by neck chains, have great freedom of motion, but can not quarrel. A gutter to conduct off the urine runs along behind each range of stalls, and there are well secured traps, one in about every 15 feet, through which the manure is dropped to the cellar. The letter *C*, wherever it occurs in fig. 3, indicates a trap-door for a manure drop. Wherever there are doors which, in the engraving might be taken for windows, the letter *D* is placed.

The cattle pass to the yards through doors in the ends of the wings. The south yard is nearly upon a level with the floor, sloping gradually away toward the south and east, but the large barn yard is on the level of the manure cellar, and an inclined way gives access to the yard on the east side from the cow stalls. Three roomy, loose boxes are provided, one for horses, and two for lying-in stables for cows; and from the satisfaction which Mr. Lyman takes in these, we think, if he could be brought to admit, that the barn is not perfect, he would arrange to have several more. Near the points marked *W*, and *F*, stand the hydrant for flowing water, and the trough for mixing feed, and here, too, the shutes for grain and cut feed discharge from the floor above.

VENTILATION AND LIGHT.—Four immense ventilating trunks, 4 feet square, rise from the feeding floor straight to the roof. These are capped by "Emerson's Ventilators," of the largest size, and cause a constant change of air in the stables, the draft being ordinarily sufficient to be felt like a fresh breeze by raising the hand anywhere within a few feet of the open-

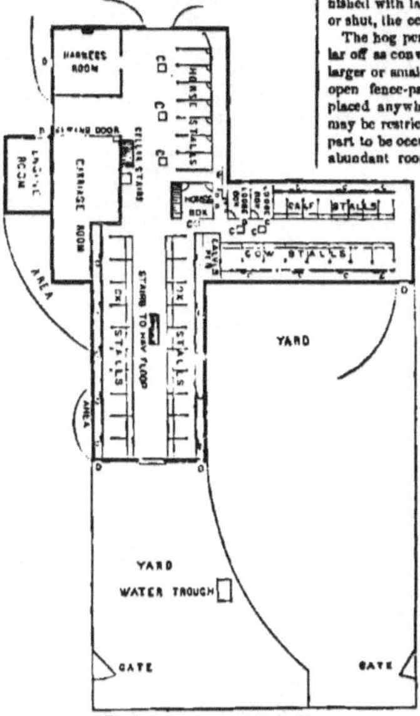

Fig. 3.—PLAN OF FEEDING FLOOR.

ings. This keeps the air in the whole establishment sweeter and purer than in most dwellings. The windows on all sides of this floor are of large size, with double sashes, hung with weights.

Under the main drive-way is a fire-proof room, intended for an engine, but not now in use for that purpose. When this is set and in operation, it will, we presume, do away with horse-power for elevating and carrying hay, cutting hay, stalks, and straw, grinding apples, and grain, and the boiler will furnish steam for cooking hay and cattle fodder.

THE BARN CELLAR.—This is arranged for hogs, roots, and manure. The fixed partitions in it are only two—the one enclosing the root cellar, and the other, outside of that, shutting off a wide, cemented passage way, extending from the door at the northeast corner, around two sides of the root-cellar. (See fig. 4.) The rest of the cellar is occupied by the manure, and hogs are enclosed upon different parts of it, according to convenience. That part of the cellar wall against the side-hill, is very substantial, and laid up of cement concrete. Part of the remaining walls are brick, and in these are ordinary windows; in the remaining portion of the walls wooden partitions are inserted between the posts. These, as a general rule, consist of an upper portion hinged to the sill of the building, which may be raised and hooked up against the ceiling, and of a lower part, like a solid fence-panel, which two men can take out and set at one side, affording entrance for carts or cattle from the barn yards. The upper parts of these door-like walls are, in most cases, furnished with large sashes, so that, whether open or shut, the cellar is very light.

The hog pens are formed by dividing the cellar off as convenience and necessity dictate, into larger or smaller yards, by means of substantial, open fence-panels. Thus, the hogs may be placed anywhere on the manure, or their range may be restricted, so as to allow a considerable part to be occupied by cattle. The cellar affords abundant room to work over the manure, and make regular compost heaps, if desired. The two large hog-pens are so far fixtures that platforms (2, fig. 4) are set, upon which the hogs are fed, and which prevent a waste of food.

THE YARDS are open to the south and east, and contain large troughs supplied with running water, and racks for fodder. No water flows into them except the direct rain-fall, the entire building being furnished with eave-troughs and conductors; and the wash of the yards being collected is conducted to vats where it can be pumped over the manure heaps. Even this is not sufficient to keep the immense heaps of manure in a suitably moist condition at all times, and so a hose is attached to a hydrant to wet them down occasionally. We append some memoranda received from Mr. Lyman, in response to questions proposed by us, which leave little else for us to say in regard to this most commodious and substantial barn. It is exceedingly roomy and comfortable for men and beasts, at all seasons. It thoroughly protects animals, and their fodder, with all farm products, implements, and manure, from the weather, effects great saving of labor, is subject to easy and rapid inspection, and not least, it is easier for hired men to keep it clean and in order, than to do otherwise. The barn and surroundings will well repay a visit.

Neither care nor expense has been spared to make the whole structure as substantial and convenient as possible, the material being all of the best quality. The whole subject has been under consideration, and the general plan formed, for several years. Mr. L. did not build until he felt sure he knew exactly what he wanted, and was ready to secure this to himself and his children, at any reasonable cost.

MR. LYMAN'S MEMORANDA.—*Timbers, Flooring, Siding, Roof, etc.*—Lower timbers, white oak, 12 × 14; joists, chestnut; floor, chestnut; rest of the frame, white pine, hemlock, and spruce, mainly hemlock. The long cross-beams, 55 ft. long, squared 12 × 14 inches, are pine. Threshing floors, 2½-inch pine plank, grooved, with a tongue inserted. Bay floors, 1¾-inch pine, planed and matched, laid planed side down. Siding is pine, 10 to 12 inches wide, planed and matched, with battening of this  form—costs no more than plain. The Roof is 1¼-inch, planed and matched spruce well slated. Furnished with Spratt's lightning rods. The Architect is R. G. Russell, New-Haven. The Builder, Henry E. Woodward, Thompsonville, Conn.

Size of Barn.—The building covers more than one-fifth of an acre of land, and thus there is over three-fifths of an acre under a roof. The main barn is 55 × 80 feet square; the wings, each 56 feet long, the south one being 35, and the east wing 31½ feet wide. The four points which I sought to obtain were: 1st. Economy of room under a given roof; 2d. Plenty of light; 3d. Plenty of air, and ventilation which would draw off all deleterious gas as fast as generated; 4th. Convenience, to save labor. Saving of manure, and many other things are of course included. No barn should have less thorough ventilation. The windows are all hung with pulleys, and are lowered in warm days in winter, and closed in cold days. This is important.

As to *Inspection.*—I can in five minutes see whether 75 head of cattle and 8 horses are all right, and the work of attending them well done.

The gables on the sides of the barn and south wing, give great strength to the frame, afford light to the floor, and in summer give a splendid draft of air over the floor, to say nothing of the beauty added to the building.

A cheap barn can be built on this general plan of: 1st. Basement for manure roots and hogs; 2d. Floor for stock, wagons, and tools; 3d. Floor for hay, grain, hay scales, etc. And I believe that a farmer may get for the same money one-third more room than by the old plan. If a man has no side hill, let him make an approach or drive-way, 60 feet long, for his hay story, and he is just as well off. It is an easy matter. All cement walls should be made early in the season, to have the work get thoroughly dry before frost. The mows are so large that I mow away no hay while carting, but do it the

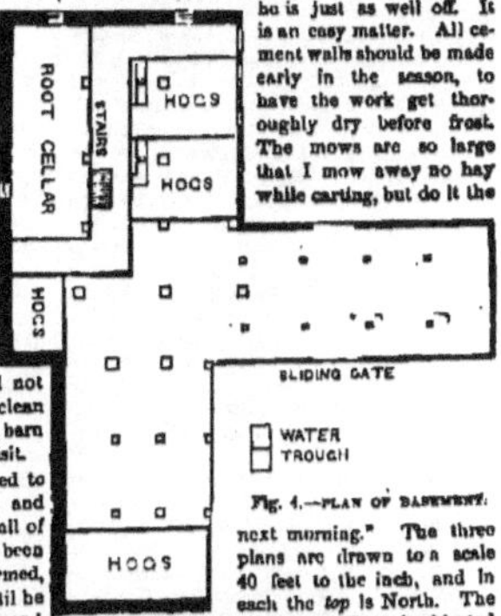

Fig. 4.—PLAN OF BASEMENT.

next morning." The three plans are drawn to a scale 40 feet to the inch, and in each the *top* is North. The storing of manure in barn-cellars is objected to by many farmers—but with the free use of dry muck, etc., as absorbents, and such perfect ventilation, we cannot take ground against it.

FEEDING GREEN FODDER.—Cattle and horses will eat an enormous amount of green fodder, if fed fresh to them in the stall. Serious evil sometimes comes from this practice, as the animals eat too much, and bloat, as when turned into rank clover. It saves labor to cut early, and let the corn, oats, clover, sorghum, or whatever else used as green fodder, wilt thoroughly, and thus lose a good part of its water, before feeding it out. Milch cows can hardly eat too much regularly; and after feeding all day in the pasture, if a cow will eat a good forkfull of green corn fodder, the result will surely be seen in the pail. Green fodder ought to be fed in racks, in the yard, and the cows yarded at night. Two-thirds of all their manure is thus saved, and the dung heaps grow almost as fast in summer as in winter.

Rotation of Crops in Eastern Pennsylvania.

There is much more uniformity in the rotation of crops in Eastern Pennsylvania than we had anticipated. The lower part of the Valley of the Lehigh, and the Valleys of the North and West branches of the Susquehanna, which we recently visited, are mainly grain growing districts, and we suspect all the best farming of the State would come under the head of cereal agriculture. Only about a fourth part of the State was put down as improved land in 1850, and with all the rapid improvement of agriculture, there is probably not more than a third of the State now under cultivation. There are still considerable tracts of unbroken forest, and vast regions of rough, mountainous land, which the lumbermen are rapidly stripping of all large trees, and leaving it to make a second or third growth. The best farming is to be found in the valleys of the rivers and creeks, where the soil is almost uniformly fertile and well adapted to grain and grass.

The rotation is a five or six years' course, beginning with corn upon a clover or timothy sod. The liming of the land, which is almost universal, takes place in connection with this crop. The lime is applied at the rate of from thirty to a hundred bushels to the acre, and is expected to last through the course. There is a difference of practice both in regard to the time of applying the lime and of turning over the sod. Some apply the lime upon the grass immediately after mowing, and turn under the sod the following spring. They say the lime strengthens the growth of the grass, and sinks into the soil, so that the spring plowing brings it to the surface where it ought to be. Others plow in the fall, and lime either in the fall or spring upon the plowed field. We found the best farmers most strongly in favor of the spring plowing, and they would only justify fall plowing where there was danger of not having help enough to finish the needed plowing seasonably in the spring. The lime and the sod are the main reliance for the corn crop, which yields from forty to sixty bushels to the acre.

The second course is either oats or a summer fallow. The best usage is in favor of the oats, for they say that it is in itself a paying crop, and does not very much diminish the subsequent crop of wheat. The third course is winter wheat, for which preparation is made by spreading all the manure of the farm upon the oat stubble or the fallow, and plowing it in. The Mediterranean wheat is the variety most commonly used, and the yield in good years is from twenty to thirty bushels to the acre. The white varieties of wheat formerly used were more productive, but were more delicate, and more liable to be destroyed by insects. At the time of sowing the wheat, timothy is sown, and clover the following spring, about the last of the frosts, when the ground is cracked with settling.

This gives clover as the fourth course, of which there are frequently two crops taken in the same season, one for hay and the second for seed, of which the yield is from one and a half to two and a half bushels. The fifth year the timothy has the ground, and this crop is continued for one or more years according to circumstances. If the grass is very good, or if manure is plenty for top dressing, it stays in grass until it is wanted to begin another rotation. Much larger areas of land are kept under the plow than is common in the dairy regions. Grain fields of from twenty to fifty acres are of frequent occurrence. Upon one 300-acre farm that we visited in the famous Buffalo Valley, we found 60 acres in wheat, 50 in corn, and 30 in oats; or more than one half the whole area of the farm. We think the farms in these valleys would average one fourth of their whole area in these three crops. Rye, which is so common in the dairy regions, is very little raised in the valley of the Susquehanna. In Eastern Pennsylvania it is much more common. This rotation is very well adapted to the wants of the grain growing districts, and perhaps can not at once be changed for the better. Lime is everywhere abundant, and with the manure made upon the farm, furnishes the ready means of keeping up the fertility of the soil. Potatoes are not much raised, except to supply the wants of the family and the nearest village market. The grain growing farmers of Pennsylvania, and of other districts also in the United States, have no faith in the cultivation of roots. They certainly could be raised profitably for stock feeding in winter, but would require additional laborers. Grain and hay are the principal products sold from these farms. There is some fattening of cattle in the winter, and some raising of pork and making of butter, but they are mainly for the home markets.

Walks and Talks on the Farm.—No. 44.

The editor of the *Agriculturist* wrote me that he had received a number of letters referring to my Walks and Talks, "some praisewise and some otherwise." I asked him to forward them, and he did so. He must have retained the "praisewise," for all of them are "otherwise." Several of them criticise my treatment of the cow we lost by milk fever. I had another cow taken sick in the same way, and gave her the same treatment, except the ergot, and she recovered. This does not prove, however, that the ergot was the cause of the death of the other, as one of my neighbors lost the best cow he had from milk fever that had not had ergot, and the Deacon says a farmer in an adjoining town lost six cows from milk fever this spring. He thinks the disease is unusually prevalent.

One writer advises me to get a breed of hogs that will not kill lambs. I have both the Suffolk and Essex, neither of which have any savage tendencies. The sows that killed the lambs were some coarse, ill-bred creatures that I bought for the purpose of crossing with the thoroughbreds. It is said that such sows are better mothers than finer animals. They certainly breed better, and the little pigs take after the sire in fineness of bone, early maturity, and fattening qualities. But they need high feeding. You can push them forward so as to be ready for the butcher in five or six months, but if half starved, when young, they rarely get over it, even if well fed afterwards. It was very annoying, however, to lose the lambs. I sold the rest of them to the butcher for $4.00 a head, and the keep of a lamb is never felt.

Another of the letters is very savage. The writer assails me on all sides, but makes no specific charges. I take him to be a city man who knows nothing of agriculture, and is annoyed because I do not represent farming in accordance with his imaginary notions. All I can say is that I tell the truth according to my experience. I do not find farm-life entirely free from care and anxiety. Perhaps I exaggerate the disappointments and annoyances. But if so, it is not a common fault of agricultural editors. We hear more of the successes than of the failures, and yet the latter, properly considered, teach more than the former. A man who really loves farming will not be discouraged by hearing of the mistakes of others. He will try to avoid them. I have had my trials, but think I shall succeed in renovating my farm. Every year affords me more encouragement. If I mistake not, we have five acres that will turn out more, and far better, barley than I got from twenty acres the first year. And I have fourteen acres of clover that will afford more good feed than could have been cut from half the farm. I have a very fair crop of wheat on land where the oats the first year only yielded 8 bushels per acre, and those hardly fit to feed the geese. I have some very promising corn on the "Deacon's duck pond," and fair grass on part of the old stump lot, where nothing ever grew before but rushes and weeds. But if I should talk in this style, it might be thought that I had quit farming, and gone back to the old editorial chair.

The more I use petroleum paint, the better I like it. A few days ago we painted an old wagon that looked as though it would tumble to pieces like the old chaise. The hubs were full of cracks, the bolsters loose, and the box decidedly shaky. We took off the nuts, oiled them, put on wide washers where the wood was rotten, and made all tight and snug, then put on all the oil the wood would absorb, going over the hubs and tires several times as fast as the oil soaked in. We got in at least two gallons of oil. The cracks closed up, the tires were tight, the box snug, and the wagon looked almost as strong as a new one. We all know that soaking wheels in water will tighten the tires, but it is merely temporary. As soon as the water dries out, the wheels are as loose as ever. The oil is absorbed more rapidly than water, and will have, I think, the same effect, and be permanent. But if not, go over the wagon again as often as needed. It is little trouble. It seems curious to me that such a use of petroleum could be patented. In Captain Cox's *Asiatic Researches* he says: "The town of Rainanghong is the centre of a district in which there are some hundred petroleum wells in full activity. * * * The annual quantity of petroleum produced by the district exceeds 400,000 hogsheads. It is used by the lower classes in lamps, instead of oil, and when mixed with earth or ashes answers the purpose of fuel. A composition of petroleum and resin is an excellent material for covering wood-work, etc." It was also used for ship bottoms to preserve them from insects, etc.

I planted potatoes this year on clover sod. The clover last year was cut for hay, and afterwards for seed. This is running the land pretty hard, but as nothing is exported from the farm except the seed, and as a bushel of oil-cake meal which costs about $1.50, contains more fertilizing ingredients than a bushel of clover seed, and as you can get five or six bushels of oil-meal for one bushel of clover seed, the farm is benefited by exchanging the clover seed for oil-cake. But unless some such plan as this is adopted, growing clover seed impoverishes your land. Last fall, in cutting the clover seed, a strip about the width of the machine was skipped, and you can now see the effect on the potatoes. They are far better than on the rest of the field. I should not be surprised if the yield was one-third or one-half greater, and this will a good deal more than pay for the clover seed. With such effects it is not surprising that so many good farmers object to raising clover seed. But I think it is nevertheless true that if the money obtained for the seed is expended in oil-cake, and the manure returned to the land, there is a decided gain. You do not see the effect, however, quite so soon as if the clover was pastured with sheep, or plowed under.

You may recollect, I asked your opinion as to whether a clover field that was cut for seed would give a good crop of clover the next season. I had such a field, and, not being willing to risk the whole, I plowed up half of it and planted potatoes, and the other half I left for hay. The clover is not quite as good as the first crop was last year, but much better than I expected. I sowed no timothy, but there is quite a sprinkling of it among the clover, and I shall have a fair crop of hay. I presume, nevertheless, that a heavy crop of seed weakens the clover plant very materially, and, as a rule, it should not be allowed to go to seed except in cases where it is to be plowed up the next season.

This morning I was up unusually early, and saw a Dominique rooster in a cherry tree picking off the fruit almost as neatly as a robin. During the day, when we are around, they do not meddle with them. The little chickens eat the strawberries, but the hens seem to know better, although they occasionally take a slice out of a Trollope's Victoria or an Agriculturist. They leave us all the Wilson's. If chickens are well fed, they do comparatively little injury in the garden. The ducks have done us the most damage this year, as they manifest a great partiality for green peas. They gobbled up a whole row of Daniel O'Rourke's, and if we had not shut them up, they would have left us scarcely a pea in the garden. I suppose the only way is to have a large yard and hen-house where you can shut up the poultry when they prove troublesome. The next best thing is to feed them all they will eat, and keep them out of the garden as much as possible. A garden with a high fence round it is not at all ornamental.

A gentleman in Huntington, Conn., writes me that he has sown twelve acres of corn, intending to plow it in for manure, but would like to know my opinion as to "whether it would not be better to cure it and feed it out." I judge from the fact that corn is the crop selected, the land is not a heavy clay, and that the object in plowing it under is simply to furnish manure, and not to loosen the soil. This being the case, the only point to be determined is, whether the feed will not pay for the expense of curing and storing the crop, and drawing back the manure. If the manure does not drain away, but is all saved, it will be worth within five per cent. as much as if the crop was plowed under. This is true, I think, even if the crop is fed out to milch cows. The milk will not carry off more than five per cent. of the nitrogen and phosphates. If fed to dry cows, the loss will be still less. And if, as is too often the case, the cows are no heavier in the spring than in the fall—if, in other words, the animals have neither grown or got fatter, I do not see where there can be any loss except in the carbonaceous matter used to keep up the animal heat. Where can there be any loss of nitrogen or phosphate? or of potash, soda, lime, magnesia, etc.? There is soda in the blood, but there is no more blood in the animal than there was at the commencement of winter. There are phosphates and lime in the bones, but there has been no increase of bones. There is nitrogen in the flesh, but for each pound of new flesh added, a pound of old flesh has been transformed, and the nitrogen from this is exactly equal to the nitrogen taken from the food. There is, therefore, no loss. The manure will contain as much plant food, except carbonaceous matter, as the food consumed by the animal. The question then is simply, what is the value of an acre of cured corn fodder, say three tons? A good-sized cow would probably eat from 30 to 35 pounds a day, and the three tons would last her about six months. Now what is it worth to winter a cow? A cow weighing from 900 to 1000 pounds will eat about 200 pounds of hay a week. With hay at $10 per ton, this would make the cost of keeping a cow six months $26. If we estimate the manure worth half the price of the hay, we have $13 as the actual value of the food given to a cow during six months. What farmer in the New England or Middle States will winter a cow for less? Now in plowing under clover or corn fodder as a green manure we lose this sum, less the cost of cutting and curing the crop and the expense of drawing back the manure. Many farmers make a great deal more than this from their food. One would think few could make less. In this section the past spring, hay was sold for a short time at $30 to $35 per ton, and it would seem in such circumstances to be worse than folly to plow under good hay or fodder, when, by feeding it to animals, we get the same benefit from the manure, and have the food in addition.

If the present drouth continues, many of us would like these twelve acres of green corn for our milch cows. But if the corn can not be used for this purpose, and if it can not be cut and cured, or used to good advantage when it is cured, why then, plow it under. It is a very low order of farming, but is a good deal better than skinning the land by selling all the hay and straw.

I am not sure that a good summer fallow would not enrich land just as much as plowing under a crop of corn. If not, why not? On very sandy soil, where some of the elements of plant food may be washed out of the soil, a crop that would organize and retain it may be better than a summer fallow. And on a very heavy soil, where you want the mechanical action of the green manure for loosening the soil, plowing under the crop may produce better results. But otherwise I do not exactly see what we gain from plowing under a crop of corn. It must be confessed, however, that we do not know enough to speak very positively on the point. It may be that the large quantity of carbonaceous matter plowed under in the green crop, may, in fermenting, form organic acids that act on the latent plant food in the soil, and render it available. Or, at all events, the carbonic acid ultimately formed, doubtless has such an effect. I have always supposed, however, that we get enough of such matter from the roots and stubble, in proportion to other ingredients, without plowing under a whole crop. So far as wheat is concerned, I have never known an application of carbonaceous matter, directly or indirectly, attended with any increase of the grain. It will give more straw. And those farmers who tell us that the reason they can not grow as good wheat as formerly, is not owing to the land being poorer, because they get straw enough for forty bushels per acre, while the crop only turns out 20 bushels, should consider whether they are not furnishing too much carbonaceous matter to the soil, and too little nitrogen and phosphates.

"What about the price of wheat?" asks an old friend. It is not safe to predict. I hope we shall have a good crop. The country needs it. Manufacturers need it, the Secretary of the Treasury is looking anxiously at the grain fields of the West, and farmers themselves need it as much as any other class to pay high wages and still higher taxes. I am inclined to think we shall have a fair crop, and I hope for fair prices. The markets of the world are bare of wheat. There is no accumulation any where. High prices have brought it all out. In such circumstances, it would seem that the new crop should command at least as much as the cost of production. Such will be the case if farmers will not sell for less. Manufacturers sometimes sell, they say, for less than cost. But they frequently make large profits. Farmers never do. Then again, a manufacturer fears to hold, because there may be a change of fashion, but the fashion for wheat does not change. It is always wanted. I am aware that consumers have much to say about the extortion of farmers. The charge is unfounded. It is vain to expect that wheat can be grown as cheaply as it was 25 or 30 years ago. In this section, I do not see, with the present cost of implements, wages, and taxes, how wheat can be grown for less than $1.50 per bushel, even if you get the land for nothing. You may on rich land raise it for less, but you take enough out of the land to make up the difference. Your land will become poorer. If means are taken to keep up the fertility of the soil, we can not grow a bushel of wheat for less than $1.50 a bushel. And if we expect an interest for the money invested in the farm, we ought to get $2.00 a bushel. At $2.50, a good farmer will get ample remuneration. But when the crop does not average over 15 bushels per acre, the profits, even at this figure, are not dazzling. I have made up my mind to sell when I can get $2.25 for red wheat. If consumers can not pay this, let them curtail their expenses in some other direction. Farmers need the money more than French milliners.

Wheat, in England, is now worth from 60s. to 75s. a quarter of eight bushels. Now, as an English shilling is 24 cents of our money, if we multiply the price per quarter by 3, we get the price in dollars and cents. Sixty shillings a quarter, therefore, is $1.80 a bushel. Seventy-five shillings a quarter is $2.25 per bushel. This is in gold. With gold at 140, $1.80 in gold is worth $2.52, and $2.25 in gold is worth $3.15. Wheat, in England, therfore, is worth in our money, from $2.52 to $3.15 per bushel.

The *Agriculturist* should tell us next month, what it costs to send wheat to Liverpool, and London, and we can then form some idea as to what prices we should expect for our wheat. As I understand it, wheat has been for several months higher here than in England, and consequently none was exported. But since the recent decline of $1.00 a bushel in New York, wheat can be exported with a profit, and as long as this is the case, it will be no lower. If we raise more wheat this year than is wanted by our own rapidly increasing population, the price will depend on the foreign demand. We certainly shall not have enough to spare to glut the markets, and farmers should insist on receiving fair prices—and sell when such are offered.

[Copyright secured.]

IMPORTED COTSWOLD RAM, "HIS ROYAL HIGHNESS." — Owned by Burdett Loomis, Windsor Locks, Ct.

Cotswold Sheep.—Mutton and Wool.

When the whole community of sheep raisers is running wild, almost, after fine-wool sheep, it may seem strange to some that we should continually advocate mutton breeds. Perhaps it would not be so if these were the favorites of the speculative class of breeders. We can, and do, raise as good mutton in this country as they do in England, but our people are not such mutton eaters, and, though mutton raising pays quite as well, in fact better usually, than beef raising, yet our market is not a discriminating one, and the most profitable sheep to buy and fatten are fine-wools, if bought with judicious care. There is always sale for South-down and Coltswold mutton, and the difference in price is not what it ought to be, though remunerative.

Of late there has been a remarkable change in the value of the combing wools. They have increased in price, while fine wools rule scarcely any higher than in specie times, and, were the quotations reduced to the gold standard, they would be lower now than for many years. The reasons for the high price of long wools are several. A class of manufactures has come in vogue which requires these combing wools, and the supply from Canada is, in a good measure, cut off by the operation of the new Tariff, while in England, the home demand keeps prices up, and the wool chiefly at home. The small amount of combing wools raised in this country is not, it seems, sufficient for the demand. There seems to be an overstock of goods made from the finest wools, and manufacturers are buying but very limited quantities, hence the general depression of the fine wool market.

A few years ago long wool sold according to quality—length, fineness, strength and gloss—at 25c. to 35c. per pound. Now it sells at 50c. to 75c. The clip of a flock of equal purity and excellence with those shown in our engraving, recently sold, unwashed, at 50c. to 55c., which is equal to 75c. to 82c., according to the usual calculation—deducting one-third as loss in washing. It is not to be expected that these relative prices will continue, but it is certain that these beautiful combing fleeces have gained, and will hold, a value far above carpet wools.

For the real wool raiser, no doubt the best policy will ever be to raise the finest and best wool, free from excess of grease; but for small farmers who have rich farms on which a few sheep, 50 to 100, will do well, none present so great attractions now as do the Cotswolds. They grow to an immense size, Christmas mutton carcasses weighing over 200 pounds being almost every year brought to New York, and sell at the highest prices. They make large early lambs. The grades, half-bred, are very strongly marked, and the three-quarters pure are often hard to tell from the full-blood Cotswolds, except by the accurate and distinctive marks of purity of blood.

The fine ram in the engraving was drawn by our artist at the New England and Vermont Fair last fall, at which he was a first prize winner, and was imported from one of the best, if not the very best flock in Great Britain—that of Robert Garne, at Aldsworth, near North Leach, Eng.

Notes on Strawberries.

The season has, on the whole, been a successful one for the strawberry grower, though in some places, as in southern New Jersey, the heavy rains, which came just as the fruit was ripe, caused considerable loss. A very fine exhibition was held by the American Institute, in New York, on June 25th and 26th, and another by Mr. Knox, at Pittsburgh, on the 26th and 27th of the same month. We attended both of these exhibitions, and give such notes on varieties as we gleaned from these and other sources.

METCALF'S EARLY.—This variety originated in Michigan. In a basket note last month, we quoted Mr. Williams and Mr. Doty for its earliness. We have since seen Mr. Parry, of Cinnaminson, and others, who do not give a very favorable account of its earliness, productiveness, or good quality. Figure 1 gives the shape of the berry, which is of a light scarlet color.

Fig. 1.

HIPPOWAM.—A variety that has been before the public a few years, but has not been extensively cultivated. It originated with Mr. J. W. Faulkner, Stamford, Conn. The engraving, Fig. 2, gives one of the exhibition berries. We have not seen it in bearing, but at several shows very large fruit has been exhibited. It has a remarkable tendency to assume the flattened, coxcomb shape, which tells strongly against its good qualities, which are a firm flesh and a very agreeable flavor. Growers of this variety differ in their accounts of its productiveness.

Fig. 2.—HIPPOWAM.

STINGER'S SEEDLING.—This berry originated with Mr W. H. Stinger, of Gray's Ferry, Pa. We give a figure of it, (fig. 3,) but from the fact that we have never seen the fruit in good condition, do not care to say much about it. There are very few berries upon which it is fair to pass judgment after they have been picked forty-eight hours. We can only say that some of our Philadelphia friends, in whose opinion we place confidence, think well of it.

Fig. 3.—STINGER'S.

SETH BOYDEN.—Mr. Seth Boyden, well known as the originator of the *Agriculturist*, exhibited at the late show of the American Institute his seedling No. 30, which, we understand, is to bear his name. Mr. B. stated that the exhibition was at least ten days too late to allow him to show his berry in perfection. As exhibited, the berry was of great promise, reminding one of the "Agriculturist," but of better color and more regular shape, (fig. 4.) We shall be glad if this proves to be a valuable variety, and one worthy to bear the name of one who has done so much for strawberry culture as has Mr. Seth Boyden, of Newark, N. J.

Fig. 4.—SETH BOYDEN.

ROMEYN'S SEEDLING. — This is a chance seedling raised from mixed seed of the Triomphe de Gand, Austin, and Wilson, grown together. The plants shown at the late exhibition were apparently very productive, though but a small portion of the fruit was ripe. It has a surface much like that of Triomphe de Gand, and its shape is shown in figure 5.

Fig. 5.

CHAS. DOWNING.—Mr. J. S. Downer, of Elkton, Kentucky, with whom originated the well known Downer's Prolific, has sent to the East a berry of remarkable excellence, and which has been named for our distinguished horticulturist, Chas. Downing. Figure 6 gives an average berry, but not one of the largest. Both Mr. Carpenter and Mr. Downing have grown it, and speak in high terms of its productiveness and other good qualities. It is certainly a berry of remarkably high character, as to flavor, and we expect a great deal from its present promise.

Fig. 6.—CHAS. DOWNING.

IDA.—We figure this variety, (fig. 7,) because so much has been said of it. It is reported as productive, but as a fruit we do not consider it as good as the Wilson. The specimens we have seen are quite indifferent. It is pistillate.

Fig. 7.—IDA.

JUCUNDA.—Very fine specimens of this variety were shown at the exhibition of the American Institute, and from all that we can learn, it is growing rapidly in favor. Mr. Knox's farm, at Pittsburgh, is the headquarters of this variety, where it is also known as "700." The show of this fruit upon his grounds was this year something wonderful to see. To say that the crop was large, would not express it—it was immense. We never before saw berries run so uniformly large. The fruit is of fine color, and that it carries well is shown by the fact that it is sold in the New York markets, after a long journey from Pittsburgh. The day we were at Mr. Knox's farm, he shipped a hundred bushels of this variety to New York, a similar quantity to Philadelphia, besides supplying the home market. We figure a good sized berry of regular shape, (fig. 8,) but it would have been easy to select a larger, if no regard were had to form.

Fig. 8.—JUCUNDA.

ABRAHAM LINCOLN.—A variety with this name was shown at the Exhibition of the American Institute. As far as the fruit is concerned, it is not easy to see how it differs from Jucunda.

LUCIDA PERFECTA.—This is a foreign sort that is attracting some attention. The fruit is medium size, (fig. 9), round, of a bright salmon color. For sweetness and richness of flavor it is scarcely surpassed by any variety. The foliage has a very robust appearance, and is of a deep green. From what we have seen of it, it does not appear to bear well enough for a market berry, but it is certainly a sort worthy the attention of amateur cultivators.

Fig. 9.

FILLMORE.—This is a variety about which there is much difference of opinion. On the strong soil of Mr. Knox it proves itself a valuable sort, being there a good bearer, early, and of excellent quality. The fruit is of good size, and its firmness allows it to carry well to market. It has the disadvantage of being pistillate.

GOLIATH, (*Kitley's*).—An old variety which the American Pomological Society placed upon their "Rejected List" some ten years ago, and the cultivation of which is generally abandoned. Yet Mr. Knox finds it to his account to grow it, and thinks more highly of it than of many newer sorts. Size and shape shown in fig. 10.

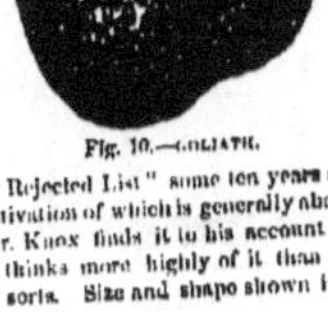

Fig. 10.—GOLIATH.

Agriculturist.—This has assumed a place among the standard varieties, and though like other sorts it is unsatisfactory in some places, there are but few first class berries of recent introduction, so really valuable. It holds its character and size in a remarkable degree. To show how difficult it is to get satisfactory information about varieties, we have before us two letters, dated only one day apart, from Washington, D. C., one of which says: "I find it, on sandy soil, large, ragged, flat, and of poor flavor," while the other writes: "For size and quantity to the stool, the Great Agriculturist stands far ahead."

Upon Mr. Knox's grounds, where it has not heretofore done itself justice, it this year gives a most abundant crop of great excellence.

Pruning the Blackberry.

We know of no plantation that, if left to itself, will become a greater nuisance than one of blackberries. We often see the bushes having their own way, with the fruit up out of reach, or the unsupported, long canes bent over and entangled in an almost impenetrable mass. By proper pruning, the plants may be kept under control, and rendered more productive.

As soon as the new canes get to the hight of four or five feet, their upward growth should be stopped by pinching off the tops. They will then throw off lateral branches freely, which, in turn, are to have their growth checked by pinching, when they reach the length of 18 inches. Bushes thus treated will have their wood better ripened, and will be much more likely to pass the winter in safety than will those that are allowed to continue their growth until it is checked by the approach of frost.

Propagation of Black Cap Raspberries.

The Black Cap Raspberry, (*Rubus occidentalis*), so common in its wild state, has sported into a number of varieties, which are quite popular with growers on account of their productiveness and the absence of suckers. Most other kinds of raspberry sucker to a degree that is annoying, and in the abundance of young plants thus formed, propagate themselves; but the Black Caps multiply by quite a different method. At the end of summer, or early in autumn, when the growth is nearly completed, the long branches bend over until their ends touch the ground, and the plant has the general form of figure 1. From the tips of the branches thus brought in contact with the ground, roots are thrown out, and finally a strong bud appears. We have only to sever the stem just above the surface, and we have a new plant. Often, after the point of the stem has taken root, the buds just above (or

Fig. 1.—Manner of growth of the black cap.

rather below,) it will throw out shoots, which will in turn take root, and thus form a cluster of plants, as in figure 2, which, of course, are to be separated when taken up the following spring. Though more or less young plants will be formed without any care on the part of the cultivator, yet as the motion caused by the winds will prevent many of the pendant branches from taking root, it is best, where plants are wanted, to slightly cover the tips with sufficient earth to hold them in place. This operation should not be performed until the wood acquires sufficient firmness, otherwise it will decay.

There are several red raspberries, of which

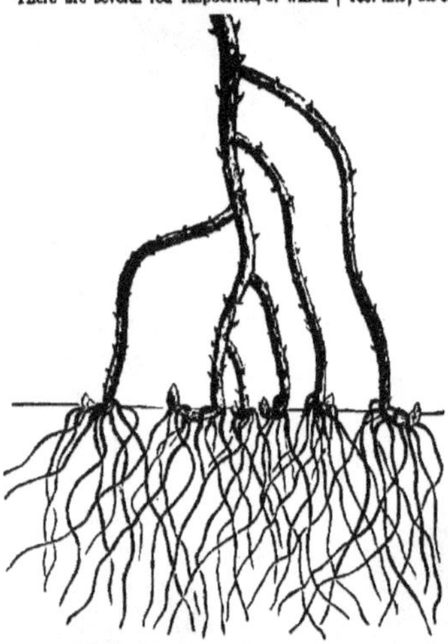

Fig. 2.—Tip of a branch rooted.

the species is doubtful, such as the Purple Cane, that are propagated in the same way. The two engravings given here are taken from Fuller's Small Fruit Culturist, a work recently published and indispensable to the grower of small fruits.

Where is the Mixing of Varieties Shown?

The question of the crossing of varieties has been considerably discussed of late, and it does not seem to be satisfactorily settled as to whether the influence of a mixture, caused by the fertilization of one variety by the pollen of another, is manifest in the fruit resulting from this operation, or if the crossing is only manifest in the progeny of the *seeds* of such fruit. There is some evidence that indicates that a cross is shown in the fruit, but Mr. Gregory, who has carefully observed squashes, plants that "mix" very readily, is quite positive on the other side of the question. In his recent excellent little treatise on squashes he says:

"All of the crossing or mixing of squashes is caused by the pollen from the male flowers of one variety being carried by the bees to the female flowers of another variety. *Squashes are crossed or mixed in their seed, and not in the fruit.* Many cultivators are in error on this point; they have the very common illustration of the crossing of different varieties of corn in their mind, where the mixture of the varieties is at once apparent to the eye, and infer from this, that the mixture between different varieties of squashes should make itself visible to the eye *the same season it occurs.* A moment's reflection will correct this; *the crossing of the first season is always in the seed*, and for this reason we see it in the corn the first season, as the seed is immediately visible to the eye, while the various colors of the different varieties also aid us in the matter. With squashes the crossing is likewise in the seed, and hence cannot be seen in them, until the seeds are planted, when the yield will show the impurity of their blood. But, though the crossing cannot be seen in the squashes themselves the first season, yet if one of the varieties planted near each other, has seed having the peculiar, thick, salmon-colored coating, so characteristic of some of the South American varieties, this indication of admixture may be detected by the eye the first season. The parallelism between the crossing of squashes and corn may be carried further, for it is oftentimes true with corn as with squashes, that there is a mixing of varieties, of which no indication can be detected in the seed by the eye the first season, which a second season will develop—what was before an eight-rowed variety, into a ten or twelve-rowed sort, or dark kernels may be replaced with white ones, and by numerous similar freaks, bring to light an admixture of varieties.

"It is of considerable practical importance, that the law of admixture should be clearly understood, that the risk, incidental to planting seed from squashes that *look* pure, should be generally known; for it will be seen from what I have written, that seed taken from squashes that externally are perfect types of their kinds, may yield a patch, where every one may show marks of impurity. Again, no matter how many varieties are planted together, no crossing from the result of that planting will be seen in the *external shape, color, or appearance* of the crop *the same* season.

To have squash seed pure, the squashes from which they are taken, must have grown isolated, and this not only for one season, but for a succession of seasons. Should several varieties of squashes be grown together, and it be desirable to keep one kind pure, it can be done by preventing any male flowers of the other varieties from maturing—no easy job, as those who have tried it know. The product of any particular blossom may be kept pure under such circumstances by covering with fine muslin, removing it only to fertilize with pollen from a male flower of its own vine."

This subject is not only one of scientific interest, but has an important practical bearing, and we shall be glad to receive carefully collected evidence on either side of the question.

The Care of Seeds.

Those who would propagate shrubs or trees, either for the interest that attends the production of new varieties, or as a matter of profit, a raising of stocks, often fail from lack of proper care with their seeds. The seeds, or pits, of peaches, plums, and cherries, we all know, are enclosed in a very hard and bony envelope, and these, though they have a large and vigorous embryo, often fail for want of proper care. The seeds of the strawberry, raspberry, blackberry, and of many of our ornamental shrubs, are enclosed in a case, which, in proportion to the size of the embryo, is scarcely less formidable than that of the peach. Most seeds with these very hard envelopes, if once thoroughly dried, are very difficult to germinate. Nature sows them at the time of ripening, but this is often very inconvenient, and the best way is, to imitate nature and not allow the seeds to dry. With all hard-shelled seeds, whether as large as that of the peach or as small as that of the raspberry, the best way is to clean the seeds from the pulp, and then put them with sand or sandy loam, in sufficient quantity to preclude all danger of heating by fermentation, and keep the mixture of sand and seeds in a place so cool that there will be no danger of the seeds starting too early in the season. This process is known in the books as "stratification," and is often performed by making a mound of alternate layers of seeds and sand, and covering the whole with earth, sloped to keep off the rain. In a small way a flower-pot answers every purpose, or, if a larger quantity of seeds are at hand, a rough box, in which the seeds and sand are to be placed and kept in a cool cellar, or buried at the north side of a fence or building. Many failures result from the seeds being kept too warm; they start with the first warm day of spring, and having no opportunity to grow, the germ withers, and the seeds of course fail.

These remarks apply to the seeds of all of our small fruits, and to all of our hardy shrubs, the seeds of which have a bony shell. Indeed the seeds of many of our trees and shrubs, such as the thorns, need to lie stratified in this way through one year. Keeping them in a mass, and exposed to the changes of temperature through one whole year, is much better than to sow them, and be at the trouble of keeping the grounds clear of weeds. Freezing and thawing does not, as a general thing, hurt the seeds of our hardy trees and shrubs, but helps them.

About Weeds.

We have—we know not how many letters asking how to kill this or that weed. If those who write us these queries would only think on the subject, they would see that there can be no specific that will kill an undesirable plant—or weed and not injure the desirable plants of the crop. Therefore, all applications, be they salt, plaster, ashes, or what not, merely to *kill* weeds, are simply absurd. Cultivation consists solely in giving the plant that we wish to grow an advantage over other plants. In an uncultivated field, where everything is left to itself, it becomes a "struggle for existence," and the strongest—which is usually the most worthless—gets the best of it. In all our cultivation, the aim is to give the crop we wish to grow sole possession of the soil, and all our cultivators, horse-hoes, hand-hoes of all kinds, etc., are used to destroy every plant except a particular one that we wish should have full possession of the soil. Now we know of no help for weeds, whether in garden or in field, except a mechanical one. If one finds a few Canada Thistles in his lawn, cuts the stems and puts some salt on each, and thus destroys them, it is no exception to the general rule. Had he put an equal amount of salt all over his lawn, he would have killed everything upon it. We have but little sympathy with a gardener who lets the weeds get the better of him. His soil should have been kept so constantly stirred that weeds could have no chance. Whoever is not able to keep down the weeds by the use of the rake, or the many weeding hoes, has more garden than he can properly care for. If weeds have got the mastery, use some of the various weeding hoes, rake them at once from the ground, and if there is a sign of a flower or a seed upon them, do not let them go the manure heap—it is all nonsense to talk of destroying their vitality by fermentation—but just spread them where they will dry, and then, with the accumulated brush and other combustible garden rubbish, burn them. With a little care, ashes, so valuable as a fertilizer, may be made in considerable quantity from properly dried refuse of the garden.

Neglected Squares in Cities and Towns.

A "Subscriber" in New York sends us the following communication upon the smaller parks and squares. We give his article place, as the fault to which he refers is found in most public grounds in large and small towns all over the country. It is very rarely that these places fall under the management of persons of either knowledge or taste. Those having them in charge order trees for them, and the nurseryman, naturally enough, sends those that he can propagate most readily. The consequence is, our public squares are planted with but a few kinds of trees, and these are almost without exception rapidly growing foreigners.

"Why should they not, the numerous parks and squares of New York, be improved and made worthy of the commercial metropolis? The Central Park is a well managed institution, and an honor to our city. Why should not a little of the wisdom which has produced so satisfactory results in that locality, be brought to bear upon Union, Madison, Tompkins, and Washington squares, which are in the heart of the city, and are within easy approach of multitudes who rarely find time to visit Central Park? We do not hesitate to say that the management of these Squares is a disgrace to the city. Tens of thousands of dollars are lavished upon granite and iron fences, as if the inclosure was of any value when there was nothing to inclose. Trees have been planted there that are a nuisance upon any soil devoted to human use. They are unsightly to the eye, and their roots are continually sending up suckers that mar the beauty of the lawn, when it is established. We would have these coarse, ugly trees, like the Abele and the Poplar, removed at once, and the others judiciously thinned, so that every tree left may have ample room to develop its natural beauty. As a rule, they are now interfering with each other, and quarreling for a share of the air and sunlight, as well as for the soil.

We would have well kept lawns mowed every two weeks. A clean, smooth sod is refreshing to the eye. At the date of this writing, June 7th, much of the grass in these squares is still untouched. There ought to have been, at least, two cuttings. Should a city square, kept ostensibly for the esthetic culture of a million of people, be conducted upon the same principle that a stingy merchant manages the lawn of his country residence—with an eye to hay rather than beauty? It would probably cost no more to have these parks kept as they should be. Men enough are employed, and if their labor was wisely directed, it would give us what we pay for—clean, attractive squares. But whatever the cost, give us clean, smooth lawns. Instead of cheap and easily raised foreign trees, we would have specimens of the beautiful natives of our own forest, and all properly labelled, so that children might learn to know the difference between an oak and a butternut. Then, we would have these places planted with more evergreens and flowering shrubs. We want something to refresh the eye in the winter as well as in summer. Our suburban nurseries are able to turn out over a hundred varieties of pines, spruces, piceas, arbor vitæs, cedars, yews and cypresses, perfectly hardy, and many of them beautiful. Why should not our citizens be permitted to make the acquaintance of the finest of them in the squares that they are obliged to frequent every day? Why should we not have rhododendrons and laurels in masses, and other beautiful flowers in their season, where we can see them with our families, without paying five dollars for a carriage, and spending two or three hours to accomplish it? Those who live in the city are heavily taxed, let them have something refreshing and beautiful for their money."

The Achilleas.

Every one knows the common Yarrow, *Achillea Millefolium*. Yet this vulgar plant—rated as a pest by cultivators, when it shows its white flowers, is, when its flowers assume a rose color, prized as a border plant, and sold at a good price by the florists. Even the common weed has a delicacy of foliage and flower that would make it prized did it not make itself too abundant, but the rose-colored one is really beautiful. We have, in years past, got much satisfaction out of the double variety of *Achillea Ptarmica*, even though it does bear the common name of "Sneeze-wort." It is perfectly hardy, and gives a long succession of pure white flowers. It is so valued among the French that they give it the name of "Silver-bud," (*bouton d'argent*). Nothing is more valuable for summer bouquets than the double *Achillea Ptarmica*. Those who like yellow flowers will be pleased with *Achillea tomentosa*, another hardy species, with foliage and flowers much like those of the common Yarrow, except that the leaves are downy, and the flowers are of a bright yellow. We wish that hardy, herbaceous plants were more generally cultivated than they now are.

Among the Wild Flowers.

It is a good thing to leave the garden occasionally with its Verbenas, Heliotropes, and all the like, and go out and see a bit of nature's gardening. In this month of July there are many fine things in bloom in the meadows and woodsides, and a ramble among them is refreshing to one who has to weed and train the exotics. If there is any thing in our gardens handsomer than our low meadows can show now, we would like to see it. The beautiful *Calopogon* now spreads its numerous pinkish, purple and fragrant flowers in all the low places, while its near relative, *Arethusa bulbosa*, too delicate to be very common, is more chary of its bloom, and gives us only a single beautifully

DEER-GRASS—(*Rhexia Virginica.*)

DWARF IRIS—(*Iris pumila.*)

fringed flower to the stalk. We have been much pleased with the abundance of these that have fallen under our observation this season, and hope in due time to give engravings of them.

Among the plants of our low lands, none makes more show than the "Deer-grass"—which, by the way, is no grass at all, but we have to accept common names as we find them. This plant is so striking in its appearance, and has been sent us so often for a name, that we have figured it. Its botanical name is *Rhexia Virginica*. The derivation of the generic name, *Rhexia*, is not well made out; the specific name *Virginica*, was applied to it before the geography of this country was well understood. The plant is not peculiar to Virginia, but is found from Massachusetts far southward. The plant belongs to the family Melastomaceæ, one which gives us many valued green-house plants from the tropics; but is only represented with us by the genus *Rhexia*. The leaves of the plants in this family are all opposite, very strongly ribbed, and the anthers burst in an unusual manner—by openings or pores at the apex, instead of by the ordinary way of a longitudinal slit. We have three species of *Rhexia* in the Northern States, but the one we have figured is the showiest. This plant was long ago cultivated in England, and we see no reason why it should not be introduced into our own gardens. The peculiar form of the four petaled, bright purple flower, with the conspicuous yellow anthers, gives it so peculiar an appearance, that if the plant were potted, no one except a practical botanist would recognize it as an inhabitant of our Eastern swamps. Later will come the most gorgeous of all our wild flowers, *Lobelia cardinalis*, the Cardinal Flower, before the intense brilliancy of whose color the exotics pale. But we can not notice now all that one will meet with in a ramble. We would merely give the advice to those who would transfer these wild beauties to their grounds, to mark the plants while in flower, and if there are many ramblers in the neighborhood, to follow the practice of one of our friends, and render the plants less conspicuous, by removing the flowers. Mark with good stakes, that can be readily recognized—a common stick with a bit of white rag tied to the top, so as to flutter in the wind, we have found to be as good as anything—and after the foliage is dead, transfer the plants to a situation in the garden as near like their natural one as may be.

The Flower de Luce.

The name Flower de Luce has been applied to some species of *Iris*, because it was assumed by Louis VII., of France, as his badge or device. It was in old French *fleur de Louis*, and the recent *fleur de lys* is a change from the original. So much for the derivation of a common name about which people who try to be correct differ. Flower de Luce is as much English, among flowers, as *avoirdupois* is in respect to weights. Every one knows our common wild Blue Flag; that is a Flower de Luce, or, botanically speaking, *Iris versicolor*. The genus *Iris* is a large one, and comprises both tender and hardy species. Our present object is to call attention to the hardy ones, as there are few hardy herbaceous perennials that will give more satisfaction than a collection of the best sorts of *Iris*; they present a great variety of color, from white, through blue and deep purple to yellows and browns.

One of the very earliest is the European Dwarf Iris, *Iris pumila*. Its leaves grow but a few inches high, and its very early flowers are borne on very short stems. We have figured this species of its natural size. Ordinarily its flowers are of a violet color, but it varies from white to pure blue. On account of the low growth of the plant and its hardiness, it is very useful for edgings. It is not at all particular as to soils, and does very well in a dry situation. We have three native species of Dwarf Iris, which, if brought into cultivation, would doubtless be as valuable as the old *Iris pumila*. These are the *Iris verna*, found on the hill-sides of Virginia and Kentucky; *Iris cristata*, which grows in similar localities, and *Iris lacustris*, another dwarf species, found along the shores of the great lakes of the West. These native species bloom in April and May, and are well worthy the attention of cultivators. Among the taller growing kinds are: *Iris Germanica*, the common Flower de Luce of the old gardens, and *Iris sambucina*, the elder-scented kind. *I. variegata* and *I. Belgica*, (of the books,) give no end of pleasing varieties, and some of them give a quite late bloom. All that we have mentioned have large and fleshy root-stocks, which are readily divided, and give an abundance of plants. The "orris root" of the drug stores, much valued for its violet perfume, is the dried root of *Iris Florentina*, a species often found in our collections.

THE HOUSEHOLD.

(☞ For other Household Items, see "Basket" pages.)

Dashes at House-Keeping with a Free Pencil.

PRIZE ESSAY BY MISS EVA M. COLLINS, ROCHESTER.

We have been canning fruit all day—plums, peaches, and pineapples. The latter were not set down in the programme for to-day. Aunt Mary brought us a half bushel after we had got well started with the peaches and plums. She said they were very ripe, and besides she wanted to attend to their canning herself, so if Ralph could be detailed for her special service in the back kitchen, she should be exactly suited. They require so much cooking to make them tender, he would be able not only to keep enough pared and sliced ahead, but assist her in putting them into the bottles. Aunt Mary has been telling us about a "Fruit Drying House," which she says we ought to have, as it would not be a quarter the trouble to prepare fruit in that, that it is to can enough to last the year around. There are a number of sizes in operation, from one intended for use in a small family, to one of sufficient size where fruit drying is made a special business for market. Father says, "Just as mother says," so probably we shall have one. Most of the berries, cherries, plums and pears, are as good for common use when dried, as canned, and green corn and many other vegetables are better so prepared. Father thinks the expense of a Drying House would soon be met by the saving of cans.

Paring fuzzy peaches all day is nervous work, so I begged an exchange with Mary for an hour or two, and scalded the milk-room shelves.

Aunt Mary came into the milk-room while I was scalding the shelves, and described a milk-rack which Uncle Charles recently brought home for her to use as a provision stand, which would be very useful for us, when, as on this occasion, we set the milk. It is a circular wire work of shelves, 6 in number. Aunt Mary says her rack stands in the center of her store-room, between the windows. She has it covered with a musquito net, which readily admits the air, while doing its duty in keeping out insects. I can readily understand that the cream would rise much better in the rack than on shelves, as Aunt Mary describes, because we always find that, however thick, and firm, and golden the cream may be in the front of the pan, which has access to the air, that on the opposite side of the pan is thin, soft, and white, in comparison. The action of the atmosphere would effect as great a miracle over the entire pan, when in the rack, as at present it does in the fore part of our milk pans, as they stand upon their shelves.

To-day, mother remarked that she learned something of value from every one she knew; so we set our wits to work, conjuring up some most incorrigible specimens of humanity; but, to our surprise, we found mother was right even in this, which we all thought a wonderfully wild remark for her. Old blind Pierre taught us years ago to leave out a portion of the coffee, until just as the coffee pot was removed from the stove, in order to secure the fragrance as well as strength of the beverage. Even the old woman whom we took into the house and employed during the great snow storm, and then sent on her way rejoicing in a comfortable wardrobe, besides her wages, because she was so very destitute, and who the next day sold our tea through the village, mother says, taught us two valuable lessons. One lesson was to let the tea toast in a warm place for fifteen minutes before steeping, and the other, to be more watchful of stragglers, and the tea chest.

We thought this case the climax, until Jennie suggested, "Ike, mother, what did Ike do?" As mother hesitated a moment, and the case seemed rather dubious, I asked Jennie "Who made her first wish-bone doll?" Ralph said this was not admissible, for mother said "lessons of value;" but he might better have let the wish-bone doll pass unchallenged, for mother turned to him immediately and said, "Ike hung the south woodshed door, which you know was impossible to be done with those heavy hinges, and we have no more substantially hung door, or gate, on the premises than that." Ralph gathered up the peach skins, and replenished the dishes all around, and before we had got ready to work again, Aunt Mary came with the pineapples, so no more cases were brought forward. After we were all at work again, grandmother told me "it was only those persons who had their eyes and ears open, who picked up valuable lessons from every one about them. Many persons go through the whole course of their existence without learning much, except what is forced upon them through their own experience, and those persons rarely profit even by such lessons."

Leaves from My Journal.—No. VI.

PRIZE ESSAY BY MRS. B. M'CLELLAN, OF OHIO.

August.—How much watching and care everything about house requires these sultry days! Mould gathers here and there, for there is moisture notwithstanding the heat. Mildew and blight take one by surprise. These are gala days for insects, spiders and flies. Brooms, brushes, and suds, are in good demand. Where does all the dust come from in the darkened and closed rooms? A house with good elevation, not too closely surrounded with trees and shrubbery, is far healthier now. I wonder if we don't greatly mistake here, filling our yards too full of trees, and covering houses and porches with too many vines. They are beautiful, and the shade grateful, but would not more of the free sunlight and air of heaven make all purer within? The flowers are in their glory. Dahlias threaten to outvie the roses. I have great respect for dahlias! They so faithfully fulfill their mission. Till the heavy frosts come, they will never weary mounting one tier of blossoms above another, perfect in form, and varied with every color. I made a great mistake with verbenas; I tried to grow them in the same bed with dahlias, and thought they would look finely together. But the poor things, like the frog in the fable, tried so hard to be like their aspiring neighbors, climbing hither and yon, that though they could not after all become dahlias, they certainly were not verbenas in any way flattering to their kind—putting out only a profusion of large, coarse leaves, and here and there a straggling, puny blossom. They want a bed to themselves, with the sun shining full in their faces, where, in every variety of color, they lovingly intertwine, serving only by contrast to show the rare beauty of each,—like two lovely sisters, the blonde and brunette, on the same parent stem.

Is it, indeed, true! that, with the country filled with sewing machines, and so many other labor-saving implements, we housekeepers are no nearer the "leisure time" we covet, than ever before? Our garments are so highly embroidered, so continuously tucked and plaited with innumerable rows of stitching, that, though quickly done, there seems no end to the doing. Are we not misusing the price put into our hands to get wisdom? Few housekeepers allow themselves time even to read the papers on their tables. There is ever another piece of work to be done, calls to be made or received, unexpected company to be entertained, or invited friends to prepare for. There are demands outside of home, upon the time as well as charity of all. But after making full allowance for all these, can not an hour or half hour be secured for self improvement and culture, on subjects of more consequence than dress or the pleasures of the table? How often have I resolved that to-morrow shall not be like to-day in this matter, only to see to-morrow's sun set upon broken promises of amendment. We are too much the slaves of fashion. Like the centurion to his servants, she says to one, come, and she cometh; to another, go, and she goeth; and still to another, do this, and she doeth it. But where shall the line be drawn, beyond which it is not safe to venture? Where is the blessed mean beyond the ever widening extremes? Who shall point out the path in which our wayward, wandering feet may walk without stumbling? A friend said to me once, "I should think I had lived long enough to find out that I never shall see the time that I have not plenty of work to do, and indeed to feel hurried about." Must we not then *take* time *as it passes*, for reading and correspondence with friends or absent members of the family? "As cold waters to a thirsty soul, so is good news from a far country." We can not afford to lose such delightful refreshment.

I made some pumpkin pies to-day. They are nice and fresh as those of last thanksgiving, and a real treat. The pumpkin was stewed and dried upon plates. If these are well greased it comes off without trouble. It must be kept in a tight bag in a dry place. Soak over night in milk before using, and prepare the same as when fresh. Hubbard squash prepared in this way, is excellent also.

I make a variety of jellies. They are always acceptable, and a great ornament to the table. Quinces, crab apples, and fall pippins, make the very best. Currant jelly should be made when the fruit *first* ripens. After straining the juice, boil gently half an hour before adding the sugar, after which it needs little more. Cool a small quantity in a dish before taking up, to see if it thickens.

Leaves from the Diary of a Young House-keeper.—No. VIII.

PRIZE ESSAY BY MRS. LAURA E. LYMAN, STAMFORD, CT.

August 3d.—For a week now, I have been pretty busy. The blackberries are ripe, and Sue and I have picked a good many, some of which I have dried, made several pounds into blackberry jam for winter use, and to-day, I made two to three bottles of cordial. For light cases of summer complaint, I know of nothing more agreeable or effectual. If I do not need it myself, some of my friends may, and there is nothing more pleasant than to have it in one's power to relieve the sufferings of friends, and add to their happiness. How grateful, in that long spell of fever I had two years ago, were the kind attentions of our neighbors! How I relished the various delicacies they sent in to tempt my appetite after I began to convalesce!

August 7th.—To-day I commenced drying corn for next winter. We have had it on the table several days, but it is just coming in abundantly. I boil it about ten minutes, then cut it off the cob and spread it on a board to dry, covering it with a piece of fly netting. Edward relished that mother sent me last winter so much, that I mean to have a plenty laid by in store.

August 15th.—The weather for a month past has been very sultry and oppressive, and some of the time very hot, so that my enterprise of converting the milk, of which we have a great deal, into cheese instead of butter, proves to have been very timely. I have now twelve cheeses which I keep on a new, clean shelf in the milk-room. The little milk and cream that I appropriate for butter, I keep on the swinging shelf at the north end of the cellar. I have a great curiosity to know how my cheeses are going to taste. They look to my eyes very tempting, and I count them over every day, when I turn them and rub them, much as a miser would twenty dollar gold pieces, and they are almost of the color.

August 17th.—I have been putting up peaches. Edward has been helping me, for the stress of farm work that has been on him ever since the middle of April, has relaxed a little at last, as haying and harvesting are over. In the preparation of my canned peaches, I followed a recipe that I found in a bound volume of the *Agriculturist* for 1860. I think it is the same one mother went by last year, and her peaches were splendid. She brought me a couple of cans when she came to visit me in June. As I have plenty of other preserves, I canned all my peaches, for I think, generally speaking, peach preserves are too rich to be wholesome.

Edward says I must go visiting a few days, that I am quite too enthusiastic a farmer's wife. But how can I be otherwise, when he is so industrious and laborious, and makes every edge cut on the place? He says now that all the workmen are gone but our soldier, who is entirely recovered, and that the weather is cool, I can be spared a few days as well as not. Sue can take care of the milk, and the cream will keep till I come back. I agree with him that it will be very pleasant to recreate awhile, but I can not go without him. Our soldier is so grateful for the attentions we paid him when he was sick, and so reliable a man, that I think Edward may feel safe in leaving everything in his care.

August 23d.—Home again! Found everything in a satisfactory condition. The weather was cool, the cream rose well, and Sue ventured to try her hand at making butter in my absence, and really succeeded very well. I told her she should have it to take down to the store and sell on her own account, but advised her to work it over once more.

We went to see an old friend of Edward's, about fifteen miles distant, and our visit was delightful. The ride through the country, now rich with all the pomps of midsummer, was truly exhilarating to the spirits of us both. It is the first journey that we have taken since our marriage. How busy, how crowded, and how happy have these eight months of our married life been! We have both been blessed with perfect health, our table has been, with the exception of tea, coffee, and salt, supplied by the labor of our own hands, and as I reflected on the past, that beautiful sentence of "the pious Hooker" was recalled to my mind, where he describes the farmer as "living nearer to God, and seeing more of His works than any of the less favored children of men, for he beholds the blessings of God blossoming out of the earth around him!"

We started just after dinner and reached the farm-house about sunset, where we received a most hearty welcome. Edward had told me, during our ride, that most of the valuable ideas which he had about farming and housekeeping, he had acquired during his residence with this family. The first year after he was of age, he worked for Mr. George during the summer and fall, and in the winter taught the adjoining district school, boarded with Mr. George, and paid his board by working before and after school. The family have always thought very highly of him ever since his residence with them, and when I made their acquaintance I could see why the respect and admiration was mutual. Their's is the best farmer housekeeping I ever saw anywhere. It is Mr. George's ambition to have the best cows and the largest milkers of any dairyman in the county, and it is his wife's to send to market the largest firkins of the most perfect, golden and fragrant butter. She took three successive prizes for butter at the October fair, and if the three handsome little silver cups and butter knives which she drew were cut out of solid amethyst, she would not think more of them. But I can see that her success is produced by the almost perfect arrangements and appliances for butter-making, as much as by the care that she herself bestows. The house is one which was planned throughout by Mr. George, who has the great advantage of knowing precisely what he wants, and possessing the ability to suit himself in everything he does.

The architecture of the farm-house is very much in the usual style, having in the main part, four rooms below and four above. It is situated on a gentle slope which looks eastward, and the house fronts westward, being on the lower side of the road. At the rear of the house and attached to the main building is a lean-to, which is also of two stories, the first being a basement, of which the walls are heavy masonry. Here in the upper part, and on a level with the first story of the main building are the kitchen, store-room and tool-house. Underneath is an ice-room, a small wash-room, back of which is the cellar door, and on the north-side is the milk-room or dairy. I was so much pleased with the arrangement that I made a plan of it, and Edward says that when he builds a new house it shall have all these conveniences.

A, is the ice-house, entered by a large trap door from the tool-room floor above; on one side of it, I, is a small ice-chamber, six feet by six, entered by a double door from B, the wash-room, and so surrounded by ice as to be a perfect refrigerator. C D is a door, also double, that opens into the cellar in the rear, which is not shown in the plan. The outer door of the wash-room has a low threshold, so that a large wheel-barrow can be trundled directly into the cellar from without, thus obviating the necessity

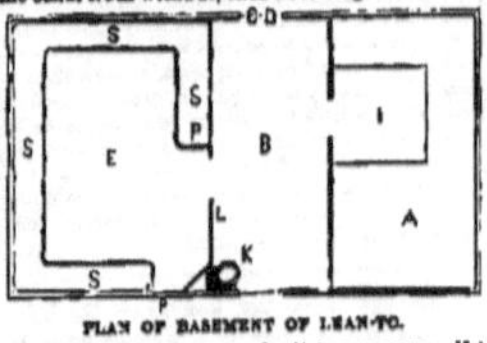

PLAN OF BASEMENT OF LEAN-TO.

of laying planks or props for it to run upon. K is a large kettle or caldron, set in masonry, and very near the outer door, so as to be convenient at hog-killing time, for soap-making, washing, cooking food for animals, and furnishing hot water for dairy purposes. L is a small lead pipe leading from a tank in the kitchen above, so that by turning a faucet, the caldron may be filled with water in two or three minutes. E is the milk-room, twenty feet square, with a shelf of masonry, S, on the top of which is a shallow trough, thoroughly lined on the inside with cement, so as to be water-tight. P is a pipe, also leading from the tank above, and throwing a small stream of water into the trough, which, after making the circuit of the shelf, and cooling all the pans alike, runs out at p, whence it passes to the barn yard. There is a fall from P to p, of a fraction of an inch, so as to give a gentle and uniform current. The room is lighted by double windows on hinges, so the amount of external air to be admitted can be easily and perfectly regulated. There is a flue in the corner, and in winter an air-tight stove is used, by which the temperature of this apartment can be so perfectly adjusted that the thermometer which hangs there does not vary ten degrees the year round. Fly screens are fitted into the windows in midsummer. The washing of milk vessels, and the churning, are all done in the adjoining room, the butter, when packed, is set into the ice chamber, and thus, whether in January or July, nothing affects the flavor, the quality, or the hardness of the butter, except changes in the food of the cows.

The water, which is so admirably economized and skillfully applied, comes from a never-failing spring on the side of the hill above the house, and is conducted in pump logs. The tank in the kitchen into which it discharges, is divided into two compartments, one of which is always full, and supplies a uniform stream to the milk-room below. The other compartment supplies the kitchen, the caldron below, and its waste passes to the barn-yard. All the labor of the house is strictly confined to these six apartments, the rooms of the main building being kept in perfect order, and pleasantly furnished with carpets, sofas, agricultural and other books, so that a visitor would never know whether Mr. George was a farmer or a gentleman retired on his fortune, unless he visited the working rooms in the rear.

I noticed that Mr. George himself, his sons, and the laborers that are hired by the year, upon coming in from their work, left their heavy farm boots in the tool-room, where were also conveniences for washing, and wore light and clean slippers when they came into the nicely carpeted rooms.

Like a model mother, Mrs. George is training her three daughters to understand every department of domestic industry. One week Mary, the elder, directs the dairy girl, and is held responsible for the quality of the butter, while Jane attends to the washing, ironing, and mending, and the clothing department generally, and Ellen presides over the management of the kitchen and pantry.

From my observations of Mrs. George's methods of conducting the housework on a large farm, I have obtained some valuable hints for my own benefit, when by our thrift and economy our stock has become much larger than it is at the present time.

A noticeable feature which I have seen also in other well kept houses is, that everything at Mrs. George's moves in an unchanging routine, which is probably the secret of her accomplishing so much, and doing everything so well.

I observe that although the labors of the farm are confined to a set of apartments, the entire house is open to her guests and the various members of the family, and their amusements, the conversation at table, the books they read, and their modes of entertaining their friends, are as high toned as in any family I have ever visited.

His sons are taught to aspire to the ownership of a well kept farm, and a thorough understanding of all departments of agriculture as their most legitimate and praiseworthy ambition; and the daughters all expect to become the wives of farmers.

I cannot but think that if all were to look upon agriculture as this admirable family does, the young men of our country would not have such a proclivity to the cities, nor girls show a preference for white handed dandies and professional men.

Reading for Boys and Girls.

A father asks our advice as to suitable reading for boys from the age of 12 to 17. He has five sons, whose education occasions him a good deal of solicitude, and wants a library of choice books for them in the departments of history, biography, travels, and natural science. This request opens a subject of great importance, and we have a few old fashioned ideas upon the subject, which are at the service of our readers. The books we had access to, at the age of twelve to fourteen, were Plutarch's Lives, Hume's History of England, Rollin's Ancient History, and works of that stamp. It was the best thing perhaps that could have happened, that we saw little of fiction until maturer years. We think many of our Sabbath School books, and works especially written for the young, run too much to fiction and small talk. There is no occasion to resort to novels for interesting reading. Historical writers have as much grace of style as the masters of fiction. Any boy or girl, of average intelligence, would be charmed with Macauley's History of England, Bancroft's History of the United States, Prescott's and Motley's historical works, Irving's Life of Washington, Irving's Columbus, Life and Letters of W. Irving, Sparks' American Biography, and the travels of Stephens, and of Bayard Taylor. These alone would make a respectable library, and would be as much as any child ought to read between 12 and 17 years of age, in addition to the drill of the school room and the reading of the papers. One of the pleasantest winters we remember was that in which Irving's Life of Washington was read aloud in the family, for three evenings in the week, the children taking turns in the readings. All of Irving's most genial works may be read with profit, at a later age.

There is much less need of private libraries now than thirty years ago; for public libraries are greatly multiplied in our cities, and villages, and the best thoughts of the best minds of the country are given to the public through our periodical literature. These papers and magazines are virtually circulating libraries, and a good selection of them should be found upon the centre table of every intelligent family. Farmers of course will see that the agricultural papers are well represented at their fire-sides, if they wish to cultivate rural tastes in their children.

Pickling Beans.—Robert Black, New Bedford. We know no better way than to pick them before they have any strings, soak in weak salt water for 24 hours; prepare vinegar with spices as for other pickles, pour it hot on the beans, and then after 3 or 4 days pour it off and re-scald it. A little alum hardens them, but is not desirable, nor is the poisonous verdigris from the brass kettle that gives such a beautiful green to the pickles cooked in that metal. It is much better to have pickles of any kind wholesome, rather than make them attractive to the eye by injurious additions.

BOYS & GIRLS' COLUMNS.

An Eventful Life.

A correspondent writing to an Exchange from Indianapolis, Indiana, says: "While passing through the Union Depot a few days ago, I was accosted by a one-armed man in faded army blue. Fourteen years ago I first saw him working at a windlass in the gold diggings of Australia. He and his three partners hoisted by that windlass, from a single shaft, more than $600,000. A few months later I bade him good-bye, as he sailed from Melbourne to New-York with $300,000 in bills of exchange in his pocket. I next saw him a wounded Rebel soldier, lying on the field of Antietam. A little more than a year later I saw him a Union soldier, lying in a hospital in Tennessee. To-day he is a helpless wanderer, dependent on public charity for a dinner." He may yet be a millionaire.

A Small Piece of Work.—A most curious and interesting model at the French exhibition is that of the rock and fortress of Gibraltar, with a fleet of ships lying in the harbor. This fleet consists of a ship of the line, a frigate and a steam corvette, a brig and a schooner, every spar and rope being faithfully represented; and yet the hulls of these little vessels were constructed out of less than the tenth part of a cherry stone. The rock and fortress of Gibraltar are in the same proportions, and the whole structure can be covered over with a florin.

Our Artist's Game.

One of our artists is very fond of hunting. Recently he made an excursion into the country, where he says he was very successful. He has made a sketch to show the results of his expedition. Somehow he appears to have mixed things up considerably, but we suppose some allowance must be made for the excitement he was under, caused by his astonishing achievements. It will be as good as a puzzle to discover which belongs to which.

A Valuable Nest.

A Brooklyn, N. Y., paper says: "Birds usually build their nests of hair, hay, feathers, etc., but an exceptional case has just come to light, in a remarkable discovery made by a lady residing in East Brooklyn. While walking in her garden she observed a neatly arranged bird's nest among the branches of a cedar bush, and on closer examination was greatly surprised to find that it was formed principally of Valenciennes lace, worth about $1 per yard. A piece seven yards in length formed the lining of the nest. The lady recognized the lace as some she had missed a month ago, and strongly suspected at the time that it had been taken by some of the servants in the house. No clue as to the whereabouts of this feathery thief has, as yet, been ascertained by the guardians of property, the bird having flown."

A Sincere Mourner.

A singular funeral occurred in this City a few days since. A horse belonging to a tradesman in Worth-st., had his leg broken, and was shot, to end his misery. Men came to remove him, but were met and resisted by a large dog that had been the companion of the horse for several years. They succeeded, however, in partially quieting him, and raised the carcass upon a cart to take it away, the dog meanwhile holding on to it with his teeth, and trying to pull it back. At last, when the cart was started, the faithful friend mounted beside the body of his dead companion, and was carried away with it, a sincere mourner. After about three hours absence, he returned, and entered the stable, showing plainly by his downcast look and whining, how much he missed his former companion. Such attachments are not rare.

A Troublesome Sliver.

Charley came to his father one day with a pitiful face, and, holding up his finger, said: "It hurts so, I wish you would see what is the matter." His father examined it carefully, noticed a small red and swollen place, and when he touched it, Charley flinched, saying, "Oh! it's sore there." "I think there must be a sliver in there," said his father, and, taking out his penknife, he carefully picked away the skin, and soon brought out a small, sharp bit of wood, which had caused the trouble. "Now, it will soon be well." "Thank you, sir, it feels better already; I must have got it in yesterday, when I was piling up boards." "Don't get a sliver in your *conscience*, my boy," said his father, and Charley started off for his play, thinking of his father's curious remark. Soon he was enjoying a lively game of base ball. Quarter to nine came, and he knew it was time to start for school, but his side had the "innings," and it would soon be his turn to strike, and he waited. Somehow, every boy before him took a long time, and after he had sent the ball flying across the field and made a good run, he waited to have another turn at it, for the game was a close one, and a few more runs would decide it in favor of his party. Boom! boom! sounded out the village clock, just as the innings were finished, and then Charley knew he must be late to school; the door would be locked, and he must wait until half past nine before he could be admitted. He gathered up his books, and slowly sauntered off, thinking what excuse he could give for tardiness. It seemed to him that half past nine would never come, as he waited before the door, and heard his companions inside singing their morning song, and he could not make up his mind what to say to his teacher. At last he entered. The teacher looked at him pleasantly, saying: "An unusual thing for you to be late, Charley; you were busy, no doubt." "Yes, sir," replied the boy promptly. "I *was* busy," thought he, pleased that his teacher had shown him how to evade the truth. "I knew it must be so, for you are a pattern for punctuality," said his teacher, and sent him to join his class in the recitation room. "I got off nicely, and I didn't tell a lie, either," was Charley's first thought; but somehow it didn't satisfy him, and he couldn't get it out of his mind, that he had done wrong. Things did not go pleasantly all day; his mind wandered from his books, he was reprimanded for want of attention, and altogether had a hard time of it. Just before school was out, while sharpening his pencil, he slightly hurt his finger, which was yet tender, and like a flash it came to his mind, "there's a sliver in your conscience." Now he knew what his father meant. "I'll have it out," bravely said he to himself. He waited until the other boys had gone, and then told his teacher the whole story about the real cause of his lateness in the morning. Then his peace returned—the "sliver" was out, and you may be sure he remembered it many times afterward, and when he had done wrong, made haste to confess it, and in this way to get rid of his trouble.

A Fair Division.

It is related that when one of our largest war vessels lay at anchor in the harbor, a man who wanted to see all the sights endeavored to go on board. The Commander warned him off, saying they were not then receiving visitors. The man called out, "That ship belongs to the people of these United States, and I am one of the people, and being an owner, I have a *right* to go on board." The Commander, who loved a joke, took out his penknife, cut a small chip from the mast and threw it over the side of the vessel into the small boat, saying, "there, take your share of the ship, and be off with you!"

A similar anecdote is told of one of the house of Rothschild, the great Bankers of Europe. During revolutionary times an excited workman called at the banking house, and demanded that a division of riches be made, saying that no one had a right to be richer than another. The banker handed him a *sou* for his portion of what was in their hands, and the man at once felt the absurdity of his demand, and left the banker undisturbed.

Counting all who *read* the *Agriculturist*, month by month, the number must be nearly a million. Once in a while a reader seems to forget that he is but a very small fraction of this number, and claims that *his* letter shall be printed, or *his* views set forth, or some thing else be done for his special gratification, as though in 1,000,000 he were the 1 and the remainder were the 000,000's. When we publish 36 pages, as in this number, a paper will contain somewhere about 500,000 letters, that is about *half a letter* to a reader, if each could claim his special share. How will you have your half-letter fixed, Mr. One-eye-dear man?

New Puzzles to be Answered.

No. 272. *Illustrated Rebus.*—For obstinate individuals.

No. 273. *Mathematical Problem*, by J. D. McGiffert.—Three neighbors, A, B, and C, whose dwellings are situated in the form of a triangle, and distant from each other 60, 75, and 90 yards, respectively, desire to dig a well, to be used in common by them, at a point, within the triangle, equally distant from the abode of each. How far from each neighbor's dwelling must the well be dug?

No. 274. *Illustrated Rebus.*—A truth worth studying.

Answers to Problems and Puzzles.

The following are answers to the puzzles, etc., in the July number, page 261. No. 269. *Puzzle Picture.*—"Nine tailors make a man." ...No. 270. *Illustrated Rebus.*—"One swallow does not make a summer." ....No. 271. *Arithmetical Problem.*—A should receive $\$20.42\frac{6}{7}$; B, $\$14.57\frac{1}{7}$. *Solution.*—A's hog weighed 400 lbs., which at ¼ cent per lb. more than the price of B's, would bring him $1 extra. This $1 subtracted from $35, the money for both hogs, leaves $34 to be divided according to the weight of the hogs; $\frac{4}{7}$ for A, and $\frac{3}{7}$ for B.

More About Breath—Experiments.

The experiments described last month on page 261, proved that breath coming from the lungs is a very different thing from the air which enters them. They showed that air supports a flame, but breath will extinguish it; and that breath is heavier than air. Very many experiments have proved that whatever will not support a flame, is not fit to be breathed, but is destructive to life. A mouse dropped into a jar filled with your breath, would die if kept there a short time. Or if it or any other animal were simply placed in an air-tight box, it would soon spoil the air by breathing it, and die unless fresh air were admitted. A close room, where the air can not enter freely, is unfit for human beings. The first symptoms of being poisoned by breathing again what has passed from the lungs, is a dull, heavy feeling, accompanied by headache; this is followed by sickness at the stomach, fainting, and by death unless relief be given. Thousands of persons are partially *poisoned* every day by the want of ventilation in rooms. Some thoughtful boy or girl may ask, "If this is true, why has not all the air in the world been spoiled long since, by the millions of human beings and animals that have breathed it?" Because the Creator has arranged a wonderful process by which the poisoned air is purified. To give a clear idea of this we must first know something of what breath is. Two experiments will help us somewhat. Take a small handful of quicklime, pour water enough upon it to slake it, and also to have a quart or two remain in the vessel after the lime is slaked; it will settle, leaving the water looking nearly as clear as before, but still containing a little of the lime dissolved. Pour this clear fluid into a wide mouthed jar. Next put some *air-slaked* lime into a bottle. Have a cork for the bottle fitted with a tube passing through it, conveniently bent, and long enough for one end to pass to the bottom of the jar containing the "lime-water," while the other end with the cork is in the bottle. Pour some vinegar into the bottle, and immediately stop it with the cork and tube, and place the other end of the tube at the bottom of the jar of lime water. Bubbles will soon begin to pass up from the tube, the lime water will lose its transparency, and become of a milky color.

Second Experiment.—Blow through a tube into the bottom of another jar of clear lime water for a minute or so, and that will also turn milky in appearance. Then it seems that what passed from the bottle through the bent tube into one jar of lime water, and what was sent through the other tube from the lungs, must be somewhat alike, for they produce similar effects upon the lime water. Find out something more about this by reading or asking questions, before we have room to tell you more about it, and you will become more interested.

The Home Guards.

Oh, such fun! Mr. Editor. You see cousin George, from the City, is spending the summer at our house, and his father, who used to be one of the Zouaves, sent him over so many fireworks, and a whole suit of soldier clothes to keep up Fourth of July with. Then George must have a "training" he said, and we, that is, his five cousins, must be his soldiers. "I can make a soldier cap," said Edward, and he soon folded one up from a newspaper, and stuck some lily leaves into it for a feather. Then he took the poker for a gun. Nate seized the shovel, Susie the tongs, Fanny the toasting fork, and I took father's cane, and at it we went *pell mell*. But Captain George soon brought us into line, and we had *regular* fun, with "shoulder arms," "order arms," "present arms," etc. Here's a picture to show how we looked "at rest." But we did not stay at rest, for soon a pig came into the garden, through the gate which we had left open, and our Commander gave the order "charge," in a hurry. Away went piggy, over flower beds, among cabbages, and through the currant bushes, retreating in great disorder, and he was soon routed out of the garden. Nobody was wounded on our side, except Fanny, who fell into a rose bush and scratched her arm. After repairing the damage done by the enemy upon our earthworks, we marched in good order into the house, where we were reviewed by father and mother, and treated to a grand complimentary dinner, which was properly disposed of. — MARY.

[We print the above lively account of the exploits of a section of Home-guards, that their comrades throughout the country, who are fond of military exercise, may enjoy their share of the sport and the glory. — ED.]

THE HOME GUARDS.—*Drawn and Engraved for the American Agriculturist.*

A Freedman from down South was lately inspecting a horse-power in operation, driving a threshing machine, when he broke out thus: "Mister, I have seen heaps of things in my life, but I never saw anything whar a horse could do his own work and ride hisself too."

Our News-boy Correspondent.

For some year or two past there have appeared from time to time articles in the *Agriculturist* from a correspondent then personally unknown to the editors. We had a pleasant call from him a few weeks ago, and as he was leaving he said: "This ground was very familiar to me some 20 years ago." Knowing that our office stands on the ground which the "Old Brick Church" occupied, we said: "You used to attend Dr. Spring's church, perhaps?"—"No," said he, "not *much*—in those days—I used to sleep in the grass inside the railing."—He went on to tell how he used to sell papers and black boots all day—spend his few pennies, some for food and the rest to get admission to some place of amusement or show in the evening, and sleep in the street at night. The narrow grass plot around the church made a very soft bed for tired boys, if the police did not notice them and drive them out. He told us, too, how he had, by avoiding bad companions and by diligence in business, acquired a competence and good education. The little boot-black he employed looked up to him with mingled reverence and wonder, when he told him that at his age he used to brush boots for one to three cents, and never thought of getting five or ten cents as boys do now-a-days. So he called to a mate, saying: "Look-er here, Big Billy, aint this a fine gent'man to ha' used to shine boots in the streets, same as us?"

The Great Family Meeting.

The newspapers for some months past have been filled with accounts of the great "Exposition," at Paris. How many of our young friends have taken pains to look out the exact meaning of that word "Exposition"? If you examine it properly you will find it has a root and branch—(prefix, the grammarians call it.)—which together signify *placing out*. When Mary invites her young friends to tea, and brings out her new doll, her china dishes, and other treasures to show them, she has an "Exposition." The Emperor Napoleon invited all the world to come and see the fine things made in France, and to bring with them what their countries could furnish to add to the show. People from every part of the globe accepted the invitation, and a very grand time they are having. Americans are proud to find that they have taken so many prizes, some of them for things which Europeans thought could be made nowhere as well as by workmen on their side of the Atlantic.

But we think the best part of the whole performance is the *family* meeting. Brothers and sisters come together there, from almost every nation and race under the sun. The brown Japanese shakes hands with the sooty African and the white Englishman; Egypt embraces Australia; the Islanders of the Pacific exchange greetings with the Tartars of Asia, and men of different manners, customs, and religions, are learning that all belong to one great family. Kings and Emperors come together and talk over national affairs, and a kindly feeling is awakened which will do much to prevent wars in the future. All are learning that the skill, the wisdom and the excellence of the world is not confined to their own country, but that each nation has its share, more or less, and so they come to respect and sympathize with each other, and acknowledge their brotherhood.

(Business Notices $[illegible] per Agate Line of Space.)

Piano for a Life Time.

Those [illegible] to find a Piano which will give entire satisfaction [illegible] tone, touch, and [illegible] will [illegible] REMAIN GOOD FOR A LIFETIME, will please call and examine, or send for a circular describing the newly invented

MATHUSHEK PIANOS,

constructed on an entirely new plan, the invention of Mr. Frederick Mathushek, who is well known among manufacturers as the "Father" of [illegible] in Pianos. By [illegible] the power and tone of the instrument [illegible] so much so, that [illegible] "Square" form, only *four feet nine inches long and two feet [illegible] inches wide*, [illegible] piano [illegible] equals the CONCERT GRAND of any other maker. The peculiar construction INSURES ITS DURABILITY. Address

BARLOW, DOEHLER & CO., [illegible] Broadway, New York.

The Howe Machine Co.'s Sewing Machines,

699 Broadway, Cor. Fourth-st., New York.

For Families and Manufacturers.

These World-Renowned Sewing Machines

Were awarded the highest premium at the World's Fair in London, and six first premiums at the N. Y. State Fair of 1866.

These machines are made under the immediate supervision of the President of the Company, ELIAS HOWE, Jr., the original Inventor of the Sewing Machine.

The Stitch invented by **MR. HOWE**, *and made on this Machine, is the most popular and durable, and all Sewing Machines are subject to the principle invented by him.*

SEND FOR CIRCULAR.

LOCK STITCH

ELLIPTIC

SEWING MACHINE

THE LATEST AND INCOMPARABLY THE BEST FAMILY SEWING MACHINE EVER INVENTED.

Combining the Greatest Simplicity with the Highest Perfection of Mechanism and Greatest Range of Work.

All the Highest Premiums of 1866.

☞ Send for Circular and Samples of Work.
ELLIPTIC S. M. CO., 543 Broadway, N. Y.

SPECIAL NOTICE.

Whereas the [illegible] Company advertise six First Premiums at the New York State Fair of 1866, we deem it justice to ourselves to publish the following certificate:

We, the Committee on Sewing Machines of the New York State Fair of 1866, hereby certify that ALL the Highest Premiums on Sewing Machines were (except one for heavy leather work) awarded to the Elliptic Sewing Machine, to wit: For "Best Family Sewing Machine, Best Double-Thread Machine, and Best Samples of Sewing Machine Work."

C. E. PETERS,
HECTOR MOFFAT, } Committee.

THE GREAT FAMILY SEWING MACHINE.

GROVER & BAKER'S

HIGHEST PREMIUM

Elastic Stitch

SEWING MACHINE.

495 Broadway, New York.

DOTY'S

WASHING MACHINE

and the

UNIVERSAL

CLOTHES WRINGER

are so well known as the best, that recommendations are not [illegible].
(see back numbers of *Agriculturist*.)
R. C. BROWNING, General Agent,
32 Cortlandt st., N. Y. (opposite Merchants' Hotel).

See EWELL & CO.'S Advertisement of "Star Drill," on page 305.

WHEELER & WILSON
ROTARY HOOK

LOCK STITCH

SEWING MACHINES.
625 BROADWAY.

"WOMAN'S GREATEST BOON. We would advise a man to forego a [illegible] and thresh wheat with a flail, rather than to see the wife wear her [illegible] away in the everlasting 'stitch, stitch, stitch,' when a Sewing Machine can be obtained. The WHEELER & WILSON is an invaluable aid to every household. We have had several different kinds [illegible] and after [illegible] years' service, the WHEELER & WILSON has taken the precedence as the best, where all kinds of sewing are to be done in a family." —*American Agriculturist*, Jan., 1865.

THE MAP

IS DONE.

THE

New Double Map

which has

A TOWNSHIP AND RAILROAD MAP

of the

GREAT WEST

on one side, and

ALL THE WORLD

on the other.

On the same side with the World Map is a New Pacific R. R. Map, [illegible] inches, and a minute map of the Mississippi River, [illegible] inches.

The best work ever made for canvassers. Size of each map, [illegible] inches. Price of the whole, $1.50. Sold only by subscription by experienced canvassers to whom Town and County Rights will be given.

H. H. LLOYD & CO.,
Publishers, 21 John-st., New York.

☞ The *American Agriculturist* says: "We have already spoken favorably of the reliable character of the House of H. H. Lloyd & Co. This is not J. T. Lloyd. Notice that the Initials are H. H."

THE LITTLE CORPORAL

Is acknowledged by the leading papers to be the

Best Juvenile Paper in America.

We offer a MAGNIFICENT LIST of PREMIUMS!
Subscribe at any time during the year.

The price of the Corporal is one dollar a year, in advance; sample copy, telling all about the premiums, ten cents.
Address ALFRED L. SEWELL, Publisher, Chicago, Ill.

HERALD OF HEALTH.

In order to let those who have never seen this excellent monthly judge of its merits, we will send it three months ON TRIAL for [illegible] cents. $[illegible] a year; 20 cents a number.

MILLER, WOOD & CO., 15 Laight-st., New York.

Fort Edward Institute, N. Y.

$183 per Year. Best sustained boarding Seminary in the nation. For $[illegible] a lady has board, carpeted and fully furnished room, fuel, and washing, with Common English, for term of fourteen weeks, beginning Sept. [illegible]. A gentleman pays $[illegible] without carpet. Classical, Scientific, Commercial, College preparatory, Normal, Painting, and Musical Departments, with eighteen Professors and Teachers.

Address, for Catalogues or Rooms,
JOSEPH E. KING, D. D., Fort Edward, N. Y.

☞ Orange Judd said [illegible] years Agriculturist: "Those who have sons and daughters to send away to school, will do well to apply for the Fort Edward Catalogue."

THE EUREKA

BRICK MACHINE

makes 2,[illegible] splendid Brick per hour, with only nine men and one pair horses, or [illegible] per hour by steam power. Has no complex machinery to be getting out of order or breaking down. Its great simplicity and marvelous power command the approval of every expert, at sight.

We challenge the world to produce its equal.

Satisfaction guaranteed to all purchasers.

ABRAM REQUA, General Agent,
No. [illegible] Broadway, New York.

FRANKLIN
BRICK MACHINE.

Justly celebrated for perfect simplicity, great strength, and immense compressing power, is GUARANTEED, with eight men and two horses, to [illegible] temper the clay and make [illegible] [illegible] J. H. RENICK, Proprietor, No. [illegible]

GRAPE VINES.

PARSONS & CO.,

FLUSHING, N. Y.,

Inform their customers and correspondents that their stock of **VINES**, the coming Autumn, will be much larger than it has yet been.

There will be large quantities of **CONCORD, IONA, DELAWARE, IVES,** and others, and prices will be lower even than those of last Spring. A Price List will be ready in August.

Strawberry Plants Grown in Pots.

We are growing a large stock of

JUCUNDA—No. 700,

and other choice varieties of Strawberries in Pots, for full fruitage next summer.

Plants ready for delivery Sept. 1st. Send 5 cents for Circular.

J. KNOX,
Box 155, Pittsburgh, Pa.

TO THE TRADE.

VINES AND PLANTS.

Our stock of **Grapes, Strawberries, Raspberries, Blackberries, Gooseberries, Currants, &c.,** is now so large, that we are able to offer special inducements to the Trade. **Nurserymen and Dealers** will find it to their interest to correspond with us, or visit our grounds. Circulars sent to all applicants enclosing five cents.

J. KNOX,
Box 155, Pittsburgh, Pa.

POMONA'S HOME NURSERY.—See large advertisement and price list in Sept. No., and send immediately for copy of "Manual of Grape Culture," with an additional year's experience in it, some new illustrations, and complete guide in the growing of small fruits, of which we have planted 12 acres in Strawberries; 6 acres of Raspberries; 8 acres of Blackberries, &c. Address J. H. FOSTER, Jr., Glendale P. O., Camden Co., N. J. (formerly W. Newton, Pa.)

Rural Improvements.

Robert Morris Copeland, author of Country Life, furnishes plans and advice for laying out or improving public or private grounds. Refers to John M. Forbes, Nathaniel Thayer, Boston; Francis G. Shaw, New York; Rufus Waterman, Providence, R. I.

Office, 40 Barristers' Hall, Boston, Mass.

To Merchants & Peddlers Everywhere!

A New and Good Thing for Every Family.

DOTY'S EVERLASTING CLOTHES-PIN!

Retail Price, 30 cents per dozen. Send two red stamps for sample Pin and wholesale terms and circulars.

DOTY'S CLOTHES PIN CO., 32 Cortlandt st., New York.

SQUIRE'S PATENT FRUIT JAR.

Fruits Preserved Without Sugar.

The Only Jar for Preserving Vegetables.

The Newest, Most Convenient and Economical Jar extant.

This Jar is constructed so that the contents can be cooked in it, and all handling of Hot Fruit or Hot Jars or Tempering of Jars avoided; the contents retain all their natural flavor, and the labor of preserving is lessened more than one-half. Pamphlets sent on application.

J. B. BARTLETT, Wholesale Manufacturer,
69 Murray-street, New York.

Important to Cider Makers.

THE JERSEY

POWER APPLE GRINDER.

(BUTTERWORTH'S PATENT.)

For grinding Apples, Peaches, Sugar Beets, and other kinds of fruit and vegetables. This greatly superior machine is rapidly growing in favor among the Cider makers and farmers of our country, and is destined soon to supersede all other mills used in the manufacture of Cider. For Illustrated Pamphlet, address, inclosing two stamps,

R. BUTTERWORTH, Trenton, N. J.
Patentee and Sole Manufacturer.

CRESYLIC SOAP.

A PERFECT DISINFECTANT
(Patented).

For Disinfecting, Deodorizing, and Purifying Cellars, Hospitals, Tenement Houses, &c. Also, for Exterminating Roaches, Bugs, and Insects of all kinds.

Manufactured solely by
JAMES BUCHAN & CO.,
[illegible] street, New York.

Advertisements, to be sure of insertion, must be received BEFORE the 5th of the preceding month.

TERMS—(cash before insertion):

Ordinary Pages, $1.50 *per line. Open Pages*—$2 *per line. Business Notices*—$2.50 per line of space, each insertion.

RIVERVIEW MILITARY ADADEMY, Poughkeepsie, N. Y.—Location healthy; Scenery unequaled; Building convenient; Teachers highly educated, earnest, working men; System of Order unsurpassed. A wide awake thorough-going School for boys wishing to be trained for Business, for College, or for West Point or the Naval Academy. For circulars address OTIS BISBEE, A. M., Principal and Proprietor.

PREMIUM CHESTER WHITE PIGS for Sale.—Sent by Express to all parts of the United States. For Circulars and Prices, Address N. P. BOYER & CO., Gum Tree, Chester Co., Pa.

STRAWBERRIES.

Our Strawberry Circular for fall of 1867, is now issued, and will be sent to all applicants enclosing five cents.

It gives complete lists of the best varieties for home use and market purposes, and contains much valuable information in reference to the Strawberry.

J. KNOX,
Box 155, Pittsburgh, Pa.

C. E. MEISSNER
RICHMOND
STATEN ISLAND, N. Y.

Would call the attention of Dealers and Planters to his extensive stock of Grape vines, and especially to the Concord and Iona varieties.

Our vines have always been unsurpassed by any in market, and our aim is not only to keep up their well known standard of excellence, but to produce, if possible, still better plants than we have had heretofore.

Having a very large number in course of propagation, we are enabled to sell at very low prices where quantities are taken, and all parties intending to purchase will find it greatly to their interest to examine our stock and prices before purchasing elsewhere. Last year the demand for our plants was so large that we were not able to fill one half of our orders. Therefore, send your orders in early to secure the best plants. Address C. E. MEISSNER, Richmond P. O., Staten Island, N. Y.

PEACH TREES AND SMALL FRUITS A SPECIALTY. RUMSON NURSERIES. Send for Circulars. A. HANCE & SON, Red Bank, Monmouth Co., N. J.

IMPORTANT TO ALL.
Another Great American Invention.

It is recommended by Surgeon Boche, of U. S. Navy, Surgeon Woodward, U. S. Army, by J. R. Chilton, the celebrated Chemist, New York, by Drs. Hayes and Jackson, State Assayers of Mass., by J. M. Maris & Co., Chemists, Philad'a., and other Chemists, and by N. Y. Tribune, American Agriculturist, N. Y. Independent, Southern Cultivator, and other leading Journals, and by thousands of families of the highest respectability who have used it.

A cheap and healthful antiseptic—the only method in the world for preserving Fruits, Juices of Fruits, Vegetables, Milk, &c., &c., without sugar, and without making air-tight.

It does away entirely with the need and use of all expensive Patent air-tight Jars, and admits of keeping the fruits, &c., in vessels of any size and kind, by simply corking them or tying paper or cloth saturated with *Paraffin*, or with Rosin and Wax over them. When opened the fruit will keep for 1 to 2 months during winter, or 2 to 4 weeks during summer—fully exposed to the air—giving ample time to use them from large vessels as wanted.

It will preserve with or without sugar. It is the only reliable method for preserving cider. Every dairyman wants it during summer to preserve milk sweet. It will preserve milk 24 to 36 hours longer than it will naturally keep—causing it to furnish more cream.

It is warranted healthful and effectual. No family should be without it. It is sold by all Druggists in every wholesale market in the U. S. Retail price, $1 per bottle. Each bottle will preserve 128 pounds of fruit, &c., and is accompanied with full directions for using.

Ask for Spear's Fruit Preserving Solution, and don't fail to try it—get it from your Merchant.

L. P. WORRALL, Gen'l. Agent, 91 Hudson st., New York.

AGENTS WANTED!—Male or Female, in all parts of the United States, to sell "Abbott's Lives of the Presidents," one of the best books for Agents ever published in this country. The work is finely illustrated, complete in one volume, ready for subscribers, and sells splendidly. Address B. B. RUSSELL & CO., Boston, Mass.

SPECIAL
ADVERTISING AGENCY.

Advertisements from reliable parties only, inserted in the Agricultural, Religious, and other first-class mediums throughout the country, by the undersigned.

An experience of several years in conducting the advertising department of the American Agriculturist, gives superior facilities for satisfactory transaction of such business.

See Notice in July No., page 242.

W. A. FITCH, 151 Nassau-st., New York.

VICTOR CANE MILL.

The leading Mill in *twenty-five* States. The out-growth of seven years previous experience in the manufacture of Cane Mills, and now only in its fourth year, yet has taken *Eighteen State Fair First Premiums.*

Over Seven Thousand

are now in use. No keys about it—no plate or bar between the rolls, hence no choking. Don't require levers or springs to ease up under pressure to prevent breaking, but is strong enough to force all kinds of Cane through same space without danger of breakage. Also,

CENTRIFUGAL SUGAR DRAINER.

Sugar Crushers, Church and Farm Bells, Star Corn Shellers, Drag Sawing Machines, Eureka Cutting Boxes, &c. Full description sent free.

BLYMYER, NORTON & CO., Cincinnati, O.

SORGO JOURNAL.

An Elegant Monthly, devoted to Northern Sugar Cane culture. Price, $1.50 per year. Address SORGO JOURNAL, Cincinnati, O.

COOK'S EVAPORATOR.

The old, reliable, and only successful Sorgo Evaporator. Is in its *ninth year*—has outlived over 200 *competitors*, and is yet *unrivaled.*

51 State Fair First Premiums have been awarded it.

Over 10,000 in use. It won't pay to boil Sorghum on anything else. It is *warranted* in every respect. Full description sent free on application to

BLYMYER, DAY & CO., Mansfield, O.

SORGO HAND BOOK.

Our Eighth Annual Sorgo Hand Book.

Giving the most reliable information on Manufacturing Sorghum Syrup, the result of 10 years personal experience, with full description of the celebrated Cook Evaporator and Victor Cane Mill.—Also, description of the Eureka Cider and Grape Mill, sent free to all applicants. BLYMYER, DAY & CO., Mansfield, O.

THE DASHER CHURN

Brings good butter regularly in SIX MINUTES time, on an average, at the farm of M. C. Weld, Associate Editor *American Agriculturist.*

It is MADE ON THE TRUE PRINCIPLES, as described in the *Agriculturist*, July number, page 243.

It WORKS EASILY, is VERY SIMPLE IN CONSTRUCTION, EASILY CLEANED, and EVERY WAY RIGHT.

At a recent trial before the Farmers' Club, in New York, it brought and gathered *good* butter in LESS THAN TWO MINUTES.

For prices, terms of Agency, purchase of territory, etc., address JOHN W. DOUGLASS, Dealer in Agricultural Implements, Sole Agent, 181 Water-st., New York.

N. B.—Agents wanted everywhere.

CONTINUAL LEVER and Screw Press, with Grinder attached, for Pressing Cheese, Wines, Cider, and Lard, &c. Address WILLIAM C. REA, Pleasant Run, New Jersey.

Fruit-Farm and Nursery for Sale.

The CELEBRATED POMONA FRUIT-FARM and NURSERY of J. W. Dodge, on the Cumberland Table Lands of East Tennessee. Unequaled as a fruit growing region. Beautiful Tract of 160 acres, with rich Prairie. Good improvements, large Orchards of Select Fruits. SEVEN FIRST PREMIUMS awarded by the State and Division Fairs, to fruit from the POMONA ORCHARDS. Fine opportunity for Nursery business. Can be made a superior stock or Dairy Farm. Must be sold immediately. Price moderate. For particular description, terms, &c., address J. W. DODGE & SON, Pomona, Cumberland County, Tennessee.

Seeds of Florists' Flowers.

FOR THE CONSERVATORY AND THE FLOWER GARDEN, FOR SOWING IN AUGUST AND SEPTEMBER.

Particular attention is invited to the following list of Seeds of Florists' Flowers, which have been carefully selected from the stocks of several of the most successful cultivators and exhibitors in Europe, and can be confidently recommended.

Calceolarias, extra select, from prize flowers	50
do. Rugosa, from the finest shrubby varieties	50
Cineraria, extra choice, from all the new varieties	50
Gloxinia, from the finest erect and drooping varieties	50
Hollyhocks, (very double,) from his unrivaled collection, (ready in August)	25
Pansy, English, extra select, saved from the finest prize flowers	50
Pansy, New Fancy, very beautiful	50
Primula sinensis fimbriata, (Chinese primrose, fringed,) various colors, mixed, extra quality	50
Pink, Tree, or Perpetual Carnation, ex. quality	50
Pink, Carnation and Picotee, celebrated German collection	50
Polyanthus, finest mixed varieties	25
Mimulus, finest mixed, golden yellow and white ground	25
Tropæolum, finest mixed var. for winter flowering	25
Stock, scarlet and white intermediate London, extra, each, (ready in August)	25
Stock, French Cocardeau, scarlet, purple and white, mixed, fine for winter flowering	25
Stock, new white wallflower leaved, a superb variety for pot culture	25
Sweet Williams, Hunt's extra select, far surpassing anything hitherto offered	25
Wallflower, extra fine double German	25

Collections of twenty varieties of HARDY ANNUALS, BIENNIALS AND PERENNIALS, for Autumn sowing, for $1.00. Address B. K. BLISS, Springfield, Mass.

GRAPE VINES
BY THE
1,000 or 10,000.
Iona, Israella and Delaware,
[the three best grapes]
A SPECIALTY.

Superior vines of all other varieties. Our vines, already well known as of first quality in every respect, this year surpass all we have heretofore grown.

The Trade are particularly invited to examine the stock.

A visit to our grounds and examination of our well trained vineyard of bearing vines, will well repay those about planting for fruit or wine, as they may here see how to **save time and money.**

Address HOLTON & ZUNDELL, Haverstraw, N. Y.

The New Strawberry.
CHARLES DOWNING.

This new Seedling was raised by J. S. Downer, of Kentucky, and is justly entitled to bear the name of this first Pomologist of America. It is a Seedling of Downer's Prolific. The plant is more vigorous and productive than its parent; fruit enormously large, solid, firm enough for market, scarlet, and of the finest flavor. The great vigor of this plant enables it to mature all its fruit to a large size. The leaves are very large, and stand a foot high; flowers perfect. A bed of this variety set out the first of Oct. last, in my garden, was picked over on the 15th of June, by John C. Thompson, of Staten Island, N. Y.; of a fair average of the berries selected, 28 weighed one pound. Mr. Downer informs me that several of his neighbors have grown them from plants one year old, weighing over one ounce each. Mr. Greeley having offered a prize of $50.00 for a better berry in every respect than the Wilson, this berry has been entered for the prize, and submitted to the Committee. Mr. Greeley requires it to be tested by two years trial, consequently the award cannot be made this season. We understand, however, that the Committee consider it far in advance of any other seedling.

Charles Downing, one of the Committee, says:

Newburgh, July 5th, 1867.

"Downer's new Seedling is certainly a very promising sort, and from what I have seen this season, think it will prove an acquisition, and for *vigor, productiveness, size and quality*, combined, think it *superior to any new sort.* The naming it Charles Downing prevents me from saying much about it."—CHAS. DOWNING. We propose sending out plants after the 15th Sept., in rotation, as ordered, at the following rates: 3 plants, $2.00; 6 plants, $3; 12 plants, $5; 100, $25; 500, $80; 1,000 plants, $150. Twenty per cent. deducted for cash orders, received this fall, plants deliverable next spring.

Address WM. S. CARPENTER, 156 Reade-st., New York.

NEW STRAWBERRIES.

PRESIDENT.—A new Seedling of very large size, productive and firm.

HARRISON.—A chance Seedling, raised in Westchester Co., fruit very large, quite equal to the Hovey in size and quality, productive and firm.

MARKET.—A Seedling from Illinois, of large size, wonderfully productive, and very early. Several days before the New Jersey Scarlet.

ABRAHAM LINCOLN.—A Seedling raised by Mr. Plattmen, of Erie, Pa., monstrous in size, productive, and of extra quality. These 4 splendid varieties, $2 dozen, each, of the collection, 1 dozen each, $6.

PERPETUAL PINE.—I have imported this remarkable berry, at a large expense. It is described by Mr. Gloede, the originator, as follows: "The kind I have the good luck to offer is a real, perpetual, large-fruited strawberry, of the pine class, which, during three years culture, not only bore an abundant crop in spring, but continued flowering and fruiting till late in the Autumn."

Plants $1.00 each, 6 for $5.00; 12 for $8.00.

The following new Seedlings have been well tested in different parts of the country, and strongly recommended.

PHILADELPHIA, very early, *Starr, Stinger, Great Eastern, Hubbard Seedling*, very fine, *Fenner Seedling, Durand Seedling*, and *Ella*, one of earliest to ripen, and very fine. Plants $1 per dozen for each variety, or the 8 varieties, $5.00.

ROMEYN SEEDLING.—This new Seedling is better than the Wilson, quite as firm and productive, and continues fruiting until August. 3 for $1; 20 for $3; 50 for $6; 100 for $10; 1,000 for $75.

AGAWAM, has proved this season to be the king of strawberries, monstrous in size, firm, exquisite flavor, and very productive. 12 plants $2.00; 100, $8.00.

Address WM. S. CARPENTER, 156 Reade-st., New York.

MAKE MONEY

FROM YOUR

TREES, VINES, AND GARDENS.

READ THE NEW BOOKS, AND THRIVE.

SMALL FRUIT CULTURIST.

By ANDREW S. FULLER.

It tells all about

STRAWBERRIES.
RASPBERRIES.
BLACKBERRIES.
BARBERRIES.
DWARF CHERRIES.
CURRANTS.
GOOSEBERRIES.
CRANBERRIES.
HUCKLEBERRIES.
CORNELIAN CHERRIES.

This book covers the whole ground of Propagation, Culture, Varieties, Packing for Market, etc.

SENT POST-PAID. - - - PRICE, $1.50.

AMERICAN POMOLOGY.

THE NEW BOOK ON APPLES.

By DOCT. JOHN A. WARDER.

HISTORY.
PROPAGATION.
BUDS, CUTTINGS.
SITE FOR AN ORCHARD.
PREPARATION OF SOIL.
SELECTION, PLANTING.
CULTURE & PRUNING.
RIPENING & PRESERVING.
CLASSIFICATION & DESCRIPTION
CATALOGUE AND INDEX

The latest and best book on Apples.

SENT POST-PAID. - - PRICE, $3.00.

GRAPE CULTURIST.

By ANDREW S. FULLER.

Growing from Seed.
Propagation from Buds.
Propagating Houses.
Cuttings in Open Air.
How to Make Layers.
Grafting the Grape.
Hybridizing, Crossing.
Soil, Situation, Planting.
Insects, Mildew, Sunscald, etc.
Valuable, & Discarded Varieties.

New Edition, revised and enlarged.

SENT POST-PAID. - - PRICE, $1.50.

GARDENING FOR PROFIT.

In the Market and Family Garden.

By PETER HENDERSON.

Everything is made perfectly plain. Read the TABLE OF CONTENTS.

Men Fitted for Gardening.
Amount of Capital Required.
Profits of Market Gardening.
Manures and Implements.
Location, Situation, Preparation
When, and Where to Sow.
Transplanting; Insects.
Varieties and Cultivation.
Packing for Shipping.
Preservation in Winter.

Find Out from this book how to make money from your Garden.

SENT POST-PAID. - - - PRICE, $1.50.

Either of the above-named books will be sent post-paid, on receipt of price, by the Publishers.

Also, many other new and valuable books for the FARM, GARDEN, AND HOUSEHOLD.

SEND FOR A CATALOGUE.

ORANGE JUDD & CO.,
41 Park Row, New York.

DRAINING FOR PROFIT

AND

DRAINING FOR HEALTH.

By GEO. E. WARING, Jr.,

ENGINEER OF THE DRAINAGE OF CENTRAL PARK, NEW YORK.

Illustrated.

TABLE OF CONTENTS:

LAND TO BE DRAINED AND THE REASONS WHY.—Indications of the need of draining.—Sources of water.—Objections to too much water.—Wet sub-soil.

HOW DRAINS ACT AND HOW THEY AFFECT THE SOIL.—Characteristics of well laid tile drain.—Surface-water and rain water beneficial, springs and soakage water injurious. Cracking of stiff clays.—Evaporation and filtration.—Rain fall.—Evaporation.—Temperature.—Drought.—Porosity or mellowness.—Chemical action in the soil.

HOW TO GO TO WORK TO LAY OUT A SYSTEM OF DRAINS.—Amateur draining.—Maps.—Levelling Instruments.—Outlets and location of drains.—Main drains. Spring water.—Fall.—Tiles. Depth and distance apart.—Direction of laterals.—Collars.—Discharge of water from drains.

HOW TO MAKE THE DRAINS.—Tools.—Marking the lines.—Water courses.—Outlet. Silt Basins.—Opening the ditches.—Grading.—Tile laying.—Connections.—Covering the tile and filling in.—Collecting the water of springs.—Amending the map.

HOW TO TAKE CARE OF DRAINS AND DRAINED LAND.—Removing obstructions.—Mistake of substituting large tiles for small ones which have become obstructed.—Heavy lands should not be trampled while wet.

WHAT DRAINING COSTS.

Draining, expensive work.—Their permanence and lasting effects.—Cheapness versus economy.—Details of cost.—(1. Engineering and Superintendence.—2. Digging the ditches.—3. Grading the bottoms.—4. Tile and tile laying.—5. Covering and filling.—6. Outlets and Silt Basins.)

WILL IT PAY?

Increased crops required to pay cost of draining.—(Corn, Wheat, Rye, Oats, Potatoes, Barley, Hay, Cotton, Tobacco.)—Instances of profit.—Benefit of draining in facilitating farm work.

HOW TO MAKE DRAINING TILES.

Materials.—Preparation of earths.—Moulding tile machines.—Drying and rolling.—Burning.—Kilns.—General arrangement of a tilery.

THE RECLAIMING OF SALT MARSHES.—Extent of marshes on the Atlantic Coast.—The English Fens.—Harlaem Lake.—The exclusion of sea water.—Removal of the causes of inundation from the upland.—Removal of rain fall and water of filtration.—Embankments.—Muskrats.—Rivers and Creeks.—Outlet of drainage.

MALARIAL DISEASES.

Fever and Ague.—Neuralgia.—Vicinity of New York.—Dr. Bartlett on Periodical Fever.—Dr. Metcalf's Report to U. S. Sanitary Commission.—La Roche on the effects of Malarial Fever.—Dr Salisbury on the "Cause of Malarial Fevers."—English experience. Reports to the British Parliament.—Cause of Malaria removed by draining.

HOUSE AND TOWN DRAINAGE.

Sewerage.—The use of pipes.—The new outfall sewers in London.—The use of steam pumps to secure outlets.—Utilization of sewage matters in agriculture.—Effects of imperfect house drainage on health.—Typhoid fever.—The Westminster fever in London.—Epidemic at the Maplewood Young Ladies Institute in Pittsfield, Mass.—Lambeth Square, London.—Back drainage.—Water supply.—General Board of Health, (England).

SENT POST-PAID. PRICE, $1.50.

ORANGE JUDD & CO.,
41 Park Row New-York.

SQUASHES.

HOW TO GROW THEM.

By JAMES J. H. GREGORY.

A most valuable little Treatise for Farmers and Gardeners. It tells about

Selecting the Soil.
How much Manure.
Preparing and Planting.
Hoeing and Cultivating.
Setting of the Fruit.
Ripening; Gathering.
Storing of the Crop.
Care During Winter.
Market Prices and Varieties.
When to Take Out Seed.

SENT POST-PAID. - Price, paper covers, 30 cts.

ORANGE JUDD & CO.,
41 Park Row New-York.

BOOKS

FOR FARMERS AND OTHERS,

PUBLISHED BY

ORANGE JUDD & CO.,

41 Park Row, New York.

Either of the Books mentioned in the following list will be sent, post-paid, on receipt of the price.

Allen's Domestic Animals $1.00

A History and Description of the HORSE, MULE, CATTLE, SHEEP, SWINE, POULTRY, and FARM DOGS, with directions for Breeding, Crossing, Rearing, Feeding, and Preparation for Market, with their DISEASES and REMEDIES. By R. L. ALLEN. Cloth, 12mo, 227 pp.

Allen's Rural Architecture $1.50

Practical Directions and Suggestions for Construction of convenient FARM-HOUSES, COTTAGES, and OUT-BUILDINGS, including Barns, Stables, Sheds, Carriage and Wagon-Houses, Work-Shops, Wood-Houses, Ash and Smoke-Houses, Ice-Houses, Poultry and Bee-Houses, Dove-Cotes, etc., together with directions for the gardens and grounds; useful and ornamental Domestic Animals, etc. By Hon. LEWIS F. ALLEN, Editor "American Herd-Book," etc. Cloth, 12mo, 378 pp.

American Bird-Fancier ...... *Paper*, .. 30.

Field, Cage, and House-Birds, breeding, rearing, etc. Paper, 12mo, 107 pp.

American Farm-Book (R. L. ALLEN) $1.50

OR A COMPEND OF AMERICAN AGRICULTURE; Being a Practical Treatise on Soils, Manures, Draining, Irrigation, Grasses, Grain, Roots, Fruits, Cotton, Tobacco, Sugar-Cane, Rice, and every Staple Product of the United States; with the best methods of Planting, Cultivating, and Preparation for Market. Over one hundred engravings. By R. L. ALLEN. Cloth, 12mo, 325 pp.

American Rose Culturist 30

(Including the Dahlia.) Being a Practical Treatise on the Propagation, Cultivation, and Management of THE ROSE, to which are added full directions for the treatment of the Dahlia. In neat paper covers. 12mo, 96 pp.

American Weeds, and Useful Plants $1.75

An Important Work for every Cultivator—Farmer, Gardener, etc.; being an Enumeration and Description, (with accurate illustrations), of the WEEDS and PLANTS found in American Fields and Gardens, which meet the observation, or require the attention of Cultivators; with practical suggestions for their Eradication when needed. While *practical* in its character, it includes both the common and botanical names and characters of the Weeds and Plants, with a Popular Account of the Structure of Plants. By WM. DARLINGTON, M.D., and Prof. GEO. THURBER. Thoroughly Illustrated with 277 Engravings. 12mo., 460 pp.

Annuals.. ....*Paper*, 50, *Cloth*, 75

THE AMERICAN HORTICULTURAL ANNUAL FOR 1867. A YEAR BOOK FOR THE GARDENER, THE FRUIT GROWER, AND THE AMATEUR. It is a beautifully illustrated volume of 168 pages. It contains an Almanac and Calendar for each month, giving hints for work in the various departments, with useful tables, and an article on Growing Grape Vines from cuttings, by William Patrick; How Horseradish is Grown for Market, by P. Henderson; Home Decorations, by A. Bridgeman; The New Apples of 1866, by Dr. J. A. Warder; New or Noteworthy Pears, by P. Barry; Small Fruits in 1866, by A. S. Fuller; Rarer Valuable Evergreens, by T. Meehan, with valuable contributions by other writers.

THE AMERICAN AGRICULTURAL ANNUAL FOR 1867. A companion volume to the Horticultural Annual, and containing, besides an Almanac with hints about work for each month, an Essay on Draining, by Col. Geo. E. Waring, jr.; articles on the Culture of Sorghum, by Wm. Clough; Some of the Newest and Best Potatoes, by Wm. S. Carpenter; How to Train a Horse, by S. F. Headley; Essential Features of a Good Barn, with Plan, by Dr. F. M. Hexamer; Recent Scientific Progress in Agriculture, by Prof. S. W. Johnson, of Yale College; The Culture of Wheat, by Joseph Harris, and other valuable essays upon subjects of interest to agriculturists. Finely Illustrated.

Bement's Rabbit Fancier............ . 30

BREEDING, REARING, FEEDING, AND GENERAL MANAGEMENT of Rabbits; their Diseases and Remedies; Full Directions for the Construction of Hutches, Rabbitries, etc.; Recipes for Cooking and Dressing for the Table. Numerous Illustrations. By C. N. BEMENT, author of *Poulterer's Companion*, etc. 12mo, 101 pp., in neat illustrated paper covers.

Boussingault's Rural Economy.... .$1.60

Rural Economy in its relations with Chemistry, Physics, and Meteorology; or CHEMISTRY APPLIED TO AGRICULTURE in the Principles of Farm Management, the Preservation and Use of Manures, the Nutrition and Food of Animals, and the General Economy of Agriculture. By J. B. BOUSSINGAULT, Member of Institute of France, etc. Translated, with Introduction and Notes, by GEORGE LAW, Agriculturist. Cloth, 12mo, 507 pp.

Breck's New Book of Flowers, or Flower Garden................ .... $1.75

In which are described the various Hardy Herbaceous Flowers, Annuals, Shrubby Plants, and Evergreen Trees, with Directions for their Cultivation. New edition, revised and corrected. By JOSEPH BRECK, Seedsman and Florist, former editor of *New England Farmer*, and *Horticultural Register*. Cloth, 12mo, 395 pp.

Buist's American Flower Garden Directory..........................$1.50

Containing Practical Directions for the Culture of Plants in the Flower-Garden, Hot-House, Green-House, Rooms for Parlor-Windows, FOR EVERY MONTH IN THE YEAR; with descriptions of most desirable plants, soils, transplanting, erecting a Hot-House, a Green-House, laying out a Flower-Garden, etc., etc. By ROBERT BUIST, a practical Nurseryman and Seed-Grower of Philadelphia. Cloth, 12mo, 342 pp.

Buist's Family Kitchen-Gardener.....$1.00

An excellent Practical work, containing Plain and Accurate Descriptions of all the Different Species and Varieties of Culinary Vegetables, with their Botanical English, French, and German Names, alphabetically arranged; with full Directions for the Best Mode of Cultivating them in the Garden or under Glass. By ROBERT BUIST. Cloth, 12mo., 216 pp.

Cobbett's American Gardener.......... 75

A Treatise on the Laying Out and Management of Gardens. Though an old work, it is one which will find a place in every considerable library, as the production of a remarkable man. While it is marked by the author's peculiarities, it is so full of plain common-sense, that it is worthy of being kept in print. By WILLIAM COBBETT. Cloth, 12mo., 230 pp.

Cole's American Fruit Book. 75

Containing Directions for Raising, Propagating, and Managing Fruit-Trees, Shrubs, and Plants, with descriptions of the best varieties of fruit, etc. 18mo, 283 pp.

Chorlton's Grape-Grower's Guide.... . 75

INTENDED ESPECIALLY FOR THE AMERICAN CLIMATE; being a practical Treatise, with Engravings, on the Cultivation of the Grape-Vine in each Department of Hot-House, Cold Grapery, etc.; with Plans for the Construction and Heating. By WM. CHORLTON. Cloth, 12mo, 204 pp.

Cole's American Veterinarian..........75

Diseases of *Domestic Animals*, showing the *Causes*, *Symptoms*, and *Remedies*, and rules for *Restoring* and *Preserving Health* by good management, with directions for *Training* and *Breeding*. By S. W. COLE. Cloth, 18mo., 288 pp.

Copeland's Country Life..........$5.00

An elegant Octavo Volume, containing 926 pages, and 250 Engravings. It is a Compendium of Agricultural and Horticultural Practical Knowledge; embracing Descriptions, Hints, Suggestions and Details of great value to every one interested in Fruit, Flowers, Vegetables, or Farm Crops. It describes and illustrates nearly the whole range of topics of interest to the Farmer, the Gardener, the Fruit Culturist, and the Amateur. By ROBERT MORRIS COPELAND. Cloth, beveled boards, 8vo., 926 pp.

Cotton-Planter's Manual.......... .$1.50

This is the only popular work published on the subject. It is a compilation of facts from the best authorities on the CULTURE OF COTTON, its Natural History, Chemical Analysis, Trade, and Consumption, with a history of Cotton and the Cotton-Gin. Cloth, 12mo, 290 pp.

Dadd's American Cattle-Doctor.. .$1.50.

To Help Every Man to be his own Cattle-Doctor. A work by GEO. H. DADD, M. D., Veterinary Practitioner; giving the necessary information for preserving the Health and Curing the Diseases of OXEN, COWS, SHEEP, and SWINE, with a great variety of original Recipes, and valuable information on Farm and Dairy Management. 12mo, 350 pp.

Dadd's Modern Horse Doctor......$1.50

CONTAINING PRACTICAL OBSERVATIONS ON THE CAUSES, NATURE, AND TREATMENT of Diseases and Lameness of HORSES; embracing the most recent and improved Methods, according to an enlightened system of Veterinary Practice, for Preservation and Restoration of Health. Illustrated. By GEO. H. DADD, M.D., Veterinary Surgeon. Cloth, 12mo., 432 pp.

Dana's Muck Manual.................$1.25

A Manual for Farmers; treating of Soils, Manures, Composts, etc., and especially of the important subject of using MUCK, the great natural fertilizer of the country. By SAMUEL L. DANA. Cloth, 12mo., 312 pp.

Downing's Landscape Gardening and Rural Architecture.........$6.50

The most complete and valuable work ever issued on Landscape Gardening in North America, for the Improvement of Country Residences; containing full Directions for everything connected with the Laying out and adorning the Rural Home, the Grounds, the Gardens, the Buildings, the Trees and Plants, etc., with principles of taste so stated as to adapt the work to all classes. Splendidly Illustrated with many Steel and fine Wood Engravings. By the late A. J. DOWNING. New Edition, Enlarged, Newly Illustrated and Revised, with Supplement, by HENRY WINTHROP SARGENT. Octavo, 534 pp. Extra cloth, gilt, beveled bds.

Eastwood's Complete Cranberry Manual 75

Giving directions for the cultivation in different localities, with illustrations and descriptions of varieties. By BENJ. EASTWOOD. Cloth, 12mo, 120 pp.

Elliott's Western Fruit Grower's Guide1.50

The previous Edition of this work was Thoroughly Revised; embracing all the new and valuable Fruits, with the latest improvements in their Cultivation; especially adapted to the wants of Western Fruit-Growers; full Illustrations. By F. R. ELLIOTT, of Ohio. Cloth, 12mo, 503 pp.

Fuller's Illustrated Strawberry Culturist.................*Paper*,.. 20

A new, practical little work, meeting with universal favor. It gives a full list of varieties, down to the latest valuable seedlings. Paper, 12mo, 48 pp.

Field's Pear Culture............. ..$1.25

THE PEAR GARDEN; a Treatise on the Propagation and Cultivation of the Pear Tree, with Instructions for Management from the Seedling to the Bearing Tree. By THOMAS W. FIELD. Illustrations. Cloth, 12mo, 286 pp.

Flax Culture.......................... 50

A new and very valuable work, consisting of full directions, from selection of ground and seed to preparation and marketing of crop, as given by a number of experienced growers. 8vo, paper.

French's Farm Drainage.......... . 1.50

The Principles, Process, and Effects of Draining Land with Stones, Wood, Drain-Plows, Open Ditches, and especially with Tiles; including Tables of Rainfall, Evaporation, Filtration, Excavation, Capacity of Pipes, cost and number to the acre. With over 100 Illustrations. The best work on Draining published. By Judge FRENCH, of New Hampshire, President of Mass. Agricultural College. Cloth, 12mo, 384 pp.

Guenon s Treatise on Milch Cows.... 75

An interesting work, giving new and peculiar directions, and many illustrative engravings, for determining by natural marks or external signs, the quality and quantity of milk a cow will give, length of time she will continue in milk, etc., with introductory remarks of forty pages on the Cow and Dairy. Sixty-third thousand. 8vo, 88 pp.

Herbert's Hints to Horse-Keepers. . $1.75

This is the best practical work on the Horse, prepared in this country. A COMPLETE MANUAL for HORSEMEN, embracing: How to Breed a Horse; How to Buy a Horse; How to Break a Horse; How to Use a Horse; How to Feed a Horse; How to Physic a Horse (Allopathy or Homœopathy); How to Groom a Horse; How to Drive a Horse; How to Ride a Horse, etc., and Chapters on MULES and PONIES, etc. By the late HENRY WILLIAM HERBERT, (Frank Forester.) Beautifully Illustrated throughout. Cloth, 12mo., 425 pp.

Hooper's Dog and Gun...... .... .30

"A Few Loose Chapters on Shooting," with some Anecdotes and Incidents, Notes on Guns, Choosing and Training Dogs; about Game, etc. By J. J. HOOPER, Montgomery, Ala. Neat paper covers; 12mo, 105 pp.

Hop Culture..........................40

PRACTICAL DETAILS fully given, from the Selection and Preparation of the Soil, SETTING and CULTIVATION of the Plants, to PICKING, DRYING, PRESSING and MARKETING the Crop. Plain Directions by Ten Experienced Cultivators. Illustrated with over forty engravings. Edited by PROF. GEORGE THURBER, Editor of the *American Agriculturist*. 8vo., paper.

Johnston's Agricultural Chemistry.. 1.75

LECTURES ON THE APPLICATION OF CHEMISTRY AND GEOLOGY TO AGRICULTURE. New edition, with an Appendix, containing the Author's Experiments in Practical Agriculture. By the late JAS. F. W. JOHNSTON, M.A., F.R.SS. L. and E., etc., etc. This is an American edition of the large and extensive English work. Cloth, large 12mo, 709 pp.

Leuchars' How to Build Hot-Houses..$1.50

GREEN-HOUSES, GRAPERIES, etc. etc., and how to Ventilate them. Illustrated with numerous Engravings. This is the only work published in this country, specially devoted to this subject. By ROBERT B. LEUCHARS, Garden Architect. Cloth, 12mo., 366 pp.

My Vineyard at Lakeview...... .$1.25

This book is especially valuable as giving an account of the processes actually followed in celebrated Grape Regions in Western New York, and on the shores and islands of Lake Erie. To any one who wishes to grow grapes, whether a single vine or a vineyard, it is full of valuable teachings. It tells just what the beginner in grape culture wishes to know, with the charm that always attends the relation of personal experience. Cloth, 12mo., 143 pp.

Onions: How to Raise them Profitably, *Paper*..............................20

Being the Practical Details, from Selection of Seed and Preparation of Ground to Harvesting and Marketing the Crop, given very plainly by *Seventeen Practical Onion Growers* of long experience, residing in different parts of the country. No more valuable work of its size was ever issued. Octavo, 32 pp. Neat paper covers.

HAVE YOU A GARDEN?

A NEW WORK.

GARDENING FOR PROFIT,

IN THE MARKET AND FAMILY GARDEN.

BY PETER HENDERSON.

Illustrated.

This is the first work on Market Gardening ever published in this country. Its author is well known as a market gardener of eighteen years' successful experience. In this work he has recorded this experience, and given without reservation the methods necessary to the profitable culture of the commercial or

MARKET GARDEN.

It is a work for which there has long been a demand, and one which will commend itself, not only to those who grow vegetables for sale, but to the cultivator of the

FAMILY GARDEN

To whom it presents methods quite different from the old ones generally practiced. It is an

ORIGINAL AND PURELY AMERICAN

work, and not made up, as books on gardening too often are, by quotations from foreign authors.

Everything is made perfectly plain, and the subject treated in all its details, from the selection of the soil to preparing the products for market. Frames, Hot-beds, and Forcing Houses, the management of which is usually so troublesome to the novice, are fully described, and the conditions of success and causes of failure clearly stated.

The success of the market gardeners near New York City is proverbial, and this is the only work that sets forth the means by which this success has been attained. Valuable hints are given to those who would raise Vegetables at the South for northern markets.

The following synopsis of its contents will show the scope of the work:

Men Fitted for the Business of Gardening.
The Amount of Capital Required and Working Force per Acre.
Profits of Market Gardening.
Location, Situation, and Laying Out.
Soils, Drainage, and Preparation.
Manures. Implements.
Uses and Management of Cold Frames.
Formation and Management of Hot-beds.
Forcing Pits or Green-houses.
Seeds and Seed Raising.
How, When, and Where to Sow Seeds.
Transplanting. Insects.
Packing of Vegetables for Shipping.
Preservation of Vegetables in Winter.
Vegetables, their Varieties and Cultivation.

SENT POST-PAID. PRICE, $1.50.

ORANGE JUDD & CO., 41 PARK ROW.

HINTS TO HORSE-KEEPERS,

A COMPLETE

MANUAL FOR HORSEMEN.

BY THE LATE HENRY WILLIAM HERBERT.

(FRANK FORESTER.)

Beautifully Illustrated.

HOW TO BREED A HORSE.—
CHOICE OF STALLION.—National Value of the Horse—The best class of Horses the cheapest for all purposes—What constitutes excellence—Blood; what it gives, should be on the side of the Sire—Breed up, not down—Diseases and Defects Hereditary—General Rules.
CHOICE OF THE MARE.—Size, Symmetry and Soundness more important than Blood—Points of the Brood Mare—Diseases Hereditary—Condition of the Mare—Should have moderate work when with Foal—Food and care during gestation—Health and temper.
MUTUAL ADAPTATION OF SIRE AND DAM.—First consideration in Improvement of "cold" Blood—Relative size of Sire and Dam—Defects in either Parent—How Remedied in Progeny—Bloods which "hit."
CANADIAN BLOOD.—The Canadian originally the French Norman—Characteristics—Hardihood—Speed—Mode of Improvement Crossing with Thorough-breds.
NORMAN BLOOD.—Origin and History of the Percheron Norman—A pure race—Characteristics and Points.
MODERN ARAB BLOOD.—English and American Thorough-breds derived from Oriental Blood—are now superior to the Modern Arabs—Nolan Arab.

PONIES — DIFFERENT BREEDS,
CHARACTERISTICS AND UTILITY.—Origin—Different Breeds—Shetlands and Scots—Galloways and Narragansetts—Mustangs and Indians—Profit of raising Ponies.

HOW TO BREED MULES.
Value of Mules—Their History and Natural History—The Mule and Hinney—Thorough-blood wasted in the Dam for Mules—The Mule in the United States—Large size not Desirable—Varieties of the Ass—The kind of Mares to be selected.

HOW TO BUY A HORSE.
Of whom to Buy it—Extraordinary Cheapness and Extraordinary Excellence not consistent with each other—Points to be regarded—How to Examine the Eye—Broken Wind—Roaring—Whistling—Broken Knees—To examine the Legs—Splints—Damaged Back Sinews—Spavins Ringbones—Curbs—How to tell the Age of a Horse.

HOW TO FEED A HORSE.
Consequences of Improper Feeding—Different Food for different conditions—Food for the Brood Mare—for the Foal—For Working Horses—Green Food—Carrots—Corn—Feeding Horses in Training—While Travelling—Summering Horses—The Best Method—Management of Omnibus Horses in New York.

HOW TO STABLE AND GROOM A HORSE.—Requisites for a good Stable—The economy of Proper Arrangements—Ventilation—Grooming; its necessity for all descriptions of Horses—How Performed—Clothing—Treatment when brought in from Work.

HOW TO BREAK, AND USE A HORSE.—What is required in a well-broken Horse—His education should commence when a Colt—Bitting—Putting in Harness—How to Use a Horse—Travelling—Working—Pleasure Horses—Punishment.

HOW TO PHYSIC A HORSE—
SIMPLE REMEDIES FOR SIMPLE AILMENTS.—Causes of Ailments—Medicines to be given only by the order of the Master—Depletion and Purging—Spasmodic Colic—Inflammation of the Bowels—Inflammation of the Lungs—How to Bleed—Balls and Purgatives—Costiveness—Cough—Bronchitis—Distemper—Worms—Diseases of the Feet—Scratches—Thrush—Broken Knees.

FARRIERY, ETC.
Castration—Docking and Nicking—Blood-letting—Treatment of Strains and Wounds—Galls of the Skin—Cracked Heels—Clipping and Singeing—Administering Medicines—Diseases of the Foot.

HOW TO SHOE A HORSE.
Unskillful Shoers—Anatomy of the Foot Illustrated—The Foot of a Colt—Preparation of the Foot—Removing the Old Shoe—Paring the Foot—The Shoe—Fitting the Shoe—Nailing—Number of Nails—Diseases of the Foot.

BAUCHER'S METHOD OF TRAINING HORSES.—What Constitutes a Well-trained Horse—To make him come at your call—The Philosophy of Training—Flexions of the Jaw—Flexions of the Neck—Flexions of the Croup—Backing—The Paces—Leaping.

HOW TO RIDE A HORSE.
The Saddle—The Girths—The Stirrups—Saddle-Cloths—The Crupper—The Martingale—The Bridle—Spurs—Mounting and Dismounting—The Seat—The Hands—The Legs—The Paces—Hints for Special Cases—The Art of Falling—Riding with Ladies.

LADIES' RIDING—WRITTEN BY A LADY.—Learning to Ride—The Side-saddle—The Girths—The Stirrup—The Bridle—The Martingale—The Bit—The Dress—Mounting and Dismounting—The Position—The Hands—The Leg and Whip—Accidents.

HOW TO DRIVE A HORSE.
The Art of Driving—Pleasure Driving—How to Hold the Reins—Driving a Pair—Four-in-hand Driving—Driving Working Horses—Plowing—Three-a-breast.

RAREY'S SYSTEM OF HORSE-TAMING.—Rarey's System a New Discovery—Previous System—Principles of this System—Instructions for practicing Rarey's Method—To Stable the Horse—To Approach the Horse—Tying up the Leg—Laying the Horse Down—Finale—Vices and Bad Habits—Rearing—Kicking—Baulking—Pulling on the Halter—Shying.

VETERINARY HOMŒOPATHY.
Principles of the System—Table of Remedies—General Directions—Treatment of a Sick Animal—Diet—Remedies for Specific Cases—Glossary of Diseases.

12mo. 425 p.—Sent by mail post-paid. $1.75.

ORANGE JUDD & CO.,
41 Park Row, New York.

NEW BOOKS.

Saunders' Domestic Poultry.

By S. M. Saunders.

New Edition Revised and Enlarged.

This Book contains Articles on the Preferable Breeds of Farm-Yard Poultry, Their History and Leading Characteristics, with Complete Instructions for Breeding and Fattening, and Preparing for Exhibition at Poultry Shows, etc., etc., derived from the Author's Experience and Observation.

The work is compact, full of valuable hints and information, and beautifully illustrated.

An appendix contains an account of *Poultry breeding on a large scale*, as practiced in the neighborhood of Paris, and is a very important addition to the work.

Price, paper 40 cts., cloth 75 cts.

ORANGE JUDD & CO., Publishers.

Money in the Swamps.

PEAT! PEAT! PEAT!

FUEL—MANURE.

WHERE TO FIND IT.

HOW TO MAKE AND USE IT.

ITS VALUE.

A NEW WORK ON PEAT,

THOROUGH AND PRACTICAL;

By PROF. SAMUEL W. JOHNSON, of Yale College.

It gives a full history of **PEAT, MUCK, etc.**, telling what they are, where found, and how to estimate their value.

It describes the various methods of using Peat for manure, as an absorbent, as an ameliorator of the soil, etc. and it is especially explicit in regard to the

USE OF PEAT AS FUEL,

describing minutely the various processes employed in preparing it to burn, from the simplest to the most complicated; such as are in use in this country, and Europe. It is illustrated with many Engravings of machines, etc.

The work is invaluable to those having Peat or Muck swamps, or wishing to invest in Peat Companies.

SENT POST-PAID. PRICE $1.25

ORANGE JUDD & Co., 41 Park Row.

THE STAR DRILL. Ewell & Co., Proprietors, Baltimore, Md.

This Machine plows the ground, seeds the grain, and rolls the surface smoothly for the Harvester, all at one operation, and in its use we claim the saving in labor of five hands and horses over the old system, (and as certificates of many Farmers will show), of at least one-third of the grain seeded per acre, and that grain seeded by this Machine is not liable to be affected by the winter frosts, but grows continuously through the same. One field-hand can plow, seed, and roll, from six to eight acres per day. Wheat seeded last Fall, in Logan County, Kentucky, by the "STAR DRILL," was examined by fifteen or twenty Farmers, on the 23d of April, of the present year, who stated, in certificates given by them, (and which are embodied in the Patentee's circular), "that it then stood twenty to twenty-four inches in hight, and full set, promising a heavy yield, with but one bushel sown to the acre, while in the same and adjoining fields, wheat sown at the same time, in the old way, with one and a half bushels to the acre, did not promise much more than half the yield, having been affected by the hard winter, and was but eight to ten inches high, which was the average of all sown in any other manner than by this Machine." Very recent certificates have been received from some of the same Farmers, stating that they saw the wheat threshed and measured in June, and that that seeded by the "Star Drill," yielded an average of twenty-nine and a half bushels per acre, which was more than double they yielded by the ordinary way, in adjoining fields. These are facts. This Machine seeds all kinds of small grain, and the [illegible] grass seeds, with perfect regularity. As a Corn Planter or Drill, for Sorghum, Peas, Beans, &c., it can not be surpassed. Its construction is very simple, and the material of which it is made, the very best, in every particular. Any laborer who can plow or drive a wagon can work it with ease. The saving of labor and economy in the various uses for which it is adapted, must make it invaluable to the Farmer. All that is asked is a fair trial. Send for Circulars. Price for each Machine complete, $125. All orders promptly attended to by EWELL & CO., Patentees, Proprietors and Manufacturers, Baltimore, Md.; Also, R. H. ALLEN & CO., Agents, 189 and 191 Water st., New York; JULIUS BARBAROUX, Louisville, Ky., [illegible] for Kentucky and Tennessee; P. MOHAN, Agent, [illegible] Main street, St. Louis, Mo.

A. N. WOOD & CO.

EATON, MADISON CO., N. Y.,

Continue to manufacture their Improved

PORTABLE ENGINES,

For Farm and Mechanical purposes. They are particularly adapted to driving Threshing Machines, Circular Saws, Mills of all kinds, [illegible], Planers, [illegible] Iron Lathes, Machinery in Cabinet or Wagon Shops, Boring Artesian Wells, Pumping Water, [illegible] &c., &c.

We warrant [illegible] [illegible] we recommend them, and [illegible] in all respects.

A. N. WOOD & CO.

BULLOCK'S Portable Cotton Press,

AS IMPROVED BY US,

is strong, simple, not easily out of order, and being made at our own manufactory of first-class material and workmanship, we can guarantee its perfect operation, if properly managed.

Portable Steam Engines, Horse-Powers, and Cotton Gins, with every variety of Agricultural Implement and Machine, Seeds and Fertilizers.

A large Illustrated Catalogue of our goods will be sent on application.

R. H. ALLEN & CO.,
189 and 191 Water st., New York.

INGERSOLL'S COTTON AND WOOL PRESSES.

INGERSOLL'S HAY AND STRAW PRESSES,
INGERSOLL'S RAG AND PAPER PRESSES,
INGERSOLL'S HIDE AND HAIR PRESSES,
BOTH HAND AND HORSE-POWER PRESSES,

for baling all kinds of material, on hand and made to order. Also, a practical machine for sawing down trees. Price $[illegible]. For price-list and full information, call on or address the manufacturers, INGERSOLL & DOUGHERTY, Greenpoint, (Brooklyn), N. Y.

The Prize Apple Parer at the Paris Exposition.

The Lightning Apple Parer, proved by two year's use, and hundreds of testimonials, to be the best invention of this class, has just received

The Highest Premium at the Paris Exposition.

It also took the **First Premiums** at the New England Fair, and the New York State Fair in 1866, at the Mechanics' Fair of the Franklin Institute, at Syracuse, in Feb., 1867, and wherever introduced is acknowledged to be ahead of all others for simplicity, speed and durability.

Sold at Wholesale by
A. H. SHIPLEY & SON, Philadelphia, Pa.
SPEAR BROTHERS, Baltimore, Md.
JAMES BOWN, Pittsburgh, Pa.
E. W. BOOTH & Co., Cincinnati, O.
J. H. VAJEN, Indianapolis, Ind.
G. HALLMAN, Louisville, Ky.
WARNE, CHEEVER & Co., St. Louis, Mo.
HORMAN & [illegible], Chicago, Ill.
BUHL, DUCHARME & Co., Detroit, Mich.
GEO. WORTHINGTON & Co., Cleveland, O.
J. W. MCKINSTRY, Rochester, N. Y.
KENNEDY & SEYMOUR, Syracuse, N. Y.
C. TREMPER, Albany, N. Y.
And by the Wholesale Hardware Trade everywhere.

SARGENT & CO.,
70 Beekman St., New York,
Manufacturers' Agents.

NORTH RIVER AGRICULTURAL "WORKS"
GRIFFING & CO. PROPRIETORS
58 & 60
CORTLANDT ST. NEW-YORK

WIND MILLS

For Pumping, and all Light Work on a Farm.

For details, see our Circular, that will be sent on application to us.

R. H. ALLEN & CO.,
189 and 191 Water st., New York City.

Eureka Cider Mill and Press.

THE BEST PORTABLE MILL AND PRESS ever built, and greatly improved for 1867. It has repeatedly taken the First Premium at State Fairs over all others, and is warranted in every respect. It does not simply crush or cut the apple, but crushes and rasps, so that at trials the pomace from this mill has yielded one quart more cider from a bushel of apples than other mills. It is a superior

GRAPE MILL.

Circular giving full description, with cut, sent free to all applicants by the manufacturers.
Liberal inducements to dealers.

BLYMYER, DAY & CO., Mansfield, O.

Sherwood's Cotton Seed Planter.

The great problem solved, and the companion of the Cotton Gin now in the field! The principles of this machine are approved by the best machinists of America. It has been in use for two seasons. Five hundred of these Planters are now ordered for the State of Tennessee. For orders or information, address S. B. SHERWOOD, Millville, Orleans Co., N. Y.; F. J. Le VALLEY, Agent, Lockport, N. Y., or JOHN W. DOUGLASS, 181 Water st., New-York.

CHEAPEST AND BEST
CIDER AND WINE MILLS,
(Hutchinson's Patent—Large and Small.)
Cheapest and Best Feed Cutters.
Best Cider Press Screws.
A variety of Best Agricultural Implements.
Send for Illustrated Circular to
PEEKSKILL PLOW WORKS,
Peekskill, N. Y.

$100 FOR A BRICK MACHINE SIMple; $160 with Tempering Box and Moulds, warranted to make 15,000 brick per day, of a superior quality. Address FREY & SHECKLER, Bucyrus, O.

GRINDING MILLS.—Cheapest and best in the world. Burr Stones from 8 inches to 4 feet.
EDWARD HARRISON, New Haven, Conn.

THE BEST MACHINERY.

COOPER'S OLD AND EXTENSIVE FACTORY HAS FOR SALE

130 Improved Portable Engines, 8 to 30 Horse-Power.

85 Improved Stationary Engines, 20 to 135 Horse-Power.

800 Circular Saw Mills, of all Sizes.

123 Patent French Burr Flour and Feed Mills, with Bolts, and complete Machinery for same.

1,000 Cooper's Patent Sugar Pans, 8 to 15 feet long. Price $22 to $75.

1,000 Cooper's Patent Union Sugar Mills, 8 Sizes. Price, Heavy One-Horse Mill, $75.

All are being erected in the most approved and substantial manner, with recent valuable improvements.

This Firm was the first to commence the practice of furnishing complete fixtures for *Saw* and *Grist Mills*, and millwrights to erect and set them in operation; hence their unprecedented success and reputation for *building the best Mills in the world*. Send for Circulars, addressing

C. & J. COOPER, Mt. Vernon, Ohio.

Well Known Implements.

Wheeler's Patent Horse-Powers and Threshing Machines; Fan Mills; Gale's Copper-strip Feed Cutter; Hutchinson's Family Wine and Cider Mill; Hickok's Keystone Cider Mills; Cider Mill Screws, (wrought and cast iron). See July No. Agriculturist. Also,

Approved Fertilizers.

Fish Guano, recommended by *American Agriculturist*, May No., page 163 as "cheapest fertilizer of the day," manufactured by Quinnipiac Co. Also, Peruvian Guano; Bone; Coe's Superphosphate, etc. All for sale by

JOHN W. DOUGLASS, 181 Water-st., New York.

For Rock Digging and Wall Laying Machines,

Address G. L. SHELDON, Hartsville, Mass.

INVENTIONS.—One which is justly deserving the attention of the people is the BREAD MIXING AND KNEADING MACHINE. Circulars describing and setting forth the merits of this household necessity can be obtained by addressing WM. FORDUSH, Agt., 60 Court-st., Boston, Mass.

GREEN-HOUSE AND HOT-BED SASH.—The undersigned would respectfully call your attention to their extensive facilities for manufacturing Sashes for Florists and Gardeners, by which means we are enabled to furnish our patrons at a much lower rate of prices than any other establishment in the city. Particular attention paid to all orders, and furnished at the shortest notice. N. B.—Hotbed Sashes constantly on hand. WM. H. COLES & CO., Office: 70 Nassau st., New York.

OFFICE OF "Passaic Carbon Works,"
159 FRONT STREET, (CORNER MAIDEN LANE).

LISTER BROTHERS,

MANUFACTURERS OF

PURE BONE DUST,

Fresh Bone Superphosphate of Lime, Animal Charcoal, Ivory Black, &c.

Orders for the above articles manufactured at our Works on the *Passaic River, N. J.*, should be addressed to

LISTER BROTHERS, 159 Front-st., New York.

TO FARMERS.

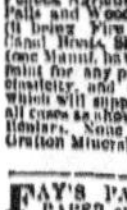

THE LODI MANUFACTURING CO. offer for sale by far the *finest* and *purest* Bone-Dust in the Market, at the same rate as a coarser article. Also a (*warranted pure, or no sale*) Flour of Bone. Samples of each sent on receipt of 3-cent postage stamp, with address.

DOUBLE REFINED POUDRETTE.

This is one of the most forcing as well as quick acting manures in market; is composed of the night-soil of New-York City, from which all the impurities have been extracted. It is then deodorized, dried, and pulverized to flour. From 400 to 500 lbs. per acre on wheat will bring a *good crop* on poor soil. Price only $25 per ton.

Apply to THE LODI MANUFACTURING CO.,
66 Cortlandt-st., New-York.

PAINTS for FARMERS and others.—The Grafton Mineral Paint Co. are now manufacturing the Best, Cheapest and most Durable Paint in use; two coats well put on, mixed with pure Linseed Oil, will last 10 or 15 years; it is of a light brown or beautiful chocolate color, and can be changed to green, lead, stone, olive, drab or cream, to suit the taste of the consumer. It is valuable for Houses, Barns, Fences, Agricultural Implements, Carriage and Car-makers, Pails and Wooden-ware, Canvas, Metal and Shingle Roofs, (it being Fire and Water proof), Bridges, Burial Cases, Canal Boats, Ships and Ships' Bottoms, Floor Oil Cloths, (one Manuf. having used 5000 bbls. the past year), and as a paint for any purpose, is unsurpassed for body, durability, elasticity, and adhesiveness. Price $6 per bbl. of 300 lbs., which will supply a farmer for years to come. Warranted in all cases as above. Send for a circular, which gives full particulars. None genuine unless branded in a trade mark, Grafton Mineral Paint. Address DANIEL BIDWELL, Proprietor, 254 Pearl-st., New York.

FAY'S PATENT WATER-PROOF ROOFING PAPER, etc. For Circular and Price List, and terms of State-Rights, address C. J. FAY, Second and Vine-sts., Camden, N. J.

The Highest Flavored, Most Productive, and Best Berry for Amateur Culture.

Combining large size, handsome appearance, and very high flavor, with great vigor, and productiveness almost equalling "Wilson's Albany."

"One of the most distinct fruits we know, and one of the best in many respects."—THOS. MEEHAN, Editor of "Gardeners' Monthly."

"Promises to be an acquisition."—A. S. FULLER, Author of "Small Fruit Culturist."

Price, (by mail, postage free), $3 per doz.; $20 per 100.

ALSO

The New Perpetual Strawberry.
"Perpetual Pine,"

recently raised and introduced by Mr. F. Gloede, Les Sablons, France, and now first offered in the United States. Mr. Gloede describes it as a "real, perpetual, large-fruited strawberry," and adds, that "during 3 years culture, it not only bore an abundant crop in the spring, but continued flowering and fruiting until late in the Autumn." The plant is very hardy, and the fruit bright vermilion, solid, juicy, sweet, and high-flavored.

We offer a very limited supply of plants of this novel and valuable variety.

Price, (by mail, postage free), 50 cents per plant; $5 per dozen. Descriptive Circulars mailed to any address.

EDW'D J. EVANS & CO.,
Central Nurseries, York, Pa.

Romeyn's Strawberry Seedling.

A DESIDERATUM SUPPLIED.

The attention of Strawberry producers is called to ROMEYN'S NEW SEEDLING—the best plant extant, for general cultivation.

This Seedling is a most prolific, as well as a late bearer—COMING INTO FRUITAGE A FORTNIGHT AFTER THE WILSON—thus giving the producer control of the market after the glut of the Wilson is past.

The flavor is equal to any grown—THE BERRY IS A FINE COLOR, AND VERY SOLID, and the size is large and uniform. The plant is unequaled for vigor and hardiness.

It received a SPECIAL PREMIUM for flavor, at the New York Institute, in 1865. The plant in fruit was exhibited at the late Queen's County Horticultural Fair, and at the Newburgh Bay Exhibition, receiving SPECIAL PREMIUMS at both places.

A limited number of plants, (deliverable on and after August 20th), are offered for sale, at the following rates:

1000	$75.00
100	10.00
50	6.00
20	3.00
5	1.00

Orders addressed to either of the subscribers will receive prompt attention:

WILLIAM H. ROMEYN,
JOSEPH FOSTER, Agent,
Kingston, Ulster Co., N. Y.
V. H. HALLOCK,
NICHOLAS HALLOCK, } Agents.
Queens, Long Island.
W. S. CARPENTER, Agent, 156 Reade-st., New York.

STRAWBERRY PLANTS

Sent out in August and September, at prices annexed, and lower, if so offered in this paper, *charges prepaid by me.* Jenny Lind, Downer, French, Wilson, Early Washington, and Russell, 20 cts. per doz.; 75 cts. per 100; Fillmore, Shaker, Buffalo, Green Prolific, and Agriculturist, 20 cts. per doz.; $1.00 per 100; Metcalf, Jucunda, Golden Queen, and Ida, 30 cts. per doz.; $2 per 100. *Enormous* quantities of all kinds of *Small Fruits at extremely low rates.* Those wanting largely to plant or sell, address

A. M. PURDY, South Bend, Indiana.

METCALF'S EARLY. 200,000 plants, of this valuable early strawberry. A large stock of grape vines, leading varieties. Blackberries, old and new. Also, Peach trees, including Van Buren's Golden Dwarf. Plants packed and delivered in Chicago, free. THOS. ARCHER, Lake Shore Nursery, St. Joseph, Michigan.

The Great European Strawberry.
"DR. NICAISE."

Said to be the largest berry known. From plants set in September last, fruit was picked and exhibited at the **Fruit Growers' Society**, held in Rochester, on the 27th of last June, which weighed 1¼ ozs., and measured 6½ inches around.

Plants very hardy, vigorous grower, and productive. From five plants imported in the Spring of 1866, we produced 600 very strong plants. This variety we have imported at a great expense, and will have a fine stock to offer our customers in August and September.

The following are extracts from European Catalogues:

"It is of enormous size, the berries weighing over 1¼ ozs., (9 to the pound), and early, of a bright red color, very glossy, the flesh white, and of fine quality."

This sort is one of the finest cultivated in Europe, and has the best characteristics of any we have ever introduced. Orders must be sent in early, as they will only be filled in rotation.

We will furnish plants, postage paid, at the following rates: $1 per plant; $10 per doz.; $75 per 100. A liberal discount to the trade. Address

FROST & CO.,
Genesee Valley Nurseries,
Rochester, N. Y.

J. KEECH'S

New Seedling Strawberries, Gen'l's. Grant, Sherman, Meade, and Sheridan. The people's choice of all berries. Plants ready by August 20th. $1 per doz.; $3 for 50; $5 per 100; $25 per 1000, cash. J. KEECH, Waterloo, N. Y.

SMALL FRUITS.—40 varieties of Strawberries, and 6 varieties of Raspberries in fruit this year—description and comparative merits in my new Price List now ready. Strawberry plants also ready and **warranted to arrive in good condition or the order duplicated.** Address with three cent stamp for Price List, JOHNSON'S NURSERY, South Bend, Indiana.

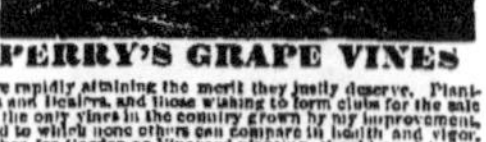

PERRY'S GRAPE VINES

Are rapidly attaining the merit they justly deserve. Planters and Dealers, and those wishing to form clubs for the sale of the only vines in the country grown by my improvement, and to which none others can compare in health and vigor, either for Garden or Vineyard planting, should send immediately for my Price List or my liberal terms to Clubs. Planters will please state about the number of each variety they wish, and whether for spring or fall planting. My Illustrated and Descriptive Catalogue contains as correct a description of the different varieties of grapes I grow, as ten years' experience in propagating and fruiting vines will admit. Price 10 cents, less than cost. Address

F. L. PERRY, Canandaigua, N. Y.

200,000 GRAPE VINES,

One and two years old.

An extra fine stock of
DELAWARE,
CONCORD,
IVES' SEEDLING,
CREVELING, HARTFORD, DIANA, IONA,
ISRAELLA, CLINTON, CATAWBA,
and many other good varieties.

At low rates by the dozen, 100, or 1,000.

Send for Price List.

Also a good stock of Fruit and Ornamental Trees, Evergreens, Small Fruit, Shrubs, Roses, &c., &c.

Osage Orange Plants, 2 years, at $5 per 1,000.

LENK & CO., Humboldt Nurseries,
Toledo, Ohio.

GEORGE PERRY & SON,

Grape Layers and Grape Vines for Fall of 1867.

We would most respectfully call the attention of Amateurs, Planters and Dealers in Grape Vines, to our very large stock of Concord Grape Layers. We shall sell cheap. We will take orders for other leading kinds of Grape Vines, Clark's and Philadelphia Raspberry, Kittatinny Blackberry, Perry's Seedling Strawberry, &c. 200,000 *Grape Buds*, (mostly Concord), for propagating. Our *Circular* sent to *all applicants* FREE. Apply without delay to GEORGE PERRY & SON, Nurserymen, Georgetown, Conn.

IVES' SEEDLING GRAPE VINES.—Ives' Seedling, Iona, Delaware and Concord, with many other kinds; [illegible] of which are new varieties from Longworth's School of Vines, selected by Dr. Jno. A. Warder, for sale, with Nursery Stock generally. Send for Circular and Price List, with history of the Ives Seedling grape, FREE.

JAMES F. MARTIN, Mt. Washington, Hamilton Co., Ohio.

EXCELSIOR NURSERIES.

MUNSON & KEIL, Zanesville, Ohio. *Now is the time* to send for a Price List. Ives' Seedling, Hartford Prolific, Concord, Delaware, Catawba, and other varieties of grapes, also, all kinds of small fruit plants, at Wholesale and Retail prices, to suit the Million. Our stock promises to be large and splendid. Price List sent free. Address at once,

MUNSON & KEIL, Zanesville, Ohio.

150,000 APPLE TREES.—Two to four years from the bud, of superior growth. 10,000 Pear Trees, one year from the bud, (very fine), popular varieties. Largely of Hale's Early.
10,000 Van Buren's Golden Dwarf Peach Trees.
50,000 Grape Vines, consisting largely of Concords, Hartford Prolifics, Ionas and Israellas.
Apple Seedlings by the acre, and much other Nursery Stock. Address

STEPHEN HOYT & SONS,
New Haven, Conn.

Seeds for Autumn Sowing.

Aquilegia 8 varieties,	per p'kt.	25c.
" Glandulosa	"	75c.
Antirrhinum, Tom Thumb	"	25c.
Clump Violet, the sweetest of all, perfectly hardy,	"	25c.
Carnation Pink, extra fine	"	50c.
" Perpetual or Tree	"	50c.
Calceolaria, extra select, from prize flowers	"	50c.
" Rugosa, shrubby varieties	"	50c.
Cineraria, extra choice, from newest varieties	"	50c.
Gladiolus, from finest erect and latest named varieties	"	25c.
Hollyhock, collection of 8 new and select varieties	"	[illegible]
" finest mixed, double	"	25c.
Mimulus, finest mixed	"	25c.
Pansy, English, saved from prize flowers	"	50c.
Primula, all the best varieties mixed	"	25c.
Polyanthus, finest mixed varieties	"	25c.
Tropæolum, finest varieties for Green house	"	25c.
Stock, [illegible] mixed	"	[illegible]
" New White Wallflower, leav'd, a superb var.	"	25c.
" Crimson "	"	[illegible]
Sweet William, Hunt's Perfection	"	25c.
" " Auricula eyed	"	25c.
Wallflower, double German, extra	"	10c.

Washburn's Amateur Cultivators' Guide, beautifully illustrated, containing a list of over 2,500 varieties of Flower and Vegetable Seeds, mailed free on receipt of 25 cents.

WASHBURN & CO.,
Seed Merchants, Horticultural Hall,
Boston, Mass.

Winter Seed Wheat for 1867,

FOR SALE BY

GEORGE A. DEITZ,

IMPORTER AND GROWER OF

SEED WHEAT & GRASS SEEDS,
CHAMBERSBURGH, PA.

Premium Red Mediterranean,	$2.[illegible] ₩ peck.		$[illegible] ₩ bush.	
Italian White	"	2.[illegible]	"	8.00
Hungarian Red	"	2.00	"	8.00
French Red	"	2.00	"	8.00
Hallet's Rough Red	"	2.75	"	8.00
German Red	"	2.25	"	8.00
Hallet's Eng. White,	"	2.25	"	8.00
Diehl's White,	"	1.50	"	6.00
Canada White,	"	1.50	"	5.50
Rappahannock White,	"	1.50	"	5.00
Soulier White,	"	1.[illegible]	"	5.50
Blue Stem White,	"	2.00	"	7.00
Premium Red Mediterranean,	"	1.50	"	5.00
Red Chaff	"	1.30	"	5.00
White Chaff	"	1.31	"	5.10
Lancaster Red Chaff	"	1.30	"	5.00

☞ Four pounds of either of the above varieties will be sent by mail (free of Postage) for one dollar. G. A. D.

SEED WHEAT.

The Subscriber offers for sale Red Mediterranean Seed Wheat, raised for Long Island, from imported seed. Price, $1.50 per peck. This wheat is much sought after, from the [illegible] Mediterranean Seed Wheat imported [illegible] years. Also, Diehl and Boughton White Wheat, price, $4 per bush. C. W. PAYNE, Sag Harbor, L. I.

BARTLETT'S REVERSIBLE SEWING MACHINE has the NEW AND LATEST PATENT Improvements. They are the best that run backward or forward [illegible], and sew equally well. They are the kind that have the [illegible] Presser foot, which turns entirely away from the needle, so convenient in setting a needle, [illegible] in taking out "work," &c. They are made for use. [illegible] $25, with table and and treadle, $30 to $[illegible]. J. W. BARTLETT, Patentee, Depot No. 569 Broadway, New York.

☞ See illustration of this Machine in Harper's Weekly, of July 6, or send for Descriptive Circular.

Stereopticons and Magic Lanterns,

With the Improved [illegible] Light, [illegible] brilliantly two [illegible] lantern [illegible] the views to [illegible] size, an [illegible] for an whole evening's exhibition. [illegible] pays well.

Illustrated priced catalogue of the apparatus, with list of over two thousand artistically colored photographic views on glass, of the War, Scripture History, Choice Statuary, etc., etc., forwarded on application. T. H. McALLISTER, Optician, late firm of McAllister & Bro., Phila., 49 Nassau-street, New York.

H. W. JOHNS'

IMPROVED ROOFING

Has been in use nearly ten years, and forms a handsome and reliable roof. Can be applied by any one. **Elastic Mineral Cement,** for Repairing Leaky Shingle and other Roofs. **Preservative Paints, Roofing, Cement,** &c. Exclusive right to sell and apply will be given. Send for descriptive circular, prices, &c., to

H. W. JOHNS, 78 William St., N. Y.

PINE APPLE, BANANA AND ORANGE LAND FOR SALE.—100 acres together or divided, of the finest land on Indian River, East Florida. Rich soil, beautiful situation, healthy and delightful climate, with abundance of game, fish, oysters, turtle, and in fact every requisite for profit or enjoyment. Access by rail, steam, or land travel. Address A. VARNO, Agriculturist Office, 41 Park Row, New York.

THE HOG BREEDERS' MANUAL.

A Treatise on Breeding, Feeding, and General Management of Hogs. Particulars of all Diseases, Remedies, &c. Sent free of postage for 25 cents. Every farmer should have a copy. Address N. P. BOYER & CO., Gum Tree, Chester Co., Pa.

BRIGHAM'S PATENT

Garment Conformator,

For fitting Dresses and other garments without the use of measures. Made of thin sheet rubber, very elastic, it adjusts itself perfectly to the form; on the line of the seams and around the neck, arms, and waist, are rows of small, sharp points or indicators. By laying thin, strong, paper over each portion of the Conformator, holding it smooth, and pressing it upon the indicators, an exact impression of the form is obtained, and by cutting out on the lines indicated, the pattern is ready for use, and a *perfect fit must result,* without any further fitting. By its use a perfect fitting garment is obtained with ease and certainty. It is very simple in its operation, can be used by any one with perfect success, and being made of very elastic material, can be used on persons of almost any size.

Price, $10.00. Sent *prepaid* by Express on receipt of price, by GOODYEAR'S I. R. GLOVE M'F'G CO., 205 Broadway, New York.

IMPORTANT TO OWNERS OF HORSES.

Advice and Prescriptions for Sick or Injured Horses given Free.

The Editor of WILKES' SPIRIT OF THE TIMES desires to inform the owners of horses throughout the United States, that he has regularly engaged upon his paper, one of the ablest and most experienced professional veterinarians in the United States, whose special duty it shall be to answer, gratis, all questions relative to sick or injured horses which may be addressed to the SPIRIT, *whether by subscribers or not.* These answers will in all cases contain a prescription for the injury described, and will be printed, in connection with the question asked, in the following number of the SPIRIT. No answers, however, will be given by mail, it being a part of the object of the editor to submit the ability of the professor who has assumed this department of the SPIRIT, to the keenest criticism of the general public. By adding this useful department to the SPIRIT, the editor contributes to those of his readers and subscribers who own horses, a horse-doctor free, and not only to his subscribers, but *to every horse-owner in the United States who may choose to direct an inquiry to the SPIRIT by mail.* The subscription price of the SPIRIT is $5 a year; but single copies may be bought from news agents from week to week by those who desire to use it temporarily only, for veterinarian questions, at fifteen cents per copy. The SPIRIT OF THE TIMES is a high-toned gentleman's paper which (with the old SPIRIT, whose business and title it inherits) is of forty years' standing, and is devoted to Hunting, Fishing, Racing, Field Sports, Literature, and the Stage. It also contains a series of articles by HIRAM WOODRUFF, on the Trotting Horse of America, and How to Train and Drive him.

GEORGE WILKES,
Editor and Proprietor,
201 William-st., New York.

☞ *Dealers will continue to procure their supplies as heretofore.*

THOMAS FITCH,
of New London, Conn.,

Breeder of *Alderney* and *Ayrshire* Stock of all descriptions, has constantly on hand and for sale the best Animals of each of the above breeds, at reasonable prices. Warranted as represented.

CHESTER WHITE PIGS

For Sale. Send for Circular. Address
H. TEMPLE & CO., Marshallton, Chester Co., Pa.

BRAHMA POOTRAS, bred from stock weighing 21 lbs. to 28 lbs. per pair, at maturity. Warranted pure. Price $8 per pair; $12 per trio. Eggs, $2 per dozen. Address N. P. BOYER & CO., Gum Tree, Chester Co., Pa.

AMERICAN STOCK JOURNAL, a first class monthly, containing 30 large double column pages, only 50 cents for 6 months. Try it! Will save every farmer many dollars, as we offer a Horse and Cattle Doctor free. Address N. P. BOYER & CO., Gum Tree, Chester Co., Pa.

FOR SALE.—*Pure* Spanish fowls, (this year's), at $3.00 per pair, $5.00 per trio, by Express to any address in the Union. *Warranted* to give satisfaction or no pay. Address JOHN BENNETT, Sunman, Ripley Co., Ind.

WHITE LEGHORN FOWLS with Yellow Legs. A few pair of the real breed for sale by JOHN SALISBURY, Jr., Box 95, Nyack, N. Y.

NEW NATIONAL RELIGIOUS PAPER.

A national religious newspaper, to be called "THE ADVANCE," will be published weekly, from the first of September, onward, in the city of Chicago. It will represent Congregational principles and polity, but will be conducted in a spirit of courtesy and fraternity towards all Christians. The form will be what is popularly termed a double sheet of eight pages, of the size and style of the *N. Y. Evangelist.* The pecuniary basis is an ample capital furnished by leading business men and others, to be expended in the establishment and improvement of the paper, which is intended to be second to none in the country, in its literary and religious character. The purpose of its projectors is indicated in the name: their aim being to ADVANCE the cause of evangelical religion, in its relations not only to doctrine, worship and ecclesiastical polity, but also to philosophy, science, literature, politics, business, amusements, art, morals, philanthropy and whatever else conduces to the glory of God and the good of man by its bearing upon Christian civilization. No expense has been spared in providing for its editorial management in all departments, while arrangements are in progress to secure the ablest contributors and correspondents at home and abroad. The city of Chicago has been selected as the place of publication, because of its metropolitan position in the section of the country especially demanding such a paper, and the fact that it is nearly the center of national population, and in a very few years will be the ecclesiastical center of the Congregational churches. Issued at the interior commercial metropolis, THE ADVANCE will contain the latest market reports, and able discussions of financial subjects, such as will make it a necessity to business men in all parts of the country. The editor-in-chief will be Rev. Wm. W. Patton, D. D., who resigns the pastorate of the leading church of the denomination at the West for this purpose, and who has had many years experience in editorial labor. The subscription price will be $2.50 in advance. Advertising rates made known on application. Address "THE ADVANCE COMPANY," P. O. Drawer 6371, Chicago, Illinois.

FRANKLIN TRACT.—20,000 ACRES on Railroad, Gloucester Co., New Jersey, 25 miles south of Philadelphia, good soil, mild, healthful climate. Low prices, in lots to suit purchasers. Pamphlets with map and full information sent free. Address MORRIS & CO., Newfield, Gloucester Co., N. J. Improved Farms for sale.

FARM WANTED in EXCHANGE for a new Valuable PATENT. To a man wanting a sure first-rate city business this is a splendid chance. No competition. Address with particulars, D. W., Agriculturist Office.

IT DON'T SCRATCH YOU,

Or Tear Your Clothes.

Davison's Thornless Black Cap Raspberry is the best, as it is hardy, productive, early, and sweet, and it is a pleasure to cultivate it. Circulars giving origin, description, prices, testimonials, &c., ready in September.

JOSEPH SINTON, Angola, Erie Co., N. Y.

STRAWBERRY PLANTS.

Jucunda, Rippowam, Durand, Metcalf's Early, Lennig's White, Agriculturist, Barnes, Wilson, and all other valuable varieties. For Catalogue and Price List, address REISIG & HEXAMER, New Castle, Westchester Co., N. Y.

Fire Engine for Every Household.—Window Washer, superior Hot-house Syringe, and Garden Engine in one, for $5. "In our opinion excels anything of the kind heretofore invented."—[*Ed. N. Eng. Farmer.*] *Free* to one agent in each town for $30. NEW ENGLAND PORTABLE PUMP CO., No. 31 Hanover-st., Boston, Mass.

WANTED 1,000 LADIES AND GENTLEMEN to sell Trees, Shrubs, Vines and Flowers. Send for Price List, with full particulars.

L. L. WHITLOCK,
"ALL NURSERIES IN ONE,"
37 Park Row, New York.

THE STOCK OF ALL NURSERYMEN sending me their list of prices by August 5th, will be advertised free, in the Horticultural Advertiser, which will be issued from this office about August 20th.

L. L. WHITLOCK,
"ALL NURSERIES IN ONE,"
37 Park Row, New York.

SEND STAMP FOR THE HORTICULTURAL ADVERTISER, which will contain a list of the things offered by "ALL NURSERIES IN ONE." Also, practical suggestions for the cultivation and management of Trees, Vines, Flowers, &c.

L. L. WHITLOCK, 37 Park Row, New York.

GET UP CLUBS FOR TREES, VINES, Shrubs, Roses, Flowers, &c. Send stamp for Terms and Price List.

L. L. WHITLOCK,
"ALL NURSERIES IN ONE,"
37 Park Row, New York.

(Business Notices $2.50 per Agate Line of Space.)

THE

GREAT AMERICAN TEA COMPANY

HAVE JUST RECEIVED

TWO FULL CARGOES

OF THE

FINEST CROP OF TEAS.

22,000 HALF CHESTS by ship *Golden State.*
12,000 HALF CHESTS by ship *George Shotton.*

In addition to these large cargoes of Black and Japan Teas, the Company are constantly receiving large invoices of the finest quality of Green Teas from the Moyune districts of China, which are unrivaled for fineness and delicacy of flavor, which they are selling at the following prices:

OOLONG (Black), 50c., 60c., 70c., 80c., 90c., best $1 ℔ lb.
MIXED, (Green and Black), 50c., 60c., 70c., 80c., 90c., best $1 per pound.
ENGLISH BREAKFAST (Black), 50c., 60c., 70c., 80c., 90c., $1, $1.10, best $1.20 per pound.
IMPERIAL (Green), 50c., 60c., 70c., 80c., 90c., $1, $1.10, best $1.25 per pound.
YOUNG HYSON (Green), 50c., 60c., 70c., 80c., 90c., $1, $1.10, best $1.25 per pound.
UNCOLORED JAPAN, 90c., $1, $1.10, best $1.25 per pound.
GUNPOWDER, (Green), $1.25, best $1.50 per pound.

COFFEES ROASTED AND GROUND DAILY.

GROUND COFFEE, 20c., 25c., 30c., 35c., best 40c. per pound. Hotels, Saloons, Boarding-house keepers, and Families, who use large quantities of Coffee, can economize in that article by using our FRENCH BREAKFAST AND DINNER COFFEE, which we sell at the low price of 30c. per pound, and warrant to give perfect satisfaction.

Consumers can save from 50 cents to $1 per pound (beside the Express charges,) by purchasing their Teas of the

GREAT AMERICAN TEA COMPANY,

Nos. 31 and 33 VESEY STREET.
Post Office Box, 5643, New York City.

We warrant all the goods we sell to give entire satisfaction. If they are not satisfactory, they can be returned at our expense within 30 days, and have the money refunded.

By our system of supplying Clubs throughout the country, consumers in all parts of the United States can receive their Teas at the same price (with the small additional expense of transportation), as though they bought them at our warehouses in this city.

Some parties inquire of us how they shall proceed to get up a club. The answer is simply this: Let each person wishing to join in a club, say how much tea or coffee he wants, and select the kind and price from our Price List, as published in the paper or in our circulars. Write the names, kinds, and amounts plainly on a list, and when the club is complete, send it to us by mail, and we will put each party's goods in separate packages, and mark the name upon them, with the cost, so there need be no confusion in their distribution—each party getting exactly what he orders, and no more. The cost of transportation, the members of the club can divide equitably among themselves.

The funds to pay for the goods ordered can be sent by drafts on New York, by Post-Office money orders, or by Express, as may suit the convenience of the club. Or, if the amount ordered exceeds $30, we will, if desired, send the goods by Express, to "collect on delivery."

Hereafter we will send a complimentary package to the party getting up the Club. Our profits are small, but we will be as liberal as we can afford. We send no complimentary package for a Club less than $30.

N. B.—All villages and towns where a large number reside, by Clubbing together, can reduce the cost of their Teas and Coffees about one-third (beside the Express charges,) by sending directly to "The Great American Tea Company."

BEWARE of all concerns that advertise themselves as branches of our Establishment, or copy our name either wholly or in part, as they are *bogus* or *imitations*. We have no branches, and do not, in any case, authorize the use of our name.

Post-Office orders and Drafts, make payable to the order of "Great American Tea Company." Direct letters and orders to the

GREAT AMERICAN TEA COMP'Y,

Nos. 31 and 33 VESEY-ST.,
Post-Office Box, 5,643, New York City.

SCALES.

THE ACKNOWLEDGED STANDARD.
Take the FIRST PREMIUMS

TWO MEDALS:

at the great PARIS EXPOSITION, and are mentioned in the award as
THE STANDARD SCALES.

FAIRBANKS & CO.,
No. 252 Broadway, New York.

MAGNIFICENT TRIUMPH!

MASON & HAMLIN

Have the honor to announce that they have been awarded a

FIRST PRIZE MEDAL!

AT THE

GREAT PARIS EXPOSITION, 1867,

FOR THE SUPERIORITY OF THEIR

CABINET ORGANS.

It is not easy to over-estimate the importance of this recognition of superiority, because this is the greatest Industrial Fair the world has witnessed, at which the best makers of all countries have competed for the honors, and because Mason & Hamlin were

Represented only by their ordinary Styles

of instruments, such as are currently sold from their warerooms. The superiority of the M. & H. Organs in substantial excellence, was universally recognized by the eminent jury, and by the musical profession of the world, as represented at Paris.

THIS IS THE FIFTY-SEVENTH MEDAL,

or other highest premium, awarded M. & H. within twelve years, completing the most emphatic and universal official record of demonstrated superiority ever realized by any maker of musical instruments in the world.

M. & H. now manufacture about twenty five styles of Organs, differing in musical capacity, from an instrument having one set of reeds of four octaves' compass, to one of twenty-two stops and nine octaves of tone. Most of these are furnished in cases of different degrees of excellence, from those which are quite plain, though neat and substantial, to others of most elaborate design and finish, comparing favorably with any furniture manufactured. They are thus adapted to a very wide range of uses, public and private, and are sold at prices from $75 to upwards of $1,000, each. They are adapted to secular as well as sacred music, occupy little space, can be easily transported all ready for use, are not liable to get out of order, and are most fully warranted in every respect.

The most important improvements used by M. & H. are patented, and cannot be employed by other makers. Circulars, with full particulars, free to any address.

MASON & HAMLIN.

WAREROOMS, { 154 TREMONT-ST., BOSTON. / 596 BROADWAY, NEW YORK.

Granville Female College.

Honorable history for 33 years. 31th year begins Sept. 12th. The best Educational facilities; location very healthy. Terms low. Send for Catalogue. W. P. KERR, Granville, Licking Co., Ohio.

Silver Tips for Children's Shoes.

They protect the toe from wear, and are highly ornamental. Applied to the most genteel shoes made. Buy no others.

FERD. F. MAYER, Chemist,

Has removed his Office to 25 Cedar-st., New York.

GRAPE VINES AT IONA.

My stock of plants the present season is large, and promises to be of surpassing quality.

All persons interested in the purchase of vines, are invited to call and inspect during the season of growth.

A Descriptive List, stating quality and price of plants will be published in August.

ALSO,

Plows for Deep Working and Thorough Trenching.

I have a set of plows designed for performing every grade of deep working, from a few inches deeper than that generally attainable by ordinary tillage plows to thorough trenching with reversal of the soil to the depth of two feet or more.

The complete set will consist of six or more, four of which are now ready for inspection or trial. For information concerning vines or plows referred to, address

C. W. GRANT,
IONA, near Peekskill,
Westchester Co., N. Y.

A NEW GRAPE.

SALEM.

The subscriber now offers for sale for the first time the above grape, No. 53 of his hybrids, named SALEM, from the place of its origin.

This grape has been withheld from sale or exhibition for various reasons until a stock of plants could be obtained. It is a variety considered not only superior to any of the former well known numbers, but also to any hardy grape at present before the public, combining, as nearly as possible, every quality desired in an outdoor grape; being one of the hardiest, healthiest and most vigorous of vines, and producing enormous crops of beautiful and high-flavored fruit.

This grape is a hybrid between the native and Black Hamburg; bunch large and compact, berry large as Hamburg, of a light chestnut or Catawba color, thin skinned, perfectly free from hard pulp, very sweet and sprightly, with a most exquisite aromatic flavor, not equaled by any other out-door grape for wine or table; as early as Delaware or Hartford, having never failed to ripen in the most unfavorable season for the past six years.

Taking all its qualities into consideration, earliness, hardiness, and great vigor of vine, size and quality of fruit, it is pronounced by a few of the best judges who have tried it, to have no equal among all the numerous varieties now before the public; and I can, with confidence, recommend it as the best of all my collection, and now offer it for sale.

E. S. Rogers, Salem, Mass.

NOTICE.—The subscriber would here state that he has disposed of his entire stock of vines and wood of the Salem Grape to J. L. WARING, of "Amenia Vineyard," Amenia, Dutchess Co., N. Y., to whom all orders for the same must hereafter be addressed. E. S. Rogers.
Salem, Mass., March 2d, 1867.

The undersigned now offers for sale, this Autumn, the above valuable Vine, in quantity, one and two year old plants, suitable for vineyard purposes. The demand for it will be large, and those wishing to secure them would do well to send in their orders early. Price List and engraving will be sent in August, on application to

J. L. WARING, Sole Proprietor "Salem" Vine,
Amenia, Dutchess Co., N. Y.

PERRY'S GRAPE VINES

are grown on high, dry ground, where **mildew is unknown**, hence the perfectly ripened canes and roots which they possess, that gave so much satisfaction to those who patronized me last season. They promise this year to be much larger than last, and worthy of particular attention. My extra selection of two year old Vines for the Garden is very desirable. My Vines for Dealers and Vineyard planting, are in quality, all that one can wish for. Prices not Advertised, but sent upon application, and found to be as low as the lowest. Address

F. L. PERRY, Canandaigua, N. Y.

NEW WATER PIPE.

WHY RUN ANY RISK!

That leaden pipes contaminate spring water, and injure the health, is beyond question. *A certain protection* is the recently invented ENCASED BLOCK TIN PIPE. Water flowing through this pipe *cannot be impregnated with poisonous solutions of lead*, as it comes in contact with pure block tin only. The Tin-lined Pipe will bear nearly double the pressure of Lead Pipe, and is sold at the same price. Pamphlets of reports, and opinions, sent *free* on application. THE COLWELLS, SHAW & WILLARD M'F'G. CO., Foot of West 27th-st., New York.

Great Economy in Painting.

DOTY'S PATENT COMPOUND PAINT OIL, four years tested. Fully as durable, covers as well, easier to spread, quicker to dry, and in no respect inferior to pure Linseed Oil, yet much cheaper! Warranted to render White Lead WHITER, either inside or outside, and FULLY AS DURABLE as Linseed Oil, and as good for all colored paints. Four years' use has fully established this.

Price, by the Barrel (40 gallons)..............$36 00
5 Gallons for trial, put up in good oak keg...... 6 10
10 " " " " 11 00

Shipped as common Railroad Freight, or by Express. Testimonials as to Durability, in Circulars. Agents wanted everywhere. Exclusive sale given.
DOTY'S PAINT OIL CO., 21 Cortlandt-st., New York.

EVERYBODY should send for THE AMERICAN STOCK JOURNAL. Only 50 cents for 6 months. Address N. P. BOYER & CO., Gum Tree, Chester Co., Pa.

AMERICAN AGRICULTURIST

FOR THE

Farm, Garden, and Household.

"AGRICULTURE IS THE MOST HEALTHFUL, MOST USEFUL, AND MOST NOBLE EMPLOYMENT OF MAN."—WASHINGTON.

ORANGE JUDD & CO., PUBLISHERS AND PROPRIETORS. Office, 41 Park Row, [illegible]

ESTABLISHED IN 1842. Published also in German at $1.50 a Year.

$1.50 PER ANNUM, IN ADVANCE. SINGLE NUMBER, 15 CENTS. 4 Copies for $5; 10 for $12; 20 or more, $1 each.

[illegible] Court of the United States for the Southern District of New-York.

VOLUME XXVI [illegible] — NEW-YORK, SEPTEMBER, 1867. — NEW SERIES—No. 248.

[COPYRIGHT SECURED.]

THE AMERICAN BUFFALO.—DRAWN BY W. J. HAYS, N. A., FROM LIFE STUDIES, FOR THE AMERICAN AGRICULTURIST.

[illegible] American [illegible] ... which they knew to be ox-like, but had never seen, gave him the name Buffalo, though in reality he bears even [illegible] resemblance to the [illegible] Buffalo than he [illegible] others. The name thus given has been popularly retained; and we might as well try to change the name of the Indians, (who are, [illegible] quite as little related to the Indians of [illegible] after whom they were named), as to call the Buffalo, "Bison." The Bison, once of Europe, now nearly extinct, very closely resembles the American Buffalo, and if our magnificent ruminant should, of necessity, bear a borrowed [illegible] that he should [illegible] called Bi[son] ... [indis]putably true. But he was not, and we do not use "Bison robes" in our sleighs, nor "Bison horn" knife-handles, and we never will. It is our Buffalo, though the pedants' Bison.

The studies from which the above striking picture was drawn, were taken by the artist upon the Plains. It strikes one as exaggerated, for the simple reason that few of the drawings of the Buffalo which we see, are made by artists who know them on their grazing grounds; they do not dare give that fullness and length to the shaggy hair of the head and jaw, nor the towering flatness to the hump. On page 323, will be found other facts concerning the Buffalo.

Contents for September, 1867.

INDEX TO "BASKET" OR SHORTER ARTICLES.

Back Volumes Supplied.—The back volumes of the *Agriculturist* are very valuable. They contain information upon every topic connected with rural life, out-door and in-door, and the last ten volumes make up a very complete library. Each volume has a full index for ready reference to any desired topic. We have on hand, and print from electrotype plates as wanted, all the numbers and volumes for ten years past, beginning with 1857—that is, Vol. 16 to Vol. 25, inclusive. Any of these volumes sent complete (in numbers) at $1.75 each, post-paid, (or $1.50 if taken at the office). The volumes, neatly bound, are supplied for $2 each, or $2.50 if to be sent by mail. Any single numbers of the past ten years will be supplied, post-paid, for 15 cents each

AMERICAN AGRICULTURIST.

NEW-YORK, SEPTEMBER, 1867.

Every year we are led to regard with thankfulness the beneficent provision which ordered the territory now occupied by this great nation, to be subject to so varied climatic and meteorological influences, yet so closely connected, and the intercommunication between its parts so intimate. This year the seaboard has been wet, and the inland States have been rather dry. If grain has been damaged for flour in one State, the well secured harvests of others easily supply the need. If we, of the East, lose our potato crop, as it seems probable that we shall, we can look to the West for a supply, and to the South for a substitute. The hay of New England may have been gathered in too poor a condition for market, and so while her farmers will lose their wonted profits, the railroads may now, thanks to improvements in hay-presses, bring the hay a thousand miles, and not make the price too high for our city markets. Eastern farmers who have been in the habit of selling hay may now learn an important lesson if they will, namely: that hay kept on the farm and fed out or made manure of, is worth a good deal more to them than if sold at any ordinary prices. The hay being unfit for sale must be used; part of it will be fed, the rest made into manure. Another lesson: —the poor hay, either that which has been wetted in curing, or that which has stood until it is hard, grown too tough, and wiry to be profitably used, must be either chaffed short and steamed, or wet down with a little meal or oil-cake, bran or other similar feed, and left to stand until incipient fermentation commences. The value of the grain thus used need not be much—the labor will not be grudged when the results are seen.

September is a happy month; it brings the golden fruits of the orchard, and the golden corn ripens under the Autumnal suns. There is, too, a harvest of greenbacks—no gold now-a-days—which September usually yields to those who have early crops to sell. During this month the prices of grain in Europe become settled, ordinarily. They may be such as to excite speculation, or the prices here may quietly settle down to what we may consider about remunerative values.

Save time to *attend the Fairs;* and be sure to take or send something to help the show. Have it in the best possible order, and don't expect so confidently to get the prize as to be made uncomfortable if you lose it. It is no shame to be beaten, but it would be shameful for a poor article to take a prize over a better one. Therefore rejoice that something more excellent than your's could be raised and that the raiser brought it. A good part of your reward should be in having contributed to make a fine show. A man seldom gains credit to himself by declaring openly that things he has, at home, are much better than those exhibited. Such statements, if made, should be said privately and generally in self condemnation for not having brought the articles. The unsuccessful competitor seldom gains more than an unenviable notoriety by openly impugning the motives of judges.

Every one is happy to receive prizes, and the hope that he may, is a great inducement to present articles in competition. The honor and credit should count for much, the money for very little, and really the unselfish motive of contributing to make a fine show, should be the chief inducement to exert one-self for the fair. An exhibitor going to the fair with these feelings will not leave his wagon loads of fruit, vegetables, and dairy products outside, while he searches through the exhibition tables to find out if he will be morally certain of the prizes, before he decides to exhibit. There is nothing criminal in this, but it is certainly not honorable and commendable.

Hints About Work.

There is a greater variety of labors to employ farmers in September than perhaps in any other month. We have manuring, plowing, sowing and harvesting, thrashing, feeding, marketing, all upon us at once, yet the labors are seldom pressing and of an anxious kind, except perhaps a little anxiety in regard to early frosts.

Animals, in general, need little care, except good pasturage or feeding. *Fattening bullocks* that are to be finished off for the autumn trade need a gradual increase of meal as the weather grows cooler. *Sheep*, also, that are to be sold, should be separated from others and fed a little grain. Examine any that it may be necessary to have in moist pastures to check the very first appearance of foot rot. Shelter all during storms, and give access to water and salt. *Swine*, to be fattened this fall, will do much better if fed a little ground old corn now while at grass, or being kept on thin swill, as is usual.

Orchard fruit collect frequently, not only for feeding swine and cows, but in order to destroy the insects which sting the fruit at the time of laying their eggs, and to prevent the development of the larvæ which causes it to become gnarly and to drop, prematurely ripe, or even green. Much good cider for vinegar may be made from windfalls.

Root crops.—All kinds of root crops having become well established and full of leaf, keep on growing until freezing weather, and often swell with prodigious rapidity, as the season becomes moister and cooler. Keep the weeds down and the ground open and loose, and pull for cow feed wherever they stand too thick.

Beans.—Pull before the ripened pods dry, and lay them up to ripen in small heaps, or, better, between two stakes driven perpendicularly about 5 or 6 inches apart. The plants being laid alternately heads and roots, and at the same time crosswise.

Grass and Clover Seeding may be done now upon land which is in order to be laid down, to very good advantage, provided we have rains. If the grass and clover can get a start this fall, so as to make an approximation to a sward, they will stand the winter well, and if the land is rich, be fit to mow next year. If not rich, the clover may be fed off in June, but not close, and cut for seed in the fall. Timothy sowed now and getting a good start of all other accidental grass on a good land, often yields a fine crop for seed two years in succession. If you need the grain or straw, sow it, but if you want grass, sow that.

Wheat.—Too much stress can not be given to having wheat land well prepared—drained rich, and mellow, also free from weeds, if possible. Sow during this month; the earlier the better. Drill rather than sow broadcast, and put the seed deep rather than shallow on all light soils.

Rye.—It is generally best to sow rye in the early part of October, as it often gets too much growth before the ground freezes if sown earlier.

Vermin in Granaries.—See article on corn-houses p. 323. Arrange to have security from mice and rats. Rats will generally clear out mice and may themselves be gotten rid of by the phosphorous paste which is a safe poison if the poultry are shut up and kept so for several weeks. The rats vomit up the poison, and the chickens eat it and die. The poison kills a few, but stampedes the vermin. Mice are not so affected; a few die, the rest remain. Use traps and cats; give the cat a sand box and punish her severely if she does not use it. A good mouser, and well trained, is almost invaluable.

Potatoes.—At the East the season has been such as to rot potatoes in some places very much. After the vines die or are thoroughly blighted, the tubers will make but little growth. They are fit for swine, but not for market. Yet many are perfectly good. It is sometimes best to dig and feed to pigs or cattle before they rot. If left in the ground the sound ones will remain good, while most of the diseased ones will become so bad that they may be detected at a glance. This, it is claimed, is a great saving of labor in picking over potatoes that rot in the bin; besides, the sound ones are not contaminated, and so more sound ones will finally be saved.

Draining and Irrigation.—These subjects are *hinted* at every month; their importance demands it. See what has been said in previous numbers and *act* upon the hints.

Manure.—Dig muck and peat, cut swamp grass, collect all weeds not in seed, and through the agency of swine, of the liquid manure of the barn-yard and the stables, of ashes and lime, and of every method of composting, start an active fermentation in the largest possible quantity of vegetable matter.

Ashes.—Send a team through the neighboring villages and wherever wood is burned, and engage the winter's ashes, agreeing to pay in soap, tin ware, wooden ware, money, or in any other way.

Bones.—Collect by paying children to gather them at the rate of 50 cents a barrel—you can afford to pay $1.00 if you use the bones in gardening or in the fruit orchard, or if the land needs phosphates.

Straw.—September is a good month to buy straw; taken direct from the thrashing machine, it often sells cheap. In most wheat regions it is worth the price of three bushels of wheat per ton for manure, and should not be sold for that of four.

Linseed Cake.—Lay in a stock in advance. It is worth all it costs simply as manure, (taking the price of Peruvian guano as a criterion of value,) and if fed, you either gain in some other way, as in milk, or get nearly the full value in the manure, with the flesh and fat of the animals, as clear profit.

Weeds.—Mow or pull while in bloom or before; if possible, use as an ingredient of compost heaps or in the pig pen. If seeds have formed, dry the weeds, burn them, and use the ashes.

Orchard and Nursery.

The question of autumn planting should be decided by the locality. In those places where winter sets in early, spring planting is preferable; but where a long, mild autumn succeeds the planting, the trees become well established, and setting them at this season is advantageous. The ground for the orchard should be prepared as early as may be, by deep plowing and subsoiling. In most cases draining also is advisable. Order trees from the nurseries before the season of taking up begins, so as to obtain them as soon as they are fit for removal.

Autumn Fruit is to be picked as it matures. This and all other fruit should be left upon the tree until it attains its full development. Peaches must be picked before they soften. Pears should be kept in a cool, dry cellar, until they show signs of ripening. Bartlett pears, kept in a cool place until the supply is nearly exhausted, bring very high prices.

Packages should be at hand in sufficient abundance to allow for the uncertainty of returns from market. For peaches, pears, and even the choicer early apples, the basket is fast giving way to a wooden crate, with two compartments that hold a half bushel each. The sides of these are made with slats which allow of ventilation, while the compact form of the package allows it to be packed to better advantage than the baskets.

Budding will continue with the peach, and pear on quince stocks. Remove or loosen the ties as soon as the buds have formed a union with the stock, which is usually in about two weeks. In cases of failure, re-bud if the bark will lift.

Preserving fruit, either by drying or canning, is to be attended to as the different sorts ripen. A drying house of some kind is useful where the quantity is large. Fruit dried out-of-doors should be covered by some open fabric to keep off flies and other insects.

Pomological Exhibitions, either those held by themselves, or in connection with State and County fairs, do much to impart a knowledge of fruits. Visit these; and if you have any fruit, go not only as a spectator, but as an exhibitor. If there are any varieties of which the name is lost, or any of doubtful identity, take specimens for comparison, and for submitting to other fruit growers.

Insects.—Much may be done to diminish the number of these by picking up all fallen fruit and feeding it to swine.

Seeds.—Secure these as the fruits ripen. Those of stone fruits must not be allowed to get too dry. See hints on page 280—last month.

Weeds must be kept down in the nursery if good plants are expected. The plow, cultivator, and pronged hoe, are the principal implements used for this purpose, and they should not be idle.

Fruit Garden.

Autumn planting is in many cases desirable, but the practice in this respect must be governed by the considerations given under "Orchard and Nursery." The secret of success in small fruit growing is in well preparing the soil, selecting good varieties, and in giving thorough cultivation. Those who think that they have done their whole duty in merely setting out the plants, will find their mistake when they come to harvest the crop.

Blackberries, if properly shortened, will have thrown out side shoots, which, when they attain the length of 18 inches, should be pinched early this month. This will cause the wood to ripen and withstand the winter better than when they are allowed to grow on until checked by frost.

Black-caps and others, that only propagate from the tips of the branches, will need to be layered. See illustrated article on page 293, last month.

Raspberries.—Keep the young canes tied up to wires and stakes, and the soil clear of weeds.

Grapes. — Market the early ripening varieties, handling carefully so as not to injure the bloom. Use scissors in gathering, and leave long stems to the bunches.

Pears are to be gathered as soon as mature, and ripened in the house. If picked too early, they will shrivel instead of ripening.

Strawberries.—If fall planting is practised this is the month in which to do it. Plants that were struck in pots are removed with little risk. With others, unless the roots are taken up with a ball of earth, it will be better to remove all the large leaves, as this diminishes the evaporating surface and increases the chances of success.

Kitchen Garden.

The gardener is now occupied with the care of his late crops, which, under good culture, should be growing rapidly.

Asparagus—It is recommended by some to plant in the fall. We have never tried it, but Meehan, of the Gardener's Monthly, says it is advisable. One year old plants have their tops cut off and are planted in a well manured bed in the usual way.

Beans.—Shell or dry all the Limas that will not be used before frost comes. They are excellent in winter. Salt string beans.

Cabbages and Cauliflowers.—Promote their growth by frequent stirring of the soil. Use lime if slugs are troublesome, or trap them by means of cabbage leaves laid on the ground. From the 10th to the 20th sow seeds of early sorts in the open ground to get plants for wintering in cold frames.

Borecole, or German greens, sow for "sprouts."

Corn. — Save seed from the best, and dry an abundance for winter use.

Cucumbers.—Gather, if large enough for pickles.

Celery.—Keep the plants cultivated and earth them up in flat culture about ten days before wanted for use. That for winter is left until later.

Endive.—Blanch as wanted for use either by tying the leaves together, or laying a piece of board or slate over the plant.

Manure.—This is the key to successful gardening, and the heaps should be increased from every available source.

Melons ripen better if a board or wisp of straw be placed between them and the earth.

Onions.—Harvest, if not already done, and cure and store as directed last month.

Radish.—The Chinese Rose-colored Winter may be sown. When not overgrown, it is tender and will keep good all winter.

Shallots.—A species of onion, and much used in the green state as a substitute for it. Divisions of the bulb are set 6 inches apart, in rows one foot distant. It is hardy and comes early in spring.

Spinach, for early spring, may now be sown, in drills 13 to 15 inches apart. It meets with a ready sale in the spring, and is a profitable crop.

Sweet Potatoes.—Carefully remove the earth and take out the largest roots for use. The smaller ones will grow until frost comes.

Squashes.—Allow the vines to root at the joints, and look out for late broods of insects.

Tomatoes.—Preserve a good supply and make catsup while the fruit is abundant. Select only the best formed and earliest for seed. The "worm," before mentioned, will still continue its depredations.

Turnips.—Sow the round sorts and give Swedes good culture.

Winter Cherry.—Gather as the fruit ripens, and use for sweetmeats, or spread in a dry room.

Flower Garden and Lawn.

A number of things may be done in preparing for next year's enjoyment. Among these one of the most important is the planting of

Bulbs.—These should be purchased as soon as the florists receive their stocks, as the best bulbs are soon bought up. All the spring-flowering ones should go in the ground the last of this month, or early in October.

Chrysanthemums.—Pot those intended for house blooming, and shade them for a few days. See that those left in the grounds are properly staked.

Dahlias should now be in their prime. Remove faded flowers and keep the stems well tied up.

Bedding Plants must have cuttings made for a new stock. Those that it is worth while to keep over, should be potted before cool weather. Seeds of

Perennials, if sown at once, will make plants strong enough to winter safely, at least if a slight protection be given them. Make preparation for

Wintering Plants.—A well drained and vermin proof pit, covered with sash, will answer for storing tender roses, carnations, and other half hardy things. A light, dry, and not too warm, cellar, will also serve for the same use.

Violets for winter blooming are to be set in a cold frame this month. The soil should be fine and rich. The frame should not be covered until frost.

Green and Hot-Houses.

Repairs and alterations of the house and heating apparatus ought to be finished, and everything ready for immediate use.

Sow Seeds of such annuals as are desirable for house blooming as well as those of cinerarias, calceolarias, Primulas, and other florists' flowers.

Cuttings, to give a stock of young plants, are to be made.

Cape Bulbs must be potted for winter blooming.

Plants out-of-doors must not be neglected. They often receive much injury in the heavy gales of autumn.

Hanging Baskets and Vases should be stocked with plants. Use plenty of Ivy for this purpose.

Cold Grapery.

When the fruit is ripe, keep the atmosphere of the house dry, but give ventilation on fine days. If rats trouble the fruit, set traps or poison for them, and look out for two-legged marauders.

Apiary for September.—As Mr. Quinby's notes have failed to reach us this month, we simply call the attention of the bee keepers among our readers to the necessity of shielding their weak colonies from the tendency of bees to rob, which increases as the season advances and pasturage yields a less abundant supply of honey. When buckwheat is in full flower, bees will busy themselves in storing honey, but when this supply fails, they will rob other hives, or take honey out of the surplus boxes. These should be watched and removed before they are attacked. The fly-holes of weak colonies should be contracted very much, and these stocks should be strengthened or broken up altogether. Look out also for queenless stocks or barren queens, and either give other queens, if the drones are not killed, eggs or young brood, or combine hives in such a way as to keep only populous ones with good queens.

A QUARTER OF

A MILLION

WANTED FOR 1868;

OR,

ALL OUR OLD SUBSCRIBERS,

AND NEARLY

100,000 MORE.

LOOK AT WHAT WE OFFER.

A Most Beautiful Paper,

The Most Liberal Terms,

Most Valuable Premiums,

And Three Months Free.

The subscription list of the *American Agriculturist* for the year 1867, is far in advance of that of any previous year. The Publishers take this opportunity to thank the hosts of friends who have not only expressed in the most emphatic terms their satisfaction with our paper, as it has made its monthly visits, but who have also swelled our subscription list by calling the attention of neighbors and others to the paper. We hope to retain all our old subscribers, and to add 100,000 to the list. And we want as many names as possible **this month.**

LOOK AT WHAT WE OFFER.

Interesting to all Readers.

1st. What You will receive for a very little money. For $1.50, or less, every one of our subscribers receives an entire volume, 12 numbers, of this paper, any one number of which contains articles, hints, suggestions, etc., worth more than the cost of a year's subscription. The engravings are of the first order, drawn and engraved by the best artists, and illustrating subjects so various that they cannot fail to interest *every member of a family.* Many a father has written to us that he must continue to take the *American Agriculturist,* not only for *himself,* but because his *children* think so much *of* it. Our determination is to make each year's issue better than that of the preceding year. Whether or not we have done this thus far, our friends who have subscribed for some years, can tell by comparing back volumes with the later ones.

LOOK AT WHAT WE OFFER.

2d. Every worker for us may secure a Premium. *All of our premiums are good,* and many of them *very valuable.* No paper can be found for which it is easier to secure subscribers than the *American Agriculturist.* This is the testimony of many who have sent us club lists. In order to give to all an equal chance, the Publishers will offer a General Premium List, in which a description of premiums is given, and also all needed information relative to getting up clubs. Among the premiums will be found Seeds, Vines, Plants, Trees, Implements, Machines, Books, Gold Pens, beautiful extra-plated Tea-sets, Pitchers, Guns, Rifles, Melodeons, Pianos, etc.

(The Premium List will soon be ready, and will be sent free to every one desiring it.) **Begin now** to make up your clubs. Every new subscriber received after September 1st, may count in the New Premium List. Extra inducements are offered to those who subscribe in September, as will be seen below.

LOOK AT WHAT WE OFFER.

3d. Look at our special offer for September. *To any new subscriber sending in the regular subscription price* **this month,** and the name marked **new,** we will send the *Agriculturist* for all of 1868, (volume 27,) **and the last three months of this year FREE.**

Notice:—This offer applies to **all** new subscribers received in September, whether single names, or members of clubs. Thus, $5 will pay for *four* subscribers for 15 months, (October 1867 to December 1868 inclusive,) and so of all other club rates. **All new subscriptions received this month, will be entered on our mail books for 15 months from October 1st.**

The Publishers will allow sufficient time after September 30th for responses to this offer to come from the Pacific States and Territories, and other distant points.

Try the American Agriculturist for a year —or 15 months, now,—three months free.

Commercial Matters—Market Prices.

The following condensed, comprehensive tables, carefully prepared specially for the *American Agriculturist,* show at a glance the transactions for the month, ending Aug. 15, 1867, and also for the same month last year:

1. TRANSACTIONS AT THE NEW-YORK MARKETS.

RECEIPTS.	*Flour.*	*Wheat.*	*Corn.*	*Rye.*	*Barley.*	*Oats.*
27 days *this* m'th	180,000	611,000	2,934,000	21,300	67,000	102,000
26 days *last* m'th	151,000	171,000	953,000	57,000	29,000	881,000

SALES.	*Flour.*	*Wheat.*	*Corn.*	*Rye.*	*Barley.*
27 days *this* month,	278,000	694,000	3,480,000	98,000	9,000
26 days *last* month,	271,500	570,000	1,889,000	161,000	71,000

2. *Comparison with same period at this time last year.*

RECEIPTS.	*Flour.*	*Wheat.*	*Corn.*	*Rye.*	*Barley.*	*Oats.*
27 days 1867....	180,000	611,000	2,934,000	21,300	67,000	102,000
24 days 1866....	351,500	31,300	3,620,000	115,000	23,000	1,203,000

SALES.	*Flour.*	*Wheat.*	*Corn.*	*Rye.*	*Barley.*
27 days 1867......	278,000	694,000	3,480,000	98,000	9,000
24 days 1866......	181,000	447,000	3,967,000	135,000	18,300

3. *Exports from New York, Jan. 1 to Aug. 15:*

	Flour.	*Wheat.*	*Corn.*	*Rye.*	*Oats.*	*Barley.*
1867.....	815,082	148,673	5,441,960	135,501	102,024	889,153
1866.....	810,728	160,900	7,946,258	287,129	211,285	25,016

4. *Stock of grain in store at New York:*

1867.	Wheat, bush.	Corn, bush.	Rye, bush.	Barley, bush.	Oats, bush.	Malt, bush.
Aug. 13...	91,174	603,721	32,785	12,276	200,519	48,672
July 15...	218,500	160,780	65,940	21,300	266,763	41,706
June 11...	574,270	217,736	117,251	60,618	379,605	16,311
May 15...	151,300	261,091	148,804	113,706	606,191	16,464

5. *Receipts of Breadstuffs at tide water at Albany, May 1st to August 7th:*

	Flour, bbls.	Wheat, bush.	Corn, bush.	Rye, bush.	Barley, bush.	Oats, bush.
1867.....	64,700	396,100	5,692,300	130,900	35,100	1,516,000
1866.....	111,400	1,460,500	11,183,000	470,000	105,300	4,194,000

Gold has advanced one or two points since our last, closing quite firmly.... Receipts of produce have been increasing, especially in the breadstuff line. New wheat has come in quite freely, chiefly by coastwise vessels, and by railway. New wheat from the South has been abundant, but not of the best average quality.... The demand for breadstuffs has been good, but holders have been eager sellers, as a rule, and prices have been generally lower, and quite irregular. Old wheat and old wheat flour have been quite scarce, and have been quoted firmer than almost any other kind of produce. They have been given decided preference over new, which has been much depressed. Quite a brisk speculative business has been transacted in corn within the past two weeks, leading to a rapid rise in prices. The export trade is kept in check by the advance. Weather and crop reports from Europe have been more favorable, and have tended to lessen the export call. Oats have been scarce and held very stiffly. Various speculative operations have been in progress in them.... Provisions have been quite active, but irregular in price, closing, as a rule, rather firmly.... Cotton has been in better demand, at higher quotations, closing buoyant.... Wool has been sparingly dealt in at declining prices. Holders have been rather eager to sell, in view of the accumulating supplies.... Tobacco has been freely purchased, especially for export, at uniform prices, quality considered.... Hay has been plenty, particularly new, which has declined materially. The demand has been moderate.... Hops have been salable and firm.... Seeds have been nominal and dull.

CURRENT WHOLESALE PRICES.

	July 15.	Aug. 15.
PRICE OF GOLD	139½	140⅜
FLOUR—Super to Extra State	$7 00 @ 11 75	$6 75 @ 11 50
Super to Extra Southern....	9 75 @ 17 00	11 00 @ 14 75
Extra Western	8 75 @ 13 50	8 50 @ 13 50
Extra Genesee	11 50 @ 13 00	11 70 @ 13 50
Superfine Western	7 00 @ 8 75	6 75 @ 8 00
RYE FLOUR	7 50 @ 9 25	7 00 @ 9 25
CORN MEAL	5 50 @ 6 10	5 25 @ 6 70
WHEAT—All kinds of White.	2 10 @ 3 00	2 25 @ 2 85
All kinds of Red and Amber.	2 00 @ 2 10	1 60 @ 2 45
CORN—Yellow	98 @ 1 11	1 10 @ 1 23
Mixed	70 @ 1 07½	1 05 @ 1 13
OATS—Western	72 @ 85	80 @ 81
State	61 @ 80	91 @ 95
RYE	1 20 @ 1 20	1 12 @ 1 35
BARLEY	Nominal.	1 00 @ —
HAY—Bale ₩ 100 lb	75 @ 1 40	75 @ 1 70
Loose	55 @ 1 55	65 @ 1 80
STRAW, ₩ 100 lb	50 @ 1 15	75 @ 1 15
COTTON—Middlings, ₩ lb ...	26 @ 27½	28½ @ 29½
HOPS—Crop of 1866, ₩ lb ...	30 @ 65	50 @ 65
FEATHERS—Live Geese, ₩ lb.	78 @ 90	75 @ 88
SEED—Clover, ₩ lb	11 @ 12½	11½ @ 12½
Timothy, ₩ bushel	3 00 @ 3 25	3 00 @ 3 25
Flax, ₩ bushel	3 10 @ 3 25	3 25 @ 3 50
SUGAR—Brown, ₩ lb	10⅛ @ 13	10¾ @ 13½
MOLASSES, Cuba, ₩ gl	37 @ 55	35 @ 55
COFFEE—Rio, (Gold price) ₩ lb	14⅜ @ 19¼	14½ @ 19
TOBACCO, Kentucky, &c., ₩ lb.	4 @ 25	4 @ 15
Seed Leaf, ₩ lb	5 @ 65	5½ @ 65
WOOL—Domestic Fleece, ₩ lb.	40 @ 70	51 @ 65
Domestic, pulled, ₩ lb	30 @ 55	31½ @ 50
California, unwashed, ...	18 @ 30	18 @ 30
TALLOW, ₩ lb	11⅛ @ 11¾	11⅛ @ 12
OIL CAKE—₩ ton	36 00 @ 38 00	36 00 @ 37 00
PORK—Mess, ₩ barrel	23 95 @ 23 12	22 12 @ 23 00
Prime, ₩ barrel	19 50 @ 19 75	19 12 @ 20 00
BEEF—Plain mess	18 00 @ 24 00	14 00 @ 21 00
LARD, in barrels, ₩ lb	12 @ 13¾	12⅜ @ 13¾
BUTTER—Western, ₩ lb	15 @ 21	15 @ 25
State, ₩ lb	11 @ 30	22 @ 35
CHEESE	7 @ 11¾	6 @ 13¼
BEANS—₩ bushel	2 00 @ 4 07	3 00 @ 4 10
PEAS—Canada, ₩ bushel	1 20 @ 1 25	1 25 @ 1 45
EGGS—Fresh, ₩ dozen	17 @ 21	23 @ 27
POULTRY—Fowls, ₩ lb	16 @ 18	20 @ 22
Turkeys, ₩ lb	16 @ 20	20 @ 22
POTATOES—Old & New, ₩ bbl,	2 25 @ 6 50	2 00 @ 2 50
APPLES—₩ barrel	1 00 @ 5 00	2 00 @ 4 50
PEACHES—₩ basket	— @ —	1 00 @ 2 50
CRANBERRIES, ₩ barrel	@	Nominal.

New York Live Stock Markets.—

WEEK ENDING.	*Beeves.*	*Cows.*	*Calves.*	*Sheep.*	*Swine.*
July 23..............	5,903	61	1,601	27,537	16,671
July 30..............	5,372	11	1,198	21,810	20,104
August 6	6,288	54	1,134	24,301	23,891
August 13............	5,997	39	1,450	27,718	10,781
Total in four Weeks....	23,562	165	5,376	101,375	81,867
Average per Week......	5,890	41	1,491	25,806	20,167
do. do. *last Month*...	5,325	51	2,141	24,112	10,652
do. do. *prev's Month*.	5,119	65	2,020	14,464	10,815
Average per Week, 1866.	5,718	94	1,299	20,000	13,000
do. do. do. 1865.....	5,255	118	1,500	16,091	11,023
do. do. do. 1864.....	5,161	115	1,511	15,313	12,676
do. do. do. 1863.....	5,150	129	694	9,941	21,670
Total in 1866	298,880	4,885	62,420	1,040,000	672,000
Total in 1865........	270,271	6,161	77,991	836,733	573,197
Total in 1864........	267,609	7,083	75,621	782,462	660,270
Total in 1863........	264,091	6,470	35,705	519,316	1,101,617

Beef Cattle.—Our report covers four weeks of exceedingly variable weather, part of the time very hot and moist—bad weather both for animals and for butchers. Irregularity of supply, at this season, influences the prices promptly, and consequently there has been rather more than the ordinary fluctuations in the ruling prices.

At the last two markets, the average price was determined more perhaps by the quality than by the supply, for most of the stock was very poor and badly treated. We quote extra beef 16½c., and from that to 15c. for good fair steers. The general average of the market was not more than 14½c., and the lowest grade of cattle sold for about 10 to 12c. These prices are per pound for the estimated weight of the dressed meat in the quarters. . . **Milch Cows.**—Little demand and small supply; prices $50 to $85 with calves. . **Calves.**—Fat calves sell at about 11c.@12c. per lb. live weight. Common ones at 8 to 9c.; poor, 4½ to 6c. A good many grass calves are reported as sold to neighboring farmers, at an average price of $12.50 per head. **Sheep.**—The last market leaves prices about as follows: Prime sheep, 6@6½c. per lb. live weight; medium, 5¼c.; poor, 4½c. Lambs, 7½@9½c., according to quality. Really extra mutton sheep will bring better prices than quoted, say 7@7½c. per lb.; but it takes remarkably fine lambs to sell for over 9 or 9½c. .

Swine.—As we close our report, the prices have been unusually uniform for some time. The supply is abundant and steady, though less than for two weeks past; prices 7½ and 7¾c. per lb. live weight, a few extra lots going a little above the highest figures.

The Fairs for 1867.

State Agricultural Fairs.

New England	Providence, R. I.	Sept. 3-7
California		Sept. 9-18
New Hampshire	Nashua	Sept. 10-13
Michigan	Detroit	Sept. 10-13
Wis. Ag'l & Mech.	Milwaukee	Sept. 10-13
Vermont	Brattleboro	Sept. 10-13
International State Fair, Del. and Md.	Eastern Pa., N. J. Norristown, Pa.	Sept. 11-17
N. Y. State, Trial of Plows, etc.,	Utica	Sept. 11
American Institute	N. Y. City	Sept. 12, Oct. 26
Iowa Central	Des Moines	Sept. 15-27
New Jersey	Newark	Sept.
Kentucky	Louisville	Sept. 17-20
Ohio	Dayton	Sept. 23-27
Wisconsin	Madison	Sept. 23-27
Canada	Kingston	Sept. 23-27
Kansas	Lawrence	Sept. 24-27
Pennsylvania	Pittsburgh	Sept. 24-27
Indiana	Terre Haute	Sept. 30-Oct. 4
Illinois	Quincy	Sept. 30-Oct. 5
New York	Buffalo	Oct. 1-4
Minnesota	Rochester	Oct. 1-4
Iowa	Clinton	Oct. 1-4
Missouri	St. Louis	Oct. 7-12
Tenn. Ag'l & Mech. Ass.	Clarksville	Oct. 15-19
Maryland	Baltimore	Oct. 29-31
Louisiana	Baton Rouge	Nov. 5-9
Louisiana Ag'l & Mech. Ass.,	New Orleans	Nov. 19-30

Horticultural Meetings and Fairs.

American Pomological	St. Louis, Mo.	Sept. 11-14
Delaware Horticultural	Wilmington	Sept. 19-21
Ill. State Hort'l Soc. Southern Ill. Fruit Growers Association.	South Pass	Sept. 4—
Mass. Hort'l Soc.	Boston	Sept. 24-27
Queens Co., N. Y.	Mineola, L. I.	Sept. 25-27
Worcester Co. (Mass.)	Worcester	Sept. 7-10

Horse Fairs.

U. S. Horse Exhibition	Springfield, Mass.	Aug. 27-30
Wisconsin Mech. and Ag. Soc.'s Horse Fair	Milwaukee	Sept. 10-13
Orange Co. Horse Fair	Goshen, N. Y.	Sept. 11-13
Hudson Co. Ag. Soc. Horse,	Hoboken, N. J.	Sept. 17-20
Horse Show	Kalamazoo, Mich.	Oct. 1-4
National Horse Fair.	Washington, D. C.	Oct. 28—

County and Local Fairs.

MAINE.

Aroostook Co	Houlton	Sept. 25-26
Franklin Co	Farmington	Oct. 1-3
Hancock Co	Ellsworth	Oct. 1-3
Somerset Co	Central Skowhegan	Sept. 25-27
Waldo Co	Belfast	Sept. 25-27
West Penobscot.	Kenduskeag	Sept. 24-26
West Washington	Jonesboro	Oct. 2-3
York Co	Saco and Biddeford	Oct. 8-10

NEW HAMPSHIRE.

Connecticut River	Keene	Sept. 17-19
Essex Co.		Oct. 1-2
Merrimack Co.	Concord	Sept. 24-26
Rockingham Co.		Sept. 18-19

MASSACHUSETTS.

Barnstable Co.	Barnstable	Oct. 8-9
Bristol Co.	Taunton	Oct. 1-3
Berkshire Co.	Pittsfield	Oct. 1-3
Essex Co.	Haverhill	Sept. 24-25
Housatonic Co.	Great Barrington	Sept. 25-26
Hampshire, Franklin & Hampden,	Northampton	Oct. 3-4
Hampshire Co.	Amherst	Sept. 24-25
Hampden Co.	Springfield	Oct. 1-2
Hampden East.	Palmer	Oct. 8-9
Highland Co.	Middlefield	Sept. 12-13
Hoosic Valley Co.	North Adams	Sept. 17-18
Middlesex Co.	Concord	Oct. 3-4
Middlesex South	Framingham	Sept. 17-18
Middlesex North	Lowell	Sept. 26-27
Martha's Vineyard	West Tisbury	Oct. 15-16
Nantucket	Nantucket	Sept. 25-26
Norfolk Co.	Dedham	Sept. 19-20
Plymouth Co.	Bridgewater	Sept. 26-27
Southboro Farmers' Club,	Southboro	Sept. 26
Worcester Co.	Worcester	Sept. 19-20
Worcester West	Barre	Sept. 26-27
Worcester North	Fitchburg	Sept. 24-25
Worcester South	Sturbridge	Oct. 3
Worcester Southeast	Milford	Sept. 24-25

VERMONT.

Bennington Co.	Bennington	Sept. 25-26
Caledonia	St. Johnsbury	Sept. 24-26
Franklin	Richford	Sept. 18-19

RHODE ISLAND.

Woonsocket Co.	Woonsocket	Sept. 11-12

CONNECTICUT.

Fairfield Co	Norwalk	Sept. 24-27
Hartford Co.	Hartford	Oct. 1-3
Housatonic Co.	New Milford	Oct. 1-3
Litchfield Co.	Litchfield	Sept. 10-11
Milford and Orange Co.	Milford	Oct. 2-3
New London Co.	Norwich	Oct. 8-11
Ridgefield (Town)	Ridgefield	Oct. 1-3
Woodstock (Town)	Woodstock	Sept. 18-19

NEW YORK.

Albany Co.	Albany	Sept. 16-19
Cattaraugus Co.	Little Valley	Sept. 11-13
Cayuga Co.	Auburn	Sept. 17-19
Chenango Co.	Norwich	Sept. 24-26
Duchess Co.	Washington Hollow	Sept. 17-20
Delaware Co.	Walton	Sept. 17-19
Erie Co.	Springville	Sept. 17-19
Monroe Co.	Rochester	Sept. 25-27
Oneida Co.	Rome	Sept. 24-25
Ontario Co.	Canandaigua	Sept. 21-23
Otsego Co.	Cooperstown	Oct. 1-3
Putnam Co.	Carmel	Sept. 18-27
Queens Co.	Mineola	Sept. 25-27
St. Lawrence Co.	Canton	Sept. 24-26
Ulster Co.	Kingston	Sept. 20-22
Washington Co.	Salem	Sept. 10-12
Wyoming Co.	Warsaw	Sept. 24-25

TOWN AND INDEPENDENT FAIRS—NEW YORK.

Brookfield	Clarkville	Oct. 1-3
Garrattsville (Otsego Co.)		Sept. 18-19
Gouverneur Ag'l & Mech. Soc.,	Gouverneur	Sept. 18-20
New York (City) German Ag. and Hort.	Hamilton Park, 69th St. & 3d Av.	Sept. 30, and Oct. 1 and 2
Oswego Falls	Oswego Falls	Sept. 24-26
Palmyra Union	Palmyra	Sept. 23-24
Susquehanna Valley	Unadilla	Sept. 25-27

NEW JERSEY.

Burlington Co.	Mt. Holly	Oct. 1-3
Central Co.	near Trenton	Sept. 17-20
Cumberland Co.	Bridgeton	Sept. 25
Hunterdon Co.		Sept. 24-26
Passaic Co.	Patterson	Oct. 1-3
Vineland—Ag'l & Hort.	Vineland	Sept. 18-20

PENNSYLVANIA.

Bucks Co.	Newtown	Sept. 24-26
Chester Co.	Westchester	Sept. 20-24
Crawford Co.	Meadville	Sept. 24-26
Cumberland Co.		Oct. 1-4
Doylestown Co.		Oct. 1-3
Lehigh Co.	Allentown	Sept. 24-27
Susquehanna Co.	Montrose	Sept. 11-12
Wickhill Co.	Jacksonville	Sept. 25-26
Union Co.		Oct. 2-4
Warren Co.	Youngsville	Sept. 18-20
Westmoreland Co.	Mt. Pleasant	Sept. 17-19
York Co.	York	Oct. 1-4

OHIO.

Ashtabula Co.	Jefferson	Oct. 9-11
Athens Co.	Athens	Oct. 3-4
Belmont Co.	St. Clairsville	Sept. 25-27
Champaign Co.	Urbana	Oct. 1-4
Clarke Co.	Springfield	Sept. 10-13
Clermont Co.	Boston	Sept. 17-20
Clinton Co.	Wilmington	Sept. 18-20
Cuyahoga Co.	Newburgh	Oct. 8-11
Defiance Co.	Defiance	Oct. 15-17
Delaware Co.	(Fair Grounds)	Oct. 2
Erie Co.	Sandusky	Oct. 1-4
Franklin Co.	Columbus	Sept. 10-13
Fulton Co.	Ottokee	Sept. 25-27
Geauga Co.	Burton	Sept. 18-20
Geauga, (Free)	Claridon	Sept. 23-25
Greene Co.	Xenia	Sept. 4-6
Guernsey Co.	Cambridge	Oct. 1-2
Hamilton Co.	Carthage	Sept. 3-6
Hancock Co.	Findlay	Oct. 3-5
Harrison Co.	Cadiz	Oct. 2-4
Huron Co.	Norwalk	Oct. 2-4
Jackson Co.	Jackson	Oct. 3-4
Knox Co.	Mt. Vernon	
Lake Co.	Painesville	Oct. 2-4
Lake Shore Grape Growers' Ass.,	Elyria	Oct. 15-17
Lawrence Co.	Ironton	Sept. 25-27
Lorain Co.	Elyria	Oct. 1-4
Lucas Co.	Toledo	Oct. 2-4
Madison Co.	London	Sept. 18-20
Marion Co.	Marion	Oct. 1-4
Medina Co.	Medina	Oct. 2-4
Miami Co.	Troy	Oct. 3-5
Morgan Co.	McConnellsville	Oct. 1-3
Morrow Co.	Mt. Gilead	Oct. 2-4
Meigs Co.	Racine	
Pickaway Co.	Circleville	Sept. 11-13
Plymouth Co.		Oct. 8-10
Portage Co.	Ravenna	Oct. 18-20
Preble Co.	Eaton	Sept. 17-20
Putnam Co.	Ottawa	Oct. 2-4
Richland Co.	Mansfield	Oct. 2-4
Sandusky Co.	Fremont	Oct. 2-4
Seneca Co.	Tiffin	Oct. 9-12
Stark Co.	Canton	Oct. 1-4
Trumbull Co.	Warren	Sept. 17-19
Tuscarawas Co.	Canal Dover	Sept. 25-27
Union Co.	Marysville	Oct. 9-11
Van Wert Co.	Van Wert	Oct. 3-5
Warren Co.	Lebanon	Sept. 11-13
Wayne Co.	Wooster	Oct. 9-11
Williams Co.	Bryan	Oct. 1-3
Wyandotte Co.	Upper Sandusky	Oct. 1-3

TOWN, OR INDEPENDENT FAIRS.

Jamestown "Union,"	Greene Co.	Aug. 28-30
Urichsville	Tuscarawas Co.	Sept. 10-13
Richfield	Summit Co.	Sept. 18-20
Blanchester	Clinton Co.	Sept. 24-27
Orwell	Ashtabula Co.	Sept. 24-26
Conneaut	Ashtabula Co.	Sept. 25-27
Southern O. Union	Manchester	Oct. 1-4
Garrettsville	Portage Co.	Oct. 1-3
Union, Greene Co.	Marysville	Oct. 9-11

ILLINOIS.

Boone Co.	Belvidere	Oct. 1-3
Bureau Co.	Princeton	Sept. 17-19
Carroll Co.	Mount Carroll	Sept. 25-27
Champaign Co.	Urbana	Sept. 10-13
De Kalb Co.	De Kalb	Sept. 25-26
Edwards Co.	Albion	Sept. 17-19
Fulton Co.	Canton	Oct. 8-11
Franklin Co.	Benton	Oct. 9-12
Greene Co.	Carrollton	Oct. 15-18
Grundy Co.	Morris	Oct. 8-11
Henry Co.	Cambridge	Sept. 3-6
Henderson Co.	Biggsville	Oct. 9-11
Jefferson Co.	Mt. Vernon	Sept. 23-25
Jo Daviess Co.	Galena	Sept. 24-27
Knox Co.	Knoxville	Oct. 8-11
Kane Co.	Geneva	Sept. 25-28
Kendall Co.	Bristol	Oct. 8-10
Lake Co.		Sept. 24-26
Lasalle Co.	Ottawa	Oct. 9-11
Macoupin Co.	Carlinsville	Oct. 15-18
McLean Co.	Bloomington	Sept. 3-6
Madison Co.	Edwardsville	Sept. 3
Marshall Co.	Henry	Sept. 10-13
Marion Co.	Near Salem	Oct. 14-17
McHenry Co.	Woodstock	Sept. 17-19
Mercer Co.	Millersburgh	Sept. 24-26
Montgomery Co.	Hillsboro	Oct. 1-4
Peoria Co.	Peoria	Sept. 17-20
Pike Co.	Pittsfield	Sept. 24-27
Pope Co.		Sept. 3-5
Randolph Co.	Sparta	Sept. 25-27
Richland Co.		Sept. 25-27
Rock Island Co.	Rock Island	Sept. 2-6
Schuyler Co.	Rushville	Sept. 24-26
Stark Co.	Toulon	Sept. 24-26
St. Clair Co.	Belleville	Sept. 10-13
Stephenson Co.	Freeport	Sept. 24-27
Tazewell Co.	Tremont	Sept. 25-27
Union Co.	Jonesboro	Sept. 18-20
Whiteside Co.	Sterling	Sept. 10-12
Woodford Co.	Versailles	Aug. 15-19

INDIANA.

Decatur Co.	Greensburgh	Sept. 17-20
Dearborn Co.	Fairgrounds	Sept. 23-28
Elkhart Co.	Goshen	Oct. 3-5
Harrison Co.	Corydon	Sept. 10-13
Marion Co.	Bridgeport	Sept. 25-27
Morgan Co.	Martinsville	Sept. 3-7
Posey Co.	New Harmony	Sept. 10-13
Spencer Co.	Rockport	Oct. 2-5
Rush, Hancock, and Henry Counties	Knightstown	August 27-30

KENTUCKY.

Barren Co.	Glasgow	Oct. 1-5
Breckenridge Co.		Oct. 1-3
Boone Co.	Burlington	Aug. 27-31
Bourbon Co.	Paris	Sept. 3-6
Boyle Co.	Danville	Sept. 10-13
Clarke Co.	Winchester	Aug. 28-30
Daviess Co.	Yelvington	Oct.
Fayette Co.	Lexington	Sept. 24-28
Green Co.	Greensburgh	Oct. 8-11
Harrison Co.	Cynthiana	Sept. 10-13
Madison Co.	Richmond	Aug. 13-16
Mason and Bracken Co.	Germantown	Sept. 10-14
Mercer Co.	Harrodsburgh	Sept. 3-6
McCracken Co.	Paducah	Oct. 8-11
Montgomery & Bath Co.	Mt. Sterling	Aug. 21-23
North Kentucky	Florence	Aug. 28-31
Nelson Co.	Bardstown	Sept. 3-6
Salvisa Stock Fair	Salvisa	Sept. 3-6
Scott Co.	Georgetown	Aug. 27-29
South Kentucky	Glasgow	Oct. 8-11
Shelby Co.	Shelbyville	Aug. 27-30
Washington Co.	Springfield	Oct. 1-4
Woodford Co.	Versailles	Aug. 20-23

IOWA.

Benton Co.	Vinton	Sept. 25-28
Bremer Co.	Waverly	Oct.
Crawford Co.	Dennison	Sept. 27-28
Chickasaw Co.	New Hampton	Sept. 26-27
Cedar Co.	Tipton	Sept. 17-19
Clayton Co.	Farmersburg	Oct. 1-3
Clinton Co. Union	Wheatland	Sept. 24-27
Cedar Valley Co.	Cedar Falls	Oct. 15-17
Des Moines Co.	Burlington	Sept. 25-27
Hardin Co.	Eldora	Sept. 25-26
Jasper Co.	Newton	Oct. 9-11
Jones Co.	Anamosa	Sept. 25-27
Jefferson Co.	Fairfield	Oct. 9-11
Kossuth Co.	Algona	Sept. 25
Louisa Co.	Wapello	Sept. 17-20
Linn Co.	Marion	Sept. 17-20
Madison Co.	Winterset	Oct. 18-19
Mahaska Co.	Oskaloosa	Sept. 11-13
Marshall Co.	Marshalltown	Sept. 25-27
Muscatine Co (Un. Dist).	West Liberty	Oct. 8-10
Poweshiek Co.	Brooklyn	Sept. 20-21
Scott Co.	Davenport	Sept. 9-14
Tama Co.	Tama City	Oct. 10-13
Union Co.	Afton	Oct. 11-12
Van Buren Co.	Keosauqua	Sept. 25-27

WISCONSIN.

Columbia Co.	Columbus	Sept. 18-20
Green Lake Co.	Berlin	Sept. 19-20
Outagamie Co.	Grand Chute	Sept. 17-19
Ripon (Town)	Ripon	Oct. 1-3
Union Co.	Warren	Sept. 10-13
Vernon Co.	Viroqua	Oct. 3-4
Walworth Co.	Elkhorn	Oct. 8-10

MINNESOTA.

Goodhue Co.	Red Wing	Oct. 16-18

KANSAS.

Shawnee Co.	Topeka	Sept. 18-19

MISSOURI.		
Andrew Co.	Savannah	
Boone Co.	Columbus	Sept. 30, Oct. 8
Cole Co.	Jefferson City	Sept. 17-20
Clark Co.		Sept. 25-28
Jefferson Co.	De Soto	Sept. 25-27
Lewis Co.	Canton	Oct. 14-17
Linn Co.	Hannibal	Sept. 25-29
Monroe Co.	Paris	Sept. 9-10
Pike Co.	Ashley	Sept. 17-20
Randolph Co.		Sept. 24
Ray Co.	Richmond	Oct. 8-11
St. Louis Ag'l & Mech.	St. Louis	Oct. 7-13
NEBRASKA.		
Douglass Co.	Omaha	Sept. 24-26
Nemaha Co.		Sept. 25-27
TENNESSEE.		
Maury Co.	Columbia	Oct. 8-12
West Tennessee, Union City, Obion Co.		Sept. 30, Oct. 5
CALIFORNIA.		
San Joaquin Co.	Stockton	Sept. 17-21
CANADA.		
East Riding Durham Ag. Soc., Port Hope		Oct. 0
Northumberland, East	Brighton	Oct. 2
Norwich	Norwich	Oct. 8-9
South Grenville		Oct. 2-4
South Ontario	Whitby	Oct. 1-2
West Durham	Bowmanville	Oct. 4
West Durham	Darlington Branch	Oct. 11
Victoria Co.	Lindsay	Oct. 10-10

Containing a great variety of Items, including many good Hints and Suggestions which we throw into smaller type and condensed form, for want of space elsewhere.

WHY FOR NOTHING? "Why Do You Give Three Months' Papers for Nothing?" some of our readers may ask.

1st. Because we feel sure that thousands of families who may be induced by our offer to take the *American Agriculturist*, will give their testimony to the benefit received from reading it; and thus, through them, we shall gain many other friends and new subscribers.

2nd. Because there is a very large amount of labor to be done near the close of a year, and at the beginning of a new year, in entering on our books, and properly arranging, the great number of names of subscribers whose subscriptions are renewed at that time; and we are willing to offer these extra inducements for the sake of getting some of this large amount of work done earlier in the season. *Help us swell the list.*

How to Remit:—Checks on New-York Banks or Bankers are best for large sums; make them payable in all cases to the order of Orange Judd & Co.

Post Office Money Orders may now be obtained at nearly every county seat, in all the cities, and in many of the large towns. We consider them perfectly safe, and the best means of remitting fifty dollars or less, as many hundreds have been sent to us without any loss.

Registered Letters, under the new system, which went into effect June 1st, are a very safe means of sending small sums of money where P. O. Money Orders cannot be easily obtained. *Observe*, the Registry fee, as well as postage, must be paid in stamps at the office where the letter is mailed, or it will be liable to be sent to the Dead Letter Office. *Buy and affix the stamps both for postage and registry, put in the money and seal the letter in the presence of the postmaster, and take his receipt for it.* Letters sent in this way to us are at our risk.

Three New Grape Books.—If our people fail in grape culture, it will not be for lack of a sufficient number of teachers. The literature of the subject is becoming voluminous, and one who would have all that is written upon grape culture must invest in a moderate sized library. The books on grape culture since Fuller, are so much alike, that, as a general thing, one is about as good as another, and we find a dreary sameness about them. The fact is, if one only comprehends the structure and mode of growth of the vine, he can easily follow any of the many systems of training. We have now before us three books, which we mention in the order of their publication:

AMERICAN GRAPE CULTURE AND WINE MAKING, by Peter B. Mead, N. Y. Harper & Brothers. pp. 483. 8vo. Price, $3.00. This is by far the most sumptuous grape book that has yet appeared, good paper and type, a most liberal margin, and illustrated by engravings that are, for the most part, of great excellence. In all the practical part we find scarcely anything that has not been told before. In this case the story is clearly and well told, and the book will doubtless be a safe guide. The chapter on varieties will attract attention. As there are few grapes commended save the Iona, Israella, and Eumelan, the book is open to the criticism of having been written in the interest of the originator and owner of those varieties. We are not aware that this makes it any better or any worse; books and grapes must stand on their own merits. In one point we must dissent from the author. He introduces a new word for lateral—*thallon*, and from this derives *athallise*, *dethallise*, etc. This appears learned, but is useless, for the reason that the word lateral has become well understood as applied to the grape vine, and people will not unlearn it to substitute so uncouth a word as thallon. There is just as much need of a new word for stake or post as for lateral. Despite a rather extravagant use of adjectives, the work is generally well written, and will be acceptable not only to the many personal friends of the author, but to those grape growers who wish to read all sides of the subject.

VINEYARD CULTURE, by A. Du Breuil, with notes by John A. Warder. Cincinnati, Robert Clarke & Co. pp. 337. 12mo. Price, $4.00. This is a translation of a work by one of the highest European authorities, and is brought out in a remarkably neat and beautiful style. The original was written for a different climate, and other vines than ours, but the very copious notes of Doctor Warder have quite naturalized it. We should have preferred that Dr. W. had given us a work entirely his own; as it is, he has embodied a great deal in his notes, and the work cannot fail to have a large sale.

THE GRAPE VINE, BY FREDERICK MOHR. Translated by Horticola. New York, Orange Judd & Company. pp. 129. 12mo. Price, $1.00. This work takes up its subject quite differently from any other, and devotes more attention to the structure of the vine and its manner of growth than it does to particular methods of training, though it is not by any means deficient in practical instructions. One who fully masters the teachings of Doctor Mohr will be able to work among his vines understandingly. The translator, (Dr. Chas. Siedhof,) has added a chapter on the propagation of American varieties, as the practice with these is different from that followed in Europe with their vines. We think that this will prove a most useful little book, and it will, doubtless, in its English dress, take the same high stand here that the original holds in Germany.

"An Opinion as is an Opinion."—Some horticultural Jack Bunsby, in the American Journal of Horticulture, answers a "subscriber," who asks, "Can good wine be made from grapes grown at the North?" as follows: "We very much doubt it; what are or have been called native wines, are fixed-up stuff—grape juice and water sweetened, not wine." What did its "Western Editor" think when he read this? What do the Hammondsport people think? What do the members of the Lake Shore Wine Growers' Association say to this? Can Mottier and the Longworth Wine House subscribe to the statement that native wines are fixed-up stuff?—Oh, we forgot—"the North" means the country within sight of Boston State House.

The Strawberry Chas. Downing.—In describing this berry in our August No., we omitted to say that the engraving was from fruit borne upon young plants, set out in October last. The illustration, therefore, fails to do justice to the fruit, which on old plants attains a much larger size than is there represented.

Exhibition of the American Institute.—The American Institute will hold its thirty-seventh Annual Exhibition in New York at the armory on 14th st., near 6th avenue, beginning on September 12th, and closing on October 29th. The programme, which is well arranged, and a marked improvement on those of former years, as well as all necessary information, may be had by addressing Prof. S. D. Tillman, Corresponding Secretary. The Department of Agriculture and Horticulture includes all products of the farm and garden, as well as all the tools and implements used in cultivating them. Liberal premiums will be offered, and we hope to see this department better filled than it has been of late years. The Institute seems to have taken a turn in the right direction, and as we see a disposition to shed its shell of old fogyism, we shall try to second its efforts.

Gardening for Profit.—The sale of this book has been something unprecedented, and shows that it was just the work that was needed. It gives the experience of a practical market gardener, who, cultivating valuable land, was obliged to make it pay. While it is written by a market gardener, its teachings are none the less applicable to the family garden, as the best mode of culture in one place is the best in another, and if it will pay a market gardener to get two or three crops a year from the same soil, it will be profitable for the farmer or owner of a town or village lot to do the same. If the doctrine of this book, high manuring and thorough cultivation, should find an application outside of the garden, we do not think that the farmer would suffer. No one who raises vegetables of any kind for sale, can afford to do without this book, and indeed the same remark will apply to those who have only private gardens. Those who intend to try market gardening, should begin this autumn. The work covers the whole ground, from selecting and preparing the soil to marketing or storing the crops. It has a particularly valuable chapter on the construction of houses for forcing vegetables and propagating plants. The demand has been such that our stock has several times been exhausted. We have made arrangements for a constant supply. Price, $1.50 by mail.

What will Secure the Agriculturist?—$1.50 pays for a copy of the *American Agriculturist* for the whole of 1868, and a new subscriber sent us this month, (September,) will receive the paper *free* the last three months of this year.

$5.00 pays for *four* copies for 1868, and each *new* subscriber will receive the paper for the rest of this *year free.* The same rates for five, six, seven, eight, or nine copies.

$12.00 pays for *ten* copies for 1868, and each *new* subscriber will receive the paper for the rest of this year *free.* The same rates for any number of subscribers up to nineteen. A free copy to the sender of the club.

$20.00 pays for *twenty* copies for 1868, and each *new* subscriber will receive the paper for the rest of this year *free.* The same rates for all copies over twenty. A free copy to the sender of the club.

The American Pomological Society.—The President of the Society, Col. Marshall P. Wilder, writes us from Paris that he shall sail from Europe in company with Mr. Barry, in time to be present at the meeting at St. Louis, on the 11th of this month. This promises to be a largely attended and important meeting. All interested in pomology should join the society, attend its meetings, and get its Transactions.

The Practical Entomologist.—We regret to learn that this most excellent monthly is about to cease, unless adequate support be immediately tendered. The journal is devoted entirely to the interests of cultivators, and we should hope that there might be enough of these, sufficiently awake to the importance of the subject, to sustain it. The price is only 50 cents a year. E. T. Cresson, Philadelphia, receives subscriptions.

Sundry Humbugs.—Letters received during the last month, with reference to various swindling operations, though numerous, indicate a decided falling off in this line of business. We have reason to believe that our blasts are telling upon them, and the sums of money which, we are assured by correspondents, have been saved to their owners by our timely warnings, would be sufficient to set up several respectable establishments in Wall-street, and leave enough to buy out the whole stock in trade of a hundred or two of these villainous sneaks, who filch money from the unwary by means of confidential circulars, nice little tickets put up in nice little envelopes, as if they were worth something, offering valuable articles for one tenth, or less, of what they are reported to be worth. Respectable dealers don't do business in this way, and those parties who have written us in the last month for special aid in their particular cases, because they have sent money, and got no returns, are advised to take the *Agriculturist*, heed our general warnings, and in future save their money.... Clark, Webster & Co. come out as follows: "A CARD to the Ticket Holders and Agents of the Bankers' and Merchants' Grand Presentation Enterprise. We are sorry to say that we have been obliged to extend the time of drawing to August 24, 1867, on account of the city authorities claiming that the enterprise was a violation of the law, so we have at a great deal of trouble and expense secured a United States License to carry the enterprise through, and we have obligated ourselves to make the Grand Distribution of Prizes on the evening of the 24th of August, 1867. As we have the United States License in our possession, we will guarantee that there will be no further delay in bringing this stupendous scheme to a close." The claim of the city authorities is just, and, we think, will be sustained. The *United States license* is no protection, and gives them no authority to carry on their illegitimate business. A decision from Chief Justice Chase, published in the city papers July 21st ult., settles this question. We cannot quote the whole of this lengthy document; a few lines are sufficient. Speaking of the U. S. License Law, as to giving authority to carry on business against State laws, he says: "But it is not necessary to regard these laws as giving such authority. *So far as they relate to trade within State limits, they give none, and can give none.*" Clark, Webster & Co. are still under bonds for trial, and, we hope, they will get their deserts. Their new *obligations* and *guarantees*, we suppose, are as good now as they were before; that is, good for nothing. ...A. A. Kelley & Co. are still operating, and assure the public that the Gift Concert will positively *come off*. Please keep in mind that this concert was to have been given July 5th, 1866, then September, 1866, then November 17th, 1866, then January 27th, 1867, then July 4th, 1867, and now at some *indefinite* time. Let fools send in their money for tickets. ...Matthew Westbrook & Co. would like to send more of their cheap Greenbacks, Watches, Jewelry, several hundred Pianos, Organs, Sewing Machines, etc., etc.; that is, they would like to get your money on their promises to do such things. Matthew says he runs one end of this town—give him a wide berth. He is under bonds for trial. ...H. Ballou Carter, Hampstead, N. H., pretends to want to furnish counterfeit greenbacks done in the best style, $3 for $1, $12 for $5, and 4 V's for $10. If you want to *throw away* your money, it can easily be done nearer home. ...R. H. Foster & Co., Chas. Miner & Co., S. Curtis, and others, offer to send Watches, Chains, Jewelry, etc., etc., $30 to $100 worth, for from $4.50 to $10. Curtis don't want money orders or registered letters sent to him. What is the matter? It will not injure an honest man to sign his name at the post office for such documents. ...We are glad to announce that an Association for the Suppression of Gamblers has been formed in this city, and we understand that their attention has already been turned to these Gift Enterprises and other swindles. We wish them God speed in their truly Herculean task.

The Death of Wm. N. White.—Mr. Wm. N. White, editor of the Southern Cultivator, died at Athens, Ga., on July 14th. The Southern Cultivator was the only agricultural paper that sustained itself during the rebellion, and it was maintained mainly by the great energy of Mr. White. While we had occasion to differ with Mr. W on many points, we never lost our admiration for his agricultural and horticultural knowledge, nor for his personal character. The cause of agriculture in the South has, in Mr. White, lost a zealous and intelligent advocate, and the horticultural community, one of its most devoted members.

Bread Kneading is well done by a machine advertised on another page. This, in large families, especially, will be appreciated. The machine is simple, works on the right principle, and is very durable.

Cotswold Sales in England.—Cotswold sheep breeders in this country look with interest for the reports of the annual ram sales. Private letters state that fifty rams of the flock of Wm. Lane, of Broadfield Farm, sold, July 24th, for an average of £21 17s. 11d., and fifty of Robert Garne's flock, of Aldsworth, brought an average of £24 14s. 8d., on the following day.

Begin on your Clubs this Month.—The Premium List for 1868 is not quite ready, but the Publishers will complete it this month, and send to all who may desire it. Do not wait for this, but **start your clubs at once**. You can choose the premium after the new list comes out. Both old and new names will be counted in the premium clubs. The special offer to *new* subscribers will aid you greatly in securing names, as the extra numbers will be sent to all *new* subscribers on your list, **provided** *they are thus marked when received by us.*

N. B.—*Mark every list* of names designed for a premium club, *when you send it in*. This insures its entry to the credit of the sender in our Premium Book.

State Bank Bills.—There are still in circulation some of the old State bank bills. The charters of some of these banks have already expired, and their bills are sold at a discount, or are entirely worthless. Many others will soon follow. Some bank notes that were good yesterday, last week, or last month, are worthless to-day. We advise the sending in for redemption at once the notes of ALL STATE BANKS. Take the greenbacks—as many as you can get honestly.

Fuller's Small Fruit Culturist.—Now that the small fruits are receiving deserved attention, the work of Mr. Fuller comes most opportunely. Those who wish to embark in this most profitable culture, can have no safer guide. Much preparatory work has to be done in autumn, and in many places, planting at this season is advisable. Nowhere else can such complete directions be found as in the work under notice. It has been very favorably noticed by the press. The Gardener's Monthly, a periodical that is always very discriminating in its book notices, and never given to undue praise, says in its August number: "A well-printed and illustrated octavo of 276 pages, giving the results of Mr. Fuller's experience and observations on the culture of small fruits. It is a common proverb that "Doctors disagree," and especially is this true of fruit Doctors, no two of whom agree as to the best way of treating anything, if we are to judge by reports of discussions at fruit meetings. But after a careful perusal of Mr. Fuller's book, we can say we think he has been fortunate in hitting on the true medium or common ground wherein most of the best practical men will agree with him; and thus has been fortunate enough to produce a work which will prove generally acceptable alike to those who believe they know, and to those who want to know the best general way to grow small fruits."

Report of Central Park.—The Tenth Annual Report of the Commissioners of the Central Park has been received from A. H. Green, Esq., Controller. We are always glad to get these reports, as they not only advise us of the progress of this great work, but they give many useful details concerning road making and similar matters. A set of them will be invaluable to a person undertaking any work of this kind. The present volume is illustrated by several maps, and plans, and photographs of scenes in the park. Among the latter is a representation of some noticeably fine designs for stone carving, by J. Wrey Mould, the well known Architect.

Fruit Notes from Ohio.—Mr. G. W. Campbell, Delaware, Ohio, sends us the following notes on fruits in his locality: "Most kinds of grapes are doing well this season. The Iona is doing better than ever before. Fruiting vines perfectly free from rot and mildew. Concords, near by, rotting slightly; the first time I have had any rot upon this variety. Catawbas, I am told, are rotting pretty badly about Sandusky, and upon the Islands—to the extent of one-fourth to one-half of the crop. Delawares are doing better than last season, wherever I have heard from or seen them, and seem to be increasing in favor among the vineyardists of the Lake Shore region. The Agriculturist and Jucunda have proved the finest of all strawberries on my grounds this season, the former much the stronger and more vigorous plant. The Clarke Raspberry promises well here. Stood 25° below zero perfectly uninjured, in several localities, all fully exposed, and without protection.

The Horticultural Indelible Pencil.—The Indelible Pencil Co., Northampton, Mass., make a pencil for the use of gardeners, nurserymen, etc., with which we are much pleased. Ordinary wooden labels are moistened with a solution of soda or saleratus, and the pencil is used like an ordinary lead pencil. We have had labels out during three months of the rainiest of seasons, and cannot see any change in the writing.

Pickled Grapes.—Drop grapes into hot spiced vinegar. The better the grapes, the better the pickles. Put up a jar of these, and you will be sorry you had not put up more.

Catalogue of Agricultural Implements, etc., etc.—We have received from R. H. Allen & Co., 189 Water St., New-York, one of the largest, and best illustrated catalogues we have ever seen, we presume the most complete ever published in this country.

The Size of a Peach Crate.—The crate used for sending peaches and some other fruits to the New York market is 24 inches long, 8 inches high, and 14 inches wide. The end pieces and central partition are of half-inch stuff. The sides are of quarter-inch boards. The top and bottom are covered by five slats, 24 inches long, 2½ inches wide, and ¼ inch thick.

Sending by Express.—Good natured Mr. A., living in Illinois or Wisconsin, has some apples of which he would like to know the name, and he puts up a few dozen in a box, and sends them by express, at the same time writing us a polite letter, informing us that he has sent the apples, and asks the name. We have been too good-natured to inform Mr. A. that we had to pay from $2 to $3 express charges, and that the apples were of a common sort that would have been readily recognized by the nearest nurseryman or orchardist. This thing has become a little extravagant, and an item of expense which we wish to stop. Most of the things sent for our inspection are for the purpose of eliciting information for the benefit of the sender. We submit that it is not fair that we should pay the charges.

Rye for Early Feeding.—"Young Farmer," Cumberland Co., Ill. Rye makes excellent and the earliest spring feed, but if pastured it is very rapidly fed off and destroyed. The best plan is to mow it, and feed to cattle or swine in the stall or pen. Though, if fed off first by cattle, and then by swine, it might be economically consumed. How early it will do to feed it off, we cannot say, but it is making its most rapid growth just about the time that grass begins to be fit for grazing. The period for the most economical cutting and feeding is between the first appearance of the heads and their full growth before blossoming. Rather, perhaps, after the heads begin to show, and before wheat arrives at the same stage. Wheat comes later, but makes better feed, because so much more leafy. Sow the wheat earlier than the rye in autumn.

LOOK AT THIS.—Fifteen Months for One Year's Subscription.—The attention of all our readers is called to the very liberal offer made on a preceding page. It will be seen that the *American Agriculturist*, for the last three months of 1867, will be **given** to all *new* subscribers for 1868, whose subscriptions are received in September. Will *all our friends* make this offer known to *all their friends!* This offer is only for September.

Salt and Plaster Mixed, for Grass Land.—"B. Z." The theorizers are, and have been, at loggerheads about these two articles, in trying to settle how they act as manure, and in endeavoring to give us rules for the application of each by itself. As yet, no one has troubled himself much about the mixture. Practically they may be applied separately or mixed, and in such proportions as one's judgment shall dictate. Experiments are always instructive, and, in the absence of sound bases to found opinions on, always try different quantities in making the mixture, or the application of any fertilizer; also use each ingredient alone, and keep a record of everything in black and white.

The Crops and the Weather.—The solicitude of the public, and especially of the mercantile community, in regard to the crops has been in a great measure relieved, and though business is still dull, the hopes of people seem to presage prosperous times in the near future. The Monthly Report of the Department of Agriculture opens with the statement that never before has the Department been able to report so favorable a prospect for uniformly good crops. There are, indeed, localities in which some crops are a comparative failure, or much damaged by the insects or the weather, but, on the whole, our information up to the middle of August, gathered from correspondents, exchanges, and personal observation, (which has been quite extensive, covering a good portion of New York, Pennsylvania, New Jersey, Ohio, Indiana, and New England,) confirms the view taken by the Department of Agriculture.

The great *Wheat* crop of the country has been secured in unusually good condition, and if well thrashed and marketed, will meet high expectations as regards quality; and in respect to the amount of wheat raised this year, though early for accurate estimates, the opinion is general that the crop will prove very heavy. The rains which have affected the seaboard, caused some injury to grain, but this will not influence the general result.

Rye, where much raised, has turned out well on the whole, the lightness of the grain being, in general, compensated by the excellence of the straw.

The *Corn* crop of the West is looking finely; localities which feared drought have generally been relieved, and the reports are numerous that not a curled leaf has been seen this season in *many* localities. At the East, the crop is still backward. At the South, the abundant crops both of small grain and corn have relieved the pressure of hunger on the part of many of the poor and improvident, so that now, if we may credit newspaper reports, in Texas, corn, which was worth $4.00 per bushel, is selling as low as 25 cents.

Oats.—The crop will probably be an average one. It is as yet too early to learn accurately, as the crop is not cut throughout the most extensive oat producing regions.

Grass.—The product has been very large, the late and continuous rains having thickened it up by a short undergrowth, which has added largely to the bulk and quality of the hay. A large part of that of New England and the seaboard was harvested well, but much in bad condition.

Potatoes.—The promise of a very fine crop is still held out throughout the West, Central New York, and Pennsylvania; but the rot has affected many localities quite seriously, and fears are entertained that the malady will affect the general crop of the country.

Sorghum.—*Tobacco.*—The product of syrup will be less than that of last year, and the tobacco crop will be less than the average.

Cotton.—The reports are generally very favorable. Central Louisiana seems to be the most marked exception, though in many sections a deficiency of labor allowed the grass to get such a start during the wet weather, that the crop is not nearly so good as it should have been.

Fruit.—Apples are a failure in the Middle States, east of the Alleghanies, but good in parts of New England and the West. Peaches are most abundant.

Brinckle's Orange Raspberry Blighted.—A. S. Jack, Province of Quebec, Canada. You do not say whether your vines were protected in winter or not. From your description of the blight we should infer that it was caused by a cold and wet spell, just at blossoming time. This is a most critical period with all fruits, and unfortunately we cannot control the weather. A cold rain, just when bushes or trees are in flower, prevents fertilization, and as a consequence we get very little, or no fruit. English gardeners often cover their dwarf pear trees with a screen or tent while in bloom.

Musquito Nets or Bars for Windows.—These can easily be manufactured at home, and the pest of autumn be effectually barred out. First make a frame for the netting, that will just fit into the lower part of the window. If you have a pine board, a saw, and a jack plane, make them yourself; if not, you can buy mouldings about 1¼ inches wide, by ⅜ thick, for one to two cents a foot. With a knife, a fine saw and a few tacks or wooden pegs, the frame can be joined together at the corners. Now stretch over it the mosquito netting, and fasten with tape and tacks, and your work is done. It is light and handy, and a great comfort in all regions where these insects flourish. We have just completed four, and are ready for dog days. The netting cost sixteen cents each, and the material for the frames about twenty cents each. A boy or girl can readily make the frames, and sleep all the better for it.

Sheep Raising at the West.—A gentleman in Illinois, after four years' experience in this business has discovered that his practice does not correspond with the theory of the papers. He says in the Prairie Farmer: "My losses have been greater; my percentage of lambs less; my weight of clip less; the price obtained for my wool less, and I have been generally and particularly disappointed. Sheep bite so close that when a drouth comes it uses up a pasture much worse than when stocked with cattle. I have about come to the conclusion that one sheep will eat, of grass, as much as two steers." If his former conclusions are as reliable as this last, they will not be likely to damage sheep raising on the prairies very much.

Wiegela Nivea.—Under this name, Mr. Geo. Such, South Amboy, N. J., sends us a Wiegela with pure white flowers.—Very beautiful.

Making Vinegar.—P. T. S. Hard cider will turn to vinegar very soon, by exposing it to the atmosphere in a warm place. Allowing it to run slowly from one vessel into another, over a platform covered with oak shavings, will hasten the process. A few drops of red cabbage water will make the color a deeper red, if people desire it.

Massachusetts Agricultural College.—Prof. Chadborne has resigned the Presidency. Prof. Wm. S. Clark, of Amherst College, has been elected President by the Trustees. Prof. E. S. Snell, also of Amherst College, has been offered the Chair of Mathematics and Engineering, and Prof. H. H. Goodell, of Williston Seminary, East Hampton, Mass., has been appointed instructor in French, Gymnastics, and Military Science.

A Tree Swindle.—L. Newton, Washington, Iowa, sends a leaf of a tree which some nurserymen are selling for "Silver Maple." The leaf is that of the Silver Poplar, or Abele—one of the worst nuisances among trees. It suckers so badly that it is unfit for any place except a paved street. The Silver-leaved Maple is *Acer dasycarpum*, also called White Maple, and in some places at the West, Soft Maple. The Soft Maple of the East is *Acer rubrum*, also called Red and Swamp Maple.

Nutritive Value of Corn of Different Colors.—Wm. Brummer, of Iowa, asks, "What is the nutritive value of our white western corn compared with the yellow or mixed?" Color is no indication of nutritive value, except as it is a feature of a particular variety. The only reliable guide is *weight*, when the varieties compared are of about the same degree of dryness, or have been exposed to the same conditions of temperature, circulation of air, etc., for several weeks. The heaviest corn will be found to be the most nutritive, provided both can be equally well digested.

Much Land to be Possessed.—New York, the great dairy State of the Union, is said to produce less than a ton of hay to the acre on an average. The pastures are still less productive, for it is the best land that is kept in meadow. The Eastern States average still less. There are large tracts that do not yield a dollar's worth of grass to the acre. We know of a twelve hundred acre farm that rents for a thousand dollars, and we suppose the rent is some criterion of its value. It is a sad sight to travel through such farms—often situated within a half hour's ride of good markets, and behold the neglect and slovenly farming. What a good time there will be when these farms are redeemed, and made to yield their increase! He who has skill and capital, need not go West to find a profitable field for his investment. New England and New York can be more cheaply fed from their own soil, than from the prairies of the West and from the shores of the Pacific. California wheat for sale in Rochester! Ohio butter and cheese in New England! What a comment upon our husbandry!

English Market Reports.—*£. s. d.* "E. E.," of Philo, Ill., reads the reports of foreign markets, and asks the value of Pounds, Shillings, and Pence, Sterling. *Sterling* is the name applied to the currency of Great Britain, and means hard money. A *pound* Sterling (£) is worth, at par, $4.84; a *shilling* (*s*) is one-twentieth of a pound, hence worth 24 cents 2 mills; a *penny* (*d*) is one-twelfth of a shilling, hence is worth a little more than 2 cents. All these values are in gold, with exchange at par. Now our gold values are very different from paper or currency values, and this difference must be included in the calculation of values of grain, etc. Besides, the state of trade varies—at one time making the merchants of this country in debt to England, at which time the pound sterling is worth here more than $4.84; at another time the merchants of England are in debt to us, and then exchange is said to be in our favor, and the pound is worth less than its par value. A "quarter" is 8 bushels, and wheat is calculated at 60 pounds to the bushel; hence the quarter of wheat is 480 pounds.

Holcus Tartaricum.—This year, a new cereal has been advertised in England, under the name of *Holcus Tartaricum* and *Sorghum Tartaricum*. The London Field has tried seed from three sources, and thus records its opinion: "Here then we have one of the gigantic humbugs of modern times; but we ought to be thankful that the puffs were so big, and the seed so dear that little soil was wasted in the trials; at the same time it is most devoutly to be wished, for the good of all, that matters of this kind should not be so lavishly extolled without due trial, or very good evidence on the part of those by whom they are so authoritatively recommended." We quite agree with the Field, and give its caution for the benefit of our readers, as this "new cereal" will probably make its way here. From all we can learn, it deserves a place along side of *Bromus Schraderi*.

Value of Farms in Indiana.—In Marion County, in which the capital of the State is situated, farms will average $75 to the acre. This county is about twenty miles square, and contains some of the best land in the world. Nothing can exceed the fertility of the White River bottoms. The clay lands are not so valuable for some purposes, and much better for others. Excellent farms, with comfortable buildings, can be bought in this State for $50 an acre, which would be worth $200 an acre in any part of Connecticut or Rhode Island. In Benton County, 24,000 acres of land were bought for about $6 an acre, and in this and the adjacent counties, wild lands are still to be had for about that price. In Allen County, within a few miles of Fort Wayne, improved lands can be bought from $15 to $30 an acre. We were informed that farms with improvements upon them could be bought cheaper in this county than in any other part of the State. There are plenty of cheap farming lands in Indiana, and it is unquestionably one of the best States for thriving Eastern people to go to. The land is superb, and only needs skill and capital to make its owners independently rich.

Price of Land in Pennsylvania.—A subscriber inquires for the price of land in the Valley of the Susquehanna, Pa. In Buffalo Valley, which comes down upon the Susquehanna, at Louisburg and Milton, a district about ten miles broad by twenty long, the value of farms will average $150 per acre. In the Paradise Valley, on the opposite side of the river, the price of land is about the same. These lands are probably as productive as any in the State. In the immediate vicinity of the large towns and villages, where there is a prospect of selling building lots, land is worth from $500 to $3000 an acre. Good land in all the Valley of the Susquehanna is worth from $75 an acre upwards. The farms run large, and would probably average 150 to 200 acres to the farm. Back on the hills, remote from railroads and other privileges, land can be had much cheaper, say from $15 to $30 per acre, and is dearer than land that costs ten times more.

Salmon Culture in Australia is entirely successful. The eggs were carried 16,000 miles, packed in ice, and successfully hatched three years ago. This year they have a fine run of salmon up the Derwent river, and a promise of abundance for home use and export. These eggs were a magnificent present to that island continent. Let us profit by this example.

Chess—the Crucial Test.—On page 244, (July No.,) we say: "When we can be shown a plant that is part wheat and part chess, we shall be willing to discuss the subject." Mr. P. P. Severance, of Greenfield, Mass., sends us two specimens of plants of wheat and chess, growing with their roots so intertwined as to appear to be but one plant. On putting them under a stream of water, and washing all the dirt off, the roots slipped apart, and showed no sign of connection. If this is the best the transmutationists can do, we must still decline to "discuss the subject,"—of wheat turned to chess.

Barn Cellars.—In a recent trip through Connecticut and Massachusetts, we were struck with this almost universal appendage of new barns. They are generally built in the most substantial manner, and well supplied with muck. Farmers who economize as closely as New Englanders generally do, would hardly make this investment unless it paid. We noticed also, that the best farms invariably were those that had the barn cellars. These are the stomachs of the farms, indispensable in the North, and soon to be so on the new farms of the West.

Willow Trees About Wells.—A subscriber wishes to know if these will injure the water. The popular belief that they will is well founded. The roots will go very far and deep to find the water, and will impart vegetable matter to it which affects the taste. The leaves also will be likely to fall into the well and defile it. All trees should be kept away from it, and the mouth of the well should have ventilation. The old sweep with an oaken bucket was useful in keeping away trees.

Insects' Eggs.—Geo. Surface, Upshur, Ohio. The eggs are those of the tent caterpillar. We have more than once figured them. Remove all you can find. They do not hatch until spring, and are readily seen in winter.

The State Alms-house at Palmer, Mass., is a model institution of a model State, and well worth visiting for its lessons of economy in farming. A poor worn-out farm has gradually been brought up to a high state of productiveness, by utilizing every thing that too often runs to waste in public institutions. The privies, the styes, the barn-yard, the waste water from the house, are all made to pay tribute to the soil. It stands on a beautiful eminence overlooking the village, and the meadows and gardens looked greener than ever, as we recently passed them. The inmates are not exactly self-supporting, but the cost of their maintenance is very much diminished by their location upon this farm.

Salmon in the Connecticut.—Satisfactory laws, we are informed, have been passed by the Connecticut Legislature, just adjourned, for the protection of this fish, according to the programme laid down by the New England Fish Commissioners. The eggs placed in the upper waters of the stream were hatched, and the young *fry* are said to be now making their first visit to the sea, in large numbers. In three years more we hope to be eating this fish from the Connecticut, whence it disappeared more than fifty years ago. Cheap salmon is a great desideratum in our markets, and with suitable legislation it can once more be realized.

A Cheese Factory in England.—A meeting was held in Cheshire, June 22d, to discuss a cheese factory, at which American example was quoted with favor. A committee was appointed to investigate the factory system and report. We are astonished at this. John is so confident that he can do everything better than his neighbors, that he seldom looks abroad for a new idea. He has been over thirty years trying to get so simple a thing as the connecting of a train of steam cars by a bell rope, through his head, and does not see it yet. If he sees a cheese factory before the millenium, we shall be happily disappointed.

Elms and Evergreens.—G. W. W., Green Castle, Ind. There is no elm equal to the American, or White Elm. It bears removal better than any other tree, and we have seen trees twenty to thirty feet high successfully transplanted. Of course, the tops must be cut back, in proportion to the shortening of the roots. They grow with great rapidity, and we should prefer trees of smaller size, say ten to fifteen feet high. As to the best evergreen for a door yard, our taste inclines to Hemlock, though the Norway Spruce is more generally planted. Whatever one is chosen, always keep the upper branches from overhanging, and stifling the lower ones.

Notes on Farming in Indiana.—We have heard much of the dairies of the Western Reserve of Ohio, of the blue grass pastures of Kentucky, of the boundless prairies of Illinois, and its seas of Indian corn, but whoever heard of anything remarkable in the agricultural line in the State of Indiana? That there were farms there, tilled by thinking people, our large list of subscribers testified; but beyond this we looked upon the State as a sort of *terra incognita*, that needed exploring. Approaching Indianapolis, the capital of the State, by rail, from Columbus, Ohio, our first impressions were of a new level country, half subdued and imperfectly tilled, yet everywhere giving evidence of the overflowing riches of its soil. Along the line of the road, one is rarely out of sight of broken forests, dead trees and stumps, luxuriant meadows burdened with grass, oats, and corn. The breadth of wheat sown is less than in former years, but is everywhere good, and the yield is considered satisfactory, though but about one half what better husbandry would give. The weather has been everything that the farmers could desire during the wheat harvest, clear and sunny, and there will probably be very little sprouted or unsound wheat in the market this year.

INDIANAPOLIS.—We rubbed our eyes as we stepped out of the depot amid a bustling population of 40,000, into wide streets, with great warehouses and imposing public buildings. This is the railroad center of the State, and here seven lines daily discharge their passengers and freight. The city has grown quite rapidly in population and wealth during the war, and the thousands that the necessities of the war brought hither seem still to linger. It is a large market town for agricultural produce, and grain is shipped in large quantities, in favorable seasons, to various points East and South. A railway connects it with Michigan City, upon the lake, and with Jeffersonville, upon the Ohio river, nearly opposite Louisville. We found old corn selling at 63 cents a bushel upon the cob, reckoning 68 pounds to the bushel; and new wheat at $2 a bushel. A farmer's wagon, loaded with wheat, is said to be quite a novel sight in the streets, the last two years having given very poor crops of this grain. The farmers are thrashing the wheat as fast as possible, eager to realize good prices while they can. The expectation is general that wheat will be lower as soon as the harvest is gathered.

THE STATE AGRICULTURAL SOCIETY has its headquarters here in the State House, and is much ahead of the State authorities in its enterprise. It issued several interesting volumes of transactions previous to the war, receiving appropriations from the State to foot the bills. These were widely distributed through the State, and did much to quicken the zeal of the people in agricultural improvement. When the war broke out, this appropriation was withheld in a spasm of very short-sighted economy, and no volume has been published since that of 1859 and 1860. One has been authorized for the present year. The State Society owns thirty-six acres of land in the suburbs of the city, which has been fitted up as a fair ground. Buildings were put up, and about $9000 were expended upon them last year. They have a like sum on hand, and are making preparations for a State Fair at Terre Haute, in September. There are ninety-two counties in the State, of which fifty-three have organized societies. Twenty-two were discontinued during the war.

FARM OF F. M. CHURCHMAN.—This gentleman is a banker in the city, and resorts to farming in the suburbs, for recreation and health. He has about 200 acres, threaded by a brook, which is a pleasant feature in any farm, and much more so here, where clear streams are not abundant. The home is a neat white cottage, about twenty feet above the water. The bank furnishes a living spring, which has been utilized for a milk-house, and to supply in part a fish pond in the valley below. This valley is shaded with magnificent trees, which have been left from the primitive forest. We found here under the Sugar Maples and Burr Oaks, well bred Devons from the herd of E. Faile, of Westchester Co., N. Y. Cotswold sheep from the flock of Mr. Loomis, of Hartford, Conn. Chester White pigs and Brahma fowls.

THIS IMPROVED STOCK flourishes at the West, and is not likely to lose any of its good points under the supervision of the present owner. The only danger is that the Devons may become too fat for breeding in the very abundant food which the Indiana lands furnish. The Shorthorns usually attain their best development in the adjoining State of Kentucky, and the beef families of this breed are probably the most profitable for Indiana farmers. The Cotswold and Chester Whites are at home here, and the soil and climate, with good breeding, will unquestionably perpetuate their best points. Improved stock of all kinds is very much needed in the State. The want is generally felt among intelligent farmers, and there is a disposition to invest in this line of improvement. Mr. Churchman has made a good beginning. We noticed with great interest the commencement of *tile draining* upon this farm—an improvement more needed in this State than almost anything else. The drains were put down about three feet, and were working well. Though there is very little swamp land in this State, there are millions of acres of heavy clay loams, that can never be made to yield more than half a crop until they are drained. They have a compact soil, and cannot be worked in the spring on account of water. Fortunately the material for making tile is very widely distributed, and the coal and wood for burning them is abundant. One of the best enterprises that could be started in the suburbs of this city would be a manufactory of tile. The transforming power of good drainage is so wonderful, and the remuneration is so large, that a few examples would set the whole region in a blaze of excitement upon this subject. We expect to hear of forty bushels of winter wheat to the acre, and one hundred bushels of corn upon clay loams, when this improvement is generally introduced.

STEAM THRASHERS are a prominent feature in Western husbandry. The horse thrashers are still in use, but are as certainly doomed as the scythe or the hand rake. They are altogether too slow for this age. The steam thrasher is mounted upon wheels, and is drawn by horses from place to place, as it is wanted. It costs about $1700, with all the apparatus necessary for running. The power may also be used for chaffing straw, hay, and corn stalks, for sawing wood, and other purposes. It takes fourteen hands to work it, where the wheat is brought in from the shocks, and it will clean, ready for market, 800 bushels of wheat in a day. The price of thrashing is eight cents a bushel. Wheat straw is sold in town for $10 a ton for paper making and for bedding, and forms an important item in the farmer's profits. The great advantage of the steam thrasher is that it puts the wheat harvest so much into the power of the farmer. As a rule, wheat stands in the shock until it is thrashed, and the first good weather is availed of to clean the crop, and send it to market. As yet, there is no adequate provision made for storing wheat in first hands, and this is one great disadvantage that the producer must labor under until he secures better barns. He cannot hold on to his wheat for a rise, unless he keeps it in stack, and there it is exposed somewhat to the weather, and still more to the depredations of rats and mice. Tens of thousands of bushels of this precious grain are lost almost every year by sprouting and moulding.

THE WHITE RIVER BOTTOMS are a splendid corn region, and the sun shines upon no richer land. We saw a single field of three hundred acres, where we were informed corn had been planted from the first settlement of the country, and the yield was still from sixty to one hundred bushels per acre, in good years. The land is annually overflowed, and needs no other fertilizer than the deposit of the river. This is the general experience upon all the bottom lands of the White and Wabash rivers and their tributaries that are subject to overflow. When the great length of these rivers and the breadth of their bottoms is recalled, we have some conception of the vast extent of the corn lands of the State, which must be inexhaustible while water runs.

Notes on Farming in the Grain Districts of Pennsylvania and New Jersey.—Traveling toward Easton, through Morris and Warren Counties, New Jersey, one of the first things that strikes the eastern farmer, is the greatly *increased size of the fields*. The one and two acre lots so common in his observation, have expanded to ten and twenty acres, and thirty and forty acres are not uncommon. Farming is manifestly pursued upon a much larger scale. There is a clean sweep for the sulky cultivators and harrows among the corn, and for the reapers and mowers among the grain and grass. In some cases the fields have always been upon this generous scale, in others, the stone walls and hedges have been removed, in order to enlarge them. We found one farmer who had just cleaned out the old fences, and made several smaller fields into one of 60 acres. Very little time will be lost in turning round at the ends of the rows, and little corn trampled in cultivation. Another noticeable feature of the farming here is the much *larger proportion of plowed land*. From a fourth to one-half of the land is kept in grain. On one farm we saw 80 acres in corn, 25 in wheat, and as much more in oats. On another 200-acre farm, we found 80 in wheat, 50 in corn, and 30 in oats. Grain fields of from 20 to 50 acres are common. Probably not less than a fourth part of all the cleared lands in the valley of the Susquehanna is in these three grains, the present season.

THE VALLEY OF THE LEHIGH, which we enter at Easton, is one of the richest in the State. The soil is fertile, and is well cultivated at the lower part, with the usual grain crop. Rye stands side by side with the winter wheat, and is nearly as extensively cultivated. The soil is full of limestone and iron ore, and the coal is near at hand. The leading business in the villages below Mauch Chunk is the smelting of iron ore, and the manufacturing of the metal. The foundries and rolling mills support a large population, and one is hardly ever out of sight of the smoke stacks of these institutions. We were surprised to see the extent and thrift of these iron cities and villages. By giving variety to the industry of the region, they are a great advantage to its agriculture. Almost everything that can be raised upon the adjacent farms finds a ready market at good prices in these villages. At Mauch Chunk, the coal mines first begin to disgorge their contents, and a new industry absorbs the whole attention. The mines are several miles back from the river, and the coal is brought by rail to the top of the bluff at a very moderate grade, whence it is either discharged into a shoot that conducts it into canal boats, or sent down in cars by a wire rope attached to a windlass, the loaded cars drawing up the empty ones. All the Lehigh coal mines in this basin send their freights to market down this valley, either by rail or by canal. Above the coal district there is an extensive lumber region, and vast quantities of peeled hemlock logs are seen in the ponds, made by damming the river. There are vast tracts of forest above White Haven, with very few clearings, poor, rough land, that will probably pay better to grow timber for generations to come than for any other purpose. Two rival railroads have found their way through this wild region to the

WYOMING VALLEY, for the traffic of which both are struggling. Much has been said and sung of this charming valley, but, with all this in mind, we were not prepared for the vision of beauty that burst upon us as we emerged from the wilderness on the crest of the mountain, some twelve hundred feet above. One gets glimpses of it through the rifts in the forest all the way down until the depot at Wilkesbarre, on the banks of the Susquehanna, is reached. Coal of an excellent quality underlies the whole region for a distance of forty-four miles long, by about three in width, and by its superior value has spoiled one of the finest farming districts in the State. Unimproved coal lands are worth from $300 to $500 an acre for mining purposes, and have been bought up extensively by companies, who care very little for the surface of the soil. It is estimated that not one-fourth of the land is tilled by people who own it. It is very generally leased, and the tenant looks for present profit without much regard to the future of the soil. In some parts of the valley, where the land has been bought up on speculation, the farmhouses are abandoned and the fences are broken down. Mining also works to the disadvantage of the farmer in enhancing the price of labor. During the war, skillful miners were making from $8 to $10 a day, and even now they make $5, working about nine hours. Those who work with them to break up the coal, and load it into the cars, make about $1.75 per day, which is too high for farming. Of course, it is somewhat difficult to get labor, and agriculture has to give place to mining. But notwithstanding these drawbacks, there is some good husbandry in the valley. The bottom lands of the river are very productive, and though overflowed in the freshets almost every year, are frequently sown with winter grain. There is a County Agricultural Society organized in the valley, which has its exhibition grounds, and holds an annual fair at Wyoming.

Our Exhibitions of Poultry.

The only poultry shows that we have, so far as we are aware, in this country, are held in connection with, and as part of our State and County Agricultural Fairs, with the single exception of those of the Worcester Co. (Mass.,) Poultry Club. At these fairs, fowls, geese, turkeys, ducks, and fancy poultry, pigeons, etc., are arranged in the utmost disregard of order, except so far as to group the coops and cages of each exhibitor by themselves. One would suppose that for his own convenience, and to show off his birds to the best advantage, an exhibitor would have his coops made nearly alike, and of one or two definite sizes, but we often find every imaginable form of box, coop, and cage, some neat and convenient, others dirty and inconvenient; though some exhibitors do better.

The judges are, no doubt, selected conscientiously by the managing officers, but as they frequently know little or nothing of the points of excellence in fancy poultry, they err in judgment, make poor awards, and help to establish false notions about the different breeds, to poor specimens of which they give value by awarding high and entirely unmerited premiums.

The American Poultry Society begins its career by announcing its intention to do what it can to correct these things. It has decided that each entry shall consist of one pair only, and that each pair, except of turkeys and pea-fowls, shall be exhibited in coops 3 feet in width, 2 feet in depth, and 2½ feet in hight, perpendicularly slatted on the front, and provided with boxes and cups for food and water. We presume that these coops might be divided so as to accommodate two pairs of bantams, or small ducks, but they are none too large to show off a fine cock and hen of any of the larger breeds, and barely large enough for geese.

The most tasteful and convenient exhibition cages we have ever seen, were of wickerwork, and the space allowed by the Society, viz.: 2 × 2 feet on the shelf, and 2½ feet high, would be abundant for such a basket-work coop. Any basket weaver could make one in a short time, and with little explanation. A good size and shape would be 18 inches in diameter at the base, the sides 20 inches high, flaring to exactly 2 feet in diameter, outside measure, the top coming to a point with a handle upon it, so that the whole hight should be not more than 2½ feet. The willow rods forming the sides should stand up and down, 2 inches apart, and the top should

BASKET-WORK COOP.

be formed of the same rods bent and drawn together. Unless the rods are very stiff, they will need a narrow band woven around the middle to prevent their being spread apart. The bottom is movable, and may be made of a round piece of board, or of basket-work, which is much lighter, covered with a piece of floor oilcloth, or canvas, for cleanliness. There need be no door, the birds and their food being put in from beneath. The bottom is pinned in securely when the coop is moved.

Would it not be well for Agricultural Societies to take some uniform stand in regard to the manner in which birds should be exhibited? If the size of coops adopted by the American Poultry Society is right, then let it be generally adopted and the rule strictly adhered to.

Thorough Draining—The Secret of Success in a Nutshell.

The present practice in regard to thorough draining has not been arrived at simply by the reasoning of engineers and physicists, but by a long course of practical experiments, guided by sound philosophy. If any man says that open drains are good enough, we can now show him in thousands of cases that covered ones are vastly better; if one claims that 2-foot drains are deep enough, we can refer him to farms where 2-foot drains gave place to 3-foot ones, with a great increase of good results, and where, keeping pace with the march of ideas, the use of 3-foot has given place to that of 4-foot drains. Stones, wherever used, and no matter what the necessity for getting rid of them, give way to tiles—for the whole cost of digging, laying and filling 4-foot tile drains on any ordinary land is not so great as the handling of the stone alone, as stone drains are usually made; besides this, their shallowness, liability to fill up, and the fine harbor they present for vermin, ensure their condemnation. Nevertheless, a badly laid tile drain is worse than a stone one. So true is this, that we can name an excellent Connecticut farmer of large means who had tiles replaced by stone drains, at a heavy expense, and who rejoices now in much better drained land than before, with fewer stoppages and trouble from imperfect drainage. The reason was that the tiles were poorly laid and much too near the surface, so becoming filled with roots at some places, and deranged by receiving surface water at others, they failed adequately to drain the land.

There are places where drains must be laid shallow, not more than 20 or 30 inches deep. For such spots, wherever the roots of grass might cause obstruction, we prefer to use *brush drains*, for they last a long time, are no more likely to fill up than stone ones, are cheap, and easily dug out and mended, if repairs are needed.

No one should undertake the drainage of farm lands without thoroughly understanding the principles on which good drains act, and are made. We have prepared a diagram to illustrate these principles. It is a section of the ground, crossing a drain, showing the drain tile (*C*) laid in collars at a depth of 4 feet, with a packing of clay (*E*) well rammed down above it, to prevent surface water finding its way downwards to the tile, and any water entering from above. It shows the level at which water (*W*) stands in the ground, and the drops of water (*D*) trickling down through the soil and blending with the water of the soil at the level of the drain. Were there no drain there, the water level would rapidly rise until it reached the surface, but as fast or almost as fast as it rises the drain carries it off. The upper part of the filling of the drain trench (*B*) is porous and permits the rain to enter, but it is stopped and the water turned off to either side by the clay-filling, or hard-rammed soil below. Water which *rises* into the tile can bring with it but little silt, but that which flows downward into it brings, of necessity almost, sand and much fine silt. How absurdly wrong, then, is the practice of filling-in the lower part of the trench

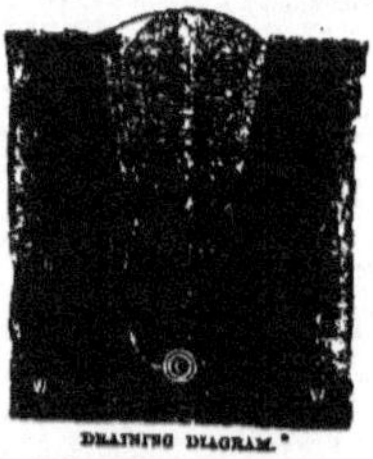

DRAINING DIAGRAM.*

directly above the tiles or stones with loose materials such as swamp grass, sods, shavings, etc.

If the drain be properly constructed, it is almost an impossibility for the occurrence to take place which we have figured at *F*, namely, for a passage to be formed for surface water down to the tile. To obviate all chance for anything of this kind, before the loose filling of the upper part of the trench becomes compacted and like the rest of the soil, no surface water should be allowed to stand or flow over the newly laid drains for a year at least, if it is possible to prevent it, but if impossible, then the trench for its entire depth should be filled with well rammed earth, and the filling raised some inches above the surface. Surface furrows on each side of the drain are effective, if they carry off the water.

We should really wrong our readers did we close an article on draining without alluding to that most excellent book by Col. G. E. Waring, Jr., which was issued the past summer from the press of Orange Judd & Co. We regard the fact that water should always enter the drain from below, and that it does so in all good drains, as the very foundation of successful drainage. In this nutshell is the secret of success. Col. Waring's book is full of just such "nuts."

Hexamer's Wide-Pronged Hoe.

Dr. Hexamer, (Reisig & Hexamer, Ivy Hill Nurseries, New Castle, N. Y.,) has such a sure way of making his investigations and coming at his facts, that we accept his results with almost the same confidence we would have in our own. He makes use of expensive labor, and the month-

WIDE-PRONGED HOE.

ly pay-roll is so large as to lead him to employ his men to the very best advantage. The problem was, what tool to place in the hands of his laborers for hoeing out between rows of strawberries, or other small fruits, root crops, nursery stock, etc. The common hoe is a slow, hard, old-fogy tool, and, of course, its use out of the question. The potato hook, or pronged hoe, with round prongs, good, but not sufficiently rapid for the outlay of strength, yet vastly superior to the hoe for the same purposes, except after weeds have grown large, which ought rarely or never to occur. After having made numerous experiments with tools made expressly for him, he decided upon the implement of which we present an engraving. The six teeth or prongs are eight inches in length, the outer ones being ten inches apart, which is the width of the actual cut. The prongs are square, of the best steel, and inserted in pairs into a malleable iron head, in which they are firmly wedged. They are delicate, but very strong and elastic.

The tool is used by a man walking backwards. It stirs the soil thoroughly more than a foot wide, and from two to four inches deep, killing all small weeds, lifting out stones of small size, removing weeds, and all obstructions as effectually as a rake. On light soil, it is as easily worked as a hoe, and on heavy soils, if dry enough to work at all, very much easier. It is safe to say, that a man with one of these can do several times as much work as with a hoe. We think it will prove more useful as a potato digger, in light soils, on account of its breadth, than the implement made for the purpose.

The American Gray Wolf

This is the wolf of the exciting tales of our childhood, the destroyer of sheep and calves of the frontier settler, the wolf which followed benighted or snow-bewildered travelers in the old colony times. Moreover, it is the White Wolf of the north-western border, the Black Wolf and the Red Wolf of the South, the Dusky Wolf of the West, etc. The tendency of the species to vary is remarkable, and the common European and Asiatic wolves are by some naturalists considered, we believe, as belonging to the same species. The Dog closely resembles the Wolf in some of its varieties, and these species have been very closely studied by naturalists, with the result that they are undecided as to whether the dog is a tamed wolf or not. Some claim that the dog is a distinct species; others, that certain varieties of the dog are descended from wolves, while other varieties sprung from the jackals of Asia. Certain it is that wolves and dogs, and jackals and dogs, will breed together, and their progeny will be fertile with either of the parent species, and, we believe, after the first generation, among themselves. It is said that the northern Indians are in the habit of crossing their sledge dogs with wolves, to gain strength and fleetness.—The picture which accompanies this article is the portrait of a fine animal in the possession of a gentleman of Manchester, N. H., drawn upon the wood by Herrick. We know of no other engraving of the Gray Wolf equal to it. It exhibits all the prominent peculiarities of the animal so accurately, that a further description on our part seems unnecessary. Still we must call attention to the general gauntness so characteristic of wolves, the sharp, snappish muzzle, the convexity of the forehead, the wicked, oblique-set eye, the erect, pointed ears, the powerful muscular development of the forequarters, the protection furnished to the throat and neck, (perhaps the wolf's and dog's most vulnerable part,) by the length and abundance of the hair, and, lastly, to the drooping of the tail, which character is the only one which will enable an unscientific observer to decide at sight between wolves and dogs; for the tails of all dogs have a greater or less tendency to curl up.

The Latin name of the European Wolf is *Canis lupus*, that of the American Wolf *Canis occidentalis;* the Dog is *Canis familiaris*, and the best known of the oriental Jackals, is *Canis aureus*.

Wolves are no longer the terror of farmers over a large part of the older States. They still exist in the densely wooded mountain ranges, and in general wherever deer are found, as these form their principal food. They were formerly so numerous as to warrant the high bounties, amounting often to $15 or $20 each, offered by States, counties, and towns, for their heads. The usual size of the wolf is 3½ to 4½ feet from nose to tail, which is 17 to 20 inches long. The female has 4 to 9 whelps at a birth in the spring, and conceals them so thoroughly in holes and burrows that it is very difficult to get at them. Where wolves are abundant, they hunt in packs, seldom attacking man or animals that will resist them when single; but when pressed by hunger, they are rendered savage and fearless, and at those times devour any animal they can master, singly, or by overpowering numbers. The weaker ones of their own pack are often victims of the ravenous appetite of the rest. Their traits of character are maliciousness, cowardice, treacherousness. They are often so overcome by abject fear, that, when taken in situations which they consider hopeless, they will allow themselves to be handled freely, and killed like sheep. Hunters have been known to jump without harm into pits containing several wolves, seize them by the hind legs, and throw them out to have their throats cut by their companions.

THE AMERICAN GRAY WOLF.—(*Canis occidentalis.*)

Meadow Mice.

These little animals, of which we give an engraving, are familiar to most of our readers, and universally regarded as enemies of the farmer. We know of no plea to set up for their defense; they destroy very considerable quantities of grain and grass seed, frequently penetrating the granary, and taking up their abode in barns. They are often pressed for food in winter, and gnaw the bark of young trees, especially if they gain easy access to them beneath the snow. When numerous during the winter, they often cause a very serious damage to the grass crop by eating the roots. We believe they eat grubs and insects when pressed by hunger, but not from choice. The largest of the group represents a very beautiful and long haired variety of the meadow mouse, two-thirds the natural length. The fur is dark-brown above and ashy beneath, very long and soft—whence it is called the Beaver mouse—and the ears, which are very delicate and membranaceous, but not very small, are almost entirely concealed. These mice are 5 to 5½ inches long, and the tail less than half that length. The one on the left, the common meadow mouse, (*Arvicola riparia*,) is usually found in moist meadows throughout the northern States. It is tawny and very glossy above, and

GROUP OF MEADOW MICE.

of a light lead color below, 4 to $4^{1}/_{2}$ inches long, the tail being about $^{1}/_{2}$ the length of the body. The engraving also shows the light colored meadow mouse, described in the New York State Natural History, which is probably only another variety of the same species.

Walks and Talks on the Farm.—No. 45.

We finished thrashing wheat yesterday. There were 316 bushels from 17 acres of Amber Michigan, and 204 bushels from 12 acres of White Whittaker. The latter yielded the better, but the Amber was the larger and plumper berry, and I think it will make the whiter flour. The White Whittaker wheat, if mine is the genuine article, is not white at all. It is no whiter than good Amber. The chaff is white, and it has large heads, and looks very handsome when it is growing, but the berry is rather small, and the miller would pay no more for it than for the Amber. In fact, two or three of our best millers pronounced the latter the better wheat. I sold the whole crop for $2.50 per bushel. Some of my neighbors who thrashed early got $2.75 for Soule's wheat.

One reason why the white wheat yielded the better, is owing to the fact that three years ago the land received a dressing of five or six hundred pounds of bone-dust per acre, applied to corn. It did comparatively little good on the corn the first year. But the land was full of thistles, and we planted it to corn another year, followed by barley, and then with wheat seeded down. I think the bone-dust helped the corn the second year, and also the barley, and now the wheat has yielded about 4 bushels per acre more than that on land, in the same field, not dressed with bone-dust. And I expect the clover will show a still greater difference. Phosphatic manures, as a general rule, have a better effect on clover than on the cereals. Last year my wheat that was dressed with an ammoniated superphosphate gave a fair crop, due entirely, I think, to the manure. Still the effect was by no means as decided as it is this year on the following crop of clover. A heavier crop of clover is seldom grown, and the second growth is now very fine, promising a good yield of clover seed. The increase of the wheat may hardly pay for the manure, but taking clover and all, the application will be quite profitable.

Mr. Wade, of Port Hope, C. W., was here a few days since, and he thought my clover very fine, but says we do not cut the first crop early enough. One of his neighbors last year raised 70 bushels of clover seed from ten acres, and sold it for $7.00 a bushel in gold. Five bushels per acre is the largest crop I ever heard of before.

"Will not these ammoniacal manures run out your land?" asked a gentleman from Virginia, who was here last week. Such, he said, was found to be the case in his section before the war. Farmers in Virginia who used Peruvian guano, got excellent crops for a few years, but it left the land poorer than it was before. On the other hand, a mixture of Peruvian guano and a phosphatic guano like Swan Island, gave equally good results, and kept up the fertility of the land. Peruvian guano, he thought, contains too much ammonia in proportion to the phosphates, and it was better to add more phosphates in the form of bone-dust or Swan Island guano. It is not improbable that such is the case, and if so, use the mixture. It is cheaper than Peruvian guano. But buy the guanos or bone-dust separately, and *do your own mixing.* In manipulated guanos you are not always sure of getting just what you bargain for.

But in regard to guano impoverishing the land, there is a good deal of misconception, and more or less prejudice. You *can*, of course, impoverish your land by the use of guano. Take the field where I sowed 300 lbs. per acre of the ammoniated superphosphate on wheat, two years ago this fall. It gave probably an extra yield of eight or ten bushels of wheat per acre. Two crops of clover would probably give two tons of hay extra. Then plow it up and plant corn, and there would be still some increase from the extra amount of clover roots in the soil. After the corn, sow barley, followed by wheat in the fall. Now, then, suppose I sell all the wheat and the straw, and also all the clover hay from the two crops, together with the seed. Suppose, too, I sell the next crop of corn and the stalks, and serve the barley and straw in the same way, and also the next crop of wheat and straw, would it be surprising if the next crop of clover is hardly worth cutting? Would not such a course impoverish the land? And the larger the crops at first obtained from the 300 lbs. of ammoniated phosphates, the more plant food I should export from the farm, and the more rapidly would the land be impoverished. But, on the other hand, if I sell only the wheat and make the straw into manure; if I plow under the clover, or feed it out and return the manure; or if the corn and stalks are all consumed on the farm, and the barley straw is also fed out and made into manure, and this carefully preserved and returned to the land, will not the extra amount of wheat straw, and the extra crops of clover, and the extra crop of corn make an extra amount of manure, and will not the land, after the manure is returned, give me an extra crop of clover, and this in turn supply a large quantity of plant-food for the following crop of wheat, and if the system of growing clover is continued,—of making it and the straw, and corn, and stalks, with an occasional crop of peas, into manure,—will it not greatly increase the fertility of the soil? The guano will give me more clover, and this will make more manure, and when the yards are filled with rich manure in the spring, it will not be long before larger barns will be required to hold the crops in the fall. So that while an injudicious use of artificial manures may impoverish your land, their proper application, coupled with a judicious rotation of crops, and a right system of feeding animals, and saving and applying manures, will prove permanently advantageous. The principle is equally true in regard to the use of plaster. Whenever plaster increases the growth of clover, it affords the opportunity of making more manure, and of enriching the land. But sell the clover and all the grain and straw, and the use of plaster will tend to impoverish the farm.

John Johnston's remarkable success as a farmer might be attributed to his underdraining, and to the large quantity of plaster he used for many years on clover. But this would only be a partial statement of the truth. His success is owing, first, to the man himself—to his rare good judgment, combined with indomitable energy, persevering industry, close observation, and prompt, intelligent action. Second, to underdraining. Third, to the free use of plaster on clover. Fourth, to consuming all the clover, straw, and corn, on the farm. He has raised 9,000 bushels of corn in a year, but none has ever been exported from the farm except some which he gave to be sent to Ireland at the time of the famine. *He never sold a bushel.* It has all been fed out with the clover, straw, stalks, etc., raised on the farm. In addition to this, he has bought large quantities of oil-cake to feed to sheep and cattle, and this has added greatly to the quality of the manure heap. Fifth. He bestowed great care on his summer-fallows. They were not allowed to grow up to weeds, but were repeatedly plowed and harrowed, and rolled and cultivated, until the stiffest clay was reduced almost to as fine a tilth as an English turnip field. Such thorough tillage is itself more than equivalent to a heavy dressing of our common strawy manure.

Underdraining enabled him to work his land thoroughly and in good season. This thorough tillage set free the latent plant-food in the soil. The clover took it up and organized it into good food for sheep. The sheep extracted the fat from the clover hay, and left the nitrogen and mineral matter in the manure heap. So of the corn, straw, and stalks. They all found their way back to the land, with oil-cake in addition. It is easy to understand why his land is vastly more productive than when it first came into his possession. Underdraining, good culture and good manure will make any land rich.

A few days since I received a letter from a subscriber of the *Agriculturist* in Kentucky, who wished to get for himself and half a dozen of his neighbors, some of our leading varieties of wheat. Their plan was for each to sow one variety, and if it proved good, to distribute the product among the others. The idea is a capital one. He says they have been raising the "New York Premium" wheat. When they first got the seed from this State, the crops were excellent, sometimes 40 bushels per acre, but they have grown it so long on the same land that it has degenerated, and the yield is now very light and the quality poor.

A miller and farmer in Maryland writes to the same effect. He has introduced a great many varieties of wheat, and for a few years they do well, and then run out. Is such really the case? Do not farmers, when they get a new kind of wheat from a distance, select their best land, give it extra care and culture, and consequently get good crops; while after a few years, when the seed is common, they bestow only ordinary culture, and get only ordinary crops?

John Johnston writes me, July 23*d*: "My Delhi wheat is pretty good. One field may yield about as well as last years; the other, not. Cause: *Not manured for many years.*" The variety has degenerated on the one field, but not on the other! Mr. J. adds: "If plenty of manure were applied, there would be less loss from midge. All that is needed to insure good crops is more and better manure. Delhi wheat is excellent for rich land, but not good for poor." This is not a popular doctrine, but it is true. Breeders of improved stock tell us that it costs no more to raise a good animal than a poor one. The nurserymen assert that it is as easy to raise a choice variety of fruit as a common, inferior kind; and some farmers appear to think if they send to a distance for a celebrated kind of grain, they are sure of good crops. Now, the truth is, if we want any thing that is really good, we must work for it. But when we get it, it will be so *very good* that we shall esteem the extra care and labor nothing. We ought not to expect to raise a barrel of large, well grown, highly colored Northern Spy apples as easily as we can a barrel of common seedlings, or even Baldwins. We can not raise Sheldon as easily as a Choke pear. I question if the

Agriculturist strawberry will stand neglect as well as Wilson's Albany; certainly Triomphe de Gand will not. We have a tree that bears every year bushels of small insipid peaches. If we should wake up some morning and find them all turned into Royal Kensington's, I should conclude the millennium had come, and send word to the good people in the Dutch Settlement, who have had a sharp fight with the weeds, that they might bring their baskets to gather the fruit, but leave their hoes at home.

As things now are, it is easier to raise a crop of thistles than a crop of wheat, and we can raise poor wheat more easily than good. But what of it? It is far better to raise wheat than thistles, and better to raise good wheat than poor. It is a mistake to suppose that any real farmer or intelligent horticulturist will be discouraged by a knowledge of the fact that if he wants well bred animals, or the best grains, or the choicest fruits, he must bestow the requisite care and attention. For 25 years, Thomas Bates did not show an animal at any of the fairs. He was quietly at work. But when he did exhibit, at the Royal Agricultural Fair, at Oxford, in 1839, he swept all before him. One thousand guineas were offered for one of his bulls—and he was worth it. And to-day, all our high-priced short-horns can be traced back to this twenty-five years of care and labor of the Yorkshire farmer. It is always so. Bakewell, Ellman, Webb, other agricultural worthies, paid an honest price for their success. It was no lucky hit, but the result of persevering and intelligent effort.

The *Agriculturist* for July calls attention to the value of corn husks for making paper. If there is a demand for them at good prices, it will be an additional reason why we must have a machine for husking. I have great hopes of "French's American Corn-Picker and Husker." From what I saw of its operation, at the New York State Fair, last year, I shall be disappointed if it does not husk corn to perfection. All that is now needed is some method of operating it by horse-power in the field. This machine separates the husks from the stalk as well as from the corn, and they could easily be gathered up, pressed, and sent to market. Out West, I was once offered shelled corn for "ten cents a bushel in trade, or nine cents cash." I do not know how they husk it. Here it costs me at least twelve cents a bushel to husk and shell corn. I pay five cents for husking a bushel of ears, and by the time we get it to the barn and shelled, it will cost at least a cent more, and it takes nearly two bushels of good corn to make a bushel of shelled corn. We need a good machine for husking, and I hope this fall will not pass by without giving us one. If French's will do it, let it be introduced. The person who exhibited it at the fair seemed more anxious to sell "rights" than machines, which is not a hopeful sign; if it worked well, it would be for sale.

We may as well make up our minds, first as last, that we must fight insects and fungi. It will not do to fold our hands, and wait till they pass over. Study their habits, find out their weak spots, foster their natural enemies, and we shall soon conquer.

One reason why we have so much fungus is owing to the slovenly practice of throwing the branches of trees, etc., into fence corners, and allowing them to decay, instead of burning them. No wonder that so many varieties of pears and apples are specked and cracked by fungus growth. I have an orchard of Virgalieu pears, and I do not think there is a single specimen free from specks. And even the Louise Bonne de Jersey begins to show symptoms of the disease. Flemish Beauty and Seckel have been liable to it for two or three years. Several varieties of apples crack as badly as the Virgalieu pears. We ought to be careful to remove all the fallen fruit, and to keep our gardens neat and clean, and especially should all the affected fruit be removed from the trees before winter. Because it is worthless, it is not unfrequently allowed to stay on the trees as long as it will hang. We could not devise a better plan for propagating the disease.

We do not use lime as freely as we should in our gardens and fruit orchards, or, for that matter, on our fields either. It would not only enrich the land, and give us larger crops, but they would be of better quality, and not so affected by disease. This is the experience of all who have used it. If we could burn our own lime, so that it would not cost more than ten cents a bushel, we could well afford to use it freely, at the rate of 150 to 200 bushels per acre. Large dressings at once, are better, I think, than small quantities more frequently applied. We want enough to change the character of the soil, liberate its potash, decompose the organic matter, and destroy fungus. We have plenty of limestone in this section, and there is more or less rough wood that could be used to burn it. What we want is a method of building a cheap kiln, or some plan of burning without kilns. As the lime is to be used for manure, it is not at all important that it should be free from charred sods or burnt clay. In fact, both these substances make excellent manure.

The probabilities are that we shall have a great deal of immature corn this fall. Where the corn and stalks are both fed out to cattle, sheep, and horses on the farm, why is it not just as well to cut the crop while rather green, cure it, and feed the stalks and corn together? We do not let our timothy get ripe, and then thrash out the seed, giving the horses the timothy straw in the rack, and the seed in the manger. Why should we do so in the case of oats or corn? If my corn matures, I shall husk it, and feed it out separately, because this is the orthodox way. But if it does not mature, I shall cut up the crop, and make it into fodder, and shall try and persuade myself that the method is in strict accordance with the teachings of science.

The Deacon says, in old times, when they sowed wheat after corn, and it was desirable to get the crop off as early as possible, he frequently put the stalks, while quite green, into the barn, and by putting a layer of six inches of dry straw between every two or three layers of corn stalks, they never mildewed, and the whole made excellent fodder.

The Use of Steam for Farm Work.

In this country we concede great advantage in the use of steam on large farms where stationary engines, or those used as such, may be placed and do a variety of work, such as cut wood, hay, and stalks, thrash, and grind, pump water, etc., and where the steam may also be used to cook feed for swine and other stock, but so far we have not used this power much in plowing and otherwise cultivating the land. In Great Britain, where steam tillage is more in vogue, it is, except on a few very large estates, accomplished by joint-stock companies, the shareholders consisting chiefly of farmers. The directors employ competent engineers and hands who go about with their different machines to do the work required, thrashing or plowing as the case may be. Some of these steam cultivating companies are quite successful, and declare handsome annual dividends; others are less prosperous. Much is found to depend upon the character of the country, much upon the hands employed, and also upon the superintending engineers. First class hands are needed, but they can not be employed at all seasons, as there are many days when they can not work on account of the condition of the soil, and the men must have some other employment.

Where the engines are well managed, and the fields are of a character to allow of their being profitably employed, the companies find no lack of custom, for the work is done more thoroughly and better than it could be by horse-power, and it costs less. The company usually furnishes every thing except coal and water for the engine. This requires a boy with a horse and cart, furnished by the farmer.

Ordinary surface plowing and tillage even upon farms where steam is regularly employed, are done by horse-power, but the steam plows are used for subsoiling and deep working, and for accomplishing deep tillage by powerful cultivators adapted to the purpose, which, by once or twice working a field over, will accomplish more towards the reduction of a stiff fallow than four or five times plowing and harrowing. Some of the managers have employed their engines at mole-draining with marked good results, the drainage being at the depth of two feet, and the drains four feet apart. The opinion of the Secretary of one of the most successful companies is that before declaring any dividends, 10 per cent. of the whole capital should be reserved as a sinking fund, besides 10 per cent. of all earnings thereafter, and 5 per cent. for interest on the investment. The engines used are Howard's, and Fowler's, and between these public opinion seems divided.

We have no doubt that there are many districts in this country where a similar system would prove most advantageous, and are waiting to learn particularly in regard to some experiments now being conducted on the prairies, before giving our readers pointed advice in regard to either English or American steam plows.

Drilling Wheat.

We found the practice of drilling wheat almost universal in the grain districts of Pennsylvania and New Jersey, and the only exceptions are among the small farmers who do not feel that they can afford a drill. At the West, the practice of drilling is coming rapidly into favor. Those who have their farms sufficiently cleared of stumps, and can own a drill, generally use the instrument. There are many patented drills, which cost from $90 upwards. Some, drawn by two horses, sow eight inches apart, and make eight drills at a time. We found at Terre Haute, Ind., a sulky cultivator and drill combined, costing $35. In that neighborhood the sale of drills is increasing very fast. The advantages of the drill are that it saves seed, which in the case of wheat is a very important item; that it gives the growing grain more air and sunlight, and guards against winter killing. It plants the seed at a very uniform depth in the bottom of a narrow trench, the sides of which crumble under the action of the frost, and cover the roots of the plant, if they are thrown out. The conviction is universally in favor of the practice, and a good drill will prove a good investment.

How Lime Is Burned.

The simplest method of preparing lime for agricultural uses is by burning it in stacks, very much in the same way as charcoal is prepared. (Fig. 1.) The spot selected for the burning is the quarry, which should be a soft variety of stone cleaving naturally into small fragments or being easily broken. The heap is usually in the form of a parallelogram, about a rod wide,

Fig. 1.—STACK OF LIME BURNING.

and of any desirable length. The first thing is a ground-work of wood about eighteen inches in thickness, of the size of the proposed stack. The wood may be old stumps or any coarse material, and the dryer it is the better. The wood is surrounded with a layer of earth and sods, leaving holes about fifteen inches square, at intervals of five or six feet, for firing the wood, and for regulating the combustion. These ventilators should run back into the mass of wood several feet, and be filled with dry kindling wood at the time of firing the heap. Upon this foundation of wood, a layer of the broken stone is placed, about six inches thick, then a layer, two inches thick, of fine anthracite coal, called culm in the coal districts. This is what is screened out in preparing the merchantable coal for market. It can generally be had for the cost of carting or freight at the shafts, where it often accumulates in large quantities. It adds very much to the heat of the fires, and reduces the expense of burning. The heap is then carried up six or eight feet high with alternate layers of culm and limestone, the stone layers increasing a little in thickness toward the top. The whole mass is covered with a layer of dirt at the sides, and at the top as soon as the heap is well ignited. A heap containing several thousand bushels will burn down in about six days. It is calculated that one ton of the coal will burn about 150 bushels of lime. Any one who has skill enough to burn a coal pit, can prepare lime by this method. It is principally of use where the limestone is in small fragments or easily broken. Of course, good coal and wood can be substituted for the refuse anthracite, if that is not to be had. Under favorable circumstances for obtaining fuel, lime is burnt in this way for one or two cents a bushel.

The harder varieties of limestone require a kiln for burning them. This is usually placed

Fig. 2.—LIME-KILN.

upon a side hill for convenience in delivering the stone and fuel for charging. (Fig. 2.) A convenient size for a farmer's use would be about twelve feet across at the top, sixteen at the bottom, and eighteen feet high. The outer walls should be laid in masonry, and the walls of the inner chamber that holds the charge, (Fig. 3.,) should be lined with fire brick, or with some refractory or infusible stone. The chamber is nearly in the shape of an egg, the small end downward, about three feet across at the bottom, seven at the top, and sixteen feet deep. There is a flue at the bottom,

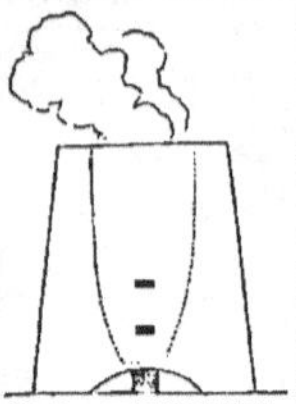

Fig. 3.—SECTION OF KILN.

two feet or more square, and extending completely under the chamber, for the purpose of giving draft for the fire, and it also serves for discharging the lime when it is sufficiently burned. The small holes above the flue, in figures 2 and 3, are for the purpose of thrusting in an iron rod, when needed to hold up the mass of stone and fuel within. In charging such a kiln as this, about a cord of dry wood would be placed upon the bottom, and on top of this three or four bushels of refuse anthracite, then a layer of the broken stone about one foot in thickness. Three inches of coal would be placed upon this, and so on until the chamber was filled, the layers of stone increasing in thickness toward the top. The burnt lime would be drawn

Fig. 4.—KILN FOR OYSTER SHELLS.

out at the bottom twice a day, about thirty-five bushels at each drawing, and fresh layers of coal and lime added on top. Such a kiln can be kept going for months until any desired quantity of lime is burned. It is calculated that by this method a ton of coal will burn a hundred bushels of lime. The culm is carried on the railroads considerable distances, and delivered at the depot for just the cost of freight. At two dollars a ton at the kiln, it is probably cheaper than wood cut upon the premises. The cost of the lime to the producer would not be, under favorable circumstances, more than four or five cents a bushel. This very cheap lime is one of the secrets of its almost universal use in Pennsylvania and western New Jersey. Of course, where fuel costs more, lime will be dearer; but we think wherever lime rock and wood are plenty, lime can be economically made and applied to the soil. The experiment certainly ought to be tried over a much wider region. Figure 4 shows the process of preparing oyster shell lime in our cities and villages. The refuse of coal yards, now so often used for road making or grading, might be applied to burning oyster shells with great economy. This lime is usually considered better for agricultural purposes than that prepared from stone.

Willow Stakes for Fences on Bottom Land.

BY HOOSIER.

Spring freshets and floods prove very destructive to farmers living along water courses, by washing away fences. Stakes without roots will decay, and wash out, letting the rails take a free ride on the swift and turbid waters. Almost every farmer knows what a disagreeable task it is to reset fences, and it is particularly so after freshets, when the rails are all coated over with mud and slime. To make rail fences compar-

Fig. 1.—WILLOW FENCE POSTS.

atively permanent, you must have self-supporting stakes, that is, stakes that will firmly support themselves, and also the weight of the fence and waters. To make a stake self-supporting, it must have roots to enable it to retain a firm hold of the earth. The willow, white, or yellow, is for this purpose about as near being "the right thing in the right place," as any tree we can find. It grows without trouble, and is a natural denizen of wet, marshy grounds; therefore it is well adapted for stakes through bottom lands. The stakes may be cut from three to ten feet in length, and from three inches to a foot in diameter. They may be set in holes made with a post auger, about two feet deep, firmly ramming the earth around them; or they may be pointed, and driven into the ground. In one season they will be well rooted, thrifty trees, well able to resist, and hold the fence against, the impetuosity of the rushing water.

The willow grows easily from cuttings, and when properly pruned, makes a beautiful tree. From its rapid growth it is rendered valuable as a shade tree for pasture lands. It grows almost as well on the hill top as in the valley, unless the former be very dry or rocky.

Perhaps a willow hedge through bottom lands would be better than staking rail fences. The only trouble would be the closeness of the hedge, making too much "back-water," but that might be obviated. As to the size of the cuttings it may be said that they will grow from a small twig to a limb as large as a man's body. Keep stock from browsing them for the first year or two, and after that there will be no trouble.

[The cuts represent two light fences made altogether of willow. In fig. 1, the posts are two

Fig. 2.—WILLOW FENCE WITH RIDGE.

stakes, driven perpendicularly, and bound with withes which form the support of the rails. It is best to nail besides. Fig. 2 shows a fence made by turning four furrows together on the line of the fence, then driving stakes crossing so as to support rails over these furrows, the lower rails "breaking joints," as the carpenters say, with the upper ones. Such a fence is strong, and one not likely to be broken through by common cattle, if the rails are stout.—Eds.]

Cost of Raising Corn by the Old and New Methods.

The sight of a man on a Sulky Cultivator, sweeping through a cornfield astride the rows, and leaving scarcely a live weed behind him, has led us to speculate a little upon the cost of raising corn by the old and new methods. We will take a piece of 80 acres, 160 rods long and 80 rods wide, and calculate four rows to the rod running one way. If the breaking up and harrowing cost two dollars per acre, we have $160, as the cost of preparing the ground for the crop. There will be 320 rows in the plot, and with a drill drawn by one horse, the corn may be dropped 1 foot apart, and covered in four days, the horse walking 20 miles a day. At $2.50 a day, this would be $10. It will take a man and pair of horses four days to cultivate once, which at $3.50 per day, will cost $14, and for cultivating five times, $70, making the whole cost $240. The 80 acres with this attention, on good land, would produce 40 bushels to the acre or more, say 3,200 bushels. The corn fodder, we think, would be a fair offset against the expense of harvesting and storing, as it is now generally admitted that, well cured and cared for, it is worth two-thirds as much as the best hay. This would make the cost of the corn a trifle less than eight cents a bushel.

Cultivating the same piece by the old method, the cost of preparing the ground would be the same, $160; marking out the ground both ways, with plow, $20; planting at $1 an acre, $80; cultivating or plowing between rows, both ways, six times, $84; hand-hoeing three times, at $1.50 an acre each time hoeing, $364; making the expense about $708, or 22 cents—nearly three times as much as by the new method—the proportions, if not the figures, being nearly accurate.

There are variations of these methods, increasing or diminishing the cost. Some do not use any drill or planter, but make rows both ways and plant by hand, covering with the hoe, and do all the cultivation by horse-power. The hand planting increases the cost. The use of fertilizers increases the expense, but adds to the yield enough to make up the difference. If the land is poor and the yield is less, of course the corn costs more. On some farms the cost of raising corn is probably a dollar a bushel. On the prairies, under favorable conditions, it does not probably exceed ten cents per bushel. There is, on an average, we think, a difference of two hundred per cent. in favor of the new methods. Farmers at the east, with their eyes open, should invest early in rock and stump pullers, and beat their hoes into sulky cultivators.

How the Paper Pays.

A good many farmers are still shy of agricultural papers. They say it don't pay to take them. They never made an experiment but they lost money by it. The same men will talk about crops by the hour with their neighbors, comparing their own practice with what they see and hear of in others. The agricultural paper does for its readers, on a much larger scale, simply what these men do for themselves, at much greater expense. It gathers up from a thousand sources the details of farm experience all over the country, and gives them in a condensed form. These results, surely, are no worse for being printed. They are generally stated with as much accuracy as the farmer would give them in his own language. To most cultivators these details of experience are instructive, and are most prized by those who know the most. They furnish important hints to all. They serve to quicken thought, and to make the practice of farmers more profitable. A single suggestion acted upon often makes a difference of dollars in the productiveness of every acre under the plow. Here it guards against loss, there it makes large gains. It leads the farmer to study his business, and puts him in the way of learning much more from his own observation and experience. He gets out of the ruts, and thinks as he works. He uses his brains and grows as a man, and as a consequence, therefore, makes everything else grow that he touches.

Corn Cribs.

Whatever temporary expedients the grower of Indian corn may resort to for storing his crop, he at last comes to a crib as a prime necessity. The rail pen is a very insecure inclosure, much exposed to damage from the storms, and an invitation for any thief to plunder. Storing in the garret is a very laborious business, and unless spread very thin, it is exceedingly liable to

Fig. 1.—CONNECTICUT CORN CRIB.

injure by mould. Spread upon the barn floor, it is always in the way, and free plunder to all the rats and mice upon the premises. This grain is more liable to injury from imperfect curing than any other that we raise. Wheat, oats, rye, barley, and buckwheat are easily

Fig. 2

cured in the field, so that a few days or weeks after cutting they can be thrashed there, and immediately stored in bins or sent to market. But Indian corn has a much larger kernel, and grows upon a thick stout cob from which it takes months to expel the moisture after it is fully ripe. Each section has its peculiar contrivances for storing this grain on the cob. In the South it is quite common to store husks and all in the barn or some other outbuilding. In the North they have buildings put up especially for storing the husked ears.

The Connecticut corn crib, (Fig. 1,) is the common type at the East, and has many good qualities. It sets upon posts covered with inverted tin pans, (Fig. 2,) to make it inaccessible to rats and mice. These posts are a foot or more in diameter, and two or three feet from the surface of the ground to the bottom of the building. Sometimes flat stones, two or three feet broad, are substituted for the tin pans, but the latter are preferred. The sides of the build-

Fig. 3 Fig. 4.

Fig. 5.—TWO CRIBS ROOFED OVER.

ing are made of slats nailed to sills and plates at bottom and top, and to one or more girders between. The bin upon the inside is made by a board partition, three or four feet from the siding. The boards are movable, and are put up as the crib is filled. The remaining space between the bins is used for shelling corn or as a receptacle for bags and barrels, and the back part is sometimes used for a tool-house, or fitted with bins for storing shelled corn or other grain.

Fig. 3 represents the end view of the model Pennsylvania corn crib, and Fig. 6 the side view showing the mode of construction. Fig. 4 shows the same thing with a more economical roof. Fig. 5 shows two of these cribs with a roof thrown over them to form a convenient shed or shelter for carts, wagons, and farming tools. Sometimes the passage is boarded up at one end, and furnished with doors at the other. These cribs are entered at one end by a narrow door, and the whole space is occupied by the corn. They are from three to five feet in width, and give very perfect ventilation to the ears. They have usually a stone foundation with a sill and board floor above. They are not usually rat proof. They are made of any desirable size, and cribs holding from five hundred to a thousand bushels are common. In case the farm enlarges, and more room is wanted, the roof of Fig. 3 is extended downward on one or both sides; or other cribs are added, and more room is made for carts.

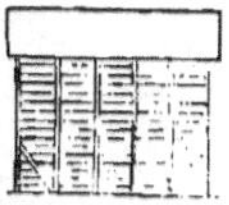

Fig. 6.—SIDE OF CRIB.

The American Buffalo.

The fine picture on our first page introduces this magnificent and valuable animal to the notice of the reader, but the arrangement of our pages forbid our writing but very briefly in connection. No one can look into the history of the Buffalo on this Continent, its rapid extirpation east of the Mississippi, and wherever civilization really sets her foot, without a feeling of pain. With the Indians, these splendid herds are rapidly approaching extinction. The present range of the Buffalo is the Great Plains between the northern part of Texas and the Red River of the North, and between the Missouri River and the Rocky Mountains. Here they exist in immense numbers, so great that parties crossing the plains have sometimes been a week and more in passing through a herd. Mr. Hayes, the artist, writes: "The Buffalo is a timid animal, and generally will run from a man; but when parties are in the neighborhood of one of these herds, the great danger is from a stampede, in which case it requires the utmost care and watchfulness to prevent the mass of frightened animals from running over the camp, or making the cattle break from the corral, and join the terror stricken herd, leaving the traveler to pursue the remainder of his journey on foot.

The cows bring forth in the spring, producing one and sometimes two calves, at which time the herds break into small bands, of from half a dozen to fifty; and remain so until the autumn, when they come together again.

Many attempts have been made to cross the Buffalo with the domestic cattle. The Buffalo bull has been crossed with the domestic cow, and the heifer calf from this union has bred with both the Buffalo and domestic bull; no attempt has succeeded in crossing the domestic bull with the Buffalo cow. The Buffalo has been broken to the yoke, but is said to be unreliable and dangerous.

The hump is caused by the prolongation of the processes of the spine, commencing at the first dorsal vetebra. The second, which is longest, sometimes measures twenty-two inches in length. Across the top of these processes runs the strong ligament which serves to raise the enormous head. This hump gives a formidable appearance to the animal, and when coming directly towards you, with the head down, presents a similar outline to the fresh water sunfish. The flesh of the Buffalo bears about the same relation to beef that venison does to mutton.

The Buffalo is the main dependence of the Indians, and it is a low estimate that half a million are destroyed yearly. About fifty-five thousand robes are annually brought to market, the skin of the cow only being saved for that purpose, that of the bull being too thick to dress. This operation is performed by the squaws."

The destruction of the Buffalo, as now carried on, is sheer wantonness in the exercise of the ability to kill. Often only the tongues are taken; often not even these, but the animals counted as they roll in mortal agony, that their destruction may be boasted of by the hunters. This certainly calls for action on the part of the Government to prevent it, and preserve some representatives of these great herds for future generations to make use of, if we cannot.

The Crops—Editorial Correspondence.

One of our editorial corps is up in one of the New England States—we won't say which one—fishing for his health. He sends us the following: "When I went off, it was with the injunction not to put pen to paper while I was gone, so I will write in pencil. While I have caught fish, the weight of which "averaged well," (*i. e.* the boy with me caught a $6\frac{1}{4}$ pound pickerel, while mine was only $\frac{3}{4}$ of a pound, making the average $3\frac{1}{2}$ pounds,) I could not help between spells having an eye to the crops, and I give the result of my observation.

"MULLEIN promises fair, and though rather late, there is a good stand, and no fear of scarcety of seed for next year.

"WILD PARSNIPS.—I am surprised at the abundance of this crop. In some fields it grows with such luxuriance that the fence cannot restrain it, and it has run over and fills the roadside. There will be no lack of Wild Parsnips at this point, and probably the breadth of land devoted to it will increase each year.

"VIPER'S BUGLOSS.—Some fine patches of this are to be seen. It is a rather local crop, but I do not see why it should be. A small patch of it in a meadow or pasture will soon run everything else out, and in a few years the field will be covered with its beautiful blue flowers, and the plant will become so well established that there need not be the least fear of losing the stock. Botanists call it *Echium vulgare*.

"CANADA THISTLE.—This seems to be the staple crop of the farms hereabouts, and, on the whole, promises well. In some fields I noticed that the crop is interfered with by a few oats, but notwithstanding this, I think there will be an average yield. The farmers in these parts economize every available foot of land, and devote the roadsides to the Canada Thistle. This, I believe, is from purely benevolent motives, for while their fields supply seed for home use, the plants by the roadside are sure to give the neighbors all the seed they want.

"These seem to be the principal growths of this neighborhood, though some of minor importance are to be found. Elecampane is grown to some extent, as are Ox-eye or White Daisy, Tansy, etc., but they are fast being superseded by the Canada Thistle. Wild Carrot, so abundant in York State, seems to receive but little attention here, but it will doubtless come in. Corn, oats, and the like are grown to some extent, but the land is mainly devoted to the crops I have mentioned above, of which I see not the least reason to fear a reduced yield."

A Western Grazing Farm.

The immense consumption of beef cattle in the great seaboard cities, has built up a great business extending clear across the Mississippi Valley into Texas. There are at least four distinct branches of this business: the raising of the cattle in districts where there are no inclosures, and where ear-marks are the only badge of ownership; the purchase and removal of these cattle to the more thickly-settled regions where there are inclosed pastures, and beef is higher; the fattening of these animals; and their forwarding to the eastern markets.

There are many farms in the West, some of them of vast extent, whose chief product is fat beeves. The whole farm is managed with reference to this result. If grain and grass are raised it is to feed to cattle. If hogs are kept it is to consume what the cattle do not perfectly digest, and to gather up the waste. If wheat is raised, it is for the purpose of subduing the soil, and getting it into better condition to produce grass. Messrs. Fowler and Earl, of Lafayette, Ind., have a farm of 24,000 acres in Benton Co., of that State, which is worked exclusively to prepare cattle for market. The enterprise was begun some three years ago, and, as will be seen, has involved a large expenditure of capital. The land alone, at six dollars an acre, must have cost nearly $150,000. The tract lies upon Mud and Sugar creeks, and is about eight miles long, by five broad, and is well watered by these streams. The first step toward improvement was the inclosure and subdivision of 13,000 acres of the prairie with a board fence. This was made with cedar posts, seven and a half feet long, three feet in the ground, and placed at a distance of six feet apart. Upon these, boards were nailed, making a fence four and a half feet high. The 13,000 acres were divided into eleven fields, making in all about forty-three miles of board fence, at a cost of $850 a mile, or $36,550. The remaining 11,000 acres have just been furnished with seventy-seven miles of Osage Orange hedge, which will be in condition to turn cattle, in three years from planting. The farm and the improvements are under the efficient management of A. D. Raub, Esq., who resides upon the place.

It is found that the cultivated grasses are more nutritious than the wild, and the aim is to bring about a thousand acres a year into meadow. This requires at least two years of cropping. The prairie is broken in May and June with five yoke of cattle and a plow which turns a furrow from eighteen to twenty-two inches wide, and about three inches deep. This is planted with corn, which receives no cultivation, and yields about forty bushels to the acre. The corn is followed by wheat, either of the fall or spring variety, and with the wheat is sown a mixture of four parts of herds-grass and one of red clover, at the rate of one bushel to five acres. This is mowed the first season after it takes possession, and after that it is turned into pasture. The tendency of the pasturing, it is thought is to run out the herdsgrass and red clover, and to bring in the blue grass and white clover, which need no seeding. It is expected that these pastures once established will be permanent, and fully equal in value to the celebrated blue grass pastures of Kentucky. It seems to flourish quite as well here as in Kentucky, and it only needs good husbandry to make their pastures quite as famous.

It is expected, when the whole tract is brought into grass, that it will carry 8000 cattle a year, and its present productiveness justifies this estimate. The cattle of three or four years of age are bought of drovers and small farmers, from January to April, wherever they can be bought to the best advantage. The corn is drawn from the field where it was raised, and where it has stood in shocks through the winter, and is fed out to the cattle upon the open prairie. They eat the corn quite clean, and the leaves from the stalks. They are also fed with hay of which about nine hundred tons were cured last year. The cattle come to grass in high condition, and by June or July the best of them are ripe for the butcher, and they are sold off in lots to suit purchasers, as they fatten through the summer and fall. A lot of 176 bullocks, averaging a little over 1400 pounds each, was sold the last of July at seven and a half cents a pound. The custom is to sell by live weight, twelve hours after the cattle have been last fed and watered. This sale amounted to over $18,000. There were 1250 acres in corn last year, and the yield was about forty bushels to the acre; 500 acres were sown in winter wheat, much of which was winter killed; 550 acres were sown with spring wheat of the Italian and Tea varieties which were a decided success. Thus far much more money has been expended than received in this enterprise, but there can be no doubt that it will prove a good investment. Other items of interest upon this farm are noticed elsewhere.

Forwarding Beeves to the Eastern Markets.

The great demand for beef in our seaboard cities is felt in the Mississippi Valley and beyond, and millions of capital are invested in supplying it. Chicago alone has about two millions invested in fixtures for carrying on this business, and sends east about a thousand cattle a day. But these are not all fat cattle, nor do they immediately reach their destination. Many tarry for a year or more, and change hands several times before they reach the consumer. The large towns further east become centers of a cattle trade, where they are collected from the pastures in which they have been fattened, and from whence they are forwarded to market. We came upon traces of this trade at Lafayette, Indiana, and made some inquiries of Col. W. J. Templeton, who is engaged in it, as to the mode of sending fat cattle to market. On an average he forwards about three hundred head every week during the year. The cattle are bought, generally of the large farmers, or at large markets, and are forwarded in open slat cars by rail. They are well fed and watered before starting, and the first stop on the journey is at Toledo, where they are taken out of the cars for feeding, and rest for twenty-four hours. They have a similar stop at Buffalo, and another at Albany, whence they come through to New York, and are discharged from the cars into the cattle pens to be sold to the butchers. It takes about six days to transport a lot of cattle from Lafayette to New York, with the necessary rest. This is very important, as it brings the cattle to the butcher without much loss of weight and in good condition. The cost of transportation, by special contract with the railroad companies, is about eleven dollars a head. Without this arrangement, the cost would be sixteen dollars or more. If the bullocks averaged eleven hundred pounds each of beef, it would cost only a cent a pound to get them to market. This is about the real difference between beef in Indiana and in this city, and all that is paid over that goes to the shipper, the butcher, and the retailer, each of whom makes a respectable profit. Is it necessary for the consumer to pay from twenty to thirty-five cents a pound for beef, to keep these gentlemen thriving and good-natured?

Raising Corn on the Prairie Sod.

Corn is usually the first crop put into the virgin soil, whether upon the prairie or in the fresh clearings of the forest at the West and South. It prepares the way for cotton, and for wheat and grass as well. There is some variety in the methods of handling the crop, but in most cases it is a very simple process. The practice of breaking the sod in May and June, and turning it over in a very thin, broad slice, about three inches thick, is almost universal. The ranker the grass at the time of breaking, the better for the rotting process. Very strong plows are used to break this sod, and it requires about five yoke of oxen, or their equivalent in horses or mules, to do it well. The shallow plowing is found in experience to do better than the deeper upon the virgin sod. The sod rots better, and the corn grows with luxuriance. The planting immediately follows the breaking. This is done with a variety of appliances, but upon the large farms always with machinery. At the farm of Messrs. Fowler and Earl, in Benton Co., Ind., it is done with a large, heavy drill, something like Brown's Corn Planter. It plants two rows at a time, three feet eight inches apart, and eighteen inches apart in the row, three kernels of corn in the hill. The drill is made about six inches deep, with sharp steel cutters, which sever the sod and drop the corn, which is covered by a roller. It takes four horses abreast to draw the machine and two men to manage it, and it will plant about twenty acres a day. This machine works very well, and is considered an improvement upon anything yet tried. It cuts the sod so clean that it is not much disturbed. The deep planting of the corn is considered a safeguard against drought. The vegetable mold is so loose above it that it is not smothered as it would be in older and more compact loams. After the planting, the ground is gone over with cutter harrows, and rolled with a heavy roller. There are no weeds upon the sod, and there is no cultivation. The yield is about forty bushels to the acre. We think if the rows were four feet apart, and the stalks two in a hill, there would be more corn. Cultivation with a light harrow or cultivator, just to disturb the surface of the inverted sod, would also probably increase the yield. There are machines that plant two rows at a time, and with such regularity in the hills as to make rows running both ways. This is a great advantage in older soils, where there are weeds to be subdued by cultivation. Cultivation on old ground is performed with a great variety of implements, but almost always with horse-power. There are shovel-plows and double shovel-plows and bar-plows, cultivators, and harrows, and last, but not least, the sulky cultivator, which goes astride the row with two horses, and finishes the cultivation at once. With this implement cultivation becomes a genteel business, and a lady, handy with the reins, might clean out her dozen acres in a day, with no more fatigue than in riding to market. Some M. D., who is not a quack, we suspect will soon be recommending this as a substitute for the water-cure in nervous diseases. We know it would be good for the corn, and it might help a certain class of invalids just as much.

When the corn is well glazed, it is cut near the roots, and shocked in bunches made up of sixteen hills each. Here it remains until it is wanted for fodder, when it is drawn out upon the sod, and fed to cattle, if grazing is the style of the farm. If pork is the chief product, the swine are often turned into a field of standing corn, and left to do their own harvesting. Of course, there is some waste in this process, but where corn costs less than 20 cents a bushel, the waste does not keep people awake o' nights.

Specialties in Farming—Hops.

The age of Homespun is past, and the tendency of society is now very strongly in the direction of the division of labor. Men confine themselves more and more to the doing of one thing as a means of livelihood. This is more manifest in other callings than in that of husbandry, but it is beginning to be felt even in this. Fifty years ago, the farmer mainly clothed as well as fed his family, furnished lights and fuel, and did the most of his own tinkering and cobbling. One by one mechanics and manufacturers have come to his aid, until he has little else to do but till the soil. Long ago, the spinning wheel, cards and loom disappeared from the kitchen, and are now only looked for in the lumber of the garret. Tin candle moulds drove out candle rods and dips, and whale oil and petroleum banished tallow candles. Anthracite has taken the place of wood at many a farmer's fireside, and the forest is only valued for timber. He no more sleds wood in winter, and his wife goes wool gathering among magazines and quarterlies rather than among Saxony and South Down fleeces. Instead of the general farming which was once almost universal in the North and East, we have now many specialties in husbandry, which are becoming more clearly defined. This, no doubt, has its advantage in pecuniary results, but we are not so clear about its influence upon manhood. The old style farming gave a wonderfully varied discipline to all the powers of body and mind. The modern gymnasium could hardly put the body into more postures, and better discipline every muscle. It sharpened the wits, and developed the inventive faculties, so that the graduate of the farm was prepared for every emergency in life. He was not likely to find any new obstacles or difficulties that had not been met and overcome in his early discipline. Possibly some substitute may be found for this training, but we are a little skeptical. However that may be, there is no mistaking the tendency of farm life in our country to a division of labor. In the vicinity of all our large towns and villages, there has sprung up, within a few years, a distinct business, known as truck farming. A man buys a few acres, often less than ten, raises vegetables for the city markets, educates his family, gets a competence, and if the city grows fast enough, leaves a fortune to his heirs by the rise of his real estate. Nearly allied to this, and sometimes united with it, is fruit farming. Then there are whole farms devoted mainly to the production of some one article, as hay, onions, hops, tobacco, etc. Then there is the production of milk for the supply of the city; cheese farming and butter farming, and both combined; sheep farming, and grazing to make beef. In the grain districts, the chief business is the production of wheat, oats, and corn for sale. This style of farming, no doubt, simplifies the business, and generally pays better. There will come, however, bad years, and defective crops, and if the farmer stakes everything upon one product, he is liable to lose a year's labor. This is a thing which never happens in a varied husbandry.

Sometimes these specialties are enormously profitable. We recently visited the hop farm of M. C. Wetmore, near Rochester, who makes hops his main product. There are thirty acres in the farm, and he has this year fifteen acres in hops—four on poles by the old method, and eleven on strings, about seven feet from the ground. He sold last year, from fourteen acres, $10,000 worth of hops, and this year, judging from the look of the vines, the product will be still larger. Hops sold last year for sixty-five cents a pound. This article can be raised at a profit for ten cents a pound. He gets about 1100 pounds to the acre in good years. He finds the strings very much better than the poles; they cost about one-eighth as much, and make a yield of 200 pounds more to the acre, and save a good deal of labor in the picking. These are facts worth knowing among our hop growing friends. A small farm, well tilled, with a single crop, will keep a man out of the almshouse.

Agricultural Improvement.

It has always been our custom to accept from every source suggestions bearing in however slight a degree upon improvement in agriculture, and using them as best we can for the good of the public. We get a great variety of letters, but rarely have we had a communication so sensible and suggestive as the following, from so humble a source. We commend it to certain of our readers who will no doubt sympathize with our correspondent in his sentiments.

Editors of the American Agriculturist:—That you may understand me the better, and be less surprised at my suggestions, I must tell you at the outset that I am one of a troupe of performers who have been for some years traversing this broad and beautiful land, seeing and being seen. It is our highest ambition to imitate as well as we can the actions of mankind, and the kind gentlemen who conduct us over the country exact no other reward. They furnish us, as you know, both ponies and dogs for horses; they

RACE FOR THE ALL-WIN PURSE OF THE JOCKO CLUB.

INTENSELY EXCITING AND GREAT MORAL ATTRACTION OF THE MUTUAL BENEFIT AGRICULTURAL UNION.

clothe us like human beings, and we do the best we can to *act* like men in all the different circumstances in life in which we see them. We find it a very great aid to us in successful imitation, to study the motives of men, and by these we judge of their actions.

This is what leads me to write to you,—and now to come directly to the point. It appears to us that to make people take an interest in the things which are of most value to them, is a great art. Thus subjects of no use interest everybody, but only the wise among men are interested in matters which promise lasting benefit to mankind, or even to themselves.

We have been repeatedly engaged to perform at some of the minor Agricultural Fairs and Cattle Shows, and the general features of those exhibitions have impressed us most favorably, but it seems to us passing strange, while a town is full of strangers attracted by the fair, and the grounds surrounding are quite crowded, that so few people enter the enclosure until the time for the horse-race, the balloon ascension, or our monkey-show. Once in, these people see and learn a great deal of use to them. In our innocence, we supposed that the horse-races were really trials of speed, and tended to improve the breeds of that fine animal, but from what we learn from the horses, this is not so, for they seldom are allowed to exhibit their good qualities, being held back or urged forward, according to their jockey's whims, and these jockeys or drivers are influenced by pay received from various parties, and so make the honest horses lose or win the race, not on their merits, but according as they are paid by their employer or by those inimical to him; or, as it often happens, the owners arrange the race between themselves, and, winning or losing, divide the purse.

Now monkeys are good riders, and so far as they know, they are honest, and money is of no value to them; and, besides, being morally irresponsible, the employment of Jocko for a jockey would prevent the distressing moral corruption to which these drivers and riders are subjected. Why not then, I ask, employ monkeys and apes at these "agricultural fairs" more extensively?

Moreover, as this racing, instead of being beneficial, is injurious to horses, we would suggest the employment of dogs, as less liable to injury, and answering well, with monkey-riders, the sole purpose of horse-races, as conducted by agricultural societies,—that of drawing a crowd.

One point more:—In many parts of this country it is very discreditable to have anything to do with the running or trotting of horses, so by all artfully selected names the Fair managers cover up the real character of the horse-races which they superintend. They are, they say, "tests of speed," "trials of wind, bottom, and endurance," and simply, the best means for the judges to decide upon the relative merits of different horses. This, we see, is all a pretence. The truth is, they want an exciting scene, and though they regret the betting and gambling which always attends horse-races, (at any rate after the first year or two,) yet they know of no other way to draw a crowd, to fill up their treasury, pay their premiums, and so do all the good they can with their Agricultural Society. The employment of us and our dogs will give all the excitement, draw the same crowd, and interest more people, while it will neither foster gambling, betting, calling things by false names, nor immorality of any sort. Moral or immoral, it is all one to us, yet even we dislike to have the good people wound their consciences, and play the hypocrite to no good purpose. Please observe that we require no race-course, but only a smooth bit of turf or tan-bark. Where race-courses, (called "tracks,") cannot be afforded, "female equestrianism" has, I believe, been tried with entire success, so far as gathering the crowd, (to do them good,) is concerned, but the effects upon the females are said to be anything but good, from the moral and modest stand-point from which we poor monkeys are forced to view these things for the reasons stated.

I enclose a picture of what might, I think, take the place of horse-racing and of all immoral and indelicate shows at fairs. Let your readers see it, and then judge for themselves.

Yours, jocularly, JOCKO THE JOCKEY.

Petunias Then and Now.

Do any of our old horticultural friends recollect their first Petunia? Over thirty years ago, we cherished our first one as a prized house plant. It was the old *Petunia nyctagyniflora*, the first one introduced into cultivation. It had coarse white flowers, but then it produced them abundantly, and it was altogether a pleasing plant. Great was our surprise when we found that the plant could be grown as a garden annual, and greater still when we discovered that it would grow from self-sown seeds, and in fact become, in some places, a weed. After the common white species, came the purple one, greatly superior to the other. Then began a course of improvement by the crossing of these two and with other species, and now we have the Petunia ranking as a florist's flower, presenting a great number of named varieties, both single and double. Some of the single ones are beautifully veined or blotched, and the habit of the plant is greatly improved as well as the texture and fineness of the flowers. For bedding purposes we much prefer the finer single varieties to the double ones. The choice kinds are propagated from cuttings, which strike root with the greatest ease, but seeds of good sorts will produce nice plants, and there is a chance of getting fine varieties in this way.

The double varieties are now becoming numerous. Some of the flowers are enormous in size, beautiful in color, and very fragrant. The variety, Abraham Lincoln, is one of the most generally distributed and best known. Something after the same style is a new variety sent out this year by Mr. J. Kadletz, Staten Island, and named by him Mrs. Peter Henderson. The flower is large, of good shape, and very brilliant, the ground white, with a purple blotch on the tip of each petal. Mr. K. considers this the best of his numerous seedlings. Messrs. Frost & Co., of the Genesee Valley Nurseries, Rochester, N. Y., have also sent us specimens of a fine new seedling, called Edward Beach, from the gentleman with whom it originated. The flowers were full, rich in color, and quite equal to any that we have seen. Messrs. F. & Co. state that they have had blooms measuring over six inches in diameter.

DOUBLE PETUNIA—MRS. PETER HENDERSON.

Tree Planting by the Road-Side.

What traveler in the summer has not blessed the thoughtful man who planted, or spared from the original forest, the roadside tree, where he found rest and shelter for himself and his jaded beast? Why should we not have continuous rows of such trees planted through every farm? Why should not every village or town in a town form its tree planting association, and line its streets with the beautiful indigenous trees that are to be had for the cost of digging in the neighboring forests? Why should not these rows of trees extend every year, along every thoroughfare, until the villagers meet in the honorable rivalry of mending their ways, and beautifying the country? We have a good many model avenues in New England and in the older parts of the country, where the present generation is enjoying the results of the good taste and toils of their forefathers. Trees were planted when the village streets were first laid out, and their branches are now a crown of glory, affording shelter from the summer heats.

We admire the arrangement of those early settled towns in the Connecticut River Valley, and elsewhere, where they had a common a mile long, and twelve rods wide or more, the houses arranged upon the sides, and looking out upon the village green beneath the shadows of noble elms. These trees are now the glory of the village, fondly cherished by the residents, and forming beautiful pictures never to be effaced from the mind of the stranger who visits them.

We find hundreds of villages and towns in our occasional visits, and they are by no means confined to the more recent settlements, where the work of planting the road-side is yet to be done. One or two generations have gone by without developing public spirit enough to attend to this enterprise. The church, the academy, the school-house, the inn, and the dwellings that cluster around them, stand through all the scorching heats of summer unblest with shade. And this is the case too, where there is no want of refinement among the people. The desirableness of the improvement is admitted, but there is great lack of public spirit, and no one provokes his neighbor to this kind of good works. It is time something was done, and we propose a familiar talk with the reader upon his personal responsibilities in the matter. If you live in one of these neglected districts, you have missionary work before you, and it will require a good degree of faith to undertake this ministry of the beautiful. You may not meet with violent opposition and personal abuse, but the big pagan, Indifference, will resist you at every step. The place has stood for fifty years, they will tell you, without any shade trees, and they have got along pretty well. They would give money or volunteer their men and teams if they could see any use in it. But they don't see the need of it. This, and much more like it, will be your first salutation. Never mind. "There is no impossibility to him who wills." Get one man enlisted on your side, and if possible let that man be a woman. Take the matter up and make a business of it. If you have a sewing society in the parish, get the ladies interested. While they are laboring for the heathen, and for the starving South, and trying to make the wilderness bud and blossom, let them have an eye to the wilderness along their own street. Buds and blossoms are wanting there, and the desolate wayside can be made "a thing of beauty and a joy forever." This is a home enterprise that has been neglected quite too long. Talk with the minister about it, and if he be a man of taste, as he is apt to be, get him to preach a sermon on the moral uses of beautiful things, text, St. Paul, "Whatsoever things are lovely," or, better yet, the Great Preacher, "Consider the lilies." There is a great deal of unapplied truth in the Bible that touches upon this matter of tree planting. Stir up the Farmers' Club if you have one, and if not, form one. Get the Horticultural Society or County Agricultural Society to offer premiums for planting wayside trees. One resolute man in a place can carry this much needed reform, and make his name immortal. Hillhouse Avenue, in New Haven, with its lordly elms, will preserve the name of the planter long after his monument has crumbled and his career as a Senator is forgotten.

EDGINGS AND EDGING PLANTS.—Recently we saw some cast iron edgings in use around beds cut in a lawn; they were of a rustic pattern, but being painted of a bright red, the effect was anything but pleasing. Had they been of a subdued or neutral tint, it would have been much better, as a scarlet edging detracts from whatever may be in the bed. To the list of plants already suggested for edging purposes, we have to add *Sedum spurium*, a dwarf growing and hardy species. It spreads rapidly, and will need to be kept within bounds. A variegated Thyme has been introduced that makes a very neat edging. It is like the common Thyme except that each leaf has a delicate white line upon the margin. Its general effect is subdued and quiet. We have not yet tested its hardiness.

Seedling Strawberries.

BY B. HATHAWAY, LITTLE PRAIRIE RONDE, MICH.

The remarks of Mr. Boyden, in the July *Agriculturist*, although correct in the main, contain some erroneous statements.

He says, "The strawberry seed, like several other seeds, remains until the following spring before it germinates." How he could adopt such an hypothesis, that analogy and observation must alike refute, seems unaccountable. It is well known that the strawberry is almost cosmopolitan in its character and habits. Its geographical range covers three zones, and it is alike at home in Lapland, Mexico, South America, and the islands of the Pacific.

For some years I have given attention to the improvement of this fruit, and I have never failed to get the seed to grow by putting it in the ground at once, without previous preparation, giving plenty of water, with shade. I have at this date—July 14th—hundreds of plants up, many of them showing the third leaf, from seed sown since the 1st inst.

For ten years, or more, I have been experimenting with seedling strawberries—have had a thousand or more new sorts fruiting in a season.

Several years were spent in random experiments, before developing anything like improvement. I sowed seed from the largest and best berries, without regard to class or the sexual character of the plant. It was only after discovering that seedlings from hermaphrodites, or from foreign sorts, or from hybrids in which the foreign element predominated, whatever might be their sexual character, were of little or no value, that I conceived of the true theory of progress.

It is this: our native scarlet strawberry must be the basis of any improvement that will be permanent and valuable. While we may get size and, possibly, flavor from foreign sorts, in our native kinds alone lies the germ of productiveness.

Only from the time when I first grew seedlings from the old Virginia scarlet, that were purely pistillates, do I date any real progress.

These were fertilized by the old sorts—Wilson, Triomphe de Gand, Boston Pine, etc., and the best of the pistillates grown were used as the maternal parents of the next generation.

Last year I set a small plot of ground—about thirty square rods—to several of my new kinds, and the leading older sorts, for the purpose of testing their relative value and productiveness, and the result was as surprising to myself and friends as it was gratifying, in disclosing the fact that I had several new seedlings that proved more productive than the world-renowned Wilson even, besides being possessed of other qualities that make them of greater value.

In order to give a more definite idea of the test, I will give my plan more in detail.

The plants were propagated by rooting them into thumb-pots, and were put out as they were grown, a row or two at a time, in July, August, and some as late as September, and consisted of the following sorts:

3 rows of No. 1 Seedling, 5 of No. 9, 2 of No. 6, 1 of No. 8, 1 of No. 10, 1 of No. 3, 1 of No. 2, 2 of Wilson, 1 of Agriculturist, 1 of Brooklyn Scarlet, 1 of Monitor, 1 of Russell's Prolific.

The plants were set two feet by four, two plants to the hill, and had good culture.

My most valuable seedlings are identified by numbers, and are known as No. 1, 6, 9, and, possibly, 8. It was no unusual thing to gather a heaping quart of ripe berries from a hill at one picking of either of these numbers, except 6, which is not quite so prolific.

No. 1, for field culture, will probably take the lead. The berry is a light scarlet in color, about the size of the Wilson when the latter is not overgrown, with fewer small ones, and it will hang on the vines for a week after it is ripe, if the weather is dry, without spoiling, a quality by no means to be overlooked, and as for fruitfulness—it is a marvel to behold.

No. 8 is about as productive as No. 1, late—ten days later than the Wilson. It is a large berry, dark colored, juicy, and sour, which is equivalent to saying that it will not keep, and though hill after hill, set in August last, yielded its quart at the first picking, the finer flavor and better keeping qualities of the other numbers nearly or quite neutralize its value.

No. 6 is probably the most taking sort to the eye, and, possibly, to the majority of people, to the taste also, that I have. The fruit is large, light scarlet, conical, slightly necked, very uniform in size and shape. While none of the berries are as large as you will occasionally find a Wilson, the average will be as large or larger, giving the appearance of having been assorted.

As to quality, it is a rich acid, with just sufficient of the pine aroma to give it flavor, while it does not possess the insipid sweetness that is the characteristic of that class.

No. 9 has also a very distinctive character.

It is the strongest growing sort I have on my grounds. The berries are medium to large, with no small ones; in color, deep scarlet or purple crimson, which adds much to its beauty; in shape, long—about the form of an overgrown blackberry, and in quality it has few compeers. It will hang on a long time, if the weather is favorable, and will do what I never saw another strawberry do before—literally dry into a sweet delicious pulp, like a raisin.—Of the other numbers it is needless to speak, though twenty years ago they would have been great acquisitions.

Of the older sorts, the Russell is of no value—large, productive, soft, and sour—too many small ones—all on the ground, and the plant sun-scalds. The Monitor, too tender. The Brooklyn Scarlet—healthy, hardy, a good grower, sweet fruit—too sweet, but only moderately productive. The Agriculturist is the best of our recently disseminated kinds, so far as I have tried. It produced some of the largest berries on my grounds. It is about as productive as the Wilson under the same treatment—hill culture—and of much better quality, and will keep better than that variety, but not so well as is desirable. Its greatest faults are a want of uniformity in the size of the fruit, and its tendency to cockscomb, and irregular shape.

Of the Wilson it is hardly necessary to speak. That its introduction began a new era in strawberry growing, will not be denied; but it will be superseded, or, at least, hold a divided realm.

Very many of the growers of this fruit found to their cost, the past season, that it was not wise to set all their eggs under one hen, and we think hereafter the later and earlier varieties will command the attention that they deserve.

I will say that none of these new sorts are offered for sale. Although they may be found valuable on my own grounds, and in comparison with the best, this is not a sufficient guarantee that they are adapted to universal cultivation. They will be put into the hands of leading and reliable horticulturists to be pronounced upon.

In the mean time, that the progress of experiment may not stop with these results, the best plants from the seed of best varieties I have yet grown will go into experimental grounds.

A Trial of Early Peas.

The number of peas named in the catalogues of seedsmen, each claiming to be the earliest, led the Royal Horticultural Society, (England), to institute a comparative trial in 1865. The results of this trial we gave in May, 1866; these were severely criticised, not only by interested seedsmen, but by some of the English Horticultural Journals. This year another trial has been made at the Society's gardens at Chiswick, and we condense the following from a report in the Gardeners' Chronicle:

"The earliest Pea was long considered to be the Early Frame, which varied slightly, although its variations could scarcely be made out as permanently distinct. Sometimes differences were indicated by the designations of Double-Blossomed and Single-Blossomed Frames, and Early Nimble; there was, indeed, no Express in those days, but there was the Early Racehorse, a name indicative of a pea that would quickly become fit for use; and there were more than twenty others which ultimately proved synonymous. From amongst these arose the Early Kent, Early Emperor, Prince Albert, and subsequently Sangster's No. 1, or Daniel O'Rourke.

Among a number of samples, consisting of varieties with differences almost imperceptible, some in the course of repeated sowings exhibited a more luxuriant habit than others; and luxuriance militates against earliness. On the contrary, Dillistone's Early, Carter's First Crop, and Sutton's Ringleader, &c., at the expense of luxuriance, have gained earliness over Early Frame and Early Emperor. Vegetables of all kinds raised from seed are liable to degeneration. Much depends on a careful selection of the plants from which to save the seed; for if the most vigorous plants are selected and grown in succession in rich soil, a more luxuriant but later progeny will result. In this way a variety which is found to be the first in point of earliness this season, may become only second, third, or fourth in the next or subsequent years.

The Committee, at their meeting held on the 25th inst., decided that Dillistone's Early, Carter's First Crop, Sutton's Ringleader, and Veitch's Early, were identical. There can not be any doubt on that point; they were all sown on the same day, and they respectively bloomed, slatted, and became fit for use on the same day. They were, moreover, all injured by the frost more than any others, but all in an equal degree; while Sangster's No. 1, Dickson's First and Best, &c., under the same conditions, were not injured in the slightest degree.

Dwarf Waterloo is ten days later than Sangster's No. 1; from 12 to 18 inches high, producing large pods, well filled, excellent, earlier than, and an improvement on, Bishop's Long-pod.

Sudbury A 1, and Nutting's No. 1 wrinkled, are identical. This is a very excellent early white wrinkled marrow, three days earlier than Alliance, and with larger and better filled pods; about 18 inches high.

Carter's Improved Emperor is very similar to Dickson's First and Best; free bearing, and a very excellent stock.

Sangster's No. 1 and Daniel O'Rourke are synonymous.

Taber's Perfection and Early Perfection (Brown) are identical; a day or two later, and producing more haulm than Sangster's No. 1.

Young's No. 1 (Veitch) is a capital early Pea, of about the same earliness as Sangster's No. 1, but taller and stronger; a good cropper. The ripe seed of a pale olive color; darker than any of the others in the same class.

Washington is the same as Early Emperor.

Carpenter's Express is a run-out mixed stock.

Hooper's Early Rival is a much mixed stock of Sangster's No. 1.

London Conqueror is a third-rate stock of the old Early Frame.

Taber's 08, a shade dwarfer, but is in other respect identical with Dickson's Favorite.

Essex Rival (Eley) is seven to eight days later than Sangster's No. 1; a large pale-podded white marrow, with blotched foliage, about four feet high, of the old Ringwood Marrow class. The peas when cooked are of a nice green color; it is a very productive and most excellent pea.

Sutton's Long-podded Tom Thumb seems very much like the Old Spanish Dwarf.

Carter's Improved Tom Thumb shows no improvement.

Little Gem (Turner), a blue wrinkled marrow, is truly a little gem, coming into use but a few days after Sangster's No. 1, having very large pods, very productive, and of excellent quality. This can not be too highly recommended.

Multum in Parvo (Nutting) resembles Little Gem, but with somewhat broader pods, and is a few days later than that variety."

The Garden and the Farm.

In a somewhat extended journey we have had our eyes open to see the farmers' gardens. We have seen the poor patches, called gardens, in which peas and beans were struggling with mustard and other weeds, and, as far as we could see, the weeds generally had the best of it. Peas, beans, cabbages, cucumbers, beets, squashes, and, rarely, tomatoes, make up the usual variety. How rarely we see an asparagus bed, while spinach, egg plant, salsify, okra, and even sweet corn are seldom met with. How a farmer can do without asparagus and sweet corn, is beyond our comprehension. The one, when once established, will yield for years a supply in early spring, just at the time when all green things are scarce, and therefore the more acceptable; the other, as easily raised as any other corn, and no one who has once tasted its delicious kernels will ever again go to the field for roasting ears. We must mention one notable exception to this general neglect. Not far from Glen's Falls, N. Y., we passed a farm which attracted attention from the excellent condition of its fences and the neat appearance of its fields. Upon nearing the house, our eyes were delighted with the sight of a large and well kept kitchen garden, in which there appeared to be an extensive variety of esculent vegetables. Had it not rained torrents, we should have tried to ascertain the name of this exemplary farmer—we know from the looks of his garden that he reads the *Agriculturist*, and we congratulate him and his family that they can enjoy so many of the good things that earth affords to those who will take a little trouble to procure them. If farmers would grow a few acres less of corn or wheat, and devote the labor required for these to a good kitchen garden, it would pay in the saving of meat, and doubly pay in the amount of satisfaction and contentment it would bring. Farmers, do you know that the sameness and unattractiveness of the table has much to do with the desire of your sons to leave home? Contentment with daily pork and potatoes, with an occasional variation to cabbage, is hardly to be expected. A family garden is humanizing.

Why Transplanted Trees Die.

"WORTH KNOWING—TRANSPLANTING TREES.—If the Commissioners of the Central Park would give strict orders to mark the north side of trees with red chalk before they are taken up, and when set out to have the tree put in the ground with its north side to the north in its natural position, a large proportion would live. Ignoring this law of nature is the cause of so many transplanted trees dying. If the north side is exposed to the south, the heat of the sun is too great for that side of the tree to bear, and therefore it dries up and decays."

These worthy gentlemen who are engaged in adorning our Central Park, will be grateful for this bit of advice. They have lost a great many trees there. They die by the hundred every year, and many thousands in all have been lost, and all for the want of "a piece of red chalk." We quote this as a sample of the "profane and old wives' fables" that are circulated in the farmer's column of some of our cotemporaries. The assertion that the change of the side of a tree from north to south in transplanting affects the chances of its living, is without any basis of facts sufficient to support it. It may or may not be true. We believe it has as little to do with the life of a tree as the phase of the moon at the time of transplanting, and the assertion is calculated to do injury by diverting attention from the causes which do make new plantations failures. These are the loss of too many of the fine rootlets in taking up the tree, the drying of the roots in removal, the want of drainage and preparation of the soil, careless handling and planting, want of mulching, and the prevalence of severe drying winds immediately after planting. These evils are not to be remedied by a piece of red chalk or the skin of a black cat.

Horticulture in Indiana.

We were agreeably surprised in our recent visit to see so many evidences of progress in this delightful art. Indiana has not only a State Society with its volume of transactions, but several auxiliary societies in the larger towns, which have frequent meetings, and are doing much, with fine fruits and flowers, to awaken an interest in gardens. The State Society is in the sixth year of its existence, and holds two sessions annually of several days each, which are well attended, and occupied with lively discussions. These meetings, reports of which are published in the papers, are diffusing a knowledge of the better varieties of fruit, and encouraging the planting of orchards and vineyards. The influence of these discussions is apparent in all the older parts of the State, especially in the suburbs of the large towns.

The climate and soil of this State are favorable to fruit culture, and nearly all the small fruits flourish in the greatest luxuriance, with ordinary care. The apple and pear are at home, and can be raised in any desired quantities. Apples are abundant this season throughout the State. We saw but one orchard that had any appearance of disease, or was not well filled with fruit, if it had reached bearing age. There are many young orchards a few years out, or just planted, that are looking in perfect health. Pears are not as extensively planted, but flourish quite as well, and in the opinion of a gentleman of large experience, do quite as well as the apple, and bear with more uniformity. Grapes are cultivated to some extent, and many in the vicinity of the cities are planting vineyards. The Concord is unquestionably the most popular grape in the State, and the vines that have been planted are now so generally in bearing condition, that fruit growers understand whereof they affirm. The Hartford Prolific stands next, but drops its berries from the bunch. The Delaware and Rebecca are superb, but are poor growers. We found one fruit grower who cultivated the latter in the shade, to prevent it from casting its leaves, a calamity to which it is exceedingly liable. The newer varieties are in cultivation, and their merits for the climate and soil of the State will soon be decided. They have a flourishing local Society at Terre Haute, of which Hon. D. H. Scott is President; also at Laporte, of which Hon. A. L. Osborne is President. Monroe, Indianapolis, Danville, Plainfield, Bridgeport, and Fort Wayne, also have flourishing horticultural societies.

Notes on Grapes and Grape Culture.

So much was said last year about grapes that we have but little to add upon the subject until the season of ripening shall have given us more knowledge concerning the merits or demerits of varieties. Many of our contemporaries have opened their columns to a lively discussion of the award of the Greeley Grape Prize, and as about an equal amount of abuse has characterized both sides of the dispute, we assume that the account is square. It seems to us that no good can come from the further agitation of this subject, for no one, with even a limited knowledge of fruits, would expect to find any one variety of any fruit that will be the best in every locality. The mistake was not so much in the award of the Committee, as that they should consent to act at all upon so impracticable a proposition.

As we write, (early in August,) we hear some accounts of mildew and rot, and in some localities the Concord, which is usually free from disease, has rotted and dropped badly. In the only case of this which has come under our observation, the vines were not closely pinched, but allowed to keep on growing; while in those places where the vines were systematically pruned, and the laterals pinched, no rot was visible.

We believe that the early establishment of a strong and robust foliage, by pinching the bearing shoot at three or four leaves beyond the last bunch of grapes, and persistently pinching back the laterals, has much to do with the vigor of the vine, and its ability to resist rot and mildew.

We cannot learn that it has caused much trouble where sulphur and other remedies were promptly applied. One of our editors, finding that mildew had appeared upon his vines, followed the suggestion of Mr. Lazaris, of Athens, Greece, which was published in the *Agriculturist*, for August, 1866. Mr. L. proposed the use of dry clay or any other fine dust, as a substitute for sulphur. He considered that when used in the open air, sulphur acted merely as an absorbent of moisture, and if this were the case, any other dry powder thrown upon the mildew would dry it up and destroy it. He found dry and sifted clay and fine road dust were equally efficacious with sulphur. Without asserting that the fact is proven, the instance above cited shows that, in that case at least, the use of dust arrested the mildew, and that the matter is one deserving the attention of grape growers. The fact that some cultivators find that a mixture of air-slaked lime and sulphur is better than sulphur alone, seems to point to the same conclusion. Overbearing is also a common fault; it serves to weaken the vine, and while a larger number of bunches may be obtained, they will be inferior in both size and quality.

In some places there is complaint of the failure of the grapes to set well, very large clusters often having but three or four fertilized and growing berries upon them, all the others remaining abortive. This may be owing to heavy rains or cold, and damp weather just at the critical period of blossoming. We look forward with much interest to the grape harvest this autumn, as the status of many of the newer kinds will be better known; and it is our intention to keep our readers advised of all that is likely to interest them in relation to this increasingly important branch of horticulture.

VARIEGATED PELARGONIUMS.—The Pelargoniums, (often called Geraniums,) with variegated leaves, are now very numerous, and the number is rapidly increasing. Some of them have leaves of such beautiful colors that they have all the brilliancy of flowers. In England, these plants are much employed in bedding, and very fine effects are produced by them. With us their use in this way is attended by very indifferent success, and those who would enjoy the beauty of such fine varieties as Mrs. Pollock, Sunset, and others of that elegant class, must grow them in-doors. Our hot sun is too much for the delicate foliage of these variegated kinds, and the leaves soon curl up, and drop off. Besides this, caterpillars make sad havoc among them, and they need looking over every day to remove these pests. Among a large number tried this year out of doors, the most satisfactory were the Mountain of Snow, which has a dark-green leaf with a broad and well-marked white margin, and the Cloth of Gold, the leaf of which is of yellowish green, bordered with yellow, the two not very distinctly defined. We hope that some of the more richly colored ones will be found that will endure our summer heats.

KEYES' EARLY PROLIFIC TOMATO—was advertised as being thirty days earlier than any other variety—a claim so extravagant that we have watched it in widely different localities with much interest. H. J. Rudisell, of Fort Wayne, Ind., grew them in his market garden, side by side with the Early York, of Henderson, and the Eureka, and they ripened at the same time with these varieties. The plants were all forced in the usual manner, and the first specimens were picked July 17th. On the other hand, Chas. Downing, as well as cultivators near New York, finds it to be at least ten days earlier than any other variety. Even this is a great advance, and had it been put out as being ten days earlier than others, instead of thirty, the public would have accepted it as a probable statement, and have been more disposed to try it.

THE RABBIT-FOOT CLOVER.—(*Trifolium arvense.*)

The Rabbit-foot Clover.—(*Trifolium arvense.*)

In poor and sandy soil, and in old fields, there is found a plant, the peculiar softness of which, with its dull, gray appearance, is very apt to attract attention. It has many popular names, among which are Rabbit-foot and Hare's-foot-Clover, Pussy-Clover, Stone-Clover, etc. Its botanical name is *Trifolium arvense*, and though in its general appearance it is unlike the other clovers with which we are familiar, its structure in the main corresponds with theirs. It is a much branched annual, that grows from 5 to 10 inches high, and produces upon the ends of its branches flower heads that are at first globular, but which soon elongate and become cylindrical. The engraving, taken from a small plant, gives its general appearance. The three-parted leaves are quite small, the flower heads being the most conspicuous part of the plant. The whole plant is covered with silky hairs, and the heads are especially soft to the touch. A close examination shows to what this softness is owing. At the lower left hand side we have given a single flower, very much magnified. The corolla, which in other clovers is so showy, is here very small, while the points of the calyx are much elongated, thickly clothed with silky hairs, and the most conspicuous parts of the flower. Though so common with us from Canada to Florida, it was introduced from Europe. It can hardly be ranked as a troublesome weed, as it is, like other annual weeds, readily exterminated by cultivation.

A WORD FOR THE CURRANT.—It is very strange that so little attention is paid to this most acceptable fruit. It is easily raised, and brings a good price in market, the supply always being short of the demand. We shall have something to say about varieties and propagation for those who wish to make new plantations. At present we give the experience of the author of "Walks and Talks," for the benefit of those who have old and unproductive bushes: "We have had a splendid crop of currants this year. There was quite a quantity of old bushes on the farm when we came here, but the worms had stripped off every leaf, and they were in a forlorn condition. We set out a number of new ones, and in the meantime undertook to renovate the old ones by pruning and manuring. The old bushes have produced this year five times as many currants as the new ones, and are good for years to come. Currants bring six dollars a bushel in the city, and it would seem that at such prices the crop would be a profitable one. If you have old bushes of good varieties, dig about them and dung them. Cut out all the suckers except one or two that may be needed to take the place of the old, decayed branches. Keep a sharp lookout for the worms soon after the leaves are formed. You will find the eggs on the under side of the lower leaves, and they can be crushed between the thumb and finger in a moment. And then, especially, look out for the second brood, after the fruit is gathered, and serve them in the same way. It is here where so many fail. Destroy this second brood, and you will have comparatively few to kill next spring. If any escape, dust the bushes with *white* hellebore powder; but don't forget to destroy the eggs."

INCREASE OF FORESTS IN FRANCE.—The forests in France are under the care of the government, and under the new laws for their protection, they have increased nearly one million of acres. Less than one sixth of the area of the kingdom is covered with woodland. This is much less than is desirable for the best interests of the husbandman. It is estimated that from twenty to twenty-five per cent. of a country should be covered with forest, in order to secure uniformly good crops. Our forests, now disappearing at the rate of 8,000,000 of acres annually, demand the attention of government

THE HOUSEHOLD.

(☞ For other Household Items, see "Basket" pages.)

Dashes at House-Keeping with a Free Pencil.

PRIZE ESSAY BY MISS EVA M. COLLINS, ROCHESTER.

THE PLAY-ROOM MADE OVER.

Jennie thinks she is getting to be too large a girl to have a play-room any longer, and quite surprised me a few days ago by asking if I could not help her convert it into a spare bedroom for her. Little

Fig. 1.—PLAY-ROOM CONVERTED.

cousin Helen is coming to spend her vacation here, and probably that was what put the idea into Jennie's head; but at that moment the little black-eyed lady did not occur to me, nor did the possibility of bestowing any of our friends there seem very feasible, so I could only echo the last of her sentence, "bedroom for me," as Miss Betsy Lavender would have done. The play-room is six feet by nine, or would be of those dimensions, only that a chimney occupies a third of one end of the room, protruding eighteen inches into the apartment, which makes it appear even smaller than it is in reality. It was originally a large closet, but had been from time immemorial, so far as I am concerned, given up to the little girls for a play room, and had now for years belonged exclusively to the baby. And so the baby wanted to convert the play-room into a spare room. "Well! what next?" Whereupon little sister explained herself. It would make such a nice little room, just large enough for Helen—and herself—and very likely the spare rooms will all be in requisition for larger company, especially while the boys are at home. She is sure she and Helen will like the room all the better for its small size, and it will seem like keeping house in earnest to have the room where she has always pretended to live, for her own. Dim visions of the possibility of having to take one of the children into my room had been hovering in the distance for several days, but this disposition of the play room dispelled them at once, though I should never have thought of it. Ralph was, as usual, our right hand man. He brought down the oldest cot-bed from the garret, and by shortening it half a foot, removing a large rent in the foot of the canvas, and made the bed fit in the short way of the room, so Jennie has still a passage way from the door to the window, fig. 1, besides the spaces each side of the chimney. In the space back of the door, Ralph has put up a number of hooks, and by hanging a curtain in front of them, it makes quite a respectable wardrobe. For the other space, the one near the window, Ralph has contrived a toilet table, which

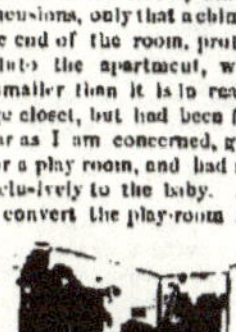

Fig. 2.—TOILET TABLE.

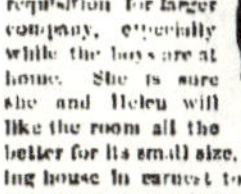

Fig. 3.—TOILET CASE.

Jennie declares is just the thing. It is a board securely fastened over cleats with a curtain in front, and a cloth over the top, fig. 2. Over the toilet table and near the window we hung a case for combs and brushes, made of pasteboard and covered with tissue paper, fig. 3. I tell Jennie she and Helen will have to be very neat, or they will make a deal of washing, as everything in the room is white—bed, window curtains, wardrobe, and toilet table. Jennie thought she wanted a place for a few books, so we hung a little shelf, fig. 4, at the foot of her bed, opposite the "Lord's Prayer," which hung over the head of it. Then she thought "nothing was wanting but a light stand which would not take up any room." Ralph has suited her exactly, fig. 5, and has made the bottom of the stand so much heavier than the top, that it will not easily tip over. The room is cunning enough. The small red and white squares in the matting look brighter than ever before, and the view from the window is lovely either in winter or summer, as it looks off down one of the most beautiful valleys in the world.

Fig. 4.—BOOKCASE.

Two little sets of hands to keep out of mischief this summer! Jennie has a box at the bottom of her wardrobe, where I am to put work for her and Helen, as I come across anything that will answer for them, the only conditions being that no work placed in the box can be undertaken before the article under way is completed, except by permission. Jennie, and I believe children generally, likes the plan of being obliged to decide for herself, and then of being held to her own decision, even though some different course may appear more attractive. Grandmother has taught her that little girls who are driven about by every passing fancy, almost always grow up into wavering, weak minded, silly women, while it is the privilege, the right, the duty of each little girl to grow into a noble, beautiful woman. It will be entirely optional with the children whether any work in this box shall be commenced or not, but if begun, it must be finished unless there is some very good reason why it can not be done; therefore the pro's and con's must all be considered beforehand. This piece of thick Bristol-board, six inches by eight, will make them a transparency to hang in their window. If I draw the design lightly with a pencil, they can cut it upon a board with a penknife, wherever it is marked, bend all the points out, and paste a narrow ribbon around the edge, fig. 6. Jennie called us last evening to see how the moonlight shadowed the grotesque figures in the window curtains over the bed and wall. The cross among the leaves will form an agreeable variety. Here is a bundle of bright cambric and silk for linings to muslin bags, which have long been waiting to be made. I will roll the white cotton yarn with this parcel, and put it into the children's work-box. A pattern in the roll, fig. 7, will show them what this is intended for, and please them better than verbal instruction. It seems a little sad to see the play-room thus "converted," as Jennie calls it. I really almost wish I could have dressed the little people's dolls for one more Christmas, in the play-room; but after all, Jennie is right; it is only the play-room still in a different dress—not very materially different, because suddenly clothed anew. Real changes are slow in their growth, necessarily, because growth requires time. The little room will be the play-room probably for some time to come. Mothers! do not hastily wrest the play-room from the children. It has a mission to fulfill. It teaches them by constant practice how to make the most of every thing; to cover over neatly the most outlandish shapes; to make homely things pretty, and to see all the naughty traits in themselves in their true light, as they are reflected in their imaginary little ones. The lessons learned in the play-room, more than elsewhere, are industry, patience, gentleness, economy, and accuracy, while the taste is cultivated, and affection sacredly cherished. No matter if the hundredth attempt is still rude and unsuccessful, it is yet a step in the right direction. A suggestion now and then will not be lost. The child may be taught, but the lessons can be learned only by itself. The most beautiful painting was, in its first stage, a mere daub, and so the child, in its first endeavors, can not be expected to foreshadow the ingenious woman, which, in a congenial atmosphere, its mature growth may unfold.

Fig. 5.

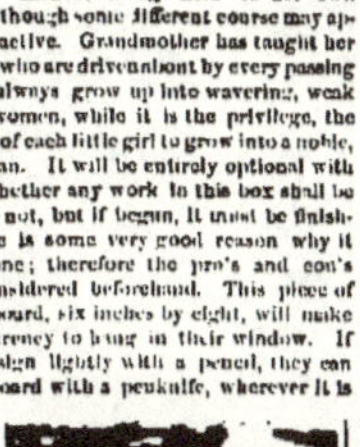

Fig. 6.—TRANSPARENCY.

Fig. 7.—BAG.

Leaves from the Diary of a Young Housekeeper.—No. IX.

PRIZE ESSAY BY MRS. LAURA E. LYMAN, STAMFORD, CT.

Sept. 7th.—On our way home from our delightful visit to Mr. and Mrs. George, I expressed to Edward my unbounded admiration for a farmer's life, such as we saw it in their establishment, and I thought over in my mind some improvements I might make in housekeeping, and especially in the care of my milk, cream, and butter. The secret of Mrs. George's splendid success in the production of butter is, that she has every facility for preserving nearly a uniform temperature in every part of her dairy establishment, the year round. Since coming home I have endeavored to imitate her so far as the arrangements of my house will, as yet, permit. I have no ice chamber for keeping my cream in as she has, but talking the matter over with Edward, he suggested that in one corner of the cellar the soil is damp and cool, and that a little pit might be made there to answer the purpose. So he took his spade and made a little hole about eight inches deep, where I place my cream jar and fill it round with the moist, cool earth, so that I can preserve it at nearly a uniform temperature. My last churning showed the difference; it was as good September butter as I ever saw. I have also put less milk in a pan than I used to, and find the cream rises more perfectly.

Sept. 12th.—The past week has been a very busy one. The apples and tomatoes are ripening rapidly and must be cared for in their proper time; so, early and late, Sue and I have kept our knives in motion, and in the evening Edward has kept the paring machine running. Instead of the old mode of quartering and coring them, we find slicing them in thin pieces, uniform in thickness, is a better and more expeditious way of preparing them. As apples, when drying, very readily absorb flavors, I have observed the utmost care in keeping them where they could acquire no taint. Edward made me a scaffolding of hemlock boards upon which I spread some old sheets that were perfectly clean, and laid over the apples some fly netting to preserve them from the contact of insects of all kinds.

These hot days of September I thought best to improve in drying tomatoes, in imitation of dried figs. After making a rich syrup and cooking them till they were done, which takes fifteen or twenty minutes, I spread them on plates to dry. Thus prepared they are almost equal to dried figs. My cans are of glass, with India rubber stoppers, and require no cement of any kind to make them air-tight. After using cans of various kinds, mother at last settled upon these as the best, and I use no other. As tomato preserve is so very sweet, I decided to fill but a small jar, and can nearly all I put up. My recipe is half a pound of sugar to a pint of water. This makes the tomato sufficiently sweet, and its flavor is not so much disguised by the syrup as when more sugar is used. I have made a large jar of green tomato pickle, which Edward likes so much, and which is not a very common dish, and after the early frosts, I shall make another of the green tomatoes left upon the vines. No pickle is more easily made, and none better than this. To a peck of tomatoes, sliced about a quarter of an inch thick, add sufficient vinegar to cover them, and of whole spices, one ounce each of pepper, cloves, allspice, cinnamon, and white mustard seed, and two medium sized onions chopped fine. Bring them all to the boiling point for a minute, and then pour into a jar and set in a cool place. In two weeks they will be ready for use. The finest looking of my ripe tomatoes I preserve and dry; the others make excellent catsup.

Sept. 18th.—For a week we have been reveling in ripe grapes, and I have used all my skill in endeavoring to preserve them in jellies, with sugar and by other modes, so as to prolong our enjoyment of them into the winter months. Edward has picked some of the finest clusters, and I prepared several dozen strings of uniform length, with which we tied them to long poles and hung them in the wood-house loft, taking special care to remove all that were imperfect, and not to bruise any or break them from the cluster. Here we will let them remain until freezing weather, when they can be transferred to the cellar without disturbing them on the poles. I feel quite confident that we shall have some delicious clusters to lay upon our table at New Year's, and perhaps as late as February. We experimented also upon the French mode of preserving grapes, with what success remains to be seen next winter. It seems as though it must succeed, and it is very simple. Edward made a thick whitewash of the consistency of cream, straining it, and taking pains to crush all the little pieces of lime. We then dipped a number of the very finest clusters into this whitewash, taking them out very slowly. The dipping was repeated two or three times, until a firm white crust, looking like a rough egg shell, was formed all over each grape, and the stem to which they are attached. We hung these clusters with the others in the wood-house loft.

Sept. 20th.—Three or four days since Edward's sister, Jane, came to visit us. She looked pale and worn, and I found upon conversation with her that she had been sitting in the house all day, instead of breathing this delightful September air under the open sky, and burning the lamp late at night, reading some new French novels, which a friend had sent her. Edward and I talked the matter over and determined to initiate her, unconsciously to herself, into the delight and the wholesomeness of ample out-door exercise and early hours of sleep at night. So every day since she came, we have planned some excursion or some pastime, which has given us all full draughts of this boundless ocean of air the Creator has poured above and around us. The roses are beginning to bloom on her cheek, and she has ceased to inquire constantly for "some interesting book." If our American women would but spend an hour or two every day in the open air, how much should we as a nation gain in health and happiness. The exercise of housework is not sufficient; it is monotonous and liable to become mere drudgery. The wife and mother, if she would ever keep fresh in feeling and firm in health, if she would be always cheerful and a bright and radiant center of home delight, must daily leave her cares and the little routine of her domestic activities and place her spirit in harmony with the perpetual calm and the annual round of nature.

Sept. 27th.—Yesterday and to-day we have made a lounge for our sitting room, and we shall find it a great addition to our comfort this fall and winter. Edward got out the frame and legs, fastened them securely together and nailed some slats on the under side of the long side pieces. Into these, at regular intervals, we put some second hand springs he found at an upholsterer's, and tacked over them an old quilt, tying each spring with twine to the quilt to keep it in place. Then I made a mattress case of tow cloth and filled it with the shucks we saved when we were drying corn, and some others, which were all carefully picked over, and covered the whole with brown calico, and a very presentable article of furniture it makes. I priced a lounge the other day at the store, and the cheapest article I could find, and that a very poor one, was thirteen dollars, so I determined to make one myself. We reckoned up the cost, and find it amounts to just six dollars and fifty cents. The frame timber is worth fifty cents, the springs cost thirty, the ten yards of tow cloth came to three dollars and a half, and the calico cover two dollars and twenty cents. Jane made the cover while I made the mattress, and we finished the whole thing up very quickly.

Sept. 30th.—I thought it would do Jane good to see a little of Sue White's housekeeping, and her excellent management of her boys, so she consented to stop on her way home to visit my excellent friend, if I would go with her. I was curious to learn too, how Sue, who at school had been noted for her love of Plato and the classics, had become so thoroughly practical a woman in all domestic matters. Our conversation naturally fell on the routine of household duties, and I expressed to Sue my surprise at the perfect familiarity she seemed to have with all the little details of nice cookery, and every department of family industry. "It is very true," said she, "that at school I reveled in the ideal world. I dreamed with Plato, I delighted in Shakespeare and the poets, but after marriage my husband placed Bacon's Novum Organum in my hands for me to read, and it effected an entire revolution in my daily life. I saw the beauty of utility, and determined to become as Baconian in my practice as a housewife as I had been Platonic in my previous modes of thinking. From that time I have made it a principle and a study to have every article on my table prepared in the very best manner possible, and to perform every task in the most thoroughly practical and sensible manner."

October 4th.—For two days I have been engaged in a task that would have been very heavy had not Edward assisted me. We assorted the wool that we reserved from the spring clipping, taking a few pounds of the best for stocking yarn, washed and dried the remainder, and made it into a mattress, which has cost us only the price of the ticking.

Mrs. George told me of an excellent and cheap way of making a spring bed, by purchasing three or four dozen of spiral coils of wire at an upholsterer's establishment, and setting them into the slats of the bedstead. She has a set of them that have been in use many years, and are now as good as ever. The upper end of the wire is fastened to the last turn of the coil, and the wires covered with an old quilt upon which the mattress is laid.

Leaves from My Journal.—No. VII.

PRIZE ESSAY BY MRS. E. MC'LELLAN, OF OHIO.

September.—There is much sickness in town from typhoid fever. That is always tedious, distressing, and alarming. When sickness comes, how vain appear our worldly cares and anxieties. We resolve never to be so engrossed by them again. And yet we could hardly bear always to carry about the heavy heart we have now. Nursing the sick seems especially to belong to woman, but man's stronger arms and nerves are quite as indispensable. "Oh," said a daughter, after recovering from a long and dangerous illness, "I felt *so at rest* when father was in my room." What little things will annoy and distress the sick! The mind is weak with the body, and must be as tenderly cared for and indulged. Some displacement of furniture, a spider hanging from its web in some corner, music on the street, noise of the children, bread burned instead of nicely toasted, tea not boiling hot, water not just from the well, jar upon the sensitive nerves and create suffering and complaint, which, to one never or rarely sick, appear childish in the extreme. I remember when Nellie was but four, she was sick with a disease affecting the head. The room to which she was confined had a window containing in the lower sash but two frames in depth, while the upper one had three. She often said aloud, "three and two, three and two!" We supposed her mind wandering, but at last discovered it was the incongruity of the window, from which she could not divert her attention. At another time a friend whose shoulder had been dislocated, and who was obliged to lie in one position, suffered greatly from a stray hair that was under the shoulder. I laughingly told her it was only her fancy, until seeing the tears in her eyes, I found and removed it. In health we may call such things foolish—in sickness we had better not. Fresh air and water work wonders in the sick room. Cover the patient, head and all, with the bed clothes, adding more if the weather is cold, and open wide the windows for two or three minutes, when the day is fine. Every time the patient drinks, let the water be fresh. The nerves of taste and smell become as sensitive as any others. Fresh linen is a luxury, and everything about the person and bed should be kept strictly clean.

It becomes, of course, no light task to take care of the sick, and calls for a large stock of patience and endurance. Lost sleep must be made up at odd times, as far as possible, a bath often taken, and fresh air without stint. A good meal, too, is an excellent disinfectant. A cheerful face, a cheerful tone of voice, *never a whisper*, rather quick and decided movements, instead of timid and lingering, all tend to inspire the patient with hope, and produce happy results. These are small things in themselves, but being usually left by the physician to the good sense of the nurse, should not be overlooked by her, or even considered less important than medicine towards effecting a cure.

Our dear father has gone to his rest. Though robust for one of his age, he had not strength to rally again from so long and wasting a fever. My husband was the younger of his children, and his home has been with us for a few years past. We shall miss his gentle quiet ways, his hat by the door, his cane in the corner. His chair at the fireside will be vacant now. No more stories for the children, of the times when he was a little boy, about which they never wearied of hearing. He didn't seem old as he was, for his heart was warm and young. His age was seventy-five. To the child, how far in the future! To him it was "but a span." Has life to him opened again, where death never comes? We trust "All is well."

To-day I was made glad with the sight of Lizzie's dear face peering in through my blind, while she called me to take a view of Georgy, who, without ceremony, had seated himself under an apple tree, and after filling his lap with apples, had commenced the work of eating them all up. How he has grown! I venture to say that grandmother thinks there never was such a child before, though she may have a dozen of her own. Ah, yes, I see it now! Those little socks so gaily shaded and ribbed, are her work, I know. The apron with long sleeves, fitting closely about the neck, and substantial shoes, have come from her good motherly advice. But can it be that baby Georgy has gone, and this stout boy has taken his place? Mr. Beecher says: "Nothing on earth grows so fast as children." I should know, if he had said no more, that his own were leaving the home circle; that he too was growing old! But Lizzie has improved in looks. The rest from care awhile has been just what she needed. Home, too, will seem dearer now than ever, and with new energy she will enter upon its duties. Of one thing I am pretty sure. Her mother never before found an ear more ready to listen to instruction. In all her girlhood days she learned not so much about housekeeping as in these few weeks under her mother's tuition. How often she had heard the same things before! Now they have a real value.

BOYS & GIRLS' COLUMNS.

Breath—How Air is Purified.

In our last talk about the breath, we showed that what passed from the lungs, and the bubbles which rise from the lime and vinegar, are similar; both make clear lime-water turn milky. Such air, or, more properly speaking, such *gas*, is called *carbonic acid gas*. It forms the largest part of the breath which leaves the lungs, and is a poison if breathed again. Freshly burned lime will absorb this gas from the air, and become "air-slaked." If strong vinegar or other acid be poured upon air-slaked lime, it will unite with the lime, and let the carbonic acid gas pass off again. Wood, coal, and most combustibles are largely made up of *carbon*. When they are burned, *oxygen* from the air unites with the carbon and forms carbonic acid. When air is drawn into the lungs, it mixes with the blood, and its *oxygen* unites with carbon contained in the blood, forming carbonic acid, which is expelled by breathing out. Then the atmosphere around the house is being constantly spoiled by all the fires that are burning, and by every living creature that breathes, for they are all pouring out the poisonous carbonic acid gas. There must be some very extensive apparatus to purify the air, for it has received millions of tons of carbonic acid every day for thousands of years. There is such apparatus. It is found in every leaf of the trees, in every blade of grass, in every weed that grows under the water, in all vegetable productions. For these are so made, that they take carbonic acid from the air, keep the carbon to increase their growth, and send out the oxygen into the atmosphere again. The wood of forest trees, the stalk of waving corn, the flowers, and all the innumerable parts of vegetable growth, are mostly made of carbon thus drawn from the air. The breath from your lungs to-day may ere long be part of the rose which will bloom in the garden. The wood consumed in your stove will find its way back to the forests; the coal will help to nourish the harvests of coming years. The wheat will be eaten, its carbon will help form living muscle, this, when worn out, will be taken into the blood, oxygen from the air will enter the lungs, find the worn-out particle, and unite with it, the gas will go forth to enter some other form of growth—and thus ceaselessly the wonderful round of growth, change, decay, and new life will be continued to the end of time, as it has since its beginning, ever bearing testimony to the wondrous skill of the Creator, and his goodness in providing for the life of his creatures, and calling for their gratitude.

Ready and Willing to Work.

On the roof of a high building at the corner of a street in the city of New York, stands the statue of a boy leaning against the trunk of a tree. He seems in a watchful, waiting mood; not idly wasting time, but all ready for a call to duty,—hoping for it and expecting it. The boy represented there has grown to be a prosperous and wealthy man. When a boy he was very poor. A tree stood upon that street corner then, and there he would go and wait, sometimes leaning for rest against the tree, but always on the alert; always ready for work, and prompt to answer the first call of any who would employ him. Years passed by and he became the rich owner of that corner and the buildings on it. But he was not ashamed of the days of his honest poverty, and he caused this statue to be made from the old tree, and placed where it is, to show what he had been in his boyhood. And now the statue is constantly proclaiming from its lofty place to all the passers by, what industry and perseverance can accomplish.—There is nothing wonderful in that boy's success. He was *not ashamed to work*, and was *always ready* for it. Here, boys, is a lesson for you. Most of you will probably have to work for a living. Do not regard that as a misfortune. Make up your minds to go at it like *manly* boys; always wide-awake, always willing to do your part as fast as you find out what that is. Such boys make noble men.

UNCLE PAUL.

Terriers vs. Cats.—A sharp-eyed correspondent, "G. H. C.," thus comments on the answer to the "Cat Problem," (No. [illegible]). "Mathematically it is answered correctly, but practically, it is incorrect, for the reason that a cat rarely, if ever, kills two rats in immediate succession. As soon as one rat is vanquished, it is carried to a place of safety, or to the house to be exhibited, or more frequently the cat begins to devour it. Had the problem named *terriers*, there would have been no such doubts as to practicability." We print this note, to encourage all to keep their eyes open, to closely observe every thing going on around them; the above fact in the habits of cats was probably known to most of those who answered the problem, but only one seems to have thought of it in connection with the problem.

New Puzzles to be Answered.

No. 275. *Figure Puzzle.*—What well-known plant can the number four be made to exactly represent?

No. 276. *Double Puzzle.*—The picture below is first a puzzle for the eye. When all it contains is discovered, you may find a rebus to be read, giving a word that has some fame in history. It will be interesting to read the history describing and giving an account of it, and thus you may get the whole benefit of the puzzle.

No. 277. *Enigma.*—Contributed to the *American Agriculturist* by Mehitable Duncan. I have a tongue, but never eat; I have a voice, but never speak; I'm sometimes young, and sometimes old, but rarely number more than twelve; and 'though all over the world I roam, I very seldom go alone; at home, abroad, in every place, I wear no stays, but often lace; I have eyes, but never see, and the "Wellspring of Life" is contained in me.

No. 278. *Study in Horsemanship.*—This is not difficult to solve, as it is only required to get the boys off their horses. Almost any boy can easily tell how that is done.

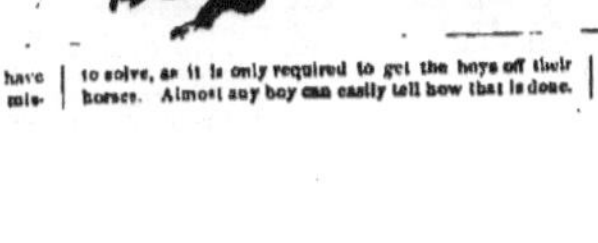

No. 279. *Illustrated Rebus.*—For the young to remember.

Answers to Problems and Puzzles.

The following are answers to the puzzles, etc., in the August number, p. 297. No. 272. *Illustrated Rebus.*—To be over-tenacious in trifles indicates little understanding.... No. 273. *Arithmetical Problem.*—No correct answers received; left open for another month..... No. 274. *Illustrated Rebus.*—Keep malice in your heart, and you harbor a viper there.... The following sent in correct answers to the puzzles, etc.: Clara L. Rice, Jas. Crockett, Susie and Hannah Otis, J. R. Land, Henry Weber, J. F. B., P. J. Umsted, Isaac T. McLain, Stephen Hait, Enos Stoneback, Sarah E. Adkins, Joseph Rawson, Wm. A. Smith, "L. A. C.," Mamie and Lena Close, Samuel F. King, J. Milton Snyder, Sarah L. Tyler, Etta Wilson, John H. Coffin, Andrew Jackson, Henry J. Meixell, Eugene A. Baumann, Hugh U. Kay, M. Campion, S. M. Wright, George E. Clarke, "A. P. C.," Julius M. B. Larabee, Stanford Swords, E. Leonard, T. Gurnee, Frank Botsford, Wm. P. Powell, Student, Beckie R. Morse, William Wilkenson, William H. Rowe, Mary R. Child, Jay Clark, H. J. Porter, F. W. Earl, Frank H. Marston, Anice Cochran, Lebbie Stephens, James D. Marshall.

True Courage.

Bishop Simpson relates the following incident: Before the war, while General Sherman was living in San Francisco, there was a great celebration of Independence Day. The General was Grand Marshal, and presided at an immense gathering at the theatre, where the Declaration was to be read, a poem delivered, with other exercises appropriate to the occasion. Just as the poem was commenced, one of the General's aids advanced to the platform, looking ghastly pale, and beckoning Sherman to him, whispered in his ear that the side-walls of the building had settled under the great pressure from the crowd within, and there was danger of their giving way and overwhelming them in the ruins. The General instantly directed him to be seated where the audience could not see his frightened countenance, ordered another aid to watch the walls and report if any further settling was noticed, and then calmly took his seat and apparently gave his entire attention to the exercises. He judged that any violent commotion among the assembly would be likely to increase the danger, while if they dispersed slowly, no harm might follow. For an hour or more he remained at his post, and at last the crowd retired safely, entirely ignorant of the great peril they had escaped.

[COPYRIGHT SECURED.]

COMMENCEMENT OF HOSTILITIES.—FROM A PAINTING BY ZACHARIE NOTERMAN.—*Engraved for the American Agriculturist.*

A Lively Time in Prospect.

An exciting battle is about commencing, as anybody can see by one look at the picture. As usual, greediness and selfishness are the moving causes, and the innocent, as well as the guilty, must suffer. If anybody does not believe animals feel and think much like human beings, let him study the expression of the enraged cat, whose motherly passion is aroused, and who is ready to meet any odds in repelling the invaders of her home. A few vigorous strokes from pussy's claws will send Fido yelping from his intended feast. He certainly counted without his host. No doubt he had often made the cat scamper at a lively rate, when she came near his premises at dinner time, and he foolishly thought she was a poor, cowardly animal, that would submit to anything. Probably he felt encouraged to make this attempt by his rough play-fellow that he became acquainted with in the street; bad company makes bad manners. That is very much like human nature. Perhaps it would be more correct to say, that human nature, left to itself, is, in many, respects very much like dog and cat nature.

Looking through Grandpa's Spectacles.

"Now, I'll be grandpa," said little Charley Wright. He had climbed into his grandfather's easy chair near the window, wrapped himself in the old gentleman's dressing gown, and clapped on his spectacles, which had been left lying on the window sill. "What a funny little grandpa!" shouted his sister Kate, who was busy with her new building blocks on the floor. "Hush, child, you disturb me," said Charley, looking over the spectacles, and trying to keep very sober and to speak in a heavy and slow voice. He was laughing all over inside his plump little body, and his eyes twinkled with the fun he was having. Kate enjoyed the sport, and "made believe" she was very sorry she had interrupted his meditations, and Charley settled himself back in the chair "to think of old times," he said. In a few minutes he was much surprised to see how different everything looked through the spectacles. His hands appeared large, bony and wrinkled; his feet seemed grown to four times their former size, and in place of his little buttoned gaiters, there were a pair of worked slippers, just such as he had often put on to his grandfather's feet. He started up and stared into the looking glass, where he saw a thin wrinkled face, with sunken cheeks and mouth, and a large head thinly covered with grey hair. "I am grandfather, sure enough," thought he, for his hand trembled as he passed it over his face, and as he walked a twinge of the rheumatism in his limbs made him step very carefully. "Kate, my child, will you please bring some water," said he, turning to the little girl, who was still playing with her blocks. "Yes, pretty soon, grandpa; wait till I finish this church." "I would like it now, dear." "Well, *I'll go*," said she, pettishly, and left the room. "I'm sorry Kate is so thoughtless and rude," said he, to himself, "she cannot know how such conduct pains me." Just then, a boy came bounding into the room, whom he at once recognized as his former self, little Charley. "O, grandpa, I want a ride on your back," shouted he. "Not this afternoon, Charley, my rheumatism hurts me to-day." "Give me a penny then to buy candy." "You have just had dinner, and should not eat anything more now." "Stingy grandpa," replied the boy. He would not have said it if he could have known how the words hurt. The old man sighed, but said nothing. Just then Kate came in with a glass of water in one hand and a large apple in the other. "Oh, I want an apple," cried Charley, trying to snatch it from her hand. "You can't have this," said Kate, holding it out of reach. "Go ask Susan, she will give you one." "I want that one," persisted Charley, struggling to get it. The old gentleman here interfered, but Charley turned upon him, and would have struck him, but his arm was firmly held, and he was led to the door, put out, and told to stay out until he could behave himself properly. "Why will children be so thoughtless and selfish," said the old man sadly, as he sank back in his chair. "They make themselves unhappy, and disturb all around them. If they could only feel for a little while as they will when they are older, I am sure they would try to do better." "What did you say?" said Kate. Charley started up from the easy chair, the spectacles fell from his nose—he had been asleep. "Oh, Kate," said he, "*such* a dream I've had. I'm never going to speak naughty to Grandpa again. You don't know how bad it makes him feel." Then he told all that had happened, and Kate could hardly help crying, for she remembered how she had often spoken crossly to her "dear grandfather," as she called him, and when the old gentleman did come in, it would have done you good, as it did him, to see how pleasantly they greeted him, and to hear them say how sorry they were that they had ever made him any trouble by their thoughtlessness.

Charley's Question.—A correspondent writes to the *American Agriculturist*: "Our five-year old Charley asked me the following question: 'If at the icy north they have six months day and six months night—do they have any Sunday?'" How is this, boys and girls?

Queries.—Does a Walrussian go barefoot when he has snow-shoes on? Could a bear-footed animal catch him? And when caught would he say "its snow joke?"

Advertisements, to be sure of insertion, must be received BEFORE the 5th of the preceding month.

TERMS—(cash before insertion):

Ordinary Pages, $1.50 per line. *Open Pages*—$2 per line. *Business Notices*—$2.50 per line of space, each insertion.

New York College of Veterinary Surgeons.

Incorporated 1857.

370 Lexington Avenue. Session 1867-8.

The regular course of Lectures in this Institution will commence the first week in October, '67, and continue until the latter part of February, 1868.

Professors (Emeritus) J. Busteed, M. D., Histology; L. D. Mason, M.D., Physiology; F. Nkuti, D. Weiss, M.D., Surgical Pathology; Samuel I. Perry, M. D., Chemistry, Materia Medica and Therapeutics; A. T. Liautard, M. D., V. S., Comparative Anatomy and Operative Surgery; A. Large, M. D., M. R. C., V. S., Theory and Practice of Medicine of the Horse and other Domestic Animals. Address for particulars, Dr. J. Busteed, President of Faculty, 179 Lexington Ave.; A. T. Liautard, M. D., V. S., Registrar.

HUDSON RIVER INSTITUTE, CLAVERACK, Columbia county, New York.—Eighteen instructors, eight departments, $2[illegible] a year. No extras, except piano music. Term opens Sept. 2. Lewis' gymnastics for ladies; military drill for gents. Every facility for the very best Christian education. Rev. ALONZO FLACK, A.M., Principal.

CREVECŒUR FOWLS FOR SALE.—A few pairs bred from best imported stock, from Zoological Garden of Acclimatation, Paris, and described in May number *Agriculturist*. Price $20 per pair. Address

W. A. FITCH, *Agriculturist Office*, New York.

IT DON'T SCRATCH YOU,

Or Tear Your Clothes.

Davison's Thornless Black Cap Raspberry is the best, as it is hardy, productive, early, and sweet, and it is a pleasure to cultivate it. Circulars giving origin, description, prices, testimonials, &c., ready in September.

JOSEPH SINTON, Angola, Erie Co., N. Y.

A GREAT SUCCESS!!

Donwill's Shoe-String Fastener! But one end of string used in lacing! Tied or untied in a moment! No knots! Strings one-third shorter and never work loose from wearing! Is attached to shoe, wears as long, and can be put on by any one! Suitable for any kind of laced shoe! Pays for itself in saving of strings! No disfigurement! Only 5 cts. per pair! Send price and stamped envelope for a sample to Dr. WM. G. DONWILL, Patentee and Genl. Agent, Dover, Delaware. Agents wanted. Patented June 25th, 1867.

G. E. MEISSNER

RICHMOND

STATEN ISLAND, N.Y.

Would call the attention of Dealers and Planters to his extensive stock of Grape Vines, and especially to the

CONCORD AND IONA.

Our Concord vines this year, are pronounced by those who have examined them to be far superior to those ordinarily grown, and we challenge comparison with any other reliable establishment, both in price and excellence of plants.

By our system of growing and in our soil the roots of the vines attain the highest point of perfection, and it is to this in particular that we would direct the attention of purchasers and planters.

PRICE OF CONCORD VINES.

1st Class, 25c. each; $2.00 per doz.; $6.00 per 50; $10 per 100; $75 per 1,000; $700 per 10,000.

2d Class, 20c. each; $1.50 per doz.; $4.50 per 50; $8 per 100; $60 per 1,000; $550 per 10,000.

Our stock of IONA vines is also of the highest excellence, and will compare favorably with those of any other grower.

This excellent variety is fast gaining a reputation which promises to supersede all others. No person setting out a vineyard should fail to plant it extensively. The reports which we hear this year from nearly all parts of the country are of the most favorable character. We can furnish vines of this variety in any quantity, by the single vine or 10,000, at as low rates as equally good plants can be obtained from any *reliable* grower. We warrant all our plants *true to name, and of the quality stated.*

Of all the other leading varieties we have a well selected stock, which we offer at the lowest rates, for which we refer to our Price List. We would here only mention a beautiful lot of **Hartford Prolific**, which is undoubtedly the most reliable and profitable *early* market grape which we have.

Also a very superior lot of Diana vines, both 1 & 2 years old.

CLINTON VINES.—Of this excellent and profitable wine grape we have a choice lot of plants. Price: 1st Class, 25c. each; $2.00 per doz.; $6 per 50; $8 per 100; $65 per 1,000; $600 per 10,000.

For further information send for Price List, and address

G. E. MEISSNER, Richmond P. O., Staten Island, N. Y.

UNIVERSAL CLOTHES WRINGER.

THE

Cannot be surpassed or equaled by any other Wringer for durability, till the expiration of the patent for the "COG WHEEL REGULATOR" or "STOP-GEAR." *No other Wringer is licensed under this Patent.* It being now universally conceded that Cogs are necessary to prevent the Rolls from being broken or torn loose, many attempts have been made to get a Cog-Wheel arrangement which shall equal the UNIVERSAL, and yet avoid the "Stop-Gear" patent, but *without success.*

Any Cog-Wheel Wringer having Cogs, whether at one or both ends of the roll, which can play apart and *fly* out of gear when a large article is passing through, is COMPARATIVELY WORTHLESS, as the Cogs are then of no aid *when most needed*, and an arrangement of Cog-Wheels in *fixed* bearings, the upper one acting on a roll in *movable* bearings, must prove a *mechanical failure* in use, and we warn all persons not to purchase such Wringers as an "improvement on the Universal," which they are sometimes represented to be by the salesmen.

Many who sell the UNIVERSAL WRINGER keep also the

DOTY WASHING MACHINE,

which, though but recently introduced, is really as great a LABOR and CLOTHES SAVER as the Wringer, and is destined to win public favor and patronage everywhere.

It washes *perfectly*, without *wearing* or *rubbing* the clothes at all.

Those keeping the Wringer for sale, order the Washer for customers, if they have not got a supply on hand. On receipt of the Retail price, *from places where no one is selling*, we will send either or both machines from New York.

Prices—Family Washer, $14. No. 1½ Wringer, $10. No. 2 Wringer, $8.50.

A supply of the Wringers and Washers is always kept on hand in Chicago, Cincinnati, Cleveland, Janesville and St. Louis, boxed ready for shipment, at about New York prices.

Large profits are made selling these machines. Exclusive right of sale given, with no charge for the patent right.

Circulars, giving Wholesale and Retail prices, sent free.

☞ These Machines are adopted by the *American Agriculturist* as Premiums, and endorsed by its Editors as the best in market—for recommendations see back numbers.

R. C. BROWNING, General Agent,
No. 32 Cortlandt-st., New York,
(Opposite Merchant's Hotel.)

Choice Fruits for the Garden.

A splendid stock of **Standard and Dwarf Trees, Grapes, Small Fruits,** &c. Send for our

AMATEUR'S PRICE LIST,

containing especial inducements to planters.

EDW'D. J. EVANS & CO.,
Central Nurseries, York, Pa.

Plows for Deep Working,

Designed specially for the preparation of ground for Orchards and Vineyards. Patent secured. Description and Prices sent for a stamp.

C. W. GRANT, Iona,
near Peekskill, Westchester Co., N. Y.

SPEAR'S PRESERVING SOLUTION

For Fruits, Cider, etc. Sold by all dealers. See previous Nos. Agriculturist.

L. P. WORRALL, Gen'l. Agent,
91 Hudson st., New York.

TREES.—TREES.—TREES.

VINES, &c.

Peach Trees.—An immense stock. Prices reduced.

Grape Vines.—Concord, Clinton, Hartford Prolific, &c., at low rates.

Roses.—Several thousands, pone budded, unusually strong.

Hedge Plants.—Osage Orange and Honey Locust, at low rates.

Our stock of *Apples, Cherries, Plums, Apricots, Nectarines, Rhubarb,* &c., &c., is exceedingly heavy and well grown. Wholesale and Retail Descriptive Catalogues furnished gratis.

HOOPES, BROTHER & THOMAS,
Cherry Hill Nurseries, Westchester, Pa.

P.S.—Especial notice is requested to our beautiful collection of *Double Flowering* and *Dwarf Peaches.*

STRAWBERRIES.

After a trial of eight years, we unhesitatingly say that for

Uniform and large size,
Beauty of Form and Color,
Enormous Yield,
Long Continuance in bearing,
Health and Vigor of Plant,
Adaptation to Shipment,
Great Profit,

and other desirable qualities, the

JUCUNDA—Our No. 700,

is much the most valuable Strawberry of which we have any knowledge.

Plant the Best.—It is poor economy to grow *inferior varieties*, when the *best* can be obtained, though the plants could be had for nothing. We can make more money on *one* acre of **Jucunda—Our No. 700**, than we can on *five* of **Wilson.**

For full information in reference to this wonderful Strawberry; its uniformly immense crops, fine shipping qualities and high market value; testimonials from different parts of the country; opinions of Dr. Jno. A. Warder, Author of *American Pomology*, Prof. Geo. Thurber, Editor of *American Agriculturist*, Thos. Meehan, Editor of *Gardeners' Monthly*, M. B. Batcham, Sec'y of *Ohio Pomological Society*, Geo. Beeler, late Sec'y of *Indiana Horticultural Society*, A. W. Harrison, and many others, see the

NEW EDITION OF OUR CATALOGUE,

which also contains **Complete Lists** of best **Early, Medium,** and **Late** varieties, for both **Home use,** and **Market purposes.** Prices of plants **grown in Pots** and otherwise—by **Mail** and **Express,** and much other valuable information in reference to the Strawberry.

We will furnish strong plants of

JUCUNDA—Our No. 700,

this fall, at following prices:

By Mail, $1 per dozen; $6 per 100.

By Express, $5 per 100; $40 per 1000.

Pot grown Plants for Bearing a full crop of fruit next season:

2-inch Pots	$2.00 per dozen;	$12 per 100;	$100 per 1000.
3 " "	$2.50 " "	$15 " "	$125 " "
4 " "	$3.00 " "	$20 " "	$150 " "

For prices of other varieties, See **Catalogue,** which will be sent to all applicants enclosing 10 cents.

J. KNOX,
Box 155, Pittsburgh, Pa.

GRAPE VINES, ROSES, WILSON'S EARLY and Kittatinny Blackberries, Currants, Gooseberries, Strawberries, Evergreens, &c., at wholesale prices. Send for a Catalogue.

MAHLON MOON, Morrisville, Bucks Co., Pa.

PEACH TREES AND SMALL FRUITS A SPECIALTY.

UMSOM NURSERIES. Send for Circulars.

A. HANCE & SON,
Red Bank, Monmouth Co., N. J.

A NEW WORK.

SMALL FRUIT CULTURIST.

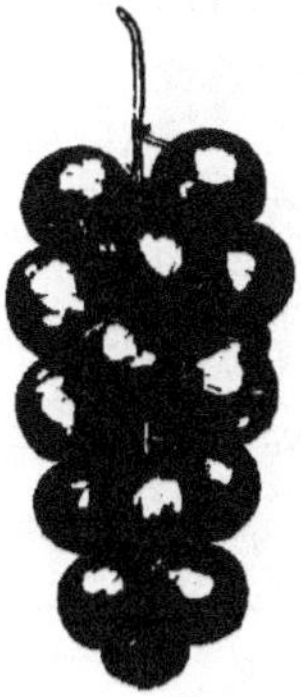

By ANDREW S. FULLER,

PRACTICAL HORTICULTURIST, RIDGEWOOD, BERGEN CO., N. J.

A new work, and the only one devoted to **Small Fruits.** Special treatises of this kind have the advantage that the author can more thoroughly discuss his subject, and go into greater detail, than in a work embracing both large and small fruits. The work covers the whole ground of Propagation, Culture, Varieties, Packing for Market, etc.

CONTENTS: INTRODUCTION—I. BARBERRY—II. STRAWBERRY—III. RASPBERRY—IV. BLACKBERRY—V. DWARF CHERRY—VI. CURRANT—VII. GOOSEBERRY—VIII. CORNELIAN CHERRY—IX. CRANBERRY—X. HUCKLEBERRY—XI. SHEPHERDIA—XII. PREPARATION FOR GATHERING FRUIT.

We predict that this work will bring Mr. Fuller many enemies, as he has given his opinion about varieties without reserve. On the other hand it will the more strongly endear him to all true lovers of horticulture, as these wish to have the merits of fruit given without reference to the persons who introduce them.

While very full on all the small fruits, the Currants and Raspberries have been more carefully elaborated than ever before, and in this important part of his book, the author has had the invaluable counsel of Charles Downing. The chapter on gathering and packing fruit is a valuable one, and in it are figured all the baskets ad boxes now in common use. The book is very finely thoroughly illustrated, and makes an admirable anion to his Grape Culturist.

POST-PAID. PRICE, $1.50

NEW YORK:

'ANCE JUDD & CO.,

41 PARK ROW.

DRAINING FOR PROFIT

AND

DRAINING FOR HEALTH.

By GEO. E. WARING, Jr.,

ENGINEER OF THE DRAINAGE OF CENTRAL PARK, NEW YORK.

Illustrated.

TABLE OF CONTENTS:

SENT POST-PAID. PRICE, $1.50.

ORANGE JUDD & CO.,

41 Park Row New-York.

MAKE MONEY

FROM YOUR

TREES, VINES, AND GARDENS.

AMERICAN POMOLOGY.

THE NEW BOOK ON APPLES.

By DOCT. JOHN A. WARDER.

HISTORY.
PROPAGATION.
BUDS CUTTINGS.
SITE FOR AN ORCHARD.
PREPARATION OF SOIL.
SELECTION PLANTING.
CULTURE & PRUNING.
RIPENING & PRESERVING.
CLASSIFICATION & DESCRIPTION
CATALOGUE AND INDEX.

The latest and best book on Apples.

SENT POST-PAID, - - - - PRICE, $3.00.

GRAPE CULTURIST.

By ANDREW S. FULLER.

Growing from Seed.
Propagation from Buds.
Propagating Houses.
Cuttings in Open Air.
How to Make Layers.
Grafting the Grape.
Hybridizing, Crossing.
Soil Situation, Planting.
Insects, Mildew, Sunscald, etc.
Valuable, & Discarded Varieties.

New Edition, revised and enlarged.

SENT POST-PAID, - - - - PRICE, $1.50.

GARDENING FOR PROFIT

In the Market and Family Garden.

By PETER HENDERSON.

Everything is made perfectly plain. Read the TABLE OF CONTENTS.

Men Fitted for Gardening.
Amount of Capital Required.
Profits of Market Gardening.
Manures and Implements.
Location, Situation, Preparation
When, and Where to Sow.
Transplanting; Insects.
Varieties and Cultivation.
Packing for Shipping.
Preservation in Winter.

Find Out from this book how to make money from your Garden.

SENT POST-PAID, - - - - PRICE, $1.50.

SQUASHES;

HOW TO GROW THEM.

By JAMES J. H. GREGORY.

A most valuable little Treatise for Farmers and Gardeners. It tells about

Selecting the Soil.
How much Manure.
Preparing and Planting.
Hoeing and Cultivating.
Setting of the Fruit.
Ripening; Gathering.
toring of the Crop.
Care During Winter.
Market Prices and Varieties.
When to Take Out Seed.

SENT POST-PAID, - Price, paper covers, 30 cts.

Either of the above-named books will be sent post-paid, on receipt of price, by the Publishers.

Also, many other new and valuable books for the FARM, GARDEN, AND HOUSEHOLD.

SEND FOR A CATALOGUE.

ORANGE JUDD & CO.,

41 Park Row, New York.

ARCHITECTURE. AGRICULTURE. HORTICULTURE.

NEW AND PRACTICAL STANDARD PUBLICATIONS OF

GEO. E. & F. W. WOODWARD,

37 Park Row, New York.

Todd's Young Farmer's Manual. Vol. 1.
The Farm and the Work-shop, with Practical Directions for laying out a Farm, erecting Buildings, Fences, Farm Gates, selecting good Farm and Shop Tools, and performing Farm Operations. Fully Illustrated. One handsome post octavo volume, beveled boards, 460 pages. New edition, ready Sept. Post-paid....................$2.50

Todd's Young Farmer's Manual. Vol. 2.
How to make Farming pay, with full practical details of Farm Management, Character of Soils, Plowing, Management of Grass Lands, Manures, Farm Implements, Stock, Drainage, Planting, Harvesting, &c. One handsome post octavo volume, beveled boards, upwards of 400 pages. Ready Sept. Post-paid....................$2.50

Jacques' Manual of the Farm:
Or, how to Cultivate all the Field Crops. Post-paid..$1.00

Jacques' Manual of the Barn-Yard:
Or, how to Rear Domestic Animals. Post-paid......$1.00

Jacques' Manual of the Garden, Farm and Barn-Yard. Complete in one vol. Post-paid..$2.50

Woodward's Country Homes.
150 Designs and Plans of Country Houses, with illustrated description of the manner of constructing Balloon Frames. Post-paid....................$1.50

Woodward's Annual of Architecture and Rural Art. No. 1, for 1867. Original Designs and Plans of Cottages, Farm Houses and Out-buildings. New and enlarged edition, Cloth. Post-paid....................$1.50

Woodward's Annual of Architecture and Rural Art. No. 2, for 1868. With Designs and Plans of Country and Suburban Houses, and numerous examples of the French, or Chateau Roof. Ready October. Cloth. Post-paid....................$1.50

Wheeler's Rural Homes.
Houses suited to American Country Life. Illustrated with original plans and designs, and full directions for designing, building, heating and furnishing, and form of contract and specification. Post 8vo, beveled boards, 300 pages. Ready Sept. Post-paid....................$1.50

Wheeler's Homes for the People.
For the Suburb and Country. The Villa, the Mansion, and the Cottage, with examples showing how to alter and remodel old buildings. One hundred original designs, with full descriptions and constructive and miscellaneous details. Post octavo, beveled boards, 440 pages. Ready Sept. Post-paid....................$3.00

Jacques' Manual of the House:
Or, how to Build Dwellings, Barns, &c. 126 Designs and Plans. Post-paid....................$1.50

Woodward's Graperies and Horticultural Buildings. A practical work on the design and construction of Buildings for Growing Plants and Ripening Fruit under glass. 60 designs. Post-paid..............$1.50

Woodward's Record of Horticulture.
No. 1, for 1868. Edited by Andrew S. Fuller. An original and valuable illustrated record of Horticultural Progress. Post-paid....................$1.00

Elliott's Lawn and Shade Trees.
Popular Deciduous and Evergreen Trees and Shrubs for planting in Parks, Gardens, Cemeteries, &c. Fully illustrated. Ready December. Post-paid....................$1.50

Fuller's Forest Tree Culturist.
A new illustrated work on the Cultivation of Forest Trees, for Shade, for Shelter, for Fuel, for Timber and for Profit. Post-paid....................$1.50

Husmann's Grapes and Wine.
A new and practical work on the Cultivation of the Native Grape and Manufacture of American Wine. Fully illustrated. Post-paid....................$1.50

Jacques' Manual of the Garden.
Or, how to Cultivate Vegetables, Fruits, Flowers, Trees, and Shrubs. Post-paid....................$1.00

The Horticulturist Almanac for 1867.
Post-paid....................10 cents.

The Horticulturist Almanac for 1868.
Post-paid....................10 cents.

CUMMINGS' & MILLER'S Architectural Details, Exterior and Interior, 714 Illustrations to scale. Post-paid....................$10.00

SLOAN'S HOMESTEAD ARCHITECTURE, Villas, Cottages, and Farm Houses, 200 Illustrations. Post-paid....................$4.50

GEO. E. & F. W. WOODWARD, Publishers, 37 Park Row, New York.

SUPPLY ALL BOOKS ON AGRICULTURE, HORTICULTURE, AND ARCHITECTURE. CATALOGUE SENT FREE.

A Great National Work on the Horse.
Will be ready for delivery in September.

WALLACE'S

AMERICAN STUD BOOK,

BEING A COMPILATION OF THE PEDIGREES

Of American and Imported Blood Horses, from the earliest records, with an Appendix of all named animals without extended Pedigrees prior to the year 1840. And

A SUPPLEMENT containing a History of all Horses and Mares that have trotted in public from the earliest trotting races till the close of 1866.

By J. H. WALLACE.

In one royal 8vo, volume of over 1,000 pages.

Illustrated with 20 original Portraits of Celebrated Racers and Trotters, finely engraved on Steel, from paintings and drawings by distinguished artists.

TO BE SOLD EXCLUSIVELY BY SUBSCRIPTION.

AGENTS WANTED TO CANVASS FOR SUBSCRIBERS *in every County in the Union.*

Published by W. A. TOWNSEND & ADAMS,
No. 434 Broome-street, New York.

GUIDE TO AUTHORSHIP, a valuable aid to all who desire to engage in Literary Pursuits of any kind, for pleasure or profit. With interesting and valuable chapters on Newspaper Editing, &c. 50 cents.

Secrets Worth Knowing, tells how to make medicines, perfumery, toilet and dental articles, soaps, vermin remedies, candies, wines, cordials, cheap and delicious home beverages, veterinary remedies, manufacturers' secrets, and many articles in universal demand, made at small cost and sold at large profits. 25 cents.

Rogues and Rogueries, exposing all tricks and traps of cities, and all swindles and humbugs. Illustrated. 25 cts.

Hand-book of Ventriloquism, and how to make the Magic Whistle. For imitating Birds, Animals, &c. 15cts.

How to Make Bad Memory Good and Good Better, valuable to everybody. 15 cents.

Phonographic Hand-book, for Self-Instruction in the modern improved and simplified art as used by practical reporters. The only *good* "cheap" book. 25 cents.

Haney's B. B. Reference Book, by Henry Chadwick. The standard authority on all points of the game, with much important matter not elsewhere published. Endorsed by Convention and principal Clubs. Numerous illustrations, 141 pages, only 15 cents.

May be had of most Booksellers, or by sending price *at any time* to
HANEY & CO., 119 Nassau-st., New York.

BEAR IN MIND

That on receipt of the advertised price, I will mail to your address any Book, Magazine, or cheap publication that may be advertised or issued by any respectable publisher in the United States. A Catalogue will be sent on receipt of a postage stamp. Address C. A. ROORBACH, 122 Nassau-st., New York.

HOW TO BUY, TAME, and DOCTOR HORSES. 3 Vols.; 50 cts. W. C. WEMYSS, 575 Broadway, N. Y.

NEW NATIONAL RELIGIOUS PAPER.

A national religious newspaper, to be called "THE ADVANCE," will be published weekly, from the first of September, onward, in the city of Chicago. It will represent Congregational principles and polity, but will be conducted in a spirit of courtesy and fraternity towards all Christians. The form will be what is popularly termed a double sheet of eight pages, of the size and style of the *N. Y. Evangelist.* The pecuniary basis is an ample capital furnished by leading business men and others, to be expended in the establishment and improvement of the paper, which is intended to be second to none in the country, in its literary and religious character. The purpose of its projectors is indicated in the name: their aim being to ADVANCE the cause of evangelical religion, in its relations not only to doctrine, worship and ecclesiastical polity, but also to philosophy, science, literature, politics, business, amusements, art, morals, philanthropy and whatever else conduces to the glory of God and the good of man by its bearing upon Christian civilization. No expense has been spared in providing for its editorial management in all departments, while arrangements are in progress to secure the ablest contributors and correspondents at home and abroad. The city of Chicago has been selected as the place of publication, because of its metropolitan position in the section of the country especially demanding such a paper, and the fact that it is nearly the center of national population, and in a very few years will be the ecclesiastical center of the Congregational churches. Issued at the interior commercial metropolis, THE ADVANCE will contain the latest market reports, and able discussions of financial subjects, such as will make it a necessity to business men in all parts of the country. The editor-in-chief will be Rev. Wm. W. Patton, D. D., who resigns the pastorate of the leading church of the denomination at the West for this purpose, and who has had many years experience in editorial labor. The subscription price will be $2.50 in advance. Advertising rates made known on application. Address "THE ADVANCE COMPANY," P. O. Drawer 6374, Chicago, Illinois.

Short-Hand without a Master, by which the art of taking down Sermons, Lectures, Speeches, Trials, etc., may be attained in a few hours. Fifty-fourth edition, WITH SUPPLEMENT. Price 25 cents. Send orders to
C. A. ROORBACH, 122 Nassau-st., New York.

A PORTRAIT OF HORACE GREELEY.

The publishers of THE TRIBUNE having received many inquiries from time to time for a good likeness of the Editor of THE TRIBUNE, have made an arrangement with Messrs. Derby & Miller to furnish copies of Ritchie's fine steel engraving, size 14x18 inches, from a photograph by Brady, which will be sent to such subscribers to THE TRIBUNE as wish it on the conditions below. This is much the best likeness of Mr. GREELEY that has been engraved. The print sells for $1. Each subscriber who sends $10 for THE DAILY, $4 for THE SEMI-WEEKLY, or $2 for THE WEEKLY TRIBUNE, the paper to be sent by mail, *and who requests the engraving* AT THE TIME OF SUBSCRIBING, will have a copy carefully mailed, post-paid, to his address. This is not proposed as a *premium,* but to gratify the many friends of THE TRIBUNE, who feel a desire to possess a good likeness of its founder.
Address THE TRIBUNE, New York.

THE CHURCH UNION.

The largest and best Religious Family Newspaper in the World.

It is to be enlarged to twice its present size.

It is devoted to the Unity of the whole Church of Christ, and opposes Ritualism in every form.

It is the organ of no sect, and it advocates free communion and a free pulpit.

It will print Sermons from Rev. Henry Ward Beecher in every issue.

Terms, $2.50 yearly. $1.00 to Agents for every subscriber. Sold by the American News Company, New York.

Address CHARLES ALBERTSON,
Sup't. Church Union, 143 Fulton-st., New York.

CARPENTERS.—SEND FOR CATALOGUE of New and Practical Architectural Works, enclosing stamp.
A. J. BICKNELL, Publisher, TROY, N. Y.

SOLDIERS' CHECK BOOKS, (or if lost, the amount they call for), and all other claims promptly collected by C. S. TREVITT, (late of the Pay Department), Washington, D. C. Send for Circular.

AGENTS WANTED

for J. T. HEADLEY'S Great Work on our Navy, entitled "FARRAGUT AND OUR NAVAL COMMANDERS," comprising the early Life and Naval Career of Admirals Farragut, Porter, Foote, Dupont and a host of others—the only work of the kind published. It is highly recommended by the leading Naval Officers, and endorsed by Secretaries Seward and Wells, Governors Fenton, Buckingham and Burnside, and leading men of the country. Our Agents in connection with this work can take orders for four other standard works by the same author. Our terms are nowhere excelled.
E. B. TREAT & CO., Publishers, 654 Broadway, N

Plants by Mail, post-paid, at Retail I
M. H. LEWIS & CO., Sandusky

PARSONS & CO.

OFFER FOR THE FALL TRADE:

	Each.	Fifty.	Per 100.	Per 500.	Per 1000
ADIRONDAC	40c.	$15.00.	$20.00.		
ALLEN'S HYBRID	40c.	$15.00.	$20.00.		
CONCORD, 1 year, No. 1	25c.	$ 7.50.	$10.00.	$45.00.	$ 75.
do. do. No. 2		$ 5.00.	$ 7.00.	$32.00.	$ 55.
do. 2 years,	35c.	$12.00.	$18.00.	$85.00.	$150.
do. 3 years,	50c.	$20.00.	$35.00.		
CREVELING	35c.	$15.00.	$20.00.	$90.00.	$150.
DELAWARE, 2 and 3 years	50c.	$17.00.	$25.00.	$115.00	$200.
do. 1 year, No. 1	40c.	$15.00.	$20.00.	$90.00.	$150.
do. do. No. 2		$10.00.	$15.00.	$65.00.	$120.
DIANA, 1 year	30c.	$15.00.	$20.00.		
do. 2 years	50c.	$17.00.	$25.00.	$115.00	$200.
HARTFORD PROLIFIC, 1 yr, No. 1	25c.	$10.00.	$15.00.	$65.00.	$120.
do. do do. No. 2		$ 7.50.	$10.00.	$45.00.	$ 75.
do. do. 2 years	35c.	$17.00.	$25.00.		
IONA, 1 year, No. 1	40c.	$15.00.	$20.00.	$90.00.	$150.
do. No. 2		$10.00.	$15.00.	$65.00.	$120.
ISRAELLA, 1 year, No. 1	50c.	$18.00.	$25.00.	$115.00	$200.
do. No. 2		$12.50.	$20.00.	$90.00.	$150.
IVES' SEEDLING, 1 year	40c.	$15.00.	$20.00.	$90.00.	$150.
do. do. 2 years	50c.	$17.00.	$25.00.	$115.00	$200.
MILES	50c.	$20.00.	$30.00.		
NORTON'S VIRGINIA	50c.	$17.00.	$25.00.	$115.00	$200.
REBECCA	35c.	$17.00.	$25.00.		
ROGERS' HYBRIDS	50c.	$20.00.	$30.00.		
UNION VILLAGE	35c.	$12.50.	$20.00.		

Those who wish to obtain 10,000, or more, can correspond, and will be furnished at still lower prices.

All the vines we offer are grown from well ripened wood, and in good, deep soil, not injured by extra manuring.

In classifying we make no *extras*. Our No. 1 plants are the largest and best of our stock, and their average quality is not allowed to be diminished by selecting the largest for retailing as *extras*.

Our vines must speak for themselves, and those who wish to purchase largely are sufficiently wise to accept the evidence of the vines rather than the assertion of the grower. To account for the abundant roots of our plants it is only necessary to say that ours is the *open border culture*, and that we aim to obtain the model roots of our figure.

Our mode of propagation is that by single eyes of well ripened wood, without the forcing caused by bottom heat. Plants thus naturally brought forward have good roots, and when planted in the open ground, commence growing at once. They thus make their growth during the summer, and in September and October are ready to mature their wood and roots. By other modes the plants are late in starting, and thus have a shorter time for growth and maturing their wood and roots.

We can especially recommend our **DELAWARE** of two and three years of age. The success of this variety in New England, and in the lake region of the Western States, renders unnecessary any assertion of its merits.

The **IONA** is succeeding better this season than the last, and in many localities is winning golden opinions.

Of the **IVES** we cannot speak too highly. Its freedom from rot or mildew, and its very rapid, hardy growth, make it one of the most reliable varieties, one of the few which are absolutely safe.

For Catalogues address

FLUSHING, near New York.

IVES' SEEDLING GRAPE VINE

That never fails. The wine sells to Longworth's Wine House at $1.25 per gallon. 75,000 vines of superior growth for sale at lowest prices. Send for its History and Price List, FREE. Also all leading kinds with wine, new varieties from Longworth's School of Vines, selected by Dr. John A. Warder, with nursery stock generally. JAS. F. MARTIN, Mt. Washington, Hamilton Co., Ohio.

GRAPE VINES.

All the best varieties, including Salem and Martha. Price and quality of vines are worthy of the special attention of Dealers and Planters. Price Lists free to all applicants.
C. L. HOAG & CO., Lockport Grape Nurseries, Lockport, N. Y.

SALEM and Rogers' Hybrids, numbers 1, 2, 3, 4, 5, 9, 14, 15, 19, 22, 28, 30, 33, 33, 34, 39, 41, 44, Diana, Hamburg, Martha, Black Hawk, Christine, Sigiar, Kraka. $5,000 was offered for 10,000 buds of this last named sort last fall. The above varieties are grown by F. L. PERRY, Canandaigua, N. Y. *See advertisement on page 341.*

GRAPE VINES OF BEST KINDS AND qualities, at low rates. J. W. HELMER, Lockport, N. Y.

NATIVE GRAPE VINES.

A large stock of the most approved varieties, *very low*, by the 100 or 1000. SEND FOR PRICE LIST.
JOSEPH KIFT, WESTCHESTER, PA.

Woodside Garden.

My Annual Catalogue of Small Fruits is now ready, and will be sent free to all applicants. Those in want of Blackberries, Raspberries, Currants, Gooseberries, Strawberries, Grapes, etc., etc., should send their orders, early, to
A. S. FULLER, Ridgewood, Bergen Co., N. J.

MIAMI BLACK CAP RASPBERRY.

Superior to Doolittle in every respect, but a week later and keeps in fruiting two weeks longer, thus keeping up the Raspberry season until Blackberries come. Habit, a *very strong, stocky* grower, with scarcely any thorns. ☞ I will give fifty dollars for 1 doz. plants of *any* Raspberry that combines more valuable qualities. Price of Plants $1 per doz.; $4 per 100; $25 per 1,000.—Doolittle and Purple Cane, both *very early*, productive and valuable, $1 per doz.; $3 per 100; $15 per 1,000.—Ohio Everbearing, $1.50 per doz.; $4 per 100; $25 per 1,000.—Golden Cap, $1 per doz.; $5 per 100; $30 per 1,000.—Catawissa, $2 per doz.; $10 per 100.—DAVISON'S THORNLESS, $1 each; $10 per doz.—Philadelphia, $1 per doz.; $10 per 100.—BLACKBERRIES, Dorchester, $1 per doz.; $5 per 100.—New Rochelle or Lawton, $1 per doz.; $3 per 100; $15 per 1,000.—Wilson's Early, 75 cts. each; $4 per doz.; $30 per 100.—Kittatinny, 50 cts. each; $5 per doz.; $20 per 100.—Crystal White, delicious, beautiful, and fine yielder, $2 per doz.; $10 per 100.—HOUGHTON SEEDLING GOOSEBERRY, never mildews, $1 per doz.; $5 per 100.—RED DUTCH CURRANT, 1 year old, finely rooted, $1 per doz.; $5 per 100; $30 per 1,000. Cherry, White Grape and La Versaillaise, $1.50 per doz.; $8 per 100.—GRAPES, CONCORD, *good roots*, $10 per 100; *best*, $15 per 100.—Creveling, Ives' Seedling, and Norton's Virginia, 1 year old, strong, $20 per 100; 2 years old, *extra strong*, $30 per 100.—Delaware, Hartford Prolific, Diana, Iona, Israella, and Adirondac, *fine roots, as low as offered in this paper*.—ORANGE QUINCE, *very strong, fine rooted plants*, $3 per doz.; $20 per 100.—☞ STRAWBERRY PLANTS in *large quantities at low rates*, see advertisement in August No. of *Agriculturist*. *Wholesale List* sent on application. Instructive Catalogue, giving information how to plant, etc., sent on receipt of 10 cents.

If any of the above is offered lower in this paper, *we will sell for the same.* 6 of each at the doz. rate, 50 at 100 rate, 500 at 1,000 rate. Remember, Raspberries and Blackberries *should be set in the fall.* We have had *very bad* luck with spring setting, and *no failures* when set in the fall.

Address A. M. PURDY, South Bend, Ind., or M. B. PURDY, Box 125, Palmyra, N. Y.

☞ P. S.—*We will prepay Express charges* on all cash orders to any point North of Washington or Memphis, and East of St. Joseph, Mo.

Kittatinny Blackberry at the West.

Among the many testimonials received by the subscriber, the following in regard to this splendid berry from a gentleman in Fulton Co., Ill., may suffice:—

"The Kittatinny plants got of you, spring of '66, fruited this season most abundantly,—one week earlier than my Lawtons on the same grounds and location, and the smallest branch withstood the winter without any injury whatever."

The subscriber and several others here have also fruited it thoroughly and most satisfactorily the past season. Strong Plants $20 per 100, $150 per 1,000. F. K. PHOENIX, Bloomington, Ill.

THE BEST RASPBERRY

Is now acknowledged by all to be the CLARKE RASPBERRY. Strong plants, warranted genuine, $2 per doz.; $5 for 50; $9 per 100; $25 per 500; $40 per 1,000.
LYMAN BASSETT, North Haven, Conn.

THE EARLY WILSON BLACKBERRY.—The *largest, most productive, and valuable of all Blackberries; early, and ripening rapidly. Twice as profitable this year as either Lawton or Dorchester.* My stock is pure and grown in the open field, and all sent out shall have *good and abundant roots*, averaging six inches in length. Also the *Philadelphia Raspberry*, which retains all its laurels wherever heard from. Also *Kittatinny, Lawton*, and *Dorchester Blackberries*, and *Strawberries*, etc., in great variety.
SAMUEL L. ALLEN, Cinnaminson, N. J.

VERY EXTRA STANDARD PEAR.

Parties wanting, for their own planting, Pear-trees of an *Extra Choice Quality*, or any other kind of Fruit trees of the best quality, will be supplied in quantities to suit, by the half dozen or ten thousand. Prices low. Trees freshly dug, true to name, and securely packed for any distance. Write for particulars, references and Catalogue. Trade supplied as usual. T. T. SOUTHWICK, Commercial Nurseries, Dansville, Liv. Co., N. Y.

NOW READY.—Washburn's Autumn Catalogue of splendid Flowering Bulbs, containing a list of the choicest Hyacinths, Tulips, Crocuses, Lilies, etc., with full and explicit directions for their culture. It also contains a beautiful colored plate, and many other fine engravings. It will be forwarded post-paid upon receipt of 10 cents, to all applicants. Address WASHBURN & CO., Hort'l Hall, Boston.

BLOOMINGTON NURSERY.

10th year, 10 Green-houses, 330 Acres Fruit, Ornamental and Nursery Stock, General Assortment.

1,000,000 Apple, 1 to 4 years, superb yearlings, 1000, $30.
150,000 Pear, Stand. and Dw'f. *Dw'f. Apple*, all sizes.
40,000 Cherry, largely Richmond or May, 100, $15 to $25.
30,000 Peach, Hale's Early, &c., 1000, $125.
300,000 Grape, strong Concord layers, 1000, $85; Hartford layers, 1000, $150; Ives, $170; Rogers, Iona, &c.
5,000,000 Osage Orange, 1st class, 100,000, $300.
55,000 Currant, Gooseberry and Raspberry.
30,000 Kittatinny Blackberry, warranted genuine, strong, first class every way, 1000, $150. (See separate advertisement.)
1,000,000 Apple Stock, extra, selected 1 year, 1000, $10.
50,000 Pear Stock, fine, 1 year, 1000, $25; Quince, Cherry.
30,000 Roses, all classes, Marshal Neil, fine plants, $0 per doz.; Evergreens, immense stock, Tulips, Hyacinths, and other Hardy Bulbs. Send 2 red stamps for New Descriptive and Trade List.
F. K. PHOENIX, Bloomington, Ill.

Select Vegetable Seeds for Market Gardeners and Others.

			per oz.	per lb.
Cabbage,	Jersey Wakefield	(own growth),	$1.20	$16.00
"	" "	(imported),	1.00	10.00
"	Flat Dutch,	(own growth),	50	6.00
"	Early York,	. . .	25	3.00
Cauliflower,	Early Paris,	. . .	1.50	16.00
"	Early Dwarf Erfut,	. .	3.00	30.00
Lettuce,	Curled Simpson,	(own growth)	50	6.00
"	Hardy Green,	" "	50	6.00
"	Butter,	" "	50	6.00
Spinach,	Round and Prickly,	. . .	10	75

Sent free by mail, for the prices affixed.

HENDERSON & FLEMING,
Seedsmen and Market Gardeners,
67 Nassau-st., New York.

THE NEW STRAWBERRY.

CHARLES DOWNING.

Raised by J. S. Downer, of Kentucky, promises to be far in advance of any other berry known. I have fruited it two years. The vigor of the plant is very remarkable, its leaves are immensely large, and of great substance, which enables it to mature every berry to a large size; all are perfect in shape, no coxcombs or ill-shaped fruit. The berry is of the largest size, the productiveness quite astonishing, and the flavor superior to any large berry known. The berry of the Charles Downing, represented in the August No. of this paper, was picked from a young plant set out in Oct. last, and does not represent half the size of the largest berries. Charles Downing, of Newburgh, has fruited it one or two years, and gives it a high character. For further description and letter from Charles Downing, see advertisement in August No. I am now ready to deliver plants at the following rates: 3 for $2.00; 6, $3.00; 12, $5.00; 100, $25; 500, $85; 1,000, $150. 2 plants of Gloede's Perpetual Pine for $1.00.

A large lot of that remarkable berry, *Brumagin's Seedling*, also, *President, Harrison, Market, Abraham Lincoln, Perpetual Pine, Philadelphia, Starr, Stringer, Great Eastern, Hubbard Seedling, Fraser Seedling, Durand Seedling, Fillmore*, and the *Great Rippowam*, the king of berries. For description and prices of all these new berries, see advertisement in August No.
WM. S. CARPENTER, 156 Reade-st., New York.

Bulbous Roots for the Trade.

Our **Wholesale Catalogue of Imported Dutch Bulbous Roots**, for the autumn of 1867, is now ready for mailing to applicants enclosing a postage stamp.
J. M. THORBURN & CO., 15 John-st., New York.

Strawberry Plants.

For retail prices see August No.—Jenny Lind, Downer's Prolific, Early Washington and French, $4.50 per 1,000. Wilson's Albany and Russell, $4 per 1,000. Crimson Cone, Foust's Fillmore, Austin's Shaker, New Jersey Scarlet, Ida, Buffalo, and Green Prolific, $5 per 1,000; 10,000 for $40. Metcalf, Golden Queen, and Jucunda, or "Knox's 700," $10 per 1,000; 500 of each at 1,000 rate.—☞ *Charges prepaid by us.* Prices lower if so offered in this paper.
Address A. M. PURDY, South Bend, Ind., or M. B. PURDY, Box 125, Palmyra, N. Y.

STRAWBERRY PLANTS.—A few good, strong plants of the Agriculturist, Russell, Buffalo Seedling, Negro, and others. $1.00 per 100. A. M. HALSTED, Rye, N. Y.

HARDY CLIMBING ROSES.

Prairie Queen and Baltimore Belle, strong, 1 year plants, $1 per 100; $30 per 1000. Also, a fine stock of the most popular varieties of *Everblooming Roses*, very low by the 100 or 1000. Send for Price List.
JOSEPH KIFT, Westchester, Penn.

STANDARD AND DWARF PEAR TREES can be obtained of F. L. PERRY, Canandaigua, N. Y. Trees are perfect in form, carefully lifted and well packed. Call and see them, or send for Price List. *See advertisement on page 344.*

WANTED 1,000 LADIES AND GENTLEMEN to sell Trees, Shrubs, Vines and Flowers. Send for Price List, with full particulars.
L. L. WHITLOCK, "ALL NURSERIES IN ONE," 37 Park Row, New York.

Strawberry, Raspberry and Blackberry plants. Doolittle's Black Cap, $10 per 1000. Wilson, Downer, French, and May Queen, $1 per 1,000 for 5,000 plants. SAMUEL T. DUFFELL, Vardville, N. J.

HEXAMER'S PRONG-HOE.

Price, per piece, **$2.50**; per dozen, **$24.**
All orders must be accompanied by Cash, or Draft on New York. Address
REISIG & HEXAMER, New Castle, Westchester Co., N. Y.

THE BEST MACHINERY.

COOPER'S OLD AND EXTENSIVE FACTORY HAS FOR SALE

150 Improved Portable Engines, 8 to 30 Horse-Power.
85 Improved Stationary Engines, 20 to 125 Horse-Power.
800 Circular Saw Mills, of all Sizes.
123 Patent French Burr Flour and Feed Mills, with Bolts, and complete Machinery for same.
1,000 Cooper's Patent Sugar Pans, 8 to 15 feet long. Price $22 to $75.
1,000 Cooper's Patent Union Sugar Mills, 6 Sizes. Price, Heavy One-Horse Mill, $73.

All are being erected in the most approved and substantial manner, with recent valuable improvements.

This Firm was the first to commence the practice of furnishing complete fixtures for *Saw* and *Grist Mills*, and millwrights to erect and set them in operation; hence their unprecedented success and reputation for *building the best Mills in the world.* Send for Circulars, addressing
C. & J. COOPER, Mt. Vernon, Ohio.

A score of First Premiums taken. Cuts Turnips, Carrots, Beets, Potatoes, Pumpkins, &c. Suitable for an Ox or a Lamb.

The most durable and efficient Cutter made. Easily transported to any part of the country. Sold by most agricultural dealers, and Wholesale and Retail by A. H. WELLINGTON & CO., Sole Manufacturers, Woodstock, Vermont. Send for a Circular.

For Rock Digging and Wall Laying Machines,

Address G. L. SHELDON, Hartsville, Mass.

DUANE H. NASH,

MANUFACTURERS' AGENT.
Shares' Coulter Harrows.
Hay and Stalk Cutters.
Horse Powers and Threshers.
Stump Pullers, &c., &c.
Agricultural Implements at Manufacturers' prices.
53 Cortlandt-st., New York.

HUTCHINSON'S PATENT

Cider and Wine Mill with Press.

Grinds Fine, Fast and Easy—Large and Small. *Best Cast Cider Press Screws*, fine thread, very stout and powerful. *Grinders and Presses separate.* *Best and Cheapest Feed Cutter.* Gale's Copper Strip, all sizes and length of cut. Send for Illustrated Circular to
PEEKSKILL PLOW WORKS, Peekskill, N. Y.

Premium Farm Grist Mill.—Cheap, simple, and durable—adapted to all kinds of Horse-Powers, and grinds rapidly.
Send for Descriptive Circular, and address
WM. L. BOYER & BRO., Philadelphia, Pa.

Important Aid to Cane Growers.

D. W. Shares' Patent Cane Stripper, warranted to save more labor than anything of the kind in the country for preparing Sorghum or any kind of Cane for the mill. For further particulars send for a Circular.
D. W. SHARES, Hamden, Conn.

(Business Notices $2.00 per Agate Line of Space.)

THE
GREAT AMERICAN TEA COMPANY

HAVE JUST RECEIVED

TWO FULL CARGOES

OF THE

FINEST CROP OF TEAS.

22,000 HALF CHESTS by ship *Golden State*.
12,000 HALF CHESTS by ship *George Shotton*.

In addition to these large cargoes of Black and Japan Teas, the Company are constantly receiving large invoices of the finest quality of Green Teas from the Moyune districts of China, which are unrivaled for fineness and delicacy of flavor, which they are selling at the following prices:

OOLONG (Black), 50c., 60c., 70c., 80c., 90c., best $1 ℔ ℔.
MIXED, (Green and Black), 50c., 60c., 70c., 80c., 90c., best $1 per pound.
ENGLISH BREAKFAST (Black), 50c., 60c., 70c., 80c., 90c., $1, $1.10, best $1.20 per pound.
IMPERIAL (Green), 50c., 60c., 70c., 80c., 90c., $1, $1.10, best $1.25 per pound.
YOUNG HYSON (Green), 50c., 60c., 70c., 80c., 90c., $1, $1.10, best $1.25 per pound.
UNCOLORED JAPAN, 90c., $1, $1.10, best $1.25 per pound.
GUNPOWDER, (Green), $1.25, best $1.50 per pound.

COFFEES ROASTED AND GROUND DAILY.

GROUND COFFEE, 20c., 25c., 30c., 35c., best 40c. per pound. Hotels, Saloons, Boarding-house keepers, and Families who use large quantities of Coffee, can economize in that article by using our FRENCH BREAKFAST AND DINNER COFFEE, which we sell at the low price of 30c. per pound, and warrant to give perfect satisfaction.

Consumers can save from 50 cents to $1 per pound (beside the Express charges,) by purchasing their Teas of the

GREAT AMERICAN TEA COMPANY,

Nos. 31 and 33 VESEY STREET.
Post Office Box, 5643, New York City.

We warrant all the goods we sell to give entire satisfaction. If they are not satisfactory, they can be returned at our expense within 30 days, and have the money refunded.

By our system of supplying Clubs throughout the country, consumers in all parts of the United States can receive their Teas at the same price (with the small additional expense of transportation), as though they bought them at our warehouses in this city.

Some parties inquire of us how they shall proceed to get up a club. The answer is simply this: Let each person wishing to join in a club, say how much tea or coffee he wants, and select the kind and price from our Price List, as published in the paper or in our circulars. Write the names, kinds, and amounts plainly on a list, and when the club is complete, send it to us by mail, and we will put each party's goods in separate packages, and mark the name upon them, with the cost, so there need be no confusion in their distribution—each party getting exactly what he orders, and no more. The cost of transportation, the members of the club can divide equitably among themselves.

The funds to pay for the goods ordered can be sent by drafts on New York, by Post-Office money orders, or by Express, as may suit the convenience of the club. Or, if the amount ordered exceeds $30, we will, if desired, send the goods by Express, to "collect on delivery."

Hereafter we will send a complimentary package to the party getting up the Club. Our profits are small, but we will be as liberal as we can afford. We send no complimentary package for a Club less than $30.

N. B.—All villages and towns where a large number reside, by Clubbing together, can reduce the cost of their Teas and Coffees about one-third (beside the Express charges,) by sending directly to "The Great American Tea Company."

BEWARE of all concerns that advertise themselves as branches of our Establishment, or copy our name either wholly or in part, as they are *bogus* or *imitations*. We have no branches, and do not, in any case, authorize the use of our name.

Post-Office orders and Drafts, make payable to the order of "Great American Tea Company." Direct letters and orders to the

GREAT AMERICAN TEA COMP'Y,

Nos. 31 and 33 VESEY-ST.,
Post-Office Box, 5,643, New York City.

TO

The Young and Middle Aged Men of the Country.

THEIR START IN LIFE AND THE WORK BEFORE THEM.

Start in Life.—To get a start in life has perplexed the young men of every age. How can I obtain a foothold? What shall I do? Where shall I go? have been problems not easily solved. These obstacles no longer exist.

An Opportunity.—To the many young men of the country starting in life or seeking successful, honorable employment, and to the middle aged men living by small wages and desiring to better their situations by engaging in active, successful business, I offer (at my Institution at Poughkeepsie, N. Y., on the Hudson,) better advantages, at a more reasonable expense than was ever before presented to the people of this country, and guarantee situations in first class business houses, to graduates of merit, who desire assistance.

Farmers and Planters.—My course for FARMERS as well as MERCHANTS, and for those from the plantations and manufactories, is the best in the world, it being THE SHORTEST, THE MOST PRACTICAL, AND THE MOST REASONABLE.

I refer not only to the two hundred distinguished citizens who have just presented me with a complimentary testimonial expressing their appreciation of my services in founding this Institution and introducing practical instruction, and patrons in every State, but to more than TWO THOUSAND GRADUATES, who owe their success as Merchants, Bankers, Clerks and Business Men, to the situations obtained for them on the completion of their course here.

Work Ahead! Men Wanted!—The nation, in its new start in wonderful, unprecedented prosperity, calls for new men of practical skill, and great business gifts. They are wanted everywhere. The country is full of money waiting for practical talent to use it. The avenues of Commerce, Agriculture, Trade, and Finance are open wider and more inviting than ever before. Vast crops are being gathered, and their great money value, amounting to more than four hundred millions of dollars last year, will give an activity to trade seldom witnessed in our history.

This Institution, then, with its *common sense* course of business training, is a natural necessity.

The West and South.—The closing of the Western College at Chicago and its removal here is increasing largely our number of Western and South-western students. The expenses here is more than one-third less than at Chicago, and this difference in many cases more than pays railroad fare and expenses of the Western students coming here. Particularly is this the opportunity for the young men of the South in this important period of their history.

Full information and valuable reading matter in College paper, sent free of charge.

Address the President, H. G. EASTMAN, LL. D., Eastman Business College, Poughkeepsie, N. Y., on the Hudson.

NOTE.—The regular Fall exercises, celebrating the fourteenth year of this, the oldest Commercial Institution in this country, will take place Tuesday and Wednesday, Sept. 17th and 18th. Hon. Horace Greeley, Hon. Mark D. Wilber, Rev. Samuel D. Burchard and others will address the College on that occasion.

Gov. Fenton and staff, Gen. Woodford, Hon. Lewis L. Parsons, of Alabama, and other distinguished gentlemen have been invited to be present.

This occasion will afford to those who desire to enter the College at that time or thereafter, an opportunity of witnessing the practical workings of the Institution. This invitation is extended to any Young and Middle Aged Men who desire to educate themselves at a small cost for better positions in life, that they may inform themselves by a personal examination of the superior facilities this College presents over other Commercial Institutions.

It will also be a favorable time for Parents, Teachers and others to visit our beautiful City of Schools, now the Educational Metropolis of the country.

For a programme of exercises address as above.

PERRY'S GRAPE VINES

are worthy of every Planter's and Dealer's particular attention. By the use of my improvement in rooting and transferring vines to the open ground without in the *least checking their growth, or disturbing the roots or soil in which that they are growing*, enables me to keep far ahead of all others in the production of vines best suited for future vigorous growth and productiveness.

Notice the few extracts from letters received from my patrons. See Illustrated and Descriptive Catalogue for a number of pages of the same character; these are given to show those unacquainted with my vines, *their real superiority over those grown in the ordinary way*.

From Dr. S. Parker, Ithaca, N. Y., April 4, 1867.
"I have had vines from a dozen different propagators of late, but none equal yours. When I saw your propagation last season I was convinced that yours was the true way to propagate."

From W. L. Strond, Oshkosh, Wis., April 10, 1867.
"I must say that I am not only satisfied but delighted with your vines. My conclusion is that you are the man to buy vines of if one wants his money's worth."

From E. A. Thompson, Cincinnati, O., May 13, 1867.
"The Dianas are fine vines; Rogers' first-rate; Ionas the best roots I have ever seen."

From A. T. Bilsbee, Watkins, N. Y., April 20, 1867.
"Your vines are splendid and more than answer my expectations."

From I. S. Horton, Council Bluff, Iowa, April 19, 1867.
"I never saw better rooted vines. The Club were *all satisfied*. Shall send you a much larger order in the fall."

From H. Houghton, West Boylston, Mass., April 12, 1867.
"I like the appearance of your vines very much."

From I. B. Kauffman, Strasburg, Pa., April 18, 1867.
"I must say your vines are *greatly superior* to those sent me by * * * * * * Those marked extra for the garden are REALLY SPLENDID."

From W. D. White, Wheeling, W. Va., April 16, 1867.
"The roots of your vines are wonderfully developed and of remarkable excellence."

I have a class of vines two and three years old that will fruit next season, if planted this fall, and from which the *best results may be expected*. The number of this class is limited, and for the garden of the most desirable character. Although my vines come in direct competition with an immense stock of Hotbed or Glass-frame grown vines, I propose to sell at as low prices as are advertised in the columns of this paper.

I can furnish twenty thousand very fine Standard and Dwarf Pear Trees, two, three, and four years old.

10,000 Clarke Raspberry (True).—The best hardy Raspberry yet introduced. I can furnish splendid plants that will give a good crop next season, at the advertised price of others.

Price List sent to all applicants gratis.

Illustrated and Descriptive Catalogue 10 cents. This is much less than actual cost. Address

F. L. PERRY, Canandaigua, N. Y.

GRAPE VINES at IONA.

My stock comprises all of the leading kinds, including Ives' Seedling, but principally consists of

IONA, ISRAELLA and DELAWARE.

The performance of the Iona and Israella generally throughout all of the vine-region of the country, leaves no doubt in the minds of those best informed that upon these now rests chiefly the prospect of the eminent success of grape culture in America.

My stock of these kinds is very large, and of surpassing quality. My unequaled facilities and the result of the past years warrant the belief that I can make more advantageous terms to buyers than can be done by any other propagator. Price List sent on application with stamp.

Prices for best vines for Garden or Vineyard, as low as can be afforded.

C. W. GRANT,
IONA, near Peekskill,
Westchester Co., N. Y.

STAMMERING CURED

by BATES' PATENT APPLIANCES. For Pamphlets, &c., address SIMPSON & CO., 277 West 23d-st., New York.

"HINTS TO BEE-KEEPERS," a *Practical Pamphlet*, Sent Free *to any address*. Also AGENTS wanted to sell Italian Queen-bees. "The Bee-Keeper's Text Book, (3d Revised Ed.), and the American Bee Hive." For the free Pamphlet, address

H. A. KING & CO., Nevada, O.

HEALTH AND ECONOMY.

PATENT LEAD ENCASED TIN PIPE. Recommended by the medical faculty and approved by WATER COMMISSIONERS. COSTS LESS THAN LEAD PIPE AND IS MUCH STRONGER. Recent improvements enable us to supply THIS pipe at a less price per foot than common lead pipe.

To furnish the cost per foot, please give the head or pressure of water and bore of pipe. Pamphlets sent FREE on application. Address THE COLWELLS, SHAW & WILLARD MANUFACTURING CO., Foot of West 27th-st., New York.

Rural Improvements.

Robert Morris Copeland, author of Country Life, furnishes plans and advice for laying out or improving public or private grounds. Refers to John M. Forbes, Nathaniel Thayer, Boston; Francis G. Shaw, New York; Rufus Waterman, Providence, R. I. Office, 40 Barristers' Hall, Boston, Mass.

Choice Grape Vines at Right Prices.—See G. E. MEISSNER'S Advertisement, page 336.

AMERICAN AGRICULTURIST

FOR THE

Farm, Garden, and Household.

"AGRICULTURE IS THE MOST HEALTHFUL, MOST USEFUL, AND MOST NOBLE EMPLOYMENT OF MAN."—WASHINGTON.

ORANGE JUDD & CO., PUBLISHERS AND PROPRIETORS. OFFICE, 245 BROADWAY.

ESTABLISHED IN 1842. Published also in German at $1.50 a Year.

$1.50 PER ANNUM, IN ADVANCE. SINGLE NUMBER, 15 CENTS. 4 Copies for $5; 10 for $12; 20 or more, $1 each.

[illegible] by ORANGE JUDD & CO., [illegible] the Clerk's Office of the District Court of the United States for the Southern District of New-York.

VOLUME XXVI—No. 10. NEW-YORK, OCTOBER, 1867. NEW SERIES—No. 249.

[COPYRIGHT SECURED.]

THE FLUSHED PARTRIDGE.—*Drawn and Engraved for the American Agriculturist.*

W[illegible] —B[illegible] Bang.—Not a feather touched! [illegible] a fair a shot, yet we do not envy him who [illegible] pick up the still warm bird—its flight for life and freedom cut short, without an emotion of regret blending with the pleasure [illegible] having made a good shot, and bagged the game. Our sympathies for it, as it wings its whirring flight over some barrier the sportsman cannot pass, [illegible] the pang of regret at having [illegible] the trigger with too nervous or careless a finger.

This beautiful dweller in the mountains and forests, common [illegible] in the woodlands and along the [illegible] of New England and the Middle States, is familiar to [illegible] every one, either in the woods or in the markets. It is the Partridge of New England, the Pheasant of the Middle States, and is properly called the Ruffed Grouse, (*Bonasa umbellus*). The dark neck feathers, when spread, form a ruff almost like Queen Elizabeth's, and the tail is banded with black and gray. The motions of these birds, when in the wild woods and unsuspicious of harm, are charmingly graceful and courtly, blending dignity and ease. The step is proud, light, and free, and they daintily poise themselves a second on each foot, as they trip along. During the spring and summer the males are [illegible] and lusty, and are apparently fond of [illegible] log or fallen tree, and beating it with their wings in a way to produce a peculiar sound, which begins slowly and ends like the roll of a drum, and is called "drumming." It may be heard a long distance. The young, until several weeks old, are strikingly like little chickens, and the hen partridge has the same maternal ways as a common hen, as she leads about her downy brood. They remain in or near their haunts the year round, occasionally descending into the orchards and farm enclosures for food in severe winters. They often dive into light snow, burrowing rapidly to escape pursuit, and also shelter themselves in this way from very severe cold during winter nights.

Two Months for Nothing.

All new subscribers to the American Agriculturist whose names are received during the month of October for the year 1868, **will receive the paper for the last two months of this year FREE.** *This offer applies to all new subscribers received in October, whether single names or members of clubs. Thus, $1.50 sent us now will secure one copy of the Agriculturist for 14 months, (November 1867 to December 1868 inclusive); $5 will pay for four copies for the same time, and so of all our club rates. N. B.—This offer is only for October, except for names from the Pacific Coast, and other points too distant to respond by the close of the month.*

Contents for October, 1867.

INDEX TO "BASKET" OR SHORTER ARTICLES.

AMERICAN AGRICULTURIST.

NEW-YORK, OCTOBER, 1867.

October is pre-eminently the month for Agricultural Fairs. We hope all our readers will be able to visit one or more. The problem with many a farmer will be how to get ahead with work enough to enjoy the few days spent away from the farm. To accomplish this—prepare for three or four rainy days, and then noting down, clearly, directions for your hands to follow, rain or shine, throw the responsibility of good work and diligence upon their honor, and leave.—They will not disappoint you.

Make a pencil memorandum of every thing you see, or hint you get, which may be of future use, not as a newspaper reporter jots down everything, but classify what is seen. Some things you can afford to buy at once, others you wish to inquire about. Some tools are better than you now use, and when yours are worn out, you will be glad to remember where they may be bought. So there will be knowledge and useful ideas in a perfect stream flowing into the mind, and your memorandum book may catch a great portion if you will.

No weeds should be cut in dry weather. Clean culture is every man's theory. After a wet season like that experienced along the Atlantic Coast, practice and theory do not agree very well. Almost every farmer will need to mow and burn some weeds. In wet weather the seeds will shell out but little. In dry weather many hedge rows may be burned without cutting. Any use of fire is attended with danger. Take care lest it gets into the grass, or into the woods, or burns beyond control. A high wind may spring up without warning.

Feed the land well, and it will feed you. Manure will not run to waste on most soils; but for all our common crops, except corn, it is an advantage to have it several months in the soil. It becomes more easily assimilable by the plant, and, besides, influences decompositions, which increase the amount of plant food yielded by the soil itself.

Feed stock well. Reduce the amount of live stock to a winter footing as soon as possible. If pasturage is suddenly cut off, a large number of animals will be rushed into market and prices will fall. Stock taken up in good flesh are half wintered, and such animals are not on overstocked pastures.

Hints About Work.

Buildings.—Certain repairs ought to be done before frost, such as require work upon walls, and cement floors, etc., brick laying or plastering. If such work is not greatly needed for the comfort of the family or one's stock, we advise delaying until spring, for it will be rare good luck if it has not all to be done over next season. Done after this month it will hardly stand at all.

Cement Cisterns may be set if below the reach of frost. Bring water to the house for the comfort and convenience of housekeepers and servants.

Fences.—Poor fences are a temptation to cattle, and induce bad habits. Look especially to those around grain fields, which will be attractive.

Fattening Animals of all kinds lay on flesh very rapidly as the weather grows cooler. Keep beeves and sheep in pasture as long as the feed is good, but yard them at night, and feed twice a day with grain, if they are to be marketed soon; otherwise simply feed so as to be sure they are constantly gaining. Pigs should have cooked food, and plenty of it. Push forward their fattening as rapidly as possible, for at no season will they gain faster. Keep them clean and give warm sheltered nests. Poultry also gain very rapidly, and it is best to fatten them on scalded meal, with corn, wheat screenings, and other food in addition, at daylight in the morning, and late in the afternoon.

"Store" Animals and Young Stock often get poor usage and no attention till snow falls, and the ground freezes solid, or the pastures give out, so that they begin the winter scrawny and down in flesh. This is very poor policy. If the stock must be half fed before spring, let it be at the close of the season. Perishable fodder, such as pumpkins, soft corn, common turnips, should be provided in abundance, so that the "stores" and young animals can lay on a good stock of flesh, if not fat. Animals in good condition proverbially winter much more easily than thin ones.

Cows and Butter.—Fall butter may be nearly as good as that made in June. As the pastures fail, feed a little grain, with turnips and pumpkins, removing the seeds, which act on the kidneys and almost uniformly decrease the flow of milk.

Sheep.—The present is often the most favorable time to secure a stock of sheep for fattening, though from the number of sheep marketed in August, it is possible that prices may be higher than usual in proportion. Still, sheep for this purpose should be bought early, while they will have the benefit of several weeks' feeding. Select those in good condition. Provision should be made this month for market lambs to be dropped in March, by crossing a good mutton ram with hardy, good constitutioned ewes. The lambs of such will be strong, grow quickly, and fatten easily. The ewe's time of gestation averages 152 days.

Roots.—Beets, mangels, and carrots, may be dug as soon as the tops show that there is no longer vigorous growth; at all events, before severe freezing. Preserve in cellars, after topping, drying, and laying in heaps, protected by the tops or bagging, a few days, to sweat. If not stored in cellars, put them in dry trenches covered with straw, and banked over with earth. Cabbages may be preserved in the same way. Rutabagas and turnips may stand out longer, but not until the ground freezes. The tops of all these roots are worth feeding to stock.

Grain.—Sow Rye throughout the month, wheat in the early part only, soaking in strong brine to prevent smut, and dry by rolling in lime.

Manure.—Apply, and plow under for spring crops; and dig muck for use in the yards and stables as an absorbent, or get out as much as possible to be pulverized and ameliorated by the frosts of winter.

Plowing done at this season costs usually about two-thirds as much as if done in April and May, and on stiff soils for all crops except corn is just as good, or better. In ordinary shallow plowing, turn sod ground over flat. If in breaking up you plow eight or ten inches deep with the single plow, it makes little or no difference whether flat or lap furrows are turned, as the sod will probably be well covered, and thus rot thoroughly.

Corn.—See article on page 362. After the grain is cured, husk it, and bind the stalks in small bundles. They cure most rapidly when set up in two double rows leaning against poles held in crotched stakes, about 3½ feet high. The poles should run north and south, that the bundles may be better exposed to the sun. When dry, stack, protect under straw-sheds or barracks, or bring into the barn.

Timber.—Cut for building purposes, for fence posts, rails, etc., and for whatever purpose durability is required, and lay it up for seasoning.

Water.—Bring water to house and barn by pumps or by pipes from springs. The pipes must be sunk below freezing, and the pump or spout also protected.

Sorghum.—Strip, top, and cut that not cut last month. Haul at once to the mill, and have it ground as soon as possible. Do not strip or top before cutting, and when cut, bind with two strong bands in bundles of a size for easy handling. The leaves and suckers are good fodder; the seed may be ground and fed to sheep, swine, or cattle.

Soiling Crops.—Sow both wheat and rye for soiling in the spring. The land should be dry and well covered with manure; plow deeply, cross-plow, and harrow in nearly twice the quantity of seed—say 2 bushels of rye and 2½ to 3 bushels of wheat. The wheat should be sown first, and that early in the month; in fitness for cutting it will be fully two weeks later than the rye. One square rod per day to each cow is the common rule. It is a very liberal one, if no failures occur. Very late sowed rye does well to follow that sowed early, but is not so good as wheat, which excels in amount of leaf and sweetness.

Draining.—As men can be spared from other work, and as others can be hired, get at the drains. There is hardly a farm in the United States, except those on gravel banks, or with leachy subsoil, that might not, in spots at least, be underdrained to advantage. Calculate to drain permanent meadows at least three feet deep, better deeper, and all land that will ever be plowed, not less than four feet on an average. See article in the September number.

Granaries.—Clean out, and make vermin proof in some way—best by setting them on posts capped with flat stones or tin pans. After grain is in, care must be incessantly exercised, lest by some heedlessness the steps are left down, or in some other way mice get in. After that trapping, fumigation, etc., must be resorted too, and these are always uncertain in operation.

Orchard and Nursery.

The late ripening fruits will need attention. Apples and pears, while they should be left on the tree as long as they derive any benefit from it, ought not to be exposed to frosts. The appearances that attend perfect maturity are easily learned by a little observation. The tree ripens its wood and leaves, and the latter part from the twig with a slight pull. So with the fruit; its stem readily severs its connection with the tree. Careful picking is necessary to good keeping. None but a vandal will ever pull the stem from a fruit. Ladders and fruit pickers have heretofore been described in great variety. Whether the fruit is picked into baskets or bags, assort it at once into barrels, putting in the fruit as closely as possible. Avoid all unnecessary handling, as the waxy exudation or bloom natural to many varieties not only improves the appearance, but aids in the keeping of the fruit. The practice of using packing material is now generally abandoned. The barrels are filled about an inch above the chine, and the head brought down by pressure. A simple lever press will accomplish this, or some of the screw presses sold for the purpose may be used. The fruit, after being packed, should be kept as cool as possible without freezing. We have before insisted on the advantage of assorting fruit. Of apples, intended for sale, never put but one kind in a barrel. Treat winter pears in the same way.

Draining.—Nothing is more essential to success in orchard culture than draining, and nothing is more generally neglected. Drains may be made between the rows in young orchards and in land intended to be set with trees next spring.

Autumn Planting is advisable in localities where a mild season may be depended upon. At all events, order trees in the autumn, as a better assortment is to be had, and there are fewer risks in transportation at this season. If the land is not in readiness, or it is not thought best to plant this fall,

Heel in the trees, and they will be at hand for setting in early spring. In heeling-in, select a dry and rather sheltered place, and open a trench. In this put the trees in a sloping direction, and as they are placed in the trench, fill all the spaces among the roots with fine, mellow soil. Bank up the earth to a depth that will protect the roots from freezing, and slope it to carry off rain.

Cider, to be good, should be made from perfectly clean and sound fruit. Cleanliness is to be observed in every step of the process. Ferment slowly in a cool cellar, and when fermentation is over, bung tightly, and when the cider becomes clear, rack it off into clean casks. Where vinegar is the object, so much pains need not be taken. After the cider is fermented, the addition of some old vinegar, or "mother," and free access of air in a warm place, will hasten the conversion into vinegar.

Apple Jelly may be made by carefully evaporating unfermented apple juice. Some of the sorghum pans are found useful for this.

Drying of Fruit should be hurried up. If there is no drying-house, it will pay to put up a stove in a spare room, and subject the fruit to a fire heat on rainy and cloudy days.

Buds are to be looked to, as in a warm autumn the stocks will continue to grow, and the bandages must be loosened.

Nursery Stock should receive a fall manuring. In the best nurseries a plow is run between the rows, and manure is placed in the furrow, and covered.

Seeds are saved from the pomace where a large quantity is wanted. Wash out, dry in thin layers, stirring now and then, and keep in a cool place. For the home nursery let all the family save the seeds of the apples and pears they consume. Have a box of sand in some handy place where they may be deposited, and a large quantity will accumulate.

Orchards may receive a top-dressing of compost.

Ornamental Deciduous Trees are to be planted or heeled-in as suggested above for fruit trees.

Labels are to be looked to, and if any are so weather-worn that they are likely soon to be effaced, replace them by new ones.

Fruit Garden.

Prepare the ground for new plantings. Drain, work deep with the spade or plow, manure, and get the land in the best possible condition.

Planting may be done or not; this is a question of locality. In mild regions, cultivators prefer autumn for blackberry and raspberry, for the reason that the shoots start so early in the spring that there is danger of breaking them in handling.

Currants and Gooseberries are readily propagated by cuttings. These are to be made as soon as the leaves are off. Cut them about 6 inches long, and place them in shallow trenches. Put the cuttings about 4 inches apart, with an inch or so above the surface. Press the earth firmly around the lower end, and when the earth is filled in, cover them with litter or leaves to prevent injury by frosts.

Grapes are to be picked, whether for market or for wine, according to hints given on subsequent pages. As soon as the leaves fall, the vines may receive their fall pruning. If it is desired to use the prunings for propagation, cut them into suitable lengths and bury them in an accessible place.

Root Cuttings of blackberries and raspberries may be made. Cut the roots in pieces 2 or 3 inches long, place them in a box with alternate layers of soil, and bury the box below the reach of frost in a well drained place. See article in October last for details.

Raspberries of the tender sorts should not be laid down too early; delay it until there is danger that the ground may become frozen.

Kitchen Garden.

The gardener will find plenty to do this month in securing and marketing his crops, or in storing them for winter, and in preparing his land for spring.

Preserving Vegetables from frost and decay during the cold months is next in importance to producing them. Small quantities of roots may be kept in a cool cellar, and will be all the better if they are covered with earth or sand. When a large quantity is to be kept it is best to make pits out-of-doors. Select a dry spot and dig a pit 3 or 4 feet deep, 6 feet wide, and of the necessary length. The roots, when dug, are thrown into heaps and covered with a few inches of soil to prevent freezing. When heavy frosts occur, pack them in the pit; put in two feet of roots, leave a space of six inches, and then put in a section of two feet more of roots and so on. The spaces left between the sections are to be filled up with earth, so that the trench will be filled with alternate layers of roots and earth. Cover the whole with a mound of earth about two feet high, so rounded as to shed water. A pit of this kind can be opened, and a portion of its contents removed without disturbing the rest. In this manner beets, turnips, carrots, parsnips, horseradish, etc., may be kept until wanted. Success, however, will in good part depend on thoroughly draining all the water away from the pit.

Preparation of Soil.—If land now in sod is to be used for a garden next spring, spread on a liberal dressing of manure and turn over the sod with a shallow, flat furrow. Other lands, especially if at all stiff, may be plowed into ridges and left to the ameliorating influence of winter.

Draining is almost always needed, and if the soil is at all wet, will be an imperative necessity.

Asparagus.—Cut and burn the tops and cover the beds with coarse manure.

Beets should not be exposed to hard frosts. Store in the cellar, or in pits, as directed above.

Cabbages.—Set the young plants, from seed sown last month, in cold frames. A simple frame is made of planks nailed to posts, the planks at the rear being 1 foot wide, and those at the front 8 inches. It should be wide enough for the sash at hand, and as long as desirable; of course the ends must be closed and the earth banked around the outside of the frame. Set the plants 2½ inches apart each way, down to the first leaf, to cover all the stem. The sash should not be put on until freezing weather. Winter cabbages are best preserved by pulling them before the ground freezes, inverting them on a level piece of ground, and then covering the heads with earth by use of the plow or spade, to the depth of 4 or 6 inches.

Cauliflowers.—Set young plants of early sorts in frames, as directed for cabbages. Store in a light cellar those which have not yet developed their heads.

Celery.—Finish earthing up. Towards the end of the month put the roots away in trenches a foot wide, and deep enough to contain the plants. Pack them closely, and as the weather becomes colder, cover gradually with straw or leaves.

Leaves.—Gather as many as possible to use in hot-beds next spring, and to increase the manure heap.

Lettuce for an early crop next spring is to be had from young plants wintered as directed for cabbage.

Parsnips.—Dig what are wanted for winter use and preserve in the cellar or in pits, and leave the rest in the ground until spring.

Horseradish.—Dig and preserve as other roots, first taking off the small roots to plant next spring. These are to be preserved in boxes with sand.

Rhubarb.—Plantations are better made now than in spring; divide the old roots so as to leave a bud with each. Plant in rich soil, 3 feet apart each way.

Salsify.—Dig what will be needed during the severe weather, and leave the rest in the ground.

Spinach and other crops, to be wintered in the field, should be kept clear of late weeds.

Squashes.—Gather as soon as ripe, and avoid exposure to frost. Keep spread out for a few days to the sun before storing. Handle carefully. Store in a dry place where they will not freeze.

Sweet Potatoes.—Dig on a warm day, as soon as the vines are touched by frost, and allow them to dry off before housing. Handle carefully. Those for winter should be packed in dry, cut straw, or perfectly dry sand, and be kept where they will be at an uniform temperature of about 60°.

Flower Garden and Lawn.

October usually brings us just the weather for all out-door work. New beds, walks, and other improvements in the grounds may be made, ground prepared for spring planting, deciduous trees set, draining and other heavy work done.

Perennials of which the clumps have become too large should be taken up, the mass divided into several parts by means of a sharp spade, and reset. This affords an excellent opportunity to exchange with, or give to, friends. Pæonies, especially, should be moved at this time, if at all.

Bulbs in plenty will be appreciated next spring. A good, deep soil, enriched with cow manure is best. See an article on page 366.

Chrysanthemums.—Keep neatly tied up or they will become straggling. Pot for blooming in doors. Some prefer to delay potting until they are in bloom, thinking that the plants receive less check at this time than when it is done earlier.

Larkspurs.—We seldom see beds of the Rocket Larkspur now-a-days. Seeds sown now will give a fine show in the spring. Indeed, most of the

Hardy Annuals do better if seed be sown in autumn. Every one must have noticed that plants from self-sown seeds are stronger and finer every way than those of the same kind sown in the spring.

Dahlias succumb to the first smart frost unless protected. After the stems are killed, allow the roots to remain a week or more in the ground. Take them up carefully on a dry, warm day, label, and when they have dried somewhat, store in a place that will keep potatoes well.

Hardy Shrubs may be transplanted, and divided if needed, and plants for

Deciduous Hedges, such as Privet, Buckthorn, etc., may be set in well prepared ground.

Bedding Plants and all tender things that are to be kept over winter should be potted preparatory to removal to the green-house, cold frame, or cellar. Provide a good supply of materials for

Winter Protection.—Leaves should be gathered from the lawn and roadsides. These make an excellent covering and are kept in place by a slight sprinkling of earth upon them. Where Red Cedar boughs can be had they will be found most useful to lay over half hardy shrubs and other plants.

Green and Hot-Houses.

Previously to removing plants to the house, they should be put in complete order. Cleanse the pots from dirt and moss, and remove the hardened and weedy top soil, and replace it with a layer of fresh compost. See that no

Insects are taken in with the plants. If proper vigilance be exercised from the start, the task of keeping a mastery over insects will be lessened.

Plants for Forcing should be potted. Many of our common plants force very finely; among these *Dicentra spectabilis*, *Deutzia gracilis*, *Astilbe Japonica*, and Lily of the Valley, make most desirable decorations for the green-house in early spring.

Annuals should be sown for winter blooming, always taking care to have a good stock of Mignonette and Candytuft on hand for bouquet uses.

Bulbs, too, will be needed, and should be potted now and kept in the dark until the pots are well filled with roots.

Rustic Stands and hanging baskets for parlor decoration are to be filled. Some plants suitable for this purpose are mentioned on page 365.

Ventilation must be given freely whenever the weather will allow, and fire heat used only when cold or damp weather makes it necessary.

Cold Grapery.

It is a bad practice to strip the leaves from the vines. They are needed to perfect the wood, and when they have done their work they will drop of their own accord. The ripening of the wood may be aided by keeping the house rather warm, which may be accomplished by keeping the lower ventilators closed and using only the upper ones. Close up all the ventilators on cold and damp days.

Apiary in Oct.—*Prepared by M. Quinby.*

By correspondence from nearly all the States of the Union, I find the honey crop more generally good than last year. Bees have usually swarmed well, and are prepared for winter. Yet so many bees were lost last season, that there is a less number in the country now than a year ago. This will make it desirable that all good stocks should be wintered. Ascertain the amount of honey by weighing hive and contents, and subtracting the weight of an empty hive of similar size, thickness of boards, etc., and six pounds for weight of bees, wax, and bee-bread. Call the remainder honey, and you will not be far from the mark, unless the combs are very old. Then a little more should be added. Less than 20 or 25 pounds of honey is not enough. Too much is as detrimental as too little. With movable frame hives, if any combs are filled with honey throughout, they should be alternated with such as are empty. If any stock is too light and has too few combs to hold sufficient stores, at this season, it should be taken up at once. If the combs are sufficient, but bees are few, and there is no condemned colony to reinforce them, they should receive the same treatment. Such hives, after the dead bees have been taken from between the combs, will be of most account set away for use next year. Set right side up, keep dry, and stop all holes that will admit a bee.

Two weak colonies united make a strong one, and may be put together if there is honey sufficient. To prevent quarreling, smoke them out of the combs with puff-ball, tobacco, or what will answer just as well, have every bee fill itself with honey. When a stock has bees and combs, and lacks honey, it may be fed up to the required weight. October is the time, or as soon as the brood is all hatched. Feed all that is required in the shortest possible time, or the bees may use too much in rearing brood. Honey should be fed when it is to be had. West India honey is good and much cheaper than Northern. To be safe from disease, add a quart of water to ten pounds, scald thoroughly, and skim. Feed in a dish on the top of the hive by opening a few holes, and covering with a box to keep out robbers. Put cut straw or shavings in the dish to keep the bees from drowning. See that the sides of the dish are rough enough for them to creep up and down. If honey in the comb is preferred, the caps of sealed honey should be shaved off with a knife. All winter stores should be in the apartment with the bees. They might starve in cold weather with an abundance in the boxes. Where two light, weak stocks in the movable comb hives have enough bees, combs, and honey, for one good one, they may all be put together. Select the combs with honey, and put them into one hive. With bees in box hives after smoking or feeding them into quietude, turn both hives bottom up. Trim off the bottom edges of the combs in one, square across; take off the side of the other, cut loose the edges of the first comb, take it out and set it into the first hive, fitting it upon the base of the first comb; then proceed with the others in the same way, keeping the combs in the same relative position and at a proper distance apart. Rolls of paper between will hold them until the bees can fasten them. Put a stick across the edges as a support when the hive is turned over; let it touch all, and fasten each end of the stick to the side of the hive. Cover, and let it stand bottom up, a week or two, or until a short time before putting to winter quarters.

Any stocks one year old, that have not been examined relative to foul brood, should be attended to at once. On no account allow a hive with foul brood to be robbed. You have no right to let it stand exposed to be plundered by your neighbors' bees. Honey from such hives should never be allowed to go into healthy stocks without scalding. Strain honey before cold weather. See directions in previous numbers and volumes of the *Agriculturist*.

Commercial Matters—Market Prices.

The following condensed, comprehensive tables, carefully prepared specially for the *American Agriculturist*, show at a glance the transactions for the month ending Sept. 16, 1867, and also for the same month last year:

1. TRANSACTIONS AT THE NEW-YORK MARKETS.

RECEIPTS.	*Flour.*	*Wheat.*	*Corn.*	*Rye.*	*Barley.*	*Oats.*
27 days this m'th	218,500	639,000	3,291,000	39,300	58,000	570,000
27 days last m'th	189,000	611,000	2,954,000	21,900	67,000	102,000

SALES.	*Flour.*	*Wheat.*	*Corn.*	*Rye.*	*Oats.*
27 days last month,	281,000	1,079,000	4,181,000	151,000	1,387,000
27 days this month,	279,000	694,000	3,469,000	95,000	739,000

2. *Comparison with same period at this time last year.*

RECEIPTS.	*Flour.*	*Wheat.*	*Corn.*	*Rye.*	*Barley.*	*Oats.*
27 days 1867...	218,500	639,000	3,291,000	39,300	58,000	570,000
26 days 1866...	387,000	436,000	3,254,000	111,000	165,000	1,281,000

SALES.	*Flour.*	*Wheat.*	*Corn.*	*Rye.*	*Oats.*
27 days 1867......	284,000	1,079,000	4,181,000	151,000	1,387,000
26 days 1866......	279,100	790,000	3,138,000	319,000	1,011,000

3. *Exports from New York, Jan. 1 to Sept. 14:*

	Flour.	*Wheat.*	*Corn.*	*Rye.*	*Oats.*	*Barley.*
1867....	395,063	980,749	4,391,173	185,141	103,173	208,290
1866....	676,165	230,854	9,089,815	191,199	969,309	184,924

4. *Stock of grain in store at New York:*

1867.	Wheat, bush.	Corn, bush.	Rye, bush.	Barley, bush.	Oats, bush.	Malt, bush.
Sept. 10...	130,732	1,151,872	770	9,526	183,797	61,503
Aug. 13...	9,174	968,144	[illegible]	17,370	200,319	[illegible]
July 15...	215,509	109,290	64,926	21,200	268,703	34,700
June 11...	578,219	211,798	111,237	67,843	[illegible]	16,311
May 15...	331,330	261,094	105,401	115,706	608,191	16,161

5. *Receipts of Breadstuffs at tide water at Albany, May 1st to September 7th:*

	Flour, bbls.	Wheat, bush.	Corn, bush.	Rye, bush.	Barley, bush.	Oats, bush.
1867....	91,100	764,100	9,313,[illegible]	171,100	62,000	2,833,[illegible]
1866....	187,100	1,639,300	[illegible]	641,800	118,100	5,022,800

Gold has been much more active since our last, especially within the past week. It was as high on Thursday, Sept. 12, as 140⅞. It has since been down to 141⅛. The demand has been almost exclusively from speculative buyers.... Diminished estimates of the harvest product are now gaining currency, and are tending to stimulate speculation in Breadstuffs, which latter have been in more active request, and generally at higher prices. The inquiry for flour has been mainly from regular buyers for home use and export. Desirable grades have been in very moderate supply, closing firmly. Wheat has been more sought for home and foreign use; as also on speculative account, closing buoyantly. Prime spring wheat is scarce and wanted. Corn has been in lively demand, largely on speculation, at decidedly buoyant, but quite variable, prices. Rye has been quiet, closing steadily. Oats have been more freely offered and purchased, but at lower rates.... Provisions have attracted more attention, the leading articles closing firmly, on reduced supplies.... Cotton has been less active and has declined materially, closing in favor of purchasers.... Wool has attracted more attention. Desirable lots of high grades of fleece have been comparatively scarce and held with increased firmness. Other descriptions have been steadier as to price than during the preceding month, though they have been in fair supply.... Tobacco have been active and firm. The export and speculative demand have been brisk.... Hay has been plenty and depressed, with a moderate inquiry. .... Hops have been in demand, and steady.

CURRENT WHOLESALE PRICES.

	Aug. 15.	Sept. 16.
PRICE OF GOLD	140[illegible]	144[illegible]
FLOUR—Super to Extra State	$8 75 @ 11 50	$8 25 @ [illegible]
Super to Extra Southern	11 60 @ 14 25	[illegible]
Extra Western	8 85 @ 15 50	[illegible]
Extra Genesee	11 60 @ 13 50	[illegible]
Superfine Western	[illegible]	[illegible]
RYE FLOUR	[illegible]	[illegible]
CORN MEAL	[illegible]	[illegible]
WHEAT—All kinds of White	[illegible]	[illegible]
All kinds of Red and Amber	[illegible]	[illegible]
CORN—Yellow	[illegible]	[illegible]
Mixed	[illegible]	[illegible]
OATS—Western	73 @ 80	67 @ 68¾
State	84 @ 85	67 @ 68
RYE	1 40 @ 1 53	1 33 @ 1 50
BARLEY	1 00 @ —	[illegible]
HAY—Bale ₩ 100 lb	[illegible]	[illegible]
Loose	[illegible]	[illegible]
STRAW, ₩ 100 lb	[illegible]	[illegible]
COTTON—Middlings, ₩ lb	[illegible]	[illegible]
HOPS—Crop of 1866, ₩ lb	[illegible]	[illegible]
FEATHERS—Live Geese, ₩ lb	[illegible]	[illegible]
SEED—Clover, ₩ lb	11½ @ 17½	[illegible]
Timothy, ₩ bushel	3 00 @ 3 25	2 75 @ 3 00
Flax, ₩ bushel	3 20 @ 3 50	[illegible]
SUGAR—Brown, ₩ lb	10¼ @ 13¾	10¾ @ 13¾
MOLASSES, Cuba, ₩ gal	[illegible]	[illegible]
COFFEE—Rio, (Gold price) ₩ lb	11½ @ 19	14¾ @ 19
TOBACCO, Kentucky, &c., ₩ lb	[illegible]	[illegible]
Seed Leaf, ₩ lb	[illegible]	[illegible]
WOOL—Domestic Fleece, ₩ lb	[illegible]	[illegible]
Domestic, pulled, ₩ lb	[illegible]	[illegible]
California, unwashed	[illegible]	[illegible]
TALLOW, ₩ lb	[illegible]	[illegible]
OIL CAKE—₩ ton	[illegible]	[illegible]
PORK—Mess, ₩ barrel	[illegible]	[illegible]
Prime, ₩ barrel	[illegible]	[illegible]
BEEF—Plain mess	[illegible]	[illegible]
LARD, in barrels, ₩ lb	[illegible]	[illegible]
BUTTER—Western, ₩ lb	[illegible]	[illegible]
State, ₩ lb	[illegible]	[illegible]
CHEESE	6 @ 13½	[illegible]
BEANS—₩ bushel	[illegible]	[illegible]
PEAS—Canada, ₩ bushel	[illegible]	[illegible]
EGGS—Fresh, ₩ dozen	[illegible]	[illegible]
POULTRY—Fowls, ₩ lb	[illegible]	[illegible]
Turkeys, ₩ lb	[illegible]	[illegible]
POTATOES—Old & New, ₩ bbl.	[illegible]	[illegible]
APPLES—₩ barrel	[illegible]	[illegible]
PEACHES—₩ basket	1 00 @ 2 50	[illegible]
CRANBERRIES, ₩ barrel	Nominal.	Nominal.

New York Live Stock Markets.—

WEEK ENDING.	*Beeves.*	*Cows.*	*Calves.*	*Sheep.*	*Swine.*
August 20	5,784	65	1,241	[illegible]	[illegible]
August 27	6,994	45	1,316	[illegible]	[illegible]
September 3	6,397	35	[illegible]	[illegible]	[illegible]
September 10	[illegible]	53	1,181	[illegible]	20,314
Total in four Weeks	26,176	175	5,201	[illegible]	91,793
Average per Week	6,544	44	1,300	[illegible]	[illegible]
do. do. *last Month*	5,896	47	1,404	[illegible]	[illegible]
do. do. *prev's Month*	5,323	51	2,141	[illegible]	[illegible]
Average per Week, 1866	5,715	91	1,200	[illegible]	13,000
do. do. do. 1865	5,255	118	1,500	[illegible]	[illegible]
do. do. do. 1864	5,161	115	[illegible]	[illegible]	[illegible]
do. do. do. 1863	5,150	179	[illegible]	[illegible]	[illegible]
Total in 1866	298,880	4,885	[illegible]	[illegible]	[illegible]
Total in 1865	[illegible]	6,161	[illegible]	[illegible]	[illegible]
Total in 1864	267,609	7,600	[illegible]	[illegible]	[illegible]
Total in 1863	264,091	6,170	[illegible]	[illegible]	[illegible]

Beef Cattle.—Considering that since early in the month reported upon, the weather has steadily improved, it is not strange that with largely increased supplies there should be also an improvement in prices—at least, no falling off. Prime cattle have decidedly improved, and are in [illegible]. The shortness of pastures forces a good deal of [illegible] stock upon the market, and this, of course, tends to keep prices down. Our citizens are [illegible] from the country, and there [illegible] a larger home demand for good beef. The law relative to slaughtering animals within the city limits has had its influence also in determining the price of beef. Now, however, we [illegible] more [illegible] season, and the usual [illegible] the market will operate naturally. [illegible] of prices may be stated now as [illegible] per pound, estimated dressed weight, for very fine beef [illegible] about the average; poor, thin, travel-[illegible] ...**Milch Cows** are [illegible] **Calves** are [illegible] sold by the head, and [illegible] each. They are thin, but big and [illegible] veal is worth [illegible]c. per pound, live [illegible] **Sheep.** The supply has been remarkably [illegible] large, prices about as follows: Prime [illegible] live weight; medium to poor, 4½c.@5c. [illegible] per pound; common, [illegible]c. Many [illegible] have been bought by the farmers and driven into the country for feeding, while the pastures of this vicinity remain good. **Hogs.**—There has been considerable variation in the quality of the swine, and a proportionate one in prices. Little really good pork comes to market now and this is quickly taken. Good to prime sell at [illegible]c.@7[illegible]c. per pound live weight; ordinary 6½c.@7c.

The Fairs for 1867.

[We give below a list of all the State and National Fairs yet to take place, and of such County, Town, and District Fairs, not yet held, as were not included in our list in the September number of the *Agriculturist*. A few are added which have changed their dates.]

State Agricultural Fairs.

American Institute	N. Y. City	Sept 12, Oct. 20
[illegible]	Terre Haute	Sept. 30-Oct. 4
[illegible]	[illegible]	Sept. 30-Oct. 5
New York	[illegible]	Oct. 1- 4
[illegible]	[illegible]	Oct. 1- 4
[illegible]	[illegible]	Oct. 1- 4
[illegible]	St. Louis	Oct. 7-12
[illegible] Ag'l & Mech. Ass.	Clarksville	Oct. 15-19
Maryland	Baltimore	Oct. 29-31
New Jersey	Betw. Newark and Elizabeth	Oct. 8-11
[illegible]	Denver	Oct. 9-12
Louisiana	Baton Rouge	Nov. 5- 9
Louisiana Ag'l & Mech. Ass., New Orleans		Nov. 19-26

Horse Fairs.

Horse Show	Kalamazoo, Mich	Oct. 1- 4
National Horse Fair	Washington, D. C.	Oct. 8–
Del. Horse Show	Newcastle	Oct. 15-16

County and Local Fairs,

not in the list published in the September number.

NEW HAMPSHIRE.		
Exeter (Town)		Oct. 1- 2
[illegible] Co	(Time changed to)	Oct. 8- 9
Strafford Co	Dover	Oct. 1- 3
VERMONT.		
Addison Co	Middlebury	Oct. 1- 3
Windham Co	New Fane	Oct. 2- 3
CONNECTICUT.		
Meriden (Town)		Oct. 9-10
Pequabuck	Bristol	Oct. 9
NEW YORK.		
Chemung Co	Elmira	Oct. 8- 9
Dundee Union (Town)		Oct. 15 17
Montgomery Co	Fonda	Oct. 9 10
[illegible] Co	[illegible]	Oct. 1- 2
Oneida Town	Madison Co	Oct. 8 5
Warren Co		Oct. 8-11
Yates Co.	Penn Yan	Oct. 9-11
PENNSYLVANIA.		
Beaver Co		Oct. 2- 4
Bedford Co	Bedford	Oct. 2 4
Clearfield Co	Clearfield	Oct. 1- 4
Clarion Co	Clarion	Oct. 2- 4
Columbia Co		Oct. 9 11
[illegible] Valley	Blairsville	Oct. 9 11
Cumberland Co	Carlisle	Oct. 1 4
Doylestown (Town)	Doylestown	Oct. 1- 4
Hartford (Town)	Susquehanna Co.	Oct. 2- 3
Huntingdon Co	Huntingdon	Oct. 2- 4
Indiana Co	Indiana	Oct. 2- 4
Washington Co	Washington	Oct. 8 10
Wayne Co	Honesdale	Oct. 9 11
OHIO.		
Ashtabula (Town)	Ashtabula Co.	Oct. 2- 4
Auglaize Co	Wapakoneta	Oct. 2- 4
Augusta (Town)	Carroll Co	Oct. 9-10
Greenfield Union (Town)		Oct. 16-18
Lake Shore Grape Growers' Ass., Elyria		Oct. 15-17
Mahoning Co.	Canfield	Oct. 1- 3
Marion Co.	Marion	Oct. 9-11
Muskingum Co	Zanesville	Oct. 9-11
Plymouth (Town)	Richland Co.	Oct. 8-10
Union (Greene Co.)	Marysville	Oct. 9-11
INDIANA.		
Allen Co	Fort Wayne	Oct. 10
Jefferson Co	North Madison	Oct. 7
Kosciusko Co	Warsaw	Oct. 2
[illegible] Co		
[illegible] Co	Peru	Oct. 2
[illegible] Co	Ligonier	Oct. 3
[illegible]wick Co.	Boonville	Oct. 15-17
Wayne Co	Centerville	Oct. 15-18
IOWA.		
Blackhawk Co.		Oct. 9-11
Butler Co	Shell Rock	Oct. 9-11
Fayette Co	West Union	Oct. 1- 3
Henry Co.	Mt. Pleasant	Oct. 9-11
Madison Co	Winterset	Oct. 1- 3
Winneshiek Co.	Decorah	Oct. 3- 4
MINNESOTA.		
Le Sueur Co	Cleveland	Oct. 10-11
WISCONSIN.		
Beaver Dam Ag. and Mech. Ass.		Oct. 15 17
Racine Co	Burlington	Oct. 1 3
Richland Co.	Richland Centre	Oct. 3- 4
Sauk Co.	Baraboo	Oct. 2- 4
Fond du Lac Co.	Ripon	Oct. 1- 3
Juneau Co	Mauston	Oct. 2- 3
Lodi Union (Town)	Lodi	Oct. 2- 4
Lafayette Co	Darlington	Oct. 3- 5
ILLINOIS.		
Clay Co	Louisville	Oct. 2- 4
Clark Co	Marshall	Oct. 9-12
Edgar Co	Paris	Oct. 8-11
Marion Co.	Salem	Oct. 14-17
Monroe Co	Waterloo	Oct. 16-19
Pope Co.	Golconda	Oct. 3- 5
Shelby Co.	Shelbyville	Oct. 9-12
Sandwich Union (Town)	Sandwich	Oct. 1- 4
Washington Co.	Nashville	Oct. 2- 4
Vermillion Co	Catlin	Oct. 8-11
MICHIGAN.		
Calhoun Co	Marshall	Oct. 9-11
Central Michigan	Lansing	Oct. 8-10
Genesee Co.	Flint	Oct. 2- 4
Livingston Co.	Howell	Oct. 8-10
Macomb Co.	Romeo	Oct. 2- 4
Ottawa Co	Lamont	Oct. 7- 9
Saginaw Co.	E. Saginaw	Oct. 2- 4
MISSOURI.		
Audrian Co	Mexico	Oct. 14-19
Boone Co	Columbia	Sept. 30, Oct. 8
Clay Co	Liberty	Oct.
Carroll Co.	Carrollton	Oct. 1- 5
Gentry Co.	Albany	Oct. 1- 4
Moniteau Co.	California	Oct. 1- 5
Montgomery Co	Montgomery	Oct. 21-24
Saline Co.	Marshall	Oct. 16-20
Scotland Co	Memphis	

The Results of the Harvest.—We go to press just in the beginning of the corn harvest over most of the country, and still in the midst of one of the most remarkable "spells of weather" that has ever been experienced here. It seems really that the sunshine and showers, and tempests too, have been spellbound—the one to glow and burn, the others to rain and blow, each over a particular region. The seaboard has been rained upon till the farmers begin to feel almost amphibious, while the interior has been suffering from a severe drought. These sections of country have been relieved —the one by a day or two of sunshine almost every week, and the other by occasional showers which have held out hope of relief. To some parts happy relief has come; others still suffer. The result is, that it is very difficult to come at a just estimate of the harvest.

At present the fate of the corn crop is regarded with considerable solicitude. We hear of rains coming just in time to save it in isolated localities throughout the region which has been suffering from drought, which includes Central New York, and westward, especially the southern portions of the great corn and wheat raising States of Ohio, Indiana, Illinois and Missouri. By the time this reaches our readers, we hope that these rains may be general. The corn of the Eastern and Middle States is in danger now from frosts which have already touched the leaves in exposed places. The crop is backward, and shocking can not be done as early as common without serious loss of weight. On the whole, a less than average crop may be looked for. The great wheat region has profited by the dry weather so far as to have its wheat threshed in excellent order. The crop is decidedly less than average in quantity, but of a very superior quality. Oats have not filled well where the dry weather was severest, but as we usually hear the croakers first we can hardly judge of the results—and very much the same report must be made of barley and spring wheat. Potatoes have rotted distressingly at the East, especially those early planted and well manured; while in the interior the dry weather causes a short yield. Root crops generally look remarkably well wherever it has been sufficiently moist, and on good soils everywhere the crops will be remunerative.

The hay of the dry section is not abundant, while in the wet it has been poorly cured, so that everywhere the corn-stalks should be well secured if possible.

Apples are abundant over the great apple regions of the central and western parts of the Middle States, Ohio and Indiana; but many localities at the East are almost altogether without this fruit.

Tobacco has had too much rain for its good in the Connecticut Valley, and a full crop has not set. It is in danger from the frost, also. From the great tobacco region south of Mason and Dixon's line we have, as a rule, unfavorable reports. The cotton region of the Atlantic board has suffered from rain and an inordinate growth of grass. The crop of Arkansas, part of Louisiana, Texas, and Mississippi is quite good. The general crop is estimated as considerably larger than that of last year on account of the greater breadth planted, but the yield per acre will prove discouraging.

The effect of the season on Dairying is what might have been expected. The supply of butter for the New York market was essentially diminished by the drought affecting the greater part of the State and the great dairy region of Northern Ohio, and prices rose accordingly. The same cause affects the cheese products. New England, New Jersey and Pennsylvania pastures have produced abundantly, but the quality of the grass was poor and watery. The amount of milk was large, but the butter not so good as common.

We shall doubtless have an abundance of all staples for home consumption, and a good deal for export. Prices of almost all farm produce are ruling high. Speculation, in part influences this gradual advance, but with the menacing attitudes of European powers towards each other, a possibility that the wheat supplies of the Black Sea region will be cut off, crops falling below the average in Western Europe, and only a moderate crop here, farmers will be foolish if they do not get remunerative prices.

Containing a great variety of Items, including many good Hints and Suggestions which we throw into smaller type and condensed form, for want of space elsewhere.

245 BROADWAY.

After October 1st, the Office of the

AMERICAN AGRICULTURIST

will be at

245 BROADWAY,

with a Branch Office at the old place,

41 PARK ROW.

In our next number we shall say more on this subject.

Mark All Subscriptions sent in, as *New* or *Old*.

The American Agriculturist, 245 Broadway, N. Y.—It will probably seem as strange to our correspondents to write the above, as it does the figures of the new year; yet by the time this sheet reaches the majority of our readers, the *Agriculturist* and all its belongings will have been transferred from 41 Park Row to 245 Broadway. The distance is not great, the two locations being within sight of one another; yet the removal is accompanied by the regrets that one always feels at leaving a long familiar spot for a new and untried one. It was at 41 Park Row that the *Agriculturist* attained its majority. It came here a successful paper, and leaves it as an institution. It was here that the important part of our business, the publication of agricultural books, had its beginning, and has become a channel for distributing agricultural and horticultural information second only in importance to the paper. Here new relations have been formed in our business and editorial departments, and here we have had the pleasure of meeting face to face with so many of those whom we monthly visit through the medium of the paper. But the *Agriculturist* has outgrown its old home, and notwithstanding these pleasant associations, it must go to a new and more commodious one. We are glad that this change is made while Mr. Judd is abroad, as he would feel it more keenly than any one else. In his absence, we may say that when he compares the five-story brown stone store on Broadway with the obscure rooms on a second floor in Water street, from which the earlier volumes were issued, he may properly congratulate himself on the success that has attended well directed energy and unceasing devotion to business. We hope to carry to our new quarters all our old friends, and shall be prepared to receive large accessions to their number. With increased facilities for producing the paper, we hope that we shall more certainly than ever attain our constant aim—to make each volume better than the last.

Pasturing Clover the First Year.—"Will a field sown with clover in the spring furnish pasturage for cows during the summer?"—If the ground is well manured, clean, and the season moist, and the clover gets a good start, it will be fine, rich feed by July, and, if not fed off close, will not be injured. On ordinary land the practice is never advisable, and is seldom best,

Fatal Disease among Poultry.—Lemuel D. Dobbs, of Brownsville, Texas, writes: "My young chickens, ducks, and turkeys are all dying. I have just lost two entire broods. A swelling commences around the eyes, nostrils, and the skin on the under part of the bill. These places rise up like great warts, and in from one to three days from the time that the disease first appears, the chickens die. I think it is the biting of mosquitoes, and have tried to prevent it by cooping them at night under a mosquito bar, but it does no good. All my neighbor's chickens are affected the same way." Whether our subscriber's suspicions are well founded or not, we would recommend the application of warm pine tar, smearing it over all the affected parts, but not stopping up the nostrils. If this does not cure, we would try painting the parts with a solution of nitrate of silver, (*lunar caustic*,) applied with a feather.

Incubators, or Artificial Egg Hatchers.—We have several inquiries for these articles, or for descriptions of them. It is, perhaps, enough to say, we know of none which we believe it worth while to attempt to use. There are several advertised, and used more or less abroad, but none that we know of in this country. It seems to be a fair subject for experiment. What is needed is a tolerably uniform temperature, not far from 100° Fahrenheit, a certain slight degree of moisture in the air, and daily turning of the eggs. Tegetmeier, in The Poultry Book, speaks highly of Manad's Patent Incubator. The French plan is taking hen turkeys, forcing them to sit on false eggs a few days, and, when they are contented, putting good ones under them, as many as they will cover. The chicks are removed as fast as hatched, and other eggs substituted. This plan has been tried by one of our neighbors, with success. A turkey covers twice as many eggs as a hen.

What Birds are "Fowls."—There is an article "going the rounds" of the press, distinguishing fowls as birds which take their young to their food. The absurdity of this definition is apparent on a moment's thought; for, though applicable to farmyard poultry, in distinction from the birds of the hedge, it will not bear a more extensive application. It is unfortunate that, in English, we have no single *word* for our barn-door or dung-hill fowls. Even the names cock and hen they share in common with a score of other birds from Cock-robin to Cock-turkey—(Cockroach and Hood's Cock-mermaid included)—Hen Sparrow and Pea Hen as well. Poultry fanciers have, of late, with an unanimity which is remarkable, confined the use of the word *fowl* to this, in English, nameless bird—*Gallus domesticus*.

Killing Animals at the Paris Abattoirs.—Mr. Judd writes: "To-day, (July 18th.) I visited the extensive new Abattoirs, or slaughter houses, now partly completed, within the city walls, but beyond the thickly-settled portion, on the north-northeast side of Paris. The grand market, not yet finished, is an immense iron structure, with iron and glass roof, supported on iron columns, and to remain open on the sides, I believe. A strict prohibition to visitors, at present, prevented my examining it fully. The roof covers several acres; the pens are small and low, and arranged in streets and avenues, and the bottom is as hard and smooth as rough cut stone. The slaughter-houses near by are nice blocks of stone and stucco building, each apartment opening at either end into the avenues running between the blocks. The whole looks like a village of tasteful houses, joined side to side along the streets, which are bent at a small angle frequently, so as to diminish the sight of too many operations at one view. The floors of both buildings and streets are solid cement, with an inclination to frequent drains, opening into subterranean sewers. Water is arranged to wash the whole surface neat and clean, as often as it becomes soiled. Ladies can walk through the whole establishment without soiling their dresses, except in the vicinity of the actual operations of cleaning the offal. Two masters or journeymen butchers occupy each killing room with two assistants, and dressing eight to twelve beef cattle is a day's work, according to the size of the animal and the activity of the market. I watched the entire process of killing and dressing a bullock, which was as follows. The animal was driven in at one door, the other being closed; a rope was lassoed over his horns, and the other end put through a ring in the floor. When his nose was drawn to the floor, so as to to curve his neck, a short, spear-like knife was thrust into the spinal column, just back of the horns. It was done in an instant, and the animal dropped as suddenly as if struck with a cannon ball, and scarcely moved a muscle. A moment or two after, the front of the head was struck with an appropriate long-handled hammer several heavy blows; the animal lay almost perfectly still. Next, the operator cut into the neck, as near the shoulders as possible, and opened the arteries at or near the heart, apparently to give the best outlet to the blood, which flowed off into an opening in the floor, and was all saved in a clean condition. The animal was then moved and pushed about to promote the entire expulsion of *all* the blood. One man then skinned the legs up to the gambrel joint, and cut them off. The other, in the mean time, made one small opening through the skin on the belly, just back of the forelegs, and another between the hind legs. Into these apertures he thrust a round-pointed half-inch steel rod, a little curved, and made openings along under the skin in different directions. A large hand bellows was then thrust into each of the openings, and one long lever arm was worked, while the other was held upon the floor with the foot. The air was thus driven in with great power and permeated every part under the skin and throughout the entire flesh and internal fat. The carcass swelled to nearly double size, and when beat with a stick to promote the circulation of the air, the skin sounded like a heavy, loosely strained, bass drum. When the inflation was complete, the skinning was easily and quickly performed. Great tact was exercised in running the knife along so as to have its curved point leave the surface of the meat slightly gashed in stripes, at various angles. A small iron windlass, with ratchet wheel and pulleys, served to raise the carcass as fast as it was skinned. Napkins or towels were kept at hand to remove the slightest trace of filth or blood. The puffiness of the flesh, its clearness from blood, and the line cutting where the red integument appeared, together with the neatness everywhere exercised, gave an exceedingly beautiful appearance to the dressed sides as they were conveyed to the store-room, and hung up for sale. One can eat meat in Paris without any qualm from slaughter-house recollections or associations. The entire absence of apparent pain or motions in the dying animal, and the inflation of the meat, though often read of, were novelties to me in actual observation. Calves and sheep are dressed in the same manner. I priced some of the meats to-day as follows: The *best* sides of beef, 142 francs per 100 killogrammes—equal to about 12 cents per pound in gold, or 16@17 cts. per pound U. S. currency. Other qualities ran down to 110@105 francs per 100 killogrammes. Very good carcasses of sheep were selling at 15 sous per livre, (about 15 cents gold per pound, equivalent to 21 cents currency;) and dressed pork at 17 sous per livre.

Miami Raspberry.—Mr. W. Johnston, South Bend, Ind., dissents from Mr. Fuller's estimate of this variety, and gives his own experience as follows: "I fruited it in connection with seven other varieties; the time of ripening first berries was as follows: Kirtland, June 30th; Golden Cap and Miami, July 3d; Doolittle and Philadelphia, July 4th; Ohio Everbearing and Catawissa, July 7th. Thus, it has a very favorable season. Compared with the Doolittle, which, Mr. F. says, is 'very large and very productive, and a profitable market berry,' its superiority over it was, in all respects, quite noticeable—the bush larger, more hardy and thrifty, the berry larger, more abundant, flavor decidedly superior, and berry much firmer. I had the Philadelphia in its perfection, I believe, and it is a magnificent berry, giving more fruit during the best days of its season than the Miami, but as the season of the latter is from eight to ten days longer, I think it will yield full as much fruit, and is a more profitable market berry, as the Philadelphia is quite too soft for long transportation. Thus we know of no raspberry superior to the Miami, and if Mr. F. does, we wish he would name it, for it is wanted."

The Kittatinny Blackberry.—We, two years ago, described and figured this berry. This year it has quite warranted all that we have said of it. Some specimens brought us in August from E. Williams, Montclair, N. J., show it to be the very best berry that is now in cultivation. We have seen plants in localities north of New Jersey, fruiting finely.

Black Caps from Seed.—Wm. Lawrence writes: "I have a cluster of vines that produce much larger and finer fruit than any other that I have seen," and asks if they can be propagated from the seed. They can be readily grown from seed, but there is no certainty that the same qualities will be reproduced. The resulting plants may produce better fruit, but are more likely to give that of inferior quality. The only sure way is to layer the tips of the branches as soon as they get somewhat firm. See *Agriculturist* for August, page 291.

The One-leaved Strawberry.—Every one knows that the leaf of the strawberry is three-parted. In 1761, a variety with a single leaf was brought to notice, and afterwards figured in the Botanical Magazine as *Fragaria monophylla*, or One-leaved Strawberry. Just one hundred years after this appearance, Mr. A. S. Fuller, author of the Small Fruit Culturist, found (in 1861,) a similar freak among his seedlings, from the Boston Pine, and now Gloede, the great French strawberry grower, gets a similar form from seeds of Napoleon III. These departures from the normal type are interesting: they, however, show a general debility in the plant, as in neither of the three recorded cases was the fruit of any value.

Grasses Named.—H. A. Slater, N. Manchester, Conn.—Blue Joint-Grass, *Calamagrostis Canadensis*. ..R. F. Roberts, Woodworth, Wis.—*Eragrostis poaeoides*, an introduced weed, for which we know no common name ...New Egypt, N. J. (can't read the name)—*Triticum repens*, the Couch, Quack, Quick, or Twitch Grass. Valued in some places for pasturage, but a terrible pest in cultivated lands ..."Subscriber," St. Paul, Minn.—The purple specimen is Barn-yard Grass, *Panicum Crus-galli*; the long one is Indian Grass, *Sorghum nutans*; that of which two specimens were sent, is a Beard Grass, *Andropogon furcatus*; and the most delicate of all is *Sporobolus heterolepis*. When more than one specimen is sent, they should be numbered. With the exception mentioned in reference to Couch Grass, none of them are of any agricultural value, and many of them are so little noticed that they have received no popular names.

Grand Old Plants.—Recently we visited the grounds of a gentleman near Newburgh, N. Y., and were delighted to see a *Gardenia*, or Cape Jessamine, some six feet high, and well furnished with branches to the base. It had good company in some Pomegranate and Lemon and Orange trees, all of which showed that they had been objects of care for years. We have a great affection for these old plants, as we have for old furniture, old china, and old pictures. These plants are venerable, and it is pleasant to think of the kindly care of several generations that is incorporated with their growth.

Red and White Clover.—Prof. Way, of the Royal Ag'l. Society, made several analyses of clover hay with a view to determine what substances clover crops extracted from the soil, and thus, if possible, to come at the cause of what in England is called "clover sickness." This is a condition of the soil when it refuses under ordinary treatment to yield good crops of clover—and so is called "sick" or "tired" of clover. We are not, as yet, troubled with this failure of the crop upon land where it once did well, except as we lose the influence of plaster on the crop, which frequently occurs. The analyses show that clover makes great drafts upon the soil for alkalies, especially potash, and no doubt it is the gradual exhaustion of this ingredient which causes the failure of the crop. The great benefit of applications of wood ashes and of plaster to clover are matters of universal experience, and we may safely say that so long as we continue them we will live in ignorance of clover sickness.

Clover in Mercer Co., Ill.—"E. L. M." writes that in this hot dry summer the red clover is killed out, so that they have to give it up as a farm crop. This is also the case farther south, in many places, and no kind of red clover will grow. Neither will the ordinary grasses, that form the greensward of the Northern States. The only chance to get clover to stand under such disadvantages is to sow it in time for the usual early autumn rains. Thus early sown, it may send its roots deep enough to withstand the summer droughts.

Double Pelargonium—Gloire de Nancy.—We were gratified to receive from Mr. John Saul, Florist, of Washington, D. C., some flowers of this new variety. It has made quite a sensation abroad, and, apparently, deservedly so. The flowers are very double, and of a brilliant deep rose color. It is greatly superior to the Ranunculiflora, figured in December last. Mr. Saul says: "It is a noble plant, strong and vigorous in its growth, and luxuriates in our hot bright sun, blooming freely. The flowers are thrown up well above the foliage, and, being double, are more enduring than single kinds."

Plants with Gray Foliage.—In the present popular "bedding out" planting, a plant with a gray or silvery tint is very desirable to set off the more brilliant *Coleus* or *Achyranthes*, (*Iresine*,) *Herbstii*. *Centaurea ragusina*, also called *candidissima* is one of the best for this purpose, but it does not propagate fast enough to suit the florists, who prefer to sell the freer growing *Cineraria maritima*, or "Dusty Miller." We have tried this latter, this summer, for a bed in the lawn, and find that by cutting it back freely, it may be made to grow bushy, and we are rather pleased with it. The English gardeners are talking about one of our wild plants for this purpose—*Antennaria margaritacea*, or Life Everlasting. We have never seen it in cultivation, but think it worth a trial. Mr. Peter Henderson has shown us this season a new plant of this style, *Centaurea gymnocarpa*, and from what we have seen of it with him and elsewhere we think that it will become popular—provided that it favorably answers the florists' great question—"will it cut?"

Toad Flax. "Snap Dragon." —"Butter and Eggs."—E. Stowe, of Wis., asks: "Will you be kind enough to state the best method of destroying that pest of farmers, Snap Dragon.—There is more or less of it in Wisconsin; I have mowed it in blossom, and tried digging it out; this last seems to spread it and make it grow more vigorously. —*Answer:* We know of no way easier than to smother the plant. Make a pile of fresh cut grass or weeds, 5 inches thick, well trodden down over and around the infested locality. If on a lawn or in a garden, after cutting up the plants, cover with old boards, laid close together, and covered with hay to prevent their warping. This is said to be a sure cure in one season, and is the easiest one we know.

L'Illustration Horticole.—This is a most elegantly illustrated monthly, published by A. Verschaffelt, the horticulturist of world wide reputation, and contains beautifully colored plates of all the floral [illegible]. The June number is especially interesting to Americans, as it contains a new Passion Flower from Panama, *Tacsonia Buchanani*, in compliment to our [illegible] friend, J. Buchanan, of this city, who first cultivated it. The same number contains a colored representation of our native Bird-foot Violet, *Viola Pedata*, one of our common plants which we pass by unheeded, but [illegible] in which our friends over the water lavish a great deal of elegant French.

The Revue Horticole.—This periodical is published semi-monthly, in Paris, under the able editorship of M. Carriere. Its "Chronique Horticole" is an admirable resume of horticultural news, and we cordially recommend the journal to those who read French, and wish to keep advised of European horticultural doings. The Revue has one feature which we would commend to the attention of certain American journals—when it copies, as it often does, articles and figures from the *Agriculturist*, it gives full credit for them.

"Sunshine and Showers."—This is a most fascinating subject. It engages everybody's attention, because it affects everybody's comfort. An English barrister has written a very instructive popular book on the weather, giving it the above attractive title. No doubt the [illegible] which govern the weather of Great Britain prevail over the whole world, and, with a little allowance for the different climatic influences, would form a correct basis for judging of its changes, provided we could give proper relative weight to the indications. Everybody believes that it may be possible to predict the weather with some degree of certainty and Mr. Steinmetz believes that he can do so generally, and that man ought to do it as well as the lower animals. In a very pleasant way he mentions the premonitions which storms and showers give of their approach. Certain it is that many birds know when storms are coming, and frogs and leeches perceive it also. The Old Salt has no better reason for predicting a storm than that he "smells it," and the old rheumatic aunty, than that she "feels it in her bones." Hence we fully believe that if we, who are neither old salts nor rheumatic, only knew enough, we could do the same. The little book before us has helped us so much towards gaining knowledge about these things, that we have placed it on our book list. It is printed in London but imported in sheets, and neatly bound by Roberts Bros., Boston, Mass., and is for sale at our counter, or will be sent by mail on receipt of price.

The Osage Orange as a Tree.—Those who have only seen the Osage Orange as a hedge plant, can have no idea of its beauty when allowed to grow into a tree. There are fine specimens at Iona Island, (Dr. Grant's,) and at the place formerly owned by the late A. J. Downing, at Newburgh. It grows to the height of twenty or thirty feet, and has a remarkably clean appearance. The leaves are of a bright green, and its fruit, which grows to the size of a large orange, is very conspicuous. It is put down by botanists as a diœcious tree, i. e., one having staminate and pistillate flowers on separate plants. Our French friends are discussing this point, as they find that trees bear fruit when there is no staminate one in the neighborhood, and suppose that, as is very likely to be the case, it is only imperfectly diœcious. We hope to see this very beautiful tree more generally introduced in ornamental planting.

The Vegetable World, by Louis Figuier, New York. D. Appleton & Co. A handsomely printed volume of 576 pages, and intended to give a popular account of the structure, and some general ideas of the classification, of plants. Unfortunately it was translated from the French by one who apparently had no knowledge of the subject, and the work is so full of mistakes as to seriously interfere with its value as a popular teacher. The illustrations are many of them very beautiful, but as some blunderer has in several instances put the wrong names to them, they are sometimes calculated to mislead rather than to instruct. It is painful to see so handsome a work marred by so many blemishes. While those who have sufficient botanical knowledge to see the errors, will find much instruction in it, we cannot recommend the work as an introduction to the study of plants.

Our Annuals.—The American Agricultural and Horticultural Annuals are in course of preparation, and will be issued before the close of the present year. As these works are in part devoted to recording the progress in Agriculture and Horticulture during the past year, they cannot, on this account, be brought out as early as if they were made up of miscellaneous articles that could be written at any time. The work has mainly to be done when the growing season is over. The favorable reception given to the volumes of 1867 is an incentive to make those for 1868 worthy of general approval.

Conn. Board of Agriculture, 1866.—The First Report of the Conn. State Board of Agriculture has been for some time on our table, through the politeness of Hon. E. H. Hyde, Vice President of the Board. The chief value of the book consists in the report of the lectures and discussions at the annual meeting in January last, a brief account of which was given in the *Agriculturist* for February. The Board, between their meetings for business, listened to lectures which were open to the public. The report of them is so full as to give the volume a permanent value to all agriculturists. They are, one by Prof. Johnson, on The Source of Nitrogen in Plants; one by Prof. Brown, on Irrigation in California, and two, by the same gentleman, on Diseases of Plants Caused by Fungi. Discussions took place in regard to Draining, Irrigation, and Fruit Culture, and responses to a circular, sent out by the Secretary, asking information based on personal experience on these subjects. The information thus given is of notable value. The Secretary has little to tell about the town and county societies which are known to exist, except their names, and the fact that they spend the $1800 appropriated for premiums by the State, and it appears as if he collected this meagre information about them much as a newspaper reporter would do. This ought not to be, and the State bounty should, we think, be appropriated only to those societies presenting a detailed report of all their doings, and the amount paid should be graduated according to the degree of excellence of these reports.

Gray's Manual of Botany.—Fifth Edition. N. Y.: Ivison, Phinney, Blakeman & Co.—About twenty years ago, the first edition of this work appeared, and immediately took the position it has since maintained—that of guide and hand-book to those who wish to gain a knowledge of the plants of the Northern States. That our first botanist should be so mindful of the wants of students as to prepare for them a series of books unequalled by any in the language, is something to be thankful for—a good which those of us, who, in our early studies, struggled along with incomplete and unsatisfactory text-books, can better appreciate than can the student of the present day. We are indebted to the publishers for an advance copy of the new edition, which is in the same neat and attractive style that characterized the former manuals. The present one embodies all the recent discoveries, and contains such alterations as the advance of the science demands. Gray's Manual for the Northern States, Chapman's Flora for the South, and Brewer's forthcoming Botany of California, gives us a series of admirable hand-books for all parts of our extended territory—except, perhaps, "Walrussia,"—and the botanist will be likely to find but few plants not recorded in one or the other of these standard works.

Plants Named.—Mrs. C. L. Mabbit, Vineland, N. J.—*Veronica spicata*, the blue; and the white is the delicate Fringed Orchid, *Platanthera blephariglottis*. ..Mrs. Robuck, Herkimer Co.—*Dicentra Canadensis*, the Squirrel-corn; less common than the closely related *D. Cucullaria*, or Dutchman's Breeches, and worth cultivating....F. W. Earl, Tawas, Mich.—*Kalmia angustifolia*, the Low, or Sheep Laurel.. A. Williams, Hillsdale, N. Y.—The common Wiegela rosea, properly *Diervilla Japonica*, a fine ornamental shrub....C. J. Brane, Wabash Co., Ind.- *Solanum Dulcamara*, Bittersweet, a pretty climber but the berries are suspected of poisonous qualities.

Salmon Fisheries in England.—The work of restoring this noble fish to the rivers of England is in successful progress, though it meets with obstacles from defective legislation, from the refuse of factories poured into the streams, from badly constructed fish ways, and from illegal fishing. Notwithstanding these hindrances, the fish appear in increasing numbers in all the streams that have been restocked, and best cuts of salmon are quoted in the *London* market at twenty cents a pound, or about half the price it commands here, in the cheapest part of the season. When we get our rivers restocked, we hope to turn the tables on our British cousins, and quote salmon at ten cents a pound. The best style of passes or ladders at the mill dams is now a theme of lively discussion. One writer proposes "rough rock work, the rougher the better, built against the dam on an incline." He has seen fifteen fish pass such a ladder in three quarters of an hour. The idea may be valuable.

Hatching Shad at Holyoke, Mass.—Mr. Seth Green, of Mumford, N. Y., is supervising the work of stocking the Connecticut River with shad, at Holyoke. By his system, 93 per cent. of the spawn is hatched while in the river. It is estimated that not more than 5 per cent. live, the most being destroyed by fish and by unfavorable changes in the temperature of the water. He will turn into the river this season more than 100,000,000 of these fish. If they return to their birthplace as their instinct prompts them, there will be fine fishing in that stream next season. Under the new regulations of the New England Fish Commissioners, the fish will be able to visit the upper waters of the River, and Vermont and New Hampshire can eat home-bred shad again. Fish breeding is now as easily managed as the breeding of land animals, and measures should be taken to restock all our streams.

Damp Houses.—"W. B." These are occasioned quite as often by the surroundings as by the materials of which they are made. An undrained cellar, or too many shade trees, will make a damp house. If brick or stone is used, fill out the walls, and ventilate. The house is then as dry as if made of wood, and cooler in summer as well as warmer in winter.

Longworth's Wine House.—Some samples from this establishment show that it maintains its well established reputation, and are of a quality to convince even the writer in the Boston Journal of Horticulture that "pure wines" can be produced in the North.

Ox-bows and Yokes.—H. A. S., of Manchester, Conn., criticises the ox-yoke, figured in the August number, page 284, on the ground that the holes for the bows are too close together. Such narrow bows may do, he says, to draw in, but cattle will not back well in them. Narrow bows chafe the roots of the ears in backing or holding back, going down hill. He formerly used yokes with bows only 10 inches wide, but never found his cattle to back easily until he put the bow-holes 12 inches apart. Cattle will not back well if the yoke hurts them.

Prof. Glover's Work on Entomology.—Aside from his labors in the Museum of the Department of Agriculture at Washington, Prof. Glover is carrying on his elaborate work on insects, which, one would think, is of itself sufficient to occupy all his time. His plan appears to be as admirable in design as his figures are beautiful in execution. The work is needed, and we hope that a way will soon be found to publish it.

Mosquitoes in Water-troughs.—A few little brook or pond fish keep water-troughs, open cisterns, water barrels, ponds, etc., entirely free from the larvæ of mosquitoes, by eating them almost as soon as the eggs hatch.

Pickling Cucumbers.—B. G. B. We have never found any substitute for salting cucumbers. A bag of spices is usually tied up, and put in the vinegar for those who like it. More commonly the vinegar is applied hot upon the cucumbers, but some housekeepers of unquestioned gumption apply the vinegar cold. Cider vinegar, however, is always used, and has a snap to it. Mem.—It is some trouble to have anything nice.

Influence of Climate in North and South America.—Prof. John Disturnell has given to the public, through the publishing house of D. Van Nostrand, New York, a work with the above title, discussing the climate and climatic changes and influences which prevail in this Western Hemisphere, and their influence upon vegetation, animals, man, diseases, civilization, etc. It is accompanied by an agricultural and an isothermal map of North America. The former shows the limits of profitable culture of our staple crops; the latter, the lines of equal mean, summer and winter temperatures. The work contains a great array of carefully collected facts and observations, with free citations of the opinions of travelers and writers upon the climate. It is an octavo of 334 closely printed pages.

Twelve More Than We Promise.—The reader will notice that this month's issue of the *Agriculturist* contains 44 pages. In our prospectus we offer a sheet of 32 pages, but in no month of this year have there been less than 36, and for a greater part of the time we have given 40 pages. This month we have so much reading and advertising matter that we increase the size as far as possible, and not exceed legal weight.

Reliable Advertisements. — From every quarter we receive commendation for the rule strictly and impartially adhered to of admitting "no advertisements into our columns except from parties believed to be reliable and able, and willing to perform what they advertise to do." During the present month several hundred dollars' worth has been rejected, which we see appearing conspicuously in the columns of otherwise respectable papers, both secular and religious. Our course in this respect proves of great value to those who do advertise in good faith, as the public are not afraid to send their orders to those admitted under this rule. Of course, mistakes will occur, and blame should not hastily be bestowed. Mail clerks and express agents are not infallible, and failure to receive goods ordered is often chargeable to their account, if not to that of the person ordering.

A Nursery in every Town.—The numerous offers made in our advertising columns of vines, plants, etc., to be forwarded by mail, in effect, bring the best nurseries almost to the door of every man. A very large business has been satisfactorily transacted in this way, since the reduction of postage to a point admitting of it. Every family, having the use of ground enough for the purpose, should avail themselves of these facilities to secure a good supply of fruit for home use. Send your orders early, that the nurserymen may provide in time for expeditiously forwarding the articles wanted.

The American Pomological Society.—The 11th meeting of the Society commenced at St. Louis, on Wednesday, September 11th, the President, Col. Marshall P. Wilder in the chair. Fourteen States were represented by delegates, and it was supposed that several other delegations would come in. A very large show of fruit is upon the tables, grapes being especially numerous. The first day was occupied mainly with preliminary matters. Addresses of welcome were made by Mr. Mudd, President of the Missouri State Horticultural Society; Mr. Bryant, President of the Illinois State Society, and by Doctor Spaulding, in behalf of the Grape Grower's Association of the Mississippi Valley. President Wilder briefly and feelingly responded to these salutations. In the afternoon, the President gave his address, and the election of officers was held. We regret that we have not space for the address. The remaining days will be given to discussions which are likely to be interesting, as such men as Wilder, Downing, Barry, Warder, Knox, Ellwanger, Meehan, Husmann, and a host of other well known pomologists will take part in them. New or interesting facts will be noted for the benefit of our readers.

Grapes at Pittsburgh.—A visit to Mr. Knox's vineyards shows a condition of the crop in marked contrast with the reports from the grape region of the Lakes and other parts of the West. The main crop is, of course, of the Concord, which, for health of foliage and productiveness, is so much superior to all other varieties that we do not wonder at Mr. Knox's advocacy of it. He planted his vineyard for the purpose of getting fruit, and has it by the ton. Delaware has a good crop, but the leaves have suffered, though enough remain to ripen the fruit. Iona is fruiting, but the foliage in about the condition of the Delaware. Diana shows a good crop, with some rot. Catawba and Isabella very full, and scarcely any trouble. Hartford Prolific and Creveling now, (Sept. 7th,) being marketed. These are two very prolific grapes. The Hartford, as grown here, hangs to the bunch as well as any other grape. The Creveling surprised us with its yield, and pleased us with its quality. It has the fault of not making a compact bunch, but it will nevertheless be a salable grape when known.

The New England Fair.—Fine weather, proximity to the second city of New England, unusually fine grounds and buildings, and the hearty enthusiasm with which the people of Rhode Island welcomed the society to their State, united in making the Fair a grand success in a pecuniary point of view. The exhibition was well worthy of the society. The show of Ayrshires was remarkably fine; Jerseys were also numerous and excellent, and the cross-bred Jersey-Ayrs of Mr. Fitch, of New London, Conn., noticed some time since in the *Agriculturist*, attracted deserved attention. The Shorthorn stables were graced by most excellent stock, and by none superior to that noble animal, 8th Duke of Thorndale. If His Grace is not the best bull in this country, we would be glad to see his better. The Lieut.-Governor of Connecticut, Mr. E. H. Hyde, of Stafford, a prominent candidate for Commissioner of Agriculture, was present with the choice of his fine herd of Devons, and took the herd sweepstakes premium. The show of Devons was good, better than can be made in this country, outside of New England. The Dutch cattle of Mr. Chenery, of Belmont, were also exhibited, and Burmese cattle by Mr. Clark of the same town. The horses did not equal those shown in Vermont last year, either in numbers or quality. Among the mutton sheep, Cotswolds were predominant, and very fine, but the fine wools did not make much show. The swine and poultry classes disappointed us, as did also the implements, though there was a good display of mowers and small tools. On the whole, the fair was a very gratifying one, and not by any means so given up to fast horses as was expected, nor as has been represented by the Associated Press' dispatches.

Investments of Money. — We advise farmers to invest their money in farm improvements, mechanics in better tools and facilities, merchants in advertising. But there is much money which cannot be invested in these ways. Public improvements, really needed and of great utility next to securities for which the faith of the State or Nation is pledged, ought to be the safest and best paying investments. So they are, if well managed. The first mortgage bonds of the Central Pacific Railroad Co. are regarded as first class securities. These bonds are sold by our friends Fisk & Hatch, No. 5 Nassau st., whose representations are thoroughly reliable.

Seed Store at the Agriculturist Office—or rather at the place where the Office of the *Agriculturist* was. As announced elsewhere, we have entered our new quarters, 245 Broadway. 41 Park Row, so long associated with Agricultural and Horticultural matters, is, however, to be most worthily filled. It has been rented by Mr. B. K. Bliss, of Springfield, Mass., for a Seed and Horticultural Warehouse. Most, if not all, of our readers have long known Mr. Bliss as a most enterprising, reliable and obliging dealer. By [illegible] advertising, thorough system, and indefatigable attention to the details of his work, he has built up a business extending all over the United States, and demanding larger facilities. To secure these, he has formed a partnership with his son, S. B. Bliss, under the firm of B. K. Bliss & Son, and made their headquarters here in the Metropolis. Their business at Springfield, Mass., will also be conducted under the same firm. We are greatly pleased that one whom we know to be fully worthy the confidence of the public, which he has already largely secured, is to occupy the premises so long devoted to kindred pursuits, and which otherwise we should more regret leaving. With the numerous friends of Mr. Bliss we wish him success commensurate with his increased facilities.

Egyptian Corn.—"H. G. C.," Bennington, Vt.—The advertisement of F. E. G. Lindsey, of Virginia, about Egyptian corn which bears ears as large as maize, and yields 150 bushels to the acre weighing 63 pounds to the bushel is, on the face of it, calculated to deceive. Nevertheless we have written to F. E. G. L. to send us some seeds, and receiving no answer, know what to conclude. Let it alone; the story is better than the crop.

The Boulevard Skirt.—The ladies of the household are greatly pleased with this article just introduced into the fashionable world. It is made of all wool, without seam, is light, warm, and of every desirable color. The fabric resembles thick but light French cloth. It is a decided improvement over the "Balmoral."

Draining for Profit.—Peter Henderson, Esq., the well-known market gardener, thus writes to the author of this recently published work on Draining: "There would have been no necessity for my troubling you with the draining queries if I had carefully read your work, as all my questions are there fully anticipated. Allow me to most sincerely congratulate you on your production. I never before picked up a book on draining that I could read with interest enough to keep me at it ten minutes. Business drives me so that I have little time to read anything; and to wade through a bushel of chaff to get at a grain of wheat is so discouraging that I rarely make the attempt. But 'Draining for Profit' is straight to the point, without a superfluous word." See advertisement of this book on page 370.

Fair of the American Institute.—This great exhibition of American industry opened in the city of New York, on the 12th. It is certainly the best arranged one we ever saw, and in this particular as well as in the entire exclusion of all large signs, the managers are to be highly commended, and the exhibition regarded as an example to all industrial fairs. The rule which, rigidly enforced, secures this very desirable result, is this, that while the articles exhibited shall be confined to the allotted space, no sign shall appear *above* them. The result is that exhibitors are advertised by their wares, and not by flaming paint and canvas. The fair is a great success, being so systematized that any one can go directly to any Department, of which there are seven, viz.: 1. Fine Arts and Education; 2. The Dwelling; 3. Dress and Handicraft; 4. Chemistry, etc.; 5. Machinery, etc.; 6. Intercommunication, (Carriages, Telegraphs, Boats, etc.;) 7. Agriculture and Horticulture, each being divided into groups.

The Use of Plaster.—"W. W. Fuller," of Michigan, proposes a practical question under cover of a theoretical one. Letting the theory go, he admits that by means of plaster he gets greatly increased crops. Those crops contain a proportionately increased quantity of ash constituents drawn from the soil, which, of course, is by just so much the poorer. Hence impoverishment of the soil is certain if the practice is continued long enough. How soon it will come depends on the richness of the soil, both in available plant food and in that which may be developed by tillage and the action of the weather. An equivalent must in some way be returned, if the soil be kept as it is. Plaster works good to the land in several ways, and the wise ones cannot agree upon a theory.

Apples in England.—A recent Gardener's Chronicle gives a tabular report, occupying several pages, showing the state of the fruit crop in the various counties in England. While there is plenty of small fruits, there is a general scarcity of pears and apples, the latter crop being so bad that it may be set down as a total failure. It is not unlikely that large shipments of apples will be made from this country; which, judging from the appearance of the orchards in the Western States, we shall be abundantly able to do.

Have Done With It.—Either the Farmers' Club or the New York Weekly Tribune is guilty of a disregard of the health of the community that deserves the severest reprobation. The two form a sort of reciprocally irresponsible concern. Whenever we blame the [illegible] we are told that they are not responsible for the reports, and when the Tribune is called to account, it says [illegible] reports the proceedings of the Club. In the report [illegible] meeting of August 28th, we find people encouraged to tamper with so dangerous and fatal a disease as [illegible], by the use of a decoction of bark and roots, and what is worse, if possible, to try the cure of consumption by [illegible] so violent a poison as Lobelia. We see by the reports of the Club that a large proportion of those who take part in the proceedings are Doctors. Can it be possible that they so disregard the safety of the community as to allow these things to go by without a protest? Gentlemen of the Club, you have it in your power to do much good when you stick to matters belonging to Agriculture, but when you meddle with medicine you weaken your influence, and your [illegible] become dangerous.

Feed Cutters.—[illegible] or chaffing, wetting, and flavoring with meal [illegible], make good fodder go much farther than otherwise, and [illegible] very poor fodder palatable and useful. This [illegible] no little labor, but a good machine makes light work of it, compared with any other. We bought [illegible] Strip Feed Cutter, made by the Peekskill (N. Y.) [illegible] Works, several months ago, and use it with great satisfaction, in cutting hay and cornstalks, knowing of none better. The past season has been so peculiar that many farmers, who rarely are so unlucky have this year damaged hay, and that cut after having become old and wiry. The diligent use of the hay cutter is the only alleviation of this state of things. Cut fine, wet down, and, at least, flavor with oil or corn meal, bran, or some ground feed.

Documents Acknowledged. — Our list of these has been crowded out from month to month. If the friends who have favored us with Reports, Catalogues, and other documents, will for this once accept a general acknowledgment, we will try to do better in future.

How to Cook a Ham.—We dine occasionally at the table of Mrs. K., and until we tasted it there, we did not know what a ham was capable of. It being too nice to remain a family secret, we asked the recipe for the benefit of our readers. Boil a ham for three hours, remove the skin, and trim it nicely, and then rub into the fat a pound of powdered sugar, or as much as it will take up. The ham is then placed in a dripping pan, in which is put a pint of sherry, or other good wine, and put into the oven, and baked very slowly for two hours. During the baking it is frequently basted with the wine. Try this, and we are confident you will say that you have never before eaten ham in its greatest perfection.

AMERICAN AGRICULTURIST.

ORANGE JUDD & CO., Publishers, 245 Broadway, N. Y. City.

ANNUAL SUBSCRIPTION TERMS (always in advance): $1.50 each for less than four copies: Four to nine copies, $1.25 each: Ten to nineteen copies, $1.20 each: Twenty copies and upwards, $1 each. Papers are addressed to each name.

EIGHTY-SIX

Valuable Premiums.

We Invite Everybody

To secure one or more of the valuable articles offered as Premiums on our List. All of these Premiums are good and useful, and some are costly and elegant.

Look at the List, and make up your mind to obtain some of the Premiums.

The American Agriculturist, with its 32 to 40 large quarto pages, its profuse and costly illustrations, its practical, reliable, and condensed information, obtained and prepared at great expense, is furnished to its subscribers at a price but very little above the cost of the paper on which it is printed. This can be accounted for,

First, by the fact that but one corps of Editors, one set of Engravings, one setting of type, and one Publishing House managing the business affairs of the paper, suffice for supplying its great army of subscribers; and

Again: While the funds received for subscriptions are expended in preparing the paper and delivering it to subscribers, its immense circulation secures a very large and valuable advertising patronage. For every premium obtained a list of new subscribers is sent in, and the more subscribers of course the more valuable our columns for advertisers.

We are willing, therefore, to pay well, in *good Premiums*, those who get up clubs for us. While it is true that many persons send to us the names of their friends and acquaintances without premiums, merely from good will and their confidence that they are thus conferring a favor upon their friends, it is also true that we most cheerfully bestow all premiums that are earned, and in every proper way encourage *everybody* to get up clubs, with the remuneration to be secured in view.

Everybody may be an Agent.—We have no special agents. Instead of this we have made up a list of valuable articles, many of which have been suggested by individuals who have worked for us, and all of which are good and useful; and from this list any one who gets up a club can select the premium desired, and obtain it by sending us the required number of subscribers.

We can Pay much more in Premiums than in Cash.—Our purchases by Wholesale, our arrangements with Manufacturers and Dealers for advertising, etc., enable us to do this. It will be noticed that we give each premium article at the regular price which the purchaser would pay for the same.

Every Premium on our list is to be secured by sending us a definite number of subscribers. There need be no mistake, therefore, on this point; and there can be no favoritism in the matter, since the same number of subscribers for any particular premium is required from every one who secures it.

No person need fail of obtaining some one of our many Premiums. Those who make the attempt to raise a club are often surprised at the ease with which names of subscribers are secured. The paper is very attractive in appearance, (notice the great number of beautiful and costly engravings in the Oct. paper, which is a fair specimen,) and the most hasty glance at its contents often satisfies one of its value. We have many times received subscriptions at our counter from persons who came in for books or on other business, and who, on looking over the paper for a few moments, have decided that they *must have it*.

You can make money in canvassing for the *American Agriculturist*. Many persons take hold of the work as a business. If you do not wish the Premium secured for your own use, it can always be sold; and you will see, upon looking over our Premium List, that but a small number of names obtained each day gives you good wages, while for 10 names or more a day, you will receive very handsome returns. A lady obtained subscribers enough in seven months to secure one of the magnificent Steinway Pianos, worth $650, and this, too, while attending to the cares of a family.

Beautiful and valuable Presents may be secured by working for us. You will find on our Premium List many articles which are most useful in a family; articles suitable for presents from husband to wife, brother to sister, children to parents, scholars to teachers. Here are opportunities for giving a pleasant surprise to your pastor and his wife, by sending them a handsome tea set, a valuable library, or a sewing machine. Sunday school classes, or scholars in other schools, may secure a beautiful present for their teachers in this way, or a good melodeon for their school room. Several Agricultural Societies have paid for a large club of subscribers, given away the subscriptions as prizes at their exhibitions, or supplied them to members, and sold the premium articles, at auction, for the benefit of the treasury.

Only good articles.—We are careful not *to place upon our list anything for a Premium which is not the best, and, in all respects, what is claimed for it. All, therefore, who secure premiums, may be sure that they are not running the risk of getting poor or indifferent goods.*

Send in the names of subscribers as fast as you obtain them, not waiting to complete your list; and to save mistakes in accounts, send the exact subscription money with each list; and **every name** *designed for a premium list, must be so marked* **when sent in.**

Begin Now to raise your clubs. It is not necessary that all the papers of Premium Clubs should go to one office. You can get them anywhere.

Old and New Subscribers will be counted in premium lists, but some should be new names, as it is to obtain such that premiums are in part offered. The extra copy, usually offered to clubs of ten or twenty, will not be furnished when a premium is called for.

How to Remit:—Checks on New-York Banks or Bankers are best for large sums; make them payable to the order of Orange Judd & Co.

Post Office Money Orders may be obtained at nearly every county seat, in all the cities, and in many of the large towns. We consider them perfectly safe, and the best means of remitting fifty dollars or less, as many hundreds have been sent to us *without any loss*.

Registered Letters, under the new system, which went into effect June 1st, are a very safe means of sending small sums of money where P. O. Money Orders cannot be easily obtained. *Observe*, the *Registry fee*, as well as postage, must be paid in stamps at the office where the letter is mailed, or it will be liable to be sent to the Dead Letter Office. *Buy and affix the stamps both for postage and registry, put in the money and seal the letter in the presence of the postmaster, and take his receipt for it.* Letters sent in this way to us are at our risk.

Specimen Numbers of the Agriculturist, Cards, and Showbills, as may be needed, will be supplied to canvassers. These should be economically used, as each extra copy of the paper, with postage, (2c.,) which must be pre-paid, costs about 12 cents.

☞ *Every Premium article is new and of the very best manufacture. No charge is made for packing or boxing any of the articles in our Premium List. The forty-four Premiums,* **Nos. 1, 2, 6,** *and from* **30** *to* **39,** *and from* **50** *to* **86** *inclusive, will each be delivered* **FREE** *of all charges, by mail or express, (at the Post-Office or express office nearest recipient), to any place in the United States or Territories, excepting those reached only by the Overland Mail.—The other articles cost the recipient only the freight after leaving the manufactory of each, by any conveyance that may be specified.*

Table of Premiums and Terms,
For Volume 27—(1868).

Open to all—No Competition.

No.	Names of Premium Articles.		Price of Premiums.	Number of Subscribers required at $1.50	at $1.
1	Garden Seeds for a Family (40 kinds)		[illegible]	[illegible]	[illegible]
2	Flower Seeds for a Family (100 kinds)		[illegible]	[illegible]	[illegible]
3	Nursery Stock (Any kinds desired)		[illegible]	[illegible]	[illegible]
4	Iona Grape Vines (12 of No. 1)		[illegible]	[illegible]	[illegible]
5	Concord Grape Vines (100 of No. 1)		[illegible]	[illegible]	[illegible]
6	Japan Lilies (12 Bulbs)		[illegible]	[illegible]	[illegible]
7	Sewing Machine (Grover & Baker)		[illegible]	[illegible]	[illegible]
8	Sewing Machine (Howe Machine Co.)		[illegible]	[illegible]	[illegible]
9	Sewing Machine (Singer's Tailoring)		[illegible]	[illegible]	[illegible]
10	Sewing Machine (Florence)		[illegible]	[illegible]	[illegible]
11	Sewing Machine (Willcox & Gibbs)		[illegible]	[illegible]	[illegible]
12	Sewing Machine (Finkle & Lyon)		[illegible]	[illegible]	[illegible]
13	Sewing Machine (Wheeler & Wilson)		[illegible]	[illegible]	[illegible]
14	Washing Machine (Doty's)		[illegible]	[illegible]	[illegible]
15	Clothes Wringer (Best—Universal)		[illegible]	[illegible]	[illegible]
16	Tea Set (Hart's best Silver Plated)		[illegible]	[illegible]	[illegible]
17	Castor and Fruit Basket (do. do.)		[illegible]	[illegible]	[illegible]
18	Ice or Water Pitcher (do. do.)		[illegible]	[illegible]	[illegible]
19	One Dozen Tea Spoons (do. do.)		[illegible]	[illegible]	[illegible]
20	One Dozen Table Spoons (do. do.)		[illegible]	[illegible]	[illegible]
21	One Dozen Dining Forks (do. do.)		[illegible]	[illegible]	[illegible]
22	Tea Knives and Forks (Patterson Bros.)		[illegible]	[illegible]	[illegible]
23	Table Knives and Forks (do. do.)		[illegible]	[illegible]	[illegible]
24	Carving Knife and Fork (do. do.)		[illegible]	[illegible]	[illegible]
25	Musical Box (Shell Case)		[illegible]	[illegible]	[illegible]
26	Melodeon, 4-octave (G. A. Prince & Co.'s)		[illegible]	[illegible]	[illegible]
27	Melodeon, 5-octave (do. do.)		[illegible]	[illegible]	[illegible]
28	Colibri Piano (Barlow, Doehler & Co.)		[illegible]	[illegible]	[illegible]
29	Piano, Splendid 7-oct. (Steinway & Sons)		[illegible]	[illegible]	[illegible]
30	Ladies' Gold Watch (Beautiful)		[illegible]	[illegible]	[illegible]
31	Silver Watch (Valuable Time-Keeper)		[illegible]	[illegible]	[illegible]
32	Double Barrel Gun (Cooper & Pond)		[illegible]	[illegible]	[illegible]
33	Repeating Shot Gun (Roper Rifle Co.)		[illegible]	[illegible]	[illegible]
34	Spencer's Breech-loading Rifle (Hunting)		[illegible]	[illegible]	[illegible]
35	Tool Chest (Patterson Bros.)		[illegible]	[illegible]	[illegible]
36	Case of Mathematical Instruments		[illegible]	[illegible]	[illegible]
37	Case of Mathematical Instruments		[illegible]	[illegible]	[illegible]
38	Gold Pen, Sil. Case, E (Warren & Spadone)		[illegible]	[illegible]	[illegible]
39	Gold Pen and Silver Case, F (do. do.)		[illegible]	[illegible]	[illegible]
40	Barometer (Woodruff's Mercurial)		[illegible]	[illegible]	[illegible]
41	Barometer (Woodruff's Mercurial)		[illegible]	[illegible]	[illegible]
42	Buckeye Mowing Machine, No. 2		[illegible]	[illegible]	[illegible]
43	Allen's Patent Cylinder Plow, etc.		[illegible]	[illegible]	[illegible]
44	Pump and Sprinkler (Page's)		[illegible]	[illegible]	[illegible]
45	Family Scales (Fairbanks & Co.)		[illegible]	[illegible]	[illegible]
46	Building Blocks (Crandall)		[illegible]	[illegible]	[illegible]
47	Pocket Lanterns, One Dozen		[illegible]	[illegible]	[illegible]
48	American Cyclopedia (Appleton's)		[illegible]	[illegible]	[illegible]
49	Worcester's Great Illustrated Dictionary		[illegible]	[illegible]	[illegible]
50	Any Back Volume Agriculturist	In clean new Nos. Post-paid—Unbound.	[illegible]	[illegible]	[illegible]
51	Any Two Back Volumes do.		[illegible]	[illegible]	[illegible]
52	Any Three do. do. do.		[illegible]	[illegible]	[illegible]
53	Any Four do. do. do.		[illegible]	[illegible]	[illegible]
54	Any Five do. do. do.		[illegible]	[illegible]	[illegible]
55	Any Six do. do. do.		[illegible]	[illegible]	[illegible]
56	Any Seven do. do. do.		[illegible]	[illegible]	[illegible]
57	Any Eight do. do. do.		[illegible]	[illegible]	[illegible]
58	Any Nine do. do. do.		[illegible]	[illegible]	[illegible]
59	Any Ten do. do. do.		[illegible]	[illegible]	[illegible]
60	Vols. XVI to XXVI do.		[illegible]	[illegible]	[illegible]
61	Any Back Volume Agriculturist	Neatly Bound, Sent Post-paid.	[illegible]	[illegible]	[illegible]
62	Any Two Back Volumes do.		[illegible]	[illegible]	[illegible]
63	Any Three do. do. do.		[illegible]	[illegible]	[illegible]
64	Any Four do. do. do.		[illegible]	[illegible]	[illegible]
65	Any Five do. do. do.		[illegible]	[illegible]	[illegible]
66	Any Six do. do. do.		[illegible]	[illegible]	[illegible]
67	Any Seven do. do. do.		[illegible]	[illegible]	[illegible]
68	Any Eight do. do. do.		[illegible]	[illegible]	[illegible]
69	Any Nine do. do. do.		[illegible]	[illegible]	[illegible]
70	Any Ten do. do. do.		[illegible]	[illegible]	[illegible]
71	Vols. XVI to XXVI do.		[illegible]	[illegible]	[illegible]
72	Downing's Landscape Gardening	All sent paid through, by Mail or Express.	[illegible]	[illegible]	[illegible]
73	Cummings & Miller's Architect.		[illegible]	[illegible]	[illegible]
74	A $10 Library (Your Choice)		[illegible]	[illegible]	[illegible]
75	A $15 Library do.		[illegible]	[illegible]	[illegible]
76	A $20 Library do.		[illegible]	[illegible]	[illegible]
77	A $25 Library do.		[illegible]	[illegible]	[illegible]
78	A $30 Library do.		[illegible]	[illegible]	[illegible]
79	A $35 Library do.		[illegible]	[illegible]	[illegible]
80	A $40 Library do.		[illegible]	[illegible]	[illegible]
81	A $45 Library do.		[illegible]	[illegible]	[illegible]
82	A $50 Library do.		[illegible]	[illegible]	[illegible]
83	A $60 Library do.		[illegible]	[illegible]	[illegible]
84	A $75 Library do.		[illegible]	[illegible]	[illegible]
85	A $100 Library do.		[illegible]	[illegible]	[illegible]
86	A Choice of Good Books (See Terms below.)			..	..

Description of the Premiums.

No. 1—Garden Seeds.—A valuable selection of **40** varieties of the best seeds for a family garden, each parcel large enough for a garden of ordinary size. This premium and the next are put up for us by Messrs. B. K. Bliss & Son, Seed and Horticultural Warehouse, 41 Park Row, (old *Agriculturist* office,) whose seed establishment is well known as one of the best in the country. This premium will be of great value and convenience to many, especially to those distant from good seed stores, as we shall send the seeds post-paid to any part of the United States (☞ except to those points reached only by the Overland Mail.)—In many cases the recipient will have enough in each package for his own use, and some to spare to members of the club, or others.

No. 2—Flower Seeds.—Like No. 1, this is a valuable premium. It consists of **100** different kinds of beautiful flower seeds, all in separate papers, and includes not only the finer common varieties, but many of the newer and rarer kinds that are costly when bought by the single paper. Each parcel contains the usual amount, and they are *delivered free*, the same as No. 1.

No. 3—Nursery Stock—Plants, etc.—This premium can be selected *in anything desired*, from the Catalogues of Parsons & Co., Flushing, N. Y., or of F. K. Phœnix, Bloomington, Ill. Both are well known, very reliable parties, having extensive Nurseries, Green-Houses, Ornamental Trees and Plants, Grape Vines, Shrubs, etc., etc. Send a stamp direct to either of them, for their regular catalogues, stating that it is to look into the value of this premium, and they will be furnished free. Any one choosing this premium can select from the catalogues $20 worth, or more in proportion, if more names are sent us, and we will send an Order for the amount on either party named above, in fall or spring, as desired.

No. 4—Iona Grape Vines (12).—This valuable new variety is becoming so well known that we need not describe it here. Only No. 1 Vines will be sent. They will be forwarded by express either this fall or next spring, or by mail, if so desired, and postage is furnished.

No. 5—Concord Grape Vines (100.)—"*The Grape for the Million.*"—This excellent, hardy, early, prolific, grape, is popular almost everywhere, and though not so highly flavored as the Iona and Delaware, its easy culture, vigorous growth, earliness, and productiveness, make it one of the best *for general cultivation*. It is now so abundant that we can offer a large number of No. 1 Vines. They will be sent by express, well packed, in fall or spring, as noted above for the Iona Vines.

No. 6—Japan Lily Bulbs.—A most beautiful flower, one of the few flowering bulbs that do well even when planted early in spring. Most kinds of bulbs require to be planted early in autumn. One can easily multiply his stock after getting a few to start with. We send them, post-paid, by mail to any place in the United States. We got them of B. K. Bliss & Son.

Nos. 7, 8, 9, 10, 11, 12, 13—Sewing Machines.—We are glad to be able to offer this year *a choice* of the leading kinds of good Sewing Machines. We can recommend any one of them as of great value. Each of these seven machines has some peculiarities in which it is superior to the others. We have used them all at home during the last half dozen years, except the Tailoring Machine, and that we have watched carefully in the hands of tailors. One has been tried several months, and then another, and so round; and they are all so valuable that we prefer to recommend all, instead of in the slightest degree hindering the speedy introduction of this important household implement by even a comparative word of discredit to any one of them. We would not part with the last one of these, whichever it might be, and be without any Sewing Machine, for $500! Here are the reasons: The $500 at 7 per cent. interest, would yield, less taxes, about $32. Most families require, at the lowest, four months of steady hand-sewing a year, costing, if all hired, not less than $21 a month, board included, or $96 a year. With a Sewing Machine a woman can certainly sew as much in one month as in four months by hand. Here is a clear saving of $74, or of $60 if you call the seamstress' work only $20 a month, including board—leaving a net annual saving of $30 to $40 above the interest, while any good machine will wear a dozen years. But far above this and all questions of money saving, is that of *health*. The everlasting "Stitch, stitch, stitch," with form bended over work, and the loss of sleep, have brought tens of thousands to early graves, broken down millions more at an early age, and entailed an enfeebled constitution upon many millions of infants. We say to *every* man, get *your* wife a Sewing Machine, even if you have to sell a favorite horse or an acre or two of land. A Sewing Machine costing $55 to $65 involves an interest of only $3 or $4 a year: it will, in the long run, save you five, if not a hundred, fold, in Doctor's bills alone. Get the Sewing Machine any way. If you can get one through our premium list, well and good; it will help you, will enlarge our circulation, and benefit those you induce to read and think more; but get the machine.——Every machine given is boxed and delivered free to any railroad station, or express office, or other place in this city, and costs the recipient only the freight after leaving the city. They go safely as railroad freight. Full printed instructions go with each, and the machine is supplied with a Hemmer. Further particulars may be obtained by sending for circulars to:

Grover & Baker M'f'g Co., 495 Broadway, N. Y. City.
Howe Machine Company, 699 Broadway, N. Y. City.
Florence Sewing Machine Co., 505 Broadway, N. Y. City.
Singer Manufacturing Co., 458 Broadway, N. Y. City.
Willcox & Gibbs M'f'g Co., 508 Broadway, N. Y. City.
Finkle & Lyon Sew'g M. Co., 587 Broadway, N. Y. City.
Wheeler & Wilson M'f'g Co., 625 Broadway, N. Y. City.

No. 14—Washing Machines.—For a long time we have annually tried half a dozen or more new Washing Machines. Some of them have promised well at first, but no one has continued in so much favor as the "Doty's Paragon," which we have now used nearly three years. It is the only one the "help" will use without being required to do so. Some new improvements have been added within the present year. It is neat, compact, and convenient. Full Descriptive Circulars can be had of R. C. Browning, 32 Courtlandt-st., New York, or of the Metropolitan Washing Machine Co., Middlefield, Conn. The machine packs in small compass, and can be sent cheaply as freight or by express.

No. 15—Clothes-Wringing Machine.—A very useful, time-saving, strength-saving, clothes-saving implement, that should be in every family. The wringing of clothes by hand is hard upon the hands, arms, and chest, and the twisting stretches and breaks the fibres with lever power. With the Wringing Machine, the garments are passed between elastic rollers which press the water out better than hand wringing, and with no wrenching of the fibres. It is done as fast as the left hand can pick up the garments, while the right hand turns the crank. It is so easily done that a child of 10 or 12 years can quickly wring out a tub-full of clothes, dropping them from the machine set upon the side of the wash tub directly into a clothes basket, ready to hang out. We offer the family size, "Universal Wringer," provided with *Cogs* which make the rollers turn together, and which we consider essential to prevent injury to the fabrics, loosening of the rubber, etc. We used a single one of these Wringers, one of the first make, several years without any repairs, and with the greatest satisfaction.—It weighs only 15 lbs., and can be readily carried by hand, or sent by express, or as freight, to any part of the country, ready to be set upon any form of tub, and used at once. We have given over a thousand of these as premiums, with almost universal satisfaction. At least a thousand families may get one this year as a premium. They are made by the Metropolitan Washing Machine Co., Middlefield, Conn.

No. 16—A Tea Set.—This premium has given the greatest satisfaction for the last two years. There are six pieces, viz.: *A Coffee Pot*, two *Tea Pots*, a *Creamer*, *Sugar*, and *Slop Bowl*—all of beautiful, uniform pattern, and new style, with raised and embossed figure work. They are not the common silver-*washed* articles, but the heaviest plate, equal to "Sheffield Plate," the foundation being white metal, so as not to show, even when the heavy silver-coating may chance to be worn off in any spot by long hard usage.——These Sets are made by Lucius Hart & Co., of Nos. 4 and 6 Burling Slip, N. Y. City. Mr. Hart, "the veteran Sunday School man," has been in the same place and business for nearly a quarter of a century. We have known him and his work for many years, and take pleasure in commending and guaranteeing its value to be as represented. The amount of silver on plated ware depends wholly upon the will and integrity of the manufacturer. We could give nearly as *good looking* plated ware for less than half the money. The Sets given as premiums will be boxed without charge, and sent to any place by express or otherwise as desired. (See remarks under No. 20 below.)

No. 17—Castor and Fruit or Cake Basket Combined.—This is a new pattern, both novel and beautiful. It can be used as a large, showy, Castor, with six cut glass bottles, or be instantly changed into a complete Castor, with Call Bell, and a separate Cake or Fruit Basket, with a colored glass dish inside. Every one receiving it will be delighted. It is from the same maker as No. 16, and of the same metal, plating, etc., and will be sent in the same way. Many cheaper and less beautiful Castors could be obtained, but, desiring only the *best* things in our premium list, we selected this.

No. 18—Ice or Water Pitcher.—A large and ornamental article, just such as we recently selected for our own use. It is of the same metal, plating, etc., and by the same maker, as No. 16. For 35 subscribers at $1.50 each, we will add a round Salver of pattern to correspond (value $6); or, for 47 subscribers, a large 18-inch oval Salver, (value $14,) large enough for two goblets with the Pitcher; and for 55 subscribers, the Pitcher, large Salver, and a pair of beautiful Goblets, silver-plated without, and gilded within (value $28). This complete Set is exceedingly desirable, though the Pitcher alone, or that and the smaller Tray or Salver, will answer a good purpose both for use and ornament.

No. 19—One Dozen Teaspoons.—These are of fine pattern, "figured tips," Olive-leaf Pattern, and of the same metal, plating, etc., and from the same maker, as No. 16. They are *far cheaper* than any thing we have found at half the price.

No. 20—One Dozen Table Spoons.
No. 21—One Dozen Table Forks.—The same description and remarks apply to these as to No. 19. We select as premiums only such articles as we can warrant every way in quality and price. As we explained in Volume XXV, page 147, a silver dollar can by the galvanic process be spread over many yards of surface so as to deceive the eye completely. Plated ware is valuable when we can trust to the honesty of the manufacturer to put on a coat of silver of given weight and thickness, and to do it on a good white metal. All these articles come from Messrs. Lucius Hart & Co.

Nos. 22, 23, 24—Knives and Forks.—This premium is an addition to our list of really useful and valuable articles. A dull knife, with a shabby handle, and a broken or crooked fork, will injure greatly, if it does not spoil, the taste of even a rare beefsteak, but it is next to impossible to keep a poor iron or steel knife and fork in a passably neat condition, and a *shine* will not come with any amount of brick dust and rubbing. The knives offered in this premium are manufactured by the most celebrated makers of cutlery in the world, Joseph Rodgers & Sons, Sheffield, England, whose corporate mark is dated 1764, and whose wares are known in every part of the world open to foreign commerce. They are of the best refined steel, with ivory balanced handles, and stamped with the full address of the makers, and are of the size known as table knives. The table forks are manufactured by Holmes, Booth & Haydens, on genuine albata, and warranted double plated with coin silver. The tea knives and forks are by the same makers, but of smaller size. The carving knife and fork are both steel, made by Rodgers & Sons, best ivory balanced handles. *For 29 subscribers, at $1.50 each*, we will send the tea knives, of the same make and material, *double silver plated*, forks the same, (value $20.) *For 45 subscribers*, at $1.50 each, we will send the table knives, *double silver plated*, with same forks, (value $30.) These articles are furnished to us by Messrs. Patterson & Brothers, 27 Park Row, agents for the manufacturers, and a thoroughly established and reliable house, who will furnish the above articles at prices named, and express charges paid to any one who may wish to purchase, and any other goods in the hardware line.

No. 25—Musical Box.—Something for the **Boys and Girls.** A new and beautiful Premium, and we have provided it specially for our young friends. Come, now, BOYS and GIRLS, we know you all love music, and we have made it easy for you to obtain a beautiful, shell-cased musical box, 2¼ inches cylinder, which will perform four tunes, making what we believe you will say is the sweetest music you have ever heard. We wish you could have been with us and listened while we selected these Premiums for you at the importers. We are sure you would have felt like making haste to get up the necessary club, only 22 subscribers, at $1.50, to make this most pleasing premium your own.

Nos. 26, 27—Melodeons.—These are excellent and desirable instruments, for the Home Circle, for small Churches, for Sunday Schools, for Day Schools, Academies, etc. Instrumental and Vocal music in a school has a beneficial influence upon the pupils. We have seen the whole tone and character of the pupils of a school improved by the introduction of a Melodeon.——Set the pupils to work and they will raise a club of subscribers, and obtain this premium easier than they can get money subscribed for it. We offer GEO. A. PRINCE & Co's. Melodeons, for we know them to be good. A large one in our own Sunday School room has been in use for eight years, and is to-day just as good as when first purchased, though used from time to time by a large number of persons.—Several clergymen have obtained this premium for themselves, their Churches, or Sunday School rooms. The premium clubs of subscribers were quickly raised among the members of their parishes.——Many others can get this premium for their own home use. We have given these instruments as premiums in the past few years, and we believe they have invariably been highly esteemed. Send a postage stamp to Geo. A. Prince & Co., Buffalo, N. Y., and get their illustrated descriptive circular, giving full particulars of forms, sizes, and prices. The premium Melodeons will be shipped direct from the manufactory at Buffalo, ready boxed for safe transportation by Railroad, Steamboat, or by Express, as may be ordered. They go just as safely by freight, as by express, and much cheaper, though not so quickly.

No. 28—Colibri Piano.—This is a newly invented Piano, the work of Mr. Frederick Mathushek, who has for many years been known among manufacturers as the author of some of the best improvements introduced into this instrument. A particularly novel feature of this piano is its size, being only four feet nine inches long, two feet three inches wide, of the square form, yet having seven full octaves. Before its adoption as a premium, some of the most eminent musicians examined it at our request, and pronounced it an instrument of remarkable power, brilliancy, and sweetness, entirely worthy to rank with the full-sized piano of other makers. H. Mollenhauer, Director of the Conservatory of Music, New York, says: "Their tone is truly astonishingly sweet, pure, and powerful, and so greatly superior to all others, that they must be heard to form a just conception of their superior excellence." Mr. Theodore Hagen, editor of the leading musical paper of this country, says of the Colibri Piano: "It is a thorough square piano-forte, only very small, but at the same time very proportionate and beautiful—and can speak to such an extent, with such power and sonority, that we must see as well as hear it to believe it possible." Its peculiar construction not only secures improvement in sounding qualities, but seems to insure great durability and long continuance in tune. It is finished in handsome style, with rosewood case, large round corners, fancy scroll desk, legs, lyre, etc., and will be an ornament in any parlor, besides being entirely satisfactory as a musical instrument. Other styles are made by the same firm, but this was selected as especially adapted to the wants of many of our readers. Messrs. Barlow, Doehler & Co., 694 Broadway, New York, are the agents, and will send circulars, giving full particulars, to applicants.

No. 29—Steinway Piano.—SEVEN OCTAVE, ROSEWOOD CASE; SOLID ROSEWOOD DESK, LARGE FRONT, ROUND CORNERS; OVERSTRUNG BASS, FULL IRON FRAME, PATENT AGRAFFE TREBLE, GOTHIC LEGS, AND CARVED LYRE.—This is one of the most elegant Premiums ever offered; regular and only price $450. That this magnificent instrument comes from the celebrated establishment of Messrs. STEINWAY & SONS, Nos. 71 and 73 East 14th street, is enough to say: but it is due to these enterprising manufacturers to state that, while their pianos have repeatedly received the FIRST PREMIUMS by the award of the most competent judges the world can produce, the crowning triumph has recently been achieved. At the Universal Exposition, in Paris, Steinway & Sons received the FIRST GRAND GOLD MEDAL for American Pianos in all three styles exhibited, viz.: Grand, Square, and Upright. The following is a copy of the official certificate, which was signed by the President and the five members of the International Jury: "Paris, July 20th, 1867. I certify that the First Gold Medal for American Pianos has been unanimously awarded to Messrs. Steinway by the Jury of the International Exhibition. First on the List in Class X." Besides all this, and second only to it in importance, is the fact that the Society of Fine Arts, in Paris, unanimously awarded to Steinway & Sons their *only* annual Testimonial Medal for 1867. The President of the Musical Department of that society says, in his report: "The Pianos of Messrs. Steinway appear to me, as well as to all the artists who have tried them, superior to all that have been made to this day in the entire world." This is to be added to abundant testimony from the best judges in America and other lands. We are able to speak from personal knowledge of the excellence of these instruments, as each of our partners has one at home, and desires no better. This splendid premium may be secured by many persons. Only 580 subscribers are required to do it. The last successful canvasser was a lady—a wife and mother—who, though with the care of a family, and among them at least one bright little child to our knowledge, found time to secure one of these magnificent pianos within seven months. Others, more at liberty, might obtain subscribers enough in 2 or 3 months; and for even a year's labor the compensation would not be small for some persons. Classes of young ladies at school might unite in effort, and thus obtain a present for a Teacher, or a Piano for their schoolroom. We shall be glad to give this premium to a large number. Who will try for it? Send to Messrs. Steinway & Sons for a free circular describing it.

No. 30—Ladies' Gold Watches.—At the request of canvassers, we add this and No. 31.——The Lady's Watch offered is one of the prettiest watches we have seen. It is in a "hunting" or closed case, beautifully engraved, and inlaid with enamel, and is warranted a good time-keeper by Messrs. Benedict Bros., 171 Broadway. (See No. 31, below.) This is a beautiful and appropriate present to a Teacher from the members of a School, who can easily divide among themselves the number of subscribers to be raised. It is also a very neat and beautiful gift for a companion. Not a few gentlemen can get this in time for a Holiday Present. Several have taken this premium and are delighted with it.

No. 31—A Good Watch.—For years past we have been urged to offer a good, reliable, Watch as a premium, and can now do so. We have arranged with Messrs. Benedict Brothers, of 171 Broadway, Dealers in Watches and Jewelry, to supply us with two kinds, and such watches as they will put in first-rate order and *warrant*. These parties we know to be in every way upright and reliable gentlemen, governed in their dealings by Christian principles, and with *their* guarantee we unhesitatingly offer these articles with confidence. (As is generally known, Messrs. Benedict Brothers are entrusted with the keeping of the N. Y. City time, and they furnish time to a large number of Railroads and Steamers.) Every watch we send as a premium will be first put in running order by them, and thoroughly tested, and warranted for one year.—No. 31 is a patent lever, full jewelled, in engine turned hunting case of Coin Silver, and manufactured by the justly celebrated Arnold Adams, of London. This premium will give very many a chance to obtain a *really valuable, reliable time-piece*, and at the cost of only a little effort. We have given a large number of these watches this year, and they have proved as recommended.

No. 32—Double Barrel Gun: OR FOWLING PIECE.—These guns are the genuine London "Twist" barrel, Patent Breech, Bar Lock, ebony ramrod, and in all respects desirable. Their calibre and length of barrel vary, and may be ordered to suit the kind of shooting to be done. As a special favor they are furnished to us for this premium, by Messrs. Cooper & Pond, of 177 Broadway, and well known as one of the most reliable and best houses in their line of business, and they highly recommend this particular gun, and guarantee it in every respect. It is from one of the oldest and most favorably known English manufacturers, and of a kind which Mr. Cooper assures us he has had so long, and found so good, that it is just the gun he should take if he were going out for a day's shooting. The price is not put on in fancy carving, and useless plating for show, but in the gun itself. We could get almost as good looking guns for half the sum, but we offer only real, substantial, reliable articles, those *cheap* at the price named in our table. This premium includes the Gun, Powder-Flask, Shot-Pouch, and Wad-Cutter.

No. 33—Roper Repeating Shot Gun.—Bang, Bang, Bang, Bang—four times in as many seconds, or even less! What a luxury to a sportsman! With a good flock of ducks, prairie chickens, quails, or snipe, the bag may be filled at once. This gun seems to meet all the wants of the sportsman. It is a splendid shooter, it can be fired four times without re-loading, the cost of ammunition is no more than for a muzzle loader, it is very light, (6¼ lbs.,) and the charges are waterproof. The barrel is steel, 25 inches long, with a receiver at the breech, into which four charges, each in a steel case, are placed at once, and are carried into the barrel separately, simply by cocking the piece. A Belt, 21 Shells, Wiper, Loader and Loading Block, accompany the Gun. This gun is highly recommended by distinguished sportsmen, and our boys, not accustomed to the use of a gun, found it a very pleasant companion in their summer recreations, showing that there is no difficulty in the management of it. The gun is manufactured by the Roper Repeating Rifle Company, Amherst, Mass., under the supervision of C. M. Spencer, Esq., inventor of the famous Spencer Rifle, who will furnish circulars with full descriptions.

No. 34—Spencer Repeating Rifle.—This Premium is one of Spencer's Repeating, Sporting or Hunting Rifles. It carries 7 charges inside of the stock, which are successively thrown into the barrel and fired, simply by pressing out the trigger guard, pulling it back, cocking and pulling the trigger itself. One can do all this lying behind a log without rising to scare his game. The seven shots can be readily fired *in less than half a minute*, and then you have only to slip seven more ready made charges into the stock—in half the time you can load a common rifle once at the muzzle—to be ready to fire seven times more, and so on.—An exceedingly interesting statement of what this rifle has done during the war, and of what it is, and is capable of, may be obtained by addressing WARREN FISHER, JR., *Treasurer of Spencer Repeating Rifle Company, Tremont-street, Boston, Mass.*—Our premium includes the $45 Rifle, and $10 more for the Globe and Peep-sights, including 100 rounds of prepared ammunition, boxing and shipping. These are the Company's cash prices. The addition of the Globe and Peep-sight adapts the gun for the longest ranges, for sharp-shooting, etc. Each charge contains powder, conical ball, and fulminate, all in a copper case, and is waterproof. No ramrod, no cap, and little or no cleaning of the gun barrel is required.——The regular size is: bore or calibre, 44-100 of an inch; length of barrel, 20 inches. Any one preferring a length of 26 or 30 inches, can have it for $1 or $2 extra.

No. 35—Chest of Good Tools.—For the present year, we have, through the special favor of Messrs. PATTERSON BROTHERS, of 27 Park Row, arranged for a few chests of the *very first quality of tools* of the kinds and prices named below. The same kinds of tools could be purchased for about half the money, but these are all A No. 1, and cannot be procured at any less price. They are for practical use, and worth a dozen common articles. For this we have the word and guarantee of Messrs. Patterson, which is amply sufficient for us, and for all who know them. They make up assortments of these, or any part of them that may be ordered of them, at the prices affixed, and any one can purchase of them what they desire. We make up only a single premium, which contains a full assortment for all common purposes. The tools are of regular size, and but few additions would be required for a Journeyman Carpenter. The assortment of our premium is as follows: Plain chest, 31×16¼×16 inches, with sliding compartment box, $7; Jack Plane, $1.60; Smooth Plane, $1.45; Jointer Plane, $2.25; Hand Saw, 22 inches, $1.75; Compass Saw, 10 inch., 70c.; Compasses, 6 inch., 60c.; Warner's Hammer, (adz eye,) $1.30; Hammond's Hatchet, 85c.; Drawing Knife, $1.25; Try Square, 6 inch., 65c.; Bevel, 8 inch., 70c.; Chalk Line and Spool, 45c.; Mallet, 25c.; Pair of Pliers, (pinchers,) 85c.; Sliding Tongs, (pinchers,) 55c.; Calipers, 3½ inch., 35c.; Brace, 65c.; Augur Bitts for Brace, ¼ inch, 24c.; ½ inch, 40c.; ¾ inch, 72c.; Center Bitts, ½ inch, 21c.; ¾ inch, 23c.; 1 inch, 25c.; 1¼ inch., 35c.; 1½ inch., 40c.; Six Gimlet Bitts, assorted sizes, 30c.; Three Gimlets in Handles, assorted Sizes, 36c.; Screw-driver Bitt, 25c.; Flat Countersink Bitt, 25c.; Rose do. do., 25c.; Snail do. do., 25c.; Octagon Reamer, 30c.; Taper Bitt, 50c.; 3-inch Screw-driver in Handle, 30c.; 6 inch., do. do., 40c.; ½ inch Handled Gouge, 50c.; ¾ inch do. do., 56c.; ½ Handled Chisel, 35c.; ¾ inch do. do., 40c.; 1 inch do. do., 50c.; 1½ inch, do. do., 60c.; ¾ inch heavy Framing Chisel, $1.10; 1 inch do. do., $1.25; 1½ inch, do. do., $1.50; ¾ inch Augur, 60c.; 1 inch do. do., 70c.; 2 inch do. do., $1.20; full set of Bradawls, $1.25; Common 2 feet Measuring Rule, 30c.; File, 3-cornered, 20c.; do. do., 25c.; Flat File, 30c.; Wood Rasp, 50; Soldering Iron, (copper,) $1.15; Solder, Nails, etc., $1.; Total, $44.50.——The Chest will be locked, and sent as freight or otherwise, and the key sent by mail.

Nos. 36, 37—Mathematical Instruments, for Draughting, Drawing, etc.—Very convenient not only for Architects and Mechanics, but for farmers and others, and for Boys and Girls. These are neatly fitted in beautiful Rosewood Cases, having dividers with flexible joints, and points, semi-circles, pencil and penholders, rulers, etc., etc. All the pieces in No. 36, are finished in brass and steel; those in No. 37, are German silver and steel. The pieces are the same in each, but No. 37 is of extra beauty and workmanship. They are useful in making drawings, plans of buildings, fields, etc. They are valuable to children, to cultivate a taste for, and habit of observing and sketching farms, plotting fields, orchards, buildings, for drawing, etc., etc. Such "playthings" not only keep them from "mischief," but develop their minds, and make them "handy." These premiums will be sent by mail, post-paid, to any place in the United States.

Nos. 38, 39—Dawson, Warren & Hyde's Gold Pens:—WITH EVER POINTED PENCILS, IN EXTENSION COIN SILVER CASES. Premium No. 38 contains the best E Gold Pen, and No. 39 the best F Gold Pen, which is the same style, but larger. These pens are made by Messrs. Warren & Spadone, No. 4 Maiden Lane, N.Y., successors to Dawson, Warren & Hyde, whose pens obtained so wide and good a reputation that the original firm name is the Trade Mark, and is still stamped upon every pen made. We have known the makers and their goods for many years, and can recommend both to our readers. Messrs. W. & S. are the largest manufacturers of Gold Pens, Silver and Gold Pencil Cases and Holders in the country, and their wares are fully equal to any manufactured. In ordering, state whether a stiff or limber point is desired, and if the Pen received is not suited to the hand, it may be exchanged at a trifling expense for postage. If a larger desk pen is desired, we will send the G (very large,) style, with ebony and silver holder, in leather case, in place of E with Pencil Case, or the H, (largest,) same style, in place of F, with Pencil Case.

Nos. 40, 41—Mercurial Barometers.—WOODRUFF'S PATENT, made by CHAS. WILDER, Peterboro, N. H. These are the most convenient and portable Mercurial Barometers made. (Send to Mr. Wilder for a circular giving engravings and descriptions of the instruments.) The peculiar form of Mercury cup invented by Mr. Woodruff renders these far more portable than any Mercurial Barometer previously known. They are so easily carried that Mr. Wilder *guarantees the safe delivery of every Barometer given by us as a Premium*, if not to be sent beyond the Rocky Mountains. The instruments are beautifully made, are about 3 feet long, and are packed and sent direct from the factory, with no expense save the express charges. We offer two forms which differ mainly in the style of case, both being supplied with *Thermometer* and *Vernier*. A Barometer is to farmers, or others on land, what it is to sailors at sea—an indicator of the weather to be looked for. Many who have received this premium from us in former years have given us definite statements touching its great value to them. We have tested these instruments thoroughly, and have confidence in them as weather indicators. Aside from its direct utility, the *habit* of observation and of scientific study, cultivated in children where a Barometer is used, is important.

No. 42—Buckeye Mowing Machine.—The gratification expressed by those who received this premium last year, and the request of others who wish to get it this year, lead us to continue it on the same terms. The Buckeye Mower is so widely and favorably known throughout the country that we need not describe it particularly. Any one writing to the Manufacturers, Messrs. Adriance, Platt & Co., 165 Greenwich-st., N. Y. City, will receive a circular giving full description, engravings, etc. The experience of last year showed that many a farmer can easily secure this premium by a very few days', or odd hours' and evenings', canvassing for subscribers. A few can unite their efforts, each getting a part of the subscribers, and then own the machine in common, if they do not each need the entire use of a mower.——It would pay a man well to canvass for this premium, and sell it afterward. Ten subscribers a day for 13 days would secure the premium, which sells regularly for $125.—Many can, at town meetings, fairs, elections, and other gatherings, or during the evenings, secure this premium club without much, if any, loss of time.

No. 43—Cylinder Plow (Allen's Patent).—We hear very good reports from those who received this premium last year. It is named from the peculiar form of the mould-board. Several improvements have been made upon it within a year or two past. It is an Ohio invention, we believe, but is manufactured by the well known and reliable firm, R. H. Allen & Co., 189 & 191 Water-st., New York City, to whom application may be made for further description, etc. There are several sizes and prices, with a greater or less number of attachments. The kind we offer for premiums is the "Two-horse size, cutting a furrow 12 to 14 inches wide, and 5 to 8 inches deep." It is also provided with wheel, and with a "skim plow," that is, a smaller plow attached under the beam, like the double "Michigan plow."

No. 44—Page's Patent Pump and Sprinkler.—This apparatus combines most of the advantages of a Hand Watering Pot, a Green-house Syringe, a light Force Pump, and Garden Engine. It is very simple in construction, light to carry, easy to operate, and adapted to a great variety of uses. In every household it will be found most convenient for washing windows, or window blinds. It throws a small stream with considerable force about *forty feet*, and will be invaluable in case of fire, where places otherwise inaccessible can be easily reached. In the stable it will be valued for washing carriages, horses, etc. In the garden, it gives the readiest means for watering plants. By a very simple arrangement, the stream can be instantly changed to drops, spray, or mist. It is manufactured by the New England Portable Pump Company, 11 Hanover-st., Boston, Mass.

No. 45—Family Scales.—These scales combine the advantages of counter and platform scales, and are peculiarly adapted to household purposes. They weigh from *one-half ounce* to *two hundred and forty pounds*. They are provided with a scoop or pan for weighing flour, sugar, and other house stores, and also with a platform for heavier articles, and are, in short, just such an apparatus as is needed for in-door or out-door use, occupying less than two feet square. The advantages of such an apparatus will be appreciated by every housekeeper. In cooking, preserving, keeping the weight of the grocer, butcher, etc., up to its proper mark, and in weighing meats, butter, and other produce sold from the farm, they will save much more than the cost of obtaining them as a premium. These scales are manufactured at the well known establishment of Fairbanks & Co., whose weighing apparatus has for many years been ranked as the standard, and to whom were awarded the highest premiums, two medals, at the Paris Exposition.

No. 46 — Crandall's Improved Building Blocks furnish a most attractive amusement for children. They are very simple in construction, will stand years of children's handling without breaking, and give renewed pleasure daily. Churches, Dwellings, Barns, Mills, Fences, Furniture, etc., in almost endless variety, can be built with them, and when finished, the structure remains firm so that it can be carried about without falling to pieces. For developing the ingenuity and taste of children they are unequaled. Having given these blocks a practical trial in our own families, we are so well pleased with them that we have placed them on the Premium List. The Blocks are put up in neat boxes, each box containing 130 pieces, and a card giving various designs of buildings. The sets used for this Premium are plain. The same blocks may be had painted red, white, and blue, by sending to us 3 more subscribers, at $1.50 each, or 10 more, at $1 each, than are required for the plain set.

No. 47—Pocket Lanterns.—This new premium is a very ingenious as well as valuable Yankee invention. It is a complete *Lantern*, large enough to afford light for walking or other purposes, and yet in half a minute it can be *folded* into a parcel 8 by 4 inches long, and ¾ of an inch in thickness, or small enough to set into the vest pocket, and yet contain 3 little sperm candles, matches, etc. We have used one for twelve months, carrying it in the pocket whenever going out at night, ready for use at any moment. It is manufactured by the Merriam Manufacturing Company, (Julius Ives & Co., Agents, 40 Maiden Lane, N. Y. City.) The manufacturers enable us to make the special offer in our Premium List, in order to introduce specimens of these lanterns to general use. A dozen pack in a box 8¼ by 8½ by 8¼ inches.

No. 48—American Cyclopedia.—APPLETON'S NEW.—We can hardly commend this great work too highly. We wish it could be placed in every family in the country. Several were fortunate in securing it through our premium list last *year*, and we hope many more will do so this. Scholars at our Academies and Seminaries, and members of Library Associations, can easily unite their efforts and secure this important work for their Libraries. Many young men ought to devote their evenings and spare hours to canvassing, and obtain this magnificent and useful work for their own use. ☞ The Cyclopedia *is a whole Library of itself*, consisting of *sixteen* very large octavo volumes, well bound, averaging **800** large two-column pages in each book, or in the whole, **12,804** pages! They treat upon over **25,000** different subjects. It is hardly possible to name any subject, any country, any person of note, in past or recent time, concerning which pretty full information may not be found in the Cyclopedia. It embraces every topic of human knowledge, alphabetically arranged for convenient reference.——The British Cyclopedia, though less comprehensive, and not coming down to recent dates, costs more than twice as much as our better American Cyclopedia. This premium is worth a year's effort in raising subscribers. The lowest price is $80.

No. 49—The Great Dictionary.—WORCESTER'S LARGE PICTORIAL, UNABRIDGED EDITION, containing **1854** three-column pages, with a multitude of illustrative engravings. (The work is 12 inches long, 10 inches wide, and nearly 4 inches thick, and weighs about 10 lbs.!) Many of the most thoroughly educated men of the country consider this as far the best Dictionary in the English Language. It gives the spelling and pronunciation of every word in the language with full explanations, and as a source of general information stands next to the Cyclopedia. The Dictionary can be called for at our Office, or be sent by express or otherwise, to any part of the country. We have given away hundreds of copies as premiums, many of them obtained by quite young boys and girls. It should be in every family. It is published by Brewer & Tileston, Boston.

Nos. 50 to 60—Volumes of the American Agriculturist (Unbound). — There amount to a large and valuable Library on all matters pertaining to the Farm, Garden, and Household, and contain more varied information on these subjects than can be obtained in books costing three times the money. We have stereotype plates from the Sixteenth to the Twenty-fifth Volume complete, and will have Volume 26 soon after Dec. 1st. From these plates we print as needed. The price of the volumes is $1.50 each, at the office, or $1.75 if sent by mail, as they must be post-paid. They are put up in clean numbers, with the Index to each volume. ——They are profusely Illustrated, the Engravings used in them having alone cost about Twenty Thousand Dollars! Those obtaining premiums for from one to ten volumes, can select any volumes desired, from XVI to XXVI, inclusive. For ordinary use, the sets of numbers unbound will answer quite well.—Many hundreds of these volumes are taken every year as premiums.

Nos. 61 to 71—Bound Volumes of Agriculturist.—These are the same as Nos. 50 to 60 above, but are neatly *bound* in uniform style, and cost extra for binding and postage. Sent post-paid.

No. 72—Downing's Landscape Gardening, and Rural Architecture.—This is a most beautiful Octavo volume, in extra binding, and will be an ornament to the best center table in the land, as well as be practically useful. It contains 108 fine engravings on Wood, Steel, and Stone. It will be sent post-paid.

No. 73—Architecture: A NEW AND PRACTICAL WORK ON ARCHITECTURE, containing Designs for Street Fronts, Suburban Houses, and Cottages, etc., etc., giving in detail Designs and Working Drawings for both the exterior and interior of buildings; also a great variety of Details not in the Designs. It is 11 by 14 inches in size, and contains engravings of **382** Designs, and **714** Illustrations, that would separately cost Hundreds of Dollars. By Cummings & Miller. Sent post-paid.

Nos. 74 to 85—GOOD LIBRARIES.—In these premiums, we offer a choice of **Books** for the **Farm, Garden, and Household.** The person entitled to any one of the premiums 74 to 85, may select any books desired from the list below, to the amount of the premiums, and the books will be forwarded, *paid through* to the nearest Post Office, or Express office, as we may find it most convenient to send them. We need not enlarge upon these premiums; every one knows the value of good books. Twenty-five or Fifty dollars worth of books on subjects pertaining to the farm will give the boys new ideas, set them to thinking and observing, and thus enable them to *make their heads help their hands*. Any good book will, in the end, be of far more value to a youth than to have an extra acre of land, on coming to maturity. The thinking, reasoning, observing man, will certainly make more off from 49 acres, than he would off from 50 acres without the mental ability which reading will give him.——Our premiums will enable many a family to secure a larger or smaller Library. ☞ This is a good opportunity for the farmers of a neighborhood to unite their efforts and get up an Agricultural Library for general use.

No. 86—General Book Premium.—Any one not desiring the specific Book premiums, 74 to 85, on sending any number of names above 25, may select Books from the list below, to the amount of 10 cents for each subscriber sent at $1; or to the amount of 30 cents for each name sent at the (ten) club price of $1.20 each; or to the amount of 60 cents for each name at $1.50. *This offer is only for clubs of 25 or more. The books will be sent by mail or express, prepaid by us.*

BOOKS FOR FARMERS AND OTHERS.

(For sale at the office of the *Agriculturist*, or they will be forwarded by mail, *post-paid*, on receipt of price. ☞ *All these are included in our Premiums, Nos. 74 to 86, above.*)

Allen's (L. F.) Rural Architecture	$1 50
Allen's (R. L.) American Farm Book	1 50
American Agricultural Annual, 1867, paper, 50c.; cloth	75
Allen's Diseases of Domestic Animals	1 00
American Horticultural Annual, 1867, paper, 50c.; cloth	75
American Bird Fancier	30
American Pomology—Apples—By Dr. John A. Warder.	3 00
American Rose Culturist	30
American Weeds and Useful Plants	1 75
Architecture, by Cummings & Miller	10 00
Barry's Fruit Garden	1 75
Bement's Poulterer's Companion	2 00
Bement's Rabbit Fancier	30
Bommer's Method of Making Manure	25
Boussingault's Rural Economy	1 60
Breck's New Book of Flowers	1 75
Buist's Flower Garden Directory	1 50
Buist's Family Kitchen Gardener	1 00
Chorlton's Grape Grower's Guide	75
Cobbett's American Gardener	75
Cole's (S. W.) American Fruit Book	75
Cole's Veterinarian	75
Copeland's Country Life ... $5.00 cloth	[illegible]
Cotton Planter's Manual (Turner)	1 50
Dadd's (Geo. H.) Modern Horse Doctor	1 50
Dadd's American Cattle Doctor	1 50
Dana's Muck Manual	1 25
Dog and Gun (Hooper's) ... paper, 30c. ... cloth	60
Downing's Landscape Gardening (new Edition)	6 50
Draining for Profit and Health, by G. E. Waring, Jr	1 50
Eastwood on Cranberry	75
Elliott's Western Fruit Grower's Guide	1 50
Flax Culture	50
Field's (Thomas W.) Pear Culture	1 25
French's Farm Drainage	1 50
Fuller's Grape Culturist, (Revised Edition)	1 50
Fuller's Strawberry Culturist	20
Fuller's Small Fruit Culturist	1 50
Gardening for Profit, by Peter Henderson	1 50
Gregory on Squashes ... paper	30
Guenon on Milch Cows	75
Harris' Rural Annual. Bound, 8 Nos., in 2 Vols. Each	1 50
Herbert's Hints to Horsekeepers	1 75
Hop Culture	40
Johnston's Agricultural Chemistry	1 75
Johnston's Elements of Agricultural Chemistry	1 50
Leuchar's How to Build Hot-Houses	1 50
Mohr on the Grape Vine	1 00
My Vineyard at Lakeview	1 25
Norton's Scientific Agriculture	75
Onion Culture	20
Our Farm of Four Acres (bound) 60c. ... paper	30
Pardee on Strawberry Culture	75
Peat and its Uses, by Prof. S. W. Johnson	1 25
Pedder's Land Measurer	60
Quinby's Mysteries of Bee Keeping (new)	1 50
Randall's Sheep Husbandry	1 50
Randall's Fine Wool Sheep Husbandry	1 00
Rivers' Miniature Fruit Garden	1 00
Richardson on the Dog, paper 30c. ... cloth	60
Saunders' Domestic Poultry (new), paper, 40c., bound	75
Schenck's Gardener's Text Book	75
Skillful Housewife	75
Stewart's (John) Stable Book	1 50
Thompson's Food of Animals	1 00
Tobacco Culture	25
Todd's (S. E.) Young Farmer's Manual	1 50
Warder's Hedges and Evergreens	1 50
Youatt and Spooner on the Horse	1 50
Youatt and Martin on Cattle	1 50
Youatt on the Hog	1 00
Youatt on Sheep	1 00

Editorial Jottings in Europe.

Since his absence in Europe, Mr. Judd has written frequently, with permission to publish such portions of his letters as we chose. Several of his notes of travel have been crowded out by other matter, and we briefly say that, after visiting Great Britain, France, and Holland, he is now in Russia, and will go by way of Germany and Switzerland to Southern Europe. We give some of his notes on the northern countries:

"STOCKHOLM, Sweden, August 10th.... We have had an interesting journey of 450 miles up through Sweden, from Malmo, which lies opposite Copenhagen. Around Malmo is quite a fertile section, and we saw some good farms between lakes Wenner and Wetter, and at other points, but the country is generally either wet or rocky. Yet there is a neatness and American look about the farm-houses and the villages that is very pleasing—indeed, rather surprising. In this city (Stockholm,) and its surroundings, we are very agreeably disappointed. The finish and style of the buildings, and the form, physiognomy, and dress, of the people, are more like those of a first class American city of 80,000 inhabitants than we have found anywhere else in our journey through France, Belgium, Holland, Germany, Prussia, and Denmark, and we will not except even Great Britain. In politeness and general good manners the citizens of Stockholm apparently excel us. The city is most beautifully located on a number of islands, divided by small lakes and narrow, swift running streams. The ground of each island rises high above the water, in the center especially, so that the city, as a whole, has a diversified appearance, the houses rising rapidly, one above the other, from the water's edge to the middle. At a little distance, the dividing waters are not seen, and the city appears as a compact mass of buildings. Outside of the city are seen some beautiful fields with growing crops, though the surface is much broken with rocky hills or immense granite boulders, with lakes or lakelets every mile or two. What surprises me most, is a field of tobacco just north of the city, which exhibits as vigorous a growth of leaf and stem as I have ever seen even in the most favored regions. Every hill is perfect, the leaves of immense size, and not a plant is under four feet in hight to the curve of the top leaves. This, remember, is nearly up to latitude 60°, or about the same as the southern part of Greenland, the northern end of Labrador, and the middle of Hudson's Bay.. "

"HELSINGFORS, Finland, August 13th. ..The passage hither from Stockholm is the most charming one in my experience. I have traveled hundreds of miles to see the "Thousand Islands" of the St. Lawrence, but they sink into insignificance in comparison with what we have seen during the past two days. With the exception of a narrow space of open sea between the Swedish outer coast and Aland, and again between that island and the outer Finnish coast, there is one continued succession of little islands, between which the steamer threads her way for over two hundred miles in coming from Stockholm to this place. Some of these islands are mere rounded granite rocks of an acre or two, more or less; many of them have evergreen and other shrubs or trees, with grass plots. Some of them have dwellings and cultivated fields. Often there are fifty to one hundred of those beautiful islands in sight at a time. The water channels between them vary from three or four rods to a mile or more in width. The passages are so narrow and tortuous, and the under-water islands are so numerous, that no steamer or sailing vessel moves at night. Our steamer left Stockholm at daylight, (two o'clock A. M. here, now!) and made Abo, (pronounced Obo.) in Finland, by 8 P. M., and stopped until 4 A. M., giving us several hours of daylight to tramp around the town, and climb the old Lutheran church tower, to gain a view of a dozen miles in every direction. In the vaults beneath the church, we examined bodies deposited hundreds of years ago, yet still preserving their forms and features. In this high, dry latitude, they literally dried up, or changed to enduring matter without decay. Abo, like Stockholm, much resembles an American town in its buildings, and the dress and physiognomy of the people. But here, at Helsingfors, the capital of Finland, our surprise has reached its climax. The neat, well-built city is as lovely an one, at this season, as I ever saw. We find green parks, broad, clean, well-paved, beautiful streets, thriving business stores and shops, magnificent churches, a flourishing University, with its library of 200,000 volumes, etc., etc. The people are vigorous and intelligent, and equal in physique our best class of native Americans. The "guide books" say little of this region; travelers come here but seldom, and so we hear little of Finland, and think of it only as a cold, bleak region, inhabited by a semi-savage race. It is far, very far, otherwise, and I would advise every American traveling abroad, to visit Holland, Denmark, Sweden, and Finland. A single voyage through the "Ten Thousand Islands" will repay a voyage from New York to Stockholm, and a visit to Finland will exceed in interest that usually made to Middle and Southern Europe. A trip up by rail-road, lake, and canal, into middle Finland, is easily accomplished in July or August, and from all I can learn here, is one of perfect safety and of great interest. I only regret that our large company, including small children, and engagements abroad, will prevent my going further north now. We came from Stockholm in the fine steamship Aura, whose captain, Mr. LARS KROGIUS, of Helsingfors, Finland, is a model Christian gentleman. He has been in America, speaks our language well, and he has done everything possible to make us comfortable, and aided us greatly in seeing and understanding the various points of interest on the route...."

"WYBORG, Finland, August 16th.... Leaving Helsingfors at 6 A. M., we passed, at the mouth of its spacious harbor, the powerful fortifications at Sweaborg, which are of historic interest, and are well styled the 'Gibraltar of the North.' To-day's sail has been mainly among a succession of beautiful islands, like those met with all the way from Stockholm. At 4 P. M., we passed the Russian war fleet at anchor, and counted among the ships at least nine large turreted 'Monitors,' similar to our own. We then entered through a narrow channel, guarded by extensive batteries, into the eight mile harbor, at the head of which stands Wyborg, a city of 7,000 inhabitants. This, too, is, in many respects, a beautiful town. About 1½ miles north-east of the fortified city is located 'Mon Repos,' (My Repose,) the former residence of Baron Nicolai. This delightful retreat is on the shore of a large lake, and nearly shut in by hills; the grounds are interspersed with little lakes and streams, valleys, and hillocks, which are mainly of immense granite boulders or ridges, covered with patches of trees and green verdure. Bridges, summer-houses, green-houses, graperies, arbors, walks, arched by living trees, extensive flower plots, all in beautiful bloom, etc., abound. Taken altogether, the combination of natural and artificial scenery at Mon Repos excels anything of the kind that we have ever seen elsewhere. It is doubly interesting from the fact that we find it above latitude 60°, away up in Finland. The pen of a Downing, aided by an artist's pencil, is needed to justly describe this exquisite retreat...."

"ST. PETERSBURG, Russia, August 20th.... After leaving Wyborg, on Friday, we had a slightly rough passage, caused by a stiff western breeze over the Gulf of Finland, which sent sundry passengers to their berths. At 2 P. M., we neared the renowned fortifications and ship-yards at Cronstadt, eighteen miles west of St. Petersburg, and our hearts were gladdened, and our eyes fairly glistened with tears of joy, as we saw flying from beautiful ships the 'Star-spangled Banner,' and Admiral Farragut's square, five-starred, blue Pennant, at the main-mast head of one of them. After so long journeying—always, thus far, in foreign ships—the sight of our own flag gaily floating in the breeze, awakened such emotions as none but those who have experienced them can appreciate. We wonder not at the devotion of the seaman to the flag of his country.....Further on, we passed some Russian ships, and then the fleet of Sweden, (the native land of Ericsson,) and here, too, were ten or a dozen monitors—the smoke from a salvo of artillery of all the vessels and fortifications just then fired in honor of a visit from the Russian Grand Duke to our fleet prevented our counting the ships accurately.... Eighteen miles more, and we come to anchor in the Neva, in the midst of the Great City of the North, and, in many respects, the City of the World. The bug-bear of rough, searching Russian custom house and other officials, so graphically written down in the English guide books, was not found. The fact that we were American travelers, with our necessary baggage, secured us a polite reception, and an unsearched and unmolested passage to our hotel. At the 'Grand Hotel,' we found as spacious, clean, and well furnished rooms, as good, well prepared food, as careful, prompt, and polite attendance, and at quite as reasonable rates, as we have secured anywhere else since crossing the Atlantic. No 'Russian bears' walk the streets, in official or other garb, but every class, official, mercantile, shop-keepers, market men—indeed all classes, down even to the cab-men, if not including them also, are as polite and well-bred as we have anywhere found, not excepting Paris itself. I wish to note here, that everywhere on the continent we have seen among *all* classes a degree of politeness—a touch of the hat, a 'thank you' for the slightest favor, that might well be copied by us Americans far more generally than it is.... During three days past, we have rode 20 miles through some of the broad, beautiful streets, and in one of the parks; have taken a full survey of the whole city, from the top of Isaac's Cathedral, have visited the 'Hermitage,' with its infinite treasures of art, modern and ancient—and from what we have seen and know is to be seen, we are almost ready to write down St. Petersburg as a city more interesting, more instructive, and more pleasing than any we have seen after traversing, (now, or previously,) every country of Europe, north of Spain and Italy. We Americans have seen and known northern and north-eastern Europe too much through English and French eyes. For myself, though I came hither with much desire, and with many expectations, I confess that what I have already seen, far surpasses my very highest conception. Even an enthusiastic French gentleman, a fellow traveler hither, who has all the way been loud in his praises of Paris, to-day, voluntarily, remarked to us, 'St. Petersburg is a second Paris.' Perhaps after three days more, he may say, 'Paris is almost a second St. Petersburg.'...."

Walks and Talks on the Farm.—No. 46.

We have had one of the most severe drouths I have ever known. I have always been partial to a dry, hot summer—it gives such a splendid chance to kill weeds—but this is rather too good. At the East, I understand, they have had a very wet summer, and the papers complain that the potatoes are rotting in consequence. Here we shall have few or none to rot. Corn will not be half a crop. I did not sow any corn for fodder, but we have been obliged for some time to cut up corn for the cows. As it was drilled in, and was a little too thick, I do not begrudge it the cows as much as if it was planted in hills. There is a heavy growth of stalks, and I am astonished to see how little ground we have to go over for a day's supply. Another season I will not be without a piece of corn fodder, on rich land, near the barn-yard, to be cut up in August for milch cows. Some of my neighbors had a piece this year, but it was sown broadcast, and the dry weather parched it up. In moist seasons, corn sown broadcast sometimes does well, but, as a general rule, it should be sown thickly in drills, and thoroughly cultivated, and the more highly it can be manured, the better. Rich land, thick seeding in drills, say three bushels per acre, and thorough cultivation, are the essentials in raising corn fodder. And in such circumstances it is astonishing how much food can be obtained from an acre.

How much land does an old-fashioned fence occupy? I have always thought it took up a good deal of land, but never had the curiosity to measure. But this summer we have been building a stone wall along the whole west side of the farm, and after it was completed, and the old fence removed, I was surprised at the quantity of land we had gained. The ground, of course, might have been plowed closer to the fence, but taking the case as it actually was, the old rail fence, with stones, weeds, rubbish, etc., occupied a strip of land one rod wide. A field, 31 rods long and 31 rods wide, contains about six acres. If surrounded by such a fence, it would occupy a little over three quarters of an acre of land. A farm of 160 acres so fenced would have twenty acres of land taken up in this worse than useless manner. Not only is the use of the land lost, but it is, in the majority of cases, a nursery of weeds, and, in plowing, much time is lost in turning, and the headlands and corners are seldom properly cultivated.

But will it pay to use more capital in farming? If we could calculate on getting present prices, there can be no doubt that it would pay well. And, at all events, you cannot have good farming without the use of a large working capital, or of liberal credit, and it is quite certain that, if good farming will not pay, poor farming will not. And as agriculture is the main business of the nation, farming will pay in the long run, if anything pays.

This question, so often asked, and so seldom answered, "Does farming pay?" is a very absurd one. Of course farming pays. Farmers *do* get a living, and it is rare that one of them falls. I have three neighbors. One came from the eastern part of the State, when the country was new. He took up 160 acres of land, cleared it, fenced it, lived, probably, at first in a log house, worked hard, but enjoyed himself. He is a capital farmer, up early in the morning, attends to his stock, always has his crops sown in good season, treats his land liberally, and gets ample returns. He commenced with little, has brought up a large family, given them a first-class education, and he is probably to-day worth $25,000 to $30,000. True, it has taken him 40 years to accumulate this amount of property, and nearly all of it has been derived from the advance of real estate. Still he has had a good living, has enjoyed life, is an intelligent, public-spirited, energetic, and generous-minded gentleman, and enjoys the respect of all his neighbors. I am sure such farming pays. I have another neighbor who has a farm of equally good land. He is a well educated man, and seems to work hard, but he is always behind with his work. He occasionally gets a good crop, but the general yield is hardly sufficient to pay even for the little labor bestowed in preparing the land. He is in debt, and seems to depend more on chopping and selling wood to meet his payments than on raising crops. His fences are out of repair, and the land is full of weeds. Still he gets a living for himself and a large family, and, I suppose, even in his case, we must conclude that "farming pays." I have another neighbor, whose land is low, but would be very productive if attention was paid to surface drainage. The same creek runs through it that runs through the south end of my farm. It is choked up with old logs, branches, and fallen trees. The water sets back in the spring, and floods his land. But he makes no effort to clean out the creek. I offered to do it for him, if he would give me the wood, but no, he intended to do it himself. I presume he has been intending to do it for years. A good portion of his land does not produce enough to pay the taxes, and the dryer portions are not half worked, and yield the most meagre returns. I passed his house this morning. He was cutting some coarse hay on the low land. His oats were harvested, but nearly half of them were still lying on the ground among the clods, and his wife was thrashing the other half in the barn with a flail. Now this is rather poor farming, but as the family gets a living, I suppose it "pays."

But *how much* does it pay? Does he make as much as he would if his son and himself worked as hard for some other farmer as they do for themselves, to say nothing of the wife? I do not believe they make half as much, and certainly their land is not improving, though they probably persuade themselves that, owing to the improvements of others, it is increasing in value.

Now, I have no doubt that an intelligent, enterprising man, with the necessary capital, could take this farm, and increase its productiveness fourfold. But such a man cannot live in the style of its present occupant, and his wife would not want to thrash in the barn. And so the real question is whether farming will afford sufficient profits to enable an educated man to live in a style suited to his necessities. *I think it will*, but there are those who contend that it will not.

Can an educated man get a suitable living by making boots? Can he make much more than the illiterate man who sits on the adjoining bench? Can an educated farmer dig more potatoes in a day than a good stalwart Irishman? Can he chop more wood than a French Canadian, or plow better than a Scotchman? Can General Grant fight in the ranks any better than Patrick O'Flannagan?

The educated shoemaker, as soon as he had learned the trade, would have others helping him, and by and by, if made of the right kind of stuff, he would be the proprietor of a large boot and shoe factory, and call to his aid all the contrivances for saving labor that modern science and invention can afford.

"This is all very well. I see the point. But you cannot make money by farming, unless you work yourself." Very true. I never supposed you could. Neither can the educated shoemaker. He probably works harder than any man in the establishment, although he does not wax his own strings, or hammer out his sole on the lapis. He knows how to do all these things. And so must a farmer be acquainted with all the details of his business, and must give them his undivided attention. But must he necessarily do his own plowing, dig his own ditches, and husk his own corn? Work he must, and so must a manufacturer and a professional man. But what work shall he do? If he has men husking corn by the bushel, he should see that they husk clean, and tie up the stalks well, and make the bundles into stooks that will shed rain, and not blow down in the first wind. He must see that he is not cheated in measuring the corn, and that it is properly sorted. He can make more by attending to such things than by husking himself. And so it is in nearly all the operations of the farm. Especially must he see to his stock. He will find ten men that can dig potatoes, husk corn, hoe, plow, cultivate, and even build a stack, and dig underdrains, to one that can be entrusted to feed pigs or take care of the cows. To neglect to feed regularly and properly—to starve this week, and surfeit the next, will cost you half the feed.

But I am wearying you. I am satisfied, however, that this subject must receive the attention of farmers. Those who intend to make agriculture their business should study it thoroughly, and make themselves masters of every detail. They must know how to do all kinds of farm work, and should study especially how to direct others. It is frequently easier to do the work one's self than to show another how to do it, but it is better, in the end, to bear with a bungler, than to let him stand idle while you do the work. John Johnston is employing contrabands on his farm, and likes them well, though he says, "they cannot set themselves to work." That is precisely my idea. A man with a large farm must know how to set others to work, and see that they do it properly, and he will find that this will give him enough to do without going into the field to plow himself. Nearly all the labor we can now command is unskilled, and this state of things will continue. There are now thousands of Chinese at work on the Pacific Rail-road, and when we think that one-third the population of the globe is in the Chinese Empire, it will not be surprising if the high wages paid in this country, should induce hundreds of thousands to emigrate to San Francisco, and from there over the Pacific Rail-road to the mines of Colorado and the prairies of the Great West. They will not be able to "set themselves to work," and the young farmers of the country should educate themselves for the task. There is not one farmer's son in a hundred that could do it at present. They have not been trained to direct others, and it is time this part of a farmer's education received attention.

If the drouth continues much longer, it will be difficult to get in the usual quantity of winter wheat. It is almost impossible to plow heavy land. I have heard of several farmers who have abandoned the attempt. We are plowing up an old meadow, which, although somewhat mucky, is so hard on the dryer portions that a new cast iron point will not last longer than a day. The men say the point gets so hot from the friction that it will almost burn your hand. The high price of cast iron points will compel us to use steel points. These can be sharpened by a blacksmith at little expense, and although the first cost is about three times as much as an iron point, they are cheaper in the end, and work easier. By taking a cold chisel, and putting it in a vise or having some one to hold it on the top of a large stone, you can, by putting the point on the chisel, cut or break off the worn end of the point, and it will then do almost as good work as when new. Cutting it off square with a cold chisel is far better than trying to break it off with a hammer or a stone, as some do.

I think I told you that I proposed to seed down this old meadow in September, as soon as it was plowed and harrowed. It makes rather a rough job of it, but then it is a rough piece of land, and at any rate it will be far better than it was before.

I have been consulting Flint's valuable work on "Grasses and Forage Plants" in regard to the quantity of seed that should be sown per acre, but he merely advises liberal seeding, without saying how much. This is a too common fault among agricultural writers, and I should have been apt to conclude that the author was not as "practical" as I had supposed, but for the following sentence. Speaking of the improvement of waste land, he says: "The difficulty with most small farmers is to begin. Well begun is half well done; for the moment any real improvement is begun in earnest, the interest is excited, the mental activity is increased, the desire for improvement partakes of the nature of a passion; and hence, though the beginning may be small, the end may be the renovation of the owner as well as the land." This is well said, and eminently true, and the man that wrote it, must have himself tasted something of the pleasure of renovating waste land.

The chemistry of the book is a little out of date. For instance, he says: "Every keeper of stock knows that to feed an animal oilcake, *which is but slightly nitrogenous*, might fatten him, but it would not give him strength of muscle, or size; while, if the same animal be kept on the cereal grains, as wheat or Indian corn, alone, his size rapidly increases, his muscular system develops, and he gains flesh without increasing his fat in proportion." Now, the fact is, of all the foods used for stock, oilcake is the most nitrogenous. It contains more than twice as much nitrogen as Indian corn or wheat.

In the same connection it is stated that Timothy contains more nitrogenous matter than red clover. This may be so in the fresh state, because the clover is more succulent than Timothy, and contains more water. But clover hay contains a good deal more nitrogen than Timothy hay—in fact, nearly double. It is for this reason that clover hay makes so much richer manure than Timothy hay. But it does not follow that it is more nutritious. The old notion that a food is nutritious in proportion to the nitrogen which it contains, proves unfounded. Peas and beans contain twice as much nitrogen as Indian corn and wheat, but they are not twice as nutritious. But they make manure twice as valuable, and this is one of the chief reasons why they deserve to be more extensively cultivated.

The Common Seal.

In introducing the interesting family of the seals to the readers of the *Agriculturist*, we are happy in being able to present so beautiful and accurate an engraving. It represents the common seal of our own coast, so abundant on the coast of Labrador, on the ice islands which, in the breaking-up of the northern winter, float along the north-east coast of America, and the most abundant of the Greenland seals. This seal, (*Phoca vitulina*,) is the type of the natural family *Phocidæ*, which includes those animals which have the same general form — the Walrus, Sea-Elephant, Sea-Lion, Harp Seal, Hooded Seal, etc. It has a fish-like form, the fore feet projecting from the sides like fins, and the hind feet being nearly united at the hinder end of the animal, and appearing much like the tail of a fish, or the flukes of a whale or porpoise. The tail extends down to the hind feet, and appears as an inconspicuous appendage between them. The body, which is of a brownish or yellowish-gray color, is cylindrical for a short distance below the neck and shoulders, but tapers rapidly to the tail. The head is much like that of an intelligent dog, and the voice resembles the barking of a dog also; hence the name Sea-Dog is not inappropriate. The great intelligence of the seal is well known, and might be inferred from the size of its brain, which is proportionately larger than that of any other animal, except man and the most intelligent monkeys. The eye is most noticeable for its lustrous brilliancy and calm look, expressive of intelligence far above other brutes. The ears are simple orifices, closed by valves or lids which shut water-tight, and a similar arrangement closes the nostrils, so that, when under water, none can enter to interfere with either hearing or breathing, when they come out again. Besides, the ear valves have the additional advantage of giving seals the ability to hear with great acuteness, while submerged. They have also the power of diving and remaining down fifteen or twenty minutes, and by their accuracy of hearing they regulate the length of time they stay below, and the place where they come up. The lips are thick, and the large stiff and knotted bristles, or whiskers, which grow upon them, are exceedingly sensitive, and aid them greatly in catching fish, which is their almost exclusive diet. The neck, though short, is very lithe, and a seal can move its head about with the ease and facility of a duck, though lacking in grace.

THE COMMON SEAL.—(*Phoca vitulina.*)

The limbs of the seal are like those of other quadrupeds, so far as this,—they consist, in general, of the same bones, similarly placed; but, with the exception of the feet, they are concealed beneath the skin of the body. It is curious to observe, when the seal moves its "flippers," the motions of the apparently well-formed arm slipping about under the tight fitting coat. The home of the seal is the sea; on the land it is awkward, and comparatively helpless. In fact, a seal on the land appears to be in a straight-jacket, and as if, could one enlarge the arm-holes of its coat, he would do the animal a lasting service. The extremities are fin-like feet, with webs between, and nails upon the toes. In swimming, the fore feet are used only in turning, while the hind feet and tail propel the body forward, with a sculling motion, and great power. The skins of all seals are valuable; they make good leather, and many are covered with a very fine and beautiful fur, beneath a complete covering of longer, coarse hair, which is removed when the fur is used. Some seals yield a valuable oil in great quantity, and these products are the basis of "fisheries" of vast importance. The seals are usually taken upon the ice and in the water, and many are captured by the Esquimaux. To these people they are as important as our flocks and herds are to us, for from them they obtain food, skins for tents, boats, and clothing, and leather for boots, their most important merchandise, from some of the membranes, window panes, from the sinews, thread and cord, and from the bones, utensils, etc.; besides, they use the oil for light and for fuel, and are fond of drinking it.

The males are polygamous, having three or four wives, to which they are very devoted. During the time of gestation, the seals remain on shore chiefly, and, if pressed by hunger, feed on vegetables. They have one or two young at a birth, with which they early take to the water. A common seal will often yield eight to twelve gallons of oil; the size of adult animals varies, however, from three to six feet.

THE CINNAMON BEAR.—(*Ursus Americanus, var.* [illegible])

Cinnamon Bear.

The animals of that remarkable region of North America, embraced between the different ranges of the Rocky Mountains, are subject to many diverse climates and conditions of life. It is wet and cold, dry and hot, within the compass of comparatively few miles. It is not strange then, as it seems to us, that variations in color and other characteristics should occur which justify the hunters in considering the animals as different species from those they have known elsewhere, though they may be the same. The Cinnamon bear of the Rocky

Mountains is a variety of the American Black bear, (*Ursus Americanus*,) which has a reddish fur, varying also considerably in different individuals, but generally of a cinnamon color. It is, besides, usually more slender than the common black bear, but otherwise has the same habits and characteristics. Baird describes the fur of a specimen from Oregon as longer and softer than that of the black bear, and says that the color is of a nearly uniform dark chestnut or cinnamon hue, with a purple reflection in certain lights.

The Use of the Plow in Draining.

After such a season as we have just experienced—wet in one section, and dry in another—farmers consider thorough draining, to see if the claims of its advocates are really true, and if the distressed tillers both of wet and dry soils may not find in it a panacea for their troubles.

We encounter one stubborn fact at the outset, namely, that draining is expensive, even if we put the drains barely below the reach of frost and the plow. Next, we are forced upon another fact, which no sophistry can budge, and that is, that the most expensive draining is shallow draining. As we make up our minds to do deep draining, the fact is turned up with each spadeful of earth, which, if we heed it, teaches that thoroughness and cheapness in the long run are identical. That is, reasonable expense for thoroughness' sake is the strictest economy.

Referring our readers to arguments in favor of deep laid tile drains, in former numbers of the *American Agriculturist*, and the works on Drainage in our book list, we discuss now the cheapest way of placing a course of drain tiles, four feet deep on an average, in an ordinary soil. Every farmer who wants to dig a ditch, thinks of his plows, for they will turn out the soil ten inches deep with comparative ease. If a man is to have a ditch four feet deep dug with spades, he ought to try to move as little earth as possible, and as sixteen inches has been found about the least width that a man can work in, he should try to have his ditch no wider. If he can use plows to facilitate his work, he need not be so particular about this, although a narrow ditch—the narrowest possible—is best under all circumstances.

We prefer to use, to cut the sod, a plow that will cut eight inches, and lay the slice over true and flat. Then we take a stout stick, like a short bean pole, as long as the plow beam, lash one end to the beam at the nigh handle, brace the other end out sixteen inches from the landside of the beam, and attach a short chain to this end. The brace is a half-inch strip, three inches wide, made fast by the clevis bolt, and, if necessary, a big iron washer. In plowing, the team is driven so that the chain will drag along the edge of the first furrow, and aids the judgment of the plowman materially in determining the width of the slice. Men must follow and throw the sods out. The trench will now take a plow of the largest size, and it should be drawn by two yokes of oxen, or two pairs of horses, working so as to tread neither in the trench nor on the sod near the edge. This is accomplished in either of two ways. Each team may draw independently, one upon each side of the ditch, being attached to the plow by a log-chain, and the chains being braced apart, so that the draft shall be reasonably true, that is, parallel to the line of draft. The other way is to work the oxen upon ten-foot yokes, and the horses of each pair upon long eveners, they being driven by outside reins only, and the heads of each pair being held apart by a stick.

The large plow may be run in the ditch two, three, or four times, according to the soil, or it may be best to use a smaller one, and as comparatively little earth can be thrown out by the plow, men must follow, and shovel as fast as the soil is loosened. After the loose earth is removed to the depth of twelve to eighteen inches, according to its character, a sub soil plow will be found of more service than a surface plow. With this, we can work down, little by little, into the hard pan. So large a force of hands is not needed when the sub soil plow is used, for the earth broken up by this plow does not interfere with its deeper working as is the case when a surface plow is used. The successful employment of the sub soil plow is limited both by the difficulty of plowing in very hard ground with the plow two or three feet below the team, and in the handles interfering with the sides of the ditch. There are, however, plows constructed to run deep enough to be of very essential service to a depth of about three feet.

This use of the power of animals greatly lessens the expense of digging the ditches, and various forms of scrapers expedite the filling, so that, after a little experience, the formidable difficulties which at first may appear as insurmountable obstacles to a poor man's doing much thorough draining, disappear, especially when we consider that a moderate outlay of money or labor, expended with discretion, almost immediately begins to make large returns, fifty per cent. per annum being not uncommon.

Earth Closets vs. Water Closets.

The manure wastes of civilization are vastly greater than those of savage or nomadic life. Even on most farms we lose more or less ashes, bones, and other valuable fertilizers. Much of value escapes from the fermenting manure heaps, much is washed away, while four-fifths of all human soil and liquid is lost; and we think if we were to say nine-tenths, we should be nearer the truth. In the cities almost the whole is virtually lost, and were the system of water closets, now so much in vogue, to extend, *all* would be washed out to sea. Among savages and wandering tribes, the wastes are left upon the surface of the ground, or slightly buried, and so the earth is not robbed to benefit the ocean. The manurial value of the sewage of cities, which is emptied into the rivers and flows out to sea, consists chiefly in the urine and soil of the inhabitants. A great reform has been commenced in England in regard to this subject, and the long known deodorizing and purifying effects of *dry* earth are systematically applied not only to rendering human excrements inoffensive, but at the same time preserving them for manure, in a form which may be economically transported many miles. This principle has been already explained in the *Agriculturist*, but the way of operating the "earth closets" was not described, the closets being a source of profit to somebody, and hence involved in a little mystery.

A Sewage Congress has lately been held at Leamington, Eng., and at this meeting a paper was read by a Mr. James, in regard to some simple closets which have been introduced upon the estate of the Jewish banker, Baron Rothschild, at Halton. These consist of simple boxes or shallow, tight vaults, which receive the soil and liquid of the family, and into which, at evening, enough thoroughly dried earth is thrown to cover all, being about a pound and a half per day to each adult. This quantity is found to be sufficient to deodorize the soil and absorb the liquid. The accumulations, when these boxes and vaults become full, are dried in the sun without any unpleasant odor, and when dried and pulverized, may be used again and again, the substance becoming a more concentrated form of manure with each repetition. The author of the paper alludes to the natural instincts of animals, cats for example, and to the instructions of the great Jewish lawgiver to his people, (Deut. xxiii, 12 and 13,) as both precept and example in favor of using dry earth in this way. The advantages claimed are, increased cleanliness, freedom from bad odors, that the waters of wells are not contaminated by privy vaults in the vicinity, that brooks and rivers are not rendered too impure for valuable fish to frequent them, that the closets may even be in the house, without offence, and the saving of great quantities of valuable manure.

These seem to be strong and rather startling propositions, but the writer is able to cite his own experience during the heat and wet of the past summer, to corroborate many of the claims of the advocates of earth closets in England. A privy was built with a simple draw of 2 inch planks, well put together, and on runners set beneath the seats, and the deposits kept constantly covered with sun-dried and sifted garden soil, which entirely suppresses all odors. We have not thought it necessary to re-dry the earth, as fresh soil must be more easily prepared; besides, fresh earth is a more agreeable substance to handle, if one is inclined to humor his prejudices, as most of us are. We secure in this way a rich and concentrated manure, though proportionally more bulky than if passed several times through the closet. This manure is free from weed seeds of course, and may be applied immediately, or, if desired, dried and kept under cover a long time.

Improvement of Land by Grazing.

If the soil can have all its crops returned to it in kind, or in the shape of manure made from feeding them to animals upon it, it will constantly improve. A worn-out soil left to grow up to forest will recover its fertility in due time. Cow pastures decline in productiveness because the cows are usually yarded at night, and a large part of the manure, as well as milk and calves, is removed from the soil. It is different with the grazing of beeves or of fattening sheep. Where the object is to make beef for market, bullocks of three or four years of age are bought in the spring in good condition, and turned into the pasture as soon as the grass is sufficiently grown to support them, and are sold off in the fall. It is considered a matter of great importance by graziers that the pasture should be large, and should have only so many cattle as it can carry through the season. It has been found in experience that the changing of beeves from one pasture to another has a bad influence upon them. They become restless and lose flesh. In many districts where ground plaster does well, it is sown at the rate of a bushel or two to the acre every spring. Even in this small quantity the effect is often astonishing, bringing in white clover, and on pastures where it has not been applied before, it will sometimes increase the feed four-fold. With this cheap dressing and grazing beeves, many run down farms have been brought up to a high degree of productiveness. Some boast that their meadows will carry a bullock to the acre. With good judgment in buying and selling, this is an easy way of getting rent from land. The stock require very little attention after they are turned into the pasture, until the drover comes in the fall, or they are otherwise marketed.

Sheep are said to improve land more rapidly than bullocks. The manure is more evenly distributed if the land is level; and if it is broken, the most of it is dropped where it is most needed, upon the tops of the knolls. They also crop bushes much more closely than beeves, but in order to keep brush under, all the brush should be cut with the scythe at the start, and the pasture should be heavily stocked as long as the sprouts push. In Harrison County, Ohio, and in other parts of the State, where the winter wheat has become an uncertain crop, we are informed that many of the farmers have resorted to wool as a substitute. This crop has several important advantages over wheat. It involves much less labor, and improves, rather than exhausts the soil. It is found that the sheep pastures are growing more productive. Wool at fifty cents a pound can be carried to market profitably, much farther than wheat at the ordinary prices. A pound of wheat is now worth but three or four cents, and freight on grain is about as expensive as on wool. The latter, moreover, is one of the few products of the farm that can be held over without serious risk of loss. Some of the finest wool in the State is produced in this County, and has been sold from fifty to sixty cents a pound this season. In considering the question of abandoning sheep husbandry, as some may be tempted to do, under temporary reverses or falling prices, we think due credit should be given to sheep as improvers of the soil. The farmer can hardly grow poor whose soil is constantly growing rich.

Barn Plan for a Small Farm.

Small barn plans interest directly many more people than very large ones, and we do not mean to be remiss in presenting too many of the latter in proportion. This month we give one, in the devising of which it would seem that many of the teachings of the *Agriculturist* had been observed. It is convenient, compact, well built, neat, roomy, and economical, but not without its faults. That is, with the same outlay of money and labor, we think it might have been better. This barn was built by Mr. Christian Braunle, of Coudersport, Potter Co., Pa., and as he has great satisfaction in its use, and as it meets the high approval of his neighbors, he sends us the plan. The figures represent the ground plan, and two sections through the center. Enough of the framing is shown to give an idea of the construction. The barn is 36 feet wide and 40 feet long. The thrashing floor crosses the barn in the middle, with stalls for horses and cattle on each side, but on lower and different levels. Fourteen feet above the thrashing floor, but below the level of the plates, are two platforms with a space between them, and above these a space of 14 feet intervenes below another floor framed into the posts just below the purline plates. This forms the granary, up in the very peak of the gambrel roof. It is easily made rat proof, is hot, and dry, if the roof be tight. A pulley (*L*, figs. 2 and 3,) enables a horse to draw up the clean grain, or corn in the ear, which can be returned to the floor through the conductor, *k*, in the same figures.

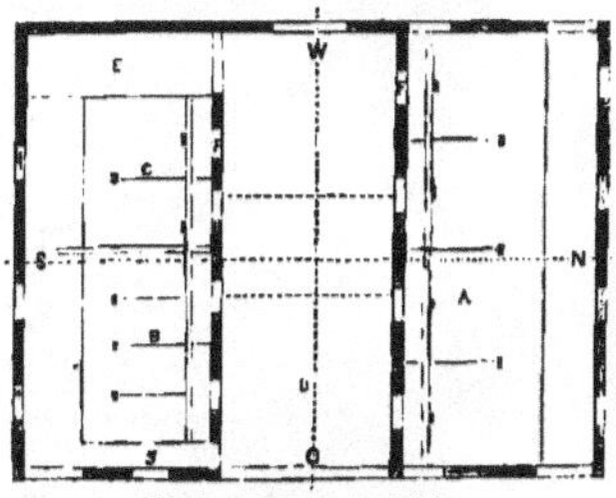

Fig. 1.—GROUND PLAN OF BARN.

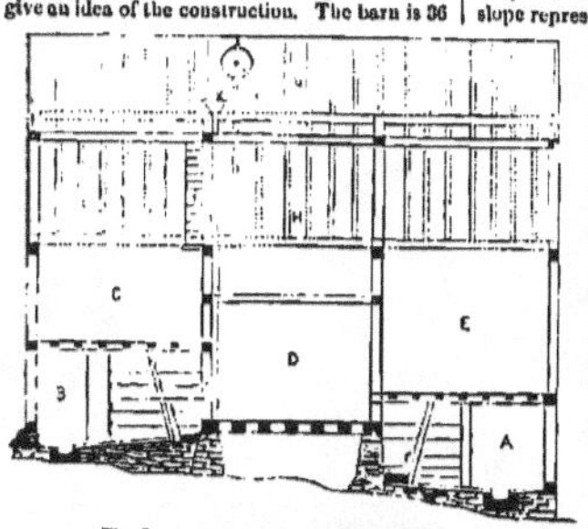

Fig. 2.—EAST AND WEST SECTION OF BARN.

There is an excellent place for a root cellar below the thrashing floor, but this was not in our correspondent's plan, and so he did not carry it out, though he makes the suggestion.

Figure 1 is the ground plan. *A* represents a stable for one pair of oxen and six cows. There is a door at each end, and a gutter for liquid manure, as seen in fig. 2. *B* represents the horse stable, 16 feet wide, containing four stalls. *C* shows double stalls for young cattle. *G* is the passage way from the thrashing floor, which is 14 feet wide. *E* is a room open to the thrashing floor, for bins of feed for daily use, for tools, etc. *F*, *F*, are openings from the thrashing floor into the mangers, for feeding the stock.

Figure 2 is a section from east to west. Fig. 3 a cross-section, and so far as possible, the lettering in each corresponds. *C* and *E* are hay bays over the stalls, extending to the roof. *D* is the thrashing floor, *H* the space above the two platforms, over the thrashing floor. Two dotted lines crossing this floor in the ground plan, (fig. 1), indicate the position of these platforms and the space between them for pitching up hay, grain, or straw. *M* and *I* are ladders which are boxed for safety, and *P* is a platform landing between them. *T*, *T*, in figure 3, corresponds with *E* and *C*, in fig. 1.

It will strike those familiar with side-hill barns having barn cellars, or stables for stock beneath the main floor, that this barn is arranged ingeniously to lose the advantages of a side-hill, by having the thrashing floor run across the slope. But the cattle stable being so much below the floor, the great object of a side-hill barn, namely, low hay bays, is in part gained. Still we prefer the old plan, and think with the fine slope represented, it would have been better to have had the barn stand facing the south instead of the east, with the whole main floor on one level, and that about as high as the floor above the stable, *A*. This would give four deep bays and a spacious cattle floor besides. We have no doubt the barn is a convenient one as it is, but it needs ventilation, and a sheltered place for making manure. The ability to drive through the barn would be a great advantage. No doubt sheds and yards, sheep barns, and hog pens, are located near and conveniently.

How Long to Milk Cows.

Some cows settle the question for their owners, and such, unless they are fine large animals, and calf raising is the chief use of the cow, should be fatted and killed at 4 or 5 years old, or sold. As a general rule, it is a poor cow that does not need to be dried off before calving. As

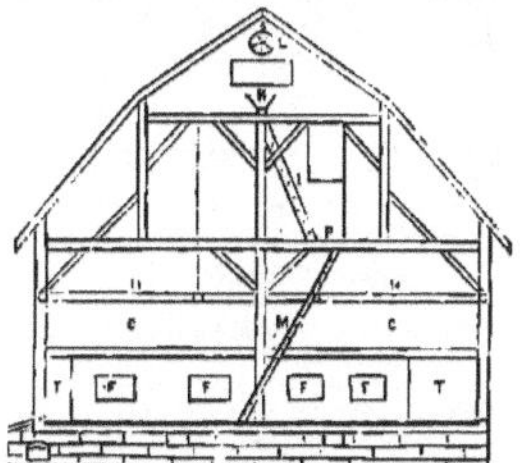

Fig. 3.—CROSS-SECTION OF BARN.

to how little milk will pay for the trouble of milking, that depends upon the number of cows, and the amount required for family use or for sale. If the milk is worth 3 or 4 cents a quart, it will pay to milk every cow that will average two quarts a day. If less than that quantity is obtained, we would advise to dry off the cow. The practice of half-feeding dry cows is execrable. All cows that are worth keeping should be well kept, and any animal with young should be as well fed as when giving milk, though the food need not be so rich (oleaginous) as when the milk is set for cream or used for butter-making. It does not hurt cows to grow fat while dry; but they should not be very fat, as a general rule. The rapid taking-on of flesh at this period is an indication of sound health. When the time of calving approaches, cut off oilmeal or any such rich addition to the feed if the cow is in good flesh; give plenty of sweet hay, and a few, say 3 or 4, ears of corn, daily. If you expect to value the calf enough to raise it, or even to fatten it for veal, stop milking, at all events, six weeks before the cow will come in; but if the calf has little or no value to you, milk two weeks longer before you begin to dry her off.

Some cows will give milk the year round, if you will let them, and it is hard to dry them before they make bag anew; but this should always be done. Even in large dairies it will be found profitable to feed cows well, curry them twice a week thoroughly, and milk them *ten months*. This gives eight weeks instead of six before calving, and the amount of milk given the next season will be essentially greater than if the common course be followed. The practice of drying cows early in the winter, and calculating to milk them only about 8 or 9 months of the year, has its origin not in a desire to benefit the cows or coming calves, but in the desire to have easy work during the winter, in taking care of dry cows. Its fruit is a decrease of ability in the herd to give as much milk as otherwise. Especially is this true of young cows, whose milk secreting tendencies should be encouraged as much as possible. To this end also, heifers should come in young; Alderneys at 18 months, Ayrshires and other milch breeds at 2 years.

GROUP OF HOUDAN PRIZE FOWLS.

Prize Fowls of the Great French International Exhibition.

We have already devoted considerable space to the more prominent breeds of French fowls, yet the interest of the poultry raising public in them is so great that we would be inexcusable did we not present new facts and instructive portraits when it is in our power. An enterprising American poultry fancier, Mr. James E. Mallory, of Tarrytown, Westchester Co., N. Y., secured and shipped at once to this country the prize trios of the three prominent French breeds of fowls, namely: Crevecœur, Lafleche, and Houdan, and the prize trio of Rouen Ducks. All arrived in poor flesh, but good health, and are doing very well. Though not in the best plumage, we had drawings made of them, and present engravings of the Houdan and Lafleche trios. They are well formed, the size of all is large, that of the Lafleches especially so. The color of these is black, with white ear-lobes, and slate-colored legs; that of the Houdan is black and white, speckled or spangled, (whichever term is best understood.) The latter have topknots, and throat-ruffles, a triple comb, lead colored legs, and five-toed feet, like the Dorkings. We congratulate the fanciers of these attractive breeds of fowls on the possession in this country of these fine birds which will, we hope, furnish excellent crosses with the different strains of blood of the same breeds already in their possession.

GROUP OF LAFLECHE PRIZE FOWLS.

The Crevecœurs Fifteen Years in this Country.—We found, a few days since, with surprise and pleasure, a fine flock of fowls, bearing an unmistakable likeness to the fashionable "Creves," on the farm of Mr. J. P. Swain, of Westchester Co. The Johnnie-Crapeau style and air of the cocks, their split combs, the topknots, the tendency to muffle or ruffle, the color, and the character of the hens as persistent layers, class them unmistakably as, at least, closely akin to the Crevecœurs. The original stock was purchased by Capt. Funk, of the old line of Havre packets, under the name of "Layers," (*Pondeuse*,) at Havre. Two importations were made of twenty and thirty-six birds respectively, but few of either importation survived, or long survived, the passage. Their descendants, however, are hardy and healthy, and Mr. S. gives them the credit of being the hardiest and best hens for eggs he has ever had, although he has bred almost all the famous varieties, importing them from both Europe and Asia. We learn that it is the common experience of importers of fowls that the original birds frequently fail and die, soon after coming here, and they are lucky if they secure a dozen or two good eggs. The trouble is roup, contracted from the long confinement and exposure. These French hens have been distributed to some extent through the country, but Mr. S. advises persons to get them from the more recent importations, as the custom in France has been to take the largest eggs from the handsomest hens, from which to raise "layers." As long as Mr. S. continued this practice, eight of the French hens' eggs were nearly equal in weight to ten of ordinary fowls, but the egg-shells became thin, and grow thinner constantly.

Harvesting Corn.

In cutting up corn, either cut *close* to the ground, or leave stubs six or eight inches long. The buts are worth nothing for feeding, and though good for manure, may be ignored, since they are turned-under at the first plowing. Corn stubs eight inches long, with the great, gnarly root attached, are in the way of subsequent cultivation. If the land is put in grain, and grass follows, they often interfere with the haying for a year or two. To remedy this, either cut close, or, as we said, leave long stubs. These may be broken off by hauling some flat drag over the field after the ground is frozen. If the piece is to be plowed this autumn, cut close to the ground. We have used various implements for cutting up corn, and the public has settled upon two or three patterns of corn knives as the best. The writer prefers a good little hoe, ground sharp, with a handle about 14 inches long. The clip should be made a little upward, as it cuts easier, but no great outlay of strength is required, even if the cut be made square across.

When the corn is all well glazed, cut and set

up in shocks, spread out at the buts so as to brace the shock against high winds from whichever way they may come. If the shocking jack or "corn shocker" is not used, it saves time to make the shock around a standing hill.

The shocking jack is a smooth pole 12 feet long, with two legs about 4 feet from the but end, spread so as to brace it well. This will stand firmly with its small end on the ground. The big end should be about four feet from the ground, and a foot from this end a hole is bored, through which a stout pin, two feet long, is put. This pin forms a support around which the corn stalks are set up, and when the shock is finished and bound at the top, the pin is pulled out and the jack taken away. It is very desirable that the shock should be very tightly bound, as it is otherwise liable both to blow over and to become wet inside. A straw band can not be put on tight enough, generally, and several contrivances to aid in binding are illustrated in the *Agriculturist*. See page 343, (Nov.,) 1865. The difficulty is not in tight binding so much as in gathering the tops in closely before the band is put around. To do this perhaps the best contrivance is a hickory pin with a crank on one end, and a rope attached near the crank. There are knots on the rope at about the distance required to go around the top of the shock. The pin is thrust through the shock, the rope passed around and made fast by one of the knots holding in a slot in the end which passes through the handle. The crank being turned, the rope is tightened up and the shock made ready to be bound with straw.

Silk Culture—New Silk Worms.

Textile fabrics are essential to our present civilization; trade in them constitutes a large part of the commerce of the world, and their manufacture creates and sustains varied and extensive industries, both among the most enlightened, and among semi-barbarous nations. Silk goods are of all such fabrics the most beautiful, the most costly, and the most durable. It is probable also that in their manufacture there is employment given to proportionally more people and more capital than in making any other class of goods. For several years, a terrible epidemic disease has destroyed the silk worms of France, and this extended into Spain, spread over Piedmont, then Lombardy, and the rest of Italy; then it attacked the establishments of Turkey, Asia Minor, and Syria, and from these countries on it spread, and continues to diffuse itself among the silk-growing countries of Asia. The French and others obtained healthy eggs from each of these countries in succession before the disease occurred in them, and thus their manufactures are sustained, but bringing the eggs into the contaminated feeding buildings, the worms are infected, and though they produce silk, yet it is diminished in quantity and quality, and the eggs of the moth, if laid at all, are worthless. The disease is called "Pebrine," and no little anxiety is beginning to be felt for the fate of silk industries, as it appears probable the time will soon come that no more eggs can be obtained. This has led to the close study of all other silk-spinning caterpillars, spiders, etc. The result has been the introduction into France of two insects which give some promise—the Ailanthus and the Tussch moths. The former of these, under the name of Ailanthus silk-worm, has been repeatedly alluded to in the *American Agriculturist*, and numerous experiments were made with it in this country, with such poor success, however, that the culture has been abandoned by most experimenters, so far as we are informed. (See Vol. XX, 1861, page 81; also Vol. XXIV, 1865, pages 76 and 238.)

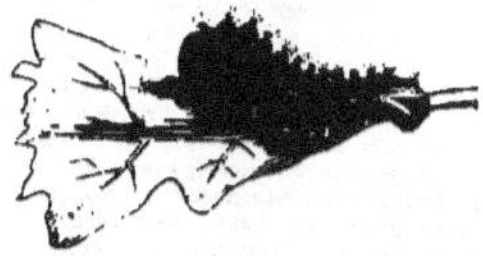

Fig. 2.—WORM AFTER SECOND MOULTING.

Fig. 3.—FULL-GROWN CATERPILLAR.

The Japanese variety of the Tussch moth, (*Antheræa Yama-mai*,) coming, as it does, from a cool country, is the one held in most esteem by M. Guerin Meneville, who has done more towards this important investigation than any one else. The silk of both of these insects is used in China and Japan in the manufacture of an inferior class of goods to that made from the true silk-worm, (*Bombyx mori*.) It is of a brownish color, lacking in brilliancy, and, as usually prepared, the goods made from it have a fuzzy exterior, but are possessed of great durability. Still it is silk, and as such, could it be profitably raised, the fabrics would find an important place among our manufactures. Some qualities of it are carded, mixed with cotton, and spun on cotton machinery into a very durable and handsome cloth.

Fig. 1.—PERFECT INSECT.

The cocoons of these two kinds of silk-worms are quite different, and while the silk of the Ailanthus is very hard—almost impossible—to reel off without constantly breaking, and can only be prepared for spinning by carding, that of the Japanese Tussch moth is much more easily wound off. Considerable success has attended the domestication of the Ailanthus silk-worm in France, and an Ailanthus farm has been sanctioned by the emperor, and conducted by M. Guerin Meneville. A few years ago, this gentleman felt a good deal discouraged about acclimating this insect, but from the reports of the Paris Exposition, we infer that he has had, of late, better success. Experiments enough have been made to prove the Japanese Tussch moth hardy in France, and hopes are entertained that it may be domesticated upon the low oaks, and live upon them as the Ailanthus worm does upon the tree, the name of which it bears. Should it prove that either of these insects will do well anywhere in this country, with comparatively little care, and that, when once established in an Ailanthus or Oak plantation, the trees will year after year bear their crop of cocoons, we may yet raise silk instead of wool, and be independent of dog-laws, except to protect the interests of our mutton raisers. It will be a long time, however, before we shall substitute silk for wool for economy.

Fig. 1 represents the perfect Tussch moth of Japan; Fig. 2 the worm in the third month after its second moulting; Fig. 3 the full grown caterpillar of the natural size, and Fig. 4 shows the cocoon. We believe that successful efforts have been made to breed this silk-worm in the United States, but at present have no facts to present in regard to the results. We copy the engravings, and are indebted for some of the statements to Andrew Murray, Paris exhibition correspondent of the Illustrated London News.

Fig. 4.—COCOON.

A Milking Stool.

The following description of a milking stool is sent by Mr. Benj. F. Wilbur, whose address we have mislaid. He considers it preferable to any other he has tried.

Take a piece of 1½ inch pine plank, 10 or 12 inches wide, and 2 feet long. Put in four legs, in such a manner as to bring the surface of one end of the plank 4 inches, and the other 6 inches high. Then take two strips, 10 inches long, 2

MILKING STOOL.

inches wide at one end, and 3 inches wide at the other. Nail these strips on the edges of the high end of the plank, putting the narrow end of the strips at the upper end of the plank. On these strips nail a board for a seat. This brings the seat level, and leaves a clean platform for the pail, and by its being slanting, inclines the pail towards the cow. It brings the pail at a convenient distance from the ground, relieves the milker from holding it between his knees, and gives freedom to the feet and legs.

INCOME FROM THE DOG TAX IN ENGLAND.—The licenses numbered nearly 700,000 in 1867, against nearly 409,000 in 1866, and in Scotland 80,000 against 36,000 in 1866. This increase in the number of licenses is not to be attributed to any increase in the number of the dogs, but to the more faithful execution of the law. Estimating the taxed dogs in Ireland at 220,000, it would make the whole number for the United Kingdom about 1,000,000. As the tax is twelve shillings, it would make the income about $3,000,000 in gold. The number of dogs in this country is estimated at 7,000,000, and a like tax, ($3 each,) upon them by our national government, would give us $21,000,000 of revenue. This would help pay our national debt, and be a great relief to sheep owners.

Remedy for the Worn-Out Lands of the West.

The cultivator of the river bottoms and of the prairies, where corn has been grown for fifty years in succession, may smile at the idea of exhausted lands, and yet they are to be found in his region, if not in his immediate vicinity. There is much land in Ohio and Indiana, back from the bottoms, that will not yield, this year, more than thirty or forty bushels of corn to the acre—lands that when they were first cleared were good for seventy or eighty bushels. They are not so much exhausted as the New England hill-sides, where nothing but Mullein and Johnswort, Penny Royal and Five-fingers, will grow, yet much of their fertility has gone, and they yield small profit to the owners. The land that produces only half a crop, is what we call worn-out or exhausted. A large part of the cultivated farms in the older Western States, is already in this condition. It has been brought about by constant cropping with grain, and returning no manure. Corn, wheat, oats, and grass, have followed each other in constant succession, and nothing has been done to improve the soil. The whole management has been with reference to immediate profit, and the expectation of soon selling the farm.

The remedy for this is permanent occupation and a course of husbandry that looks to the increasing productiveness of the soil. We commend to the careful study of this class of farmers, the rotation of crops followed in Pennsylvania, and noticed in our August issue. For the kind of farming pursued in the grain districts of the West, we know of nothing better, and we would only change it in introducing barn cellars or sheds, for the saving and composting of manures.

Lime comes in as a part of this rotation, and in many parts of the West lime rock is quite as abundant as in Pennsylvania, and it can be manufactured quite as cheaply. The same kind of lime rock exists along the line of the railroads in Ohio, where cuttings had been made, and more than half of the State of Indiana is underlaid by lime. Coal, too, abounds, often in the same districts, and where it does not, wood is plenty, and often burned in immense piles to get it out of the way. As we have shown in our September issue, the burning of lime is a very simple process, and any one who can manufacture charcoal, can manage a lime stack. This article is needed upon these partially worn soils, and would work very beneficial changes. In connection with this, or without it, if lime cannot be had, clover should be used as a part of the course. We were surprised to see so few clover fields in the West. The value of the plant as a renovator of the soil is not at all understood in that region. For the class of lands indicated, it is the most remunerative crop that can be sown. It makes good fodder. The seed brings a good price in market. Above all, it is a most valuable renovator of the soil, whether it be fed off or turned under with the plow. More clover means more wheat, more corn, more cattle; and more cattle means more manure and richer land, if the farmer will see to it. Any one who can estimate the difference between thirty and seventy bushels of corn to the acre can tell whether this kind of farming will pay.

The Osage Orange as a Hedge Plant.

This plant has been more extensively tried for hedges at the West, than any other, and with fair success. The verdict of the people is by no means unanimous in its favor, nor was this to be expected in a region where labor is very scarce, and where the training of hedges was an art to be learned. North of forty-two degrees of north latitude, the plant is tender and is liable to be injured during the winter, making sad breaks in the hedge row. We recently passed through the State of Indiana, and were agreeably surprised to see the popularity of this hedge. The plant everywhere seemed in perfect health, and the only fault noticeable was the rampant growth of the hedges. In many cases they had been left to their own course, and had formed a dense screen twenty or thirty feet high. The only fault found with it that we heard of was that it did not make a tight hedge—to keep out pigs and fowls. This we think is entirely owing to the neglect of training in the early stages of growth. It is thought entirely practicable by the friends of this hedge to make it hog proof. Messrs. Fowler & Earl, of Lafayette, Ind., have recently planted many miles of this hedge upon their large farm in Benton County, pursuing the following method:

As the farm was located in a new country, they put the line of the outside hedge 30 feet from the line of ownership, to make room for a highway. The turf was broken as for corn in the month of June, for ten feet on each side of the proposed hedge. The following May it was harrowed and back furrowed, and one-year-old plants set out on the line, 9 inches apart. The ground for the whole twenty feet is kept cultivated for three years. Then the plants are about one-half cut off, 3 or 4 inches above the surface of the ground, as shown in the illustration. They are bent over at an angle of 45 degrees, and new shoots start from the stumps, crossing the inclined stems and making a very compact fence. This method was pub-

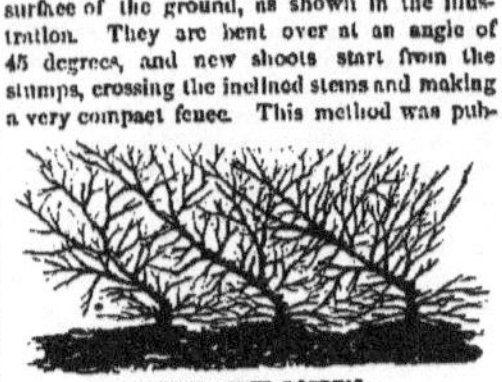

HEDGE AFTER LOPPING.

lished in the *Agriculturist* several years ago, and it is pretty good evidence of its value that it has been adopted by these gentlemen on so large a scale. The Osage Orange hedge can be planted for twenty-five cents a rod, including the preparation of the soil. At three years old it is estimated that the hedge will cost 63 cents a rod. This makes a cheap and durable fence, and answers the purpose of a screen as well.

Storing Root Crops.

Heavy frosts often come the last of this month, and it is quite important that sugar beets and mangels should be housed before the crowns are frozen. Carrots and turnips are not damaged by light freezing, and often grow through the month of November in this latitude, and the only risk in leaving them out is in the sudden setting in of winter. The earlier potatoes are put in a dark cellar after they get their growth the better. They should be stored in small bins where they can be examined easily for the first indications of rot. The tops of turnips, beets, and carrots, make excellent feed for cows, and if the pastures fail they will be found a welcome addition to their bill of fare. They will pay for curing, as one cannot turn the cows into the field where they are grown. The practice of feeding roots in the winter is steadily gaining in all the Eastern States.

Sauer Kraut.

Our native Americans turn up their noses at this preparation of cabbage, and many do at the article itself, no matter how it may be dressed for the table. Yet cabbage is a great institution, and is growing in favor among all classes of laboring people. As an adjunct of the farmer's boiled dinner it is indispensable. The Sauer Kraut is a convenient preparation of the article, easily made, and easily preserved for use where the fresh article cannot be had. By our German fellow citizens it is generally preferred to the cole-slaw, or boiled cabbage.

To save the labor of cutting it by hand, various machines are employed, one of which, simple, and easily made at home, is thus described by a German correspondent: "Common corn knives are used for the cutting part of the machine, and are fitted into a bed plate, or frame, fig. 1. This consists of a heavy oak plank with ledges, shown also in end view in fig. 3, upon the sides,) and a hole beneath the knives to allow the cut cabbage to drop through. A suitable notch is cut in the ledges to allow of fastening in the knives, which are fixed at the desired angle by means of wooden plugs or wedges. The corn knives, figure 2, are ¼ of an inch thick on the back, and are preferred to a piece of scythe, as they do not bend. Fig. 3 gives the complete machine in perspective; *A* is a box, upon each side of which are the slats, *b*, *b*. It will be seen by the examination of the end view of fig. 3, that the parts *b*, *b*, belong to the box, and those marked *c*, *d*, are attached to the frame. This box enables one to hold the cabbage firmly, and should run freely backward and forward." It is well, though our correspondent does not mention it, to have a wooden follower to fit the box, and thus avoid all danger to the hands when the cabbage is pressed down. The box should be of the size to hold a large cabbage, and the frame long enough to go across a barrel or tub.

Fig. 1.—FRAME WITH KNIVES.

Fig. 2.—CORN-KNIFE.

Fig. 3.—MACHINE COMPLETE.

For making the kraut, select the most solid and perfect heads, and after splitting them, remove the stalks and the green leaves. They are then passed over the knives and cut fine. A tight barrel, perfectly clean, is then lined with cabbage leaves at the bottom, and a little way up the sides. A layer of about three inches of the sliced cabbage is then put in and pressed with the hand, and about four tablespoonfuls of salt are sprinkled over it. After four layers are put in and salted in this way, it is pressed down with a wooden rammer as closely as it can be packed. Then follow four more layers and a ramming, and so on until the barrel is nearly full. It should be pounded so hard that the juice of the cabbage and the melting salt will appear on top. Cover with cabbage leaves and with a board or follower, and press down with a heavy stone. Set the barrel away to ferment, and in about three weeks remove the top scum and brine, and add enough water to keep the kraut covered. In four weeks it will be fit for use. It needs a little looking to occasionally, and will keep good for a year or more. The taste is a little peculiar at first, but is much relished by people who have become accustomed to it.

Notes on Grapes and Grape Culture.

These notes are written just at the close of a season, which, at the East, has been an unprecedentedly rainy one. This unusually humid state of the atmosphere and soaked condition of the soil has not only had the effect to retard ripening, but it has given every advantage to rot, mildew, and some kinds of insects. Fortunately this moist condition has not extended far inland, and whatever of ill may befall the crops there will not be entirely due to this cause. We hear of disastrous rot to the Catawba, and to a considerable extent to the Concord, while the Delaware promises better than it has for several years. A letter from Hammondsport informs us that the prospect for the grape crop is unusually fine at that point, and no complaint is made of rot. It is worth while to consider if this exemption is not due to the remarkable natural drainage of the land at Hammondsport. A loose soil of indefinite depth, intersected every few rods by deep ravines, presents natural advantages rarely to be found. It is, however, too early to judge of the general grape crop, as we usually hear of the failures sooner than we do of the successes.

In looking over a file of letters, all asking questions upon some points in grape culture, we find that the majority of them indicate that the writer has an insufficient knowledge of the way in which a vine grows and bears its fruit. It is impossible for us to give space to answer these individual cases. Every one who has vines should have one of the many excellent works now before the public. There is scarcely any one of them that does not set forth the essential principles of vine pruning, though some do it more in detail than others. To one fond of horticulture, we can conceive no more interesting amusement than the systematic training of a few vines by different methods.

Two correspondents have vines that have blossomed for two or more years, but have failed to bear fruit. As we are not given the names of the varieties, we infer that some peddler has imposed upon them some of our wild vines, which are very often infertile. The shortest way is to dig up the barren vines and put good ones in their places. We have often referred to the dangerous practice of over-bearing, and repeat the caution in view of a letter now before us in which the writer boasts that some of his vines, two years planted, have sixty bunches of fruit upon them. What wonder would it be if we should hear next year that these vines are poor growers and poor bearers?

Grapes are too often prematurely picked; they should be left on the vine until thoroughly ripe. The coloring alone should not be relied upon, as many kinds become colored before they are within a week or two of perfect ripeness. The taste must aid the eye in this matter, and each variety should be left upon the vine until it has acquired the sweetness and flavor and tenderness of pulp belonging to it—characters which will differ in degree according to the quality of the grape. Fruit for wine-making should be left on the vines as long as it is safe to do so, on account of frosts.

Preserving grapes in winter is a point asked about by many. The grapes must be well ripened and laid for a week or two in a cool room. They should not be allowed to shrivel, but only to part with a share of their moisture. The skin becomes tough, and they are then ready to pack in small boxes holding five or ten lbs. The room in which they are kept should be at a low and uniform temperature, as low as may be, without danger of freezing. Grape packers have houses for the purpose, built like an ice-house, with double walls filled with some non-conducting materials. Some varieties will not keep at all, while the Catawba, Diana, Iona, and Isabella, (if well ripened), may be kept for several months in excellent condition. To inquirers about raisin grapes, we reply, that we have not as yet any native grape that may be profitably made into raisins.

Packing Nursery Trees.

In the best nurseries the trees are packed in boxes instead of in bales, in the old way. Mr. J. W. Haggard sends us a model of a contrivance for facilitating packing. It consists of a standard, fig. 1, which has an iron foot to go under the box, and at the upper end a slot is cut, through the sides of which passes an iron pin which can be moved higher or lower as needed. This standard is placed near one of the cross cleats of the box, the trees put in, and then pressed down by a long lever which hooks under the pin in the standard, as shown in figure 2. A smaller lever is attached to the long one, and has a curved end. By pressing down on this, its curved end will crowd against the sides of the box and bring them together, so that the cleats on which the cover is to be nailed can be fastened in place. Mr. H. states that he finds this a great improvement over the usual method of bringing the sides of the box in place by means of a screw clamp.

Fig. 1.

Fig. 2.—LEVER FOR PACKING TREES.

A Group of Orchids.

Many who look at the engraving on the next page will probably think that the artist has indulged in caricature, and attempted to present a group of flowers as unlike flowers as he could, and has even tried to make some of them assume the shape of insects. But this is no fancy sketch. It is a copy of a faithful painting, made by the well known artist Hayes, and could we give the colors as well as the forms, the picture would be still more striking. Most of the flowers, if not all, from which Mr. Hayes made his studies, were from the Orchid House of our friend I. Buchanan, at Astoria, Long Island.

For the Orchis family, or Orchids, there is no popular name, though, as many of them grow upon limbs of trees, and will flourish without any connection with the earth, they are often called air-plants—a name which is not distinctive enough, as other plants live in the same manner, and many of the Orchids are terrestrial. *Orchis*, the genus which gives its name to the family, retains its ancient Greek name. The family contains some four hundred genera, and numbers its species by thousands. In the Northern States we have about fifty species, all of them terrestrial; some of these are of great beauty, such as the Showy Lady's Slipper, figured in July last. The warm, moist regions of the East and West Indies, and the dense forests of Central and South America furnish the species that are so prized in cultivation, and which astonish us with the brilliant color and strange shapes of their flowers, and often delight us with the delicacy of their odor. Some of our own orchids are found in cultivation in Europe, but we have seldom seen them in collections here. Our *Arethusa bulbosa* and *Calopogon pulchellus* are really beautiful, as are all the *Cypripediums*. Several of the *Platantheras* are showy.

It would require too much of a botanical description, to show the peculiarities that distin-

A GROUP OF ORCHIDS.—ENGRAVED FOR THE AMERICAN AGRICULTURIST, AFTER A PAINTING FROM NATURE BY W. J. HAYES,

guish the Orchids. In a general way, it may be stated that the flowers are irregular, and that one of the petals is usually of a form strikingly different from the others. This is called the lip, and it is often fringed, cut, or curiously dilated. In the Lady's Slipper, already referred to, it forms a large bag or sac. There is usually but one stamen (sometimes two), which is curiously joined with the pistil, and forms what is called the *column*. The pollen, instead of being a fine powder, as in most plants, is all united into a coherent pear-shaped mass.

The mimetic tendency of the flowers of some Orchids is remarkable, and they imitate the shapes of insects and spiders so closely, that those strong in the belief that animals originally sprung from plants, might look upon some of the Orchids as plants well on their way towards developing as spiders, butterflies, etc. One of the most conspicuous is the Butterfly Orchis, *Oncidium*, of which two species are shown, one in the lower part of the picture, and the other at the right hand, as well as at the top. The parts of the flower represent an insect's wings, and long feelers. Still more striking, as well as more rare, is the white flower in the upper part of the engraving; here the parts of the flower form a shell-like cup of the purest white, within which is the column, shaped so like a dove as to require no imagination to help out the resemblance. In Central America, this is called El Spirito Santo, or Holy Ghost plant, from the association of the form of the dove with the artistic attempts to represent the Holy Spirit.

It was formerly supposed that Orchids could only be grown in a house of high temperature, but of late years it has been found that many of these do as well, or even better, under what is called the cool treatment, and now some very fine species are successfully cultivated at the ordinary green-house temperature. This being the case, we hope to see them less rare.

Going into Winter Quarters.

Every lover of flowers looks with regret upon his pets as the cool nights warn him that frosts will soon desolate them, and naturally wishes to prolong the enjoyment of them through the winter. So he pots his favorites, and at the approach of cold weather, brings them indoors, in anticipation of a continued bloom. Soon the leaves drop, the buds wither, and the plant is an object of pity rather than of admiration. It is in vain to expect roses, etc., to bloom all summer and all winter too; the plants must have rest. So with the half shrubby things, such as geraniums, heliotropes, and the like; if taken up just as they have grown during the summer and transferred to the house, they are pretty sure to bring disappointment. All such plants should have been trained in a compact, bushy shape, with a view to their removal, and should have been potted early enough to have become established before taking them in. Those who have plants which they intend to keep in the dwelling during winter, should make the removal gradually. First place them under a veranda or other shelter, then remove them to a room where there is no fire, and only subject them to a heated atmosphere when there is danger of the temperature of the room falling below 45 or 40 degrees.

Those who are tired of trying to flower plants in the dry air of our often over-heated dwellings, can still derive much enjoyment from growing plants for foliage only. These can be grown in pots, window boxes, rustic or other stands, and hanging baskets. In either or all of these ways they will give a room an air of cheerfulness, and if the foliage be kept clean, a well developed mass of it will be much more satisfactory than poorly grown flowers.

Fig. 1.—IVY-LEAVED GERANIUM.

Fig. 2.—TRADESCANTIA ZEBRINA.

We have often alluded to the use of Ivy for this purpose, than which nothing can be more satisfactory not only for its hardiness but for its beauty. In all these internal decorations it should be freely used. We have before noted other suitable plants for this purpose, and now have a few to add to the list. A very good plant is the old Ivy-leaved Geranium or Pelargonium, (*P. lateripes*), fig. 1, which in its trailing habit and smooth, Ivy-like leaves is so dissimilar to other geraniums. In good soil, and with plenty of sun, it will grow luxuriantly and give pleasure not only by the beauty of its foliage, but by its neat, though not very showy flowers.

Another plant often used for hanging baskets is the Moneywort, (*Lysimachia nummularia*). Its round, bright green leaves are produced abundantly along the flexible stems, and it makes a pleasing effect where the room is not too warm. Figure 3 shows a stem in flower, but does not represent as abundant foliage as is borne on those which do not flower.

We give in figure 2, a small branch of the natural size of a common green-house plant, *Tradescantia zebrina*. This will grow in our hottest rooms, and will endure everything but freezing. It has a remarkable tenacity of life, and as its branches root at every joint, it is propagated with ease. The foliage is of a silvery-green, marked with brownish stripes. This is one of the most useful plants for growing indoors. By the tasteful use of these and similar plants, the dwelling will have a cheerful look, an appearance which may be enhanced by the introduction of a Wardian case, some styles of which are given on page 360, while others can be made of panes of glass set in a frame.

Market Gardening at the South.

The cultivation of vegetables at various points in the Southern States had become established before the war; but like many other kinds of industry, it was totally prostrated. It is now reviving, and only needs capital and intelligent labor to make it a leading interest in those States. Thanks to the wide diversity of climate our country presents, and the ready means of transportation furnished by steam, the season of fresh vegetables and fruits is, in our large cities, greatly prolonged, if not doubled. New York, for instance, draws its supplies from a long distance—beginning with far off Bermuda, then, a little later, from South Carolina, Georgia, Maryland, and Delaware, and finally Southern New Jersey pours in its products before the market gardens near the city are able to supply the demand. A gentleman familiar with the subject, writes us the following concerning the peculiar advantages presented by Norfolk, Va., to those who would engage in market gardening. What is said about Norfolk will apply to many other localities both south and north of that point. "The advantages for this kind of farming which Norfolk presents, are somewhat peculiar and very attractive. The season is about three weeks earlier than that of New York, from which it is only twenty-four hours distant by the regular steamers, and still nearer Philadelphia and Baltimore. Norfolk has the command of three of the best markets in the country, and is connected with them by lines of steamers and in part by rail.

Fig. 3.—MONEYWORT.

It can put all its early products into these markets in the best condition, and realize very high prices for them. Then the soil about Norfolk is a sandy loam, and matures its products with great rapidity. A glance at the map will show that the bay has many arms and creeks running up into the land for several miles. These creeks are navigable for scows and lighters, so that it is very easy for a farmer having a front upon the water to transport his vegetables many miles, and put them immediately on board the steamer, within a few hours of the time of her sailing. This materially diminishes the cost of marketing. Such rare natural advantages have been to some extent appreciated, and a large business has been done. But the demand for early vegetables and fruits is so great, and the prices are so remunerative that, with sufficient skill and capital, the business may be increased many fold, to the advantage of both consumer and producer.

Owing to the desolations of the war and the uncertainty that has hung over Virginia politics, land is still cheap in this region. It can be bought sufficiently near the city for truck farming from $50 to $300 an acre, according to the character of the improvements upon it. Land can be rented for about ten dollars an acre, though the owners generally prefer to sell. Cultivators need both more skill and more capital to make their business pay better. The season of renting begins with the year, and the plowing and other preparations for a crop commence as soon after as the weather will admit. The plowing is performed in pleasant weather all through the winter. The manure most used is of the most expensive kind, street and stable manure, and much of it is brought from Baltimore in vessels. This is applied at the rate of about five full cords to the acre. As this article costs a dollar and a quarter a load in Baltimore, and as much more for freight, it becomes a very expensive fertilizer by the time it is delivered upon the field. Stable manure can be had in Portsmouth and in Norfolk for about a dollar and a quarter a load, the carting to be done by the purchaser, but the supply is quite limited. Guano is sometimes used for forcing, and bone-dust on special crops, which pays well. A good article of superphosphate and fish guano would pay much better on these lands than stable manure. Night soil, sea weed, and sea mud, which might be had easily, are not much used. The great want of this whole region is more manure and of better quality.

The planting season opens early in February, and peas are put in as soon as the soil is fit, and early potatoes immediately follow. These, with cucumbers, tomatoes, beans, cabbages, squashes, and strawberries, are the crops most largely raised. Melons are grown a good deal, but are exceedingly liable to depredations on the way. The farmer begins to forward articles to market by the 1st of May, and by the 15th of August the season is mainly over, and he begins to look around him and plan for another year. Hay, oats, and corn, do well enough, and there is no difficulty in growing what forage is needed for stock. The products of the farm are generally sold in the cities that we have named, on about ten per cent. commission, and the commission merchant makes his returns once a week. This makes a cash business, and the farmer is not out of pocket for his outlay in manures more than four or five months. A part of the help is employed by the year, but in the picking season large numbers of women and children are employed by the job. Good laborers can be had for about twenty dollars per month, with house-rent and fire-wood. Horses and mules are principally used for teams. There are many details of the business that vary so much with different individuals, that no satisfactory account of them can be given here. The profits are considered very satisfactory by those engaged in the business.

Where is the Mixing of Varieties Shown?

Some remarks on this subject in the August *Agriculturist*, have called out the following note from the botanist whose initials will be readily recognized. We know of no one more able to thoroughly investigate this subject, and hope it will receive his attention. It is one of immediate practical interest to every fruit grower.

"As to where the mixing of varieties is shown, I would first ask, why should it be in the seed rather than in the seed-vessel or fruit? Of course we expect the mixture to be shown in the offspring, that is, in the next generation, the principle being that the offspring inherits from both parents. But the seed is not the offspring; it only contains the offspring in an embryo state. If the alien pollen may impress some peculiarity on the coats of a seed—which are a part of the mother-plant—why not upon the seed-vessel as well?

So much for the likelihood of the case. It appears to be well settled that the coats of beans are thus affected. It is generally supposed that the fruits or seed-vessels of melons and squashes are similarly affected. Careful observation and experiment ought to determine the question.

Now in the case of certain plants of the squash family, Naudin found, if I remember correctly, that alien pollen which would not act on the ovules so as to cause an embryo to be produced at all, would yet cause the fruit to set and grow apparently to full size, though not a seed matured within. Does not this prove that the pollen may somehow act on the ovary or pistil as well as on the contained ovules?" A. G.

Apples—American Pomology.

BY LEWIS F. ALLEN, BLACK ROCK, N. Y.

As Doct. Warder's work on Apples was published by the proprietors of the *Agriculturist*, we have not noticed it at the length its importance demands, and we give place to the following communication from so well-known a writer as the Hon. L. F. Allen, the more readily, that while it is an entirely unsolicited tribute to the value of the work, it is a forcible and seasonable plea for apple culture.

"We like this book—for several reasons: It is written by one who knows whereof he writes; it takes the seed, and plants, grows, and cultivates it into a tree for transplanting; it selects the soil, prepares it in the proper way, takes the tree from the nursery, plants it and trains it until it bears; it then shows to what particular uses either variety of the fruit is best applied, how to pick it, and how to preserve it till it is used. All these are told in a practical, thorough manner, that the merest neophyte may understand, and work upon. It also describes the proper soils, elevations, and positions for orchards,—the modes of draining, where it is needed, and the whole system in all its minutest parts.

The book also talks of insects; and not only talks of, but describes them, and the best ways of preventing, or getting rid of them. It classifies the different varieties of the fruits as to size, shape, color, taste, and quality, and also the habits of the different trees—all essential to be understood by the orchardist. In short, it tells the whole story throughout, in all that is necessary to be known by either the professed grower of apples for market, the amateur, or the small lot owner who grows only for family use.

This is an *apple* book only, and we like it all the better for that, because it is mixed with nothing else, and one's attention in reading is not diverted to a dozen or twenty other fruits, which, in our opinion, are much better to be treated distinctly, by themselves. Apples are not only an important staple in our agricultural productions, but are growing more important every year; and the time is not far distant when even large farmers in our country will make orchards their *specialty*, and rely upon them, as others do on their grain crops, their neat stock, their wool, and their dairies, for a living and revenue.

There are already well known sections of our wide spread country where apple orchards are much more productive, to the acre, and steadily productive too, than any other crops the farmer can raise, let the crop or the price fluctuate as it may; and knowing these facts, the fortunate holders of such land will appropriate considerable portions of them to apple growing. There are also other extended regions where apples are a precarious or contingent crop, and where they will only be grown for family use. Orchards, as a crop, will pay little or nothing on such soils, and with such fitful bearing that it will be no object to attend to them. These facts, with observation and experience, will become better known than now, and the more men observe, and read, the sooner will they know to what extent, and with what success and profit they can cultivate them.

To come to the thing practically, he who lives far from water communication, or a rail-way, or where rail-ways are not likely to be made—no matter how applicable his soil and climate may be for the purpose, will not go extensively into apple growing, unless for cider or vinegar, for the reason that he cannot get his fruit to market cheaply, nor, from the jolting of wagons, with safety to its good keeping; while he who enjoys such advantages can just as safely embark in the business as in any other branch of cultivation. Every one need not suppose he can do so successfully, even with the best advantages of soil and locality. Every one has not a taste for the pursuit. A good pomologist must be somewhat of an enthusiast. He must have a natural taste for the pursuit primarily, and then a fund of acquired knowledge to be a successful apple grower. He must know what varieties best suit his soil, and that is to be ascertained by observation and trial. Let him see what good varieties flourish and give the best and surest crop in his vicinity. Some kinds flourish well in one soil and position, while others, perhaps equally good, do not succeed at all.

The apple, in many of its best varieties, like almost every kind of fruit, is somewhat capricious in its preference, not only of soil, but of position, and climate; and of this fact too many of those who strive to be orchardists on a considerable scale, appear to have been profoundly ignorant in their early attempts at planting. They looked upon an apple simply as an apple, irrespective of what variety it might be, or in what climate or soil it originated. Our best varieties have originated in various parts of the United States. Pretty much all of them were *American* seedlings, for we have not a dozen kinds which came across the Atlantic that are worth propagating. The nearer a really *good* apple is grown to the place of its origin, the better, as a rule, it is. For instance, the Newtown Pippin, once the best apple in our New York markets, originated on Long Island, and was chiefly cultivated there, and along the lower section of the Hudson River, and the contiguous parts of New Jersey, and seldom grows anywhere else in perfection. It is now the scarcest *good* apple to be found with us. It has been introduced, to be sure, and grows extensively, east, north, south, and west of us. In those distant localities it has ceased to be *the* Newtown Pippin *of Long Island*, but is quite another thing, hardly to be recognized in either appearance or flavor, by those not intimately acquainted with its original character. So with the Swaar, of Ulster Co., N. Y., the Greening, of Rhode Island, the Roxbury Russet, the Westfield Seek-no-further, of Massachusetts, and many other varieties which originated and flourished in peculiar localities, and of great local excellence and fame. Still, there are many good varieties which hold their original qualities over a wide diversity of soil, climate, and position.

Thus it is that we have so many varieties, sundry of which are favorites in separate markets, each the best for a given locality, and worth very little, as profitable fruits for the cultivator, far beyond them. It becomes a matter of necessity, then, for the orchardist to know what are the best apples for him to grow; and when he ascertains such fact, to take his proper kinds, and cultivate them with all his might.

Those who aspire to become orchardists are prone to grow too many varieties. Ten or a dozen, to range through the various seasons of ripening, are enough for the most ambitious cultivators to plant. Two or three of early, three or four of autumn, and as many of the winter kinds, are sufficient, for the profit of any apple grower who rears them as a market crop, and if the bulk of his winter crop be confined to not more than two varieties, all the better. For early apples, the season is short, and the market limited. One good sweet, and another tart, is enough for the brief time they are in season. Three or four, from September until the middle of November, or the first of December at latest—sweet and tart—will fill the range of demand, when the winter kinds will come in use, from December until the next June or July; and half a dozen of the later varieties will fill the entire season.

We do not say what these varieties should be, for the very reason we have given, that soils, climates, and positions so differ as to make an apple which is quite good for one locality, altogether an indifferent one for another. Find out a few of the very best kinds for the place you occupy, and the market you are to sell in, and then confine your attention to them. A man with fifty things in his orchard, all good *somewhere*, will, perhaps, on trial, hardly find a dozen which give him either profit or satisfaction in their production, and at the end of a dozen or twenty years cultivation, he has to re-graft three-fourths of them, and begins the world again in fruit growing—all too expensive, vexatious, and heart-breaking, to be borne with equanimity.

We might expand into several pages of these remarks, but have not the space. We can only throw out hints for reflection. We started with Doctor Warder's book, and pronounce it a capital one of its kind, full of instruction to every one who wants to know anything of apples, or apple growing. He gives a list and description of apples, and of the best ones all over the United States, where they originated, and where they best grow. He names some twelve or fourteen hundred varieties. One quarter in number, of the best, would be quite enough, for hundreds of them have been thrown out by the growers, as not of much account, and it is useless to keep a further record of such anywhere. Yet he names a great many of unimpeachable excellence from which every one may select and apply to his own locality with success.

We wish to say more on this prolific subject, but must forbear, merely commending this book to every orchardist. Study it well, and closely. We have no interest in it other than what relates to our brother orchardists, and the welfare of good apples. We are glad that it has been written, and hail its appearance as an indication that its subject is drawing the attention of our pomologists to a degree commensurate with its great economical importance among our agricultural staples."

New Fruits and New Names.

It seems a great pity that the introduction of new fruits, or at least fruits with new names, could not in some way be regulated. It is, of course, a subject beyond the reach of any other law than that which fruit growers make unto themselves. Each year brings such an addition to our "new fruits," or rather new names, that one almost despairs of keeping pace with them. We are not to be supposed as deprecating novelties, for we like them, but we do desire, and the public have a right to claim, that these new fruits have some qualities superior to old varieties. There is too much looseness in the way in which varieties are introduced, and no nurseryman who is a true pomologist will put forth a variety that has not been thoroughly tested, or which has not been decided upon by some pomologist or pomological body competent to judge of its quality.

There is one practice that seems to be increasing among introducers of new fruits, to which we decidedly object, as tending to make confusion, and fill our books with useless synonyms. It is that of sending a fruit out under one name, and then changing it to another. A strawberry that has been offered as Abraham Lincoln, now comes to us as the President; a grape that was exhibited as the Carpenter, is now known as the Out-Door Hamburgh, and we can call to mind other instances of the like. There should be no change of name for any possible reason, save that the first one had already been given to another plant, to which it belongs by right of priority. Gentlemen fruit growers, give us as many good fruits as you can, but trouble us with as few useless names as possible.

GUARD AGAINST FROSTS.—It usually is the case that after the first few frosts we have a long succession of golden autumn days, just made for ripening fruit and bringing out the late blooming flowers. A very slight covering will protect a plant, and those who have a choice grape or tomato that is late in ripening, or Dahlias or other plants that are just in the hight of their bloom, should have at hand some screen to protect them from the first frosts. A sheet or other cloth put up tentwise, or stretched in any way over the plant, will be all that is needed. In England the amateur fruit growers have regular fixtures, upon which a covering may be stretched when the trees are in flower, as well as when the fruit is ripening.

Wine-Making on the Small Scale.

Those who wish to make wine in any considerable quantities, will, of course, study up the subject in books devoted to it. But there are many, who, having a few grapes, would like to convert them into wine for their own use, or to test the wine-making qualities of some particular variety. If the grapes contain sufficient sugar to make a good wine, the process requires but little care, as the wine will make itself, but with grapes deficient in sugar the process becomes less easy. The theory of wine-making may be briefly summed up thus: Grape juice contains sugar; fermentation converts this sugar into alcohol. If the amount of sugar and the resulting amount of alcohol be small, then further changes take place, and vinegar is the result. If, on the other hand, the grape juice or must be naturally rich in sugar, so much alcohol is produced that the liquid does not readily pass into vinegar—but remains as wine—and if there is a very large amount of sugar, more than is converted into alcohol before fermentation ceases, there will be a sweet wine—a thing not at present likely to occur with us. The first requisite is good grapes. These must be as thoroughly ripened as possible. They are to be carefully freed from defective berries, removed from the stems and crushed. With small quantities this may be done with the hands, or with larger ones, in a barrel with a wooden pounder. The steps after this will depend upon the character of wine desired. The juice may be at once pressed out and placed in the keg or demijohn in which it is to ferment, or, if it be desired to extract color and aroma from the skins, then the unpressed mass is put in a tub or other vessel, covered with a cloth over which some boards are laid, and allowed to ferment for two or three days, or until the color of the skins is sufficiently extracted. At the end of this time, press out the must, and transfer it to the vessel in which the fermentation is to be completed. This will take place in from ten days to several weeks, according to the richness of the grape, and it will go on more or less rapidly, according to the temperature of the room. A weak must will ferment readily at 60°, while a heavier one will require a higher temperature. With rich grapes, the only thing necessary is to fill the vessel to the bung or mouth, allowing the froth to be thrown over. The loss must be supplied from must kept for the purpose. If the must is poor, it is better to close the vessel with a tight bung or cork, with an India rubber tube inserted in its center. This tube, which may be a foot or two long, should have its free end dip below the surface of water in a cup conveniently placed. As fermentation goes on, the liberated gas will bubble through the water, but no air can enter.

When fermentation is complete, which will be known by the liquid becoming quiet, the vessel is to be closed and allowed to remain until the wine becomes clear. It should then be carefully racked off, or transferred to another and perfectly sweet and clean cask or vessel. Another fermentation, less violent than the first, will take place when warm weather returns, after which the wine may be bottled. If sufficient care be used, these experiments may be made on a small scale, but they need careful watching. The best specimen of American wine we ever saw was made from the Iona, by Doct. Grant, who used a demijohn for a cask, and his dining-room for a wine-cellar. The richer the must is in sugar, the more successful will these small operations prove.

Spring-flowering Bulbs—The Scillas.

There is such a freshness and delicacy about the flowers of the early blooming bulbs, that we naturally associate them with the soft showers and gentle breezes of spring, and a garden from which they are absent seems only half

SCILLA HYACINTHOIDES.

enjoyable. Those who plant bulbs seldom go beyond the usual assortment of Hyacinths, Tulips, and Crocuses. The old Crown Imperial is much less frequently met with than formerly, yet it is a grand old plant. Its bulbs and leaves, it is true, are far from fragrant, but then it throws up such a vigorous stem, and when it puts on its coronet of flowers it looks withal so stately, that we like it, even if it is not among the "novelties." We began to say a word about the Scillas, or—despite the medicinal smack the name has—the Squills. These are for the most part hardy, early blooming bulbs, with flowers of some shade of blue, or, sometimes, white. The spikes are but a few inches high, and to produce much of a show, they are best planted in a bed by themselves. The bulbs, which are quite small, are to be planted this month or next, in good, light, rich, earth, at a depth of about two inches, in the same manner that other bulbs are planted. Though most of the kinds are hardy, yet, like other bulbs, they do all the better if the bed be covered with leaves or coarse littery manure. We enumerate below the species usually kept by the bulb dealers.

S. hyacinthoides is one of the tallest species, free flowering, and of a soft, subdued blue. We saw last spring in the grounds of B. K. Bliss, at Springfield, Mass., a large bed, the effect of which was very pleasing. From this garden we obtained the specimen from which the accompanying engraving was made.

S. Sibirica is a hardy and much smaller species, with flowers of an intense blue.

S. amœna is also deep blue, and is a rather later bloomer than the preceding.

S. Peruviana is another blue species, of which there is a white variety. It is less hardy than the others, and well adapted to pot culture.

The bulbs of the Scillas do not need to be disturbed oftener than once in four or five years, when it will be necessary to take them up and divide the clumps and replant the bulbs.

Ichneumon Flies.—Pimpla Lunator.

BY EDWARD NORTON.

[Some time ago, we received from a correspondent in Indiana a specimen of an insect, which, he supposed, was injuring his trees. Indeed, from the formidable appendage borne by the insect, a stranger to its ways might be warranted to regard it with suspicion. Knowing that Mr. Norton was an enthusiastic student of this family of insects, we gave him the specimen, requesting him to furnish some notes upon it, which he does as follows.—ED.]

An insect sent from Indiana to the *Agriculturist*, for a name, by Mr. ——, proves to be a friend to the farmer instead of an enemy, as was supposed. It belongs to that large family of insects, the Ichneumonidæ, all the members of which occupy themselves in destroying other injurious insects. They are so called from the Ichneumon, formerly supposed to be a parasite upon the crocodile, and to deposit its eggs within its body, which served as food for the young when hatched. No tribe of insects is free from these parasites, which are created to keep down the excessive increase of injurious species, and are each fitted with an apparatus suited for the end proposed, as in the case before us. The borers, (or their grubs,) in trees, make their passages, in many cases, so far below the outer surface that they can be reached in no ordinary way. But certain Ichneumon flies are provided with boring instruments, long enough to probe these tunnels. These borers are hollow, and through them, when the proper spot is reached, the insect places its eggs in or near the grub, upon which the young Ichneumons may feed.

The *Pimpla* or *Rhyssa lunator* (fig. 2), belonging to the group *Pimpla* and genus *Rhyssa*, and called *lunator* from the yellow crescents across its ab-

Fig. 1.—INSECT AT WORK.

domen, is one of the largest of these. It has an ovipositor, sometimes as much as five inches in length, which, when not in use, extends straight out behind the insect, which is not more than two inches long itself, and is enclosed in two hollow sheaths of the same length. This ovipositor and borer combined is apparently quite smooth and solid, but is really composed of three parts, two of which have fine saw teeth and rasps near the end, which are used when boring. When by some wonderful instinct the insect discovers its prey within the tree, often the grubs of the *Tremex columba* or Pigeon Borer, it takes its position, (fig. 1), the head downward, and raising its abdomen as high as possible, curves its end, and bends the ovipositor so that its point touches the desired spot. As this is too long to be applied with power at once, the extra length is coiled at this time in a transparent membrane, which lies between the two last segments of the back, (marked *e* in fig. 1,) and which pushes out like a thin elastic piece of rubber, vibrating with the severe strain upon it from below. The two sheaths do not enter the tree, but rising above the back, pass down upon each side of the ovipositor to give it strength. They are held in position, and stiffened by the hinder thighs between which they pass. In this way, the ovipositor is sometimes introduced four or five inches into solid wood, although it is often pushed wholly or in part into crevices, or more or less decayed trees, such as borers inhabit. Sometimes it becomes so firmly fastened in the tree that the insect cannot withdraw it, and dies there. A friend tells me that when he could not draw this out without breaking it, he has known the insect to succeed in extracting it when left alone.

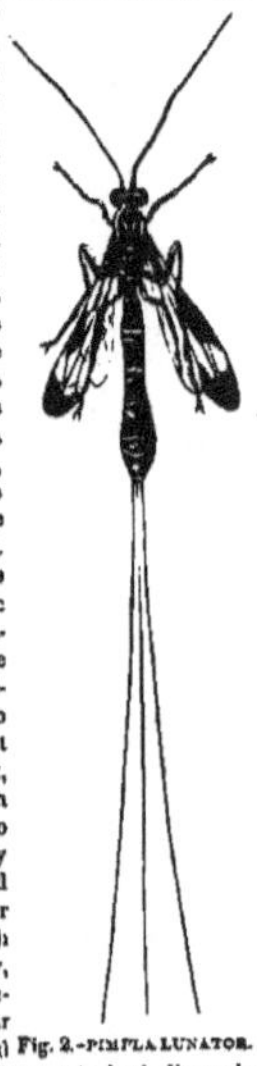

Fig. 2.—PIMPLA LUNATOR.

I had the pleasure of seeing this whole operation, as above described, performed by three insects, a few days ago, August 15th, 1867, on an oak tree in the City Park, Brooklyn. Two of them, which I captured, were smaller, with the terebra about two inches long, and worked quite rapidly, depositing the eggs in a few minutes. One, which I took, was much longer about it, and I was forced to use some strength to draw out its borer. The wood was dead, and perforated with small holes in many places, but was too solid to be penetrated with the point of a knife. The third insect which escaped, was much larger, and appeared to work more slowly from the inconvenient length of its ovipositor.

This is one of the "wheels within wheels" which we constantly see in nature. Trees, from various causes, die, and their decay is hastened by insects which tunnel the hard wood, and open it to the air, and to other insects. But lest these should become too numerous, they are followed in their deepest hiding by insects, which are parasitic in their habits, and these are often, in their turn, the prey of others.

THE HOUSEHOLD.

(☞ *For other Household Items, see "Basket" pages.*)

Household Ornaments.

The Wardian Case is one of the most entertaining and instructive of home ornaments. It is an ingenious device to keep plants in a thriving and at-

Fig. 1.—WARDIAN CASE.

tractive condition, without the constant attention which a bouquet in a vase, or growing plants in pots require. The glass which is put over the little bed of plants retains the moisture of the atmosphere and constantly returns it to the bed, so that no extra watering is required for weeks. For stocking a case, plants are usually selected that flourish in deep woods or in moist, secluded places. The fine velvety mosses which grow upon rocks, along water courses, and all the smaller ferns, especially the Maiden's hair, are admirable for this purpose. One who enters upon the study of suitable material for stocking a case will be surprised at the number and beauty of the mosses and ferns that grow in wet, unfrequented woods. The Twin or Partridge berry, (*Mitchella repens*), a trailing evergreen, with flowers growing in twos, and bright scarlet berries holding on all winter; the Adder's Tongue, *Erythronium Americanum*, with its curiously blotched leaves; the Wintergreen, *Gaultheria procumbens*; the Prince's Pine, *Chimaphila umbellata*; the Trailing Arbutus, *Epigæa repens*, fairest and sweetest of all the children of the early spring, are suitable plants for this purpose. The catalogue might be greatly extended, for almost all the plants that flourish in wet, shady localities, do well in the case. Many bulbs flourish here, and you may have your Crocuses anticipate their spring blooming out

Fig. 2. WARDIAN CASE.

of doors by planting the bulbs among the mosses.

The first thing needed is a suitable frame to hold the case. This may indeed be set upon a table or shelf, but it is much more elegant to have a stand made for the purpose, even if it be very rough rustic work. Fig. 1 shows a stand made principally with the turning lathe. The top piece is made concave so as to hold the plate of plants without showing it. The plate fits in closely, and the edge is concealed by the wooden rim of the stand. Three rounds unite the top piece and the shaft below, and this is furnished with three legs. In fig. 2 a platform under the legs makes a nice place for a pot of ivy, which may be trained gracefully about the legs or suffered to climb along the window case. A common earthen plate or shallow tin pan will serve to hold the bed for the plants. The preparation of the soil is a matter of considerable importance. Nothing is better than leaf mould or rotten wood, which is usually found in abundance with the plants. With this, pounded charcoal should be mixed in about equal parts, and a handful of sand be added. The surface should be left evenly convex to show the plants to the best advantage. The moss now goes on as the background of the picture, and the other plants are arranged according to the taste of the operator. When finished, the glass case is put over it, and you have an ornament for the fireside that will give you a fresh bit of summer all through the dreary winter. The divinity who presides in our household adds, "be sure and take off the glass case every day when you are dusting, for the space of five minutes by the clock, and no more." As this injunction is very emphatic, and her case is always the finest in the town, we advise our readers to take heed. The glasses may be had in city stores. A small aquarium, made in a jar or vase, is shown in Fig. 3. Clean white pebbles are put in the bottom of the jar, in which are placed some of the plants that live entirely under water, and which may be found in almost every pond or slow stream. *Anacharis* and *Valisneria* are very good, but any with fine foliage will do. A few small gold fish may be put in after the plants have been established for a few days. This will make a handsome ornament for the center or dining table, and may also be used to hold a bouquet.

Fig. 3.—AQUARIUM.

Leaves from the Diary of a Young House-keeper.—No. X.

PRIZE ESSAY BY MRS. LAURA E. LYMAN, STAMFORD, CT.

October 2d.—I always hail with enthusiasm the coming of this month! The air is so bracing, and Nature wears her most gorgeous livery of russet and brown and gold. She has just put on the mellow, warm tints that presage the coming frosts. Summer still lingers lovingly in the lap of autumn, arraying herself in her most fascinating garb, that we may more sadly mourn her departure. All the morning I have been in the garden gathering seeds for next spring; they are wrapped up in little packages, carefully secured with twine, labeled and put away in the seed basket for future use. Taking the hint from Edward's practice, I selected the seeds from the largest and most perfect plants, so as to improve the varieties. By continuing thus, I hope in two or three years to have the very best seed of everything which the garden produces.

October 12th.—I am in the midst of my preparations for the Fair which is to take place next week, and find myself absorbed in the very natural housewifely ambition to carry off some of the prizes which have been offered. If I fail it will not be for want of effort on my part, but because some more successful competitor has more knowledge, skill, and experience than I possess. For several days the cows have been turned into the wheat fields to feed upon the young clover that has sprung up there since harvest; this will give the butter a richer flavor and a more golden color to the butter than the pasture they have been in lately.

The abundant care I have always taken of my milk and cream is redoubled. Every day I scald my pans in hay water that they may be perfectly sweet, and watch my milk carefully, using my best judgment in removing the cream from it at just the right moment. This morning I churned, and more fragrant, golden, delicious butter I never saw in my life. I have worked it over once, and just before dark shall do so again, and mould it into the shape of a pineapple. Four of the lumps will just fill a little shallow hemlock firkin Edward bought for me, to put them in to carry to the fair. They will weigh about three pounds each. Besides my butter, I am going to take to the fair some Boston brown bread, which is quite a novelty in these parts, and my parlor rug.

October 14th.—To-day I made my brown bread. Last night I sifted two quarts of corn meal, and wet it in warm buttermilk from my last churning, and set it to soak over night. This gives it full time to swell, and extracts all the sweetness of the meal, which is fresh ground, and of this year's growth. This morning I added a pint of the best molasses, two pints and a half of rye meal, some salt, buttermilk sufficient to moisten the whole, and soda to neutralize the acid of the buttermilk. After mixing all the ingredients thoroughly, I put it into a large earthen pan and baked it three hours in a moderately heated oven, being careful to preserve the heat at a uniform temperature. A little of the dough I put in a smaller pan, and Edward declares it is the best brown bread I ever made, but suggests that, as many object to the hard crust formed over the top of the loaf by this long baking, I had better make another loaf to-morrow, and steam it in my pudding pan. There is no crust at all upon bread cooked in this way, and its flavor, too, is different from that which is baked.

My rug, which has been so much admired, and which resembles tapestry carpeting so closely that everybody takes it for an imported article, I made of carpet thrums, purchased at a carpet factory. They cost only two dollars, but such a rug as I made of them could not be purchased for less than ten dollars. My own labor in its manufacture I never count; it was a recreation from the routine of household duties. The pattern, which I made myself, is a double cornucopia, filled and overflowing with flowers of all hues and every variety. I took them from worsted patterns and varied the figure to suit my taste.

Edward is going to take two of the largest and fattest of the Chester Whites we raised with so much care last spring, and we shall carry also some of the handsomest clusters of our grapes, and the largest and finest flavored of our apples.

October 20th.—We returned last evening from the Fair, and a most delightful time we had. My butter, my bread, my rug, each drew a prize. For the butter, I received a beautiful silver cup; for the bread, a silver fruit knife; and for the rug, a silver dessert spoon. They shine on the table as I write, and much as I prize them for their intrinsic value, the honor of which they are the pledge, I rate of far more worth. My butter was pronounced by the judges as at once more beautiful in appearance, and excellent in quality, than any other at the Fair, and it was beautiful; four magnificent golden pineapples in a setting of green leaves; they looked like fruitage from the trees of Eden! The silver cup I shall keep, but the butter that took the prize I have sent as a gift to our excellent pastor.

When our hired man brought back the articles we sent to the Fair, I missed the two pigs from the farm wagon, and saw in it a big square box of pine occupying their place. Inquiring of Edward about it, he smiled in a queer way, and said, "women mustn't be too curious; the box was a little private affair of his own." I said no more, but this morning when I went down stairs, I found in the corner of my sitting room, near my sewing chair, the very same sewing machine I saw and admired so much, and which took the prize at the fair. It is a Wheeler & Wilson, just such an one as I have been wishing for. Edward came in and found me standing over it with happy tears of surprise in my eyes. "How do you like the looks of your Chester pigs?" said he. "They are more of an ornament to my sitting room than I thought pigs could be," I replied; and then he told me that the two little pigs had sold for enough, with the prize they took at the fair, to pay for the sewing machine, that I had earned it, and called me a prize wife, and other names which I shall remember, but won't write down here. Ever since I made him that vest, he said, he had intended this surprise for me in the fall, before the time for winter sewing to be done. Now I can make all his clothes, except his Sunday coats, and perhaps I shall in time learn to make even those.

Edward's sister Jane writes me a very pleasant letter, and, among other things, remarks that she has taken, since her visit to us, regular daily exercise in the open air, and is trying to learn how to keep the house in order and have a little more system in their family arrangements. I am afraid she will have a hard time, and accomplish but little in that line. Habits of order and system will be slowly superinduced upon long years of carelessness and disorder. But it is better to begin now than not at all, and she may inspire the younger members of the family with something of her own ambition, which will lead to happy results in their future households.

Sue has become almost invaluable to me; she is learning all the domestic arts, and I find her perfectly reliable. Reliability I regard as among the very first of social virtues, and, in one sense, the corner stone of them all.

October 25th.—I have been collecting for some time all the pieces of calico and woollen dress goods to make some quilts for winter use. For several days I have been busy piecing the calico into squares, and have nearly enough run together for a quilt. I shall line it with partly worn domestic, colored with tea; that is the easiest and quickest way of coloring I know of. The tea grounds of two or three days must be saved, and when there are a bowlful or so, I shall put them into my porcelain kettle, fill it with water and boil it, and after wringing the domestic in alum water to set the color, dip it in the tea dye, wring it out and hang it to dry. When ironed it will be ready for use.

Instead of marking off my quilt with chalk lines, I will do as one of my neighbors suggested: pin a piece of white domestic where I wish to quilt, and run along the edge; this saves the fingers very much in quilting. There are plenty of woollen pieces to make a quilt, and I have given them to Sue to make up for her bed. She will thus become initiated into the mystery of quilt making, and find that she can, by economy and thrift, by and by furnish her own bed by her own labor.

October 28th.—We have a few quinces this year which I have been preserving to-day. There was not more than a peck in all, so I put up a small jar only of pure quince, and selecting twice as many hard russet apples as there were quinces left, and as near the same size as I could find, I cut them up in just the same shape as the quinces, and preserved them together, and the apple is so flavored with the quince that one can hardly distinguish the two.

October 30th.—Edward brought in eight or ten pounds of honey to-day, and after putting about six pounds away in a jar, I made the rest into a delightful honey syrup for family use, which is even more agreeable than pure honey. My recipe is as follows: Dissolve ten pounds of sugar in four pounds, or two quarts of water; when melted, add two pounds of honey, mix well together, and when cooling, stir in a few drops of essence of peppermint or other flavoring, according to taste.

Leaves from My Journal.—No. VIII.

PRIZE ESSAY BY MRS. B. M'CLELLAN, OF OHIO.

October.—Henry and Lizzie Mason have well-defined ideas in regard to the discipline necessary for little Georgy, I see. I suppose they have formerly said, (like all the rest of us,) that a child of theirs should be made *to mind*, at any rate. About the propriety of this there can be no question, but only in regard to the best means for producing the result. How quietly and lovingly some parents, with a simple word, gain obedience! Others, worried and angered, it may be with a long contest, obtain at last but a sullen and very imperfect compliance with their wishes. Young parents often err here in judgment, rather than in motive. Though pained to punish a child, they honestly believe it must be done. "The rod and reproof give wisdom, but a child left to himself bringeth his mother to shame." "Chasten thy son while there is hope, and let not thy soul spare for his crying." The admonitions rest upon their hearts like huge weights, that can only be thrown off by administering the punishment. But is not the trouble a more radical one? Do not parents often misjudge as to the *true cause* for correction? For instance: a little child, half in fun, and half in willfulness, disobeys some command. The parent at once threatens punishment. The child, in alarm, runs from the danger. Now, surely, the parent reasons, this obstinacy must be subdued, this dreadful temper conquered. The child, suffering in every delicate nerve, and well nigh beside itself with terror, is in no fit condition to understand what is required, or even to think what wrong thing it has done. Some children have become idiotic, some epileptic, some deaf, and some blind, from such treatment. Positive untruth, and deliberate, willful disobedience, doubtless demand prompt and decisive punishment, but let not every trifling fault, every accidental failure or delay, be exaggerated into abundant cause for correction. How common for the parent to urge the child, to "be a man," or "be a lady." *Oh, let children be children!* Let them act, and think, and speak, and play, and dress, as children should. Childhood will swiftly pass, and worldly wisdom and questionable maxims, and fashion, and guile, and strong temptations, will soon enough surround them. Ah, let not the sanctuary of home be so darkened by unreasonable and exacting demands, that it shall not furnish a dear retreat from the snares and pitfalls of this earthly way. Jesus blessed little children, and is not Our Father infinitely patient with His disobedient family?

I have been canning tomatoes and quinces to-day. These about close up that labor for the season, and I am not sorry when it is over. Tomatoes are nicer if cooked for some time. No water should be added, as they contain a superabundance of juice.

Sweet corn and lima beans will find ready market in winter, if put up in generous quantity. The former has been prepared before this, but the latter claim attention now. They are better to be gathered while green, well scalded in water, and dried on plates by the stove, but can be left to ripen on the vines. Both corn and beans should be kept, when dried, in a tight bag. Before cooking, cover well with cold water, and soak over night. One teacupful of beans to two of corn is a good proportion, and sufficient for a family of five or six. Boil two and a half or three hours. Just before taking up, add butter, salt, and pepper, to taste. Some sweet cream is an improvement, and as the corn loses some of its sweetness in the process of drying, two or three teaspoonfuls of sugar will give the original flavor.

As washing was about to-day, and by little and little we are doing something at house cleaning, I thought I would wash the windows, and clean the paint in the bedroom. The tubs were at hand, and plenty of hot suds. "Nothing like killing two birds with one stone," as my dear old grandfather used to say. After washing one window, I tipped it upon the corner to drain, with good exposure to the sun and air. But how the wind blows! It is almost a hurricane out there. That window may go over, I ought not to leave it so, but I'll hurry with the other, and soon have all in safe quarters. Hark, a crash, an ominous rattling of broken glass! "What's that?" said Hannah. Ah, that unlucky window—*I* have no trouble in knowing the place of the disaster. I could find it in the dark! I dislike to be called careless, or be obliged to pronounce such humiliating judgment upon myself, but, Mrs. Frisby, with the most charitable construction, you must plead guilty to the charge here.

It is no small accomplishment for a lady to be a neat sewer. A costly garment, shabbily made, is never ornamental, while a plain one, well fitted and put together, is always becoming.

Instruction in this department should commence in early childhood. The patchwork must be prepared with exactness, and the little girl patiently taught how to set stitches. As she grows older, she must not be allowed to sew carelessly. Dresses, as well as other garments, sometimes get sadly torn. Shall they be thrown aside now? Rather let them be mended so neatly that, if noticeable, it shall only call forth admiration for the way in which it is done. "Why," said a young lady who dressed with refined taste, after examining a rent thus repaired, "I should consider that ornamental rather than otherwise."

I was taught while at school, how to "set in a patch," and probably have never once done it since without thinking of my teacher with gratitude. Cut a square piece out from the place of the rent. Notch each corner diagonally, the notch being just of the depth required for turning down the raw edge, which should be overcast with fine thread. The piece to be put in must be cut enough larger than the one taken out, to allow for the turning down of both sides, and also be overcast. Sew together on the wrong side, over and over, with fine thread or silk of the color of the material. Let the stitches be quite close together, but not deep. The corners, which are now square, must be tightly sewed. If striped or figured, take pains to match. When finished, dampen and press upon the wrong side.

No wonder that Tommy, with great, round, staring patches on elbows and knees, hides behind mother's chair, when fine ladies so splendidly dressed call to see her. No wonder, if, while at play in the yard, some sweet girls going by, peer at him through the railing and try to make his acquaintance, he scampers away behind the wood-pile, wishing all the while, *oh! so much*, that his father was rich, and he might wear his Sunday suit every day. But now let those patches be put in with more painstaking, (for even the Sunday suit, if worn every day, would soon need them), so that these same ladies will notice and praise the neat work, and the dear little girls say they wish their mothers could mend like Tommy's. Won't he stand erect now? Won't his bright, open face beam like sunshine? Won't he think his mother the most wonderful woman in the world?

Preserve Ripe Cucumbers.—Mrs. L. E. L. Take large yellow cucumbers, pare them, take out the cores, and soak in salt water two days. Then take them from the brine, pour over them boiling water, and let them stand over night. Pour off this water, and they are ready for the pickle, which prepare thus: For each quart of sharp vinegar take one pint of hot water, two large cups of sugar, and one tablespoonful of each of the following spices: cinnamon, cloves, allspice, black pepper, mace or nutmeg. Add one handful of raisins or ripe grapes. Scald all together, and boil until the cucumbers are easily penetrated with a fork. Use as little of the vinegar to boil them in as possible, and pour the rest over them when done.

Jelly Roll.—Four eggs, one teacup of sugar, one of flour, one teaspoonful of soda, two of cream of tartar. Spread thin on bread pans; bake quickly. When done, spread on jelly and roll.

BOYS & GIRLS' COLUMNS.

About Perpetual Motion.

Men have spent fortunes trying to invent a machine that would run of itself, without winding up or any other help when it had once been started. Probably some are now trying to put wheels and springs and levers together, so that they will make their own power, and somebody will be likely to succeed when he can take hold of his boot straps and lift himself over a fence. If this seems too discouraging to hopeful but inexperienced inventors, we will say they may expect to make a "perpetual motion" machine, when they first discover something which is not already in motion, or when they learn how to keep anything from perpetual motion. "Why, everything keeps still if nobody moves it," says a young friend whose tongue is always ready to move. What will you show us to prove it? Take that stone lying by the roadside. It has lain there, you say, ever since you can remember; it has not moved a single inch. We know it *looks* so, but when we are seeking to know the exact truth, we have sometimes to use other instruments as well as our eyes. First, we will take the microscope. All over the rough surface we discover that small particles of that stone are missing. They have left marks in the places which they once occupied, but they have gone on their travels. Some have mounted into the air and gone flying through space as dust; some have escaped in the drops of water which fell from the clouds, and carried them down to the ground, where hungry roots of grass and other plants were waiting to draw them in and send them circulating through their veins. If the stone had been accurately measured many years ago, an exact measure of it now would show that many particles on the outside had moved or been carried away. Another examination many years hence would show more to be missing; so we must conclude that they are now in motion, very slowly perhaps, but yet moving. We will apply another test. During a hot day hold the thermometer against the stone; the mercury rises in the tube; the stone is heated more than the air around it. Now we know that heat makes stone as well as other things expand. The little particles of which it is made separate slightly—they move when heat is applied from the sun, or anything else. When the air around the stone grows cooler, then the heat will pass out, the stone will contract, its particles will move up closer together. Now, as the temperature of the air is continually changing from hour to hour, the stone keeps moving, and its particles are never wholly at rest; there is perpetual motion in it. Shall we examine some other object? Do so for yourself, until we have space to say something more about this subject in the *Agriculturist*.

Rats.

Gnaw, gnaw,—nibble, nibble,—day and night, in sheds, cellars and garrets! Surely there are no creatures so greedy as rats: bread, cheese and meat, or books, papers and cloths carefully packed away—nothing comes amiss. Even the hard wood of boxes, floors and doors is not safe from their sharp teeth. This gnawing propensity is therefore very troublesome to us, but perhaps if we could change mouths with the rats we should be quite as greedy: *for* in truth, this propensity is not only excusable in a rat but actually necessary to his existence. And this is true of many other animals besides rats and mice, namely: rabbits, squirrels, and all the "gnawers," or "rodents," as they are called scientifically.

Instead of chewing on side teeth as we do, the gnawers use *four* little front teeth with bevelled edges,—that is, with one side sharper than the other, like a chisel, and so they file or nibble their food.

The teeth of most animals, once grown, remain of a certain size; but the teeth of rats and other rodents continue to grow like our finger nails, so that constant gnawing is necessary to keep them down to the right length. We cannot, therefore, blame a rat *for* spoiling our papers and wood, since his comfort, and even life, depends upon it. We are always sorry enough to lose a tooth, but to a rat such a loss is a far more serious misfortune, *for* the opposite tooth, having nothing to file against, grows longer until it bars the mouth. If both upper or under teeth were lost, the poor creature could not eat, and in a very short time would certainly die of starvation.

A Wonderful Pump.

The heart of an animal is a miniature force-pump, having supply and discharge pipes, and complete sets of valves. It has a world of work to do during a lifetime of seventy years. Each minute the human heart beats about seventy times, at each beat receiving and discharging two and one half ounces of blood. Thus, it must distribute 175 ounces per minute, 656 pounds per hour, 7¾ *tons* per day; and in 70 years about 200,000 tons. No pump ever constructed by man has continued to work so steadily, without derangement, and without repairs—though that is saying too much; *for*, by its wonderful mechanism, it repairs its own wear, until the end of life.

Use Plain Words.

Little boys sometimes put on their fathers' boots or their big brothers' clothes, and act as though that had made them larger and more important; but nobody is deceived, and they are only laughed at. Young writers and speakers should remember this when clothing their thoughts with language. Never try to find large or high sounding words. They are not natural, they will be awkwardly used, will often show misfits, and expose the author to ridicule. An ambitious young student, in writing his composition, thus attempted to describe a very dark night; "tenebrious gloom obscured the darkening shade." The teacher, on reading it, remarked, "this being translated into plain English, means 'dark darkness darkened the darkening dark;' that is, I suppose, it was very dark." A young lady thus expressed the idea of a fine sunrise; "the royal king of day, clad in glorious golden panoply of dazzling effulgence, flooded the earth with gorgeous brightness." "It is easier to swallow a dictionary than to digest it," remarked the teacher, on reading that outburst. In all writing, strive to express the thought most clearly. Nobody cares to unwrap a dozen or more coverings to get at a small parcel of candy. If you have a pleasant idea, out with it in as few and plain words as possible, and not oblige the reader to strip off a pile of waste word wrappers. Use the language in which you think and converse; *that* will be entirely natural. In time you may learn to make it elegant. Strive for excellent thoughts, and to express them *clearly*; they will be valuable even in the homeliest words, just as a beautiful face is attractive in the plainest garb.

No. 280. *Illustrated Rebus.*—This is a difficult puzzle; it will require considerable study to solve it.

New Puzzles to be Answered.

No. 281. *Illustrated Rebus.*—What order of nobility is here represented?

No. 282. *Riddle.*—With two hands, no finger or thumb, I speak plainly, yet have no tongue; my face is attractive, much looked at, yet has neither mouth, nose, or eyes. I go almost constantly, having neither feet nor wings, but never advance a step without company.

No. 283.

No. 283. What way of cooking bivalves is shown in the above engraving?

No. 284. How does the *foot* in the engraving below represent that its owner is determined on success?

Answers to Problems and Puzzles.

The following are answers to the puzzles, etc., in the September number, page 333.

No. 284.

No. 275. *Figure Puzzle.*—Ivy (IV)... No. 276. *Double Puzzle.*—A cat may be found concealed over the bird's nest. She has the old bird in her mouth. The rebus is "*Catacombs.*" The combs in the beehives, on the fowls, making the fence, and the curry-comb on the ground, fully supply the latter part of the word... No. 277. *Enigma.*—A Shoe, (*understanding* is a well-spring of life.)... No. 278. *Study in Horsemanship.*—Turn the picture sidewise and the boys will evidently be thrown... No. 279. *Illustrated Rebus.*—As twigs are bent, trees are inclined... No. 273. *Arithmetical Problem.*—(August number, page 279.) 45.85 yds.

The Catacombs.

In the September *Agriculturist*, page 333, it was stated that the word formed in the puzzle picture was of historical interest, and our young readers were requested to find out what they could about the "Catacombs." As many of them may have no books at hand containing the information, we give the following brief sketch. They were rooms cut under ground in the rocks for the reception of bodies of the dead. The first Catacombs were probably made in Egypt. In that country it was customary to embalm the dead, and the "mummies," as the embalmed remains were called, were then placed in the Catacombs. An entire chain of mountains in the neighborhood of Thebes, is mined by these chambers for the dead. Those belonging to the royal families and wealthy classes were splendidly decorated with costly paintings. Valuable ornaments of gold and silver were also used to adorn the mummies, but these have been despoiled long since by hostile invaders. Many of the paintings yet remain, their colors as bright as when first put on. These paintings represent scenes in the daily lives of the Ancient Egyptians, and give a complete history of their manners and customs. It is estimated that not less than 400,000 mummies were entombed in the Catacombs of Egypt, which gives some idea of their vast extent. The most interesting Catacombs are those of Rome, which are also immensely large, running under ground for miles. In the times of persecution, the early Christians found refuge in their intricate windings, and lived and worshipped unmolested by the enemies of Christ. On this account these places are held in great reverence by the Catholic population of Rome. The Catacombs of Naples are of still greater extent than those of Rome. At Paris, a large part of the city had been undermined in quarrying stone for building purposes, leaving extended galleries and rooms. They were not used for burial places until 1784, when the remains taken from a cemetery were deposited there. Frequent additions have been made from other burial grounds, until it is computed by good authorities that the bones of at least 3,000,000 people rest there

[COPYRIGHT SECURED.]

THE LOVING SISTER.—FROM A PAINTING BY MERLE.—*Engraved for the American Agriculturist by J. L. Langridge.*

How lovingly this sister clasps her baby brother in her arms! How naturally and sweetly the artist has told the story! The child's little troubles have given place to peaceful and happy dreams. The little fellow sleeps securely in his place of refuge. He has told his sister his childish grief, and has been consoled. He still holds tenaciously the apple she has given him, and we imagine we can almost see the traces of her kisses upon his pure forehead and plump cheeks. The day will come, perhaps, when his strong arm may support and protect her in turn. It is a fine thing to have a big brother—some one to protect and care for you—but we are sorry to say that big brothers are apt to be selfish and domineering, to have grand ideas of their own personal dignity, and to be very jealous lest their smaller brothers and sisters assume in any respect an equal footing with themselves. This is much less often the case with an older sister, who, if she is a good girl, can sympathize with the little ones and understand them much more readily than any brother, even if he is disposed to be kind and attentive. If you have a sister, return her love with kindness and affection, and you will always find her a true friend.

Serious Disturbance.—A few nights since, a family in Brooklyn, N. Y., were alarmed by a noise. Several burglaries committed in the neighborhood had made them nervous, and now they thought their turn had come for a visit from the housebreakers. The father of the family attempted to get a light by turning on the gas, but in his trepidation turned it off. The women, now more frightened than ever, ran screaming to the windows, and the whole neighborhood was aroused. A man armed himself with a broadsword, others seized various weapons, and the police came with their clubs. The family were afraid to venture down stairs, so the crowd below broke open the front door, and entered to capture the robbers. On entering the kitchen they found the faucet to the water-works open, and a full stream rushing out, and right behind this faucet, the rascal that had caused all the disturbance. A large cat had thrust his head into a milk pitcher, but could not get it out. It had "thrashed round" furiously in trying to extricate itself, thus making the alarming noises, and finally got fastened in the place where it was found, its struggles having turned the faucet. The fright ended in a hearty laugh.

(Business Notices $2.00 per Agate Line of Space.)

EXPOSITION UNIVERSAL,

Paris, 1867.

The Howe Machine Co.,—Elias Howe, Jr.,—699 Broadway, New York, awarded, OVER EIGHTY-TWO COMPETITORS, the

Only Grand Cross of the Legion of Honor,

AND GOLD MEDAL,

given to American Sewing Machines, as per Imperial Decree, published in the "Moniteur Universel," (Official Journal of the French Empire), Tuesday, 2d July, 1867.

Exposition Universelle,

Paris, 1867.

WHEELER & WILSON,

625 Broadway, New York.

AWARDED OVER EIGHTY-TWO COMPETITORS, THE HIGHEST PREMIUM,

A GOLD MEDAL,

FOR THE PERFECTION OF

SEWING MACHINES, and BUTTON-HOLE MACHINES.

The only **Gold Medal** for this Branch of Manufacture.

WHEELER'S HOMES for the PEOPLE.

Villas, Mansions, and Cottages, post-paid, $3.

Wheeler's Rural Homes,

Houses for Country Life, post-paid, $2.

Woodward's Architecture & Rural Art, Nos. 1 & 2, $1.50 each, post-paid. Numerous Designs and Plans for Cottages, Country Houses and Stables.

GEO. E. WOODWARD,

Publisher & Importer of ARCHITECTURAL BOOKS, 191 Broadway, New York.

Complete Illustrated Catalogue mailed FREE.

"—Fighting against Wrong,

and for

The Good, the True and the Beautiful."

THE

Little Corporal

Is acknowledged by Press and People almost universally to be THE BEST PAPER for Boys and Girls ever published in this country.

It is edited by ALFRED L. SEWELL, and EMILY HUNTINGTON MILLER.

Volumes begin July or January. Back Nos. supplied. Terms, One Dollar a year; Sample copy ten cents.

GREAT INDUCEMENTS are offered to those who wish to raise clubs.

Address, ALFRED L. SEWELL, Publisher, Chicago, Ills.

All New Subscribers for 1868 sent to *The Little Corporal* during October, will receive the November and December numbers of 1867 FREE.

GRAPE VINES

In Large Quantities and at Low Prices.

PARSONS & Co. call attention to their advertisement of VINES in the September number of the Agriculturist, and to the remarkably low prices detailed therein. The Vines offered are of the finest quality, and are offered low because the stock is large.

Address for Catalogue,

PARSONS & CO.,

Flushing, N. Y.

ACROSS THE SIERRA NEVADAS.

THE CENTRAL PACIFIC RAILROAD.

The Western Half

OF THE

GREAT NATIONAL TRUNK LINE

Across the Continent,

Being constructed WITH THE AID AND SUPERVISION OF THE UNITED STATES GOVERNMENT, is destined to be one of the most important lines of communication in the world; as it is the *sole link between the Pacific Coast and the Great Interior Basin,* over which the immense Overland travel must pass, and the

Principal Portion of the Main Stem Line between the Two Oceans.

Its line extends from Sacramento, on the tidal waters of the Pacific, eastward across the richest and most populous parts of California, Nevada and Utah, contiguous to all the great Mining Regions of the Far West, and will meet and connect with the roads now building east of the Rocky Mountains. About 100 miles are now built, equipped and in running operation to the summit of the Sierra Nevada. Within a few days 35 miles, now graded, will be added, and the track carried entirely across the mountains to a point in the Great Salt Lake Valley, whence further progress will be easy and rapid. Iron, materials, and equipment, are ready at hand for 300 miles of road, and 10,000 men are employed in the construction.

The local business upon the completed portion surpasses all previous estimate. The figures for the quarter ending August 31, are as follows, in gold:

GROSS EARNINGS.	OPERATING EXPENSES.	NET EARNINGS.
$187,579.61	$86,548.47	$101,031.17

or at the rate of about two millions per annum, of which more than three-fourths are net profit, on less than 100 miles worked. This is upon the actual, legitimate traffic of the road, with its terminus in the mountains, and with only the normal ratio of government transportation, and is exclusive of the materials carried for the further extension of the road.

The Company's interest liabilities during the same period were less than $125,000.

Add to this an ever-expanding through traffic, and the proportions of the future business become immense.

The Company are authorized to continue their line eastward until it shall meet and connect with the roads now building east of the Rocky Mountain ranges. Assuming that they will build and control half the entire distance between San Francisco and the Missouri River, as now seems probable, the United States will have invested in the completion of 803 miles $48,504,000, or at the average of $35,000 per mile—not including an absolute grant of 10,000,000 acres of the Public lands. By becoming a joint investor in the magnificent enterprise, and by waiving its first lien in favor of the First Mortgage Bond holders, THE GENERAL GOVERNMENT, IN EFFECT, INVITES THE CO-OPERATION OF PRIVATE CAPITALISTS, and has carefully guarded their interests against all ordinary contingencies.

The Company offer for sale, through us, their

First Mortgage Thirty-Year Six Per Cent. Coupon Bonds,

Principal and Interest Payable in Gold Coin,

in New York city. They are in sums of $1,000 each, with semi-annual gold coupons attached, and are selling for the present at 95 per cent. and accrued interest from July 1st added, in currency, at which rate they yield nearly

Nine Per Cent. Upon the Investment.

These Bonds, authorized by Act of Congress, are issued only as the work progresses, and to the same amount only as the Bonds granted by the Government; and represent in all cases the *first lien* upon a completed, equipped, and productive railroad, in which have been invested Government subsidies, stock subscriptions, donations, surplus earnings, etc., and which is worth more than three times the amount of First Mortgage Bonds which can be issued upon it.

The Central Pacific First Mortgage Bonds have all the assurances, sanctions and guaranties of the Pacific Railroad Acts of Congress, and have, in addition, several noticeable advantages over all other classes of railroad bonds.

First—They are a *first lien* upon altogether the most vital and valuable portion of the through line.

Second—Beside the fullest benefit of the Government subsidy, which is a subordinate lien, the road receives the benefit of a large donation from California.

Third—Fully half the whole cost of grading 150 miles eastward of San Francisco is concentrated upon the 150 miles now about completed.

Fourth—A local business already yielding three-fold the annual interest liabilities, with advantageous rates payable in coin.

Fifth—The principal as well as the interest of its Bonds is payable in coin, upon a legally binding agreement.

Having carefully investigated the resources, progress and prospects of the road, and the management of the Company's affairs, we cordially recommend these Bonds to Trustees, Executors, Institutions and others as an eminently *sound, reliable and remunerative form of permanent investment.*

Conversions of Government Securities

INTO

CENTRAL PACIFIC

FIRST MORTGAGE BONDS

now *realize for the holders from*

Twelve to Eighteen Per Cent. Advantage,

WITH THE SAME RATE OF INTEREST.

The exchange is effected at the following rates to-day, (September 9th), subject, of course, to slight fluctuations from day to day. We receive in exchange:

U. S. Sixes, 1881, coupon, and pay difference	$152.40
U. S. Five-Twenties, 1862, coupon, and pay difference	150.49
U. S. Five-Twenties, 1864, coupon, and pay difference	138.69
U. S. Five-Twenties, 1865, coupon, and pay difference	143.69
U. S. Five-Twenties, 1865, (new), coupon, and pay difference	130.99
U. S. Five-Twenties, 1867, (new), coupon, and pay difference	130.99
U. S. Ten-Forties, coupon, and pay difference	99.49
U. S. Seven-Thirties, (2d series), and pay difference	128.19
U. S. Seven-Thirties, (3d series), and pay difference	123.19

on each one thousand.

For sale by Banks and Bankers generally, of whom descriptive Pamphlets and Maps can be obtained, and by

FISK & HATCH,

BANKERS

And Dealers in Government Securities,

AND

Financial Agents of the C. P. R. R. Co.,

No. 5 Nassau St., N. Y.

HERALD OF HEALTH.

This Magazine has met with a great success during 1867. Those who subscribe for this Journal for 1868, NOW, shall get the Oct., Nov., and Dec. Nos. of 1867 free. A Wheeler & Wilson Sewing Machine premium for 30 subscribers, $60. Those who have never seen this Magazine can have it three months on trial for 30 cents—$2 a year; 20 cents a number.

MILLER, WOOD & CO.,

No. 15 Laight-st., New York.

Rural Improvements.

Robert Morris Copeland, author of Country Life, furnishes plans and advice for laying out or improving public or private grounds. Refers to John M. Forbes, Nathaniel Thayer, Boston; Francis G. Shaw, New York; Rufus Waterman, Providence, R. I. Office, 40 Barristers' Hall, Boston, Mass.

FRANKLIN BRICK MACHINE.

Justly celebrated for perfect simplicity, great strength, and immense compressing power, is GUARANTEED, with eight men and two horses, to self-temper the clay and make 3,000 to 3,500 elegant bricks per hour. J. H. RENICK, Proprietor, No. 71 Broadway, New York, Room 26.

FEED CUTTERS.—Gale's Copper Strip is the cheapest and best. Cuts Hay, Straw, or Stalks. Suitable for one horse or a hundred, *(not to be paid for till tried).* Agents wanted. Send for Circulars to PEEKSKILL PLOW WORKS, Peekskill, N. Y.

Advertisements, to be sure of insertion, must be received BEFORE the 5th of the preceding month.

TERMS – (cash before insertion).

Ordinary Pages, $1.50 *per line.* *Open Pages*—$2 *per line.*
Business Notices—$2.50 per line of space, each insertion.

The Best Advertising Paper in the U. S. is THE NEW YORK TRIBUNE.

THE NEW YORK TRIBUNE has the largest circulation of any Newspaper, among the Intelligent Agricultural, Horticultural, Stock Raising, Wool Growing, and Implement using classes.

All who want to sell **Lands, Farms, Machinery, Inventions, Trees, Plants, Seeds, Tools, Books,** or anything that contributes to the happiness, comfort, or enjoyment of the great Agricultural and Manufacturing Public, from Maine to California, will do well to advertise in THE NEW YORK TRIBUNE.

TERMS OF ADVERTISING:
DAILY TRIBUNE, 25 cents a line.
WEEKLY TRIBUNE, $1.50 a line.
SEMI-WEEKLY TRIBUNE, 25 cents a line.

Address THE TRIBUNE, New York.

PEACH TREES AND SMALL FRUITS A SPECIALTY.
RUMSON NURSERIES. Send for Circulars.
A. HANCE & SON,
Red Bank, Monmouth Co., N. J.

NORTON'S VIRGINIA SEEDLING GRAPE VINES, 2 years, for sale, $150 per 1000. Terms cash in advance, or collected by Express on delivery.
GEORGE NESTEL, Mascoutah, St. Clair Co., Illinois.

UNIVERSAL CLOTHES WRINGER.

THE

Cannot be surpassed or equaled by any other Wringer for durability, till the expiration of the patent for the "COG WHEEL REGULATOR" or "STOP-GEAR." *No other Wringer is licensed under this Patent.* It being now universally conceded that Cogs are necessary to prevent the Rolls from being broken or torn loose, many attempts have been made to get a Cog-Wheel arrangement which shall equal the UNIVERSAL, and yet avoid the "Stop-Gear" patent, but *without success.*

Merchants who sell the UNIVERSAL WRINGER keep also the

DOTY WASHING MACHINE,

which, though but recently introduced, is really as great a Labor and Clothes Saver as the Wringer, and is destined to win public favor and patronage everywhere.

It washes *perfectly, without scouring or rubbing* the clothes at all.

Those keeping the Wringer for sale, can order the Washer for customers, if they have not got a supply on hand. On receipt of the retail price, *from places where no one is selling*, we will send either or both machines from New York.

Prices—Family Washer, $14. No. 1½ Wringer, $10. No. 2 Wringer, $8.50.

A supply of the Wringers and Washers is always kept on hand in Chicago, Cincinnati, Cleveland, Janesville and St. Louis, boxed ready for shipment, at about New York prices.

Large profits are made selling these machines.
Circulars, giving Wholesale and Retail prices, sent free.

☞ These Machines are adopted by the *American Agriculturist* as Premiums, and endorsed by its Editors as the best in market—for recommendations see back numbers.

R. C. BROWNING, General Agent,
No. 32 Cortlandt-st., New York,
(Opposite Merchant's Hotel.)

Bliss' Seed and Horticultural Warehouse.

B. K. BLISS & SON,

41 PARK ROW, NEW YORK,

(Old Office of American Agriculturist,)

Also, 231 Main Street, Springfield, Mass.

The Subscriber is happy to inform his patrons and the public generally, that, in order to better accommodate his numerous customers in New York and vicinity, as well as his rapidly increasing trade in other sections of the country, he has formed a business connection with his son, S. D. BLISS, under the above-named firm, and leased the well-known premises of the AMERICAN AGRICULTURIST, 41 PARK ROW, NEW YORK, where it is their intention to keep a well assorted stock of the various articles required by the **Farmer, Gardener, and Amateur Cultivator.** Among these may be found every desirable variety of **Garden, Field, and Flower Seeds, Dutch Bulbous Roots, Summer Flowering Bulbs, Hardy and Exotic Grape Vines, Small Fruits, Roses, and Flowering Plants,** both for the **Conservatory** and **Flower Garden, Agricultural and Horticultural Implements, Fertilizers,** and other requisites for the **Farm and Garden.**

The Seed Department will receive that special attention which its importance demands. Every effort will be made to sustain the favorable reputation which his seeds have already acquired wherever they have been introduced. With an experience of upwards of Twenty Years in the business, and possessing unrivaled facilities for procuring both Foreign and Home-grown Seeds, he feels no hesitation in guaranteeing perfect satisfaction to those who may favor them with their orders.

He would take this opportunity to return his sincere thanks to his friends for their liberal patronage, and respectfully solicits a continuance of the same for the New Firm.

B. K. BLISS.

OUR NEW

Catalogue of Dutch Bulbous Roots,

beautifully illustrated, with special directions for the culture of each variety therein enumerated, is now ready, and will be mailed, post-paid, to all applicants enclosing 10 cents.

OUR CELEBRATED

Seed Catalogue and Guide to the Flower and Kitchen Garden,

Containing One Hundred and twenty-five pages of closely printed matter, beautifully illustrated with upwards of *One Hundred Engravings*, and a Descriptive List of upwards of *Two Thousand varieties of Vegetable and Flower Seeds*, with special directions for their culture, will be mailed to all applicants enclosing 25 cents. Orders may be addressed to

41 Park Row, New York,
Or, 231 Main-st., Springfield, Mass.
B. K. BLISS & SON.

ECONOMY!
A FIRST-RATE COOK BOOK.
WHAT TO DO WITH THE COLD MUTTON.
A BOOK OF RECHAUFFES.

Containing nearly 400 practical receipts for plain dishes of all kinds, Soups, Fish, Beef, Poultry, Game, Salads, Puddings, Pastry, Cake, Pickles, etc. The great feature of the book is that it suggests very many ways of re-cooking cold meats, other than as the inevitable hash.

Send us $1.00 and you will get a copy neatly bound in cloth by return mail, postage paid.

F. J. HUNTINGTON & CO.,
459 Broome-st., New York.

Get up Clubs
AND
BUY VINES CHEAP.

Almost any man will join with his neighbors in buying a few choice grape vines.

For $5.00
I will send by mail, post paid,
5 Iona Vines, 5 Concord Vines,
5 Hartford Prolific Vines,
and one of each kind to the party getting up the Club.

For $10.00
I will send by mail, post-paid,
10 Iona Vines, 10 Concord Vines,
10 Hartford Prolific Vines,
and three of each kind to the party getting up the Club.

All the above will be No. 1 vines, from my well known stock. Orders filled in rotation as received. Address
GEORGE E. MEISSNER, Richmond, Staten Island, N. Y.

New York College of Veterinary Surgeons.

Incorporated 1857.

179 Lexington Avenue. Session 1867–8.

The regular course of Lectures in this Institution will commence the first week in October, '67, and continue until the latter part of February, 1868.

Professors (Emeritus) J. BUSTEED, M. D., Histology; L. D. MASON, M.D., Physiology; FAIRFIELD WEISSE, M.D., Surgical Pathology; SAMUEL R. PERRY, M. D., Chemistry, Materia Medica and Therapeutics; A. T. LIAUTARD, M. D., V. S., Comparative Anatomy and Operative Surgery; A. LARGE, M. D.; M. R. C., V. S. L., Theory and Practice of Medicine of the Horse and other Domestic Animals. Address for particulars, Dr. J. BUSTEED, President of Faculty, 179 Lexington Ave.; A. T. LIAUTARD, M. D., V. S., Registrar.

COTTAGE HILL SEMINARY,

POUGHKEEPSIE, N. Y.—An English and French School for Young Ladies. Very select, delightfully situated, and affording unusual advantages for a solid and elegant education. For the prospectus, address, early, the
REV. GEORGE T. RIDER, A. M., Rector.

NOTICE.

Our Strawberry Catalogue of 16 pages, for fall of 1867, contains instructions for the selection of varieties. Gives their sexual character—a full description, and illustration, of

JUCUNDA—Our No. 700,

greatly the most valuable of all our Strawberries. Also, of Fillmore, next in value, and all other desirable kinds. Complete Lists of Early, Medium, and Late varieties, both for family and market purposes—our favorites—prices of plants grown in pots and otherwise, by mail or express.

OUR SMALL FRUIT CATALOGUE

of 24 pages, for fall of 1867, contains descriptions of the leading varieties of Grapes, Raspberries, Blackberries, Gooseberries, Currants, &c. Considerations which should influence in the selection of varieties. Complete lists of the most desirable kinds. Illustrations of Hornet Raspberry; Ives' Grape; White Grape, and Cherry Currant. Complete assortments of SMALL FRUITS by mail. Mr. Batcham's Circular, &c.

OUR ORDER LIST

for 1867, contains the plainest instructions for making out an order. It will be found a great convenience, and guard against mistakes. Both Catalogues, with Order List, and directed envelope, will be sent to all applicants enclosing 10 cents.

J. KNOX,
Box 155, Pittsburgh, Pa.

Choice Fruits for the Garden.

A splendid stock of Standard and Dwarf-Trees, Grapes, Small Fruits, &c. Send for our
AMATEUR'S PRICE LIST,
containing especial inducements to planters.
EDW'D. J. EVANS & CO.,
Central Nurseries, York, Pa.

500,000 GRAPE VINES.

Superior layers, 1 and 2 years old, mostly Concord, Hartford, Catawba, Norton's Virginia, Delaware, Ives, and others, *cheaper than anywhere else*, for sale. Also, Roses, Currants, Rhubarb and Raspberry Plants very cheap. Send stamp for Catalogue and Essays on Grape Culture, to
Dr. H. SCHROEDER, Bloomington, Illinois.

CROSSMAN BROTHERS & COMPANY,

Manufacturers of Fire Brick, Glazed Drain Pipe, Land Tile, &c.

DEALERS IN FIRE CLAY, FIRE SAND AND KAOLIN,

On Raritan River, 2 1-2 Miles above Perth Amboy, Woodbridge, N. J.

We invite public attention to an enterprise having for its object a combination of *practical, successful*, business operations, and valuable inventions; the working of which will have a tendency to revolutionize present systems of drainage, *greatly diminish its cost*, and increase its efficiency by *being done in a* SUPERIOR MANNER; add to the prosperity, profits, and *certainty* of agricultural operations, and by thus increasing the National Wealth in Agricultural Products, the prosperity of all other interests and business of the country will be promoted and insured; the volume and cash value of our National Exports will be increased, and tend to avert those monetary crises that succeed poor crops, and consequent diminished cash value of our exports and over trading on credit principles.

In our Brick-making business we found and secured a worn-out farm containing inexhaustible quantities of common brick, DRAIN TILE, Pipe and Fire Brick Clay, that make goods of such SUPERIOR quality as the clays of Woodbridge, N. J. are celebrated for. These different kinds of valuable Woodbridge Clays overlie and successively *dovetail each other*. They lie accessible and exposed above the level of our Railroad, and *reach almost to the surface* of the ground.

They are connected with Factory, Ship Channel, and excellent shipping facilities, by a Railroad of about 3,000 feet, with a slight *down grade* to the river. It is a combination of natural and artificial advantages for manufacturing *superior goods of vital importance* to the country, and for exhibiting our valuable machinery for sale in practical, profitable working operation, that is not known to exist in any other locality.

The machinery that is of such importance to the agricultural and other interests of the country consists in part of the inventions of Mr. Geo. S. Tiffany. They are the only machines known that take unprepared clay from the bank, grind it to *plasticity*, and drive it out at any *desired rate of speed*—not as simple mud—but in continuous streams of very dense, strong, and *polished* round tile, that are only equaled in smoothness by the Glass Tile of Holland. They are precisely the goods that every intelligent and scientific Drainer in the country will have whenever obtainable. They are manufactured stiff enough to wheel direct from the machine, *the only hand labor* required being to shovel clay, handle and wheel away the *ready made* tile, to be dried and burned, &c., &c. We counted 43 ready made polished tile issuing per minute, in a continuous stream from the machine of Sword Bros., in Michigan. The different strata in our clay hills that can thus be rapidly made into *valuable and superior goods* by our combination of water and rail transportation and valuable machinery, were formerly thrown away to get the more valuable clays beneath.

Another invention of great importance to this Company and to the country is the Patent of Mr. Henry C. Ingraham. It is probably the first *efficient*, practical, economical, light draft Ditching Machine ever invented *and practically used*. With such little work as it has already done, under *great disadvantages*, and with limited means to develop it, we already have *practical proof* that it will, with a single team of horses, dig from ¼ of a mile to ½ mile, 2 to 3 feet deep, of Ditch per day, with the bottom of the Ditch hardened, *graded, and shaped to precisely fit round tile*, in a manner *far superior* to hand labor. It is self-adjustable and self grading. By driving it a few times across the roughest plowed ground, the bottom of the Ditch becomes smooth and graded, with no loose dirt left in the Ditch. The dirt is deposited on each side in the smallest possible quantities, because the Ditch is cut *precisely of uniform width*, without waste by irregularities in digging. The operator rides as in a Mowing Machine, and it is believed to be of greater value to the country to *increase* Agricultural Products than Mowing Machines, or any other implement, are to secure the crops after being produced. It is difficult to estimate the value of a machine by which farmers can now drive teams and *thoroughly* perform the hitherto disagreeable, expensive, and slow, work of Ditching.

This Company is as yet composed exclusively of the working men and inventors that have developed this combination of business and advantages. The business will be managed by them, and their production will be still improved and developed to a higher standard of perfection, and kept in advance of the times, if the Inventors now comprising the Company should live. These Inventors are young men of integrity, and have not yet attained their proper positions in life.

The Company is not absolutely organized, but it is under consideration to name it the CROSSMAN CLAY AND MANUFACTURING COMPANY, and to be formed of the following Officers:

JACOB H. CROSSMAN, President.
GEORGE S. TIFFANY, Treasurer.

TRUSTEES.

JACOB H. CROSSMAN,
ALONZO G. CROSSMAN,
HENRY C. INGRAHAM.

The Company now possess and are working yards that can produce from two million to five million brick per year. We enclose estimates of what is now being done by Sword's Brick Machine. It made 80 Brick per minute while we stood by and timed it by watch.

EXHIBIT OF ONE WEEK'S WORK.

Though we can, with ease, with the same number of men, make 180,000 in Six *Days* of ten hours, we here state the average Week's Work at 130,000.

COST.

2 men at the clay bank	$27.00
2 men on the platform feeding the Machine	27.00
1 man taking off brick from the Machine	13.50
2 men, (or three boys,) wheeling	27.00
1 man helping unload barrows in yard	13.50
1 engineer	21.00
4 setters	60.00
3 burners	45.00
130 bushels nut coal, for engine	7.50
2 horses, keeping	10.00
1,050 bushels Coke and Coal, to burn a kiln of 130,000 brick	121.50
Oil for machinery	3.50
Delivering kiln of brick	225.00
Manager of yard, and contingent expenses	50 00
	$637.00

PROFIT.

130,000 brick at $12 per 1,000	$1,560.00
Deduct cost of making	$557.00
Net profit of yard for one week	$1,118.00

Admitting what every one knows cannot possibly occur, that brick fall to half present prices, and wages remain as high as at present, still, a Machine in a brick market, is a fortune.

The above estimates of cost are much higher than will be found true of many localities. They are above the actual working expenses of our own yard, but we wish to be entirely on the safe side!

The clay that is now made into common brick, can, by the Tiffany Tile Machine, be rapidly made into superior Tile, for a great demand exists at the following prices:

1¼ inch, without bands,	$17	1¼ inch, with bands,	$23.
2 " " "	20	2 " " "	28.
3 " " "	35	3 " " "	45.
4 " " "	50	4 " " "	56.

To show the comparative cost of Brick and Tile made from the same clays, we extract from the work by Geo. E. Waring, entitled "Draining for Profit and Health," page 183, as follows:

"**The Cost of Tiles.**—It would be impossible, at any time, to say what should be the precise cost of tiles in a given locality, without knowing the prices of labor and fuel; and in the present unsettled condition of the currency, any estimate would necessarily be of little value. Mr. Parker estimated the cost of inch pipes in England at 6s., (about $1.30) per thousand, when made on the estate where they were to be used, by a process similar to that described herein. Probably they could at no time have been made for less than twice that cost in the United States,—and they would now cost much more; though if the clay is dug out in the fall, when the regularly employed farm hands are short of work, and if the same men can cut and haul the wood during the winter, the hands hired especially for the tile making, during the summer season, (two men and two or three boys,) cannot, even at present rates of wages, bring the cost of the tiles to nearly the market prices. If there be only temporary use for the machinery, it may be sold, when no longer needed, for a good percentage of its original cost, as, from the slow movement to which it is subjected, it is not much worn by its work.

"There is no reason why tiles should cost more to make than bricks. A common brick contains clay enough to make four or five 1¼-inch tiles, and it will require about the same amount of fuel to burn this clay in one form as in the other. This advantage in favor of tiles is in a measure offset by the greater cost of handling them, and the greater liability to breakage."

It will readily be seen there is room for immense profits in Tile manufactures by our combination and application of machinery, even at a large reduction in the price of tile.

Orders for Ditching and Tile Making Machines are solicited, and their satisfactory working will be guaranteed by our Company.

It is proposed to raise $50,000 Cash Working Capital to develop and extend our enterprise. To do so, the property and business of the Company will be represented by shares of $50 each. One Thousand such shares are now offered to capitalists and consumers, with the firm belief as practical men that no enterprise in this country holds out equal inducements for investment. Inventories, full explanations, and satisfactory references, will be furnished applicants by addressing or calling on

CROSSMAN BROTHERS,
Woodbridge, N. J.

Three Months for Nothing.

THE METHODIST,

A First-Class Religious Newspaper.

VIIIth Volume Commences Jan. 1st,

1868.

NOW is the time to subscribe, as by doing so you will get the paper for the remainder of this year **For Nothing.**

THE METHODIST

is an eight-page Weekly Newspaper, now in its eighth year of highly successful publication. It is Religious and Literary: Independent, Fraternal, Loyal, and Progressive.

As a Family Paper it is unsurpassed. It commands some of the best Literary ability of the

Methodist Episcopal Church,

and of *other Christian Denominations*, and is largely patronized by all classes of Christians, as a Family paper.

It is *Edited*, as heretofore, by

REV. GEORGE R. CROOKS, D.D.

Assisted by the following able Editorial Contributors:

REV. ABEL STEVENS, LL.D.
REV. JOHN McCLINTOCK, D.D. LL.D.
REV. B. H. NADAL, D.D.
REV. H. B. RIDGAWAY, and
PROF. A. J. SCHEM.

Sermons by

HENRY WARD BEECHER,

every Fortnight.

Also, Sermons from

Eminent Methodist Pulpit Orators,

Among whom are the

Bishops of The Methodist Episcopal Church.

Other experienced writers contribute to the various special departments, rendering it one of the most original, thorough, and comprehensive religious periodicals of the day.

In typographical appearance THE METHODIST is unrivaled, being printed on good paper, with the best of ink, from the clearest of type.

It has a valuable Correspondence, both Domestic and Foreign; a *fresh* Story every week for the Children; a Financial, Commercial, Mercantile, and Agricultural *Department*; a *valuable* Religious and Secular News' Summary brought up to the hour of going to press.

Altogether, as a Religious and literary Weekly Newspaper, THE METHODIST has been pronounced, by disinterested judges, to be without a superior in point of talent, beauty, and punctuality. Its visits to any family will pay back its price, to every careful reader, a hundred fold.

Terms to Mail Subscribers, Two Dollars and Fifty Cents per Year, in Advance; to all Ministers, for their own Subscription, Two Dollars.

Postage prepaid at the Post-office where received, Twenty Cents per year. Twenty Cents must be added by Canada subscribers, to prepay postage. Fifty Cents additional if served by Carrier in New York City.

Any one sending THREE SUBSCRIBERS and $7.50, will receive a Fourth copy free for one year.

Subscriptions received at any time during the year.

Liberal Premiums and Commissions to persons getting up Clubs. Send for Premium Circular.

Specimen copies sent *free* on application.

Address

THE METHODIST,
114 Nassau Street,
New York.

H. W. DOUGLAS,
Publishing Agent.

25,000 Norway Maple, 3 to 15 Feet.

5,000 Horse Chestnut,	3 to 10 feet.
1,000 Tulip Trees,	8 to 15 feet.
1,000 Magnolia Acuminata,	3 to 10 feet.

Also, a general Nursery Stock at extremely low rates.
J. A. LEWIS, Willimantic, Conn.

DAVISON'S THORNLESS BLACK RASPBERRY plants for sale. Send for Circular. JOHN W. MEAD, Waterford, Camden Co., N. J.

THE CHURCH UNION.

"The Freest Organ of Thought in the World."

Owing to the unprecedented reception of this paper, it has been enlarged to double its original size, and is now the largest, best, and most liberal, as well as cheapest, family newspaper in the world.

It is the Organ of No Sect,

but will aim to represent every branch of the Church of Christ, as well as every society organized for the purpose of Evangelizing the world.

It is Trinitarian in Creed,

but favors free discussions of all subjects not already settled by the universal consent of the Church in all ages. It will oppose Ritualism and Infidelity, and advocate a free pulpit for Christ's ministers and a free communion table for all the Lord's people.

It will favor universal suffrage and equal rights

to every man and woman of whatsoever nationality, and will oppose all human instruments contrived by men for the enslavement of the consciences of men.

It will publish a sermon by Rev. Henry Ward Beecher every Monday

at 12 o'clock. This sermon is not copyrighted, nor does it come under the eye of Mr. Beecher before publication, and will be a faithful report of the utterances of the Great Preacher of Freedom. Writers and editors of every branch of the Church are engaged on this paper.

Terms $2.50; $1.00

TO AGENTS FOR EVERY SUBSCRIBER.

The usual premiums of sewing-machines, etc., will be offered.

FOR SALE BY THE

American News Company, for 5 Cts.

Address

C. ALBERTSON, Supt.,

103 Fulton St., N. Y.

Important Music & School Books

JUST PUBLISHED BY

MASON BROTHERS,

596 Broadway, N. Y.

THE ANALYTICAL SCHOOL READERS.—First Reader, 25 cents; Second Reader, 50 cents; Third Reader, 75 cents; Fourth Reader, 90 cents; Fifth Reader, $1.25; Sixth Reader, $1.50. By RICHARD EDWARDS, LL.D., President of the Illinois State Normal University, and J. RUSSELL WEBB, author of the Word Method. With elegant Illustrations by THOS. NAST. Fresh, new, practical books by practical men, embodying modern improvements. Teachers and pupils will like these books. Send for a Circular with description and specimen pages.

THE TEMPLE CHOIR.—A new collection of Church Music for Choirs and Singing Schools. By Theo. F. Seward, assisted by Dr. Lowell Mason and Wm. B. Bradbury. This is the first time these two most popular musical authors in the country have been united in one book. THE TEMPLE CHOIR has a very full Singing School Department, with 150 Glees, Rounds, Part Songs, etc., over 500 tunes of all meters, a large number of Anthems, Set Pieces, etc., for special occasions, social use, etc.; and is altogether one of the most complete collections of music ever published. Price, $1.50 each; $13.50 per dozen; $100 per hundred. A single copy will be sent for examination to any teacher of music, or leader of a choir, post-paid, for one dollar.

A NEW METHOD FOR THE PIANO FORTE, by WILLIAM MASON and E. S. HOADLY, 230 pages, large quarto; illustrated. Price, $4.00. Very full, complete, progressive, clear and comprehensible; embodying important improvements in teaching, and having those minute directions which the best teachers are accustomed to give orally, written out in full, as far as possible. Retaining all that is valuable in previous methods, it embodies the improvements used by the best living teachers.

APPLES OF GOLD IN PICTURES OF SILVER.—A new book of Hymns and Tunes for Sunday Schools, by R. ROBERTS. It has the best of the old songs, with a rich variety of new hymns and tunes. An admirable book, which can hardly fail to commend itself to all. It has many new, beautiful songs, (about 300 hymns and 200 tunes) and none which are not in good taste. Price, in paper covers, 30 cents, or $25 per hundred; in board covers, 35 cents, or $30 per hundred. A copy will be sent for examination to any person remitting 20 cents. Published by

MASON BROTHERS, 596 Broadway, N. Y.
MASON & HAMLIN, Boston.

HANDSOME AND CHEAP.

Globe Edition of Dickens' Works, the cheapest legible edition ever published. Large clear type, fine paper. Illustrated by Darley & Gilbert. To be completed in 13 volumes, 8 of which are now ready. Price per volume, in cloth, $1.50.

Riverside Edition of Dickens' Works. The very best library edition ever published, containing all the *English and American Illustrations* by Phiz, Cruikshank, Darley, Gilbert, and others. To be completed in 25 vols., crown 8vo, 8 of which are now ready. Price per volume, in cloth, $2.50.

Household Edition of Dickens' Works. An elegant library edition, now complete in 53 vols. Price per volume, in cloth, $1.25, the set complete in Crape cloth, price $65.25.

Illustrated Library Edition of Cooper's Works. Illustrated by Darley, handsomely printed on fine paper. Complete in 32 vols., crown 8vo. Price in cloth per volume $2.00. In complete set of 32 vols., uniform cloth $64.

People's Edition of Cooper's Works. Complete in 32 vols. Price per volume $1.75.

Household Edition of Cooper's Works. The cheapest edition published. Complete in 32 vols., elegantly bound in Crape cloth. Price per volume $1.25, or the complete set 32 vols., $40.

Sent by mail on receipt of prices annexed.

HURD & HOUGHTON, Publishers,
459 Broome-st., New York.

ACTIVE AGENTS,

Male and Female, wanted for permanent employment in selling the new and popular subscription book, the PHILOSOPHY OF HOUSEKEEPING; by Mr. and Mrs. Joseph B. Lyman. The latter is the well known Prize Essayist in the Household Department of this Journal.

This work was written to meet a want that the community has long felt, and the fidelity, thoroughness, and skill with which all the departments of housekeeping are taken up and treated, have produced a most valuable work. For this reason it is the most rapidly selling book of the season.

For terms and Circulars giving full description of the work, apply to
GOODWIN & BETTS,
91 Asylum-st., Hartford, Conn.

TO AGENTS.

Experienced Book-Canvassers can now pre-engage territory for *the best book of the year*. A new National Work entitled

The History of the Great Republic,

from the Discovery of America to the present time, considered **from a Christian Stand-point.**
By JESSE T. PECK, D.D.

Address, with testimonials, BROUGHTON & WYMAN, 13 Bible House, New York.

AGENTS WANTED.

The Book for the Million. "THE BOYS IN BLUE; or, HEROES OF THE RANK AND FILE," by Mrs. A. H. Hoge, of the United States Sanitary Commission. It is not a History of the War, or of any Campaign or General, but a full and gallant record of the sacrifice and sufferings of the Rank and File, who by their heroism conquered for us a glorious and honorable peace.
E. B. TREAT & CO., Publishers, 654 Broadway, New York.

ALL WORKS ON "THE WATER CURE," with prices, Illustrated Catalogue sent on receipt of two stamps, by S. R. WELLS, Publisher, No. 389 Broadway, New York. Agents wanted.

WINE MAKING

Grape Growing and Wine-Making, by George Husmann. A practical book by a practical man. Price $1.50, post-paid.
F. W. WOODWARD, Publisher,
37 Park Row, New York.

Nearly Ready for Delivery.

WALLACE'S
AMERICAN STUD BOOK.

One Royal 8vo volume, 1,070 pages.

Illustrated by 20 original Steel Portraits. Price $10.

Published by W. A. TOWNSEND & ADAMS,
434 Broome-st., New York.

Agents Wanted.

KEEP COPIES OF ALL YOUR LETTERS in the PENN. LETTER BOOK. No copying press or water needed. This valuable invention saves labor, time, and money; and is not for a day only, but for all time. Local and General Agents wanted. Address Penn. Manufacturing Works, 702 Chestnut-st., Philadelphia, Pa., Box 217.

BOOK AGENTS WANTED FOR "THE AMERICAN CONFLICT."

Mansfield, Ohio, August 11, 1867.

Messrs. O. D. CASE & CO.—GENTLEMEN:—Since my return home I have read the 2d volume of Greeley's "American Conflict." It is not only a wonderful monument of the industry of the author, but it is admirably arranged—clear and very accurate—and as interesting as any history can be. On some mooted points, I have carefully compared it with official documents and find that Mr. Greeley tells the truth fairly and distinctly. I regard the work as altogether the best history of our remarkable struggle, and one that ought to be in every household in the United States.

I am very truly yours, JOHN SHERMAN.

The undersigned have also just published an elegant edition of "CRUDEN'S CONCORDANCE TO THE HOLY SCRIPTURES"—a work which every family needs, and which is selling very rapidly.

For Circulars and full information, address O. D. CASE & CO., Publishers, at Hartford, Conn., Cleveland, Ohio, or Detroit, Mich.

AGENTS WANTED.

SUPERB NATIONAL WORK.

A Pictorial History of the United States,

By BENSON J. LOSSING.

Now being issued in Serial form, and beautifully illustrated by *Steel Plates*, from *original designs* by Stephens, and several hundred engravings on wood by Lossing & Barritt.

It will be comprised in *one volume* of about 800 pages, in the most *perfect* and *elegant form*, and at a *moderate price*. Every family and library should possess a copy.

Agents Wanted in every Town. Send for a Circular.
T. BELKNAP & CO., 102 William-st., New York.

"**W**ORKS ON MAN."—For New Illustrated Catalogue of best Books on Physiology, Anatomy, Gymnastics, Dietetics, Physiognomy, Short-hand Writing, Memory, Self-Improvement, Phrenology and Ethnology, send two stamps to S. R. WELLS, Publisher, No. 389 Broadway, New York. Agents wanted.

MME. DEMOREST'S MAMMOTH BULLETIN PLATE OF LADIES' FASHIONS, for the fall and winter of 1867-8, with 10 full size Cut Patterns of the principal figures on the plate. Now Ready. Price $2.50. Also Mme. Demorest's Bulletin Plate of Children's Fashions, with 10 full size Patterns, either or both with full descriptions, mailed free on receipt of price.
473 Broadway, New York.

Games, all kinds, sample and Catalogue, - -	25 cents.
Books, " " " " " - -	25 cents.
Photographs, " " " - -	25 cents.
How to Train and Doctor Horses, 2 Books, -	50 cents.

Sent post-paid. W. C. WEMYSS, 575 Broadway, N. Y.

A NEW VOLUME, ENLARGED.—With July the ILLUSTRATED PHRENOLOGICAL JOURNAL commenced the 46th volume. Forty quarto pages, and 70 engravings of men, women, monkeys, gorillas; Ethnology, Physiognomy, Phrenology, Psychology. Adapted to Clergymen, Lawyers, Physicians, Editors, Parents, Teachers, Artists, Business Men—indeed, everybody may read it with profit. Only 30 cents, or $3 a year. Address S. R. WELLS, No. 389 Broadway, New York. Sent six months for $1.50.

Short-Hand without a Master, by which the art of taking down Sermons, Lectures, Speeches, Trials, etc., may be attained in a few hours. Fifty-fourth edition, WITH SUPPLEMENT. Price 25 cents. Send orders to
O. A. ROORBACH, 122 Nassau-st., New York.

CARPENTERS.—SEND FOR CATALOGUE of New and Practical Architectural Works, enclosing stamp.
A. J. BICKNELL, Publisher, TROY, N. Y.

A GOOD THING: Send Two Stamps for Illustrated Catalogue of Works on Physiognomy, Phonography, Gymnastics, Anatomy, Dietetics, Psychology, etc., etc. S. R. WELLS, 389 Broadway, N. Y.

10,000 RICHMOND or EARLY MAY Cherry Trees, thrifty and handsome, 3 to 8 feet—$15 to $25 per 100. $100 per 1,000 for best class, 4 to 6 feet. $1,000 Concord grape vines! $20 to $25 per Thousand.
HENRY AVERY, Burlington, Iowa.

PURE BRAHMA FOWLS For Sale, (*pea-combed*).
B. F. HOLBROOK, Natick, Mass.

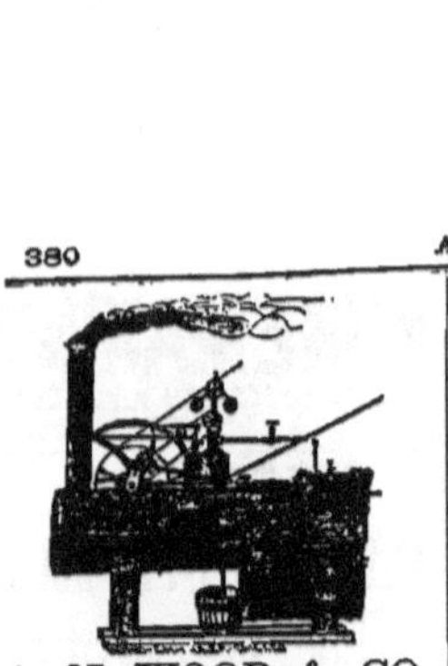

A. N. WOOD & CO.,

EATON, MADISON CO., N. Y.,

Manufacturers of their Celebrated

PORTABLE ENGINES,

For Farm and Mechanical purposes. They are particularly adapted to driving Thrashing Machines, Circular Saws, Mills of all kinds, Printing Presses, Wood or Iron Lathes, Machinery in Cabinet or Wagon Shops, Boring Artesian Wells, Pumping Water, Corn Shellers, &c., &c.

They are mounted either on legs, like the above cut, for stationary use, or on wheels, with a pole, ready for attaching a team for moving from place to place.

Mr. W. N. Fassy, of Rushville, Yates Co., N. Y., says in the Country Gentleman of Aug. 29th, 1867: "By the way, we are thrashing by steam, using a six-horse portable engine. It works to a charm, just the thing to do a nice job; it does the work of ten horses on a sweep power, and very much better."

The American Agriculturist, in editorial notes, on page 317, Sept. number, 1867, says: "Steam Thrashers are a prominent feature in Western husbandry. The horse thrashers are still in use, but are as certainly doomed as the scythe or the hand rake. They are altogether too slow for this age. The steam thrasher is mounted upon wheels, and is drawn by horses from place to place, as it is wanted. The great advantage of the steam thrasher is that it puts the wheat harvest so much into the power of the farmer. As a rule, wheat stands in the shock until it is thrashed, and the first good weather is availed of to clean the crop, and send it to market."

The Manufacturers take pleasure in referring to the following parties, some of whom have used their Portable Engines for years:

Wm. Porter & Son, 271 Pearl-st., New-York.
E. B. Osborne, Poughkeepsie, N. Y.
F. M. Hegan, Dobbs Ferry, N. Y.
A. S. Webb, Hudson, N. Y.
D. E. Teal & Co., Norwich, N. Y.
D. J. Woolworth, Yorkshire, N. Y.
Hancock Bros., Deposit, N. Y.
John Greenway, Syracuse, N. Y.
J. T. Nicks, Elmira, N. Y.
White & Fuller, Binghamton, N. Y.
John Schuyler, Bloomingdale, N. J.
C. H. Raymond, Franklin, Pa.
Wm. Stilzel, McEwensville, Pa.
Worts & Co., Toledo, Ohio.
A. W. Copeland, Detroit, Mich.
Cook & Thomas, Kalamazoo, Mich.
Moses H. Lee, Edwardsburg, Mich.
O. S. Colby, Niles, Mich.
J. H. Kiefer, E. Saginaw, Mich.
Deane & Bingham, Alpena, Mich.
J. F. Bonebrake, Mishawaka, Indiana.
Geo. A. Wood, Richardson, Indiana.
Prairie Farmer Co., Chicago, Illinois.
Geo. & C. W. Sherwood, Chicago, Illinois.
Geo. Lineberger & Co., Elwood, Ill.
G. H. Sanford, Griggsville, Ill.
J. Whiting, Elpaso, Ill.
E. Ford, Bada, Ill.
D. M. Conkey, Homer, Ill.
Wm. Illingworth, Polo, Ill.
Myres & Co., Bloomington, Ill.
E. P. Allis & Co., Milwaukee, Wis.
W. H. Amidon, Rubicon, Wis.
Owen Whitney & Co., Footville, Wis.
Daily Gazette Co., Davenport, Iowa.
Chandler & Frost, Monticello, Iowa.
Timothy Allen, West Point, Iowa.
Pioneer Printing Co., St. Paul, Minn.
Gardner & Meloy, Hastings, Minn.
Cyrus Stoner, Leitersburg, Md.
Parkersburg Mill Co., Parkersburg, W. Va.
Chisolm Bros., Charleston, S. C.
Isaac D. Spear, Mobile, Ala.
E. M. Ivens & Co., New Orleans, La.
John P. Dale, Nashville, Tenn.
Plant Bros., St. Louis, Mo.
J. C. Austin, Cosumnes, Cal.
R. G. Bradley, Cotton Plant, Ark.

Descriptive Circulars and Price Lists sent on application to
A. N. WOOD & CO.

DO YOU WANT THE AGENCY, (or for your own use), of the fastest, easiest worked, and most durable Self-Feeding Hay, Straw and Stalk Cutter. *Not to be paid for until tried.* Price, at your nearest railroad station, $10 to $20. Send for Illustrated Circular to
PEEKSKILL PLOW WORKS, Peekskill, N. Y.

Hexamer's Prong-hoe.

Price, per piece, $2.50; per dozen, $24. All orders must be accompanied by cash, or the bills will be collected on delivery, including return charges.
Address,
REISIG & HEXAMER,
New Castle, Westchester Co., N. Y.

Premium Farm Grist Mill.—Cheap, simple, and durable—adapted to all kinds of Horse-Powers, and grinds rapidly.
Send for Descriptive Circular, and address
WM. L. BOYER & BRO.,
Philadelphia, Pa.

PLOWS, PLOW CASTINGS, Caldrons, Sugar Pans, Gin Gear, Agricultural Implements, and Plantation Machinery. J. R. DECATUR, 197 Water-st., New York.

THE FARMER'S STEAM BOILER AND CALDRON.

COME AT LAST; an apparatus so long needed by Stock growers, Pork raisers, Milk men, Dairymen, and in fact, all classes where cooking in quantities, heating, steaming, boiling, distilling, &c., are required. This new boiler combines all the advantages of the best *Portable Caldron and Furnace* with the steam boiler. *No Farmer can afford to be without one.*

Numerous testimonials from some of the most noted men in the country who have them in use, can be furnished if desired. A splendid life picture at a glance from a large new Lithograph, designed for *Dealers* and *Agents*, can be sent by mail free, of postage, at 25 cents; the same framed and mounted, by Express, at 75 cents. Four sizes are now ready for the fall trade. *Circulars giving details, testimonials, prices, sent free.* D. R. PRINDLE, *Patentee and Proprietor*,
Sept. 1, 1867. East Bethany, N. Y.

THE BEST MACHINERY.

COOPER'S OLD AND EXTENSIVE FACTORY HAS FOR SALE

150 Improved Portable Engines, 8 to 30 Horse-Power.

85 Improved Stationary Engines, 20 to 125 Horse-Power.

200 Circular Saw Mills, of all Sizes.

123 Patent French Burr Flour and Feed Mills, with Bolts, and complete Machinery for same.

1,000 Cooper's Patent Sugar Pans, 8 to 15 feet long. Price $22 to $75.

1,000 Cooper's Patent Union Sugar Mills, 8 Sizes. Price, Heavy One-Horse Mill, $75.

All are being erected in the most approved and substantial manner, with recent valuable improvements.

This *Firm* was the first to commence the practice of furnishing complete fixtures for *Saw* and *Grist Mills*, and millwrights to erect and set them in operation; hence their unprecedented success and reputation *for building the best Mills in the world.* Send for Circulars, addressing
C. & J. COOPER, Mt. Vernon, Ohio.

NORTH RIVER AGRICULTURAL "WORKS"

GRIFFING & CO. PROPRIETORS

58 & 60

CORTLANDT ST. NEW-YORK

Clif's Aerating Churn.

(FORMERLY CALLED THE "DASHER.")

Needs only to be tried to be appreciated; saves time, labor, and patience; makes good butter in five minutes' time.
Send stamp for Circular.
JOHN W. DOUGLASS, Sole Agent,
Dealer in Agricultural Implements, Seeds, and Fertilizers.
181 Water-st., New York.

AMERICAN BASKET CO. NEW BRITAIN, CONN.

The most economical Crate and Basket in use. Neat, strong, compact, and well ventilated.
Agents wanted in all the fruit growing districts.
For sale, the right to manufacture for the Western and Southern States. CIRCULARS SENT FREE.

H. W. JOHNS'

IMPROVED ROOFING

Has been in use nearly ten years, and forms a handsome and reliable roof. Can be applied by any one. **Elastic Mineral Cement,** for Repairing Leaky Shingle and other Roofs. **Preservative Paints, Roofing Cement,** &c. Exclusive right to sell and apply will be given. Send for descriptive circular, prices, &c., to
H. W. JOHNS, 78 William St., N. Y.

$100 FOR A BRICK MACHINE SIMple; $150 with Tempering Box and Moulds, warranted to make 12,000 brick per day, of a superior quality. Address
FREY & SHECKLER,
Bucyrus, O.

IMPROVED FOOT LATHES.—Elegant, durable, cheap and portable. Just the thing for the Artisan or Amateur. Send for descriptive circular.
S. K. BALDWIN, Laconia, N. H.

For Rock Digging and Wall Laying Machines,

Address G. L. SHELDON, Hartsville, Mass.

PURE FERTILIZERS.

Bone Dust..........................$1.00 per 100 lbs., $60 per ton.
Peruvian Guano..................$4.00 " " " $100 " "

HENDERSON & FLEMING,
SEEDSMEN AND MARKET GARDENERS,
67 Nassau-st., New York.

THE SUNDAY SCHOOL.—Girls' and Boys' Music Box, playing "Love at Home," "Happy Land," and other familiar airs. *Price $3.00.* Manufactured expressly for LEWIS P. TIBBALS, 478 Broadway, New York. Children's Bazaar for Hobby Horses, Carriages, Swings, Skates, Sleds, and Toys.

BREAD

MIXING AND KNEADING MACHINE.

SOMETHING NEW.

These Machines *insure great saving of labor, Perfect Cleanliness, Certainty of Good Bread, and are Cheap.* From first to last, the hands do not touch the flour or other ingredients. The perspiration and other impurities of the hands and arms need no longer constitute an ingredient of the bread. By simply turning a crank, (which a child can do,) the dough is thoroughly mixed and kneaded in from 5 to 7 minutes.

For sale by the New York Bread Machine Company, No. 765 Broadway, New York.

Massachusetts Agricultural College.

Applicants for admission to the Freshman Class will be examined Oct. 1st. For further information apply to
W. S. CLARK, President.
Amherst, Mass., August 12, 1867.

MT. PLEASANT INSTITUTE.—*Private classes for Boys,* Amherst, Mass., H. C. Nash, A. M., Principal. Established 1846. Commercial and Classical. Number limited. Terms $100 per year. Circulars upon request.

ATTENTION! ALL WANTING FARMS.—Several thousand acres of superior farm and fruit land for sale cheap, at Glassboro, 18 miles south of Philadelphia, at the junction of the West Jersey and Cape May R. R. Information sent free. Address WM. ABBOTT, Glassboro, N. J.

A First Prize Medal at the

PARIS EXPOSITION has been awarded to the MASON & HAMLIN CABINET ORGANS, being the FIFTY-SEVENTH highest premium awarded them within a few years.

Sixty styles of these Organs are made, varying from $75 to $1,000 each. They are believed to be not only the best, but considering their quality, durability, &c., the cheapest instruments of the class in the world.

Circulars with full particulars free to any address.
MASON & HAMLIN,
596 Broadway, New York; 154 Tremont-st., Boston.

OFFICE OF "Passaic Carbon Works,"
159 FRONT STREET, (CORNER MAIDEN LANE).

LISTER BROTHERS,

MANUFACTURERS OF

PURE BONE DUST,

Fresh Bone Superphosphate of Lime,

Animal Charcoal, Ivory Black, &c.

Orders for the above articles manufactured at our Works on the *Passaic River, N. J.*, should be addressed to
LISTER BROTHERS, 159 Front-st., New York.

FISH GUANO.

The cheapest and best fertilizer in use, manufactured and sold by the "Mystic Oil Company," Mystic Bridge, Conn. It is pressed very dry, put up in barrels, and sent to any part of the United States for $30 per ton, in quantities less than 25 tons. For 25 tons and upwards, $25 per ton. A dried and fine ground article is sold at $40 per ton, for ten tons and upward, and for $50 per ton in smaller quantities, delivered on board vessel or R. R. at Mystic. Admirable for market gardening, grain, cotton, and other crops. Orders may be addressed to WM. CLIFT, Jr., 50 East 20th st., N. Y., or D. S. MILLS, Pres't., Mystic Bridge, Conn.

INVALIDS' WHEEL CHAIRS,

for in or out-door use, $20 to $40. INVALIDS' CARRIAGES to order. PATENT CANTERING HORSES, $12 to $75. CHILDREN'S CARRIAGES, Swings, etc. Send for Circulars.
S. W. SMITH,
90 William-st.,
NEW YORK.

Stereopticons and Magic Lanterns,

With the Improved Lime Light, illuminating brilliantly two hundred square feet of canvas, and magnifying the views to that size, at an expense of less than one dollar for a whole evening's exhibition. Easily managed and pays well.

Illustrated priced catalogue of the apparatus, with list of over two thousand artistically colored photographic views on glass, of the War, Scripture History, Choice Statuary, etc., etc., forwarded on application. T. H. McALLISTER, Optician, (of late firm of McAllister & Bro., Phila.,) 49 Nassau-street, New York.

A DESIRABLE COMPANION with a good temper and perfection in every point, and will stick by you through thick and thin—MME. DEMOREST'S DIAMOND NEEDLES.

The Iona and Israella Grapes.

ARE THEY HARDY, HEALTHY, EARLY, and PRODUCTIVE?

[illegible] has nearly ceased to be a question.

At the great meeting held at Northeast Pa., Aug. 28, consisting of about 300 members, coming from an extent of several hundreds of miles, but one only was present "with whom the Iona did not succeed." The general voice was emphatic in its favor in all points, and often where those reported most hardy had partially or wholly failed. Secretary Champlin reported "3,000 in his vicinity, all very satisfactory." These reports I have very extensively verified by my own travels and personal observations through the principal vine regions the current season.

The coloring generally has already (Aug. 29th) demonstrated that even on young vines the ripening is as early as claimed, but the most interesting sight to all lovers of good grapes and pure wine, was Mr. Griffiths' vineyard of 10,000 Ionas, which, for evenness, sturdy vigor, perfect health and keeping, left nothing to be desired. His 2,000 Israellas were in no degree inferior.

Few, comparatively, have yet had opportunity to verify by their own eating the essential and radical difference which constitutes the distinctive excellence of the Iona for table and for wine, and separates it widely from all other native grapes.

Many thousands will have that opportunity this year, and will also learn that the pure juice of ripe Iona grapes, under the [illegible] treatment in every family, will afford pure red [illegible] wine that has no disposition to acetic fermentation, [illegible], and that is vastly better than the Catawba has ever afforded under the most favorable circumstances.

I [illegible] letters as specimens of reports from as widely different points as possible. (See Pamphlet accompanying Price List, for further statements.)

MADISON, Wisconsin, Aug. [illegible], 1867.

DR. C. W. GRANT,

DEAR SIR: The Iona grape has been grown here under different management three years. That the vines will grow and sustain the winters here does not admit of question. Mr. Gill, of this city, is fruiting a considerable number of vines this season, and both his vines and fruit are satisfactory in the highest degree. We are in latitude 43 degrees.

WM. BROOKS.

[EXTRACT.]

PULTENEY, N. Y., Aug. 28, 1867.

DR. C. W. GRANT,

DEAR SIR: My Israella grapes commenced to ripen on the [illegible], Iona on the 12th, and Delaware the 20th inst. The [illegible] No. 1 Ionas purchased of you, and planted last spring [illegible] taken from one house, are perfectly splendid, all [illegible] who see them. They will prove a good standing advertisement of vines from your nursery. Many of them have already grown [illegible] six feet high, with canes at the ground as large as my finger.

Yours truly, D. S. WAGENER.

HARTFORD, Conn., Aug. 24, 1867.

C. W. GRANT, Esq.,

DEAR SIR: Not having reported to you this summer, I thought it might perhaps interest you to learn how the Iona and other [illegible] are doing with me.

The [illegible] other variety. * * * The vines set in spring of 1865 are growing splendidly, and a [illegible] crop of fruit, which seems to be entirely free from [illegible].

[illegible] Iona, now, the second year, have a good [illegible] fruit, and canes sixteen feet long and more than [illegible] in diameter.

[illegible] Iona vine (planted 1863), I am glad to notice one [illegible] "as the vines grow [illegible] ripen fruit earlier." It would now seem they will [illegible] same time as Delaware. Israella, Ad[illegible] at Hartford, began to color at the same time.

[illegible] fall off; we shall hardly have a [illegible] grafted upon Concord last winter [illegible] two canes each more than ten feet, and I fear I shall be [illegible] all my Concord and Diana in the same way, to get any fruit from them. They are nothing but [illegible]. Delaware are as good as I expected, but the crop will be small.

Yours truly, C. M. BEACH.

My [illegible] of these kinds is very large and of surpassing quality. [illegible] for Garden or Vineyard as [illegible], and my unequaled facilities and the results of past years warrant the belief that I can make more advantageous terms to buyers than can be done by any other [illegible].

Price List with Pamphlet, containing "Present State of Grape Culture," and "Batcham's What Kinds to Plant? etc.," sent on application with stamp.

C. W. GRANT,
Iona, near Peekskill, Westchester Co., N. Y.

200,000 GRAPE VINES. One and two years old.

An extra fine stock of
**DELAWARE,
CONCORD,
IVES' SEEDLING,
CREVELING, HARTFORD, DIANA, IONA,
ISRAELLA, CLINTON, CATAWBA,**
and many other good varieties.

At low rates by the dozen, 100, or 1,000.

Send for Price List.

Also a good stock of Fruit and Ornamental Trees, Evergreens, Small Fruits, Shrubs, Roses, &c., &c.

Osage Orange Plants, 2 years, at $4 per 1,000.

LENK & CO., Humboldt Nurseries,
Toledo, Ohio.

Vines and Small Fruits by Express, Prepaid.

No charge for Packing, Boxes or Delivery. Plants of 1st quality one and two years, and of every desirable variety.

Mail and Express Lists at $1, $5, $10, $25, &c.

Illustrated Circular and Price List free.

M. H. LEWIS & CO., Sandusky, Ohio.

First Class Grape Vines.

Iona, Israella and Delaware, A Specialty.

A large stock unsurpassed for quality, at the lowest rates for which good vines can be grown. Cheaper than inferior vines at no price.

All other varieties, equally well grown.

Send for Price Lists.

We shall be pleased to have parties call and examine stock.

HOLTON & ZUNDELL,
Haverstraw, Rockland Co., N. Y.

THE NEW GRAPE.

"SALEM."—THIS GRAPE IS THE MOST successful result of the Hybridizations originated and carried on by Mr. E. S. Rogers, of Salem, Massachusetts, whose well known character for probity and modesty of statement affords every guarantee for the unsurpassed excellence of this, his favorite variety. His published statement is as follows:

"The subscriber now offers for sale for the first time, a New Grape, named Salem from the place of its origin. This is a variety considered not only superior to any of the former well known numbers, but also to any hardy grape at present before the public, combining as nearly as possible every quality desired in an out door grape, being one of the hardiest, healthiest and most vigorous of vines, and producing enormous crops of beautiful and high flavored fruit.

Like other well known kinds, Nos. 4 and 15, this is a hybrid between a native and the Black Hamburg; bunch large and compact, berry large as Hamburg, of a light chestnut or Catawba color, thin skinned, perfectly free from hard pulp, very sweet and sprightly, with a most exquisite aromatic flavor, not equaled by any other out-door grape for wine or table; as early as Delaware or Hartford, having never failed to ripen its fruit, in the most unfavorable season, for the past six years.

Taking all its qualities into consideration, earliness, hardiness, and great vigor of vine, size and quality of fruit, it is pronounced by the best judges who have tried it, to have no equal among all the numerous varieties now before the public; and I can, with confidence, recommend it as the best of all my collection, and now offer it for the first time."

Salem, Feb., 1867. E. S. ROGERS, Salem, Mass.

NOTICE.—The subscriber would here state that he has disposed of his entire stock of vines and wood of the Salem Grape to J. L. WARING, of "Amenia Vineyard," Amenia, Dutchess Co., N. Y., to whom all orders for the same must be hereafter addressed. E. S. ROGERS.

Salem, Mass., March 3d, 1867.

In addition to the high merits of the "Salem," the undersigned is able to say, from personal experience and knowledge, that the claims put forth in favor of the Salem are in no respect exaggerated. During the present season it has made uniformly a most vigorous and healthy growth, and proved itself impervious to mildew, where vines of most of the new and high priced varieties growing by its side and receiving equal care in culture, have been seriously affected. It is believed that, as a paying grape, especially for market purposes, the Salem is without a competitor among out-door varieties. J. L. WARING.

I take pleasure in announcing that, since purchasing the Salem Vine, I have disposed of my Vineyard and Propagating Establishment, including the entire stock of the Salem, to JAMES A. BEQUA, Esq., who will hereafter carry on the business with every facility for its successful prosecution.

Amenia, N. Y., August 21, 1867. J. L. WARING.

Having purchased the above, and having secured the services of a most experienced and successful Propagator, with able assistants, I design to make the growing of vines for sale a specialty, and hope to furnish the public with a class of plants unsurpassed in quality, and in every instance warranted up to standard and true to name.

August 21, 1867. JAMES A. BEQUA,
Amenia, Dutchess County, N. Y.

One Thousand very extra DELAWARE LAYERS.

One Thousand very extra DIANA LAYERS.

Also a few well-grown GENUINE SALEM vines, propagated from stock bought of Mr. Rogers by F. C. Brehm, before his sale to Miss Waring. Also, Iona, Delaware, and others. Send for Price List. R. P. KENDIG,
Waterloo, Seneca Co., N. Y.

Wanted to Exchange.

A general supply of Nursery Stock wanted in exchange for Grape Vines, principally Concord, Iona and Clinton.
Address, GRAPE, Box [illegible], P. O., New York.

J. W. CONE & CO.,
Vineland, N. J., offer for Sale
700,000 CONCORD,
40,000 HARTFORD PROLIFIC,
15,000 CLINTON,
3,000 IVES' SEEDLING
GRAPE VINES.

And a large stock of CLARKE RASPBERRY plants.
Price List sent free.

1867. **To Nurserymen and Grape Growers.** 1868.

RICHARDSON & BELLOWS, (successors to Moore & Richardson,) Geneva, N. Y., offer for sale a large stock of Dwarf Pear Trees, Plum and Cherry Seedlings and Grape Vines. Send for Price List.

TO GRAPE VINE PURCHASERS!—*Grape Vines only propagated!* At the celebrated "*Mira Grape Vine Nurseries,*" immediately adjoining the Gardens of *Charles Downing, Esq.*, Newburgh, N. Y. Knowing that *good vines will always sell*, we have propagated according to our capacity, not for *large quantities* but for *good quality*. Having had a good propagation this season, we therefore particularly invite an examination and comparison of our stock before purchasing, consisting of all the known varieties, all of which will be sold low. For Circulars and Price List address JOHN W. HANMORE, Box 91, Newburgh, N. Y.

GRAPE WOOD.—We offer for sale from 3 to 5 million Concord, and 200,000 Ives' Seedling eyes.
J. W. CONE & CO.,
Vineland, N. J.

**C. E. MEISSNER
RICHMOND
STATEN [illegible] AND N.Y.**

Would call the attention of Dealers and Planters to his extensive stock of Grape Vines, and especially to the

CONCORD AND IONA.

Our Concord vines this year are pronounced by those who have examined them to be far superior to those ordinarily grown, and we challenge comparison with any other reliable establishment, both in price and excellence of plants.

By our system of growing, and in our soil, the roots of the vines attain the highest point of perfection, and it is to this in particular that we would direct the attention of purchasers and planters.

PRICE OF CONCORD VINES.

1st Class, 25 c. each; $2.00 per doz.; $6.00 per 50; $10 per 100; $75 per 1,000; $[illegible] per 10,000.

Our stock of IONA vines is also of the highest excellence, and will compare favorably with that of any other grower.

This excellent variety is fast gaining a reputation which promises to supersede all others. No person setting out a vineyard should fail to plant it extensively. The reports which we hear this year from nearly all parts of the country are of the most favorable character. We can furnish vines of this variety in any quantity, by the single vine or 10,000, at as low rates as equally good plants can be obtained from any *reliable* grower. We warrant all our plants *true to name, and of the quality stated.*

Of all the other leading varieties we have a well selected stock, which we offer at the lowest rates, for which we refer to our Price List. We would here only mention a beautiful lot of **Hartford Prolific**, which is undoubtedly the most reliable and profitable *early* market grape which we have.

Also a very superior lot of Diana vines, both 1 & 2 years old.

CLINTON VINES.—Of this excellent and profitable wine grape we have a choice lot of plants. Price: 1st Class, 25c. each; $2.50 per doz.; $5 per 50; $8 per 100; $65 per 1,000; $600 per 10,000.

For further information send for Price List, and address
G. E. MEISSNER, Richmond P. O., Staten Island, N. Y.

Mead's American Grape Culture,

AND WINE-MAKING.

Extract from Secretary Batcham's Review.

"I have commended it highly on its *general* merits, and also on very important *special* merits entirely its own. I have heard a number of our most experienced grape-growers speak of the work in terms of very high praise, all concurring in the opinion that it is by far the best work on the subject that has yet appeared. The very clear and independent manner in which he treats the subject of varieties of grapes, defining which are really good, bad, or indifferent, and the reasons why they are one or the other, is one of the most timely features of the book, and will be the saving of thousands of dollars to planters. No other author has given half so much sound information in regard to varieties in so little space as Mr. Mead. Indeed, on all points he is rich in information, and there are single chapters that many will find worth the price of the book. The questions as to the 'Morality' and 'Profits' of grape-culture and wine-making must be met and answered by every one who engages in it as a business, and Mr. Mead gives the result of his examination of them."

The book is a very handsome octavo volume, of nearly 500 pages, and nearly 200 most life-like engravings. It is suitable for parlor or library, and interesting for family or student, and is essentially new in manner and matter.

PRICE $3.00.

I fully concur in Mr. Batcham's high opinion of it, and have made arrangements with Messrs. Harpers, the publishers, by which I can furnish it to Clubs at very liberal rates, and also to single subscribers by mail, where there are no Bookstores. C. W. GRANT,
Iona, near Peekskill, Westchester Co., N. Y.

Grape Vines & Small Fruits.

Delawares,	1 and 2 years old,	$10,	$15,	$25	per hundred.	
Iona,	1 and 2 " "	$15,	$20,	$30	"	"
Israella,	1 and 2 " "	$15,	$20,	$30	"	"
Adirondac,	1 and 2 " "	$20,	$25,	$30	"	"
Ives' Seedling,		$15,	$25,		"	"
Concord,		$10,	$15,	$25	"	"
Rogers' Hybrids, all the good Nos.,				$15	"	"
Kittatinny Blackberries,				$15	"	"
Clarke Raspberries,				$25	"	"

Also large vines for immediate bearing, which would have borne the present season if permitted. Our Vines are equal to any in the market. Descriptive Catalogue and Price List of above and other varieties sent on application to
HUSTED & HAZELTON, Delaware, Ohio.

GRAPE VINES.

Iona, Israella, Delaware and Allen's Hybrid. From one year single eye plants to four years old plants with arms. Also, Hartford Prolific, and Alvey, one and two years old. Ranging in price from 25 cents to $5, according to age and size. My vines are grown from bearing wood, and for quality I can refer to those who have purchased them the past two years. CHARLES M. MASON,
West Hartford, Conn.

50,000 one year old Concord Vines from long cuttings for sale low.
JOHN B. CALKINS, New Market, N. J.

Dutch Bulbous Roots.

J. M. THORBURN & CO.,
15 JOHN STREET,
NEW YORK.

Have now in Store and imported by them from Holland in the finest condition

HYACINTHS, TULIPS, LILIES, CROCUS, SNOWDROPS, CROWN IMPERIALS, NARCISSUS, SCILLAS, ETC., ETC., ETC.

Priced Catalogues of Bulbs, containing directions for their management, mailed on application. Also:

BEAUTIFUL COLLECTIONS OF BULBOUS ROOTS.

No. 1.—ASSORTMENTS OF (If by mail, add 14 cts.)

- 6 Fine Named Double and Single Hyacinths, *for pots, glasses or open border*
- 1 Polyanthus Narcissus
- 6 Early Tulips
- 12 Fine Mixed Crocus
- 1 Persian Iris

$2.00

No. 2.—ASSORTMENTS OF (If by mail, add 30 cts.)

- 6 Fine Named Double and Single Hyacinths, *for pots, glasses or open border*
- 6 Fine Double Tulips
- 15 Beautiful Named Early Tulips
- 25 Fine Mixed Crocus
- 3 Polyanthus Narcissus
- 6 Double Narcissus
- 3 Bulbocodium Vernum
- 3 Persian Iris
- 25 Double Snowdrops

$5.00

No. 3.—ASSORTMENTS OF (If by mail, add 75 cts.)

- 10 Fine Named Double and Single Hyacinths, *for pots, glasses or open border*
- 50 Fine Mixed Crocus
- 25 Beautiful Named Early Tulips
- 12 Fine Named Double Tulips
- 4 Polyanthus Narcissus
- 12 Double Narcissus
- 6 Persian Iris
- 6 English Iris
- 1 Crown Imperial
- 6 Bulbocodium Vernum
- 50 Double Snowdrops

$10.00

ALSO:

Fresh Mahaleb Cherry Pits, 35 cts. per lb. **Pear Seed**, deliverable in December, at $3 per lb. Rates for large quantities on application.

J. M. THORBURN & CO.,
Seed Warehouse,
15 JOHN STREET, New York.

NEW AUTUMN CATALOGUE OF Imported Dutch Bulbous Roots,

With descriptions and directions for their cultivation, now ready for mailing.

J. M. THORBURN & CO.,
15 John-st., New York.

Bulbous Roots for the Trade.

Our **Wholesale Catalogue of Imported Dutch Bulbous Roots,** for the autumn of 1867, is now ready for mailing to applicants enclosing a postage stamp.

J. M. THORBURN & CO.,
15 John-st., New York.

50,000 HYACINTHS, TULIPS, CROCUS, Snowdrops, and other Dutch Bulbs, at low rates.—New Strawberries, Chas. Downing, (plants received direct from Mr. Carpenter, and at his prices), Lady of the Lake, Great Hippowam, Agriculturist, and 20 other new and standard sorts. 1,000 pounds fresh Pear, Apple, Cherry, Quince, and Mahaleb seed. Also stock of all kinds. Flower and Garden seed. All at low rates. Agents wanted. Catalogues now ready. B. M. WATSON, Old Colony Nurseries and Seed Establishment, Plymouth, Mass.

Adirondac Grape Nursery and Vineyard.

We offer at greatly reduced prices, a large stock of grape vines, one, two, and three years. All desirable varieties—including the two new Hybrids, "SALEM," and "DIANA HAMBURG." Quality of vines unsurpassed. Our autumn Price List and Descriptive Catalogue, or Wholesale Price List for the trade, sent on application.

JOHN W. BAILEY & CO., Plattsburgh, Clinton Co., N. Y.

THE MUSCOGEE GRAPE.—Small, black grape. Large, handsome bunch—sweet enough for wine without sugar. The vine a good grower, a good bearer, and fully matures its fruit. Can be had (price $2.50) of

N. RICHARDS, (11 Maiden Lane, New York,)

who has also other varieties of vines.

READ the opinion of the "*Scientific American*," concerning the *Favorite Washing Machine*. Send stamp for Illustrated circular. Address S. H. JENNINGS, Deep River, Conn.

Dutch Bulbous Flower Roots.

Sent by Mail, Post-paid, at Catalogue Prices.

B. K. BLISS & SON

Offer for sale a large and well selected assortment of the above, just received from Holland, embracing the most desirable varieties of DOUBLE AND SINGLE HYACINTHS; POLYANTHUS NARCISSUS; DOUBLE AND SINGLE EARLY AND LATE TULIPS; DOUBLE AND SINGLE NARCISSUS; JONQUILS; CROCUS, CROWN IMPERIALS; IRIS, SNOW-DROPS; SCILLAS, HARDY GLADIOLUS; RANUNCULUS; ANEMONES, JAPAN AND MANY OTHER LILIES. Also a fine assortment of GREENHOUSE BULBS, comprising CYCLAMENS, IXIAS, OXALIS, SPARAXIS, TRITOMAS, ACHIMENES, GLOXINIAS, &c., &c.

Particular attention is invited to their

New Illustrated Autumn Catalogue,

(containing an accurate description of each variety, with particular directions for culture, so that any person, however unacquainted, can not fail to succeed,) which will be mailed to all applicants enclosing ten cents.

Collections containing a fine assortment of all the leading varieties of the above will also be mailed post-paid, as follows: Collection No. 1, $20; No. 2, $10; No. 3, $5.00; No. 4, $3.00. For the contents of each collection and further particulars, see Catalogue.

The following varieties will be sent by mail, post-paid, upon receipt of prices affixed. Selection of varieties to be left with us. When less than the specified number are ordered, an additional price will be charged.

	Per doz.
Hyacinths, double or single, fine named varieties	$4.50
Hyacinths, double or single, fine unnamed varieties	2.00
Hyacinths, Parisian, double and single, mixed	1.50
Tulips, early double, fine named varieties	1.50
Tulips, early double, fine mixed unnamed	75
Tulips, early single, fine named varieties	1.50
Tulips, early single, fine mixed unnamed	75
Tulips, Parrot, fine mixed, unnamed	1.00
Tulips, Byblоemen, bizarres and rose, fine named	3.00
Tulips, Bybloemen, fine mixed	1.00
Tulips, various sorts mixed, unnamed	75
Crocus, mixed, blue, white, yellow, and striped	25
Crocus, finest named varieties	40
Polyanthus Narcissus, finest named varieties	2.50
Polyanthus Narcissus, fine mixed unnamed	1.50
Jonquils, double	1.50
Jonquils, single, sweet-scented	75
Iris, English, fine mixed varieties	1.00
Iris, Spanish, fine mixed varieties	75
Ranunculus, fine mixed varieties	50
Anemones, fine mixed varieties	50
Gladiolus, hardy fine mixed varieties	1.00
Snowdrops, double	60
Snowdrops, single	30
Hyacinthus, fine mixed varieties	75
Lilium Auratum, a new superb variety from Japan, *each*	$3, $4, and 5.00
Japan Lily, red and white, *each* 50 cents	5.00
White Lily, (Lilium candidum.)	1.15
Lily of the Valley	2.00
Lilium longiflorum	2.00
Peonies, twelve varieties	4.00

Orders may be addressed to

B. K. BLISS & SON,
41 Park Row, New York,
Or, 231 Main-street, Springfield, Mass.

Grape Wood and Osage Orange Vines

At wholesale, *extremely low*. No extra charge when cash is advanced on orders at retail rates. Plants 1st quality and *warranted genuine*. We will supply planters and the Trade with Ives', Concord, Hartford, Delaware, Clin, Iona, Rogers' Nos. 1, 3, 4, 15 and 19, Creveling, Norton's Va., Herbemont, Cynthiana, Salem, Martha, &c.; with the three best Currants, Raspberries, Blackberries and Goodrich potatoes. Illustrated Circular and Price Lists *free*.

M. H. LEWIS & CO., Sandusky, Ohio.

IVES' SEEDLING GRAPE VINE

That never fails. The wine sells to Longworth's Wine House at $4.25 per gallon. 75,000 vines of superior growth for sale at lowest prices. Send for its history and Price List, FREE. Also all leading kinds with nine new varieties from Longworth's School of Vines, selected by Dr. John A. Warder, with nursery stock generally. JAS. F. MARTIN.

Mt. Washington, Hamilton Co., Ohio.

VINES AT WHOLESALE

To Dealers. For sale this fall, in one lot, about 5,000 very choice vines. Layers and transplants 2 and 3 years old of Iona, Israella, Adirondac, &c., first-rate plants for the retail trade. Also, a large quantity of Grape Wood for sale.

Address A. F. TAIT, Woodstock Vineyard,
Morrisania, Westchester Co., N. Y.

GRAPE VINES.

Extra Strong Vines at Common Prices.

Special attention is invited to our stock of 2 year Concord, Ives', Hartford, and other varieties. Also a fine stock of one year plants of all the leading kinds. Send for Price List.

I. H. BABCOCK & CO., Lockport, N. Y.

VINES.

IONA..........50c. each; $70 per hundred; $130 per 1000.
CONCORD.......15c. " $10 " " $75 " "

Delaware, Hartford Prolific, Adirondac, Allen's Hybrid, 3 yrs. Iona, &c. C. W. CLAPP, Wappingers Falls, N. Y.

ROSES, $120 per 1,000.

CAMELLIAS, $20 per 100.

RHODODENDRONS, $100 per 100.

PARSONS & CO.,
Flushing, N. Y

Rochester Commercial Nurseries,

Established 1830.

W. S. LITTLE, Proprietor,

(FORMERLY H. E. HOOKER & CO.)

The NEW CIRCULAR OF PRICES, (by the Dozen, Hundred and Thousand,) for the Fall Trade, is JUST PUBLISHED and will be sent FREE TO ALL APPLICANTS.

I have grown and offer for sale this year, an unusually large and fine assortment of Nursery Products, containing every description of

Hardy Trees and Plants,

INCLUDING STANDARD AND DWARF FRUIT TREES, VINES, &c.

With all the varieties of latest introduction, and

HARDY ORNAMENTAL TREES, SHRUBS AND ROSES,

BESIDES MANY SPECIALTIES AND NOVELTIES,

For a description of which, see "Circular." Send for the Circular. Address

WM. S. LITTLE,
COMMERCIAL NURSERIES, ROCHESTER, N. Y.

BLOOMINGTON NURSERY.

16th year, 10 Green-houses, 350 Acres Fruit, Ornamental and Nursery Stock, General Assortment.

1,000,000 Apple, 1 to 4 years, superb yearlings, 1000, $50.
150,000 Pear, Stand. and Dw'f. *Dw'f. Apple*, all sizes.
40,000 Cherry, largely Richmond or May, 100, $15 to $25.
30,000 Peach, Hale's Early, &c., 1000, $125.
300,000 Grape, strong Concord layers, 1000, $85; Hartford layers, 1000, $150; Ives, $180; Rogers, Iona, &c.
5,000,000 Osage Orange, 1st class, 100,000, $250.
50,000 Currant, Gooseberry and Raspberry.
30,000 Kittatinny Blackberry, warranted genuine, strong, first class every way, 1000, $150. (See separate advertisement.)
1,000,000 Apple Stock, extra, selected 1 year, 1000, $10.
50,000 Pear Stock, fine, 1 year, 1000, $25; Quince, Cherry.
30,000 Roses, all classes, Marshal Neil, fine plants, $9 per doz.; Evergreens, immense stock, Tulips, Hyacinths, and other Hardy Bulbs. Send 2 red stamps for New Descriptive and Trade List.

F. K. PHOENIX, Bloomington, Ill.

Atlantic Small Fruit Nurseries.

Grape Vines, Strawberries, Raspberries, Blackberries, &c., &c. The largest and most complete stock in the country to order from. Every article WARRANTED TRUE TO NAME. Plants, &c., imported to order. We offer inducements to cash buyers unsurpassed, if equaled, elsewhere, especially for large quantities. Price List one stamp. Address

C. K. & J. B. FRITTS, Elwood, N. J.

☞ Grape Wood wanted in quantity.

IONA AND ISRAELLA VINES.

A large and fine stock of these new grapes, 1 and 2 years old, strongly rooted; also, Framingham, Delaware, Adirondac, and other kinds. The trade supplied on liberal terms.

Address HOVEY & CO.,
53 North Market-st., Boston, Mass.

GRAPE VINES.

Delaware, Iona, Israella, Adirondac, and all other leading varieties of vines AT LOW RATES to Dealers and those who wish to plant vineyards. Send for Circular.

J. W. HELMER, Lockport, N. Y.

1,500,000 Superior Grape Vines, 1, 2 and 3 years old, 150 varieties. 2,500,000 Raspberry, Blackberry and Strawberry plants, all varieties. Cheapest good stock extant. Send stamp for Price List. Grape Wood of all kinds for sale. L. E. DAKE, Rochester Grape Nurseries, N. Y.

To Wine Growers!

Grape Sugar Syrup for sale by HARTMANN & LAIST, 47 East Second-st., Cincinnati, Ohio.
Pamphlets and Price List furnished gratis on application.

50,000 1 and 2-year Cherry trees; 10,000 3-year Apple; 30,000 1-year Apple; 50,000 fine Apple stocks, and a general Nursery stock. W...PLER & TILLOTSON, Trotwood, Ohio.

Just Published

A NEW WORK ON APPLES.

AMERICAN POMOLOGY.

APPLES.

By DOCT. JOHN A. WARDER,

PRESIDENT OHIO POMOLOGICAL SOCIETY; VICE-PRESIDENT AMERICAN POMOLOGICAL SOCIETY, ETC.

293 Illustrations.

To pomologists a work by Dr. Warder will need no commendation. Though a citizen of Ohio, he is so sure to be at any pomological gathering, be it East or West, that the whole country claims him, and if any one has a right to entitle his work *American* Pomology it is certainly Dr. Warder. The present is the first instalment of a work intended to cover the whole ground. In it the author has attempted the difficult task of bringing apples into something like order.

This volume has about 750 pages, the first 375 of which are devoted to the discussion of the general subjects of propagation, nursery culture, selection and planting, cultivation of orchards, care of fruit, insects, and the like; the remainder is occupied with descriptions of apples. With the richness of material at hand, the trouble was to decide what to leave out. It will be found that while the old and standard varieties are not neglected, the new and promising sorts, especially those of the South and West, have prominence. A list of selections for different localities by eminent orchardists is a valuable portion of the volume, while the Analytical Index or *Catalogue Raisonné*, as the French would say, is the most extended American fruit list ever published, and gives evidence of a fearful amount of labor.

This differs from any fruit book heretofore published in this country, in its complete classification of apples. The author gives the principal European systems and modestly puts forth his own to be tested by practice. He divides apples into four classes, according to their forms. Each of these classes is sub-divided by other obvious characters, and it would seem that any apple described in the book might be easily identified. We trust that this will prove a great help to the pomologist.

Fruit-growers will welcome this book as a valuable and long-wished for addition to pomological literature, and it will be found equally useful to the novice and the experienced orchardist. The work has 293 illustrations, is printed on good paper and well bound.

SENT POST-PAID, PRICE $3.00.

ORANGE JUDD & CO.,
245 Broadway and 41 Park Row, N. Y.

A NEW WORK.

GARDENING FOR PROFIT,

IN THE MARKET AND FAMILY GARDEN.

BY PETER HENDERSON.

Illustrated.

This is the first work on Market Gardening ever published in this country. Its author is well known as a market gardener of eighteen years' successful experience. In this work he has recorded this experience, and given without reservation the methods necessary to the profitable culture of the commercial or

MARKET GARDEN.

It is a work for which there has long been a demand, and one which will commend itself, not only to those who grow vegetables for sale, but to the cultivator of the

FAMILY GARDEN

To whom it presents methods quite different from the old ones generally practiced. It is an

ORIGINAL AND PURELY AMERICAN

work, and not made up, as books on gardening too often are, by quotations from foreign authors.

Everything is made perfectly plain, and the subject treated in all its details, from the selection of the soil to preparing the products for market. Frames, Hot-beds, and Forcing Houses, the management of which is usually so troublesome to the novice, are fully described, and the conditions of success and causes of failure clearly stated.

The success of the market gardeners near New York City is proverbial, and this is the only work that sets forth the means by which this success has been attained. Valuable hints are given to those who would raise Vegetables at the South for northern markets.

The following synopsis of its contents will show the scope of the work:

Men Fitted for the Business of Gardening.
The Amount of Capital Required and Working Force per Acre.
Profits of Market Gardening.
Location, Situation, and Laying Out.
Soils, Drainage, and Preparation.
Manures. Implements.
Uses and Management of Cold Frames.
Formation and Management of Hot-beds
Forcing Pits or Green-houses.
Seeds and Seed Raising.
How, When, and Where to Sow Seeds.
Transplanting. Insects.
Packing of Vegetables for Shipping.
Preservation of Vegetables in Winter.
Vegetables, their Varieties and Cultivation.

SENT POST-PAID. PRICE, $1.50.

ORANGE JUDD & CO.,
245 Broadway and 41 Park Row, N. Y.

SQUASHES;

HOW TO GROW THEM.

By JAMES J. H. GREGORY.

A most valuable little Treatise for Farmers and Gardeners. It tells about

Selecting the Soil.
How much Manure.
Preparing and Planting.
Hoeing and Cultivating.
Setting of the Fruit.
Ripening; Gathering.
Storing of the Crop.
Care During Winter.
Market Prices and Varieties.
When to Take Out Seed.

SENT POST-PAID, - Price, paper covers, 30 cts.

Either of the above-named books will be sent post-paid, on receipt of price, by the Publishers.

Also, many other new and valuable books for the FARM, GARDEN, AND HOUSEHOLD.

SEND FOR A CATALOGUE.

ORANGE JUDD & CO.,
245 Broadway and 41 Park Row, N. Y.

GRAPE CULTURIST.

By ANDREW S. FULLER.

This is the best Book published on Hardy Grape Culture.

CONTENTS.

INTRODUCTORY.—BOTANICAL CHARACTER OF THE Vine, Propagation by Seed.—4 *Illustrations.*

GROWING FROM SEED—GATHER WHEN FULLY RIPE.

PROPAGATION BY SINGLE BUDS.—MODE OF OPERATION, Planting in Beds, Single Buds in Open Air, Starting in Hot-Beds, Form of Single Bud Cutting—3 *Illustrations.*

CUTTINGS OF UNRIPE WOOD.—THOUSANDS OF VINES are Annually Produced from Green Cuttings.—4 *Illus.*

PROPAGATING HOUSE.—PERFECTION SHOULD BE our Aim, Span Roofed Propagating House, Lean-to Propagating House, Single Roofed House, Flues.—2 *Ill.*

CUTTINGS IN OPEN AIR.—TIME TO MAKE CUTTINGS, Selection of Cuttings, Form of Cuttings, Mallet Cuttings.

LAYERING THE VINE.—THIS IS ONE OF THE MOST Certain and Convenient Methods in Use.—1 *Illustration.*

GRAFTING THE GRAPE.—THIS IS AN OLD BUT VERY Uncertain Mode of Propagating the Grape, but Can be Used Successfully.—4 *Illustrations.*

HYBRIDIZING AND CROSSING.—THESE ARE OPERATIONS that Should Demand the Attention of Every One Who Undertakes to Produce New Varieties, Mode of Operation.—3 *Illustrations.*

TRANSPLANTING—VINES WILL OFTEN REQUIRE ONE Season of Nursery Culture before being Planted in the Vineyard, Heeling-in.—3 *Illustrations.*

SOIL AND SITUATION.—MUCH DEPENDS UPON THEM. Preparing the Soil, Manures and their Operations

STEM APPENDAGES.—SPINES, HAIRS, LATERALS. Forms of Leaves, Tendrils, Buds.—7 *Illustrations.*

PLANTING THE VINE.—A GREAT DIVERSITY OF Opinion, My Own Rule, Root Pruning, How to Plant.

GRAPE TRELLISES.—2 *Illustrations.*

TIME TO PRUNE VINES.—PRUNING AND TRAINING. Opposite Arms, Oblique Arms, A Plan for Poor Soils.

GARDEN CULTURE.—POSITION OF BORDER, TRAINING the Vines, Four Tiers of Arms, Double Stem, Trellises in Gardens, Training to Stakes, Girdling the Vine, Removing the Leaves.—9 *Illustrations.*

GATHERING THE FRUIT.—PRESERVING THE FRUIT. Wine Making, Pruning Shears.—1 *Illustration.*

INSECTS.—ROSE CHAFER, GRAPE VINE FLEA BEETLE, Spotted Pelidnota, Tree Beetle, Caterpillars, Yellow Bear, Hog Caterpillar, Grape Vine Sphinx, Blue Caterpillar, Procris Americana, Leaf Rollers, Thrips, Aphis, Red Spider, Vine Scale, Diseases, Mildew, Sun Scald.—18 *Illus.*

DESCRIPTION OF (*nearly Seventy*) VARIETIES.

REVIEW OF VARIOUS SYSTEMS OF PRUNING AND Training, Reversing the Arms, Single Arm System, Bow System, Long Rod Spur System, Upright Canes, Thomery System.—Index.

SENT POST-PAID. - - - PRICE $1.50

ORANGE JUDD & CO.,
245 Broadway and 41 Park Row, N. Y

AMERICAN AGRICULTURIST

FOR THE

Farm, Garden, and Household.

"AGRICULTURE IS THE MOST HEALTHFUL, MOST USEFUL, AND MOST NOBLE EMPLOYMENT OF MAN."—WASHINGTON.

ORANGE JUDD & CO., PUBLISHERS AND PROPRIETORS. Office, 245 BROADWAY.

ESTABLISHED IN 1842.
Published also in German at $1.50 a Year.

$1.50 PER ANNUM, IN ADVANCE.
SINGLE NUMBER, 15 CENTS.
4 Copies for $5; 10 for $12; 20 or more, $1 each.

VOLUME XXVI—No. 11. NEW-YORK, NOVEMBER, 1867. NEW SERIES—No. 250.

[COPYRIGHT SECURED.]

THREE MEMBERS OF THE TEMPERANCE SOCIETY.—FROM A PAINTING BY J. F. HERRING.—*Engraved for the American Agriculturist.*

We [illegible] Mr. Herring appreciated water in its [illegible] purity, in its invigorating freshness, [illegible], joy-giving, life-giving [illegible], showered upon us as one of H[illegible] best boons, welling up from [illegible] depths; making glad the pastures, [illegible] the cattle, reviving the faint, refreshing the [illegible].—The group of heads before us is a [illegible] conception, and the picture [illegible] from different points of view. The artist's name for his production is the same which we have given it above, and in this age of excess and whiskey frauds we may well ponder upon the superiority of this natural beverage to all others, and perhaps join the horses in a draught. The characters exhibited by the three animals are very different. The nearest drank his sip from habit, was not thirsty, and is a little cross. The next has filled himself to satiety and enjoys it to the full; while the later comer, in the earnestness of thirst, is pumping the big draughts down his throat with a real gusto. We see in the first horse a hypochondriac who has joined the temperance society, partly to get some good if he can, partly to have society, and to be able to talk, to carp and criticise. He bears about him the marks of former years of excess. The middle one portrays the member who never committed an excess in his life, and never will. He is a member of the society by nature, genial, honest, good, strong in the right, and by precept and example wishes to keep others so. Black Hawk is Young America on the right track, now wildly enthusiastic as a temperance reformer, as he was gay among the clicking glasses. He goes in for water on his own account and on everybody's else, and withal is just as good, honest, and exemplary as his friend by his side. Our friends will agree with us that the above is a successful reproduction of one of Herring's most admired pictures. There are many artists who can paint a horse's head with anatomical accuracy, but there are very few who, like Herring, can give the expression that indicates the character of the animal. Every lover of the horse can judge quite correctly of his disposition by looking at his face and eye.

Contents for November, 1867.

INDEX TO "BASKET" OR SHORTER ARTICLES.

AMERICAN AGRICULTURIST.

NEW-YORK, NOVEMBER, 1867.

There is a chilly sound in the word November, yet to Americans it is a cheerful month. We read Hood's lines, "No sun, no moon, no dawn, no noon," and so on, through his description of an English fog, to his conclusion, *No vember*, while we rejoice in the bland noons of our "Indian Summer," and in the mellow sunlight, dusky and softened by the thin smoke which veils the distant hills. The brown leaves are in windrows by the fences; the mornings are frosty, but bright and bracing, and the sunsets have that ruddy glow which promises other days as perfect as the one just passing. So the early part of the month goes by, giving time for all necessary labors before the days and nights are colder, and the plastic and crumbly soil becomes stone, and the storm clouds give us snow instead of showers, and the ringing of the skates, and the shouts of the skaters, come up from the ponds.

The labors and pleasures of the month are various, being in part a continuation of those of the past month, but chiefly those of that preparation for winter, which it is dangerous to postpone.

The harvests are gathered and secured. In part, no doubt, they are already marketed, and paid for. The country has been doing, of late years, much more a "cash business" than used to be the case, and it especially behooves producers promptly to check the tendency to any other course. "Short credits make long friends," and the payment on the spot for value received is better still.

The winter brings with it pleasure to those prepared for it, but suffering to the improvident, and to those who, from sickness or no fault of their own, are not provided to meet its rigors. If our hearts rise in thankfulness to the All-Father for His mercies to us, let our hands and hearts go out to His children, our brethren, who are likely to suffer. He trusts us with good things this year, and we should be the almoners of His bounty, good stewards, kind, tender, and judicious in sharing our surplus, if we would enter into the joy of our Lord, be more widely useful, and more trusted by Him in the future.

Hints About Work.

Buildings.—It is of prime importance that the fair weather of the early part of this month should be employed to put the farm buildings and their surroundings in good order for winter, and it is well to be a little ahead with such work. Go carefully over old buildings, tightening weather boards, renewing eaves-troughs and spouts. Clear surface ditches, to keep water out of the barn-yards, and away from the foundations. Roofs may be temporarily patched without much, if any, nailing, by simply driving shingles here and there between the courses to carry water over actual holes. Old roofs are often more damaged than benefited by mending, unless it is very thoroughly done. A little careless hammering and nail driving will split shingles and start nails, and open more holes than it closes.

Roads that are to be used during the winter must be put in order before frost; the stones picked off, gravel or earth put on where they have washed, good side drainage made,—on both sides, if possible,—the surface well rounded to turn water, and to make easy turn-offs for the wash that follows the wheel tracks down the hills.

Bridges.—If the rains and freshets have moved stones in the brooks and runs, and deposited an unusual amount of gravel anywhere, it will most likely be where they are contracted to pass through bridges or culverts. These should be carefully examined and cleaned out, for when ice forms, and an unusual flow of water comes, serious damage may result. It is more important that there should be a chance for water to flow off rapidly in passing and after passing a bridge, than that it should have easy access; a single stone will dam up a stream greatly.

Plowing.—Plow lands that will not be subject to wash. The more plowing is done in the fall, the more will the hurry of spring work be relieved, and, as a general rule, the better will the land be prepared for the crops. Fall plowing kills weeds; it kills grubs; it exposes the soil to the action of the frost, and if manure be plowed in, which is best if the land is prepared for root crops or corn, it becomes better incorporated with the soil. Clay lands and heavy loams are especially benefited by fall plowing; the action of the frost, or rather thawing and freezing, benefits such land as much as many loads of manure. Plow such land in ridges, turning two furrows together. Good loamy soils may be plowed with flat or lap furrows. We prefer the former, and sandy or light land, or rich and dark mould, should be plowed flat

Grain Fields.—In plowing furrows to carry off surface water, where this may be necessary, take care that their direction is such that they will not collect too much, wash deep gullies, and thus do more harm than good.

Draining.—So long as we do not have real winter weather, the work of underdraining may be pushed forward. It is more important to keep well up with the tile laying, for we may be caught by heavy freezing rains and snow-storms, and so all work be stopped suddenly

Manure.—Bring in all muck sods, surface parings, forest soil, and leaves, that you can, to be used in composts, and lay up good even heaps of these materials, alternated with stable manure, in layers, using at least twice as much vegetable mould in whatever form you have it, as of the stable manure. The compost heaps should be of assorted materials, all, of course, vegetable matter, like potato tops and swamp grass, or other long litter, put together with a sufficiency of manure to make the whole ferment, or leaving the nitrogenous stable manure out, and adding instead freshly dry-slaked lime, or wood ashes, at the rate of about one bushel to the cart-load. Composts of coarse, porous, materials, not made with lime or ashes, should stand over a sunken hogshead or other vat for containing liquid. This should be pumped every few days over the heap, and allowed to run back again to the vat, which should be supplied with water if there is any lack. In all composts, hog manure goes further than that of the horse, which is much more powerful in starting and maintaining fermentation than that of milch cows and young cattle, but hardly equal to that of fattening cattle or well fed oxen.

Fences.—We cannot too strongly present the evils of bad fences. The freezing and thawing of winter will almost surely develop the weak spots in old lines of fences, and breachy cattle will be sure to find them, if they are allowed either in the highway or in the fields. Grain fields are a strong attraction. The fences, therefore, should be looked to, weak posts staked up or renewed, sound rails or boards put in place of failing ones, and all secured against cattle, wind, and frost.

Horses, if well fed, enjoy cold weather. Although they show a natural preference for the sheltered side of the barn-yard, they seldom manifest any dislike to exposure to severe cold, unless they have been blanketed, and habituated to warm stables. When horses are warm, always blanket them, either in stables or in the open air; take care that they are exposed to no draughts. When cooled off, remove the blanket. Carriage horses, which it is desirable should have a shiny coat, may wear linen covers buttoning round the breast, and having a crooper attached. Give good daily grooming, plenty to eat, water regularly, provide good ventilation, and let the sunlight into the stable.

Beeves.—Feed freely, but uniformly, all they will eat with a relish, changing character of the feed according to your judgment, if there be any failure of appetite. Keep salt always before them or accessible. Prepare the feed in another apartment from the one in which the cattle stand, and be punctual to the minute in feeding. In increasing the amount of grain or oil-meal, do it gradually, watching the effect. Use the card and brush frequently, and litter freely. Beeves need pure air and clean stables as much as horses; warmth is more important than light to them, as to all fattening stock.

Cows, however, need light, clean, stables, with good ventilation. Warmth is desirable also, as well as great quiet. Give them an hour or two in a sunny yard daily, if the weather be pleasant.

Young Stock.—Keep in warm sheds or stables, with the range of yards exposed to the south and east. Feed, water, and salt, regularly.

Sheep.—See "Walks and Talks" on sheep feeding. Keep in dry, roomy, sheds and yards; give plenty of litter, but accommodate them with some hard ground. Feed in racks and troughs protected by sheds. Increase the feed gradually. Oil-cake will probably be found as economical as any feed, more so than any other you can purchase. Sheep feeders are satisfied if they get the manure clear, the sheep selling for their cost with the value of the feed added.

Hogs may be pushed forward as rapidly as possible, and marketed according to the feeder's best judgment. Prices often rule much higher early in the month than later, but the difference is often made up by the increase in the manure pile. The value of manure is in almost direct proportion to the quality of the food of animals. That of fattening hogs is very rich.

Poultry.—See article on page 408. Keep in warm, light, houses, and feed a little meat or scrapcake daily, and hens will soon begin to lay.

Orchard and Nursery.

In a mild November, planting may advantageously be done, but if the weather be very frosty, it is better to postpone it until spring.

Heel-in trees received from the nursery after cold weather sets in, rather than attempt to plant them in half frozen ground.

Fruit in barrels should be kept as cool as possible without freezing. Do not close up the cellar of the fruit room, except there is danger of frost. A detached cellar, or one under an out-building, is much preferable for the storage of fruits or vegetables to that under the dwelling, as fruit, in ripening, gives off a quantity of unwholesome gas.

Cider should be made from good fruit only, as suggested last month. Where vinegar is the object, so much pains need not be taken. See page 410.

Labels will need looking to, and the defaced ones replaced. Go over the newly planted trees, and see that the nursery labels are not wired on so tightly as to injure the limb. Do not trust entirely to labels, but have a record of every orchard.

Cions may be cut, labelled, and stored in sawdust in the cellar.

Stocks for root grafting are to be taken up, assorted, tied in bundles, or packed in boxes, and put away in the cellar.

Nursery Rows should have the plow run between them. See that surface water will run off.

Plowing, Draining, and other preparatory work, may be done as long as the ground is not frozen.

Fruit Garden.

Most of the general directions given under "Orchard," apply here. Much may be done to prepare for next spring's planting, and in many favorable localities plants may be put out now.

Covering of tender raspberries with earth, mulching of strawberries, and such work of protecting, is usually done too early, and the plants suffer from being smothered. It is better to defer the operation until freezing weather.

Fruit should be kept cool. Grapes, if kept at a low and even temperature, may be preserved for a long time in an eatable condition.

Blackberries and Raspberries may be propagated from cuttings of the roots. These should be prepared before the ground freezes. Cut the roots in pieces two or three inches long, and place them in a box with alternate layers of soil. The box should have holes in the bottom to allow any superfluous moisture to pass off, and should be buried in a dry spot below the reach of frost.

Grape Vines.—Prune when the leaves have fallen. Those who wish to propagate vines from cuttings should try the plan given on page 409. It is not practical to give directions for pruning in these brief notes. There are now many excellent treatises giving the philosophy and practice of grape culture.

Currant Cuttings may be set, if the ground is not frozen; otherwise they may be tied in bundles, and treated as noted for grape cuttings, on page 409.

Kitchen Garden.

It will be necessary to hurry up all unfinished work, secure the crops that are still in the ground, and put everything in order for winter.

Plowing and Spading can continue as long as the ground is open. Land upon which the sod was turned over early in the fall, may, if the sod has sufficiently decayed, be cross-plowed.

Level inequalities as far as practicable, put down drains where needed, and get through with as much preparatory work as possible.

Roots should be dug before frost has injured the tender ones, and stored in pits, as noted last month, or, where the quantity is small, in the cellar. Do not cover the pits until there is danger of freezing. Horseradish, salsify, and parsnips, being perfectly hardy, may be left until the last.

Manure will be needed in large quantities in spring, and the stock should be on the increase. Accumulate not only stable manure, but brewers' and sugar-house waste, muck, leaves, and every available fertilizer. See that sinks and privies are in condition to save all the soil.

Cover asparagus and rhubarb beds with several inches of coarse manure or other litter; the crop next spring will be enough earlier and better to pay.

Cold Frames, containing cabbage and lettuce plants, will need to be covered on cold nights, but the sashes must be removed in the day time, or the plants will start to grow, and become tender. They will endure a moderate freezing without harm.

Soil for Hot-beds.—Get ready a supply for use in February, by mixing good loam with one third its bulk of well rotted manure. Place it near the place where the hot-beds are to be made, and cover with boards or sods, to keep it in good order.

Celery.—Store in trenches a foot wide, and deep enough to contain the plants. Pack the plants in upright and close together without any soil between them. When hard frosts occur, put on a covering of leaves or straw.

Cabbages.—Invert as directed last month, and cover with earth when freezing weather comes.

Rhubarb.—As long as the ground is open, new plantations may be made; cut the old roots with a sharp spade into as many pieces as there are eyes, and set three feet apart each way in rich soil.

Spinach.—In exposed places, or where the climate is severe, it will be necessary to put on a covering of leaves or straw to protect it.

Flower Garden and Lawn.

It is one of the advantages of a light soil that work can be continued well towards winter. New walks and borders may be made, and if the weather continues suitable, deciduous trees and hardy shrubs may be set. The grounds should always present a neat appearance, and all decayed stems, useless stakes, and other rubbish, be removed.

Bulbs.—Plant all the spring sorts that are still left out. Take up Tuberoses, Tigridias, Gladioluses, and the like, before hard frosts. Japan Lilies are perfectly hardy, and need not be lifted; these and the other bulbs will bloom all the better if they have a covering of coarse manure by freezing time.

Chrysanthemums.—See that they are not beaten down by heavy storms, and note, while in flower, those that it is desirable to propagate from next spring. Those that have been potted for house blooming, when past flowering, may be set in a cool, dry, cellar, or turned out into the grounds.

Dahlias.—If the roots still remain in the ground, take up as directed last month. Label, and handle carefully, as the freshly dug roots are very brittle.

Frames and Pits.—Half hardy plants, placed in these, should at present only be covered at night. See that the drainage is good, and that the pits are mice-proof. Set poison if any get in.

Lawns will be benefited by a top dressing of well rotted manure, to be applied as soon as convenient.

Leaves.—Accumulate a good stock of these from lawn, roadsides, and the woods.

Roses.—Lay down the half hardy varieties, and cover with sods placed grassy side upwards.

Climbers, such as Roses, Wistarias, and others not remarkably hardy, should be taken down, and covered with earth.

Perennials, even the hardy ones, will bloom all the finer next year, if a forkful of littery manure is put over them. Protect half hardy shrubs by laying cedar or other evergreen boughs over them.

Green and Hot-Houses.

The temperature of the house will demand the attention of the gardener. The heat of the sun will for a good part of the month enable him to do without fire. Everything should be ready to start a fire in case of a cold night or a sudden change. The thermometer should be consulted. Plants merely stored in the green-house, may get as cool as 40°, or even 35°, but if flowers are wanted, the temperature should not be less than 60°. Collections of tropical plants, of course, require more heat.

Bulbs.—Continue to pot, and keep in a cool place until they have formed an abundance of roots.

Camellias.—Syringe frequently, and look out for the first appearance of insects. Keep rather cool unless early flowers are wanted.

Propagate stock for winter blooming, especially of climbers for decorating the house. Tropæolums, Lophospermums, Maurandias, etc., will grow quickly and their flowers soon make a fine display.

Seeds.—Sow annuals for winter blooming, if not already done. Candytuft, Sweet Alyssum, and Mignonette are always wanted for bouquets. Nemophilas, Lobelias, and other annuals, soon flower.

Cold Grapery.

If any fruit remain upon the vines, look to it, and remove any berries that show a tendency to decay. Keep the atmosphere of the house as dry as possible, by closing entirely in damp weather.

Apiary in Nov.—*Prepared by M. Quinby.*

The cool weather of this month renders the bees more stupid than they usually are in much colder weather. Consequently, anything heretofore neglected, should now be attended to. All empty surplus boxes, or those containing so little honey as not be worth removing for the table, should be taken from the hive. Leave the combs whole, except the edges that are near the glass, if in glass boxes. These should be trimmed off, the glass scoured clean, replaced, and the boxes set away, holes down, making it impossible for the mice to enter. Hives standing out for the winter should be fully protected from mice by wire cloth, nailed on with small tacks, over all passages, leaving room for the bees only. Ample ventilation must be secured. Holes equal to two or three square inches must be made—if possible, at the bottom. Mr. Coe says, "It should be in the center of the bottom board." When covered with wire cloth, some device to prevent dead bees from falling on, and covering it, is needed. A box, two or three inches deep, of the same size as the bottom of the hive, put under it, is very good. The hole in one of its sides, covered with wire, will do. Let it be on the back side, or where the wind will not drive directly through.

Hives may be painted now, with the bees inside; take a day cool enough to keep the bees at home. Use several colors for the hives, such as nearly white, light green, lead, yellow, etc., that each bee, another year, may know its own hive at a glance, and avoid mistakes by making visits out of place.

AMERICAN AGRICULTURIST.

ORANGE JUDD & CO., Publishers, 245 Broadway, N. Y. City.

ANNUAL SUBSCRIPTION TERMS (always in advance): $1.50 each for less than four copies: Four to nine copies, $1.25 each: Ten to nineteen copies, $1.20 each: Twenty copies and upwards, $1 each. Papers are addressed to each name.

A FEW WORDS FOR

EVERYBODY

WHO WOULD LIKE TO OBTAIN

Our Valuable Premiums.

More than $20,000 is expended every year by the Publishers in procuring the best, most reliable, and practical reading matter and beautiful and instructive engravings for this paper. The cost of producing the *American Agriculturist* is divided among so great a host of subscribers that it amounts to but a trifle to each above the cost of the white paper on which it is printed.

Tens of thousands of persons, old and young, in city and country, and in all the various trades and professions,—owners of farms and those who never have owned a foot of ground,—gardeners, fruit growers and others,—have not only subscribed for the first time, but continued to be subscribers for years thereafter, and remain so to-day. No better proof than this fact is needed of its great value. The circulation to actual subscribers is doubtless larger than that of any monthly journal in the world.

Every paper contains from 30 to 50 beautiful engravings, all of them by the best draughtsmen and engravers, and many of them very costly. Special attention is called to the engravings in the volume for the present year. All who are at all familiar with the difficulty and expense attendant upon the production of such pictures will, we are sure, acknowledge that the subscribers to the *Agriculturist* receive **much for a little.** And while these engravings are in the highest style of the art, they are so varied in character as to interest every member of a family, even the youngest.

A great amount of interesting and instructive reading matter is provided for all.

Farmers find here thousands of hints and suggestions about all kinds of farm work.

Mechanics find much that interests them in the engravings and descriptions of implements and machinery; also in the directions for culture of their garden lots, if they have them.

City Merchants find a large amount of valuable information for the management of their country places, or which at least helps to keep bright in their minds the pleasing ideal of a beautiful place in the country, to which so many are looking forward when they shall retire from business.

Country Merchants keep the paper in their stores where customers can see it, and many of them secure large clubs.

Children are delighted with the sketches and beautiful engravings found in the Boys' and Girls' Department.

Everybody finds something to please, interest and instruct; and by the constant and thorough exposure of humbugs in this paper, it is not too much to say that thousands of dollars have been saved to the unwary from their being thus put upon their guard.

Now Look at our Premiums.

DO YOU WANT A finely assorted lot of Garden Seeds, 40 kinds; or a lot of Flower Seeds, 100 kinds, just such as your wife or daughter would select; or that most useful article, Page's Patent Pump and Sprinkler, which combines most of the advantages of a Hand Watering Pot, a Green-house Syringe, a light Force Pump, and Garden Engine? You can have either one of these three Premiums by sending to us 13 names with their subscriptions for one year, at $1.50 each. Eleven subscriptions at the same rates will secure *for you* a first-rate, F. Gold Pen, with silver case, from one of the best manufactories in the country; 14 subscriptions, at $1.50 each, give you the F. Gold Pen, which is larger, and by the same makers. ☞ The right hand column of the Table gives the number of names required at the lowest club prices, ($1 a year), to get any of the Premiums referred to.

DO YOU WANT A dozen best plated Tea Spoons, or Table Spoons, or Knives and Forks? Do you want a set of Tea or Table Knives and Forks of Rodgers & Sons' make, or an elegant Ice Pitcher, or Castor and Fruit Basket? Look at the list and notice that for a comparatively small amount of labor you can obtain any one or all of these. Many have received these Premiums, and others are working for them. A lady who has already secured a part of them writes us that she means to have the rest. We are all ready; and for only 66 subscribers at $1.50 each, we will give one of those beautiful, extra-plated Tea Sets made by Lucius Hart & Co., and comprising six pieces, viz.: Coffee Pot, two Tea Pots, a Cream-er, Sugar, and Slop Bowl, of uniform pattern, new style and embossed figure work.

DO YOU WANT Something which shall at once lessen the necessary labor of your family, and which will be a pleasant surprise at home when it reaches there? Look over the list of first quality Sewing Machines which we offer as Premiums. Here, too, are the Washing Machines, and the best Clothes Wringers. Many a husband and father has made glad hearts at home and brought rest to weary hands by a little effort in bringing the *American Agriculturist* to the notice of persons who only needed that little effort to induce them to subscribe for it.

DO YOU WANT To provide for yourself and your family a library of most useful Books,—the latest and best for the Farm, Garden, and Household;—Books which will do more to interest your sons and daughters in Agriculture and Horticulture than could be done by any other means? Or do you want to secure a set of the Back Volumes of the *Agriculturist* for the last eleven years, or any part of the set,—each volume being most valuable for its thousands of hints, suggestions, and items of information, and for the pleasure and instruction it will give to your children? Look at the 37 Premiums, No. 50 to No. 86, and see how easily you can obtain such a Library. See Book List, page 421.

DO YOU WANT Music in your home? Who does not? You can have it; for among our Premiums you will find the beautiful little Musical Box;—the Melodeon, for the Home Circle or for the Hall; the Colibri Piano, an instrument of remarkable power and sweetness; and the elegant Seven Octave, Rosewood Case, Steinway Piano. Which will you take?

DO YOU WANT Any one of the Eighty-Six valuable Premiums on our List? *Then make up your mind to have it.* Go out among your friends. Sit down beside them and tell them what the *Agriculturist* is, and show them a paper. We will give a specimen number to any one who asks for it, in order to obtain subscribers.

Table of Premiums and Terms, For Volume 27—(1868).

Open to all—No Competition.

No.	*Names of Premium Articles.*	*Price of Premiums.*	Number of Subscribers required at $1.50	at $1.
1	*Garden Seeds for a Family* (40 kinds)	$5 00	13	37
2	*Flower Seeds for a Family* (100 kinds)	$5 00	13	37
3	*Nursery Stock* (Any kinds desired)	$20 00	30	97
4	*Iona Grape Vines* (12 of No. 1)	$18 00	27	90
5	*Concord Grape Vines* (100 of No. 1)	$12 00	19	65
6	*Japan Lilies* (12 Bulbs)	$6 00	15	45
7	*Sewing Machine* (Grover & Baker)	$55 00	60	210
8	*Sewing Machine* (Howe Machine Co.)	$60 00	67	210
9	*Sewing Machine* (Singer's Tailoring)	$80 00	85	320
10	*Sewing Machine* (Florence)	$63 00	70	210
11	*Sewing Machine* (Willcox & Gibbs)	$55 00	60	240
12	*Sewing Machine* (Finkle & Lyon)	$60 00	67	210
13	*Sewing Machine* (Wheeler & Wilson)	$55 00	60	210
14	*Washing Machine* (Doty's)	$14 00	21	70
15	*Clothes Wringer* (Best—Universal)	$10 00	18	58
16	*Tea Set* (Hart's best Silver Plated)	$50 00	66	275
17	*Castor and Fruit Basket* (do. do.)	$30 00	44	140
18	*Ice or Water Pitcher* (do. do.)	$18 00	27	90
19	*One Dozen Tea Spoons* (do. do.)	$6 00	13	45
20	*One Dozen Table Spoons* (do. do.)	$12 00	19	65
21	*One Dozen Dining Forks* (do. do.)	$12 00	19	65
22	*Tea Knives and Forks* (Patterson Bros.)	$20 00	30	97
23	*Table Knives and Forks* (do. do.)	$24 00	37	120
24	*Carving Knife and Fork* (do. do.)	$6 50	17	50
25	*Musical Box* (Shell Case)	$13 00	22	75
26	*Melodeon, 4-octave* (G. A. Prince & Co.'s)	$67 00	73	295
27	*Melodeon, 5-octave* (do. do.)	$112 00	138	400
28	*Colibri Piano* (Harlow, Doehler & Co.)	[illegible]	[illegible]	1150
29	*Piano, Splendid 7-oct.* (Steinway & Sons)	[illegible]	540	1600
30	*Ladies' Gold Watch* (Beautiful)	$100 00	130	400
31	*Silver Watch* (Valuable Time-Keeper)	$32 50	48	158
32	*Double Barrel Gun* (Cooper & Pond)	$30 00	46	150
33	*Repeating Shot Gun* (Roper Rifle Co.)	$60 00	67	270
34	*Spencer's Breech-loading Rifle* (Hunting)	$55 00	70	275
35	*Tool Chest* (Patterson Bros.)	$44 50	60	196
36	*Case of Mathematical Instruments*	$9 00	15	52
37	*Case of Mathematical Instruments*	$15 00	23	75
38	*Gold Pen, Sil. Case, E.* (Warren & Spadone)	$4 50	11	35
39	*Gold Pen and Silver Case, F.* (do. do.)	$5 50	14	42
40	*Barometer* (Woodruff's Mercurial)	$12 00	19	65
41	*Barometer* (Woodruff's Mercurial)	$18 00	27	90
42	*Buckeye Mowing Machine, No. 2*	$125 00	150	450
43	*Allen's Patent Cylinder Plow, etc.*	$20 00	31	100
44	*Pump and Sprinkler* (Page's)	$5 00	13	37
45	*Family Scales* (Fairbanks & Co.)	$10 00	18	58
46	*Building Blocks* (Crandall)	$2 00	6	20
47	*Pocket Lanterns, One Dozen*	[illegible]	12	[illegible]
48	*American Cyclopedia* (Appleton's)	[illegible]	96	[illegible]
49	*Worcester's Great Illustrated Dictionary*	$12 00	19	65
50	*Any Back Volume Agriculturist*	[illegible]	[illegible]	[illegible]
51	*Any Two Back Volumes* do.	[illegible]	[illegible]	[illegible]
52	*Any Three* do. do. do.	[illegible]	13	[illegible]
53	*Any Four* do. do. do.	[illegible]	15	47
54	*Any Five* do. do. do.	[illegible]	[illegible]	[illegible]
55	*Any Six* do. do. do.	[illegible]	[illegible]	[illegible]
56	*Any Seven* do. do. do.	[illegible]	[illegible]	[illegible]
57	*Any Eight* do. do. do.	[illegible]	[illegible]	[illegible]
58	*Any Nine* do. do. do.	[illegible]	[illegible]	[illegible]
59	*Any Ten* do. do. do.	[illegible]	[illegible]	[illegible]
60	*Vols. XVI to XXVI* do.	[illegible]	[illegible]	[illegible]
61	*Any Back Volume Agriculturist*	[illegible]	[illegible]	[illegible]
62	*Any Two Back Volumes* do.	[illegible]	[illegible]	[illegible]
63	*Any Three* do. do. do.	[illegible]	[illegible]	[illegible]
64	*Any Four* do. do. do.	[illegible]	[illegible]	[illegible]
65	*Any Five* do. do. do.	[illegible]	[illegible]	[illegible]
66	*Any Six* do. do. do.	[illegible]	[illegible]	[illegible]
67	*Any Seven* do. do. do.	[illegible]	[illegible]	[illegible]
68	*Any Eight* do. do. do.	[illegible]	[illegible]	102
69	*Any Nine* do. do. do.	[illegible]	[illegible]	110
70	*Any Ten* do. do. do.	[illegible]	[illegible]	118
71	*Vols. XVI to XXVI* do.	[illegible]	[illegible]	[illegible]
72	*Downing's Landscape Gardening*	[illegible]	[illegible]	[illegible]
73	*Cummings & Miller's Architect.*	[illegible]	[illegible]	[illegible]
74	*A $10 Library* (Your Choice)	[illegible]	18	[illegible]
75	*A $15 Library* do.	[illegible]	[illegible]	[illegible]
76	*A $20 Library* do.	[illegible]	31	106
77	*A $25 Library* do.	[illegible]	[illegible]	[illegible]
78	*A $30 Library* do.	[illegible]	[illegible]	[illegible]
79	*A $35 Library* do.	[illegible]	[illegible]	[illegible]
80	*A $40 Library* do.	[illegible]	[illegible]	[illegible]
81	*A $45 Library* do.	[illegible]	[illegible]	[illegible]
82	*A $50 Library* do.	[illegible]	[illegible]	[illegible]
83	*A $60 Library* do.	[illegible]	[illegible]	[illegible]
84	*A $75 Library* do.	[illegible]	100	[illegible]
85	*A $100 Library* do.	$100 00	125	500
86	*A Choice of Good Books* (See Terms below.)	..	..	..

(Nos. 50–60: *In clubs over Nos. Postpaid—Unbound.* Nos. 61–71: *Neatly Bound, Sent Postpaid.* Nos. 72–85: *All sent paid through, by Mail or Express.*)

Only good articles.—**We are careful not** *to place upon our list anything for a Premium which is not the best, and, in all respects, what is claimed for it. All, therefore, who secure premiums, may be sure that they are not running the risk of getting poor or indifferent goods.*

Send in the names of subscribers as fast as you obtain them, not waiting to complete your list; and to save mistakes in accounts, send the exact subscription money with each list; and **every name** *designed for a premium list, must be so marked* **when sent in.**

Begin Now to raise your clubs. It is not necessary that all the papers of Premium Clubs should go to one office. You can get them anywhere.

Old and New Subscribers will be counted in premium lists, but some should be new names, as it is to obtain such that premiums are in part offered. The extra copy, usually offered to clubs of ten or twenty, will not be furnished when a premium is called for.

☞ *Every Premium article is new and of the very best manufacture. No charge is made for packing or boxing any of the articles in our Premium List. The forty-four Premiums,* **Nos. 1, 2, 6,** *and from* **36** *to* **39**, *and from* **50** *to* **86** *inclusive, will each be delivered* **FREE** *of all charges, by mail or express, (at the Post-Office or express office nearest recipient), to any place in the United States or Territories, excepting those reached only by the Overland Mail.—The other articles cost the recipient only the freight after leaving the manufactory of each, by any conveyance that may be specified.*

Commercial Matters—Market Prices.

The following condensed, comprehensive tables, carefully prepared specially for the *American Agriculturist*, show at a glance the transactions for the month ending Oct. 17, 1867, and also for the preceding month:

1. TRANSACTIONS AT THE NEW-YORK MARKETS.

RECEIPTS.	Flour.	Wheat.	Corn.	Rye.	Barley.	Oats.
27 days this m'th	437,000	2,316,000	1,750,000	180,000	845,000	1,210,000
27 days last m'th	215,000	925,000	3,231,000	36,500	53,000	570,000

SALES.	Flour.	Wheat.	Corn.	Rye.	Oats.
21 days this month,	411,000	1,902,000	2,911,000	830,000	2,016,000
25 days last month,	281,000	1,773,000	4,181,000	131,000	1,767,000

2. *Exports from New York, Jan. 1 to Oct. 16:*

	Flour.	Wheat.	Corn.	Rye.	Oats.	Barley.
1867	993,920	891,887	6,481,108	319,771	196,215	860,667
1866	111,161	311,135	10,323,616	192,880	1,018,753	101,116

3. *Stock of grain in store at New York:*

1867.	Wheat, bush.	Corn, bush.	Rye, bush.	Barley, bush.	Oats, bush.	Malt, bush.
Oct. 15	147,608	961,861	7,970	91,790	881,987	57,977
Sept. 10	120,382	1,154,942	349	9,318	183,737	64,494
Aug. 15	[illegible]	989,721	32,780	17,078	980,179	10,511
July 15	215,780	160,720	65,946	21,090	396,764	31,700
June 11	[illegible]	211,291	112,357	16,511	310,403	10,201
May 15	151,380	911,991	146,471	115,196	608,191	16,791

4. *Receipts of Breadstuffs at tide water at Albany, May 1st to October 8th:*

	Flour, bbls.	Wheat, bush.	Corn, bush.	Rye, bush.	Barley, bush.	Oats, bush.
1867	160,200	2,261,800	11,857,000	337,200	485,100	1,086,500
1866	181,700	2,148,100	21,117,000	713,800	957,300	6,485,800

Gold has been as high as 146⅝, since our last, closing yesterday at 143⅜.... Breadstuffs have been in much better request for home use, shipment, and on speculation; and prices have advanced materially. The foreign inquiry is unexpectedly active for flour, wheat, corn, and rye; and but for the very marked rise in ocean freights, an unusually extensive anti-raid movement would have been fairly begun by this time. As it is, despite the scarcity and dearness of freight room, the shipments are increasing rapidly, encouraged by the highly favorable market reports from England and the West of Europe. The break in the Canal seriously checked receipts at the seaboard, but these are now comparatively liberal.... Provisions have been quiet, and depressed in price. ...Cotton has fallen materially, but closes in favor of sellers, on a reviving demand.... Tobacco has been actively sought after at full prices.... Wool has been in light request, and tending downward.... Hay, Hops, and Seeds, have been in moderate demand, at about steady rates.

CURRENT WHOLESALE PRICES.

	Sept. 16.	Oct. 17.
PRICE OF GOLD	[illegible]	[illegible]
FLOUR—Super to Extra State	$ 8 25 @ 10 70	$ 8 50 @ 11 30
Super to Extra Southern	9 75 @ 13 75	11 00 @ 15 50
Extra Western	9 50 @ 13 75	10 50 @ 16 [illegible]
Extra Genesee	11 25 @ 13 50	11 50 @ 14 50
Superfine Western	8 25 @ 9 75	9 25 @ 10 00
RYE FLOUR	[illegible]	[illegible]
CORN MEAL	[illegible]	[illegible]
WHEAT—All kinds of White	[illegible]	[illegible]
All kinds of Red and Amber	[illegible]	[illegible]
CORN—Yellow	[illegible]	[illegible]
Mixed	[illegible]	[illegible]
OATS—Western	[illegible]	[illegible]
State	[illegible]	[illegible]
RYE	[illegible]	[illegible]
BARLEY	[illegible]	[illegible]
HAY—Bale ₩ 100 ℔	[illegible]	[illegible]
Loose	[illegible]	[illegible]
STRAW, ₩ 100 ℔	[illegible]	[illegible]
COTTON—Middlings, ₩ ℔	[illegible]	[illegible]
HOPS—Crop of 1867, ₩ ℔	[illegible]	[illegible]
FEATHERS—Live Geese, ₩ ℔	[illegible]	[illegible]
SEED—Clover, ₩ ℔	[illegible]	[illegible]
Timothy, ₩ bushel	[illegible]	[illegible]
Flax, ₩ bushel	[illegible]	[illegible]
SUGAR—Brown, ₩ ℔	[illegible]	[illegible]
MOLASSES, Cuba, ₩ gal	[illegible]	[illegible]
COFFEE—Rio, (Gold price) ₩ ℔	[illegible]	[illegible]
TOBACCO, Kentucky, &c., ₩ ℔	[illegible]	[illegible]
Seed Leaf, ₩ ℔	[illegible]	[illegible]
WOOL—Domestic Fleece, ₩ ℔	[illegible]	[illegible]
Domestic, pulled, ₩ ℔	[illegible]	[illegible]
California, unwashed	[illegible]	[illegible]
TALLOW, ₩ ℔	[illegible]	[illegible]
OIL CAKE—₩ ton	[illegible]	[illegible]
PORK—Mess, ₩ barrel	[illegible]	[illegible]
Prime, ₩ barrel	[illegible]	[illegible]
BEEF—Plain mess	[illegible]	[illegible]
LARD, in barrels, ₩ ℔	[illegible]	[illegible]
BUTTER—Western, ₩ ℔	[illegible]	[illegible]
State, ₩ ℔	[illegible]	[illegible]
CHEESE	[illegible]	[illegible]
BEANS—₩ bushel	[illegible]	[illegible]
PEAS—Canada, ₩ bushel	[illegible]	[illegible]
EGGS—Fresh, ₩ dozen	[illegible]	[illegible]
POULTRY—Fowls, ₩ ℔	[illegible]	[illegible]
Turkeys, ₩ ℔	[illegible]	[illegible]
POTATOES—New, ₩ bbl	[illegible]	2 00 @ 3 [illegible]
APPLES—₩ barrel	[illegible]	2 00 @ 4 00
PEACHES—₩ basket	[illegible]	[illegible]
CRANBERRIES, ₩ barrel	Nominal.	7 00 @ 11 00

New York Live Stock Markets.—

WEEK ENDING.	Beeves.	Cows.	Calves.	Sheep.	Swine.
September 17	[illegible]	66	[illegible]	26,800	24,801
September 24	7,391	75	[illegible]	26,705	21,780
October 1	7,843	41	2,001	34,820	25,711
October 8	5,761	37	1,616	35,016	63,274
October 15	[illegible]	23	1,488	33,153	22,199
Total in five Weeks	35,087	212	8,757	168,750	116,308
Average per Week	7,017	41	1,751	33,750	31,302

A glance at the above table will show that there has been a very large increase in all kinds of live stock destined for slaughter, except beef, and the same is probably true of the receipts of slaughtered meats and poultry. The wonder is that prices have not seriously fallen off.

Beef Cattle.—The supply has been fully up to the demand of the market and prices have fluctuated but very little, except during the first week of October, when the receipts (reported on the 8th,) were very large, and of a quality not to sustain the previous prices. They came up again promptly with the smaller receipts of the next week, the last that we report, and we may now put them down about as follows: The very best steers, well fattened, sell at 17c.@17¼c. per pound, estimated dressed weight; excellent beef, 16c.; general average, a little above 14c.; poorest, 9c.@11c..... **Milch Cows.**—The market seems a little more active, especially for family cows for citizens returning from the country, though most of these purchase in the country. $80 to $100 is paid for a really good cow, readily... **Calves.**—Those classed as prime sell at 11c.@11½c. per pound, live weight. Fat calves bring 12c.@12½c., while grass fed ones bring 9c.@10c., according to quality. "Hog dressed" veal sells at 14c.@17c. A good many calves are sold by the head, some to farmers for raising, others to butchers at prices all the way from $4 to $25 each.... **Sheep.**—The rush of sheep to this market has been unprecedented though hardly unexpected. Prices have come down somewhat, but hardly in proportion. Extra sheep bring this week, 6½c., good, fat sheep, 5½c.@6c., while the poorer qualities range from 4c. to 5¼c. Common lambs bring about 6c.@6½c., prime, 7c.@7½c. **Swine.**—The supply has been most extraordinary, a great part of the hogs being of very poor quality, entirely unfit for slaughter. Such brought only 5c. per pound on the 4th week reported, when the receipts were so much in excess of the demand that all grades fell off in price. The closing quotations this week are about as follows: Prime, heavy hogs, 7¼c.@7¾c., good, 7¼c.@7⅜c., common to poor, 6½c.@7c. per pound, live weight. The cause is the shortness of the corn crop.

Containing a great variety of Items, including many good Hints and Suggestions which we throw into smaller type and condensed form, for want of space elsewhere.

13 Months in a Year.

All new subscribers to the Agriculturist for 1868, whose names are received during November, will receive, **free of charge,** *the December number, which will be beautifully illustrated, and very valuable. This will give* **13 months** *for a year's price. The offer applies to* **all** *new subscribers, singly, in clubs, in premium lists, etc. Sufficient time will be allowed for responses to this offer to come from the Pacific States and Territories, and other distant points. All new names must be marked* **new** *to secure the extra number.*

Mark All Subscriptions sent in, as *New* or *Old*.

How to Remit:—Checks on New-York Banks or Bankers are best for large sums; make them payable to the order of Orange Judd & Co.

Post Office Money Orders may be obtained at nearly every county seat, in all the cities, and in many of the large towns. We consider them perfectly safe, and the best means of remitting fifty dollars or less, as many hundreds have been sent to us *without any loss*.

Registered Letters, under the new system, which went into effect June 1st, are a very safe means of sending small sums of money where P. O. Money Orders cannot be easily obtained. *Observe*, the *Registry fee*, as well as postage, *must be paid in stamps* at the office where the letter is mailed, or it will be liable to be sent to the Dead Letter Office. *Buy and affix the stamps both for postage and registry, put in the money and seal the letter in the presence of the postmaster, and take his receipt for it.* Letters sent in this way to us are at our risk.

Specimen Numbers of the Agriculturist, Cards, and Showbills, as may be needed, will be supplied to canvassers. These should be economically used, as each extra copy of the paper, with postage, (&c.,) which must be pre-paid, costs about 12 cents.

Cheap Ice-House.—"H. W. B.," Windsor Locks, Conn. In former years we have given plans. Select a *dry* spot having perfect natural drainage, if possible. Throw out the earth not more than a foot deep, over 14 feet square. Lay a foundation of brick, about 18 inches high; on this lay sills 14 feet long, 10 inches wide, and 8 inches thick, halved and pinned together at the ends; on the sills set posts or uprights, 7 feet high on the sides, and higher on the gables. For these use two-inch spruce or hemlock planks, 10 inches wide, nailing them to the sills, and also to the plates. Board up, nailing to the uprights on both sides. Fill in with tan bark, dry sawdust, planing mill shavings, etc. Put on a roof shingled or thatched, and board on the under side of the rafters, filling with sawdust, if you please. There must be a sliding shutter in the gable for ventilation, and the earth thrown out of the cellar should be banked around the foundation. There must be perfect drainage, and if a drain is laid opening in the floor of the ice-house it must be covered by a bed of gravel or a trap. The outside boarding may be spruce boards, the inside two-inch hemlock. Bank up against the foundation with earth so that no draft of air shall have access. The door should be in the gable end, some feet up from the ground, and double; or movable boards may be used instead of an inner door. The house will be 12 feet square on the inside, and will keep ice enough for any ordinary family.

Postage.—To our *published terms* for the *American Agriculturist*, postage must in all cases be added when ordered to go out of the United States. For Canada, send twelve cents besides the subscription money with each subscriber. In the United States, *three cents*, each quarter, or *twelve cents, yearly*, must be prepaid at the post office where the paper is received.

Subscription Letters.—Write the Name, Post Office, County, and State, plainly, and *separately from all remarks, questions*, etc. Any communications for the editors should be on a different part of the sheet, or on another piece of paper.

Renew Subscriptions Now.—Many of the subscriptions expire with the next number, December. It will secure prompt delivery for January, 1868, to renew *now*; besides, it will aid us much in getting the names all properly on our books in good season.

State and other Fairs.—Some representative of the *Agriculturist* has been present at most of the important exhibitions held this autumn. While we present brief notes on several of these, our space does not allow of extended reports. We visit these fairs to gather information for the benefit of our readers in all parts of the country; this is used from time to time much more to their advantage than it could be in a single report. Besides the brief sketches of those given this month, we have been obliged to leave out several already in type, including those of the Pennsylvania Horticultural Society, Illinois and Pennsylvania State Fairs, and Fair of the American Institute, New York.

Sundry Humbugs.—The list of humbug letters for the last month is quite long, but most of them have been previously shown up in the *Agriculturist*, and others are so precisely similar that it would seem to be impossible for any one to mistake their character. Follow our advice, and do business, as far as possible, with those only who are well known and reliable dealers.... Wright Bros. & Co. are filling the country with their circulars, offering rare chances to obtain fine watches valued at from $15 to $1000 for only a $10 greenback, and a trifle for a case and postage. Among other styles is a Silver Hunting Chronometer, valued at $100, recommended as a splendid article. With a pocketful of tickets we "dropped in" to their place, or rather, we climbed up, and found their very small rooms on the *top floor*, and examined some of their stock. It is the kind known among dealers as *bogus*, and that word *means* the same all over the country, though it may not be in the dictionaries,—that is, not what it is represented to be. We purchased the Hunting Chronometer, valued at $100, as a curiosity. It has a little silver in the case, perhaps two dollars worth; the movement is very showy, and it will tick a few times if shaken very hard, and kept bottom upwards; turn it over, and it is dead as a hammer, and as a time-keeper it is utterly useless. The "American Watch," described as retailing at $35 to $45, with 2 oz. solid silver hunting cases, we saw, and "the man" told us that both case and movement were made in this city; it was stamped "Union Watch Company, New York." There is no such institution in the city, and no such watches were ever made here. An importer in Maiden Lane examined our $100 Duplex, and offered to sell the same article, which he had in stock and showed to us, for $6.75 gold, or $9.50 greenbacks. The Union Watch Company's Watch in Hunting Case, precisely like the one at W. B. & Co.'s, and which we were informed was *white metal*, and not silver, was offered for $8.25 greenbacks.... We warn our readers again, that those parties who are induced by *private* circulars and tickets to buy watches or other articles, represented as worth several times the price asked, will find their money gone and themselves SOLD....C. L. Van Allen, who told us a while ago that *his* name was A. D. Dowman, now assures us that there is *no such person*. He is advertising, however, in the name of A. D. Bowman & Co. Mr. Van Allen advertises also to sell rights to make "Eureka Oil," which is represented as very cheap, not explosive, can be made by everybody, etc. We received a letter from a chemist, stating that this article is very dangerous, so we obtained a sample bottle of the "Eureka Oil." It is simply benzine with, perhaps, slight additions, and *explodes as readily as gunpowder*. Any man who recommends the manufacture of such stuff by unskilled hands, deserves the gallows or the penitentiary for life. Don't touch it, or the advertiser of it, in any way....Kelley & Co.'s Grand Gift Concert is *again postponed*. Keep the tickets as a warning to make no more such investments, which not only reduce capital, but generally good nature too....We have numerous inquiries about Concerts for Soldiers' Widows and Orphans, Libraries, etc., where tickets are sold and prizes drawn by some means "strictly honest," and "entirely legal," etc. We class them all together, without any exception, as *lotteries*, and all *lotteries* as *humbugs*....Beware of parties who take *great pains* to assure the public that they are "licensed by United States authority." All respectable business men pay for U. S. license, and many who are not respectable, and *such license gives no authority to disregard State laws*, as has been decided over and over again....The medical humbugs are still extant, though we have not given them much attention of late. The most recent demonstration that we have seen is that of Dr. H. R. Barner, whose four page circular is a curiosity in its way. It informs us that the "Union Combination Medical Association of Great Britain" has invested $275,000 "in the United States, to aid and assist suffering humanity," which is a very handsome thing of them to do. They publish a certificate from "the Executive Department, Washington, D. C.," signed "G. F. Attendon, General Surgeon." Now we would like to know just what the "Executive Department" does with a surgeon, though if it must have one, "Attendon" is a good name for him. "Remember," says the circular, "he, (Dr. Barner,) is not to be classed with the Traveling Impostors of the land." Very likely not, but as he "guarantees a cure in every case undertaken," we class him with those belonging abroad. This Doctor B. is endorsed by the "President" of the "Union Combination Medical Association," "branch office, No. 209 Broadway." The seeker after this office on Broadway would appropriately bring up in St. Paul's Church-yard, which is where 209 would be, if there were such a number. The superstitious might think this indicative of the fate of those who take the "French Remedies," or try to prove the statement of the circular that "the Doctor has a balm *for* every wound."

Personal Inquiries.—We have had of late more than the usual number of letters asking questions of interest only to the writer. We usually answer as many of them as possible, but the absence of the editors during the season of fairs, together with the interruption caused by our removal, has made it necessary to leave many unanswered. Every one must see that we cannot occupy half a day in looking up information for his benefit, and that many letters are for this reason unanswerable.

Safe Pipe for Drinking Water.—Lead poisoning from water brought in lead pipe is the often unsuspected cause of disease and death. Galvanized iron pipe, wood, and cement pipe, are expensive and inconvenient substitutes, so that people will risk their lives and use lead. The Lead-encased Block Tin pipe is even cheaper than lead, and we believe perfectly safe. Our faith in it has led us recently to lay some 80 feet of it, through which all our drinking water is drawn.

Shade in Pastures.—"Welchman."—Certain trees, like Elms, Maples, Basswoods or Lindens, Willows, etc., interfere with the growth of grass or any crop, their roots being near the surface. Hickories, Oaks, Pepperidges, and Beeches, send their roots deep, and grass grows well in their shade. Still we would not cut down the former class. Cows give milk better the more quiet and comfortable they are, and cool shade contributes essentially to their comfort. Cattle will soon fill themselves if the pasturage is good; then they want shade to chew their cuds under, and do proportionally better for it.

Horse with his Foot in his Mouth.—Dr. G. W. Booth, of Harrison Co., Ind., relates the following singular occurrence in a letter to the *Agriculturist*: "A neighbor, passing the stable, observed that one of my riding horses was lying down, and appeared to be in distress. He came to the house and told me. We immediately went, and found that he had his left hind foot fast in his mouth, the outside calk of the shoe buried in the roof. I ran to the blacksmith shop to get something to pull off his shoe, and just as I got back to the stable door, the horse made a violent effort, and jerked the foot out, loosing one tooth, and tearing his mouth badly, and cutting his foot just at the top of the hoof, so that he was lame for several weeks. I had to shell his corn, and feed him cut-feed for three weeks, till his tooth grew fast."

When to Plow for Corn.—W. S. K. A rolling field of mellow soil, long in grass, is to be broken up, and put in corn next spring. The corn will do quite as well if planted on a fresh turned sod. Grub worms will suffer if the plowing be done late this fall. What shall be done? We think it depends on the answers to two questions. Will the land wash if the winter is open and we have hard rains? If so, let it lie in sod. Will you have plenty of time to do the plowing next spring, or will you be crowded with work?

Bringing up Sandy Land.—"R. W. C.," Carroll Co., Ark. You say your sandy land has a red clay subsoil. The means of renovation are then close at hand, provided you can touch the clay with the plow. All you have to do is to bring it up and mingle it with the surface. If the clay lies too deep, then try green manures. Sow rye now and plow it under in the spring, then sow Indian corn and plow that under after about three months. If you can not trust corn after the rye, sow buckwheat. Lime alone would probably be of little or no benefit, unless the clay comes up.

Broom-corn Seed—Value.—"J. W.," Westmoreland Co., Pa.—Good seed should weigh about 50 pounds to the bushel, and it may be used on the farm to take the place of oats for sheep and poultry, and ground, it is good feed for pigs and milch cows. Plump seed will go as far as oats, and probably farther, but unripe seed is very inferior. Chickens eat it as a variety, but are not fond of it. The probable reason why there is so poor a market for it is that *the quality* is so variable.

A Well in a Quicksand.—Lafayette Erskine, Oneida Co., N. Y., anticipates trouble in digging a well in a quicksand. His neighbors have used a plank curbing, but this makes the water taste. What can be do? He can surely brick up inside a curbing of plank, lay in the bricks in cement, but leaving the bottom open and finally draw out the planks one at a time. Will not our readers suggest better ways?

Coal Tar and Gas Tar.—"H. N. S." Substances composed in whole or in great part of hydrogen and carbon, such as bituminous coal, rosin, or even wood, when exposed to high temperatures, are usually decomposed, becoming part gas, part tar and oils, and part a thick or coaly residuum, according to the degree and continuance of the heat. The presence of water and of oxygen causes other substances to be produced, wood vinegar, etc., and there is frequently nitrogen enough to cause the formation of a notable quantity of ammonia. The gas formed is a mixture of several gases; the tar is a very complex mixture, varying in its composition not only with the substances heated, but with the temperature. From whatever source these tars come, they possess peculiar and similar properties. Among others, remarkable anti septic qualities. So far as we are aware, there has been very little difference found in the relative values of the various coal or gas tars for preserving timber, painting, etc., and we presume that tar from rosin is just as good as that from Cannel coal, for these purposes. If not, we hope to be set right.

How to Get Rid of Briars.—Blackberry bushes, both the high and the running kinds, wild rose bushes, and other briars, are, when young, very palatable to sheep, and if they are cut close in the winter or in the spring, and sheep are turned on to the land before the thorns become stiff and woody, a single season will nearly eradicate them. This will not do upon very wet land, for the sheep will not thrive. On such ground mowing in August must be resorted to in addition to the winter or spring cutting.

Value of Bones.—W. P. E. Ground bones are worth about $40 a ton. The uncrushed article bears various prices. Shin bones and some other pieces are used in the arts, and bring high prices. Such as are thrown out from the kitchen bring what the boys can get for them. We have paid twenty-five cents a barrel for a great many barrels, delivered at the barn, and should have considered them cheap at twice the price. We would rather pay $10 a ton for old bones than be without them. They are indispensable in planting fruit trees in the older parts of the country, and are good for all crops. A pile of them should be kept constantly under the shed, and if a bone-mill is not handy, break them with a sledge or stone hammer on rainy days. Such rainy days, we think, will pay the farmer better than clear ones.

Destruction of Horses.—In the annual report of the Belt Railroad, in this city, it is stated that 279 horses out of 983 died during the year. The average life of a horse in this service is said to be only 3¼ years. The city is a great market for horses. The average price paid by this company was about $156. For those sold in a broken down condition, it received a trifle over $80 each.

Rotting Stumps Speedily.—There is an idea abroad that oil of vitriol poured upon a stump or into an auger hole in one, will cause it to decay rapidly. So far as we can ascertain there is no ground for such a notion. Nitric acid, *aqua fortis*, as a highly corrosive body containing much oxygen, would appear to be better adapted to this purpose, for decay is oxidation. The surest way to promote the quick decay of stumps we should think would be to gash the main roots with an ax or bore holes into them, and also into the top of the stump, which might be cut dishing with a few well directed blows, in order that water might settle in the holes and work into the heart of the tree. This will surely cause more or less rapid decay, and substances like the droppings of birds and little animals, or even leaf-mould, would soon wash in, and expedite the process.

Short-horns Homeward Bound.—Eight of these animals, from the herd of James O. Sheldon, of Geneva, N. Y., were recently shipped from this port to England. John Bull cannot resist the temptation of fine cattle even in America. Third Duke of Geneva, who heads the list, will be heard from across the water.

"Chicken Cholera."—"S. V." recommends the following remedy, and has the good sense not to call it infallible. "Take two eggs, a tablespoonful of powdered alum, and a sufficient quantity of flour to make a thin paste. Force the fowl to take a portion of it, if it will not eat voluntarily. Powdered alum, mixed in the food, is a good preventive. Feed no swill or sour messes."

Churning in Cold Weather.—Mrs. Spicer, of Peoria Co., Ill., gives the following sound directions: "Procure a common thermometer, costing from fifty cents to one dollar. Set the cream in a warm place, and stir occasionally, until the thermometer indicates a temperature of 64°; rinse the churn in hot water, put in the cream, and churn immediately. Do not let the hot water stand in the churn, as the heat from it should not raise the cream over 65°, or the butter will "come soft." We practised the above during the past winter, and were not detained at the 'crank' over *ten or twelve* minutes, on an average, securing good hard butter in every case—while under the same circumstances in other respects we have previously been from one to five hours churning during the cold months.

Dogs.—It is estimated that 6,000 dogs are legally drowned in this city annually. Vermont, one of the best protected States in the Union, lost 500 sheep by dogs last year in five counties.

Questions Proposed by Readers to Readers.—1. *Milk-house.*—"What is the best mode of building a *Milk-house* above-ground. One that can be put up on a cheap plan by a common carpenter or ingenious farmer himself?"

2. *Spring-house.*—"J. W." asks for the best way of employing the water of a spring that would fill a three-quarter-inch pipe in a farm dairy or milk-cellar, or in a house built for the purpose over the spring?

3. *Bake Oven.*—A plan for a Pennsylvania "Out-oven" is called for. That is, we presume, a brick oven large enough for the wants of a large family.

The European Rook for Insects.—Is there any objection to the introduction of this bird into this country? With all our warfare upon insects, they are increasing. "Aliquis," of Michigan, writes: "I think that a remedy, (for insects,) is to be found in the English rook. This bird may be considered entirely insectivorous. The only exception I ever knew was in a severe and long continued snow-storm, when some of them paid a visit to a solitary wheat-stack. I am aware that they are badly accused, and many a day I have kept watch with a gun to keep them off the newly sowed grain, and many of them I have dissected, but I never found anything but insects in their crops. They are constantly in attendance on newly stirred land, and hundreds may be seen following the plow and harrow within two or three yards of the plowman's heels. Indeed, if they were a grain-eating bird, no grain could be raised in the neighborhood of rookeries, where millions are congregated. I believe the intelligent part of Scotchmen do not believe they eat grain, and they won't touch carrion. I was told by a relation that, (it must now be 80 or 100 years ago,) he was one of those employed to kill off the rooks, which they nearly effectually accomplished, but ere many years they were glad to get them back, the land having become entirely overrun with grubs and wire-worms."

Fine Bulbs.—The stock of J. M. Thorburn & Co. is this year very full and fine. We have no doubt that of other dealers is fine also, but we happened to see theirs just as it was opened, and were struck with the great variety and the excellent quality of the bulbs.

Coal Ashes.—I. F. H. Will pay for carting a short distance. They contain the mineral constituents of the plants from which the coal was made, and as they are usually found in cities and villages, small quantities of potash and lime from the wood and charcoal used in kindling. Judging from the rapid disappearance of kindlings in our kitchen, this must be an important item. We have often used them for top dressing for moist grass lands. They are particularly good for muck lands and for heavy clays, serving to make the soil more friable.

Compost of Forest Leaves.—"Crawford." Gather the leaves in dry weather, use them as litter for cattle or penned hogs, and compost them with manure. If you have not enough manure, pile leaves by themselves with a small quantity of wood ashes or lime.

House Drains.—The best are glazed earthen pipes with socket collars, (each pipe fitting into the next,) with cement mortar filling around the joints water tight. The pipe for an ordinary family should be the smallest that comes, which is two inches in diameter. Small pipes will keep themselves clean. They should be laid not less than two feet deep. Large pipes give space for filth to accumulate. All house drains should be as small as will carry the water, and be laid in cement, so that all the water will run through, and should be uniformly inclined as much as one inch in 10 feet, that the flow may be rapid, and wash out all sediment.

A Request Repeated.—Advertisers are always gratified by learning in what paper their notice was seen by parties writing for circulars or sending orders. We repeat the request that our readers will please give information, when writing in answer to advertisements in our columns.

Coal Tar for Fence Posts.—Immerse them in coal tar, as far as they go in the ground, and sand afterwards; it will make them much more durable.

About Lime.—A. R., McVeytown, Pa., asks: "Does lime made from stone gathered on the surface of the ground possess the same fertilizing properties as that made from stone taken from the quarry?" Undoubtedly, if the stone found in the two places is the same. Some limestone contains much silex and other impurities, and these may occur more abundantly in the surface stone than in that taken from below. As far as the mere fact of exposure goes, it can make no difference.

Cheap Lands in Virginia.—In Fauquier, Culpepper, and Albemarle Counties, are some of the finest lands of the State. Here the devolations of the war were severely felt, and the farmers are anxious to sell a part of these lands to get money to work the balance. This is a good field for the northern capitalist.

The Trapper's Guide.—This is a neat octavo volume of 416 pages, illustrated with a large number of good engravings of the fur-bearing and game animals of America, together with articles of the hunter's outfit. It is written by Mr. S. Newhouse, an experienced trapper, and published by the Oneida community. Mr. N. is the manufacturer of a very good style of steel traps, and "The Trapper's Guide" was originally written to extend their sale by instructing in their use; now it is much enlarged. There is so much in the book likely to interest many of our readers that we place it upon our list: but must say that neither Mr. Newhouse or his editors have much of the spirit of true sportsmen when they recommend the practice of taking in traps animals which the world over are recognized as "noble game," and entitled to a chance for their lives. Trapping deer is heathenish. It is far worse than taking trout in nets, which is justly punished by heavy penalties in some of the States.

Plants Named.—E. S. Resh, Pa. No. 1. *Mitchella repens*, or Partridge-berry; it could only be cultivated in a shady place. No. 2 is our commonest blue Violet. *Viola cucullata*....J. J. E., Afton, Maine. The Cockspur Thorn, *Cratægus Crus-galli*, one of the finest of our native thorns. The Buckthorn is a widely different plant....E. H. Stiles, Lake Mills, Wis. The Pasqueflower, *Anemone Pulsatilla*, not known east of Wisconsin; very beautiful....Mrs. A. A. McElwee, Ulster Co., N. Y. Two species of *Trillium*; the purple one is *Trillium erectum*, and the white one with purple stripes on the petals is *Trillium erythrocarpum*....J. H. Clendenin, Gallipolis, Ohio. The common English Plantain, *Plantago lanceolata*, often called Rib-grass, though it is no grass at all; neither is the one sent us "a grass." It is one of the Sedge Family, of a species too young to determine....O. W. Fuller, Blackstone, Mass. No. 1 is Velvet Grass, *Holcus lanatus*; No. 2 is Reed Canary Grass, *Phalaris arundinacea*; neither of them of any great value....M. W. Philips, Chatawa, Miss. *Arrhenatherum avenaceum*, or Oat Grass, both specimens the same, though unlike in appearance, probably from differences of situation. Not valuable at the North.

Beautiful Lobelias.—Messrs. B. K. Bliss & Son have sent us specimens of some very fine hybrid Lobelias. They are hybrids between *Lobelia cardinalis* and *L. syphilitica*, our two most showy native species; the flowers present every gradation of shade between the intense scarlet of the one and the equally intense blue one of the other. These hybrids have attracted much attention in England, and are a fine addition to our list of hardy herbaceous perennials.

Pond Lilies.—P. L., New York, wishes to know how to destroy "Pond Lilies that infest fresh water ponds." If he means the white lily, (*Nymphæa odorata*,) we cannot conceive how he can have too many. If the yellow ones are in question, (*Nymphæa advena*,) a few would content us. To get rid of these or any other water plants is an easy matter, if the pond can be drawn off, and the bottom cleaned. The roots of the lilies are large, and might be dredged up without much difficulty.

Osage Orange Seed. — Machine Wanted.—A. D. Chase writes from the Chickasaw Nation, that the old method of getting out Osage Orange seed is very tedious, and asks if there is any machine for the purpose. We never heard of one, and the demand for such is likely to be so small that there is little inducement for machinists to get up one. Some of the mills for crushing grapes do the work without breaking the seeds, and we should think that a mill like the "Improved Buckeye" might, with a little adjustment, do the work.

Ditching Plows.—We know of two which give good promise; neither is yet fairly offered to the public, we believe, but both will be as soon as their owners are satisfied that they cannot essentially improve them, that they will do good work, and the demand can be supplied. One of these plows, which is intended for swampy or boggy land of a peaty character, cuts the whole ditch at a single furrow, and lays the slice at one side like a wall. The other is for any land not very stony, and will cut a ditch about three feet deep.

Substitute for Stable Manure in Market Gardening.—"A. M. R.," Poultney, Vt. You can probably, by exercising reasonable vigilance, pick up many fertilizers which now go to waste in your vicinity. The muck and ashes compost with guano would be good, but no doubt you can secure the contents of privy vaults for the trouble of clearing them out, and perhaps even be paid for doing it. Then, too, there is probably a brewery, paper mill, tannery, or some similar establishment near, in the wastes of which you may strike a mine. The first and last have each peculiarly fertilizing wastes which must be used with care. Make friends with the butcher for blood and offal useless to him, and so before you buy much guano, exhaust home resources.

Soap Suds on Melon Vines.—Walter S. Knight, Ohio. Your fault doubtless was the deluging the cucumber and melon vines with soap suds once a week, during the drouth, and doing little else. If you had dug about the hills and thoroughly mellowed the soil, and then poured the water into one or two depressions near each hill where it would gently soak away, wetting the ground not so much on the surface as at a depth below, the vines would probably have thriven. Soap suds from the tubs on washing day, has with it much scum which will not follow the water into the ground. This should be raked, or stirred into the soil in some way, or it will be very likely to form an incrustation impervious to air and moisture upon the surface.

Rats.—Mr. Langstroth, (see May number, p. 178,) catches rats easily after getting the first one. Alex. H. Haller says, he will find no difficulty in taking the first rat, if he will try a little of the oil of Rhodium on his bait. We know this is very attractive to many animals.

American Poultry Society.—At a recent meeting of this society, the following officers were elected for the ensuing year. *President*, O. C. Poole, Metuchin, N. J.; *Vice President*, S. M. Saunders, New York; *Recording Secretary*, J. H. Fry, Staten Island, N. Y.; *Corresponding Secretary*, A. M. Halsted, Rye, N. Y.; *Treasurer*, W. A. Fitch, 151 Nassau-street, New York; *Auditor*, J. G. Finnie, 11 Wall-street, New York. As will be seen by advertisement, in another column, the first exhibition is to be held the third week in November. Arrangements are made for a very successful show.

Ice-House in a Cellar.—R. M. M. This arrangement is often more convenient than any other, and fails generally from imperfect ventilation and drainage. If these matters are properly attended to, ice will keep well in a cellar. The ventilation should be with the air from the outside of the cellar. If otherwise, it would make the atmosphere damp, and affect the temperature in the rooms above. The drainage is the most difficult thing to manage in a cellar. The side walls of an ice-house here should be made with the same care as above-ground. We recently saw a very ingenious device to turn the drainage water to practical account. The bottom of the ice-house was made tight, and a little sloping, with gutters to conduct all the water into a trough in an adjoining room. The trough was made large enough to hold a dozen milk-pans or more. It was exceedingly convenient in keeping cream, butter, and other perishable articles. The temperature of the room in which the trough was kept was also very much reduced, which made it a safer place for fruits and meats. We prefer an ice-house wholly or in part above-ground where it can be had.

Where to Locate?—Wants a Farm.—We have large numbers of letters, of which the above is the purport—some of them accompanied by a strong personal appeal. Advice as to where to locate is very difficult to give, as so much depends upon individual peculiarities, capabilities, prejudices, and previous occupation. Were we to advise one who had never raised a strawberry or a blackberry in his life, that Southern New Jersey was a favorable locality for small fruits, he would probably go there, fresh from rough farming, or from some mechanical or mercantile occupation, try it a year or two, fail, and then blame us for our advice. All this matter of location for fruit and vegetable growing is mainly a question of markets. A small sum expended in personal exploration will be more satisfactory than any advice a stranger can give. As to undertaking the buying or selling farms, that is not in our line; either can be readily accomplished through the medium of advertising.

Hop Culture.—A dozen or so ask us to send them by letter a detailed statement of the methods of hop culture. To meet this very want of information concerning special crops, we offered liberal premiums for practical essays on Hop, Tobacco, Onion, and Flax culture. The best essays, several on each subject, we have published in the pamphlet form, and offer them at a low price. The work on Hop Culture is 40 cents, and contains, (as do the other essays,) fuller information than is to be found elsewhere. We could not afford to write out the matter for as many dollars as we ask cents for the treatise. As to the sets, they are frequently advertised in our columns, and we doubt not that any of the writers of these essays would furnish them.

Gypsum.—C. G. Reed, Wayne Co., Pa. Gypsum is sulphate of lime. Agricultural plaster is ground gypsum, more or less impure. It will keep indefinitely if not subjected to the action of rains or water, for it is unalterable in the air at common temperatures, but soluble in water, 400 to 500 pounds of water being capable of dissolving one pound of gypsum. Gypsum contains a little more than 20 per cent. of water, and this it loses if heated for a time, at a temperature much less than a red heat. When unground gypsum is thus heated, it crumbles to a powder. Ground gypsum heated or "boiled," as it is termed, becomes Plaster of Paris. It gradually absorbs water from the air and becomes gypsum again. Plaster of Paris then is damaged by keeping, though unhurt for agricultural purposes.

"Do you believe Toads, Fish, and Worms, rain Down?"—Ralph G. Pratt, Minn. There is every reason to suppose that fish, worms, etc., are occasionally sucked up with water by the force of water-spouts, and whirlwinds. Ponds and river beds are often emptied of water almost in an instant, by a whirlwind passing over. The same power has often lifted men, women, and children, sometimes conveyed them long distances, and set them down unharmed. After the passage of whirlwinds or hurricanes, fish are frequently found still alive on either side, and perhaps miles away from its track. Toads and worms might, and very likely would be taken up and suspended a much longer time.

THE NEW STORE OF ORANGE JUDD & COMPANY, 245 BROADWAY, NEW YORK.

The New Building, 245 Broadway.

This month we present a "Basket Item" of unusually large size—a view of our present quarters. Last month's *Agriculturist* announced our intended removal, and the present issue dates from 245 Broadway. At the present time we feel like a boy with a new pair of boots, as we are undergoing the process of "breaking in." We shall, however, soon be at home in the new place, which is as far superior for our purposes to the old one, as that was to the quarters occupied in the early days of the paper.

In the *American Agriculturist* for October 1860, seven years ago last month, Mr. Judd wrote as follows:—"The friends of this Journal will be pleased to learn that we have secured and removed into large and beautiful rooms, in one of the most eligible positions in this city." This was on the occupancy of 41 Park Row, as the office of the *Agriculturist*.

He little thought, at that time, that a change would be made so soon, but the increase of the business of the *Agriculturist* has required new partners and an enlarged working force, and now its necessities demand enlarged room. Since the time the above quoted remark was written, we have added an entirely distinct branch of business, that of book publishing, to that of the paper; this alone requires a large space, and removal became an imperative matter. The new store is a fine brown-stone building, directly opposite the old one, across City Hall Park. Every one at all familiar with New York knows that the Park is the center of the business part of the city, that it is the point of arrival and departure for most of the local travel. Indeed, so central is the situation that the U. S. Government has selected it as the best site for

THE VICINITY OF CITY HALL PARK.

the new Post Office soon to be built. The diagram will give an idea of the relations of our new building to the City Hall and new Post Office. Its situation is such as to face the open space between these two edifices, and is just below Murray-street, on Broadway. Our friends from abroad will have no difficulty in finding us, while the thousands of our city subscribers can reach us more readily than they could when on Park Row.

It will be seen, from the view on the opposite page, that the new store is five stories in hight; it has a front of 25 feet, a depth of 114½ feet, with an L projection, which gives us a wide entrance on Murray-st., with a spacious basement extending under the whole. The front portion of the main floor is occupied as a sales-room for our large stock of Agricultural and Horticultural works, where we have ample room for this important and increasing branch of business. Farther to the rear are the subscription and other business desks, while the basement is devoted to the important work of folding and mailing the paper. The printers' room, engravers' room, and editorial "sanctum" are on an upper floor.

If the change to our new location has made this month's issue a few days later than usual, we trust that our friends will overlook it. We are sure that they will be glad to know that we have such ample facilities for serving them all the better hereafter. We do not entirely give up the old place, though it is leased to B. K. Bliss & Son as a seed store. We still retain there a desk for subscriptions, and a counter for the sale of our books, to accommodate those who find it more convenient to call there.

At our new home, we shall be glad to see all our old friends, and to make hosts of new ones, and we hope that to our increasing thousands of readers, 245 Broadway will become, as 41 Park Row has been, "familiar in their mouths as household words."

Fair at Staten Island.—The Richmond County Agricultural Society had their horse trotting show at the race-course of the Richmond Club, in Southfield. Mr. R. W. Cammeron showed excellent Short-horn and Jersey stock. Mr. Saunders had a number of coops of poultry, including Brahmas, Buff Cochins, Houdans, Crevecœurs, and Gray Dorkings of great excellence, also Bremen Geese and Aylesbury Ducks, and other good poultry was shown. The manager of the County Farm, (poor-house,) made a fine display of vegetables, grain, etc. The open selling of "pools" at the race-course was permitted as on any other race day, and the show was little besides a horse-race with plenty of liquor and its accompaniments. We plead in behalf of the farmers of Richmond County and their families for a festival free from these corrupting associations.

Justice to the Partridge.—When the cock partridge drums, standing upon a log, he does it by beating his body with his wings, as we knew from personal observation, yet we carelessly allowed an old and incorrect impression that he beat the log, to sway the pen, in the November number, and were not a little chagrined to discover the error too late to change it. We ask Mr. Grouse's pardon, and are much obliged to those friends who so promptly suggested that he had a right to demand the *amende honorable*.

The New York State Fair at Buffalo.—This was held from the 1st to the 4th of October, and, notwithstanding the jealousy of other parts of the State, and the location at the extreme west end of New York, was a marked success. Some 40 or 50 acres were inclosed for the exhibition, and ample provision was made for the feeding and shelter of the animals, and for the display of fruits and vegetables. The show of fruit was not what it ought to have been in Western New York, but was creditable, especially in the department of grapes. The Pleasant Valley Grape Growers' Association, from Hammond-port, had fine samples of wine, both bottled and in the original packages, and took the first premium. They exhibited eleven samples of wine and twenty varieties of grapes. The show of agricultural implements was particularly large, as might have been expected, and was some index of the rapid progress making in improved husbandry. Horse hoes and cultivators were of numerous and excellent patterns, and among the prominent exhibitors were F. F. Holbrook, of Boston, and Alden & Co., of Auburn. In Pennsylvania and the West, these have long been popular, and in New York and New England, they must soon drive out the hand hoe. If stones and stumps are in the way, they must be cleared out. The reduction in the cost of raising corn by the use of these implements is so great that no farmer can afford to do without them. Gov. Holbrook's Universal Plow attracted much attention. They are in various styles to admit of different kinds of work. Each plow changes its moldboard for stubble, for sod, and for subsoil plowing, and for turning flat and lap furrow slices. This saves both the money and the time of the farmer. An admirable feature of the fair was the arrangement for addresses and discussions. Too often the evenings of the fair days are lost. Thousands of people come together to learn, and there is no suitable opportunity for the interchange of experience. The show of ideas is always the best part of an agricultural fair. Maj. Brooks' address upon the apple, and the discussion that followed, were worth far more to the public as an incentive to apple growing than the whole show of apples upon the tables. The attendance upon the great day of the fair, Thursday, were estimated at 35,000, and the receipts for the whole four days were $21,500, which is said to be more than has been taken in any year since 1859, at Albany. This vindicates the wisdom of our Buffalo friends in insisting upon having the fair there. We hope it paid them as well as the society.

Sheep in Oregon.—N. O. This promises to be one of the best wool-growing States. Sheep are very healthy, and the wool is of excellent quality. Crosses of the South Devon and Merino are abundant, and sell for a little over a dollar a head. Six woolen factories are established, or under way, in the western part of the State.

Weight of Merino Fleeces.—In a recent number of the *Country Gentleman* a report is given of a public shearing this spring, under the auspices of the Springfield, (Vermont,) Agricultural Society, which took place April 25th, and is remarkable for the great weight of cleansed wool reported as yielded by some of the animals. The sheep were all merinos or merino grades. One two year-old ram, weighing 110 lbs., sheared 17 lbs. 8 oz., which, cleansed, weighed 7 lbs. 8½ oz.; fleece 360 days old. Another, two years old, weighing 120½ lbs., sheared 18 lbs. 8 oz., which cleansed 6 lbs. 12 oz.; 365 days old. A four year-old, weighing 123 lbs., sheared 20 lbs. 6 oz., cleansed 6 lbs.; 365 days. Not less remarkable is the weight of cleansed ewes' fleeces, of which the heaviest three weighed 5 lbs. 14¼ oz., 5 lbs. 1½ oz., and 4 lbs. 11 oz. The average shrinking of rams' fleeces was 67.75 per cent.; that of ewes' fleeces 51.32 per cent. Why have we not reports of equally heavy fleeces where different breeds and families are shorn in competition? Part of the fleeces were cleansed at one mill, but, on account of a misunderstanding between one of the committee and the proprietor, they went to another factory to have the rest cleansed. It would be interesting to know, in connection, which fleeces were washed at the first mill.

The Agricultural College of Pennsylvania.—The circular of this institution has been sent to us, containing its programme and list of officers. We are glad to see in the faculty a number of men who have a well established reputation, and as the college seems to have made an effort to become a first class institution, we wish it all success. We are quite surprised to read one thing, however. The circular says: "For the benefit of the farming community, an Agricultural Journal, under the editorship of members of the College Faculty, will be commenced in the course of the current year. In the journal will be published the experiments made at this college." Now we advise the "Board of Trustees" to consider, in the first place, how much money they have to lose in amateur publishing, and whether, with the extensive courses laid down, their professors have not quite enough to do without editing a paper. If the professors have anything to say that is of value, there is no lack of channels of communication by which they can reach the public much more effectually than by any publication like that proposed. We advise the trustees to confine their "experiments" for the present to the establishment of the college in the favor of the people of Pennsylvania, before they experiment in Journalism.

The Drought at the West has been very severe. They are shipping stock hogs from Illinois to Western Missouri, on account of the scarcity of corn. The estimate of the Agricultural Bureau is that Illinois will be 14 per cent short of the previous year, Indiana 17, Kentucky 28, and Ohio 30. These are the great corn-growing States, and the large crops of the Southern States will hardly make good the deficiency. Corn was worth 20 cents a bushel more in Cincinnati than in Nashville October 1st, and this difference in price led to large shipments.

Wheat on Wet Land, Drained.—Wet clay lands, when drained, make the best wheat lands. In mucky soils, the plant, especially the winter varieties, would not probably do as well, as the surface would sooner feel atmospheric changes. Spring wheat does well on black prairie soils where winter wheat fails, and we should not hesitate to try that variety on reclaimed swamp, if thoroughly dry. The wheat should be sown early in the spring, before the deep frost is out, even if you have to get it in with a harrow. Early sowing is regarded as a matter of the first importance by those who have thoroughly tried it.

Rye for Spring Feed.—The sowing of rye early in the fall, for this purpose, is quite common at the West, and can be introduced with advantage in all the dairy districts. The rye can be sown among corn at the last hoeing or cultivating, and still later, by plowing specially for the purpose. It starts very early, and gives the cows their first bite of green fodder in the spring.

New Jersey State Fair.—The State Agricultural Society held its exhibition at its new grounds, at Waverley, midway between Elizabeth and Newark. We have rarely seen grounds better adapted to such purposes. They are gently rolling, include a grove, a beautiful lake, and a hill of considerable hight, upon which is level land enough for the exhibition tents and buildings, and where everybody can see the whole trotting course, and all the rest of the show. The future exhibitions, if well managed, ought to be among the most interesting people's festivals of this part of the country. The show was a very pleasant one to visit, but very small. The Jerseys were the only breed of cattle present in any force, and of these there were very fine specimens. The show of poultry included most excellent Rouen Ducks, Black Polands, White Dorkings, very good Brahmas, Black Spanish, and Silver-spangled Hamburghs, and other varieties above mediocrity. There was one hog and six sheep. The horticultural tent, in charge of Mr. P. Quin, was arranged with great taste, and contained a very fine display of pears. Other fruits, flowers, and vegetables were good, and all were well labelled. The other departments of the exhibition contained, of course, much to instruct and interest, and would compare favorably with a good county fair in New England, New York, or Ohio. We were interested in a Buckeye Mowing Machine, shown by the President, which has been in use ten years on his farm, cutting, annually, over 100 acres, and having, as he testified, required but $5.88 for repairs. Of one thing we think the public have a right to complain, and that is the almost entire absence of the names and addresses of exhibitors attached to the articles of most interest to farmers. This forced some of the exhibitors to withdraw their articles from competition, in order that they might display their names. This is done, we suppose, to make the judges honest. Well—they know their men probably; other societies appoint as judges men they think they can trust. At any rate, a great part of the interest and value of the fair, both to the public and to exhibitors, is thus lost by the suppression of the names even of successful exhibitors. The practice is all wrong.

The Ohio State Fair, held at Dayton, the same week, was in almost every respect a splendid success. It came much nearer to our ideal of a State Fair than anything we visited the present season. The grounds were so near the city that almost every one could walk, and most people preferred walking to the exactions of the hackmen, who were only half as brazen as their thrifty cousins of Madison. The grounds, belonging to the Montgomery County Agricultural Society, were ample, embracing forty-six acres, and were fitted up with everything needed except water, which was so poorly distributed that multitudes suffered from thirst, and other multitudes were driven to the drinking saloons. There were 104 sheep pens, 70 for swine, 329 stalls for horses, 43 for mules and horses, 108 for cattle, and these were nearly all full. The show was worthy of a great Agricultural State. The poultry pens were not full, and the show was not very good. The select breeds may not have had their day, but they do not make much sensation at the fairs. Horticultural Hall had a good display of fruit, though it was not so full as we had anticipated. Apples were very fair, what there were of them. These were mostly from the northern part of the State, where this fruit is quite abundant. In other parts, the crop has been injured by the drouth. Grapes were more abundant than any other fruit, and in these the fruit growers of the Lake Region bore off the palm. There was a good show of vegetables, and the potatoes, as was meet, took the front rank. L. D. Scott & Co., of Huron, exhibited a large number of varieties, and had 71 named sorts, which they offer for sale. This is a little too much of a good thing. We are glad to see, however, that our gardeners are not content with the old favorites, most of which are hopelessly diseased. The display of agricultural implements was large, as might have been expected in this great State. Mowing machines and reapers, horse hay rakes, plows and grain drills, covered a large area, and men who appreciated their excellences were generally on hand to explain. Conspicuous among these for its perfect finish was the Champion mower and reaper, a self-raker, which passes the bundles off of the apron of any desirable size. There were several patterns of self-rakers upon the ground, and this is getting to be a very necessary attachment to the reaper. It saves greatly in labor, and is one step in the right direction. The machine will not meet the wants of the harvest field until it binds the bundles. Besides these, there was an almost endless variety of contrivances for aiding the housekeeper's work, washing machines and wringers, fruit dryers and clothes dryers, all very ingenious and helpful to human muscles. The house will soon keep itself, and go by steam, if Yankee wit can accomplish it. It was a goodly sight to see the tens of thousands swarming here, and enjoying the show beneath the shade of the grand old trees. There could not have been less than fifty thousand people in attendance, and the receipts were over $20,000. The managers certainly know how to get up a fair, and we congratulate them upon their success.

The Wisconsin State Fair was held at Madison, the capital of the State, on the 23d, 24th, 25th, 26th, and 27th of September. In location nothing can be more charming than this city, on high land between two crystal lakes, overlooking them both, and a wide sweep of territory beyond. The view from the top of the State University is one of the finest in the West. The fair grounds are just on the edge of the city, perhaps a mile from the center, and about the same distance from the depot. The omnibus drivers charged fifty cents for this brief distance, which we should have considered extortion, if we had been obliged to pay it; but, being blessed with an excellent apparatus for locomotion, we fell back upon Nature's own, and went up to the show, independent, with mild meditations upon human nature, and without putting down the hackmen of Madison among the "extortioners and unjust," where they, no doubt, belong. The fair grounds were admirably arranged, and the stables and pens for the accommodation of horses, cattle, sheep, and swine, all that could be asked. The fair ran quite too much to horse flesh. Premiums of $100 to $200 for fast horses, and only from $20 to $25 for cattle, are out of proportion. We like to see Short-horns put upon the same footing with Black Hawks, and swine and sheep fairly encouraged. Large halls were put up for the display of horticultural products, and for domestic goods and the fine arts. The show of agricultural implements was uncommonly good for so young a State. Among the best things on exhibition in this department was a binder, attached to one of Marsh's reapers. It is the invention of S. D. Carpenter, of Madison, and represents five years of hard work to bring it to perfection. The straw is cut, passed up on an endless apron to the back part of the machine, where it falls into a hopper, and when a sufficient quantity is gathered, it is bound with a wire, and thrown out behind. It is a self-raker and binder, and in addition to this, saves in the hopper several bushels of seed daily, which is lost in the ordinary mode of gathering. A pound of the annealed wire, costing twenty-five cents, will bind about 800 bundles. As it takes about eight men to rake and bind after a reaper, this machine must save the farmer about $10 a day. If this machine works as well as it promises, it cannot fail to make a revolution in the harvest fields of the West, almost as great as the introduction of the reaper itself. It ought to make flour a good deal cheaper. The West is making rapid strides in the improvement of agricultural implements, and will soon drive the Eastern manufacturer out of its markets. The receipts of the fair were about $10,000, and were quite satisfactory to the managers.

The Michigan State Fair was held at Detroit from the 10th to the 13th of October. The vicinity of a large city, and the ease of access by rail and steam, and the fine weather, conspired to make the attendance large. Had there been better facilities for reaching the ground from the city, the multitudes would have been much greater. By water, old tugs and propellers of the most moderate speed were employed, and by land, horse railroads running half way, and omnibuses the other half. A little more enterprise would have put the rails up to the grounds, and accommodated everybody. With all the defects of arrangement and of material, there was a grand show, and the people were paid for going. The representation of horses eclipsed everything else upon the ground, and shows the continuance of the horse fever. There were 200 stalls for horses, and 300 animals in them and outside. There were only 90 for cattle, and 144 for sheep and swine, and many of these were empty. The racing was quite too prominent, and attracted the principal attention. Large numbers of light horses, whose chief excellence was speed, were exhibited, and the fast men had it on the track their own way. There were, however, some good farm and carriage horses, by whose legitimate use a farmer could make much more money than by betting. In the cattle pens, the Devons were well represented. Mr. Cole, of Batavia, N. Y., showed a herd of them, and there were about fifty in all. Mr. Cole took six of the prizes. There were several very fine Short-horn bulls, and some showed their offspring in adjoining stalls, which was a very good feature. David Uhl, of Ypsilanti; H. A. Pitlotson, of Marshall; T. Dinsmore, of Danville; P. C. Bush, of West Jersey, were among the exhibitors in this department. The Michigan State Agricultural College showed a Galloway Bull, weighing 1,900 pounds, and several other good animals. The feature of the cattle stalls, however, that attracted most attention, was a lot of eighteen fat cattle, exhibited by Wm. Smith, a west-end butcher of Detroit. They were gotten up for the occasion, and were manifestly a butcher's ideal of what a ripe beef ought to be. They were triumphant animals, and we all enjoyed the sight, and Mr. Smith as much as any of us. They were grand to look upon, but we thought a little too fat to eat, considering them from the consumer's point of view. The same gentleman also made a fine show of Suffolk pigs. The Chester Whites were well represented, and there were specimens of the Essex and the Berkshire. There were many more of the long-wool varieties of sheep than we expected to see—Canada was on hand with her Cotswolds and Leicesters, and the show of these animals was one of the best we have ever met with. Even the Southdowns outnumbered the fine wools. We ought not, perhaps, to infer from this that the fine wools are on the decline, but that mutton sheep are better appreciated. The show of agricultural implements was uncommonly good. In this department alone there were 473 entries. The fruit was not at all up to the mark, though there were some fine grapes, and specimens of apples and pears. We have seen a better show at County societies. In the hen coops there was abundant evidence that the hen fever has subsided. There were a few good Brahmas, and these fowls seem to be at all the fairs the most popular of all the Asiatic importations. There were quite too many small shows, monkeys, cross-eyed puppies, fat women, and things of that sort, to suit the public convenience. The room was needed for something else, and the time and money spent on mal-formations were wasted. The receipts at the gate were about $10,000, and from other sources, we understood, nearly enough would be realized to cover expenses.

The Kentucky State Fair was held near Louisville, at the grounds of the Louisville and Jefferson County Association, about three miles from the edge of the town. Some forty acres or more had been enclosed with a fence, embracing among other fixtures an old farm-house with its accompanying buildings. A few of the primitive forest trees were still left, and other fruit and ornamental trees adorned the grounds. A large amphitheater, capable of accommodating ten thousand or more people, was admirably arranged for the display of horses and other stock. The ring was well lined with tan bark, and here the famous horsemen of Kentucky displayed their not less famous steeds. This was the chief attraction of the fair, as might have been expected, and though not at all to be compared with the displays before the war, as we were informed, was still very fine, and well worth the journey of a thousand miles to see. There was much less trial for speed than we had expected to see. The judges occupied the center of the ring, and the competitors for the premium drove or rode their horses round the track, under the direction of the judges, until they were satisfied. The object seemed to be to display the action and all the good points of the horse as well as his speed. The audience took a lively interest in the awards made, and announced their approbation with loud acclaim if they were pleased with the decision. The points of a good horse are so well known and appreciated in this State, that the audience almost invariably decided with the judges. We like this association of the people with the verdict of the judges. It is eminently fair, it fixes the attention, and improves the taste of the multitudes who come to the exhibition for the purpose of learning something useful. We understood that the merits of the neat stock were decided upon in the same way, though we were not present on the first day of the fair, when they were exhibited. This confining of the show cattle to a single day is not a good arrangement. The majority who attend a fair can go only one day, and they want to see every department well represented. Arrangements should be made to keep all the animals upon the ground until the last day. A few good Short-horns were exhibited, but the display was not at all what the State ought to have afforded. There were a few good pens of Long and Middle Wool sheep. The show of swine was small. The arrangements for exhibiting them were not good. There was a great want of good pens, both for sheep and swine. The show of fruit, though small, was of superior quality. C. C. Cary, H. S. Duncan, and L. Young were prominent among the exhibitors. The fruit of Mr. Young was not only very fair, but of high color, said to be secured by enclosing the specimens in muslin, while ripening upon the tree. This enhances their value for show, but would hardly pay for market purposes. The peaches were magnificent for size, and in quality superior to any thing grown upon the sea-board, where the excessive rains of the season have made all peaches deficient in flavor. Specimens of the White Head Heath and of the Grand Admirable, both clings, were about twelve inches in circumference. There appeared to be a considerable confusion in the names of the pears, but that difficulty time will remedy, especially if the society follows the very good practice of distributing standard books upon fruit growing for premiums. Although the arrangements for reaching the fair by railroad were very good, the attendance was quite limited, showing that the State has not yet recovered from the effects of the war. There were probably not more than five thousand people present on the best day of the fair. But these were Kentuckians, fine specimens of men and women, that would have made any fair a success. When the next one comes off, may we be there to see.

Nijni-Novgorod Fair—Moscow—General Notes about Russia.

[Our readers will doubtless be interested in the following extracts from Mr. JUDD's home letters, the first dated at Nijni-Novgorod, August 24th. This place is on the Volga River, near the eastern boundary of Europe, in latitude 56° north, and longitude 44° east of Greenwich, or 118° east of New York.]

....."If Americans generally knew how easily and cheaply one can travel, more of them would visit the Old World. The money that many families expend on extra carriages, furniture, and dress, during a year or two, for mere show, would pay the expenses of a trip across the Atlantic, and a considerable distance into the continent. ....If many of those who do come knew how comfortable and convenient are the traveling facilities, they would not stop merely at London, Paris, and Switzerland, but would strike farther east, and get a glimpse of the Oriental people and customs. I am now nearly seven hundred miles east-southeast of St. Petersburg, and have with me a lady, and children of 8, 11, and 13 years of age, and we have come the last 700 miles with just as much ease as in traveling the same distance anywhere in America, and with better facilities for obtaining good food at the rail-road stations than we should find there.....Here we see a condensed picture of eastern manners or customs. At this point, or near here, for 500 or 600 years past, there has been an annual fair, lasting from four to six weeks, at which the people of the East and the West have met for the sale or exchange of their respective productions and manufactures. The great Volga River, as you will see by the map, empties into the Caspian Sea, 1600 miles below this point. That sea has no outlet to the ocean for communication with the outer world; so the various peoples and tribes around the Caspian Sea, as well as the Chinese, from the east, and the Siberians, from the northeast, or northern Asia, bring their products here, and meet the western people, who bring their goods from Western Russia, Germany, France, and Great Britain. The sales amount to from $70,000,000 to $100,000,000 worth annually. The River Oka, from the west, here unites with the Volga, and the locality of the fair is on the point of land between the north shore of the Oka and the southwest or right bank of the Volga. The city of Nijni-Novgorod is on a high bluff, between the Volga and Oka, on the south side of the latter. The rivers are full of boats of all descriptions imaginable, many of which have been poled up the whole length of the Volga. From the tower on the bluff, I can, at one view, see thousands of these boats, many of them landing or taking in merchandise. For three or four miles up the right or west bank of the Volga, there are immense piles of goods, covered with mats or skins. I never before saw such quantities of merchandise collected in one place; it is as if you should remove all the buildings in New York, and expose the contents upon the banks of the rivers. The bales of cotton and hogsheads of sugar, (beet sugar from Europe,) seem innumerable. The trading ground consists of hundreds, perhaps thousands, of one-story bazaars, arranged along regular streets, running at right angles. Each nation has its own quarter, or streets, but during the hours of trade the different peoples are of course much commingled. Each nation adopts its own peculiar style in the construction and arrangement of the bazaars. In the Chinese quarter, for example, all the bazaars are in the pagoda form, and all the people coming here retain their peculiar modes of dress. As we walked around the fair, our intelligent polyglot guide pointed out the different races, and interpreted for us as we chaffered and made some small purchases as souvenirs of our visit. Here were Siberians with minerals, precious stones, furs, etc.; there were Chinese, with their stocks of Oolong and Souchong, their ivory and wood work, cloths, silks, etc.; here were Persians, with their richly wrought gold and silver fabrics; there were Tartars, Kalmucks, and so on—an endless variety—Georgians, Circassians, Caucasians, Cossacks, Arabs, Armenians, Syrians, Turks, Russians, Germans, French, English, etc., etc.,—making all together the most novel gathering in the world, I suppose. The jargon of languages scarcely falls below what must have been heard around the tower of Babel itself. These fairs usually extend from July 23d to September 22d of each year. The second class fare, (fully equal to the American first class,) by railroad, from St. Petersburg to Moscow, (400 miles,) is 13 Roubles; and from Moscow to Nijni-Novgorod, (273 miles,) 9¼ Roubles. A Rouble of Russian paper money is at present worth about 68 or 70 cents of American gold, or a little less than $1 of United States currency. The Rouble is divided into 100 Kopecks, so that the Russian Roubles and Kopecks correspond with our dollars and cents, but 5 gold Roubles are just about equal to 4 gold dollars, when the paper money of both nations is on a par with gold."

"Moscow, Russia, August 26th.... Taken all in all, this is the most interesting city we have visited. We have been out to the 'Sparrow Hills,' two or three miles west, on to the high ground, where Napoleon's army, in 1812, caught their first glimpse of the city, after the long, tedious march of more than a thousand miles, the latter part of it fighting their weary way over the vast plains of Lithuania or Western Russia. No wonder the poor fellows shouted in wild delight, 'Moscow! Moscow!' Few of them lived to carry home the vivid impression made upon them by their first view of the goal of their toilsome pilgrimage.... The view from these hills is grand, glorious! Spread out over a wide plain, which is encircled by the serpentine Moskva River, lies the curious city of 400 churches, mostly with green roofs, and each surmounted by from one to a dozen domes or minarets. Of these domes I counted 506, visible from one point. A large number of them are covered with gold and silver, and the reflection of the setting sun gives a resplendency exceeding my highest previous conceptions of even the 'new Jerusalem' itself!.... Near the center of the city is the far famed Kremlin. This is a semi-circular space, enclosed by a high wall, nearly 1½ miles in length, surmounted with curiously shaped towers, a hundred yards or so apart, besides which there are five large gateways. Within this wall are the three ancient palaces, the treasury building, four gorgeous churches, the high tower of Ivan Veliki, (John the Great,) at the foot of which is the Great Bell or Tsar Kolokol, (Tsar of bells.) Within the Kremlin, also, is the arsenal, around the outside walls of which are arranged over 800 cannons, the trophies of war—a larger part of them taken from or left behind by Napoleon; the Senate House, some smaller buildings, and paved open spaces fill up the rest of the Kremlin. The treasury building contains an immense amount of curiously mingled gold and silver plate and precious stones, presented by the sovereigns of many nations, the crowns, and thrones, and regal insignia, not only of ancient and modern Russia, but of captured and subjugated nations, as Poland, Kasan, etc. The larger one of the three palaces, built by the late Emperor Nicholas, excels even the palaces of St. Petersburg and Paris, in the gorgeous decorations of some of its larger rooms. Of the four Kremlin churches, the Cathedral of the Assumption, where all the emperors of Russia have been crowned, is the most noted. Its walls, its ceilings, and even its interior columns, are entirely covered with richly gilded paintings, most of them full size portraits of prelates of the church, saints, and scripture characters. Standing within the great nave, one has peculiar sensations when he finds himself thus gazed upon, from every point above and around, by so many renowned personages, whose real presence is so well represented by the artist's brush and pencil. In the second church, St. Michael's Cathedral, the main floor is largely occupied with the tombs of the Emperors down to Peter the Great, since which time they have been buried at St. Petersburg. In the third, the Cathedral of the Annunciation, the Czars have long been baptized and married. The floor is paved with jasper and agate. In the fourth church, the Metropolitan, is manufactured the holy oil which is distributed throughout the empire, and which is used in the baptism of every child born in the Greek or National Church. In this cathedral, also, is shown a great number of robes, mitres, diadems, etc., wrought with costly pearls, diamonds, and other precious stones of untold value. One robe alone contains over 50 pounds weight of these precious stones and gems. These few items must suffice to give you a faint idea of the immense treasures contained within the Kremlin. The great bell is worthy of its name and fame. It is now raised upon a circular stone wall, five feet high. Its proportions are perfect, its hight over 20 feet, and I measured 68 feet around its base. (To get a full idea of its size, drive down a center stake, and with a cord, 11 feet long, as a radius, mark out a circle 22 feet across. A 20-feet pole, set up in the center, will help the conception of its great size.) It weighs 444,000 pounds, or 222 tons! A fragment, about 7 feet high and 6 feet wide, is broken out of the rim, and stands down against the wall, so that by climbing upon the wall, one can walk in through 'the crack of the bell,' as it is called. The Ivan Veliki tower, from which one has a good view of all the city, contains 40 bells, one of them half the size of the great bell, and others of somewhat smaller proportions. The chiming of only six of these, of medium size, produced painful emotions in our heads, and gave a benumbing jar to the whole body.... Some distance outside the Kremlin wall is another, the old city wall, and beyond this, the city extends two to three miles each way from the center. There is everywhere an odd commingling of spacious public and private edifices, and the mean abodes of the poor. Log structures, neatly framed and trimmed at the corners, however, are frequently seen within the city. There is everywhere an ancient air and slowness of movement, with beggars and people in rags unpleasantly frequent—quite different from the thrift and activity visible at St. Petersburg."

"St. Petersburg, August 29th.... Of this city I have already written somewhat. Returning here two days since, we have been around the public parks, and to Peterhof, etc., and my first impressions of the city are fully confirmed. Taking into account its inland position, its high northern latitude, its comparatively recent foundation, and the natural difficulties to be overcome in its low alluvial soil, it is a marvel of enterprise, unequaled elsewhere in the world! The palaces and public buildings are spacious, and exhibit within a solid magnificence hardly to be found elsewhere in Europe—not even in Paris. With a continuance of the policy and plans of the present Czar, Russia must continue to advance rapidly in civilization and refinement. The education of the masses now emerging from slavery and serfdom, and a shaking-off of the more superstitious or idolatrous rites and ceremonies of the established church, are most needed, and the tendency is in this direction. Great freedom of religious belief and worship is already granted, and education is making rapid strides."

General Notes on Russia...."Granitza, Southwestern Russia, August 31st.... During the last two days, we have come down from St. Petersburg, nearly 800 miles, to this point, stopping only a night in Warsaw, as the cholera is somewhat prevalent there. I am now awaiting the train that will take us across the Austrian border, and out to Cracow, to visit the salt mines... I have traveled over 2000 miles in Russia during the present month—with all the ease, comfort, and convenience, and with as much personal freedom as I have ever found in America or Western Europe, and any American can do the same. The espionage of our passports and luggage has been merely nominal, and at only two points—viz.: on entering Finland, and on passing through Warsaw.... European Russia, throughout, is more level than I expected to find it. In its general surface it corresponds with our Western prairies, but is generally covered with forests where not under cultivation. The trees are mainly white birch, spruce, and pines, though other kinds are frequently met with. From St. Petersburg, via Moscow, to Nijni-Novgorod, I estimate that about half the land visible from the railroad is under cultivation. From St. Petersburg southwest, for the first 400 miles perhaps, one third of the country is still in forests. Russian Poland is almost one vast fertile field. Wheat is the staple crop everywhere, though pasture lands abound on the route southeast from St. Petersburg. Highly fertile soils are apparently of rare occurrence, and pine lands of a somewhat sterile character are frequent; yet, on the whole, I judge that four or five times the present population could be readily sustained with improved modes of tillage. There are many indications of the introduction of a better class of agricultural implements, and I believe American inventors and manufacturers will find in Russia an excellent opening, not only to improve their own financial interests, but to benefit this country as well. The hand sickle, everywhere seen in the harvest fields at this season, as well as the rude hay scythe, will readily yield to the mowing and reaping machines; and the same may be said of the rude plow and other implements. The policy of the government is liberal towards all foreign improvements ...The relics of serfdom are everywhere visible, though rapidly dying out. As a rule, the small huts of the serfs are gathered in clusters or villages around or near the more stately dwellings of their former proprietors, and the smaller or larger Greek church, with its green roof and gilded dome, is close at hand. The liberated serfs generally work for their former masters, a part of the time at least, at mutually agreed upon wages, though every one is at liberty to go and come at pleasure. Mutual interest is at present the only bond that keeps these people in their original localities. Each peasant is allowed a plot of ground of his own, in fee simple, and without any payment except the past services of himself or ancestors, and each can purchase as much more as his accumulated earnings and savings supply the means for. Schools are opened in most of the serf villages. As far as I can gather from observation and from frequent conversation with intelligent Russians, I judge that the political and educational condition of the Russian people is being rapidly assimilated to that of our own country, though, of course, still far behind us in the degree of advancement. A generation or two will do much to lessen the difference. I look forward to the period as not far distant when Russia will become, in many respects, the United States of the Old World. ..."

The Use of Plaster on New Land.

The announcement in our August issue, in an article on "Top Dressing Grass Land," that two bushels of plaster produced over two tons of hay, by accurate measurement made at the State Agricultural College of Michigan, took most of our readers by surprise, and awakened in others a strong feeling of incredulity. The sentiment was not much softened by the statement that the cuttings were made twice a year, and the experiment extended over two seasons. We are not surprised at this, for we have used plaster by the sea shore, without the slightest perceptible effect. This is the general testimony of sea shore farmers. Probably, the soil gets gypsum, or its equivalent, from the sea manures so commonly used near the shore, or blown inland from the sea itself, for sulphate of lime is contained in sea water. In the grazing districts, remote from the shore, on the contrary, plaster is highly valued, and produces wonderful results, even when applied at the rate of one bushel to the acre.

Michigan is greatly blessed in its supplies of plaster. Besides the extensive deposit at Grand Rapids, a new bed has recently been opened at the town of Alabaster, in Josco County, on Saginaw Bay. This deposit has remarkable facilities for quarrying and marketing. It lies immediately upon the shore of one of the best harbors in the State; it has no overlying rock, and but little earth to be removed above it; it is split into small masses, making a great saving of labor and powder; it is of remarkable richness and purity, and is practically inexhaustible. Prof. S. P. Duffield, of Detroit, has analyzed it, and gives the following results: Lime, 00.08; Sulphuric Acid, 54.25; Water, 8.80; Impurities, 0.78. The use of plaster in this State is rapidly on the increase, as its value becomes better understood. About 14,000 tons from the mine referred to were sold last year, and the sales are much larger, thus far, the present season. We have seen the idea advanced that the use of plaster is likely to exhaust soils. There is very little ground for this fear, though the use of small quantities annually, without other manure, and without proper tillage, would tend finally to exhaustion. In plaster we add only two articles of plant food, namely, lime and sulphuric acid. The effect of plaster upon the soil is said to be stimulating, that is, it enables larger crops to be secured, than could be removed otherwise, without the use of much manure. With these large crops much plant food is taken from the soil, and in time this will tell against the land, if it is not in some way made good by manure. It is found that grazing lands are for many years increased in productiveness by its use. The plaster brings in clover, and stimulates the growth of all the grasses. Exhausted lands have been brought up to a high state of productiveness by the use of plaster and grazing alone. The roots of the plants strike down into the soil with greater vigor, and a good portion of the inorganic matter of the soil, which would constitute their ashes, if burned, is returned to the land in the droppings of the stock. Over a very large portion of our country, remote from the sea, plaster is no doubt the cheapest fertilizer that can be applied to pastures. It is easily transported, and a small application of two bushels to the acre broadcast on the surface has usually all the immediate effect of a much larger quantity.

The Side-hill or Swivel Plow.

This implement, invented to avoid the difficulty of turning furrows up hill, is likely to be as great a boon to the plain as to the hill-side. It affords great facilities to the farmers who have uneven soil to cultivate. The plow turns on a swivel at the bottom, and the mold-board may be changed in a moment from one side of the team to the other, and held tight to its place by a hook. Any plowman can do this while the team is turning round at the end of the furrow. The plowing is begun at the bottom of the hill, and the furrow is turned alternately to the left and to the right, as the team moves back and forth. All the furrows are turned down hill, and the surface is left smooth as upon the plain.

In plowing level land in the ordinary way, we have the disadvantage of making dead furrows in the middle of each land plowed, and at the diagonal lines where the team is turned. These dead furrows yield scanty crops, and are unpleasant obstructions to the mower and reaper, besides marring the beauty of the meadows. They may be mainly avoided by the use of a swivel plow. With this, you begin at one side of the field, and plow the whole length, turning all the furrows in one direction. At the next plowing you begin where you left off, reversing the furrows, and leaving the field as level as before it was plowed. All dead furrows are avoided, and time is saved in the turning of the team at the ends of the lands. These plows are exhibited in much larger numbers at the fairs, and are coming rapidly into favor. They are made of any desirable pattern, embrace most of the good points of other plows, and have the advantage of turning the furrow to the right or to the left, according to the wish of the plowman.

The Manufacture of Fish Oil and Guano.

The use of fish as a fertilizer in this country is of early origin. The Aborigines are said to have understood their value and to have applied them to the old fields where they raised their limited crops of Indian corn. The colonists along the shore began to use them as soon as their exhausted farms showed the need of fertilizers. Large seines were owned by companies of shore farmers, and every interval in the cultivation and gathering of their crops was improved in fishing. The fish were applied to the land broadcast, and either immediately plowed in, or left to decompose upon the surface and to be turned under in the fall. This was a very wasteful process, but it produced such wonderful effects upon the crops that every farmer within reach of the shore was eager to secure fish. It was not, however, until a very recent period that the attention of the fishermen was turned to the value of the oil. Perhaps the waning of the whale fishery and the increasing price of the oil first suggested the idea of extracting the oil from the fish commonly used as fertilizers.

GROUP OF MENHADEN.

The *Alausa menhaden*, of Mitchell, known under the various names of Bony-fish, White-fish, Moss Bunker, and Menhaden, swarms along our coasts from the Carolinas to Maine, in immense shoals, numbering millions. The average weight is about a pound, being lighter in the spring and heavier in the fall, when they are most valuable for the manufacturer's purpose. Other fish are frequently caught in small numbers in the seines, such as blue-fish, mackerel, bass, sturgeon, shark, and stingrays. Those which are not valuable for food are thrown into the common mass and pass through the factory. As fish guano is rapidly coming into use and is considered one of the best of our fertilizers, it will be interesting to our readers to learn something of the process of manufacture, and of the statistics of the business. Let us look in upon one of these establishments. Here, on the Long Island Sound, are plain substantial buildings, sheds, boilers, tanks, railways, and the boats and seines necessary for carrying on the business. The fishing is a business by itself. The company furnish the boats and seines, and take one-half of the catch of fish as a compensation. The rest they purchase at the market price, which is from $1.50 to $3.00 a thousand, according to the season. As the yield of oil is four or five times greater in the fall than in the spring, the fall catch is much the more valuable to the manufacturer. As the factories are usually established near each other, the fishermen have the advantage of competition and fair prices. This company employs four gangs of men with five boats to each. The seines used are from six to seven hundred feet long, and from eighty to ninety feet deep. With such a breadth of net-work, it is easy to surround a large shoal of fish and capture them in the midst of the Sound. The seines are contracted at the bottom after the fish are surrounded, and all escape is prevented. When the fish are drawn into a sufficiently small compass, they are thrown into the boats with scoop nets, and the whole catch is carried to the factory. Here the fish are transferred to a carriage upon a rail track upon which they are drawn directly to the tanks, into which they are dropped for the purpose of steaming. The tanks hold about 20,000 fish each. The fish are covered with water, and the steam is let on by a pipe at the bottom of the tank. After cooking ¾ of an hour, the water is drawn off and the fish are put into cylindrical curbs, made of ¼-inch boiler iron, lined with stout wooden slats, and placed within a hydraulic press of 1200 tons capacity. A curb holding 3000 fish is deprived of its oil in about five minutes. The average yield of oil is from 4 to 8 gallons a thousand. The mingled oil and water from the fish is conveyed by gutters from the press into a large wooden tank, where, after settling, the oil is skimmed off and conveyed by a pipe into the bleaching tanks, holding about 200 gallons each. Here it remains about 24 hours exposed to sun and rain, which makes it of a lighter color. It is then drawn off into the casks in which it is sent to market. At the bottom of the bleaching tanks a substance remains called "gurry," which is used for making a coarse kind of soap, chiefly employed in factories for cleansing wool.

The refuse thrown out from the curb is pressed a second time, and is then carried to a shed where it lies in a large heap until the fall or winter, when it is barreled or bagged for market. The barrels hold about 250 lbs. of the green scrap, and are sold by this weight, though they grow lighter by the evaporation of water.

This company also prepares a fine ground article by the following process. The green scrap is taken immediately from the curb and thrown into a picker making 1600 revolutions a minute, where the flesh and bones are torn into very fine shreds. It is then spread upon a platform a hundred feet square, and exposed to the sun and air until it is dry. By this process about forty per cent. of the weight is evaporated, and the mass is nearly pure flesh and bone. It is then put into a mill and ground very fine. This makes a concentrated fertilizer of great value, admirable for drilling with the seed.

There are about one hundred of these fish oil manufactories along the coast from Newbern, N. C., to Mt. Pleasant Bay, Me., producing not far from 80,000 barrels of oil, worth about a half million of dollars, and about 20,000 tons of guano, worth nearly as much more. It is a thriving and increasing branch of our industry, and as it is immediately helpful to good husbandry, we wish it the best success.

Flying Quadrupeds—Bats.

These little animals, which are more innocent and friendly in their relations to mankind than any other of the untamed species with which we are acquainted, are unfortunately very commonly regarded with a sort of superstitious dread, or, at least, strong antipathy. No one can accuse them of any evil deed. They require, although small, a large amount of food, and, living entirely upon insects, which they take upon the wing, are the means of destroying vast numbers of the most annoying kinds. They fly in the night, or dusky twilight, and so are especially the foes of mosquitoes, which they often follow even within our dwellings. Bats belong to the class *Mammalia*, because their young are born alive, and are suckled. Their anatomical structure is very peculiar and interesting, and they are possessed of some most wonderful faculties, especially an acuteness of the senses of smell, feeling, and hearing, which renders the deprivation of sight, as it would seem, of comparatively little moment. They all have small, clear, beadlike, eyes, with which they can see tolerably well even in broad daylight. From observations made originally, we believe, by Spallanzani, it appears that bats whose eyes have been put out will catch insects, fly about, avoiding obstacles, and even fly through narrow spaces without touching. This remarkable faculty is attributed by some to the extraordinary delicacy of the nerves in the membranes which are used as wings, by others to their very acute sense of smell and of hearing. The species which we figure is one of the most common in all parts of this country, and is appropriately called the Little Brown Bat, (*Vespertilio subulatus.*) Our engraving was taken from one which was arrested, a few nights since, in its useful career of fly catching, for the benefit of the readers of the *Agriculturist*. Observe its little body covered with long, soft, brownish gray fur; notice the great development of the muscles of the chest, used in flying; see, also, that the almost useless hind legs, if we may so call them, are the merest sticks, with apparently neither muscles nor joints, except the little five-toed feet. The forward or upper extremities are the most remarkable. Tracing the bony frame from the shoulder, we follow a perfect arm-bone, (or *humerus*,) to the elbow, from the elbow to the next joint—"wrist," if you please—there are the two bones of the fore-arm. There, just at this wrist joint, is the little thumb, projecting upward, and terminating with a strong hook; from this point, the long, slender, regularly jointed fingers spread out, tapering to the minutest little threadlike bones at the tips. The little bones corresponding to the first and second fingers of our hand are close together, forming the stiff upper rim of the wings, and from these the delicate, double, nearly transparent, skin which forms the wings extends to the next finger, and the next, and then it spreads out from the last finger on each side to the body, the legs, and the tail. This membrane is filled with a multitude of blood vessels, which, as our artist has indicated, causes the whole to appear to be covered with the finest net-work, like a spider's web. The ears are, proportionally, very large, and directly in front of each there is a long, stiff, point, called the anterior lobe of the ear, which seems to have been placed there to prevent insects lodging in the ears, should any escape the mouth in the rapid flight of the bat. The eyes are very small and bright, and deep set; the nose rather broad at the tip, and the nostrils peculiarly dilated. The mouth opens wide, and displays an efficient though minute set of very sharp, pointed, teeth. When taken, the bats all bite fiercely. The specimen from which the drawing was made measured nine inches from tip to tip of the wings, and weighed only 80 grains—that is, it would take more than eighty similar ones to weigh a pound. When at rest, bats fold their "wings" very closely, and suspend themselves by their little hooked thumbs. In winter, they collect in great clusters in hollow trees, deserted buildings, or caves, and thus hibernate. They have two young at a birth, which cling to the mother in her flights.

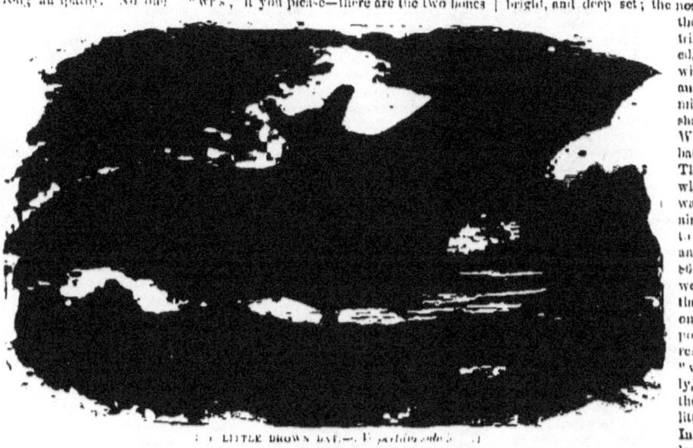

LITTLE BROWN BAT.—(*Vespertilio subulatus.*)

The American Otter.—(*Lutra Canadensis.*)

The Otter produces the most valuable fur of any animal now found in the older States of the Union, and though its range is wide, extending, or having formerly extended, through all parts of the Union east of the great plains, it is now becoming exceedingly scarce. Among our native furs the skins of the beaver, if fine, are alone superior to those of the otter. It is an animal of considerable size, weighing often from 20 to 25 pounds, and measuring three to four feet in length, exclusive of the tail, which is 15 to 18 inches long. The otter lives altogether upon fish, which it takes in the water with great adroitness. It possesses great intelligence, and is capable of very thorough domestication, and it is probable that, like its European congener, (*Lutra vulgaris*,) it will breed in confinement, and that the young may be trained to hunt for fish, and to be of essential service in fishing. The otter of India is used, as is learned from the journals of

THE AMERICAN OTTER.—(*Lutra Canadensis.*)

travelers, by fishermen much as dogs are in hunting. A peculiarity of the American otter is its habit of making smooth tracks upon steep banks, down which it slides into the water. In the summer time, clay banks are preferred to any other, and in the winter they do not forego this pleasant recreation, for they have their sliding pastime upon the snow-banks as systematically as the boys have their coasting parties. Traps are usually placed at the foot of these slides, in the water, or near the entrance of frequented burrows which always open under water, at ordinary stages. The fur of the otter is of two kinds, one fine and dense, the other coarse and glossy. The color is brown, varying somewhat, being nearly black in summer, and in autumn and winter quite dark and very glossy, the head light colored, and the chin and throat often whitish. Otters bring forth two young early in spring.

More Barn-room Wanted.

Shifts are allowable in the early history of the farm that ought not to be tolerated later. The farmer in the clearing, or upon the prairie, has everything pressing upon him at once, and must meet his most imperious wants first. He must have shelter for his family, and food for himself and stock. The log-house and barn upon the most limited scale will answer for a while, but both are temporary expedients to be superseded at the earliest moment by something better. The new house and barn are not merely matters of taste, but of economy. An ample barn for the storage of crops and the shelter of stock should be regarded as a necessary investment of capital in all farming in the Northern and Eastern States. This is better understood in Pennsylvania than in any other part of the country, and the barn that bears the name of the State is, in many respects, a model. It contemplates the shelter of all stock, and the storage of all crops raised upon the farm; and if it also provided shelter for manure, it would, with abundant light and free ventilation, meet every want.

Such a barn upon every farm where mixed husbandry is pursued would soon pay for itself. It prevents the deterioration of crops and of manure. The loss from this source is immense in all parts of the country. Even in thrifty New England, where a barn of some kind is found upon every farm, a large part of the hay and corn fodder is stored in stacks, and the open yard is still often met with as the only receptacle for manure. There is waste of labor in the topping and securing of stacks, and waste of fodder in all that part of the stack that is exposed to the ground and to the weather, and, judging from the fact that barn hay always brings the higher price, there is deterioration through the whole mass. In the West there is much more loss from this source, for there is much less barn-room, and, in addition to this, great damage from the exposure of the grain crops to the weather. The wheat crop for this year has been gathered in excellent condition, for very little rain fell in all the grain growing districts during harvest. But this is an exceptional season. If those districts had been visited with the rains and cloudy weather that have prevailed along the seaboard, we think the grain crop would have been damaged to the amount of one-third of its value. This sometimes happens, and there is much more damaged than sound wheat in the market. Ordinarily the wheat is left in small shocks, with two bundles laid crosswise for a cap, until the thrashing machine comes, which may be within two weeks or two months after cutting. If the weather is bad, the grain moulds and sprouts, and the market is crowded with damaged wheat. The straw also is injured for feeding purposes. The loss to the country from this source amounts annually to many millions of dollars. If it could be saved, it would pay all the taxes laid upon farmers.

Then, a good barn saves immensely in the expense of keeping stock and in the convenience of feeding them. It is a common estimate that shelter saves one-third in fodder. This estimate is certainly not too high for the northern half of the Northern States. The consumption of food to keep up animal heat in freezing weather is very great, and this does not benefit the farmer. He wants an increase of flesh and fat, articles that a stack-yard regimen rarely gives. With a plenty of grain, an animal will thrive out of doors, but he does not thrive as he would under shelter. It is too expensive, even in the grain districts, to substitute corn for boards. Without barns, also, the farmer is very much at the mercy of the grain speculator. With them, he can store his hay and grain, and sell when the market suits. The speculator knows the situation, and visits the regions where the barns are yet to be built. He knows the farmer must sell, for he has no place to store his grain. He generally prefers the tender mercies of the speculator, whom he knows, to the commission merchant in the city, whom he does not know. He wants the cash in hand and takes what he can get. As wheat often advances fifty per cent. in a season, the farmer ought to be able to take advantage of the rise. If grain could be kept more in first hands, it would benefit consumers, for it would tend to make uniform prices. Nobody but speculators would suffer. In the plans of barns that we frequently present in these pages, some of them giving the results of years of study by practical farmers to meet their own wants, our readers will find many profitable suggestions.

What Shall the South Do for Manure?

The great want of Southern Agriculture is manure. It is the want of systematic agriculture everywhere. Some land gains fertility, if left fallow, or from crops which may be turned under for manure, or if left in grass, which forms a sward of matted roots that readily decay when plowed under. For land too poor for grass to make a good sward, and too light to bear tillage without a crop, (clay land will be improved by simple tillage,) manure is an absolute necessity. Unskilled laborers must be employed usually at coarse, common, field work; hence there is a tendency to cultivate a few, chiefly market, crops. This makes the demand for manure the more imperative, and the call from the Southern States is at present absolutely painful; this is the universal need. The eagerness with which manures have been bought the past season, in the hope of making or saving a crop of corn, of cotton, or tobacco, has opened wide the door for extensive frauds, ruinous to many of the victimized planters. We are gratified to learn that some of these purchasers of fraudulent manures are combining to institute suits against those who make and deal in them.

The question presents itself, then, with peculiar force, "What shall the South do?" The problem has a simple solution, but the cure is applicable at first over but a small area upon each farm. It is, to make more manure. This may be done. The labor of the place may be profitably employed during a considerable part of the year, in taking care of, working over, and increasing, the amount of manures and composts.

Keep hogs confined. The northern farmer saves himself the expense of guano by keeping his hogs always penned and supplied with all kinds of weeds and litter, thus making tons of excellent manure every year. Five tons of manure, worth not less than $5 per ton, if Peruvian guano is worth $80, may be made from one hog in a year, provided a sufficiency of muck, straw, or litter of any kind, be supplied. A fair proportion of the manure thus made should be saved for fertilizing ground for a large crop of pumpkins or squashes, corn sowed in drills, yams, or whatever else will grow rapidly and produce surely and freely, good feed for the hogs, whose numbers should be each year increased, until large quantities of manure are made.

Control all the Poultry, at least so far as to make them roost always in convenient places where their manure may be saved and composted with dry muck, gypsum, coal ashes, or other good absorbent. Thus a fertilizer may be obtained in moderate quantities of exceeding richness, admirable for exactly those purposes for which Peruvian guano is employed.

Make dead animals into compost. Many an old horse is actually worth more in the compost heap than in the stable or pasture. One dollar a hundred pounds is a low estimate of the value of any living animal for manure alone. Every farmer who is buying fertilizers can well afford to pay that, and usually the carcasses may be had for their removal. The way to handle them is to cut them up, using axes and butchers' saws, into pieces of, say 20 pounds weight, and then to compost them in layers with plenty of swamp muck, crumbly peat, grass sods, or loamy soil. Do this in an out of the way place, and while it is attractive to dogs, be on the lookout with a rifle and add to the heap every dog that comes near. Otherwise drive stakes around the place, making a compost yard, inaccessible to those "vermin." It is some little trouble, but will stand the financial test, and surely *pay.* Within six months or a year, the heap may be overhauled, mixed, the hard bones thrown out, and these put into the next heap, or into any manure, or compost heap. The hardest will become soft in a year or two, so that they may be mashed with a shovel.

Make poudrette. Hints are given in previous numbers of the *Agriculturist* on the subject of earth closets. Offer to the foremen of gangs of hands, to those who keep the houses where the hands are boarded and lodged, and to such as have their own cabins, a moderate price per barrel or per load for all the poudrette of good quality which they will make, using a definite quantity of dry earth or muck. So far as our observation extends, every particle of human soil is lost to the agriculture of the South, and we hesitate not to say that were this saved it would have ten times the value of all the high priced fertilizers which the people of the Southern States import from year to year.

How to Yoke Oxen.

The hints we drop now and then in regard to the sounder philosophy in working oxen by the head instead of by neck yokes, bring occasional responses of corroborative views, one of which we give below, from Mr. Josiah M. Hubbard, of Middletown, Conn. Until we can fairly try the experiment ourselves, which may not be for years, we wait patiently for a fair test of the two systems on the same cattle. Mr. H. writes:

"Your remarks concerning the defects in the

usual apparatus for working oxen call to mind the case of a German neighbor of mine in Kansas, whose one pair of oxen were trained to draw by the forehead. His apparatus was quite simple, consisting of a padded stick placed across the forehead of each ox just below the horns, and kept in place by straps around them, the ends of the stick extending a few inches each way beyond the head. The draft was by means of a rope on each side of the animal, passed through a hole in the end of the stick and knotted in front, hitched to the whiffle-trees and evener, and kept in place by a strap over the back and another under the belly of the animal. I do not recall his method of fastening his animals together, or of supporting the tongue when worked on a wagon; but I do recollect that his animals worked with much more ease and freedom than oxen in the ordinary yoke; and also that their owner was very confident that they could pull (or as he phrased it) 'push' a much heavier load than if yoked by the neck."

The Wheat and Chess Question.

The position taken by intelligent agriculturists that such a thing as wheat turning to chess is impossible in the nature of things, hence not a question to be argued (like the assertion that 2 and 2 make 5,) is entirely unacceptable to many sensible farmers. They think they have the evidence of their senses that it does happen. We are firmly and kindly remonstrated with for taking the position that we will not argue the point. We know 2+2=4; and so decline to discuss the matter. However, one of our German readers, Mr. Geo. Kunz, has worked out this problem much more correctly than many American farmers, who claim to have tried experiments which convinced them that the change takes place. We invite attention to his reasoning.

"As the wheat last winter was more or less winter-killed, we could only count upon half a crop; but some farmers have from one-quarter to one-half chess in their wheat, which causes a great many to think that wheat is changed into chess. After many years of experience, I can say that it is an error, and, if held, of injury to the farmer. He who asserts that wheat changes to chess, is not anxious to have his seed free from chess. The superficial observers who assert that wheat turns to chess, (three-quarters of the farmers belong to that class,) say they do not sow chess; they also say that chess changes into Timothy, etc. If such is the case, why do we pay $2 and $3 per bushel for Timothy seed? Why not sow chess, for which we only pay 5 cts. per bushel for thrashing? If wheat could produce chess, it would long since have run out, and we would have as many varieties of chess as of wheat. Why we have more chess when wheat is winter-killed may easily be shown. Take one bushel of wheat and mix with it one quart of chess; the latter can hardly be detected. Supposing the wheat is sown and produces 20 bushels, and chess also 20 quarts, it cannot be detected any more than before; but then, suppose the wheat is winter-killed badly and yields only 5 bushels instead of 20, the chess is not affected, gives every year a full crop, and increases more than wheat; therefore, more chess could be seen after gathering the crop in the 5 bushels of wheat, than there could be seen in the 1 bushel before sowing. If every farmer would convince himself that chess does not come from wheat, all disputes would cease upon that point. Sow clean seed on clean soil, and you will have no more chess; and if everybody was to do so, in five or six years very little would be found in the wheat fields of the country."

Canada Thistles and Railroads.

In our recent travels to attend the State Fairs, we noticed almost everywhere in the West, the steady advance of this scourge. The West had once clean fields; but now, in many sections, the pastures and meadows are as foul as in the oldest part of the country. Most of the older railroads are already well stocked with the Canada thistle at their northern extremities, and every year carries them farther south. The seed is furnished with a tuft of down, which makes it float in the air like a feather. Growing in close proximity to the railroad track, these winged seeds are drawn into the current of air made by the passing trains, and every year distributed more widely over the country. The railroad embankment becomes thickly stocked with them, and from this line they are distributed over all the adjoining fields.

This is a great evil, and demands the immediate attention of all our State legislatures. If it is left unchecked, the thistles will spread over a wider territory every year, until they take possession of the whole country. The cost of every crop cultivated will be increased, pastures will be diminished in value, and the quality of hay will be depreciated. It is true, there is some nutriment in thistles, and asses are said to be fond of them, but these are not the wisest of beasts; and if they were, they are not likely to become popular stock in America. It is an unmitigated curse in cultivated fields, increasing the cost of farm produce to all consumers. More Canada thistles means dearer corn, wheat, rye, oats, and potatoes. They increase the cost of living to every man in the country. Railroads are a great blessing, but they have no right to spread this pestilence over our fields.

Legislation is needed to compel the railroads to keep their tracks clean. The State Commissions, which have the oversight of these institutions, should be instructed to see that this pest is kept under. If there were frequent mowings to prevent the seeding of the plant, it would soon disappear from the tracks. And while the legislatures are considering the case of the railroads, they may as well take in hand those slovenly farmers who allow these weeds to overspread their fields without hinderance. What right has a man to make his farm a seed bed of Canada thistles? What right has he to make himself a nuisance among his neighbors? The harboring of this pest should subject the farmer to fines and penalties. We must have legislation, or Canada thistles will possess the land.

A National Dog Law.

Congress is soon to assemble, and the great interest of the nation will be likely to receive just so much attention from our legislators as the people compel them to bestow. There is no money for Congressmen in this measure unless they happen to be sheep owners, but a good deal of money for their constituents. On the contrary, our honorable Senators and Representatives, who affect dogs and sporting circles, might find their taxes slightly increased. We have shown, in our past issues, the great necessity of this law to the sheep interests of the nation. England taxes her dog owners three dollars for each dog, and raises a revenue of $3,000,000 from this source. In England, mutton is a great institution by reason of this very efficient protection. If we want like protection, we must legislate against dogs. Wool-growers' associations should take the lead in this matter, and make their influence felt at Washington. Agricultural societies and farmers' clubs should start their petitions, and send them up by the cart-load to the Capitol. Sheep owners who have political influence should write to their representatives, urging the measure. By timely effort we may secure what we need. Wool and mutton can have no secure basis until the relations of sheep and dogs are permanently reconstructed.

Fattening Poultry for the Table or for Market.

The difference between the flesh of a well-fattened fowl and one that has not been cooped is so great that we venture to say that no one who really enjoys this excellent food, and raises his own poultry, will allow those destined for the table to run at large for some two or three weeks, at least, before killing them. Young birds grow finely with a free range and plenty to eat, but we have never found rapidly growing fowls or turkeys to take on *fat* readily when confined. They grow rapidly, perhaps, for a while, but then are very apt to pine, and often even lose flesh. As soon as the rapid growth peculiar to the first four or five months of chickenhood has been made, and the young birds begin to have a mature look, they may be put up in airy coops for fattening. The coops should be such as can be kept clean easily, and in which they will have some chance to move about; while all should be able to get at their food, when fed, without crowding. The two long sides, at least, should be of slats, and the bottom made of split poles, half round, about three inches wide, put on round side up, and with two-inch spaces between them. On such a floor, the birds will keep cleaner than on any other. Turkeys ought to be cooped upon the ground, and the coops shifted every few days. Geese should be in close boxes, with plenty of litter, which should be frequently changed, and the geese allowed a run of half an hour, and a bath every morning. Ducks should be penned, but let out daily to run to the pond, and take their regular "ducking," and eat a little grass.

As to food, it is a mistake to suppose because poultry usually prefer whole grain, especially corn, that it is best for them. Boiled potatoes mashed, with the addition of about one-sixth part Indian meal, make excellent feed for all kinds of poultry. If the proportion of Indian meal is increased, a little suet added, together with stale bread or crusts, soaked soft, it will be the more relished, and of much higher fattening quality. Chickens and turkeys should have some grass frequently, and occasionally some meat scraps chopped fine. Almost any raw vegetables may be substituted for grass, like cabbage leaves, beets, the inside parts of pumpkins, etc., chopped quite fine. Geese ought to have grass daily. Ducks do better, also, for similar green food, but for the water fowls, meat is unnecessary. The food for all may be greatly varied, but ground and cooked grain will go much farther than the same fed whole or raw. Birds confined for fattening, should be fed all that they will eat, as often as four times a day, and fresh water should be always before them. Every two or three days it is well to make one meal actually red with Cayenne pepper, sprinkled on in powder, and mixed with the food. A few drops of Chloride of Iron in the water, occasionally, has a beneficial tonic effect.

In case there is the least suspicion of lice, we advise to take out the fowls, and dust them thoroughly with the "Persian Insect Powder," holding them each by the legs, and sprinkling it in among the feathers. We have found this cheap, innocuous, and efficient, in removing lice from nests and sitting hens, and presume it would be equally efficacious in other cases.

Thus treated, in general, all poultry will fatten very fast. The fatness of a fowl may be ascertained, generally, by feeling the rump, and judging of its general plumpness and weight. When killed for one's own table, it makes little difference how it is done, provided it be well done. The bird must be fasted 8 to 12 hours; the head may be chopped off, and the fowl hung up to bleed, or the throat may be cut from the outside, passing a narrow, sharp blade through the neck crosswise, just below the chaps. The blade being pressed backward, and moved a little, will sever the veins. This is the common New York market practice. It is poor policy to wring the necks, for, though the most agreeable way, there being no spirting and splashing of blood, nevertheless the bleeding is not so perfect, and the bird will not keep so long. When killing for market, the neatest way is to take a straight, sharp, knife, pass it into the mouth, and cut across the back of the throat on either side. This quickly severs the large veins and arteries, and if the fowl be tied by the legs, and hung on a peg, the feathers even will not be much besmeared with blood. When plucked, a fowl, so killed, shows no mark of the knife. Pick dry, while still warm, then dip in scalding water, just enough to shrink the skin tight all over the body. This gives a very plump look, and secures a better price or quicker sale, while it is of no injury to the keeping, unless the fat is melted.

Draining Facilitated and Cheapened.

The cost of underdraining lies chiefly in the necessarily great amount of *skilled* labor required to do good work. If any common hand could be economically employed to dig trenches, it would be a great saving. Many of us have been forced to try the experiment, and know if such labor is paid by the day, as it usually must be, the draining is very expensive. Unless digging the trenches can be done by contract, the work must be overseen by the proprietor himself, or by a very trustworthy foreman. When the digging is done by the rod, the finishing must be under the immediate inspection of the foreman, and to this end it should be understood that the last inch or two of the ditch should not be dug until he directs.

As soon as the bottom is graded ready for the tiles, (which operation, as it requires care and time, will not be done by common trench-diggers on a contract, without compensation by the hour), the tiles must be laid and the trench partly filled. The care requisite in the first filling of the ditch prevents the employment of scoops or scrapers worked by horse-power; but as soon as about 18 inches have been filled with clay or stiff loam, and rammed down hard, some form of scraper will come into play.

More real farm drainage is done in the autumn than at any other time of the year, and the present season is a peculiarly favorable one for this work. We of the seaboard have had much wet, and that followed by an autumn, dry in its beginning and very likely to be so in its continuance, and so long as real winter weather holds off, draining may profitably be done.

Some time since, at a time when subjects more appropriate to the season crowded our columns, we received a communication from Asa Engle, of Gloucester Co., N. J., containing useful hints and a description of his own practice. He writes:

"In return for valuable ideas from the *Agriculturist*, I suggest an idea or two that I have proved to be advantageous in underdraining.

"My manner of laying tiles is to begin by breaking a plastering lath in half, and laying it in the bottom of the ditch. Then take whole laths and place them side by side upon the floor, thus, so as to break joints, laying the tiles immediately upon them. In this section drain tiles are all made with flat bottoms. The laths cause the tiles to settle on a line, and by the time the laths decay, the tiles are so firmly bedded that they are not likely to get out of place. After the tiles are laid, I shovel in a few inches of earth, treading it down firmly as I proceed. I then take a scraper or reversed "snow plow," made by bolting two planks to the inside of an A harrow, (see figure,) long enough to extend outside the ditch on both sides. I hitch a *quiet* horse to each end, and start the "plow" backward astride of the ditch, having a rope attached to the point by which to guide the machine and keep the open space between the ends of the planks immediately over the ditch. After passing a few times back and forth, it will expedite matters to take a horse and plow and loosen the earth on the bank, as by this operation it will have become somewhat packed."

DITCH-FILLING SCRAPER.

Convenient Farm Hooks.

The difference between what "will do well enough," and what is really convenient and exactly adapted to its use, may be measured by hours and days even of useless labors, and miles of travel on many farms every year. We were struck with the simplicity of a hook for use as a clevis attached to a harrow, cultivator, stone boat, or any such thing. It is a strong flat hook, (Fig. 1,) having a flat eye with a small hole for a bolt with a large flat head, to attach it to the implement. The point of the hook is drawn out, bent back, and welded fast, enclosing a harness ring of such a size that, when it lies in the bend of the hook, it cannot be brought out. This is well seen in the little engraving. When the hook is put on, it is, of course, turned upward, and it will be seen that the ring of the whiffletree, or ox-chain, will easily slip in, but of itself cannot slip out again. This hook may be attached to many articles, and used for sundry purposes, but is especially convenient for the use suggested, for it takes a good deal of time to undo a clevis every time the team is attached to, or taken from, the harrows and other tools. Then, too, the clevis is in two independent parts, and often three, (clevis, bolt, and ring,) either of which is liable in careless hands to be lost or out of the way.

Fig. 1.—CLEVIS HOOK.

The almost universal custom of using hooks upon the end of farm whiffletrees indicates some superiority to other contrivances for attaching the traces. Still, going down rough roads, in the woods, and on other uneven ground, there is a liability of the traces getting unhooked, accompanied, at times, by no little danger. Figure 2 represents an unpatented hook which we have attached to a new whiffletree that is now on probation; the hook, however, proves itself. As clearly shown in the cut, the eye is large and open, the bend short, the point coming back nearly opposite the middle of the eye, where it is bent at right angles towards it, and left just so close to the eye that a ring or trace-eye of the usual size will slip, when held at right angles, into the hook. It appears to be impossible for a trace to become detached of itself from this simple contrivance.

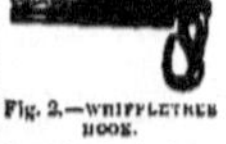

Fig. 2.—WHIFFLETREE HOOK.

Fences Across Streams.

Among the many minor perplexities which in the aggregate are serious hinderances to the farmer's peace of mind, are fences across streams. When a brook is so large that a single length of fence will not span it, and especially if at times this 12-foot "creek" becomes a torrent, bearing large trees and logs upon its turbid tide, then the problem how to put a fence across becomes a formidable one. Cattle must not pass it at low water, and it must not be swept away at any time. Mr. Matthew M. Campbell appeals to the editors and readers of the *Agriculturist* in his perplexities. A large creek flows through his farm, which will be greatly increased in value to him if he can fence it across. He describes the "Kentucky crossing," which is thus made: "One, two, or three, large logs are laid on the bottom of the creek, and the ends made fast in the banks on either side, and weighted down with stones. Rails, with sharpened ends, are then driven into the bottom of the creek above the logs, and project above them from 12 to 18 inches. This, if three feet high, or less, is a good fence so long as it can be kept from floating." Another plan suggested is that of stretching a three-quarter inch iron rod across the creek between two trees, and suspending thereon a succession of light gates reaching down to the water at ordinary stages. Yet another plan is to stretch the rod across close to the surface of the water, and hang battoned planks upon the rod, just so that they will touch the water at its lowest stage, but be floated when the water is high enough to bring down much flood-wood. We quite agree with our correspondent that "neither hog, horse, nor cattle, would be likely either to jump over, or dive under, such a fence,"—but think it would be subject to a strain, when the water is high, to which it would assuredly succumb after a short time.

Some time since, an acquaintance, in following a suggestion of ours, stretched a rod across a small stream which annoyed him by carrying off the poles which were placed across it as a fence. To this rod, which was of about three-quarter inch iron, as we judge, he suspended three small trees, the smaller branches and twigs of which had been cut off and the boughs sharpened with a drawing knife. The trees were hung so that a natural curve in them caused the limbs to point down stream, and any that pointed directly against the current were cut off. The result has been that at high water the fence floats up more or less, and the swiftness of the current keeps it entirely free from everything except an occasional bush which gets entangled, but does no damage. All large things pass along unhindered. We propose, therefore,

A FENCE ACROSS A STREAM.

to Mr. Campbell to try hanging small trees or branches of larger ones in the way we suggest. The engraving shows a combination of the hanging gates and trees, the latter being where the current is swiftest, the stream deepest, and where, almost certainly, the heavy drift will come down. The rod is attached on one side to a tree, on the other it passes through one, and is continued at an angle to a stump, where it is fixed, making a very strong anchorage. Provision is also indicated for tightening up the rod in case it stretches or slackens, which is important.

Cultivation of Corn.

A LESSON FROM NORTH CAROLINA.

We passed over a fine farm in Westchester Co., N. Y., a few days since, in company with its proprietor, a liberal minded farmer, who showed with great satisfaction a fine field of corn in which no hoe had been used this season. It was remarkably free from weeds, and that, rather than the condition of the corn, (except on wet land), is the test of good culture this season. The few weeds were good vigorous specimens, however, showing that they were such as the plow had not covered entirely at the last plowing. Once passing through to pull these weeds would be a small job, and then the field would be clean. Our friend says he

MANNER OF PLOWING CORN.

learned during the war the practice which we describe from a North Carolinian refugee.

The corn was planted in hills a little less than four feet apart—the proper distance depends upon the variety—and as soon as it was well up, it was cultivated with Share's horse-hoe, in one direction. Any good horse-hoe or cultivator will do. This cleans the land well, but does not destroy the weeds in the hills. After about a fortnight, or as soon as the weeds began to grow pretty well among the corn hills, and the brace roots began to show rows of little points around the lower joints, boys were sent through to *pull* out all the weeds in or near the hills. This is work which would have to be done by hand, were the corn hoed. The simple pulling, without previous plowing, and without hoeing at the same time, is not a labor requiring much skill, faithfulness being especially necessary. As soon as this was done, the field was plowed in the direction opposite to the way the horse-hoe was used, turning the furrows towards the corn, going four times to each row, and thus turning all the ground between the rows, and leaving the land ridged. The plow was run pretty deep, and nearly all the weeds were thoroughly buried under a heavy mass of mellow soil. This is exactly the place where weeds are wanted, and it is much better than to leave them on the surface, where some seeds may mature, and where, if wet weather follows, many will surely root again. The only chance for weeds to live is if they are not thoroughly covered up, and in the field we passed through, such were the only ones seen.

The accompanying diagram shows a section of two rows of corn, plowed as described; the corn plants with the brace roots (*b*) thrown out into the fresh turned soil, the main roots in the undisturbed portion of the soil. The line, *a*, *a*, indicates the general level of the ground.

The past wet summer has been one to put to the severest test any method of killing weeds among corn. The contrast between the field we refer to, and another treated in the usual way, is most notable. Last year an experiment, to ascertain the actual difference between the two systems, was faithfully, but rather roughly, made. Half a large piece, which was all manured and planted uniformly, was hand-hoed (three times we presume); the other half was treated as above described. The result was that five bushels per acre more corn was harvested from the ridge-plowed part of the field than from that which was hand-hoed; the larger yield with least labor.

The good effects in dry weather are explained, first, by the thorough removal of the weeds close to the corn, then by the conversion of those that are left standing into a green manuring, as they rapidly decay, and finally, by the broad mass of mellow soil which the ridge presents for the brace roots, and for the others also, to riot and revel in. The corn so quickly covers the ground after this that seedling weeds starting upon the fresh turned furrows have little chance of life, and none of vigorous growth.

A Double Entrance Gate.

An impracticable gate, one difficult to open and equally troublesome to shut, is a very common thing, but its frequent occurrence makes it none the less annoying. There are several "self-opening" gates upon the construction of which a great deal of ingenuity and machinery have been expended. Some of these work well enough *for* a while, but we never saw one that, from some derangement of its parts, was not, after a few months' use, opened by hand in the old fashioned way.

A correspondent, Doct. Henry Breiner, Allegheny Co., Pa., finding no gate to suit him, had one constructed after a plan of his own, of which he sends us a sketch. Having but one entrance from the road to his grounds, it was necessary to make a gate that should answer for carriage, horse, or foot passengers, and one of which either half could be opened independently.

The gate presents no improvement over the ordinary double gate, except in its fastening, which is simple, easily made, and apparently efficient. It will be readily understood from the engraving, with but a brief description. A bolt (*a*) of oak, ¾ inch thick and two inches wide, runs the whole length of the style of the gate, and slides freely through staples. To the upper end of the bolt is attached a lever (*b*) by which it is raised. This lever works through a mortise in the style of the gate, and a tenon on the end of it enters a mortise in the bolt. To support the lever a piece of wood is mortised into the upper rail of the gate opposite the first pale, having a mortise to receive the lever, which is held in its place by a wooden pin. This is the only fastening the lever needs. The lower ends of the bolts are received in a mortise in a piece of 2-inch plank (*c*), 20 to 24 inches long, which is spiked to two locust posts set in the ground at the proper point. The plank is bevelled in two directions and kept well oiled, so that when the gate shuts, the bolts will readily slide over it and drop into the mortise, which should be half an inch wider than the bolts. The hole in the plank should be over the space between the posts to which it is spiked, to facilitate clearing it from dirt. The gate is hung to swing either

DOUBLE ENTRANCE GATE.

way, and is easily unfastened by depressing the handle of the lever; it will fasten itself when it swings to again. Doct. B. says if there is any better fastening for a double gate he would like to have it communicated to our readers.

How to Get the Boys to Stay on the Farm.

The exodus is not yet arrested. We have been doing our best for ten years to make the labors of the farm attractive and profitable, so that the old homestead might at least retain one of the sons, and remain in the family. The labor has not been lost, for no business in the country has made more substantial and visible progress during this period. We have our State and County Fairs well organized and doing a good work in all parts of the Northern States; we have model farms and farmers, better drainage, better implements, better tillage, and larger crops, in part as a consequence of the good seed that has been sown in these pages. Yet the outflow from the farm goes on, and about as many boys are strapping their trunks and saying good-bye to the farm, this fall, as ever. Some few of the number have their faces turned in the right direction, but many, we know, are making a great mistake, and have before them much less of thrift and happiness than they could find in the calling of their fathers. This restless spirit is owing somewhat, doubtless, to the general diffusion of education among the masses, to that love of adventure which is a characteristic of the Yankee race, and to the apparent profitableness of other callings.

But with all due allowance for these things, there are causes still at work upon the farm that early alienate the affections of the boys, and drive them to other pursuits. The boys catch new ideas much more rapidly than their fathers, and, with the impulsiveness of youth, want to test them. They go to the fairs, and see the fine stock, the new tools, the premium fruits and vegetables. They read the papers, if they have them at home, and if they have not, they borrow them. Agricultural papers are greatly multiplied, and no religious or political paper quite does its duty without furnishing a column or two, weekly, of agricultural matter for its readers. People who read at all cannot very well keep themselves in the dark in regard to the changes that are coming over our husbandry. If the father keeps up with the times, has agricultural papers and books, reads, thinks, and practices, he retains the confidence of his boys, and can readily guide them. But if he is a man of routine, and keeps in the ruts, the boys soon become disgusted with farming. They do not want to break their backs over the scythe, when a mowing machine can do the work better, and at a tithe of the expense. They want tedders, horse-rakes, and horse hay-forks. They want subsoil plows, tile drains, and barn cellars. They want blood stock in the stable, and in the sty. They want to move a little faster, and to do business on a little larger scale. The boys have the facts and the argument on their side, and if you want to retain them upon the farm, you must keep up with the times, and make farming a live business. The subsoil plow has spoiled the ruts for this generation.

Another thing, the boys want an interest in the business, and the sooner you give them an investment in the farm or its stock, the more likely you will be to make farmers of them. It is true, the law gives you a right to the avails of their labors until they reach their majority. It may be true that these services are no more than a fair compensation for the expenses of their childhood. The intercourse of parents and children should not always be graduated by the legal scale. You do not want your son for a servant, but for a companion, and a support in your declining years. You want to attach him by affection and interest to the soil that he cultivates. Begin, then, early to identify his interests with your business, as if he was under no obligations to you. If he fancies stock, give him what he likes, and let the increase be his. Especially encourage him to plant orchards or vineyards of the finest varieties of fruit. Teach him to bud, graft, prune, ripen, and market, all the fruits of your climate. Furnish him with all the books and facilities that he needs to study and to practice pomology and horticulture. If properly encouraged, he will take an interest in these things very early, and before he is old enough to think of leaving your roof, his tastes will be formed, and his course in life will be determined. His heart will go down into the soil with the roots of every fruit tree that he plants, and the orchards and gardens of the old homestead, or of another close by, will be his paradise, from which nothing but necessity can drive him.

Walks and Talks on the Farm.—No. 47.

Sheep can be bought in this section for nearly half what they could be sold for at this time last year. And yet, low as wool is, it is worth nearly as much as it was a year ago. Then the depression in the wool market was thought to be merely temporary, and wool growers hoped for remunerative prices in the future. Now, however, there is a general feeling that wool will rule low for some years, and many farmers are selling their sheep at any price that is offered. Butter and cheese pay better than wool growing, and thousands will quit the business in disgust. Observing men predicted such a result during the sheep fever, and were laughed at as old fogies.

If the best time to engage in a business is when others are leaving it, the present is a good time to buy sheep. It would be strange if the United States, with its almost unlimited extent of territory, should not raise its own wool, and if we are to raise wool, we can hardly expect to see a time when sheep can be bought at lower rates. The duty on wool is now as high as we can reasonably ask for, and if there is any business in which we can compete with the cheap labor of foreign countries, it is in wool-growing. There is less labor required to raise a dollar's worth of wool than to raise a dollar's worth of any other farm product. It is not so much the cheap labor of other countries that the wool-grower has to fear, as the cheap land, and the low rates at which so concentrated an article as wool can be transported. And this competition with cheap land we cannot escape from. Those of us who have farms that cost $100 to $150 per acre must compete with the farmer on the prairie, who paid only $1.25. If we cannot compete with him in growing wool, we must grow something else, the freight on which affords us sufficient protection. Buffalo skins are high, but I do not think, when land is worth $100 an acre, we can raise buffaloes, and feed them for four or five years simply for the skins. If we wish to engage in this kind of business, we must seek cheaper land.

I do not say that we cannot keep sheep on land worth $100 an acre, simply for their wool, for the probabilities are that the profits cannot be very large. Take one of my three year old Merino wethers that I sold the other day for $2.75, and how much do you suppose it has cost to feed him? He sheared four pounds the first year, and five pounds the next, and five pounds this year—say fourteen pounds. I sold the first two clips for 60 cents. The last clip is not sold, but would not bring more than 40 cents. This sheep therefore has brought me in, say $2.40 for the first year, $3.00 for the second year, and $2.00 for the third year—$7.40 in all. The sheep sold for $2.75, so that the gross receipts for three and a half years' keep amount to $10.15. Washing, shearing, tying up the wool, and marketing the three clips, would cost 50 cents, and it will be liberal to say that I have received $9.65 for feed and attendance. Now, such a sheep would probably consume in three years and a half, a ton of hay, or its equivalent. Of course he was not fed exclusively on hay, and I only put it in this form to enable us to get some idea of the amount of food such a sheep would eat. An acre of good clover would furnish food enough for half a dozen of such sheep for a year—part mown and part grazed. To keep a sheep three years and a half, therefore, we should need as much food as seven twelfths of an acre would produce in a year. In other words, this sheep which has brought me $9.65, has eaten food equal to what could be obtained from a little over half an acre of good clover. This makes a better show for the profit of wool-growing than I expected, and when we take into consideration the fact that the manure will do nearly as much good as if the clover had been plowed under, I am not sure that there is any kind of stock which, for the care and labor bestowed, will pay much better.

The time has arrived in our agriculture, however, when we must bestow more care and labor in feeding stock, and enriching our land. I think farmers are becoming convinced of this. High prices are a great incentive to improvement. We can all see that if our farms were in condition, we could make money. I was on a farm the other day, where the wheat crop went 37½ bushels per acre, and being very clean and nice, was all sold to the neighbors for seed, at $2.75 per bushel. Most of us, on land naturally just as good, only raise 15 bushels per acre, and that not of the best quality. In a ride of some twenty-five miles, through two of the best towns in this county, in search of some good seed wheat, this was the only wheat I found that was clean! It may be that I did not happen to fall in with the right men. One farmer, who has always been noted for careful culture, and who, I was told, would have clean seed if it was to be found, had wheat no better than my own. "I have had such dirty wheat," he said, and I do not doubt it, for, on going to the barn, where he had been cleaning some thirty or forty bushels for seed, there were lying on the floor five or six bushels of stricken grains and foul stuff that had been cleaned out. This was on one of the best wheat farms in the State. Unfortunately such cases are not rare. Where one farm has improved during the past five years, ten have run down. Uncertainty in regard to future prices, and the scarcity and inefficiency of laborers are among the chief causes of this deplorable state of affairs. I did not see during the whole ride a *single clean piece of corn.* Most of the corn was cut up, and in every case the rows could be traced by weeds running to seed, and not unfrequently the whole land was covered with weeds from six inches to three feet in hight. In a dry season, like the present, it is not easy to understand how land could get so foul, where even nothing more than ordinary cultivation is employed. Next spring, this land will be sown with barley, followed by wheat in the fall. Is it to be wondered at that clean wheat is so scarce? Many farmers plow their land twice for wheat after the barley is off, and harrow, roll, and cultivate their land very nicely, in order to get it clean and mellow. But this does comparatively little good. The time to clean land for wheat is while it is in corn. If it cannot be made thoroughly clean with one corn crop, plant it two years in succession, and cultivate it every week or ten days from the time the rows can be traced, till the corn is set. You will then have clean wheat.

There are two objects in working land. First, to kill weeds, and second, to enrich it by promoting decomposition, and rendering it capable of absorbing ammonia from the atmosphere. These chemical changes require time. If you have two heaps of manure piled up last spring, and one heap has been turned over three times during four or five months, and the other has not been turned at all, the one would be well rotted, and in fine condition to put on the land, while the other would most likely be lumpy, with some parts heated too much, and others not fermented at all. Now then, if you should make a spasmodic effort to get this last heap into good condition, and should turn it over a few days before you wished to use it, three times or even six times, do you suppose the heap would be as fine, and as well rotted, and as rich as the other? So far as enriching the land is concerned, stirring it over three or four times in as many days, does comparatively little good. Such treatment may be necessary to get the land ready for the seed, but by doing the work all at one time, you lose one of the chief advantages of working the land. It should be understood that decomposition or oxidation in the soil or in a manure heap is a kind of slow combustion. Now, any good housewife who bakes in an old-fashioned brick oven proceeds in strict accordance with scientific principles. She turns the fire from one side in the oven to the other, and thus exposes the black embers to the air, and when there are all aglow, she exposes another portion. If she should neglect to do this till the bread was all ready, and then should knock the fire back and forth half a dozen times in as many minutes, she would exhibit no more sense than her husband, who is, with plows, harrows, and cultivators, trying to get his land ready for wheat in a hurry. In heating the oven, the fire heats the opposite side from that on which the wood is placed, and so in the field the effect of working the land is not felt wholly on the first crop, but on those which follow. Cultivating corn benefits the crop. This is not all; its effects will be felt for two or three years.

The Doctor says, he "never knew a man to sell his farm who did not regret it." This is perhaps stating it a little too strong. But being one of the oldest pastors in Western New York, he has had good opportunities for observation. I think men engaged in other pursuits, who buy farms, expecting to find nothing but pleasure and profit in agriculture, are generally very glad of an opportunity to dispose of them. Such men seldom regret selling. But with a farmer the case is very different. He either sells because he thinks he can buy a better or cheaper farm, or because he is tired of farming, and proposes to live in the city. In the latter case he is almost certain to wish himself back again on the farm. I heard of such a case the other day. A farmer was offered last spring what he thought a high price for his farm, and accepted the offer, thinking he could live comfortably in the city on the interest of the money. After trying it six or eight months, he offered the purchaser $1000 to let him have the farm back again, giving him the summer crops and the wheat into the bargain. A farmer who sells expecting to buy another farm, finds it not so easy to suit himself as he expected. If you must sell the better plan is to know beforehand where you are going.

Like some of the other editors of the *Agriculturist*, I have been enjoying a rather long vacation the past summer. I took it at home—in the "stump lot!" We have had a right good time, pulling up stumps, piling old logs, tearing up the bushes, and making lots of bonfires. We have cleared about twenty-five acres of land that was chopped over fifteen or twenty years ago, and which has been allowed to run pretty much to waste ever since. It had never been plowed, and probably never seeded. The drier portions afforded good sweet pasture, but not much of it. The low, mucky parts were occupied almost exclusively with tall, rank weeds, sedge, rushes and logs. It was a rough looking place to take a plow and team into, but we managed to strike out a couple of furrows and then worked on both sides of them, removing stumps, rotten logs, etc., and piling them in heaps on the plowed land. I believe I knew what a "rolling hitch" was before; at all events I do now! But my performances did not escape good-natured criticism from some of the old settlers. It was said that I should burn up all the land, and even the Deacon thinks the new ditch I am digging through it, from the creek, "will drain the creek instead of the land." There *may* be some truth in this. But what of it? The only outlet for the water is the creek. It can go no where else, and if when the creek is high the water flows on to me, when it lowers it will flow off rapidly. It will not be as stagnant as it was before the ditch was dug. I *have* burnt some of the land—did it on purpose. I had three acres of the roughest land, where it was almost impossible to turn over the tough sod, and where the plow pulled up the old sedge roots and much soil into heaps. I set fire to the whole thing and the "burnt district" is now the smoothest land in the field. "But will it not spoil the land?" I think not. "Paring and Burning" is an old practice for enriching land. Hundreds of acres are burnt, or charred, every year in England. At all events the land produced nothing of any value before, and it can scarcely be any worse now. I have sown the drier portions of the field to wheat, sowing Timothy seed with it, and the rest I have sown with Timothy alone, at the rate of a peck per acre. The work could doubtless have been done better, but at all events it is done. And if I had let it lie as it was for another twenty years, it is not probable that I should have done it then to the entire satisfaction of every passer-by. The whole, I think, has not cost me over $10.00 an acre, and if the drier portions of the land produce a fair crop of wheat, it will more than pay the whole expense, and I am mistaken if the low land will not yield some tall Timothy.

This low land was in front of the house, and was an eyesore. There were three or four "knolls" in the field, but they were hid by brush. Since we have pulled up the bushes and cut down some of the young trees, this rising ground comes into view, and the whole field seems to have risen up ten or fifteen feet! I dare not tell an old farmer so, but between you and me I think this effect as viewed from the front piazza is worth at least $20 a year, or more than the interest on the whole cost. A fine view has a cheering, invigorating influence on any man who can appreciate it. It gives tone to the mind. A farmer, more than most men, needs pluck, faith in himself and in nature, and above all patience. He must wait for results, and while doing so it is important that his surroundings should be as pleasant as he can afford to make them. A cheerful, healthy location, is of more value than a fine house.

"I thought you advocated small farms and thorough cultivation," said a visitor some time since, in a tone that implied a doubt as to my consistency. "That field of corn," I replied, "has been cultivated ten times. Is not that thorough cultivation?" "Yes, but you have a large farm." "That depends upon circumstances. A 'truck' grower near New York, who finds ten acres enough, would call it large, while Mr. Alexander, of Illinois, would call it a mere paddock for young calves, to run and graze in." It is a mistake, however, to class me with those who indiscriminately advocate small farms. I have never said that it was better to have a small farm than a large one, provided you have sufficient capital and experience. The cost of fences on a small farm is far greater per acre than on a large one. The amount of land occupied by them is proportionally much greater. You cannot plow, harrow, cultivate, mow, or reap, (with a machine,) to as great advantage. In cultivating corn on a small field, you injure a greater proportion in turning at the headlands than you would in a large field. One of my Dutchmen, to whom I was paying $1.50 per day, said he must have $1.75. I asked him how much he got in the old country, and, after considerable cross-questioning, he admitted that that he only received $8.00 a month and board. Now, hitherto the price of many of our farm products, such as wheat, corn, cheese, butter, and pork, has been determined by the price in the European markets, and we have received for them what they will sell for there, less the cost of transportation, commission, insurance, dockage, etc. In other words, we have to compete with the cheap labor of Europe. How can we do this? We have had cheap land, and we have been able to grow crops without paying much attention to manure. This is still true of a considerable extent of country in the Western States at the present time. But as compared with the States on the Atlantic, this advantage is in part counterbalanced by the expense of transportation. Much of our land is now no richer or better in any respect than that in Europe. We shall have to manure as highly as they do, pay at least double the wages, and sell our produce in the same market. True, we have cheaper land, but this is in part counterbalanced by a higher rate of interest for money. The only advantage we have is that we make our labor more efficient by the use of better tools, implements, and machinery, directed by active and intelligent men.

We cannot use machinery to its fullest extent and with the greatest economy on a small farm. We shall have larger farms. The tendency is already apparent. We may deplore it, and argue against it, but cannot stop it. Fortunately we have a country almost boundless, and we can have large farms here, if anywhere.

It is certainly far better to have a small farm highly cultivated than to have a large one half tilled. But a large farm *may* be cultivated as highly as a small one—and at less expense per acre. In England, as a rule, the largest farmers are the best farmers. One of the most highly cultivated farms I ever saw contained over 3000 acres, and I do not recollect ever seeing a farm of fifty acres or less, that would at all compare with the more liberally managed large farms. This is very different from what it is here, and one main reason is, a deficiency of working capital.

Peart, the butcher, who is a close observer, and has gone the rounds for a great many years, thinks the permanent meadows in this section are rapidly deteriorating. "It will not do," he says, "to keep them down so long. When Benjamin bought his farm, it had been in grass for fifteen years, and the meadows produced a kind of June grass with a little Timothy not over a foot high, hardly worth mowing. I told him the farm was not run down, only neglected. He plowed it up, worked it well, put on plenty of plaster, and now see what a lot of stuff he raises! I know of several such cases, and you will find, this year especially, that all the heavy grass is on the meadows most recently seeded."

[COPYRIGHT SECURED.]

SHORT-HORN BULL "CONJURER," 5476.—FROM A PHOTOGRAPH.—*Engraved for the American Agriculturist.*

Short-horn Cattle.

Our engraving is from a photograph lately taken of the magnificent Short-horn bull Conjurer, A. H. B., 5476, owned by Mr. Geo. F. Wilson, of East Providence, R. I. He is a red roan, was bred by Mr. T. L. Harison, of Morley, St. Lawrence Co., N. Y., was three years old Jan. 20th, and weighs now, in moderate flesh, 1930 lbs. His sire is Hotspur, 4030; dam, Curls, by Barington, 1220, etc. Hotspur was by Duke of Gloster, (11,382) 2763, one of the best bulls ever imported, out of Daphne, by Harold.

We have never before attempted to engrave a Short-horn from a photograph. The one from which the above is copied was sent to us. It shows in a measure the distorted foreshortening so common in large photographs, yet has so much of the grandeur and nobility of the animal in it that we have essayed to reproduce it as accurately as possible. The bull is not coarse in the head, and his muzzle is remarkably fine.

The visitor at our State and County Fairs, is always attracted by some representatives of the Short-horn breed. This can perhaps boast a less antiquity than any other distinct race of British cattle, and has, besides, more decidedly artificial characteristics. The stock from which the improved breed has sprung was that of the counties of York, Lincoln, Northumberland, and Durham. These cattle were famous for their early maturity, large size, quick fattening, and smallness of offal, and large yield of milk. They became famous, and were taken to all parts of the kingdom, while the breeders of that and other regions were stimulated to still more careful selection and judgment in breeding.

The aim with Short-horn breeders has ever been to raise animals which would grow rapidly, attain a large size, and fatten easily. It is, therefore, preëminently a beef producing race. Deep milkers are occasionally found among the Short-horns, but the production of milk has been ignored by eminent breeders, in perfecting the beef points. Crosses of the Short-horns with common stock or other breeds, are often very large milkers, and almost always quick feeders.

The Short-horn bull is the noblest and most majestic of his kind. The cow is the most queenly, the most perfect in form, and, considering her great size, the finest in bone; and as the race excells in "handling" qualities, it has, naturally, more admirers than any other.

Animals of a very similar character to the Short-horns, were introduced into this country as early as 1783, but it was not until 1791 that the first authentic importations were made. Since that time, until the rinderpest laws were passed, frequently, and, latterly, almost every year, some of these animals have been imported. Much of this stock has been carefully bred, and the animals are as good as any of their race, while some of it has run out to a great extent, so that, though sprung from the best blood, many of the animals are really inferior.

The Short-horns are of large size, red, white, or white and red, in color, the mixture being most common and most prized. The head is small, the muzzle moderately fine, the nose nearly white, the horn waxy, small, and, in cows, usually turned downward, or pointing forward and toward each other. The brisket projects forward, is very deep, and almost free from dewlap. The neck is fine, and free also from superfluous skin. The chest has great depth and width. The shoulder is very well developed, and covered with muscle, and the lines from the shoulder over the crops, back and loin are very full and fine. The carcass is round, the ribs extending far back, the hips wide, pelvis large and broad, the tail at the roots strong, but rapidly tapering, and very fine at the brush. The lines of the back and belly are nearly straight. The hide is soft and mellow, yielding and elastic to the touch, and the hair is soft and abundant. The beef of the Short-horns is not equal to that of several of the other breeds, but they are very profitable animals to the feeder, because they grow and fatten so rapidly, and to the butcher and consumer, because they have so little offal. The breeders have endeavored constantly to increase the most valuable parts, and to reduce those of the least value.

The Hoop-petticoat Narcissus.

(*Narcissus Bulbocodium.*)

Among the bulbs enumerated in the books and catalogues, there are some that we very seldom see in cultivation; one of these is the little *Narcissus Bulbocodium.* The reason for its rare occurrence may be that the dealers in their catalogues usually say "fine for pot culture," which leads to the inference that it will not do well out of doors. It is true, it is an excellent bulb for pots, but it will flower if treated like other spring bulbs, where the climate is not very severe. Our figure is taken from a plant that we found last spring in the collection of Mr. I. Buchanan. Mr. B. has a great fancy for old things which have, for the most part, gone out of fashion, and we seldom visit his place without seeing something that is novel because it is so old.

The engraving gives the leaves and flowers of the natural size. The flower is of a lively yellow, very delicate in texture, and of a shape that is well expressed by its popular name. Those who limit their list of spring bulbs to Hyacinths, Tulips, and Crocuses, are not aware how much it may be extended.

Grape Cuttings in the Open Air.

Mr Wm. Patrick, of Terre Haute, Ind., furnished us for the Horticultural Annual for 1867, an account of his method of starting grape cuttings without the aid of artificial heat. Several have experimented with this process, and have been much pleased with the results. At Mr. J. M. M'Cullough's, near Cincinnati, we saw good plants of Norton's Virginia —a variety notoriously difficult to start even in the propagating house—successfully grown by this method. As the present month is the one in which the cuttings are to be prepared, we reproduce here the substance of Mr. Patrick's article:

"Before the ground freezes, I make the cuttings, from four to six inches long, with one or two eyes on each. I prefer to have two eyes, as such cuttings seem to be better able to withstand the drouth we are apt to have the last of May or the first of June. The cuttings are tied in bundles of about fifty each, and their lower ends are puddled by dipping them half their length in mud made of loamy soil mixed with water to about the consistency of cream. A cold frame has been previously prepared with good sandy loam, but not rich. In this I place the cuttings, *top end down*, and sprinkle in fine earth, so as to fill all the spaces in and between the bundles. The crevices all being filled, sufficient earth is put over the cuttings to cover them about four inches deep, and they are left in this condition until they have been rained upon, and it begins to freeze. I then cover the bed with a mulch of leaves or straw, and over this put a shelter of boards. If I wish to plant early in the spring, I remove the boards and mulch, and place a sash over the bed, taking care to leave an opening for ventilation; water is to be given as needed. In about five weeks the cuttings will almost all be found to have formed roots from one to three inches long, while the buds are just ready to burst.

"The cuttings are now in a condition in which they require careful handling, and they should not be allowed to dry. I usually set them, as they are taken from the frame, in a bucket containing some water, and in this way carry them to the place where they are to be planted. In planting, I set the cuttings so that the upper eye is just below the surface, and press the soil firmly around them. Treated in this manner they will nearly all grow and make very strong vines.

"If there is no cold frame at hand, another plan may be followed. The cuttings, being prepared as above directed, are buried, *lower end up*, and four inches deep, in some place sloping towards the south, with the ends inclining towards the south; they are to be covered with a mulch, in the same manner as described for those in cold frames. The mulch is removed in the spring and the earth exposed to the sun. Cuttings treated in this way will not be quite so early as those in frames, but I think they are about as good. There is some danger that those in frames may get too much advanced before the ground is ready to receive them.

"By either of the above plans, Delawares can be grown, and make fine plants.

"Sometimes, when roots have not started on the cuttings, I remove, with a sharp knife, a small strip of bark, one or two inches long, from opposite sides of the cutting at its lower end. This is done just as they are planted, as they should not be exposed to the air. Cuttings so treated will usually throw out a mass of roots along the edge of the cut, if the surface of the wood is not injured, and make strong plants."

Mr. Knox is very successful with the Concord and such freely rooting kinds, by simply setting out the cuttings in rows and heavily mulching during winter to prevent the frost from throwing them out. The cuttings are of two eyes each, and set with the upper bud just at the surface of the ground. We should judge from the appearance of the bed that the failures were less than ten per cent.

THE HOOP-PETTICOAT NARCISSUS.—(*Narcissus Bulbocodium.*)

What Trees to Plant on the Roadside.

No better rule can be given than to choose the best varieties that flourish in the neighboring forests. The White Elm, (*Ulmus Americana,*) and the Sugar Maple, (*Acer saccharinum,*) are more commonly planted in New England than others, because they are very fine trees, and bear removal well. They can be taken from the forest without previous preparation, and with careful handling are quite sure to live. But tap-rooted trees are quite as sure to die, unless they are taken from the nurseries, or have a previous root pruning in the forest. Nursery grown trees are much more likely to live, and in the end are generally cheaper if they are in the immediate vicinity. They are much better furnished with fine, fibrous roots, and are already accustomed to the sun. We would add to the list of trees for the wayside the White Oak, (*Quercus alba,*) the White-wood, (*Liriodendron Tulipifera,*) the White Beech, (*Fagus Americana,*) the Black Walnut, (*Juglans nigra,*) the Hickories, etc., and, where it is possible to protect them, the Evergreens, especially the Spruces. The White and Norway Spruces and the Hemlock, where they can be kept from the depredations of cattle, make a very beautiful border to the highway. The most of these trees flourish in the West, besides others nearly or quite as desirable.

The Kentucky Coffee-tree, the Catalpa, with its snowy white blossoms, the Sweet Gum or Bilsted, the deciduous Magnolias, are admirable trees for the West. The South has treasures peculiar to itself, as well as many of the magnificent trees that flourish in our northern climate. What could be a more appropriate adornment for the village street, or the plantation avenue, than the *Magnolia grandiflora*, or the live oaks, which flourish in their bottom lands, and are every year destroyed by the new clearings for cotton, as if they were rubbish? The South would be rich in ornamental trees if it had nothing more than these, which are worth a journey across a continent to see.

We by no means advise a restriction to the trees we have named, but have simply indicated them as available for the planter's purposes. Variety is as desirable by the roadside as in the park or pleasure ground. It is by no means a difficult thing to make an arboretum of deciduous trees along the wayside. If a whole neighborhood could be waked up to the enterprize, it would be quite desirable to attempt it. There are more than a hundred desirable deciduous trees upon our nursery catalogues, many of them foreign ones, quite as hardy and beautiful as our native trees, and no more expensive. And if the nursery is to be the source of supply, it is better to have a variety. The Norway and Sycamore Maples are quite as fine trees as our native maples, and the oaks and elms of British soil flourish quite as well here as at home. It would do much for the intelligence and good taste of a town to undertake an enterprise of this kind. It would redeem many a waste by the wayside. The wilderness and solitary place would be glad for such labors. Future generations will rise up and call the planters blessed.

APPLES FOR VINEGAR.—The high revenue tax upon whiskey has made a change in vinegar making. When whiskey was at a low price, it was largely converted into vinegar, and cider vinegar was a rarity. Now Pomona claims her own again, and cider vinegar with all its superior aroma is in demand. Some apple growers find it more profitable to convert the greater part of their crop into vinegar in preference to barreling it as fruit.

Mr. J. D. G. Nelson, of Indiana, stated at the recent meeting of pomologists, at St. Louis, that he never allowed windfalls to remain on the ground in his orchard more than one day. This not only prevented the increase of insects, but the fruit being converted into vinegar yielded him profitable returns. Whenever apples brought less than a dollar a bushel, he preferred to make vinegar rather than sell the fruit.

Clapp's Favorite Pear.

This variety was at first extolled by some in a manner that seemed extravagant, and by others denounced as a nearly valueless addition to our list of fruits. It has proved to be nearly, if not quite, all its introducers claimed for it, and now that the trees may be obtained at comparatively moderate prices, we can commend it to those who wish to increase the number of their choice varieties. This pear originated in Dorchester, Mass., and is supposed to be a cross between

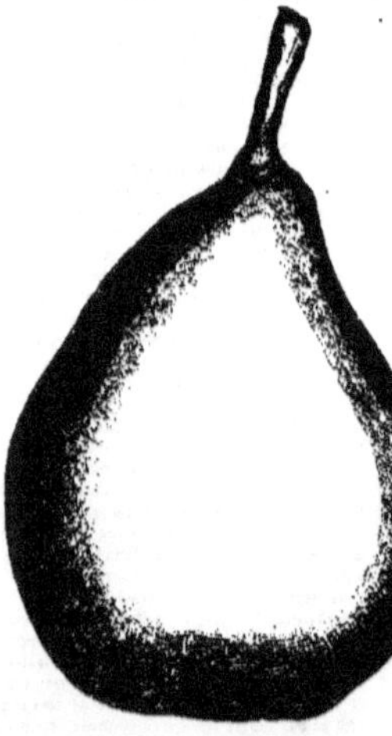

CLAPP'S FAVORITE PEAR.

the Bartlett and Flemish Beauty. The tree is a fine grower and strongly resembles the Flemish Beauty in habit. The fruit is of good size, somewhat resembling the Bartlett in shape, being frequently broader at the neck than the one from which our drawing was taken. The skin, when fully ripe, is yellow, with a red shade on the sunny side, making it a very showy fruit. In quality it is much better than the Bartlett, being very sweet, and perfumed, without the disagreeable muskiness that variety so often has, and besides it ripens about a week or ten days earlier.

A Raid Into Missouri.

The meeting of the Pomological Society, at St. Louis, allowed those from the East to see something of Missouri as a fruit growing State. That many parts of the State present superior advantages for vine culture has been made known through the writings of Husmann, Münch, and others, but probably few were prepared to see other fruits in such perfection. We speak not only of the specimens on exhibition, but of the unselected fruit as we saw it in the markets, and on the trees in the orchards.

A large party visited the fruit farm of E. R. Mason, Esq., at Webster Grove, about nine miles from St. Louis. The grapes were mainly in excellent condition, though some vines, as well as most of his apple and pear trees, had suffered from the attacks of grasshoppers. Concord, Creveling, Delaware, and other standard varieties, were grown for market, but the chief interest centered in his specimen vines of kinds less generally known. We noticed particularly fine Alvey, Maxatawney, and Rogers' No. 4. The last named variety is properly regarded by Mr. Mason, as it is by most other growers, as one from which much is to be expected.

The gentlemen who visited Mr. Mason gave expression to their gratification at his success in fruit culture, as well as to their appreciation of the hospitality with which they were entertained. Through the combined courtesies of Mr. Husmann and the Pacific R. R. Co., a party of nearly a hundred visited Hermann, which has long been known as one of the principal centers of grape culture in this country.

Hermann is about 80 miles from St. Louis, among the bluffs of the Missouri River, and seems to be a most favored spot for fruit growing. Were it not celebrated for its grapes, it would be for its peaches, and were its peaches less fine, we could sound the praises of its apples and pears. There may be such peaches elsewhere as grow at Hermann, but we have yet to see them. Mr. Husmann's vineyards and wine cellars were duly inspected, nor were his orchards neglected; probably not since General Price visited Hermann, has there been such a raid upon its products. Mr. H.'s grape crop was generally good, his favorites, the Norton's Virginia and Concord, being the leading varieties. Here, as at the other vineyards we visited, we made notes for future use. Mr. Rommel's vineyard showed the finest crops of Norton and Catawba that we saw, and here were also specimens of some new varieties. We visited also the grounds of Melchior Poeschel, Poeschel & Scherer, and Mr. Lassal, where the grape was being successfully grown. A sail up the Missouri, then very low and full of snags, of sixteen miles, brought us to Bluffton, where a large tract of land has been secured by the Bluffton Wine Company. This company, of which Mr. Husmann is President, is composed of some of the responsible capitalists of the State, and has for its object the development of grape growing on easy terms to actual settlers. It owns some of the best grape lands in the State, which are situated upon a singularly romantic portion of the river. Already extensive propagating houses are built, and the enterprise is being pushed with energy. Of course, at a new place like this, matters were a little in the rough, but the exertions of Mr. Sam. Miller, the Superintendent, and Mr. Wesselhoft, the Agent, were equal to the disposal and care of a large party.

The Ailanthus, Economically and Horticulturally Considered.

This journal has been one of the few, if not the only one, that has defended the Ailanthus from indiscriminate condemnation; and we are glad to find that evidence in favor of our position is accumulating. We do not claim that it is the best tree to grow everywhere, but do hold that its merits—those of growing in the poorest soil, and of tenacity of life, are qualities that give it a real value in many places. Many years ago the steep hills near Cincinnati were sown with Ailanthus by the direction of the late Nicholas Longworth. The prime object was to prevent the washing down of the hill-sides, which was accomplished, but another purpose was served. In a year of fuel famine, the growth afforded a most welcome supply of firewood to the poorer people who dwelt on the outskirts of the city, and this without interfering with the original object, as it is scarcely possible to kill an Ailanthus by cutting it down—it rather likes it.

Mr. J. M. M'Cullough, nurseryman of Cincinnati, informs us that he depended upon the Ailanthus for fuel all one winter, and states that it burns readily when green or dry, with a bright cheerful flame, gives off a great deal of heat, and never throws out sparks. There is another use to which Mr. M'C. puts the wood, which is worth knowing—he finds it to make most excellent vineyard stakes. He says: "For grape stakes it should be cut when of suitable size, and allowed to season, and before setting, the part coming in contact with the ground should be well charred. When this is done, its durability will compare favorably with any other grape stakes in use."

A Live Horticultural Society.

We found a society of this stamp at Fort Wayne, Ind., and as it is managed very much to our taste, we hold it up as a model. It has about two hundred members, fruit growers and farmers of Fort Wayne and vicinity. They have a reading-room, library, and lecture-room in the Court-house, where meetings are held weekly on Saturday afternoons. The exercises consist of essays or reports on horticultural topics, followed by discussions. A good collection of books has already been placed in the library, and steps have been taken to procure a collection of birds, insects, etc., natives of the country, that are injurious to the farmer and horticulturist. They will be nicely prepared, named, classified, and arranged in cases, for the instruction of members. The President of this Society is Hon. J. D. G. Nelson, and the Secretary is H. J. Rudisill. The average attendance at the meetings is about twenty-five, though in the winter, when farmers are at leisure, it is much larger. The influence of such a society, with its frequent meetings and exhibitions, in cultivating the horticultural taste of a people, must be happy, and we heartily wish that every city and village in the country had such an association. Every fruit grower has his peculiar experience and difficulties, and it would be a great help to him to have easy access to the experience of his fellow workers. In such an association much knowledge would be thrown into common stock, and made available for all. It only needs about a dozen men or women in a village, with a decided taste for horticulture, to start such a society, and to make it go. A room for meetings, and the exhibition of fruits, flowers, and vegetables, will be the largest item of expense. We think it exceedingly desirable that there should be weekly free exhibitions, at least during the summer and fall, where the members could show their best products in their greatest perfection. These would attract attention, excite interest, and spread the knowledge of new horticultural products in the community. In the winter, a course of lectures in the cities would be very desirable. Such a society, once organized, would almost take care of itself.

A "New" Old Violet.—(*Viola cornuta.*)

It is curious to see how fashions rule in floriculture as well as in other matters. Over three-quarters of a century ago, the old Botanical Magazine figured an unpretending looking violet, from the Pyrenees,—*Viola cornuta.* For the past two or three years the advertising columns of the English horticultural papers have been eloquent in the praise of this old plant, each

VIOLA CORNUTA.

seedsman claiming that his was the "Original Jacobs." Knowing that, in the words of the advertisers, "no place could be complete" without a bed of this plant, we tried it this summer, and, much to our surprise, were pleased with it. It remained in bloom from June to October, and was in all respects satisfactory. There was no day in which there was not a profusion of modest mauve-colored flowers. The past season has, however, been an unusually moist one, and we cannot infer from this year's experience what it would do in our very dry summers. Gen. Negley, of Pittsburgh, informs us that he has been much pleased with this violet, while Peter Henderson, of New Jersey, does not give it high praise. The individual flowers do not amount to much, though we figure one that our readers may see what they are like. The great merit of the plant is its free blooming character, and the modest tone of its flowers.

Notes on Grapes and Grape Culture.

In our visits to numerous vineyards, East and West, such a mass of notes has accumulated that we are obliged to omit those relating to the less known and less promising varieties, and give only such as will interest the general cultivator.

Creveling.—We hear uniformly good accounts of this wherever it has fruited. Mr. Knox had a very large crop ready for market early in September. The finest specimens were at the vineyard of Mr. E. R. Mason, Webster Grove, Mo., where the bunches were more compact than we have seen them elsewhere. Mr. Husmann predicts that the Creveling will be one of our leading wine grapes. It is certainly one of the best, healthiest, and most prolific, early varieties.

Norton's Virginia.—This is pre-eminently the red wine grape of all those that have been fully tested, though it requires a long season to perfect it, and it will be limited to particular localities. Vine healthy, bears abundantly, but not so great a weight of fruit as some others. Mr. Rommel, of Hermann, had particularly fine specimens. The fruit sold last year in St. Louis at 23½ cts. per lb. for wine-making.

Cynthiana.—In general appearance this resembles Norton, but the berry is larger and more juicy. Good judges consider that it makes a better wine than that variety.

Ives' Seedling.—Perhaps no grape at present excites more attention than this. It originated with Mr Ives, an amateur, in Cincinnati, some thirty years ago. Col Waring, of Indian Hill, cultivated the vine for fifteen years, allowing the grapes to be picked before they were ripe. By accident a bunch was allowed to remain until fully matured, and it so commended itself to him that he commenced propagating it, and soon established a vineyard. Since it became well known, it has spread with remarkable rapidity, and a great number of acres have been planted with it. The vine propagates easily, is hardy, healthy, and very productive. The grape has some resemblance to the Isabella, when fully ripe is intensely sweet, and somewhat foxy. Though a recent writer has expressed his doubts about its making wine, the Ohio people think differently, and esteem it highly as a wine grape. We asked an old German vigneron if he were to plant a vineyard of a hundred acres what vines he should set, and he replied "25 acres each of Delaware and Norton's Virginia, and the rest in Ives' Seedling."

Martha.—We saw this in bearing at both Pittsburgh and Hermann. In growth and healthfulness of foliage it much resembles the Concord, of which it is a seedling. It appears to be a good bearer; bunch medium or small, berry medium, round, pale yellow, intensely sweet and rather foxy.

Rogers' No. 4.—Those who have experimented with the Rogers' Hybrids seem to be settling upon a few numbers as being desirable varieties, and where a preference is expressed for a single number, in the majority of cases it is for No. 4. It is a large black berry, and makes a good sized bunch; sweet, and of very good quality. Should it prove healthy and hardy over a wide range of country, it will become a formidable rival to the now popular Concord, as it is a more showy and a better fruit.

Iona.—This year, the record of this, the best of our native grapes, is all favorable. Except in some localities, where from the excessive rains, grapes have generally failed, the Iona has done well. The poorest specimens we have seen were in Missouri. In our talks with western grape growers we found that plantations of young vines had generally done well, and we cheerfully accord to Doct. Grant great praise for this contribution to American grapes. We once told him that it was equal to the best Catawba we ever saw. We now say that it is better than the best Catawba, as we have (without his knowledge,) tried them side by side,—the only test that any native grape need fear is a comparison with a well-ripened Catawba.—As to the vine, previous years have given an adverse report. This year the reports are much better. Our position has always been that the standing of any fruit should not be governed by its success or failure in a single locality.

Concord.—This has generally done well, and while we cannot put it in the list of best grapes, it has a hardiness and prolific character that entitle it to commendation. If one wishes to raise grapes by the ton, the Concord will more generally give the weight than any other that we know of. On a given space of ground, one can almost as surely calculate on a certain yield of Concord grapes as he can of a yield of corn. Concords at five cents a pound will pay.

PROPAGATING THE BLACKBERRY AND RASPBERRY.—Those who wish to increase their stock of plants can do it much more rapidly by making root cuttings than by waiting for the natural formation of suckers, and besides obtain much better plants. In February (page 61) of the present volume we gave a detailed account of the manner of preparing the roots, and now wish to call timely attention to that article, as the present is the proper season to prepare for a stock of young plants next spring. So valuable was the information contained in this article considered by the owner of a new raspberry, that he sent Mr. Fuller a hundred dollars' worth of his plants as an acknowledgment of the benefit he had derived from it.

THE PEACH AND ITS VARIETIES.—It was only a few years ago that horticulturists were brought to admit that the Nectarine was only a variety of the peach. M. Carriere, editor of the Revue Horticole, had already suggested that the Almond was also a variety of the peach, and he now states that there are specimens at the Paris Museum which prove this to be the fact.

Green-house Shrubs in Common Culture.

There is one class of house plants that we see much less frequently than we did many years ago—the larger green-house shrubs that are not very particular as to their treatment, and which, being kept from year to year, become as much a part of the household as the furniture. It used to be common to see large plants of Orange, Lemon, Oleander, Pittosporum, Laurestinus, etc., in both city and country houses. Our modern modes of heating have done away with most of these. They will endure rough treatment of almost every kind, save drying up. Those who have rooms that can be kept about 45°, without the dry heat of a coal stove or furnace, can do very well with the above named, and even with Camellias. Summer blooming shrubs are easily managed by wintering them in the cellar. Among the most satisfactory shrubs of this kind are the Oleander, Pomegranate and Crape Myrtle. The Oleander, so well known and so easily raised, is more generally grown than either of the others. In St. Louis it is a common plant on the market stands. The Pomegranate is fine, both in foliage and flower, and though less common in cultivation than the Oleander, is much more frequently met with than the Crape Myrtle. Any one who has visited New Orleans and other Southern cities in summer must have noticed the great profusion of this plant in the door yards and on the verandas. It will not stand the winter with us, but it may be enjoyed here if given proper protection during that season. The Crape Myrtle, *Lagerstræmia Indica*, is a native of Southern Asia; it is not a Myrtle, as its popular name would indicate, but belongs to the Loosestrife Family (*Lythraceæ*). Its foliage is very clean and neat in appearance, and its flowers, which are borne in clusters at the ends of the branches, are of a lively rose color, with purple and white varieties. The petals are six, each on a long claw or stalk, with the broad part singularly crumpled in such a manner as to give the flowers an exceedingly beautiful appearance. The engraving shows a flowering branch of the natural size, but of course lacks the color which gives to the plant so lively an appearance. In the Southern States it needs no protection, but at the North it must be wintered in the cellar and somewhat closely pruned. The Coral Tree, *Erythrina Crista-galli*, is another very showy plant that only needs winter protection to make a grand show in the summer. The Oleander, Crape Myrtle, Pomegranate, and Coral Tree, may be put in the open ground in summer, but they particularly commend themselves to those city dwellers who have no "grounds," as they may be grown in tubs or boxes, to decorate the veranda in summer, and allowed to pass their season of rest in the cellar.

Books and Papers as Premiums.

We are glad to notice the increase of this pleasant and profitable custom. In the arrangement of the horticultural premiums, what could be more appropriate than a "Warder" for the best collection of apples, or the *Agriculturist* for one year for the best show of butter, or "Gardening for Profit" for the best collection of vegetables? The money secured in successful competition at the fairs is pocketed, and soon forgotten. But a live book, treating of practical matters, lying upon the shelf or the center table, is a perpetual fountain of pleasure. The paper that comes weekly or monthly, freighted with profitable suggestions, is a happy reminder of our success, and an incentive to do better next year. Much as our farmers need money, they need knowledge more. Nothing pays so well as the knowledge of the best way of doing things. The societies that disseminate the most knowledge by means of their exhibitions and their premiums will have the most zealous supporters, and do most for agricultural improvement. In the arrangement of the premium lists for another year, let us have a liberal sprinkling of agricultural books and papers.

CRAPE MYRTLE.—(*Lagerstræmia Indica.*)

A Curious Experiment in Grafting.

In the Revue Horticole, for Sept., M. Verlot gives an account of an experiment in grafting that is so novel that we think it will interest our readers. Two pear trees on quince roots were united by inarching, and the roots (quince) of one of the trees left exposed to the air. Of course, in order to reach the quince roots of the tree thus exposed, the sap had to go from the other tree and traverse the tissues of the one grafted upon it in a reverse direction. This it did, and the quince root then put out quince shoots three to four inches long. Upon the branches of this root, now for a year exposed to the air, pear grafts have been placed. Two of these grafts have succeeded, so that now this curious tree consists: 1st, of a quince root; 2d, a Beurre d'Arenburg pear; 3d, a Beurre de Charneu pear that was inarched into No. 2; 4th, of quince roots; 5th, of pear grafted upon these quince roots. Should these last named grafts bear fruit true to its kind, it will puzzle those who claim that the stock has an influence upon the graft, as the sap will have passed through the tissues of four other trees before these grafts were reached, and in two instances through inverted tissues. The experiment is also interesting in showing that roots may adapt themselves to circumstances, and being exposed to the air, become to all intents and purposes like branches. We hope that M. Verlot will keep watch of this remarkable tree and let us know more of the results of one of the most interesting experiments ever made in practical horticulture.

The American Pomological Society.

The meeting held at St. Louis, in September, was both a success and a failure. Socially, it was a success, as it afforded an opportunity for long separated pomologists to meet and exchange greetings; it afforded eastern men a view of one of the fine cities of the West, and gave them a taste of western hospitality, but beyond these its results were meagre. In no spirit of fault finding, but with the desire to avoid a similarly unsatisfactory result at the next meeting, we would make a few suggestions. Let there be no exhibition of fruit in connection with the meeting; it serves only to distract attention. If any member has a new fruit, let him bring it up at the meeting, and exhibit specimens at the same time. We can see quite as good fruit shows without going so far. Essays, papers, or communications upon particular points in pomology, should be referred to a publishing committee, and, if acceptable, printed in the transactions. An essay, however able, is at such times a bore. Let nurserymen forget their avocation for once, and be pomologists. A good share of the time of the last meeting was consumed in advertising the small fruits, to such an extent that pears were briefly mentioned, and apples, the most important of all fruits, omitted altogether. We should not so much regret this had the discussion on small fruits elicited anything new, but it was the same talk that we have heard over and over again, and merely went to show that certain fruits did well in some places, and not in others. In view of the unsatisfactory results of the St. Louis meeting we would suggest that in future the business be arranged long beforehand, and that all branches of pomology be allowed an equal share in the deliberations. Two and a half days are all too short a time in which to discuss new fruits. In future, let us have no more essays, no more advertising, and just a little pomology.

RICINUS SANGUINEUS.—The common Palma-Christi, or Castor-oil Plant, is an exceedingly ornamental object when well grown, but it is far eclipsed by the varieties introduced within a few years. *Ricinus sanguineus*, whether a garden variety or a species, is a most stately and pleasing plant. Its stems are of a dark red color, and its long spikes of flowers and fruit of a lighter red, while its leaves have a tropical luxuriance that is quite charming. This, as well as the other varieties, only attains its best development in the long seasons of the Middle and Southern States, though if started under glass, it proves very satisfactory at the North.

THE HOUSEHOLD.

(☞ For other Household Items, see "Basket" pages.)

Household Ornaments.

Fig. 1 shows a very neat card basket made of paper. The material is cut in pieces from half an inch to an inch square, according to the size of the basket wanted. Each piece is made into a double roll, as shown at *A*, the paper being kept rolled by applying a little gum arabic. The rolls are then

Fig. 1.—PAPER CARD BASKET.

gummed together by their sides, and set up endwise for the bottom of the basket. The sides are built up in the same manner, laying one roll upon another. By using paper of several colors, a pleasing variety of figures may be wrought into the sides.

Fig. 2 represents the manner of covering a box with mosaic of colored straw. The straws are first dyed of various bright hues, then carefully split

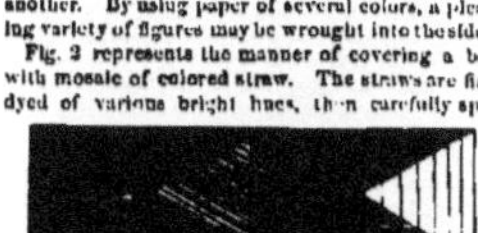

Fig. 2.—MOSAIC BOX COVER.

and pressed flat. A plain wooden box may be marked with any patterns to please the fancy; the straws are then cut of suitable lengths and gummed on. This is very neat work for young people on winter evenings. Many pleasing articles for sale at Ladies' Fairs may be easily made in this way.

Leaves from the Diary of a Young Housekeeper.—No. XI.

PRIZE ESSAY BY MRS. LAURA E. LYMAN, STAMFORD, CT.

November 2d.—At intervals for two weeks past I have been learning to work my Wheeler & Wilson. My excellent neighbor has one of the same patent, and whenever I have been puzzled, has helped me out of my difficulties. I have already made Edward two shirts, and yesterday I cut out for him a pair of pantaloons which are now nearly done. In half an hour I stitched up seams that would have occupied me with hand sewing nearly half a day; the making of clothes after they are cut out and fitted is reduced to almost nothing, and the relief of mind it gives to know that in a short time a big piece of work can be accomplished even better than by the old slow mode of stitching by hand, is immense. I can appreciate the remark of a recent writer, who says: "If a man has but three acres of land, he had better sell one and buy a sewing machine." In a family of children it is quite indispensable. Slavery to the needle need no longer be the sad lot of woman, and many a wife and mother can devote the time thus saved her by the ingenuity of this wonderful invention, to the improvement of her own mind, and the minds of her children, and to the cultivation of social and domestic enjoyments. How many families seem to live only to work, work, work! It is true that Adam was commanded to earn his living by labor, and that lot is upon most of us, but who believes that when Adam came in from his daily toil he did not *enjoy* the society of "the fairest of her daughters, Eve," and try to reproduce in some faint degree the happiness of their lost Eden; that he did not play with his twin boys, Cain and Abel, and tell them wonderful tales of the beauty of Nature, before thorns and thistles marred its perfection? Every wife and mother should strive to make home a happy place, sunny, cheerful, attractive; and the numerous labor-saving inventions of these modern times afford her far more leisure than she formerly enjoyed, which she ought to devote to that very sacred object, family happiness.

I never made a pair of pantaloons before, but Edward got the pattern of a tailor, and with his best pair as a model, and the advice of my neighbor, I had but little difficulty. The best way to cut them out is to fold the cloth double, if there is no nap to it, as is the case with the Harris goods which I am making up, and after having the patterns ironed out smoothly, pin them all down upon the cloth before using the shears at all. In this way one can cut to the best advantage, and save the residue in as large pieces as possible; they are useful not only for mending, but for slippers, caps, and gaiters. Mother made all the boys' caps from pieces saved in this way. Pockets are put in first, then the "dress" of the pants finished, then the seams stitched up and pressed, then the waistbands put on, and last and most difficult of all, the part around the foot lined and hemmed. I find that pressing a long time makes a great difference in the "finish" they have. A "goose" would no doubt be the best thing to press with, but a heavy flat-iron answers very well, if it is used long enough.

November 10th.—There is an old fashioned fireplace in the sitting room, and Edward says we shall have the luxury this winter of sitting before an open hickory fire. So I have got down an old pair of brass andirons that were stowed away in the attic when Edward bought the place, and Sue has rubbed them up with silver soap until they shine like gold. "The wrist is parted from the hand," probably, that polished them last, and they are most refreshingly old style in their appearance, so suggestive of big log fires, of glowing warmth and radiant cheer in the happy olden time, before Franklin ever thought of stoves. These last are a wonderful convenience and great economizers of fuel, and must continue to be in universal demand, but they are very dull as companions, and hopelessly black and uninteresting, while the open fire is a fountain of light, and warmth, and cheerfulness, to all in the house. One of our neighbors has thirty cords of wood cut and rotting on the ground, yet he and his family sit all the long winter evenings around a great, ugly, black, iron box, filled with burning coal. Surely they cannot know what *fireside* enjoyment is! A recent writer inquires in a very happy article about home happiness, "who ever heard of men fighting for a stove or a big black hole where heat comes up into the room?" The thrilling appeal of Bozzaris to his Greeks, "Fight for your altars and your fires," loses its force in these days of modern improvement.

Many, I know, must economize and cannot afford an open fire, but those who prefer to go without some other article of luxury and indulge in this, will find health of body and mind much promoted, and their home enjoyment vastly increased.

We shall use our sitting room this winter much more than we did last. It seems better to us, upon talking the matter over, to use our house more; we have a very pleasant sitting room, and why should we stay all day and all the evening in the same room? The custom is a very prevalent one when a family occupy an ample house, to keep all the rooms shut up and use only an ell, perhaps, or some snug room in the rear of the house, when the general comfort and health of the family would be much increased if they permitted themselves to expatiate in an ampler space, and allowed the hospitable firelight to gleam through the front windows not too closely curtained.

November 25th.—In the midst of preparations for Thanksgiving, which is to-morrow, Edward purchased a beef's heart and a large hock, and I have made up mince meat enough to last until spring. Reserving what I wish for immediate use, the rest is packed down in a large jar, and covered over the top with molasses, to exclude the air, and put away down cellar.

We have been fattening a turkey for two weeks to grace the occasion. Sue is picking him now. I have directed her to save the quills carefully, for I vastly prefer a good turkey quill to all the steel pens, and even to Morton's celebrated gold ones. Some skill is required in making a good quill pen, but one soon learns.

We shall have a chicken pie for dinner, among other things, and I shall try and make it digestible as well as palatable. Rich pastry is always dyspeptic, and I shall use as little lard as possible in my crust, and yet have it tender and flaky. We shall certainly feel more thankful with stomachs filled with food that they can digest, and which is adapted to our bodily wants, than when they are overloaded with a rich and indigestible mass, pleasant in the mouth, perhaps, but ruinous to digestion. Edward bottled some cider two months ago, and we shall indulge in a glass of our own manufacture. The grapes we preserved with so much care repay all our trouble, and some of the clusters are almost as beautiful and fresh as when they were taken from the vine. This evening, Edward will carry to our excellent pastor a basketful of good things—a chicken, some grapes, a glass of currant jelly, a couple of mince pies, and a dozen eggs. He ministers to us so graciously in spiritual things that it is a delight to send him these tokens of our appreciation of his labors. Sue will take a basket of "goodies" home to her mother and the children, to make Thanksgiving a happy time for them. Some day I may be poor and unable to give, but while I have the power I will enjoy the luxury of beneficence.

November 30th.—It is now a year since we commenced housekeeping, and I have this morning been looking back over twelve months of busy, industrious, and successful life. Though I can see points in which my housekeeping can be improved, and in which I am determined it shall be, I cannot regard my first year's experience at all in the light of a failure. My success, such as it is, and certainly I have some very tangible proofs of it, is attributable to three causes.

First: I am under unspeakable obligations to my excellent mother for having drilled her daughters, almost from the cradle, in habits of economy, neatness, and dispatch. Her instructions were as incessant as they were valuable. For instance, if we went down cellar for anything, as butter, she would remind us to think if there were not something else we needed to bring up at the same time, so as to save steps. When we took off our bonnets and cloaks, she insisted upon our putting them at once in place; when breakfast was over she gave us half an hour as the time in which the dishes were to be washed, wiped, the knives scoured, and everything put away in good style; and all the time we were at work, the principles that should guide us in matters of economy and thrift were constantly reiterated in such homely, but valuable proverbs as

"*Once well done is twice done.*"
"*A place for everything, and everything in its place.*"
"*A time for everything, and everything in its time.*"
"*Waste comes to want.*"
"*Keep a thing and in seven years it will come in use.*"
"*Any slut can clean, but it takes a neat woman to keep clean.*"

Second: No young housekeeper was ever sustained in all her plans and wishes by a husband more thoughtful, more provident, or more apt in all matters about the house, than I have been. Edward's philosophy on this subject is, I think, eminently sound. He says that the policy of good farming and bad housekeeping is one that is tight at the bung and leaks at the tap, and that he has seen farmers' wives that could "throw out with a spoon as fast as the man could throw in with a shovel." Thinking thus, he is just as ready to assist me to make good butter as he is to cut clover hay for the cows in winter; for he says it is better to gain five cents a pound on account of superior quality of the article sent to market, than to have another cow and make more, but poorer, butter.

Third: I believe I am an enthusiast in housekeeping. I love it. "The mental exercise of keeping all the interests of my household in my mind and making all the ends meet; the skill to be evinced in extracting the greatest amount of comfort from supplies on hand; the ability to make every hour of my time tell upon the happiness of those I love, or the growth of our fortunes—these seem better to me, and happier, than all the fashions of cities, the delights of theatres, the vanities of dress, or the splendors of wealth.

The substantial results of my first year's industry I can sum up as follows: With Edward's rainy-day assistance, I have made a mattress, and an extremely neat and comfortable sitting room lounge. My needle and sewing machine have done my own sewing and made all my husband's and my own new winter clothing. I have made three hundred and twenty pounds of butter, and twelve fifteen-pound cheeses. I have four dozen and a half cans of preserved fruit. On the lower shelf of my store closet there is a large jar of tomato preserve, a smaller one of strawberry, one of quince, a large jar of quince and apple, and several quarts of manufactured honey. A large paper bag I have filled with dried corn, and another with dried apples. The pigs we saved from infantile death stand in my sitting room in the form of one of Wheeler & Wilson's best. A rag so handsome that every one considers it bought at the store, lies before our sitting room fire. Two quilts add warmth to Sue's bed, and that of our hired man.

Have I been happy? I've been too happily busy to think whether I was enjoying myself or not, but upon retrospect, I must pronounce it by far the most delightful year of my life.

Leaves from My Journal.—No. IX.

PRIZE ESSAY BY MRS. B. M'CLELLAN, OF OHIO.

November.—The glory of the Dahlias has departed. They look as if mourning that their reign is over. But they have well performed their part, and given us some useful lessons. Now, some fine day, let the bulbs be exposed to the sun and air until well dried, and then put in the cellar for safe keeping until another season of flowers. Roses need not be covered yet. They bear the cold well. Even the choice monthlies designed for the winter sitting room, must not be hurried into close, warm, quarters. They had better stand on the porch awhile. But notice the Chrysanthemums. Now is their time of triumph. Jack Frost cannot make them bend to him. Among the early snows they blossom still. What a bright "good morning" they give us after one of these biting nights. What mysterious principle of life is theirs? So frail and yet so strong! Emblems of immortality. Thus the good man's soul, when its surroundings die, plumes its pinions for that clime where "everlasting spring abides, and never fading flowers."

The cars furnish a good place for the study of human nature. How involuntarily we sit in judgment upon the characters of our fellow travelers! How trifling an act will cause them to rise or fall in our esteem! Is there some strange magnetic influence by which we are attracted or repelled, or is it only the offshoot of plain common sense?

I was on board for a night trip. In the absence of sleeping cars, the passengers had arranged themselves as best they could. Some had generously appropriated two entire seats, and with the aid of coat, shawl, carpet bag, etc., seemed likely to pass a comfortable night. Others sat crowded and erect.

One little company soon attracted my attention. The man had evidently taken good care of number one. Stretched at full length upon the seat he was enjoying a serene snooze. Opposite sat his wife and baby. How tired she looked as the hours went on! Occasionally she would snatch a nap, but all the while holding the little one in her arms,—with such a care at her heart she could not sleep long. I had no patience with Lazybones, as I inwardly named him, and put it down in my own mind that he ought not to have a wife or baby either. At length, opening one eye dreamily, it chanced to fall upon them in the corner, when presto, change! He rose at once, gave one good stretch to his cramped limbs, prepared upon part of his seat a nice bed for baby, took it tenderly from its mother's arms, and laid it down without waking it. Then, arranging coats and shawls with dispatch, his weary wife sank down upon them with such a trusting, grateful look that I knew her burden was gone—and so it proved. Till broad daylight she slept, apparently without one anxious thought. And well she might. Did baby wake,—strong arms were ready for it, and gently was it soothed to rest. Faithful, untiring sentinel that he was! I really felt like shaking hands and begging pardon for my harsh judgment at first. But considering that this would place me in an embarrassing situation, I resolved to be more deliberate in forming an opinion of the character of others, and write this down to deepen the impression.

I have been turning a pair of sheets to day. It is good economy, as they will last a third longer. After they become thin and worn in the middle, rip open the seam, sewing the opposite sides together. My good, prudent mother, taught me this, and I can never feel quite easy until it is done.

Graham bread should be freely eaten through the winter months. If rightly made it is both healthy and palatable. It should not be stiff enough to mould, but only so thick as to be conveniently stirred with a spoon. Set a sponge as for other bread. After rising, add one half teacupful of molasses, (some prefer it not so sweet,) and one teaspoonful soda, to sponge sufficient for one loaf. Thicken with flour as above. If kept moderately warm it will soon be ready for baking. It is even better when fresh sour milk can be had, to be stirred up with that, (adding more soda,) and baked at once.

Composition Cake.—Three eggs, one-half teacupful of butter, one and a half of sugar, two and a half of flour, one-half cupful sweet milk, one teaspoonful of cream of tartar, one-half teaspoonful of soda, a little salt. This is sufficiently rich for almost any occasion. Flavored and frosted it is a good loaf cake. Baked in shallow pans it is nice for jelly cake, or in patty pans for fancy cake. It is a convenient and reliable rule for the housekeeper.

A favorite and simple cake is the raised cake. Take one coffee cup of light bread dough, add one egg, one cup of sugar, one-half cup of butter, a little salt and nutmeg, one-half teaspoonful of soda, and raisins, if desired. Mix all together with the hand very smooth. Let it stand half an hour, and bake.

I have received some brackets and a card rack from Nellie, which are very pretty. They are made of cigar boxes, [I am glad these, for once, can be put to a respectable use,] cut with a knife into fanciful shapes, and varnished. They can be arranged in clusters, or scattered about the walls, surmounted with a delicate vase of flowers, choice shells, or anything ornamental. Her letter gives a description of a Sabbath School she had visited. It is held in a pleasant hall in town, secured for the purpose. Brackets adorn the walls, with vases of flowers in their season. Wreaths and mottoes of evergreen here and there—"Get wisdom;" "He shall gather the lambs in His arms;" "Enter His gates with thanksgiving;" "Love one another." A recess in one part of the room for the infant class. Above it this motto—"The Bird's Nest." A fountain in front of the desk. Three or four instruments accompany the voices in their songs of praise. It is refreshing thus to see the beautiful made to serve the good.

Dreary, desolate, chill, November. The verdure has gone from the meadow, the trees have doffed their royal robes, the skies are gray and leaden. We shiver about, saying winter has not yet come, and knowing too well we are not prepared for its coming. Young people linger to chat upon the streets, but with blue lips, and red noses, and chills that curdle the blood. Benny runs in from his play, and though stoutly protesting he is not cold at all, his fingers are red as cherries, and he joins the rest encircling the stove, no doubt to keep *that* warm. True winter has not come. It is not summer, neither is it spring. Can it be autumn? It is not sleighing, neither is it decent wheeling. There is no pleasure in riding, none in walking. Well, well, can nothing be said in its praise? Do neither moon nor stars appear? Ah, nestled somewhere among its thirty revolving suns is one dear day, so bright and gladsome, that with a halo of beauty, it illumes the rest, redeeming the whole to the rights and honors of the sisterhood of months. Thanksgiving Day! How timely its coming, how beneficent its mission! How fitting that with grateful hearts we enter into the courts of the Lord, and "sing praises unto Him with the timbrel and harp!" "Let everything that hath breath praise the Lord." The native born New Englander, though thousands of miles, it may be, from the old homestead, welcomes and celebrates its annual return. How busy are his thoughts with the memories of childhood! Father and mother, brothers and sisters, again surround the family board. The portly turkey has the chief place of honor, while at its right the chicken pie of ample dimensions modestly bides its time. Vegetables of all kinds send up their grateful incense, and cranberry sauce, jellies, pickles and celery give variety to the scene. But to the child the next course has a more thrilling pleasure. Plum pudding now has the place of the turkey, while circled about it are choice flaky pies of every conceivable kind. Willie has often before been put off with the smaller half of one piece. Now look at his plate! He thinks he will take some of each, and mother replies he shall have just as much as he wants. Of course he can't dispose of it all, but how sagely he reasons that it might make him sick, and he'll not be such a fool as to spoil all the fun in that way. Now hurrah for play! With pants tucked into boots, with mittens and muffler, with sled and skates too, was there ever a boy so happy as he! The young people of the neighborhood come in for the evening, and gathering round the fireside crack nuts and jokes together. Little Lucy, with the blue eyes and flaxen curls, whom Willie in his own mind pronounces by far the handsomest lady (?) in the room, he gallantly offers to draw home on his sled, and thus ends the programme of Thanksgiving Day years ago. We care not to draw a parallel between it and that of the present. Its delights seem ever new, and each return demands a richer and more grateful offering for the mercies of another year.

Now, surely, winter *is* just at hand. Flannel wrappers and drawers, woolen stockings, and substantial shoes and boots, must forthwith be put into service. They cost something indeed—but not so much as a cold and cough that no doctor's skill can arrest, not so much as a new made grave among the snows, the vacant place at the table, and the broken hearts of the bereaved.

But how fares it with the poor and unfortunate? Cannot a few garments be spared from our comfortable stock? Cannot words of tender sympathy and encouragement be spoken, or useful hints, that shall stimulate to truer economy, and more hopeful, persevering labor.—"Inasmuch as ye have done it unto one of these, ye have done it unto Me."

An Old Housekeeper's Advice to all young housekeepers in the country is to furnish their rooms with good Ingrain carpets, (all wool). Don't deceive yourself with the economical idea of rag or hemp carpets. The clean floor is greatly preferable. Those who are averse to scrubbing could have painted floors. The shade of newly planed pine boards, it seems to me, would be appropriate for the floor of the common room, dark colors showing the dust, and giving a gloomy appearance to the room. For the same reasons, select a carpet not too dark.

Graham Bread.—To every quart of unbolted wheat meal add one cup of molasses, and one tablespoonful of lard or butter. Make it up with milk and yeast. When risen, work in a little soda, make it into loaves, raise again, and bake.

Ginger Drops.—Two tablespoonfuls of molasses, one of lard, half a cup of sour milk, one teaspoonful of soda. Will be better with one egg, but can be made without. Flour enough to make a batter that will drop easily. Bake quickly.

Poor Man's Cake.—One tablespoonful of butter, one egg, one cup of sugar, one of sweet milk or cream, one teaspoonful of soda and two of cream of tartar, mixed dry in two cups of flour.

BOYS & GIRLS' COLUMNS.

Which Premium Will You Take?

The wide-awake boys and girls who read these columns have probably looked over the list of valuable premiums in the first part of the paper. The most energetic among them have already commenced taking subscribers, that they may secure that music-box, or a watch, a gun, a melodeon, perhaps some aim as high as one of the pianos. Such go-ahead characters need no encouragement from us. In a few weeks their lists will be complete, and they will have the satisfaction of owning some choice article honorably earned by their own efforts, which will be far better than to have asked father or some other friend for the money. Some, however, are still looking and longing, but have not yet mustered up courage to undertake the work. They dislike to ask for subscriptions, they say, because it looks like begging. That is a great mistake. Whoever induces another to subscribe for a good paper does him a favor. The thousands of good hints and suggestions, the beautiful engravings, the interesting stories, and other good things which the *Agriculturist* brings to its readers every month, will confer on each a benefit worth many times the subscription price. We ask no one to beg, but to offer the money's worth and more. So take heart, young friends. There are many in almost every neighborhood who will readily subscribe if you will let them examine a number and point out to them its many attractive features. It always gives us great pleasure to send premiums to our young friends, and we have remembered hundreds of them in this way. Who will earn a piano within the next three months? If you should fail to find enough for that, the melodeon or some other valuable premium will be reached—there will surely be good pay for all you accomplish.

A Faithful Sentinel.

Nearly 1700 years ago the city of Pompeii was buried by ashes and lava thrown out from the volcano Vesuvius. Since its discovery under the mound where it had lain so long undisturbed, an immense number of interesting relics have been brought to light—household utensils, works of art, tools of the trades, and remains of the former inhabitants. Among the latter was a skeleton that might be called a monument of fidelity. It was that of a Roman sentinel stationed at the gate of the city. Military law required him to remain at his post until ordered away, no matter what should come. He might have properly said: "The eruption of a volcano is an exception to all common law. I have a right now to run for my life." But no, that, he thought, would bring dishonor, and he preferred death. He stood firm, the ashes falling thick around him, deeper and deeper they gathered, slowly burying him, yet he stirred not, and there he found his tomb! After seventeen centuries they found his skeleton standing erect, clad in its rusty armor, the helmet on his empty skull, and his bony fingers still grasping his spear, his own monument to his faithfulness.

Our Old Boys and Girls.

It is pleasing to notice the great number of men and women who, on receiving the *American Agriculturist*, open first to the Boys' and Girls' Department. This is true of at least five-sixths of those we have noticed who call at the office for their monthly numbers. Another indication of the same fact is the large number of answers to problems that come from adults. We have published puzzles made by Presidents of Colleges and Judges of Courts, showing that they have not forgotten to be young. It is in every way desirable to keep a young heart as long as possible. Americans are probably the oldest of civilized people. The proverb "Care killed a cat" (which, you know, is said to have nine lives) is at least partly realized here. The cares and perplexities of business are suffered to take too much time and attention, and people grow old fast. An hour a day of downright play would lengthen the lives of most people and make the life itself richer in enjoyment and in power. We invite our friends who are old in years but young in feeling, and those who desire to become so, to take a frolic occasionally with the young folks in these columns. Tell them a good story (let it be short), set them to puzzling over some ingenious problem, show them how to make a new toy—in short amuse them and yourselves at the same time, and thus secure a welcome benefit all around.

A Boy with his Eyes Open.

Many years ago, a lad thirteen years old was sent to school in a town on the coast of Ireland. Like other boys he often roamed by the seashore, collected shells, caught insects, picked up seaweed and gathered flowers, but, unlike most, while others forgot or threw them away, or only half observed them, he bore them in his thoughts, compared one with another, kept and reconsidered them, asked questions and looked at books, and so, by degrees, acquired information and a *habit of observation* which influenced the course of his whole life. Any boy could have done the same, but none of his companions did it, and so he only gained the distinction which such a course persevered in is sure to bring. One day he found a plant differing from any he had seen in all his careful observation of the surrounding country. He looked in botanical works, but could find no description of it, so at last he sent it to a distinguished botanist to learn its name. The gentleman not only cheerfully gave the information, but complimented him on his sharp-sightedness and close observation, which, of course, inspired him to new effort. Although he was soon called to enter business life, he continued to study nature with open eyes, and was soon rewarded by discovering new species of shells and plants. From one step to another he passed on, until he became the distinguished naturalist, Dr. W. H. Harvey, whose death is recorded in our recent foreign exchanges, accompanied by a sketch of his life. In the course of his studies he visited many parts of the globe, discovered and described a great number of new species, and enjoyed the highest respect of the scientific world. Boys, and girls too, *keep your eyes open*. There are thousands of undiscovered facts all over the world waiting for some careful sighted observer to note them, and by so doing to distinguish himself and benefit the race.

New Puzzles to be Answered.

No. 286. *Mathematical Problem.* Contributed to the *American Agriculturist* by A. J. Pierce.—A man has a spring at the bottom of an irregular hill. To reach it, he first descends by 6 steps, each 8 inches high and 6 inches wide; then walks along a level plane 21 feet, then descends an inclined plane 30 feet, depressing at an angle of 10 degrees from the horizontal; then descends another inclined plane 19½ feet in which at every 5 feet slope he descends 3 feet. Required, 1st, the whole horizontal distance; 2d, the perpendicular distance; 3d, the distance in a direct line; 4th, the angle of depression.

No. 287. *Illustrated Rebus.*—Very good advice to all.

No. 288. *Puzzle Picture.*—Why should there be eleven animals more of the same kind shown in this pen?

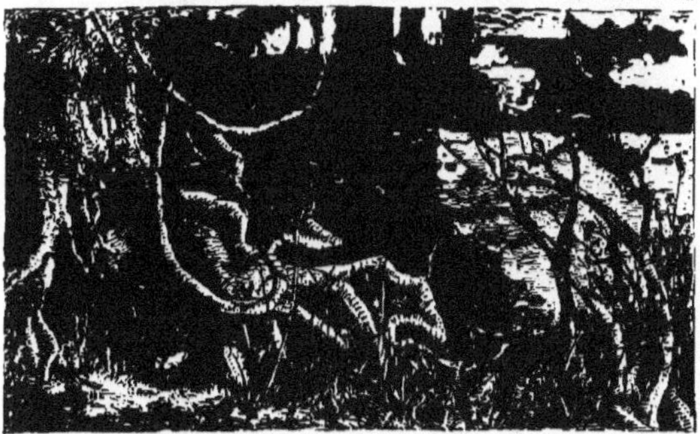

No. 289. *Puzzle Picture.*—The hare is evidently afraid to venture from his hole. Look carefully at the picture, and find where the danger lies; if successful, you can then enjoy seeing others of your friends look for it.

Answers to Problems and Puzzles.

The following are answers to the puzzles, etc., in the October number, page 373. No. 280. *Illustrated Rebus.*—

A man intent on charity,
Above base fear or discontent,
Twixt man and man sees nought amiss,
Nor sees a Judas in a kiss.

No. 281. *Illustrated Rebus.*—Baronet. No. 282. *Riddle.*—A Watch. No. 283. *Puzzle Picture.*—Oyster stew, (Oysters two). No. 284. *Puzzle Picture.* It is sole, (soul) is bent on it. The following have sent in correct answers to puzzles, etc., in October and former numbers. Alm. Lutz, Robert J. Phillips, L. W. Bridgers, S. M. Hunter, James Redwood, R. Baird, Wapsier, "Nubia," Benjamin Doe, (we don't know the article,) James W. Grath, J. A. Dawson, Augustus C. Beazby, "A. B. C.," M. H. Kelsey, R. L. Selden, John Ober, Ezra Hainbey, Adam Snyder, Matthew Simpson, J. R. Wilkinson, School Miss, Wilbur Buzzell, S. M. Hertzler, Frederic E. Willits, E. and Ellen L. Rankin, Andrew Jackson, "E. W.," "A. M.," "A. L. W. S.," Ollie M. Sake, Emma Davis, "Wide-asleep," W. H. Carter, Laura Dickson, Hugh C. Kay, George H. Lawrence, Samuel Dwight Drury, "Old Dominion," Thomas W. Raine, "G. H. C.," L. M. Wright, Mrs. George Bresner, E. T. Bell, J. Milton Snyder, Mary Vandegrist, Aaron B. Leach, Frank H. Marston, Cyrus T. Fox, C. Baker, John Kinsey, D. O. Jones, John McNeal, H. J. Mekel, M. G. Mullonry, E. Leonard.

"Papa," said a bright-eyed little girl one day, "I believe mamma loves you better'n she does me." Papa had his doubts upon the subject, but concluded it was not best to deny the charge. She meditated thoughtfully about it for some time, evidently construing her father's silence as unfavorable to her side of the question. "Well," said she at last, "I 'spose its all right; you're the biggest, and it takes more to love you."

Waiting, but not Watching.

It will take that jar a long time to fill, my little man, at the present rate. As long as it will for Mr. Spend-easy to get rich, or Mr. Fun-lover to grow learned. Things are not apt to prosper in this world unless they are properly watched on all sides, and the out-go as well as the income looked after. Evidently the boy is in no hurry; he appears very comfortable—by his looks we should say he had eaten a very good dinner. Perhaps, though, he is thinking of something more important than his water jar. Perhaps he is in a day dream, imagining himself riding in some fine coach he has watched passing his cottage home, or a tall soldier with gay clothes. We cannot read his thoughts, but whatever they are, our advice to him is: "Attend to the business in hand; let that be well done first." A boy who does this will gain a character that will almost insure success in whatever he undertakes. Think of this when there are chores to do, or lessons to learn, or an errand to attend to. If tempted to turn aside from the business in hand, think of the water-jar that was so long being filled.

[COPYRIGHT SECURED.]

WAITING, BUT NOT WATCHING.—*Drawn and Engraved for the American Agriculturist.*

About Bells.

Who invented bells? Perhaps Jubal and Tubal Cain. These brothers are mentioned in the Bible as being the first musicians, and the first metal workers. We only know, however, that bells were used very early in the history of man. They are mentioned by old Hebrew writers as being used by the priests in religious services. They have been associated with worship in almost all countries, being used mostly to call the people together. Among some sects bells receive a baptism with much ceremony before being used for the church service. Names have long been given to large bells in some parts of Europe. The tones of bells are associated with so many events, marriages, deaths, alarms, rejoicings, etc., it is not strange that they should awaken superstitious feelings and beliefs among the ignorant. In former times they were rung when thunder storms were approaching, to frighten away the evil spirits that were supposed to control the winds and the lightning.

Bells are made principally of copper and tin. Silver and gold have been employed, and iron has also been cast into bell form. They are also manufactured from steel, but thus far those of "bell metal," or copper and tin, are most numerous. In this country there are no bells of very large size, compared with the monsters that have been cast in Europe. The largest one here is said to be that once used for a fire bell at the City Hall Park, New York. It weighs about 20,000 lbs. It is said that when the bell previously used, weighing about 10,000 lbs., was broken, a proposition to replace it was opposed in the Common Council, because of the great cost of so large a one. Finally a member, by way of joke, moved that a bell of 20,000 lbs. be cast. One and another voted for it in sport, until the motion was carried; the Mayor approved it, and the bell was made. It had a deep, mellow, far reaching tone, being heard miles away, and in the night its voice telling of danger was solemn and impressive. It was cracked sometime since, and has recently been broken to pieces to be recast into four bells to weigh 5000 each. A bell weighing 29,400 lbs. hangs in the Notre Dame Cathedral in Montreal. Several bells in Europe weigh from 25,000 to 40,000 lbs. The Great Bell of Moscow, the largest ever cast, is estimated to weigh 443,772 lbs. The metal alone is worth over $300,000. It was cast in 1653, by order of Empress Anna, but was never hung. While yet in the pit where it was cast, the foundry above it was burned in the great conflagration of Moscow, while hot, water was poured upon it and a large piece was cracked out. It remained there for many years, until, in 1837, the Emperor Nicholas caused it to be raised and placed upon a granite pedestal. It has been consecrated as a chapel; the door is in the opening made by the piece falling out. Since the above was written, we have received some further particulars about this bell from Mr. Judd, who visited it.

Danger of Hasty Words.

A gentleman relates the following, which he witnessed recently while traveling in a stage in New Jersey. A man entered, followed by his wife and three children. It was easy to see by the flushed face and nervous manner of the lady that she had been greatly hurried to get herself and children ready. Presently the fare was asked for, and the lady began looking for her purse. It seems that the family were going in different directions at the end of the stage ride, and they had divided their funds accordingly. The purse could not be found. "I have left it on the table in my room," said the lady meekly. "Just like you," snarled out the man, "I do wish you'd be more careful." The poor woman said nothing, but her quivering lip spoke her feelings, and awakened the sympathies of all present. Meantime the man was fumbling for his pocket-book, first in one pocket, then another—three times he "went through" his clothes, but no money could be found. "I declare," exclaimed he, "if I haven't left my money at home too! So much for being in a hurry." A quiet twinkle took the place of the tear that had been struggling in the eye of his wife, and a hearty laugh burst from the passengers, who greatly enjoyed his discomfiture. The matter was at last arranged by a loan from a friend who knew the parties, and they went on their way with something to remember.

A Lesson in Politeness.

An elderly gentleman recently entered a street car in which the writer was riding. The seats were all occupied, and the new comer after glancing up and down the sides and finding no vacant place, took a position to stand as comfortably as possible. Just then a lad about twelve years old arose and insisted on the gentleman taking his seat, which the latter did, thanking the boy for his politeness. After riding a short distance, the gentleman took from his pocket a passage ticket and presented it to the boy, who at first declined it, but afterward took it, more to please the gentleman than to save his fare. "I want to encourage the boy in his politeness," remarked he, "by showing him that it is appreciated." Not long after an elderly woman with a little girl, probably her grand-daughter, entered the car. The old gentleman who was sitting near the door, immediately arose and gave her his place, which she took as a matter of course, without even saying "thank you." Presently a man sitting next to this woman left the car, and she immediately tried to pull her little girl into the vacant seat, although the old gentleman who had so gallantly yielded his place was now about to sit down again. "Madam," said he, sternly, "that is so piggish, I will not allow it!" and took the seat. The rebuke was severe, but well deserved. The contrast of politeness and selfishness, and the assertion of the claims of courtesy by the old gentleman, caused a smile to go around the car, and furnished a good lesson. It is in little things like this that real character is shown: he who is of kind disposition and refined feelings, will manifest it in his conduct even in trifles.

(Business Notices $2.50 per Agate Line of Space.)

HERALD OF HEALTH
FOR 1868.

THREE NUMBERS FREE!

Every person who values good habits, temperance, fine health, and who would secure for his or her children beauty, symmetry, fine vigorous constitutions, should subscribe.

The N. Y. Tribune says:

THE HERALD OF HEALTH well sustains the high standard it has held forth since the commencement of the new series.

Dr. DIO LEWIS, writes:

Dear Dr. Holbrook:—THE HERALD OF HEALTH delights us. The friends of Physiological Christianity must make it in circulation what you have made it in scope and spirit—cosmopolitan. I am deeply gratified with its broad, genial, catholic spirit.

MOSES COIT TYLER writes:

Everybody to whom I have shown it, of late, expresses astonishment and delight. People say: "Why, it's a grand Magazine—racy, practical, liberal, strong, and full, too, of all kinds of most important information!"

Our Monthly has been a great success in 1867. Those who subscribe at once for 1868 will get OCTOBER, NOVEMBER, and DECEMBER NUMBERS FREE. Those who send a Club of Thirty Subscribers for 1868 and $60 will get a Wheeler & Wilson Sewing Machine worth $55 as a premium. $2 a year; samples 20 cents.

MILLER, WOOD & CO.,
15 Laight St., New York.

THE NORTHWESTERN MUTUAL LIFE INSURANCE CO.,

OFFICE No. 410 MAIN STREET, MILWAUKEE, WIS.

HAS 18,000 MEMBERS AND $2,500,000 ASSETS;

thus ranking among the 25 New York companies *third* in number of members, *fifth* in amount of insurance, and *sixth* in amount of assets.

IT IS A PURELY MUTUAL COMPANY:

that is an ASSOCIATION OF POLICY-HOLDERS, managed by men selected BY THEMSELVES, FROM THEMSELVES, FOR THEMSELVES. Thus all officers and members are ALIKE INTERESTED, each one is a PARTNER in the whole business, entitled at any time to his share of the Company's funds, but by provisions of the charter is not liable beyond the premiums he has already paid. It thus adapts its plans to the benefit of its members, adopts all real improvements, and aims to be

A MODEL LIFE INSURANCE COMPANY.

It was one of the first to adopt the popular feature known in insurance circles as the NON-FORFEITING PLAN, and now APPLIES IT TO ALL the POLICIES IT ISSUES.

IT IS THE ONLY COMPANY that adopts the full benefit of the Note System, without doing a credit business or destroying the cash principle; and also gives the note privilege to the poor man, who needs it most and takes a small policy.

IT IS THE ONLY COMPANY (with one exception) that makes the FIRST payment on a ten premium policy secure its TENTH of the policy as well as each other payment.

IT IS THE ONLY COMPANY which gives a PROPORTIONATE amount of full-paid insurance after TWO annual premiums (if other premiums are not paid) on ordinary life and endowment policies.

IT WILL LOAN A MEMBER a sum equivalent to the surrender value of his policy; and thus often helps a member in extremity to keep his policy in force. Policy-holders permitted to travel anywhere in the United States or in Europe, but risks in the far South not sought.

Few appreciate the ADVANTAGE OF ITS LOCATION at the West, where the money can be SAFELY loaned at higher rates than at the East.

$1,000 LOANED FOR	50 YEARS AT	6	PER CENT.	PRODUCES	$	18,420 15.
$1,000 "	" 50 "	" 8	"	"		46,901 61.
$1,000 "	" 50 "	" 10	"	"		117,390 85.

And thinking men know that money can be loaned with care at the West (where nearly all property is rapidly enhancing in value) quite as SAFELY, if not MORE SAFELY, than in older communities. Therefore, as the rate of mortality is also low at the West, its

DIVIDENDS MUST BE LARGE.

Dividends made annually, to commence three years after date of the policy, but to equal in number the years of insurance, and

DISTRIBUTED TO POLICY-HOLDERS ONLY,

there being no Stockholders to absorb the Surplus or control the Company for selfish purposes.

AGENTS WANTED AT THE EAST.

For a Policy or an Agency apply to the officers.

HEBER SMITH, Gen'l Agent. S. S. DAGGETT, Pres't.
A. W. KELLOGG, Sec'y.

Exposition Universelle, *Paris, 1867.*
WHEELER & WILSON,
625 Broadway, New York.

AWARDED OVER EIGHTY-TWO COMPETITORS, THE HIGHEST PREMIUM,

FOR THE PERFECTION OF
SEWING MACHINES, and BUTTON-HOLE MACHINES.

The only Gold Medal for this Branch of Manufacture.

THE TEMPLE CHOIR.

A new collection of Church Music for Choirs and Singing Schools. By THEO. F. SEWARD, assisted by Dr. LOWELL MASON and WILLIAM B. BRADBURY. This is the first time these two most popular musical authors in the country have been united in one book. THE TEMPLE CHOIR has a very full Singing School Department, with 150 Glees, Rounds, Part Songs, etc., over 500 tunes of all meters, a large number of Anthems, Set Pieces, etc., for special occasions, social use, etc.; and is altogether one of the most complete collections of music ever published. Price, $1.50 each; $13.50 per dozen; $100 per hundred. A single copy will be sent for examination to any teacher of music, or leader of a choir, post-paid, for one dollar.

Published by MASON BROTHERS,
596 Broadway, New York.

CLIFTON SPRINGS, N. Y., May 7th, 1867.

Agent Florence Sewing Machine Co., Sir:—Having used the Florence Sewing Machine in our family for the past two years, we feel fully justified in pronouncing it the best family machine now in use. R. CASE.

Office and Sales Room, 505 Broadway, New York. Brooklyn Office, 431 Fulton-street.

THE ADVANCE,

The new national religious paper, has already secured a character and circulation worthy of its name. Rev. W. W. Patton, D.D., is its editor-in-chief, and among its special and its regular contributors are Rev Jos. P. Thompson, Rev Horace Bushnell, Prof. Tayler Lewis, Rev. J. P. Gulliver, Pres. G. F. Magoun, Rev. John Todd, Prof. Edwards A. Park, Rev. N. J. Burton, Pres. J. M. Sturtevant, Rev. Lyman Whiting, Rev. Leonard W. Bacon, Rev. Isaac P. Langworthy, Grace Greenwood, Sydney E. Holmes, Mrs. Julia P. Ballard, etc., etc.

SPLENDID PREMIUMS!

Are offered for Clubs of any size. Canvassers receive TWO DOLLARS in premiums for each subscriber. The Premium List includes *Solid Silver Ware, Ticknor & Fields' Books, Prang's Chromos, Anthony's Stereoscopes and Views, Mason & Hamlin's Organs, Gold and Silver "Elgin" Watches, Steck's Pianos, Bradley's Croquet Sets, Willcox & Gibbs and Florence Sewing Machines, Webster's Dictionaries, Craig's Microscopes, Lamb's Knitting Machines, etc.* Clubs are rushing in from all parts of the country. Those who start soonest do the best. Specimen copies sent free.

Address THE ADVANCE COMPANY.
25 Lombard Block, Chicago.

"FIGHTING AGAINST WRONG, and for THE GOOD, THE TRUE AND THE BEAUTIFUL."

THE Little Corporal

Is acknowledged by Press and People almost universally to be THE BEST PAPER for boys and GIRLS ever published in this country.

It is edited by ALFRED L. SEWELL, and EMILY HUNTINGTON MILLER.

Volumes begin July or January. Back Nos. [illegible] Terms, One Dollar a year; Sample copy ten cents.

GREAT INDUCEMENTS are offered to those who wish to raise clubs.

Address, ALFRED L. SEWELL, Publisher, Chicago, Ill.

All New Subscribers for 1868 sent to The Little Corporal during November will receive the December number of 1867 FREE.

A First Prize Medal at the

PARIS EXPOSITION has been awarded to the MASON & HAMLIN CABINET ORGANS, being the FIFTY-SEVENTH highest premium awarded them within a few years.

Sixty styles of these Organs are made, varying from $75 to $1,000 each. They are believed to be not only the best, but considering their quality, durability, &c., the cheapest instruments of the class in the world.

Circulars with full particulars free to any address.

MASON & HAMLIN,
596 Broadway New York; 154 Tremont-st., Boston.

SEE ADVERTISEMENT ON PAGE 42?—Valuable Plantation for Sale, and show it to your neighbors

A NEW BOOK.

THE GRAPE VINE.

By FREDERICK MOHR,

DOCTOR OF PHILOSOPHY AND MEDICINE.

Translated from the German, and accompanied with Hints on the Propagation and General Treatment of American Varieties.

By HORTICOLA.

This work is mainly devoted to the most elementary matters. It explains the structure and mode of growth of the vine so clearly that no intelligent person who reads it need be in doubt what to do with his vines. It has been well translated, and a chapter on the propagation of American varieties has been substituted for the original one on multiplying the European grape. As anatomy is the foundation of surgery, so is a knowledge of the structure of the vine to the vine dresser. In both cases it is as important to know when and where to cut, and how.

CONTENTS.

Development and Structure of the Grape Vine.
The Node; The Branch; Reasons for Pruning; Pruning.
Training on Trellises; Treatment in Summer; Plantations.
Vines Trained along the Garden Walk.
Trellises on Walls; Tree Trellises.
Vines Trained to Trellises; Brouner's Method.
Time Required for Covering a Trellis.
Manuring the Vine; Age of Vineyard.
The Rising Sap in the Vine; The Grape Disease.
Treatment of Vines Injured by Frost.
Implements; Proper Time to Perform Work on the Vine.
Constituents of the Vine and their Distribution.
Propagation of the Vine: By Layers; By Cuttings; By Grafting; By Inarching; By Seeds.
Hybridization.
American Varieties—General Management; Planting; Pruning; Pinching; Covering in Fall.

SENT POST-PAID. . . . . PRICE, $1.00.

ORANGE JUDD & Co.,
245 Broadway and 41 Park Row, N. Y.

A NEW WORK.

SMALL FRUIT CULTURIST.

By ANDREW S. FULLER,

PRACTICAL HORTICULTURIST, RIDGEWOOD, BERGEN CO., N. J.

A new work, and the only one devoted to Small Fruits. Special treatises of this kind have the advantage that the author can more thoroughly discuss his subject, and go into greater detail, than in a work embracing both large and small fruits. The work covers the whole ground of Propagation, Culture, Varieties, Packing for Market, etc.

CONTENTS: INTRODUCTION—I. BARBERRY—II. STRAWBERRY—III. RASPBERRY—IV. BLACKBERRY—V. DWARF CHERRY—VI. CURRANT—VII. GOOSEBERRY—VIII. CORNELIAN CHERRY—IX. CRANBERRY—X. HUCKLEBERRY—XI. SHEPERDIA—XII. PREPARATION FOR GATHERING FRUIT.

We predict that this work will bring Mr. Fuller many enemies, as he has given his opinion about varieties without reserve. On the other hand it will the more strongly endear him to all true lovers of horticulture, as these wish to have the merits of fruit given without reference to the persons who introduce them.

While very full on all the small fruits, the Currants and Raspberries have been more carefully elaborated than ever before, and in this important part of his book, the author has had the invaluable counsel of Charles Downing. The chapter on gathering and packing fruit is a valuable one, and in it are figured all the baskets and boxes now in common use. The book is very finely and thoroughly illustrated, and makes an admirable companion to his Grape Culturist.

SENT POST-PAID. PRICE, $1.50

NEW YORK:

ORANGE JUDD & CO.,
245 BROADWAY and 41 PARK ROW.

DRAINING FOR PROFIT

AND

DRAINING FOR HEALTH.

By GEO. E. WARING, Jr.,

ENGINEER OF THE DRAINAGE OF CENTRAL PARK, NEW YORK.

Illustrated.

TABLE OF CONTENTS:

LAND TO BE DRAINED AND THE REASONS WHY.—Indications of the need of draining.—Sources of water.—Objections to too much water.—Wet sub-soil.

HOW DRAINS ACT AND HOW THEY AFFECT THE SOIL.—Characteristics of well laid tile drain.—Surface-water and rain water beneficial, springs and soakage water injurious.—Cracking of stiff clays.—Evaporation and filtration.—Rain fall.—Evaporation.—Temperature.—Drought.—Porosity or mellowness.—Chemical action in the soil.

HOW TO GO TO WORK TO LAY OUT A SYSTEM OF DRAINS.—Amateur draining.—Maps.—Levelling instruments.—Outlets and location of drains.—Main drains.—Spring water.—Fall.—Tiles.—Depth and distance apart.—Direction of laterals.—Collars.—Discharge of water from drains.

HOW TO MAKE THE DRAINS.—Tools.—Marking the lines.—Water courses.—Outlet.—Silt Basins.—Opening the ditches.—Grading.—Tile laying.—Connections.—Covering the tile and filling in.—Collecting the water of springs.—Amending the map.

HOW TO TAKE CARE OF DRAINS AND DRAINED LAND.—Removing obstructions.—Mistake of substituting large tiles for small ones which have become obstructed.—Heavy lands should not be trampled while wet.

WHAT DRAINING COSTS. Draining, expensive work.—Their permanence and lasting effects.—Cheapness versus economy.—Details of cost.—(1. Engineering and Superintendence.—2. Digging the ditches.—3. Grading the bottoms.—4. Tile and tile laying.—5. Covering and filling.—6. Outlets and Silt Basins.)

WILL IT PAY? Increased crops required to pay cost of draining.—(Corn, Wheat, Rye, Oats, Potatoes, Barley, Hay, Cotton, Tobacco.)—Instances of profit.—Benefit of draining in facilitating farm work.

HOW TO MAKE DRAINING TILES. Materials.—Preparation of earths.—Moulding tile machines.—Drying and rolling.—Burning.—Kilns.—General arrangement of a tilery.

THE RECLAIMING OF SALT MARSHES.—Extent of marshes on the Atlantic Coast.—The English Fens.—Harlaem Lake.—The exclusion of sea water.—Removal of the causes of inundation from the upland.—Removal of rain fall and water of filtration.—Embankments.—Muskrats.—Rivers and Creeks.—Outlet of drainage.

MALARIAL DISEASES. Fever and Ague.—Neuralgia.—Vicinity of New York.—Dr. Bartlett on Periodical Fever.—Dr. Metcalf's Report to U. S. Sanitary Commission.—La Roche on the effects of Malarial Fever.—Dr. Salisbury on the "Cause of Malarial Fevers."—English experience.—Reports to the British Parliament.—Cause of Malaria removed by draining.

HOUSE AND TOWN DRAINAGE. Sewerage.—The use of pipes.—The new outfall sewers in London.—The use of steam pumps to secure outlets.—Utilization of sewage matters in agriculture.—Effects of imperfect house drainage on health.—Typhoid fever.—The Westminster fever in London.—Epidemic at the Maplewood Young Ladies Institute in Pittsfield, Mass.—Lambeth Square, London.—Back drainage.—Water supply.—General Board of Health, (England).

SENT POST-PAID. PRICE, $1.50.

ORANGE JUDD & CO.,
245 Broadway and 41 Park Row, N. Y.

COPELAND'S COUNTRY LIFE.

A Compendium

of

Agricultural & Horticultural

Practical Knowledge.

Embracing Descriptions, Hints, Suggestions and Details of great value to every one interested in Fruit, Flowers, Vegetables, or Farm Crops. It contains 926 *large Octavo Pages*, and 250 *Engravings*. Describing and Illustrating nearly the whole range of topics of interest to the FARMER, the GARDENER, the FRUIT CULTURIST, and the AMATEUR.

It is adapted not only to those owning large and Elegant Estates, but contains directions for the best arrangement of the smallest Plot, down to the *City Yard*, the *Roof* or Window Garden, or the simple Flower Stand. It also gives an abstract of the Principles, Construction and Management of Aquariums. Among numerous other matters it treats of

Draining. Giving best methods, estimates of cost, trenches, tiles, etc., thus enabling almost any one properly to perform this important work.

Cattle are carefully noticed with reference to the special merits of different breeds for dairying or fattening.

Sheep Management, including Breeding, Feeding, Prices, Profits, etc., receives attention, and a very full treatise on the Merinos is given.

Grape Culture occupies a large space, embracing the opinions of men in all parts of the country, as to best sorts, planting, training, diseases, and general management for house use or for market.

Full Lists of Ornamental Trees and Shrubs, Fruits, Flowers, Green and Hot-house Plants, etc., are given, with directions for management each month in the year.

The Kitchen Garden receives particular attention, with reference to the best way to grow and preserve each kind of Vegetable.

In short, as its name indicates, the book *treats of almost every subject that needs consideration by those* living in the country, or having anything to do with the cultivation of the soil.

SENT POST-PAID. PRICE $5.00.

ORANGE JUDD & CO.,
245 Broadway and 41 Park Row, N. Y.

New Book of Flowers.

By JOSEPH BRECK, Practical Horticulturist.

Beautifully Illustrated.

This work, while preserving scientific accuracy, is written in a familiar style, and with the enthusiasm of a life-long lover of flowers. Its teachings are eminently practical, and cover all branches of out of door gardening.

Bulbs.

The cultivation of bulbs, whether in-doors or in the open ground, is clearly described, and such instructions are given as will insure success with these favorite plants.

Annuals.

All the finer annuals are described, and the peculiar treatment necessary for each given in full.

Herbaceous Perennials.

This justly favorite class of plants is given here more at length than in any work with which we are acquainted.

Bedding Plants.

The treatment of the popular kinds of bedding plants is given, together with that of Dahlias, Chrysanthemums and such as usually fall under the head of florist's flowers.

Flowering Shrubs.

A separate section is devoted to the hardy flowering shrubs, including a very full chapter upon the

Rose.

We have no work which is so safe a guide to the novice in gardening, or that imparts the necessary information in a style so free from technicalities. Not the least interesting part of the work is the author's personal experience, as he tells not only how he succeeded, but the mistakes he committed. Thus far it is

"The Book of Flowers."

SENT POST-PAID. PRICE, $1.75.

ORANGE JUDD & CO., Publishers.

WARDER'S
Hedges and Evergreens.

This is the only book wholly devoted to the cultivation, pruning, and management of plants suitable for American hedging, especially the Maclura, or OSAGE ORANGE; illustrated with engravings of plants, implements, and processes; to which is added a *Treatise on Evergreens*, their varieties, propagation, culture, etc. By J. A. WARDER. 12mo, 291 pp.

SENT POST-PAID. PRICE $1.50.

ORANGE JUDD & CO., Publishers.

BUIST'S
American Flower-Garden Directory.

Containing Practical Directions for the Culture of Plants in the Flower-Garden, Hot-House, Green-House, Rooms or Parlor Windows, FOR EVERY MONTH IN THE YEAR, with descriptions of most desirable plants, soils, transplanting, erecting a Hot-House, a Green-House, laying out a Flower-Garden, etc., etc. By ROBERT BUIST, a practical Nurseryman and Seed-Grower of Philadelphia. Cloth, 12mo.

SENT POST-PAID. PRICE $1.50.

ORANGE JUDD & CO., Publishers.

BOMMER'S
Method of Manure Making

COMPLETE AND CLEAR IN ITS DIRECTIONS.

Carries Conviction of its usefulness, and the correctness of its principles

GIVES GREAT SATISFACTION.

Abundance of Good Manure depends simply upon systematic and well applied labor.

ENGLISH AND GERMAN. PRICE, [illegible]

ORANGE JUDD & CO.,
245 Broadway and 41 Park Row, N. Y.

BOOKS FOR FARMERS and OTHERS.

[Published and for sale by Orange Judd & Co., 245 Broadway, New York. Any of these books will be forwarded by mail, post-paid, on receipt of price.]

Allen's (L. F.) Rural Architecture	$1 50
Allen's (R. L.) American Farm Book	1 50
Allen's (R. L.) Diseases of Domestic Animals	1 00
American Agricultural Annual, 1867, pa., 50 cts., cloth	75
American Horticultural Annual, 1867, pa., 50 cts., cloth	75
American Bird Fancier	30
American Pomology, by Dr. J. A. Warder	3 00
American Rose Culturist	30
American Weeds and Useful Plants	1 75
Architecture, by Cummings & Miller	10 00
Bement's Rabbit Fancier	30
Bommer's Method of Making Manures	25
Boussingault's Rural Economy	1 60
Breck's New Book of Flowers	1 75
Buist's Flower Garden Directory	1 50
Buist's Family Kitchen Gardener	1 00
Chorlton's Grape Grower's Guide	75
Cobbett's American Gardener	75
Cole's (S. W.) American Fruit Book	75
Cole's Veterinarian	75
Cotton Planter's Manual (Turner)	1 50
Country Life, by R. M. Copeland	5 00
Dadd's (Geo. H.) Modern Horse Doctor	1 50
Dadd's American Cattle Doctor	1 50
Dana's Muck Manual	1 25
Dog and Gun (Hooper's) ... paper, 30c ... cloth	60
Downing's Landscape Gardening	6 50
Draining for Profit and Health, by G. E. Waring Jr.	1 50
Eastwood on Cranberry	75
Elliott's Western Fruit Grower's Guide	1 50
Field's (Thomas W.) Pear Culture	1 25
Flax Culture	50
French's Farm Drainage	1 50
Fuller's Grape Culturist	1 50
Fuller's Small Fruit Culturist	1 50
Fuller's Strawberry Culturist	20
Gardening for Profit, by Peter Henderson	1 50
Grape Vine, by Prof. F. Mohr	1 00
Gregory on Squashes ... paper	30
Guenon on Milch Cows	75
Herbert's Hints to Horsekeepers	1 75
Hop Culture	40
Johnston's Agricultural Chemistry	1 75
Johnston's Elements of Agricultural Chemistry	1 50
Leuchar's How to Build Hot-houses	1 50
Miles on the Horse's Foot	75
My Vineyard at Lakeview	1 25
Norton's Scientific Agriculture	75
Onion Culture	20
Our Farm of Four Acres ... paper, 30c ... cloth	60
Pardee on Strawberry Culture	75
Peat and Its Uses, by Prof. S. W. Johnson	1 25
Pedder's Land Measurer	60
Quinby's Mysteries of Bee keeping	1 50
Randall's Sheep Husbandry	1 50
Randall's Fine Wool Sheep Husbandry	1 00
Richardson on the Dog ... paper 30 cents ... cloth	60
Rivers' Miniature Fruit Garden	1 00
Rural Annual, by Joseph Harris	25
Rural Annual (Harris) 8 Nos., bound, 2 Vols. ... Each	1 50
Saunders' Domestic Poultry ... paper, 40 c. bound	75
Schenck's Gardener's Text Book	75
Skillful Housewife	75
Stewart's (John) Stable Book	1 50
Thompson's Food of Animals	1 00
Tobacco Culture	25
Todd's (S. E.) Young Farmer's Manual	1 50
Warder's Hedges and Evergreens	1 50
Youatt and Spooner on the Horse	1 50
Youatt and Martin on Cattle	1 50
Youatt on the Hog	1 00
Youatt on Sheep	1 00

O. J. & Co. keep in Stock the following Books:

Art of Saw Filing (Holly)	75
Barry's Fruit Garden	1 75
Bement's Poulterer's Companion	2 00
Bridgeman's Young Gardener's Assistant	2 50
Brandt's Age of Horses, (English or German)	50
Burr's Vegetables of America	5 00
Carpenter's and Joiner's Hand Book (Holly)	75
Dead Shot; or Sportsman's Complete Guide; Engravings from Frank Forester	1 75
Downing's Cottage Residences	3 00
Downing's Fruits and Fruit Trees of America	3 00
Downing's Rural Essays	5 00
Flint (Charles L.) on Grasses	2 50
Flint's Milch Cows and Dairy Farming	2 50
Frank Forester's Horse and Horsemanship, 8vo., gilt backs, 2 vols	20 00
Frank Forester's Field Sports, 8vo., tinted paper, gilt backs, 2 vols	7 50
Frank Forester's Fish and Fishing, 8vo., gilt back, 100 engravings	5 00
Frank Forester's Complete Manual for Young Sportsmen, Crown 8vo., gilt back	3 00
Fuller's Forest Tree Culturist	1 50
Gray's How Plants Grow	1 25
Gray's Manual of Botany and Lessons in one Vol.	4 00
Haraszthy's Grape Culture and Wine Making	5 00
Harris' Insects Injurious to Vegetation, plain 4.00, col'd	5 00
Hatfield's American House Carpenter	3 50
Husmann's Grapes & Wine	1 50
Jennings' Horse Training Made Easy	1 25
Jennings on Cattle	1 75
Jennings on Sheep, Swine, and Poultry	1 75
Jennings on the Horse and his Diseases	1 75
Johnson's (Prof. S. W.) Essays on Manures	1 25
Kemp's Landscape Gardening	2 00
Langstroth on the Honey Bee	2 00
Mayhew's Illustrated Horse Doctor	3 50
Mayhew's Illustrated Horse Management	3 50
Mayhew's Practical Book-Keeping for Farmers	90
Blanks for do. do.	1 20
McMahon's American Gardener	2 25
Morrell's American Shepherd	1 75
Parkman's Book of Roses	3 00
Parsons on the Rose	1 50
Quincy, (Hon. Josiah) on Soiling Cattle	1 25
Rand's Bulbs	3 00
Rand's Flowers for Parlor and Garden	3 00
Rand's Garden Flowers	3 00
Register of Rural Affairs ... (bound) ... 4 Vols. ... each	1 50
Scribner's Ready Reckoner and Log Book	30
Silloway's Modern Carpentry	2 00
Strong's Grape Culture	3 00
Ten Acres Enough	1 50
The Dog, By Dinks, Mayhew, and Hutchinson.—Edited by Frank Forester, Crown 8vo.	3 00
Tucker's Register of Rural Affairs	30
Vaux's Villas and Cottages	3 00
Watson's American Home Garden	2 00
Woodward's Annual, 1867 ... Paper, 75c., cloth,	1 00
Wheeler's Homes for the People	1 50
Woodward's Graperies, &c	1 50
Youmans's Household Science	2 00

HINTS TO HORSE-KEEPERS,

A COMPLETE

MANUAL FOR HORSEMEN.

BY THE LATE HENRY WILLIAM HERBERT.

(FRANK FORESTER.)

Beautifully Illustrated.

HOW TO BREED A HORSE.—

CHOICE OF STALLION.—National Value of the Horse—The best class of Horses the cheapest for all purposes—What constitutes excellence—Blood: what it gives; should be on the side of the Sire—Breed up, not down—Diseases and Defects Hereditary—General Rules.

CHOICE OF THE MARE.—Size, Symmetry and Soundness more important than Blood—Points of the Brood Mare—Diseases Hereditary—Condition of the Mare—Should have moderate work when with Foal—Food and care during gestation—Health and temper.

MUTUAL ADAPTATION OF SIRE AND DAM.—First consideration in Improvement of "cold" Blood—Relative size of Sire and Dam—Defects in either Parent—How Remedied in Progeny—Bloods which "hit."

CANADIAN BLOOD.—The Canadian originally the French Norman—Characteristics—Hardihood—Speed—Mode of Improvement—Crossing with Thorough-breds.

NORMAN BLOOD.—Origin and History of the Percheron Norman—A pure race—Characteristics and Points.

MODERN ARAB BLOOD.—English and American Thorough-breds derived from Oriental Blood—are now superior to the Modern Arabs—Nolan Arab.

PONIES — DIFFERENT BREEDS,

CHARACTERISTICS AND UTILITY.—Origin—Different Breeds—Shetlands and Scots—Galloways and Narragansetts—Mustangs and Indians—Profit of raising Ponies.

HOW TO BREED MULES.

Value of Mules—Their History and Natural History—The Mule and Hinney—Thorough-blood wasted in the Dam for Mules—The Mule in the United States—Large size not Desirable—Varieties of the Ass—The kind of Mares to be selected.

HOW TO BUY A HORSE.

Of whom to Buy it—Extraordinary Cheapness and Extraordinary Excellence not consistent with each other—Points to be regarded—How to Examine the Eye—Broken Wind—Roaring—Whistling—Broken Knees—To examine the Legs—Splents—Damaged Back Sinews—Spavins—Ringbones—Curbs—How to tell the Age of a Horse.

HOW TO FEED A HORSE.

Consequences of Improper Feeding—Different Food for different conditions—Food for the Brood Mare—for the Foal—For Working Horses—Green Food—Carrots—Corn—Feeding Horses in Training—While Travelling—Summering Horses—The Best Method—Management of Omnibus Horses in New York.

HOW TO STABLE AND GROOM A HORSE.—Requisites for a good Stable—The economy of Proper Arrangements—Ventilation—Grooming; its necessity for all descriptions of Horses—How Performed—Clothing—Treatment when brought in from Work.

HOW TO BREAK, AND USE A HORSE.—What is required in a well-broken Horse—His education should commence when a Colt—Bitting—Putting in Harness—How to Use a Horse—Travelling—Working—Pleasure Horses—Punishment.

HOW TO PHYSIC A HORSE—

SIMPLE REMEDIES FOR SIMPLE AILMENTS.—Causes of Ailments—Medicines to be given only by the order of the Master—Depletion and Purging—Spasmodic Colic—Inflammation of the Bowels—Inflammation of the Lungs—How to Bleed—Balls and Purgatives—Costiveness—Cough—Bronchitis—Distemper—Worms—Diseases of the Feet—Scratches—Thrush—Broken Knees.

FARRIERY, ETC.

Castration—Docking and Nicking—Blood-letting—Treatment of Strains and Wounds—Galls of the Skin—Cracked Heels—Clipping and Singeing—Administering Medicines—Diseases of the Foot.

HOW TO SHOE A HORSE.

Unskillful Shoers—Anatomy of the Foot Illustrated—The Foot of a Colt—Preparation of the Foot—Removing the Old Shoe—Paring the Foot—The Shoe—Fitting the Shoe—Nailing—Number of Nails—Diseases of the Foot.

BAUCHER'S METHOD OF TRAINING HORSES.—What Constitutes a Well-trained Horse—To make him come at your call—The Philosophy of Training—Flexions of the Jaw—Flexions of the Neck—Flexions of the Croup—Backing—The Paces—Leaping.

HOW TO RIDE A HORSE.

The Saddle—The Girths—The Stirrups—Saddle-Cloth—The Crupper—The Martingale—The Bridle—Spurs—Mounting and Dismounting—The Seat—The Hands—The Leg—The Paces—Hints for Special Cases—The Art of Falling—Riding with Ladies.

LADIES' RIDING—WRITTEN BY A LADY.—Learning to Ride—The Side-saddle—The Girths—The Stirrup—The Bridle—The Martingale—The Bit—The Dress—Mounting and Dismounting—The Position—The Hands—The Leg and Whip—Accidents.

HOW TO DRIVE A HORSE.

The Art of Driving—Pleasure Driving—How to Hold the Reins—Driving a Pair—Four-in-hand Driving—Driving Working Horses—Plowing—Three-a-breast.

RAREY'S SYSTEM OF HORSE-TAMING.—Rarey's System a New Discovery—Previous Systems—Principles of this System—Instructions for Practicing Rarey's Method—To Stable the Horse—To Approach the Horse—Tying up the Leg—Laying the Horse Down—Finale—Vices and Bad Habits—Rearing—Kicking—Baulking—Pulling on the Halter—Shying.

VETERINARY HOMŒOPATHY.

Principles of the System—Table of Remedies—General Directions—Treatment of a Sick Animal—Diet—Remedies for Specific Cases—Glossary of Diseases.

12mo. 425 pp.—Sent by mail post-paid. $1.75.

ORANGE JUDD & CO.,

245 Broadway and 41 Park Row, N. Y.

NEW BOOKS.

Saunders' Domestic Poultry.

By S. M. SAUNDERS.

New Edition Revised and Enlarged.

This Book contains Articles on the Preferable Breeds of Farm-Yard Poultry, Their History and Leading Characteristics, with Complete Instructions for Breeding and Fattening, and Preparing for Exhibition at Poultry Shows, etc., etc., derived from the Author's Experience and Observation.

The work is compact, full of valuable hints and information, and beautifully illustrated.

An appendix contains an account of *Poultry breeding on a large scale*, as practiced in the neighborhood of Paris, and is a very important addition to the work.

Price, paper 40 cts., cloth 75 cts.

ORANGE JUDD & CO., Publishers.

Money in the Swamps.

PEAT! PEAT! PEAT!

FUEL—MANURE.

WHERE TO FIND IT.

HOW TO MAKE AND USE IT.

ITS VALUE.

A NEW WORK ON PEAT,

THOROUGH AND PRACTICAL;

By PROF. SAMUEL W. JOHNSON, of Yale College.

(It gives a full history of **PEAT, MUCK**, etc., telling what they are, where found, and how to estimate their value.

It describes the various methods of using Peat for manure, as an absorbent, as an ameliorator of the soil, etc. and it is especially explicit in regard to the

USE OF PEAT AS FUEL,

describing minutely the various processes employed in preparing it to burn, from the simplest to the most complicated; such as are in use in this country, and Europe. It is illustrated with many Engravings of machines, etc.

The work is invaluable to those having Peat or Muck swamps, or wishing to invest in Peat Companies.

SENT POST-PAID. - - PRICE $1.25

ORANGE JUDD & CO.,

245 Broadway and 41 Park Row, N. Y.

The Miniature Fruit Garden,

OR THE CULTURE OF

Pyramidal and Bush Fruit Trees.

BY THOMAS RIVERS.

Nothing is more gratifying than the cultivation of dwarf fruit trees, and this work tells how to do it successfully.

Dwarf Apples and Pears

are beautiful ornaments, besides being useful in giving abundant crops of fruit; they can be grown in

Small Gardens and City Yards,

and be readily removed. The work also gives the manner of training upon walls and trellises.

Root Pruning

is fully explained, and methods of protection from frosts are given.

Dwarf Cherries and Plums

are treated of as are other dwarf trees. Directions are also given for growing

Figs and Filberts.

This little work is full of suggestions to the cultivator, and like all the writings of its venerable author, bears the marks of long experience in the practice of fruit growing.

SENT POST-PAID. - - - PRICE, $1.00

ORANGE JUDD & CO., Publishers.

My Vineyard at Lakeview;

Or, Successful Grape Culture.

To any one who wishes to grow grapes, whether a single vine or a vineyard, this book is full of valuable teachings. The author gives not only his success, but what is of quite as much importance, his failure. It tells just what the beginner in grape culture wishes to know, with the charm that always attends the relation of personal experience.

It is especially valuable as giving an account of the processes actually followed in

Celebrated Grape Regions

in Western New York and on the shores and islands of Lake Erie.

This book is noticed by a writer in the Horticulturist for August last as follows: "Two works very different in character and value have just been published and seem to demand a passing notice. The better and less pretentious of the two is 'My Vineyard at Lakeview,' a charming little book that professes to give the actual experience of a western grape grower, detailing not only his successes, but his blunders and failures. It is written in a pleasant style, without any attempt at display, and contains much advice that will prove useful to a beginner—the more useful, because derived from the experience of a man who had no leisure for fanciful experiments, but has been obliged to make his vineyard support himself and his family."

SENT POST-PAID. - - - PRICE $1.50.

ORANGE JUDD & CO.,

245 Broadway and 41 Park Row, N. Y.

SUBSCRIBE NOW FOR 1868 AND GET REMAINDER OF 1867 FREE.

THE HORTICULTURIST.

TWENTY-THIRD ANNUAL VOLUME, 1868.

A MONTHLY MAGAZINE DEVOTED TO

Horticulture, Agriculture and Architecture.

400 Royal Octavo Pages Annually --- Ably Edited and Splendidly Illustrated.

OUR TERMS FOR 1868 ARE AS FOLLOWS:

One Copy one Year - -	$ 2.50
Three Copies - - -	5.00
Ten Copies - - -	15.00
Vol. 1867, bound and post-paid, and Nos. 1868 - -	$4.00
Vols. 1866 and 1867, bound and post-paid, and Nos. 1868.	5.50
Vols. 1865, 1866 and 1867, bound and post-paid, and Nos. 1868 - - - -	7.00

PREMIUMS.

We will send the *American Agriculturist* one year, or any book or periodical of the value of $1.50, to any person who remits us Five Dollars for three new subscribers.

We will send *Harpers' Weekly* or *Monthly* or the *Atlantic Monthly* one year, or any books or periodicals of the value of $4.00, to any person who remits us Fifteen Dollars for ten new subscribers.

We will send a $55.00 *Wheeler & Wilson* or *Howe* Sewing Machine to any person who remits us $60.00 for twenty-four subscribers, at $2.50 each; or $90.00 for sixty subscribers at $1.50 each; or $125.00 for one hundred subscribers at $1.25 each.

Parties desiring other premiums will please say what they wish; we will state the number of subscribers necessary to procure them.

F. W. WOODWARD, Publisher.

37 Park Row, New York.

ARCHITECTURE

& Rural Art, No. Two, post-paid $1.50

NEW DESIGNS for COUNTRY HOUSES.

GEO. E. WOODWARD, 191 Broadway, N.Y.

All Books on Architecture. Catalogue Free

A WHEELER & WILSON SEWING MACHINE for nothing. An extraordinary Premium of a new Wheeler & Wilson Sewing Machine for only 20 subscribers to DEMOREST'S MONTHLY MAGAZINE.

HEADQUARTERS

FOR

Original Kittatinny

BLACKBERRY PLANTS.

The very BEST Blackberry extant.

We have also the WILSON EARLY, and a good stock of the best Raspberries, Strawberries, Currants, Grapes, &c.

Price list gratis. Address

E. & J. C. WILLIAMS,
Montclair, N. J.

NEW RASPBERRY,

The AUTUMN BLACK.—A new Seedling of great promise, producing a fine crop of fruit in July, and a bountiful one in the fall, continuing until winter. Plants, by mail, $1 each. Send for descriptive Circular.

H. D. LUM, Sandusky, O.

Adirondac Grape Nursery and Vineyard.

We offer at greatly reduced prices, a large stock of grape vines, one, two, and three years. All desirable varieties—including the two new Hybrids, "SALEM," and "DIANA HAMBURG." Quality of vines unsurpassed. Our autumn Price List and Descriptive Catalogue, or Wholesale Price List for the trade, sent on application.

JOHN W. BAILEY & CO., Plattsburgh, Clinton Co., N. Y.

DOOLITTLE RASPBERRY PLANTS—800,000 for sale, low.

OSBORNE & SONS,
Benton Harbor, Mich.

BLOOMINGTON NURSERY.

16th year, 10 Green-houses, 350 Acres Fruit, Ornamental and Nursery Stock, General Assortment.

1,000,000 Apple, 1 to 4 years, superb yearlings, 1000, $50.
150,000 Pear, Stand. and Dw'f. *Dw'f. Apple*, all sizes.
40,000 Cherry, largely Richmond or May, 100, $15 to $35.
30,000 Peach, Hale's Early, &c., 1000, $125.
300,000 Grape, strong Concord layers, 1000, $85; Hartford layers, 1000, $150; Ives, $150; Rogers, Iona, &c.
5,000,000 Osage Orange, 1st class, 100,000, $200.
50,000 Currant, Gooseberry and Raspberry.
30,000 Kittatinny Blackberry, warranted genuine, strong, first class every way, 1000, $150. (See separate advertisement.)
1,000,000 Apple Stock, extra, selected 1 year, 1000, $10.
50,000 Pear Stock, fine, 1 year, 1000, $25; Quince, Cherry.
30,000 Roses, all classes, Marshal Neil, fine plants, $9 per doz.; Evergreens, immense stock, Tulips, Hyacinths, and other Hardy Bulbs. Send 2 red stamps for New Descriptive and Trade List.

F. K. PHŒNIX, Bloomington, Ill.

REID'S NURSERIES,

Elizabeth, New Jersey.

For sale at low prices, the following trees, which are first class in every respect.

200,000	Standard and Dwarf Pears, 1, 2 & 3 yrs. old,	extra fine.		
50,000	Standard and Dw'f Apples, 1, 2 & 3 yrs. old,	"	"	
50,000	Standard and Dw'f Cherries, 1, 2 & 3 yrs. old,	"	"	
50,000	Peaches, . . . 1 year old,	"	"	
20,000	Kittatinny Blackberries, 1 year old,	"	"	

Also, a large collection of Currants, Raspberries, Gooseberries, Grapes, Asparagus, &c., &c. A large and complete stock of Ornamental Trees, Shrubs, &c., &c.

An examination of the above stock by dealers and others who wish to purchase in quantities, is respectfully solicited.

Catalogues just published with prices annexed, forwarded on application.

DAVID D. BUCHANAN,
Successor to Wm. Reid.

GRAPE VINES.

A large assortment of Strong, Healthy Vines, propagated in open air. Also, Grape Wood. Prices *low*. Send for Circular.

S. J. ALLIS, North East, Pa.

Early Goodrich and Harison Potatoes.

Warranted pure, for sale in large or small quantities, by

JAMES THORNTON, Byberry, Philadelphia, Pa.

YOUNG FARMERS MANUAL

Vol. 1. The Farm and the Work Shop. Fully illustrated, handsomely bound. New edition, post-paid, $1.50.

Vol. 2. Just published. How to Make Farming Pay. Post-paid, $2.50. F. W. WOODWARD, Agricultural Book Publisher, 37 Park Row, New York.

FOREST TREES

A new work on the Cultivation of Forest Trees for profit. Post-paid, $1.50. F. W. WOODWARD, Agricultural Book Publisher, 37 Park Row, New York.

IONA AND ISRAELLA GRAPES.

It is a fact worthy of the attention of all who are about to plant vines, that the Iona and Israella Grapes have been rapidly gaining in reputation despite of all adverse interests and consequent efforts at disparagement, while all others have been losing in comparison.

The few adverse reports of last season should have included all other kinds also, for all of the same age suffered equally, and none would have suffered at all under the proper course of management as directed in "The Manual."

From all the great West, (with exception only of part of Missouri), as well as from all other quarters generally, we have the same favorable reports, (from good plants under fair treatment), while the quality of the fruit distances all competitors for table and for wine. Israella is also an excellent wine-grape, as shown by trial.

I offer vines for garden and vineyard of excellent quality at most favorable rates to purchasers.

For Price Lists and account of performance as shown by testimonials from all quarters, send stamp.

"Manual of the Vine," a full, thorough treatise, most profusely illustrated, sent for fifty cents.

C. W. GRANT,
Iona, near Peekskill, Westchester Co., N. Y.

Spring Valley Nurseries.

The best stock of grape vines I have ever grown, at very low prices for the quality of the plants.

Send for prices or Catalogue. J. F. DELIOT,
Vine Grower, Sing Sing, N. Y.

BUIST'S GARDEN MANUAL AND

ALMANAC for 1868, is out. This is an indispensable little work, and should be had by every cultivator of the garden; 50,000 copies were published for 1867, which did not supply more than half the demand. Copies mailed gratis—enclose red stamp for postage to

ROBERT BUIST, JR.,
Seed Warehouse 922 & 924 Market-st.,
PHILADELPHIA, PA.

SMALL FRUITS EXTREMELY LOW,

AND CHARGES PREPAID BY EXPRESS.

KITTATINNY and PHILADELPHIA Raspberry, $3 per doz.; $20 per 100. EARLY WILSON Blackberry, $6 per doz.; $45 per 100. CLARKE Raspberry, $3 per doz.; $20 per 100. DAVIDSON'S THORNLESS, $3 per doz.; $20 per 100. CRYSTAL WHITE Blackberry, fine yielder, hardy, and extremely beautiful and delicious, $9 per 100. MIAMI BLACK CAP Raspberry, $20 per 1000. RED DUTCH Currants, $30 per 1000. *See Sept. No. of Agriculturist* for other stock, and *remember* these low prices are *only for this fall trade*. Prices will be higher next spring. Address PURDY & HANCE, South Bend, Ind., or Purdy's Fruit Farm, Palmyra, N. Y.

1,500,000 Superior Grape Vines, 1, 2 and 3 years old, 130 varieties. 2,500,000 Raspberry, Blackberry and Strawberry plants, all varieties. Cheapest good stock extant. Send stamp for Price List. Grape Wood of all kinds for sale. L. E. DARE, Rochester Grape Nurseries, N. Y.

PLANT THE BEST VINES.

Being acquainted with most of the Grape Propagators in this country, and having seen many of the stocks of vines this season, I am prepared to judge where the best can be obtained, and give reliable information about prices, quality, etc. Planters and dealers are invited to correspond with me, stating the number they expect to want, etc.

M. B. BATEHAM,
Sec'y *Lake Shore Grape Growers' Ass'n*, Painesville, O.

ANY KIND YOU WANT.—GRAPE VINES, STRAWBERRIES, RASPBERRIES, BLACKBERRIES, etc., in any quantity, sent by Mail or Express, *as low as the lowest*. Close buyers, in or out of the trade, should SEND NOW for Price List.

C. E. & J. S. FRITTS,
Atlantic Small Fruit Nurseries, Elwood, N. J.

GRAPE VINES.

Our Catalogue of Grape Vines, embracing all the approved varieties, (mostly two years old), is now ready. Many of the Concords have made ten feet of wood. Send stamp for Price List. FERRIS & CAYWOOD, Poughkeepsie, N. Y.

VINES AT WHOLESALE

To Dealers. For sale this fall, in one lot, about 5,000 very choice vines. Layers and transplants 2 and 3 years old of Iona, Israella, Adirondac, &c., *first-rate* plants for the retail trade. Also, a large quantity of Grape Wood for sale.

Address A. F. TAIT, Woodstock Vineyard,
Morrisania, Westchester Co., N. Y.

Agents Wanted. Address H. C. WITT, 37 Cedar-st., New York.

Stereopticons and Magic Lanterns,

With the Improved Lime Light, illuminating brilliantly two hundred square feet of canvas, and magnifying the views to that size, at an expense of less than one dollar for a whole evening's exhibition. Easily managed and pays well.

Illustrated priced catalogue of the apparatus, with list of over two thousand artistically colored photographic views on glass, of the War, Scripture History, Choice Statuary, etc., etc., forwarded on application. T. H. McALLISTER, Optician, (of late firm of McAllister & Bro., Phila.,) 49 Nassau-street, New York.

THE PERPETUAL (WATCH CHARM) CALENDAR—size of a two cent piece—with plain, masonic and temperance emblems, needed by everybody everywhere. Price by mail, electroplate, plain, with enameled figures and letters, 50 cents, gold, with emblem, ditto, $1.50. Address

E. MADEN, 161 Broadway,
Room 3, New York, P. O. Box, 5878.
Active Agents wanted everywhere.

$100 FOR A BRICK MACHINE SIMple, $150 with Tempering Box and Moulds, warranted to make 15,000 brick per day, of a superior quality. Address FREY & SHECKLER, Bucyrus, O.

Swift's Patent Farm Mill

For both HAND and POWER. Very efficient and durable. Price low. Send for Circular. Manufactured by LANE BROS., Washington, N. Y.

GALE'S COPPER STRIP FEED CUTTERS, the Best in the World. For Sale at Wholesale or Retail by JOHN W. DOUGLASS, Dealer in Agricultural Implements, etc., 181 Water-st., New York.

METZLER'S Patented Leaping Horse, best in use. Send for Circular to LEWIS P. TIBBALS, 478 Broadway, New York.

Thoroughbred Premium Chester White Pigs.

Progeny of Hogs that have taken State and United States Premiums. For sale Singly or in Pairs (not akin), of any age. Carefully boxed and shipped by Express to any part of the United States. *Their safe arrival insured.*

Our Pigs have always taken the highest premium wherever exhibited. They have all the good qualities desirable in a Hog; they are quiet, kept easily, have a good square form, deep and wide chest, very heavy hams and shoulders, broad in the back, short head and legs, and without exception always white; they readily fatten while young, or at any age, and will grow to weigh from 500 to 800 lbs., at 14 or 18 months old. They will make more pork in a given length of time, with a given quantity of food, than any other breed of Hogs. We have had them to weigh 1,250 lbs. at 21 months old.

We always have a large stock of Hogs on hand, of all ages, from 1 to 23 months old, and can fill orders at any time.

We insure the safe arrival of the Pigs.

They are carefully boxed, with feed and trough; the Express or Railroad Agents feed and water them.

For Circulars and Prices, address

N. P. BOYER & CO.,
Gum Tree, Chester Co., Pa.

CASHMERE GOATS!!!

I offer for sale a very superior and beautiful lot of CASHMERE KIDS, of 1867, ready to ship early in November. I have bred my flock of CASHMERE GOATS with *great care*, using *superior males* each year, since my purchase of the "Davis importation" in 1853. *For purity of blood and fineness and value of fleece*, my flock is unsurpassed by any in America.

RICHARD PETERS, Atlanta, Ga.

Cashmere! Cashmere!

We have just received direct from the district of Angora, in Asia Minor, a new importation of Angora (Shawl) Goats, (known in this country as Cashmere), which we offer for sale at moderate prices.

For Circulars and Prices, address N. P. BOYER & CO., Gum Tree, Chester Co., Pa.

MARK THIS.—Our reputation for shipping CHESTER WHITES of pure blood, and of fine quality, is established beyond a doubt. *We have never shipped a Pig that was condemned.* We doubt if there is any other breeder in the country who can say the same. *We guarantee satisfaction.* Circular sent free. JAMES YOUNG, Jr. & CO., Marshallton, Chester Co., Pa.

IMPROVED STOCK, consisting of pure Short-horns, with Herd Book Pedigrees, Alderneys, Devon's, Ayrshires, Southdown and Cotswold Sheep, pure Chester Co. swine, (premium stock), also choice breeds of poultry. Sent by Express to all parts of the United States. For Circulars and Prices, address N. P. BOYER & CO., Gum Tree, Chester Co., Pa.

SWINE.—27 pages devoted to Breeding, Feeding, and the general management of swine, sent to any address on receipt of 25 cents. Worth ten times its cost. Every farmer should have it. Address JAMES YOUNG, Jr., Marshallton, Chester Co., Pa.

Premium CHESTER White Pigs,

Bred and for sale by GEO. B. HICKMAN, West Chester, Chester Co., Pa. ☞ Send for Circular and Price List.

Superior Berkshire Swine.

Old and Young, from recently imported stock. Enquire of J. S. CLARK, Tivoli, N. Y.

ALDERNEYS AND CHESTER WHITES for sale by C. W. FAHLER, Cresskill, N. J., on Northern R. R., one hour from New York.

A BLOODED STALLION will be exchanged for four pairs of working oxen; is warranted sound and kind. Address E. T. PHILLIPS, Plainfield, New Jersey.

POULTRY of all desirable breeds, from first-class stock constantly on hand. New Importations arriving. Send for circular. A. M. HALSTED, Rye, N. Y.

POULTRY OF ALL BEST BREEDS for sale by JOHN W. DOUGLASS, Dealer in Ag'l Implements, Fertilizers, &c., 181 Water-st., New York.

SIX TRIOS of pure Rouen ducks for sale at $8 per trio. Also, fine Brahma cocks. A. W. MARSHALL, Metuchen, N. J.

MRS. SAUNDERS HAS A FEW BRAHMA POOTRAS (February and March chickens, from an Imported Cock,) to sell. Address Port Richmond, Staten Island, New York.

SEND STAMP for 16 Pages Description of a great variety of the finest *Thoroughbred Imported Animals and Fowls in America.* L. B. SILVER, Salem, Ohio.

PLOWS, PLOW CASTINGS, Caldrons, Sugar Pans, Gin Gear, Agricultural Implements, and Plantation Machinery. J. H. DECATUR, 197 Water-st., New York.

The American Paint—For Roofs.

Tin or Shingle, New, Old, or Leaky. Will not corrode metals, exposure has no effect. Warranted pure. Furnished or applied by CHARLES DIMON, 191 Pearl-st., New York. Send for Circulars. P. O. Box 4694.

VALUABLE PLANTATION FOR SALE, near ALBANY, GA., one of the most healthy locations in America, where consumptives *regain their health*; the winters are *delightfully* mild; yet a combination of breezes, peculiar to this section, makes the summer day and night singularly comfortable. White men can labor on land as well as in any part of the North, sun-stroke never occurs here, water is excellent, the Plantation has two sets of buildings, and can be divided into two farms. The land and location are the most desirable in all the South, in a district where families from the North are safe in every respect, and find plenty of good, kind neighbors. The hatchet is buried *deep* here, not to be *disinterred*. The writer is from the far North, and has enjoyed perfect health here, and has made more on this place this year raising cotton and cane than can be made in 10 years in the North, with the same ease. Sugar-cane is exceedingly profitable here. Choice Fruits, the Peach, Fig, Pomegranate, etc., etc., are abundant; see Aug. *Agriculturist*. This is the best place in the world to keep cattle, they *never* need feeding and keep fat nearly all the year. The beef is the *best quality*. An abundance of butter is also obtained with no expense, with as good a market for both, within 11 miles on a fine road, as New York City. The Savannah Railroad Depot is 12 miles from this Plantation, soon to be built within 2 miles. Present fare from here to New York, by New York and Savannah Steamers, three times a week, and Railroad to Albany, Ga., $31; time 4 days. 50 Cattle for sale with the place, at $4 a head. Excellent and experienced laborers can be obtained for $15 a month, *without* board. Religious Privileges and society excellent. One Church, and Baptist and Methodist Preaching *close* by. This is a rare opportunity; from $5000 to $10,000 will be needed.

Call on L. C. SHAW, Express Agent, Albany, or, address J. W. HUNTEEN, Albany, Ga.

ATTENTION!—ALL WANTING FARMS!—Cheap Farm and Fruit Lands, Village Lots, Water Powers for manufacturing, for sale at Bricksburg, Ocean Co., New Jersey, 44 miles from New York, on railroad to Philadelphia.

Soil, fine loam, superior for all crops. Country just rolling enough for beauty and utility. Climate mild and proverbially healthy. Water soft and pure. No fever and ague. Sold only to actual settlers on easy terms. Price per acre $25 and upward. For circulars and maps, address ROBT. CAMPBELL, President, No. 153 Broadway, New York. V. S. HOLT, Agent, Bricksburg.

FOR SALE.—Farm of 234 Acres, with good improvements, 16 miles from Baltimore, Md., fronting on the Frederick Turnpike, above Ellicott's City. Will be sold *very low, say 45 dollars per acre.* Also, 300 Farms and Country seats for sale. Apply to "Maryland and Virginia Land Office," Northwest corner of St. Paul and Lexington sts., Baltimore, Md. E. LIVEZEY.

WANTED—Farms and Village Property, for which 20 per cent. cash and balance in good farming lands in Iowa will be paid. 7000 acres to choose from, in eight different counties, in the Des Moines Valley. Address, giving particulars, A. S. WHITE, Goshen, Ind.

FARMERS AND DAIRYMEN, if you want to economize in feed, use the *Eureka Cutting Box* for Straw and Fodder. It has taken more first premiums than any other. Also, A NEW TREAD POWER on entirely a new principle, which will meet the objections made to others now in the field. All warranted in every particular.

Send for Circular. BLYMYER, DAY & CO., Mansfield, Ohio.

Torrey's Patent Weather Strips

Exclude *Wind, Rain, Snow* and *Dust* from Doors and Windows of every description.

They save in fuel one half, and preserve health by the prevention of drafts, so productive of colds.

Cheap, simple, effective, durable, ornamental, and warranted for five years.

E. S. & J. TORREY & CO., Sole Manufacturers, 72 Maiden Lane, New York.

CARPENTERS.—SEND FOR CATALOGUE of New and Practical Architectural Works, enclosing stamp. A. J. BICKNELL, Publisher, TROY, N. Y.

FRANKLIN TRACT.—20,000 acres on railroad, New Jersey.—25 miles south of Philadelphia, good soil, mild, healthful climate. Low prices; in lots to suit buyers. Some improved farms. Map and full information sent free. Address MORRIS & CO., Newfield, Gloucester Co., N. J.

ENDLESS AMUSEMENT

FOR

BOYS AND GIRLS.

Crandall's Improved Building Blocks, described in April number of the *American Agriculturist*, page 147, furnish a most attractive amusement for children. They are very simple in construction, will stand years of childrens' handling without breaking, and give renewed pleasure daily.

CHURCHES,
DWELLINGS,
BARNS,
MILLS,
FENCES,
FURNITURE, etc.,

in almost endless variety, can be built with them, and when finished, the structure remains firm so that it can be carried about without falling to pieces.

For developing the ingenuity and taste of children they are unequaled. Having given these blocks a practical trial in their own families, the publishers of the *Agriculturist* were so well pleased with them, that they consented to take the general agency for their sale.

The Blocks are put up in neat boxes, each box containing a set, and a card giving various designs of buildings. Price per Set; Plain, $2.00; Painted, red, white, and blue, No. 1, $3.00; No. 2, $2.00; No. 3, $1.50. A liberal discount will be made to dealers. Address

ORANGE JUDD & CO.,
245 Broadway and 41 Park Row, N. Y.

A RARE CHANCE!

GENESEE FARMER.

BACK VOLUMES COMPLETE,

from 1858 to 1865 inclusive.

A RARE CHANCE!

There are among the readers of the *American Agriculturist*;
1st.—Many old readers of the Genesee Farmer whose sets of back volumes and numbers are incomplete.—

WE CAN FILL THEM.

A RARE CHANCE!

2d.—Many who did not keep their numbers.—

WE CAN SUPPLY FULL SETS from 1858 to 1865.

A RARE CHANCE!

3d.—Thousands of reading Farmers who know the value of such *sets* as reference works. They may have the *Agriculturist* from first to last, and if so, they will be the more likely to want the Genesee Farmer.—

WE CAN SUPPLY IT.

A RARE CHANCE!

4th.—Others who do not know the great value of old volumes of an agricultural journal of such sterling merit as the Genesee Farmer, which stood second to none in America, for soundness of doctrine and practical sense.

We Would be Glad to Supply it to Them.

A RARE CHANCE!

The opportunity of obtaining so valuable a set of Back Volumes, well bound, at so low a price, ought not to be neglected.

Single Numbers, Post-Paid	10
Unbound, Single Vols., Post-Paid	$1.00
" Sets, Eight Vols., Post-Paid	6.50
Bound, Single Vols., "	1.50
" Sets, Eight Vols., "	9.00

ORANGE JUDD & Co.,
245 Broadway and 41 Park Row, N. Y.

AMERICAN AGRICULTURIST

FOR THE

Farm, Garden, and Household.

"AGRICULTURE IS THE MOST HEALTHFUL, MOST USEFUL, AND MOST NOBLE EMPLOYMENT OF MAN."—WASHINGTON.

ORANGE JUDD & CO., PUBLISHERS AND PROPRIETORS. Office, 245 BROADWAY.	ESTABLISHED IN 1842. Published also in German at $1.50 a Year.	$1.50 PER ANNUM, IN ADVANCE. SINGLE NUMBER, 15 CENTS. 4 Copies for $5; 10 for $12; 20 or more, $1 each.

[illegible] in the Clerk's Office of the District Court of the United States for the Southern District of New-York.

VOLUME XXVI—No. 12. NEW-YORK, DECEMBER, 1867. NEW SERIES—No. [illegible]

THE INTERRUPTED SUPPER.—After a Painting by Ludwig Beckman, Dusseldorf.—[illegible]

One of the pests of European agriculture is the rabbit, which breeds seven times in a year, and [illegible] it produces [illegible] it is estimated that the progeny of a single pair would in four years amount to the enormous number of 1,274,480. It is fortunate that they have so many enemies, besides man, to keep them in check. Rabbits and hares are much alike, but differ in their habits—the hare is a solitary animal, and makes its nest or "form" on the ground, while the rabbit burrows and lives in large colonies. Naturalists place all our animals that are usually called rabbits among the the hares, of which we have in our entire territory some twenty species. Our common species is the *Lepus sylvaticus*, found throughout the greater part of the United States. It retains its brown color all winter, while the Northern Hare, *Lepus Americanus*, which has a more northern range, is brown in summer, and white in winter. Both hares and rabbits are [illegible] timid, and for their safety from their enemies rely upon their fleetness. Our domestic rabbits are supposed to be varieties of the European *L. cuniculus*. The above group admirably represents characteristics common to these animals—contentment when no danger is suspected, and great timidity when alarmed,

Contents for December, 1867.

AMERICAN AGRICULTURIST.

NEW-YORK, DECEMBER, 1867.

Hail winter, the resting time of vegetable life. We gather strength in sleep, and by repose. So do the animals, to which man is so close akin in his physical and even intellectual structure. Plants also undergo internal changes which fit them for the new life of the spring. The maple stem contains little sugar during the season of growth, but gains it from the changes which occur to the contents of its cells during the period of rest. The grasses and winter grains *ripen* their roots, so to speak, and we presume that no vegetables which maintain their vitality through the cold season, approach the spring unchanged, but they are better prepared to commence a new growth. The soil firmly bound by the frost fetters is no exception to the rule of improvement. Simple freezing is very beneficial, freezing and thawing still more so, and the more thorough the exposure to the action of the elements, the greater the advantages. Particles of plant food, before unavailable, are brought into a condition to be dissolved by water, and taken up by the plants. Stiff clays are ameliorated, peaty soils are made friable, and a volume might be written on the good effects of frost on the soil. It makes up to the dwellers in the temperate and frigid zones the lack of the intenser action of warm airs, moisture, fermentation, and decay upon the soil and its constituents, occurring in the tropics.

Rest is not a folding of the hands in idleness, that is *rust*, or its equivalent. A change is more resting than a cessation of labor. If the hands rest, let us set the brain at work, and let the social qualities find useful employment, for thus shall we be invigorated in body and mind, and all the better prepared for hard work when it comes. After all, the rest of winter, to most farmers, is more in change of work than in anything else. Work enough may be done in the shortest day to give any man good digestion, and to soften even a bed of straw.

The interest in Farmers' Club meetings, and in other similar gatherings, will flag, if especial efforts be not made by those who have the ordering of them to make every meeting attractive by drawing out from the members facts useful to all, imparting some practically useful knowledge, giving away seeds, grafts, roots, duplicate catalogues and circulars, etc. Here let us drop a hint, which, in our experience, has always worked well. If the secretary, at each meeting, distributes *all* the articles of the kinds enumerated that he has on hand to the members present, be they many or few, saving *none* for delinquent or absent ones, the meetings will be much better attended.

The Retrospect.—The last month of the year is upon us. Our volume closes with it, but we neither shut our books, nor lay down our pens. The Sabbath of the year is for our readers, not for us, with whom every month is like its fellows. Yet these brief halts upon the march are pleasant, as we cast the eye back over the way we have come, and take our bearings, and make ready to move forward into the unknown but hopeful future. The year has been one long to be remembered as presenting the anomaly of a parching drought and most damaging rains, sweeping hand in hand, as it were, across the continent; yet our prosperity, as an agricultural people, is great. Most of our products are sought for at high prices, and we have much to sell. The diseases which have threatened our stock, have passed away, means of intercommunication have greatly increased, so that access to markets, with remunerative prices are offered even to the corn growers and herdsmen of our out-most borders. The peaceful conquests of labor and of the strifes of trade are noticeable everywhere. Each section is being bound to the other by cords of iron, and bonds of commercial intercourse. The mutual dependence of each portion of the country upon the other for real prosperity, is every day more strongly apparent.

Hints About Work.

The winter evenings have come, and it is a matter of the first importance that a portion of them should be devoted to the cultivation of the mind. The summer has necessarily been devoted to labor. In the winter, Nature puts a barrier upon many of our labors, and we should take advantage of the interval to read upon topics that have been deferred for want of time to discuss them. The mind needs cultivation as much as the soil, and it is generally the state of the mind that makes farming profitable or otherwise. The brain is more and more showing its power every year in economizing farm labor, and no man can afford to remain in ignorance of the manifold appliances that help his industry. Keep the mind improving, and make all your farm operations a means of mental culture. Look back over the past year, and see wherein you have made bad plans, or failed to carry out good ones. Determine what practices have been profitable and what ought to be abandoned. Every year's operations ought to have its lessons for the thinking farmer, and settle some principles.

Books.—These are becoming more and more necessary upon the farm. The more a man knows, the more he needs to know in every calling in life. "A little learning is a dangerous thing." There has been a great mental quickening upon the farm within the past ten years, and multitudes of workers have got smattering of the science of agriculture. They have got out of the ruts in which they were comparatively safe, and have ventured upon experiments. They need more light to guide them; and to this end they must read the writings of men farther advanced than themselves, and thus avail themselves of their knowledge. The books made by practical farmers, gardeners, and fruit-growers, embody the experience of a life-time and are invaluable to those who come after them. The man who masters this experience saves himself from a multitude of losses, and puts himself in the way to make large gains. "Draining for Profit" is a book that ought to be in every farmer's hands. Get the best books on your business, and study them with a view to following such teachings as are adapted to your soil and climate.

Periodicals. — These are indispensable now to keep a man abreast of his times. No investment pays better than a few dollars in the best agricultural and horticultural journals. Farming is progressive like the other arts, and there is money saved and gained in the hints which these papers drop in their monthly or weekly visits.

Circulating Libraries, will furnish much that one is not able to purchase for himself. These should be established in every town, and provision made for their regular increase. At least exchange books and periodicals with your neighbors. They are great educators. Your children will read something, and you may as well direct their education as to leave it to others. A home well supplied with good books and papers is rarely deserted for places of vicious resort.

Schools.—Keep your children in the best schools. Make the free schools as good as they can be, but if there are better, use them. There is no compensation for the loss of the advantages of education.

Accounts.—Have everything settled up by the close of this month, and ascertain definitely the result of the year's transactions. *Know* whether you have gained or lost, and how much. Farmers are more negligent than any other class in this matter. They have much barter with their neighbors, and at the store or market town, and often accounts run for years without any settlement. They do not know how they stand with the world, and cannot tell whether any crop they cultivate is a loss or gain to them. This is bad farming, and often leads to bad morality. Keep accounts and settle them once a year, for your own sake as well as your neighbors'. Begin the next year with a clean balance sheet.

Protection against Frost.—The cellar may be made frost-proof originally, by good underpinning and double glazed windows. If this has not been done, make a thick bank of earth, tan-bark, sea weed, or straw. The roots have cost quite too much labor to be ruined by frost. A well protected cellar makes the whole house warmer and saves fuel. Protect water pipes and pumps, and if the pipes chance to get frozen, wrap them in flannel and pour hot water upon them to thaw them out. Save plumbers' bills by timely attention.

Fodder.—This has cost money to raise and should be carefully used. Feed regularly, and only so much as an animal eats up clean. There is waste in irregular, or over-feeding. If you fodder in the yard let it be under a shed, with racks to put the hay in. Stocks should be brought to the barn and foddered there. It is wasteful to scatter hay upon the ground. Much of it is trampled and lost.

Live Stock of all kinds should have the owners' daily supervision. If others do the work, his eyes should see that it is well done. Few hired men can be trusted to do things constantly according to directions. In the very cold weather there is a constant temptation to consult his own ease rather than the comfort of the animals entrusted to his care. Feed and water regularly, and shelter all cattle in barns or sheds. Pine boards are cheaper than hay and grain. Keep salt within reach of horses, cattle, and sheep. A large lump of rock salt is best for this purpose. If they can lick when they please, they will not take it in excess. Attend to ventilation in barns and stables, and give the animals the benefit of the sun for a while on clear days. Keep all animals in a thriving condition.

Colts and Steers.—Improve the leisure of the season to break them in to work. The smooth snow path makes light loads, and their strength should not be much taxed at first.

Horses.—The horse above all animals wants careful handling. See that the shoes are well put on, and the caulks sharpened as icy weather approaches. Warm blankets save fodder and promote health. If the young folks go on a sleigh ride, insist upon the horse blanket to keep company with the robes for Tom and his sweetheart. There will be bills enough to settle without a sick horse in the stable to be doctored.

Working Oxen should be kept shod and caulked, if used. Keep up the flesh by generous feeding. A lean working ox is poor property.

Cows.—Keep the stables clean and well bedded at night. Sprinkle plaster or dried peat upon the floors when cleaned out, to save the ammonia and to avoid injury to the eyes of the cows. Ventilate thoroughly, and from the top of the barn if possible. Give them an opportunity to exercise an hour or two in the warmest part of the day. Keep the horns ornamented with balls, if they are inclined to be quarrelsome. Plan to have one or more farrow, or new milch cows for winter. There is no substitute for a plenty of good milk in the family.

Hogs ought to be well fattened by Christmas. Pork is made much more economically in warm than in freezing weather. Pay great attention to the quarters of the animals. Good sties with plenty of straw are cheaper than meal to keep up the animal heat. The pig is cleanly in his habits, and will keep himself clean if you give him a dry lodging place and straw. Corn meal is high this year, and the root crop is short, and pork will probably cost the Eastern farmer about all it comes to. Cooked food pays best.

Poultry is one of the most attractive features of the barn-yard, and when well cared for nothing pays better. In fattening geese and ducks, give them a pen for two weeks before killing. Hens and turkeys we have thought fattened quite as well at large. But they should be fed frequently with a variety of food, and have all they can eat. Arrange to have eggs in winter. A room on the south side of a hill, with plenty of glass, is almost indispensable. The birds must have animal food in some form, broken shells, and dust to roll in. Eggs in winter always bring a high price in city markets. Select for layers the early pullets of last spring. For plans of poultry houses see back numbers.

Manure.—Attend to its manufacture early and late, in summer and winter. Your success in husbandry depends mainly upon this article. It pays even upon good lands by making them better, and securing larger and more economical crops. Be avaricious of fertilizers. It is often convenient to draw muck and peat from the banks of ditches that have been dug in the summer. We have found it quite practicable to dig muck in winter after the surface is frozen hard enough to bear teams. Some swamps are accessible at this time that cannot be approached in summer. A farmer can never have too much muck on hand, if he has an acre of meadow that does not produce three tons of hay.

Wood-cutting and Lumber.—Now is the time to lay in a stock of wood for the year. Well-seasoned wood saves fuel, time, money, and the temper of the housewife. Much of the comfort of a family depends upon the kitchen fire. Rails have also to be provided upon many farms. Posts are wanted, and joists, planks, and boards. Saw-mill logs are much more easily carried upon sleds than upon carts. Improve the first good snow to move them.

The Ice Harvest.—Secure this as soon as the ice is six inches thick. This sometimes comes in December, and does not come again. If an ice-house is wanting, build one. See plans of inexpensive ice-houses, in back volumes. Ice is at once a luxury and a necessary in summer. The dairy is better managed with it, and many perishable articles can be preserved that would otherwise be lost.

Tools.—Now that the season is ended, overhaul all implements and vehicles. Repair damages, and if new tools are wanted, secure them, to be ready for next year's operations. If these have no abiding place, build a tool-house without delay, and illustrate that motto: "A place for every thing, and every thing in its place."

Seeds.—Get a complete assortment for next year. Much of the success of farming depends upon this item. For corn select sound ears, and those growing two ears upon a stalk. Keep the ears in a dry, warm room, until thoroughly cured. Much poor seed corn is planted every year, and people wonder why it does not come up. Early seed potatoes should be secured now. It often makes a difference of half in price whether a crop is marketed in July or October. Burn up the old garden seeds and get a new stock from some reliable seedsman. Our present postage law brings a seed store to every man's door, and he has no excuse for planting seed that are most too good to throw away, but not quite good enough to come up. Doubtful seeds will not pay when good ones can had for love or money.

Work in the Horticultural Department.

Now that cold weather has well-nigh put a stop to out-of-door work, it is well to take a look ahead and, before the present year has expired, give thought to the labors of the one that is so soon to open. It is a pleasant thing about horticulture that it is always progressive, and that perfection is never attained in any department. That which we now consider the perfect fruit or flower will, in ten years, be looked upon as unworthy of cultivation. It is this succession of novelties, this striving after improvement, that lends such a charm to horticultural pursuits. Each year's experience teaches better ways of cultivation, and gives us new knowledge of the things we cultivate. Fortunate is he who makes use of each year's teachings, and still more fortunate if he has the means and the will to add to them the experience of others. Now at this season, when one can be a student without feeling that he is neglecting other matters, it is well to gather up the scattered hints that are hidden in papers that were laid aside in the busy season, and to look at the recent books that have been written in his particular department. It is not possible that men like Warder, Thomas, Fuller, Henderson, and others, can write a book upon matters to which their lives have been devoted, without giving some information that may be turned to practical account. Commending the horticulturist to his books and journals, we give the few items of out-door work that belong to the month.

Orchard and Nursery.

In the Southern States, and in favorable seasons at the North, much of the work of plowing and subsoiling, and making ready for spring planting, may be done. Every favorable opportunity of this kind should be seized upon. Planting an orchard implies a promise to take care of it; trees set last fall should be occasionally looked to, to see that they are safe from domestic animals.

Fences must be in a condition to keep out horses, cattle, and sheep, as well as those thoughtless people who, when snow covers the ground, strike a straight line for their destination without regard to the damage they may do.

Rabbits are often destructive to young orchards, and various preventives have been from time to time proposed. The simplest of these, and the one largely followed at the West, is to sprinkle the trunks of the trees with blood, or, what answers the same purpose, rub them with a piece of fresh liver.

Mice like to work under cover, and if dead weeds or other litter lie close to the trees, they will be very apt to bark them. Clear away all rubbish, and after a snow fall, go around and press the snow firmly around the trunks. Surrounding the base of the trunk with a cylinder of tin or sheet iron may be practised where there are not many trees. A solid, smooth mound of earth, about a foot high, will protect them; but when snow covers this, the mice will work under it if it is not trampled hard.

Standing Water in the orchard must be prevented by opening surface drains where they are needed.

Cions may be cut any time, provided the twigs be not frozen. Choose good, well ripened shoots, of last season's growth; tie in bundles and label with the greatest care. To insure against the loss of the tag, it is well to mark one of the cions in each bundle also. Whittle a flat place at the large end of the twig, and then cut a number in Roman numerals, which shall serve as a reference to a memorandum. Saw-dust is better than sand for preserving the cions; keep in a cool place.

Catalogues should be consulted, and the list of trees for spring planting made out. Our advice is to always buy of the nearest reliable nurseryman.

Manure may be applied to the orchard—not a little near the tree, but over the whole surface.

Fruit in store is to be kept at as low and even a temperature as practicable, without freezing. Choice pears that have been well kept bring a good price, especially as the holidays approach.

Nursery stock can now be propagated by [illegible] grafting. This work is done in-doors, in unpl[illegible] weather; while the mild days are employed in bending back and shaping the last season's growth of young trees. Look to trees that were

Heeled-in for the winter, and see that no water stands around them and that the banking of earth is not washed away by heavy rains.

Fruit Garden.

The general directions for the orchard are for the most part applicable here.

Protection of those plants that need it is usually done too soon; when the ground becomes crusted is time enough. Tender raspberries may be bent down and covered with earth, and a mulch put over the strawberry beds, as noted on page 450.

Snow, if it accumulates in the heads of dwarf trees, should be shaken out while it is yet light.

Grape Vines, if yet unpruned, may be attended to on mild days. Even the hardiest do all the better if laid down and covered with earth. Make cuttings and bury them, or callus them by the process recommended last month on page 409.

Pruning of dwarf trees may be done, provided no large wounds are made.

Kitchen Garden.

Wherever the condition of the ground will allow of the use of the plow and spade, a great deal may be done to save valuable time in the spring. To this end all rubbish should be cleared up, and everything made snug and neat.

Roots that are already in pits should be covered as the cold increases, and when winter fairly sets in, the pits should be banked over with about two feet of soil, neatly rounded off, to shed rains. Hardy roots, such as horse-radish, parsnips, and salsify, may have some litter thrown over them, and thus prolong the season during which they may be dug.

Celery, stored in trenches as heretofore directed, will also need to be covered gradually, commencing with a few inches of leaves or litter, and as the cold increases, adding a covering of earth.

Covering of standing crops of kale, shallots, spinach, etc., will need to be done in localities where the winter is severe. Near the coast, salt hay is used for this purpose, and is an excellent material, but straw or leaves are more generally available.

Cabbages and other plants in cold frames will require constant attention, and are more likely to suffer from heat than from cold. Give them air by lifting the sash even in freezing weather, and on mild days remove the sashes altogether.

Seeds should be in a place secure from mice and moisture as well as great extremes of temperature. Have every parcel correctly marked with its contents as well as date of growth. Destroy all seeds of doubtful identity or vitality.

Tools may be overhauled and repaired, and everything put in working order for spring.

Manure.—This is the key to successful gardening, and its accumulation is one of the kinds of hoarding that we advocate. In most large towns there are waste fertilizers that are worth carting away.

Flower Garden and Lawn.

With the departure of the Chrysanthemums, the borders are bare of flowers. Those who have been thoughtful enough to introduce Rhododendrons, Kalmias, and other evergreens for winter effect, can now enjoy their cheerful appearance.

Protection must be given to many tender shrubs. Where the case admits of it, laying down and covering with earth is the readiest as well as one of the best ways. Half hardy Roses, Clematises, Wistarias, (in very cold places,) and the like, winter nicely under a covering of earth, provided the spot is so well drained that water cannot settle about them.

Evergreen boughs, especially those of the red cedar, may be placed over low shrubs to protect them.

Lawns should have a good top dressing of rich compost.

Evergreens, as well as dense clumps of shrubbery and evergreen hedges, not of proper form, are very apt to get bent out of shape if not broken down by heavy accumulations of snow. Such accidents should be prevented by removing the snow while it is still light and can be readily shaken off.

Green and Hot-Houses.

The management of fires will require some judgment, especially in a month in which a fine, mild day is often succeeded by a very cold night. In the greenhouse, the thermometer should not go below 38° at night, and reach 55° or 60° in the day-time. Give air wherever it is safe to do so.

Arrange the plants to the best advantage. Renew sticks and labels, and have all in complete order.

Insects must be fought at the start. At the first appearance of the green fly, or aphis, make a smoke with tobacco. The syringe will keep the red spider in check. Page's Sprinkler is excellent for this.

Cacti, and all plants that are in a state of rest, need but very little water, while growing ones should not be allowed to lag for the want of it.

Bulbs that were potted for house decoration may be brought into a warm place, a few pots at a time, to keep up a succession of flowers.

Hanging Baskets, so much in demand for the holidays, should be filled. Ivy is the ground work, and it is better to fill a basket with this alone than to crowd a lot of unsuitable things into it.

Apiary in Dec.—*Prepared by M. Quinby.*

Give the bees liberty to fly during the last warm days, and when the weather is too cool to allow of their flight, they may be put into winter quarters. Strong stocks should be selected for storing, especially if there are but few hives. Poor stocks do not generate heat enough to prevent them from perishing. If kept in a room, which should be perfectly dark, it requires about 50 stocks to produce sufficient heat. Smaller numbers may be kept in a dry cellar, or be buried. In September, 1865, we gave an article on burying hives, with an illustration. Very strong stocks will winter on the stand, and better in the straw hive than in any other. In any case, there should be proper ventilation. Wooden hives should be well protected by straw. If the entrance to the hive is so large that mice can get in, cover it with wire cloth, leaving room for the passage of the bees. Now is a good time to make hives, and to study up the subject of bee culture. The works of Quinby and Langstroth should be in the hands of every apiarian, as they not only give full direction for practice, but discuss the curious habits, and remarkable physiology of the bee.

Commercial Matters—Market Prices.

The following condensed, comprehensive tables, carefully prepared specially for the *American Agriculturist*, show at a glance the transactions for the month ending Nov. 18, 1867, and also for the preceding month:

1. TRANSACTIONS AT THE NEW-YORK MARKETS.

Receipts.	Flour.	Wheat.	Corn.	Rye.	Barley.	Oats.
26 days *this m'th*	444,000	3,533,000	3,194,000	877,000	1,169,000	3,718,000
27 days *last m'th*	487,000	3,310,000	1,750,000	180,000	805,000	1,310,000

Sales.	Flour.	Wheat.	Corn.	Rye.	Oats.	Barley.
26 days *this m'th*	376,000	3,314,000	3,330,000	187,000	2,818,500	317,000
27 days *last m'th*	411,000	1,802,000	2,911,000	520,000	3,916,000	813,000

2. *Comparison with same period at this time last year.*

Receipts.	Flour.	Wheat.	Corn.	Rye.	Barley.	Oats.
26 days 1867...	408,000	3,283,000	2,491,000	877,000	1,169,000	2,718,000
27 days 1866...	331,000	1,312,000	1,446,000	107,000	2,184,000	840,000

Sales.	Flour.	Wheat.	Corn.	Rye.	Oats.	Barley.
26 days 1867..	376,000	3,311,000	3,334,000	188,000	2,818,500	317,000
27 days 1866..	383,000	2,015,000	5,678,000	476,000	1,343,000	3,185,000

3. *Exports from New York, Jan. 1 to Nov. 10:*

	Flour.	Wheat.	Corn.	Rye.	Oats.	Barley.
1867.....	898,028	5,252,946	4,980,470	848,196	111,970	844,985
1866.....	811,083	345,765	14,556,000	182,480	1,067,897	434,581

4. *Stock of grain in store at New York:*

1867.	Wheat, bush.	Corn, bush.	Rye, bush.	Barley, bush.	Oats, bush.	Malt, bush.
Nov. 12...	911,169	1,051,706	151,518	361,033	2,216,752	52,156
Oct. 15....	177,826	987,861	7,300	82,738	833,097	67,917
Sept. 10...	170,558	1,151,898	500	9,878	155,737	61,308
Aug. 13...	61,171	973,723	35,355	12,370	300,819	45,072
July 15...	843,808	198,750	60,866	31,880	388,763	84,700
June 14...	274,279	817,285	111,357	58,815	879,865	16,311
May 15...	781,830	901,091	186,904	145,706	668,691	10,461

5. *Receipts of Breadstuffs at tide water at Albany, May 1st to October 31th:*

	Flour, bbls.	Wheat, bush.	Corn, bush.	Rye, bush.	Barley, bush.	Oats, bush.
1867...	398,800	3,188,100	11,829,100	620,100	2,372,300	3,919,100
1866...	315,300	8,988,000	25,125,900	817,800	3,210,600	7,786,400

Gold has been much depressed since our last. It has been down to 138¾, and thereafter up to 141. It closed on Saturday, Nov. 16th @ 139¾....The breadstuff market has been rather more active, but, under increased supplies, and the decline in gold, prices have been quoted lower generally. The home trade have been buying freely. The export demand has also been good, particularly for low grades of flour, and for spring wheat. Prices of wheat closed in favor of buyers. Corn has not been much sought after, save for home use. It has generally ruled at figures above the limits of shippers, and comparatively few foreign orders have been executed. The market for it closed weak and drooping. Rye and Barley have been held quite firmly, and have been in fair request. Oats have been mostly controlled by speculators, who hold about two-thirds of the stock here, and under whose management the market prices have been subject to frequent and extreme fluctuations. The closing transactions on the 16th inst. were of considerable magnitude, but mainly on speculative account at higher and rising prices....Provisions have been generally lower, and less inquired for, though Lard, Bacon, and Butter attracted more attention towards the close, and were quoted stronger in price....Cotton has been in better supply and less active demand at easier and drooping rates....Wool has been freely offered at reduced figures, and toward the close has been in rather better demand, especially fine fleece, largely on speculation....Hay, Hops, and Tobacco have been in good demand, and buoyant.

CURRENT WHOLESALE PRICES.

	Oct. 17.		Nov. 18.	
Price of Gold	143½		139¾	
Flour—Super to Extra State	$ 9 00	@ 11 80	$ 8 [illegible]	@ [illegible] 80
Super to Extra Southern	11 00	@ 16 50	9 65	@ 15 75
Extra Western	10 50	@ 16 55	9 [illegible]	@ 15 50
Extra Genesee	11 50	@ 14 [illegible]	10 40	@ 13 50
Superfine Western	9 25	@ 10 00	8 00	@ 9 20
Rye Flour	7 [illegible]	@ 9 50	7 00	@ 9 15
Corn Meal	6 50	@ 7 75	6 15	@ 7 15
Wheat—All kinds of White	3 00	@ 3 30	2 75	@ 3 15
All kinds of Red and Amber	2 [illegible]	@ 2 75	2 15	@ 2 40
Corn—Yellow	1 41	@ 1 45	1 35	@ 1 36
Mixed	1 42	@ 1 43	1 [illegible]	@ [illegible]
Oats—Western	83½	@ 84½	78	@ 79½
State	84	@ —	78	@ 79
Rye	1 55	@ 1 75	1 55	@ 1 60
Barley	1 57	@ 1 85	1 41½	@ 1 63½
Hay—Bale ⅌ 100 lb	70	@ 1 45	65	@ 1 30
Loose	85	@ 1 30	55	@ 1 15
Straw, ⅌ 100 lb	60	@ 90	70	@ 95
Cotton—Middlings, ⅌ lb	19	@ 21	17½	@ 18½
Hops—Crop of 1867, ⅌ lb	40	@ 65	35	@ 65
Feathers—Live Geese, ⅌ lb	75	@ 90	75	@ 87½
Seed—Clover, ⅌ lb	12½	@ 13½	11½	@ 12½
Timothy, ⅌ bushel	2 50	@ 2 75	2 50	@ 3 75
Flax, ⅌ bushel	2 70	@ 2 80	2 70	@ 2 80
Sugar—Brown, ⅌ lb	11½	@ 14	11½	@ 13½
Molasses, Cuba, ⅌ gal	38	@ 55	34	@ 50
Coffee—Rio, (Gold price) ⅌ lb	15	@ 18¼	15½	@ 18
Tobacco, Kentucky, &c., ⅌ lb	5½	@ 20	6	@ 20
Seed Leaf, ⅌ lb	3½	@ 65	5½	@ 65
Wool—Domestic Fleece, ⅌ lb	37	@ 62	35	@ 60
Domestic, pulled, ⅌ lb	30	@ 55	35	@ 55
California, unwashed	15	@ 30	16	@ 28
Tallow, ⅌ lb	12	@ 12½	11½	@ 11¾
Oil Cake—⅌ ton	52 00	@ 55 00	51 00	@ 53 00
Pork—Mess, ⅌ barrel	21 00	@ 21 05	20 97	@ 21 10
Prime, ⅌ barrel	18 00	@ 18 50	17 75	@ 19 25
Beef—Plain mess	16 00	@ 18 00	14 00	@ 19 00
Lard, in barrels, ⅌ lb	13½	@ 14½	12½	@ 13½
Butter—Western, ⅌ lb	19	@ 35	18	@ 36
State, ⅌ lb	20	@ 45	34	@ 50
Cheese	9	@ 17	8	@ 16½
Beans—⅌ bushel	3 25	@ 4 50	3 50	@ 4 50
Peas—Canada, ⅌ bushel	1 40	@ 1 50	1 40	@ 1 50
Eggs—Fresh, ⅌ dozen	30	@ 35	30	@ 33
Poultry—Fowls, ⅌ lb	14	@ 18	10	@ 16
Turkeys, ⅌ lb	16	@ 20	12	@ 18
Potatoes—New, ⅌ bbl	2 00	@ 2 75	2 25	@ 3 75
Apples—⅌ barrel	2 00	@ 4 00	2 75	@ 4 25
Cranberries, ⅌ barrel	7 00	@ 11 00	10 00	@ 11 50

New York Live Stock Markets.—

Week ending.	*Beeves.*	*Cows.*	*Calves.*	*Sheep.*	*Swine.*
October 21	6,549	67	1,232	24,012	36,149
October 28	7,033	58	1,083	29,374	27,769
November 5	5,879	94	1,347	34,707	41,801
November 12	7,187	81	1,175	31,281	30,107
Total in four Weeks	26,251	293	4,877	121,332	135,846
Average per Week	6,559	71	1,219	30,333	33,951

While beeves have fallen off about 430 per week, as compared with the previous month, the supply has still exceeded the demand. Sheep, too, have been less freely offered, but swine more than make up for the deficiency. In fact, meats of all kinds have been, and still continue to be, a drug upon the market. Cheap poultry is a strong competitor of beef, mutton, and pork.

Beef Cattle.—For the last month but very few really good cattle have come forward, owners holding such for the holidays when fat beeves are in demand. In their places are large numbers of thin steers, dry cows, and old oxen, sent to market when out-door feed failed, the expense of feeding hay and grain being heavy. The majority of those who bought cattle in the high markets last spring, and grazed them during the summer, lost all the cost of pasturage, and in many cases more, the decline in price being fully equal to the gain in weight. The market continues in a depressed condition, with too much stale poultry, selling by the ton at 6 @ 10 cts. per lb, to cause a quick demand for beef. On the 12th, the date of our last cattle report, immense quantities of soft turkeys and chickens were sold at 5 cts. per lb, the weather being rainy. At the present time, 16 cts. per lb net weight is the outside price for extra fat steers, while good to prime are selling at 13 @ 15 cts., and common to fair at 8 @ 12 cts., the average being about 13¼ cts.... **Milch Cows.**—These are in quick demand, with a scarcity of good milkers. Ordinary cows are little called for, the high price of milk and increased expense of keeping, causing buyers to select only good cows. For such they pay $90 @ $110, and when something extra is offered, $125 is frequently obtained. We noticed a large native cow, with perhaps one-fourth Durham blood, reputed to give 20 quarts per day, sold at $140, without the calf, which of itself was worth $15. Ordinary to fair cows are selling at $65 @ $85.... **Calves.**—Fat veals for the butcher are scarce, and will sell readily at 12½ @ 13 cts. per lb, live weight. Common to fair calves are worth 9 @ 11 cts. Some large and very fat calves, six months old, were sold at $31 each.... **Sheep.**—These continue to come forward faster than they can be sold. Instead of going upon winter feed, they are rushed into market. The decline of wool, too, is leading farmers to diminish their flocks. They are ½ cent per lb lower than last month, fat sheep of 95 @ 100 lbs. selling at 5¼ @ 5½ cts. per lb, live weight, while common to fair go off at 4 @ 5 cts. Choice lambs bring 7 cts., ordinary to good, 6 @ 6½ cts. per lb, weighed alive.... **Swine.**—Hogs have been coming in faster than at any time since the fall of 1865, but prices are no lower than they were the last of December, and the beginning of the present year; but fully ½ cent lower than one month ago. The quality is improving, most of the poor trash having been sent off. Prime hogs are now worth 7 @ 7½ cts., with fair at 6¾ cts., and common at 6 @ 6¼ cts. per lb, live weight.

AMERICAN AGRICULTURIST.
ORANGE JUDD & Co., Publishers, 245 Broadway, N. Y. City.
ANNUAL SUBSCRIPTION TERMS (always in advance): $1.50 each for less than four copies: Four to nine copies, $1.25 each: Ten to nineteen copies, $1.20 each: Twenty copies and upwards, $1 each. Papers are addressed to each name.

HARVEST TIME

FOR PREMIUMS.

GOOD WORK AND SURE PAY.

If any proof is needed that canvassing for this paper pays, we can refer to the large number of persons who have already sent us subscribers' names enough for volume 27, (1868,) to secure valuable Premiums, and many of whom are still at work, determined to obtain more of them. **Just now is the harvest time for canvassers.** We want both new and old subscribers' names on premium lists. With the present number, about 100,000 subscriptions expire. These subscribers may be found in almost every city and town and village. While a large number will renew their subscriptions as a matter of course, without waiting for an invitation from any quarter, there will still be tens of thousands who will need a reminder which they will gladly receive, and subscribe as soon as their attention is called to it. All that is needed to secure large clubs in any town of considerable size, and many subscribers, too, in the smaller places, is **energy and civility.** With these, names enough can readily be obtained for one or more of the valuable articles named in our Premium List in the next column. (See October *Agriculturist* for description of articles, or send for a printed Premium List, which will be forwarded *free* to all applicants.)

Don't be afraid to start a Club because a small one has already been made up in your town. There is room for more as long as there is a family to be found without the paper. And remember, besides, that the names of your club need not all be at your own Post-Office. Get them wherever they can be got.

Your work will be well paid for in Premiums. Look over the list, and see how small a number of subscribers secures a very valuable and useful article. Thousands of persons have received these Premiums. **Your name** can be added to the number of successful canvassers. Will you make money in this way?

Read over again, and think and act upon the suggestions in the "Few Words for Everybody," on page 3[illegible], November *Agriculturist*.

Notice the word at the head of the illustrated column, on page 4[illegible] of this number, and the remarks which follow; and if you are an old subscriber, whose subscription **now expires**, please send us your name for the next year, and, if possible, several new names, or a Premium Club, or at least one other name.

You can recommend the paper with confidence. No person, who has seen a copy, will doubt that our regular rates are very low for a paper so expensive to the publishers. You need not hesitate to promise much for the future, for we give the assurance that it shall be worth far more than our readers have to pay for it.

We can Pay much more in Premiums than in Cash.—Our purchases by Wholesale, our arrangements with Manufacturers and Dealers for advertising, etc., enable us to do this. It will be noticed that we give each premium article at the regular price which the purchaser would pay for the same.

Every Premium on our list is to be secured by sending us a definite number of subscribers. There need be no mistake, therefore, on this point; and there can be no favoritism in the matter, since the same number of subscribers for any particular premium is required from every one who secures it.

Table of Premiums and Terms, For Volume 27—1868.

Open to all—No Competition.

No.	Names of Premium Articles.	Price of Premiums.	Number of Subscribers required at $1.50	at $1
1	Garden Seeds for a Family (40 kinds)	[illegible]	[illegible]	[illegible]
2	Flower Seeds for a Family (100 kinds)	[illegible]	[illegible]	[illegible]
3	Nursery Stock (Any kinds desired)	[illegible]	[illegible]	[illegible]
4	Iona Grape Vines (12 of No. 1)	[illegible]	[illegible]	[illegible]
5	Concord Grape Vines (100 of No. 1)	[illegible]	[illegible]	[illegible]
6	Japan Lilies (12 Bulbs)	[illegible]	[illegible]	[illegible]
7	Sewing Machine (Grover & Baker)	[illegible]	[illegible]	[illegible]
8	Sewing Machine (Home Machine Co.)	[illegible]	[illegible]	[illegible]
9	Sewing Machine (Singer's Family)	[illegible]	[illegible]	[illegible]
10	Sewing Machine (Florence)	[illegible]	[illegible]	[illegible]
11	Sewing Machine (Willcox & Gibbs)	[illegible]	[illegible]	[illegible]
12	Sewing Machine (Finkle & Lyon)	[illegible]	[illegible]	[illegible]
13	Sewing Machine (Wheeler & Wilson)	[illegible]	[illegible]	[illegible]
14	Washing Machine (Doty's)	[illegible]	[illegible]	[illegible]
15	Clothes Wringer (Best—Universal)	[illegible]	[illegible]	[illegible]
16	Tea Set (Hart's best Silver Plated)	[illegible]	[illegible]	[illegible]
17	Castor and Fruit Basket (do. do.)	[illegible]	[illegible]	[illegible]
18	Ice or Water Pitcher (do. do.)	[illegible]	[illegible]	[illegible]
19	One Dozen Tea Spoons (do. do.)	[illegible]	[illegible]	[illegible]
20	One Dozen Table Spoons (do. do.)	[illegible]	[illegible]	[illegible]
21	One Dozen Dining Forks (do. do.)	[illegible]	[illegible]	[illegible]
22	Tea Knives and Forks (Patterson Bros.)	[illegible]	[illegible]	[illegible]
23	Table Knives and Forks (do. do.)	[illegible]	[illegible]	[illegible]
24	Carving Knife and Fork (do. do.)	[illegible]	[illegible]	[illegible]
25	[illegible]	[illegible]	[illegible]	[illegible]
26	Melodeon, 4-octave (G. A. Prince & Co.'s)	[illegible]	[illegible]	[illegible]
27	Melodeon, 5-octave (do. do.)	[illegible]	[illegible]	[illegible]
28	[illegible] (Shoninger & Co.)	[illegible]	[illegible]	[illegible]
29	Piano, Splendid 7-octave (Steinway & Sons)	[illegible]	[illegible]	[illegible]
30	Ladies' Fine Gold Watch (Beautiful)	[illegible]	[illegible]	[illegible]
31	Silver Watch (American Watch Co.)	[illegible]	[illegible]	[illegible]
32	Double Barrel Gun (Cooper & Pond)	[illegible]	[illegible]	[illegible]
33	Repeating Shot Gun (Roper Rifle Co.)	[illegible]	[illegible]	[illegible]
34	Spencer's Rifle (Repeating Rifle)	[illegible]	[illegible]	[illegible]
35	Tool Chest (Patterson Bros.)	[illegible]	[illegible]	[illegible]
36	Case of Mathematical Instruments	[illegible]	[illegible]	[illegible]
37	Case of Mathematical Instruments	[illegible]	[illegible]	[illegible]
38	Gold Pen, Sil. Case, E (Warren & Spadone)	[illegible]	[illegible]	[illegible]
39	Gold Pen and Silver Case, F (do. do.)	[illegible]	[illegible]	[illegible]
40	Barometer (Woodruff's Mercurial)	[illegible]	[illegible]	[illegible]
41	Barometer (Woodruff's Mercurial)	[illegible]	[illegible]	[illegible]
42	Buckeye Mowing Machine, No. 1	[illegible]	[illegible]	[illegible]
43	Allen's Premium Cylinder Plow, etc.	[illegible]	[illegible]	[illegible]
44	Pump and Sprinkler (Page's)	[illegible]	[illegible]	[illegible]
45	Family Scales (Fairbanks & Co.)	[illegible]	[illegible]	[illegible]
46	Building Blocks (Crandall)	[illegible]	[illegible]	[illegible]
47	Pocket Lanterns, One Dozen	[illegible]	[illegible]	[illegible]
48	American Cyclopedia (Appleton's)	[illegible]	[illegible]	[illegible]
49	Worcester's Great Illustrated Dictionary	[illegible]	[illegible]	[illegible]
50	Any Back Volume Agriculturist	[illegible]	[illegible]	[illegible]
51	Any Two Back Volumes do.	[illegible]	[illegible]	[illegible]
52	Any Three do. do. do.	[illegible]	[illegible]	[illegible]
53	Any Four do. do. do.	[illegible]	[illegible]	[illegible]
54	Any Five do. do. do.	[illegible]	[illegible]	[illegible]
55	Any Six do. do. do.	[illegible]	[illegible]	[illegible]
56	Any Seven do. do. do.	[illegible]	[illegible]	[illegible]
57	Any Eight do. do. do.	[illegible]	[illegible]	[illegible]
58	Any Nine do. do. do.	[illegible]	[illegible]	[illegible]
59	Any Ten do. do. do.	[illegible]	[illegible]	[illegible]
60	Vols. XVI to XXVI do.	[illegible]	[illegible]	[illegible]
61	Any Back Volume Agriculturist	[illegible]	[illegible]	[illegible]
62	Any Two Back Volumes do.	[illegible]	[illegible]	[illegible]
63	Any Three do. do. do.	[illegible]	[illegible]	[illegible]
64	Any Four do. do. do.	[illegible]	[illegible]	[illegible]
65	Any Five do. do. do.	[illegible]	[illegible]	[illegible]
66	Any Six do. do. do.	[illegible]	[illegible]	[illegible]
67	Any Seven do. do. do.	[illegible]	[illegible]	[illegible]
68	Any Eight do. do. do.	[illegible]	[illegible]	[illegible]
69	Any Nine do. do. do.	[illegible]	[illegible]	[illegible]
70	Any Ten do. do. do.	[illegible]	[illegible]	[illegible]
71	Vols. XVI to XXVI do.	[illegible]	[illegible]	[illegible]
72	Downing's Landscape Gardening	[illegible]	[illegible]	[illegible]
73	Cummings & Miller's Architect	[illegible]	[illegible]	[illegible]
74	A $10 Library (Your Choice)	[illegible]	[illegible]	[illegible]
75	A $15 Library do.	[illegible]	[illegible]	[illegible]
76	A $20 Library do.	[illegible]	[illegible]	[illegible]
77	A $25 Library do.	[illegible]	[illegible]	[illegible]
78	A $30 Library do.	[illegible]	[illegible]	[illegible]
79	A $35 Library do.	[illegible]	[illegible]	[illegible]
80	A $40 Library do.	[illegible]	[illegible]	[illegible]
81	A $45 Library do.	[illegible]	[illegible]	[illegible]
82	A $50 Library do.	[illegible]	[illegible]	[illegible]
83	A $60 Library do.	[illegible]	[illegible]	[illegible]
84	A $75 Library do.	[illegible]	[illegible]	[illegible]
85	A $100 Library do.	[illegible]	[illegible]	[illegible]
86	A Choice of Good Books (See Terms below.)			

(Nos. 50–59: In cloth ... Post-paid ... Unbound. Nos. 61–71: Neatly Bound, Sent Post-paid. Nos. 72–85: All sent paid through, by Mail or Express.)

Only good articles.—**We are careful not** *to place upon our list anything for a Premium which is not the best, and, in all respects, what is claimed for it. All, therefore, who secure premiums, may be sure that they are not running the risk of getting poor or indifferent goods.*

Specimen Numbers of the Agriculturist, Cards, and Showbills, as may be needed, will be supplied to canvassers. These should be economically used, as each extra copy of the paper, with postage, (&c.,) which must be pre-paid, costs about 12 cents.

Begin Now to raise your clubs. It is not necessary that all the papers of Premium Clubs should go to one office. You can get them anywhere.

Old and New Subscribers will be counted in premium lists, but some should be new names, as it is to obtain such that premiums are in part offered. The extra copy, usually offered to clubs of ten or twenty, will not be furnished when a premium is called for.

☞ *Every Premium article is new and of the very best manufacture. No charge is made for packing or boxing any of the articles in our Premium List. The forty-four Premiums,* **Nos. 1, 2, 6,** *and from* **36** *to* **39,** *and from* **50** *to* **86** *inclusive, will each be delivered* **FREE** *of all charges, by mail or express, (at the Post-Office or express office nearest recipient), to any place in the United States or Territories, excepting those reached only by the Overland Mail.—The other articles cost the recipient only the freight after leaving the manufactory of each, by any conveyance that may be specified.*

Nos. 50 to 60—Volumes of the American Agriculturist (Unbound). These amount to a large and valuable Library on all matters pertaining to the Farm, Garden, and Household, and contain more varied information on these subjects than can be obtained in books costing three times the money. We have stereotype plates from the Sixteenth to the Twenty-fifth Volume complete, and will have Volume 26 soon after Dec. 1st. From these plates we print as needed. The price of the volumes is $1.50 each, at the office, or $1.75 if sent by mail, as they must be post-paid. They are put up in clean numbers, with the Index to each volume. They are profusely Illustrated, the Engravings used in them having alone cost about Twenty Thousand Dollars! Those obtaining premiums for from one to ten volumes, can select any volumes desired, from XVI to XXVI, inclusive. For ordinary use, the set of numbers unbound will answer quite well.—Many hundreds of these volumes are taken every year as premiums.

Nos. 74 to 85—GOOD LIBRARIES.—In these premiums, we offer a choice of **Books** for the **Farm, Garden, and Household.** The person entitled to any one of the premiums 74 to 85, may select any books desired from the list below, to the amount of the premium, and the books will be forwarded, *paid through* to the nearest Post-Office, or Express office, as we may find it most convenient to send them. We need not enlarge upon these premiums, every one knows the value of good books. Twenty-five or Fifty dollars' worth of books on subjects pertaining to the farm will give the boys new ideas, set them to thinking and observing, and thus enable them to *make their heads help their hands.* Any good book will, in the end, be of far more value to a youth than to have an extra acre of land, on coming to maturity. The thinking, reasoning, observing man, will certainly make more off from 40 acres, than he would off from 50 acres without the mental ability which reading will give him.—Our premiums will enable many a family to secure a larger or smaller Library. ☞ This is a good opportunity for the farmers of a neighborhood to unite their efforts and get up an Agricultural Library for general use.

BOOKS FOR FARMERS AND OTHERS.

[For sale at the office of the *Agriculturist,* or they will be forwarded by mail, *post-paid,* on receipt of price. ☞ *All these are included in our Premiums, Nos. 74 to 85, above.*]

Allen's (L. F.) Rural Architecture	$1 [illegible]
Allen's (R. L.) American Farm Book	1 [illegible]
American Agricultural Annual, 1868, paper, 50c.; cloth	[illegible]
Allen's Diseases of Domestic Animals	1 [illegible]
American Horticultural Annual, 1868, paper, 50c.; cloth	[illegible]
American Bird Fancier	[illegible]
American Pomology—Apples—By Dr. John A. Warder	3 [illegible]
American Rose Culturist	[illegible]
American Weeds and Useful Plants	1 [illegible]
Architecture, by Cummings & Miller	10 [illegible]
Barry's Fruit Garden	[illegible]
Bement's Rabbit Fancier	[illegible]
Boussingault's Method of Making Manures	[illegible]
Boussingault's Rural Economy	[illegible]
Breck's New Book of Flowers	[illegible]
Bridgeman's Gardener's Assistant	[illegible]
Buist's Family Kitchen Gardener	[illegible]
Chorlton's Grape Grower's Guide	[illegible]
Cobbett's American Gardener	[illegible]
Cole's (S. W.) American Fruit Book	[illegible]
Cole's Veterinarian	[illegible]
Copeland's Country Life	[illegible]
Cotton Planter's Manual, (Turner)	[illegible]
Dadd's (Geo. H.) Modern Horse Doctor	[illegible]
Dadd's American Cattle Doctor	[illegible]
Dana's Muck Manual	[illegible]
Dog and Gun (Hooper's) paper, 30c.; cloth	[illegible]
Downing's Landscape Gardening (new Edition)	6 [illegible]
Draining for Profit and Health, by Geo. E. Waring, Jr.	1 [illegible]
Eastwood on Cranberry	[illegible]
Elliott's Western Fruit Grower's Guide	[illegible]
Flax Culture	[illegible]
Field's (Thomas W.) Pear Culture	[illegible]
French's Farm Drainage	[illegible]
Fuller's Grape Culturist	[illegible]
Fuller's Strawberry Culturist	[illegible]
Fuller's Small Fruit Culturist	[illegible]
Gardening for Profit, by Peter Henderson	[illegible]
Gregory on Squashes	[illegible]
Guenon on Milch Cows	[illegible]
Harris' Insects Injurious to Vegetation	[illegible]
Herbert's Hints to Horsekeepers	[illegible]
Hop Culture	[illegible]
Johnston's Agricultural Chemistry	[illegible]
Johnston's Elements of Agricultural Chemistry	[illegible]
Leuchar's How to Build Hot Houses	[illegible]
Miles on the Horse's Foot	[illegible]
Mohr on the Grape Vine	[illegible]
My Vineyard at Lakeview	[illegible]
Norton's Scientific Agriculture	[illegible]
Onion Culture	[illegible]
Our Farm of Four Acres (bound)	[illegible]
Pardee on Strawberry Culture	[illegible]
Peat and its Uses, by Prof. S. W. Johnson	1 [illegible]
Pedder's Land Measurer	[illegible]
Quinby's Mysteries of Bee-keeping (new)	[illegible]
Randall's Sheep Husbandry	[illegible]
Randall's Fine Wool Sheep Husbandry	[illegible]
Rivers' Miniature Fruit Garden	[illegible]
Richardson on the Dog, paper 30c.; cloth	[illegible]
Saunders' Domestic Poultry (new), paper, 40c.; bound	[illegible]
Schenck's Gardener's Text Book	[illegible]
Skillful Housewife	[illegible]
Stewart's (John) Stable Book	[illegible]
Thompson's Food of Animals	[illegible]
Tobacco Culture	[illegible]
Todd's (S. E.) Young Farmer's Manual	[illegible]
Warder's Hedges and Evergreens	[illegible]
Youatt and Spooner on the Horse	[illegible]
Youatt and Martin on Cattle	[illegible]
Youatt on the Hog	[illegible]
Youatt on Sheep	[illegible]

THE AMERICAN

HORTICULTURAL ANNUAL for 1868.

The second number of this serial will be ready about the holidays, and will contain a popular record of horticultural progress during the past year, besides valuable articles from

EMINENT HORTICULTURISTS.

Among those who contributed to its pages are

Hon. Marshall P. Wilder,	Doctor John A. Warder,
Peter Henderson,	S. B. Parsons,
Thomas Meehan,	Jas. J. H. Gregory,
Josiah Hoopes,	George Such,
Wm. S. Carpenter,	Andrew S. Fuller,
Geo. W. Campbell,	John Saul,
Doctor Van Keuren,	James Vick, and other well-

known pomological and floricultural writers.

The engravings which have been prepared expressly for the work, are numerous, and of a character that will make it the

MOST BEAUTIFULLY ILLUSTRATED

work of its kind ever published in this or any other country. Tables, Lists of Nurserymen, Seedsmen, and Florists, and other useful matters of reference.

Price, in fancy paper covers, 50 cts.; in cloth, 75 cts.

THE AMERICAN

AGRICULTURAL ANNUAL for 1868.

The volume will be ready toward the close of the present month, and will contain much of interest to every agriculturist. Besides the general record of agricultural progress, it will contain a valuable article on

Factory Dairy Practice, by Gardner B. Weeks, Esq., Secretary of the American Dairymen's Association, in which he discusses the reasons *for* the best practice and the most approved apparatus, buildings, etc., fully illustrated, and is equally interesting to the practical dairyman and to the novice;—an article on

Sewers and Earth Closets *in their relations to Agriculture*, by Col. Geo. E. Waring, Jr.;—one upon

Winter Wheat, describing, with engravings, new and valuable varieties, by John Johnston;—one upon

Scythes and Cradles, by John W. Douglas, (fully illustrated;) also articles on HORSE BREAKING and on DRIVING COLTS, by Sam. F. Headly, Esq., (illustrated.) ON RECENT PROGRESS IN AGRICULTURAL SCIENCE, by Prof. S. W. Johnson; on Commercial Fertilizers, Veterinary Medicine and Jurisprudence, Farm Architecture, Progress of Invention Affecting Agriculture, etc.

It is intended that the work shall be practical, excellent in beauty of its illustrations, and in its adaptation to the [illegible] of American Farmers, superior to anything of the [illegible] heretofore published.

In its general features it will be like the Agricultural Annual for 1867, containing an Almanac and Calendar, and there will be added a list of dealers in Agricultural Implements, Seeds, etc. Price, fancy pa., 50c.; clo., 75c.

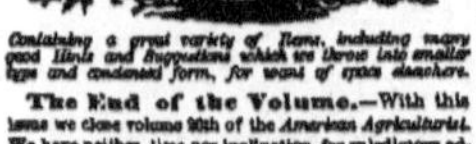

Containing a great variety of Items, including many good Hints and Suggestions which we throw into smaller type and condensed form, for want of space elsewhere.

The End of the Volume.—With this issue we close volume 26th of the *American Agriculturist*. We have neither time nor inclination for valedictory addresses to our readers. We believe that we can, however, congratulate ourselves on having not only done all we agreed to, but more. Our prospectus promises only thirty-two pages, and we have in every month given more than that, and we believe that we have in good part fulfilled our pledge to make the paper better than ever before. The next number will begin volume 27—(how fast we grow old!) and we enter upon it with increased facilities for meeting our obligations to our readers. A new building gives us the long needed room, and with an abundant working force in the business, editorial and mechanical departments, we are warranted in saying that the coming volume will be better than any of its predecessors. We feel that our old readers are well enough satisfied to continue with us, and that many will express their satisfaction by an early renewal of their subscriptions, and also in making the *Agriculturist* known to their friends. The publishers offer remarkable inducements to personal effort, as will be seen by the premium lists on another page. With all pleasant holiday greetings to old and young, we turn our attention to preparing them a brilliant and varied number for the new year.

A New Work upon Cotton Culture, by J. B. Lyman. This work has been prepared to meet a growing want, and is a complete manual of cotton growing, intended for those who are unfamiliar with the production of this crop. It discusses climate, the farm, stock, implements, preparation of soil, and planting, cultivation, picking, ginning, baling, and marketing. A calendar of monthly operations, a discussion of the extent of the cotton lands, the varieties of the cotton plant, and the insects and diseases that molest it, form the second part of the work, which also includes valuable statistics and suggestions. An additional chapter has been prepared by J. R. Sypher, Esq., upon Cotton-Seed and its Uses, giving the details of manufacturing the oil; the whole forming a handsome, illustrated volume of about 275 pages. Ready this month. Price, by mail, $1.50.

Louisiana Fair.—The State Fair at Baton Rouge was postponed on account of the prevalence of yellow fever, until after frosts should have stopped the disease, and rendered the State salubrious. It is now announced for the the 23d of December and days following. The similar postponement of the Mechanical and Agricultural Fair at New Orleans, to January 7th, will render it possible for exhibitors to attend both fairs. A great object which the managers of these fairs have in view is the introduction of labor-saving machinery of all kinds, especially such as under the old regime found little favor. Substitutes for manual labor are the great need of the South now. These States are almost entirely destitute of those little conveniences found in the North, such valuable auxiliaries to household economy—washing machines, wringers, improved churns, improved pumps, etc. The popular idea among manufacturers that such things would not sell was well founded when Dinah and Pompey, "Uncle" and "Auntie," had to do the work. Now, the case is different, and the easier Phillis and Cato work, and the more they can do, the less care and labor come upon the heads of the household. We hope these departments will soon be well filled, and there will be abundant time for many of our readers, who have wares to exhibit, if they start after reading this.

Castor Beans and Broom-Corn.—Numerous inquiries have come from Tennessee and other States concerning the cultivation of these articles. We are glad to see our friends there turning their attention to a varied husbandry, and shall always be glad to aid them. The subjects mentioned have been put into competent hands, and articles upon their culture will shortly appear.

Boston Fun.—Boston is the embodiment of "down East." We like Boston, we like its people, and above all we like its Horticultural Journals, as we are sure of a laugh at least once a month. Now, who would suspect the staid and dignified Hovey's Magazine of provoking a smile?—But it does. In January last our Horticultural Annual was published, and in September this journal notices it. That is funny enough, but see what it says: "Much or the greater part of this has appeared previously in our pages, but is here condensed for the use of those who like the rapid path to knowledge and have no time to obtain really valuable information."—Oh, Hovey! You didn't find that where the most of your good things come from—in the Gardener's Chronicle—did you? This venerable magazine is getting so lively that its young rival, the American Journal of Horticulture, is becoming funny also. It takes pains to inform us in Italics as follows: "*The illustrations which we shall use will be made for the subjects which they represent. They are paid for by us, and the description given will be our own.*" As this is in the announcement for 1868, the question naturally occurs, were not former illustrations "made for the subjects which they represent?" and were they not "paid for?" It is too much of a conundrum for us—we give it up.

A Good Religious Newspaper.—In addition to the *Agriculturist*, every family should have the help which a good religious newspaper will give in forming the character of the children, and keeping the minds of the older ones alive to the progress and the wants of the world. We cheerfully commend the Methodist, published in this city, as a first class paper of its denomination, wide awake, progressive, and conducted with eminent literary ability.

Russian Sweet Potato.—Several of our Western friends have been swindled by chaps selling the seed of the "Russian Sweet Potato" at $2 a package. One of the seed papers and a few of the seeds have been sent us. The directions for planting are signed by "Frank Delaine, Gardner, Long Island," who gives as references A. T. Stewart, S. S. Fitch, M. D., and G. V. Bigelow, New York. The seeds are apparently millet. Why cannot people exercise a little common sense about such things and know that novelties do not first make their appearance in the hands of peddlers? New things are always talked about in the papers long before they become common enough to be hawked about the country.

Mathushek Pianos.—We are pleased to notice that these pianos, which were selected for our premium list after careful examination, received the highest premiums at the late fair of the American Institute.

No Grafts, No Seeds.—We have more than once expressed our inability to comply with requests for grafts and seeds. We scarcely ever publish an illustration of a new plant or fruit but we have several applications for cuttings or seeds. It would give us pleasure to comply with these requests were it in our power, but it often happens that the things described are entirely new, and we do not even possess a plant ourselves. We mention the source from which our illustrations are obtained, and applications should be made there.

Poultry Exhibition.—The first Annual Exhibition of the American Poultry Society will be held in this City, commencing Tuesday, Dec. 3d, instead of during the last week in November, as previously announced. We understand arrangements have been made to insure a large and interesting Exhibition. The Premium List, which is very attractive, and all other information on the subject will be furnished by Mr. A. M. Halsted, Secretary, 68 Pearl-street, New York.

The Pennsylvania Horticultural Society.—Our report of the annual show of this society was crowded out last month, and we can now only briefly record its success, and congratulate the thoroughly alive association on the completion of its new and beautiful hall. The exhibition was very strong in specimen plants, and we doubt if so fine a show could be made elsewhere in the country. Grapes were well represented, and other fruits moderately so. One of the most noticeable things in the fruit line was a collection of apples from Franklin Davis & Co., Richmond, Va. This comprised 163 kinds, and took the first premium. The display of vegetables was fine, as it always is here, where they have an equal chance with Pineapples and other costly luxuries.

Sundry Humbugs.—There seems to be little that is new in the humbug line, but many of the old schemers that have been "shown up" in the columns of the *Agriculturist* are still at work, sometimes in new places and sometimes under different names, but with the same old story, told in flattering and golden words to deceive the unwary. Has any one of our readers, who, "just for the fun of the thing," has tried his hand in some one of these wonderfully sure and rapid ways of making money, ever received satisfactory returns? We have not been advised of such a circumstance in a correspondence amounting to thousands of letters. The lottery scheme leads, in swindling humbugs, and everything with tickets to be drawn should be avoided by all honest people. Clark, Webster & Co., who have before appeared in the columns of the *Agriculturist*, are now sending out circulars, advising parties that one of their tickets has drawn a prize valued at $200, and on paying an *assessment* of $10 the prize will be forwarded. Singularly enough, *all* the prizes drawn, so far as heard from, are valued at $200, and consist of two hundred shares in the "SAND RIVER PETROLEUM COMPANY." We are not informed as to when this company was chartered, or who are the principal stockholders. It does not appear in the stock lists, but the same article was given out a year or two ago by one J. D. Miller, a humbug, at No. 526 Broadway. Any one sending $10 for this drawn prize, will get in return, if anything, about *one-eighth of a cent's worth of printed paper*, and will find that he has "Struck Ile" more explosive than "Bowen's Eureka," which needs fire to "blow it up." "Sand River" is "bust" when you get it. This will be a fair representation of any one of the swindling lottery schemes, circulars of which are being sent all over the country. "Gettysburg Asylum Association" is a lottery, and consequently a humbug, and should be avoided. One would not be excused for stealing money, though *a part* of it might be given to the poor. As the holidays approach, the watch and jewelry swindle circulars are on the increase. We advise all our readers not to waste their money or insult their friends by buying or presenting the bogus stuff that is offered by these swindlers. See the November number of the *Agriculturist* for a fair exposition of all this class of dealers. Temple, Richardson & Co., (bogus,) send out circulars to advertising agents, containing advertisements of many firms in this city of high standing, and ask the price for inserting in different papers. On receiving a reply, the advertisement of Wright, Brothers &

Co., dealers in bogus watches, is sent instead of any of those of the respectable firms whose names have been used without authority. It is better to buy a ten dollar watch or any other article that is worth the money, of a dealer whom you know, than to send it to a villain expecting to get a hundred dollar article in return, and get nothing, or a bogus thing of no value. *A Chicago Dodge.* —"E. C. S.," Franklin Co., Me., sends us a letter, which he received from a Chicago sharper. Said sharper writes that he has bought out the business of a firm in Ann Arbor, and finds by their books that "E. C. S." has sent money for an obscene publication, which had not been forwarded. He asks for sixty-four cents to pay the postage, when he will send the book. "E. C. S." hopes you may get it Mr. Chi-*Cargo*. There are villains so wretched as to send circulars to respectable people of both sexes too vile to be mentioned in a public journal. In most cases the overdose is its own antidote, but lest some invalid and unwary persons should catch at these straws, we advise all to burn at sight every paper that savors of quackery or villainy. Of this class are C. D. Murphy & Co., L. J. Merion & Co., Kuhn & Co., Reeves & Tuttle, Hosea B. Carter, Charles Elmer. Many parties send humbug tickets and notices of prizes drawn, etc., to us for collection, offering liberal commissions, or half the proceeds for collection. Money could be made more rapidly and more honorably by gathering rags in the streets than by running after one of these villainous schemes, and we include lotteries, gift sales and gift enterprises of every kind. We have the assurance from hundreds, that our exposures of humbugs during the year have saved thousands of dollars, mostly to the poor, and themselves from many regrets. Our efforts in this line will be continued, and we invite all our readers to assist us by sending information, circulars, etc., with responsible names (not for publication), and by calling attention to our articles on this subject, and thus saving thousands more.

Letters Once More.—We have requested that those who send postage for a reply should send a stamp and no more. We do not write letters for pay, and when 50 cents or a dollar is sent, it is only a letter to return the change. Letter writing is done when it will not interfere with other matter. We answer all we can, but some are quite unanswerable—such as those entirely without the scope of this paper.

Fine Marigolds.—Mr. John Hague, an English gardener who has made his home at Clinton, Iowa, sent us some specimens of his French Marigolds. For richness of color and regularity of form, they are superior to anything we have seen. Mr. H. has made them a specialty for ten years, and his flowers are an interesting illustration of what can be done by careful cultivation and selection, with a flower that, in its ordinary form is not very highly prized.

Plants in Rooms.—"Reader." We have answered this once before. Plants, as many as can be kept in a sleeping or sitting room, will not vitiate the air as much as an extra person or a burning lamp. The odor of some flowers is often unpleasant to sensitive persons and invalids. So far as that goes, they are injurious. We know a person who is made very sick by the smell of cheese, another who cannot tolerate the odor of vinegar, and two who cannot sit comfortably at a table where there are green peas. These things are "injurious" to these particular persons.

Nebraska Plums and Cherries.—L. Bails, Mich. We do not know which particular things Mr. R. O. Thompson describes, nor do we much care. All these western curculio-proof plums are varieties of the common wild plum, of which there are a plenty in your State. The cherry, two feet high, is the sand cherry, worthless as to fruit, but pretty as a bush.

Tree Seeds.—We can answer some twenty letters by saying that J. M. Thorburn & Co., 15 John st., New York, issue each year a catalogue of tree seeds, and that Thomas Meehan, Germantown, Penn., also sells tree seeds, and makes a specialty of seeds of evergreens and hedge plants.

"**Some Pumpkins**" is the heading under which Mr. F. W. Livingston, of Illinois, sends a description of a specimen of a young plant that was found within a sound pumpkin. The radicle is 3 inches long, has seed leaves and a well developed plumule. It is not a very rare occurrence, and we have several times noticed it in pumpkins that had been left for some weeks on exhibition in our office, and we have many times seen seeds of oranges that had germinated within the fruit. Warmth, moisture, and air, are the conditions that induce germination. We can readily see how the first two may be present, and from what we now know of the diffusion of gases, it is easy to see that air is readily supplied. There are some plants the seeds of which always germinate before the fruit is severed from its connection with them.

Water Cress.—R. D. Overton. The cress sent to market is generally cultivated. Running water with a gravelly bottom is required, and the plantation is made by putting in pieces of the plant, and securing them in place by means of stones. It spreads rapidly, and will take care of itself.

Strawberry Tree.—W. J. Brown. A species of *Euonymus*, or Spindle tree, is sometimes called Strawberry-bush or strawberry-tree, from the color and appearance of its fruit. No tree bears *strawberries*.

Herbaceous Perennials.—S. C. P. By these we mean those plants the roots of which live from year to year, while the top dies down in winter. The common Peony, Columbines, Rhubarb, and Horse-radish are familiar examples.

Balsam Fir.—M. A. Runyon. The cones are not to be planted, but the small seeds contained between the scales. Keep the seeds in the cones, and remove them in spring, and sow as soon as the frost is out.

Fuchsias Wont Bloom.—"Subscriber," Tullytown.—The want of success in blooming Fuchsias is a common complaint. There are very few varieties that are winter bloomers. The best way to treat them is to allow them to rest in the fall, in a cool cellar where they will not freeze. They will need but very little water, but should not get absolutely dry. In February or March, bring them to a warm room, and previously pruning into shape, give water, and they will soon begin to grow. When they once start, give them all the water they need and all the light you can.

Heating Small Green-Houses.—Several ask by letter if a green-house cannot be warmed by gas, kerosene, and gasoline stoves. Leaving out of consideration the expense in case of gas, and the risk attending the use of the other things, we say *yes, provided* the stove has a flue to carry off the products of combustion. Do not think that, because the combustion of these is not attended with smoke, that nothing results from it. Either of them, burned without ample provision for carrying off the invisible gases thus produced, will be sure to kill the plants. Putting a pan of water on the stove, as one suggests, will be of no use as far as this goes.

Barn Cellars.—Uncle David says that, the manure made in his barn cellar, by forty hogs, in six months, is worth more than the hogs themselves. Study it up, farmers. We have great confidence in what Uncle David says, for he is great on barns.

Ground Vinery.—W. L. wishes those who have tried the ground vinery to give their experience. In England, this manner of growing grapes is followed with success. We gave in June, 1866, an account of it with an illustration.

Grape Trellis or Arbor.—"Subscriber," Archibald, Pa., proposes to build an arbor with old gas pipe, and asks: "Will not the iron injure the vines in severe winters?" Not at all; the iron is no colder than the vine. It only feels so, because it is a better conductor. Old telegraph wire will answer for your trellis, provided it is not weakened by rust. Best to try it first with a powerful strain.

Vergalieu Pears.—Mr. J. W. Davis, of Hammondsport, N. Y., sent to our *Grape Show* some specimens of this fine old pear. They were perfect—and nothing can be better than this variety in its best estate—and recalled the time when this was the leading variety at the East. No cracks and bitter rot at Pleasant Valley.

Propagating the Oleander.—W. B. R., Elk River, Minn. This roots very readily. For your purpose, the old way of putting cuttings of the past season's growth in a bottle of water will answer. Several things are called myrtle, and we do not know which one you mean.

Barberry for Hedges.—Mrs. M. A. B., Mass. This shrub makes a very attractive and effective hedge, and would undoubtedly do well in your region. It should be thoroughly cultivated until it is well established.

Jujube.—S. O. Chase, R. I. The Jujube is a tree, growing in the Mediterranean countries, and as it is not hardy in the north of France, it would probably not succeed with you. Formerly its acid fruit was used in making the Jujube paste. The article now sold under that name is made of sugar and cheap Gum Arabic, (Gum Senegal,) flavored and colored. We are told that the cheaper kinds are only sugar and gelatine.

Agricultural College, at Amherst, Mass.—N. F. This institution opened in October with 54 scholars. The course of study extends over four years, and promises to give a good literary and scientific education at moderate cost. W. S. Clark is the President, and will give you any further information you desire.

Large Beets.—Joseph Bridge, of Detroit, took the premium at the Michigan State Fair, for Turnip Rooted Blood Beets, weighing 11½ pounds each, and for Mangel wurzels, weighing 18 to 22 pounds each. The seed of the Mangels were sown June 5th.

Lake Mahopac.—Uncle David says that the medical institution, located at this beautiful place, is a real boon to the afflicted, being only the second asylum of the kind in the world. He has been there with one of his friends, and staid quite long enough to satisfy himself that the establishment is of the right kind, properly conducted, and calculated greatly to relieve, and in many cases absolutely cure epileptic and paralytic diseases. We have great confidence in what Uncle David says, and besides that, we know that Doct. Echeverria has a good reputation among medical men, and is well known as a writer upon the forms of disease to which he gives special attention.

Lilies in D. C.—Mrs. Brooks. The Martagon and other lilies you mention should succeed with you. We can only account for your failure by supposing that the bulbs had been too long out of the ground. They will not bear a great deal of drying.

Planting Corn in Drills.—John Johnston, of Geneva, has proved that this practice secures about one-fourth more corn, and twice as much fodder as when the corn is planted in rows both ways. About eighteen acres are planted in a day, with two horses and a drill.

Winter Mulch for Grass Lands.—B. F. G. Nothing is so cheap as grass, and it is pretty well settled by our best farmers that pastures and meadows should not be fed closely in the fall. Give them time to make their own covering. Coarse manure or straw is good, but more expensive.

Feeding Fowls.—K. G. The old birds as well as the chickens should be fed frequently, or, what is better, let them have access to food and water constantly. If allowed to feed themselves, they will eat a [illegible] time, and frequently, and this is much better for [illegible] to cram their crops full. Give them corn on the [illegible] in a platform box, where the weight of the hens will lift the cover, and they can help themselves.

Buckwheat Short-cake.—B. F. C. Two cups of buttermilk, one teaspoonful of soda-saleratus, a piece of shortening the size of a butternut, and buckwheat flour to make a stiff batter. Bake in a moderately-heated oven 20 minutes. This makes one tin full.

Tainted Barrels.—People, will still salt their meat in this kind of package, and spoil it for food. Some think that they succeed in cleansing them by thorough soaking, others char them, but the only really infallible remedy is a new barrel. The cooper will tell you he never knew it fail, and he knows. Not that a tainted cask cannot be cleansed; but we know no way that will be surely successful. Who does?

When to Take Up Old Meadows.—G. F. N. If a mowing field does not yield a ton of hay to the acre, either plow and manure or top dress. It does not pay to cut hay from it in its present condition.

Wheat Crop of England.—J. B. Lawes, of Rothamsted, Eng., estimates it as twenty per cent. short of the average.

Yeast.—Pare six good-sized potatoes, and boil with them three handfuls of hops; also put into an open vessel one cup of sugar, half a cup of salt, half a cup of ginger; pour the boiled hops and potatoes, while hot, through a sieve, rubbing a little, making, when strained, one gallon. When lukewarm, add one cup of good yeast, and when a froth rises, put all in a jug, and cork tight. This will keep good for three months. Use one cup for five or six loaves.' No flour! Sent by Lois Strole

Mark all subscriptions sent in as *New* or *Old*.

How to Remit:—Checks on New-York Banks or Bankers are best for large sums; make them payable to the order of Orange Judd & Co.

Post-Office Money Orders may be obtained at nearly every county seat, in all the cities, and in many of the large towns. We consider them perfectly safe, and the best means of remitting fifty dollars or less, as many hundreds have been sent to us *without any loss.*

Registered Letters, under the new system, which went into effect June 1st, are a very safe means of sending small sums of money where P. O. Money Orders cannot be easily obtained. *Observe*, the *Registry fee*, as well as postage, *must be paid in stamps* at the office where the letter is mailed, or it will be liable to be sent to the Dead Letter Office. *Buy and affix the stamps both for postage and registry, put in the money and seal the letter in the presence of the postmaster, and take his receipt for it.* Letters sent in this way to us are at our risk.

Now Increase Clubs begun early in the autumn. This may be done at any time by sending with each new name the club price. If any reader started with the intention of getting a particular premium, and he has obtained it, he may still go on, and add to his club at the same rates as before, and secure another premium. All names sent by one person, though at different times, and from different places, are counted in the premium club if for the same volume of the paper, and if each list of names is marked "for premium," when sent in; or the rates may be decreased. For example: Any one having sent 10 subscribers for $12, may afterwards add 10 names more for $8, making a club of 20 subscribers for $20, and so of other club rates.

Profitable Investments. — Good Books.—The books which are to be found upon our list, (see advertisements in this and other numbers,) *are such as pay the reader*. They have been prepared with great care, and by men who understand what they write about. It is easy to convince any one that expenditure in this direction must prove a profitable investment. Take, for example, the work entitled "Gardening for Profit." It was written by a practical, successful gardener, who gives, in detail, the results of many years' experience in his business, and in a clear, common sense way which all can understand. The cost of this book, $1.50, is a mere trifle when compared with the valuable information received. Mr. Henderson, the author, is not satisfied unless his gross receipts are $1000 from an acre on the average, and this amount, he informs us, he often receives. Take another, "Draining for Profit and Health," a book which fully explains the subject of Land Drainage; telling what land should be drained; how to do it; what it costs; what it pays, etc., etc.,—a book costing only $1.50, and which ought to be in [illegible]mer's hands. Take the "Small Fruit Culturist, [illegible] "Grape Culturist," costing $1.50 each; or the larger book, "American Pomology," for $3.00. No one interested in Fruit Culture, can read those works without getting hints or information which he will value far beyond their cost. Here, too, are works on the management of Stock of all kinds, on Architecture, Chemistry, Plants, Flowers, Trees, and many other subjects connected with work on the Farm, and in the Garden and Household. This is a kind of reading that not only puts money in a man's pocket, but makes him and his family wiser, happier, and better. These are books that pay.

Good Papers.—Money paid for a good family paper is well invested. In what way could the small sum of $1.50 be made to return so much as to invest it in a periodical, as richly freighted with valuable information, fresh every month, as is the *American Agriculturist*?—designed *for every member* of the Household.

Bound Volumes—Covers.—Now that the last number of Volume 26 is out, we shall bind up a supply of this volume in our regular style, neat black cloth covers, with gilt title on back, complete index, etc. Price, per volume, $2, at our store, or $2.50, if to be sent by mail. We can furnish any of the previous ten volumes, (16 to 25,) at the same rate; or we will supply them *unbound* for $1.50, at the store, 24 cents extra if to be sent by mail. Volumes sent to the office are bound in our uniform style for 75 cents each, and missing numbers will be supplied at 12 cents each. We keep the covers or "jackets" on hand, into which any bookbinder can easily insert the numbers. Price of covers, 50 cents each; or 60 cents, if sent by mail.

Save Your Index Sheet.—The Index and Title page of this volume will be found in this number, put in *loose* to save cutting the threads. It is thus all ready to be placed in front of the January, (1867,) number in stitching or binding the volume.

A New Year's Present for the Boys and Girls.—We ask all fathers and mothers to notice that the *American Agriculturist* is a paper for the *Farm*, *Garden*, and HOUSEHOLD, and that it contains a special and interesting Department for CHILDREN and YOUTH. What more pleasing or useful present could a father, mother, or other friend give to the boys and girls than a copy of this paper, with its beautiful engravings and instructive articles? Said a father to us, "My children watch eagerly every month for the coming of the *Agriculturist, and I never have to look that paper over before putting it into their hands for fear it will contain something I would not have them read.*" This would be a New Year's gift received each month.

Clubs of Subscribers need not all be at one Post-Office.—We wish to encourage the getting up of large lists, and it costs much less to mail a large number in one package than separately. This induces us to make the reductions in our terms to clubs of four or more names. But we are quite willing to receive names from several post-offices, if sent by the same canvasser; for such names often become the centers of new clubs.

A Good Dictionary should be in every household, and be kept where it is always readily accessible. Although not as costly as some of our premiums, we consider it one of the most valuable, because it is one of the most useful. It can be obtained by procuring nineteen subscribers to the *Agriculturist*, at the regular rates, or sixty-five at the club rates. The dictionary we offer is Worcester's Large Illustrated, and this was selected because it is the one we should choose for ourselves if we were limited to a single dictionary. This is one of our popular premiums, and we should be glad to send out a great many more of them.

Chromo-Lithography.—This is a term applied to a process of printing in colors which has within a few years been brought to great perfection. We have seen some specimens from the New York Chromo-lithographic Company which in color and execution so closely resemble oil paintings, that an unskilled person would never suppose them to be produced by any process of printing. We would suggest to the publishers that as this process is intended to popularize works of art, they give us subjects that are not so purely foreign as those they have thus far brought out.

Send us the Specimens.—Benjamin Mize—locality not given—writes that "We have perfect wheat and chess on the same head." This is just one of the things that we have long wanted to see, and will thank Mr. M. if he will allow us the opportunity of doing so.

The Newsboys' Lodging House.—If a New York newsboy should make his appearance in a country village he would be as much of a curiosity as an elephant. Ragged and dirty, yet bright and shrewd, an infant in years, but old in experience—homeless, and often friendless, he is altogether a character the like of which is only found in large cities, and nowhere of the genuine type save in New York. Several years ago, the Children's Aid Society did a good thing in establishing a lodging house, where these homeless boys could get a good meal and a lodging for a small sum, and those who wished to, could save their earnings. This has been a most useful institution, and now the Society, feeling the need of a permanent location, wish to procure a building. We have not room for their appeal for aid in this work, but we commend this charity to those who are looking for some way in which to do good. Mr. C. L. Brace, at the office of the Children's Aid Society, No. 8 East 4th street, will give all information concerning it.

Bottling Cider.—R. H. E., Lafayette, Ind. Cider for bottling should be fermented at a low temperature, and racked off from the sediment after it is clear.

Hanging Baskets.—"Minnie," Grampion Hills. The hanging baskets sold in the city are mainly of three kinds: those made of pottery, those of wire, to be lined with moss, and what are called rustic baskets, which are made of wooden bowls, ornamented by tacking on bits of vines, knots, burs, cones, etc. A deep wooden bowl, an old oyster keg cut down, a child's toy pail, or some similar receptacle may be used—anything that will hold enough earth. Those sold are generally too shallow. The vessel need not be water-tight; a little moss put over the cracks will make all right. The outside may be "rusticated" by tacking on split twigs, pieces of bark, vines, or whatever suits the fancy. These may be left of their natural color, or painted brown and varnished. Handles may be of willow or rattan.

Abdominal Tumor in a Horse.—Dr. G. W. Booth, of Harrison Co., Ind., writes: "If you will allow me a space in your paper, I will relate a very singular case which will probably interest farmers and horsemen generally. It is that of a horse of Mr. J. C. Lopp, of this place. This spring, while plowing for corn, Mr. Lopp noticed that his horse began to lose his appetite, and grow thin, and soon noticed that he passed his urine with difficulty. After trying the various diuretics usually resorted to, he called in several of the horse-wise men of the neighborhood, and had their opinions as to the nature of the disease, and its treatment. The horse gradually grew worse, and in two or three weeks died. At the post mortem, upon cutting him open, we found a tumor lying in the right side, to which were attached the right kidney and liver. The tumor would have filled a half bushel measure, and was composed of lobules from the size of a walnut up to the size of a man's double fist, attached by a pedicle to each other. When cut into, the lobules presented the shining appearance of kidney structure, but were of a grayish color."

Cows Holding Up Their Milk.—C. E. Pond, Kansas. It seems as if there must be some way of influencing a cow to give down her milk, but we know of no specific remedy. The usual causes are, we think, jealousy for her calf, and nervousness. A cow always used to kind treatment should not be jealous of her milker. One which does not suckle her own calf at all will not be jealous on its account. One of a nervous temperament may be quieted if fed or "messed" in a stall or loose box at the time of milking. A nervous cow ought to be handled by a quiet, gentle person. Boisterousness in the yard or stable, and rough usage, will get cows into all sorts of bad habits.

Ventilation of the Soil.—"S. B.," of Long Island. The suggestion made is not new. Experiments in artificial aeration of the soil have been made, and by means of pipes, and the advantages, if not imperceptible, found to be unremunerative. The passage of wind over the surface, and the property of infinite diffusion which air and its constituents, in common with all gaseous bodies, possess, is equivalent to thorough ventilation, as far down into the soil as good drainage exists.

Watering-Troughs on Highways.—A common thing in New England—less frequently found in the Middle States, and very rare at the West or (as the new phrase is) "Interior." Why is this?

Asphaltum Floors for Stables.—These may be made without fear of injury from frost, if not laid in very cold weather.

Chess.—A. W. B., West Meriden. The German told you an old tradition. This, and all other ways of converting wheat into chess, was tried by a committee of the New York State Society, several years ago. Cutting off the roots of wheat is about as likely to convert it into chess as cutting a horse's tail is to make a donkey of him.

Salt and Lime.—We hold it as settled that for most, if not all, manurial purposes, lime slaked with a strong brine is decidedly superior to simply slaked lime, with or without a separate application of salt.

Sorghum and its Products.—An account of recent investigations concerning the value of Sorghum in sugar production, etc., by F. L. Stewart, 220 pages, 12mo., J. B. Lippincott, Phila. We consider it a valuable contribution to our literature on this subject. Price $1.50.

Facts about Peat.—As an article of fuel, etc., by T. H. Leavitt, 2d Edition, 316 pages, 12mo., published by Lee & Shepard, Boston. A neat work, exhibiting commendable research, and of general interest. Mr. Leavitt is practically familiar with his subject, and the inventor of a condensing mill. For sale at the *American Agriculturist* Office. Price, $1.50.

A Soldering Iron, a bar of solder, and a little pulverized rosin, will be found a good investment for farmers. Many leaks can be stopped, much time saved, and also many dimes. The art of soldering is an easy one to acquire.

Farm Boiler and Steamer.—"J. H. D.," Hampden Co., Mass. The apparatus, invented by D. K. Prindle, of East Bethany, N. Y., is a neat and effective apparatus for cooking feed, steaming roots or coarse fodder, boiling water in vats or tubs, for scalding hogs, steaming timber, and many other purposes for which either a caldron set on a furnace or on an arch, or a low pressure steam boiler is employed. It has been used, and has the approval of many of our best farmers.

Cost of Keeping Sheep at the South.—In Union County, S. C., it is estimated at 37½ cents a head to winter a flock, and the profits at two dollars a head per year.

Feeding Cabbages, Stumps and All.—"J. L.," Westchester Co., N. Y., says: "In feeding cabbages, I have found the stumps cut in small pieces nearly down to the roots and slightly steamed and mixed with bran, very much relished and eaten clean."

Plowing with One Line and with Left-hand Plows.—Our pictures in the July number have been the subjects of so many and so differing criticisms, that we are forced to think they are pretty near right. Still the common usage, which is a very safe guide, differs a little from our representations. Instead of attaching the line from the head of the off horse to the head of the nigh one, it is usually attached to the girth. J. D. Smalley, of Stark Co., O., says the single rein should be buckled into a ring in the bridle rein, and recommends passing the rein through a ring attached by a short strap to the crupper, in order to hold it up better.

Clotty Milk in One Teat.—"F. C. C.," Wisconsin, has a cow which gave clotty milk from one teat at a time, different teats being affected. This is a mild stage of garget, and the cow should probably be cured by a dose of 1 lb. of epsom salts, and ½ oz. of ginger mixed with molasses. If the cow manifests feverishness, add half an ounce of saltpeter, and be very thorough about milking. If more than one teat is affected, or if the bag is sore, milk several times a day, and washing it with warm water, knead it gently each time. Warm grease is often applied with advantage after the washing. The farmers' remedy is Garget-root, or Poke-root, of which a few ounces are given, shaved up with the feed. It is laxative, and usually efficacious, but not always at hand.

"J. B. J." says: "Take a handful of Poke-root, chop it fine, boil till tender, and give it to the cow in feed or slops." He has never known it to fail.

Oysters and Salmon at Salt Lake.—M. M. Oysters reach their perfection only in tide-water streams and bays where they have a constant alternation of salt and fresh water. We are not aware that they will thrive under any other conditions. There is no chance for them at Great Salt Lake. Salmon must have access to the varied fare of the ocean in order to do their best. They frequently add threefold to their weight on their first visit to the sea. It is not at all probable that they would do well in the streams of the Great Basin. But *the artificial propagation of fish* that do not require these conditions can be carried on to any extent in those waters. The hatching of fish eggs is represented by experts in the business to be much more sure than the hatching of the eggs of the domestic fowls. They are easily transported. There is no conceivable limit to their multiplication but the want of rivers, and food for them. We were told that the whole expense of putting fifty millions of shad into the Connecticut River did not exceed fifty dollars. Black bass, salmon, trout, pike, pickerel, and white fish, are desirable sorts to propagate in fresh-water streams and lakes. Dr. Garlick's little work on fish culture is the best that has fallen under our notice, but this work is out of print. A new edition, with the latest information, should be immediately issued.

Cheap Homes.—"J. W." Under the Homestead Law, one hundred and sixty acres of land can be obtained in Missouri for $18. Improved farms can be bought at from $5 to $10 per acre. Churches, schools, and good society are not guaranteed.

The Early Goodrich Potato.—"R. P." We have good reports of this seedling from all quarters. It is very productive, not liable to rot, and of good quality. It is a good time to lay in your seed now.

The Wheat Crop of the United States is estimated at 225,000,000 of bushels, the largest ever raised, and of good quality. There will be little sprouted or musty grain in market.

The Crops in Europe.—There is a short crop of wheat in France, Belgium, Spain, and Poland. A good deal of wheat, flour, and corn is already sent out from this country, and breadstuffs will be one of our large items of export for the year.

The Farmer's Home Journal is one of the best of the young agricultural papers of the West. It is published at Lexington, Ky., by our friend, J. J. Miller, Esq. We wish him the largest success in his labors.

Journal of the Farm.—The first number of a journal of 16 pages, with the above title, has reached us. It is published by Baugh & Sons, Philadelphia, who say, "the proprietors wish it distinctly understood that it is published for the express purpose of making more generally known, and thereby increasing the sale of *Baugh's Raw Bone Phosphate*, of which they are sole manufacturers." Now, there is no misunderstanding this, and it is much more open and fair than those sheets published in the interest of some particular establishment, and which make believe all the time that they are not. We are not informed how often the journal is to be issued. If there is any virtue in Phosphate, the first issue contains enough of it to make its circulation grow rapidly, but besides its "phosphatic diathesis," as the doctors say, it presents much well-considered reading matter.

Cotton Culture and Manure.—A. B. This crop has been very generally cultivated without manure, and the product has been from one-third of a bale to one bale per acre, according to the quality of the soil. A subscriber expresses his surprise that we should recommend so much as a ton of fish guano to the acre for this crop, costing perhaps fifty dollars delivered. Dr. N. B. Cloud, of Alabama, demonstrated twenty years ago that two and three bales even per acre could be raised more economically than the same quantity on five or six acres. It is mainly a question of manure and thorough cultivation. We are aware that two hundred pounds to the acre is used, with a crop of one-half to three-fourths of a bale. It is much better husbandry to use more manure, and get more cotton.

500 Loads of Well Weathered Muck.—A. Halett, of Portage Co., Ohio, has 500 loads of well weathered muck, and proposes to send to New York for superphosphate of lime, at $60 per ton, to compost with it. Don't do it. Spend your money for something nearer home. Perhaps you can buy stable manure; with one load of this, and three of the muck, you may make fully three loads of manure, worth as much as good yard manure next spring. Perhaps you can get bone dust, or burnt bones, cheaply. If you can add 50 pounds to the load of compost. The woolen waste of factories, the wastes of soap boilers, of paper makers, horn turners, etc., are all valuable, and may often be used without a basis of animal manure with the muck. Pen your hogs on the muck, (under cover, if possible,) and throw out the contents of the pen upon a compost heap, as often as it is well worked over. Mingle muck with the manure in the barn-yard, so that it shall thoroughly pervade the whole. Throw it under the horses and cattle in the stables, taking it out clean at least once a week. Any way to impregnate it with the fermenting principle of animal manure, urine, or barn-yard leachings will make good manure of it. The compost will be all the better if bones, wood-ashes, and other inorganic substances of manurial value are added and thoroughly intermingled with it.

Selecting Seed Corn.—G. F. [illegible] ears from the stalks that bear two or three, taking the best. Hang them up to dry in a room that has the full benefit of the sun or a fire. If once thoroughly dried, it is easily kept. Much labor is saved by having well cured seed corn.

Mowing Machines and John Bull.—They cut grass well, John admits, but they also cut off the heads of sitting pheasants and partridges. What can John do without his game? What is an estate worth if it does not afford shooting for the aristocracy? Mowers and reapers are democratic institutions.

Vinegar from Sorghum Juice.—It can be made in a few weeks, treated as cider, without evaporation. But it is better to boil it, so as to bring the impurities to the surface, and skim. The more it is exposed to the air the sooner it will become good vinegar.

The Harison Potato.—The reports from this variety are wonderfully favorable. It has withstood both drouth and wet better than any other potato. It has everywhere given good crops. Cut in single eyes and planted singly, it has yielded fully 160 for one, and in some cases, no doubt, 200 for one. J. T. Mapes, of Orange Co., reports an increase of 160 good marketable potatoes, besides some small ones, for one planted.

Farming in Colorado is said to be making rapid progress, considering the obstacles they have to contend with. In Pueblo County, every spot that can be watered is plowed and cultivated. They have already spent a hundred thousand dollars for dams and ditches. About 800,000 acres are under cultivation in the whole territory. Not a very attractive country, where every foot of land has to be irrigated to produce a crop.

Native Woods.—In the prize list of the late Nova Scotia Agricultural and Industrial Exhibition, we find several unusual and very sensible premiums offered. Among others is one for the best collection of native woods, prepared to show the bark, as well as longitudinal and transverse sections, polished and plain. But very few are familiar with the appearance of our native woods, other than the few kinds that have a commercial value. Such a collection at any fair would be far more instructive than many things for which prizes are given.

Clearing Heavily Timbered Land.—Some of our readers are anxious for information about new and good ways of clearing land, handling the timber, and cultivating of the cleared forest.

Difficulty with Tile Drains.—"Pennsylvanian" writes that he has trouble with his drains. The water finds its way from the surface into the drains directly during hard rains. They are tile drains, laid four feet deep, two rods apart, in stiff clay hard pan soil. He finds, besides, that drains laid two and a half feet deep answer fully as well. Our correspondent has exactly the soil in which *well laid* tile drains, four feet deep, would pay best. His drains, we doubt not, were laid thus. The ditch was dug, the tiles laid, sods placed upon the tiles; stones upon the sods followed, and finally it was filled up with the soil. Such a drain is, of course, little or no better than a two-foot one. The joints of the tiles should have been protected with scraps of tin, leather, or regular collars; the clay, free from big hard lumps, should have been thrown upon the tiles to the depth of a foot or sixteen inches, and rammed down so hard that not a drop of water could flow down into the tiles. It must all flow up, as explained on page 418, (Sept.). N. B. Always run the drains straight down hill.

Machines for Lifting Stones.—D. I. A. Belles' machine is a good one, moving with two wheels. Packer's is a more recent patent, and has some improvements. Either will lift stones weighing six tons or more, and place them in a wall. Any first class agricultural warehouse will put you in the way to find them. The price is $200 and upward.

Fattening Food for Horses.—"W. C. R." asks, "What are the merits of corn meal, ground coarse, and then boiled or cooked into a sort of mush, mixed with cut feed, as a food for fattening horses?"—We know of nothing that will fatten a horse quicker than corn meal on cut hay, unless it be the same with the addition of a little oil-cake daily, which is most excellent. Cooking the meal is, no doubt, an improvement, and it would probably be better yet to cook hay and all.

Indiana State Fair.—This came off at Terre Haute, the first week in October, and was the most [illegible]l fair ever held in the State. The grounds se[illegible]r the exhibition were about forty acres, on the National road, a mile or more east of the city. It was a charming spot, shaded with black walnuts, sugar maples, and oaks of magnificent proportions. The arrangements were very good for the display of farm products, and the show was a credit to the State. The fruits and vegetables showed the effects of the drought, but there were enough fine specimens to make a good show. The fair ran quite too much to horse-racing, and displeased many of the sober-minded citizens, who could not quite see the propriety of this part of the fair. Perhaps they will make their influence felt more at the annual meeting, when the arrangements are made for the next fair. The receipts were about $21,000, and the expenses $15,000, which makes a good show financially.

Vault Supplied with Coal Ashes.—"If a shallow privy vault is well supplied with sifted coal ashes, and the contents removed once a month, will that be sufficient?" Yes, if it be well worked over. If frozen, it should be laid in a heap till spring, and then mixed.

Iowa State Fair.—This was held at Clinton, and for so young a State, the show was creditable, exceeding, we understand, all former State fairs. The receipts very nearly reached $8,000. A leading feature of the first day was the trial of cultivators. A field of corn had been planted a few weeks previous that the competitors might have a fair opportunity to show what work their machines could do. It shows the strong hold which the improved cultivators have taken upon the farming public, that there were twenty competitors with walking and riding machines for one horse or two. They all did their work well, completely stirring the ground and burying all weeds. Deere & Co., of Moline, Ill., took the first prize for sulky cultivator. The question of dispensing wholly with the hand-hoe in the cultivation of field crops, is one in which all parts of the country have a deep interest. The West has solved the problem, and we have now several styles of cultivators that will completely take care of a crop from the time it is planted until it may safely be laid by. The inevitable result of this improvement will be that field crops will be much more frequently and faithfully cultivated, and that corn and potatoes will be cheaper. The cattle were not out in large numbers, and the sheep attracted little notice. The hogs were good, especially the Chester Whites, which seem to take the lead at all the State fairs. The display of fruit and flowers was uncommonly good. Apples, pears, and grapes were well represented. The dairy products were not what we had a right to expect. In the Fine Art Hall there was a fine display in Natural History, and Secretary Schaffer made broad his phylacteries with the fowls of the air, insects, mammals and reptiles. We once heard murder treated as one of the fine arts, and there is no impropriety perhaps in putting scorpions, spiders, hen hawks, and rattlesnakes in the same category. The multitudes had to go home in the rain, but this failed to damp their ardor. They had a jolly good time and are ready for the next one of the same sort.

A Correction.—Some of our fine drawings are from the facile pencil of Mr. W. J. Hayes, and in indicating this fact, we have sometimes put "N. A." after his name. As Mr. H. is not a member of the National Academy, and does not wish to appear to assume titles that do not belong to him, we cheerfully admit that the mistake was our own. There is a growing feeling among artists that "N. A." is a title of very little value.

Fruit Preserving House in New York.—At our Grape Show, Mr. W. S. Carpenter exhibited specimens from a new fruit house which has been erected under the Nyce patent. Peaches, early sorts, were only tolerably well preserved, but early pears were in very fine condition. Bartletts were as green as when picked from the tree, and Washington, a pear that matures in August, was in fine eating condition and of excellent quality. We understand that those interested in this enterprise are well pleased with its success thus far.

American Pomological Society.—The Secretary, F. R. Elliot, of Cleveland, Ohio, has issued a circular to members, asking each "to aid the making up of the Society's biennial report by contributing immediately any information you have relative to new seedlings, and the values of different fruits, diseases, soils, etc., in your section of the country. You are also invited to forward samples of any new seedling or unnamed fruits by express, to the address of the Secretary, that he may make comparison, drawings and descriptions. Any fruits thus forwarded, the names of which are unknown to him, will be again transmitted to pomologists for the desired information. The American, United States, and Merchants Union Express Companies have generously offered to transport all sample packages of fruit for this purpose FREE. Due credit will be given to contributors."

Are Hickory Nuts Seeds?—D. D., Minfield, Ind., asks if there "is yet any decision as to whether or not Hickory nuts are mailable as *seeds*." Some one some time ago decided that they were *not* seeds. We have forgotten now who it was that gave the opinion, but it was some official who probably knows better than nature does. It is a great pity that our friends living on the prairies, where trees are needed, cannot get certain tree seeds by mail, because they happen to be called nuts, while potatoes are mailable in any quantities, yet they are neither seeds, roots nor cuttings.

A Grape Growers' Meeting.—The Grape Show, noticed elsewhere, brought together quite a large number of pomologists, not only from the immediate vicinity, but from considerable distances. Several having expressed a desire to hold a discussion on grapes, a meeting was called for Friday, October 25th, in the spacious room on the second floor of the *Agriculturist* building. The Hon. Marshall P. Wilder was chosen chairman by acclamation, and Mr. James Hogg was elected secretary. Col. Wilder, on taking the chair, expressed his gratification at meeting so many interested in grape culture. He was recently from the grape countries of Europe, and felt confident that our own country would before many years be not only a great grape-growing, but a wine producing country. He believed that the value of a grape should be estimated by its wine producing capabilities.

Doctor E. Van Keuren, of Hammondsport, Steuben Co., gave an account of the Pleasant Valley region. We have already given a sketch of this grape region, and omit Dr. V. K.'s description of the locality. There are three companies organized for the purpose of cultivating the grape and making wine, and $300,000 are invested in this industry. Four-fifths of the crops are Catawba. Vines are always healthy, almost entirely free from rot, and very slightly affected with mildew. The past season was very dry, and fruit ripened well. Concord healthy, occasionally rotting. Delaware hardy, and holds its foliage. Diana sensitive to cold, rots in some places. Allen's Hybrid first fruited this year, and ripened well. No experience with Roger's Hybrids. Lydia promises well. Rebecca good. Israella later than Hartford Prolific. Alvey and Norton's Virginia are somewhat grown for wine, and give a must of 90°. Iona has been extensively planted, is a good grower, and ripens its fruit later than Delaware.

Gen. J. S. Negley, of Pittsburgh, Pa., representing Mr. Knox. Pittsburgh is a favorable locality for the grape. Have tried all varieties. Catawba does well, Concord and Hartford Prolific, the most robust. Creveling hardy and productive, but with a loose bunch. Delaware gives a good crop once in three years. It is fickle, and requires good culture. It ables to ripen its crop even when the vines have been defoliated by mildew. Iona ripens unevenly, and is no better than a good Catawba. Israella no better than Isabella. Adirondac, a complete failure. Maxatawney, Anna and Martha are the best white grapes. Elsinburgh and Alvey, the best for wine. Several of Rogers' Hybrids are very promising, differing in aroma and character of flesh.

Mr. J. W. Bailey, of Plattsburgh, N. Y. His fruit set ten days later than usual, otherwise the season had been favorable. No mildew except on Allen's Hybrid. Adirondac colored August 25th, and bore large crops, one vine had from 300 to 400 pounds. A frost about September 20th prevented their attaining their full flavor. Hartford ripens perfectly, and the Delaware generally. None of Rogers' Hybrids are first quality, though some are valuable at the North. Concord, though healthy and vigorous, is too late, and entirely unsatisfactory.

Doctor C. W. Grant stated that in his locality the season had been very unfavorable to fruit growing. The Iona and Israella had done better than any others. Comparisons as to time of maturing should be made between vines of equal age. The Israella was the first to ripen, and the last to fall from the vines; its must stood at 75°, and upwards, that of Iona, 80° to 88°.

Remarks were also made by Messrs. Beach, Townsend, Cornell, Bushnell, Dr. Trimble, and several others, but we are not able to give a more extended report.

Early Potatoes.—S. M. The Early Goodrich and the Sebec are very popular varieties.

Grapes from California.—Probably most of our readers are aware that the climate of California allows of the open air culture of those varieties of European grape that with us can only be grown in glass structures. We were much interested in the results of an experiment of shipping a quantity of those grapes to New York. They were sent by Mr. Wm. McP. Hill, of Sonoma, Cal., on October 10th, arrived in New York on October 30th, and were opened on November 2d. Two methods of packing were tried, each bunch was wrapped in paper, one lot packed in chaff, and a corresponding lot packed in sawdust. The Rose of Peru, a black and most lusciously sweet grape, was in both cases nearly spoiled. Muscat of Alexandria came better in sawdust than in chaff, but not particularly well in either. Flame colored Tokay bore carriage better than the others, and those packed in sawdust came in fine condition. The transportation of grapes from California presents difficulties, which will doubtless be overcome, and we hope to see the magnificent clusters from its vineyards abundant in our eastern cities.

The Lake Shore Grape-growers' Meeting.—Engagements elsewhere prevented our attending this meeting, and we are indebted to George W. Campbell, Delaware, Ohio, for the following summary. The Annual Exhibition of the Lake Shore Grape-growers' Association, at Elyria, Lorain Co., Ohio, on the 15th, 16th, and 17th of October, was well attended, the tables well filled with specimens of grapes and wines, and the show of grapes of unusual excellence in all the leading varieties in cultivation. There were 146 entries for the several premiums offered on grapes, and 187 plates of grapes on exhibition. For the premiums on wines, there were 23 entries, and 47 bottles exhibited. Catawbas were in great profusion, of very large size, finely colored, and of quality never surpassed in this region. Notwithstanding the rot in the early part of the season, the crop will be large in the aggregate, and it is expected the wine of this season will be of the finest quality. Delawares were also largely exhibited, and of size of bunches and berries absolutely unequaled at any previous exhibition in Ohio. The quality this season is also unusually good. Repeated tests of must from a quantity pressed at Cleveland, for wine, gave, by Oechsle's scale, the unparalleled weight of 110°. The first premium for "the best 10 bunches of one variety, quality to rule," was unanimously awarded to the Delaware; the second to the Catawba; the Iona and Diana also competing. A magnificent single cane of Delaware was exhibited, about 8 feet high, bearing 71 well developed and perfectly ripened bunches. Ionas were not largely exhibited, and specimens were generally rather inferior; bunches loose and straggling, and imperfectly ripened. A few fair bunches from Lockport, N. Y., and from Erie Co., Ohio, were the best on exhibition, tolerably well ripened, but not equal to samples shown in former years. Reports in discussion and from private sources indicated that this variety had not generally met the expectations of planters. A few handsome, compact clusters of Israella and Adirondac were exhibited, about equal to those shown on former occasions. Dianas of remarkable size and excellence, with very heavy shouldered, compact bunches, beautifully colored, were shown, both from the Lake Shore region, and also from Crooked Lake, N. Y. The Detroit grape was again on exhibition; but it was difficult to see any material difference between it and the Catawba, though the specimens shown were a little smaller, and the bunches a little more compact than the average of Catawbas. The general impression seemed to be that it was the Catawba, grown with some favorable advantages of location or position. The Lydia was represented by some fair specimens; bunches medium, compact; quality good. Cuyahoga was also shown of rather better quality than for two or three years past. Several plates of Rebecca from the vicinity of Cleveland were very handsome; bunches large, compact, and fine. The sandy soil of that region seems well adapted to the growth of this variety. The Lorain grape was again on exhibition this season; a very handsome grape, closely resembling the foreign white Chasselas, though its foliage is decidedly native. Bunch medium to large; berry large, slightly oval, semi-transparent; slightly pulpy, with pleasant sub-acid flavor. A seedling, evidently from the Delaware, originated at Dansville, N. Y., received the first premium for best unnamed seedling native grape. It resembles the Delaware in color and general appearance; berries about the same size, bunches smaller; more pulpy; pleasant flavor, but quite strong, foxy odor. In no respect superior to Delaware. In addition to the single case of Delaware before mentioned, very fine cases of Catawba, Isabella, Concord, Diana, and some others, were exhibited, indicating extraordinary productiveness, with great size and beauty of bunches and berries. The Walter was not on exhibition—its originator being, perhaps, better satisfied with publishing *pictures* exaggerating it about *four times* larger than any specimens yet exhibited. Rogers' Hybrids were not largely represented, and the specimens were mostly rather indifferent. Some fine No. 15, were on exhibition from Cleveland. No other numbers were shown worthy of special notice. The Wines on exhibition were good samples of still and sparkling, of various kinds, though generally not of any remarkable excellence above those exhibited in former years. Some Ives' Seedling wine from Cincinnati received special attention, and was really a fine, red wine of high character. Some pure sparkling Delaware, bottled during natural fermentation, and without the addition of sugar, was also regarded as very superior.

The Grape Exhibition at 245 Broadway.—The occupancy of the new office was fitly "solemnized" as the French say, by a magnificent show of native grapes,—a display that would be fine at any season, but at the late date of Oct. 24th was something remarkable.

As no general notice was given of our intention to hold an exhibition, some explanation is due to the many friends who were unable to participate in it. After our October issue had gone to press, we received an application from Mr. Knox for permission to show his grapes at our new office, on Oct. 17th; this was readily acceded to, but the carpenters' work being delayed, the time was postponed to the 24th. As it was too late to extend a general invitation to grape-growers, we sent circulars by mail to such as we thought might be able to get their fruit here in time, and these were responded to by a sufficient number to make up, in addition to Mr. Knox's collection, one of the finest displays ever seen in the city. In addition to the fruit, there was a large exhibition of vines, which gave an opportunity for comparing the products of different nurseries. Although we did not ask for contributions of wines, or other fruits than grapes, a few specimens of each were brought in, and are noticed elsewhere. In this exhibition no prizes were offered and no determinations made by any other committee than the public. Each exhibitor was at liberty to advocate his own fruits or vines—a plan which seemed to be satisfactory to all concerned. At the exhibitions of the Imperial Horticultural Society of France there are no prizes offered, and the same thing is being advocated in England. From our experience in October, we feel sure that it will bring out a larger number of contributors, and on the whole avoid much dissatisfaction. At the late meeting of the Lake Shore Grape-growers' Association, there were 25 samples of Catawba so nearly alike, that the committee excused itself for its award on the plea that it must be made to somebody, and regretted that they had no more premiums to give to others equally deserving with the recipient.

The exhibition was open for three days, and was each day visited by thousands of interested spectators. On the 25th, at the suggestion of several grape-growers, an impromptu meeting was held for discussion. An abstract of its proceedings will be found in another item. Subjoined is a list of entries in the order in which they were taken by the entry clerk, and on page 450 will be found notes upon many of the varieties.

J. Knox, Pittsburgh, Pa., by Gen. J. S. Negley: Concord, Hartford, Creveling, Ives, Delagburgh, Herbemont, Martha, Anna, Taylor, Manhattan, Clinton, Rogers' Hybrids Nos. 1, 2, 3, 4, 5, 9, 13, 14, 15, 19, 22, 30, 33, 35, 34, 38, 39, 41, 43, 44, Salem, Rachel, Cuyahoga, Miner's Seedling, Northern Muscadine, Mary Ann, North Carolina Seedling, Oporto, Perkins, Cigar Box, Diana, To Kalon, Union Village, Norton's Virginia, Logan, Adirondac, Louisa, York Madeira, Isabella, Mottled, Catawba, Iona, Israella, Alvey, Rebecca, Delaware. Besides samples in plates, many of the varieties were exhibited in 5-lb. boxes. Large fruiting canes of Concord, Delaware and Herbemont were shown.—C. M. Beach, West Hartford, Conn.: Iona, Israella.—Jno. A. Requa, Amenia, N. Y.: Salem.—Chas. Siedhof, North Hoboken: Weehawken, Union Village, Jersey Black, Alvey.—Jno. W. Bailey & Co., Plattsburgh, N. Y.; Adirondac.—L. Phillips & Son, Berlin Heights, O.: 2 plates Iona.—B. F. Hopkins, Brownhelm, O.: 1 box Iona.—B. Summers, Vermillion, Erie Co., O.: 2 plates Iona.—J. H. Ricketts, Newburgh, N. Y.: Iona, Clinton, Cuyahoga, Herbemont, Allen's Hybrid, Israella, Rebecca, Creveling.—Leander Clark, Newburgh, N. Y.: Isabella, Montgomery, Delaware.—Charles Downing, Newburgh, N. Y.: Iona, Delaware, Israella.—J. F. Lowry, Berlin Heights, O.: 2 plates Iona.—C. W. Grant, Iona, near Peekskill, N. Y.: Several plates Iona, amounting in all to about 30 lbs., 5 plates Israella.—H. Cornell, Newburgh, N. Y.: 2 plates Iona.—Pleasant Valley Wine Co., Hammondsport, N. Y., by R. Van Keuren,: Catawba, Diana, Delaware.—D. S. Wagener, Crooked Lake, near Hammondsport, N. Y.: Diana, and Catawba, in five-pound boxes, and Iona.—Otis Brothers, Springfield, Mass.: 2 Unnamed Seedlings.—Jacob Newkirk, Hudson City, N. J.: Raspberries.—Chas. Arnold, Paris, Canada; Seedlings 1, 2, 16, 5 (white).—Geo. W. McDowell, Crooked Lake, N. Y.: Keuka.—Vines. The following were exhibited and many of them sold:—Peter De Pew & Son, Nyack, N. Y.; Ionas and Allen's Hybrid, 1 year; the latter in pot.—F. F. Merceron, Catawissa, Pa.: Creveling, Concord, Delaware, Clinton, Taylor, Franklin.—Richardson & Bellows, Geneva, N. Y.: Ionas and Israellas, 1 year.—J. F. Martin, Mt. Washington, O.: Ives' Seedling.—Lyman Bassett, North Haven, Conn.: Concord and Hartford Prolific.—L. L. Whitlock, 37 Park Row, N. Y., had seventy entries of vines, showing the manner in which he unites "all nurseries in one." We have not space for the list, but it includes both standard sorts and novelties.—J. W. Hanmore, Newburgh, N. Y.: Salem, Iona, Israella, a large and fine assortment of various grades.—J. F. Deliot, Sing Sing, N. Y.: Iona, Israella, Adirondac, Delaware, Creveling, Rebecca, Allen's Hybrid, several numbers of each sort. J. W. Bailey, Plattsburg, N. Y.: Adirondac, 1, 2, and 3 year vines.—N. H. Lindley, Bridgeport, Conn.: Salem, Rogers' No. 15, Rogers' No. 19, Ionas.—C. S. Mason, West Hartford, Conn.: Iona Nos 1 and 2, Allen's Hybrid, Israella, and very fine Iona wood.—A. F. Tait, Morrisania, N. Y.: Iona and Adirondac transplants and layers, Concord layers, Iona grafted, Concord, Israella, Iona and Adirondac wood.—C. W. Grant, Iona, N. Y.: Iona, 1 year.—Besides Grape-vines, L. L. Whitlock presented an interesting collection of young evergreens, and Lyman Bassett, New Haven, Conn., exhibited the Clarke Raspberry, with canes 10 feet high, large in proportion, and remarkably healthy, vigorous, and well-ripened.

Editorial Jottings in Europe.

"....CRACOW SALT MINES, Sept. 2....A vivid description of these wonderful mines, read in a school-book of my boyhood days, produced a strong desire to visit them that has never left me, and which to-day, nearly forty years afterward, has been gratified. At Trzebinia, about 200 miles south of Warsaw, on the route to Vienna, we turned aside 27 miles to Cracow, which is in Austrian Poland, and about 270 miles northeast of Vienna. Cracow is an old city, formerly containing 80,000 inhabitants, but reduced to less than half that number since the dismemberment of Poland. There are many fine buildings, the relics of former days, but everything is in a decaying condition. The people themselves look sad and dispirited, and I could not but feel sorrowful for them as I looked at the graves of Kosciusko, Sobieski, and of other heroes, and recalled the valor of this people who stemmed and broke the tide of Mohammedanism, when its immense armies seemed about to overflow all Europe. ..

The chief Salt Mines are at Wieliczka, 7 miles southeast of Cracow . . A party of fifteen of us, men, women, and children, enveloped in long white frocks, and flannel caps, and supplied with two dozen Bengal lights to illuminate the caverns, and accompanied by six guides carrying large lamps, descended first through the shaft about 250 feet. Each one was seated in a rope sling, and the sling ropes were arranged in two clusters, one above the other, all the ropes being bound together above our heads into one immense cable that was wound upon a windlass turned by horse-power—a comical sight, resembling two huge bunches of grapes, (or white ghosts) let down by a string. Landing upon the firm salt bed we quickly clambered out of our slings, and found ourselves in a large artificial cavern, the walls of which were solid rocks of pure salt, but of a dark color. From this point we wandered some two miles or more, descending by steps cut in the salt here and there, or through inclined passages, until we were 800 or 900 feet below the surface, and we could have gone down 1,800 feet. Above, around, and under our feet, there is nothing but the rocks of salt as hard and firmer than compact white chalk, but without any cracks or seams, save here and there a slight bed or layer of stone or clay. Immense rooms, halls, chapels, a dance hall, and altars, statues, obelisks, chandeliers, etc., cut in salt instead of marble, were visited in various parts of the mine, which extends nearly two miles from east to west, and over ½ mile north and south. Some of the passage ways, high enough to walk in, and wide enough for small hand-cars on iron rails, were 30 to 50 rods in length. At one point we crossed a lake, perhaps 200 feet in diameter, in a large boat—the only water, or dampness even, that we met with. Our visit was very opportune, as we were preceded by a large party of wealthy gentlemen and ladies who had caused the preparation of thousands of lighted lamps, candles, Chinese lanterns, extensive fire-works, cannon, rockets, that echoed and re-echoed through the caverns like a hundred peals of deafening thunder. They had with them a large brass band, which, on learning that a party of Americans were approaching, struck up one of our national airs, as we entered a large cavern. The effect upon us was thrilling beyond measure. Those not too much affected tried to join in "My Country 'tis of thee, Sweet land of liberty, etc."—and this, 800 feet beneath the soil "where Kosciusko fell,"—away in Austrian Poland! You can imagine our emotions better than I can describe them! .. After wandering for hours, and having seen but a small part of the mines, but enough to satisfy us fully, we returned to the surface in the same novel manner as we had descended. The most timid ladies in our company fully enjoyed the whole excursion, excepting the firing of the cannon....These mines have been worked for at least 800 years. The salt grows purer or more transparent the further downward it is penetrated. In some places the workmen blast out large blocks, but usually it is worked out the same as stone or marble from the quarries. Great pieces are undermined with the pick-axe, and then split off with wedges. These are broken into cubic blocks of a foot, more or less. [illegible] place we saw them hewing salt blocks into the [illegible] barrels, and putting the staves and hoops around the blocks. The chips of salt were beaten into a compact mass in other barrels. The salt is a government monopoly, and the amount taken out depends upon the demand. More than a million of centners of salt per year have been quarried during many years past . . "

" . . VIENNA, Austria, Sept. 6th, . . I have been pleasantly disappointed in this city. The buildings are generally in excellent style, and, except in the central part or the old city—the streets are wide, and all are neat and well kept. There is an intelligent look in the countenances of all the people, an elasticity of step, and an air of business activity and thrift visible on all sides, such as I have not seen anywhere else in Central Europe.. I have not noticed a single beggar here, (always excepting the hotel employees, who crowd around you at your departure, each with an outstretched hand for "pour boire," or "drink-money"—though you have paid your bill in full, "service" included,) and nowhere else have I seen so few people in poor dress, wearing apparel so cheap, and other articles also—excepting the charges at the hotels, the proprietors of which seem to be proud of the reputation of charging higher than is done anywhere else in Europe.... I forgot to tell you that for 250 miles of the route from Cracow here, we passed through a most charming agricultural region. In clean, thorough culture, and in good crops and abundant fruit, I have seldom seen a region superior to this. Fine pears were offered by women at many of the stations, three, four, or five for the kreutzer (of ½ cent!). Large orchards of heavily loaded plum trees were frequent, and so abundant was this fruit that you could get your hat full of splendid great plums for a penny or two. The Curculio is evidently a stranger in this region. I don't wonder at the thrift of Vienna, when it is backed by such a rich farming region as the long and wide Valley of the March River."

Convenient Horse Manger.

There have been many contrivances suggested, and used indeed, to prevent horses throwing their hay and other food out of their mangers, to preserve the fodder from contamination by the breath of the animals, and always to maintain in the manger a sufficient supply, but no excess. Such a contrivance, hampered by no patents, and easy to make, we present the

HORSE MANGER.

readers of the *Agriculturist*. It strikes us as convenient and practical, and a person with any facility in the use of tools can construct one. The engraving shows the manger, (A,) extending the width of the stall, but not of necessity so large, two feet wide, and two feet deep, made of two-inch plank, and iron bound. It has a box, (F,) for feeding grain at one end, and above the other a trunk, (B,) for hay, descends from the floor above. This is the peculiar feature of the arrangement. The hay-trunk is eighteen inches wide, and a foot deep. It descends four inches below the top of the manger, and the end is slanting, as shown in the engraving. A lid, hinged to the back and lowest part of the trunk, shuts up into it, where it may be fastened by a pin or button. When the lid is let down it rests on the two bars, (d, e,) and the hay will slide down within reach of the horse. The opening between the front edge of the trunk and the lid being only about five or six inches, the horse can draw out but little hay at a time, yet he can get at all that is thrown into the trunk at one time. If the animal drops any hay, the tendency is to drop it into his manger, and not waste it. The trunk is made of inch stuff, and iron bound about the bottom and corners if necessary. The lid shuts in the way it does to prevent the horse gnawing upon it as he would otherwise be very likely to do.

Walks and Talks on the Farm.—No. 48.

One of the most interesting experiments I have seen for some time was made last year at the Michigan Agricultural College, by Professors Miles and Sanford Howard to ascertain whether an animal eats less or more food in proportion to live weight as it grows older, and whether we get less or more increase from the food consumed.

Three thoroughbred Essex pigs were weighed when 11 days old. They then weighed 14¾ pounds, or 4.88 pounds each. They were then allowed all the milk they would eat, and consumed the first week 79.10 pounds. They then weighed 23½ pounds, or an average of 8¼ pounds each. The next week they eat 106.94 pounds milk. At the end of the second week they weighed 39 pounds, or 13 pounds each. The next week they eat 129.94 pounds of milk, and at the end of the week weighed 50 pounds, or 16.66 pounds each. The next week they eat 141.81 pounds milk, and at the end of the week weighed 64 pounds, or 21.33 pounds each. They gained on an average 3.66 pounds each the first week, 4.5 pounds the second week, 3.66 pounds the third week, and 4.66 pounds the fourth week.

The average amount of milk consumed for each pound of live weight was: 1st week, 3.96 pounds; 2d week, 3.32 pounds; 3d week, 2.92 pounds; 4th week, 2.49 pounds. This is a very remarkable *falling off in the rate of consumption in proportion to live weight*, as the animal grows older.

At this point the experiment terminated "for want of suitable facilities for weighing the mixed food." Shame to the State of Michigan, shame to a nation of Farmers, that our oldest and best Agricultural College should be compelled to stop such an important experiment for want of a pair of scales!

The gain for each 100 pounds live weight was: 1st week, 75.86 pounds; 2d, 50.92 pounds; 3d, 28.20 pounds, and 4th, 28 pounds.

The amount of milk consumed to produce one pound of increase of live weight was: 1st week, 7.20 pounds; 2d, 7.92 pounds; 3d, 11.81 pounds; and 4th, 10.13 pounds.

So far as these experiments go, they sustain a principle which I have long supposed was true, that, other things being equal, the more you can get an animal to eat in proportion to its live weight, the more it will gain in proportion to the food consumed. If this is true, the aim of breeders should be to produce animals that are "great eaters"—and, of course, they should also aim at the same time to reduce the offal parts, so that nearly all the food shall be turned into valuable meat.

For the first two weeks it took only 7½ pounds of milk to produce one pound of increase, and for the next two weeks, 11 pounds, or 46½ per cent. more. This is an enormous falling off in the meat-producing power of the food, and as the pigs grow larger there would doubtless be less and less increase from the food consumed. And this is really the point which we wish to ascertain experimentally.

The experiment terminated August 18th. The best pig of the three was then five weeks and four days old, and weighed 24½ pounds. He was then gaining at the rate of 28 per cent. per week. Although no record was kept of the amount of food consumed, the pig was weighed at the end of the week, (August 25th,) and weighed 29¾ pounds. This is a gain for the week of 20 per cent. He was not weighed the next week, but was the week after, (September 8th.) He then weighed 45⅞ pounds. This is also a gain of a little over 20 per cent. per week. Now, if he could be kept on growing at that rate, he would weigh the next week, (September 15th,) about 57 pounds, and the next, (September 22d,) 71 pounds, and the next week, (September 29th,) 89 pounds. He would then be between ten and eleven weeks old, and would probably dress, if as fat as such a rapid-growing pig must be, about 65 pounds. If we keep him longer than this, the proportion of increase will rapidly grow less. This very hog, at 5½ months old, weighed 154 pounds; which, if we assume that he weighed 89 pounds when 11 weeks old, is a gain of only between 4 and 5 per cent. per week.

Only give us a breed of pigs that will gain for ten or eleven weeks, in proportion to live weight, as rapidly as this one gained for eight weeks, and nothing more could be desired, so far as the supply of fresh pork is concerned. In London, the pig most in demand by the butchers, and most profitable for the farmers, is one dressing between 60 and 70 pounds.

The real point I want to enforce is this. It takes some 75 per cent. of all the food an ordinary animal eats to keep him alive, and the increase is derived from the other 25 pounds. Now, if you can get him to eat 125 pounds, or only one-fourth more, you double your increase; if 150 pounds, you get *three* times the increase, and with 175 pounds, *four* times, and with 200 pounds, *five* times, while your food is only doubled. Now, will not a little, well bred pig, eat as much again in proportion to live weight as he will at an older age, and will he not consequently give more than double the increase in proportion to the food consumed? And if this is so, should not our aim be to get animals having immense digestive powers embodied in a small frame? I believe breeders have never turned their attention to this point.

In Mr. Lawes' experiments on the "Comparative Fattening Qualities of the Different Breeds of Sheep," the sheep that gained the most on the same kind of food had the *largest stomachs*. Thus, of 20 Cotswold sheep, the five that gained the most were found, on killing them, to have stomachs weighing on the average, 4 lbs. 14¾ oz.; while the stomachs of the five that gained the least averaged only 4 lbs. 4¼ oz.

Of the Leicesters' the four that gained the most had stomachs averaging 4 lbs. 1¾ oz., and the four that gained the least, 3 lbs. 2½ oz.

Of the Hampshire Downs, the four that gained the most had stomachs averaging 4 lbs. 8½ oz., and the four that gained the least, 3 lbs. 8½ oz.

Of the Sussex Downs, the four that gained the most had stomachs weighing 3 lbs. 4 oz., and the four that gained the least, 2 lbs. 11½ oz., and so it was in other cases which I have not time to mention.

You say that this would naturally be so; that the sheep that gained the most were the largest animals, and consequently had the largest stomachs. But while this is true of the sheep at the termination of the experiment, it was not so when the animals were put up to fatten. And this is the real point. Thus, at the commencement of the experiment, the five Cotswold sheep that afterward gained the most weighed 122 lbs. each, and the five that gained the least, 123 lbs. At the end of the experiment the latter weighed 167 lbs. each, and the former, 202 lbs. So much for big stomachs! To anticipate another objection, I may add that the dressed weight of the five that gained the most was 117 lbs. each, and that of the five that gained the least, 93 lbs.

In Mr. Lawes' Pig Experiments, one of the pigs, considered a fair representative of the others, was killed at the commencement of the experiment. His "fasted" live weight was 94 lbs.; carcass, 63¾ lbs. The stomach of this pig weighed 1 lb. 3.08 oz.

After the pigs had been fattened for ten weeks, another pig of the same litter was killed. His fasted live weight was 185 lbs.; carcass 140¾ lbs. The stomach of this pig weighed 1 lb. 3.48 oz.—less than two-tenths of an ounce more than the pig killed 10 weeks before. The older pig weighed nearly as much again as the other, (and dressed 220 per cent. more,) and yet the stomach was no larger. You can draw your own conclusion from the fact. To me it seems to confirm the views I have endeavored to set forth.

(*Continued on page 442.*)

Fruit-eating Bats—Flying Foxes.

In the last number of the *American Agriculturist*, we introduced to our readers a member of the very interesting order of animals—flying mammals—or bats. From what we then wrote it might well be supposed that all bats live upon insects chiefly, and altogether upon animal food, but this is not the case, though all occurring in this country do. There are about forty species inhabiting the warmer parts of A[illegible] and Africa, which live upon fruit, and do great damage to the orchards, especially to plantations of figs. These are generally bats of very large size, and to impress the fact that there are vegetarians even among bats, as well as to show the manner in which they close their [illegible] pinions when in repose, we present an engraving of the largest of the well-known bats, the Flying Fox of India, (*Pteropus* [illegible]). This animal measures five feet from tip to tip of its expanded wings, and its head and body together are about one foot in length. Unlike the Vampire bat, which is not more than half as large, it is not dangerous to man or animals, except when attacked, when it defends itself as well as it can. The damage which flocks of these animals might do may easily be imagined when we consider the losses which we experience from birds. The Flying Foxes will work their way under or through nets, and unless trees are enclosed in bamboo [illegible], they can hardly be excluded. The [illegible] are made among them [illegible], which renders it still more difficult to guard against them. Their name is given them from their [illegible], and from the foxlike shape of their head.

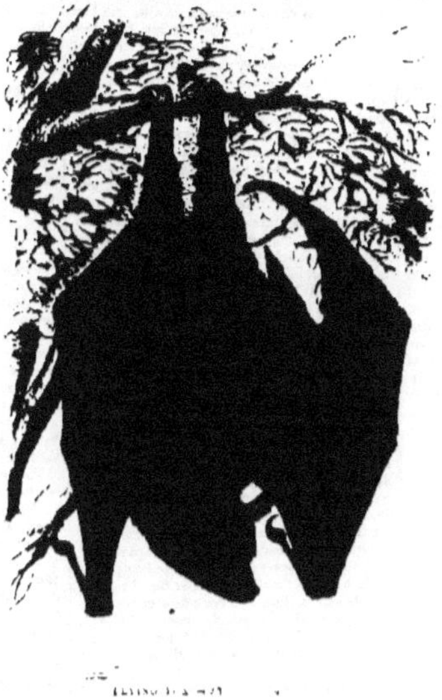

FLYING FOX—[illegible]

The American Sable.—*Mustela Americana.*

This beautiful animal, [illegible] we [illegible] careful and well executed engraving, is entirely different from the Sable of Siberia, the fur of which is so highly prized. Still, the American Sable approaches its namesake somewhat in the beauty of its coat, but is a much larger animal. It is so closely related to the Pine Marten of Europe as to have been regarded as identical by several naturalists. The home of this animal is in the trees of densely wooded regions where birds and squirrels abound, which constitute its chief food, and to which it is a very destructive enemy. It will pursue almost any of the smaller animals, and easily overtake and kill them; the red squirrel and some of the weasel tribe alone being agile enough to escape. It [illegible] attacks owls, crows and other [illegible] in their nests, [illegible] the year. [illegible] 20 [illegible] [illegible]ored, and the throat and sides of the neck are white. The head is long and pointed; the somewhat pointed ears, broad and short. The tail is bushy and club-shaped. The geographical range of the Sable is across the continent, between the 40th and 68th parallels of latitude, and throughout this [illegible] it is diligently hunted. Trappers establish what is called a "Sable line," often 60 or 70 miles in length. This [illegible] series of traps, [illegible] to the [illegible] made [illegible] stakes into the ground to form three [illegible] a hollow [illegible]; over the [illegible] side, one end of a log or trunk of a young tree is [illegible] being held up by a [illegible] stick [illegible] another which is baited with a [illegible], partridge, or piece of venison. The least disturbance of the bait causes the stick to roll, and the log to fall. It often happens that wolverines, [illegible], and occasionally foxes, tear [illegible] traps, destroying bait and game for miles along the "line." The trapper passes continually back and forth, spending some part of his time in hunting other game, but visiting all his sable traps as often as once in two weeks. The fur is best between the last of October and the first of April. The female [illegible] takes possession of an [illegible] bird's nest in a hollow tree, or ousts the occupants, and [illegible] brings forth six or eight young. Were it not for the persistence with which these animals are hunted, they would be much more numerous; [illegible] they hardly hold their own from year to year in those parts where they are abundant enough to pay for hunting them, for they [illegible] very little [illegible] [illegible] the natural [illegible] of the animal [illegible] ever be so far overcome as to render it [illegible] to [illegible] in destroying birds.

AMERICAN SABLE.—(*Mustela Americana.*)

Tim Bunker on Base Ball Clubs.

"Don't you think they are running on't into [illegible]," asked Seth Twiggs, as he stopped [illegible] fence, when I was [illegible] squashes this morning. "I declare [illegible] clean out [illegible] body to work, [illegible] [illegible]. We [illegible] [illegible] among the [illegible], where the women do all the drudgery, and the men play all the time they ain't fishin'. I hired Kish Frink and another White Oaker to come down and help me husk, and they had to leave right away after dinner to go to a base ball match. They said they wouldn't stop for double wages, for they could make more money on the ball ground betting. They knew which side was gwine to win. Pretty state of things!" Seth thought the case was so clear that he didn't wait for an answer, but walked off in his usual cloud of smoke. This evening, Mrs. Bunker took up the Hookertown Gazette, and read, "Shadtown victorious! the White Oaks nowhere!! The score stood 27 to 9. Great interest has been taken in this match from the well-known fact that both parties had been training for it for a month past, and large sums had been staked upon the result. It is said that the White Oakers practiced by moonlight while they were burning their coal pits, and the picked nine of the Shadtown Club have made a business of playing ball six days in a week for the last month. Of course, they bore off the honors."

"Honors!" exclaimed Sally, lifting her gold bowed spectacles to the top of her forehead, and looking over to me. "When we were young, Timothy, it used to be an honor for a young man to lay a straight furrow, or to mow a wide swath. But now they've beat their plowshares into ball clubs, and the loafers that can play ball best carry off all the honors. It seems to me, Timothy, that we are getting considerable ahead of the days of prophecy. The plowshares and pruning hooks is the Bible ideal of a perfect state of society. When grown up men exchange plowed fields and orchards for the ball ground, and make a bat stick their coat of arms, I think they are progressing the wrong way."

This set me to thinking about this base ball business. For it has ceased to be a mere amusement, and, with some people, has got to be as much of a business as catching fish or making brooms. I believe in the division of labor and in new kinds of business, but it is a question whether this is going to add anything to the common wealth or happiness. I believe in athletic sports and games of skill, and have no doubt that there is a place for them in every well-regulated society. Base ball, as we used to play it when I was a boy at school, was a very healthful recreation. It was a change from sedentary habits that the boys needed. I should think it might be a good thing for college boys and clerks in the city. But what do people want of it whose lives are already full of labor? It can only add to their weariness, and detract from the interest and pleasure that every man should take in his daily toil. After a man has spent three or four hours in a game, he is pretty well used up for the day, and is in rather poor trim for work next morning. Base ball, as it is played now, is getting to be a great nuisance.

It seriously interferes with the business of life. Seth Twiggs' case is just what has happened to me a dozen times this summer, and is happening all over the country. When I get a gang of men into the hay field, and have the hay all ready to go into the barn, I do not want to have half of them quit at three o'clock in the afternoon for a ball match. It breaks up all my plans for the day, and necessarily leaves a part of my hay to stand out over night. Over in Shadtown, they build ships, and when a man gets a contract to drive his ship through in a given time, it's a great vexation to have a part of his force absent two or three days in a week, to attend a ball match. Many kinds of mechanical labor are done by contract, and it subjects a contractor to very serious loss if he cannot depend upon his laborers.

It is a great waste of time and money, and few men can afford it. Most laboring men need the avails of their six days' work for the support of their families and for the accumulation of capital enough to carry on business for themselves. One day in the week is a serious loss to them. But if a man joins a base ball club, the loss of time is only a small item. He must have a suit expressly to play ball in, costing, say twenty-five dollars. Then, there must be a club-room, nicely fitted up, where the members meet for business, and on state occasions, when they receive guests from abroad. Then they must have their entertainments—which means sprees. Then they must, of course, accept all invitations to attend matches, no matter at how great a distance. Come to foot up the invitation fees, taxes, traveling expenses, sprees, and lost time, a young man finds himself three or four hundred dollars out of pocket at the close of the year. This may be all very agreeable pastime, but how few can afford it even in the city! And if they could, there are still more serious objections to it.

It leads very naturally to bad company. I know the young men that make up the ball clubs of Hookertown, Shadtown, and the White Oaks, and I have seen their guests. They are not such men as I should want my John to associate with. Some of them are what they call gentlemen's sons, with plenty of money and no business, which is very bad. Others have business, and neglect it to play ball, which is still worse. Some are average farmers and mechanics, rather green at the play, not yet spoiled, but in a fair way to be. Others are confirmed loafers, rather seedy, and far on the downhill road. They are vulgar and profane; but pitch, bat, and catch splendidly, for the game is their only business. It can't do a young man much good to be brought in contact with such characters. The manners and morals of the ball ground are much more likely to mar than to mend him. The tendency of the game, as now managed, is toward idleness, gambling, and dissipation. It makes good ball players, but bad farmers and mechanics, bad husbands and fathers. I am not ready to have the plow beams whittled into ball clubs just yet.

Then it is rather a low aim in life. There is something noble in making a first-rate farmer. That means cheaper bread and meat for the nation. To be a good mechanic is praiseworthy. It means better homes for the people, and better tools to do their work. But to be a first-rate ball player, or to be one of a champion nine, —what does it amount to? If Shadtown beats the White Oakers all hollow, who is the better for it? General Trowbridge came through Hookertown last week in his splendid turn-out, and when opposite the widow Taft's, a little noisy cur came out, and barked at his carriage, as if he thought he could stop it. He succeeded, and the general jumped out, and walloped the cur soundly, and sent him yelling through the gate. This brought the widow to the door in a somewhat excited state; "Wall, gineral, that's a big victory for you! You've whipt a one-eyed cur." It strikes me that the base ball victories are about on a par with the general's. Shadtown is triumphant, but the White Oakers still live. Yours, to command,

TIMOTHY BUNKER, Esq.

Hookertown, Oct. 25th, 1867.

THE KIDNEY VETCH.—The Kidney Vetch, (*Anthyllis Vulneraria*,) one of the wild plants of England, having been proposed as a valuable forage plant, was analysed by Prof. Voelcker. The plant was examined in the form of hay, with the result that it was found to contain scarcely half the amount of fatty matters, was poorer in flesh-forming compounds, and had a great deal more indigestible woody fibre than either clover hay or good meadow hay. Prof. V. thinks it might be more valuable if fed green.

Walks and Talks on the Farm.—No. 48.

(*Continued from page 440.*)

We have a cheese factory in successful operation here in the wheat district, and another is about to be established. This is what I have always wished. I do not see why we cannot make as good cheese here as is made in Herkimer County or the Western Reserve. We can raise just as good grass, and more of it. With plenty of wheat, barley, and oat straw, corn stalks, pea and bean haulm, and clover hay so abundant that many farmers still plow it under for manure, we can winter our cows much cheaper than in the dairy districts. On my farm I can winter three times as much stock as I keep through the summer. In the dairy districts, where the farms are devoted almost exclusively to grass, and where, consequently, the cows must be wintered principally on hay, the number of cows to be kept must be determined by the ability of the farmer to carry them through the winter.

The cost of feeding a cow on hay through the winter must form a large item in the expense of keeping a dairy, and yet it is strange that nearly all our writers on dairying say little on this point. They give us very minute directions as to feeding the cows in the spring, after they come in, but say nothing in regard to feeding them during the winter. And yet it seems to me the latter is, if anything, the more important point. The cow needs to accumulate strength during the winter to enable her to stand the great strain on her constitution during calving, as well as through the long period of milking.

A cow will eat 3 pounds of hay a day to each 100 pounds of her live weight. If she weighs 800 pounds, she will eat 24 pounds of hay, or 168 pounds a week. If fed on hay alone from December 1st to May 1st, (22 weeks,) she would consume 3,696 pounds. A cow weighing 1000 pounds would eat in the same time 4,620 pounds, or a little over $2\frac{1}{3}$ tons. Horsfall, the best authority we have on feeding dairy cows, says it requires 20 pounds of hay a day for the maintenance of a store cow. In other words, it takes this amount merely to support the vital functions—the cow will give no milk, nor increase in weight. She will merely live. According to this, it requires a little over a ton and a half of hay to keep a cow from December to May, without getting anything in return. When cows are fed three per cent. of their live weight, of good hay, per day, we may reasonably expect more or less milk, or an increase in flesh or fat.

If it takes 20 pounds of hay a day to keep a cow alive, we should never forget that *all* our profit comes from the food the cow consumes over and above this amount. Mr. Horsfall had a cow that, for the sake of the experiment, he fed on hay alone. She was a rather small cow, but noted for her usefulness as a good milker. At the time of calving her third calf, November 12th, she was in rather high condition, and gave 17 quarts of milk a day. On the 1st of January, at the commencement of the experiment, she weighed 980 pounds, and was giving $13\frac{1}{2}$ quarts of milk a day. She was allowed all the hay she would eat, and consumed, on an average, 28 pounds per day. On March 5th, her yield had fallen off to $9\frac{1}{2}$ quarts per day, and the cow then weighed only 896 pounds—a loss of 84 pounds. On the average, during the experiment of nine weeks, she gave $12\frac{1}{2}$ quarts per day.

Another cow fed according to Mr. Horsfall's system on steamed food, gave 18 quarts per day at the time of calving, October 8th, and at the commencement of the experiment, January 1st, 13¼ quarts per day. She then weighed 1093 pounds. She gave, on the average, 14 quarts per day, and at the end of the experiment weighed 1170 pounds—a gain of 56 pounds.

Mr. Horsfall figures up the result as follows:

No. 1. Average yield of milk per day 18¼ quarts @ 4 cents		$3.50
Deduct loss of flesh, 8¼ @ 12 cents		1.12
		$2.39
28 pounds of hay per day, @ $17.14 per ton		1.69
Profit per week		$0.70
No. 2. Average yield of milk per day 14 quarts, @ 4 cents		$3.92
Gain of flesh 6¼ pounds, @ 12 cents		75
		$4.67
Hay, 63 pounds per week	54c.	
Straw and oat shells	30c.	
Mangel wurzel	24c.	$1.08
Rape-cake, 35 pounds; Bran, 19¼ pounds; Malt combs, 10¼ p'nds; Bean meal, 10¼ pounds	97	2.65
Profit per week		$3.02

"The richer quality of the manure," Mr. H. well observes, "will probably compensate for the extra labor, cooking, and attention bestowed." The profits from the cow fed on hay are 70 cents per week, while from the cow fed on rich food they are $3.02 per week. It is true, if we take merely the cost of the food and the value of the milk, the profit from the two cows is nearly identical, or $1.8[illegible] from the hay-fed cow, and $1.67 from the high-fed cow. And there are many people who would figure in this way. They would leave out of the question the gain or loss of flesh.

The 9¼ pounds of flesh which the cow lost per week either went to make milk or to support the animal. It was equivalent to a certain amount of food. Thanks to the investigations of Lawes and Gilbert, we know what this flesh which an animal lost is composed of, or, at all events, we know what the flesh which an animal gains is composed of, and we may well suppose that within certain limits they are identical.

One hundred pounds *increase* of beef cattle is composed of:

Water	24.6	pounds
Mineral matter	1.47	"
Nitrogenous compounds	7.69	"
Fat	66.2	"

Now it is very evident that 12 cents per pound is rather a low estimate of the value of such animal food.

The *carcass* of a half-fat ox is composed of—

Water	54.00	per cent.	
Mineral matter	5.56	"	"
Nitrogenous compounds	17.6	"	"
Fat	22.4	"	"

Even the carcass of a "fat ox" contains 45.6 per cent. of water; and such beef sells in New York for 17 cents per pound, and I think it would not be difficult to show that butchers and consumers really pay us from 20 to 25 cents for every pound of *increase* we put on a well bred, half-fat ox. What does a thin steer sell for in New York, and what a fat one? I have frequently seen "extra" cattle quoted at 18 cents, and "inferior" at 8 cts. But let us assume that a "half-fat ox" brings 12 cents per lb. "estimated dressed weight for the four quarters," and the "fat ox" 17 cents. The "half-fat ox," analysed by Lawes and Gilbert, weighed, alive, after fasting, 1233 pounds; the carcass, 797¾ pounds. At 12 cents per pound, he would bring $95.73.

The "fat ox," analysed by Lawes and Gilbert, weighed, alive, after fasting, 1419 pounds, and dressed 930¾ pounds. At 17 cents per lb. this ox would bring $140.71.

Now, the difference between the two, in live weight, is 187 pounds. One was kept fatting till he had *increased* 187 pounds more than the other. Mr. Horsefall reckons this increase of flesh at 12 cents per pound. What do the New York butchers estimate it at? At 12 cents per pound, it comes to $22.44. But the butchers will pay $95.73 for the one animal, and $140.71 for the other. In other words, they pay for this 187 pounds of increased live weight $53.98, or over 28⅞ cents per pound.

This 9¼ pounds of flesh which the cow lost each week would contain over 6 pounds of fat, equivalent to over 7 pounds of butter. There is no record of how much butter the 12¼ quarts of milk contained, but it would be of full average quality if it gave a pound a day, and consequently the whole of the butter obtained might have come from the fat which had been stored up in the cow previous to calving. But this 9¼ pounds of flesh, so called, would contain only about 12 ounces of nitrogenous compounds, while the milk obtained during the week contained probably six or seven pounds. Nearly the whole of this must have come from the food. And this will account, in some measure, for the well known fact that milch cows require a more nitrogenous food than fattening animals.

But excuse me. You have been out in the cold all day, and I know that a warm stove and a talk about "nitrogenous food" will put any farmer to sleep.

The matter has, however, a very important practical bearing, and a *young farmer*, at least, should make himself acquainted with the subject. The old people may be excused. It is just as easy to learn the difference between nitrogenous food and carbonaceous food as it is to learn the difference between haw and gee. But I will not use the terms any more than is necessary. In short, it may be said that theory and practice both indicate that it is most economical to feed milch cows high enough to enable them to give all the milk they can secrete, and to lay on fat at the same time.

The drouth still continues in this section, and fears are entertained that winter may set in before we have rain enough to start the springs. Should such be the case, we shall surely be troubled to get water for the stock. Many farmers now have to drive their cattle to the canal or to the nearest stream; and water for the hogs has to be carried in barrels. It has been vain to think of fall plowing. Heavy soil is as dry and as hard as a rock—and it is this kind of land, rather than the sandy loams, that is most benefited by fall plowing. Wheat has come up very unevenly. Where the ground is loose and moist, the wheat is too rank; while on the dry, lumpy "clay spots," much of it is barely out of the ground. It has been splendid weather for doing fall work—digging potatoes, husking corn, etc. But the stalks are so dry and brittle, that it is almost impossible to tie up the bundles. Pigs that are well fed grow rapidly this mild weather, but corn is so high that farmers are selling them before they are half or quarter fat. Buyers are picking them up at about 5 cents per pound. One of my neighbors was selling cider the other day, and was asked if he had put any water in it. "Water," said he, "no, *sir;* not *this year.* Water is a good deal scarcer than cider."

The Cotton Moth.—(*Ophiusa xylina.*)

Again the destructive larvæ of this insect have done great damage to the cotton crop.

Of late years their reappearance has been more frequent, and at shorter intervals, although not always over the entire cotton-growing region.

It is strange that so little has been published of their nature and habits; and that of that little still less has been at all correct. Here is a representation of the parent moth, as nearly correct as it is possible to make wood cuts which must be printed on ordinary paper by a power press. Few of the beautiful and delicate markings can be shown; but in form, true proportions, and general markings, the likeness is correct. So of the larva, or *Cotton worm*, and the chrysalis.

The insect has never been even authoritatively named.

Fabricius describes an entirely different insect under the name of *Noctua xylina.*

Jay gives a pretty good description of the true Cotton-moth, styling it *Noctua xylina*, "which name," the late Dr. T. W. Harris remarks in a letter to the writer of this, "was a good and proper name for the insect, as the subject was understood by Mr. Jay, who did not pretend to know much of the *Lepidoptera*. *Ophiusa xylina* better accords with the present state of the science." That name, first published by myself, on the above authority, seems now to be adopted. I will spare you any lengthy history of the previous appearances of the insects, or any attempt at a scientific disquisition, and confine myself to a familiar sketch of their habits, and their effects upon the crop, probable manner of hybernating, and possible means of heading them off.

It is difficult, nay, well-nigh impossible, to speak positively as to the *where* or *when* of the first appearance of an insect which spreads itself over so vast an extent of country, and possesses such wonderful powers of migration for a thing so frail.

This present year, I heard of them early in June, as being then at work in a small crop of Sea Island or Long-stapled Cotton on the [illegible] of Judge Jones, at Virginia Point, on the [illegible]and opposite the city of Galveston—the extreme southern portion of the main-land at that point.

Although doubts were expressed as to their being the real "*Simon pure,*" I found they were so. They were few in number, and thinly spread over a scattering crop of cotton. They had been reported on the extreme southern plantations at the mouth of the Brazos and of Old Caney rivers, some 50 or 60 miles west and south of Virginia Point, several days before. They soon spread northward, utterly destroying the crops in some localities, doing partial damage to others, and in some places appearing only in small numbers. In old times, the injury would have been deemed quite serious wherever they appeared, but now, all of the cotton the worm spared will not be picked.

And this has been the invariable history of their advent each season of their appearance. They first show themselves to the extreme south and south-west, and thence spread rapidly into the interior.

The *worm* cannot exist without a plentiful supply of its only food. The egg is extremely fragile, and deposited, I believe, invariably on the leaf of the cotton plant. In no instance have I been able to keep the chrysalis long beyond the time of the appearance of the perfect insect. It is the *Moth*, then, that *hybernates.*

The winters upon the Texas seaboard are mild and of short duration. Very frequently the cotton plant is in leaf all winter. I was shown a prodigiously tall and strong stalk of cotton, cut from a *stool* of the plant, which had become perennial, or had at least held its own for many winters, in the lovely Valley of the Guadaloupe, not far from the village of Cuero, throwing up these immense shoots each spring. Now, under these circumstances, the life of the moth would need to be preserved but a very few weeks, to enable it to perform its errand, in perpetuating its species. The first deposited eggs and the first larvæ would be exposed to many casualties; yet, a very few escaping these, would soon produce untold millions. I have never been able to preserve the moth alive longer than from three to seven days. But the period of the existence of all such insects depends so greatly upon the degree of moisture and heat of the atmosphere, their supply of food, etc., that that is no criterion.

Fig. 1.—WORM.

During the lifetime of the moth, in summer, they may be seen in the evening, flitting from blossom to blossom of the cotton plant, the cow-pea, etc., feeding upon the nectar of the flowers.

The female deposits from four to six hundred eggs, thinly scattered over the under side of the leaves of the cotton plant. The egg is minute, round, flattish, and of a whitish-green color.

The *larvæ* are hatched forth in from two to five days; almost invariably in two days of moist, warm weather. When hatched, they are very minute. About the fifth and sixth days, they begin to increase rapidly in size, and are voraciously destructive. From the tenth to the fifteenth day, generally about the eleventh and twelfth, they enter the *chrysalis* state. The worm draws the edge of a leaf over itself, by means of numerous silken threads, until completely enveloped, and there, if undisturbed, undergoes its transformation. Fig. 1 represents a full-grown worm. Fig. 2 is an outline of a moth, to show its natural size, and fig. 3 a moth enlarged to show its markings more distinctly.

A very few days are required by the worm of the second or third crop to devour not only every leaf, blossom bud, and blossom, but the *calyx leaves*, also, at the base of the *bolls*, fully and partially grown; when the *lobes* which hold the cotton open entirely back, and allow the cotton to drop on the merest touch.

From this sketch of the nature and habits of these insects, it will be seen how difficult, if not impossible, would be the task of destroying them by the use of the finger and thumb or scissors, as in the case of the tobacco worms, which are of great size and few in number comparatively. I have experimented with every means that has been suggested through an active outdoor life; and the conclusion arrived at, is: Destroy the moth, as you may, with fires and lights, or pick off and kill the worm; if a single cotton grower in a large district neglects to do the same, your labor is in vain.

Fig. 2.—MOTH.

The plant must be rendered obnoxious to the moth, so that she will not deposit her eggs upon it. Then your indolent or indifferent neighbor suffers for his neglect instead of yourself.

Investigations and experiments recently made, at home and in Europe, to find a cure for *Scab* and *Foot-rot* in sheep, led me to the discovery that, of all known substances, the comparatively recently discovered acid, known as *Carbolic*, formed into a saponaceous compound, was *the most obnoxious to all insect life*.

I brought home a moderate quantity of *McDougall's Sheep Dip*, and first experimented with that. It is, in fact, a *Carbolic soft soap*, into a solution of which sheep are dipped, and thereby cured of scab.

But I found that the insects in our clear, warm, dry climate possess a strength, vitality, and power of revivication, if I may use the expression, unknown to the same species in England; and that to destroy the scab insect, fleas on dogs, etc., a much stronger solution had to be used here than there, and under different treatment.

But in the yet more recently discovered *Cresylic Acid* we have the very thing that was wanted.

I will leave the manufacturers of this soap to speak for themselves,—except as to our present subject. I found that upon the cotton plants sprinkled with a solution of this soap, *no cotton moth thereafter deposited an egg!*

Is not this fact worthy of further experiment, not only on the cotton plant, but upon all other vegetable life threatened by insects,—the plum by the curculio; the apple and pear by the canker-worm; the grape and the rose by the rose-bug; all young plants by aphides, and, above all, the wheat by the fly? Soon after the Cotton-worm first appeared, this season, I urged that others should try similar experiments. Many did so, and almost every experimenter made the same report—"If the mixture is used in sufficient strength *to kill the worm*, it also destroys the leaf of the plant." Exactly. But there is no necessity for trying *to destroy the worm*. Let him go, if any are there, but *prevent the moth depositing any more eggs*. Yours, T. A.

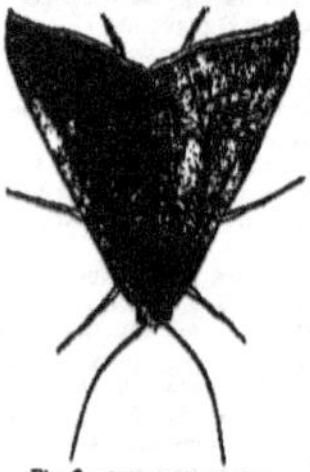
Fig. 3.—MOTH ENLARGED.

Poultry—Close Breeding, etc.

It is gratifying to observe the rapid increase of a very *healthy* interest in poultry and poultry breeding, which is manifesting itself almost all over the country. An American Society has been formed, which it is hoped will take high ground, uniting the various clubs, societies, and individual poultry breeders in various parts of North America, and being by them used for advancing their own interests by exchange of birds, information, etc., besides the advantage in having a certain uniformity of rules and standards. Writing to the *Agriculturist* on this general subject, Mr. S. B. Heiyes, of York Co., Pa., remarks:

"A greater interest than heretofore has recently been manifested in poultry, because of the great number of reliable persons who have gone into importing and rearing valuable varieties of poultry, both for ornament and use.

That the general interest is greater is plainly seen from the crowds assembling around the poultry coops at our County fairs, where a greater and better variety of all domestic fowls has been placed upon exhibition than our State fairs could boast of a few years ago.

While this is the fact, there are a great many truths which can be promulgated only by the *united* action of individuals, as a society. The majority of breeders are ignorant of the many evils (and of the few good results) attending close, or in-and-in, breeding. They start out with a few noble specimens, and in a very few years their darling fowls have lost size and good qualities; they become discouraged, and abandon every effort to raise fine poultry. Proper instruction from well organized societies would obviate this.——Permit me to state two remarkable phenomena, results of close breeding, that were submitted to my consideration lately. Jos. Shuman, near York Co., Pa., a gentleman who raises nothing but Sumatra game, (having procured his stock from Albertus Welsh, who bought of Bennett's imported stock,) by continually breeding from the same strain has produced perfectly white Sumatras; a change from black to white. They are beautiful specimens, with dark legs, and compact bodies containing greater weight in small superficies than any other breed with which I am familiar. Samuel Dick, Esq., of the same County, from a stock of Buff Shanghaes, which I have also traced back to importation, has also produced fine specimens of pure *white*. May not the White Leghorn have been produced by breeding from the same strain of Black Spanish? They possess all their characteristics, and, if bred *closely*, will produce *black* offspring, which I know beyond a doubt. That good may result from this practice, I do not deny, but that "like will produce like," is not always true when we overstep the bounds of nature.

It is conceded that all of our varieties of turkeys have sprung from the wild bird. Domestication and in-and-in breeding have given us fowls differing widely from the original in color, bearing, and size, and possessing traits unknown in the original, as the custom of the White Holland turkey to lay extensively in the fall."

Breeding of Swine.

The careless way in which swine are bred entails upon them enfeebled constitutions, proneness to disease, inability to make the best use of their food, grow rapidly, fatten rapidly, and make hard, firm flesh, with little offal. Close attention to breeding and to health will quickly develop in this plastic race an astonishing aptitude to take on fat, rapid change of form, approaching nearer and nearer whatever may be taken as a standard, and a soundness of constitution which is increasingly hereditary. We have not a doubt that many of the ills from which mankind suffer come directly or indirectly from pork eating. Nevertheless, we believe that reasonable attention to the health of swine would result in so much greater healthfulness of pork, that it might be eaten by persons able to take so hearty food, with impunity. Jefferson Co., N. Y., has long been noted for its fine hogs. The State fairs have repeatedly witnessed fine exhibitions coming from that County, and we have almost come to regard any Jefferson Co. farmer as authority on hogs. Mr. M. Pierson, who dates thence, writes:

"I was glad to see something in the *Agriculturist* in regard to breeding this indispensable, yet most neglected, carelessly fed and bred, of all domestic animals—the hog. Messrs. Bidwell Bros., of Minnesota, speak well in their suggesanother good in these particular points in which the former fails, and always keep our breeders after they have been tested and found to be what we want as long as they will breed. And always keep them fleshy, as flesh will become a natural condition after a few generations, if they are not allowed to run down. I believe we may just as well have a breed that will mature in eight or ten months and dress from 300 to 400 lbs., and this done too, on three-fourths the food that it would require to attain the same weight with our "old-fashioned hogs" in eighteen or twenty months, and an inferior quality of pork at that. I am not a swine breeder, but I know how it is done, and how it should be done, for I have a neighbor who has put the foregoing practical rules to the test for the past ten years, and his pigs are easily made to dress 350 to 400 lbs. at nine months, as hundreds of pork makers in this county can affirm. And I have no doubt that this County alone is more than ten thousand dollars better off for his enterprise in this direction. He is rewarded by having made a fortune in the business. Not only this County but this State and many others, as well as Canada, are greatly benefited by one man conducting this business in a sensible way, and as every other sensible farmer should."

[We can mention other good farmers who are doing much in the same way, and are making hog-raising for pork, profitable even at the East. For ourselves we very well know that there is no profit in raising hogs for pork alone, unless prices of corn rule low, and those for pork, high. It is not for their flesh alone that *we* raise hogs, but for their service as manure makers, and this should be borne in mind by the farmer.—Ed.]

Killing Time for Hogs and Beef.

The subject of killing domestic animals for food comes directly home to every farmer and farmer's wife in the country. Slaughtering is not so pleasant to the farmer as the preliminary labors of breeding, raising, and fattening, neither are the labors it imposes upon the good-wife so agreeable as preparing the fat spare-ribs and sirloin roasting pieces for the table, yet both are equally necessary.

It is very desirable to have cold weather for the operation, and as our cold days are very likely to come in threes or fours, there seldom being more than four consecutive very cold days, and usually but three, it is best to be ready, and take the first clear cold day for the work, and trust to the two following to freeze what meat is to be kept fresh. In regard to pork, that is almost all to be salted or smoked, this is not very important, yet it is much more convenient and pleasant to handle meat that is firm and cold than that which is flabby.

The most convenient way for a farmer to handle

In cutting up beef, it is important to remember that the object is not simply to get it all into small pieces, but to have the pieces of such shape, and so cut with relation to the bones, that the meat will cook to the best advantage, cut up well, appear well on the table, and more than all, be most palatable and nutritious. All this depends much upon the cutting up of the carcass.

There are many approved ways of doing this, and we cannot now discuss them, but may give two general hints, which, if followed, will be satisfactory to everybody. *First*, cut so that the pieces, when brought to the table, may be cut *across the fibre*, as squarely as possible. *Second*, so divide the carcass that each part shall have its due proportion of bone. This is difficult indeed, for the shins and knuckles will have much bone and little meat, the end of the ribs too, and the piece including the great bones of the hip and pelvis will be disproportionately bony, and pieces cut from the leg for smoked beef and salting may properly be quite free from bone; nevertheless, retail butchers know they must ever *try* to make a fair division of the bone among their customers, and the result is much more satisfactorily shaped pieces than if this principle were not heeded.

Indian Corn—Fertilization—How to Gain Two Ears to a Stalk.

A few weeks since a gentleman handed us two neatly made sections of ears of Western corn, from the farm of Wm. F. Thompson, Logan County, Ill. In themselves they were not very extraordinary, but the sections were carefully cut, and the corn being of a bright yellow edged with white, in one, and clear yellow in the other, contrasted beautifully with the red scales on the outside of the cob, and with the clear white within. We have not a doubt that many of the readers of the *Agriculturist* will be struck with the beauty of the rosette-like figures, and be surprised to find out what they are, for there are many among them familiar with the Dent or Horsetooth corn only as it comes to market, and with whom a 10-rowed or 12-rowed variety of corn is a rarity. The corn of the North-eastern States is the 8-rowed white or yellow flint, the season generally being too short for the Dent varieties. In the smaller figure, (2,) at several points, the filament connecting the kernel with the pith in the center of the cob may be distinctly traced. In all, it might have been dissected out, with a little care. At the opposite end of the kernel there is a little elevated point at which another filament, the silk, was attached. Through the silk, as is well known, the fertilizing influence of the pollen, coming from the "spindles" or "tassels," at the tops of the corn stalks in the field, descends to the kernels. Now, inasmuch as a

that, as the kernel actually derived its origin, as we have described, from two different plants

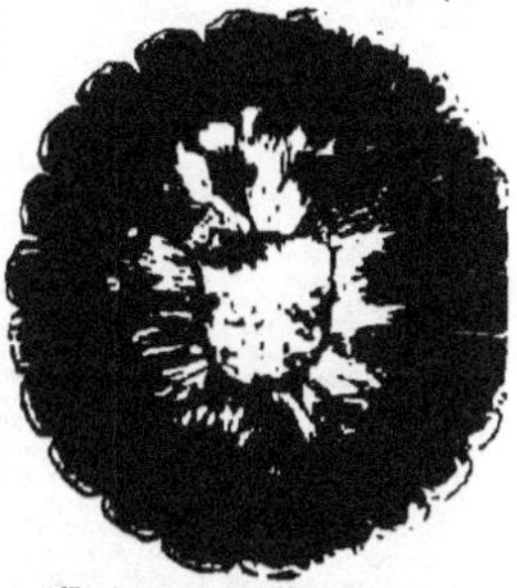

Fig. 1.—Section of 24 rowed corn.

saving the seed corn from stalks bearing two ears was not enough; he must see to it that the kernel germs were fertilized by similar stalks. So he planted every year a special patch for seed, and carefully cut off all the spindles on stalks where two or more ears were not set. The result was an improvement year by year in the quantity of corn, as well as in the manner in which it grew. The principle has a wide application in the improvement of the different kinds of farm and garden produce. In the breeding of animals, the qualities expected from the male, and those which usually are inherited from the dam, are to a degree understood, and the application of similar principles in breeding

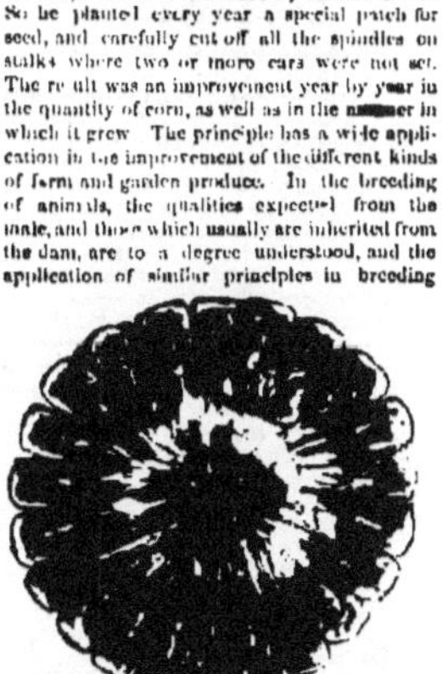

Fig. 2.—Section of 22 rowed corn.

vegetables is certainly legitimate. The fact above stated has so good a foundation in sound reasoning, that we give it to our readers, anticipating its publication in the "American Agricultural Annual," which is now in press.

THE NEW SEEDLING POTATOES.—This has been a season to test the new varieties of potatoes. The long continued rains have induced rot, and the disease has prevailed to a much greater extent than for several years. We planted the Cuzco on gravelly loam, and had a good crop, with no appearance of disease. A neighbor planted the Peachblow on the same kind of soil, and did not get his seed back again. A second neighbor, in an adjoining field, planted the same, and did not get enough to pay for his labor. The disease was probably owing entirely to the varieties of the potato planted. The Cuzco is one of Goodrich's Seedlings which we have planted for six years with uniform success. The Garnet Chili and Pink-eyed Rusty Coat are equally free from rot, yield well, and are of fair quality. The Early Goodrich and the Harison are also sound, and very productive. The new seedlings are generally much more free from rot than the old varieties, and ought to be universally adopted. Millions of dollars would have been saved to the country if these seedlings had been planted this season. Get your stock of seed potatoes early, while they are plenty and comparatively cheap.

Smoking Meats in a Small Way.

Economical farmer folks and others are often put to their wits to arrange for smoking the small quantities of meat they require for their own households, and to have at the same time a safe place to keep such meats away from flies. Barrels are occasionally used to smoke meat in, and they do very well to give the flesh the smell and flavor of smoke, but that is all. Long exposure heats the meat, and often repeating the operation is apt to cause decay at the centre, the smoke not penetrating, and the warmth affecting the meat. We are inclined to adopt, at least to make trial of, the following suggestion, and propose it to our readers as susceptible of such modifications as may be deemed expedient. The figure represents one of the casks in which British hardware is imported, though any hogshead will do. They are made of heavy, hard wood, thick and strong, and very strongly hooped. The heads are easily removed, and the casks may be made tight by pitching the seams, if not by simply tightening the hoops.

APPARATUS FOR SMOKING MEATS.

We mention these because they are cheaply obtained in most of our large cities. Take out one head of the cask, and set in it a number of hooks, upon which to hang the hams, shoulders, or sausages, cut a hole in the top in which to insert a 2-inch tin pipe, extending half way or more to the bottom, and, replacing this head, take out the other. If the position of the hoops is such that it can be done, a door may be cut, as shown in the engraving, through which the interior may be reached conveniently. If we dig a channel in the ground some 8 or 10 feet in length, and lay a course of 3-inch drain tiles in it, putting in a piece of old stove pipe in which to make the smoke-fire at one end, and turning the last tile up perpendicularly out of the ground at the other, the smoke will be sufficiently cooled in its passage through the tiles, not to affect the meat. Should the draft be too great or the smoke too warm, a flat stone might be laid over the end of the tile, and an inch above it, being supported on stakes or bricks. Our cask may be set over this; the smoke will rise and fill it, the tin pipe drawing it off when filled down to its end, and providing a draught, which, if excessive, may be checked by pressing the conical top on tight. Should a door be cut it would be necessary to have it close as snugly as possible, and if one cannot conveniently be made, the plan is still feasible, for by a block and tackle the cask may be lifted and held upright, and meat put in or taken out.

The cask should be set in a cool shed, or out-building, with an earth floor, so that in warm weather, when it will remain some days unopened, the earth may be brushed up around the chine to keep flies and insects away more effectually. During the warm weather an occasional "smudge" would, we think, enable us to keep well cured meat without difficulty.

Tight Embankments in Draining—Security against Muskrats.

The great obstacle to success in reclaiming salt marshes is the muskrat, as every one knows who has much experience in this business. You can shut out the water very readily by making your embankment high enough and thick enough. Perfect security against the encroachments of water is only a question of a little more earth taken from the inside ditch. But while you are glorying in the completeness of your work, a family of muskrats locate generally near the outlet or tide-gate, and commence their mining operations. They burrow above and below the tide-gate, and meeting in the middle the water immediately follows, and a breach is made in your dyke, the first spring-tide. To head them off various devices have been suggested and tried; concrete walls, filling a section with clay and ramming, iron plates, planks, and lastly, plates of burnt clay. This last is suggested by a correspondent who asks: "Why could not the tile men make and sell suitable tiles—a merchantable article, say 1 foot by 3 feet, and a half-inch thick? To facilitate the driving of these brick plates into the mud, an iron driver might be made with a blade a foot wide to cut through the sods and the mud. Do you not think these could be made cheaply, and that they would answer even better than iron?" No doubt brick plank could be made and put in position, but we do not see the need of them. For making the dyke tight immediately around the tide-gate, we doubt if anything can be found cheaper and more effectual than good hemlock or chestnut plank. These will last fifty years or more, and if the instincts of the muskrat be studied a little, we may guard against his assaults.

Col. Waring, in his able work upon Draining for Profit, says: "The bed of the creek should be filled in back of the dam for a distance of at least fifty yards, to a hight greater than that at which water will stand in the interior drains—say to within three feet of the surface—so that there shall never be a body of water standing within that distance of the dam. It should be a cardinal rule with all who are engaged in the construction of such works, never to allow two bodies of water, one on each side of the bank, to be nearer than twenty-five yards of each other, and fifty yards would be better. Muskrats do not bore through a bank, as is often supposed, to make a passage from one body of water to another, (they would find an easier road over

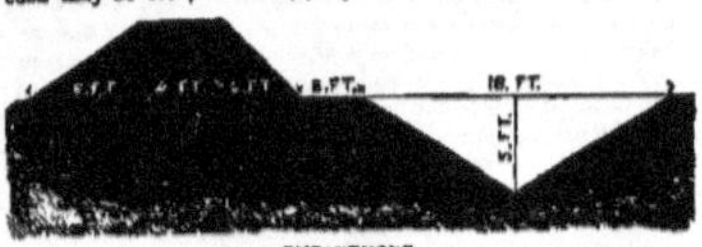

EMBANKMENT.

the top;) but they delight in any elevated mound in which they can make their homes above the water level, and have its entrance beneath the surface, so that their land enemies can not invade them. When they enter for this purpose, only from one side of the dyke, they will do no harm, but if another colony is at the same time boring in from the other side, there is great danger that their burrows will connect, and thus form a channel for the admission of water, and destroy the work. A disregard of this requirement has caused thousands of acres of salt marsh that had been enclosed by dykes having a ditch on each side, (much the cheapest way to make them,) to be abandoned, and it has induced the invention of various costly devices for the protection of embankments against those attacks." These the author condemns.

We have, then, only to keep in mind this instinct of the muskrat to make a dyke perfectly secure. In fig. 1, we have a view of a dyke and an inside ditch well adapted to ordinary locations. The only change we would make in it, suggested by our experience, is the enlargement of the border between the dyke and the ditch. This is put at three feet. We should prefer twenty, for greater security against the muskrats, and for better drainage. The rats would probably be content with the ditch border and would not touch the bank at all. The drainage nearest the ditch is most perfect, and the meadow would have the benefit of it, instead of the bank which does not need it. The strip between the bank and the ditch is as good as any part of the reclaimed land, and could be more conveniently mowed and raked with machines if it were twenty feet wide, than if it were only three. It would cost a little more to make this broad border, but it would be the cheaper in the end.

The greatest inconvenience we ever suffered from muskrats was their attacks upon the ditch borders and upon the tide-gate. The borders, in some places, were honeycombed, and the tide-gate was repeatedly eaten through until we lined it with yellow metal, which proved a little too tough for them. But with all their assaults, the gate that was put in, in November, 1855, is still doing good service. The idea of resorting to iron plates, to dam out the sea water from the Hackensack meadows, is simply ridiculous. That great improvement needs no such costly outlay. The clay or tenacious mud found just beneath the surface of a salt marsh is usually as good a material as could be desired for an embankment. For a fuller discussion of this very important matter we refer our readers to Col. Waring's work.

Pear Culture on the Connecticut Coast.

A correspondent from near Stonington, Conn., sends us the following notes upon pears:

"Stonington, Mystic, and other places near L. I. Sound, have felt very strongly the recent impulse given to fruit-growing, and during the last ten years much progress has been made, especially in the cultivation of the pear. It is rare to find out of the vicinity of Boston so many private gardens so well stocked with good fruit. The pear does even better near the shore than the apple. In no one of the last ten years has there been a general failure of the crop. It has contributed not a little to the success of pear culture that the old pastures of this early settled town are quite well stocked with pear trees. Many seedlings come up in by-places, and these, in many instances, have been transplanted, and make the best of stocks for grafting. We have sometimes taken up these seedlings, six or eight inches in diameter, by the frozen ball method, and by gradually grafting them with desirable fruit have got it early and in great abundance.

"The Flemish Beauty, for the early part of the period mentioned, was a first-rate variety. The trees grew with sufficient rapidity, came early into bearing, gave a fair russet pear with a red cheek, and it was thought to be one of the best for this region. But of late years it cracks so badly that the fruit men are quite out of patience with it and are grafting it with better sorts. It will have to be abandoned. The Beurre Diel cracks to some extent, and is considered doubtful. The Duchesse d'Angouleme does well on the lighter soils, but is hardly worth cultivating in heavy loams. The Bartlett sustains its well-earned reputation. The Julienne, on a dry, warm soil, is a first-rate summer pear, bearing regular and abundant crops. The Tyson is superb, beautiful in color, and tastes better than it looks. The Paradise of Autumn is of the most exquisite flavor, bears abundantly every year, and has this remarkable quality that the imperfect specimens are nearly deficient in flavor. It is worthy of much more general cultivation. The St. Ghislain is also about as good as it can be, and bears regular and abundant crops. It has a very sprightly, vinous, flavor, that leaves nothing to be desired. The Belle Lucrative is an early and abundant bearer upon the quince, and good enough for those who like a rich, saccharine fruit. The Muskingum is perhaps the most popular pear of this region. It comes in about a week or ten days earlier than the Bartlett, is nearly as large, is a much better fruit, and bears uniformly good crops every year. The Vicar of Winkfield, always a good baking pear, is here, when well grown, good enough for any man's table. We have eaten it in January when it was quite equal to the White Doyenne. The Bloodgood is very poor, or we have been exceedingly unfortunate in the specimens produced. The Dearborn's Seedling improves as the trees get age, but at its best estate is hardly up to its reputation. The Glou Morceau very generally cracks as badly as the White Doyenne. But we saw a large basket of them at Mystic, this fall, the product of a single tree, worthy of their highest fame. Pear culture has taken deep root here, and will be likely to spread into orchard culture. The crop is so generally reliable that it could not fail to be largely profitable."

FROZEN PLANTS.—When plants in pots become frozen, they may often be saved by judicious treatment, provided the freezing is not very severe. The way to complete the work of the frost is to bring the plant into a warm room, or, still worse, to attempt to thaw it with warm water. Leave it in a cool place where the thawing will be very gradual, and where the sun will not reach it. Trees frozen in transportation are to be treated in a similar manner. Place the box or parcel in a dark, cool cellar, or, if it be not convenient to do that, cover it thickly with straw or coarse hay, or bury it in the earth—any way to avoid a sudden change.

The Papaw.

The Papaw, (*Asimina triloba*), called also the *Custard Apple*, is widely distributed over the Western and Southern States. Its favorite localities are the bottom lands, though it grows readily on higher ground, and thousands of the young seedlings are seen springing up in the fresh clearings. The tree grows to the hight of thirty feet, and begins to bear fruit quite early, when it may be called a shrub. The fruit is three or four inches long, and more resembles the fig banana in shape and size than any thing we are acquainted with. It is less regular in its form and more rounded at the ends. It is of a greenish-yellow color when ripe, has a thin, delicate skin, and a sweetish pulp, in which are imbedded a dozen or more seeds, looking like thin, brown beans. The engraving represents one of the natural size. The leaf, flower and fruit are illustrated in Jan., 1864, page 20. The fruit is highly relished by some persons, and we have even heard it eulogized as the most delicious of all. But to most tastes it is lacking in character. It is even more neutral than fresh ripe figs, which many consider insipid. It is abundantly offered for sale, with other fall fruits, in the markets of Louisville and other Western cities. We occasionally noticed trees standing in the yards of that city, and near the farm-houses in Indiana, but we are not aware that any systematic attempts have been made for its cultivation, or that any departures have taken place from the native type of the forests. The original fruit is much more promising than many of those which have been so long cultivated and are now so highly prized. If it were taken in hand by the pomologists we have no doubt it could be made to break into rich and palatable varieties and become as popular as the banana, which is now quite as common and cheap in the New York market as the pear. The tree is as ornamental as the cherry, which it somewhat resembles in general contour. Though a native of regions lying south of forty degrees of North latitude, it would probably bear removal and become acclimated several degrees further north, and keep company with the peach and the cherry. Could the Horticultural Societies of the Western States do better than to offer a handsome premium for the first new variety of the Papaw?

PAPAW SEED.

Constitution of a Horticultural Society.

Numerous requests have been made for a form of constitution for a Horticultural Society. The best we have seen is that of the Warsaw, Ill., Hort. Society, because it is the briefest. We are indebted to Mr. F. Starr for a copy of this constitution, to which we have made some slight amendments. When a body of live horticulturists meet for the promotion of the cause, they will, if animated by the right spirit, prefer to be troubled with as little constitution as possible. There are in every community certain individuals who like to belong to societies for the opportunity it gives them to show their powers in expounding the constitution. We have known more than one society broken up because it had too strong a constitution. Another great trouble in all such societies is the everlasting talker, who occupies time, but never says anything. The hard work in all such associations falls upon a few, and it is well to put those in office who have horticulture at heart, and will work for the love of it.

CONSTITUTION. — Sec. 1. This Association shall be known as "—— Horticultural Society."

Sec. 2. Its object shall be the advancement of the science of Pomology, and of the art of Horticulture, and the collection and preservation of statistics of fruit culture in —— County.

Sec. 3. Its members shall consist of annual members, paying an annual fee of one dollar, and of honorary members, who shall consist only of persons of distinguished merit in horticulture or kindred sciences, who may, by vote, be invited to participate in the privileges of the Society. The wives of members shall be members without fee. Membership shall cease with the expiration of the year for which the fee is paid.

Sec. 4. Its officers shall consist of a President, Vice-President, and Secretary, who shall also act as Treasurer; all of whom shall be elected at the December meeting in each year, and serve until their successors are elected. These shall constitute the Executive Committee.

Sect. 5. The Executive Committee shall have charge of the property of the Society, have power to call special meetings, and attend to any executive business not otherwise provided for in the By-Laws or by especial vote of the Society.

Sec. 6. This Society shall hold monthly or other meetings as may be determined by By-Laws or resolution.

Sec. 7. This Constitution may be amended at any regular meeting by two-thirds vote of the members present, notice having been given at the preceding regular meeting.

FOREIGN ITEMS.—We glean the following notes from our recent French journals:

Thornless Gooseberry.—The Billiard Gooseberry, the fruit of good quality, the bush rather a slow grower, but without thorns.

Japanese Maples, with much divided and colored leaves, are figured in rival journals, which disagree about names. We have known the same things for several years in the collection of Mr. James Hogg, of this city, who always has some rare Japanese or other plants.

Camellia-flowered Double Peach.—This very ornamental peach, which we figured two years or more ago, fruits quite freely in France, and is said to bear a cling-stone peach of good quality.

Forcing Lilacs.—For the Paris market alone Lilacs are forced to bloom in winter by the hundred thousand. With the necessary heat and not much light, the common lilac blooms white.

Unseasonable Flowering.—Near Lyons, and in other parts of France, the unusually dry season followed by rains, caused the apple, pear, and plum trees to flower in great numbers.

The Sweet Potato as a Window Plant.—This is recommended as a plant for the dwelling, on account of the fine green of its leaves. We have seen it now and then in use in this country.

[COPYRIGHT SECURED.]

A MEMBER OF THE HUMANE SOCIETY. — *Engraved for the American Agriculturist, after a Painting by Sir Edwin Landseer.*

The Newfoundland Dog.

We know it is heretical for an agricultural paper now-a-days to see much that is good in dogs, but we cannot help it, especially when one is presented to our consideration like this in the engraving, which is a portrait by Landseer, of the full-blooded Newfoundland dog which received the medal of the Humane Society of London, for saving the lives of several drowning persons. It is certainly an astonishingly faithful representation of a good Newfoundland.

This variety is usually classed with the Spaniels, and is probably in some degree related to the Esquimaux dogs. There are two quite distinct families, the large and the small, and these have indefinitely intermingled. All are marked by a long body, broad chest, pointed head, large and fully webbed feet, great intelligence, dignity of demeanor, excessive fondness for water. The coat is always shaggy or closely curling. They are animals of great power and endurance, and by the natives of the island whence they come, were extensively used for hauling wood from the back country to the shore; a pack of four or six traveling off with what would be a good load for a horse. The Newfoundland makes an excellent watch-dog, unless he has been taught to make friends with everybody, after which he is nearly worthless for this purpose. Kept chained, he becomes very alert, and often unfriendly, though he seldom inflicts serious injuries. These dogs are possessed of a peculiar instinct, which leads them to bring out of the water almost everything which falls into it. Hence the endeavor to rescue drowning persons, in which they have been successful in numerous instances. In point of intelligence the Newfoundland ranks, among dogs, second only to the Scotch Cooley or Shepherd dog. They are the safest of dogs to have as play-mates for children, and nothing can exceed the gallant care and attention one will pay his mistress or her children if allowed to walk with them, or otherwise act as their protector.

In a careful enumeration of canine virtues, we think all familiar with this noble breed will accord to it almost every one. The attachment of a Newfoundland to his master is great, but it is remarkable that any person in real distress need not call in vain upon the dog for aid that he can give. In the water, with great sagacity he holds up the drowning man's head and swims to shore; men or children floundering and freezing in deep snows are dragged out and brought to notice; in fact, wherever he finds a human being is in distress he serves him if he can. These noble dogs have repeatedly been known to undergo great hardships in order to bring succor to entire strangers. On their native island, the dogs used to be hard worked during the winter and turned loose in the spring in a half-starved condition. Preferring mutton and game to codfish heads and offal, they are naturally inclined to the sports of the chase, and it is said that flocks often suffer. No doubt a natural proclivity thus strengthened is hard to correct in subsequent generations, — still we do not think that Newfoundland dogs are worse sheep-killers than others. Dogs of the large breed of Newfoundlands often stand 30 to 32 inches high, while the smaller ones, sometimes called St. John's dogs, measure only about two feet— a notable difference. In character they are much alike. As a watch-dog the cross with the Mastiff is greatly valued. When the Setter is crossed with a dog of the smaller breed, an animal of great service to the sportsman as a retriever, is produced, the dog retaining that faculty of the Newfoundland which leads it to bring things out of the water, to fetch and carry so naturally and handily—while it has some of the lightness and agility of the Setter.

Upon the island of New Foundland little attention has been paid to breeding these dogs, and the best animals have been sold freely for prices very small in comparison with what they will readily bring in England or the United States; the result is that the breed of the island has not improved, and it is probable that better dogs may be obtained elsewhere. The larger breed is common upon the coast of Labrador, and here fine specimens have been obtained.

BLACK ALDER—(*Ilex verticillata.*)

Our Showy-fruited Shrubs.

There are many shrubs that are quite as effective, (if not more so), in fruit as in flower, and which, upon the shedding of their leaves prolong our enjoyment of them by the pleasing colors of their berries. Leaving the exotics out of the question for the present, we find that our own shrubs present us with a great range of color, from the pure white of the Snowberry of the West, through the rich purple of the *Callicarpa* of the South, and the intense scarlet of the Black Alder, to the black of the Viburnums. Our present object is to call attention to one that is so common everywhere that its value as an ornamental plant has been overlooked. In early winter we find, in many places, the swamps in a blaze of scarlet, in strong contrast to the general dreariness of the landscape. This brilliant appearance is due to the fruit of the Black Alder, *Ilex verticillata.* By the older botanists it was called *Prinos verticillatus*, but it is now regarded as an *Ilex* or Holly, with deciduous leaves. The shrub is very common, grows from five to ten feet high, and in cultivation can easily be made to assume a symmetrical form. The flowers are small, white, and not very showy, both sterile and fertile ones being borne on the same bush. The berries are bright scarlet, very numerous, and contain six or eight seeds. The above engraving gives the size and shape of the leaves as well as of the berries.

"Solomon in all his Glory."

We are told that "Solomon in all his glory" was not arrayed like one of the "Lilies of the field." While writers have perplexed themselves in the endeavor to determine what particular plant is referred to as the lily of the field, we think that the figure has sufficient force if we accept it as applying to our garden lilies, for some of these have a gorgeousness and a glory truly regal, and they are "lilies of the field" in some parts of the world. We are at a loss to account for the comparative rarity of lilies in our gardens, when the majority of them possess every element of popularity. They present a great variety in coloring, hight, time of flowering, and most of them are quite hardy and need not be replanted for several years. It is true that some of the rarer sorts are expensive; the catalogues give a wide range of prices, from 15c. to $3.00 per bulb. Those who do not strive to possess every new thing can forego the more rare and costly ones, and at an expense of from 30 to 50c. procure sorts that will be well worth the money, and which will in a few years multiply to such an extent that one will soon have an abundance of bulbs to give to less fortunate friends. Our admiration was greatly excited over a box of lilies sent us last summer by Mr. James Vick, of Rochester, N. Y., which presented some shades of color we had not before seen. Mr. V. not only deals in seeds and bulbs, but raises them, not in a garden, but on a farm, and his many acres, all aglow with the choicest flowers, form one of the notable sights to be seen near that most beautiful of inland cities—Rochester. All the lily requires is to be planted in a good, deep, rich, mellow soil, and be let alone, except to supply a stake to support the taller kinds. Most of the bulbs will the first season, make two that will flower the next year, and each of these will again subdivide. Besides this, numerous small bulbs or offsets will be formed, which, after growing a year or two, will give flowers. When the clump becomes too crowded, the bulbs may be lifted in the fall or very early in the spring, divided and replanted. This natural multiplication is usually rapid enough for ordinary cultivators, but the florist who has to supply them by hundreds and thousands must work faster. The lily bulb is covered with scales overlapping one another, and each one of these scales, which is in reality the thickened base of the leaf of the previous season, is capable, when placed under proper conditions, of producing a new plant. The scales are carefully broken off from the bulb and planted in sand or sandy earth in boxes, taking care to have at least a third of the upper part of the scale above the surface. The boxes are kept in a cool green-house, and not too moist, until a small bulb, (and sometimes two), is found at the base of each scale. When these bulbs push out roots, they are potted in richer earth. The outer scales are generally used for the purpose, and the bulb is still left in a salable condition. We

TURK'S CAP LILY—(*Lilium Martagon.*)

enumerate a few of the desirable sorts, with the remark that they may be planted as long as the ground remains open in the autumn, and as soon as the frost leaves it in the spring.

WHITE LILY, *Lilium candidum*, one of the oldest and commonest, as well as the best, of the genus. Long ago chosen as an emblem of purity, it has in it those elements of beauty, that, as old and as common as it is, have enabled it for nearly two centuries to hold a place in our gardens against all new comers. There are double and striped-leaved varieties of this, but they all appear like monsters when contrasted with the simple dignity and purity of the original. It grows about four feet in hight.

THE LONG-FLOWERED LILY, *Lilium longiflorum*, is also white flowered and fragrant, but it has fewer and much longer flowers than the foregoing, and grows only about 18 inches high.

THE TURK'S CAP LILY, *Lilium Martagon*, grows from 3 to 5 feet high, bears a great many flowers, and perhaps varies more in color than any other species,—from white to deep purple. Our engraving is taken from a lilac colored specimen, with dark purple spots, from Mr. Vick.

THE CHALCEDONIAN LILY, *Lilium Chalcedonicum*, is another tall-growing species with most brilliant scarlet flowers, the petals of which are more strongly recurved than those of the species shown in the engraving. Omitting many other equally fine species, we notice the

JAPAN LILIES, *Lilium speciosum*, or *L. lancifolium* of the catalogues. These, which formerly sold for $3 a bulb, can be had now for 50 cents or less, and we do not know how the same amount can be expended in flowers to produce more satisfaction. There are several varieties, varying in their marking, and even a pure white one. Most are, however, white, with more or less abundant red or rose-colored spots. It is difficult to convince one unacquainted with this lily that so beautiful a flower is as hardy as a horseradish root. *Lilium giganteum*, *L. Brownii*, and *L. auratum*, are among the high priced bulbs. We must not forget to say a word for our native species, of which *L. Canadense*, *L. Philadelphicum*, and *L. superbum*, are the most common. If these be marked when in flower, and the bulbs transferred to the garden when the foliage has withered, they will repay the trouble.

A Self-closing Gate or "Stile."

In last month's *Agriculturist*, (page 405,) is an illustration of a self-closing double entrance gate. A recent number of the (English) Journal of Horticulture gives a single gate, or, as it

Fig. 1.—GATE CLOSED.

is called there, a "Sommersetshire Stile;" though a stile, properly speaking, is a set of steps to pass over a fence or hedge. The construction is quite simple, and there are probably many places in which it would be found more useful than a swinging gate, as it is self-closing and self-fastening. Fig. 1 represents the gate closed, and fig. 2 gives it half open and open; the letters refer to the same parts in both. Two posts are set, united by a cross-piece below; one of the posts, *b*, has at its top a slit to receive the cross-bar, *a*; this bar at one end passes in-

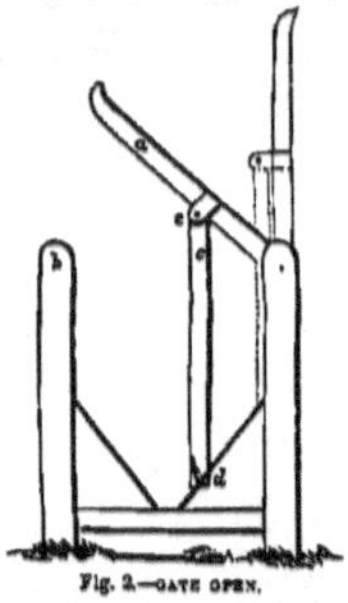

Fig. 2.—GATE OPEN.

to a mortise in the other post, and is fixed by a pin upon which it moves, and the other end is made long enough to be shaped into a projecting handle. A perpendicular piece, or pendant, *c*, is attached to the cross-bar, *a*, by means of a pivot, at *e*, and at the lower end it has a ring which runs upon the iron rod, *d*. The action of the different parts in opening is shown in fig. 2. In the description no dimensions are given, nor are there any particulars beyond what are here stated. It is thought of sufficient utility in England to patent it. We have no doubt that some one here will patent this, as has been done with several sliding gates and other simple contrivances that we have published.

Covering Strawberries in Winter.

The object of covering strawberries at the approach of winter is often misapprehended. It sometimes happens that a novice covers his plants and finds a large portion of them dead in spring. He has overdone the thing, and taken too much care of his favorites. The object is not so much to keep frost from the plant, as to protect both tops and roots from the disastrous effects of alternate freezing and thawing. Hence the covering should be put on with discrimination, and while it may be quite thick between the rows, it should not be more than an inch or so in depth over the plants themselves. In all good cultivation the plants are covered, and this serves the double purpose of protecting them from injury by alternate heat and cold, and when left on, as it should be, it keeps down the weeds and prevents the fruit from becoming soiled by contact with the earth. As to the material to be used, that will depend much upon the resources of the locality. Probably the worst materials are tan-bark and saw-dust, not that they do not afford sufficient protection, but because they soil the fruit quite as much as if it were exposed to damage from the earth. Near the coast, "salt hay" is much used, and where it is obtainable, nothing can be better. It is made from a wiry kind of grass, that preserves its elasticity in a remarkable degree. Perhaps the most generally used material is straw. Oat straw, thrashed by the flail, is preferred by some cultivators, but any kind will answer. With machine-thrashed straw it is well to throw a sprinkling of earth over it to hold it in place until the snows and frosts secure it. Do the same when leaves are employed to cover the plants; these make an excellent mulch, as do spent hops from the breweries. Pine straw—fallen pine leaves—where they are abundant, are capital for the purpose. Corn-stalks are used in some parts of the West with success, and lastly, nature's own covering—snow, if we could but secure its permanency, is, as far as winter protection goes, the best covering of all.

Improvement in Tomatoes.

There are now before the public some twenty or more kinds of tomatoes; several of these have been produced within a few years, and have been put forth with great claims to superior quality, earliness, and productiveness. We find that people try one or more of these new kinds every year, and go back to the Early Smooth Red. We cannot suppose that those who "originate" these varieties are not honest in their statements concerning the superiority of their favorites. The readiness with which the tomato varies is well known by all who have had any experience in growing it, and the trouble is that any particular sort does not have its peculiarities sufficiently fixed by a number of years' careful selection before it is put before the public as a new variety. Carelessness in saving seed, that is, in not selecting typical specimens, is sufficient in some cases to destroy the distinctive character in a single year. If a kind with some marked peculiarity were propagated from cuttings, there would not be such different opinions concerning varieties, but with a plant having so strong a tendency to variation, it is hardly to be expected that it should remain true when raised from the seed each year, unless the greatest care were taken in selecting for seed only those fruits that presented the desired form and other qualities in the strongest degree.

Two of the varieties most prominent just now are Tilden's and Keyes'. Tilden's, which is usually fine at the West, is not generally successful at the East, where it is disposed to depart from the typical form. Keyes' is said to be, in some parts of Massachusetts, "thirty days earlier than any other variety," while Mr. Gregory finds it at Marblehead, in the same State, later than several others, and at the Michigan Agricultural College, it stands third on the list in regard to earliness. Prof. Prentiss, of the above named institution, reports to the Prairie Farmer the results of his experiments with twenty-three varieties. He says: "Estimating their value by their average qualities, the finest, most desirable tomatoes now before the public, are the Tilden, Red Valencia, Collins, and Foard, these being mentioned in the order of their merit; and to these four should be added the old-fashioned Early Smooth Red, as being the earliest good variety yet produced." Another equally careful cultivator in another locality would probably make a different list. We hope that no more names will be added to our catalogues unless the varieties have some marked qualities that have become so well fixed by a course of careful breeding, so to speak, that they may be in a measure permanent. Any one who has a good sort, like the Early Smooth Red, to start with, can, by selecting the earliest good specimens from the most fruitful plants, obtain an improved variety. By continuing to do this from year to year, the superior quality of plants from such seed will be so manifest that he will have little need to run after new sorts.

Notes on Grapes and Grape Culture.

Our notes on grapes in Missouri and Ohio must give way to those gathered at the Grape Exhibition held at the office of the *Agriculturist*, on the 24th of October—an account of which will be found in our "Basket" columns.

Rogers' Hybrids.—Here are 20 varieties of these grapes, all grown by Mr. Knox. We have gone over them carefully, and our mouth burns smartly after the operation. We never see these grapes without regretting that so many of them were ever offered for sale. Their general characters are a small bunch and a large berry that readily falls from the stem. A thick skin and tough pulp are found in many, but to all these defects there are some exceptions. Some of the numbers will no doubt acquire a permanent standing, while the majority may be classed as too good to throw away, and not good enough to keep. Of the earlier numbers, 4, 9, and 15 seem to us the best. No. 4 was noticed last month, and we have nothing to add to our description. No. 9 is a dark Catawba color, smaller than No. 4, and much less showy. A very sugary grape, but not tender enough to be first class. No. 15, large berry and good-sized bunch, nearly black; flesh very "meaty," and resembles a Black Hamburgh as far as this quality goes. Not so sweet as No. 9. Of the later numbers, 33, 39, 41, 43 and 44, are all large, black, berries, and in character of flesh resemble No. 15, but some are sweeter and more vinous. From the specimens before us we should say that 39 is better than the others. The bunches from young vines are small, but if a large one can be obtained this will become a favorite.

Salem.—Only small and indifferent bunches were sent, and it is not fair to judge from these.

If what we have is a fair sample, we consider it inferior to No. 89, but we wait another year before forming a definite opinion of this.

Keuka.—Exhibited by Geo. W. McDowell, of Crooked Lake, Steuben Co., N. Y. It is an early black grape, and claimed to be a seedling. Judging from the fruit alone, we cannot see in what it differs from the Logan, which variety it resembles in being very seedy. But little is known of it outside of its place of origin.

Martha.—Mention was made of this in last month's notes. We cannot agree with the high estimate which some put upon this variety, but we have no doubt it will please a large class who like a very sweet grape, without sprightliness. The flesh of the Martha is peculiarly buttery, and the skin very tender.

There are three grapes which much resemble each other in general characters, that are especial favorites with us: the Herbemont, Elsinburgh, and Alvey. They deserve to be better known, as they are first class fruits in every respect save that of size.

Herbemont.—A large, very compact bunch; berry medium, black, with a fine bloom. Vine too tender for general cultivation at the North. Mr. Knox exhibited fine specimens and a cane with the grapes upon it to show its abundant bearing. It requires a still more favorable locality than his to reach its full development, the specimens shown by him not being equal in quality to those we tested in Missouri.

Elsinburgh.—A looser bunch and smaller berry than Herbemont. Vine quite hardy; fruit very spirited and vinous. Excellent for amateur culture, but not sufficiently attractive in appearance to be a market sort.

Alvey.—This is a larger berry than either of the two foregoing. Ripens perfectly around New York, and is, if possible, still better further south. Mr. Fuller says, "too small for a table grape," in which we cannot agree with him, as the berries are larger than those of the Delaware. Mr. Mead thinks it the same as the Lenoire, but if we have the true Lenoire, the two are quite distinct. Tender, sweet, rich, sprightly, with a very thin skin, on which account it can never be a market grape, but for family use it hardly has a superior.

Iona.—Through the exertions of Dr. Grant, a fine show was made of this variety, embracing specimens from Ohio, New York, and Connecticut. Those from Ohio were the best ripened, but suffered somewhat from long carriage. The specimens exhibited by Mr. Beach, of Hartford, Conn., were very handsome, but were picked too soon, in anticipation of a frost. Our opinion of the high character of this grape was expressed in our notes last month.

Adirondac.—No specimens were equal to what we have seen in previous years. Those from Mr. Bailey were far from the standard, on account of continued wet weather. It is a great pity that so fine a grape is not more reliable.

Catawba.—Mr. Knox exhibited specimens of a depth of color and beauty of bloom hardly to be excelled in the celebrated Lake Shore Region.

North Carolina.—A showy grape, somewhat after the style of Hartford Prolific, but with larger and better berries, and nearly as early as that variety. A good market sort.

Muscogee.—Exhibited by Mr. Richards, of Fordham, N. Y. A small fruit, of the Herbemont class. It much resembles that variety in quality, but ripens earlier. We have never seen the fruit except from the gentleman above named.

Weehawken.—A seedling by Doct. Siedhof from a Crimean grape. The specimens were shown under great disadvantage, as, from a misunderstanding as to the time of the exhibition, they had been packed a week. It is a white grape, with all the characters of the European varieties, very productive, and with Doct. S., healthy in a locality where mildew is abundant.

Unnamed Seedlings.—Olm Brothers, Springfield, Mass., sent two; one a grape much like the Elsinburgh, and the other resembling the Catawba. The last named has all the appearance of a good Catawba, and is quite as good, with a rather loose bunch, but it ripens perfectly before that variety is colored.

Mr. Arnold, of Paris, Canada, sent two of his seedlings, obtained, as we understand, by hybridizing the Clinton with exotic sorts. No. 5 is a white, or rather green grape, inclining to amber; a long bunch without shoulders; small sized berry, sprightly in flavor, and of good character. No. 2 is a compact bunch, usually with a large shoulder; berry of medium size, black, with a fine bloom; flesh tender, very juicy, and rather acid, but vinous. Mr. A. states that the specimens are not in their best condition, as the vines were nearly defoliated by a hail storm before the fruit ripened. He has certainly reason to be pleased with his success in raising seedlings, and we look with interest to the reports of their trial in localities further south.

The Profits of a Small Place.

A correspondent, M. S., in a New England town, is so much pleased with the results of his attempts at gardening that he desires to give his experience for the encouragement of others. We give his letter as a specimen of many we receive of similar purport. It is not practicable for us to publish many accounts of this kind, but we are, as our readers know, as much interested in the success of small gardens as in that of large ones.

"About ten years ago I purchased a house and a small parcel of ground about fifty rods from the principal business street in N——; said ground located on the east side of a steep hill, dimensions 225 ft. × 30 ft., surrounded on the north and west by a bluff of rocks, 30 or 40 feet high. This land was considered worthless by former owners. I found on it two old apple trees, which bore only a few gnarly apples; these I had thoroughly scraped, washed with soft soap, tops cut off, and grafted with Baldwin apples.

I had the ground dug over to the depth of a foot and a half or two feet, the stones taken out (small ones buried, larger put into wall,) and the land thoroughly supplied with manure. About half of the ground was terraced and set out with fruit trees, the rest devoted to vegetables.

As a result we have annually of vegetables,—early peas, potatoes, green corn, cucumbers, beets, tomatoes, pole beans,—from one to three bushels each; of asparagus, pie plant, onions, carrots, parsnips, summer squashes, winter squashes, rock turnips, cabbage, a supply for family use; of fruits we have, (on an average), two bushels of strawberries and currants; from two to five bushels of grapes; one bushel of quinces; from four to six barrels of apples; and pears from twenty-five trees, half of them bearing, the oldest yielding about half a bushel. These embrace sixteen varieties, so arranged as to ripen monthly from August to March. We also have a limited supply of cherries and peaches.

A word in conclusion with regard to *expense* and *profits*, the former of which, in any undertaking of this kind, is a *bugbear* to so many, being, as they say, so much greater than the profits. I would prove the contrary from my own experience. 1st. The profits from a small pear nursery, 20 × 80, pay the expense of fertilizing and preparing the ground for planting. 2nd. The benefit in point of health gained by garden labor more than repays all necessary toil; to say nothing also of the pleasure which one feels in watching for the anticipated results of all his care and labor. 3rd. The expense of supplying the tables from one's own garden is much less than the cost of purchasing from the market, which would average a dollar a day during the greater part of the season."

Earth Worms in Flower Pots.

Sometimes horticultural troubles seem to be epidemic, and we have a succession of letters all of the same purport, as is now the case with reference to the common Earth or Angle-worm in flower pots. There is a difference of opinion in regard to the food of worms, some claiming that they actually eat the roots of plants, while others hold that they live upon the decaying matter contained in the soil. Whichever may be the case, there is no doubt that they do much injury to potted plants; in passing through the soil in all directions they not only perforate it with small channels, but they so compact it that is difficult to water a plant thoroughly, as the water will run off by the worm holes before the mass becomes wetted through. Worms should be kept from entering the pots, and those already in them should be removed. Those who, in taking up plants, use common garden soil for potting, are quite apt to introduce the trouble themselves. Potting soil should be prepared beforehand and frequently worked over, during which operation the worms may be seen and picked out. Worms frequently enter pots that are set outdoors for the summer, or are plunged in the borders. We have frequently cautioned against this in our "Notes for the Month." The pots should be set upon a layer of coal ashes, and when they are plunged, a quantity of ashes should be placed in the bottom of the hole made for the reception of the pot.

When a pot is infested by them, it is not very difficult to remove them. We have found that if the earth is allowed to get as dry as may be without injury to the plant, the worms will usually collect together, probably attracted by the moisture of one another, at the bottom or sides of the pot. By turning the ball of earth out of the pot they may be removed. This turning out the earth from a pot seems to those who have never practised it, a difficult operation as well as one dangerous to the plant. It is very easily done, and will not disturb the growth of any but very recently potted plants, in which case the roots have not sufficiently permeated the earth to hold it together in a ball. Spread the fingers of the left hand over the surface of the earth, invert the pot, and hold it in the right hand; then give the edge of the pot a slight downward rap upon the edge of a table, shelf, or the like, and out will come the ball, which must be carefully received in the left hand. A few pickings in this way will soon free the pots of worms. Where the trouble occurs with plants in boxes or in tubs, some other means must be resorted to. An infusion of soot is very disagreeable to them, and will drive them to the surface; this, to many plants, will act as a manure. Lime water will kill the worms; it is made by slaking a lump of lime of the size of one's fist, and stirring it in a pailful of water. When the liquid has become perfectly clear, it may be used in moderate quantity upon the earth containing robust shrubs. We have no experience in its use upon tender plants, and that must be a matter of experiment.

The Lizard's-tail.

One of the most pleasing of our aquatic plants is the Lizard's-tail, (*Saururus cernuus.*) It is very common in wet places, from New York westward and southward, where it forms large masses of pale-green foliage against which are

LIZARD'S-TAIL—(*Saururus cernuus.*)

contrasted the graceful spikes of white flowers, which are interesting from the simplicity of their structure; they have neither calyx or corolla, but are made up entirely of stamens and pistils, sheltered by a little bract or scale. These flowers are very much crowded upon the stem, and together make quite a show. They have a very pleasing fragrance, and as they open gradually, the period of flowering lasts for a long while. The engraving is from a small specimen, but it shows the shape of the leaves and the drooping character of the flower spike, the peculiar form of which, somewhat resembling a Lizard's tail has given it its common name as well as its botanical one—*Saururus*. Those who have a pond or stream of water on their grounds, should introduce this plant to ornament the margins.

Judging of Fruits at Fairs.

There are two sorts of fruit committees—those who do their work faithfully and conscientiously, and those who merely look at the fruit and make their award at once. We place very little reliance upon fruit premiums at fairs, unless we know who awarded them. A very good instance of thoroughness in a committee, though not exactly on fruits, came under our notice at the autumnal Exhibition of the Pennsylvania State Horticultural Society. The committee on vegetables had some fifteen varieties of potatoes to decide upon; instead of going by the eye alone, samples of each were boiled and thoroughly tested, each member of the committee making his marks as to flavor, texture, etc. It would be an excellent thing if an uniform system of marking or "points" could be established for fruit judges. It often happens that the largest fruit is by no means the best—and an award made upon size alone would be unfair, as others might excel it in form, color, and flavor. What we need is a comparison which shall take all the characters into account. English pomologists are very much exercised just now upon the subject of grape judging, and column after column appears in their different journals, until one is tired of so much talk upon a simple question, which, after all, is only this: Shall grapes be tasted by judges, or shall the flavor be inferred from the color? One would think that some national issue was at stake, so earnestly are both sides advocated. One writer suggests something like what we would have adopted for all fruits. For grapes he proposes the following marks as standard of perfection: Color and bloom, 5; flavor, 5; size of bunch, 2; form of bunch, 1; size of berry, 2; total, 15. According to this scale a grape perfect in every respect, would be marked 15. As perfection is seldom attained in every particular, each quality is marked by itself and the whole added up. Thus a sample of grapes is submitted to a committee. One member marks in this way: Color and bloom, 4; flavor, 2½; size of bunch, 1; shape of bunch, ½; size of berry, 2; total, 10. If every member of the committee makes the same total, very well; if not, the various totals are added together and divided by the number composing the committee. We hope to see something of this kind adopted for all fruits. When awards are made for the "best exhibited," we get very little idea of what was the character of the fruit that took the prize.

Peat Moss and its Uses.

Almost every one is familiar with the peat bog, usually a cold, low, wet place, covered with moss of a very pale green color, and of a peculiar, spongy, nature, and furnishing, besides the moss, a number of shrubs and other plants that are rarely met with in other localities. The Peat Mosses proper belong to the genus *Sphagnum*, of which we have in the United States about 20 species, some of them very local in their range, while others extend from New England to the Gulf States, and some of our most abundant ones are found also in Europe. The figure shows one of the commonest species, and gives an idea of the general appearance of them all—the distinctions between the species being founded on characters that would be noticed only by the botanical student. The long, weak stem is furnished with clusters of short branches, which at the top of the stem are crowded into a sort of head. The branches are covered with leaves, which are so very small that in our engraving they appear like minute scales upon the branches. Under a strong magnifier the leaves are interesting objects, most of the cells of which they are composed containing a spiral filament, which gives them a very pretty marking. The spores, or reproductive dust, are contained in small globular capsules, about the size of a pin's head, which at the time of their maturity open by a lid and liberate the spores. A short distance below the surface of the bog we find the moss in a decaying state, gradually being converted into peat. Sufficient has recently been said on the subject of peat, the production of which is the most important use of the moss, but it renders no mean service to the horticulturist, and we mention it on this account. Moss is one of those minor aids to the horticulturist of which he seldom knows the value until deprived of it. From its spongy character it absorbs water readily, and parts with it slowly. This, together with the fact that it is one of the few vegetable substances that can be kept moist for a long time without fermenting or decaying, renders it the most valuable packing material we possess. Indeed for surrounding the roots of living plants during their transportation, there is nothing that can replace it. Its softness and elasticity make it an agreeable material to work with. In Europe, the moss rubbed to a coarse powder is used to pack those seeds which it is desirable to prevent from becoming too dry. Some bog plants, such as *Sarracenias*, and some Orchids, are most successfully grown in pots filled with *Sphagnum*, and it is often used over the "crocks" that are placed in the bottom of a flower pot for drainage. Hyacinths and such bulbs as are grown in water, succeed admirably in pots or baskets filled with it. Nurserymen and florists who live near the bogs usually collect the moss themselves, but large quantities of it are sent from New Jersey to those portions of the West where it does not grow. We have no statistics upon the subject, but suspect that in the aggregate the trade in this plant must amount to a considerable sum. When first gathered the moss is quite heavy, on account of the water it holds, and if it is to be transported to any great distance, it should be spread thinly and dried.

SPHAGNUM.

THE MINER PLUM.—Several have sent us specimens of this fruit. It seems to be a seedling of our common native plum, of rather larger size than the wild fruit. It has a very thick skin which is said to be curculio proof, though its immunity from curculio is more probably due to its late blooming. It is of fair flavor, and is a showy fruit, which would, no doubt, sell well in the market. We are glad to welcome this improvement in one of our native fruits.

THE HOUSEHOLD.

(For other Household Items, see "Basket" pages.)

What to Do with a Person apparently Drowned.

Many lives are annually lost by drowning, which might be saved did those present at the recovery of the body know just what to do. These casualties usually occur in places where medical aid is long in reaching the patient, and he suffers often from neglect, but perhaps more frequently from the rude, though well-meant, endeavors of the spectators to restore life. The Royal National Life-boat Association, of England, has published a series of brief directions for the treatment of those apparently drowned. These are compiled by some of the most eminent medical men in England, and are distributed throughout the navy and at all the army stations of that country. Now that the skating season, a time at which accidents are very frequent, is at hand, we think we shall do a timely service

FIG. 1.—MANNER OF INDUCING INSPIRATION.

in reproducing the essential portions of these directions with the accompanying illustrations. In accidents of this kind, as well as in others, it is important to keep spectators from crowding about the patient and thus preventing free access of air.

I.—Send immediately for medical assistance, blankets, and dry clothing, but proceed to treat the patient *instantly* on the spot, in the open air, with the face downward, whether on shore or afloat; exposing the face, neck, and chest to the wind, except in severe weather; remove all tight clothing from the neck and chest, especially the braces.

The points to be aimed at are—first and *immediately*, the RESTORATION OF BREATHING; and secondly, the PROMOTION OF WARMTH AND CIRCULATION.

The efforts *to restore breathing* must be commenced immediately and energetically, and persevered in for one or two hours, or until a medical man has pronounced that life is extinct. Efforts to promote *Warmth and Circulation*, beyond removing the wet clothes and drying the skin, must not be made until the first appearance of natural breathing; for if circulation be induced before breathing has recommenced, the restoration to life will be endangered.

FIG. 2.—MANNER OF INDUCING EXPIRATION.

II.—TO RESTORE BREATHING.—*To Clear the Throat.*—Place the patient on the floor or ground with the face downwards, and one of the arms under the forehead, in which position all fluids will more readily escape by the mouth, and the tongue itself will fall forward, leaving the entrance into the windpipe free. Assist this operation by wiping and cleansing the mouth. If satisfactory breathing commences, use the treatment described below to promote warmth. If there be only slight breathing — or no breathing — or if the breathing fail, then—

To Excite Breathing.—Turn the patient well and instantly on the side, supporting the head, and excite the nostrils with snuff, hartshorn, and smelling salts, or tickle the throat with a feather, etc., if these are at hand. Rub the chest and face warm, and dash cold water, or cold and hot water alternately, on them. If there be no success, lose not a moment, but instantly—

To Imitate Breathing.—Replace the patient on the face, raising and supporting the chest well on a folded coat or other article of dress. Turn the body very gently on the side and a little beyond, and then briskly on the face, back again, repeating these measures cautiously, efficiently, and perseveringly, about fifteen times in the minute, or once every four or five seconds, occasionally varying the side. By placing the patient on the chest, the weight of the body forces the air out; when turned on the side, this pressure is removed, and air enters the chest. On each occasion that the body is replaced on the face, make uniform but efficient pressure with brisk movement, on the back, between and below the shoulder-blades or bones on each side, removing the pressure immediately before turning the body on the side. During the whole of the operations let one person attend solely to the movements of the head and of the arm placed under it. The first measure increases the expiration — the second commences inspiration. The result is Respiration or Natural Breathing; and if not too late, Life.

Whilst the above operations are being proceeded with, dry the hands and feet, and as soon as dry clothing or blankets can be procured, strip the body, and cover or gradually reclothe it, but taking care not to interfere with the efforts being made to restore breathing.

FIG. 3.—SILVESTER'S METHOD OF INDUCING INSPIRATION.

III.—Should these efforts not prove successful in from two to five minutes, proceed to imitate breathing by Dr. Silvester's method, as follows:—

Place the patient on the back on a flat surface, inclined a little upwards from the feet; support the head and shoulders on a small, firm cushion, or folded coat placed under the shoulder blades.

Draw forward the patient's tongue, and keep it projecting beyond the lips; an elastic band over the tongue and under the chin will answer this purpose, or a piece of string or tape may be tied round them, or by raising the lower jaw, the teeth may be made to retain the tongue in that position. Remove all tight clothing about the neck and chest.

To Imitate the Movements of Breathing.—Standing at the patient's head, grasp the arms just above the elbows, and draw the arms gently and steadily upwards above the head, and *keep them stretched upwards* for two seconds. (*By this means air is drawn into the lungs.*) Then turn down the patient's arms, and press them gently and firmly for two seconds against the sides of the chest. (*By this means air is pressed out of the lungs.*) Repeat these measures alternately, deliberately, and perseveringly, about fifteen times in a minute, until a spontaneous effort to respire is perceived; then immediately cease, and proceed to INDUCE CIRCULATION AND WARMTH.

FIG. 4.—SILVESTER'S METHOD OF INDUCING EXPIRATION.

IV.—TREATMENT AFTER NATURAL BREATHING HAS BEEN RESTORED.—*To Promote Warmth and Circulation.*—Commence rubbing the limbs upwards, with firm, grasping pressure, and energy, using handkerchiefs, flannels, etc. The friction must be continued under the blanket or over the dry clothing.

Promote the warmth of the body by hot flannels, bottles, or bladders of hot water, heated bricks, etc., at the pit of the stomach, the armpits, between the thighs, and at the soles of the feet. If the patient has been carried to a house after respiration has been restored, be careful to let the air play freely about the room. On the restoration of life, a teaspoonful of warm water should be given; and then, if the power of swallowing has returned, small quantities of wine, warm brandy and water, or coffee, should be administered. The patient should be kept in bed, and a disposition to sleep encouraged.

GENERAL OBSERVATIONS.—The above treatment

should be persevered in for some hours, as it is an erroneous opinion that persons are irrecoverable because life does not soon appear, persons having been restored after persevering for many hours.

CAUTIONS.—Avoid rough usage, and do not allow the body to remain on the back unless the tongue is secured. Under no circumstances hold the body up by the feet. On no account place it in a warm bath unless under medical direction, and even then it should only be employed as a momentary excitant.

Extracts from Miss Collins' Prize Essay.

We housekeepers know that this is really the busiest season of the year, but the work is so agreeable and is interspersed with so much that is delightfully mysterious, we never think of its being work at all, and only regret we have not each two pairs of hands, that we might accomplish more. Christmas is so near, and then—well—Charlie is coming home from Chicago, and Willie from New York. They will come so late, we must have the tree all trimmed, the presents hung, and the candles ready to be lighted before they arrive. What a pity we cannot have gas out here in the country, and so have a Christmas tree drop-light, like the one cousin Tom has in Liverpool! The most vivid imagination could scarcely convert our little candles and lamps (I beg their pardon for mentioning it. May their shadows never be less,) into the fifty bright jets which illuminated their tree; or transform Jennie's doll, which will hover with outstretched arms over our tree, suspended from the ceiling by a string around her waist—a contrivance of Ralph's—into the silver Christ-child nestling in the upper branches, "all radiant with light as with a flood of glory," as Tom described it in his letter to Ralph. Father says if the Petroleum Oil Gas Co. gets to work, and does as well as he thinks it will, we shall have our house lighted with the gas before another Christmas. I don't suppose father would get us a drop with fifty lights, but one with six or eight, as in figures 1 and 2, would be very nice among our candles and lamps. Yes, eight, opened to the best advantage, as shown in figure 1, would quite set off a tree.

Fig. 1. TREE LIGHTED WITH GAS.

Fig. 2.—DROP.

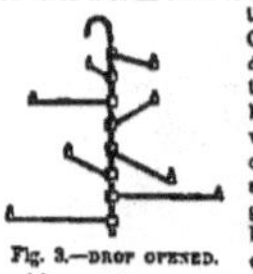
Fig. 3.—DROP OPENED.

Our new stove came to-day. It is an Empire Gas Burner, just like the one we have in the sitting-room, only this has a door in front. Ralph always makes such an ado about putting in the coal, because he has to lift off the urn from the top of the stove, and get some one to hold up the inside lid, while he empties the scuttle. This lid is opened by means of a damper just outside, which is always hot. I have burned my fingers many a time, and my handkerchiefs too, and scorched my dress into the bargain, holding the damper for Ralph. It would stay open itself when we first bought the stove a year or two ago, but will not now. I will ravel Jennie's old black worsted hood, and knit some holders diamond-shaped or octagonal in form, (figs. 4 and 5,) and embroider a wreath or cluster of flowers in the middle on canvas, (fig. 6); then pull out the canvas threads, crochet a bright border and line them with old silk. No; it will be better to let Jennie make them, and then put them on the tree for mother. She was just telling me she had finished stitching the strawberry seeds into the emeries, and wanted another job. She made most of the emeries. I cut out the strong cotton bags, and let her sew them up over a similarly shaped woolen sack filled with emery. She made the red silk sacks, and fastened them on, ready for the green leaves and the cord. She stitched in the seeds with yellow saddler's silk. I think they are very pretty, and she is delighted with them. (See figures 7, 8, 9, and 10.)

Fig. 4.

Fig. 5.

Fig. 6.

Fig. 7.

Fig. 8.

Mother has been making a jar of mince meat to-day for the winter. Father said he would remain at home this morning and chop mince meat, if Ralph preferred to go for the drain tiles, and so they are progressing famously. Sister Kate, who is somewhat of an invalid, stoned the raisins, and chopped half of them, and washed the currants. Mother cooked the meat yesterday. She is very particular to have it put into boiling water, and to keep it boiling briskly all the time, in order to preserve all the juices in the meat. Mother thinks the jar will last all winter. We chop the apples, a few at a time, as we want to make the pies, and mix well together with cold water or clean snow. Ralph says he believes every one in the house had a hand in the mince meat except Jennie and grand-father; but Katie says grand-father did most of her chopping for her, and she is sure Jennie had a hand in the raisins pretty often. Mother uses considerable snow and ice water in cooking, always wetting the pie-crust with one or the other.

Fig. 9.

Fig. 10.

Leaves from the Diary of a Young Housekeeper.—No. XII.

PRIZE ESSAY BY MRS. LAURA E. LYMAN, STAMFORD, CT.

December 10th.—We have had a busy week of it, but our butchering is done, the pork salted down, some of it packed in snow to be eaten fresh, the lard put down, and sausage meat prepared. We do not either of us believe much in the use of pork, but where the animals are young, and killed soon after they attain their growth, we think they are less injurious than when they are allowed to live a year in a low condition, and then suddenly fattened for slaughter. Edward has been very careful of their food, that it be wholesome and well cooked, and has not permitted them to root in the ground, believing that the disease which has injured the pork market so seriously is aggravated by their eating earth-worms, of which they are very fond. In rendering the lard, which was a matter that I considered strictly in my department, I was very careful to keep the fire at all times moderate, so as to entirely prevent that scorching which so much damages the flavor of this important ingredient in cookery, and the most scrupulous cleanliness was observed in every part of the process. When the lard was partly cool, I dipped it into large earthen jars or crocks, holding about four gallons, and set it away in the pantry, carefully covered. It is as white as snow and cuts like butter. Edward chopped my sausage meat and I put it into little bags made of old clean domestic, which I rolled until they were round, and then dipped them in hot lard and set them into a firkin. These bags or rolls are five inches in diameter, and ten or twelve in length. I added some flour to the meat when I spiced and salted it, so that I can cut these rolls into slices and fry them without their breaking into pieces. Mother tried putting sausage meat into skins and making it into cakes, but at last settled down upon this mode as at once the least troublesome and the most satisfactory of all. If during the January thaw they should become mouldy and threaten to spoil, I have but to put them into a baking-pan and scald them thoroughly. I spiced them with sage, summer savory, a little thyme and black pepper. As a breakfast dish they are very convenient, and quickly prepared for the table.

The pigs' heads and feet I made into head-cheese. After scalding and scraping them carefully, I put them all into a large pot, salted them, and let them boil until they fell all to pieces. When partly cool I picked the whole mass over carefully, excluding the bones and everything unpalatable, and then added pepper, sage, summer savory and vinegar, until it was quite sour, and put it away to cool. Cut in slices it makes a very good dish for supper or lunch, and is a pleasant change from dried beef and cold tongue. The longer I keep house the more I am impressed with the desirableness of abridging, as far as possible, the daily task of preparing meals. This I am doing by baking in large quantities, now it is cold weather, enough bread at a time to last a week, and pies and cakes for two or three. I try to have something always ready for breakfast, so that meal can be prepared in the shortest time possible, and while Sue is getting it ready I make any preparations that may be necessary for dinner, a tapioca pudding, perhaps, so that Sue can do all the rest and leave me undisturbed to work on my machine. This I find is a great saving of time, and by being beforehand with my cooking, I do not find it burdensome, and my meals are always ready in season. The best way of keeping bread is to put it when cool from baking into a tin box or trunk with a tight cover, and set it in the cellar or in a cool closet. The bread box should be frequently scalded and kept perfectly sweet. Bread in this way may be made to last a week without injury to its flavor. When it becomes a little stale I toast it, and with butter melted in warm milk and poured over it, it is very palatable, and a quick breakfast dish.

December 15th.—My husband returned from town the other day, where he had been with a load of produce, and brought home among other things a dozen yards of heavy gray flannel to be made up into underclothing. He is a great believer in flannel, particularly for farm laborers, to be worn next the skin at all seasons of the year. When he was in the army, (for he served a year under Banks in the Southwest,) he wore it constantly, and attributes his unbroken health in a great degree to that precaution. Since his return he has kept up the excellent practice, and has persuaded me to adopt it also, and I have never suffered so little from colds as so far during this season. During these long winter evenings Edward has been reading aloud, and among other valuable practical suggestions we have both been very much impressed by an article on "The Health of Farmers and Farmers' Wives," printed in the Patent Office Reports for 1863. How much good Congress could do if it would take this excellent article and print it in a pamphlet form for general distribution! It would do so much more good than the electioneering documents which are so profusely scattered at the national expense. It seems to me that any well-informed person after reading this piece would adopt flannel as the material to be worn next the skin for the rest of his life. The remarks of the author, too, about the discomfort and the danger to health that attend the usual manner of washing, particularly in winter, made such an impression upon Edward's mind that he determined immediately to investigate the claims of the different washing machines. When we were at the fair we saw a number and observed their operation. It seemed to us that the principle upon which Doty's washer proceeds is the best; his patent does not attempt what nearly all the others do, to rub the clothes between fluted surfaces of wood, which must wear them more or less. I told Edward I liked the Doty washer, and he purchased one. We are delighted with it, and wonder how we ever got along without it.

BOYS & GIRLS' COLUMNS.

A Curious Box.

A few days since we were much interested and not a little puzzled in examining a box procured at one of the toy stores. It was so constructed that a drawer, occupying the whole of the inside, could be pushed out from either of the four sides. How one drawer could thus cross another was the mystery. Upon taking it apart,

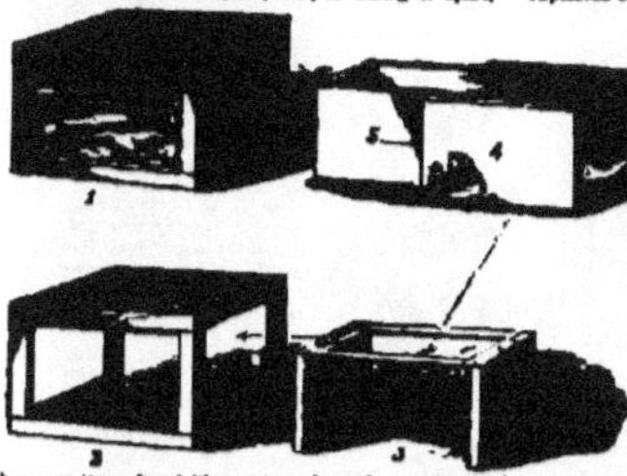

however, it was found, like most puzzles, to be very simple when you once know how it is done. We here give engravings representing the various parts. The arrows show the direction in which one piece is to be introduced to the other parts. Thus a square box, (5,) is to be placed in a box open at each end, (4). The skeleton box, (3,) is to be placed in 2, then 5 and 4 can be slid into the opening, and the box is complete. The parts need to be made to exactly fit, and will exercise your care with tools as well as your ingenuity in making it.

Christmas Presents.

We trust the custom of making presents on Christmas day will never cease. Our young friends are all of the same mind, without doubt. Many of them are already imagining the good things they will receive, and planning pleasant surprises for their friends. The shop-keepers are laying in their stock of toys, books, games, etc., with which to supply the demand for presents, and Santa Claus is making up his famous pack for the great occasion. What to give is often a perplexing question. A gift will be all the more valued, if it is appropriate. We should hardly think of selecting a Bible as a present to a minister, though it is often thoughtlessly done. It is to be supposed that one of his profession is already supplied with that book. Better add a new Encyclopædia, or some recent historical works to his library; or better still make up a purse and let him select the articles he most needs. A periodical like the *Agriculturist*, or some favorite magazine for a year, is almost always a pleasing gift. It will remind the recipient of your affection each time it comes to hand. In general, select useful articles for presents. Even children are better pleased with such things, especially if they are also ornamental, than with toys which will soon be broken or cast aside as tiresome. Perhaps a clothes wringer or washing machine would please mother much better than a gold ring, while father would prize a new umbrella or some other serviceable article. Consult both the wants and the tastes of your friend, in selecting a gift. Especially should the poor be remembered during the holiday season. In no way can we better commemorate the event which brought Heaven's great gift to men. See that the heart of every poor widow and orphan is made glad by abundant bounty. Their smiles and gratitude will give greater satisfaction than the reception of costly presents, and a blessing is promised to those who remember the friendless. May a Merry Christmas gladden the hearts and brighten the lives of all our large *Agriculturist* family from Maine to California.

An Ignorant Engineer.

What would be thought of an engineer who was ignorant of the number of wheels and springs in his engine, which he had run for fifteen years or more, and of the uses of many of them? You would expect that the apparatus would soon be out of order, and that a fearful explosion or other calamity would occur, bringing the whole machinery into ruin. Well, then, my young friend of fifteen years old, there is no more wonderful piece of machinery than the one you are to have the care of as long as you live—your own body. How many pieces in the frame work? How many springs? What goes on inside of the works? How are they to be kept in good running order? What will injure the stomach? What will hurt the brain? What will increase the power of the muscles, and how may the nerves be kept steady? For want of such knowledge hundreds of calamities are daily taking place. There is a man who says he is dyspeptic. He is thin, sallow, and miserable; every thing he eats disagrees with him. His machinery runs badly—it must be mended, or it will soon cease running. When a boy he used to stuff himself with good things, not only at meal times, but whenever he could find any thing that tasted good. He overworked his machinery. There goes a man limping with rheumatism. His springs are rusty. He did not know how to use them properly. Another is red, bloated, nervous, unsteady in his walk, dim of sight, and ready to break down all over. He has spoiled his machinery with alcohol. It would be as wise to pour oil of vitriol among the wheels of a watch, to brighten them, as to try to sharpen up the faculties of men by stimulants. Whatever book you read or neglect, always excepting the Bible, do not fail to buy or borrow one on Physiology. Learn the parts of your body, their uses, how to take care of them, and put your knowledge into practice. Don't be an ignorant engineer, when your engine is so precious.

A Ride by Wind-Power.

At the Fair of the American Institute just closed in this city, a new apparatus was exhibited, for conveying passengers and freight, called the Pneumatic Railway. A large tube, seven feet in diameter, was laid across the room from one gallery to another, a distance of about one hundred feet. Tracks were laid on the bottom of the tube, and a car placed on them, large enough to hold twelve persons. We joined a company of passengers, and presently found ourselves passing through the tube at considerable speed, and then back again to the entrance. There was no smoke, nor steam, nor machinery in connection with the car. The power which moved the vehicle, however, was produced by a steam engine in another part of the building. By means of shafts and belts, connected with the engine, a large wheel, in front of one end of the tube was made to turn rapidly. This wheel was made something on the plan of a boy's windmill. The blades were set [illegible], so that, when turned in one direction, it drew the air out of the tube. When this was done, the air in front of the car being partly exhausted, the air behind it pressed against the car, and so forced it along. The principle was the same as that by which any thing is pumped or sucked through a tube. When the motion of the wheel was reversed, the air forced into the tube against the car, caused it to move in a contrary direction, and so the vehicle was driven back and forth. The inventors claim that this plan will work through very long tubes, and that in this way passengers may be rapidly and cheaply carried from place to place. If the invention succeeds, some of you may live to be blown through from New York to Washington.

New Puzzles to be Answered.

No. 290. *Illustrated Rebus.*—A very cheering truth.

Send New Puzzles.

We are always pleased to receive new puzzles, and to publish them if they are of sufficient merit. Where engravings are necessary, make a drawing if you can, but that is not indispensable, if the description is clear. Do not be discouraged if your contributions do not appear. The mental exercise required to originate a good problem will of itself be worth making a trial. We do not want puzzles you have seen published elsewhere, or which are old in your neighborhood. Hundreds of such have been rejected. Always send the answers with the puzzles. The kind of puzzles is left to your own fancy. A good mathematician can amuse and instruct our readers with interesting problems. Practical ones are preferred. Whatever will call out thought, and also amuse, will find a welcome place.

No. 289. *Labyrinth.*—Find your way from the entrance to the fortune in the center, without crossing a line.

Answers to Problems and Puzzles.

The following are answers to the puzzles, etc., in the November number, page 415. No. 285. *Puzzle Picture.*—A fox is watching for the hare. His outline may be traced by following the lower branches on the right hand side of the picture. No. 286. *Mathematical Problem.*—[illegible] ft.; 2d, 16.71 ft.; [illegible] ft.; 4th, [illegible] very nearly. No. 287. *Illustrated Rebus.*—Bear this in mind; with [illegible] and misfortune and [illegible] will stay not with you. No. 288. *Puzzle Picture.*—Because every pound should contain at least twelve ounces.

Our Railroad.

Such a journey! Frank was chief engineer, after the train was built. George superintended that, and Susie, who is now tired out by her labors and her ride, helped, by bringing the pot-lid and the sieve, when we were all wondering where to get wheels for our locomotive. "We'll call it the Grand Trunk Rail-Road," said Robert, who remembers what he reads, and has been studying about the Pacific Rail-Road. At last we had it all fixed. There were two first class carriages, made of chairs from the parlor; a second class, which the great arm-chair furnished; a roll of Tribunes answered for a stove-pipe—"it's a first-rate 'blower,'" said George. Then we set Dolly where she could see us start, and, waving her good-bye, off we went full steam for California. Now you who have traveled thousands of miles on real rail-roads will smile at our make-believe, but I don't think you ever had half the fun that we did on our journey. We could have just such weather and just such scenery as we pleased. Sometimes we made the snow block up the track, and then had a grand time shoveling out, snowballing, shaking off the snow from our clothes, and going ahead all right again. Then we ran down a herd of buffaloes, but did not get off the track; and occasionally we passed through a long tunnel, by drawing the curtains over the windows and making it very dark. If you want the pleasure without the pains of traveling, just try our plan once, and if you know how to make it work, you will agree that there is no road like it in the world. FANNIE.

Garibaldi.

Few names in modern history rank above this illustrious hero of Italy. Without titled rank or money, by the power of his own character, he shakes the thrones of Europe. He was born in Nice, Italy, July 4th, 1808, and was educated as a sailor by his father, who followed that calling. He was remarkable for his affection for his parents, his sincerity to his companions, and his generosity and bravery to those needing help. When twenty-eight years old, a visit to Rome so impressed him with hatred of tyranny, that he joined those who sought to revolutionize the government, and was, in consequence, ere long exiled from his native land. After various wanderings he went to South America, where he was soon engaged in aiding the Republic of Uruguay in achieving her independence of Brazil. In this war he was severely wounded and made prisoner, but escaped, and continued to render great service to those whose cause he had espoused. While there he married a South American woman of great energy, who became his companion in all his dangers by sea and land. In a subsequent war with Buenos Ayres, by his skill and bravery he saved Montevideo from capture. In 1848 Garibaldi returned to Europe, and was soon in command among the republicans in Italy, who had expelled the Pope and were striving to establish a new government. With the greatest heroism he fought the French and Austrians who joined to restore the ancient dynasty, until he was overpowered by numbers, and compelled to flee in disguise. During these disasters his wife died, and he was left almost heartbroken. Banished again from Italy, he came to New York, and supported himself by making candles in a factory on Staten Island. Next he resumed his former occupation as sailor, made several voyages in the Pacific, and finally returned in command of a Peruvian bark. Then being invited to return to his native city, Nice, he lived there in retirement until the breaking out of the war with Austria, in which he engaged with his usual resolution and spirit, and contributed largely to the success of the Italian arms, and the establishment of Victor Emanuel upon the throne. Now we find him moving again for the deliverance of the Roman States from the government of the Pope, and the eyes of the world are upon him. Whatever may be his success in this enterprise, his fame is secure, and his name will be remembered as one of the most unselfish and heroic of patriots.

THE RAIL-ROAD RIDE.—*Engraved for the American Agriculturist.*

Little "Tot."

A correspondent to the *American Agriculturist* writes; "I once knew a little fellow whose real name was 'Obadiah,' but who, having a decided objection to that name, insisted on being called 'Tot.' He had a wise little head full of queer thoughts, and used, when a very little fellow, to ask very odd questions. He was about five years old when I one day took him out to ride. We had a very pleasant drive over a quiet country road, and 'Tot' who was a city child, little accustomed to country life or scenes, sat drinking in the beauty of the landscape without a word until he broke out with an abrupt 'Hello!' 'Well, Totty,' said I. 'I say, do'es sheepses hairs grow on trees?' He had noticed tufts of wool which had been left by some passing flock of sheep, on the thorns of a hedge opposite us. I explained the matter to him and told him what windfalls these bits of wool were to the little birds who wove from them warm linings for their nests. Tot said no more, but appeared very thoughtful. I had business to transact in a neighboring town, and it was quite dark before we returned. It was a beautiful night, and the heavens shone with stars. 'I say,' exclaimed Totty, pointing his chubby hand upward as he uttered his favorite phrase, 'I say, Uncle James, I knows what stars is.' 'You are a wise infant, Tot,' I replied. 'Perhaps you will condescend to enlighten your uncle on the subject?' 'I knows what stars is,' repeated Tot, disdaining to notice what I said. ''Cause you see the great big sun he goes clean across the sky and some of him sticks to the rough places like the sheepses hairs sticks to the tree, and' concluded Totty triumphantly, 'them's stars, them is.' Tot has signed the pledge. He can just write enough to write his name, but he insisted on signing with the rest of the family, and sign he did. One of the farm hands, (for Tot now lives in the country), who had signed it, went on a journey into the lowlands along the lake shore where the farm is situated. While returning he became very thirsty and called for a glass of water at a house by the wayside. He was told that the water in the well had been spoiled by a large piece of meat which had accidentally fallen into it but that he was welcome to a glass of cider. Being very thirsty indeed, he so far forgot himself as to drink it. When he returned home he related the circumstance. When he had finished, Tot, with his eyes filled with tears came up to his knee and said: 'I say, Phil., how far was you from the lake?' 'A full ten mile,' said Philip, looking a little conscience-stricken. 'Well, Phil.,' said the child, with a tremor in his voice, 'I'd have walked there and back again 'fore I'd a broken the pledge.'"

A Bully Rebuked.

The Springfield Republican relates the following as having occurred in a railroad car in Massachusetts. As the train was about starting, a well dressed, gentlemanly appearing, but very black man came in and took a vacant seat beside a white man. The latter at once sprang up and, with an oath, exclaimed, "Do you suppose I am going to sit by a nigger?" Then pushing rudely past he sought another place in the seat with a young student who was just returning home from his university. He had no sooner taken his new place than the young man sprang up, saying, "Do you suppose I will sit with you?" and went and sat down by the colored man. "Would you rather sit by a nigger than a white man?" shouted the enraged individual whose company he had left. "I prefer to sit with a gentleman," replied the student. "Do you say I'm not a gentleman?" quickly asked the other. "Gentlemen do not use profane language, neither do they insult people on account of their color," was the answer. "You shall be taken care of, you impudent young jackanapes," said the first speaker shaking his fist menacingly. "I will take care of him," quietly remarked the colored man, who until this time, had remained silent. The tone of voice was so full of meaning, and the powerful frame of the speaker so full of muscle, that the bully at once sneaked quietly into his seat, to digest as best he might his inglorious defeat and the unconcealed scorn of his fellow-travelers. It is to be hoped that he learned the lesson that to be a gentleman one must do something more than merely assume the name; actions speak much louder than words.

Herald of Health for 1868.

3 Numbers Free.

The objects of this Journal are:

TO PREVENT DISEASE

AND

TO RESTORE HEALTH.

It aims to effect this by teaching

HOW TO LIVE.

It presents the laws of Health, and the proper way to observe them, points out the manner in which they are most liable to be broken, suggests the means of recovering from the penalties of their violation; in short, gives attention to all topics affecting the

PHYSICAL CONDITION.

It numbers among its contributors some of the

Most Eminent Writers.

Among these are

HORACE GREELEY,
HENRY WARD BEECHER,
DIO LEWIS,
MOSES COIT TYLER,
DR. H. W. BELLOWS,
ALICE and PHŒBE CARY,
MRS. GLEASON,
PROF. RUFUS K. BROWNE,

and many others.

Every number contains facts, hints, and suggestions that will, if properly followed,

Save Many Years Subscription IN DOCTORS' BILLS.

The press and individuals throughout the entire country have given the most cordial testimony in favor of the worth of the

HERALD OF HEALTH.

The New York Tribune says:

THE HERALD OF HEALTH well sustains the high standard which it has held forth since the commencement of the new series. In fulfilling its task as a "preacher of righteousness" in the department of Physical Culture, it enjoys the aid of numerous sound thinkers and able writers, whose contributions give popular interest and, in many cases, permanent value to its contents.

HON. GERRITT SMITH writes:

"I value this periodical very highly. Were it thickly scattered over the whole land, what a power it would prove!

"Professor Tyler's 'Athletic Club' is worth more than the price of each number it appears in. By the way, he is one of the most brilliant and racy of all our writers.

A LIFE SAVED BY READING THE HERALD OF HEALTH.—"SPRINGFIELD, O., *December* 21, 1866. MILLER, WOOD & CO. —*Gents*: I would inform you that I have not received my HERALD for November, and as I have preserved them through all its changes for about eighteen years, I wish to have it.

"I was a poor dyspeptic, pronounced by my physician to be in the last stage of consumption—had night sweats, a violent cough, was given up as incurable, and I made my will, supposing I would die in a few weeks. I settled with my physicians and everybody else, and was expecting that a few days would close up my earthly career. At that time I got your publications, and without any other information I treated myself as well as I could from reading those works, and in less than six months my health was quite good, and in twelve months I had good health, and have had, with but slight exceptions, ever since. I am now in my 67th year, and I farm, and did husk corn day after day this fall with young men and made a full hand, and I found I could lead the most of them. I credit the above works with my good health, though I have quite a library of books on the system you advocate in your Journal. I expect to read it while it advocates its present principles.

A. MOORHOUSE."

Those who subscribe at once for 1868 will get OCTOBER, NOVEMBER, and DECEMBER NUMBERS FREE. Those who send a Club of Thirty Subscribers for 1868 and $60 will get a Wheeler & Wilson Sewing Machine worth $55 as a premium. $2 a year; samples 20 cents.

MILLER, WOOD & CO.,
15 Laight St., New York.

NEW-YORK TRIBUNE

The Great Farmers' Newspaper.

THE

NEW-YORK WEEKLY TRIBUNE

is printed on a large sheet, making eight pages of six broad columns each. It contains all the important News published in THE DAILY TRIBUNE, except of merely local interest; also, Literary and Scientific Intelligence, Reviews of New Books, Letters from our large corps of correspondents; the latest news by Telegraph from all parts of the World; a Summary of all important intelligence in this city and elsewhere; a Synopsis of the proceedings of Congress and State Legislature when in session; Foreign News received by steamer; Full Reports of the Proceedings of the Farmers' Club of the American Institute; Talks about Fruit, and other Horticultural and Agricultural information essential to country residents; Stock, Financial, Cattle, Dry Goods and General Market Reports; making it, both for variety and completeness, altogether the most valuable, interesting, and instructive WEEKLY NEWSPAPER published in the world.

The Full Reports of the American Institute Farmers' Club, and the various Agricultural Reports, in each number, are richly worth a year's subscription.

TERMS:

Single copy, 1 year—52 numbers	$2.00
Clubs of five	9.00
Ten copies or over, to names of subscribers, each	1.70
Twenty copies, to names of subscribers	34.00
Ten copies, to one address	16.00
Twenty copies, to one address	30.00

An extra copy will be sent for each club of ten.

THE NEW-YORK SEMI-WEEKLY TRIBUNE,

Published every TUESDAY and FRIDAY, contains in addition to all enumerated above, the

BEST AND LATEST POPULAR NOVELS,

by living authors, carefully selected from the ENGLISH MAGAZINES. Nowhere else can so much current intelligence and permanent literary matter be had at so cheap a rate as in THE SEMI-WEEKLY TRIBUNE. Those who believe in the principles and approve of the character of THE TRIBUNE can increase its power and influence by joining with their neighbors in forming clubs to subscribe for THE SEMI-WEEKLY Edition. It will in that way be supplied to them at the lowest price for which such a paper can be printed.

1 copy, 1 year—104 numbers	$4.00
2 copies, do. do.	7.00
5 copies, or over, for each copy	3.00

Persons remitting for 10 copies $30 will receive an extra copy for six months.

Persons remitting for 15 copies $45, will receive an extra copy one year.

For $100 we will send thirty-four copies and THE DAILY TRIBUNE.

THE NEW-YORK DAILY TRIBUNE

Is published every morning (Sunday's excepted) at $10 per year; $5 for six months.

PORTRAIT OF HORACE GREELEY.

On receipt of $2 for THE WEEKLY, $4 for THE SEMI-WEEKLY, or $10 for THE DAILY TRIBUNE, we will send a copy of Ritchie's fine Steel-engraved Portrait of HORACE GREELEY to any person who asks for it at the time of subscribing.

TO ADVERTISERS.

All who want to sell Lands, Farms, Machinery, Inventions, Trees, Plants, Seeds, Tools, Books, or anything required by the great Agricultural and Manufacturing Public, from Maine to California, will do well to advertise in THE NEW-YORK TRIBUNE.

TERMS OF ADVERTISING.

DAILY TRIBUNE 25 cents a line.
WEEKLY TRIBUNE $1.50 a line.
SEMI-WEEKLY TRIBUNE 25 cents a line.

Terms, cash in advance.

Drafts on New-York, or Post-Office orders, payable to the order of THE TRIBUNE, being safer, are preferable to any other mode of remittance. Address

THE TRIBUNE, New-York.

THE BEST IS THE CHEAPEST!

IF YOU WANT A FIRST-CLASS
AGRICULTURAL PAPER,
HORTICULTURAL PAPER,
WOOL GROWERS' PAPER,
STOCK GROWERS' PAPER,
FAMILY PAPER,
LITERARY PAPER,
YOUNG PEOPLE'S PAPER,
GENERAL NEWS-PAPER,

—(AND ALL OF THESE COMBINED IN ONE.)—

THEN SUBSCRIBE FOR

MOORE'S RURAL NEW-YORKER,

A WEEKLY JOURNAL,

Established in 1850,—which is the Leading and Largest-Circulating RURAL, FAMILY, LITERARY and GENERAL NEWSPAPER on the Continent—most conclusive evidence that it is THE BEST PAPER OF ITS CLASS!

THE RURAL IS ABLY EDITED,
PROFUSELY ILLUSTRATED,
NEATLY PRINTED.

IT IS PRACTICAL,
IT IS SCIENTIFIC,
IT IS USEFUL.

MORAL IN TONE,
PURE IN SENTIMENT,
HIGHLY ENTERTAINING.

THE RURAL is unequaled in Value and Variety of Contents, and unique in Appearance. It embraces a greater variety of Agricultural, Horticultural, Scientific, Educational, Literary and News Matter, interspersed with many Engravings, than any other journal—rendering it by far the most complete combination of PRACTICAL, INSTRUCTIVE, ENTERTAINING and TIMELY Journalistic Reading in America. Its ample pages comprise Departments devoted to or including

Agriculture,	Choice Literature,
Horticulture,	Science and Art,
Sheep Husbandry,	Education,
Grazing, Dairying,	Youth's Reading,
Rural Architecture,	General News,
Domestic Economy,	Commerce, Markets,

With Illustrations, Tales, Essays, Music, Poetry, Rebuses, Enigmas, &c., &c.

THE RURAL EMPLOYS THE BEST TALENT
IN ALL DEPARTMENTS,
Practical, Scientific and Literary.

Among its EDITORS, CONTRIBUTORS and CORRESPONDENTS are many of the most experienced and successful Farmers, Planters, Wool Growers, Horticulturists, Gardeners, Scholars, &c.,—including eminent Soil Cultivators, Breeders and Graziers, Scientists, Litterateurs, LL. D.'s, D. D.'s, M. D.'s, Presidents and Professors of Colleges, and others of note and decided ability. For example, its SHEEP HUSBANDRY Department is Edited by the Hon. HENRY S. RANDALL, LL. D., (author of "*The Practical Shepherd*," "*Sheep Husbandry in the South*," &c., and Pres't. of the National Wool Growers' Association,) the best authority on the subject in this country.

Whether located in Town or Country
YOU WANT THE RURAL,
YOUR FAMILY WANT IT,
YOUR NEIGHBORS WANT IT,

For it is adapted to the wants of all, and has thousands of readers in Cities and Villages in addition to its immense circulation among the Rural Population of the whole Country,—East and West, North and South.

THE RURAL NEW-YORKER

Is a **National Journal**, having enthusiastic friends and admirers in every State and Territory of the Union, and also in Canada, Europe, &c. And while "*Excelsior*" is its glorious Motto, and "*Progress and Improvement*" its laudable Objects, it will fully maintain its position as the most Popular and Meritorious Weekly in its Sphere of Journalism. In judging of its price, &c., remember that MOORE'S RURAL is not a monthly, but a Large and Beautiful *Weekly*.

FORM, STYLE, TERMS, &c.

THE RURAL comprises Eight Double Quarto Pages,—published in superior style, with Copper-faced Type, Good Paper, and many Appropriate and Costly Engravings, (it being the most profusely illustrated Weekly in its sphere of Journalism.) A Title Page, Index, &c., given at close of each Volume, complete for binding.

TERMS—Only $3 a Year; Five Copies for $14, Seven for $19; Ten for $25, &c. A new Quarter commences Oct. 5, and Volume XIX in January. **Now is the Time to Subscribe and form Clubs.** The most liberal inducements to Local Agents, Clubs, &c., but no traveling agents are employed. Specimens, Show-Bills, Premium Lists, &c., SENT FREE—or we will send the 13 numbers of this (Oct. to Jan.) or any preceding Quarter of this year, on trial, or as specimens, for ONLY FIFTY CENTS.

Address **D. D. T. MOORE, Publisher,**
UNION BUILDINGS, ROCHESTER, N. Y.

JAMES BUCHAN & CO.,

190 ELIZABETH STREET,

NEW-YORK,

MANUFACTURE AND SELL

THE CRESYLIC ACID COMPANY'S

SAPONACEOUS COMPOUNDS.

DISINFECTING SOAPS.

Soft Soap.—Dark, for floors, ships' decks, etc., in 5 lb. canisters, $1.25; 10 lb. do., $2.25; in 50 lb. kegs, at $10; and in 200 lb. barrels, $35.

For all the purposes intended, these have double the cleansing powers of ordinary soaps.

No. 1 Soap.—In bars. For all common uses in the house and laundry, for floors, closets, clothing, linens, woolens, bedding, etc., which it thoroughly disinfects and renders obnoxious to all insects.

In 24 lb. boxes, at 13 cents per lb.; and in 60 lb. boxes, at 12½ cents.

Laundry.—A finer soap, for similar purposes, and for the bath, etc.

In 60 lb. boxes, 14 cents per lb.; in 24 lb. boxes, and in 10 paper boxes, containing 6 lbs. each, packed in a case, 15 cents per lb.

Laundry women should not object to the peculiar and not unpleasant smell of the soap. This very odor protects them from any possibility of catching disease from foul or infected clothing; and disappears when the clothes are dried.

These soaps possess a **Bleaching** quality which none others do; and without the slightest damage to the fibre of the cloth.

The **Black Bar-soap,** for destroying vermin on horses, cows, pigs, dogs, etc., and to protect them from flies, in neat cakes enveloped in tin foil, in a cheap and convenient form, in boxes containing 20 cakes, $2.

The **Death to Screw-worm.**—A soft and very effective ointment, or may be used as a soap; will destroy all insect life or render the locality most obnoxious to them, and forms the best of all washes and ointments for foul and putrid or other sores. The *altering* and *marking of young stock* may be done with safety even in the extreme south, at any season of the year, by immediately anointing with this preparation.

To that pest of the Southern Stock-breeder, the *Screw-worm*, it is certain death, and is the cheapest and safest remedy ever applied. It not only destroys the worm, but cleanses and quickly heals up the offensive sores made by them. In ordinary cases, a piece of the ointment, as large as the first joint of the finger, pushed into the wound, will effect an immediate cure. But, in serious cases, best to inject a solution two or three times, and then insert the ointment. It is rare that a second application will ever have to be made. Sheep, which rarely recover the attack of the worm under the ordinary treatment of Calomel, various Liniments, etc., are quickly cured by this application.

Sold in canisters containing one pound, at 50 cents, or three pounds, at $1.

The **Sheep Dip** is sold in canisters of 5 pounds, at $1.25; 10 pounds, at $2.25; 50 pound kegs, at $10; and in barrels, containing 200 pounds, at $35.

The proportions for dipping large and heavily-fleeced sheep, are *one pound of the composition to five gallons of water for five sheep.* When a number exceeding fifty are dipped, the bath must be replenished after 25 sheep are dipped, with five pounds of the composition dissolved in one gallon of boiling water, added to 24 gallons of water. But *for the average of sheep* in the United States, and especially if recently shorn, it will be found that this quantity, in these proportions, will suffice for nearly, if not quite, *double the number.* The liquid is placed in an oblong vessel, of sufficient size to immerse two sheep at a time conveniently. The animals are carefully dipped, so that every part is immersed, protecting only the ears, nose and mouth from contact with the liquid. Each sheep should remain a full minute in the bath, and then stand on the *drainer*, or sloping platform alongside the bath-tub, until all the liquid that will, has drained off. Do not turn out during a rain, immediately after dipping. The hands and arms may be freely put in the bath, as it will injure neither skin nor clothes. But, if the sun is shining brightly, it is best to protect the arms by a loose sleeve or other wrapping; otherwise some smarting may be felt. If the smarting is severe, the bath had best be somewhat diluted with water; and especially for weakly sheep or lambs. When *Scab* is actually present, a little of the pure *Dip*, or better still, of the *Death to Screw-worm* should be rubbed on the spots or diseased parts. If first rubbed not too harshly, with a corn-cob, so much the better. There is no danger of reinfection, even in pastures or lots known to be infected with the scab insect. If the lots, pastures, &c., are limited in extent, and badly infested with the *Scab-insects*, wash over with the *Dip*, the stems of trees, posts, &c., against which the sheep have been in the habit of rubbing themselves; as the insects will live there for a long time, ready to attack again these sheep not thoroughly protected by dipping.

A profitable business could be done by

PROFESSIONAL DIPPERS,

charging so much per head, and who could do the work more thoroughly, and at a less actual cost than could be done by those less practical.

Messrs. Buchan & Co. will be glad to treat with parties who desire to engage in the business.

Foot-rot Ointment thoroughly cures and prevents the return of this dangerous disease. Let the animals to be treated, stand for five minutes or so, in the ordinary solution of sheep-dip; which will soften and cleanse the hoofs. Pare and cut away all of the diseased portion; but expose no more fresh surface than can be avoided. Anoint well with the ointment, and especially every diseased part, rubbing a little into the hair as high as the knee. Keep the animals in a dry, clean pasture or lot for a few days, and a cure will not only be affected, but the animal guarded from reinfection for a considerable period.

Sold in canisters of 3 pounds, at $1.

The **Plant-Protector** is sold in lb. canisters at 50 cts.; 3 lb. do., $1.00; 5 lb. do. $1.25; 10 lb. do., $2.25; 50 lb. kegs, $10.00, and in barrels, containing 200 lbs., at $35.

The strength of the solution must be determined by the age and condition of the trees and plants to which it is to be applied. For strong growing plants and trees, out of doors, 5 pounds to 50, or even 100 gallons of water will suffice.

To sprinkle over a crop of wheat, or to be forced in a spray, over and through the growing cotton plants, a still weaker solution would probably have the desired effect of driving off the parent insects.

The Hide Preserver.—This article, dissolved in sufficient boiling water, adding cold water until about the consistency of rich milk, or say five pounds to 30 gallons of water, will, if green or dried hides are coated on both sides with it, completely prevent the attacks of insects. And will cure green hides more thoroughly and in less time than by salt or any other antiseptic.

Sold in canisters of 5 pounds, at $1.25; 10 pounds, at $2.25; 50-pound kegs, at $10; and in barrels containing 200 pounds, at $35.

Soaps for the **Toilet and Bath,** and for **Surgical Uses,** are in course of manufacture, and will soon be offered.

The Cresylic Acid Company,

No. 62 Cedar St., New York,

MANUFACTURE AND SELL

GRANULATED DISINFECTING POWDER.

A powerful disinfectant and purifier; and at same time obnoxious to all insect and fungus life.

Cleanly, odor pleasant, convenient for use, effects continuous and lasting.

Sprinkled over the floor before nailing down carpets, matting, or oil-cloth, it absorbs foul smells, contributes to health, and kills or drives off all insects.

Strewn over the yard, in stables, sinks, water-closets, &c., it purifies and deodorizes.

Placed in and about the poultry yard and in the nests, the little pests which usually harrass the poultry can no longer exist.

If scattered lightly over the stalls, when dressed up, each morning, foul odors are absorbed and causes of disease destroyed amongst live stock; and hoof-ail, foot-rot, &c., prevented.

Strewn over seed beds in the garden or field, it gives complete protection to young plants, from insects.

A little of this powder placed in saucers around the sick room, will purify and disinfect the air, without offending the sick by its odor.

And, if put in the vessels used, will prevent unpleasant smells, and all infection from that most fruitful of causes, the excreta of the sick.

A few pounds placed in the coffin will check decay and the consequent offensive odors, for two weeks or more. And if the entire vacant space under, and around, and above the body be filled in with this powder, all decomposition will be arrested for months.

Sold in neat packages at 50c.; in large boxes with sliding tops at $1.25. And in barrels for stable use, &c.

Insect-Proof Paper

for lining closets to contain furs, woolens, &c.; and closets, pantries, &c., infested by or exposed to ants, cockroaches, or other insects. For spreading under carpets for their more perfect preservation. Being manufactured.

Advertisements, to be sure of insertion, must be received BEFORE the 5th of the preceding month.

TERMS—(cash before insertion):

Ordinary Pages, $1.50 *per line. Open Pages*—$2 *per line.*
Business Notices—$2.50 per line of space, each insertion.

Neat Present for the Holidays.

THE YANKEE BLADE

Is a Patent Sewing Ripper.
Eraser for the Desk.
Letter Opener.
Paper Cutter.
Nail Cleaner and Trimmer.

Is good for all these uses. As a Ripper it will take out a seam faster than a Sewing Machine can make it. 30 cents each, by mail, 4 for $1, 2.50 per dozen.

W. A. FITCH, 151 Nassau-st., New York.

THE BEST ORGANS AND MELODEONS. PRINCE & CO.'S ! !

Address WHITING BROS., 814 Broadway, N. Y.
Also, SPLENDID PIANOS *at low prices.* Price Lists free.

AGENTS WANTED!—Male or Female, in all parts of the United States, to sell "Abbott's Lives of the Presidents," one of the best books for Agents ever published in this country. The work is finely illustrated, complete in one volume, ready for subscribers, and sells splendidly. Address B. B. RUSSELL & CO., Boston, Mass.

ALL WANTING FARMS—Good soil, mild climate, 34 miles south of Philadelphia. Price only $25 per acre. Also improved farms; hundreds are settling; information sent free. Address C. K. LANDIS, Vineland, New Jersey.

The Ladies' Christian Monitor

Commences its Seventh January 1868.
Terms $1.00 per annum. *Specimen numbers sent free.*
Address MRS. M. M. B. GOODWIN, Indianapolis, Ind.

WANTED, AGENTS to sell Boardman's Patent Lamp-wick Inserter, and Cast Handle Knife. Samples sent post-paid on receipt of 40 cents for knife, and 10 cents for Inserter. W. Y. A. BOARDMAN, New Haven, Conn.

Fuller & Barnum's New Tuck Creaser and Self-Guide and Baster combined, for all Sewing-Machines, $1. No. 663 Broadway, New York.

CONCORD VINES.

A Rare Chance.

I offer of my large and well selected stock of vines, the best quality of Plants.
20,000 No. 1 Concord, $7.50 per 100; $60 per 1000; $250 per 5,000
25,000 " No. 2 " $6.50 per 100; $45 per 1000; $200 per 5,000
The above are offered at these rates for cash for immediate delivery only. Address

G. E. MEISSNER, Richmond P. O., Staten Island, N. Y.

B. K. BLISS & SON,

Seed and Horticultural Warehouse

Nos. 41 Park Row, and 151 Nassau-st., N. Y.
Late Office of American Agriculturist,
Also, 231 Main-st., Springfield, Mass.,

would inform their Patrons that the *Fourteenth Edition* of their Celebrated Seed Catalogue and Guide to the Flower and Kitchen Garden is now in press, and will be published in January. It will contain about *One Hundred and twenty-five pages* of closely printed matter, beautifully illustrated with *One Hundred Engravings of Flowers and Vegetables*, and a descriptive list of upwards of 2,500 *varieties of Garden, Field, and Flower Seeds*, with special directions for their culture. Mailed post-paid to all applicants upon receipt of 25 cents. Regular customers supplied without charge. Orders addressed either to New York or Springfield, as above, will be promptly attended to.

B. K. BLISS & SON.

JEROME PARK,

May 25th, 1867.

E. F. BAKER, ESQ.,

DEAR SIR,—We take pleasure in stating that your HOOF LINIMENT has cured the Running Horse "Fleetwing," of Quarter Cracks. He ran Two and Three-Quarter Miles yesterday, and Three Miles again to-day, carrying One Hundred and Twenty-eight Pounds, without starting his feet to Crack in the least, and we now consider it a PERFECT CURE.

GEORGE C. WALDEN,
Trainer for Forbes & Jerome.

Manufactured only by

E. F. BAKER & CO.,
141 Maiden-Lane, New York.

Sold by Druggists, Saddlers, Horse-Shoers and Feed Stores everywhere.

SCHOOL DESKS

Of first quality, and new styles.
SUPERIOR PHILOSOPHICAL INSTRUMENTS on hand, and made to order, at the LOWEST PRICES.
For cuts and prices, direct to

N. C. BOARDMAN,
No. 21 John-st., New York.

"KNOW THYSELF." FOR 1868.

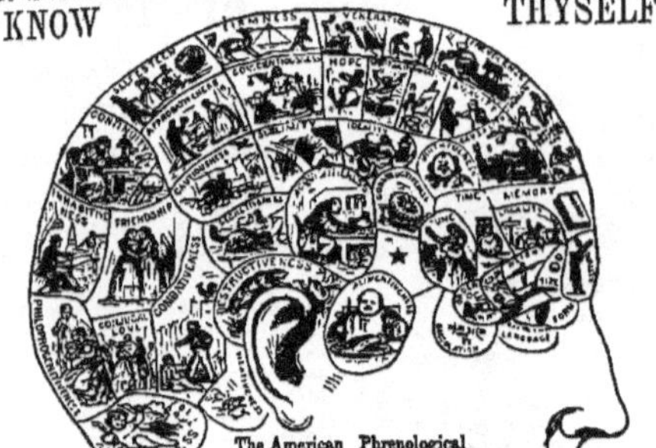

The American Phrenological Journal and Life Illustrated.

Devoted to Ethnology, Physiology, Phrenology, Physiognomy, Psychology, Sociology, Biography, Education, Art, Literature, with Measures to Reform, Elevate and Improve Mankind Physically, Mentally and Spiritually. It is a standard authority in all matters pertaining to Phrenology and the Science of Man. Edited by S. R. WELLS. Published monthly, at $3 a year, 30 cents a number. A new volume begins now.

Address S. R. WELLS, 389 Broadway, New York.

DOTY'S WASHING MACHINE

Washes perfectly without the least injury to clothes, and with great ease to the operator. It is the first and only Clothes Washer which has proved a GREAT SUCCESS, and sells rapidly wherever introduced. This, with the UNIVERSAL CLOTHES WRINGER (the best) does away with the wash tub and rubbing board, and saves clothes, time, and money. Descriptive circulars sent free.

To introduce these machines, we will send either or both to places where no one is selling, *and will pay the freight charges*, on receipt of the retail price. Family Washer, $14. Universal Wringer, "Extra," $9. Also, the new LIGHTNING MEAT CHOPPER, $7.

Send for Wholesale Terms Circular.

R. C. BROWNING, General Agent,
No. 5 Cortlandt-st., New York.
(Opposite Merchants' Hotel.)

HEALTH AND ECONOMY.

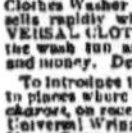

PATENT LEAD ENCASED BLOCK TIN PIPE. Recommended by the medical faculty and approved by WATER COMMISSIONERS. COSTS LESS THAN LEAD PIPE, AND IS MUCH STRONGER. Recent improvements enable us to supply THIS pipe at a less price per foot than common lead pipe.

To furnish the cost per foot, please give the head or pressure of water and bore of pipe. Pamphlets sent FREE on application. Address THE COLWELLS, SHAW & WILLARD MANUFACTURING CO., Foot of West 27th-st., or 165 Beekman-st., corner of Pearl, New York.

FRANKLIN BRICK MACHINE.

Justly celebrated for perfect simplicity, great strength, and immense compressing power, is GUARANTEED, with eight men and two horses, to self-temper the clay and make 3,000 to 3,500 elegant bricks per hour. J. H. RENICK, Proprietor, No. 71 Broadway, New York, Room 28.

Torrey's Patent Weather Strips

Exclude *Wind, Rain, Snow* and *Dust* from Doors and Windows of every description.
They save in fuel one half, and preserve health by the prevention of drafts, so productive of colds.
Cheap, simple, effective, durable, ornamental, and warranted for five years.

E. S. & J. TORREY & CO., Sole Manufacturers,
72 Maiden Lane, New York.

IT DON'T SCRATCH YOU,

Or Tear Your Clothes. Davison's Thornless Black Cap Raspberry is the best, as it is hardy, productive, early, and sweet, and it is a pleasure to cultivate it. For origin, description, prices, testimonials, &c., send for Circular. JOSEPH SINTON,
Angola, Erie Co., N. Y.

LOOK AT THIS!

$1.50 WILL PAY FOR THE MONTHLY

NEW ENGLAND FARMER

from this date to January 1, 1869!

14 Months for only One Dollar and Fifty Cents—in advance.

48 Pages of reading in each number, handsomely illustrated, and largely composed of original contributions.

588 Pages of valuable and interesting Agricultural and Horticultural reading in the volume for 1867.

40 and upward extremely Liberal Premiums offered for new subscribers.

1 new name for our list will entitle you to a premium.

3 cent stamp pays for specimen and circular.

34 Merchants' Row, Boston, the place of publication, and all letters should be addressed to

R. P. EATON & CO.,
Publishers N. E. Farmer.

☞ Any paper copying the above and calling attention to it shall receive the numbers for 1868 without charge.

We quote the following from the Semi-Weekly Times of Nov. 5, 1867, believing it will be of interest to thousands who want all the Horticultural stock they can buy for the money they have to spare for that purpose.

Whitlock's Horticultural Advertiser.

This is a 12mo. pamphlet of seventy-four pages, gotten up in an attractive style, by L. L. WHITLOCK, No. 37 Park Row, New York City, who proposes to act as a judicious and trusty "middle-man" between farmers and gardeners and those who raise trees, vines and shrubs for sale. This is a new arrangement to supply the million with choice vines and trees at low prices. The *Horticultural Advertiser* is WHITLOCK's medium of communication. Producers offer their stock of trees and vines to him at exceedingly low prices—perhaps twice as low as they will sell to customers direct. Those in want of trees or vines send their orders to him, and thus receive all the advantage of the low prices by simply paying WHITLOCK a small per centage. As the advantage is all on the side of farmers and gardeners, let us look into the practical operation of the system, that the doubting may understand how to take still greater advantage of the facilities for procuring trees. A farmer, for example, near Rochester, N. Y., wants $300 worth of fruit trees. He desires to superintend digging them himself. Producers hold the same trees at $1,000; but by writing to New York and paying the middle-man $25, the farmer saves $[illegible]. This is a liberal advertisement of the agency; but the information imparted to the million by disclosing these honest tricks of the trade seems to be a sufficient excuse for telling those who want trees and vines how to obtain them cheaply and at the same time procure as good ones as if they were to get them by retail. Besides this, the *Horticultural Advertiser* contains much valuable information on the subject of horticulture and pomology. (See Adv.)

"Unquestionably the best sustained work of the kind in the world."

HARPER'S MAGAZINE.

The most popular Monthly in the world.—*New York Observer.*

We can account for its success only by the simple fact that it meets precisely the popular taste, furnishing a pleasing and instructive variety of reading for all.—*Zion's Herald, Boston.*

"A complete Pictorial History of the Times."

Harper's Weekly.

AN ILLUSTRATED NEWSPAPER.

The model newspaper of our country.—*N. Y. Evening Post.*

This paper furnishes the best illustrations. Our future historians will enrich themselves out of HARPER'S WEEKLY.—*N. Y. Evangelist.*

The articles upon public questions which appear in HARPER'S WEEKLY from week to week form a remarkable series of brief political essays.—*North American Review.*

"A Repository of Fashion, Pleasure, and Instruction."

Harper's Bazar.

HARPER'S BAZAR, besides being the leading Fashion Journal in this country, also presents the very best specimens of Household Literature. No subject of domestic interest is excluded from its columns.

Terms for Harper's Periodicals.

HARPER'S MAGAZINE,	One Year	$4.00
HARPER'S WEEKLY,	One Year	4.00
HARPER'S BAZAR,	One Year	4.00

HARPER'S BAZAR, HARPER'S WEEKLY, and HARPER'S MAGAZINE, to one address, for one year, $10.00.

An Extra Copy of either the MAGAZINE, WEEKLY, *or* BAZAR *will be supplied gratis for every Club of* FIVE SUBSCRIBERS *at $4.00 each, in one remittance, or, Six Copies for $20.00.*

YOUR "SWEETHEART" would thank you for THE PHRENOLOGICAL JOURNAL. In it she would find the means by which to judge character correctly.

THE GREAT FAMILY PAPER.

THE FIRESIDE COMPANION,

IS A GIANT AMONG THE WEEKLIES.

IT CONTAINS

THE BEST STORIES,
THE BEST SKETCHES,
THE BEST ILLUSTRATIONS,
THE BEST ADVENTURES,
THE BEST POETRY,
THE BEST JOKES,
THE BEST EDITORIALS,
THE BEST EVERYTHING.

The BEST AUTHORS write for the FIRESIDE COMPANION, and all the BEST PEOPLE will be DELIGHTED TO READ IT. For sale by all newsdealers, price 6 cents; subscription price, $3 per year.

GEO. MUNRO & CO., No. 137 William-st., New York.

OUR SCHOOLDAY VISITOR

is one of the very best, cheapest and handsomest Boys' and Girls' Magazines in the world! **Volume XII commences January, 1868. Form Clubs now for new Volume. PREMIUMS FOR EVERYBODY.**—$1.25 a year. $1.00 to clubs. Specimen numbers and full instructions to Agents, 10 cents. **Agents wanted at every Post-Office and School District in the United States.** Address J. W. DAUGHADAY & CO., 424 Walnut-street, Philadelphia, Pa.

MERCHANTS should read THE PHRENOLOGICAL JOURNAL to learn how to select trusty clerks.

PIERCE EGAN'S EXCITING NARRATIVE of his Adventures among the BRIGANDS OF ITALY, is now being published in

FRANK LESLIES'

Chimney Corner.

With No. 120 is given away a magnificent picture, 22 by 28, entitled STOP THIEF; OR, THE MONKEY'S GRIP. For sale by all Booksellers.

LAWYERS should read THE PHRENOLOGICAL JOURNAL, that they may read clients and culprits.

GOODRICH'S

History of the United States.

RE-WRITTEN, AND BROUGHT DOWN TO THE PRESENT TIME (1867).

BY WM. H. SEAVEY, A. M.,

Principal of the Girls' High and Normal School, Boston.

This edition of Goodrich's "History of the United States" has been prepared from the latest and most trustworthy authorities. It has been attempted, by brevity of statement and an economical arrangement of matter, to bring the story of our history through the war of the rebellion, without making it so meagre as to be useless or swelling the work to an inconvenient size. To do this, it has been necessary to re-write nearly the whole work, which, exclusive of an Appendix of [illegible] pages, including maps, portraits, and many other illustrations, useful chronological tables, and tables of analysis, is comprised in [illegible] pages 12mo.

The book may be used as three separate histories, or each may be made to assist the other.

The work forms a carefully prepared work, arranged so as to facilitate the labor of the learner, and fix the facts stated in the mind of the pupil by various [illegible] to the memory, the importance of which the practical teacher can well understand.

The book is illustrated by [illegible]. The design has been [illegible] every part in the United States mentioned in the history. Much care has also been taken to give acceptable PORTRAITS of the most distinguished historical personages.

From D. B. Hagar, Principal State Normal School, Salem, Mass.

I consider it a text-book of extraordinary merit. Its style is clear, concise and interesting; its matter is judiciously selected and arranged; its illustrations are numerous, appropriate, and well executed; its [illegible] analyses, chronological reviews and contemporary [illegible], are of great practical value, and its typographical appearance is highly attractive.

We take pleasure in announcing the publication of the above, and solicit correspondence with School Committees and Teachers with regard to the introduction of the same into schools under their charge.

BREWER & TILESTON, *Publishers*,

May, 1867. 131 Washington-st., Boston.

Whitlock's Horticultural Advertiser.

50 cts. per year, 10 cts. for Specimen Copy.

All Nurseries in One. 37 Park Row, New York.

Containing Premium List, Prices of Trees, &c., in 300 Nurseries.

MECHANICS should read THE PHRENOLOGICAL JOURNAL, and learn how to select boys to learn trades.

IMPORTANT TO OWNERS OF STOCK.

The American Stock Journal

AND

FARMERS' AND STOCK BREEDERS' ADVERTISER.

A First-class Monthly Journal, devoted to Farming and Stock Breeding. Each number contains 36 large double-column pages, illustrated with numerous engravings. Only $1 a year. Specimen copies free, for stamp, with list of splendid Premiums to Agents.

HORSE AND CATTLE DOCTOR, FREE.

The publishers of the *American Stock Journal* have established a Veterinary Department in the columns of the Journal, which is placed under the charge of a distinguished Veterinary Professor, whose duty it is to receive questions as to the *ailments or injuries of all kinds of stock*, and to answer in *print*, in connection with the question, how they should be treated for a cure. These prescriptions are given gratis, and thus every subscriber to the Journal has always at his command a Veterinary Surgeon, *free of charge*. Every Farmer and Stock Breeder should subscribe for it.

Sent Free. Three Months for Nothing.

Every new subscriber for 1868, received by the 1st of January, will receive the October, November, and December numbers of 1867, *free*, making over 500 large double-column pages of reading matter in the 15 numbers. All for the low price of $1.00. Address

N. P. BOYER & CO., Gum Tree, Chester Co., Pa.

WALLACE'S AMERICAN STUD BOOK

Now Ready to Subscribers.

Price $10.

W. A. TOWNSEND & ADAMS, Publishers, 434 Broome-st., New York.

EDITORS should read THE PHRENOLOGICAL JOURNAL and learn how to make perfect newspapers.

Our Young Folks

Will contain early in the volume for 1868 the first part of CHARLES DICKENS'S New Story, "A Holiday Romance," written *expressly* for this Magazine, and *elegantly* illustrated by JOHN GILBERT. Besides this, the volume will contain a large variety of the best and most entertaining reading, especially adapted to the capacities and tastes of young folks. Profusely illustrated. Music in every number. Capital Puzzles, Charades, Rebuses, &c. Send 20 cents for Specimen Number with Prospectus for 1868. TERMS: $2.00 a year. Liberal discount to clubs.

TICKNOR & FIELDS, Publishers, Boston.

YOUR WIFE will thank you for THE PHRENOLOGICAL JOURNAL, with its suggestions for training children. Only $3 a year by post. Address S. R. WELLS, N. Y.

Good Pay for Doing Good.

Magnificent Premiums.

A good active man or woman wanted in every neighborhood to canvass for the weekly PRAIRIE FARMER. The oldest and best *Agricultural, Horticultural, and Family Paper* published in the great Northwest. Price only $2.00 per year. Splendid PREMIUMS are given to agents, and gratuities to all new Subscribers.

Address for full particulars,

THE PRAIRIE FARMER CO., Chicago, Ill.

WANTED—AGENTS—

FOR DR. GEO. H. DADD'S AMERICAN HORSE AND CATTLE DOCTOR.

This work, as its name indicates, is a full and reliable treatise on all the Diseases of Horses, Cattle, Sheep and Hogs, and embraces Breeding, Rearing, Management, Improvement, and Preservation of Live Stock. It is, therefore, a Complete Stock Manual, and as such is without a rival worthy the name. This work is gaining an immense popularity, and must eventually crowd out all others. Territory open in all parts of the country, on our usual liberal terms. H. W. CARROLL & CO., Publishers, Cincinnati, O.

IONA GRAPE VINES

AND

The American Agriculturist.

$5.00 will pay for 10 No. 1 Iona Grape Vines, and *American Agriculturist* for 1 year.

$10.00 will pay for 25 No. 1 Iona Grape Vines and *American Agriculturist* for 1 year. Address

G. E. MEISSNER, Richmond, Staten Island, N. Y.

The Vanishing Picture Trick, 25 cents. Photographic, Sample and Catalogue, 25 cents. Tame, Train and Doctor Horses, 2 Books, 30 cents. Duncan's Masonic Monitor, [illegible] $2.50. Pearl Cuff Buttons and Studs, [illegible] only $2.00. Correct Letter Writing, Conversation, [illegible] Etiquette, 4 books for 60 cents. Courtship Made Easy, Wooing and Wedding, Bridal Etiquette, 3 books, 45 cents. [illegible] 30 cents each—500 Puzzles, 500 Home Amusements, Fireside Games,—Parlor Theatricals, Parlor Magician, Parlor Dialogues—Parlor Pantomimes—novels and [illegible] all kinds. Dealers supplied. W. C. WEMYSS, 575 Broadway, N. Y.

YOUR DAUGHTER would thank you for THE PHRENOLOGICAL JOURNAL, with its instructions on health and beauty. Only $3 a year. Address S. R. WELLS, N. Y.

THE HOLIDAY JOURNAL

Of Parlor Plays, Magic Sports, Fireside Games, Pleasing Experiments, Practical Jokes, Queer Problems, Puzzles, Riddles, Charades, Rebuses, Enigmas, Anagrams, Transpositions, Conundrums, &c., SENT FREE. Address ADAMS & CO., Publishers, Boston.

"The Teacher of Penmanship"

tells "how to *write*," "how to *flourish*," and "how to *draw*." Subscribers for 1868 receive the October, November and December numbers, for 1867, *free*. Valuable and attractive premiums offered to subscribers and those who raise clubs. Only $1 per year. Send 5 cents to pay postage for sample numbers, to L. S. THOMPSON, Sandusky, Ohio.

BEAR IN MIND

That on receipt of the advertised price, I will mail to your address any Book, Magazine, or cheap publication that may be advertised or issued by any respectable publisher in the United States. A Catalogue will be sent on receipt of a postage stamp. Address O. A. ROORBACH, 122 Nassau-st., New York.

CARPENTERS. SEND FOR CATALOGUE of New and Practical Architectural Works, enclosing stamp.

A. J. BICKNELL, Publisher, TROY, N. Y.

SCHOOL TEACHERS should read THE PHRENOLOGICAL JOURNAL, and learn to classify their students. Also to govern them wisely. $3 a year.

Stereopticons and Magic Lanterns,

With the Improved Lime Light, illuminating brilliantly two hundred square feet of canvas, and magnifying the views to that size, at an expense of less than one dollar for a whole evening's exhibition. Easily managed and pays well.

Illustrated priced catalogue of the apparatus, with list of over two thousand artistically colored photographic views on glass, of the War, Scripture History, [illegible] Statuary, etc., etc., forwarded on application. T. H. McALLISTER, Optician, (of late firm of McAllister & Bro., Phila.,) 49 Nassau-street, New York.

YOUR SON would be greatly benefited by reading THE PHRENOLOGICAL JOURNAL. He would learn how to make the most of himself. $3 a year.

EXHIBITION OF

DITCHING, BRICK, PIPE, AND TILE MACHINES.

PEREMPTORY, CASH AUCTION SALE.

$100,000 REAL ESTATE, PERSONAL PROPERTY, AND STOCKS,

WILL BE SOLD AT AUCTION DECEMBER 12, PRECISELY AT 10 1-2 O'CLOCK,

ON THEIR RIVER PROPERTY, TO CLOSE UP THE BUSINESS OF

CROSSMAN BROTHERS, OF WOODBRIDGE, MIDDLESEX COUNTY, NEW JERSEY.

One good farm of 65 acres, with one good residence and two tenant houses thereon; together with out buildings, crops, carriages, furniture, 24 horses, 30 head of cattle, and various implements connected with farming, mining, and manufacturing business. Also, a quantity of fire brick; 400,000 common brick: several thousand feet of first quality and damaged drain pipe; several thousand tons of fire clay, suitable *for* No. 1 fire brick, stove linings, stone ware, drain pipe, alum manufactories, foundry purposes, &c., &c. Five pipe machines that make drain pipe from 3 inches to 22 inches diameter; three clay tempering wheels and circular pits, well paved with blocks of wood set endwise; two substantial common brick machines, (and soak pits), capable of grinding and moulding ordinary clays, at the rate of 4,000 to 6,000 brick per hour, with two horses and six men. Also a water-power flour and grist mill, with two run of stone; turbine water-wheel and new machinery lately fitted up. This mill is located on the property where the business of the company, and the surrounding clay, mining, and manufacturing business, and the facilities for freighting grain to the mill by water, give advantages over distant mills for an excellent custom trade. Also,

TWELVE HUNDRED SHARES

OF

$50 EACH

IN STOCK OF

The Crossman Clay and Manufacturing Company,

whose capital stock is $250,000, free from all assessments. The real estate consists of factories, houses, wharf, railroad, connecting all with ship channel; 177 acres of land of which ¼ to ¾ is underlaid with beds of a variety of such valuable fire clays as are unequaled in quality and value anywhere, excepting in the Woodbridge Clay Mines. Careful estimates show that an acre of our fire clay land produces over half a million dollars' worth of manufactures, or even double the amount in some places. Two responsible members of our company offer to manufacture the more valuable goods at 25 per cent. of their value, and for 50 per cent. of the value of the cheaper goods.

The price of Woodbridge clays constantly and slowly increases, and the price of clay lands rapidly increases. Before clay is freighted, its price is greater than coal after the freight is paid. Consequently good fire clay property is among the best real estate investments of the country.

In addition to the unequaled manufacturing and transportation advantages that this property possesses, another very important and valuable peculiarity of these clay beds is, that they overlie each other up to the surface dirt for a depth of 10 feet to 40 feet thickness. The small quantity of surface dirt is cheaply removed to uncover the fire clay, and leveled off into brick yards, capable of producing next year from 5,000,000 to 10,000,000 bricks to be made from the surface clays. Our other factories and other clay strata produce an equal value of fire brick, drain pipe, etc.

The business of manufacturing these upper strata is profitable; it also uncovers valuable fire clay to be cheaply transported and manufactured into fire brick. In other places upper strata are removed and piled up in the banks at heavy expense, to become a nuisance in obstructing the drainage and proper working of the beds of fire clay, and making the clay costly. The whole present process of stripping, mining, transporting, and manufacturing fire clay, is clumsy, discreditable, and costly, to the loss of all consumers, and all connected with it, excepting that the manufacturers and owners of Woodbridge fire clays become wealthy in spite of the present awkward, anti-progressive system.

Many manufacturers of fire brick and drain pipe adhere so firmly to the old-fashioned systems they learned when young, as constituting "experience," and are so opposed to increase of knowledge, under the fear of affecting prices, as not to admit strangers or suspected competitors in their works to see brick made by hand, (or worse made,) or to see drain pipe clumsily and badly made in plunger machines invented and used a lifetime ago. Again, such parties will ignore the inexorable laws of trade, of supply and demand, and vainly endeavor to sustain prices and remove competition by combinations. Again, as will happen in all trades, the most crafty operate against the majority of their honorable competitors and the consumer in fixing prices, by influencing with commissions, and otherwise, such masons, superintendents, captains, or officers, that act *for* brick consumers, each consumer seeming to think his employees will not accept outside favors, or be influenced by them. While these systems of acquiring wealth prevail in different degrees among clay manufacturers, there are *true* and great progress and improvements being made by mechanics and inventors of genius in their workshops and in other arts. While the sewing machine and watch manufacturers are rapidly producing their valuable goods by machinery, those classes that must work in the dirt and mud are left behind the age to dig ditches with such spades as Amos made years ago; with such plunger pipe and tile machines as were used a lifetime ago, and are still advocated in treatises on drainage, and make brick with machines no better than Hall's expired brick machine patents, and often with such machines as ruin all that use them. It is as important to secure genius *for* the unpleasant duties of perfecting inventions to work in dirt and mud, as in the more pleasant duties of perfecting other arts in the workshop. But in such dirt and clay business where physical strength rather than genius has been employed, principally radical improvements have slept, while the *whole country and every branch of business suffers thereby. Every branch of trade needs good crops;* and still one may ride a thousand miles in some seasons and see one-half the crops thinned out and injured by wet lands capable of being underdrained. Hoping to do our share toward practical improvement *for* the benefit of ourselves and others, we have purchased three patents of the most radical practical improvements of the age, in the ditching, pipe, and tile business; also the agency of Sword's brick machine *for certain districts.* They are all from the same workshop of H. Brewer, in Tecumseh, Michigan. We also secured the assistance of two of the inventors of these unequaled machines. They are undoubtedly the best inventors of their day in their line for practical results. These inventors have become acting members of the Crossman Clay and Manufacturing Co. All parties will cheerfully be granted *free* access to our works, (as yet in a rude state,) to examine our principles: the use and sale of the ditching, tile and brick machines, for the benefit of our company and others; and we do not yet see why these patents and machines will not *alone be as much benefit to our company and the country,* as any sewing machine or mowing machine, or any great improvement benefits any company and the country. As yet we place the *drainage of lands, increase of crops,* and decreased price of brick building material, *before all other* improvements, to benefit all classes. These inventors' machines are of the original and not imitation invention class, that cease when no more ideas can be borrowed. If they live, the company will directly and indirectly receive further benefits, that cannot now be foreshadowed.

In addition to the great benefit to the company of the sale of pipe and tile machines that belong directly to the company, and the indirect help by co-operating with the ditching machine, we have located our regular business on the most valuable clay beds known in this country. Our whole combination of stripping, mining, carting, manufacturing, and shipping advantages of clay goods, has been practically tested one by one for eight years, and our present incomplete business was built up from nothing meantime. To secure the benefits of the future better development of legitimate business, the company get the clay property at far less cost than it would bring at auction if the improvements had not been placed on it. This company can manufacture cheaper than all others, it can compete in all markets, but cannot be driven out of all markets; and the company could any time make a profit by selling it at auction, as there is not a fire brick maker in the country that could safely let his competitor get it. This *alone* practically puts the stock above par at the outset, aside from all benefits from sales of machines and our *combination of all advantages.* Any reliable dealers and consumers that become stockholders directly or indirectly on account of themselves or friends, will naturally have influence and preference over others in the buying and selling our goods in distant markets. We believe we shall in future make goods of quality and price to place our customers beyond the reach of injurious competition. We believe it will be the interest of buyers of fire brick, drain pipe and tile, and common brick, to take an interest in our company and buy direct from the factory and clay property; also the interest of individuals, clubs, and committees, to take interest with us in starting combined brick and tile yards in country places where clay lands make drainage necessary. By selecting proper men, machinery, and by industry, competence can be attained from clays now lying idle—a gain not appreciated in many places. A Sword's brick machine, and one Tiffany tile machine could, together, make a handsome business in many places where one alone would be less remunerative. Such a tile maker would have no competitors if he secured the agency of Ingraham's ditching machine, as digging cheap and good ditches is equivalent to cheap tile. As an investment for capitalists, this fire clay property, constantly increasing in value, possesses advantages over any other investment yet seen by us or any one else that has yet examined it so far as is yet known. To develop the business, to give consumers, buyers, and investors, a chance, and to exhibit the machinery on the same day to public inspection in these days of locating enterprises behind the Alleghanies and Rocky Mountains, we shall have an auction of from $50,000 to $75,000 of our personal stock and much other personal property. $50,000 of the stock for working capital of the company will be held for sale to secure desirable associates, and, perhaps, sold at the same auction. From one-half to three-fourths of the remaining capital will be principally held by us, the inventors and workers of the company. Not one cent has been or will be spent for influence or personal assistance. The company has more than the full benefit of our former labor and development. Every article put up must be absolutely and rapidly sold by an energetic auctioneer, to enable parties to decide whether or not to bid without delay. The Steamer Magenta will leave Barclay street, New York City, at 7 A. M., Nov. 11th, land at our wharf, and remain long enough to examine everything thoroughly. Also, at the same time and place, Nov. 12th. We do not compete with customers buying clay of us. Tickets out, 50 cents. Excursion tickets to return, 50 cents. For sale at the Astor House. Meals provided on board by giving notice at the Astor House the previous day.

Applications to manufacture machines solicited from machinists.

Wanted a young man of superior ability to assist in the office and out-door work of introducing our machinery, and starting tile yards in various sections.

CROSSMAN BROTHERS,

WOODBRIDGE,

MIDDLESEX CO., NEW JERSEY

BOOKS FOR WINTER EVENINGS.

GOOD BOOKS FOR FARMERS AND OTHERS,

PUBLISHED BY

ORANGE JUDD & CO.,

245 Broadway, New York.

Improve the long Winter Evenings by reading the new Books for the Farm, Garden, and Household.

Either of the Books mentioned in the following list will be sent, post-paid, on receipt of the price.

A VALUABLE HOME LIBRARY.

BACK VOLUMES

OF THE

AMERICAN AGRICULTURIST.

The publishers of the *American Agriculturist*, having preserved the electrotype plates of the back volumes of that paper, from the Sixteenth to the Twenty-sixth Volume complete, can supply any or all of these as may be desired. These volumes contain more varied and interesting information on all matters pertaining to the Farm, Garden, and Household, than can be obtained in books, costing three times as much money. They are profusely illustrated with the best of engravings, and in addition to the large amount of instructive reading matter for the older members of the Household, they contain a Special Department for the Boys and Girls. They, therefore, constitute in themselves a

Most valuable Library for the Farmer's Family or for any other Home.

The price of these volumes, unbound, is $1.50 each, at the office, or $1.75, if sent by mail, as they must be post-paid. The price of the same volumes, in neat cloth binding, with gilt title on the back, is $2.00, at the office, or $2.50, if sent by mail.

Address, ORANGE JUDD & Co., Publishers, 245 Broadway, New York City.

BOOKS FOR FARMERS and OTHERS.

[Published and for sale by Orange Judd & Co., 245 Broadway, New York. Any of these books will be forwarded by mail, post-paid, on receipt of price.]

- Allen's (L. F.) Rural Architecture
- Allen's (R. L.) American Farm Book
- Allen's (L. F.) Domestic Animals
- American Agricultural Annual, 18[illegible], pa. [illegible]; cloth
- American Horticultural Annual, 18[illegible], pa. [illegible]; cloth
- American Bird Fancier
- American Pomology, by Dr. J. A. Warder
- American Rose Culturist
- American Weeds and Useful Plants
- Architecture, by Cummings & Miller
- Barry's Fruit Garden
- Boussingault's Method of Making Manures
- [illegible]'s Rural Economy
- Brown's New Book of Flowers
- Buist's Flower Garden Directory
- Buist's Family Kitchen Gardener
- [illegible]
- Cobbett's American Gardener
- [illegible]
- Cole's Veterinarian
- Cotton Planter's Manual (Turner)
- Country Life, by R. M. Copeland
- Dadd's (Geo. H.) Modern Horse Doctor
- Dadd's American Cattle Doctor
- Dana's Muck Manual
- [illegible] paper, [illegible] cloth
- [illegible]
- Draining for Profit and Health, by G. E. Waring, Jr.
- [illegible]
- Elliott's Western Fruit Grower's Guide
- [illegible]
- Flax Culture
- French's Farm Drainage
- [illegible] Grape Culturist
- Fuller's Small Fruit Culturist
- [illegible]
- Gardening for Profit, by Peter Henderson
- Grape Vine, by Prof. F. Mohr
- [illegible] paper
- Guenon on Milch Cows
- [illegible]
- Hop Culture
- Johnston's Agricultural Chemistry
- Johnston's Elements of Agricultural Chemistry
- [illegible]
- [illegible]
- My Vineyard at Lakeview
- [illegible]
- Onion Culture
- Our Farm of Four Acres ... paper, [illegible] cloth
- [illegible]
- Peat and its Uses, by Prof. S. W. Johnson
- Pedder's Land Measurer
- Quinby's Mysteries of Bee-keeping
- Randall's Sheep Husbandry
- Randall's Fine Wool Sheep Husbandry
- [illegible] paper [illegible] cloth
- Rivers' Miniature Fruit Garden
- Rural Annual, by Joseph Harris
- Rural Annual (Harris) 8 Nos., bound, 2 Vols. ... Each
- [illegible] paper, [illegible] bound
- Schenck's Gardener's Text Book
- [illegible]
- Stewart's [illegible] Stable Book
- [illegible] of Animals
- Tobacco Culture
- Todd's (S. E.) Young Farmer's Manual
- Warder's Hedges and Evergreens
- Youatt and Spooner on the Horse
- Youatt and Martin on Cattle
- Youatt on the Hog
- Youatt on Sheep

O. J. & Co. keep in Stock the following Books:

- Art of Saw Filing ([illegible])
- [illegible]'s Fruit Garden
- [illegible]
- Bridgeman's Young Gardener's Assistant
- Brandt's Age of Horses, (English or German)
- Burr's Vegetables of America
- Carpenter's and Joiner's Hand Book (Holly)
- Dead Shot: or Sportsman's Complete Guide; Engravings from Frank Forester
- Downing's Cottage Residences
- Downing's Fruits and Fruit Trees of America
- Downing's Rural Essays
- [illegible]
- Flint's Milch Cows and Dairy Farming
- Frank Forester's Horse and Horsemanship, 8vo., gilt backs, 2 vols. ... 10 00
- Frank Forester's Field Sports, 8vo., tinted paper, gilt backs, 2 vols. ... 7 50
- Frank Forester's Fish and Fishing, 8vo., gilt back, 100 engravings ... 5 50
- Frank Forester's Complete Manual for Young Sportsmen, Crown 8vo., gilt back
- Fuller's Forest Tree Culturist
- Gray's How Plants Grow
- Gray's Manual of Botany and Lessons in one Vol.
- Haraszthy's Grape Culture and Wine Making
- Harris' Insects Injurious to Vegetation, plain [illegible], col'd
- Hatfield's American House Carpenter
- Husmann's Grapes & Wine
- Jennings' Horse Training Made Easy
- Jennings on Cattle
- Jennings on Sheep, Swine, and Poultry
- Jennings on the Horse and his Diseases
- Johnson's (Prof. S. W.) Essays on Manures
- Kathrina. By Timothy Titcomb
- Langstroth on the Honey Bee
- Mayhew's Illustrated Horse Doctor
- Mayhew's Illustrated Horse Management
- Mayhew's Practical Book Keeping for Farmers
- Blanks for [illegible] do.
- McMahon's American Gardener
- Morrell's American Shepherd
- My Farm of Edgewood
- Parkman's Book of Roses
- [illegible] on the Horse
- Quincy, (Hon. Josiah) on Soiling Cattle
- Rand's Bulbs
- Rand's Flowers for Parlor and Garden
- Rand's Garden Flowers
- Register of Rural Affairs ... bound ... 4 Vols. ... each
- Rural Studies
- Scribner's Ready Reckoner and Log Book
- Silloway's Modern Carpentry
- Strong's Grape Culture
- Ten Acres Enough
- The Dog, By Dinks, Mayhew, and Hutchinson.—Edited by Frank Forester, Crown 8vo.
- Tucker's Register of Rural Affairs
- Vaux's Villas and Cottages
- Watson's American Home Garden
- Woodward's Annual, 18[illegible] ... Paper, 75c., cloth
- Woodward's Country Homes
- Woodward's Graperies, etc.
- Youmans's Household Science

www.ingramcontent.com/pod-product-compliance
Lightning Source LLC
Chambersburg PA
CBHW022106300426
44117CB00007B/601
9783337716752